HANDBOOK OF HUMAN-COMPUTER INTERACTION

Second, Completely Revised Edition

HANDBOOK OF HUMAN-COMPUTER INTERACTION

Second, Completely Revised Edition

Edited by

MARTIN G. HELANDER

Linköping Institute of Technology
Linköping, Sweden

THOMAS K. LANDAUER

University of Colorado at Boulder
Boulder, Colorado
U.S.A.

PRASAD V. PRABHU

Human Factors Laboratory
Eastman Kodak Company
Rochester, New York
U.S.A.

1997
ELSEVIER
AMSTERDAM – LAUSANNE – NEW YORK – OXFORD – SHANNON – TOKYO

ELSEVIER SCIENCE B.V.
Sara Burgerhartstraat 25
P.O. Box 211, 1000 AE Amsterdam, The Netherlands

ISBN hardbound: 0 444 81862 6
ISBN paperback: 0 444 81876 6

This book is printed on acid-free paper.

Printed in The Netherlands.

EDITORIAL BOARD

CONTRIBUTORS

Albert J. Ahumada, Jr.
NASA Ames Research Center,
Moffett Field,
California, USA

Robert B. Allen
Bellcore,
Morristown,
New Jersey, USA

John R. Anderson
Department of Psychology and
Computer Science,
Carnegie Mellon University,
Pittsburgh, Pennsylvania, USA

Benjamin B. Bederson
Computer Science Department,
University of New Mexico,
Albuquerque, New Mexico, USA

Durand R. Begault
NASA Ames Research Center,
Moffett Field,
California, USA

Rachel K.E. Bellamy
Apple Computer, Inc.,
Cupertino,
California, USA

Philip Bernick
New Mexico State University,
Las Cruces,
New Mexico, USA

Stephen J. Boies
IBM Research Center -Hawthorne,
Yorktown Heights,
New York, USA

Guy A. Boy
European Institute of Cognitive
Sciences & Engg. (EURISCO),
Toulouse, France

Ahmet Çakir
ERGONOMIC Institute,
Berlin, Germany

John M. Carroll
Computer Science Department,
Virginia Tech,
Blacksburg, Virginia, USA

Mark H. Chignell
Dept. of Industrial Engineering,
University of Toronto,
Toronto, Canada

Frank T. Conway
Department of Industrial Engg.,
University of Wisconsin-Madison,
Madison,
Wisconsin, USA

Nancy J. Cooke
Department of Psychology,
New Mexico State University,
Las Cruces,
New Mexico, USA

Albert T. Corbett
Human Computer Interaction
Institute,
Carnegie Mellon University,
Pittsburgh, Pennsylvania,USA

Sara J. Czaja
Department of Industrial Engg.,
University of Miami,
Miami, Florida, USA

Tom Dayton
Somerset,
New Jersey, USA

Thomas A. Dingus
Virginia Polytechnic Institute and
State University,
Virginia, USA

Wolfgang Dzida
GMD,
Sankt Augustin, Germany

Ken Eason
HUSAT Research Institute,
Loughborough University,
Leicestershire, U.K.

Ray E. Eberts
Purdue University,
West Lafayette,
Indiana, USA

Pelle Ehn
Department of Informatics,
Lund University,
Lund, Sweden

Michael Eisenberg
Department of Computer Scince,
University of Colorado
Boulder, Colorado, USA

Stephen R. Ellis
NASA Ames Research Center,
Moffett Field,
California, USA

George Engelbeck
U S WEST Advanced
Technologies,
Boulder, Colorado, USA

David M. Frohlich
Hewlett-Packard Laboratories,
Bristol, England

William W. Gaver
Royal College of Art,
Kensington Gore,
London, UK

Andrew W. Gellatly
Virginia Polytechnic Institute and State University,
Virginia, USA

John D. Gould
IBM Research, Emeritus
New York, USA

Joel S. Greenstein
Clemson University,
Clemson,
South Carolina, USA

Peter Gregor
University of Dundee,
Dundee, Scotland

Jonathan Grudin
Information and Comp. Science,
University of California, Irvine
Irvine, California, USA

Mats Hagberg
National Institute for Working Life,
Solna, Sweden

Sture Hägglund
Dept. of Comp. and Info. Science,
Linköping University,
Linköping, Sweden

Jean Hallewell Haslwanter
Wandel & Goltemann,
Eningen u. A.,
Germany

Martin G. Helander
Linköping Institute of Technology,
Linköping, Sweden

Jonathan I. Helfman
AT&T Research,
Murray Hill,
New Jersey, USA

Charles Hill
Apple Computer, Inc.,
Cupertino,
California, USA

James D. Hollan
Computer Science Department,
University of New Mexico,
Albuquerque, New Mexico, USA

Stephanie Houde
Apple Computer, Inc.,
Cupertino, California, USA

Robin Jeffries
Sun Microsystems, Inc.,
California, USA

Clare-Marie Karat
IBM T.J. Watson Research Center,
Hawthorne, New York,USA

John Karat
IBM T. J. Watson Research Center,
Hawthorne,
New York, USA

Wendy A. Kellogg
IBM T.J. Watson Research Center,
Yorktown Heights,
New York, USA

David Kieras
University of Michigan,
Michigan, USA

Jonathan K. Kies
Department of Industrial and Systems Engineering,
Virginia Tech,
Blacksburg, Virginia, USA

Karl H. E. Kroemer
Department of Industrial and Systems Engineering,
Virginia Tech,
Blacksburg, Virginia, USA

Kenneth R. Koedinger
Human Computer Interaction Institute,
Carnegie Mellon University,
Pittsburgh, Pennsylvania,USA

Thomas K. Landauer
University of Colorado at Boulder,
Boulder,
Colorado, USA

Clayton Lewis
Department of Computer Science and Institute of Cognitive Science,
University of Colorado at Boulder,
Boulder, Colorado, USA

James R. Lewis
IBM Corp.,
Boca Raton,
Florida, USA

Gerald Lee Lohse
University of Pennsylvania,
Philadelphia,
Pennsylvania, USA

Jonas Löwgren
Dept. of Comp. and Info. Science,
Linköping University,
Linköping, Sweden

Holger Luczak
Inst. of Ind. Engg. and Ergonomics,
Aachen University of Technology,
Germany

Regis L. Magyar
Magyar and Associates,
Chapel Hill, North Carolina, USA

Jane T. Malin
NASA Johnson Space Center,
Houston, Texas, USA

Aaron Marcus
Aaron Marcus and Associates,
Emeryville, California, USA

Monica A. Marics
U S WEST Advanced Technologies,
Boulder, Colorado, USA

M. Lynne Markus
Programs in Information Science,
The Claremont Graduate School,
Claremont, California, USA

Richard E. Mayer
University of California,
Santa Barbara,
California, USA

Michael J. Muller
Boulder,
Colorado, USA

Bonnie A. Nardi
Apple Computer,
USA

Dennis C. Neale
Virginia Polytechnic Institute and State University,
Blacksburg, Virginia, USA

Alan F. Newell
University of Dundee,
Dundee, Scotland

Raymond S. Nickerson
Tufts University,
Massachusetts, USA

William C. Ogden
New Mexico State University,
Las Cruces, New Mexico, USA

Dan R. Olsen Jr.
Computer Science Department,
Brigham Young University,
Provo, Utah, USA

Gary M. Olson
University of Michigan,
Michigan, USA

Judith S. Olson
University of Michigan,
Michigan, USA

Kenneth R. Paap
Department of Psychology,
New Mexico State University,
Las Cruces, New Mexico, USA

Misha Pavel
Oregon Graduate Institute,
Portland,
Oregon, USA

Annelise Mark Pejtersen
Risø National Laboratory,
Denmark

David L. Post
Armstrong Laboratory,
Wright-Patterson Air Force Base,
Ohio, USA

Kathleen M. Potosnak
Independent Consultant,
Kingston,
Washington, USA

Girish V. Prabhu
Eastman Kodak Company,
Rochester,
New York, USA

Prasad V. Prabhu
Eastman Kodak Company,
Rochester, New York, USA

Jens Rasmussen
Consultant,
Denmark

Stephen J. Reinach
The University of Iowa,
Iowa, USA

David Rempel
Univ. of California San Francisco - Univ. of California at Berkeley
Ergonomics Program,
California, USA

Emilie M. Roth
Westinghouse Science and Technology Center,
Pittsburgh,
Pennsylvania, USA

Mary Beth Rosson
Department of Computer Science,
Virginia Polytechnic Institute and State University,
Virginia, USA

Joan M. Ryder
CHI Systems Incorporated,
Lower Gwynedd,
Pennsylvania,USA

Debra L. Schreckenghost
Metrica Inc.,
Houston,
Texas, USA

Thomas B. Sheridan
Massachusetts Institute of Technology,
Massachusetts, USA

Murray F Spiegel
Bellcore,
Morristown,
New Jersey, USA

Michael J. Smith
Dept. of Industrial Engineering,
University of Wisconsin-Madison,
Madison,
Wisconsin, USA

Johannes Springer
Institute of Industrial Engineering and Ergonomics,
Aachen University of Technology,
Germany

Lynn Streeter
US West Advanced Technologies,
Boulder,
Colorado, USA

Thomas S. Tullis
Fidelity Investments,
Boston,
Massachusetts, USA

Jacob Ukelson
IBM Research Center -Hawthorne,
Yorktown Heights,
New York, USA

Mary Van Deusen
InterMedia Enterprises,
Wrentham,
Massachusetts, USA

Robert A. Virzi
GTE Laboratories Incorporated,
Waltham,
Massachusetts, USA

Pawan R. Vora
U S WEST Communications,
Denver,
Colorado, USA

Yvonne Wærn
Dept. of Communication Studies,
Linköping University,
Linköping, Sweden

John A. Waterworth
Department of Informatics,
Umeå University, Sweden

Jennifer C. Watts
The Ohio State University,
Columbus,
Ohio, USA

Elizabeth M. Wenzel
NASA Ames Research Center,
Moffett Field,
California, USA

Cathleen Wharton
U S WEST Advanced
Technologies,
Boulder,
Colorado, USA

Beverly H. Williges
Department of Industrial and
Systems Engineering,
Virginia Tech,
Blacksburg, Virginia, USA

Robert C. Williges
Department of Industrial and
Systems Engineering,
Virginia Tech,
Blacksburg, Virginia, USA

Chauncey Wilson
FTP Software Inc.,
North Andover,
Massachusetts, USA

Dennis Wixon
Digital Equipment Corporation,
Nashua,
New Hampshire, USA

David D. Woods
The Ohio State University,
Columbus,
Ohio, USA

Wayne W. Zachary
CHI Systems Incorporated,
Lower Gwynedd,
Pennsylvania,USA

PREFACE

The Handbook of Human-Computer Interaction is concerned with principles for design of the Human-Computer Interface. This is the second edition of the Handbook. The first edition was published in 1988.

The handbook has both academic and practical purposes. It is intended to summarize the research and provide recommendations for how the information can be used by designers of computer systems. There is an interest from academia in using this volume as a reference for teaching and research. The handbook can also be used by professionals who are involved in design of HCI, such as: Computer scientists, Cognitive scientists, Experimental psychologists, Human factors professionals, Interface designers, Systems engineers, Managers and Executives working with systems development.

Much information may be used outside the traditional field of HCI. With increased computerization we will find that there is a broad interest in HCI and usability. Many new users will not sit in front of a regular computer - for example users of smart consumer products, users of medical equipment, and car drivers who use automation in automobiles. Others will be interacting with very large computer applications, such as decision support in process industries and nuclear power plants, and software for product data management to name a few. Although we supply little direct information or research concerning these applications, the information in the handbook can be generalized to these areas. The main limiting factor in HCI is usually the cognitive limitations of the operator, and the implications of these for interface design. These are valid across all domains of application; to the extent that we can formulate theories of HCI these will be applicable in many areas.

Some readers may be interested in a definition of Human-Computer Interaction. We reluctantly supply a definition below. We are reluctant because it is generally difficult to capture a large investigative field with just a few words. Another problem is that there are a multitude of alternative definitions depending upon ones interest and goal. A professional interested in the organizational impact of software would have a different focus and framing of HCI than someone interested in, say, natural language understanding. Our general interest is to improve design of HCI., so our definition is also general.

"In human-computer interaction knowledge of the capabilities and limitations of the human operator is used for the design of systems, software, tasks, tools, environments, and organizations. The purpose is generally to improve productivity while providing a safe, comfortable and satisfying experience for the operator".

The contents of this edition of the handbook are fundamentally different compared to 1988. In the first edition there were 52 chapters. In this edition there are 62. Fourteen chapter titles remain since the first edition. Some of these have new authors and the remaining chapters have been rewritten or extensively modified to reflect the development in the field. The remaining 48 chapters are new. This reflects the development of the field: the continued search for new theories, new applications of HCI, and the fact that there has been a tremendous amount of new research since 1988. In the first issue of the handbook, there were some 5,000 references - now there are about 7,000, and most of them were published after 1988.

There are nine sections in the Handbook:

1. Issues, Theories, Models and Methods in HCI
2. Design and Development of Software Systems

3. User Interface Design
4. Evaluation of HCI
5. Individual Differences and Training
6. Multimedia, Video and Voice
7. Programming, Intelligent Interface Design, and Knowledge-Based Systems.
8. Input Devices and Design of Work Stations.
9. CSCW and Organizational Issues in HCI

Several of the topic areas that were hot issues in the first edition are not included or are less emphasized here. Examples of chapters that are no longer represented are: command names, text editors, and query languages. These topic areas are still of interest for HCI. However, the chapters in the 1988 edition provide authoritative reviews and they are still current. The problem in retaining them here is that most of the research was done before 1988, and little has been done after 1988. We recommend the reader of this text to consult the previous edition for such information. Below is a list of chapters from the first 1988 edition that are still current and deserve reading:

Table 1. Chapters in the 1988 edition of the Handbook, that are still current and have become classics in the field.

Chapter 1. D. D. Woods and E.M. Roth. Cognitive Systems Engineering

Chapter 2. J.N. Carroll and J.M. Olson. Mental Models in Human-Computer Interaction

Chapter 9. J. Rasmussen and L.P. Goodstein. Information Technology and Work.

Chapter 11. P.J. Barnard and J. Grudin. Command Names

Chapter 12. P. Reisner. Query Languages

Chapter 16. J. Elkerton. Online Aiding for Human-Computer Interaction

Chapter 20. H. L. Snyder. Image Quality

Chapter 24. D.E. Egan. Individual Differences in Human-Computer Interaction

Chapter 28. P. Wright. Issues in Content and Presentation in Document Design

Chapter 29. T.L. Roberts. Text Editors

Chapter 30. S.T. Dumais. Textual Information Retrieval

Chapter 36. J. Whiteside, J. Bennett. and K. Holtzblatt. Usability Engineering: Our Experience and Evolution.

Chapter 51. R.R. Mackie and C.D. Wylie. Factors Influencing Acceptance of Computer-Based Innovations.

In this edition there are several missing areas, which would have been interesting to address, but they were not included because the chapters were either refused in the review process, or the authors did not deliver in time, or these areas were not included by the editors because there was not enough research. Here are some examples. Two chapter on the Internet were refused. Unfortunately, due to the tight time schedule in the production process they could not be replaced by other authors. Several chapters were not delivered by designated authors including a chapter on Display Image Quality. A potential chapter on HCI of software modules residing on the web was never considered, since this area has not been well researched. We therefore take exception to any potential comments by reviewers of this handbook that some important areas were not included. There were in most cases good reasons.

Each chapter was reviewed by two outside reviewers. The following individuals kindly contributed to the review process:

Håkan Alm
Thomas J. Armstrong
Roy Berns
Randolph Bias
Sara Bly
Guy Boy
Stuart K. Card
Sherry Perdue Casali
Stephen M. Casner
Donna L. Cuomo
Sara Czaja
Deborah Boehm-Davis
Gunilla Derefelt
Mark Detweiler
Susan Dray
K.D.Eason
Mike Eisenberg
Steven Ellis
Ray Eberts
Doug Gillan
Björn Granström
Anand Gramopadhye
Wayne Gray
Jonathan Grudin
Irene Greif
Stephanie Guerlain
Joerg Haake
Martin Helander
Tom Hewett
Ed Hutchins
Ellen Isaacs
Patricia M. Jones
Clare-Marie Karat
John Karat
Christopher Koch
Thomas K. Landauer
Gerald (Jerry) L. Lohse
Eva Loven
Jonas Löwgren
Arnie Lund
Aaron Marcus
Robert L. Mack
Richard Mayer
Andrew Monk
Lena Mårtensson
Judy Olson
Girish Prabhu
Prasad Prabhu
Ben Shneiderman
Andrew Sears
David Smith
Harry L. Snyder
Lee Sproull
Loren G. Terveen
David Travis
Gregg C. Vanderheiden
Robert A.Virzi
Pawan Vora
John Waterworth
Gunnela Westlander
Cathleen Wharton
Robert C. Williges
Dennis Wixon

Several other individuals participated in the review process, and they are listed in the acknowledgments section of individual chapters.

We would like to acknowledge the contributions of the Department of Mechanical Engineering, Linköping Institute of Technology, Sweden, which paid for some of the travel expenses and telephone costs in coordinating the handbook. Thanks also to Dr. Anand Gramopadhye, of Clemson University, USA, for valuable help during the production editing of the handbook.

We are also grateful to Dr. Kees Michielsen of Elsevier Science. He found economic resources to organize the work on the handbook. He encouraged us throughout the production process and displayed great patience in waiting for the final product.

Most of all our thanks go to Davis Jebaraj, our production editor. He formatted and assembled the chapters, coordinated the subject index, and finally printed the text. He spent many long hours on this monumental task, and we owe him our sincere gratitude.

January, 1997

Martin Helander
Linköping
Sweden

Thomas K. Landauer
Boulder, Colorado
USA

Prasad Prabhu
Rochester, New York
USA

CONTENTS

Part I

Issues, Theories, Models and Methods in HCI

Handbook of Human-Computer Interaction
Second, completely revised edition
M. Helander, T.K. Landauer, P. Prabhu (eds.)

Chapter 1

Human–Computer Interaction: Background and Issues

Raymond S. Nickerson
Tufts University
Massachusetts, USA

Thomas K. Landauer
University of Colorado at Boulder
Boulder, Colorado, USA

One of us—we will not say which—writes these words with the help of a desktop computer that five years ago was as good as the industry had to offer, but that could be replaced today by a machine with 8 times as much RAM, 30 times as much hard disk capacity, 8 times the processing speed, and assorted additional capabilities (e.g., CD ROM, sound), at about 75 percent of its cost. The museum piece is retained because it is more than adequate to its user's needs; besides, why upgrade now when the machine that would be purchased is likely to be obsolete almost before it is unpacked? Information technology has been, and is, moving rapidly indeed.

The uses to which computers are put and the ease and effectiveness with which people interact with them have also changed over the past few years, but at nothing close to the same rate. Moreover, as we shall see, although many industries have invested heavily in computer-based tools for their workers, compelling evidence that the investment has paid off, either in terms of anticipated gains in productivity or increased satisfaction of most workers with their jobs, or most people with their lives, is wanting.

A major assumption that motivates this handbook and the work described in it is that the potential that information technology represents for helping people to attain their individual and corporate goals can be realized only if sufficient effort is made to discover and understand what determines whether a system will be useful and usable, or, better, how useful and usable a system will be. By information technology, we mean communication and computer technologies in combination.

Our purpose in this chapter is to help set the stage for what is to follow by discussing, briefly and in broad terms, the history, state, and prospects of information technology, to consider a representative sample of HCI issues relating to the uses of this technology, and to raise some questions for future research, innovation and development. The focus of the handbook is on people interacting with—using—computers, and information technology more generally, so there is relatively little emphasis on hardware per se; our intent is to say only enough to provide a sketchy account of the technological context in which the issues of interaction arise.

1.1 Historical Background

1.1.1 Communication Technology

Until late in the 19th century the speed of long-distance communication was limited by methods of transportation. To transmit a message from point A to point B, one put it on some physical medium, and transported that medium from the one point to the other. Various methods were devised to obviate the transporting of messages, including the use of smoke signals, flashing lights, or sounds that could be sent and resent through a series of appropriately spaced relay stations. Such systems had severely limited message-carrying capacity and could be effective only over relatively short distances.

The inventions of the telegraph and the radio constituted major advances in communication technology. Both made it possible to send messages over very long distances extremely rapidly. The telegraph, and later the telephone, became the means of choice to effect long-distance communication between individuals. The radio, as it evolved, and later television, were used predominantly for broadcasting. As a matter of historical interest, when radio was first used, it was seen primarily as a means of point-to-point communication; only later did its broadcast possibilities become widely recognized and this mode of operation become the dominant one; Alexander Graham Bell and his early supporters thought the telephone would be primarily a broadcast medium, sending musical performances far and wide. Now, with the rapid spread of cellular (radio) telephony, and cable connections with their potential for interactive use, the association of media with role and content is again in the process of change.

1.1.2 Computer Technology

Precursors to modern computer technology can be seen in ancient devices used to facilitate computation (the abacus or soroban) as well as in less ancient inventions (Pascal's 17th century mechanical calculator, Jacquard's 18th century loom, Babbage's 19th century analytic engine, Hollerith's tabulating machinery used in the census of 1890), but the beginning of the age of the electronic digital computer is probably best marked at roughly the middle of the 20th century. One might debate which of several events most deserves to be considered the starting point; among the possibilities would be the completion of Howard Aiken's Mark I by IBM in 1944, that of J. Presper Eckert and John Mauchly's ENIAC with its 17,000 vacuum tubes in 1946, the invention of the transistor by John Bardeen, Walter Brattain and William Shockley in 1948, and the first commercial sale of an electronic digital computer—a Univac—in 1951.

The important point, for present purposes, is that the electronic digital computer is only about half a century old. Despite this fact, it has already had an enormous impact on our lives, and the technology is still in a phase of rapid development; what its further impact will be is unclear, but who can doubt that it will be very great? The speed with which computer technology has advanced since the middle of the century is remarkable by any standards, and "predictable" only with the benefit of hindsight. Few, if any, of even the most clear-sighted visionaries of fifty years ago imagined in their wildest speculations how things would develop over the next few decades.

The most apparent trend that has characterized progress in the technology over that time has been the ever-decreasing size of computing components ("active element groups," such as logic gates and memory cells), which has allowed the packaging of ever-larger amounts of computing power into less and less space. With the miniaturization have come also great increases in the speed and reliability with which components operate, and commensurate decreases in their costs and power requirements. The aggregate effect has been to make much greater amounts of computing power than were available to major corporations even 20 years ago affordable today to individuals of modest means

The surprising nature of what has transpired may be illustrated by the juxtaposition of two observations published in the Scientific American, one in 1949 and the other in 1994. In 1949 George Gray, citing Warren McCulloch as the source of his estimates, noted that "if a calculator were built fully to simulate the nerve connections of the human brain, it would require a skyscraper to house it, the power of Niagara Falls to run it, and all the water of Niagara to cool it." Forty-five years later, Marvin Minsky (1994), noting that the brain is now believed to contain on the order of 100 trillion synapses, speculated that "[s]omeday, using nanotechnology, it should be feasible to build that much storage space into a package as small as a pea" (p. 112). Minsky's speculation is admittedly a little noncommittal as to when this is likely to be feasible, but even a claim that it would ever be so would have seemed absurd in 1949.

Other indications of the spectacular rate of change in computer technology are not difficult to identify. The cost of a logic gate went from about $10 in 1960 to about $0.0001 in 1990. The estimated number of active element groups in the average U.S. home went from about 10 in 1940 to about 100 in 1960 to about half a million in 1990.

1.1.3 Software

From the beginning, the development of software has been at least as great a challenge as the continual improvement of hardware, but progress has been more sporadic and more difficult to judge objectively. In the early days of computers, most users were programmers as a matter of necessity. Prewritten programs did not exist in abundance, so if one wanted to use a computer to accomplish some task, one had to write the required program oneself. Today, commercially available applications programs abound.

The nature of programming has changed more or less continuously since computers first appeared on the scene and had to be programmed in machine code. The variety of languages and operating systems that exist make it difficult to say much about programming that is applicable in all contexts. At the highest level of abstraction, programming can be thought of as a two-phase process: (1) specifying in detail the steps that are necessary to accomplish some task, and (2) expressing those steps in a language of a particular operating system. In practice, the two phases may be so closely coupled that they cannot be distinguished, but they are conceptually different; the same procedure specification may be represented in different languages so as to be executable on different systems.

Programming today can be done at a variety of levels. Systems programmers develop operating systems like DOS, Windows and UNIX that represent operating environments in which other programs can run. Applications programmers produce programs to be used for specific purposes, like maintaining payroll information, scheduling airline travel, composing and editing text, doing mathematics, helping to diagnose illness, and designing industrial products. Starting with the invention and dramatic evolution of compilers, programming languages have evolved in several ways: by taking over more of the chores originally done by programmers, such as translating abstract symbols, words, control instructions and operators into detailed sequences of basic operations by which they are achieved; by providing bookkeeping and organizational aids, such as automatic memory allocation, configuration management, and version control; and by enabling and enforcing various notational schemes, systems for expressing logical relations or procedures, and disciplines for the expression of relations and ideas, such as are represented by LISP and object oriented languages.

As a result of these developments, much bigger, more complicated programs became easier to construct, and the rate at which new software systems could be developed increased greatly. Now, even relatively unsophisticated computer users can write their own programs, if they wish, using specific languages provided with most desktop or laptop computers for that purpose; however, probably only a small minority of personal computer users actually exercise this option. Basic HCI efforts such as user-centered design and iterative evaluation have played little role in the development of programming languages, although such efforts might be richly rewarded, especially, perhaps, in the case of the expanding availability of programming facilities for nonprofessional users.

1.1.4 The Blending of Communication and Computer Technologies

Information technology, as the term is generally used today, and as it is used here, connotes a blending of communication and computer technologies that has been so thorough that it is no longer possible to tell where the one ends and the other begins. The most obvious and significant result of this blending has been the building of computer networks, beginning only a little more than a quarter of a century ago, that link computers from different geographical locations around the world (Cerf, 1991).

Computer networks combine computer and communication technologies in the obvious sense that they connect computers through communication channels, but the blending of the technologies goes much deeper than that. The communication networks are themselves permeated with computational capabilities that are essential to their operation. The blurring of the distinction between computer and communication technologies is seen not only in the implementation of computer networks, per se, but in many of the capabilities and services that such networks provide. These include electronic mail and bulletin boards, computer-mediated teleconferencing, multifeature phones and voice mail, facsimile store-and-forward capabilities, digital encryption systems, information utilities, and many others.

1.1.5 Worldwide Connectivity

The first computer networks were implemented on an experimental basis in the mid 1960s (Davies and Barber, 1973; Marrill and Roberts, 1966). The ARPAnet, the immediate predecessor of the Internet, began in 1969 as a four-node system funded by the Advanced Research Projects Agency of the U. S. Department of Defense in 1969 (Heart, 1975; Heart, McKenzie, McQuillan and Walden, 1978); it became and remained the largest operational network in the world for many years. Its successor, the Internet connected an estimated 1.7 million host computers and had an estimated 5 to 15 million users as of 1993 (Pool, 1993). The 1995 special issue of Time on Cyberspace reported 4.8 million hosts (Elmer-DeWitt, 1995).

Traffic on the NSFnet backbone of the Internet increased 100-fold between 1988 and 1994, and as of 1994, traffic on all federally funded networks and the number of new local and regional networks connecting to them was doubling annually (OSTP, 1994). Of course all of these numbers are estimates, and any of them could be in error. Even allowing for some inaccuracies, however, it seems safe to assume that the community of users of computer networks is growing very rapidly and is likely to continue to do so for the foreseeable future.

China got its first direct link to the Internet in May, 1994; it was used to support 2000 terminals at the Chinese Academy of Sciences and two of its major universities. Two more links were scheduled to be established early in 1995 (Plafker, 1995). These are thought-provoking events both because China is the most populous country on the planet and because, as a society, it has, for a long time, been relatively isolated from much of the rest of the world. One can only guess what the effects will be—on China and the rest of the world—of the international communication that easy access to the global networks would make possible. More generally, what the eventual implications (psychological, social, economic, political) will be of the kind of worldwide connectivity we anticipate is very difficult to say. The one point on which technologists clearly agree is that they are very likely to be profound (Hiltz and Turoff, 1978; Licklider and Vezza, 1978). For HCI, the most obvious implication is that the number and diversity of users of computers is likely to continue to grow rapidly over the period during which this book will serve its audience. And the majority of the vast numbers of new users are likely to be less sophisticated than those of the past, at least for the next several years, if not permanently. The challenge to HCI is apparent.

How long it will take is anybody's guess, but it seems likely that eventually information will be moved around from place to place by an integrated technology that will incorporate the capabilities now provided by the telephone, radio and television, and computer terminals that are linked to networks. With the same device one will be able to send and receive text, voice and video, and to do so to and from other people as well as to and from information resources and services of many types. Ensuring that the functions and interfaces for that system are useful and usable, given the enormous heterogeneity of the user population and its goals, will be a major task for the HCI community.

1.2 Expectations

1.2.1 Basic Technology

Electronic computing and storage devices can be improved beyond present capabilities—in terms of switching speed and storage capacity—before fundamental limits to progress are met. Further increases in speed are being sought through the making of transistors of materials other than silicon, such as gallium arsenide and alloys of silicon and germanium (Meyerson, 1994) as well as through further reductions in scale.

Memory chips with a billion bits of storage capacity and microprocessors capable of performing more than a billion instructions per second are currently being designed. This is a 1000-fold increase over the technology of the early 1980s in both cases (Stix,

1995). The smallest dimensions on the most recent memory chips are about 0.35 micron and are expected to reach 0.2 if not 0.1 micron ("point one") by early in the coming decade. At about .05 microns, dimensions are approaching those of some biological molecules and devices are beginning to be subject to disruptive quantum effects, so miniaturization probably cannot advance much beyond this point without a shift to new principles of operation.

The ability to store very large amounts of information in very small spaces is, of course, already being exploited for the purpose of making information in encyclopedic quantities more readily available to specialists and general consumers alike. *The Journal of the American Chemical Society* was made available on CD ROM in 1994. "The 1994 edition of Microsoft Bookshelf contained on one searchable CD ROM the complete text of the *American Heritage Dictionary*, *Roget's Thesaurus*, the Columbia *Dictionary of Quotations*, the *Concise Columbia Encyclopedia* (15,000 entries and 1,300 images), the *Hammond Intermediate World Atlas* and the *World Almanac and Book of Facts 1994*—not to mention tricky pronunciations of foreign places in digital stereo" (Eisenberg, 1995, p. 104).

One vision of what will be available to the individual computer user by the end of the century or soon thereafter includes a battery operated 1000-by-800-pixel high-contrast display, a fraction of a centimeter thick and weighing about 100 grams, driven by a low-power consumption microprocessor that can execute a billion operations per second and that contains 16 megabytes of primary memory, augmented by matchbook size auxiliary storage devices that hold 60 megabytes each, and larger disk memories with multiple gigabyte or even terabyte capacity (Weiser, 1991).

As this technology based on electronics continues to advance, alternative types of devices are being researched that promise eventually to go beyond what electronics can deliver. Devices that use photonics instead of electronics, for example, have existed in experimental forms for several years and may be available commercially before many more, and ones based on biological molecules may not be too far behind (Birge, 1994, 1995; Horgan and Patton, 1994; Parthenopoulos and Rentzepis, 1989). One implication of these predictions is that HCI design may continue for the foreseeable future to be predicated on successive waves of extraordinary changes in the capacities of the underlying technologies that support our inventions and designs.

Most of the speculation about the nature of human–computer interaction in the future is based on the model of a person using a device that obviously is a computer. Although this model is likely to continue to be appropriate for much of human–computer interaction, at least in the near-term future, it is also certain that in many instances the computers with which people will interact in the future will not resemble computers as we think of them today. They will be invisible—embedded in the woodwork, as it were. As a direct consequence of the spectacular success that designers have had in packaging enormous amounts of computing capability in tiny devices that can be manufactured at very little cost, computational capability is being incorporated not only in "large ticket" items like automobiles and major appliances, but in furniture, games, toys and clothing. This increasing distribution of computing capability is likely to have implications for the study of human–computer interaction that we have not yet imagined.

1.2.2 Software Development

Software continues to be a major challenge. According to Gibbs (1994), underestimation of the difficulty (as measured by time and money) of developing new systems and bringing them to the point of operation is a chronic problem. "Studies have shown that for every six new large-scale software systems that are put into operation, two others are canceled. The average software development project overshoots its schedule by half; larger projects generally do worse" (p. 86). Gibbs describes several very large and highly visible software development projects the costs of which escalated to several times the original estimates before the projects were terminated or forcefully scaled down. Although development managers sometimes believe that adding usability engineering activities and user testing to projects will cost even more, a case can be made that the opposite effect, saving time by simplifying requirements and avoiding costly revisions, is a more common result (see Landauer, 1995, p 320–322)

Programs containing millions of lines of code have become commonplace. Such programs are sufficiently complex that no individual understands them in their entirety. Guaranteeing that they are error-free, or that whatever errors they contain will not lead to catastrophic malfunctions, is very difficult—perhaps impossible. Techniques are needed that will provide reasonable estimates of probabilities of malfunctions and of their likely consequences. Quite good methods exist for estimating interface flaws (Landauer,1995, p 310–313). Research into (programmer-) user-centered methods and tools for *preventing* programming errors is also needed.

Despite the difficulties involved in software development, a lot of useful software is being produced, much of which is readily available to anyone who wishes to acquire it. This is not to suggest that all, or even most of, the software that gets to the commercial market is useful, or that it delivers what its promotional literature claims, but some of it is, and does, and more is being developed all the time. However, as we will elaborate below, the greatest barrier to usefulness has been too little effective attention to how, for what purposes, and with what results the technology is being put to use.

1.2.3 Users and Uses

When computers first appeared on the scene, users were not, for the most part, garden-variety folk. They tended to be technically trained, or at least technically oriented, and to find programming to be an intrinsically interesting activity. Many were willing to invest large amounts of time in learning what was necessary to use these machines and to endure all sorts of inconveniences to get a modicum of the machines' time to execute their programs.

Although computer professionals and hobbyists still form a large segment of the most frequent users of computers and networks, today's computer users include people from all walks of life, many of whom are neither technically trained nor even interested in technology per se. They use computers not for the purpose of developing the technology, but as a means to other ends: document preparation and editing, accounting and bookkeeping, information access, decision aiding, music composition, designing (buildings, industrial equipment, consumer products), and for countless other purposes. People who use computers more or less daily in their work include, sales people, scientists, hotel clerks, engineers, librarians, gas station attendants, secretaries, stock brokers, airline reservation personnel, bankers, physicians, supermarket cashiers, law enforcement officers—it might be easier to list people who do not make use of computers.

Computer technology now pervades the workplace, and its applications here continue to increase rapidly (Sproull and Kiesler, 1991a, b). Many jobs have changed significantly as a consequence of its introduction; some have been transformed beyond recognition. In many cases, the workplace itself has been relocated to the home or, in effect, to wherever one cares to take a portable computer. According to Jaroff (1995), three million employees of American companies were telecommuting, at least part of the time, for purposes of work as of 1995, and this number was increasing by about 20 percent per year. The transient and long-term implications—economic, psychological, social, technical and for HCI—of this change remain to be understood.

Computers are used not only for work, but for avocational and educational purposes, for entertainment, for communication, for personal information management, and, unfortunately, for crime and various types of mayhem as well. Users include very smart people and less smart people, people of all ages, people who are able bodied and people who are disabled in one or another way, people of all ethnic origins and every conceivable political persuasion, urbanites, suburbanites, and people from relatively isolated parts of the world; in short, it is hard to imagine a more heterogeneous community than that constituted by computer users today. Indeed, the user community that has to be considered is already so heterogeneous and expanding so rapidly that, for design purposes, we would not go far wrong in assuming that it includes essentially everyone.

One of the major surprises to follow on the implementation of government and commercial computer networks was the degree to which they were used for purposes of person-to-person communication via electronic mail and associated resources. This was not the use that was intended or expected by the original network implementors; nevertheless within two years of the installation of the ARPAnet, electronic mail was its major source of traffic (Denning, 1989) and, so far as we know, it (along with the closely associated electronic bulletin boards and forums) remains the primary use today, at least if usage is measured in terms of numbers of users or occasions of use, rather than in terms of amount of computing resources—storage and processing cycles—utilized. Whether person-to-person communication will continue to be the most common reason for using computer networks, there can be little doubt that it will remain among the more common uses.

Steinberg (1994) identifies, as the four major uses of the Internet, email, electronic bulletin boards, real-time conversations, and retrieval of information from electronic databases and libraries. Real-time conversations take place within IRCs (Internet Relay Chats) or MUDs (Multi-User Dimensions) which link people who are on line at the same time and, in the case of MUDs, provide them with virtual places or environments (virtual rooms and other imaginary places) that are thematically suited to the real-time interaction that takes place. IRCs and MUDs appear to be used primarily for casual conversation. More generally, Steinberg claims that "most people who inhabit the Net use it chiefly for human-to-human contact, not for gathering information from computer databases" (p. 29). If, as Steinberg surmises, a major reason for this is the fact that information on the net is hard to find, this situation might change with the development of more effective information finding aids, of which programs like Gopher, Archie, Mosaic, Netscape and others may be considered promissory notes awaiting, at least in part, advances based on HCI research and on more attention to user-centered design and evaluation.

In the most recent explosion of network usage, graphic user interfaces (GUIs) and associated search software, formatting, and message-passing standards have spawned an enormous interest in the World Wide Web (WWW), a method for connecting computer networks everywhere. Individuals, institutions and commercial organizations rushed to establish presence on the national and international network scene by creating "home pages" for themselves and stocking them with information and decorations to appeal to others. Network-based ventures such as flower shops, virtual vineyards, movie recommenders, telephone service desks and email order catalogue sales are, as of this writing, sprouting like mushrooms after rain. New interfaces, browsers, search engines and other facilities and accessories are becoming available at a bewildering rate.

The topsy-turvy race to create these new resources is at once impressive and daunting. While there are ever more marvelously large and heterogeneous information sources, services and facilities to choose among, there is an ever more difficult problem of search and choice. This issue of making the networks provide ease and quality to individual users, as compared to sheer quantity of access, may be the single greatest challenge facing HCI in the near future.

1.2.4 Tools and Services

As the users of computers have grown in number and the uses to which computers are put have become increasingly diverse, the number and diversity of tools and services that the industry has to offer have increased apace. All systems and software packages come with users' guides and handbooks; many, if not most, also offer on line instruction and tutorial aids. The usability of this material varies considerably from system to system, but our impression is that it is not easy, as a general rule, to become an adept user of any nontrivial system simply by consulting instructional material, whether packaged in book form or presented interactively on line. The proliferation of third-party how-to books, courses and consulting services to help users of popular applications programs is evidence of this problem. (Perhaps this fact should be taken as a challenge for HCI; after all, "how-to" books are not in great demand for users of telephones, cars, or household appliances.) Learning from experienced users appears to remain a favored and relatively effective approach.

1.2.5 Increasing General Awareness of Information Technology

Human–computer interaction is not a subject that one was likely to have learned anything about through the mass media until very recently. Within the last few years, however, this has begun to change. Significant amounts of space are now being devoted to the topic by major news magazines and periodicals; it is not uncommon for some aspect of the topic to be a cover story, and occasionally it accounts for an entire issue, to wit the Spring, 1995, special issue of Time on Cyberspace. The topic is even receiving explicit recognition in political agendas.

Many terms that would have been considered esoteric technical jargon a short time ago—RAM, modem, cyberspace, email, Internet—have made their way into common usage. Elmer-DeWitt (1995) reported a Nexis search of newspapers, magazines, and television transcripts on the word "cyber" that turned up 167 mentions in January 1993, 464 in January 1994, and 1,205 in January 1995. Daily newspapers now run regular columns providing information and advice to prospective users of the Internet and other computer-based resources.

1.2.6 Information Access and Exchange

The use of computer networks for the dissemination of scientific information has been growing steadily. Research scientists, especially those located at universities, were among the first professionals who, as a group, used computer networks to distribute information on a large scale. Distribution techniques have been informal, for the most part, but today news of major developments in many fields typically is transmitted almost instantaneously to the major players in those fields via networks, and much of the scientific debate that once occurred at a leisurely pace on the pages of conventional journals now takes place at a much accelerated rate in cyberspace long before any of it finds its way into print media.

What this method of information distribution will eventually mean for the traditional peer-reviewed scientific journal remains to be seen. The idea of electronic journals that preserve some of the benefits, such as quality control, of the traditional system, but that greatly increase the speed with which findings become available to the research community and the ease of access to "publications," and that decrease the cost of that access, is receiving increasing attention and experimentation (Taubes, 1996). The 1994 edition of the *Directory of Electronic Journals, Newsletters* and *Academic Discussion Lists* listed 440 such facilities (Stix, 1994). According to a Science article, over 100 peer-reviewed science, technical, and medical journals were available on the Internet by the end of 1995. Increasingly, too, mainstream newspapers, periodicals and popular magazines are making their publications available electronically through CompuServe, Prodigy, WWW, or other information services in increasing numbers.

How are people to cope with the plethora of information riches that technology is beginning to provide, especially in view of the fact that all too often the treasures are completely commingled with an endless mass of infojunk and empty pointers? How will this technology change the role of the library, and of the librarian? What new information brokering services will it spawn? What sorts of new filtering and filing schemes will users need?

In February 1993, the U.S. Government announced a "High Performance Computing and Communications Technology Initiative" intended to be a major force in the development of a new National Information Infrastructure (NII). The vision for the NII is that it "will consist of computers and information appliances (including telephones and video displays), all containing computerized information, linked by high speed telecommunication lines capable of transmitting billions of bits of information in a second (an entire encyclopedia in a few seconds)" (OSTP, 1994, p. 8). The vision includes "[a] nation of users...trained to use this technology" (p. 8). "This infrastructure of 'information superhighways' will revolutionize the way we work, learn, shop, and live, and will provide Americans the information they need, when they need it, and where they need it—whether in the form of text, images, sound, or video. It promises to have an even greater impact than the interstate highways or the telephone system" (p. 8).

Targeted application areas for the HPCC and NII include several "National Challenge" problems, which are "major societal needs that computing and communications technology can help address in key areas such as the civil infrastructure, digital libraries, education and lifelong learning, energy management, the environment, health care, manufacturing processes and products, national security, and public access to government information" (p. 2).

This is a very optimistic vision. We believe that the degree to which it is realized will depend, in no small measure, on the care with which fundamental questions of HCI are addressed. We need to understand much better than we now do about how to ensure that the technology and tools that are developed are both useful—in the sense of meeting human needs—and useable. As a consideration of the question of how information technology has affected productivity to date will show (see below), it is not safe to assume that making powerful technology available guarantees that the anticipated desirable effects will follow.

1.2.7 Summary of Expected Trends

Many of the expected trends for the foreseeable future are continuations of those that have been apparent for some time. With respect to computer hardware, these include continued decreases in component size, power requirements, and unit costs accompanied by further increases in speed, reliability, bandwidth and storage capacity. Computing resources will be increasingly distributed, as will computer-based processes and the control of them. Applications and uses of this technology will continue to multiply and to become evermore diverse.

What is being called the "information age," or the "fifth wave," is expected to be characterized by a decreasing emphasis on heavy industry, mass production, and long-term stability of processes and products and an increasing dependence on flexible small-lot manufacturing, a greater emphasis on services, and growing recognition of information as a major commodity. Television, the telephone, and other communication media are expected to become increasingly integrated with computer network resources. More and more functions are likely to make use of, and become dependent on, information technology. The moving of bits in the form of electrons and photons could replace, to some significant degree, the transporting of people and material, although the extent to which this possibility will be realized will depend on factors other than technical feasibility. For example, will, or under what conditions will, people—basically social creatures—find substitutes for physical togetherness desirable?

There are many questions that are impossible to

answer now regarding how information technology will impact the quality of life in the future. Some of these questions have to do with aspects of work and life that traditionally have been considered within the domain of human factors science and engineering—the designs of the functions and interfaces of the information systems that people will use, the effects of the introduction of new technologies in the workplace on work efficiency and worker satisfaction, the allocation of functions between people and machines. Many involve social, political, legal, or ethical matters that have psychological aspects and represent challenges both to system design and to applied cognitive and behavioral science broadly defined.

1.3 Human–Computer Interaction

1.3.1 A New Area of Research and Engineering

Human–computer interaction did not exist as a field of scientific inquiry or engineering fifty years ago—not surprising given the fact that electronic digital computers hardly existed fifty years ago. In the earliest days of computers, HCI was not a topic of interest, because very few people interacted with computers, and those who did generally were technical specialists. Excepting a few visionary essays, like that of Vannevar Bush (1945), papers on the subject began to appear only in the 1960s. Several seminal articles were written by J. C. R. Licklider (1960, 1965, 1968; Licklider and Clark, 1962) and Douglas Englebart (1962; English, Englebart and Berman, 1967).

Having gotten a start with papers like these, interest in HCI began to grow; as more and more people found themselves using computers for a broadening variety of tasks, the topic soon became an important focus of research. Articles appeared with increasing frequency in *Human Factors*, *Ergonomics*, the *International Journal of Man–Machine Studies*, *IEEE Transactions on Human Factors in Electronics* and elsewhere. The journal *Human–Computer Interaction* was founded in 1985. Other subsequently founded journals that focus primarily if not exclusively on this topic include *Interacting with Computers*, and the *International Journal of Human–Computer Studies*.

HCI has now been, for some years, a major area of research in computer science, human factors, engineering psychology, ergonomics, and closely related disciplines. Annual conferences are devoted exclusively to the topic, articles on it are regularly published in many broad spectrum journals—Baecker and Buxton (1987) estimated that by 1987 over 1,000 papers relevant to the field were being published annually—and it is the special interest of groups within traditional societies and a standard colloquium topic at professional meetings attended not only by computer scientists, human factors specialists and research psychologists, but by anthropologists, physical designers and other specialists as well.

1.3.2 Why Study HCI?

The argument could be made—the argument has been made—that research on HCI is not only unnecessary, but futile. The technology is moving so rapidly, according to this argument, that research has little chance of affecting it. By the time the results of research find their way into peer-reviewed journals, they are no longer of use to system designers. The systems for which that research was relevant are already obsolete. The only approach that will work in such a fast-moving area is a Darwinian one: throw lots of designs into the arena and let competition in the marketplace sort them out.

One need not accept or reject the argument—although we reject it—to note that it assumes that the only reason for doing research on HCI is to influence the design of future systems. We believe that that is one motivation for research in this area, but not the only one. First, we believe research can have its most significant effect on future design not by comparing designs or design elements, but by revealing the aspects of human tasks and activities most in need of augmentation and discovering effective ways to provide it. We believe that such research can be fundamental, and foundational to the synthesis and invention of computer applications that simply would not occur by intuition or trial and error.

Another reason for doing HCI research is to increase our understanding of the technology and its effects, to discover what impact computers (or uses of computers) are having on people's productivity, job satisfaction, communication with other people, and the general quality of their lives. Another is to increase our ability—although this will always be limited—to anticipate, and steer, future developments and effects. We think another important reason for studying HCI is to have some influence not just on the continuing development of the technology—to increase its usefulness and usability—but also, and perhaps more importantly, to help increase the chances that it will be put to uses that are constructive and humane.

What should be the goals of HCI research? We

would like to know what makes systems more of less easy to learn to use, and what makes them more or less effective in the hands of experienced users; we would like to know how they could be more useful to people, more helpful in people's work, and more effective in facilitating their avocational and recreational pursuits. We would like to understand better what effects, good and bad, this technology could have on our lives and on future generations, and what can be done to maximize the desirable effects and minimize the undesirable ones.

It is generally believed that this technology, already powerful, has the potential to change life on the planet profoundly. We need to know how to think about it and its potential effects. We need to know how to relate it, in our reflections and planning, to other major agents of change. We need to understand better its potential implications for world peace, for environmental change, for fighting the age-old problems of disease, poverty, and political repression. We should be concerned too to understand its potential for criminal, antisocial and inhumane applications. Only by understanding the various possibilities can we hope to influence effectively which of them are realized or to what extent.

1.3.3 Productivity

Among the many reasons for studying HCI, a particularly compelling one relates to productivity—a primary concern of any industrialized society, because it is believed to be a major determinant of a country's ability to compete in world markets and of the general standard of living that its citizens can maintain. Technological innovation is considered by many economists to be the most effective means for increasing productivity (Baily and Chakrabarti, 1988; Cyert and Mowery, 1989; Klein, 1988; Mokyr, 1990; Solow, 1959; Young, 1988). Many corporations have made huge investments in information technology on the assumption that such investments would more than pay for themselves by the productivity gains that would result from them. Unfortunately, there is compelling evidence that computer applications have not had the expected general and major beneficial effects on labor productivity.

Bad News

It appears that, despite the enormous gains in hardware power and software versatility, and the widely held belief that computers are very effective productivity tools for business and related applications, the efficiency with which everyday humans perform everyday tasks has not been greatly improved by computer aids. On the contrary, the evidence is that, on average, the effects of computer aids on worker efficiency and economic productivity is relatively slight. A detailed review of a wide spectrum of data that converge on this conclusion has been provided by Landauer (1995, pp. 1–78). We will summarize only a few highlights here.

First, national economic productivity, measured as constant dollars' worth of output per hour of labor expended, has grown less than half as fast since the introduction of widespread computing than in any previous period for which data exist. Dating the widespread use of computers from the mid–1970s, by which time, for example, over 90 percent of banks were using them heavily, by 1995 over $5 trillion had been spent in the United States on computing hardware, software, and support. Meanwhile U. S. productivity grew at a little over 1 percent a year, compared to 2–3 percent annually over the previous century. The same story repeats itself in slightly altered form in all the other major industrialized nations. The picture is darkest in the service industries—banking, insurance, restaurants, transportation…—where most information workers are found. Although it is often argued that the problem is with the measurement of productivity in services, most of the "service" industries involved actually are subject to reasonable measurement, and economists who have studied the situation do not believe that much of the deficit in productivity growth can be accounted for this way. Moreover, productivity in service industries had been increasing steadily by the usual measures before their move into computers as their main capital investment (for a thorough review of this issue, see Landauer, 1995, pp 95–101).

Other data regarding computers and productivity include comparisons among major industrial groups, like banking, insurance, communications, transportation, and retail stores. Those groups that have invested more heavily, that have provided their workers with the greater amounts of information technology, have not fared better, generally speaking, in terms of either productivity as usually measured or business success indexed by return on investment, than have those that did less in this regard. The same holds for particular firms within major industries: firms that computerized vigorously during the 1980s and early 90s showed no better returns, on average, than those that did not. Indeed, with some exceptions, econometric analyses, of which there have been about a dozen, show either slightly negative effects of computerization or very small positive gains. This situation can be compared with similar analyses for investments in buildings and machinery, which, on average, show returns of about 13 percent. Several economists and management experts have commented that most businesses would apparently have been much better off had they been able to invest their capital in bonds at market prices instead of computers (e.g. Baily and Chakrabarti, 1988; Franke, 1987; Loveman, 1990; Strassman, 1990).

But caveats to all this must be stated. Manufacturing was becoming a smaller and smaller part of the advanced economies and service industries a larger part during the period mentioned. Service industries have always had lower productivity than manufacturing, as traditionally measured, and slightly lower productivity growth. Thus, there was no necessary reason why productivity should have continued to grow at historical rates as the mix of industries changed. It could be that computerization has allowed movement into services as manufacturing declined, forestalling an even greater potential stagnation of productivity growth. In short, the fact that productivity has increased at a slower rate since computers became prevalent in the workplace than it did before does not prove that the introduction of computers was the cause of the change; on the other hand, the fact that the increased rate of productivity growth that many industrialists anticipated was not realized challenges the assumption that large expenditures for computing resources are easily justifiable in terms of resulting productivity gains. Of course, there may be other justifications, and there are important psychological and cultural value questions to ask about whether economic productivity is the right or most important goal of progress, matters on which we will comment later.

Whether computers have caused a slowing of productivity growth, or have mitigated what would otherwise have been a worse situation, they have brought no great leap forward in productivity and in standards of living comparable to those caused by previous technological revolutions (which often also accompanied major shifts in economic activity—think of what happened in agriculture) Revolutions that exploited new sources of inanimate power, new mechanical and chemical technologies, new agricultural techniques, and, more recently, technologies for communication and transportation, have had major overall economic consequences. For example, a significant improvement in national productivity can be traced quantitatively to introduction of the electric motor alone (David, 1990). Information technology and computers certainly seem to be just the right technologies to multiply the efficiency of service work, yet it appears that they have not done so.

The most discouraging and, to HCI professionals, challenging, evidence has yet to be mentioned. This is the fact that relatively small gains in individual work efficiency have resulted when people have moved from old ways to new computer-aided ways of doing things. Word processing, for example, is the most widespread use of computers in service industries, with the possible exceptions of point-of-sales transactions and inventory control. Text production work has been studied both in the laboratory and in the field. Generously credited, there is at most a 50 percent increase in the amount of work produced per hour (Landauer, 1995 pp. 50–56). While this may seem a lot, such an efficiency advantage is often not enough to pay for the increased equipment and the organizational and technical support, and educational efforts, required. Moreover, whether it can be considered increased efficiency, in strictly economic terms, is questionable when one takes into account the fact that people who operate word processors are paid at a higher rate than those who simply type.

Many more drafts of a document are likely to be produced with word processing resources than without them, and much more paper is likely to be printed, but evidence of greater quality or markedly quicker end-to-end throughput is missing. There have been several studies of the quality and time taken to compose business letters and student essays with and without word processors (e.g., Card, Robert and Keenan, 1984; Gould, 1981; Vacc, 1991). The box score slightly favors paper and pencil for quality, and shows mixed results for time efficiency depending on user skill and the type of application. Often word-processor technology is used to move document preparation from document specialists—typists, compositors, etc.—to highly paid professionals with lower document preparation skills who would otherwise be more productively employed.

The work aids brought in by other technological and economic revolutions had hugely greater effects. The equipment for spinning thread produced a 30,000 percent (i.e. a 300 to 1 ratio) output-per-labor-hour improvement over a period of approximately the same length of time that computers have been around (Mokyr, 1990). Even since computers have been here, the productivity of textile manufacture has gone up by over 200 percent. Total gains in output per worker hour in agriculture were on the order of 3,000 percent before the computer era and have continued to grow at about the same rate since.

Thus, the size of the work efficiency gains attributable to information technology and computing are tiny compared to those that have been the engine of progress in modern industrialized societies. It takes much more than a 50 percent or even 200 percent gain in individual efficiency to translate into great improvements in overall productivity of a single company, or an industry, or a nation, because individual improvements, which generally apply only to parts of a business, have to be effectively deployed and woven into organizational fabrics (National Research Council, 1994). And gains happen only when technology is actually applied to increase productivity; much computer power, for example, has gone into purely competitive activities, like security market manipulations, complex insurance and investment instruments, and airline seat marketing strategies, that shift business share from one firm to another but do not materially increase total output value.

Good News and Challenge

The challenge to HCI is to help change the bad news to good. Usefulness and usability are where many basic problems lie, and this is the province of HCI. Computers are spectacularly wonderful machines, extraordinarily well suited to being the basis of better tools for intellectual—thus service—work, and for a host of yet-to-be imagined ways to enhance everyday life. We need to find out why they have not been having a greater beneficial impact and how to make them do so.

Landauer (1995) suggests that the root cause of the problem is an inadequate engineering design discipline for applications software. In particular, the usefulness and usability of software have usually not been subjected to the regular and systematic testing of actual utility that underlies improvement in most other technologies. Evaluation has concentrated on the internals of the systems themselves: how fast they calculate, how much data they store, how flawlessly they run, how many features they support, the quality of their graphics, the impressiveness of their tricks. Too often, insufficient attention has been paid to measuring how well and in what ways systems do and do not actually help people get work done. Even when usability evaluation is extensive, it rarely measures or aims directly at improving work efficiency, it is primarily concerned with superficial aspects of ease of use as they will affect sales appeal. Commercial development efforts have almost never compared the efficiency of people using computer methods with those using state-of-the art noncomputer techniques.

The good news is that techniques exist for improving things and using them can and does make a great difference. Gathering together all reports of development projects in which software intended to aid a job has been informatively evaluated, redesigned and tested again, disclosed stunning results. The average gain in the efficiency of work done with the help of a computer system as a result of one short cycle of empirical user-centered design is over 50 percent. Empirical user-centered design means tests with real users doing real work, or some equivalent assessment method that allows observation of what the strength and weaknesses of the technology are for its real users' real purposes (see, e.g. Landauer, 1995 p 221–227; Nielsen 1993 and many chapters in this volume.) From data of experiments by Nielsen (Nielsen and Landauer, 1993), it can further be shown that the benefit-to-cost ratio—where the benefit is for the end users—from such activities is simply enormous, almost always over 20-to-1, and often in the 200-to-1 range. Moreover, to get substantial effects often requires very minor amounts of effort, only days of effort by a few people (Nielsen, 1989). Thus, to put it bluntly, there is a bone-simple way to improve products immensely.

The immediate challenge, then, is to get user-centered design—empirical evaluation and observation and iterative improvement—actually in place so that it can do its job (Nickerson and Pew, 1990). The result could be much more than improvement of individual products. It could also bring us closer to the general principles and methods that could eventually help us to design better in the first place. Bridge designers can do good initial designs from first principles. However, they have learned the engineering science behind their craft largely from analyses of successes and failures over a long period of time. Bridge designers have the advantage of a relatively obvious criterion of success and failure. For mind tools, effective feedback requires special assessment methods and effort. But regular practice of iterative formative evaluation would provide an enormous amount of the needed data. The challenge facing HCI is to be able to use knowledge about actual effectiveness in helping people achieve their goals to make new applications not only novel, exciting, and technically impressive, but useful, usable and socially valuable as well.

We have stressed productivity here, because it is an issue of great concern, and rightly so, we think. In its broadest connotation, increasing productivity means, among other things, getting more out of less—making more efficient use of resources. This seems like something we, as individuals and corporately, should want to do. On the other hand, we think also that this emphasis on productivity needs to be qualified in two ways. How productivity is best measured in a "post-industrial" economy is a persisting and difficult question. Second, we do not mean to argue that increasing productivity should be our only, or even necessarily our major concern. It would be a dubious gain if we managed to get everyone producing more and enjoying life less. Presumably increased productivity is considered a desirable goal because it is assumed to be a way to raise the standard of living—to enhance the quality of life—not only for those people in the segment of an economy whose productivity is at issue but for others as well. It seems a reasonable assumption, but we need to consider the possibility that there are conditions under which it would not be true.

This is a complicated subject and we do not propose to pursue it here, beyond noting that a major determinant of the quality of workers' lives is the satisfaction (or dissatisfaction) they get from their jobs. When productivity is increased at the expense of making jobs less interesting or intrinsically less rewarding, it is not clear that progress has been made. We think that the enhancement of job quality should be a major objective of HCI along with increasing productivity.

More generally, as mentioned earlier, we need to go beyond economic measures of the effects of technological advances to assess their effects on the quality of workers' and consumer's lives and their influences on families, communities and nations. Some research effort has been exerted in this direction, as well as considerable popular speculation. The research literature has tended to be inconclusive (see Attewell and Rule, 1984, for a survey, Kraut, Dumais and Koch, 1989, for an exemplary controlled study), and the opinion expressers fiercely divided (for example compare Clifford Stoll's, Silicon Snake Oil, and the Tofflers' Third Wave). Our own conclusion is that much more thought and research on these matters is needed. HCI researchers and designers have a major role in choosing what results to strive for and to assess. We would not maintain that the economic efficiency gains that have motivated much of the computer revolution are either hopeless or unworthy, but we would urge that other goals—the augmentation of human competence and satisfaction, and of societal harmony—are of at least equal importance.

1.3.4 Increasing Importance of Topic

We believe that, as a research and design activity, HCI will become increasingly important. This belief rests on some of the expectations mentioned above, including a continued decrease in the cost of computing hardware, continued expansion of computer networks and increasing access to them, increasing use of computer technology in the workplace, increasing availability of software that is potentially useful or entertaining for the general consumer, increasing use of computers in education, and a growing assortment of on-line services available through computer networks. The true value of all of this will depend critically on the quality of the interaction of humans with computers.

In short, the size of the population of computer users and the variety of uses to which information technology is put are both likely to grow rapidly for the foreseeable future, as they have been doing in the recent past. The challenges to research and design are many and extraordinarily diverse. Although the topic has already received considerable attention, we believe that the surface of possibilities has hardly been scratched, that many of what will prove to be the most significant challenges have yet to be conceived, and that the field could benefit not only from the articulation of some new questions but from the development of some new approaches to investigation and innovation.

1.4 How to Study HCI?

How can research help to push HCI forward? The literature review cited earlier demonstrated that systems that have the benefit of evaluation and redesign are usually much better than those that do not. It seems clear, then, that some form of research can guide progress. What kinds of research are practicable and effective in this field? The general endeavor is what is usually called applied research, yet there does not appear to be a great deal of relevant basic science ready to be directly applied. Perhaps it is more appropriate to HCI (as to many other fields of invention and design) to speak of "engineering research," meaning investigations into what functions to build for desired effects and how to build them. Among published accounts of successful efforts to improve the objectively measured utility of computer applications, many research methods are described; indeed, unless one classifies the methods quite broadly, no two projects appear to have used exactly the same method. Adopting one such broad categorization, we give the following partial list of techniques that have been involved in significant achievements and that seem to us especially sound and promising.

1.4.1 Task Analysis

Task analysis is a loose collection of formal and informal techniques for finding out what the goals are to which a system is going to be applied, and what role new technology might play in helping to achieve them. The center of attention is not the computer system, but the goals of the activity (business, education, entertainment, social interaction...) that is contemplated. Indeed, the best attitude is to assume that non–computer solutions are at least equally welcome, and to let analysis and imagination roam freely over possible, and maybe even seemingly impossible, approaches.

The first step in task analysis is always to go to the place of work and see what is being done now. Analysts watch people and ask questions, talk some to executives, managers, and marketers, a lot to the people doing the activity. The way work (or play) is actually done is seldom the way it is officially prescribed. Many analysts try to get people to talk aloud as they go about what they are doing. The context brings things to mind that are not thought of or mentioned in an interview. In a technique sometimes called video ethnography, analysts make inconspicuous video tapes that can reveal how work is actually done and how it depends on social norms and processes. Footage of struggling workers can be especially valuable for converting unbelieving executives and designers. Analysts measure how long people spend doing specific tasks and notice what kinds of errors they make. How much time does each subprocess take? What contributes to variability in performance? Are some workers faster than others, some kinds of tasks finished more quickly than others? When speed is a priority, how might slow jobs or slow people be converted into fast jobs and fast people?

1.4.2 Consultation of Potential Users

When it comes to jobs, it is hard to be wiser than the people doing them, perhaps not wise to try. What is sometimes called the "Scandinavian School" of system design prescribes going out into the work environment in which a system is to be used and bringing users into the process at every step. The emphasis is on personal, social and organizational factors in the introduction and use of new technology. While one might not ordinarily think of such activities as research, in the HCI context they are. Traditionally, computer applications have been largely, sometimes entirely, technology driven. Seeking knowledge about desirable characteristics of systems from a source other than the technically sophisticated but application-naive developer's perspective is thus an important kind of research. Often the naturalistic data that can be acquired from workers simply by asking is sufficiently precise and reliable for the purpose at hand. Improving understanding of the organizational, social and motivational milieu in and for which an information system is to work is one such purpose.

A caveat is necessary with respect to both task analysis and user consultation. The introduction of information technology in the workplace often changes the nature of the jobs that are performed in unanticipated ways. Although the intent may be to increase the effectiveness with which one can perform a particular task, the result may be to modify, perhaps profoundly, the tasks that the worker will perform and the interpersonal, social and business processes of which it is part. Analysis of an existing task may fail to provide a clue to the transformation that the new technology will effect, and neither workers nor managers may be able to imagine the ways in which activities and relationships will change before they have had any experience using that technology. What this suggests is that task analysis and user consultation should be thought of, not as activities that are carried out once at the beginning of a design project, but as dynamic processes that must be ongoing, in one or another guise, over the entire course of the design and development effort and over the life of the system's deployment. This is part of what the notion of "iterative design" involves.

1.4.3 Formative Design Evaluation

The term "formative evaluation" originated in the development of instructional methods, where it is contrasted with "summative evaluation." Formative evaluation is used to guide changes, summative to determine how good something is. Unfortunately, in the past most usability testing for computer systems has been merely summative, and rarely produced useful design guidance or generally applicable principles. The idea of formative evaluation is not to just decide which is better, A or B, but to learn what does and does not work and why.

The need for formative, as opposed to summative, evaluation in computer system development has been recognized by many writers (Carroll and Rosson, 1984; Eason, 1982; Gould, Boies and Lewis, 1991; Sheil, 1983), and it stems from the fact that computer systems and user interfaces are compounded of myriad interacting details any one of which can potentially defeat or enhance usability and utility, while few of their effects can be reliably anticipated, and also, in part, from the fact, just mentioned, that new technology can change tasks in unanticipated ways. The idea that both exploration and evaluation need to occur more or less in parallel throughout the development process is reflected in the notion of "guided evolution" (Nickerson, 1986).

1.4.4 The Gold Standard: User Testing

Only if we study real workers doing real jobs in real environments, can we be sure that what we learn is truly relevant to design. User testing tries to get as close to this ideal as is practical by testing people like those for whom the system is intended with tasks like those they will most often do, using a mock-up, a "Wizard-of-Oz" simulation in which a human plays the role of system, or a prototype or early version, either in situ or in a laboratory setting that is similar to the intended office, home or other place of use. Experience suggests that such compromises are usually, if not always, good enough. Information gained from user tests has been the most frequent source of major usability improvements. User testing is straightforward. Users try, the tester watches, notes errors, times tasks, later asks questions. Many practitioners urge the users to talk aloud as they work. Some make videotapes to review and analyze in detail, although there is debate about the cost-effectiveness of this time-consuming process. On initial design, the average interface has 40 unsuspected but identifiable flaws. Testing two trial users on average reveals half of the flaws, tests with four users reveal three-quarters, and so forth (Nielsen and Landauer, 1993). Most of the flaws are fixable, and observing the test users often leads to creative insights that feed innovation.

1.4.5 Performance Analysis

The goal of performance analysis is deeper understanding on which to base innovation and initial design rather than assessment and improvement of existing designs. Broadly speaking, performance analysis studies people doing information-processing tasks in an attempt to understand what they can do well and what they typically do poorly, where help is needed and, if possible, how that help might best be provided. Performance analysis is done either in the laboratory with somewhat abstracted tasks, such as suggesting titles or key words for information objects, or with an existing technology for the performance of some real job. Performance analysis, when successful, leads to the identification of a human performance limitation that a computer can ameliorate. Computers are sufficiently powerful and flexible that finding the right problem is often harder than finding its solution. The unlimited aliasing technique described by Furnas, Landauer, Gomez, and Dumais (1987) illustrates the point. Once it had been discovered that people typically refer to "information objects" such as files, records and commands, by many more names than systems usually recognize, providing an effective solution—many more "aliases"— was straightforward.

Performance analysis pays special attention to time, errors, and individual differences, all of which can provide important clues to deficiencies in present technologies and processes and opportunities for improvement. In computer-based tasks, mistakes often lead to extreme difficulties that are very costly in user time, lost work, propagated erroneous information or irretrievable records. Computers also often greatly amplify the differences in efficiency between different people (Egan, 1988.) Studying the sources of errors and the abilities that are demanded can lead to insights on which HCI progress can be based.

1.4.6 Science

It is tempting to think that fundamental research in psychology might provide the basis for improving HCI. To some extent it can and already has, and one hopes that eventually it will do more. But we believe the extent of direct help is modest at the present time. Psychology has provided some real advances in understanding human behavior, but only in limited domains, usually represented by relatively narrow problems that have been brought to the laboratory. A few well established fundamental principles speak to system design: the Hick–Hyman law, according to which decision time is proportional to the log of the number of equal alternatives, implies that a single screen with many choices is better than a series of screens with a few choices each (Landauer and Nachbar, 1985); Fitts' law, which tells how long it takes to point to an object depending on how large and far away it is, helps in designing pointing devices and laying out mouse targets on a screen; the power law of practice, which tells how response speed increases over time, can sometimes predict how well experts with a new system will perform relative to those using an old system; the facts of working memory limitations suggest that users should have to keep very few new, unorganized, pieces of information in mind at once; human factors principles and tables for color combinations and font size/distance requirements help designers avoid suboptimal displays; and there are more examples. A noteworthy effort to apply the results of basic research in the HCI domain is the work of Card, Moran and Newell (1983).

A fairly representative example of both the success and limitations of basic science in HCI can be found in early efforts to provide underpinnings for the design of command languages. Are "natural" words and syntax an advantage? Experiments found that for small systems, say a basic text editor, the choice of words , e.g. using "allege," "cipher" and "deliberate" instead of "omit," "add" and "change" was inconsequential (Landauer, Egan, Remde, Lesk, Lochbaum, and Ketchum, 1993; Landauer, Galotti and Hartwell, 1983.) Using "normal" English word order sometimes made some difference, but not a great deal. Using a consistent word order—verb before object, for example—sometimes was helpful, but not universally so (Barnard and Grudin, 1988; Barnard, Hammond, Morton, Long, and Clark, 1981.) The user–language research with the best payoff was on how to construct abbreviations; it turned out that using a consistent rule was more important than what rule was used (Streeter, Acroff, and Taylor, 1983).

These and other examples show that research aimed at better understanding of the cognitive underpinnings of the use of information systems can pay off. However, it will take time, and much greater volume than the current trickle, to make a major contribution. We believe there is much to be gained by applied research aimed more specifically at developing a better understanding of the complex dynamics of interactions between human intellects and powerful information-processing computers, inasmuch as it is just these highly complicated and nonlinear characteristics of HCI that it is most important to accommodate in system design. In the short term, we are more optimistic about the opportunities for direct engineering research than about the promise of new basic research creating a significantly useful applied science of HCI. On the other hand, we recognize that research that is focused narrowly on the details of a specific system's design may lack generalizability. There is a happy medium: research that is addressed to specific aspects of HCI but that is sufficiently generally conceived to have applicability across many systems, and that is done within the conceptual framework of some psychological theory so that it can have theoretical import as well.

Before leaving this topic, it is important to note that the domain of HCI has sometimes provided a fertile ground for the elaboration and testing of cognitive theories, a development in the opposite direction from "applied science" as usually conceived, but a direction that is not unusual in science and technology (Kuhn, 1977; Mokyr, 1990). Good examples include the work of Card, Moran and Newell cited earlier, that of Polson and Keiras (1985) on production system models of problem solving and transfer, and of Singley and Anderson (1989) and Pennington and her colleagues (Pennington, Nicholich and Rahm, 1995) on transfer. Another recent example is the progression from the studies and innovations in information retrieval methods at Bellcore to a new model of human word learning and memory representation (Landauer and Dumais, 1996).

1.5 Some Specific, and Some Broader Issues

The psychological and social aspects of HCI are many and diverse. Questions of interest run the gamut from those pertaining to the layout of keyboards and the design of type fonts, to the nature of effective navigation aids and information displays, to the configuration of virtual workspaces that are to be shared by geographically dispersed members of a work team. They involve the effects that computer systems can have on their users, on work, on business processes, on furniture and building design, on interpersonal communication, on society and social processes, and on the quality of life in general. Some research is motivated by an interest in making computer-based systems easier to use and in increasing their effectiveness as tools; some is driven by a desire to understand the role, or roles, this technology is likely to play in shaping our lives. Here we can do no more than comment briefly on some of the specific issues we think will be among those most important to consider for workers in human–computer interaction in the near-term future.

1.5.1 Equity

The question of equity in relation to computer technology takes many forms. Much of the discussion of the question has focused on economic aspects of the issue. Will computer technology be differentially available to the haves and the have-nots, where this distinction sometimes pertains to individuals and sometimes to nations? Will the increasing globalization of network facilities give third-world scientists greater access to the rest of the scientific world, or will it increase the isolation of those in countries lacking the communications infrastructure on which ready access to the Internet depends (Gibbs, 1995)?

Questions of these sorts have been of concern for

some time, but they have not been a burning issue. As long as the large majority of people did not have computers and ownership of them was not considered to be especially beneficial, the nature of the concern was the possibility that a small minority of people had some advantage over the majority and the likelihood that that small minority did not include a proportionate share of low income people or other disadvantaged groups. The concern is likely to increase considerably as more and more of the people who can afford to purchase computers do so and the use of these machines plays increasingly significant roles in their daily lives. If access to computers and computer-based resources becomes a critical determinant of how effectively one can function in society, as it seems almost certain to do, the question of equity will become a very serious one indeed. In the U.S. the disparity in computer ownership and use between the richest and poorest quarters of the population was almost eight to one in 1993, and had grown in the previous five years. Differences between urban and rural dwellers, those over 60 or below, and those with or without high-school educations, and of differing ethnic or racial origins were less pronounced, although still large, and had also grown (Anderson, Bikson, Law, and Mitchell, 1995).

There is another sense in which equity is an issue, that has not received much attention, and this is the question of the possibility that computer technology will differentially benefit the can-dos and cannots. "Cannots" in this context refers to individuals who, perhaps because of lack of training or limitations of ability, are not able to make effective use of a computer system even if one is available. Will this technology tend to be an equalizer or to amplify differences in knowledge and ability? Maybe it will create new opportunities for everybody, in principle, but will also, in practice, give an enormous advantage to those who are capable of making the most of those opportunities. If this is what it does, is that bad? How one answers this question is likely to depend on one's system of values and one's concept of justice. But we suspect that most people would agree that one worthy goal would be to find ways to ensure the usefulness of computer technology to people who have to cope with one or another type of disadvantage or disability.

1.5.2 Security

Schiller (1994) points out that much of what eventually became the Internet was designed with only trustworthy users in mind and that, consequently, privacy-invading intrusions on network communications and resources are not difficult. As the numbers of individuals and institutions using network facilities to work with and transmit sensitive information have steadily increased, efforts to develop measures to ensure security have increased apace. Encryption techniques are now commonly used for data transmission, and safeguards have been implemented to restrict access to private files. None of the approaches that have been developed is foolproof in all respects, however, and it seems unlikely that any of those that will be implemented soon will be. The possibility of unauthorized access to information residing in a computer that is connected to a network will remain a fact of life for the foreseeable future.

Much of the current debate about security and what should be done about it focuses on the question of what constitutes an acceptable compromise between security and freedom of access (Germain, 1995). Ideally, one wants to maximize freedom of access by legitimate users of systems and databases while making access by intruders impossible, but the two goals may not be simultaneously realizable. To prevent access by intruders, or even to impede such access significantly, it may be necessary to inconvenience legitimate users to some extent as well; assuming this to be the case, the question is how to make this tradeoff in an acceptable way.

Impersonation and forgery are special problems for electronic mail. As Wallich (1994) puts it, "virtually no one receiving a message over the net can be sure it came from the ostensible sender" (p. 91). "A message from 'president@whitehouse.gov' could as easily originate from a workstation in Amsterdam as from the Executive Office Building in Washington, DC" (p. 99). Technologists are keen on finding a solution to this problem that does not impede freedom of access to the net.

1.5.3 Function Allocation

There are many issues relating to the question of who (or what) is to do what in a system that includes both humans and computers. At one time it was fashionable to construct lists showing which functions could be performed better by people and which could be done better by computers. This is a somewhat risky venture, however, because the capabilities of computers have been changing fairly rapidly, whereas those of human being are little, if any, different from what they were 50 years ago.

As it happens, many functions can be performed either by people or by computers; more specifically, the list of things that people can do and computers cannot has been growing smaller over time and is likely to continue doing so. This does not mean that people are going to have less and less to do; that would be the case only on the assumption that if a computer can be made to perform some function, it *ought* to be given that function to perform.

We believe that the question of what tasks should be assigned to computers is of fundamental importance and that it will be the subject of debate more and more as the capabilities of computers continue to expand. The basis on which the decision should be made will itself be a matter on which opinions are likely to diverge; what is clear is that whether or not a function is within a computer's capability is only one of the factors that will figure in the debate. What functions do we want computers to perform? What do we want them to do with our help or guidance? What do we want them to help us do? And what do we want to do without their involvement? What do we want to be made easy for us, and how easy, and what do we want to remain a challenge to special skills that grant satisfaction in their execution in part because of their difficulty; we think of such skills as musical performance, art and chess? Such questions can only grow in importance as the technology and the potential it represents continue to advance.

1.5.4 Effects and Impact

We have already noted that companies have spent a great deal of money to acquire large amounts of computing power in the expectation of realizing cost-cutting efficiencies and increases in productivity, and that evidence that the expected benefits have been realized is at best equivocal. One hypothesized reason for the failure of corporate investments in computing resources to have yielded the expected returns is mismanagement, and, in particular, the tendency by managers to acquire much more computer power than their companies know how to use effectively (Leutwyler, 1994). However, we believe that even more important is lack of usefulness and usability, caused by failures to evaluate and design systems well enough to produce their intended effects of enhancing the ease, efficiency and waste-free coordination with which work is accomplished by individuals and organizations (Landauer, 1995).

The issue of productivity aside, there can be little doubt that the introduction of computer technology in the workplace has changed the nature of many jobs, including many that have—or had—little if anything to do with technology. At least as important as the question of the effect of these changes on productivity is that of the effect the new technology has on people's satisfaction with their work. Given that work is not only a means of making a living, but an important part of living, it should be intrinsically satisfying, and we need to know much more about whether and how technologically driven changes in work tend to make it more so or less.

An area of application of information technology that many have long believed to have great potential, but that has not had the expected impact to date, is education. Many believe the potential is still there and even increasing as the technology continues to advance (Nickerson and Zodhiates, 1988; Tinker and Kapisovsky, 1992), and examples of what can be accomplished have been reported (Bruce and Rubin, 1993; Lajoie and Derry, 1993; Larkin and Chabay, 1992; Perkins, Schwartz, West, and Wiske, 1995; Psotka, Massey, and Mutter, 1988; Ruopp, Gal, Drayton, and Pfister, 1993). The success of efforts to apply information technology to education is likely to depend on a variety of factors, not all technological, but the extent to which systems intended for use by students and teachers are well designed from an HCI perspective must be among the more important of them.

As we have already noted, information technology is a resource of enormous potential for constructive and destructive uses alike. The same technology that can bring us unprecedented access to information, educational resources of many types, greater participation in debate about issues of local, national, or international interest and policy, aids to creative pursuits, personal contact with people around the world...has also the potential to bring us electronic surveillance, privacy invasion on a grand scale, crime and mayhem of epic proportions, degrading and exploitive forms of entertainment.... But all technologies can be used for bad purposes as well as good, and the more powerful the technology, the greater its potential for good and bad alike. It is a continuing challenge to people of good will to ensure that the good uses of information technology exceed the bad by a large margin.

Perhaps even more challenging than the problem of limiting the technology's "affordances" to people who intend to use it to work mischief is that of trying to anticipate and avoid undesirable effects that no one intends. This requires giving some thought to what the effects of various developments could be, and perhaps challenging assumptions that are sometimes made uncritically to justify moving the technology in one or another direction or using it in one or another way.

What, for example, will be the effect of efforts to engage the entire citizenry of a country in decision making on national policy issues through instant polling and electronically conducted referenda? Will government be more immediately responsive to the will of the people if democracy is made more participatory, or is it the case, as Ted Koppel (1994) has argued, that "nothing would have a more paralyzing impact on representational government?" Will interactive advertising help people make better informed purchasing decisions, or will it increase the ease with which advertisers can convince people to buy what they neither need nor really want? Might information technology make people become more isolated? Less likely to come into face-to-face contact? How fully can remote contact satisfy social and psychological needs?

Such questions, of which a very large set could be generated, are difficult, perhaps impossible, to answer in the abstract. It is possible, however, to collect data on effects as systems begin to be used for various purposes and thereby to gain some fact-based understanding of what the effects of specific uses are. This understanding should help guide further developments.

1.5.5 Users' Conceptions of the Systems They Use

Users develop mental models of the systems they use. These models may be consistent with reality to greater or lesser degrees. A common reaction of people interacting with systems that display some modicum of cleverness is to impute to these systems more capability or intelligence than they have. Observations of users of Weizenbaum's ELIZA (1966), a rather crude simulation of an interacting human by today's standards, revealed this tendency in sometimes unsettling ways. The complexity and richness of the world of information resources that is approachable from computer terminals today will support the development of very fanciful models of what lies at the other end of the wire. Models that fail to correspond very closely to reality may or may not cause difficulties of various types. It would be good to understand better the factors that determine what types of models users develop and how to facilitate the development of adequately accurate and useful ones. How one conceptualizes the world of information to which the technology provides access may determine how effectively one is able to navigate in that world; conversely, the types of navigation aids that are provided for users will undoubtedly influence the mental models they develop.

1.5.6 Usefulness and Usability

Usefulness and usability are the twin goals of HCI research and development. First and foremost a system must do something that is helpful or pleasing. Although it may bring sales success, in the long-run it is not enough that a system does something that is novel, clever or impressive; what it does should provide significant advantage over what we had before. The challenge of design for usefulness starts with understanding what people need, what they would like to do that they find difficult, and proceeds to finding ways to make the impossible possible, the difficult easy, the slow fast. How to take an individual or family, at their convenience, from home to workplace, relative's house or distant vacation land was the usefulness challenge of transportation. It was answered by the invention of trains, autos and airplanes. What do people want to do or do better, and how can computers help them satisfy this desire; these are the pressing questions.

Usability is the next issue. Once we have identified a useful function and learned how to provide it, we must find a way to make its operation easy to invoke and control and its output easy to understand, verify and alter; in short to make the computer's interaction with its human master serve the master rather than the slave. By now there has been enough experience in the design of interfaces and interactive processes to ensure the availability of scores of effective devices and techniques and of considerable expert judgment and creativity. Nevertheless, the complexity of humans and computers and their joint behaviors, depending as they do on natural cognitive processes in the one and artificial ones in the other, insures that first-try drawing-board solutions will rarely be good enough. Many approaches to the complexity of HCI design have been taken, and many are described in this handbook. They range from theory and modeling of thought and action sequences to methods for simulating human–computer transaction protocols and their outcomes. Progress and successes have come from such efforts, and more are to be expected. Still, at the end of the day, system designs, like bridge designs, must be tested and revised both early and often to assure usability. Among the techniques to achieve usability the most useful and promising are methods to simplify, speed and increase the accuracy of the iterative test-and-fix cycle, and ways to make test findings more helpful for future design.

It is clear that usefulness and usability are closely related, that it is hard to have one without the other. To be sure, extremely useful machines—we think of jet liners and backhoes—may justify long years of training of skilled operators, and there is a necessary tradeoff between utility and complexity. But as a general rule, making a tool easier to use will, *ipso facto*, make it more useful. And, given the rapidity with which computer applications multiply and change, thereby limiting the time available for learning, trying hard to maximize usability is not a luxury but a necessity.

Still, usefulness and usability, essential as they are, and even when synergistically combined, are not quite the whole story. Systems must be desirable as well. A technology will be of little benefit if few use it. Word processors were at first used to centralize document preparation. As a result secretaries lost their knowledge of office context and jargon, and could not fix problems by conversations with the authors of the documents on which they were working. Consequently, word-processing centers lost their popularity (Johnson and Rice, 1987).

A desirability failure that degrades the user's life is especially serious. Centralized word processing in businesses often has this unwelcome effect as well. Typists and their supervisors usually intensely dislike this style of work, its social isolation from the life of the office, its artificial work-flow control procedures, its separation from the real consumer. High on the list of issues to be addressed by HCI efforts should be that of making system design intentionally and systematically improve the lives of individuals and the functioning of the groups to which they belong.

1.5.7 Interface Design

Displays

One aspect of hardware the future progress of which is particularly important to HCI is displays. Computer screens in popular use offer a much smaller viewing and interaction space than does paper and print technology. Although computers can partially compensate for this disadvantage by serial presentation of text and graphics in multiple overlapping windows, and by provision of dynamic displays not possible in print, they do not exploit very well the human's wide field of vision and action in space.

Thus, many desks that hold computers are still littered with paper, books and notes, and users have difficulty maintaining perceptual, memory and attentive continuity between components of complex tasks on the screen, e.g., the relation between entries in multiple spreadsheet pages or reference, text, footnotes and figures for a document. A back-of-envelope calculation suggests that a viewing space roughly four to six times that of current one-page screens would be desirable, if not optimal, because it would accommodate most of the space in which text can be read conveniently by moving just the head and eyes.

Display resolution is also still suboptimal. At normal reading distance, the human visual system can usefully resolve detail of about an order-of-magnitude greater density than current displays provide. More research is needed into the parameters of size and resolution for visual displays that are required to optimize computer-aided human performance.

Visual displays have been the predominant means of communicating from computer to user in the past and are likely to continue to be so for the foreseeable future, if not indefinitely. This should not obscure the fact, however, that the possibilities for communicating via other modalities—especially hearing and touch—have hardly begun to be realized.

Input Devices

Keyboards and mice now provide the means for almost all input. Despite great optimism over many years, effective technology for general-purpose speech and handwriting input remains elusive. Some observers question the desirability of these modes for many purposes. Speech is frequently imprecise and can be hard to edit. After learning to type, many people prefer keyboarding to (the originally even harder-to-learn method of) handwriting or dictation.

The question of which input modes are best for what tasks and which people is another issue much in need of research. One would not want to control a violin or a car by either typing or speech. What about all the other jobs in which a computer might eventually intercede between people and their work? Speech has been of great interest as a possible input mode for a long time. Progress, from some perspectives, has been slow; but the problems have been very difficult, and, although they need not all be completely solved before the technology can be applied effectively, sufficient progress must be made to get them over the threshold of usefulness. Speech recognition systems with limited ability are now on the market, and the technology is improving. How effective speech will be as an input mode, and under what circumstances it will be preferred to other possibilities, if and when the technology becomes sufficiently robust to support extensive use, remain to be seen. Much will depend on the degree to which the introduction of speech is guided by careful studies of users' needs and preferences.

Work on other modes—use of pointing devices other than the mouse, grasping of virtual objects, eye-fixation tracking—continues apace. A more mundane concern, but one of immediate practical interest is the need for a solution to the conflicting demands of mouse and keyboard.

Intelligent Interfaces

The development of intelligent system interfaces is part of the plan of the U. S. government's 1993 High Performance Computing and Communications (HPCC) initiative. "In the future, high level user interfaces will bridge the gap between users and the NII. A large collection of advanced human/machine interfaces must be developed to satisfy the vast range of preferences, abilities, and disabilities that affect how users interact with the NII. Intelligent interfaces will include elements of computer vision and image understanding; understanding of language, speech, handwriting, and printed text; knowledge-based processing; and multimedia computing and visualization. To enhance their functionality and ease of use, interfaces will access models of both the underlying infrastructures and the users" (OSTP, 1994, p. 52). The interest in variety in interfaces stems, one assumes, from the intention that the NII be a resource that is available to, and approachable by, essentially the entire population.

1.5.8 Augmentation

Among the possibilities for more fundamental and dramatic advances we find the prospect of new tools to augment human intellectual and creative processes especially exciting. Consider three examples: math, writing, and art and music.

Math

Tools for mathematical problem solving are of two kinds: those that facilitate the application of mathematical principles and methods, as appropriate, to the problems to be solved, and mechanical aids to computation. Problems can be difficult either for conceptual reasons or because of computational demands, or because of the way the two types of factors are intertwined. Suppose you want to solve a compound-interest problem; specifically, you want to know the monthly payments on a $112,000 30-year mortgage at 7.25 percent. There is a conceptually simple method for working the problem with pencil and paper: propose a trial monthly payment, calculate the interest for the first month, subtract it from the monthly payment and the result from the outstanding balance, and repeat the process for 360 payments, when you will find the error in your trial payment. Then pick a new payment value that will make a change in the right direction, say by splitting the difference between bracketing errors, until you get it right. Although this method is correct and foolproof, it obviously is very tedious and the mechanics are highly error prone.

Calculus provides a much less computationally intensive method for solving such problems, but the conceptually difficult principles of calculus elude the majority of people who pay mortgages (even if they have learned them in high school and applied them to just such problems). So they are left without a usable intellectual tool.

It seems at least plausible that most people would find the iterative trial and error method easier to grasp and apply because the correspondence between the problem and the solution method is more direct (see Nathan, Kintsch, and Young, 1992). It turns out that most spreadsheet programs contain methods to set up and execute iterative hill climbing methods and compute the answers quickly and accurately. Suppose high school students were taught these methods, and the HCI of the spreadsheet methods were improved, might this, perhaps, cause a leap forward in the practical intellectual competence of the average person, just as the provision of calculators can enhance the ability of people to do arithmetic?

We should note too that computers are being used by mathematicians today in the doing of pure, as well as applied, mathematics (Appel and Haken, 1977). Software now exists that can facilitate the doing of mathematics by mathematicians at all levels of competence, and some of it has the potential to be very useful in the teaching and learning of mathematics as well.

Writing

Currently available computer tools for writing augment primarily the superficial mechanics of a creative process performed as always; they help with typographic editing, formatting and layout of documents, facilitate the organization, alphabetization and formatting of footnotes and references, give some assistance with spelling and a little with vocabulary and grammar. The more important aspects of composition and expression—generating information and ideas, creating clear and compelling arguments, composing efficient and effective narrative, or evocative and beautiful description, and ensuring discursive coherence and grace—are almost untouched.

There are promising avenues to be pursued in all these directions. Computer systems could help to find examples to quote, paraphrase or be inspired by, provide word and expression-finding aids more advanced than simple synonym lists and thesauri (e.g. type or mouse-select a phrase and get back words with related meanings and paragraphs from great literature or sections from textbooks or encyclopedias), evaluate and suggest improvements in coherence.

Art and Music

Most children love to draw until they "find out" that they are not good at it. Many adults like to invent tunes, so long as there is no danger of anyone else hearing them. Computer-aided tools for drawing, composition and performance are available that can be effective in the hands of experts (the first fully animated film, Toy Story, required years of effort by expert programmers and artists as well as enormous computing power and software sophistication); but the facilities currently available to the average computer owner are still crude toys, offering primarily mechanics for doing art or music in ways that mimic how it is done without the computer's help. New methods of creation and composition are needed that can make it easier for the average person to take advantage of new computer-based execution to produce things of satisfying originality and beauty.

So far, art creation systems have received very little user-centered design attention, almost no systematic analysis of what it is that ordinary people would want to do, find too hard to lead to satisfaction, and what would help them. When it has happened, we might, should we want to, all be able to draw lifelike portraits of our loved ones, animations and cartoons of our pets, produce good quality home movies, compose songs, set them to music and sing or play them with feeling and vivacity. We believe that the primary impediment to the realization of this vision is not technological limitations but a lack of understanding of users' needs and preferences with respect to artistic expression, and of the ways in which the technology presents the potential to meet them—e.g. to what extent it is good to make things easy, where does the optimum lie, for different folk, between a better color pallette and "paint-by-numbers?"

What will deeper HCI advances require? A primary need is the invention of new functions based on effective analyses of the cognitive processes involved in doing math, writing, and creating art, analyses that would reveal which parts of what processes are difficult and which are easy, which are desirable to make easier—or, perhaps more difficult—for whom and when, what alternative techniques could be enabled with new computer-aided mechanics and tools. Second, newly invented "cognitive tools" need to be implemented and then subjected to authentic formative evaluation involving actual trials with real people doing real work or play, trials from which what works and gratifies and what does not can be determined, and from which insights for better ideas can be gleaned.

The goal of all this, the hope for the future, is for computer systems to make it possible for ordinary people to perform intellectual and creative tasks at a markedly higher level than they can now, and the reason for that is to provide, through the interactive possibilities of computer mediation and augmentation, not only more effective and productive work tools, but, equally important, more active and productive avocational and recreational activities, activities that are at once more fulfilling and more growth-enhancing than the passive entertainment of television or the superficial excitement of current computer games.

The resources that already are available to the user of the Internet can represent a bewildering plethora of possibilities. To exploit the opportunities that are there, users, especially new users, need help. Steinberg (1994) identifies several tools that have been developed to help users find their way around the Internet and provides instructions as to how to avail oneself of each of them. The tool mix is changing rapidly, however, and we can expect it to continue to do so for the foreseeable future. As of this writing, nothing has become adopted by a sufficiently large segment of the user community to be considered an industry standard. Studies aimed at determining the kinds of help that users most need can contribute useful information to the process, as can studies of the tools that have been developed and efforts to discover ways that their effectiveness can be improved.

1.5.9 Information Finding, Use, and Management

Finding information is a generic problem that we all face, more or less constantly. One wants to discover what job opportunities exist for a specific vocation in a given geographical area, what houses are available for purchase in a particular town and within a specific price range, what universities have first-rate programs in applied mathematics, what is known about a new medication that one has been advised to try to combat a stubborn allergy.... At a more day-to-day level, one might want to know what specials the local supermarket is running this week, where to find a replacement for a worn-out part to a household appliance, how to fix a leaky faucet....

When information of the type that people often want is stored electronically, what is needed are effective search programs that can quickly find within the electronic databases just the information one seeks. This is a difficult problem in part because distinguishing between what is within the category of interest and what is not is typically a nontrivial task to automate. However, systems and tools that succeed in making it much easier for people to find the kinds of information that they often spend significant amounts of time seeking are clearly desirable objectives for research and development.

Harnad (1990) has noted the capability that electronic mail provides for researchers to distribute findings or prepublication drafts of scientific articles to individuals, groups, or even an entire discipline for comment and interactive feedback, and has referred to this medium as "scholarly sky writing." In Harnad's view, "sky writing offers the possibility of accelerating scholarly communication to something closer to the speed of thought while adding a globally active dimension that makes the medium radically different from any other" (p. 344). Levinson (1988) sees teleconferencing technology enabling what he refers to as "the globalization of intellectual circles." The idea of such circles is contrasted with Marshall McLuhan's "global village," the inhabitants of which receive common information from television but usually are not able to create or exchange it. "The computer conferencing network establishes on a geographically irrelevant basis the possibilities for reception and initiation and exchange of information that heretofore have existed only in in-person, localized situations. The result is that members of these electronic communities know each other much as members of a real-life local intellectual community such as a university do, but as members of a global television audience do not" (p. 205).

Complementary to the idea of sky writing is that of casting "does anybody know ..." questions on a network. Electronic bulletin board readers find such questions on many subjects addressed to the community at large in the hope that someone will have an answer and be willing to share it. One small study of the use of a corporate electronic bulletin board found that roughly one-quarter of 1000 messages posted during a 38-day period were either requests for information or posted replies to those requests (Nickerson, 1994). (Replies that went directly to the requestors instead of being posted on the bulletin board were not counted.) Requests for information covered a wide range of topics: Where can I rent a hall for a wedding reception? Find costumes for a masquerade party? Buy firewood? How do I send a message to a particular network host? Supplement heat from an oil furnace in an old drafty house? Convert home movies to VCR tape? Who can recommend an agent/company from whom to obtain an automobile/homeowner's insurance policy? How does one initiate a small claims court case? Please recommend hotels, inns, B&Bs, campgrounds, hiking trails, . . , in New England, in Montreal, in Oaxaca. What are some good hiking possibilities within one-and-one-half hours of Boston, not more than five hours up and down, and not mobbed? What is the origin of the Olympic torch?

This study focused on the bulletin board used primarily—though not exclusively—by the employees of a single technology-oriented company of modest size. When casting "Does anybody know ...?" questions on a large network, it probably makes sense to post them on specific bulletin boards whose communities of readers would be considered most likely to include some who knew the answers. There are many anecdotal reports of people who do just this and often to good effect. The Internet provides users with access to Usenet, which can be thought of as a collection of special-interest bulletin boards or discussion groups. As of 1994, Usenet was posting about 40,000 messages a day (Steinberg, 1994).

Although there are many tools and resources that can help one find information through the Internet—directories, bulletin boards, World Wide Web searchers—learning how to use these resources effectively can be a nontrivial task. There are many instruction and reference manuals that provide useful guidance both to the beginner and to the occasional user, but real expertise is acquired only through experience. Useful advice and guidance can be gained from other more experienced users on line; the casting of "does anybody know ..." questions can be productive in this regard.

An expected effect of the continuing development of information technology is much greater availability of information to the average person. We assume that this is a good and desirable thing. But this benefit could bring with it some unanticipated problems. Without effective tools that will help people deal with it, the greatly increased access could complicate life. What can be done to help people handle information glut? What can help them to keep from becoming paralyzed by a surfeit of choices? Programs that can search large databases or that can filter datastreams for information of interest to particular users are one approach to this problem that is being tried.

There is considerable interest in the development of electronic "agents" (personal digital assistants, gophers, alter-egos...) that can continuously scan large databases on behalf of individuals, finding and organizing the information they would want to have. There is some concern, however, that consumers are likely to have unrealistic expectations regarding the types of services that personal agents will be able to perform in the foreseeable future, especially if encouraged to do so by industry hype. As an antidote to the building of such unrealistic expectations, Browning (1995) has suggested that whenever one sees the phrase "intelligent agent" one should substitute "trainable ant" because that is a more appropriate model of what is likely to be available at least in the short term. In any case, the general question of how to make very large collections of electronically accessible information really useful to the average person presents a wealth of research, development and evaluation opportunities.

1.5.10 Person-to-Person Communication

We note again that, although it was not the purpose for which computer networks were developed, electronic mail, broadly defined to include electronic bulletin boards, discussion groups, and similar interperson-communication facilities, has turned out to account for a surprisingly large fraction of the total traffic over computer networks. Programs to permit the sending and receiving of messages were initially written to facilitate communication among engineers working on the development of network technology, but the potential inherent in this means of communication soon became apparent and motivated the development of formal email software for more general use. Advantages of electronic mail over more traditional communication media were pointed out by early enthusiasts (Bair, 1978; Lederberg, 1978; Uhlig, 1977). Possible disadvantages, or problems that the new capability might cause, received less attention.

According to Ratan (1995) the total volume of mail delivered by the U.S. post office has increased by about 5 percent since 1988, but the volume of business-to-business mail has decreased by 33 percent during the same period. Much of the decrease is assumed to have been lost to fax machines. At the present time, fax machines are much more likely to be found in offices than in homes, but they could become much more common in homes in the future. If they do, it seems reasonable to expect that much person-to-person mail will go the way that business-to-business mail seems to be going. The fax machine itself may be a temporary thing, however; in time affordable computer systems could provide all the capabilities now provided by PCs, phones and fax machines, and some others as well. Many uses of fax involve printing a document from a computer, transmitting it in facsimile, then rekeying or scanning some or all of its information into another computer. Obviously email, especially when it becomes more nearly universally available, is a considerable improvement over this process.

What are the implications for human communication of the fact that with email and related means of computer-mediated communication the impression one forms of people is based on what and how they communicate with these media and not on how they sound or look? Are people more likely to reveal their "true personalities" with computer-mediated communication than in face-to-face encounters, or does the email venue encourage and facilitate masquerading and the presentation of false identities? How will the character and quality of the communication change when voice and video are standard options?

One of the more thought-provoking findings to date on the difference between electronically mediated and face-to-face communication is that social status is a less important determinant of behavior, perhaps because status differences are less apparent in electronic communication. The proportion of talk and influence of higher status individuals is less when communication is via electronic mail, for example, and impediments to easy participation in meetings—soft voice, physical unattractiveness—seem to be less important factors in electronically mediated communication (Sproull and Kiesler, 1991a, b). This is not to suggest, that electronically mediated communication is to be preferred to face-to-face communication in any general sense, but only to point out that it may have advantages under certain circumstances.

It may of course have certain disadvantages as well. Email does not provide, for example, the rich context of nonverbal cues that carry nuances of meaning and affect. Kiesler, Siegel and McGuire (1984) identify "(a) a paucity of social context information and (b) few widely shared norms governing its use" (p. 1126) as two of the more interesting characteristics of computer-mediated communication from a social psychological point of view.

Face-to-face communication appears to follow certain rules even though most of us are probably not sufficiently aware of many of them—even though we follow them—to be able to articulate them very clearly. These rules have to do with selecting forms of address that are appropriate to the relationship between the conversing parties, keeping the affective qualities of the conversation within acceptable bounds, using changes in eye-fixation to signal changes in speaker–listener roles, filling intervals where a pause in the conversation would be awkward, terminating a conversation in an inoffensive way, and so on. Most of the conversational rules that we follow were not invented, like the rules for chess, but evolved over time, and it is not clear that all of them are yet well understood, despite considerable research directed at discovering them. Some of the rules that govern face-to-face conversations will probably transfer to computer-mediated conversations, and some will not; moreover, it is to be expected that rules unique to the computer-mediated situation will evolve over time, and that they too will be discovered only by research.

The question of control will be an important one as the patterns of use of electronic bulletin boards continue to evolve. There appears to be a fairly strong preference among most users for a system to be completely uncontrolled, but there is also a recognition that the lack of constraint sometimes results in the degeneration of effective discussions into intemperate shouting matches or worse. This is not unique to electronically mediated discussions, of course, but we have had considerably longer to work out some commonly accepted rules of etiquette for face-to-face discussions; it is likely to take a while to get to a comparable place with respect to discussions that occur in cyberspace.

1.5.11 Computer-Mediated Communication and Group Behavior

How will the greater person-to-person access that computer-mediated communication provides across different levels of an organizational hierarchy affect organizational structures of the future? It is generally assumed that the communication that occurs via computer networks is more lateral than that that occurs face-to-face or with other media. Perhaps because, as already noted, status differences are less apparent, the fact that communicants do not occupy the same level within an organizational hierarchy has less influence on communication within a network context than elsewhere. In any case, the network medium seems to foster a more egalitarian attitude among users than other communication media, and especially than face-to-face situations (Kiesler, Siegel, and McGuire, 1984).

To the extent that these perceptions are true, they raise the question of whether networks will tend, in general, to stimulate and facilitate the formation of groups of people with common interests (values, goals, ideologies) or to inhibit and impede the same. The question also arises as to how groups formed via network communication will resemble, and how they will differ from, groups formed in more traditional ways. Will they be more or less cohesive? More or less effective in realizing their group goals? More or less easily influenced by nonmembers? More or less open to change?

People with email access probably number in the tens of millions today. What will it mean when that number increases to hundreds of millions, as it is may well do in the foreseeable future, or to billions, which is not out of the question. In principle, everyone with a telephone—100 million in the U. S. alone—could have email as well. What should we make of Smolowe's (1995) claim that "[a]n estimated 80 percent of all users [of the Internet] are looking for contact and commonality, companionship, and community?"

How will computer-mediated communication compare with mass media in terms of the effectiveness with which it can be used for purposes of mass persuasion? For the dissemination of propaganda? Will it prove to be a useful tool for demagogues, or will it weaken demagoguery, in general, by making it easier to expose faulty arguments and false claims? All of these questions are challenges to research and innovation.

1.6 Summary and Concluding Comments

In a somewhat cynical assessment of the computer revolution and the "utopian fantasies" about the future course of it, Hughes (1995) has warned that "We will look back on what is now claimed for the information superhighway and wonder how we ever psyched ourselves into believing all that bulldust about social fulfillment through interface and connectivity" (p. 76). The picture he paints of the course the revolution could take presents the technology that is symbolized by computers and interactive multimedia as a powerful means of removing ourselves from reality, turning our heads to mush, and entertaining ourselves to death—more or less continuing the worst aspects of television but much more effectively. "Interactivity may add much less to the sum of human knowledge than we think. But it will deluge us with entertainment, most of which will be utter schlock" (p. 77). The picture is not as implausible as one would like it to be, in our view. We hope it proves to be wrong, but only time will tell.

Another possibility is that of what Dertouzos (1991) has referred to as the "hopeful vision of a future built on an information infrastructure that will enrich our lives by relieving us of mundane tasks, by improving the ways we live, learn and work and by unlocking new personal and social freedoms" (p. 62). This exciting and optimistic vision was expressed in the lead article of a special issue of Scientific American on "Communications, Computers and Networks," Other contributors to the issue also expressed generally optimistic expectations regarding the future impact of information technology on our lives, but they also showed some sensitivity to the fact that such a happy future is not assured. Noting that the new technologies could widen the gap between rich and poor, inundate us with "infojunk," and increase the incidence of white-collar crime and violations of privacy, Dertouzos noted the importance of efforts on the part of designers and users of this technology to attempt to steer it in useful directions. We agree with this and believe that efforts in HCI can play a consequential role in that steering.

1.7 References

Anderson, R. H., Bikson, T. K., Law, S. A., and Mitchell, B. M. (1995). *Unviversal Access to E-mail: Feasibility and Societal Implications*. Santa Monica CA: RAND.

Appel, K., and Haken, W. (1977). The solution of the four-color-map problem. *Scientific American, 237(4)*, 108–121.

Attewell, P., and Rule, J. (1984). Computing and Organizations: What we know and what we don't know. *Communications of the ACM, 27*(12), 1184–1191.

Baeker, R. M., and Buxton, W. A. S. (Eds.) (1987). *Readings in Human–Computer Interaction: A Multi-Disciplinary Approach*. Los Altos, CA: Morgan Kaufman.

Baily, M., and Chakrabarti, A. K. (1988). *Innovation and the Productivity Crisis*. Washington D.C.: The Brookings Institute, Washington, D.C.

Bair, J. H. (1978). Communication in the office of the future: Where the real payoff may be. *Proceedings of the International Computer Communications Conference*, 733–739, Kyoto, Japan.

Barnard, P. J., and Grudin, J. (1988). Command Names. In M. Helander (Ed.), *Handbook of Human–Computer Interaction*. Amsterdam: North Holland.

Barnard, P. J., Hammond, N. V., Morton, J., Long, J. B., and Clark, I. A. (1981). Consistency and compatibility on human–computer dialogue. *International Journal of Man–Machine Studies, 15*, 87–134.

Birge, R. R. (1994). Three-dimensional memory. *American Scientist, 84*, 348–355.

Birge, R. R. (1995). Protein-based computers. *Scientific American, 272(3)*, 90–95.

Browning, J. (1995). Agents and other animals: Good software help is hard to find. *Scientific American, 272(2)*, 28–29.

Bruce, B. C., and Rubin, A. (1993). *Electronic Quills: A Situated Evaluation of Using Computers for Writing in Classrooms*. Hillsdale, NJ: Erlbaum.

Bush, V. (1945, July). As we may think. *The Atlantic Monthly*.

Card, S. K., Moran, T. P., and Newell, A. (1983). *The Psychology of Human–Computer Interaction*. Hillsdale, NJ: Erlbaum.

Card, S. K., Robert, J. M., and Keenen, L. N. (1984). On-Line Composition of Text. In *Proceedings of Interact '84*, 1 (pp. 231–236). London: Elsevier.

Carroll, J. M, and Rosson, M. B. (1984). *Usability specifications as a tool in iterative development*. Report No. RC 10437. Yorktown Heights, NY: IBM Watson Research Center.

Cerf, V. G., (1991). Networks. *Scientific American, 265(3)*, 72–81.

Cyert, R. M., and Mowery, D. C. (1989). Technology, employment and U.S. competitiveness. *Scientific American, 260*)(5), 54–62.

David, P. A. (1990). The dynamo and the computer: An historical perspective on the modern productivity paradox. *The American Economic Review, 80*(2), 355–361.

Davies, D. W., and Barber, D. L. A. (1973). *Communications Network for Computers*. New York: Wiley.

Denning, P. J. (1989). The science of computing: The ARPANET after 20 years. *American Scientist, 77*, 530–534.

Dertouzos, M. L., (1991). Communications, computers and networks, *Scientific American, 265*(3), 62–69.

Eason, K. D. (1982). The process of introducing information technology. *Behavior and Information Technology, 1*, 197–213.

Egan, D. E. (1988). Individual differences in human computer interaction. In M. Helander (Ed.), *Handbook of Human-Computer Interaction* (pp. 543–568). Amsterdam: North–Holland.

Eisenberg, A. (1995). Scientists and their CD-ROMS. *Scientific American, 272(2)*, 104.

Elmer-DeWitt, P. (1995). Welcome to Cyberspace: What is it? Where is it? And how do we get there? *Time* (Special issue: Welcome to Cyberspace) (pp. 4–11).

Englebart, D. C. (1962). *Augmenting human intellect: A conceptual framewark.* No. AFOSR–3223) Stanford Research Institute (SRI) Menlo Park, CA

English, W. K., Englebart, D. C., and Berman, M. L. (1967). Display-selection techniques for text manipulation. *IEEE Transactions on Human Factors in Electronics, HFE–8*, 5–15.

Franke, R. H. (1987). Technological Revolution and Productivity Decline: Computer Introduction in the Financial Industry. *Technology Forecasting and Social Change, 31*, 143–154.

Furnas, G. W., Landauer, T. K., Gomez, L., M., and-Dumais, S. T. (1987). The vocabulary problem in human system communication. *Communications of the ACM, 30*(11), 964–971.

Germain, E. (1995). Guarding against Internet intruders. *Science, 267*, 608–610.

Gibbs, W. W. (1994). Software's chronic crisis. *Scientific American, 271(3)*, 86–95.

Gibbs, W. W. (1995). Lost science in the third world. *Scientific American, 273(2)*, 92–99.

Gould, J. D. (1981). Composing letters with computer-based text editors. *Human Factors, 23*, 593–606.

Gould, J. D, Boies, S. J. and Lewis, C. (1991) Making usable, useful, productivity-enhancing computer applications. *Communications of the ACM*, 34, 75–85.

Gray, G. W. (1949) The great ravelled knot. *Scientific American.* Also in *Scientific American Reader* (pp. 493–508). New York: Simon and Schuster, 1953.

Harnad, S. (1990). Scholarly sky writing and the prepublication continuum of scientific inquiry. *Psychological Science, 1*, 342–344.

Heart, F.E. (1975, September). The ARPANET network. In R.L. Grimsdale and F.F. Kuo (Eds.), *Computer communication networks: 1973 Proceedings of the NATO Advanced Study Institute.* Leyden, The Netherlands: Noordhoff International Publishing.

Heart, F., McKenzie, A., McQuillan, J., and Walden, D. (1978, January). *ARPANET completion report.* Cambridge, MA: Bolt Beranek and Newman Inc.

Hiltz, S. R., and Turoff, M. (1978). *The Network Nation: Human Communication via Computer.* Reading, MA: Addison-Wesley.

Horgan, J., and Patton, R. (1994). More bits from pits. *Scientific American, 271(2)*, 87–88.

Hughes, R. (1995). Take this revolution.... *Time* (Special issue: Welcome to Cyberspace) (pp. 76–77).

Jaroff, L. (1995). Age of the road warrior. *Time* (Special issue: Welcome to Cyberspace) (pp. 38–40).

Johnson, B. M., and Rice, R. E. (1987). *Managing Organizational Innovation: The evolution from word processing to office information systems.* New York: Columbia University Press.

Kiesler, S., Siegel, J., and McGuire, T. (1984). Social psychological aspects of computer-mediated communication. *American Psychologist, 39*, 1123–1134.

Klein, L.R. (1988). Components of competitiveness. *Science, 241*, 308–313.

Koppel, T. (1994). The perils of info-democracy. *New York Times* (Op-Ed page).

Kraut, R., Dumais, S., and Koch, S. (1989). Computerization, productivity, and quality of work-life. *Communications of the ACM, 32*(2), 220–238.

Kuhn, T. S. (1977). *The Essential Tension: Selected Studies in Scientific Tradition and Change.* Chicago, IL: University of Chicago Press.

Lajoie, S. P., and Derry, S. J. (Eds.) (1993). *Computers as Cognitive Tools.* Hillsdale, NJ: Erlbaum.

Landauer, T. K. (1995) *The Trouble with Computers: Usefulness, Usability and Productivity.* Cambridge, MA., MIT Press.

Landauer T. K.,and Dumais, S. T. (1996). How come you know so much? From practical problem to theory, In C. McEvoy, P. Hertel and D. Hermann, *Memory in Context: The Theory Practice Nexus,* Erlbaum, Hillsdale, NJ.

Landauer, T. K., Egan, D. E., Remde, J. R., Lesk, M. E., Lochbaum, C. C., and Ketchum, R. D. (1993). Enhancing the usability of text through computer delivery and formative evaluation: the SuperBook project. In A. Dillon and C. McKnight (Eds.), *Hypertext: A Psycho-*

logical Perspective (pp. 71–136). London: Ellis Horwood Limited.

Landauer, T. K., Galotti, K. M., and Hartwell, S. (1983). Natural command names and initial learning: a study of text editing terms. *Communications of the ACM, 26,* 495–503.

Landauer, T. K., and Nachbar, D. W. (1985). Selection from alphabetic and numeric menu trees using a touch screen: breadth, depth and width. In *Proceedings of the CHI'85 Conference on Human Factors in Computing Systems.* Gaithersburg, MD: ACM.

Larkin, J. H., and Chabay, R. W. (Eds.) (1992). *Computer-Assisted Instruction and Intelligent Tutoring Systems: Shared Goals and Complementary Approaches.* Hillsdale, NJ: Erlbaum.

Lederberg, J. (1978). Digital communications and the conduct of science: The new literacy. *Proceedings of the IEEE, 66,* 1314–1319.

Leutwyler, K. (1994). Productivity lost: Have more computers meant less efficiency? *Scientific American, 271(5),* 101–102.

Levinson, P. (1988). *Mind At Large: Knowing in the Technological Age.* Greenwich, CT: Jai Press.

Licklider, J. C. R. (1960). Man-computer symbiosis. *Institute of Radio Engineers Transactions on Human Factors Electronics,* HFE–1, 4–11.

Licklider, J. C. R. (1965). Man-computer partnership. *International Science and Technology, 41,* 18–26.

Licklider, J. C. R. (1968). Man-computer communication. In C. A. Cuadra (Ed.), *Annual Review of Information Science and Technology* (Vol 3). Chicago: Encyclopedia Britannica.

Licklider, J. C. R., and Clark, W. E. (1962). On-line man-computer communication. *AFIPS Proceedings, 21,* 113–128.

Licklider, J. C. R., and Vezza, A. (1978). Applications of information networks. *Proceedings of the IEEE, 66,* 1330–1346.

Loveman, G. W. (1990). *An Assesment of the Productivity Impact of Information Technologies.* Cambridge: MA. MIT Sloan School of Management.

Marrill, T., and Roberts, L. A. (1966). Cooperative network of timesharing computers. *Proceedings of the AFIPS 1966 Sprint Joint Computer Conference,* 425–431.

Meyerson, F. (1994). High-speed silicon-germanium electronics. *Scientific American, 270(3),* 62–67.

Minsky, M. (1994). Will robots inherit the earth? *Scientific American, 271(4),* 108–113.

Mokyr, J. (1990). *The Lever of Riches: Technological Creativity and Economic Progress.* New York: Oxford University Press.

Nathan, M.J., Kintsch, W., and Young, R.(1992). A theory of algebra word problem comprehension and its implications for the design of computer learning environments. *Cognition and Instruction,* 9(2), 329-389.

National Research Council (1994). *Organizational Linkages: Understanding the Productivity Paradox.* Panel on Organizational Linkages, Committee on Human Factors. Washington, DC: National Academy Press.

Nickerson, R. S. (1986). *Using Computers: The Human Factors of Information Systems.* Cambridge, MA: MIT Press.

Nickerson, R. S. (1994). Electronic bulletin boards: A case-study in computer-mediated communication. *Interacting with Computers, 6,* 117–134.

Nickerson, R. S., and Pew, R. W. (1990, July). Toward more compatible human–computer interfaces. *IEEE Spectrum* (pp. 40–43).

Nickerson, R. S., and Zodhiates, P. P. (Eds.). (1988). *Technology in Education: Looking Toward 2020.* Hillsdale, NJ: Lawrence Erlbaum Associates.

Nielsen, J. (1989). Usability engineering at a discount. In G. salvendy and M. J. Smith (Eds.), *Designing and Using Human-Computer Interfaces and Knowledge Based Systems* (pp. 394-401). Amsterdam: Elsevier.

Nielsen, J. (1993). *Usability Engineering.* Boston, MA: Academic Press.

Nielsen, J., and Landauer, T. K. (1993). A mathematical model of the finding of usability problems. In *INTERCHI'93, ACM Conference on Human Factors in Computer Systems* (pp. 206–213). Amsterdam: ACM.

NIST (1994). *Putting the information infrastructure to work: Report of the Information Infrastructure Task Force Committee on Applications and Technology.* Washington, DC: National Institute of Standards and Technology, U. S. Department of Commerce.

OSTP (1994). *High performance computing and communications: Toward a national information infrastructure.* Washington, DC: Office of Science and Technology Policy (Federal Coordinating Council for Science, Engineering , and Technology).

Parthenopoulos, D. A., and Rentzepis, P. M. (1989).

Three-dimensional optical storage memory. *Science, 245*, 843–845.

Pennington, N., Nicholich, R., and Rahm, J. (1995). Transfer of training between cognitive subskills: Is knowledge use specific? *Cognitive Psychology, 28*, 175–224.

Perkins, D. N., Schwartz, J. L., West, M. M., and Wiske, M. S. (Eds.) (1995). *Software Goes to School: Teaching for Understanding with New Technologies.* New York: Oxford University Press.

Plafker, T. (1995). China to triple Internet links with commercial hookups. *Science, 267*, 168.

Polson, P. G., and Kieras, D. E. (1985) A qualitative model of the learning of text-editing knowledge. In C. Borman and B. Cutris (Eds) , *Proceedings of the CHI 1985 Conference on Human Factors in Computing Systems*, (pp. 207–212), New York, ACM.

Pool, R. (1993). Beyond databases and e-mail. *Science, 261*, 841–843.

Psotka, J., Massey, L. D., and Mutter, S.A.,(Eds.) (1988). *Intelligent tutoring systems: Lessons Learned.* Hillsdale, NJ: Erlbaum.

Ruopp, R., Gal, S., Drayton, B., and Pfister, M. (Eds.) (1993). *LabNet: Toward a Community of Practice.* Hillsdale, NJ: Erlbaum.

Ratan, S. (1995). Snail mail struggles to survive. *Time* (Special issue: Welcome to Cyberspace) (p. 40).

Schiller, J. I. (1994). Secure distributed computing. *Scientific American, 271(5)*, 72–76.

Sheil, B. (1983). Power tools for programmers. *Datamation, 29*(2), 131–144.

Singley, M. K., and Anderson, J. R. (1989) *The Transfer of Cogntive Skill.* Cambridge, MA. Harvard University Press.

Smolowe, J. (1995). Intimate strangers. *Time* (Special issue: Welcome to Cyberspace) (pp. 20–21, 24–26).

Solow, R. M. (1959). Investment and technical progress. In K. J. Arrow, S. Karlin, and P. Suppes (Eds.), *Mathematical methods in the social sciences* Stanford, CA: Stanford University Press.

Sproull, L., and Kiesler, S. (1991a). Computers, networks and work. *Scientific American, 265(3)*, 116–123.

Sproull, L., and Kiesler, S. (1991b). *Connections: New Ways of Working in the Networked Organization.* Cambridge, MA: MIT Press.

Steinberg, S. (July, 22, 1994). Travels on the net. *Technology Review* (pp. 20–31).

Stix, G. (1994). The speed of write. *Scientific American, 271(6)*, 106–111.

Stix, G. (1995). Toward "Point one." *Scientific American, 272(2)*, 90–95.

Strassmann, P. (1990). *The Business Value of Computers: An Executive's Guide*. New Canaan, CT: The Information Economics Press.

Streeter, L. A., Acroff, J. M. and Taylor, G. A. (1983). On abbreviating command names. *The Bell System Technical Journal, 62*, 1807–1826.

Taubes, G. (1996). Science journals go wired. *Science, 271*, 764–766.

Tinker, R. F., and Kapisovsky, P. M. (Eds.) (1992). *Prospects for Educational Telecomputing: Selected Readings*. Cambridge, MA: The Educational Research Center.

Uhlig, R. P. (1977, May). Human factors in computer message systems. *Datamation* 120–126.

Vacc, N. N. (1991). Word processing and handwriting: writing samples Produced by At-Risk Freshman. *Journal of Educational Technology Systems, 19*(3), 233–250.

Wallich, P. (1994). Wire pirates. *Scientific American, 270(3)*, 90–101.

Weiser, M., 1991, The computer for the 21st century, *Scientific American, 265*(3), 94–104.

Weizenbaum, J. (1966). Eliza—A computer program for the study of natural language communications between man and machine. *Communications of the ACM, 9*, 36–45.

Young, J.A. (1988). Technology and competitiveness: A key to the economic future of the United States. *Science, 241*, 313–316.

Handbook of Human-Computer Interaction
Second, completely revised edition
M. Helander, T.K. Landauer, P. Prabhu (eds.)

Chapter 2

Information Visualization

James D. Hollan
Benjamin B. Bederson
Computer Science Department
University of New Mexico
Albuquerque, New Mexico, USA

Jonathan I. Helfman
AT&T Research
Murray Hill, New Jersey, USA

2.1 Introduction

Computation provides the most plastic representational medium we have ever known. It can be employed to mimic successful mechanisms of earlier media but it also enables novel techniques that were not previously possible. Computationally-based information presentations promise to dramatically enrich our understandings as well as assist us in navigating and effectively exploiting rapidly growing and increasingly complex information collections. In this chapter we survey a sample of recent information visualization research.

Information visualization has a long history, dating to the earliest forms of symbolic representation, and can be approached from multiple perspectives, ranging across psychology, epistemology, graphic design, linguistics, and semiology to newer perspectives emerging from cognitive science. There are numerous introductory surveys of information visualization. Examples include popular books by (Tufte, 1990) practical work on data visualization (Keller and Keller, 1993), and work applied to specific fields such as statistics (Cleveland and McGill, 1988). Information visualization research has grown dramatically in the last few years. Well-designed visualizations can be tremendously helpful but are still very challenging to create. There is an increasing amount of work on automating the production of visualizations (Mackinlay, 1996) and on providing tools to assist in designing effective interactive information visualizations. The Sage and Visage work of Roth and his colleagues (Roth, Kolojejchick, Mattis, and Chuah, 1995) is particularly noteworthy.

Our goal in this chapter is not a comprehensive survey of information visualization but rather to provide a glimpse of current research and attempt to communicate the exciting potential of new dynamic representations. To accomplish this we profile selected recent work from our research group and others. We then step back from the details of specific projects to discuss what we see as the beginnings of a paradigm shift for thinking about information, one that starts to view information as being much more dynamic and reactive to the nature of our tasks, activities, and even relationships with others.

2.2 Lenses As Information Filters

Consider the series of screen snapshots in Figures 1-4. They depict movable lenses (Stone, Fishkin, and Bier, 1994) that combine arbitrarily-shaped regions with filtering operators. They can be moved over objects to dynamically change the views presented. Figure 1 depicts placement of a pair of lenses over a section of text. The upper lens highlights text with special properties. In this example, it has highlighted Middle and Right and thus has provided additional information, regions that can be selected with the mouse, that would

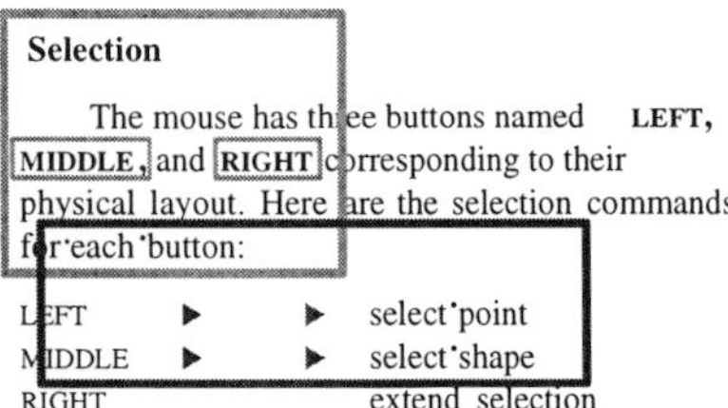

Figure 1. ***Pair of movable lenses.*** *Upper lens reveals special properties of text and the lower lens shows tabs and formatting.*

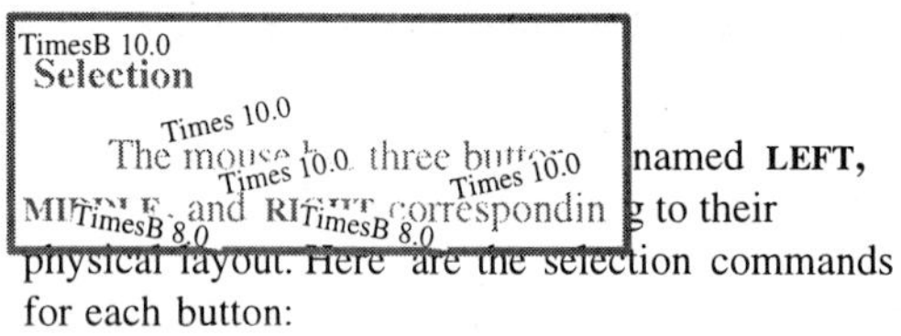

Figure 2. ***Font identification lens.*** *Shows fonts used in regions it is postponed over.*

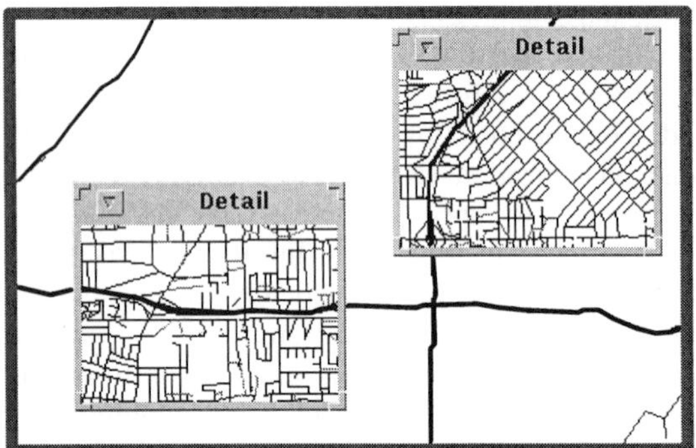

Figure 3. ***Detail lenses.*** *Here placed over the starting and ending location of a journey to assist in planning.*

Selection

The mouse has three buttons named LEFT,
MIDDLE
physical layout. Here are the selection commands
for each
selleclton *n.* **1. a.** The act of selecting or the fact of being selected; choosing; choice. **b.** That which is selected.

Figure 4. ***Definition lens.*** *Clicking through this lens displays the definition of a word.*

normally be invisible. The lower lens similarly shows whitespace and formatting codes such as tabs (here indicated by triangles).

The lens in Figure 2 allows the identification of fonts used in a portion of text. Figure 3 uses lenses to provide greater detail about sections of a map. In this particular example, lenses have been placed over the starting and ending locations of a journey to assist with planning. One, for example, typically needs much more detail about streets in the areas around the beginning and end of a journey. Figure 4 demonstrates a lens that one can click through to display the definition of a word.

These examples of simple interactive information visualization techniques employ a metaphor based on physical lenses but allow for creation of lenses with dynamic functionality that goes beyond mere magnification. They are movable regions that provide alternative representations of objects within an overall context.

There are a number of research groups exploring the use of lens-like interfaces to support information visualization. The work described above comes from researchers at the Xerox Palo Alto Research Center (Bier, Stone, Pier, Buxton, and DeRose, 1993). Earlier work at the MCC Human Interface Laboratory investigated similar interface mechanisms for selectively viewing information in large knowledge bases (Hollan, Rich, Hill, Wroblewski, Wilner, Wittenburg and Grudin, 1991). This technique, also termed lenses, provided for access to alternative perspectives on knowledge base entries. Related work on *brushing* to link data across different views has been very valuable for analyzing multi-dimensional data (See Cleveland and McGill, 1988). For the last several years we have also been exploring lens-like filters as part of the Pad++ dynamic multi-scale interface research effort that we describe next.

2.3 Pad++: A Zoomable Graphical Sketchpad

Imagine a computer screen made of a sheet of a miraculous new material that is stretchable like rubber, but continues to display a crisp image, no matter what the sheet's size. Imagine further that vast quantities of information are represented on the sheet, organized at different places and sizes. Everything you do on the computer is on this sheet. To access a piece of information you just stretch to the right part, and there it is. If you need more work room in some location, you just stretch the sheet to provide it.

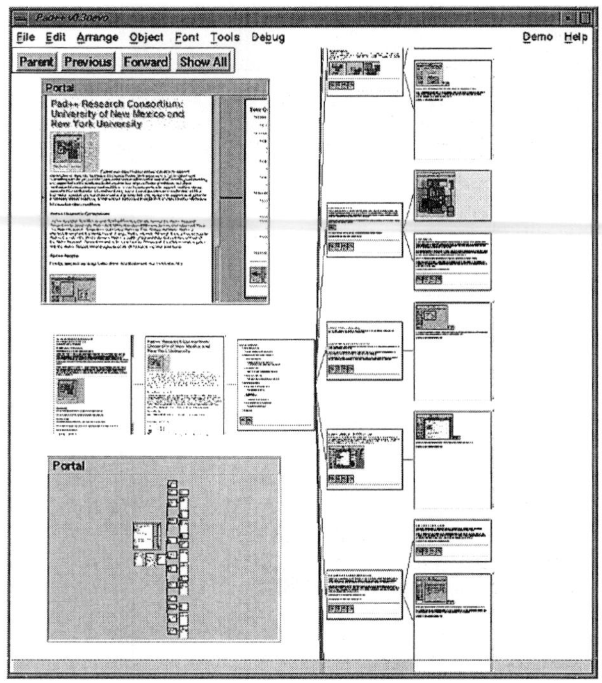

Figure 5. Pad++ Web Browsing. *This depicts use of Pad++ for browsing the World Wide Web. Here we are looking at the Pad++ home page (www.cs.unm.edu/pad++). There are two portals providing views onto the same surface. In the top portal we have zoomed into the Pad++ home page. The lower portal shows a zoomed out view that allows us to see all the pages that have been traversed.*

In addition, special lenses come with this sheet that let you look onto remote locations. With these lenses, you can see and interact with many different pieces of data that would ordinarily be quite far apart. The lenses can also show different representations of the same underlying data and can even filter the data so that, for example, only data relevant to a particular task appears.

Imagine also new mechanisms that provide alternatives to scaling objects purely geometrically. For example, instead of representing a page of text so small that it is unreadable, an abstraction of the text, perhaps just a title that is readable, can be presented. Similarly, when stretching a spreadsheet, instead of showing huge numbers, it might be more effective to show the computations from which the numbers were derived or a history of interaction with them.

Pad++ (Bederson, Hollan, Perlin, Meyer, Bacon, and Furnas, 1996) provides the beginnings of an interface like this. We don't really stretch a huge rubber-like sheet, we simulate this with panning and zooming. By tapping into people's natural spatial abilities, Pad++ tries to increase users' intuitive access to information. Figure 5 depicts a view of the World Wide Web. Pad++ uses *portals* to provide lens-like features and also to support scaling data in non-geometric ways that we term *semantic zooming* or *context-sensitive rendering*.

One simple example of lenses in Pad++ is to support alternative views of numerical data. For certain tasks numerical data may be more effectively viewed as a scatter plot, bar chart, or some other graphic. The advantage of lenses is that they allow users to dynamically choose between alternative views of the information. By selecting a lens, users can chose a particular view of the data that best supports their current task. As Cleveland and his colleagues have demonstrated, some graphical depictions are better for supporting certain types of data comparisons. Lenses provide a technology that empowers users to participate in this representational choice. In addition, lenses make such displays available *when* and *where* needed rather than clutter the display with multiple representations.

As shown in Figure 6, we can also use lenses to change the behavior of objects seen through them, allowing design at a more abstract level. For example, we have implemented a pair of data entry lenses that can change a numeric depiction into a slider or dial, as the user prefers. By default, the entry mechanism allows input by typing. However, dragging the slider lens over a numeric entry changes the representation from

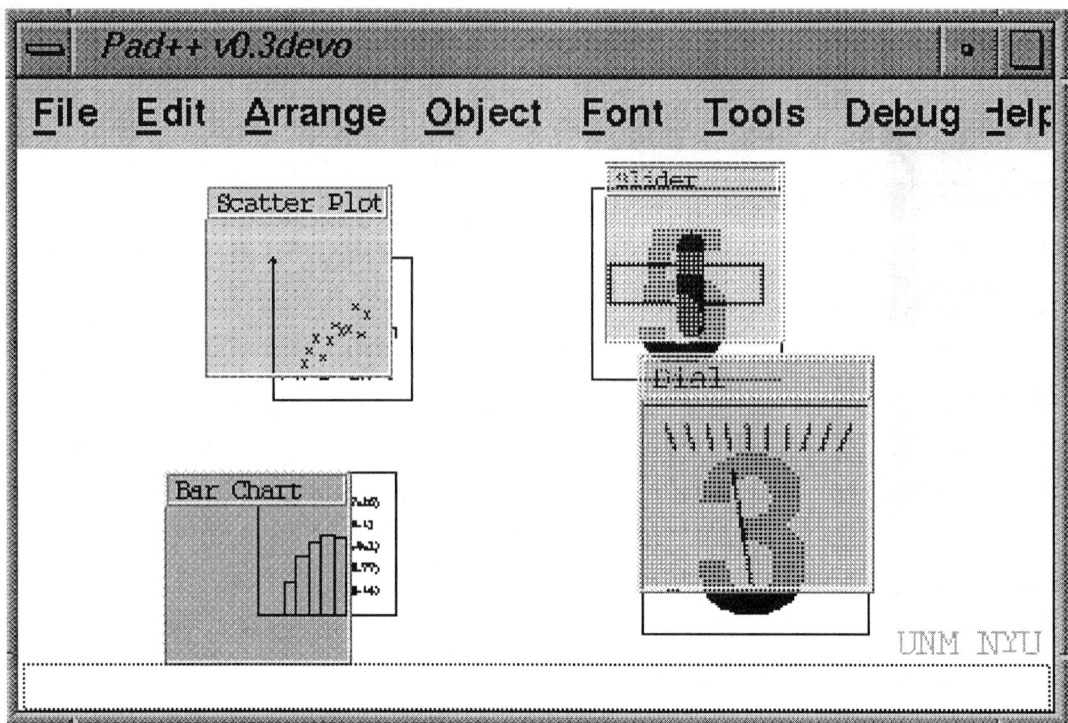

Figure 6. Example Pad++ lens. *The lenses on the left depict numerical data as a bar chart or as a graph. The examples on the right demonstrate how lenses can be used to change methods of interaction. They allow numeric data to be changed using either slider or dial mechanisms.*

text to a slider, and then the mouse can be used to change the value by moving the slider. Another lens shows the data using a dial and permits modification by manipulating the dial's needle.

While it is effective to use lenses to see data in place, it is also sometimes useful to see different representations of data simultaneously and to be able to position these views at arbitrary locations. Portals are graphical objects that, in addition to acting as lenses, can provide a view of any portion of the Pad++ surface. Although a lens is used by dragging it over objects, a portal is used by panning or zooming within it to change where it is looking.

Easily finding information on the Pad++ surface is obviously very important since intuitive navigation through large dataspaces is one of its primary motivations. Pad++ supports visual searching with direct manipulation panning and zooming in addition to traditional mechanisms, such as content-based search. Some applications animate the view to the found items. These animations interpolate in pan and zoom to bring the view to the specified location. If the end point is further than one screen width away from the starting point, the animation zooms out to a point midway between the starting and ending points, far enough out so that both points are visible. The animation then smoothly zooms in to the destination. This gives a sense of context to the viewer, helps maintain object permanence, and speeds up the animation since most of the panning is performed when zoomed out.

We are exploring several different types of interactive visualizations within Pad++, some of which are described elsewhere (Bederson, Hollan, Perlin, Meyer, Bacon, and Furnas, 1996). Here we give one example: using Pad++ to develop a browser and navigation aid for the World Wide Web. It takes advantage of the variable resolution available for both representation and interaction. Layout of graphical objects within a multi-scale space is an interesting issue, and is quite different than traditional fixed-resolution layout. Deciding how to visually represent an arbitrary graph on a non-zoomable surface is extremely difficult. Often it is impossible to position all objects near logically related objects. Also, representing the links between objects often requires overlapping or crossing edges. Even laying out a tree is difficult because, generally speaking, there are an exponential number of children to fit in a fixed size space.

Traditional layout techniques use sophisticated it-

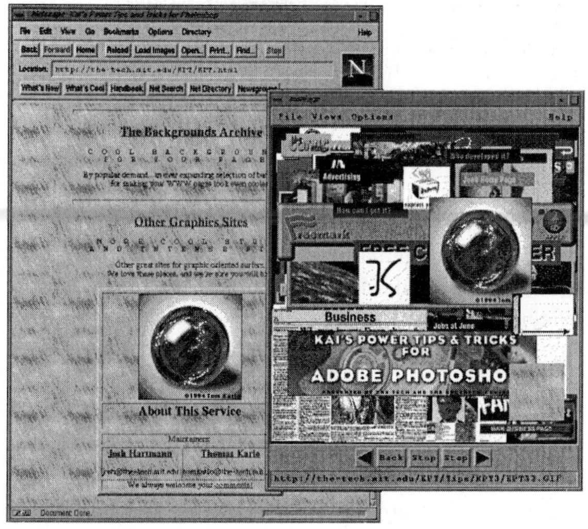

***Figure 7. Montage.** Montage application (on right) with regular browser (in back).*

erative adaptive algorithms for laying out general graphs, and can still result in graphs that are hard to understand. Large trees are often represented hierarchically with one sub-tree depicted by a single box that references another tree. Using an interactive zoomable surface, however, allows very different methods of visually representing large data structures. The fact that there is always more room to place information gives more options. Of course there are trade-offs involved in these representational decisions too. Pad++ is particularly well suited for visualizing hierarchical data because information that is deeper in the hierarchy can be made smaller. Accessing this information is accomplished by zooming.

In traditional window-based systems, there is no graphical depiction of the relationship among windows even when there is a strong semantic relationship. For example, in many hypertext systems, clicking on a hyperlink brings up a new window with the linked text (or alternatively replaces the contents of the existing window). While there is an important relationship between this linked information (parent and child), this relationship is not represented.

We are experimenting with a variety of multi-scale layouts of hypertext document traversals in which relationships between linked pages are represented visually. In one experimental viewer when a hyperlink is selected, the child document is shown to the side and smaller, and the view is animated to center the new object. After many links have been followed, zooming out gives an overview of the data, and the relationships between links is retained in the layout. In another viewer, tree relationships are explicitly depicted by edges between the pages of an html document. An alternative viewer provides the user with a camera that can be moved around the tree and the nodes it is looking at are show via a Pad++ portal.

We have also constructed facilities so that tree visualizations of web traversal can be pruned and annotated. Currently we are adding the ability for such trees to be checked periodically to see if the information they point to has changed. Annotations can be added to the tree to indicate changed sections. We are also investigating animations to take a user to places on pages they have saved that have changed since the last time they visited. This type of history-based information is discussed further in the section on history-enriched digital objects. We now turn to an information visualization system that provides image montages to assist in finding relevant and interesting web pages.

2.4 Montage

Web browsing is popular because hypertext is recognized as an easy way to access complex and interrelated information. But hypertext structures are often complex and their designers can't anticipate the particular needs and interests of every reader. Getting lost in hyper-space is all too common. Web browsers that only display one or two pages at a time don't provide enough context to help people stay oriented. The Pad++ web browser allows one to see many more pages and provides a focus plus context view so that one can see a page in the context of local traversals. Imagine instead, if there were an effective way to see hundreds of web pages at once.

Montage is a new way to surf the web by watching hundreds of images from web pages. Figure 7 shows a Montage application. Select an image that looks interesting to drive your regular web browser to the associated page. Montage is a fast way to visualize the landscape of the web because it utilizes the human capacity to recognize patterns in many images at once. Montage is effective because a large percentage of web images have content that is either explicitly textual or in some way relevant to the text on the associated web page.

Montage changes the nature of web navigation, avoiding some of the problems associated with hypertext navigation. By removing images from their associated web pages, Montage flattens the hypertext structure of the web. Similar images begin to form relationships, clusters, and streams. Relationships among images may only exist in the user's mind or the images may, in fact, have come from related pages. It hardly matters. Since hypertext structures are usually designed by someone who couldn't anticipate the particular needs and interests of all users, the actual hypertext structure is far less relevant than the relationships imposed on the information by a user through their own process of searching and browsing.

Before Montage can display images, it must first determine a mapping of images to associated web pages. A mapping of images to web pages can be obtained from many sources. In one version of Montage, the mapping is obtained from a local proxy server log file (and the images are obtained directly from the proxy server cache). Caches of HTML pages and images are meant to minimize access delays, but Montage reveals the cache as a community-wide resource. Images in the cache illustrate how a community uses the web and what subset of the web they find important. Montage monitors the cache, displaying any new images as they appear. When images are ordered by access time, streams of similar images identify active hypertext trails. Several images of new cell phones, for example, probably indicate that someone in your community is searching for information about purchasing a new cell phone. If this is of interest, select a cell phone to follow that hypertext trail.

It is also possible to obtain a mapping of images to associated web pages by parsing HTML pages and searching for embedded image tags. Although parsing HTML is not as fast as the proxy-server approach, it may be more generally useful. For example, imagine submitting a query to your favorite search engine on the web, but instead of having to read through the typical textual representation of the web pages that match your query, you can sit back and watch a Montage of images taken from the web pages that match your query. It should be easier to pick out the relevant images in the Montage than it is to pick out the relevant URL's in a large page of text. As another example, you may want to see a Montage of images taken from the pages listed in your hotlist or bookmarks file that have changed since you last saw them.

A snapshot of any portion of a Montage may be saved, annotated, and shared with others on the web. Montage snapshots are stored as imagemaps. Imagemaps, which have become a de-facto standard for implementing graphical menus on the web, are single images with associated coordinate files that maps regions of an image to a URL. When a user selects an imagemap, the coordinates of the selection point are sent to the web server, which searches through the associated coordinate file, determines which region was selected, and drives the user's web browser to the associated URL.

A Montage snapshot is a composite of all the images that were visible in the original Montage when the snapshot was created. The coordinates of each Montage image and the URL of its associated web page are stored in the imagemap coordinate file. Although Montage snapshots are static, when installed on a web server as an imagemap they retain the interactive quality of the original Montage. Select any region of the imagemap to drive your browser to the associated web page, just as if you had selected the image in Montage.

It's easy to add annotations to snapshots. Since imagemaps are designed to appear on web pages with text, annotations take the form of arbitrary HTML. Annotated snapshots seem particularly useful when the Montage images are ordered by internet site. Snapshots of images from the same site form a visual preview, or Postcard, of the site. Postcards are useful for illustrating bookmarks and hotlists. Annotated Postcards are useful for sharing information about web sites. An example of one particularly useful application is a shell script that automatically illustrates "surf reports" by converting email site reviews into web pages with interactive Postcards.

When Montage installs a Postcard on a web server it gives it a unique URL. To share the Postcard with a friend, send them the Postcard's URL via email. When they drive their browser to the URL they can see your snapshot and read your annotations. If your friend wants to visit the actual web site all they have to do is select an image on the snapshot. Surely something one can't do with a cardboard postcard!

Perhaps the most important idea embodied by Montage is that it shows people what is available on the web and it makes it easy to access web pages about things that seem interesting or relevant. We call this sort of activity "Passive Surfing" because it makes web surfing dramatically easier than clicking through irrelevant hypertext structures. But while Montage focuses exclusively on images, there are in fact many other types of multimedia files on the web: audio, MIDI, video, animation, etc. Like images, many of these multimedia files are associated with textual web pages that contain associated information. Future systems for Passive Surfing will play audio and MIDI files while displaying video and animation files and continuing to make it easy to access the associated web pages for things that seem interesting or relevant.

But why limit ourselves to the web? Even without the web, our computers are typically loaded with information that that is difficult to use for two major rea-

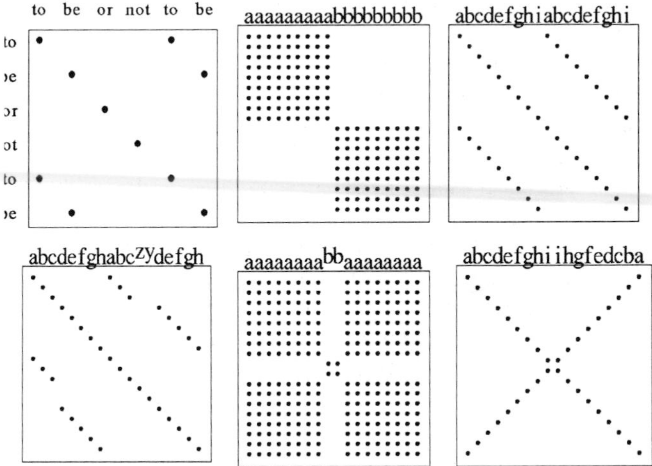

Figure 8. Dotplot. *a)Six words of Shakespeare, b)Squares, c)Diagonals, d)Broken Diagonals, e) Light Cross, f) Palindrome.*

sons: 1) we don't know what's available, and 2) we don't know how to access it. There seems to be a pressing need for a general class of systems for *Passive Browsing*: a lazy way to access information that uses animation to illustrate what is available and which actions are possible. Like trailers for motion pictures and demo modes for arcade games, a Passive Browser entices with snippets of representative action. Unlike trailers and demos, however, a passive browser affords user interaction. Users can pause or replay the animations and select images to obtain additional information. Each user's selections can be collated to build a profile of that user's interests, which can in turn be used to guide the creation of the animations. A passive browser might take the form of an interactive screen saver that illustrates available on-line services and responds to gestures by providing additional information or launching applications. Most screen savers cause our computer screens to either display no images or to display completely gratuitous graphics. Instead, why not seize this opportunity to show people what sorts of information is available, while at the same time making it easy for them to access the information that they find interesting and relevant?

Montage exploits our ability to see patterns in information. A Montage of a web site provides a graphical overview of the available information. We turn now to a novel information visualization technique specifically designed to assist us in seeing patterns and structure in large quantities of information.

2.5 Dotplot

Dotplot is a technique for visualizing patterns of string matches in millions of lines of data, text, or code. Dotplots were originally used in biology to study similarities in genetic sequences (Maizel and Lenk, 1981; Pustell and Kafatos, 1982). Since then, the Dotplot technique has been extended and improved (Church and Helfman, 1993). Dotplot patterns may now be explored interactively, with a Dotplot Browser, or detected automatically with a variety of image processing techniques. Current applications include text analysis (author identification, plagiarism detection, translation alignment, etc.), software engineering (module and version identification, subroutine categorization, redundant code identification, etc.), and information retrieval (identification of similar records in results of queries).

Dotplot patterns reveal a hidden, unifying structure in the digital representations of information. Information is always encoded in a particular representation: programs and texts are stored in a particular language; data is stored in a particular format; DNA is represented by sequences of nucleotides, etc. Whatever the representation, streams of information can be tokenized and matching tokens can be plotted. The patterns that appear in the plots reveal universal similarity structures that exist in all digital objects at multiple scales and levels of representation.

The Dotplot technique is illustrated in Figure 8a. A sequence is tokenized and plotted from left to right and top to bottom with a dot where the tokens match. Dots off the main diagonal indicate similarities. While Figure 8a shows six words of Shakespeare, Figure 9a shows "The Complete Works". Grid lines show the boundaries between concatenated files. Dark areas show a high density of matches, while light areas show

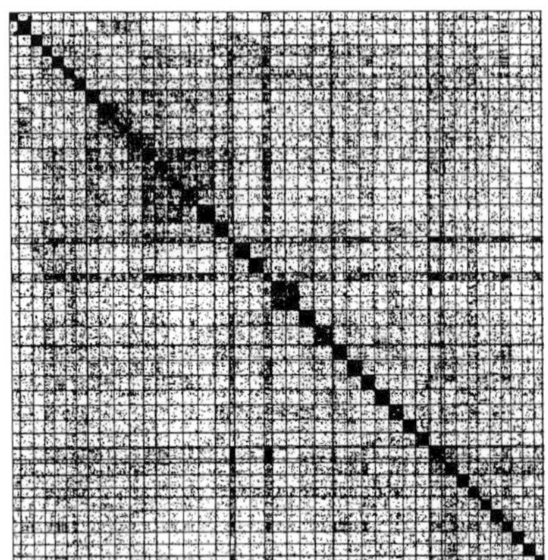

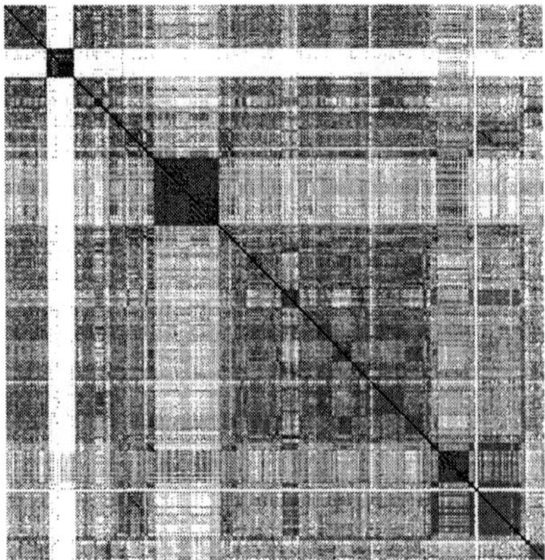

Figure 9. Dotplot. *a) A million words of Shakespeare, b) About two million lines of C code: an entire module of telecommunications switching program.*

a low density of matches. Weighting and reconstruction methods are used to display matches from more than one pair of tokens in a single pixel. Weighting prevents matches between frequent tokens from saturating the plot. Additional details of the dotplot technique are described elsewhere (Church and Helfman, 1993).

Previous approaches to detecting similarity do not reveal the richness of the similarity structures that have been hidden in our software, data, literature, and languages. Information retrieval techniques that model documents as distributions of unordered words, can identify similar documents, but can not identify copies, versions or translations. Dynamic programming techniques (e.g. the UNIX *diff* utility) and algorithms that identify longest common substrings have difficulty dealing with noisy or reordered input. In contrast, the Dotplot technique is remarkably robust and insensitive to noise because it relies on the human visual system for identify patterns.

Dotplot patterns are interpreted though a visual language of squares and diagonals (Church and Helfman, 1993). Figures 8b-f show Dotplots of artificial character sequences that have been tokenized into characters and plotted with a dot where the characters match. Figure 8b shows that squares identify unordered matches (documents with lots of matching words or subroutines with lots of matching symbols), while Figure 8c shows that diagonals identify ordered matches (copies, versions, and translations). Although dotplots often appear complex, they can always be interpreted in terms of their constituent squares and diagonals.

The Dotplot technique scales up to very large data sets. No matter how many matches are plotted, the interpretation of squares and diagonals is still the same. For example, the small, dark squares along the main diagonal of Figure 9a are caused by the names of the casts of characters in each of Shakespeare's plays, which generally match within a single play, but not across different plays. There are also dark squares along the main diagonal of Figure 9b, a Dotplot of about two million lines of C code. The input to Figure 9b (and the other dotplots of C code, Figures 10 and 11a) has been tokenized into lines and plotted with a dot where entire lines of code match. The squares in Figure 9b identify submodules of a large telecommunications switching system; comments and statements generally match within a single module, but not across different modules. In both Figures 9a and 9b, squares identify unordered matches. As another example, in Figure 10a, a Dotplot of about 3000 lines of C code (from the same telecommunications switching system shown in Figure 9b), diagonals identify groups of several hundred consecutive lines of code that were copied at least four times. In Figure 10b, a Dotplot of about 67,000 lines of C code, the long, broken, diagonals identify different versions of the same program. In each case, diagonals identify ordered matches. Broken diagonals, shown synthesized in Figure 8d, identify insertions of unordered tokens into otherwise ordered matches. In Figure 10b, each discontinuity in the diagonals indicate lines of code that were added to the new version of the program.

The Dotplot technique reveals similarity structures at multiple levels of representation. For example, the grid-like texture of Figure 11a is formed by repeated "break" tokens in a C program "switch" statement. This pattern is not due to a particular programmer, but rather to the designers of the C programming language itself, who chose to require an explicit syntactic struc-

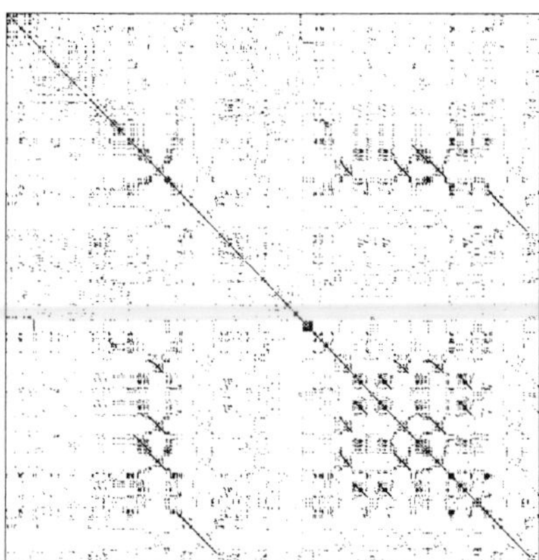
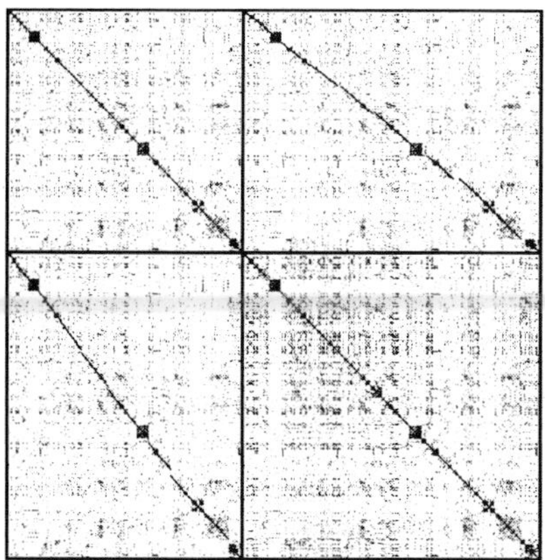

Figure 10. Dotplot. *a)Copies in 3400 lines of C code, b)two versions of the X Toolkit (66,600 lines of C code).*

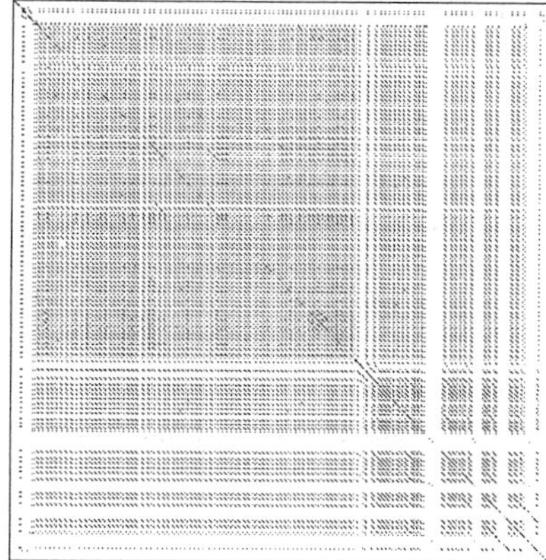
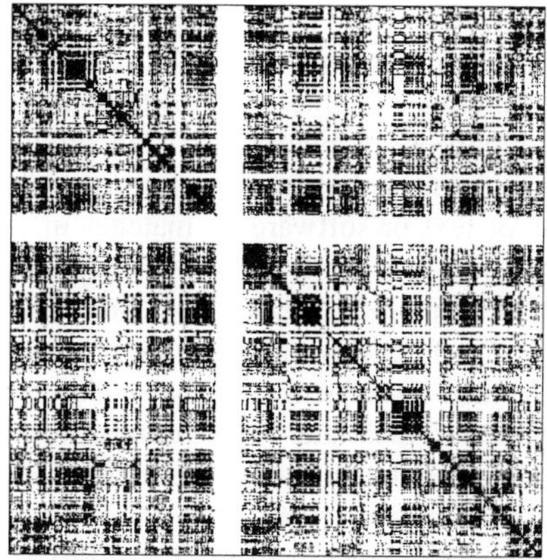

Figure 11. Dotplot. *a) A 1000 line C switch statement, b) 290,000 file names.*

ture ("break") to achieve a commonly needed function (terminate a switch statement). As a result, grid-like textures occur frequently in Dotplots of C code.

The analysis of string matches might seem to be limited, static, and literal. If you analyze only matching strings in a program's code or data, you might expect to learn about the program's syntax, but you might not expect to learn anything about the program's semantics, how it works, runs, or is used. However, in some cases at least, the similarity structure of data related to a program does reveal aspects of how the program is used, and how it works. For example, Figure 11b is a Dotplot of several hundred thousand file names, each of the files on our laboratory's file server one particular afternoon. The file names appear in *inode* order (the order in which they were created) and a dot appears wherever two file names match.

The large white cross that spans Figure 11b is modeled by the character sequence of Figure 8e in which a sequence of *b*'s is inserted into a larger sequence of *a*'s. In general, light crosses indicate insertions into unordered sequences. The light cross in Figure 11b is caused by several thousand files with unique names that were created at about the same time. These file names were in fact generated by the UNIX *split* utility. Someone was in the process of sending the X Window System to Spain via email! Near the center of Figure 11b is a dark square, which when plotted with greater resolution (see Figure 12a), is shown to be formed by a pattern of equally-spaced diagonals. This pattern indicates that the file system is used to store many sets of files with exactly the same names, in exactly the same order---in fact, the file system is being used to store many different versions of the same, large program.

It is important to emphasize that both Figures 11b and 12a plot data associated with a particular program (i.e. file names). The code for the file system program

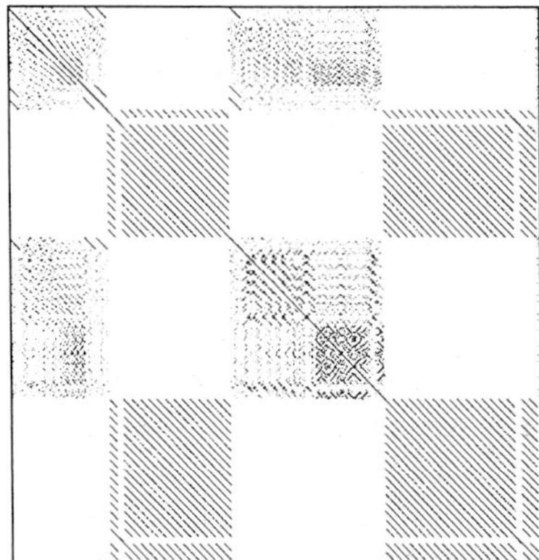

Figure 12. Dotplot. *a) Versioning in 8000 file names, b) Palindromes in 900 file names.*

itself is not plotted. Yet Figures 11b and 12a identify two different ways in which the file system program is used (as temporary storage while transferring large programs and as permanent storage for versions of large programs). An even more stunning example is shown in Figure 12b (a detail of Figure 12a). Figure 12b shows reverse diagonals, a rare form of diagonal that is hardly ever seen in dotplots of text or software (yet quite frequent in dotplots of music). A reverse diagonal, modeled in Figure 8f, indicates a palindrome, a sequence that is the same forwards as it is backwards. In Figure 12b the palindromes are formed by sequences of file names that appear first in one order, then later in the reverse order. These files were generated by the UNIX *make* utility that was used to quickly free several inodes ("make clean") and then reallocate them ("make"). The file system evidently stores inodes in a stack (i.e. a data structure with a Last-In-First-Out or LIFO access policy) so that they are reallocated in an order that is the reverse of the order in which they are freed. In this case, the Dotplot identifies a design decision in the file system code itself (which isn't even being plotted!).

Although understanding the similarity structure of large, complex Dotplots (such as the one shown in Figure 9b) is straightforward, it can be tedious. In an attempt to make large, complex Dotplots even easier to understand, we have begun experimenting with interactive Dotplot tours by combining Dotplots with Pad++. A Dotplot can be analyzed automatically and regions of the plot that contain high densities of matches can be precomputed at different resolutions along with textual representations of the input tokens most responsible for the matches. The precomputed plots can then be automatically scaled and positioned over an image of the original Dotplot in Pad++. Animations can be generated that zoom through the precomputed plots while updating a textual view of the associated matching tokens. At any time, users watching the animated tour can pause the animation to obtain additional information about the data set, compute additional plots, etc.

In summary, we have shown that although dotplots are primarily a technique for plotting literal string matches in static data, they are remarkably general, robust, resolution independent, representation independent, and can even reveal dynamic information about how programs are used and designed. In addition, we have described some preliminary experiments that promise to make Dotplots even more dynamic and interactive.

2.6 Information Visualizer

Card and colleagues have developed the *Information Visualizer* as part of an effort to attempt to better understand information workspaces. The system is based on the use of 3D/Rooms (Henderson and Card, 1986) for increasing the capacity of immediate storage available for the user, what they term the *Cognitive Coprocessor Scheduler-Based* user interface interaction architecture for coupling the user to information agents, and the use of visualization for interacting with information structure. (Card, Robertson, and Mackinlay, 1991).

The system is motivated by looking at information-based work in terms of cost structure. While it is widely appreciated that it costs to acquire, organize, and store information, the designers of the Information Visualizer emphasize that it also costs to access information and that a most important potential benefit of information visualization is that it can lower the cost structure of information access. For example, effective information visualizations often make aspects of in-

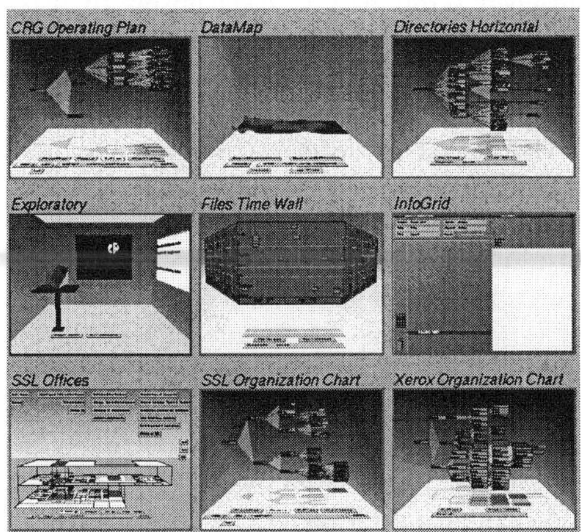

Figure 13. Information Visualizer. *This depicts a variety of Information Visualizer applications. These include visualization techniques for browsing hierarchical structure (Cone Trees and Cam Trees) and linear structure (Perspective Wall). See Card, Robertson, and Mackinlay for more detail about these and other Information visualizer applications.*

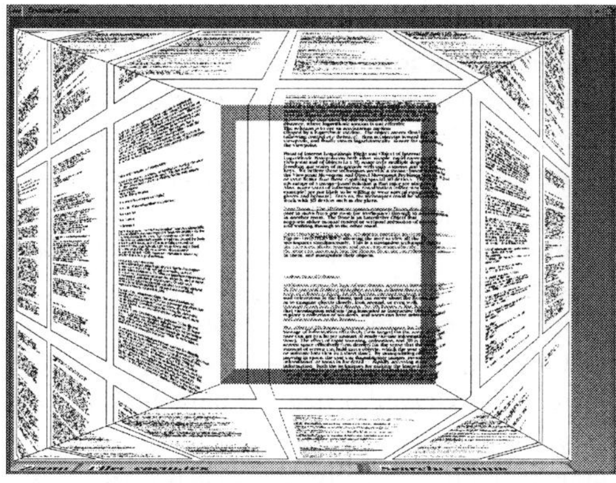

Figure 14. Document Lens. *This example of a document lens uses a rectangular lens with elastic sides that produces a truncated pyramid. The sides of the pyramid contain the portions of the document not visible in the rectangular area. This is another example of use of the focus plus context information visualization technique first explored in Furnas work on fisheye lenses.*

formation that would normally have required inference directly perceptually available. Turning what would have required inference into direct perception is an example of changing the cost structure of information.

Card, Robertson, and Mackinlay make an analogy to the cost structure of sources of information for a typical office worker. Such an office worker can access a variety of information sources ranging from a computer terminal to files in a filing cabinet or books in a bookcase. They argue that each piece of this information has a cost structure associated with finding and accessing it and point out that what is normally meant by an "organized office" is one arranged so as to have a low cost structure.

Figure 13 gives a schematic overview of Information Visualizer projects. Main features of this work are the use of 3D perspective to provide focus plus context views of information and the use of double-buffering and other animation techniques to provide smooth interaction. Of central importance is a cognitive coprocessor architecture. This architecture is designed to increase the information interaction coupling with users. The architecture is based on a scheduler that continuously tries to support a level of interactivity appropriate for particular taks. The system will, for example, degrade rendering if that is needed to be able to maintain an appropriate level of responsiveness.

Figure 14 depicts lenses used with the Information Visualizer. In this case it is a document lens, a rectangular lens with elastic sides, that provides a focus plus context view of a document. Figure 15 shows two alternative techniques for depicting hierarchical structure. The figure at the top shows a cone tree visualization of a hierarchical directory structure. The visualization at the bottom shows an alternative layout. Again, notice the use of 3D perspective to provide fisheye views. Also when a node is selected the tree smoothly rotates so that nodes on a path to the root node are brought to the front. Animation is at a rate such that object constancy is maintained and thus the cognitive cost for the user of reorienting to the new layout is minimized.

2.7 History-Enriched Digital Objects

In addition to visualizing the information structure inherent in objects, we can also visualize the history of interaction with digital objects. By recording the interaction events associated with use of objects (e.g. reports, forms, source-code, manual pages, email, spreadsheets) makes it possible on future occasions, when the objects are used again, to display graphical abstractions of the accrued histories as parts of the objects themselves. For example, we depict on source code its copy history so that a developer can see that a particular section of code has been copied and perhaps be led to correct a bug not only in the piece of code being viewed but also in the code from which it was derived.

The basic idea behind history-enriched digital ob-

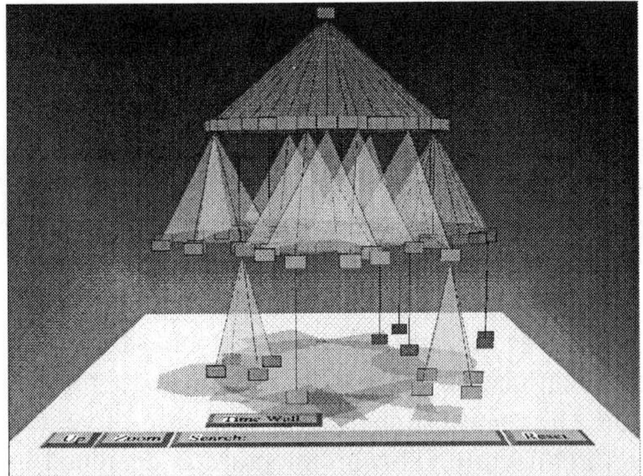

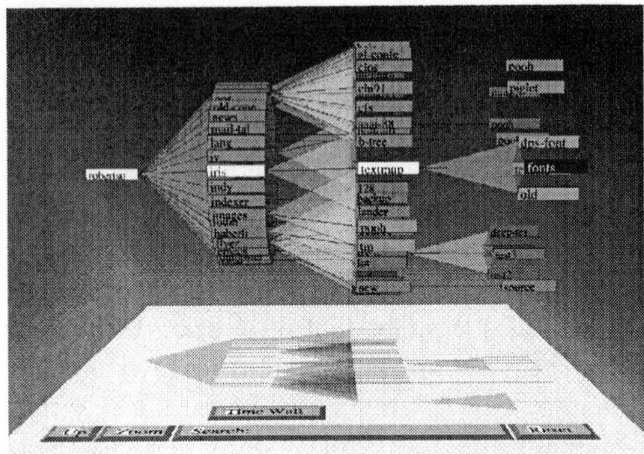

Figure 15. Cone Trees. *Use of three dimensions to view hierarchies. At the top is a simple cone tree. When a note is selected the tree rotates so that nodes on the path to the top node are brought to the front.. Animation is at a rate that object constancy is maintained. The lower figure shows an alternative layout.*

jects is to record the history of use on interface objects. We maintain a history of interactions and then attempt to display useful graphical abstractions of that history as parts of the objects themselves. In our interaction with objects in the world there are occasions when the history of their use is available to us in ways that support our interaction with them. For example, the well worn section of a door handle suggests where to grasp it. The binding of a new paper back book is such that it opens to the place we stopped reading last time. The most recently used pieces of paper occupy the tops of piles on our desk. The physics of the world is such that at times the histories of our use of items are perceptually available to us in ways that inform and support the tasks we are doing. We can mimic some of these mechanisms in interface objects. Of more importance we can also look for new types of mechanisms we can exploit in a computational media that have similar informative and supportive properties.

One of our first efforts was to explore the use of attribute-mapped scroll bars as mechanisms to make the history of interaction with documents and source code available. We have modified various editors to maintain interaction histories. Among other things, we recorded who edited or read various sections of a document. The history of that interaction was then graphically made available in the scroll bar. Figure 16 shows a history of editing of a file of code. We can see which sections have been edited most recently and who has edited various sections. A feature of representing this in the scroll bar is that it makes good use of limited display real estate. To investigate any particular section, users need only point at click at that section of the scroll bar.

We have explored a variety of other applications of the idea of history-enriched digital objects. For example, one can apply the idea to menus so that one might see the accrued history of menu choices of other users of a system by making the more commonly used menu items brighter. Or one can present spreadsheets such that the history of changes of items are graphically available. Thus, one easily can see which parts of a budget were undergoing modification. We have also explored applications that record the time spent in various editor buffers to allow one to see a history of the amount of time spent on the tasks associated with those buffers. We also record the amount of time spent reading wire services, netnews, manual pages, and email messages. This type of information can then be shared to allow people to exploit the history of others interaction with these items. One can, for example, be directed to news stories that significant others have already spent considerable time reading or to individuals who have recently viewed a manual page that you are currently accessing.

Of course, there are complex privacy issues involved with recording and sharing this kind of data. In our view, such data should belong to users and it should be their decision what is recorded and how it might be shared.

2.8 Toward a New View of Information

We hope this brief survey of recent informational visualization research has expanded your view of the possibilities for new dynamic information entities. We think the future holds an ever richer world of computationally-based work materials arrayed in multiple spaces that exploit representations of tasks, semantic relationships explicit and implicit in information and in our interactions with it, and user-specified tailorings to

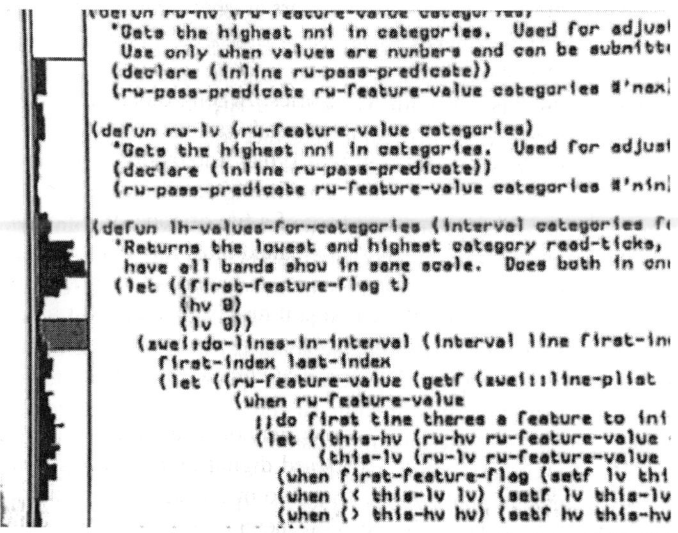

Figure 16. Attributed-Mapped Scroll Bar. *The scroll bar depicts a graphical summary of the history of editing this code.*

provide effective, enjoyable, and beautiful places to work. Underlying this work is the beginnings of what we think is a paradigm shift for thinking about information, one that starts to view information as being much more dynamic and reactive to the nature of our tasks, activities, and even relationships with others.

In our view, this paradigm shift is evidenced in interfaces starting to move beyond mimicking mechanisms of earlier media to more fully exploit computationally-based mechanisms. While there is clearly much to be gained from continuing to explore traditional approaches, we see this new paradigm as expanding the space of interface possibilities. It also brings with it major challenges associated with developing new dynamic representations.

While interface designers have traditionally followed a metaphor-based approach, we see these new areas of the design space as arising from what we term an *informational physics* approach to interface design. Viewing information as being more dynamic and operating according to multiple alternative physics highlights a shift in focus to exploration of new representational mechanisms that do not necessarily have origins or analogues in the mechanisms of earlier static media. While an informational physics strategy for interface design certainly involves metaphor, we think there is much that is distinctive about a informational physics approach. Traditional metaphor-based approaches map at the level of high-level objects and functionality. They yield interfaces with objects such as windows, trash cans, and menus, and functions like opening and closing windows and choosing from menus. While there are ease-of-use benefits from such mappings, they also orient designers towards mimicking mechanisms of earlier media rather than towards exploring potentially more effective computer-based mechanisms. Semantic zooming is but one example mechanism that we think more naturally arises from adopting an informational physics strategy.

We are not the first to propose a physics-inspired view of interface design. It derives, like many interface ideas, from the seminal work of Sutherland on Sketchpad. Simulations and constraint-based systems that fostered the development of direct manipulation style interfaces are other examples of this general approach. They too derive from Sutherland and continue to inspire developments. Recent examples include the work of Borning and his students (Borning, 1979 and Borning, 1981). Witkin (Harada, Witkin, and Baraff, 1995) in particular has taken a *physics-as-interface* approach to construction of dynamic interactive interfaces.

Smith's Alternate Reality Kit (Smith, 1987 and Smith, 1996) and languages such as Self (Ungar and Smith, 1987) are also examples of following a physics-based strategy for interface design. These systems make use of techniques normally associated with simulation to help "blur the distinction between data and interface by unifying both simulation objects and interface objects as concrete objects" (Chang and Unger, 1993). More importantly, they are based on implementation of mechanisms at a different level of abstraction than is traditional. Smith, for example, gives users access to control of parameters of the underlying physics in his Alternate Reality Kit. With this approach comes the realization that one can do much more than just mimic reality. As Chang and Unger point out in their discussion of the use of cartoon animation mechanisms in Self, "adhering to what is possible in the physical world is not only limiting, but also less effective in achieving *realism*."

One aspect of our argument here is that it is important to look at the costs as well as the benefits of traditional metaphor-based strategies. We think it is crucial to not allow existing metaphors, even highly successful ones, to overly constrain exploration of alternative interface mechanisms. While acknowledging the importance and even inevitability of the use of metaphors in interface design, we feel it is important to understand that they have the potential to limit our views of possible interface mechanisms in at least four ways.

First, metaphors necessarily pre-exist their use. Pre-Copernicans could never have used the metaphor of the solar system for describing the atom. In designing interfaces, one is limited to the metaphorical resources at hand. In addition, the metaphorical reference must be familiar in order to work. An unfamiliar interface metaphor is functionally no metaphor at all. One can never design metaphors the way one can design self-consistent physical descriptions of appearance and behavior. Thus, as an interface design strategy, physics, in the sense described above, offers more design options than traditional metaphor-based approaches.

Second, metaphors are temporary bridging concepts. When they become ubiquitous, they die. In the same way that linguistic metaphors lose their metaphorical impact (e.g., *foot of the mountain* or *leg of table*), successful metaphors also wind up as dead metaphors (e.g. file, menu, window, desktop). The familiarity provided by the metaphor during earlier stages of use gives way to a familiarity with the interface due to actual experience.

Thus, after a while, it is the actual details of appearance and behavior (i.e. the physics) rather than any overarching metaphor that form much of the substantive knowledge of an experienced user. Any restrictions that are imposed on the behaviors of the entities of the interface to avoid violations of the initial metaphor are potential restrictions of functionality that may have been employed to better support the users' tasks and allow the interface to continue to evolve along with the users' increasing competency.

Similarly, the pervasiveness of dead metaphors such as files, menus, and windows may well restrict us from thinking about alternative organizations of interaction with the computer. There is a clash between the dead metaphor of a file and newer concepts of persistent distributed objects.

Third, since the sheer amount and complexity of information with which we need to interact continues to grow, we require interface design strategies that *scale*. A traditional metaphor-based strategy does not scale. A physics approach, on the other hand, scales to organize greater and greater complexity by uniform application of sets of simple laws. In contrast, the greater the complexity of the metaphorical reference, the less likely it is that any particular structural correspondence between metaphorical target and reference will be useful. We see this often as designers start to merge the functionality of separate applications to better serve the integrated nature of complex tasks. Metaphors that work well with the individual simple component applications typically do not smoothly integrate to support the more complex task.

Fourth, it is clear that metaphors can be harmful as well as helpful since they may well lead users to import knowledge not supported by the interface. Our point is not that metaphors have not useful but that as the primary design strategy they may well restrict the range of interfaces designers consider and impose less effective trade-offs than designers might come to if they were to consider a larger space of possible interfaces.

There are, of course, also costs associated in following a physics-based design strategy. One cost is that designers can no longer rely as heavily on users' familiarity with the metaphorical reference (at least at the level of traditional objects and functionality) and so, physics-based designs may take longer to learn. However, the power of metaphor comes early in usage and is rapidly superseded by the power of actual experience. One might want to focus on easily discoverable physics. As is the case with metaphors, all physics are not created equally discoverable or equally fitted to the requirements of human cognition. Still, the new dynamic representations we are now starting to explore as part of an informational physics strategy may well serve as the metaphorical basis for future interfaces.

2.9 Acknowledgments

Our views of information visualization and an informational physics approach to interface design have benefited from many discussions with the members of our research groups over the years. We particularly acknowledge Scott Stornetta, Will Hill, Ken Perlin, Larry Stead, Kent Wittenburg, Jon Meyer, Mark Rosenstein, Dave Wroblewski, and Tim McCandless.

2.10 References

Bederson, B. B., and Hollan, J. D. (1994). Pad++: A Zooming Graphical Interface for Exploring Alternate Interface Physics. *Proceedings of 1994 ACM User Interface and Software Technology Conference, UIST'94*, 17-26.

Bederson, B. B., Hollan, J. D., Perlin, K., Meyer, J., Bacon, D., and Furnas, G. W. (1996). Pad++: A Zoomable Graphical Sketchpad for Exploring Alternate Interface Physics. *Journal of Visual Languages and Computing, 7*, 3-31.

Bederson, B. B., Hollan, J. D., Stewart, J., Rogers, D., Vick, D., Grose, E., and Forsythe, C. (1997). A Zooming Web Browser. Submitted to *CHI'97*.

Bier, E. A., Stone, M. C., Pier, K., Buxton, W., and DeRose, T. D. (1993). Toolglass and Magic Lenses: The See-Through Interface. *Proceedings of 1993 ACM SIGGRAPH Conference*. 73-80.

Borning, A. (1979). *Thinglab: A Constraint-Oriented Simulation Laboratory*. Xerox PARC Technical Report SSL-79-3.

Borning, A. (1981). The Programming Language Aspects of Thinglab: A Constraint-Oriented Simulation Laboratory. *Transactions on Programming Language and Systems. 3 (4),* 353-387.

Borning, A. (1986). Defining Constraints Graphically. Human Factors in Computing Systems. *Proceedings SIGCHI'86.*

Card, S. K., Robertson, G. G., and Mackinlay, J. D. (1991). The Information Visualizer: An Information Workspace. *Proceedings of 1991 ACM SIGGHI conference.* 181-188.

Card, S. K., Robertson, G. G., and York, W. (1996). The WebBook and the Web Forager: An Information Workspace for the World-Wide Web. *CHI'96 Conference Proceedings*, 111-117.

Chang, B. and Unger, D. (1993). Animation: From Cartoons to the User Interface. *UIST'93*, 45-55

Church, K. W., and Helfman, J. I. (1993). Dotplot: A Program for Exploring Self-Similarity in Millions of Lines of Text and Code. *Journal of Computational And Graphical Statistics*, American Statistical Society and Interface Foundation. 2 (2), 153-174.

Cleveland, W. S. and McGill, M. E. (1988). *Dynamic Graphics for Statistics.* Cole Advanced Books Software: Wadsworth & Brooks.

Donnelson, W. C. (1978). Spatial Management of Information. *Proceedings of 1978 ACM SIGGRAPH Conference.* 203-209.

Dumais, S. T., Furnas, G. W., Landauer, T. K., Deerester, S., and Harshman, R. (1988). Using Latent Semantic Analysis To Improve Access To Textual Information. *Proceedings of CHI'88.* 281-286.

Furnas, G. W. (1986). Generalized Fisheye Views. *Proceedings of 1986 ACM SIG-CHI conference.* 16-23.

Harada, M., Witkin, A., and Baraff, D. (1995). Interactive Physically-Based Manipulator of Discrete Continuous Models. *Computer Graphics Proceedings (SIGGRAPH'95),* 1-10.

Henderson, A. and Card, S. (1986). Rooms: The Use of Multiple Virtual Workspace To Reduce Space contention in a Window-Based Graphical Interface. *ACM Transaction on Graphics. 5 (3),* 211-243.

Herot, C. F. (1980). Spatial Management of Data. *ACM Transactions on Database Systems. 5 (4),* 493-514.

Hollan, J. D., Williams, M. D., and Stevens, A. (1981). An Overview of STEAMER. *Behavior Research Methods and Instrumentation. 13*, 85-90.

Hollan, J. D., Hutchins, E. L., and Weitzman, L. (1984). Steamer: An Interactive Inspectable Simulation-Based Training System. *AI Magazine 5* (2), 15-27.

Hollan, J. D., and Stornetta, W. S. (1992). Beyond Being There. *CHI '92 Conference Proceedings*, 119-126.

Hollan, J. D., Rich, E., Hill, W., Wroblewski, D., Wilner, W., Wittenburg, K., Grudin, J., and Members of the Human Interface Laboratory. (1991). An introduction to HITS: In *Human Interface Tool Suite. Intelligent User Interfaces.* Sullivan and Tyler (Eds.), 293-337.

Hutchins, E. L., Hollan, J. D., and Norman, D. A. (1985). Direct manipulation Interfaces. *Human-Computer Interaction. 1*, 311-338.

Keller, P. R., and Keller, M. M. (1993). *Visual Cues: Practical Data Visualization.* IEEE Computer Society Press

Macinlay, J. D., (1996). Automating the Design of Graphical Presentation of Relational Information. *ACM Transactions on Graphics*, 5, 110-141.

Maizel, J. and Lenk, R. (1981). Enhanced Graphic Matrix Analysis of Nucleic Acid and Protein Sequences. In *Proceedings of the National Academy of Science, Genetics*, USA. 78 7665-7669.

Perlin, K. and Fox, D. (1993). Pad: An Alternative Approach to the Computer Interface. *Proceedings of 1993 ACM SIGGRAPH Conference*. 57-64.

Pustell, J. and Kafatos, F. (1982). A High Speed, High Capacity Homology Matrix: A Zooming Through SV40 and Polyoma. *Nucleic Acids Research*, 10 (15) 4765-4782.

Robertson, G. C., Card, S. K., and Mackinlay, J. D. (1993). Information Visualizer Explores Future of User Interfaces. *Communications of the ACM, 36 (4)* 56-72.

Roth, S. F., Kolojejchick, J., Mattis, J., and Chuah, M. (1995). SageTools: An Intelligent Environment for Sketching, Browsing, and Customizing Data Graphics. Conference Companion of the conference on *Human Factors in Computing Systems (SIGCHI '95),* 409-410.

Smith, R. B. (1987). The Alternate Reality Kit: An Example of the Tension Between Literalism and Magic. *Proceedings of CHI + GI*, 61-67.

Smith, R. B. (1996). The Alternate Reality Kit: An Animated Environment for Creating Interactive Simulations. *Proceedings of IEEE Computer Society Workshop on Visual Languages*, 99-106.

Shneiderman, B. (1983). Direct Manipulation: A Step Beyond Programming Languages. *Computer, 16 (8),* 57-69.

Stone, C. S., Fishkin, K., and Bier, E. A. (1994). The Moveable Filter as a User Interface Toool. *Human Factors in Computing Systems: CHI '94 Conference Proceedings*, 306-312.

Sutherland, I. E. (1963). Sketchpad: A Man-Machine Graphical Communications System. *Proceedings of the Spring Joint Computer conference*. Baltimore: Spartan Books. 329-346.

Tufte, E. R. (1983). *The Visual Display of Quantitative Information*. Graphics Press.

Tufte, E. R. (1990). *Envisioning Information*. Graphic Press.

Unger, D. and Smith, R. (1987). Self: The Power of Simplicity. *OOPSLA '87 Proceedings*, 227-241.

Witkin, A., Gleicher, M. S., and Welch, W. (1990). Interactive Dynamics. *Computer Graphics, 24*, 11-21.

Handbook of Human-Computer Interaction
Second, completely revised edition
M. Helander, T.K. Landauer, P. Prabhu (eds.)

Chapter 3

Mental Models and User Models

Robert B. Allen
Bellcore
Morristown, New Jersey, USA

3.1 Introduction

The expectations a user has about a computer's behavior come from *mental models* (Figure 1); while the "expectations" a computer has of a user come from *user models* (Figure 2). The two types of models are similar in that they produce expectations one "intelligent agent" (the user or the computer) has of another. The fundamental distinction between them is that mental models are inside the head while user models occur inside a computer. Thus, mental models can be modified only indirectly by training while user models can be examined and manipulated directly.

3.2 Mental Models

Models are approximations to objects or processes which maintain some essential aspects of the original. In cognitive psychology, mental models are usually considered to be the ways in which people model *processes*. The emphasis on process distinguishes mental models from other types of cognitive organizers such as schemas. Models of processes may be thought of as simple machines or transducers which combine or transform inputs to produce outputs. While some discussions about mental models focus on the representation, the approach here considers mental models as the combination of a representation and the mechanisms associated with those representations (see Anderson, 1983).

A mental model synthesizes several steps of a process and organizes them as a unit. A mental model does not have to represent all of the steps which compose the actual process (e.g., the model of a computer program or a detailed account of the computer's transistors). Indeed, mental models may be incomplete and may even be internally inconsistent. The representation in a mental model is, obviously, not the same as the real-world processes it is modeling. The mental models may be termed *analogs* of real-world processes because they incorporate some, but not all, aspects of the real-world process (Gentner and Gentner, 1983). Mental models are also termed *user's modes* (Norman, 1983) although the expression is avoided here because of confusion with the term "user models" (Section 3.3).

Because they are not directly observable, several different types of evidence have been used to infer the characteristics of mental models:

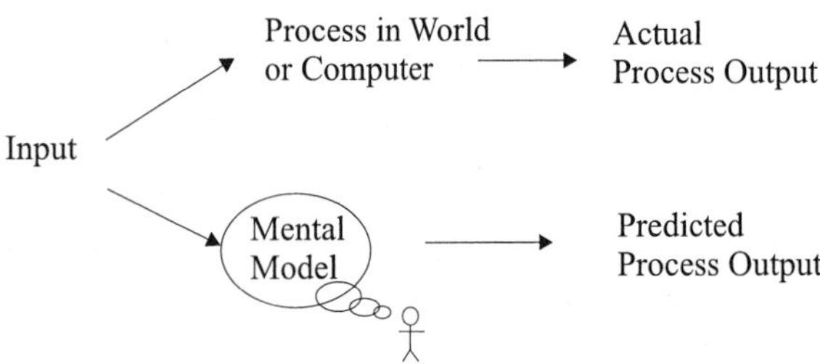

Figure 1. Process and mental model of that process.

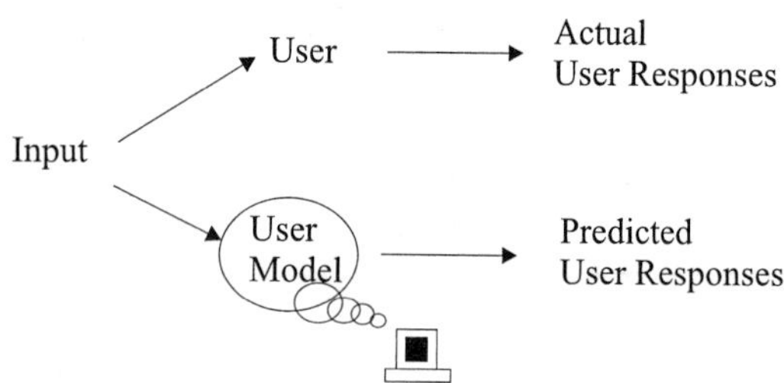

Figure 2. User responses and user model predicting those responses.

- **Predictions:** Users can predict what will happen next in a sequential process and how changes in one part of the system will be reflected in other parts of the system. However the most informative aspect of their predictions are often the errors from the model.

- **Explanations and Diagnosis:** Explanations about the causes of an event and diagnoses of the reasons for malfunctions reflect mental models.

- **Training:** People who are trained to perform tasks with a coherent account (i.e., a conceptual model, see below) of those tasks complete them better than people who are not trained with the model.

- **Other:** Evidence is also obtained from reaction times for eye movements and answering questions about processes.

3.2.1 Conceptual Models

Because mental models are in the user's head, it is helpful to have models of mental models in order to discuss them. These models of mental models may be termed *conceptual models*. Several classes of conceptual models may be identified:

Metaphor: Metaphor uses of the similarity of one process with which a person is familiar to teach that person about a different process (Carroll, 1988). For instance, a filing cabinet for paper records may be used to explain a computer file system. Indeed, the metaphor may be built into the interface (as in the use of filing cabinet icons). The ways in which a metaphor is incorporated into a mental model are difficult to examine and probably vary greatly from user to user. Moreover, a metaphor can be counterproductive because the metaphor is rarely a perfect match to the actual process and incorrect generalizations from the metaphor can result in poor performance on the task (Halasz, 1983). For instance, if word processing is introduced by analogy to typing on paper pages, word-wrapping on the screen makes little sense.

Surrogates: Surrogates are descriptions of the mechanisms underlying the process. For a pocket calculator, surrogate models would describe its function in terms of registers and stacks. As noted by Young (1983), surrogate models are not well suited to describing user-level interaction. For example, they provide poor explanations for the learnability of a system (e.g., how to use a calculator to do simple arithmetic operations).

Mappings, Task-Action Grammars, and Plans: Another class of conceptual model describes the links between the task the users must complete and the actions required to complete those tasks. Several models have this property. Young (1983) describes task-action *mappings*, which are simple pairings between tasks and actions. He compares this with the surrogate model (above) for describing the performance on simple tasks with three calculator architectures. In distinction to surrogates, he claims that mappings are suitable for describing learnability and as a basis for design.

Grammars are of interest because of their ability to describe systematic variations of complex sequences. Specifically, grammars computer dialogs are often described as a type of linguistic interaction. Grammars can be designed which specify actions as terminal nodes. TAG (Task-Action Grammars, Payne and Greene, 1986) is a framework for describing the grammars of specific command languages. It consists of definitions of tasks, categorization of tasks, and rules with schemas for combining tasks.

Planning models can also integrate tasks and actions. The GOMS model (Goals, Operators, Methods, and Selection; Card et al., 1983; Kieras, this volume) is a plan-based model which has been used widely to describe complex computer-based tasks.

Propositional Knowledge: The process assumptions of conceptual models not always explicit. Johnson-Laird (1983) has proposed that *propositional knowledge* (which he terms a "mental model") is the basis for most logical reasoning. However, his thesis has little direct application to human-computer interaction and it is not considered further here.

3.2.2 Mental Models for Computing Systems and Applications

Although mental models have been studied in physics and mathematics, the vast majority of research on them has been based on computer-human interaction. Many aspects of human-interaction with computers involve complex processes, thus people who interact with computer systems must have some type of mental model of those processes. There are several levels of processes in computing about which a person might build a model; these include a computer model such as the hardware, the operating system, software, and applications (such as text editors and spreadsheets). Indeed, an unresolved theoretical issue is whether it is possible to have multiple mental models active simultaneously and, if so, how they might interact.

Mental Models and Computing Systems: Computing systems are complex and their use and maintenance requires elaborate planning. Tasks such as system or network administration involve understanding many different subsystems. Users of computer systems also have mental models of those systems, although presumably these are very simple models compared to the system administrators. For instance, a user might have a (largely incorrect) mental model that Internet response times are based on the physical distance email messages have to travel. As noted above, training based on conceptual models about processes can lead to improved performance on tasks requiring an understanding of those processes.

Mental Models and Computing Applications: Users of computer applications have mental models of the effects of commands in operating these computing applications. For instance, users have expectations about the effects of entering values in using a spreadsheet. Halasz and Moran (1983) compared the effects of styles of training about simple calculators. Students given task-focused training were better at simple tasks than students trained with conceptual models of the calculator. On the other hand, the students trained with conceptual models were better at tasks that went beyond the initial training.

Borgman (1986) compared two styles of training on a command-based information retrieval system. In one type of training a conceptual model (what she called a "mental model") was used an analogy between the retrieval system and a traditional card catalog. The other training style was giving examples of how specific procedures would be accomplished. As in Halasz' study, the users trained by analogy performed better on tasks that required inferences beyond what was covered in the training.

When a user attempts to apply knowledge from a mental model for one task to another task, the *transfer* may show synergy or conflict. For instance, Douglas and Moran (1983) report that users familiar with traditional typewriters had more difficulty learning about electronic word processors than others. Mental models of "experts" may actually be counterproductive during transfer if they are not relevant to the task at hand. Singley and Anderson (1985) compared transfer among multiple text editors. The transfer was modeled by ACT (Anderson, 1983) in terms of the overlap in the number of rules needed to complete tasks with each of the text editors.

Designer's Mental Models: Design of complex systems requires mental models (Simon, 1969). Computer-related design tasks (as well as related design tasks such as the design of video-games, educational applications, and CD-ROMs) may involve the interaction of several different mental models. These may include models of the capabilities of the tools, models of the partially completed work and models of the user's interests and capabilities (Fischer, 1991).

Effective programmers seems to have a conceptual model of their programs as a machine for transforming inputs to outputs. Littman et al. (1986) compared two groups of programmers in a program debugging task. One group was instructed to attempt to systematically understand the program while fixing bugs. The other group was instructed to fix the bugs without attempting to form an overview of the programmer's function. The members of the first group were much better at understanding the interaction of the components of the program and they were also better at fixing the bugs.

3.2.3 Structuring Content to Improve Mental Models

The most important practical application of understanding students' mental models is for training. This section explores the issues in enhancing mental models of students with complex training programs. Section 3.3.11 examines interactive student models in which the students' knowledge is modeled to improve the performance, tutoring, and help systems.

Selection of appropriate text and graphics can aid the development of mental models. For instance, parts of a document could be highlighted to emphasize their relation to a particular concept (e.g., Kobsa et al., 1994). Training material about dynamic processes may include diagrams and other techniques for improving the learner's mental models. Hegarty and Just (1993) and Kieras (1988) have examined the optimal level of realism to present in schematic diagrams.

Beyond the local effects of media on mental models, the organization of the entire content of a manual or a course may be designed to improve the development of the user's mental models. *Scaffolding* is the process of training a student on core concepts and then gradually expanded the training. The "training wheels" approach (Carroll, 1990) is a type of scaffolding for training about computer systems.

Animation of data or scenarios which evolve over time should be especially useful for developing mental models because the causal relations in a process can be clearly illustrated. Gonzalez (1996) examined many properties of animations and found that factors such as the smoothness of the transitions were important for performance of tasks which had been presented with the animations. Because performance improved, it may be assumed that the mental models are also improved.

Interaction with a virtual environment can allow users to focus on those topics with which they are least familiar. The utility of organizers for improving the recall of information is well established. Lokuge et al. (1996) used this broad sense of mental models to develop a representation of the relationships among tourist sights in Boston. They then built a hypertext presentation which aids in the presentation of those relationships to people unfamiliar with Boston.

3.3 User Models

As indicated in Figure 2, the user model is the model computer software has of the user. In the following sections, several issues for user modeling are discussed (Sections 3.3.1-3.3.6) and then application areas are examined (Sections 3.3.7-3.3.11).

3.3.1 User Model Inputs

User models have parameters which can distinguish users. Sometimes these are set explicitly by the user and sometimes they are inferred by the computer from the user's past responses and behavior.

Explicit Profiles: In some user modeling techniques, users must create a profile of their interests. For example, in the information filtering technique know as *Selective dissemination of information* (SDI, Section 3.3.8), users must specify what terms match their interests. However, users may not have a clear memory of preferences or may not want to give an honest response. In addition, performance will be better if the user understands the model enough to select the discriminative terms (i.e., has a mental model of the user model mechanism). To some degree all entries in an explicit user profile are a type of self-categorization.

Inferences from User Behavior: An unobtrusive recording of movie preferences might simply collect information from a set-top box what movies a person had the set tuned to and how long the set stayed turned to that movie. In addition, assumptions are necessary to interpret this type of data. It is not safe to assume that a user is looking at their TV screen all the time, thus the amount of time a video is displayed on that screen may not be an accurate measure of the person's interest in that material. On the other hand, this type of data often has considerable value. Morita and Shinoda (1994) found a positive correlation between the amount of time a person spent look at a document and the ratings of interest in that document.

3.3.2 Degree of Personalization

User Models may be personalized to different degrees. They may range from baserate predictions to totally individualized predictions. All of these models should be better than random predictions.

Baserate Predictions: A *baserate* prediction is what would be expected for any individual (Allen, 1990). Baserate models might not even be considered user models since they are not differentiated across individuals. One example is of a baserate predication could follow statistical norms (e.g., that a person would like a

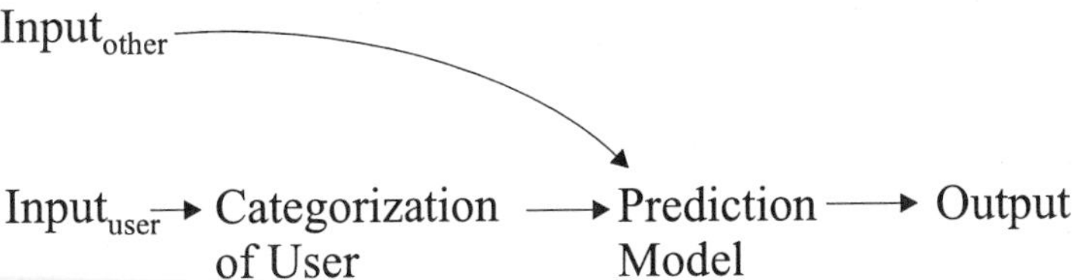

Figure 3. Categorization of user input.

best-selling book). Other types of baserate prediction could be derived from laws or social norms. In some cases, when the population is very consistent, baserates may be very accurate. In other cases, they may apply to only a small portion of the population.

User Categorization: Rather than developing separate models for each individual, users are often categorized and models developed based on those categories (as illustrated in Figure 3). Of course, the complexity of the categories may vary greatly from simple demographics (e.g., age) to complex personality constructs. There are many examples of categorization in user modeling. One example is the classification of utterances according to their function as *speech acts* (Section 3.3.10).

Another example of a user categorization is the novice-expert distinction. It might be expected that there would be consistent differences in the behavior of experts and novices which could be useful, for instance, in constructing different types of training. While there are clearly differences in the knowledge of novices and experts on a given task (e.g., Egan, 1988; Mayer, 1988), difficulties arise when attempting to classify people as novices or experts or in attempting to generalize expertise in one area to expertise in other areas. There are many dimensions of expertise and although users may be an expert on one set of commands, they may be novices in other areas. Thus, broad classification of users as experts or novices does not often seem to be helpful.

Still another example of categorization of users is a *stereotype* (Rich, 1989). Rich's "Grundy" system predicted preferences for fiction books, primarily using a user's self-descriptions (e.g., feminist) with adjectives as inputs. Unfortunately, it was difficult to tell whether Grundy's predictions were better than simple baserate predictions. To provide control conditions for a Grundy-like system for predicting book preferences, baserate predictions were found to make significantly better predictions than a random selection and a simple 'male/female' dichotomy further improved the predictions (Allen, 1990).

Kass and Finin (1991) describe GUMS (Generalized User Modeling System) in which they introduce the notion of hierarchical stereotypes and inference mechanisms based on that those stereotypes. This formalism is helpful for reasoning about users; however, it seems removed from the usual psychological notion of a stereotype. For instance, GUMS stereotypes include 'rational agents' and 'cooperative agents'. In addition, it is not clear that the stereotypes people have can be combined with or derived from other stereotypes in a systematic way.

3.3.3 User Models in Complex Systems

Blackboard Systems: A user model may be a component of more a complex system which includes other components. In some cases, a user model is said to contain all the knowledge a system has about the user. For instance, Wahlster and Kobsa (1989, p. 6) state: "A user model is a knowledge source in a NL dialog system which contains explicit assumptions on all aspects of the user that may be relevant to the dialog behavior of the system". In other cases, that knowledge is subdivided into several specific models such as task models and situation models. In training systems (Section 3.3.11), the "student model" holds task-relevant state and the "user model" applies to long-term knowledge about the user such as demographic information. This situation is similar to the suggestion that several different mental models may be active for a programming task (Section 3.2.2).

Figure 4 shows a typical collection of knowledge sources which includes user, task, and situation. The inputs are combined with data from various repositories on a blackboard. As described in the previous section, the *task expert* has information about what the user is trying to accomplish and possible strategies for accomplishing those goals. The *situation expert* contributes knowledge about the environment in which the

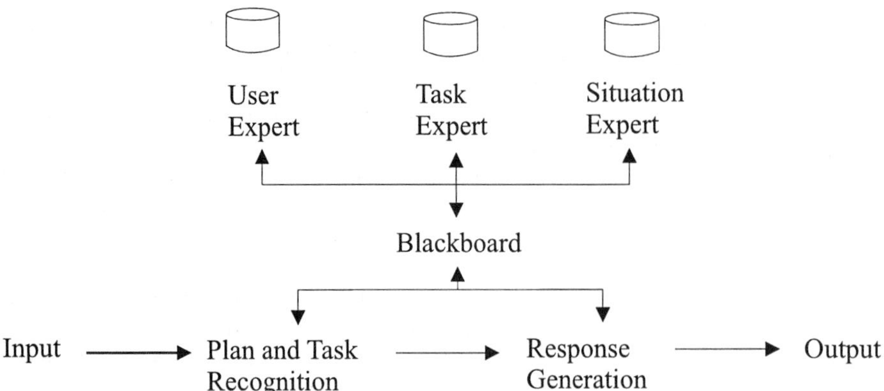

Figure 4. Typical components of a blackboard system.

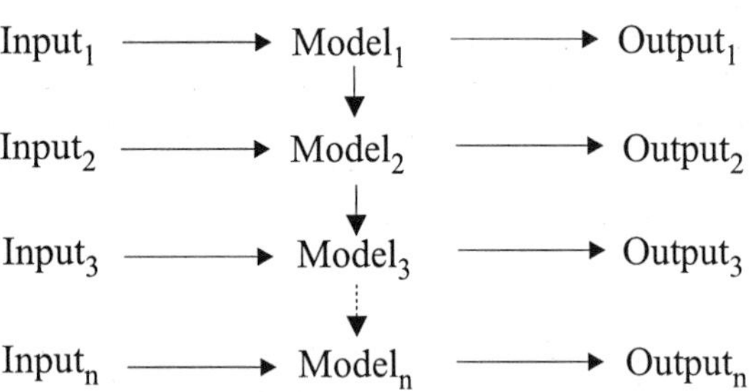

Figure 5. Adaptation of model across sequential events.

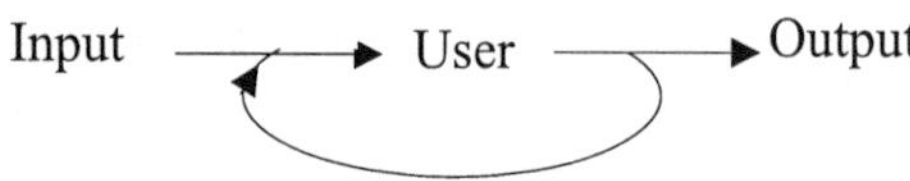

Figure 6. Model with feedback.

user is trying to complete the task. There are many possible ways of organizing the knowledge required for this type of system. Other components which have been proposed include *system, domain,* and *discourse* processors. Clearly, it is possible to partition these models in many different ways and simply proposing different sets of models is not necessarily helpful. Modularity is generally a useful design principle. Unfortunately, information about users may be very tangled and inconsistent. It may be difficult to separate the user model from the other models components. Even for Figure 3, it seems somewhat arbitrary to declare that the user model is just the categorization stage and does not include the Prediction Model.

User Agents: An *agent* may be considered as just one module of a complex system (e.g., one of the experts in Figure 4). However, a more interesting sense of the term "agent" is as modular system which acts on behalf of the user. A user agent might simply provide information about the user. For instance, it might search a database of the user's writings to answer a question on behalf of the user. An active user agent may negotiate on behalf of the user. This mean that user agents must have a model of the relative values of alternative outcomes for the user.

3.3.4 Adaptive Models, Machine Learning, and Feedback

User models are often said to *adapt* to users. However, there are different senses in which a model may be adaptive. In the simplest sense, a model is adaptive if it gives different responses to different categories of users. A more interesting sense is that a model adapts as it gains experience with an individual user. Adaptation may be within connected sequences of events or across different events. Figure 5 illustrates a model which keeps state across a sequences of inputs such as a conversation, information retrieval session, or task.

As indicated in Figure 6, *feedback* uses output from the model to refine it. This would be most common for models in which adjustments are made across a sequence of events for future trials. Most often feedback is an automatic process, however, having users refine their profiles could also be considered a type of feedback. The idea of feedback originated with control theory in which only a few parameters in the model would typically change; however, in computer models, the structure (i.e., the program) of the model itself may change.

User models which change and improve their performance as a result of greater experience are said to show *machine learning*. Some examples of machine learning algorithms are neural networks, genetic algorithms, clustering, and case-based reasoning. An important distinction is whether all training examples are maintained by the model (as in case-based reasoning) or whether other data are compressed to form a *representation* of the original training set.

3.3.5 Tasks and Planning

User models are often distinguish according to whether they apply to "short-term" or "long- term" interactions, however, this blurs several issues of adaptation and feedback. Typically, short-term models describe the user performance on specific tasks.

Tasks and Task Models: The task in which a person is engaged and plausible strategies for completing it greatly constrain the behavior of that person. Indeed, the task in which a person is engaged is often more important than individual differences for predicting user behavior (see Mischel, 1968). The interaction of tasks with behavior is so strong that there is a tendency to identify tasks or even to define new tasks to explain ambiguous behaviors. On the other hand, there are many cases in which individual differences have a major effect (Egan, 1988).

A *task model* (Sleeman, 1982) is a description of a task as well as strategies for completing that task. In some cases, the task model may include incorrect methods for completing the task. In situations when tasks are clearly defined, mental models and user models reflect the task structure. For instance, student models (Section 3.3.11) are typically focused on a student completing specific tasks.

Planning and Plan Recognition: Planning often proceeds as a cycle of determining goals or subgoals and finding methods for completing those goals. GOMS (Section 3.2.1; Kieras, this volume) is a planning model of how people complete command sequences. There are several different types of planning mechanisms and the nature of planning has been widely discussed recently. Some important dimensions for planning are whether the plans are fixed once they have been established or whether they may be modified depending on the situation.

When users complete a task they, presumably, have strategy for what they are doing. However, a human being or computer with whom they are interacting many not know what strategy the users have or even what task they are trying to accomplish. The process of *plan recognition* would involve identifying the task and the strategy. Although Figure 5 illustrated a user model in which the model is known, the figure might also be applied to plan recognition in which an observer must infer the model (i.e., the plan) and maybe the inputs (i.e., the task) given the outputs and a few contextual clues. For instance, a person who comes to a train ticket window is likely to be asking for information about trains but could, instead, be asking for other types of information. As suggested by J. Allen (1983, p. 108), "[People] are often capable of inferring the plans of other agents that perform some action."

A wide variety of techniques has been proposed for plan recognition. Most often some type of grammar is fit to responses although statistical methods such as neural networks could also be applied. Plan recognition may benefit from information about the user. For instance, knowing accents and idiosyncratic expressions may be useful for speech utterance understanding systems. The closely related problem of interpreting a student's strategy in solving a problem is an essential component of intelligent tutoring systems (Section 3.3.11).

Another tradition of inferring information about people from the context of their actions is *attribution theory* (Kelley, 1963). This describes the processes by which people make inferences about internal state of other people. For instance, *social norms* might be employed in assessing how a person might be expected to be behave in a given situation. A person who behaves differently from the norm is likely to be judged as showing an *intention* for that action.

3.3.6 Evaluation of User Models

Evaluation Criteria: The main criterion for the *effectiveness* of a user model is in predicting important behavior which facilitates the user's activities. Among the components contributing to this are:

- *Relevance* requires that models make predictions that apply to the target behavior or user goals.
- *Accuracy* requires that the models make correct predictions for at least one task and situation.
- *Generality* of the model requires robustness despite changes in tasks, situations, and users. In addition, the model should be *scaleable* with increased numbers of tasks, situations and users. Too many existing systems have been tested only on "toy" data sets.

- *Adaptability* of the model requires that it not be *brittle* in response to changes in user behavior.

- *Ease of development and maintenance* is whether the effort in maintaining the user model is worthwhile for the user. A typical factor is whether the inputs are collected unobtrusively. For instance, if the model has to be maintained by an individual, is it clear to the user how to do that?

- *Utility*: The model should improve the user's behavior. For instance, adding new commands to an interface based on a models might confuse the user.

Evaluation Techniques: While the ultimate test of a user model is how well it satisfies the criteria listed above, it is often difficult to test a model as a whole in field conditions. However, to test parts of it in limited environments. For a given set of inputs it is worth choosing the model which give the best predictions. Another standard for measuring the performance of a user model is to compare it to the performance of a human being who is given the same inputs. This is a control condition for the model. It may be called a *Turing control* condition because it is a limited type of Turing Test (Allen, 1990).

The extensive literature in psychology on techniques for assessing individual differences and personality types can be applied to the evaluation of user models. Standard assessment criteria such as *reliability* and *validity* can be adopted. Reliability is measured as the consistency by which different samples of a person's behavior are classified the same. Validity is the agreement of a model's classification with evidence from other aspects of behavior. *Incremental validity* (Mischel, 1968) is the use of the simplest set of independent variables and inference mechanisms to generate classifications.

Social Implications of User Models: Beyond the evaluation of the performance of user models, they may be evaluated in terms of their effect on individuals in society and on society itself.

Privacy may be compromised by having large amounts of detailed information about individuals stored on-line. Private information may be breached and used in unauthorized ways. An alternative is not to store sensitive information about a person but only categorical information and demographics. Another possibility is to have the most personal details of these systems stored locally and under user's control. For instance, an agent acting on behalf of the user could have access to the data and respond to inquires.

If agents (Section 3.3.3) make decisions on behalf of human beings based on user models, then the users may be removed from those actions and may not feel *responsible* for the actions of their agents. Eventually laws are likely to be developed to clarify the extent of responsibility a person has for agents acting on their behalf.

Effective user modeling may greatly affect the behavior of individuals and their *relationship to society*. For instance, information services can be tailored for individuals. Paradoxically, however, the ability to personalize highlights the similarity among people.

3.3.7 User Models for Supporting Completion of Routine Tasks

Streamlining Routine Command Sequences: It is widely recognized that the completion of tasks in HCI follows regular patterns. Several proposals have been made for systems which learn patterns of computer commands by purely statistical regulation, or inference underlying tasks (e.g., Hanson et al., 1984). From a different approach, Desmarais et al. (1991) apply plan recognition to parsing user actions in order to recognize inefficient user behavior and to suggest shortcuts. "Eager" is a programming-by-example system (Cypher, 1991) which attempted to anticipate and support the placement of widgets by GUI designers by observing patterns of their responses.

Agents and Routine Office Tasks: User agents have been applied to routine office tasks such as scheduling appointments on an electronic calendar and prioritizing email. Typically, these agents do not model goals and complex chains of events. Because the tasks being modeled are repetitive, there is sufficient data to apply machine learning to find salient attributes. The agents also often adapt across users and across tasks for a given user.

Dent et al. (1992) describe a learning apprentice and apply it to personal calendar management. The system uses decision trees to characterize previous calendar scheduling. For example, it created a rule that theory seminars were held on Mondays. After training, the model performed slightly better than rules hand coded by the researchers. Maes and Kozerick (1994) describe two interfaces with agents: an email assistant and a calendar scheduling assistant. The agents predicted meeting schedules with an inference mechanism known as case-based reasoning. Small improvements in the confidence level reported by the agents' when their predictions when those predictions were correct.

3.3.8 User Models for Information Access

Information Retrieval and Information Filtering: The most widely studied approach to information needs is *information retrieval* (IR) (Dumais, 1988). The usual paradigm in information retrieval is to find documents which match a user query. This requires representations of the document collection and the query as well as algorithms for comparing the two representations. The algorithm for comparing queries to documentation may be simple keyword matches or complex derivation of verbal associations. In terms of user models, the IR algorithms integrate input from users and produces a set of relevant documents which are, ideally, those the users would have selected for themselves.

An IR model may be tuned to improve its selections by *relevance feedback*. The user identifies the most relevant documents and terms from those are used as inputs for a revised model (see Figure 6) to use in retrieving documents from the document representation. While relevance feedback is usually thought of as refining a query this may also be seen as developing a user model (Figure 5). For instance, Foltz and Dumais (1992) represented users' interests as a points in latent-semantic indexing (LSI) space.

Although there are parallels between IR and generalized user modeling, it seems that user modeling could be used even more in IR systems. The IR task is often implicit (e.g., a research topic the user is exploring). Demographic information about the user has, typically, been little used in the IR literature (Korfhage, 1984). There have been suggestions for long-term user models as part of IR systems. For instance, a user's interest across several sessions could be recorded and used to improve responses to queries but little work has been done.

Information filtering is a variation of IR; specifically, it is a type of text categorization. Filters identify new information which matches long-term, relatively stable interests. Selective dissemination of information (SDI, Luhn, 1958) usually employs an explicit profile of keywords. In some systems, these word lists are maintained by the users and it not clear if people are good at maintaining these profiles. Feedback in SDI is accomplished by the users making changes in their profiles.

Agents (see also Sections 3.3.3 and 3.3.7) were applied to adaptive information filtering by Sheth (1994). Specifically, genetic algorithms were employed as a highly adaptive model of NetNews preferences. This agent was able to acquire initial models for several subjects. It was also able to adapt to changes in simulated preferences ratings.

Hypertext Linking: Hypertext allows users to browse text by linking information objects together. Links may be selected that would be relevant to a specific task of use or interest to a given user. One example of adaptive hypertext is from KN-AHS (Kobsa et al., 1994) in which, for instance, the fact that a user checks a term in a glossary is used to infer that the user is not familiar with that term and a full explanation of it is included if it is used in later text. Thus, tailoring links in a hypertext may be related to community ratings on web pages (Section 3.3.8), to language generation (Section 3.3.10) and interfaces for training (Section 3.3.11).

Graphical views of objects and links which have been frequently accessed have been described as "history-enriched digital objects" (Hill et al., 1993, also see Lesk and Geller, 1983). Typically, these show total counts (i.e., baserates).

On the Web, there is often a delay in accessing information, and it is helpful to predict what topics the user will browse next. The anticipated material can be *prefetched* so it will be available locally if the user decides to access it. Clearly, prefetching would be more efficient with accurate models of what the user is likely to access.

Information and Aesthetic Preferences: Information preferences may include movies a person would like to view or books or news articles they would like to read. Information and aesthetic preferences may be distinguished from information needs (previous sections) in not being associated with a particular task. Because the are based on easily-described tasks, it is difficult to model users' processes involved in aesthetic preferences.

Probably the most successful technique for predicting information and aesthetic preferences is known as *collaborative filtering* (Section 3.3.9) although other techniques for predicting information preferences have been examined. These include the stereotypes of the "Grundy" system described earlier (Section 3.3.2).
A content-based system which modeled music preferences was proposed by Loeb (1992). Songs were categorized and models developed for each category of song based on ratings made by the user just after the song had finished. This is, essentially, an IR relevance feedback mechanism.

Table 1. Hypothetical ratings of seven items by four users.

	1	2	3	4	5	6	Target
1	9	1	4	8	3	0	2
2	3	0	9	2	3	8	1
3	2	8	7	9	3	1	7
4	8	3	3	7	8	2	?

Table 2. Correlations of ratings among four users from Table 1.

	1	2	3	4
1	-			
2	-0.14	-		
3	+0.10	-0.40	-	
4	+0.74	-0.49	-0.11	-

Yet another proposal for predicting information preferences is based on "interestingness" (e.g., Hidi and Baird, 1986). This is, essentially, a baserate prediction and might work if there is consensus over what is interesting. However, where there are substantial individual differences, the problem of determining what is interesting seems no easier than the original task of predicting preferences.

3.3.9 Collaborative Filtering for Information Preferences

While most user models attempt to model the user's thought process, other mechanisms are possible. Recently, statistical mechanisms based on identifying individuals with similar preferences have been proposed (Allen, 1990). With collaborative filtering (also known as "community ratings" or "social learning"), there is no attempt to model the underlying cognitive process. Rather, the preferences of other individuals are employed, the other individuals integrate the inputs.

Example: While users may differ greatly in their preference ratings for different items, subgroups of users may be quite similar to each other. Table 1 shows hypothetical ratings by four users for seven documents. Table 2 shows the correlation coefficients of the ratings on a 10-point scale for the users. The ratings of Users 1 and 4 are similar. Thus, User 1's ratings could be a predictor for User 4's ratings (specifically, predicting a rating of 2 for the target item). Beyond the simple correlations, multivariate statistics, such as *multiple linear regression,* combine evidence from several different users into a single predictive model. For the data in Table 1, a multiple linear regression gives an $\mathbf{R}^2 = +0.77$ which is better than any of the simple correlations for that user in Table 2.

News, Videos, Movies, and Music: Allen (1990) used collaborative filtering to make predictions about preferences for news articles, however, few of those correlations were substantial. This may have been because of the small number of participants or because news preferences are not stable and are difficult to predict.

Collaborative filtering has been more successful predicting preferences for movies. Hill et al. (1995) report studies of video preference predictions with data collected from the Internet. 291 respondents made 55,000 ratings of 1700 movies. Three of four video recommendations made by the service were highly evaluated by the users of the system. In Figure 7, individualized predictions show a much stronger correlation with the user's preferences than do the predictions of the movie critics.

Collaborative filtering has also been applied to recommend music preferences. Shardanad and Maes (1995) developed the "Ringo" system (also known as "Firefly") in which ratings were collected from users by email. Modified pairwise correlation coefficients were calculated for 1000 of the people who made ratings. Predictions of preferences based on these correlations were somewhat better than the baserate predictions.

Limitations and Extensions of Collaborative Filtering: A number of constraints determine whether collaborative filtering will be effective in real-world applications. Ratings are often used to build the filtering models. Ratings are not direct measures of the target behavior and may be affected by many incidental factors. The underlying preferences must also be fairly stable. For instance, musical tastes may change depending on time of day, mood, and what is going on around a person. The ratings a person provides must not change very much while predictions are being made. If the community is heterogeneous and if there is a wide variety of opinions about the material, a relatively large number of other people must make ratings.

Beyond the basic correlational techniques described above, a number of extensions for collaborative filtering techniques may be considered. While collabo-

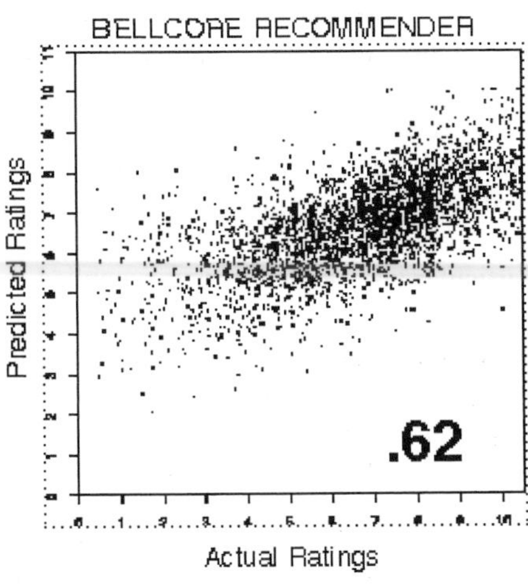

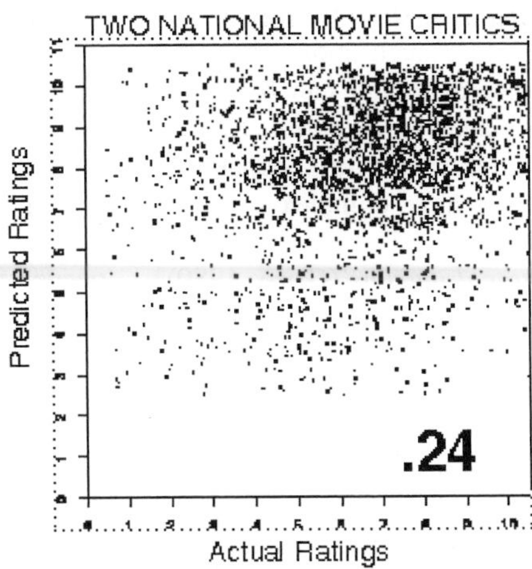

Figure 7. Video recommender scatterplots.

rative filtering is an effective technique, it seems likely that predictions with a mixture of community ratings and a limited amount of content (categorization) could be better still. Preferences in one domain (e.g., movies) could be used to make predictions across domains (e.g., books). Indeed, a generalized profile might be developed in which a wide range of a user's preferences were combined and compared with other people's preferences. In addition to matching a person with an information object, user models can also be used to match one person with another. For instance, people with similar interests might be identified based on correlations their aesthetic preference ratings. In some cases, information about users may be used to *initiate* the presentation of information to them. This would often be *targeted advertising* (i.e., personalized commercial information); however, other types of information such as health messages and community information could also be triggered.

Predictions may be made by friends of the user (Allen, 1990). In the previous section the subjects in the control condition had relatively little information about the preferences of the person for whom the predictions were to be made. Collaborative filtering might also be used to make predictions about the preferences of a group such as a family or friends attempting to find a movie which they would enjoy. If the group provides ratings as a unit, the predictions should be similar to those made for individuals. Alternatively, group prediction could be synthesized from predictions for the individuals in that group. In that case, a simple technique would be to find the item which was highest, on the average, across users. However, group dynamics such as the dominance among members of the group would be difficult to model.

3.3.10 User Models and Natural Language

Natural language processing is complex and involves many user modeling issues. This section is divided into discussion of low-level modeling issues in the speech chain and higher-level issues affecting understanding and generation. Related issues are also considered in the following section on training (Section 3.3.11) and in Section 3.3.5 under subsection on plan recognition.

Speech Chain: The activities associated with the production of speech may be said to form a *speech chain*. There are individual differences at many steps in the speech chain. These include speaker characteristics in speech recognition, word senses, complexity of vocabulary and grammar, and dialect. These differences apply to both language understanding and generation.

Speech recognition attempts to identify the words in user utterances. Because individuals differ substantially from each other in their speech, it is helpful to have a model of their characteristic speech patterns. These individualized models, known as *speaker-dependent* models, can be used to transform responses for further processing. However, a detailed review of the literature on user models for speech recognition is beyond the scope of this paper.

Neural networks were used classify gestures of a person wearing a data glove and then to produce speech based on those gestures (Fels and Hinton, 1995). The neural networks adapted to the idiosyncratic responses of the user. After 100 hours of training, a person gesturing with the data glove was able to use the system to produce speech somewhat better than a speech synthesizer.

Language Generation and Understanding: Communication between people is much more than the transmission of literal messages which can be easily deciphered with a dictionary and simple parser. Rather, communication is highly context and task dependent and both sender and receiver have complex expectations about the for the interaction. These expectations are described as *conversational maxims* (Grice, 1980). They are: Quality (truthful and accurate information), Quantity (neither more nor less information than is required), Relation (information appropriate to the task), and Manner (clear and unambiguous information).

The emphasis on the *function* of messages instead of on their literal meaning has led Austin (1962) to categorize them in terms of *speech acts*. Speech acts may be *indirect* (Searle, 1980) as in irony where is intended message is the opposite of the literal message. Purposeful conversations have a regular structure or pattern of speech acts (Winograd and Flores, 1986). For instance, we would expect a offer of help to be followed by an acceptance or rejection of that offer.

In order to engage in communication human beings may be said to have mental models of the task, the context, and the other participants. If the communication is between a human being and a computer (whether as a task-oriented dialog or as natural language dialog) then the computer may be said to have a user model of the human being. In order to fulfill conversational maxims and to initiate speech acts, in language generation, a speaker or agent must consider long-term characteristics of the listeners such as their knowledge level. In addition, the speaker may monitor the reactions of the listeners during the conversation to ensure the intended communication is received. Likewise, the listener could expect that the communicator was following conversational maxims. Recognition of speech acts by a listener may be viewed as a type of plan recognition (see Section 3.3.5). As noted earlier, plan recognition would include many aspects of user models such as the situation, the speaker's appearance, and previous experiences with the speaker.

3.3.11 User Models for Tutoring, Training, and Help Systems

Instructional interaction between a computer and a human being may be viewed as a specialized conversation. For workers using computers to complete routine tasks, the actions in which the user may be engaged are generally highly constrained. Thus, for help systems which try to give advice to those workers, little inference is about the task is needed. However, the task and the user's interpretation of it are generally less well known for training or tutoring contexts than for help system. Thus, plan recognition is an important part of training and tutoring systems.

Tutoring and training are closely related to each other although training is focused on teaching skills needed for a particular task while tutoring is applied to learning general skills such as reading and mathematics. Help systems support users who are attempting to complete tasks with a computer system. These systems differ in their style of interaction with the student. For instance, the system may interrupt the user in the middle of a task to provide advice, or it may wait for the user to request information. Similarly, the system might follow a prescribed set of tasks or it might schedule tasks for the student depending on the model of the student's knowledge.

Personalization in tutoring may be modeled by observing the conversations between tutors and students. There have been several studies of how human tutors adapt their interests to a given student and to assess the human tutors' strategies for modeling the user (e.g., Grosz 1983; Stevens, et al., 1982).

The models of users or students in training, tutoring, and help systems combine aspects of mental models, user models, and task models. *Student models* usually describe the student on a given task but generally do not include demographic information about the student. In the style of Figure 4 separate "user models" with long-term information are often included in these systems.

The key for training systems based on student models is in recognizing inefficiencies and errors in the student's performance and determining where they came from. The simplest approach to recognizing errors is to make a catalog of errors for a given task. However this is not always so easy, there may be several correct ways to solve a task.

A more general approach to recognizing errors is known as *differential modeling* (Burton and Brown, 1979). This compares a student's performance to that of an expert engaged in a similar task. The models a student has of the task may not be like a expert's models of that same task (Clancey and Lestinger, 1981). Because they are novices, students' models are generally simplified or incomplete (see Section 3.3). Indeed, the student's model may have inconsistent and even illogical strategies for completing tasks.

Determining the cause of an error can be very tricky; an error may be caused by a combination of factors. Errors may be modeled as the result of specific processes. Sleeman (1982) has proposed modeling a student's problem solving with "mal-rules" which are rules that an expert would say are false, but which reflect a student's incorrect beliefs. Similarly, Brown and Burton (1978) proposed a "theory of bugs". The "EdCoach" system (Desmarais et al's, 1993), models the task as a grammar for executing sequences of knowledge units. It then infers the student's confusions about these knowledge units by examining the methods the students actually use.

3.4 Discussion

Focusing on mental and user models in human-computer interaction highlights the intentionality of the interaction between the person and the machine. Because mental models are inside a person's head, they are not accessible to direct inspection and it is difficult to have confidence about how a mental model is constructed or how it can be modified. Indeed, a *reductionist* might assert that there are no mental models per se, but only "generalizations" from behaviorally conditioned expectations. By contrast to mental models, user models can be directly inspected and modified. Although for user models many difficult questions remain about the best way to capture and represent information about the user and the task.

Because computing is relatively cheap and widely deployed, complex networked services can increasingly be personalized Yet, few of the techniques described here are in regular use; simpler techniques non-adaptive techniques are generally preferred as being more robust. Thus, we may expect mental models and user models to expand as an area of research and innovation.

3.5 References

Allen, J. (1983). Recognizing intentions from natural language utterances. In: *Computational Models of Discourse*, M. Brady and R.C. Berwick (eds.), Cambridge, MA: MIT Press, 107-166.

Allen, R. B. (1990) User models: Theory, method, and practice. *International Journal of Man-Machine Studies,* 32, 511-543.

Anderson, J. R. (1983). *The Architecture of Cognition*, Cambridge, MA: Harvard.

Austin, J.L. (1962). *How to do Things with Words,* Cambridge, MA: Harvard.

Borgman, C. L. (1986). The user's mental model of an information retrieval system: An experiment on a prototype online catalog. *International Journal of Man-Machine Studies,* 24, 47-64.

Brown, J. S. and Burton, R. R. (1978) Diagnostic models for procedural bugs in basic mathematical skills. *Cognitive Science,* 2, 155-191.

Burton, R. R., and Brown, J. S. (1979). An investigation of computer coaching for informal learning activities. *International Journal of Man-Machine Studies,* 11, 5-24.

Card, S. K., Moran, T. P., and Newell, A. (1983). *The Psychology of Human-Computer Interaction,* Hillsdale NJ: Erlbaum.

Carroll, J. M. (1990), *The Nurnberg Funnel: Designing Minimalist Instruction for Practical Computer Skill.* Cambridge, MA: MIT Press.

Clancey, W. J. and Lestinger, R. (1981). NEOMYCIN: Reconfiguring a rule-based expert system for application teaching. *Proceedings International Joint Conference on Artificial Intelligence,* 829-836.

Croft, W. B. and Thompson, R. H. (1984). The user of adaptive mechanisms for selection of search strategies in document retrieval systems. In: *Research and Development in Information Retrieval,* C.J. vanRijsbergen (ed.), Cambridge: Cambridge University Press, 111-122.

Cypher, A. (1991). EAGER, Programming repetitive tasks by example. *Proceedings ACM SIGCHI* (New Orleans) 33-39.

Dent, L., Boticario, J., McDermott, J., Mitchell, T., and Zabowski, D. (1992). A personal learning apprentice. *Proceedings of the 10th National Conference on Artificial Intelligence,* Menlo Park, CA, AAAI Press, 96-103.

Desmarais, M. C., Giroux, L., and Larochelle, S. (1991). Plan recognition in HCI: The parsing of user actions. In: *Mental Models and Human Computer Interaction (vol.2),* M.J. Tauber and D. Ackermann (eds.), Amsterdam: North-Holland, 291-314.

Desmarais, M. C., Giroux, L., and Larochelle, S. (1993). An advice giving interface based on plan-recognition and user-knowledge assessment. *International Journal of Man-Machine Systems,* 39, 901-924.

Douglas, S. and Moran., T. P. (1983). Learning text editor semantics by analogy. *Proceedings ACM SIGCHI* (Boston), 207-211.

Dumais, S. T. (1988). Information retrieval. In: *Handbook of Human Computer Interaction,* 1st edition. M. Helander (ed.), Amsterdam: North-Holland, pp. 673-694.

Egan, D. E. (1988). Individual differences. In: *Handbook of Human Computer Interaction,* 1st edition. M. Helander (ed.), Amsterdam: North-Holland, pp. 543-568.

Fels, S. and Hinton, G. (1995). Glove-TalkII: An adaptive gesture-to-format interface. *Proceedings ACM SIGCH,* (Denver, May) 456-463.

Fischer, G. (1991). The importance of models in making complex systems comprehensible. In: *Mental Models and Human Computer Interaction* (Vol. 2), M.J. Tauber and D. Ackermann (eds.), Amsterdam: North-Holland, 3-36.

Foltz, P. W., and Dumais, S. T. (1992). Personalized information delivery: An analysis of information filtering methods, *Communications of the ACM*, 35 (12) 51-60.

Geller, V., and Lesk, M. E. (1983). User interfaces to information systems, *Proceedings ACM SIGIR* (Bethesda, June), 130-135.

Gentner, D. and Gentner, D. R. (1983). Flowing water of teeming crowds of electricity. In: *Mental Models*, D. Gentner and A. Stevens (eds.), Hillsdale NJ: Erlbaum, 99-129.

Goldstein, I. P. (1982). The genetic graph: A representation for the evolution of procedural knowledge. In: *Intelligent Tutoring Systems.* D. Sleeman and J.S. Brown (eds.), London: Academic, 59-78.

Gonzalez, C. (1996) Does animation in user interfaces improve decision making. In *Proceedings ACM SIGCHI* (Vancouver, April), 27-34.

Grice, H. P. (1975). Logic and conversation. In: *Syntax and Semantics: Vol. 3, Speech Acts*, P. Cole and J.L. Morgan (eds.), New York: Academic, 41-58.

Halasz, F. G. (1983). Analogy considered harmful, *Proceedings ACM SIGCHI*, Boston, 383-386.

Halasz, F. G. and Moran, T. P. (1982). Mental models and problem solving in using a calculator. *Proceedings ACM SIGCHI,* 212-216.

Hanson, S. J., Kraut, R. E., and Farber, J. M. (1984). Interface design and multivariate analysis of UNIX command use. *ACM Transactions on Office Information Systems,* 2, 42-57.

Hegarty, M. and Just, M. A. (1993). Constructing mental models of machines from text and diagrams. *Journal of Memory and Language,* 32, 717-742.

Hidi, S. and Baird, W. (1986). Interestingness: A neglected variable in discourse processing. *Cognitive Science,* 10, 179-194.

Hill, W. C., Hollan, J., Wroblewski, D., and McCandles, T. (1992) History-enriched digital objects. *Proceedings ACM SIGCHI* (Monterey, May), 3-8.

Hill, W. C., Stead, L., Rosenstein, M., and Furnas, G. W. (1995). Video recommender. In *Proceedings ACM SIGCHI* (Denver, May), 194-201.

Johnson-Laird, P. N. (1983). *Mental Models*, Cambridge, MA: Harvard.

Kass, R. and Finin, T. (1991). General user modeling: A facility to support intelligent interaction. In: *Intelligent User Interfaces,* J. W. Sullivan and S. W. Tyler (eds.), New York: ACM Press, 111-128.

Kelley, H. H. (1971). Attribution in social interaction. In: *Attribution: Perceiving the Causes of Behavior,* E. E. Jones., et al. (eds.), Morristown NJ: General Learning Press, 1-26.

Kieras, D. E. (1988). What mental model should be taught: Choosing instructional content for complex engineered systems, In: *Intelligent Tutoring Systems: Lessons Learned,* Psotka, J., Massey, L.D., and Mutter, S. A. (eds.), Hillsdale NJ: Erlbaum, 85-111.

Kieras, D. (this volume). GOMS Model. In: *Handbook of Human Computer Interaction,* 2nd edition.M. Helander, T. K. Landauer and P. Prabhu (eds.), North-Holland: Amsterdam.

Kobsa, A., Muller, D., and Nill, A. (1994). KN-ANS: An adaptive hypertext client of the user modeling system BGP-MS. *Proceedings User Modeling Conference,* (Hyanis, MA), 99-105.

Korfhage, R. R. (1984). Query enhancement by user profiles. In: *Research and Development in Information Retrieval*, C.J. vanRijsbergen (ed.), (Cambridge: Cambridge University Press), 122-132.

Littman, D. C., Pinto, J., Letovsky, S., and Soloway, E. (1986). Mental models of software maintenance. *Proceedings of Empirical Studies of Programmers* (Washington), 80-98.

Loeb, S. (1992). Architecting personal delivery of multimedia. *Communications of the ACM,* 35 (12) 39-48.

Lokuge, I., Gilbert, S. A., and Richards, W. (1996). Structuring information with mental models: A tour of

Boston. In: *Proceedings ACM SIGCH* (Vancouver, April), 413-419.

Luhn, H. P. (1958). A business intelligence system. *IBM Journal of Research and Development, 2,* 314-319.

Maes, P. and Kozierck, R. (1994). Agents that reduce workload and information overload. *Communications of the ACM,* 37, 31-40.

Mayer, R. E. (1988). From novice to expert. In: *Handbook of Human Computer Interaction,* 1st edition. Landauer, Helander, M. (ed.), Amsterdam: North-Holland, pp. 569-580.

Morita, M., and Shinoda, Y. (1994). Information filtering based on user behavior analysis and best match text retrieval. In *Proceedings SIGIR*, Dublin, 272-281.

Mischel, W. (1968). *Personality Assessment.* New York: Wiley.

Norman, D. (1983). Some observations on mental models, In: *Mental Models*, D. Gentner and A. Stevens (eds.), Hillsdale NJ: Erlbaum,, 7-14.

Payne, S. J., and Green, T. R. G. (1986). Task-action grammars: A model of mental representations of task languages. *Human-Computer Interaction,* 2, 93-113.

Rich, E. (1989), Stereotypes and user modeling. In: *User Models in Dialog Systems*, A. Kobsa and W. Wahlster (eds.), Berlin: Springer-Verlag, 35-51.

Searle, J. Indirect speech acts. In: *Syntax and Semantics: Speech Acts*, vol. 3. P. Cole and J. L. Morgan (eds.). New York: Academic, pp.59-82.

Self, J. (1974). Student models in CAI. *International Journal of Man-Machine Studies,* 6, 261-276.

Shardanand, U. and Maes, P. (1995). Social information filtering: Algorithms for automating "word of mouth". In *Proceedings ACM SIGCHI*, (Denver, May), 210-217.

Sheth, B. D. (1994). *A Learning Approach to Personalized Information Filtering*. MIT Media Laboratory Technical Report, 94-01.

Simon, H. A. (1969). *The Sciences of the Artificial,* Cambridge, MA: MIT Press.

Singley, M. K., and Anderson, J. R., (1985). The transfer of text-editing skill. *International Journal of Man-Machine Studies,* 22, 403-423.

Sleeman, D. (1982). Assessing aspects of competence in basic algebra. In: *Intelligent Tutoring Systems.* D. Sleeman and J. S. Brown (eds.) London: Academic, 185-199.

Stevens, A., Collins, A., and Goldin, S. (1982). Misconceptions in students' understanding. In: *Intelligent Tutoring Systems*, Sleeman, D. and Brown, J.S. (eds.), New York: Academic Press, 13-24.

Wahlster, W. and Kobsa, A. (1989). User models in dialog systems. In: *User Models in Dialog Systems*, A. Kobsa and W. Wahlster (eds.), Berlin: Springer-Verlag, 4-34.

Winograd, T., and Flores, F. (1986), *Understanding Computers and Cognition.* Norwood, NJ: Ablex.

Young, R. M. (1983). Surrogates and mappings: Two kinds of conceptual models for interactive devices. In: *Mental Models*, D. Gentner and A. Stevens (eds.), Hillsdale NJ: Erlbaum, 35-52.

Handbook of Human-Computer Interaction
Second, completely revised edition
M. Helander, T.K. Landauer, P. Prabhu (eds.)

Chapter 4

Model-Based Optimization of Display Systems

Misha Pavel
Oregon Graduate Institute
Portland, Oregon, USA

Albert J. Ahumada, Jr.
NASA Ames Research Center
Moffett Field, California, USA

4.1 Introduction

Visual displays are key components of information, communication, and computing systems. Because of the large information bandwidth required for image-based communication, displays are frequently performance bottlenecks for such systems. Display design may, therefore, determine the degree of success of such systems.

The key aspect of a successful display design is the specification of meaningfully quantifiable and measurable objectives. To be most relevant for a given application, these objectives should be based on the ability of an operator to perform his task. We can use such task-based objectives to evaluate systems, and to optimize the display parameters. An example of a task-based measure in medical domain is the accuracy of

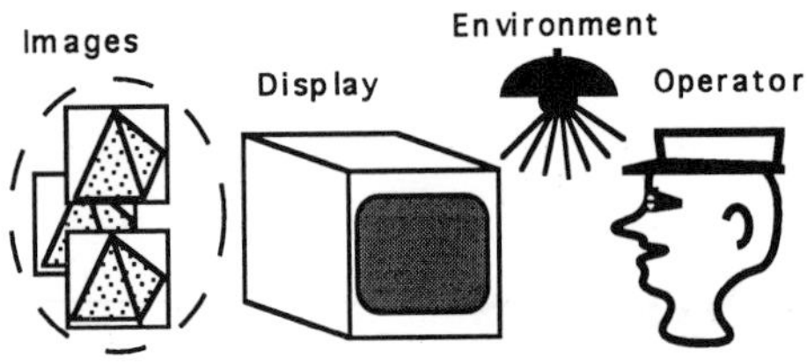

Figure 1. An overview of a display system.

detection abnormal tissue in an X-ray image. Another example, in aviation, is the accuracy with which a pilot can identify a runway from a display of an airport scene.

Given a quantitative, task-based performance measure, it is in principle possible to optimize the display by the brute-force approach of designing prototypes with different set of parameters, and measuring the performance empirically. The optimal set of parameter values is then approximated by interpolation in the design parameter space. The obvious disadvantage of this strategy is that the high cost of performance evaluation per candidate set of parameter values makes it likely that large regions of the parameter space will be left unexamined.

An alternate approach, advocated in this chapter, is to construct models of human operators and of display system, and to use these models to evaluate image quality (IQ) metrics with respect to task-based objectives. The IQ computation is typically performed in two phases: (1) using task independent models of perceptual representation, and (2) using task-dependent algorithms that relate the perceptual representation from phase (1). to human performance. We describe these two phases in sections 4.4 and 4.5 following preliminary general discussion of display systems and modeling section 4.3. In Section 4.6, we describe how the models are used to compute IQ metrics. Although, for the sake of consistency with much of the existing literature, we focus on an image discrimination task, we suggest extensions to other important tasks in the final section.

Notwithstanding scientific and engineering efforts, characterization of IQ is not yet a mature engineering field that offers tabulated answers. Therefore, rather than listing step-by-step recipes, we provide a general design framework that summarizes the methods that have been researched, describes the relationships among the methods, and provides recent references. Table 1. summarizes the different approaches. In addition, discussion of selected topics in greater detail can be found in two recent collections (Peli, 1995; Watson, 1993b).

4.2 System Description

The parameter space needed to describe a display system is large, because displays are typically complex systems. This complexity is apparent when we consider the different components involved in the display of images (Figure 1):

1. The set of possible images
2. The display, including capture, storage, communication, and display
3. The Environmental (e.g., viewing) conditions
4. The operator's visual system and tasks

We must have sufficiently detailed description of all these components if we are to evaluate the performance, of and to optimize, a display system. As in any complex system, there are many tradeoffs among the different parameters.

It is a common error made by even many accomplished designers, to assume fixed system parameters (e.g., rendering scheme), and focus on the optimization of a specific display parameter (e.g., a pixel density). The resulting designs not only are sub-optimal, but also may be unexpectedly sensitive to changes in various aspects such as types of images or compression schemes. By considering all the components simultaneously, and examining the many resulting tradeoffs with minimum implicit prior assumptions, the designer is likely to find more nearly optimal solutions.

In this section, we describe briefly the components of the complete display system illustrated in Figure 1. Except for a description of the human visual system, a detailed description of the components is well beyond the scope of this chapter. We only note selected critical aspects of each component relevant to the display system design, and, where appropriate, we describe simple models of the components.

4.2.1 Images

For the purpose of this chapter, a gray-level image is a specification of intensity as a functions of two-dimensional (2D) coordinates $I(x,y) = I(\vec{x})$, where $\vec{x} = (x,y)$ are the coordinates. A color image is typically a three-dimensional (3D) function of 2D coordinates. Each dimension of this function corresponds to a

Table 1. Summary of different research approaches to Image Quality.

		Perceptual Transformations					Metric		
Researchers	Topic	Images	Filter	N	C	A	S	Exp	Comments
Lubin, 1993	IQ	7×4	B	N	C	A	S	2.4	peripheral summation
Daly, 1993	IQ	6×6	B	N	C	A	P		
Zetzsche and Hauske, 1989	IQ	5×6	B	N	C			2	rati pyramid
Watson, 1993	IC	8×8	B	N	C			4	DCT basis
Sakrison, 1977	IC	12×9	B	N		A		6	early theory
Watson, 1987	IC	6×4	B	N				4	efficient subsampling
Watson and Ahumada, 1989	IC	3×6	B	N					hexagonal array
Daly, 1992	IQ	6×6	B	N			P		
Shlomot et al., 1987	IC	6×6	B						
Martin et al., 1992	IQ	9×3	B					4	Haar pyramid
Ahumada and Peterson, 1992	IC	8×8	B					∞	DCT basis
Klein et al., 1992	IC	8×8	B					2	DCT basis
Grogan and Keene, 1992	HT	8	B	N				2	
Burt and Adelson, 1983	IC	5	B						Laplacian pyramid
Stockham, 1972	IQ	1	B	N				2	
Mannos and Sakrison, 1974	IQ	1	B	N				2	
Ngan et al., 1986	IC	1	B		C				DCT basis
Girod, 1989	IC	1	B		C		S	2	linearized
Budrikis, 1972	IC	1	B			A		1, 2	TV quality meter
Limb, 1979	IQ	1	B			A	S	2	options compared
Griswold, 1980	IC	1	B					2	
Nill, 1985	IC	1	B					2	
Analoui and Allebach, 1992	HT	1	B					2	
Mitsa, 1992	HT	1	B					2	
Lukas and Budrikis, 1982	IQ	1	L		C	A		2, 4	
Zakhor et al., 1992	HT	1	L					2	
Chu and Watunyuta, 1992	HT	1	L					2	
Sullivan et al., 1991	HT	1	L					2	
Pappas and Neuhoff, 1992	HT	1	L					2	
Pappas, 1992	HT	1	L					2	
Kolpatzik and Bouman, 1992	HT	1	L					2	
Mulligan and Ahumada, 1992	HT	1	L					2	
Netravali and Prasada, 1977	IC	1				A		2	no CSF

Legend for Table 1: Topic indicates the application areas according to the following key: HT = halftoning, IC = image compression, and IQ = image quality. The column ``Images" indicates the number of perceptual images generated; the first is the number of spatial frequency channels, the second is the number of orientation channels. Filter shape is designated B for bandpass, L for lowpass. N designates point nonlinearities before the final metric stage, C designates local contrast computation, Contrast masking is designated by A. S indicates the use of local error summation preceding the final error aggregation step. Exp contains exponents values; probability summation is indicated by P color component — for example $(R(\vec{x}), G(\vec{x}), B(\vec{x}))$. Although, in theory, these functions may be continuous, in practice, images are sampled in space and in intensity level. An image I is, therefore, a matrix of integers.

In most applications, the description of the images is one of the more difficult aspects of the design specifications for at least two reasons. First, the designer may not know the characteristics of images that are critical for the application. Second, a useful description may not yet be known or even may not be possible.

In certain cases, an adequate description is possible. For example, images conveying text, diagrams, and graphs can be described by straight lines, edges, and regular regions. In most other cases, however, we must resort to specifications of ensembles of images in terms of images spatial-frequency content or using statistical models such as Markov fields. In a Markov field, the probability distribution of a pixel gray level depends on only the values of that pixel's nearest neighbors.

In the frequency domain we may specify the average frequency spectrum of an ensemble of images. For example, some researchers argued that the expected spatial frequency amplitude spectrum of an image will decay with the square of the frequency, approximated by:

$$S(\omega)=\frac{1}{1+\left(\frac{\omega}{\omega_0}\right)^2}, \qquad (1)$$

where $\omega=\omega_x+\omega_y$ is spatial frequency in radians per degree of visual angle computed from its two-dimensional *(2D)* components, and ω_0 is a constant (Field, 1987).

4.2.2 Display

A description of the display system includes parameters pertaining to representation, communication, storage, and rendering of images. The parameters include those that describe the physical structure of the display (e.g., geometric arrangements of pixels), gamma of the display, rendering scheme, display temporal properties, and spatial resolution. A display system also includes image-compression schemes, communication-network response and error characteristics, and storage-device characteristics. The linear aspects of the display are typically described in terms of its spatial and temporal frequency response using the modulation transfer function (MTF), which we denote by $G(\omega_x, \omega_y, \omega_t)$. The value of MTF for a display at a given spatial frequency is defined as the amplitude of a sinusoidal variation produced by the display for a constant input. In many applications, MTF is given for static signals and a single dimension — e.g. horizontal — as a function of spatial frequency f in cycles per degree, $G(f)$.

4.2.3 Environmental Conditions

The viewpoint of the observer and the range of operating environmental lighting conditions are critical determinants of what an observer can see. Environmental conditions include the physical attributes of the display device design (e.g., size), location and orientation. A complete description of the light distribution including all possible reflections of near-by objects is generally not possible, except perhaps in highly structured environments such as an airplane cockpit. The typical model, therefore, consists of a range of viewing distances, and a range of ambient lighting levels. In many design situations, the display size is combined with the viewing distances, and the spatial dimensions are specified in terms of visual angles.

4.2.4 Human Visual System

The final component of the system is the human observer engaged in the performance of a task. The ultimate output of the complete system is a response of the observer, summarized in terms of a task-performance measure. A complete characterization of a system requires a description of an observer that relates a task to an image combined with environmental conditions, and predicts an observer's response. The remainder of this chapter describes several models of the human visual system and shows how we can use them to predict observers' performance.

4.3 Approaches to Modeling of Human Performance

Before we discus specific aspects of existing models of the human visual system we consider general issues involved in the development and application of such models. In this section we cover rudimentary notions involved in perceptual and cognitive assessment of performance and modeling. Readers already familiar with these concepts can skip directly to the Section 4.4.

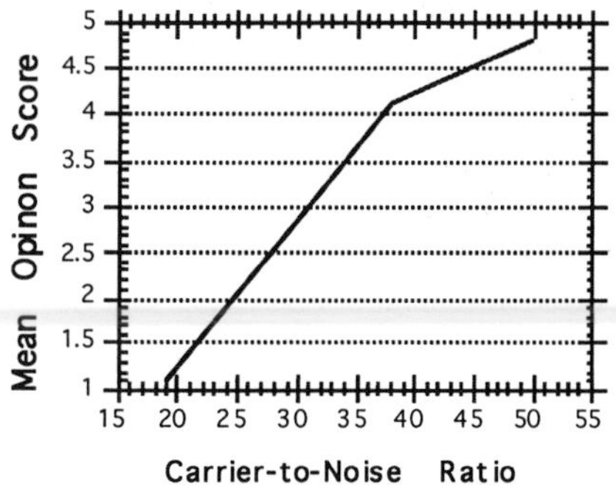

Figure 2. An example of a relationship between mean opinion scores (MOS) and image noise level.

Additional details on measurement and characterization of performance are presented in the appendix to this chapter.

Models of human performance used in assessment of display quality vary significantly in the level of details, and in their relationship to experimental data and test results. They range from purely empirical models to complex perceptual and cognitive models.

4.3.1 Empirical Models

In the simplest models, images are represented by their physical characteristics, without any consideration of the observer. These empirical models are based on fitting of computationally convenient functional forms that relate human responses to physical characteristics of the display. For example, we can relate the mean opinion scores (MOSs) obtained in subjective opinion tests to the amount of noise level by fitting an appropriate family of curves such as polynomials, power, or harmonic functions, see for example (Kayargadde and Martens, 1996).

A typical example is shown Figure 2 (c.f. Watson, 1993b, p157). The advantages of this approach include simplicity and a direct relationship to measured opinions. The major disadvantage is that this approach is difficult to generalize to new and different conditions. Thus, it is typically difficult to extend the model to the parameter values that have not been sampled experimentally, and it is virtually impossible to predict the effect of any image distortions that have not been tested previously. Therefore, this approach is typically costly, because it requires subjective testing of a large number of combinations of parameter values.

4.3.2 Perceptual Models

The cost of the empirical approach has frequently compelled designers to replace empirical performance measures by less labor-intensive image quality metrics. The intent is to specify computational procedures to predict the performance of a human observer on a variety of tasks. Achievement of this goal requires an approximation of the perceptual processes of the human visual system.

Such perceptual models incorporate aspects of the human visual system that are relevant to predicting performance. The structure of the models is based on our current knowledge of physiology and of psychological phenomena. The details are based on a variety of extensive data sets collected by visual scientists over the last century. To the extent that these models can account for a variety of data, their predictions are more likely to generalize to new situations, images, and tasks.

4.3.3 Task: Image Discrimination

The tasks that researchers used to evaluate system design range from subjective opinion judgments to objective measures such as target detectability. To facilitate our presentation of the models, we will examine a specific task: image discriminability. In a discriminability task, the observer is asked to detect a difference between two images. Performance on a discrimination task is a measure of the ability to distinguish between representations of the original and a processed, test image. This task, therefore, is considered to be useful for evaluation of various distortions introduced by communication systems or compression schemes. In the following section we overview several quantitative measures of performance, and in Section 4.7, we describe the relationship between the model representation and other tasks such as target detection, and search.

4.3.4 Performance Measures

In most practical situations, there are numerous ways to measure and summarize human performance. Image quality and performance measures can be divided into objective, e.g., probability of artifact (target) detection, and subjective, e.g., opinion scores. Because subjective measures depend frequently and critically on the visual material and on the individual observers, (see, e.g., (Ahumada and Null, 1993)) they are harder to inter-

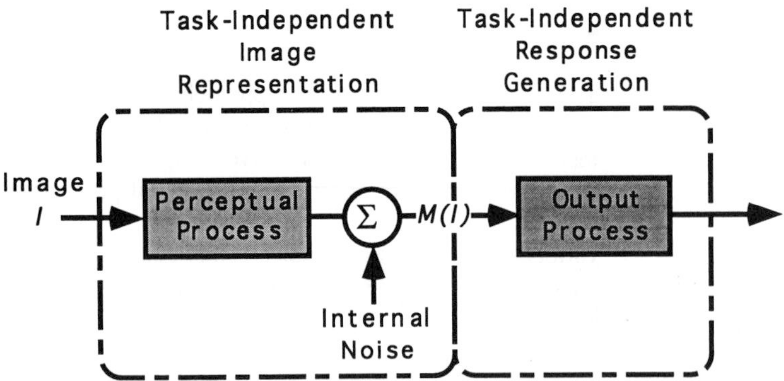

Figure 3. General structure of a perceptual model comprising two parts.

pret, and to generalize. Here we focus on models of objective measures. In principle, and for any specific case our the general approach can be extended to account for the subjective measures.

The three measures of performance that are most important for display evaluation and optimization are

1. Accuracy
2. Response time
3. Subjective opinions

These measures and their interpretations are described briefly in the appendix of this chapter. Although accuracy and response time appear to be independent measures, we urge researchers to consider — and measure — both at the same time because humans can tradeoff between speed and accuracy.

4.3.5 Structure of Perceptual Models

The details of any performance model will depend on the particular task to be modeled. Yet, there are components that are independent of task. Consequently, almost all models of human performance comprise the two parts depicted in Figure 3.

1. Computation of an image representation, $M(I)$, that is independent of the task.
2. Computation of a task-based image-quality metric.

The first component incorporates general properties of the front-end of the visual system and computes a perceptual representation of and image, $M(I)$. This representation is designed to capture the limitations of the perceptual system. We can interpret these limitations in terms of additive internal noise that is uncorrelated with $M(I)$.

The second component incorporates processes that underlie generation of responses (e.g., target detection), and is used to estimate observers' performance on specific tasks. This response component often is based on the notion of an *ideal observer* (Green and Swets, 1966).

Models vary significantly in the level of detail and in the number of perceptual phenomena that are incorporated in the computations. Their generalizability, accuracy, and flexibility vary as well. Sections 4.4 and 4.5 describe the two parts of various models of an observer: image representation and response generation.

4.4 Perceptual Image Representation

The first component of an algorithm for computation of IQ embodies transformations of viewed images to correspond more closely with the image's perceptual effect. For example, given two images, I_0 and I_1, we would like to find a representation $M(I_0)$ and $M(I_1)$ such that the difference between the representations $M(I_0)$ and $M(I_1)$ will be useful in predicting the discriminability of the images. Thus, M is the transformation of an image to its internal representation that underlies human visual performance. The transformation M that generates the representation $M(I)$ is a *model* of the human visual system.

A sufficiently complete transformation M underlying an IQ metric should incorporate the following components of the visual processing:

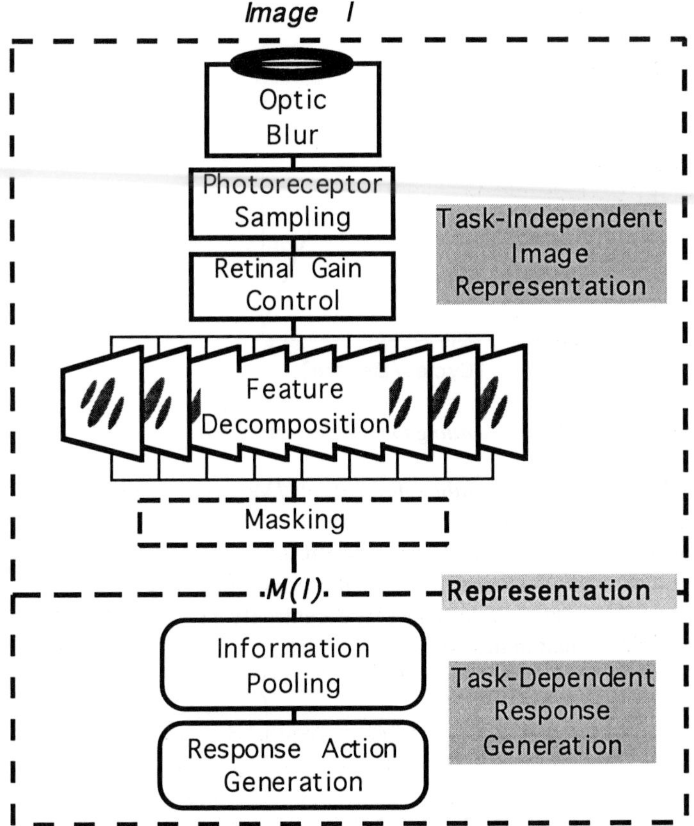

Figure 4 A model of an observer comprising two parts: image representation and task-dependent response generation process. *The main components of the perceptual image representation are shown in a typical order of information processing.*

1. Optic blur
2. Photoreceptor sampling and transduction
3. Retinal local contrast enhancement and gain control
4. Decomposition of images into features, resulting in multi-channel models
5. Masking that depends on luminance, contrast, spatial frequency, orientation, and location

A graphical representation of the components of the perceptual representation computation is shown in Figure 4.

Models of visual processing and performance are generally derived from a large number of existing data sets that originate from many different laboratory experiments. Despite the significant progress of and considerable agreement among the researchers, however, there is no single model that can account for all possible situations. In particular, current models do not capture completely the dependency of performance on images and viewing situations. For example, the blur function depends on the pupil size, and the effective sampling rate depends on whether rods are playing a role. Both of these aspects depend on the environmental conditions and stimuli present prior to the viewing of the target display.

Although most of the components — with the exception of optic blur — are to some extent nonlinear, they are often approximated by linear computations. For example, the local contrast and gain-control mechanisms are considered to be more divisive than subtractive, but are most frequently modeled by a linear filter whose response falls off for spatial frequencies below 1 cycle per degree. We now describe the different components of an image representation.

4.4.1 Optic Blur

The first stage of the human visual process comprises the eye optics, typically characterized by an optical

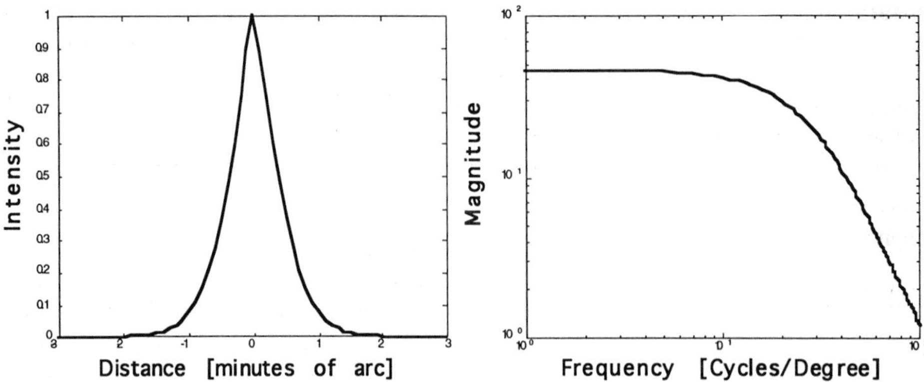

Figure 5 . An approximation of spatial blur and its spectrum computed according to (Westheimer, 1986).

transfer function that is a Fourier transform of the point-spread function (blur). This optical transfer function represents the intensity of retinal illumination as a function of spatial frequency of a fixed-amplitude sinusoidal grating.

A one-dimensional approximation to a typical point spread function h proposed by (Westheimer, 1986), and used by several models is

$$h(x) = 0.952e^{-2.59|x|^{1.36}} + 0.048e^{-2.43|x|^{1.74}}, \qquad (2)$$

where x is the distance in minutes of arc. The spatial response h, and its spectral characteristics are shown in Figure 5.

Williams and his colleagues measured the point-spread function more recently, and developed a similar, more complex approximation (Williams, Brainard, McMahon, and Navarro, 1994).

4.4.2 Retinal Sampling

The optically blurred image is sampled by the receptors in the retina. At the central portion of the retina (fovea), the average sampling frequency is approximately $N_0 \approx 120$ receptors per degree of visual angle; estimates from different individual retinas range between 100 to 160. The sampling rate decreases with increasing eccentricity (i.e., with the angle from the fovea). Accordingly, the ability to perform tasks that depend on spatial resolution decreases as a function of eccentricity.

For many tasks, decrease of spatial resolution is a linear function of eccentricity. More specifically, suppose that performance at the fovea on a spatial task can be characterized by a spatial measure, such as the *just noticeable difference* (*JND*), see appendix. Suppose, moreover, that the *JND* in the fovea, $JND = \Delta s(0)$, is measured as the distance between two vertical lines, or the period of a sinusoidal patch. Then, performance at eccentricity α can be related to that in the fovea ($\alpha = 0$) by:

$$\Delta s(\alpha) = \Delta s(0)\left(1 + \frac{\alpha}{\alpha_2}\right),$$

where α_2 is a constant equal to the eccentricity at which performance measured by *JND*s deteriorates by a factor of 2. The value of α_2 depends on the task. For example, if Δs is the spatial period of a sinusoidal signal to be detected, then $\alpha_2 = 2.5\,°$, (Watson, 1987b). On a spatial discrimination task such as vernier acuity, where Δs is the distance between two lines to be aligned, performance deteriorates with eccentricity faster than on the detection task, with $\alpha_2 = 1.3\,°$; see (Beard, Levi, Klein, and Carney, 1996).

We note that, if the degradation with eccentricity is due entirely to the to retinal sampling as implemented in some models, the corresponding equation for the inhomogeneous sampling density is

$$\Delta s(\alpha) = \frac{1}{N_0}\left(1 + \frac{\alpha}{\alpha_2}\right). \qquad (3)$$

where N_0 is the number of samples per degree. Strictly speaking, because of spatial inhomogeneity, any IQ evaluation should depend on the direction of gaze of the observer. The typical approach, however, is based either on the worst-case computation or on evaluation of average performance over number of glances.

4.4.3 Contrast Computation - Luminance Gain Control

For the human visual system image contrast is often more important attribute of an image than the absolute value of the luminance. Contrast at a point $c(x, y)$ is typically defined as the deviation from the mean, $\langle L \rangle$, divided by the mean luminance,

$$c(x,y) = \frac{L(x,y) - \langle L \rangle}{\langle L \rangle}. \tag{4}$$

Contrast is useful because of the empirical observation that the ability to detect a luminance increment is proportional to the average luminance when luminance is sufficiently high (> 100 cd/m^2). There is physiological evidence that luminance averaging is mainly a retinal process.

One implicit aspect of this formulation is the area over which the average $\langle L \rangle$ is computed. In some models, the averaging process extends over the entire image. In more complex models, however, the average luminance is computed over small neighborhoods local to the point. A general approach incorporating this local averaging is specified in terms of a multi-resolution representation, see Section 4.4.5.

When the image is has a meaningful minimum and maximum, then its maximum contrast c_m can be represented by a single number,

$$c_m = \frac{\max\{L(x,y)\} - \min\{L(x,y)\}}{\max\{L(x,y)\} + \min\{L(x,y)\}}.$$

For example, the contrast of a vertical sinusoidal grating of the form

$$L(x,y) = A\sin(2\pi x) + B,$$

with constant $A \leq B$ is given by the ratio of the sinusoidal modulation to the average (DC) component, $c_m = \frac{A}{B}$.

4.4.4 Contrast Sensitivity Function

The ability of the human visual system to detect both extremely gradual and extremely fine spatial variations is limited, and this limitation typically is characterized by the *contrast-sensitivity function* (CSF). The CSF can be interpreted— and measured empirically — as the reciprocal of the contrast of a just-detectable spatial sinusoidal image plotted as a function of its spatial frequency.

A CSF-based description is useful for representing the linear aspects of visual-system sensitivity, including the optic blur, A CSF is an empirically measured function: it depends, therefore, on many details of the psychophysical procedure, such as temporal aspects, spatial extent, and luminance.

For computational convenience, it is useful to fit a CSF with an explicit functional form. In some cases, the actual form of this CSF function may incorporate components corresponding to aspects of the perceptual system. An example of such an explicit formulation was developed by Carlson and Cohen (1980), and has been used by others including (Barten, 1990) and (Lubin, 1993). This approximation described by (Barten, 1990) is

$$H(f) = e^{-bf} af \sqrt{1 + 0.06 e^{bf}}, \tag{5}$$

where

$$a = 540\left(1 + \frac{0.7}{L}\right)^{-0.2} \frac{d(f+3)}{d(f+3)+36},$$

$$b = 0.3\left(1 + \frac{100}{L}\right)^{0.15},$$

and f is spatial frequency in cycles/degree, L is the average display luminance in cd/m^2, and d is the square root of image area in degrees of visual angle. This approximation, depicted in Figure 6, is useful for typical display dimensions, and incorporates the effects of optic blur. To give you an intuitive understanding, we plot this approximation for different display sizes and luminances. The major effects of the modulation transfer function are that the average luminance determines the high-frequency cutoff, and that the display size has an effect at only lower frequencies.

Because the CSF is determined empirically by measuring the threshold of detectability, we sometimes express it in terms the *modulation threshold function* (MTF), which is the reciprocal of the CSF,

$$\Theta(f) = \frac{1}{H(f)}. \tag{6}$$

In some models the CSF is incorporated explicitly; in others, it is implemented as a weighting factor that multiplies each the output of each spatial-frequency band by an appropriate weight.

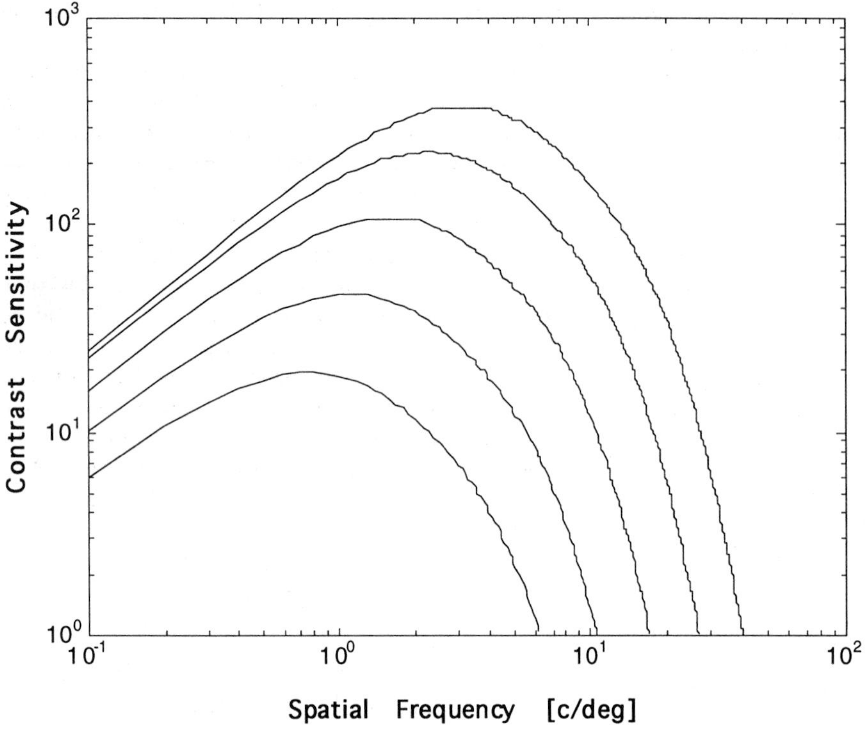

Figure 6. A theoretical contrast sensitivity function from equation (5).

4.4.5 Multi-resolution Decomposition

Consistent with physiology of the visual system and with much of psychophysical evidence, certain models decompose the retinal, sampled image into a number of perceptual-feature images. In a typical model, the retinal image is decomposed into spatial frequency and orientation-selective perceptual representations. In that case, the value of *M(i, x, y)* represents the amount of *i*th feature located at *(x,y)*.

In a typical multi-resolution representation we decomposed an image into its bandpass components by convolution with a sequence of similar filters at different scales. For efficiency and computational convenience, each bandpassed component is subsampled such that the number of samples does not unnecessarily exceed the corresponding Nyquist limit.

A detailed explanation of multi-resolution representation is given in the original papers e.g., (Burt and Adelson, 1983). (Wandel, 1990) presents an interesting exposition and point of view.

The general strategy for constructing of a multi-resolution representation consists of performing convolutions and resampling operations:

1. Low-pass filtering
2. Downsampling
3. Upsampling
4. Interpolation

In one of the earliest multi-resolution representations (Burt and Adelson, 1983) the filter is a 5-point approximation of a Gaussian impulse response. The *k*th level of the multi-resolution pyramid c_k is obtained by a sequence of *k* combinations of a convolution with the filter and subsampling by a factor of 2. Thus, the filter at level *k* is approximately given by

$$G_k(\vec{x}) = \frac{1}{k\sigma\sqrt{2\pi}} e^{-\frac{x^2+y^2}{2(k\sigma)^2}}, \tag{7}$$

where $\vec{x}$ is the pixel location in the original image and σ is a constant controlling the spatial extent of the filter. Note that this formulation is closely related to wavelet decomposition. Although the filter in equation (7) is a low-pass, we can use it to generate a band-pass filter by subtracting two different low-pass filters,

$$B_k(\vec{x}) = G_k(\vec{x}) - G_{k-1}(\vec{x}).$$

The filter specified in equation (7) is isotropic — i.e., radially symmetric — and thus processes each orientation in the same way. To account for observed effects of orientation, some models of image representation use filters that are sensitive to orientation. We can achieve orientation selectivity by modulating the Gaussian filter by a component that depends on the angular direction specified by the $\tan(y/x)$. To achieve a complete representation, we decompose each image into a number spatial-frequency bands selective to a range of orientations. We can then interpret the resulting representation $V_I(j,\vec{x})$ as the "amount" of feature j at location $\vec{x}$.

Thus, in a multi-resolution representation, an image is decomposed into a number of *perceptual images* indexed by j. The decomposition results in increased computational complexity, but embodies a number of properties of the human visual system that may influence task-based image-quality assessment. For example, models without multi-resolution representation may be unable to predict the relative independence of detection of small and large targets. Similarly, models without orientation selectivity may be unable to account for the lower thresholds for detection of energy along oblique directions. The advantageous characteristics of multilevel representations must be evaluated because there is some evidence (Ahumada, 1996) that single channel models with nonlinearities (see Section 4.6.5) may predict discrimination performance at least as well as do more complex, multi-resolution models.

4.4.6 Nonlinearity

Although most of the processes in all the models are linear, important nonlinearities must be incorporated. Perhaps the most significant nonlinearity, discussed in Section 4.4.3, is in the computation of contrast, i.e., normalization of luminance by the local mean luminance. This type of nonlinearity allows the internal representation of images to reflect that human visual sensitivity is more closely related to luminance ratios rather than to luminance differences. This computation reduces the signal in higher luminance backgrounds as compared to low luminance ones. The placement of this luminance gain control may vary in different models.

Early attempts at IQ metric construction found a need for reducing sensitivity by local variability in luminance or contrast as well as by the mean luminance (Limb, 1979). These local variance measures or edge energy measures obtained by high pass filtering and rectification were initially thought to be unnecessary for the multiple channel models with their nonlinear transformation of channel outputs. For example, (Zetzsche and Hauske, 1989) showed that such a model could predict masking in the region of a luminance edge. Psychophysical evidence for masking between spatial frequency channels (Foley, 1994) has led new versions of channel models to include nonlinear interactions among the channels (Teo and Heeger, 1994; Watson and Solomon, 1995). For example, (Teo and Heeger, 1994) used:

$$M_I(j,\vec{x}) = \frac{[V_I(j,\vec{x})]^2}{\sigma^2 + \sum_k [V_I(k,\vec{x})]^2},$$

where σ is a constant. Another example, Ahumada (Ahumada, 1996) used a formulation similar to:

$$M_I(j,\vec{x}) = \frac{V_I(j,\vec{x})}{1 + C^2[V_I]}, \tag{8}$$

where $C[V_I]$ is proportional to the average contrast of the reference image.

In addition to contrast computations, some models include other point nonlinearities before they compute the final metric. These nonlinearities are most often concave downward functions that increase dynamic range, but they can also be S-shaped functions that mimic the thresholding and saturation properties of neurons.

4.5 Response Generation

In this section, we describe several ways that a response might be generated from the representation M. The primary task that we consider is image discrimination; we extended our discussion to other tasks in Section 4.7.

In a discrimination task, an observer is asked to judge whether the test (or processed) image I_1 differs from the reference (or original) image I_0. The basic problem in modeling response generation — and therefore performance — is how to integrate local differences over space, time, and over features (e.g., multi-resolution). The result of this integration is a quantity Q that is monotonically related to the IQ.

It is possible to construct many different response generation rules; however, we describe two generally accepted classes of rules for integrating the local differences between the representations of the test and the reference images: *probability summation*, and *signal summation*. Most existing models incorporate some version of signal summation because it has greater generality.

4.5.1 Probability Summation

The probability summation rule is based on the assumption that detection of the differences is *all or none*, and that the detectors never make false-positive errors (false alarms). In that case, the probability of detecting a difference is the probability that at least one detector detects the difference — that is that the difference in the image representations exceeds the threshold at least at one location. Thus, the response summary — the probability $P\{M_1 \succ M_0\}$ of detecting a difference between the representations $M_1 = M(I_1)$ and $M_0 = M(I_0)$ — is given by

$$Q(I_1, I_0) = P\{M_1 \succ M_0\}$$
$$= 1 - \left[1 - P\{M_1(i,\vec{x}) - M_0(i,\vec{x}) > \theta(i,\vec{x})\}\right]^N$$

where $\theta(i,\vec{x})$ is a threshold for the i th feature located at $\vec{x}$, and N is the number of all relevant features at all locations. For a given representation, the performance of this rule is governed by the setting of the thresholds. Note that the threshold often is defined to be independent of the location $\vec{x}$.

4.5.2 Signal Summation

Signal-summation rules are used more frequently than the probability summation rules, because they are, in general, more flexible. The typical implementation of the signal summation rule is the *Minkowski metric* or distance (Ridder, 1992).

$$Q(I_1, I_0) = \left[\sum_{i,\vec{x}} \left|M_1(i,\vec{x}) - M_0(i,\vec{x})\right|^E\right]^{1/E} \qquad (9)$$

where E is a constant that determines the nature of the summation. In particular, for $E = 2$ this computation yields Euclidean distance, when $E = 4$ it approximates probability summation (Watson, 1979), and when $E = \infty$, it finds the maximum absolute difference.

Although a simple Euclidean distance function (e.g., RMS error) is used most frequently, some researchers, e.g., (Lubin, 1993; Peli, 1996) have found it necessary to use other exponents.

4.5.3 Model Linearization

In some optimization problems, we need to estimate the signal level — degradation or artifact level —that achieves a given performance. To find the answer using the complete models requires a search in the signal space. In some such situations where the main focus of interest is small image distortions we can approximate the nonlinear transformations by locally linear functions. A useful technique for simplifying nonlinear models so that we can evaluate the effects of small image distortions from a base image I_0 is to linearize the model M in the neighborhood of I_0. We approximate M by a linear function such that

$$M(I_0 + \Delta I) \approx M(I_0) + M'(I_0)\Delta I,$$

where $M'(I_0)$ can be thought of as the derivative of M with respect to I evaluated at I_0. If the integration rule for the quality measure Q is a function of the difference of the two images, then Q will depend only on $M'(I_0)$:

$$Q(I_0 + \Delta I) \approx Q[\Delta I\, M'(I_0)].$$

(Ahumada, 1987) discussed this technique for simplifying nonlinear vision models; (Girod, 1989) illustrated its usefulness in the application of vision models to image-quality assessment. Note that the image distortions have to be so small that they do not enter significantly into the masking process, which is assumed to be a function of only the base image I_0. For very low contrast images $M'(I_0)$ is a linear filter that depends only on the luminance as it affects the CSF function in equation (5).

4.6 Measures of Image Quality

Although we define IQ in terms of specific tasks, to maintain consistency with typical approaches to IQ metric, we discuss here IQ measures based an observers ability to discriminate between two images. Given perceptual representations of the test and reference im-

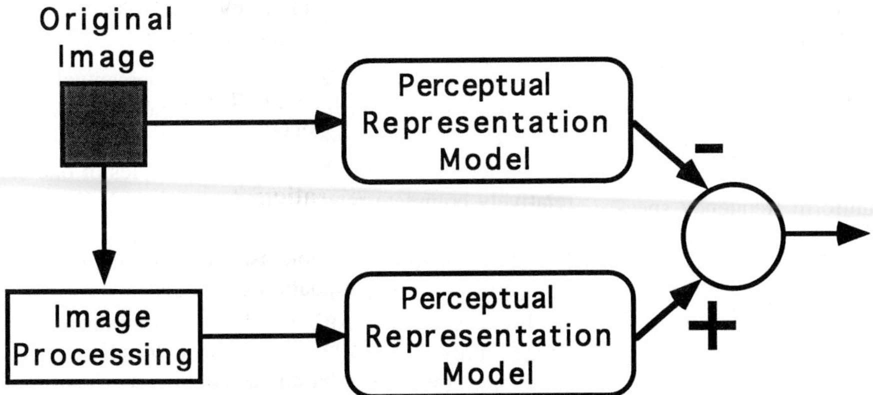

Figure 7. Use of image representation models to predict image discrimination performance.

ages, it is reasonable to assume that the ability to discriminate between them should depend on a distance measure of the difference between the two representation. If the distance measure based on the differences between representations of the two images, then we can express Q — a measure of IQ metric — in an explicit form such as

$$Q(I_1, I_0) = \left\| M(I_1) - M(I_0) \right\|. \qquad (10)$$

This assumption of a metric dictates an approach for using image-representation models to predict discrimination performance, and therefore, measure of IQ.

First we compute the representation for each image; then we evaluate the perceptual distance (Figure 7).

The simplest version of this approach is the RMS IQ metric described in Section 4.6.1. In subsequent sections, we discuss various, more complex, approaches, in order of increasing adherence to known properties of the human visual system.

4.6.1 RMS Metric

The RMS metric is based on the notions that a reference image I_0 is known, and that the displayed test image I_1 is a distorted version of the reference image. The representations I_0 and I_1 are matrices of sampled values (pixels) of the display luminance.

The RMS metric - distortion measure - Q_{RMS} is computed as the square root of the average pixel-by-pixel squared difference between the two images:

$$Q_{RMS}(I_1, I_0) = \sqrt{\sum_{\vec{x}} \frac{1}{N} \left| I_1(\vec{x}) - I_0(\vec{x}) \right|^2}, \qquad (11)$$

where $\vec{x}$ is a pixel location and N is the number of pixels in the image. The RMS metric is, therefore, the *Euclidean distance* between the two images — a particular instantiation of the Minkowski metric in equation (9)

In some cases the RMS, metric is specified for images quantized to 8-bits accuracy in terms of the peak signal-to-noise ratio (PSNR) given by

$$PSNR = 20 \log \left(\frac{255}{Q_{RMS}} \right).$$

Use of the RMS measure for display optimization is based on the assumption that performance on a number of different tasks can be characterized directly by the signal and noise levels expressed in terms of RMS deviations. Indeed, the RMS measure of an SNR is useful for characterization of discrimination performance of an ideal observer in the presence of Guassian noise.

Although it has the appeal of parsimony, the RMS-based approach often fails to predict perceptual image quality, because not all differences are equally important to the human visual system (see, e.g., (Girod, 1989)). For example the human visual system is not equally sensitive to all frequency components, and large deviations in high frequency textured segments of an image might be imperceptible. Another reason for RMS failure is that the human visual system is sensitive to image contrast — ratio of luminances — rather than the absolute value of luminance.

4.6.2 Modulation Transfer Function Area

One early attempt to incorporate characteristics of the human visual system is based on the notion that only information exceeding the *human modulation threshold* $\theta(f)$ (see Equation (6)), is useful. We must also assume that an image has a uniform frequency spectrum. Under these assumptions, we compute the modulation-transfer-function area (MTFA) by integrating over all frequencies where $G(f) > \theta(f)$,

$$MFTA = \int_{G(f)>\theta(f)} [G(f) - \theta(f)] df,$$

where $G(f)$ is the MTF of the display (see Section 4.2.2).

The main shortcoming of this measure is that, under the linearity assumption, visually useful signals are processed by the product (convolution in space) of the two spectral representations, rather than by the latter's difference. In addition, because the human visual system responds to ratios (e.g., Weber's law), the subtractive representation gives too much weight to the high frequencies (Barten, 1990).

4.6.3 Square Root Integral Model

Square Root Integral (SQRI) model is a computationally simple model that incorporates the human MTF and a nonlinear transformation to account for human's ability to discriminate similar images.

Assuming that an image has a uniform frequency spectrum, and the display has a modulation transfer function *G,* then the quality of an image is determined by the perceptible visual information available following filtering by the human CSF function.

The perceptual representation of images are in terms of spectral values; we convert them to *JND*s (see appendix) by taking the square root. The resulting measure is computed by a simple sum (integral) of the *JND* s over all frequencies,(Chapman and Olin, 1965; Snyder, 1973):

$$JND = \frac{1}{\log 2} \int \sqrt{\frac{H(f)}{G(f)}} \frac{df}{f},$$

where H is the human CSF, and G is the display MTF, see section 4.2.2. The SQRI model is limited in several ways, including that it is insensitive to any complexity arising from the 2D nature of displays and images.

4.6.4 Multiple-Channel Models

Although most of the multi-resolution perceptual and response models have the same general structure (Sakrison, 1977), the models proposed by individual researchers differ in many aspects. Examples of one of relatively complete models were developed (Watson, 1987a), (Lubin, 1993), and by (Daly, 1993). Many of the other models can be regarded as simplifications and extensions of these models.

Lubin's model incorporates all the components for image representation described in Section 4.4 see (Peli, 1995) and (Watson, 1993b). Initial stages of Lubin's model comprise optic blur and retinal sampling, described by equations (2) and (3). The multi-resolution representation is given in terms of a contrast pyramid (Peli, 1990). In particular, the multi-resolution representation in Lubin's model is given by the ratio of two consecutive levels:

$$c(k) = \frac{I * [G_k - G_{k+1}]}{I * G_{k+2}},$$

where G_k is the kernel corresponding to the *k*th level of the pyramid— see Equation (7). Following these bandpass and contrast computations, the component images are further decomposed into four orientations, each with a range of about 65 degrees. Lubin's model computes the output at each orientation *o*, *c(x,o)* by summing the outputs from the steerable filters (Freeman and Adelson, 1991) and their Hilbert transform.

To maintain consistency with psychophysical thresholds, or to *calibrate* the model, we weight the intensity at each orientation is by the maximum contrast sensitivity function [*H(f)* in equation (5)] such that the normalized intensity, *v(k,o)* is unity if the input intensity is at threshold.

The next stage of Lubin's model consists of a nonlinear (sigmoidal) transformation of the form:

$$\tilde{M}(I) = \frac{2v^a}{1+v^b},$$

where the constants $a \approx 1$ and $b \approx \frac{1}{2}$.

The final stage in computing the image representation consists of pooling (filtering) with an inhomogeneous circular filter whose diameter increases linearly from 5 pixels at the fovea towards the periphery, in accordance with the eccentricity function, Equation (3).

Response generation is computed from the difference between the test and the reference images, as illustrated in Figure 7. The difference at each location is assumed to provide the perceptually relevant difference measured in *JND* s. In order to generate a single output estimate, Lubin's model pools the *JND*s using the Minkowski metric Equation (9) with the exponent E=2.4.

4.6.5 Comparison of Single and Multiple-Channel Models

Because the multiple-channel models are computationally complex, it is critical to compare their predictive ability to the simpler, single channel models. One such comparison, using a target detection task, was performed recently by (Ahumada, 1996).

Ahumada compared a single-channel model with a multi-channel model based on the Cortex transform (Watson, 1987a). Both models had the same initial stages of processing, consisting of computation of contrast and filtering by a CSF function. He computed contrast relative to the image background and used the CSF function proposed by (Barten, 1992).

Ahumada computed the single-channel response using the Euclidean distance, normalized by function of the RMS contrast, as in equation (8),

$$d_s'(I_1, I_0) = \left[\sum_{\vec{x}} \frac{|M_1(\vec{x}) - M_0(\vec{x})|^2}{1 + C^2[M_0]} \right]^{1/2},$$

where d' is a measure of discriminability (see appendix), C is the RMS contrast

$$C[M_0] = k\sqrt{\sum_{\vec{x}} M_0^2(\vec{x})},$$

and k is a constant inversely proportional to the maximum gain of the CSF filter.

He generated the multi-channel response by computing the normalized distance as follows:

$$d_c'(I_1, I_0) = \left\{ \sum_{i,\vec{x}} \left[\frac{|M_1(i,\vec{x}) - M_0(i,\vec{x})|}{\sqrt{1 + M_0^2(i,\vec{x})}} \right]^4 \right\}^{\frac{1}{4}}.$$

In this particular comparison, the single-channel model predicted the detectability of the target as well as or more accurately than did the multi-channel model. Although the single channel model cannot predict various narrow-band masking results, it can do a good job with wide band signal and masking.

4.6.6 Discussion of Models

We summarize a variety of models with different properties and application areas in Table 1. The entries are generally listed by the names of the developers and are generally ordered by complexity. Except for the (Grogan and Keene, 1992) metric, most of the models can be regarded as simplified versions of the (Lubin,1993) model.

The number of channels or perceptual images is an indicator of the computational complexity of the model. Typically, larger numbers of channels could be used with larger images, but little change in computation occurs if the low frequency channels are adequately subsampled. The multiplicity of channels is useful to account for the strong masking within frequency and orientation bands.

Nonlinearities are often critical components of the models, and can be avoided only in specific situations where small signal approximations hold. Once again there is a tradeoff between a model complexity and its ability to account for various masking effects.

For example, there are several models that use small neighborhoods to compute contrast in the manner of (Peli, 1990) and (Duval-Destin, 1991) (designated by the entry C in the Table 1).

One obvious question is whether we need so many different models. To the extent that some are computational approximations of more complex ones, the variety seems reasonable, since different applications requiring computing simplification would be willing to sacrifice different model features.

(Farrell, Trontelj, Rosenberg, and Wiseman, 1991) reported that using a filter to represent the visibility of artifacts predicts the psychophysical performance worse than does using the RMS distance between the original images (Farrell, et al., 1991). This result suggests not that visibility can be ignored (Girod, 1993), but rather that more complex, nonlinear image-dependent metrics are required.

4.7 Extension to Other Tasks

In this section, we discuss the applicability of the performance models to other important tasks. The general strategy outlined in Section 4.3 is to use the same model front end, but to replace the response generation components. For each task, we assume the existence of a representation *M(I)*, and describe algorithms for response generation. The general approach for the development of the computational-response models is to assume, whenever possible, an *ideal observer.* An ideal observer is an algorithm that generates an optimal response based on decision theory, and given all available statistical information. For reference we first review the application of the models to the image discrimination or detection of difference task.

4.7.1 Image Discrimination

In many applications, such as communication, it is desirable for the test image to be indistinguishable from the corresponding reference image. The quality measure can, in that case, be defined in terms of the detectability of any difference between I_0 and I_1.The performance on this discrimination task should be a function f of the difference between the representations:

$$Q(I_1, I_0) = f\left[M(I_1) - M(I_0)\right].$$

Examples of *f,* discussed in Section 4.5, include probability summation and the Minkowski metric. Typical examples of applications for which this type of tasks is relevant include the design of image compression-algorithms and of image-transmission systems. The objective of the designers, in these situations, is to develop *visually lossless* systems in which the test (processed) image is visually indistinguishable from the reference one.

4.7.2 Target Detection, Recognition, and Identification

Detecting, recognizing and identifying targets are three important, closely related tasks that are supported by displays in many real systems. An observer in a *detection task* is asked to identify the presence or absence of a target in a set of possible targets at a fixed location in the visual field. The *recognition tasks* consists of classification of a given image of an object into one of several classes. Finally, in the *identification task*, the observer is asked to identify the unique object, such as, a specific aircraft model.

One way to model the detection task, as discussed in the Section 4.6.5, is to consider two images that are identical except for a target that is present in I_1 and is not present in I_0.The ability of an observer to discriminate between the two images can be then used to estimate his ability to detect the presence of the target.

In a more general approach, we can relate performance on a single target-detection task to the representation *M(I)* using statistical signal-detection and classification methods. For example, one approach uses templates or matched filters to detect the presence of a target.

A template is the internal representation of a target , and can be expressed as

$$\Delta M_1 = M(I_1) - M(I_0)\,. \tag{12}$$

We correlate the internal representation of a target t with the image representation, that is,

$$\Delta M_t M(I) = \sum_{j,\vec{x}} \Delta M_i(j,\vec{x}) M_I(j,\vec{x})\,.$$

This correlation measure can be then used as a decision variable to represent the likelihood that the target is present (Eckstein, Whiting, and Thomas, 1996; Pavel, Econopouli, and Landy, 1992a). For example, in a two-alternative forced choice the image I_1 is judged the contain a target if

$$\Delta M_t M(I) > \Delta M_t M(I_2) \tag{13}$$

Following (Ahumada, 1987) we assume that the noise that limits performance is uncorrelated with the representation, and therefore, can compute the discriminability measure as

$$d' = \frac{\Delta M_t\left[M(I_1) - M(I_0)\right]}{\sigma_v}, \tag{14}$$

where σ_v is the variance of the visual system noise. When the target t is present in I_1 then the discriminabilty measure is:

$$d' = \frac{\Delta M_t \Delta M_t}{\sigma_v} = \frac{\|\Delta M_t\|}{\sigma_v}.$$

We can extend the decision strategy in equation (13) to recognition and identification tasks by increasing the number of templates and properly combining the likelihoods for the different templates in each response group (Eckstein and Whiting, 1996; Palmer, Ames, and Lindsey, 1993; Pavel et al., 1992a). Although not ideal, the rule of selecting the response on the basis of the template closest to the sample image can provide a convenient model. A simple way to incorporate the increased uncertainty about target identity is to modify the variance term in by incorporating the increased uncertainty about target identity into the variance term in equation (14),

$$d' = \frac{\Delta M_t[M(I_1) - M(I_0)]}{\sigma},$$

where $\sigma^2 = \sigma_v^2 + \sigma_M^2$, (Peli, 1985). The term σ_M^2 is a component of variance due to the variability among potential targets. This procedure does not mirror the effect of signal strength on uncertainty, that uncertainty is very deleterious for very weak signals.

Many real-life tasks require target detection, recognition, identification, ranging from medical image (X-rays, MRIs, etc.) inspection for abnormal features to detection of camouflaged vehicles in military applications. In medical image analysis, a radiologist may be asked to classify a given region of an image as representing normal or abnormal tissue. In military surveillance, an observer may need to recognize an object as an enemy aircraft, a camouflaged vehicle, or a friendly helicopter. We note in passing that psychophysicists use detection, recognition, and identification tasks as tools to study the capabilities and limitations of the human visual system.

4.7.3 Visual Search

Visual search is an important extension of the detection, recognition and identification tasks. Typical search tasks involve higher uncertainty than do the corresponding detection task, because, in addition to the uncertainty regarding the presence or absence — or the identity of the targets — there is uncertainty about the possible object location (Eckstein and Whiting, 1996; Palmer et al., 1993; Pavel et al., 1992a).

In some search tasks the target is known exactly, but its location is unknown, such as when a user searches for a particular command (word) in a pull-down menu. In other search tasks, the observer has less prior information; for example, she may search an image for a known human face, a familiar type of automobile, or a specific aircraft type on a potential collision course. The actual target image, in this situation is not known exactly because the relative pose of the 3D object or color are unknown.

We can develop a model of a Yes-No (present-absent) search task by extending the model for target detection to incorporate unknown target location and the variability due to potential distracters (foils). We assume that during the search process the visual system computes a target representation of each possible target according to equation (12), and correlates (convolve) it with the test image representation. Then, the visual system compares the maximum over targets and locations to fixed criterion and responds Yes if the criterion is exceeded.

The main effect of uncertainty is to reduce the effective signal-to-noise ratio (Peli, 1985). The reduction in signal-to-noise ratio can be expressed in terms of increased variance as in section 4.7.2, or by reducing the effective difference between the target and the mean of potential distracters. This simple model of a search task has been shown to account for a wide range of phenomena observed in search experiments, such as the dependence of performance on the number of potential distracters (false targets) (Palmer et al., 1993; Pavel, 1990; Pavel et al., 1992a).

4.7.4 Gestures and Sign-Language Communication

The models described in this chapter are applicable to static images. In general, extending these models to sequences of images with motion would require, at the minimum, adding filtering in the temporal domain. Such filtering could be implemented by extending a 2D multi-resolution representation to 3D.

The potential of the model-based approach to account for IQ of dynamic sequences is suggested by work on gesture-based communication. One example of this type of application are systems for mediation communication among deaf individuals using the American Sign Language (ASL).

The performance of such systems is characterized in terms of an objective measure: message intelligibility. Results of prior work (Pavel, Sperling, Riedl, and Vanderbeek, 1987) suggest that, when the image impairments can be characterized in terms of additive, uncorrelated noise, then signal to noise ratio can be used to predict the intelligibility of the ASL communication.

4.8 Examples of Display Optimization

We provide here a brief list of examples of recent applications of computational image-quality models to the design of display and image processing systems. These examples are all recent projects undertaken at the Human Performance Laboratory at NASA Ames Research Center (ARC).

- The design of LCD displays is a complex process involving a large number of parameters and decisions. Construction and evaluation of prototypes is expensive. A group of researchers at NASA ARC developed a simulator that enables a designer to build a model of an LCD display using a general purpose workstation. They incorporated a version of the Lubin's computational model of image quality within the simulation software to evaluate the proposed LCD designs (Martin, A. Ahumada, and Larimer, 1992).

- Halftoning is an effective method to generate gray-level appearance using binary (black or white) pixels. The development of the most effective approach to dithering involves design decisions concerning spatial distribution of the pixels. Recently (Mulligan and Albert J. Ahumada, 1992) developed a halftoning-optimizing method that relies on a model-based metric for evaluating the quality of halftones.

- The development of visually lossless compression scheme is a natural domain for applications of model-based quality metrics. The general idea is that information that is not visible does not need to be coded. In recent extension of discrete cosine transform (DCT) image compression several investigators (Ahumada and Peterson, 1992; Watson, 1993a) used a model-based method for measuring visibility of compression artifacts.

- One way to improve the efficiency and safety of ground and airborne transportation is to provide operators with reliable information in poor-visibility conditions. We can achieve this goal by enhancing displays with combined (fused) outputs of multiple sensors, including infrared (for night operations) and millimeter radar (for fog). The optimization of fusion algorithms is a complex design problem, and benefits greatly from model-based evaluation of enhanced displays (Pavel, Larimer, and Ahumada, 1992b).

4.9 Acknowledgments

This work was supported in part by NASA grant NCC 2-811 to Oregon Graduate Institute. We are thankful for helpful feedback from Dr. B. L. Beard, and for editorial work by Lyn Dupre.

4.10 References

Ahumada, A. J., Jr. (1987). Putting the noise of the visual system back in the picture. *JOSA A, 4*, 2372-2378.

Ahumada, A. J., Jr. (1996). Simplified vision models for image quality assessment. In J. Morreale (Ed.), *Society for Information Display International Symposium Digest of Technical Papers* Playa del Ray, CA: SID.

Ahumada, A. J., Jr., and Null, C. E. (1993). Image quality: A multidimensional problem. In A. B. Watson (Ed.), *Digital Images and Human Vision* (pp. 141-148). Cambridge, MA: MIT Press.

Ahumada, A. J., Jr., and Peterson, H. (1992). Luminance-model-based DCT quantization for color image compression. *SPIE Proc.,* 1666, 365-374.

Barten, P. (1990). Evaluation of subjective image quality with the square foot integral method. *JOSA A, 7,* 2024-2031.

Barten, P. (1992). The SQRI as a measure for VDU image quality. *SID Digest, 23*, 867-870.

Beard, B. L., Levi, D. M., Klein, S. A., and Carney, T. (1996). Vernier acuity with non-simultaneous targets: The cortical magnification factor estimated by psychophysics. *Vision Research*, accepted for publication.

Burt, P., and Adelson, E. (1983). The laplacian pyramid as a compact image code. *IEE Trans., COM-31*, 532-540.

Chapman, W. H., and Olin, A. (1965). Tutorial in image quality criteria for serial camera systems. *Photographic Science and Engineering*, 9, 385-397.

Daly, S. (1993). The visible differences predictor: an algorithm for the assessment of image fidelity. In A. B. Watson (Ed.), *Digital Images and Human Vision* (pp. 179-206). Cambridge, MA: MIT Press.

Duval-Destin, M. (1991). A spatio-temporal complete description of contrast. *SID Digest*, 22, 615-618.

Eckstein, M. P., and Whiting, J. S. (1996). Visual signal detection in structured backgrounds I. Effect of number of possible spatial locations and signal contrast. *Journal of the Optical Society of America A*, 13(10), 1960-1968.

Farrell, J., Trontlej, H., Rosenberg, C., and Wiseman, J. (1991). Perceptual metrics for monochrome image compression. *SID Digest*, 22, 631-634.

Field, D. J. (1987). Relations between the statistics of natural images and the response properties of cortical cells. *Journal of the Optical Society of America A,* 4(12), 2379-2394.

Foley, J. M. (1994). Human luminance pattern-vision mechanisms: masking experiments require a new model. *Journal of the Optical Society of America A,* 11(6), 1710-1719.

Freeman, W. T., and Adelson, E. H. (1991). The design and use of steerable filters. *IEEE Transactions of Pattern Analysis and Machine Intelligence*, 13, 891-906.

Girod, B. (1989). The information theoretical significance of spatial and temporal masking in video signals. *SPIE Proc.*, 1077, 178-187.

Girod, B. (1993). What's wrong with mean squared error? In A. B. Watson (Ed.), *Digital Images and Human Vision* (pp. 207-220). Cambridge, MA: MIT Press.

Green, D. M., and Swets, J. A. (1966). *Signal Detection Theory and Psychophysics*. New York: Wiley.

Grogan, T., and Keene, D. (1992). Image quality evaluation with a contour-based perceptual model. *SPIE Proc.*, 1666, 188-197.

Kayargadde, V., and Martens, J. B. (1996). Perceptual characterization of images degraded by blur and noise: model. *Journal of the Optical Society of America*, 13(6), 1178-1188.

Limb, J. (1979). Distortion criteria of the human viewer. *IEEE Trans.*, SMC-9, 778-793.

Lubin, J. (1993). The use of psychophysical models and data in the analysis of display system performance. In A. B. Watson (Ed.), *Visual Factors in Electronic Image Communications*, MA: MIT Press.

Luce, R. D. (1986). *Response Times*. New York: Oxford University Press.

Martin, R., Ahumada, A. J., Jr., and Larimer, J. (1992). Color matrix display simulation based upon luminance and chromatic contrast sensitivity of early vision. *SPIE Proc.*, 1666, 336-342.

Mulligan, J. B., and Ahumada, A. J., Jr. (1992). Principled halftoning based on models of human vision. In B. E. Rogowitz (Ed.), *Human Vision, Visual Processing and Digital Display III* (pp. 109-121). Bellingham, WA: SPIE.

Palmer, J., Ames, C. T., and Lindsey, D. T.(1993). Measuring effect of attention on simple visual search. *Journal of Experimental Psychology: Human Perception and Performance,* 19(1), 108-130.

Pavel, M. (1990). Statistical model of pre-attentive visual search. *In 31st Annual Meeting of the Psychonomics Society*, New Orleans.

Pavel, M., Econopouli, J., and Landy, M. (1992a). Theory of rapid visual search. Invest. Opthal. *Visual Sci. Supplement*, 33.

Pavel, M., Econopouli, J., and Landy, M. (1992b). Sensor Fusion for Synthetic Vision. *SID Digest*, 23, 475-478.

Pavel, M., Sperling, G., Riedl, T., and Vanderbeek, A. (1987). The limits of intelligibility of American sign language. *Journal of the Optical Society of America A,* 4(12), 2355-2366.

Peli, E. (1990). Contrast in complex images. *Journal of the Optical Society of America*, 7, 2032-2040.

Peli, E. (1995). *Vision Models for Target Detection and Recognition.* River Edge, New Jersey, USA: World Scientific.

Peli, E. (1996). Test of a model of foveal vision by using simulations. *Journal of the Optical Society of America,* 13(6), 1131-1139.

Pelli, D. G. (1985). Uncertainty explains many aspects of visual contrast detection and discrimination. *Journal of the Optical Society of America A*, 2(9), 1508-1532.

Ridder, H. D. (1992). Minkowski-metrics as a combination rule for digital-image-impairments. *SPIE Proc.*, 1666, 16-26.

Ruthruff, E. (1996). A test of the deadline model for speed-accuracy tradeoffs. *Perception and Psychophysics,* 58(1), 56-64.

Sakrison, D. (1977). On the role of the observer and a distortion measure in image transmission. *IEEE Trans.,* COM-25, 1251-1267.

Snyder, H. L. (1973). Image quality and observer performance. In M. Biberman (Ed.), *Perception of Displayed Information.* New York: Plenum.

Teo, P. C., and Heeger, D. J. (1994). Perceptual image distortion. *In Proceedings of ICIP-94* (pp. 982-986). Los Alamitos, CA: IEEE Computer Society Press.

Wandell, B. A. (1990). *Foundations of Vision.* Sunderland MA: Sinauer Associates.

Watson, A. (1979). Probability summation over time. *Vision Res.*, 19, 515-522.

Watson, A. B. (1987a). Efficiency of an image code based on human vision. *Journal of the Optical Society of America A*, 4(12), 2401-2417.

Watson, A. B. (1987b). Estimation of local spatial scale. *Journal of the Optical Society of America*, 4, 1579-1582.

Watson, A. B. (1993a). DCTune: A technique for visual optimization of DCT quantization matrices for individual images. In J. Morreale (Ed.), *Society for Information Display International Symposium Digest of Technical Papers.* (pp. 946-949). Playa del Rey, CA: SID.

Watson, A. B. (1993b). *Digital Images and Human Vision.* Cambridge, MA: MIT Press.

Watson, A. B., and Solomon, J. A. (1995). Contrast gain control model fits masking data. *Investigative Ophthalmology and Visual Science*, 36, (4 (ARVO Suppl.)), S438 (abstract).

Westheimer, G. (1986). The eye as an optical instrument. In K. Boff, L. Kaufman, and J. Thomas (Eds.), *Handbook of Perception and Human Performance.* NewYork: Wiley.

Williams, D. R., Brainard, D. H., McMahon, M. J., and Navarro, R. (1994). Double-pass and interferometric measures of the optical quality of the eye. *Journal of the Optical Society of America,* 11(12), 3123-3135.

Zetsche, C., and Hauske, G. (1989). Multiple channel model for the prediction of subjective image quality. *SPIE Proc.*, 1077, 209-216.

4.11 Appendix: Measurement of Performance

We assume that the objective is to measure the ability of an observer to discriminate between two images: an original (reference) image and a test image that was processed or that contains a target. Actual measurement of performance is typically implemented in terms of different types of tests each comprising sequences of trials. On each trial, the observer is shown one or more images and is asked to indicate his response. In the Yes/No type of test the observer is shown a single image and is asked to respond with "yes" or "no" to a question such as "Is a target present," or "Is this a processed image?" In multiple-alternative, forced-choice (MAFC) tasks, the observer is asked to choose one of several alternatives (e.g., which of the images contains a target). In either type of test, observers can be asked to respond as fast as possible, and the response times as well as the proportion of responses are used to summarize the raw test results. The raw results are often transformed in one of several ways in order to remove biases, or to relate the results to some physical characteristics of images. For more background information see, e.g., (Green and Swets, 1966).

A1. Accuracy

Many objective performance measures are specified in terms of the accuracy of performance for tasks that must be completed in a given time interval.

Two measures generally are used to express discriminability: just noticeable differences (*JND*), and discriminability *d'*. In both cases, performance accuracy is first summarized in terms of the raw proportions of correct and incorrect responses in one of two types of discrimination tasks: two-alternative, forced-choice (2AFC) and Yes/No tasks.

In a 2AFC task, an observer is given two images and is asked to judge which of them is more likely to be the processed image. As the physical difference between two images increases, so does the probability that humans can discriminate them. A typical way to summarize the ability to discriminate the original and the processed images is in terms of *JND* s. *JND* is the value of physical difference between two images (e.g., contrast), such that observers will discriminate the two images correctly with probability of. 75%.

In a Yes/No, task the observer is shown a single image and is asked to judge whether that image is the processed image. The results of this task consist of two independent measures: the proportion of correct identification, p_s, and the proportion of false positives, p_n (false alarms). The values of these measures for a particular pair of images depend not only on the discriminability of the images, but also on the observer's criterion, or *bias*. A frequently used summary of the discriminability of images is based on the assumptions of the signal detection theory, such as that the underlying distributions are normal. Using such assumptions, we summarize the results in terms of *d,'* computed as

$$d' = \Phi^{-1}(p_n) - \Phi^{-1}(p_s). \quad \text{(A1)}$$

For an ideal detector, the *d'* measure can be interpreted as a statistical *t*-test based on a normalized difference of means as expressed by equation (14).

A2. Response Time

An alternate response measure of discriminability is the speed with which an observer can respond while maintaining a given — typically high — level of accuracy. The response time (RT) is measured on each trial and the performance is summarized by calculating the average RT on correct trials.

The motivation for collecting RTs is that the more difficult discrimination requires more processing and therefore takes more time. Under this assumption, the average response time should decrease with increase in discriminability. To develop a quantitative relationship between the RT and physical characteristics of images requires considerable modeling and experimental effort (Luce, 1986). We think that assessing discrimnability by measuring RTs is not yet practical. In some applications, however, the response time is a critical component of performance, e.g., driving, flying, etc.. In that case, RT measure of performance should be a component of the system evaluation.

The importance of considering both speed and accuracy simultaneously cannot be overstated. Consideration of only one can be misleading, because human operators can exhibit strong cognitive-strategy shifts that result in speed-accuracy tradeoffs. Typical examples of speed-accuracy tradeoffs are that observer may guess a faster response may result from easier task or from the observers decision to guess (Ruthruff, 1996). In that case, faster responses may not reflect more discriminable images. Although our concern is accuracy, for all tasks where only accuracy is measured, the observers should be limited to fixed time intervals to perform the tasks.

A3. Subjective Opinions

In addition to the tasks with objectively measurable performance (e.g., discriminability), the subjective appearance and esthetic appeal of images on displays are important components of a display systems merit. The only currently practical way to measure these subjective perceptual characteristics is by asking observers to judge the quality of each image. In typical experiment observers are asked to rate, on a numerical or adjective scale, the subjective quality of each image. The results frequently are summarized in terms of average scores, and are reported as mean opinion scores (MOSs). There are questions with respect nonlinear transformations of the resulting scales, and the appropriateness of averaging. In addition, there exist other, more sophisticated methods for summarizing and interpreting the data. For example, one such method, used in practice, involves fitting of truncated Gaussian distributions.

Handbook of Human-Computer Interaction
Second, completely revised edition
M. Helander, T.K. Landauer, P. Prabhu (eds.)

Chapter 5

Task Analysis, Task Allocation and Supervisory Control

Thomas B. Sheridan
Massachusetts Institute of Technology
Massachusetts, USA

5.1 Introduction

This chapter discusses the analysis of tasks and the allocation of tasks to computers and to humans. While these are old problems, the relation of task allocation to task analysis is sometimes not well understood. Often it is naively assumed that tasks may simply be broken into independent elements and then assigned to either computer or human, based on accepted criteria. The chapter seeks to clarify why, in the case of human-computer interaction, this is not realistic. It goes on to discuss in some detail a form of human-computer allocation ideally suited for complex, emerging human-machine systems, namely supervisory control. Supervisory control provides a continuum of different mixes of human and computer for performing tasks, which makes clear why "human-computer task allocation" may change radically with time and/or circumstance.

Task allocation is generally taken to mean the assignment of various tasks (jobs) that need to be done to resources, instruments or agents capable of doing those tasks, or the allocation of such resources to tasks, which is equivalent. Task allocation is an inherent part of system design. *Task analysis* means the breakdown of overall tasks, as given, into their elements, and the specification of how these elements relate to one another in space and time and functional relation. It is an accepted means to begin almost any human factors effort. By task one can mean the complete performance of a given procedure, or the totality of effort to design and/or build a given thing, to monitor and/or control a given system, or to diagnose or solve a given problem. Alternatively a task can mean a small sub-element such as a particular movement or measurement. Sometimes *mission* is used to connote the full task or end state to be achieved, and *subtask* used to refer to some component. Terminology for such breakdown of tasks is of no particular concern here except to note that some hierarchical breakdown is usually helpful or even necessary.

In this chapter we are concerned especially with the allocation of relatively complex tasks - ones necessarily involving sensing, remembering, decision-making and acting - which use human and machine resources available and capable of performing these functions. Moreover we are concerned with human and machine resources acting in concert, as compared to assignment of a whole task to either machine or human by itself. And we are particularly concerned with allocation between humans and intelligent machines - computers - where the capability of the modern machine now comes closer to that of the human than in the past.

Issues of task analysis and allocation to human vs. machine have continued to challenge the human factors profession for many years, but as of now, while there are many accepted techniques for doing task analysis, there is no commonly accepted means to perform task allocation. The reasons are several: (1) while tasks may indeed be broken into pieces, those pieces are seldom independent of one another, and the task components may interact in different ways depending upon the resources chosen for doing them; (2) there is an infinity of ways the human and computer can interact, resulting in an infinite spectrum of allocation possibilities from which to choose; and (3) criteria for judging the suitability of various human-machine mixes are usually difficult to quantify and often implicit. Though the chapter suggests some things to consider when allocating tasks to people and machines (including machines with "intelligent" capabilities), no attempt is made to offer a general procedure for synthesizing the task allocation.

5.2 Task Analysis and Task Allocation in the Human Factors Literature

Analysis of tasks into functional elements for performance by humans and/or machines is an old art, with little quantitative science. The early exponents of "scientific management" (Taylor, 1947) proposed qualitative analyses of production line tasks, which eventually evolved into the time-and-motion techniques of repetitive assembly-line tasks we have today. Micromotion analysis is typically in terms of elements like *position* (the hand, for example, in preparation to grasp a part), *grasp*, *transport loaded* (move the hand from A to B while grasping the part), and so on. Only much later were information processing tasks analyzed in a similar way (see, for example, Card et al., 1983).

Task analysis is now routinely performed, using any of a variety of methods to name and list sequential steps, specify probabilities or logical conditions of transition from one step to another, specify whether human or machine performs each step, and so on. Alternative methods of task analysis will be reviewed briefly in the next section.

Turning now to task allocation, Fitts (1951) proposed a list of what "men are better at" and what "machines are better at" (Table 1). This has come to be known as the Fitts MABA-MABA List, or simply the Fitts List. It is often referred to as the first well-known basis for task allocation.

Jordan (1963) criticizes use of the Fitts List by people who assume that the goal is to compare men

Table 1. The Fitts (1951) MABA-MABA list.

Men are better at:

- Detecting small amounts of visual, auditory, or chemical energy
- Perceiving patterns of light or sound
- Improvising and using flexible procedures
- Storing information for long periods of time, and recalling appropriate parts
- Reasoning inductively
- Exercising judgment

Machines are better at:

- Responding quickly to control signals
- Applying great force smoothly and precisely
- Storing information briefly, erasing it completely
- Reasoning deductively

and machines, then decide which is best for each function or task element. He quotes Craik (1947a,b) who had earlier pointed out that to the extent that man is understood as a machine, to that extent we know how to replace man with a machine. Early studies by Birmingham and Taylor (1954) revealed that in simple manual control loops performance can be improved by quickening, wherein visual feedback signals are biased by derivatives of those signals, thereby adding artificial anticipation (what the control engineer would call proportional-plus-derivative control) and saving the human operator the trouble of performing this computation cognitively. Birmingham and Taylor concluded that "man is best when doing least" in this case. Jordan suggests that this is a perfect example of Craik's tenet. He also quotes Einstein and Infeld (1942) who discuss the development and then the demise of the concept of ether in physics, and how when empirical facts do not agree with accepted concepts it is time to throw out the concepts (but retain the empirical facts). Jordan's point is that we should throw out the idea of comparing man and machine but keep the facts about what people do best and what machines do best. Jordan's idea of what we should espouse, and the main point of retaining the Fitts List, is that people and machines are *complimentary*.

Meister (1971) suggested a straightforward procedure for doing task allocation:(1) write down all the salient mixes of allocation; (2) write down all the applicable criteria. Following this, one should rank order all combinations of allocation mix and criteria, thus determining a rank order score. Alternatively one could weight the relative importance of each criterion, rate each mix by each criterion, multiply by the weight, and add up the scores for each allocation mix. However, there are serious difficulties with any such direct method, as implied at the very beginning of this chapter: hidden assumptions, unanticipated criteria situations, non-independence of tasks, non-independence of criteria, non-linearities which invalidate simple multiplication of weight by rating and addition of products, and most of all the fact that a very large number of possible interactions between human and computer compete for consideration, not simply "human vs. computer".

Price (1985) asserts that in order to make use of the Fitts MABA-MABA list, one needs data which are context dependent, but these data are mostly not available. Acquisition of these data is exacerbated by the fact that the status of the machine is not static, and that the capabilities of machines to perform "intelligent" acts such as automation and decision-support are ever improving. But, claims Price, automation can "starve cognition" if the human is not kept in sufficient communication with what the automation is doing or intending. He seems to agree with Jordan when he points out that human performance and machine performance are not a zero-sum game, implying that the combination can be much better than either by itself. Kantowitz and Sorkin (1987) and Price (1990) provide recent reviews of the literature in task allocation.

The public (and unfortunately too many political and industrial decision-makers) have been slow to realize that task allocation does not necessarily mean allocation of a whole task to either human or machine, exclusive of the other. For example, in the space program, it has been common to consider that a task must be done by either an astronaut or a "robot", that if a spacecraft is manned then astronauts must do almost everything, and that if a spacecraft is unmanned every task must be automated. In fact, on manned spacecraft many functions are automatic, and on unmanned spacecraft many functions are performed by remote control from the ground. In later sections of this chapter an effort is made to show how various combinations of human and machine can function interactively and cooperatively.

5.3 The Relation of Task Allocation to Task Analysis

Task analysis and task allocation are highly interrelated. It is sometimes asserted that task analysis is the "what" and task allocation is the "how". This unfortunately is not a helpful idea, because "what" and "how" are not separable. The difference between task analysis and task allocation can better be characterized as the difference between specification and clarification of the constraints which are given initially, and specification of additional constraints which determine a demonstrably best (or acceptable) final solution or design to the problem (task) in terms of available resources. Sometimes the "givens" are not accepted, and the task is redefined to accommodate the resource allocation.

Let us elaborate. In defining task analysis above the term given was repeatedly used. What is given are the task constraints, and task analysis is really a matter of articulating these constraints and making them visible. The task analyst's first duty is to list the salient independent variables (inputs) which must be considered when doing the task, and the dependent variables (outputs) the measures of which constitute task performance. The constraints are properties of the independent and dependent variables.

Constraint properties can take several forms. (1) they can be fixed numbers, which might, for example, set the mean values or ranges of the variables. (2) they can be functional relations between two or more variables, e.g., laws of nature such as those of Newton (force = mass times acceleration) or Ohm (voltage = current times resistance), or economic statements of the dollar or time cost of certain objects or events. (3) finally, they can be objective functions of two or more variables which define the relative worth (goodness, utility) of particular states (combinations of variables).

For an extremely simple example, suppose the task is to move a given object from A to B, and the only salient variables are time and dollar cost (see Figure 1). Lines 1a and 1b may be fixed constraints of the first form specifying what is acceptable. Line 2 may be an economic constraint of the second form, which states that a (T,$) solution to get from A to B in time T costs at least $ because of, for example, some theoretical fuel efficiency - thus a (T,$) solution must lie on or above line 2. Curves 3a, 3b and 3c are lines of constant utility (third form). In this case the task is completely specified to the point where the ideal solution is to find the lowest (greatest utility) point which still satisfies the given constraints. The best solution, a (T,$) combination specified by point S is tractable by simple mathematical tools such as linear programming. The allocation or design stage in this case is automatic; it is contained in the task specification. There is nothing more to decide. If, however, an objective function is not given *as part of the task specification*, then any

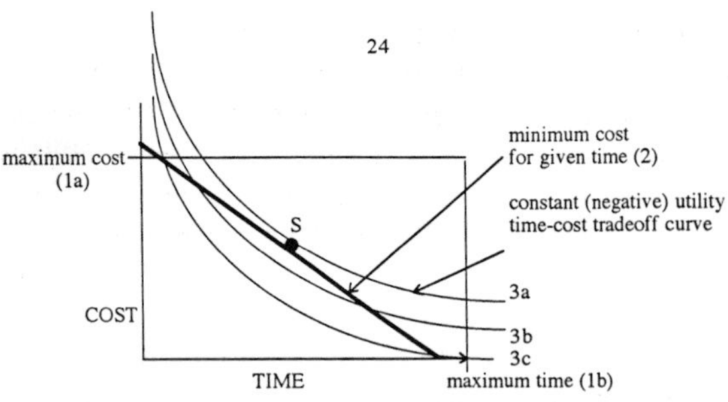

Figure 1. Three kinds of constraints.

solution which accommodates the given task constraints is equally acceptable. In that case other allocation costs judged relevant (e.g., safety, aesthetics, justice), which may not be given initially, will then be brought to bear to influence the (T,$) solution.

If only specification of task constraints were so simple as in the above example. The first form of constraint - a constant or fixed range of a variable - is simple enough to understand, if indeed there are such constraints.

The second form is often much more difficult, where the essential relations between variables are "if--then--else--" rules, more like those in a computer program than like simple analytical functions. Sometimes such rules take the form of a time-ordered series of steps, a *procedure*. Sometimes they take the form of a graph with logical criteria (e.g., Boolean ANDs and ORs; or IF some condition is true, THEN some task element is required, ELSE some other task element). When these are specified for going from one node in the graph (task element) to another, this is variously called a *logic tree* or a *process flow chart*. Sometimes the nodes on the graph of task elements are just connected by probabilities, indicating the state-determined probabilities of various task sequences. The latter is variously called an *event tree*, a *transition matrix*, or more generally a *Markov process*. Sometimes the task can be specified as the achievement of some final condition or physical and geometric configuration, such as is specified by a mechanical drawing with material specification, and even (perish the thought!) verbal description of what is to be done, where other means are not sufficient to communicate the ideas unambiguously. These are all standard rendering media used by the task analyst.

The various first- and second-form relations between and among variables are almost always accompanied by some third-form time, economic, legal, or other criteria for getting the job done, i.e., some objective function, however incompletely stated.

Task analysis for human-machine systems means analysis of tasks which combine seeking information, sensing various displays, detecting patterns of information, abstracting, remembering and recalling parts of that information, making decisions, and taking control actions. These are all steps that can be done by either human or machine. It is important at the task analysis stage to stay relatively abstract and refrain from implying either human or machine until the constraints of what is to be done are clearly specified.

When performing a task analysis it is all too easy to start the allocation process before the constraints are completely specified. For example, let us assume one seeks to improve a particular system which presently consists of various displays and controls. The redesign can include some machine sensing and some automatic control, or at least a redesign of the displays and controls. There is a tendency to fall into the trap of analyzing the task as a series of steps for a human to look at particular existing displays and operate particular existing controls - the very displays and controls which constitute the present interface one seeks to improve upon or automate. The correct way to analyze the task is with each named step, to specify the information to be obtained and/or stored, the decisions to be made, and the actions to be taken - independent of the human or machine means to achieve those steps.

There is one additional consideration which should be mentioned in conjunction with analyzing human-computer tasks. Human-computer tasks tend to be of two types. One type includes information processing tasks where the information does not, during the particular processing of concern, interact with the physical world except the human user. Examples are people using computers to do word processing or spread sheets, or getting spoken information from telephone query systems. In these cases one can arbitrarily stop and later resume the task, and nothing will have changed during the recess. The second type of human-computer task is where there is a dynamic system on the other side of the computer from the human user (e.g., airplane, manufacturing plant, etc.) which is tied to the physical world in a dynamic sense, and the human is monitoring or controlling the dynamic process through a computer intermediary. In this latter case the human cannot arbitrarily stop and later resume the task and expect the state of the task to be exactly where he left it. Forces in the physical world will have changed the task (assuming of course that the recess time is not negligible relative to the time constants of the real-world dynamic process.)

5.4 How to Consider Task Allocation

It was emphasized earlier that human-computer task allocation is not simply a matter of assigning independent task elements to either human or computer based on accepted criteria. The task elements are seldom independent, there is an infinite variety of ways the human and computer can interact to perform task elements, and the human element certainly cannot be turned on and off like a machine (making the stages of human participation far from independent of one another), and many salient criteria cannot be easily quantified (though some can and should be). Thus the task allocation problem is really a systems design problem of the most general sort where an infinite variety of solutions are possible, not at all like a well-defined operations research problem of assigning independent task elements to a small number of independent resources according to a given objective function.

What then are some special considerations in coping with the human-computer task allocation problem? Such consideration should help reduce the size of the search space which must be evaluated.

*1. **Go back and check for over-constraining in the task analysis:*** The task analysis should be complete, but constraints that are not really necessary make the allocation step that much more difficult. Factors of safety can be added later, as dictated by resource availability. Note which constraints are the firmest and which may be regarded as fuzzy, where some adjustment may be made. A common bit of naiveté is to specify that a system be "100% safe", which of course means that no allocation is feasible.

*2. **Judge what are obvious allocations:*** Given the various admonitions that human-computer task allocation is a complex design task not normally amenable to simple deductive procedure, there nevertheless may be some obvious pointers to allocation. Some tasks may be easy to computerize and this may be obviously acceptable according to Fitts' MABA-MABA list. Some non-repetitive tasks may be done much more simply by a human who is already available and knows what is required, whereas communicating the task requirements to the computer would take more time and be more trouble than it is worth. And some tasks may be so complex that programming a computer to do them would be too difficult or too time consuming compared to any advantage to be gained.

*3. **Look at the extremes:*** A common engineering approach is to look at the extremes of a situation. A pro-computer extremist (perhaps in hopes of maximizing speed and reliability and avoiding messy training requirements) would ask what can possibly be automated - what prevents doing everything by computer? And then what is left for the human to do? That would push the allocation as far as it could go in the computer direction. In contrast, a pro-human extremist (perhaps with zeal to maximize job satisfaction and minimize change from what already exists) would ask what tasks can possibly be done by the human, and for what tasks is there no choice but to give the human some computer help? That would push the allocation as far as it could go in the human direction. Asking such questions helps to set the range of the "solution space" or the "allocation space".

*4. **Consider various degrees between the extremes:*** Table 2 (Sheridan, 1987) offers a ten-point scale of degrees of automation/computerization from zero to one hundred percent. It is worthwhile examining some of the intermediate stages when considering allocation for the particular set of tasks at hand.

*5. **Ask how fine an allocation makes sense:*** The coarsest allocation is to have the human do everything or the computer do everything, but in modern systems this is less and less often the best answer. On the other hand to allocate tasks to too fine a degree makes no sense because, regardless of how finely the task can be divided into elements, human attention and cognition cannot be partitioned arbitrarily, or simply turned on or off. Human memory seems to prefer large chunks, relatively complete pictures and patterns, and tends to be less good at details. This empirical fact strongly suggests that insofar as it is feasible and practical, the human should be left to deal with the "big picture" while the computer copes with the details.

*6. **Consider trading vs. sharing:*** Trading means the human and computer perform their duties one after the other, each handing the task back to the other when finished with any one part. Sharing means human and computer work on the task at the same time, possibly handling different variables but perhaps acting on the same variables with some other human or machine device comparing their decisions/actions to determine if they are consistent. Human and computer can cooperate in either mode. Which is best depends upon task context.

*7. **Consider many salient criteria:*** There are many criteria for judging one allocation to be better than an-

Table 2. Scale of degrees of automation.

1. The computer offers no assistance: the human must do it all.
2. The computer offers a complete set of action alternatives, and
3. narrows the selection down to a few, or
4. suggests one alternative, and
5. executes that suggestion if the human approves, or
6. allows the human a restricted time to veto before automatic execution, or
7. executes automatically, then necessarily informs the human, or
8. informs the human only if asked, or
9. informs the human only if it, the computer, decides to.
10. The computer decides everything and acts autonomously, ignoring the human.

other, and the designer should naturally consider most of them without being reminded. Nevertheless it is important to write them down and even try to rank order them, though there is doubt that criteria can simply be weighted in the sense that Meister suggested, since some are more important for some parts of the task and some are more important for other parts. A relatively small number of criteria should emerge as most important for a given task.

5.5 Supervisory Control: The New Challenge for Task Allocation

The remainder of this chapter puts forth a perspective for considering how computers and computer users are coming to interact in a broad range of tasks that can be called supervisory control tasks. The *supervisory control* perspective, or framework or paradigm, can encompass any task wherein the computer is assigned to receive information about the ongoing state of some ongoing physical process and, based upon such sensed information as well as information programmed into it by a human supervisor, direct actions on that process. The human supervisor works through the computer to effect what needs to be done in the physical world. The computer is then seen as a mediator - communicating upward to the supervisor, and communicating downward to the physical process, whatever it may be.

Does that include all conceivable tasks? Perhaps, but the concept of supervisory control has found most currency in control of aircraft, spacecraft, ships and other vehicles, control of chemical and electrical power generating plants, and industrial and other robotic devices. Computer word processing and "number crunching" are not normally considered supervisory control, since the physical process beyond the computer itself is relatively trivial. There is little doubt that the paradigm could be extended to just about all computer-interactive tasks.

Obviously the supervisory control paradigm is but one of many perspectives that may be useful; others are described in this book. But useful for what? For predicting behavior of human or computer or both? Unfortunately there are few, if any, current models of supervisory control with much predictive value. Supervisory control models refined to that point exist now only for a very narrow range of tasks, such as well defined aircraft piloting or industrial plant operations where given procedures are being followed and well defined global criteria apply. In the present context the usefulness of the supervisory control perspective, it is argued, is for classifying human functions with respect to computer functions, and for gaining insight into ways in which computers can aid people in doing jobs.

Much of what follows will be devoted to presenting a scheme by which human activities in supervising physical processes can be categorized. Twelve detailed functions are discussed, under five broader categories, and for each function the computer will be shown to have a role to play in aiding the human operator. For each of these functions it will be asserted that the human operator carries a (hypothetical) mental model in his head, and corresponding to each component mental model there can (should) be a computer-based representation of knowledge.

The rest of the chapter will also consider issues of the timing of human operator attention-giving to supervisory tasks, and what are the attributes of these tasks which demand attention. Problems of modeling supervisory control are considered, including what factors limit our ability to model these kinds of systems.

Finally the chapter discusses the question of "who is in charge (or should be), when." Some social implications of supervisory control are mentioned, both gratifying and threatening, since, when the computer is directly connected through sensors and effectors to the world, the computer is granted the power of control, beyond mere information processing.

The chapter does not purport to be a comprehensive review of the subject of supervisory control, monitoring, attention, or related topics. For other reviews the reader is referred to Moray (1986) or Sheridan (1987, 1992).

Some Definitions. Supervisory control may be defined by the analogy between a supervisor of subordinate staff in an organization of people, and the human overseer of a modern computer-mediated semi-automatic control system. The supervisor gives human subordinates general instructions which they in turn may translate into action. The supervisor of a computer-controlled system may do the same.

Defined strictly, *supervisory control* means that one or more human operators are setting initial conditions for, intermittently adjusting, and receiving information from, a computer that itself closes a control loop in a well-defined process through artificial sensors and effectors.

By a less strict definition "supervisory control" is used when a computer transforms human operator commands to generate detailed control actions, or makes significant transformations of measured data to produce integrated summary displays. In this latter case the computer need not have the capability to commit actions based upon new information from the environment, whereas in the first it necessarily must. The two situations may appear similar to the human supervisor, since the computer mediates both his outputs and his inputs and the supervisor is thus removed from detailed events at the low level.

A supervisory control system is represented in Figure 2. Here the human operator issues commands c to a human-interactive computer capable of understanding high level language and providing integrated summary displays of process state information y back to the operator. This computer, typically located in a control room or cockpit or office near to the supervisor, in turn communicates with at least one, probably many (hence the dotted lines), task-interactive computers, located with the equipment they are controlling. The task-interactive computers thus receive subgoal and conditional branching information from the human-interactive computer. Using such information as reference inputs, the task-interactive computers serve to close low-level control loops between artificial sensors and mechanical actuators, i.e., they accomplish the low level automatic control.

The low level task typically operates at some physical distance from the human operator and his human-friendly display-control computer. Therefore the communication channels between computers may be constrained by multiplexing, time delay or limited bandwidth. The task-interactive computer, of course, sends analog control signals to and receives analog feedback signals from the controlled process, and the latter does the same with the environment as it operates (vehicles moving relative to air, sea or earth, robots manipulating objects, process plants modifying products, etc.).

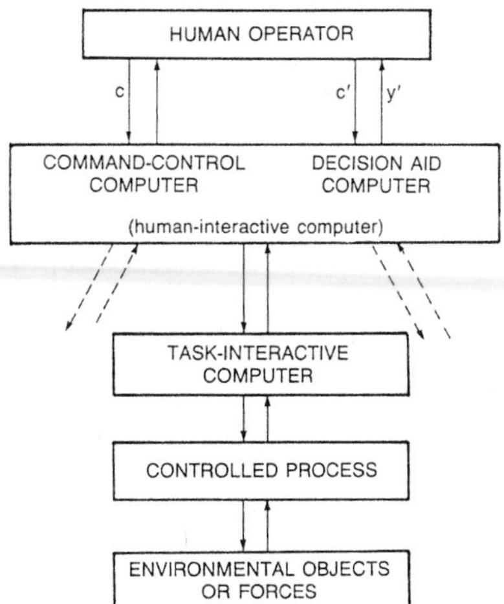

Figure 2. A supervisory control system.

Supervisory command and feedback channels for process state information are shown in Figure 2 to pass through the left side of the human interactive computer. On the right side we represent the decision-aid functions, with displayed output $\mathbf{y'}$ being advice relevant to operator requests for auxiliary information $\mathbf{c'}$. Customarily the latter interaction has not been recognized explicitly as part of a supervisory control system. New developments in computer-based "expert systems" and other decision aids for planning, editing, monitoring and failure detection have changed that. Reflection upon the nervous system of higher animals reveals a similar kind of supervisory control wherein commands are sent from the brain to local ganglia, and peripheral motor control loops are then closed locally through receptors in the muscles, tendons or skin. The brain, presumably, does higher level planning based on its own stored data and "mental models", an internalized expert system available to provide advice and permit trial responses before commitment to actual response.

A Brief History of the Concept. Theorizing about supervisory control began as aircraft and spacecraft became partially automated. It became evident that the

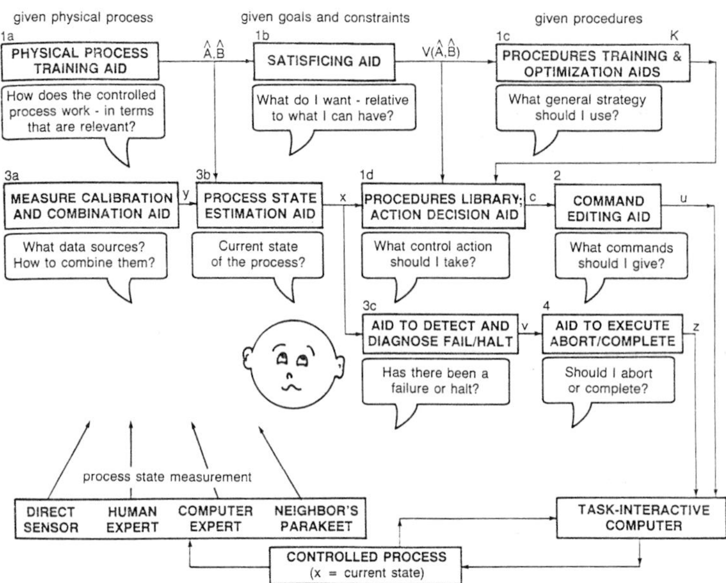

Figure 3. Computer decision aids (boxes) and mental models (thought balloons) corresponding to each of the supervisor's functions.

human operator was being replaced by the computer for direct control responsibility, and was moving to a new role of monitor and goal-constraint setter (Sheridan, 1960). An added incentive was the US space program, which posed the problem of how a human operator on earth could control a manipulator arm or vehicle on the moon through a three-second communication round-trip time delay. The only solution which avoided instability was to make the operator a supervisory controller communicating intermittently with a computer on the moon, which in turn closed the control loop there (Ferrell and Sheridan, 1967).

It became evident that the rapid development of microcomputers was forcing a transition from manual control to supervisory control in a variety of industrial and military applications. The design of display and control interfaces was seen to require a number of new developments (Sheridan and Johannsen, 1976; Sheridan, 1984). The National Research Council (1983, 1984) recognized supervisory control as one of the most important areas in which new human factors research is needed.

5.6 Twelve Functions of the Human Supervisory Controller

Categories of human supervisor functioning are listed in Table 3 (twelve in all, considering all the subordinate a's and b's). They are presented in the order in which they normally would occur in performing a supervisory control task. Figure 3 presents a similar sequence of nine of these functions in pictorial flowchart form, where for each of the nine functions the corresponding mental model is shown as a "thought balloon" of what the supervisor might be asking himself, and the potential computerized decision aid is shown as a rectangular box. It can be argued that functions 4a and 4b can be combined as one function, and the same for 5a and 5b, reducing the functions to ten. It can be argued further that 5a and 5b actually operate as parts of the other functions, resulting finally in a minimum of nine functions, represented as pairs of boxes and balloons (human functions and corresponding computer-aiding functions) in Figure 3.

The various functions are cross-referenced to Table 3 by numbers and letters over each corresponding block in Figure 3. Normally for any given task the first three functions are performed only once, off-line relative to the automatic operation of the system, while the remaining functions are done iteratively, and therefore are shown within two nested loops, as will be explained below. The functions in detail are:

1. Plan. Starting at the top of Table 3, and in the order in which the supervisor would perform the functions, the first broad category of functions is PLAN. The functions under PLAN engage only the human-interactive computer.

Table 3. The categories of human supervisory functions.

Supervisory Step	Associated Mental Model	Associated Computer Aid
1. PLAN		
a) understand controlled process	physical variables: transfer relations	physical process training aid
b) satisfice objectives	aspirations: preferences and indifferences	satisficing aid
c) set general strategy	general operating procedures and guidelines	procedures training and optimization aid
d) decide and test control actions	decision options: state-procedure-action; results of control actions	procedures library; action decision aid (in-situ simulation)
2. TEACH		
decide, test, and communicate commands	command language (symbols, syntax, semantics)	aid for editing commands
3. MONITOR AUTOMATION		
a) acquire, calibrate, and combine measures of process state	state information sources and their relevance	aid for calibration and combination of measures
b) estimate process state from current measure and past control actions	expected results of past actions	estimation aid
c) evaluate process state: detect and diagnose failure or halt	likely modes and causes of failure or halt	detection and diagnosis aid for failure or halt
4. INTERVENE		
a) if failure: execute planned abort	criteria and options for abort	abort execution aid
b) if normal end of task: complete	options and criteria for task completion	normal completion execution aid
5. LEARN		
a) record immediate events	immediate memory of salient events	immediate record and memory jogger
b) analyze cumulative experience; update model	cumulative memory of salient events	cumulative record and analysis

1a. A first specific supervisor function under PLAN is *understand controlled process*, which means to gain some understanding of how the given physical thing, equipment or system operates, and what are the relations by which inputs to it become outputs. Understanding of the process is usually the first consideration in training an operator. The idea is to build into the operator a mental model of the controlled process which is appropriate to his role - enough knowledge of the appropriate variables and their input-output transfer relations to be able to control and predict what the process will do in response to various inputs, but omitting details that are irrelevant to operation. The current research on mental models (de Kleer, 1979; Gentner and Stevens, 1983) has tended to concentrate on this function. A new generation of computer-based training aids has been developed recently which includes computer representation in terms of production rules, semantic nets, frames or other AI manifestations (Holland et. al., 1984; Harmon and King, 1985).

1b. A second specific function under PLAN is *satisfice objectives*. To control engineers this corresponds to obtaining an objective function, a closed-form analytical expression of "goodness" which is a scalar function of all relevant variables or *performance attributes* or *objectives*. To a mathematical decision theorist it may correspond to a *multiattribute utility function*, which specifies the global and unchanging relative goodness or badness of any point in the hyperspace of all relevant attributes (Keeney and Raiffa, 1976). However, the behavioral decision scientist knows that neither of the above models of human preference works very well in practice. People find it extremely difficult to consider levels of attributes that they have never experienced, and hence they cannot provide reliable data from which to generate global objective or utility functions.

What appears much closer to the way people actually behave is what has been termed *satisficing* (March and Simon, 1958; Weirzbicki, 1982), wherein a tentative aspiration point in attribute space is set and the decision-maker considers whether he can achieve this. But upon discovering that constraints will not permit this, or that he can achieve something more than what was aspired to, he will set a new aspiration level and consider whether he can achieve that, eventually deciding on the basis of time and energy spent in thinking about it that he is satisfied with some one set of objectives, some single point or small region of indifference in attribute space.

In this case the computer may provide aid to the operator by determining for any aspiration point whether that condition can be achieved, or whether or in what direction the operator can do better, all the while reminding him what set of options are *Pareto optimal*, i.e., not dominated by a point in attribute space which is not worse in any attribute and is better in one or more. Charny and Sheridan (1986) describe the development of an interactive computer-graphic aid to help a supervisor satisfice. The tool allows the user to set range constraints on the attributes, set weights, or set partial solutions. The aid then displays the implications in terms of what is feasible and what is not, what are "optimal" solutions, and how the selected "optimum" relates to other decision possibilities in multiattribute space. Perhaps most interesting, the aid reveals how much the weights or constraints must change in order for a different optimum to emerge - in other words it provides a running sensitivity analysis.

Using such a tool the supervisor may be expected to be influenced at least to some degree by goals given "from above" by his employer, by professional training, by laws of the government, by his early upbringing, or by social/cultural mores. Nevertheless, even though other aspects of systems become more automated in their actual control, the free-will "tuning" of task goals by the supervisory operator (which could also be called objective function setting by a satisficing process) is the one human role that would seem impossible to automate.

1c. A third specific function under PLAN is set general strategy. The supervisory operator is usually given some procedures or operating guidelines which he is to follow generally (or to deviate from as required for the particular task at hand). This function is also (normally) performed off-line, before the automatic system starts up. It is the second activity usually addressed formally in training programs (objective function setting is typically not addressed formally, though it might well be). The mental model here is that of the highest level operating procedures and guidelines which must be committed to memory (where detailed procedures can be accessed and read as needed). The corresponding computer aid here is one for broad procedures training. To help the supervisor relate the strategy planning to the satisfied objectives there might also be an aid for optimization in a broad sense, particularly when the general procedures are not already formulated and where certain general goals are given and are not supposed to be modified. Any of a number of common operations research techniques might be applied here, depending upon the class of tasks.

1d. A fourth specific function under PLAN is *decide and test control actions*. Control actions are events such as opening a valve or starting a pump in a plant, braking or accelerating or turning a vehicle-events which amount to physical forcing of the controlled process (not human behavioral responses, which here are called commands , see step 2). To decide control actions, of course, is by definition the essential function of any controller, and the supervisory controller is no exception. On the first pass of stepping through the supervisory functions this step would consist of deciding what actions are necessary to start up the automatic systems (and thus legitimately be part of PLAN), but on successive passes the specific control decisions must necessarily be based on feedback of state (necessarily follow block 3b in Figure 3). The supervisor's job then is to decide what procedures are appropriate to the estimated state in consideration of process dynamics and satisficed objectives as mentally modeled in steps 1a, 1b and 1c.

One form of decision aid for this function, already employed in some modern nuclear power and process control plants, is a computerized system which, based upon its algorithm for estimation of process state, displays to the operator the pre-planned control actions which best fit that plant condition. These are not implemented automatically, though in some cases they could be, for it is deemed important to give the human supervisor some room for interpretation in light of his knowledge about process or objectives that are not shared by the computer. Kok and Van Wijk (1978) modeled this decision function in a simple supervisory control context. Baron et. al (1980) developed a decision model of aircrew supervisory procedures implementation which they term PROCRU and which is built on their earlier optimal control model.

Since supervisory control is discontinuous and because each control action constitutes a commitment for some period of time or even a sequence of process responses, it is appropriate that the supervisor test out his commands on some form of off-line simulator before committing them to be executed in the real system. Part of the mental activity for this function is the exercise of an internal model to yield expected results of hypothetical control actions, i.e., "what would happen if--?" (where "happen" means both physical response of the controlled process and resulting goodness of performance relative to objectives). The internal model prediction may then be compared to the results from the computer simulator test. Early models of supervisory control embodied this idea (Sheridan and Johannsen, 1976). Yoerger (1982) implemented such a test capability in his supervisory manipulation interface, whereby the operator could see a graphic display of just where a manipulator arm would move relative to a workpiece in response to any control action which might be taken. The idea of testing out potential actions before committing to them has had many antecedents, both in computer control and in behavioral models. For example, Rasmussen (1976) included a dynamic world model in an early version of his multilevel model of behavior.

2. Teach. The second general category of supervisory function is TEACH, which means to *decide, test,* and *communicate commands* to the computer sufficient that it be able to cause or implement the intended control actions. Commands are the operator's own movements of analogical computer interface devices such as joysticks, master manipulator arms, or computer screen cursor controls, and his stroking of symbolic alphanumeric and special function keys. This could also be called programming. Now both the human-interactive computer and the task-interactive computer become involved.

It is essential to distinguish between commands, the operator's responses, and control actions, which force the process. Applying muscle force to the steering wheel or brake pedal are commands; turning or braking are control actions. With the computer involved, key presses are commands, while what the computer does to modify the text of a document or the flight path of an airplane is a control action. The novice may know what control action is to be taken but not know what command will produce that control action. To the experienced operator, the command is the control action (but only because the causality is both reliable and well learned).

The mental model in this case is the command language (the set of syntax or rules for their combination, and the semantics or meanings of both individual symbols and combinations). The computer aid in this case is an editing aid, an iterative means to help the user say to the computer what it needs to hear in order to do what the operator wants done. This is not unlike an editing aid for word processing or for programming in general, where the computer informs the user what commands are not interpretable, and might come back and suggest what might be meant.

Many developments of supervisory command language have occurred over the last two decades, some in conjunction with industrial computer-driven machinery and robots, some in conjunction with aerospace systems. In modern aircraft, for example, there are several levels of commands for setting the autopilot (such as going to and holding a new altitude, flying to a set of latitude-longitude coordinates on the other side of the earth, or making an automatic landing (Yoerger, 1979). In industrial robotics various protocols have been developed for using "teach" pendants (shop floor portable switch boxes) to program simple instruct-move-playback routines. More sophisticated symbolic command structures have enabled the teaching of arbitrarily defined terms, conditional branching, etc. (Nof, 1985). Flexible combined analogical-symbolic command languages such as SUPERMAN (Brooks, 1979; Yoerger, 1982) have been developed to allow very fast and natural instruction of telerobots. Supervisory languages currently under development promise the user the capability to use fuzzy (imprecisely defined) commands (Yared, 1986).

3. Monitor Auto. The third general category of supervisor functions is MONITOR AUTO, meaning the human operator monitors the automatic execution of the programmed actions, the process itself being under automatic control, performed in accordance with what was just taught. Here there are three separate functions.

3a. The first function under MONITOR AUTO is *acquire, calibrate and combine measures of process state.* This requires that the supervisor have a mental model of potential sources of relevant information, their likelihood of being measurements of particular variables of interest, and their likely biases in measuring and reporting. The point is that there can be many sources which have something to tell about any one variable: real-time sensors, computerized data bases and "expert systems", human experts, and incidental sources which are likely to be unreliable but may provide some useful evidence (e.g., the neighbor's parakeet). Some sources advertise themselves as being very precise but may not be, others may be much more precise than first expected. Some may be consistently biased. If only one could sort out which sources were in fact precise and which were not, and could then remove biases and combine data sources to provide corroboration and a better statistical sample, that could be a real boon to the human supervisor. Mendel and Sheridan (1986) describe an approach for doing just that.

3b. The second function under MONITOR AUTO is *estimate process state from current measure and past control actions.* Empirical measurement (3a above) is part of state estimation, but certainly not all of it. Often the sensors are inadequate, so it is important to gain additional knowledge of which direction the system was previously known to have been headed, and what effects recent inputs ought to have had. Estimation theory provides a normative way to combine empirical measurements with this latter form of knowledge, which is why such estimation techniques are important to modern control practice. Estimation requires a good model of the physical process, which is not ordinarily available in complex systems controlled by a human supervisor. Presumably the human supervisor has some internal (mental) model of how past control actions should be affecting present process response, and tries to combine this with his best (sometimes inaccurate) direct measurement data on current process state, all in order to form a best overall estimate of current state. This is not easy for a person, especially if the system is complex. However for a computer, given a good model of the controlled process and a single best measurement of its state (which still is likely to be imperfect), it is relatively straightforward to calculate the best estimate of current state. The problem then comes in displaying this to a human operator in a way which is meaningful and useful.

Roseborough and Sheridan (1986) describe experiments wherein a human controller of a partly deterministic, partly stochastic process (which is characteristic of real supervisory control systems) is provided with such a normative decision aid. Results show that operators cannot accommodate cognitively all of the state information which a full formal estimate makes available (including the estimated multi-variable probability density of state), and suggest how operators take various shortcuts to simplify their cognitive tasks in making use of the advice given them.

Note that each of many separate measurements of process state could involve internal models (using Kalman estimation or other model-based techniques). These multiple estimates might subsequently be combined by Bayestian or other methods.

3c. The last supervisory function under MONITOR AUTO is *evaluate process state; detect and diagnose failure or halt.* This means that the operator maps state information relative to the satisificed objective (which may not be straightforward if the estimated state is outside the region of attribute space in which satisficing was done). The operator must detect and diagnose whether the process has failed (strayed sufficiently far from expected objectives) or whether it has halted (stopped before the commanded actions were all executed without getting into trouble), and to some extent the operator must diagnose where and how. The mental model accordingly incorporates, in addition to the state estimate available from 3b, the likely modes and causes of failure or halt. The computer aid in this case is an aid to the operator for detecting and diagnosing the location and cause of failure or halt. Recently there have been a number of computer aids developed for this purpose, some of which are based on statistical estimation theory (Curry and Gai, 1976), some of which are based on discrepancies between measured variables and component models (Tsach et al, 1983) and some of which are based upon production rules and other AI techniques (Scarl et al, 1985).

4. Intervene. The fourth supervisory function is INTERVENE, which is conditional upon detection of a failure or halt condition. If the latter is true, there is a second conditional branching required, depending upon whether there is a failure or a normal end-of-task. These are described below as 4a and 4b (consistent with Table 3), though, as seen in Figure 3, 4a and 4b are not really thought of as separate supervisory functions.

4a. When the state has deviated sufficiently far from what is desirable, or supervisor judgment and/or the computer-based failure detection suggests that it will, the supervisor promptly executes an already programmed abort command *(If failure: execute planned abort).* The mental model is of a relatively small number of pre-planned abort commands and their criteria for use. A computer decision aid in this case can advise the operator of which to use and how to use it.

4b. If there is no failure and the process has halted when it was expected to, the supervisor must bring the task to completion (execute an appropriate completion command). That is, if normal end of task: complete. His mental model is of a relatively small number of pre-planned commands to finish off the task, and he should have some knowledge of their criteria for use. As in 4a, the computer decision aid can advise which to use and how to use it. If there is no failure and the halt condition does not call for normal completion, the operator is not likely to have a simple pre-planned open loop command at the ready, and he must cycle back to 1d for a more considered execution of the next step. But before he does, there is one important function to perform.

*5. **Learn.*** The final broad category of supervisory function is LEARN. Because of the complexity of systems which lend themselves to supervisory control, the recording of what was considered, what was commanded, what control action was taken and what happened cannot be left to chance. It is an important function of the human supervisor not only to update his own mental models but also to ensure that some computer-based records are kept for later use. As under 4 we make use of 5a and 5b to represent contingent decisions (shown by feedback loops in Table 3) rather than essentially different supervisor functions. Because the LEARN function draws upon all of the other functions, and indeed is embodied in the aggregate mental models and computer models of all the other functions, it cannot be represented as a separate block in Figure 2.

5a. If there is neither failure nor completion and the supervisor is ready to cycle back to 1d, the LEARN function only means *record immediate events* so that there be some immediate human memory of significant events and an update of computer records. In this case it is helpful if some computer aid(s) also provide "memory jogging" displays such as a chart of recent events (as is commonly done in nuclear power plants).

5b. If the task is terminated either by abortion in response to failure or by normal completion, then it is important to exercise the LEARN function in a more extensive manner. In this case *analyze cumulative experience* means that the supervisor should recall and contemplate the whole task experience, however many command cycles there were, so as to improve his readiness when called upon for the next task. The computer aid in this case should provide some cumulative record and analysis in a form that can be accessed and used later during the PLAN phase.

To summarize this section, it is claimed that twelve functions (which can be compressed to five) characterize what a human supervisor does (or should do) in a variety of complex supervisory control systems. For each function both human and computer play specific roles, and for each there is an appropriate "mental model".

Before concluding this section it is appropriate to relate the supervisory control paradigm to the well-known Rasmussen (1986) three-level model of skill-based, rule-based and knowledge-based human behavior, Figure 4. I suggest in Figure 5 a "Rasmussen-based" alternative to Figure 3 for representing the relations between human decisions and computer aids in supervisory control.

5.7 Human Supervisor Attention Allocation and Timing

Given the functions both human and computer may play in supervisory control systems, what are the strategies and tactics by which the human supervisor should share his attention among these different functions, assuming he can engage in but one at a time? Insofar as the attention of the computer is concerned, it is safe to assume that the computer functions can be performed in parallel by essentially different computers, or that there is plenty of time for a single computer to time-share. But the same cannot be said about the human operator. He (she), relatively, is very slow, and cannot shift attention rapidly from one function to another. Yet attention sharing must be done.

It might be expected that the supervisory operator would rotate attention in a regular round-robin pattern among the functions. But that would not be efficient if the task demands within each functional role varied.

Supervisor attention demands, at a first approximation, may be characterized as having four attributes:

1. What human resources need be assigned to perform each task (particular senses, memory, decision, motor capabilities)?
2. How long it will take to do each task, and how much mental and physical effort?
3. How much time is available to get the task done?
4. What is the reward for successfully completing each task, or part of it, or what is the cost of not doing it?

Clearly this simple characterization treats attention/task demands as though they are independent of one another, which they almost never are, as though they are instantly apparent and obvious in terms of their attributes, which is seldom true (you have to be "into" the task to learn what is required), and as though they are deterministic, when we all know that there are great uncertainties about all of these attributes.

Nevertheless one can think of attention/task demands in a computer-game format of assigning one's own (human or computer) resources from a limited

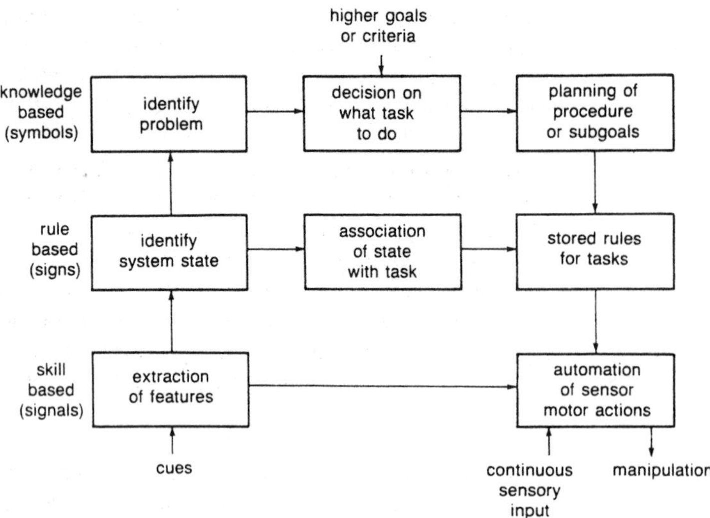

Figure 4. Simplification of Rasmussen's qualitative model of human behavior.

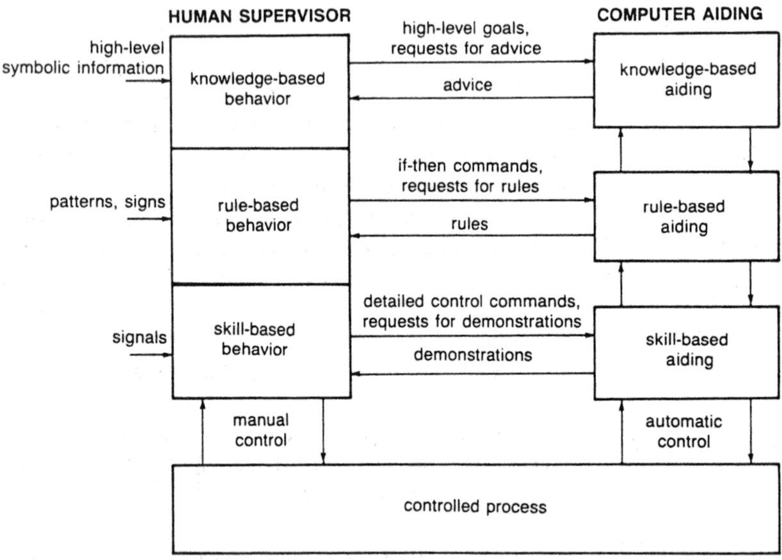

Figure 5. Supervisor interactions with computer decision aids at knowledge, rule and skill levels.

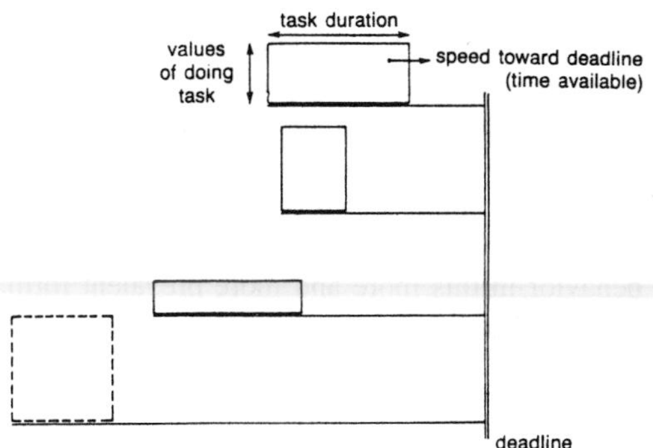

Figure 6. Experimental representation of attention/task demands and their attributes.

pool of such capabilities in response to random attention/task demand "inputs" as represented in Figure 6. This might be displayed on a computer screen, where blocks represent different tasks which occur at random times and positions on the screen and move at uniform speed toward a "deadline" at the right. Width of each block represents effort or time required of that task, block height represents relative reward, and distance to the "deadline" at right represents time available. Though not shown here, each block could specify different resources to "do" it.

Tulga and Sheridan (1980) ran experiments using such a display and compared subjects' decision behavior to what was optimal (an algorithm which itself took considerable effort for the authors to figure out in this case). Results indicated that subjects' choices were not too far from optimal when they had plenty of time to plan. As the task demands became heavier and the "mental workload" grew there came a point where the strategy switched from "plan ahead" to "put out bonfires", i.e., do whatever needs to be done that there is still time to do, never mind that some long-term very important task could be done "ahead of time" before there is no time remaining. Interestingly, the subjects found that as pace and loading increased, and "planning ahead" finally had to be abandoned in favor of "do what has an immediate deadline", subjective mental workload actually *decreased*!

Some kinds of attention demands are simply to observe, and insofar as the resource constraint is the effort of switching attention (including focusing and reading from one relatively simple display to another, it may be assumed that observation time is constant across displays. In this special case the strategy for attending becomes one of relative sampling frequency, that is, checking each of many displays often enough to ensure that no new demand is missed and/or sampling a continuously changing signal often enough to be able to reproduce the highest frequency variations present (the bandwidth). This latter is called the Nyquist frequency and is precisely twice the highest frequency component in the signal. Senders et al. (1964) showed that experienced visual observers do tend to fixate on each of multiple displays (of varying frequency) in direct proportion to each maximum signal frequency. However subjects tend to oversample the lowest frequency signals and undersample the highest frequency signals - the same kind of "hedging toward the mean" that is found in other forms of operator decision behavior.

At the instant an operator observes a display the information may be regarded as perfect (unless of course the instrument is noisy or he reads poorly), but as time passes after one observation and prior to a new one the information becomes stale, eventually converging to some statistical expectation. Sheridan (1970) suggested how one may compute the optimal sampling interval. The procedure assumes a given model of how, following an observation, the standard deviation of expectation increases from zero and converges on some constant. The method further assumes an expected cost of taking a sample.

Assume $\mathbf{x}$ is an independent time-varying signal that one wishes to keep track of, that it has a known prior density function $\mathbf{p(x)}$, that $\mathbf{x_0}$ is its precise value at the time of sampling, and that $\mathbf{p(x_t, t)}$ is a best available model of expectation of $\mathbf{x}$ at time $\mathbf{t}$ following a sample, i.e., given $\mathbf{x_0}$ and $\mathbf{t}$. Assume u is a control action one takes, and $\mathbf{V(x,u)}$ is the reward for taking action u when the signal has a value $\mathbf{x}$. Clearly, without any sampling the best one can do is adjust u once and for all in order to maximize expected value of reward i.e.,

$$\text{EV for no sampling} = \max_u \Sigma_x\, p(x)\, (V|x,u)$$

If one could afford to sample continuously the best strategy would be to continuously adjust $\mathbf{u}$ to $\max_u (V|x,u)$, so that on average

$$\text{EV for continuous sampling} = \Sigma_{x0}\, p(x_0) \max_u (V|x_0,u),$$
where $p(x_0) = p(x)$.

For an intermediate rate of sampling, expectation is
$E(V|x_0,t)$ at t after sample $x_0 = \max_u \Sigma_{xt}\, p(x_t\, |x_0,t)\, (V|x_t,u)$.

Then $E(V|t) = \Sigma_{x0}\, p(x_0)\, E(V|x_0,t)$,

remembering again that $p(x_0) = p(x)$.

Finally, for any sampling interval **T** and sampling cost **C**,

$$EV^* = 1/T \, \Sigma^{T}_{t=0} \, E(V|t) - C/T$$

So the best one can do is to maximize EV^*.

That is equivalent to finding the best tradeoff between (1) sampling too often, to the point of diminishing returns, while incurring a high cost per sample, and (2) sampling too seldom, having only a rough idea what the input **x** is doing, and therefore not selecting a control action **u** at each instant which gives a very good return. The experienced human supervisor mostly allocates his attention to various monitoring needs on an intuitive basis. If suitable value functions (**V**) were available his monitoring strategy might be improved, but making **V** explicit is a problem.

5.8 Factors which Limit Our Ability to Model Supervisory Control Systems

Our ability to model supervisory control systems is limited by two factors.

A first factor is the same as that which makes any cognition difficult to model. As compared to simpler manual control and other perceptual-motor skills, the essence of supervisory control is cognition, or mental activity, particularly including objectives and command/control decisions made at least partly by the free will of the supervisor. The problem is that such mental events are not directly observable; they must be inferred. This is the basis for the ancient mind-body dilemma, as well as the basis for the rejection, by some behavioral scientists, of mental events as legitimate scientific concepts. Such "behaviorism", of course, is out of fashion now. Computer science motivated "cognitive science," and by indirect inference made computer programs admissible representations of what people think. However, the limits on direct measurement of mental events do not seem to want to go away.

The second factor is more specialized to supervisory control. It is a result of wanting to combine mental models internal to the human operator and external computer decision aids. If the operator chooses to follow the aid's advice what can be said about his exercising of his own mental model? If he claims to "know" certain facts or have a "plan" which happens to correspond to the knowledge or plan communicated by the computer, can the normative decision aid be considered a convenient yardstick against which to measure inferred mental activity? Where there is free will and free interaction between the two it is difficult to determine what is mental and what is computer. Mental and computer models might more easily be treated as a combined entity which produces operator decisions.

We must continue efforts to model and predict human behavior in this more and more prevalent form of control system in spite of these difficulties mentioned above.

5.9 Social Implications of Supervisory Control

The relentless drive of new technology results in takeover of more and more functions from the human operator by the computer. Many decades ago the operator's muscles were relieved by mechanization, so that he needed only to provide guidance for the movements of aircraft, lathe, or whatever, and the machine followed without his having to exert much physical effort. Then, two decades ago, stored program automation allowed the operator to indicate movements only once, and the machine would dutifully repeat those movements forever, if necessary. Then the operator was bumped up to a higher level, so that he could give the computer goal statements, branching instructions, production rules, and "macro" information, and the computer would dutifully oblige. All these advances have elevated the stature of the human operator in "motor" activities.

This elevation has also been taking place in sensory and cognitive activities. Artificial sensors now feed data into computers, which process the data and give the operator graphic displays of summary assessments, formatted in whatever manner is requested. "Intelligent" sensory systems draw attention when "something new" has occurred, but otherwise may leave the operator alone. Newer computer systems build up "world models" and "situation assessments". "Expert systems" can now answer the operator's questions, much as does a human consultant, or whisper suggestions in his ear even if he doesn't request them.

How far will or should this "help" from the computer go? Are there points of diminishing returns? Already the aircraft pilots have an expression they use to refer to new computer cockpit automation and advisory aids: "killing us with kindness".

There is another problem of supervisory control, apart from the matter of trust *per se*. That is, even if the computer were quite competent and reliable, there may be other reasons for not having it assume so much subordinate responsibility. This problem may be summarized by the word "alienation". Elsewhere (Sheridan, 1980) I have discussed in some detail seven factors contributing to alienation of people by computers, and I will mention them here only briefly:

1. People worry that computers can do some tasks much better than they themselves can, such as memory and calculation. Surely people should not try to compete in this arena.

2. Supervisory control tends to make people remote from the ultimate operations they are supposed to be overseeing - remote in space, desynchronized in time, and interacting with a computer instead of the end product or service itself.

3. People lose the perceptual-motor skills which in many cases gave them their identity. They become "de-skilled", and, if ever called upon to use their previous well-honed skills, they could not.

4. Increasingly, people who use computers in supervisory control or in other ways, whether intentionally or not, are denied access to the knowledge to understand what is going on inside the computer.

5. Partly as a result of factor four, the computer becomes mysterious, and the untutored user comes to attribute to the computer more capability, wisdom or blame than is appropriate.

6. Because computer-based systems are growing more complex, and people are being "elevated" to roles of supervising larger and larger aggregates of hardware and software, the stakes naturally become higher. Where a human error before might have gone unnoticed and been easily corrected, now such an error could precipitate a disaster.

7. The last factor in alienation is similar to the first, but all-encompassing, namely the fear that a "race" of machines is becoming more powerful than that of the human race.

These seven factors, and the fears they engender, whether justified or not, must be reckoned with. Computers must be made to be not only "human friendly" but also "human trustable". Users must become computer-literate at whatever level of sophistication they can deal with.

There is no question but that supervisory control puts more and more power into the hands of fewer people, and human engineering to make this kind of human-computer interaction safe and productive for all is a challenge.

5.10 Conclusions

It is naive to assume that tasks may simply be broken into independent elements and then assigned to either human or computer based on accepted criteria. While there are many techniques now used for task analysis, it is still very much an art. So too is human-computer task allocation, because there are infinitely many design options for human computer interaction and cooperation to be considered, not simply human or computer by itself. Further, there are many salient criteria for evaluating the alternatives. The emerging dominant form of human-computer cooperation is supervisory control, applicable to both pure information tasks as well as monitoring and control of vehicles, factories and other complex dynamic systems. There are multiple functions or roles of the human supervisor, and for each the computer has a function in assisting in decisions and actions. However, because humans are human, there are dangers in removing them too far from direct involvement with tasks.

5.11 References

Baron, S., Zacharias, G., Muraldiharan, R., and I. Craft (1980). "PROCRU: a model for analyzing flight crew procedures in approach to landing." *Proceedings of 16th Annual Conference on Manual Control,* 488-520. Cambridge, MA: MIT.

Birmingham, H. P. and Taylor, F. V. (1954). A design philosophy for man-machine control systems. *Proc. I.R.E., 42,* 1748-58.

Brooks, T. L. (1979). *Superman: a system for supervisory manipulation and the study of human-computer interactions.* SM Thesis. Cambridge, MA: MIT.

Card, S. K., Moran, T. P. and Newell, A. L., (1983). *The Psychology of Human-Computer Interaction,* Hillsdale, NJ: Erlbaum.

Charny, L., and Sheridan, T. B. (1986). *Satisficing decision-making in supervisory control.* Unpublished paper. Cambridge, MA: MIT, Man-Machine Systems Laboratory.

Craik, K.J.W. (1947a). Theory of the human operator in control systems: 1. The operator as an engineering system. *British J. of Psych., 38,* 56-61.

Craik, K.J.W. (1947b). Theory of the human operator in control systems: 2. Man as an element in a control system. *British J. of Psych., 38*, 142-8.

Curry, R.E., and Gai, E.G. (1976). Detection of random process of failures of human monitors. In T. Sheridan and G. Johannsen, (Eds.), *Monitoring Behavior and Supervisory Control*, New York: Wiley, 205-220.

deKleer, J. (1979). *Causal and Teleological Reasoning in Circuit Recognition.* Ph.D. Thesis. Cambridge, MA: MIT, AI-TR-529.

Einstein, A. and Infeld, L. (1942). *The Evolution of Physics*. NY: Simon and Schuster.

Ferrell, W.R. and Sheridan, T.B. (1967). Supervisory of remote manipulation. *IEEE Spectrum, 4-10*, 88.

Fitts, P.M. (1951). Human engineering for an effective air navigation and traffic control system. *Ohio State University Research Foundation Report,* Columbus, OH.

Genter, D., Stevens, A.L. (Eds.), (1983). *Mental Models,* Hillsdale, N.J.: Erlbaum Press.

Harmon, P., and King, D. (1985). *Expert Systems*, Wiley.

Holland, J.D., Hutchins, E.L., and Weitzman, L. (1984). Steamer, an interactive, inspectable simulation-based training system. *Al Magazine*, 5-2.

Jordan, N. (1963). Allocation of functions between man and machines in automated systems. *J. of Applied Psych., 47,* 161-5.

Kantowitz, B. and Sorkin, R. (1987). Allocation of functions. Chapter in G. Salvendy, Ed., *Handbook of Human Factors.* NY: Wiley, 365-9.

Keeney, R.L., and Raiffa, H. (1976). *Decisions with Multiple Objectives: Preferences and Value Tradeoffs.* NY: Wiley.

Kok, J.J., and Van Wijk, R.A. (1978). *Evaluation of Models Describing Human Operator Control of Slowly Responding Complex Systems.* Delft, The Netherlands: DUT, Laboratory of Measurement and Control.

March, J.G., and Simon, H.A. (1958). *Organizations.* NY: Wiley.

Meister, D. (1971). *Human Factors, Theory and Practice*. NY: Wiley.

Mendel, M., and Sheridan, T.B. (1986). *Optimal Combination of Information from Multiple Sources.* Cambridge, MA: MIT Man Machine Systems Laboratory.

Moray, N (1986). Monitoring behavior and supervisory control. In: K. Boff, L. Kaufmann, and J.P. Thomas (Eds.), *Handbook of Perception and Human Performance.* NY: Wiley.

National Research Council (1983). *Research Needs for Human Factors.* Washington, DC, National Academy Press.

National Research Council (1984). (Sheridan, T.B., and Hennessy, R., Eds). *Research and Modeling of Supervisory Control Behavior.* Washington, DC: National Academy Press.

Nof, S.Y., (Ed), (1985). *Handbook of Industrial Robotics.* NY: Wiley.

Price, H. (1990). Conceptual system design and the human role. Chapter 6 in H. Booher, Ed., *Manprint.* NY: Van Nostrand.

Price, H.E. (1985). The allocation of functions in systems. *Human Factors 27 (1),* 33-45.

Rasmussen, J. (1976). Outlines of a hybrid model of the process plant operator. In T.B. Sheridan and G. Johannsen (Eds.), *Monitoring Behavior and Supervisory Control.* NY: Plenum, 371-384.

Rasmussen, J. (1986). *Information Processing and Human-Machine Interaction.* NY: Elsevier/North Holland.

Roseborough, J., and Sheridan, T.B. (1986). *Aiding Human Operators with State Estimation.* Cambridge, MA: MIT Man-Machine Systems Laboratory.

Scarl, E.A., Jamieson, J.R., and Delaune, C.I. (1985). Process monitoring at the Kennedy Space Center. *SIGART Newsletter, 93*, 38-44.

Senders, J.W., Elkind, J.E., Grignette, MC., and Smallwood, R.P. (1964). An Investigation of the Visual Sampling of Human Observers. *NASA Report CR-434.* Cambridge, MA: Bolt, Beranek and Newman.

Sheridan, T.B. (1960). Human metacontrol. *Proceedings of Annual Conference on Manual Control.* Wright Patterson, AFB, OH.

Sheridan, T.B. (1970). On how often the supervisor should sample. *IEEE Trans. on Systems, Man and Cybernetics. SSC-6*, 140-145.

Sheridan, T.B. (1980). Computer control and human alienation. *Technology Review, 83(1),* 60-75.

Sheridan, T.B. (1984). Supervisory control of remote manipulators, vehicles and dynamic processes. In W.B. Rouse (Ed), *Advances in Man-Machine Systems Research, 1,* 49-137. NY: JAI Press.

Sheridan, T.B. (1987). Supervisory control. In G. Salvendy (Ed.), *Handbook of Human Factors /Ergonomics*. NY: Wiley.

Sheridan, T.B. (1992). *Telerobotics, Automation and Human Supervisory Control.* Cambridge, MA: MIT Press.

Sheridan, T.B., and Johannsen, G. (Eds.) (1976). *Monitoring Behavior and Supervisory Control.* NY: Plenum Press.

Taylor, F.W. (1947). *Scientific Management.* NY: Harper Brothers.

Tsach, U., Sheridan, T.B. and Buharali, A. (1983). Failure detection and location in process control: integrating a new model-based technique with other methods. *Proceedings on Americal Control Conference*, San Francisco.

Tulga, M.K. and Sheridan, T.B. (1980). Dynamic decisions and workload in multitask supervisory control. *IEEE Trans. on Systems, Man and Cybernetics. SMC-10,* 217-132.

Wierzbicki, A.P. (1982). A mathematical basis for satisficing decision-making. *Math, Modeling, 3,* 391-405.

Yared, W. (1986). Informal memo, *MIT Man-Machine Systems Lab*. Cambridge, MA.

Yoerger, D.R. (1979). *Man-Machine Performance for a Simulated Aircraft with Multi-level Automatic* Control System. SM thesis. Cambridge, MA: MIT.

Yoerger, D.R. (1982). *Supervisory Control of Underwater Telemanipulators: Design and Experiment.* Ph.D. Thesis. Cambridge, MA: MIT.

Handbook of Human-Computer Interaction
Second, completely revised edition
M. Helander, T.K. Landauer, P. Prabhu (eds.)

Chapter 6

Models of Graphical Perception

Gerald Lee Lohse
University of Pennsylvania
Philadelphia, Pennsylvania, USA

6.1 Introduction

Graphical perception investigates the mechanisms by which humans perceive, interpret, use, and communicate graphical information. Models of graphical perception explain how people process information from graphs and heighten our understanding of the underlying psychological processes. This knowledge facilitates the design of graphics by providing robust quantitative predictions for evaluating alternative graphic designs or for automating the design of graphics entirely. Algorithmic models of graphical perception and cognition enable quantitative predictions about the effectiveness of a graph for a specific task. The ultimate goal for future versions of commercial graphics software is to automate graphic design processes in a manner that is transparent to the user. Embedded intelligence would reduce the amount of time users spend creating graphs and presentations. Furthermore, many casual users could then create graphics that follow certain rules for effective graphic presentation.

This chapter discusses models of graphical perception and the design of graphic presentations. The next section presents an overview of the literature on graphs and tables. It documents important uses of graphics. Then, section two provides insights about contemporary graph usage through a history of graphics. Section two also summarizes a large body of empirical research on the presentation of graphical information. The third section describes the psychology of graphical perception and cognition and explains how people acquire information from graphs. The fourth section briefly highlights seven models of graphical perception for evaluating graphic design or automating the design of graphics. The last section considers opportunities for future research.

6.2 An Overview of the Graphics Literature

6.2.1 Use of Graphics

The adage "A picture is worth a thousand words" aptly expresses the value of a graph to aid our information-processing. Scientists and engineers in medicine, geophysics, space exploration and other areas use graphics to visualize complex computations and to simulate physical processes. Graphics provide insights to understanding phenomena that are not afforded by looking at the numbers alone. Recent advances in microcomputers,

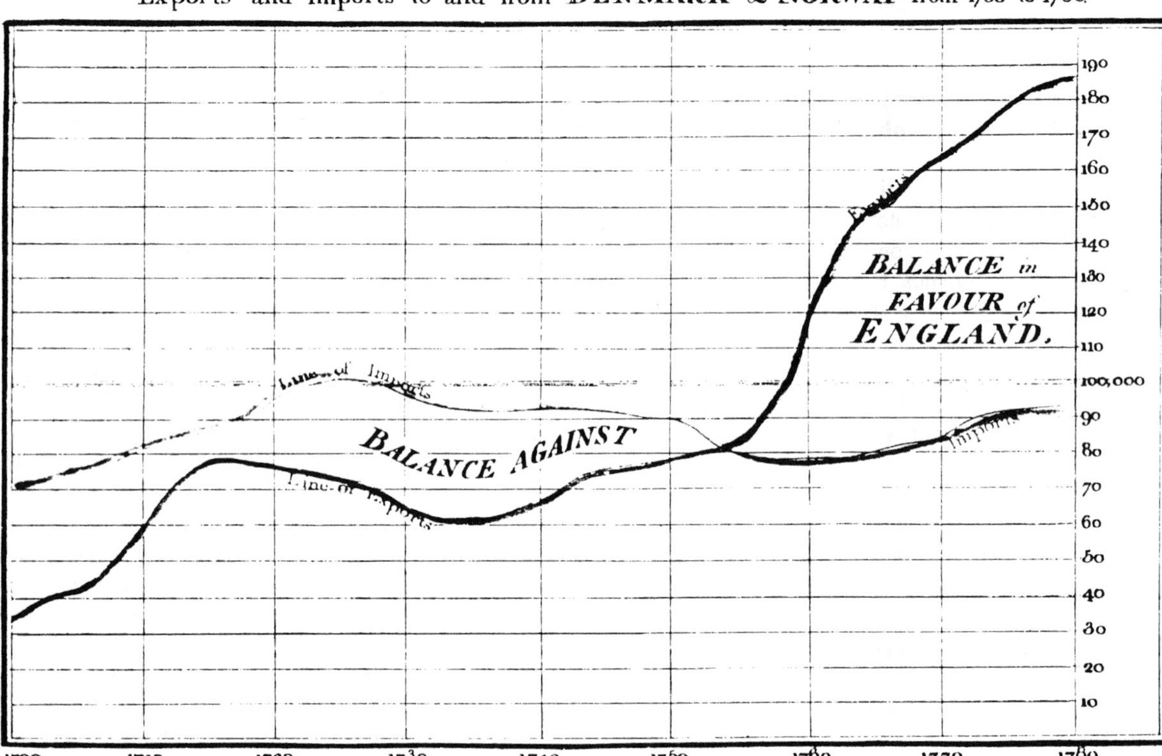

Figure 1. One of the early graphs by Playfair depicting imports and exports of England to and from Denmark and Norway (Tufte, 1983).

workstations and graphics software provide new and creative ways to generate useful images.

Graphics are a powerful tool for the discovery of ideas. Exploratory data analysis helps identify relevant information from a set of data as well as gain new insight or understanding of a problem. Graphics aid problem-solving. Often verbal and numeric cues are insufficient to trigger some insight into the specific nature of the problem (Larkin and Simon, 1987). Drawing a picture or a graph often helps break a mental block by providing a memory structure to aid the decomposition of information in the problem. Graphics also allow users to digest a lot of information quickly. Decision accuracy and decision speed have always been important reasons to use graphics. Graphs aid data reduction, data summary, improve information search (Robertson, Card, and Mackinlay, 1993) and facilitate computation. Graphics, diagrams, and pictures transcend language barriers. Icons and international signs are examples of symbols used to communicate across language barriers. Cognitive psychologists found that visual information can benefit observable behaviors such as recall, comprehension, and retention of information. (Arnheim, 1969; Umanath and Scamell, 1988). Graphics enhance persuasion (Vogel, Lehman, and Dickson, 1986). The audience perceives speakers as more professional and more knowledgeable if they incorporate graphics into their overhead transparencies. The audience tends to agree more with speakers using graphics and have higher attention levels as well as increased retention and comprehension of the information presented. Vogel et al. (1986) also found that color overheads increased comprehension and retention of information when compared to black and white. Graphics improve recall for presented information, reduce working memory (WM) loads during problem solving (Lohse, 1995), provide information about the state of a problem solution, and help organize knowledge about a particular task or problem.

6.2.2 An Historical Perspective of the Evolution of Graphs and Charts

A historical perspective of the evolution of graphics provides insights about contemporary graphics usage (Daru, 1989). Playfair is considered the founding father of quantitative graphics. His intent was to improve the general understanding of facts normally shown in tables. line graph depicting time-series data of imports and exports of England to and from Denmark and Norway is shown in Figure 1.

It took over a half century after Playfair's death before graphs gained acceptance among even a small group of economists and statisticians. An additional twenty years passed before governments used graphs in widely circulated publications. Since the turn of the century, the display of data has been a widely discussed topic among scholars of many fields. Throughout this period, many experiments examined the effectiveness of different types of graphs and tables for displaying data (Eells, 1926; Von Huhn, 1927; Croxton, 1927; Croxton and Stryker, 1927; Washburne, 1927).

Quantitative graphics gained widespread support during the First World War because graphs helped summarize a vast quantity of strategic data in a clear and concise manner. Brinton believed ' . . . the feverish demand for prompt and reliable data during war time did more to stimulate the use of graphic chart techniques than anything that has happened since 1920.' (Daru, 1989). After the First World War, graphs became a tool for data analysis and decision-making. The planning of work was done better using graphs than using lengthy lists with descriptions. Businesses increased the use of visual means for advertising and presenting their products. According to Riggleman (1936), "In many up-to-date plants at the present time executives and managers value their charts as highly as engineers value their drawings." Graphics also gained wide acceptance in the mass media.

As early as 1915, the American Society for Mechanical Engineers set standards for graphic presentation (Joint Committee on Standards for Graphic Presentation, 1915). Standardization remains a preoccupation for some scholars in the field (e.g., Jarett, 1983). From the 1940s through the 1960s, scholars compared the relative effectiveness of presenting numerical data by the use of graphs and tables (Carter, 1947; Feliciano et al., 1963; Schutz, 1961a, 1961b; Vernon, 1950, 1953, 1962).

In the early 1900s, scholars associated graphics with manual training, while mathematics and the sciences were considered more academic. Graphics emerged as a specialized field called drafting or graphics design. Computers returned graphics to the masses by automating the manual drafting components. Although computers automated the mechanics for producing a graph, computers have not automated the task of choosing the right kind of graph that best conveys the information. As a result, many people are unable to produce pleasing, ergonomically correct, substantially true and statistically valid graphs (Johnson *et al.*, 1980). Indeed, Cleveland (1984) found that 30% of the graphs reported in the 1980 volume 207 of *Science* contained one or more errors in at least one of these four categories: items on the graph could not be distinguished, something on the graph was not explained, some part of the graph was missing, or there was a error in the construction of the graph (mislabeling, wrong scales, etc.).

In summary, three major points arise from this historical review of graphics. First, graphs are a tool for reasoning about information. At some point in the evolution of science, the transformation of knowledge into visual and graphical representations ought to be considered an advancement of the thinking tools of the time. Second, people invented graphs on an *ad hoc* basis as the need arose. The final point is that despite a relatively long history, there is not a common theory for testing the effectiveness of graphic data displays. While it is easy to invent a new graph type, it is hard to invent one that works well.

6.2.3 Designing graphs and charts

Books on Designing Graphs: Bertin (1967) provides a structural taxonomy of graphs, network charts and cartograms (graphical maps). One section of this seminal work on the semiology of graphics shows 100 different presentations for the same data. Bertin defined efficiency criteria to judge the quality of competing graphic designs. All other things being equal, if one graph requires a shorter viewing time than another, Bertin hypothesized that it is more efficient for that particular question. Ideally, the answer to a question posed to a graph should be perceivable instantly. One should not need to engage in an arduous deciphering task to decode the answer from the graph.

In his taxonomy, retinal variables and perceptual approaches express the structure of the data (Figure 2).

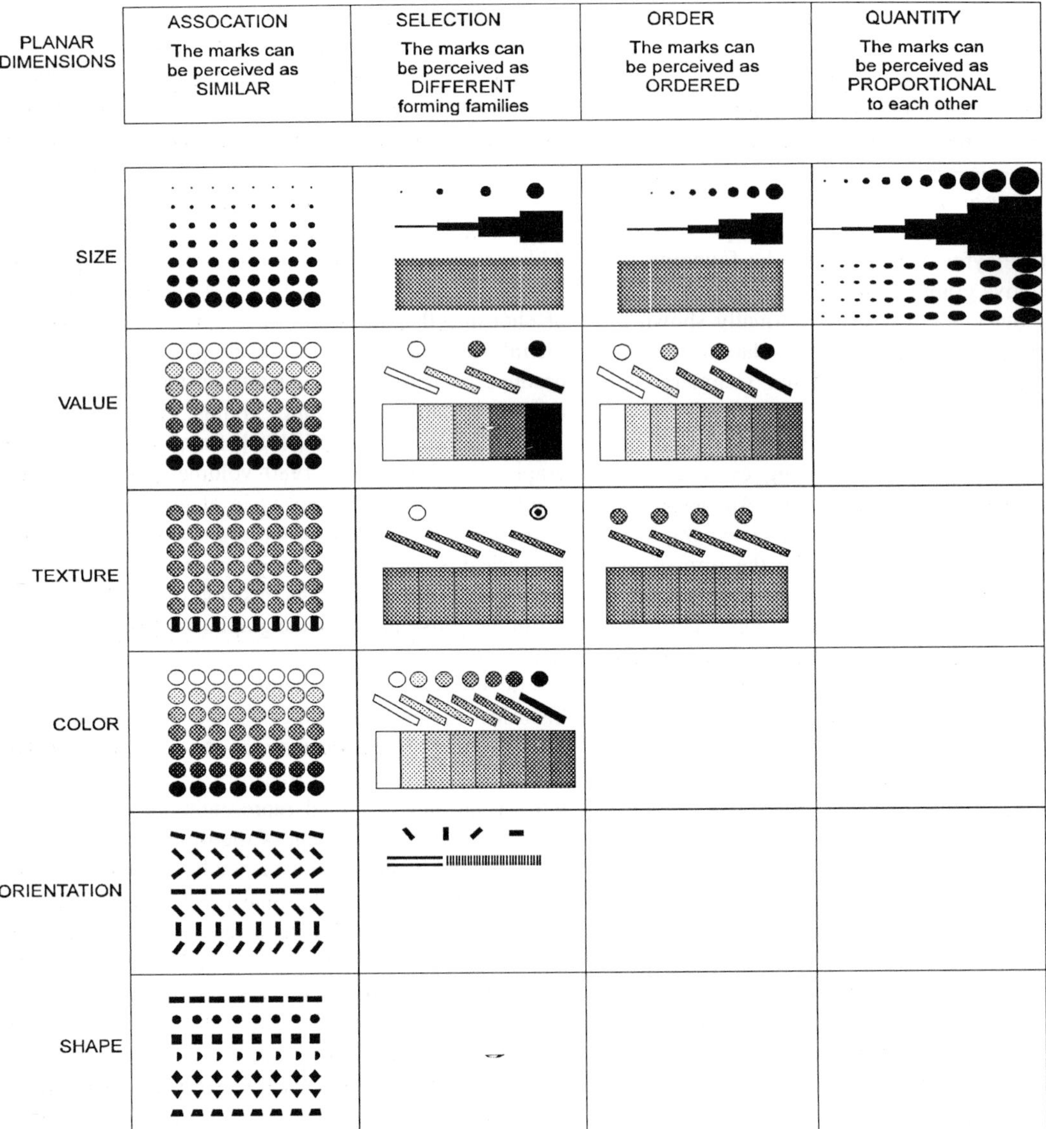

Figure 2. Level of retinal variables and perceptual approaches from Bertin (1983).

These retinal variables include position, size, value (saturation), texture, color, orientation, and shape. Each retinal variable or combinations of retinal variables express variations in the data. Bertin uses four perceptual approaches: quantitative, ordered, associative, and selective. Mapping retinal variables to perceptual approaches identifies ways for graphing data. For example, changes in size best express quantitative differences; colors show perceptual groups. Each graphic should convey a single message to the reader.

Tufte (1983, 1990) presents a fascinating collection of illustrations and graphics. Tufte discusses graphic design quality and develops empirical measures of graphic performance. The metrics suggest why some graphics might be better than others. Tufte packages numerous generalisms into a series of suggestions to aid graphic design. His central tenet was that well designed, powerful graphics are the simplest. Tufte defines simple graphics as those that reduce the non-data ink. His novel ideas for well-designed graphics are supported by excellent examples; however, Tufte does not offer any empirical support for his design guidelines.

Most 'how-to' graphics handbooks rely solely on

the author's intuition and experience. While these intuitions have yielded valuable insights, some of the broad generalizations in handbooks are not supported by empirical research. For example, Tufte (1983, p96) advocates erasing non-data ink that carries no information. In an empirical study, Spence (1990) found that extraneous dimensions not carrying variation (e.g., 3-D bar charts that show 1-D or 2-D data) do not effect the speed and accuracy of decision performance. Thus, Tufte's conjecture was not supported. Although some handbooks are based on empirical research (Kosslyn, 1989), recent research in visual psychophysics discredits some of the sweeping generalizations suggested by other graphics handbooks (Legge, Gu, and Luebker, 1989; Spence, 1990; Spence and Lewandowsky, 1991).

Empirical research: The literature is rife with experimental data assessing differences in graphic design (e.g., tables, line graphs, grouped bar graphs, etc.). Experimental variables that influence performance include: characteristics of the task, graphic display design variables and expertise of the decision maker (Ives, 1982; DeSanctis, 1984; Jarvenpaa and Dickson, 1988; Jarvenpaa, 1989; Kleinmuntz and Schkade, 1993). Table 1 highlights selected research studies within five sub-areas: graphs versus tables, task complexity, color usage, multidimensional data displays, and features of tables.

Color deserves special notice because of its overwhelming preference by users. Christ (1975) provides an excellent review of 42 empirical studies, published between 1952 and 1978, on color coding research for visual displays. Other reports also provide color usage guidelines (Kinney and Huey, 1990). Color influences observable behaviors such as the retention and recall of information (Dwyer 1971; Gremillion and Jenkins, 1981). People retain information presented in color longer and prefer it more than information presented in monochrome (Tolliver, 1973; Ehlers, 1985). Further, color coding increases attention span in instructional situations (Dooley and Harkins, 1970; Dwyer, 1971).

Two goals of this empirical research are to identify some universal principles to aid designers (e.g. use graphs to show trend over time; Jarvenpaa and Dickson, 1988; p. 772) and to evaluate which graph format is best for particular tasks. The brute force empirical methodology involves assessing the effectiveness of graphs by comparing several experimental variables at a time. However, it is neither possible nor desirable to resolve each and every graphic design issue with an empirical study. The experimental factors approach has not allowed researchers to make convincing *a priori* predictions about the expected study results. Furthermore, researchers did not relate differences among the treatments to the perceptual and cognitive processes used to complete the task. If a graph or table improves performance, it must have a concomitant effect on the efficiency of some underlying elementary perceptual and cognitive information processes.

Without a theory for predicting results, it should come as no surprise that this literature is fraught with conflicting outcomes and a paucity of robust findings. Empirical research has shown that the effectiveness of a particular graph is contingent upon the task, the decision maker, and the graph. However, the results are difficult to code into an algorithm that provides quantitative predictions about the effectiveness of a graph for a specific task. The cognitive psychology literature provides a theoretical basis for developing models of graphical perception that predict the efficacy of different presentation formats for specific tasks.

6.3 A Theory of Graphical Perception and Cognition

6.3.1 The Psychology of Graphical Perception and Cognition

Models of perception and cognition from cognitive psychology provide insight about the underlying human information processing mechanisms we use to understand a graph. Figure 3 presents a model of perception and cognition for graph comprehension from Pinker (1990). This classic model contains three major components: perception, WM, and long-term memory (LTM). These components support several processes: pre-attentive visual processes, visual encoding processes, recognition, interrogation, and inferencing.

When viewing a graph, early visual processes detect and encode visual primitives such as shape, position, color, and length. Visual primitives such as texture (Julesz, 1981) and color (Kahneman and Henik, 1981) are detected and organized in parallel; other visual primitives such as shape, area and containment are detected and organized less efficiently via serial scanning (Figure 4). Images remain in a store for a fraction of a second after shifting one's gaze (Card et al., 1983). Visual primitives must be a certain minimum size to be detected. If visual primitives are too small or too dim, they cannot be seen during an initial glance. Once detected, the viewer must discriminate and separate the visual primitives. Variations in size, texture, color,

Table 1. Selected empirical studies of graphics research.

Reference	Study Summary	Key Findings
Dickson, Senn, and Chervany (1977) on comparing graphs and tables.	Two experiments studied the effect of report format on the effectiveness of decision making in a production management simulation. Subjects controlled labor, material, and inventory costs by making decisions.	Subjects using tables had lower costs than subjects using graphs. Subjects using graphs took longer to complete the task. Subjects using graphs had performed better and used fewer reports than subjects using tabular reports.
Zmud (1978) on comparing graphs and tables.	Tested effect of line and bar graphs and tables on perception and perceived usefulness of different formats to show data.	Subjects perceived line graphs as most relevant and accurate. Bar graphs were least relevant and accurate. Tables in between.
Lusk and Kersnick (1979) on comparing graphs and tables.	Subjects viewed five formats. Answers to a 20 question quiz measured comprehension.	Performance decreased as perceived complexity increased. From low to high complexity tables > histogram > frequency graph of raw data > frequency graph of percentages.
Lucas and Nielsen (1980) on comparing graphs and tables.	Subjects used graphs or tables to make decisions about shipments, and inventory levels.	Information format had no effect on decision performance.
Lucas (1981) on comparing graphs and tables.	Subjects used graphs and tables to select reorder quantities for an importer under conditions of uncertain demand.	Graphs helped understand the underlying demand probabilities; subjects enjoyed graphs more than tables. Tables were better for understanding the simulation output.
Tullis (1981) on comparing graphs and tables.	Compared four formats: narrative, table, monochrome graphs, and color graphs.	Time to answer question decreased 40% versus narrative. Subjects preferred color graphics.
Powers, Lashley, Sanchez, and Shneiderman (1984) on comparing graphs and tables.	Tested whether more usable information could be conveyed and comprehended using tables *and* graphs than by using either format by itself.	Tables are less complex and easier to understand than graphs; users are more familiar with tables. Tables were faster and improved comprehension measures. Tables and graphs combined were more accurate.
Remus (1984) on comparing graphs and tables.	Compared the effectiveness of line graphs and tables on decision performance in a production scheduling problem.	Tables resulted in lower production costs than line graphs (using composite rules). Tables were better than line graphs.

Table 1 Selected empirical studies of graphics research(Continued).

Reference	Study Summary	Key Findings
Umanath and Scamell (1988) on comparing graphs and tables.	Two experiments studied the effect of bar graphs and tables on recall ability for trends, patterns, and specific facts using data from work center load profiles.	Bar graphs were better than tables for trend and pattern recall; no difference between display formats for specific fact recall.
DeSanctis and Jarvenpaa (1989) on comparing graphs and tables.	Compared numeric, graphical, and both formats on users' judgment heuristics and accuracy in forecasting financial information. Practice effects were measured.	Accuracy was better for the combined group; tables were least accurate; bar graphs were intermediate. Practice improved performance for subjects using graphs but not for subjects using tables.
Umanath, Scamell, and Das (1990) on comparing graphs and tables.	Compared the effect graphs or tables and presentation order (top, middle, bottom) had on recall performance in a capacity planning/production scheduling simulation.	Tables were better than graphs for recall of specific point values; graphs were better than tables for recall of patterns. Material processed from the bottom was retained better than items at the top.
Spence and Lewandowsky (1991) on comparing graphs and tables.	Four experiments compared the accuracy of pie graphs, bar graphs and tables to display portions and percentages.	Prejudice against pie graphs is misguided. Pie graphs were not found to be inferior to bar graphs. Either graph format outperformed tables.
Ghani and Lusk (1982) on task complexity.	Subjects used color line graphs or tables to help make inventory ordering decisions in a simulated stochastic market environment.	Switching report formats increased total time and decreased performance. There were no differences in decision performance for subjects in the unswitched condition.
Zmud, Blocher, and Moffie (1983) on task complexity.	Studied effects of task complexity and information format. Subjects identified invoices as high or low risk using cumulative risk scores across 5 or 9 cost categories.	With low complexity tasks, subjects performed better using graphs; with high complexity tasks, subjects performed better using tables.
Schwartz and Howell (1985) on task complexity.	Two experiments measured how information formats affects evacuate-stay decisions in a hurricane-tracking scenario under three levels of time pressure.	Under time pressure, subjects made faster decisions with graphs than with tables. Tables forced the subjects to consider too much information.
Remus (1987) on task complexity.	Compared the effectiveness of lines graphs and tables on performance in a production scheduling problem with two levels of complexity.	Tabular displays were better in low task complexity environments; line graphs were better in high task complexity environments.

Table 1. Selected empirical studies of graphics research(Continued).

Reference	Study Summary	Key Findings
Dwyer (1971) on color usage.	Nine types of illustrations with increasing levels of photorealism were used to test student achievement on five performance measures for 261 college students.	Despite realistic illustrations, students were not able to attend to the additional information. Color improved achievement in many conditions.
Gremillion and Jenkins (1981) on color usage.	620 undergrads viewed 9 overhead transparencies either in color or in black and white. A control group did not view any overhead transparencies.	Knowledge was tested using a quiz. Color significantly enhanced the ability of subjects to recall the information presented in lecture.
Benbasat and Dexter (1985) on color usage.	Assessed the influence of line graphs, tables, or both in color or monochrome on decision performance in a simulated business task. Field dependence was assessed using the group embedded-figures test (GEFT).	No differences in decision performance. Field-dependents (low GEFT score) achieved 37% of the potential profit with monochrome and 64% using color displays. Color aided field-dependents more than field-independents.
Benbasat and Dexter (1986) on color usage.	Assessed the influence of line graphs, tables, or both in color or monochrome on decision performance under time pressure. There were six treatment groups in a between-subjects design.	A combined format using line graphs and tables led to superior performance. Tables led to the slowest performance. Color is more beneficial if the decision maker is under time pressure.
Benbasat, Dexter, and Todd (1986a, 1986b) on color usage.	Assessed the influence of line graphs and tables in color or monochrome on decision performance in a simulated business task. There were four treatment groups in a between-subjects design with 16 subjects per treatment.	Line graphs facilitated rapid search for an optimum solution; tables helped locate the exact data values of the optimum solution. Color reduced the number of simulation periods required to complete the task.
Ware and Beatty (1988) on color usage.	3 experiments explored the usefulness of color for displaying five-dimensional data using 2 spatial and 3 color dimensions.	Color enhanced cluster separation and the perception of unique clusters for exploratory data analysis.
Hoadley (1990) on color usage.	Subjects answered multiple choice questions posed to monocolor and multicolored tables, pie, bar, and line graphs.	Color improves time performance for pie and bar graphs, accuracy for pie and line graphs but not bar graphs. Accuracy and time performance of tables did not improve with color.

Table 1. Selected empirical studies of graphics research(Continued).

Reference	Study Summary	Key Findings
Watson and Driver (1983) on dimensionality of presentation format.	Using graphs and tables, the study compared immediate and delayed recall of the location information.	Graphic data superimposed on a 3D map projection was not better than a tabular presentation of these data.
Yorchak, Allison, and Dodd (1984) on dimensionality of presentation format.	Compared 2D and 3D depictions of satellite altitude and coverage area in a space navigation scenario.	Subjects preferred 3D displays. Navigation patterns are strongly affected by information presentation order. No difference times or errors.
Lee and MacLachian (1986) on dimensionality of presentation format.	Studied the effectiveness of 3D presentations for answering questions about multivariate data using standard business graphics.	3D continuous data improved performance over 2D views. 3D presentations of discrete data did not improve performance over 2D.
Barfield and Robless (1989) on dimensionality of presentation format.	Investigated performance of novice and expert managers using 2D or 3D graphs displayed on paper or on the computer.	Novice subjects performed better using 2D graphs on paper. Expert subjects performed better using 3-D graphs on the computer.
Spence (1990) on dimensionality of presentation format.	Examined the accuracy and speed of judgments made from various graphs to assess whether 2D or 3D presentations impact performance.	Judgments from graphs carrying extraneous dimensions that do not carry quantitative variation were judged as accurately as their 1D counterparts.
Haskell and Wickens (1993) on dimensionality of presentation format.	Examined the accuracy of judgments made from 2D or 3D displays for aviation.	3D had superior lateral and altitude flight-path tracking accuracy, whereas 2D displays had superior airspeed tracking accuracy.
Kolers, Duchnicky, and Ferguson (1981) on features of tables.	Compared eye movements and reading speeds as a function of 2 line spacings, two character densities, and five scrolling rates.	People read double-spaced text faster than single-spaced text. Scrolling text is processed slower than fixed text.

shape, value, and orientation convey information. If the variations are too subtle, the information encoded in the visual primitives will not be conveyed (Cleveland, 1985). Clustering forms Gestalt units or perceptual groupings of visual primitives.

Some graph information must be retained in WM while other information is apprehended from the display. Later **visual encoding processes** organize and map retained information to a coordinate grid that identifies the locations of regional patterns. Local re-scanning permits a finer decomposition of regional patterns in the graph. Gradually, WM builds a visual description of the graph from localized re-scanning. WM retains this visual description for about 7 seconds. Only a small fraction of graphic information (four chunks) can be held in WM at one time. Thus, reorganization and re-interpretation of the information decoded from a graph is subject to capacity and duration limitations in WM.

Information held in WM triggers an association to a kind of memory trace in LTM called an instantiated graph schema. Locating stored information is necessary for recognizing the graph type, graphic elements of the display, and the interrelationships that aid com-

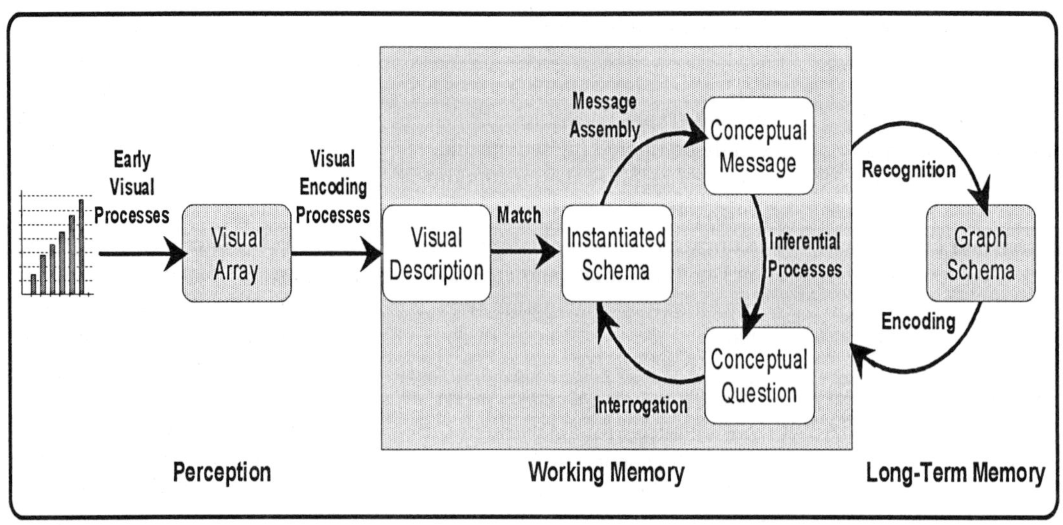

Figure 3. Model of perception and cognition for graph comprehension from Pinker (1990).

parallel detection

color red orange yellow green blue

value

angle

slope

length

texture

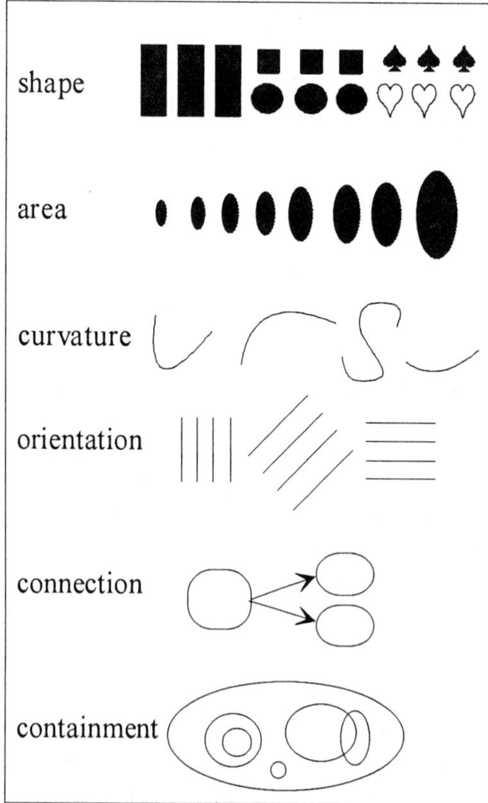

Figure 4. Examples of visual objects detected in parallel and in serial.

prehension. **Recognition** of the graph type facilitates understanding. Graph schemata contain standard, learned procedures for locating and decoding information presented in the graph. For example, a bar graph schema would contain declarative knowledge about the location of information in bar graphs as well as procedural knowledge used to extract information from different exemplars of bar graphs. Graph schemata contain slots for knowledge about the information encoded in a graphic. The slot for maximum value may contain a procedural rule that states the tallest bar is the maximum value. For a table, the slot for maximum value may contain a procedural rule that requires a serial scan of each value in the display while comparing the current table entry to the maximum value found up to that point in the search. Thus, schemata can direct subsequent scanning and decomposing to answer a question from a graph or table.

Each display type has its own schema for extracting information from the display. Some slots contain output from a graphical perception task; other slots require additional **interrogation** and **inferential** processing to answer a specific question posed to a graph. WM capacity limits the amount of interrogation and inferential processing. As a result, a graph can have significantly different comprehensibility from the viewpoint of two users with different WM capacities. The greater the extent of the interrogation and inferential processing required, the more difficult it will be to extract the information from the graph. Thus, each graphic has an inherent advantage for displaying a certain type of information with a minimal amount of additional interrogation and inferential processing.

Graphics users vary greatly. Some people have faster perceptual processors, or a larger WM capacity, more powerful inferential processes, or more learned patterns (e.g., musicians). Most of the variation is contingent upon the type of user, the degree of expertise with graph conventions, and the nature of the task. Novices may lack the necessary schemata to understand the symbolic notation of the graph. Practice and training can improve recognition of the schemata as well as the ability to decode information from a graph (DeSanctis and Jarvenpaa, 1989).

6.3.2 How do we Acquire Information from Graphs?

An example illustrates the workings of this classic model of visual information processing. Suppose we use the line graph shown in Figure 5a to answer the question, "In 1981, did zinc cost less than copper?". Unlike causal viewing of a graph that allows each viewer to generate some insights about any of the relationships depicted in the graph, the question specifies one goal and structures the graphical information processing task. The efficiency criteria described by Bertin (1983, p. 9) succinctly states this important aspect of graphical perception.

> "If, in order to obtain a correct and complete answer to a given question, all other things being equal, one construction requires a shorter period of perception than another construction, we can say that it is more efficient for this question."

Given the question posed to a specific graph or table, there exists a shortest path sequence for decoding the information presented graphically that enables the viewer to answer the question in the least amount of time. This is an important premise underlying most quantitative models of graphical perception.

Let us assume that we have learned to recognize line graphs and have a specific procedure in LTM for decoding information from line graphs. This procedure tells us how to extract semantic information from line segments presented in a Cartesian coordinate system. We will also assume that in understanding the question, we have extracted the important semantic cues "zinc", "copper", and "1981", which are then retained in WM.

Given the nature of the question, we first direct our attention to the legend. The legend contains the syntactic elements used to represent copper and zinc in the graph. A quick scan of the legend would identify copper first. Using the gestalt principle of proximity, we associate the closest symbol, an 'X', to copper. The process is repeated, associating a 'I' to zinc.

Next, we direct our attention to the "1981" located near the center of the graph. From 1981, we scan up from the X-axis looking for either an 'X' (copper) or a 'I' (zinc). The question asks for which is more, not specific values. This can be ascertained from the relative vertical position along the Y-axis. We do not have to scan the Y-axis for actual numbers.

Unfortunately, discrimination among the symbols is somewhat difficult because the shapes overlap. To discriminate among these shapes, we use the gestalt principle of continuation to follow the line toward a pair of shapes that do not overlap. While processing this additional visual information, the association of an 'X' to copper and a 'I' to zinc may become lost if WM is overloaded. If that occurs, we need to reread the legend.

It is important to note that information lost from

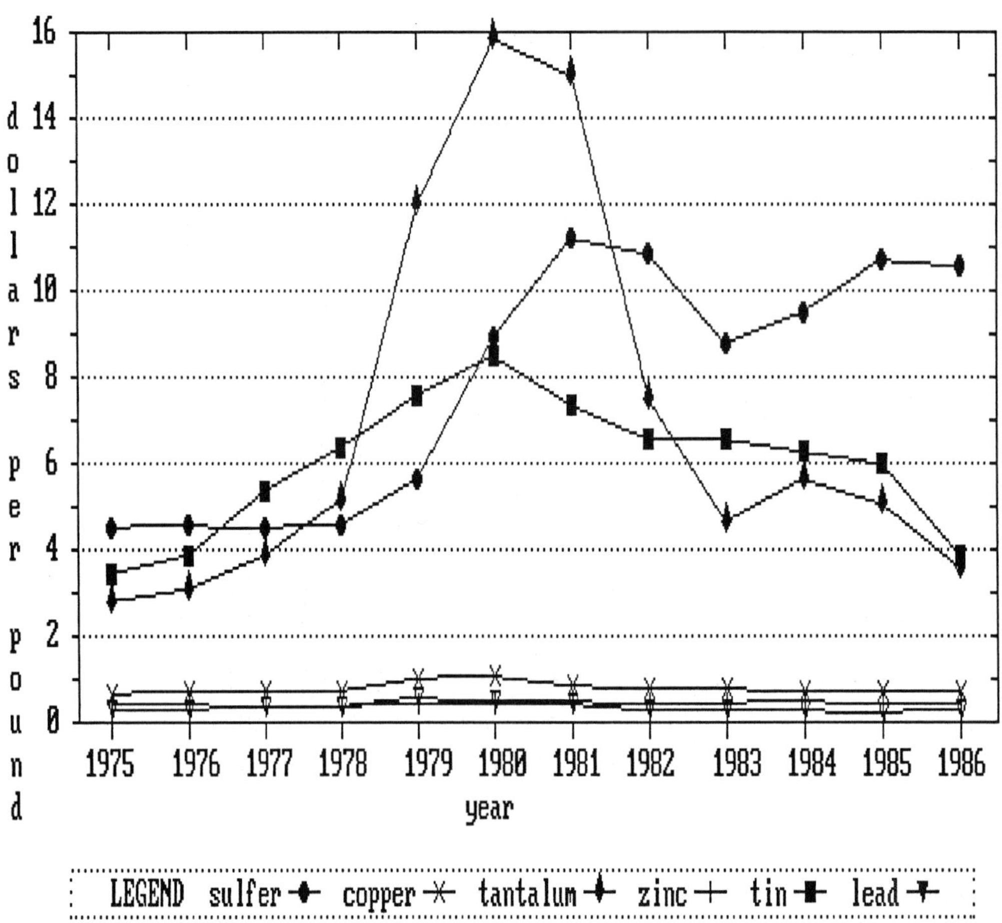

Figure 5a. A line graph showing mineral prices for the USA. Semantic trace for the question, "In 1981, did zinc cost less than copper?".

WM results from additional information processing imposed by the discrimination task. Once we engage in an arduous serial scanning of an image, our ability to process complex visual information decreases. The problems arise from WM bottlenecks.

We could facilitate this stage of decoding by making it easier to discriminate among the visual primitives used in the graph. We know that people perceive some visual primitives more readily than others. For example, texture (Julesz, 1975) and color (Kahneman and Henik, 1981) are detected and organized in parallel during pre-attentive visual processing. Other visual primitives such as shape, area and containment (such as in Venn diagrams) are detected and processed via less efficient serial scanning (Treisman, 1982, 1985). Since shape is detected serially, it is slow. We could use a redundant coding scheme that encodes the mineral data using color. Color coding of these data reduces the information processing load on WM, because color is apprehended in parallel.

In sum, the process of answering the question involves reading the legend, scanning the X-axis for 1981, moving up to find the right symbols, discriminating among the shapes, and comparing the relative vertical position of the shapes representing zinc and copper. In this example, discrimination among the monochrome shapes imposes an additional load on WM, interfering with the information held in WM.

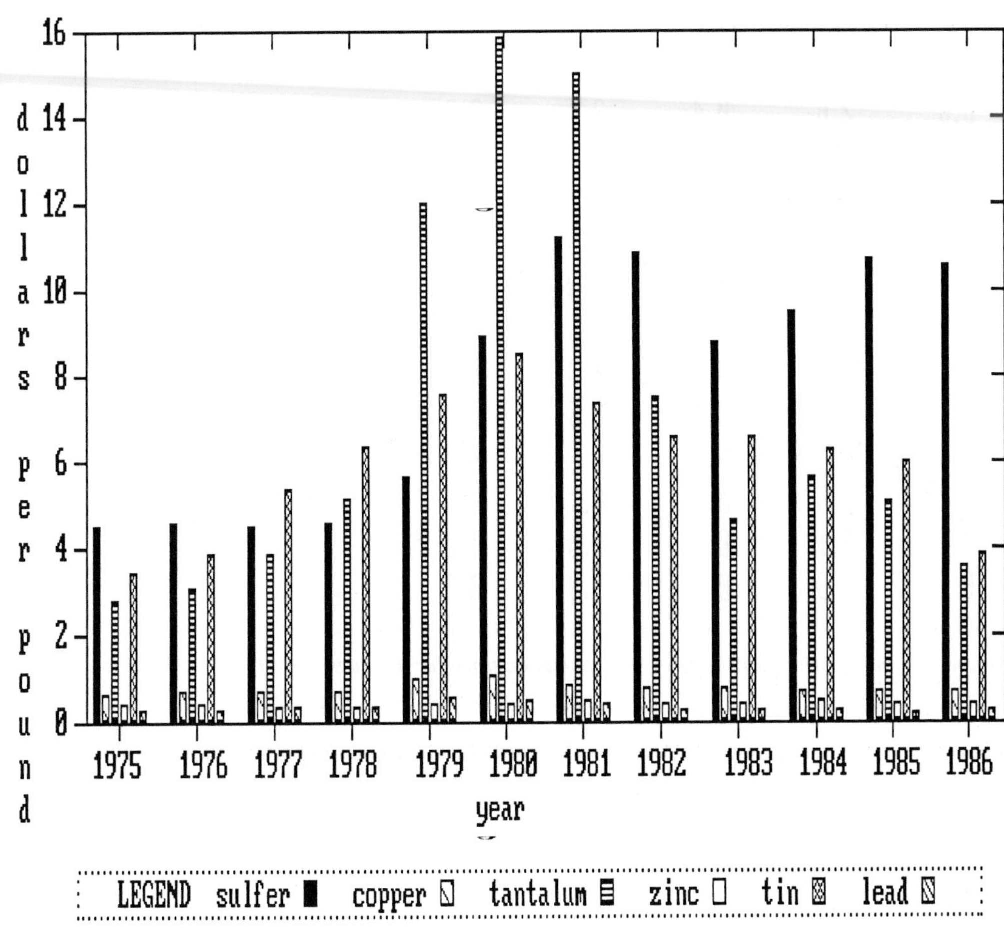

Figure 5b. A bar graph showing mineral prices for the USA. Semantic trace for the question, "In 1981, did zinc cost less than copper?".

Some information may become lost. This forces the viewer to reread the legend or some part of the graph, incurring additional processing time or setting the basis for an error.

Figures 5b and 5c provide two additional examples to illustrate this model of visual information processing. Both figures use the same data set as Figure 5a. Both contain the answer to the same question, "In 1981, did zinc cost less than copper?" These examples compare the perceptual and cognitive information processing required to answer the question using different presentation types.

The bar graph in Figure 5b uses bar height to represent cost for zinc and copper in 1981. The legend associates mineral names to textures much as it did for the symbols in the line graph. Then, the year 1981 is located on the X-axis. Next, the bars are matched against the texture patterns held in WM. After identifying the bars, their heights are compared. Adjacent bars are easier to compare than non-adjacent bars. Reaction time is similar to that of the line graph. Much of the time involves discriminating among the textures and comparing the relative vertical position of the bars.

The table in Figure 5c presents the same data. Tables are void of the abstract symbolic notation found in the line and bar graphs. Tables contain a matrix of alphanumeric data. People use well-learned spatial patterns for extracting information from a table. Assuming an

MEAN MINERAL PRICES

year	sulfer	copper	tantalum	zinc	tin	lead
1975	4.5	0.6	2.8	0.4	3.4	0.2
1976	4.6	0.7	3.0	0.4	3.8	0.2
1977	4.4	0.7	3.8	0.3	5.3	0.3
1978	4.5	0.7	5.1	0.3	6.3	0.3
1979	5.6	0.9	12.0	0.4	7.5	0.5
1980	8.9	1.0	15.8	0.4	8.5	0.4
1981	11.1	0.8	14.9	0.4	7.3	0.4
1982	10.8	0.7	7.5	0.4	6.5	0.3
1983	8.7	0.8	4.6	0.4	6.6	0.2
1984	9.4	0.7	5.6	0.5	6.2	0.3
1985	10.6	0.7	5.1	0.4	6.0	0.2
1986	10.5	0.7	3.6	0.4	3.8	0.2

Figure 5c. A table showing mineral prices for the USA (A). Semantic trace for the question, "In 1981, did zinc cost less than copper?".

English reading order of left to right and top to bottom, subjects viewing a matrix screen display tend to read row-wise (Tullis, 1988; Galitz, 1985). Also, people locate information by scanning the row and column labels. To answer the cost question posed above, people would match the column label to copper and zinc, and then proceed to the correct row indexed by 1981.

Tables do not require a complex mapping of syntactic symbols to semantic information. Tables contain semantic information that people extract directly from the table. This greatly reduces the information load in WM when the queries are simple. However, for complex comparisons of trends, tables require the reader to look up several entries in the table and make mental calculations and comparisons among these values. These intermediate values are held in WM during the comparison. In contrast, Figure 5a, show trend information without the scanning and interpolation of line graphs, like those in intermediate data. Slopes are perceived readily from a line graph.

Obviously, as these examples illustrate, some graphs are better at conveying certain kinds of information than others. Models of graphical perception and cognition provide insights about how a graph conveys information to a user. The next section describes models of graphical perception that evaluate graphic design or automate the design of graphs.

6.4 Models of Graphical Perception

Intelligent software for graphics presents a combination of text and graphics that best conveys the information desired by the user. An automated system eliminates the need for end-users to specify, design and arrange the graphic elements of a display. Instead, users focus their attention on the tasks of determining and describing the content of the information to be expressed by the graphic display. This section describes research (Table 2) that facilitates the evaluation of graphic displays (Gillan and Lewis, 1994), automates the evaluation of graphic displays (Tullis, 1983, 1988; Lohse, 1991, 1993; Kieras and Meyer, 1994), or automates the design of a graphic (Mackinlay, 1986; Casner, 1991).

6.4.1 MA-P - Gillan and Lewis

Gillan and Lewis (1994) developed a componential model of human interaction with graphs called the mixed

Table 2. Summary of models of graphical perception and cognition.

Graphical Perception Model	Type of Model
MA-P Gillan and Lewis, 1994	Regression model of graphical information processing
DAP Tullis 1983, 1988	Evaluating screen design
UCIE Lohse 1991, 1993	Evaluating design of graphs and tables
APT Mackinlay 1986	Automating graphic design
BOZ Casner, 1991	Automating graphic design with task analysis
GOMS Card, Moran, and Newell, 1983	General purpose cognitive model
EPIC Kieras and Meyer, 1994	General purpose cognitive model

arithmetic - perceptual model (MA-P). MA-P derives a model of the user from task analyses of users performing graphical perception tasks. The component processes identified in the task analyses are similar to elementary information processes (EIP) used in other research (Newell and Simon, 1972; Bettman, Johnson, and Payne, 1990; Simkin and Hastie, 1987). An EIP is a basic cognitive operation such as reading a value. A sequence of EIPs provides a strategy for completing a task.

The task analysis used in MA-P identified five component processes. *Search* locates the value of a variable. *Encode* stores the value of a variable in memory. *Arithmetic operations* are component processes for performing addition, subtraction, multiplication or division on values. *Spatial comparisons* rank the relative heights of bars, or lengths of line segments encoding data values. *Respond* is a component process for typing an answer in a message box. MA-P assumes (1) subjects execute component processes in a sequence of processing steps, (2) each component process requires the same amount of time to execute, and (3) total time to complete the task increases linearly as a function of the number of component processes required to complete the task. Also, MA-P predictions do not reflect WM capacity or duration constraints.

A graph user might answer the question, "What is the sum of A, B, and C?". Using a stacked bar graph, the user would simply identify the value C at the top of the stack. The sequence of component processes is Search C, Encode C, Respond. Using a line graph, the user would derive the sum. The sequence of component processes is Search A, Encode A, Search B, Encode B, Search C, Encode C, Add A+B+C, and Respond. Task completion time is a function of the number of component processes. In this example, there were three component processes for the stacked bar graph and eight for the line graph. Thus, the theory predicts it would take almost three times as long to complete the task using a line graph as compared with a stacked bar graph.

An empirical study compared actual performance to MA-P predictions over a range of three graph types and eight question types for each of 12 subjects. Overall, a simple linear regression model of the form, (reaction time = intercept + Y * number of component processes), explains 90% of the variance in mean reaction times (N=24). Gillan and Lewis also derived timing parameters for each of the five functional components from another regression. Process times for each component (search, encode, arithmetic operation, spatial comparison, and respond) varied as a function of question type and graph type. Subjects took longer to answer arithmetic questions from stacked bar graphs than predicted by MA-P. Also, subjects took the same amount of time comparing five values as for comparing two or three - again suggesting that subjects used a different information processing strategy. Overall, this relatively simple approach provides a good account for the variance in these data.

However, like GOMS, the predictions are invariant to subtle variations in discrimination tasks. MA-P yields an identical prediction for color or monochrome displays with or without grid lines. In some cases, MA-P is invariant to the graph type. For example, predictions for scatter plots are identical to predictions for line graphs, and horizontal bar graphs. Thus, MA-P would need more detailed process operators for detection, discrimination, and perceptual grouping to explain performance for subtle differences in graphical presentation formats.

6.4.2 DAP - Tullis

Tullis developed one of the first tools for automating the evaluation of displays (1983, 1988). He identified six parameters for objectively evaluating screen formats. These parameters include: (1) the overall density of characters on the screen, (2) the local density of other characters near each character, (3) the number of

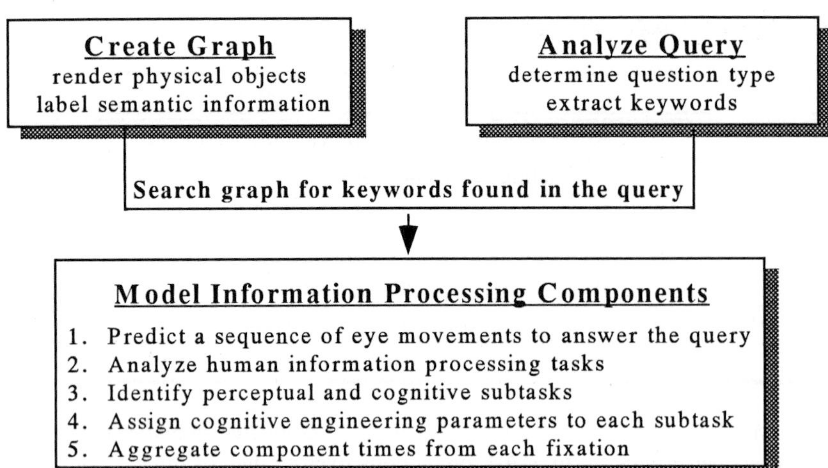

Figure 6. Major inputs and processing components of UCIE.

visual groups of characters, (4) the visual angle subtended by those groups, (5) the number of labels or data values, and (6) a measure of alignment of the screen elements.

Based on a usability analysis of these six parameters from 520 displays, Tullis developed regression equations to predict average search time and display quality. Using these regression estimates, Tullis developed a program to analyze screen displays. The program reads an ASCII file containing a copy of the screen to be analyzed. The display analysis program (DAP) automatically measures the six parameters described above, makes an assessment of usability, recommends improvements in the screen layout, and calculates an average visual search time and a subjective rating of overall quality.

Predictions generated by the program rely heavily on the Gestalt principle of proximity. Although the predictions generated by DAP are quite good (r = .71), DAP only analyzes monochrome, alphanumeric tables whereas graphical displays afford more determinants of grouping in addition to spatial proximity. These determinants include color, graphical borders, highlighting, type faces and multiple fonts. Items coded with the same color are a perceptual group. Rectangular boundaries also help form groups, although not as effectively as color since containment is detected serially. Highlighting, using reverse video, increased brightness, flashing, underlining or color, can be very effective in attracting user attention. For graphical displays, DAP needs to be extended to include these other display features.

6.4.3 UCIE - Lohse

UCIE (Lohse, 1991, 1993) not only provides a research tool for understanding visual cognition and perception- but also provides graphic designers a metric for measuring display quality that evaluates information processing time for alternative display layouts. Figure 6 shows the major inputs and processing components of UCIE (Understanding Cognitive Information Engineering). During the creation of a graph, UCIE notes the location, syntactic and semantic properties of each object in the graph. By comparing the keywords in the query to the semantic information in the graph, the model predicts a sequence of eye fixations that contains the information needed to answer the query. Within each fixation, UCIE identifies the perceptual and cognitive sub-tasks. Next, UCIE assigns each component task a known cognitive engineering time parameters reported in the literature (e.g., 300 msec to process a 6-letter word; John and Newell, 1990). UCIE, like other human performance models, predicts total task execution time by summing the known cognitive engineering time parameters over all the component tasks.

UCIE simulates how people answer certain questions posed to bar graphs, line graphs, and tables. It can process three types of queries: point reading, comparison, and trend. Point reading questions refer to a single data point. Comparison questions refer to a pair of adjacent data points. Trend questions refer to a range of successive data points. Queries define the top-level goal of answering a question posed to a graphic dis-

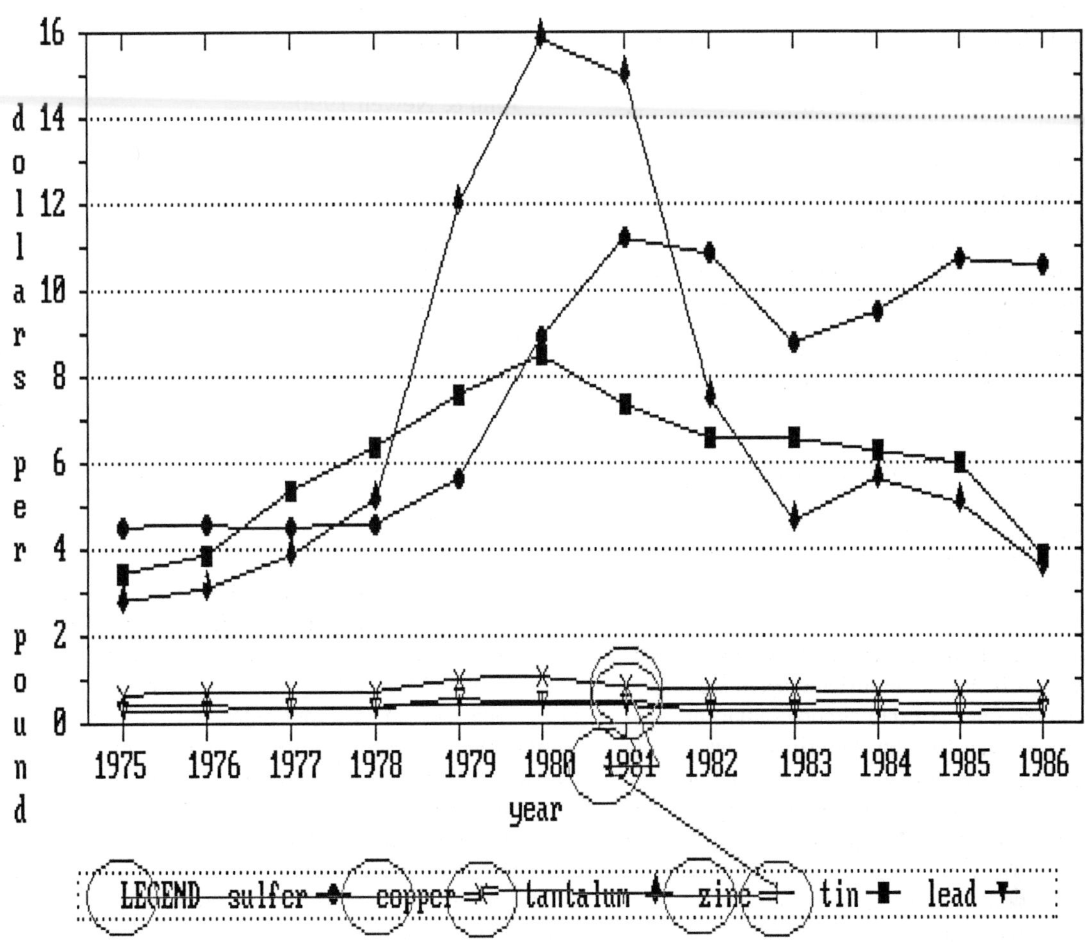

Figure 7. Sequence of eye movements to answer a question posed to a line graph. (In 1981, did zinc cost less than copper?)

play. Decomposition of the query identifies important sub-goals of the task such as mapping legend symbols to category labels. These component tasks determine the number and location of eye fixations (Figure 7).

Like GOMS (Card, Moran, and Newell, 1983), UCIE contains many perceptual and cognitive operations that have known approximate times associated with them. These are commonly referred to as cognitive engineering time parameters (Figure 8). The rightmost column in Figure 9 shows the GOMS component times for the comparison question posed to the line graph in Figure 7 (In 1981, did zinc cost less than copper?). The total GOMS prediction is 4,417 msec. While the prediction seems similar to the values generated by UCIE (4,166 for a monochrome display and 3,493 for a color display), GOMS is invariant to different presentation formats. GOMS yields an identical prediction for color or monochrome displays with or without grid lines. GOMS also is invariant to the actual question posed to the display as long as the question was of the form 'In *YEAR*, did *CATEGORY1* have more *BLANK* than *CATEGORY2*?' For example, the GOMS prediction for the question, "In 1981, did tin cost less than sulfur?", would also be 4,417 msec. Furthermore, if we had posed the question to a bar graph of these data, GOMS would still give a prediction of 4,417 msec.

Of course actual human performance is a function of both the question and the format of the display. Thus, in the spirit of previous research that has sought

Time msec	Parameter	Reference
372	keypunch an entry	Card, Moran & Newell 1983
1200	compare two units in memory	Olson & Olson 1990
1180	interpolate on a linear scale	Boff & Lincoln 1988
300	recognize a 6-letter word	John & Newell 1990
230	make a saccade (travel + fixation time)	Russo 1978
70	execute a mental step	Olson & Olson 1990
92	perceptual judgment	Welford 1973
33	compare two digits in working memory	Cavanaugh 1972
38	compare two colors in working memory	Cavanaugh 1972
40	compare two letters in working memory	Cavanaugh 1972
47	compare two words in working memory	Cavanaugh 1972
50	compare two shapes in working memory	Cavanaugh 1972
68	compare two forms in working memory	Cavanaugh 1972
4	per degree of visual arc scanned assuming no head movement	Kosslyn 1983

Figure 8. Cognitive engineering time parameters used by UCIE.

to extend the GOMS model to slightly different tasks (e.g. Olson and Nilsen, 1988; John and Newell, 1990), UCIE refined the GOMS keystroke-level model. UCIE time predictions reflect subtle differences in similarity, proximity, color, and overlap among adjacent non-target objects in each fixation. Discrimination time in UCIE depends on how difficult it is to discriminate the target object from other objects in the fixation. Discrimination time increases as the number, proximity, percentage overlap and similarity of non-target objects within the fixation increase. The additional level of detail for discrimination tasks provides a better account of the variance in actual human performance (Lohse, 1993).

UCIE also simulates the flow of information through WM (Kosslyn, 1985). UCIE assumes that in understanding a question, people extract the necessary semantic cues. These cues occupy a storage slot in WM. Each storage slot is a chunk. UCIE assumes WM has a capacity of four chunks. WM holds chunks for a duration of seven seconds or until incoming information displaces old information from WM. UCIE does not use a contemporary spreading activation model of memory (e.g. Anderson, 1983). Occasionally WM becomes overloaded causing information needed for certain sub-goals of the task to become lost. Then, the display must be rescanned to reprocess information or reread the question to understand the task. This increases the predicted time to complete the task.

An empirical study compared actual performance to UCIE predictions for 576 combinations of presentation formats and question types from 28 subjects (N=16,128). Each subject participated in eight replications, viewing three kinds of graphs (bar, line and tables), each with and without color and grid lines, answering three types of questions (point reading, comparisons, and trends) with two levels of difficulty. For conditions that predominantly involve serial processing, zero-parameter predictions from UCIE explained 60% of the variance in reaction times. Overall, a zero-parameter model explains 37% of the variance in average reaction times (N=1,128). The largest predictive component is the number of fixations, explaining 31 percent of the variation by itself. The zero-parameter model only explains about 10% of the individual variation in reaction times across 28 subjects (N=15,200). While UCIE provides an objective metric for evaluating display quality that could be incorporated into current research tools for designing graphical presentations of data automatically, additional research is needed to explain individual differences in performance.

6.4.4 APT - Mackinlay

Mackinlay (1986) developed a compositional algebra for systematically generating a wide variety of graphics from a small set of presentation elements. The theoretical model was incorporated in a computer program called APT (A Presentation Tool). Constraints define the

Fixation	Parameter	UCIE (mono)	UCIE (color)	GOMS
1	process from Legend to copper	94	94	
	scan to copper	39	39	230
	discriminate copper	115	57	47
	read copper	300	300	300
2	scan to 'X'	5	5	230
	discriminate 'X'	171	100	50
3	scan to zinc	32	32	230
	discriminate zinc	115	57	47
	read zinc	300	300	300
4	scan to '|'	5	5	230
	discriminate '|'	171	98	50
5	scan to 1981	30	30	230
	discriminate 1981	119	87	47
	read 1981	300	300	300
6	scan to 'X'	15	15	230
	discriminate 'X'	267	130	47
7	scan to '|'	5	5	230
	discriminate '|'	511	267	47
	Comparison: Is '|' greater than 'X'?	1200	1200	1200
	Keystroke	372	372	372
	Total time	4166	3493	4417
	Actual	6725	4693	
	Minimum	4660	2910	
	Maximum	11810	7580	
	Standard Error	541	490	

Figure 9. Comparison of UCIE and GOMS for the monochrome line graph in figure 6 and a color presentation of the same graph *(not shown) to answer the question " In 1981, did zinc cost less than copper?". All times are in milliseconds.*

solution space for generating graphics with APT. Two major constraints are the output medium (printer, monitor, plotter) and the structure of the raw data (nominal, ordinal, quantitative).

Mackinlay uses two design criteria, expressiveness and effectiveness, to design graphic displays automatically. For each information component to be displayed in a graph, APT selects a set of visual primitives capable of expressing that information. For example, length encodes quantitative relations (e.g., largest) whereas color does not express quantity well. In contrast, color facilitates perceptual grouping among nominal data categories whereas length does not readily promote perceptual grouping.

Once APT selects an appropriate set of relations, APT selects the single primitive that best expresses a particular relation. Table 3 shows which visual primitive best expresses the type of data capable of being displayed by his system. Once APT satisfies expressiveness and effectiveness criteria, compositional operators design a graphic presentation of these data.

APT provides two important advances for automating graphic design. First, nearly every graphic presentation tool designed after APT, including BOZ (Casner,

Table 3. Ordering of elementary graphical perception tasks (from Cleveland and McGill (1984, 1985)).

Quantitative*	Ordinal	Nominal
position	position	position
length	gray saturation	color hue
angle	color saturation	texture
slope	color hue	connection
area	texture	containment
volume	connection	gray saturation
gray saturation	containment	color saturation
color saturation	length	shape
color hue	angle	length
texture	slope	angle
connection	area	slope
containment	volume	area
shape	shape	volume

* from Cleveland and McGill (1984, 1985)

1991) uses APT's formal graphical language. Second, APT designs graphics with a minimal amount of input from the graphic designer. Thus, APT is a prescriptive theory of how to design a graphic.

Although APT generates a wide variety of bar graphs, pie graphs, and line graphs, and scatter plots, it has some limitations. It has no empirically proven theory for all of the expressiveness criteria. Cleveland and McGill (1984) provide empirical evidence to support the rankings for quantitative perceptual tasks. However, the rankings of visual primitives for ordinal and nominal data in Table 3 are based on intuition and conjecture. Further research must verify the expressiveness criteria used by APT. APT also lacks a tremendous amount of knowledge about choosing font sizes, selecting line widths, and positioning objects for rendering the graphic design. Additional research should explore how these features influence the communication of intended information. Finally, the design algorithm relies on an analysis of the raw data to be graphed. APT does not consider the end user task of answering some question posed to the data. This prevents APT from generating different graphic presentations of the same data to support different questions.

6.4.5 BOZ - Casner

BOZ renders graphs from raw data and a task analysis of a specific question posed to the data (Casner, 1991). BOZ replaces demanding logical operators in the codified task description with less-demanding visual operators that reduce visual search. BOZ identifies an equivalent perceptual task by substituting perceptual inferences in place of logical inferences. For example, BOZ might replace a comparison of numeric values with a perceptual judgment comparing the heights of two bars. By focusing on the task posed to a graphic presentation, BOZ renders multiple presentations of the same data customized to different task requirements.

The graphical presentation language for BOZ has five components. A *logical task description language* allows the user to describe the task. A *perceptual operator substitution component* contains a catalog of perceptual operators that can substitute for logical operators in the task description. A *perceptual data structuring component* determines an appropriate perceptual grouping of multiple operators. A *perceptual operator selection component* determines which mapping of visual operator to logical operator minimizes the end user's information search across competing graphic designs. A *rendering component* translates the logical facts and graphic constraints into a graphic design on the computer screen.

Using BOZ, Casner and Larkin (1989) create four displays of one set of complex airline reservation data (Figure 10). Display 1 uses a table to show flight origin and destination city, seating availability, price, and departure and arrival times. Display 2 places the departure and arrival times on a horizontal number line. Each flight is a box along the number line. The length of the box encodes the length of the flight. Distance between boxes encodes layover time. Display 3 is identical to display 2 except shading encodes the availability of flights. Display 4 is identical to display 3 ex-

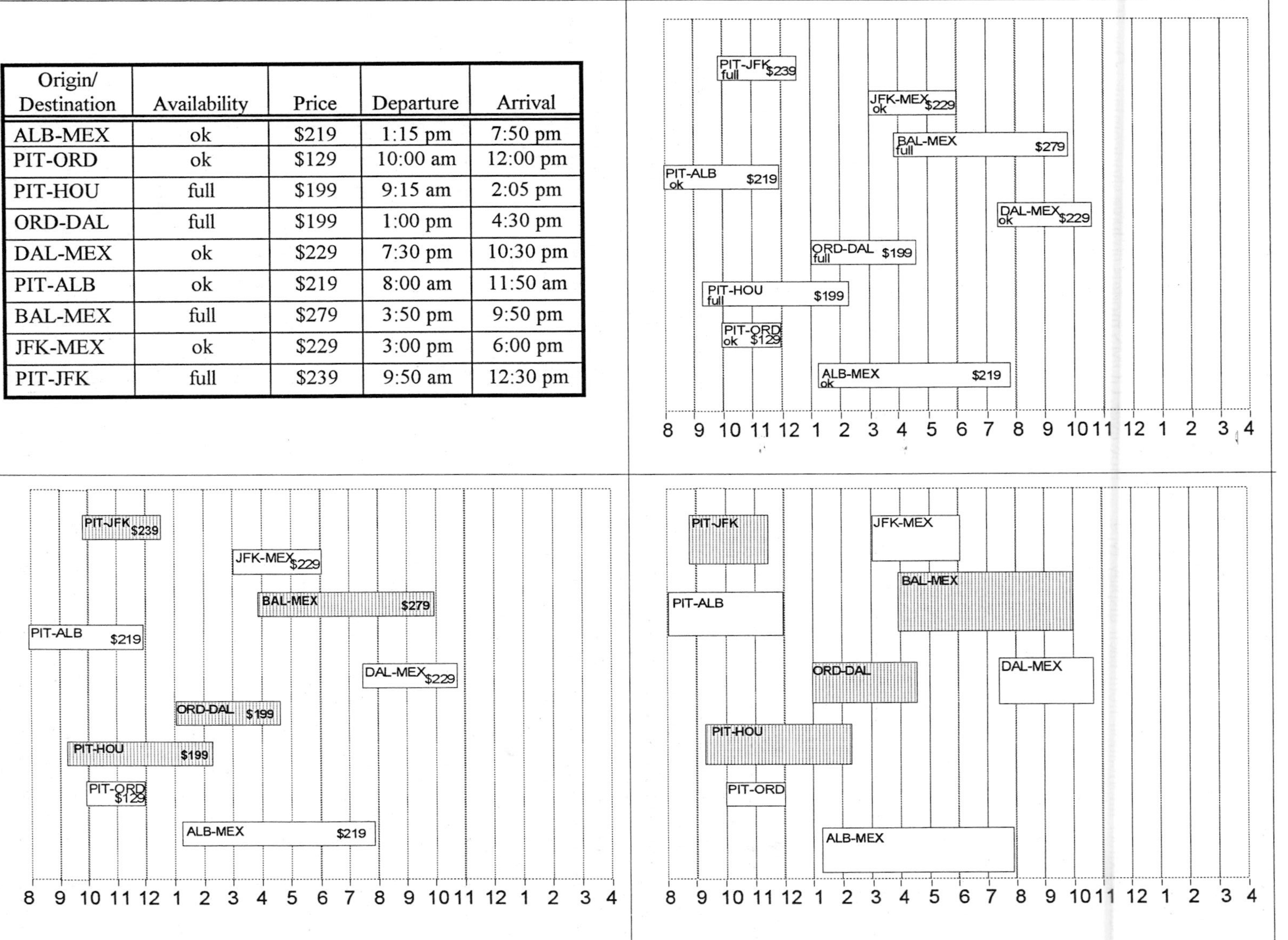

Origin/ Destination	Availability	Price	Departure	Arrival
ALB-MEX	ok	$219	1:15 pm	7:50 pm
PIT-ORD	ok	$129	10:00 am	12:00 pm
PIT-HOU	full	$199	9:15 am	2:05 pm
ORD-DAL	full	$199	1:00 pm	4:30 pm
DAL-MEX	ok	$229	7:30 pm	10:30 pm
PIT-ALB	ok	$219	8:00 am	11:50 am
BAL-MEX	full	$279	3:50 pm	9:50 pm
JFK-MEX	ok	$229	3:00 pm	6:00 pm
PIT-JFK	full	$239	9:50 am	12:30 pm

Figure 10. Airline reservation task: a) table; b)horizontal distance codes time; c) shading codes availability; d) height codes cost.

cept box height encodes cost of the flight. The taller the box, the greater the cost of the flight.

Casner and Larkin postulate what specific procedural mechanisms people use to extract information from tabular displays. Casner and Larkin predict the efficacy of the four displays using a LISP simulation of the search procedure used to extract information from each display type. The authors verify the simulation using a lab experiment to measure the time required to extract information from each of the four display types. Except for display 4, each visual operator reduced visual search time in the manner predicted by the simulation. Detailed data analyses suggest that overall time improvements were due to operator substitution and the use of visual cues that reduce search time, but not due to restructuring of the search.

BOZ does have several limitations. It does not consider fonts, typeface, or color. The graphical presentation language does not compute task completion time. "Time" is simply an intuitive ranking of the execution time for graphical perception tasks. BOZ also does not consider general conventions (left - to right reading order, spatial numbering patterns, etc.) BOZ ignores real-world artifacts that do not express data (e.g., aisles for airline seating chart). While it is unlikely that BOZ will create any new graphic designs (for example, Minard's chart of Napoleon's march to Moscow in Tufte 1983, p 41), BOZ does create "customized" graphic presentations that support a specific task. This is a major contribution in the development of tools for automating graphic presentation.

6.4.6 GOMS - John

GOMS models a sequence of user actions in tasks of routine cognitive skill (e.g., text-editing, building a spreadsheet, operating an ATM machine). GOMS models have four components: (1) a set of goals, (2) a set of operators to perform actions, (3) a set of methods to achieve the goals, and (4) a set of selection rules for choosing among competing methods for goals (Card, Moran, and Newell, 1983). An analyst decomposes high-level goals into various sub-goals. Next, an analyst identifies methods to perform each sub-goal. Finally, by assigning mean times to operators, GOMS predicts task duration. GOMS assumes that routine cognitive skills are a serial sequence of perceptual, cognitive, and motor activities. Each of these actions has a time parameter that is independent of the particular task context and is constant across all tasks. The ability to use cognitive engineering calculations for predicting how users will interact with proposed designs is a useful tool for the system designers of computer interfaces.

GOMS models exist for a wide variety of tasks (Olson and Olson, 1990). The most notable application has been for a telephone operator workstation that saved millions of dollars (Gray, John, and Atwood, 1993). However, GOMS models do have shortcomings. One of these is its suitability for a limited range of domains. In particular, except for Lohse's work (1991, 1993) there has been little or no effort directed towards extending GOMS to model graphical perception tasks. However, recent extensions of GOMS to model low level perceptual, cognitive, and motor operators (John, 1990) facilitate the use of GOMS for modeling the efficacy of various graphical and textual layouts.

Chuah, John, and Pane (1995) used GOMS to model the airline flight reservation tasks (Figure 10) used by Casner and Larkin (1989) and Casner (1991). Rather than examine all possible search methods, Chuah, John, and Pane used one information search algorithm for each display. They also made three additional assumptions. First, all information grouped within a five degree visual angle represents one eye fixation. Second, scanning begins in the upper left corner and proceeds from left to right and from the top to the bottom. Third, they assumed the user would point to requisite information with their finger and attend to it directly without any additional information search. These assumptions enabled precise predictions about the number of eye movements required to complete the information acquisition task.

Chuah, John, and Pane compared zero-parameter predictions from the GOMS model to the empirical data collected by Casner and Larkin (1989). The average absolute error was 8%. These results are preliminary because of the limited scope of the comparison. Only four GOMS predictions were compared with the mean actual search times from these four displays. However, the early results are very encouraging. They demonstrate that GOMS models provide accurate measures of performance for a relatively complex graphical perception task.

6.4.7 EPIC - Kieras and Meyers

The EPIC (Executive Process, Interactive Control) architecture is a computational modeling environment for simulating a range of human perceptual-motor and cognitive tasks (Kieras and Meyers, 1994). EPIC has visual, auditory, motor, and cognitive processors. EPIC requires, as input, a set of production rules that specify what actions must be performed to do the task.

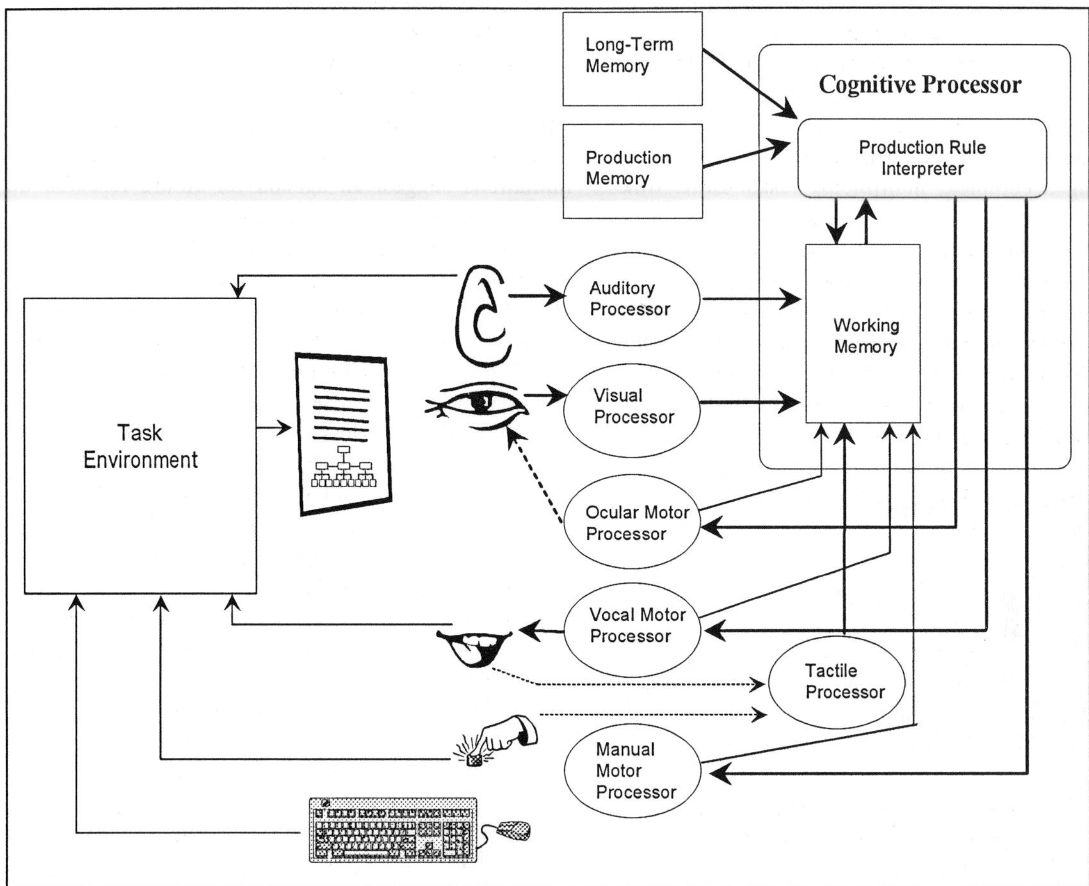

Figure 11. Overall structure of the EPIC architecture.

A simulated human with generalized procedural knowledge of the task interacts with the simulated task environment. The model generates a specific pattern of activities necessary to perform the task. EPIC also predicts total task time. EPIC time predictions are very good. Model simulations of various dual-tasks (e.g., pressing keys in response to lights and saying words in response to tones) explain specific patterns of effects in quantitative detail (Meyers and Kieras, 1995).

The structure of the processing mechanisms in EPIC mimic those of the most recent empirical studies, especially studies on multitask performance. Physical sensors in EPIC send signals to visual, auditory, and tactile perceptual processors. The perceptual processors send outputs to a central WM. A cognitive processor uses a production-rule interpreter to perform various tasks based on the contents of WM. Vocal, ocular motor, and manual motor processors handle responses. Figure 11 shows the overall structure of the EPIC architecture.

EPIC uses a production rule system coded in Common LISP of the form IF CONDITION, THEN ACTION. EPIC incorporates the interpreter from the Parsimonious Production System (PPS) (Bovair, Kieras, and Polson, 1990). PPS allows any number of rules to fire and execute their actions. Unlike other production rule systems, EPIC executes multiple actions in parallel. At the start of each cognitive cycle, EPIC updates the contents of WM with new inputs from perceptual and motor processes. WM does not include any mechanism for rehearsal, decay, or overflow. WM capacity and duration are sufficient for multitask performance. The production rule interpreter tests the contents of WM against all conditions of rules stored in the production-rule memory. At the end of the cycle, EPIC executes associated actions in parallel. Thus, there are no central-processing bottlenecks in EPIC.

EPIC is a general purpose architecture useful for modeling a range of auditory, motor, visual search, and multiple task situations. As noted above, EPIC predictions for dual-tasks are quite accurate (Meyer and Kieras, 1995). Kieras, Wood, and Meyer (1995) used EPIC models to predict the time of telephone operators performing a complex, multimodal tasks. EPIC time predictions were accurate within 10% of actual times. The EPIC architecture also accommodates more graphical information-processing tasks. Extensions of the visual processor will allow EPIC to handle such tasks as answering a question posed to a line graph. Thus, EPIC provides very detailed predictions about micro-level perceptual and cognitive activities needed to complete graphical information-processing tasks.

6.5 Future Directions

Empirical research identifies universal graphic design principles and recommends graphs for particular tasks. This literature has shown the effectiveness of a particular graph is contingent upon the task, the decision maker, and the graph. Unfortunately, general qualitative principles and guidelines are difficult to apply in the context of designing a specific graphic for a given task. Further, very little empirical graphics research could be codified into an algorithm to provide robust quantitative predictions about the effectiveness of a graphic design for a specific task.

Keen (1980) cautioned others against using qualitative theories because they are untestable, hard to challenge and difficult to apply to real problems. The results are always subject to caveats regarding potential interactions among other factors. This does not deny the value of qualitative theories. In fact, there are many ordinal statistics for evaluating these data and phenomena. In Newell's view (Card, Moran, and Robertson, 1992), if psychological theories are to be usable, the mechanisms underlying performance should be teased out using computational models of behavior. Computational cognitive models should emphasize detailed task analysis, quantitative calculation, and zero-parameter predictions to make them useful for real applications. GOMS models are one example of such an approach (Card, Moran, and Newell, 1983).

Of course, no algorithmic model always chooses the most effective or accurate graphic design. The computational model would need to generalize over different users, graph formats, and tasks. Each of these factors can strongly alter performance, thus making generalizations difficult. Subtle variations in the data or graph format can have an overwhelming effect on the ability of a model of graphical perception to predict performance. For example, noisy data impact our ability to interpret trends from line graphs. Further, the signal/noise ratio is not explicitly address by any of these models of graphical perception. These kinds of limitations suggest an agenda for future research on models of graphical perception and cognition.

Table 4 compares some of features supported by the graphical perception models reviewed in this chapter. All models, except APT, stem from detailed analyses of the user's task. All models, except APT and BOZ, predict task completion time. Time predictions using MA-P can be invariant to the graph type. For example, MA-P lacks detailed operators to predict processing time differences between two bar graphs of the same data with and without grid lines. Tullis designed DAP for analyzing screen designs. DAP does not handle charts and graphs. UCIE only models information processing from bar graphs, line graphs or tables. EPIC incorporates a model of WM, although the WM component of the EPIC architecture is in the early stages of development. CPM-GOMS and EPIC are designed specifically for parallel tasks.

None of the models fully examine individual differences in user capabilities. Individual differences include levels of skill, practice acquiring information from particular graph formats, knowledge of the graphical perception tasks, learning to process information from new or novel graph formats, age, and culture (e.g., most Asian reading patterns are not left to right). In addition, all models only consider skilled, error-free behavior. These models do not explain errors that occur frequently in skilled behavior. Another aspect of the models that seems missing is the ability of the user to vary their information seeking strategy and conceptualization of the displayed information in ways that total alter their processing, much as an expert chess player "sees" the chessboard in a totally different way than a novice. For example, subjects eye movement patterns change contingent upon changes in their perceptual organization when viewing ambiguous pictures (e.g., old woman with gnarled chin and nose and young woman seen with eyelash extending from the silhouette; Stark and Ellis, 1981).

All of the models function in the domain of static, two-dimensional, graphic displays. Animation and dynamic displays are beyond the scope of current models. Such extensions would be difficult for two reasons. First, little is known about the perception and cognition of animated displays. Second, models would need to incorporate episodic memory.

Table 4. A comparison of features supported by models of graphical perception.

Model feature	MA-P Gillan	DAP Tullis	UCIE Lohse	APT Mackinlay	BOZ Casner	GOMS John	EPIC Kieras
based on task analysis	■	■	■		■	■	■
time predictions	■	■	■			■	■
screen layout and tables		■	■	■	■	■	■
general purpose tasks						■	■
automatic designs				■	■		
color			■	■			■
individual difference			■				■
WM limitations			■				■
parallel tasks						■	■
font size							■
errors							
typeface							
animation							
practice/skill effects							
learning new schemata							

This chapter motivates a computational cognitive engineering approach for quantifying the effectiveness, efficiency and quality of graphic designs. Unlike empirical graphics research, a quantitative cognitive modeling approach can provide robust objective predictions using an algorithm that could be incorporated into software for automated graphic design. Quantitative models provide a falsifiable theory of graphical perception and cognition that can be tested empirically by comparing decision time predictions from the model with actual decision times. The next generation of graphics research not only should enhance our understanding of graphical perception and cognition but also provide quantitative predictions that facilitate the objective evaluation of the effectiveness, efficiency and quality of graphic displays. Clearly, models of graphical perception are still in their infancy. Quantitative processing time predictions are for a limited range of graphics within each model domain. Much work remains in extending the basic foundation to an understanding on all of the underlying graphical perception phenomena.

6.6 References

Anderson, J. R. (1983). A spreading activation theory of memory. *Journal of Verbal Learning and Verbal Behavior*, 22, 261-295.

Arnheim, R. (1969). *Visual Thinking*. Berkeley, CA: University of California Press.

Barfield, W., and Robless, R. (1989). The effects of two- or three-dimensional graphics on problem-solving performance of experienced and novice decision makers. *Behaviour and Information Technology*, 8(5), 369-385.

Benbasat, I. and Dexter, A. S. (1985). An experimental evaluation of graphical and color-enhanced information presentation. *Management Science*, 31(11), 1349-1364.

Benbasat, I. and Dexter, A. S. (1986). An experimental evaluation of graphical and color-enhanced information systems under varying time constraints. *Management Information Systems Quarterly*, 10(1), 59-81.

Benbasat, I., Dexter, A. S., and Todd, P. (1986a). The influence of color and graphical information presentation in a managerial decision simulation. *Human-Computer Interaction*, 2, 65-92.

Benbasat, I., Dexter, A. S., and Todd, P. (1986b). An experimental program investigating color-enhanced and graphical information presentation: an integration of the findings. *Communication of the ACM*, 29, 1094-1105.

Bertin, J. (1967). *Sémiologie Graphiques*, (2nd ed.) Paris, France: Gauthier-Villars. [English translation: W. J. Berg, 1983. *Semiology of Graphics*. Madison,

Wisconsin: University of Wisconsin Press].

Bettman, J. R., Johnson, E. J., and Payne, J. W. (1990). A componential analysis of cognitive effort in choice. *Organization Behavior and Human Performance,* (45)1, 111-139.

Boff, K. R. and Lincoln, J. E. (1988) *Engineering Data Compendium: Human Perception and Performance.* AAMRL, Wright-Patterson AFB, OH.

Bovair, S., Kieras, D. E., and Polson, P. G. (1990). The acquisition and performance of text editing skill: A cognitive complexity analysis. *Human-Computer Interaction,* 5, 1-48.

Card, S. K., Moran, T. P., and Newell, A. (1983). *The Psychology of Human-Computer Interaction.* Hillsdale, NJ: Lawrence Erlbaum Associates, Inc.

Card, S. K., Moran, T. P., and Robertson, G. (1992). Remembering Allen Newell. *SIGCHI Bulletin*, 24(4), 22-24.

Carter, L. F. (1947). An experiment of the design of tables and graphs used for presenting numerical data. *Journal of Applied Psychology*, 31(6), 640-650.

Casner, S., and Larkin, J. H. (1989). Cognitive efficiency considerations for good graphic design. Eleventh Annual Conference of the Cognitive Science Society, August 16-19, 1989. University of Michigan, Ann Arbor, MI. Hillsdale, NJ: Lawrence Erlbaum Associates, Publishers, 275-282.

Casner, S., (1991). A task-analytic approach to the automated design of graphic presentations. *ACM Transactions on Graphics*, 10(2), 111-151.

Cavanaugh, J. P. (1972). Relation between the intermediate memory span and the memory search rate. *Psychological Review*, 79, 525-530.

Chuah, M. C., John, B. E., and Pane, J. (1994). Analyzing graphic and textual layouts with GOMS: Results of a preliminary analysis. *CHI'94 Proceedings of the ACM Conference on Human Factors in Computing:* Companion Volume, Boston, MA, May 7-11, 1994. Catherine Plaisant (ed.) New York, NY: ACM Press, 323-324

Christ, R. E. (1975). Review and analysis of color coding research for visual displays. Human Factors, 17(6), 542-570.

Cleveland, W. S. (1984). Graphs in scientific publications. *The American Statistician*, 38, 261-269.

Cleveland, W. S. (1985) *The Elements of Graphing Data.* Monterey, CA: Wadsworth Publishing, first edition.

Cleveland, W. S. and McGill, R. (1984). Graphical perception: theory, experimentation, and application to the development of graphical methods. *Journal of the American Statistical Association*, 79, 531-554.

Cleveland, W. S. and McGill, R. (1985). Graphical perception and graphical methods for analyzing and presenting scientific data. *Science*, 229, 828-833.

Croxton, F. E. (1927). Further studies in the use of circles and bars. *Journal of the American Statistical Association*, 22(157), 36-39.

Croxton, F. E. and Stryker, R. E. (1927). Bar charts versus circle diagrams. *Journal of the American Statistical Association*, 22(160), 473-482.

Daru, M. (1989). The culture of quantitative graphicacy. *Information Design Journal*, 5(3), 191-208.

DeSanctis, G. (1984). Computer graphics as decision aids: directions for research. *Decision Sciences*, 5(3), 463-487.

DeSanctis, G. and Jarvenpaa, S. L. (1989). Graphical presentation of accounting data for financial forecasting: an experimental investigation. *Accounting, Organizations, and Society*, 14(5/6), 509-525.

Dickson, G., Senn, J. A., and Chervany, N. L. (1977). Research in management systems: the Minnesota experiments. *Management Science*, 23, 913-922

Dooley, F. M. and Harkins, L. E. (1970). Functional and attention-getting effects of color on graphic communication. *Perceptual and Motor Skills*, 31, 851-854.

Dwyer, F. M. (1971). Color as an instructional variable. *AV Communication Review*, 19, 399-416.

Ehlers, H. J. (1985). The use of color to help visualize information. *Computing and Graphics*, 9(2), 171-176.

Eells, W. C. (1926). The relative merits of circles and bars for representing component parts. *Journal of the American Statistical Association*, 21 119-132.

Feliciano, G. D., Powers, R. D., and Kearl, B. E. (1963). The presentation of statistical information. *AV Communication Review*, 11, 32-39.

Galitz, W. O. (1985). *Handbook of Screen Format Design.* QED Information Sciences, Inc. Wellesley, MA.

Gillan, D. J. and Lewis, R. (1994). A componential model of human interaction with graphs: I. Linear regression modeling, *Human Factors*, 36(3), 419-440.

Ghani, J., and Lusk, E. J. (1982). The impact of a change in information representation and a change in the amount of information on decision performance.

Human Systems Management, 3, 270-278.

Gray, W. D., John, B. E., and Atwood, M. E. (1993). Project Ernestine: A validation of GOMS for prediction and explanation of real-world task performance. *Human-Computer Interaction*, 8(3), 237-309.

Gremillion, L. L., and Jenkins, M. A. (1981). The effects of color enhanced information presentations. In C. A. Ross (ed.), *Proceedings of the Second International Conference on Information Systems*, December 7-9, Cambridge, MA: ACM Press, 121-134.

Haskell, I. D., and Wickens, C. D. (1993). Two- and three-dimensional displays for aviation: A theoretical and empirical comparison. *International Journal of Aviation Psychology*, 3(2), 87-109.

Hoadley, E. D. (1990). Investigating the effects of color. *Communications of the ACM*, 33(2), 120-125.

Ives, B. (1982). Graphical user interfaces for business information systems. *MIS Quarterly*, special issue, 15-47.

Jarett, I. M. (1983). *Financial reporting using computer graphics*. New York: John Wiley and Sons.

Jarvenpaa, S. L. (1989). The effect of task demands and graphic format on information processing strategies. *Management Science,* 35, 285-303.

Jarvenpaa, S. L. and Dickson, G. W. (1988). Graphics and managerial decision making: research based guidelines. *Communications of the ACM*, 31(6), 764-774.

John, B. E. (1990). Extensions of GOMS analyses to expert performance requiring perception of dynamic visual and auditory information. *CHI'90 Proceedings of the ACM Conference on Human Factors in Computing,* Seattle, WA, Los Alamitos, CA: ACM Press, 107-115.

John, B. E. and Newell, A. (1990). Toward an engineering model of stimulus response compatibility. In R. W. Gilmore and T. G. Reeve (Eds.) *Stimulus-response Compatibility: An Integrated Approach.* North-Holland: New York, NY. 107-115.

Johnson, J. R., Rice, R. R., and Roemmich, R. A. (1980). Pictures that lie: the abuse of graphs in annual reports. *Management Accounting*, 62(4), 50-56.

Joint Committee on Standards for Graphic Presentation. (1915). Preliminary Report. *Journal of the American Statistical Association*, 14, 790-797.

Julesz, B. (1975). Experiments in the visual perception of texture. *Scientific American*, 232(4), 34-43.

Julesz, B. (1981) Textons, the elements of texture perception and their interactions. *Nature*, 290, 91-97.

Kahneman, D., and Henik, A. (1981). Perceptual Organization and attention. In Micheal Kubovy and James R. Pomerantz, editors, *Perceptual Organization*, 181-211; Hillsdale, NJ: Lawrence Erlbaum Associates.

Keen, P. G. W. (1980). MIS Research: Reference disciplines and a cumulative tradition. In *ICIS Conference Proceedings*. Philadelphia, PA. Los Alamitos, CA: ACM Press, 9-18.

Kieras, D. E., and Meyer, D. E. (1994). The EPIC architecture for modeling human information processing and performance: A brief introduction. EPIC Technical Report No. 1 (TR-94/ONR-EPIC-1). University of Michigan, Ann Arbor, MI.

Kieras, D. E., Wood, S. and Meyer, D. E. (1994). Predictive engineering models using the EPIC architecture for a high-performance task. *CHI'95 Proceedings of the ACM Conference on Human Factors in Computing,* Denver, CO, May 7-11, 1995. Katz, I. R., Mack R., and Marks, L. (eds.) New York, NY: ACM Press, 11-18.

Kinney, J. S. and Huey, B. M. (1990). *Application Principles for Multicolor Displays*. Washington, D.C: National Academy Press.

Kleinmuntz, D. N., and Schkade, D. A. (1993). Information displays and decision processes. *Psychological Science,* 4(4), 221-227.

Kolers, P. A., Duchnicky, R. L., and Ferguson, D. C. (1981). Eye movement measurement of readability of CRT displays. *Human Factors*, 23, 517-527.

Kosslyn, S. M. (1983). *Ghosts in the mind's machine*. New York: Norton.

Kosslyn, S. M. (1985). Graphics and human information processing. *Journal of the American Statistical Association*, 80, 499-512.

Kosslyn, S. M. (1989). Understanding charts and graphs. *Applied Cognitive Psychology*, 3, 185-225.

Larkin, J. H., and Simon, H. A. (1987). Why a diagram is (sometimes) worth ten thousand words. *Cognitive Science*, 11, 65-99.

Lee, J. M., and MacLachian, J. (1986). The effects of 3D imagery on managerial data interpretation. *Management Information Systems Quarterly*, 10(3), 257-269.

Legge, G. E., Gu, Y., and Luebker, A. (1989). Efficiency of graphical perception. *Perception and Psychophysics*. 46(4), 365-374.

Lohse, G. L., (1991). A cognitive model for the perception and understanding of graphs. *CHI'91 Conference Proceedings,* New Orleans, LA, April 28 - May 2, 1991. Robertson, S. P., Olson G. M., and Olson J. S. (eds.) Los Alamitos, CA: ACM Press, 131-138.

Lohse, G. L. (1993). A cognitive model for understanding graphical perception, *Human-Computer Interaction,* 8(4), 353-388.

Lohse, G. L. (1995). Designing graphic decision aids: the role of working memory, Working paper, Operations and Information Management Department, The Wharton School of the University of Pennsylvania.

Lucas, H. C. (1981). An experimental investigation of the use of computer-based graphics in decision making. *Management Science*, 27, 757-768.

Lucas, H. C. and Nielsen, N. R. (1980). An experimental investigation of the mode of information presentation on learning and performance. *Management Science*, 26, 982-993.

Lusk, E. J., and Kersnick, M. (1979). Effects of cognitive style and report format on task performance: The MIS design consequences. *Management Science*, 25, 787-798.

Mackinlay, J. D. (1986). Automating the design of graphical presentations of relational information. *ACM Transactions on Graphics*, 5(2), 110-141.

Meyer, D. E., and Kieras, D. E. (1995). A computational theory of human multiple-task performance: The EPIC information-processing architecture and strategic response-deferent model. *Psychological Review*.

Newell, A. and Simon H. (1972). *Human Problem Solving*. Englewood Cliffs, NJ: Prentice Hall.

Olson, J. R. and Nilsen, E. (1988). Analysis of the cognition involved in spreadsheet software interaction. *Human-Computer Interaction*, 3, 309-350.

Olson, J. R. and Olson, G. M. (1990). The growth of cognitive modeling in Human-Computer Interaction since GOMS. *Human-Computer Interaction*, 5, 221-265.

Pinker, S. (1990). A theory of graph comprehension. In R. Freedle, (ed.) *Artificial Intelligence and the Future of Testing*. Hillsdale, NJ: Lawrence Erlbaum Associates.

Powers, M., Lashley, C., Sanchez, P. and Shneiderman, B. (1984). An experimental comparison of tabular and graphic data presentation. *International Journal of Man-Machine Studies*, 20, 533-542.

Remus, W. E. (1984). An experimental investigation of the impact of graphical and tabular data presentations on decision making. *Management Science*, 30, 533-542.

Remus, W. E. (1987). A study of graphical and tabular displays and their interaction with environmental complexity. *Management Science*, 33, 1200-1204.

Riggleman, J. R. (1936). *Methods for presenting business statistics*. McGraw-Hill: New York and London.

Robertson. G. G., Card, S. K., and Mackinlay, J. D. (1993). Information visualization using 3D interactive animation. *Communication of the ACM*, 36(4), 57-71.

Russo, J. E. (1978). Adaptation of cognitive processes to eye movement systems. In J. W. Senders, D. F. Fisher, and R. A. Monty, eds. *Eye Movements and Higher Psychological Functions*, 89-109, Hillsdale, New Jersey: Lawrence Erlbaum Associates.

Schutz, H. G. (1961a). An evaluation of formats for graphic trend displays. *Human Factors*, 3, 99-107.

Schutz, H. G. (1961b). An evaluation of methods for presentation of graphic multiple trends. *Human Factors*, 3, 108-119.

Schwartz, D. R., and Howell, W. C. (1985). Optional stopping performance under graphic and numeric CRT formatting. *Human Factors*, 27, 433-444.

Simkin, D. and Hastie, R. (1987). An information processing analysis of graph perception. *Journal of the American Statistical Association*, 82(398), 454-465.

Spence, I. (1990). Visual psychophysics of simple graphical elements. *Journal of Experimental Psychology: Human Perception and Performance*, 16(4), 683-692.

Spence, I. and Lewandowsky, S. (1991). Displaying proportions and percentages. *Applied Cognitive Psychology*, 5, 61-77.

Stark, L., and Ellis, S. (1981). Scanpath revisited: Cognitive models direct active looking. In D. F. Fisher, R. A. Monty, and J. W. Senders (Eds), *Eye movements, Cognition, and Visual Perception* . Hillsdale, NJ: Lawrence Erlbaum Associates, Inc.

Treisman, A. (1982). Perceptual Grouping and Attention in Visual Search for Features and for Objects. *Journal of Experimental Psychology: Human Perception and Performance*, 8, 194-214.

Treisman, A. (1985). Search asymmetry: a diagnostic for pre-attentive processing of separable features. *Journal of Experimental Psychology: General,* 114(3), 285-310.

Tolliver, D. L. (1973). Color functions in information perception and retention. *Information Storage Retrieval*, 9, 257-265.

Tufte, E. R. (1983). *The Visual Display of Quantitative Information.* Cheshire, Connecticut: Graphics Press.

Tufte, E. R. (1990). *Envisioning Information.* Cheshire, Connecticut: Graphics Press.

Tullis, T. S. (1981). An evaluation of alphanumeric, graphic, and color information displays. *Human Factors*, 25, 657-682.

Tullis, T. S. (1983). The formatting of alphanumeric displays: A review and analysis. Human Factors, 25(6), 657-682.

Tullis, T. S. (1988). Screen Design. In M. Helander (ed.) *Handbook of Human-Computer Interaction.* Amsterdam; New York: North Holland; New York: Elsevier Science Publishers, Inc., 377-411.

Umanath, N. S., and Scamell, R. W. (1988). An experimental investigation of the impact of data display format on recall performance. *Communications of the ACM*, 31, 562-570.

Umanath, N. S., and Scamell, R. W. Das, S. R. (1988). An examination to two screen/report design variables in an information recall context. *Decision Sciences, 21, 216-240.*

Vernon, M. D. (1950). The visual presentation of factual material. *British Journal of Educational Psychology*, 3, 19-23.

Vernon, M. D. (1953). Presenting information in diagrams. *AV Communication Review*, 1, 147-158.

Vernon, M. D. (1962). *The psychology of perception.* London: Penguin.

Vogel, D., Lehman, J., and Dickson, G., (1986). The impact of graphical displays on persuasion: an empirical study. *Proceedings of the Seventh International Conference on Information Systems*, San Diego, 240-254.

Von Huhn (1927). Further studies in graphic use of circles and bars: A discussion of the Eells experiment. *Journal of the American Statistical Association*, 22, 31-36.

Ware, C., and Beatty, J. C. (1988). Using color dimensions to display data dimensions. *Human Factors*, 30(2), 127-142.

Washburne, J. N. (1927). An experimental study of various graphic, tabular, and textual methods of presenting quantitative material. *Journal of Education Psychology*, 18(6), 361-376.

Watson, C. J., and Driver, R. W. (1983). The influence of computer graphics on the recall of information. *Management Information Systems Quarterly*, 7, 45-53.

Welford, A. T. (1973). Attention, strategy, and reaction time: A tentative metric. In S. Kornblum, ed., *Attention and Performance IV*, New York: Academic Press, 37-54.

Yorchak, J. P., Allison, J. E., and Dodd, V. S. (1984). A new tilt on computer generated space situation displays. In Proceedings of the Human Factors Society 28th Annual Meeting. Santa Monica, CA: Human Factors Society, 894-898.

Zmud, R. W. (1978). An experimental investigation of the dimensionality of the concept of information. *Decision Sciences*, 9, 187-195.

Zmud, R. W., Blocher, E., and Moffie, R. P. (1983). The impact of color graphic report formats on decision performance and learning. In *Proceedings of the Fourth International Conference on Information Systems*, 179-193.

Handbook of Human-Computer Interaction
Second, completely revised edition
M. Helander, T.K. Landauer, P. Prabhu (eds.)

Chapter 7

Using Natural Language Interfaces

William C. Ogden and Philip Bernick
New Mexico State University
Las Cruces, New Mexico, USA

7.1 Introduction

A goal of human factors research with computer systems is to develop human-computer communication modes that are both error tolerant and easily learned. Since people already have extensive communication skills through their own native or natural language (e.g. English, French, Japanese, etc.) many believe that natural language interfaces (NLIs) can provide the most useful and efficient way for people to interact with computers.

Although some authors express a belief that computers will never be able to understand natural language (e.g. Winograd and Flores, 1986), others feel that natural language processing technology needs only to advance sufficiently to make general purpose NLIs possible. Indeed, there have been several attempts to produce commercial systems.

The goal for most natural language systems is to provide an interface that minimizes the training required for users. To most, this means a system that uses the words and syntax of a natural language such as English. There is, however, some disagreement as to the amount of "understanding" or flexibility required in the system.

Systems have been proposed that permit users to construct English sentences by selecting words from menus (Tennant et al., 1983). However, Woods (1977) rejects the idea that a system using English words in an artificial format should be considered a natural language system, and assumes that the system should have an awareness of discourse rules that make it possible to omit easily inferred details. In further contrast, Perlman (1984) suggests that "naturalness" be determined by the context of the current application and urges the design of restricted "natural artificial" languages.

Philosophical issues about the plausibility of computers understanding and generating natural language aside, it was widely believed that the number of NLI applications would continue to grow (Waltz, 1983). Since then, work in graphical user interfaces (GUIs) has solved many of the problems that NLIs were expected to solve. As a result, NLIs have not grown at the rate first anticipated, and those that have been produced are designed to use constrained language in limited domains.

Research into NLIs continues, and a frequently asked question is how effective are these interfaces for human-computer communication. The focus of this chapter is not to address the philosophical issues of natural language processing. Rather, it is to review empirical methods that have been applied to the evaluation of these limited NLIs and to review the results of user studies. We have not included the evaluation of speech systems, primarily due to space limitations. Readers interested in speech system evaluations should consult Hirschman et al. (1992), and Goodine et al. (1992).

This discussion of empirical results is also not limited to a single definition of natural language. Instead, it uses the most liberal definition of natural language and looks at systems that seek to provide flexible input languages that minimize training requirements. The discussion is limited to two study categories that report empirical results obtained from observing users interacting with these systems. The first category consists of prototype system studies developed in research environments. These studies have been conducted both in laboratory settings and in field settings. The second category consists of simulated systems studied in the laboratory that are designed to help identify desirable attributes of natural language systems. Before reviewing these studies, some criteria for evaluating NLIs are presented.

7.1.1 Habitability

Habitability is a term coined by Watt (1968) to indicate how easily, naturally, and effectively users can use language to express themselves within the constraints of a system language. A language is considered habitable if users can express everything that is needed for a task using language they would expect the system to understand. For example, if there are 26 ways that a user population would be likely to use to describe an operation, a habitable system will process all 26.

In this review of studies, at least four domains in which a language can be habitable should be considered: conceptual, functional, syntactic, and lexical. Users of a NLI must learn to stay within the limits of all four domains.

***Conceptual*:** The conceptual domain of a language describes the language's total area of coverage, and defines the complete set of objects and the actions covered by the interface. Users may only reference those objects and actions processable by the system. For example, a user should not ask about staff members who are managers if the computer system has no information about managers. Such a system would not understand the sentence:

1. What is the salary of John Smith's manager?

Users are limited to only those concepts the system has information about. There is a difference between the conceptual domain of a language and the conceptual domain of the underlying system. The conceptual domain of a language can be expanded by recognizing concepts (e.g. manager) that exceed the system's coverage and responding appropriately (Codd, 1974), (e.g. "There is no information on managers.") The query could then be said to be part of the language's conceptual domain, but not supported by the system's. However, there will always be a limit to the number of concepts expressible within the language, and users must learn to refer to only these concepts.

***Functional*:** Functional domain is defined by constraints about what can be expressed within the language without elaboration, and determines the processing details that users may leave out of their expressions. While conceptual coverage determines what can be expressed, functional coverage determines how it can be expressed. Natural language allows speakers to reference concepts many ways depending on listener knowledge and context. The functional domain is determined by the number of built-in functions or knowledge the system has available. For example, although a database may have salary information about managers and staff, a natural language interface still may not understand the question expressed in Sentence 1 if the procedure for getting the answer is too complicated to be expressed in one question. For example, the answer to Sentence 1 may require two steps; one to retrieve the name of the manager and another to retrieve the salary associated with the name. Thus, the system may allow the user to get the answer with two questions:

2a. Who is the manager of John Smith?

`System: MARY JONES`

2b. What is the salary of Mary Jones?

With these questions, the user essentially specifies procedures that the system is capable of. The question in Sentence 1 does not exceed the conceptual domain of the language because salaries of managers are available. Instead, it expresses a function that does not exist (i.e. a function that combines two retrievals from one question). Nor is it a syntactic limitation since the system might understand a question with the same syntactic structure as Sentence 1, but that can be answered with a single database retrieval:

3. What is the name of John Smith's manager

Other, more formal, languages vary on functional coverage as well. Concepts like square root can be expressed directly in some languages but must be computed in others. A habitable system provides functions that users expect in the interface language. Since there will be a limit on the functional domain of the language, users must learn to refer to only those functions contained in the language.

Syntactic: The syntactic domain of a language refers to the number of paraphrases of a single command that the system understands. A system that did not allow possessives might not understand Sentence 1, but would understand Sentence 4:

4. What is the salary of the manager of John Smith?

A habitable system must provide the syntactic coverage users expect.

Lexical: The lexical domain of a language refers to words contained in the system's lexicon. Sentence 1 might not be understood if the language does not accept the word "salary" but accepts "earnings." Thus, Sentence 5 would be understood:

5. What are the earnings of the manager of John Smith?

A natural language system must be made habitable in all four domains because it will be difficult for users to learn which domain is violated when the system rejects an expression. A user entering a command like Sentence 1 that is rejected by the system, but does not violate the conceptual domain, might be successful with any of the paraphrases in Sentence 2, 4, or 5. Determining which one will depend upon the functional, syntactic, or lexical coverage of the language. When evaluating the results of user studies, it is important to keep the distinctions between habitable domains in mind.

NLIs attempt to cover each domain by meeting the expectations of the user, and interface habitability is determined by how well these expectations are met. Of course, the most habitable NLI would be one capable of passing a Turing Test or winning the Loebner Prize[1].

It can be difficult to measure the habitability of a language. To determine how much coverage of each domain is adequate for a given task requires good evaluation methods. The next section reviews some of the methodological issues to consider when evaluating natural language interfaces.

7.2 Evaluation Issues

When evaluating the studies presented in this chapter there are several methodological issues that need to be considered: user selection and training, task selection and presentation, so-called Wizard-of-Oz simulations (Kelley, 1984), parsing success rates, and interface customization. Here we present a brief discussion of these issues.

User Selection and Training: Evaluating any user-system interface requires test participants who represent the intended user population. For natural language evaluations, this is a particularly important factor. A language's habitability depends on how well it matches user knowledge about the domain of discourse. Therefore, test participants should have knowledge similar to that held by the actual users in the target domain. Some studies select carefully, but most have tried to train participants in the domain to be tested. It is likely, however, that participants employed for an experiment will be less motivated to use the NLI productively than existing users of the database. On the other hand, a measure of control is provided when participants are trained to have a common understanding of the domain.

Training ranges from a minimal introduction to the domain to extensive training on the interface language that can include instructions and practice on how to avoid common traps. Obviously, the quality of training given to users significantly affects user performance. Therefore, the kind and amount of training users receive should represent the training that users are expected to have with the actual product.

Task Generation and Presentation: The goal of studies designed to evaluate the use of natural language is to collect unbiased user expressions as they are engaged in computer-related tasks. These tasks should be representative of the type of work the user would be expected to accomplish with the interface and be presented in a way that would not influence the form of

---

1.In the 1950's Turing proposed a test designed to challenge our beliefs about what it means to think (Turing, 1950). The Loebner variant involves computer programs with NLIs that have been designed to converse with users (Epstein, 1993). Users do not know whether they are communicating with a computer or another user. Winning the prize involves fooling the users into thinking they are conversing with another human, when, in fact, they are communicating with a computer.

expression. In most studies, tasks are generated by the experimenter who attempts to cover the range of function available in the interface. Letting users generate their own tasks is an alternative method, but results in a reduction of experimenter control. This method also requires that users be motivated to ask appropriate questions.

Experimenter-generated tasks are necessary if actual users are not available or need prior training. These tasks can simulate a hypothesized level of user knowledge and experience by presenting tasks assumed to be representative of questions that would be asked of the real system. The disadvantage of experimenter-generated tasks are that they do not allow for assessment of the language's conceptual habitability because experimenters usually generate only solvable tasks.

User-generated tasks have the advantage of being able to assess the language's conceptual and functional coverage because users are free to express problems that may be beyond the capabilities of the system. The disadvantage of user-generated tasks is that a study's results may not generalize beyond the set of questions asked by the selected set of users; no attempt at covering all of the capabilities of the interface will have been made. Another disadvantage is that actual users of the proposed system must be available.

How experimenter-generated or user-generated tasks are presented to test participants has strong influence on the expressions test participants generate. In an extreme case, participants would be able to solve the task merely by entering the task instructions as they were presented. At the other extreme, task instructions would encourage participants to generate invalid expressions.

Researchers usually choose one of two methods for overcoming these extremes. One method presents the task as a large generally-stated problem that requires several steps to solve. This method not only tests the habitability of the language, but also the problem-solving ability of the participants. Participants are free to use whatever strategy seems natural and to use whatever functions they expect the interface to have. Like user-generated tasks, this method does not allow researcher to test all of the anticipated uses of the system because participants may not ask sufficiently complicated questions.

An alternative method has been used to test more of a system's functions. In this method, participants are given items like tables or graphs, with some information missing, and are then asked to complete these items by asking the system for this missing information. This method gives an experimenter the most control over the complexity of expressions that participants would be expected to enter. However, some expressions may be difficult to represent non-linguistically, so coverage may not be as complete as desired (c.f. Zoeppritz, 1986). An independent measure of how participants interpreted the questions should also be used to determine whether participants understood the task. For example, participants may be asked to do the requested task manually before asking the computer to do it.

Wizard-of-Oz (WOz) Simulations: WOz studies simulate a natural language system by using a human to interpret participants' commands. In a typical experiment a participant will type a natural language command on one terminal that will appear on a terminal monitored by an operator (the Wizard) hidden in another location. The Wizard interprets the command and takes appropriate actions that result in messages that appear on the participant's terminal. Usually the Wizard makes decisions about what a real system would or would not understand. It is likely that the Wizard will not be as consistent in responding as the computer would, and this problem should be taken into account when reviewing these studies. However, WOz simulations are useful for quickly evaluating potential designs.

Evaluation of Parsing Success Rates: An often reported measure of habitability is the proportion of expressions that can be successfully parsed by the language processor returning a result. But studies that report parsing success rates as a global indicator of how well the system is doing assume that all commands are equally complex when they are not (Tennant, 1980).

A high success rate may be due to participants in the study repeating a simple request many times. For example, Tennant observed a participant asking "How many NOR hours did plane 4 have in Jan of 1973," and then repeating this request again for each of the 12 months. This yields 12 correctly parsed questions. On the other hand, another participant trying to get the information from all 12 months in one request had two incorrectly parsed requests before correctly requesting "List the NOR hours in each month of 1973 for plane 4." The second participant had a lower parse rate percentage, but obtained the desired information with less work than the first participant. In fact, Tennant found that successful task solution scores did not correlate with parsing success rates. Therefore, a user's ability to enter allowable commands does not guarantee that they can accomplish their tasks.

Parsing success rates need to be interpreted in light of other measures such as number of requests per task, task solution success, and solution time. Since these measures depend on the tasks users are given, which vary from study to study, it would be inappropriate to compare systems across studies.

Interface Customization: Finally, how a system is customized for the application being evaluated is an important methodological issue. Each NLI requires that semantic and pragmatic information about the task domain be encoded and entered. Evaluation results are significantly affected if researchers capture and enter this information poorly. Since most evaluations have been conducted on systems that were customized by system developers, these systems represent ideally adapted interfaces. However, most operational systems will not have the advantage of being customized by an expert, so performance with the operational system may be worse.

7.3 Evaluations of Prototype and Commercial Systems

The feasibility of the natural language approach is usually shown by building and demonstrating a prototype system prior to delivering it to the marketplace. Very few of these prototype systems have been evaluated by actually measuring user performance. The few that have been evaluated are reviewed here, beginning with a review of evaluations done under controlled laboratory conditions, and followed by a review of field studies.

7.3.1 Laboratory Evaluations

LADDER: Hershman et al. (1979) studied ten Navy officers using LADDER, a natural language query system designed to provide easy access to a naval database. The goal of this study was to simulate as closely as possible the actual operational environment in which LADDER would be implemented. To accomplish this, Navy officers were trained to be intermediaries between a hypothetical decision maker and the computer's database in a simulated search and rescue operation. Officers were given global requests for information and were asked to use LADDER to obtain the necessary information. Training consisted of a 30 minute tutorial session that included a lengthy discussion of LADDER's syntax and vocabulary, followed by one hour of practice that involved typing in canned queries and solving some simple problems. Compared to participants in other studies, these participants were moderately well trained.

Participants were largely successful at obtaining necessary information from the database, and were able to avoid requests for information not relevant to their task. Thus, it seems that participants were easily able to stay within the conceptual domain of the language. Hershman et al, however, report that LADDER parsed only 70.5 percent of the 366 queries submitted. Participants also used twice the number of queries that would have been required by an expert LADDER user. Almost 80 percent of the rejected queries were due to syntax errors. Apparently, LADDER's syntactic coverage was too limited for these moderately trained users. However, a contributing factor may have been the wording of information requests given to the participants. These requests were designed not to be understood by LADDER and this could have influenced the questions typed by the participants.

Hershman et al. concluded that the system could benefit from expanded syntactic and lexical coverage, but that users would still require training. Apparently, the training that was given to participants in this study was adequate for teaching the system's functional and conceptual coverage, but not for teaching its syntactic and lexical coverage.

PLANES: Tennant (1979) conducted several studies of prototype systems and came to similar conclusions. However, Tennant also provides evidence that users have trouble staying within the conceptual limits of a natural language query interface. Tennant studied users of two natural language question answering systems: PLANES and the Automatic Advisor. PLANES was used with a relational database of flight and maintenance records for naval aircraft, and the Automatic Advisor was used to provide information about engineering courses offered at a university. Participants were university students who were unfamiliar with the database domains of the two systems. Participants using PLANES were given a 600-word script that described the information contained in the database. Participants using the Automatic Advisor were only given a few sentences describing the domain. Participants received no other training. Problems were presented either in the form of partially completed tables and charts or in the form of long descriptions or high-level problems that users had to decompose.

Problems were generated either by people familiar with the databases or by people who had received only the brief introduction given to the participants. The purpose of having problems generated by people who had no experience with the system was to test the conceptual completeness of the natural language systems. If all of the problems generated by inexperienced users could be solved, then the system could be considered conceptually complete. However, this was not the case. Tennant does not report statistics, but claims that some of the problems generated by the inexperienced users could not have been solved using the natural language system, and consequently participants were less able to solve these problems than the problems generated by people familiar with the database.

Tennant concluded that the systems were not conceptually or functionally complete and that without extending the conceptual coverage beyond the limits of the database contents, natural language systems would be as difficult to use as formal language systems.

NLC: Other laboratory evaluations of prototype systems have been conducted using a natural language programming system called NLC (Biermann et al., 1983). The NLC system allows users to display and manipulate numerical tables or matrices. Users are limited to commands that begin with an imperative verb and can only refer to items shown on their display terminals. Thus, the user is directly aware of some of the language's syntactic and conceptual limitations.

A study conducted by Biermann et al. (1983) compared NLC to a formal programming language, PL/C. Participants were asked to solve a linear algebra problem and a "grade-book" problem using either NLC or PL/C. Participants using NLC were given a written tutorial, a practice session, the problems, and some brief instructions on using an interactive terminal. Participants using PL/C were given the problems and used a batch card reading system. The 23 participants were just completing a course in PL/C and were considered to be in the top one-third of the class. Each participant solved one of the problems using NLC and the other using PL/C. Problems were equally divided among languages.

Results show that 10 of 12 (83 percent) participants using NLC correctly completed the linear algebra problem in an average of 34 minutes. This performance compared favorably to that of the PL/C group in which 5 of 11 (45 percent) participants correctly completed this problem in an average 165 minutes. For the "grade-book" problem, 8 of 11 (73 percent) NLC participants completed the problem correctly in an average of 68 minutes while 9 of 12 (75 percent) PL/C participants correctly completed the problem in an average of 125 minutes The reliability of these differences was not tested statistically, but it was clear that participants with 50 minutes of self-paced training could use a natural language programming tool on problems generated by the system designers. These participants also did at least as well as similar participants who used a formal language which they had just learned.

The system was able to process 81 percent of the natural language commands correctly. Most of the incorrect commands were judged to be the result of "user sloppiness" and non-implemented functions. Users stayed within the conceptual domain when they were given an explicit model of the domain (as items on the display terminal) and were given problems generated by the system designers. However, users seemed to have difficulty staying within the functional limitation of the system and were not always perfect in their syntactic and lexical performance.

The idea of referring to an explicit conceptual model that can be displayed on the screen is a good one. Biermann et al. also pointed out the necessity of providing immediate feedback via an on-line display to show users how their commands were interpreted. If there was a misinterpretation, it would be very obvious, and the command could be corrected with an UNDO instruction.

In another study of NLC, Fink et al. (1985), examined the training issue. Eighteen participants with little or no computer experience were given problems to solve with NLC. To solve these problems, participants had to formulate conditional statements that the system was capable of understanding. Participants received no training, nor were they given examples of how to express these conditions. In other respects the experimental methodology was the same as Biermann et al. (1983). The following is an example of an allowable conditional statement in NLC.

For i = 1 to 4, double row i if it contains a
positive entry

Fink et al. reported large individual differences in the participants' abilities to discover rules for generating conditional statements. One participant made only one error in solving 13 problems, whereas another participant could not solve any problems. In general, participants made large numbers of errors solving the first few problems and made few errors after discovering a method that worked. These findings support the conclusion that training is required for these kinds of natural language systems.

A Commercial System: Customization can make it difficult to study prototype natural language interfaces. The flexibility of commercial systems demands customization, but a system's usability depends on its natural language processor and on how well the interface has been customized for the application. When usability problems occur, evaluators may have trouble determining whether the natural language processor or the customization is responsible.

Ogden and Sorknes (1987) evaluated a PC-based natural language query product that allowed users to do their own customizing. The evaluation goal was to assess how well a commercially available NLI would meet the needs of a database user who was responsible for customization, but who had no formal query training. The interface was evaluated by observing seven participants as they learned and used the product. They were given the product's documentation and asked to solve a set of 47 query-writing problems. Problems were presented as data tables with some missing items, and participants were asked to enter a question that would retrieve only the missing data.

The interface had difficulty interpreting participants' queries, with first attempts resulting in a correct result only 28 percent of the time. After an average of 3.6 attempts, 72 percent of the problems were answered correctly. Another 16 percent of the problems users thought were correctly answered were not. This undetected error frequency would be unacceptable to most database users.

The results also showed that participants frequently used the system to view the database structure; an average of 17 times for each participant (36 percent of the tasks). This indicates that the system's natural language user needed to have specific knowledge of the database to use the interface. Clarification dialog occurred when the parser prompted users for more information. This occurred an average of 20 times for each participant (42 percent of the tasks). The high frequency of undetected errors, coupled with the frequent need for clarification dialogs, suggests that users were struggling to be understood.

The following is an example of how undetected errors can occur:

* User: How many credits does "David Lee" have?

```
System: count: 2
```

* User: What are the total credits for "David Lee"

```
System: total credits: 7
```

Here the system gives a different answer to paraphrases of the same question. In the first case, the phrase "How many" invoked a count function, and "2" is the number of courses the student took. In the second case, the word "total" invoked a sum function. The system did not contain the needed semantic information about credits to determine that they should be summed in both cases. Thus, to use this system, users would need to know the functional differences between saying "How many..." and "What are the total..." The language was not habitable for the participants in the study who did not know these differences due to limitations in the system's functional coverage. The conclusion is that users need specific training on the functional characteristics of the language and database in much the same way as users of formal languages do. Without this training, users cannot be expected to customize their own language interface.

Harman and Candela (1990) report an evaluation of an information retrieval system's NLI. The prototype system, which used a very simple natural language processing (NLP) model, allowed users to enter unrestricted natural language questions, phrases, or a set of terms. The system would respond with a set of text document titles ranked according to relevance to the question. This system's statistical ranking mechanism considered each word in a query independently. Together these words were statistically compared to the records in an information file. This comparison was used to estimate the likelihood that a record was relevant to the question.

The system contained test data already used by this study's more than 40 test participants. The questions submitted to the system were user-generated and relevant to the participant's current or recent research interests. Nine participants were proficient Boolean retrieval system users, and five others had limited experience. The rest of the participants were not familiar with any retrieval systems. All participants were very familiar with the data contained in the test sets.

Evaluating results from this and other text retrieval systems is problematic in that the measure of success is often a subjective evaluation of how relevant the retrieved documents are, and this makes it impossible to determine how successful the interaction was. However, Harman and Candela report that for a select set of text queries, 53 out of 68 queries (77 percent) retrieved at least one relevant record. The other reported results were qualitative judgments made by Harman and Candela based on the comments of the test participants. Generally, this study's participants found useful information very quickly, and first time users seemed to be just as successful as the experienced Boolean system users. While the study did not test a Boolean system, Harman and Candela point out that, in contrast, first time users of Boolean systems have little success.

Harman and Candela conclude that this type of NLI for information retrieval is a good solution to a difficult Boolean interface. Whereas some queries are not handled correctly by statistically based approaches, such as queries requiring the NOT operator, these problems could be overcome. A study by Turtle (1994) that directly compares results of a Boolean and NLI information retrieval system are reviewed later in this chapter.

Summary: Laboratory studies of natural language prototypes make possible the observation that users do relatively well if they 1) are knowledgeable about the domain or are given good feedback about the domain, 2) are given language-specific training and 3) are given tasks that have been generated by the experimenters. Users perform poorly when 1) training is absent, 2) domain knowledge is limited, or 3) the system is functionally impoverished.

Tennant's studies suggest that user-generated tasks will be much more difficult to perform than experimenter-generated tasks. Since actually using an interface will involve user-generated tasks, it is important to evaluate NLIs under field conditions.

7.3.2 Field Studies

Field studies of prototype natural language systems have focused on learning how the language was used, what language facilities were used, and identifying system requirements in an operational environment with real users working with genuine data. Two of these evaluations (Krause, 1980; Damerau, 1981) are discussed here. Harris (1977) has reported a field test that resulted in a 90 percent parsing success rate, but since no other details were reported the study is hard to evaluate. Three other studies, one that is a field study of a commercial system (Capindale and Crawford, 1990), a second that compares a prototype natural language system with a formal language system (Jarke et al., 1985), and third that describes a field test of a conversational hypertext natural language information system (Patrick and Whalen, 1992) will also be examined.

USL: Krause (1980) studied the use of the User Specialty Language (USL) system for database query answering in the context of an actual application. The USL system was installed as a German Language interface to a computer database. The database contained grade and other information about 430 students attending a German Gymnasium. The users were teachers in the school who wanted to analyze data on student development. For example, they wanted to know if early grades predicted later success. Users were highly motivated and understood the application domain well. Although the amount of training users received is not reported, the system was installed under optimal conditions: by its developers after they interviewed users to understand the kinds of questions that would be asked.

The system was used over a one-year period. During this time, about 7300 questions were asked in 46 different sessions. For each session, a user would come to a laboratory with a set of questions and would use the system in the presence of an observer. Study data consisted of the session logs, observer's notes, and user questionnaires. The observer did not provide any user assistance.

The results reported by Krause come from an analysis of 2121 questions asked by one of the users. Generally, this user successful entered questions into USL. Overall, only 6.9 percent of the user's questions could be classified as errors, and most of these (4.4 percent) were correctable typing errors. Krause attributes part of this low error rate to the observation that the user was so involved in the task and the data being analyzed that there little effort spent to learn more about the USL system. This user may have found some simple question structures that worked well and used them over and over again. This may be very indicative of how natural language systems will be used. It is unclear whether the user actually got the wanted answers since Krause provides no data on this. However, Krause reports two observations that suggest that the user did get satisfactory answers: 1) the user remained very motivated and 2) a research report based on the data obtained with USL was published.

A major finding by Krause was that syntactic errors gave the user more difficulty than semantic errors. It was easier to recover from errors resulting from "which students go to class Y?" if it required a synonym change resulting in "which students attend class Y?" than if it required a syntactic change resulting in "List the class Y students." From these observations, Krause concludes that broad syntactic coverage is needed even when the semantics of the database are well understood by the users.

TQA: Damerau (1981) presents a statistical summary of the use of another natural language query interface called the Transformational Question Answering (TQA) system. Over a one year period, a city planning department used TQA to access a database consisting of records of each parcel of land in the city. Users, who were very familiar with the database, received training on the TQA language. Access was available to users whenever needed via a computer terminal connected to the TQA system. Session logs were collected automatically and consisted of a trace of all the output received at the terminal as well as a trace of system's performance.

The results come primarily from one user, although other users entered some requests. A total of 788 queries were entered during the study year, and 65 percent of these resulted in an answer from the database. There is no way to know what proportion of these answers were actually useful to the users. Clarification was required when TQA did not recognize a word or when it recognized an ambiguous question, and thirty percent of the questions entered required clarification. In these cases, the user could re-key the word or select among alternate interpretations of the ambiguous question.

Damerau also reports instances of users echoing back the system's responses, and this was not allowable input in the version of TQA being tested. The TQA system would repeat a question after transforming phrases found in the lexicon. Thus, the phrase "gas station" would by echoed back to the user as "GAS_STATION." Users would create errors by entering the echoed version. TQA was subsequently changed to echo some variant of what the user entered which would be allowable if entered.

The results reported by Damerau are mainly descriptive, but the researchers were encouraged by these results and reported that users had positive attitudes toward the system. Evaluating this study is difficult because no measures of user-success are available.

INTELLECT: Capindale and Crawford (1990) report a field evaluation of INTELLECT, the first commercial NLI to appear on the market. INTELLECT is a NLI to existing relational database systems. Nineteen users of the data, who had previously accessed it through a menu system, were given a one-hour introduction to INTELLECT. They were then free to use INTELLECT to access the data for a period of ten weeks. Users ranged in their familiarity with the database but were all true end-users of the data. They generated their own questions, presumably to solve particular job-related problems, although Capindale and Crawford did not analyze the nature of these questions. The capabilities and limitations of INTELLECT are summarized well by Capindale and Crawford, who make a special note of Martin's (1985) observation that the success of an INTELLECT installation depends on building a custom lexicon and that "To build a good lexicon requires considerable work" (p. 219). Surprisingly, no mention is made of the effort or level of customization that went into installing INTELLECT for their study. This makes it difficult to evaluate Capindale's and Crawford's results.

Most of the reported results are of questionnaire data obtained from users after the ten week period and are of little consequence to the present discussion except to say that the users were mostly pleased with the idea of using a NLI and rated many of INTELLECT's features highly. Objective data was also recorded in transaction logs which Capindale and Crawford analyzed by defining success as the parse success rate. The parse success rate was 88.5 percent. There was no attempt to determine task success rate as is often the case in field studies.

Comparison to Formal Language: Since no system can cover all possible utterances of a natural language, they are in some sense a formal computer language. Therefore, these systems must be compared against other formal language systems in regard to function, ease of learning and recall, etc. (Zoeppritz, 1986). In a comprehensive field study that compared a natural language system (USL) with a formal language system (SQL), Jarke et al. (1985) used paid participants to serve as "advisors" or surrogates to the principal users of a database. The database contained university alumni records and the principal users were university alumni officers. This could be considered a field study because USL and SQL were used on a relational database containing data from an actual application, and the participants' tasks were generated by the principal users of these data. However, it could also be considered a laboratory evaluation because the participants were paid to learn and use both languages, and they were recruited solely to participate in the study. Unfortunately, it lacked the control of a laboratory study since 1) participants were given different tasks (although some tasks were given to both language groups), and 2) the USL system was modified during the study. Also, the database management system was running on a large time-shared system; response times and system availability was poor and varied between language conditions.

Eight participants were selected non-randomly

from a pool of 20 applicants who, in the experimenter's judgment, represented a homogeneous group of young business professionals. Applicants were familiar with computers, but only had limited experience with them. Classroom instruction was given for both SQL and USL, and each participant learned and used both. Instruction for USL, the natural language system, was extensive and specific, and identified the language's restrictions and strategies to overcome them.

Analysis of the tasks generated by the principal users for use by the participants indicated that 15.6 percent of the SQL tasks, and 26.2 percent of the USL tasks were unanswerable. The proportion of these tasks that exceeded the database's conceptual coverage versus the proportion that exceeded the query language's functional coverage is not reported. Nevertheless, Jarke et al conclude that SQL is functionally more powerful than USL. The important point is, however, that principal users of the database (who knew the conceptual domain very well) generated many tasks that could not be solved by either query language. Thus, this study supports the findings suggested by Tennant (1979); users who know the conceptual domain but who have had no experience with computers, may still ask questions that cannot be answered.

SQL users solved more than twice as many tasks as USL users. Of the fully solvable tasks, 52.4 percent were solved using SQL versus 23.6 percent using USL. A fairer comparison is to look at the paired tasks (tasks that were given to both language groups), but Jarke et al. do not present these data clearly. They report that SQL was "better" on 60.7 percent, that USL was "better" on 17.9 percent and that SQL and USL were "equal" on 21.4 percent of the paired tasks. They do not indicate how "better" or "equal" performance was determined. Nevertheless, the results indicate that it was difficult for participants to obtain responses to the requests of actual users regardless of which language was used. Furthermore, the natural language system tested in this study was not used more effectively than the formal language system.

In trying to explain the difficulty users had with natural language, Jarke et al. cited lack of functionality as one main reason for task failure. Of the solvable tasks, 24 percent were not solved because participants tried to invoke unavailable functions. Apparently, the USL system tested in this study did not provide the conceptual and/or functional coverage that was needed for tasks generated by the actual users of the database.

Many task failures had to do with the system's hardware and operating environment. System unavailability and interface problems contributed to 29 percent of the failures. In contrast, system and interface problems contributed to only 7 percent of the task failures when SQL was used. This represents a source of confounding between the two language conditions and weakens the comparison that can be made. Therefore, little can be said about the advantage of natural language over formal languages based on this study.

It is clear, however, that the prototype USL system studied in this evaluation could not be used effectively to answer the actual questions raised by the principal users of the database. It should be noted that the system was installed and customized by the experimenters and not by the system developers. Thus, a sub-optimal customization procedure might have been major contributor to the system's performance.

COMODA: Patrick and Whalen (1992) conducted a large field test of COMODA, their conversational hypertext natural language information system for publicly distributing information about the disease AIDS to the public. In this test, users with computers and modems could call a dial-up AIDS information system and use natural language to ask questions or just browse.

Whalen and Patrick report that during a two month period the COMODA system received nearly 500 calls. The average call was approximately 10 minutes, and involved an average of 27 exchanges (query-response, request) between the user and the system. Of these, approximately 45 percent were direct natural language queries, and though they provide no specific numbers, Whalen and Patrick report that the system successfully answered many of them.

Users were obtained by advertising in local newspapers, radio, and television in Alberta, Canada. A close analysis of the calls for the final three weeks of data collection was done that evaluated not only those inputs from users that the system could parse, but success rates of system responses. Correct answers were those that provided the information requested by the user or gave a response of "I don't know about that." when no information responding to the request was available. Incorrect responses were those that provided the wrong information when correct information was available, provided wrong information when correct information was not available, a response of "I don't know about that." when correct information was available, or when the query was ambiguous so that a correct answer could not be identified. Whalen and Patrick report a 70 percent correct response rate.

Patrick and Whalen were surprised by the number of requests to browse since the system was designed to enable users to easily obtain information about a particular topic area. However, since topic focus requires knowledge of the domain by a user, and since there is no way for the experimenter to know how knowledgeable users were, the request for browsing might be explained by the novelty of the system, and users' interest in exploring the system in conjunction with learning about the information it contained.

It also isn't clear from the study whether users thought they were interacting with a human or a computer. Previously, Whalen and Patrick have reported that their system does not lead users to believe that they are interacting with a human (Whalen and Patrick, 1989). However, Whalen went on to enter a variant of this system in the 1994 Loebner competition where he took first prize. Though his system fooled none of the judges into thinking it was a human (which is the goal of the competition) he did receive the highest median score of all the computer entrants. An important difference between Whalen's entry and other systems is that it contains no natural language understanding component. Like COMODA it is limited to recognizing actual words and phrases people use to discuss a topic.

The result of this work contributes significantly to the notion that NLP is not an essential component of successful NLIs, and that NLIs are useful for databases other than relational databases.

Summary: Field studies are not usually intended to be generalized beyond their limited application. Only the relative success of the implementations can be assessed. The studies that have been presented offer mixed results. In general, the results of the field studies tend to agree the laboratory study results. If users are very familiar with the database, their major difficulties are caused by syntactic limitations of the language. However, if the system does not provide the conceptual or functional coverage the user expects, performance will suffer dramatically. If this is the case, it appears that training will be required to instruct users about the functional capabilities of the system, and the language must provide broad syntactic coverage. The type of training that is required has not been established.

7.3.3 Natural Language Versus Other Interface Designs

A first issue concerns the question of whether a natural language would really be any better for an interface than a formal artificial language designed to do the same task. The previously discussed studies that compared prototype languages with artificial languages reported mixed results. In the case of a database application, Jarke et al. (1985) showed an advantage for the artificial language, whereas in a programming application Biermann et al. (1983) showed an advantage for the natural language. This section reviews other studies that compare natural and artificial languages.

Small and Weldon (1983) simulated two database query languages using WOz. One language was based on a formal language (SQL) and had a fixed syntax and vocabulary. The other allowed unrestricted syntax and free use of synonyms. However, users of both languages had to follow the same conceptual and functional restrictions. Thus, users of the natural language had to specify the database tables, columns, and search criteria to be used to answer the query. For example, the request "Find the doctors whose age is over 35." would not be allowed because the database table that contains doctors is not mentioned. Thus, a valid request would have been "Find the doctors on the staff whose age is over 35." Because Small and Weldon were attempting to control for the information content necessary in each language, this study compared unrestricted syntax and vocabulary to restricted syntax and vocabulary while trying to control for functional capabilities.

The participant's task was to view a subset of the data and write a query that could retrieve that subset. Although it is unclear how much of the required functional information (e.g. table and column names) was contained in these answer sets, this method of problem presentation may have helped the natural language participants include this information in their requests. Participants used both languages in a counterbalanced order. Ten participants used natural language first and ten participants used the artificial language first. The natural language users received no training (although they presumably were given the names of the database tables and columns) and the artificial language users were given a self-paced study guide of the language. The participants were then given four practice problems followed by 16 experimental problems with each language.

Results showed that there was no difference in the number of language errors between the two languages. It appears that the difficulty the natural language users had in remembering to mention table and column names was roughly equivalent to the difficulty artificial language participants had in remembering to mention the table and column names while following the syntactic and lexical restrictions. The structured order of the formal language must have helped the participants remember to include the column and table names. Thus, it is likely that it was more difficult for the natural language participants to remember to include table and column information than it was for the formal language participants. This analysis is based on the assumption that the participants in the formal language condition made more syntactic and lexical errors than the participants using natural language. However, Small and Weldon only present overall error rates, so this assumption may be incorrect.

The results also show that participants using the structured language could enter their queries faster than those using the natural language, especially for simple problems. Small and Weldon use this result to conclude that formal languages are superior to natural languages. However, the tested set of SQL was limited in function compared to what is available in most implementations of database query languages, and the speed advantage reported for SQL was not as pronounced for more complicated problems. Thus, a better conclusion is that NLIs should provide more function than their formal language counterparts if they are going to be easier to use than formal languages. To provide a flexible syntax and vocabulary may not be enough.

Shneiderman (1978) also compared a natural language to a formal relational query language. However, unlike Small and Weldon (1983), Shneiderman chose not to impose any limits on the participant's use of natural language. Participants were told about a department store employee database and were instructed to ask questions that would lead to information about which department they would want to work in. One group of participants first asked questions in natural language and then used the formal language. Another group used the formal language first and then natural language. In the formal query language condition, participants had to know the structure and content of the database, but in the natural language condition they were not given this information. The results showed that the number of requests that could not be answered with data in the database was higher using natural language than when using formal language. This was especially true for participants in the natural language first condition. This should not be surprising given that the participants did not know what was in the database. However, the result highlights the fact that users' expectations about the functional capabilities of a database will probably exceed what is available in current systems.

In another laboratory experiment, Borenstein (1986) compared several methods for obtaining on-line help, including a human tutor and a simulated natural language help system. Both allowed for unrestricted natural language, but the simulated natural language help system required users to type queries on a keyboard. He compared these to two other traditional methods, the standard UNIX "man" and "key" help system and a prototype window and menu help system. The UNIX help system was also modified to provide the same help texts that were provided by the menu and natural language systems. The participants were asked to accomplish a set of tasks using a UNIX-based system but had only prior experience with other computer systems. As a measure of effectiveness of the help system, Borenstein measured the time these participants needed to complete the tasks.

The results showed that participants completed tasks faster when they had a human tutor to help them, and slowest when they used the standard UNIX help system. But Borenstein found little difference between the modified UNIX command interface, the window/menu system, and the natural language system. Because all of the methods provided the same help texts, Borenstein concluded that the quality of the information provided by the help system is more important than the interface.

Hauptmann and Green (1983) compared a NLI with a command language and a menu-based interface for a program that generated simple graphs. Participants were given hand-sketched graphs to reproduce using the program. The NLI was embedded in a mixed initiative dialog in which the computer or the users could initiate the dialog. Hauptmann and Green report no differences between the three interface styles in the time to complete the task or in the number of errors. However, they do report many usability problems with all three interfaces. One such problem, which may have been a more critical problem for the NLI, was a restrictive order in which the operations could be performed with the system. Also, the NLI was a simple keyword system that was customized based on what may have been a too small of sample. The authors concluded that NLIs may give no advantage over command and menu systems unless they can also overcome rigid system constraints by adding flexibility not contained in the underlying program.

Turtle (1994) also compares a NLI to an artificial language interface. He compared the performance of several information retrieval systems that accept natural language queries to the performance of expert users of a Boolean retrieval system when searching full-text legal materials. In contrast to all other studies described in this section, Turtle found a clear advantage for the NLI.

In Turtle's study, experienced attorneys developed a set of natural language issue statements to represent the type of problems lawyers would research. These natural language statements were then used as input to several commercial and prototype search systems. The top 20 documents retrieved by each system where independently rated for relevance. The issue statements were also given to experienced users of a Boolean query system (WESTLAW). Users wrote Boolean queries and were allowed to iterate each against a test database until they were satisfied with the results. The set of documents obtained using these queries contained fewer relevant ones than those sets obtained by the NLI systems.

This is impressive support for using an NLI for searching full text information, and amplifies the earlier results of Harman and Candela (1990). The weakness of this study, however, is that it did not actually consider or measure user interactions with the systems. There is little detail on how the issues statements were generated and one can only guess as to how different these might have been had they been generated by users interacting with a system.

Another study presents evidence that an NLI interface may be superior to a formal language equivalent. Napier et al. (1989) compared the performance of novices using Lotus HAL, a restricted NLI, with Lotus 1-2-3, a menu/command interface. Different groups of participants were each given a day and a half training on the respective spread-sheet interfaces, and then solved sets of spread-sheet problems. The Lotus HAL users consistently solved more problems than did the Lotus 1-2-3 users. Napier et al. suggest that the HAL users were more successful because the language allowed reference to spread-sheet cells by column names. It should be pointed out that Lotus HAL has a very restricted syntax with English-like commands. HAL does, however, provide some flexibility, and clearly provides more functionality than the menu/command interface of Lotus 1-2-3.

Walker and Whittaker (1989) conducted a field study that compared a menu-based and a natural language database query language. The results they report regarding the usefulness of and problems with a restricted NLI for database access are similar to those of the studies previously summarized (e.g. high task failure rates due to lexical and syntactic errors). An interesting aspect of their study was the finding that a set of users persisted in using the NLI despite a high frequency of errors. Although this set of users was small (9 of 50), this finding suggests the NLI provided a necessary functionality that was not available in the menu system. However, the primary function used by these users was a sort function (e.g. "... by department"). This function is typically found in most formal database languages and may reflect a limitation of the menu system rather than an inherent NLI capability. Walker and Whittaker also found a persistent use of coordination, which suggests another menu system limitation. Coordination allows the same operation on more than one entity at a time (e.g. "List sales to Apple AND Microsoft"), and is also typically found in formal database languages. Thus, it seems that this study primarily shows that the menu system better met the needs of most of the users.

Summary: With the exception of Turtle (1994) and Napier et al. (1989), there is no convincing evidence that interfaces that allow natural language have any advantage over those restricted to artificial languages. It could be effectively argued that some of these laboratory investigations put natural language at a disadvantage. In the Small and Weldon (1983) study, natural language was functionally restricted, and in the Shneiderman (1978) study users were uninformed about the application domain. These are unrealistic constraints for an actual natural language system.

When the NLI provides more functionality than the traditional interface, then clearly —as in the case of Lotus HAL— an advantage can be demonstrated. What needs to be clarified is whether added functionality is inherently due to properties of natural language, or whether it can be engineered as part of a more traditional GUI. Walker (1989) discusses a taxonomy of communicative features that contribute to the efficiency of natural language and suggests, along with others (e.g. Cohen et al, 1989), that a NLI could be combined with a direct manipulation GUI for a more effective interface. The evidence suggests that a well-designed restricted language may be just as effective as a flexible natural language. But what is a well-designed language? The next section will look at what users expect a natural language to be.

7.4 Design Issues

Several laboratory experiments have been conducted to

answer particular design issues concerning NLIs. The remainder of the chapter will address these design issues.

7.4.1 What Is Natural?

Early research into NLIs was based on the premise that unconstrained natural language would prove to be the most habitable and easy-to-use method for people to interact with computers. Later, Chin (1984), Krause (1990), and others observed that people converse differently with computers (or when they believe that their counterpart is a computer) than they do when their counterpart is (or they believe their counterpart to be) another person. For example, Chin (1984) discovered that users communicating with each other about a topic will rely heavily on context. In contrast to this, users who believed they were talking to a computer relied less on context. This result, as well as those of Guindon (1987), suggests that context is shared poorly between users and computers. Users may frame communication based upon notions about what computers can and cannot understand. Thus, 'register' might play an important role in human-computer interaction via NLIs.

Register: Fraser (1993) reminds us that register can be minimally described as a "variety according to use." In human-human conversation, participants discover linguistic and cognitive features (context, levels of interest, attention, formality, vocabulary, and syntax) that affect communication. Combined, these features can be referred to as register. Fraser points out that people may begin communicating using one register, but, as the conversation continues the register may change. Convergence in this context refers to the phenomenon of humans adapting, or adopting the characteristics of each other's speech, in ways that facilitate communication. Fraser suggests that for successful NLIs it is the task that should constrain the user and the language used, not the sublanguage or set of available commands. In other words, it would be inappropriate for a NLI interface to constrain a user to a limited vocabulary and syntax. Rather, users should be constrained in their use of language by the task and domain.

Register refers to the ways language use changes in differing communication situations, and is determined by speaker beliefs about the listener and the context of the communication. Several laboratory studies have been conducted to investigate how users would naturally communicate with a computer in an unrestricted language. For example, Malhotra (1975) and Malhotra and Sheridan (1976) reported a set of WOz studies that analyzed users' inputs to a simulated natural language system. They found that a large portion of the input could be classified into a fairly small number of simple syntactic types. In the case of a simulated database retrieval application, 78 percent of the utterances were parsed into ten sentence types, with three accounting for 81 percent of the parsed sentences (Malhotra, 1975). It seems that users are reluctant to put demands on the system that they feel might be too taxing.

Malhotra's tasks were global, open-ended problems that would encourage a variety of expressions. In contrast, Ogden and Brooks (1983) conducted a WOz simulation study in which the tasks were more focused and controlled. They presented tables of information with missing data, and participants were to type one question to retrieve the missing data. In an unrestricted condition, Ogden and Brooks found that 89 percent of the questions could be classified into one global syntactic category[2]. Thus, participants seem to naturally use a somewhat limited subset of natural language. These results have been replicated by Capindale and Crawford's (1990) study of INTELLECT. Using the same syntactic analysis, they found 94 percent of the questions fell into the same category identified by Ogden and Brooks. Burton and Steward (1993), also using the same method, report 95 percent of the questions to be of the same type.

Ringle and Halstead-Nussloch (1989) conducted a series of experiments to explore the possibilities for reducing the complexity of natural language processing. They were interested in determining whether user input could be channeled toward a form of English that was easier to process, but that retained the qualities of natural language. The study was designed to test whether feedback could be used to shape user input by introducing an alternative to an ordinary human-human conversation model that would maintain users' perception of natural and effective question-and-answer dialogue. Nine college undergraduates who were classified as casual computer users of email and word processors were participants in this study. The task was to use an unfamiliar electronic text processor to edit and format an electronic text file to produce a printed document that was identical to a hard-copy version they had been given. The computer terminal was split into two areas, one for editing an electronic document, and a second dialog window for communicating with a human tutor. Human tutors used two modes of interac-

2. See section 'Restrictions on Syntax' for a description of this type.

tion; a natural mode where tutors could answer questions in any appropriate manner, and a formal mode in which tutors were instructed to simulate the logical formalism of an augmented transition network (ATN). For example, in simulating the ATN, response times should be longer when input was ill formed or contained multiple questions. Each participant had two sessions, one in formal mode, and one in natural mode. Four participants began with formal mode sessions, and five with natural. The study's two measurement factors were tractability (how easily the simulated ATN could correctly parse, extract relevant semantic information, identify the correct query category, and provide a useful reply), and perceived naturalness by the user. Tractability was measured by analyzing and comparing the transcripts of natural versus formal user-tutor dialogs for fragmentation, parsing complexity, and query category. Perceived naturalness was determined by looking at users' subjective assessments of usability and flexibility of natural versus formal help modes.

Of the 480 user-tutor exchanges in the experiment, 49 percent were in the natural mode, and 51 percent in the formal. Dialogue analysis for fragmented sentences found a rate of 21 percent in natural mode versus 8 percent in formal mode. This suggests that feedback in the formal mode may have motivated queries that were syntactically well formed. A five point scale was used for evaluating utterance parsing complexity; 1) could be easily handled by the hypothetical ATN parser; 2) contained some feature (misspelling, sentence fragment, unusual word) that might make parsing difficult; 3) had two or more difficult parsing features; 4) had features that would probably be handled incorrectly; 5) could not be handled at all. Ringle and Halstead-Nussloch report that complexity ratings were significantly lower for formal dialogues than for natural. More interesting are their results that indicate that both group's complexity level fell after the first session. This result was used to suggest that the shaping of user queries accomplished in the first formal session held. Another explanation might be that the difficulties users were having with the system became less complex. Numerical values of the users' subjective evaluations of system usability and usefulness are not given. It is reported that users rated both natural and formal modes very highly, and much higher than users would rate 'conventional' on-line help.

Ringle and Halstead-Nussloch's results seem to support their conclusion that user input can be shaped in ways that could be more tractable for natural language interfaces, though their result would be stronger had their study used an actual ATN system. Further, it appears that differences in register between formal and informal language can be used to effect this shaping. Because their study used so few participants it is difficult to evaluate the claim that the perceived naturalness does not decrease as a result of switching from natural to formal dialog modes. However, the perceived usability of the system did not appear to change for users in this study.

These results are encouraging for the prospect of defining usable subsets for natural language processing. Less encouraging results are provided by Miller (1981). He asked computer-naive participants to write procedural directions intended to be followed by others. They were given six file-manipulation problems and were required to carefully enter into the computer a detailed procedure for solving the problems. Their only restriction was that they were limited to 80 characters of input for each step in the procedure.

The participants in Miller's study did not provide the type of specific information a computer would require to be able to solve the problems. Participants left out many important steps and were ambiguous about others. They were obviously relying on an intelligent listener to interpret what was entered. Different results may have been obtained had the participants been interacting with a simulated computer, and thus, would have been writing instructions intended for the machine instead of for other people. However, the study shows that a true natural language programming environment would need to provide very broad conceptual and functional domains.

Another study that investigated how people naturally express computer functions was conducted by Ogden and Kaplan (1986). The goal of the Ogden and Kaplan study was to observe participants' natural use of AND and OR in the context of a natural language query interface.

Thirty-six participants with word-processing experience, but with little or no database experience, were given an explanation of the general concept of a database and were told that they would be testing a database program that could answer English questions. For each problem, participants were given a table shown on a computer screen. This table consisted of hypothetical student names followed by one or more columns of data pertaining to the student (such as HOMESTATE and MAJOR). Each table contained missing names. The participant was to enter a question that would retrieve the missing names by identifying them using the information in the other columns of the table. Thus, by controlling the information in the additional columns, Ogden and Kaplan controlled the type of set relationships that were to be expressed.

Results showed that participants always used OR correctly to indicate union, but AND was used to indicate both union and intersection. For problems that required union, participants used OR on 60 percent of the problems, used AND on 30 percent and used neither AND nor OR on the remaining 10 percent. On the other hand, participants almost always used AND when they wanted to specify intersection (97 percent). The use of OR to specify intersection was very rare (1 percent). Thus, programs written to accept natural language can safely interpret OR as a logical OR but will need to process additional information to interpret AND correctly.

The data showed that participants tended to use 'and' to conjoin clause groups in the context of union problems, but not in the context of intersection problems. For example, for a union problem, participants would type, "Which students live in Idaho and which major in psychology?" For an intersection problem they would type, "Which students live in Idaho and major in psychology?" In the first case two clauses were conjoined, and in the second case two adverbial phrases were conjoined. Thus, Ogden and Kaplan were able to identify a consistent pattern of using 'and' that could be used to clarify its meaning. Their conclusion was that without training, users would not be able to specify the meaning of 'and' clearly enough for unambiguous natural language processing. Processors will need to be able to recognize an ambiguous 'and' and prompt users to clarify the meaning.

The studies by Malhotra and by Ogden and Brooks suggest that users impose natural restriction on themselves when interacting with a computer while the studies by Miller and by Ogden and Kaplan suggest that natural language is too informal to clearly communicate with the computer. A natural language subset that people would find easy to use seems possible, but formal constraints required for clarity may cause problems. The next sections review work that was designed to understand the restrictions users can be expected to learn.

7.4.2 Restrictions on Vocabulary

Several studies have shown that participants can be effective communicators with a restricted subset of English. For example, Kelly and Chapanis (1977) identified a 300-word vocabulary that allowed participants to communicate as effectively as participants who had an unrestricted vocabulary. Kelly and Chapanis first determined what words were used by unrestricted two-person teams when solving particular problems while communicating via a teletype. They then restricted a subsequent group to the 300 words most commonly used by the unrestricted group and found that the restricted group solved the same set of problems as quickly and as accurately as the unrestricted group. In another set of studies, Ford, Weeks and Chapanis (1980) and Michaelis (1980) encouraged groups of participants to restrict their dialog to as few words as possible and compared their performance to groups who were given no incentive to be brief. They found that the restricted-dialog group performed a problem solving task in less time than the unrestricted group.

While Kelly and Chapanis (1977) used a vocabulary restricted to an empirically determined sub-set, Ogden and Brooks (1983) tested a group of participants who were restricted to a vocabulary defined by an existing database. In this condition, participants had to enter questions using only those nouns contained in the database as table names, column names, or data. The participants were given (and always had available) a list of these nouns that showed the structure of the database. Other verbs, prepositions, articles, etc. were allowed, and no syntactic restrictions were imposed. On the first attempt at solving a new problem, 23 percent of the questions that participants entered contained non-allowed words. It can be concluded that this type of lexical restriction was not very natural. However, by the third attempt at a question, these errors were reduced to 7 percent of the questions entered.

Summary: The findings from restricted lexicon studies support an observation by Krause (1980) that users of USL could recover easily from errors caused by omissions in USL's lexicon. Thus, it can be concluded that users can adapt to a limited vocabulary, especially if it is has been derived on the basis of empirical observations. However, Krause and others (e.g. Hershman, et. al., 1979) provide evidence that users have a difficult time recovering from syntactic errors. The next section reviews work related to this issue.

7.4.3 Restrictions on Syntax

While the studies outlined above show that humans can communicate with each other within a restricted vocabulary, these results may not generalize to restricted human-computer communications. There are, of course, many syntactic constructions in which a restricted vocabulary could be used. However, the evidence cited previously suggests that users could be comfortable using a restricted-English syntax (Malhotra, 1975; Malhotra and Sheridan, 1976; Ogden and Brooks, 1983).

Hendler and Michaelis (1983) followed a methodology similar to Kelly and Chapanis (1977) to study the effects of restricted syntax natural language dialog. Participant pairs were to solve a problem by communicating with each. Communication was effected by entering messages into a computer terminal. One participant pair group was allowed unrestricted communication while another group had to follow a limited context-free grammar. This grammar was selected to be easily processed by a computer. The restricted group were told to use a limited grammar, but was not told what the grammar rules were. Each group received three problems in a counterbalanced order. The results showed that the restricted participant pairs took longer to solve the problems than the unrestricted participants in Session 1, but that this difference went away in Sessions 2 and 3. It appears that these participants adapted to the restricted syntax after solving one problem.

Ogden and Brooks (1983) also imposed a syntactic restriction on a group of 12 participants entering questions into a simulated query language processor. They imposed a context-free pragmatic grammar where the terminal symbols of the grammar referred to attributes of the database. The grammar restricted users to questions that first allowed for an optional action phrase (e.g. "What are..." or "List...") followed by a required phase naming a database retrieval object (e.g. "...the earnings...") which could optionally be followed by any number of phrases describing qualifications (e.g. "...of the last two years"). Unlike the participants in the Hendler and Michaelis study, participants were informed of the constraints of the grammar and were given several examples and counter-examples of allowable sentences.

Results showed that 91 percent of the first attempts at a question were syntactically correct, and this improved to 95 percent by the third attempt. Participants had the most trouble avoiding expressions with noun adjectives (e.g. "Blue parts" instead of "Parts that are blue"). These results are limited in that the syntactic constraints were not very severe, but they do suggest that users can control input based on these types of instructions.

Jackson (1983) imposed a set of syntactic restrictions on participants who were using a command language to perform a set of computer tasks. Each task involved examining and manipulating newspaper classified ads stored and displayed by the computer. Participants were given a description of a function the computer was to perform. They were then told to enter commands having a single action and a short description of the objects to be acted upon. For half of the participants, commands were to be constructed in an English-like order with an action followed by an object description (e.g. "Find the VW ads"). The other participants were asked to reverse the order and specify the object first followed by an action (e.g. "VW ads find"). It was hypothesized that the more natural English-like action-object construction would be easier to enter than the unnatural object-action construction.

Commands were collected from 30 experienced and 30 inexperienced computer users who were fully informed about the syntactic restriction. Comparisons between the two conditions were made on the basis of the command entry time. Experienced users were faster than inexperienced users, but both groups could enter object-action commands as quickly as action-object commands. This suggests that the experience of using natural English does not transfer to learning and using a computer command language. It also suggests that the experience of using an action-object command language (the experienced group) does not negatively transfer to learning and using an object-action command language. Syntax does not seem to matter for constrained languages like this.

Jackson also reports that users had little difficulty generating constrained commands that had only one action and noun phrase while leaving out common syntactic markers like pronouns. The participants had more trouble including all the necessary information in their requests than they did in getting the words in a particular order. Participants tended to leave information out of commands that could be inferred from context. Over half (53 percent) of the initial commands omitted the type of object from the object's description. For example, participants would enter "Find VW" instead of "Find VW ads." The language was not habitable because of functional limitations; the language processor could not infer object types.

Burton and Steward (1993) also analyzed the use of ellipsis, (e.g., asking "Pens?" after asking "How many pencils?") and compared it to an NLI with a feature that allowed the previous question to be edited and re-submitted. When participants had both features available, re-editing a previous query was chosen twice as often as using ellipsis. However, an interface with both features seemed to be harder to use than an interface that had only one. They reported few differences in success rates when using either the ellipsis or edit interfaces.

Summary: The results of these laboratory studies of syntactic restrictions suggest that people adapt rapidly to these types of constraints when interacting with a computer. None directly investigated the observation that syntactic errors are hard to correct, although the Ogden and Brooks study indicates an ability to recover. However, in the language they tested, specific syntactic errors could be detected by the computer, and error messages could indicate specific solutions to the participants who were fully informed about the syntactic restrictions of the language. The issue of feedback is discussed in a later section. However, Jackson's findings suggest that functional restrictions will be harder to adapt to than syntactic restrictions. The next section looks at this issue.

7.4.4 Functional Restrictions

Omitting information that can be inferred from context has been referred to as a functional capability of natural language. A habitable language will be able to infer information that users leave out of their natural language. At issue is the match between the user's expectations and the language's capabilities. Either users must be taught the language's capabilities, or the language must be customized to provide capabilities users expect. The customization issue is reviewed in a later section. This section will look at the user's ability to learn and adapt to functional limitations.

In a follow-up study based on the Ogden and Brooks methodology, Ogden designed a functionally limited natural language query system and attempted to teach computer-inexperienced participants the limitations of the language. Twelve participants were told to follow the restricted grammar described by Ogden and Brooks (see above), but participants also had to include all needed references to existing database attributes. For example, the request, "Find the salary of David Lee.", would need to be rephrased as, "Find the salary of the employee named David Lee." and the request, "List the courses which are full.", would need to be rephrased as "List the courses whose size equals its limit." This is similar to the restriction imposed by Small and Weldon (1983).

Participants were fully informed of the restrictions and were given several examples and counter-examples of allowable questions. They were also given the necessary database information and always had it available while entering questions.

The results showed that it was difficult for participants to learn to express the needed database functions using natural language. Particularly difficult were expressions that required calculations, especially when they had common synonyms that were not allowed (e.g. "... a 10 percent raise..." vs. "...salary times 1.1..."). Further, expressions that required identifying necessary data relationships were usually left out (e.g. "...staff ID is equal to salesman ID..."). The total percent error rate for this condition was 29 percent on participants' first attempts. This was much worse than for the syntactic restriction reported by Ogden and Brooks (9 percent). The results indicated that participants have a difficult time recovering from these errors as well (19 percent errors on the third attempt).

Summary: These results are consistent with previously reported findings: it may be difficult for people using natural language to be specific enough for the system to clearly understand them. (e.g. Jackson, 1983; Miller, 1981; Ogden and Kaplan, 1986). Next, studies that use feedback to help the user understand system limitations are examined.

7.4.5 Effects of Feedback

Zolton-Ford (1984) conducted a WOz simulation study that examined the effects of system feedback on the participants' own input. Zolton-Ford systematically varied two system feedback characteristics; the vocabulary used (high frequency or low frequency) and the system feedback phrase length (complete sentences or only verbs and nouns). Two input characteristics were also varied: the communication mode (keyboard or voice) and the amount of restriction placed on participants' language (restricted to phrases matching the system's feedback language, or unrestricted). Zolton-Ford's question was to what extent would the participants imitate the system's feedback language. The participants in the restricted condition were not informed of the restrictions they were to follow. Instead, to introduce participants to the system's communication style and to the functions available in the system, all participant groups were guided by the program during the initial portion of their interactions. Participants were asked to solve 30 problems concerning input, update, and retrieval functions of an imaginary inventory database.

Results showed that the restricted participants generated significantly more output-conforming entries than did unrestricted participants. This was especially true when the feedback language was simple (verbs and nouns) rather than complex (complete sentences). System message word frequency had no effect. Zolton-Ford suggested the following design criteria:

1. Provide a consistently worded program feedback because users will model it.
2. Design the program to communicate with tersely phrased outputs because users will be able to more easily model it than more verbose outputs.
3. Include error messages that reiterate the vocabulary and syntax that is understood by the program because users will alter their vocabulary and syntax to be like those provided in the error messages.

Support for Zolton-Ford's conclusion comes from a study reported by Slator et al. (1986). Slator et al. used a WOz simulated NLI to an existing software package that produced computer-generated graphs to measure the effects of feedback. Participants were asked to construct a graph by entering English commands. The Wizard interpreted and entered translated commands into the graphics package. Participants were divided into two feedback groups. The control group received no feedback other than the feedback that resulted from changes in the graph. The feedback group saw the translated commands entered by the experimenter. Results show that the feedback group made significantly fewer semantically ambiguous utterances than did the control group (7.9 percent and 22.4 percent, respectively). According to Slator et al., the reason the feedback group did so much better was that they began to imitate the feedback. They provide this example:

Participant: For X axis lable only every tenth year.

Which is translated to a computer command (ignoring the misspelled word "label")

```
Feedback: XAXIS MAJOR STEP 10
```

The participant immediately recognizes a shorter way to say what was wanted which is reflected in the next statement.

Participant: Y axis major step 2000.

Just as in the Zolton-Ford study, the users modeled the system's output. Slator et al. also suggest that by showing the formal-language translations of the natural language input, users will more quickly learn an abstract system model that will help them understand how to use the computer. Of course, this depends on how well the formal language reflects the underlying system model. The formal language design must be coherent or users may have trouble imitating it.

Summary: It is clear from these two studies that feedback in a NLI will strongly influence user performance with the system. Feedback should be formed to reflect the simplest input language acceptable to the system. Certainly another role for feedback is to let users know how their input was interpreted by the interface. This has been the recognized role of feedback in many systems. These two studies suggest that training may be a more important role for feedback in natural language systems.

7.4.6 Empirically Derived Grammars

An important issue for NLIs is the effort required to install a new application. Each application of a natural language interface will require encoding semantic and pragmatic information about the task domain and the users' linguistic requirements in that domain. For most prototype systems, a great deal of effort is required to capture, define, and enter this information into the system. This customization process requires a person who knows how to acquire the information and how to translate it into a form usable by the natural language program. Very little research has been conducted to investigate methods for collecting the necessary application data so it could be used to customize the interface. Customization is important because the functional capabilities of the end-user interface will be determined by how well the domain-specific linguistic information is gathered and encoded. The following two studies described an approach to building domain-specific information into the system. These studies started with systems with no linguistic capability and used WOz simulations to demonstrate how domain-specific information could be empirically derived and incorporated into a natural language program.

Kelley (1984) developed a NLI to an electronic calendar program using an iterative design methodology. In the first phase, participants used a simulated system whose linguistic capabilities were totally determined by the Wizard simulating the system. Then the inputs collected during the first phase were used to develop language processing functions, and 15 additional participants used the program. During this phase, the Wizard would intervene only when it was necessary to keep the dialog going. After each participant, new functions were added to the language that would make it possible to process the inputs whenever an input required operator intervention. Care was taken to prevent new changes from degrading system performance. Finally, as a validation step, six more participants used the program without experimenter intervention.

Kelley used a widely diverse participant population, and most had very limited computer experience. They were given a brief introduction on using the display terminal and were then asked to enter whatever appointments they had over the next two weeks. They were specifically asked to enter at least ten appointments and were prodded by the experimenter during the course of their work only if they failed to exercise storage, retrieval and manipulation functions against the database on their own.

System performance improved rapidly during the intervention phase. The growth of the lexicon and new functions reached an asymptote after only ten participants (iterations). During the validation phase, participants correctly stored 97 percent of the appointments entered. Other interpretation errors occurred, but either the user or the system was able to recognize and correct them. Even if these corrected errors are included, participants were understood 84 percent of the time.

The data suggest that the system provided an interface that was easy to use for novice computer users. The input language covered by this "empirically derived" grammar is very distant from grammatical English. A typical input to this system was:

remind me 8/11/82 send birthday card to mama

This finding provides further support for Slator et al.'s (1986) conclusion that users care more about brevity than grammatical correctness.

The quickness by which most of the lexicon and phrase structures could be captured indicates that the users in the study had a clear and homogeneous knowledge of the application domain. An important issue is whether this technique would work as well in wider domains, for example, those domains covered by most databases. The following study can be used to address this issue. It uses the same technique as Kelley in an electronic mail application domain.

Good et al. (1984) conducted a study similar to Kelley (1984), but with five important differences. First, the Wizard intervened only when the input was judged to be simple enough to be parsed, and error messages were sent to the participants when it was not. Second, the initial prototype system was based on existing mail systems, not on a user-defined system as it was in the Kelley study. Third, the system was not modified after each iteration, but only at periodic intervals. Fourth, Good et al. presented a fixed set of tasks whereas Kelley's tasks were user-generated. Fifth, Good et al. used 67 participants during the iterative development phase compared to the 15 participants used in the Kelley study. Despite the differences, the results were similar. Good et al. focus the discussion of their results on the improvement in parse rate obtained from changes made to the system based on user input. The initial performance of the system could only parse 7 percent of the commands issued by users, but after 67 participants and 30 changes to the software, 76 percent of the commands could be parsed. The study does not report all the data, but participants were not able to complete all of the tasks with the initial system but were able to complete all of them within one hour with the final system.

Summary: It is difficult to compare the results obtained by Kelley to those obtained by Good et al. Kelley reports a better parse rate with fewer iterations, but the task sets given and the amount of modification done to the system may have been quite different. What can be generally concluded is that user-defined systems can be created that will allow users to get work done in a natural way without any training or help.

7.5 Design Recommendations

Two things people must learn in order to use any system are 1) the system's capabilities, and 2) a language to invoke those capabilities. With formal computer languages, people learn the capabilities of the system as they learn the language. With natural language, they are spared the burden of learning the formal language and consequently lose an opportunity to learn the capabilities of the system. The evidence presented here suggests that users have difficulties with natural language systems when they either have not had enough experience to know what the capabilities of the system are, or the system has not been built to anticipate all of the capabilities users will assume. People tend to enter incomplete requests (e.g. Miller, 1981; Jackson, 1983) or attempt to invoke functions the system does not have (e.g.: Jarke et al., 1985; Ogden and Sorknes, 1986; Tennant, 1979).

There are two approaches to correcting this mismatch between users' expectations and the system's capabilities. The first approach can be considered an artificial intelligence approach. Its goal is to provide a habitable system by anticipating all of the capabilities users will expect. It requires extensive interface program customization for each application domain. Unfortunately, the methods for collecting and integrating domain-specific information have not been well developed or tested. For large domains, like database applications where the pragmatic and semantic information is often complex, customization methods have been proposed (e.g. Grosz et al., 1987; Hass and Hendrix, 1980; Hendrix and Lewis, 1981; Manaris and Dominick, 1993), but these methods have not been empirically evaluated. It is clear, however, that as the complexity of the NLP system increases, users' expectations for the system increase, as do the difficulties involved with customizing the system for other domains. For systems based on very simple NLP techniques, like statistically-based full text retrieval systems, the customization problem becomes much simpler or at least more well defined.

For smaller domains, the procedures used by Kelley (1984) and Good et al. (1984) are promising. The disadvantage of their approach is that the solution is not guaranteed. The performance of the system will depend on the availability of representative users prior to actual use, and it will depend on the installer's abilities to collect and integrate the relevant information.

The second approach might be considered a human engineering approach. It depends on more training for the users, coupled with an interface language whose capabilities are more apparent. The primary goal of this approach is to develop a system that allows users to develop a consistent conceptual model of the system's domain so they will understand the system's capabilities. One aspect of a more apparent language is the use of feedback. Zolton-Ford (1984) and Slator et al. (1986) have shown the effectiveness of feedback in shaping a user's language. Another example of the use of feedback and an apparent language model is provided by the NLC system described by Biermann et al. (1983). Extreme examples of this interface type are systems that provides natural language in menus (Tennant et al., 1983; Mueckstein, 1985). The disadvantage of this second approach is that users will need to be trained. To keep this training to a minimum (i.e., less than what would be required for an artificial language), the language should provide more function than would be provided by an artificial language. Thus, domain-specific information would still need to be collected and integrated into the interface.

The solution lies in a combination of artificial intelligence and human engineering approaches. The following set of recommendations represents a synthesis of these two approaches based on the results of the reviewed user studies. The recommendations concern the design and development of NLIs, but could easily apply to the design of any user-system interface.

Clearly Define an Application Domain and User Population: It would be desirable to offer a list of characteristics that could describe the users and the domains best suited for natural language technology. However, there has been far too little work done in this area to provide this guidance. What is certain, however, is that NLIs can be built only when the functional and linguistic demands of the user can be determined. Therefore the domain and user population must be well defined.

Plan for an Incremental Adaptation Period: It is recommended that application-specific linguistic information be gathered empirically and that the system be designed to easily accept this type of data. Representative users should be asked to use the interface language to generate data for system customization. The system must be built to incorporate incremental changes reflecting use over a period of time. There is no evidence to suggest how long this period may be. Methods for collecting and integrating domain-specific information need to be established. The verdict is still out on whether these systems can be installed and customized for a new application by people other than the system developers.

Provide Access to Meta-Knowledge: The data that have been reviewed here suggest that the most difficult problem people have when using natural language interfaces is staying within the language's conceptual and functional limitations. Because users are not required to learn a formal language, there is less opportunity to learn the capabilities of the system. Systems must therefore provide mechanisms that allow users to interrogate the system for its knowledge. Few of the reviewed prototype systems provide this kind of mechanism.

Provide Broad (or Well-Defined) Syntactic Coverage: Evidence obtained from user evaluations of prototype systems suggest that a primary problem for users is limited syntax, whereas laboratory experiments suggest that people can adapt fairly rapidly to some syntactic restrictions, especially when the restrictions can be defined. More studies should be conducted to investigate the possibility that broader syntactic coverage will encourage users to expect even more coverage. Current findings suggest that the broader the syntactic coverage, the better.

Provide Feedback: Feedback in a NLI can have two functions. One is to play-back the user's expression in a paraphrase or visible system response to demonstrate how it was interpreted. Another is to show the user the underlying system commands to inform the user of a more concise expression. Evidence strongly suggests that users will echo the feedback's form so paraphrases should be constructed to be allowable as input expressions. Concise feedback should be provided for training purposes if the syntactic coverage is very limited. Visible system responses as well as concise paraphrases should be provided where possible. In database queries, concise paraphrases may be ambiguous, so in this case, long unambiguous expressions should be used. Nevertheless, they should be constructed as allowable system input.

7.6 Conclusion

No attempt has been made to identify characteristics of specific technologies used in the various natural language systems that contribute to usability. Thus, no conclusions can be made for or against any particular natural language technology. This is not to imply that differences in technology are not important. They certainly are. But the focus has been to review the existing empirical evidence of how NLIs are used.

The evidence gathered with existing natural language prototypes and products does not provide an encouraging picture. There has been just one well documented case of a single user having success working with a NLI on self-generated questions in an actual application (Krause, 1980). Damerau's (1981) results may or may not be taken as an example of successful use. The other successes (Biermann et al., 1983; Hershman et al., 1979) can be attributed to well-designed experimental tasks and trained users. More studies show users having problems when tasks are user-generated, or when users have not had extensive experience with the task domain or with the system's capabilities (Jarke et al., 1985; Ogden and Sorknes, 1986; Tennant, 1979). Experience with prototype systems suggests that much more research needs to be done.

From the experimental studies, it is clear that users do not need and do not necessarily benefit from grammars based on natural language. When communicating with a computer, users want to be as brief as possible. These studies suggest that users will benefit from a natural language system's ability to provide broader conceptual and functional coverage than that provided with an artificial language. The use of synonyms and the ability to leave out contextual information (ellipsis) would seem to provide the most benefit. However, to provide this coverage requires the collection of application domain-specific information. How this information is gathered and represented will determine the usability of the NLI. The methods for accomplishing this are not well established, and, in the eight years since this review appeared in the first edition of the Handbook of Human Computer interaction, these methods are still not forthcoming. There is no doubt that with enough hard work and iteration, good NLIs can be developed that provide the usability enhancements we expect. Given that the most impressive recent NLI successes have been in text-based information retrieval applications, the key may lie in using simple models of NLP resulting in simpler domain customization methods. For example, statistically-based text retrieval systems have well specified indexing methods for acquiring the linguistic domain knowledge required by the system. This may represent the most important area for further research into NLIs.

7.7 Acknowledgments

The authors are indebted to comments from an anonymous reviewer and Rhonda Steele on earlier drafts of this chapter.

7.8 References

Biermann, A.W., Ballard, B.W., and Sigmon, A.H. (1983). An experimental study of natural language programming. *International Journal of Man-Machine Studies*, 18, 71-87.

Borenstein, N.S. (1986). Is English a natural language. In K. Hopper and I.A. Newman (Eds.), *Foundation for Human-Computer Communication*, (pp. 60-72). North-Holland: Elsevier Science Publishers B.V.

Burton, A. and Steward, A.P. (1993). Effects of Linguistic Sophistication on the Usability of a Natural Language Interface. *Interacting with Computers*, 5 (1), 31-59.

Capindale, R.A., and Crawford, R.O. (1990). Using a

Natural Language Interface with Casual Users. *International Journal of Man-Machine Studies*, 20, 341-361.

Chin, D. (1984). An Analysis of Scripts Generated in Writing Between Users and Computer Consultants. In *National Computer Conference*, (pp. 637-642).

Codd, E.F. (1974). *Seven steps to RENDEZVOUS with the casual user* (IBM Research report J1333). San Jose, CA: San Jose Research Laboratory, International Business Machines Corporation.

Cohen, P.R., Sullivan, J.W., Dalrymple, M., Gargan, R.A., Moran, D.B., Schlossberg, J.L., Pereira, F.C.N., Tyler, S.W. (1989) Synergistic Use of Direct Manipulation and Natural Language. In *Proceedings of CHI'89*: (pp. 227-232). New York: Association for Computing Machinery.

Damerau, F.J. (1981). Operating statistics for the transformational question answering system. *American Journal of Computational Linguistics*, 7, 30-42.

Epstein, R. (1993). *1993 Loebner Prize Competition in Artificial Intelligence: Official Transcripts and Results*. Technical Report, Cambridge Center for Behavioral Studies.

Fink, P.K., Sigmon, A.H. and Biermann A.W. (1985). Computer control via limited natural language. *IEEE Transactions on Systems, Man, and Cybernetics*, 15, 54-68.

Ford, W.R., Weeks, G.D. and Chapanis, A. (1980). The effect of self-imposed brevity on the structure of didactic communication. *The Journal of Psychology*, 104, 87-103.

Fraser, N.M. (1993). Sublanguage, Register and Natural Language Interfaces. *Interacting with Computers*, 5 (4) 441-444.

Good, M.D., Whiteside, J.A., Wixon, D.R., and Jones, S.J. (1984). Building a user-derived interface. *Communications of the ACM*, 27, 1032-1043.

Goodine, D., Hirschman, L, Polifroni, J., Seneff, S. and Zue, V. (1992). Evaluating Interactive Spoken Language Systems. In *Proceedings of ICSLP-92* (Vol. 1, pp. 201-204). Banff, Canada.

Grosz, B.J., Appelt, D.E., Martin, P.A., and Pereira, F.C.N. (1987). TEAM: An experiment in the design of transportable natural-language interfaces. *Artificial Intelligence*, 32, 173-243.

Guindon, R. (1987) Grammatical and ungrammatical structures in user-adviser dialogues: evidence for sufficiency of restricted languages in natural language interfaces to advisory systems. In *Proceedings of the 25th ACL*: (pp. 41-44). Stanford University.

Harman, D. and Candela, G. (1990) Bringing Natural Language Information Retrieval Out of the Closet. *ACM SIGCHI Bulletin* 22 (1), 42-48.

Harris, L.R. (1977). User-oriented database query with ROBOT natural language query system, *International Journal of Man-Machine Studies*, 9, 697-713.

Hass, N. and Hendrix, G. (1980). An approach to acquiring and applying knowledge. *First National Conference on Artificial Intelligence* (235-239). American Association for Artificial Intelligence.

Hauptman, A.G. and Green, B.F. (1983). A comparison of command, menu-selection and natural-language computer programs. *Behaviour and Information Technology*, 2 (2) 163-178.

Hendler, J.A. and Michaelis, P.R. (1983). The effects of limited grammar on interactive natural language. In *Proceedings of CHI '83. Human Factors in Computing Systems* (pp. 190-192). New York: Association for Computing Machinery.

Hendrix G. and Lewis W. (1981). Transportable natural language interfaces to databases. In *Proceedings of the Annual Meeting of the Association for Computational Linguistics*. (pp. 159-165). Menlo Park: Association for Computational Linguistics.

Hershman, R.L., Kelly, R.T., Miller, H.G. (1979). *User performance with an natural language query system for command control* (Technical Report NPRDC-TR-797). San Diego, California: Navy Personnel Research and Development Center.

Hirschman L., et al. (1992). Multi-Site Data Collection for a Spoken Language Corpus. In *Proceedings of ICSLP-92* (Vol. 2, pp. 903-906). Banff, Canada.

Jackson, M.D. (1983). Constrained languages need not constrain person/computer interaction. *SIGCHI Bulletin*, 15(2-3), 18-22.

Jarke, M., Turner, J.A., Stohr, E.A., Vassiliou, Y., White, N.H., and Michielsen, K. (1985). A Field evaluation of natural-language for data-retrieval. *IEEE Transactions on Software Engineering*, 11, 97-114.

Kelley, J.F. (1984). An iterative design methodology for user-friendly natural-language office information applications. *ACM Transactions on Office Information Systems*, 2, 26-41.

Kelly, M.J., and Chapanis, A. (1977). Limited vocabulary natural language dialog. *International Journal of*

Man-Machine Studies, 9, 479-501.

Krause, J. (1980). Natural language access to information systems. An evaluation study of its acceptance by end users. *Information Systems*, 5, 297-319.

Malhotra, A. (1975). *Design Criteria for a Knowledge based English Language System for Management: An Experimental Analysis*, (Project MAC Report TR146). Cambridge MA: Massachusetts Institute of Technology.

Malhotra, A. and Sheridan, P.B. (1976). *Experimental determination of design requirements for a program explanation system* (IBM Research report RC 5831). Yorktown Heights, NY: International Business Machines Corporation.

Martin, J. (1985). *Fourth Generation Languages*, vol. 1, Principles. Englewood Cliffs: Prentice-Hall Inc.

Michaelis, P.R. (1980). Cooperative problem solving by like and mixed-sex teams in a teletypewriter mode with unlimited, self-limited introduced and anonymous conditions. *JSAS Catalog of Selected Documents in Psychology*, 10, 35-36 (Ms. No. 2066).

Miller, L.A., (1981). Natural language programming: Styles, strategies, and contrasts. *IBM Systems Journal*, 20, 184-215.

Mueckstein, E.M. (1985). Controlled natural language interfaces: *The best of three worlds. In Proceedings of CSC '85: ACM Computer Science Conference* (pp. 176-178). New York: Association for Computing Machinery.

Napier, H.A., Lane, D., Batsell, R.R., and Guadango, N.S. (1989). Impact of a Natural Language Interface on Ease of Learning and Productivity. *Communications of the ACM*, (pp. 1190-1198). 32 (10). New York: Association for Computing Machinery.

Ogden, W.C. and Brooks, S.R. (1983). Query languages for the casual user: Exploring the middle ground between formal and natural languages. In *Proceedings of CHI '83: Human Factors in Computing Systems* (pp. 161-165). New York: Association for Computing Machinery.

Ogden, W.C. and Kaplan, C. (1986). The use of AND and OR in a natural language computer interface. In *Proceedings of the Human Factors Society 30th Annual Meeting*, (pp. 829-833). Santa Monica CA: The Human Factors Society.

Ogden, W.C. and Sorknes A. (1987). What do users say to their natural language interface? In *Proceedings of Interact'87 2nd IFIP conference on Human Computer Interaction*. Amsterdam: Elsevier Science.

Patrick, A.S. and Whalen, T.E. (1992). Field Testing a Natural Language Information System: Usage Characteristics and Users' Comments. *Interacting with Computers*, 4(2), 218-230.

Perlman, G. (1984). Natural artificial languages: low level processes. *International Journal of Man-Machine Studies*, 20, 373-419.

Ringle, M.D., and Halstead-Nussloch, R. (1989). Shaping User Input: A Strategy for Natural Language Dialog Design. *Interacting with Computers*, 1 (3), 227-44.

Shneiderman, B., (1978). Improving the human factors aspect of database interactions, ACM *Transactions on Database Systems*, 3, 417-439.

Slator, B.M., Anderson, M.P., and Conley W. (1986). Pygmalion at the interface. *Communications of the ACM*, 29, 599-604.

Small, D.W. and Weldon, L.J. (1983). An experimental comparison of natural and structured query languages. Human Factors, 25, 253-263.

Tennant, H.R. (1979). *Experience with the Evaluation of Natural Language Question Answerers* (Working paper 18). Urbana, IL: University of Illinois, Coordinated Science Laboratory.

Tennant, H.R. (1980). *Evaluation of natural language processors* (Report T-103). Urbana, IL: University of Illinois, Coordinated Science Laboratory.

Tennant, H.R., Ross, K.M., and Thompson, C.W. (1983). Usable natural language interfaces through menu-based natural language understanding. In *Proceedings of CHI '83: Human Factors in Computing Systems* (pp. 154-160). New York: Association for Computing Machinery.

Turing, A.M. (1950) Computing Machinery and Intelligence. *Mind*, 54, 433-460.

Turtle, H. (1994) Natural Language vs. Boolean Query Evaluation: A Comparison of Retrieval Performance. In *Proceedings of the Seventeenth Annual International Conference on Research and Development in Information Retrieval*, (pp. 212-221). London: Springer-Verlag

Walker, M. and Whittaker, S. (1989). *When Natural Language is Better than Menus: A Field Study*. Technical Report, Hewlett Packard Laboratories, Bristol, England.

Waltz, D.L. (1983). Helping computers understand natural language. *IEEE Spectrum*, November, 81-84.

Watt, W.C. (1968). Habitability. *American Documentation*, July, 338-351.

Whalen, T. and Patrick, A. (1989). Conversational Hypertext: Information Access Through Natural Language Dialogues with Computers." in *Proceedings of CHI'89: ACM Human Computer Interaction Conference*, New York: Association of Computing Machinery.

Winograd, T and Flores, C.F. (1986). *Understanding Computers and Cognition*. Norwood NJ: Ablex.

Woods, W.A. (1977). A personal view of natural language understanding. *Special interest group in artificial intelligence*, Newsletter, 61, 17-20.

Zoeppritz, M. (1986). Investigating human factors in natural language data base query. In J. L. Mey (Ed.), *Language and discourse: Test and protest: A Festschrift for Petr Sgall. (Linguistic and Literary Studies in Eastern Europe 19)* (pp. 585-605). Amsterdam, Philadelphia: John Benjamins.

Zolton-Ford, E. (1984). Reducing variability in natural-language interactions with computers. In *Proceedings of the Human Factors Society 28th Annual Meeting*, (pp. 768-772). Santa Monica CA: The Human Factors Society.

Handbook of Human-Computer Interaction
Second, completely revised edition
M. Helander, T.K. Landauer, P. Prabhu (eds.)

Chapter 8

Virtual Environments as Human-Computer Interfaces

Stephen R. Ellis, Durand R. Begault and
Elizabeth M. Wenzel
NASA Ames Research Center
Moffett Field, California, USA

8.1 Communication and Environments

8.1.1 Virtual Environments are Media

During the past 10 years, highly interactive computer graphics simulations have become widely known through the development of increasingly, inexpensive position sensing devices and miniature visual displays. Instrumented gloves now exist that can quickly measure, for example, the shape and position of users' hands to communicate these signals to a graphics computer. The computer may then display a graphical representation of the users' hand through a head-mounted display so that the graphical image of the hand changes shape and position in a manner almost identical to that of the users' real hand. Those wearing the display are consequently able to behave within a synthetic environment created within the computer as they would act within the real world.

When adequate computational speed and perceptual detail is available in these displays, users may spontaneously feel "present" within the simulated environment. Such an experience of displaced presence in a synthesized environment is not unique to virtual display technology; it can be mimicked by a good novel. But when the virtual displays act as a human interface to an interactive, graphical computer simulation, they make this duplicity of parallel experiences more concrete through the merging of remote viewing and sighting technology, vehicle simulation equipment and interactive 3D graphics.

The virtual environments created through computer graphics, as their preceding text based computer interfaces once were, (Licklider, Taylor, and Herbert, 1978) are new communications media. They are generally experienced through head-coupled, virtual image, stereoscopic displays that can synthesize a coordinated multisensory presentation of a synthetic environment. The development of these displays as human interfaces to simulation and telerobotics systems can be traced back approximately 30 years (Ellis, 1990; Ellis, et al., 1991; 1993; Brooks Jr., 1988; Kalawsky, 1993; Pimentel and Texeira , 1993; Barfield and Furness, 1995; Carr and England, 1995).

8.1.2 Optimal Human-Machine Interface Design

A well-designed human computer interface gives the user an efficient, effortless flow of information between the device and its operator. When users are given sufficient control over the pattern of this interaction, they themselves can evolve efficient interaction strategies that optimize their communications to the machine. (Zipf, 1949; Mandelbrot, 1982; Ellis and Hitchcock, 1986; Grudin and Norman, 1993). But successful interface design should strive to reduce this adaptation period by analysis of the users' task, interaction metaphor, their performance limitations and strengths.

The dominant interaction metaphor for the human computer interface changed in the 1980's. Modern graphical interfaces, like those first developed at Xerox PARC (Smith et al., 1982) and used for the Apple Macintosh, transformed the "conversational" interaction in which users "talked" to their computers to one in which they "acted out" their commands within a "desktop environment".

8.1.3 Extensions of the Desk-top Metaphor

Virtual environment displays represent a three-dimensional generalization of the two dimensional "desk top" metaphor. The central innovation of the concept, first stated and elaborated by Ivan Sutherland (1965; 1970) and Myron Krüger (1977; 1983) was that the pictorial interface generated by the computer could become an illusory, synthetic but apparently physical environment. These synthetic environments may be experienced from egocentric or exocentric viewpoints. That is to say, the users may appear to actually be immersed in the environment or see themselves represented through an apparent window. The objects in this synthetic space, as well as the space itself, may be programmed to have arbitrary properties. However, the successful extension of the desk-top metaphor to a full "environment" requires an understanding of the necessary limits to programmer creativity in order to insure that the environment is comprehensible and usable. These limits arise from human experience in real environments and illustrate a major connection between work in telerobotics and virtual environments. For reasons of simulation fidelity, previous telerobotic and aircraft simulations, which have many of the aspects of virtual environments, also have had to take explicitly into account real-world kinematic and dynamic constraints. Thus, they can provide guidelines for to

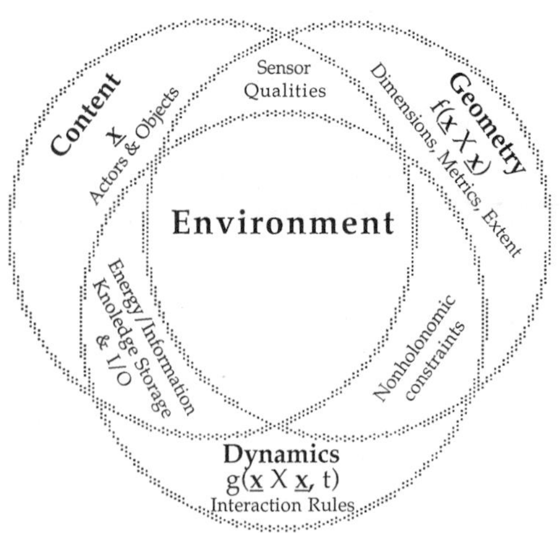

Figure 1. Decomposition of an environment into its abstract functional components. *Actors and objects are described by position vectors x. Geometric characteristics are defined as functions or relations on the Cartesian product, x X x, of elements of the position vectors. The rules of dynamic interaction are defined as functions over the interaction space described by the Cartesian product. Some aspects of environments which share features of the three basic components are listed in the intersections of the Venn diagram.*

tally synthetic environments (Hashimoto, Sheridan, and Noyes, 1986; Bussolari, Young, and Lee, 1988; Kim[1], Takeda, and Stark, 1988; Tachi, Hirohiko, Maeda, 1989; Bejczy, Kim, and Venema, 1990; Sheridan, 1992; Cardullo, 1993; See also volumes 1-5 of the journal Presence).

8.1.4 Environments

Successful synthesis of an environment requires some analysis of the parts that make up the environment. The theater of human activity may be used as a reference for defining an environment and may be thought of as having three parts: a content, a geometry, and a dynamics. (Figure 1.) (Ellis, 1991).

Content

The objects and actors in the environment are its content. These objects may be described by their position, orientation, velocity, and acceleration in the environ-

[1] Higher dimensional displays have also been described. See Inselberg (1985) or Feiner and Beshers (1990) for alternative approaches.

mental space, as well as other distinguishing characteristics such as their color, texture, sound and energy content. These are the properties of the objects. Though the actors in an environment may for some interactions be considered objects, they are distinct in that they have capacities to initiate interactions with other objects. The basis of these initiated interactions is the storage of energy or information within the actors, and their ability to control the release of this stored information or energy after a period of time. The self is a distinct actor in the environment which provides a point of view establishing the frame of reference from which the environment may be constructed. All parts of the environment that are exterior to the self may be considered the field of action. As an example, the balls on a billiard table may be considered the content of the billiard table environment and the cue ball controlled by the pool player maybe considered the "self." The additional energy and information that makes the cue ball an actor is imparted to it by the cue controlled by the pool player and his knowledge of game rules.

Geometry

The geometry is a description of the environmental field of action. It has dimensionality, metrics, and extent. The dimensionality refers to the number of independent descriptive terms needed to specify the position of every element of the environment. The metrics are systems of rules that may be applied to establish an ordering of the contents and to establish the concept of geodesic or the loci of minimal distance or default motion paths between points in the environmental space. The extent of the environment refers to the range of possible values for the elements of the position vector. The environmental space or field of action may be defined as the Cartesian product of all the elements of the position vectors over their possible ranges. An environmental trajectory is a time-history of an object through the environmental space. Since kinematic constraints may preclude an object from traversing the space along some paths, these constraints are also part of the environment's geometric description.

Constraints manifest themselves in terms of the specific perceptual modality simulated for the virtual environment. For example, in terms of virtual acoustics, the geometry involves simulation of an environmental context in which the physical properties of surrounding objects and surfaces influences the character and spatial disposition of reverberant energy.

Dynamics

The dynamics of an environment are the rules of interaction among its contents describing their behavior as they exchange energy or information. Typical examples of specific dynamical rules may be found in the differential equations of Newtonian dynamics describing, for example, the responses of billiard balls to impacts of the cue ball. For other environments, these rules also may take the form of grammatical rules or even of look-up tables for pattern-match-triggered action rules. For example, a syntactically correct command typed at a computer terminal can cause execution of a program with specific parameters within the command. In this case the meaning and information of the command plays the role of the energy, and the resulting rate of change in the logical state of the affected device, plays the role of acceleration. An important aspect of the dynamic rules for virtual acoustic objects is that the phenomenon of visual capture usually ties a sound to the most logical visible or proximate object. If there is no corresponding visual object, then the sound's location is assumed to be out of the visual field-of -view. In this case, auditory cues and cognitive modification based on memory and expectation are used to localize a sound.

The analogy between energy and semantic information suggests the possibility of developing a semantic or informational mechanics in which some measure of motion through the state space of an information processing device may be related to the meaning or information content of the incoming messages. Further development of this analogy may lead to a theory of simulation that could help organize further research on virtual environments.

The usefulness of analyzing environments into these abstract components, i.e. content, geometry, and dynamics, primarily arises when designers search for ways to enhance operator interaction with their simulations. For example, this analysis has organized the search for graphical enhancements for pictorial displays of aircraft and spacecraft traffic (McGreevy and Ellis, 1986; Ellis, McGreevy and Hitchcock, 1987; Grunwald and Ellis, 1988; 1991; 1993). However, it also can help organize theoretical thinking about what it means to be in an environment through reflection concerning the experience of physical reality.

8.1.5 Sense of Physical Reality

Our sense of physical reality is a construction derived from the symbolic, geometric, and dynamic information directly presented to our senses. But it is noteworthy that many of the aspects of physical reality are only presented in incomplete, noisy form. For example, though our eyes provide us only with a fleeting series of snapshots of only parts of objects present in our visual world, through a priori "knowledge" brought to perceptual analysis of our sensory input, we accurately interpret these objects to continue to exist in their entirety. (Gregory, 1968; Gregory, 1980; Gregory[2], 1981; Hochberg, 1986). Similarly, our goal seeking behavior appears to filter noise by benefiting from internal dynamical models of the objects we may track or control (Kalman, 1960; Kleinman, Baron, and Levison, 1970). Accurate perception consequently involves considerable a priori knowledge about the possible structure of the world. This knowledge is under constant re-calibration based on error feedback. The role of error feedback has been classically mathematically modeled during tracking behavior (McRuer, and Weir, 1969; Jex, McDonnell, and Phatak, 1966; Hess, 1987) and notably demonstrated in the behavioral plasticity of visual-motor coordination (Welch, 1978; Held, Efstathiou, and Greene, 1966; Held, and Durlach, 1991) and in vestibular and ocular reflexes (Jones, Berthoz, and Segal, 1984; Zangemeister, and Hansen, 1985; Zangemeister, 1991).

Thus, a large part of our sense of physical reality is a consequence of internal processing rather than being something that is developed only from the immediate sensory information we receive. Our sensory and cognitive interpretive systems are predisposed to process incoming information in ways that normally result in a correct interpretation of the external environment, and in some cases they may be said to actually "resonate" with specific patterns of input that are uniquely informative about our environment (Gibson, 1950; Heeger, 1989; Koenderink, and van Doorn, 1977; Regan, and Beverley, 1979). In addition to underlying coordinated interaction with the physical world these interpretive processes give rise to a subjective sense of presence within our environment. The costs and benefits of attempting to synthesize this subjective sense are a matter of current discussion (Sheridan, 1992b; 1996; Slater, Usoh and Steed, 1992; Schloerb, 1995; Ellis, 1996).

These discussions recognize that the same constructive processes are triggered by the displays used to present virtual environments. However, since the incoming sensory information is mediated by the display technology, the constructive processes producing a sense of presence will be triggered only to the extent the displays provide high perceptual fidelity. Accordingly, virtual environments can come in different stages of completeness, which may be usefully distinguished by their extent of what may be called virtualization.

8.2 Virtualization

8.2.1 Definition of Virtualization

Virtualization may be defined as the process by which a viewer interprets patterned sensory impressions to represent objects in an environment other than that from which the impressions physically originate. A classical example would be that of a virtual image as defined in geometrical optics. A viewer of such an image sees the rays emanating from it as if they originated from a virtual point rather than from their actual location (Figure 2).

8.2.2 Levels of Virtualization

Three levels of virtualization may be distinguished: virtual space, virtual image, and virtual environments. These levels represent points on a design continuum of virtualization as synthesized sensory stimuli more and more closely acquire the sensory and motor characteristics of a real environment. Virtually all displays, including reality itself, fall somewhere along this continuum. As the process of virtualization becomes more complete, the resulting impression from the display becomes indistinguishable from that of physical reality.

Virtual Space

The first form, construction of a virtual space, refers to the process by which a viewer perceives a three-dimensional layout of objects in space when viewing a flat surface presenting the pictorial cues to space, that is, perspective, shading, occlusion, and texture gradients (Figure 3). This process, which is akin to map interpretation, is the most abstract of the three. Viewers must literally learn to interpret pictorial images

[2] This "knowledge" should not be thought of as the conscious, abstract knowledge that is acquired in school. It rather takes the form of tacit acceptance of specific constraints on the possibilities of change such as that are reflected in Gestalt Laws, e.g. common fate or good continuation. Its origin may be sought in the phylogenetic history of a species, shaped by the process of natural selection and physical law, and documented by the history of the earth's biosphere.

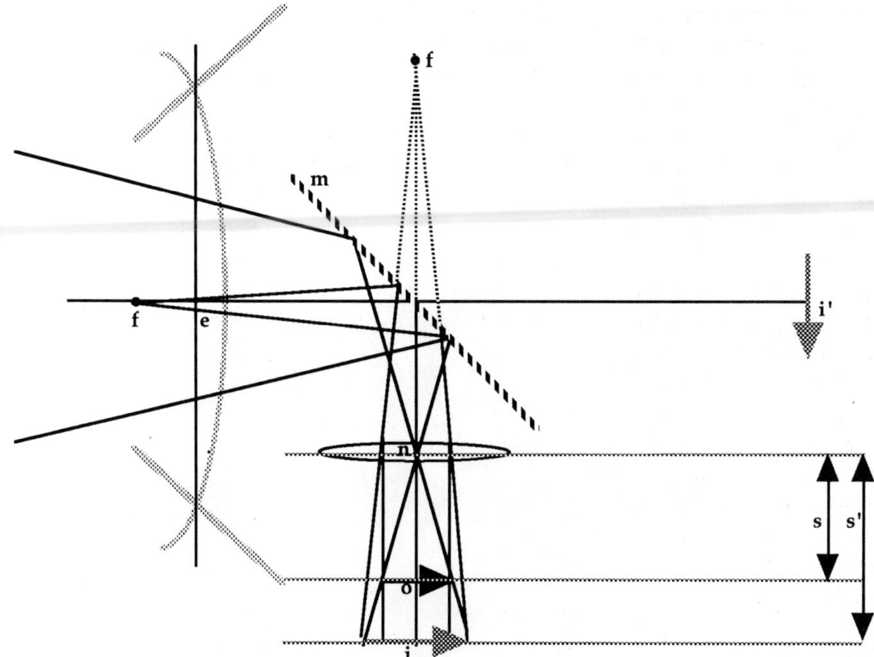

Figure 2. ***Virtual image created by a simple lens placed at n with focal point f and viewed from e through a half-silvered mirror appears to be straight ahead of the viewer at i'.*** *The visual direction and accommodation required to see the virtual image clearly are quite different that what would be needed to see the real object at o which could be produced on a display surface there: An optical arrangement similar to this would be needed to superimpose synthetic computer imagery on a view of a real scene as in at heads up display.*

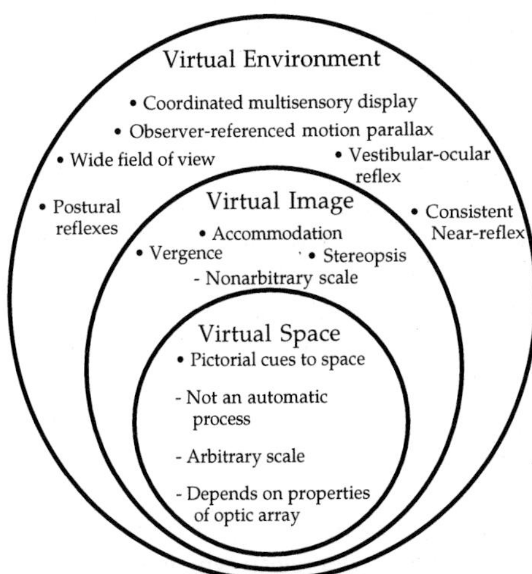

Figure 3. Levels of virtualization. *As displays provide richer and more varied sources of sensory information, they allow users to virtualize more and more complete theaters of activity. In this view, the virtual space is the most restrictive and the virtual environment is the most inclusive having the largest variety of information sources. Only the bulleted entries indicate characteristics of each level of virtualization.*

(Gregory and Wallace, 1974; Senden, 1932; Jones, and Hagen, 1980). It is also not an automatic interpretive process because many of the physiological reflexes associated with the experience of a real three-dimensional environment are either missing or inappropriate for the patterns seen on a surface. The basis of the reconstruction of virtual space must be the optic array, the patterned collection of relative lines of sight to significant features in the image, that is, contours, vertices, lines, and textures. Since scaling does not affect the relative position of the features of the optic array, perceived size or scale is not intrinsically defined in a virtual space.

Virtual Image

The second form of virtualization is the perception of a virtual image. In conformance with the use of this term in geometric optics, it is the perception of an object in depth in which accommodative, ocular vergence, and (optionally) stereoscopic disparity cues (Bishop, 1987) are present, though not necessarily consistent. Since, virtual images can incorporate stereoscopic and ocular vergence cues, the actual perceptual scaling of the

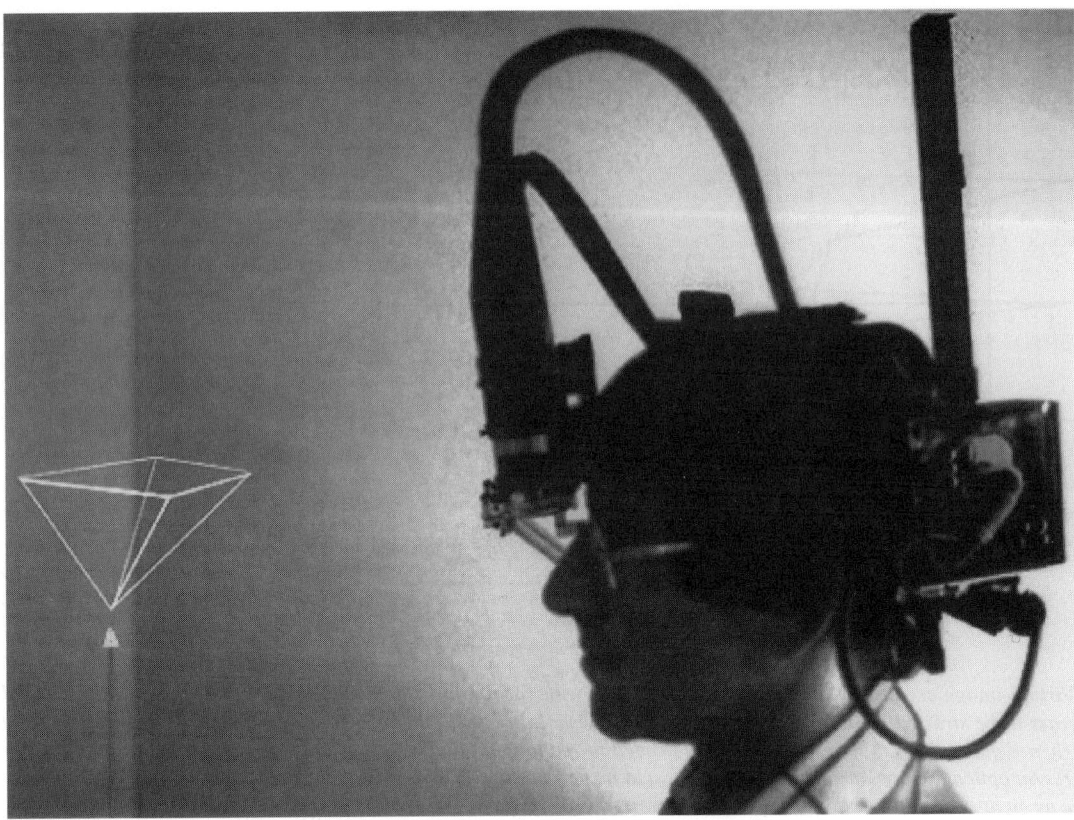

Figure 4. See-through, head-mounted, virtual image, stereoscopic display allow users to interact with virtual objects such as *a tetrahedron synthesized by computer graphics and superimposed in their field of vision; however, the perceived depth of the stereo overlay must be adjusted for perceptual biases and distortions (Ellis and Bucher, 1992). The above electronic haploscope, redesigned in collaboration with Ramon Alarcon, is currently being used to study these biases (Photograph courtesy of NASA).*

constructed space is not arbitrary but, somewhat surprisingly, not always simply related to viewing geometry (Zuber, 1965; Foley, 1980; Foley, 1985; Collewijn, and Erkelens, 1990; Erkelens, and Collewijn, 1985a; Erkelens, and Collewijn, 1985b) (Figure 4).

Virtual Environment

The final form is the virtualization of an environment. In this case the key added sources of information are observer-slaved motion parallax, depth-of-focus variation, and wide field-of-view without visible restriction of the field of view. If properly implemented, these additional features can be consistently synthesized to provide stimulation of major space-related psychological responses or physiological reflexes such as accommodative vergence and vergence accommodation of the "near response" (Hung, Semlow, and Cuiffreda, 1984; Deering. 1992), the optokinetic reflex, the vestibular-ocular reflex. (Feldon, and Burda, 1987), and postural reflexes (White, Post, and Leibowitz, 1980) These features, embellished by synthesized sound sources (Wenzel, Wightman, and Foster, 1988; Wenzel, 1991; Wightman, and Kistler, 1989a; Wightman, and Kistler, 1989b; Begault, 1994) and other sense modalities, i.e. haptic (Hannaford and Venema, 1995), can substantially contribute to an illusion of telepresence (Bejczy, 1980), that is, of actually being present in the synthetic environment.

Measurements of the degree to which a virtual environment display convinces its users that they are present in the synthetic world can be made by measuring the degree to which these environmental responses can be triggered in it (Figure 5) (Nemire, Jacoby and Ellis, 1994). This approach provides an alternative to the use of subjective scales of "presence" to evaluate

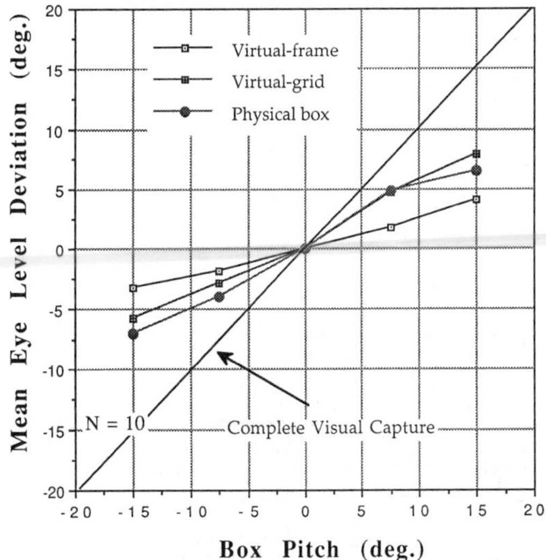

Figure 5. Observers who view into a visual frame of refer- *ence such as a larger room or box that is pitched with respect to gravity, will have their sense of horizon, biased towards the direction of the pitch of the visual frame (Martin and Fox, 1989). An effect of this type is shown for the mean of ten subjects by the trace labeled "physical box". When a comparable group of subjects experienced the same pitch in a matched virtual environment, simulating the pitch using a stereo head-mounted display, the biasing of effect as measured by the slope of this displayed function was about half that of the physical environment. Adding additional grid texture to the virtual surfaces, increased the amount of visual-frame-induced bias, i.e. the so-called "visual capture" (Nemire and Ellis, 1991). Recent work shows that more detailed virtual environments presented by higher power graphics computers can simulate perceptual responses indistinguishable from those evoked by matched real environments (Proffitt, Bhalla, Grossweiler, and Midgett, 1995).*

the simulation fidelity of a virtual environment display. Such subjective evaluation scales such as the Cooper-Harper rating (Cooper and Harper, 1969) have been used to determine simulation fidelity of aircraft. Related subjective scales have also been used for workload measurement (Hart and Staveland, 1988).

Though virtualization may be developed with respect to visual information, direct analogs of virtual space, virtual images and virtual environments exist for other sensory modalities. Acoustic signals may be processed, for example, to reproduce the binaural filtering and shadowing effects introduced by the pinnae and the head (i.e. the Head Related Transfer Function, or HRTF). Signal processing with HRTFs can produce an acoustic stimulus which can produce a sound source display analogous to the presentation of virtual images, conveying both position and distance of virtual acoustic objects. The reverberation of a real or simulated environmental context can also be included. Finally, the dynamic variation of these sources in a manner responsive to a listeners' head position can trigger space-related, vestibular-acoustic reflexes such as acoustically stimulated vection, the illusion of self motion, allowing movement within a virtual acoustic environment. Thus, acoustic stimuli can play a role analogous to visual stimuli used to stimulate vection. Interestingly, the problems associated with synthesizing virtual acoustic space described above are not as acute as corresponding visual issues, partly because of the historical and cultural experience of most persons with audio representation. For example, most people have heard more music over a loudspeaker than in a concert hall. More problematic is the ability to create a consistent virtual acoustic image between multiple persons. Acoustic localization differs considerably between different people; particularly with respect to elevation and distance perception (Begault and Wenzel, 1993; Begault, 1994).

The fact that actors in virtual environments interact with objects and the environment by hand, head, and eye movements, tightly restricts the subjective scaling of the space so that all system gains must be carefully set. Mismatch in the gains or position measurement offsets will degrade performance by introducing unnatural visual-motor and visual-vestibular correlations. In the absence of significant time lags, humans can adapt to these unnatural correlations. However, time lags do interfere with complete visual-motor adaptation (Held and Durlach, 1991; Jones and Durlach, 1984), and when present in the imaging system can cause motion sickness (Crampton, 1990; Presence, 1992).

8.2.3 Environmental Viewpoints and Controlled Elements

Virtual spaces, images or environments may be experienced from two kinds of viewpoints: egocentric viewpoints, in which the sensory environment is constructed from the viewpoint actually assumed by users, and exocentric viewpoints in which the environment is viewed from a position other than that where users are represented to be. In this case, they can literally see a representation of themselves (McGreevy and Ellis, 1986; Grunwald et al., 1988; Barfield and Kim, 1991). This distinction in frames of reference results in a fundamental difference in movements users must make to track a visually referenced target. Egocentric viewpoints classically require compensatory tracking, and exocentric viewpoints require pursuit tracking. This distinction also corresponds to the difference between inside-out and outside-in frames of reference in the aircraft simulation literature. In the former case the display only presents the tracking error that the operator is trying to null. In the later case both the position of the target and the operators' cursor is presented. The substantial literature on human tracking performance in these alternative reference frames, and the general literature on human manual performance, may be useful in the design of synthetic environments (Poulton, 1974; Wickens, 1986; Wickens and Prevett, 1995). Studies in this area can help to identify the kinds of spatial judgments that specifically benefit from either exocentric or egocentric frames of reference. Judgments of global spatial configurations, for example, tend to benefit from exocentric, non-immersing formats (McCormick and Wickens, 1995).

8.2.4 Breakdown by Technological Functions

The illusion of immersion in a virtual environment is created through the operation of three technologies which may be functionally isolated:

1) Sensors, such as head position or hand shape sensors, to measure operators' body movements, 2) Effectors, such as stereoscopic displays or headphones, to stimulate the operators' senses and 3) Special purpose hardware and software to interlink the sensors and effectors to produce sensory experiences resembling those encountered by inhabitants immersed in a physical environment (Figure 6). In a virtual environment this linkage is accomplished by a simulation computer. In a head-mounted teleoperator display the linkage occurs through robot manipulators, vehicles, control systems, sensors and cameras at the remote work site. The functional similarity of teleoperator displays and virtual environments, in fact, allows imagery from both to be intermixed.

The successful interaction of a human operator with virtual environments presented by head and body referenced sensory displays depends upon the fidelity with which the sensory information is presented to the user. The situation is directly parallel to that faced by the designer of a vehicle simulator. In fact, since virtual environments extend flight simulation technology to cheaper, accessible forms, developers can learn much from the flight simulation literature (e.g. Cardullo, 1993; Rolfe and Staples, 1986).

Virtual environments are simulators that are generally worn rather than entered. They are personal

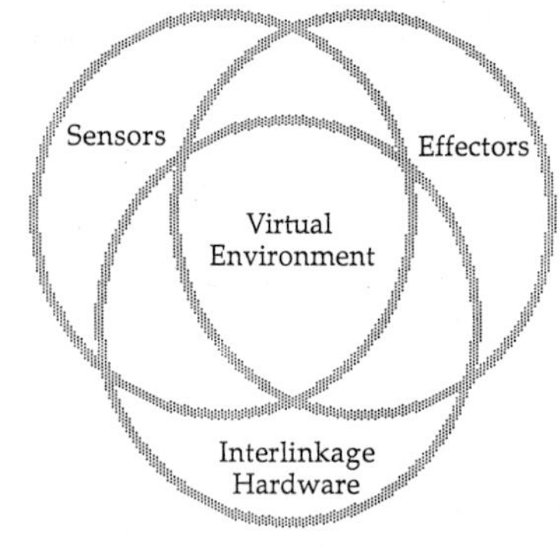

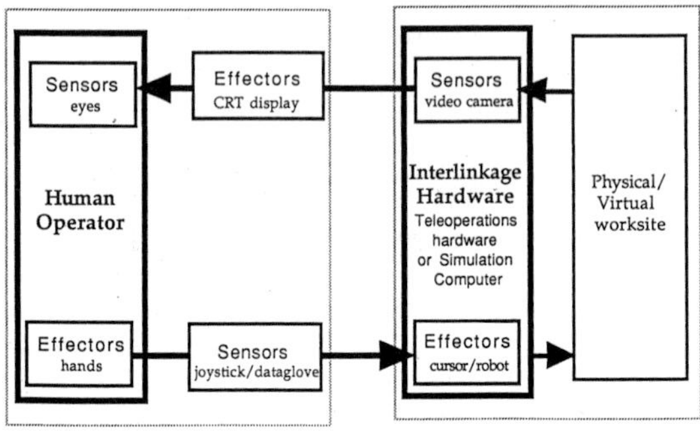

Figure 6. Technological breakdowns of virtual environments (upper panel) and the information flows within virtual environment simulations or telepresence systems (lower panel).

simulators. They are intended to provide their users with a direct sense of presence in a world or space other than the physical one in which they actually are. Their users are not in a cockpit that is within a synthetic environment, they are in the environment themselves. Though this illusion of remote presence is not itself new, the diffusion and rapid drop in the cost of the basic technology has raised the question of whether such displays can become practically useful for a wide variety of new applications ranging from video games to laparoscopic surgical simulation.

Unfortunately, at the composition time of this chapter, users of many display systems staying in virtual environments for more than a few minutes have been either legally blind, i.e. their visual resolution is effectively 20/200, stuck with an awkwardly narrow field of view(~30° horizontal), suffering from motion sickness, headed for a stereoscopic head-ache, and have been suffering from unmistakable pain in the neck from the helmet weight. Newer displays promise to reduce some of these problems, but performance targets necessary for a variety of possible applications

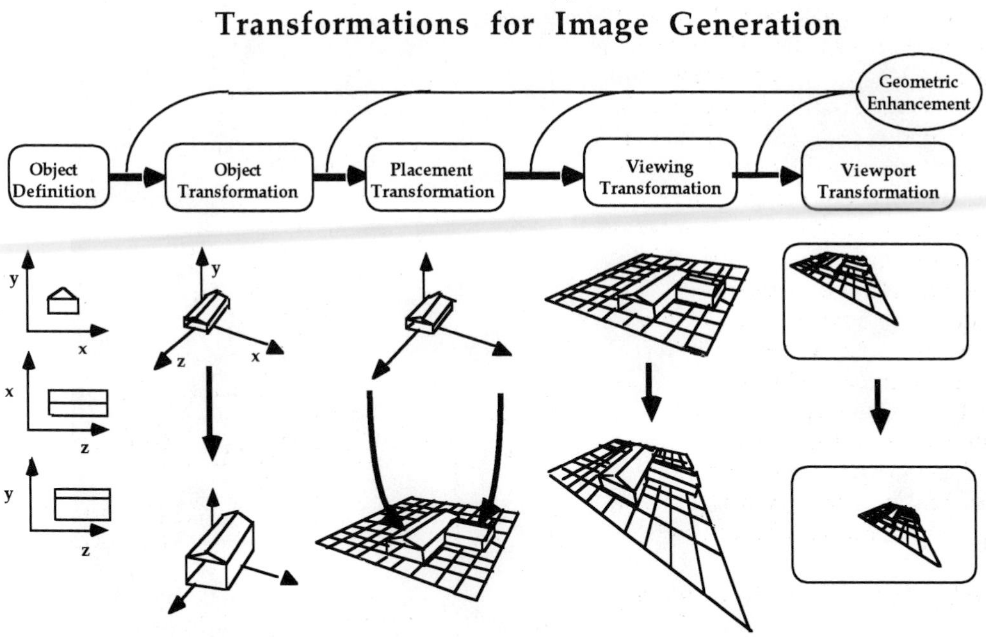

Transformations for Image Generation

Geometric Enhancement

Object Definition → Object Transformation → Placement Transformation → Viewing Transformation → Viewport Transformation

Figure 7. The process of representing a graphic object in virtual space allows a number of different opportunities to introduce informative geometric distortions or enhancements. *These may either may be a modification of the transforming matrix during the process of object definition or they may be modifications of an element of a model. These modifications may take place (1) in an object relative coordinate system used to define the object's shape, or (2) in an affine or even curvilinear object shape transformation, or (3) during the placement transformation that positions the transformed object in world coordinates, or (4) in the viewing transformation or (5) in the final viewport transformation. The perceptual consequences of informative distortions are different depending on where they are introduced. For example, object transformations will not impair perceived positional stability of objects displayed in a head-mounted format, whereas changes of the viewing transformation such as magnification will (For transformation details see : Robinett and Holloway, 1995).*

are only currently being determined as seen from recent general reviews of human performance in virtual environments (Ellis, 1994; Barfield and Furness, 1995, Carr and England, 1995).

8.2.5 Spatial and Environmental Instruments

Like the computer graphics pictures drawn on a display surface, the enveloping synthetic environment created by a head-mounted display may be designed to convey specific information. Thus, just as a spatial display generated by computer graphics may be transformed into a spatial instrument by selection and coupling of its display parameters to specific communicated variables, so too may a synthetic environment be transformed into an environmental instrument by design of its content, geometry, and dynamics (e.g. Ellis and Grunwald, 1989). Transformations of virtual environments into useful environmental instruments, however, are more constrained than those used to make spatial instruments because the user must actually inhabit the environmental instrument. Accordingly, the transformations and coupling of actions to effects within an environmental instrument must not diverge too far from those transformations and couplings actually experienced in the physical world, especially if disorientation, poor motor coordination, and motion sickness are to be avoided (Figure 7). Thus, the advent of virtual environment displays provides a veritable cornucopia of opportunity for research in human perception, motor- control, and interface technology.

8.3 Origins of Virtual Environments

The obvious, intuitive appeal that virtual environment technology has is probably rooted in the human fascination with vicarious experiences in imagined environments and has a long history in art and technology. Caroll, 1872; Huxley, 1938; Sutherland, 1965; Sutherland, 1970; Krueger, 1977; Greenberg and Woodhead, 1980; Lipton, 1982; Krueger, 1983; Gibson, 1984; Krueger, 1985; Fagan, 1985; Laural, 1991; Cruz-Neira, Sandin, DeFanti, Kenyon, and Hart, 1992).

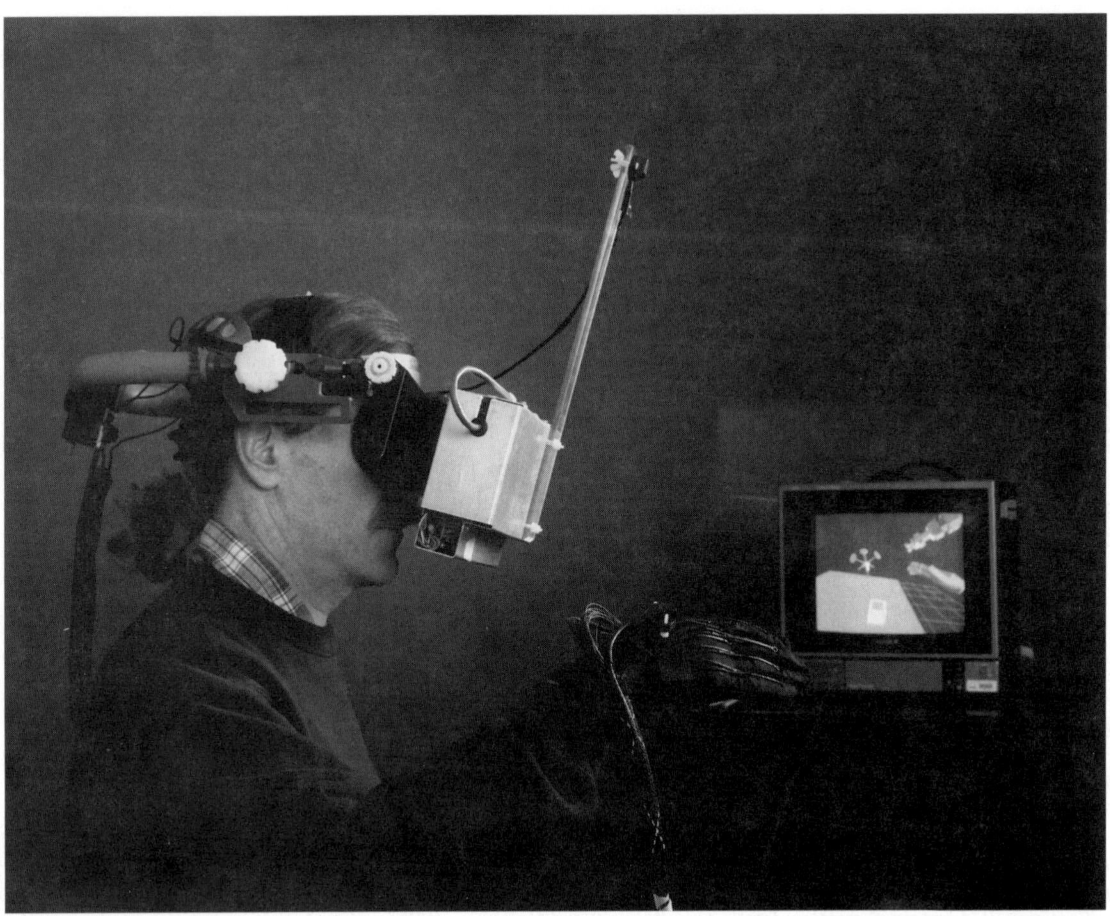

Figure 8. This head-mounted, stereo, virtual environment display system at the Ames Research Center Advanced Displays *and Spatial Perception Laboratory which has been used to control a remote PUMA robot in the Intelligent Mechanisms Laboratory. The simulation update rate now varies from 20 to 60 Hz depending on the complexity of the graphics. A local kinematic simulation of the remote work site could aid the operator in planning complex movements and visualizing kinematic and operational constraints on the motion of the end effector. (Photograph courtesy of NASA).*

8.3.1 Vehicle Simulation and Three-Dimensional Cartography

Probably the most important source of virtual environment technology comes from previous work in fields associated with the development of realistic vehicle simulators, primarily for aircraft (Rolfe and Staples; 1986; CAE Electronics, 1991; McKinnon, and Kruk, 1991; Cardullo, 1993) but also automobiles (Stritzke, 1991) and ships (Veldhuyzen, and Stassen, 1977; Schuffel, 1987). The inherent difficulties in controlling the actual vehicles often require that operators be highly trained. Since acquiring this training on the vehicles themselves could be dangerous or expensive, simulation systems synthesize the content, geometry, and dynamics of the control environment for training and for testing of new technology and procedures.

These systems have usually cost millions of dollars and have recently involved helmet- mounted displays to recreate part of the environment (Lypaczewski, Jones, and Vorhees, 1986; Barrette, et al., 1990; Furness, 1986; Furness, 1987; Kaiser, 1990). Declining costs have now brought the cost of a virtual environment display down to that of a workstation and have made possible "personal simulators" for everyday use (Foley, 1987; Fisher, McGreevy, Humphries, and Robinett, 1986; Kramer, 1992; Bassett, 1992; Amadon, 1995, W. Industries, 1991) (Figures 8 and 9).

The simulator's interactive visual displays are made possible by advances in computer graphics hardware and software. Development of hardware ma-

Figure 9. As in many current relatively inexpensive, head-mounted virtual environment viewing systems using LCD arrays, *the view that the operator actually sees using a LEEP® view finder is significantly lower resolution than that typically seen on the graphics monitors (background matched in magnification). The horizontal pixel resolution through the view finder is about 22 arcmin/ pixel, vertical resolution is 24 arcmin / line. Approximately 2 arcmin / pixel are required to present resolution at the center of the visual field comparable to that seen on a standard Macintosh monochrome display viewed at 57 cm. The lower inset shows a part of the user's actual field of view photographed through the display optics and exhibiting spatial aliasing, distortion and visible contrast (Photograph courtesy of NASA).*

trix multiplication devices, were an essential first step that enabled generation of real-time 3D graphics (Sutherland, 1965; Sutherland, 1970; Myers, and Sutherland, 1968; more recent examples ; the "reality engine" of Silicon Graphics). New "graphics engines" now can project literally millions of shaded or textured polygons or other graphics primitives per second (Silicon Graphics, 1993) and new efficient software techniques and data structures have been shown to dramatically improve processing speed for inherently volumetric or highly detailed structure of graphics objects that also may be given simulated physical attributes (Jenkins, and Tanimoto, 1980; Meagher, 1984; Netrovali and Haskell, 1988; Cowdry, 1986; Hitchner and McGreevy, 1993; Witkin, A., Fleisher, K., and Barr, A. 1987) (Figure 10).

Since vehicle simulation may involve moving-base simulators, programming the appropriate correlation between visual and vestibular simulation is crucial for a complete simulation of an environment (Figure 11). Moreover, failure to match these two stimuli correctly can lead to motion sickness (AGARD, 1988; Presence, 1992) Paradoxically, however, since the effective travel of most moving base simulators is limited, de-

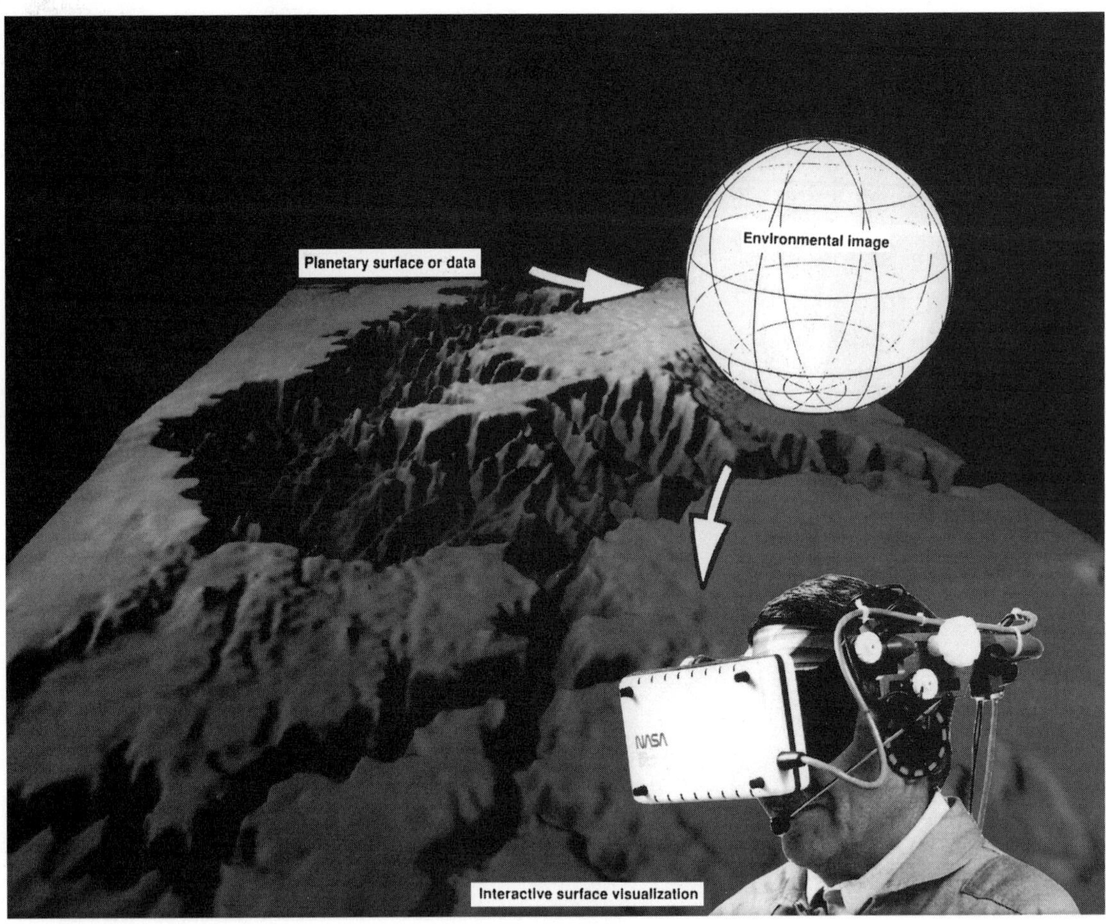

Figure 10. When high-performance computer display technology can be matched to equally high resolution helmet display *technology, planetary scientists will be able to use these systems to visualize remote environments such as the surface of Mars to plan exploration and to analyze planetary surface data. (Photo courtesy of NASA).*

signers must learn to introduce subthreshold visual-vestibular mismatches to produce illusions of greater freedom of movement. These allowable mismatches are built into so-called "washout" models (Bussolari, et al., 1988; Curry, Hoffman, and Young, 1976) and are key elements for creating illusions of extended movement. For example, a slowly implemented pitch-up of a simulator can be used as a dynamic distortion to create an illusion of forward acceleration. Understanding the tolerable dynamic limits of visual-vestibular miscorrelation will be an important design consideration for wide field-of-view head-mounted displays.

The use of informative distortion is also well established in cartography (Monmonier, 1991) and is used to help create a convincing three-dimensional environments for simulated vehicles. Cartographic distortion is also obvious in global maps which must warp a spherical surface into a plane (Cotter, 1966; Robinson, Sale, Morrison, and Muehrcke, 1984) and three-dimensional maps, which often use significant vertical scale exaggeration (6-20X) to clearly present topographic features. Explicit informative geometric distortion is sometimes incorporated into maps, cartograms presenting geographically indexed statistical data and visualizations of scientific data (Tobler, 1963; Tobler, 1976; Tufte, 1983; Tufte, 1990; Bertin, 1967/1983; Wolfe and Yeager, 1993), but the extent to which such informative distortion may be incorporated into simulated environments is constrained by the user's movement-related physiological reflexes. If the viewer is constrained to actually be in the environment, deviations from a natural environmental space can cause disorientation and motion sickness

Figure 11. Moving base simulator at the NASA Ames Research Center pitched simulating acceleration (left), Cockpit view (right). (Photo courtesy of NASA).

(Crampton, 1990; Oman, 1991). For this reason, virtual space or virtual image formats are more suitable when successful communication of the spatial information may be achieved only through spatial distortions (Figure 7). However, even in these formats the content of the environment may have to be enhanced by aids such as graticules to help the user discount unwanted aspects of the geometric distortion (McGreevy, and Ellis, 1986; Ellis, McGreevy, and Hitchcock, 1987; Ellis, and Hacisalihzade, 1990).

In some environmental simulations the environment itself is the object of interest. Such simulations combine surface altitude data with surface photography and have been used to synthesize fly-overs of planets through positions never reached by the spacecraft cameras (Hussey, 1990). These simulations promise to provide planetary and earth scientists with the new capability of virtual exploration (NASA, 1990; Hitchner, 1992; McGreevy, 1993) (Figure 10).

8.3.2 Physical and Logical Simulation

Visualization of planetary surfaces suggests the possibility that not only the substance of the surface may be modeled but also its dynamic characteristics. Dynamic simulations for virtual environments may be developed from ordinary high-level programming languages like Pascal or C, but this usually requires considerable time. Interesting alternatives for this kind of simulation have been provided by simulation and modeling languages such as SLAM II, with the graphical display interface, TESS (Pritsker, 1986; Cellier, 1991).

Another alternative made possible by graphical interfaces to computers is a simulation development environment in which the simulation is created through manipulation of functional icons representing its separate elements, such as integrators, delays, or filters, so as to connect them into a functioning virtual machine. Microcomputer programs Pinball Construction Set published in 1982 by Bill Budge and Rocky's Boots (Robinett, 1982) are widely distributed early examples of this kind of simulation system.

The dynamical properties of virtual spaces and environments may also be linked to physical simulations. Prominent, non-interactive examples of this technique are James Blinn's physical animations in the video physics courses, The Mechanical Universe and Beyond the Mechanical Universe (Blinn, 1987; Blinn, 1991). These physically correct animations are particularly useful in providing students with subjective insights into dynamic three-dimensional phenomena such as magnetic fields. Similar educational animated visualizations have been used for courses on visual perception (Kaiser, MacFee, and Proffitt, 1990) and computer-aided design (Open University, 1991). Particularly interesting are interactive simulations of anthropomorphic figures moving according to realistic

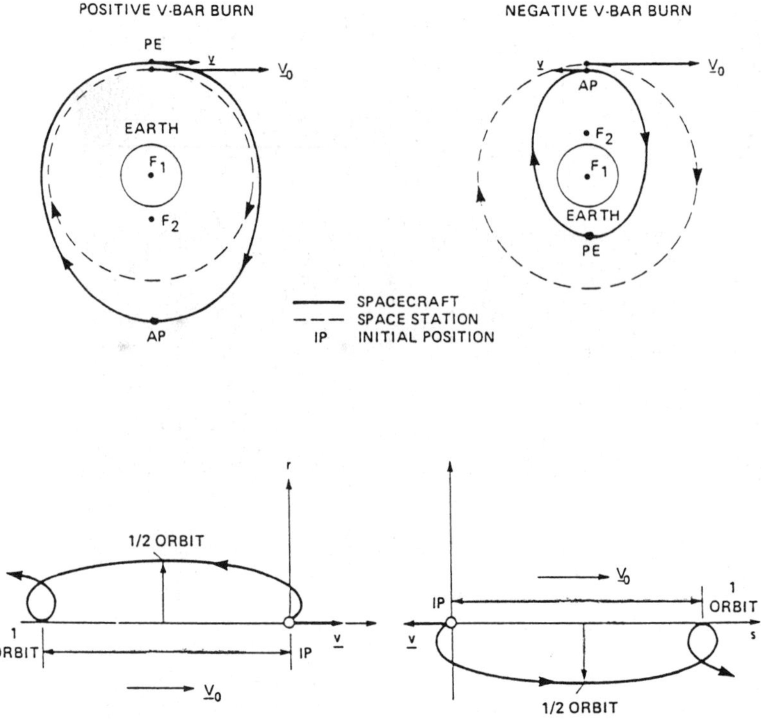

Figure 12. Unusual environments sometimes have unusual dynamics. *The orbital motion of a satellite in a low earth orbit (upper [panels) changes when thrust v is made either in the direction of orbital motion or, Vo, (left) or opposed to orbital motion (right) and indicated by the change of the original orbit (dashed lines) to the new orbit (solid line). AP and PE represent apogee and perigee respectively. When the new trajectory is viewed in a frame of reference relative to the initial thrust point on the original orbit, (Earth is down, orbital velocity is to the right, see lower panels), the consequences of the burn appear unusual. Forward thrusts (left) cause non-uniform, backward, trochoidal movement. Backward thrusts (right) cause the reverse.*

limb kinematics and following higher level behavioral laws (Zeltzer and Johnson, 1991).

Some unusual natural environments are difficult to work in because their inherent dynamics are unfamiliar and may be nonlinear. The immediate environment around an orbiting spacecraft is an example. When expressed in a spacecraft-relative frame of reference known as local-vertical-local-horizontal, the consequences of maneuvering thrusts becomes markedly counter-intuitive and nonlinear (NASA, 1985). Consequently, a visualization tool designed to allow manual planning of maneuvers in this environment has taken account of these difficulties (Grunwald, and Ellis, 1988; Ellis, and Grunwald, 1989; Grunwald and Ellis, 1991; Grunwald and Ellis, 1993). This display system most directly assists planning by providing visual feedback of the consequences of the proposed plans. Its significant features enabling interactive optimization of orbital maneuvers include an "inverse dynamics" algorithm that removes control non-linearities. Through a "geometric spreadsheet," the display creates a synthetic environment that provides the user control of thruster burns which allows independent solutions to otherwise coupled problems of orbital maneuvering (Figures 12 and 13). Although this display is designed for a particular space application, it illustrates a technique that can be applied generally to interactive, operator-assisted optimization of constrained nonlinear functions. It is also noteworthy that this particular display is an instance in which an immersive visual display mimicking the appearance of the actual situation would be more confusing than an abstracted display not providing a strong sense of presence in the simulated environment.

8.3.3 Scientific and Medical Visualization

Insight into the meaning of physical theories that deal with three dimensional phenomena are often best provided by 3D visualizations as shown by Figure 14

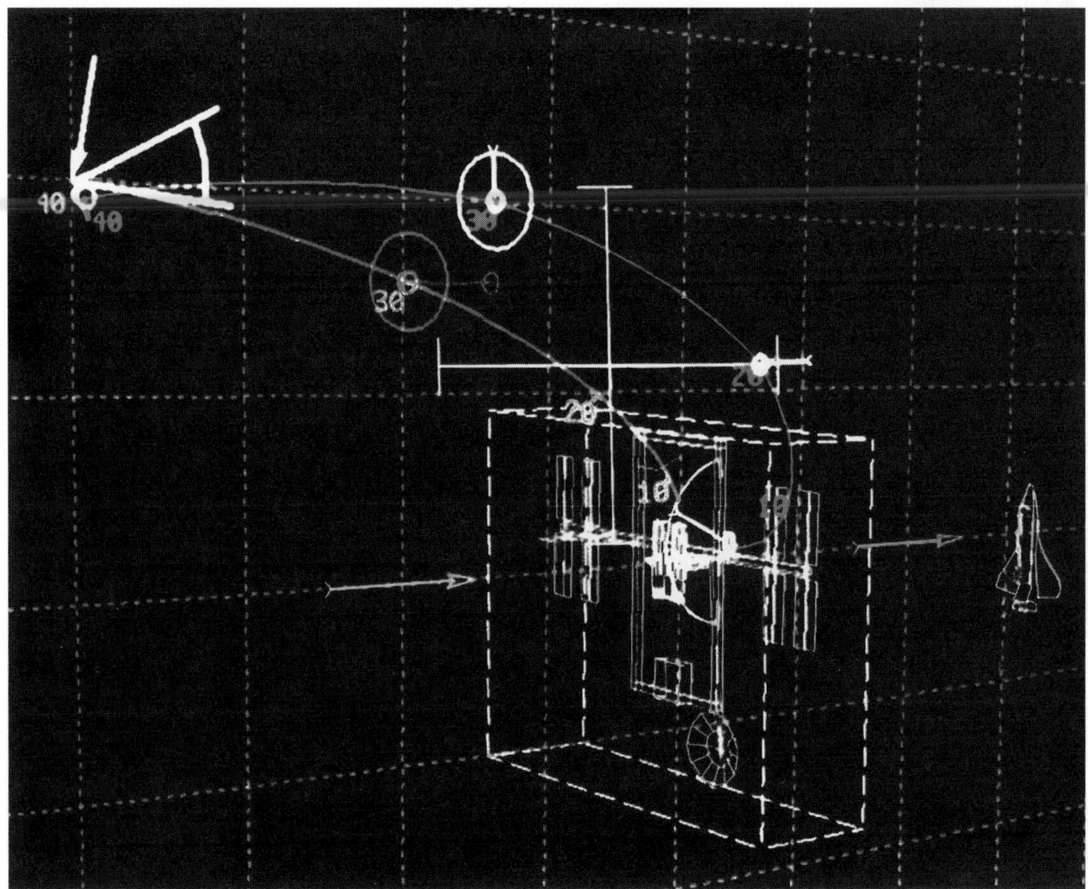

***Figure 13. Proximity operations planning display presents a virtual space that enables operators to plan orbital** maneuvers despite counter-intuitive, nonlinear dynamics and operational constraints, such as plume impingement restrictions. The operator may use the display to visualize his projected trajectories. Violations of the constraints appear as graphics objects, i.e. circle s and arcs, which inform him of the nature and extent of each violation. This display provides a working example of how informed design of a planning environment's symbols, geometry, and dynamics can extend human planning capacity into new realms. (Photo courtesy of NASA).*

which shows a theoretical display of air flow patterns surrounding the Space Shuttle Orbiter. Whether such visualizations are best appreciated from an immersing egocentric viewpoint as illustrated or whether an exocentric, panel mounted displays presentation is better is a question still to be resolved.

Another application for which a virtual space display already has been demonstrated some time ago in a commercial product has been the visualization of volumetric medical data (Meagher, 1984). These images are typically constructed from a series of two-dimensional slices of CAT, PET, or MRI images in order to allow doctors to visualize normal or abnormal anatomical structures in 3 dimensions. Because the different tissue types may be filtered digitally, the doctors may perform an "electronic dissection" and selectively remove particular tissues. In this way truly remarkable skeletal images may be created which currently aid orthopedic and cranio-facial surgeons to plan operations (Figure 15). These volumetric data bases also are useful for shaping custom-machined prosthetic bone implants and for directing precision robotic boring devices for precise fit between implants and surrounding bone (Taylor, et al., 1990). Though these static data bases have not yet been presented to doctors as full virtual environments, existing technology is adequate to develop improved virtual space techniques for interacting with them and may be able to enhance

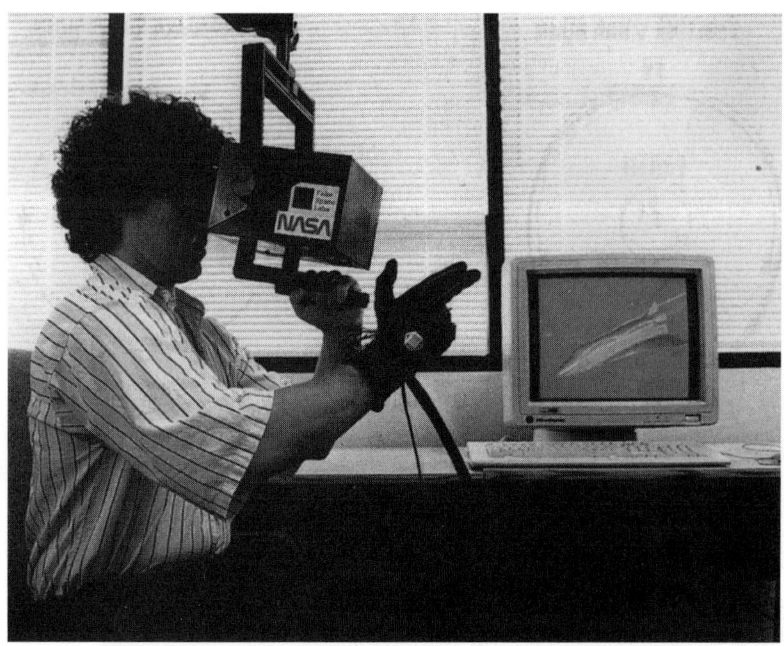

Figure 14. Virtual environments technology may assist visualization of the results of aerodynamic simulations. *Here a DataGlove is used to control the position of a "virtual" source smoke in a wind-tunnel simulation so the operator can visualize the local pattern of sir flow. In this application the operator uses a viewing device incorporating TV monitors (McDowall, Bolas, Pieper, Fisher, and Humphries, 1990) to present a stereo view of the smoke trail around the test model also shown in the desk-top display on the table (Levit and Bryson, 1991). (Photo courtesy of NASA).*

the usability of the existing displays for teleoperated surgery and anatomy instruction (Green, Satava, Hill, and Simon, 1992; UCSD Medical School, 1994). The visible human database just released on the Internet now represents the most complete source of models for these medical purposes (National Library of Medicine, 1990). Related scene-generation technology can already render detailed images of this sort based on architectural drawings and can allow prospective clients to visualize walk-throughs of buildings or furnished rooms that have not yet been constructed (Greenberg, 1991; Airey, Rohlf, and Brooks Jr., 1990; Nomura, Ohata, Imamura, and Schultz, 1992).

8.3.4 Teleoperation and Telerobotics and Manipulative Simulation

Another major technical influence on the development of virtual environment technology is research on teleoperation and telerobotic simulation (Goertz, 1964; Vertut, and Coiffet, 1986; Sheridan, 1992; Kazerooni and Snyder, 1995). Indeed, virtual environments have existed before the name itself as telerobotic and teleoperations simulations. The display technology, however, in these cases was usually panel-mounted rather than head- mounted. Two notable exceptions were the head-controlled/head-referenced display developed for control of remote viewing systems by Raymond Goertz at Argonne National Laboratory (Goertz, Mingesz, Potts, and Lindberg, 1965) and a head-mounted system developed by Charles Comeau and James Bryan of Philco (Figure 16) (Comeau and Brian, 1961). The development of these systems anticipated many of the applications and design issues that confront the engineering of effective virtual environment systems. Their discussions of the field of view/image resolution trade-off is strikingly contemporary. A key difficulty, then and now, was lack of a convenient and precise head tracker. The current popular, electromagnetic, six-degree-of-freedom position tracker developed by Polhemus Navigation (Raab, Blood, Steiner, and Jones, 1979) also see (Ascension Technology Corp, 1990; Polhemus Navigation Systems, 1990; Barnes, 1992), consequently, was an important technological advance but interestingly was anticipated by earlier work at Philco that was limited to electromagnetic sensing of

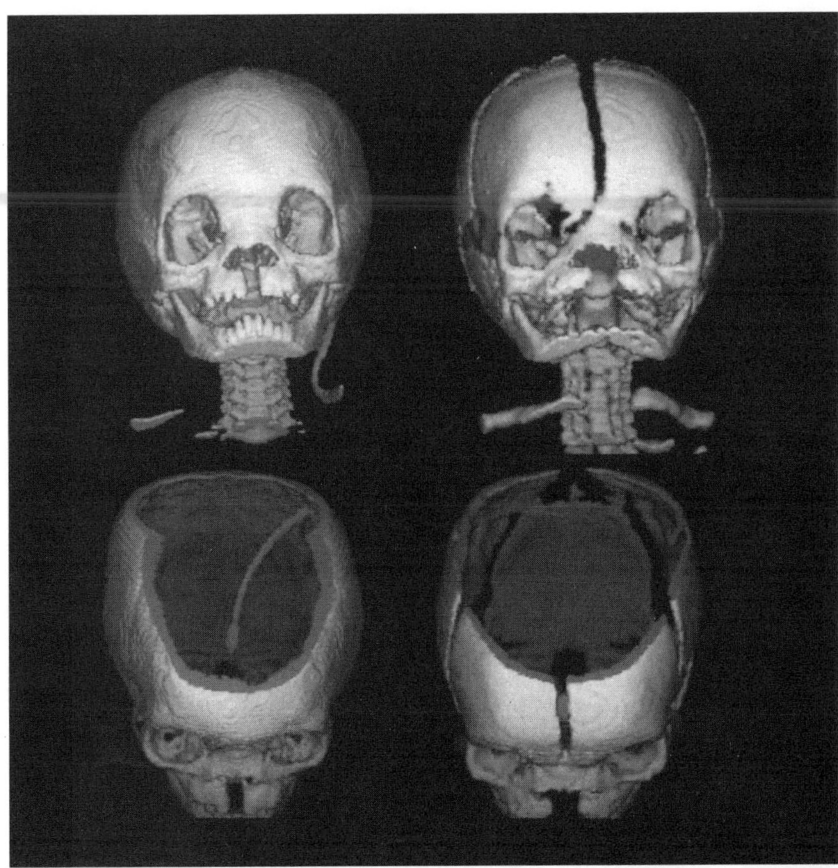

Figure 15. Successive CAT scan x-ray images may be digitized and used to synthesize a volumetric data set which then may be electronically processed to identify specific tissue. *Here bone is isolated from the rest of the data set and presents a striking image that even non-radiologists may be tempted to interpret. Forthcoming hardware will give physicians access to this type of volumetric imagery for the cost of a home computer. Different tissues in volumetric data sets from CAT scan X-ray slices may be given arbitrary visual properties by digital processing in order to aid visualization. In this image tissue surrounding the bone is made partially transparent so as to make the skin surface as well as the underlying bone of the skull clearly visible. This processing is an example of enhancement of the content of a synthetic environment. (Photo courtesy of Octree Corporation, Cupertino California).*

orientation. In other techniques for tracking the head position, accelerometers optical tracking hardware (CAE Electronics, 1991; Wang, Chi, and Fuchs, 1990), or acoustic systems (Barnes, 1992) may be used. The more modern sensors are much more convenient than those used by the pioneering work of Goertz and Sutherland, who used mechanical position sensors, but the important, dynamic characteristics of these new sensors have only recently begun to be fully described (Adelstein, Johnston and Ellis, 1992; Jacoby, Adelstein and Ellis, 1995).

A second key component of a teleoperation work station, or of a virtual environment, is a sensor for coupling hand position to the position of the end-effector at a remote work site. The earlier mechanical linkages used for this coupling have been replaced by joysticks or by more complex sensors that can determine hand shape, as well as position. Modern joysticks are capable of measuring simultaneously all three rotational and three translational components of motion. Some of the joysticks are isotonic (BASYS, 1990; CAE Electronics, 1991; McKinnon and Kruk, 1991) and allow significant travel or rotation along the sensed axes, whereas others are isometric and sense the applied forces and torques without displacement (Spatial Systems, 1990). Though the isometric sticks with no moving parts benefit from simpler construction, the users' kinematic coupling within their hands make it

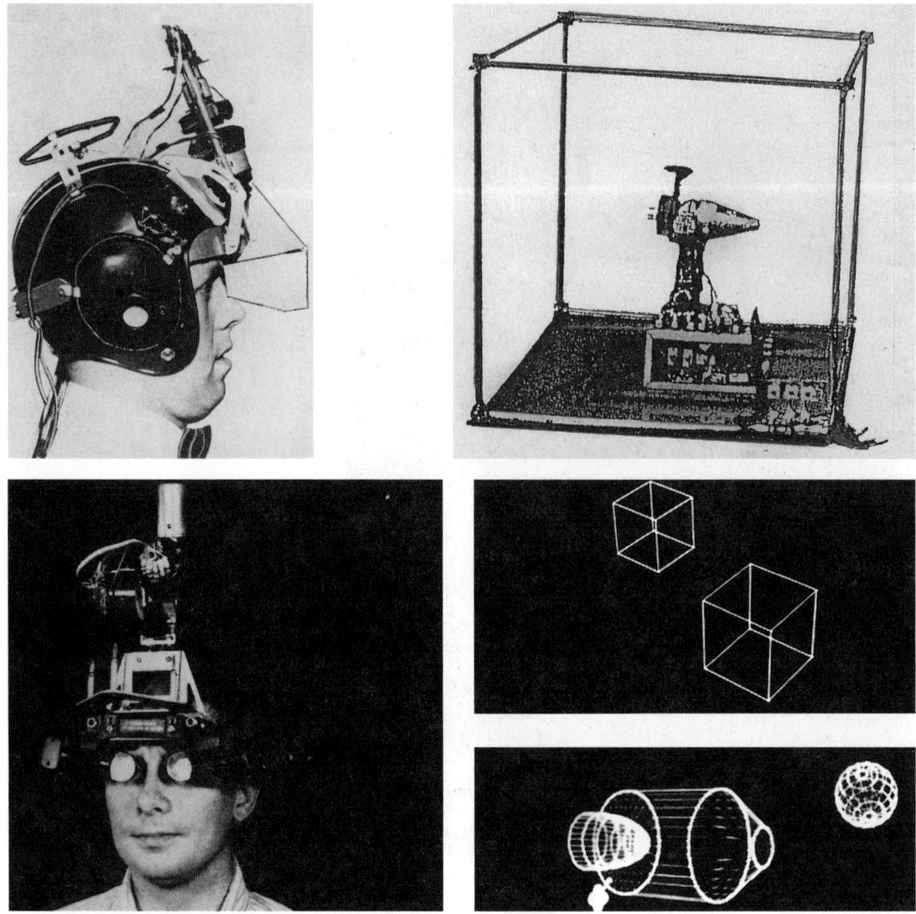

Figure 16. Visual virtual environment display systems have three basic parts*; a head referenced visual display, head and / or body position sensors, a technique for controlling the visual display based on head and / or body movement. One of the earliest system of this sort (upper left panel) was designed by Philco engineers (Comeau and Bryan, 1961) using a head-mounted, binocular, virtual image viewing system, a Helmholtz coil electromagnetic head orientation sensor, and a remote TV camera slaved (upper right panel) to head orientation to provide the visual image. Today this would be called a telepresence viewing system,. The first system to replace the video signal with a totally synthetic image produced through computer graphics (lower panels), was first demonstrated by Ivan Sutherland for very simple geometric forms (Sutherland, 1965).*

difficult for them to use them to apply signals in one axis without cross-coupled signals in other axes. Consequently, these joysticks use switches for shutting down unwanted axes during use. Careful design of the breakout forces and detents for the different axes on the isotonic sticks allow a user to minimize cross-coupling in control signals while separately controlling the different axes (CAE Electronics, 1991; McKinnon and Kruk, 1991).

Although the mechanical bandwidth might have been only of the order of 2-5 Hz, the early mechanical linkages used for telemanipulation provided force-feedback conveniently and passively. In modern electronically coupled systems force-feedback or "feel" must be actively provided, usually by electric motors. Although systems providing six degrees of freedom with force-feedback on all axes are mechanically complicated, they have been constructed and used for a variety of manipulative tasks (Bejczy and Salisbury, 1980; Hannaford, 1989; Jacobson et al., 1986; Jacobus et al., 1992; Jacobus, 1992). Interestingly, force- feedback appears to be helpful in the molecular docking work at the University of North Carolina (Figure 17) in which chemists manipulate virtual images of molecular models of drugs in a computer graphics physical simulation in order to find optimal orientations for binding sites on other molecules. The provision of haptic feedback associated with virtual objects that would

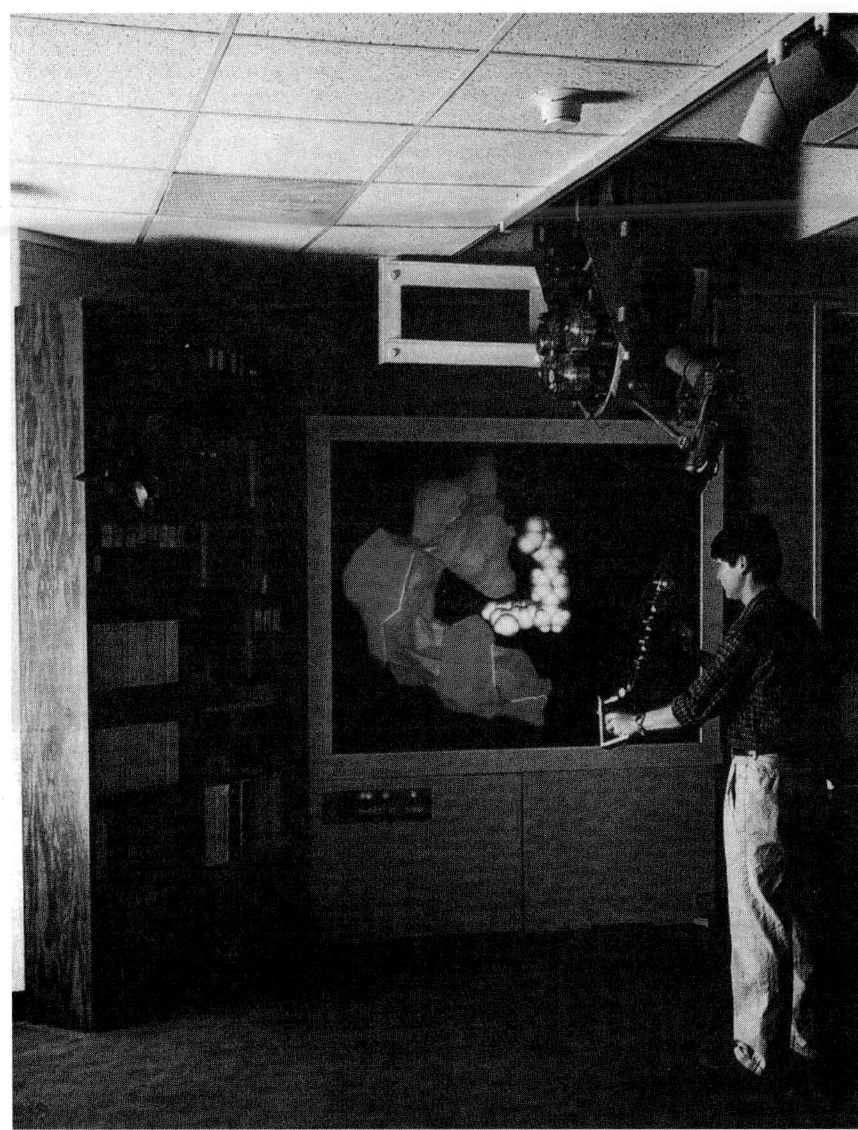

***Figure 17. A researcher at the University of North Carolina uses a multidegree-of-freedom manipulator** to maneuver a computer graphics model of a drug molecule to find binding sites on a larger molecule illustrating a novel medical application. A dynamic simulation of the forces is computed in real time so the user can feel them through the force-reflecting manipulator and use this feel to identify the position and orientation of a binding site (Photograph courtesy of University of North Carolina, Department of Computer Science).*

otherwise appear as insubstantial phantoms appears to be practically beneficial but further quantification of this benefit is needed to understand its generality (Ouh-young, Beard, and Brooks Jr., 1989).

High-fidelity force-feedback requires electromechanical bandwidths over 30Hz Most manipulators do not have this high performance. A mechanical force-reflecting joystick with these characteristics has been designed and built (Figure 18) (Adelstein and Rosen, 1991; 1992; See Fisher, Daniel, and Siva (1990) for some descriptions of typical manual interface specifications; also Brooks, and Bejczy (1986) for a review of control sticks; Maffie and Salisbury, 1994).

Manipulative interfaces may provide varying de-

Figure 18. A high-fidelity, force-reflecting two-axis joystick designed to study human tremor. (Photo courtesy of B. D. Adelstein).

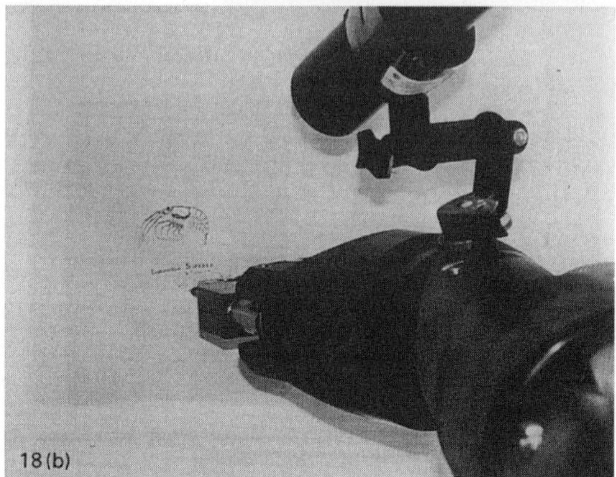

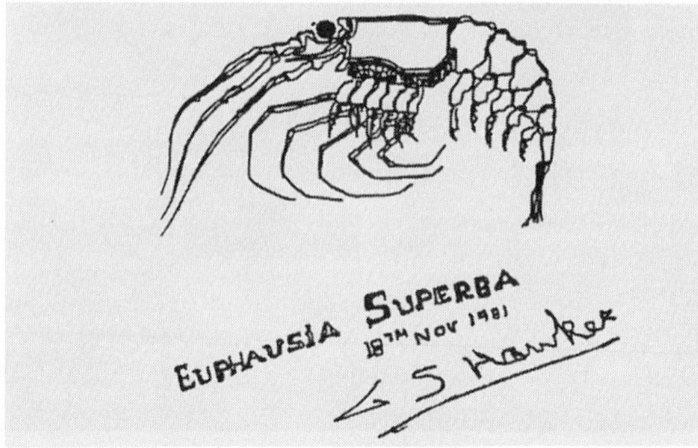

Figure 19. Experienced operators of industrial manipulator arms (center) can develop great dexterity *(see drawing on bottom) even with ordinary two-degree-of-freedom, joystick interfaces (top) for the control of robot arms with adequate mechanical bandwidth. Switches on the control box shift control to the various joints of the arm. The source of the dexterity illustrated here is the high dynamic fidelity of the control, a fidelity that needs to be reproduced if supposedly more natural haptic virtual environment interfaces are to be useful. (Photo courtesy of Deep Ocean Engineering, San Leandro, California).*

grees of manual dexterity. Relatively crude interfaces for rate-controlled manipulators (Figure 19) may allow experienced operators to accomplish fine manipulation tasks. Access to this level of proficiency, however, can be aided by coordinated displays of high visual resolution, by use of position control derived from inverse kinematic analysis of the manipulator, by more intuitive control of the interface, and by more anthropomorphic linkages on the manipulator.

An early example of a dexterous, anthropomorphic robotic end effector is the hand by Tomovic and Boni (Tomovic, and Boni, 1962). A more recent example is the Utah/MIT hand (Jacobson, Knutti, Biggers, Iversen, and Woods, 1984). Such hand-like end effectors with large numbers of degrees of freedom may be manually controlled directly by hand-shape sensors; for example, the Exos, exoskeleton hand (Exos, 1990) (Figure 20).

Significantly, the users of the Exos hand often turn off a number of the joints suggesting the possibility that there may be a limit to the number of degrees of freedom usefully incorporated into a dexterous master controller (Marcus, 1991). Less bulky body shape measurement devices have also been developed using

***Figure 20. An exoskeleton hand-shape measurement system** in a dexterous hand master using accurate Hall Effect flexion sensors which is suitable to drive a dexterous end-effector. (Photo courtesy of Exos, Inc., Burlington, Mass.).*

fiber optic or other sensors (Zimmerman, Lanier, Blanchard, Bryson, and Harvil, 1987; W Industries, 1991). (Figures 21 and 22); however, use of these alternatives involves significant trade-offs of resolution, accuracy, force-reflection and calibration stability as compared with the more bulky sensors. A more recent hand shape measurement device had been developed that combines high static and dynamic positional fidelity with intuitive operation and convenient donning and doffing (Kramer, 1992).

As suggested by the possibility of unneeded degrees of freedom in the Exos hand shape sensor, the number of needed degrees of freedom can become an important general research question. For example, it is possible to examine the performance implications of reducing the number of degrees of rotational freedom used in tracking the head positions of inhabitants of virtual environments. Some viewing systems such as the Fakespace Boom, a periscope-like devices used for high-resolution viewing, significantly constrain their users' ability to roll their heads. This device primarily provides them with only pitch and yaw movements, roll requires extra effort to produce. Questions, thus, arise regarding the impact of this kind of constraint.

Some anecdotal answers from observations during the use of head-mounted displays for architectural walk-throughs, suggest roll may not be necessary to record (Nomura, 1993). These observations have indicated that head position sensors could dispense with tracking roll since the system lag in updating the visual image made the users especially uncomfortable, sometimes nauseous, if their visual image rolled. Accordingly, one might reasonably ask if there are spatial awareness benefits provided by systems with head-roll tracking that might offset these costs of user discomfort (Figure 23).

This question has been investigated for manipulative interaction with targets placed within arms length of a user. The results show that if large head-torso rotations (> ~ 50°) with respect to the torso are not required, head roll tracking provides only minor improvements in the users' accuracy of positioning objects in a virtual environment (Adelstein and Ellis, 1993). Thus, roll-tracking/roll-compensation telepresence camera platforms may be unnecessary if the users' interface to the control of the remote device does not require large head-torso rotations. This conclusion, however, does depend upon the specific gymbol kinematics and the hemispheres of regard to be used.

8.3.5 Role of Engineering and Physiological Models

Since the integration of the equipment necessary to synthesize a virtual environment represents such a technical challenge in itself, there is a tendency for groups working in this area to focus their attention only on collecting and integrating the individual technologies for conceptual demonstrations in highly controlled settings. The videotaped character of many of these demonstrations of early implementations often suggested system performance far beyond actually available technology. The visual resolution of the cheaper, wide field displays using LCD technology was, for example, implicitly exaggerated by presentation techniques using overlays of users wearing displays and images taken directly from large-format graphics monitors. Accomplishment of specific tasks in real environments, however, places distinct real performance requirements on the simulation of which visual resolution is just an example. These requirements may be determined empirically for each task, but a more general approach is to use human performance models to help specify them. There are good general collections that can provide this background design data (e.g. Borah et al., 1978; Boff et al., 1986; Elkind

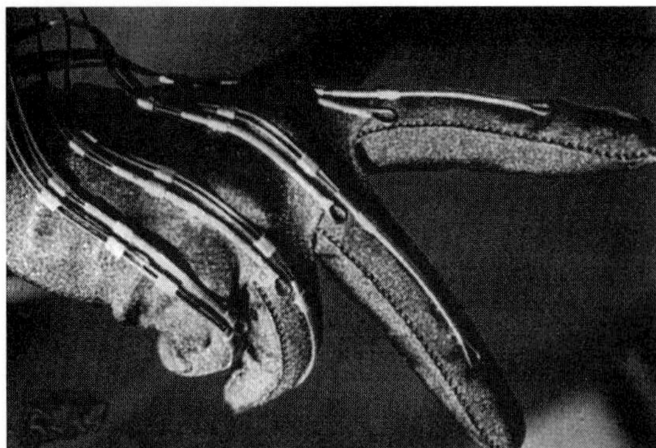

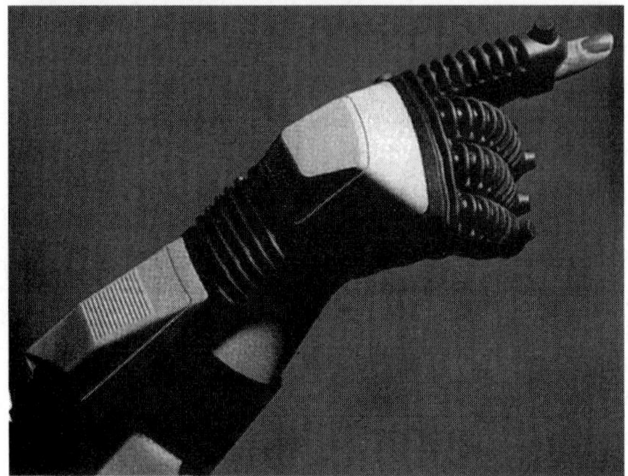

Figure 21. Less bulky hand-shape measuring instruments using flexible sensors *(upper panel: courtesy of VPL, Redwood City, California; (lower panel) courtesy of W. Industries, Leicester, UK).*

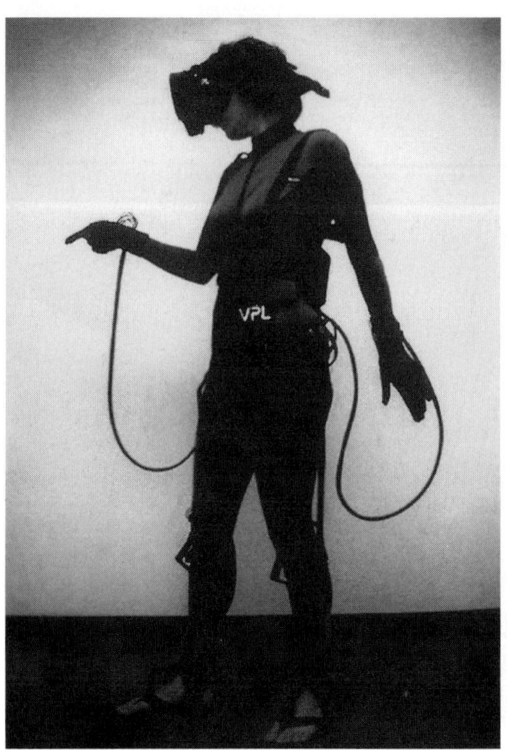

Figure 22. Fiber-optic flexion sensors used by VPL in the DataGlove have been incorporated in to a body-hugging suit. *Measurements of body shape can be used to dynamically control a computer graphics image of the body which may be seen through the head-mounted viewing device. (Lasko-Harvill, Blanchard, Smithers, Harvill, and Coffman, 1988). (Photo courtesy of VPL, Redwood City, California).*

et al., 1989) and there are specific examples of how scientific and engineering knowledge and computer-graphics-based visualization can be used to help designers conform to human performance constraints (Figure 24) (Monheit and Badler, 1990; Phillips et al., 1990; Larimer et al., 1991). Useful sources on human sensory and motor capacities relevant to virtual environments are also available (Howard, 1982; Brooks and Bejczy, 1986; Salvendy, 1987; Blauert, 1983; Goodale, 1990; Durlach et al., 1991; Ellis et al., 1993). Because widely available current technology generally limits the graphics and simulation update rate in virtual environments to less than 30 Hz, understanding the control characteristics of human movement, visual tracking, and vestibular responses is important for determining the practical limits to useful work in these environments. Theories of grasp, manual tracking (Jex, et al., 1966) spatial hearing (Blauert, 1983; Wenzel, 1991; Begault, 1994), vestibular response, and visual-vestibular correlation (Oman, 1991; Oman, Lichtenberg, Money, and McCoy, 1986) all can help to determine performance guidelines.

Predictive knowledge of system performance is not only useful for matching interfaces to human capabilities, but it is also useful in developing effective displays for situations in which human operators must cope with significant time lags (Smith and Smith, 1987), i.e. those exceeding 250 msec., or other control difficulties. In these circumstances, accurate dynamic or kinematic models of the controlled element allow the designer to give the user low latency control over a predictor which he may move to a desired location and which will be followed by the actual element at a later time (Hashimoto, et al., 1986; Bejczy, et al., 1990; McKinnon and Kruk, 1993) (Figure 25). Predictive filters that have been used in virtual environment simulation, however, have not yet benefited from incorporation of significant dynamical models (Azuma and Bishop, 1994) and likely can be considerably improved.

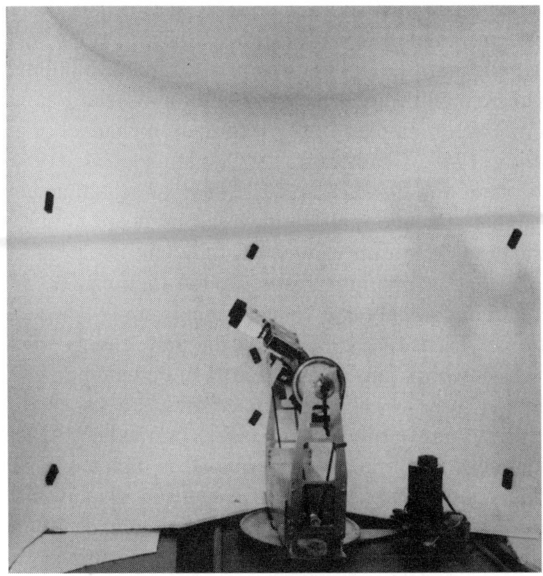

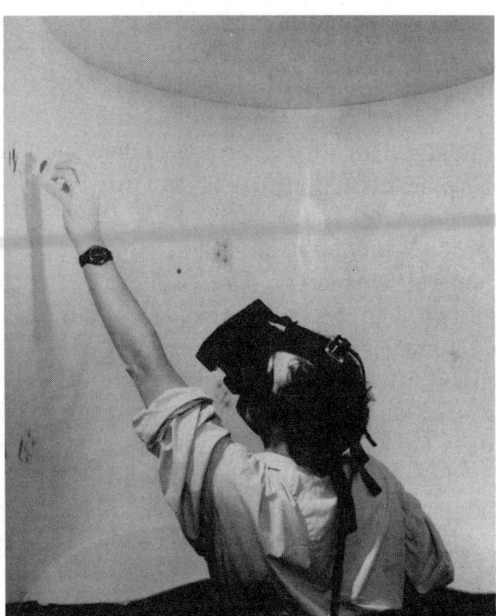

Figure 23. Apparatus used to study the benefits of incorporating head-roll tracking into a head-mounted telepresence display. *The left panel shows a stereo video camera mounted on a 3 dof platform that is slaved in orientation to the head orientation of an operator wearing a head-mounted video display at a remote site. The operator sees the video images from the camera and uses them to reproduce the orientation and position of rectangular test objects distributed on matching cylindrical work surfaces.*

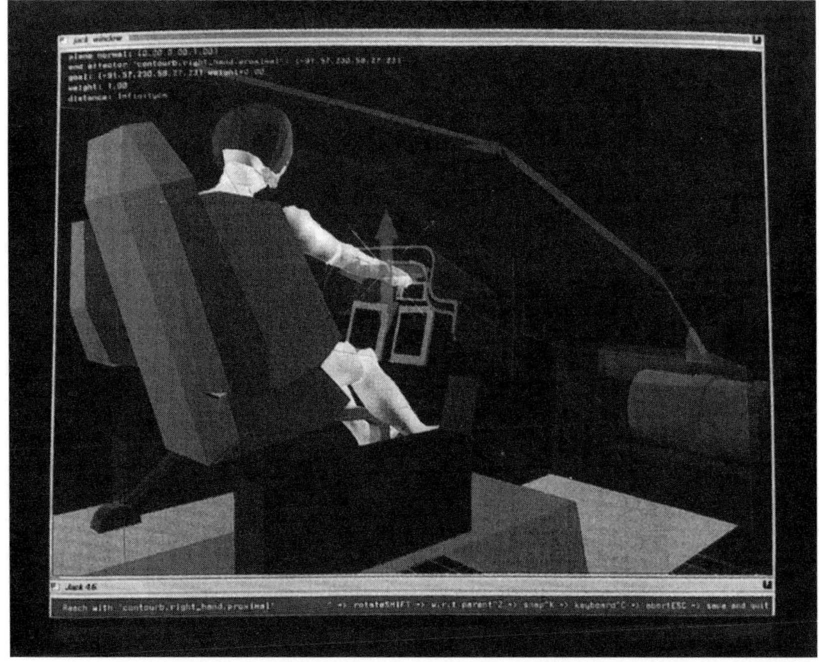

Figure 24. "Jack" screen (Phillips, et al., 1990; Larimer, et al., 1991) example of a graphics display system *that is being developed to assist cockpit designers to determine whether potential cockpit configurations would be consistent with human performance limitations such as reach envelopes or visual field characteristics. (Photo courtesy of NASA).*

Demonstrated Systems as Sources of Guidelines

Other sources of guidelines are the performance and designs of existing high fidelity systems themselves (Figures 26 and 27). Of the virtual environment display systems, one of the best visual display is the CAE Fiber Optic Helmet Mounted Display, FOHMD, (Lypaczewski, et al., 1986; Barrette, et al., 1990) which is used in military aircraft simulators. One of its earlier models presented two 83.5° monocular fields of view with adjustable binocular overlap, typically in early versions of about 38°, giving a full horizontal field-of-view up to 162°. Similarly, the Wright-Patterson Air Force Base Visually Coupled Airborne Systems Simulator or VCASS display, also presented a very wide field of view, and has been used to study the consequences of field-of-view restriction on several visual tasks (Wells, and Venturino, 1990). Their results support other reports indicating that visual performance improves with increased field of view, but that this effect wanes as fields of view greater than 60° are used (Hatada, Sakata, and Kusaka, 1980).

Towards the Design of Multimodal Virtual Environments: Audio Displays

Engineering models and scientific theories concerning human perception and interaction with the physical world can not only enhance interaction with virtual environments within single sensory channels but also assist development of multimodal systems. Auditory virtual environments provide a good recent example of how such multimodal virtual environment simulations can be developed. Research over the last decade has established the base technologies for virtual acoustic displays, sometimes termed "3-D sound systems." Specialized digital signal processing hardware for these devices has been developed to simulate salient spatial auditory cues that are provided by the HRTF (Head Related Transfer Function) and the environmental context in everyday listening.

The binaural advantage can be roughly categorized into two areas likely to improve human-machine interfaces for communication, telepresence, and simulation/training: (1) a 360 degree system for situational awareness, allowing the monitoring of positional information in all dimensions, without the use of the eyes; and (2) an increased ability to segregate multiple signals and increase intelligibility against noise, compared to one-ear listening. In many previous display contexts, the only modalities available for interacting with complex information systems have been visual and manual. When audio is present, it is usually monaural, and implemented for non-spatial functions such as simple alarms. But many investigators have pointed out the potential of the spatial auditory system as an alternative or supplementary information channel (e.g., Garner, 1949; Deatherage, 1972; Doll, et al., 1986; Buxton, et al., 1989). Useful features of spatial acoustic signals include that (1) they can be heard simultaneously in three dimensions, (2) they tend to produce an alerting or orienting response, (3) they can be detected more quickly than visual signals, and (4) we are extremely sensitive to them when they change over time (Mowbray and Gebhard, 1961; Patterson, 1982; Kubovy, 1981). These characteristics are especially useful in inherently spatial tasks, particularly when visual cues are limited and workload is high; e.g., air traffic control rooms. A virtual acoustic display also allows the auditory system to use its inherent ability to segregate, monitor, and switch attention among simultaneous streams of sound. This is known as the Cocktail Party Effect (Cherry, 1953). See Begault and Erbe (1994) for a description of how this advantage is applied to speech communications hardware. The name of this effect comes from a vivid example of the binaural advantage: at a cocktail party with many people speaking at once, it is still possible to listen to a single conversation, but is much more difficult with one ear listening. Spatial presentation of multiple sound sources allows greater intelligibility of a desired signal from a noisy background and allows a listener to use selective attention.

Techniques for Creating Spatial Auditory Displays

The success of spatial synthesis relies on understanding the acoustical cues that are used by human listeners to locate sound sources in space. In the duplex theory of sound localization based on experiments with pure tones (sine waves), interaural intensity differences (IIDs) were thought to determine localization at high frequencies because wavelengths smaller than the human head create an intensity loss or head shadow at the ear farthest from the sound source (Lord Rayleigh, 1907). Conversely, interaural time differences (ITDs) were thought to be important for low frequencies since interaural phase (delay) relationships are unambiguous only for frequencies below about 1500 Hz (wavelengths larger than the head.) The duplex theory, however, cannot account for the ability to localize sounds on the vertical median plane where interaural cues are minimal. Also, when subjects listen to sounds over headphones, they usually appear to be inside the

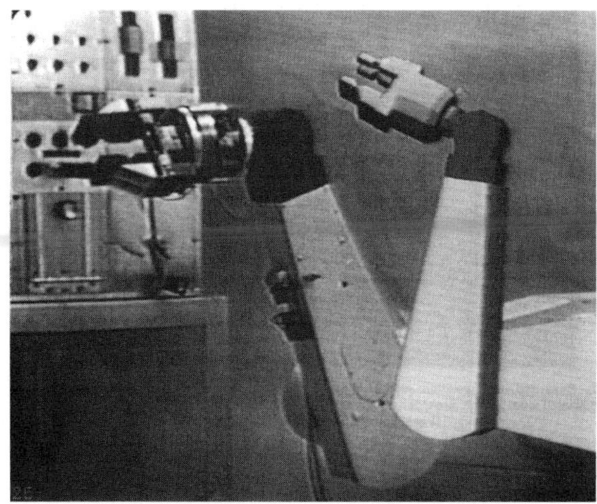

Figure 25. ***Graphic model of a manipulator arm electronically superimposed on a video signal from a remote work site to assist users who must contend with time delay in their control actions (Photograph courtesy of JPL, Pasadena, California).***

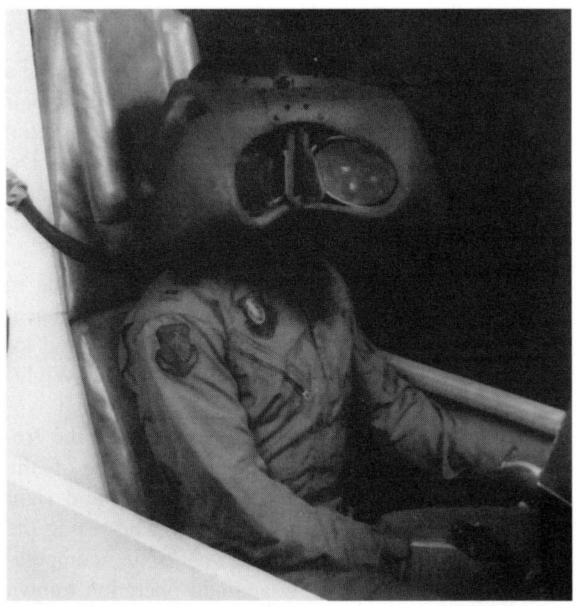

Figure 26. Visually Coupled Airborne Systems Simulator of *the Armstrong Aerospace Medical Research Laboratory of Wright-Patterson Air Force Base can present a wide field-of-view stereo display (120^0 X 60^0) which is updated at up to 20 Hz Head position is measured electromagnetically and may be recorded at a slower rate Visual pixel resolution 3.75 arcmin/ pixel. (Photograph courtesy of AAMRL, WPAFB).*

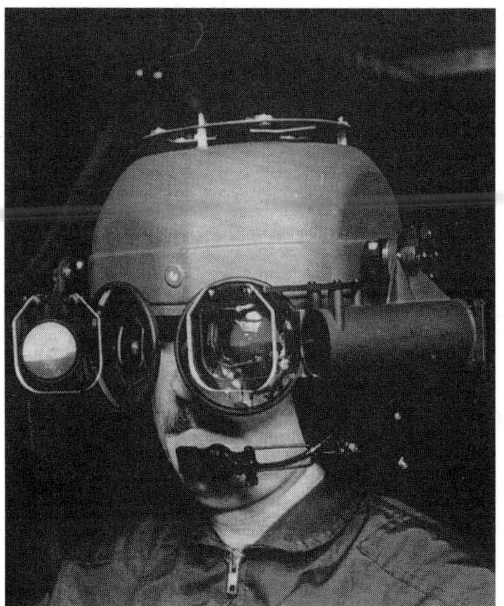

Figure 27. Though very expensive, the CAE Fiber Optic *Helmet Mounted Display, FOHUD (upper panel), is one of the highest-performance virtual environment systems used a head-mounted aircraft simulator display. It can present an overall visual field of 162^0 X 83.5^0 with 5 arcmin resolution with a high resolution inset of 24^0 X 18^0 of 1.5 arcmin resolution. It has a bright, full-color display, 30 Foot- Lambert, and a fast, optical head-tracker, 60 Hz sampling, with accelerator augmentation. The Kaiser WideEye® display (lower panel) is a roughly comparable, monochrome device designed for actual flight in aircraft as a head-mounted HUD. It has a much narrower field of view (monocular : 40^0 , binocular with 50% overlap 40^0 X 60^0 ; visual resolution is approximately 3 arcmin) (Photographs courtesy of CAE Electronics, Montreal, Canada; Kaiser Electronics, San Josè).*

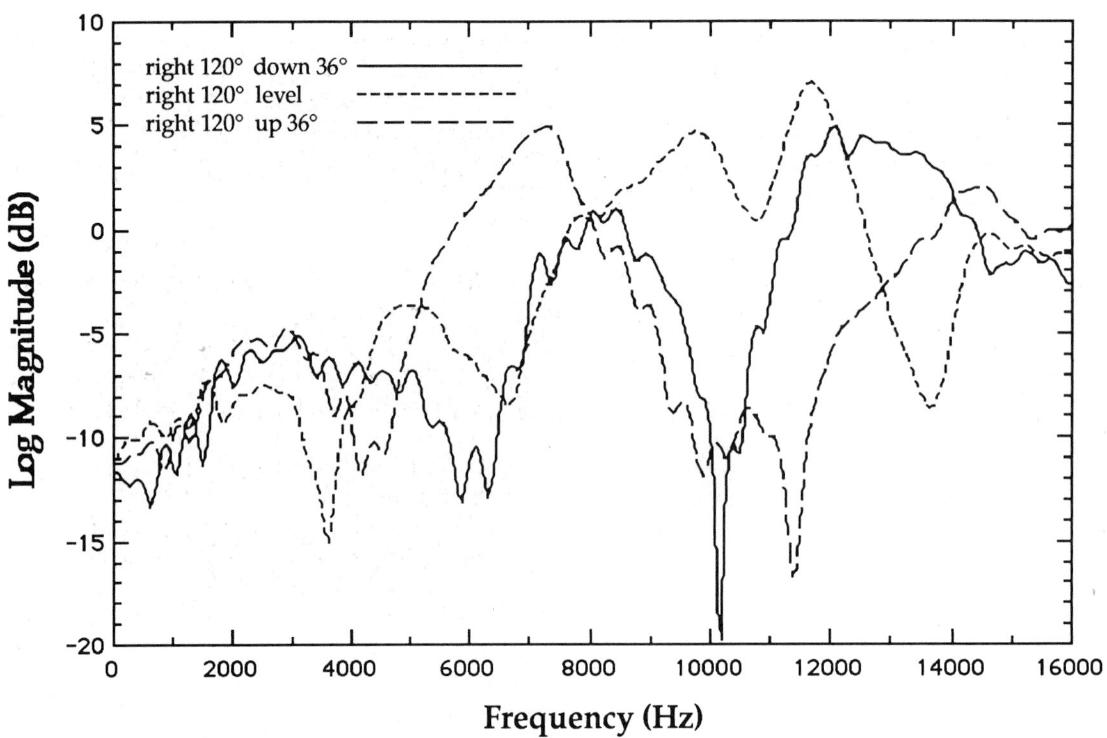

Figure 28. The Head-Related Transfer Function (HRTF) for three different elevations, measured at one ear. *The differences in intensity as a function of frequency are imparted on an incoming sound source. The different characteristics of the transfer function as a function of elevation are considered to provide perceptual cues to elevation.*

head even though ITDs and IIDs appropriate to an external source location are present. Many studies now indicate that these deficiencies of the duplex theory reflect the important contribution to localization of the direction-dependent filtering that occurs when incoming sound waves interact with the outer ears. Experiments have shown that spectral shaping by the pinnae is highly direction-dependent (Shaw, 1974), that the absence of pinna cues degrades localization accuracy (Gardner and Gardner, 1973), and that pinna cues are at least partially responsible for externalization or the "outside-the-head" sensation (Plenge, 1974). See Figure 28 for an example of the spectral shaping caused by the pinnae.

The synthesis technique typically used in creating a spatial auditory display involves the digital generation of stimuli using location-dependent filters constructed from acoustical measurements made with small probe microphones placed in the ear canals of individual subjects or artificial heads for a large number of different source (loudspeaker) locations (Wightman and Kistler, 1989a; Begault, 1994). These measurements are converted into a pair of "HRTF filters" (one for the left ear, one for the right) that are used to filter an arbitrary sound source for use within a virtual acoustic display. Acting something like a pair of graphic equalizers, the HRTFs capture the essential cues needed for localizing a sound source; the ITDs, IIDs, and the spectral coloration produced by a sound's interaction with the outer ears and other body structures.

Using these HRTF-based filters, it is possible to impose spatial characteristics on a signal such that it apparently emanates from the originally-measured location (Wenzel, Wightman and Foster, 1988; Wightman and Kistler, 1989b; Wenzel, 1992). Spatial synthesis can be achieved either by filtering in the frequency domain, a point-by-point multiplication of the spectrum of the input signal with the left and right HRTFs, or by filtering in the time domain, using the FIR representation and a somewhat more computationally-intensive, multiply-and-add operation known as convolution. Of course, the localization of the sound will also depend on other factors such as its original spectral content; narrow band sounds (sine waves) are generally very difficult to localize while broadband, impulsive sounds are the easiest to locate. The use of HRTF-based filters cannot increase the bandwidth of the original signal; they can only transform the energy and phase of the frequency components that are initially present.

In most recent real-time systems such as the Convolvotron[3], from one to four moving or static sources can be simulated (with varying degrees of fidelity) in an anechoic (free-field or echoless) environment by time-domain convolution of incoming signals with HRTF-based filters chosen according to the output of a head-tracking device. The head-tracking device allows the display to update the directional filters in real time to compensate for a listener's head motion so that virtual sources remain stable within the simulated environment. Motion trajectories and static locations at finer resolutions than the empirical data are generally simulated either by switching, or more preferably, by interpolating between the measured HRTFs (Wenzel and Foster, 1993). Also, in some systems, a simple distance cue can be provided via real-time scaling of amplitude.

It should be noted that the spatial cues provided by HRTFs, especially those measured in free-field environments, are not the only cues likely to be necessary to achieve accurate localization (Blauert, 1983; Durlach, et al., 1992; Wenzel, 1992). Research indicates that synthesis of purely anechoic sounds can result in perceptual errors; in particular, increases in apparent front-back reversals, decreased elevation accuracy, and failures of externalization. These errors tend to be exacerbated when virtual sources are generated from non-personalized HRTFs, a common circumstance for most virtual displays. Other research suggests that such errors might be mitigated by providing more complex acoustic cues from reverberant environments. For example, acoustic features such as the ratio of direct to reflected energy in a reverberant field can provide a cue to distance (closer sources correspond to larger ratios) as well as enhance the sensation of externalization (Begault, 1992).

While nonreal- time room modeling (termed "auralization") has been implemented for some time (see Kleiner, 1993), recently some progress has been made toward interactively synthesizing reverberant cues. For example in the Convolvotron, the walls, floor, and ceiling in an environment are simulated by using HRTF-based filters to place the "mirror image" of a sound source behind each surface to account for the specular reflection of the source signal (Foster, Wenzel, and Taylor, 1991). The filtering effect of surfaces such as wood or drapery can also be modeled with a separate filter whose output is delayed by the time required for the sound to propagate from each reflection being represented.

[3] The Convolvotron is a commercially available spatial synthesis system developed at NASA Ames in collaboration with Crystal River Engineering.

Reviews of Human Factors Guidelines

Adequate technical descriptions with performance data for fully integrated virtual environment display systems have not been generally available or accurately detailed for many of the early systems. (e.g. Fisher, et al., 1986; Stone, 1991ab). This situation should change as reports are published in a number of journals, i.e. IEEE Computer Graphics and Applications, Computer Systems in Engineering, Presence: the Journal of Teleoperations and Virtual Environments, Pixel, the Magazine of Scientific Visualization, Ergonomics, Human Factors. Recent technical books have cataloged the technology and its human factors design issues (Ellis, et al, 1993; Kalawsky, 1993; Barfield and Furness, 1995, Carr and England, 1995). But due to the absence of standards and the novelty of the equipment, developers are likely to find current assessments incomplete and premature. Consequently, users of the technology must often measure the basic design impact of its components' characteristics for themselves (e.g. Adelstein et al., 1992).

8.4 Virtual Environments: Performance and Trade-Offs

8.4.1 Performance Advances and Customizability of the Technology

With the state of off-the-shelf technology, it is unlikely that a fully implemented virtual environment display will today uniquely enable useful work at a price accessible to the average researcher. Those systems that have solved some of the major technological problems, that is, adequate head-tracking bandwidth, viewing resolution comparable to existing CRT technology, do so through special purpose hardware that is very expensive. The inherent cost of some enabling technologies, however, is not high and development continues, promising improved performance and flexibility, (e.g. optical head tracking (Wang, et al., 1990) and high quality detailed volumetric display hardware for medium cost workstations stations (OCTREE Corporation, 1991)). Medium cost complete systems costing on the order of $200,000 have currently proved commercially useful for visualizing and selling architectural products such as custom kitchens (Nomura, et al., 1992). However, no matter how sophisticated or cheap the display technology becomes, there will always be some costs associated with its use. With respect to practical applications, the key question is to identify those tasks that are so enabled by use of a virtual environment display, that users will choose this display format over alternatives. This comparison is particularly important in applications for which most of the benefit arises from the underlying simulation itself. In these cases panel mounted displays providing good global spatial information should generally prove cost effective when compared to head-mounted alternatives.

Clearly, there are many possible applications, beside flight simulation and cockpit display design, which may soon become practical. In addition to the obvious video game applications, the technology could help CAD/CAM designer visualize their final product, telerobotic programmers debug the planning algorithms, teleoperation controllers deal with time lags, laparoscopic surgeons plan and execute procedures, customers design and select custom kitchens. The list of possibilities could go on and on. The difficulties with such lists is that for each application a very particular set of static and dynamic task demands needs to be satisfied and its satisfaction involves the definition of a livable, but specially tuned environment.

The apparent general applicability of virtual environments to practically anything is, in reality, a significant difficulty. Technology derives its power from its specificity and its customizability (Basalla, 1988). The first LINK trainer which taught an aircraft's response to control stick and pedal inputs was a commercial failure, but the later model designed for the more specific purpose of relating control inputs to flight instrument readings was a success. An aircraft simulator is valuable not because it can simulate an aircraft but because it can simulate a Boeing 747SP!

This requirement for specificity is really quite an order as the developers of flight simulator know full well, and it is where a good portion of development resources need to be committed. In fact, even in flight simulation we are only beginning to be able to create head-mounted simulators with adequate fidelity to avoid nausea, allow protracted use, and enable useful training. The motion sickness problem (Presence, 1992) is only one of many human factors issues yet to be resolved with this technology as both the serious applications as well as entertainment applications are fielded.

The wide array of application possibilities can be a distracting design issue, since the apparent applicability of virtual displays to everything can obscure the best applications. In fact, virtual environments are probably almost uniquely useful for telerobotic-like tasks. But for other applications the egocentric frame of reference provided by head-mounted displays may not provide significant added performance over much cheaper, publicly viewable, panel-mounted alternatives. Research needs to be done to identify what level of virtualization is most appropriate to which applications and to understand how to match specific aspects of the display to needs of the human users. Some suggestions of appropriate matches for a variety of sensory and motor communication channels exist (Figure 29) but these have not been systematically tested or validated and only represent informal engineering opinion. Some visual aspects of the difficulties of matching human perceptual needs in virtual environment are discussed in more detail below. In general, the visual specifications for heads-up aircraft displays (HUDs) are a good first place to look for visual specifications for virtual environments (Weintraub and Ensing, 1992) and the specific visual consequences of virtual environment displays deviating from these specifications have begun to be specifically investigated (Mon-Williams, Wann and Rushton, 1993). Designers of helmet-mounted displays for military applications have known that field use of stereoscopic displays is difficult because careful alignment is required to avoid problems with visual fatigue (Edwards, 1991; Melzer, 1991). Accordingly, stereo eye strain is a possible difficulty for long-term use of stereo virtual environments, especially because most stereo displays of near objects significantly violate the normal relationships between vergence and accommodation by presenting only a single plane of focus (Ciuffreda, 1992; Mon-Williams, et al, 1993). However, new devices for measuring acuity, accommodation, and eye position (Takeda, Fukui, and Lida, 1986) may help improve designs. Development of a self- compensating display that adjusts its accommodative demand or of a display that actually presents multiple focal planes is one possibility (Kollin, 1993; Holgren and Robinett, 1993). But it is currently well beyond fieldable technology. As with eye strain, the neck strain caused by the helmet's mass is likely to be relieved by technical advances such as miniaturization. But, as Krueger has consistently emphasized, there will always be a cost associated with required use of head gear and the simple solution to this problem may be to avoid protracted use.

Another cost associated with head-mounted displays versus panel mounted alternatives, is that though

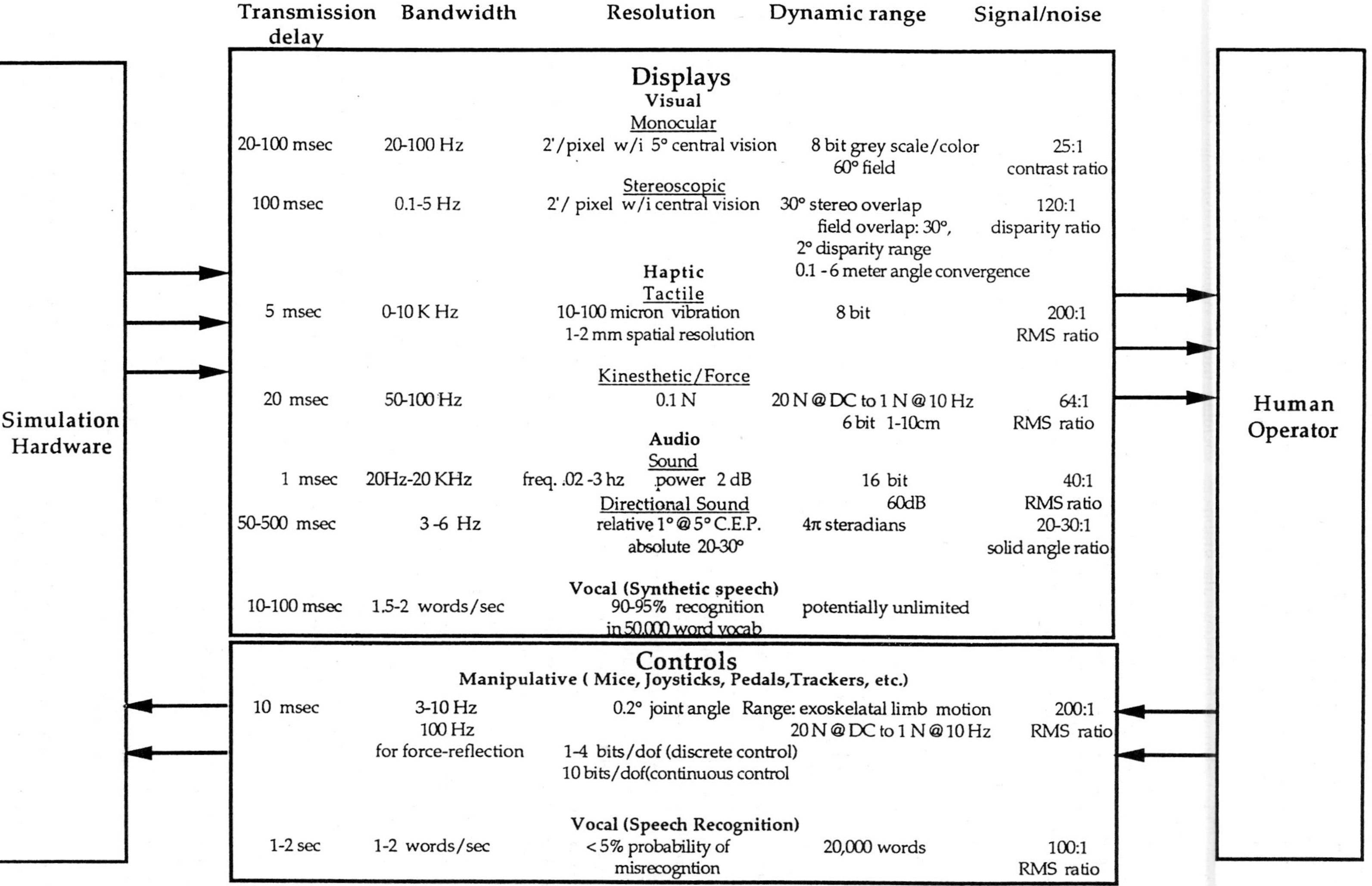

Figure 29. This block diagram describes some characteristics of the communicating channels that must be opened between a user of a virtual environment and the underlying simulation program. *These are simulation-specific and will vary for different applications, but the values in the table are based on human perceptual; and note on performance characteristics that have allowed useful performance in at least one specific application. They enumerate a vocabulary of performance targets that simulation hardware may need to achieve for the development of useful virtual environments (Eliis, 1994).*

they may generally have larger fields of view than the panel-mounted alternative, they will typically have correspondingly lower spatial resolution. Eye movement recording technology has been used to avoid this trade-off by tracking the viewer's current area of fixation so that a high-resolution graphics insert can be displayed there. This technique can relieve the graphics processor of the need to display high- resolution images in the regions of the peripheral visual field that cannot resolve it (Cowdry, 1986). Reliable and robust eye tracking technology is still, however, costly, but fortunately may be unnecessary if a high resolution insert of approximately 30° diameter may be inserted. Since in the course of daily life most eye movements may be less than 15° (Bahill, Adler, and Stark, 1975), a head-mounted display system which controls the viewing direction of the simulation by head position, need not employ eye tracking if the performance environment does not typically require large amplitude eye movements.

8.4.2 Unique Capabilities

In view of these and other costs of virtual environment displays, what unique capabilities do they enable? Since these systems amount to a communications medium, they are intrinsically applicable to practically anything...education, procedure training, teleoperation, high-level programming, remote planetary surface exploration, exploratory data analysis, and scientific visualization (Brooks Jr., 1988). One unique feature of the medium, however, is that it can enable multiple, simultaneous, coordinated, real-time foci of control in an environment. Tasks that involve manipulation of objects in complex visual environments and also require frequent, concurrent changes in viewing position, for example, laparoscopic surgery (SAGES, 1991) are tasks that are naturally suited for virtual environment displays. Other tasks that may be mapped into this format are also uniquely suitable, for example, maintenance training for complex machinery such as jet engines which may be manually "disassembled" using virtual environment displays. The common element of all these applications is that benefits arise from offloading of a viewing control function from the hands to the head, thereby achieving some degree of hands-free operation.

In conclusion it's important also to note that in addition to the physiological and psychological aftereffects that prolonged use of virtual environments displays can produce e.g. disturbances of visuo-motor coordination, use of these displays may also have sociological effects, especially if the high level of violence in existing video games is transferred into this new medium. Thus, the future design of virtual environments might provide not only technical, but also social and possibly political challenges as well. Consequently, significant research into costs of extensive societal use of virtual environments needs to be conducted (See Presence, 1993).

8.5 References

Adelstein, B. D. and Ellis, Stephen R. (1993). Effect of head-slaved visual image roll on spatial situation awareness. *Proceedings of the 37th Meeting of the Human Factors and Ergonomics Society,* October 11-15, 1993.

Adelstein, B. D., and Rosen, M. J. (1991). *A high performance two degree of freedom kinesthetic interface. Human machine interfaces for teleoperators and virtual environments.* Santa Barbara, CA, NASA CP 91035, NASA Ames Research Center, Moffett Field, CA, 108-113.

Adelstein, B. D., and Rosen, M. J. (1992). *Design and Implementation of a Force Reflecting Manipulandum for Manual Control Research.* Anaheim, CA. American Society of Mechanical Engineers, New York. 1-12.

Adelstein, B. D., Johnston, E. R., and Ellis, S. R. (1992). A test-bed for characterizing the response of virtual environment spatial sensors. *The 5th Annual ACM Symposium on User Interface Software and Technology. Monterey,* California. ACM, 15-20.

AGARD. (1988). Conference Proceedings N. 433: Motion Cues in Flight Simulation and Simulator Induced Sickness, (*AGARD CP 433*) Springfield, VA. NTIS.

Airey, J. M., Rohlf, J. H., and Brooks Jr. (1990). Towards image realism with interactive update rates in complex virtual building environments. *Computer Graphics*, 24(2), 41-50.

Amadon, Gregory (1995). President, Virtual I/O, 1000 Lenora St. #600, Seattle, WA 98121, personal communication.

Apple Computer Co. (1992). Newton Technology: An Overview of a New Technology from Apple. Apple Computer Co, 20525 Mariani Ave, Cupertino, CA 95014.

Ascension Technology Corp. (1990). Product description. *Ascension Technology Corporation*, Burlington, VT 05402.

Azuma, R. and Bishop, G. (1994). Improved static and dynamic registration in an optical see-through HMD. SIGGRAPH 94, *Computer Graphics Proceedings, Annual Conference Series*. pp. 197-204.

Bahill, A. T., Adler, D. and Stark, L. (1975). Most naturally occurring human saccades have magnitudes of 15 degrees or less. *Investigative Ophthalmology*, 14, 468-9.

Barfield, W and Kim, Y. (1991). Effect of geometric parameters of perspective on judgments of spatial information. *Perceptual and Motor Skills*, 73(2), 619-23.

Barfield, W. and Furness, T. A. (eds.) (1995). *Virtual Environments and Advanced Interface Design*. New York: Oxford University Press.

Barfield, W. and Furness, T. A., (Eds.) (1995). *Virtual Environments and Advanced Interface Design*. Oxford: Oxford University Press.

Barnes, J. (1992). Acoustic 6 dof sensor. *Logitech*, 6505 Kaiser Dr., Fremont CA 94555.

Barrette, R., Dunkley, R., Kruk, R., Kurtz, D., Marshall, S., Williams, T., Weissman, P., and Antos, S. (1990). Flight simulation advanced wide FOV helmet mounted infinity display (AFHRL-TR-89-36). *Air Force Human Resources Laboratory*.

Basalla, G. (1988). *The Evolution of Technology*. New York: Cambridge University Press.

Bassett, B. (1992). Virtual reality head-mounted displays. *Virtual Research*, 1313 Socorro Ave, Sunnyvale CA, 94089.

BASYS. (1990). Product description, *Basys Gesellschaft für Anwender und Systemsoftware mbH*, Nürnberg, Germany.

Begault, D. R. (1992). Perceptual effects of synthetic reverberation on three-dimensional audio systems. *Journal of the Audio Engineering Society*, 40(11), 895-904.

Begault, D. R. (1994). *3-D sound for Virtual Reality and Multimedia*. Cambridge, MA: Academic Press Professional.

Begault, D. R., and Erbe, T. (1994). Multichannel spatial auditory display for speech communications. *Journal of the Audio Engineering Society*, 42(10), 819-826.

Begault, D. R., and Wenzel, E. M. (1993). Headphone Localization of Speech. *Human Factors*, 35(2), 361-376.

Bejczy, A. K. (1980). Sensor controls and man-machine interface for teleoperation. *Science*, 208, 1327-1335.

Bejczy, A. K. and Salisbury Jr, K. S. (1980). Kinesthetic coupling between operator and remote manipulator. Advances in Computer Technology. *Proceedings ASME International Computer Technology Conference*. San Francisco, Calif. 197-211.

Bejczy, A. K., Kim, W. S., and Venema, S. C. (1990 May 13-18). The phantom robot: predictive displays for teleoperation with time delay. *Proceedings of the IEEE International Conference on Robotics and Automation*. IEEE. 546-551.

Bertin, J. (1967 / 1983). *Semiology of Graphics: Diagrams, Networks, Maps*. Madison, WI: University of Wisconsin Press.

Bishop, P. O. (1987). Binocular vision. In R. A. Moses, and W. M. H. Adlers., Jr. (Eds.), *Physiology of the Eye* (pp. 619-689). Washington, D.C.: C.V. Mosby.

Blauert, J. (1983). *Spatial Hearing*. Cambridge, MA: MIT Press.

Blinn, J. F. (1987). The mechanical universe: an integrated view of a large animation project (Course Notes: Course #6). *Proceedings of the 14th Ann. Conference on Computer Graphics and Interactive Techniques*. Anaheim, Ca.. ACM SIGGRAPH and IEEE Technical Committee on Computer Graphics.

Blinn, J. F. (1991). The Making of the Mechanical Universe. In S. R. Ellis, M. K. Kaiser, and Grunwald (Eds.), *Pictorial Communication in Virtual and Real Environments* (pp.138-155) London: Taylor & Francis.

Boff, K. R., Kaufman, L., and Thomas, J. P. (1986). *Handbook of Perception and Human Performance*. New York: Wiley & John.

Borah, J., Young, L. R., John and Curry, R. E. (1978). *Sensory Mechanism Modeling* (USAF ASD Report AFHRL TR 78-83). Air Force Human Resources Laboratory.

Brand, S. (1987). *The Media Lab: Inventing the Future at MIT*. New York: Viking.

Brehde, D. (1991). CeBIT: Cyberspace-Vorstoss in eine andere Welt (Breakthrough into another world). *Stern*, 44(12), 130-142.

Brooks Jr., F. (1988 May 15-19). Grasping reality through illusion-interactive graphics serving science. *Proceedings CHI'88*. Washington, D. C. 1-12.

Brooks, T. L., and Bejczy, A. K. (1986). Hand controllers for teleoperation (*NASA* CR 175890, JPL Publication 85-11). JPL.

Bussolari, S. R., Young, L. R. and Lee, A. T. (1988). The use of vestibular models for design and evaluation of flight simulation motion. *AGARD Conference Proceedings N. 433:* Motion cues in flight simulation and simulator induced sickness. NTIS, Springfield, VA (AGARD CP 433).

CAE Electronics. (1991). Product literature. *CAE Electronics, Montréal*, Canada

Cardullo, F. (1993). *Flight Simulation Update 1993.* Binghamton, New York: Watson School of Continuing Education, SUNY Binghamton.

Carr, K. and England, R. (Eds.) (1995). *Simulated and Virtual Realities.* London: Taylor & Francis.

Carroll, Lewis (1872). *Through the Looking Glass: and What Alice Found There.* London: Macmillan and Co.

Cellier, F. (1991). *Modeling Continuous Systems.* New York: Springer-Verlag.

Clark, J. H. (1980). A VLSI geometry processor for graphics. *IEEE Computer*, 12, 7.

Clark, J. H. (1982). The geometry engine: a VLSI geometry system for graphics. *Computer Graphics*, 16(3), 127-133.

Collewijn, H. and Erkelens, C. J. (1990). Binocular eye movements and the perception of depth. In E. Kowler (Ed.), *Eye Movements and their Role in Visual and Cognitive Processes* (pp. 213-262). Amsterdam: Elsevier Science Publishers.

Comeau, C. P. and Bryan, J. S. (1961). Headsight television system provides remote surveillance. *Electronics*, (November 10, 1961), 86-90.

Cooper, G.E. and Harper, R. P. Jr. (1969) The use of pilot ratings in the evaluation of aircraft handling qualities. *NASA* TN D 5153.

Cotter, C. H. (1966). *The Astronomical and Mathematical Foundations of Geography.* New York: Elsevier.

Cowdry, D. A. (1986). Advanced visuals in mission simulators In Flight Simulation. NTIS Springfield VA (*AGARD*). pp. 3.1-10.

Crampton, G. H. (1990). *Motion and Space Sickness.* Boca Raton, FL: CRC Press.

Cruz-Neira, C., Sandin, D. J., DeFanti, T. A., Kenyon, R. V., and Hart, J. C. (1992). The cave: audiovisual experience automatic virtual environment. *Communications of the ACM,* 35(6), 65-72.

Cuiffreda, Kenneth J. (1992) Components of clinical near vergence testing. *Journal of Behavioral Optometry,* 3, 1, 3-13.

Curry, R. E., Hoffman, W. C. and Young, L. R. (1976 December 1). Pilot modeling for manned simulation (AFFDL-TR-76-124). Air Force Flight Dynamics Laboratory Publication.

D'Arcy, J. (1990). *Re-creating Reality.* MacCleans, 103(6), 36-41.

Deering, Michael (1992). High resolution virtual reality, *Computer Graphics*, 26(2) 195-201.

Durlach, N. I., Rigopulos, A., Pang, X. D., Woods, W. S., Kulkarni, A., Colburn, H. S., and Wenzel, E. M. (1992). On the Externalization of Auditory Images." *Presence*, 1, 251-257.

Durlach, N. I., Sheridan, T. B., and Ellis, S. R. (1991). Human machine interfaces for teleoperators and virtual environments (*NASA* CP91035). NASA Ames Research Center.

Edwards, O. J. (1991). Personal communication. S-TRON, Mountain View CA 94043 S- TRON, Mountain View CA 94043.

Elkind, J. I., Card, S. K., Hochberg, J. and Huey, B. M. (1989). Human Performance Models for Computer-Aided Engineering. National Academy Press Washington, D. C: National Academy Press.

Ellis, S. R. (1990). Pictorial Communication. Leonardo, 23, 81-6.

Ellis, S. R. (1991). Prologue. In S. R. Ellis, M. K. Kaiser and A. J. Grunwald (Eds), *Pictorial Communication in Virtual and Real Environments.* (pp. 3-11). London: Taylor & Francis.

Ellis, S. R. and Grunwald, A. J. (1989a) Visions of visualization aids: design philosophy and observations. *Proceedings of the SPIE OE/LASE'89*, 1083, Symposium on three- dimensional visualization of scientific data. Los Angeles, CA. SPIE Bellingham. Washington, 220-227.

Ellis, S. R. and Hacisalihzade, S. S. (1990). Symbolic enhancement of perspective displays. *Proceedings of the 34th Annual Meeting of the Human Factors Society.* Santa Monica, CA.

Ellis, S. R. and Hitchcock, R. J. (1986 May/June). Emergence of Zipf's Law: spontaneous encoding optimization by users of a command language. *IEEE Transactions on Systems Man and Cybernetics*, SMC-16, 423-7.

Ellis, S. R., and Grunwald, A. J. (1989b). The dynamics of orbital maneuvering: design and evaluation of a visual display aid for human controllers. NTIS, Springfield, VA (*AGARD FMP symposium* CP 489, pp. 29-1 - 29-13).

Ellis, S. R., Kaiser, M. K. and Grunwald, A. J. (1991; 1993 2nd ed.). *Pictorial Communication in Virtual and Real Environments.* London: Taylor & Francis.

Ellis, S. R., McGreevy, M. W. and Hitchcock, R. (1987). Perspective traffic display format and airline pilot traffic avoidance. *Human Factors*, 29, 371-82.

Ellis, Stephen R. (1994). What are virtual environments?. *IEEE Computer Graphics and Applications*, 14(1),17-22.

Ellis, Stephen R. (1996). Presence of mind: commentary on Sheridan's 'Musings on telepresence'. *Presence* (accepted for publication).

Ellis, S. R. and Bucher, U. J. (1994). Distance perception of stereoscopically presented virtual objects superimposed by a head mounted see through display. *Proceedings, 38th Annual Meeting of the Human Factors and Ergonomics Society,* Santa Monica CA, 1994. pp. 1300- 1305.

Ellis, S. R. and Menges, B. M. (1995). Judged distance to virtual objects in the near visual field. *Proceedings of the Human Factors and Ergonomics Society, 39th Annual Meeting.* San Diego, CA, 1400-1404.

Erkelens, C. J. and Collewijn, H. (1985a). Eye movements and stereopsis during dichoptic viewing of moving random dot stereograms. *Vision Research*, 25, 1689-700.

Erkelens, C. J. and Collewijn, H. (1985b). Motion perception during dichoptic viewing of moving random dot stereograms. *Vision Research*, 25, 583-88.

Exos (1990). Product literature. *Exos*, 8 Blanchard Rd., Burlington, MA.

Fagan, B. M. (1985). *The Adventures of Archaeology.* Washington, D. C: National Geographic Society, p. 245.

Feiner, S. and Beshers, C. (1990). Worlds within worlds: metaphors for exploring n-dimensional virtual worlds. *Proceedings of 3rd Annual Symposium on User Interface Technology.* Snowbird, Utah, 3-5 October 1990. ACM 429902.

Feldon, S. E. and Burda, R. A. (1987). The extraocular muscles: Section 2, The oculomotor system. In R. A. Moses and Moses W. M. H. (Jr. Ed.), *Adler's Physiology of the Eye* (pp. 122- 68). Washington, D.C.: Mosby.

Fisher, P., Daniel, R. and Siva, K. V. (1990). Specification of input devices for teleoperation. *IEEE International Conference on Robotics and Automation.* Cincinnati, Ohio. IEEE. 540-5.

Fisher, S. S., McGreevy, M., Humphries, J. and Robinett, W. (1986). Virtual Environment Display System. *ACM 1986 Workshop on 3D Interactive Graphics.* Chapel Hill, North Carolina. 23-24 October 1986. ACM. pp. 77 - 87.

Foley, J. D. (1987). Interfaces for Advanced Computing. Scientific American, 257(4), 126-35.

Foley, J. M. (1980). Binocular Distance Perception. *Psychological Review*, 87, 411-34.

Foley, J. M. (1985). Binocular Distance Perception: Egocentric Distance Tasks. Journal Experimental Psychology: *Human Perception and Performance*, 11, 133-49.

Foster, S.H., Wenzel, E.M., and Taylor, R.M. (1991, October). Real-time synthesis of complex acoustic environments [Summary]. *Proceedings of the ASSP (IEEE) Workshop on Applications of Signal Processing to Audio and Acoustics*, New Paltz, NY.

Furness, T. A. (1986). The supercockpit and its human factors challenges. *Proceedings of the 30th Annual Meeting of the Human Factors Society.* Dayton, OH. 48-52.

Furness, T. A. (1987). Designing in virtual space. In W. B. Rouse, and K. R. Boff (Ed.), *System Design*, Amsterdam: North-Holland.

Gardner, M. B., and Gardner, R. S. (1973) Problem of Localization in the Median Plane: Effect of Pinnae Cavity Occlusion. *Journal of the Acoustical Society of America*, 53, 400-408.

Garner, W. R. (1949). Auditory signals. In *A Survey Report on Human Factors in Undersea Warfare* (pp. 201-217). Washington, D.C.: National Research Council.

Gibson, J. J. (1950). *The Perception of the Visual World.* Boston: Houghton Mifflin.

Gibson, William(1984). *Neuromancer.* New York: Ace Books.

Goertz, R. C. (1964). Manipulator system development at ANL. *Proceedings of the 12th RSTD Conference. Argonne National Laboratory.* 117-36.

Goertz, R. C., Mingesz, S., Potts, C. and Lindberg, J. (1965). An experimental head-controlled television to provide viewing for a manipulator operator. *Proceedings of the 13th Remote Systems Technology Confer-*

ence. *American Nuclear Society*, La Grange Park IL 60525, pp.57-60.

Goodale, M. A. (1990). Vision and Action: *The Control of Grasping*. Ablex Publishing Corp. Norwood, N. J: Ablex.

Gore, A. (1990). Networking the future. *Washington Post,* (July 15), B3.

Green, P., Satava, R., Hill, John and Simon, I. (1992). Telepresence: advanced teleoperator technology for minimally invasive surgery. *Surgical Endoscopy,* 6, 62-67.

Greenberg, D. P. (1991). Computers and architecture. *Scientific American*, 264(2), 104-109.

Gregory, R. L. (1968). Perceptual Illusions and Brain Models. *Proceedings of the Royal Society*, B, 171, 278-296.

Gregory, R. L. (1980). Perceptions as Hypotheses. *Philosophical Transactions of the Royal Society*, B, 290, 181-197.

Gregory, R. L. (1981). *Mind in Science*. London: Weidenfeld and Nicolson.

Gregory, R. L., and Wallace, J. G. (1974). Recovery from early blindness: a case study. In R. L. Gregory (Ed.), Concepts and mechanisms of perception (pp. 65-129). London: Methuen.

Grudin, J. and Norman, D. (1993). Language evolution and human-computer interaction. (manuscript submitted for publication).

Grunwald, A. J. and Ellis, S. R. (1991). Design and evaluation of a visual display aid for orbital maneuvering. In S. R. Ellis, M. K. Kaiser, and A. J. Grunwald (Ed.), *Pictorial Communication in Virtual and Real Environments.* London: Taylor & Francis.

Grunwald, A. J., and Ellis, S. R. (1988). Interactive orbital proximity operations planning system (*NASA TP* 2839). NASA Ames Research Center.

Grunwald, Arthur J. and Ellis, Stephen R. (1993). A visual display aid for orbital maneuvering: experimental evaluation. *AIAA Journal of Guidance and Control,* 16, 1, 145-50..

Grunwald, Arthur, and Ellis, Stephen R. and Smith, Stephen R.(1988) Spatial orientation in pictorial displays. *IEEE Trans. on Systems Man and Cybernetics* , 18, 425-436.

Hannaford, B. (1989). A design framework for teleoperators with kinesthetic feedback. *IEEE Transactions* on Robotics and Automation, 5(4), 426-34.

Hannaford, B. and Venema S. (1995) Kinesthetic displays for remote and virtual environments. In W. Barfield and T. A. Furness (eds.) *Virtual Environments and Advanced Interface Design.* New York: Oxford University Press.

Hart, S. G. and Staveland, L. E. (1988) Development of the NASA TLX, T ask Load Index: Results of empirical and theoretical research In *Human Mental Workload.* P. A. Hancock and N. Meshkati (Eds) New York: North-Holland.

Hashimoto, T., Sheridan, T. B. and Noyes, M. V. (1986). Effects of predictive information in teleoperation with time delay. *Japanese Journal of Ergonomics*, 22, 2.

Hatada, T., Sakata, H. and Kusaka, H. (1980). Psychophysical analysis of the sensation of reality induced by a visual wide-field display. *SMPTE Journal*, 89, 560-9.

Heeger, D. J. (1989). Visual perception of three-dimensional motion. *Neural Computation*, 2, 127-35.

Heilig, M. L. (1955). El cine del futuro (The cinema of the future). Espacios, Apartado Postal Num 20449, Espacios S. A. , Mexico(N0. 23-24, January - June),

Held, R., and Durlach, N. (1991). Telepresence, time delay and adaptation. In S. R. Ellis, M. K. Kaiser, and A. J. Grunwald (Ed.), *Pictorial Communication in Virtual and Real Environments.* London: Taylor & Francis.

Held, R., Efstathiou, A., and Greene, M. (1966). Adaptation to displaced and delayed visual feedback from the hand. *Journal of Experimental Psychology*, 72, 887-91.

Hess, R. A. (1987). Feedback control models. In G. Salvendy (Ed.), Handbook of human factors New York: John Wiley.

Hirose, M., Hirota, K. and Kijma, R. (1992). Human behavior in virtual environments. *Symposium on Electronic Imaging Science and Technology.* San Jose, CA SPIE.

Hirose, M., Kijima, R., Sato, Y., and Ishii, T. (1990 October). A study for modification of actual environment by see-through HMD. *Proceedings of the Human Interface Symposium*. Tokyo.

Hitchner, L. E. (1992). Virtual planetary exploration: a very large virtual environment (course notes). *SIGGRAPH'92*. Chicago, IL, ACM. 6.1-16.

Hitchner, Lewis E. and McGreevy, Michael W. (1993) Methods for user-based reduction of model complexity for virtual planetary exploration. In *Human Vision,*

Visual Processing and Digital Display IV, Proceedings SPIE 1913, 622-636.

Hochberg, J. (1986). Representation of motion and space in video and cinematic displays. In K. R. Boff, L. Kaufman, and J. P. Thomas (eds.), *Handbook of Perception and Human Performance*. 1, 22:1-63. New York: John Wiley.

Holgren. D. E. and Robinett, W. (1993) Scanned laser displays for virtual reality: a feasibility study. Presence, 2(3), 171-174.

Howard, I. (1982). Human Visual Orientation. New York: John Wiley.

Howlett, E. M. (1991). Product literature. *Leep Systems*, 241 Crescent Street, Waltham, Massachusetts Leep Systems, 241 Crescent Street, Waltham, MA.

Hung, G., Semlow, J. L., and Cuiffreda, K. J. (1984). The near response: modeling, instrumentation, and clinical applications. *IEEE Transactions in Biomedical Engineering,* 31, 910-19.

Hussey, K. J. (1990). Mars the Movie (video), Pasadena, CA: JPL Audiovisual Services.

Huxley, Aldous (1938). *Brave New World.* London: Chatto and Windus.

Inselberg, A. (1985). The plane with parallel coordinates. *The Visual Computer*, 1, 69-91.

Jacobson, S. C., Iversen, E. K., Knutti, D. F., Johnson, R. T. and Biggers, K. B. (1986). Design of the Utah/MIT Dexterous hand. *IEEE International Conference on Robotics and Automation.* San Francisco, California. IEEE. 1520-32.

Jacobson, S. C., Knutti, D. F., Biggers, K. B., Iversen, E. K. and Woods, J. E. (1984). The Utah/MIT dexterous hand: work in progress. *International Journal of Robotics Research*, 3(4), 21-50.

Jacobus, H. N. (1992). Force reflecting joysticks. CYBERNET Systems Corporation Imaging and Robotics, 1919 Green Road, Suite B-101, Ann Arbor, MI 48105 *CYBERNET Systems Corporation Imaging and Robotics*, 1919 Green Road, Suite B-101, Ann Arbor, MI 48105,

Jacobus, H. N., Riggs, A. J., Jacobus, C. J., and Weinstein, Y. (1992). Implementation issues for telerobotic hand controllers: human-robot ergonomics. In M. Rahmini, and W. Karwowski (Ed.), *Human-Robot Interaction* (pp. 284-314). London: Taylor & Francis.

Jacoby, R., Adelstein, B.D. and Ellis, S. R. (1995). Improved temporal response in virtual environments through system hardware and software reorganization. *SPIE abstract*, work in progress.

Janin, A. L., Mizell, D. W., and Caudell, T. P. (1993) Calibration of head-mounted displays for augmented reality applications. *Proceedings of the IEEE VRAIS* '93. Seattle, Washington.

Jenkins, C. L. and Tanimoto, S. I. (1980). Oct-trees and their use in representing three-dimensional objects. *Computer Graphics and Image Processing*, 14(3), 249-70.

Jex, H. R., McDonnell, J. D. and Phatak, A. V. (1966). A critical tracking task for man- machine research related to the operators effective delay time (*NASA CR* 616). NASA.

Jones, G. M., Berthoz, A. and Segal, B. (1984). Adaptive modification of the vestibulo-ocular reflex by mental effort in darkness. *Brain Research*, 56, 149-53.

Jones, R. K. and Hagen, M. A. (1980). A perspective on cross cultural picture perception. In M. A. Hagen (Ed.), *The Perception of Pictures* (pp. 193-226). New York: Academic Press.

Kaiser Electronics (1990) Product literature, *Kaiser Electronics*, San Jose, CA 95134

Kaiser, M. K., MacFee, E., and Proffitt, D. R. (1990). Seeing beyond the obvious: Understanding perception in everyday and novel environments. *NASA Ames Research Center* Moffett Field, Calif: NASA Ames Research Center,

Kalawksy, Roy S. (1993). *The Science of Virtual Reality and Virtual Environments.* Reading, MA: Addison-Wesley.

Kalman, R. E. (1960). Contributions to the theory of optimal control. *Boletin de la Sociedad Matematico* Mexicana, 5, 102-19.

Kazerooni, H. and Snyder, T. J. (1995). Case study in haptic devices: human induced instability in powered hand controllers. *Journal of Guidance, Control and Dynamics*, 18(1), 108-113.

Kim, W. S., Takeda, M. and Stark, L. (1988). On-the-screen visual enhancements for a telerobotic vision system. *Proceedings of the 1988 International Conference on Systems Man and Cybernetics.* Beijing 8-12 August, 126-30.

Kleiner, M., Dalenbäck, B.-I., and Svensson, P. (1993). Auralization-an overview. *Journal of the Audio Engineering Society*, 41(11), 861-875.

Kleinman, D. L., Baron, S., and Levison, W. H. (1970). An optimal control model of human response,

Part I: Theory and validation. Part II: Prediction of human performance in a complex task. *Automatica*, 6, 357-69.

Koenderink, J. J. and van Doorn, A. J. (1977). How an ambulant observer can construct a model of the environment from the geometrical structure of the visual inflow. In G. Hauske and E. Butenandt (Ed.), *Kybernetik.* Munich: Oldenburg.

Kollin, J. (1993) A retinal display for virtual environment applications. *Proceedings of the SID*, 24, p. 827.

Kramer, J. (1992). Company literature on head-mounted displays. *Virtex/Virtual Technologies*, PO Box 5984, Stanford, CA 94309 Virtex/Virtual Technologies, P.O. Box 5984, Stanford, CA 94309,

Krueger, M. W. (1977). Responsive environments. NCC Proceedings. 375-385.

Krueger, M. W. (1983). *Artificial Reality.* Reading, MA: Addison-Wesley.

Krueger, M. W. (1985 April). VIDEOPLACE--An artificial reality. *SIGCHI '85 Proceedings*, ACM. 35-40.

Larimer, J., Prevost, M., Arditi, A., Bergen, J., Azueta, S. and Lubin, J. (1991 Feb). Human visual performance model for crew-station design. *Proceedings of the 1991 SPIE.* San Jose, CA. 196-210.

Lasko-Harvill, A., Blanchard, C., Smithers, W., Harvill, Y. and Coffman, A. (1988 29 February - 4 March). From DataGlove to DataSuit. *Proceedings of IEEE CompConn88.* San Francisco, CA, 536-8.

Laural, B. (1991). *Computers As Theatre.* Reading, Mass.: Addison-Wesley.

Levit, C. and Bryson, S. (1991 Feb). A virtual environment for the exploration of three dimensional steady flows. SPIE 1457. pp. 161-168.

Licklider, J. C. R., Taylor, R. and Herbert, E. (1978 April). The computer as a communication device. *International Science and Technology*, 21-31.

Lippman, A. (1980). Movie maps: an application of optical video disks to computer graphics. *Computer Graphics,* 14(3), 32-42.

Lipton, L. (1982). Foundations of Stereoscopic Cinema. New York: Van Nostrand.

Lord Rayleigh [Strutt, J. W.] (1907). On Our Perception of Sound Direction. *Philosophical Magazine*, 13, 214-232.

Lypaczewski, P. A., Jones, A. D. and Vorhees, M. J. W. (1986). Simulation of an advanced scout attack helicopter for crew station studies. *Proceedings of the 8th Interservice/Industry training Systems Conference.* Salt Lake City, Utah., 18-23.

Maffie, T. H. and Salisbury, J. K. (1994) The "Phantom" haptic interface: a device for probing virtual objects. *Proceedings A. S. M. E.* , Winter Meeting, Chicago, Ill.

Mandelbrot, B. (1982). *The Fractal Geometry of Nature.* San Francisco: Freeman.

Marcus, O. B. (1991). Personal communication. *Exos*, 8 Blanchard Rd., Burlington, MA Exos, 8 Blanchard Rd., Burlington, MA.

McCormick, E. P. and Wickens, C.D. (1995) Virtual reality features of frame of reference and display dimensionality with stereopsis: their effects on scientific visualization. *Aviation Research Laboratory*, Univeristy of Illinois at Urbana-Champaign, Savoy, Illinois,ARL-95- 6/PNL-95-1.

McDowall, I. E., Bolas, M., Pieper, S., Fisher, S. S. and Humphries, J. (1990). Implementation and integration of a counterbalanced CRT-base stereoscopic display for interactive viewpoint control in virtual environment applications. *Stereoscopic Displays and Applications II.* San Jose, CA. SPIE.

McGreevy, M. W. (1993). Virtual reality and planetary exploration. In A. Wexelblat (Ed.), *Virtual Reality Applications: Software.* New York: Academic Press.

McGreevy, M. W. and Ellis, S. R. (1986). The effect of perspective geometry on judged direction in spatial information instruments. *Human Factors*, 28, 439-56.

McKinnon, G. M. and Kruk, R. (1991). Multiaxis control of telemanipulators. In S. R. Ellis, M. K. Kaiser and A. J. Grunwald (Ed.), *Pictorial Communication in Virtual and Real Environments* (pp. 247-64). London: Taylor & Francis.

McRuer, D. T. and Weir, D. H. (1969). Theory of manual vehicular control. *Ergonomics*, 12(4), 599-633.

Meagher, D. (1984). A new mathematics for solids processing. *Computer Graphics World*, November, 75-88.

Mon-Williams, M., Wann, J. P. and Rushton, S. (1993) Binocular vision in a virtual world: visual deficits following the wearing of a head-mounted display. *Ophthalmological and Physiological Optics*, 13, 387-392.

Monheit, G. and Badler, N. I. (1990 August 29). *A Kinematic Model of the Human Spine and Torso* (Technical Report MS-CIS-90-77). University of Pennsylvania. Philadelphia.

Monmonier, M. (1991). *How to Lie with Maps.* Chicago: University of Chicago Press.

Myers, T. H. and Sutherland, I. E. (1968). On the design of display processors. *Communications of the ACM*, 11(6), 410-4.

NASA. (1985). *Rendezvous/Proximity Operations Workbook*, RNDZ 2102. Lyndon B. Johnson Space Center, Mission Operations Directorate Training Division.

NASA. (1990). Computerized reality comes of age. *NASA Tech Briefs*, 14(8), 10-12.

National Library of Medicine (U.S.) (1990) Board of Regents. Electronic imaging: Report of the Board of Regents. U.S. Department of Health and Human Services, Public Health Service, National Institutes of Health, *NIH Publication* 90-2197. Also see: http://www.nlm.nih.gov/extramural_research.dir/visible_human.html

Nemire, K. and Ellis, S. R. (1991 November). Optic bias of perceived eye level depends on structure of the pitched optic array. *32nd Annual Meeting of the Psychonomic Society*. San Francisco, CA.

Nemire, Kenneth, Jacoby, Richard H., and Ellis, Stephen R. (1994). Simulation fidelity of a virtual environment display. *Human Factors*, 36, 1, 79-93

Netrovali, Arun N. and Haskell, Barry G. (1988). *Digital Pictures: Representation and Compression,* New York: Plenum Press.

Nomura, J. (1993). personal communication.

Nomura, J., Ohata, H., Imamura, K. and Schultz, R. J. (1992). Virtual space decision support system and its application to consumer showrooms. in T. L. Kunii (ed.) *Visual computing,* Tokyo, Springer Verlag., pp. 183-196.

Octree Corporation. (1991). Product literature. Octree Corporation, Cupertino, CA 95014 *OCTREE Corporation*, Cupertino, CA 95014.

Oman, C. M. (1991). Sensory conflict in motion sickness: an observer theory approach. In S. R. Ellis, M. K. Kaiser and A. J. Grunwald (Ed.), *Pictorial Communication in Virtual and Real Environments* (pp. 362-76). London: Taylor & Francis.

Oman, C. M., Lichtenberg, B. K., Money, K. E., and McCoy, R. K. (1986). MIT/Canada Vestibular Experiment on the SpaceLab 1- Mission: 4 Space motion sickness: systems, stimuli, and predictability. Experimental Brain Research, 64, 316-34.

Open University, and BBC. (1991). Components of reality Video #5. 2 for Course T363: *Computer Aided Design.* Walton Hall, Milton Keynes, England MK7 6AA.

Ouh-young, M., Beard, D. and Brooks Jr, F. (1989). Force display performs better than visual display in a simple 6D docking task. *Proceedings of the IEEE Robotics and Automation Conference*, May 1989. 1462-6.

Pedotti, A., Krishnan, V. V. and Stark, L. (1978). Optimization of muscle force sequencing in human locomotion. *Mathematical Bioscience*, 38, 57-76.

Phillips, C., Zhao, J. and Badler, N. I. (1990). Interactive real-time articulated figure manipulation using multiple kinematic constraints. *Computer Graphics*, 24(2), 245-50.

Pimentel, Keneth and Teixeira, Kevin (1993). *Virtual Reality, Through the New Looking Glass.* Summit, PA, USA: Windcrest/McGraw Hill.

Plenge, G. (1974). On the difference between localization and lateralization. *Journal of the Acoustical Society of America*, 56, 944-951.

Polhemus Navigation Systems. (1990). Product Description. *Polhemus Navigation Systems,* Colchester, VT 05446.

Pollack, A. (1989). What is artificial reality? Wear a computer and see. *New York Times*, (April 10, 1989), A1L.

Poulton, E. C. (1974). *Tracking Skill and Manual Control.* New York: Academic Press.

Presence (1992) Spotlight on simulator sickness. *Presence*, 1, 3, 295-363.

Presence (1993) Spotlight on social issues, *Presence*, 2, 2, 141-168.

Proffitt, Dennis R., Bhalla, Mukul, Grossweiler, Rich, and Midgett, Jonathan (1995) Perceiving geographical slant. *Psychonomic Bulletin and Review*, 2, 409-428.

Pritsker, A. A. B. (1986). *Introduction to Simulation and SLAM II 3rd. Ed.* (3rd ed.). New York: John Wiley.

Raab, F. H., Blood, E. B., Steiner, T. O. and Jones, H. R. (1979). Magnetic position and orientation tracking system. *IEEE Transactions on Aerospace and Electronic Systems, AES-* 15(5), 709-18.

Regan, D. and Beverley, K. I. (1979). Visually guided locomotion: psychophysical evidence for a neural mechanism sensitive to flow patterns. *Science*, 205, 311-13.

Robinett, W. (1982). *Rocky's Boots*. Fremont, CA: The Learning Company.

Robinett, W. and Holloway, R. (1995) The visual display transformation for virtual reality. *Presence,* 4(1) 1-24.

Robinson, A. H., Sale, R. D., Morrison, J. L. and Muehrcke, P. C. (1984). *Elements of Cartography,* (5th ed.). New York: John Wiley.

Rolfe, J. M. and Staples, K. J. (1986). *Flight Simulation.* Cambridge University Press London: Cambridge University Press.

Rolland, Jannick, Ariely, D and Wibson, W. (1994) Towards quantifying depth and size perception in virtual environments. *Presence,* 4(1) 24-29.

SAGES. (1991). Panel on future trends in clinical surgery. *American Surgeon,* March.

Salvendy, G. (1987) *Handbook of Human Factors,* New York: Wiley.

Schloerb, David W. (1995) A quantitative measure of telepresence. *Presence,* 4(1) 64-80.

Schuffel, H. (1987). Simulation: an interface between theory and practice elucidated with a ship's controllability study. In R. Bernotat, K.-P. Gärtner and H. Widdel (Ed.), *Spektrum der Anthropotechnik Wachtberg-Werthoven,* Germany: Forschungsinstitut für Anthropotechnik.

Senden, M. V. (1932). *Raum und Gestaltauffassung bei operierten Blindgeborenen vor und nach Operation.* Leipzig: Barth.

Shaw, E. A. G. (1974) The External Ear. *Handbook of Sensory Physiology,* Vol. V/1, Auditory System, edited by W.D. Keidel and W.D. Neff, 455-490. New York: Springer-Verlag.

Sheridan, T. B. (1992). *Telerobotics, Automation and Human Supervisory Control.* Cambridge, MA: MIT Press.

Sheridan, T.B. (1992) Musings on telepresence and virtual presence. Presence, 1(1), 120-125.

Sheridan, T.B. (1996). Further musings on the psychophysics of presence. *Presence,* 5(2), 241- 246.

Silicon Graphics. (1993). Product literature. *Silicon Graphics Inc.,* Mountain View CA.

Slater, M., M. Usoh, A. Steed (1994) Depth of presence in virtual environments, *Presence,* 3(2) 130-144.

Smith, D. C., Irby, C., Kimball, R. and Harslem, E. (1982). The Star User Interface: an overview. Office *Systems Technology* (pp. 1-14). El Segundo, CA: Xerox Corp.

Smith, T. J and Smith, K. U. (1987) Feedback control mechanisms in human behavior. In G. Salvendy (Ed.), *Handbook of Human Factors.* New York: John Wiley.

Spatial Systems. (1990). Spaceball product description. *Spatial Systems Inc.,* Concord, MA 01742.

Stewart, D. (1991). Through the looking glass into an artificial world via computer. *Smithsonian Magazine,* (January), 36-45.

Stone, R. J. (1991a). Advanced human system interfaces for telerobotics using virtual reality and telepresence technologies. *Fifth International Conference on Advanced Robotics.* Pisa, Italy. IEEE. 168-73.

Stone, R. J. (1991b). personal communication. The National Advanced Robotics Research Centre, Salford, United Kingdom.

Stritzke, J. (1991). *Automobile Simulator.* Daimler-Benz AG, Abt FGF/FS, Daimlerstr. 123, 1000, Berlin 48, Germany, 1991.

Sutherland, I. E. (1965). The ultimate display. *International Federation of Information Processing,* 2, 506.

Sutherland, I. E. (1970). Computer Displays. *Scientific American,* 222(6), 56-81.

Tachi, S., Hirohiko, A. and Maeda, T. (1989 May 21-24). Development of anthropomorphic tele-existence slave robot. *Proceedings of the International Conference on Advanced Mechatronics.* Toyko. 385-90.

Tachi, S., Tanie, K., Komoriya, K. and Kaneko, M. (1984). Tele-existence (I): design and evaluation of a visual display with sensation of presence. in *Proceedings of the 5th International Symposium on Theory and Practice of Robots and Manipulators.* Udine, Italy 26-29 June 1984 [CISM-IFToMM-Ro Man Sy'84]. 245-53.

Takeda, T., Fukui, Y. and Lida, T. (1986). Three dimensional optometer. *Applied Optics,* 27(12), 595-602.

Taylor, R. H., Paul, H. A., Mittelstadt, B. D., Hanson, W., Kazanzides, P., Zuhars, J., Glassman, E., Musits, B. L., Williamson, B. and Bargar, W. L. (1990). An image-directed robotic system for hip replacement surgery. *Japanese R. S. J.,* 8(5), 111-16.

Tobler, W. R. (1963). Geographic area and map projections. *The Geographical Review, 53,* 59-78.

Tobler, W. R. (1976). The geometry of mental maps. In R. G. Golledge, and G. Rushton (Ed.), *Spatial Choice and Spatial Behavior.* Columbus, OH: Ohio State University Press.

Tomovic, R., and Boni, G. (1962). An Adaptive Artificial Hand. *IRE Transactions on Automatic Control*, AC-7, April, 3-10.

Tufte, E. R. (1983). *The Visual Display of Quantitative Information.* Cheshire, CO: Graphics Press.

Tufte, E. R. (1990). *Envisioning Information.* Cheshire, CO: Graphics Press.

UCSD Medical School, *Abstracts of the Interactive technologies in Medicine II,* Medicine meets virtual reality, San Diego, CA., January 27-30, 1994.

Veldhuyzen, W., and Stassen, H. G. (1977). The internal model concept: an application to modeling human control of large ships. *Human Factors*, 19, 367-380.

Vertut, J., and Coiffet, P. (1986). *Robot Technology: Teleoperations and Robotics: Evolution and Development Vol. 3A* and *Applications and Technology Vol. 3B* (English Translation). Englewood Cliffs, New Jersey: Prentice-Hall.

W Industries. (1991). Product literature. *ITEC House* 26-28 Chancery St., Leicester LE1 5WD, U.K.

Wang, J.-F., Chi, V., and Fuchs, H. (1990). A real-time optical 3D tracker for head-mounted display systems. *Computer Graphics*, 24, 205-215.

Weintraub, D. J., and Ensing, M. (1992). *Human Factors Issues in Head-up Display Design: The Book of HUD.* Wright Patterson AFB, Ohio: CSERIAC.

Welch, R. B. (1978). *Perceptual Modification: Adapting to Altered Sensory Environments.* New York: Academic Press.

Wells, M. J., and Venturino, M. (1990). Performance and head movements using a helmet- mounted display with different sized fields-of-view. *Optical Engineering*, 29, 810-877.

Wenzel, E. M. (1992). Localization in virtual acoustic displays. *Presence*, 1(1), 80-107.

Wenzel, E. M., Wightman, F. L., and Foster, S. H. (1988 October 22-24). A virtual display system for conveying three-dimensional acoustic information. *Proceedings of the 32nd Meeting of the Human Factors Society.* Annaheim, CA. 86-90.

Wharton, John (1992) personal communication.

White, K. D., Post, R. B., and Leibowitz, H. W. (1980). Saccadic Eye Movements and Body Sway. *Science*, 208, 621-623.

Wickens, C. D. (1986). The effects of control dynamics on performance. In K. R. Boff, L. Kaufman, and J. P. Thomas (Ed.), *Handbook of Perception and Human Performance.* New York: Wiley.

Wickens, C. D. and Prevett, T. (1995) Exploring the dimensions of egocentricity in aircraft navigation displays: influences on local guidance and global situation awareness. *Journal of Experimental Psychology: Applied*, 1, 110-135.

Wightman, F. L., and Kistler, D. J. (1989a). Headphone simulation of free-field listening I: stimulus synthesis. *Journal of the Acoustical Society of America*, 85, 858-867.

Wightman, F. L., and Kistler, D. J. (1989b). Headphone simulation of free-field listening II: psychophysical validation. *Journal of the Acoustical Society of America*, 85, 868-878.

Witkin, A., Fleisher, K., and Barr, A. (1987). Energy constraints on parameterized models. *Computer Graphics*, 21(4), 225-232.

Witkin, A., Gleicher, M., and Welch, W. (1990). Interactive dynamics. *Computer Graphics*, 24(2), 11-22.

Wolfe, Robert S. and Yaeger, Larry (1993) *Visualization of Natural Phenomena.* Springer- Verlag, New York.

Zangemeister, W. H. (1991). Voluntary presetting of the vestibular ocular reflex permits gaze stabilization despite perturbation of fast head movement. In S. R. Ellis, M. K. Kaiser, and A. J. Grunwald (Ed.), *Pictorial Communication in Virtual and Real Environments.* (pp. 404-416). London: Taylor & Francis.

Zangemeister, W. H., and Hansen, H. C. (1985). Fixation suppression of the vestibular ocular reflex and head movement correlated EEG potentials. In J. K. O'Reagan, and A. Levy- Schoen (Eds.), *Eye Movements: From Physiology to Cognition* (pp. 247-256). Amsterdam- New York: Elsevier.

Zeltzer, David and Johnson (1991) Motor planning: specifying the behavior and control of autonomous animated agents. *Journal of Visualization and Computer Animation*, 2, 2.

Zimmerman, T., Lanier, J., Blanchard, C., Bryson, S., and Harvil, Y. (1987 April 5-7). A hand gesture interface device. *Proceedings of the CHI and GI.* Toronto, Canada. ACM. 189-192.

Zipf, G. K. (1949). *Human behavior and the Principle of Least Effort.* Cambridge, Mass: Addison-Wesley.

Zuber. B. (1965) Physiological control of eye movements in humans. *Ph.D. thesis at MIT,* Cambridge, Mass. p. 103.

Handbook of Human-Computer Interaction
Second, completely revised edition
M. Helander, T.K. Landauer, P. Prabhu (eds.)

Chapter 9

Behavioral Research Methods in Human–Computer Interaction

Thomas K. Landauer
University of Colorado at Boulder
Boulder, Colorado, USA

9.1 Introduction: For Whom and Why and What

This chapter discusses the conduct of research to guide the development of more useful (performing helpful functions) and usable (easy and pleasant to learn and operate) computer systems. Experimental research in human–computer interaction involves varying the design or deployment of systems, observing the consequences, and inferring from observations what to do differently. For such research to be effective, it must be "owned"—instituted, trusted and heeded—by those who control the development of new systems. Thus, managers, marketers, systems engineers, project leaders, and designers, as well as human factors specialists, are important participants in behavioral human–computer interaction research. This chapter is intended for those with backgrounds in computer science, engineering, or management at least as much as for human factors researchers and cognitive systems designers.

9.1.1 Why Behavioral Research is Important in Human–Computer Interaction

Development With and Without Behavioral Research

Even when the goal is to improve usability, current computer system development makes little use of behavioral research to guide design. Although usability evaluations are popular, especially among major software suppliers, most efforts are primarily summative, used to ensure that the final product is up to standard, not to shape the design and development processes. However, there is ample evidence that expanded task analysis and formative evaluation can, and almost always do, bring substantial improvements in the effectiveness and desirability of systems. On one hand, it has become clearer that informal intuitive evaluations by designers, managers, marketers, press critics and even users do not provide sufficiently accurate feedback. For example, Nielsen (1989) found that traditionally trained programmers were unable to choose the better of two interfaces by informal examination. On the other hand, it has also become clear that objective methods for evaluative feedback work wonders. Landauer (1995) reviewed all 16 published reports on quantitative results of systematic empirical user-centered design efforts available in 1994. He found that user task efficiency with an application was improved, on average, by over 50%. Nielsen and Landauer (1993), based on a analysis of a variety of systems and evaluation methods, estimated that the benefit to cost ratio of formal efforts devoted to evaluation and redesign ranged from a *low* of 20:1 up to 100:1 or more when measured by downstream effects on user productivity. Nielsen and Landauer found that the average interface has about forty significant flaws, and that two user tests or two expert heuristic evaluations will usually reveal about half of them.

So why is formative evaluation still so seldom practiced? Part of the reason is resistance by management that "doesn't get it". I know of exploratory development projects funded by technically sophisticated organizations that have been explicitly forbidden to do usability testing. However, in my opinion, another contributor to resistance has been that many usability practitioners have demanded greater resources and more elaborate procedures than are strictly needed for effective guidance—such as expensive usability labs rather than natural settings for test and observations, time consuming videotaping and analysis where observation and note-taking would serve as well, and large groups of participants to achieve statistical significance when qualitative naturalistic observation of task goals and situations, or of disastrous interface or functionality flaws, would be more to the point. But there are other, more insidious causes rooted in the cognitive psychology of software development and management.

The Egocentric Intuition Fallacy

A major source of resistance to formative evaluation is the egocentric intuition fallacy. One part is the compelling illusion that one knows the determinants of one's own behavior and satisfaction. Users and critics say things such as "What made it hard was the poor choice of command names." Unfortunately people do not have direct access to many of the important functions of their own minds. For example, they cannot observe how their brains retrieve facts from memory or perform logical operations. Even when a system is obviously difficult to use, intuition may not reveal the true reasons. For example, GUI text-editors rapidly replaced command-based editors; they were obviously better. Many people, including editor designers (e.g., Joy, 1984) believed that the advantage was that the user would immediately see the results of edits, "what you see is what you get" or make use of "direct manipulation" (Shneiderman, 1983). But analytic research by Egan and Gomez (1985) found that other reasons were more important, and a command-based editor designed with extensive formative evaluation at DEC tied the best GUI of its era on benchmark tasks (Good, 1985).

A second part of the fallacy is equally troublesome. We all tend to greatly overestimate the degree to which what is true for us will be true for others; we greatly underestimate variability in performance and preferences. Possibly this is because we put too much faith in a special sample of one, ourselves. It is a fundamental fact that behavior is extremely variable from one occasion to the next, and from one individual to the next. Moreover, variability in performances is often much greater in computer-based tasks then in other domains (see Egan, 1988); differences between the performance of two equally trained users are often 10 to 1 or more! Unfortunately, the extent of behavioral variability is virtually impossible to evaluate without systematic observation and measurement.

These fallacies make it hard for programmers, development managers, and purchasers to appreciate the need for more rigorous methods for ensuring usefulness and usability. Thus, the introduction of good research methods is a pressing and immediate practical concern, not just a step toward a firmer scientific base.

9.1.2 What this Chapter Says

In what follows it is argued that the special goals and difficulties of human–computer interaction research make it different from most psychological research, as well as from traditional computer engineering research. The main goal, the improvement of complex, interacting human-computer systems, requires behavioral research, but is not sufficiently served by the standard tools of experimental psychology such as factorial controlled experiments on pre-planned variables. On the other hand, different more observational and exploratory methods have been developed that offer proven, powerful help. Chief among these are techniques for human performance analysis and iterative testing. Going along with the shifted emphasis in research methods are somewhat different needs for data collection and analysis. The chapter contains about equal quantities of criticism of inappropriate general research methods, description of valuable methods, and prescription of specific useful techniques.

The chapter is organized as follows. First, there is a discussion of the variety of different goals for research in human–computer interaction. Second, there is a brief discussion of the special problems of doing research in this area. Third, the design and conduct of research to meet the several goals is discussed. Fourth, measurement issues are considered. Finally, analytic and statistical methods for evaluating and summarizing results are briefly discussed.

9.2 Goals for Research in Human–Computer Interaction

The goals of human–computer interaction research can be divided into four categories:

1. Evaluation or comparison of existing systems or features.
2. Invention or design of new systems or features, that is, determining what a new system should do and how.
3. Discovering and testing relevant scientific principle.
4. Establishing guidelines and standards.

Let us consider each in turn.

9.2.1 Relative Evaluation of Systems or Features

Often, the goal for human–computer interaction research is the relative evaluation of two or more systems, or of two or more options for the design of a function, a feature or an interface. The main research issues are in finding measures that will accurately predict differences in actual use, and data collection methods that are sufficiently informative, quick and economical.

9.2.2 Determining What a System Should Do

The question of what system with what functions to build in the first place deserves a more user-centered answer than it often receives. Too frequently we attempt to build things that will use technology, rather than trying to use technology to solve known human problems. Special kinds of information are needed to make good judgments as to what functions and methods of operation will be most effective in helping people to get results that are valuable to them. Gaining such information requires systematic observation and analysis of situations, tasks and users.

9.2.3 Discovering Relevant Scientific Principles and Testing Models

Another goal of research is to gain more general understanding of the determinants of human behavior in settings like those for which computer tools are designed. It seeks knowledge, theories and models about what makes cognitive and social tasks easy or difficult: how various demands on thinking and performing trade off against one another: how quickly things can be looked up or entered, how long will selection of a menu item take depending on the structure of the menu, what parts of a shared task are done best separately and which in close interaction. Results of this kind of research ordinarily do not feed directly into a specific design, but knowledge of them informs and deepens the thinking of designers and human factors specialists.

9.2.4 Establishing Explicit Standards or Guidelines for Design

A final goal for research is the explicit generation of guidelines or standards. This kind of research activity is, of course, closely related to all the others. However, the decisions toward which it is directed have two special properties. One is that guidelines and standards should only be promulgated when an appropriate level of certainty is achieved. The other is the question of how much consistency is important in the particular aspect of design. Different kinds of evidence are needed to establish the effects of lack of standardization than are needed to establish the effectiveness of a single variable or the relative quality of a system.

9.2.5 Being Clear About a Goal is the First Step

The logic and mechanics of research method, as outlined in the remainder of this chapter, are only means to ends. Different methods will be suitable for different goals. For example, the classical experimental-control comparison can be useful in deciding whether to add a particular feature to a system, and in answering critical theoretical questions, but it produces very little information, and requires too much to be known in the choice of experimental variables, to be of much use in exploring the functions needed by humans in a novel task.

9.3 Special Problems of Research in Human–Computer Interaction

There are special difficulties in doing behavioral research not found in other kinds of research. The three most important are the unreliability of intuition and the variability of behavior, as discussed above, and the very large and subtle effects of unintended biases on the part of both researchers and participants in behavioral studies.

Intelligent people often believe they understand behavior by virtue of their thoughtfulness and insight and the fact they themselves are people. This belief is almost never lost until one tries to study people scientifically, predicting, then measuring. *More often than not, intuitions are wrong*. Short of providing laboratory experience, the best we can do is to call attention to the fact that many computer systems are advertised in the first pages of their multi-hundred page manuals as being "transparent", "user friendly", or "requiring no learning". No doubt, its designers find the system easy to use. But without systematic research they have no way of knowing whether it is so for others.

Some part of the problem arises from an important fundamental aspect of human cognition. The way one perceives the world is intimately entwined with what one already knows and can do. Once you have seen a hidden figure, you can't avoid seeing it again; what is at first invisible becomes unavoidably obvious. In much the same way, it is nearly impossible for someone who has worked with a system day after day to tell how difficult it is to use. Its concepts have become familiar, its once novel terminology transparent, and its procedures automatic and largely unconscious.

Other problems lie in the nature of the particular kind of behavior studied in human–computer interaction. Computer technology, and user interfaces, are complex and subject to frequent change. A user is often required to learn several new concepts, procedures or skills all at once, and to operate in a rich environment with many conflicting demands and possible sources of confusion. One consequence is that isolating a given feature or procedure for study can be misleading. The fact that a particular procedure is easy to learn by itself may not mean that is easy to learn in the context in which it is usually embedded. The opposite may also be encountered; a difference in design that in isolation causes learning difficulties may, when embedded in the learning of the whole system, have no appreciable consequences (Landauer, Galotti and Hartwell, 1983, Landauer and Galotti, 1984). Therefore, research that aims at understanding important design differences needs to study them in a place in full systems, and needs to study their effects on complete tasks that users will actually perform, rather than only in isolated subtasks. All this, of course, makes research harder and requires more ingenuity on the part of the researcher.

The rapidity with which technology is changing is also difficult. We want research methods that will tell us things we can use before evolution has taken us beyond them. Evolution against the selective forces of the marketplace can be seen as a kind of natural experimental procedure (albeit often distorted by marketing and economic factors). Various vendors try various features or combinations of functions, and users reject or accept them. Eventually better configurations of features will usually win out over less good ones, but not always, because features come in bundles and the first to gain market can dominate indefinitely. Market decision may well occur before systematic research has been able to show which, what, if and why. Thus, we must focus on the kinds of problems for which research will be helpful, and the kinds of research methods that can yield useful and timely answers.

9.4 Research Designs and General Methodology

Research design means deciding what kinds of information to obtain and how to obtain it in an accurate, unbiased and efficient way. It includes issues such as whether to use controlled laboratory experiments, naturalistic or participant observations, survey questionnaires, or model simulations, and so forth. It also involves issues of how to maximize the bearing of the results on the question it is intended to answer.

The appropriate design or method often depends on the question or goal, so we break down the discussion by the goals categories set out in the last section. We begin with design issues common to most of the goals, then specialize to those particularly relevant to invention of new functions, choice among design alternatives, and elucidation of underlying principles.

9.4.1 Bias

There are some general issues of strategy that should be discussed before moving on to specific methods. First and foremost, we need to deal with the issue of bias. Because of the fundamental nature of human perception and thinking, a human judgment is never made solely on the basis of the evidence at hand. It is always intimately dependent on personal interpretation of events, which, in turn depends on what the person knows, believes and desires. A very common example of these phenomena is in the opposing evaluations that loyalists on either side give of performances in a political debate, evidence in a public trial, or a penalty in a football game. The same event can be honestly and fervently believed to have opposite qualities depending on the beliefs and desires of the observer. The same happens in judging whether an observed user is having trouble or succeeding when using the system you or someone else designed. Thus, when you take a system that you designed or implemented to the usability lab and watch it used, you can be assured that you will think it does better than will most other observers. There is overwhelming evidence that this kind of *experimenter bias* affects even apparently objective human judgments. For example, psychologists have had students do experiments on the effect of different kinds of music on plant growth (Rosenthal, 1976). When the students believe one kind should be more helpful and know which plants get it, they *measure, with a ruler,* greater growth; when they don't know which plant got what, no differences are found. The experimenter bias problem is subtle and insidious; it often works by simple, unintentional, "unconscious" shifts in attention or interpretations, sometimes by differences in what data are rechecked or rerun.

The bias problem does not end here. When you introduce your new system or feature to users, many will guess that you think it's an improvement. Most of them will try to please you by making it work well because most people want to please others, especially if the other is perceived to be smart or important or in control of the money.

The bias problem does not end here. Most people who volunteer in studies of technology like new technology. They assume that what is being tried on them must be new and better, and they tend to like it. Rare is a trial in which users don't report overall subjective liking. A report of dislike is a serious matter; one of liking means next to nothing unless it can be compared in magnitude to a carefully controlled alternative.

The bias problem does not end here. In many situations in which computers are employed, their use involves supervision, instruction, or cooperative interaction between users and a facilitator—a consultant, a systems administrator, a teacher, or a supervisor. How enthusiastically and well the facilitator does the job can impact how well the system works. Usually, first adopters, or those who undertake beta tests, are favorably inclined, if not outright proponents. They are bound to make things go better than later adopters, who may be neutral or even hostile. A frequent and egregious example of this problem is met in the introduction of new educational methods. A good and enthusiastic teacher can make students learn with almost any method. Enthusiasm itself is important, providing motivation for teacher and student. Focused application of skill on a process the teacher believes in is another factor, and the subjective evaluation of how well it is all working, which amplifies gains in a positive feedback loop, also helps. As a result, almost all new educational methods work wonders in the hands of their developers, proponents, and early adopters. But the same methods seldom have large positive effects when passed on. This situation holds equally for computer-based methods. It simply is no proof of the advantage of someone's new MUDS-based constructive cooperative interactive learning scheme that when they try it with a group of volunteer offspring of their technical colleagues and the offsprings' friends that the users are delighted and teacher and designer see wonderful results.

The only way to avoid these bias it is to use double-blind procedures; always have a comparison system and ensure that the experimenter, facilitator, and participant know which is the new and which is the comparison system. Merely having comparison systems helps somewhat to make judgments less biased, but adequate control groups and double-blind administration, data collection and analysis are the only way for researchers to avoid fooling themselves. Certainly, one doesn't need to do that for the earliest trial trials, when one is more interested in detecting flaws. But before you convince yourself that you have a competitive winner, taking pains to avoid bias will help insure that you do.

9.4.2 Statistical Significance: Surprise, It's Not So Important

Second, in engineering-oriented applied research, traditionally defined "statistical significance" will not usually be a concern. What is important is some measure to improve a particular decision between designs or help predict its importance. Traditional significance testing is intended as a quality control on scientific decisions about whether there is any effect of some variable. Often such decisions carry weight in explanations of phenomena or in rejecting theories. In engineering or purchase, one is more interested in knowing how much difference there probably is to guide cost–benefit strategy. In science decisions can be postponed if the evidence is not good enough. In engineering or purchase, we usually have to decide on whatever evidence is at hand. In neither case is it very interesting simply to know whether there is a "statistically significant" effect according to some conventional and strict cut-off percentage point. On the other hand, calculating the "significance", that is, estimating the probability that the result could have been due to chance, can add additional useful information for certain kinds of decisions. Later we will discuss some ways to do that and advocate using the "odds-ratio" as an especially good way to state the conclusions in practical terms.

Note also that the customary significance test ritual is aimed at protecting us from concluding that there was an effect when there might not have been one. For practical problems it is often just as important to avoid concluding that there is no effect when there might have been one; and the usual strict levels of significance will *necessarily* cause us to make such errors (unhelpfully called Type II) quite often. The matter is closely related to decision and signal detection theory. Given the same quality of evidence, choosing to lower the probability of "false positive" errors means simultaneously raising the probability of "false negative" conclusions. Gary McClelland tells a story of an airline task force that wanted to urge pilots to reduce the number of unnecessary takeoff aborts until consulting statisticians explained this inexorable tradeoff.

9.4.3 Generality and Transfer

Third, we are intensely interested in questions of generality, that is, to what potential user populations and to what tasks and applications, and to what variations in the systems studied will the findings of our research be applicable? In some kinds of engineering research, finding that a machine runs as intended in the lab or field test is sufficient proof of a solution. In usability issues, one always has to add the question of whether the people using the machine in the test will give the same results as those who will use it for real. The first rule of this kind of research, then, is to somehow find participants with whom to test the ideas or designs who are similar in background, occupation, ability, age, and variability to those for whom it is destined. Moreover, the test must be in a situation, and embedded in work, that embodies the range of situations in which it is to be used. Most important it must test the tasks and goals, and mixes of tasks and goals, that real individuals, organizations and communities will use it for.

Sometimes otherwise excellent developmental research inadvertently results in systems that are extremely easy for their first half hour with novice users, but not very effective thereafter, because the usability testing was done only in "first-use" settings for which appropriate participants are easy to find. We come back to this problem later. A related problem is transfer between applications with similar purposes. Experts with one application almost always find it easier to learn a new application than novices do, but that they also often encounter annoying interference from conflicting ways of doing the same thing (Singley and Anderson, 1985, 1989; Pennington and Rehder, 1995). Since those who use a system most and whose productivity is most influenced by it include those most vulnerable to this problem, its economic consequences urge careful evaluation. One needs to be careful about generalizing results from a subject population that knows too much, too little, or the wrong thing. The ticket is to test subjects who are representative of target users, ideally a random sample from a population actually expected to use the new system or version.

When research is intended to guide design in many different systems, the problem becomes even more difficult. Here the ideal solution would be to sample from all possible systems and applications, but clearly this is impossible. One escape from this dilemma is to gain "robustness in variation" (Furnas, Landauer, Dumais and Gomez, 1983). Rather than testing a principle in one instantiation for one group of users, try to test it in as many potentially relevant settings as possible. If the same qualitative conclusions emerge in all tests, then one can conclude that the effect is not special to one particular set of circumstances, and thus a safer bet for wide generality. Following this approach, Furnas et al. studied the number of keywords needed for successful access to information items in six very different environments, and found that in all cases many more—two to thirty times as many—were needed than usually provided. The fact that this held true for command names, superordinate categories for classified ads, key words for documents, and index terms for cooking recipes, and with experienced system designers, expert and novice cooks, homemakers, scientists, librarians, and college students yields a certain degree of confidence—although not logical certainty—that the effect lies in a general property of knowledge, language, and cognition rather than in a spurious detail of one or another experimental task or subject population.

Another basic consideration arises from the dual problems of rapid changes in computer technology and the large and complex space of possible system feature sets and designs. There are too many variables, too many different possible designs, too many possible design parameters, too many different kinds of users and tasks to test out all combinations. Picking any one comparison to test can be a high risk gamble. Unless previous research and experience indicate that a critical design or theory question is at stake, such a one-question study is unlikely to be cost-effective. What is needed is research methods with much richer information yield. The idea of richness in a research design is that the set of observations and conditions used be such that a large number of possible outcomes, unexpected as well as expected, are allowed to occur, be noticed and be measured.

9.4.4 Comparisons With Prior Computer and Noncomputer Methods

In my opinion, this issue is of paramount importance. In order to make real progress in using computers we have to monitor and understand the progress we do and don't make, An especially critical aspect is evaluating whether a new computer aid for a task improves the speed, quality and pleasure of its accomplishment over that provided by pre-existing methods that do not rely on computers. There have been astonishingly few such comparisons, and the results of those that have been made have frequently been disappointing (see Landauer, 1995, for review). One example was the comparisons made by both key-stroke analysis and user tests on an apparently well motivated and implemented system for telephone company service representatives studied by Gray, John and Atwood (1992). They found that the new system decreased throughput relative to the old system it was designed to replace. Often such effects are hard to notice without systematic study because the new system speeds up or improves the vast majority of operations but there is a defect that produces occasional problems or errors that have costs that overwhelm the benefits. For example, user disorientation in hypertext or deep menu search schemes can result in extremely long recovery times, certain rare typing errors with powerful editors or data entry devices can make horrendous messes or cause system failures that require rebooting, what were easily corrected run-of-the mill data errors in paper can be propagated far and wide and nearly impossible to chase down and fix in an integrated system. A homely example is checkout counter barcoding, which, usually faster than keying, creates long delays when it fails, undoing its speed advantage (Cutler and Rowe, 1990). Another example was a new system for repair crew dispatch that neglected to include a phone number directory for occasionally needed supervisors: the time spent off the system on that one sub-task cost more than the system saved.

These examples are of seemingly minor details, but in HCI and interface design details can make all the difference. Moreover, sometimes comparisons with old methods are needed to understand deeper principles as well. Take the on-line public access terminal that has replaced card catalogues in most libraries. I hazard a guess that careful comparative studies of how each differentially affects people's ability to find the kinds of things they want—astonishingly, such studies have never been done (but see Borgman, 1986, for an illustrative sad case)—would have led to greatly improved designs, as they did in Egan's studies of systems for scholarly access to the content of books and journals (Egan et al. 1991, Landauer et al. , 1993).

9.4.5 A Model for Research

One useful model of research that achieves most of the aforementioned aims is as follows. Before engaging in extensive research:

1. Set up a situation in which it is easy to instrument the computer system to keep a timed log of all keystrokes. This is not done with the intention of always analyzing all these data; that would be a

self-defeating waste of resources. Rather, the idea is to have detailed data available in case something comes up for which its examination might prove revealing. For example, if some users, or some users on some occasions or with some tasks, experience special difficulty or unusual success, such data will allow tracking down the reasons. Note that a "laboratory" for our purposes need not be a special place set up to do research; indeed there is considerable advantage in conducting research in a normally functioning office or home environment as the case demands, so long as the necessary means for observation and/or control can be arranged.

2. Acquire a large panel of potential participants who vary in as many relevant ways as is feasible, and in which there are representatives of many potential classes of users.

3. Try to acquire background data on subjects, and if possible administer batteries of standard cognitive, perceptual and typing tests prior to participation.

4. Keep track of the previous studies in which subjects have participated, so that appropriate ones can be selected, and the effects of particular prior experiences controlled and studied.

5. Arrange that participants can be observed unobtrusively and, when appropriate, questioned while working.

6. Whenever possible have one of the intellectually sophisticated members of the research team (including, especially, responsible designers, developers and managers) present during many test sessions to observe.

7. Use questionnaires or interviews to see what participants thought of what was happening, and what ideas they might have that you don't.

8. Try to combine several questions in the same study; if you're interested in options on both feature A and feature B, include counter-balanced and factorially crossed variations on both within the same experiment. As Fisher (1935) long ago pointed out, the informational gain from studying many factors at once rather than in independent experiments can be enormous, and is even more important in this field where interactions (synergistic or limiting effects) between factors are often strong.

Doing all of this may not be expensive. Few of these suggestions require elaborate equipment, expensive analysis or procedures. They do require a little planning and the intent to produce a rich yield from studies, including, especially allowing opportunity for serendipitous discoveries.

The next sections address methods relevant to particular research goals. This classification is not intended to be exclusive. Methods suitable for one goal are often modifiable for use with others, and many appropriate variants on the methods are not discussed.

9.4.6 Invention and Specification Oriented Methods

If one wishes to design a new system to help people perform a task better, it is important to start by understanding what that task is and how it should be performed. This is traditionally the realm of task analysis, and should be a major component of systems engineering. The general procedure usually followed is some variant of the following. A team of engineers and human factors experts study the way a function is currently performed, ask managers what problems there are and what they would like to accomplish, watch and interview operators of current systems, and pay serious attention to users' observations and suggestions. Then they sit around and think, dream up ideas and plausible designs, and write a preliminary description of the system they intend to build. Then they go back to the workers and managers and get their opinions on whether the ideas will work. The importance of watching and talking to actual workers, rather than only "experts" and purse-string holders, cannot be overestimated. Often actual work problems and processes are markedly different from official job descriptions and management prescriptions (see Brown, 1991 for a telling case), and real workers have different skills and habits from supervisors and executives, who may have done the job involved, if ever, long ago, and differently.

There is no agreed on formal methodology for task analysis, and perhaps it is unrealistic to hope for one, because the appropriate procedures will differ depending on the problem at hand. However, any reasonably systematic empirical task analysis will almost certainly prevent one or more design disasters. Let me give but one example. I once selected two carpets in a retail store, along with pads. The salesman had to enter my name, address, credit and charging information and several other items of information four times: on a form for each rug, and on a form for each pad. He said that this was necessary because the order system had just been "computerized." Apparently, the design process had foregone watching salespeople at work or discussing their needs with them.

Thorough, thoughtful observation and analysis of the whole task in its natural context will accomplish much. Ethnographic methods involving close observation of social, cultural and communicative processes in the application environment generalize the value of naturalistic observation and, together with careful analysis of the organizational structure of work integration and its formal and informal control, greatly improve the chances of understanding the possibly novel and effective roles that a new system may play and avoiding dangerous pitfalls where superficially attractive features or methods may inadvertently undermine important work or social processes. With increasing interconnection and integration of both business and personal applications, new and extremely important opportunities for effective system design are rapidly emerging. In order to capitalize on them, the focus of "task" analysis needs to be very wide, to include all of what has traditionally been called systems analysis but now including the much wider scope of systems.

Human-problem Oriented Invention

A different approach to the creation of new technology may be needed. Rather than starting with an idea for a system-based on what technology can do, and then trying to determine whether people and organizations will be able and willing to use it, instead start with people's needs and abilities; and find a technology that they will be able to use to fulfill a need. The main steps in such a strategy are the following:

1. First identify a goal, a kind of effect on the world that people would like to have but currently have difficulty producing. Observations are necessary. Just asking people will not suffice, because it is extremely hard to break the frame of reference of how things are now. (Asking people in 1870 what they would like in transportation would not have elicited air transport as a desideratum.)

2. Then find what causes the difficulty. Techniques for these two steps will be discussed in more detail in the following sections.

3. Then, if possible, invent a way to help people around the difficulty. Test and develop to see that they can use the proposed method.

4. Then incorporate it in a system. If the function people wanted to perform but couldn't do well is made more available, chances are you'll have a winner (provided, of course, that it can be done at an acceptable price, is well marketed, etc.).

Failure Analysis

This leads us to the description of kinds of methodology that bear on the problem of invention of new computer-based methods. One such method, just alluded to, is to find out where people go wrong or slowly. We may call this "failure analysis." For example, in the case of information retrieval, by observing people trying to find information in a variety of different places, Furnas et al. (1987) discovered that people never had very high initial success rates, commonly below 20% on their first try. The lack of success was (almost always) due to a failure of the system to recognize a word that the user tried as a referent for the desired object. In this case it was a relatively easy step to invent a method by which systems could avoid this failure, simply recognizing many more words that users used.

The essence of failure analysis is to identify a task in which people often engage in unsuccessful subtask attempts, then carefully study what happens when these attempts fail. The use of many different instantiations will lead to greater robustness. The observations have to be made with the whole range of users of current technology, working on real problems, not with experts who have learned how to work around the deficiencies of current technologies. Note how different this kind of research is from traditional hypothesis testing experiments, or even from common focused task analysis.

Individual Difference Analysis

If we can find that certain kinds of people, ones with certain background characteristics, experience, or abilities, find systems easy while others find them difficult, we are on our way to understanding wherein the difficulties lie. For example, Greene, Gomez and Devlin (1986) found that formulating logical queries in standard data base query languages, such as SQL can usually be mastered with little training by young people with high scores on logical reasoning tests, but hardly ever by older or less able people. They also found, however, that an alternative form of query formulation, selecting rows from a truth table, allowed correct specification of queries by almost everybody, independent of their abilities. By redesigning a system to use a method that did not require special abilities, they found they could bring up the performance of the less able without diminishing that of the more able.

The general logic of the individual difference method is as follows: Try to have the users who are to be studied measured on as many different relevant characteristics and abilities as is feasible. Then have them engage in the task as now done while measuring their performances. If people with certain abilities or backgrounds find the task especially difficult, or especially easy, the next step is to try to understand their reactions. The goal is to find sub-components or aspects of the task that correlate most strongly with the ability in question, then try to manipulate those components so as to reduce the need for unusual ability. For example, by simulating various subtasks with paper-and-pencil tests, Egan and Gomez (1985) were able to decompose text editing into error location, description of the needed text changes, and formulation of syntactically correct commands. Performance with a word processor was highly predictable from the paper-and-pencil tests, establishing that the decomposition captured the essential skills of the task. In addition, the specific individual characteristics most strongly associated with successful editing—in this case spatial memory and age—were primarily associated with only one sub-task, command formulation. Egan and Gomez subsequently were able to show that word-processors with appropriately redesigned methods for specifying editing operations had reduced dependency on the individual characteristic in question, and were easily mastered by many more people.

Time Profiling

Another way to identify targets for redesign or invention is to analyze the way time is spent on tasks. Time profiling consists of measuring the amount of time spent on all isolatable components, including training, reference manual consultation, performance of various functions, and recovery from errors. Components that occupy large amounts of time are obvious candidates for new methods. While a remedy will not necessarily be available, the opportunity for significant gain at least exists.

It is also useful to measure the *variability* of time. If a component task is sometimes done quickly and sometimes slowly, further analysis will often reveal what goes wrong in slow cases, or is especially effective in fast cases, and design around, or for, it. A real example: times to record an order were extremely variable. A few observations and questions revealed that the customer's telephone number was not always posted on the screen occasioning a lengthy search. Easy fix.

9.4.7 Design-Oriented Research Methods

If one knows what function a system is to support, certain other research methods become more directly applicable. These methods divide fuzzily into two overlapping sets: full-scale comparative evaluation studies, and formative evaluation or iterative design methods.

Full-scale Evaluation Studies

Sometimes it is of interest to simply compare the overall effectiveness of two or more systems, or two or more variants of the same system. The research design for this kind of study is fairly standard and obvious. One gets or finds a group of representative naive subjects to learn or experts to use each of the systems and compares them on a pertinent set of performance measures.

The biggest problems arise in the cost of such studies and in the selection of the sample of participants. If interest is just in how much trouble people have during the first hour of use on the system, there's not much problem. Unfortunately this is seldom the only goal of a design choice; one wants to know what will happen to real users over the period of time they will really use it. It is rarely feasible to study 30 or more people participating on a full time basis for six months or a year in each comparison group. There is no completely adequate way around this problem, but there are some approximations. One method is to study use by people who are already experienced users of each of the different kinds of systems. The deficiency here is that the different users of different systems may have selected the equipment to suit their own differing abilities. Also, the user of certain kinds of systems (e.g., EMACS vs. WordPerfect editors) may come from very different populations (e.g., academic vs. business backgrounds), and have different talents. Another issue in such a comparison is what to measure. In order to choose one system over another it is necessary to know how good it is for the task for which it will be used. One approach (Roberts and Moran, 1983) is to use a set of "benchmark" tests that are chosen to represent the important functions performed with a system.

Another approach is to study strengths and deficiencies of systems already long in use. Accumulate data on the frequency with which various subtasks and features are used. Finding that a powerful feature goes unused may suggest that it needs careful redesign.

When it comes to feature comparisons rather than full system comparisons, we are in better shape. Here the classical machinery of experimental design is of value. If the researcher is in the enviable position of being able to field-test two or more designs in which features can be varied, for example giving half the users labels as well as icons in a menu, then a perfectly respectable experiment can be run. (But note, that a feature superiority established in such an experiment is not guaranteed to hold when embedded in a different system. Many such comparisons are needed to judge robustness.)

Experiments

"Respectable experiments" consist of the following:

1. Assignment of one feature or other to different users must be random, where random means really using a pseudo-random number generator (spreadsheet programs have them) or table. Just haphazardly assigning conditions, or alternately assigning one and the other will not do; there are many horror stories in the statistical literature about unwarranted conclusions resulting from such procedures.

2. Confounding of features with other factors must be avoided (e.g., feature A should not be tried first, or late in the day, or in a quiet room, or with an enthusiastic experimenter, any more or less often than feature B).

3. Measurements must be accurate and statistical analysis sound.

4. There must be a sufficient number of "independent" subjects in each test group. "Independence" may be hard to achieve, given that systems tend to be used by several communicating people in the same office. The fact that all three people in one office find a system easy does not mean that three independent measurements have been made; the users may have been helping each other, yielding just one instead of three cases. The statistical sampling unit should be a group, office, or individual whose performance is not affected by that of any other sampling unit.

5. The outcome measures must be accurate, reliable and unbiased.

6. As discussed above, participants must not be exposed to subtle biases such as the experimenter's (unstated) opinion that one method is better than another (Rosenthal and Rosnow, 1984). The nitty-gritty of experimentation, measurement and statistics are treated more fully below.

An appealing experimental design for choosing features is the factorial experiment (or a variant like partial or fractional factorial design), one in which several different variables are studied, with the different subject groups in the experiment being exposed to different combinations of the values or levels on each factor. For example, to study the effect of menus versus commands, the use of icons versus verbal labels, and differences between novice and experienced users, an experiment would test 8 different conditions representing all combinations of these three factors. Such a design estimates the effect of all three factors with the same precision using approximately the same number of subjects as would be needed to study just one of the them, and as an extra bonus estimates the degree to which the effect of one factor is different for different levels of the other. For example, it would show whether the advantage of menus over commands is general, or different for novices and experts.

The factorial experiment as a method in human–computer interaction research has sometimes been maligned, and sometimes for good reason. Its main drawback is that the factors and their different values must be important variants for design, else the experiment will yield no interesting results. In the huge space of possible features and feature combinations, it is not feasible to try to sort through all possible design alternatives by formal experiments on the effects of predetermined variables. Once it has been established that a mouse works better than cursor keys, then it might be necessary to study whether a mouse with three buttons instead of one works better than cursor keys with menus, and so forth. The point is not that factorial experiments are not useful; they are, indeed, an extremely effective and efficient research tool. The point is that their use to search the entire space of design options is a futile strategy. (Unfortunately, some early critics of behavioral research in HCI appear to have mistakenly equated it with this strategy.)

There are powerful research designs other than the fully crossed factorial experiment. We cannot go into them here; rather the interested reader is referred to standard texts in research design for behavioral experimentation (e.g., Atkinson and Donev, 1992; Box, Hunter and Hunter, 1978; Judd and McClelland, 1989; Judd, McClelland and Culhane, 1995; Kirk, 1982; Lunneborg, 1994; Maxwell and Delaney, 1990; Mead, 1988; Rosenthal and Rosnow, 1991). There are also sophisticated methods for setting up and making the best use of data in studies where only partial control over the assignment of conditions is feasible; see Cook and Campbell (1979) for a thorough treatment.

Formative Evaluation (aka Iterative Testing)

The best strategy for good design is to try various options (suggested, of course, by experience with previous similar systems, guidelines, and available principles), test them, and be guided by the failures, successes and comments garnered in watching their use, redesign trying new options, and iterate. This is called formative (or developmental) evaluation. The idea is simple enough. The barriers to its more frequent use are largely lack of will (organizational resistance), lack of time, or lack of ingenuity.

Organizational resistance often comes as demands that the designer or human factors specialist be able to specify good designs without research, or with little. This comes from a lack of realization that there is no reliable way to find out what works other than to test, and a lack of an appreciation for the high cost-effectiveness of formative evaluation if done right. An argument that sometimes wins is to point out that system performance would never be left untested. Designing a computer system without early user testing is akin to designing an aircraft without wind-tunnel tests.

As summarized earlier, experience shows that formative evaluation can be effective and economical, where as a single test is rarely enough, neither are dozens of iterations of the whole system required. There are many reports in the literature, and in the halls of good development organizations, of dramatic improvements in usability in cases where two or three iterations were made on each important interface design problem, each requiring less than a dozen hours of human testing and an equivalent amount of reprogramming. For example, in designing an interface for a prototype voice store and forward system, a first attempt—by an expert human factors team—produced around 50% unrecoverable errors in attempts to use the service. After four weeks of testing and three revisions in the protocol, field tests found the procedure to result in less than one error for every hundred uses (personal communication, Riley, 1982). The development of the much acclaimed user interface for the Apple Lisa computer (later incorporated into the Macintosh) was accomplished by almost continuous formative testing during system and interface development. The testing was done by the manager of the interface programming group (Tesler, 1983, and personal communication). The tests were relatively informal. Tesler selected a particular issue, for example where to put an "exit" icon on the screen, for semi-formal evaluation, (i.e., for some subjects it was in one place and for others in another), for each small experiment. Then he would have a few subjects try each of the two options. Most of the gain was not, however, from the comparison of the options but merely from observing the difficulties experienced by the users, and from the participants' comments and suggestions. According to Tesler the formal comparison served primarily to ensure a common and appropriate task focus. Difficulties were then either taken back to the design team for immediate alterations and retest, placed on a wish list for later solution, or ignored for practical reasons. Iterating this step every time an interesting design question arose, and after every significant milestone in the interface development, required running only about a dozen potential users per week through trials of the system, and caused no delay in the total development process because fixes were made concurrently with the normal course of programming and averted more costly fixes later. For many more examples see Landauer (1995) (where evidence is presented that the superior usability of the Macintosh was probably a result of this process rather than the GUI features and consistency it is usually attributed to.)

It is often possible to do user tests on important design and function options before any system is built at all. One way is to use paper or video mock-ups, for example of screen layouts or information organization, and have users try comparable tasks to those the system will support An especially useful technique is the so-called "Wizard-of-Oz" experiment, in which a hidden human plays the part of the not-yet-extant computer system, allowing dynamic interaction features to be studied (see Gould, Conti, and Hovanyecz (1983) for an early and excellent example).

9.4.8 General Principle-Oriented Methods

There are too many different ways of searching for and describing generalities for us to outline appropriate methods for each. The general methods of data collection and analysis to be described in the next section are relevant to all. Nonetheless, there are some problems special to applied areas, and to complex computer systems, that do not usually arise in theoretically oriented psychological or cognitive science research. Some of these have already been alluded to (e.g., the necessity of trying several different tasks and sets of user populations to assure robustness, and the need to choose trial users like those for whom real systems will be designed).

One of the most important issues is that of the degree of abstraction. It is standard procedure in scientific research to try to isolate a small number of variables to study in the laboratory. This makes the elucidation of cause and effect much easier. One is not caught in a hopeless web of tangled interacting or correlated factors. Unfortunately, whenever one abstracts, one runs the risk that what is learned will not be important when brought back into its real context. It is not that principles discovered in isolation are likely to be wrong, but that they will often be incomplete, or will be dominated by other considerations in practice. For example, some early studies concerned with command name choice were performed by having college students memorize associations between printed names and prose description of functions (e.g., Black and Sebrechts, 1981, who found that popular names were easier to memorize). The standard laboratory learning experiment isolated the difficulty of learning particular facts from all the other aspects of learning to use a text editor. Unfortunately, the conclusions of such "paper-and-pencil" studies have not always held up when applied to system design. For example, Landauer et al. (1983) and Grudin and Barnard (1984), found no learning advantage for popular names when used for commands in basic text editors. Thus, if one wants to discover general principles that are useful for design across a wide range of applications, then the studies that establish them must be embedded in representative full scale systems and environments. If it becomes desirable, in order to understand some particular issue, to abstract it to a simpler laboratory situation, then it will always be essential to try out the new knowledge in its full context to see if it is still valid. An ideal long-term strategy is 1) identify important variables by observations in fully contextual use, 2) elucidate their causative effects and mechanisms in simplified controlled experiment, 3) test the completeness of resulting understanding by trying to design or predict effects in full context; loop.

9.5 Measurement and Analysis

First we must consider what we really want to measure. The needed level of sophistication of measurement can be slight or great depending on the goal. For many important usage issues we may need nothing more than total time or errors. On the other hand if we are interested in basic understanding of the mechanisms of cognition or visual-motor reaction underlying a certain kind of performance, then we will have to find measures that reveal such mechanisms. Typically these have involved response times, or errors measured either over some distance metric (e.g., distance of a pointer from a target) or categorically as in a confusion matrix in which the number of occurrences of each response is tallied for each situation in which it occurs incorrectly (e.g., editing commands over text-correction types). The methodological, measurement and statistical issues involved in this kind of work can be extensive, and sometimes deep, and have been treated well elsewhere (good starting places, depending on the depth of treatment desired can be found in Judd and McClelland, in press; Luce, 1995; Luce and Krumhansl, 1988; Michell, 1990). Indeed, the theory of measurement is probably nowhere better developed than in the study of psychophysics (the relation of physical input to perceived quantity) and psychomotor response time (e.g., Luce, 1986). The reader who wants to set forth on the difficult waters of empirical analysis of mental processes would be well-advised to first read deeply in the area; there are treacherous problems and sophisticated solutions to be known about. However, for the other goals of HCI research, we can offer here at least an introduction and some useful elementary techniques.

9.5.1 Preliminaries: What to Measure and How Many Observations

What should be measured and how? In exploratory studies designed to find the source of difficulties and errors, the best start is to observe performance in common tasks in a free and open-ended way, and to talk to the users. From such naturalistic observations the researcher might proceed to a classification or taxonomy of the acts and errors that can be reliably observed, and that occupy users' time. The next step might be to count the number of failures of each kind over a sample of performance, and/or measure the times required to perform actions or complete subtasks.

All of this seems straightforward, but requires some care. A few rules of thumb may help plan such studies. Because behavior is variable, it is necessary to observe enough occasions to allow stable statistical estimate. Just as one would not try to predict the outcome of an election by polling ten potential voters, one should not try to measure the expected proportion of errors on a computerized procedure by observing ten occasions on which they might or might not occur. How many observations is enough? It depends on the degree of precision that is required for the kinds of conclusions to be drawn and the variability of the behavior being measured. Note that the optimal strategy is not always to assign the same number of participants to each condition; for example, to generalize to a stratified population it may be better to sample proportionally to strata membership, and when some condition has higher than average measurement variability it may be more efficient to make more observations on it (see Atkinson and Donev, 1992; or Mead, 1988 for detailed guidance.)

Power

If the concepts of standard error and confidence intervals are unfamiliar, the reader is advised to study the next-following section on statistical analysis or one of the referenced texts, before proceeding. Often errors in human performance can be approximated by a binomial distribution, for which the standard error, se = $(pq/n)^{1/2,}$ where p is the probability correct q = (1 - p), and n is the number of independent observations. If the experimenter has preliminary data or a good guess about the expected value of p, then a value of n, the number of observations to be taken, can be set such that the standard error of the collected data is expected to be less than or equal to some chosen value.

For convenience we can rewrite the equation as n = p $(1\text{-p})/(\text{se})^2$. For example, if preliminary data suggests that there will be 10% errors, then getting 36 independent observations would achieve a theoretical variability of the estimate (se) of 5%. This gives a 95% confidence interval (plus or minus 1.96 se for a large sample) of 10% ± 10%. This means that assuming the sample is from a true binomial distribution, 95 out of 100 times the true mean would lie between 0 and 20%. If that sort of conclusion were sufficient to the purposes of the study, then 36 independent observations would be reasonable for the experiment. (Of course, everything has to be recalculated once the data are in and the value of p and the estimate of variance can actually be obtained from the data rather than from an educated guess based on an assumed distribution. This part is covered in the next section. Also notice that, somewhat counter-intuitively, the worst situation for the sensitivity of an experiment with binomially distributed data, and one unfortunately often unwittingly arranged for by researchers, is when the average probability is .5, for then p*(1-p), in the equation is maximized at .25, whereas at a probability of, say 1%, p*(1-p) = .01.)

This kind of preliminary calculation is related to the concept of the *power* of an experiment. Power means the ability of the experiment to detect differences of a certain size, or to make measurements at a certain level of precision. It is determined by the kind and accuracy of the measurements that can be made, by the amount of variability in the performance, and by the size of the sample of observations that is collected.

As errors are approximated roughly by a binomial distribution, response times are often approximated very roughly by an exponential (or gamma or log normal) distribution (Luce, 1986). In carefully set up experiments with well practiced subjects and accurate time measurement the standard deviation in human response times is usually around 0.2 times the mean for responses under 0.5 sec., rising to about 0.5 times the mean for reactions of a second or more (Luce, 1986; Card Moran and Newell, 1983).

The standard error (precision) of a mean varies inversely with the square root of n (i.e., sem = $(\text{var})^{1/2}/(n)^{1/2}$). As a result of the central limit theorem (see any of the statistics textbooks) if we use for each individual data point not a single observation but the mean of a large group of observations (e.g., those of several subjects in a condition), the distribution of the data points will tend to be normal no matter what distribution the original observations came from. For many purposes this allows us, with appropriate caution, to ignore the issue of what the underlying distribution is and use conveniently available tables or calculations of the normal distribution for modeling chance.[1] Referring to the normal probability distribu-

[1] If the underlying distribution has a very long tail, as does the gamma, there will likely be a few extreme observations that have large effects on the mean. For some purposes, notably statistical significance tests (and the related odds ratios advocated here), these extreme values cause problems. A common statistical cure is to transform the data in such a way that it becomes normally distributed, e.g. by taking logs of response times (than transforming back at the end for natural interpretation.) Second, because we can't easily tell true extreme values from gross measurement errors (e.g. the computer clock failed to stop with the response), they can distort conclusions. Therefore, in many cases it is prudent, and not

tion then lets us specify what proportion of values are to be expected within a given number of standard errors from the mean. For example, 95% fall between the mean minus 1.96 se and the mean plus 1.96 se, and 99% within ± 2.33 se of the mean. Thus if one expects average response times to be in the second to half minute range, and one wants to be 95% confident that the mean of the measurements is within 10% of correct, obtaining 96 observations, (e.g., about a dozen independent measurements from each of 8 independent users[2]) will probably be about the right number: 0.10 m = (expected std = 0.5 m) * 1.96 / $(96)^{1/2}$. To get similar confidence of 20% accuracy, probably only about 24 independent observations would be required to be 99% sure of being within 1%: 0.01 m = 0.5 m * 2.33 / $(13{,}572)^{1/2}$.

The point of such rule-of-thumb guides is just to give the experimenter some preliminary planning guesses. Note that for exploratory studies accuracies good to plus or minus 10%, or even 50%, in times or errors are sometimes good enough. Knowing that the system fails to recognize users' spontaneous keywords on 70 - 90% of attempts is sufficient to point the finger of blame. So is knowing that 10 to 30 (20 plus or minus 50%) minutes of every hour of text editing is devoted to recovery from mistakes.

Let us now consider some measurement issues relevant to evaluation studies. In an evaluation study we are interested explicitly in the expected performance of a program or system, or in the influence of a particular feature. This requires that the measurements reflect the quality or quantity of performance that the experimenter or designer is really interested in. It is critically important to think carefully about just what that is, rather than simply choosing an outcome measure that is convenient to observe. Take, for example, the case of text editing. Suppose we want to know whether voice input or a mouse will be more effective. We might be tempted to measure the amount of time it takes to position the cursor over the beginning of a specified word using one or the other of the two devices. But this would be a mistake. We are really interested in how long it takes an average user to edit an average text to a desired level of correctness. It is conceivable that positioning a mouse to a word is much faster than telling the machine where to go unambiguously, but that moving hand to mouse disrupts the flow of typing or thinking and degrades the overall performance of the operator. Thus if we measured only the partial performance associated with the device we would not get the answer we really want.

The only guarantee that we will know the effect on overall performance is to measure overall performance. The needed measurement is "end-to-end." That is, one measures from the beginning of the performance of the user/system to the desired end of that performance.

In most cases, as in the text editing examples, users are interested in achieving some goal in as short a time as possible. Therefore, one measurement that is almost always pertinent is the amount of time required to achieve adequate completion of common tasks. Sometimes, of course, the goal has several natural measures (e.g., reducing the number of errors, decreasing time, and increasing subjective satisfaction). In this case it is necessary to measure each of the different outcomes in an end-to-end fashion. A problem arises if a particular variable has opposite effects on two of the measures, for example decreasing time but increasing errors. Unless there is some way to weigh the importance of the two outcomes, for example an economic rationale for trading time for errors, the results can be ambiguous.

There are some useful ways to disentangle effects on outcome measures that trade off. One is to use some method to hold one of the variables constant. For example, in spreadsheet use one might give the user only a set amount of time to complete a task and count the residual errors at the end of that time, or make users find and correct all errors and measure total time.

Lest the concentration on time and errors in the examples give the wrong impression, I do not wish to

"cheating" so long as done appropriately, to exclude them or treat them specially (see, e.g., Chapter 9 of Judd and McClelland, 1989). However, in applied research we need to be especially wary of transforming or throwing out data. In scientific psychological (or other) research we are often interested in the performance of the normal, typical subject, the properly functioning individual or task we seek to understand or model. For that purpose it is appropriate to transform data to a form required by a model or throw out data from abnormal, diseased, inattentive, etc. objects of study. But if our purpose is to estimate, for example, the number of hours of labor that will be needed to compute budget scenarios, we want the arithmetic mean hours of work; and so long as the working conditions, the tasks and the subject pool from which our participants are fairly sampled are genuinely representative of the population that will use the program, which will also contain abnormal, diseased, inattentive, etc. participants, we want to use all the data.

[2] To be precise, 13 independent observations from each of 9 independent users might be needed in a typical design for statistical reasons we won't go into here; moreover, several measures for a given user may well not be independent unless appropriate care is taken (e.g. taking each as a difference from the user's personal mean and checking that the within and between subject distributions are the same). However, such niceties are not needed at this stage of planning so long as these estimates are viewed as approximate lower bounds on the number of observations planned.

imply that these are the only or necessarily most important things to observe. They have the virtue of being nicely measurable and quantifiable, and are usually of practical interest. However other candidates and other issues may be significant. In studying programming, one might want to look at the number of residual bugs, or the running time or memory load required by the resultant program, or, in the use of spreadsheets, the profit margin of the best solution found. Or, perhaps more importantly, one might assess what giving all relevant parties in an organization or community the new facility does to overall outcomes and satisfaction.

Subjective satisfaction is an important measure. There is a sense in which the end goal of all systems is to have them satisfy their users. There are cases in which systems that give faster and more accurate results are not liked and not used. In "cognitive work load analysis," relevant to control system configuration for airplane cockpits for example, it has sometimes been found that systems that allow people to get more work done per unit time are rated as less desirable.

Often in early research stages, when trying to understand where the problems are, "verbal protocols" are collected. Subjects trying to use a system are asked to think aloud as they work. While there is some debate as to the proper scientific interpretation of such reports, there is no doubt that they are practically useful.[3]

In the last section we mentioned the important use of measures of individual differences. There are thousands of tests of psychological abilities, motives and so forth, available on the market. Among those useful in research on human–computer interaction are several measures taken from the "French Kit" of cognitive ability measures (Ekstrom, French and Harman, 1976). These tests, distributed by Educational Testing Service, Princeton, NJ, consist of a number of carefully constructed, validated and statistically analyzed subtests that measure partly independent mental skills. The spatial memory and logical reasoning subtests have been found to be good predictors of several kinds of computer skill acquisition (Egan and Gomez, 1985; Greene, Gomez and Devlin, 1986). Background observations on age, sex, education and previous experience are easy to collect and often valuable. Age seems often to be strongly correlated with the acquisition of computer-based skills. (See chapter by Czaja). Choice of courses in school (e.g., number of mathematics courses taken) is often another valuable predictor. Such measurements or observations not only offer an avenue for discovering the soft spots in systems, but provide useful statistical controls for variability in experiments. If one of these measures is found to correlate strongly with performance in the measured task, then methods such as analysis of covariance (see below) can make the results less noisy by statistically removing the influence of the "nuisance" variable.

Finally, let us not neglect evidence from contexts other than formal experiments, measures obtained during the marketing or use of a system. Sales figures are an important measure for several purposes. Work or productivity, measured as lines of code written, letters produced, or number of typists required in the word processing center are others. One might count the residual errors in documents produced by two organizations that use different word processors, for example, or the number of modification requests or bug reports lodged against development or maintenance organizations using different software tools. To repeat a point made above, richness in the evidence obtained from a study is an important goal. Thinking of multiple measurements, and especially ones directly related

---

[3] Much of the argument revolves around how much of the important aspects of thinking, problem solving and performance are open to conscience awareness or are reflected in what people report, how well people can express and describe what is going on in these processes, and how well experimenters are able to interpret what subjects say. There is surely truth on both sides of the argument. For simple reactions that take less than a second to perform, for example deciding which of two digits (e.g. nine or three) is the largest, there is little content to human introspecting (how did you do it?) The stories that people will tell about how they solve such problems sometimes flatly contradict observable characteristics of what they do. (e.g. a 9-3 inequality judgment is faster than 9-8; does that match your initial ideas of how you did it?) Similarly, the pattern recognition process by which you recognize a face is not open to your introspection. There must be a great deal of processing going on, but you cannot observe and report what it is. A great deal of human cognition relies on just this sort of automatic complex pattern recognition. Moreover, what one often gets from introspective reports is a cultural or personal theory of how problem solving is accomplished, rather than what the mind actually did. (see Nisbett and Wilson, 1977).

On the other side of the argument (see Ericsson and Simon, 1980), the claim is that for more deliberate processes that take times much in excess of one second, especially during the early stages of learning a new task, or when extensive formal problems solving is required, much more of the process is accomplished by "working memory" and is available to introspective report. What people report often reveals much about the steps in their thinking processes, and the sources of errors they make. Protocol reports can provide good evidence of what people have noticed, though not necessarily of what they have not noticed. For an example of protocol data collection methods see Lewis and Mack (1982).

to the ultimate improvement of the system, is an important part of the researchers' problem.

9.5.2 Data Quality

Before thinking of numerical manipulations for analyzing data, it's important to consider the inherent data quality. First let us re-emphasize the danger of inadvertent bias; honesty and carefulness are not enough to prevent errors and bias. In copying or adding up figures, even with calculators and spreadsheets, the best, most careful workers make errors; and if they believe the sum should be large the errors will tend to be positive. Errors that violate expectations ("sensibility checks") are easier to detect. Welcome errors tend to go uncorrected more often than unwelcome ones.

Whenever possible, data recording and analysis should be fully automatic. Care must be taken that the mean for one treatment is not confused with that of another. When extensive data are recorded, copied, or calculated by hand, it is essential that a second person, working alone, does the same calculations, preferably in a different order and if possible by a different method. There will *always* be errors, even when using fully automatic data collection and statistical packages for analysis. It is easy to transpose the rows and columns in a data matrix or to mislabel printouts or graphs. In calculating standard error it is easy to divide by the square root of *n* twice instead of once. Such errors are especially likely when the task is delegated. The only way to avoid errors is to take excessive caution; always hand check a sample of calculations. Programmers are accustomed to checking the first, last and some intermediate value in a loop to guard against errors that they know better than to make but do anyway. The same thing holds for data analyzed with a package, or by other means; hand check some important extreme values and some representative ones, always run an analysis on a miniature data set where the correct answer is known. Like people, programs written and used by people do not always do what we think they will.

9.5.3 Reliability

Another issue of data quality of particular importance in behavioral research is reliability. Many of the measures one wants to take require a human observer or judge. Whenever humans make observations, measurements or judgments, they are subject to random as well as bias errors. If the outcome measure of interest is something like the quality of a composed letter, or the readability of a section of code, or the ease of use of a spreadsheet, the human judgment involved is likely to be of low precision. It is essential to assure that such measurements are made with adequate repeatability. The standard approach in psychological research is to have observations made by two different people working independently for a sizable random or representative subsample of the occasions. Alternatively two independent but presumably equivalent measures are taken, for example the odd versus even numbered items in a reasoning test. Then a product-moment correlation coefficient is computed across the pairs of measurements. Ordinarily, with training, it is possible to get two human judges to agree sufficiently to generate a correlation coefficient of around $r = .7$ -.8. For psychological tests, "reliability coefficients" of this size are customarily required (see Judd and McClelland, in press, for details and the latest methods.).

If reliability is lower than one wants, there are a few strategies available to increase it. One is to revise the way in which the judgments are made, to have a more explicit set of rules, or to train the judges more thoroughly, giving them practice and feedback on a large number of cases. One problem with doing this is that the resulting judgments will not be based on an easily interpretable naive view of what the quality of performance was. That is, the more training the judges have, the less likely they are to be judging in the same way that the reader of the report would have judged.

Another way of increasing reliability is to use more than one judge for each measurement. If unreliability is due to random sampling error, then it will decrease with the square root of n, so for example, the average of four estimates of the legibility of a program will on the average be subject to half as much random error as estimates based on one judge. Another way to increase reliability is to strive for some more objective measure, for example in program comprehensibility to have people read and answer questions based on the program, rather than just giving an opinion.

Statistical Analysis

The point of statistical analyses is simply to be able to see clearly and say concisely what variable data have to tell. The great intrinsic variability of behavior, and especially of behavior of people using computers (Egan, 1988) means that overall patterns of results will always be at least partly obscured by noise. Thus statistical analysis is an extremely important component of HCI research. The use of statistics divides into four overlapping categories: summary of noisy data, estimating the size of effects, exploring data patterns, and fitting quantitative models. We discuss each, describing the intent, rationale, and general methods used, providing a few simple methods that the reader could use, and pointing to more complete reference sources.

Summarizing Results Accurately

The point of collecting data is to describe what happened in the investigation. The most important description is usually a set of central tendency measures for the various conditions or occurrences observed. These are the measures that predict what will happen later. It's good practice, before calculating any measure of central tendencies, such as a mean or median, to rank and plot the data points along a line (or if the tools are available, to do a quantile-quantile plot against some reasonable assumed distribution, see Wilk and Gnanadesikan, 1968). Looking at this will reveal whether the data are distributed in some fairly regular manner, for example approximating what one would expect from a normally distributed population (the familiar and useful bell-shaped curve). If the data seem reasonably well behaved, and one is willing to assume that the values can be treated as having the arithmetic properties of real numbers, (e.g., $z * (x + y) = zx + zy$) then one can proceed to calculate a mean for each condition. If the numbers are wickedly strange, for example if there are some very extreme outliers, there is a great bunching up in one or two parts of the distribution, or you don't believe that the difference between a 5 and a 10 is more significant than the difference between a 4 and a 7, then the mathematical nature of the problem becomes much deeper and more difficult. However a good deal of attention has gone into the creation of so-called "robust" statistical methods, in which the existence of outliers, peculiar distributions, or violations of measurement assumptions will not usually affect the conclusions to be drawn from the results. Again, for the serious, full time researcher, I can do no better than note some good sources (Chambers and Hastie, 1992; Hastie and Tibshirani, 1990; Hoaglin, Mosteller and Tukey, 1983; Siegal, 1956; Tukey, 1977;). (And see footnote 1.)

However, there are some easy methods that will get around most of the problems. One is trimming; in calculating the average; don't use a certain proportion (e.g., 5% of the values at either extreme). This does *not* imply throwing out individual pieces of intuitively suspicious data or data from particular nonconforming subjects, a good way to introduce bias; we are talking here only about different ways to calculate an average. A convenient and demonstrably robust central tendency measure is the mid-mean, calculated by lopping off the top and bottom quarter of the observations before calculating a mean.

Having gotten a measure of central tendency, one has achieved a lot. In it one has probably the best characterization of what happened (e.g., of differences between treatments). The best estimate as to how much faster one cursor-key arrangement is than another is the difference in the mean times needed to operate the system with one and the other. If you have to choose between the two features, and the only consideration is average performance, you need no more.

Of course, if there is any cost to the choice, one also wants to know how confident to be in the answer, how large the difference really is. The problem is acute if there have been only a few observations on each method. Suppose you give three people in your drafting department package A and three package B, and measure their output for a week. The B's do more work. Because of the large variability of human performance, the mean difference in such a small sample may be due to the chance assignment of better users to one condition. If one traded in a thousand packages of type A for a thousand of type B and measured performance for a year, the final results could be disappointing.

In essence what one wants to do with the results of any study is to extrapolate to expected effects in the real world. To do this sensibly we need some way of estimating the likely amount of error in our estimates. The most common technique is to calculate both means and variability estimates, and by comparing them to what is expected on the basis of some mathematical theory of how the numbers would fall by chance, arrive at "a confidence interval." A confidence interval is a statement of the form: if the study were repeated an infinite number of times, 95 times in 100 the true mean (the one we would obtain with infinite data) would be in the interval X_1 to X_2.

In the case of data that justifies the calculation of an ordinary mean the measure of variability is usually the *variance*, the average squared deviation of individual observations from the mean. The variance, and its square root, the *standard deviation*, is easily obtainable with your favorite spreadsheet or statistics package and with many hand-held calculators. This measure has some nice mathematical properties that we will mention briefly later on. For now its importance lies in its relation to a theoretical probability distribution, for example, the normal distribution, which is a useful approximation to reality for a large number of common cases. The sample standard deviation quantifies the variability of the individual samples points. What we want to estimate is our certainty of the value of the mean. To do so we use the measured mean and variance of the observed points to estimate corresponding parameters of the theoretical distribution, then use statistical theory to tell us about the expected values of means of samples drawn from that distribution.

The final step is to notice that the probability of a mean deviating by a certain amount from the true mean can be derived from the probability distribution. This is how we get to the confidence interval. The practitioner should consult a statistics textbook or package manual for procedure details. However the calculational steps are quite easy and are given directly below.

1. Find the mean, x and variance, var of the sample.

2. Compute the standard error of the mean, sem: sem = $(\text{var}/n)^{1/2}$

3. Consult a table of the cumulative normal distribution for the number of sem units (often called z, or normal deviates) corresponding to the desired degree of confidence: For example, 99% of true means lie between x-2.58 sem and x+2.58 sem; 95% of true means lie between x-1.96 sem and x+1.96 sem; 50% of true means lie between x-.68 sem and x+.68 sem.

Using the normal distribution assumes you have a large sample (i.e., 30 or more independent observations). For smaller samples a t distribution may be more appropriate.

Confidence intervals calculated this way can be too broad to make the conclusion useful. For example if you try to decide whether to replace one system with another, and the 50% confidence interval on one estimate includes the 50% confidence interval of the other, there is at least a 50-50 chance of getting no improvement from the big expense, and you might not want to undertake it.[4] (A more precise way to evaluate differences of means from small samples is the t-test; see Judd and McClelland, 1989; Kirk, 1982, Lunneborg, 1994; Maxwell and Delaney, 1990; Pedhazur and Schmelkin, 1991, Rosenthal and Rosnow, 1991; Winer, 1971). The other implication, and often the more important one for research, is that you may want to increase the precision of your study either by tuning up its methods or by gathering more observations. Remember that the expected error in the estimate of the mean goes down as the square root of the number of observations goes up.

Take note. When one increases the number of observations to increase reliability, there is no guarantee that the size or the direction of the differences between conditions will stay the same. The estimate of the true difference will become more precise, but the conclusions may be altered. It is common to see people excuse away inconclusive results of experiments done with a small number of observations by claiming that had they collected more data the conclusion would be reliable. The fact that the original data were noisy means only that if more had been collected the means would probably have changed noticeably in one direction or the other, but there is no way to tell which.

Estimating Effect Size: The Most Important Step

Most often in applied research what we are most interested in is the magnitude of the effect of a difference. If changing the key arrangement is going to make 0.1 % difference in the speed of operation, then unless we have a huge multiplier (as is sometimes present in systems used by thousands of operators), we may not be interested. What we are usually looking for is a large "effect size." The estimation of effect size takes almost exactly the same course as just indicated for central tendency. If each subject has tried each of two systems, we measure the difference in time between the two systems for each subject, treat those differences as the observations and get a central tendency measure and confidence interval for the size of the difference. (For small samples, a "matched-pair" t-statistic is appropriate here). We may then wish to express this as a percentage of the original time, if this makes sense in the context. If different groups of subjects have been used in the two circumstances, the formula for the standard error of the difference between the two means is as follows:

$$\text{sem of difference} = \{(\text{var}^1/n^1) + (\text{var}^2/n^2)\};$$

Sometimes it makes more sense to normalize an effect size by the standard deviation ($(\text{var})^{1/2}$) of the observations, rather than as a percentage of the abso-

[4] Stated more precisely: assume both means come from samples of the same normal distribution, nonoverlap of the two Y% confidence intervals is to be expected no more than (1-Y)% of the time.

lute value. This occurs especially in behavioral measures such as desirability ratings. Suppose users switch from system A to B. It would make no sense to describe a change in desirability rating from 5 to 6 on a 7 point scale as a 20% increase. On the other hand if the scale in use has a population standard error of one point, there are sensible interpretations associated with describing such a change as a "one standard deviation change." One such interpretation is that the mean rating on B is as high as 84 percent of ratings on A (x+1 sem contains 84% of a normal population).

Now suppose that subjects rated two features (e.g., voice input and mice), and that on the average mice rank 7 and voice 6, with standard deviation of the difference = 0.5. If you must choose, the best bet is to choose the mouse. But suppose the client's manager thinks voice input would work better. You may not want to make the decision dictated by your data unless the odds on being proven right by performance over the next year are good. How do you figure those odds? There is a lot of statistical machinery around to do this; it is called inferential statistics. One of the simplest tests is called a "critical ratio." Divide the observed difference between the two mean ratings, 1.0 in our example, by the estimate of the standard error of that difference, 0.5; 1/0.5 = 2.0. The probability of observing a critical ratio of a given size under the assumption that the samples are drawn from the same normal distributed population is given in the back of most elementary statistics textbooks, and in the handbook of physics and chemistry, and is available on-line in many spreadsheet and statistics packages. (It is sometimes called a "normal deviate" or "standard score" or "z," or "t" with small samples.) One finds the probability of having observed a critical ratio at least as big as the one observed. In this example the probability is .04. That is, if there were really no difference, the probability of observing a value at least as big as the one obtained is .04, and the probability of a smaller difference is .96. Thus the odds are 96:4 = 24 to 1 against there really being no difference, that is, of obtaining such a big difference merely by chance. You can reasonably assume that a year of experience on a thousand machines will give the essentially true answer about the *direction* of the difference (i.e., the same as an infinite amount of data would give) so, you can take the 24:1 odds ratio as the chance of at least some improvement in performance, provided conditions stay the same.

An odds ratio is very good complement to mean values and effect sizes for summarizing the results of an investigation. It makes an intuitively appealing interpretation of confidence in the results. A nice characterization of the data is to give the means for the different conditions and their confidence intervals and add a statement of odds that there is at least some difference favoring A over B. To my mind, this kind of statistical summary is usually the best in applied research. It gives an estimate of importance and how certain one can be about it, and simultaneously gives guidance on the likely outcomes of a choice based on the data.

With a small amount of arithmetic one can also get the odds that the difference is at least X%, often especially useful formulation for cost/benefit analysis. Usually what one wants to know is not whether the change makes *any* difference, but to know how likely it is that the difference will be big enough to justify the cost of purchase or programming, or will make enough profit to justify investment. If you can estimate the cost of making the change, or the benefit associated with a particular difference in performance, then with the help of the odds ratio you can play simulation games with a spreadsheet program to trace out probable bottom line scenarios. (See Abelson, 1995, for more on using statistics to support practical decisions.)

Some readers may have noticed and were perhaps puzzled by the relation between the odds ratio analysis and the "significance test." I postponed discussion of significance tests because they have been misunderstood, overused, and abused. For most applied work one wants to make design or purchase decisions; for these, effect sizes, confidence intervals and odds ratios are the proper tools. The significance test is simply a way of making a particular binary decision, that there is at least some difference between two or more conditions. By itself, such a decision is rarely of interest in applied work. However, the critical ratio described above can be used as a significance test. There are a wide variety of other significance tests (which, by the way, can always be used to obtain probability numbers from which the odds ratio can be calculated) such as the t-test, analysis of variance, and so forth (see any of the statistics texts referenced elsewhere).

Significance tests usually involve setting some arbitrary level of confidence, say 95 or 99%, and declaring there to be "no significant difference" unless the difference is big enough to justify the statement that the two are different at that level. To repeat—and it needs repeating— this procedure has merit only for some purposes. In sorting out variables of theoretical interest in cause-isolating laboratory experiments, it is often the right method. If the question is "does this variable have any effect?" (e.g., does print quality affect lexical decisions more than semantic decisions?), and the answer bears important theoretical weight, then significance tests with conventional confidence levels assure that the science marches along on ground of known solidity. (But note: that the difference between the means of A and B is *not* significant at some level, even just .10, *does not* translate into "there is no difference between A and B," an unfortunately common error found in our literature; it means only that we cannot be confident that a difference will usually be found.) However, for exploratory work or decisions based on evaluation research, the question answered by a conventional significance test alone is almost never of much interest (see Tukey, 1960, and Abelson, 1995, for related discussions).

Exploration

Often what is most useful for finding what is going on are methods called "exploratory data analysis." A simple and important example is plotting of data. Graphical displays of data, such as bar charts and scatter plots and fitted functions of various kinds, are powerful tools for discovering unexpected facts or relationships, or for evaluating ideas. Many computer systems and programs make plotting easy. Researchers should get used to plotting and re-plotting their data in every which way to see what they can find. Excellent books setting forth a number of useful graphical techniques are Chambers, 1993, and Chambers, Cleveland, Kleiner and Tukey, 1983. One danger to look out for if you use statistics or graphing packages, is this: you can easily be given an erroneous impression by two graphs that have automatically been scaled differently. It is good practice to tell the application what to make scale ranges in absolute numbers rather than letting it decide for itself. It is also a good idea to try some rough graphs by hand to see what is going on—analogous to hand checking a few calculations. Surprisingly often, simple graphs, either by hand or machine, alone are enough for practical decisions.

There are more complex statistical analyses, of descriptive and inferential form, which help one understand data. For example, the analysis of variance, familiar to most students of experimental psychology, is a common tool to analyze a factorial experiment (Judd and McClelland, 1989; Hoaglin, Mosteller and Tukey, 1991; Kirk, 1982; Lunneborg, 1994; Maxwell and Delaney, 1990; Winer, 1971, give good introductions at various levels.) When levels of a factor have been orthogonally crossed in the design, the effects of each factor can be extracted by fitting a model in which effects and variances add. The result often allows one to make inferences about the degree to which variations in overall performance are attributable to one factor versus another or to various combinations of factors. This kind of decomposition is useful. Recently, advances have been made to analyze similar complex experiments that yield frequency data for which the usual assumptions (e.g., that the underlying variability is the same for data with different means) is likely to be too far wrong. For these cases logistic or other models often provide a more rational and revealing analysis (see McCullah and Nelder, 1983; Neter, Wasserman and Kutner, 1990).

Another useful technique is regression, including multiple regression (see Judd and McClelland, 1989; McCullah and Nelder, 1983; Mosteller and Tukey, 1977). (Mathematically, traditional analysis of variance techniques are just computationally—and sometimes conceptually—simple special cases of regression analysis.) Regression techniques are used to correlate observations. When one has measured individual differences in background variables and in performance, the correlation between each variable and each other is calculated. Another useful common procedure that relies on regression analysis is the analysis of covariance, a method by which nuisance variables, such as user age, can be more-or-less held constant by a statistical correction applied to an ordinary or a factorial experiment.

If one wishes to estimate how well overall performance can be predicted on the best combination of background variables, multiple regression is the usual tool of choice. A special form of it provided by many statistical packages is the stepwise regression. In this technique the variable that makes the largest difference in prediction is found and its effect estimated and removed, then the next most influential variable, and so forth.

Another class of techniques to decompose or simplify a complex pattern of data is structural analyses (e.g., factor analysis, multidimensional scaling, hierarchical clustering; see Carroll and Arabie, in press; Kruskal and Wish, 1978) useful for analyzing measurements or judgments of the similarity of different objects to each other when the needs of research suggest simplifying the pattern of relationships. One might have observed the editing errors made by many typists of different backgrounds and want to explore underlying patterns in the data. One way to do this would be to estimate the similarity between any two errors by the probability that the same person or task produced both. From a matrix of such similarity measures, a hierarchical or multidimensional scaling can be made. In these techniques some underlying structure (e.g., some type of graph or some type of metric space) is assumed and numerical methods are employed to fit the structure to the data. In multidimensional scaling an attempt may be made to embed the initial observed distances in a lower dimensional space (related to common techniques in signal processing and pattern recognition), and then try to interpret the important dimensions in the simpler representation. INDSCAL is a method that helps in interpreting dimensions. In hierarchical scaling the data are fitted to a tree structure. In "structural equation" modeling or analysis, regression statistics are used to estimate the most likely relations in a postulated set of causally interrelated variables. LISREL is a program for the purpose (Jöreskog and Sörbom, 1993.)

All of these methods have considerable technical content, and are well beyond the scope of this chapter. They are mentioned here to raise awareness that sophisticated methods for decomposing, analyzing and representing complex data are available. It is always good practice to seek out printed or oral consultative advice on the analytic and statistical methods to be used in a study early in the planning stages so that the combination of data and analysis will be most powerful.

Modeling

Theory and models often help to analyze, make sense of, and apply the results of research. Examples of models will be found in other chapters in this volume. The idea is to build a mathematical theory that can generate data like those observed. If a simple and plausible model can be developed that does a reasonable job of prediction, and in which one or more of the parameters correspond to variations that are produced by changes in design or technology, then the model can be used to estimate the effects of such changes. For examples, in the key-stroke model of Card, Moran and Newell (1983), error-free performance times for various tasks performed by experienced users of text editors can be simulated to a useful degree of accuracy; in the Landauer and Nachbar (1985) model of choice from well ordered menus, the response time for different numbers of alternatives is closely predicted. The effects of changing a system so that different numbers of different actions are required can be estimated by running calculations on these models. The hope for such models is that they can be used to evaluate design alternatives before they are actually built and tested, thus giving a quick and cheap preliminary filter.

9.6 Conclusions and Summary

Every field of science and technology needs unique, appropriate research methods. Human–computer interaction combines work in computer science and human factors engineering, and has borrowed heavily from the research traditions of both. Some of the familiar techniques have proven more valuable than others. Only in the last few years have the methodological approaches best suited to human–computer interaction begun to be identified. This chapter reviewed and critiqued many borrowed standard methods and described the important characteristics of old and new approaches that appear promising. Among approaches inherited from computer science, we are most critical of "seat-of-the pants," "intuitive" methods devoid of systematic behavioral data and showed the much greater danger in HCI research than in traditional engineering research of fallible intuition and the importance of the extreme intrinsic variability of human behavior. (Clearly, intuition is indispensable in the inventive aspects of design; the argument is on research.) Among the borrowings from psychology, we are skeptical of the practical value of classical comparative experiments to determine the relative merits of two or more features or systems and of conventional testing of significance. (Although these are often correct for theoretically oriented research where differences between human–computer interaction and psychology disappear.)

For the central objective of inventing, designing or redesigning computer systems for human use, the main problem is that the objects of study are large and complicated. Human-computer systems have many sub-components and facets: in hardware, in software, in their operation, and in the tasks for which people use them. Because the parts can interact in subtle and unpredictable ways, it is not sufficient to study them in isolation. Yet, whole systems are slow to build, and sometimes hard to evaluate effectively. Despite these difficulties, some extremely promising research methods have been identified. Two major classes are stressed here, human performance analysis and formative evaluation.

A number of dramatic human–computer interaction design successes, some of which are cited in this and other chapters, have already occurred as a direct result of systematic research—as contrasted with intelligent creativity alone. As powerful and appropriate research methods are further developed and, especially, more consistently applied, we can expect to see much more rapid and significant advances in the creation of effective computer tools for human use.

9.7 Acknowledgment

Gary McClelland of the University of Colorado, Boulder, provided extensive and valuable advice on the experimental design and statistical considerations discussed in this chapter and recommended many of the sources given for reference on statistical methods. I thank him greatly.

9.8 References

Abelson, R. P. (1995). *Statistics as principled argument.* Hillsdale NJ: Erlbaum.

Atkinson, A. C., and Donev (1992). *Optimum experimental designs.* Oxford, UK.: Oxford University Press.

Black, J.B. and Sebrechts, M.M. (1981). *Facilitating human-computer communication.* 149-178.

Borgman, C. L. (1986). Why are on-line catalogs hard to use? Lessons learned from information–retrieval studies. *Journal of the American Association for Information Science, 37*(6), 387-400.

Box, G.E.P., Hunter, W.G. and Hunter, J.S. (1978). *Statistics for experiments.* New York: John Wiley.

Brown, J. S. (1991). Research that reinvents the corporation. *Harvard Business Review* (January–February), 102-111.

Card, S., Moran, T.P., and Newell, A. (1983). *The psychology of human–computer interaction.* Hillsdale, New Jersey: Lawrence Erlbaum.

Carroll, J. D., and Arabie, P. (In press). Multidimensional scaling. In M. H. Birnbaum (Eds.), *Handbook of perception and cognition, Vol. 3: Measurement, judgment and decision making.* San Diego, CA: Academic Press.

Chambers, J.M., Cleveland, W.S., Kleiner, B. and Tukey, P.A. (1983). *Graphical methods for data analysis.* Belmont, CA: Wadsworth.

Chambers, J. M., and Hastie, T. J. (1992). *Statistical models in S.* Pacific Grove, CA: Wadsworth.

Cook, T.D. and Campbell, D.T. (1979). *Quasi-experimentation: Design and analysis issues for field settings.* Chicago: Rand McNally.

Cleveland, W. S. (1993). *Visualizing data.* Summit, NJ: Hobart.

Cutler, K., and Rowe, C. (1990). Scanning in the Supermarket: for Better or Worse? A case study in Introducing Electronic Point of Sale. *Behaviour and Information Technology, 9*(2), 157-169.

Egan, D. E. (1988). Individual differences in human–computer interaction. In M. Helander (Eds.), *Handbook of Human–computer Interaction.* Amsterdam: North–Holland.

Egan, D.E. and Gomez, L.M. (1985). Assaying, isolating, and accommodating individual differences in learning a complex skill. In R. Dillon (Ed.), *Individual differences in Cognition (Vol. 2).* New York: Academic Press.

Egan, D. E., Lesk, M. E., Ketchum, R. D., Lochbaum, C. C., Remde, J. R., Littman, M., and Landauer, T. K. (1991). Hypertext For the Electronic Library? CORE Sample Results. In *Hypertext '91 Proceedings,* (pp. 1-14).

Ekstrom, R.B., French, J.W. and Harman, H.H. (1976). *Manual for kit of factor-referenced cognitive tests.* Educational Testing Service, Princeton, New Jersey.

Fisher, R.A. (1935). *The design of experiments.* New York: Hafner Press.

Furnas, G.W., Landauer, T.K., Gomez, L.M. and Dumais, S.T. (1983). Statistical semantics: Analysis of the potential performance of key-word information systems. *Bell System Technical Journal, 62,* 6, 1753-1806.

Furnas, G.W., Landauer, T.K., Gomez, L.M. and Dumais, S.T. (1987). The vocabulary problem in human-system communication. *Communications of the ACM, 30.*

Gould, J.D., Boies, S.J., Levy, S., Richards, J.T., and Schoonard, J. (1987). The 1984 Olympic message system: A test of behavioral principles of system design. *Communications of the ACM, 30,* 758-769.

Gould, J.D., Conti, J. and Hovanyecz, T. (1983). Composing letters with a simulated listening typewriter, *Communications of the ACM 28,* 3, 295-308.

Good, M. (1985). The iterative design of a new text editor. *Proceedings of the Human Factors Society 29th annual meeting 1985,* 571-574.

Good, M.D., Whiteside, J.A., Wixon, D.R. and Jones, S.J. (1984). Building a user-derived interface. *Communications of the ACM, 27,* 10, 1032-1043.

Gray, W. D., John, B. E., and Atwood, M. E. (1992). The precis of project Ernestine, or, an overview of a validation of GOMS. In *Proceedings CHI'92, Human Factors in Computing Systems*, Monterey: ACM.

Greene, S.L., Gomez, L.M. and Devlin, S.J. (1986). A cognitive analysis of database query production. Annual Meeting of the Human Factors Society. Dayton, Ohio.

Grudin, J. and Barnard, P. (1984). The cognitive demands of learning and representing names for text editing. *Human Factors, 26*, 407-422.

Grudin, J. (1986). Designing in the dark: Logics that compete with the user. In M. Mantei and P. Oberton (Eds.), *Human Factors in Computing Systems, Proceedings of CHI'86*, ACM, 281-284.

Hastie, T. J., and Tibshirani, R. (1990). *Generalized additive models*. London: Chapman and Hall.

Hoaglin, D.C., Mosteller, F., Tukey, J.W. (1983). *Understanding robust and exploratory data analysis*. New York: John Wiley and Sons.

Hoaglin, D. C., Mosteller, F., and Tukey, J. W. (Ed.). (1991). *Fundamentals of exploratory analysis of variance*. New York: Wiley.

Jöreskog, K. G. and Sörbom, D. (1993) LISREL8: The SIMPLIS command language. Chicago: Scientific Software.

Joy, W. (1984). An introduction to display editing with Vi. *Unix User's Manual*. Berkeley, CA: USENIX Association.

Judd, C. M., and McClelland, G. H. (1989). *Data analysis: a model comparison approach*. San Diego: Harcourt Brace Jovanovich.

Judd, C. M., and McClelland, G. H. (In press). Measurement. In D. Gilbert, S. Fiske, and G. Lindzey (Eds.), *Handbook of Social Psychology*

Judd, C. M., McClelland, G. H., and Culhane, S. E. (1995). Data analysis: Continuing issues in the everyday analysis of psychological data. *Annual Review of Psychology, 46*, 433-465.

Kernighan, B.W. and Cherry, L.L. (1978). A system for typesetting mathematics. *UNIX User's Manual: Supplementary Documents*. Berkeley, CA: USENIX.

Kirk, R. (1982). *Experimental design: Procedures for the behavioral sciences*. Monterey, CA: Brooks-Cole.

Krantz, D.H., Luce, R.D., Suppes, P. and Tversky, A. (1971). *Foundations of measurement*. New York: Academic Press.

Kruskal, J.B. and Wish, M. (1978). *Multidimensional scaling*. Beverly Hills, CA: Sage Publications.

Landauer, T.K. (1995). *The trouble with computers: Usefulness, usability and productivity*. Cambridge, MA. MIT Press.

Landauer, T. K., Egan, D. E., Remde, J. R., Lesk, M. E., Lochbaum, C. C., and Ketchum, D. (1993). Enhancing the usability of text through computer delivery and formative evaluation: the SuperBook project. In C. McKnight, A. Dillon, and J. Richardson (Eds.), *Hypertext: A Psychological Perspective* (pp. 71-136). New York: Ellis Horwood.

Landauer, T.K., Galotti, K.M. and Hartwell, S. (1983). Natural command names and initial learning: A study of text-editing terms. *Communications of ACM, 26*, 495-503.

Landauer, T.K. and Galotti, K.M. (1984). What makes a difference when? Comments on Grudin and Barnard. *Human Factors, 26*, 423-429.

Landauer, T.K. and Nachbar, D.W. (1985). Selection from alphabetic and numeric menu trees using a touch screen: Breadth, depth and width. *CHI'85 ACM conference on human factors operating systems*, New York: ACM.

Luce, R.D. (1986). *Response times: Their role in inferring elementary mental organization*. New York: Oxford University Press.

Luce, R. D. (1995). Four tensions concerning mathematical modeling in psychology. *Annual Review of Psychology, 46*, 1-26.

Luce, R. D., and Krumhansl, C. L. (1988). Measurement, scaling, and psychophysics. In R. C. Atkinson, R. J. Herrnstein, G. Lindzey, and R. D. Luce (Eds.), *Steven's Handbook of Experimental Psychology (2nd Ed.) Volume 1: Perception and Motivation*. New York: Wiley.

Lunneborg, C. E. (1994). *Modeling experimental and observational data*. Belmont, CA: Duxbury Press.

Maxwell, S. E., and Delaney, H. D. (1990). *Designing experiments and analyzing data: A model comparison approach*. Belmont, CA: Wadsworth.

McCullah, P., and Nelder, J. A. (1983). *Generalized linear models*. London: Chapman & Hall.

Mead, R. (1988). *The design of experiments: Statistical principles for practical application*. Cambridge, UK: Cambridge University Press.

Michell, J. (1990). *An introduction to the logic of psy-*

chological measurement. Hillsdale, NJ: Lawrence Erlbaum Associates.

Mosteller, F. and Tukey, J.W. (1977). *Data analysis and regression*. Reading, MA: Addison Wesley.

Neter, J., Wasserman, W., and Kutner, M. H. (1990). *Applied linear statistical models (3rd Ed.)*. Homewood, IL: Richard D. Irwin.

Nielsen, J. (1989). Usability engineering at a discount. In G. A. S. Salvendy M.J. (Eds.), *Designing and Using Human-Computer Interfaces and Knowledge Based Systems* (pp. 394-401). Amsterdam: Elsevier Science Publishers.

Nielsen, J., and Landauer, T. K. (1993). A mathematical model of the finding of usability problems. In *INTERCHI'93, ACM Conference on Human Factors in Computing Systems,* Amsterdam, ACM, 206-213.

Pedhazur, E. J., and Schmelkin, L. P. (1991). *Measurement, design and analysis: An integrated approach,*. Hillsdale, NJ: Lawrence Erlbaum Associates.

Pennington, N., and Rehder, B. (1995). Looking for transfer and interference. In D. L. Medin (Ed.), *The psychology of learning and motivation.* Boston: Academic Press.

Roberts, T.L. and Moran, T.P. (1983). The evaluation of text editors: Methodology and empirical results. *Communications of ACM, 26*, 4, 265-283.

Rosenthal, R. (1976). *Experimenter effects in behavioral research*. New York: Halstead.

Rosenthal, R. and Rosnow, R.L. (Eds.) (1991). *Essentials of behavioral research methods and analysis.* New York: McGraw-Hill.

Shneiderman, B. (1983) Direct manipulation: A step beyond programming languages. IEEE Computer 16, 8, 57-69.

Siegal, S.S. (1956). *Nonparametric Statistics*. New York: McGraw-Hill.

Singley, M.K. and Anderson, J.R. (1985). The transfer of text-editing skill. *International Journal of Man-Machine Studies, 22*, 403-423.

Singley, M. K., and Anderson, J. R. (1989). *The transfer of cognitive skill.* Cambridge: Harvard University Press.

Smith, S. and Mosier, J.N. (1986). *Guidelines for designing user interface software*. Bedford, MA: Mitre Corp.

Tesler, L. (1983). Enlisting user help in software design. *SIGCHI Bull., 14*, 5-9.

Tukey, J.W. (1960). Conclusions vs. decisions, *Technometrics, 2*, 423-433.

Tukey, J.W. (1977). *Exploratory data analysis*. Reading, MA: Addison Wesley.

Wilk, M.B. and Gnanadesikan, R. (1968). Probability plotting methods for the analysis of data. *Biometrika, 55*, 1-17.

Winer, B.J. (1971). Statistical principles in experimental design (2nd ed.), New York: McGraw-Hill.

Part II

Design and Development of Software Systems

Handbook of Human-Computer Interaction
Second, completely revised edition
M. Helander, T.K. Landauer, P. Prabhu (eds.)

Chapter 10

How To Design Usable Systems

John D. Gould
IBM Research, Emeritus
New York, USA

Stephen J. Boies and Jacob Ukelson
IBM Research Center -- Hawthorne
Yorktown Heights, New York, USA

10.1 Abstract

This chapter summarizes a process of system design that, if you follow it, will help you create usable computer systems for people -- systems that are easy to learn, easy to use, contain the right functions, and are liked. There are four key points in this usability design process: early focus on users; empirical measurement; iterative design; and integrated design, where all aspects of usability evolve together from the start. We review 20-30 informal methods to carry out these four points. Many of the methods can be used without extensive training in human factors. In the second half of this chapter we summarize how we used this design process to develop a new comprehensive software development system, called ITS. We created ITS to make it easier for developers to carry out this design process particularly incremental, iterative design. As part of iteratively developing ITS, we used ITS to build serious applications, particularly multimedia ones, used by thousands and millions of users. We describe these case studies, with emphasis upon the human factors methods used and our iterative, incremental approach.

10.2 Introduction

The first half of this chapter contains recommendations on how to design usable systems. This design process was published in the first edition of this Handbook (Gould, 1988), has stood up to the passage of time, and is summarized here. The second half summarizes our experiences in following the process advocated here in creating a software development system and then using it to implement about ten serious computer applications, ranging from traditional transaction systems to leading-edge multimedia ones used by millions of people. While the applications created with these software tools have been largely successfully, the tools themselves have not yet become widely used.

The focus of this chapter is again on how to design computer systems. It is aimed at system designers who want to know more about how to design useful, usable, desirable computer systems -- ones that people can easily learn, that contain the functions that allow people to do the things they want to do, and that are well liked. Throughout, "good computer systems" mean ones with these characteristics.

The intended audience, or users, of this paper are expected to be (1) human factors people involved, or getting involved, in system design; (2) experimental psychologists and other discipline-oriented people who may want to learn how to do behavioral system design work; and (3) system designers who are not trained in human factors but who are concerned about usability of systems. This latter group is particularly important since it is impractical for trained human factors people to work on all aspects of usability. There are not enough of them. Usability is too broad. And, besides, as a result of reading this paper, systems people can learn how usability people ought to work.

"There is no comprehensive and generally accepted manual on how to design good human factors into computer systems," wrote Shackel (1984). While not comprehensive, we hope this paper will at least be useful. It is intended to be tutorial, to identify and explain the main things you must do to design a good system. The earlier version provided indications of where to go for more information, and what you can expect to find when you get there. Here we give you our experiences in the 1990's in following the approach that we recommend below.

10.2.1 Overview

In this Introduction, we first note that usability consists of many pieces. Second, we briefly mention a process for system design which addresses all these pieces. We have argued for over fifteen years that the four key points ("principles") of this process are the required cornerstones for designing good systems. Third, as a means of showing where these principles fit into system design, we divide the design process into four rough phases. These sections are summaries of what we previously wrote. Next, we describe our own group's experiences in using this approach to create an integrated set of system development tools, and our experiences in using these tools to develop about ten serious customer applications in the 1990's.

10.2.2 Usability Has Many Aspects

There are many aspects to usability which must be taken into account if a system is to be good (Table 1). Generally designers focus on only one aspect of usability, e.g., knitting pre-given functions together into an user interface. This narrow focus almost guarantees missing the point that usability is made up of many important factors which are often mutually dependent (see Gould, Boies, Levy, Richards, and Schoonard, 1987 for a detailed example).

To illustrate the importance of the various aspects of usability, consider several of those shown in Table 1 that are perhaps least discussed in the literature.

System reliability and responsiveness are the sine qua non elements of usability. If the system is unavailable, it cannot be used. If the system is unreliable, users will avoid it regardless of how good it may be when it works. A survey of 4,448 computer users found that response time was the most important variable affecting their happiness (Rushinek and Rushinek, 1986). With increased system responsiveness user productivity goes up (Doherty and Kelisky, 1979; Doherty and Thadhani, 1982; but see Martin and Corl, 1986). Usability factors go deep, as well as being broad. System reliability and responsiveness go to the heart of system configuration.

It is often alleged that people buy systems for their functions, rather than for their user interface characteristics. (While this is probably historically true, the popularity of Macintosh reflects the increased value users place on user interfaces.) In the Usability Design Process section below we address how to determine required functions.

Language translation is a serious and time- consuming process. Just the usability detail of putting all the messages in one file, rather than burying them in the code, eases the language translation process -- even makes it possible (see Gould et al., 1987 for a behavioral approach to language translation).

Table 1. Components of usability.

Components
System Performance
Reliability
Responsiveness
System Functions
User Interfaces
Organization
I/O Hardware
For end-users
For other groups
Reading Materials
End-user groups
Support groups
Language Translation
Reading materials
User interfaces
Outreach Program
End-user training
On-line help system
Hot-lines
Ability for customers to modify and extend
Installation
Packaging and unpacking
Installing
Field Maintenance and serviceability
Advertising
Motivating customers to buy
Motivating user to use
Support-group users
Marketing people
Trainers
Operators
Maintenance workers

Unpacking and installing computer systems have been greatly improved and speeded up by work of human factors psychologists (Comstock, 1983; Granda, Personal Communication, 1980; Green, 1986).

What we call outreach programs, which include user training, reading materials, on-line help, and hot-lines, often do not reflect the general observation that people learn by doing and by observing others doing.

It is easy to overlook the fact that several other groups, besides the primary users, also need user interfaces, reading materials, and training. These include user trainers, system operators, maintenance workers, and salespeople. Ultimately, usability is seriously affected by the usability of what these people are taught and given. We have observed sales people who avoid giving demonstrations of even simple products (dictating equipment was one example) because of uncertainty about how the products work.

10.2.3 Usability Design Process — The Four Principles

To design good systems, we believe that you must follow the four principles of system design shown in Table 2. These steps have been developed at IBM Research (Gould et al., 1987; Gould and Lewis, 1983; 1985). They will be discussed in the next main section.

Table 2. Four design process principles.

- Early -- and continual -- focus on users
- Empirical measurement
- Iterative design
- Integrated design -- wherein all aspects of usability evolve together

10.2.4 Usability Design Phases

As a chronological framework for discussing what you must do to carry out the four steps in Table 2, we divide the work roughly into four phases: a gearing-up phase, an initial design phase, an iterative development phase, and a system installation phase.

Gearing-Up Phase. This is mainly an information gathering and conceptualization phase. Here you look for good starting points, e.g., learn about related systems. You familiarize yourself with existing user inter-

Table 3. Comments we have informally heard from system designers.

"We didn't anticipate THIS."
"But that's not how I thought it worked."
"What do users REALLY want"?
"I'm too pooped to change it now -- it took so long to get here."
"The manual and the user interface are different"!
"Even simple changes are hard."
"Why is user testing so late"?
"Why does user testing take so long"?
"Why don't we do user testing"?
"I would've tested, but...."
"We are surprised that..."
"It worked before..."
"The manual will take care of this..."
"The help system will take care of this..."
"A hot-line will take care of this..."
"We'll take care of it in the NEXT release."
"It's not broken; that's how it's supposed to work."

face standards, guidelines, and any development procedures and development tools that your organization may have. You study existing systems, familiarize yourself with new influential systems and new technologies. You can study journals, proceedings, attend user interface conferences, talk to attendees (in our experience almost all of these people are approachable and friendly), demonstrations, workshops, short courses, and perhaps hire consultants.

Initial Design Phase. Early focus on users takes center stage here. Here you need to collect critical information about users and their work. You need to make a preliminary specification of the user interface, drawing upon existing and leading systems, standards, guidelines, and user interface styles where appropriate. If you are considering using prototyping tools that are different from the actual tools that will be used to implement your system (i.e., prototype tools that do not scale up), you need to carefully consider the relation between the two. You need to develop testable behavioral goals, and organize the work to be done. Integrated design, in which all aspects of usability are considered at the outset and evolve together, begins in this phase and is carried into the iterative development phase. All of this is elaborated on below.

Iterative Development Phase. With testable behavioral goals and ready access to user feedback established, continuous evaluation and modification of all aspects of usability can be achieved, as described below.

System Installation Phase. Here concentration centers on techniques for installing the system in customers' locations, introducing it to users, employing the training materials you developed earlier, ascertaining and assuring customer acceptance. (In the case of vendor products, this phase assumes successful marketing has occurred.) The work done on installation, customer support, and system maintenance now receives the ultimate test. For most systems, delivery to the customer should not signal the end of the road, since there are the inevitable follow-ons. Thus, it is just another iteration. If data logging programs to record user performance and acceptance have been incorporated, they will prove useful here. This phase is not discussed further in this chapter.

10.3 The Usability Design Process

Table 3 contains revealing comments made by system designers. Behind them is the realization that relying on a blend of designers' own experiences and following standards, guidelines, or various rational and analytic design philosophies is not sufficient to arrive at good computer systems. Too many systems end up being hard to learn and use, have arbitrary inconsistencies with other systems, and lack the sparkle of insight into what users could really benefit from. From these experiences, several general points shown in Table 4 emerge.

In response to these problems, several human factors people, apparently working independently, pro-

Table 4. General observations about system design.

Nobody can get it right the first time.
Development is full of surprises.
Developing user-oriented systems requires living in a sea of changes.
Making contracts to ignore them does not eliminate the need for change.
Designers need good tools.
You can have behavioral design targets, just as you have other capacity and performance targets for other parts of the system, e.g., memory size, calculation time (Gould and Lewis, 1985).
Even if you have made the best system possible, users -- both novices and experienced -- will make mistakes using it.

Table 5. Generally required steps in designing good systems.

Define the problem the customer wants solved
Identify tasks users must perform
Learn user capabilities
Learn hardware/software constraints
Set specific usability targets (in behavioral terms)
Sketch out user scenarios
Design and build prototype
Test prototype
Iteratively incorporate changes and test again until:
Behavioral targets are met
A critical deadline is reached
Install system at customer location
Measure customer reaction and acceptance

vided in the 1980's relatively similar recommendations about how to do better (Bennett, 1984; Bury, 1984; Chapanis and students, e.g., Sullivan and Chapanis, 1983; Damodaran, Simpson, and Wilson, 1980; Meister, 1986; Reitman-Olson, 1985; Rubinstein and Hersh, 1984; Shackel (1984), the Usability Engineering group at DEC, e.g., Good, Spine, Whiteside, and George, 1986; Wixon and Whiteside, 1985; a group at IBM Research, Gould and Lewis, 1985; Gould, et al., 1987. Shackel (1985) has provided a historical summary. All this work represents a coming together of many earlier experiences. For example, the "application of empirical methods to computer-based system design" was the title of an experimental paper more than thirty years ago (Grace, 1966). There are many common procedural steps in the recommendations of all these people, summarized in Table 5, which should be used in carrying out the usability design process.

10.3.1 Design Principle 1. Early — and Continual — Focus On Users

Your Job. Your job is to design a system that has the right functions in it so people can do their work better and like it. You can't figure out what people want, need, can do, and will do without talking with them.

Decide Who the Users Will Be. A first step in designing a system is to decide (a) who the users will be and (b) what they will be doing with the system. This should be done either before starting to design the system, or at a very early stage after obtaining some general ideas about it. Having done this, subsequent decisions, e.g., about system organization, required functions, user interface, must reflect these answers. The user population may ultimately be broader or more heterogeneous. If so, there is no a priori rule for aiming at the "lowest common denominator" or at the "average" user. Rather, your system will have to be tailored and tested for the other groups as well, and design tradeoffs may be required. But establishing one user set is much better than letting this decision continue to slip, as it forces design decisions that otherwise remain open too long. Open decisions about the intended users reflect slipperiness, not flexibility. We believe that the single best way to move advanced technology toward useful applications is by defining an intended user population and what they will do with it.

Designers Often Avoid This. We have observed two serious types of reluctance: one a reluctance to define the users, and the other a reluctance to take the definition seriously. First, as strange as it may seem, designers often avoid coming to grips with the question of who the users will be. This is due in part to the strong (and appropriate) effect the answer will have on subsequent design decisions. For example, designers cannot maintain that they are designing a toolkit system for non-programmers and make it so complicated ("powerful") that even their programming colleagues recognize the contradiction. Reviewers have suggested that this example is a paper tiger -- that no one would believe it. We did not make it up. The reluctance seems to be greatest in research environments, where people's goals are often mixed, e.g., advance the discipline of speech recognition versus build a listening typewriter, advance the discipline of expert systems versus build one to aid human operators or schedulers.

Second, even where designers define early who the users will be, the implications of this decision do not always drive subsequent design decisions in as powerful a way as they should. For example, setting out to design a picture editor for secretaries is laudable, but then building it so that only programmers can use it is inappropriate. We know of one advanced technology interface that was developed for a specific list of executive users. Yet the designers never talked with or visited the offices of these executives -- even though they worked in the same building. The result was that when completed, the system was never used. Often without iterative user-designer interaction there is little relation between what designers build and what intended users are likely to ever use.

We have learned that people, even those who should know better, often avoid taking seriously the implications established once the intended user group is identified. This seeming inability to recognize the resulting design constraints occurs with all kinds of systems and organizations, in addition to computer systems. For example, in a book of invited chapters on various aspects of human factors, the authors (mostly well known human factors themselves) in preliminary meetings hammered out who the intended audience would be. The audience, it was agreed, was different from their usual ones. Despite this agreement, nearly all the authors subsequently wrote their individual chapters for different audiences (generally, their usual research audiences). Later reviews in which the authors were reminded of the characteristics of the intended audience did not lead to appropriate major revisions

Even Shorter Development Cycles. Development cycles have become dramatically shorter in the last ten years. There is no time to talk with users, we often hear. But the key point is that with even shorter development cycles, there is even greater need to get as close as possible to a usable system as soon as possible.

You Can't Rely Upon Descriptive Data. Even if a description of the intended users were as complete as it possibly could be, it would not be an adequate basis for design. It would not substitute for direct interaction and testing. For example, while developing a system to replace an existing one for a major insurance company we were told by the data processing department that the intended users were "heads-down" data entry clerks. Weeks later we learned that the users were actually professional underwriters whose work greatly determined the profit and loss of the company.

10.3.2 Methods For Doing Early Focus On Users

Table 6 summarizes several methods for focusing on users. These are explained with examples in the first edition of this Handbook (Gould, 1988). Several of these methods apply to more than one principle. For convenience, however, we have grouped methods under the principle to which they are probably most relevant.

Table 6. Methods for focusing on users.

- Talk with users.
- Visit customer locations.
- Observe users working.
- Videotape users working.
- Learn about the work organization.
- Have users think aloud.
- Try it yourself.
- Participative design.
- Have expert on design team.
- Use task analysis.
- Use surveys and questionnaire.
- Make testable behavioral usability goals.

Table 7 is a checklist to help you carry out early -- and continual -- focus on users.

Table 7. Checklist for achieving early -- and continual -- focus on users.

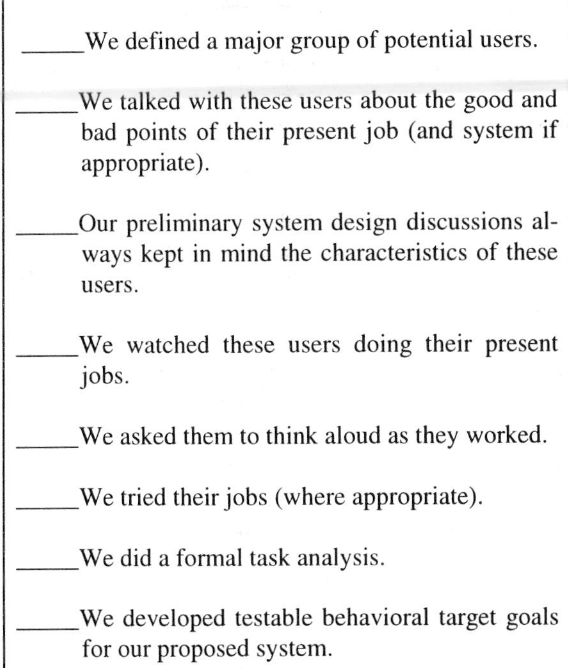

_____We defined a major group of potential users.

_____We talked with these users about the good and bad points of their present job (and system if appropriate).

_____Our preliminary system design discussions always kept in mind the characteristics of these users.

_____We watched these users doing their present jobs.

_____We asked them to think aloud as they worked.

_____We tried their jobs (where appropriate).

_____We did a formal task analysis.

_____We developed testable behavioral target goals for our proposed system.

10.3.3 Design Principle 2. Early — and Continual — User Testing

Remember, your job is to design a system that works and has the right functions so that users can do the right things. You won't know whether it is working right until you start testing it. From the very beginning of the development process, and throughout it, intended users should carry out real work using early versions of training materials and manuals, and simulations and prototypes of user interfaces, help systems, and so forth. The emphasis here is upon measurement, informal and formal.

The basic premise is that you cannot get it right the first time, no matter how experienced or smart you are. This observation is not limited just to computer system designers. Heckel (1984), in writing about software design, asks "If Ernest Hemingway, James Michener, Neil Simon, Frank Lloyd Wright, and Pablo Picasso could not get it right the first time, what makes you think you will?" Heckel quotes others: "Plan to throw one away" (Fred Brooks). Rewrite and revise...it is no sign of weakness or defeat that your manuscript ends up in need of major surgery" (William Strunk and E. B. White). "The two most important tools an architect has are the eraser in the drawing room and the sledge hammer on the construction site" (Frank Lloyd Wright). If you measure and then make appropriate changes you can hill-climb toward an increasingly better system.

10.3.4 Methods To Carry Out Early — and Continual — User Testing

Table 8 summarizes the methods, explained and described with examples in the first edition (Gould, 1988), to carry out early and continuous focus on users.

Table 8. Methods for user testing.

- Printed or Video Scenarios.
- Early User Manuals.
- Mock-ups.
- Simulations.
- Early prototyping.
- Early Demonstrations.
- Thinking Aloud.
- Make Videotapes.
- Hallway and Storefront Methodology.
- Computer Bulletin Boards, Forums, Networks, and Conferencing.
- Formal Prototype Tests.
- Try-to-Destroy-It Contests.
- Field Studies.
- Follow-up Studies.

A Checklist. Table 9 is a checklist to help you carry out early -- and continual -- user testing.

10.3.5 Design Principle 3. Iterative Design

The key requirements for iterative design are shown in Table 10.

The required or recommended changes can be identified with measurements made on intended users and the results compared against previously established behavioral goals. To make these changes, however, requires that designers have good tools, and that the work is organized in a way that enables them to be responsive. When you find a problem, what to do about it may not be clear. There is no principled method to determine what the solution is. There are only empirical methods -- to be used after careful analysis, critical

Table 9. Checklist for achieving early user testing.

_____	We made informal, preliminary sketches of a few user scenarios -- specifying exactly what the user and system messages will be -- and showed them to a few prospective users.
_____	We have begun writing the user manual, and it is guiding the development process.
_____	We have used simulations to try out the functions and organization of the user interface.
_____	We have used mock-ups to try out the functions and organization of the user interface.
_____	We have done early demonstrations.
_____	We invited as many people as possible to comment on on-going instantiations of all usability components.
_____	We had prospective users think aloud as they used simulations, mock-ups, and prototypes.
_____	We used hallway and storefront methods.
_____	We used computer conferencing forums to get feedback on usability.
_____	We did formal prototype user testing.
_____	We compared our results to established behavioral target goals.
_____	We met our behavioral benchmark targets.
_____	We let motivated people try to find bugs in our systems.
_____	We did field studies.
_____	We included data logging programs in our system.
_____	We did follow-up studies on people who are now using the system we made.

thinking, and innovation have been applied. The empirical methods can either be used during system development or they, in effect, will be used after the system is delivered -- which is usually an inopportune time. Sometimes you may make changes that will cause other problems. You will only know if you test for them.

Table 10. The key requirements for iterative design.

- Identification of required changes.
- An ability to make the changes.
- A willingness to make changes.

10.3.6 Methods To Carry Out Iterative Design

Table 11 summarizes the key methods for carrying out iterative design.

Table 11. Methods for carrying out iterative design.

- Collect the required improvements during user testing.
- Organize the development work in a way that improvements can be made.
- Have software tools that allow you to make the needed improvements.

A Checklist. Table 12 is a checklist to help you carry out iterative design.

Table 12. Checklist for carrying out iterative design.

_____	All aspects of usability could be easily changed, i.e., we had good tools.
_____	We regularly changed our system, manuals, etc., based upon testing results with prospective users.

10.3.7 Design Principle 4. Integrated Design

As explained in Gould et al. (1987), we recommend that all aspects of usability evolve in parallel. At the outset, work should begin on planning an user interface, the language translation approach, the help system, user guides, other reading materials, and so forth. In order for this to happen successfully, all aspects of usability should be under one focus or person. Usability cannot be coordinated otherwise. This one-focus recommendation presumes line-management responsibility, and is thus different from Usability Committees (Demers, 1981).

A project can be managed to only a few goals, e.g., low cost, processing speed, compatibility with the past, reliability, short development schedule, usability. With the methods described in this paper, you can measure usability, therefore control it, and therefore manage it. Integrated design is an essential approach if one of the goals of your project is usability.

10.3.8 Methods To Carry Out Integrated Design

The methods just outlined under early focus on users and user testing must be brought to bear on all aspects of usability. Technically, these methods are sufficient to guarantee an acceptable system. The main difficulty in carrying out integrated design will be organizational. Integrated design requires a departure from fractionated development practices where various aspects of usability are developed in different loosely-related departments, divisions, cities, companies. Integrated design assumes a recognition at the very outset that usability is important, that it includes many factors (Table 1), and that work must begin on it from the start. Integrated design requires a sincere dedication to manage for usability.

Integrated design requires that one group, at the very beginning, be given sufficient resources (money, personnel, time, authority) to drive and control usability, and to invent what is needed to make usability good. This organization must have critical mass early enough to be an effective lobby for usability -- to assure that usability gets its share of the resources of the project. Integrated design requires that this group sign up to *guarantee* good usability. With these resources comes serious responsibilities to make a usable system. Development of the functions, user interface, manuals, help system, training materials, etc. are often each done in separate departments in large projects, or are vended out. Because of these traditions integrated design may be tough to carry out in many organizations. It requires that the usability people be outstanding, be given the responsibility (and accountability), and have good tools. Integrated design is not just a plug for more jobs for human factors people. The responsibility is extremely demanding, especially on large systems. Very special people are required. We have been told that no one person could possibly control all aspects of usability on large systems. This is simply not logical, since there is generally one person in charge of the whole system (of which usability is only a part).

Table 13. Checklist for achieving integrated design.

_____We considered all aspects of usability in our initial design.

_____One person (with an appropriate number of people) had responsibility for all aspects of usability.

_____User manual

_____Manuals for subsidiary groups, e.g., operators, trainers, etc.

_____Identification of required functions

_____User interface

_____Assure adequate system reliability and responsiveness

_____Outreach program, e.g., help system, training materials, hot-lines, videotapes, etc.

_____Installation

_____Customization

_____Field Maintenance

_____Support-group users

A Checklist. Table 13 is a checklist to help you carry out integrated design.

10.3.9 Comparison To Other Approaches

Gould and Lewis (1985) compared usability design with other design approaches, e.g., getting it right the first time. You simply cannot fully specify a system in advance -- even when using a methodology that tries to do so (Swartout and Balzar, 1982). Further, Gould and Lewis (1985) explicitly raised, and then addressed, several reasons why this process of usability design is often not used, e.g., belief that the development process will be lengthened, belief that iteration is just fine-tuning. Human factors is more than just frosting that can be spread on at the end. "What if the development schedule is so tight that you cannot afford the luxury of talking to users," we are sometimes asked. Talking to users is not a luxury; it is a necessity. The methods described here should help with achieving a schedule. They introduce reality into the schedule, since you must do all these things eventually anyway. "Can't talking to just a few people be misleading," we are sometimes asked. Yes, possibly -- but you will be far, far better off than if you talk to none. Talking to no one is a formula for failure.

Necessary, But Not Sufficient. Using the methods advocated here does not guarantee a GREAT system. The methods are necessary but not sufficient, as pointed out in Gould et al. (1987), to achieve acceptable usability. As in all other professions, designers have a range of ability. By definition, most systems are designed by average designers. Practicing usability design greatly increases the probability that average designers will design systems with acceptable usability. Good starting points further help. To go beyond this and design GREAT systems requires innovation and creativity, as in the invention of the electronic spreadsheet. Also required is an outstanding leader and very good, committed people, dedication, hard work, and lots of self-imposed pressure.

10.3.10 Status Of The Usability Design Process

So far we have summarized the usability design process described about ten years ago (Gould, 1988).

Stood the Test of Time. There is little need, ten years later, to change what was said then, despite the fact that many things have changed in the development process in the last decade. Among the most important changes are the widespread of use of personal computers, powerful new application development tools, shorter development cycles, and the potential to exploit (rather than compensate for) the limits of computers.

The Customer is King. Today there is a widespread belief that preoccupation with customers pays off in all businesses. This is a generalization of the design principle of early and continual focus on users, since the ultimate customers of system designers are the users.

Successful Systems Use It -- And Brag About It There are two common threads that run through 15-20 published case studies described in the first edition (Gould, 1988): the need for using and the effectiveness of using the design methods described here. When designers follow the process advocated here, they brag about it. Not so with most other design approaches. Indeed, we have even heard presentations where designers claim to have done much of what is advocated here, but clearly have not.

Controlling The Tradeoffs. Design is a series of on-going tradeoffs among hardware, software, usability, economic, and scheduling factors. The usability design process must be followed if usability is to receive its due.

10.3.11 So Why Not Use It?

If all of this is so good, why doesn't everybody use it? We previously thought that the principles of the usability design process were almost trivially simple to follow -- they are so common sensical, and they are not difficult technically to carry out. We were wrong. They are not common sensical to many designers (Gould and Lewis, 1985). They are hard to carry out, not only for organizational and motivational reasons, but largely for lack of powerful system development tools that facilitate iterative design by letting designers make serious changes easily.

To some, user testing and iterative design may seem like a pessimistic design philosophy. Do I always have to start from scratch? When will we have a scientific, analytic approach that leads to getting a good user interface the first time? User testing and iterative design will probably always be necessary to be sure you did get it right the first time. Even expert bridge players do not always make their bids.

We have met designers who are certain that the development process will be lengthened and more expensive if they practice the usability design process. They would be adding on more work, they reason, and therefore more time and effort would be required. This view fails to recognize that you learn things with this approach which eliminate a lot of work that would otherwise go on (see Gould and Lewis, 1985; Gould et al., 1987). Imagine building a house without knowing pretty much what you wanted when you started. Without a plan, you would save time getting started, but it would certainly cost you later.

Practicing usability design is especially difficult for managers. Being willing to live in a sea of changes, which the usability design process requires, on very large projects with hundreds of people presents a significant stumbling block. Groups that report practicing the usability design process typically have a strong, committed manager. These groups are often, but not always, relatively small.

Experimental psychologists sometimes see some of our recommended methods as requiring inordinate drudge work. "I don't want to sit and watch people for hours in the experiments." Observing, listening, and making notes provide valuable insights that can be gained no other way. "Why not just completely automate, using computer-controlled experiments"? This automation itself requires iteration; usually there is not enough time.

Engineers and scientists in the early stages of work on a new and innovative technology (a relatively rare situation in most environments, since most systems are really follow-on systems) usually concentrate on demonstrating the feasibility of their new technology, e.g., a new form of automatic recognition of people, objects, or whatever. They sometimes find it hard to map these methods of usability design onto their work. The most important thing to do at this stage is to identify a potential user group. Once this is defined, everything becomes easier because this definition, if taken seriously, is so powerful in guiding design and testing thereafter.

Designers always seem to be in the middle of something -- and never at the beginning of something with time to think about global issues. Taking the opportunity to think about the process with which you will design something rather than the design of that something, is difficult for many people, especially those who feel that they do not have the time or freedom to do so.

Probably the biggest reason, however, that computer system developers, who otherwise have the will to do so, do not follow the design process advocated here is that they simply do not have the technical software tools that makes iterative design possible. And this brings us to the second half of this chapter, which describes our creation of a software development system that make iterative design possible.

10.4 Our Experiences In Creating the ITS Software Tools

The remainder of this chapter summarizes our group's experiences in following this recommended design process as we invented and developed a new, integrated, powerful set of software development tools, and then used these tools to develop about ten serious applications, several of which have been very successful. (ITS is now a commercially available IBM software product called Customer Access Development Tool Set (CADT)).

Software tool design represents an even more difficult challenge than application design because of the need to worry about both (a) the usability of the tools and (b) the usability that can be achieved in the application that can be created with the tools (since tools set limits on the applications they are used to build). What follows is, to our knowledge, the first description of human factors applied to the development of application development tools for serious applications, and therefore it can serve as a model to be improved upon in the future.

10.4.1 Problems to be Solved

It was clear ten years ago that there were several major technical obstacles to carrying out iterative design, thus affecting usability in a negative way.

- Without an ability to do iterative design, continual user testing makes little sense, since required improvements cannot be made. Existing software development tools, capable of doing serious applications, did not, however, allow developers to make changes and improvements easily. Where possible, given the way application code was generally (un)organized, it was often risky to make changes because of unknown side-effects.

- Where changes were possible, usability people generally lacked the skills to make them; they had to ask developers to do so. And there is limited coin in that realm.

- Usability people were using prototyping tools, but they (the tools, anyway) lacked power. Hardly any of them connected to real data bases. User interfaces created with them could not be simply incorporated into real application code because that was done with a different language and approach.

- Good interaction techniques existing in one application could not be easily imported into another application.

- There was little code re-usability. Every application seemed to be created from scratch. Applications took long times to create, and they were therefore expensive to create. Application development productivity was therefore poor. Iterative design, it was thought, even if possible would only add more expense.

In 1987 we began inventing and implementing a comprehensive approach to application development and iterative design (called ITS) that would address these problems. (See Boies, Bennett, Gould, Greene, and Wiecha, 1989; Wiecha, Bennett, Boies, Gould, and Greene, 1990 for early descriptions of ITS. See any of the case studies of using ITS to implement applications listed below for additional descriptions.)

10.4.2 Brief Summary of The ITS Approach

ITS provides workstation software tools for user interface and application development, libraries of human-computer interaction techniques, and a run-time environment for application execution. There are several key concepts.

Separate the Content from the Style of an Application. ITS separates the content of a particular application (e. g., what makes the application a payroll one or a medical one) from the user-interface style in which that application will work (e.g., the Macintosh style, IBM's CUA style, a touch-screen kiosk style, etc.). The content of an application includes an application's functions and its data bases. A user-interface style includes what the screen looks like, the human-computer interaction techniques, and the interaction devices (e.g., mouse, touch screen). A particular user-interface style is used with many applications. In ITS, styles are rule-based. The strategy here is to make it possible for many applications to run in the same style, thus eliminating over half the work in every application that uses an existing style.

Work Roles. ITS envisioned four general work roles (content experts, content programmers, style designers, and style programmers). We had learned that most customers feel that they understand their own business, but have a hard time communicating this expertise to their data processing people. They are often surprised by what gets created for them by developers. Hence, we set out to make it possible for such content experts to play an active, technical role in making their computer application.

Software Tools. ITS has created software tools appropriate for each work role (described in Boies et al., 1989; Wiecha et al., 1990).

10.4.3 Focus on Users and User Testing of ITS

In making software tools, one has to be concerned with (a) the user groups who use the tools ("applications developers") , (b) user groups who use the applications created with the tools (the "end-users"), and (c) user groups who maintain the applications. We will talk about the first group ("application developers") here, and about "end-users" under ITS-made applications later on. We organize this by discussing some of the methods listed in Tables 6 and 8, and providing examples of how we used some of them. The evidence shows that the usability design process that we recommended and successfully used in application development is also valuable for developing a software development environment, which in turn can be used to create applications.

Expert on Design Team. Although three of us in the initial ITS design group had worked together in creating applications previously, we (and subsequent members) would agree that one member was truly an expert on system design (accurately called here the ITS chief designer). He was not a consultant, as we have had in mind for this role previously, but rather the day to day leader of the group.

After demonstrating the feasibility of the ITS approach, we quickly added an established graphic designer, a technical expertise which we were lacking (see comments below under Style Designers).

Use ITS Ourselves. Our group members were the first users of the tools which we were creating for others. From the very beginning we put great pressure on ourselves to do this. For example, at a time when everyone else used viewgraphs, we used ITS to prepare a description of our ITS project for our group's first annual review with our Director. We presented an on-line interactive talk, made with ITS, about ITS and *demonstrated* initial feasibility that ITS could do the challenging things we set out to accomplish, e.g., separate content and style. (Researchers we know do not like to fail in these annual reviews!) As the capability of ITS increased, we used ITS ourselves to create real applications (see below). Some of us who were not as capable as others had embarrassing moments in early public demonstrations, but these motivated us all the more to get things right.

After one-two years of design, implementing, recruiting additional people, and some initial feasibility demonstrations, we forced ourselves to use ITS to create significant applications. This was much earlier in the design process than typical of other tool groups. We wanted to develop an application of someone else's requirements. We were aware that if we selected an application of our own requirements we could be influenced too heavily by the presently existing status of ITS and could avoid the difficulties encountered if someone else was our task master. That is why we did the joint development project with Continental Insurance mentioned below. Rather than speculate about what a good application development environment needed, our strategy was to learn by doing. We also used ITS to create more ITS. When impossible, this of course identified what was needed, and we made it. Recently, our group has grown to about twenty people, nearly all of whom use ITS to create new applications for business and government customers.

Early User Manual for ITS. During the first year, we had almost daily design meetings. One of us was in charge of incorporating the ideas into a user manual, aimed primarily at describing the general approach of ITS and the command language for content experts. This manual served as a memory of what had already been decided in our meetings, identified contradictions and inconsistencies in our thinking, and was a communication device among ourselves and for newcomers to our group. The manual, which also served as a design document, was usually ahead of the implementation of the described function in the first year or two. As time passed, this was our main document for others to learn about ITS.

Later on, as we emphasized on-line documentation over paper documentation, we made it possible to print an up-to-the-minute latest version of the command language directly from the computer-based implementation of it. That is, the command language became self-documenting.

Early Prototype of ITS. We quickly made it possible for end-users of our tools (at first ourselves playing the role of content experts) to create toy applications using ITS. We did this by developing enough code on the style side to display traditional interaction techniques, e.g., radio buttons, check-boxes, lists, tables. The tools we created for content experts to use are similar to mark-up, or tag, languages that skilled word processing people use. Content experts were then able to use this language, for example, to specify in their content files that end-users could have Water, Coffee, or Milk to drink and could select only one alternative. ITS would pick a user-interface style (only one ran at first) and show these alternative drinks on an end-user's screen in an attractive window of radio buttons and text. (Another style might render this same content as images of three cups that suggested the three drinks.) Later on ITS had the capability to actually enter values into data-base fields, thus beginning to allow for more serious prototypes. With time, we implemented additional function for content experts that we learned was needed as a result of using ITS to build real applications (some of which are described below). Of powerful importance, unlike all other prototyping tools, which require the user interface to be re-written for the final application, with ITS this prototype is used "as is" in the final application. ITS "prototypes" are essentially "proto-applications."

On the style side, with time, we created all of the 15-20 standard human-computer interaction techniques of the 1980's (see Ukelson, Gould, Boies, and Wiecha, 1991). From then on, new, re-usable ones were added to existing style libraries mainly as a result of creating them for real applications that we were using ITS to build (see below). Examples include touch screen interaction techniques of finger painting, and setting time by moving clock hands created for the EXPO'92 application (described below).

Identify ITS User Groups. There four work roles in creating applications with ITS:

- Content experts,
- Style designers, and
- Content programmers and Style Programmers (C-language).

We found time and again that each business has people with expertise in that business (ITS so-called *content experts*). Unlike what we had initially hoped, however, they never became part of a development team and actually implemented anything -- despite much support from us. They are busy with what they already do. Organizationally, they are in different departments from application developers. There are powerful boundaries between these departments. For example, the content expert for a time and attendance application that we were jointly creating (see below), would meet with us, view our ITS-made prototype screens, and tell us what needed to be changed. But he would not make these changes himself. He was paid more than programmers, had a better office, and was not about to regress. In developing business applications over the years (e.g., see Touch Illinois below) we have learned we must continually visit customers' locations, learn about their businesses by talking with people there, create models and get their reactions to them, implement ourselves a part of content, get their feedback, and iteratively improve this evolving application.

We envisioned the need for graphic *Style Designers* to be involved in defining general purpose user interface styles containing attractive screens and attractive human-computer interaction techniques. Recruiting them ten years ago was difficult, since there were very few trained graphic designers who were designing user interfaces. Hiring them full-time also presented problems. Most graphic designers do not work for a single employer for long periods of time. Rather each is typically self-employed in a number of short-term work assignments, and is tied into career-oriented networks of other graphic designers. Further, we found that hiring a graphic designer as a professional, full-time employee in a major company presented problems because they are thought of by administrative personnel as support people ("illustrators"). There was no professional job description that placed them equivalent with engineers, researchers, etc. With effort, patience, and grace our initial graphic designer overcame this. The graphic designer in our group, and other graphic designers whom she has since hired have with assistance from other group members created screens that are very attractive. They have made re-usable human-computer interaction techniques that are very responsive and effective. These interaction techniques have since been used by millions of end users (in applications described below). We envisioned correctly that since styles, including human-computer interaction techniques, are re-usable there would be a need for fewer style designers than content experts.

Content Programmers and *Style Programmers* use the C-programming language to create their re-usable routines. They also select routines from the ever increasing, sharable, library of re-usable routines. Understandably, we try to hire the best people available to us, and therefore the people in our group doing this work are skilled C-programmers. Management pressure, group encouragement, and tutoring are required to get new programmers to write their routines in a general, re-usable way. We have also found in training people to create ITS routines that its difficult to think sufficiently abstractly to write general, re-usable C-routines. For example, one programmer was working very hard on a routine that would quickly compare, as each keystroke was entered, a password being entered with a known one, and quickly provide appropriate user feedback. The programmer proudly showed his work to the ITS chief designer who had him throw it away! And then had the programmer write a general purpose string compare routine that would work not only for passwords but for all other string compare operations.

What role do *usability people* play in making applications with ITS? Usability people outside our group have wondered where they fit into the ITS approach. There have always been human factors people in our group. Initially, we concentrated on designing the tools. Later, during application development (see below), we iterated with content experts to learn about their businesses and then did the implementation work that we had hoped content experts would do themselves. We now expect that usability people will continue this role and also work jointly with style designers. Outside our group, usability people have not been quick to use ITS for prototyping, preferring instead to use less powerful commercially available packages.

Like others, many usability people are enamored with prototyping tools with which they can quickly prepare a demonstration of a few WYSIWYG screens. We lose out here, despite the facts that nearly all these tools cannot connect to real databases, cannot scale up, and once real application development work begins, the development team uses a different development language that generally does not allow the user interface to look and work like that of the prototype. Over these years, a number of tools that these people once favored, and that others compared with ITS during it development, have dropped from site and sight. We had also envisioned that human factors people would use ITS to experimentally evaluate, in laboratory experiments, new human-computer interaction techniques and develop a library of well-tested ones. This has not happened outside of our group. Such work, should it be done, needs to realize that a good user interface style is made up of many individual, but consistent, human-computer interaction techniques, and that such experiments must take this into account. The goal is to optimize an entire user-interface style, not just a particular human-computer interaction technique.

Talk With Users of ITS. We constantly talked with users of ITS, which for the most part have been members of our own expanding group. Our group is characterized by daily close interactions, and therefore we could learn from people using ITS how the tools for each work role could be improved.

Visit Customer Locations. We visited many customer locations, often because we were proposing to use ITS to create an application for them or were actually creating an application for them. Our motivation for doing this was to let real applications empirically guide what needed to be added to or changed in ITS -- not what we merely thought was needed. We learned first-hand about application development organizations and how they relate to the commercial or business organizations. From early on we tried using commercially available prototyping and software development tools, and regularly found that the claims of what they could do, more often by enamored potential users than by the vendors themselves, exceeded what they could actually accomplish. We visited software tool conventions, so we could make comparative judgments of what actually existed (separate from the claims of what existed), and we presented ITS at national and international professional meetings, almost always with live demonstrations (at first risky) rather than just talks (safe, very robust, and possibly misleading).

Teach ITS to Others. We began this about one year after we started (very early for a tools project). This was very time-consuming for our (then) small group. Logistically, we had to find a spare room, good workstations (not as plentiful in the late 1980's as now), create tutorial materials, make sure everything ran reliably, find people who were willing to use this new approach to build their own applications (actually prototypes at first), and then help them afterwards. But, as always, all of this focused work energy in the right places. We taught these small courses about every month or two, and also used them to identify what were the most critical things to add to ITS.

Hallway and Storefront Methodology. Due to space shortages, we began doing our development work in a large hallway. This helped maintain group communication. The ITS chief designer set up in the middle of this hallway, and other group members liked being where the action was. As more space became available, we continued this approach, using our offices for other functions. Management and other research groups could see that something exciting was happening. As we began building applications with ITS, we took over more hallways (see below). Nobody escaped seeing our work on their way to lunch; later it seemed that these hallways were simply our group's turf and other building occupants found other avenues to get where they were going.

Testable Usability Goals for ITS. A main goal of ours was to improve application development productivity. We wanted to make it possible to build computer applications more quickly than previously possible, with higher quality, responsive user-interfaces that did not require end-users to be trained to use them. The ITS-made applications mentioned below show that we accomplished this (see Gould, Ukelson, and Boies, 1993 and 1996). For example, in using ITS to build a typical database transaction system for insurance underwriters, we did it many times more quickly and created a much superior user interface than did a vendor working in parallel with a traditional approach (Boies, Ukelson, Gould, Anderson, Babecki, and Clifford, 1993).

Field Studies of ITS. Doing significant field studies to test the value of new software tools requires that one uses the tools to build real applications (not just toy ones). We did this, as described below.

In addition to the methods just described, others are described a few pages below where we talk abut some applications made with ITS.

10.4.4 Iterative Design of ITS

All of these findings provided a steady stream of required changes to ITS. Our development strategy for ITS, summed up in one sentence, was an iterative, incremental strategy based upon implementing empirically determined, required improvements, and integrating each improvement with the rest of the system. We identified many of these requirements by using ITS to make real applications, adding functions to ITS as each application demanded. (See section below on Our Experiences Using ITS to Create New Applications.) We provided a discipline for implementing these iterations through our Promote Policy, which differs from the more typical Release approach. With the latter, the owners of a system make a series of changes, but make these improvements available to the public (i.e., release them) only a few times over the life time of the system. In contrast, with our Promote policy we "released" a set of improvements to the ITS platform rapidly, typically 2-3 times per week, even during the World's Fair application that millions of people were using (see below).

In doing this, we met the key requirements for iterative design mentioned in Table 10. We empirically *identified* needed improvements (rather than speculate what they should be); we had (because we created it) a technical *ability* to make these improvements; and we had a strong *willingness* to make them. To our knowledge, no other software development system has been created by following this iterative strategy. The development and improvement of ITS, and ITS use in creating new applications continues today.

Organizing the work into the four work roles described above led to well-organized applications, even though content experts do not directly implement their applications. This facilitates iterative design of ITS made applications.

10.4.5 Integrated Design of ITS

Unlike what we recommended earlier (Gould, 1988), the responsibility for the usability of ITS was shared among several group members, rather than having just one person responsible. This was primarily due to the still on-going, almost decade long development of ITS, the fact that several people assumed serious responsibility for usability, and to our group being relatively small and highly communicative. A story illustrates the problems that can arise without such communication, however. Once two of us were asked by a major airline to make comments on a new workstation-based executive information system that they had just "completed" for their top executives. We told them we would make the trip if they had the person who would demonstrate the system to and train the executives run through this in our presence, and videotape the process. The developers balked at this; besides they did not know who was going to do the training, even though the planned installation was only a few days away. They simply never realized that all the person-years of their work were in the hands of the person who would have at most one hour with each of these top executives (with whom the developers had never talked). We said: no simulated run-thru on your part, no trip on our part. They relented. Upon our arrival, people responsible for the various parts of usability met for the first time. Understandably, with one of us playing the role of the president of that airline, the run-through revealed many things they had to coordinate and fix in the next few days.

10.5 Our Experiences Using ITS to Create New Applications

We have just described a few methods we used in creating a new software development system called ITS. Here we describe how we ourselves used ITS to develop several applications. The characteristics of several of these applications, listed roughly chronologically, are shown in Table 14.

Besides the motivation to identify needed improvements in ITS, we carried out the first three case studies to test the technical feasibility of using ITS, and how ITS affected development productivity. The Spreadsheet Package application (Sitnik, Gould, and Ukelson, 1991) tested whether the content and style of an application could actually be separated in a well-know application that others thought it would be hard to do. The Continental Insurance joint study (Boies, Ukelson, Gould, Anderson, Babecki, and Clifford, 1993) was our first attempt at a joint study to implement someone else's business application. The IBM CUA study (Ukelson, et al., 1991) tested the feasibility and developer productivity of using ITS to produce a reusable style that looked and worked like the prevailing IBM user-interface style, designed by others. The Time and Attendance application was a joint development effort inside IBM that was nearly completed, but then not put into use. The EXPO'92 Multimedia application was our first attempt to use ITS to produce a leading edge multimedia application, and this was a resounding success with millions of visitors to the World's Fair in Seville, Spain using it (see Gould, Ukelson, and Boies, 1996), for a brief description). The Illinois Department of Employment application (called "Touch Illinois") was completed and is in use.

Presently our group is using ITS to create a variety of new kiosk-based, multimedia business and government applications, including auto-finance and retail sales, and extending existing ITS-made applications to other customers.

Case Studies. These applications just mentioned were primarily developmental efforts, essential in our view to iteratively improving ITS. But we turned them into case studies as well, which made us spend the extra effort to really think about what we were learning

Table 14. Summary of key points from several applications developed with ITS.

General-Purpose Spreadsheet Package (See Sitnik, et al., 1991)

- Lab study with college work-study student as participant.
- With ITS, created much of a general-purpose spread sheet package in 2 person-months.
- Successfully separated the content and the style of this application.
- Implemented application in one style; used it in another style.

IBM-Continental Insurance Underwriting Application (see Boies, et al, 1993)

- Field study jointly carried out by Continental Insurance and IBM ITS group.
- Traditional data-base transaction-oriented application.
- Results compared with ongoing traditional Continental development method.
- ITS led to 25 times productivity improvement, higher quality user interface, anticipated lower application maintenance.

IBM CUA User Interface Style (See Ukelson, et al., 1991)

- Two ITS group members kept a diary as they used ITS to implement IBM's CUA user interface style.
- Implemented all 14 human-computer interaction techniques and 9 others in 7 person-weeks.
- This style is reusable, and several ITS-made applications have used it.

Time and Attendance Recording Application (See Gould, et al., 1996 for a brief summary)

- Three-site development effort using ITS to make a workstation version of existing mainframe time and attendance recording system.
- ITS workstation version to run with same back-end code as the mainframe version used.
- Workstation version ran on both OS/2 and AIX, and in multiple graphic standards.
- Project ultimately terminated because customer eliminated need for this application.

EXPO'92 Multimedia Visitor Services Applications (See Gould, et al., 1996 for a brief summary)

- 1992 World's Fair in Seville, Spain, attended by 42 million visitors.
- International development team used ITS to make integrated set of advanced multimedia applications that visitors used from touchscreens.
- Applications included allowing visitors to send multimedia messages, take their pictures, create art, study hours of entertaining interactive multimedia stories on the 100 participating countries, read the daily news in multiple national languages, learn about lottery results, make restaurant reservations.
- Thirty-three kiosk buildings dedicated to, and networked for, these applications.
- This was the largest, most diverse multimedia system ever developed; it demonstrated the value of ITS for making leading-edge applications.
- Data-logged results showed 5-15 million visitors used these multimedia applications.

Illinois Department of Employment Security

- 600,000 unemployed people in Illinois and 1 million unemployment claims filed annually.
- ITS group made highly graphic, "sit down and use" touch-screen user interface.
- Citizens can now directly file their unemployment claims and search jobs databases instead of filing paper and waiting for available employment department staff members.
- Application ties into several existing very large government databases.
- Additional huge databases used to facilitate novel human-computer interaction techniques.

and then publish, with attendant peer review, the process and results. This requires time to reflect, structure, write, and iteratively respond to suggestions for improving the manuscript.

Over the years, we gave talks about and demonstrations of ITS at many professional meetings on human factors, human-computer-interaction, and computer science, often reporting one or more case studies. Oftentimes we would be followed by a speakers who would describe the tool they were making and conclude their talk by indicating that they would soon carry out a serious case study of their own tool. To put into perspective how unusual it is to do such case studies with new tools, we are unaware of any published case study, by them or anyone else, that aimed at evaluating or iteratively improving new software tools by using them to develop a serious application that people actually used.

10.5.1 Focusing on Users and User Testing

In carrying out the case studies we used nearly all the methods that we recommended above to get the initial ideas about what each application should be, and then to get ideas on how to improve each successive implementation. To avoid redundancy, we will mention here only observations that are a bit different from those already mentioned above and previously (Gould, 1988).

Visit Customer Locations. In the early stages of the work with the State of Illinois, for example, we made 10-20 trips to employment offices there. We talked with unemployed people; observed the waiting lines (and decided we could design a system to eliminate them); talked with citizens who wanted to get a better job (and decided we could help them by making sit-down, kiosk-based workstations and connect them to employment data-bases throughout the U. S.); talked with employers who get the names of potential employees from these offices and hire some of them (and decide we could make a system the would help with this match-making process); talked with staff members and were surprised at their dedication to assisting their clients (and decided that we could make a system to reduce the amount of paper work they did, thus freeing them to spend more time counseling their clients); talked with office managers (and learned they were willing to help us if we really wanted to make a difference); talked with the Illinois Director of Employment Security and learned how supportive she was of our vision (we like this). We came away from these visits, which ranged from the South Side of Chicago to affluent suburban offices, with a view that we could use technology to create a more dignified way for citizens and staff to interact, and to empower these citizens, unemployed and employed, to get better jobs.

Expert on the Design Team. As noted before, even though ITS is organized so that application experts can directly take control of the implementation of their applications, they have not done so to date. In the CUA study, we would show our style (basically a collection of 15 or so human-computer interaction techniques) to CUA style experts whose job it was to inspect new applications in IBM before they were released to sure they conformed to the style standards book. We would make their suggested changes. Interestingly, they sometimes disagreed among themselves -- which shows how hard it is to specify in a book all the details of how a human-computer interaction technique should look and behave in a variety of contexts. In the Time and Attendance application, the application expert with whom we worked in this joint study first taught us the business requirements of the existing application (of which there were many rules), as well as about the existing databases to which we would ultimately connect and the on-going activities to change it. Every week or so, for several months, he and his colleagues would evaluate our user interface against their requirements, and then we would make changes. We were unsuccessful in getting them to make these changes themselves, despite a number of attempts to facilitate it.

Hallway and Storefront Methodology. We used this methodology, for example, to construct a prototype kiosk at our Research Center, capable of working in the desert-like temperatures and sun of Seville, Spain where the World's Fair would be held. One challenge was to make our display screens visible and attractive to passer-bys, yet shield the screens from the bright sun so they could be seen. Another challenge was that we wanted people, ranging in height from children to tall adults, to be able to take video pictures of themselves without having to sit on a stool (as in photo booths) or adjust their height in some other way. Further, they had to be able to take these pictures in all outdoor light conditions, from the brightest midday to the darkest night (the Fair ran for 180 days, opening at 9 a.m. and closing at 4:00 a.m. each night). We first built cardboard mockups, and simulated the bright conditions of Spain in the snow of New York on sunny days. Colleagues watched us playing in the snow, as they did once we began construction of an 8-foot high plywood model in the hallway. Colleagues and management knew we were again up to something exciting. With weeks of effort, we solved the camera problem, making it possible for children and adults to take their pictures by remotely controlling the position of the camera associated with each display via software buttons on that same touchscreen display that the entire EXPO'92 application used. In this process, lots of colleagues and their children, passing through the hallway, stopped to take their pictures, laugh, and go on their way. These were all data for us. Later, at the World's Fair, thirty-three circular kiosk buildings (about 11 meters in diameter), each with seven outdoor guest stations around the circumference and a round roof that shaded them, were built for us. These kiosks worked successfully throughout the Fair. In contrast, every other outdoor attraction at the Fair involving video screens could not be used by visitors during the day. The sun was just too bright.

Today, the hallways around our group's offices contain several kiosks, each different, each containing a running application that we have made, or are in the process of making for other customers. These demonstrations are much better at telling the story of our multimedia applications than, unfortunately, are journal articles or book chapters like this.

User Training. We have tried for over twenty years, starting with voice messaging systems in the 1970's, to make user interfaces for workstation and kiosk-based applications that users can use without any training. We did this successfully for the millions of users of the EXPO'92 application and for the thousands of users of the Touch Illinois application. Basically, consistent with the way we iteratively designed these applications, they learned by doing and by observing peers.

Early User Manuals. Using ITS, we have tried in the last several years to make user interfaces for workstation and kiosk-based applications so that users do not need paper manuals. We did this successfully for the millions of users of the EXPO'92 application and for the thousands of the Touch Illinois application.

Help Systems. In the last few years we have been developing multimedia systems that people can use without the need even for on-line help systems of the usual sort (e. g., a user gets help messages by selecting a HELP button). We did this successfully in the EXPO'92 application and the Touch Illinois application.

New Interactive Ways to Aid Users. On the other hand, using ITS we have been inventing new ways to assist users. We try to aid users each time they interact with an application, e.g., make a reservation. One of the most important experiences we have had in this regard is the first-hand realization of the important dependent relationship among

- The ability to successfully provide innovative human-computer interaction techniques.
- Fast system response time,
- The structure of existing data bases, and
- Data-base access methods.

For example, in the Time and Attendance application, a mainframe version had been running for years. Employees recorded their Attendance, vacation, sick days, contract-assigned work, travel mileage, etc. for a particular day. Each week the Payroll Department automatically collected the results. In a planned new version employees could use either a mainframe display (in about the same way) or a workstation. Our job in this joint development effort was to use ITS to make a graphic user interface for the workstation version. We made a prototype which displayed a month of data in calendar form. For us, this was just another use of a general calendaring application that was in the ITS sharable library. Employees, we thought, could flip through months of their attendance history, project ahead what days they intended for vacation, keep a running total of actual and expected vacation days, etc. While waiting for the backend work to be completed (by another group) so we could have access to these data, we placed our version in the cafeteria, let employees use it with dummy data, and kept iteratively improving it. This is the end of the good news. When our user interface was finally connected to the existing data base, which turned out not to be organized as we had been led to believe, our user interface worked poorly. Far too much time was required for the backend system, basically capable of handling only a week's worth of data at a time, to fill in a calendar month of data. If, for example, users scrolled backwards to review their Attendance from several months before -- changes in their user interfaces were painfully slow. In the end, we had to eliminate many of the already-tested good features or our user interface to conform to the limits of the existing data base and backend system limits.

Fortunately, happier examples exist, and many of them involved using available huge databases and innovative, very fast responding human-computer interactions. In the Touch Illinois application, we wanted, for example, to aid users while they entered their names and addresses. The huge U. S. Post Office data base (inexpensive to obtain) contains all of the mailing addresses in the U. S. We incorporated this database, together with our own access routines, into the application. After users entered each digit of their zip codes, for example, the user interface provided feedback, if appropriate, before they entered the next number -- without slowing down users. If the system was slow in doing this, users would be confused when using this interaction technique, known as autocompletion.

In the EXPO'92 application, there were 5,000 images stored for the multimedia educational stories and thousands of other video images from the many people who had taken pictures of themselves. We wanted near instantaneous response when users requested an earlier photo of themselves, and, remarkable, we achieved this using ITS.

Prototypes. With ITS, a prototype grows smoothly into a proto-application and then into the actual application. Within ITS, the actual application differs from the prototype only in that more C-routines (either reusable, already existing ones or newly written ones by Content Programmers) are called in a content expert's tag-language file; or new interaction techniques are created by the Style Designer and Style Programmer. To illustrate, consider the integrated set of multimedia applications that we made with ITS for EXPO'92. We first made a prototype of one application (e.g., letting people take video pictures of themselves), and installed this in Seville for visitors to the construction sites to use. We would get feedback from really excited users, and iteratively improve this prototype-application. This was the process of growing it into a full-fledged application. Later we installed the communication ability for visitors to send these pictures as part of messages they were composing to visitors at another other kiosk. Same situation. Here we could study the messaging prototype that was growing into that application. Eventually, for communication among all kiosks, we installed the largest LAN ever installed in Europe.

We used this same prototyping approach for other applications in this set, e.g., an educational application containing entertaining multimedia stories based about the one-hundred participating countries; an art application; a restaurant reservations application. In each case we integrated each newly implemented application with the existing ones, "seamlessly" as they say. This led to what we call an iterative, incremental development strategy (see below).

Try-To-Destroy Tests. In the EXPO'92 work, turning each new version over to excited children and older child-like visitors at the construction sites (as well as the severe weather there) gave us plenty of opportunities to test the robustness of each new version.

Video Tapes. Long before the World's Fair started, we videotaped visitors using our prototypes on the construction sites in Seville so that our colleagues in the U.S. could see the results. Two years later, midway into the Fair, we realized that there was no adequate way in print that we could convey to people the success of what was happening. Usage statistics, although impressive (e.g., 250,000 users on an average day, which made this application perhaps the most widely used multimedia one ever), did not capture the excitement and joy users experienced, many using a computer for the first time. So used videotape in a different way. We made a professionally-produced videotape of visitors at the Fair using this system for later showing, which much better captures the scope, excitement, and success of what was going on than anything we can say here.

Multiple National Languages. With ITS, developers need a file of messages for each national language that they want the application to have. Nothing but the messages are in each file. If a developer wants to use three national languages, as we did for EXPO'92, then they create three files and provide a mechanism (e.g., a set of radio buttons or its equivalent) on the user interface for users to select the national language they want.

Field Studies. Increasingly, as we have entered the business of application development, we do most of our observations during field studies, i.e., at locations selected by our customers. For example, we installed an early prototype in one Illinois Employment Office that had limited function (i.e., let citizens browse for job openings), watched them use it, and then iteratively improved that function. Then we added another function (i.e., let citizens register for interviews on the job openings they liked), tested and improved it, and continued this process with more functions, e.g., filling out unemployment claims on this aided, electronic graphical user interface rather than with paper and pencil. With ITS, probably 75% of our development effort is spent after real users start using a new fledgling application. This contrast with the traditional approach wherein perhaps 5% or so of development occurs after real users start their work.

Research in the Marketplace. As a result of our experiences, we have added a new research method to the already mentioned ones, consistent with present day trends. This goes beyond field studies. The motto here, which may not be much of an exaggeration, is "If you aren't doing it for someone else (i.e., generally getting paid and even making a profit) then you aren't doing it for real."

10.6 New Thoughts on Iterative Design

From these experiences we have learned more about the effects of iterative design -- so essential to usability.

Iterative, Incremental Development Strategy. Our basic strategy in making each of these applications has been to make a proto-application, give it to users, collect ideas for improving it, implement these ideas, and see if they meet customer requirements and if end-users like them. Then we repeat this process. This is what we have called iterative design.

In addition using ITS, we have developed an "incremental" approach of building, testing, and improving one piece, then building, testing, and improving a second piece (integrated with the pieces that already exist). An example was described under "Prototypes" above.

This iterative, incremental approach, made possible with ITS, contrasts with the traditional development approach of trying to do it all at once. The latter, the so-called "Release" approach, has two drawbacks. It can be overwhelming in very large endeavors, such as our EXPO'92 application, to begin prototype testing all at once. Two, over the life of most applications there are only a few "releases." In the case of EXPO'92, we made about sixty new field-ready versions that replaced earlier ones. With the State of Illinois, once we had installed a prototype, we replaced it with improved versions about three times each week. With time, this dwindled to three times per month, then three times per year.

The management of EXPO'92 very much liked this iterative, incremental strategy. It gave them at least one workable thing to show the thousands of visitors to the behind-schedule construction sites more than a year before the Fair started. As we added more function to our working prototype/application, EXPO'92 management had a more exciting thing to show thousands more visitors to the still very much behind schedule construction site. When the Fair did start, they had a reliable, responsive integrated set of multimedia applications working in kiosks located across the completed construction site of the World's Fair that they could proudly show to millions of visitors and the world's media.

Uncertainty -- A New Reason Not to Like Iterative Design. In the last few years we have entered the commercial market of developing applications for paying customers. As commercial developers we have found that, once the work is nearly completed, being able to make iterative improvements in an application has some drawbacks. The customer keeps wanting more than we had agreed to do at a given price. This "scope-creep," as it is called, puts us in a dilemma. We want to be helpful, but the requests seem never ending and can go way beyond what was originally promised. On the other hand, the customer observes that we have already done much more than they ever expected, and so why stop here. It is hard for us to declare that we are done.

Potential customers for our services see, for example, what we have done in the past. They talk with us about making a new, very advanced, multimedia user interface for an existing application of theirs. So, we talk and speculate about what this might look like, and about adding additional related function. Just as avant garde architects of buildings have found, we have found that only if a customer trusts us and has a shared vision of what is possible and good do we get a contract to build a new application. Understandably, this trust is often lacking, because customers do not like the Uncertainty of living with our iterative approach. They are uncomfortable with giving up control and not feeling that they know exactly what they will get at the end (which of course is usually false security, anyway).

Contracts for Sequential Steps. To address these problems, we have developed a 5-stage contract system, and ask customers to sign up for only as many stages as they feel comfortable with at that time. The stages are:

- Consulting -- we study their business and provide a work product that tells them our understanding of it, and our proposal of what we would do for them.

- Proof of Concept -- we make a running prototype, sometimes connected to a real database.

- Pilot Project -- we install the application in one office, for example, and we and they can observe its use.

- Deployment -- we put the application in the remainder of that customer's offices, for example.

- Replication -- we sell the application to other similar customers.

Trust and Vision. Consider three general classes of applications. (1) Standard, traditional ones, e.g., editors, data managers, next versions of already existing applications. (2) New market niches, wherein software entrepreneurs see a potential niche and they try to fill it, e.g., desk top publishing. (3) Applications that change the way an industry does business, e.g., the SABRE airline reservations system of American Airlines and IBM in the 1950's and 1960's; Ticketron; CNN 24-hour news; ATMs in banks and elsewhere. It is in this third domain that we are currently using ITS to build applications. It stretches customers' trust to visualize the possibilities and to carry out a joint project with a software vendor because, at least in their eyes, we are modifying greatly the way they will run their business (e.g., as in the case of unemployed citizens filling out unemployment claims without even coming into an unemployment office). That is risky to a businessperson. The relevance of all this to human factors is that such innovation has the potential to improve people's quality of life.

Hint of the Vision. To address this trust problem, we sometimes have created a small proto-application to demonstrate the possibilities of a new vision for a potential customer's business. This sometimes helps the customer visionary to handle organizational pressures to resist, e.g., from existing data processing departments. This concreteness about how a system and the resulting business might work sometimes helps them in interacting with their bosses, colleagues, or whoever they are accountable to or work with who find it hard to imagine a radical new approach to running their business. It is also a feasibility demonstration of our group's capability.

Iterative Design Requires Costly Tools. IBM Research invested much money in our activities over the last decade to bring ITS to where it is today. Any software development tool that lets developers do iterative design as well as can be done with ITS is bound to be very expensive. Assume that our group's costs can be assigned either to *Enhancing ITS* or to creating a *Specific Application*. In the first year of our work, all our expenses went to *Enhancing ITS*. In about the third year, when we carried out the Continental Insurance study (see above), approximately 65% of the costs of that effort went to the *Particular Application* and approximately 35% of the costs went to *Enhancing ITS*. This 35% was like putting money in the bank, from which we would draw a high rate of interest again and again each time we made another application. Today, several years later, we have repeated this process with several additional applications, each time using a significant proportion of the cost of making an application for *Enhancing ITS*. Consequently, the ITS development system becomes increasingly valuable.

Simultaneous Iterative Development of Tools and Applications. Assume that it would take our group about as long to create a new application as it would take any other development team. But we have ITS, and we estimate that, because of reuse of existing ITS functions, it takes us only about 25% of the effort it would otherwise take us without ITS. This is a 400% savings. But note how even today this 25% effort is assigned. We do not spend all of this effort on the *Particular Application*. We continue to spend 25% of this 25% for the *Particular Application* on which we are working, and 75% of this 25% on *Enhancing ITS*. That is, the 75% can be written in a general way so that it can be reused either in general or for other applications in that domain. Thus, on the one hand, we keep reducing the amount of new effort (i.e., costs) required to create a new application, whereas on the other hand we keep enhancing the worth of our development tool (at an unprecedented rate of dividend re-investment!).

10.7 Status of ITS

The usability work on ITS centered (a) on the *usefulness* of ITS by providing enough power to developers using ITS so they can be very productive in making applications ranging from the traditional to leading-edge multimedia ones; and (b) *ease of use* of ITS for skilled programmers. The applications mentioned above showed great success on the usefulness criterion. With respect to ease of use, the evidence shows that ITS enhances development productivity (Gould, Ukelson, and Boies; 1993; 1996). In that sense, ITS is easy to use. However, we have not been successful in making ITS inviting or possible for non-programmers to use ITS to create serious new applications.

Despite the evidence that ITS is productivity enhancing, can be used to create both traditional and leading edge applications, pressure from IBM management that other groups use ITS to create commercial applications, and many attempts by ourselves to facilitate this (e.g., teaching classes in a variety of places, telephone support, joint programs, etc.) other development groups besides ourselves have been slow to use ITS. Recently, however, ITS has become commercially available IBM software product, call Custom Access Development Tool Set (CADT), which can be used to develop workstation application.

Our research group continues to use and improve ITS while making four types of commercial applications for paying customers -- all aimed at empowering people in this information age:

1. Secure transaction systems that individuals use quickly and frequently, e.g., multi-functional ATMs.

2. Secure transaction systems that individuals use quickly and occasionally, e.g., retail kiosks for ordering products.

3. Secure transaction systems that individuals use only periodically and for longer periods of time, e.g., filling out electronic forms for unemployment benefits.

4. Systems that encourage individuals to explore, linger, and learn, e.g., museum systems.

10.8 Summary

The design process that we recommended a decade ago (Gould, 1988) was summarized in the first part of this chapter. It has stood the test of time pretty much "as is." In developing software tools and then using them to develop traditional and innovative applications, we followed the design process that we recommended earlier. The usability work on ITS centered mainly on testing our tools (a) on ourselves by using them to create a variety of applications used by others; (b) by getting feedback from end-users of these applications; (c) by getting feedback as a result of demonstrating them to developers and university people, by talking about them at professional meetings, and publishing about them in professional journals and books; and (d) by teaching others to use them. All of these approaches have provided a continuous stream of required improvements, which we used to iteratively improve ITS. We used similar, appropriate methods for developing applications, collecting users' reactions through a variety of methods, changing the prototypes and applications accordingly, and then repeating this cycle.

10.9 References

Bennett, J. L. (1984). Managing to meet usability requirements: establishing and meeting software development goals. In J. Bennett, D. Case, J. Sandelin, and M. Smith (Eds.) *Usability Issues and Health Concerns*, (pp. 161-184). Englewood Cliffs, New Jersey: Prentice-Hall.

Boies, S. J., Bennett, W. E., Gould, J. D., Greene, S. L., Wiecha, C. (1989). The Interactive Transaction System (ITS): Tools for Application Development. IBM Research Report, RC-14694, IBM Corp, Yorktown Hts, N.Y. 10598. Published in 1992 as "ITS Tools for Application Development", in R. Hartson and D. Hix (Ed.) *Advances in Human-Computer Interaction. Volume III*. Norwood, New Jersey: Ablex 229-276.

Boies, S. J., Ukelson, J. U., Gould, J. D., Anderson, D., Babecki, M., and Clifford, J. (1993). Using ITS to Create an Insurance Industry Application -- A Joint Case Study. *Human-Computer Interaction, 8,* 311-336.

Bury, K. F. (1985). The iterative development of usable computer interfaces. In *Human-Computer Interaction -- Interact '84*, (pp. 343-348).

Comstock, E. (1983). Customer installability of computer systems. In *Proceedings of the Human Factors Society Annual Meeting*, (pp. 501-504). Santa Monica, California: Human Factors Society.

Damodaran, L., Simpson, A., Wilson, P. (1980). Designing Systems for People. Manchester, England: NCC Publications.

Demers, R. A. (1981). System design for usability. *Communications of the ACM, 24*, 494-501.

Doherty, W. J., Kelisky, R. P. (1979). Managing VM/CMS system for user effectiveness IBM System Journal, 1, 143-163.

Doherty, W. J., Thadhani, A. J. (1982). The economic value of rapid response time. IBM Technical Report Publication #GE20-0752-0 (Available from author at IBM T. J. Watson Research Center.)

Good, M., Spine, T. M., Whiteside, J., George, P.

(1986). User-derived impact analysis as a tool for usability engineering. In *Human Factors in Computing Systems CHI'86 Proceedings*, (pp. 241-246). New York: ACM.

Gould, J. D., Lewis, C. H.. (1983). Designing for usability--key principles and what designers think. In *Proceedings of the 1983 Computer-Human Interaction Conference*, (pp. 50-53).

Gould, J. D., Lewis, C. H.. (1985). Designing for usability - -key principles and what designers think. *Communications of the ACM*, *28*, 300-311.

Gould, John D. (1988). How to design usable systems. In M. Helander (ed.) *Handbook of Human-Computer Interaction.* North-Holland:Elsevier Science Publishers, 757-789.

Gould, J. D., Boies, S. J., Levy, S., Richards, J. T., and Schoonard, J. W. (1987). The 1984 Olympic Message System--A Test of Behavioral Principles of System Design. *Communications of the ACM, 30(9)*, 758-769.

Gould, J. D., Boies, S. J., and Lewis, C. (1991). Making Usable, Useful, Productivity-enhancing Computer Applications. *Communications of the ACM. 34(1)*, 74-85.

Gould, J. D., Ukelson, J. P., Boies, S. J. (1993). Improving Application Development Productivity by Using ITS. *International Journal of Man-Machine Studies, 39,* 113-146.

Gould, J. D., Ukelson, J. P., Boies, S. J. (1996). Improving user interfaces and application productivity by using the ITS application development environment. In M. Rudisill, C. Lewis, P. Polson, and T. McKay (Eds.) *Human-Computer Interface Design: Success Cases, Emerging Methods, and Real-World Context.* Morgan Kaufmann: San Francisco, pp 173-197.

Grace, G. L. (1966). Application of empirical methods to computer-based system design. *Journal of Applied Psychology*, *50*, 442-450.

Granda, R. (1980). Personal Communication. IBM Corporation, Poughkeepsie, New York.

Green, P. (1986). Customer setup of the NCR PC-8 personal computer: a case study. The University of Michigan Transportation Research Institute Report, UMTRI-86-25. Ann Arbor, Michigan.

Heckel, P. (1984). *The Elements of Friendly Software Design*. New York: Warner Books.

Martin, G. L., Corl, K. G. (1976). System response time effects on user productivity. *Behaviour and Information Technology, 5(1).*

Meister, D. (1986). *Human Factors Testing and Evaluation*. Amsterdam, Netherlands: Elsevier.

Reitman-Olson, J. (1985). Expanded design procedures for learnable, usable interfaces. In *Proceedings of the ACM-SIGCHI Human Factors in Computing Meeting,* (pp. 1-3). New York: ACM.

Rubinstein, R., Hersh, H. (1984). *The Human Factor: Designing Computer Systems for People.* Burlington, Massachusetts: Digital Press.

Rushinek, A. Rushinek, S. F. (1986) What makes users happy? *Communications of the ACM*, *29*, 594-598.

Shackel, B. (1984). The concept of usability. In J. Bennett, D. Case, J. Sandelin, M. Smith (Eds.), *Visual Display Terminals: Usability Issues and Health Concerns,* (pp. 45-87). Englewood Cliffs, N.J.: Prentice-Hall.

Shackel, B. (1985). Human factors and usability -- Whence and whither? *Software Ergonomics '85*, 13-31.

Sitnik, E., Gould, J.D., and Ukelson, J. P. (1991). Case Study: Using ITS to Make a General Purpose spreadsheet Package. IBM Research Report, RC-16696, IBM Corp, Yorktown Heights, N.Y. 10598.

Sullivan, M. C., Chapanis, A. (1983). Human factoring a text editor manual. *Behavior and Information Technology, 2(2),* 113-125.

Swartout, W., Balzer, R. (1982). On the inevitable intertwining of specification and implementation. *Communications of the ACM*, *25*, 438-440.

Ukelson, J.P., Gould, J. D., Boies, S. J., and Wiecha, C. (1991). Case Study: Using ITS Style Tools to Implement IBM'S CUA-2 User Interface Style. *Software Practice and Experience 21(12),* 1265-1288.

Wiecha, C., Bennett, W., Boies, S., Gould, J., and Greene, S. (1990). ITS: A Tool for Rapidly Developing Interactive Applications. *ACM Transactions on Office Information Systems, 8,* 204-236.

Wixon, D., Whiteside, J. (1985). Engineering for usability: Lessons from the user derived. In *Human Factors in Computing Systems CHI'85*, (pp. 144-147). New York: ACM.

Handbook of Human-Computer Interaction
Second, completely revised edition
M. Helander, T.K. Landauer, P. Prabhu (eds.)

Chapter 11

Participatory Practices in the Software Lifecycle

Michael J. Muller
Boulder, Colorado
USA

Jean Hallewell Haslwanter
Tübingen
Germany

Tom Dayton
New Jersey
USA

11.1 Introduction

Participatory design has become increasingly important over the past several decades. Early work in Scandinavia (for review, see, e.g., Bjerknes and Bratteteig, 1995; Ehn and Kyng, 1987) has recently been complemented by work in other countries (e.g., Muller et al., 1991; Schuler and Namioka, 1993). There are many important contributions in areas of theory, research, practice, assessment, and analysis.

In this chapter, we focus on practices: Our goal is to help practitioners find methods, techniques, and procedures that they can use for participatory work. For this purpose, we have limited our scope to methods and techniques that are relatively well-defined as courses of action, suitable for adoption by practitioners without a great deal of additional research. Our concern is to help practitioners introduce (or to expand) their participatory practices in conventional software lifecycles. We hope that, in this way, we may become part of a growing community that is expanding the space for democratic principles and practices in the workplace. For these reasons, we have restricted our scope to approaches that are more than the use of a particular technology, or the creation of a particular artifact or representation. We believe that vital work is taking place in these areas, and we hope to contribute to these areas ourselves. Where that work included a component of guidance for new practitioners, we have attempted to include it.

11.1.1 The Plan of This Chapter

We begin with a brief introduction to what has come to be known as *participatory design*, including some of the questions that have arisen concerning the boundaries of participatory practice. We expand the discussion from the important—but limited and limiting—concept of design per se, toward a recognition that almost every phase of the software lifecycle may be improved through direct participation by users. This broad notion of the lifecycle serves as the context for the rest of the chapter.

We then describe a taxonomic space of participatory activities (see Table 1). In guiding the reader through that space, we note participatory practices that may be useful at different points within the software lifecycle. We also organize the practices in terms where they are likely to be used: in users' world, in the software professionals' world, or in a space intermediate between the two. Because many of the practices

Table 1. Taxonomy of Participatory Methods, Organized by Phase of Lifecycle and by Site of Activity

	Problem Identification & Clarification	Requirements & Analysis	High-Level Design	Detailed Design	Evaluation	End-User Customi-zation	Re-Design
Users' World	• Forum Theatre • Ethnography • Mock-Ups • Search Conference • Starting Conference	• Artifact Walkthrough • Blueprint Mapping • CARD • Ethnography • Forum Theatre • Mock-Ups • PICTIVE • PictureCARD	• Artifact Walkthrough • Lunchbox	• Artifact Walkthrough	• Forum Theatre • Interface Theatre	• Buttons	
Between Worlds	• Future Workshop • Graphical Facilitation • Layout, Organization, & Specification Games • Scenarios • Storytelling Workshop • Translators	• CISP • Collab. Design Workshop • Coop. Reqmts. Capture • CUTA • Future Workshop • Graphical Facilitation • Layout, Organization, & Specification Games • Participatory Ergonomics • Scenarios • Translators • Work Mapping	• ACE • CARD • Graphical Facilitation • Metaphors Game • Mock-Ups • Scenarios • Translators	• CISP • Collaborative Design Workshops • Critics • Graphical Facilitation • Icon Design Game • Scenarios	• CISP • Collab. Design Workshop • Cooperative Evaluation • Mock-Ups • Participatory Heuristic Evaluation • Participatory Ergonomics • Pluralistic Walkthrough • Scenarios • Storyboard Prototyping • Translators • Work Mapping	• Critics	• Critics • Priority Workshop
Software Profes-sionals' World	• Workshop for O-O GUI Designing	• KOMPASS • Prototyping • TOD • Workshop for O-O GUI Designing	• HOOTD • KOMPASS • PrOTA • Prototyping • TOD • Workshop for O-O GUI Designing	• BrainDraw • HOOTD • PICTIVE • PrOTA • Prototyping • Video Prototyping	• CARD • PICTIVE • Prototyping • TOD • Workshop for O-O GUI Designing		
Methods that span *Multiple* Lifecycle Phases	• ACOST • CESD • Codevelopment • Conceptual Toolkit in CSCW Design		• Contextual Design • Contextual Inquiry • Diaries • ETHICS • FIRE		• Florence • Group Elicitation Method • Hiser Design Method • JAD • ORDIT	• SSADM • SSM • STEPS • UTOPIA	

may be used at multiple phases in the lifecycle, we postpone detailed descriptions of the practices until the Appendix.

Our taxonomy may be used by readers to select one or more participatory practices to incorporate into software lifecycle activities. We also describe some models of the software lifecycle that are themselves organized, at least in part, around the concept of participation. These participatory whole-lifecycle models may provide better *continuity of participation* than the less ambitious piece-part strategy of selecting one or two participatory practices for incorporation into a conventional lifecycle model. Practitioners may wish to consider the risks and benefits of whole-lifecycle approaches versus piece-part approaches.

We then briefly review the evidence for the success of participatory approaches, and conclude by reviewing problems that remain to be solved.

We especially encourage the reader to tell us about other practices that we have omitted, or about new applications of old practices of which we are unaware.

11.1.2 Participatory Design

There is no single definition of "participatory design" (PD) that satisfies all researchers and practitioners in this field. The core of the term as it is used in this chapter on human-computer interfaces, is that the ultimate users of the software make effective contributions that reflect their own perspectives and needs, somewhere in the design and development lifecycle of the software. By this we mean active participation—something more than being used as mere data sources by responding to questionnaires or being observed while using the software. User participation is no longer restricted to designing per se; it has proven valuable in activities throughout the entire software lifecycle. We will not offer a more precise definition, in deference to the diversity of principled positions that have been developed by our colleagues. For some sense of the disagreements about the definition and the nature of PD, see Hallewell Haslwanter and Hammond (1994), and the debates in *Communications of the ACM* (1993) and in *Scandinavian Journal of Information Systems* (1994).

In this section, we consider three convergent motivations for participatory approaches:

- **Democracy.** The first theme was stated clearly in the original Scandinavian formulation of participatory design. That work was conceived and undertaken in the context of a movement toward workplace democracy, and the development of workers'competence and power to influence decisions that would affect their work and their workplaces (e.g., Ehn and Kyng, 1987). This motivation remains strong today in both Scandinavian practice (e.g., Beck, 1996; Bjerknes and Bratteteig, 1995) and in some non-Scandinavian practice (e.g., Bernard, 1996; Blomberg, Suchman, and Trigg, 1995; Boy, in press; Floyd, Züllighoven, Budde, and Keil-Slawik, 1992; Greenbaum, 1996; Greenbaum and Sclove, 1996; Muller, 1996b; Segall and Snelling, 1996).

- **Efficiency, Expertise, and Quality.** A second theme has emerged from North American practice (e.g., Holtzblatt and Beyer, 1993; Noro and Imada, 1991; Wixon, Holtzblatt, and Knox, 1990). Effectiveness of software design and development is improved by including the users' expertise. Efficiency is improved by getting users to collaborate in design instead of merely to provide input for other designers or feedback on a completed design; and by involving users early in the design process, before much investment has been made in any design. Quality of the design and the resulting system is improved through better understanding of the users' work, and better combination of the diverse and necessary backgrounds brought by various participants (e.g., Braa, 1996). One way to restate this theme is in terms of *epistemological effectiveness*: That is, no single person or discipline has all the knowledge that is needed for system design. Direct participation by end-users is seen, in this context, as a means of enhancing the process of gathering (and perhaps interpreting) information for system design.

- **Commitment and Buy-In.** A third theme occurs in the area of *organizational development*. In this view, a system is more likely to be accepted by its "downstream" end-users if those users are involved in certain "upstream" formative activities (e.g., Macaulay, 1995).

There have been related developments in other areas. Participatory *action research* shares—and in some ways improves on—the democratic motivations of participatory *design* (e.g., Burkey, 1993; Reason and Rowan, 1981). Several participatory design practices have explicitly developed from practices in the fields of community planning (e.g., Jungk and Mullert, 1987; Nisonen, 1994) and social system and policy development (e.g., Ackoff, 1974; Boy, in press; Warfield, 1971). Developments in areas of labor theory (e.g.,

Braverman, 1984), activity theory (Bødker, 1990), feminist analysis in general (Albrecht and Brewer, 1990; Balka, 1991, 1993; Balka and Doucette, 1994; Benston and Balka, 1993; Greenbaum and Kyng, 1991; Linn, 1987; Suchman and Jordan, 1988), feminist constructivism in particular (Belenky, Clinchy, Goldberger, and Tarule, 1986), and critical theory (for a starting point, see Muller, 1995a, 1996b) have also contributed to participatory theory and practice. These relationships are not surprising. Indeed, participatory design emphasizes the combining of dissimilar knowledges. It would be surprising if theory and practice in this area did not communicate with theory and practice from dissimilar fields.

Individual theorists and practitioners disagree on the relative importance of the three themes described in this section. We have argued that the three themes are often convergent (Kuhn and Muller, 1993; Muller et al., 1991), and one of us has collected evidence showing that the economic and political motivations have sometimes been included in the same project (Hallewell Haslwanter, 1995). In brief, democratic work at the level of design has the potential to improve both knowledge gathering *and* "downstream" commitment and buy-in—both within the software development process and within the users' work. In this analysis, democracy, epistemology, and commercial effectiveness go hand-in-hand.

11.1.3 Participation and Its Discontents

The increasing popularity of participatory work has led some researchers and practitioners to be wary of the phrase "participatory design" itself, and of the ways in which that phrase has been interpreted by others. To varying extents, we share their discomforts. In a review chapter such as this, we prefer to phrase these discomforts as questions—for example:

- Some knowledge elicitation techniques emphasize "participation" by workers for the purpose of increasing the knowledge that will be used primarily by the analyst or by a knowledge engineer (e.g., in the development of expert systems). What is the meaning of "participation" in describing practices in which the users give up their work-oriented knowledge without receiving in return any effective decision-making role in design? When does "participation" become exploitation?

- Certain well-known usability-testing practices in human-computer interaction treat users as measurement indicators of the productivity associated with a product, without considering the users' needs for comfort, dignity, respect, or a quality work environment. What is the meaning of "participation" when someone other than the users chooses which attributes of the users' experience are relevant? When does "participation" become objectification?

- Some practitioners have developed highly effective methods for participation by potential customers, in determining the most attractive attributes of mass market products. What is the meaning of "participation" when people contribute to activities that are then used to develop more effective advertising campaigns? When does "participation" become manipulation?

- Certain organizational development approaches have reassured managers that problems may be solved at a lower level in the organization, while decisions about those problems are retained at a higher level in the organization. What is the meaning of "participation" without decision-making? When does "participation" become illusion?

We three authors have worked together to varying extents, and yet we have come to somewhat different answers to these difficult questions (for related sets of questions, see Mackay, 1995; Muller, 1995a, 1995b). In this chapter, we will not attempt to provide examples of our own or others' answers to these questions. We hope that readers will consider the ethical and political dimensions of their own practices as they select from the techniques that we describe in this chapter.

11.1.4 Against Methods

Some practitioners believe that the methods-oriented approach we have taken here is inappropriate (e.g., Blomberg et al., 1995; in some ways, Bødker, Christiansen, and Thüring, 1995; see also the general disinclination to provide precise methodological descriptions in the Scandinavian work, as evidenced in many contributions to Greenbaum and Kyng, 1991).

In this view, methods are problematic for two reasons. First, this view's engineering assumptions regarding a "method" are that a method is a straightforward, usually linear or sequential, series of well-understood steps that will lead to a predictable and relatively guaranteed outcome. These assumptions do not hold in the area of participatory methods, because any methodological description in our field provides merely a scaffold or an infrastructure for a complex group process that is neither linear nor well-understood. Of course, the complex group process is essential, and is in fact the heart of participatory work. All of the details of methods that we present in this chapter are intended as support for this fundamental human-to-human communication.

A second objection to a methods-oriented approach is that some practitioners may be able to *name* a participatory method that they claim to have applied, but they may *apply* that method in a way that is contrary to the goals of participatory design. For example, two of us have been present when human factors analysts claimed to have done "participatory design with the developers—we used PICTIVE." Yet there were no users present in these allegedly participatory activities. This story is an example of an appropriation of the language of participatory design for a non-participatory activity. Some of our colleagues cite such problems as examples of the dangers of presenting participatory methods for use by people who may not agree with the democratic motivations of participatory design[1].

We have nonetheless decided to pursue a methods-oriented approach, because (1) We believe in the value of iterative, flexible, loosely guiding methodological approaches in general (Dayton, 1991; Karat and Dayton, 1995), including non-participatory ones; and (2) We believe that a clear "guide to participatory methods" can aid in the piecemeal, incremental, experimental introduction of participatory approaches in organizations that have previously relied on non-participatory software methods. Good practitioners of every background look for improved methods. We offer these participatory practices in the hope that practitioners will try at least *one* appropriate method in their work, and see the values of participation. They may then be able to use this chapter to find other methods that may apply to other aspects of their work. In this way, we hope that this chapter may help to bring greater and greater participation to work within a conventional software lifecycle. Recent analyses of the state of information engineering (Mulder, 1994) and HCI (Strong, 1994) agree on the need to introduce more participatory practices.

We agree with our colleagues about the dangers of misapplication of participatory methods in non-participatory work (see, e.g., the question that we listed in the preceding section). However, we are convinced that these dangers and problems will require searching inquiries, discussions, and reflections (see, e.g., Muller, 1995b). Making methods available to practitioners may in fact be a way of hastening these needed discussions.

We hope that these discussions will include a clarification of the concept of participation. During our preparations for this chapter, some practitioners pressured us to include practices that we considered to be borderline participatory at best. With mixed feelings, we have generally decided to err on the side of being too inclusive, rather than not inclusive enough. Perhaps the inclusion of borderline cases will help the participatory community to develop a clearer definition of its own concepts. We trust that future versions of this chapter, prepared by others or ourselves, will correct any mistakes that we have made.

There are alternatives to this piecemeal approach of adding one or more participatory practices to conventional lifecycle models. A later section of this paper briefly reviews what we have called *participatory whole-lifecycle models*. We encourage practitioners to consider a wholesale adoption of participatory practice through such lifecycle models. We believe that, even with a participatory lifecycle model, practitioners may need to search for additional methods. Thus, we hope that this chapter will be useful for practitioners who work within either conventional lifecycle models or participatory lifecycle models.

11.1.5 History of This Work

Work on this collection of participatory practices began in collaboration with Ellen White and Daniel Wildman. Conference participants at the CHI '92 conference were invited to write their own contributions to a "participatory poster of participatory practices" (Muller, Wildman, and White, 1992). The resulting, early view of participatory practices was published in Muller, Wildman, and White (1993).

One of us conducted a survey of participatory

---

[1]We believe that methods from participatory design may be useful in non-participatory domains. In fact, all of us have been involved in such activities (e.g., Muller, Hallewell Haslwanter, and Dayton, 1995; Nielsen et al., 1992). However, we recommend that practitioners use very clear language regarding such applications of methods. In Muller, Hallewell Haslwanter, and Dayton (1995), we distinguished between the *participatory analysis methods* that we were borrowing for the purposes of a non-participatory *collaborative analysis* that, for organizational reasons, excluded the end-users. In Nielsen et al. (1992), we borrowed a method from *participatory design* for the purpose of helping developers to understand concepts in graphical user interfaces. Our purpose here was education of developers, not codevelopment of systems with end-users. In both of these examples, we believe that the methods contributed to our work. In both of these examples, we were clear that the methods were being used in a non-participatory fashion, and that they therefore should be described in non-participatory terms.

methods and outcomes as part of her thesis research (Hallewell Haslwanter, 1995). In connection with that survey, the participatory poster was presented for further codevelopment at conferences in Australia, Europe, and North America in 1994 and 1995 (Hallewell Haslwanter, Muller, and Dayton, 1994; Muller, Hallewell Haslwanter, and Dayton, 1994, 1995).

This chapter is, then, a report of a continuing work-in-progress that is being carried out by members of the field of participatory design. The "authors" of this chapter serve only as the current facilitators of that process.

11.2 Taxonomies of Participatory Practices

This chapter presents the many participatory methods labeled by their places in several dimensions, such as the sizes of the groups the methods can handle, and the points in the software lifecycle where the methods are used. We hope that this organization will help readers understand the universe of participatory methods, and quickly find methods that are appropriate to the readers' particular situations.

11.2.1 Practices in the Lifecycle?

Early work in participatory design tended to treat the participatory activity as the overwhelming focus of the endeavor. It was often difficult—if not problematic—to situate the participatory work in the context of a software lifecycle or software development organization. We know of two responses to that set of problems:

- **PANDA.** The 1992 taxonomy of participatory practices was organized across a dimension of the relevant phases of the software lifecycle. Our original motivation for this organization was to help practitioners find useful practices. An unintentional outcome was a very clear demonstration that "participatory design" practices in fact are used in many more phases of the lifecycle than just in design. One of us discovered in her survey of practitioners that participatory activities were used most often in design, but also in the following phases: requirements, prototyping, system design, and system test. Her research also showed that over 50% of respondents used participatory activities in *all* lifecycle phases (Hallewell Haslwanter, 1995). One of us is exploring a broader treatment that can be rendered as a pronounceable term as PANDA, for Participatory ANalysis, Design, and Assessment (Muller, 1996b). This formulation highlights participatory activities that contribute to the *analysis* of work and to the *assessment* of computer systems and work systems, as well as to issues of *design*.

  However, as we will show, the PANDA description is in fact too narrow. There are participatory methods falling outside of the limited domain addressed by a literal interpretation of the PANDA formulation.

- **Tools for the Toolbox.** In 1992 and 1993, Kensing and Munk-Madsen (1993) developed an analysis of participatory methods that they termed "tools for the toolbox" (recently extended as the MUST conceptual organization for participatory work by Kensing, Simonsen, and Bødker, 1996). Their spirit was very much in keeping with our position as described above in section 11.1.4 ("Against Methods"): to provide practitioners with tools that could be applied in conventional software lifecycle models.

  Kensing and Munk-Madsen went beyond our own 1992 and 1993 work, however, by including in their analysis both participatory methods and formal methods. Their analysis considered both the relatively concrete and end-user-accessible methods of participatory design *and* a subset of the relatively formal and end-user-inaccessible methods that are used by software professionals for communication *within* their own profession. Their analysis suggested that there may be pairs of methods—one participatory method and one formal method—that complement one another. We have attempted to include this component of analysis in this chapter.

More generally, there has been concern to make usability methods more usable in the software lifecycle (Dayton, 1991; Dray, Dayton, Mrazek, Muckler, and Rafeld, 1993; Hefley et al., 1994; Hix, Hartson, and Nielsen, 1994; Kensing and Munk-Madsen, 1993; Olson and Moran, 1993; Strong, 1994). The critique of Olson and Moran is particularly apt. They suggested that each method be described in terms of problem to be solved, materials, process, and result. In this chapter, we have extended their proposed descriptors in directions that appear to us to be consistent with participatory design[2].

In the remainder of this section, we describe our

[2]For a different conceptual organization of a space of methods, see Braa (1996).

revised analytical space of participatory methods. Table 1 provides one organization of the methods. The Appendix provides more details on each method.

11.2.2 Describing Practices

Our analytical space is organized according to nine major attributes:

- **Abstract:** What is the practice supposed to do? Why might a practitioner choose this practice? In some ways, this attribute is related to the question of the phase or phases of the software lifecycle.

- **Object Model:** What materials are used in the practice?

- **Process Model:** What do people do to communicate with one another? How do they make decisions? What do people do with the materials in the Object Model?

- **Participation Model:** Who is involved in the work? Are people with specific roles needed for the practice to work well?

- **Results:** What tangible or intangible benefit is produced as a outcome of the work? How is this result used?

- **Phases of the Lifecycle:** In many cases, participatory methods were developed to meet a particular need within a particular phase of the software lifecycle. Where this is the case, we have indexed the method to that phase.

  However, some methods were developed for application to multiple lifecycle phases. In other cases, practitioners have discovered that a method originally developed for one particular phase can be applied with little modification to other phases. In these cases, we have indexed the method to multiple lifecycle phases. To avoid multiple descriptions, we have placed all of the detailed descriptions of method not in the sections on lifecycle phases, but rather in a single omnibus appendix to this chapter. In many cases, a single method description in the appendix is indexed from several lifecycle sections.

  The span of lifecycle activities in our analysis may be surprising to some North American practitioners. Following the Scandinavian approaches and also the persuasive analysis of Floyd (1987), we begin our lifecycle model with very early activities that are concerned with problem identification and problem clarification (e.g., Is there a problem to be solved? What is it? Would a computer system help to solve the problem?). Conventional North American lifecycle models often treat this phase as *external* to the lifecycle. Experiences from Scandinavia, from participatory action research, and from some of the pragmatically-oriented research and application, have shown the importance of end-user participation in this early phase of understanding and decision-making.

  We also extend the span of lifecycle activities somewhat later than some North American models, to include customization of computer systems in the field, and participatory redesign of existing systems.

- **Complementary Formal Methods:** Can the practice work in conjunction with a formal lifecycle method that might be known to software professionals?

- **Group Sizes:** Many participatory practices were designed for work with small groups. A few practices appear to require a pair of people with well-defined roles (e.g., user and developer). Other practices were designed for work with larger groups, or in a few cases with very large groups. We have attempted to indicate the group sizes for which each practice appears to work well.

- **References:** How may the reader find out more about this practice? Where possible, we list formal publications that are likely to be available in research libraries. When necessary, we resort to tutorial notes or position papers at conference workshops, recognizing that these resources will be more difficult for readers to obtain. In a few cases, there is no documentary record available: In these cases, we have provided contact information for the originator of the practice.

11.3 Participatory Whole-Lifecycle Models

Our focus in this chapter is on specific methods, techniques, and procedures for participatory work, which can be applied within existing, conventional software lifecycle approaches. We therefore can only briefly mention several promising approaches toward a *par-*

ticipatory model of the software lifecycle (specific references to each of the approaches named in this section may be found in the Appendix). The ETHICS, STEPS, and CESD models for lifecycle-spanning participatory approaches are being developed in the United Kingdom, Germany, and Denmark, respectively. For Denmark, see also the Conceptual Toolkit project. The US has seen a much more restricted experiment in the Codevelopment project at Xerox.

Several people have developed integrated approaches that provide participatory continuity *across* a significant subset of lifecycle phases. Early phases (i.e., from problem identification through design) have been spanned by the UTOPIA project in Denmark, by Contextual Inquiry and Contextual Design in the US, by the Hiser Design Method in Australia, and by Soft Systems Methodology and ORDIT in the United Kingdom. The FIRE project in Norway has begun to integrate the later phases of the lifecycle.

Many of these lifecycle-oriented approaches provide conceptual, organizational, and political frameworks within which specific participatory practices may be located. Thus, several of the practices that are described by themselves (e.g., workshops, prototyping) also serve as components of the more integrated, continuous participatory approaches.

11.4 Approaches from Other Domains

We briefly note several other domains that may be of value to readers who do not find in this chapter, methods to suit their purposes. Participatory action research has been concerned with developing co-investigatory relationships between researchers and the people whom they study (e.g., Burkey, 1993; Reason and Rowan, 1981). Feminism has explored ways of reducing the objectification and exploitation of the people who are studied in social science research (e.g., Reinharz, 1992; see also Belenky et al., 1986). Grounded theory may provide a means of developing theoretical contributions directly from the social systems that are studied, as contrasted with the more traditional approach of fitting observations into a theoretical structure that was developed independently of those observations (e.g., Glaser and Strauss, 1967; for methods, see especially Strauss and Corbin, 1990). Finally, activity theory has recently been argued to have potential value to the field of human-computer interaction (e.g., Nardi, in press) and specifically participatory design (Bødker, 1990).

11.5 Does Participation "Work?"

The readers of this chapter may reasonably wish to ask whether participation in software activities by end-users is worth the time and apparent trouble? In this section, we briefly address that question.

First, we note that different methods, practices, and procedures have different time-courses. Ethnography, for example, typically involves a long relationship. At the other extreme, some participatory practices can be begun and concluded within a single session. We wish to emphasize that participatory activities do not necessarily require more time than conventional practices: Some participatory activities, in fact, take much less time than corresponding or complementary formal software lifecycle methods. The strengths and weaknesses of these different approaches must, of course, be considered as practitioners and researchers choose practices that fit within their particular constraints.

In an earlier section, we introduced several convergent motivations for participation. Economic motivations included the incorporation of user expertise, and increases in the efficiency and quality of knowledge gathering. Organizational motivations included improved communications, and earlier understanding and commitment by "downstream" staff and organizations). Political motivations included the enhancement of workplace democracy, and the direct articulation of end-users' needs by the end-users or their organization. Several researchers have examined each of these areas of potential contribution. An early study of user "involvement" in lifecycle activities showed no reliable effects (Ives and Olson, 1984). However, the concept of "involvement" appears in retrospect to have been too broad. It included direct participation, but it was large determined as a subjective estimate of the users' sense of involvement, ascertained as a unidimensional numerical response to a survey item. Moreover, the survey respondent was usually a manager in the user organization, rather than an end-user. Thus, this early study has less to tell us about the effects of user *participation* than we might have thought. More recent studies have shown complex but reliable positive effects of user participation (not just "involvement") in lifecycle activities. Cotton, Vollrath, Froggatt, Lengnick-Hall, and Jennings (1988) studied multiple dimensions of participation, and multiple outcome measures. Their results showed that certain forms of user participation were beneficial for certain economic and organizational outcomes. Saarinen and

Saaksjarvi (1989) showed a similar, complex set of relationships. Their study helped to tease apart to separate but equally valuable contributions of end-users as participants and of analysts as participants. Thus, careful studies of end-user participation have shown both (a) the value of end-users' contributions to economic and organizational goals, and (b) the value of the contributions of analysts and other professionals to those same goals.

These three studies—and especially the later two—provide some support for our first two motivations: economic and organizational. We also note that some of the work on individual methods, techniques, and procedures has included assessments of their effectiveness. Case studies of participatory design are provided by Greenbaum and Madsen (1993), Hallewell Haslwanter (1995), Mumford (1993), Thoresen (1993), and URCOT (1993).

Outcomes regarding the third motivation—workplace democracy—are more difficult to measure. Good qualitative summaries of these complex outcomes in Scandinavia are provided by Ehn and Kyng (1987) and by Bjerknes and Bratteteig (1995). We know of no similar omnibus summaries for participatory practices in software activities outside of Scandinavia.

11.6 Some Outstanding Research Problems in Participation

In this section, we briefly provide our perspective on unsolved problems in the area of participatory work with end-users in software lifecycles.

11.6.1 Relationships Between Participatory Practices, Formal Software Methods, and Contractual Models

As we noted earlier, it has been difficult to integrate participatory activities into the software lifecycle. Kensing and Munk-Madsen (1993) made progress in this area by suggesting correlative participatory and formal methods. We have attempted to continue their approach in this chapter. Nonetheless, we believe that there are many more relationships between participatory and formal methods that remain to be discovered or created. Establishing these relationships and their syncretic benefits may require modification to both participatory and formal methods: We anticipate that working through these tradeoffs will be a complex, difficult, and rewarding undertaking.

A more significant problem arises with certain formal lifecycle methods that are gaining in popularity. We outline two problems in this section, to provide a sense of the challenges facing participatory theorists and practitioners:

- **Use cases.** Certain object-oriented methodologies encourage the construction of use cases as scenarios of user activities related to the software system (e.g., Jacobson, 1995, and more generally Jacobson, Christersson, Jonsson, and Övergaard, 1992). There are several problems with these approaches. First, the use case model is almost always written with the software system as the overwhelming focus of attention. The use case model is thus an example of a *product-oriented paradigm*, which gives too much priority to the software, and too little priority to the end-users' work or life processes (see Floyd, 1987, for an influential distinction between product-oriented and process-oriented paradigms in software engineering). At a deeper level, each use case is a definition of user actions by system designers: Its words carry a connotation of end-user focus and work analysis, but its substance is in fact centered on software features that may or may not be related to end-users'needs. In practice, we have seen development organizations utilize the use case model as a replacement for work with end-users. The problem, then, is to make effective user participation an integral part of the use case model and its related practices.

- **ISO 9001.** The ISO 9001 standard for quality assurance encourages an agreement or contract between a software development organization and a user organization. In the analysis of Braa and Øgrim (in press), the standard focuses entirely on technical quality, as contrasted with other potential quality areas such as use quality, aesthetic quality, symbolic quality, and organizational quality. The standard also omits any formal relationship between the development organization and an organization that might represent the needs of the end-users (i.e., as contrasted with the needs of their managers, as reflected in the user organization). Thus, the standard may be unethical, according to Braa and Øgrim. It may also explain recent informal reports from Scandinavia, of end-user constituencies being omitted from discussions of new or revised systems, despite the fact that they had been primary participants in earlier discussions with the same employers. As the ISO 9001 and 9003 standards become more widely used, we may find a need to modify them so that they explicitly include end-user participation as part of the assurance of quality, and, perhaps more crucially, end-user organizations (e.g., unions or other forms of representation) as among the parties who are directly involved in contractual relationships with developers and with user organizations.

11.6.2 Non-Organized and Contingent Workers

Participatory activities are easiest to conduct when the end-users are organized and self-represented through an autonomous organization, such as a union (e.g., Greenbaum, 1993; Grudin, 1990; Muller, 1996a). Nonetheless, many practitioners and organizations are engaged in participatory activities with workers who do not have formal representation. There are different problems and obstacles for these participatory venues (Bruce and Kirup, 1987; Carmel, Grudin, Juhl, Erickson, and Robbins, 1994; Darwin, Fitter, Fryer, and Smith, 1987; Greenbaum, 1993; Grudin, 1990). The problems are perhaps most difficult when the workers go from one temporary job to another (e.g., Greenbaum, Snelling, Jolly, and Orr, 1994; Greenbaum and Orr, 1995). Effective participation by non-organized or contingent workers presents a number of daunting challenges for which we are still searching for solutions. These problems are magnified when we consider the constituencies for on-line or distance educational services (Muller, 1995a).

11.6.3 Finding Partners and Structuring Relationships

Participation involves risks—especially for less powerful participants and constituencies. In the introductory section, we outlined several ethical questions. From the perspective of the practitioner's perspective, these questions may seem to be related to fairness, or even efficiency. From the perspective of end-users, these questions may seem to be related to exploitation, or even betrayal. Decision-makers in end-user organizations, such as unions, must weigh the risks of participation to their constituencies and also to themselves—for instance, as elected leaders who will be held responsible for their commitments by their membership. There is some work in Scandinavia toward reducing these risks (e.g., Bjerknes and Bratteteig, 1995; Ehn and Kyng, 1987). There appears to be less work outside of Scandinavia that addresses this difficult area.

If the risk is considered worthwhile, then there arises the question of the form of relationship that is to develop. In one sense, the diverse participants form a team. In another sense, each participant remains—and *should* remain—a member of her or his group of origin. Feminists working in multi-cultural contexts have explored differences among concepts of *coalitions*, *alliances*, and other forms of inter-organizational relationship (e.g., Albrecht and Brewer, 1990). We are unaware of similarly detailed analyses in the software area.

11.6.4 Balancing Group and Individual Activities

Participatory work is by definition shared among group members. However, there are other work components that are best done by individuals, or by subgroups. Examples include a human factors worker applying a detailed style guide to a rough design, and a union stewards' group developing a work force position with respect to a job design decision.

In the more formal constructs of Clement and Wagner (1995), subgroups and individuals have needs both of aggregation (working together, sharing data and experiences) and disaggregation (working alone, keeping data and experiences private). Much of the research literature has concerned needs for, and technologies in support of, aggregation. Aside from work on privacy and censorship, there is little research in the software area into needs for, and technologies in support of, disaggregation. Clement and Wagner argued that this area requires more subtle concepts than sharing "versus" privacy, or expression "versus" censorship, and they have provided a starting point for researchers who want to pursue these questions.

11.7 Conclusion

In this chapter, we have attempted (a) to provide a set of guideposts to the considerable progress that has been made in practices in participatory activities, and (b) to outline some of the problems that remain to be solved. Because of the extraordinary diversity of the communities that work toward effective participation, we feel the need to review our efforts to work beyond our own limited perspectives. The materials that we have summarized in this chapter have been gathered on three continents over a period of as many years. Nonetheless, most of the venues at which we conducted our "participatory posters" were professional meetings for privileged, salaried members of the managerial and academic social classes (and students who aspired to join their ranks). Our information-gathering has thus been biased, despite our best intentions. We look forward to the next iteration of this summary of participatory methods, techniques, and procedures, and we hope that the people who prepare that summary can do so in a more inclusive manner than we have been able to achieve.

11.8 Acknowledgments

We thank Heather Shepherd and Anne McClard for helping find references; Ellen White and Danny Wildman for co-authoring the early participatory posters used to collect and present these data; Judy Hammond and Peter Petocz; and the many people who have contributed information about methods in the several years of this ongoing project.

11.9 References

Ackoff, R. L. (1974). *Redesigning the future—A system approach to societal problems.* New York: Wiley.

Albrecht, L., and Brewer, R. M. (Eds.). (1990) *Bridges of power: Women's multi-cultural alliances.* Philadelphia: New Society.

Balka, E. (1991). *Womantalk goes on-line: The use of computer networks for feminist social change.* Doctoral thesis, Simon Fraser University, Burnaby, British Columbia, Canada.

Balka, E. (1993). Cappuccino, community, and technology: Technology in the everyday life of Margaret Benston. *Canadian Woman Studies Journal / Les Cahiers de la Femme, 13*(2), 62–65.

Balka, E., and Doucette, L. (1994). The accessibility of computers to organizations serving women in the province of Newfoundland: Preliminary study results. *Electronic Journal of Virtual Culture, 2*(3).

Beck, E.E. (1996). P for political? Some challenges to PD towards 2000. In *PDC'96 Proceedings of the Participatory Design Conference*, 117-125.

Belenky, M. F., Clinchy, B. M., Goldberger, N. R., and Tarule, N. M. (1986). *Women's ways of knowing: The development of self, voice, and mind.* New York: Basic Books.

[3] Michael J. Muller, 1969 Joslyn Court, Boulder, Colorado 80304, USA; muller.chi@xerox.com
Jean Hallewell Haslwanter, Weilerburgstrasse 3, 72072 Tübingen, Germany; jean.hallewell@wago.de
Tom Dayton, 41C Franklin Greens South, Somerset, New Jersey 08873, USA; tdayton.chi@xerox.com

Benston, M., and Balka, E. (1993). Participatory design by non-profit groups. *Canadian Woman Studies Journal / Les Cahiers de la Femme, 13*(2), 100–103.

Bernard, E., (1996). Power and design: Why unions and organizations matter. In *PDC'96 Proceedings of the Participatory Design Conference*, 207.

Bjerknes, G., and Bratteteig, T. (1995). User participation and democracy: A discussion of Scandinavian research on system development. *Scandinavian Journal of Information Systems, 7*(1), 73–98.

Blomberg, J., Suchman, L., and Trigg, R. (1995). Back to work: Renewing old agendas for cooperative design. In *Conference proceedings of Computers in Context: Joining Forces in Design* (pp. 1–9). Århus, Denmark: Aarhus University.

Boy, G. A. (in press). Group elicitation method. To appear in *interactions.*

Braverman, H. (1984). *Labor and monopoly capital.* New York: Monthly Review.

Bruce, M., and Kirup, G. (1987). An analysis of women's roles under the impacts of new technology in the home and office. In G. Bjerknes, P. Ehn, and M. Kyng (Eds.), *Computers and democracy: A Scandinavian challenge.* Brookfield, VT, USA: Gower.

Braa, K. (1996). Influencing qualities of information systems — Future challenges for participatory design. In *PDC'96 Proceedings of the Participatory Design Conference*, 163-172.

Braa, K., and Øgrim, L. (in press). Critical view of the application of the ISO standard for quality assurance. *Information Systems Journal.*

Burkey, S. (1993). *People first: A guide to self-reliant participatory rural development.* London: Zed.

Bødker, S. (1990). *Through the interface: A human activity approach to user interface design.* Hillsdale, NJ, USA: Erlbaum.

Bødker, S., Christiansen, E., and Thüring, M. (1995). A conceptual toolbox for designing CSCW applications. In *COOP '95: Atelier international sur la conception des systèms coopératifs* [International workshop on the design of cooperative systems] (pp. 266–284). Sophia Antiipolis, France: INRIA.

Carmel, E., Grudin, J., Juhl, D., Erickson, T., and Robbins, J. (1994). Does participatory design have a role in software package development? *PDC '94: Proceedings of the Participatory Design Conference*, 33–35.

Clement, A., and Wagner, I. (1995). Fragmented exchange: Disarticulation and the need for regionalized communication spaces. In *Proceedings of the Fourth European Conference on Computer-Supported Cooperative Work* (pp. 33–49). Stockholm: Kluwer.

Communications of the ACM. (1993). *36*(10).

Cotton, J. L., Vollrath, D. A., Froggatt, K. L., Lengnick-Hall, M. L., and Jennings, K. R. (1988). Employee participation: Diverse forms and different outcomes. *Academy of Management Review, 13*(1), 8–22.

Darwin, J., Fitter, M., Fryer, D., and Smith, L. (1987). Developing information technology in the community with unwaged groups. In G. Bjerknes, P. Ehn, and M. Kyng (Eds.), *Computers and democracy: A Scandinavian challenge.* Brookfield, VT, USA: Gower.

Dayton, T. (1991). Cultivated eclecticism as the normative approach to design. In J. Karat (Ed.), *Taking software design seriously: Practical techniques for human-computer interaction design* (pp. 21–44). Boston: Academic Press.

Dray, S., Dayton, T., Mrazek, D., Muckler, F. A., and Rafeld, M. (1993). Making human factors usable. *Proceedings of the Human Factors and Ergonomics Society 37th Annual Meeting*, 863–866.

Ehn, P., and Kyng, M. (1987). The collective resource approach to systems design. In G. Bjerknes, P. Ehn, and M. Kyng (Eds.), *Computers and democracy: A Scandinavian challenge* (pp. 17–57). Brookfield, VT, USA: Gower.

Floyd, C. (1987). Outline of a paradigm change in software engineering. In G. Bjerknes, P. Ehn, and M. Kyng (Eds.), *Computers and democracy: A Scandinavian challenge* (pp. 191–210). Brookfield, VT, USA: Gower.

Floyd, C., Züllighoven, H., Budde, R., and Keil-Slawik, R. (1992). (Eds.). *Software development and reality construction.* Berlin: Springer Verlag.

Glaser, B., and Strauss, A. (1967). *The discovery of grounded theory.* Chicago: Aldine.

Greenbaum, J. (1996). Post modern times: Participation beyond the workplace. In *PDC'96 Proceedings of the Participatory Design Conference*, 65-72.

Greenbaum, J. (1993). A design of one's own: Towards participatory design in the United States. In D. Schuler and A. Namioka (Eds.), *Participatory design: Principles and practices* (pp. 27–37). Hillsdale, NJ, USA: Erlbaum.

Greenbaum, J., and Kyng, M. (Eds.). (1991). *Design at work: Cooperative design of computer systems.* Hillsdale, NJ, USA: Erlbaum.

Greenbaum, J., and Madsen, K. H. (1993). Small changes: Starting a participatory design process by giving participants a voice. In D. Schuler and A. Namioka (Eds.), *Participatory design: Principles and practices* (pp. 289–298). Hillsdale, NJ, USA: Erlbaum.

Greenbaum, J., and Orr, J. (1995). Participatory panel: Re-divided work—Implications for work and system design. In *Conference proceedings of Computers in Context: Joining Forces in Design* (p. ii). Århus, Denmark: Aarhus University.

Greenbaum, J., and Sclove, R. (1996). Beyond participatory design. In *PDC'96 Proceedings of the Participatory Design Conference*, 63.

Greenbaum, J., Snelling, L., Jolly, C., and Orr, J. (1994). The limits of PD? Contingent jobs and work reorganization. *PDC '94: Proceedings of the Participatory Design Conference,* 173–174.

Grudin, J. (1990) Obstacles to participatory design. *Proceedings of CHI '90*, 142–143.

Hallewell Haslwanter, J. D. (1995). *Participatory design methods in the context of human-computer interaction.* M. Sc. thesis, University of Technology, Sydney, Sydney, Australia.

Hallewell Haslwanter, J. D., and Hammond, J. (1994). Survey of cross-cultural differences in participatory design. *OZCHI '94 Proceedings*, 317–318.

Hallewell Haslwanter, J. D., Muller, M. J., and Dayton, T. (1994). Participatory design practices: A classification. *OZCHI '94 Proceedings*, 319–320.

Hefley, W. F., Buie, E. A., Lynch, G. F., Muller, M. J., Hoecker, D. G., Carter, J., and Roth, J. T. (1994). Integrating human factors with software engineering practices. *Proceedings of the Human Factors and Ergonomics Society 38th Annual Meeting,* 315–319.

Hix, D., Hartson, H. R., and Nielsen, J. (1994). A taxonomy for developing high impact formative usability evaluation methods. *SIGCHI Bulletin, 26*(4), 20–22.

Holtzblatt, K., and Beyer, H. (1993). Making customer-centered design work for teams. *Communications of the ACM, 36*(10), 92–103.

Ives, B., and Olson, M. (1984). User involvement and MIS success: A review of research. *Management Science, 30*(5), 586–603.

Jacobson, I. (1995). The use-case construct in object-oriented software engineering. In J. Carroll (Ed.), *Scenario-based design: Envisioning work and technology in system development* (pp. 309–360). New York: Wiley.

Jacobson, I., Christersson, M., Jonsson, P., and Övergaard, G. (1992). *Object-oriented software engineering—A use-case driven approach.* Reading, MA, USA: Addison-Wesley.

Jungk, R., and Mullert, N. (1987). *Future workshops: How to create a desirable future.* London: Institute of Social Invention.

Karat, J., and Dayton, T. (1995). Practical education for improving software usability. *Proceedings of CHI '95,* 162–169.

Kensing, F., and Munk-Madsen, A. (1993). PD: Structure in the toolbox. *Communications of the ACM, 36*(6), 78–85.

Kensing, F., Simonsen, J., and Bødker, K. (1996). MUST — A method for participatory design. In *PDC'96 Proceedings of the Participatory Design Conference*, 129-140.

Kuhn, S., and Muller, M. J. (1993). Introduction to the issue on participatory design. *Communications of the ACM, 36*(6), 24–28.

Linn, P. (1987). Gender stereotypes, technology stereotypes. *Radical Science Journal, 19,* 127–131.

Macaulay, L. (1995). Cooperation in understanding user needs and requirements. *Computer Integrated Manufacturing Systems, 8*(2), 155–165.

Mackay, W. E. (1995). Ethics, lies and videotape. *Proceedings of CHI '95,* 138–145.

Mulder, M. C. (1994). *Educating the next generation of information specialists.* Washington, DC: National Science Foundation.

Muller, M. J. (1996a). Defining and designing the Internet: Participation by Internet stakeholder constituencies. *Social Science Computing Review* 14(1), 30-33.

Muller, M. J. (1995a). Ethnocritical heuristics for HCI work with users and other stakeholders. In *Conference proceedings of Computers in Context: Joining Forces in Design* (pp. 10–19). Århus, Denmark: Aarhus University.

Muller, M. J. (1995b). Ethnocritical questions for working with translations, interpretations, and their stakeholders. *Communications of the ACM* 38(9), 64-65.

Muller, M.J. (1996b). *Participatory activities with users and others in the software lifecycle.* Tutorial at CHI 96.

Muller, M. J., Blomberg, J. L., Carter, K. A., Dykstra, E. A., Greenbaum, J., and Halskov Madsen, K. (1991). Panel: Participatory design in Britain and North America: Responses to the "Scandinavian challenge." *Proceedings of CHI '91,* 389–392.

Muller, M. J., Hallewell Haslwanter, J. D., and Dayton, T. (1994). Updating a taxonomy of participatory practices: A participatory poster. *PDC '94: Proceedings of the Participatory Design Conference,* 123.

Muller, M. J., Hallewell Haslwanter, J. D., and Dayton, T. (1995). A participatory poster of participatory practices. In *Conference proceedings of Computers in Context: Joining Forces in Design* (p. i). Århus, Denmark: Aarhus University.

Muller, M. J., Wildman, D. M., and White, E. A. (1992). *Taxonomy of participatory design practices: A participatory poster.* Poster at CHI '92, Monterey, California, USA.

Muller, M. J., Wildman, D. M., and White, E. A. (1993). Taxonomy of PD practices: A brief practitioner's guide. *Communications of the ACM, 36*(6), 26–27.

Mumford, E. (1993). The participation of users in systems design: An account of the origin, evolution, and use of the ETHICS method. In D. Schuler and A. Namioka (Eds.), *Participatory design: Principles and practices* (pp. 257–270). Hillsdale, NJ, USA: Erlbaum.

Nardi, B. A. (Ed.). (1996) *Context and consciousness: Activity theory and human computer interaction* (pp. 387–400). Cambridge, MA, USA: MIT Press.

Nielsen, J., Bush, R. M., Dayton, T., Mond, N. E., Muller, M. J., and Root, R. W. (1992). Teaching experienced developers to design graphical user interfaces. *Proceedings of CHI '92,* 557–564.

Nisonen, E. (1994). Women's safety audit guide—An action plan and a grass roots community development tool. *CPSR Newsletter, 12*(3), 7.

Noro, K., and Imada, A. S. (Eds.). (1991). *Participatory ergonomics.* London: Taylor and Francis.

Olson, J. S., and Moran, T. P. (1993). *Mapping the method muddle: Guidance in using methods for user interface design* (Technical Report No. 49). Ann Arbor, MI, USA: University of Michigan, Cognitive Science and Machine Intelligence Laboratory.

Reason, P., and Rowan, J. (Eds.). (1981). *Human inquiry: A sourcebook of new paradigm research.* Chichester: Wiley.

Reinharz, S. (with Davidman, L.). (1992). *Feminist methods in social research.* New York: Oxford University Press.

Saarinen, T., and Saaksjarvi, M. (1989). The missing concepts of user participation: An empirical assessment of user participation and information system success. In *Proceedings of the 12th IRIS (Information System Research in Scandinavia)* (pp. 533–553). Århus, Denmark: Aarhus University.

Scandinavian Journal of Information Systems. (1994). 6(1).

Schuler, D., and Namioka, A. (Eds.). (1993). *Participatory design: Principles and practices.* Hillsdale, NJ, USA: Erlbaum.

Segall, P., and Snelling, L. (1996). Achieving worker participation in technological change: The case of the flashing cursor. In *PDC'96 Proceedings of the Participatory Design Conference*, 103-109.

Strauss, A., and Corbin, J. (1990). *Basics of qualitative research: Grounded theory procedures and techniques.* Newbury Park, CA, USA: Sage.

Strong, G. W. (with Gasen, J. B., Hewett, T., Hix, D., Morris, J., Muller, M. J., and Novick, D. G.). (1994). *New directions in human-computer interaction education, research, and practice.* Washington, DC: National Science Foundation.

Suchman, L., and Jordan, B. (1988). Computerization and women's knowledge. In *Women, work, and computerization: IFIP conference proceedings.* Amsterdam: Elsevier.

Thoresen, K. (1993). Principles in practice: Two cases of situated participatory design. In D. Schuler and A. Namioka (Eds.), *Participatory design: Principles and practices* (pp. 271-287). Hillsdale, NJ, USA: Erlbaum.

URCOT. (1993). *Systems development in the ATO: Staff participation in the HURON pilot* (Project briefing). Melbourne, Australia: Union Research Centre on Organisational Technology Ltd. (URCOT).

Warfield, J. N. (1971). *Societal systems: Planning, policy, and complexity.* New York: Wiley.

Wixon, D., Holtzblatt, K., and Knox, S. (1990). Contextual design: An emergent view of system design. *Proceedings of CHI '90*, 329–336.

11.10 Appendix: Summaries of Participatory Practices

11.10.1 ACE (Amsterdam Conversation Environment)

Abstract: Low-tech simulation/enactment of e-mail communication patterns to support conversation among participants, by using paper airplanes as a vehicle for discussion.

Object Model: Notepad, pencils and paper airplanes to carry notes. Streamers stapled to the planes carry the semantics of the message openness: If the streamer is exposed it is traceable; if it is tucked in it is anonymous.

Process Model: Series of face-to-face meetings, where participants discuss the proposed system by: (1) Writing notes. (2) Sending notes. (3) Receiving notes. (4) Replying to notes.

Participation Model: Users, developers, testers.

Results: (1) Understanding of communication patterns. (2) Envisionment of a system to support these.

Phases of the Lifecycle: Requirements, analysis.

Complementary Formal Methods: Prototyping.

Group Sizes: Designed to support 21 people, can be used for groups greater than 2 people.

References:

Dykstra, E. A., and Carasik, R. P. (1991). Structure and support in cooperative environments: The Amsterdam Conversation Environment. *International Journal of Man-Machine Studies, 34*, 419–434.

11.10.2 ACOST Project

Abstract: Technique used in groupware environment to let people generate ideas and vote anonymously during requirements, prototyping and evaluation.

Object Model: Group decision support system environment.

Process Model: Discussion takes place through a groupware environment. Stages include: (1) Analysis of current situation in terms of problem and possible solutions. (2) Group requirements identification process, including identification of critical success factors, activities, processes, information requirements, data elements, and so on. (3) Prototype including user comments. (4) Piloting of the prototype. (5) Evaluation. (6) Rollout.

Participation Model: Process facilitator, developers, users, key players and "technical chauffeurs" (some of these may participate anonymously).

Results: (1) Prioritized list of critical success factors. (2) Information requirements with data elements and functions. (3) Prioritized list of modifications needed for each iteration.

Phases of the Lifecycle: Problem identification, requirements, evaluation.

Complementary Formal Methods: None known.

Group Sizes: 8–15.

References:

Coleman, D. (Ed.). (1994). *Proceedings of GroupWare '94 Europe.* San Mateo, CA, USA: Morgan Kauffman.

De Vreede, G. J., and Sol, H. G. (1994). Combating organized crime with groupware: Facilitating user involvement in information system development. In D. Coleman (Ed.), *Proceedings of GroupWare '94 Europe.* San Mateo, CA, USA: Morgan Kauffman.

11.10.3 Artifact Walkthrough

Abstract: Users utilize artifacts from their work environment to reconstruct and review a specific example of their work process.

Object Model: Artifacts from the users' environment, such as documents and tools. A large wall display (whiteboard, blackboard, brown paper) on which the facilitator can write.

Process Model: Participants, as a group, retell a narrative of a specific example of a work process. A model of that work process is constructed "on the wall" by the facilitator. "Focus areas," such as time to complete steps and information needed, are called out as the model is constructed. The constructed model is cleaned up by the facilitators, and reviewed using additional scenarios by the users. Qualifications and extensions are noted at the time.

Participation Model: End-users (any stakeholder in the work process being described), human factors worker as facilitator, human factors worker as recorder, developers, managers.

Results: A process or work flow diagram with descriptions of scenarios of work and conclusions about that work (e.g., usability goals, general design objectives, constraints).

Phases of the Lifecycle: Requirements, analysis, high-level design, detailed design (provides a basis for prototype construction and testing).

Complementary Formal Methods: Task analysis, use case analysis, cognitive walkthrough, Joint Application Design, prototype testing, usability engineering.

Group Sizes: 6–8.

References:

Wixon, D. R., Pietras, C., Huntwork, P., and Muzzey, D. (in press). Changing the rules: A pragmatic approach to product development. In D. Wixon and J. Ramey (Eds.), *Field methods casebook for software design.* NY: Wiley.

Wixon, D. R., and Raven, M. B. (1994, April). *Contextual inquiry: Grounding your design in user work.* Tutorial at CHI '94 conference, Boston.

11.10.4 Blueprint Mapping

Abstract: Onto a large map of the workplace (the blueprint), participants attach pictures of work sites, work tools, and workers. The acts of placing these representations serve as a series of triggers for participatory analysis.

Object Model: Large map of the workplace, attached to a display surface. Photographs or drawings of work sites, tools, and people. Post-it[4] notes as annotations or as surrogates for illustrations that were not prepared ahead of time.

Process Model: Ultimately, the plan is for workplace participants to place the small representations onto the large map, and to discuss the work that is done at each site on the large map (the "current situation") as they perform the placements. Subsequently, the same or different participants review the current situation by talking about how the work is performed at the illustrated sites on the map. In practice, it may be useful for the facilitators to do some initial placing of the small illustrations.

Participation Model: People from the workplace who

[4] Post-it is a trademark of 3M Corporation.

carry out the daily work activities.

Results: Map with illustrations placed at "correct" sites. Understandings of how each group perceives the work to be organized. Recognition of diverse viewpoints. Discussions of both ordinary, every-day work flows and exceptions.

Phases of the Lifecycle: Analysis.

Complementary Formal Methods: Requirements analysis. Tracking of persons or artifacts through a task flow.

Group Sizes: Small, but not specified.

References:

Klær, A., and Madsen, K. H. (1995). Participatory analysis of flexibility. *Communications of the ACM, 38*(5), 53–60.

11.10.5 BrainDraw

Abstract: Graphical round-robin brainstorming[5] for rapidly populating a space of interface designs.

Object Model: Paper and pens. These may be arranged in a series of drawing stations (e.g., easels placed in a circle), or they may be assigned to seated team members.

Process Model: Each participant draws an initial design at that participant's initial drawing station. At the end of a pre-stated time interval, each participant moves left to the next drawing station, and continues the design found there. At the end of a pre-stated time interval, each participant again moves left to the next drawing station and again continues the design found there. The process continues until the participants are satisfied that they have worked with one another's' ideas.

Alternatively, the participants may stay still, the designs rotating from participant to participant.

Participation Model: Users, designers, artists.

Results: Many candidate designs. Each design has received contributions from many or all of the team members. Thus, each design is potentially a fusion of the participants' ideas. However, each design has a different starting point, so the fusions are not necessarily identical.

Phases of the Lifecycle: Detailed design.

Complementary Formal Methods: None known.

Group Sizes: 2–8, perhaps more.

References:

Dray, S. M. (1992, October). Understanding and supporting successful group work in software design: Lessons from IDS [Position paper]. In J. Karat and J. Bennett, (Chairs), *Understanding and supporting successful group work in software design.* Workshop at CSCW '92 conference, Toronto.

See also the entry on *Group Elicitation Method.*

11.10.6 Buttons Project

Abstract: For the support of shared end-user customizations, a software system supports end-user design (and automatic implementation) of customized functions. Each design takes the form of a button. End-users may share their customizations by sending buttons to one another.

Object Model: Experimental software system.

Process Model: End-users use a template-based approach to specify functionality in buttons. End-users mail buttons to one another. Recipients of buttons may modify them further. A social intervention in workplace culture may be required before certain end-user constituencies are willing to take the initiative to perform customizations.

Participation Model: End-users, by themselves.

Results: New functionality, shared among end-users. A software record of the innovations, in the form of executable customizations.

Phases of the Lifecycle: End-user customization.

Complementary Formal Methods: None known.

---

[5]There are cultural differences in the ways in which brainstorming is conducted. In our experience, the largest cultural different occurs between academia and industry, at least in the US. In corporate cultures, and perhaps in Scandinavia in general, brainstorming is understood to be the free contribution of ideas, without any critique or evaluation (those come in subsequent activities). In US academia, brainstorming is often understood to include critique by other participants, and/or evaluation of the contributed ideas by the facilitator. All of our references to brainstorming in this paper are intended to follow the model of free contribution without fear of critique or evaluation, and with the assumptions that the group will commonly own *all* of the ideas from the brainstorming activity, and will conduct a critical evaluation of those ideas *as a group* during a subsequent activity.

Group Sizes: Typically one end-user works alone, then shares the resulting customizations with any number of other end-users.

References:

MacLean, A., Carter, K., Lovstrand, L., and Moran, T. (1990). User-tailorable systems: Pressing the issues with buttons. *Proceedings of CHI '90*, 175–182.

11.10.7 CARD (Collaborative Analysis of Requirements and Design)

Abstract: Participants use a deck of cards to lay out or critique task flows. The cards represent work components, including computer-based functionality, non-computer events and objects, cognitions, motivations, goals, and people.

Object Model: Cards representing work components, often arranged in a class hierarchy of components. A background sheet of paper onto which the cards can be attached, and onto which flow arrows, choice points, decision criteria, and so on, can be written.

Process Model: (1) Introductions that include each participant's expertise, contribution to the shared work, organization and constituency, and what that constituency is expecting from the participant (i.e., personal and organizational stakes). (2) Mutual education through "mini-tutorials," if needed. (3) Working together to explore the task domain (in the form of analysis, design, or assessment). (4) Brief walkthrough of the group's achievements during the session, preferably recorded on videotape.

Participation Model: End-users and one or more of the following: human factors workers, software professionals, marketers, technical writers, trainers, perhaps clients or customers of the end-users, other stakeholders in the system.

Results: Representations of task flows, recorded in sequences of cards, plus annotations and (optionally) task flow arrows, branch points, decision criteria, and so on, recorded on the background sheet.

Phases of the Lifecycle: Analysis, design, evaluation.

Complementary Formal Methods: Object-oriented analysis and modeling.

Group Sizes: Up to 8.

References:

Muller, M. J., and Carr, R. (1996). Using the CARD and PICTIVE participatory design methods for collaborative analysis. In D. Wixon and J. Ramey (Eds.), *Field methods casebook for software design.* NY: Wiley.

Muller, M.J., Tudor, L.G., Wildman, D.M., White, E.A., Root, R.W., Dayton, T., Carr, R., Diekmann, B., and Dykstra-Erickson, E.A. (1995). Bifocal tools for scenarios and representations in participatory activities with users. In J. Carroll (Ed.), *Scenario-based design for human-computer interaction.* New York: Wiley.

Tudor, L. G., Muller, M. J., Dayton, T., and Root, R. W. (1993). A participatory design technique for high-level task analysis, critique, and redesign: The CARD method. *Proceedings of the Human Factors and Ergonomics Society 37th Annual Meeting,* 295–299.

See also the entries on *CUTA*, *Layout Kit*, *Metaphors Game*, and *PictureCARD*.

11.10.8 CESD (Cooperative Experimental System Development)

Abstract: CESD provides a framework in which to conduct a participatory lifecycle (however, it does not provide a model as such).

Object Model: Prototypes and prototyping are the most salient attributes of the work. Other Scandinavian techniques, such as workshops and Mock-Ups , may also be used.

Process Model: CESD provides a process "in the large"—at the level of the software lifecycle. At this level of granularity, there are two major differences from conventional lifecycle approaches: End-users participate in most or all phases of the work, and implementation (or realization) activities begin much earlier in the lifecycle, and are much more open to end-user participation).

Participation Model: End-users, software professionals.

Results: Completed systems, deeply informed by end-user and union concerns and perspectives.

Phases of the Lifecycle: CESD is a lifecycle approach, with application to all phases of the software lifecycle.

Complementary Formal Methods: Other software lifecycle models.

Group Sizes: Variable by activity.

References:

Grønbæk, K., Kyng, M., and Mogensen, P. (1995). Cooperative experimental System development: Cooperative techniques beyond initial design and analysis. In *Conference proceedings of Computers in Context: Joining Forces in Design* (pp. 20–29). Århus, Denmark: Aarhus University.

See also:

Grønbæk, K., and Mogensen, P. (1994). Specific cooperative analysis and design in general hypermedia development. *PDC '94: Proceedings of the Participatory Design Conference*, 159–171.

See also the entries on *Mock-Ups* and *Prototyping*.

11.10.9 CISP (Cooperative Interactive Storyboard Prototyping)

Abstract: A small team of developer(s) and user(s) cooperatively generate and modify user interface designs, evaluate existing interfaces, and compare interface alternatives, sometimes using computerized tools.

Object Model: CISP software tool, or HyperCard[6].

Process Model: Iterations of the following steps: (1) Explore storyboard (the user does the task, the interface tool records the user's steps). (2) Evaluate storyboard (play back the storyboard's record of the user's activities, and discuss within the user-developer team). (3) Modify storyboard.

Participation Model: One or a few users and one or a few developers.

Results: Enhanced storyboard or prototype; recordings of users' interactions with the storyboard or prototype.

Phases of the Lifecycle: Detailed design, assessment/evaluation.

Complementary Formal Methods: Design, usability inspection.

Group Sizes: 2–4.

References:

Madsen, K. H., and Aiken, P. J. (1992). Cooperative Interactive Storyboard Prototyping: Designing friendlier VCRs. In S. J. Andriole (Ed.), *Rapid application prototyping: The storyboard approach to user requirements analysis* (2nd ed., pp. 261–233). Boston: QED.

Madsen, K. H., and Aiken, P. (1993). Experiences using cooperative interactive storyboard prototyping. *Communications of the ACM, 36*(6), 57–64.

See also the entry on *Storyboard Prototyping*.

11.10.10 Codevelopment

Abstract: End-users and software professionals form a long-term working relationship to share the responsibilities for specifying and implementing a custom software system for the end-users and their organization. End-users collaborate at nearly every phase of the project.

Object Model: General meeting facilitation materials. Mock-ups. Prototypes. A large Wall area that holds artifacts (mostly paper) of varying formality (from scribbled notes, drawing, and photographs to finished reports) arranged along the project's timeline.

Process Model: Complex. Some work is done at the end-users' work site. Some work is done at the software professionals' work site. Specific processes within work sessions are tailored to the needs of each session.

Participation Model: End-users and software professionals.

Results: Working system. Formal documents. Informal, graphical, contextualized record of the project and its rationale in the form of the Wall.

Phases of the Lifecycle: This is a model for a participatory lifecycle. It spans all phases of the lifecycle.

Complementary Formal Methods: Other software lifecycle models.

Group Sizes: Perhaps as many as 20.

References:

Anderson, W. L. (1994). The wall: An artifact of design, development, and history. *PDC '94: Proceedings of the Participatory Design Conference*, 117.

Anderson, W. L., and Crocca, W. T. (1993). Engineering practice and codevelopment of product prototypes. *Communications of the ACM, 36*(6), 49–56.

[6] HyperCard is a trademark of Apple Computer.

11.10.11 Collaborative Design Workshops

Abstract: Scenarios are combined with low-fidelity prototypes for a task-centered walkthrough.

Object Model: Low fidelity paper prototypes; videotaping equipment.

Process Model: Guided by a contextualized work scenario, two users discuss work practices, variations, and alternatives while manipulating the low-fidelity prototype. The users' work with the materials (but not their faces) plus additional group discussions are recorded on video.

Participation Model: "Key players" — for example, two users, a designer, and a domain expert; a developer, a documenter, and a requirements analyst may be included upon need.

Results: The evolving paper mock-up and informal notes, sometimes formalized as a "design memo" or an illustrated scenario.

Phases of the Lifecycle: Analysis and design.

Complementary Formal Methods: None known.

Group Sizes: Small — four people in the most representative case.

References:

Bloomer, S., Croft, R., and Wright, L. (in press). Collaborative design workshops: A case study. To appear in *interactions* magazine.

See also *Artifact Walkthrough*, *Hiser Method*, *PICTIVE*, *Pluralistic Walkthrough*, and *Scenarios*.

11.10.12 Conceptual Toolkit in CSCW Design

Abstract: The toolkit supports communication during design-by-doing, through the use of checklists and scenarios.

Object Model: Scenarios of work. Artifacts from work. Checklists to support analysis and communication.

Process Model: Participants discuss work situations described in scenarios, using role-specific checklists (e.g., a work-oriented checklist and a technical checklist) to support and extend communications across different perspectives. This process occurs within a broader participatory scheme, including workshops and prototyping.

Participation Model: End-users. Software professionals.

Results: Annotated scenarios that particularize problems to be solved.

Phases of the Lifecycle: Requirements, analysis, high-level design.

Complementary Formal Methods: Requirements analysis, task analysis.

Group Sizes: Small.

References:

Bødker, S., Christiansen, E., and Thüring, M. (1995). A conceptual toolbox for designing CSCW applications. In *COOP '95: Atelier international sur la conception des systèms coopératifs* [International workshop on the design of cooperative systems] (pp. 266–284). Sophia Antiipolis, France: INRIA.

See also the entries on *Prototyping* and *Scenarios.*

11.10.13 Contextual Design

Abstract: Contextual *design* uses contextual *inquiry* as its first step, to gather user data. Those data are analyzed in a teamwork approach by a team that appears to consist, for the most part, of members other than end-users, to produce a user interface design. Steps along the way focus on analyzing the work flow aspects of the user data.

Object Model: Room dedicated to the project, viewgraphs shown on its wall, and its walls and table covered with flip chart paper, diagrams, and Post-it notes; paper prototypes of the user interface.

Process Model: Users are interviewed with contextual inquiry, by the product designers, at the users' work sites. The resulting user data are utilized in the forms of the product designers' understanding and notes, to inform the designers and other relevant personnel (excluding users) as they go through several specific steps to analyze the user work flow and produce an appropriate user interface design. All these post-interview activities are done by the entire team, together, in the dedicated project room. Several teamwork methods are used, such as brainstorming and group memory in the form of paper notes on walls. The understandings may then be structured in a bottom-up process to put the information into conceptual groupings to form an affinity diagram.

Participation Model: Users, product designer, usability engineer, developer, system engineer, product manager. Users participate in the initial contextual inquiry step, but may be involved as co-designers only in the limited sense of responding to prototypes that the design team has created (Holtzblatt and Beyer, 1993).

Results: User interface design, prototyped in paper.

Phases of the Lifecycle: Requirements, analysis, high-level design.

Complementary Formal Methods: Writing of formal requirements documents to put the design into a format more suitable for system engineers, developers, and testers.

Group Sizes: Up to 10.

References:

Holtzblatt, K., and Beyer, H. (1993). Making customer-centered design work for teams. *Communications of the ACM, 36*(10), 93–103.

Whiteside, J., Bennett, J., and Holtzblatt, K. (1988). Usability engineering: Our experience and evolution. In M. Helander (Ed.), *Handbook of human-computer interaction* (pp. 791–817). New York: North-Holland.

Wixon, D., Holtzblatt, K., and Knox, S. (1990). Contextual design: An emergent view of system design. *Proceedings of CHI '90*, 329–336.

See also the entry on *Contextual Inquiry*.

11.10.14 Contextual Inquiry

Abstract: The ethnographically-based contextual inquiry gets data from users by having product designers observe and interview users in their workplace, as they do their work. This is used as the first step in the method called contextual *design*.

Object Model: Users use all the artifacts they normally use to do their work. Interviewers take private notes, though they may show and explain the notes to users. Video recordings of people at work may also be used.

Process Model: Interviewers observe users doing their real work in their real workplace. Interviewers have permission to interrupt users at any time to ask questions, and to converse about the work. Interviewers also ask users' opinions on the interviewers' design ideas, and may ask users for their ideas for improvements in their work and current interface. An affinity diagram may be used to organize the findings[7].

Participation Model: Users and interviewers, the latter preferably being the product's designers. "Designers" can be anyone on the cross-functional team, such as a usability engineer, developer, system engineer, or product manager.

Results: The product's designers get detailed understanding and notes of the users' work and needs, fully contextualized in the real work situation. The resulting user data can be input to a design process.

Phases of the Lifecycle: Problem identification, requirements, analysis, some high-level design.

Complementary Formal Methods: Preliminary survey to identify appropriate samples of users and work.

Group Sizes: Usually 2; perhaps as many as 4.

References:

Bennett, J., Holtzblatt, K., Jones, S., and Wixon, D. (1990, April). *Usability engineering: Using contextual inquiry*. Tutorial presented at CHI '90, Seattle, WA.

Holtzblatt, K., and Jones, S. (1993). Contextual inquiry: A participatory technique for system design. In D. Schuler and A. Namioka (Eds.), *Participatory design: Principles and practices* (pp. 177–210). Hillsdale, NJ, USA: Erlbaum.

Wixon, D. R., and Comstock, E. M. (1994). Evolution of usability at Digital Equipment Corporation. In M. E. Wiklund (Ed.), *Usability in practice: How companies develop user-friendly products* (pp. 147–193). Boston: AP Professional.

See also the entry on *Contextual Design*.

11.10.15 Cooperative Evaluation

Abstract: An evaluation team is formed of one end-user and one developer. Together, they explore a prototype and develop a critique.

Object Model: Software system or prototype, using the *York Manual* to guide the analysis.

Process Model: Elaborate—provided in the *York Manual*.

Participation Model: One end-user and one developer.

---

[7]Holtzblatt and Beyer (1993) excluded from the label "Contextual Inquiry" all activities after the actual field interview. However, Holtzblatt and Jones (1993) discussed affinity diagramming and related analysis as part of contextual inquiry.

Results: Critique of prototype or system.

Phases of the Lifecycle: Assessment.

Complementary Formal Methods: Usability testing, discount usability evaluations.

Group Sizes: 2.

References:

Wright, P., and Monk, A. (1991). A cost- effective evaluation method for use by designers. *International Journal of Man-Machine Studies, 35*(6), 891–912.

11.10.16 Cooperative Requirements Capture

Abstract: Informed by a broad analysis of who are the stakeholders (or interested parties) in a computer system design problem, software professionals enter a six-step process to determine the requirements for that design. Three steps involve direct work with users as active participants. Four other steps provide context within the software professionals' lifecycle.

Object Model: None. The work involves a series of workshops with users and other stakeholders.

Process Model: Six steps, really seven. (0) The pre-process step is an analysis of the stakeholders, in terms of four broad categories that are described below under "participation model." (1) Identify the business problem that needs to be solved; no direct user participation occurs in this step. (2) Formulate the team from among the four classes of stakeholders described in the "participation model," below (no direct user participation occurs in this step). (3) Explore the user environment through a User Workshop. (4) Validate understanding of user environment, *perhaps* through consultations with the users, but *perhaps* through market research or the team's confidence in what it already knows. (5) Identify scope of proposed system, including usability goals, through a User Workshop. (6) Validate scope with stakeholders via user participation in one of various venues (e.g., focus group, survey, interview, mock-up).

Participation Model: Four stakeholder groups are considered in the selection of representatives: (1) Software professionals who are responsible for design and implementation. (2) Business and marketing analysts with a financial concern for the design and system. (3) Managerial and support staff responsible for introduction and maintenance of the system. (4) Users, who should be drawn from three categories: primary (frequent users), secondary (occasional users), and tertiary (people affected by the system or its purchase, but who are not direct users of it).

Results: Paper documents, including a User Document after Step 3, "Explore the user environment," and an Initial Requirements Document after Step 5, "Identify scope of proposed system."

Phases of the Lifecycle: Requirements, analysis.

Complementary Formal Methods: This approach includes formal methods—or in any event, methods for software professionals only—*within* its six steps.

Group Sizes: 6–8.

References:

Macaulay, L. (1995). Cooperation in understanding user needs and requirements. *Computer Integrated Manufacturing Systems, 8*(2), 155–165.

11.10.17 Critics to Support End-User Customization

Abstract: A software system provides means for customization by end-users. Through specialized software entities called "critics," the system inspects the end-users' customizations for unusual properties, such as apparent violations of design rules. When a critic encounters an unusual customization, it queries the end-users who originated those changes, and records their rationale for later use by software professionals. Subsequent redesign of the system is guided in part by end-users' customizations and by their recorded rationales for those customizations. Critics may also be activated during software professionals' design and redesign activities.

Object Model: Experimental software system.

Process Model: Here is one version, which is more a scenario than a formal process model: (1) Requirements are established through an unspecified participatory process. (2) Software professionals create initial user interface design. (3) Software critics inspect the initial design according to standard design heuristics, noting apparent violations of those heuristics. Software professionals may record their rationales for their design decisions, or may modify their designs. (4) End-users engage in an unspecified collaborative activity to select system attributes for customization, and use customization capabilities that are part of the system to accomplish these customizations. Software critics inspect the end-users' customizations according to standard design heuristics, noting apparent violations of those heuristics. End-users may record their rationales for their customization decisions, or may modify their customizations. (5) During the next iteration of the lifecycle, software professionals consult the end-users' customizations and their recorded rationales as part of their redesign activities.

Participation Model: During development: End-users and software professionals. During usage: End-users. During redesign: Software professionals and end-users.

Results: End-user-initiated customizations to the working system. Recorded rationales for all unusual customizations and design features.

Phases of the Lifecycle: Design. Customization in the field. Redesign.

Complementary Formal Methods: None known.

Group Sizes: Unspecified.

References:

Malinowski, U., and Nakakoji, K. (1995). Using computational critics to facilitate long-term collaboration in user interface design. *Proceedings of CHI '95,* 385–392.

11.10.18 CUTA (Collaborative Users' Task Analysis)

Abstract: CUTA is a variation on the CARD method. Participants use cards to lay out a task analysis. The cards consist largely of photographs of actual members of the workplace conducting work tasks, plus photographs of objects and items in the workplace, plus more abstract "wild card" drawings that represent less specific instances of work. Each card also contains a task analysis data template.

Object Model: Cards. Each card contains a photograph of an actual worker (who is known to the participants) or a workplace object or item (which is familiar to the participants). More abstract cards may contain drawings of categories of events, such as temporal events, meetings, and a person thinking. Each card contains a template that requests the number of this card's component in the task sequence, the duration of the activity represented by this card, and the frequency with which the action is done (e.g., "once per participant").

Process Model: Participants lay out the cards, filling in the required template information. Repeating sequences or other non-linear flows may be color coded.

Participation Model: End-users and software professionals.

Results: Cards as documentation of task flows. Estimates of task durations and frequencies of task occurrences.

Phases of the Lifecycle: Analysis.

Complementary Formal Methods: More formal task analyses.

Group Sizes: Up to 6.
References:

Lafreniere, D. (1995). CUTA: A simple, practical, and low-cost approach to task analysis. To appear in *interactions*.

See also the entries on *CARD, Layout Kit, metaphors Game,* and *PictureCARD.*

11.10.19 Diaries

Abstract: Diaries are maintained by the design group as a record and point of access for users and others who wish to understand the design rationale.

Object Model: Various system documents and system versions. On-line diaries.

Process Model: Informal notes are kept of design decisions. They are made accessible in an on-line system.

Participation Model: Designers and users.

Results: Improved understanding. Decisions recorded in diaries.

Phases of the Lifecycle: Potentially, throughout design and implementation.

Complementary Formal Methods: Other design rationale techniques.

Group Sizes: Unclear.

References:

Braa, K. (1992). Influencing system quality by using decision diaries in prototyping projects. *PDC '92: Proceedings of the Participatory Design Conference,* 163–170.

Kautz, K. (1992). Communications support for participatory design projects. *PDC '92: Proceedings of the Participatory Design Conference,* 155–162.

11.10.20 ETHICS (Effective Technical and Human Implementation of Computer-based Systems)

Abstract: Participatory systems development method that balances social and technical aspects to ensure an optimized system. This is a participatory lifecycle approach.

Object Model: Paper, flip charts, pens.

Process Model: (1) Describe current work situation. (2) Clarify business mission. (3) Identify problems in present work organization that are reducing the efficiency. (4) Set human objectives for new system (e.g., job satisfaction and quality of working life). (5) Set business objectives for new system (e.g., efficiency). (6) Consider changes that are likely occur and that the system will have to accommodate. (7) Consider alternatives for the system in terms of social system (e.g., job design and work organization) and technical/administrative system (e.g., hardware, software, work procedures, information flow). (8) Set objectives for the new system by matching objectives for human and business, and considering alternatives, problem areas, and likely changes. (9) Redesign organizational structure. (10) Choose technical system. (11) Prototype organizational and technical systems. (12) Change job design to match new system. Each job should represent an enhancement of the previous work and take account of the challenge, responsibility, autonomy, and so on. (13) Implement the system in the workplace. (14) Evaluate the system in terms of the human and technical/business sides. For the human side, job satisfaction of the users should be compared to the level before the new system was introduced, in terms of the knowledge, psychological, efficiency, task structure, and ethical fit. For the business side, the number of problems that have been controlled or eliminated should be identified.

Participation Model: Facilitator; representatives from user group, development, and management.

Results: (1) New or modified computer system. (2) Modified work organization that fits computer system. (3) List of changes that are likely to occur during life of system, and which can be accommodated by the new or modified system. (4) List of variances to be used to help increase efficiency and minimize problems. (5) Questionnaire to assess job satisfaction before and after introduction of system.

Phases of the Lifecycle: Entire lifecycle: requirements, analysis, high-level design, and evaluation.

Complementary Formal Methods: Prototyping. More broadly, other software lifecycle models.

Group Sizes: Up to 40.

References:

Mumford, E. (1983). *Designing human systems for new technology: The ETHICS method.* Manchester, UK: Manchester Business School.

Mumford, E. (1991). Participation in systems design—What can it offer? In B. Shackel and S. J. Richardson (Eds.), *Human factors for informatics usability* (pp. 267–290). Cambridge: Cambridge U. Press.

Mumford, E. (1993). The participation of users in systems design: An account of the origin, evolution, and use of the ETHICS method. In D. Schuler and A. Namioka (Eds.), *Participatory design: Principles and practices* (pp. 257–270). Hillsdale, NJ, USA: Erlbaum.

Mumford, E. and Weir, M. (1979): *Computer systems in work design—The ETHICS method: Effective technical and human implementation of computer systems.* New York: Wiley.

11.10.21 Ethnographic Practices

Abstract: We include ethnographic practices in this chapter on a very tentative basis. Ethnographic practices have been highly influential in participatory design. However, many practitioners have stated quite clearly that these are not simple techniques that can be picked up and used by anyone. Rather, ethnography requires extensive training in both specific practices, and more importantly, in the perspectives and disciplines that underlie those practices. In this sense, the word fragment "methodology" in "ethnomethodology" should be understood as being *different in kind* from more conventional engineering methods[8]. Thus, this item in the taxonomy is intended as an access point, to help potential practitioners find descriptions of ethnographic work in participatory design, and to help them begin to appreciate the complex requirements of this type of work.

---

[8]In general, participatory "methods" are different from engineering "methods" along a number of dimensions. Ethnomethodology is perhaps the furthest of all participatory practices from an engineering "method."

Object Model: The users' workplace. Representations of the end-users' work, including (but not limited to) video recordings, where possible, of the end-users' work.

Process Model: A variety of ethnographic practices that are difficult to summarize in the telegraphic style required for our chapter.

Participation Model: End-users. Ethnographers. Possibly software professionals, facilitated by ethnographers.

Results: A detailed description of the end-users' work.

Phases of the Lifecycle: Requirements, analysis.

Complementary Formal Methods: Requirements, analysis.

Group Sizes: Generally small. Varies by ethnographer.

References:

Blomberg, J., Giacomi, J., Mosher, A., and Swenton-Wall, P. (1993). Ethnographic field methods and their relation to design. In D. Schuler and A. Namioka (Eds.), *Participatory design: Principles and practices.* Hillsdale, NJ, USA: Erlbaum.

Nardi, B. (1995). Some reflections on scenarios. In J. Carroll (Ed.), *Scenario-based design: Envisioning work and technology in system development.* New York: Wiley.

Rose, A., Shneiderman, B., and Plaisant, C. (1995). An applied ethnographic method for redesigning user interfaces. In *Proceedings of DIS '95* (pp. 115–122). New York: ACM.

See also:

Blomberg, J., Suchman, L., and Trigg, R. (1994). Reflections on a work-oriented design project. *PDC '94: Proceedings of the Participatory Design Conference,* 99–109.

Blomberg, J., Suchman, L., and Trigg, R. (1995). Back to work: Renewing old agendas for cooperative design. In *Conference proceedings of Computers in Context: Joining Forces in Design* (pp. 1–9). Århus, Denmark: Aarhus University.

Hughes, J., King, V., Rodden, T., and Anderson, H. (1995). The role of ethnography in interactive systems design. *interactions, 2*(2), 56–65.

Hughes, J., Randall, D., and Shapiro, D. (1992). Faltering from ethnography to design. *Proceedings of CSCW '92,* 115–122.

McClard, A. P. (1995). Borderlands: Ethnography in the technical industries. *Proceedings of the American Anthropological Association 1995 Annual Meeting.*

Orr, J. and Crowfoot, N. C. (1992). Design by anecdote—The use of ethnography to guide the application of technology to practice. *PDC '92: Proceedings of the Participatory Design Conference,* 31–37.

Suchman, L. (Ed.). (1995). Representations of work [Special issue]. *Communications of the ACM, 38*(9).

Suchman, L., and Trigg, R. (1991). Understanding practice: Video as a medium for reflection and design. In J. Greenbaum and M. Kyng (Eds.), *Design at work: Cooperative design of computer systems.* Hillsdale, NJ, USA: Erlbaum.

Wall, P., and Mosher, A. (1994). Representations of work: Bringing designers and users together. *PDC '94: Proceedings of the Participatory Design Conference,* 87–98.

See also chapter 15 of this handbook.

11.10.22 FIRE (Functional Integration through Redesign)

Abstract: Organizational principles and techniques for continuous redesign of computer-based systems that are conceived to be integrated with work and other technologies.

Object Model: None.

Process Model: System versions are redesigned in a planned and organized way, including user participation at specified points in the process.

Participation Model: All users at all levels (including management) and all development staff.

Results: Redesign decisions and suggestions.

Phases of the Lifecycle: Problem identification, requirements, analysis, high-level design, redesign.

Complementary Formal Methods: SSM. Object-oriented analysis and design.

Group Sizes: About 20.

References: A series of reports has been issued by the FIRE project. Contact FIRE, Department of Informatics, University of Oslo, P.O. Box 1080 Blindern, N-0316 Oslo, Norway, +47 2 85 24 10 (voice), +47 2 85

24 01 (fax), fire@ifi.uio.no.

11.10.23 Florence Project

Abstract: This project concentrated on communication with the users during the development process to find out what sort of computer system, if any, the users need.

Object Model: Paper and pens to record observations; materials for electronic prototyping.

Process Model: (1) Observe users in their place of work to gain understanding of current work procedures. (2) Develop prototypes to try out ideas and clear up misconceptions.

Participation Model: Users and computer scientists.

Results: (1) Mutual learning: Computer scientists learn about the work of the users; users learn about computers in relation to their work. (2) Envisionment of the computer system, if any, that is needed.

Phases of the Lifecycle: Problem identification, requirements, high-level design.

Complementary Formal Methods: None known.

Group Sizes: Not specified.

References:

Bjerknes, G. and Bratteteig, T. (1987): Florence in Wonderland: System development with nurses. In G. Bjerknes, P. Ehn, and M. Kyng (Eds.), *Computers and democracy: A Scandinavian challenge* (pp. 279–295). Brookfield, VT, USA: Gower.

11.10.24 Forum Theatre

Abstract: A troupe of actors (stakeholders) acts out a scenario with an undesirable outcome, as an informal theatrical production. The audience (other stakeholders) has the opportunity to change the script, after which the actors again act out the scenario. This entire process iterates until the outcome is more desirable.

Object Model: None. Forum theatre has its roots in street and guerrilla theatre. There are few props, and the script is rather conceptual.

Process Model: A group of active designers develops a description of a situation that, in their view, ought to be changed. They develop their description into a scenario. They perform this scenario for other stakeholders, and ask those stakeholders to find ways of modifying the events in the scenario so that the outcome is improved. The process is very spontaneous.

Participation Model: End-users and other stakeholders (loosely defined).

Results: Improved understanding. A sense of drama.

Phases of the Lifecycle: Problem identification and clarification, analysis, assessment.

Complementary Formal Methods: None known.

Group Sizes: Large.

References:

In the political domain:

Boal, A. (1992). *Games for actors and non-actors* (A. Jackson, Trans.). London: Routledge.

In the software domain, forum theatre was informally presented at an IRIS (Information systems Research symposium In Scandinavia) conference by Finn Kensing and Kim Halskov Madsen. Forum theatre was listed as a participatory practice in:

Kensing, F., and Munk-Madsen, A. (1993). PD: Structure in the toolbox. *Communications of the ACM, 36*(6), 78–85.

11.10.25 Future Workshop

Abstract: A three-part workshop addresses a critique of the present situation, a fantasy of an improved future situation, and the question of how to move from the critiqued situation to the fantasy situation.

Object Model: None. Some common meeting supports are useful (e.g., blackboards or whiteboards, Post-it notes).

Process Model:

- *Critique Phase:* Participants engage in structured brain-storming focused on the current work problems. Problems may be recorded on a wall-chart or other medium that is accessible to all participants. Participants then break into small groups. Each group works with a subset of the problem statements to develop a concise critique of a subset of issues in the current work situation. Specific facilitation techniques that may be useful in this phase include exploration of metaphors about the current work situation, and strict limits on the time for each comment by any participant.
- *Fantasy Phase:* Participants envision a future work

situation that is better than the present. Specific facilitation techniques that may be useful in this phase include inversion of the Critique Phase's negative statements into positive statements, drawing pictures of the envisioned future, multivoting[9] to select the most desirable future attributes, and (as in the Critique Phase) metaphors and strict limits on the time for each comment.

- *Implementation Phase:* Each small group presents a report on their envisioned future. The workshop conducts a plenary discussion to evaluate whether the envisioned future can be achieved under current circumstances. If not, what changes need to be made? How can those changes be planned?

Participation Model: End-users and other stakeholders, generally not software professionals. One or more facilitators.

Results: An implementation plan, including specific action items to be completed by specific persons.

Phases of the Lifecycle: Problem identification and clarification. Requirements. Perhaps other phases.

Complementary Formal Methods: None known.

Group Sizes: Medium to large.

References:

In German municipal planning, and for a detailed procedural account:

Jungk, R., and Mullert, N. (1987). *Future workshops: How to create a desirable future*. London: Institute of Social Invention.

In software design:

Kensing, F., and Madsen, K. H. (1991). Generating visions: Future workshops and metaphorical design. In J. Greenbaum and M. Kyng (Eds.), *Design at work: Cooperative design of computer systems* (pp. 155–168). Hillsdale, NJ, USA: Erlbaum.

See also:

Greenbaum, J., and Madsen, K. H. (1993). Small changes: Starting a participatory design process by giving participants a voice. In D. Schuler and A. Namioka (Eds.), *Participatory design: Principles and practices* (pp. 289–298). Hillsdale, NJ, USA: Erlbaum.

11.10.26 Graphical Facilitation

Abstract: A facilitator aids a group in clarifying its analysis or design (or other shared purpose) by reflecting the group's words and ideas back to the group in the form of quickly-drawn graphical images.

Object Model: Flip charts, blackboards, whiteboards, colored markers, chalk.

Process Model: Facilitator listens, sketches, queries the group for clarification.

Participation Model: One or two facilitators work with a group of project stakeholders.

Results: Graphical images are the only physical artifact that is produced. The major "product" is the enhancement of shared understanding among the stakeholders, and their movement toward a shared purpose.

Phases of the Lifecycle: (1) Problem identification. (2) Requirements, analysis, high-level design.

Complementary Formal Methods: None known.

Group Sizes: Up to 40.

References:

Crane, D. (1990). *Graphic recording in systems design*. Workshop at PDC '90: Conference on Participatory Design, Seattle, WA, USA.

Sibbet, D., Drexler, A., et al. (1993). *Graphic guide to team performance: Principles/Practices*. San Francisco: Grove Consultants International.

11.10.27 Group Elicitation Method

Abstract: A six phase workshop provides decision support to a method for sharing ideas in a brainstorming format.

Object Model: Nothing specific.

Process Model: (1) Issue statement and formulation: State the problem clearly and recruit relevant domain experts (see Participation Model, below). (2) Viewpoints generation (round-robin brainstorming, or "brainwriting"): Participants write ideas on a sheet of paper, and then pass the sheet to the next participant. Upon receiving another participant's ideas, each participant may then agree, disagree, or state a new viewpoint. This phase continues until all participants have

9 In multivoting, each participant has a number of votes that can be cast in any arrangement—that is, each vote on a different item, or all votes on a single item, or any other assignment. The group casts their votes on a number of topics are typically candidates for future, more focused work. The topics with the most votes are selected.

seen all other participants' ideas once. (3) Reformulation into more elaborated concepts: The group reduces the large list of ideas to a smaller number of more central concepts. (4) Generation of relationships among the concepts: Each participant completes a cross-product table, stating that participant's perception of the relative importances (greater, equal, lesser) among all pairs of concepts. (5) A "consensus" is calculated from the relative importance pair ratings. (6) Critical analysis of the results: The group considers the calculated results, and modifies them as necessary.

Participation Model: End-users and perhaps designers. A facilitator.

Results: Lists of ideas. Lists of concepts (refinements and combinations of ideas). Importance ranking of concepts. Critical analysis of importance ranking.

Phases of the Lifecycle: Problem identification and clarification. Requirements.

Complementary Formal Methods: None known.

Group Sizes: Up to 7.

References:

Boy, G. A. (in press). The group elicitation method for participatory design and usability testing. To appear in *interactions*.

See also:

Boy, G. A. (1991). *Intelligent assistant system.* London: Academic Press.

Warfield, J. N. (1971). *Societal systems: Planning, policy, and complexity.* New York: Wiley.

See also the entry on *BrainDraw*.

11.10.28 Hiser Design Method

Abstract: User interface design method that incorporates aspects of HCI to develop usable systems within real-world constraints.

Object Model: Papers and pens, normal office materials for paper prototyping and videotaping materials. Materials for electronic prototypes may also be used.

Process Model: Iterations of: (1) Analysis, which takes place through contextual field studies and informal evaluation of current systems. (2) Design, which takes place through collaborative design sessions, paper prototyping sessions, and electronic prototyping. (3) Evaluation, which is done through collaborative design and testing, heuristic evaluation, and usability testing.

Participation Model: Interface designer, analyst or user representative, and two or more users from different groups.

Results: (1) User profile document that gives information about the users, their activities, and their work environment. (2) Scenarios to envision system usage. (3) Design document. (4) Prototypes of system. (5) Style guide or user interface specification. (6) Usability goals and test findings.

Phases of the Lifecycle: User requirements, user interface design.

Complementary Formal Methods: None known.

Group Sizes: 3–4.

References:

Bloomer, S. (1993): Real projects don't need user interface designers: Overcoming the barriers to HCI in the real world. *Proceedings of OZCHI '93*, 94–108.

See also *Collaborative Design Workshop*, *Contextual Inquiry*, *PICTIVE*, and *Scenarios*.

11.10.29 HOOTD (Hierarchical Object-Oriented Task Decomposition)

Abstract: Participants decompose a task description into the information objects acted upon and the actions taken on them, and assign groups of those objects to interface windows.

Object Model: Index cards.

Process Model: All participants, in parallel, write each task (noun and verb) on its own index card. Duplicate cards are discarded. Then all the participants work as a group to sort the cards into piles, using whatever criteria the participants think appropriate. That clustering scheme is recorded, the participants re-sort the cards according to any other criteria, and finally choose one of the sorting schemes as the best. Each pile in that scheme becomes one task domain, with one of the eventual graphical user interface windows serving that task domain by containing all the objects and actions in that pile of task cards.

Participation Model: Users, usability engineer, system engineer, developer, subject matter experts in the relevant business processes and information systems, developers of documentation and training, managers of all these people.

Results: Definitions of all the user interface windows and the information objects contained in them.
Phases of the Lifecycle: Analysis, high-level design.

Complementary Formal Methods: Task analysis and design to ensure participants are aware of all the relevant tasks.

Group Sizes: Up to 8.

References: Contact Robert W. Root, Bellcore, RRC 1B-127, 444 Hoes Lane, Piscataway, NJ 08854, USA, +1-908-699-7763, broot@ctt.bellcore.com.

11.10.30 Icon Design Game

Abstract: One participant (the sketcher) draws informal icons while other participants attempt to guess at the concept that the sketcher is trying to express. The drawings become *first drafts* (not finished artwork) for the development of icons. The game can be played co-operatively (with a single team) or competitively (with multiple teams).

Object Model: Sketching surface, pens.

Process Model: (1) The sketcher selects a concept to attempt to communicate to the team. (2) The sketcher draws pictures of the concept. (3) The team attempts to guess the concept that the sketcher is trying to express. (4) Optionally, an observer takes notes on drawings that appeared to be particularly effective or particularly confusing. (5) The best drawings are delivered to a graphic artist or other professional for further development into polished, professionally designed icons.

Participation Model: End-users and one or more of the following: human factors workers, software professionals, marketers, technical writers, trainers, perhaps clients or customers of the end-users, other stakeholders in the system.

Results: Rough sketches of icons, for further development.

Phases of the Lifecycle: Detailed design.

Complementary Formal Methods: None known.

Group Sizes: Up to 20 people per team, though smaller teams probably work better.

References:

Muller, M. J., Wildman, D. M., and White, E. A. (1994, April). *Participatory design through games and other group exercises.* Tutorial at CHI '94 conference, Boston.

11.10.31 Interface Theatre

Abstract: Interface Theatre is an experimental practice to support a design walkthrough and critique by a very large group of end-users and other stakeholders. Working on a stage with human-scale theatrical props, the design team acts out the appearance and dynamics of the user interface and its system. Actors are guided by "object-oriented scripts" that describes the functionality of interface components. The audience of end-users and other stakeholders critiques the appearance and actions, transforming the design. The troupe of actors re-enacts the interface until they and the audience are satisfied.

Object Model: A stage. "Costumes" for the actors, in the form of human-scale interface objects (e.g., a 0.7 1 m cardboard dialog box). Object-oriented scripts, which specify the behavior of each interface object (as portrayed by an actor) in terms of the messages that might be sent to that role, the methods that the character (interface component) may execute in response to the messages, and any visible side-effects. "Behind the scenes" representations of system components without a direct representation in the user interface (e.g., buffers, databases, communication ports).

Process Model: (0) Prior to the theatre, the design team develops the theatrical props, such as dialog boxes, cursor images, and other interface components. The design team also develops object-oriented scripts. They may, as well, write a scenario to begin the drama. (1) Guided by three process characters (the audience agent, the critic, and the spirit—see steps 2–5), the characters (portrayed by members of the design team) introduce themselves to the audience of end-users and other stakeholders. (2) The audience agent works with the audience (a communal "user") to tell the cursor character and perhaps the keyboard character how to input to the system. Following their scripts, the cursor and keyboard characters send messages to other roles. (3) The other roles respond with methods and their own messages. (4) The critic works with the audience to critique the design. (5) The spirit attempts to highlight design and work questions, and to keep track of everyone's needs. (6) The play is re-enacted, with changes, until everyone is satisfied.

Participation Model: Actors (design team) and audience (end-users and other stakeholders). Perhaps the process characters (audience agent, critic, and spirit) should be external facilitators.

Results: Modified interface-component theatrical props. Modified object-oriented scripts. Improved understanding of developers' visions and users' visions.
Phases of the Lifecycle: Assessment.

Complementary Formal Methods: Object-oriented design, object-oriented programming.

Group Sizes: Very large.

References:

Muller, M. J., Wildman, D. M., and White, E. A. (1994, April). *Participatory design through games and other group exercises.* Tutorial at CHI '94 conference, Boston.

11.10.32 JAD (Joint Application Design, or Joint Application Development)

Abstract: Selected user representatives are involved with many other people in highly structured, disciplined sessions. A neutral, skilled leader/facilitator is important, even more than users. The goal usually is not political or philosophical, but is to speed the design of, and improve the quality of, information systems. Users at the meeting need not be representative of the user population, because they are invited for their expertise. There is no single JAD method, but a family of methods descended partly from work by Chuck Morris and Tony Crawford of IBM in 1977. Other names for members of this family of methods are Joint Application Requirements, Joint Requirements Planning Interactive JAD, Interactive Design, Group Design, Accelerated Design, Team Analysis, Facilitated Team Techniques, and Rapid Application Development (RAD).

Object Model: Flip chart paper on walls, overhead projector transparencies, magnet board, flow charts, text, and sometimes CASE tools.

Process Model: The leader/facilitator enforces a strict agenda and time limit, controls who speaks publicly and who writes on the public surfaces, and often has the sole writing privilege. Public memory is the writing on walls, or a wall projection of CASE tool displays being produced by the scribe or leader/facilitator. There are several kinds of activities, including brainstorming and issue resolution.

Participation Model: A neutral leader/facilitator who is trained specifically in JAD, and who often is considered to be the key to the entire process, even more so than the users; "users," who can be either real end-users or their managers; sometimes the executives who have the power to define the entire project and its resources; scribe; the information system project's staff: analysts, project managers, database personnel, and technical experts.

Results: An information system design.

Phases of the Lifecycle: Requirements, analysis, high-level design, perhaps detailed design.

Complementary Formal Methods: This *is* a rather formal method, because of the strict and strictly enforced agenda, and the required formal and standardized training of the leader/facilitator.

Group Sizes: Commonly 14, though many other sizes are possible.

Reference:

Carmel, E., Whitaker, R. D., and George, J. F. (1993). PD and Joint Application Design: A transatlantic comparison. *Communications of the ACM, 36*(6), 40–48.

11.10.33 KOMPASS

Abstract: Participatory method for function allocation, job design, and socio-technical design for the complementary development and evaluation of design options for highly automated work systems.

Object Model: No special materials.

Process Model: Series of six steps: (1) Define system objectives and requirements through discussions with users. (2) List the functions the work system is to perform. (3) Flag functions according to decision requirements, type of activity, process transparency, and automation potential. (4) Decide on allocation based on function characteristics: human only, machine only, or joint human and machine. (5) Develop allocation options for functions done jointly by humans and machines. (6) Evaluate options based on three different levels: human-machine system, individual work tasks, and work systems.

Participation Model: Current operators, future operators, managers, system designers.

Results: Development options for system.

Phases of the Lifecycle: Analysis, high-level design.

Complementary Formal Methods: None known.

Group Sizes: Unspecified.

References:

Grote, G. (1994). A participatory approach to the complementary design of highly automated work systems. In G. Bradley and H. W. Hendrick (Eds.), *Human factors in organizational design and management—IV*. Amsterdam: Elsevier.

11.10.34 Layout, Organization, and Specification Games

Abstract: Games in which users get the chance to see operations from other points of view, to determine desired changes in layout and organization.

Object Model: (1) Layout Game: Large sheet of paper with layout of building, wood cards with different tools and accessories. (2) Organization Game: Set of situation cards describing market opportunities, new technological possibilities, and economic or political changes. (3) Specification Game: Large piece of paper, pens.

Process Model: Series of three games: (1) **Layout Game:** Users place the cards with the tools and accessories in the rooms in the building. This allows for an understanding of the present state. The finished layout can then be used to identify problems and design new alternatives for individual workplaces and the overall business layout. (2) **Organization Game:** Users take turns choosing situation cards and reacting as managers. Users take one of three roles: the tycoon, the stingy manager, and the enlightened owner. After the game, the outcome is discussed, focusing on the relationship between quality, business ideas, and the design of technology and work. (3) **Specification Game:** Results from the Layout and Organization Games are structured and refined. Users discuss aspects of the product, technology, organization, and work that have been made in the past. Through discussion about quality, users develop their own demands in these areas.

Participation Model: Users and software professionals.

Results: (1) Layout of business with proposed changes. (2) Proposed changes in the product, technology, organization, and work, to help increase quality. (3) Increased understanding about work of users, managers, and software professionals.

Phases of the Lifecycle: Problem identification, requirements, analysis.

Complementary Formal Methods: Mock-ups, prototyping.

Group Sizes: 2–8.

References:

Ehn, P., and Sjögren, D. (1991). From system descriptions to scripts for action. In J. Greenbaum and M. Kyng (Eds.), *Design at work: Cooperative design of computer systems* (pp. 241–268). Hillsdale, NJ, USA: Erlbaum.

Klær, A., and Madsen, K. H. (1995). Participatory analysis of flexibility. *Communications of the ACM, 38*(5), 53–60.

See also the entries on *CARD*, *CUTA*, *Metaphors Game,* and *PictureCARD*.

11.10.35 Lunchbox Project

Abstract: The lunchbox project used drawings and collages to understand children's ideas about what they would like their lunchboxes to look like. Similar exercises were used, on a tutorial basis, to design bedside alarm clocks.

Object Model: (1) Drawing materials. (2) Collage images drawn from graphical images in magazines and suchlike are color-photocopied and treated with a temporary (removable) adhesive.

Process Model: (1) Draw the design that you would like. (2) Assemble and arrange images that suggest the desirable attributes of the design (i.e., attributes and connotations, rather than specific features and interface objects).

Participation Model: End-users or consumers, facilitators.

Results: Graphical drawings and images that are suggestive (rather than definitive) of what the design should be.

Phases of the Lifecycle: Requirements.

Complementary Formal Methods: None known.

Group Sizes: Perhaps as many as 20.

References:

Nutter, E. N., and Sanders, E. B. N. (1994). Participatory development of a consumer product. *PDC '94: Proceedings of the Participatory Design Conference,* 125–126.

Sanders, E. B. N. (1992). Participatory design research in the product development process. *PDC '92: Proceedings of the Participatory Design Conference,* 111–112.

Sanders, E. B.-N., and Nutter, E. H. (1994). Velcro[10]-modeling and projective expression: Participatory design methods for product development. *PDC '94: Proceedings of the Participatory Design Conference,* 143.

11.10.36 Metaphors Game

Abstract: This game helps to develop a systematic metaphorical model for a complex system domain, with the goal of providing a potential mental model to make it easier for end-users to understand the system. A team explores one or more metaphor domains and attempts to match their attributes to the current design problem, using a card game and a board game to structure their work.

Object Model:

- *Card Games:* Formatted template cards. Each card indicates the metaphoric domain (or system domain), at least one attribute of that domain, and some notes on how the attribute relates to other attributes.
- *Board Game:* The playing boards are spaces in which to organize and interrelate the cards from the preceding card games.

Process Model: (1) The team explores one or more metaphorical domains, writing down the attributes of each domain on cards, one card per attribute. (2) The team explores the system or work domain, writing down its attributes on cards, one card per attribute. (3) The team explores potential matches of metaphorical attributes with the system's attributes, aligning the card on a board.

Participation Model: End-users and one or more of the following: human factors workers, software professionals, marketers, technical writers, trainers, perhaps clients or customers of the end-users, other stakeholders in the system.

[10] Velcro is a registered trademark of Velcro USA, Inc.

Results: Informal understanding of the extent of match of several metaphorical domains onto the system domain. Materials (cards aligned on boards) that can easily be transcribed into a table that pairs metaphorical attributes with system attributes.

Phases of the Lifecycle: Analysis. High-level design.

Complementary Formal Methods: Requirements analysis. Development of "mental models."

Group Sizes: Up to 8.

References:

Muller, M.J., Wildman, D.M., and White, E.A. (1994, April). *Participatory design through games and other group exercises.* Tutorial at CHI '94 conference, Boston.

See also the entries on *CARD*, *CUTA*, *Layout Kit,* and *PictureCARD.*

11.10.37 Mock-Ups

Abstract: Computer technology is symbolized, and perhaps simulated, using coarse-granularity mock-ups (e.g., cardboard boxes for workstations and printers) or fine-granularity mock-ups (e.g., detailed screen images on cardboard boxes, with smaller boxes simulating mice). Developers and users walk through contextualized work scenarios, referring to the mock-up technologies as appropriate, to explore the potential changes of new computer technologies.

Object Model: Plywood, paper, overhead projectors, slide projectors, boxes, pencils, and so on, to simulate tools used in work. Most importantly, the users' workplace.

Process Model: Iterative process: (1) Develop models of potential solutions, which can be used in simulations. These should start out very simple and get more realistic with successive iterations. In later iterations electronic prototypes may also be used. (2) Simulate work with the solution. Allow the user to do the work that is to be supported, step-by-step with the model. This helps illustrate what information is needed. At the same time the systems designer should point out possibilities and limitations of the proposed solution. (3) Change the model based on information gained through the simulation.

Participation Model: End-users, developers, designers, perhaps facilitators.

Results: (1) Models of possible systems to support the

work. (2) Mutual learning.

Phases of the Lifecycle: Problem identification and clarification, requirements, analysis, high-level design, implementation, assessment, redesign.

Complementary Formal Methods: Prototyping.

Group Sizes: 2–40.

References:

Bjerknes, G., and Bratteteig, T. (1987) Florence in Wonderland: System development with nurses. In G. Bjerknes, P. Ehn, and M. Kyng (Eds.), *Computers and democracy: A Scandinavian challenge* (pp. 279–295). Brookfield, VT, USA: Gower.

Bødker, S., Ehn, P., Kyng, M., Kammersgaard, J., and Sundblad, Y. (1987): A UTOPIAN Experience: On design of powerful computer-based tools for skilled graphic workers. In G. Bjerknes, P. Ehn, and M. Kyng (Eds.), *Computers and democracy: A Scandinavian challenge* (pp. 251–278). Brookfield, VT, USA: Gower.

Ehn, P. (1988). *Work-oriented design of computer artifacts*. Falkoping, Sweden: Arbetslivcentrum/Almqvist and Wiksell International (2nd ed.: Hillsdale, NJ, USA: Erlbaum).

Ehn, P., and Kyng, M. (1991). Cardboard computers: Mocking-it-up or hands-on the future. In J. Greenbaum and M. Kyng (Eds.), *Design at work: Cooperative design of computer systems* (pp. 169–196). Hillsdale, NJ, USA: Erlbaum.

11.10.38 ORDIT (Organizational Requirements Definition for IT systems)

Abstract: Process and tools to support communication between problem owners and developers, to generate and evaluate alternative socio-technical options for the future.

Object Model: Materials for modeling; materials for prototyping.

Process Model: Support debate between interested parties during iterative process to capture emergent requirements: (1) Get input from a wide range of task and user analysis methods, to determine user and task requirements. (2) Model situation to help generate solution options. Useful techniques include scenarios, enterprise models, and requirements reference models. (3) Generate socio-technical solutions. (4) Evaluate solutions through prototyping. This generates discussion about requirements. (5) After iterations are complete, capture the requirements that have emerged through the process.

Participation Model: User organization; may also include external developers, consultants, end-users, and so on.

Results: (1) Increased understanding of organizational and technical constraints and opportunities. (2) Jointly agreed statement of user requirements, including organizational and non-functional requirements.

Phases of the Lifecycle: Problem identification, requirements.

Complementary Formal Methods: SSADM, IE, and so on.

Group Sizes: Varies by activity.

References:

Harker, S. (1993) Using case studies in the iterative development of a methodology to support user-designer collaboration. *Adjunct Proceedings of INTERCHI '93,* 57–58.

11.10.39 Organization Game

See the entry on *Layout, Organization, and Specification Games.*

11.10.40 Participatory Ergonomics

Abstract: Using conventional quality process methods, workers contribute to the solution of usability problems, usually on the shop floor.

Object Model: Actual work.

Process Model: Standard quality process methods (brainstorming, fishbone charts, etc.).

Participation Model: Users/workers by themselves, sometimes with a facilitator.

Results: Proposals to management for changes to work processes and conditions, documented in quality process formats.

Phases of the Lifecycle: Assessment, perhaps problem identification and clarification.

Complementary Formal Methods: Total quality management.

Group Sizes: Variable.

References:

Noro, K., and Imada, A. S. (Eds.). (1991) *Participatory ergonomics*. London: Taylor and Francis.

11.10.41 Participatory Heuristic Evaluation

Abstract: Inspectors use an extended set of heuristics—some product-oriented, some process-oriented—to assess potential problems of a design, prototype, or system, in terms of both usability and appropriateness to the end-users' work.

Object Model: The design, prototype, or system to be evaluated. The set of heuristics.

Process Model: (1) The inspectors are oriented to the task of heuristic evaluation, including an exploration of the 14 heuristics used in this practice. (2) Inspectors carry out a free exploration or a scenario-guided exploration of the design, prototype, or system; one person keeps a list of problems found.

Participation Model: End-users, human factors workers, development team, other stakeholders.

Results: A list of potential problems in terms of usability or work-appropriateness, from the combined perspectives of end-users, human factors workers, developers, and other stakeholders.

Phases of the Lifecycle: Assessment.

Complementary Formal Methods: Inspection methods, discount usability methods, especially heuristic evaluation.

Group Sizes: Up to 10, but better with smaller sets.

References:

Muller, M. J., McClard, A., Bell, B., Dooley, S., Meiskey, L., Meskill, J. A., Sparks, R., and Tellam, D. (1995). Validating an extension to participatory heuristic evaluation: Quality of work and quality of work life. *CHI '95 Conference Companion,* 115–116.

11.10.42 PICTIVE (Plastic Interface for Collaborative Technology Initiatives through Video Exploration)

Abstract: Using low-tech materials, participants prototype the appearance and—at a descriptive level—the dynamics of a system with a textual or graphical user interface. The technique is most useful for design, but can also be used for assessment of a simulated paper-prototyped system, or for analysis.

Object Model: Common office supplies (colored pens, scissors, Post-it notes, colored acetate for highlighting). Customized, pre-printed materials (e.g., interface components that conform to a particular style guide or development environment, icons from the work domain).

Process Model: (1) Introductions that include each participant's expertise, contribution to the shared work, organization and constituency, and what that constituency is expecting from the participant (i.e., personal and organizational stakes). (2) Mutual education through "mini-tutorials," if needed. (3) Working together to explore the task domain (in the form of analysis, design, or assessment). (4) Brief walkthrough of the group's achievements during the session, preferably recorded on videotape.

Participation Model: End-users and one or more of the following: human factors workers, software professionals, marketers, technical writers, trainers, perhaps clients or customers of the end-users, other stakeholders in the system.

Results: (1) Paper artifacts representing the appearance of the system. (2) Paper artifacts that can be used to reconstruct the group's ideas about the dynamics of the system. (3) Videotaped walkthrough showing the appearance, dynamics, and summary rationale.

Phases of the Lifecycle: Design and assessment. Analysis, to a lesser extent.

Complementary Formal Methods: Prototyping.

Group Sizes: Up to 8 people, if the furniture allows all of them to work on the same set of shared materials.

References:

Muller, M. J. (1991). PICTIVE—An exploration in participatory design. *Proceedings of CHI '91,* 225–231.

Muller, M. J. (1992). Retrospective on a year of participatory design using the PICTIVE technique. *Proceedings of CHI '92,* 455–462.

Muller, M.J., Tudor, L.G., Wildman, D.M., White, E.A., Root, R.W., Dayton, T., Carr, R., Diekmann, B., and Dykstra-Erickson, E.A. (1995). Bifocal tools for scenarios and representations in participatory activities with users. In J. Carroll (Ed.), *Scenario-based design for human-computer interaction*. New York: Wiley.

For related approaches (which did not adopt an explicitly participatory agenda), see:

Rettig, M. (1994). Practical programmer: Prototyping for tiny fingers. *Communications of the ACM, 37*(4), 21–27.

Virzi, R. (1989). What can you learn from a low-fidelity prototype? *Proceedings of the Human Factors Society 33rd Annual Meeting*, 224–228.

11.10.43 PictureCARD

Abstract: In situations in which end-users and software professionals do *not* share a common language, they communicate using highly pictorial cards to develop a representation of work.

Object Model: Cards using almost exclusively pictures (digital images reduced to line drawings) of objects and events in the users' world. Cards are grouped into six major categories: Person, Action, Season, Tool, Event, Location (PASTEL).

Process Model: Cards are arrayed in a linear sequence, beginning with the general PASTEL categories and then refining those categories into specific subclasses.

Participation Model: End-users and software professionals.

Results: Stories told by the users, initially expressed through the cards, and subsequently translated into text.

Phases of the Lifecycle: Analysis.

Complementary Formal Methods: Object-oriented analysis and design.

Group Sizes: Very small: the storyteller, the card-provider, and perhaps observers.

References:

Tschudy, M.W., Dykstra-Erickson, E.A., and Holloway, M.S. (1996). PictureCARD: A storytelling tool for task analysis. In *PDC'96 Proceedings of the Participatory Design Conference*, 183-191.

See also the entries on *CARD, CUTA, Layout Kit, Metaphors Game.*

11.10.44 Pluralistic Walkthrough

Abstract: End-users participate in an inspection team that evaluates a user interface or system design. The inspection sessions are designed to highlight and emphasize end-users' perspectives.

Object Model: The system or design to be inspected.

Process Model: The team inspects the system or design. End-users and their comments and perspectives are assigned the primary and most privileged position in the team's inspection agenda.

Participation Model: End-users and software professionals.

Results: Critique of the design or system.

Phases of the Lifecycle: Assessment.

Complementary Formal Methods: Software inspections, usability testing.

Group Sizes: Not specified, but manageably small for a team effort.

References:

Bias, R. (1994). Pluralistic usability walkthrough: Coordinated empathies. In J. Nielsen and R. L. Mack (Eds.), *Usability inspection methods.* New York: Wiley.

Bias, R. G. (1991). Walkthroughs: Efficient collaborative testing. *IEEE Software, 8*(5), 58–59.

11.10.45 Priority Workshop

Abstract: Users and developers collaborate on redesign of a system or systems, usually in a matrix of multiple stakeholder organizations. The practice follows a sequence of eight activities in a workshop format.

Object Model: None. The work involves a series of workshops with users and other stakeholders.

Process Model: Eight stages: (1) Introductory discussion on the aim of the workshop. (2) Users' presentations of system attributes characterized as positive, negative, and desirable. (3) Developers' presentation of plans and priorities concerning the system. (4) Exploration of alternatives through prototypes and mock-ups, conducted in small groups. (5) Plenary discussion of alternatives in light of users' presentations from Stage 2. (6) Summary of priorities and qualities, subjected to rank ordering through users' ratings of "+" or "-." (7) Discussions of organizational consequences (for the users) of the changes selected in Stage 7, including modes of further user participation. (8) Closing discussion and summation, including plans for further such workshops.

Participation Model: Users and developers; also, project leader and/or manager. There is a need for a moderator and for a recorder, who may need specialized skills. In any event, the moderator appears not to be a member of the stakeholder organizations.

Results: Decisions regarding features and capabilities to be included in the redesign. The decisions are informed by an understanding of the implications for the users' organizations.

Phases of the Lifecycle: Redesign, involving multiple, interrelated user organizations, and potentially multiple, interrelated software modules.

Complementary Formal Methods: Requirements, perhaps analysis.

Group Sizes: 10–20 (tentative estimate).

References:

Braa, K. (1995). Priority workshops: Springboard for user participation in redesign activities. In *Proceedings of the Conference on Organizational Computing Systems: COOCS '95*. New York: ACM.

11.10.46 PrOTA (PRocess Oriented Task Analysis)

Abstract: Takes a set of task steps arranged in a flow, and reorganizes them for sensibility of expression in a user interface. In this way, PrOTA is a bridge between high-level and detailed designs of a process, and so can be used in between (for example) the CARD and PICTIVE methods.

Object Model: Index cards and Post-it notes.

Process Model: Participants break the input task flow into (1) individual tasks, and (2) individual contexts (environments) in which those tasks are done. Each task step is written on an index card. A taxonomy of tasks is created by clustering those index cards into piles, each pile representing a common environment in which those tasks are done.

Participation Model: Users, usability engineers.

Results: Clusters of task steps, each cluster being an environment common to the task steps within it. These environments can be input to methods such as PICTIVE that design details of interfaces. If a set of physical equipment was being designed instead of a computer interface, each environment might become a room containing that equipment. For a GUI design, each environment might become a GUI window or menu.

Phases of the Lifecycle: Bridge between high-level design and detailed design.

Complementary Formal Methods: None known.

Group Sizes: 2–4.

References: Contact Susan Hornstein, Bellcore, Room PY1 1L-175, 6 Corporate Place, Piscataway, NJ 08854, USA, +1-908-214-9631, susanh@cc.bellcore.com.

11.10.47 Prototyping

Abstract: Prototyping has been used in many ways in participatory activities. This brief entry in this appendix provides a starting point for exploring the various approaches. Note, first, that low-tech prototyping is covered elsewhere (see BrainDraw, CARD, CUTA, Mock-Ups, PICTIVE). Note also the full methodological descriptions of Storyboard Prototyping and CISP (Cooperative Interactive Storyboard Prototyping). This entry on Prototyping, then, lists points of access for prototyping initiatives that are not as fully detailed as the practices described elsewhere in this appendix.

Object Model: Software system, usually programmed in a flexible environment that supports rapid changes.

Process Model: Varies from one prototyping approach to another, and from one phase of the lifecycle to another.

Participation Model: Users, developers, and perhaps other stakeholders. Sometimes a computer-literate human factors worker replaces, or works with, the developer.

Results: One or more of: (1) Improved software. (2) Improved requirements. (3) Documentation of users'needs.

Phases of the Lifecycle: Potentially all of the following: Requirements, analysis, high-level design, detailed design, implementation, assessment, customization, redesign.

Complementary Formal Methods: Software design and development. Sometimes object-oriented methods and technologies.

Group Sizes: Usually quite small.

References:

Bødker, S., and Grønbæk, K. (1991a). Cooperative prototyping: Users and designers in mutual activity. *International Journal of Man-Machine Studies, 34,* 453–478.

Bødker, S., and Grønbæk, K. (1991b). Design in action: From prototyping by demonstration to cooperative prototyping. In J. Greenbaum and M. Kyng (Eds.), *Design at work: Cooperative design of computer systems* (pp. 197–218). Hillsdale NJ, USA: Erlbaum.

Bødker, S., Grønbæk, K., and Kyng, M. (1993). Cooperative design: Techniques and experiences from the Scandinavian scene. In D. Schuler and A. Namioka (Eds.), *Participatory design: Principles and practices* (pp. 157–175). Hillsdale NJ, USA: Erlbaum.

Budde, R., Kautz, K., Kuhlenkamp, K., and Züllighoven, H. (1992). *Prototyping: An approach to evolutionary system development.* Berlin: Springer Verlag.

Budde, R., Kuhlenkamp, K., Mathiassen, L., and Züllighoven, H. (Eds.). (1984). *Approaches to prototyping.* Berlin: Springer Verlag.

Floyd, C., Züllighoven, H., Budde, R., and Keil-Slawik, R. (Eds.). (1992). *Software development and reality construction.* Berlin: Springer Verlag.

11.10.48 Scenarios

Abstract: Descriptions of work move from the abstract and decontextualized toward the concrete and situated, through the usage of specific stories about specific workplace events. These stories, or scenarios, can work as triggers for other participatory activities.

Object Model: None.

Process Model: Observe, or if necessary construct, very specific, contextualized scenarios. Use these in discussions with users and others.

Participation Model: Users and software professionals; perhaps other stakeholders.

Results: Increased understanding.

Phases of the Lifecycle: Various.

Complementary Formal Methods: None known.

Group Sizes: Small.

References:

Bødker, S., Christiansen, E., and Thüring, M. (1995). A conceptual toolbox for designing CSCW applications. In *COOP '95: Atelier international sur la conception des systèms coopératifs* [International workshop on the design of cooperative systems] (pp. 266–284). Sophia Antiipolis, France: INRIA.

See also the entry on *Storytelling Workshop.* More generally, see chapter 17 of this handbook, and:

Carroll, J. (Ed.). (1995). *Scenario-based design: Envisioning work and technology in system development.* New York: Wiley.

11.10.49 Search Conference or Starting Conference

Abstract: Participants from multiple, interrelated organizations, at multiple levels of management and power, meet together to analyze current working relationships, future opportunities, and how to move from the current to the future. Participants at different levels of power are partially protected from risks due to exposing their ideas or perspectives to their own organizations.

Object Model: None.

Process Model: In general, the workshop is structured so that the high-risk discussions take place among people who are at the same organizational level. Medium-risk discussions take place among people who are at different organizational levels, but who are *not* in direct reporting relationships with one another. It is only in the low-risk discussions that participants work directly with their own direct supervisors.

Participation Model: Members of the organizations from (usually three) levels of labor and supervision. Facilitators.

Results: Improved understanding (1) among organizations, and (2) among levels in each organization. An action plan to transform the current situation into the desired future situation.

Phases of the Lifecycle: Problem identification and clarification.

Complementary Formal Methods: None known.

Group Sizes: Large—multiple organizations in conversation with one another. This is a conference-scale workshop.

References:

Palshaugen, O. (1986). *Method of designing a starting conference.* Oslo: Work Research Institute.

11.10.50 Specification Game

See the entry on *Layout, Organization, and Specification Games.*

11.10.51 SSADM (Structured Systems Analysis and Design Method)

Abstract: Method developed to help overcome problems that are encountered in the design (such as cost and schedule overruns), while maintaining quality. User involvement during analysis and design ensures the system is based on the "real world" and can meet changing requirements.

Object Model: Paper, flipcharts, pens.

Process Model: Series of six steps, with quality assurance reviews at the end of each step: (1) Analyze system operations and current problems. This is done using data flow diagrams and logical data structures. (2) Specify requirements using data flow diagrams, logical data structures, entity life histories, and logical dialog outlines. (3) Select technical options. (4) Design data. This is done using relation data analysis (third normal form) and composite logical data design. (5) Design processes using entity life histories, logical dialog outlines, and process outlines. (6) Design physical system.

Participation Model: Users and developers.

Results: (1) File/database design. (2) Program specifications. (3) Manual procedures. (4) Operating schedules. (5) System testing and implementation plans.

Phases of the Lifecycle: Analysis, design.

Complementary Formal Methods: Interviews with users, user-interface design methods.

Group Sizes: 2–8.

References:

Longworth, G. (1992). *A user's guide to SSADM* (Version 4). Oxford: N. C. C. Blackwell.

11.10.52 SSM (Soft Systems Methodology)

Abstract: A well-known general methodology for handling problem situations, where all stakeholders are included to gain multiple perspectives to derive feasible and desirable solutions.

Object Model: Paper, flipcharts, pens to create rich pictures and models

Process Model: (1) Analyze the cultural situation as a group to create rich pictures about the problem situation. This involves brainstorming about the planned intervention, as well as about the social and political systems that exist. (2) Develop conceptual models of relevant systems to make different perspectives explicit, and to show activities that are to be supported by the technical system. (3) Examine differences between the models created and the real world. (4) Identify changes that are both feasible and desirable; this may include a precise list of system objectives. (5) Take steps to improve the situation, in this case partially through a technical system.

Participation Model: All stakeholders, including users, managers, developers.

Results: (1) Models of systems relevant to the problem situation. (2) Plan of action to improve the situation.

Phases of the Lifecycle: Problem identification, requirements, analysis, evaluation.

Complementary Formal Methods: Data-flow models to represent supporting technical systems.

Group Sizes: Any size.

References:

Checkland, P. (1981a). *Systems thinking, systems practice.* New York: Wiley.

Checkland, P. (1981b). Towards a systems-based methodology for real-world problem solving. In Open Systems Group (Eds.), *Systems Behaviour* (3rd ed., pp. 288–314). London: Harper and Row.

Checkland, P., and Scholes, J. (1990). *Soft Systems Methodology in Action.* New York: Wiley.

Vidgen, R., Wood-Harper, T., and Wood, R. (1993). A soft systems approach to information systems quality. *Scandinavian Journal of Information Systems, 5,* 97–112.

11.10.53 STEPS (Software Technology for Evolutionary Participative System development)

Abstract: Framework for user-oriented cooperative development, which integrates technical and social concerns to provide high quality products that can be adapted to changing needs.

Object Model: No special materials.

Process Model: Iterations of: (1) Establishment of project or revision. At this stage, a system concept and project strategy are developed. (2) Production of system. This stage includes cooperative system design, development of a system specification, software realization by developers, and embedment preparation by users. (3) Implementation of system version. (4) Application of system. This stage involves system use by users, and maintenance by developers.

Participation Model: Users and developers.

Results: (1) Design specification, including functional specification and changes required in the user organization. (2) System version, including hardware, software, documentation, and guidelines for work organization. (3) Mutual learning.

Phases of the Lifecycle: Lifetime of a project

Complementary Formal Methods: Other software lifecycle models.

Group Sizes: Variable by process stage.

References:

Floyd, C. (1993). STEPS—A methodical approach to PD. *Communications of the ACM, 36*(6), 83.

Floyd, C., Reisin, F.-M., and Schmidt, G. (1989). STEPS to software development with users. In C. Ghezzi and J. A. McDermid (Eds.), *ESEC '89: Lecture notes in computer science Nr. 387.* Berlin: Springer Verlag.

11.10.54 Storyboard Prototyping

Abstract: Users and others evaluate and use a prototype that exists only as a storyboard—a series of still images. This type of prototype is often faster and cheaper to create than prototypes created with traditional programming languages, so iterations of design and evaluation are faster. Some versions of the method, such as CISP (Cooperative Interactive Storyboard Prototyping), involve users in codeveloping the prototype instead of just evaluating a version so other people can go off on their own to create the next version.

Object Model: Drawings made by hand or with software, presented on paper or computer screen. The lowest-tech variety of the method uses hand drawings on sheets of paper, each drawing showing one state from a succession of states of the interface. A higher-tech variety uses software for drawing and for presenting the images in sequence. Perhaps the highest-tech variety (e.g., CISP) creates *interactive* software storyboards, in which the user's actions on the screen (e.g., using a mouse to click an on-screen button) control which image appears next.

Process Model: (1) For each scenario of use of the interface, develop a "storyboard": a series of cartoon images of the interface states as they would occur during the task's steps. These storyboards may or may not be codeveloped by the users, as in the CISP method. If users do not codevelop the initial storyboards, then a prior step is necessary: Gathering information on users' basic needs, including fundamental goals and objectives, functions to be performed, relevant data elements and relationships, and any problems to be solved by system. (2) Present the storyboards to the interested parties, including users and/or managers. Participants review the succession of images. Comments may be elicited by asking "what if" questions. In some cases, participants can control the succession of images by pointing at interface controls in the pictures, with the appropriate next image being chosen either by a human or by software. (3) Iterate between developing storyboards and presenting them, until all participants deem them satisfactory.

Participation Model: Users, usability engineers, prototypers, graphic artists, maybe developers, maybe managers and marketers.

Results: Iteratively evaluated and redesigned storyboard or prototype. Improved understanding of requirements.

Phases of the Lifecycle: High-level design, detailed design, implementation (in the sense of prototyping).

Complementary Formal Methods: Programming of fully functional software prototypes that behave as the storyboard appears.

Group Sizes: 2 to perhaps 20.
References:

Andriole, S. J. (1989). *Storyboard prototyping: A new approach to user requirements analysis.* Wellesley, MA, USA: QED.

Andriole, S. J. (Ed.). (1992). *Rapid application prototyping: The storyboard approach to user requirements analysis* (2nd ed.). Boston: QED.

See also the entry on *CISP*.

11.10.55 Storytelling Workshop

Abstract: Participants bring to a workshop two short oral stories about computer usage. The invitation to participate includes the request that one story be positive, and one story be negative, with respect to usage and outcome. Participants share their stories.

Object Model: None.

Process Model: Participants tell their stories, comment on one another's stories, and comment on commonalties and contrasts.

Participation Model: End-users, facilitator(s).

Results: (1) Increased cohesion among the end-users. (2) Recognition among the end-users that the difficulties that each of them has faced as an individual are not in fact unique.

Phases of the Lifecycle: Problem identification and clarification.

Complementary Formal Methods: None known.

Group Sizes: Medium (perhaps up to 40).

References:

Greenbaum, J., and Madsen, K. H. (1993). Small changes: Starting a participatory design process by giving participants a voice. In D. Schuler and A. Namioka (Eds.), *Participatory design: Principles and practices* (pp. 289–298). Hillsdale, NJ, USA: Erlbaum.

See also:

Erickson, T. (1995). Notes on design practice: Stories and prototypes as catalysts for communication. In J. Carroll (Ed.), *Scenario-based design: Envisioning work and technology in system development* (pp. 37–58). New York: Wiley.

Orr, J. E., and Crowfoot, N. C. (1992). Design by anecdote—The use of ethnography to guide the application of technology in practice. *PDC '92: Proceedings of the Participatory Design Conference,* 31–37.

11.10.56 TOD (Task Object Design)

Abstract: Participants design a complete set of units of information that are needed and desirable for a worker to do a task that has already been documented in a flow chart. Each object is represented by an index card. These task information objects serve as a stepping stone from the task flow to an object-oriented user interface design.

Object Model: Index cards, Post-it notes, felt-tipped pens

Process Model: Initially the task objects are just extracted from the previously documented task flow by writing each task step's noun on an index card, and each step's verbs on a Post-it note attached to that card. But participants then start designing the details of the objects, by listing (on more Post-it notes) each object's attributes and hierarchical relations to other objects. Participants also usability test the set of objects for its ease of use in doing the task flow. This is an iterative process in which objects are discarded or drastically redesigned, new objects are designed, and the task flow itself changed. All activities are done by all the participants, who are seated around a small round table, with the materials on the table.

Participation Model: Users, usability engineer, system engineer, developer, subject matter experts in the relevant business processes and information systems, developers of documentation and training, managers of all these people.

Results: A complete set of abstract information objects for doing the task flow. These "task objects" are to be used in other methods, for bridging that task flow to the designing of any object-oriented user interface for doing that task flow. For example, the task objects might be translated into GUI objects such as windows.

Phases of the Lifecycle: Analysis, high-level design, assessment.

Complementary Formal Methods: Formal requirements-document writing to put the objects with their attributes and relationships into a format more suitable than index cards, for system engineers, developers, testers, and project managers.

Group Sizes: 2 to 6.

References:

Dayton, T., Kramer, J., McFarland, A., and Heidelberg, M. (1996). Participatory GUI design from task models. *CHI '96 Conference Companion.*

McFarland, A., and Dayton, T. (1995). A participatory methodology for driving object-oriented GUI design from user needs. *Proceedings of OZCHI '95.*

See the entry on *Workshop for O-O GUI Designing*

from User Needs for a context in which TOD is used.

11.10.57 Translators

Abstract: End-users and developers find common ground through a mediator (the translator) who understands both the users' and the developers' domains.

Object Model: None.

Process Model: The translator translates between the users' way of doing work and thinking about work, and the developers' way of doing work and thinking about work.

Participation Model: End-users, developers, one translator.

Results: Increased mutual understanding. Development of improved translation techniques.

Phases of the Lifecycle: Problem identification, requirements, analysis, assessment.

Complementary Formal Methods: None known.

Group Sizes: 6–8.

References:

Williams, M. G. (1994). Enabling schoolteachers to participate in the design of educational software. *PDC '94: Proceedings of the Participatory Design Conference*, 153–158.

Williams, M. G., and Begg, V. (1993). Translation between software designers and users. *Communications of the ACM, 36*(6), 102–103.

11.10.58 UTOPIA Project—Training, Technology, and Products From the Quality of Work Perspective

Abstract: This project concentrated on the development of computer-based tools for skilled workers. The tools were designed to be skill-enhancing tools which would lead to high-quality products.

Object Model: Plywood, paper, and such, to build Mock-Ups of different tools.

Process Model: A focus on work processes rather than data flow analysis, through a series of steps: (1) Learn about the work process of the user. (2) Visit other work places doing similar work as a group. This helps to gather information about technology and work practices. (3) Develop plywood and paper mock-ups to simulate different tools. This enables developers learn about existing technology and to develop use models, while users learn about the technical possibilities. (4) Use games (see Layout, Organization, and Specification Games) to learn about the work organization. (5) Develop requirement specification. At the same time, build alternative models for work organization. (6) Organize training for users. (7) After development is complete, pilot the system at one location to see how it works.

Participation Model: Users, trade unions and developers.

Results: (1) Specification for system to be implemented. (2) Plans for new work organization. (3) Design methods appropriate for designing systems with users. (4) Mutual learning about each other's domain.

Phases of the Lifecycle: Problem identification, requirements, high-level design, evaluation.

Complementary Formal Methods: None known.

Group Sizes: Variable.

References:

Bødker, S., Ehn, P., Kyng, M., Kammersgaard, J. and Sundblad, Y. (1987). A UTOPIAN experience: On design of powerful computer-based tools for skilled graphic workers. In G. Bjerknes, P. Ehn, and M. Kyng (Eds.), *Computers and democracy: A Scandinavian challenge* (pp. 251–278). Brookfield, VT, USA: Gower.

See also the entry on *Mock-Ups*, and on *Layout, Organization, and Specification Games.*

11.10.59 Video Prototyping

Abstract: Develop a representation of the dynamics of the user interface using paper-and-pencil materials and stop-action (cartoon) animation techniques

Object Model: Video recorder; paper-and-pencil materials to sketch interface components.

Process Model: The group's ideas about how the interface should behave (the dynamics of the interface) are recorded by working through the interface events using the paper-and-pencil materials to show each component and each event involving that component. The video camera is run while the participants are moving the interface objects. When the paper computer "screen" changes (for example, when a menu is pulled down from the menu bar), the camera is stopped, the pull-down menu is placed on the paper "screen," and the camera is restarted. The cursor is often represented as a hand-drawn arrow, which is moved across the paper "screen" on a sheet of transparent plastic or acetate. Sound effects, such as clicks and beeps, may be included. The resulting video record is an animated version of what the design would look like if it were programmed. Voice-over narration may be included.

Participation Model: An expert animator and a design team.

Results: Videotape of interface dynamics, suitable for showing others how the design is supposed to behave. Because the "interface components" in the videotape are made of paper, the videotape cannot be mistaken for a real, computerized artifact; it is a representation of the intended artifact.

Phases of the Lifecycle: Detailed design.

Complementary Formal Methods: GUI description languages.

Group Sizes: 2–8.

References:

Young, E. (1992, May). *Participatory video prototyping*. Poster at CHI '92 conference, Monterey, CA, USA.

11.10.60 Work Mapping

Abstract: Method for information analysis and modeling that can help to understand work practices important to the redesign of business processes and computer systems.

Object Model: Paper, pens, mock-ups of work environment, business systems, and computer systems.

Process Model: (1) Develop models of current work processes. (2) Enrich and test models by acting out with mock-ups. (3) Identify problems and areas for efficiency improvement in work by analyzing work models. Things that may considered at this phase include bottle necks, decisions points, computer support, information sources, business objectives, and feedback mechanisms. (4) Examine impact of changes through simulations with mock-up. (5) Update model and develop action plan.

Participation Model: Facilitators from development team; staff and management to represent different functions in work area.

Results: (1) Systematic models of work, documenting existing work processes. (2) Action plan to improve work organization and supporting technology. (3) Commitment to implement changes to work organization.

Phases of the Lifecycle: Analysis, evaluation.

Complementary Formal Methods: Prototyping; The HURON Way

Group Sizes: Up to 40

References:

URCOT. (1994). *Work mapping: Possible application in the Australia Taxation Office* (Working Paper No. 4). Melbourne, Australia: Union Research Centre on Organisation and Technology Ltd. (URCOT).

11.10.61 Workshop for O-O GUI Designing from User Needs

Abstract: Participants use index cards to analyze and design task flows, and paper prototyping to design a graphical user interface (GUI) that is good for users to do those task flows. The bridge between those two steps is the index-card based TOD (Task Object Design) method.

Object Model: Flip chart paper, index cards, Post-it notes, felt-tipped pens, Post-it transparent adhesive tape, scissors.

Process Model: There are three major steps, with iteration within and among steps. For more details of the CARD, TOD, and PICTIVE methods that are components of the Workshop, see their descriptions in this chapter. Usability testing is done frequently within and after each step. All activities are done by all the participants, who are seated around a small round table, with the materials on the table.

The three major steps are (1) A tailored version of CARD is used for producing documented user requirements. The output is a flow chart of a desirable but feasible, detailed but somewhat abstract, set of steps that a user will take when using the new user interface. (2) TOD is then used to design a set of task objects that are well usable for a worker executing the task flow from the first step. (3) The fundamental GUI design is then produced by translating the task objects into GUI objects, via a succession of small steps, a multi-platform GUI design guide, and a tailored version of PICTIVE.

Participation Model: Users, usability engineer, system engineer, developer, subject matter experts in the relevant business processes and information systems, developers of documentation and training, managers of all these people.

Results: Paper prototype of an object-oriented, style-guide compliant, usability tested, graphical user interface, and documentation of the task flow in which the user will employ that interface.

Phases of the Lifecycle: Problem identification, analysis, requirements, high-level design, assessment.

Complementary Formal Methods: Formal requirements-document writing to put the objects with their attributes and relationships into a format more suitable than index cards and paper prototypes, for system engineers, developers, testers, and project managers.

Group Sizes: 2–6.

References:

Dayton, T., Muller, M. J., McFarland, A., Wildman, D. M., and White, E. A. (in press). Participatory analysis, design, and assessment. In J. Nielsen (Ed.), *Handbook of user interface design*. New York: Wiley.

McFarland, A., and Dayton, T. (1995). A participatory methodology for driving object-oriented GUI design from user needs. *Proceedings of OZCHI'95*.

Handbook of Human-Computer Interaction
Second, completely revised edition
M. Helander, T.K. Landauer, P. Prabhu (eds.)

Chapter 12

Design for Quality-in-use: Human-Computer Interaction Meets Information Systems Development

Pelle Ehn
Department of Informatics
Lund University
Lund, Sweden

Jonas Löwgren
Department of Computer and Information Science
Linköping University
Linköping, Sweden

12.1 Introduction

Our aim is to illustrate how human-computer interaction (HCI) and information systems development (ISD) have evolved from similar backgrounds, via largely independent paths, to a common point of intersection. The evolution is organized around different conceptualizations of usability and what it means to design systems with high quality. We will show that the intersection point takes us beyond usability to the notion of quality-in-use, which in turn prompts a reconsideration of HCI and ISD in terms of design work.

One suitable starting point to illustrate the problem is the concept of "user". In HCI and ISD, we have grown accustomed to discussing user-centered systems development. But who is this user? As we shall see throughout the following sections, many answers have been explicitly proposed or implicitly assumed:

- a representative person in the statistical or pragmatical sense;
- an individual person in a unique context;
- a person working in a collaborative setting;
- a component of a work system;
- an organization;
- a stakeholder;
- an end-user;
- an organization representing users;
- a customer.

The list is extensive; the question of defining the user is obviously more or less futile, since the concept is problematic in itself (Bannon, 1991; Grudin, 1993a). In this paper, we shall explore the alternative of focusing on the use situation rather than on the user *per se*. We will show how developments in HCI as well as in ISD can be understood as an evolution in this direction. The resulting view can be properly characterized as *use-centered systems development*, oriented towards achieving *quality-in-use*. We will argue the importance of understanding that power has a rationality that tra-

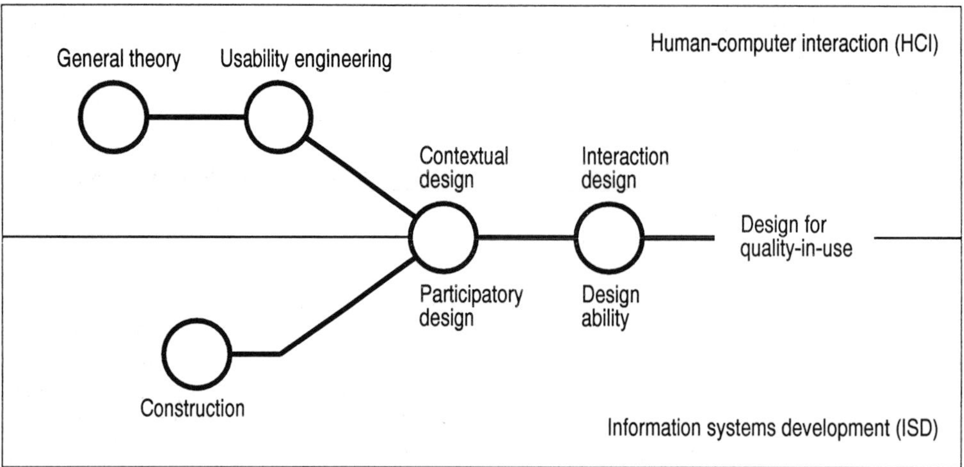

Figure 1. Overview of the conceptual evolution in HCI and ISD.

ditional rational engineering cannot understand, but also that design for quality-in-use has a rationality beyond power and user participation.

12.1.1 Overview

The first parts of the paper outline two parallel developments: the evolution of the usability concept in HCI, and the methodological evolution in the field of ISD, with a particular focus on participatory design in Scandinavia. Our presentation is by necessity oversimplified, but we hope to capture accurately an essential feature of the two parallel threads: the move from an exclusively rationalistic and objective perspective to the inclusion of interpretative social and subjective aspects. Next, we bring the two threads together and introduce the concept of quality-in-use, by which we attempt to provide a more appropriate foundation for understanding the quality of information technology artifacts. The paper closes by identifying the crucial implications of adopting quality-in-use as a guiding concept in HCI and ISD. Figure 1 illustrates the concepts and the evolution we wish to present.

12.2 Usability in HCI

There can be no doubt that the concept of usability is central to the area of HCI. Arguably, the aim of most efforts by HCI researchers and practitioners is to achieve more usable computer systems. In this section, we examine the concept of usability within HCI. We will illustrate how the perspectives within the field have developed, from general psychological theory via usability engineering to what we have termed the experiential view of usability. The point of this historical survey is to emphasize a line of conceptual development within the field of HCI that moves across ISD and towards a new synthesis. A more detailed version of the account in this section can be found in Löwgren (1995b).

12.2.1 General theory

HCI has its roots in what was in the 70s called software psychology (Shneiderman, 1980), a discipline with a solid basis in experimental psychology and scientific traditions (Carroll, 1993). The phenomenon under study was a human interacting with a computer; the intention was to accumulate pieces of empirical knowledge by controlled experiments. The scientific methodology would ensure that the knowledge was true (within statistical limits) and applicable to other instances of human-computer interaction. The number of studies performed in this way and reported in the literature is considerable; for example, the well-known collection of theory-based design guidelines by Smith and Mosier (1986) contains no less than 173 references, even though it was compiled, fairly selectively, 10 years ago.

HCI as an experimental science is not content with accumulating pieces of knowledge. In order to provide general and useful knowledge, theories are induced from the available data. A proposed theory should obviously account for the data, but also be general enough to predict outcomes for new situations. One highly recognized example in the HCI literature is the work by Card, Moran and Newell in *The psychology of human-computer interaction* in 1983, in which the cognitive theory of the Model Human Processor and the GOMS model are presented as a way to analyze and predict expert-level human interaction with computer systems. Since then, numerous refinements, extensions and competing theories have been proposed (a recent survey is given by John, 1995). The general theory perspective is strongly represented in scientific HCI journals and conferences to the present day.

How, then, is usability viewed from a general theory perspective? Returning once again to the work of Card et al. (1983, p.1),

> "The domain of concern to us ... is how humans interact with computers. A scientific psychology should help us in arranging this interface so it is easy, efficient, error-free — even enjoyable."

The same notion of usability as a maximally good fit with general human characteristics can be found in subsequent work on cognitive engineering and human factors (e.g., Woods and Roth, 1988).

12.2.2 Usability Engineering

The impact of general HCI theory on professional software development has regrettably been rather limited. The reasons are not central to our purposes; we will instead concentrate on the new perspective on usability that emerged from the "failure". It draws upon the methodological foundations of general theory but orients itself towards a paradigmatic model of applied science and engineering.

> "Usability engineering is a process, grounded in classical engineering, which amounts to specifying, quantitatively and in advance, what characteristics and in what amounts the final product to be engineered is to have. This process is followed by actually building the product and demonstrating that it does indeed have the planned-for characteristics.
>
> Engineering is not the process of building a perfect system with infinite resources. Rather, engineering is the process of economically building a working system that fulfills a need. Without measurable usability specifications, there is no way to determine the usability needs of a product, or to measure whether or not the finished product fulfills those needs. If we cannot measure usability, we cannot have a usability engineering." (Good et al., 1986, p. 241)

Usability engineering as a process is typically described as consisting of three main steps. The first is a user and task analysis, in which the intended user population is investigated along with the work tasks the system is intended to support. Next, a usability specification is negotiated in analogy with a requirement specification, detailing a number of measurable usability goals. This specification is then used as the control instrument for an iterative process, in which a prototype is designed, usability-tested and redesigned until the goals are met. In this view of usability, measurements are very important. Based on general HCI theory as well as practical experience, many operationalizations of usability have been suggested (e.g., Roberts and Moran, 1982; Carroll and Rosson, 1985; Shackel, 1986; Whiteside et al., 1988; Dumas and Redish, 1993; Löwgren, 1993; Nielsen, 1993). Examples of measurable aspects of usability include:

- user performance on specified tasks (measured in terms of task completion rate, completion time, or number of errors made);
- flexibility of the design (proportion of users in a heterogeneous population able to perform the test tasks);
- learnability (completion rate, time, errors, retention, use of documentation or help desk);
- user's subjective preference or degree of satisfaction (questionnaires, interviews).

One, perhaps surprising, trait of usability engineering is that the usability of the system is divorced from its utility (Nielsen, 1993, is particularly explicit on this topic). It is as if usability engineering is primarily concerned with the users' efficient and error-free access to the services of the system, but not with the appropriateness of the services. Grudin (1993b) points out that one factor contributing to this divorce of usability and utility can be the origins of usability engineering in product development settings, where the services afforded by new products are planned by managers and marketing long before product development. Hence, the utility of the system — which is determined by the appropriateness of its services — is not used as a factor in product development. Another explanation is that it is very hard to formulate measurable utility goals in a lab setting beyond the obvious self-estimates (compare Landauer's (1995) discussion of the productivity paradox and the lack of relevant utility measures).

12.2.3 Experiential Usability

Critics of the usability engineering perspective have gradually voiced concerns that a strong focus on measurability always runs the risk of concentrating on easily measurable aspects at the expense of perhaps more important considerations. Two of the originators of the usability engineering perspective, John Whiteside and Dennis Wixon, were also among the first to clearly articulate its limitations. They wrestled with the inadequacies of regarding usability as an objective property:

> "For us, software usability refers to the extent to which software supports and enriches the ongoing experience of people who use that software. This direct emphasis on experience is at variance with 'standard' definitions of usability that concentrate on, as primary, measurable manifestations of usability such as productivity, preference, learnability or throughput. Although these may be interpreted as important properties of usability, for us they are not primary. Primary is the person's experience at the moment experienced." (Whiteside and Wixon, 1987, p. 18)

Thus, usability becomes a purely subjective, experiential property of the interaction between a specific user and the computer at a specific moment in time. Moreover, there is no question that usability in the experiential perspective comprises utility as well:

> "If the [usability] goals are not grounded in something really meaningful to the users, the resulting product will be useless to them." (Ibid., p. 20)

The experiential view of usability formed the basis for a software development approach known as *contextual design* (Whiteside et al., 1988; Wixon et al., 1990; Holzblatt and Beyer, 1993; Holzblatt and Jones, 1993; Beyer and Holzblatt, 1995). Essentially, contextual design is described as a cyclic process of requirements generation, design, implementation and evaluation, similar to Boehm's (1986) spiral model. A suite of techniques are used to ensure that the developers understand the users and customers, and that this understanding is reflected in the system. A contextual data collection method called contextual inquiry, based on ethnographic field research techniques, is used to acquire the necessary understanding of users' work. Diagrams and modelling languages are used to produce a coherent interpretation of the collected data, the work is redesigned in a participatory effort and evaluated using further contextual inquiry. The conceptual structure of the system is designed, followed by a mapping to the user interface. The conceptual design is tested using mock-ups; as the shared understanding grows, the prototypes can be more detailed. The emerging understanding also prompts further contextual inquiry and work redesign in an iterative manner.

As will be shown, the contextual design process bears striking similarities to methods and techniques formulated within the participatory design tradition. In a sense, the experiential perspective on usability with its methodological implications provides a place where HCI concepts can fruitfully intersect with participatory design within the area of information systems development.

12.2.4 Beyond Usability in HCI: Interaction Design

In recent years, there has been a growing interest in the HCI community to think about the development of usable systems as design work, rather than as science or engineering. "Design" should be understood as in industrial design or urban design, i.e., a creative activity that is concerned with the shaping of possible future realities. In HCI, the primary design considerations are, of course, the situations of ultimate use, involving users as well as system.

The increasing interest in design is apparent in the journals and conferences in the HCI field (see Winograd, 1995, for a survey). There is an emerging body of experience reports and empirical studies to show that the process of software development in practice is not amenable to descriptions in terms of application of scientific theory or engineering transformations (Löwgren, 1995a). Moreover, with the ubiquitous adoption of computer technology, it has been argued that new foundations are needed to replace the productivity-oriented usability concepts of earlier phases:

> "... a maturing technology reaches a wide audience of 'discretionary users' who choose it because it satisfies some need or urge. The emphasis is not on measurable cost/benefit analyses, but on whether it is likable, beautiful, satisfying or exciting. The market attractiveness of a product rests on a mixture of its functionality, its emotional appeal, fashion trends and individual engagement... The huge new markets of the future — the successors to the productivity markets conquered by IBM and Microsoft in the past — will be in this new consumer arena, responsive to different dimensions of human need." (Winograd, 1995, pp. 66-67)

It is clear that the design perspective on HCI requires a reconceptualization of the guiding values. In the latter part of this paper, we will introduce the concept of quality-in-use and show how it can be used to further our understanding of contemporary software development.

12.3 Users in Information Systems Development

The historical development in the HCI field is, however, not an isolated phenomenon. In interesting ways it parallels both a more general development of approaches, methodologies and theories across "design" disciplines and more specifically also developments in the field of information systems development (ISD). In this section we will introduce the parallel history of ISD, with a special focus on one development branch known as Scandinavian participatory design. We begin with the background in the still dominating rational systems thinking and engineering tradition: Construction — a technical approach. The understanding of use and users in this tradition was criticised from the emerging participatory design (PD) tradition for not understanding that *power has a rationality that rationalistic systems thinking does not understand.* PD started out as a "political" approach, but soon also became a theoretical attack on the reduction of human competence to what can be formally described. Hence, one can say that the proactive critique of the political rationality of the design process also led to a transcending critique of the scientific rationality of methods for ISD. Active user participation in the design process became both a means for better systems and a democratic ends in itself. This also called for new methods and techniques, and the PD tradition had to learn the hard way that *design has a rationality to which not even democratic participation is a sufficient answer.* To contribute to really useful systems, PD had to be concerned not only with the social side of participation, but also with the subjective. This led to the emergence of a complementary, more aesthetical orientation: Design ability — a subjective approach.

12.3.1 Construction — a Technical Approach

In a famous lecture at M.I.T. in 1968, Herbert A. Simon outlined a programme for a science of design, and a curriculum for training of professional designers. He did this with engineering as an example, but argued that it was just as relevant for, e.g., management science or computer science, fields from which he had personal experience. In a broader perspective he concluded that "the proper study of mankind is the science of design, not only as the professional component of a technical education but as a core discipline for every liberally educated man." (Simon, 1969, p. 83)

Simon based this statement on his experiences from having lived close to the development of the modern computer and the growing communication among intellectual disciplines taking place around the computer. The ability to communicate across fields does not come from the computer as such, he argued, but from the need to "be explicit, as never before, about what is involved in creating a design and what takes place while the creation is going on." (Ibid., p. 83)

On the one hand, Simon took the position that what was traditionally known about design was "intellectually soft, intuitive, informal, and cookbooky"(Ibid., p. 57), and that this was scientifically unsatisfactory. At the same time he claimed that design of the artificial is really what most professions are about. Thus it cannot be replaced by mathematics, physics, etc. This understanding of a fundamental dilemma for the design sciences was an important observation by Simon.

The alternative that Simon suggested was a science of design of the artificial, a genuine science of its own. His elegant solution was to pose the problem of design of the artificial in such a way that we can apply methods of logic, mathematics, statistics etc., just as we do in the natural sciences.

In summary we learn from Simon's science of design of the artificial that computers are complex hierarchical systems, as are the users and the use organizations, and as is ISD — together they are sub-systems of a bigger system, and we can define their various functionalities separately. In designing these systems we can use many scientific methods (based on theory in formal logic, mathematics and statistics) for evaluation of designs and in the search for alternatives.

Concerning computer artifacts, the science of design of the artificial informs us that computers are systems "of elementary functional components in which, to a high approximation, only the function performed by those components is relevant to the behaviour of the whole system." (Ibid., p. 18)

Scientifically they can be studied both as abstract objects by mathematical theory and as objects in an empirical science of the behaviour of computers as complex systems. At the same time the computer artifact is also seen "as a tool for achieving a deeper understanding of human behaviour." (Ibid., p. 22). This is, Simon argued, because of its similarity in organization of components with the "most interesting of all artificial systems, the human mind." (Ibid., p. 22)

This approach was not without problems from a user and usability point of view. Theoretically we were stuck with design as a process of *problem-solving by individual decision-makers among sets of possible worlds*. It may be that this transformed the question of design into the rationalistic scientific vein, but at the same time many essential aspects of design seemed to be lost. What about the social and historical character of the design process — the conflicting interests, the differences in skill, experiences and professional languages? What about the creativity of professional designers and users; does design not by its very nature refuse to be reduced to formalized decision-making? However, such questions emerged only later in the history of ISD.

In the coming years Simon's programme and the rationalistic tradition appeared in many guises. One was the branch of rationalistic design formulated as the first programme for software engineering (Naur and Randell, 1969). This was the idea of understanding computer programs as formal mathematical objects derived by formalized procedures from an abstract specification. The correctness of programs was to be ensured by methods for successive transformations from specification texts to executable code. However, this product-oriented view left the relationship between programs and the living human world entirely open.

Another important appearance of the rationalistic tradition was the "theoretical analysis of information systems" (Langefors, 1966). Here, the idea was to define the elementary abstract information needs of an organization, and then redesign an optimal or at least sufficient information system. Based on this information systems analysis, specifications for implementation of computer-based information systems could be derived. This development was a reaction to the confusion of programming and data-structures with information needs in organizations. However, this approach remained entirely within the rationalistic realm. The relation between people in an organization and their information needs was a question of objective facts to be discovered by the analyst.

This rationalistic approach has been dominating in ISD ever since (e.g., DeMarco, 1978; Jackson, 1983; Yourdon, 1982; Lundeberg et al., 1978). For all their other merits, later object-oriented approaches in ISD have not changed the rationalistic picture (e.g., Coad and Yourdon, 1990).

In summary, the first ISD approaches were rationalistic and can be characterized by a strong belief in systematic design methods founded in mathematical-logical theories. These were design approaches guided by the research interest in technical control. A common assumption behind most of these objective ISD approaches in the IT design field seems to be that the users must be able to give complete and explicit descriptions of their demands.

12.3.2 Participation — a Social Approach

Partly as a reaction to the rationalistic ISD approaches, a "second generation" of ISD approaches developed in the 1970s. They focused on user participation, communication and democracy in the design process.

In the ISD field, participatory design approaches have been especially strong in Scandinavia (for an overview see Bjerknes et al., 1987; Ehn, 1988; Floyd et al., 1989; Greenbaum and Kyng, 1991). This new understanding of the role of users and designers in ISD as participatory design has been summarized as follows (Ehn, 1988):

- Participatory design is a learning process where designers and users learn from each other. Truly participatory design requires a shared social and cultural background and a shared language. Hence, participatory design is not only a question of users participating in design, but also a question of designers participating in use. The professional designer will try to share practice with the users.

- By understanding design as a process of creating new design practices that have family resemblance with the daily practices of both users and designers, we have an orientation for really doing design as skill based participation; a way of doing design that may help us transcend some of the limits of formalization. To set up these design practices is a new role for the designer. Hence, the creative designer is concerned with the practice of the users in organizing the design process, understanding that every new design practice is a unique situated design experience. However, paradoxical as it may sound, there are no requirements that the design practice makes the same sense to users and designers, only that the designer sets the stage for a design practice so that participation makes sense to all participants.

- Practical understanding is a type of skill that should be taken seriously in a design practice, since the most important rules we follow in skilled performance are embedded in that practice and defy formalization.

- Creativity depends on the open-textured character of human "rule-following" behaviour — how we enact and sometimes even invent the rules in a certain context as we go along. Hence, focus on traditional skill is not at the cost of creative transcendence, but a necessary condition. To support the dialectics between tradition and transcendence is at the heart of design.

- Traditional systems descriptions are not sufficient in a skill-based participatory design approach. Design artifacts should not primarily be seen as means for creating true or objective pictures of reality, but as means to help users and designers discuss and experience current situations and envision future ones.

- No matter how much influence participation may give in principle, design practices must transcend the boredom of traditional design meetings if the design work is to be a meaningful and involving activity for all participants. Hence, formal democratic and participatory procedures for designing computer artifacts for democracy at work are not sufficient. Design practices must also be organized in a way that makes it possible for ordinary users not only to utilize their practical skill in the design work, but also to have *fun* doing this.

- To set the stage for shared design practices using engaging design artifacts makes it possible for ordinary users to express their practical competence when participating in the design process. With "design-by-playing" approaches, such as the use of organizational games, designers can make useful interventions into the social interaction and social construction of an organizational reality. With "design-by-doing" approaches, such as the use of mock-ups and other prototyping design artifacts, it is possible for users to get practical "hands-on" experiences of the technology being developed.

This view of ISD was not there from the beginning. Scandinavian participatory design emerged from a strong political commitment to the idea of democracy at work. The pioneering research work of Kristen Nygaard and the Norwegian Metal Workers' union — the NJMF project — began in 1971, and the social definition of results was unique (Nygaard, 1979, p. 98):

> "as a result of the project we will understand actions carried out by the Iron and Metal Workers' Union, centrally or locally, as a part of or initiated by the project. In this strategy knowledge was acquired when actions had made the need for new knowledge clear. It was realised that successful initiatives at the national level had to be based on discussions and actions at the local level. The strategy towards design and use of information technology aimed at creating a process which would build up knowledge and activities at all levels, with the main emphasis at the local level."

One of the most tangible, and certainly the most widely studied and publicized outcome of the NJMF project was the *data agreements*. These agreements primarily regulate the design and introduction of computer-based systems, and in particular the acquisition of information. They also introduced so-called data shop stewards, a new kind of shop steward (NAF/LO 1975):

> "Through the shop stewards the management must keep the employees oriented about matters which lie within the area of the agreement, in such a way that the shop stewards can put forward their points of view as early as possible, and before the management puts its decisions into effect. The orientation must be given in a well-arranged form and in a language that can be understood by non-specialists. It is a condition that the representatives of the employees have the opportunity to make themselves acquainted with general questions concerning the influence of computer-based systems on matters that are of importance to the employees. The representatives must have access to all documentation about software and hardware within the area of the agreement."

The NJMF project inspired several new research projects throughout Scandinavia. In Sweden the DEMOS project on "trade unions, industrial democracy and computers" started in 1975 (Ehn, 1988). A parallel project in Denmark was the DUE project on "democracy, education and computer-based systems" (Kyng and Mathiassen, 1982). As the NJMF project, these projects emphasized democratization of the design process.

Although growing, the extent and impact of these activities did not meet the initial expectations. It seemed that one could only influence the introduction of the technology, the training, and the organization of work to a certain degree. From a union perspective, important aspects such as the opportunity to further develop skill and increase influence on work organization were limited. Societal constraints, especially concerning power and resources, had been underestimated, and in addition the existing technology constituted significant limits to the feasibility of finding alternative local solutions which were desirable from a trade union perspective.

At this instance the main idea of the first projects, to support democratization of the design process, was complemented by the idea of really *designing tools and environments for skilled work and good use quality products and services*. To try out the ideas in practice, the UTOPIA project was started in 1981, in cooperation between the Nordic Graphic Workers' Union and researchers in Sweden and Denmark with experience from the earlier projects (Ehn, 1988).

The NJMF, DEMOS, DUE and UTOPIA projects were followed by a number of projects jointly forming what became known as the Scandinavian participatory design approach. However, this approach changed focus over time. In the 1970s the researchers' interest was driven by a political commitment to the idea of *democracy at work*. Focus was on contact with local unions as the key players in ISD. At the same time there was an attempt to establish a link to the society level by trying to influence laws and agreements to be more supportive of democratic local change processes. It was an approach driven by a clear social change strategy, but it was weak on design methods. It is not a coincidence that the results focused on struggle, negotiations, laws and agreements. The approach was basically *ethical*, in the sense that it applied technology to achieve the quality of function.

In the 1990s the picture has changed. Much has been learnt about participatory design methods in numerous projects during the last decade. To make worker and management participation possible in ISD, a number of methods have been developed based on prototyping, full scale mock-ups, organizational games, role playing, future workshops, and so forth (see Greenbaum and Kyng, 1991). The inspiration for this change came from many sources.

One major source of inspiration was the theoretical reflections on what kind of phenomenon the design of computer artifacts actually is — a reframing of the rationalistic understanding of computer artifacts. The point of departure was what people do with computers in concerned human activity within a tradition. This also means an emphasis on differences in kinds of knowledge between on the one hand human practical understanding and experience, and on the other, knowledge representation in computers understood as "logic machines" or "inference engines". In design, focus was on concerned involvement rather than on correct descriptions. Design becomes a process of anticipating possible breakdowns for the users in future use situations with the computer artifacts being designed; anticipation in order to avoid breakdowns, as well as enabling users to recover from them. Two people have been particularly influential in the development of this tradition: the philosopher Hubert L. Dreyfus (Dreyfus, 1972; Dreyfus and Dreyfus, 1986) and the computer scientist Terry Winograd. Dreyfus argues for the relevance and importance of skill and everyday practice in understanding the use of computers. His investigations are based on the philosophical positions of existential phenomenology in the tradition of philosophers like Heidegger and Merleau-Ponty, and the positions on ordinary language and language-games taken by Wittgenstein. Winograd brought this view into computer science and the design of computer artifacts for human use. To Winograd it is in involved practical use and understanding, not in detached reflection, that we find the origin of design. Design is the interaction between understanding and creation. Winograd's arguments were first put forward in the by now classical book *Understanding computers and cognition* (Winograd and Flores, 1986). A complement to those reflections was the ethnomethodological approach to plans and situated actions formulated by the anthropologist Lucy Suchman (1987).

There was also the paradigmatic shift of primary point of view from design of software as formal mathematical objects derived by formalized procedures from abstract specifications, towards a *process-oriented* view. This new orientation in software engineering was suggested by people who were closely associated with the early software engineering programme. Particularly influential was the historically important paradigm shift paper by Christiane Floyd (1987). Also Peter Naur, one of the founders of the software engineering tradition, made comments in a similar direction (Naur, 1985). In this new paradigm, the software engineering focus is on human learning and communication in the design process, and the *relevance, suitability and adequacy in practical use situations of the software being designed*, not just on the correctness and efficiency of the piece of code being produced.

A more general source of inspiration were *social system design methods* which included *the role of subjectivity* in design of systems. Theoretically, the different approaches to social systems design have their origin in rationalistic systems thinking, but transcend this framework philosophically by including the subjectivity of the users. The different approaches are well developed and based on extensive practical experience. However, these approaches are fundamentally "pure" methodology. A challenge was to investigate how they could be integrated with, or supplemented by, substantial theory of the social situations in which they are to be used. Another challenge was how they could be refined to more specifically deal with design of computer artifacts and their use. Here, we want to concentrate on three design researchers who have developed challenging alternatives to Simon's systems engineering. They are C. West Churchman, Russell Ackoff, and Peter Checkland. To Churchman, a designer is engaged in detached reflection over the possibilities for developing and implementing good systems. In this he is guided by the *systems approach* (Churchman, 1968). This is a special development of ideas from American pragmatism, and in particular Churchman's philosophical mentor, E. A. Singer (Churchman, 1971). Ackoff, another of Singer's disciples, had a major influence on social systems thinking in operations research (see, e.g., Ackoff, 1974). As Churchman, he includes subjectivity in objectivity. But whereas Churchman was basically interested in ideas, Ackoff argued the crucial role of *participation*. To him, objectivity in design is the social product of the open interaction of a wide variety of individual subjectives. Ideally the design process involves as participants all those who can be directly affected by the system, its stakeholders. Ackoff's designer is not like a doctor who diagnoses organizational messes and prescribes cures; rather, he is like a teacher. The designer uses encouragement and facilitation to enable the participants and stakeholders to deal more effectively with their organizational messes — and have fun while doing it. Finally, Checkland, like Ackoff and Churchman, also started out in the tradition of rationalistic systems engineering. Like them he found that systems engineering simply was not appropriate for practical intervention in the complex and ambiguous "soft" problem situations in social practice. His systems development methodology is focused on the importance of the dialectics between the many and different world views involved. With Checkland, a step was also taken away from rationalistic systems thinking towards interpretation and phenomenology (cf. Checkland, 1981).

Finally we will mention the inspiration from the general history of design methodology. Computers are not the only artifacts that are designed. How did design methodology develop in more mature design fields, such as architectural and industrial design? Why was there a shift from rationalistic, formal and mathematically oriented approaches towards both more participatory approaches and more design-like ways of thinking? Why did theoretically influential designers react so strongly against their own rationalistic approach "to fix the whole of life into a logical framework" (industrial designer Christopher Jones) that they even advised us to "forget the whole thing" (architect Christopher Alexander) and started experimenting with art and chance in the design process? A fine collection of major papers in the design methodology movement was edited by architect and design researcher Nigel Cross (1984). To summarize briefly, the movement has developed through three generations since the early 60s. The first, rationalistic generation, up to the early 70s, included important contributions like Alexander (1964), Simon (1969) and Jones (1970). As a reaction to the expert role of the designer, a participative second generation of design methods developed in the 70s (Rittel, 1984). The focus shifted again in the 80s, and a third generation emerged, concerned with trying to understand what designers really do (Broadbent, 1984). The new transcending positions taken by early important members of the design methodology movement is illustrated by Alexander (1984) and Jones (1984). ISD in general as well as Scandinavian participatory design seem to have followed a similar pattern and the researchers from the Scandinavian participatory design tradition have become designers rather than politicians. At the same time the research has become more *aesthetical*, in the sense that it concentrates more on the quality of experience: What is it like for the worker to use the technology?

To conclude the historical survey, we may observe that participatory design today presents a well-established tradition, with a biannual international conference (PDC) and a broad literature (e.g., Schuler and Namioka, 1993; *Communications of the ACM,* 1993).

12.3.3 Design Ability – A Subjective Approach

Since the late 1980s a "third generation" of ISD has emerged. The specific competence of the designer has come more into focus, not least the importance of "tacit" and contextual knowledge in design and of conditions for creativity. These aspects emerged already in the participatory design approaches, but current research is now focusing on aesthetic values and a search for a missing complementary design rationality beyond construction and participation. Donald Schön (1983, 1987) made major contributions across design

Table 1. The developments in HCI and ISD in terms of Habermas' (1985) forms of knowledge interests.

	Objective	Social	Subjective
HCI	General theory; Usability engineering	Experiential	Interaction design
ISD	Systems theory; Software engineering	Participatory design	Design ability

disciplines to this third aesthetic-expressive generation of design approaches.

The approach, however, is still in its infancy in the ISD field. Adler and Winograd (1992) suggested a step in the direction of transcending design rationality by arguing that we must articulate new criteria of usability that are appropriate to the use situation.

> "The key criterion of a system's usability is the extent to which it supports the potential for people who work with it to understand it, to learn and to make changes. Design for usability must include design for coping with novelty, design for improvisation, and design for adaptation." (Ibid., p. 7)

The examples of design of everyday artifacts-in-use collected by Norman (1988) is another major source of inspiration for bringing this new design orientation to ISD.

In Scandinavia, several new approaches have been suggested. Lundequist (1992a, 1992b) proposed "design as language games", and Stolterman (1991) formulated the concept of "ideal-oriented design". Another similar example, that we shall elaborate below, is the "quality-in-use" approach to support the designer's design ability. This is based on a repertoire of paradigmatic cases of the interplay between technical, social and subjective aspects of information technology in use (Ehn et al., 1995).

12.4 Quality-in-use

The descriptions above make it fairly clear that both HCI and ISD have gone through a similar development. Based on Habermas' (1985) discussion of rationality in communicative action, we can characterize three phases in terms of the system developer's main interests as objective, social and subjective.

- The *objective* interests are based on a cognitive-instrumental rationality, concerned with the evaluation of objective facts. They lead to focusing on observation, empirical analyses and instrumental control for the purposive rational design of systems.
- *Social* interests are oriented towards a moral-practical rationality, related to evaluations of social action and the norms and practices of social interaction. Interpretation, communication and the establishment and expansion of action-oriented understanding become the main foci.
- *Subjective* interests stem from an aesthetic-practical rationality, addressing the sincerity in emotional and artistic expression. They emphasize emotional experiences and creativity.

Using these three categories, the developments we sketched above can now be summarized (Table 1).

For HCI, it is clear that general theory as well as usability engineering are guided primarily by objective interests. The methodology emerging from the experiential perspective is characterized by communication and understanding, and thus belongs primarily to the category of social interests. Finally, the interaction design perspective includes subjective interests (while certainly not neglecting the other two categories).

First generation ISD focused on systems theory and software engineering and emphasized methods to support knowledge elicitation by means of requirement specifications and transformations between different system descriptions. The relation between users and designers was guided by a cognitive-instrumental rationality. These approaches addressed the design process and the "world" of objective facts. Second generation ISD — participatory design — focused on user participation, communication and democracy in the design process. These were design approaches guided by the research interest in practical understanding. They addressed the design process and our social "world". The third generation of ISD illustrate the aesthetic-expressive interest designers' and users' design ability and experience of use. These new design approaches address the design process and our subjective "world" (again while hopefully not neglecting the other two categories).

Our discussion so far has concentrated on the dialectic evolution of ideas, and presented a simplified progression from objective via social to subjective interests. However, in looking back it is perfectly clear that all three types of interests are highly relevant for the theory and practice of system design. Although we may think of rationalistic design as an exclusive approach, an objective interest in instrumental control is relevant for the determination of a system to be implemented. At the same time, the process is undeniably one of dialogue and participation between all those concerned with the system — hence the social interest. Finally, any system that is in fact used in the world causes emotional use experiences and thus motivates a subjective interest. The question becomes one of formulating a design rationality that goes beyond objectivity and power in accounting for all the different interests.

Our response is to focus on the actual use situation and to assess the *quality-in-use* of the designed system. To account for the different interests means (by applying concepts from architecture) to study a system in use from three different standpoints: structure, function and form.

- The *structure* of a system is its material or medial aspects, the technology in terms of hardware and software. The structural aspects of a system are objective in the sense that they are inherent in the construction of the system, and less dependent on context and interpretation.

- The *functional* aspects of a system concern its actual, contextual purpose and use. Typically, different users have different purposes for and usage of a system. Organizational dynamics and impacts belong to the functional aspects, as do functions beyond the simple utilities of the system: one example is symbolic functions, such as the use of a laptop to signal personal effectiveness.

- Finally, the *form* of a system expresses the experience of using the system. Form is not a property of the system, but rather a relation between system and user. This further means that it is subjective, contextual and contingent on the individual user's previous experience.

To judge the quality of a system in use according to structural, functional and formal aspects means to apply three quality perspectives: construction, ethics and aesthetics.

The *constructional* quality of the system is expressed in terms of correctness, as is readily exemplified within the field of software engineering. Concepts such as performance, robustness, maintainability and portability are routinely developed and used to talk about the constructional quality of systems, typically in a way that is independent of the current use context.

The *ethical* quality of the system concerns whether it is used in the right way. Ethical questions are typically related to utility and power: Who benefits from the system? Who loses, who wins? Whose purpose is the system fulfilling? Ethical quality is obviously contextual, and — as shown above — fairly well developed in the ISD literature.

The *aesthetical* quality of the system is probably the hardest to explain and the least well-developed in the literature. To many individuals, aesthetics is associated with superficial beauty. For instance, a painting is perceived as beautiful, or a dress as pretty. But to take the form aspects of a computer system in use seriously requires more than merely assessing the beauty of the user interface. Again, form is not a property of the system but a relation between system and user. Aesthetic judgment is based on a repertoire of previous experiences ("This word processor feels like a cheap radio"), ideas, values and aesthetical concepts such as appropriateness ("the toolbar offers an appropriate set of tools") and comfort.

A well developed aesthetical sense, and the ability to continuously improve the feel for quality, are crucial in designing for use. In the design disciplines (such as architecture and industrial design), it is seen as necessary for the designer to have a thorough understanding of exemplars, traditions, epochs and styles of the discipline: classicism, functionalism, modernism, postmodernism, and so forth. However, our concept of quality-in-use adds another dimension to the style concept, namely the explicit focus on artifacts-in-use. To illustrate this distinction, consider the case of early functionalism in architecture as exemplified by the Bauhaus, which programmatically advocated the principle of social utility. However, the Bauhaus had an element of elitism and paradoxically a set of artifact-related aesthetic values that seemed unrelated to social utility. The social utility principle of the Bauhaus grew out of a political and emancipatory standpoint: by industrial production, good applied art could be made available to the general public. The Bauhaus, however, dictated what was good. Hence the elitist image and the lack of focus on artifacts-in-use. From our perspective, it would be necessary for a designer to concentrate on use experiences: to find out what it was like to, say, live in a Mies van der Rohe villa or attend a service in Corbusier's church at Ronchamps, and to incorporate that knowledge into the aesthetic value system.

To summarize, the quality-in-use of a computer system is determined by its constructional, ethical and aesthetical quality. These are three aspects on one phenomenon, and have to be dealt with concurrently. Actual use situations are the focal points where the perspectives meet; to assess quality-in-use means to describe and critique a use situation from all three perspectives in a holistic way. Within our discipline, constructional and ethical quality perspectives are comparatively well-developed (but not integrated) whereas the aesthetical quality perspective is merely beginning to form. We would argue that the further development of the aesthetic perspective and, perhaps most importantly, the integration of the three perspectives is needed for a proper understanding of use-centered systems development.

12.5 Implications for Information Systems Development

Going back to the evolutionary aspects of the first part of this paper, we noted a dialectical shift from the product-orientation of the first generation and the process-orientation of the second generation to a use-orientation beyond the product-process dichotomy. This concluding section discusses *use-centered systems development:* the development of systems for quality-in-use.

Our main message is simply the following: to design for quality-in-use, it is necessary to consider all three quality perspectives holistically: constructional quality for the structure, ethical quality for the function and aesthetical quality for the form. To elaborate, we will indicate what this could mean in terms of systems development practice and research.

12.5.1 Information Technology Criticism

On a fairly general level, the notion of assessing quality-in-use implies the emergence of *information technology criticism* and the scientific and societal role of *system critic*. Computing magazines often publish evaluations of the latest products. These reports, however, are typically intended to form the basis for a decision to purchase rather than evaluating quality-in-use. We can imagine a branch of system design research concerned with studying systems in use in more principled ways.

Traditional criticism, such as in art, literature or architecture, has to some extent focused on the artifacts in themselves. With our focus on quality-in-use, other sources are needed to provide the foundations for understanding the role of the system critic. The research tradition known as "social construction of technology" can provide useful starting points (see Latour and Woolgar, 1979; Bijker et al., 1987). A study of a system in use from a social construction perspective may enhance the reflective ability of a system designer in several ways. First, it may present the story of the system from several perspectives — users, managers, interest groups, etc. — and demonstrate how the system is actually continually constructed in discourse, which can be a valuable ethical insight on behalf of the designer. Secondly, the attention to detail and intimacy with actual use provides good material for conveying form aspects of the system in use (compare the current debate on ethnography in system design, e.g., Anderson, 1994). Thirdly, a social construction study can provide a language (categories, metaphors, etc.) to enable further debate of the system and its use. To summarize, the task of the system critic is to report his findings in a way that stimulates public debate and furthers the growth of applicable design knowledge, to the benefit of the designers and ultimately the users.

12.5.2 Design Ability

What skills, then, does a system developer need to have to design for quality-in-use? It is clearly outside the scope of this paper to enumerate all knowledge and skill requirements; we will focus on some specific implications of our approach. To do this, we need to introduce some preliminary concepts from design methodology.

Lundequist and Ullmark (1993) have formulated a conceptualization of the design process, intended to facilitate the understanding of what happens in design and how designers use different kinds of knowledge. It consists of three non-sequential steps or modes of operation: conceptual, constitutive and consolidatory.

- The *conceptual* step is guided by the designer's vision, which is typically not very distinct: unclear in parts, hard to communicate. To clarify the vision, the designer matches it to a repertoire of known structures, which are called formats. The matching process is a physically tangible activity, in which externalizations of different kinds are used to guide the work and to communicate with users and other stakeholders.

- In the *constitutive* step, the concept from the conceptual step is confronted with typical use situations in order to raise questions about requirements and constraints. The concept is modified and extended, and possibly abandoned in favor of a new wave of conceptual activity.

- The *consolidatory* step is concerned with refining a proposed solution in terms of simplicity, elegance and appropriateness for long-term use. Value-based judgment and experience are crucial components of consolidation.

As can be seen from the short description, the notion of quality-in-use has two main implications for this account of the design process. The first concerns the designer's repertoire of formats. In order to do good design, it is absolutely crucial for the designer to have a broad and reliable repertoire. The formats are significant not only in the conceptual step, where they shape the expression of the vision, but also in the constitutive step — good formats are robust with respect to the gradually uncovered constraints — and the consolidatory step, where the initial choice of format affects the appropriateness of the design for long-term use. This means that a good designer must be able to learn from observations and experiences of systems in use, and to operationalize his learning in new formats to use in future design situations.

The second implication concerns the value judgments being made throughout the design process: Is this a good choice of format? How serious is the constraint that we have discovered? Is the solution appropriate for actual use? The point we wish to make here is that all such judgments must be holistically made from constructional, ethical and aesthetical standpoints. It is highly unlikely that any significant design decision is purely constructional, ethical or aesthetical. The notion of quality-in-use provides the designer with a tool to ensure that the relevant values are brought to bear on the problem at hand. Phrased in terms of design ability, a good designer must have strong value systems in all three quality dimensions and be able to use them in an integrated way.

12.6 Acknowledgments

We are grateful to the editors for helpful comments and suggestions. This work was sponsored in part by the Swedish Board for Industrial and Technical Development (Nutek).

12.7 References

Ackoff, R.L. (1974). *Redesigning the future.* John Wiley.

Adler, P., and Winograd, T. (1992). The usability challenge. In Adler, P., and Winograd, T. (eds.) *Usability: Turning technologies into tools*, pp. 3-14. New York: Oxford University Press.

Alexander, C. (1964). *Notes on the synthesis of form.* Cambridge: Harvard University Press.

Anderson, R. (1994). Representations and requirements: The value of ethnography in system design. *Human-Computer Interaction* 9(2):151-182.

Bannon, L. (1991). From human factors to human actors: The role of psychology and human-computer interaction studies in system design. In Greenbaum, J., and Kyng, M. (eds.) *Design at work: Cooperative design of computer systems*, pp. 25-44. Hillsdale, NJ: Lawrence Erlbaum.

Beyer, H., and Holzblatt, K. (1995). Apprenticing with the customer. *Communications of the ACM* 38(5):45-52.

Bijker, W., Hughes, T., and Pinch, T. (1987). *The social construction of technological systems.* Cambridge, Mass.: MIT Press.

Bjerknes, G., Ehn, P., and Kyng, M. (1987). *Computers and democracy: A Scandinavian challenge.* Aldershot: Avebury.

Boehm, B. (1986). A spiral model of software development and enhancement. *IEEE Computer* 21(5):61-72.

Broadbent, G. (1984). The development of design methods. In Cross, N. (ed.) *Developments in design methodology.* Bath: John Wiley & Sons.

Card, S., Moran, T., and Newell, A. (1983). *The psychology of human-computer interaction.* Hillsdale, NJ: Lawrence Erlbaum.

Carroll, J. (1993). Creating a design science of human-computer interaction. *Interacting with Computers* 5(1):3-12.

Carroll, J., and Rosson, M. (1985). Usability specifications as a tool in iterative development. In Hartson, H.

(ed.) *Advances in human-computer interaction*, pp. 1-28. Norwood, NJ: Ablex.

Checkland, P. (1981). *Systems thinking, systems practice*. Chichester: John Wiley & Sons.

Churchman, C.W. (1968). *The systems approach*. New York: Delta.

Churchman, C.W. (1971). *The design of inquiring systems — Basic concept of systems and organization*. New York: Basic Books.

Coad, P. and Yourdon, E. (1990). *Object-oriented analysis*. Englewood Cliffs, NJ: Prentice-Hall.

Communications of the ACM (1993). Special issue on participatory design, 36(6).

Cross, N. (1984). *Developments in design methodology*. Bath: John Wiley & Sons.

DeMarco, T. (1978). *Structured analysis and system specification*. Englewood Cliffs, NJ: Prentice-Hall.

Dreyfus, H. L. and Dreyfus, S. D. (1986). *Mind over machine — The power of human intuition and expertise in the era of the computer*. Glasgow: Basil Blackwell.

Dreyfus, H. L. (1972) *What computers can't do — A critique of artificial reason*. New York: Harper & Row.

Dumas, J., and Redish, J. (1993). *A practical guide to usability testing*. Norwood, NJ: Ablex.

Ehn, P. (1988). *Work-oriented design of computer artifacts*, Stockholm: Almqvist och Wiksell.

Floyd, C. (1987). Outline of a paradigm change in software engineering. In Bjerknes, G. et al. (eds.) *Computers and democracy — A Scandinavian challenge*. Aldershot: Avebury.

Floyd, C., Mehl, W.-M., Reisin, F.-M., Schmidt, G., and Wolf, G. (1989). Out of Scandinavia: Alternative approaches to software design and system development. *Human-Computer Interaction* 4:253-350.

Good, M., Spine, T., Whiteside, J., and George, P. (1986). User-derived impact analysis as a tool for usability engineering. In *Human factors in computing systems (CHI'86 Proceedings)*, pp. 241-246. New York: ACM Press.

Greenbaum, J., and Kyng, M. (1991). *Design at work: Cooperative design of computer systems*. Hillsdale, NJ: Lawrence Erlbaum.

Grudin, J. (1993a). Interface: An evolving concept. *Communications of the ACM* 36(4):110-119.

Grudin, J. (1993b). Obstacles to participatory design in large product development organizations. In Schuler, D., and Namioka, A. (eds.) *Participatory design: Principles and practices*, pp. 99-119. Hillsdale, NJ: Lawrence Erlbaum.

Habermas, J. (1985). *Theorie des kommunikativen Handelns*. Frankfurt: Suhrkampf.

Holzblatt, K., and Beyer, H. (1993). Making customer-centered design work for teams. *Communications of the ACM* 36(10):93-103.

Holzblatt, K., and Jones, S. (1993). Contextual inquiry: A participatory technique for system design. In Schuler, D., and Namioka, A. (eds.) *Participatory design: Principles and practices*, pp. 177-210. Hillsdale, NJ: Lawrence Erlbaum.

Jackson, M. (1983). *System development*. Englewood Cliffs, NJ: Prentice Hall.

John, B. (1995). Why GOMS? *interactions* 2(2):80-89.

Jones, J.C. (1970). *Design methods — Seeds of human futures*. New York: Wiley.

Kyng, M., and Mathiassen, L. (1982) Systems Development and Trade Union Activities. In Bjørn-Andersen, N. (ed.) *Information society, for richer, for poorer*. Amsterdam: North-Holland.

Landauer, T. (1995). *The trouble with computers — Usefulness, usability and productivity*. Cambridge, Mass.: MIT Press.

Langefors, B. (1966). *Theoretical analysis of information systems*. Lund: Studentlitteratur.

Latour, B., and Woolgar, S. (1979). *Laboratory life: The construction of scientific facts*. Princeton, NJ: Princeton University Press.

Lundeberg, M., Goldkuhl, G., and Nilsson, A. (1978). *Systemering [Systems analysis]*. Lund: Studentlitteratur. In Swedish.

Lundequist, J. (1992a). Designteorins teoretiska och estetiska utgångspunkter [Theoretical and aesthetical foundations of design methodology]. Department of Architecture, Royal Institute of Technology, Stockholm. In Swedish.

Lundequist, J. (1992b). Projekteringsmetodikens teoretiska bakgrund [The theoretical background of architectural planning]. Department of Architecture, Royal Institute of Technology, Stockholm. In Swedish.

Lundequist, J., Ullmark, P. (1993). Conceptual, constituent and consolidatory phases — New concepts for the design of industrial buildings. In Törnqvist, A., Ullmark, P. (eds.) *Appropriate architecture: Workplace design in post-industrial society*, pp. 85-90. IACTH 1993:1, Chalmers University of Technology, Sweden.

Löwgren, J. (1993). *Human-computer interaction: What every system developer should know*. Lund: Studentlitteratur.

Löwgren, J. (1995a). Applying design methodology to software development. In *Proc. Symp. Designing interactive systems (DIS '95)*, pp. 87-95. New York: ACM Press.

Löwgren, J. (1995b). Perspectives on usability. Research report LiTH-IDA-R-95-23, Department of Computer and Information Science, Linköping University, Sweden.

NAF/LO: Norwegian Employers Federation and Norwegian Federation of Trade Unions (1975). *General agreement on computer based systems*.

Naur, P., and Randell, B. (1969). *Software engineering*. Report from a conference sponsored by the NATO Science Committee. Brussels.

Naur, P. (1985). Intuition and software development. In *Formal methods and software development*, Lecture Notes in Computer Science no 186. Berlin: Springer Verlag.

Nielsen, J. (1993). *Usability engineering*. Boston: Academic Press.

Norman, D. (1988). *The psychology of everyday things*. New York: Basic Books.

Nygaard, K. (1979). The iron and metal project: Trade union participation. In Sandberg, Å. (ed.) *Computers dividing man and work*. Malmö: Swedish Center for Working Life.

Rittel, H. (1984). Second-generation design methods. In Cross, N. (ed.) *Developments in design methodology*. Bath: John Wiley & Sons.

Roberts, T., and Moran, T. (1982). Evaluation of text editors. In *Human factors in computing systems (CHI'82 Proceedings)*, pp. 136-141.

Schuler, D., and Namioka, A. (1993). *Participatory design: Principles and practices*. Hillsdale, NJ: Lawrence Erlbaum.

Schön, D. (1983). *The reflective practitioner — How professionals think in action*. New York: Basic Books.

Schön, D. (1987). *Educating the reflective practitioner*. San Francisco: Jossey Bass.

Shackel, B. (1986). Ergonomics in design for usability. In Harrison, M., and Monk, A. (eds.) *People and computers: Proc. 2nd conf BCS HCI specialist group*, pp. 45-64. Cambridge: Cambridge University Press.

Shneiderman, B. (1980). *Software psychology: Human factors in computer and information systems*. Cambridge, Mass.: Winthrop Publishers.

Simon, H. (1969). *The sciences of the artificial*. Cambridge, Mass.: MIT Press.

Smith, S., and Mosier, J. (1986). Guidelines for designing user interface software. Report ESD-TR-86-278, Mitre Corp., Bedford, Mass.

Stolterman, E. (1991) Designarbetets dolda rationalitet [The hidden rationality of design work]. UMADP-RRIPCS 14.91, Department of Information and Computer Science, University of Umeå, Sweden. In Swedish.

Suchman, L. (1987). *Plans and situated actions — The problem of human-machine communication*. Wiltshire: Cambridge University Press.

Whiteside, J., Bennett, J., and Holzblatt, K. (1988). Usability engineering: Our experience and evolution. In Helander, M. (ed.) *Handbook of human-computer interaction*, pp. 791-817. Amsterdam: Elsevier.

Whiteside, J., and Wixon, D. (1987). The dialectic of usability engineering. In Bullinger, H.-J., and Shackel, B. (eds.) *Human-computer interaction — Interact '87*, pp. 17-20. Amsterdam: Elsevier.

Winograd, T. (1995). From programming environments to environments for designing. *Communications of the ACM* 38(6):65-74.

Winograd, T., and Flores, F. (1986). *Understanding computers and cognition — A new foundation for design*. Norwood, NJ: Ablex.

Wixon, D., Holzblatt, K., and Knox, S. (1990). Contextual design: Our experience and evolution. In *Human factors in computing systems (CHI'90 Proceedings)*, pp. 329-336. New York: ACM Press.

Woods, D., and Roth, E. (1988). Cognitive engineering: Human problem solving with tools. *Human Factors* 30(4):415-430.

Yourdon, E. (1982). *Managing the system life cycle*. New York: Yourdon Press.

Handbook of Human-Computer Interaction
Second, completely revised edition
M. Helander, T.K. Landauer, P. Prabhu (eds.)

Chapter 13

Ecological Information Systems and Support of Learning: Coupling Work Domain Information to User Characteristics

Annelise Mark Pejtersen
Risø National Laboratory
Denmark

Jens Rasmussen
Consultant
Denmark

13.1 Abstract

This chapter presents a framework for design of work support systems for a modern, dynamic work environment in which stable work procedures are replaced with discretionary tasks and the request of continuous learning and adaptation to change.

In this situation, classic task analysis is less effective and a framework is therefore presented for *work* analysis, separating a representation of the work domain, its means and ends, its relational structure, and the effective task strategies among which the user may choose, from a representation of the users' general background, resources, cognitive style and subjective preferences. The aim is to design work support systems that leave the freedom open to a user to choose a work strategy that suites the user in the particular situation.

An important feature of this ecological approach to system design for support of effective learning under changes in a dynamic environment is therefore a human-work interface directed towards a transparent presentation of the action possibilities and functional/intentional boundaries and constraints of the work domain relevant for typical task situations and user categories.

13.2 Introduction

Behavior during work is oriented towards the objectives of the work domain as perceived by the individual actor. These objectives, that is, what should be done, are usually well established, whereas when and how are left to the discretion of the user. The options for action will be defined by the work environment and the users are faced with a space of possibilities defined by the limits of functionally prescribed work performance, by limits of acceptable efficiency and, finally, by the knowledge and experience of the particular user and the work load accepted by the individual. Within this space of work performance, many action possibilities are left for the individual to explore and learn. Users' opportunities to learn and plan in a new territory depend on their knowledge of goals, work requirements and constraints, action possibilities and functional properties of the work environment. User knowledge is in particular critical for the initial planning of an activity and for the exploration of action possibilities and the boundaries of possible or acceptable performance.

The basic point of view taken here is to consider work and work organization in a dynamic environment to be a self-organizing and learning process. Learning is distributed across all individuals, teams and groups of an organization. In other words, a distributed, self-organizing feature will shape the functional and intentional structure of work, the role allocation to people, and the performance of the individuals. It is important that work support systems remain effective in this organic process and allow for evolutionary work performance.

To effectively support learning in a dynamic environment the human-work interface must be transparent and present action possibilities and functional/ intentional boundaries and constraints of the work domain relevant for typical task situations and user skill levels.

13.3 System Design and Work Analysis

Traditional work environments are planned for efficient performance through long periods. In for example manufacturing, product models are more or less standardized and change rather slowly. Planning criteria are efficiency, economy, and reliability. The human actors are tool users, they are involved in the transformation of work items. Their performance depends on know-how and skills which can evolve through long stable periods. In this situation, quite naturally, analysis and description of work are in terms of 'task analysis' decomposing the flow of activity into a sequence of modular elements, so called 'acts.' These express human activities on work objects by means of tools. Some workers become specialists on an individual tool or a set of tools. The specialization is high and time-and-motion studies can be used for planning. Work procedures are typically trained by apprenticeship. In stable systems, even the higher level coordination of activities can be based on stereotype and passing of forms, work schedules and orders.

Changes during such stable periods occur typically one-at-a time; the system has the opportunity to adapt to individual changes, as they propagate through the relational network of the organization. This, in turn, implies that the effects of changes can be generalized to entire branches of enterprises. This gives the opportunity to identify factors of influence and consequences by the use of questionnaires and interviews. Changes in work conditions and organizations can be analyzed using statistical, factorial analysis without the need for detailed studies of functional mechanisms and relationships affected by the initial change.

In a modern, dynamic organization, advanced information technology is the origin of many fundamental and simultaneous changes: Increasing mechanization and automation of the physical work processes imply that new skills and competence are required by actors. Knowledge and skill in the physical work process will be replaced by skills in diagnosis, operations analysis and planning of contingency control. Computer integration of activities offers a high degree of flexibility of planning and lead to systems, which are able to respond quickly and effectively to changing requirements. Design, work planning and production can no longer be a rather slow sequence of separate processes in different departments, but will be simultaneous, integrated activities of a task-force. Such organizations require decision support systems, centralization of data bases, and advanced communication systems which must be designed from a reliable analysis of the future needs of the individual actor in the individual, planned organization. In such systems, the effects of one drastic technological change will not have stabilized before another change appears and the many influences of the technological development can no longer be considered separately. We are no longer faced with the application of new technological means for solving problems which are empirically identified in the present systems. Instead, a continuous flux of simultaneous changes is found from introduction of new tools which place established functions in completely new relationships, together with changes caused by dynamic markets and legal environments.

New technology means new ways of doing things. If, however, the action possibilities offered by such new technology are not identified and formulated explicitly together with the necessary set of criteria of choice, there is a severe danger that the blindness from tradition and practice will prevent proper exploitation.

It is clear, that the design problem is not a human-computer interface problem, but the problem of designing effective human-work interfaces by means of new information technology.

From this discussion it is concluded that a systematic framework for analysis of the work domain includes a description of objectives, resources, and options for decisions is mandatory for design of information systems. Such systems should guide the users during the efforts to explore the work domain, to acquire expertise and skill. It must support users with very different levels of skill: it should support the novices without frustrating the experts.

13.4 The Approach To Analysis

A framework for analysis will be able to support dynamic analysis only if the constraints guiding this learning process are explicitly represented and can be modified.

Such an analysis of a modern dynamic work environment cannot be based on a classic task analysis, but must lead to a representation of the landscape of work within which actors are free to navigate according to their discretionary decision. This analysis will involve two paths of representation, as illustrated by figure 1. One path of analysis serves to identify the activities which an actor is faced with, another serves to identify the role and characteristics of the individual actor - as described in more detail in the subsequent paragraphs. In addition, the mutual relationships between these two concurrent aspects of an analysis should be kept in mind.

13.4.1 Identification of Activities

This is concerned with the 'work requirements,' which are to be compared to the actor's - user's - resources and preferences in order to determine the individual actor's likely choice of work strategy. It is important to stress that this analysis will not lead to a normative prescription, but to an identification of a repertoire from which actors can choose. Therefore, the analysis should be based on an ethnographic analysis of the scenario and involve hermeneutic interpretations of the actors' statements. It includes the selection of the performance variants, the formulation of tasks and strategies, the actors' subjective formulation of their goal, the way they view their tasks, and their subjective preferences. This is done by considering a repertoire of *'possible'* task strategies which are relevant and *can be used* by an actor dependent on the subjective interpretations.

The aim of the activity analysis then is to identify the characteristics of a work domain in such a way that

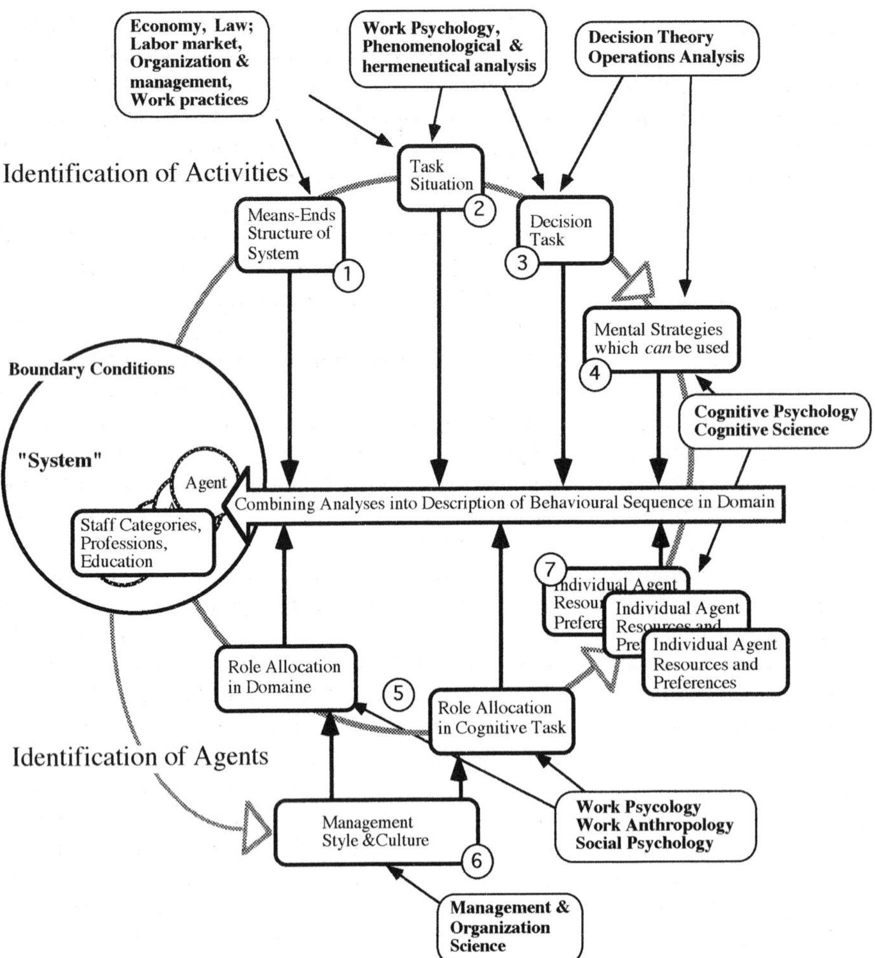

Figure 1. Illustrates the perspectives of a cognitive work analysis. *Two lines of analysis are used: The upper path of the figure shows the identification of activities. This is concerned with the 'work requirements', which are to be compared to the individual actor's resources and preferences and likely choice of performance. The lower path shows the identification of the actor. This line of analysis is aimed at a description of the role, the resource profile, and the subjective preferences of the individual actors and an identification of the cooperative structure. Also the scientific disciplines involved in the various analyses are indicated. The figure shows the cross-disciplinary disciplines required for a phenomenological and hermeneutic analysis of a work situation.*

they can be matched to the cognitive resources and subjective preferences of an actor. That is, the world of objectives, resources and constraints of the work content, expressed in terms belonging to the particular domain, should be related to the user characteristics expressed in psychological terms. This requires an analysis passing through several levels each with its particular language of representation. The strategy involves a step-wise zooming-in on the repertoire of action alternatives from which an actor can freely choose.

13.4.2 Identification of the Actor

The other line of analysis is aimed at a description of the role, the resource profile, and the subjective preferences of the individual actors and an identification of the cooperative structure. The work domain is considered to be controlled by the distributed decision making of cooperating actors. The analysis is focused on a determination of the criteria which control the dynamic distribution of work, i.e., the role allocation, and the *content* of the communication necessary for concerted action. In addition, the preferred *form* of communication as influenced by the adopted management style is analyzed. The point of view of the analysis is the evolutionary nature of the actual (informal) cooperative structures and work organizations. The organization is considered an open, self-organizing network, in accordance with the management and organization theories such as those presented by Thompson (1967). For a comprehensive review, see Scott (1987).

The interaction between the two lines of analysis is complex and iterative. *Role allocation* interacts with the description of the structure of the work domain and the nature of the task situation. The description of the mental strategies which *can* be used must be compatible with the description of the individual's resources and preferences. Finally, when a match between possible strategies and preferences has identified the chosen strategy, it has to be 'folded back' onto the higher levels of analysis and the work domain in order to determine the actual behavioral sequence. The individual will put meat on the conceptual bones; it is necessary to add details of the actual situation, which have been removed during the conceptual analysis. When a cognitive strategy is identified, the implications for the decision task and the related information requirements will be inferred. Next, the relevant set of cognitive activities involved in an actual situation will be determined to establish the likely work procedure in actual work domain terms and, finally, the involved means-ends structure in the work domain can be identified as well as the coupling to other activities and actors.

13.5 The Dimensions of the Framework

The different levels of analysis and their significance for system design are briefly described in the subsequent sections with reference to figure 1 (for more details, see Rasmussen et al. 1994).

13.5.1 Work Domain, Task Space

This dimension of the framework serves to *delimit* the system to be analyzed and thus to represent the landscape within which work takes place. It serves to make explicit the goals and constraints which must be respected in meaningful work activities independent of particular situations and tasks in order to have a first delimitation of an actor's action possibilities. This analysis of the basic means-ends structure is particularly well suited to identify goals and constraints which have been hidden in established practice and to find possible alternatives. In addition, it gives structure to the description by decomposition in modular elements along the part-whole dimension and by identification of the potential means and ends at several levels of abstraction covering physical form and anatomy, physical processes, general functions, abstract value functions and, finally, of the goals and constraints with reference to the environment, see Figure 2. At the lower levels, elements in the description represent the material properties of the work domain. When moving from one level of abstraction to the next higher level, the change in domain properties is not merely a removal of detailed information about physical or material properties, but information is added on at higher-level principles governing the co-functioning of the various elements at the lower level. These higher-level principles representing co-functions are derived from the purpose of the work domain, i.e., from the reasons and intentions behind.

An important feature of this complex means-ends network is the many-to-many mapping found among the levels. If this was not the case, there would be no room or need for human decision or choice (Rasmussen, 1985). Analysis within this dimension identifies the structure and general content of the global knowledge base of the work domain that is, the functional territory within which the actors will navigate. Analysis of the organization of the work and coordination functions in the various levels of means-ends relationships will greatly support the identification of the actors' needs for retrieval of information as well as the information that will be presented in interfaces. The means-ends structure explicitly will identify the *why*, *what* and *how* attributes of information items, see figure 3. This dimension of the analysis is also important for the categorization of work domains and the approach to work support and we will return to this issue in detail below in the section called "kinds of work domains".

13.5.2 Activity Analysis in Domain Terms

This dimension further delimits the focus of analysis to the possibilities left for meaningful work activities as these are bounded by the constraints posed in time and in functional or intentional space. It instantiates that subset of the basic means-ends network which is relevant for a particular task. It is important to realize that 'a typical task sequence' will not normally exist in a modern, advanced work setting. In consequence, generalization cannot be made in terms of work procedures found by a classical task analysis. Generalization should be made at the level of the individual decision

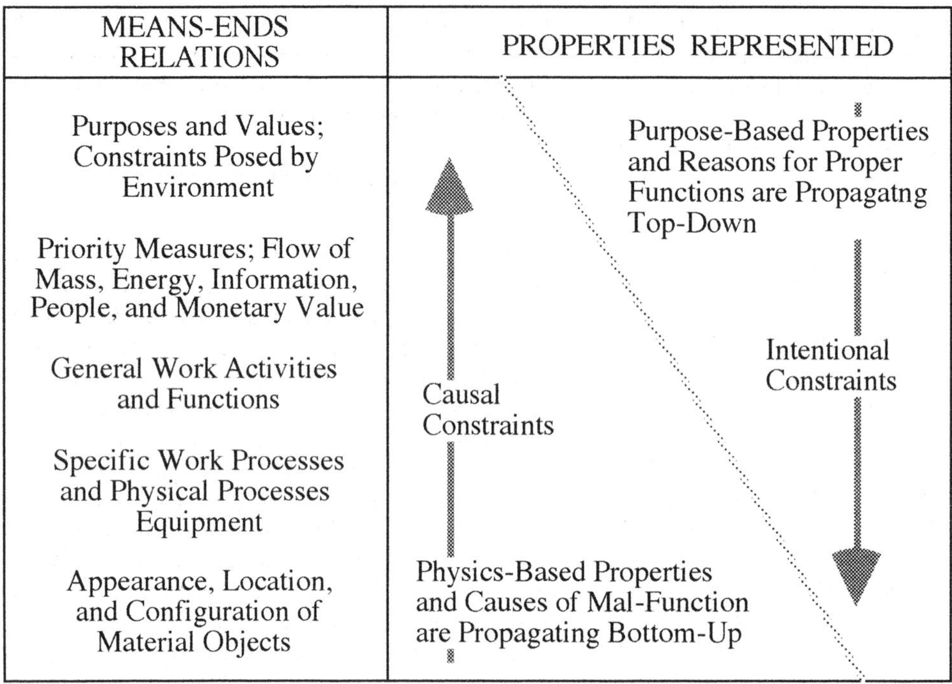

Figure 2. Any system can be described at several levels of functional abstraction adding up to a means-ends hierarchy. *Lower levels are related to the physical configuration and processes. Higher levels to general functions and priority measures. Reasons for proper functions propagate top-down while causes of functional changes propagate bottom-up. The need and potential for human decision making depend on a many-to-many mapping among the levels of representation.*

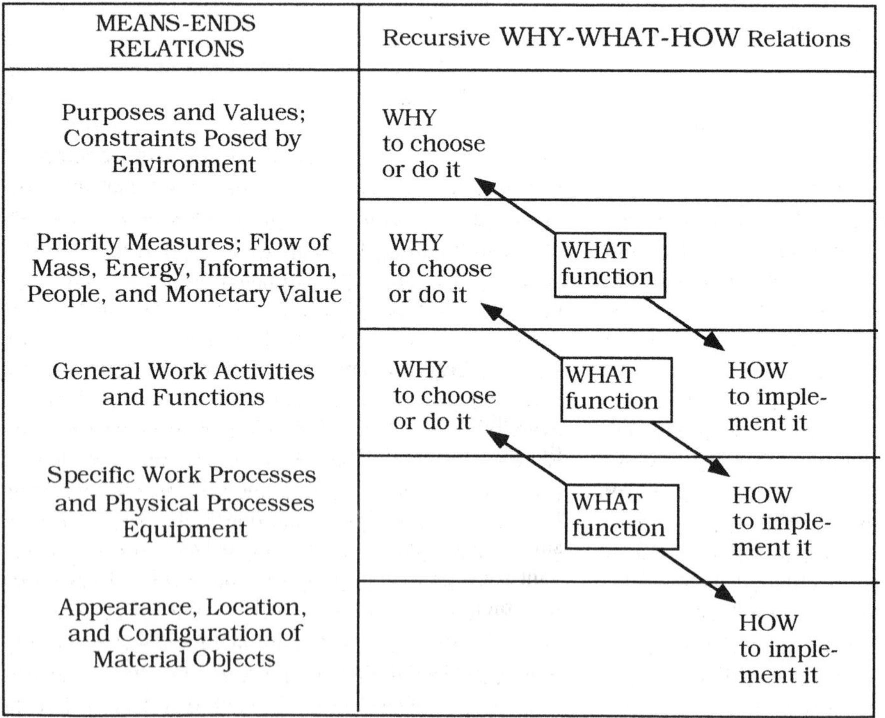

Figure 3. WHY, WHAT and HOW in the means-ends space.

situation and be expressed in *domain terms* thereby identifying a set of prototypical task situations which can be used to represent activities to be considered in information system design.

For the interface design, this part of the analysis separates from the global knowledge base the particular information that will serve a user and the information necessary to serve an integrated set of tasks and to coordinate the support of cooperating actors.

13.5.3 Decision Analysis in Information Terms

For this analysis a shift in representational language is necessary. For each of the activities defined above under dimension 2, the relevant tasks in terms of decision making functions, such as situation analysis, goal evaluation, or planning, are identified. This representation serves to break down work activities in subroutines which can be related to cognitive activities and, at the same time, it punctuates activities by "states of knowledge," which separate different information processes and which are normally the nodes used for communication in cooperative activities.

The information gained in this analysis will identify the knowledge items from the work domain representation, which are relevant for a particular decision task, together with the required information about their functional relationships. In addition, it identifies the quest-ions posed by decision makers.

13.5.4 Information Processing Strategies

Further analysis of the decision functions requires a shift in language in order to be able to compare task requirements with the cognitive resource profile and the subjective performance criteria of the individual actors. For this purpose, the mental strategies which *can* be used for each of the decision functions are identified by detailed analysis of actual work performance of several individuals in different situations. *Strategies* are categories of cognitive task procedures each based on a particular mental model and the related interpretation of information, and on a particular set of tactical rules. The characteristics of the various strategies are identified with respect to subjective performance criteria such as time needed, cognitive strain, amount of information required, cost of failure, etc.

Analysis of the available effective strategies is important for the interface design because it supplies the designer with several coherent sets of mental models, data formats, and tactical rule sets which can be used by actors of varying expertise and competence. In the following phases of analysis, constraints on meaningful activities depending on the role and preferences of the individual actor are analyzed.

13.5.5 Allocation of Decision Roles

The first step in the analysis of the degrees of freedom for subjective choice within the work given constraints, is an identification of the principles and criteria determining the allocation of roles among the groups and individuals involved. The work domain is considered to be under control of a set of cooperating actors, and allocation of roles can refer to sub-spaces of the work domain or roles in decision functions. This allocation of roles to actors is dynamically depending on the circumstances and is governed by criteria such as actor competency, their access to information, the need for communication for coordination, sharing of work load, compliance with regulations (e.g., Union agreements) and so forth.

This phase of the analysis identifies the scope of the information window which should be available for an actor during a particular work situation and the information exchange with cooperators needed for coordination. The constraints posed by the work domain and the criteria for role allocation specifies the *content* of communication necessary for concerted activity.

13.5.6 Management Structure, Social Organization

While the role allocation determines the content of communication necessary for coordination, the "management culture" of the organization determines the form of communication, i.e., whether the coordination depends on orders from an individual actor, on consensus in group decision making, or on negotiation among the involved actors. The management structure will heavily influence subjective performance criteria and the formulation of goals and constraints of the individual actor. The identification of the communication conventions underlying the social organization is necessary to determine the communication formats of an integrated information system. In particular, identification of the actual role of the communication of social values, subjective criteria, and intentions for coordination of activities, for resolution of ambiguities, and for recovery from misinterpretation of messages, is very important for the allocation of functions to an information system and to face-to-face communication, and for the design of the information communication formats.

13.5.7 Mental Resources, Competency, and Preferences of the Individual Actor

At this stage, the action possibilities available in the individual actor's work performance have been delimited by identification of the work depending constraints and the mental strategies which *can* be used for the decision functions that are allocated the individual actor. In order to judge whether a given actor is able to meet the requirements and to determine the approach to work which might be chosen, the level of expertise and the performance criteria of the individual actors should be analyzed.

When planning field studies for system design, cross-disciplinary studies should be carefully considered up front including ethnographic methods for observations and interviews and hermeneutic and pheno-menological approaches to analysis and interpretation of field data. This analysis requires expertise in the particular work domain, both with respect to the core technology and the work practices, and competence in operations analysis, work psychology, decision theory and cognitive psychology (Rasmussen et al., 1974; Pejtersen, 1979; Rochlin et al., 1987; Bucciarelli, 1984, 1988).

13.6 Ecology of Work and Direct Perception

Accepting the role of learning for effective performance there are implications for the design of the information environment. Work is more effectively supported by an information environment which makes visible the ecology of work with direct perception of its internal functional and intentional relationships, rather than by giving advice with respect to preconceived ideas by the designer about the proper way of approaching a task.

According to Gibson (1979) the basis for direct perception is said to be the invariant relationships in the ecology that are made available to the observer via invariants in the optical array. The notion of an affordance, an invariant combination of variables that demands or invites appropriate behaviors, was introduced to account for goal-oriented behavior. Basically, an affordance represents attributes of the environment that are relevant to the organism's purposes; it specifies a possibility for action. An object's affordances are perceived via the invariants through a process of direct attunement. Thus, perception is viewed as a means of selecting the appropriate action to attain a goal, and the concept of an affordance relates perception to action. The result is goal-oriented behavior. Gibson claimed that in normal cases the meaning and value of the objects are directly perceived, not only the individual characteristics of these objects.

It is useful to consider the hierarchy of levels at which direct perception of the environment can take place. Gibson provides some examples to explain how the world is actually composed of a hierarchy of affordances. An interesting property of this hierarchy is that the relation between levels is one of means-ends relations, which makes it plausible that the concept of affordances can be described with the means-ends structure of the framework described above (see figure 2). This has important implications for the design of 'ecological information systems.' Perception of affordances at the various levels has different roles in the control of human activity. Selection of goals to pursue are related to perception of value features at the highest level, the planning of activities to perception at the middle levels, while the detailed control of movements depends on perception at the lowest level of physical objects and background.

This implies that the interface can be processed without any mediating decision making; the information in the relational means ends structure would be perceived as affordances that would specify what action to take.

Displaying the invariant structure and the affordances of the work domain is a more effective way to support discretionary tasks than procedural guides. In other words, in a world of dynamic requirements, a map supports navigation more effectively than route instructions. This approach will lead to an information system which presents for actors a complex, rich information environment.

Designers are often warned not to create cluttered, complex displays. However, complexity in itself is not a problem, Users can be overloaded by presentation of many separate data, whereas meaningful information presented in a coherent, structured context may not be perceived as cluttered. Skilled actors in work are not subject to information input; they are actively asking questions to the environment, based on their perception of the context. They are able to consult even a very complex environment perceptively, given a meaningful organization.

13.7 Kinds of Work Domains

It appears from this discussion that to support ecological decision making, system designers should focus on the action possibilities, boundaries and con-

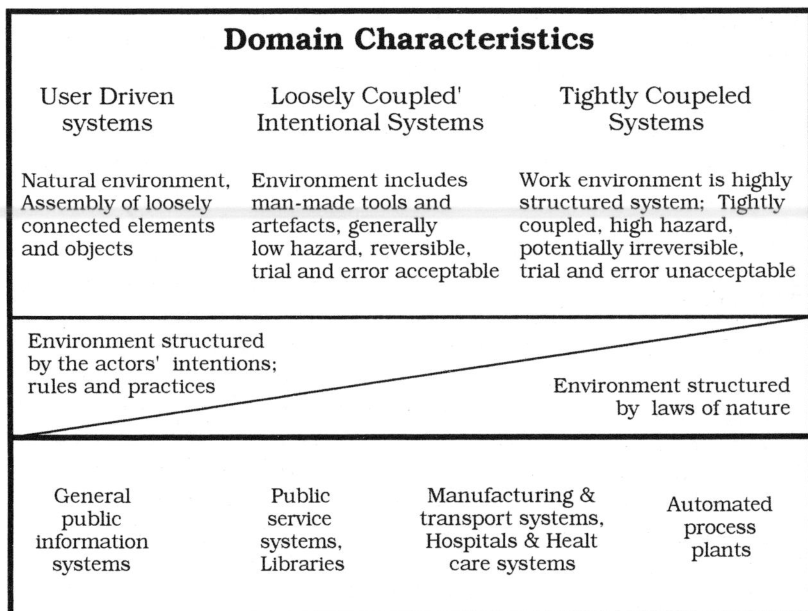

Figure 4. Some basic properties of different work domains. *The properties of work domains and tasks vary along many dimensions which underlie the work framework. However some of the properties can be gathered together to generate typical cases. Thus the figure illustrates a continuum stretching from domains constituted by "natural environments" with loosely coupled assemblies of objects on the one hand to highly structured and tightly coupled technical systems at the other extreme. System design considerations at these two extremes will, of course, have to be very different.*

straints in a work domain and on the information requirements of experts as well as novices during work. Only a thorough understanding of the deep structure of the work domain can be a basis for meaningful, complex interfaces.

This understanding can be based on the means-ends structure which is described above in the framework for work analysis. The levels of abstractions are illustrated in figure 2. The higher levels of abstraction represent properties connected to the purposes and intentions governing the work domain, whereas the lower levels represent the causal basis of its physical elements. Consequently, perturbations of the work domain in terms of changes in company goals, management policy, or general market conditions will propagate downward through the levels. In contrast, the effect of changes of the material resources, such as introduction of new tools and equipment or break down of major machinery will propagate up-wards, being causes of change. To achieve the intended goal any actor striving to control or change the state of affairs within a work domain will have to take changes of the internal constraints and their possible effects into consideration. This involves operation on the *causal constraints* of the physical part of a work domain, or on the *intentional constraints* of the functional task requirements originating in the other actors of the work domain. Whether one or the other mode of control is appropriate, depends on the task situation and the characteristics of the work domain.

The weight of intentional constraints compared with functional and causal constraints can be used to characterize different work domains. In this respect, the properties of different work domains represent a continuum from tightly coupled, technical systems where the intentional properties of the work domain is embedded in the functions of a control system, through systems where intentionality is represented by social rules and values, to systems in which the entire intentional structure depends on the actual users' subjective preferences, see figure 4. The relationship between the causal and intentional structuring of a work system, and the degree to which the intentionality of the system is embedded in the system or brought to work by the individual actor is an important characteristic of a work domain to be considered in the design of ecological information systems.

In the following sections, some examples are discussed to illustrate the influence of the work domain characteristics on design of work support systems.

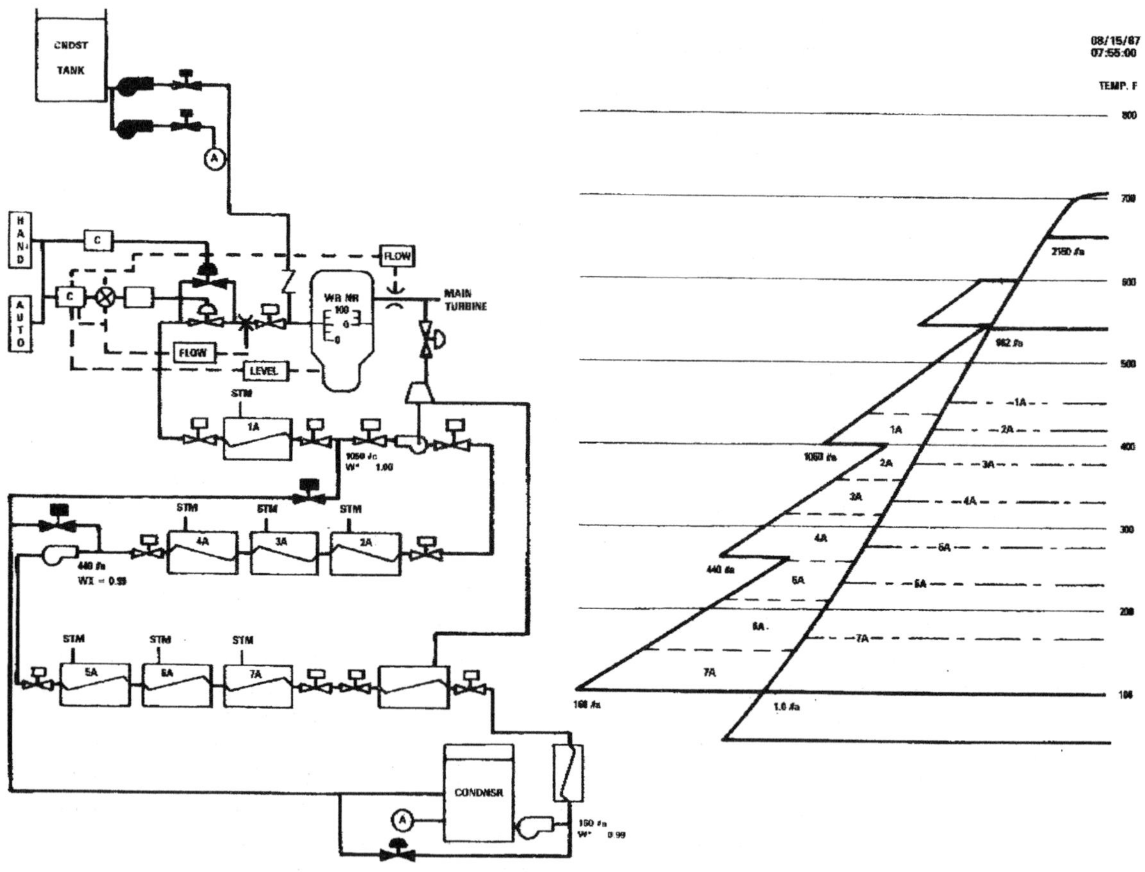

Figure 5. ***Symbolic display for operation of the feed-water system of a power plant.*** *The display combines a configural representation of the measured process variables with reference to the intended operation (Rankine symbols) with a mimic diagram for resource management. The display is based on primary measuring data used to modulate the shape of graphical patterns which support perception of higher level functional features. (For a detailed description see Beltracchy, 1984, 87, 89; Rasmussen et al., 1994). Courtesy Leo Beltracchi.*

13.7.1 Tightly Coupled Technical Systems

The regularity of behavior of some systems such as industrial process plants, manufacturing machinery, automatic tools, etc., depends on physical processes obeying *laws of nature* within boundary conditions created by the technical equipment. The *content* of the information environment to be created for system users or *'operators'* depends on the physical laws from which the processes of the system and the limit conditions of the confinement are determined.

Visual support of work in systems with a stable and well defined functional structure, and with work processes which can be quantitatively modeled, can be given by displays which represent the actual, functional state (the relationships among measured variables), and the intentional target and limit states in a compatible fashion. Consequently, the representation of invariants will often be in terms of diagrammatic representations of relationships among quantitative variables, for an example see figure 5. (For a detailed discussion of ecological interfaces for this category of systems see Rasmussen and Vicente, 1990; Rasmussen and Goodstein, 1987, Vicente and Rasmussen 1993).

The functionality of the process systems to a large degree is implemented in the configuration of the tightly coupled production equipment. The intentional structure will be hard-wired into a complex, automatic control and safety system, serving to maintain the functions of the production equipment in accordance with the high level, stable design goals, e.g., to produce power as requested by customers, and to do it as eco-

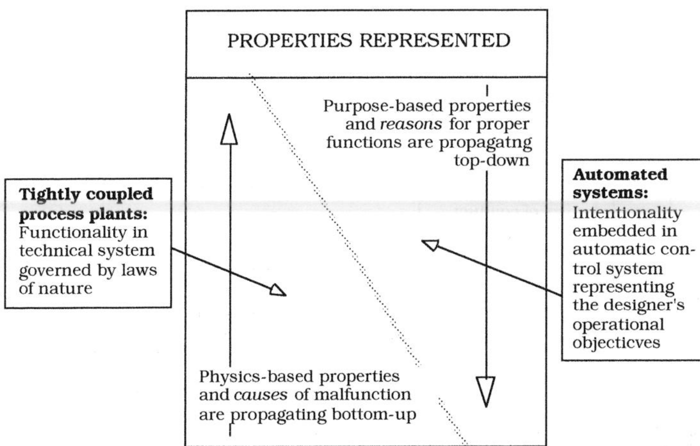

***Figure 6. In a technical system, such as, e.g., a power plant, the functionality is implemented in the configuration of the** tightly coupled production equipment and the intentional structure shown will be hard-wired into an, automatic control system. The subjective intentions of the operators are irrelevant.*

nomically and safely as possible through the lifetime of the system. The task of the operating staff is basically to make sure that the function of the automatic control actually represents the intentionality of the original design. In this type of systems, the user is an 'operator' serving the system, see figure 6.

Reasoning of operators in process plants is generally supposed to be causal reasoning from an understanding of the functionality of the system. However, for the understanding of the control system functions, intentional reasoning is necessary. Unfortunately, in process plant control rooms, little attention has been given the communication of design intentionality to the operating staff by designers of support systems (Rasmussen, 1987).

13.7.2 Loosely Coupled or Intentional Systems

Another kind of systems is found when regularity of system behavior is related to human intentions such as policies, plans, and regulations. This category includes many important examples such as offices, manufacturing workshops and hospitals. In these systems, the functional coordination is not brought about directly by a tightly coupled production system but depends on the activities of the staff, see figure 6. The intentionality originating from the interpretation of environmental conditions and constraints by management of for example a manufacturing company, propagates dynamically downward and becomes implemented in more detailed policies and practices by members of the staff. Making intentions operational and explicit during this process requires instantiations by a multitude of local details. Therefore, choice among many action possibilities remains to be resolved by situational and subjective criteria by the staff at the intermediate levels of an organization. This in turn implies that the individual actor faces a work environment in which the regularity to a considerable degree depends on the intentionality brought to bear by colleagues. The intentional structure is much more complex and dynamic than for the industrial process systems, see figure 7.

In a stable work environment, the odds are that intentionality can be embedded in a common work practice. However in a modern, flexible work organization, the exchange of intentional information among cooperating actors becomes an important function of an information system. Dynamic and verbal as well as nonverbal communication of intention among cooperating individuals become very important. Reasoning in intentional systems generally will be based on intentions and motives, capability and power, not causality. When replacing direct face-face contact in cooperative activities by 'advanced work stations,' the role of non-verbal perception of the intentions of colleagues must be very carefully considered.

In contrast to systems governed by laws of nature, intentional systems are normally represented by qualitative models in terms of objects and chains of events rather than relations among quantitative variables. Case handling in offices is normally described in terms of a transaction sequence. The invariant structure governing the sequencing can be represented by an event tree representing planning policies and regulatory rules and describing the possible paths of a case through a system. In this tree, the branching points reflect the deci-

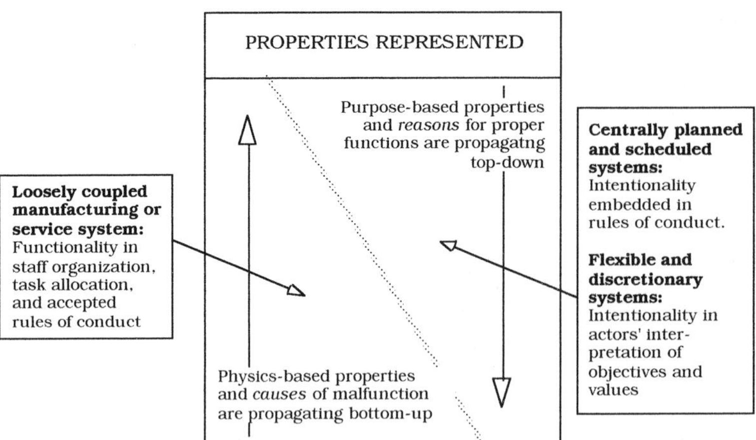

Figure 7. In a loosely coupled system such as e.g., and office, the functionality propagates upward by the activities of the staff. *The institutional intentionality propagates downwards but many degrees of freedom are left to the actors and subjective interpretation adds intentional constraints to the work environment of the individual actors. The intentional structure is very complex and dynamic. Direct verbal and non-verbal communication of intentions is important.*

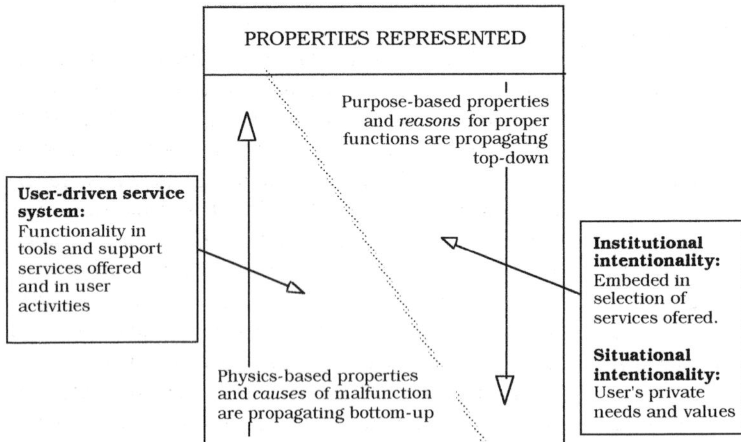

Figure 8. Illustrates the sources of functionality and intentionality in a library system. *The institutional intentionality is only represented in the selection of the book stock. The intentionality in the situation is defined by the user. The semantics of a support system should match the intentions of the users and the functionality the user's preferred search strategies.*

sion points in which it is possible to change the course of events.

Acceptance of the learning nature of modern organizations implies that office activities cannot be modeled by general transaction concepts. Analysis of the substance matter of the administrative activities is necessary. Office work actually takes place within a functional and intentional network shaped by the structure and content of the productive activities of the organization. Therefore, local and subjective criteria is an important object of analysis. Unfortunately, identification of such criteria from analysis of the present and observed work practice is a difficult matter.

13.7.3 User Driven Systems

Another kind of work system located further to the left in the map of figure 4 is the user-driven work system, i.e., a system designed for support of the personal (private or professional) needs of a user. In this case, the intentionality governing the use of the system is brought to work by the individual user within the space defined by the institutional policies, see figure 8. Like intentional systems, user driven systems can best be represented by qualitative models in terms of objects and chains of events. The focus in design of support systems has traditionally been on providing factual in

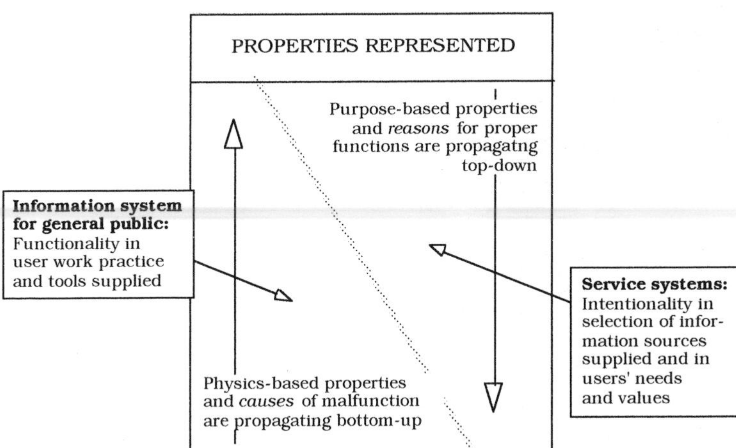

Figure 9. For some systems, the users' task situation is unknown and a metaphor based approach is chosen to system design. *That is, system functionality is organized to match the intentions and skills governing user behavior in another, familiar environment.*

formation about the state of affairs in the work domain and about functional relations. Little effort has been spent on intentional information which is an increasingly important issue for system design.

An example of this category is the system for information retrieval in public libraries described in the last section of this chapter. In this example, the aim of the design has been to impose a functional structure on the retrieval system which matches the preferred search process of the user. The semantics of the search to be represented by the interface should represent the invariants and affordances which map onto the users' intentional structure and their explicitly or implicitly formulated information needs. How this can be done in general depends on the degree to which the categories of users and their intentional structure can be analyzed and formulated.

13.7.4 Systems for the Autonomous, Casual Users

For some information systems, such as lexicographic data bases, information services for the general public, etc., the task situation and intentions of the casual users in general is considered to be unknown. The systems normally include a set of generally useful information sources and data bases coming from many different public services, institutions, and commercial companies, see figure 9. No generally relevant intentional structure or task situation is normally formulated as a design basis to structure system function or interface design. The intentionality of the task situation is entirely defined on occasion by the actual user. Not even the higher level means-ends structure of a system is formulated except in very general terms of making information available to the public.

For such systems without structural invariants (when the user situation cannot be defined in advance), an artificial structure can be imposed on the interface to help the user to navigate and to remember the location of previously consulted items. In general, a cover-story can be found which makes it possible for a user to transfer intuition and skill from another familiar situation, i.e., a *metaphor* can be used, such as the desk-top metaphor for office systems. The metaphorical approach is also the basis for the Japanese "21st Century Personalized Information Environment" project (Fri-end'21, 1991) which is based on transfer of features of a familiar medium (news-paper, TV news, albums, etc.) to the computer-based medium in terms of two principles: the *multiple metaphor* and the *multiple actors* principles.

13.7.5 Conclusion

In most modern domains the goal-relevant domain properties are not directly observable unless modern information technology provide users with the capability to visually explore, learn and manipulate the objects of the work environment. The nature of the work domains and the source of their internal boundaries and constraints that shape actor behavior and are to be learned by the actor, basically defines the knowledge base supplying the *content* of the interface presentation. The interface content is derived from the analysis of work situations, decision tasks and applicable

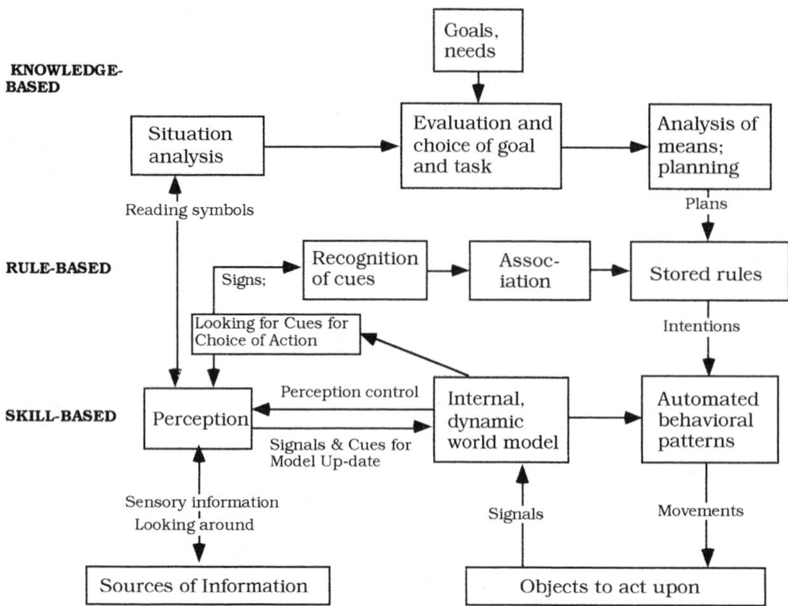

Figure 10. Schematic map illustrating different levels in cognitive control of human behavior. *The basic level represents the highly skilled sensori -motor performance controlled by automated patterns of movements. Sequences of such sub-routines will be controlled by stored rules, activated by signs. Problem solving in unfamiliar tasks will be based on conceptual models at the knowledge based level which serve to generate the necessary rules ad-hoc. - skill-based behavior depending on a repertoire of sensori-motor patterns rule based behavior, involving attention on cue-classification and choice among alternative responses or recall of past scenarios to prepare for future action and, finally, knowledge-based behavior based on situation analysis and action planning based on a mental relational model.*

mental strategies. The *form* in which the information should be presented depends very much on the level of expertise and cognitive style that a user will bring to work in a given situation.

13.8 Coupling the User's Expertise to the Work Content

The aim of ecological information systems is to reflect the deep structure of the work environment that enables the actor to utilize all the cognitive levels of expertise also in work domains where the relational means ends structure is hidden from normal direct perception. This involves the creation of - not a virtual reality - but a virtual ecology "making the invisible visible."

We are concerned with the dynamic coupling of the cognitive processes of the actor with varied levels of expertise to the relational means ends structures and sources of regularity of the work domain (natural laws, social policies, user intentions). This complex coupling is related to several levels in the means-ends representation, to several modes of cognitive control and to different time horizons - each of which may change with the actual work domain, even within the same task situation.

To do this, we have to consider in detail the basis for the users' cognitive control, the related mental representations, and the interpretation of observations, that is the skill-, rule-, knowledge model of cognition, (Rasmussen, 1983, 1985). In this effort we have to consider that humans are not subject to information 'input' but are goal-oriented creatures who actively select their goals and seek the relevant information.

The particular aspect of interest is that this model conceives human information processing as being based in an internal 'dynamic world model' representing the dynamic interaction of the body and senses with the environment. This dynamic world model can be seen as a structure of objects and their functional and intentional properties: what they can be used for, their potentials for interaction and what can be done to them. These elements of behavior are updated and aligned according to sensory information acquired while interacting with the environment, see figure 10.

During very *familiar situations* involving a high degree of sensori-motor skill, such as car driving, this model is synchronized to the environment. It controls effectively the behavior of the body, and directs the perception toward environmental features that need attention for up-dating of the internal model. During a familiar situation, in a normal 'real world' environment, the internal world model represents and guides perception at all the levels of the means-ends hierarchy. Consider for example the reaction of a tennis player to a oncoming ball. This is not controlled by the slow perception of the path of the ball, but on the anticipation based on direct perception of the opponent's intention. Evolution has created a particular sensitivity which makes it possible directly to perceive the intention of an actor. Direct perception at all levels of means-ends abstraction is very effective in a familiar, real world social context and, likewise, when faced to pictorial representations of such a context.

When the environment is *less familiar,* as when it deviates from the prediction of the internal world model, an interrupt to a more or less conscious attention occurs, and the environment is consulted to find a cue for choice of a proper response or set of responses, a rule of action that has previously been successful in a similar, unusual situation, see figure 10. If no suitable response is found, situation analysis becomes necessary, and conscious deliberation based on declarative knowledge and a mental model of the relational structure of the environment is activated to analyze the problem, understand the situation and plan a suitable action. We have, thus, three basically different levels of control of the interaction with the environment as described below.

13.8.1 Skill-based Behavior

Skill-based behavior represents sensory-motor performance during activities which, following a statement of an intention, take place without conscious control as smooth, automated, and highly integrated patterns of behavior. In most skilled sensory-motor tasks, the body acts as a multivariable continuous control system synchronizing movements with the behavior of the environment. The senses are subconsciously directed towards those aspects of the environment needed to update and orient the internal world model. The flexibility of skilled performance is due to the ability to compose, from a large repertoire of automated subroutines suited for various familiar purposes.

Representations at the skill-based level. Performance at the skill-based level depends on a dynamic world model which has a perceptual basis. The model is structured with reference to the space in which the person acts and is controlled by direct perception of the features of relevance to the person's immediate needs and goals.

Interpretation of information. For the skill-based behavior the sensed information is perceived as complex patterns monitoring and up-dating the world model and observation in terms of time-space *signals,* continuous quantitative indicators of the time-space behavior of the environment. These signals have no "meaning" or significance.

13.8.2 Rule-based Behavior

At the next level of *rule-based behavior,* the composition of a sequence of subroutines in a familiar work situation is typically controlled by recall of the response to a situation in the past, a kind of *stored rule* or *know-how.* The boundary between skill-based and rule-based performance is not quite distinct, and much depends on the level of training and on the attention of the person. For an expert in a familiar situation the rule-based performance may roll along without the person's conscious attention, and she will typically be unable to make explicit the cues consulted; very often these are convenient, informal cues or stereotypes, not situation defining attributes. For a less trained person in an unfamiliar situation, some higher level, rule-based coordination is based on explicit knowledge, and the rules are consciously used and can be reported by the person.

Representations at the rule-based level. At the rule-based level, work domain properties are only implicitly represented in the empirical mapping of cue-action patterns representing states of the environment and related, normally successful responses. This representation does not qualify as a mental 'model' since it does not support the anticipation of responses to new acts or events which have not been previously encountered, and it will not support an explanation or understanding, except in the form of references to prior experience.

Interpretation of information. At the rule-based level, the information is typically perceived as *signs.* The information perceived is defined as a sign when it serves to activate or modify predetermined actions or manipulations. *Signs* indicate a state in the environment with reference to certain conventions for acts, and cannot be used for relational reasoning.

13.8.3 Knowledge-based Behavior

During unfamiliar situations, faced with an environment for which no know-how or rules are available from previous encounters, the behavior must move to a higher conceptual level, in which performance is goal-controlled and *knowledge-based.* In this situation, the goal must be explicitly formulated, based on an analysis of the environment and the overall aims of the person. Then a useful plan is developed—by selection—such that different plans are considered, and their effect tested against the goal, physically by trial and error, or conceptually by means of understanding the causal and intentional properties of the functional means ends environment, and prediction of the effects of the plan considered. At this level of functional, causal and intentional reasoning, the internal structure of the domain is explicitly represented by a "mental model" which may take several different forms.

Representations at the knowledge-based level constitute proper 'mental models' of the means ends domain structure and of the causal or intentional and functional invariants of the work content. Many different kinds of relationships are put to work during reasoning and inference at this level - all depending on the circumstances; for example whether the task is to analyze a new situation, to evaluate different aspects of possible goals or to plan appropriate actions. Situation analysis and planning implies causal and intentional reasoning in a complex functional network, which is mentally very demanding.

Interpretation of information. At the knowledge-based level, reasoning will require presentation of symbolic information. To be useful for intentional and causal functional reasoning in predicting or explaining unfamiliar behavior of the environment, information must be perceived as *symbols.* Symbols refer to concepts tied to causal, intentional and functional properties, and are defined by and refer to the internal conceptual representation which is the basis for reasoning and planning, which by conventions can be related to features of the external world.

13.9 Implications for Ecological Design

Learning serves several important functions which influence effective system design: learning in *the longer run* is necessary for the evolution of expertise. An information system must be able to support a novice without frustrating the expert. Consequently, to conform to the evolution of expertise, an interface must be able to support different cognitive control modes at the same time. The information presented to the user will have at least three distinct functions. Information must be available in terms of signals for control of sensory-motor routines; in terms of signs to guide of the course of actions and, finally, in terms of symbols to support analysis in unfamiliar situations and evaluation of the result of an activity. It is essential that an interface be able to support performance at different cognitive levels because users with different levels of training may use the same system, and because learning to meet new requirements will require different interactions between cognitive levels. The demands of the task, the actor's experience, and the form in which information is presented combine to determine which level of cognitive control is activated.

In *the short run,* learning will lead to frequent shift of mental strategy during one task. In most cognitive tasks, several different mental strategies can be used requiring different resources by the user, who therefore will be able to shed work load and circumvent local difficulties by shifting strategy. As a result, user acceptance will depend on an information system's capabilities for supporting all the relevant strategies.

The form of the information must meet certain requirements for each level. Skill-based behavior can be activated only when information is presented in the form of objects that can be manipulated dynamically in space, therefore the spatial-temporal signal loop must be intact. Rule-based behavior, on the other hand, is triggered by familiar perceptual cues and affordances for action. And finally, knowledge-based behavior is activated by meaningful relational structures of the work domain. This is discussed in more detail next and in the example of the library system.

13.9.1 Interface Support at the Skill-based Level

To allow the development of a high degree of manual skill, the interface must be designed in such a way that the aggregation of elementary movements into more complex routines corresponds with a concurrent integration of visual features into higher level cues for these routines. Thus, for a particular domain, the display of information should for example be isomorphic to the part-whole structure of movements rather than being based on an abstract, combinatorial code like that of command languages. For supporting skill-based operation, the visual composition should be based on visual patterns which can be easily separated from the background and perceptively aggregated/decomposed to match the formation of patterns of movements at different levels of manual skill.

13.9.2 Interface Support at the Rule-based Level

The rule-based level governs the choice of action alternatives. The display provides the user with signs that she/he uses as cues for the selection of an appropriate action. Typically, the action alternatives consist of a set of task procedures and routine strategies. Ecological design attempts to develop a unique and consistent mapping between the symbols that govern the behavior of the task process, and the signs, or cues, that the interface displays. A display of cues for action should not just be convenient signs, they should be integrated patterns based on defining attributes and provide, at the same time, a symbolic representation necessary for functional, causal and intentional reasoning and understanding of performance. This will reduce the frequency of errors due to procedural traps because the cues for action will be uniquely defining the proper action.

At the rule-based level, we are also concerned with supporting memory for sign-rule correlation of items, acts, and data which are not part of an integrated domain structure.

13.9.3 Interface Support at the Knowledge-based Level

Knowledge-based behavior consists of abstract reasoning based on a mental model of the task domain. Knowledge-based reasoning can be supported by externalization of the effective mental models required for situation analysis and evaluation. Presentation of information should then be imbedded in a structure that can serve as an externalized mental model, effective for the kind of reasoning required by the task. Because the work domain is best described in terms of an abstraction hierarchy, the work domain will actually be described in terms of a hierarchy of higher-order invariants at various levels of abstraction. Since the mental process adopted for problem solving in a unique situation cannot be predicted, support should not aim at a particular process, but at an effective strategy, i.e., a category of processes related to a particular form of mental model.

Support of this level of cognitive control takes place through the mapping of signs onto symbols. This mapping turns out to be very complex because the symbolic reference can be to several different abstraction levels. This means that, in addition to serving as cues for action, the same display configuration can also be interpreted in several ways as symbols for reasoning. Thus, if the display configuration is interpreted symbolically, it presents the user with a visible model of the task domain that can support thought experiments and other planning activities. In addition, it is suggested that such a mapping will also support functional understanding necessary for error recovery. If signs can also be interpreted as symbols, then this may force the user to consider informative aspects when looking for action cues.

For knowledge based reasoning, the visual form serves as a symbolic representation - that is, an externalized mental model of the relational network representing the work content at the appropriate means-ends level(s). The form of the displays should not be chosen to match the mental models of actors found from analyses of an existing work setting. Instead they should induce the mental models which are effective for the tasks at hand in the new work ecology. If they exist, established graphical designs which have been used for decades in textbooks for teaching are probably the best sources for these representations.

13.9.4 Navigation and Mental Models during Task Performance

To support learning it is important that a user can shift both between different levels of cognitive control and different mental strategies. This will allow a user to circumvent resource-demand conflicts by shifting strategy and work approach. Strategies depending on recognition and intuitive classification are based on skill-based control and, therefore, on parallel processing and feature identification. Empirical strategies depend on rules and cues for their selection and, finally, analytical strategies based on conceptual situation analysis and planning depend on symbolic mental models of work domain functions. Therefore, mental models applied for cognitive control during an actual work situation will be a kind of a semantic network which evolves and changes as the situation progresses. Since shifts among strategies are frequent, the mental model used will consist of many fragments replacing each other repeatedly.

In general, the relation of information presentation to users' mental models of the system depends much on the work domain considered. For tightly coupled technical systems where users have to cope with rare events, the mental model must be based on system processes and their causal structure. From here, interface formats have to be designed that will lead the operators to adopt the proper mental model. In contrast, in user driven systems designed to serve the casual user in public information domains, interfaces have to be based on the actors' intentional structures and designed to match the mental models the actors' have acquired by activities in their work place and every day life context.

A set of display formats related to different mental models is required to support users' navigation in the system in order to avoid them "getting lost." The problem is to create in the users a *cognitive map of the navigational* displays including their present location, without constraining any possibility for them to develop and choose their own preferred work trajectories. Thus a limitation of task support to the normative approach preferred by the designer should be avoided.

13.9.5 Types of Display Composition and Interpretation

More concrete remarks can be made in the matter of display composition and interpretation. For example, there exist several generic ways of mapping information onto displays. Pepler and Wohl (1964) describe four such types. These comprise:

scalar: the basic coding is *geometric* that is, magnitude-length, angle, area. The underlying data is quantitative and can be discontinuous (discrete) or continuous in nature. Reference information identifying coordinates, scales and units is alphanumeric. There are many variations on this theme. The time dimension can be explicit or implicit.

matrix: the basic coding is *positional* that is, data-cell in a 2D row-column array-like arrangement. Cell coding can consist of any of the other types.

diagram: the basic coding is *representational* and/or *relational*. Diagrams comprise connected elements coded as lines, symbols, text., etc. to reflect structure, function etc..

symbolic: everything from narrative-like formats employing words and numbers to pictorial, analogical or abstract entities (*icons*) serving as symbols or signs relating to domain or task.

composite: a format which combines one or more of the above.

The general applicability of the basic types should be obvious. Scalar displays are indispensable for quantitative data. However certain variations will be domain-dependent. Likewise matrix-type arrays are widely employed for depicting spatially organized information (e.g. spreadsheets). Moreover they form the basis for menu arrangements, groupings of command icons and the like.

Where relevant, diagrams play an indispensable role in supporting mental models of structure and function, while symbolic representations are of course commonplace. One difference between display types is the semantic content and relations in the underlying information base and the resultant depiction, behavior and significance of the perceived entities.

13.9.6 Representation of Invariants and Affordances

For direct perception interfaces, some guidance can be drawn from the concepts of invariants and affordances. To sum up: The aim of ecological information systems is to present to the user relevant information about the state of affairs in the work environment structured according to its invariant properties. The regularity of behavior of a work domain comes from a combination of causal, functional and intentional factors and consequently the invariants and constraints to be depicted in an interface depend on the type of system considered.

The constraints forming the system's invariant structures have been discussed by Hansen (1994). These constraints should strongly shape the displayed representations of the system in order to deal with important features of persistence and change, that is, the visualization of persisting constraints and the invariants in the changes which occur. A preliminary overview of invariant types would include items such as:

relations: for example causal, intentional, empirical, organizational.

boundaries: for example physical, intentional, formal, legal, resource.

sequences: time and order.

behavioral paths: for example system performance trajectories, footprints of a strategy

The second ecologically relevant parameter to consider has to do with the object's, system's and/or event's affordances. This includes the possibilities offered for the actor to exert control in some sense within the limits of his/her capabilities. This of course is of prime importance, if there is no affordances, there will be no possibilities for response. Thus designers will have to identify what it is their users are supposed to pick up and gain a possibility to act on, and thereafter ensure that these facilities appear on the displays. It is also possible to list general classes of affordances:

maintain something

adjust, modify something

reconfigure something

The list and their connotations will of course have to be expanded depending on the domain application. However, some general guides can be given for their display.

13.9.7 Information about Invariants:

Information about invariants can be displayed as informtion about the system's actual state versus the intended goal state and as constraints and limitations to be considered by the actor.

Actual vs. goal state:

map as a configural "goodness": use linearity, symmetry, balance, alignment; take advantage of persistence with the onset of deviations to enhance the detection and identification of invariant "no-good" configurations.
map as graphical (scalar) figure from established repertoire of candidates include comparative coding of "is/should be", "is/was" and/or "is/will be" where possible and relevant. The time dimension can also be coded.
map as graphical symbol, that is as mimic or analog: use position, size, area, outlining, texture with/without text to discretely or dynamically depict state, result or outcome.
map connections between entities as geometric lines, intersections, coincidences; use width, texture, direction to code connective attributes.

Constraints, Limits:

map as background containment, boundaries, areas.
map as text message use size, framing, texture etc. to denote type, urgency.

As Hansen (1994) points out, a useful display will probably consist of an appropriate integration or overlapping of these items.

13.9.8 Information on Affordances

Information on affordances display potentials for user actions:

map as a track, pattern or other geometric entity which "affords" adjustment, i.e. straightening, turning, lifting, moving, connecting, etc. via some kind of direct manipulation.
map as a set of alternatives which "afford" selection (operation, manipulation). These alternates can utilize iconic, textual or geometric representations and they can also be conditionally visible and available.

Michaels and Carello (1981) point out that it is important that there also exists an invariant relation between the distal object, system, place or event and *detectable information* about it. To this one must add the obvious need for an invariant relation between this information and its visual representation on the display screen.

13.10 The Ecology of the Library Domain

An example of the use of ecological design principles is found in the icon based Book House retrieval system for public libraries discussed in the following. The structural content of the composite displays are based on a cognitive work analysis applying the framework described in the previous sections, and the visual form chosen for coding corresponds to the level of cognitive control for which the support is intended. Examples can serve to illustrate the complex coupling of the relational structure of information sources of the work domain to system functions and several modes of users' cognitive strategies and mental resources.

13.10.1 Work Domain Characteristics

The work domain in libraries is very loosely coupled, constituted by a large collection of similar information carrying items in dissimilar media and a set of separate tools, such as computers, catalogues, printed and multimedia materials. Relational structures originating in causal laws, therefore, are only to be found at the lower means-ends levels - in the anatomy and processes of the separate items of equipment and tools and their related work processes. The functionality at the higher levels depends on human activities and the predominant sources of regularity related to the coordination of the work processes can only be found in an intentional structure derived from institutional policies, legislation, socially established rules of conduct, and so forth. The institutional intentionality is derived from financial constraints and legislation concerning the role of libraries in public education and their mediation of information and cultural values. This intentionality is reflected in the selection of information media, materials and equipment, and in the objective and subjective

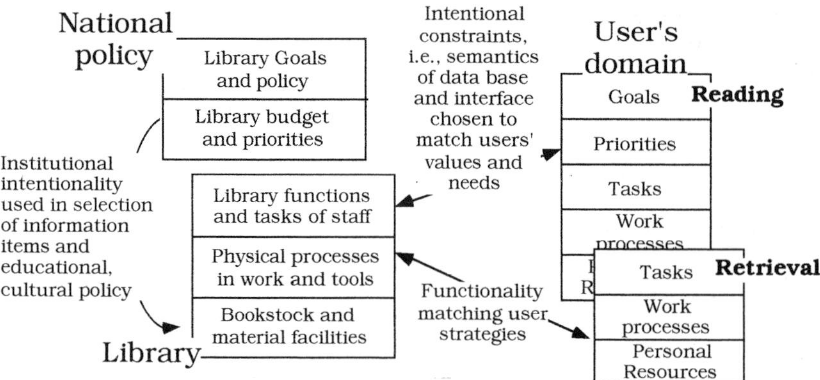

Figure 11. An ecological information system is organized so as to match the semantic dimensions of the information sources to the intentions of the users. *Tthe functionality of the system is designed to match to the search strategies which are natural to the users for a given problem situation. For the library system the functionality built into the retrieval system has been identified by an extensive analyses of users' search behavior and an explicit formulation of the dimensions of the expressed reading needs. The dimensions of the user needs define the structure of the database. The semantics, the indexing of the items of the data base, match the users' query language while the search strategies define the search dialogue and the retrieval functions.*

contents of the instructions from the librarians to the users on the basis of their training, instructions and personal experience.

In work systems designed for meeting the personal needs of a user in work, education and leisure, the intentionality governing the use of computer systems within the institutional policies and constraints, is exercised entirely by the user. Many action alternatives underlie the choice of 'what, when and how to do', and these are left to the discretion of the users. The 'work space' activated within the domain is basically a collection of information items with no natural functional structure. Accordingly, special means are necessary to support retrieval in terms of making the actual object of work explicit and visible and to support exploration of the relational structures and boundaries of the subject domains. The representation of the field in which the search is done, that is, the semantics of the content of the information items must match user values and needs(see figure 11).

Making information about book contents available in computer interfaces at multiple intentional levels according to the user's needs in fact means making the affordances of the information directly visible in interfaces for direct manipulation.

13.10.2 Task Situation, Decision Tasks

Based on an analysis of users' queries and verbal statements during information retrieval tasks, the relational structure of users' needs and intentions has been identified in terms corresponding to various levels of the abstraction hierarchy. This representation was used to develop a classification scheme to organize and classify information and employed as the data base structure. (Pejtersen, 1979, 1983, 1988. 1992, 1993).

Major cognitive decision task elements during information retrieval in libraries include:

Why the search: what is the user's problem? This in volves situation analysis, goal setting and prioritization of user goals, tasks, functions and reading capabilities with reference to the work and leisure context of the user domain and reading activity

How to search:? This involves exploration of system content, search activity planning, execution and control of activity, strategies and procedures.

How satisfying is the result:? This involves comparison and verification of match between the search result and the user's need and subsequent revision of the search.

These decisions are iteratively carried out by knowledge based reasoning and by a number of rule based observations and procedures that involve identification of the state of affairs, action to take, objects to use, goals to pursue, actors involved etc. Figure 12 lists these decision tasks together with examples of interface displays that support these different tasks. A similar figure can be made with respect to displays that support the task strategies reviewed below.

13.10.3 Task Strategies

To support exploration and search in a work environ-

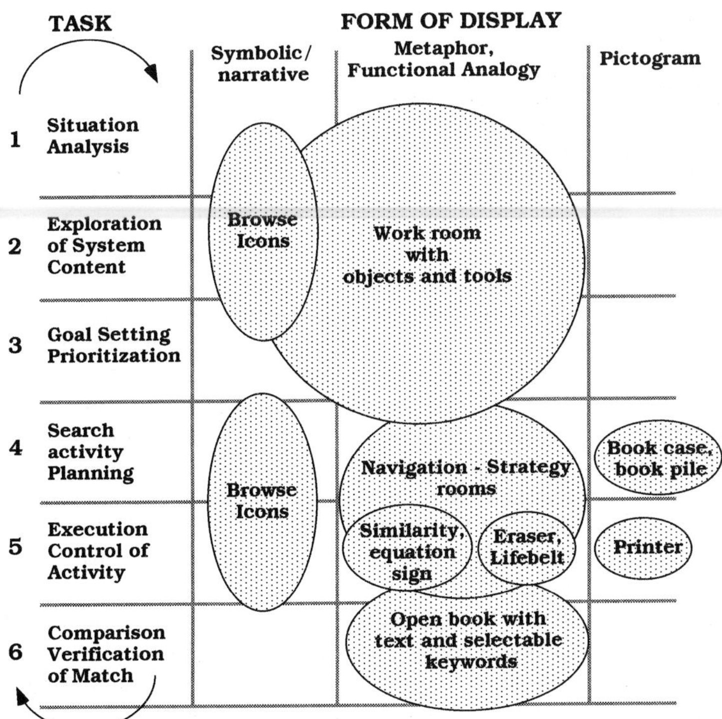

Figure 12. Shows the task decisions during information retrieval and the different visual forms of displays: *symbols, the meaning of which is determined by a reference to population stereotypes. Metaphors, i.e., representations with objects, persons, actions, states, concepts etc., the meaning of which is determined by an analogy between the current work domain and another familiar context. Pictograms, i.e. pictures of objects or persons having a literal meaning which is determined by their resemblance with the real thing.*

ment essentially without any inherent structure, the functionality of the work system must be designed to match as well as possible the work processes and search strategies, relevant to the task and preferred by the users. Analysis of information processing strategies applied by users and librarians during decision making and the underlying mental models supplied several coherent sets of mental models, data formats, and tactical rule sets used by searchers with varying expertise and competence. The most important search strategies which are effective for retrieval and which match the resource profiles and preferences of the users are:

Browse: appropriate if the user need is so ambiguous that no search specification is possible and, instead, the bookshelves or databases are scanned for recognition of cues for intuitive matching of book contents with one's current reading need.

Search by analogy: an associative problem solving strategy appropriate if the user has a muddled idea of important aspects to be included in a query and limits the verbalization to something similar to author/title examples.

Search analytically: a rational problem-solving approach appropriate if the user explicitly can verbalize a query with the relevant combination of book aspects by an explicit specification of needs.

These were used to design a user system dialogue with free access through multiple search strategies and flexible shift among strategies.

13.10.4 User Characteristics

Library users are typically autonomous casual and/or professional users belonging to a defined group (defined by age, sex, profession, nationality. etc.) sharing common knowledge, experience and cultural prototypes. Library systems must cater to a wide range of casual and professional users, children and adults, with varying backgrounds, experience, needs and temperaments - e.g. the amount of time they are willing to spend, their expertise of technology, etc.. An analysis of users' characteristics, cognitive resource profiles is necessary to meet the resource requirements of the

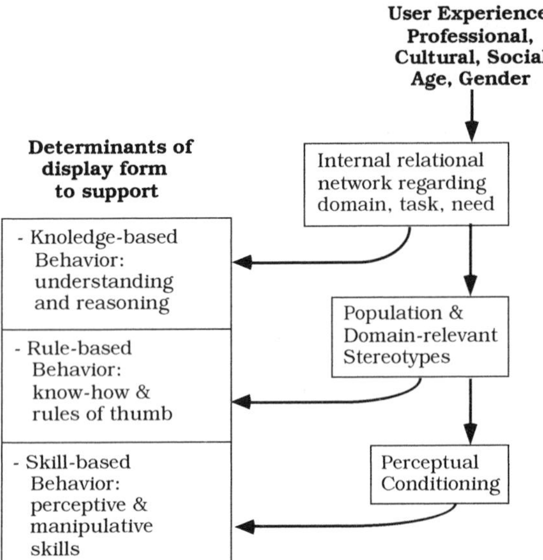

Figure 13. Determinants of display form in a user-driven domain. *A number of field studies of the user population in libraries including questionnaires, laboratory tests, association tests, observations and evaluation of users' perception of the displays were conducted to determine the form of the Book House displays.*

various strategies and the level of expertise and the performance criteria of the individual users.

13.11 Coupling Work Domain to Content and Form of Displays

It follows that the functionality, the syntax, of the library system is derived from these analyses of users' preferred work processes and their strategies, while the semantics of the system is based on users' formulation of their subjective values and reading intentions as identified in work studies. Both the syntax and the semantics define the *content* of the necessary interface displays, (see figure 11) while the knowledge background and culture of the user population will determine the *form* of information in the displays. In addition, the *form* of the interface, should allow the user to interpret the representation according to the level of expertise activated in a particular situation (see figure 13).

The overall *architecture* of such an information system, its purpose and functions as well as the *form* of the required displays cannot be derived solely from the functionality identified from the users' intentions and individual search strategies. The users in a library represent a wide selection of the general public and therefore an overall organizing principle cannot be related to a particular problem space and its related knowledge structure as is the case for systems such as process plants and manufacturing systems. Unlike with a power plant, there is no object system in the background to structure the context of the search and its pictorialization. Therefore, one must seek a more universal means and a higher level organizing principle must be found which is familiar to users from another context. A suitable *metaphor* has to be found. A ware-house metaphor can support users' memory and navigation by location of information about the functionality and content of the system in a coherent and familiar spatial representation, which is easily understood and remembered. As Miller (1968) states: "Information is a question of *'where'*."

The Book House concept relates the information in the data base, the various strategies, and task procedures to locations in a virtual space. The many dimensions of information are allocated to rooms or sections of rooms within a house. Such an approach should be flexible enough to cope with the wide range of library users - novice, casual, professional, children and adults - with more or less analyzable needs and intentions.

13.11.1 Design of Icons

There are various representational problems in designing icons: the features of the action to be "iconized" and how these features will be represented. It is important to realize that the interpretation of the content of the icon depends on the current context from which it is viewed as well as the users' level of expertise. In any single situation, a user's response depends on a host of factors - need, available time, training, and, in our case particularly, the repertoire of heuristics and skills. How a user interprets an icon in a given situation depends on his/her intentions/experience at the given moment. The challenge for the designer is to provide a match between the context of the information retrieval task, displayed as icons, and the context of the intentions and needs of users' problem space, so that the user perceives the icons in the intended fashion.

One way of achieving meaningfulness and suggestiveness would be to study the conventional use and repertoire of icons for directing action in the users' work environment and everyday life. This pictorial form can be based on a pictogram (a realistic reproduction), an analogy or an arbitrary representation (Lodding 1983). The possibilities are enormous and there are no rules or guidelines for making the best (or avoiding the worst) selection. A study for the Book House project indicated

1. State of affairs needing attention
Everyday context: Traffic signs, a locomotive informs about crossing trains. Be careful. BookHouse context: Books put aside as interesting candidates for later perusal: "Pile of books" icon
2. The actors who should care
Everyday context: Icon: Lady's and gents on rest room doors BookHouse context: Adults and children in search of books matching their age. Icon: Adults and children searching the book shelves
3. Action to perform
Everyday context: Icon: Man walking on stairs. BookHouse context: Put aside interesting candidates of books for later perusal. Icon: Hand putting a book aside on a table
4. Object to use
Everyday context: Garbage can icon. BookHouse context: Delete a search term. Rubber icon
5. Target State to reach
Everyday context: "Light on" icon. BookHouse context: Get more books. Icon: Book case full of books
6. State to avoid
Everyday context: "Flame" icon informs about open fire to be avoided. BookHouse context: None
7. Symbolic reference
Everyday context: "Hammer and Sickle " icon informs about Socialism. BookHouse context: Books dealing with religion. Icon: The bible
8. Pure Convention
Everyday context: Red light at street crossing. BookHouse context: Keywords displayed in red and black text

Figure 14. Design of icons can be based on different reference to items in an action scenario.

that the interpretation of the links between action / intentions and icons can be structured in a systematic way several scenarios (Pejtersen and Rasmussen, 1987) and the visual *content* chosen for an icon may refer to any of the underlined elements in the following sequence:

1. If State - 2. Then Actor - 3. Does Act - 4. With object - 5. to reach goal-state

The design of icons was based on the items in this action scenario. Each icon was determined by testing the users' and librarians' interpretation of their meaning during the design process (see figure 14).

In addition to the referent in the action scenario, the pictorial *form* of an icon is chosen to enhance fast learning and recognition. In the following, the form of the individual icon will be characterized as 1). symbols, the meaning of which is determined by user testing and population stereotypes 2). metaphors, i.e., representations with objects, persons, actions, states, concepts etc., the meaning of which is determined by an analogy between the current work domain and another familiar context and 3). pictograms, i.e. pictures of objects or persons having a literal meaning which is determined by their resemblance with the real thing. The strength of the association of the picture with the real device rather than with an analogy is in focus here (see figure 12 for examples of these three different display forms and their support of decision tasks).

13.12 Ecological Display Examples from a Library System

13.12.1 Display for Need Situation Analysis

Figure 15 shows the interface display designed to support a user's explicit formulation of reading needs by presenting a model of the relational domain structure

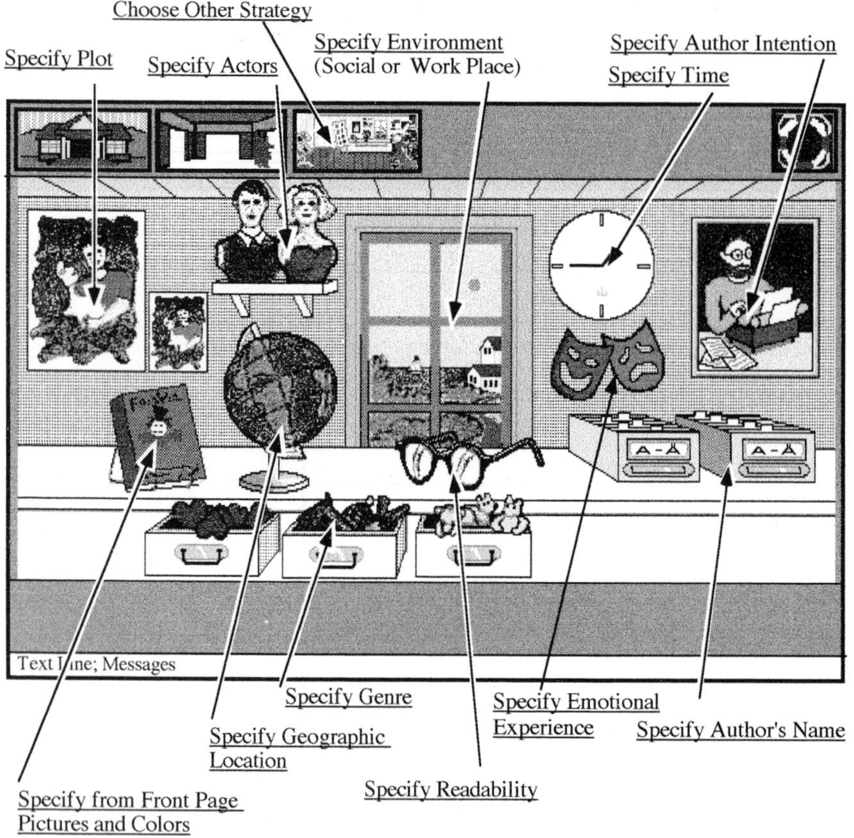

Figure 15. The intended level of cognitive control is to support knowledge- and rule based action. *The users' explicit formulation of reading needs is supported through the display of icons which identify the various needs. By making these dimensions explicit, the display probes the user's memory for aspects to consider. At the same time, the icons supports action which allows the specific dimensions to be used for search to be specified by direct manipulation.*

of user intentions imposed on the work space of book contents.

This display has implications for both knowledge-based, rule-based, and skill-based search.

Knowledge-based Support: Intentional Domain Structure in Work Space

The display in figure 15 represents the domain structure during search for information. It incorporates users' intentions at several levels of means-ends abstractions including the users' overall goals, the attributes of their information needs (including their reading ability) and a matching information about the contents of documents along these dimensions. This user centered structure is embedded in the database and is used to organize domain knowledge as well as to make the semantic retrieval attributes of the document collection immediately transparent to the user. The attributes are important for mapping the user's domain to the authors' domain in task decisions involving *situation analysis of users' information needs*, *goal setting and prioritization* and formulation of search query. The attributes enable the user to analyze the means ends abstraction level of documents, determine the relevant dimensions and decide the goal of the search. In ecological terms, the display supports knowledge-based reasoning by providing an external mental model of the work space, and by making these dimensions explicit. The display also probes the user's memory for aspects to consider and supports analytical search strategies.

When trying to build a mental model of their problem space and its representation in the system, novices and casual users of the library system are likely to interpret information as symbols. At the same time, the icons function as signs for action which allow the specific dimensions to be used for search and to be specified by direct manipulation. Selection of an iconic object is the only action needed to execute a search.

Rule-based Support

In general, the menu line in the upper and lower parts of the display in figure 15 support routine tasks to be executed to progress from problem analysis to evaluation of system responses and planning of next step. Hence the menu lines represent work domain properties at the rule-based level.

In the upper menu line the overall *navigation* in the information system is facilitated via indications of the rooms which have been previously visited and which can be revisited by direct manipulations on the room icons displayed at the top of the screen. Therefore, once visited, a room always appears on the top menu line together with the other rooms of the house which have been visited.

Planning of a search and choice of an appropriate strategy is an iterative process, and the strategies will change as the search progresses. A *shift of strategy* and *database* can be performed at any level of the search at any time by choice of the appropriate icon. Request for help is activated by the Life belt icon.

In the menu line at the bottom of the display, the number of retrieved books in any current set is displayed in a book case. Information about the *state of a search* is used to plan the next step of a search.

As a general principle, these rule-based representations appear on every single display, when appropriate for the current stage of the task, with the same functional content and iconic form. Therefore, they will not be discussed further.

Skill-based Support

Efficient learning of the domain knowledge in a data base is greatly enhanced when the data base structure is embedded in its context which is represented directly on the interface display surface. This makes it possible even for a casual user to quickly develop efficient skills in communicating through the interface without the need for complex mental juggling to convert one representation to another. Therefore the abstract attributes of the items in the database are consistently recoded as physical objects to positions in various spatial arrangements as tools on the desk and posters on the wall to reinforce the development of manual skills involving a device such as a mouse to cope with the spatial-temporal working space. This principle for skill based support is adopted for every single display and will not be discussed further.

Visual Form

A symbolic representation of objects, concepts and events representative of the categories within the relational structure of the user's problem space relevant for need situation analysis as well as for the analytical strategy are displayed in a work room as familiar metaphors to be perceived as signs for action. On and around the work table are icons giving a pictorial link to the semantics of the topical dimension they represent like the posters on the wall. They are based on an analogy to common population knowledge such as objects to use like the globe on the table and tools with reference to previous technology in the library.

The icons in the menu line direct the user's attention to the user's current mode and previous choices, and at the same time displays alternative action possibilities through the functional analogy of a room with objects that afford action.

13.12.2 Display for Domain Exploration

Figure 16 shows the display for intuitive exploration of pictorial representations. Below we will explore the implications of this display for rule-and skill-based intuitive exploration.

Rule-based support: Users' Associations as Work Space.

Domain exploration is typically used when the user has a need which is so ambiguous that an explicit situation analysis and goal setting and prioritization is impossible. Instead, the objects of the work domain is explored for recognition of possible matches between the intuitive need and the available items. Figure 16 shows a pictorial representation of objects, concepts and events representative for the categories within the relational structure of users' intentions. This representation is particularly relevant for *implicit,* rule-and skill-based *intuitive domain exploration.* The picture association with icons can provide a quick birds eye view of the semantic content of the data base and is intended to probe the user's tacit knowledge. It supports intuitive recognition of vaguely specified needs by evoking memories and experiences.

The available, elementary textual information about document contents was used to develop a consistent transformation of concepts for integration in

Figure 16. Display for intuitive search by browsing pictorial representations of prototypical concepts, objects, events, *emotions, and situational relationships with reference to population stereotypes based on an analysis of the intuitive associations in a multiple choice association test of the target group of end users. While exploring pictorial representations of book content, users' recognize attributes of needs. When an icon is selected the category of books is retrieved.*

higher level representations appropriate for the recognition of familiar concepts.

The pictorial representation of a document was used as a source for an association test with library users, who commented on abstract concepts, objects, events, situational relationships, colors, and the emotional experiences conveyed by the pictures. Therefore, each icon represents a semantic network of topics belonging to several different abstraction levels of the users' intentional structure. However, selection of an icon is the only action necessary to search the semantic network.

The icons are then typically designed to support rule-based reasoning during domain exploration for familiar topics. But due to their combination of several underlying abstraction levels of the users' domain structure, some of the icons can also support knowledge based analysis.

Visual Form

Pictures for intuitive domain exploration and browsing are implemented in the form of a "photo album" metaphor.

The icons were designed as *signs* and refer to users' prototypical concepts and needs. When drawing an appropriate pictorial analogy the designers tried to predict the potential system users' experience and knowledge of symbols, conventional signs and books. Traditionally used forms were chosen such as hammer and sail for communism, hearts for love, and so forth. Unique and original symbols were invented to signify abstract concepts, such as identity problems and narcissism. The effectiveness of these icons in supporting prediction and symbolic reasoning depends on the user's familiarity with their content and form. To support signs for action, metaphors were chosen with functional analogies to a familiar context of conventional signs such as traffic signs and cars for books about car accidents.

A controlled multiple choice association test was conducted among library users, children and adults, as well as librarians to evaluate icons and determine the associative meaning. The purpose was to identify icons that were recognized as familiar concepts, representative of information needs and providing cues for action during browsing. Only those icons whose meaning was clear to naive users in two seconds or less were ac cepted for system design. The naive users could identify the underlying conceptual relations and associate to previous experiences, and later spontaneously used the icons.

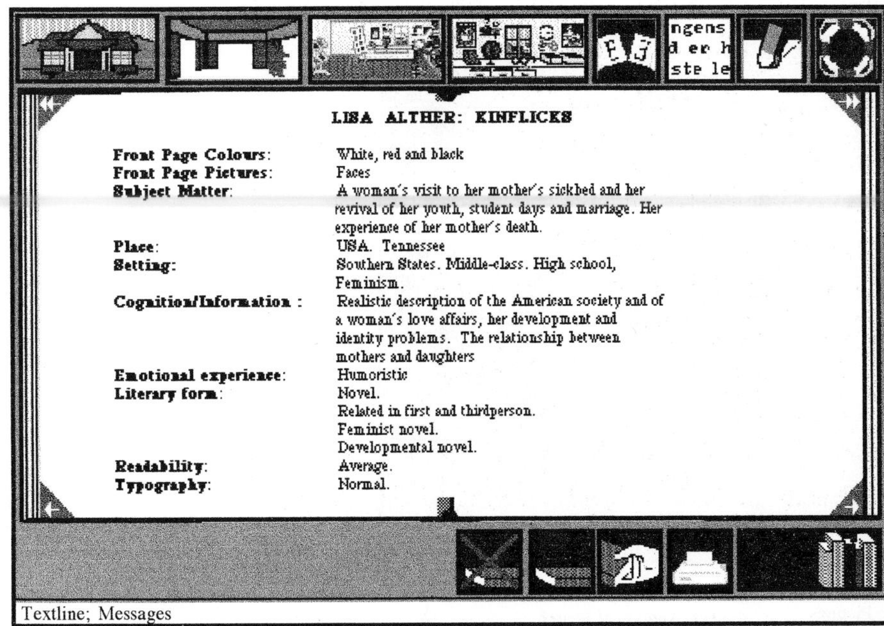

Figure 17. Knowledge-based representation: Document content at different means ends abstraction levels.

13.12.3 Display for Evaluation, Comparison of Match, Revision

Figure 17 illustrates the information content of a document represented according to the intentional structure of the user domain. The representation in this display supports knowledge and rule-based behavior.

Knowledge-based Support: Intentional Domain Structure in Work Space

The standardized format of the display enables the task of *comparing* and *evaluating* the appropriateness of retrieved books considering users' needs and goals at each of the means ends abstraction levels. The order of abstraction levels is established in empirical studies of users' focus and preferences.

The display can furthermore support iterative reformulations of need based on relevance feedback. The text reflects authors' intention, subscription to paradigms, subject matter, time, place, social setting, language, typography etc..

Groupings of the contents are used to display five levels of the abstraction hierarchy. The visibility of this internal user structure embedded in the textual representation of the document contents and made explicit through a highly structured representation supports knowledge based reasoning.

Rule-based Support

For *execution and control of the search,* a host of options and search tools are selectable. These includes representations of the previous modes, the current state, and responses from the system such as strings of searched keywords, navigational paths, and search tactics.

The user can repetitively select among these options —including shift of strategy— without entering a previous room. By clicking on the corners of the book the user can browse through the retrieved set of books, one after the other in both directions or in large leaps.

The upper menu line: The current need can be *modified by adding or removing search terms* from the current search profile by means of an erazer icon. Keyword icons are displayed as searchable keywords in the current book description. The minus icon can be used to operate a Boolean "Not" search to indicate a keyword that is not wanted.

The lower menu line: Searching for books is a dynamic and iterative process during which a user will learn about the content of the system and recognize and *revise* his/her own need and value criteria repetitively as the search progresses. Therefore the user can save interesting candidates for later browsing and thus *plan the search* appropriately. The number of books put aside during searches for later consideration is displayed as books in a contemporary pile. By selecting

Figure 18. Shows the room for choice of search strategy for control, preparation, planning and execution of a search. *A particular search strategy can be activated by selecting one of four work places in the strategy room. Separate 'rooms' are available to support the various decisions which have to be made during use of a search strategy.*

the icon with a pile of books put aside on a table, the user can get descriptions of previously searched books and compare how well they match with the user's need. Activation of the printer icon prints book descriptions. Two *strategies* represented as action icons can be selected any time a book description is displayed. The strategy choice is then made visible to support the comparison and verification of match between book content and the user's need. The result of the comparison may provoke a *shift of strategy,* which can then be performed immediately as either a *search by analogy* or an *analytical search*. While the room for choice of search strategy (figure 18) supports the overall planning of the search approach, these icons represent lower level rules and procedures executed by these strategies and performed by the system without the user's change of level.

Visual Form

The mapping between symbols and signs of the book content display is achieved through highlighting semantically important keywords as well as headlines of means-ends levels. Both complements the user's need formulation. The keywords and headlines are highlighted in red, a convention which has to be learned like the meaning of colors in a traffic light. This makes it possible that the semantic book content can be perceived as cues for action.

Signs govern the user's choice among the action possibilities. The upper and lower parts of the display show a selective repertoire of icons to be perceived as signs for *action*. The form of icons were designed to ease novice users' ability to understand, learn, and distinguish among the numerous possibilities for control actions at the lowest level of a search. The icons refer to possible *actions* to perform. *objects* to use and *states* and *goals* to reach. Perceptually strong metaphors are chosen as iconic signs for action possibilities. They also support analogical reasoning in a familiar context for the general, public novice user. Many design features improve novices' learning of system functionality. In particular the book metaphor can display *a task sequence* with its individual familiar routines like taking books in and out of book cases, and putting books in piles.

The *search by analogy strategy* is displayed as a metaphor with an equation mark that indicates that choice of this icon will lead to similar books.

13.12.4 Display for Choice among Task Strategies

Figure 18 shows the room for choice of search strategy for control, preparation, planning and execution of a search. A particular search strategy can be activated by selecting one of four work places in the strategy room, which will give access to. separate rooms available to support the various decisions which have to be made during use of a retrieval strategy.

Rule-based Support

The display of several search strategies supports the user's selection of the problem solving path most appropriate for the task at hand. The search strategy display offers tools for analytical search, search by analogy, and search by browsing. The analytical tools support a well structured and systematic exploration of dimensions of the user's needs. Search by analogy gives access to a search based on examples of earlier books, which the user has to identify, in order to make the system find "something similar". Browsing gives access to either randomly displayed pictorial representation of all the subjects available in the data base or descriptions of all the books in the data base. Different display formats for each strategy are required to support users' navigation and avoid "cognitive overload," (see figures 15, 16 and 17).

The direct manipulation feature allows the user to click directly on the figure of interest.

Visual Form

A particular *search strategy* can be activated by selecting one of four work places in the "strategy room," on figure 18. The room metaphor for choice of search strategy includes representations of the four available strategies as combinations of people and books, people and icons or people and retrieval tools. The display is formatted as a functional analogy to mimic search in a library. It provides sufficient information to support free choice of strategy. The icons refer to *users,* who perform different *actions* characteristic of each strategy. The icons then display different mental models of users' intentions for the different search strategies. For example: 1) a person sitting at a table analyzing and combining information items from the intentional user structure used in the database for classifying books; 2) a person browsing through books taken randomly from the shelves; 3) a person looking through the shelves for book topics similar to those currently in the user's mind; 4) a person browsing through icons reflecting book contents. This is similar to looking at pictures on front pages when scanning the contents.

These metaphors primarily support the cue-action perception of signs, but as they also display mental models of users' intentions underlying search strategies, they can be perceived as symbols and support knowledge based reasoning.

As mentioned previously, overall navigation in the Book House system was supported by access to several search strategies via indications of the rooms in the upper menu line which have been previously visited and which can be revisited by direct manipulation on the room icons.

13.13 Visual Form and Mental Models

It is an important requirement that interference between mental models is to be avoided since the user is likely to have various mental models of the process at various levels of abstraction. The Book House metaphor serves to create a mental model of the retrieval system through the functional analogy to a library, while the display in figure 15 showing the relational work domain structure reflecting the users' intentional structure serves to create a mental model of the book stock domain. The displays of figure 15, 16 and 17 illustrates how different visual forms are chosen to avoid interference between different mental models of the book stock domain that are appropiate for different task situations and strategy categories.

13.14 Symbols and Signs

In addition, these display figures illustrate the identical configuration in each display of icons that serve several different functions. Multi purpose icons or in ecological terms, icons that at the same time represent the invariants of the domain and the affordances for action. They are intended to be interpreted as symbols that support knowledge based reasoning and development of mental models of the invariant, relational structure of the book domain. At the same time, they should be perceived as signs that support rule based behavior and direct perception of cues for action. They are situated in the middle of the display and support situation analysis, goal setting and prioritization, and domain exploration.

Secondly, icons designed to guide the use of search tools by acting as signs which afford rule-based action with no symbolic reference to an invariant, relational domain structure. They are displayed in the top and bottom menu lines and support search activity planning, and execution and control of the search.

13.15 Automation and Adaptation of Lower Level Tasks

Any decision process involves the identification of the state of affairs, that is, interpretation and reformulation of the primary information at the level of concern; analysis, planning of actions and evaluation of results. Basically, the subjective complexity of a task is significantly increased when the actor has to operate at several levels of abstraction. Therefore one way to support a user is to take over some of the information processing tasks more or less completely. For instance, the designer could let the interface system take care of the lower level data integration and action coordination tasks. Thus information is presented at the level which is most appropriate for decision making.

For example, search strategies are made easily available for users, because the computer provides the necessary support by automation and adaptation. The user can then delimit the search space to a partial selection of the semantic database network, which can then be further manipulated without excessive mental workload. As an example, keywords are related to an icon as semantic networks and are automatically searched, when the icon is selected. Each selection of icons in the work room, in the photo album display and so forth generates an automatic Boolean search. The size of the retrieved book set and the first book description in the new set is displayed automatically.

13.16 Learning by Doing and Trial and Error

Learning can be evolutionary. It is not planned by the rational analysis of a particular user within the work domain, but happens to a large degree as a result of trial and error experiments, planned and unplanned, conscious and unconscious. To support learning it is necessary to accept that users need to experiment to develop knowledge and optimize skill. During this learning, the effects of erroneous acts must be observable and reversible. This is necessary to allow effective exploration of the work domain and the search for boundaries of acceptable performance, as well as for the peace of mind of the users. Criteria for error tolerance must be formulated to guide system design. Thus, interface design should both aim at making the action possibilities visible to the users in a way which matches human perception depending on their individual level of expertise, while the effects of their actions should be immediately observable and reversible.

Typically, the action possibilities consist of a set of familiar alternatives (select keywords, display retrieved set, get help, print etc.). A common problem with conventional interfaces is that the cues they provide the users are not unique with respect to the current operational state. This difficulty is overcome in the Book House by developing a unique and consistent mapping between the symbols that represent the semantic contents of a database and the signs, or cues, provided by the interface. This will reduce the frequency of errors due to procedural traps because the cues for action, based as they are on retrieval process properties and visualized as analogies, pictograms, and so forth., will uniquely define the related action. In addition, if the signs can also be interpreted as symbols, they can support functional reasoning while looking for action cues.

One interesting error recovery strategy has been observed during the actual operation of the system: Whenever a user ran into difficulties due to errors, mistakes, or misunderstanding, they simply walked around their problem by shifting to another search strategy. Consequently, they never seemed to get lost and even novices very rarely used the help system.

13.17 Ecological Design Considerations

From this discussion, some basic considerations for ecological interface design can be concluded:

- The basic consideration for system design to draw from this discussion is to accept that learning through experiments are necessary for system users in order to be able to develop knowledge and optimize skills. Thus, interface design should aim at a 'learning' work system, making the relational work domain structure and/or boundaries and limits of acceptable performance visible to the users, while the effects are still observable and reversible.

- For tightly coupled technical systems where users have to cope with rare events, the work domain structure must be based on system processes and their causal structure. In user driven systems designed to serve users in public information domains, interfaces have to be based on the users' intentional structures.

- Information should be embedded in a structure that can serve as an externalized mental model, effective for the kind of reasoning required by the task. Since the mental process adopted for problem solving in a unique situation cannot be predicted, support should not aim at a particular process, but at an effective strategy, i.e., a category of processes. In user driven systems the interface should be designed to match the mental models users have acquired by activities in their work place and every day life context. For tightly coupled technical systems the mental model should match the causal structure of the system.

- The form of the displays should not be chosen to match the mental models of actors found from analyses of an existing work setting. Instead they should induce the mental models which are effective for the tasks at hand in the new work ecology.

- At the knowledge-based level, interference between mental models is to be avoided. This is an important requirement since the user is likely to have various mental models of the process at various levels of abstraction.
- To support learning, a display should be designed so as to make cues for action not only convenient signs, but defining attributes, not to lead the user into traps during unfamiliar work situations. This implies that signs should map faithfully onto the relational work domain structure, that is, also have symbolic content necessary for functional analysis.

- To support skill-based operation, the visual composition should be based on visual patterns which can be easily separated from the background and perceptively aggregated/decomposed to match the formation of patterns of movements at different levels of manual skill.

- Use the available, elementary domain information to develop consistent transformation of concepts for integration in higher level representations of invariants and affordances. This will enable the interface to present information at the level which is most appropriate for decision making and user expertise.

- Support of human mental resources for knowledge-based, functional reasoning can be given in different ways. One way is to take over some of the information processing tasks more or less completely. For instance, the designer could let the interface system take care of the lower level data integration and action coordination tasks. Another way to support knowledge-based reasoning is to support the human resources by, for instance, externalizing the mental model required for analysis and evaluation.

- Learning will lead to frequent shift of mental strategy during a task in order to shed work load and circumvent local difficulties. User acceptance will depend on an information system's capabilities for supporting all the relevant strategies. Strategies should therefore be visible and explicitly represented in the interface.

- A map supports navigation more effectively than route instructions. A set of displays related to different mental models is required to support users' navigation in the system in order to avoid them "getting lost" and to create in the users a *cognitive map of the navigational* displays including their present location, without constraining any possibility for them to develop and choose their own preferred work trajectories. Thus a limitation of task support to the normative approach preferred by the designer should be avoided.

- Situation analysis, planning and evaluation implies causal and intentional reasoning in a complex functional network, which is very demanding upon mental resources. Thus, it is imperative that this activity be supported.

13.18 References

Beltracchi, L. (1984). A Process/Engineering Safeguards Iconic Display, *Symposium on New Technologies in Nuclear Power Plant Instrumentation and Control,* Washington, D. C. 28-30 Nov.

Beltracchi, L. (1987). A direct manipulation interface for water-based rankine cycle heat engines. *IEEE Transactions on Systems, Man, and Cybernetics*, SMC-17, pp. 478-487.

Beltracchi, L. (1989). Energy, Mass, Model-Based Displays and Memory Recall. *IEEE Transaction on Nuclear Science*, 36, pp. 1367-1382

Bucciarelli, L. L. (1984). Reflective Practice in Engineering Design. *Design Studies*, 5, (3)

Bucciarelli, L. L. (1988). An Ethnographic Perspective on Engineering Design. *Design Studies*, 9, (3), pp. 159-168.

Friend'21 (1989). *Proceedings of the International Symposium on Next Generation Human Interface Technologies*, September November 1991, Tokyo: Institute for Personalized Information Environment.

Gibson, J. J. (1966). *The Senses Considered as Perceptual Systems*. Boston: Houghton-Mifflin.

Gibson, J. J. (1979). The ecological approach to visual perception. Boston: Houghton-Mifflin.

Hansen, J. P., (1994). Representation of System Invariants by Optical Invariants in Configural Displays. In: Flach, J., Hancock, P., Caird, J. and Vicente, K. (Eds.): *The Ecology of Man-Machine Systems*. Lawrence Erlbaum. pp.

Lodding, K.N. (1983). Iconic Interfacing. *IEEE Computer Graphics and Applications*, 3, pp. 11-20.

Michaels, C. F. and Carello, C. (1981): Direct Perception, Prentice-Hall, Englewood Cliffs, NJ.

Miller, G. A. (1968). Psychology and Information. *American Documentation*, 19, pp. 286-289.

Pejtersen, A. M. (1979). Investigation of search strategies in fiction based on an analysis of 134 user-librarian Conversations. In: IRFIS 3. Henriksen, T.(Ed.) p. 107-132.

Pejtersen, A. M. (1988). Search Strategies and data base design for information retrieval in Libraries. In: Goodstein, L. P. et al.(eds): *Tasks, Errors and Mental Models*. Taylor & Frances, 1988.

Rasmussen, J. (1983). Skill, Rules and Knowledge; Signals, Signs, and Symbols, and other Distinctions in Human Performance Models. *IEEE Transactions on Systems, Man and Cybernetics*. SMC-13, (3) 1983.pp.

Rasmussen, J. (1985). Role of Hierarchical Knowledge Representation in Decision Making and System Management. *IEEE Transactions on Systems, Man and Cybernetics*. SMC-15, (2) pp. 234-243.

Rasmussen, J. (1987). Risk and Information Processing. In: W. T. Singleton and J. Hovden (Eds.): *Risk and Decisions*. New edition, 1995. John Wiley & Sons Ltd.

Rasmussen, J. and Jensen, A. (1974). Mental Procedures in Real Life Tasks: A Case Study of Electronic Trouble Shooting. *Ergonomics*, 17, (3) pp. 293 307.

Rasmussen, J. and L. P. Goodstein (1987). Information Technology and Work. In: Helander, M. (Ed.): *Handbook of Human-Computer Interaction*. New York: North Holland.

Rasmussen, J., and Vicente, K. J. (1990). Ecological interfaces: A technological imperative in high tech systems? *International Journal of Human-Computer Interaction*, (2) pp.93-111.

Rasmussen, J., Pejtersen, A. M. and Goodstein, L. P. (1994). *Cognitive Systems Engineering*. New York: Wiley.

Rochlin, G. I., La Porte, T. R., and Roberts, K. H., (1987). The Self-Designing High-Reliability Organization: Aircraft Carrier Flight Operations at Sea, *Naval War College Review*.

Scott, W. R. (1987). *Organizations: Rational, Natural, and Open Systems*, Prentice-Hall, Englewood Cliffs, New Jersey.

Thompson, J. D. (1967). Organizations in Actions. New York: McGraw-Hill.

Handbook of Human-Computer Interaction
Second, completely revised edition
M. Helander, T.K. Landauer, P. Prabhu (eds.)

Chapter 14

The Role of Task Analysis in the Design of Software

Robin Jeffries
Sun Microsystems, Inc.
California, USA

14.1 Introduction

Task analysis is one of the most useful tools in the human factors repertoire. It has been used for everything from identifying problems that would cause repetitive strain injuries to improving safety procedures in nuclear power plants (Kirwan and Ainsworth, 1992). This chapter will discuss three areas where task analysis can be useful to the user interface designer: an overall task analysis of the domain of interest, done early in the life cycle to determine features and task flow for the product; the use of *task scenarios* to explore specific user interface decisions in the product, both at the design stage and as an evaluation methodology; and the use of micro-task-analysis as a way of managing specific user interface requests throughout the life cycle of the product.

The focus of this chapter is on using task analysis to help design software for complex unstructured tasks, where there isn't a specific order in which tasks are performed, where a great deal of human judgment goes into what happens next. Examples of such tasks include: managing one's personal finances, coding and debugging a computer program, showing video tapes to students to enhance a lesson. In such situations, it's probably impossible to do a complete analysis of all possible tasks and task variations, because every time the task is done, it represents a new combination of the infinite ways to accomplish one of a large set of goals. In such cases, the analyst's goal is to understand the tasks well enough to enumerate their steps and choice points, and to constrain the set of task variations to something that is cognitively manageable but also covers the critical functions that the software will support.

For a broader perspective on task analysis, covering a much wider range of domains and methods, see (Kirwan and Ainsworth, 1992).

14.2 Initial Overall Task Analysis

The purpose of an initial task analysis is to get a broad overview of the tasks users do in the domain. While it can be done before any concrete ideas have formed about how a software system would assist work in the target domain, it is usually combined with moderately well-formed ideas about relevant technology with the goal of determining how best to design a user model and user interface for the domain of interest.

The goal of the task analysis is to enumerate all of the tasks that need to be done in the domain, whether they can be done with the software system or not. The analyst needs to decide on an appropriate level of detail. This will depend on what the goals of the analysis are. An admittedly vague rule of thumb is: if a lowest level task in the analysis were to be further decomposed, one wouldn't expect to find any "interesting" new sub-tasks in it.

14.2.1 How to Collect the Data

The enumeration of tasks should involve people who work in the domain of interest as informants. An initial list can often be developed by the system designers and/or user interface designers, based on their knowledge of the task domain. However, stopping with this intuitively developed list is dangerous, even if some of the people creating the initial list are members of the target population. There are always biases in such lists, ranging from idiosyncrasies in the working style of a single individual to systematic memory failures to spurious tasks that represent capabilities of the software technology, but are not tasks people currently do. The intuitive list can be helpful as a starting point to develop the data acquisition strategy and to establish the granularity of sub-tasks. For example, if the domain were personal finance, and informants were interviewed in June, the interviewers might not discover many tasks related to income tax preparation. However, with a well-constructed initial set of tasks, the interview could be designed to get informants to focus on income tax-related tasks, if that were important. Or, if information is needed that is more detailed than informants are likely to be able to recall, then consider using one of the techniques that enable analysts to observe informants doing a task rather than interview them.

Interviews

The most commonly used method of gathering task data is to interview people who work in the domain. Both single interviews and group interviews (focus groups) can be helpful. The interviews need to be semi-structured; initially informants should describe the task as they do it, without any suggestions from the interviewer about how it should be done. Interviews will need to probe, however, to find more details about specific sub-tasks, to understand whether sub-tasks not mentioned are optional or simply overlooked, and to learn how sub-tasks interrelate. For example, if there is a sub-task that involves searching for an item of interest, it will be important to find out what features are used to guide the search. An excellent example of a set of interview questions can be found in the Appendix of Johnson and Nardi (1996).

Often there is an official, "correct" way to do some tasks, but a more informal "quick and dirty" way that those tasks are really done. Whenever the description of a task seems very process-heavy or more constrained than seems realistic, suspect that you are hearing the official, idealized procedure rather than the procedure used in practice. This may be because people actually believe they do the task in this idealized way (i.e., they have become oblivious to the exceptions that occur), or because the procedure they use would not be acceptable to their management. First, ask the user to recall a specific instance of doing the task and to walk you through what they did in that specific case (if they can use the actual artifacts — the paperwork or other data and tools used to do the task — it will be even more realistic). If they describe their example as "having a lot of exceptions", suspect that exceptions are perhaps the rule, and probe more deeply in this area. Second, try asking other users (individual contributors will often give you a different story than managers). Finally, if you suspect that the informant is uncomfortable sharing the true procedure with you, make clear the level of confidentiality you provide, assuming you can assure the informant that her statements will not be revealed to her management or in any way used against her.

If the interviewer wants to cover new capabilities of the future software product (as tasks that users might do), it is important to separate these topics from the current ways of doing the task. When informants speculate about what they would like to see in the future, what they say is very different and much less reliable than when they report on the work they do regularly. If the two types of questions are intertwined, it will be difficult to determine when users are responding from their personal memories and when they are speculating. Leave the questions about potential new tasks to their own section of the interview, and make it clear that you are now asking about how they would like the task to be, not what they currently do.

Surveys

In some cases, task information can be acquired from surveys sent to domain practitioners. This can be a very useful method when it is important to get information from a wide range of informants; moreover, it can be a fast turnaround, low-cost method. However, there are many drawbacks to gathering task data via surveys. People will not spend as much time answering a survey as they will in an interview, so the amount of data collected per informant will necessarily be less. Very open-ended questions are not likely to elicit much information, either because informants don't understand the question or are not motivated to think deeply about it. Thus, the survey approach is unlikely to uncover new sub-tasks. However, if there is wide variation in the ways the task is performed, and a need to understand some aspects of that variation (e.g., which sub-tasks commonly co-occur or which sub-tasks most need to be supported by the software due to their frequency), a survey can be an effective method.

Surveys are often a good follow-on method to interviews. Interviews tell you the details of the domain, but are subject to problems of bias and small samples. After distilling information from interviews, it is good to see whether your interpretations hold up with a larger sample by surveying a larger, more diverse group to test your major conclusions.

Retrospectives and Diaries

When an analyst is concerned about informants' memory for task details, interested in getting more detailed information about specific instances, or interested in the relative frequencies of particular sub-tasks, retrospectives or diary studies can be more appropriate than interviews, but they are much more labor intensive. A retrospective asks informants about specific instances of doing a task shortly after the task is done. It can be done with a questionnaire (often quite free-form) or by an interview (a telephone interview can be effective). For example, informants might be questioned at the end of a task episode specifically about what they did on that episode, or questioned at the end of a day about a specific episode during that day. Diaries are an attempt to get multiple such reports very close to the time the event occurred. Informants might be asked to fill out a template at regular time intervals, or after each episode. Each report is of necessity quite short, since people have work to do beyond informing the analyst, but in the aggregate, broad coverage is possible. Furthermore, if the information is analyzed in a timely manner, the analyst can often go back to the informant and get additional details or clarifying information, while the memory (jogged by the diary entry) is still fresh in the informant's mind.

It can be difficult to get informants to fill out diaries regularly. It is important to get them committed to the importance of the information they are providing, as their motivation is critical to the success of such a study. It's also important to make the work requested as unobtrusive as possible. The critical challenge is to jog their memory so that they remember to do the diary task at the appropriate time. Some examples of diary regimens:

- Have people enter information twice a day — before lunch and at the end of the work day. If those times are not busy times, this can be effective.
- Call informants at a set time each day.
- Each time the user does a task of interest, perhaps using the existing version of the software, have them create a short diary entry. An effective way of doing this, assuming the task is done with a software system, is to instrument the system to bring up a short dialog box with the response template, either before or after the task.
- For a manual task, a tape recorder can be effective. In one case, the analyst had the informant turn on the tape recorder every time someone came to their office to ask a question (Berlin and Jeffries, 1992). A excellent log of the questions asked was acquired, costing only the effort of remembering to turn the tape recorder on and off. Interviewing the informant to get more details of the task that resulted from particular questions resulted in a fairly detailed understanding of this person's tasks.

Observation and Shadowing

Observation involves watching users doing the task of interest. Shadowing consists of following users during their daily work including, but not limited to, the tasks of interest. Both are much more labor intensive methods of gathering data for task analysis. In some situations, they are well worth the cost. They are generally used when the task is cognitively demanding enough that informants are likely to overlook important sub-tasks in their reports. For example, if one were to ask doctors about their daily tasks in order to inform the design of an information management system for medical record keeping, it would be hard to get the needed information from interviews. Given the large number of patients doctors see in a single day, they are likely to bias their accounts with the more salient (interesting) patients, when the important tasks to capture may well be the mundane, common situations. In addition, it is most likely inappropriate for the doctor to make judgments about which of his or her tasks are information management tasks — this is a part of the task analysis that needs to be done by the analyst, not the informant. When we take into account the cost of the doctor's time to participate in an interview relative to the cost of the analyst's time to do the observations, the task analysis can better be done by shadowing doctors in their work than by interviews or diaries (Fafchamps, 1991).

Formal Analyses

GOMS (see Kieras, this volume) is an example of a formal HCI method that can be used as a form of task analysis. Related methods, such as PUMS (Young and Whittington, 1990), cognitive complexity analysis (Kieras and Polson, 1985) and keystroke level models (Card, Moran, and Newell, 1983) have also been used to better under stand how a user does a task (see also Olson and Olson, 1990). These are often useful when the microstructure of the task or its timing characteristics are of interest. GOMS stands for *Goals*, *Operators*, *Methods* and *Selection Rules*. It represents a methodology for breaking a task into the users' goals, the operations needed to achieve these goals, the methods for accomplishing various operators, and the strategies for selecting among methods. An understanding of these components of the task can provide more complete and detailed information than other methods, but because of their complexity, formal methods are generally only used when the unique information they provide is critical to issues at hand. Gray, John, and Atwood (1993) is an excellent example of the use of GOMS in a real world situation (designing a workstation for telephone operators). In this study, informal analyses suggested that a particular workstation design would be best. However, carefully analysis of time consuming subtasks (particularly when the operator has to wait for either the caller or the computer system to respond), showed that a different design could improve performance significantly.

Contextual Inquiry

While all task analysis methods to some extent involve interaction with and/or observation of potential users of the system, contextual inquiry (Holtzblatt and Jones, 1993) involves observing and working with users in their normal environment to better understand the tasks they do and the flow of their work. Its goal is not only to analyze the specific tasks to be computerized, but how those tasks fit into the larger context of work. Contextual inquiry can include many of the methods mentioned above, and those methods can, even if not embedded in a contextual inquiry, focus on the broader situations into which specific tasks fit. What distinguishes a contextual inquiry is the emphasis on that broader context; what an analyst is likely to discover studying a task in isolation will be at best a small portion of and at worst contradictory to the understanding that can be achieved by situating the task in the cultural, organizational, and other contexts that it is necessarily a part of.

A full exploration of contextual inquiry is beyond the scope of this chapter. The methods used range from having the analyst spend an extended period working with the potential users to much more light weight methods that fit the schedule constraints to typical development projects. See Holtzblatt and Jones, (1993) for more information.

Participatory Design

It is useful to contrast task analysis with participatory design (Schuler and Namioka, 1993), where users participate as co-designers of the software intended for their use. A task analysis involves users as informants; it may or may not be part of a larger design methodology where users are involved as co-designers, both for determining what tasks are covered by the software system, and how the software fits into the larger context of their work. If a task analysis is used within a participatory design methodology, it is important that the informants understand that they are not acting as designers in this context. It is critical that the task analysis not be biased by design issues that occur when one adapts a manual task to a software system, and users are as susceptible to these biases as developers are.

14.2.2 The Result

Any of these methods will produce voluminous data that the analyst must now weed through to extract mentions of tasks and subtasks. Extracting the list of tasks and categorizing it in a useful way (which will depend on the domain) is a skill that comes with practice. It may help to categorize the tasks in multiple ways; different schemes will lead to different tasks being merged or possibly eliminated from the final list.

The typical result of a task analysis is a list of all the tasks people do in this domain. In other situations, there can be more — a chronological ordering, information about interdependencies, durations of various sub-tasks — but for the sorts of domains of interest here, it is generally difficult to produce more than a list of tasks with perhaps some partial ordering and identification of the most frequent tasks.

Figure 1 shows a fragment of a task analysis done for a system to supply video on demand (VOD) technology to teachers showing educational video material in the classroom. The full analysis for this task is about twice as long as what is shown in the figure. Notice

Choosing Videos for Viewing:

View list of main topics.
View list of all videos matching given criteria: title (whole or part), topic, keywords, date-range, grade-level, length, usage-level, rating level, producer, distributor.
Print list of videos (with or without summaries).
View teacher-specific list
  View list of previously shown videos.
  View list of previously shown videos of another teacher.
Preview possible videos to decide whether to show them in class.
Decide to show a video.
Nominate a video for inclusion in catalog.

Preparing to Show a Video:

Second preview of video to determine where to pause, freeze, parts to show/skip, etc..
Rewind.
  to beginning.
  to specified location.
Create custom show from segments of several videos.
Create representation of which segments of source videos go where in custom show. Two possible approaches:
  "Watch what I do": Start record mode, then play videos, starting and stopping them "manually", system records segment list or actual video bits to custom show file.
  "Here's what to do": Write (text) file indicating video segments list of (video-ID, start-location, end-location) to include.
Schedule use of video room and system.
Check system to make sure it's working and ready to show video.

Non-system setup

Arrange monitors and chairs for optimal viewing.
Set lighting in room as necessary.
Bring kids to viewing room.

Showing a Video:

Showing stock video.
  Start.
  Pause/unpause.
  Restart.
    at beginning.
    at specified location.
    visual rewind until I say stop.
  Stop, "eject", terminate showing.

Post-Showing Activities:

Save ID of stock video for future reference.
Save custom video (however it's represented) for future use.

***Figure 1.** Task analysis of Video-On-Demand system for use in school settings.*

that some tasks in the list will clearly not be part of the software system (e.g., bring kids to viewing room), some clearly will be (e.g., rewind), and some might or might not be done using the software (e.g., nominate a video for inclusion in a catalog). Many tasks exist only because of the software system (e.g., create custom show), but other tasks that the system is likely to require but are incidental to the task are not included (e.g., logging into the system). Some tasks one might expect the teachers to be doing are missing, because they aren't relevant given this technology (e.g., dealing with videos being unavailable at the desired time). This task analysis was created from individual interviews with four teachers and a focus group of six additional teachers (Johnson, Young and Keavney, 1993). It is organized hierarchically, showing the five main tasks and their many subtasks.

14.2.3 Applying the Task Analysis

A task analysis such as the one in Figure 1 will be useful in many ways throughout the life cycle of a project. In the early stages (and it should be done as early as possible into the project), it can help answer questions such as:

- Are there tasks that could be done by the system that have been overlooked? Is this software solving people's main problems in this task domain, or just attacking small problems on the fringes? If the latter, it's likely that users will be dissatisfied with the result, and if they have other options, may avoid using the software. Perhaps the system's goals need to be rethought.
- What tasks will be covered by the software system, and which ones will continue to be done manually? Will it be possible to perform all tasks smoothly, or will there be problems going back and forth between the tasks done with this software and those done another way? It may be possible to change what the system does to improve the user's overall productivity and flow (Sometimes the improvement comes from having the computer system do *less*.)
- Are the common tasks well covered by the proposed software? When schedules don't permit that all desired functionality be provided in a single release, priorities can be determined on the basis of the tasks discovered in the analysis, especially the most common and most central to accomplishing the overall task.
- Is redundant work required? If a user does a sequence of tasks that require overlapping information, will the information entered for an earlier task be available to later tasks, or does the user have to re-enter the same information? What if no earlier task has requested that information; does the user have to break the task flow to make sure the required information is available? The task analysis will provide data about the information the user has and when she is likely to have it, so the user interface can be designed to minimize redundant data entry and interruptions to find information not at hand.
- Are there interactions among tasks? Does doing one make it more difficult to do other tasks? This may lead to a restructuring of how tasks are accomplished with the system, so that they can be done in the user's preferred order, without having to take into account how the current task will complicate doing a future task.

The task analysis can be useful in designing the user interface and the user model. For example:

- A commonly used tool for establishing a user model in a complex domain is an objects and actions analysis (Card, 1996) This is a list of all objects within the system that the user needs to be aware of and the actions the user can do on those objects. The task analysis is a good starting place for determining a set of objects and actions that are natural to the domain.
- Are there tasks that will not be obvious to users because they are required by the software but not part of the user's model of the task? (e.g., the need for setup or calibration). How can the user interface help users to remember to do these steps?
- The task analysis can help determine the grouping of functionality. For example, there may be a variety of search activities, which might be consolidated into a single interaction window or into a consistent way of doing searching across the various parts of the application. On the other hand, the analysis may indicate that a single system-level task should be broken into several tasks at the user level, because people think of the different variants as distinct operations. For example, the system might have only one way to schedule a video, but the teachers may consider scheduling for their own

classroom to be a different task from scheduling for a shared room with a large viewing screen.

- Differences within the expected population can be exposed by a task analysis. For example, a task analysis involving users from multiple countries can bring out culturally specific aspects of a task, such as the fact that different countries consider the week to start on different weekdays, which would be important in a calendar manipulating task. Or in the video-on-demand example, videos might be used very differently by secondary school teachers vs. elementary school teachers or by teachers who employ cooperative learning experiences vs. teachers who don't. Task analysis is generally the only place in the development cycle where such factors can be discovered; however, they are only likely to be uncovered if the analysis includes multiple cultures or multiple sub-populations of the intended users.

14.3 Task Scenarios

As the user model and functionality of a software system are being developed, *task scenarios* can help make and evaluate user interface decisions. A task scenario is a concrete instance of a complete task plus the context surrounding it (the *situation*) and a detailed description of how the task would be carried out using the software of interest (the *resolution*). (While task scenarios are not identical to the notion of *scenario-based design* (Carroll, 1995), there are many similarities when task scenarios are used for design.) For example, a sample task scenario situation from the video-in-the-classroom domain is:

> On the day before her lesson on Egypt, a teacher decides to show a video about the construction of the pyramids. She needs to find one that covers the social, economic, and political implications of the labor used to build these structures, and that is at an appropriate level for her seventh grade class. The one she finds is an hour, and she only wants to allot 15 minutes for this, so she has to figure out if she can extract a useful 10-20 minute segment. She is not sure whether she will show the video before or after lunch.

The scenario sets a context that will influence user interface decisions. Since this is the day before, the teacher does not have a lot of time to find the video. (We could be even more concrete about how rushed she is, if we wanted to stress the aspects of the system that make it possible to do things quickly). A number of constraints will influence how she interacts with the system — e.g., showing only part of the video, and being uncertain about the starting time.

In addition to the situation, a task scenario needs to include a resolution — a detailed set of steps chronicling how the task is completed using the proposed software. All steps involving interacting with the system, as well as critical ones that are outside the system, need to be included. For instance, in the example above, suppose there were a system requirement that the teacher give a starting time for the video that would only "hold" the video for 30 minutes. This might either force the teacher in this scenario to select one of the two viewing times or request the video twice — once for the morning time and once for the afternoon time. In either case, this part of the resolution raises an issue about the usability of the software system.

Scenarios like these can be useful in many situations during the design and evaluation of a user interface. Here are some of the situations where I have found them useful.

- In the early stages of the design of the functionality and user interface of a software system. In this case, someone, perhaps the person who did the initial task analysis, provides the situation portion of the scenario. The design team works out the interactions with the software system — doing the resolution portion of the scenario is a way to design the functionality and user interface of the application. In this use, the scenarios should represent the most commonly used functionality that the application is intended to support. While it will be important to support unusual situations in the software, focusing on corner cases too early in the design can lead to software that supports those special uses well, but at the cost of making it harder for users to do the mainstream tasks.

- Once a design, or the outline of a design, is in place, task scenarios can be used to check that the design handles a broader range of tasks than were used to develop the design and to extend the original design. Here a large number of scenarios, covering both common tasks and unusual situations, are useful. The resolution is initially developed as if the user interface were already determined — how would the user do this task, given the user interface we have so far? If that leads to usability problems, then modifications can be made, keeping in mind both the current task and other tasks that require access to this functionality.

- Task scenarios are often a good way to expose others to the user interface and the decisions behind it. In fact, useful evaluations (by other human interface engineers, by marketing personnel, by potential users) can occur if the evaluators are provided with the situation description, some form of the user interface (even a paper mockup can be useful), and asked to figure out the resolution themselves. People will invariably provide feedback about problems they had doing the task and about the relevance of the situation described. It's important to attend carefully to both kinds of feedback, since some of the hardest feedback to get is whether a product solves the right set of problems.

- Task scenarios are good input to any sort of user interface evaluation. They can make a starting point for tasks in a usability test, they can be used in a cognitive walkthrough or another type of usability walkthrough, or they can be given to heuristic evaluators, especially if the evaluators are not familiar with the task domain, and hence are less likely to be able to create task scenarios informally Nielsen, 1992).

14.3.1 Creating the Situation

Discovering useful tasks is a critical part of many usability evaluation methods (Jeffries, Miller, Wharton, and Uyeda, 1991). The need to carefully select task situations is equally important to the quality of task scenarios. An existing task analysis is very helpful. Situations can be constructed from actual examples given in interviews or from diaries, or from combining sub-tasks described in the task analysis with context information. If a task analysis is not available, task situations can be constructed from whatever form of user feedback might exist. In a recent project, we used actual examples given by users of the previous version of the software — they would send email saying "I just needed to do X, and I couldn't figure out how to do it with your software". Compelling situations became driving scenarios that got named after the users who created them, leading to statements like "Will that work in the Ellen scenario?", or "But if we extrapolate from the Douglas scenario, he would want <capability X> in this situation also."

Generally, situations need to cover both common, mundane operations and more unusual operations. They need to involve more than a single operation, since many of the most useful results from analyzing a scenario come at the transitions between sub-tasks. On the other hand, a single scenario shouldn't be too complex. About ten user interface steps (where filling out a dialog box might be a single step) is the maximum for a tractable scenario.

Adding concrete details (such as the fact that the teacher is doing this at the last minute, or that she is interested in the construction of the pyramids) adds a great deal to the situation. First, the additional information typically will generate additional constraints on the user's goals or behavior, which will influence the way she does the task. Second, concreteness is highly motivating for the resolution — when a scenario is described too abstractly, there is a strong temptation to give a high level description of the resolution, which is likely to miss important details (e.g., the mistakes made by a teacher who is in a hurry, because she does not wait for slow parts of the system).

For a complex system, developing a set of scenarios that cover all the tasks in the system and their variants is unrealistic. On the other hand, relying on only a few scenarios that don't cover the full set of tasks within the domain can lead to a system that is optimal for the scenarios considered, but not particularly useful for the full set of activities users generally carry out. The challenge is to create an appropriate mix of task situations that cover the tasks of interest and focus the most attention on the common tasks in the domain, but not to the exclusion of less common but important situations. It's useful to start with a list of the high priority tasks, another list of other tasks that would be nice to include, and a third list of aspects that are less common, but can be part of many tasks (e.g., dealing with unusually large data objects; or discovering that critical information is missing in the middle of a task and requires a detour to acquire the missing information). Situations can be created taking one or more items from each list. It's also important that the situations include multiple core tasks. The most insidious user interface problems come at transitions between tasks; it's often easy to design for ease of use within a well understood task, but harder to keep that perspective as the user goes from one task to another. Including those transitions within the task scenarios helps designers focus on this difficult component. Thus, the example at the start of this section covers tasks of selection, developing a custom video, and scheduling. It could expose potential problems such as the need to know the length of the video before scheduling, which would be a problem if the teacher did the scheduling before extracting the portion of the video she wanted to show, or if the information about the length of the selected portion was lost from the screen by the time the teacher did the scheduling.

User perspective also can be added to task scenarios. In fact, it is often useful to look at the same scenario from the perspective of different users — a new user vs. a power user; a user in a hurry vs. a user who is concerned about making a mistake; a user who wants to set up the system to match her working style vs. the user who does not want to be burdened with setting up preferences. My favorite contrast is between the optimistic user, who prefers to assume that all will go well and will backtrack to recover from unanticipated problems and the pessimistic user, who is reluctant to go forward until he has assurances that an action will have no unintended side effects.

14.3.2 Creating the Resolution

Once you have the set of task situations, it's necessary to construct their resolutions.

This involves listing every step the user would go through to accomplish this task. Be sure to include steps that don't involve the software application (e.g., the need to look up information in another document). Keep the context of the scenario in mind and the way that affects the user's approach to the task — is she in a hurry? is she very knowledgeable about the application? Such issues can impact the steps a person would take.

Common Problems

Here are some common problems that arise when constructing a resolution, with advice on how to deal with them.

At various points the user will have multiple ways to accomplish the goal. Choose the option that makes the most sense given the concrete information the scenario contains about this user; this will ensure that the scenario has the most coherence. However, it is worth considering other options available at this point for at least one step. If another choice leads to interesting issues, it may be useful to work out a variant scenario where you pursue that option more fully.

A more complex variant of the above situation is where the user might have any one of several subgoals. The most frequent version is where the subtasks the user needs to complete depend on the data involved. (The U. S. 1040 income tax forms are an excellent example of this). The scenario situation will typically describe the context relevant to deciding which subgoal will best accomplish the overall goal, but if it does not, it is important to pursue multiple branches. If the scenario writer was unaware that specific information would be necessary to the scenario, its pretty likely that the user will be equally unaware of the choice point, and might make any of the available choices. To continue the income tax example, the user might not, at the beginning of doing his taxes, recognize the need to decide whether to use the short tax form or the long one. The scenario resolution should examine what happens in both cases (for the tax situation described in the scenario), particularly focusing on how the user recovers when he discovers that he made the wrong choice — in a good design, the data does not have to be entered a second time.

As evaluators work through multiple scenarios, there will be actions that have already been covered by a previous scenario. There is often a strong temptation to skip over such parts of the later scenarios, because they are seen as redundant. It is important to at least partially examine these redundant aspects, determining whether the user would likely make the same choices in the different context (perhaps this time, some other option would be more attractive), and whether the choices made will cause problems with other goals or actions that are part of the later scenario.

An important problem that occurs relatively often, especially when resolutions are worked out before the application is implemented, is that there is vagueness in how a particular step is accomplished. It might be that accomplishing that step requires access to functionality that has not yet been designed, or that the designers have assumed that something is a trivial step that doesn't need fleshing out at this point. (For example, the designers might assume that a straightforward Open step is enough to bring the object of interest into the document, when further examination would show that there is a significant challenge for the user to figure out which object they want.) There is a tension between the need to flesh out all the component parts — many later problems can be traced back to superficial assumptions about details that were seen as too trivial to explore in detail — and the need to pursue a single coherent train of action, without losing track of relevant assumptions about users' goals and contexts. One way to deal with this is to note any aspects that seem vague, either at the time they are noticed or by making a second pass through the resolution. Those aspects can be fleshed out as mini-scenarios in a separate pass, and then the larger scenario reexamined to make sure there are no problematic interactions or rough edges at the transition points.

14.3.3 Scenario Results

What sorts of information will come out of the scenario resolution process will depend on what point in the development process it is used. When used as part of the original design, it's a useful tool for getting at large problems that can make the difference between an application being useful or unusable. Scenarios can point out missing functionality, the interactions between different sub-systems, the need to enter information redundantly, entire tasks that cannot be accomplished with the system, functionality that's not useful, a user model that doesn't cover important tasks, etc.

When used as part of an evaluation, after the functionality has been completely designed, the resolution process tends to find more detailed problems — a required step that is likely to be overlooked, an awkward transition between steps, lack of consistency, functionality that is hard to find, or a conflict with other goals — e.g., a need for privacy. In this case, the scenarios help find the numerous small details that the designers need to iterate over.

Working out a task scenario can be a usability evaluation in itself; in addition, the task situation can be used as a starting point for other evaluation methods, such as cognitive walkthroughs or heuristic evaluations. Cognitive walkthroughs (Polson, Lewis, Rieman, and Wharton, 1992) start with a task situation, but defining the tasks to evaluate is outside the cognitive walkthrough methodology; thus some task analysis method is needed to create the tasks. Heuristic evaluation (Nielsen, 1995) is not typically task-focused, but providing evaluators with tasks to work through, especially if it would be difficult for them to construct such scenarios on their own, can improve the quality of the evaluation.

Task situations make excellent tasks to give to usability test participants. The advantage of doing a set of task scenarios before usability testing, rather than creating tasks with only the usability test in mind, is that the broader task analysis provides the usability engineer with a better understanding of what portion of the tasks in the domain are covered by the usability test. This is very different from making sure the usability test covers the full range of functionality of the system. Focusing on system functionality may overemphasize rare tasks, while focusing on tasks can allow for multiple ways to exercise the core functionality, possibly exposing different usability problems each time.

14.4 Micro-task Analysis for Design Improvements

A third use of task analysis is to evaluate proposed changes/enhancements to an existing design. As a software design proceeds in development, there are frequent requests for improvements. Some of these will come from usability tests, some from use of early versions of the software (or the previous version of the software), some from kibitzers who see the demo of the software, and some from the developers. Design changes that come late in the process are always subject to additional scrutiny, particularly related to their impact on the schedule and their potential to destabilize the implementation. Even before these constraints come into consideration, it is important to examine whether the proposed change will improve the product. Task analysis can be an effective tool in determining whether an enhancement makes sense, and if it does not, the analysis can expose a different modification that might more effectively solve the same problem.

People generally describe an enhancement in terms of a change to the software (a solution), rather than in terms of the problem the change is intended to solve. For example, "We need to add a menu item that does X." rather than "In situation A, there is no way to modify Y." However, both users and software engineers are quite good at identifying problems (tasks that are not well accomplished), and relatively poor at identifying optimal solutions to those problems, especially if they are not particularly steeped in the user model for this software. And all too often, the change request is motivated more by the fact that something is possible, rather than the need to support a user's task. For example, we developed an application that allowed users to advance through a series of compiler errors using next and previous keys, to examine and modify the source code associated with each error. A user asked for menu items to take him to the first and last errors. Task analysis showed that going directly to the first error was a bona fide task, especially since the log of errors could accumulate over several compiler runs, so going to the first error of the current run wasn't a simple matter of scrolling back to the beginning of the list. However, going to the last error didn't map onto any realistic user task. Compiler errors tend to cascade; an error made early in the program may produce several spurious error messages later in the program, because the compiler can't correctly interpret later lines without information it missed due to the first error. Thus, the likelihood of the last error being of interest to the programmer is very small. Furthermore, there was already a gesture to move to approximately the last error — scrolling to the end of the list. Getting the user to describe his request in terms of the task he wanted to perform elicited a pretty good description of the task associated with "go to first error", and the statement "well, you need 'go to last error' for symmetry," but no description of a context in which he would actually use the last error capability.

Generally, the tasks covered by such requests are "micro-tasks" — subtasks that may be part of one or more common tasks. Often they are like the above request, where a user is asking for a shortcut to functionality that is accessible, but not convenient. Others will have to do with eliminating unneeded steps, making functionality more visible, allowing more flexibility, or providing a way to do a new task. The task, once elicited, can provide useful fodder for determining how important the change is relative to other constraints such as schedule pressures. The task analysis should make clear how common the task is, whether it is one done by all users or only a subset, whether it is a shortcut to other functionality or something that simply can't be done in the current system, etc. This is the sort of information needed to prioritize this modification relative to other work.

Sometimes a request seems superficially to be reasonable, but the task analysis shows that details of the task would suggest a different approach. For example, in the programming environment we were developing, a user asked for a drop-down list of all available functions in situations where a function name must be typed. She said it was hard to remember the spelling of function names, and consulting a list would be easier than looking them up in the program. The task analysis brought out that, for typical programs, 1000 functions is not uncommon. Ignoring performance issues (which are not to be discounted — such a list would only be useful if it were more quickly available than the brute force search users do now), finding the function of interest in a list of 1000 items is not likely to make the user's task easier. The request here is task-based — a need to produce a valid function name when the exact name may not be known — but the proposed solution would probably be used rarely, because it doesn't make the task any easier. In this case, some sort of name completion would be more effective, allowing the user to type the first few characters of the name, and the system responding with as much of the name as can be predicted from those initial characters.

One area to be particularly sensitive to is whether a proposed solution serves all users or only those who have a particular work style. There are many situations where different people approach a task quite differently, and a single solution cannot support them all. A task analysis needs to determine whether the user's description of how they do the task is one of several approaches, or whether it is the one used by a majority of users. A common situation is that people will want to do things in different orders. Sometimes the user interface can be made neutral with respect to these different approaches (e.g., by providing a form that can be filled out in any order), but in other circumstances, only one approach can be supported at a time. At this point, it is important to determine whether the differences are due to variations in work style (i.e., each individual will choose the same approach repeatedly) or subtle variations in tasks (i.e., an individual will do the task differently depending on the circumstances). In the former case, an option that lets the user make a choice once and forget it is most likely the best approach; in the latter case, the choice needs to be more immediately available, and, more importantly, available at the point in the task where the user is likely to know which path they need to take.

For users and engineers who are not used to thinking about software features in terms of the associated task, describing a request in task-oriented terms (the first step of the micro task analysis) is unnatural. The designer will need to probe, asking what they were doing when they realized they needed this feature, or in the case of developers, what task they think users would be doing. Figure 2 gives a list of questions that need to be answered to do an effective micro-task analysis. The original requester will most likely not know the answers to all of the questions; finding the answers may require going back to an earlier task analysis or getting new information from additional informants.

The micro-task analysis can be useful throughout the life cycle of the product, dealing with problems ranging from usability bugs to new features. It should be relatively obvious when a proposed change is too large for this approach, and a more detailed and structured task analysis is needed.

14.5 Conclusions

Task analysis is a methodology that can be useful throughout the product development life cycle, from the initial understanding of requirements to the analysis of bug reports and enhancement requests during the

1. What is the larger task the user is doing at the point they need this enhancement?
2. How often will they do this step?
3. Are there alternate ways of doing this step already? How does the proposed approach relate to the existing methods?
4. Is this way of doing the task common to all users, or can we expect different users to take different approaches? What are the other ways of approaching the task?
5. How will users decide among the different ways of doing the task — will it be a matter of user preference, or a function of other attributes of the task?
6. How does the proposed solution relate to the requirements of the task (e.g., is it fast enough, will it be discovered by users)?

Figure 2. List of questions to answer for a micro-task analysis.

maintenance phase. Almost any question about making functionality available to users will be better answered if we stop and ask: "what's the task here?" This chapter has described a few areas where I have used task analysis in the design and evaluation of user interfaces. These are only a small sampling of the many ways task analysis can be applied. As you become more familiar with a task-oriented way of looking at things, ways of using informal and formal task analyses will be apparent in many situations.

This chapter has described a best practices approach to the three methods described. In actual practice, under the time pressures of tight development schedules, it may be necessary to settle for less than this. While a task analysis that covers the domain well will always yield better results than one that only covers a few core tasks, a partial task analysis will provide enough benefits over no task analysis at all to justify the resources spent on it. At the very least, it can showcase the improvements obtained in the areas where the task analysis was done, which might get you more time and resources to do a better task analysis for the next release. At the same time, you are building a repertoire of task analysis skills and task knowledge in a particular domain, which you can build on to make the next analysis more effective and less labor intensive.

14.6 Acknowledgments

Thanks to Jeff Johnson for some of the examples included here; to Don Gentner, Ellen Isaacs, Jeff Johnson, and Rob Mori for reading earlier drafts; and to Susan Dray for moral support.

14.7 References

Berlin, L. and Jeffries, R. (1992). Consultants and Apprentices: Observations about Learning and Collaborative Problem Solving. *Proceedings of the ACM Conference on Computer Supported Cooperative Work*, CSCW'92, Toronto, Canada, 1992.

Card, S. K. (1996). Pioneers and settlers: Methods used in successful user interface design. In Rudisill, M., Lewis, C., Polson, P. G., and McKay, T. D. (Eds.) *HCI Design: Success Stories, Emerging Methods and Real-World Tasks.* Morgan-Kaufman: San Francisco.

Card, S. K., Moran, T., and Newell, A. (1983). *The Psychology of Human-Computer Interaction*, Earlbaum: Hillsdale, NJ.

Carroll, J. (1995) *Scenario-Based Design.* Wiley & Sons: New York.

Fafchamps, D. (1991). unpublished study.

Gray, W. D., John, B. E., and Atwood, M. E. (1993). Project Ernestine: Validating a GOMS analysis for predicting real-world task performance. *Human-Computer Interaction*, (6) 287-309.

Holtzblatt, K. and Jones, S. (1993). Contextual Inquiry: Principles and Practices. In Schuler, D. and Namioka, A. (Eds.) *Participatory Design: Principles and Practice.* Earlbaum: Hillsdale, NJ.

Jeffries, R. Miller, J. R., Wharton, C. and Uyeda, K. M. (1991). User interface evaluation in the real world: A comparison of four techniques. *Proceedings of the ACM Conference on Human Factors in Computing Systems,* CHI'91. ACM: New York, pp. 119-124.

Johnson, J., Young, E., and Keavney, M. (1994). unpublished data.

Johnson, J. and Nardi, B. (1996). Creating presentation slides: A study of user preferences for task-specific versus generic application software. *ACM Transactions on Computer-Human Interaction,* (3), pp. 38-65.

Kieras, D. and Polson, P. G. (1985). An approach to the formal analysis of user complexity. *International Journal of Man-Machine Studies,* (22), pp. 365-94.

Kirwan, B. and Ainsworth, L. K. (1992) (Eds.) *A Guide to Task Analysis.* Taylor & Francis: London.

Nielsen, J. (1992) Finding usability problems through heuristic evaluation. *Proceedings of the ACM Conference on Human Factors in Computing Systems, CHI'92.* ACM: Monterey, CA. pp. 373-380.

Nielsen, J. (1995) *Usability Evaluation.* Wiley and Sons: New York.

Olson, J. R. and Olson, G. M. (1990) The growth of cognitive modeling in human-computer interaction since GOMS. *Human-Computer Interaction,* 5, pp. 221-265.

Polson, P. G., Lewis, C., Rieman, J., and Wharton, C. (1992) Cognitive walkthroughs: A method for theory-based evaluation of user interfaces. *International Journal of Man-Machine Studies,* 36, pp. 741-773.

Schuler, D. and Namioka, A. (1993). (Eds.) *Participatory Design: Principles and Practice.* Earlbaum: Hillsdale, NJ.

Young, R.M. and Whittington, J. Using a knowledge analysis to predict conceptual errors in text-editor usage. In *Proceedings of the ACM Conference on Human Factors in Computing Systems,* CHI'90. ACM: New York, pp. 91-97.

Handbook of Human-Computer Interaction
Second, completely revised edition
M. Helander, T.K. Landauer, P. Prabhu (eds.)

Chapter 15

The Use of Ethnographic Methods in Design and Evaluation

Bonnie A. Nardi
Apple Computer
USA

15.1 Introduction

"You can see a lot by observing" — Yogi Berra

Anthropologists and sociologists employ ethnographic methods to study people "in the wild," as they go about their everyday activities in offices, homes, schools, gardens, laboratories, or wherever they live their lives. The experimental methods of psychology, by contrast, call for measuring how people perform on predetermined tasks undertaken by subjects in a laboratory. The point of ethnography is to find out not how people respond to a constructed situation in which narrowly pinpointed variables are studied, as in experimental psychology, but to learn how people actually work and play. For an excellent overview of ethnographic methods, see Blomberg et al. (1993).

Although both anthropologists and sociologists use ethnographic methods, the methods are mainly associated with anthropology. Since I am an anthropologist, I will take an anthropological perspective here.

15.2 How do Ethnographers Conduct their Studies?

The chief ethnographic methods are interviews, observations and participant-observation. Participant-observation involves spending a great deal of time with and participating in the everyday lives of the natives. Participant-observation was developed in the 19th and early 20th centuries when anthropologists went abroad or to Native American societies to investigate cultures which at the time were unfamiliar and completely undocumented. A goal of anthropology is to learn about every aspect of a culture. Living with the natives was critical to this endeavor. When the researcher is actually living with a group, it becomes socially necessary to participate. Anthropologists found that they could learn a lot through participation—helping herd sheep, weaving a basket, tilling the fields, building an igloo. Participant-observation gives a good feel for the rhythms and challenges of the lives of those the researcher is studying. It helps the researcher to see the world through native eyes. While technology studies usually do not require actually living with the natives, the method is still useful when spending lengthy periods of time with informants. For example, I recently conducted a five month study in a local school, and found myself assisting students, commiserating with the teacher, helping to tidy the room.

One of the greatest strengths of ethnography is its flexible research design. The study takes shape as the work proceeds. People are such surprising creatures that it is impossible to know what may be of interest in a research setting before the work is done. Following up unexpected but important events and areas of interest is fully supported by the ethnographic method. A researcher may study a focused area of interest as set forth in the original study design but, unlike an experiment, interesting material can and should be explored when it is encountered. See Nardi et. al (1996) for a study of a multimedia installation in which a crisis surrounding issues of privacy was studied, though it was not intended as part of the study. Our design recommendations were affected by what we learned by investigating the privacy issues.

Anthropologists also use quantitative methods including surveys, time-motion studies, interaction analysis (Jordan and Henderson, 1995), enumerations, and censuses.

15.3 Ethnography in Design and Evaluation

It is remarkable how many products are designed and brought to market with very little idea of how people will use them or whether they will use them at all. A good ethnography provides a basis on which to judge a product's potential impact and can be a fertile source of design ideas. Building up a series of careful case studies and understanding how they fit into one's business model is valuable in short and long range planning. An ethnography that exposes cultural themes can lead to more effective marketing of products (Ireland and Johnson, 1995).

An important tenet of anthropology is "holism," the idea that any and all aspects of a culture are related. Not all aspects of a culture are smoothly integrated, but they do connect to one another, sometimes in relations of conflict and contradiction. In human-computer interaction studies it is important to recognize that variables such as office space in the home, union politics in schools, organizational hierarchies, the cost of telephone lines and so forth, can affect the way a technology is deployed (or not deployed). Looking holistically beyond the narrow scope of technically focused design criteria opens up a vast new field of concerns that can help pinpoint good solutions as well as stimulate technical creativity.

Understanding what the natives are really up to is useful in a number of places in the design cycle, but in particular at two points: (1) Before the design has taken shape and (2) when a robust prototype is available for testing. A design informed by consideration of the users' tasks and context is invaluable, as has been recognized in the human-computer interaction community (Suchman and Winn, 1984; Blomberg, 1993; Kidd, 1994; Rogers and Ellis, 1994; Hughes, 1995; Johnson, Johnson and Wilson, 1995; papers in Nardi, 1996a) .

In the evaluation phase, testing is not "user testing" in a laboratory, but the careful study of what happens after the installation of the prototype into a setting where the real users of the system (not researcher colleagues) can use it (see Nardi et al., 1996).

In many corporate settings, it is useful to follow an ethnographic study with a quantitative study focusing on particular questions for which statistically sound predictions can be made. The qualitative research brings to life crucial areas of interest that should be pursued, avoiding the expensive (and futile!) "fishing expedition" approach of large unfocused quantitative studies. A good qualitative study provides "ecological validity" to a quantitative study, giving wider latitude for interpreting numerical data.

15.3.1 The Role of the Ethnographer in Design and Evaluation

As a member of a design team, ethnographers are useful for the following tasks:

1. conducting specific studies for a given project or product
2. project management
3. acting as the "first user" of a prototype
4. informing usability studies
5. keeping up with the literature
6. injecting the users' perspective throughout the project

Point number six is especially critical. It is useful to have an ethnographer on the design team to be an advocate for the non-computer-professional user, i.e., the end user of the products being designed or modified. Programmers have many wonderful gifts and talents, but in the heat of coding, it is easy to forget how unlike they themselves end users are. It is easy to assume that end users will find that button that's been moved, or write that easy little AppleScript, or set all those preference variables. The ethnographer can be helpful in making sure products are really easy to use, that they meet important user needs, that they are pleasing to customers.

15.3.2 How Long does it Take to do an Ethnography?

The classic anthropological study is a year in the field. This is in part an artifact of an academic system in which graduate students who do not know much are sent to a foreign country to study another culture. They usually have to learn a new language (often a very difficult one, with no cognates). They get sick and can't work for long periods of time because they are in places with malaria or dysentery (or both). They work slowly because they are lonely (or squabbling with a spouse under the pressures of living under difficult circumstances). It's hard to stay clean. They are overwhelmed by the challenges of dirt, diet, climate and culture.

If the job is to understand office procedures or how work gets done in an intensive care nursery or the use of computers in schools, a year in the field is not necessary. There are not the same constraints a graduate student faces going to the field for the first time. As little as six weeks can produce very good results— for a trained ethnographer. Even shorter, very highly focused studies are often appropriate and useful for pursuing well-defined questions of design or evaluation for a particular product. It is entirely possible to effectively use ethnographic methods even in tight product cycles.

In some settings more than six weeks is needed. For example, in a school, it may take an entire semester to understand how the school works. In an accountant's office, it's important to be around at tax time and when it is not tax time. Each setting has its own contours that must be considered.

15.4 Who Conducts an Ethnography?

I often hear people say that ethnographic studies are too expensive, too difficult, too time-consuming for the everyday workaday world of industry. True enough, unless you have an experienced ethnographer doing the work. The ethnographer knows how to pace the work, and, most important, *what to do with all that data.*

It is easy to collect a lot of data. It is especially easy to collect a lot of bad data. Good or bad, it is hard to analyze the data once you've got them. Any one who has tried will own up to this. As I have watched untrained people attempt naturalistic studies, I have seen how much they miss, how bad their sampling techniques are, how many leading questions they ask, how few probe questions they follow up with, how naively they accept superficial answers to their questions and how they flounder trying to analyze their data and how unable they are to weave together data from disparate sources such as interviews, observations, videotape, artifacts, surveys. Studying the least predictable, most complex phenomena we know of (people) is not an easy task. As Gregory Bateson, an eminent anthropologist, is supposed to have said of anthropology, "There are the hard sciences and then there are the difficult sciences."

Training does matter. Ethnographers learn through a lengthy apprenticeship. They intensively study many ethnographies, with the guidance of their teachers. They design and conduct small ethnographic studies, and they usually experience a full year in the field, when doing dissertation work, an important immersion into another culture that provides a critical training experience. Anthropology is an experiential science, much like clinical medicine.

An important part of the training ethnographers receive concerns recognizing and accounting for one's own biases. It is never possible to completely eliminate bias, but it is possible to recognize it and to open yourself up to new ways of thinking. Understanding why someone prays to a dead ancestor requires a realignment of Western thought. It can be just as trying to comprehend unfamiliar settings in one's own culture. For example, in the multimedia study I have referred to (Nardi et al., 1996), the strict staff hierarchy in the hospital produced a great deal of tension and hostility among staff members. The hierarchy had to be understood by the researchers in the larger context of the work that goes on in the hospital. It could not be dismissed out of hand as undemocratic or elitist (though it was certainly both). It sometimes takes emotional resources to cope with the unfamiliar. These resources develop over time through ethnographic training. They allow one to deal with some level of objectivity in situations where one's perspectives or beliefs are different than those of the natives.

Untrained people sometimes sentimentalize the natives, rather than rejecting or ridiculing them. This leads just as surely to bad science. It is common among well-intentioned amateurs to romanticize others as "noble," "closer to nature," "unspoiled by Western thought" and so forth. This is more likely to happen to researchers in non-Western cultures, and as companies begin to think globally, it is an important consideration for studies of foreign markets.

15.5 Where does Ethnography go Wrong?

The most commonly made mistake in ethnographic research is generalizing beyond the study's sample population. Ethnographers who are not trained in statistical methods make this mistake over and over again. It is crucial in a corporate setting to be confident that those studied are truly representative of the customers one wishes to reach.

15.6 Finding Ethnographers

When ethnographic methods are appropriate, if you do not have ethnographers on staff, contact your local university and rouse up some enthusiasm for your project. Many younger social scientists are more interested in technology than their tenured elders and welcome the chance to work on cutting edge projects. Funding is tight in universities these days and you can get a lot of quality work done at standard consulting rates.

Train your own people through apprenticeships (again try your local university). Wonders can be worked through regular email contact and well-managed infrequent face-to-face meetings. Your ethnographer may not be able to converse in Derrida- and Latour-speak, but that isn't necessary for what's useful in industry. If I had to choose between a 2-3-day course in ethnographic methods (offered by some consulting companies) and helping support a graduate student's or professor's research in exchange for apprenticeship time, I would choose the latter. Or I would choose to put one of my people in an apprenticeship relationship with an anthropologist if that were possible.

Another reason not to "roll your own" ethnographer, without training from an experienced ethnographer, is that there are serious and abiding ethical issues when conducting ethnographic research. Anthropologists and sociologists have developed ethical guidelines that help prevent abuse. Students learn about case studies where decisions had to be made. They study guidelines and get practice submitting human subjects reviews.

It is surprisingly easy for well-intentioned people to do unethical things in the belief that the value of their research is an appropriate tradeoff for questionable practices. It is easy not to see the practices as questionable. It also frequently happens in ethnographic research that the ethnographer sees and hears things that should not be revealed (highly political and personal things for example) and restraint must be exercised in dealing with such material.

Being inculcated and socialized into a culture in which unethical behavior is off limits enables a good researcher to feel ashamed of lowering his or her standards. Shame is a far more effective deterrent to ethical abuse than all the human subjects committees in the world. There is an important place for human subjects review however, as a continuing symbol of the need to be vigilant. But it is being part of a culture that cares about ethics that produces the best results.

15.7 Communicating Ethnographic Results to those Who Need Them

Ethnographers working in industry have been heard to grumble about the difficulty of getting designers to listen to them. I have heard both engineers and ethnographers use exactly the same word to describe each other: "arrogant."

One solution to this problem is to have a single ethnographer on the design team, from the outset of the project. Having a single ethnographer prevents the formation of the "social science corner" where the ethnographers form a subgroup that is easily isolated in the larger technical culture in which they are outnumbered. My personal experience is that being the ethnographer on the design team is a lot like going to the field by yourself, which you are trained to do. The natives more or less have to find a way to deal with you. I have found that engineers rise to the occasion admirably once the common goals of the project are established and shared among all group members.

Outside of research labs it is economically unfeasible, in most cases, to have more than one ethnographer on a project anyway. Just as there is probably one user interface designer, one manager, one marketing person, and so forth, one ethnographer must suffice.

Of course there are times when there is more work than one ethnographer can do. Summer interns and contractors come to the rescue here. A significant contribution to the multimedia study (Nardi et al., 1996) was made by a summer intern. I am not saying that it is never appropriate to have more than one ethnographer on a project; only that there are often advantages, social and economic, to a single ethnographer who is a key part of the team from the initial stages of a project.

When the ethnographer cannot be personally on hand, a new medium, interactive ethnography, may be useful (Nardi and Reilly, 1996). Interactive ethnography, in which the results of the research are communicated in visual and textual form on interactive CD-ROM, is in its infancy but shows promise of reaching people who would not read a research report.

15.8 Theory

It is impossible to conduct an ethnographic study without a theoretical perspective. With the rich stimuli of the real world setting, it is necessary to filter and focus. Those who lack a perspective can be expected to cobble together a perspective on the fly, one that may be uninformed, fraught with investigator bias.

The leading theoretical perspectives for ethnographically-oriented human-computer interaction studies are activity theory (Nardi, 1996a), distributed cognition (Hutchins, 1994; Rogers and Ellis, 1994), and situated action (Suchman, 1987). For a comparison of the three approaches, please see Nardi (1996b).

An illustrative example of work in the situated action area is Suchman and Trigg (1993) who considered the everyday activities of artificial intelligence researchers. Based on an analysis of the situated action evident in one and a half hours of videotape of two AI researchers working at a whiteboard, the authors argued that artificial intelligence research is a form of "craftwork" materially involving the "eyes and hands," rather than the kind of idealized mentalistic reasoning which is what the AI researchers themselves take it to be. In situated action accounts the investigator is interested in the minute particulars of interactions between people and artifacts, often in a short time frame such as the 1.5 hours at the whiteboard.

An exemplar of distributed cognition research is Hutchins' (1993) paper on navigation aboard naval ships. Hutchins described how the "robust" and redundant knowledge distributed across people and instruments on a ship enabled the complex task of piloting the ship. He called the shipboard team a "flexible organic tissue" that responds to potential breakdown in one part of the tissue by the rapid response of the another part of the tissue. In distributed cognition, the idea is to work at the systems level rather than the level of the individual. Distribution cognition theorists make the point that no matter how well you understand the capabilities of an individual in a system (whether a person or an instrument), it is impossible to understand how work actually gets done without looking at the system as a whole.

Nardi (1996) contains several papers in which activity theory is used to study problems of HCI. Christiansen (1996), for example, investigated how Danish homicide detectives used and modified a software system to handle their casework. Bødker (1996) applied video analysis to a study of a large software project used by the Danish National Labor Inspection Service (yes, activity theory is heavily represented in Scandinavia). Holland and Reeves (1996) studied three teams of student programmers, following their progress during the course of a semester. In all these studies the investigators studied the history of the activity, the changing goals and objectives of study participants and the larger context in which the activity was embedded -- all hallmarks of an activity theory analysis.

While distributed cognition and activity theory share many perspectives (see Nardi 1996b), situated action is more readily differentiated. It is committed to the study of "moment-by-moment" interactions, usually involving the study of segments of video tape, such as the Suchman and Trigg study of AI researchers. In these studies it is *interactions* between study participants that are the focus of investigator's attention. Activity theory and distributed cognition, by contrast, are more focused on longer term activities, the use of artifacts to "distribute" and "regulate" knowledge and action, and the personal objectives, beliefs and knowledge of study participants.

Each approach is useful for its own set of problems.

15.9 If You Want to Know More...

It is a common experience for ethnographers in industry to be asked "What book should I read if I want to learn about ethnography?" This is like asking what book you should read to learn about programming or physics, but here are some titles that provide good introductory material.

Glaser and Strauss (1967) is a classic and is very short. It is highly recommended. As mentioned, Blomberg et al. (1993) is an excellent introduction to ethnographic methods from a human-computer interaction perspective. See also Hammersley and Atkinson (1983).

If you want to read some traditional ethnographies, Colin Turnbull (1961) and Bronislaw Malinowski (1922) are prominent in the anthropological canon. Turnbull wrote about African Pygmies in a very accessible style. Malinowski's lengthy tome about life in the Trobriand Islands is more difficult but very rewarding. *Tiwi Wives* (1971) by Jane Goodale is excellent. *East is a Big Bird* by Thomas Gladwin (1970) is a literary and ethnographic delight.

Happy reading, and good luck in your interaction with the ethnographic enterprise.

15.10 References

Blomberg, J. et al. (1993). Ethnographic field methods and their relation to design. in D. Schuler and A. Namioka, Eds. *Participatory Design.* Lawrence Erlbaum. pp. 123-155.

Bødker, S. (1996). Applying activity theory to video analysis: how to make sense of video data in HCI. In Nardi, B. Ed. Context *and Consciousness: Activity Theory and Human Computer Interaction.* Cambridge: MIT Press. Pp. 147-174.

Christiansen, E. (1996). Tamed by a rose: computers as tools in human activity. In Nardi, B. (Ed.), *Context and Consciousness: Activity Theory and Human Computer Interaction.* Cambridge: MIT Press. Pp. 175-198.

Gladwin, T. (1970). *East is a Big Bird.* Cambridge: Harvard University Press.

Glaser, B. and Strauss, A. (1967). *The Discovery of Grounded Theory: Strategies for Qualitative Research.* New York: Aldine.

Goodale, Jane. (1971/1994). *Tiwi Wives.* Prospect Heights, Ill.: Waveland.

Hammersley, M. and Atkinson, P.(1983). *Ethnography Principles in Practice.* London: Tavistock Publications.

Hughes, J. et al. (1995). The role of ethnography in interactive systems design. *interactions.* April .

Hutchins, E. (1993). Learning to navigate. In *Understanding Practice.* Seth Chaiklin and Jean Lave, eds. Cambridge: Cambridge University Press.

Hutchins, E. (1995). *Cognition in the Wild.* Cambridge: MIT Press.

Ireland, C. and Johnson, B. (1995). Exploring the Future in the Present. *Design Management Journal* . Spring Issue. Pp. 57-64.

Johnson, P., Johnson, H., Wilson, S. (1995). Rapid prototyping of user interfaces driven by task models. In *Scenario-Based Design*, J. Carroll, ed. New York: Wiley.

Jordan, G. and Henderson, A. (1995). Interaction Analysis: Foundations and Practice. *The Journal of the Learning Sciences 4*(1): 39-103.

Kidd, A. (1994). The marks are on the knowledge worker. In *Proceedings CHI'94.* 24--28 April, Boston.

Malinowski, B. (1922/1984). *Argonauts of the Western Pacific.* Prospect Heights, Ill.: Waveland Press.

Nardi, B. (1996a). (Ed.), *Context and Consciousness: Activity Theory and Human Computer Interaction.* Cambridge: MIT Press.

Nardi, B. (1996b). Studying context: A comparison of activity theory, situated action models and distributed cognition. In *Context and Consciousness: Activity Theory and Human Computer Interaction.* B. Nardi, Ed. Cambridge: MIT Press.

Nardi, B., Kuchinsky, A., Whittaker, S., Leichner, R. and Schwarz, H. (1996). Video-as-data: technical and social aspects of a collaborative multimedia application. *CSCW 4*, 1: 73-100 (Computer Supported Cooperative Work).

Nardi, B. and Reilly, B. (1996). Interactive Ethnography. *Innovation*, Summer Issue.

Rogers, Y. and Ellis, J. (1994). Distributed cognition: An alternative framework for analyzing and explaining collaborative working. *Journal of Information Technology* 9, 119–128.

Suchman, L., and Trigg, R. (1993). Artificial Intelligence as Craftwork. In *Understanding Practice.* Seth Chaiklin and Jean Lave, eds. Cambridge: Cambridge University Press.

Suchman, L. and Wynn, E. (1984). Procedures and Problems in the Office. *Office Technology and People*, Vol 2, pp. 134-154.

Turnbull, C. (1961/1987). *The Forest People* . New York: Touchstone.

Handbook of Human-Computer Interaction
Second, completely revised edition
M. Helander, T.K. Landauer, P. Prabhu (eds.)

Chapter 16

What do Prototypes Prototype?

Stephanie Houde and Charles Hill
Apple Computer, Inc.
Cupertino, California, USA

16.1 Introduction

Prototypes are widely recognized to be a core means of exploring and expressing designs for interactive computer artifacts. It is common practice to build prototypes in order to represent different states of an evolving design and to explore options. However, since interactive systems are complex, it may be difficult or impossible to create prototypes of a whole design in the formative stages of a project. Choosing the right kind of more focused prototype to build is an art in itself, and communicating its limited purposes to its various audiences is a critical aspect of its use.

The ways that we talk, and even think, about prototypes can get in the way of their effective use. Current terminology for describing prototypes centers on attributes of prototypes themselves, such as what tool was used to create them, and how refined-looking or -behaving they are. Such terms can be distracting. Tools can be used in many different ways, and detail is not a sure indicator of completion.

We propose a change in the language used to talk about prototypes, to focus more attention on fundamental questions about the interactive system being designed: What role will the artifact play in a user's life? How should it look and feel? How should it be implemented? The goal of this chapter is to establish a model that describes any prototype in terms of the artifact being designed, rather than the prototype's incidental attributes. By focusing on the purpose of the prototype—that is, on *what it prototypes*—we can make better decisions about the kinds of prototypes to build. With a clear purpose for each prototype, we can better use prototypes to think and communicate about design.

In the first section we describe some current difficulties in communicating about prototypes: the complexity of interactive systems; issues of multi-disciplinary teamwork; and the audiences of prototypes. Next, we introduce the model and illustrate it with some initial examples of prototypes from real projects. In the following section we present several more examples to illustrate some further issues. We conclude the chapter with a summary of the main implications of the model for prototyping practice.

16.2 The Problem with Prototypes

Interactive computer systems are complex. Any artifact can have a rich variety of software, hardware, auditory, visual, and interactive features. For example, a personal digital assistant such as the Apple Newton has an operating system, a hard case with various ports, a graphical user interface and audio feedback. Users experience the combined effect of such interrelated features; and the task of designing—and prototyping—the user experience is therefore complex. Every aspect of the system must be designed (or inherited from a previous system), and many features need to be evaluated in combination with others.

Prototypes provide the means for examining design problems and evaluating solutions. Selecting the focus of a prototype is the art of identifying the most important open design questions. If the artifact is to provide new functionality for users—and thus play a new *role* in their lives—the most important questions may concern exactly what that role should be and what features are needed to support it. If the role is well understood, but the goal of the artifact is to present its functionality in a novel way, then prototyping must focus on how the artifact will *look and feel*. If the artifact's functionality is to be based on a new technique, questions of how to *implement* the design may be the focus of prototyping efforts.

Once a prototype has been created, there are several distinct audiences that designers discuss prototypes with. These are: the intended *users* of the artifact being designed; their *design teams*; and the supporting *organizations* that they work within (Erickson, 1995). Designers evaluate their options with their own team by critiquing prototypes of alternate design directions. They show prototypes to users to get feedback on evolving designs. They show prototypes to their supporting organizations (such as project managers, business clients, or professors) to indicate progress and direction.

It is difficult for designers to communicate clearly about prototypes to such a broad audience. It is challenging to build protoypes which produce feedback from users on the most important design questions. Even communication among designers requires effort due to differing perspectives in a multi-disciplinary design team. Limited understanding of design practice on the part of supporting organizations makes it hard for designers to explain their prototypes to them. Finally, prototypes are not self-explanatory: looks can be deceiving. Clarifying what aspects of a prototype correspond to the eventual artifact—and what don't—is a key part of successful prototyping.

16.2.1 What is a Prototype?

Designing interactive systems demands collaboration between designers of many different disciplines (Kim, 1990). For example, a project might require the skills of a programmer, an interaction designer, an industrial designer, and a project manager. Even the term "prototype" is likely to be ambiguous on such a team. Everyone has a different expectation of what a prototype is. Industrial designers call a molded foam model a prototype. Interaction designers refer to a simulation of on-screen appearance and behavior as a prototype. Programmers call a test program a prototype. A user studies expert may call a storyboard which shows a scenario of something being used, a prototype.

The organization supporting a design project may have an overly narrow expectation of what a prototype is. Shrage (1996) has shown that organizations develop their own "prototyping cultures" which may cause them to consider only certain kinds of prototypes to be valid. In some organizations, only prototypes which act as proof that an artifact can be produced are respected. In others, only highly detailed representations of look and feel are well understood.

Is a brick a prototype? The answer depends on how it is used. If it is used to represent the weight and scale of some future artifact, then it certainly is: it prototypes the weight and scale of the artifact. This example shows that prototypes are not necessarily self-explanatory. What is significant is not what media or tools were are used to create them, but *how they are used by a designer* to explore or demonstrate some aspect of the future artifact..

16.2.2 Current Terminology

Current ways of talking about prototypes tend to focus on attributes of the prototype itself, such as which tool was used to create it (as in "C", "Director™", and "paper" prototypes); and on how finished-looking or -behaving a prototype is (as in "high-fidelity" and "low-fidelity" prototypes). Such characterizations can be misleading because the capabilities and possible uses of tools are often misunderstood and the significance of the level of finish is often unclear, particularly to non-designers.

Tools can be used in many different ways. Sometimes tools which have high-level scripting languages (like HyperCard™), rather than full programming languages (like C), are thought to be unsuitable for producing user-testable prototypes. However, Ehn and Kyng (1991) have shown that even prototypes made of cardboard are very useful for user testing. In the authors' experience, no one tool supports iterative design work in all of the important areas of investigation. To design well, designers must be willing to use different tools for different prototyping tasks; and to team up with other people with complementary skills.

Finished-looking (or -behaving) prototypes are often thought to indicate that the design they represent is near completion. Although this may sometimes be the case, a finished-looking prototype might be made early in the design process (e.g., a 3D concept model for use in market research), and a rough one might be made later on (e.g., to emphasize overall structure rather than visual details in a user test). Two related terms are used in this context: "resolution" and "fidelity". We interpret resolution to mean "amount of detail", and fidelity to mean "closeness to the eventual design". It is important to recognize that the degree of visual and behavioral refinement of a prototype does not necessarily correspond to the solidity of the design, or to a particular stage in the process.

16.3 A Model of What Prototypes Prototype

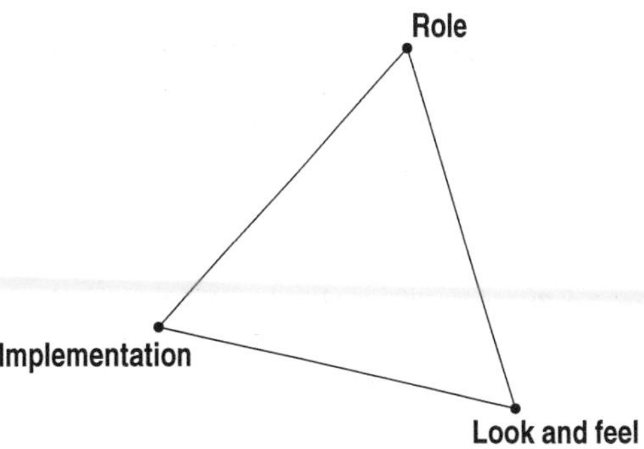

Figure 1. A model of what prototypes prototype.

16.3.1 Definitions

Before proceeding, we define some important terms. We define *artifact* as the interactive system being designed. An artifact may be a commercially released product or any end-result of a design activity such as a concept system developed for research purposes. We define *prototype* as any representation of a design idea, regardless of medium. This includes a pre-existing object when used to answer a design question. We define *designer* as anyone who creates a prototype in order to design, regardless of job title.

16.3.2 The Model

The model shown in Figure 1 represents a three-dimensional space which corresponds to important aspects of the design of an interactive artifact. We define the dimensions of the model as *role*; *look and feel*; and *implementation*. Each dimension corresponds to a class of questions which are salient to the design of any interactive system. "Role" refers to questions about the function that an artifact serves in a user's life—the way in which is it useful to them. "Look and feel" denotes questions about the concrete sensory experience of using an artifact—what the user looks at, feels, and hears while using it. "Implementation" refers to questions about the techniques and components through which an artifact performs its function—the "nuts and bolts" of how it actually works. The triangle is drawn askew to emphasize that no one dimension is inherently more important than any other.

Goal of the Model: Given a design problem (of any scope or size), designers can use the model to separate design issues into three classes of questions which frequently demand different approaches to prototyping. Implementation usually requires a working system to be built; look and feel requires the concrete user experience to be simulated or actually created; role requires the context of the artifact's use to be established. Being explicit about what design questions must be answered is therefore an essential aid to deciding what kind of prototype to build. The model helps visualize the focus of exploration.

Markers: A prototype may explore questions or design options in one, two or all three dimensions of the model. In this chapter, several prototypes from real design projects are presented as examples. Their relationship to the model is represented by a marker on the triangle. This is a simple way to put the purpose of any prototype in context for the designer and their audiences. It gives a global sense of what the prototype is intended to explore; and equally important, what it does not explore.

It may be noted that the triangle is a relative and subjective representation. A location toward one corner of the triangle implies simply that *in the designer's own judgment*, more attention is given to the class of questions represented by that corner than to the other two.

16.3.3 Three Prototypes of One System

The model is best explained further through an example from a real project. The three prototypes shown in Examples 1-3 were created during the early stages of development of a 3D space-planning application (Houde, 1992).

The goal of the project was to design an example of a 3D application which would be accessible to a broad range of non-technical users. As such it was designed to work on a personal computer with an ordinary mouse. Many prototypes were created by different members of the multi-disciplinary design team during the project.

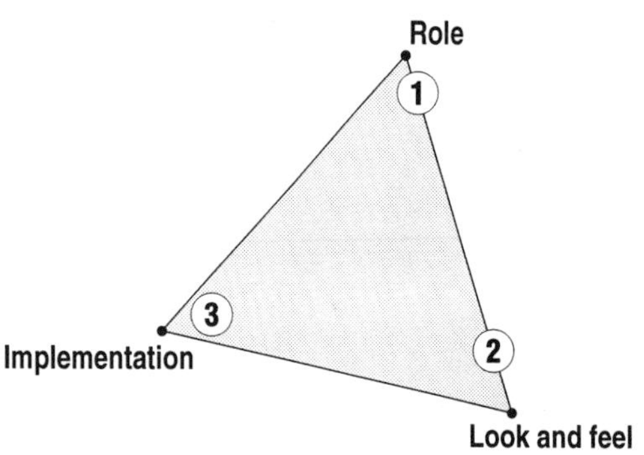

Figure 2. Relationship of three prototypes (Examples 1 - 3) to the model.

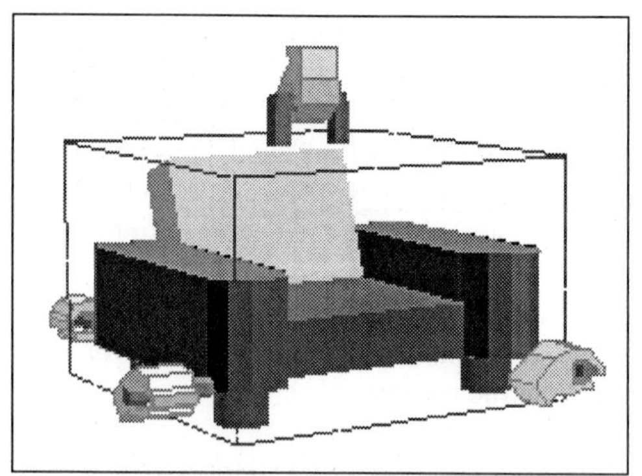

Example 2. Look and feel prototype for 3D space-planning application [E2: Houde 1990].

Example 1. Role prototype for 3D space- planning application [E1: Houde 1990].

The prototype shown in Example 1 was built to show how a user might select furniture from an on-line catalog and try it out in an approximation of their own room. It is an interactive slide show which the designer operated by clicking on key areas of the rough user interface. The idea that virtual space-planning would be a helpful task for non-technical users came from user studies. The purpose of the prototype was to quickly convey the proposed role of the artifact to the design team and members of the supporting organization.

Since the purpose of the prototype was primarily to explore and visualize an example of the role of the future artifact, its marker appears very near the role corner of the model in Figure 2. It is placed a little toward the look and feel corner because it also explored user interface elements in a very initial form.

One of the challenges of the project was to define an easy-to-use direct manipulation user interface for moving 3D objects with an ordinary 2D mouse cursor. User testing with a foam-core model showed that the most important manipulations of a space-planning task were sliding, lifting, and turning furniture objects. Example 2 shows a picture of a prototype which was made to test a user interface featuring this constrained set of manipulations. Clicking once on the chair caused its bounding box to appear. This "handle box" offered hand-shaped controls for lifting and turning the box and object chair (as if the chair was frozen inside the box). Clicking and dragging anywhere on the box allowed the unit to slide on a 3D floor. The prototype was built using Macromedia Director (a high level animation and scripting tool). It was made to work only with the chair data shown: a set of images pre-drawn for many angles of rotation.

The purpose of the Example 2 prototype was to get feedback from users as quickly as possible as to whether the look and feel of the handle-box user interface was promising. Users of the prototype were given tasks which encouraged them to move the chair around a virtual room. Some exploration of role was supported by the fact that the object manipulated was a chair, and space-planning tasks were given during the test. Although the prototype was interactive, the programming that made it so did not seriously explore how a final artifact with this interface might be implemented. It was only done in service of the look and feel test. Since the designer primarily explored the look and feel of the user interface, this prototype's marker is placed very near the look and feel corner of the model in Figure 2.

A technical challenge of the project was figuring out how to render 3D graphics quickly enough on equipment that end-users might have. At the time, it was not clear how much real-time 3D interaction could be achieved on the Apple Macintosh™ II fx computer — the fastest Macintosh then available. Example 3

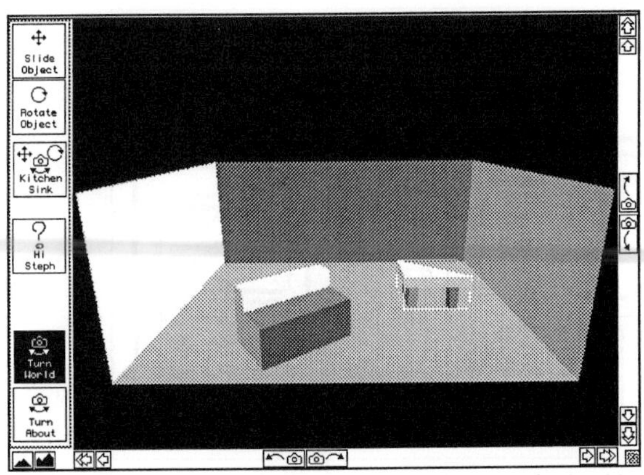

Example 3. Implementation prototypes for 3D space-planning application [E3: Chen 1990].

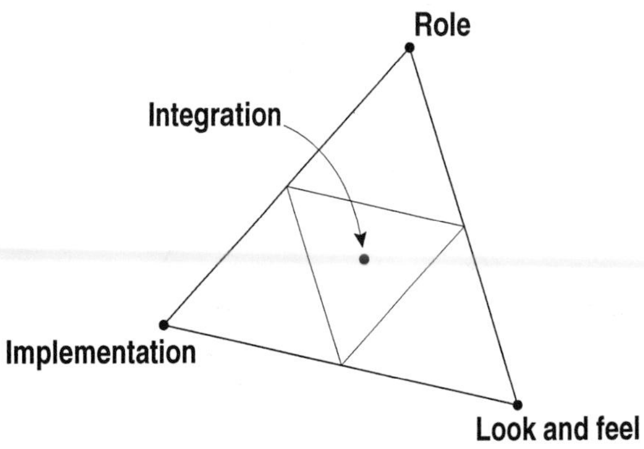

Figure 3. Four principal categories of prototypes on the model.

shows a prototype which was built primarily to explore rendering capability and performance. This was a working prototype in which multiple 3D objects could be manipulated as in Example 2, and the view of the room could be changed to any perspective. Example 3 was made in a programming environment that best supported the display of true 3D perspectives during manipulation. It was used by the design team to determine what complexity of 3D scenes was reasonable to design for. The user interface elements shown on the left side of the screen were made by the programmer to give himself controls for demonstrating the system: they were not made to explore the look and feel of the future artifact. Thus the primary purpose of the prototype was to explore how the artifact might be implemented. The marker for this example is placed near the implementation corner (Figure 2).

One might assume that the role prototype (Example 1) was developed first, then the look and feel prototype (Example 2), and finally the implementation prototype (Example 3): that is, in order of increasing detail and production difficulty. In fact, these three prototypes were developed almost in parallel. They were built by different design team members during the early stages of the project. No single prototype could have represented the design of the future artifact at that time. The evolving design was too fuzzy—existing mainly as a shared concept in the minds of the designers. There were also too many open and interdependent questions in every design dimension: role, look and feel, implementation.

Making separate prototypes enabled specific design questions to be addressed with as much clarity as possible. The solutions found became inputs to an integrated design. Answers to the rendering capability questions addressed by Example 3 informed the design of the role that the artifact could play (guiding how - many furniture objects of what complexity could be shown). It also provided guiding constraints for the direct manipulation user interface determining how much detail the handle forms could have). Similarly, issues of role addressed by Example 1 informed the implementation problem by constraining it: only a constrained set of manipulations was needed for a space-planning application. It also simplified the direct manipulation user interface by limiting the necessary actions, and therefore controls, which needed to be provided.

It was more efficient to wait on the results of independent investigations in the key areas of role, look and feel and implementation than to try to build a monolithic prototype that integrated all features from the start. After sufficient investigation in separate prototypes, the prototype in Example 3 began to evolve into an integrated prototype which could be described by a position at the center of our model. A version of the user interface developed in Example 2 was implemented in the prototype in Example 3. Results of other prototypes were also integrated. This enabled a more complete user test of features and user interface to take place.

This set of three prototypes from the same project shows how a design problem can be simultaneously approached from multiple points of view. Design questions of role, look and feel, and implementation were explored concurrently by the team with the three separate prototypes. The purpose of the model is to make it easier to develop and subsequently communicate about this kind of prototyping strategy.

16.4 Further Examples

In this section we present twelve more examples of

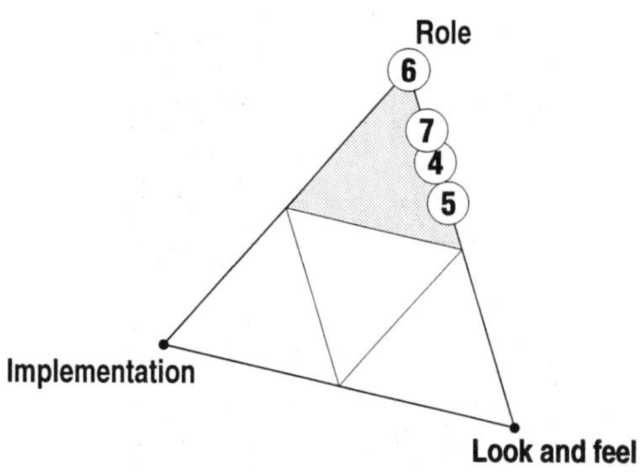

Figure 4. Relationship of role prototypes (Examples 4 - 7) to the model.

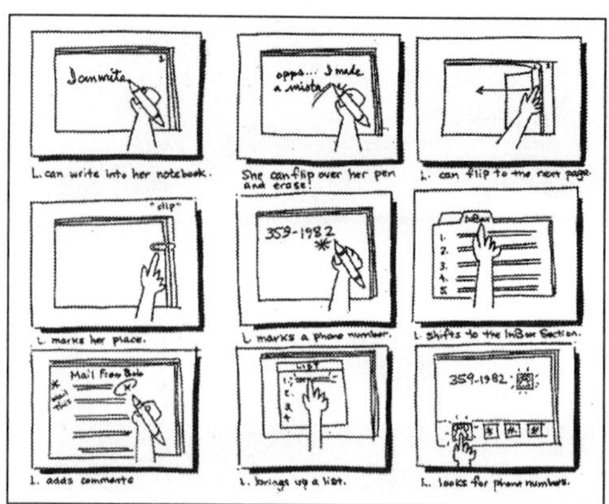

Example 4. Storyboard for a portable notebook computer [E4: Vertelney 1990].

prototypes taken from real projects, and discuss them in terms of the model. Examples are divided into four categories which correspond to the four main regions of the model, as indicated in Figure 3. The first three categories correspond to prototypes with a strong bias to-ward one of the three corners: *role*, *look and feel*, and *implementation* prototypes, respectively. *Integration* prototypes occupy the middle of the model: they explore a balance of questions in all three dimensions.

16.4.1 Role Prototypes

Role prototypes are those which are built primarily to investigate questions of what an artifact could do for a user. They describe the functionality that a user might benefit from, with little attention to how the artifact would look and feel, or how it could be made to actually work. Designers find such prototypes useful to show their design teams what the target role of the artifact might be; to communicate that role to their supporting organization; and to evaluate the role in user studies.

A Portable Notebook Computer: The paper storyboard shown in Example 4 was an early prototype of a portable notebook computer for students which would accept both pen and finger input. The scenario shows a student making notes, annotating a paper, and marking pages for later review in a computer notebook. The designer presented the storyboard to her design team to focus discussion on the issues of what functionality the notebook should provide and how it might be controlled through pen and finger interaction. In terms of the model, this prototype primarily explored the role of the notebook by presenting a rough task scenario for it. A secondary consideration was a rough approximation of the user interface. Its marker, shown in Figure 4, is therefore positioned near the role corner of the model and a little toward look and feel.

Storyboards like this one are considered to be effective design tools by many designers because they help focus design discussion on the role of an artifact very early on. However, giving them status as prototypes is not common because the medium is paper and thus seems very far from the medium of an interactive computer system. We consider this storyboard to be a prototype because it makes a concrete representation of a design idea and serves the purpose of asking and answering design questions. Of course, if the designer needed to evaluate a user's reaction to seeing the notebook or to using the pen-and-finger interaction, it would be necessary to build a prototype which supported direct interaction. However, it might be wasteful to do so before considering design options in the faster, lighter-weight medium of pencil and paper.

An Operating System User Interface: Example 5 shows a screen view of a prototype that was used to explore the design of a new operating system. The prototype was an interactive story: it could only be executed through a single, ordered, sequence of interactions. Clicking with a cursor on the mailbox picture opened a mail window; then clicking on the voice tool brought up a picture of some sound tools; and so on. To demonstrate the prototype, the designer sat in front of a computer and play-acted the role of a user opening her mail, replying to it, and so forth. The prototype was used in design team discussions and also demonstrated to project managers to explain the current design direction. According to the model, this prototype primarily explored the role that certain features of the operating

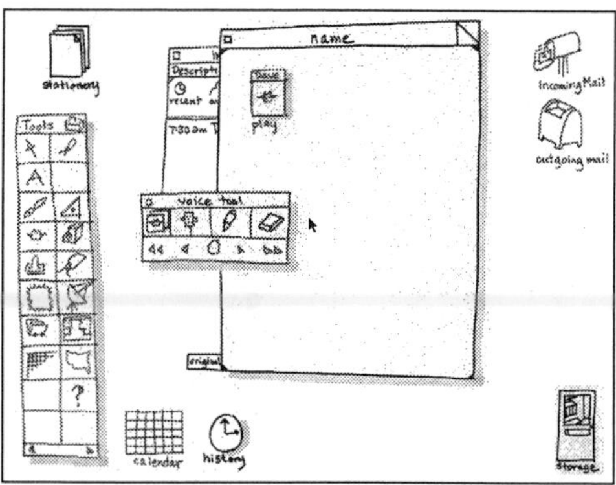

Example 5. Interactive story for an operating system interface [E5: Vertelney and Wong 1990].

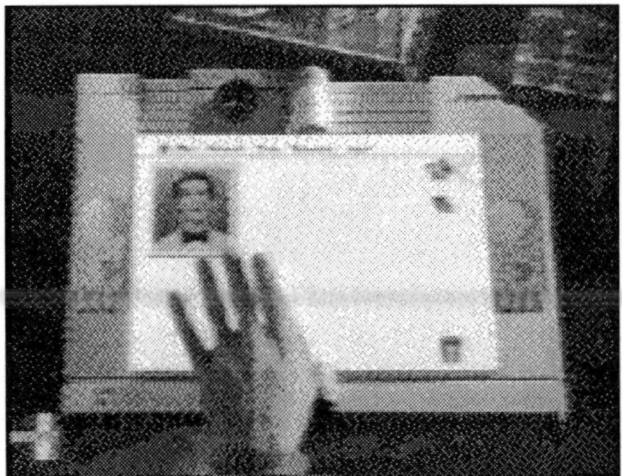

Example 6. Knowledge Navigator™ vision video for a future notebook computer [E6: Dubberly and Mitch 1987].

system could play in a user's daily tasks. It was also used to outline very roughly how its features would be portrayed and how a user would interact with it. As in the previous example, the system's implementation was not explored. Its marker is shown in Figure 4.

To make the prototype, user interface elements were hand-drawn and scanned in. Transitions between steps in the scenario were made interactive in Macromedia Director. This kind of portrayal of on-screen interface elements as rough and hand-drawn was used in order to focus design discussion on the overall features of a design rather than on specific details of look and feel or implementation (Wong, 1992). Ironically, while the design team understood the meaning of the hand-drawn graphics, other members of the organization became enamored with the sketchy style to the extent that they considered using it in the final artifact. This result was entirely at odds with the original reasons for making a rough-looking prototype. This example shows how the effectiveness of some kinds of prototypes may be limited to a specific kind of audience.

The Knowledge Navigator: Example 6 shows a scene from Apple Computer's Knowledge Navigator™ video. The video tape tells a day-in-the-life story of a professor using a futuristic notebook computer (Dubberly and Mitch, 1987). An intelligent agent named "Phil" acts as his virtual personal assistant, finding information related to a lecture, reminding him of his mother's birthday, and connecting him with other professors via video-link. The professor interacts with Phil by talking, and Phil apparently recognizes everything said as well as a human assistant would.

Based on the model, the Knowledge Navigator is identified primarily as a prototype which describes the role that the notebook would play in such a user's life. The story is told in great detail, and it is clear that many decisions were made about what to emphasize in the role. The video also shows specific details of appearance, interaction, and performance. However, they were not intended by the designers to be prototypes of look and feel. They were merely place-holders for the actual design work which would be necessary to make the product really work. Thus its marker goes directly on the role corner (Figure 4).

Thanks to the video's special effects, the scenario of the professor interacting with the notebook and his assistant looks like a demonstration of a real product. Why did Apple make a highly produced prototype when the previous examples show that a rapid paper storyboard or a sketchy interactive prototype were sufficient for designing a role and telling a usage story? The answer lies in the kind of audience. The tape was shown publicly and to Apple employees as a vision of the future of computing. Thus the audience of the Knowledge Navigator was very broad—including almost anyone in the world. Each of the two previous role design prototypes was shown to an audience which was well informed about the design project. A rough hand-drawn prototype would not have made the idea seem real to the broad audience the video addressed: high resolution was necessary to help people concretely visualize the design. Again, while team members learn to interpret abstract kinds of prototypes accurately, less expert audiences cannot normally be expected to understand such approximate representations.

The Integrated Communicator: Example 7 shows an appearance model of an Integrated Communicator created for customer research into alternate presentations of new technology (ID Magazine 1995). It was one of three presentations of possible mechanical configurations and interaction designs, each built to the same

Example 7. Appearance model for the integrated communicator [E7: Udagawa 1995].

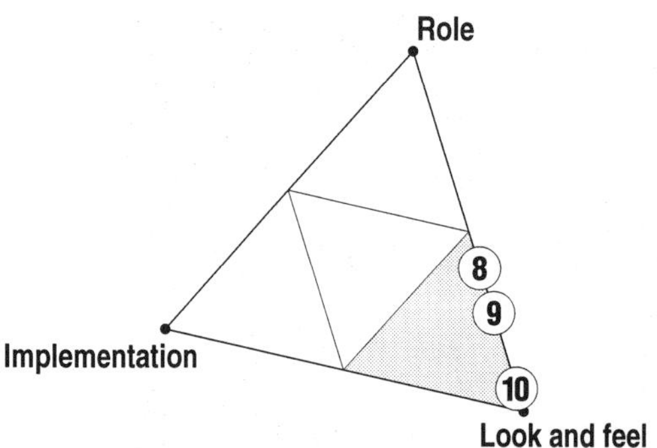

Figure 5. Relationships of the look and feel prototypes (Examples 8-10) to the model.

high finish and accompanied by a video describing on-screen interactions. In the study, the value of each presentation was evaluated relative to the others, as perceived by study subjects during one-on-one interviews. The prototype was used to help subjects imagine such a product in the store and in their homes or offices, and thus to evaluate whether they would purchase such a product, how much they would expect it to cost, what features they would expect, etc.

The prototype primarily addresses the role of the product, by presenting carefully designed cues which imply a telephone-like role and look-and-feel. Figure 4 shows its marker near the role corner of the model. As with the Knowledge Navigator, the very high-resolution look and feel was a means of making the design as concrete as possible to a broad audience. In this case however it also enabled a basic interaction design strategy to be worked out and demonstrated. The prototype did not address implementation.

The key feature of this kind of prototype is that it is a concrete and direct representation, as visually finished as actual consumer products. These attributes encourage an uncoached person to directly relate the design to their own environment, and to the products they own or see in stores. High quality appearance models are costly to build. There are two common reasons for investing in one: to get a visceral response by making the design seem "real" to any audience (design team, organization, and potential users); and to verify the intended look and feel of the artifact before committing to production tooling. An interesting side-effect of this prototype was that its directness made it a powerful prop for promoting the project within the organization.

16.4.2 Look and Feel Prototypes

Look and feel prototypes are built primarily to explore and demonstrate options for the concrete experience of an artifact. They simulate what it would be like to look at and interact with, without necessarily investigating the role it would play in the user's life or how it would be made to work. Designers make such prototypes to visualize different look and feel possibilities for themselves and their design teams. They ask users to interact with them to see how the look and feel could be improved. They also use them to give members of their supporting organization a concrete sense of what the future artifact will be like.

A Fashion Design Workspace: The prototype shown in Example 8 was developed to support research into collaboration tools for fashion designers (Hill et al, 1993; Scaife et al, 1994). A twenty-minute animation, it presented the concept design for a system for monitoring garment design work. It illustrated in considerable detail the translation of a proven paper-based procedure into a computer-based system with a visually rich, direct manipulation, user interface. The prototype's main purposes were to confirm to the design team that an engaging and effective look and feel could be designed for this application, and to convince managers of the possibilities of the project. It was presented to users purely for informal discussion.

This is an example of a look and feel prototype. The virtue of the prototype was that it enabled a novel user interface design to be developed without having first to implement complex underlying technologies. While the role was inherited from existing fashion design practice, the prototype also demonstrated new options offered by the new computer-based approach. Thus, Figure 5 shows its marker in the look and feel area of the model.

One issue with prototypes like this one is that inexperienced audiences tend to believe them to be more

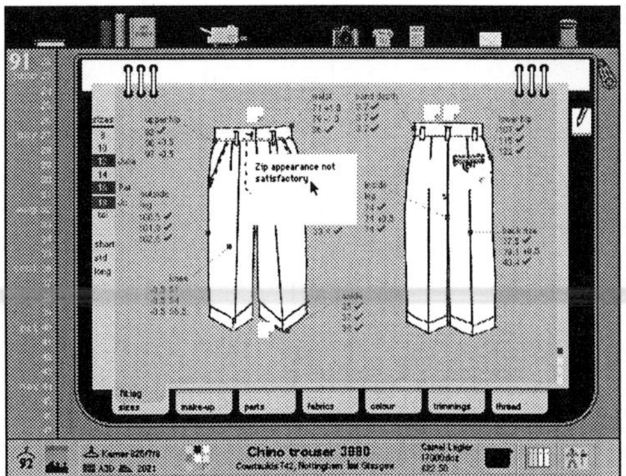

Example 8. Animation of the look and feel of a fashion design workspace [E8: Hill 1992].

Example 9. Look and feel simulation prototypes for a child's toy [E9: Bellman et al, 1993].

functional than they are just by virtue of being shown on a computer screen. When this prototype was shown, the designers found they needed to take great care to explain that the design was not implemented.

A Learning Toy: The "GloBall" project was a concept for a children's toy: a ball that would interact with children who played with it. Two prototypes from the project are shown, disassembled, in Example 9. The design team wanted the ball to speak back to kids when they spoke to it, and to roll towards or away from them in reaction to their movements. The two prototypes were built to simulate these functions separately. The ball on the left had a walkie-talkie which was concealed in use. A hidden operator spoke into a linked walkie-talkie to simulate the ball's speech while a young child played with it. Similarly, the ball on the right had a radio-controlled car which was concealed in use. A hidden operator remotely controlled the car, thus causing the ball to roll around in response to the child's actions.

As indicated by the marker in Figure 5, both prototypes were used to explore the toy's look and feel from a child's viewpoint, and to a lesser extent to evaluate the

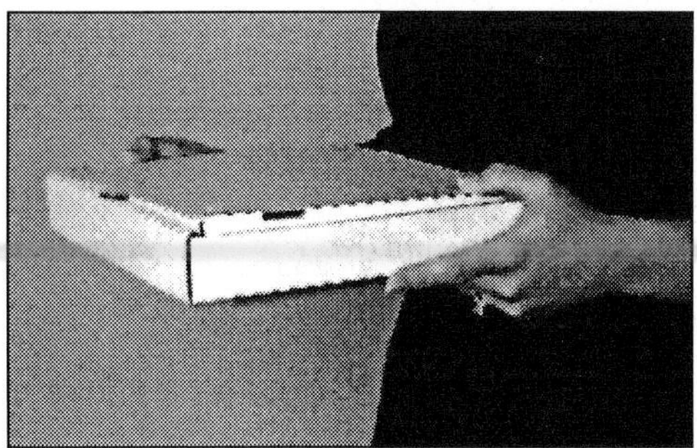

Example 10. Pizza-box prototype of an architect's computer [E10: Apple Design Project, 1992].

role that the toy would play. Neither seriously addressed implementation. The designers of these very efficient prototypes wanted to know how a child would respond to a toy that appeared to speak and move of its own free will. They managed to convincingly simulate novel and difficult-to-implement technologies such as speech and automotion, for minimal cost and using readily available components. By using a "man behind the curtain" (or "Wizard of Oz") technique, the designers were able to present the prototypes directly to children and to directly evaluate their effect.

An Architect's Computer: This example concerned the design of a portable computer for architects who need to gather a lot of information during visits to building sites. One of the first questions the designers explored was what form would be appropriate for their users. Without much ado they weighted the pizza box shown in Example 10 to the expected weight of the computer, and gave it to an architect to carry on a site visit. They watched how he carried the box, what else he carried with him, and what tasks he needed to do during the visit. They saw that the rectilinear form and weight were too awkward, given the other materials he carried with him, and this simple insight led them to consider a softer form. As shown by its marker, this is an example of a rough look and feel prototype (Figure 5). Role was also explored in a minor way by seeing the context that the artifact would be used in.

The pizza box was a very efficient prototype. Spending virtually no time building it or considering options, the students got useful feedback on a basic design question—what physical form would be best for the user. From what they learned in their simple field test, they knew immediately that they should try to think beyond standard rectilinear notebook computer forms. They began to consider many different options

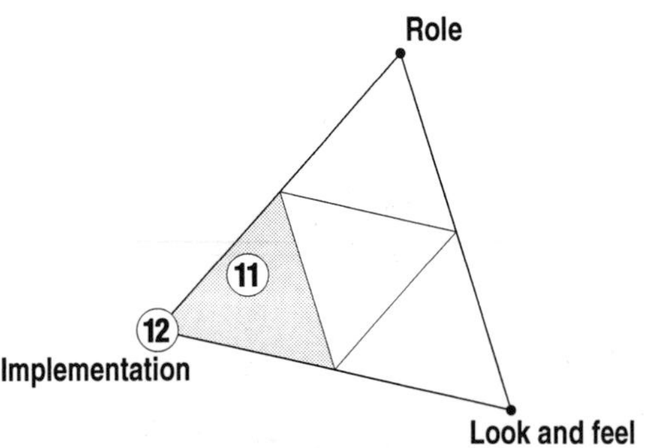

Figure 6. Relationships of implementation prototypes (Examples 11 and 12) to the model.

including designing the computer to feel more like a soft shoulder bag.

16.4.3 Implementation Prototypes

Some prototypes are built primarily to answer technical questions about how a future artifact might actually be made to work. They are used to discover methods by which adequate specifications for the final artifact can be achieved—without having to define its look and feel or the role it will play for a user. (Some specifications may be unstated, and may include externally imposed constraints, such as the need to reuse existing components or production machinery.) Designers make implementation prototypes as experiments for themselves and the design team, to demonstrate to their organization the technical feasibility of the artifact, and to get feedback from users on performance issues.

A Digital Movie Editor: Some years ago it was not clear how much interactivity could be added to digital movies playing on personal computers. Example 11 shows a picture of a prototype that was built to investigate solutions to this technical challenge. It was an application, written in the C programming language to run on an Apple Macintosh computer. It offered a variety of movie data-processing functionality such as controlling various attributes of movie play. The main goal of the prototype was to allow marking of points in a movie to which scripts (which added interactivity) would be attached. As indicated by the marker in Figure 6, this was primarily a carefully planned implementation prototype. Many options were evaluated about the best way to implement its functions. The role that the functions would play was less well defined. The visible look and feel of the prototype was largely incidental: it was created by the designer almost purely to demonstrate the available functionality, and was not intended to be used by others.

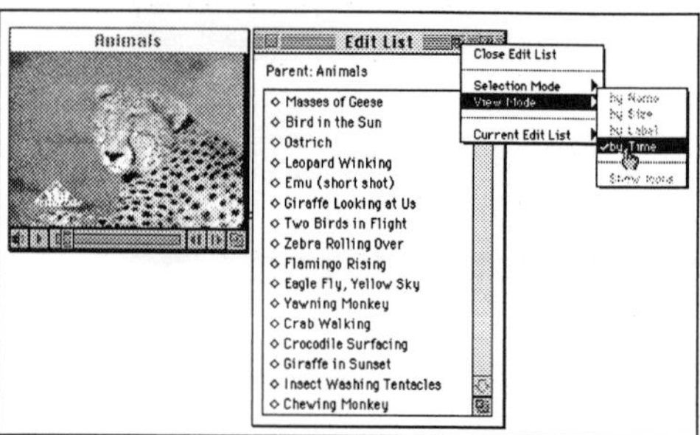

Example 11. Working prototype of a digital movie editor [E11: Degen, 1994].

This prototype received varying responses when demonstrated to a group of designers who were not members of the movie editor design team. When the audience understood that an implementation design was being demonstrated, discussion was focused productively. At other times it became focused on problems with the user interface, such as the multiple cascading menus, which were hard to control and visually confusing. In these cases, discussion was less productive: the incidental user interface got in the way of the intentional implementation.

The project leader shared some reflections after this somewhat frustrating experience. He said that part of his goal in pursuing a working prototype alone was to move the project through an organization that respected this kind of prototype more than "smoke and mirrors" prototypes—ones which only simulate functionality. He added that one problem might have been that the user interface was neither good enough nor bad enough to avoid misunderstandings. The edit list, which allowed points to be marked in movies, was a viable look and feel design; while the cascading menus were not. For the audience that the prototype was shown to, it might have been more effective to stress the fact that look and feel were not the focus of the prototype; and perhaps, time permitting, to have complemented this prototype with a separate look and feel prototype that explained their intentions in that dimension.

A Fluid Dynamics Simulation System: Example 12 shows a small part of the C++ program listing for a system for simulating gas flows and combustion in car engines, part of an engineering research project (Hill, 1993). One goal of this prototype was to demonstrate the feasibility of object-oriented programming using the C++ language in place of procedural programs written in the older FORTRAN language. Object-oriented programming can in theory lead to increased

```
IntList& IntList::operator=(const IntList& oldList)
{
register long n = oldList.size;
  if (n != size) setSize(n);
  register int* newPtr = &values[n];
  register int* oldPtr = &oldList.values[n];
  while (n--) *--newPtr = *--oldPtr;
  return *this;
}
```

Example 12. C++ program sample from a fluid dynamics simulation system [E12: Hill, 1993].

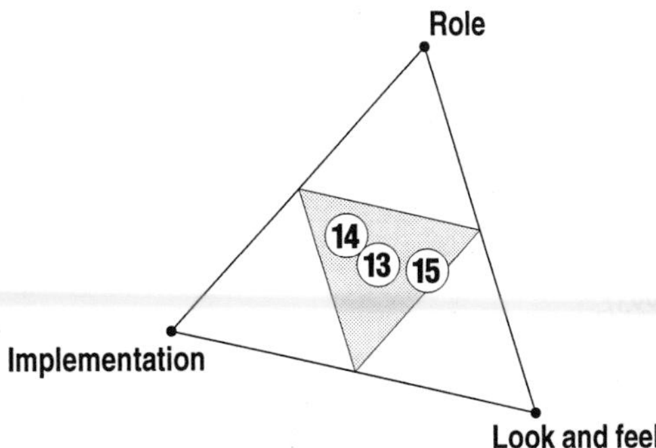

Figure 7. Relationships of integration prototypes (Examples 13 - 15) to the model.

software reuse, better reliability and easier maintenance. Since an engine simulation may take a week to run on the fastest available computers and is extremely memory-intensive, it was important to show that the new approach did not incur excessive performance or memory overheads. The program listing shown was the implementation of the operation to copy one list of numbers to another. When tested, it was shown to be faster than the existing FORTRAN implementation. The prototype was built primarily for the design team's own use, and eventually used to create a deployable system. The marker in Figure 6 indicates that this prototype primarily explored implementation.

Other kinds of implementation prototypes include demonstrations of new algorithms (e.g., a graphical rendering technique or a new search technology), and trial conversions of existing programs to run in new environments (e.g., converting a program written in the C language to the Java language).

Implementation prototypes can be hard to build, and since they actually work, it is common for them to find their way directly into the final system. Two problems arise from this dynamic: firstly, programs developed mainly to demonstrate feasibility may turn out in the long term to be difficult to maintain and develop; and secondly, their temporary user interfaces may never be properly redesigned before the final system is released. For these reasons it is often desirable to treat even implementation prototypes as disposable, and to migrate successful implementation designs to a new integrated prototype as the project progresses.

16.4.4 Integration Prototypes

Integration prototypes are built to represent the complete user experience of an artifact. Such prototypes bring together the artifact's intended design in terms of role, look and feel, and implementation. Integrated prototypes help designers to balance and resolve constraints arising in different design dimensions; to verify that the design is complete and coherent; and to find synergy in the design of the integration itself. In some cases the integration design may become the unique innovation or feature of the final artifact. Since the user's experience of an artifact ultimately combines all three dimensions of the model, integration prototypes are most able to accurately simulate the final artifact. Since they may need to be as complex as the final artifact, they are the most difficult and time consuming kinds of prototypes to build. Designers make integration prototypes to understand the design as a whole, to show their organizations a close approximation to the final artifact, and to get feedback from users about the overall design.

The Sound Browser: The "SoundBrowser" prototype shown in Example 13 was built as part of a larger project which investigated uses of audio for personal computer users (Degen et al, 1992). The prototype was built in C to run on a Macintosh. It allowed a user to browse digital audio data recorded on a special personal tape recorder equipped with buttons for marking points in the audio. The picture shows the SoundBrowser's visual representation of the audio data, showing the markers below the sound display. A variety of functions were provided for reviewing sound, such as high-speed playback and playback of marked segments of audio.

This prototype earns a position right in the center of the model, as shown in Figure 7. All three dimensions of the model were explored and represented in the prototype. The role of the artifact was well thought-out, being driven initially by observations of what users currently do to mark and play back audio, and then by iteratively designed scenarios of how it might be done more efficiently if electronic marking and viewing functions were offered. The look and feel of the prototype went through many visual design iterations.

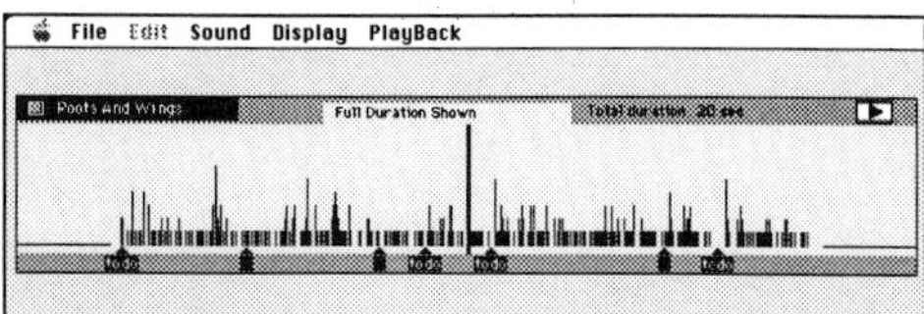

Example 13. Integrated prototype of a sound browser [E13: Degen, 1993].

The implementation was redesigned several times to meet the performance needs of the desired high-speed playback function.

When the SoundBrowser was near completion it was prepared for a user test. One of the features which the design team intended to evaluate was the visual representation of the sound in the main window. They wanted to show users several alternatives to understand their preferences. The programmer who built the SoundBrowser had developed most of the alternatives. In order to refine these and explore others, two other team members copied screen-shots from the tool into a pixel-painting application, where they experimented with modifications. This was a quick way to try out different visual options, in temporary isolation from other aspects of the artifact. It was far easier to do this in a visual design tool than by programming in C. When finished, the new options were programmed into the integrated prototype. This example shows the value of using different tools for different kinds of design exploration, and how even at the end of a project simple, low-fidelity prototypes might be built to solve specific problems.

The Pile Metaphor: The prototype shown in Example 14 was made as part of the development of the "pile" metaphor—a user interface element for casual organization of information (Mander et al, 1992, Rose et al, 1993). It represented the integration of designs developed in several other prototypes which independently explored the look and feel of piles, "content-aware" information retrieval, and the role that piles could play as a part of an operating system. In the pile metaphor, each electronic document was represented by a small icon or "proxy", several of which were stacked to form a pile. The contents of the pile could be quickly reviewed by moving the arrow cursor over it. While the cursor was over a particular document, the "viewing cone" to the right displayed a short text summary of the document.

This prototype was shown to designers, project managers, and software developers as a proof of concept of the novel technology. The implementation design in this prototype might have been achieved with virtually no user interface: just text input and output. However, since the prototype was to be shown to a broad audience, an integrated style of prototype was chosen, both to communicate the implementation point and to verify that the piles representation was practically feasible. It helped greatly that the artifact's role and look and feel could be directly inherited from previous prototypes. Figure 7 shows its marker on the model.

Example 14. Integration prototype of the "Pile" metaphor for information retrieval [E14: Rose, 1993].

A Garment History Browser: The prototype in Example 15 was a working system which enabled users to enter and retrieve snippets of information about garment designs via a visually rich user interface (Hill et al, 1993; Scaife et al, 1994). The picture shows the query tool which was designed to engage fashion designers and provide memorable visual cues. The prototype was designed for testing in three corporations with a limited set of users' actual data, and presented to users in interviews. It was briefly demonstrated, then users were asked to try queries and enter remarks about design issues they were currently aware of.

This prototype was the end-result of a progression from an initial focus on role (represented by verbal usage scenarios), followed by rough look and feel prototypes and an initial implementation. Along the way various ideas were explored, refined or rejected. The working tool, built in Allegiant SuperCard™, required two months' intensive work by two designers. In retrospect the designers had mixed feelings about it. It was highly motivating to users to be able to manipulate real user data through a novel user interface, and much was learned about the design. However, the designers also felt that they had had to invest a large amount of time in making the prototype, yet had only been able to support a very narrow role compared to the breadth shown in the animation shown in Example 8. Many broader design questions remained unanswered.

Example 15. Integrated prototype of a garment history browser [E15: Hill and Kamlish, 1992].

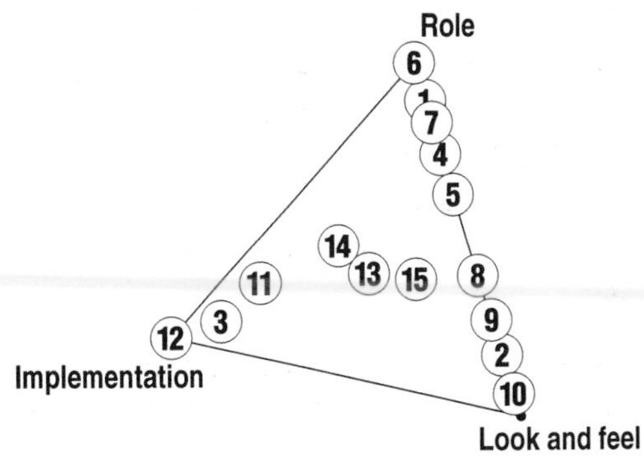

1. 3D space-planning (role)
2. 3D space-planning (look and feel)
3. 3D space-planning (implementation)
4. Storyboard for portable notebook computer
5. Interactive story, operating system user interface
6. Vision video, notebook computer
7. Appearance model, integrated communicator
8. Animation, fashion design workspace
9. Look and feel simulation, child's toy
10. Pizza-box, architect's computer
11. Working prototype, digital movie editor
12. C++ program listing, fluid dynamics simulation
13. Integrated prototype, sound browser
14. Integrated prototype, pile metaphor
15. Integrated prototype, garment histor browser

Figure 8. Relationships of all examples to the model.

16.5 Summary

In this chapter, we have proposed a change in the language used by designers to think and talk about prototypes of interactive artifacts. Much current terminology centers on attributes of prototypes themselves: the tools used to create them, or how refined-looking or -behaving they are. Yet tools can be used in many different ways, and resolution can be misleading. We have proposed a shift in attention to focus on questions about the design of the artifact itself: What role will it play in a users life? How should it look and feel? How should it be implemented? The model that we have introduced can be used by designers to divide any design problem into these three classes of questions, each of which may benefit from a different approach to prototyping.

We have described a variety of prototypes from real projects, and have shown how the model can be used to communicate about their purposes. Several practical suggestions for designers have been raised by the examples:

- *Define "prototype" broadly.* Efficient prototypes produce answers to their designers' most important questions in the least amount of time. Sometimes very simple representations make highly effective prototypes: e.g., the pizza-box prototype of an architect's computer [Example 10] and the storyboard notebook [Example 1]. We define a prototype as any representation of a design idea—regardless of medium; and designers as the people who create them—regardless of their job titles.

- *Build multiple prototypes.* Since interactive artifacts can be very complex, it may be impossible to create an integrated prototype in the formative stages of a project, as in the 3D space-planning example [Examples 1, 2, and 3]. Choosing the right focused prototypes to build is an art in itself. Be prepared to throw some prototypes away, and to use different tools for different kinds of prototypes.

- *Know your audience.* The necessary resolution and fidelity of a prototype may depend most on the nature of its audience. A rough role prototype such as the interactive storyboard [Example 4] may work well for a design team but not for members of the supporting organization. Broader audiences may require higher-resolution representations. Some organizations expect to see certain kinds of prototypes: implementation designs are often expected in engineering departments, while look-and-feel and role prototypes may rule in a visual design environment.

- *Know your prototype; prepare your audience.* Be clear about what design questions are being explored with a given prototype—and what are not. Communicating the specific purposes of a prototype to its audience is a critical aspect of its use. It is up to the designer to prepare an audience for viewing a prototype. Prototypes themselves do not necessarily communicate their purpose. It is especially important to clarify what is and what is not addressed by a prototype when presenting it to any audience beyond the immediate design team.

By focusing on the purpose of the prototype—that is, on what it prototypes—we can make better decisions about the kinds of prototypes to build. With a clear purpose for each prototype, we can better use prototypes to think and communicate about design.

16.6 Acknowledgments

Special thanks are due to Thomas Erickson for guidance with this chapter, and to our many colleagues whose prototypes we have cited, for their comments on early drafts. We would also like to acknowledge S. Joy Mountford whose leadership of the Human Interface Group at Apple created an atmosphere in which creative prototyping could flourish. Finally, thanks to James Spohrer, Lori Leahy, Dan Russell, and Donald Norman at Apple Research Labs for supporting us in writing this chapter.

16.7 Prototype Credits

We credit here the principal designer and design team of each example prototype shown.

[E1] Stephanie Houde [E2] Stephanie Houde[E3] Michael Chen (1990) © Apple Computer, Inc. Project team: Penny Bauersfeld, Michael Chen, Lewis Knapp (project leader), Laurie Vertelney and Stephanie Houde.

[E4] Laurie Vertelney. (1990), © Apple Computer Inc. Project team: Michael Chen, Thomas Erickson, Frank Leahy, Laurie Vertelney (project leader).

[E5] Laurie Vertelney and Yin Yin Wong. (1990), © Apple Computer Inc. Project team: Richard Mander, Gitta Salomon (project leader), Ian Small, Laurie Vertelney, Yin Yin Wong.

[E6] Dubberly, H. and Mitch, D. (1987) © Apple Computer, Inc. The Knowledge Navigator (videotape.)

[E7] Masamichi Udagawa. (1995) © Apple Computer Inc. Project team: Charles Hill, Heiko Sacher, Nancy Silver, Masamichi Udagawa.

[E8] Charles Hill. (1992) © Royal College of Art, London. Design team: Gillian Crampton Smith, Eleanor Curtis, Charles Hill, Stephen Kamlish, (all of the RCA), Mike Scaife (Sussex University, UK), and Philip Joe (IDEO, London).

[E9] Tom Bellman, Byron Long, Abba Lustgarten. (1993) University of Toronto, 1993 Apple Design Project, © Apple Computer Inc.

[E10] 1992 Apple Design Project , © Apple Computer, Inc.

[E11] Leo Degen (1994) © Apple Computer Inc., Project team: Leo Degen, Stephanie Houde, Michael Mills (team leader), David Vronay.

[E12] Charles Hill (1993). Doctoral thesis project, Imperial College of Science, Technology and Medicine, London, UK. Project team: Charles Hill, Henry Weller.

[E13] Leo Degen (1993) © Apple Computer Inc., Project team: Leo Degen, Richard Mander, Gitta Salomon (team leader), Yin Yin Wong.

[E14] Daniel Rose. (1993). © Apple Computer, Inc. Project team: Penny Bauersfeld, Leo Degen, Stephanie Houde, Richard Mander, Ian Small, Gitta Salomon (team leader),Yin Yin Wong

[E15] Charles Hill and Stephen Kamlish. (1992) © Royal College of Art, London. Design team: Gillian Crampton Smith, Eleanor Curtis, Charles Hill, Stephen Kamlish, (all of the RCA), and Mike Scaife (Sussex University, UK).

16.8 References

Degen, L., Mander, R., Salomon, G. (1992). Working with Audio: Integrating Personal Tape Recorders and Desktop Computers. *Human Factors in Computing Systems: CHI'92 Conference Proceedings.* New York: ACM, pp. 413-418.

Dubberly, H. and Mitch, D. (1987). *The Knowledge Navigator.* Apple Computer, Inc. videotape.

Ehn, P., Kyng, M., (1991) Cardboard Computers: Mocking-it-up or Hands-on the Future., Design at Work: *Cooperative Design of Computer Systems* (ed. Greenbaum, J., and Kyng, M.). Hillsdale, NJ: Lawrence Erlbaum. pp. 169-195.

Erickson, T., (1995) Notes on Design Practice: Stories and Prototypes as Catalysts for Communication.

"Envisioning Technology: The Scenario as a Framework for the System Development Life Cycle" (ed. Carroll, J.). Addison-Wesley.

Hill, C. (1993) *Software Design for Interactive Engineering Simulation.* Doctoral Thesis. Imperial College of Science, Technology and Medicine, University of London.

Hill, C., Crampton Smith, G., Curtis, E., Kamlish, S., (1993) Designing a Visual Database for Fashion Designers. *Human Factors in Computing Systems: INTERCHI'93 Adjunct Proceedings.* New York, ACM, pp. 49-50.

Houde, S., (1992). Iterative Design of and Interface for Easy 3-D Direct Manipulation. *Human Factors in Computing Systems: CHI'92 Conference Proceedings.* New York: ACM, pp. 135-142.

I.D.Magazine, (1995) Apple's Shared Conceptual Model, *The International Design Magazine: 41's Annual Design Review, July-August 1995.* USA. pp. 206-207

Kim, S. (1990). Interdisciplinary Collaboration. *The Art of Human Computer Interface Design* (ed. B. Laurel). Reading, MA: Addison-Wesley. pp.31-44.

Mander, R., Salomon, G., Wong, Y.Y. (1992). A 'Pile' Metaphor for Supporting Casual Organization of Information. *Human Factors in Computing Systems: CHI'92 Conference Proceedings.* New York: ACM, pp. 627-634.

Rose, D.E., Mander, R., Oren, T., Ponceleón, D.B., Salomon, G., Wong, Y. (1993). Content Awareness in a File System Interface: Implementing the 'Pile' Metaphor for Organizing Information. *Research and Development in Information Retrieval: SIGIR Conference Proceedings.* Pittsburgh, PA: ACM, pp. 260-269.

Scaife, M., Curtis, E., Hill, C. (1994) Interdisciplinary Collaboration: a Case Study of Software Development for Fashion Designers. *Interacting with Computers,* Vol 6. no.4, pp. 395-410

Schrage, M. (1996). Cultures of Prototyping. *Bringing Design to Software* (ed. T. Winograd). USA: ACM Press. pp.191-205.

Wong, Y.Y. (1992). Rough and ready prototypes: Lessons from graphic design. *Human Factors in Computing Systems: CHI'92 Conference, Posters and Short-Talks*, New York: ACM, pp.83-84.

Handbook of Human-Computer Interaction
Second, completely revised edition
M. Helander, T.K. Landauer, P. Prabhu (eds.)

Chapter 17

Scenario-Based Design

John M. Carroll
Computer Science Department
Virginia Tech
Blacksburg, Virginia, USA

17.1 Introduction

There was a time when it seemed reasonable to see computers chiefly as electronic devices and circuits, as embodiments of computational algorithms. However, through the 1980s computing broadly permeated nearly all arenas of human activity. Computers were transformed from strictly technological artifacts – the remote, arcane, and unique province of engineers and programmers – into ubiquitous cultural artifacts that are embedded in nearly everything that people do, indispensable, or at least inescapable, to the general public.

There are many facets to this transformation, and many debates have been and should be provoked and focused by it. One of these is a fundamental rethinking of the goals and methods of system design and development: As technological artifacts, computers must produce correct results; they must be reliable, run efficiently, and be easy – or at least possible – to maintain (that is, technicians must be able to understand how they work well enough to diagnose problems and to add or enhance functions). But as artifacts of general culture, computer systems must meet many further requirements: They must be accessible to non-technologists (easy to learn/easy to use); they must smoothly augment human activities, meet people's expectations, and enhance the quality of life by guiding their users to satisfying work experiences, stimulating educational opportunities, and relaxation during leisure time.

These latter requirements are far more difficult to specify and to satisfy. We do not now (and in fact may never) understand human activities in enough detail to merely list the attributes computer systems would have to incorporate in order to meet these requirements: precisely what kind of computer will help people learn microbiology, choose a new job, or relax? Indeed, human society and psychology develop in part as a consequence of the contemporary state of technology, and technology is precisely what is running ahead of our understanding so rapidly now. Thus, we have little prospect of developing "final" answers to questions about the nature of human activity — certainly not at the level of detail that would provide specific guidance to designers. Our best course is to develop rich and flexible methods and concepts, to directly incorporate descriptions of potential users and the uses they might make of an envisioned computer system into the design reasoning for that system — ideally by involving the users themselves in the design process.

Opening up the design process to intended users and descriptions of their projected use entails many technical issues. We need to develop new vocabularies for discussing and characterizing designs in terms of the projected activities of the intended users. These vocabularies should be accessible to the users them-

- Harry, a curriculum designer, has just joined a project developing a multimedia information system for engineering education. He browses the project video history. Sets of clips are categorized under major iconically-presented headings; under some of these are further menu-driven subcategories.

- He selects the Lewis icon from the designers, the Vision icon from the issues, and an early point on the project time-line. He then selects Play Clip and views a brief scene in which Lewis describes his vision of the project as enabling a new world of collaborative and experience-based education.

- Harry selects Technical Issues (instead of Vision) and from its menu, he selects Course Topic, and then Play Clip. Lewis explains why bridges and bridge failures is a good choice: it's a concrete problem, accessible to anybody and yet seriously technical; it can be highly visual Q as in the Tacoma Narrows film.

- Harry selects a point on the time-line further along on the project history. In the new clip, Lewis explains why nuclear power plants are such a good choice for the course topic: socially urgent and seriously technical.

- Harry selects Walter from the designer icons, and then requests a video clip. Walter appears in a window and explains his reasons why nuclear power plants is a good course topic: lots of good video, lots of popular-press text, and lots of technical debate.

- Harry selects various combinations: other designers besides Walter and Lewis on these same issues and times, and other times and issues for Walter and Lewis. He begins to appreciate the project vision more broadly, attributing some of the differences to individual interests and roles in the project team. He begins to see the course topic issue as a process of discovering and refining new requirements through active consideration of alternatives.

Figure 1. Browsing project history scenario: *A new project member uses a design history system to understand the evolution of the project's vision and content domain.*

selves, so that they can help to define the technology they will use. We need also to be able to integrate and coordinate such use-oriented design representations with other representations produced in the course of system development. We need to be able to assess design alternatives with use-oriented criteria and to integrate and coordinate such assessments with those we make on traditional grounds, like correctness, reliability, efficiency and maintainability. We need to develop new sorts of tools and techniques to support the development and use of use-oriented representations and methods in design. We need to produce education to help system developers understand the need for use-oriented approaches and to help them adopt such methods in their work. This is a lot to ask for, but to do anything less is to risk losing sight of the line between human beings using and controlling their technology and its antithesis.

17.2 The Scenario Perspective

A substantial amount of current research and development activity is focused on creating a more use-oriented perspective on the design and development of computer systems. One key element in this perspective is the user interaction scenario, a narrative description of what people do and experience as they try to make use of computer systems and applications. Computer systems and applications can be viewed, and should be viewed as transformations of user tasks and their supporting social practices. In this sense, user interaction scenarios are a particularly pertinent medium for representing, analyzing and planning how a computer system might impact its users' activities and experiences. They comprise a vocabulary for design and evaluation that is rich and yet evenly accessible to all the stakeholders in a development project (Carroll and Rosson, 1990; Clausen, 1993).

Figure 1 presents a simple example, a textual sketch of a situation in which a person interacts with a video information system. The person is browsing a database of video clips in which the individual members of a project team describe episodes and issues that were salient to them at various points in time during the development project. The person is particularly interested in the evolution of the project vision and the

the scenario perspective:	*the "establishment" view:*
concrete descriptions	abstract descriptions
focus on particular instances	focus on generic types
work driven	technology driven
open–ended, fragmentary	complete, exhaustive
informal, rough, colloquial	formal, rigorous
envisioned outcomes	specified outcomes

Figure 2. Contrasting perspectives on system development: The scenario perspective (left-hand side) and the establishment view (right-hand side).

choice of a content domain, as these bear on the curriculum design role this person will play in the project team. The person pursues these interests by selecting among control icons to request a series of video clips (Carroll, Alpert, Karat, Van Deusen and Rosson, 1994a,b).

The scenario identifies the person as having certain motivations toward the system, describes the actions taken and some reasons why these actions were taken, and characterizes the results in terms of the user's motivations and expectations. In practice, a scenario like that in Figure 1 might be developed to help envision various further aspects of the user's activity and experience: precisely which controls were selected, just what the user concluded from whatever video was presented, and so forth. The focus of these descriptions, however detailed they might be, is on the user, what the user does, what the user perceives, what it all means to the user.

Scenario narratives need not be presented in text, as in Figure 1. They can be represented in story-boards of annotated cartoon panels, video mock-ups, scripted prototypes, or physical situations contrived to support certain user activities. Scenarios also can be couched at many different levels of description and many grains of detail. The example in Figure 1 is a very high-level usage scenario, suggesting the overall motives that prospective users might have when they come to the system and general kind of interaction they might experience. But that scenario could be articulated at a much finer grain to specify precisely the system's functionality, including the interactions among system components (hardware, software, and user interface elements) that occur in the course of the scenario.

The defining property of a scenario is that it projects a concrete narrative description of activity that the user engages in when performing a specific task, a description sufficiently detailed so that design implications can be inferred and reasoned about. Using scenarios in system development helps keep the future use of the envisioned system in view as the system is designed and implemented; it makes use concrete — which makes it easier to discuss use and to design use.

Empirical studies of system design have frequently noted the spontaneous and informal use of scenarios by system developers (Carroll, Thomas and Malhotra, 1979; Guindon, 1990; Rosson, Maass and Kellogg, 1988). And in the current state-of-the-art, a set of user interaction scenarios is required for designing user training and documentation as well as usability tests (Mack, Lewis and Carroll, 1983; Roberts and Moran, 1985). These observations raise many questions and possibilities: Can system development occur without scenarios? How might the "upstream" creation and use of scenarios be more directly encouraged and supported, and more broadly exploited? What savings might be obtained by generating training, documentation and testing scenarios relatively early in the development process, and then referring to them continuingly throughout the process? Taking scenarios as a focal object for software and system development indeed yields an alternative perspective on the nature and objectives of the system development process relative to the current "establishment" view in software and systems engineering (Figure 2).

Scenarios seek to be concrete; they focus on describing particular instances of use, and on a user's view of what happens, how it happens, and why. Scenarios are grounded in the work activities of prospective users; the work users do drives the development of the system intended to augment this work. Thus, scenarios are often open-ended and fragmentary; they help developers and users pose new questions, question new answers, open up possibilities. It's not a problem if one scenario encompasses, extends, or depends upon another; such relations may reveal important aspects of use. They can be informal and rough, since users as well as developers may create and use them, they should be as colloquial, and as accessible as possible. They help developers and their users envision the outcomes of design — an integrated description of what the system will do and how it will do it — and thereby better manage and control these outcomes.

Specifications seek to be abstract; they focus on describing generic types of functions, and on the data processing that underlies functions. Specifications are driven by the technology they specify; they are grounded in logic. They are intended to be complete and exhaustive. They do not omit even predictable details; they do not duplicate information. They are rigorous; ideally, they are formal. They specify design outcomes by enumerating conditions that the system must satisfy. They precisely document what is designed.

The scenario perspective is not a call for a Kuhnian "paradigm shift"; the authors of this book do not take the position that the establishment view needs to be overthrown by a scenario-based system development paradigm. Our view is that current system development practice needs to be augmented to include use-oriented system development activities and artifacts. It is simply not enough to enumerate functions that a system will provide; the same function set may augment human work or obstruct it; it may stimulate and enrich the imagination or stifle and overwhelm. We need to be able to specify systems to ensure that they are logically coherent. But we need to envision the use of systems to ensure that they actually can support human activities. Our point is that neither consideration guarantees the other.

17.3 Scenario-based Design: An Example

If we agree that the scenario perspective on system development is a potentially valuable enhancement of current development practice, we must ask how the use of scenarios in system development can be evoked, supported, and brought to bear on various activities within the system development lifecycle — and with what effects. I will address these questions through an example, the development of the Raison d'Etre system. In the early Fall of 1991, a group set out to build a video information system of designers telling their stories, a documentation system containing informal material about a development process as it occurred through time. We wanted to explore how such a system could serve as a tool for managing the historical nature of design (Carroll, 1991).

Our initial direction was to build a system similar to one worked on by our colleagues, Frishberg, Laff, Desrosiers, Koons and Kelley (1991). Their project, "John Cocke: A retrospective by friends," consists of a database of stories about John Cocke told by his friends in video clips. The stories are indexed in various ways to support specific navigation and query (e.g., finding out about the development of the RISC architecture), but users could also just browse and gradually see a picture of John Cocke, the man, emerge from the various views.

Such systems create a new kind of history. Traditionally, people have gathered around campfires and kitchen tables to listen to a single telling of a tale, perhaps by someone who had directly experienced the events in the tale, but perhaps by someone who had heard the tale before and was merely passing it along. In hypermedia folklore, we hear many different tellings of the tale, each from the perspective of one of the principals in the events of tale. This is truly revolutionary; it democratizes history by eliminating singularly privileged perspectives. The John Cocke application brings a man's story to life in a way that could only be achieved if one were to travel the world interviewing the people who knew John Cocke and shared his life.

We decided to use these ideas to develop a kind of design history. Instead of purely retrospective approach, as in the John Cocke application, we wanted to collect materials starting from the inception of a system development project, focusing on designers' reflections about what they were doing when they were still engaged in planning and doing it. We want to use this material as a resource to support design reasoning and collaboration.

We quickly identified an interesting and amiable design team to work with, a group seeking to create a multimedia platform for network-delivered engineering education. The team incorporated specialists in multimedia, natural language processing, human-computer interaction, object-oriented software, as well as educational technology consultants outside IBM and a large publishing company as a customer-partner. In the first few days of October 1991, we initiated a round of videotaped interviews to document the project near its inception. We queried the designers not only about their current activities and concerns, but also about

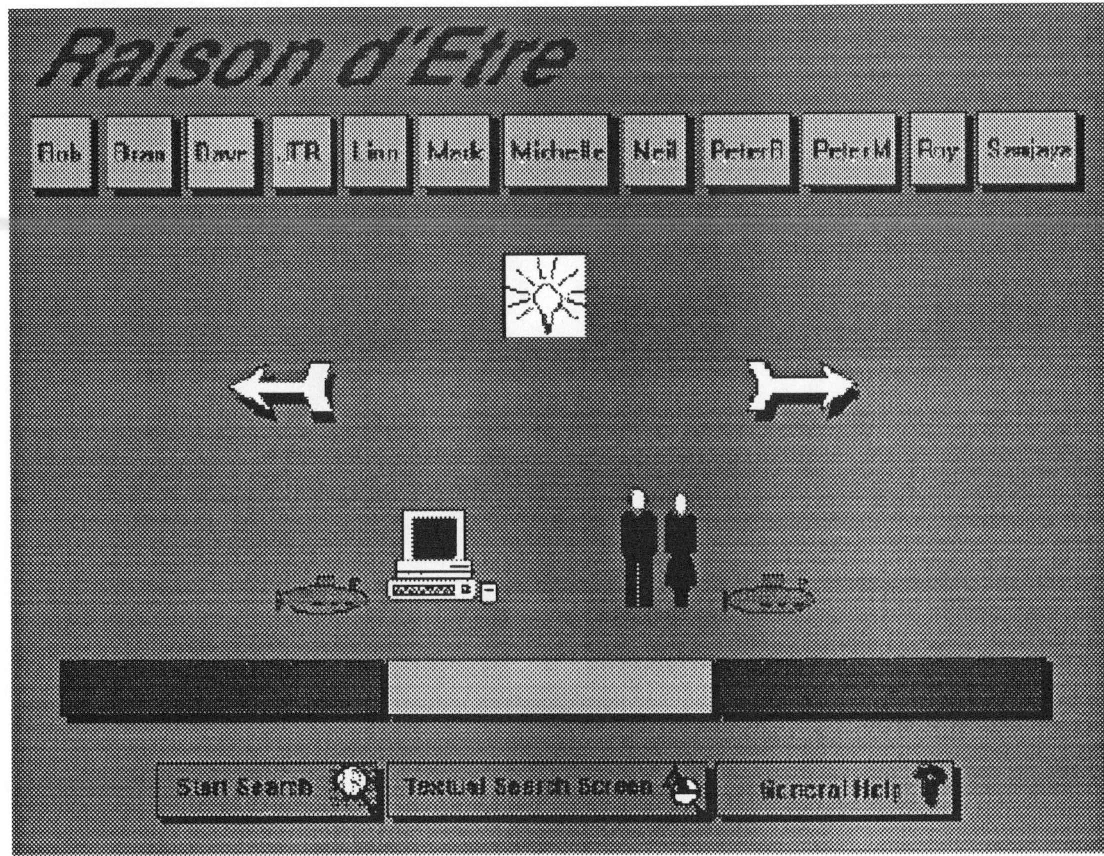

Figure 3. Layout for main menu of Raison d'Etre system

how they saw the prospects and directions of the project, and its accomplishments thus far from that point in time.

We classified and rated the thousands of video clips we collected through the next year. We were impressed throughout with the good will and the candor of the designers. It was fascinating stuff: because each interview was couched in the present tense, reviewing clips across interview rounds created a kind of persistent present that seemed to make the data more vivid and intrinsically interesting.

We created a simple presentation system for our video database: Raison d'Etre (Carroll, Alpert, Karat, Van Deusen and Rosson, 1994a,b). The home screen is shown in Figure 3. Across the top are buttons representing each of the design team members. Across the bottom is a color-spectrum time-line: red (to the left) corresponds to the inception of the project under study, violet (to the right) to its end (we had expected the project to last longer than it eventually did — it was canceled midstream; we thereby wound up with only three interview time periods). In the middle of the screen are five buttons depicting our five top-level database topics. Clockwise from the leftmost arrow these represent Looking Backward, Vision, Looking Forward, Human Issues, and Technical Issues.

Looking Backward provides access to database entries bearing on project accomplishments and the reflections of team members on previous points in the design process. The Vision topic accesses specific technical views of the project (e.g., its potential impact on its users; its possible significance vis-à-vis computer science) as well as high-level views of the project's potential impact on groups of people or on society. Looking Forward includes what still lies ahead, anticipated problems, changes, and outcomes. Human Issues refers to data bearing on group dynamics, personal relationships, communication, and collaboration. Technical Issues consists of design history and rationale in the more conventional sense, that is relating to specific design characteristics and concerns, such as the possibly alternative views regarding specific design

Figure 4. Video playout from Raison d'Etre.

points and their resolution. Due to the obvious richness in such broad categorizations, we also developed subtopics for Technical Issues and Human Issues.

The user selects sets of buttons to build a graphical query. For example, one or more team members can be selected and one or more reference times; then queries including any of the five topics will retrieve only clips relevant to those topics and spoken by any of the selected persons and occurring in any of the selected phases of the project. At any point in the query specification, the user can ask for clips; Figure 4 illustrates the playout of a video clip in Raison d'Etre.

Raison d'Etre did seem to give us interesting access to project history. For example, the set of key issues for the project we studied changed over time. In part, we were led to the five database categories because finer-grained taxonomies of our materials seemed ephemeral. In the first round of interviews, for instance, the chief technical issue discussed by the team was the nature of the initial proof-of-concept prototype. However, Prototype did not seem to be a lasting major category: subsequently the team articulated the more detailed and lower-level technical concerns that came up in the course of developing the prototype and follow-on development.

The watershed events that create a team out of a collection of diverse individuals and that create a project vision out of sometimes disparate motivations and goals are profoundly important, yet they are ephemeral. In the first round of interviews, many of the designers told us the story of a dinner they had shared after a particularly long and tiring team meeting. In the dinner conversation, it came out that all of those present were deeply concerned about that state of education in our society, and that in their different ways each saw the project they were working on as a personal commitment to contribute something to the future of education. This was expressed with intensity that really comes across in the video clips.

In subsequent interview rounds, new, more contemporaneous events were naturally more salient to the designers. They were moving on to technical issues involving databases, information retrieval, and user interface presentation and controls. The educational vision was still "there", still galvanizing the team mem-bers, but it was part of their shared history by that point, and as such not likely to be talked about. Time is critical: One has to capture history as it happens to capture it easily or, in many cases, to capture it at all.

In the first round of interviews we collected several accounts of how the team had selected a sample content domain for their proof-of-concept prototype: nuclear power plant engineering. These accounts were personalized in interesting ways: from a team member more identified with project vision and management, we got a rationale in terms of social and pedagogical values; from a team member more identified with implementation, we got a rationale in terms of availability of multimedia data and amenability of available data to the mechanisms of the prototype.

Interestingly, only a month later the team changed their sample domain due to problems with data availability and worries about social controversy. In the second round of interviews we were able to gather a solid and broad-based rationale for the new sample domain — the previously tight rationale for the now-rejected domain was no longer observable with the fidelity observed in the first round. In fact, some designers' stories seemed to forget that there ever had been another domain That early rationale became a priceless moment in the history of this design project; yet, if we had conducted retrospective interviews at the close of the project only, we would not have seen it.

17.4 Clarifying Concerns and Objectives of Use

From the very start, everyone on the team we studied was enthusiastic about the notion of a design history system. This enthusiasm seemed to have three sources: First, they seemed to share our intuition that encouraging and supporting reflection and a sense of history within a design team would create the possibility of better collaborations and better design results. Second, everyone was especially excited about pursuing this through a database of video clips — notably perhaps, the project we studied was itself focused on supporting video information systems. Indeed, we joked at one point that our project history system should be implemented on the system platform produced by the team whose project history was being documented. Third, the project members simply enjoyed talking about their accomplishments, their collaborative interactions, their goals, etc.; they seemed to enjoy our attention and the sanctioned opportunity to explicitly sort some of it out. As the team members told their stories, they would often stop to comment that these reflections were useful to them , that is, that they had not yet fully appreciated the significance of their own experiences until they made them explicit.

Our team — the one creating the design history system — experienced similar scenario-based epiphanies. We had started with a fairly vague vision: the notion that project history could be a resource for designers and the "model" of the John Cocke system. Our own design work focused immediately on enumerating potential scenarios of use, and within these, potential issues and opportunities. The list of scenarios in Figure 5 is drawn directly from the first page of our design notes. It was literally the first thing we did.

Creating and developing these scenarios helped us in several ways. First, the scenarios helped us to become a design team. Our project was essentially exploratory; we were seeking problems and solutions at the same time. It was also a skunk works, that is, no one on our team had the design history system as his or her principal job responsibility. The project was never officially chartered, and it had no budget or staffing. Indeed, only two of the five people on the team had a line management relation. We were participating out of interest, not management direction. Projects like this can wander and dissipate very easily. The scenarios quickly gave us a "What we are doing," they helped our early brainstorming hang together between meetings.

The scenarios also helped us by making it easier for us to plan what we would do, instead of prematurely diving into its execution. From the start, we felt enormous pressure. We did not know exactly what we wanted to do. We interviewed the members of the multimedia education project, but were still uncertain just what piece of their needs corresponded to support for project history. Yet we could see that the history of their project was well underway; they were having meetings and developing plans, and we were not capturing any of it! The scenarios allowed us to get going, to develop and explore our design space, but with the least possible degree of commitment. They gave us something concrete to work on, while at the same time keeping us from wastefully diving in before we understood what we needed to do.

how does one create a work group that works? — the user is interested in the collaborative dynamics of design teams, perhaps in relating this example to social psychological abstractions

how do design projects get done? — the user is interested in seeing system development exemplified with more concrete detail than the idealized descriptions of textbooks

what type of system is this, what might it do for me, why would I want to use it?— the first-time user may be unsure what goals are appropriate, and needs to be able to discover this from the system itself

what is the role of lexical networks in the project? — seeking information pertaining to a specific technical issue, which may in fact have its own sub history and a set of related topics

why did the design team abandon the bridge failure domain? — focus is a particular design decision, though in this case a major event in the design process

what was Bonnie's role in September 1991? — the user selects the "people" button, and then selects the "Bonnie" button and an early point on the project timeline

how did Bonnie's role change between September and December 1991? — query Bonnie's role at two points on the timeline, as above (perhaps we need an absolute scale on the timeline for such scenarios, but I think that users will care more about relative times within the project lifecycle)

how did Ben and Bonnie work together during the spring of 1992 (e.g., on what problems and issues)? —

compare what Peter said the November 1991 prototype would be like in September 1991 with what he said it was like in December 1991 —

what was the consensus view was about the project in October 1991? — the user selects an early point in the timeline and then browses around under various topics and people

compare the consensus view about the project in October 1991 with the consensus view in June 1992 — the user selects and browses two points on the timeline, as above

compare Mike's attitude toward Donna's tools with Donna's attitude toward Mike's tools — the user pursues Mike's attitude (for example) and then initiates another search for the comparable information about Donna (perhaps finding a bit of data the explicitly contrasts the two, but more likely having to integrate the information for him or herself)

compare the change in Mike's attitude toward Donna's tools between October 1991 and June 1992 with the change in Donna's attitude toward Mike's tools during the same time period —

make a report on a search episode — the user wishes to create a report, perhaps just saving the results of a query or a set of queries with a name or description, perhaps designing a presentation sequence (will people want to do this?)

Figure 5. Early design scenarios for Raison D'Etre: *This figure is drawn directly from the first page of our design notes, created in september 1991.*

Creating scenarios also helped us get technically focused. At the outset of the project, we sounded the mantra of supporting design team reflection. But when we brainstormed possible usage scenarios, we quickly generated major reformulations in our own vision. For example, many of the scenarios of Figure 5 address the use of Raison d'Etre in design education: the system presents an explorable case study. Looking back, it seems that we might have been led to "discover" these educational scenarios both by the fact that the multimedia education project we were studying was itself focused on scenarios like these, and by our worries that our project would lag theirs too much to provide a timely information system to the design team itself.

One of the most important uses of the these early scenarios was to help us design interview questionnaires for collecting video clips. We wanted to allow members of the multimedia education project to speak about the issues and episodes important to them. But we also wanted to exert some guidance, both to ensure broad coverage of each individual's perspectives and experiences, and to make sets of clips among different individuals more comparable. The scenarios helped us with both: We prepared an open-ended set of questions about individual perceptions of project roles, attitudes toward collaboration, the overall project vision and its evolution, the current prototype, the domain for the test module, and specific technical issues like multimedia tools and lexical networks; these are evident in Figure 5.

This first phase of scenario development occupied our first couple meetings; it easily fit into the slack time involved in setting up videotaping sessions with the team members.

17.5 Envisioning Alternative Situations

In the initial videotaping session, we collected over 11 hours of material from the 10 principal team members. The interviewing process itself, and the many hours we spent as a group screening and discussing this videotape immersed us in the technical problems and social interactions of the multimedia education project. It both grounded us and encouraged us in developing our starting set of scenarios. We tried to sketch out in more detail the things users might do with a project history system, the ways they might go about doing those things, and the contrasts between such possibilities and the current practices we could see. As the initial set grew, we revisited these scenarios, testing our conception of what we were doing, trying to stretch it to help us better articulate the "design problem" and the means and solutions we were developing.

For example, we became very impressed at how easy it is to collect relatively huge amounts of video, and at how difficult video is to handle — it cannot be conveniently searched in the way that a textual database can be, and each clip must be viewed in real time. This led us to develop the scenarios in Figure 5 with a presumption that for most user queries, there would be a relatively large number of hits. Thus, we identified the management of large sets of hits as a key technical issue: how to report/display such sets, how to allow users to browse them, whether to provide preview access to sets of hits, and so forth. We identified and developed new scenarios to describe these issues, such as the "Looking for the fast-forward button" scenario in Figure 6.

We began to consider user interface presentations and interactions more specifically. For example, in "Orienting to the project" in Figure 6, a first-time user is learning what kinds of information the system can provide, what kinds of queries can be put to it. We presumed a somewhat sophisticated user, but one for whom using the system would be casual. Thus, we were led to envision a simple, iconic interface in which queries are visually specified by selecting combinations of team members (that is, the speaker in a clip), topics (looking backward, looking forward, project vision, and various technical and human issues), and points along a project timeline.

Working with these scenarios helped us discover new functional requirements for the project history system. For example, "What is the project all about?" in Figure 6 is a further development of "Orienting to the project" but it focuses on a particular issue: a sequence of individual queries and returned video clips might not integrate into a coherent concept of the project. The user might still be wondering what the point of the project was even after hearing many specific stories and reflections from team members. This scenario motivated us to consider incorporating a series of system demonstrations in the video database, that is, we decided to include a formally narrated, integrative project demonstration for each time period, a kind of official progress report. This could both provide integrative context for the individual stories and reflections, and serve as a sounding board for the various personal perspectives.

The fourth scenario in Figure 6, "Creating a perspective on the design history" is an authoring scenario, not a browsing scenario. The user marks clips relevant to a specific interest, and creates a new subtopic in the database. This actually changes the system that subsequent users would experience. In September, we had listed a variant of this scenario with a parenthetical question "will people want to do this?" However, by November, when the scenarios in Figure 6 were generated, we were growing more confident of our design concept, enough so to take the possibility of user authoring more seriously.

The course of scenario development illustrated in

Looking for the fast-forward button:
Walter has been browsing some clips pertaining to the project manager's views of the lexical network, as they developed through the course of the project. One clip in particular seems to drag a bit, and he wonders how to fast forward through the rest of it Q perhaps he can just stop the playout?

Orienting to the project :
Harry has just joined the project team; his manager suggested that he should work with the project history to get familiar with what has happened up to now, and what the current challenges are. Looking at the home screen, Harry sees a set of labeled person icons across the top, a group of five icons in the middle Q labeled Project Vision, Technical Issues, Human Issues, Looking Forward and Looking Backward, and a rainbow ribbon along the bottom, labeled with project phases. All of these appear to be selectable buttons. In the upper-right-hand corner of the display is a button labeled Find Clips.

What is the project all about?:
Betty is a designer, but not a member of the project team. She is browsing the technical issues with the goal of learning something from the way various technical issues were handled in the project. She finds a variety of interesting tidbits on lexical browsers, multimedia authoring tools, and so on. But she has difficulty seeing how the different pieces fit together as a coherent project.

Creating a perspective on the design history:
Paul is browsing clips related to the use of Smalltalk as a prototyping tool. He notices that several of these refer to a software framework for user interface prototyping; apparently, this was a side-effort or some related work carried out by members of the project team. Paul marks these clips and assigns the new group the name "Interface Framework." He continues adding clips to the group, and then add the group name to the Technical Issues sub-menu.

Figure 6. Envisioning the scenarios more vividly to develop interface and interaction ideas (based on design notes from November 1991).

Figure 6 involves elaborating initial scenario sketches, as in Figure 5, and expanding the initial set of scenarios envisioned. A systematic approach to doing this is to generate before and after scenarios for the "same" user goals, in order to force out the design issues that differentiate them (Carroll, 1994a,b). Consider again scenarios for "orienting to the project" The scenario in Figure 7 is a more detailed view of how this scenario might run before the deployment of a project history system.

In the scenario, a new design team member attends his first team meeting and hears the project leader run through an overview pitch. The scenario is a vivid and succinct description of a person getting oriented to the work in progress of a design team. One can use it as part of a requirements analysis, to identify problem areas and opportunities for design work. For example, the new team member leaves the meeting with a clear understanding of the project vision, but a one-sided understanding. The other team members were excited and supportive of the manager's project pitch, but not at all skeptical or critical. This raises the design question of how the person might have been supported in the goal of getting a more balanced or more complete introduction to the project.

Having observed or conjectured the "development team meeting" scenario, we would search deliberately for further scenarios that complement or compete. In this case, we generated the "meet various team members" scenario in which the new team member meets first with the project leader and then subsequently with the various other team members, but in each case in a one-on-one meeting (Figure 8). This is a very different experience than the "Development team meeting" scenario: the new member hears many differing views of the project needs and priorities. At the end, he probably has gathered a much richer picture of the project, but a far less clear impression of what to do. Indeed, at the end of the sequence of meetings, he may feel the need to schedule a second round of meetings to clarify questions raised by one person about something another person had said in a prior meeting.

As we designed the Raison d'Etre system to support the work of development teams, these two scenarios and

- Harry, a curriculum designer, has just joined a project developing a multimedia information system for engineering education. Lewis, the project manager, has suggested that he attend the design team's weekly meeting to start getting up to speed on project status and direction.

- Lewis is reviewing a presentation he will make to upper management. Lewis sketches the project vision as a new world of collaborative and experience-based technical education via the use of media across high-bandwidth networks. In this vision, engineering students work on case studies incorporating social as well as technical issues from the very start of their education.

- The talk develops a walkthrough in which two engineering students collaborate across a high-bandwidth network, using a multimedia database to study a variety of technical, legal and social details pertaining to an accident at a nuclear power plant. After analyzing the case study, the students create a multimedia report, including recommendations for improving the power plant's design and operation.

- The discussion is highly animated; everyone is offering suggestions about the presentation. Some of it seems a bit quixotic, but it's very inspiring as to the future of engineering education. Harry notes that there is little detail on the students' curriculum, and clearly sees how he can begin contributing to the project.

Figure 7. The development team meeting scenario.

- In his first meeting with Lewis, Harry gets an overview. He learns that the reason for selecting nuclear power plants as a content domain for the prototype course module is social relevance and timeliness. The earlier content domain was bridges, which seemed somewhat dry by contrast. Lewis sketches the project vision as a new world of collaborative and experience-based technical education via the use of media across high-bandwidth networks. In this vision, engineering students work on case studies incorporating social as well as technical issues from the very start of their education.

- A few days later, Harry meets a team member, Walter, to discuss the state of work on the video database and the collection and scanning of new video materials. Walter mentions that the change of content domain from bridges and bridge failures to nuclear power plants was motivated chiefly by the availability of better video and other information. He reveals that the first candidate domain was searching and sorting algorithms, which was amenable to visualization through animation, but not rich enough in terms of extant text and video sources.

- To Walter, the project is a great opportunity to make his work concrete. He explains, in some detail, the challenges of integrating text from diverse sources (in diverse formats) and of collecting and organizing video to press laser disks.

- Harry is somewhat confused about what the project is really seeking to accomplish. What should he read up on to prepare? He worries about balancing the objective of working social issues into the instructional exercises with that of emphasizing browsing and authoring multimedia documents. After a few days, he decides to schedule a meeting with Lewis to get more guidance. In the office, he hears that the content domain has now changed to airport design.

Figure 8. The meet various team members scenario.

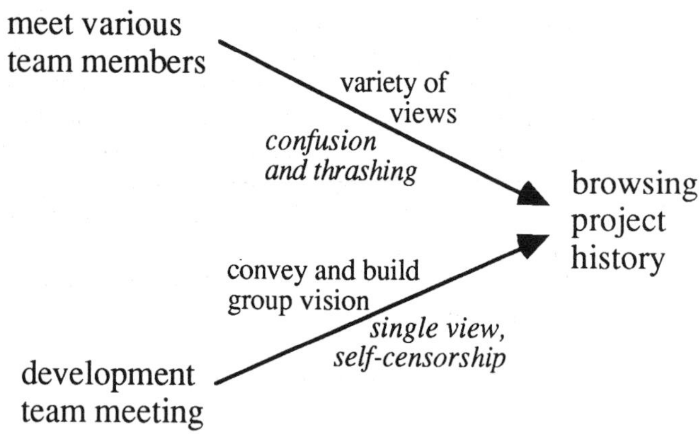

Figure 9. Scenario-based design argument.

the task-level conflicts and tradeoffs they embody provided a very different type of guidance than purely functional requirements like "search by author" even though the same underlying issues are at stake: the contrast between the "Development team meeting" and the "Meet various team members" scenarios clearly involves the question of who is the "author" of the information the new member is exposed to, but it is so much more than merely a question of the syntax for specifying queries. This is precisely the point of a scenario-based perspective on design.

We use a set of scenarios to reason toward a scenario specification of a design. Thus, we used the "Development team meeting" and the "Meet various team members" scenarios to clarify requirements (such as the problems of getting information only from the team leader or of getting information from various members but thrashing) and then tried to construct further scenarios that could address these requirements. In this manner, we constructed the "browsing project history" scenario in which the new team member accesses stored video of various team members commenting on the project vision, status, needs and current direction. The video clips he browses were created at various points through the history of the project, so the new team member can gather an impression not only of where things stand currently in the project — from each of the individual perspectives of the various team members — but also of how these individual views evolved, and what people in the team thought about various issues before events overtook them.

This specification scenario addresses the issues raised in the two requirements scenarios. The "Development team meeting" issue of hearing only the manager's perspective — and the possibility that this creates a normative bias among the team members, implicitly suppressing divergent views, is addressed by making it just as easy to access the perspectives of other team members. Yet the desirable property of conveying, and potentially strengthening the group's vision, is preserved. The "meet various team members" issue of thrashing is addressed by making it easy to switch back and forth among the video clips from various team members. Indeed, access to a variety of views is enhanced; one can switch among time frames as well as team members to explore historical factors in the project, something one could never do without such an information system. This scenario-based design "argument" is visualized in Figure 9.

This is an example of the task-artifact cycle (Carroll, Kellogg and Rosson, 1991). The "Meet various team members" and "Development team meeting" scenarios are descriptions of current tasks. By analyzing the issues implicit in these tasks — as schematized in Figure 9 — we can reason toward new artifacts that help address these issues by enabling transformations of current tasks. Ultimately, of course a project history system will enable tasks and practices beyond those its designers imagined, and will raise new issues too.

17.6 Managing Consequences and Tradeoffs

Every design move has many consequences. Scenarios are good at vividly capturing the consequences and tradeoffs of designs at various levels of analysis and with respect to various perspectives. Any given scenario text leaves many things implicit, for example, the "looking for the fast-forward button" scenario in Figure 6 does not tell us why Walter felt that the video clip dragged. This property of being concrete but rough is one reason scenarios are so useful.

However, in many cases it can be important to be able to explicitly enumerate the causal factors and relations that are left implicit in scenario narratives. In the "looking for the fast-forward button" scenario, one of the most important causal relations is relegated to the background of the actual text. It is the dual nature of video data: very rich and intrinsically appealing to viewers, yet difficult to search or scan.

We can isolate such relations in a simple schema:

{in a given usage situation, a given design feature}
...causes {desirable consequences}
...but also {undesirable consequences}

The schema make salient the tradeoffs associated with a design feature in a given scenario context by enumerating its upside and downside consequences.

The schema can be instantiated for the "looking for the fast-forward button" example:

Video Information Claim: video information
...is a very rich, intrinsically appealing medium
...but is difficult to search, and must be viewed linearly in real time

We call these schemas "claims" — they are implicitly asserted by designs in which they are embodied; we call the approach of developing causal analyses of usage scenarios "claims analysis" (Carroll and Rosson, 1991, 1992). One can identify claims by systematically posing elaboration questions about the events in a scenario (Carroll and Rosson, 1992). Thus, we can ask why the clip seems to drag; an answer is that the video must be viewed linearly in real time, even if the clip is lengthy. This raises the question of how viewers can streamline lengthy interactions, for example, through search. But searching noncoded data like video is not a solved problem, indeed, the lack of search mechanisms for video data comprises another downside.

These questions, in turn, lead us to ask why we would want to use video data in the first place, and an answer here is that it is rich and appealing to viewers. In Raison d'Etre we wanted to show how team members felt about the stories and reflections they contributed to the project history, not merely say how they felt. For this, we needed to use video.

Other elaboration questions we can pose about the "looking for the fast-forward button" scenario motivate further claims. For example, why would the user want to fast-forward through the playout of a clip? An answer is that adding such a capability mitigates the downside that video information must be viewed in real time. But it is not a comprehensive solution, since fast-forwarding typically accelerates speech to the point of intelligibility and destroys the "feel" of the real time visual information. Would the fast-forwarding capability be effective for mitigating the real time playout constraint? The relevant tradeoffs are summarized in the Fast-forward Claim:

***Fast-forward Claim*:** fast-forwarding video information
...allows the viewer to more rapidly scan and evaluate clips
...but destroys intelligibility of the sound-track and the "feel" of the real time visual information

We could go on, for example, elaborating the "Looking for the fast-forward button" scenario with respect to the particular implementation of user interface controls for fast-forwarding: a button, a slider, a frames-per-second prompter. These alternatives each raise further questions about causal relations implicit in the scenario, which in turn could be articulated as further claims.

The claims we develop as answer to elaboration questions are hypotheses about the underlying causal relations in the scenarios, the analyst's hypotheses about why and how an observed or envisioned scenario of use could occur. The objective of raising these questions and articulating hypothesized causal relations is to open up a process of critique and refinement, to help designers interrogate and explain key scenarios in enough detail that they can be interpreted, revised, perhaps discarded as the design proceeds. This analysis is not intended to merely rationalize the personal intentions of the designers. A simple way to guard against this is to make sure that claims brainstorming forces out at least some upsides and downsides for every design feature that is analyzed. At the worst, one will generate some trivial upsides for fundamentally problematic scenarios and some trivial downsides for essentially unproblematic scenarios.

Any scenario can be unpacked in this way. For example, "What is the project all about?" in Figure 6 raises questions about how a pool of separate video clips can be used to build an understanding of a project" technical rationale and design process:

Stand-alone Clips Claim: decomposing the project history into a pool of stand-alone video clips

...facilitates analysis of the system from diverse perspectives
...engages the user by allowing him/her to "construct" an overall view of the technical rationale and design process from diverse pieces
...but users may find it difficult to integrate conflicting bits of information into a coherent overall concept

The "orienting to the project" scenario in Figure 6 raises a variety of potential elaboration questions: What might Harry's manager be expecting him to gain through interaction with the project history system? Why are the various buttons grouped as they are in the interface? What do the labeled person buttons convey to users? Is the issue of choosing between Mike's and Donna's multimedia authoring tools a technical issue or a human issue, or both? What does the timeline ribbon convey to users? Where is October 10, 1991, on the timeline? How would a user find information relating to current project challenges? What will people expect to happen when they select Find Clips? The tradeoffs that bear on addressing these questions, can be organized into claims, for example:

Control Panel Interface Claim: a simple control panel interface
...directly conveys the content categories of the database
...encourages direct interaction
...but precise and/or complex queries may be difficult to directly articulate

Human Issues Claim: the Human Issues button, the team members' buttons, and the appearance of team members in the clips
...suggest questions about collaborative dynamics among team members
...but may evoke questions for which there is no information in the database

***Timeline Claim*:** the timeline interface control
...encourages the user to take a historical perspective, to consider historical or process issues
...the time periods may not resolve the history finely enough
...but the relative model of time may not support the user's concerns (e.g., a "when" question)

Causal claims analysis of scenarios is a refinement of the more informal, more purely scenario-based design analysis sketched in Figure 9 above. In the Raison d'Etre project, we used claims analysis for relatively more detailed consideration of critical scenarios, or for cases in which a scenario analysis left open questions. The claims in Figure 10 more explicitly highlight the issues raised earlier in the purely scenario-based analysis of Figures 1, 7 and 8. These three scenarios, and their claims analyses, are particularly interesting because they comprise a kind of focused design argument. They emphasize the continuity between the before and after scenarios, and the design transformation that relates them.

For each individual scenario, we can pose a set of elaboration questions. For the "development team meeting" scenario, we could ask how the talk builds group vision?, why the manager does all the talking?, whether everyone in the project team really agrees?, and so forth. And from these, we can build claims as possible explanations for why the scenarios run as they do. There may be a tendency to see the before scenarios as problem statements, that is, as mainly downsides, and the after scenarios as solutions embodying upsides. For this reason, it is very useful to ensure a balanced analysis of all the scenarios. Having done that, we can extract cross-scenario themes for the entire ensemble: it is important to convey and build a group vision, but troublesome if any one team member exerts too much influence on the vision; it is useful to be exposed to a variety of views, but it takes time and effort to do this, and there is no guarantee that the various views will "add up."

Making such design arguments explicit, and making the transformation of the issues (e.g., in the envisioned "Browsing project history" scenario) explicit, helps make the design of scenarios more cumulative and auditable. We can directly view and compare the considerations that motivated the design work and the hypothesized result of the design work: normative averaging and power bias distortions, search time and effort, potential for confusion and thrashing. As we develop and begin to implement the new design, we can evaluate it with respect to the specific claims we analyzed. We have also found that making a causal analysis of one scenario can often clarify the need for considering and designing one or more other scenarios, thus helping to elaborate the overall design.

Finally, this type of approach emphasizes the open-endedness of the design process. Design does not stop with a project history browser. Some of the issues addressed in the design may turn out to have been addressed inadequately. And new issues may arise; in Figure 10 we noted the concerns our group had that the amount of information to be browsed might quickly overwhelm users, and that the query categories

Overview Pitch Claim: An overview pitch of project status and direction
... efficiently conveys and builds the group vision
... but creates normative averaging and power bias distortions

Piecemeal Understanding Claim: Pursuing questions of project vision, status, and direction through a series of interactions with colleagues
... accesses a variety of views
... but takes a lot of time and effort
... but can cause confusion and thrashing

Browsing History Claim: Browsing a video database of statements, stories and reflections of team members
... conveys/builds group vision
... accesses a variety of views
... provides direct and flexible access to views
... clarifies and enriches answers to queries via lots of collateral information
... but the query categories may not fit the user's goal
... but the amount of information to be browsed may overwhelm users

Figure 10. Causal relations implicit in the three scenarios.

(looking forward, project vision, and so forth) might not fit users' actual goals.

It is important to stress that claims analysis provides only heuristic explanations of user interaction. Their utility in system design derives from directly linking features of a designed situation with user activities and experiences. However, this can be an oversimplification: some causal relations between features of situations and consequences for people in those situations may not be first-order, they may derive from interactions and side-effects, but be important nonetheless. Our hope is that when such interactions arise, we might improve our chances of noticing them and of beginning to fathom what's going on if we are keeping explicit account of what we expected would happen. If something is clearly working or failing, we have a basis for making credit/blame attributions, we have a starting point for systematically revisiting our decisions, and for understanding other situations that guided us to those decisions. (See Jones, 1970: 316-324, for discussion of a system design method quite similar to claims analysis).

17.7 Creating and Using Design Knowledge

Design reasoning is often quite local; designers address subsets of known requirements and then set aside tentative reasoning and partial results in order to explore other, hopefully converging subproblems. Creating an explicit analysis of the causal relations in scenarios can extend the scope and depth of a scenario analysis. It provides a working design representation to preserve and integrate interim considerations and conclusions. Indeed, the scope of such reasoning can extend beyond the current design project: we can view and reconsider the causal analyses of prior projects that might be relevant to what we currently doing.

In this way, scenarios support a principled approach to the traditional technology development paradigm of craft evolution. Our design of Raison d'Etre was in many ways a direct emulation of the John Cocke application. However, the evolutionary process in this case was not articulated only at the level of the artifact itself, it was self-consciously guided by analytic consideration of the scenarios we wanted to address and those we wanted to enable. We managed these scenarios and claims to systematically elaborate our design, for example, coming to recognize it as an "educational" design tool, as well as a documentation tool. In the end, we had made a "deliberated" evolution of John Cocke, a explicit development of the prior system backed up with extensive use-oriented rationale.

A designer's chief interest must be the project at hand, and therefore, in claims analysis for scenarios pertaining to that particular design. But it is clear that some of the analytical work one does in any particular design context is more widely applicable. For example, the Video Information Claim expresses general relations regarding the use of video, relations not specifically bound to the "Looking for the fast-forward button" scenario, or to the Raison d'Etre system. The next time we consider incorporating video information into a system design, the tradeoffs enumerated in this claim will be relevant. The work we did, or that someone else did, to understand and articulate these relations can be of direct use in the future. Some aspects of even the most specialized computer systems are general, if we take the trouble to draw out the generalizations.

We can generalize scenarios or claims developed for specific design projects by trying to see them as instances of types. For example, the "What is the project all about?" scenario can be seen an example of opportunistic interaction: the user explores information about people and issues by responding to whatever buttons or other interface mechanisms are encountered, trying to construct an understanding through a series of experiments. We can contrast opportunistic interaction scen-arios with scenarios in which the user has a guiding goal and takes a series of actions intended to attain the goal. Thus, search scenarios contrast with opportunistic interaction scenarios in that the user is by definition seeking something in particular.

If one makes an analysis of an opportunistic interaction scenario, some part of the work one has done may generalize to other instances of the type. Indeed, this was precisely our own experience with opportunistic interaction scenarios. We had identified opportunistic scenario patterns in our user studies with office systems years before we worked on Raison d'Etre (e.g., Carroll and Mazur, 1986; Mack, Lewis and Carroll, 1983). Because of this prior work, we expected that one common usage scenario for Raison d'Etre would be one in which people directly browsed and experimented with the interface controls to discover what information and functionality was available in the system. This generalized opportunism scenario is one that is always in the back of our minds in designing user interfaces and applications.

Claims also can be generalized. Claims about similar user consequences or similar artifact features can be grouped together. We have already discussed the Video Information claim as a potentially general relation with implications for any video information system. The Control Panel Interface claim can also be seen as an instance of a more general claim, one about simple, direct manipulation interfaces: such interface designs are cognitively transparent and invite user experimentation, on the other hand, it is not possible to express much variety or subtlety through such interfaces. This is a very general design tradeoff that impinges on most contemporary user interface design.

The Stand-alone Clips claim can be seen as an instance of a more general claim about piecemeal information: when the chunks of available information are quite small and only loosely structured, the user has the opportunity to actively construct meanings, to put together diverse views of the data in potentially novel ways. On the other hand, the user may not always be able to make satisfactory sense of a vast and unstructured field of data. Again, this is a highly prototypical tradeoff in design; there is a fine line between challenging and engaging the user with stimulating cognitive tasks, and overwhelming the user with tasks that are too difficult.

Integrating the generalization and refinement of knowledge employed and attained in design with design work itself is perhaps the strongest implementation of Schn's (1983) view of design as inquiry. The design argument behind the "Browsing project history"scenario provides a good illustration. One generalization of the Overview Pitch claim in Figure 10 is the Social Conformity claim:

Social Conformity Claim: Articulating one's beliefs and engaging in action in a social context

...provides a highly responsive setting for testing and refining one's beliefs and behavior, and for building group consensus

...but encourages actions and beliefs that are group-normative and consistent with the actions and beliefs of powerful others (e.g., group leaders), and thereby can inhibit diversity

...Couching the relation at this level engages a huge research literature from social psychology detailing a variety factors that create social influences (Allport, 1920; Asch, 1958; Cartwright, 1968; Latane, 1981; Lewin, 1953; Milgram, 1968; Schein, Schneier and Barker, 1961).

Being able to generalize a design argument in this way can be useful in that it provides a framework for adducing relevant science. Perhaps even more importantly though, it provides a framework for adducing the results of design inquiry to science. Thus, a current theoretical formulation of social influence states that the pressure to change one's attitudes or actions is proportional to the product of the strength, the immediacy, and the number of social interactions aligned with change (Latane, 1981). In this formulation, of course, the concept of "immediacy" does not provide for electronic immediacy, as in a video information system or electronic conferencing system. Thus, the design and use of a system like Raison d'Etre can directly bear on extending the science base of social psychology to new types of social interactions made possible by new technologies.

The point of generalizing scenarios and claims is not to undermine the creativity of design, to presume to reduce design to mere instantiation of general scenarios and claims. As we tried to emphasize earlier, making design too simple is not the problem. The problem is making it manageable at all. The purpose of generalizing scenarios and claims is to enhance the tractability of design, to provide a way of learning from design experiences, from prior design results. Technical knowledge always underconstrains design. It does this even in relatively well-worked realms, such as the design of a new word processor. It does this even more severely in the design of novel systems, such as our design of Raison d'Etre. Nevertheless, there are always existing situations, general scenarios, relationships involving potential user consequences. If we can manage this prior knowledge, and bring it to bear on our design problems, we can increase our chance for success.

Our claim is that scenario-based design facilitates generalizing and reusing design knowledge at the right level of abstraction for productive design work: the level of tasks that are meaningful to the people who perform and experience them. In this sense, the roughness of scenarios is a useful kind of abstractness — it allows scenarios to be both concrete and generalizable.

17.8 Staying Focused on Users and Use

Generalizing and reusing design knowledge at the scenario level helps keep designers focused on the tasks that will be facilitated (or impeded) by the systems they design. Our use of scenarios in the design of Raison d'Etre helped keep us focused on users and use of the system throughout the project. We never construed our project as principally a video system, though at the time, that was a popular niche for exploratory system development. Indeed, our first prototype was implemented purely with text: we recognized that many of scenarios we wanted to support could be implemented and evaluated with text transcripts standing in place of their video clips. This allowed us to finesse building the digital video database, and to get concrete feedback on the interface design in Figure 3. We did this in the spring of 1992 — months before we were able to obtain enough disk storage to begin building the digital video database!

Later, when we had a running video-based prototype, we returned to our scenarios to evaluate the performance of the system in the kinds scenarios for which it had been designed (Karat, Carroll, Alpert and Rosson, 1995). Because of delays in our own work, and the short life of the project we studied, this evaluation actually proved to be quite retrospective: 18 months after the target project had been canceled! But we were interested to find whether a system like Raison d'Etre could possibly be a tool for designers to manage their collaborations, could support communication of information and perspectives among team-members, could enhance collaborative dynamics.

Our study was a 2-hour think aloud experiment; we asked eight of the original team members to work with the system while making a running commentary of their goals and plans, actions and reactions. First, we asked each designer to recall information on selected topics; we prompted them, What did you think about <some issue>?, What did <someone else> think about it? Next, we asked each to explore this topic using the system. Finally, we asked each to assess the information provided by the system on the particular topic, and the access to and presentation of that information in the system.

Our plan was to guide the designers to explore a range of topics in this manner, including at least one technical issue, at least one human issue, and at least one general issue (for example, How did the issues identified when team members looked ahead in the project actually work out?). However, we observed more spontaneous use than expected, and often did not need our pre-planned task suggestions. In general, team members liked the system and suggested many ways in which something like it might support their design work. They created their own stories by moving between speakers, topics, and times in a variety of ways.

Many of the behaviors and judgments we observed bear out and elaborate the claims we identified. Recall, for example, the Video Information Claim. There was abundant evident that the designers appreciated the richness of video. After reading the text of a clip, one of the designers said "Let's see with what conviction he says this," and then viewed the video. Another read the transcript, and then viewed a "frustration" clip, commenting "You couldn't get 'frustration' out of that unless you sat down and looked at it." Another said: "I learn a lot looking at myself;" still another said that the video "made the information worthwhile."

However, the designers also emphasized the

downside content of the Video Information Claim: "It is more informative to see people, but it takes longer." Most designers developed a strategy of initially scanning at least some of the transcript, before deciding to view the video. Some referred to the length of clips, more readily viewing briefer clips, but first reading the transcript for more lengthy ones. Some referred to the content of clips, tending to read technical clips ("I'm more interested in what they are saying than how they said it."), but to view human issues clips ("some stuff I just want to see").

The prominent timeline in the user interface did call attention to project history, and seemed to be easily understood and controlled (cf. the Timeline Claim). However, the very coarse and purely relative model of time presented through this interface control was in other respects not satisfactory. In many cases, the designers had trouble deciding within which of the three interview rounds a clip or topic might have occurred, but at the same time were able to produce lots of temporal information (the approximate date, various contemporaneous events, etc.). This convinced us to use absolute, not relative time (e.g., a time period labeled as First Quarter 1992, instead of just as "second of three") and incorporate temporal landmarking (e.g., to indicate in the timeline dates of certain watershed events) in a subsequent design history system (Carroll, Rosson, Cohill and Schorger, 1995).

A variety of observations bear out and elaborate aspects of the Browsing History Claim. The team members we studied felt that Raison d'Etre could help teams manage a variety of their activities. Interestingly, one of the chief roles they saw for systems like Raison d'Etre was in design education. They judged that using such a tool could "significantly" decrease the time it takes new members to attain familiarity with technical issues and social aspects (personalities, collaborative dynamics), that it could "speed the transition to productivity" as one person put it. One designer, playing the role of a new member, explored a technical issue and discovered a somewhat negative comment about the approach to that issue advocated by another member. He commented that if he were in fact new to the project, he "Would want to go and talk to him about that as soon as possible."

The designers felt that Raison d'Etre could enhance communication between management and other members of the team. We observed clear tendencies for non-manager team members to explore what their managers had to say, particularly about the project vision, and for managers to see what the people reporting to them had to say, often checking what their frustrations were. Most team members agreed that these were things people would find out by directly asking, but it seemed clear that this did not happen in every case. "I never knew he thought that" (a response to a clip from one of the managers) and "That may have been more of a problem than I thought" (a response by one of managers to a clip from a designer reporting to him) were examples.

The designers also agreed that the system could help maintain focus and group vision in a distributed team. They commented that Raison d'Etre might help "to make sure people understood what the project direction was," that is, to help keep a team focused on common goals, and that the system would be useful in "keeping track of issues that were outstanding." They particularly emphasized the potential utility of such a system for supporting reflection within the context of design work: "There are times when you want to go back and remind yourself what was said and done. Seeing people talking about it themselves adds an extra dimension, a feel for the process leading up to the decision.

Because scenarios are rich descriptions, they may be better at evoking images, reactions, and new lines of thought in designers than function-level requirements. We have found it very natural to use scenarios generatively. Even a relatively small set of such scenarios can provide lots of direction in a design project (e.g., Carroll and Rosson, 1990). Just a single scenario is an obvious and immediate design resource: It highlights the goals of people in such a situation, some of the things a person might do, aspects of the activity that are successful and erroneous, what interpretation people make about what happens to them.

17.9 Scenarios as a Fulcrum for the System Development Lifecycle

The Raison d'Etre system was an exploratory design project. Our main challenges were to specify our own vision (i.e., regarding the role of project history as a design resource), to develop it in conjunction with an understanding of our users' needs and concerns, and to cooperate effectively and congenially with our users. Our use of scenarios helped us make concrete progress in envisioning and developing our design, while postponing commitment to particular approach or implementation. It helped us to balance reflection and action in our design work, to recognize and manage design tradeoffs, to manage diverse and interacting consequences. And throughout it kept us focused on the use of the system.

The possibility is now being considered that scenarios can serve as integrative working design repre-sent-ations for managing the full range of activities that constitute the system development lifecycle (Carroll, 1995). For example, one might develop training, documentation and testing scenarios relatively early in the development process, and then referring to them continuingly throughout the process: to analyze requirements, to develop specifications, to design and implement object-oriented software models.

Requirements Analysis: People using current technology can be directly observed to build a scenario description of the state-of-the-art and to ground a scenario analysis of what subsequent technology might be appropriate: the requirements scenarios embody the needs apparent in current work practice. A heuristic variant of this approach is to interview users about their practices or to stage a simulated work situation. A supplemental approach is to hypothesize scenario descriptions; this is less responsive to users' immediate needs but may facilitate discovering user needs that are not obvious in actual situations, or even apparent to users. Many proposals have been made for managing the discovery and refinement of requirements through a variety of scenario representations (e.g., Carroll and Rosson, 1990; Holbrook, 1990; Hooper and Hsia, 1982; Kuutii and Arvonen, 1992; Malhotra et al., 1980; Nardi, 1993; Wexelblat, 1987). For example, Johnson et al. (1995) gathered requirements for a medical workstation by visiting their users' workplace, observing what was done and how it was done, even trying themselves to carry out the domain activities. The designers and the users explicitly negotiated the scenarios and descriptions of the domain.

User-designer Communication: The intended users of a system can contribute scenarios illustrating design issues that are important to them, specific problems or strengths in the current technology, or the kinds of situations they think they would like to experience or avoid. The system designers and developers can also contribute scenarios to such a discussion, since the users can speak this language. Users and designers together evaluate possibilities for usability and functionality. A heuristic variant is to include user representatives. Scenarios are couched in the "lingua franca" of end-user action and experience, and therefore they can be a meeting ground for communication and collaboration between developers and users. Ehn and Kyng (1991) illustrate this property of scenarios in their discussion of the cooperative use of mock-ups (see also Muller, 1991). Kyng (1995) describes how communication between users and designers can be focused through design workshops in which designers and users jointly explore usage scenarios with a mock-up of the system being designed. Erickson (1995) notes that stories make it easy to involve people. In their case study, Johnson et al. (1995) stress the point that their early joint work with the users to develop overview scenarios and scenarios for particular tasks established a working relationship that helped throughout the development process. Muller et al. (1995) emphasize how "low-tech" scenario exercises with physical objects like cards can help stakeholders "problem-atize," that is, to transform their assumptions into open questions, and thereby better articulate their concerns and ideas.

Design Rationale: Scenarios can be a unit of analysis for developing a design rationale. The rationale would explain the design with respect to particular scenarios of user interaction. Alternative scenarios can be competitively analyzed to force out new issues and new scenarios. Because such a rationale focuses on particular scenarios, it can be a resource for guiding other lifecycle activities with respect to those scenarios. Scenarios can be evaluated by users or analyzed by designers to bring to light further issues and perhaps further scenarios. For example, the users and designers might contrast a query scenario with the browsing scenario to clarify their assumptions about envisioned use of the system. These discussions would comprise part of design rationale for the video information system by presenting the capabilities of the system in terms of what users can do with them, and in that sense justifying and explaining why the capabilities are what they are (Carey et al., 1991; Carroll and Rosson, 1991; 1992). MacLean and McKerlie (1995) used scenarios as means to generate and identify specific issues and tradeoffs in a design. On the one hand, they develop and analyze scenarios to identify new design options or criteria with which to evaluate options. On the other hand, they extract the issues, options and criteria from particular scenarios to construct a generalized view of the design

Envisionment: Empirical studies of system design have frequently noted the spontaneous and informal use of scenarios by system developers (Carroll et al., 1979; Guindon, 1990; Rosson et al., 1988). Scenarios can be a medium for working out what a system being designed should look like and do. The scenarios can be detailed to the point of assigning specific user interface presentations and protocols for user actions. Such scenarios can be embodied in graphical mock-ups such as storyboards or video-based simulations; they can themselves be early prototypes for the actual system (Nielsen, 1987; Vertelney, 1989). The open-endedness, incompleteness, or roughness of scenarios makes them especially suitable for design envisionment. Erickson (1995) notes that scenarios often encourage creative thinking by leaving some details out. Nielsen (1995) describes his experience working with a group brainstorming electronic presence applications in which a large set of micro-scenarios were generated. Each scenario was very briefly sketched, just enough to hold its place relative to the other scenario-ideas. At a later stage, the group selected a smaller set of scenarios to be envisioned in detail. Kyng (1995) makes the point that by couching the requirements, the design rationale, and the envisionment all as scenarios one coordinates design work to avoid developing technical solutions to irrelevant problems.

Software Design: A set of user scenarios can be analyzed to identify the central problem domain objects that would be required to implement those scenarios. These scenarios can then be developed with respect to articulating the state, behavior and functional interactions of the design objects. Further scenarios can be "run" against such a problem domain model to test and refine the design. Envisioning concrete situations in the problem domain guides the identification of the central computational objects — most clearly in responsibility-driven (Wirfs-Brock et al., 1990) and use-case driven (Jacobson et al., 1992) approaches to object-oriented analysis and design, though these approaches have now been assimilated into most object-oriented software engineering methods.

Implementation: The problem domain objects identified and defined in software design can be implemented and run as scenarios. Developing the implementation of one scenario at a time can help to keep developers focused on the goal of supporting that specific user activity while at the same time producing code that is more generally useful. In this way, scenario-based analysis directly supports the implementation of the application functionality. Rosson and Carroll (1993, 1995) descri-bed an environment that supports a highly interleaved process of scenario-based software design and rapid prototyping implementation.

Documentation and Training: There is a gap between the system as an artifact presented to users, and the tasks that users want to accomplish using it. This gap is bridged by documentation and training structured into scenarios of interaction that are meaningful to the users. People better understand and can make better use of documentation and training if it is presented in the context of the typical and critical tasks they actually want to accomplish (e.g., Carroll, 1990). In the current state of practice a set of user interaction scenarios is developed for designing user training and documentation. Karat (1995) described a system development project in which early envisionment and specification scenarios were directly used in the design of their documentation and training material. Thus, the same scenario-design effort was leveraged across several system development activities.

Evaluation: A system must be evaluated against specific the user tasks it is intended to support. Hence it is important to have identified an appropriate set of such tasks for the evaluation of the functionality, usefulness, and usability of systems (e.g., Mack et al., 1983; Nielsen, 1990; Roberts and Moran, 1985). Of course, it is useful to know what these tasks are throughout the development process. Nielsen (1995) described scenario-based formative evaluation of systems in which screen designs were presented to prospective users who were then asked to explain what they thought they could do and with what effects from that screen. Muller et al. (1995) and Kyng (1995) describe similar early-stage evaluation through mock-ups of systems. Karat (1995) describes how his team discovered that speech navigation would be of limited use without general speech input capability: working through the implications of this evaluation scenario early in the project completely changed its direction. Later, the team conducted workshops with potential customers in which current work practices were queried and discussed, and then future possibilities (envisioned in brief video clips) were presented and discussed. This gave Karat's team detailed information on how the customers perceived speech recognition, what they thought about alternative microphone arrangements, processing delays, error rates, and error correction and enrollment procedures.

Abstraction: It is often possible to generalize the lessons learned in the design of a given system to design work within a class of domains. Conversely, it is important to develop and evaluate candidate generalizations across a variety of user task domains in order to understand the boundary conditions for a given generalization. Thus, it is important to develop techniques for describing similarities and categorizations among scenarios. Design is more than a work process and an application context. It is a context for inquiry; one learns and one must learn in order to do design work. It is an important though difficult task to try to make what is learned explicit so that others can share in what was learned. One way of doing this is to generalize scenarios. For example, in a "search" scenario, a person is browsing data with a fairly specific objective in mind (Brooks, 1991; Carroll and Rosson, 1992). Making the generalization of a search type of scenario creates the possibility of mapping whatever might have been learned in a particular case to issues that may arise in subsequent projects. Several approaches to theory-building in human-computer interaction take scenarios as the basis for their empirical taxonomy of phenomena (Carroll et al., 1992; Young and Barnard, 1987, 1991). Kuuttii characterizes scenarios as an abstract vocabulary that allows us to speak about activity, the use of computers within work processes, while still preserving situational complexity — thus avoiding one of the typical pitfalls of abstractions. Carey and Rusli (1995) extracted underlying scenarios from sets of particular scenarios to reduce actual evaluation data, in their case scenario descriptions of particular usage situations, to "composite scenarios." Their vision is that a library of such composites could serve as a summary of an evaluation and as a resource to guide further design work. Nielsen (1995) summarized patterns in data logs for an electronic door application as scenario stereotypes.

Team Building: Developing and sharing a set of touchstone stories is an important cohesive element in any social system. Design teams tend to do this and some of the stories they share are the scenarios that motivated and directed their design work. Gathering, dis-cussing and sharing these stories as a group can be an effective means to team building. Design also is a social process; many projects can only succeed if a viable social system is created in which a variety of skills, and an even greater variety of personalities, can achieve a state of mutual respect and commitment (Karat and Bennett, 1991). Jointly creating a set of touchstone "stories" is a powerful factor in this. Some of the stories pertain to how the design project originated, oriented itself, progressed, and finally prevailed, other stories pertain to what the design project is all about or how to work around the shortcomings of current situations. Orr (1986) discussed how technicians tell each other stories about usage episodes as a means of mutual learning. Carroll et al. (1994) described the role that shared stories played in maintaining the continuity of two long-term design projects. Erickson (1995) emphasizes that stories support communication; his discussion focuses on facilitating the communication among various groups within the organization developing a system, particularly in the early stages of exploration and refinement, and at the crucial junction of transition or transfer from an advance technology group to a development group. Karat (1995) recalls that at the earliest stage of the speech recognition system design, generating and discussing scenarios helped the team decide what it was that they wanted to do, to articulate a shared understanding of what they were working towards: they imagined the consequences of performing everyday tasks without a keyboard or pointing device.

In the 1950s, C. Wright Mills (1959) complained that social science was failing in its obligation to provide effective guidance for the development of social policies, practices and institutions. His book, The Sociological Imagination, criticized the penchant of social scientists for "grand theory": precise, formal, intellectually awesome, but also low-level, limited in scope, and impossible to apply. Mills was understandably concerned that a grand science, which failed nonetheless to guide practical decision-making, might on balance be worse than no science at all. He called for a new perspective, for the development of "middle-level abstractions" that would be better grounded in social reality and better suited to application in actual social contexts. He suggested that this pursuit be called "social studies" to more clearly differentiate it's concrete aspirations from those of its more ambitious and prideful complement.

System development is now in need of a guiding middle-level abstraction, a concept less formal and less grand than specification, but a concept that can be broadly and effectively applied. Scenarios are not formal; they are not scientific in any fancy sense. We know that they can be used because they already do play many roles in the system lifecycle. Perhaps the time has come to consider how a more integrative scenario perspective for system development can be constructed. Design methods must live on a razor's edge between creative intuition and grounded analysis. Perhaps scenarios can help balance the need for flexibility and informality with the need to progress systematically toward creating effective and usable computer systems and applications.

17.10 Acknowledgment

This paper is adapted from the Introduction to the book Scenario-Based Design: Envisioning Work and Technology in System Development, cited below as Carroll (1995), and from an early draft chapter of a book in progress. I am grateful to Jonas Löwgren for comments on an earlier version.

17.11 References

Allport, F. H. (1920). The influence of the group upon association and thought. *Journal of Experimental Psychology, 3*, 159-182.

Asch, S. E. (1958). Effects of group pressure upon the modification and distortion of judgments. In E. E. Maccoby, T. M. Newcomb, and E. L. Hartley (Eds.), *Readings in Social Psychology* (3rd edition). New York: Holt, Rinehart and Winston, pages 174-183.

Brooks, R. (1991). Comparative task analysis: An alternative direction for human-computer interaction science. In J. M. Carroll (Ed.), *Designing interaction: Psychology at The Human-Computer Interface.* New York: Cambridge University Press, pages 50-59.

Carey, T., McKerlie, D., Bubie, W. and Wilson, J. (1991). Communicating human factors expertise through design rationales and scenarios. In D. Diaper and N. Hammond (Eds.), *People and Computers VI.* Cambridge: Cambridge University Press, pages 117-130.

Carey, T. and Rusli, M. (1995). Usage representations for reuse of design insights: A case study of access to on-line books. In J. M. Carroll (Ed.), *Scenario-Based Design: Envisioning Work and Technology in System Development.* New York: John Wiley & Sons, pages 165-182.

Carroll, J. M. (1990*). The Nurnberg Funnel: Designing Minimalist Instruction for Practical Computer skills.* Cambridge, MA: M. I. T. Press.

Carroll, J. M. (1991). History and hysteresis in theories and frameworks for HCI. In Diaper, D. and Hammond, N.V. (Eds.), *People and Computers VI.* Cambridge: Cambridge University Press.

Carroll, J. M. (1992). Making history by telling stories. In *Papers from the ACM CHI'92 Research Symposium.* (May 1-2, Monterey). Unpaged.

Carroll, J. M. (1994a). Making use a design representation. *Communications of the ACM*, 37/12, 29-35.

Carroll, J. M. (1994b). Designing scenarios for human action. *Performance Improvement Quarterly, 7/3*, 64-75.

Carroll, J. M. (ed.) (1995) *Scenario-Based Design: Envisioning Work and Technology in Systems Development*, New York, NY: John Wiley & Sons.

Carroll, J. M., Alpert, S. R.., Karat, J., Van Deusen, M. S.., and Rosson, M. B. (1994a) Raison d'Etre: Embodying design history and rationale in hypermedia folklore — An experiment in reflective design practice. *Library HI TECH, 48(12),* 59-70, 81.

Carroll, J. M., Alpert, S. R.., Karat, J., Van Deusen, M. S.., and Rosson, M. B.. (1994b) Raison d'Etre: Capturing design history and rationale in multimedia narratives. *Proceedings of the ACM CHI'94 Conference.*(Boston, April 24-28). New York: ACM Press, pages 192-197, 478.

Carroll, J. M., Kellogg, W. A., and Rosson, M. B. (1991). The task-artifact cycle. In J.M. Carroll (Ed.), *Designing Interaction: Psychology at the Human-ComputerInterface.* New York: Cambridge University Press, pages 74-102.

Carroll, J. M. and Mazur, S. A. (1986). LisaLearning. *IEEE Computer*, 19/11, 35-49.

Carroll, J. M. and Rosson, M. B. (1990). Human-computer interaction scenarios as a design representation. In *Proceedings of the 23rd Annual Hawaii International Conference on Systems Sciences.* (Kailua-Kona, HI, January 2-5, 1990). Los Alamitos, CA: IEEE Computer society Press, pages 555-561.

Carroll, J. M. and Rosson, M. B. (1991). Deliberated evolution: Stalking the View Matcher in design space. *Human-Computer Interaction*, 6, 281-318.

Carroll, J. M. and Rosson, M. B. (1992). Getting around the task-artifact cycle: How to make claims and design by scenario. *ACM Transactions on Information Systems, 10*, 181-212.

Carroll, J. M., Rosson, M. B., Cohill, A. M., and Schorger, J. (1995). Building a history of the Blacksburg Electronic Village. *Proceedings of the ACM Symposium on Designing Interactive Systems* (August 23-25, Ann Arbor, Michigan). New York: ACM Press, 1-6.

Carroll, J. M., Singley, M.K. and Rosson, M.B. (1992). Integrating theory development with design evaluation. *Behaviour and Information Technology*, 11, 247-255.

Carroll, J. M., Thomas, J. C. and Malhotra, A. (1979). A clinical-experimental analysis of design problem solving. *Design Studies*, 1, 84-92. Reprinted in B. Curtis, (Ed.), *Human factors in software development.* Washington, D.C.: IEEE Computer Society Press, pages 243-251.

Cartwright, D. (1968). The nature of a group's cohesiveness. In D. Cartwright and A. Zander (Eds.), *Group Dynamics: Research and Theory* (3rd edition). New York: Harper and Row.

Clausen, H. (1993). Narratives as tools for the system designer. *Design Studies, 14(3),* 283-298.

Ehn, P. and Kyng, M. (1991) Cardboard computers: Mocking-it-up or Hands-on the future. In J. Greenbaum and M. Kyng, eds., *Design at Work: Cooperative Design of Computer Systems.* Hillsdale, NJ: Lawrence Erlbaum Associates, pages 169-196.

Erickson, T. (1995). Notes on design practice: Stories and prototypes as catalysts for communication. In J.M. Carroll (Ed.), *Scenario-Based design: Envisioning Work and Technology in System Development.* New York: John Wiley & Sons, pages 37-58.

Frishberg, N., Laff, M. R.., Desrosiers, M. R.., Koons, W. R. and Kelley, J. F. (1991). John Cocke: A retrospective by friends. *Proceedings of the ACM CHI'91 Conference.(*New Orleans, April 27-May 2). New York: ACM Press, pages 423-424.

Guindon, R. (1990). Designing the design process: Exploiting opportunistic thoughts. *Human-Computer Interaction*, 5, 305-344.

Holbrook, H. (1990). A scenario-based methodology for conducting requirements elicitation. *ACM SIGSOFT Software Engineering Notes, 15-1,* January, pages 95-103.

Hooper, J. W. and Hsia, P. (1982). Scenario-based prototyping for requirements identification. *ACM SIGSOFT Software Engineering Notes, 7-5,* December, pages 88-93.

Jacobson, I., Christerson, M., Jonsson, P., and Overgaard, G. (1992). *Object-Oriented Software Engineering: A Use-case Driven Approach.* Reading, MA: Addison-Wesley/ACM Books.

Johnson, P., Johnson, H. and Wilson, S. (1995). Rapid prototyping of user interfaces driven by task models. In J.M. Carroll (Ed.), *Scenario-Based Design: Envisioning Work and Technology in System Development.* New York: John Wiley & Sons, pages 209-246.

Jones, J. C. (1970). *Design Methods: Seeds of Human Futures.* New York: John Wiley & Sons.

Karat, J. (1995). Scenario use on the design of a speech recognition system. In J.M. Carroll (Ed.), *Scenario-based design: Envisioning Work and Technology in System Development.* New York: John Wiley & Sons, pages 109-133.

Karat, J. and Bennett, J. B. (1991). Using scenarios in design meetings P A case study example. In J. Karat (Ed.), *Taking Design Seriously: Practical Techniques for Human-Computer Interaction Design.* Boston: Academic Press, pages 63-94.

Karat, J., Carroll, J. M., Alpert, S. R.. and Rosson, M. B. (1995). Evaluating a multimedia history system as support for collaborative design. *INTERACT'95: Proceedings.* Lillehammer, Norway, 27-29 June.

Kuutti, K. and Arvonen, T. (1992). Identifying potential CSCW applications by means of activity theory concepts: A case example. *Proceedings of CSCW'92: Conference on Computer-Supported Cooperative Work.* (Oct 31 - Nov 4, Toronto). New York: Association for Computing Machinery, pages 233-240.

Kyng, M (1995). Creating contexts for design. In J.M. Carroll (Ed.), *Scenario-Based design: Envisioning Work and Technology in System Development.* New York: John Wiley & Sons, pages 85-107.

Latane, B. (1981). Psychology of social impact. *American Psychologist*, 36, 343-356.

Lewin, K. (1953). Studies in group decision. In D. Cartwright and A. Zander (Eds.), *Group Dynamics: Research and Theory* (1st edition). Evanston, IL: Row, Peterson.

Mack, R. L., Lewis, C. H., and Carroll, J. M. (1983). Learning to use office systems: Problems and prospects. *ACM Transactions on Office Information Systems, 1*, 254-271.

Malhotra, A., Thomas, J. C.., Carroll, J. M., and Miller, L. A. (1980). Cognitive processes in design. *International Journal of Man-Machine Studies, 12*, 119-140.

MacLean, A. and McKerlie, D. (1995). Design space analysis and use representation. In J.M. Carroll (Ed.), *Scenario-Based Design: Envisioning Work and Technology in System Development.* New York: John Wiley & Sons, pages 183-207.

Milgram, S. (1968). Some conditions of obedience and disobedience to authority. *International Journal of Psychiatry, 6*, 259-276.

Mills, C. W. (1959). *The Sociological Imagination.* New York: Oxford University Press.

Muller, M. J. (1991). PICTIVE - An exploration in participatory design. *Proceedings of ACM CHI'91: Conference on Human Factors in Computing.* (April

27 - May 2, New Orleans). New York: Association for Computing Machinery, pages 225-231.

Muller, M. J., Tudor, L. G., Wildman, D. M., White, E. A., Root, R. W., Dayton, T., Carr, R., Diekmann, B. and Dystra-Erickson, E. (1995). Bifocal tools for scenarios and representations in participatory activities with users. In J. M. Carroll (Ed.), *Scenario-Based design: Envisioning Work and Technology in System Development.* New York: John Wiley & Sons, pages 135-163.

Nardi, B. (1993). *A Small Matter of Programming: Perspectives on End-User Computing.* Cambridge, MA: M. I. T. Press.

Nielsen, J. (1987). Using scenarios to develop user friendly videotex systems. *Proceedings of NordDATAU '89 Joint Scandinavian Computer Conference.* (Trondheim, Norway, June 15-18), pages 133-138.

Nielsen, J. (1990). Paper versus computer implementations as mockup scenarios for heuristic evaluation. *Proceedings of INTERACT'90: IFIP TC 13 Third International Conference on Human-Computer Interaction.* (Cambridge, U.K., August 27-30). Amsterdam: North Holland, pages 315-320.

Nielsen, J. (1995). Scenarios in discount usability engineering. In J.M. Carroll (Ed.), *Scenario-Based design: Envisioning Work and Technology in System Development.* New York: John Wiley & Sons, pages 59-83.

Orr, J. E. (1986). Narratives at work. *Proceedings of CSCW'86: Conference on Computer-Supported Cooperative Work.* (Austin, TX, December 3-5, 1986). pages 62-72.

Roberts, T. L. and Moran, T. P. (1985) The evaluation of text editors: Methodology and empirical results. *Communications of the ACM*, 26, 265-283.

Rosson, M. B. and Carroll, J. M. (1993). Extending the task-artifact framework: Scenario-based design of Smalltalk applications. In H.R. Hartson and D. Hix, Eds., *Advances in Human-Computer Interaction, Volume 4.* Norwood, NJ: Ablex Publishing, pages 31-57.

Rosson, M. B. and Carroll, J. M. (1995). Narrowing the specification-implementation gap in scenario-based design. In Carroll, J. M. (Ed.), *Scenario-Based Design: Envisioning Work and Technology in System Development.* New York: John Wiley & Sons, pages 247-278.

Rosson, M. B., Maass, S. and Kellogg, W. A. (1988). The designer as user: Building requirements for design tools from design practice. *Communications of the ACM, 31*, 1288-1298.

Schein, E. H., Schneier, T., and Barker, G. H. (1961). *Coercive persuasion: A Socio-Psychological Analysis of the "brainwashing" of American Prisoners by the Chinese Communists.* New York: Norton.

Schon, D. A.. (1983). *The Reflective Practitioner: How Professionals Think in Action.* New York: Basic Books.

Vertelney, L. (1989). Using video to prototype user interfaces. *ACM SIGCHI Bulletin*, 21-2, 57-61.

Wexelblat, A. (1987, May). Report on scenario technology. *Technical Report STP-139-87.* Austin, TX: MCC.

Wirfs-Brock, R., Wilkerson, B. and Wiener, L. (1990). *Designing Object-Oriented Software.* Englewood Cliffs, NJ: Prentice-Hall.

Young, R. M. and Barnard, P. B.. (1987). The use of scenarios in human-computer interaction research; Turbocharging the tortoise of cumulative science. In *Proceedings of CHI+GI'87: Conference on Human Factors in Computing Systems and Graphics Interface.* New York: ACM Press, pages 291-296.

Young, R. M. and Barnard, P. B. (1991). Signature tasks and paradigm tasks: New wrinkles on the scenarios methodology. In D. Diaper and N. Hammond (Eds.), *People and Computers VI.* Cambridge: Cambridge University Press, pages 91-101.

Handbook of Human-Computer Interaction
Second, completely revised edition
M. Helander, T.K. Landauer, P. Prabhu (eds.)

Chapter 18

International Ergonomic HCI Standards

Ahmet Çakir
ERGONOMIC Institute
Berlin, Germany

Wolfgang Dzida
GMD
Sankt Augustin, Germany

18.1 On Standardization

18.1.1 Ergonomic Versus Technical Standards

Standardization, once aimed at making bolts and nuts in a uniform size and shape has reached its most sophisticated level with ergonomic standards, the fundamental goal of which is "fitting the task to humans". In following such an ambitious approach, it is not intended to unify the equipment needed to do the task, rather, the approach is to define principles and derive requirements for human-centered design of tools, work places, and environments. The reader of an ergonomic standard may be disappointed at the vagueness of principles and requirements, since standards are expected to be precise as is often the case with technical standards which are applicable to specified products. However, if a standardized product specification is given, there is no freedom in design. Furthermore, technical standards are subject to aging similar to the aging of their objects, since aging is the most prominent feature of technology.

The difference between both approaches, ergonomic versus technical standardization, may be demonstrated by the example of constructing a piston for a machine. Customers of today's CAD systems are inclined to accept the quality of such a system, if it assists the designer in effectively creating drawings, part libraries, tables, etc. However, creating drawings or tables is not the ultimate goal when designing a piston. The real question is for example: "What features has a piston for an engine with 100 KW power running at 6,000 r.p.m.?" A pure technical standard for CAD systems would specify the user's interaction with a system to precisely prescribe how to create drawings, how to update libraries, etc. Such a standard CAD system would freeze a certain state of technology. Moreover, the ergonomic implications of the standard would be rather conservative, since it would apply to the creation of drawings or updating part libraries, instead of designing a piston. To avoid this conservatism ergonomic standards do not constrain technology, but focus on the desired performance of a user's task and take into account the user's original goals. Accordingly, the ergonomic evaluation of a product should not be restricted to a set of tasks which the product allows to perform but what it is expected to perform considering the user's goals.

Even if the standardized technical features of the system would satisfy the ergonomic requirements, the features will become obsolete when technology changes. Consequently, the ergonomics of human-system interfaces cannot depend on the current state-of-technology.

Table 1. Three types of performance.

Meaning	Example
Behaviour of an object	The selected menu option is echoed at the display as highlighted.
Process conducted by the user	The user discriminates available and unavailable menu otions.
Success a user should achieve	A user achieved to select the intended menu option within a menu panel.

Rather, the requirements of an ergonomic standard refer to the applicable current state-of-knowledge in ergonomics, not to a state of technology. An ergonomic standard thus should be expected to survive many steps of the technological evolution. Evolution in the knowledge of ergonomics is comparatively slow.

18.1.2 A Relevance Model for Standards

This paper is aimed at helping the designer (or evaluator) read and interpret ergonomic standards. The reader will be confronted with a bulk of standards and may ask which standard should be applied when? The above mentioned distinction between technical and ergonomic standards does not suffice. Here we suggest a relevance model to guide in the selection of standards. There are four levels in the relevance model, and these are explained below.

Level 1: Basic Principles of Interaction

Some requirements pertain to any interaction between human and technical environment. Let's assign these requirements to level 1: "Basic Principles of Interaction", such as "reasonable task" and "usability" (of the means to do the task). The purpose of "level 1 standards" is to define quality requirements which are technology-independent. The principles indicate fundamentals of ergonomics as regards the design of tasks, equipment, and environment. The designer of a human-machine system usually starts developing the entire system on this abstract level, being familiar with the fact that designing the system may impact the ergonomic quality of the tasks (Carroll, 1990). Conversely, a poor task design cannot be compensated by system design - no matter how well its ergonomic quality may be. A designer who bears the entirety of system design in mind will start with standards devoted to task design and a high level specification of usability (see Parts 2 and 11 in Table 1).

Level 2: Principles of HCI

A subset of interaction between human and technical environment is the user's interaction with a computer. Principles of HCI are assigned to level 2 and should correspond with the above mentioned basic principles. In other words, level 2 principles such as "readability" (of the display) or "controllability" (of the dialogue) are derived from the basic principle "usability". The designer pursues these objectives in any usability specification of information presentation or the user's dialogue with the system, irrespective of the type of information or dialogue technique (direct manipulation, menu dialogue, etc.). The standard on information presentation (Part 12, see Table 1) and the standard on dialogue design (Part 10, see Table 1) contain principles of HCI. These principles are neutral, since they do not assume any kind of interactive computer technology.

Level 3: Standard Ergonomic Requirements of HCI

With level 1 principles in mind the designer may decide for a specific dialogue technique or equipment. Considering this choice and the task requirements, the designer selects the appropriate standard, e.g. Part 14 for menu system design (see Table 1), and attempts to interpret the applicability of specific menu requirements in terms of the current task requirements. If it turns out that none of the requirements is applicable, the designer will recognize more freedom of design, and will decide for a design solution which fits with a suitable principle of dialogue (see level 2 principles). All design decisions which meet the level 3 standards should also be in compliance with at least one of the level 2 principles. Hence, keeping in mind the principles (as well as the task requirements or user needs) the designer will be able to correctly interpret a specific standard requirement.

Level 4: Standard Technical Specifications of HCI

Most designers are used to thinking on level 4, which deals with the technical feasibility of users' requirements. Technical specifications are not considered in the international ergonomic standardization groups. Nevertheless, these specifications are important, for instance, OSF/Motif (Open Software Foundation,

1990) or SAA/CUA (IBM, 1989). Level 4 requirements do not represent standards for user interfaces but rather standard interfaces, a distinction necessary (Dzida, 1995) to indicate that standards in ergonomics always rest on consensus within an international community (e.g. ISO, International Organization for Standardization), while standard interfaces rest on definition or consensus in industry. The ISO ergonomic standards rarely contain specified technical attributes. - While the level 4 specification is the most relevant level to put forward design solutions, the higher levels are relevant during the preparation and evaluation of these solutions.

The main benefit of the suggested relevance level for standards is its implied quality model of software-ergonomics. For practical purposes the different levels may serve as a guide for design decisions, either to sanction a decision when it contradicts a higher level principle, or to recommend a solution in the light of such a principle. The designer will benefit from adhering to the principles, since for each design solution a design rationale can be provided.

18.1.3 Assigning Levels to Existing or Proposed Standards

The most elaborate HCI standard is ISO 9241 ("Ergonomic requirements for office work with visual display terminals (VDTs)"). This standard is introduced and commented in this article. Since ISO 9241 is a multi-part standard, each of its parts needs to be assigned to levels 1 to 3. Level 4 is definitely not appropriate to avoid the specification of a standard interface or a standard environment.

In practice, the contents of some of the Parts of ISO 9241 can be regarded as exceptions from this rule. For example, Part 3 ("Visual Display Requirements") is generally applied for terminals with CRTs. The ISO Working group, however, is going to create a similar standard for *flat panels* (ISO 13406), an approach which is aimed at a standard equipment. Following the tradition of ergonomic standardization the group should be asked "Why not developing a standard for visual displays in general?"

Some parts of ISO 9241 cover two levels within one standard. For instance, Part 9 ("Requirements for Non-keyboard Input Devices") defines generic rules for any kind of input device, and additional specific rules for known types of input devices like a mouse or a trackball. In contrast to this, Part 4 ("Keyboard requirements") includes specific requirements such as force displacement characteristics of keys which could be mistaken for technical requirements. However, in this case, the requirements rest on proven ergonomic knowledge and the technical design options are therefore constrained. Nevertheless, the standard may not rule out that keys without displacement shall not be used, since there is no evidence to this point.

Most "level 1 standards" applicable to the HCI domain stem from areas outside this domain. The knowledge behind them originates from other scientific areas of ergonomics. Among these standards are ISO 6385 (work system design) and ISO 10075 (mental workload). Also the standard ISO 7250 (anthropometric measurements) belongs to "level 1 standards". Any HCI standard dealing with fundamentals in ergonomics should be consistent with the already existing "level 1 standards".

18.1.4 Basic Approach of ISO 9241

The requirements of ISO 9241 are mostly defined in terms of "performance" instead of attributes. Performance has a threefold meaning (see Table 1).

Attributes of equipment are rarely implicated in the requirements of ISO 9241, because definitions in terms of attributes would establish a level 4 standard. However, there are many exceptions to this rule. For instance, the first meaning of performance (Table 1) can easily be taken as an attribute of an object (see "echoed" and "highlighted" as attributes of a menu option). Nevertheless, an ergonomic standard should generally not require attributes which apply to a specific usage of a product. For example, a standard should not require characters to have a certain height; instead: "appropriate character height should be derived from readability requirements, which are formulated in terms of *visual angle*".

The "performance based" approach to ergonomic standards is often disappointing to designers, who are used to dealing with specified attributes of design. Hence, sometimes designers argue that ergonomic standards are too much like guidelines, not really standards. It can be shown, however, that all guideline-like requirements can clearly be interpreted, if, as a prerequisite, the task requirements and the user needs have been studied prior to the application of a standard. In view of these requirements the designer can be free to design, but has to prove that the attributes of design solutions comply with both the task/user requirements in a specific context of use and the standard requirement. The applicability and the interpretation of standards as well as the conformity with them almost al-

Table 2. Parts of ISO 9241, titles, status, and level of relevance (May, 1996).

Part	Title	Status	Level
1	General Introduction	IS	1
2	Guidance on task requirements	IS	1
3	Visual display requirements	IS	3 or 4
4	Keyboard requirements	DIS	3
5	Workstation layout and postural requirements	DIS	2 and 3
6	Environmental requirements	CD	2 and 3
7	Display requirements with reflections	CD	3 or 4
8	Requirements for displayed colours	DIS	3
9	Requirements for non-keyboard input devices	CD	2 and 3
10	Dialogue principles	IS	2
11	Guidance on usability	DIS	1
12	Presentation of information	CD	2 and 3
13	User guidance	CD	3
14	Menu dialogues	DIS	3
15	Command dialogues	CD	3
16	Direct manipulation dialogues	CD	3
17	Form filling dialogues	CD	3

(CD: Committee Draft, DIS: Draft International Standard, IS: Standard

ways requires the context of use (which includes the task) to be analyzed. In general, the methodology of conformance testing has been developed in line with this approach, but may vary to suit the specific subject of a standard.

The "performance based" approach may not be easily or readily understood, since it appears easier, for instance, to measure the (standard) height of a character instead of determining its readability or legibility under given circumstances. The seeming vagueness of ergonomic standards may invite the designer to utilize loopholes to avoid compliance with the requirements. This attitude, however, may be due to a misunderstanding of the ergonomic standards and their compliance testing methodology.

18.1.5 Structure of ISO 9241

The Parts of ISO 9241 can be assigned to three groups dealing with:

- *Work, organization and their role in usability specification* (Parts 2 and 11);
- *Workplace and work environment* (Parts 5 and 6);
- *Interactive equipment/tools* (see Parts 3 and 7 (on visual displays), Parts 4 and 9 (on input devices, keyboard and non-keyboard input devices), Parts 10 and 12 up to 17 (on software interfaces); Part 8 (on colour, both for visual displays and software).

Part 1 is a general introduction into the multipart standard ISO 9241 describing its scope and structure as well as the performance based approach.

Table 2 provides a list of the titles of all Parts of ISO 9241, their current status and the level of relevance to be considered in design and evaluation of work systems involving visual display terminals. The complete title of a Part of ISO 9241 reads as follows: "Ergonomic Requirements for Office Work with Visual Display Terminals (VDTs) - Part x: Title of the specific Part x" (see also list of references).

There are a number of complementary standards dealing with aspects of ergonomic design of hardware and software. A series of 8 parts is under development concerning control room design (ISO 11064), for instance, Part 2 introducing principles of control suites, Part 3 focusing on control room layout, Part 5 dealing with displays and controls. There are two software-engineering standards which include the quality concept of usability (ISO 9126 and ISO/IEC 12119). The term usability is used to refer to attributes of a product, which indicate that the software can be used easily. This concept of usability can be taken as complementary to the ergonomic definition of usability (ISO 9241-11) which essentially refers to the efficiency of user performance. Single usability attributes of the product can be tested at the software developer's workbench (ISO 9126) as far as they are valid indicators. If the performance approach to usability testing is applied, single attributes may be less relevant, but the context of use has to be considered.

18.2 The Contents of ISO 9241

18.2.1 Work, Organization and Required Usability

To design a computer system and its environment it is indispensable to understand the users' tasks. Moreover, when introducing a system at a workplace it evidently affects the performance of tasks, the organization of work and the environment. A human-centered approach of system design will therefore consider the entirety of a work system including work, organization, user needs and interdependencies (see ISO 6385). The quality of technical equipment is always relative. So is usability, a concept, devoted to the ergonomic quality of the equipment or tools within a work system. Relative to what? To the stated or implied requirements of these work system components.

Part 2: Guidance on Task Requirements

Part 2 aims at applying ergonomic principles to the design of tasks for users of VDT-based systems. When analyzing the users' work system it should be recognized that a high level goal such as "reasonability" of tasks is fulfilled. This is not the case if, for instance, the task requires undue repetitions which can lead to monotony, satiation, etc. Part 2 describes well-designed tasks, the characteristics of which should inspire the systems analyst to define the objectives of system design and derive user requirements. The standard admits that there is no single best way of designing tasks and recommends to compare and evaluate alternative task designs.

User participation is suggested as a way to obtain valid data for analysis and design. General recommendations are given for planning and implementing a system, such as discussing the potential changes of functional operations, personnel planning and training programs. The standard recommends users to be encouraged to identify existing usability problems. Furthermore, a communication channel should be implemented to help users address such problems and tell their dissatisfaction.

Part 11: Guidance on Usability

The concept of usability is defined in terms of effectiveness, efficiency and satisfaction. All these quality factors need to be satisfied for users working with a product. A product should enable the user to achieve accurate and complete results (effectiveness); the resources a user expends in relation to accuracy and completeness indicate a product's efficiency; and the product should be satisfying in use.

Part 11 emphasizes that usability depends on the context of use of a product. Hence, product design shall consider context of use and evaluate usability relative to the context requirements. The standard guides the systems analyst in describing the context of use. The evaluator is informed about performance and satisfaction measures which serve as indicators of usability, so as to transpose task and user requirements into operational measures (usability criteria). A verifiable description of the context of use and related criteria warrants that results of the evaluation (including the tests for conformity with standards) can be reproduced. This is an important methodological requirement.

18.2.2 Hardware: Displays and Input Devices

The visual display and input device (keyboard or non-keyboard input) establish the "hardware". Several ergonomic standards are devoted to this (Parts 3, 4, 7, 8, and 9). In general, the standards provide requirements in terms of design principles. However, some of the standards define requirements for single hardware attributes, Compliance with the standards can therefore be achieved by measures of performance which indicate that given attributes of the hardware meet the principles of usability. Some of the principles are unique in hardware design, for instance, the compatibility with user's biomechanical functioning; many principles developed in software-ergonomics, however, can also be applied in hardware design, especially when the software affects the usability of hardware, e.g. displayed colours.

Part 3: Visual Display Requirements

The intention of Part 3 is to specify requirements for electronic displays independent of the specific technology of the device. This part was planned to be applicable to both monochrome and multi-colour screens, but ultimately holds only for the first type of display. Conformity with this standard is tested for the legibility and readability of alphanumeric symbols (characters of the Latin alphabet and numerals). Graphics is not covered. It is not clear, however, whether the provisions of the standards apply to the entire repertoire of symbols of ISO/IEC 6967 or only to the limited set of 26 OCR-B characters.

The initial goal of this part, was to formulate performance requirements and specify methods for conformance testing. However, this approach was partly abandoned by the standards development committee during years of discussion. The standard thus contains requirements for single attributes, and the informative annex recommends a user performance test (i.e. test of legibility, readability, and comfort) which can be applied until a more suitable test method is agreed upon. Notably, the initial goal of applying this test method was to regard any design feature as in compliance with the standard as long as the performance requirements are met. This approach is considered the best, since it allows freedom of technical development - despite the standards.

The design requirements rest on the user's minimum viewing distance of 400mm which is well below the average, conveniently selected for office work (approximately 600mm), a minimum luminance of 35 cd/m^2 which is also well below the average for most (monochrome) displays of 100 cd/m^2. In addition, a minimum contrast ratio of 3:1 between characters and their background is required. The required matrix for characters, 7x9 as a minimum for text and 4x5 for superscripts, etc., is also a real minimum requirement. The display shall be flicker-free for 90% of the intended user population, and "without" jitter within the given limits.

Despite the fact that most requirements are at the "minimum" level of quality, it is not easy to meet all of them. Demonstrating conformity of single attributes with the standard requirements is even more difficult, since the measurement of all required attributes turns out to be problematic due to the required professional skills of well-equipped test agencies.

Part 4: Keyboard Requirements

This part deals with the ergonomic aspects of alphanumeric keyboard design. Some aspects that could be considered "ergonomic" (e.g. layout) are also specified in ISO 9995. However, classifying aspects as "ergonomic" or "technical" is seemingly not easy.

Part 4 contains design specifications, most of which are applicable to standard (linear) keyboard layouts. The method of compliance testing applies to any new design feature deviating from the keyboard taken as "standard". Although this standard does not deal with keyboard features alternative to the "standard", its intent is to introduce a method to test any alternative keyboard for compliance with the standard. The test criterion is defined as the performance the keyboard shall meet, given its designated purpose, i.e., the user shall be able to achieve a satisfactory level of keying performance on a given task, and to maintain a satisfactory level of comfort. Furthermore, the use of the keyboard should optimize biomechanical and physiological functioning. Comfort, while not directly measurable, is inferred from subjective ratings of comfort. Biomechanical assessment can be measured from muscle load evaluations. However, no requirements have been formulated to specify the extent of biomechanical/physiological load considered acceptable.

Many provisions in the standard are new in standardization, though well-known in keyboard ergonomics, such as keying feedback, key displacement and force. An utterly new requirement is that legibility of the key legends should be provided from the user's reference working posture(s) as defined in Part 5 of ISO 9241. In other words, a general purpose keyboard should have legends legible in both positions, seated and standing. Part 4 does not apply to products utilized for non-stationary use, e.g. keyboards of laptops.

Part 7: Display Requirements with Reflections

Part 7 deals with issues of glare and reflections from the surface of display screens. Methods of measurement and surface treatment are included. The subject of this part should have been incorporated in Part 3. The separation as a specific standard is due to the fact that there is rarely any visual display without reflection. For fulfilling visual display requirements in their entirety it is therefore necessary to comply with both parts (3 and 7) of ISO 9241.

Conformity with Part 7 is tested for legibility and comfort in use. Specifically, the requirements concerning the luminance ratio of the image shall be met; also, the ratio of the luminances between reflected images and the screen background shall be limited without the reflection control method impairing the image quality to an extent that the display cannot meet the requirements of other parts of ISO 9241. For example, if a filter is used to diminish reflections the legibility should not be affected.

Compliance with Part 7 can be qualified in terms of three classes. Class I indicates displays suitable for general office use, Class II displays are suitable for most, but not all office environments, and Class III displays are suitable only under specially controlled luminous environments.

The standard recommends an alternative test method which is not mandatory but optional (see informative annex of Part 7). However, although different methods are considered, this does not mean that any display can be tested, since the scope of the standard limits the applicability of the methods to direct-view electronic displays for office tasks, such as data entry, text processing, and interactive inquiry. Graphics applications and computer aided design are not included. Also excluded are LCD displays, ferroelectric and electrochromic displays, since the test methods of this standard are not suitable for these technologies. Rather, such technologies are dealt with in ISO 13406 (flat panel displays).

Part 8: Requirements for Displayed Colours

The requirements for monochrome displays in Part 3 are supplemented by Part 8 dealing with multi-colour displays. In contrast to other hardware-related parts of ISO 9241, this part is also applicable to software, since displaying colours on electronic screens is controlled by software. Hence, principles of information presentation (Part 12), such as detectability, identifiability and discriminability are also applicable to the design of coloured images. If colours are used for aesthetic purposes, the users' visual performance (e.g. reading information) should not be reduced. Generally, colours should not cause unintended visual effects that reduce visual performance. On the other hand, physical characteristics (like size) of images should not reduce the ability to identify and discriminate their colours.

According to the principles of information presentation, test criteria for compliance testing can be determined. However, these criteria are not as clearly defined as in other hardware-related parts of ISO 9241, and this is typical to all software-related parts. The test method does not contain a provision for measuring comfort. The test of both visual performance objectives and comfort are clear indications of usability (see Part 11) which, however, may raise incompatibilities when utilizing colours as means for displaying information.

The design requirements and recommendations of Part 8 contain provisions for a "default colour set" applying to the case that an application requires the user to discriminate or identify colours. Further requirements are addressing colour uniformity and misconvergence, object sizes and character heights of coloured symbols, and numbers of colours applied within a certain application.

The presently existing Draft of Part 8 states that the specifications of this standard hold for users with normal colour vision. Insofar Part 8 is in contradiction to a general ergonomic rule which requires that colour design be acceptable for people with colour vision deficiencies. The present draft does not address the needs of 8% of the male work population.

Part 9: Requirements for Non-Keyboard Input Devices

This part deals with ergonomic requirements for input devices, excluding keyboards, which may be used in conjunction with a visual display terminal. The specific problem considered in this standard is the fact that an alternative to a certain input device could be very different. For example., a graphic tablet could replace a mouse or vice versa. In addition, the abilities of a specific device (hardware) can be enhanced by software to perform tasks for which the hardware would not be considered adequate. Thus, the performance oriented approach taken to test devices for conformity with Part 9 requires the standard to be flexible enough for both establishing provisions for existing devices and allowing freedom of design for technologies to come.

Part 9 provides "guiding principles" for the design of input devices (different from keyboards). Principles are derived from the general concept of usability (see Part 11), such as suitability for the task and the work environment, controllability as regards device access, consistency, and compatibility with user's biomechanical functioning. Following the guiding principles, general requirements are formulated for all input devices within the scope of the standard, e.g. anchoring fingers or the hand, resolution (precision) of the device, positioning and repositioning within the workspace, ambidexterity, grasp stability of the grip surfaces, and so forth. Specific input device requirements are introduced for different input devices like mice, pucks, tablets, lightpen, etc.

To demonstrate compliance with Part 9, a device can meet either all mandatory requirements or pass the "performance test" which is based on generic tasks, so called task primitives, e.g. dragging, pointing or tracing. The performance test procedure should take account of the task, thereby interpreting the standard requirements in view of the task and then judging whether an input device complies with the requirements. In addition, compatibility with biomechanical functioning has to be assessed as well as the achievement of a satisfactory level of user comfort.

18.2.3 Workplace and Work Environment

The use of VDTs can be affected by context factors, not pertaining to "hardware", or to "software". Two standards (Parts 5 and 6) are devoted to the design of both the VDT workplace and its environment. This context should fit in well with traditional ergonomic principles of design, in order to promote the usability of VDT use. In practice, however, some of these principles may contradict each other so that the designer has to optimize the interaction between users and environmental factors. The standards guide the designer in finding a balance among trade-offs.

Part 5: Workstation Layout and Postural Requirements

This part deals with ergonomic requirements for VDT workplaces to allow the user to adopt a comfortable and efficient posture. The standard considers seated, standing, and seat-stand postures. The standard does not specify technical requirements for workplace equipment and workstation layout. Instead, principles of design are defined, such as versatility-flexibility, fit, postural change, user information, and maintainability-adaptability. Adhering to these principles, the designed workstations will enable a variety of people to perform a range of tasks with efficiency and comfort. Of course, the workstation design should be appropriate for the range of tasks to be performed at the workstation. Additionally, user characteristics, such as keyboard skills, anthropometric variation and user preferences should be considered. When designing furniture and equipment the fit between a range of task requirements and the needs of a variety of users should be considered. The concept of fit can be specified in terms of the potential to which chairs, desks, footrests, screens, input devices, etc. can accommodate to an individual user's needs. Particular fit is required for users with special needs, such as disabled persons. Fit may also be accomplished by furniture built for specified usage, or be provided in a range of sizes and forms or by adjustability. The workplace organization, the task and the furniture should encourage postural changes, because static muscular load leads to fatigue and discomfort, and may induce chronic musculoskeletal strain. It may be necessary to train users in the use of ergonomic features, such as adjusting the chair and finding a satisfactory viewing distance. Requirements for task performance shall also consider maintainability, accessibility, as well as the ability of the workplace to be adapted to changing requirements.

Conformity with Part 5 can be achieved for an intended user population. It is thus possible to restrict the target population for which the technical product is designed.

Part 6: Environmental Requirements

When designing for usability it should be taken into account that the use of a VDT can be affected by the work environment. Part 6 is applied to prevent environmental sources of stress and discomfort. In particular, environmental factors like noise, lighting, mechanical vibrations, electrical and magnetic fields as well as static electricity are considered. However, Part 6 does not specify the technical characteristics of the equipment needed to provide that environment.

Optimizing the interaction between users and environments often requires a balancing of trade-offs. For this purpose, Part 6 formulates principles to be satisfied. Basic aspects of each environmental factor are addressed, so as to provide guidance for finding a balanced solution under given circumstances. For example, a method is recommended how to control the acoustic factors for a given task and a given environment. A special annex to the standard is devoted to design of lighting and office layout. For the final version of the standard it is intended to add a technical report concerning the application of the standard in general and the consideration of ergonomic factors in the architectural design as well.

18.2.4 Software: Principles And Dialogue Techniques

The user's conceptual model of the software user interface can be structured using three aspects: the presentation of information, the dialogue and the tool. The latter aspect is highly dependent of the application and is therefore beyond the scope of standardization. Information presentation and dialogue, can be standardized (see Parts 10 and 12), since there are ergonomic design principles for both aspects which are valid across applications. The principles are formulated in terms of requirements (or recommendations), taking into account a variety of dialogue techniques (see Parts 13 -17). The standards hold for dialogues which may be generated by character-based or bit-mapped displays (often referred to as Graphical User Inferfaces, or GUIs).

Part 10: Dialogue Principles

Seven principles have been identified to form the concept of dialogue (e.g. controllability, self-descriptiveness, error tolerance; for the empirical basis see Dzida et al., 1978). For each of the principles Part 10 provides typical applications. These applications may guide the designer or evaluator to develop a common understanding of the high-level design objectives. Moreover, a common terminology can be established within the HCI community.

In contrast to the static features of information presentation (see Part 12) the dialogue is characterized by dynamic features of information exchange between user and system, such as echoing or prompting a user input, explanatory feedback to the user, interruptions of the flow of interaction, and feedback for help or error correction. The dialogue is conceptualized as the preparation, accomplishment, and completion of a user's task with the aid of the user interface. Hence, in designing the sequential or concurrent performance of a task, steps of dialogue mostly refer to typical work flow requirements, for instance, support for performing recurrent tasks, information about changes in the system status, guiding information on how to continue the dialogue, and constructive help or error messages.

The dialogue recommendations are formulated in abstract terms, so that they apply irrespective of any dialogue technique. Example: "The cursor should be where the input is wanted." It is up to the designer of a command dialogue (see Part 15) or of a form filling dialogue (Part 17) to interpret the recommendation in view of the specific dialogue technique currently under study. Part 10 includes examples to facilitate the interpretation of the recommendations.

Part 12: Presentation of Information

This Part includes principles of design similar to Part 10 for the visual presentation of information. Auditory presentation is not addressed. Principles such as discriminability, detectability and conciseness apply to both the arrangement of information on the display and the usage of coding techniques,. They improve the user's ability to find and comprehend visual information as well as increase speed and accuracy of information input. Most of the presentation principles have a long tradition in display design, whereas the dialogue principles (Part 10) have their origin in the design of interactive computers. Similar to Part 10, the principles and their applications are defined to fit any dialogue technique. The principles thus serve as high-level design objectives, which are primarily based on the psychology of human visual perception and human cognition.

Areas of the display like windows, input/output fields, or control areas are standardized as regards their appearance, location or relative position. Thereby the arrangement of information is determined in terms of groups, lists, tables, fields. Also the semantic aspects of alphanumeric coding, graphical coding and other coding techniques are addressed.

Part 13: User Guidance

Although user guidance cannot be regarded as a special kind of dialogue technique, this design issue was recognized as important to develop a separate part within the series of ISO 9241. Whatever dialogue technique a user may apply, supporting information provided by prompts or feedback as well as assistance for recovering from errors will always be required enabling the user to continue the dialogue. Part 13 introduces two concepts of dealing with errors, error prevention and error management. Although error prevention is always appropriate, the user's effort to undertake remedial actions needs specific system support, for example as undo function, history function. In addition, the conditions for automatic error correction are described. Requirements also address the design of on-line help, which may be induced by the user or the system. The standard provides criteria to guide the design of system-initiated versus user-initiated help.

Although Part 13 is relevant for designing products, the standard will even be more important for redesign and improvement of products, to enhance usability within the appropriate context of use.

Part 14: Menu Dialogues

The menu standard is the most voluminous of the standards. It was tested several times to illustrate the type of problems usability designers may encounter when applying ergonomic standards. It turned out that designers are generally too much focused on the attributes of a user-interface, whereas the standards are guideline-like. These results may saying us that designers should apply a standard in view of the product's context of use, which provides adequate information about the applicability of standard requirements and the conformity of design solutions (see section 3.1).

Part 14 roughly structures the design of a menu system into requirements of information presentation and dialogue. Presentation features are to facilitate the user's identification of an intended option, the quick recognition or discrimination of options within a menu, etc. Dialogue features should help users learn the menu structure and navigate within the structure to facilitate the access to submenus or menu options. Having in mind the type of design problem, presentation or dialogue, the designer can apply this heuristic and will rapidly find corresponding requirements. For example, the structuring of a menu system into levels, the grouping of menu options, the placement of options, and the option typography are primarily presentation problems. However, the design of navigational cues (e.g. menu titles, menu maps, quick node access, upward level movement within a hierarchical structure) as well as the design of option selection and execution are dialogue supportive. In addition to information presentation and dialogue the design of input is concerned, for instance, input for option selection and execution, guiding the input by option designators on a keyboard (key letter or number designators), the use of function keys, and the input into pointing areas on touch screens. Even the presentation and input of menu options by voice is addressed, in order to meet special user needs or unique task requirements.

Designing a menu system will usually require more information than Part 14 provides. The designer may, for instance, want to apply direct manipulation techniques and should then consult Part 16.

Part 15: Command Dialogues

A command dialogue is always initiated by the user who enters command phrases into the computer to obtain access to computer functions. To distinguish commands from other kinds of input, the nature of command representation should be considered as well as the user's memory requirements. The nature of input is language-like, and the user usually needs to recall the command name rather than recognizing it. Hence, pictorial icons are excluded from the standard, because recognition is required; also, "natural" language dialogue is omitted, since commands are elements of an artificial language.

The appropriateness of a command dialogue is judged according to a list of criteria, such as the user's typing skills, the level of training using a command syntax, the need for rapid access to specific system functions, and so forth.

Part 15 structures the requirements in four chapters, each of which deals with presentation/representation issues or the dialogue. Presentation covers problems like the structure and linkage of arguments in a command phrase, the placement of optional arguments, etc. The representation of commands is aimed at facilitating the user's memory recall, the learning of names, the distinction between the meaning of names, etc. The dialogue design is addressing controllability issues of command input, e.g. the reuse of commands, queuing, and command editing; also issues of output are considered, such as output control, echoing of typed commands as well as feedback or help.

The standard points to the need of designing the command dialogue in conjunction with other dialogue techniques, e.g. menu, direct manipulation (see the specific standards).

Part 16: Direct Manipulation Dialogues

This kind of dialogue technique (Shneiderman, 1982) is typically used to improve the user's controllability. It is the directness which makes the user feel in control when manipulating displayed objects in direct relationship to corresponding movements with a pointing device. Objects such as text, graphics, windows, and controls are considered separately in the standard, to address the specifics of controllability. Part 16 presents a long list of context criteria; the more of them are met, the greater the applicability of direct manipulation. The criteria can guide the designer in analyzing the user's context of use (see also Part 11), such as task and user characteristics,. A striking task characteristic suitable for direct manipulation is, for instance, the use of spatial data on a map. This information may be hard to transform into common language, but can easily be visualized. To visualize complex real world concepts the designer may want to use a metaphor. Part 16 provides very general recommendations to design a metaphor. The concept of direct manipulation, however, does not imply the use of metaphors, nor is this dialogue technique synonymous with graphical user-interfaces (GUIs), although manipulative objects may be displayed graphically.

Besides some requirements concerning presentation/representation issues of graphical and text objects, the standard is predominantly addressing dialogue characteristics of objects. For example, feedback should inform the user about the effects of a manipulation. Further dialogue features are concerning the selection of objects, such as sizing or resizing, dragging, scaling and rotating of objects. The specifics of CAD applications, however, have not been considered, so as to avoid developing a standardized application.

Part 16 also points to potential disadvantages of direct manipulation, e.g. the awkward step-by-step input which may require the design of compensatory techniques such as command macros (see Part 15). Supplementary or alternative techniques may be provided to enable the user to conduct the task more efficiently.

Part 17: Form Filling Dialogues

Form filling is a dialogue with an on-line form or with a dialogue box. The user selects entries of a form or a dialogue box, or fills-in, or modifies fields. Often, the designer has to consider the layout of paper source documents to develop a form filling display consistent with the source. However, if the layout of the paper document is ergonomically poor, it will have to be corrected. Some general requirements are provided to guide the design of the display, but these also apply to the design of paper forms. For instance, a limit of 40% overall information density is recommended for the display, a recommendation which should hold for paper forms, too, although this is not explicitly required by the standard.

Part 17 comprises requirements for the presentation/representation of information in displayed forms and for the dialogue design of entry fields, moving between fields, or controlling the dialogue. Typical presentation issues are the alignment of fields, field length, the amount of space for text entry fields, etc. The representation of information is considered by requirements concerning the data entry format, field labels, default values, etc. These requirements should be interpreted in line with the principles of Part 12. The dialogue with an on-line form mainly requires that the user should not input more information than is necessary for task performance. Hence, the system is required to visually indicate that fields are mutually exclusive or that choice entries are exclusive. If the user fails to sufficiently fill-in the form the dialogue should enable the user to easily recover from errors. For instance, it is required that the user should be allowed to go back to the initial state of the form, or that the field containing an error should be highlighted. Other dialogue requirements deal with system feedback allowing the user to control the dialogue; navigation methods should be provided to move between fields, to scroll within the form, etc. These requirements should be applied in view of the dialogue principles, Part 10.

18.3 Conformity with Standards

The worth of a standard can be downgraded, if it does not contain a section on conformance testing. Some standards of ISO 9241 (Parts 2, 10 and 12) will even be ignored because of lack of a conformance section, Although a specific test method is not yet recommended in the standard, it has been shown that conformity with these standards can be tested (Dzida, 1995), Testing procedures for a product can be agreed upon by negotiating partners. The proven conformity with Part 10 is then qualified with respect to the specific test approach applied. The following subsections deal with different methods for conformance testing. Since there is no conformity with a standard once and for ever the potential role of the test approaches in the process of quality assurance is addressed. Ergonomic quality assurance will become as important a label of products as the pure engineering quality labels already do. Legal implication of the international standards will promote this tendency.

18.3.1 Test Approaches

If a product is claimed to meet a standard, the procedure used in testing the product against the requirements shall be specified. Some standards prescribe a certain test method, some recommend a method, some inform the reader that the procedure used in testing is a matter of negotiation between the involved parties. Test procedures can be categorized as follows:

*1. **Attribute testing:*** test a product attribute for compliance with the technical requirement (e.g., "Designators of menu options should correspond to function key labels (e.g., F1, F2, F3)").

*2. **Performance Testing:*** test the required performance (e.g., "Any work standing upright should always be of short duration");

*3. **Criterion-Oriented Testing:*** interpret the standard requirement in view of the required task and define a test criterion to be compared with relevant product attributes (e.g., "If options can be arranged into conventional or natural groups known to users, options should be organized into levels and menus consistent with that order", Part 14, paragraph 5.1.1). The "if-clause" refers to the task/user condition to be analyzed first; in view of the kind of grouping conventions (usability criterion) the menu system is inspected for compliance with these conventions.

4. Test Against a Reference Product: take, for instance, a reference keyboard that fulfills the requirements of section 6 of ISO 9241-4 and test whether the performance of a product (which may have different features) is not worse than the reference. In this case the user's keying performance, subjective assessment of comfort, and biomechanical or physiological load are measured.

If the test procedure is not prescribed in the normative part of the standard, the tester may feel free to chose among the procedures or may combine the approaches. Cost-effectiveness will guide this decision, but the tester should consider the reproducibility of test results which is an inescapable methodical requirement regardless of the test procedure.

18.3.2 Quality Assurance Aspects

Hardware, software, the user's workplace and its environment are essential components of the work system (ISO 6385). To deliver the minimum quality of these components, tests for conformity with standards are usually conducted during the design or development phase. However, the assurance of the minimum level of quality may also be necessary concurrently to the usage of these components. In particular the software has to stand the test of exposure to real world problems after having been installed. Usually, usability problems are discovered during real usage of the software. Hence, the measures of quality assurance of software formulated in ISO 9000-3 might be appropriate to the application phase of a product to eliminate failures and defects. The improvement of software is not just a matter of software maintenance. In addition to usual quality assurance, adaptation (customization) may be necessary to cope with usability problems encountered. An adaptation of software may entail tests for conformity with ergonomic standards as regards usability features of the product.

ISO/CD 13407 is a draft of a standard dealing with processes of human centered design. This standard is expected to complement the pure software-engineering requirements of quality assurance (ISO 9000-3).

18.3.3 Legal Implications

The legal status of standards depends on the legislation of the country where the standard is applicable. In most countries, the standards themselves are not legally binding, however, the implications of specific laws (e.g. health and safety laws) may force persons or institutions to apply the standards. Especially when a law requires a "state-of-the-art" or "state-of-technology" to be respected, the standards are officially taken as representing such a state.

When conformity with standards has to be demonstrated, it is generally acceptable to provide any solution which has been proven to be equivalent, even if the solution does not comply with features required by the standard. In many countries this rule complies with high level legal principles.

In the European Union (EU) legal requirements formulated in terms of "Directives" are put into effect by so called "mandated" standards. These standards obtain specified mandates from a legislative body, thereby determining how the requirements of a Directive can be fulfilled. For example, to transpose the "Machine Directive" of the EU some machine safety standards were created to which any product shall comply, so as to warrant a free circulation of safety-critical machines throughout the EU. For all Directives specific standards can be mandated under Article 100a of the EEC Treaty. All member states are then obliged to apply these standards without any change of the quality level.

Directives concerning health and safety of workers are put into force under Article 118a of the EEC Treaty. These Directives contain minimum requirements for safety. However, any member state can introduce greater requirements. Initially, in the case of the Directives under Article 118a no mandates for standardization were planned. However, ISO 9241 was partly mandated under the "VDT Directive" (Council Directive 90/270/EEC, 1990), and the plan is to mandate the entire standard, which will become then a European standard (ISO EN 9241) that is considered to sufficiently describe the health and safety requirements of the specific national legislation. Consequently, the interpretation of ISO 9241 as a recommendation or as an obligatory requirement will be different inside and outside the EU, even if the wording of each standard is the same.

The Council Directive (1990) requires under Article 3 that employers of VDT users must inspect workstations in order to identify sources of undue physical or mental strain. The employer will have satisfied this requirement to a great extent, if the relevant components of the work system can be proven compliant to ISO 9241. Tests for conformity with standards may also be necessary as a preventive measure due to a national law.

18.4 References

Carroll, J.M. (1990). Infinite detail and emulation in an ontologically minimized HCI. In: *Empowering People - CHI'90 Conference Proc., ed. J.C. Chew and J. Whiteside*, p. 321-328. New York: ACM Press.

Council Directive 90/270/EEC, (1990). Council Directive on the minimum safety and health requirements for work with display screen equipment (fifth individual Directive within the meaning of Article 16(1) of Directive 87/391/EEC). *Official Journal of the European Communities,* No L 156: 14-18.

Dzida, W., Herda, S., and Itzfeldt, W.-D. (1978). User-perceived quality of interactive systems. *IEEE Transactions on software engineering,* SE4(4): 270-276.

Dzida, W. (1995). Standards for user-interfaces. *Computer Standards & Interfaces,* 17: 89-97.

IBM (1989). SAA/CUA advanced interface design guide.

ISO 6385. Ergonomic principles in the design of work systems.

ISO/IEC 6967. Coded graphic character set for text communication - Latin alphabet.

ISO 7250. Basic list of anthropometric measurements.

ISO 9000-3. Quality management and quality assurance standards - Part 3: Guidelines for the application of ISO 9001 to the development, supply, and maintenance of software.

ISO 9126. Information technology - Software product evaluation - Quality characteristics and guidance for their use.

ISO 9241-1 Ergonomic requirements for office work with visual display terminals (VDTs): General introduction.

ISO 9241-2. Ergonomic requirements for office work with visual display terminals (VDTs): Guidance on task requirements.

ISO 9241-3 Ergonomic requirements for office work with visual display terminals (VDTs): Visual display requirements.

ISO 9241-4 Ergonomic requirements for office work with visual display terminals (VDTs): Keyboard requirements.

ISO 9241-5 Ergonomic requirements for office work with visual display terminals (VDTs): Workstation and postural requirements.

ISO 9241-6 Ergonomic requirements for office work with visual display terminals (VDTs): Environmental requirements.

ISO 9241-7 Ergonomic requirements for office work with visual display terminals (VDTs): Display requirements with reflections.

ISO 9241-8 Ergonomic requirements for office work with visual display terminals (VDTs): Requirements for displayed colours.

ISO 9241-9 Ergonomic requirements for office work with visual display terminals (VDTs): Requirements for non-keyboard input devices.

ISO 9241-10. Ergonomic requirements for office work with visual display terminals (VDTs): Dialogue principles.

ISO CD 9241-11. Ergonomic requirements for office work with visual display terminals (VDTs): Guidance on usability specification and measures.

ISO CD 9241-12. Ergonomic requirements for office work with visual display terminals (VDTs): Presentation of information.

ISO CD 9241-13. Ergonomic requirements for office work with visual display terminals (VDTs): User guidance.

ISO DIS 9241-14. Ergonomic requirements for office work with visual display terminals (VDTs): Menu dialogues.

ISO CD 9241-15. Ergonomic requirements for office work with visual display terminals (VDTs): Command dialogues.

ISO CD 9241-16. Ergonomic requirements for office work with visual display terminals (VDTs): Direct manipulation dialogues.

ISO CD 9241-17. Ergonomic requirements for office work with visual display terminals (VDTs): Form filling dialogues.

ISO 9995. Information technology - Keyboard layouts for text and office systems.

ISO 10075. Ergonomic principles related to mental work-load - General terms and definitions.

ISO 11064. Parts 1 - 8 dealing with ergonomic requirements of control centers.

ISO/IEC 12119. Information processing - Software packages - Quality requirements and testing.

ISO 13406. Ergonomic requirements for the use of flat panel displays.

ISO 13407. Human centered design processes for interactive systems.

Open Software Foundation (1990). *OSF/Motif Style Guide*. Prentice Hall, Englewood Cliffs, NJ.

Shneiderman, B. (1982). The future of interactive systems and the emergence of direct manipulation. *Behavior and Information Technology*, 1: 237-256.

Part III

User Interface Design

Handbook of Human-Computer Interaction
Second, completely revised edition
M. Helander, T.K. Landauer, P. Prabhu (eds.)

Chapter 19

Graphical User Interfaces

Aaron Marcus
Aaron Marcus and Associates
Emeryville, California, USA

19.1 Introduction

Human-computer communication and interactivity in previous decades was a limited exchange of alphanumeric characters. Today, advanced graphical user interfaces (GUIs sophisticated interactive displays that enable novice, intermediate, and expert users to work more productively. Many of these GUIs use windows, icons, menus, and pointing devices (WIMPs) with two-dimensional or slightly three-dimensional (beveled edges and overlapping planes) to achieve their communication and interactivity goals. In particular, many classical GUIs for typical office applications simulate a "desktop" environment in the display.

To be successful, the GUI must accurately and efficiently relate to the tasks, workflow, objectives, education, personality, and culture of the user. The GUI specifically must provide the following design components in a functional and aesthetic form (also referred to as performance- and preference-oriented form):

Metaphors (essential concepts communicated through terms and images)
Mental model (organization of data, functions, tasks, and roles)
Navigation of the mental model (menus, icons, dialogue boxes, and windows)
Appearance (visual, auditory, and verbal properties of controls and ornamental background)
Interaction (behavior of interactive screen controls and physical input and output display devices).

Users can appreciate and take advantage of quality in each of these components. Good organization of contents, economical means to express each component, effective use of visual elements, and efficient interaction all lead to friendlier and more usable systems.

This chapter discusses various aspects of GUI environments focusing primarily on windowing systems, user-interface elements, and window management. Many tips and suggestions are provided at the end of the chapter that will aid in the understanding, evaluation, and development of GUI applications. A thorough discussion cross-comparing GUIs and their components is available in (Marcus, Smilonich, and Thompson, 1995). A thorough discussion of GUI design tips is available in (Marcus,1992) and (Marcus, 1995)

19.2 Applications and GUIs

Many applications present designers with a special challenge: large collections of functions that act upon very large amounts of data in complex ways. To present their data and functions, many programs have converted to one or more standard commercial GUI paradigms such as Windows, Macintosh, Motif, etc., many of which are discussed individually in this chapter.

Many multimedia applications and interactive content available on the Internet and other private online services use non-standard GUIs. Whether for standard or customized GUIs, GUI designers should be especially sensitive to how clearly the menu hierarchy is organized and to how clearly dialogue boxes are labeled and laid out, because much of the user's mental work takes place in examining and interacting with these GUI components. For many of these GUI-based products, the use of icons to represent objects, structures, or processes has become a significant feature. GUI designers also should examine how clearly icons are designed and labeled.

Current GUI building tools enable developers to construct applications more quickly than ever before. However, the tools do not ensure that the applications are automatically well-designed. To provide some background, this chapter discusses some of the standard GUI paradigms and principles of good GUI design.

The GUI windowing system is similar to an operating system. Instead of file systems or central processing-unit cycles, however, the windowing system manages resources such as screen space and input devices. In GUIs, the windowing system acts as a front end to the operating system by shielding developers, and users, from the abstract and often confusing syntax and vocabulary of a keyboard-oriented command language.

19.3 Windowing Systems

Each of the windowing systems discussed briefly below has unique features and a place in the history of GUIs. Figure 1 through Figure 6 shows applications operating within some of these GUI paradigms.

19.3.1 Macintosh

The Apple Macintosh appeared in 1984 as the first mass-marketed computer to feature a high-resolution, bit-mapped graphic display and a direct-manipulation interaction style. Its windowing system is built on top of a proprietary library of operating system and user interface tool kit routines in the Macintosh read-only memory (ROM).

The classic Macintosh GUI was a single-tasking system with a high level of responsiveness and a very simple model of the designer's tasks. Current versions permit multiple applications to be opened and operated. Apple Computer has succeeded in creating widespread acceptance among third-party software developers for their standard GUI components. As a result, knowledge about familiar Macintosh applications can ease the task of learning new ones.

The Macintosh was the first computer system with a GUI to gain widespread market acceptance and experience significant commercial success. Its popularity, particularly in non-technical market segments traditionally unreceptive toward computing, can be attributed in large part to Apple's commitment to the creation of a consistent and user-supportive user interface. Because of its historical precedence and market penetration, the Macintosh established the standard of interaction by which GUIs are judged. The degree of responsiveness to the actions of the designer demonstrates the quality of interaction that is possible when the windowing system is integrated tightly with a particular hardware and software environment.

19.3.2 NeXTStep

The NeXTStep GUI provides a windowing system and graphical desktop environment originally intended for the NeXT Computer, which began shipping in 1988, but which ceased production in 1993. Nevertheless, the NeXTStep GUI has survived and is being made available on several types of workstations. The four component modules of the NeXTStep GUI are its Window Server, Workspace Manager, Application Kit, and Interface Builder.

NeXTStep was the first in a series of products to adopt a simulated three-dimensional appearance for its standard components. The Window Server uses Display PostScript to create high-quality grayscale screen displays providing graphics that can be output on any PostScript compatible printer. The Application Kit provides a standard set of object-oriented components that can be customized by application developers. The Interface Builder is an end-user oriented tool that allows operators to link these objects to system and application level functions with no additional programming. With this tool, standard user interface components can be used to automate the designer's tasks.

Like the Macintosh user interface, NeXTStep is oriented toward the needs of the non-technical designer. A straightforward mental model (i.e., an organization of data and functions), a simple set of controls, and a well-developed collection of software tools shield the designer from the complexity of the operating system and increase the suitability of the system, especially for the initially targeted market (students and scholars in higher education). Although the sophisticated UNIX-based operating system makes some degree of complexity inevitable, the design of the NeXTStep user interface makes the system accessible even for completely UNIX-naive users.

The NeXTStep GUI is notable for, among other things, using detachable, pop-up sub-menus under the primary menu that originally appear hanging from the top of the screen and "march" to the right in successively deeper layers. For ease of reference, each sub-menu repeats at the top of the sub-menu command list, the term that called it.

19.3.3 Open LOOK

The Open LOOK GUI was developed jointly by Sun Microsystems and AT&T as the standard operating environment for UNIX System V.4. Open LOOK exists as a layer on top of a base windowing system that provides the imaging model (management of how graphical parts are displayed) and network communication services. Versions of Open LOOK have been implemented on top of both the X Window System, the base-level set of windowing functions developed by a consortium of computer companies and MIT, and Sun's Network-extensible Window System (NeWS). In 1994, further Open LOOK development was discontinued, and many applications providers are converting to other GUIs; however, Open LOOK applications continue to exist.

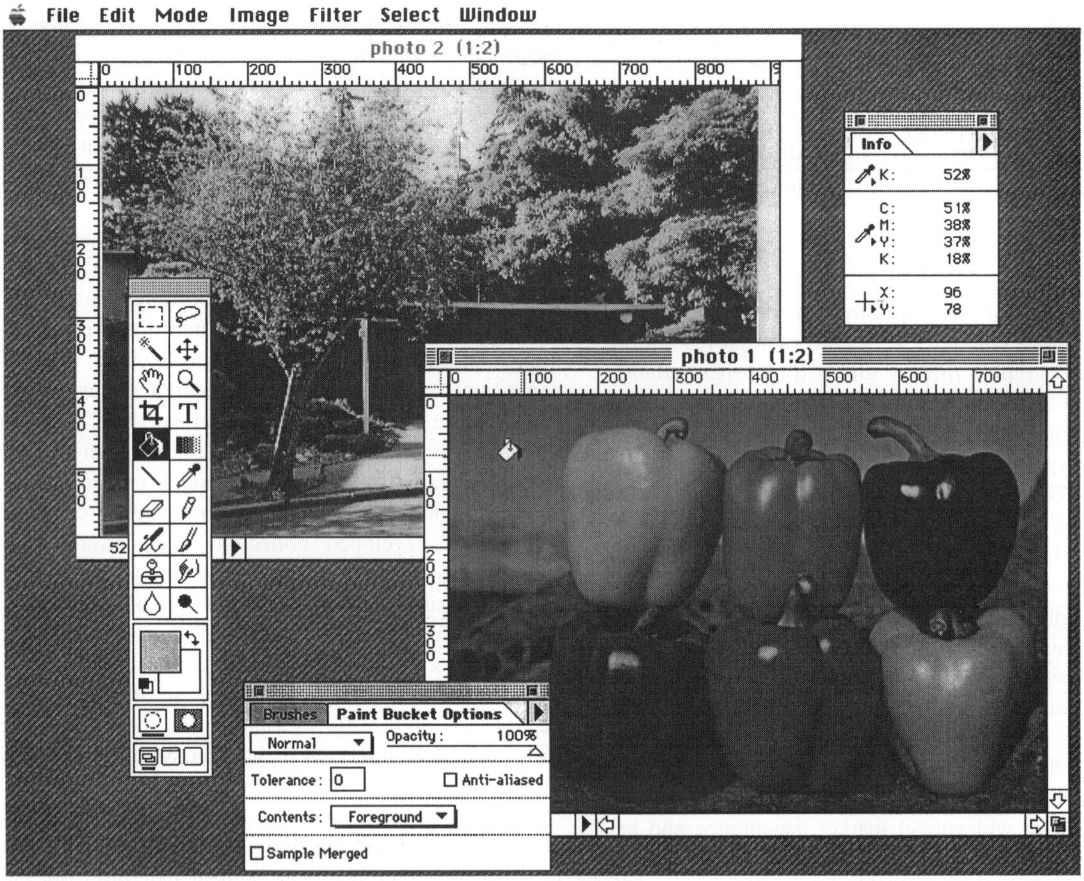

Figure 1. ***Typical applications operating in the Apple Macintosh® GUI. Single or multiple windows can be moved and resized.*** *Toolboxes and dialogue boxes can also be placed where needed. Pointer signs automatically change as required by the state of the system.*

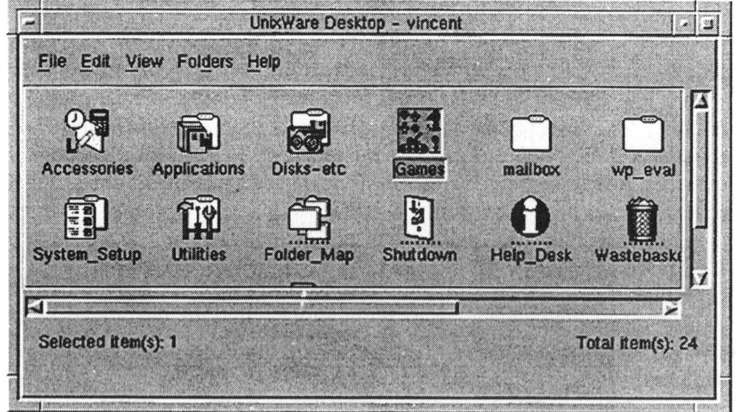

Figure 2. ***A typical application using a Motif-based GUI. On the screen is a typical window and typical icons.*** *By selecting an icon, the user can launch a background task. If the user interface is consistent across applications as well as across hardware platforms, switching among platforms is easy, and training is simplified. (Figure courtesy of Addison-Wesley)*

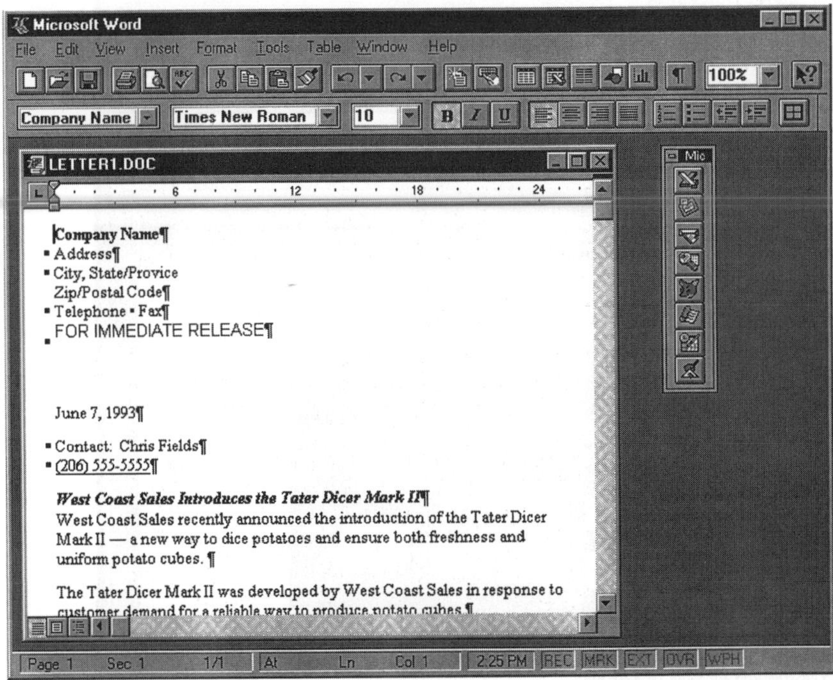

Figure 3. ***An application compliant with Microsoft Windows 95™.*** *Typical features include task bar, dialogue-box controls with visual feedback, and object linking and embedding.*

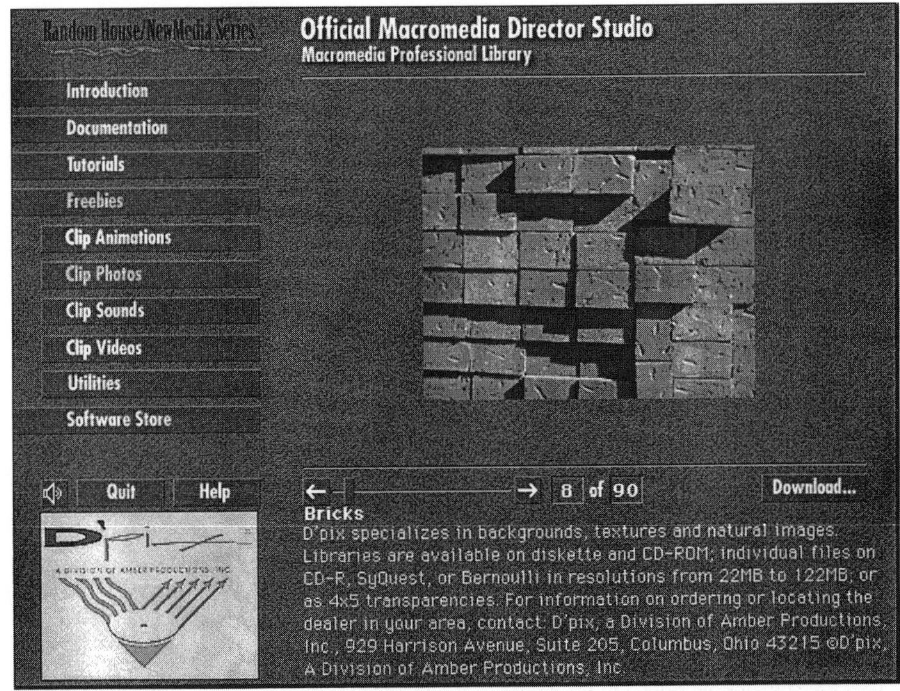

Figure 4. ***Example of an application in NeXTSTEP.*** *Note the location of icons and the use of "marching" menus. (Figure courtesy of Addison-Wesley)*

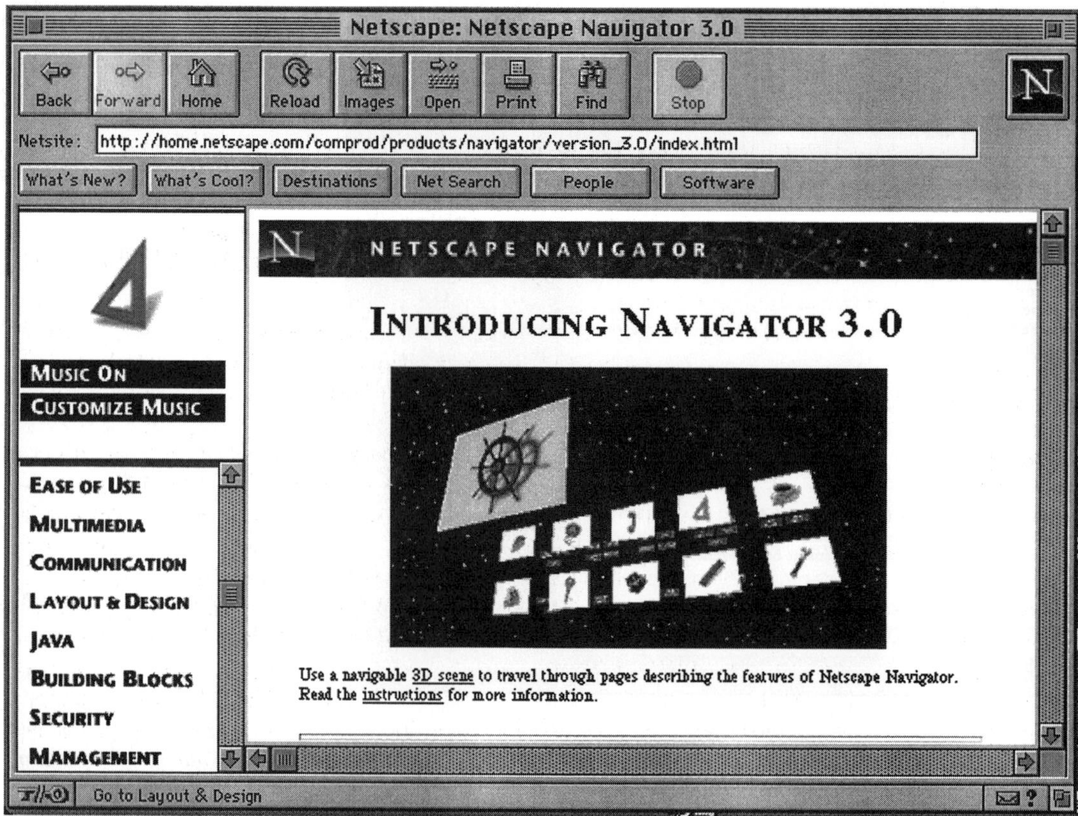

Figure 5. Example of Netscape Navigator frames.

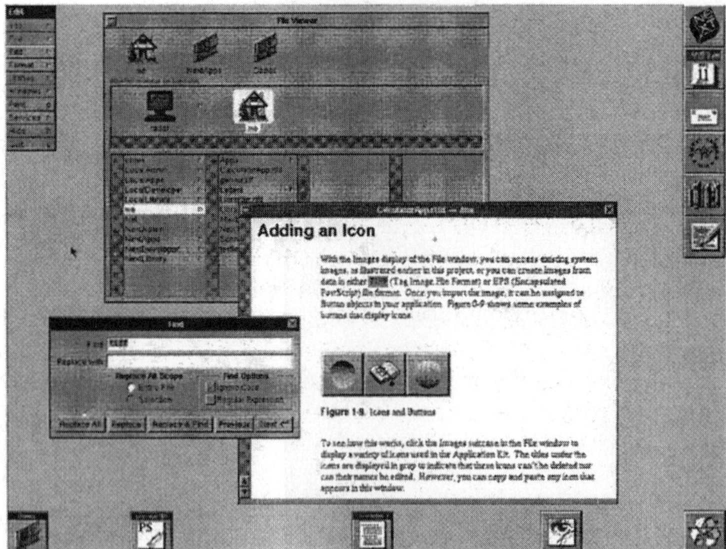

Figure 6. A custom GUI for Random House New Media CD-ROM-based multimedia application. *Menus are displayed and removed automatically as required. Menus remain on the screen for repeated selection and assist in orienting the user. Secondary controls provide appropriate manipulation of multimedia content files.*

Guidance for Open LOOK developers was provided by an exemplary functional specification and style guide. An explicit goal of the Open LOOK designers was to avoid potential legal challenges by creating innovative appearance and behavior characteristics. As a result, many of the conventions adopted deviate from the industry norm. Open LOOK adopted a contrasting appearance and approach to usability. Open LOOK was one of the earliest GUI conventions to propose muted color schemes for more effective display of complex screens. The layout of dialogue boxes and other content-full areas is often more "open" or "empty" looking than in other GUIs because of the design of the individual components.

Open LOOK's orientation toward maximum functionality is evident in the numerous context-sensitive and mode-specific operations it provides. While it, too, makes the UNIX world relatively accessible even for inexperienced users, the extended functionality of Open LOOK itself introduces an additional layer of complexity that is not seen in NeXTStep or the Macintosh human interface.

19.3.4 OSF/Motif

OSF/Motif is a window manager and GUI tool kit developed by Digital Equipment Corporation and the Hewlett-Packard Company for the Open Software Foundation (OSF). Motif provides a three-dimensional, visually dense, and often more sophisticated-looking alternative to Open LOOK that is linked to the OSF version of standard UNIX. Like Open LOOK, the Motif Window Manager exists as a software layer on top of the network-oriented X Window System. Appearance can be modified independently of the functional characteristics of the resulting system, and individual vendors are encouraged to customize the functional shell with their own proprietary widget sets.

OSF/Motif provides a GUI for a high-end, network-based computing environment whose appearance and behavior is consistent with that of Microsoft Windows and OS/2 Presentation Manager. Because of their *de facto* standardization on IBM and compatible platforms, these operating environments dominate the movement toward GUIs for PC-based systems. OSF believes that knowledge of Windows and Presentation Manager will transfer easily to Motif, making it the windowing system of choice when PC users upgrade to workstation platforms.

The implementation of Motif on top of the network-transparent X Window System allows it to leverage an emerging standard in the workstation environment as well. Motif provides a windowing system that can serve as a bridge between the PC and workstation environments. Its potential for easing this transition will increase the attractiveness of Motif for organizations integrating high-performance work stations with existing PC networks.

19.3.5 Microsoft Windows and OS/2 Presentation Manager

Microsoft Windows was created in 1985 as a multitasking, graphics-oriented alternative to the character-based environment provided by MS-DOS on PC compatible systems. The bit-mapped displays and mouse-driven menus provided by Windows first opened the door to graphics-oriented software on the PC.

Initially, Windows was limited by many of the design characteristics (640K address space, low-quality display, etc.) of the DOS environment on which it was built. Later enhancements increased the responsiveness and graphical quality of Windows, particularly on 80386- and 80486-based machines. Microsoft's Windows 95 and Windows NT environment are positioned to take advantage of Window's general approach, but with added usability features for Windows 95 and networking and multitasking capabilities for Windows NT. Windows 95 provides versions of many GUI features that Macintosh established earlier, e.g., use of icons, extensive drag-and-drop functionality, long file names, etc. Windows NT provides a GUI for high performance networked PCs and workstations.

The OS/2 Presentation Manager was developed jointly by Microsoft and IBM in 1987 and is favored by IBM and some compatible microcomputer manufacturers. The appearance and behavior of Presentation Manager are derived primarily from Windows.

Microsoft Windows and the OS/2 Presentation Manager must satisfy a very different market consisting largely of existing MS-DOS users in business and technical environments. The extensive support for keyboard-based control provided by these products reflects the heritage of the character-based DOS interface, which has historically relied heavily on keystroke combinations for selecting from menus and items in dialogue boxes.

19.3.6 Custom GUIs

Although most industry productivity tool applications are moving toward one or more standard commercial GUIs using the above mentioned windowing systems, some previous and current products utilize custom approaches. For example, touch screen applications on kiosks or multimedia-oriented, computer-based training applications may use non-standard layouts, controls, and interaction. In addition, standard GUIs may continue to include hold-over function keys or buttons from the earlier text-oriented user interfaces. Few GUI building tools prevent developers from incorporating custom deviations from standard practice. Consequently, many non-standard, semi-customized versions of commercial GUIs may be encountered, especially in multimedia and Web-oriented products.

19.4 Windowing System Architectures

Traditional windowing systems divide the display screen into multiple functional areas that provide a means of monitoring and controlling multiple application programs or manipulating multiple data objects in a graphical environment. The windows in which documents and applications are presented provide a set of well-defined visual and functional contexts that allow multiple processes to time-share a single set of input devices (mouse, keyboard, etc.) and a limited amount of physical display space. The windowing code (software architecture), the method of window management, and the base window system's method of displaying an image (image model) can have noticeable effects on the quality of the displays and the level of interaction experienced by the user. There are two types of classical windowing system architectures: kernel and client-server based in design. Each is discussed further below.

19.4.1 Kernel-Based Architecture

The location and organization of the software that implements the windowing system can influence the responsiveness, device dependence, and resource requirements of the resulting system. Kernel-based architectures provide high levels of interactivity but are dependent on the architecture and available resources of a single machine.

In kernel-based systems, windowing services are provided by some portion of the operating system itself, or by a standard add-on module that resides along with the operating system in RAM (Random Access Memory) or ROM (Read Only Memory) based libraries. Kernel-based windowing codes and operating systems share the same physical memory space and are accessed in essentially the same way.

19.4.2 Client-Server Based Architecture

Client-server based architectures allow a single instance of the windowing system software to be shared across entire networks of heterogeneous machines, but response times may be limited by the communication bandwidth of the network. A server is a computer running software that provides a particular capability to an entire network of interconnected machines. A client is a piece of software on the same network that requests and uses the capabilities provided by the server. Even the best client-server implementations incur significant communication overhead that can lead to noticeable performance degradation compared to kernel-based windowing systems. Kernel-based systems achieve higher performance at the cost of device dependence and the need to execute redundantly the same code on each machine.

19.5 Window Management

Window management facilities allow the system to maintain spatial relationships among windows as they are moved, sized, and depth-arranged. Several options are available in window control menus that feature automatic arrangement of windows. Of particular importance are tiled, overlapping, and cascading windows. While the historical controversy over the relative merits of tiled and overlapping windows continues, industry practice has favored overlapping window management; however, tiled windows may still be useful in large or high-resolution displays. These window management styles are discussed in more detail below.

19.5.1 Tiled Windows

Tiled windows are arranged automatically by the windowing system to completely fill the available display space, which may be either the entire display screen or an entire content area of a window. Windows are prevented from overlapping. When any window is resized, other windows must be sized in the opposing direction to compensate. Tiled window arrangements are often useful when investigation of users, their tasks, and the application(s) being used indicated that a tiled arrangement of certain windows will meet most users' needs most of the time during initial, intermittent, and/or frequent use. An alternative to this scheme is a single window with multiple panes, exemplified by Microsoft Window's single-document interface (SDI) concept.

19.5.2 Overlapping Windows

Overlapping windows have associated depth values that represent their distances from the viewer. At each displayed location of a visual point or pixel, only the contents of the nearest window covering that portion of the display is presented. The window with the nearest (to the viewer) depth value thus obscures the contents of any other windows occupying the same display space, creating an illusion of physical overlapping. The resulting window stack is comparable to a pile of papers on a desk and allows the designer to take advantage of existing spatial management skills to push one or more windows to the rear, or to bring one or more forward. This scheme is exemplified by Microsoft Window's multiple-document interface (MDI) concept, which can be confusing for some novice users.

19.5.3 Cascading Windows

Cascading windows are a special case of overlapping window management in which the windows are arranged automatically in a regular progression that prevents any window from being completely obscured. One corner (usually, the upper-left) of each successive window appearing "forward" of those "behind" is offset slightly in both the horizontal and vertical directions to conserve display space. Because each window's title bar at the top is visible, the user can easily see the progression of contents, while the selectability of each window simplifies the task of bringing any window to the front of the stack.

19.6 Windowing System Components

The appearance and behavior of the windowing system as experienced by the user is determined by a small group of standard windowing system components. GUIs make use of essentially the same set of these components, while the names by which they are identified vary significantly among vendors. The set of terms listed and discussed below will streamline cross-product comparisons by identifying standard components consistently and unambiguously. (A cross-comparison of all the widgets of the primary standard GUIs appears in Marcus, Smilonich, and Thompson's *The Cross-GUI Handbook for Multi-platform User Interface Design* cited in the Bibliography.)

1. Windows
2. Menus
3. Controls
4. Dialogue Boxes
5. Modeless Dialogues
6. Modal Dialogues
7. Control Panels
8. Query Boxes
9. Message Boxes
10. Mouse and Keyboard Interface

19.6.1 Windows

From the viewpoint of the window manager, a window is any discrete area of the visual display that can be moved, sized, and rendered independently on the display screen. Even though most of the components are actually implemented and managed as windows by the system, it is appropriate to consider windows from the user's point of view. The definition employed will therefore include only those display areas that allow one to change the view of the window's contents using techniques such as sizing, scrolling, or editing.

19.6.2 Menus

Menus provide a means of command execution that enables a designer to see and point instead of remembering and typing. The menu system greatly reduces problems caused by the limitations of human memory, but does so at the expense of motor performance. The benefits are substantial, particularly when the number and complexity of commonly used applications limits the user's expertise with individual command sets.

19.6.3 Controls

Any visually represented window component that can be manipulated directly with the mouse or keyboard is a control. Each of the windowing systems defines standard sets of controls that can be incorporated by applications to provide consistent interaction protocols across products.

19.6.4 Dialogue Boxes

Dialogue boxes provide a visual and functional context for presenting options from which the designer can select. Any interactive exchange of information between the designer and the system that takes place in a limited spatial context is considered a dialogue. Although three distinct classes of dialogue box are described here (control panels, query boxes, and message boxes), there may be considerable overlap among the classes. Any dialogue box can be characterized by a clearly defined scope that determines the effect on the state of the system and the subsequent operations permitted.

19.6.5 Modeless Dialogues

Modeless dialogue boxes are limited in scope and do not restrict the subsequent actions of the user. Modeless dialogues may incorporate some basic window functions such as sizing and positioning. Users can continue to work without responding, if necessary, and may be allowed to keep the modeless dialogue on display even after a response has been made.

19.6.6 Modal Dialogues

Modal dialogue boxes require the user to respond before any other action can be taken. Application modal dialogues prevent the user from invoking any application functions until the dialogue requirements have been satisfied, while system modal dialogues prevent the user from performing any operations anywhere in the system.

19.6.7 Control Panels

Control panels appear at the implicit or explicit request of the user and provide information reflecting the current state of a number of related system parameters, any of which can be changed interactively while the panel remains on display. Changes to the system state do not take effect until the user explicitly accepts the new settings.

19.6.8 Query Boxes

Query boxes appear in response to user actions, but are not requested explicitly. Query boxes prompt for a single piece of information, such as a yes-or-no answer to a single question, and provide a context in which the necessary information can be provided. Like control panels, query boxes allow the user to cancel the action that led to the query.

19.6.9 Message Boxes

Providing critical information to the user is the primary function of message boxes, which are not requested and typically appear only when the system has entered, or is about to enter, an unrecoverable and potentially dangerous state. The user's response options typically are limited to a simple yes-or-no decision, or in irreversible system states, to simple acknowledgment of the message.

19.6.10 Mouse and Keyboard Interface

GUI systems typically use a mouse and keyboard as the primary interaction devices. Each device is well-suited to certain kinds of interaction tasks. The mouse provides an efficient means of accomplishing tasks that require spatial manipulation, such as menu navigation and window sizing and positioning. The keyboard is more efficient for sequential tasks, such as text entry and changing the relative depth location of windows by bring one of them to the top.

19.7 Design Guidelines

Design Advice

The following sections provide guidance in the use of GUI windowing system components. The recommendations are intended to aid in evaluating GUIs implemented with various software packages and can be generically applied to all GUIs. If an application allows user-customization of the GUI, this advice may assist in this process as well.

19.7.1 Design Characteristics

A GUI design must account for the following characteristics:

1. Metaphor: Comprehensible images, concepts, or terms
2. Mental Model: Appropriate organization of data, functions, tasks, and roles
3. Navigation: efficient movement among the data, functions, tasks, and roles via windows, menus, and dialogue boxes
4. Appearance: Quality presentation characteristics, or look
5. Interaction: Effective input and feedback sequencing, or feel

19.7.2 Design Guidelines

Three key principles guide GUI design and user-based customization:

1. Organization: Provide the designer with a clear and consistent conceptual structure
2. Economy: Maximize the effectiveness of a minimal set of cues
3. Communication: Match the presentation to the capabilities of the user

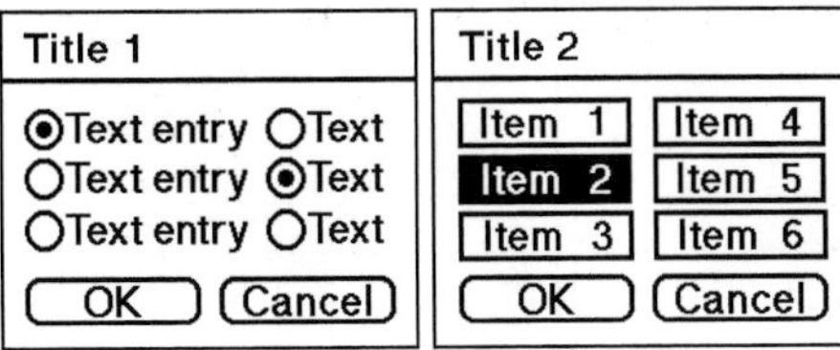

Figure 7. ***Chaotic and ordered screens.*** *The examples illustrate the difference between a disorganized and organized screen layout.*

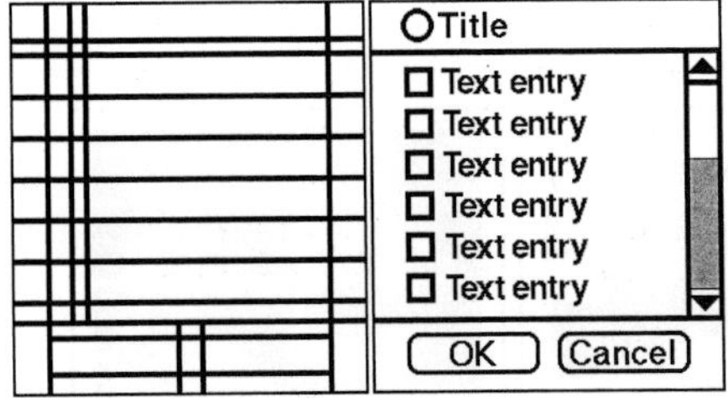

Figure 8. ***Internal consistency in dialogue boxes.*** *The examples illustrate a consistent location and appearance for titles, main contents, and action buttons.*

19.7.3 Order and Chaos

Organization lends order to a GUI, making it easier for the user to understand and navigate. Without visual and cognitive organization, the GUI becomes chaotic and therefore difficult to learn and use. Figure 7 shows an example of the trade-off between order and chaos. Organization can best be understood by examining key components such as consistency, screen layout, relationships, and navigability.

19.7.4 Consistency

The principle of internal consistency says: observe the same conventions and rules for all elements of the GUI. Figure 8 provides an example. Without a strong motivating reason, casual differences cause the viewer to work harder to understand the essential message of the display. The GUI should deviate from existing conventions only when doing so provides a clear benefit to the operator. In other words, the GUI should have a good reason for being inconsistent. GUI researcher Jonathan Grudin (1989) [3] has shown that sometimes it is impossible to avoid inconsistency, and that inconsistency can even be beneficial under certain circumstances. However, as a general rule, strive for consistency without lacking in originality.

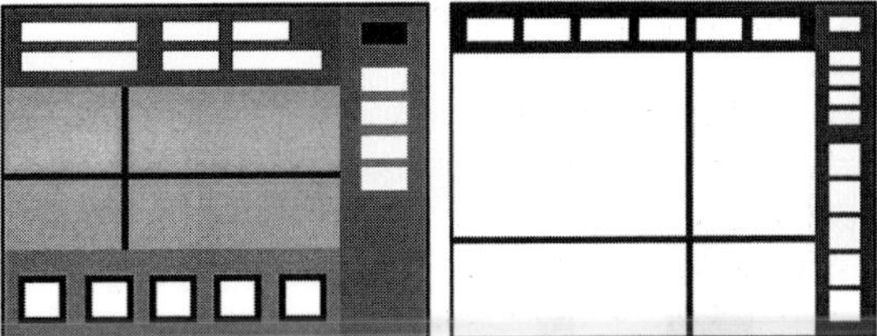

Figure 9. ***Grid and dialogue box.*** *The example illustrates a layout grid of lines that can be used to locate all visual elements of the dialogue box.*

19.7.5 External Consistency: Leverage Known Design Techniques

The GUI should be designed to match the user's expectations and task experience as much as possible rather than force users to understand new principles, tasks, and techniques. This design approach will make the user interface more intuitive and friendly.

19.7.6 GUI Screen Layout

There are three primary means of achieving an organized screen layout:

1. Use an underlying layout-grid
2. Standardize the screen layout
3. Group related elements.

Figure 9 shows examples of dialogue boxes based on a grid structure.

19.7.7 Visual Relationships

Another technique helpful in achieving visual organization is to establish clear relationships by linking related elements and disassociating unrelated elements through their size, shape, color, texture, etc. Examples of elements grouped by relationships appear in Figure 10.

19.7.8 Navigability

An organized GUI provides an initial focus for the viewer's attention, directs attention to important, secondary, or peripheral items, and assists in navigation

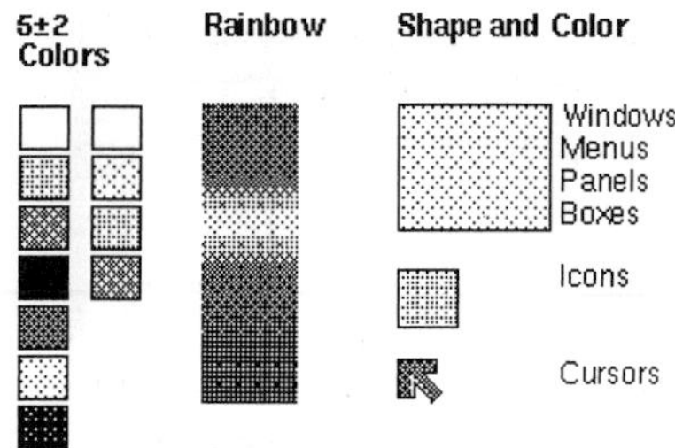

Figure 10. Relationships between grouped items. *The examples illustrate confusing and clear use of color, locations, shape, and size to visually group components of screen displays.*

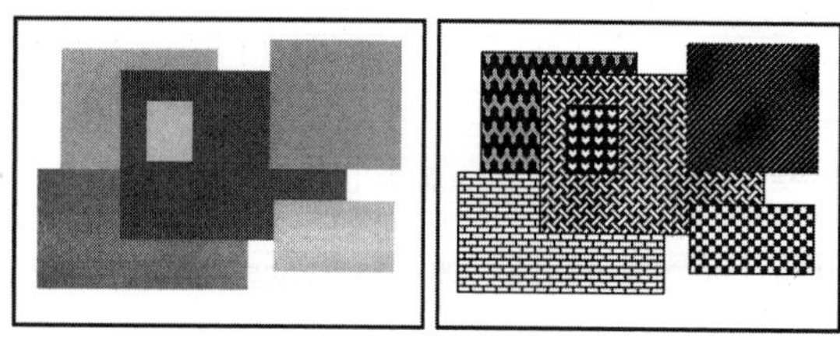

Figure 13. Distinctiveness. *Too little (at left) gives the screen a bland, uninformative look. Too much is chaotic and yields no information about how the items relate to each other.*

Figure 11. Navigability. *A viewer looking at the screen on the left would not know where to begin. The redesigned screen on the right provides clear entry points into the screen via a visual reinforcement of the hierarchy of elements.*

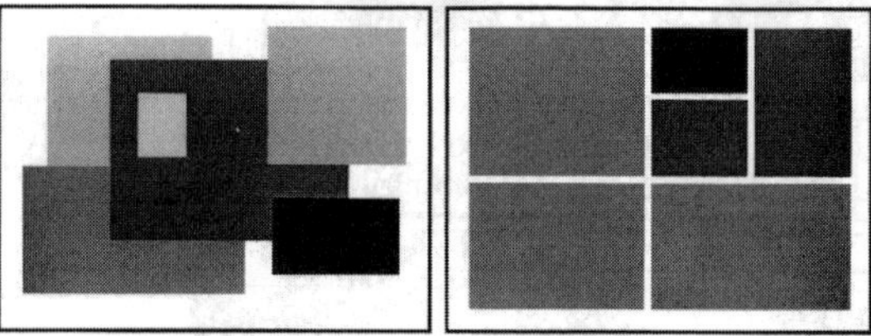

Figure 14. Emphasis. *Because every element in the figure is emphasized, the overall effectiveness is reduced. The viewer does not know what is most important. The figure at right corrects this situation, giving appropriate emphasis to each element.*

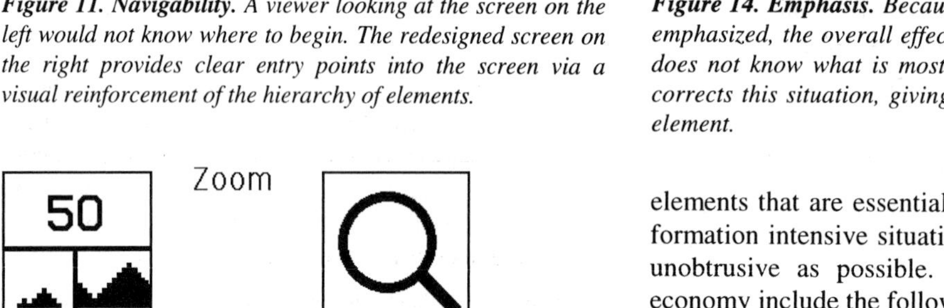

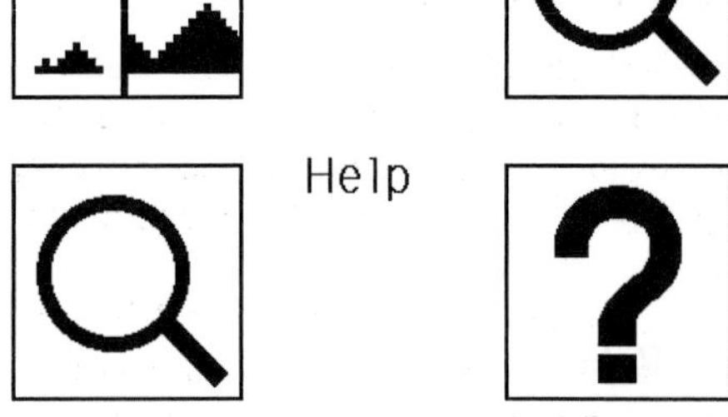

Figure 12. Clarity. *Ambiguous icons confuse and frustrate viewers. Clearly designed icons help them to understand the application.*

throughout the material. Figure 11 provides an example of a screen layout redesigned for improved navigability.

19.7.9 Economy

Economy concerns achieving effects through modest means. Simplicity suggests that including only those elements that are essential for communication. For information intensive situations, the design should be as unobtrusive as possible. Some guidelines regarding economy include the following:

1. Modesty: In general, GUI components should be modest and inconspicuous. Users should be almost unaware of the GUI working to convey meaning.
2. Clarity: Components should be designed with unambiguous meanings. Figure 12 provides a contrast of ambiguous and clearly designed icons.
3. Distinctiveness: Distinguish the important properties of essential elements. Figure 13 illustrates this technique.
4. Emphasis: In general, make the most important elements salient, i.e., easily perceived. De-emphasize non-critical elements, and minimize clutter so that critical information is not hidden. Figure 14 illustrates this point.

Text set in Old English

Text set in Univers

Large
Medium
Small

Large
Medium
Small

Figure 15. ***Legibility.*** *The decorative typeface on the left is less legible than the clean sans-serif type on the right. Size variations in text (lower left) are not distinct enough, while the text on the right clearly establishes a type hierarchy.*

Unreadable: Design components to be easy to interpret and understand. Design components to be inviting and attractive.

Readable

Design components to be easy to interpret and understand.

Design components to be inviting and attractive

Figure 16. ***Readability.*** *Centered text at the top of the figure is not as easy to interpret or as enjoyable to read as the left justified, well-spaced text below.*

19.7.10 Balanced Communication

To communicate successfully, a GUI designer must balance many factors. Well-designed GUIs achieve this balance through the use of information-oriented, systematic graphic design. This refers to the use of layout, typography, symbols, color, and other static and dynamic graphics to convey facts, concepts, and emotions.

19.7.11 Layout

The starting point for a well-designed GUI is its layout. Layout refers to the spatial organization of all dialogue boxes and windows according to an underlying grid of horizontal and vertical lines. In general, the visual field should be governed by 7±2 major lines in each orientation. These lines will regularize the appearance of all other elements, including typography, icons, charts, etc.

19.7.12 Legibility

Any GUI should be legible. Legibility refers to the design of individual characters, symbols, and graphic elements to be easily noticeable and distinguishable. Figure 15 shows some examples of legibility based on typeface (font) and size.

19.7.13 Backgrounds

Remember that dark screen backgrounds in brightly lit rooms may cause distracting reflections that can diminish screen legibility. At the other extreme, brightly lit screens in dark rooms may be too glaring and difficult to see.

19.7.14 Readability

Readability refers to a display that is comprehend, i.e., easy to identify and interpret, as well as inviting and attractive. Figure 16 presents an example of contrast in readability of texts.

19.7.15 Typography

Individual GUI elements (typefaces, such as Times Roman or Helvetica) and type styles (such as bold roman or regular italic), and their arrangement (typesetting techniques, such as line spacing) should be optimized for effective communication. The following are some guidelines to consider:

1. Within menus, dialogue boxes, control panels, forms, and other window components, adjust the point size, word spacing, paragraph indentation, and line spacing to enhance readability and to emphasize critical information.
2. Limit type variations to a maximum of 1-3 typefaces in 1-3 sizes for most applications. Lines of text should have 40-60 characters maximum, and words should be spaced correctly (usually the width of a lower case "r" for variable-width text).
3. Set text in appropriate formats, i.e., flush-left, columns of numbers flush right, avoid centered text in lists, and avoid short, justified lines of text. For fixed-width fonts, justified lines of text can slow reading speed by 12%.
4. Use upper and lower case characters whenever possible, i.e., avoid all capital lines of text, which can also slow reading speed by 12%.

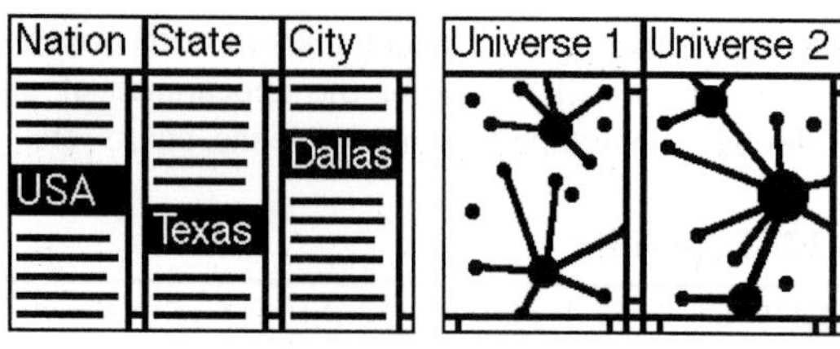

*Figure 17. **Multiple views (visual and verbal).** The examples illustrate how graphic and textual GUI components can present the viewer with different views of a single object or multiple views of different objects in order to communicate complex information effectively.*

19.7.16 Symbolism

GUI symbolism refers to signs, icons, and symbols that can help to communicate complex information and make the display more appealing. In general, keep in mind the following:

1. Use symbols or icons that are clear and unambiguous.
2. Use familiar references when possible.
3. Be consistent in the size, angles, weights, and visual density of all the signs.

19.7.17 Multiple Views

One important technique for improving communication within a GUI is to provide multiple views of the display of complex structures and processes. Figure 17 gives an example of how to present multiple views. Good GUI design makes use of these different perspectives:

1. Multiple forms of representation
2. Multiple levels of abstraction
3. Simultaneous alternative views
4. Links and cross references`

19.7.18 Advantages of Color

Color, including texture, is a powerful communication tool; so powerful, in fact, that color is easy to misuse or overuse. GUI designers must therefore understand color's functions so as to use color with proper skill and sophistication. Color refers to these dimensions: hue (combinations of wavelength), value (degree of lightness or darkness), and chroma (degree of purity or vividness). In addition, brightness refers to the amount of radiant energy in the display of color.

Color plays a significant role in communicating with a designer. Some of the most important tasks color can accomplish are these:

1. Emphasize important information
2. Identify subsystems or structures
3. Portray natural objects realistically
4. Portray time and progress
5. Reduce errors of interpretation
6. Add coding dimensions
7. Increase clarity or comprehensibility
8. Increase believability and appeal

19.7.19 Color Similarity

In general, similar colors imply a relation among objects. A viewer can sense the relatedness by color over space and over time in sequences of images. Therefore, color should be used to group related items, and a consistent color code should be used for screen displays, documentation, etc. Also, use similar background colors for related areas. This color coding can subtly reinforce the conceptual link among these areas in the viewer's mind.

19.7.20 Color Consistency

Be complete and consistent in color groupings. For example, command and control colors in menus should not be used for information coding within a work area, unless a specific connection is intended. Once color coding is established, the same colors should be used throughout the GUI and all related publications. This color continuity may require designing colors to appear in different media: CRT screens use additive color mixtures, while most hardcopy devices use subtractive color mixtures. The color gamuts (that is, available color ranges) of these two media usually are not identical.

19.7.21 Color Economy: Redundancy

The principle of color economy suggests using a maximum of 5±2 colors where the meaning must be remembered. Note that this maximum is even less than Miller's (1956) number [4] of 7±2, which refers to a human cognitive functioning limit with short term memory. If appropriate, use redundant coding based on shape as well as color.

19.7.22 Color Economy: Enhancement

Color should enhance black-and-white information, that is, in general, the display should work well when viewed as black, white, and grays. For documentation tasks and for the use of color to portray an object, the maximum number of colors needed is dependent on the application. For aesthetic purposes such as design style, emotional expression, or realism, many more colors may be required. A set of 5±2 colors may include a few grays and some strongly different hues, or the set may use only different values for a given hue.

19.7.23 Color Economy: Sequencing

To code a large set of colors, use the spectral sequence: red, orange, yellow, green, blue, and violet. Francine Frome (1983) [5], a human factors researcher has shown that CAD/CAM viewers see a spectral order as a natural one and would select red, green, and blue as intuitive choices for the front, middle, and back layers, respectively, when viewing a multi-layer display.

Note, however, that brightness can change a viewer's perception of depth. If the colors are balanced, then red seems to come forward. Use redundant coding of shape as well as color. This technique aids those with color deficient vision and makes the display more resilient to color distortions caused by ambient light changes or by converting a color display from one medium to another, such as from a CRT to slides.

Ambient light can cause changes in all dimensions of color. Conversion from one medium to another can cause unforeseen and sometimes uncontrollable changes. Remember that among Caucasian viewers, approximately 8% of males have some form of color-deficient vision.

19.7.24 Color Emphasis

Color emphasis suggests using strong contrast in value and chroma to focus the operator's attention on critical information. The use of bright colors for danger signals, attention-getters, reminders, and pointers/cursors is entirely appropriate. High chroma red alerts seem to aid faster response than yellow or yellow-orange if brightness is equal, but this also depends upon the background colors. When too many figures or background fields compete for the viewer's attention, confusion arises, as can happen in the approach to color design that makes displays look appropriate for Las Vegas (the use of many high-chroma colors).

19.7.25 Color Emphasis: Hierarchy

The hierarchy of highlighted, neutral, and lowlighted states for all areas of the visual display must be carefully designed to maximize simplicity and clarity. Here again we find the basic maxim: simplicity, clarity, and consistency are especially important for color design.

19.7.26 Color Emphasis: Viewing Differences

Older viewers may be less able to distinguish blue from white and blue-green from bluish-white light due to natural aging and change of color in the lens of the eye [6].11 Those who have viewed displays for very long periods of time may require more saturated or high-chroma colors because of changes in their visual system. Bear in mind that frequent, short-term viewing can benefit from low-chroma displays, and that very bright displays of letters, symbols or lines tend to bloom, that is, the light spreads out against the background.

19.7.27 Color Communication: Central and Peripheral Colors

Select colors appropriate to the central and peripheral areas of the visual field. The outer edges of the retina are not particularly sensitive to colors in general. Red or green should be used in the center of the visual field, not in the periphery. If they are used at the periphery, some signal to the viewer must be given to capture attention, e.g., size change or blinking. Use blue, black, white, and yellow near the periphery of the visual field, where the retina remains sensitive. These considerations are particularly important for virtual reality systems.

19.7.28 Color Communication: Combinations

Use color combinations whose color contrasts are influenced least by the relative area of each color. Use blue for large areas, not for text type, thin lines, or small shapes. Blue-sensitive color receptors are the least numerous in the retina (approximately 5%), and are especially infrequent in the eye's central focusing area, the fovea. Blue is good for screen backgrounds.

19.7.29 Color Communication: Area

If the same colors appear in objects that vary greatly in size, bear in mind that, as color areas decrease in size, they appear to change their value and chroma.

19.7.30 Color Communication: High Chroma and Spectrally Extreme Colors

Choose colors that are not simultaneously high in chroma and located at the extreme ends of the visual spectrum, e.g., red and blue.

19.7.31 Color Communication: Chroma and Value

Use colors that differ both in chroma and value (lightness). Do not use adjacent colors that differ only in the amount of pure blue, because the edge between the two colors will appear to be fuzzy. To avoid this effect, it is helpful to use other combinations, such as a dark blue and a light blue.

19.7.32 Color Communication: Combinations to Avoid

Colors of simultaneously high-chroma, spectrally extreme, strong contrasts of red/green, blue/yellow, green/blue, and red/blue can create vibrations or illusions of shadows and after-images. Unless special visual effects are needed, avoid these combinations.

19.7.33 Color Communication: For Dark-Viewing

In general, use light text, thin lines, and small shapes (white, yellow, or red) on medium to dark backgrounds (blue, green, or dark gray) for dark viewing situations. Typical low ambient-light viewing situations are those for slide presentations, workstations, and video. Video displays produce colors that are lower in chroma.

19.7.34 Color Communication: For Light-Viewing

Use dark (blue or black) text, thin lines, and small shapes on light (light yellow, magenta, blue, or white) backgrounds for light viewing situations. Typical viewing situations are those for overhead transparencies and paper. Reserve for text type the highest contrast between a figure and its background field.

19.7.35 Color Communication: Interactions

The interaction of color is a very complex subject that cannot be meaningfully covered in this limited space. The basic text on the subject is Albers' (1975) book, *The Interaction of Color* [7]. GUI designers need to become familiar with this topic, which students of art and design often study.

19.7.36 Color Symbolism: Using Color Codes

Remember the importance of symbolism in communication: use color codes that respect existing cultural and professional usage.

19.7.37 Color Symbolism: Connotations

Evoke color connotations with great care. Connotations vary strongly among different kinds of viewers, especially from different cultures. The correct use of color requires careful analysis of the experience and expectations of the viewers. For example, mailboxes are blue in the USA, bright red in England, and bright yellow in Greece. If color is used in an electronic mail icon on the screen, this suggests that color sets might be changed for different countries to allow for differences in international markets.

19.7.38 Keyboard Short-Cuts

GUIs emphasize visually oriented interaction and direct manipulation, which is often very desirable for novice or occasional users. Experts often prefer many keyboard-oriented shortcuts. In general, these should be provided for efficient operation by frequent and expert users. Their equivalencies should be made apparent in menus and on-line documentation.

19.8 Rules of Thumb

Besides the above specific guidelines for GUI's, most professionals follow general rules of thumb. (Lund, 1995) recently requested evaluation of a preliminary set via an Internet-based pole. The results (slightly edited) are summarized below. The average ratings for each of the rules of thumb, ordered from greatest relative impact on usability to least, is as follows:

4.1 Know the user, and you are not the user.

4.0 Things that look the same should act the same.

4.0 Everyone makes mistakes, so every mistake should be fixable.

3.9 The information for the decision needs to be there when the decision is needed.

3.8 Error messages should actually mean something to the user, and tell the user how to fix the problem.

3.8 Every action should have a reaction.

3.7 Don't overload the user's buffers.

3.6 Consistency, consistency, consistency.

3.5 Minimize the need for a mighty memory.

3.5 Keep it simple.

3.4 The more you do something, the easier it should be to do.

3.4 The user should always know what is happening.

3.4 The user should control the system. The system shouldn't control the user. The user is the boss, and the system should show it.

3.3 The idea is to empower the user, not speed up the system.

3.3 Eliminate unnecessary decisions, and illuminate the rest.

3.3 If the user made an error, let the user know about it before getting into real trouble.

3.3 The best journey is the one with the fewest steps. Shorten the distance between users and their goals.

3.2 The user should be able to do what the user wants to do.

3.2 Things that look different should act different.

3.2 The user should always know how to find out what to do next.

2.9 Do not let users accidentally cause themselves difficulty.

2.9 Even experts are novices at some point. Provide help.

2.9 Design for regular people and the real world.

2.9 Keep it neat. Keep it organized.

2.9 Provide a way to bail out and start over.

2.7 The fault is not in the user, but in the system.

2.5 If it is not needed, it's not needed.

2.5 Color is information.

2.3 Everything in its place, and a place for everything.

2.3 The user should be in a good mood when done.

2.0 If the user makes an error, at least let the user finish a thought before needing to fix the error.

1.7 Cute is not a good adjective for systems.

1.7 Let people shape the system to themselves, and paint it with their own personality.

1.3 To know the system is to love it.

Lund cautions: "...this survey does not guarantee that the top rated rules of thumb actually have the largest impact on usability, just that experienced professionals believe the rules do. Assessing their impact is an empirical exercise that would be worthwhile. Further, we don't know whether professionals apply the rules of thumb in the same way, or whether part of their virtue is that they represent a core principle that each expert applies in a unique way to achieve usability."

19.9 Conclusions

This chapter has introduced the major standard GUI/window manager paradigms and has provided guidance for good GUI design. GUIs present many simultaneous, complex challenges to achieving successful visual communication. This chapter has presented a basic set of recommendations that can help the designer get started in using layout, typography, symbolism and color more effectively. After these guidelines have been incorporated, consider establishing product- or company- wide style guides, templates, and color palettes so that others may adapt and benefit from previous work. Developing better communication is an important part of making applications that communicate effectively through high-quality graphic design of user interfaces.

19.10 Acknowledgments

This chapter is an edited version of an essay by Aaron Marcus, "Graphical User Interfaces," by Aaron Marcus in *Solids Modeling Handbook*, Chapter 18, Donald E. LaCourse, Editor, McGraw-Hill Publishers, New York, 1995, pp. 18.3-18.18, and is used with permission of the previous publisher. The article is based on chapters from Aaron Marcus, *Graphic Design for Electronic Documents and User Interfaces*, Addison-Wesley, Reading, 1992.

19.11 Bibliography (Including Cited References)

Albers, J. (1975). *The Interaction of Color*, Yale University Press, New Haven.

Baecker, R., and Aaron M. (1990). *Human Factors and Typography for More Readable Programs*, Addison-Wesley, Reading, Mass.

Bertin, J. (1983). *The Semiologie of Graphics*, University of Wisconsin Press, Madison.

Del Galdo, L., and Jonathan G. (1996). *Designing International User Interfaces,* Wiley.

Frome, F. (1983). Incorporating the Human Factor in Color CAD Systems, *Proceedings*, 20th Design Automation Conference, 1983, pp. 189-195.

Grudin, J. (1989). The Case Against User Interface Consistency, *Human Factors*, Vol. 32, No. 10, October (1989), pp. 1164-1173.

Hofmann, A. (1965). *Graphic Design Manual*, Reinhold Publishing Corp., New York.

Lund, A. (1995). <LUND.HORIZON@X400GW.AMERITECH.COM>, broadcast E-mail message, 28 October, 1995. Subject: "Feedback on Ratings of Usability Rules of Thumb"

Marcus, A. (1995). Graphical User Interfaces, in *The Solids Modeling Handbook*, Ed. Donald E. Lacourse, McGraw-Hill, New York, pp. 18.3-18.18.

Marcus, A. (1992). *Graphic Design for Electronic Documents and User Interfaces*, ACM Press, Addison-Wesley, Reading, MA,

Marcus, A., Nicholas S., and Lynne T. (1995). *The Cross GUI-Handbook for Multi-platform User Interface Design*, Addison-Wesley, Reading, MA.

Marcus, A. (1995). Principles of Effective Visual Communication for Graphical User Interface Design. In Baecker *et al, Readings in Human-Computer Interaction*, Morgan-Kaufman, San Francisco, pp. 425-468.

Marcus, A. (1982). Color: A Tool for Computer Graphics Communication. In Greenberg, Donald, et al., *The Computer Image*, Addison-Wesley, Reading, pp. 76-90.

Miller, G.A. (1956). The Magical Number Seven Plus or Minus Two: Some Limits on our Capacity for Processing Information. *Human Factors*, Vol. 63, pp. 81-97.

Mueller-Brockman, J. (1981). *The Grid*, Verlag Arthur Niggli, Niederteufen, Switzerland.

Ota, Y. (1987). *Pictogram Design,* Kashawi Shobo Publishers, Tokyo, Japan.

Thorrell, L. G. and W. J. Smith, *Using Computer Color Effectively*, Prentice Hall, Englewood Cliffs, 9.

Tufte, E. R. (1983). *The Visual Display of Quantitative Information.* Graphics Press, Cheshire, Conn.

Handbook of Human-Computer Interaction
Second, completely revised edition
M. Helander, T.K. Landauer, P. Prabhu (eds.)

Chapter 20

The Role of Metaphors in User Interface Design

Dennis C. Neale and John M. Carroll
Virginia Polytechnic Institute and State University
Blacksburg, Virginia, USA

20.1 Introduction

The underlying operations of computer artifacts are imperceptible to the user. What is visible is conveyed through the user interface. The user interface designed to mimic the behavior of almost any therefore, the possibilities for representing inf and actions are virtually limitless. User interface components are purely symbolic entities, and their arbitrariness is the crux of design problems (Ellis, 1993).

One common approach designers have exploited for controlling complexity is to ground user interface actions, tasks, and goals in a familiar framework of concepts that are already understood (Carroll and Thomas, 1982). Such a framework is called a user interface metaphor. The extensive use of metaphors has had a dramatic impact on user interface design practices. Understanding and improving strategies for developing user interface metaphors is one of the most important and formidable goals for human-computer interaction (HCI) design.

Lakoff and Johnson (1980) describe metaphors as "understanding and experiencing one kind of thing in terms of another," and they claim that metaphors are not only pervasive in language, but that they are a fundamental part of our conceptual system of thought and action. The proposition that all knowledge is metaphorically based has been called "the strong thesis of metaphor" by Indurkhya (1994).

In contemporary research, metaphors are conceived of as cross-domain mappings (Holyoak and Thagard, 1995; Lakoff, 1994). That is, metaphors allow the transference or *mapping* of knowledge from a *source domain* (familiar area of knowledge) to a *target domain* (unfamiliar area or situation), enabling humans to use specific prior knowledge and experience for understanding and behaving in situations that are novel or unfamiliar. Through this process, one's knowledge in the target domain is enriched by borrowing existing representations from the source domain (Collins, 1995).

In a metaphor the comparison between the source and target domains is *implicit*. Although a metaphor asserts a relationship between the two domains, it does not specify the details of the relation. The fact that the associations between the source and target are hidden is the essence of metaphor. This anomaly produces an aspect of surprise and challenge. With the details of the relationship me[illegible] it is left to the user to [illegible] the basis of [illegible] ys be discov- [illegible]).

The use[illegible] is the target domain for interface metaphors. Interface metaphors help establish user expectations and encourage predictions about system behavior. A good example is the "desktop" metaphor. This metaphor portrays the operating system of the computer as similar to objects, tasks, and behaviors found in physical office environments. Office workers have extensive and stereotypical knowledge about documents, file folders, windows, wastebaskets, and so forth; helping them to engage this knowledge can make computerized office equipment more accessible and easier to learn (e.g., Smith, Irby, Kimball, Verplank, and Harslem, 1992).

The desktop metaphor is actually a composite of many metaphors. Most systems have a global metaphor to provide the basis of interaction, which is supported by many auxiliary metaphors. Global metaphors are referred to by Dent-Read, Klein, and Eggleston (1994) as "organizing" metaphors and by Cates (1994) as primary or "underlying" metaphors. For example, the desktop metaphor provides the primary structure for representing the operating system, but it is actually comprised of many auxiliary metaphors such as the clipboard, menus, and other objects which create structure for different activities. Global metaphors serve to structure individual displays as well as sets of displays.

The ability of interface metaphors to facilitate learning is one of their most important properties (Carroll and Mack, 1985, and Laurel, 1993). In fact, Anderson (1983) has theorized that all human learning is analogically based. Metaphors provide the scaffolding for learning by making previously learned information applicable to new situations (Bruner, 1960). Learning is accelerated when metaphors are used because existing knowledge bases are borrowed when reasoning about new problems (Streitz, 1986).

The metaphor paradigm in user interface design has broadened in recent years. Metaphor terminology has always been a large part of metaphoric interfaces; however, contemporary user interfaces with abundant multimedia formats facilitate the use of an extensive variety of metaphors. For example, although visual representations afford some of the richest metaphors, auditory metaphors can be used to supplement the visual and textual aspects of metaphor (see Gaver, 1996) or to aid the visually impaired (Lumbreras and Rossi, 1995; and Mynatt and Edwards, 1995).

One significant influence of the increased reliance on metaphors in general, and on metaphors from different media specifically, has been changing notions about metaphor in the HCI community. Much of the focus on metaphors has evolved from a primarily ease-of-learning focus to include a focus on ease-of-use. The goal then becomes one of usability, rather than a focus on learnability (Kuhn and Blumenthal, 1996). Carroll and Rosson's (1994) conception that metaphorical design should be driven toward the incorporation of contexts of use reflects a more comprehensive approach to metaphor use, resulting in fundamental influences on the specification, design and implementation of tasks.

As a consequence of the thriving role metaphors play in making systems usable, designers need to understand how user interface metaphors operate, and they need systematic methods for incorporating them in their designs. Section 20.2 presents a variety of examples that illustrate metaphor use. Section 20.3 reviews classifications of interface metaphor types. Mismatches between source and target domains and circumstances that create them are described in section 20.4. The role metaphors have in communicating the designer's model, structuring users' models of the interface, and their impact on the human-machine communication process is discussed in section 20.5. Section 20.6 surveys theoretical and applied models and the design stages that can be used to implement metaphors.

20.2 Examples of Metaphor Use

Metaphors are widely used. Some of the newest developments are found in interfaces created for presenting information structures, multimedia, group work, and virtual reality. Table 1 lists some example metaphors that have been explicitly developed for various systems. Many of these metaphors offer alternatives to the desktop metaphor—metaphors other than those derived from office environment source domains—providing more appropriate real-world referents for the diverse areas listed above.

Several metaphors have been designed around physical places for representing information structures. Pejtersen and Nielsen (1991), for example, have developed a "storehouse" metaphor with different rooms for retrieving and navigating works of fiction found in public libraries. Väänänen (1993) describes a system (ShareMe) for representing multimedia information based on a "house" metaphor. Information is divided into rooms, and documents are arranged on walls. The system further supports a "library" metaphor with sections, bookshelves, books, and magazines. Henderson and Card (1986) and Savidis and Stephanidis (1995) propose using "room" metaphors for structuring information and organizing work spaces. Väänänen (1993) and Shafrir and Nabkel (1994) provide "landscape" metaphors for depicting large information structures. These metaphors tap users' prior knowledge of geo-

Table 1. Examples of user interface metaphors.

CONTEXT OF METAPHOR	TARGET DOMAIN	SOURCE DOMAIN (METAPHOR)	EXPLOITS KNOWLEDGE OF
Information Structures	Information browsing and searching	Storehouse / House / Room	stores, rooms, malls, shelves
		Library	library catalogues, books, page turning, shelves, indexes
		Landscape	roads, junctions, signs, maps, mountains, lakes
		Space, conference rooms, auditoriums, lobbies	navigation: shortcut, go to, travel between sites, links, movement.
		Travel / Tourist activities	exploring, guided tours, maps, indexes, asking questions
		Book / Dictionary	pages, bookmarks, tabs, indexes
	Organizing documents	Piles	physical piles of paper, categories
	Organizing and viewing information	Bags and viewers (filters)	bags for hold items, viewers with different filtering capabilities
Multimedia	Presenting multimedia	Television, compact disks, photographs, film	albums, photo holders, TV programs & channels, VCRs, CD tracks
	Working with large video sources	Magnifying lens	lens, changing resolution, changing viewing area, filters
Group Work	Shared work spaces, video conferencing, distance learning	Rooms, TVs, slides whiteboard, phone, video	group interaction, meeting tools, chalkboard, phones, TV
Virtual Reality	Navigating	Flying hand /Floating guide / Lean-based	physical/spatial world, flying, floating, leaning for movement
		Eyeball & Scene in hand / Flying vehicle control / Push-pull	attributes in and movement of a physical space, camera control, flying, moving objects

graphical features like mountains, lakes, roads, junctions, signs, and maps.

"Space" metaphors can help users understand information structures even if no specific visual presentation of a particular space is used. Commands and concepts found on most world-wide web browsers reflect this approach (e.g., back, forward, go to, jump, home page, path, address and others). Spatial metaphors found on the internet, though, often do include specific spaces for interacting with information and other people, such as conference rooms, auditoriums, and lobbies (Swedlow, 1995). Using spatial metaphors as a framework to design user interfaces can alleviate disorientation in computer environments by applying analogous navigational aids from real environments (Kim and Hirtle, 1995).

Other approaches to structuring information are more activity-based than place-based or object-based. Two examples include the "travel" metaphor (Hammond and Allinson, 1987) and the "tourist" metaphor (Fairchild, Meredith, Wexelblat, 1989). The travel metaphor structures the interaction as places to visit, and specific facilities support traveling around by means of tours, go-it-alone travel, maps, and indexes. Similarly, the tourist metaphor allows users to take guided tours of information.

Many metaphors use familiar objects for structuring information. BookWindow is a system based on a "book" metaphor (see Arai, Yokoyama, Matsushita, 1992). The system is equipped with bookmarks, tabs, and other features found in typical books. Benest, Morgan, and Smithurst (1987) offer a system that models a conventional library and associated activities. The metaphor uses a "dictionary" as the basis for presenting library catalogs.

Other metaphors for organizing and structuring information include the "pile" metaphor, which allows the user to create piles of documents rather than using a folder filing system (Mander, Salomon, and Wong, 1992). The "Bags and Viewers" metaphor allows database search items to be organized into metaphoric bags that can then be browsed with multi-function viewers, or metaphoric filters that allow the user to set various parameters for viewing records (Inder and Stader, 1994).

Marcus (1993b, 1994) provides many examples of objects that can be used to metaphorically represent multimedia elements: television, compact disks, photographs, film and others. Specific metaphors are being developed to manipulate these various forms of media. For example, Mills, Cohen, and Wong (1992) offer a "magnifier lens" as a metaphor for working with large video sources. Presenting functionality in familiar objects provides users with much of the knowledge for how computer systems work and how the objects in them behave.

All of the metaphors mentioned thus far are aimed at helping a single user work in a personal space. However, many new interfaces and metaphors are being developed to support group work. Fahlén, Brown, Ståhl, and Carlsson (1993) have developed a variant of the rooms/space metaphor for computer supported collaborative work that is implemented in a shared virtual environment. Users are represented by three-dimensional icons and several metaphorical real-world communication tools are used to support interaction, such as a distributed whiteboard, a conference table, a generalized portable document and a podium tool. Hämmäinen and Condon (1991) developed "Form" and "Room" metaphors for groupware that support formal and informal group tasks.

Stanney (1995) argues that new visual, auditory, and haptic metaphors specifically well suited for virtual environments need to be developed, and virtual navigation techniques being experimented with reflect this need. Fairchild, Hai, Loo, Hern, and Serra (1993) have developed "Flying hand," "Floating guide," and "Lean-based" metaphors for navigating. Ware and Osborne (1990) have implemented "Eyeball in hand," "Environment in hand," and "Flying vehicle control." Mercurio and Erickson (1990) have developed the "push-pulling" metaphor, allowing users to mimic gestures that cause the environment to move in the real world.

The examples of user interface metaphors above are only a sample of the many that exist in current commercial and research systems. Many multimedia interfaces eliminate menubar pull-down menus, windows, and standard buttons and replace them with more elaborate visuals, video, and animations (Lynch, 1994). These new formats lend themselves to rich source domains for constructing new metaphors. As hardware and software capabilities advance, and as computers are increasingly used in new ways for work, communication, and leisure, many new metaphors will make new technology more useful. These examples show how central the metaphor is to the user interface, and they illustrate how system functionality can be represented from strategies that borrow analogies from real-world systems. One of the first and most important tools for developing and evaluating new metaphors are comprehensive taxonomies. These provide designers the basis for understanding how possible metaphors generated structure the user interface.

20.3 Metaphor Classifications

Several authors have provided various schemes for classifying metaphor attributes as they relate to computers. These classifications have ranged from simple language versus visual and action versus object categories to broader distinctions that characterize how metaphors structure users' goals, tasks, and modes of interaction with the computer. Hutchins (1989) has provided one of the most comprehensive, yet more general classifications of metaphor.

1. *Activity metaphors* are determined by the users highest level goals. For example, is the user controlling a process, communicating, or playing a game?
2. *Mode of interaction metaphors* organize the fundamental nature in which the user thinks about interacting with the computer. These metaphors are task independent and determine how the user views what the computer is.
3. *Task domain metaphors* provide an understanding for how tasks are structured.

Most of the literature on user interfaces discusses metaphors only at the task domain level. However, the other two levels are always involved. In fact, designers may be using metaphors to design at the task domain level without consideration for how the metaphor operates at one of the other two levels. Hutchins urges designers to explicitly address the other two levels. For example, Hutchins (1989) describes four types of mode of interaction metaphors (number 2 above).

a) The *Conversation* metaphor creates a conversational interface (e.g., command line) that functions as an implied intermediary between the machine and user modeled after human-human conversations.
b) The *Declaration* metaphor creates an interaction where the user's commands, via a symbolic form, cause the world to somehow change. Declarations are performed on the world based on the conversational interface (e.g., delete file).
c) The *Model World* metaphor is what most in the user interface community think about when dealing with metaphors. The model world is usually based on a metaphor of the physical world. The user interacts directly on the modeled world.
d) The *Collaborative Manipulation* metaphor is a combination of the previous three.

Hutchins (1989) argues that collaboration manipulation metaphors are often appropriate because the naturalness of the model world offers great ease of interaction, while conversation and declarative metaphors offer the power of the more abstract, symbolic nature of language.

Marcus (1993a, 1994) identifies two distinctions in user interface metaphors: those of organization, and those of operation. "Organization" metaphors (structures, classes, objects, attributes) are the nouns of metaphor communication. Associations of "operation" (processes, action, algorithms) are the verbs of metaphor communication. For example, a document signifies an organization metaphor, while delete represents an operation metaphor.

Norman and Chin (1989) have identified four major metaphors used to structure interaction and mediate control over the user interface: "language" as a metaphor for command language interfaces, "printed form" as a metaphor for form fill interaction, "physical movement" as a metaphor for direct manipulation, and a "restaurant menu" as the association for menu selection.

Heckel (1991) has identified two levels of user interface metaphor operation by distinguishing between "familiar" and "transporting" metaphors. Familiar metaphors make the system familiar but do not aid functionality. Heckel claims that the critical difference between the two is that the transporting metaphor provides a framework in which real-world problems can be represented. The underlying and auxiliary metaphors (Cates, 1994) given previously are also a very broad distinction between different types of user interface metaphors.

More specific classifications include those by Collins (1995), who has classified a number of dimensions creating a catalog of metaphors. Väänänen and Schmidt (1994) give five dichotomous categories of metaphor attributes that the user interface designer should consider for hypermedia interfaces:

- Real-world metaphors (e.g., library) vs. non-real-world metaphors (e.g., UFO).
- Concrete metaphors (e.g., tree) vs. abstract/conceptual metaphors (e.g., family).
- Spatial metaphors (e.g., a house) vs. time-based metaphors (e.g., theater).
- General metaphors (e.g., book) vs. application dependent metaphors (e.g., train time table).
- Flexible and composite metaphors (e.g., desktop with recursive folder structures, or a house with books) vs. rigid metaphors (e.g., room with four walls). (Väänänen and Schmidt, 1994)

Each of the classifications given above can be useful to user interface designers for thinking about what metaphors to use and how to design them. They can do this by providing an understanding in how the different metaphor components interrelate, how they structure the interface, how they impact users' perception of the computer, and as general categories for thinking about the possibilities available. Having an exhaustive classification of metaphors that mapped user and task characteristics to different metaphor attributes would be beneficial to metaphor design. For example, is using a concrete over an abstract metaphor to represent an information structure more appropriate for certain search tasks? Also, how do different user characteristics interact with different metaphor types? The classifications given here are the starting points in creating a strategy for designing user interface metaphors.

20.4 Metaphor Mismatches

Understanding metaphor mismatches is critical to developing effective user interface design strategies because they provide much of the strength of metaphor, while posing some of the greatest challenges in getting metaphor design right. Similarities (matches) and dissimilarities (mismatches) between the source and target domains play a prominent role in how metaphors work. Matches provide direct associations between the two domains. "Matches are the sine quo non of metaphors" (Carroll, Mack, and Kellogg, 1988). Mismatches, on the other hand, can evoke greater insight into the target domain by emphasizing differences between the two domains that must be resolved. Mismatches can also intrigue the user into searching for similarities. However, mismatches can introduce problems if they are overlooked by users, inviting assumptions about the target domain that are not valid.

Mismatches can occur for several reasons. Small dissimilarities between the source and target domains cause mismatches. The combination of several metaphor source domains will typically result in mismatches among the metaphor mappings within the composite. The metaphors in the composite can be inherently different, often directly contradicting each other. Mismatches can also occur when the user's task characteristics and goals change.

Hirose (1992) differentiates static and dynamic mismatches. An example of a static mismatch for the "trash can" metaphor is that in the real world we do not have trash cans sitting on our desk. A dynamic mismatch is an inconsistency with the metaphor during task completion. For example, the trash can works well as a metaphor for throwing objects away, but as the task changes to ejecting a disk, the information provided by the metaphor breaks down. One hypothesis for the occurrence of dynamic mismatches is that the amount of information provided by the metaphor (source-target matches) changes as task and context characteristics change (Hirose, 1992). Dynamic metaphor mismatches might also be cases in which a metaphor is not adequately bound to a task context initially (Carroll and Rosson, 1994; Grudin, 1989).

Metaphor mismatches occur with aspects of computer functionality when the target domain is unable to provide a direct real-world correlate. There is an inevitable conflict between the extended functionality in a computer system and the metaphorical grounding achievable in existing functionality of real-world source domains (Streitz, 1986). Douglas and Moran (1983), for example, discovered that novice text editor learners used a typewriting metaphor for reasoning about the new domain, and that differences between typewriting and text editing lead to performance errors.

Smith (1987) has referred to this problem as the interface tension between *literalism* and *magic*. Literal features are those that are consistent with the metaphor and have real-world analogies. Magical features are those that extend beyond the metaphor and generally do not have structure found in the world. The tension between literalism and magic results because features true to the metaphor increase learnability, but powerful functionality that is not isomorphic to the source domain empowers users to perform tasks that are not possible in other mediums. Both the literal and magical aspects of computer functionality have advantages and disadvantages, requiring designers to make tradeoffs for balancing their impacts. These tradeoffs involve capitalizing on prior knowledge while offering functionality that the user is unfamiliar with, but would benefit from using.

As an example of extended functionality (magic), Smith (1987) describes features in the Alternative Reality Kit that allow users to connect buttons to other objects, requiring the user only to drag and drop a button icon on a device. If the metaphor was to remain literal, the user might have to drill a hole for the button and connect it to metaphorical wiring. This example is typical of current computer systems in the sense that it provides novel functionality relative to the physical world.

The tension between metaphorical representation based on real-world systems and the need to extend computer functionality beyond real-world source domains entails unavoidable mismatches between the source and target domains. Metaphors are needed that can span the literal-magic spectrum which create mismatches (Smith, 1987). The challenge in this problem is representing computer functionality that does not exist in the physical world with metaphors taken from real-world domains.

One of the best methods for doing this is to use composite metaphors for greater breadth to cover literal and magical properties of user interfaces. How does using more than one metaphor solve the problem? Having functionality that extends beyond a single source domain means that, by definition, the extended functionality is outside the metaphor. Even though the extended functionality being used for a particular problem domain appears quite novel and does not exist in the real world for that problem domain, the extended functionality often has analogous associations to other real-world systems or source domains.

For example, the pile metaphor is useful as a general framework for representing informal organization of document groups, particularly because users have been shown to prefer this type of organization (Mander et al., 1992). But piles of documents on physical surfaces never construct or reorganize themselves. Therefore, the extended functionality in this case is never seen in the real-world for this problem domain. There

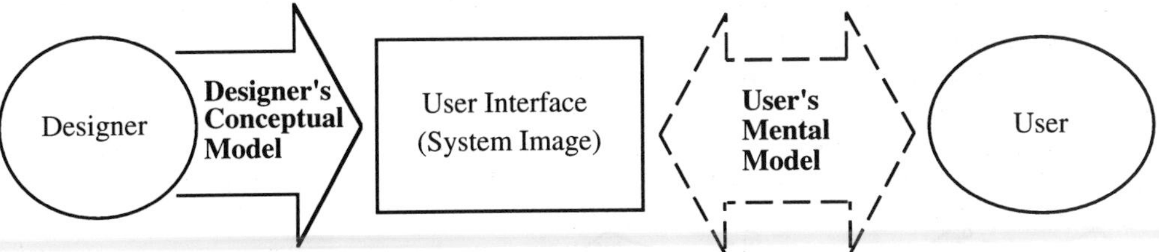

Figure 1. Model of the user interface(Adapted from Norman, 1986).

are, however, many real-world source domains outside the task of organizing documents by piles which can be used to represent construction and reorganization. For the pile metaphor, the developers chose an "assistant" as an auxiliary metaphor that helps the user perform these tasks. However, metaphors completely outside the office domain could also be used successfully.

Specific metaphors have been suggested that are claimed to be particularly well suited for making transitions from literal to magic features. For example, the metaphors that were described previously based more on sequences of events and less structured to places and things (e.g., traveling) have a less predictable structure because location and function change rapidly, allowing a wider range of possibilities to be explored in auxiliary metaphors (Cates, 1994). The travel, tourist, and other spatial metaphors given in Table 1 offer this type of flexibility. Less structure, however, may mean less of the good old matches and more of the undesirable mismatches.

Another alternative for representing nonreal-world functionality in computer systems is to use nonreal-world source domains. Terveen, Stolze, and Hill (1995) use the term "magic world" as an alternative to the model world metaphor. This magic world operates on the premise that intelligent assistance is working in coordination with, and based on, actions of the user. This type of interaction generally combines model and magic world metaphors. A good example of this is the AutoCorrect feature in Microsoft Word. The word "THe" is automatically replaced by "The." It is unclear whether this type of magic will lead to increases in superstitious skepticism already held toward computer systems by many users.

Mismatches typically enhance curiosity toward the system (Carroll and Thomas, 1987; Levialdi, 1990). Indeed, mismatches are a very powerful component of metaphors. Disparities are often more easily recognized because they are salient features that contradict the knowledge the user has about the metaphor or source domain. Mismatches raise new questions that require examining existing assumptions about the source domain based on the metaphor. When these questions are answered, dissimilarities result in further development of the user's mental model (Carroll and Mack, 1985; Rumelhart and Norman, 1978).

Metaphors need not cover every aspect of functionality nor does extended functionality necessarily undermine real-world metaphors. Adding magical features and functions that violate the basic metaphor is appropriate as long as expectations set by the metaphor do not specifically mislead users with the extended features and functions (Mayhew, 1992). For example, automatic pile reorganization in the pile metaphor does not violate the basic metaphor. Piles can be reorganized in the physical world, just not automatically. Designers will be faced with increasing demands for resolving interface tensions between literalism and magic as more novel functionality is designed into computer systems. In time, however, as more users become familiar with computers, magical properties of today will become the literal metaphors of tomorrow.

20.5 Designer, User, and System Components of Metaphor

Figure 1 presents a framework for analyzing the interaction of designers and users through the medium of the user interface and mental representations of the interface (Carroll and Olson, 1988; Norman, 1986; Staggers and Norcio, 1993; Wilson and Rutherford, 1989). The designer's *conceptual model* is the model that the designer has formulated for the system. The designer's model is a relatively complete and accurate understanding of how the system functions and should encompass an accurate understanding of the user's tasks, requirements, experience, capabilities, and limitations.

The user's *mental model* encompasses internal representations of how the user interface functions in the context of his or her tasks and goals. The user's model is determined by interaction with the system and changes in knowledge of the source domain (if the system is based on a metaphor). Ideally, the user's

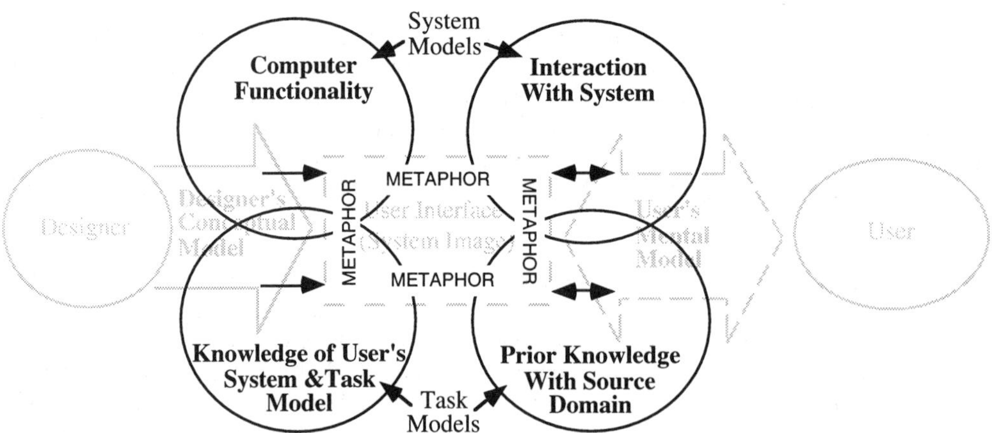

Figure 2. System and task models.

model will develop to be compatible with the designer's model. The *system image* is the physical structure designed into the user interface. It embodies the designer's conceptual model and is interpreted by the user's mental model.

Both the designer's and user's model include a model of the computer system (*system model*) and a model of the task domain (*task model*). Figure 2 is a representation of these models when the user interface is based on a metaphor. The designer's conceptual model includes (1) an understanding of the *computer functionality* (designer's system model) and (2) *knowledge of the user's system and task models* (designer's task model). The designer's system model is the abstract, conceptual understanding of how the system operates. The designers task model includes the user's predicted interaction with the system and an understanding of the user's prior knowledge with the source domain. The user's mental model is established from (1) *interaction with the system* (user's system model) and (2) the user's *prior knowledge with the source domain* (user's task model).

The metaphor is implemented through the system image to help the user construct a model that is compatible with the designer's model. The metaphor does this by bridging the designer's and user's system and task models (see Figure 2). The designer formulates a task model and system model based on the source domain of the metaphor to help the user understand the computer functionality.

20.5.1 Metaphor and the Designer's Conceptual Model

Metaphors are one of the tools used to communicate the designer's model, and a clear distinction should be made between a metaphor as a model and the designer's model (Jamar, 1986). A metaphor is often a simplified model of the designer's model (Carroll et al., 1988; Nielsen, 1990). Some debate exists over whether metaphorical models are most appropriate for communicating the designer's conceptual model. Sein and Bostrom (1989), for example, have summarized the research on several designer's conceptual models (abstract versus analogical) and conclude that which model is most appropriate for learning and mental model formation remains an open-issue.

Halasz and Moran (1981), Laurel (1993), Nardi and Zarmer (1993), and Nelson (1990) all argue that, while metaphors may have some limited usefulness, creating systems from designers' conceptual models based on metaphors will eventually impede the development of a user's mental model that more truly reflects the abstract conceptual nature of computer functionality. Metaphors in these cases are criticized for their incompleteness and inability to fully represent complex systems. These authors suggest more "abstract" representations: visual formalisms like tables and maps, activities like theater, nodes linked together with tree-like structure, and virtuality design or rich graphic expressions like movies. However, the notion of abstract in these critiques of metaphor are muddled, and these alternatives to metaphor are metaphors.

Without metaphors it is not possible from a realistic standpoint to fully represent any system with an abstract model devoid of metaphors. There is entirely too much functionality in even a relatively simple computer system. Metaphors excel in this respect because the very nature of their incompleteness leads to flexibility and power that would not be possible if simpler representations were used (Gaver, 1995).

Users do not want to learn abstract models, a difficult endeavor divorced from the tasks that motivate people to want to use computers. Metaphors, on the other hand, are embedded in task completion and in the context of user's current goals. If metaphors are viewed as a model of the underlying designer's conceptual model, the claims being made that metaphors fail to represent the full functionality of the system are not valid, as long as the user understands that the metaphor is simply a model and does not fully represent the true nature of the system (Nielsen, 1990).

Several studies have shown advantages for representing the designer's conceptual model with metaphors. Mynatt and Macfarlane (1987) showed that providing an advance organizer in the instruction manual based on a metaphor significantly improved scores on procedural and semantic knowledge transfer tests. Mayer (1976) has shown that programming constructs in BASIC are learned more easily when presented with a metaphor. Furthermore, Smilowitz (1996) found that a metaphoric interface was better than a non-metaphoric interface. She compared two world-wide web browsers. One browser used no metaphorical terminology, and the other used a library metaphor. When the user interface included metaphors, participants made fewer errors, performed tasks faster, and completed significantly more tasks successfully. Participants also perceived the metaphoric interface to be significantly easier to use than the non-metaphoric interface.

Sein and Bostrom (1989) found metaphors to be useful in training when individual differences were considered. Individual differences for training novices using either abstract or analogical models in an electronic mail filing system were compared. Visual ability and learning mode were compared for their impact on the user's mental model development. In general, the results showed that high-visual subjects performed better than low-visual subjects, and abstract learners' mental model development was better than concrete learners. Low-visual subjects performed as well as high-visual subjects when they had analogical models, but performed very poorly when learning occurred through an abstract model. Also, abstract learners performed better with an abstract model but performed worse with the analogical model. The reverse was found for concrete learners; they performed better with analogical models.

Gillan, Fogas, Aberasturi, and Richards (1995) found that users' computer experience and cognitive abilities have significant impact on their interpretation of metaphors in the interface. Computer users with more experience identified a larger number of metaphors and had more abstract interpretations than did less experienced users. Also, cognitive abilities were found to influence metaphor interpretations to some degree. People with higher nonverbal ability for attention and spatial memory were found to be more likely to identify computer metaphors.

It is difficult to imagine how underlying functionality of the system can be designed without using metaphorical associations because many of the tasks performed with a computer have the same or similar structure as tasks performed in noncomputer-based mediums. Inherently, similar tasks will have metaphorical associations to some degree. Furthermore, new users spontaneously generate metaphoric comparisons (Mack, Lewis, and Carroll, 1983; Douglas and Moran, 1983; Hutchins, 1989). Under these conditions, analogical reasoning is predominate when new material to be learned and understood is unfamiliar and abstract (Mayhew, 1992). If only abstract representations are used, and users do spontaneously generate metaphorical comparisons, how will the designer contend with the results? Will this aspect of the user's information processing be ignored; if not, how will it be mediated or prevented?

Metaphors are not simple ornaments of dialogue, limiting extended functionality not found in the real world. Nor are they mere comparisons, obstructing usability once learned. Metaphors create *ontologies* for users (Kuhn and Blumenthal, 1996). Ontologies provide a coherent structure involving a set of concepts at the user level. Metaphors allow constructivist learning of the designer's conceptual model, not possible with abstract models removed from user's prior knowledge.

20.5.2 Metaphor and the User's Mental Model

The extent to which a metaphor is used in the designer's model and supported in the system image will directly structure the user's mental model. The structure is created by linking components of the user's mental model (Collins, 1995): interaction with the system (user's system model) and prior knowledge with source domains (user's task model) (see Figure 2). A system image based on a metaphor links these components by grounding functionality the user interacts with to familiar concepts.

An attempt must be made to make user's models explicit in order for the interface design to be driven by these models (Levialdi, 1990), and this information needs to be reflected in the system image. It is also important that designers attempt to predict how user's mental models will change over time as a result of interaction with the system or changes in the knowledge of the source domain.

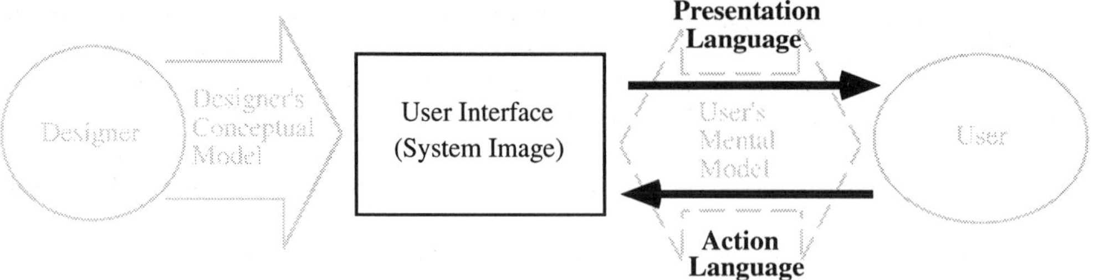

Figure 3. Languages used for communicating with the user interface (Adapted from Collins, 1995).

A great deal of research has addressed the issue of extracting and representing users' mental models, and these techniques are plagued with problems which arise because multiple mental models often coexist at different levels of abstraction (Norman, 1986). In fact, these levels often depend on the tasks and goals the user holds at a particular time. Therefore, it is important that the designer understand the user's interaction with the system, the tasks and goals associated with it, and how these relate to prior knowledge. If these two components of the user's mental model and their interaction are understood, the user interface can be designed around a metaphor that appropriately links these elements.

New techniques need to be developed that obtain valid knowledge representations (mental models) and the means for transforming those models into design specifications that are specifically useful for metaphor development and elaboration. For example, Anderson and Alty (1995) suggest using *frames* (questionnaires developed from cognitive anthropology) for eliciting user's everyday theories about metaphor referents. To utilize this information fully, designers also need to consider how metaphors affect the type of communication that occurs between the user and system.

20.5.3 Metaphor and the Human-Machine Communication Process

Collins (1995) describes a model of the user interface that includes a *presentation* and *action* language (see Figure 3). Hutchins (1989) contends that, regardless of the type of metaphor used, all interactions between humans and machines have an interface language. A presentation language is implemented by the designer in the form of visual, auditory and other cues through the system image. This language determines how all information is presented to the user and consists of expressions generated by the machine and interpreted by the user. The action language, which can be symbolic, gestural, or visual, consists of expressions composed by the user and interpreted by the machine. Response forms can include keyboard entry, mouse input, speech, etc.

Hutchins' four categories of "mode of interaction" metaphors listed previously can have a profound affect on the type of presentation and action language. The predominantly multimedia model world metaphors that exist today create interfaces that are interacted with through "direct manipulation" (see Shneiderman, 1987). These interfaces allow the user to directly manipulate visual objects on the display, reducing the need for abstract, symbolic syntax found in conversation metaphors.

These types of interfaces have gestural dialogues and visual languages. Direct manipulation interfaces, based on the model world metaphor, have a special connection between the action and presentation language (Hutchins et al., 1986). It is still a language, but one that is more direct or natural for the user. The user is not required to operate through an interface intermediary with symbolic descriptions, as is the case with conversation metaphors. Hutchins, Hollan, and Norman (1986) claim that the feeling of directness that these interfaces produce results from the user having to commit fewer cognitive resources in the communication process during task completion.

Designers often overlook how the metaphor can greatly affect the possibilities afforded to the user for communicating with the interface, and consequently, the user's resulting mental model of the system. Designers need to insure that using direct manipulation interfaces based on the model world metaphor, offering substantial power by enabling us to approach problems the way we normally do, do not restrict opportunities for novel functionality. When designing an interface metaphor, focus on a design strategy that considers the communication consequences the metaphor is imposing. By doing so, the user can be offered the optimal form of communication medium for any given situation and metaphor.

20.6 Metaphors in the Design Process

Metaphors not only provide users with a basis for reasoning about computer systems, they provide researchers and developers with concepts, criteria, and vocabulary for reasoning about designing the user interface as well. Metaphors have been shown to help designers generate creative design decisions, maintain consistency in the interface, keep the number of design decisions manageable, and provide rationale for the design decisions adopted. Johnson (1994) argues that because user interfaces mimic actions and representations in an infinite variety of ways, and because these concepts are artificial and arbitrary, metaphors of computer discourse are embedded deeply in the way computers have been thought about by developers. As a result, the process of design and the interfaces that result are metaphorical.

Metaphors directly and indirectly shape the design of user interfaces. For example, indirect influences derive from the inclination of designers to use metaphorical thinking for reasoning about their designs and for communicating with others in the design community (Hutchins, 1989). This process often occurs even without designers being aware of it; they are as predisposed to metaphorical thinking as are users. Direct influences derive from intentionally focusing design activities around supporting chosen metaphors once they have been identified (Hammond and Allinson, 1987).

Mambrey, Paetau, and Tepper (1994) found that researchers typically use metaphors in all aspects of development and design. For example, metaphors were used at the organizational level for project management, at the design group level for communication, and at the individual level as cognitive tools for creating new ideas. Dent-Read et al. (1994) interviewed twenty user interface designers and had metaphor experts identify metaphorical aspects of their designs. They found that the designers used descriptive metaphors for explaining their designs, used pictorial metaphors in depicting the displays themselves, and used organizational metaphors to structure large sets of decisions made about the user interface design process.

Gillan and Bias (1994) outline two specific uses for metaphors in aiding designers. First, metaphors increase consistency and commonality in user interfaces, and second, the number of design decisions is reduced. MacLean, Bellotti, Young, and Moran (1991) also view metaphors as the vehicles for shaping system design. Metaphors are a way to implement design functionality, generate design ideas, and as a method for justifying design decisions. Designers use analogies to develop new ideas, regardless of whether the specific metaphor under consideration becomes part of the system. Keeping track of the analogies used in generating ideas, or those analogies explicitly implemented in the system, can help challenge or justify design decisions. Furthermore, Tepper (1993) argues that metaphors facilitate creative thinking and provide a valuable communication tool in the design process.

Object-oriented design (OOD) techniques, which have been a growing force in the development of software, are a specific example of where metaphors can play a central role in the design process. Designers use metaphorical views of a problem domain as a vehicle to model the particular domain, and in fact, these metaphors are often extended beyond the design arena to be incorporated into the interface (Carroll and Rosson, 1994). One approach to OOD identifies roles which objects can assume, their responsibilities, and what relationships exist between those roles. The object-oriented metaphor is used as a heuristic to extend the real-world source domain. The idea is to view interface objects from an anthropomorphic stance as metaphorical real-world objects having responsibilities and intelligence associated with tasks (Rosson and Alpert, 1990). The object-oriented framework facilitates systems that have structures modeled similar to their real-world analogies (Pancake, 1995).

The roles of metaphors in the design process given above have been mainly from informal observations. Research needs to be conducted that pinpoints where and how metaphors facilitate the design process throughout the system life cycle. Tools also need to be developed that support metaphorical user interface design at each stage in the life cycle. For example, Young (1987) outlines a database system that automates metaphor generation, providing interactive support in creative metaphorical thinking. Some progress is being made in the development of theoretical and applied models of user interface metaphor design.

20.6.1 Theoretical and Applied Models of Metaphor

There is not a great deal of theoretical or empirical support for the design guidance found in the HCI literature, and research and design of user interface metaphors has been largely ad hoc (Carroll, et al., 1988; Kuhn, and Frank, 1991; Kuhn, Jackson, and Frank, 1991). However, the following section focuses on research endeavors that provide a theoretical basis for how metaphors function in HCI, and several have applied models with specific design guidance.

Carroll and Thomas (1982), Carroll and Mack (1985), and Carroll et al. (1988) have proposed a pragmatic, "active learning" theory of metaphor. Metaphor use is viewed as an active learner-initiated thought process because metaphors are open-ended comparisons that stimulate the learner into actively seeking explanations. Learning is viewed as an active process where computer users prefer to explore a new system, rather than learn by more traditional methods of following instructions or scripted practice (Carroll and Mack, 1985). In this model, abduction and adduction are the primary reasoning processes, generating hypotheses on the basis of limited information. Metaphors flourish under these conditions because they provide clues for these processes when the learner is developing procedural knowledge.

The active learning theory, along with Black's (1979) interaction theory and Tourangeau and Sternberg's (1982) view, claim that metaphors are more than mere descriptions of the target domain based on the source domain. Matches and mismatches between the source and target domains are both viewed as playing a significant role for the learner. "Salient dissimilarities—in the context of salient similarities—stimulate thought and enhance the efficacy of the metaphor as a learning vehicle" (Carroll and Mack, 1985).

Three distinct cognitive stages of metaphorical reasoning incorporated into a pragmatic framework have been identified: instantiation, elaboration, and consolidation (Carroll et al., 1988). Instantiation is the process of retrieving some known knowledge and is an automatic process often based on surface similarity. Elaboration, pragmatically guided by context of use and users' goals, is the more extensive process of mapping relations between the source and target domains. Consolidation, the third and final stage, forms a single representation of the target domain from mappings in the instantiation and elaboration stages. This last process results in a more intricate mental model for the user of the system.

Smyth, Anderson, and Alty (1995) and Anderson, Smyth, Knott, Bergan, Bergan, and Alty (1994) offer a pragmatic model of metaphor grounded in the psycholinguistic literature. The model was developed from research on a series of prototype telecommunication systems, and posits an active interaction between the source and target domains, much like the active learning theory. The foundation for their set intersection model is based on six components (note they use vehicle in place of source domain and system in place of target domain):

- S, system features.
- V, vehicle or source features.
- S+V+, vehicle features that map completely onto the system.
- S+V-, features of the target system that do not map to the vehicle.
- S-V+, features of the vehicle which do not map onto the system
- S-V-, features outside the system and vehicle.

Selecting metaphors is based on a design process consisting of several steps. Unique to their approach is evaluating the vehicle-system pairings using the set of characteristics given above which define the design space. Venn diagrams can be use to visualize the intersection between set components identified previously (see Smyth et al., 1995). These groupings allow designers to reason about the effectiveness of vehicle-system interactions and their associated mappings. A questionnaire allows potential users to provide agreement and confidence ratings for vehicle-system pairings (see Anderson et al., 1994). This is an empirically based design model that provides designers a mechanism for choosing among possible metaphors before the system is build based on usability and utility for representing system functionality. This model is complimentary to the active learning theory and provides some tools for evaluating and selecting user interface metaphors.

Hammond and Allinson (1987) have proposed an applications model of metaphor, which deals at the level of task domain metaphors described by Hutchins (1989). The model is based on the same premise of the two previous theories summarized: metaphor comprehension results from matches and mismatches between the source and target domains. In this model, metaphors convey information along two dimensions: *scope* of the metaphor and the *level of description.* Scope is the number of characteristics in the system that the metaphor represents, and level of description varies according to the knowledge the metaphor is intended to convey.

The model identifies two stages where users process metaphors. *Mapping abstraction* occurs when the metaphor is first encountered and represents the user trying to understand the metaphor scope and level of description. *Mapping invocation* occurs when the user relies upon the metaphor to achieve task goals. These stages correspond closely to the first two stages of metaphorical reasoning found in the active learning theory. Knowledge from the source and target domains get subdivided into four categories: task, semantic, lexical, and physical. The four categories of knowledge each represent a level of description. During the mapping abstraction, the user compares knowledge across all four levels of description between the source and target domains. Only primary entities get mapped in the mapping abstraction stage. Secondary entities get matched during mapping invocation.

When the user experiences a lack of knowledge in the target domain (system use), mapping invocation occurs. The metaphor is relied upon automatically only if mapping has occurred during the mapping abstraction. If the source domain has not provide the necessary information to use the system, a second stage occurs whereby attentional processing continues to compare primary and secondary entities. Hammond and Allinson (1987) contend that this is the active learning process that occurs with user interface metaphors described by Carroll and Mack (1985).

The model predicts that for metaphors to be successful they need not map at all levels of description, and if they are not mapped, self evident mismatched metaphors will cause more problems than mismatch metaphors that are ambiguous. Moreover, the model predicts that, if system functionality is clearly outside the metaphor, user performance will not necessarily suffer.

Gillan and Bias (1994) have proposed a dual actor/multi-function (DA/M) theory of metaphor. The theory stipulates that, through the process of knowledge transference from the source to target domain, networks of declarative knowledge are restructured. DA/M explicitly acknowledges both designers and users reliance on metaphors and is founded on theoretical constructs of human cognition relating to memory (procedural and declarative knowledge). Gillan and Bias cite Anderson's (1983) ACT theory as representative of the two-process view.

Two processes are proposed whereby the user's cognitive structures change when encountering interface metaphors and analogies: (1) procedural knowledge is mapped from the source domain to the target domain, and (2) the links between concepts in declarative memory are strengthened. The DA/M theory predicts that, when task components between the source and target domains share production rules, and when metaphorical interfaces provide clues to these shared components, a positive transfer of procedural knowledge will occur. Consequently, negative transfer is predicted when the metaphorical interface provides hints to similarity between production rules across the domains: but (1) they do not actually exist; or (2) the production rules exist under the same conditions between the training and transfer task, but different actions are required. DA/M predicts that procedural knowledge will not be mapped, regardless of whether production rules are shared, if no hints are given that a relationship exists between the two domains. Changes in declarative knowledge are also predicted. For example, new links can form between concepts and their attributes as the result of interacting with a metaphorical interface. In addition, existing links may be strengthened, weakened or eliminated.

The DA/M theory suggests that an interpretation of a metaphor will depend on a user's particular procedural and declarative knowledge structures. For example, computer experience can influence metaphor interpretation. It has been shown that experienced users interpret metaphors abstractly as where novices users interpret them concretely (Gillan et al., 1995). Concrete interpretations were found to be based on perceptual or surface similarities; however, conceptual similarities resulted in abstract interpretations.

From these findings, Gillan and Bias (1994) theorize that experienced users' declarative and procedural knowledge is relatively fixed. Based on these predictions, metaphorical interfaces will be less likely to influence experienced users' cognitive knowledge structures. Conversely, novices would be much more likely to undergo significant changes in long-term memory. Based on this theory, a specific course of action is outlined for designers in Gillan and Bias (1994).

Rieman, Lewis, Young, and Polson (1994) have also developed a model of analogical reasoning that has characteristics similar to Holland, Holyoak, Nisbett and Thagard's (1986) general model of analogy and the more specific learning theory by Carroll et al. (1988). The model views users' reasoning about metaphorical interfaces by a process of consistency between features of the system that are known and unknown. Similar to Gillan and Bias, declarative and production knowledge learning mechanisms are again addressed using the ACT-R (Anderson, 1993) and SOAR (Laird, Newell, and Rosenbloom, 1987) theories.

This model represents all knowledge by object, action, effect, and proposition types. ACT-R and SOAR are used to reason about how metaphors cause the restructuring of declarative and procedural knowledge. Evaluating the two theories in the context of metaphorical design provides a more structured understanding of consistency guidelines (Rieman et al., 1994). This approach along with the DA/M theory offer more mechanical human information processing mechanisms for evaluating metaphors than the previous theories outlined. However, they are quite complimentary and broaden the design space for evaluating metaphors.

Nonogaki and Ueda (1991) outline a cognitive approach to developing user interface metaphors called *Contextual Metaphors*. The focus of this design approach is on the use of composite metaphors. Real-world objects are utilized in building composite metaphors that are arranged to form contexts which broaden the design space, covering a greater variety of everyday activities. Two rules are used for matching metaphors to system functionality: *salience* is calculated as a measure of users' expectations of system features, and *similarity* is a measure of the match between the metaphorical source domain and the target system. Using attribute values, such as the amount of information in the metaphor and subjective probabilities for the likelihood of the metaphor being used, selection of metaphorical objects in task domains are made. Metaphors are spatially arranged, and then a scenario-based approach suggested by Carroll et al. (1988) is used to capture human activities according to users' preferences and requirements.

This type of composite metaphor approach is intended to create a gestalt scene, eliminating metaphor mismatches caused by single metaphors. This approach is unique because it suggests that composite, metaphorical aggregates will form that are something more than the sum of their parts, creating a new meaning (Nonogaki and Ueda, 1991). Many other researchers have suggested composite metaphors, but not for creating entities that extend beyond somewhat disjointed metaphors that are only intended to fill in areas where other metaphors have left off. Dent-Read et al., for example, found that designers do not systematically tie metaphors together.

Recently, database management systems (DBMSs) have been receiving a great deal of attention due to the large amounts of information being represented electronically. In addition to traditional text-based representations, visual metaphors are being used to provide data schema and query visualizations. Catarci, Costabile, Levialdi, and Batini (1995) have established metaphorical design as being the basic paradigm for visual database interaction. Catarci, Costabile, and Matera (1995) view DBMSs as layered environments where multiple metaphors are used to not only understand the database content, but also for extracting information.

Several researchers are attempting to provide a formal framework for metaphorical design tailored to DBMSs (Catarci, Costabile, and Matera, 1994; Haber, Ioannidis, and Livny, 1994). These researchers are working on developing a formal definition of visual metaphor to create mappings from the source domain to the data model and visual model. The significance of this approach in defining metaphor is it allows different visual models of the same metaphor. Many questions arise as to whether this approach has validity in other HCI areas and whether systematic relationships, based on a visual language distinction, can be distinguished between the source domain, target domain, metaphor, and the metaphors visual representation.

Kuhn and Frank (1991) and Kuhn, Jackson, and Frank (1991) have developed a method of algebraic modeling, originating from algebraic specification in software engineering, that provides a formalized cognitive theory of metaphor. Although other formal approaches to modeling metaphors exist (see Blumenthal, 1990; Gentner, 1983, 1989; Hall, 1989; Indurkhya, 1989; and Martin, 1990), Kuhn and Frank's approach specifically addresses interface metaphors by formalizing mappings between the source and target domains through algebraic expressions that consider tasks and actions. In doing so, they address what Carroll et al. (1988) refer to as the *pragmatic* aspects of metaphor, which consider the contexts of users' actual tasks. In comparison to other formalizations, Kuhn and Frank argue that this approach provides designers with specific tools to support the development of user interfaces (see Kuhn and Frank, 1991 for a detailed description of the method).

All of the theoretical and applied frameworks previously discussed attempt to model the use of metaphors from a pragmatic standpoint specifically couched in HCI. This information is invaluable to designers for understanding the fundamental mechanisms driving metaphor functioning. This work is encouraging because the majority of theories in the past on similarity and metaphor comprehension have been based exclusively on verbal and written communication. Unfortunately, most of the HCI metaphor theories are based on a single group of researches' observations and/or data and lack substantial empirical support. Accordingly, much additional theoretical and empirical work is needed from the HCI community.

20.6.2 Design Stages in Developing Metaphors

The previous section outlined several strategies which aspire to make the process of metaphor design more systematic, not only from a design standpoint but from a theoretical basis as well. This section provides a structured methodology for developing user interface metaphors consisting of five stages:

1. Identify system functionality.
2. Generate possible metaphors.
3. Identify metaphor-interface matches.
4. Identify metaphor-interface mismatches.

5. Manage metaphor-interface mismatches.

Identify System Functionality

Before metaphors can be used to model the user interface, system functionality must be specified (Erickson, 1990; Smyth, 1995). Requirements analysis and functional specification identifies the functions and features the system must have to meet the user's needs and the capabilities of the system for attaining these requirements. This may be difficult information for the designer to acquire early in the life cycle of the system, but it is imperative that this process occurs to insure that adequate information is available for mapping associations with potential source domains in the next stages.

Generate Possible Metaphors

Generating metaphors is a heuristic process, one that is highly creative and difficult to structure. However, there are several techniques which can be used to identify a set of candidate metaphors. First, predecessor tools and artifacts can be used as possible metaphors (Carroll et al., 1988; Madsen, 1994). New systems often build on existing functionality found in predecessor systems. For example, the systems which use the library and pile metaphors presented in Table 1 build on existing systems found in the physical world. Many times these systems can provide organizing metaphors since they are representative of the structure inherent in the problem domain.

A similar method is to build on existing metaphors found in computer systems the user is already familiar with using (Madsen, 1994; Smyth, 1995). In doing so, users will likely assimilated properties of the metaphor more easily. This can also provide some degree of consistency for the user across different applications. Key concepts implicit in the problem domain can also be important. For example, searching information structures has key relationships to traveling and moving through space. The landscape metaphor given in Table 1 provides a framework for representing information structures based on this key aspect.

Having designers sketch metaphors can be another useful technique for generating ideas. (Verplank and Kim, 1989; Verplank, 1990; Verplank, 1991). The designer begins by producing a list of metaphorical words that describe an existing interface. Each word is then sketched on paper. The designer continues working through the same process with metaphors for a new interface. A list is then made consisting of desirable attributes, actions, and adjectives for the interface. From the individual terms and sketches, the designer can sketch more elaborate metaphors, covering more aspects of the system. After elaboration of the metaphors' relevant and irrelevant aspects, the best ideas are further developed by constructing cardboard representations of the design.

Visual methods to developing metaphors offer a more tangible approach to visualizing possible alternatives. Further techniques for generating new ideas about metaphors can be found in Mountford (1990). The analytical techniques above can all be used by designers as starting points for brainstorming sessions. The metaphor classifications given previously are also good starting points for thinking about the range of available possibilities.

Several empirically-based methods can also be used for generating metaphors. Users can be interviewed to identify their needs, wants, tasks, terms, and images as they relate to metaphors (Marcus, 1994). Tape recording users talking about how they understand their current computer systems can also be used for identifying metaphors (Madsen, 1994). Analyzing the user's work context can be another fruitful method for developing metaphors (Marcus, 1994; Smyth et al., 1995). By observing or envisioning the way in which an application is used, the designer can understand the problem domain metaphorically and develop metaphorical terms to represent the system. For example, Moll-Carrillo, Salomon, Marsh, Suri, and Spreenberg (1994) observed how users store and organize documents and applications for developing a book metaphor to aid users in performing these tasks.

Several methods can be used to study work contexts and the social and organizational settings in which they occur. Participatory design, collaborative design, ethnography, interaction analysis, and contextual inquiry are all useful approaches for understanding work contexts. Erickson (1990) suggests identifying the user's problems with existing systems. Consider what aspects of the functionality is new to them. Observe them using similar functionality, and see if they have problems. Prototypes of new systems also can be tested on users to see if they have problems (e.g., cardboard mockups). Market feedback from customers may be another technique to get a fresh perspective. Smyth et al. (1995) claim that in the customers attempt to describe the functionality of a system, they are forced to employ rich metaphors from the source domain. The point of using all of the methods in this section is to identify metaphors from the user's point of view. This includes making explicit the user's mental model. For example, this can include empirically determining the user's semantic network and/or procedural knowledge related to the source domain (Gillan and Bias, 1994).

Table 2. Scenario components (from Carroll et al., 1988).

Tasks	*What* people do (goals and subgoals)
Methods	*How* tasks are accomplished and their component procedures, actions and objects.
Appearance	*Look* and *feel* vis-à-vis the physical elements of the domain.

Identify Metaphor-Interface Matches

Metaphor matches form the basis of the primary relationship between the source and target domains, and indeed, these properties are the core associations for generating metaphors outlined in the previous stage. Carroll et al. (1988) maintain that the key determinant for identifying matches is to express them in the context of goal-oriented user scenarios (see Carroll, 1995 for an extensive coverage of scenario-based techniques). The task, method, and appearance of the metaphor is analyzed with representative scenarios, exhausting the set of things people really do with the system.

A scenario-by-scenario comparison is performed with the template given in Table 2 (Carroll et al., 1988). A set of scenarios that exhaust the set of task contexts will provide a basis for analyzing the level of similarity of a metaphor beyond the look-and-feel to the level of user's goals and activities (Carroll and Rosson, 1994). This step is similar to the source-target pairings analysis proposed in the set interaction theory by Smyth et al. (1995), and identifying the relevant attributes and/or procedures between the source and target proposed in the DA/M theory by Gillan and Bias (1994). By using these approaches, designers can get a good feel for how user's tasks and methods will relate to plans of action for enacting goals.

Identify Metaphor-Interface Mismatches

Mismatches are inevitable, but the crux of identifying their implications is to determine when they will lead to erroneous actions, rather than leading to new insights. It is difficult to specify a priori when mismatches will lead to a greater insight into the target software domain. However, Carroll et al. (1988) hypothesize that a key condition is that the discrepancy in the software domain must be interpretable. The mismatch should be able to be isolated, and a salient alternative course of action in the target domain should be available.

Identifying metaphor mismatches can be performed with the same scenario-based technique used for identifying metaphor matches (analytical and empirical approaches can be used). Similarly, looking at mismatch pairings in the set interaction theory and identifying the irrelevant attributes and/or procedures between the source and target in the DA/M theory, provide methods for understanding mismatch implications. For example, the DA/M theory predicts that when surface similarity exists between the source and target (matches), indicating shared production rules when in fact they don't exist (mismatches), problems will occur. Pay special attention to where functionality not found in the real world is used. If the metaphor is based on real world referents, mismatches are inevitable at these areas (see section 20.4). Assuming that "good" and "bad" mismatches have been identified, the designer is faced with handling both of these conditions.

Manage Metaphor-Interface Mismatches

The discussion of composite metaphors previously applies directly to handling many types of mismatches: novel functionality and mismatches inevitable in the problem domain. Composite metaphors can create a match with one metaphor where a mismatch is occurring in another. Also, with composite metaphors offering alternative views, users can gain greater insight into understanding what the mismatch implies. The conflicting accounts stimulate users to reflect on differences (Madsen, 1994). Mismatches can also be used for indicating the boundaries of similarity. Used in this way, mismatches tell the story for when the metaphor no longer applies. Keep in mind, though, the more aspects that can be covered by a single metaphor, the better (Carroll and Thomas, 1982; Smilowitz, 1995).

In addition to using composite metaphors for handling mismatches, there are several other approaches which can be beneficial. One strategy is to teach modification rules for aspects of the system that are not represented by the metaphor. In other words, when introducing a metaphor, elaborate assumptions by making explicit what the metaphor hides and what it highlights (Carroll and Thomas, 1982; Madsen, 1994). This technique is especially useful as the metaphor that initially helped the user understand the system begins to break down. Making the limits of the metaphor explicit will circumvent problems the user may experience with functionality that is not supported by the metaphor—functionality that may not lend itself to being represented by analogies the user has with existing knowledge.

Another tactic suggested (Carroll and Mack, 1983) is to create an interface design that encourages and supports exploration of system features. Users must be able to solve the problems that arise from mismatches, and be able to recover from possible surprising system states. That is, users must be able to explore without penalty (Carroll et al., 1988).

Hirose (1992) proposes a specific strategy to assess and control dynamic mismatches. Attribute values are assigned to metaphors based on the level of matches. Then, during task completion by the user (in a formative evaluation), changes in target attribute values are measured. Hirose does not define precisely how attribute values are to be assigned, but they are intended to reflect how isomorphic the metaphor(s) is, or to what degree the source and target domains are similar. If the attribute values degrade during any portion of the task, Hirose suggests that another source domain should be chosen based on a measure of similarity and partially swapped for the old source domain.

When trying to account for mismatches, as with all the previous stages, the focus of the design must stay on communicating the functionality of the system, rather than trying to mimic ever aspect of the source domain. Smyth et al. (1995) reported that when designers focused too heavily on metaphors, they easily lost sight of communicating the system functionality. Remember that metaphors are models of the computer functionality, and the two are not the same thing. Use of metaphor is a means for the user to develop a mental model of the computer functionality.

The heuristics outlined above are derived from a synthesis of the material presented in previous sections. They offer designers a number of strategies for designing user interface metaphors. Following the approach specified above will insure that full consideration has been paid to developing a coherent, well structured metaphorical interface.

20.7 Conclusions

Metaphorical design continues to be pervasive in HCI. This is not surprising considering that metaphors are so powerful for designers and users alike. Human thought is both facilitated and limited by its reliance on metaphor. Metaphorical design must both control and exploit the relationship between matches and mismatches intrinsic to metaphor. This tension continues to be one of the most central issues for user interface metaphor research and development. Furthermore, abetting users in developing an accurate mental model of the system is the metaphor's crowning achievement. Formative and summative evaluation methods are needed to analyze metaphor effectiveness based on this dimension.

Although several theories of metaphor usage specific to the field of HCI have emerged, theoretical models pertaining to metaphors, analogies, and similes are some of the richest topics in psychology, linguistics, education and other disciplines, and much additional work is needed for incorporating these views into our current understanding and explanations of interface metaphors. Conversely, HCI as a discipline is in a unique position to contribute significantly to the understanding of metaphor, including views in other disciplines, by dissecting the "dynamic" nature of metaphor use associated with tasks found in user interfaces. In fact, this dynamic nature involving multiple media is quite different than the primarily linguistic metaphor usage focus of other research disciplines.

Highly visual, multimedia, direct manipulation interfaces are now the dominant paradigm of interaction between humans and computers. These user interfaces provide a rich environment for metaphor implementation because they offer affordances that model much of what occurs in the real world. In addition to the increased fidelity of computers to model the real world, new-sprung computer functionality detached from physical associations will only continue to flourish as we move into the 21st century. The consequences for researchers and practitioners will be an increased demand for analytical and empirical tools and methods that support creative metaphorical user interface design.

20.8 Acknowledgments

The authors would like to extend a special thanks to Vicki Neale for help in gathering background material in preparing this paper and for comments on earlier drafts. We also are thankful to Jim Alty, Tiziana Catarci, Doug Gillan, and Mike Snow for insightful reviews of this chapter.

20.9 References

Anderson, J. R. (1983). *The architecture of cognition.* Cambridge, MA: Harvard University Press.

Anderson, B., and Alty, J.L. (1995). Everyday Theories, Cognitive Anthropology and User Centered System Design. In *People and Computers X, Proceedings HCI '95* (pp. 137-150). Huddersfield, UK: Cambridge University Press.

Anderson, B., Smyth, M., Knott, R. P., Bergan, M., Bergan, J., and Alty, J. L. (1994). Minimizing conceptual baggage: Making choices about metaphor. In *People and Computers IX, Proceedings of HCI '94* (pp. 179-194). Huddersfield, UK: Cambridge University Press.

Arai, K., Yokoyama, T., and Matsushita, Y. (1992). A Window System with Leafing Through Mode: Book-Window. In *Proceedings of ACM CHI'92 Conference on Human Factors in Computing Systems* (pp. 291-292). New York: Association for Computing Machinery.

Blumenthal, B. (1990). Incorporating metaphor in automated interface design. In *Proceedings of IFIP INTERACT '90: Human-Computer Interaction* (pp. 27-31). North-Holland: Elsevier Science Publishers.

Catarci, T., Costabile, M.F., Levialdi, S., Batini, C. (1995). Visual Query Systems for Databases: A Survey - Technical Report SI/RR - 95/17, Dipartimento di Scienze dell'Informazione, University di Roma "La Sapienza."

Benest, I. D., Morgan, G., and Smithurst, M. D. (1987). A Humanised Interface to an Electronic Library, In *Proceedings of IFIP INTERACT'87: Human-Computer Interaction* (pp. 905-910). Horth-Holland: Elsevier Science Publishers.

Black, M. (1979). More about metaphor. In A. Ortony (Ed.), *Metaphor and thought*. Cambridge, MA: Cambridge University Press.

Bruner, J. S. (1960). *The process of education*. London: Oxford University Press.

Carroll, J. M. (Ed.). (1995). *Scenario-based design: Envisioning work and technology in systems development*. New York: Wiley.

Carroll, J. M., and Mack, R. L. (1985). Metaphor, computing systems, and active learning. *International Journal of Man-Machine Studies*, *22*(1), 39-57.

Carroll, J. M., Mack, R. L., and Kellogg, W. A. (1988). Interface metaphors and user interface design. In M. Helander (Ed.), *Handbook of Human-Computer Interaction* (pp. 67-85). Amsterdam: Elsevier Science Publishers.

Carroll, J. M., and Olson, J. R. (1988). Mental models in human-computer interaction. In M. Helander (Ed.), *Handbook of human-computer interaction* (pp. 45-65). Amsterdam: Elsevier Science Publishers.

Carroll, J. M., and Rosson, M. B. (1994). Putting metaphors to work. In *Graphics Interface '94* (pp. 112-119). Toronto, Ontario: Canadian Information Processing Society.

Carroll, J. M., and Thomas, J. C. (1982). Metaphor and the cognitive representation of computing systems. *IEEE Transactions on Systems, Man, and Cybernetics*, *12*(2), 107-116.

Carroll, J. M., and Thomas, J. C. (1987). Fun. *SIGCHI Bulletin*, *19*(3), 21-24.

Catarci, T., Costabile, M. F., and Matera, M. (1994). Which metaphor for which database? Submitted to the *Proceedings of Third Working Conference on Visual Database Systems VDS, 3*.

Catarci, T., Costabile, M. F., and Matera, M. (1995). Visual metaphors for interacting with databases. *SIGCHI Bulletin*, *27*(2), 15-17.

Cates, W. M. (1994). Designing hypermedia is hell: Metaphor's role in instructional design. In *Proceedings of Selected Research and Development Presentations at the 1994 National Convention of the Association for Educational Communications and Technology*, IR 016716, (pp. 95-108). Washington, DC: US Department of Education.

Collins, D. (1995). *Designing object-oriented user interfaces*. Redwood City, CA: Benjamin/Cummings Publishing Company, Inc.

Dent-Read, C. H., Klein, G., and Eggleston, R. (1994). Metaphor in visual displays designed to guide action. *Metaphor and Symbolic Activity*, 9(3), 211-232.

Douglas, S. A., and Moran, T. P. (1983). Learning test editor semantics by analogy. In *Proceedings of ACM CHI'83 Conference on Human Factors in Computing Systems* (pp. 207-211). New York: Association for Computing Machinery.

Duit, R. (1991). On the role of analogies and metaphors in learning science. *Science Education*, *75*(6), 649-672.

Ellis, S. R. (1993). Prologue. In S. R. Ellis (Ed.), *Pictorial communication in virtual and real environments* (pp. 3-11). Bristol, PA: Taylor & Francis.

Erickson, T. D. (1990). Working with interface metaphors. In B. Laurel (Ed.), *The Art of Human-Computer Interface Design* (pp. 65-73). Reading, MA: Addison-Wesley Publishing Company, Inc.

Fahlén, L. E., Brown, C. G., Ståhl, O., and Carlsson, C. (1993). A space based model for user interaction in shared synthetic environments. In *Proceedings of ACM INTERCHI'93 Conference on Human Factors in Computing Systems* (pp. 43-48). New York: Association for Computing Machinery.

Fairchild, K.M., Lee, B.H., Loo, J., Ng, H, and Serra, L. (1993). The Heaven and Earth Virtual Reality: Designing Applications for Novice Users. In *Proceedings of IEEE Virtual Reality Annual International Symposium (VRAIS)* (pp. 47-53). Piscataway, NJ : IEEE Service Center.

Fairchild, K., Meredith, G., and Wexelblat, A. (1989). The tourist artificial reality. In *Proceedings of ACM CHI'89 Conference on Human Factors in Computing Systems* (pp. 299-304). New York: Association for Computing Machinery.

Gaver, W. W. (1995). Oh what a tangled web we weave: Metaphor and mapping in graphical interfaces. In *Proceedings of CHI '95, Conference on Human Factors in Computing Systems* (pp. 270-271). New York: Association for Computing Machinery.

Gaver, W. W. (1986). Auditory icons: Using sound in computer interfaces. *Human-Computer Interaction, 2*, 167-177.

Gentner, D. (1983). Structure-mapping: A theoretical framework for analogy. *Cognitive Science, 7*, 155-170.

Gentner, D. (1989). The mechanisms of analogical learning. In S. Vosniadou and A. Ortony (Eds.), *Similarity and Analogical Reasoning* (pp. 199-241). Cambridge, UK: Cambridge University Press.

Gillan, D. J., and Bias, R. G. (1994). Use and abuse of metaphor in human-computer interaction. In *IEEE International Conference on Systems, Man and Cybernetics* (pp. 1434-1439). New York: IEEE.

Gillan, D. J., Fogas, B. S., Aberasturi, S. M., and Richards, S. (1994). Metaphors, machines, and metaphor machines. Submitted for publication.

Gillan, D. J., Fogas, B. S., Aberasturi, S. M., and Richards, S. (1995). Cognitive ability and computing experience influence interpretation of computer metaphors. In *Proceedings of the Human Factors Society 39th Annual Meeting* (pp. 243-247). Santa Monica, CA: Human Factors Society.

Grudin, J. (1989). The case against user interface consistency. *Communications of the ACM, 32*, 1164-1173.

Haber, E. M., Ioannidis, Y. E., and Livny, M. (1994). Foundation of visual metaphors for schema display. *Journal of Intelligent Information Systems, Special Issue on Advances in Visual Information Management Systems, 3*, 1-38.

Hämmäinen, H., and Condon, C. (1991). Form and room: Metaphors for groupware. *Conference on Organizational Computing Systems* (pp. 95-105). New York, NY: Association for Computing Machinery.

Hammond, N., and Allinson, L. (1987). The travel metaphor as design principle and training aid for navigating around complex systems. In *People and Computers III, Proceedings of the HCI'87* (pp. 75-90). Cambridge, MA: Cambridge University Press.

Halasz, F., and Moran, T. P. (1981). Analogy considered harmful. In *Proceedings of CHI'81, Conference on Human Factors in Computer Systems* (pp. 383-386). New York: Association for Computing Machinery.

Hall, R. P. (1989). Computational approaches to analogical reasoning: A comparative analysis. *Artificial Intelligence, 39*, 39-120.

Heckel, P. (1991). Conceptual models and metaphor in software design. In *36th IEEE Computer Society International Conference - COMPCON* (pp. 498-499). Piscataway, NJ: IEEE Service Center.

Henderson, D. A., and Card, S. K. (1986). Rooms: The use of multiple virtual workspaces to reduce space contention in a window-based graphical user interface. *ACM Transactions on Graphics, 5*(3), 211-243.

Hirose, M. (1992). Strategy for managing metaphor mismatches. In *CHI'85 Short Papers, Conference on Human Factors in Computing Systems* (p. 6). New York: Association for Computing Machinery.

Holland, J., Holyoak, K., Nisbett, R., and Thagard, P. (1986). *Induction: Processes of inference, learning, and discovery*. Cambridge, MA: MIT Press.

Holyoak, K. J., and Thagard, P. (1995). *Mental leaps: Analogy in creative thought*. Cambridge, MA: The MIT Press.

Hutchins, E. (1989). Metaphors for interface design. In M. M. Taylor, F. Neel, and D. G. Bouwhuis (Eds.), *The structure of multimodal dialogue* (pp. 11-28). Amsterdam: Elsevier Science Publishers.

Hutchins, E. L., Hollan, J. D., and Norman, D. A. (1986). Direct manipulation interfaces. In D. A. Norman & S. W. Draper (Eds.), *User centered system design: New perspectives on human-computer interaction* (pp. 87-124). Hillsdale, NJ: Lawrence Erlbaum Associates.

Inder, R., and Stader, J. (1994). Bags and Viewers: a metaphor for structuring a database browser. In *Proceedings of Advanced Visual Interfaces'94* (pp. 228-230). New York: Association of Computing Machinery.

Indurkhya, B. (1994). The thesis that all knowledge is metaphorical and meanings of metaphor. *Metaphor and Symbolic Activity*, *9*(1), 61-63.

Indurkhya, B. (1992). *Metaphor and Cognition: an Interactionist Approach.* Dordrecht, Boston: Kluwer Academic.

Jamar, P. G. (1986). Mental models for computer users. In *Proceedings of the 1986 IEEE International Conference on Systems, Man, and Cybernetics* (pp. 761-765). Piscataway, NJ: IEEE Service Center.

Johnson, G. J. (1994). Of metaphor and the difficulty of computer discourse. *Communications of the ACM*, *37*(12), 97-102.

Johnson, M. (1987). *The body in the mind.* Chicago: The University of Chicago Press.

Kim, H., and Hirtle, S. C. (1995). Spatial metaphors and disorientation in hypertext browsing. *Behaviour & Information Technology*, *14*(4), 239-250.

Kuhn, W. (1995). 7±2 questions and answers about metaphors for GIS user interfaces. In T. L. Nyerges, D. M. Mark, R. Laurini, and M. J. Egenhofer (Eds.), *Cognitive Aspects of Human-Computer Interaction for Geographic Information Systems, NATO ASI Series* (pp. 113-122). Kluwer Academic Publishers.

Kuhn, W. (1993). Metaphors create theories for users. In A. U. Frank and I. Campari (Eds.), *COSIT'93: Spatial Information theory* (pp. 366-376). Springer-Verlag.

Kuhn, W., and Blumenthal, B. (1996). Spatialization: Spatial metaphors for user interfaces. In A. U. Frank (Ed.), *Geoinfo Series*, *8*, Vienna, Austria: Technical University Vienna (Tutorial notes from the ACM Conference on Human Factors in Computer Systems (CHI '96).

Kuhn, W., and Frank, A. U. (1991). A formalization of metaphors and image-schemas in user interfaces. In D. M. Mark and A. U. Frank (Eds.), *Cognitive and Linguistic Aspects of Geographic Space* (pp. 419-434). Dordrecht, Netherlands: Kluwer Academic Publishers.

Kuhn, W., Jackson, J. P., and Frank, A. U. (1991). Specifying metaphors algebraically. *SIGCHI Bulletin*, *23*(1), 58-60.

Laird, J., and Newell, A., and Rosenbloom, P. (1987). SOAR: An architecture for general intelligence. *Artificial Intelligence*, *33*, 1-64.

Lakoff, G., and Johnson, M. (1980). *Metaphors we live by*. Chicago, IL: University of Chicago Press.

Lakoff, G. (1994). What is metaphor? In J. A. Barnden and K. J. Holyoak (Eds.), *Advances in Connectionist and Neural Computation Theory: Analogy, Metaphor, and Reminding* (Vol. 3, pp. 203-258). Norwood, NJ: Ablex Publishing.

Laurel, B. (1993). *Computers as Theatre*. Reading, MA: Addison-Wesley.

Levialdi, S. (1990). Cognition, models and metaphors. In *Proceedings of the 1990 IEEE Workshop on Visual Languages* (pp. 69-79). Piscataway, NJ: IEEE Service Center.

Lynch, P. J. (1994). The evolving interface of multimedia. *Syllabus magazine*, 8(3), 48-50.

Lumbreras, M., and Rossi, G. (1995). A metaphor for the visually impaired: Browsing information in a 3D auditory environment. In *Proceedings of ACM CHI'95 Conference on Human Factors in Computing Systems* (short papers) (pp. 216-217). New York: Association for Computing Machinery.

MacLean, A., Bellotti, V., Young, R., and Moran, T. (1991). Reaching through analogy: A design rationale perspective on roles of analogy. In *Proceedings of ACM CHI'91 Conference on Human Factors in Computing Systems* (pp. 167-172). New York: Association for Computing Machinery.

Mack, R. L., Lewis, C. and Carroll, J. M. (1983). Learning to use office systems: Problems and prospects. *ACM Transactions on Office Information Systems*, 1, 254-271.

Madsen, K. H. (1994). A guide to metaphorical design. *Communications of the ACM*, *37*(12), 57-62.

Mambrey, P., Paetau, M., and Tepper, A. (1994). Controlling visions and metaphors. In K. Duncan and K. Krueger (Eds.), *13th World Computer Congress 94*, *3*, 223-227.

Mander, R., Salomon, G., and Wong, Y. Y. (1992). A 'Pile' metaphor for supporting casual organization of information. In *Proceedings of ACM CHI'92 Conference on Human Factors in Computing Systems* (pp. 627-634). New York: Association for Computing Machinery.

Marcus, A. (1993a). Future user interface metaphors. In *Proceedings of the Human Factors and Ergonomics Society 37th Annual Meeting* (pp. 258-262). Santa Monica, CA: The Human Factors and Ergonomics Society.

Marcus, A. (1993b). Human communications issues in advanced user interfaces. *Communications of the ACM, 36*(4), 101-109.

Marcus, A. (1994). Managing metaphors for advanced user interfaces. In *Proceedings of the Workshop on Advanced Visual Interfaces: AVI'94* (pp. 12-18). New York: Association of Computing Machinery.

Martin, J. H. (1990). *A Computational Model of Metaphor Interpretation*. New York: Academic Press.

Mayer, R. E. (1976). Some conditions of meaningful learning for computer programming: Advance organizers and subject control of frame order. *Journal of Educational Psychology, 68*(2), 143-150.

Mayhew, D. J. (1992). *Principles and guidelines in software user interface design*. Englewood Cliffs, NJ: Prentice Hall.

Mercurio, P. J., and Erickson, T. D. (1990). Interactive scientific visualization: An assessment of a virtual reality system. In *Proceedings of IFIP INTERACT'90: Human-Computer Interaction* (pp. 741-745). Horth-Holland: Elsevier Science Publishers.

Mills, M., Cohen, J., and Wong, Y. Y. (1992). A magnifier tool for video data. In *Proceedings of ACM CHI'92 Conference on Human Factors in Computing Systems* (pp. 93-98). New York: Association for Computing Machinery.

Moll-Carrillo, H. J., Salomon, G., Marsh, M., Suri, J. F., and Spreenberg, P. (1995). Articulating a metaphor through user-centered design. In *Proceedings of ACM CHI'95 Conference on Human Factors in Computing Systems* (pp. 566-572). New York: Association for Computing Machinery.

Mountford, S. J. (1990). Tools and techniques for creative design. In B. Laurel (Ed.), *The art of human-computer interface design* (pp. 17-30). Reading, MA: Addison-Wesley Publishing Company, Inc.

Mynatt, B. T., and Macfarlane, K. N. (1987). Advanced organizers in computer instruction manuals: Are they effective? In *Human-Computer Interaction – INTERACT'87* (pp. 917-921). Amsterdam: Elsevier Science Publishers.

Mynatt, E. D., and Edwards, W. K. (1995). Metaphors for nonvisual computing. In A. D. N. Edwards (Ed.), *Extra-ordinary human-computer interaction: Interfaces for users with disabilities* (pp. 201-220). New York: Cambridge University Press.

Nardi, B. A., and Zarmer, G. (1993). Beyond models and metaphors: Visual formalisms in user interface design. *Journal of Visual Languages and Computing, 4*, 5-33.

Nelson, T. H. (1990). The right way to think about software design. In B. Laurel (Ed.), *The Art of Human-Computer Interface Design* (pp. 235-243). Reading, MA: Addison-Wesley.

Nielsen, J. (1990). A meta-model for interacting with computers. *Interacting with Computers, 2*(2), 147-160.

Nonogaki, H., and Ueda, H. (1991). FRIEND21 Project: A construction of 21st century human interface. In *Proceedings of ACM CHI'91 Conference on Human Factors in Computing Systems* (pp. 407-414). New York: Association for Computing Machinery.

Norman, D. A. (1986). Cognitive Engineering. In D. A. Norman and S. W. Draper (Eds.), *User centered system design: New perspectives on human-computer interaction* (pp. 31-61). Hillsdale, NJ: Lawrence Erlbaum Associates, Inc.

Norman, K. L., and Chin, J. P. (1989). The menu metaphor: food for thought. *Behaviour and Information Technology, 8*(2), 125-134.

Pejtersen, A. M., and Nielsen, F. (1991). Iconic interface for interactive fiction retrieval in libraries based on a cognitive task analysis. In H. J. Bullinger (Ed.), *Human aspects in computing: Design and Use of Interactive Systems and Work with Terminals* (pp. 753-762). Amsterdam: Elsevier Science Publishers.

Pancake, C. M. (1995). The promise and the cost of object technology: A five-year forecast. *Communications of the ACM, 38*(10), 33-49.

Rieman, J., Lewis, C., Young, R. M., and Polson, P. G. (1994). "Why is a raven like a writing desk?" Lessons in interface consistency and analogical reasoning from two cognitive architectures. In *Proceedings of ACM CHI'94 Conference on Human Factors in Computing Systems* (pp. 438-444). New York: Association for Computing Machinery.

Rosson, M. B., and Alpert, S. R. (1990). Cognitive consequences of object-oriented design. *Human-Computer Interaction, 5*, 345-379.

Rouse, W. B., and Morris, N. M. (1986). On looking into the black box: Prospects and limits in the search for mental models. *Psychological Bulletin, 100*(3), 349-363.

Rumelhart, D. E., and Norman, D. A. (1978). Analogical process in learning. In J. R. Anderson (Ed.), *Cognitive skills and their acquisition* (pp. 335-359). Hillsdale, NJ: Lawrence Erlbaum Associates.

Savidis, A., and Stephanidis C. (1995). Building non-visual interaction through the development of the rooms metaphor. In *Proceedings of ACM CHI'95 Conference on Human Factors in Computing Systems* (pp. 244-245). New York: Association for Computing Machinery.

Sein, M. K., and Bostrom, R. P. (1989). Individual differences an conceptual models in training novice users. *Human-Computer Interaction, 4,* 197-229.

Shafrir, E., and Nabkel, J. (1994). Visual access to hyper-information: Using multiple metaphors with graphic affordances. In *Proceedings of ACM CHI'94 Conference on Human Factors in Computing Systems (Companion)* (pp. 142). New York: Association for Computing Machinery.

Shneiderman, B. (1987). *Designing the user interface: Strategies for effective human-computer interaction.* Reading, MA: Addison-Wesley Publishing Company.

Smilowitz, E. (1996). *The effective use of metaphors in user interface design.* Unpublished Dissertation, New Mexico State University.

Smith, R. B. (1987). Experiences with the alternate reality kit: An example of the tension between literalism and magic. In *Proceedings of ACM CHI'87 Conference on Human Factors in Computing Systems* (pp. 61-67). New York: Association for Computing Machinery.

Smith, D. C., Irby, C., Kimball, R., Verplank, B., and Harslem, E. (1982). Designing the star user interface. *Byte, 7*(4) 242-282.

Smyth, M., Anderson, B. & Alty, J. L. (1995). Metaphor Reflections and a Tool for Thought, In M. A. R. Kirby, A. J. Dix and J. E. Finlay (Eds.), *People and Computers X, Proceedings of HCI'95* (pp. 137-150). Huddersfield, UK: Cambridge University Press.

Staggers, N., and Norcio, A. F. (1993). Mental models: Concepts for human-computer interaction research. *International Journal of Man-Machine Studies, 38,* 587-605.

Stanney, K. M. (1995). Realizing the full potential of virtual reality: Human factors issues that could stand in the way. In *Proceedings of the IEEE Virtual Reality Annual International Symposium* (pp. 28-34). Research Triangle Park, NC: IEEE Computer Society Press.

Streitz, N. A. (1986). Mental models and metaphors: Implications for the design of adaptive user-system interfaces. In H. Mandl and A. Lesgold (Eds.), *Learning Issues for Intelligent Tutoring Systems* (pp. 165-186) New York: Springer-Verlag.

Swedlow, T. (1995). Fusion in cyberspace. *VR World, 7/8,* 14-15.

Tepper, A. (1993). Future assessment by metaphors. *Behaviour & Information Technology, 12*(6), 336-345.

Terveen, L., Stolze, M., and Hill, W. (1995). From "model world" to "magic world": Making graphical objects the medium for intelligent design assistance. *SIGCHI Bulletin, 27*(4), 31-34.

Tourangeau, R., and Sternberg, R. (1982). Understanding and appreciating metaphors. *Cognition, 11,* 203-244.

Väänänen, K. (1993). Multimedia environments: Supporting authors and users with real-world metaphors. In *Proceedings of ACM INTERCHI'93 Conference on Human Factors in Computing Systems (Adjunct)* (pp. 99-100). New York: Association for Computing Machinery.

Väänänen, K., and Schmidt, J. (1994). User interfaces for hypermedia: How to find good metaphors. In *CHI'87 Short Papers, Conference on Human Factors in Computing Systems* (p. 263). New York: Association for Computing Machinery.

Verplank, B. (1990). Graphic invention for user-interface design. *CHI'90 Workshop: Conference on Human Factors in Computing Systems.* New York: Association for Computing Machinery.

Verplank, W. L. (1991). Sketching metaphors: Graphic invention and user-interface design. In *Friend 21: '91 International Symposium on Next Generation Human Interface* (pp. 1-8).

Verplank, B., and Kim, S. (1989). Graphic invention for user interfaces: An experimental course in user-interface design. *SIGCHI Bulletin, 18*(3), 50-66.

Ware, C., and Osborne, S. (1990). Exploration and virtual camera control in virtual three dimensional environments. *Computer Graphics, 24*(2), 175-183.

Wilson, A., and Rutherford, J. R. (1989). Mental models: Theory and application in human factors. *Human Factors, 31*(6), 617-634.

Wozny, L. A. (1989). The application of metaphor, analogy, and conceptual models in computer systems. *Interacting with Computers, 1*(3), 273-283.

Young, L. F. (1987). The metaphor machine: A database method for creativity support. *Decision Support Systems, 3*(4), 309-317.

Handbook of Human-Computer Interaction
Second, completely revised edition
M. Helander, T.K. Landauer, P. Prabhu (eds.)

Chapter 21

Direct Manipulation and Other Lessons

David M. Frohlich
Hewlett-Packard Laboratories
Bristol, England

The understanding of direct manipulation interfaces is complex. There are a host of virtues and vices. Do not be dismayed by the complexity of the arguments. To our mind, direct manipulation interfaces provide exciting new perspectives on possible modes of interactions with computers...We believe that this direction of work has the potential to deliver important new conceptualisations and a new philosophy of interaction.

Hutchins, Hollan and Norman 1986, pp123-4.

21.1 Introduction

What comes to mind when you think of direct manipulation interfaces? Maybe an icon in the shape of a folder or filing cabinet, a pop down menu or two, sliders and gauges, mice and windows? In short, the modern graphical interface! This impression is confirmed by searching the human computer interaction literature for articles containing the term 'direct manipulation'. Matching articles often use the term very broadly to refer to all things graphical.

In this chapter I want to move beyond this simple conception of direct manipulation as a graphical interaction style, to the more complex notion of direct manipulation as a design philosophy - as indicated in the opening quote from Hutchins, Hollan and Norman. This means I will *not* be reviewing the best ways to design screens, icons, menus or even graphical interactions in general, as these topics are all covered separately and in depth in other chapters of this volume. Instead I will return to the original definition of direct manipulation introduced by Shneiderman (1982; 1983) and to the early debate it sparked about *why* certain manual/graphical forms of interaction are more attractive than command line interfaces. The rest of the chapter will try to update this debate in the light of recent critiques and findings on direct manipulation, and of other relevant developments in the HCI field. It concludes with a re-evaluation of the direct manipulation philosophy in the modern context, and an attempt to resolve aspects of the ongoing debate which is now fuelled by concerns over the negative effects of graphical standards (Buxton 1993; Card 1995), and the rise of interface agents (Streeter 1995; Wooldridge and Jennings 1995).

Thus the main thrust of the chapter will be to guide the reader through the many twists and turns of the arguments and findings surrounding direct manipulation as a philosophy, in order to draw out some of the most valuable lessons they teach us about usability and design. The approach is similar to that recommended by Wixon and Good (1987) who argue for a deeper analysis of the dimensions of usability underlying proposed interface categories. Many of the resulting lessons *do* relate to the design of graphical interactions, but mainly at the level of deciding when to employ graphical rather than linguistic techniques at the interface. 'Other lessons' relate to the selection and use of conversational and mixed mode forms of interaction. In this sense the chapter can be seen as a compliment to others on graphical forms of interaction, and a particular companion to the chapter by Gould on The Design of Usable Systems (elsewhere in this handbook).

21.2 What is Direct Manipulation?

21.2.1 Original Definitions and Claims

Shneiderman (1982; 1983) first used the term direct manipulation to refer to an emerging class of highly usable and attractive systems of the day, including display editors, early desktop office systems, spreadsheets, CAD systems and video games. These systems had graphical interfaces which allowed them to be operated 'directly' using manual actions rather than typed instructions. Actions were mediated by special function keys, screen displayed menus and pointing devices such as mice, pens and joysticks. Such systems seemed to change the entire paradigm for human-computer interaction from *dialogue* to *manipulation* by utilizing what the programmers knew was a visual *language* in a way users believed to be an entire interactive *world.*

This illusion was the real 'magic' of the new approach which Shneiderman summarised in the following design principles:

1. Continuous representation of the object of interest.
2. Physical actions or labelled button presses instead of complex syntax.
3. Rapid incremental reversible operations whose impact on the object of interest is immediately visible.

Thus display editors showed users a full page of text exactly as it would appear when printed out ('What You See Is What You Get'), instead of in abbreviated form punctuated with formatting commands (*Principle 1*). Modifications to this 'object of interest', *the page*, could be made directly in a number of ways, including typing new text at any selected point and watching the old text shuffle up to make room, highlighting and moving blocks of text with gestures and function buttons, and removing characters in situ at the press of a button (*Principles 2 and 3).* Office systems such as the Xerox Star (Canfield, Smith, Irby, Kimball and Verplank, 1992) selected *documents* as their key 'objects of interest' and presented them to users as document icons on a virtual desktop instead of filenames in a list (*Principle 1).* Users could then open, print, file or delete documents by moving their icons around the desktop in relation to other familiar office objects such as folders, filing cabinets, wastebaskets, and printers *(Principle 2).* Such movements were continuously controlled by the user and had direct visible consequences on the documents involved *(Principle 3).* The story was similar for spreadsheets, CAD systems, video games, and early visual programming tools (e.g. Iseki and Shneiderman 1986). All presented some key set of objects in visual form which users could modify, extend, combine and otherwise manipulate.

Shneiderman claimed a number of usability benefits for these kinds of systems - the last of which has been added in a more recent publication (Shneiderman 1992). These include:

1. Learnability
2. Enhanced expert performance
3. Memorability
4. Fewer error messages
5. Better feedback
6. Reduced anxiety
7. Increased control

However, from the earliest articles, Shneiderman has always acknowledged that the *quality* of the selected graphic representation is critical to the direct manipulation effect. Simply finding a graphical alternative to a command-based interaction, in itself, will not suffice. The representation must be meaningful and accurate to users as determined by appropriate testing and evaluation. This list of benefits should therefore be seen as an idealised list representing the potential of the approach if executed well.

21.2.2 Modern Direct Manipulation Interfaces

Thirteen years later Shneiderman is still a strong advocate of the direct manipulation approach. Speaking at a panel discussion at CHI'95 he pointed to modern developments in *information visualisation* as representing where direct manipulation has got to today and indicating where it is going in the future (Streeter, 1995). Much progress has been made in extending the sheer amount of information that can be displayed to users by using 3 dimensions, stereo displays, multiple perspectives and layers, and novel data structures (e.g. Card, Robertson and Macinlay, 1991; Harrison, Ishii, Vicente, and Buxton, 1995; Strausfeld, 1995). At the same time there has been an extension of input devices and techniques for manipulating visual information, with head, eye, hand and body movements, often in combination with novel sliders, menus or gestural languages (e.g. Ahlberg and Shneiderman, 1994a; Foley, 1987; Jacob, 1991; Kurtenbach, Sellen and Buxton,

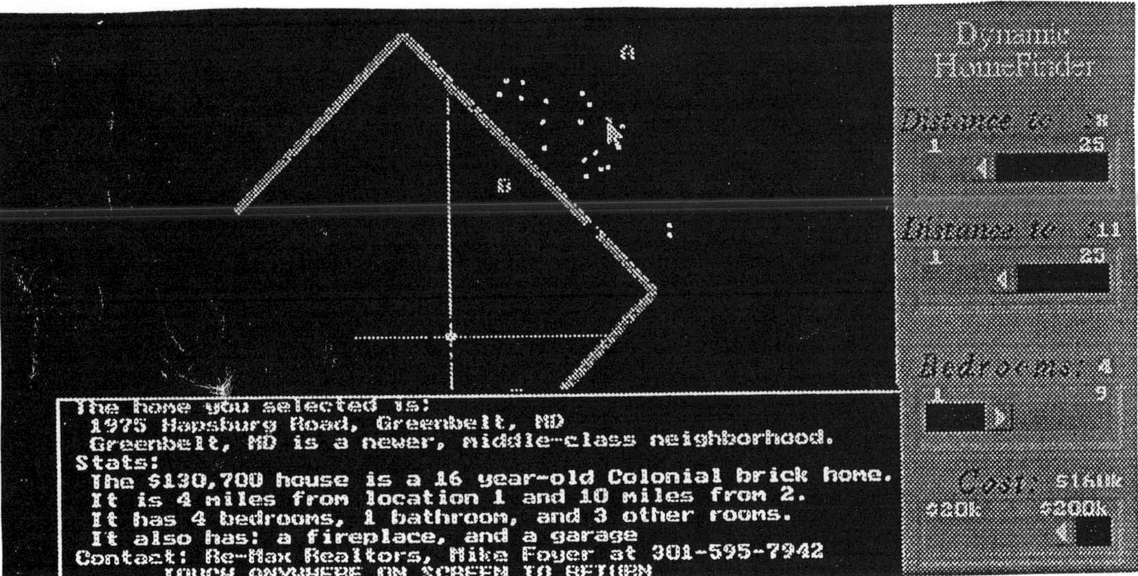

Figure 1. The dynamic homefinder interface. *(From Shneiderman, Williamson and Ahlberg, 1992; Figure 2).*

1993; Venolia, 1993; Zimmerman, Smith, Paradiso, Allport and Gershenfeld, 1995). In effect, the *scope* for finding effective graphical representations of application 'objects' has never been greater, and there is much momentum behind the approach to do so (see the chapter on Models of Graphical Perception, elsewhere in this handbook, for a more extended discussion).

A particularly compelling example of a modern direct manipulation interface is the *Dynamic Homefinder* system (Ahlberg, Williamson and Shneiderman, 1992; Shneiderman, 1994; Williamson and Shneiderman, 1992). This presents an interface to a database of houses for sale by displaying a map peppered with dots corresponding to individual homes (see Figure 1). Users constrain the range of dots that appear on the map by moving sliders for properties such as cost, number of bedrooms and distance to school or work. This system embodies all three of Shneiderman's defining principles for direct manipulation, but implementation of the rapid/incremental/reversible (*principle 3)* is particularly impressive. The distribution of dots on the map changes continuously as each slider is moved left or right, allowing the user to explore the effects of an entire range of property settings in a sweep of the hand. A similar technique is used in the interface to a database of films (Ahlberg and Shneiderman, 1994b). It is difficult to see how such 'dynamic queries' could be done at all, let alone better, in a standard query language.

21.3 What makes Manipulation Direct?

The first extensive critique of direct manipulation was written by Hutchins, Hollan and Norman (1986). The authors agreed with Shneiderman that certain graphical interfaces appear more attractive and usable than their command-based counterparts, but sought to explain when and why. In effect they were the first to ask "What makes manipulation direct?".

Their answer is rather complicated and abstract, and has to do with how the user thinks about the role of the computer in the interaction, and with the effort required to get it to do what you want. These two dimensions of *engagement* and *distance* are said to work together to conjure up the impression of directness at the interface. In short, Hutchins et al. argue that:

DIRECTNESS = ENGAGEMENT + DISTANCE

To expand, engagement refers to the perceived locus of control of action within the system (after Laurel, 1986). A critical distinction is whether users feel themselves to be the principle actors within the system or not (see Figure 2). In systems based on a conversational style of interaction the locus of control appears to reside with a 'hidden intermediary' who executes linguistic commands such as <delete filename> on the users behalf. This is like shouting through to someone in another room who then performs the requested ac-

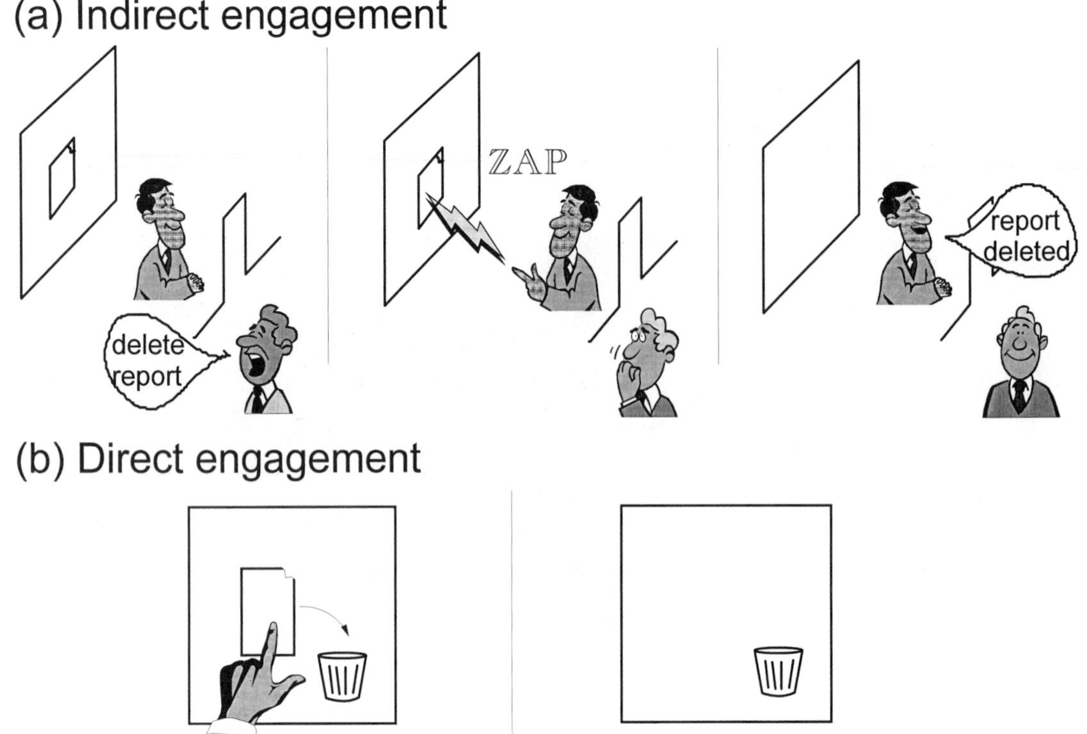

Figure 2. Two types of engagement.

tion and shouts back a response (Figure 2,(a)). This interaction is indirect in the sense that the user is not directly engaged with the actual objects of interest such as documents. In systems based on a graphical style of interaction the locus of control appears to reside with users themselves who manipulate the objects of interest within a model world. This is like reaching into the world yourself to carry out the action (Figure 2,(b)). Users act on the world in 'first-person' and are therefore said to be directly engaged with the system.

Distance refers to the mental effort required to translate goals into actions at the interface and then evaluate their effects (after Norman, 1986). Norman explains this with reference to the 'gulf' between goals and actions shown in Figure 3. This gulf is spanned through cycles of interaction in which the user does something and the system responds. Certain sorts of mental calculations have to be made by the user at the beginning of each cycle to work out what to do and bridge the 'Gulf of Execution'. Other sorts of calculations have to be made at the end of each cycle to work out what has happened and bridge the 'Gulf of Evaluation'. Systems and interfaces which make it easier for users to make these calculations are said to be more direct to operate. Use of the desktop metaphor used in the Xerox STAR system is a good example of this. By representing objects of interest as documents within a model world the designers ensured more than direct engagement with the system. They also invoked a set of ready-made expectations in users about what kinds of things could be done with documents (e.g. create, move, copy, open, delete) and what this might look like if they were. This might mean that users don't have to 'think so hard', or at least learn so much, compared to learning and using a command language for the same operations.

This analysis leads Hutchins et al. to propose a space of interfaces varying in both engagement and distance as shown in Figure 4. **Direct manipulation** turns out to be only one of four possible types in which users treat the computer as a model world *and* find it easy to translate their goals into actions. By implication, they are the best of all interfaces. The possibility of poorly designed graphical systems is acknowledged in **low-level world** interfaces which are difficult or tedious to operate despite engaging users directly in a model world. Furthermore, the lack of a model world representation is not always shown to result in poorer interaction as evidenced in **high-level language** interfaces. These may support easy and effective interactions through the type

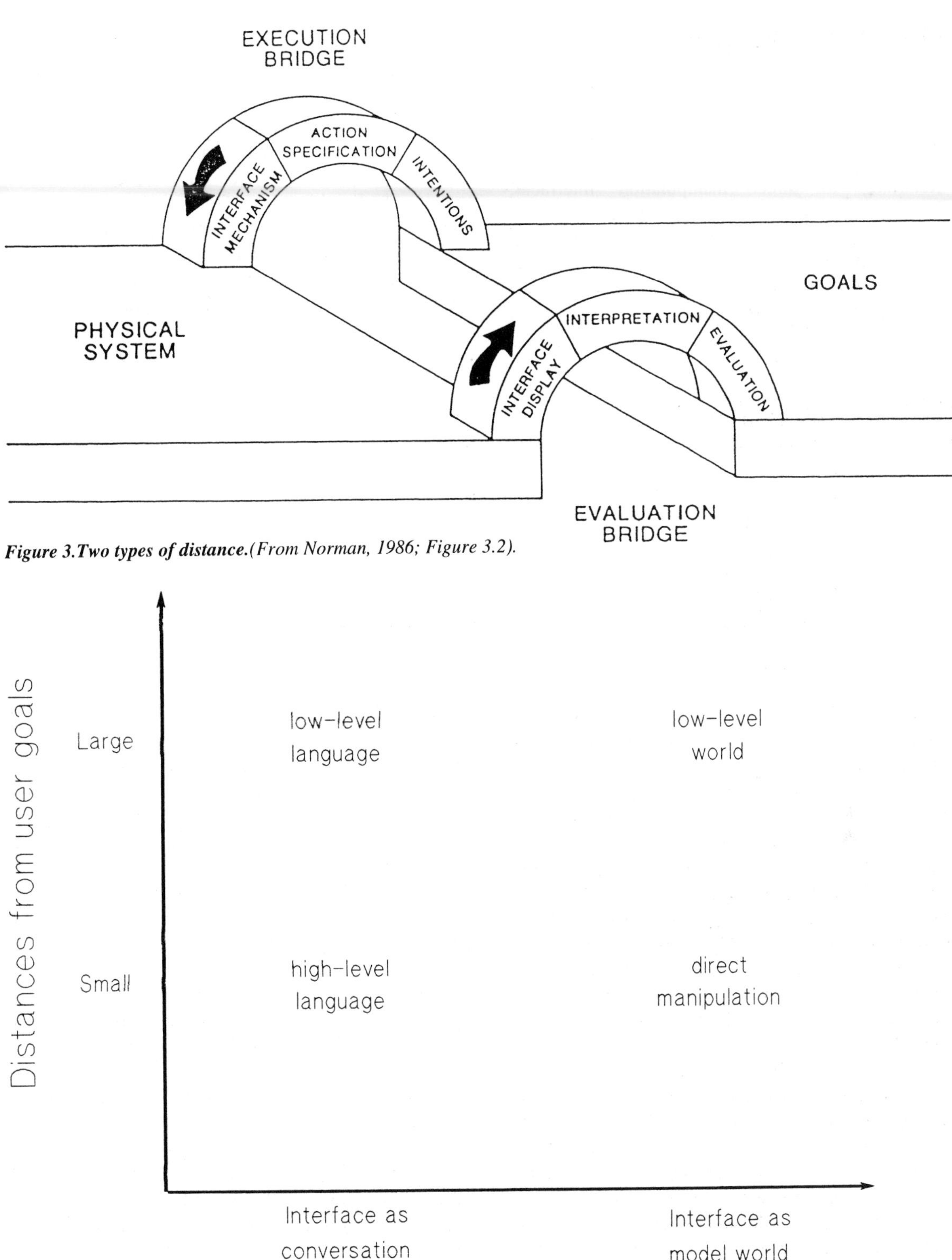

Figure 3.Two types of distance.*(From Norman, 1986; Figure 3.2).*

Figure 4. A space of interfaces. *(From Hutchins, Hollan, and Norman, 1986; Figure 5.8).*

of indirect engagement illustrated in Figure 2(a) by using commands which cor-respond closely to what users want to do. However, poor implementations of these systems result in **low-level languages**. These are the worst of all interfaces since they require users to work hard to achieve their goals through indirect engagement.

Returning to direct manipulation interfaces, Hutchins et al. go on to question some of Shneiderman's claims for them. Their *learnability* and *memorability* is said to depend upon the users prior knowledge and its semantic mapping to the system. The *need for error messages* is said to remain for task related problems, despite decreasing overall because of better feedback for the evaluation of actions. And *expert performance* is suspected to slow down rather than speed up through direct manipulation, for at least two reasons. First the loss of language involves the loss of descriptive expressions which allow the user to refer to classes of objects or actions in a single input. Second, the use of familiar real-world metaphors may lock the user into existing ways of doing things which are easy to learn and remember for the novice, but less effective than they could be for an expert in the new medium. They conclude with some force therefore that "much empirical work remains to be done to substantiate these claims" (Hutchins et al. 1986, p123).

In the next section we turn to this work, and to a related body of research on mixed mode interfaces combining elements of language and action in the same system.

21.4 Data and Developments

21.4.1 Tests

A large number of studies have tested the above claims in various ways. These tests break down into three categories:

1. Uncritical comparative evaluations - measuring the usability of a direct manipulation interface against one or more alternative interfaces

2. Critical comparative evaluations - measuring the usability of several different implementations of a direct manipulation interface, sometimes but not always against alternative interfaces, so as to separate different elements of the effect.

3. Naturalistic choice studies - measuring interactional preferences for direct manipulation and alternative methods in a mixed mode interface

The first two types of tests employ a standard experimental paradigm in which independent groups of subjects perform the same task using one of several different interfaces. Dependent measures of task performance are then used to make group comparisons. The last type of test is based on a 'Combined' condition in which subjects are faced with a mixed mode interface. A more qualitative analysis of the choice of method used by subjects throughout the session is conducted to reveal the contexts in which direct manipulation is and is not favoured. The key insights from each of these tests are as follows.

Uncritical Comparative Evaluations

Most tests of the benefits of direct manipulation fall into this category. However their key insights are difficult to summarise because of differences in the way they implement direct manipulation and contrasting interfaces, in the tasks given to subjects, and in the way they measure usability. Consequently their findings are mixed; with some studies showing clear positive advantages for direct manipulation, others showing no differences, and yet others showing clear disadvantages.

Advantages for direct manipulation have been demonstrated on word processing tasks (Card, Moran and Newell 1983; Frese, Schulte-Gocking and Altmann 1987; Jordan 1992), file manipulation tasks (Karat 1987; Morgan, Morris and Gibbs, 1991; Margono and Shneiderman, 1987), and database retrieval tasks (Egan, Remde, Landauer, Lochbaum and Gomez, 1989; Eberts and Bittianda, 1993; Te'eni, 1990, Ulich, Rauterberg, Mott, Greutmann and Strohmo, 1991). The direct manipulation interfaces here were display editors, Macintosh-style operating systems, desktop filing systems, and an interactive graphics package. The alternative interfaces were all command line interfaces, except in Ulich et al. (1991) where a menu interface was used. The studies measured different combinations of factors represented in Shneiderman's list of benefits and often found superiority of direct manipulation on only a subset of the measures used. For example, Eberts and Bittianda (1993) found benefits in speed and understanding but not accuracy; Morgan et al. (1991) found benefits in accuracy and satisfaction but not speed; Karat (1987) found benefits in speed for all but one task; while Frese et al. found performance benefits late but not early in practice.

No differences between direct manipulation and other interfaces have been found in studies of file managment (Whiteside, Jones, Levy and Wixon, 1985), drawing (Eberleh, Korfmacher and Streitz,

1992) and matching concepts and labels (Kacmar, 1989). 'Iconic' interfaces were contrasted with command and/or menu interfaces by Whiteside et al. and Kacmar, while Eberleh et al. examined the use of commands and actions on a graphics task, with and without background distractions. There were no overall performance benefits in the use of icons and no savings in 'workload' experienced by subjects using the direct manipulation graphics interface. Furthermore, Whiteside et al. and Eberleh et al. both found that subjective preferences varied across individuals and could change with the task conditions.

Disadvantages for direct manipulation have been shown in studies of table manipulation (Tullis and Kodimer, 1992), filing and retrieval (Jones and Dumais, 1986), and browsing (Egido and Patterson, 1988). Thus Tullis and Kodimer found two drag and drop methods to be slower than the use of radio buttons or a single data entry box for changing the order of fields in a table. In the other two experiments spatially arranged icons were contrasted with text labels and found to be less accurate for filing and retrieval (Jones and Dumais, 1986) and slower for navigating through a catalogue (Egido and Patterson, 1988).

The fact that the benefits of direct manipulation depend on implementation, task and measurement factors is perhaps the greatest insight provided by these tests. Taken together the tests suggest that direct manipulation interfaces do not provide a wide variety of usability benefits on any task. Rather, these interfaces seem to improve selected aspects of usability on a restricted set of tasks.

In general, the tests support Hutchins et al.'s view of a spectrum of manipulation-based and language-based interfaces varying in effectiveness (see again Figure 4). Although each study claims to have employed a direct manipulation interface, many may actually have used a low level world interface which doesn't map well to the goals users are trying to achieve with it. Depending on whether the alternative conversational interfaces are high or low level languages according to Figure 4, users may perform as well or even better with those. Hence the mixed results.

One problem here is that a surface description of a 'direct manipulation' interface doesn't ensure small 'distance' characteristics, and hence usability, because those features are dependent on the *task* the interface will be used for. This also means that the same manual interface might be classified as direct when used for one task and indirect (i.e. 'low level') when used for another. This is a problem for the direct manipulation philosophy since most interfaces support a variety of tasks or goals, some of which may be performed better through conversational rather than manual techniques.[1] A related problem is that even when manual techniques *are* appropriate to the current task, there is insufficient guidance in the original literature for designers to choose between competing implementations so as to achieve directness of manipulation in the resulting interface (Kunkel, Bannert and Fach, 1995). It is to this issue that the next set of studies are addressed.

Critical Comparative Evaluations

These tests set out to examine the effectiveness of different implementations of direct manipulation interfaces against each other and against alternative interfaces. In doing so they help to tease apart the relative importance of different elements of direct manipulation interfaces and therefore to inform design choices within and between them.

The need for such tests is underlined by Kunkel et al. (1995) who list 10 elements associated with direct manipulation interfaces in the literature. These should be recognisable from the descriptions in Sections 21.2 and 21.3:

1. Object-orientation
2. Permanent visualization
3. Extensive use of metaphors
4. Action-techniques using pointing devices
5. Window-techniques
6. Function-objects
7. Integration of different input techniques
8. Use of icons
9. Function activation by menu selection or dragging
10. User's adjustment of design features

Tests exist on the role of object-orientation (Kunkel et al.,1995), permanent visualisation (Ahlberg, Williamson and Schneiderman, 1992; Ballas, Constance, Heitmeyer and Perez, 1992; Tabachneck and Simon, 1994), metaphors (Anderson, Smyth, Knott, Bergan, Bergan and Alty, 1994; Ankrah, Frohlich and Gilbert, 1990), action-techniques (Ahlberg et al., 1992; Ballas et al., 1992) icons (Benbasat and Todd, 1993; MacGregor, 1992) and function activation (Benbasat and Todd, 1993; Kunkel et al., 1995).

[1] A version of this multiple-task problem applies to any design philosophy which promotes one style of interaction over another. However in the case of direct manipulation it is compounded by the fact that the *definition* as well as the *success* of the promoted interaction method is relative to the tasks being performed.

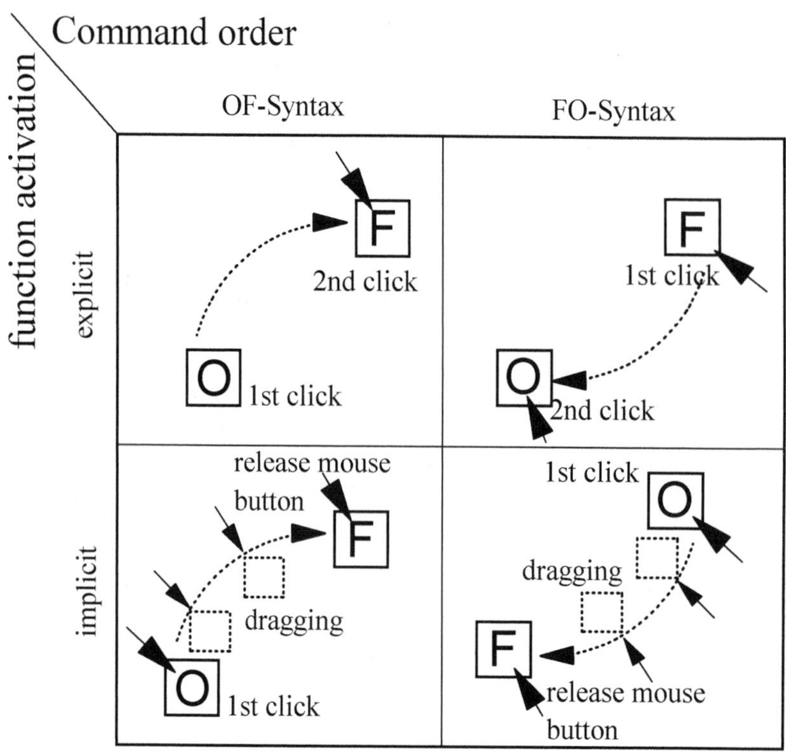

Figure 5. Four direct manipulation interface designs. *(From Kunkel, Bannert, and Fach, 1995; Figure 1).*

Thus Kunkel et al. (1995) themselves examined the relative benefits of interfaces varying in object orientation and function activation. Using the experimental design shown in Figure 5 they tested 4 independent groups of 16 subjects on one of four direct manipulation interfaces. Object orientation was varied by contrasting an object-function command order with a function-object command order. Function activation was varied by contrasting clicking with dragging selected objects. The actual system used was a graphics editor displaying triangle, circle and square objects together with icons for colour, pattern and line thickness functions. Users had to reproduce 10 abstract pictures on one of the interfaces. Command order made no significant difference to subjects performance on the task, whereas the mode of function activation did. Explicit function activation by clicking was found to be more accurate and efficient than implicit activation by dragging. There were no differences in subjects attitudes to the interfaces.

In a related experiment, Benbasat and Todd (1993) varied the method of function activation in an office system interface by supporting either clicking or dragging operations. They refer to the clicking interface as 'Menu' based and the dragging interface as 'Direct Manipulation' based. They also vary the iconic nature of each interface, by presenting actions and objects as icons or as textual labels. This leads to the four possible interfaces shown in Figure 6. Four independent groups of 12 subjects performed a meeting arrangement task on one of the interfaces. There were no significant differences between the Icon and Text conditions in speed or accuracy of performance, although dragging ('Direct manipulation') was significantly faster than clicking ('Menu'), at least on early trials.

In a direct study of the effect of icons, MacGregor (1992) tested the relative usability of the three interfaces to a Videotex information system shown in Figure 7. The 'Label' interface simply presented a menu of textual items refering to different sections of information in the system. The 'Descriptor' interface presented the same labels with textual examples next to each item, while the 'Icon' interface presented the labels with examples shown as icons. Three independent groups of 10 subjects answered 36 questions on one of the interfaces. Use of the Descriptor and Icon interfaces resulted in significantly more accurate performance than that on the Label interface, but were

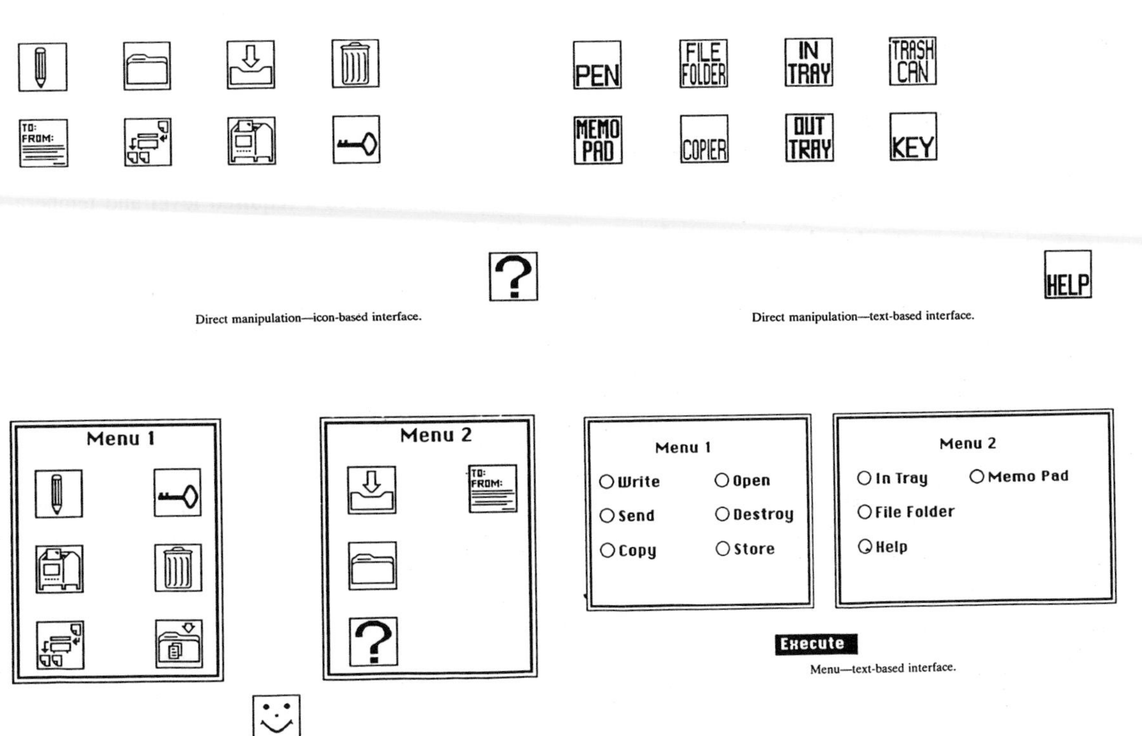

***Figure 6. Two direct manipulation and two menu interfaces.** Figures 1-4 in Benbasat and Todd (1993).*

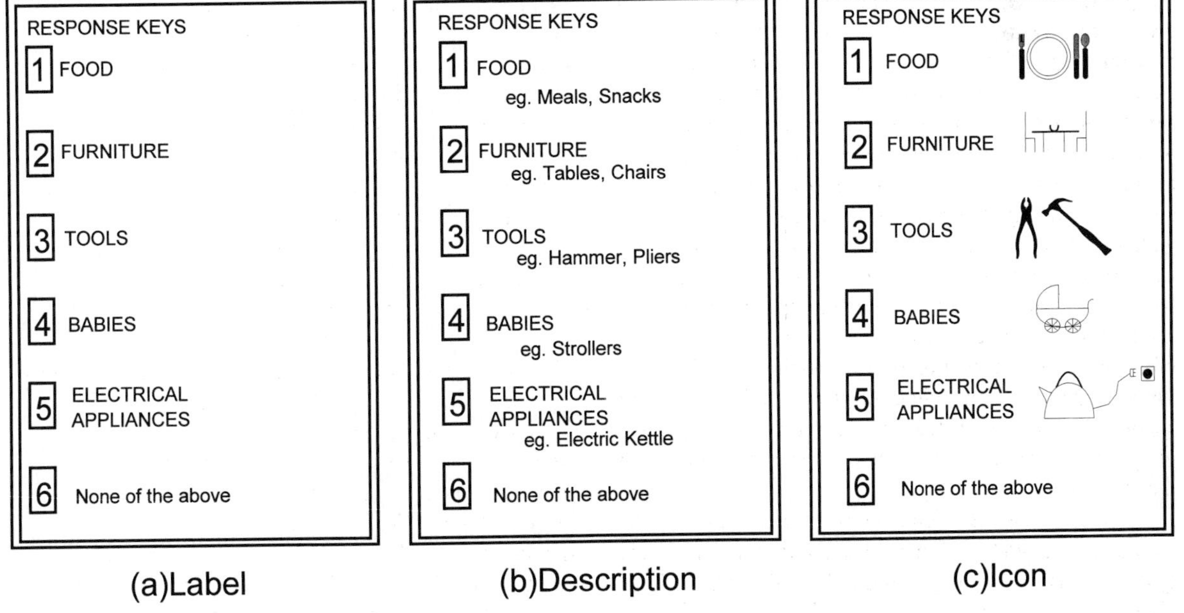

Figure 7. Three types of menu page interfaces.

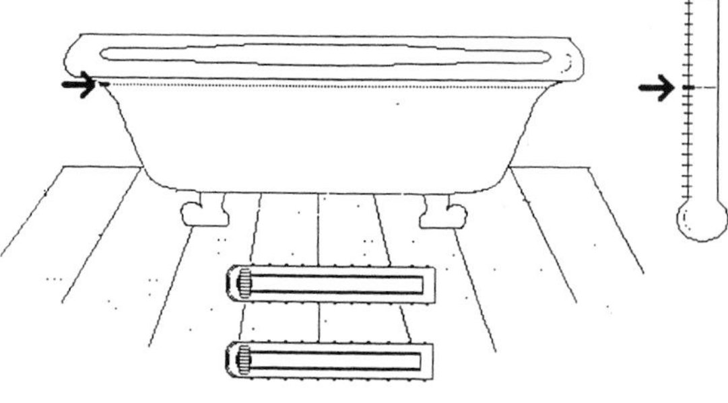

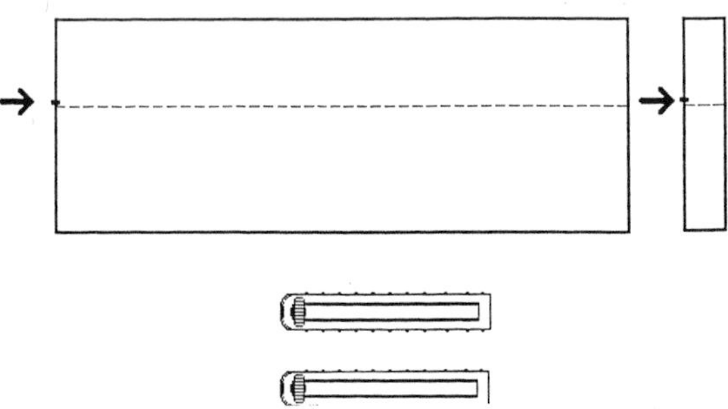

Figure 8. Two interfaces to a bath-filling task with and without the metaphor. *(From Ankrah, Frohlich, and Gilbert, 1990; Figures 1 and 2).*

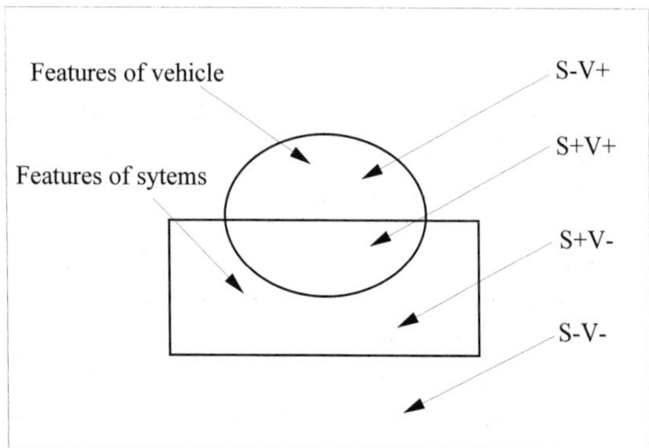

Figure 9. A model of metaphor. *(From Anderson, Smyth, Knott, Bergan, and Alty, 1994; Figure 2).*

themselves equivalent. This implies that there is no general advantage to using icons rather than textual menus, but that in particular cases icons may be better because of the additional information they carry. However, other studies have shown that poorly designed icons can actually be worse than labels because they carry less information (e.g. Franzke, 1995).

A further aspect of iconic representation is the fact that icons can convey real-world metaphors to the user. In an attempt to separate the effects of metaphor from 'directness' at the interface, Ankrah et al. (1990) chose to implement a version of Norman's (1986) example task of filling a bath to a required level and temperature (see Figure 8). In a 'With metaphor' condition users could see an iconic bathtub fill with water and watch the temperature rise in an iconic thermometer. In a 'Without metaphor' condition subjects saw only the movement of lines within two similarly shaped boxes. Within each of these interfaces directness was varied by modifying the type of tap control system embodied in two screen-displayed sliders. Following Norman's example, 'Direct' controls were supported by the use of sliders corresponding to rate of flow and temperature, while 'Indirect' controls were supported by the use of sliders for hot and cold water. Four independent groups of 10 subjects performed the process control task in one of the four resulting interfaces. Subjects performed better overall on the Direct interfaces but not on the With Metaphor interfaces. In fact the most usable interfaces were the Direct-Without Metaphor and Indirect-With Metaphor ones as revealed in a significant interaction between the factors. This effect appears to be related to the fact that the bath metaphor conveys a message not only about the task but also about the control system involved. British subjects can be expected to assume hot and cold tap controls in both the Indirect *and* Direct With Metaphor conditions, which would favour performance on the Indirect With Metaphor system only. The absence of this assumption also favoured performance on the Direct Without Metaphor interface.

In a further study of the effect of metaphor on human computer interaction Anderson et al. (1984) varied instructions in the use of a desktop videoconferencing system. Three sets of instructions were use to communicate Office Door, Dogs or Traffic Lights metaphors for system operation. Three independent groups of 6 subjects were then asked to make and receive the same connections in a communication task. A post-session questionnaire revealed that subjects made different types of errors in their reasoning about the system depending on the metaphor to which they had been exposed. Thus the Doors metaphor led subjects to believe that the system could do more than it could more often than did the Traffic Lights metaphor. Furthermore within each metaphor condition there were significant differences in the classes of reasoning mistakes made. The findings were generally consistent with a proposed model of metaphor, reproduced in Figure 9, which dis-

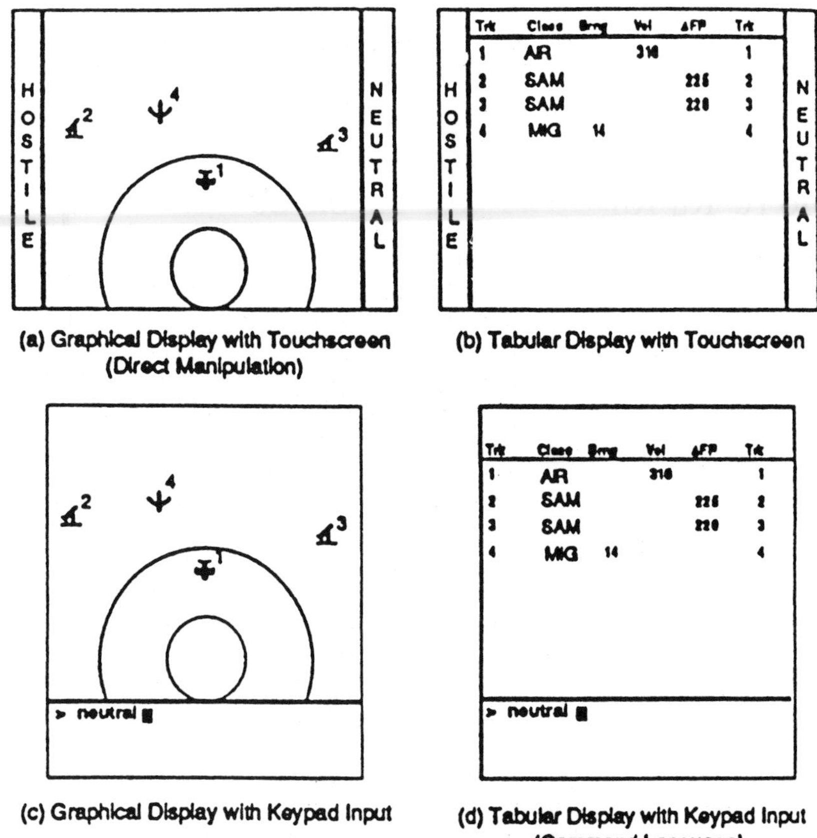

(a) Graphical Display with Touchscreen (Direct Manipulation)

(b) Tabular Display with Touchscreen

(c) Graphical Display with Keypad Input

(d) Tabular Display with Keypad Input (Command Language)

Figure 10. Four interfaces varying in distance and engagement. *(From Ballas, Constance, Heitmeyer, and Perez, 1992; Figure 2).*

tinguishes between various overlaps in the supported (+) or unsupported (-) functionality of any real-world 'vehicle' (V) and computer system domain (S).

Three studies examine the utility of data visualisation at the interface. In the first study Ballas et al (1992) attempted to vary distance and engagement in a naval command and control interface. Distance approximated to an output visualisation factor which was varied by displaying radar contact information either as a map of the spanned area (Low Distance) or as a table of contacts and properties (High Distance). Engagement approximated to an input visualisation factor which was varied by use of touchscreen (Direct Engagement) or keypad (Indirect Engagement) input devices. This resulted in the four interfaces shown in Figure 10. Four independent groups of 5 subjects performed tracking and classification tasks on the interfaces. Although there were no significant differences in the speed and accuracy of task performance across the interfaces, subjects using the graphical map displays felt themselves better able to monitor and predict changes in the tactical situation. This was confirmed by the greater ability of subjects on the map display to resume control of a previously automated activity (at least for confirmation decisions).

A similar study was carried out by Ahlberg et al. (1992) in a different domain. They varied input and output visualisation in an interface to the Periodic Table. Output varied between a tabular arrangement of highlighted element symbols (G=Graphical output) and a list of selected symbols (T=Textual output). Input varied between use of screen-displayed sliders for atomic properties (S=Slider input) and keyboard input of property values (F=Form fill-in). Although this would theoretically generate four interface designs, only the three shown in Figure 11 were evaluated in the study, with the SG combination refered to as the 'Dynamic Query' interface. An ST interface combining sliders with textual output is missing from the study. Three independent groups of 6 subjects answered

Figure 11.Two graphical and one textual interface to the Periodic Table. *(From Ahlberg, Williamson, and Shneiderman, 1992; S = Slider input, F = Form fill-in, G = Graphical output, T = Text output).*

questions about the Periodic Table each using one of the interfaces shown. Subjects using the Dynamic Query interface answered questions faster than those using the other two interfaces, and more accurately than subjects using the FT interface (with Textual output). This suggests that removal of *output* visualisation may have a more detrimental effect on (the accuracy of) performance than removal of *input* visualisation.

Finally, Tabachneck and Simon (1994) found some detrimental effects of output visualisation in a computer assisted learning task. Three independent groups of 4 economics students were given questions to answer from data displayed either in graphs, tables or algebraic expressions. Subjects using graphs were better at answering quantitative questions than subjects using equations or tables, but not at answering explanatory questions requiring underlying reasons. Two subsequent experiments appear to confirm a hypothesis that visualisation appears to induce superficial visual reasoning from the display which may compromise a deeper understanding of actual causal factors.

Taken together, these studies begin to break down the rather nebulous notion of direct manipulation into more concrete pieces. They also challange some of the unwritten assumptions about what features of graphical interfaces work best. I have described them in some detail here because they show that there are many dimensions to the concept which vary in importance and interact with each other in complex ways. From the available data we can see the following themes emerge:

- Order of command activation may not matter
- Clicking may be slower but more accurate than dragging
- Icons may be equivalent to menus with extra information
- Metaphors should be selected with a view to the device as well as the task characteristics they convey
- Choice between alternative metaphors may be informed by mapping out their applicability and inapplicability to the target computer domain
- Visualisation of output data seems critical to the benefits of direct manipulation
- Visualisation of input data may be less important

Further critical studies are needed to confirm these impressions and to address the importance of other associated features of direct manipulation such as window-techniques, function-objects, integration of input techniques and user's adjustment of design features.

Naturalistic Choice Studies

A final approach to testing the benefits of direct manipulation interfaces is to present users with a mixed mode interface incorporating elements of both manual and linguistic interaction. 'Naturalistic' choices made by users during the course of interacting with the interface would reveal not only *whether* direct manipulation methods were used more often than alternative methods but also *when* and *how*.

Unfortunately the number of studies of this kind is very limited. As we have just seen, most tests of direct manipulation interfaces vary interface type over independent groups of subjects, so that it is rare for the same subjects to experience more than one type. An exception to this was the study by Eberts and Bittianda (1993) mentioned in Section 21.4.1. They included a 'Combined' direct manipulation and command interface in two experiments testing preference for direct manipulation. However in the first experiment subjects were asked to alternate between each method in a training regime and hence had no choice open to them. In the second experiment subjects were asked to complete written tests of reasoning about the system. They found that subjects trained on the Combined interface used concepts involving direct manipulation operators more frequently than command line operators, although no analysis was conducted on *when* each type was used (personal communication).

More direct evidence regarding naturalisitic choice of interaction style comes from evaluations of a multimodal file management system called EDWARD (Bos, Huls and Claassen, 1994). EDWARD is essentially a graphical 'desktop' interface with a natural language dialogue window (see Figure 12). It supports a mixture of menu, command, direct manipulation and natural language interactions, down to the individual interface expressions (such as move this file $\rightarrow$ to this directory $\rightarrow$, where $\rightarrow$ denotes a pointing gesture). The use of EDWARD in a series of experiments is described in Huls (1995). Early feedback from 10 novice users performing file manipulation tasks on the unrestricted system revealed that

1. All users employed more than one interaction style
2. All users utilized natural language input
3. Individual users switched frequently between methods
4. Users said they liked the freedom of style choice

In a more formal experiment, 22 subjects used this 'FREE choice' condition, in contrast to 66 subjects in three RESTRICTED groups who were forced to use

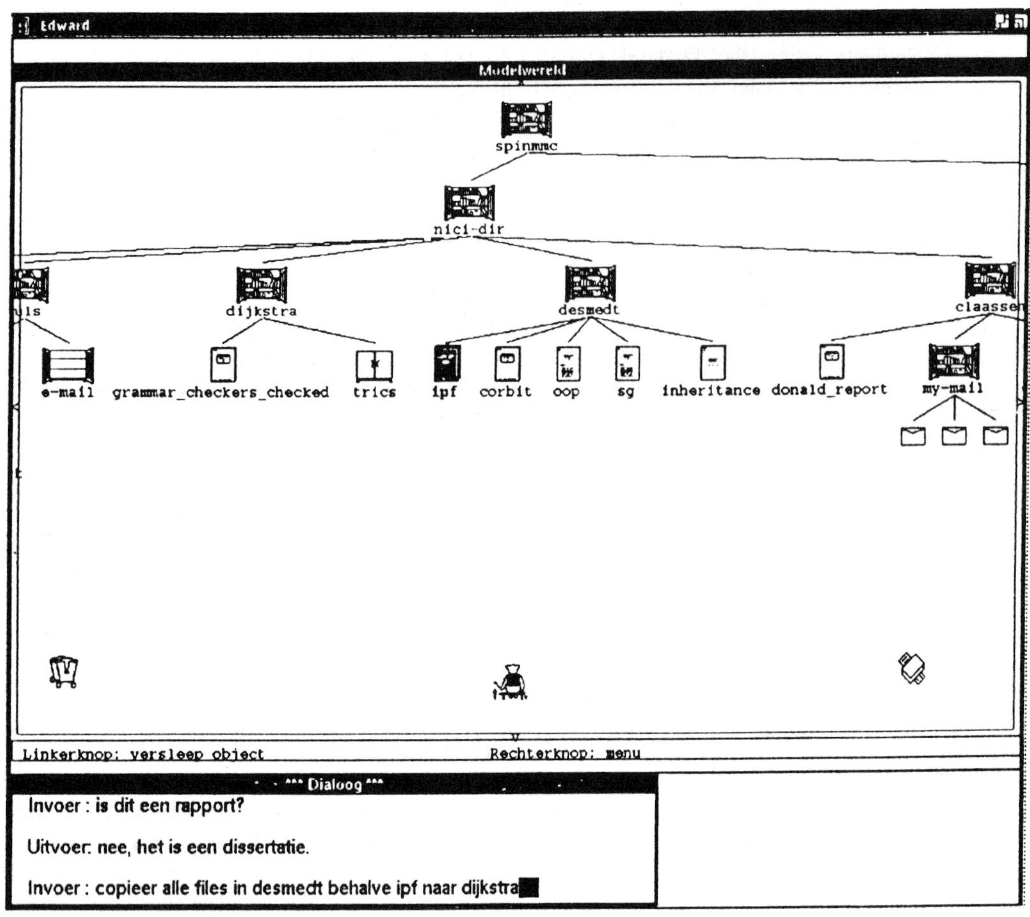

Figure 12. The EDWARD interface. *(Bos et al., 1994; Figure 1).*

natural language ('Language'), direct manipulation ('Action') or both together ('Multimodal'). Again there was a great diversity in the choice of interaction style in the FREE condition. This is shown in Figure 13 which indicates massive individual differences in preferred mode. On the whole unimodal interface expressions were preferred to multimodal expressions, although direct manipulation and natural language expressions were used selectively in the proportions shown. Analysis of when users chose these methods suggested that direct manipulation was often used to avoid typing long object names in the dialogue box, and natural language was used to refer to objects which were not visible on the screen.

Such evaluations of mixed mode interfaces are rare, perhaps because most research papers in this area concentrate on implementation rather than usage issues, while few commercial system evaluations are ever published. This is an important gap in the literature which could help to identify the limitations as well as the benefits of direct manipulation and thereby prescribe effective combinations of manual and conversational forms of interaction.

Summary

In short, the above tests confirm some but not all of the proposed benefits of direct manipulation and show them to depend on implementation, task and measurement factors. A key problem with the concept is its operationalisation in specific designs. At present, a large number of graphical features are associated with direct manipulation and a new class of tests are beginning to identify which combination of features are critical to its success. The possibility of limitations and well as benefits for direct manipulation is suggested by a small number of traditional tests which show disad-vantages to its use on certain tasks, and by an even smaller num-

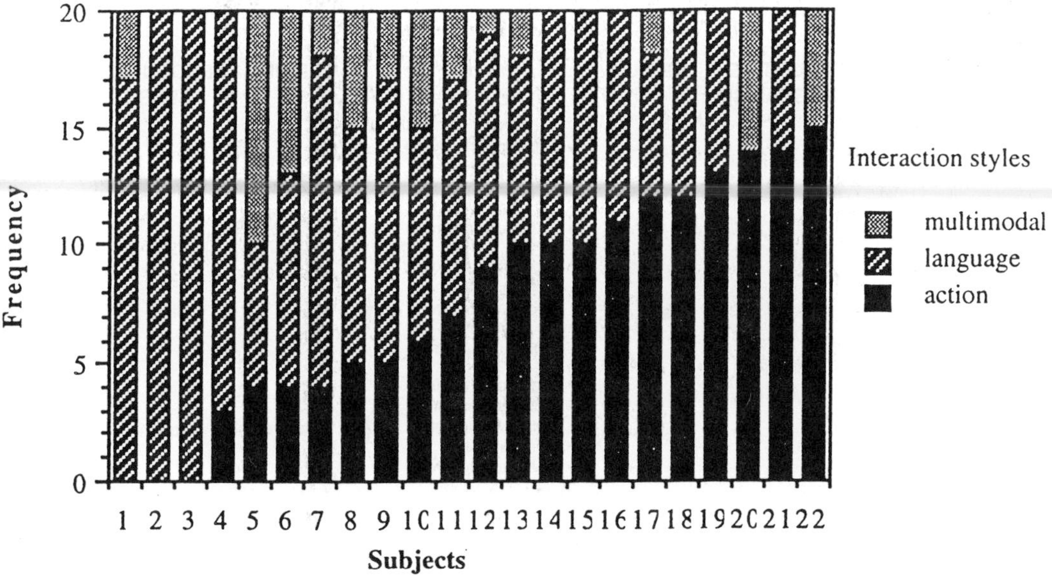

Figure 13. Free choice of alternative interaction styles in EDWARD. *(From Huls, 1995 ;Figure 2.3).*

ber of studies illustrating naturalistic choice of alternative methods in mixed mode interfaces.

21.4.2 Mixed Mode Interfaces

The design of mixed mode interfaces is a significant development for the philosophy of direct manipulation, mainly because it cannot easily accomodate them. The original insights by Shneiderman promote manual over conversational forms of interaction and do not consider how best to mix these forms in hybrid interface designs. This omission is also represented in the paper by Hutchins et al. who fail to represent mixed conversational and model-world systems in their space of interfaces (shown in Figure 4). In this section I use an alternative framework to indicate the variety of ways in which manual and conversational forms of interaction are being mixed in both prototype and commercial systems. These developments serve to shift the locus of the direct manipulation debate from *whether* direct manipulation is better than other forms of interaction to *when and how* its benefits should be combined with other forms.

Figure 14 shows an adpated version of my own 'space of interfaces' diagram, published in the context of a discussion of multimedia systems (Frohlich, 1991). This distinguishes between the input and output interfaces to any computer system and is organised around two central *modes* of interaction: language and action. These modes correspond to Hutchins et al.'s conversational and model-world interfaces, but are shown to co-exist for the same input or output interface. This allows for separate mixed mode (language/action) combinations *within* the input and output interfaces, as well as for cross-modal combinations *between* them (i.e. language in/action out or action in/language out). Furthermore, these modes are said to be subjective properties of the interface which depend on the way users intend their own inputs to be interpreted by the computer, and how they perceive the outputs of the computer. The critical distinction is whether or not they intend or interpret them as social or physical actions. Of course the expectations about whether to adopt a social or physical relationship with the machine are set by the *medium* and *style* of input allowed by the computer and the computer's own medium and style of response. In practice then, the social and physical tone of the interaction is given by the combination of interface styles employed, but differences in the balance of combinations can lead to subtle differences in the dominance of one mode over the other.

One thing this framework makes clear is that many interfaces which have traditionally been thought of as direct manipulation interfaces are themselves mixed mode. For example the Macintosh interface incorporates many elements of language as well as action through the user's use of menus, field filling and quick command gestures and the system's use of natural lan-

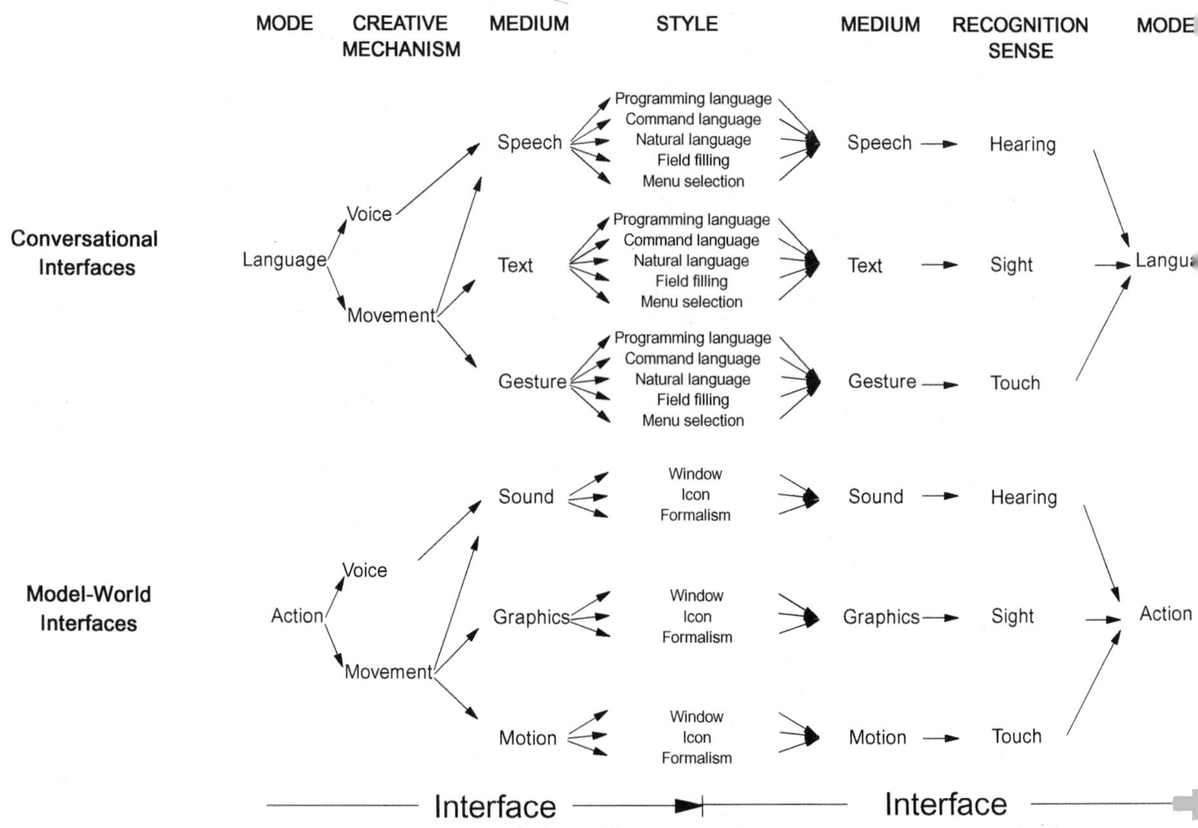

Figure 14. The design space of interfaces. (Adapted from Frohlich, 1991; Figures 1 and 2).

guage dialogue boxes containing field descriptors and menu items (see Figures 3 and 4 in Frohlich, 1991 for a full characterisation using the framework). Pure direct manipulation interfaces according to the framework would be model-world interfaces based on an Action in/Action out modality involving only the media of sound, graphics and motion. Interestingly, these are exactly the properties of information visualisation interfaces such as the Dynamic Homefinder interface described in Section 21.2.2.

Other mixed mode interfaces are those which explicitly mix model-world and agent metaphors for interaction. Hewlett Packard's own desktop office interface called NewWave does this by incorporating an 'Agent' icon on the desktop, with functionality to automate routine or background tasks such as file backup or meeting reminders (Stearns, 1989). In practice the user clicks on pre-recorded Agent 'Tasks' or can record new tasks by demonstration (see Myers, 1992 for a discussion of demonstrational interfaces). Metaphorically, the user is intended to relate to the Agent as a personal assistant in the office world of in-terest. This impression is encouraged through anima-tion of Agent actions on documents, folders and other office icons so that users can see the Agent acting on the world in much the same way as they do. The use of such interface agents as 'personal digital assitants' seems set to rise in the context of computer telephony and networking where users cannot be expected to deal manually with the vast amount of information that will become available to them (Maes, 1994).

The same kind of mixing of agent and model world attributes happens in a different way in computer mediated communication tools. In these cases the interfaces agents are other people who may act on a shared workspace or document whilst talking to you (Whittaker, Geelhoed, and Robinson, 1993).

The natural interleaving of linguistic and physical actions in human-human conversation appears to be the inspiration for a number of attempts to mix interface styles at a fine grained level in human-computer interaction (Neilson and Lee, 1994). For example, the ACORD system is a transportation monitoring application which allows users to update a knowledge base of truck positions either by dragging truck icons around a geographical map or by informing the system of truck movements in natural language (Lee and Zeevat, 1990). Both interaction styles can be combined in individual input expressions: such as typing 'This goes to Munich' after clicking on the desired truck icon. Haddock (1992) shows how these kind of referring expressions can be used to good effect in multimodal database queries in the SAMi system. Natural language follow-up questions are especially efficient when scoped by pointing to elements of the displayed output from a previous query: as in 'Which of these sales is for Walkers?', or 'Show these as a bar chart'. Cohen, Dalrymple, Moran, Periera, Sullivan, Gargan, Schlossberg and Tyler (1989) take these techniques further in the SHOPTALK system which utilizes 'natural language forms' and 'discourse tree structures' in the context of an iconic representation of a circuit-board factory.

In these last examples, conversational and manual interface styles are being mixed mainly within the input interface. Cross-modal mixing across the input and output interfaces also occurs in systems such as GeoSpace (Lokuge and Ishizaki, 1995). This is like a Dynamic Homefinder system you can talk to, since it combines natural language input with a map formalism output to give users access to a database of area and property information. Users ask for different graphical views of the information in a Language in/Action out interaction. The opposite Action in/Language out arrangement is found in certain intelligent tutoring systems which critique the user's manipulation of some world of interest in natural language output.

All these forms of mixed mode interaction show how the character of model world or conversational interfaces can be altered by introducing elements of the complementary mode into the input or output interface. The range, effectiveness and spread of such systems suggests that there is great value in choosing the middle way.

21.4.3 Theory

Further discussion of the concept of direct manipulation has continued in parallel to the studies and systems mentioned above. The same lessons are reinforced through attempts to explain the value of mixing manual and conversational forms of interaction and to further understand what makes manipulation direct. Significant contributions to each issue are reviewed in the next two sections.

The Value of Mixed Mode Interaction

In developments of their original positions, both Hutchins and Laurel promote interface agents as additions to direct manipulation interfaces.

Hutchins (1989) discusses four possible relationships a user can have with the computer which he calls 'mode of interaction' metaphors:

1. *The conversation metaphor* - where expressions have the character of utterances in a conversation about the task at hand
2. *The declaration metaphor* -where expressions take on the character of speech acts which magically cause things to happen in the world of interest
3. *The model-world metaphor* - where expressions have the character of actions taken in the world of interest
4. *The collaborative manipulation metaphor* - where expressions have the character of carrying out a task with someone elses help

Pointing out the limitations of the first three modes, Hutchins notes that conversation is limited because users have to learn a new language, maintain a mental model of the world being talked about, and converse in a manner very different from that of ordinary conversation. Declaration is limited because it depends on a practice effect in using a conversational interface which is always liable to dissipate if the user declares something that cannot be done. Model-world interaction is limited precisely because of its directness in collapsing abstract descriptions into concrete actions. Users can no longer refer to *classes* of objects but must identify each instance of a class manually. These limitations in each individual mode leads Hutchins to promote their combination in a form of collaborative manipulation in which users act within a model-world alongside an intermediary who can also act on their behalf (see Figure 15). Provision of a linguistic interface to the NewWave Agent mentioned in Section 21.4.2 would create this arrangement within a desktop office system.

Laurel (1990) makes a similar argument for the reintroduction of a conversational metaphor within a model-world context. Whereas before she had argued against the *hidden intermediary* as a primary vehicle for interaction (Laurel, 1986) she now points out the value of a *visible intermediary* (my term) within a model-world. This she refers to as an interface agent,

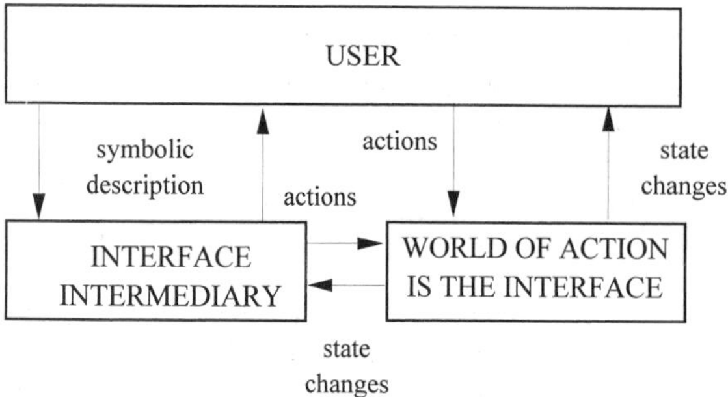

Figure 15. The collaborative manipulation interface. *(Hutchins, 1989; Figure 2.6).*

defined as "a character enacted by a computer, who acts on behalf of the user in a virtual (computer-based) environment" (p356). Like Hutchins, Laurel begins to note a number of computer-based tasks which are difficult to perform through action and might be more easily achieved by delegation through language to an interface agent. These include retrieving, sorting, organising, programming and scheduling. In addition, Laurel promotes the interface agent as a convenient new metaphor for representing the more (pro-)active and autonomous components of modern computer systems. These include various forms of agency, such as facilities to filter information, remind, help, tutor, advise, perform or play.

The same conclusions are reached via a different route by Whittaker (1990), Stenton (1990) and Walker (1989). All three authors discuss the limitations of direct manipulation in the context of desktop office systems such as the Xerox Star, Apple Macintosh, or HP NewWave systems.

Whittaker (1990) examines each of Shneiderman's three principles of direct manipulation as they apply to a desktop model world. He describes particular limitations with (*Principles 1 and 3*):

Principle 1 Continuous representation of the object of interest - This leads to the problems of locating objects that are not visible in a large or distributed system. Manual search may be inefficient even when users know the location of target documents, and completely impracticable when they don't.

Principle 3 Rapid incremental reversible operations ... - The need for incremental operations leads to inefficiencies in the execution of common compound actions which might be done faster through a single command. It also prevents automatic application of repetitive actions to a set of objects.

Principle 3 ...whose impact is immediately visible - This does not allow for processes which users may want to run in the future or while they are absent, such as reminders or mail forwarding.

These problems are said to relate to the requirement that change in the model world be a direct result of a corresponding user action. Relaxing this requirement leads to a form of agency in which the system itself takes responsibility for executing certain actions.

Stenton (1990) elaborates on this view by suggesting that the interaction between a desktop system and its user can be improved by adding an interface agent who can take the initiative from time to time. Such initiative is required to provide feedback on the kinds of delayed operations discussed by Whittaker, and could be used more generally to provide cooperative suggestions or responses for the task at hand. Without the metaphor of an interface agent to perform these actions Stenton points out that users would have to believe in a talking or listening desktop.

Walker (1989) lists a set of desktop interaction tasks that may be more suited to control through natural language than through direct manipulation. Indeed, a number of these tasks would be impossible to perform manually because they involve actions out of the 'here and now'; referring to unseen objects or to events forwards or backwards in time. The tasks are:

Definite Description - referring to objects by their attributes
e.g. Get me the messages FROM ERIK.

Discourse Reference - referring to previously evoked objects with pronouns
e.g. Get me the messages from Erik. Are any of THEM about today's meeting?

Temporal Specification - specifying future times or intervals for an event
e.g. Send a copy of the proposal to Susan EVERY WEEK.

Quantification - referring to object quantities
e.g. HOW MANY messages do I have today? Are there ANY from Erik?

Coordination - combining operations in compound phrases
e.g. print the report AND send a copy to Steve

Negation - refering to negative attributes
e.g. Are there any messages I HAVEN'T answered?

Comparatives - comparing objects by attributes
e.g. Are there any messages OLDER than two months?

Sorting Expressions - referring to the attributes by which objects should be displayed
e.g. Show me my messages BY topic

Walker is keen to recommend empirical tests which would identify which of these tasks are *actually* performed better via natural language and are valuable enough to develop as additional features of a desktop system.

A very similar argument is made by Cohen (1992) in discussing the symmetrical advantages and disadvantages of natural language and direct manipulation. Thus he identifies the following tasks as being difficult to do through direct manipulation but easy to do through natural language:

1. Description including quantification, negation and temporal information
2. Anaphora (e.g. pronouns)
3. Operations on large sets of objects
4. Delayed actions

Cohen goes on to describe features of the SHOPTALK system discussed in Section 21.4.2 which combines elements of natural language with direct manipulation. Unfortunately he fails to provide data on the *use* of SHOPTALK which would help to substantiate his own claims and the earlier ones of Walker (1989).

Further Insights on Directness

Along with the critical evaluations of direct manipulation described in Section 21.4.1 go a number of theoretical discussions of directness. These begin with those relating to the essence of good manual interaction and end with a number of attempts to apply the concept to conversational forms of interaction.

Regarding the directness of manual interaction, Johnson, Roberts, Verplank, Smith, Irby, Beard, Mackay (1989) look back at the design of the Xerox Star system to consider what made it so successful in the industry. They attribute a large part of this success to the *desktop metaphor* and everything that entailed for the direct manipulation of graphical objects on the screen, including:

- a high resolution bitmapped display
- a pointing device
- an object-oriented iconic interface
- generic commands (such as move, open, copy, delete, show properties, same)

A particular guiding principle behind the Star's design was to encourage 'seeing and pointing over remembering and typing' through the graphical interface. However, they note that one of the lessons of the Star experience is 'Don't be dogmatic about the desktop metaphor and direct manipulation' because there are things that remembering and typing are better for.

Johnson (1987) elaborates on this point in another article in which he argues that the faithfulness of the desktop metaphor depends on the individual office functions represented. Some functions are best implemented in a new way. Thus he lists a number of facilities in the Star interface which deviate from the desktop metaphor to good effect, including the sorting of files by different attributes, the nesting of folders to any depth, the shrinking of documents to icons when not in use and the tiling of windows. He also notes the absence of additional office objects such as staplers which are simply not needed on the electronic desktop where pages of documents do not naturally come apart. Johnson suggests that designers must trade off faithfulness to the metaphor with the utility of other methods, and users must learn to adapt accordingly (see also Halasz and Moran, 1981).

The role of icons in representing metaphors is explored in recent work by Familant and Detweiler (1993). An icon is defined as 'a sign that shares characteristics with the objects to which it refers' (p706), and is distinguished from other signs such as an index and a symbol. The authors show how many of the so called icons used in modern graphical interfaces have lost this property of shared characteristics with referent objects, largely because they refer to highly abstract computer facilities which have no real world counterparts (e.g. undo, find, insert frame). These do not employ metaphors and should really be called symbols. Furthermore, true icons invoking some real world metaphor can incorporate direct or indirect reference depending on various relationships between the thing depicted, the thing to which it refers, and the thing ultimately denoted or pointed to. The implications for directness of manipulation seem to be that icons will only really improve the 'fit' between user and system in cases where they depict a real world object with clear connections to the referenced computer object.

On a different tack, Desain (1988) equates distance with directness (as defined by Hutchins et al.) and applies it as a measure of the quality of both manual and conversational interfaces. In this simple move he shows how both kinds of interfaces can turn out to be direct to use. He suggests that the most direct manual interfaces are those which use a well-known graphical formalism for the application domain and support the corresponding real-world actions (such as grasping). The most direct conversational interfaces are said to be those employing natural language syntax already known to the user with the 'jargon' vocabulary of the application domain. Various strategies for minimizing semantic and syntactic distance are discussed for both types of systems, including issues of representation, abstraction, reference, error management, and precision.

Both Claassen, Bos, and Huls (1990) and Brennan (1990) adopt the same position to attack the view that conversational interfaces are necessarily indirect to use. They highlight some of the more valuable attributes of converational interfaces including the handling of error and repair, the ability to ask questions, and the range of expressions for refering to abstract properties and events. As further evidence for the directness of conversational interaction in general Brennan also cites the extremely efficient and cryptic quality of interactions between people who know each other well.

Finally in my own previous review of the area I took up this last point in a further discussion of what makes conversation direct (Frohlich, 1993). I suggested that good 'rapport' between partners is the quality to aim for; comparable to good 'engagement' within manual interactions and characterised by the kind of brief, cryptic exchanges referred to by Brennan (1990). These exchanges are a puzzle for the philosophy of direct manipulation because in one sense they are highly indirect. They increase the cognitive load on conversational partners whilst decreasing the interactional work that is done between them. Thus by making more inferences about what the other partner is saying it is possible for both partners to conduct a shorter and more efficient conversation. This observation led me to distinguish between two types of directness in human computer interaction:

1. cognitive directness already defined by Hutchins et al. as 'least cognitive effort', and
2. social directness defined as 'least collaborative effort'.

Within this view, cryptic conversations can be seen as increasing social directness at the expense of cognitive directness. To avoid too much confusion between the terms cognitive and social directness I suggested referring to social directness as gracefulness. Hence graceful interaction would be characterised by a feeling of pace and efficiency in the flow of exchanges between user and computer, whether they be through manual actions or linguisitc utterances.

Summary

In short, recent thinking on direct manipulation reinforces many of the lessons of the empirical tests and mixed mode interface designs reviewed in Sections 21.4.1 and 21.4.2. They either cast a critical eye over what accounts for the directness effect or they acknowledge that manual interaction is limited and should be combined with conversational interaction. The first line of argument results in further insights on good features of both manual and conversational interaction; such as 'seeing and pointing over remembering and typing', a clear application metaphor which is creatively implemented, icons which make sense in terms of the metaphor, words which include the 'jargon' of the domain, and a sense of gracefulness and efficiency in the flow of the interaction. The second line of argument results in discussion of the value of a 'collaborative manipulation' paradigm in which users work together with a virtual partner in the model world of interest. This allows them to use conversation with the partner to perform all those interaction tasks that are difficult or impossible to perform by manipulation alone.

21.5 Two Philosophies, Two Debates

21.5.1 Separating Directness and Manipulation

Having updated the debate about direct manipulation interfaces what can now be said about the direct manipulation philosophy?

Historically we can see that direct manipulation interfaces certainly served to break the mold of programming and command line interfaces which required users to remember and type complex phrases in an artificial language and then to hold in their heads an impression of the effects of these commands on the application. When compared to this baseline, manual interaction looked like an extremely attractive alternative which deserved much of the praise and success it received in the industry. However the industry has moved on and with it the baseline. Menu, form and natural language interfaces now constitute a fairer comparison with manual/graphical interfaces, and there are a growing number of mixed mode interfaces which

Table 1. Principles of good manual and conversational interactions.

	MANIPULATION	CONVERSATION
COGNITIVE DIRECTNESS	• Coherent real-world metaphor • Natural actions • Continuous representation	• Familiar terminology • Natural language • Personal relevance
INTERACTIONAL GRACEFULNESS	• Responsive visualisation	• Short rapid turns • Mixed initiative • Explicit repair

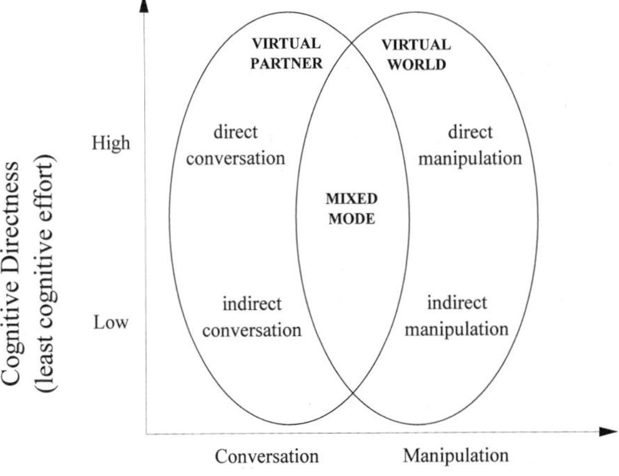

Figure 16. Interface categories partitioned by Directness and Engagement. *(Adapted from Frohlich, 1993; Figure 2).*

merge manual and conversational intearction to good effect. In line with these developments, straightforward comparisons of direct manipulation interfaces with other kinds have come up with conflicting results, while more critical tests have begun to show ways in which manual interfaces themselves can vary in design. In this modern context the old formulation of the philosophy begins to look decided shakey.

A new formulation is suggested by the progress that has been made in understanding *how* and *when* to utilize manual forms of interaction at the interface. These two questions run through the direct manipulation debate and ultimately serve to split it apart. For example, questions of how to use manual interaction are addressed by critical tests comparing different implementations of manual interfaces with each other, and by discussions of 'directness' in general (described in Sections 21.4.1 and 21.4.3). They show that some features of manual *and* conversational interaction are more effective than others. Questions of when to use manual interaction are addressed by uncritical tests comparing manual with conversational interfaces for the same task, and by the work on mixed mode interfaces (described in Sections 21.4.1, 21.4.2 and 21.4.3). They show that manual interfaces are not always better than conversational ones, and that combined interfaces can leave the choice very effectively in the hands of users.

Thus we have ended up with two distinct strands to the current direct manipulation debate relating to questions of directness and questions of manipulation. Directness is now equated with distance and manipulation with engagement. That these components are separable was first suggested by Hutchins et al.'s space of interfaces (shown in Figure 4). However, recent research has been steadily populating the space and discovering the truth of its comparisons. In addition, it has added a class of mixed mode interfaces which themselves vary in directness. This leads to a reconceptualisation of the space of interfaces shown in Figure 16 (adapted from Figure 2 in Frohlich, 1993).

Work on each dimension of this new interface space is leading to two emergent philosophies of interaction; a *directness philosophy* relating to what makes an interface easy to use, and a *manipulation philosophy* relating to why manual forms of interaction are preferable to conversational forms. In the next two sections I will suggest a characterisation of each philosophy based on the research reviewed. Each characterisation is done in terms of a set of design recommendations which can be used both to inform design and influence future research.

21.5.2 A New Philosophy of Directness

Table 1 shows a set of principles for the design of good manual and conversational interaction. The principles for manual interaction are based on a revision of Shneiderman's original principles of direct manipulation in the light of the findings about *how* to use manipulation. They are partitioned by whether or not they relate to cognitive directness in the way the user thinks about the system, or to gracefulness in the form of interaction between them. The main change is the addition of a 'Real-world metaphor' principle which seems to be associated with the most successful direct manipulation interfaces. 'Natural actions' is a development of Shneiderman's 'Physical actions' *Principle 2* which requires that the manipulations used should possess the same control dynamics as those used in the corresponding real-world task wherever possible. This serves to extend the concept of metaphor to the device as well as the task. 'Continuous representation' is Shneiderman's *Principle 1*, while 'Responsive visualisation' corresponds to his *Principle 3*, with emphasis on fast analogue change in the output visualisation as a property of the interaction.

The principles proposed for conversational interaction are derived partly from the literature reviewed, and partly from related work on the design of human-computer dialogues with conversation-like properties (e.g. Frohlich and Luff, 1990, Hayes and Reddy, 1983; Luff and Frohlich, 1991; Nickerson, 1981; Yankelovich, Levow and Marx, 1995). They are included here in response to the insight that directness (and gracefulness) can be applied to conversational as well as manual interface design, and in the hope that they might stimulate the same sort of debate as Shneiderman's original principles for manipulation. Thus, 'Familiar terminology' refers to use of application 'jargon', 'Natural language' refers to the use of a native syntax for combining and interpreting interface expressions, 'Personal relevance' refers to the use of a relationship history by the computer, 'Short rapid turns' refers to the highly interactive exchange of turns, 'Mixed initiative' refers to a switching of who is leading the conversation, while 'Explicit repair' refers to the incorporation of procedures for handling user or computer trouble in understanding.

Further research is needed to test and revise both sets of principles. Continuation of the critical tests reviewed in Section 21.4.1 for manual interfaces would help to assess the revision of Shneiderman's principles, while their extension to language-based interfaces would help to test the proposed conversational principles. Whether or not a third set of principles is required for mixed mode interaction also remains to be determined.

21.5.3 A New Philosophy of Manipulation

Table 2 presents a rough guide to the selection of interface modality. It is based on findings from the review regarding *when* to use manual and conversational forms of interaction. The essence of the new philosophy is therefore to utilize manipulation selectively! Various features of the target application can be checked off in the table. These range from high level features such as the overall activity being supported and the interaction tasks involved, to low level features such as the interaction media and technology available. An additional category of contextual factors has also been included to take into account other activities the user might be expected to perform concurrently. The designer can work through the table literally top-down or bottom-up to arrive at a set of indicators for manual or conversational interaction. If ticks appear in only one of the columns then the modality is clear. If ticks appear in both columns then a mixed mode interface is indicated, unless the designer is willing to trade-off some inefficiencies for a preferred mode.

Selective application of the manipulation modality should itself ensure a greater directness and gracefulness of manipulation when it *is* used. Whether or not these are the right features on which to base such selection remains to be tested. This will require a continuation of the uncritical tests reviewed in Section 21.4.1 together with many more evaluations of the naturalistic use of mixed mode interfaces as described in same section. In fact, the development of mixed mode interfaces itself constitutes the biggest challenge for advocates of manual interaction. This is because, in the long term, the use of language in a manual interface and the use of manipulation in a conversational one promises to extend the reach of manipulation techniques beyond their natural limits. We will only begin to see this if future tests of Manual versus Conversational interaction begin to routinely incorporate a 'Combined' condition. For many tasks this might often turn out to be the best.

21.6 Acknowledgements

Thanks to Ben Shneiderman and two anonymous referees for their helpful comments on an earlier draft of the chapter; to my colleagues in personal systems lab for numerous discussions and feedback on ideas; and to Charlotte Swain for her expert help in tracking down references.

Table 2. Modality selection checklist.

APPLICATION FEATURES	MANUAL MODE	CONVERSATIONAL MODE
ACTIVITY METAPHORS	• Looking • Browsing • Exploring • Navigating • Controlling • Monitoring • Constructing • Creating	• Informing • Requesting • Asking • Advice seeking • Understanding • Negotiating • Delegating • Problem solving
INTERACTION TASKS	• Selecting seen objects • Executing actions with immediate consequences • Responding immediately to feedback • Identifying relationships between objects	• Selecting unseen objects • Identifying sets of objects • Referring back • Scheduling forwards • Repeating actions • Combining actions • Specifying exact values
INTERACTION MEDIA	• Sound • Graphics • Motion	• Speech • Text • Gesture
INTERACTION TECHNOLOGY	• Large displays • Sound effects • Motion sensing	• Small displays • Keyboard only • Voice activation
INTERACTION CONTEXT	• Hands and eyes free • Ears busy	• Hands or eyes busy • Ears free

21.7 References

Ahlberg, C., and Shneiderman, B. (1994a). The Alphaslider: A compact and rapid selector. *Proceedings of CHI'94: Human Factors in Computing Systems,* 365-371. New York: ACM.

Ahlberg, C., and Shneiderman, B. (1994b). Visual information seeking: Tight coupling of dynamic query filters with starfield displays. *Proceedings of CHI'94: Human Factors in Computing Systems*, 313-317, New York: ACM

Ahlberg, C., Williamson, C., and Schneiderman, B. (1992). Dynamic queries for information exploration: An implementation and evaluation. *Proceedings of CHI'92: Human Factors in Computing Systems,* 619-626, New York: ACM.

Ankrah, A., Frohlich, D. M., and Gilbert, G. N. (1990). Two ways to fill a bath with and without knowing it. *Proceedings of INTERACT'90,* 73-78. North Holland: Amsterdam.

Anderson, B., Smyth, M., Knott, R. P., Bergan, M., Bergan, J., and Alty, J. L. (1994). Minimising conceptual baggage: Making choices about metaphor. In G. Cockton, S. W. Draper, and G. R. S. Weir (Eds.), *People and Computers IX*, Cambridge, UK: Cambridge University Press.

Ballas, J. A., C. L., Heitmeyer, and Perez, M. A. (1992). Evaluating two aspects of direct manipulation in advanced cockpits. *Proceedings of CHI'92: Human Factors in Computing Systems*, 127-137, New York: ACM.

Benbasat, I., and Todd, P. (1993). An experimental investigation of interface design alternatives: Icon vs. text and direct manipulation vs. menus. *International Journal of Man-Machine Studies,* 38, 369-402.

Boss, E., Huls, C., and Claassen W. (1994) EDWARD: full integration of language and action in a multimodal user interface. *International Journal of Human-Computer Studies*, 40, 473-495.

Brennan, S. E. (1990). Conversation as direct manipulation. In B. Laurel (Ed.), *The Art of Human-Computer Interface Design*, 393-404, CA: Addison Wesley.

Buxton, B. (1993). HCI and the inadequacies of direct

manipulation systems. *SIGCHI Bulletin* 25, 21-22, New York: ACM

Canfield-Smith, D., Irby, C., Kimball, R., and Verplank, B. (1992). Designing the star user interface. *Byte Magazine*, April, 210-223.

Card, S. K. (1995). The Anti-Mac: Violating the macintosh human interface guidelines. *Proceedings of CHI'95: Human Factors in Computing Systems*, 183, New York: ACM

Card, S.K., Moran, T. and Newell, A. (1983). *The Psychology of Human-Computer Interaction.* Hillsdale, NJ: Lawrence Erlbaum Associates, Inc.

Card, S. K., Robertson, G. G., and Mackinlay, J.D., (1991). The information visualizer: An information workspace. *Companion Proceedings of CHI'91: Human Factors in Computing Systems*, 181, New York: ACM.

Claassen, W., Bos, E., and Huls, C. (1990). *The Pooh way in human-computer interaction: Towards multimodal interfaces.* MMC Research Report No. 5. Nijmegen Institute for Cognition Research and Information Technology (NICI), Nijmegen, Netherlands.

Cohen, P. R. (1992). The role of natural language in a multimodal interface. *Proceedings of the 5th Annual Symposium on User Interface Software Technology*, 143-149. New York: ACM

Cohen, P. R., Dalrymple, M., Moran, D. B., Periera, F. C. N., Sullivan, J.W., Gargan, J.R., Schlossberg, J. L., and Tyler, S. W. (1989). Synergistic use of direct manipulation and natural language. *Proceedings of CHI'89: Human Factors in Computing Systems*, 227-233, New York: ACM.

Desain, P. (1988). Direct manipulation and the design of user interfaces. *Journal for the Integrated Study of AI, Cognitive Science, and Applied Epistemology,* 5, 225-246.

Eberleh, E., Korfmacher, W., and Streitz, N. (1992). Thinking of acting? Mental workload and subjective preferences for a command code and a manipulation interaction style. *International Journal of Human-Computer Interaction,* 4, 105-122.

Eberts, R. E., and Bittianda, K. P. (1992). Preferred mental models for direct manipulation and command-based interfaces. *International Journal of Man-Machine Studies,* 38, 769-785.

Egan, D. E., Remde, J. R., Landauer, J. K., Lochbaum, C. C., and Gomez, L. M. (1989). Behavioural evaluation and analysis of a hypertext browser. *Proceedings of CHI'89: Human Factors in Computing Systems*, 205-210, New York: ACM.

Egido, C., Patterson, J. (1988). Pictures and category labels as navigational aids for catalogue browsing. *Proceedings of CHI'88: Human Factors in Computing Systems*, 127-132, New York: ACM.

Familant, M. E., and Detweiler, M. C. (1993). Iconic reference: evolving perspectives and an organising framework. *International Journal of Man-Machine Studies,* 39, 705-728.

Foley, J. D. (1987). Interfaces for advanced computing. *Scientific American,* October, 83-90.

Franzke, M. (1995) Turning research into practice: Characteristics of display-based interaction. *Proceedings of CHI'95: Human Factors in Computing Systems*, 421-428, New York: ACM.

Frese, M., Schulte-Gocking, H., and Altmann, A. (1987). Direkte manipulation vs. konventionelle interaktion. Cited in Ziegler and Fahnrich (1988).

Frohlich, D. M. (1991). The design space of interfaces. In L. Kielldahl (Ed.) *Multimedia- Principles, Systems and Applications,* 53-69. Berlin: Springer-Berlag.

Frohlich, D. M. (1993). The history and future of direct manipulation. *Behaviour and Information Technology,* 12, 315-329.

Frohlich, D. M., and Luff, P. (1990). Applying the technology of conversation to the technology for conversation. In P. Luff, G.N. Gilbert, and D. M. Frohlich (Eds.) *Computers and Conversation Analysis*, 187-220. London: Academic Press.

Gittens, D. (1986). Icon based human computer interaction. *International Journal of Man-Machine Studies*, 24, 519-543.

Haddock, N. J. (1992). Multimodal database query. *Proceedings of COLING.* 1274-1278.

Halasz, F. and Moran, T. P. (1981). Analogy considered harmful. *Proceedings of CHI'81: Human Factors in Computing Systems,* 383-386. Gaithesburg, Maryland.

Harrison, B. L., Ishii, H., Vicente, K. J., and Buxton, W. A. S. (1995). Transparent layered user interfaces: An evaluation of a display design to enhance focussed and divided attention. *Proceedings of CHI'95: Human Factors in Computing Systems*, 317-324. New York, ACM.

Hayes, P.J., Reddy, D.R. (1983). Steps towards graceful interaction in spoken and written man-machine communication. *International Journal of Man-Machine Studies*, 19, 231-284.

Huls, C. (1995) *Fitting language into the picture.* Published PhD thesis. Nijmegen Institute for Cognition and Information, Technical Report No. TR 95-01.

Hutchins, E. L. (1989). Metaphors for interface design. In M. M. Taylor, F. Neal, and D. G. Bouwhuis (Eds.) *The Structure of Multimodal Dialogue,* 11-28. Amsterdam: Elsevier Science.

Hutchins, E. L., Hollan, J. D., and Norman, D. A. (1986). Direct manipulation interfaces. In D. A. Norman and S.W. Draper (Eds.) *User centered system design,* 87-124. Hillside, NJ: Lawrence Erlbaum Associates, Inc.

Iseki, O., and Shneiderman, B. (1986). Applying direct manipulation concepts: Direct Manipulation Disk Operating System (DMDOS). *ACM SIGSOFT Software Engineering Notes,* 11, (April 1986), 22-26.

Jacob, R. J. K. (1991). The use of eye movements in human computer interaction techniques: What you look at is what you get. *Transactions on Information Systems,* 9, 152-169. New York: ACM

Johnson, J. (1987). How faithfully should the electronic office simulate the real one? *SIGCHI Bulletin*, October, 21-25. New York: ACM

Johnson, J., Roberts,T. L., Verplank, W., Smith, D. C., Irby, C. H., Beard, M., and Mackay, K. (1989). The Xerox Star: A retrospective. *IEEE Computer*, September, 11-29.

Jones, W. P., and Dumais, S.T. (1986). The spatial metaphor for user interfaces: Experimental tests of reference by location versus name. *Transactions on Office Information Systems,* 4, 42-63.

Jordan, P.W. (1992). Claims for direct manipulation interfaces investigated. *Industrial Management and Data Systems*, 3-6.

Kacmar, C. J. (1989). *An experimental comparison of text and icon menu item formats.* Working paper, Texas AandM University Computer Science Department.

Karat, J. (1987). Evaluating user interface complexity. *Proceedings of the Human Factors Society 31st Annual Meeting,* 566-570. Santa Monica, CA: Human Factors Society.

Kunkel, K., Bannert, M., and Fach, P. W. (1995). The influence of design decisions on the usability of direct manipulation user interfaces. *Behaviour and Information Technology,* 14, 93-106.

Kurtenbach, G. P., Sellen, A. J., and Buxton, W.A.S. (1993). An empirical evaluation of some articulatory and cognitive aspects of making menus. *International Journal of Human-Computer Interaction,* 8, 1-24.

Laurel, B. (1986). Interface as memesis. In D. A. Norman and S. Draper (Eds.) *User Centered System Design: New Perspectives on Human Computer Interaction.* New York: Lawrence Erlbaum Associates, Inc.

Laurel, B. (1990). Interface agents: Metaphors with character. In B. Laurel (Ed.) *The Art of Computer-Interface Design.,* 355-366. CA: Addison-Wesley.

Lee, J., and Zeevat, H. (1990). Intergrating natural language and graphics in dialogue. *Proceedings of INTERACT,* 479-484. Amsterdam: Elsevier Science.

Lokuge, I., and Ishizaki, S. (1995). Geospace: An interactive visualization system for exploring complex information spaces. *Proceedings of CHI'95: Human Factors in Computing Systems*, 409-414. New York: ACM.

Luff, P., Frohlich, D. M. (1991). Mixed initiative interaction. In T. Bach-Capon (Ed.) *Knowledge Based Systems and Legal Applications,* 265-294. London: Academic Press.

Macgregor, J. N. (1992). A comparison of the effects of icons and descriptors in videotex menu retrieval. *International Journal of Man-Machine Studies,* 37, 767-777.

Maes, P. (1994). Agents that reduce work and information overload. *Communications of the ACM,* 37, 31-40.

Morgan, K., Morris, R. L., and Gibbs, S. (1991). When does a mouse become a rat? or ... Comparing the performances and preferences in direct manipulation and command line environment. *Computer Journal,* 34, 265-271.

Margono, S., and Shneiderman, B. (1987). A study of file manipulation by novices using commands vs. direct manipulation. *Proceedings of 26th Annual Technical Symposium of the Washington, D.C.Chapter of the ACM,* 57-62, Gathersburg, MD: National Bureau of Standards.

Myers, B. A. (1992). Demonstrational interfaces: A step beyond direct manipulation. *Computer*, August, 61-73.

Nass, C., Steuer, J., Henriksen, L., and Dryer, C. (1994). Machines, social attributions and ethopoeia: Performance assessments of computers subsequent to self and other evaluations. *International Journal of Human-Computer Studies,* 40, 543-559.

Nass, C., Steuer,J., Tauber,E.R. (1994). Computers as social actors. *Proceedings of CHI'94: Human Factors in Computing Systems*, 72-78. New York: ACM.

Nickerson, R. S. (1991). Some characteristics of conversations. In B. Shackel (Ed.) *Man Computer Interaction: Human Factors Aspects of Computers and People,* 53-64. The Netherlands: Sijthoff and Noordhoff.

Neilson, I., and Lee, J. (1994). Conversations with graphics: Implications for the design of natural language/graphic interfaces. *International Journal of Human-Computer Studies,* 40, 509-541.

Norman, D. A. (1986). Cognitive engineering. In D. A. Norman and S. W. Draper (Eds.) *User Centered System Design.* Hillside, NJ: Lawrence Erlbaum Associates, Inc.

Shneiderman, B. (1982). The future of interactive systems and the emergence of direct manipulation. *Behaviour and Information Technology,* 1, 237-256.

Shneiderman, B. (1983). Direct manipulation: A step beyond programming languages, *IEEE Computer,* 16, 57-69.

Shneiderman, B. (1992). *Designing the user interface: Strategies for effective human-computer interaction.* Addison-Wesley Publishing Co. (2nd Edition).

Shneiderman, B. (1994). Dynamic queries for visual information seeking. *IEEE Software*, (Nov.), 6, 70-77.

Stearns, G., (1989). Agents and the HP NewWave application program interface. *Hewlett-Packard Journal,* 40, 32-37.

Stenton, P. (1990). Designing cooperative interfaces: Tailoring the channel. In J. R. Galliers (ed.) *Proceedings of the First Belief Representation and Agent Architectures Workshop,* Computer Laboratory Technical Report No. 194, 193-197. University of Cambridge.

Strausfield, L. (1995). Financial viewpoints: Using point of view to enable understanding of information. *Companion Proceedings of CHI'95: Human Factors in Computing Systems*, 208-209. New York: ACM.

Streeter, L. (1995). Interface styles: Direct manipulation versus social interactions. *Companion Proceedings of CHI'95: Human Factors in Computing Systems,* 178. New York: ACM.

Tabachneck, H. J. M., and Simon, H. A. (1994). What you see is what you get - But do you get what you see? *Companion Proceedings of CHI'94: Human Factors in Computing Systems*, 293-294. New York, ACM.

Te'eni, D. (1990). Direct manipulation as a source of cognitive feedback: human-computer experiment with a judgment task. *International Journal of Man-Machine Studies,* 33, 453-466.

Tullis, T. S., and Kodimer, M. L. (1992). A comparison of direct manipulation, selection and data entry techniques for reordering fields in a table. *Proceedings of the Human Factors Society 36th Annual Meeting,* 1, 298-302. Santa Monica, CA: Human Factors Society.

Ulich, E., Rauterberg, M., Mott,T., Greutmann, T., and Strohmo, O. (1991). Task orientation and user-orientated dialogue design. *International Journal of Human Computer Interaction,* 3, 117-144.

Venolia, D. (1993). Facile 3D direct manipulation. *Proceedings of INTERCHI'93,* 31-36. New York: ACM.

Walker, M. A., (1989). Natural language in a desktop environment. *Proceedings of 3rd International Conference on Human-Computer Interaction,* 502-509.

Whittaker, S. J. (1990). Next generation interfaces. *AAAI Spring Symposium on KBHCC,* 127-131. Stanford, CA.

Whittaker, S. J., Geelhoed, E., and Robinson, E. (1993). Shared workspaces: How do they work and when are they useful? *International Journal of Man-Machine Studies,* 39, 813-842.

Whiteside, J., Jones, S., Levy, P., and Wixon, D. (1985). User performance with command, menu and iconic interfaces. *Proceedings of CHI'85: Human Factors in Computing Systems*, 185-191. New York: ACM.

Williamson, C., and Shneiderman, B. (1992) The Dynamic HomeFinder: Evaluating dynamic queries in a real-estate information exploration system. *Proceedings of ACM SIGIR'92*, 338-346.

Wixon D., and Good, M. (1987). Interface style and eclecticism: Moving beyond categorical approaches. *Proceedings of the Human Factors Society 31st Annual Meeting*, 571-575.

Wooldridge, M., Jennings, N. R., (1995). Intelligent agents: Theory and practice. *Knowledge Engineering Review*, in press.

Yankelovich, N., Levow, G. A., and Marx, M. (1995). Designing Speechacts: Issues in speech user interfaces. *Proceedings of CHI'95: Human Factors in Computing Systems*, 369-376. New York: ACM.

Ziegler, J. E., and Fahnrich, K. P. (1988). Direct manipulation. In M. Helander (Ed.) *Handbook of Human Computer Interaction,*123-135. Amsterdam: North Holland.

Zimmerman, T. G., Smith, J. R., Paradiso, J. A., Allport, D., and Gershenfeld, N. (1995). Applying electric field sensing to human-computer interfaces. *Proceedings of CHI'95: Human Factors in Computing Systems,* 280-287. New York: ACM.

Handbook of Human-Computer Interaction
Second, completely revised edition
M. Helander, T.K. Landauer, P. Prabhu (eds.)

Chapter 22

Human Error and User-Interface Design

Prasad V. Prabhu and Girish V. Prabhu
Eastman Kodak Company
Rochester, New York, USA

22.1 Introduction

In the realm of human-computer interaction, researchers and practitioners in the area of usability and human error are advocating the motto — "To err is human, to forgive is the role of the computer interface" — thus conferring divinity on the computer interface and putting all the pressure on the designer. In his compelling book "The Psychology of Everyday Things", Norman (1988) spells out his credo on errors "*If an error is possible, someone will make it. The designer must assume that all possible errors will occur and design so as to minimize the chance of the error in the first place, or its effects once it gets made. Errors should be easy to detect, they should have minimal consequences, and, if possible, their effects should be reversible*". Practicing this approach involves understanding a myriad of issues related to human performance and making important trade-offs related to time, resources, and task goals. This chapter is aimed at discussing some of these issues and trade-offs. The chapter will first introduce some of the theoretical underpinnings of human error and then explore the interface design issues related to human error. An attempt will be made to highlight the error management issues such as capture and recovery from human error, interface design to minimize human error, and the concept of error tolerant design.

22.2 Classifying Human Error

Two of the definitions provided by the Webster's New World Dictionary for the term "error" are (1) the state of believing what is untrue, and (2) something incorrectly done. These two definitions point to a cognitive aspect and a physical aspect of error, respectively. Furthermore, error can be defined in terms of either the *action* or the *consequences of the action*. Senders and Moray (1991) differentiate between these two definitions of error by defining error as (1) a divergence between the action actually performed and the action that should have been performed, or 2) an action or event whose effect is outside specific tolerances required by a particular system.

There are several philosophical issues involved in how error is defined. Rasmussen (1982), for example, defined human errors as experiments in an unkind environment. Reason (1990) argues that errors are the debit side of what are useful and essential mental processes. Lewis and Norman (1995) would prefer not to use the term error because to them it assigns blame. It is, however, generally agreed that errors cannot be defined by considering human performance in isolation, but have to be defined in reference to human intentions or expectations (Rasmussen, 1982). In the following sections we will look at some error classification schemes.

22.2.1 Human Error Categories

Hollnagel (1989) introduced a conceptual distinction between *error phenotypes* and *error genotypes*. Error phenotypes are defined as observable states which are deemed undesirable. Error genotypes are defined as the generative mechanisms of these observable states. Similarly, Reason (1988) distinguished between *error types* and *error forms*. Error types relate to the origin of an error within the cognitive processes (e.g., planning, storage, execution). Error forms, on the other hand, are recurrent varieties of fallibility which appear across all kinds of cognitive activity i.e., they are the recognizable manifestations of the error types. Along these lines, two approaches to classifying errors can be outlined: (1) A phenomenological classification that focuses on the error consequences (phenotypes of error or error forms), and (2) A classification that focuses upon the error causes (genotypes of error or error types).

Classification of errors by their consequences: Such a phenomenological scheme of categorizing human error describes the superficial nature of error, or the error manifestation. A typical scheme will have categories like *omissions*, *substitutions*, etc. So, for example, describing an error as the pressing of a <*shift*> key instead of a <Ctrl> key would be termed a phenomenological description of the error. Such descriptions usually point to "how" the error happened rather than "why" the error happened. For that, we have to look deeper into the cause of error.

Classification of errors by their underlying causes: Different types of human errors have different psychological origins. Dissimilar error forms could have similar causes. At this level, taxonomies of error look at either the cognitive mechanisms involved, or classify errors based on human cognitive biases. Two such classifications are discussed in the next two subsections.

22.2.2 Slips and Mistakes

When classified by the underlying causes, one of the important distinctions for human errors is that between slips and mistakes (Norman, 1981; Reason and Mycielska, 1982). The difference between these two categories is at the level of intention or planning.

- The plan for the action may be correct but the actions do not go as planned. Such errors are called *slips*. This can manifest as omission of some acts or intrusion of unwanted acts. Alternatively, the right actions get carried out in the wrong order, etc. So slips are failures of execution.
- The action may go as planned but the plan itself is wrong. Such errors at the level of intention are called *mistakes*. Mistakes are, thus, defined as planning failures. When the plan is inadequate to achieve its intended outcome, the error is one of inappropriate intention.

Rasmussen (1986) proposed that human behavior can be classified into a three-level hierarchy, namely: skill-based, rule-based, and knowledge-based (S-R-K) behavior:

- Skill-based behavior is without conscious control, representing sensorimotor performance and exhibits automated and highly integrated patterns of behavior. Examples include clicking of the left mouse button for selection, or keyboard typing for a expert typist.
- Rule-based behavior is with conscious control, in familiar work situations, using stored rules or procedures that have been previously acquired (for example, opening a document in a familiar word processor, or logging on to the Internet using a familiar on-line service interface.)
- Knowledge-based behavior is exhibited in unfamiliar situations when the environment is new and no rules or procedures are available from previous encounters (for example, learning to use a new spreadsheet application, or learning to use a new gaming program.)
- Reason (1990) identified three basic error types within the S-R-K hierarchy proposed by Rasmussen (1986):

- Skill-based slips. Errors at this level could arise due to speed-accuracy trade-offs, intrinsic variability of the human operator, capture by motor schemata, etc. These errors could occur due to fallibility at one or more of the information-processing steps like perception, attention, memory, and execution control.
- Rule-based mistakes. These involve failures in the selection or application of problem-solving rules. Thus, errors at this level can arise from application of wrong rules, incorrect recall of rules, reliance on an under-specified cue set, and interference from familiar rules.
- Knowledge-based mistakes. These arise due to the "trial-and-error" learning involved in novel situations. Errors can occur as a result of the hypothesis testing process, resource limitations, or interference in functional reasoning due to false analogies.

22.2.3 Cognitive Control and Systemic Error Mechanisms

Rasmussen and Vicente (1987) propose an error taxonomy based on cognitive control mechanisms to provide a foundation for eliminating the effects of error through effective design. They identify the following four categories of errors:

1. Errors related to learning and adaptation. The learning process can induce errors. Learning is evident even in skill-based behavior because adaptation is a continuous process which keeps performance aligned with changes in the work environment. In rule-based behavior, development of effective know-how and rules-of-thumb are developed through experiments to find shortcuts, i.e., seeking a path of least effort - such experiments can cause errors. Finally in knowledge-based behavior, users test their hypothesis as they learn about the new environment. This is a highly error-prone behavior.

2. Errors due to interference among competing cognitive control structures. In typical work environments, users will time-share several different tasks, i.e., perform multiple activities. Thus, performance will be sensitive to disruption due to interference of control mechanisms belonging to unrelated activities. These type of errors are further discussed under *Memory Limitations and Memory Aids* in the section on Error Reduction.

3. Errors due to lack of resources. These errors occur due to insufficient knowledge of basic functional principles behind the interface (system) design or a lack of mental capacity for complex causal reasoning.

4. Errors due to intrinsic human variability. Human performance is intrinsically variable. The stochastic variability can be observed via such examples as slips of memory, variability in recall of data used in reasoning, or the variability in the control of movements, or variability in attention.

22.2.4 Error-Shaping Factors

Reason (1990) notes that situational factors and psychological factors combine to shape the characteristic error forms. These error-shaping factors can operate at more than one level of cognitive control. Some of the error-shaping factors are shown Table 1. It is desirable to have an understanding of these factors while designing interfaces as they indicate probable reasons why humans could make errors. With this in mind it is an important goal of the interface/system designer to avoid (or control/provide safeguards) interface characteristics that might aid or create these error shaping factors.

22.3 Error Capture and Recovery

It is probably impossible to design systems in which people do not make errors. The classic 80-20 rule applies when considering error-free interface design -- "to design an interface which is free of errors 80% of the time takes 20% of the overall design time. To evaluate and accommodate the remaining 20% could take 80% of the time. In most practical scenarios this is not justifiable because of the cost. Lewis and Norman (1995) propose that the effort should be to maximize the discovery of error (error capture), to make it easier to recover from error (error recovery), and to minimize the incidence of error.

One of the most critical aspects of interface design is how and when errors are captured and also how the system recovers from and responds to human errors. Lewis and Norman (1995) postulate that making errors show up clearly and quickly is an important design goal. This is because delayed detection of errors results in waste of time and effort by the user as well as increases the difficulty in error diagnosis.

System Response to Human Error. Lewis and Norman (1995) have identified six possible responses that a system can provide when it cannot interpret the input provided by the user. These consist of: (1) Gag (prevent user from continuing), (2) Warn (e.g., beeps, text messages), (3) Do nothing (e.g., clicking on a disabled control provides no visible change), (4) Self-correct (e.g., word processor auto correct function, which can be used to automatically correct common typing errors such as capitalizing first letter of sentences, etc.), (5) Let's talk about it (system responds by initiating a dialog with the user - co-operative problem solving), and (6) Teach me (system asks for further clarification). Lewis and Norman provide an excellent treatment to the topic on error detection and recovery and the reader is advised to read this paper for further information.

Error Messages. The error message is one of the important ways in which the system communicates with the user. A useful error message is one which not only tells the user what went wrong, but also provides some information on how to take the right action (remedial information). Properly designed error messages help the users learn from their errors, and thus reduce the chances that the error are repeated. Frequently, errors indicate that the user's mental model of the task is wrong. In such cases, providing simple error messages (e.g., those used for syntax errors) without attempting to understand or interpret the error will not help (Eberts, 1994). Eberts notes that, in the early computer systems, error messages were conspicuously lacking in feedback effectiveness (e.g., "illegal entry") and were unfriendly (e.g., "fatal error"). Another important psychological issue is to avoid wording error messages that imply that the user is at fault. For example, use "cannot find <file name> instead of "file name error" (Microsoft). Such responses to errors can be disconcerting, as well as frustrating to users. The interface designer should try to provide as much relevant feedback as is possible and in a courteous tone.

Feedback. Rasmussen and Vicente (1989) suggest that feedback on the effects of actions should be provided to the user. Such feedback facilitates error recovery by supporting functional understanding and also helps knowledge-based monitoring. They suggest that it is important to make latent, conditional constraints on actions visible to the user. Thus, for, example, it may be better to enable/disable a control button on an interface instead of having it appear and disappear. (This is especially true if this control is available in the subsequent screens [or modes] of the interface, since this provides the advantage of maintaining a consistent position for the control. However, if this control is not available in the subsequent screen [or mode], it is better to remove it.)

Also, if the user is to learn from errors, then interface design should aim at making the limits of acceptable performance visible to the user while the effects are still observable and reversible (Rasmussen and Vicente, 1989). This can be possible at the level of skill-based slips if perceptual monitoring can be maintained. Error observability and recoverability is much harder at the rule-based level of control i.e. mistakes. This is because there is usually a time delay between the undesirable consequences of the action and the wrong intention. Also, in the immediate present, the outcome of the actions match the intentions, so the user cannot initiate the error detection.

22.4 Error Reduction: Issues and Guidelines

One of the evident goals of any good system design is the minimization of human errors. This can be done by careful consideration of the interface layout and providing good conceptual models or metaphors (if used) for the functionality of the system and its components. Using the error taxonomy based on cognitive control mechanisms (introduced earlier in this chapter), Rasmussen and Vicente (1987) provide guidelines for system design that address means of dealing with errors. Some of these guidelines are itemized below:

- Interface design should aim at making the limits of acceptable performance visible to the users, while the effects are still observable and reversible.
- Provide feedback on the effects of actions to allow the user to cope with the delay between the execution of an intention and the observation of its effect.
- Make overview displays available to avoid capture errors at the skill-based level.
- Support memory with externalization of the effective mental models.
- Develop consistent information transformation concepts for data integration to enable the interface to present information at the level that is most appropriate for decision making.
- Support of memory of items, acts, and data which are not part of an integrated 'gestalt' can be useful.

Table 1. Definitions of error-shaping factors. *(from Prabhu, Sharit, and Drury, 1992; compiled from Rasmussen, 1986, 1987; Woods et al., 1988; Hollnagel, 1988; Woods, 1989; Reason, 1990)*

KNOWLEDGE-BASED ERROR-SHAPING FACTORS	
Information Overload	• Excessive demands on memory.
Delayed Feedback	• Delays in feedback concerning execution of decisions.
Memory Cueing	• Familiar information in long term memory is cued by problem content.
Causal Series Vs Nets	• Oversimplification of causality; thinking in terms of immediate goals.
Attentional Limitations	• Finite resources of attentional process.
Biased Reviewing	• Error in reviewing planned course of action.
Illusory Correlation	• Failure to detect correlation or understand the logic of covariation.
Complexity Problems	• Problems in understanding system due to its complex nature.
RULE-BASED ERROR-SHAPING FACTORS	
Availability	• Tendency to use intuitive rules or use rules that readily come to mind.
Rigidity	• Mindset (cognitive conservatism) results in refusal to change familiar procedure.
Encoding Deficiency	• Encode inaccurately or fail to encode the properties of the problem space.
Inadvisable Rules	• Rules that satisfy immediate goals but can cause errors due to side effects.
Wrong Rules	• Rules that are wrong for the current situations.
First Exceptions	• Errors caused on the first occasion that is an exception to the general rule.
SKILL-BASED ERROR-SHAPING FACTORS	
Omissions	• Omission of actions/action sequences needed to achieve a specified goal.
Perceptual Confusion	• A familiar match is accepted instead of the correct match.
SATO	• Speed accuracy trade-offs result in errors.
Stochastic Variability	• Variability in the control of movements.
Repetitions	• Actions that are unnecessarily repeated.
Interference	• Potential problems stemming from concurrent activities.

Interface design principles that can be applied to good use for minimizing the consequences of human error include: ensuring consistency across interfaces, providing good conceptual models or metaphors, reducing or accounting for mode, capture and description errors, providing visibility through affordances, providing appropriate constraints and mapping, reducing the gap between the gulf of execution and the gulf of evaluation, appropriate communication and feedback, recognition of memory limitations and provision of memory aids, and adequate training and on-line help. We discuss some of these in the following sections.

22.4.1 Avoiding Mode Errors

These errors occur when actions appropriate in one mode are performed in another causing undesirable results. This is usually because users forget which mode they are in. This can be due to various reasons such as inadequate visual differentiation between modes, or inadequate feedback on mode change.

Microsoft-Word 6.0, for example, provides six different ways of viewing the document - normal, outline, page layout, master document, print preview, and full screen. Of these six, normal and page layout views are very similar to each other in visual appearance and so are the outline and master document views. It is easy to envisage mode errors occurring in such a scenario.

Another example of problem with modes can be seen in America On-line's (AOL) user interface, version 3.0. The AOL interface is windows-based and the user sees a new window pop up on top of the old one (since the windows are neither cascaded nor tiled, the older window is totally hidden). When the user wants to go back to the earlier window it is possible to close the current one to reveal the older window. However, the web browser interface of AOL, while also being window based, provides for navigation between windows through controls placed on fixed locations on top of the windows. Also, in this mode, if the user tries to go back to the earlier window by closing the current one (this action is available) the action results in closing the web browser itself. It is, again, easy to envisage how mode errors can occur in this scenario resulting in unwittingly coming out of the browser.

It is advisable to reduce modes or totally eliminate them if possible. If the design constraints necessitate modes then make them visible and provide adequate feedback to the users so that they are aware what mode they are currently in (for e.g., using a visible, mode indicator in the status bar on a windows interface).

22.4.2 Maintaining Consistency

Users of computer systems have certain expectancies towards what happens as a result of their actions. The concept of consistency implies that mechanisms should be used in the same way wherever and whenever they occur (Tognazzini, 1990). So, for example, pressing the return key on the keyboard or clicking the left button of the mouse for indicating an input to the system are fairly well-established action-expectation relations. Similarly, the left arrow key moves the cursor left. Maintaining such consistency with expectations is very important to avoid human errors.

Lack of consistency in the command structure, for example, can lead to a class of description errors (Lewis and Norman, 1995). Description errors occur when the actions are insufficiently specified and this ambiguity leads to wrong actions. In this case, because commands that appear related do not have equivalent command structures, users could form an inappropriate sequence of actions.

Because of the rapidly evolving nature of the computer interfaces due to market pressures, it is difficult to maintain complete consistency. Tognazzini (1990) suggests that we must pick and choose which aspects of consistency are important to maintain. Some of the guidelines for this include: (a) using published guidelines and (b) not changing something unless it really needs changing. He suggests two principles that are helpful in evolving products without seriously disrupting areas of consistency most important to users:

- Consistent interpretation of user behavior by the system is more important than consistent system objects or behaviors. The logic behind this is that if system objects change appearance, or if the system behaves in a new way (while this is not desirable), users learn the meaning of the new appearance or learn to interpret the new behavior. But if the system interprets user actions inconsistently, then the user has no basis for making stable interaction decisions. This leads to unacceptable human errors.
- If a change has to be made, make it a large and obvious one. Users develop automatic patterns of behavior after interacting with systems for a long time. For example, responses to various system queries that ask for inputs from the user are fairly unconscious as in clicking on the O.K. button to respond to the query *"Do you want to save before quitting?"* Any change in the wording of such questions has to be very large and obvious to the user, to avoid the automatic response feature.

22.4.3 Facilitating Multiple Activities

Frequently, people perform multiple activities in a given time period. This could include planned or intended activities like listening to music while typing on the word processor (parallel activities involving different sensory modes) or working with different applications such as word processing, spreadsheets, and database applications (to accomplish a given task) using office application suites. On the other hand, multiple activities may also result from interruptions of the current activity. Such interruptions could be external (from the environment) or internal (our own thought processes drawing attention from the current task) (Miyata and Norman, 1986). Human errors occur during such tasks because of limitations of memory as well as environmental disruptions. Two aspects are important—levels of cognitive control and levels of attention.

Psychological research has defined two levels of cognitive control of behavior: (1) conscious control and (2) unconscious or sub-conscious control. Conscious control is exhibited during performance of novel tasks or when tasks are not yet well-learned. Rasmussen (1986) describes this as the rule-based or knowledge-based level of control. Unconscious control or skill-based behavior is exhibited in well-practiced routine tasks.

The research on attention identifies (Wickens, 1992): (1) limits of selective attention—humans sometimes select inappropriate aspects of the environment to process, (2) limits of focused attention—humans are occasionally unable to concentrate on one source of information in the environment, and (3) limits of divided attention—humans are sometimes unable to divide their attention between multiple stimuli or tasks, all of which they wish to process.

In this context, Miyata and Norman (1986) talk about (1) current foreground activities (under conscious control), (2) current background activities (either internal under subconscious control or external by some other agency), and (3) suspended activities. So while creating a program, for example, developing the idea is a current foreground activity while typing the code is a current background activity for a skilled typist. For an unskilled typist both are foreground activities. Suspended activities can occur both due to external (change of task priority, call for help from co-worker) or internal (boredom, fatigue) interruptions. For systems where multiple activities is a significant issue, Miyata and Norman (1986) suggest the following:

- System should be designed so that it is easy to suspend an activity when it is desired.
- Sufficient information should be saved with the suspended task so that when the activity is resumed, it can be continued where it was left off.
- A reminding structure should be available so that the user does not forget the unfinished task.

Miyata and Norman (1986) suggest that *reminding* is needed if suspended activities are to be resumed at the appropriate time or place. Reminders serve to reactivate the persons memory for completing the suspended activity. Reminders can be a signal to indicate something is to be remembered (dialog box reminding user to save work before quitting) and/or they can be a description to aid in retrieving the information to be remembered (schedule listed in a calendar utility with small description of activities). The multiple documents interfaces that modern word processors provide highlight this dual aspect of the reminding function and the errors related to inadequate reminding. For example, in MS-Word, suppose you have two documents open, worked on one for a while (the autosave was disabled) and then switched to the other. Now, due to limitations of short term memory you could forget about the specific changes made to the first document that had been opened. When deciding to exit, the dialog box interface asks if you want to save changes (reminding function). However, it is possible that you have forgotten what changes you made or whether you intended to save these. Thus, a good reminder in this case should act not only as a signal but also as an aid in helping to retrieve, from memory, the information necessary for the task. It would be useful, in this instance, to also see the changes that one has made in the other document, i.e., new material highlighted, to help the decision. Miyata and Norman (1986) suggest the following characteristics for an ideal reminder:

- Remind user when conditions are ready for resuming a suspended activity.
- Remind user when something has to be done immediately.
- Do not distract from the current activity.
- Help resumption of an activity by retrieving the exact previous state of the activity and making it available to the user.
- Provide user with a list of activities that have been suspended or externally backgrounded.

22.4.4 Knowledge in the Head (KIH) versus Knowledge in the World (KIW)

Any information that must be retained in memory, to be able to perform a task, is called knowledge in the head (KIH). Interfaces that require a significant amount of KIH are more prone to errors than those that exhibit knowledge in the world (KIW) characteristics. KIW is when the information needed to perform a task resides in the task components, or in case of an interface the knowledge needed to use the interface resides in the interface itself. Designing an interface with KIW is important because it reduces the load on human memory. Norman (1988) emphasizes that precise behavior can occur if knowledge is available in the world and can be recognized (not required to recall). Knowledge in the world can be provided through design aids, memory checklists for procedural tasks, cue cards, etc.

Designs based on knowledge in the head rely on the users memory. Miller (1956) first suggested that people can easily remember seven plus or minus two items and can easily recall them. This is now generally accepted as the limit of working memory capacity. However, if different items have to remembered for similar tasks the memory fails. This indicates that "knowledge in the head" issue should not only be considered for each product but for the whole system. You should attempt to design a system that bases its operation on recognition and not recall. This reduces the chances of errors. Also, people have great difficulty in remembering specific and precise information. By designing the system to be tolerant for non-precision can reduce errors and dissatisfaction. For example, most of the earlier command line interfaces and even some current interfaces require users to enter exact commands. A wrong spelling is caught as an error. An intelligent agent trying to help the user with possible options would be a better design.

There are obvious tradeoffs between knowledge in world versus knowledge in the head. Providing all information up front (knowledge in the world) could be un-aesthetic, time consuming, and sometimes impossible due to physical constraints. However, it makes the system easy to use. Designs based on knowledge in the head could be more efficient and aesthetic but could lead to errors due to memory loss, recall problems, and also require more time to learn. A design based on hierarchy can be used in such scenarios to balance the tradeoffs. For example, in a scanner product acquire module, instead of asking the user to enter the resolution, type of image (color, gray scale, black and white), and type of document (photograph, magazine) up front, thus providing all the information in the world, part of this information can be hidden, say in preferences. When the user scans a image, it could provide the user with details about what it is scanning (such as -- "Scanning color magazine picture at 400 dpi"). The user can always go to preferences and change the setting. This makes the system more efficient for regular use, and also provides flexibility.

22.4.5 Knowledge about Users

It is critical to know who the users of the system are. This is, of course, one of the maxims of designing usable systems and is even more critical for reducing the incidence of errors. The users of computer systems come in all ages with varying levels of experience; they have different cultural backgrounds and some have disabilities that need to be considered.

Charness et al. (1995) found that older people using a mouse input device had particular difficulties with smaller targets and made a larger number of errors than younger people. Czaja (see chapter on computer technology and the older adult, in this handbook) suggests avoiding small targets, using font sizes greater than 12 and maximizing size of the icons as ways to combat the decreasing physical and visual abilities of older users Also, older people have more difficulty remembering commands and procedures, and as such would commit lesser errors with interfaces designed to place minimal demands on working memory (e.g., pull down menus, labeling icons, etc.).

People with disabilities is another group of users that are often neglected by interface designers. This is mainly due to a lack of information on how pervasive disabilities are in our society and their impact on using computers. As, Newell and Gregor point out in their chapter on Human Computer Interfaces for People with Disabilities (elsewhere in this handbook), 1 in 10 of the population have a significant hearing impairment, 1 in 125 are deaf and 1 in 100 of the population have visual disabilities. Some of the ways in which applications can help disabled users by using multiple perceptual input channels (e.g., not relying on color alone for information, avoid using only audio cues for important attention requiring information) and not requiring rapid responses to the system (Microsoft, 1992).

If the target users are not kept in mind while developing the interface, functions and more functions, controls and more controls, will creep in introducing errors without really improving functionality or usability. One such case was when a comparative benchmark of interfaces for the "acquire modules" of desktop, sheet-fed scanners indicated the mimicking of higher end flat-bed scanners. This interface worked well for people conversant with digital imaging. However, this was not the typical expertise of the target group, which was home users. Cognitive walkthroughs indicated that certain features and controls would lead to confusion and errors. This led to a modified design based on task analysis for home users, and the design also assumed progressive expertise. This, in turn, led to reduction of errors.

22.4.6 Understanding Cultural Biases

Silverman (1992) identifies cultural biases, cultural motivation, and missing knowledge as possible causes for mistakes. Shared or common knowledge of a culture could be defined by country boundaries or language. To take advantage of such knowledge, Yeo

(1996) proposed the concept of cultural user interfaces (CUI) and personal user interfaces (PUI). User interface design without considering the cultural biases could result in confusion, errors, and ultimately in the rejection of the software application.

Yeo (1996) classifies the important user interface design elements into overt and covert factors. Overt factors such as date/time formats, telephone numbers, and address formats are tangible and easily observed. An example of overt factors is the different separators used for demarcating decimals and thousands in currency formats across different cultures. In North America "," (comma) is used to separate a thousand and "." (period) is used to indicate decimals. However, in Germany, "." (period) is used to separate a thousand and "," is used to indicate a decimal. A software application dealing with pricing developed for North America when localized for Germany will result in errors, if the differences in the separators are not understood. Similarly date formats can be a major source of annoyance and errors. Different date formats such as dd/mm/yy (e.g., India, Japan), mm/dd/yy (e.g., USA, Canada) are in use. Errors can obviously occur if proper indication of the date format is not provided.

On the other hand, covert factors such as metaphors, colors, or sound are intangible. These can lead to misinterpretations and thus to errors. A good example of such an error is the infamous "trash can" icon in the Macintosh user interface. The US trash can looks similar to a UK or Japanese mailbox. Initial users of Mac in the United Kingdom or Japan could incorrectly identify the "trash can" icon as a mailbox (Fernandes, 1995). Similarly, the U.S. mailbox icon is well understood in North America but is not familiar to most Europeans or Asians. Houses here often use mail slots in the doors or the postal carrier just leaves mail at the front or hands it over personally. Thus both overt and covert factors are potential sources of error when any software application is localized for a particular culture without appropriate consideration of the implications of these factors.

22.4.7 Generating Appropriate Interface Metaphors

Erickson (1990) points out that metaphors occur throughout the interfaces that we use and design. The interface metaphor provides the user with a model of the system. They are useful for allowing novices to quickly learn the computer system by matching familiar information from the source domain (metaphor) to the new or target domain (the new system) (Eberts, 1994). Unfortunately, mismatches between the source and the target domain are inevitable, thus creating a possibility that the user has a wrong model of the new system. Any difference between the user's mental model and the actual way the system works can create problems. Mismatches can also occur as the task and context characteristics change. Neale and Carroll (see chapter on interface metaphors in this handbook)) provide the example of a "trash can" working well as a metaphor for the task of throwing objects away but when the task changes to ejecting a disk, the information provided by the metaphor breaks down.

Erickson (1990) suggests an approach to generate appropriate metaphors that includes understanding how the system works (functional definition), identifying user problems, generating the metaphor, and finally evaluating the metaphor. The following questions are suggested during the evaluation stage: (1) how much structure does the metaphor provide, (2) how much of the metaphor is actually relevant to the problem, (3) is the interface metaphor easy to present, (4) will your audience understand the metaphor, and (5) what else do the proposed metaphors buy you?

Neale and Carroll (see chapter on interface metaphors in this handbook) suggest the following guidelines for managing metaphor-interface mismatches:

- When introducing a metaphor, elaborate assumptions by making explicit what the metaphor hides and what it highlights.
- Create an interface design that encourages and supports exploration of system features i.e., users must be able to explore without penalty.

22.4.8 Selecting Interface Icons

The use of icons has become increasingly common to represent system states, system commands, or results. The meaning of an icon should be obvious to experienced users of the system and should be either self-evident or logical to inexperienced or new users. The design of icons has to be carefully analyzed as they can lead to errors. There are three distinct dimensions that have to be considered: semantic, syntactic, and pragmatic. The semantic dimension refers to the relationship of a visual image to a meaning, i.e., how well does this symbol represent the message? People can fail to understand the meaning of symbols due to differences of culture, gender, age, etc. The syntactic dimension refers to the relationship of one visual image to another, i.e., how does this icon (symbol) look and relate to other icons (symbols). Finally the pragmatic dimension refers to the relationship of a visual image to a user. Can the symbol be seen and does it remain visible? Factors affecting the pragmatic dimension could be lighting, viewing angles, and other visual noise.

22.4.9 Use of Colors

The use of color in interface design has now become pervasive. The theory and application aspects of colors in computer interfaces has been discussed in detail elsewhere in this handbook (see David Post's chapter on color). The selection of colors must be done with great care as there are numerous factors that affect how users perceive colors including the interaction of the color with its environment. Color is influenced by its location, size, and shape of the area it fills, surrounding colors, external conditions (ambient lighting, such as fluorescent, incandescent, or daylight), and physiological and cultural differences amongst individuals (Salomon, G, 1990).

If distinguishing between colors is important and the population has older viewers, higher brightness levels should be adopted for colors. The most common color deficiency is the inability to distinguish red from green. Also, the retinal periphery is insensitive to red and green, so avoid these colors in the periphery of large displays. Yellow and blue are better choices.

To address some of the problems associated with the use of colors, it is advisable to use color with a redundant coding scheme i.e., use color in combination with other cues such as shape pattern or location. A common example is the location coding used in traffic lights for red, yellow, and green lights.

22.4.10 On-line Help

Designing good help systems is one of the many ways to reduce the probability of human errors and to increase the effectiveness of error recovery. It is important to understand what help the users need. Roesler and Mclellan (1995) suggest that fancy formatting, navigational ease, etc. will not be of much use if the information in the help system is not the information that the users need. Also, help information should be delivered depending on the type of questions that the users have. Baecker, Grudin, Buxton, and Greenberg (1995) have compiled a list of questions that computer users have (from Sellen and Nicol, 1990; Baecker, Small, and Mander, 1991). Some of these question types are:

- Informational — what can I do with this program?
- Descriptive — what is this, what does it do?
- Procedural — how do I do this?
- Interpretive — what is happening/why is it happening?
- Navigational — where am I?
- Choice — what can I do now?
- Guidance — what should I do now?
- History — what have I done?
- Motivational — why should I use this?
- Investigative — what else should I know?

Roesler and Mclellan (1995) postulate that design of an efficient help system is predicated on (1) information needs and (2) help access methods. They adopt an empirical based method to suggest taxonomies for both factors. The information needs taxonomy consists of help items and types such as — what must I know first, how do I do this, what is this, what can I do next, help on help, meaning of terms, mouse and keyboard conventions, related product information, customer assistance, and version information. The access methods taxonomy addresses how to access help, and what help should be displayed and where. The focus is on minimizing the number of times the users had to leave an application and also to minimize the amount of navigation for help.

22.4.11 Training

While training is not in the control of the interface designer, it is an excellent idea to be aware of the level of training that will be available to support the user. In case the training level has not been decided, then a good thumb of rule is to assume minimal, or no training, and try to inculcate this assumption in designing the interface. This is especially true for consumer products. In other cases, an on-line training program might be made available, especially for more complicated systems. In such cases, it is important to remember that providing all the information may not be the best solution, since this can lead to errors or even discourage the user from using the training. An exploratory approach to learning is found to be effective. Guided exploration, in which learners are guided by suggestions and questions that focus attention on a set of goals appropriate for the software, can help in the active learning process.

22.5 Designing for Error Tolerance

The earlier section focused on how human error can be reduced by using appropriate interface design constructs—i.e., the focus was on eliminating errors. Another important concept in the area of human errors suggests that interfaces should be error tolerant—i.e., allow for errors but minimize their effect. Rasmussen (1990) suggests that during on-the-job training (OJT) by an individual the work processes are structured through a self-organizing, evolutionary process. This is because of the large number of the degrees of freedom existing in most work situations. In the field of human-computer interaction it is very easy to see the analogous situation, i.e., most people interacting with computers go through a similar OJT process to acquire necessary skills. Some of the knowledge is acquired from instructors, more experienced colleagues, technical manuals, and on-line help. More knowledge for the initial synchronization required to begin work is also acquired through knowledge-based reasoning. But from here on, high professional skill will evolve through an adaptation process in which "errors" are unavoidable side effects of the exploration of the boundaries of acceptable performance (Rasmussen, 1990). Rasmussen, therefore, argues that errors or near errors have a role in the development and maintaining of expertise. Along similar lines, Senders and Moray (1991) suggest that eliminating the opportunity for error severely limits the range of possible behavior, and thus inhibits trial and error learning which is helpful in discovering new ways to perform tasks. They argue that the key is to reduce the undesirable consequences of the error — not necessarily the error itself. They postulate the concept of an error-forgiving design.

Hollnagel (1990) adds another argument for why error tolerant designs are necessary. He points out that the knowledge about the limitations of human capacity (e.g., with regards to perception, attention, discrimination, memory) is used while making reasonable assumptions for system design. Such design decisions reduce the probability of system induced human errors, i.e., errors that can be traced back to particular configurations of the human-machine system (e.g., the interface design, the task design, etc.). However, Hollnagel (1990) suggests that system designers often overlook the fact that human capacity is variable and the actual variance could be larger than the expected variance in many situations. In other words, there is a category of errors that result from the variability of human cognition. One approach to address this problem is to reduce the requirements for performance until they are met by a significant fraction of the situations. However, this could mean that the system would perform below capacity in the majority of the cases. An alternate approach is to design the system with error tolerance. Hollnagel (1990) proposes the following features for an error-tolerant interface:

- Provides user with appropriate information at the appropriate time to minimize the opportunity for system-induced erroneous actions.
- Compensates for human perceptual dysfunctions by providing information in redundant and simplified forms.
- Compensates for human motor (and cognitive) dysfunctions by maintaining the integrity of input data (through anticipation, context dependent interpretation).
- Contains provisions for detection of erroneous actions in order to instigate corrective procedures.
- Allows for easy correction and recovery of erroneous actions by providing a forgiving environment.

22.6 Benefits of Reducing Error

In the overall scheme of user-interface design, the objective of designing for minimizing error/error consequences will be subsumed under the overall usability engineering effort. Thus, similar to the benefits of usability engineering, the efforts to design interfaces with an understanding of human error mechanisms will result (along with the obvious decrease in errors) in increased user productivity, decreased training costs, decreased user frustrations, decreased customer support. Mayhew and Mantei (1994) give an example how the benefits of decreased error can be calculated. Consider the case of a word-processor which had the same function key close a document in one context and cancel an edit in another (lack of consistency: increased probability of mode errors as well as description errors). Suppose, using the concept of design for errors allowed the elimination of such errors during the development of the interface. If this eliminated, say 0.2 errors per day (one error per week), each saving a recovery time of 2 minutes. Considering, say 250 users working 230 days a year at $25 per hour, the benefits would be:

Cost of error = 2 minutes/error * 1/60 * 25 $/hour
= 0.833 dollars/error

Total errors = 0.2 errors * 230 days/users * 250 users
= 11,500 errors

Therefore,

Decreased error benefits = 0.833 * 11,500
= $9,580 per year.

The costs of developing the interface can of course be calculated in terms of time spent and resources utilized in developing and testing the system. So, for the above example, in addition to the usual design time, if a human factors practitioner had evaluated the interface design and the suggestions were implemented, then the costs could be calculated as below:

Evaluation of interface:
8 hr @ $50/hr = $ 400.00

Added programming time to implement suggestions:
8 hr @ $50/hr = $ 400.00
Total cost of design = $ 800.00.

The above calculations are explicit cost/benefit comparisons in that they are directly related to the design effort. Some other benefits of minimizing errors are not as apparent. These implicit trade-offs include learning time for the user, resources spent on training, user satisfaction, and in some cases risk and safety issues.

22.7 Conclusion

In conclusion, human error cannot be separated from human performance. In some cases, errors are part of the learning process and as such systems/interfaces should be designed to be error tolerant. It should be possible for the user to explore the system without penalty, discover what the consequences are for different actions, and be able to recover from those consequences. Wherever possible, the system should capture error at the earliest feasible instance and provide the user with a feedback that is specific and useful in correcting the error.

It has to be understood that human performance is variable and that human memory is fallible. Interface design should try to minimize the necessity to carry knowledge in the head and try to make the functionality of the interface as obvious as possible. Errors at the level of incorrect intentions i.e., rule-based and knowledge-based mistakes are difficult to capture, and as such interface design should be geared towards minimizing them.

Maintaining consistency with user expectations is very important to avoid human errors. Also, providing users with the right mental model of the system with judicious use of metaphors goes a long way towards avoiding mismatches. While interface designers should not rely on *training* to alleviate errors, they should at the same time understand when and how training can be effectively used to reduce errors. With the increased trend towards globalization it is necessary to be aware of cultural biases and population stereotypes while designing software for a possible global user population. Finally, understanding the varied user population in terms of age, experience, and physical and mental abilities helps design more error tolerant interfaces.

22.8 References

Baecker, R., Small, I., and Mander, R. (1991). Bringing icons to life. In *Proceedings of CHI '91*, ACM, pp. 1-6.

Baecker, R. M., Grudin, J., Buxton, W. A. S., and Greenberg, S. (1995). Designing to fit human capabilities, In *Readings in Human-Computer Interaction: Toward the Year 2000*, R. M. Baecker, J. Grudin, W. A. S. Buxton, and S. Greenberg (eds.), pp. 667-680, San Francisco, CA: Morgan Kaufmann Publishers.

Charness, N., Bosman, E.A., and Elliot, R.G. (1995). Senior friendly input devices: Is the pen mightier than the mouse? Paper presented at the 103 Annual Convention of the American Psychological Association. New York, NY, August.

Eberts R. E. (1994). User Interface Design. Englewood Cliffs, New Jersey: Prentice-Hall.

Erickson, T. D. (1990). Working with interface metaphors. In *The Art of Human-Computer Interface Design*, B. Laurel (ed.), pp 65-73, Readings, MA: Addison-Wesley.

Fernandes, T. (1995) Global Interface Design: A Guide to Designing International User Interface. Boston, MA: AP Professional.

Hollnagel, E. (1988). Information and reasoning in intelligent decision support systems. In *Cognitive Engineering in Complex Dynamic Worlds*, E. Hollnagel, G. Mancini and D. D. Woods (eds.), pp 215-228, London: Academic Press.

Hollnagel, E. (1989). The phenotypes of erroneous actions: Implications for HCI design. In G. R. S. Weir and J. L. Alty (eds.), *Human-Computer Interaction and Complex Systems*. London: Academic Press.

Hollnagel, E. (1990). The design of error tolerant interfaces. Proceedings of *The First International Symposium on Ground Data Systems for Spacecraft Control*, Darmstadt, Germany, June 26-29, 1990.

Lewis, C. and Norman, D. A. (1995). Designing for error. In *Readings in Human-Computer Interaction: Toward the Year 2000*, R. M. Baecker, J. Grudin, W. A. S. Buxton, and S. Greenberg (eds.), pp 686-697, San Francisco, CA: Morgan Kaufmann.

Mayhew, D. J. and Mantei, M. (1994). A basic framework for cost-justifying usability engineering, In *Cost-Justifying Usability*, R. G. Bias and D. J. Mayhew (eds.), chapter 2, Boston, MA: Academic Press.

Microsoft (1992). *The Windows Interface: An Application Design Guide*. Redmond, WA: Microsoft Press.

Miller, G. (1956). The magical number 7 plus or minus 2: Some limits on our capacity for processing information. *Psychological Review*, 63, pp 81-97.

Miyata, Y. and Norman, D. A. (1986). Psychological issues in support of multiple activities. In *User Centered System Design: New Perspectives on Human-Computer Interaction*, D. A. Norman and S. W. Draper (eds.), Lawrence Erlbaum Associates: Hillsdale, NJ.

Norman, D. A. (1981). Categorization of action slips. *Psychological Review*, 88, 1-15.

Norman, D. A. (1988). *The Psychology of Everyday Things*. Basic Books Inc. Publishers: New York, NY.

Prabhu, P. Sharit, J. and Drury, C. (1992). Classification of temporal errors in CIM systems: development of a framework for deriving human-centered information requirements. *International Journal of Computer Integrated Manufacturing*, 5, 2, pp 68-80.

Rasmussen, J. (1982). Human errors: A taxonomy for describing human malfunction in industrial installations. *Journal of Occupational Accidents*, 4, pp 311-333.

Rasmussen, J. (1986). *Information Processing and Human-Machine Interaction*. New York: North-Holland.

Rasmussen, J. (1987). Reasons, causes and human error. In *New Technology and Human Error*, J. Rasmussen, K. Duncan and J. Leplat (eds.), pp 293-301, New York: John Wiley.

Rasmussen, J. (1990). The role of error in organizing behavior. *Ergonomics*, 33, 10/11, pp 1185-1199.

Rasmussen, J. and Vicente, K. J. (1987). Cognitive control of human activities and errors: implications for ecological interface design. Invited paper for *The International Conference on Event Perception and Action*, Trieste, Italy, August.

Rasmussen, J. and Vicente, K. J. (1989). Coping with human errors through system design: Implications for ecological interface design. *International Journal of Man Machine Studies*, 31, 517-534

Reason, J. and Mycielska, K. (1982). *Absent Minded? The Psychology of Mental Lapses and Everyday Errors*. Englewood Cliffs, NJ: Prentice-Hall.

Reason, J. (1988). Modeling the basic error tendencies of human operators. *Reliability Engineering and System Safety*, 22, pp 137-153.

Reason, J. (1990). *Human Error*. Cambridge University Press: Cambridge, UK.

Roesler, A. W. and Mclellan, S. G. (1995). What help do users need?: Taxonomies for on-line information needs and access methods. In *Human Factors in Computing System Proceedings*, Annual Conference Series, ACM SIGCHI, pp 437-441.

Salomon G. (1990). New uses for color. In *The Art of Human-Computer Interface Design*, B. Laurel (ed.), pp 269-278, Readings, MA: Addison-Wesley.

Sellen, A. and Nicol, A. (1990). Building user-centered on-line help. In *The Art of Human-Computer Interface Design*, B. Laurel (ed.), pp 143-153, Readings, MA: Addison-Wesley.

Senders, J. W. and Moray, N. P. (1991). *Human Error: Cause, Prediction, and Reduction*. Lawrence Erlbaum Associates: Hillsdale, NJ.

Silverman, B. (1992). *Critiquing Human Error: A Knowledge-based Human-Computer Collaboration Approach*. Academic Press: London, UK.

Tognazzini, B. (1990). Consistency. In *The Art of Human-Computer Interface Design*, pp 75-78, B. Laurel (ed.), Readings, MA: Addison-Wesley.

Wickens, C. D. (1992). *Engineering Psychology and Human Performance*. HarperCollins Publishers: New York, NY.

Woods, D. D., Roth, E. M. and Pople, H. Jr. (1988). Modeling human intention formation for human reliability assessment. *Reliability Engineering and System Safety*, 22, pp 169-200.

Woods, D. D. (1989). Coping with complexity: the psychology of human behavior in complex systems. In *Tasks, Errors and Mental Models*, L. P. Goodstein, H. B. Andersen and S. E. Olsen (eds.), pp 128-148, London: Taylor & Francis.

Yeo, A. (1996). Cultural user interfaces: A silver lining in cultural diversity. *SIGCHI Bulletin*, 28,3, pp 4-7.

Handbook of Human-Computer Interaction
Second, completely revised edition
M. Helander, T.K. Landauer, P. Prabhu (eds.)

Chapter 23

Screen Design

Thomas S. Tullis
Fidelity Investments
Boston, Massachusetts, USA

23.1 Introduction

The term "screen design" usually refers to either the *process* of determining the visual appearance and content of a single visual frame or the *end result* of that process. In the days of terminals connected to remote computers, these screens were synonymous with physical screens (i.e., presenting a new screen meant repainting the entire physical screen). As graphical user interface (GUI) systems have become common, "screen design" has taken on a somewhat different meaning. Today, in GUI applications, most people use the term "screen design" to refer to the design of a specific window or dialog box rather than the design of the entire physical screen. Consequently, the focus of this chapter is on the design of these individual frames of information.

23.1.1 Importance of Screen Design

Since the visual channel is still the predominant method of conveying information to the user, it is easy to understand why effective screen design is so important. For example, a wide variety of studies have illustrated the importance of effective screen design:

- Tullis (1981) found that redesigning a key display from a system for testing telephone lines resulted in a 40% reduction in the time required by the users to interpret the display. Based upon the very high usage rates of this particular display, that reduction in interpretation time translates to 79 person-years saved for every year the system remains in use.

- Keister and Gallaway (1983) found that redesigning a series of screens resulted in a 25% reduction in total processing time and a 25% reduction in error rates.

- In a study of over 500 screens, Tullis (1984) found that the time it took users to extract information from displays of airline or lodging information was 128% longer for the worst format than for the best.

- In a comparison of current and reformatted Space Shuttle screens, Donner, McKay, O'Brien, and Rudisill (1991) found reductions of up to 28% in the time that it took users to find the relevant information on the screen.

23.1.2 An Overview of the Literature

A large base of knowledge about screen design has been accumulated over the past thirty years or so. This knowledge is derived from several sources, including:

- Basic psychological research
- Human factors studies
- Experiences of application designers and users
- Graphic design experience

Much of this information has been compiled into a variety of guidelines addressing screen design and other human-computer interface issues. Many of the resulting guidelines are well grounded in the results of basic or applied research, but many others are not. Most of this chapter will be devoted to describing issues in screen design and the guidelines or common techniques that have arisen for addressing them. At the same time, the research evidence relevant to these issues will be described. Before describing the screen design issues, however, the two main classes of screen design literature will be summarized: (1) Guidelines, and (2) Empirical Studies.

Guidelines

The design of the visual interface to computer systems has perhaps received more attention in human-computer interaction guidelines than has any other aspect of the interface. These range from relatively short articles that discuss screen design issues in general terms (e.g., Cropper and Evans, 1968; Stewart, 1976; Pakin and Wray, 1982) to rather long technical reports that present extensive lists of specific screen design guidelines (e.g., Smith and Mosier, 1986), and, more recently, entire books (e.g., Galitz, 1993, 1994; Fowler and Stanwick, 1995).

Galitz's (1993) book on screen design contains a great deal of practical advice on designing alphanumeric screens, especially data entry screens. More recently Galitz (1994) adapted many of the same principles to GUI screens. Likewise, Smith and Mosier (1986) compiled an extensive list of very specific guidelines for the design of screens, and provided numerous references to earlier documents and empirical studies supporting the guidelines. Their guidelines for the uses of graphics are particularly extensive.

Designers of alphanumeric displays may find the Tullis (1983) review article helpful since it was an attempt to synthesize the guidelines and empirical data related to the formatting of alphanumeric displays into a well-defined framework. Likewise, designers of graphic displays may find the publications by Marcus, Arent, and Brown (1985) or Marcus (1992, 1995) particularly helpful since they touch upon a wide variety of issues related to the design of graphical interfaces.

While most of the guidelines documents are relatively application-independent, there are two exceptions: Apple's (1992) description of the Macintosh™ user interface, and Microsoft's' (1995) description of the user interface for Windows 95™. Both of these books present very detailed descriptions of the screen design rules that were adopted within their particular application domains. Where the generic guidelines state that a consistent set of screen design conventions needs to be adopted, these books describe in detail the specific conventions that were adopted. Marcus, Smilonich, and Thompson (1994) present design rules that attempt to cut across all of the major commercial GUI environments.

Empirical Studies

The apparent abundance of guidelines addressing screen design may lead one to believe that there is a corresponding abundance of empirical evidence related to screen design. While there have been quite a few relevant studies, many screen design issues remain to be addressed empirically, especially those related to GUI screens.

Most of the early empirical studies of screen design focused exclusively on alphanumeric screens (e.g., Dodson and Shields, 1978; Keister and Gallaway, 1983) since that was the predominant type of display. The most common type of performance measure used was search time (i.e., time to extract a specific data item from the screen). Many of the empirical studies have compared performance on two or more methods of displaying the same basic information. While some studies attempted to manipulate specific display variables systematically (e.g., Ringel and Hammer, 1964; Callan, Curran, and Lane, 1977), others compared screens that differed in many ways, including the use of alphanumerics vs. graphics (e.g., Schwartz and Howell, 1985; Tullis, 1981). Also included in this latter category are studies that compared an existing version of the screens for an application to a redesigned version (e.g., Burns, Warren, and Rudisill, 1986; Keister and Gallaway, 1983; Donner, McKay, O'Brien, and Rudisill, 1991). Typically, the redesigns involved a wide variety of changes to the screens, making it difficult to attribute changes in performance to specific changes in screen design.

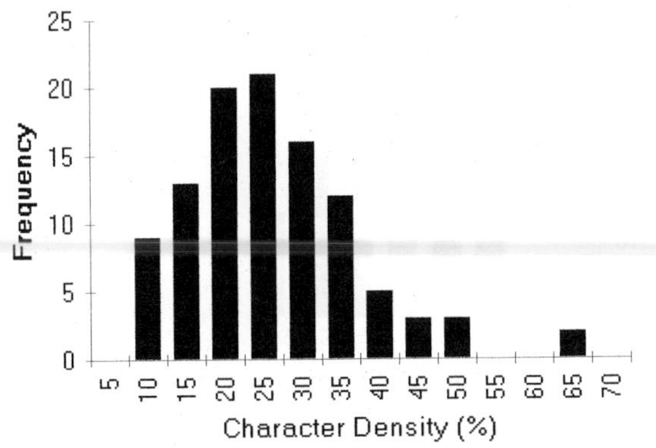

Figure1. Distribution of character densities for 104 character-mode screens from commercial PC applications. Mean = 23.7%, Standard deviation = 11.2%

An extensive investigation of alphanumeric screen formats was conducted by Tullis (1984), who studied a wide variety of alphanumeric screen formats. A computer program (Tullis, 1986a) was used to measure six characteristics of the formats: overall density, local density, number of groups, average size of the groups, number of items, and item alignment. Multiple regressions were then used to fit search times and subjective ratings of ease of use with these format variable

While it is conceivable to define a set of variables that characterize the key attributes of many alphanumeric display formats, such a task is significantly more difficult for graphic displays because of their much greater complexity. Instead, most of the studies have focused on comparing alphanumeric to graphic displays on a global level (e.g., Tullis, 1981; Schwartz and Howell, 1985), or on comparing specific types of graphic displays to each other (e.g., Yorchak, Allison, and Dodd, 1984). Other studies have begun to focus on determining the types of tasks that alphanumeric and graphic displays are best suited for (e.g., Benbasat, Dexter, and Todd, 1986; Lalomia and Coovert, 1987).

23.2 Screen Design Issues and Techniques

The following sections describe screen design issues and techniques that are relevant to a wide variety of screens and applications. In each case, an overview of the issue is presented, along with descriptions of the relevant empirical evidence, guidelines that have been developed, and specific examples of screens that illustrate the issue.

23.2.1 Amount of Information to Present

Perhaps the most basic issue that must be faced when designing a screen is how much information to present. Almost all of the guidelines specify that the total amount of information on each screen should be minimized by presenting only what is necessary to the user at that point in the interaction (e.g., Smith and Mosier, 1986, p. 98; Galitz, 1993, p. 83).

Measuring Information Density

With character-mode screens, information density is usually expressed as the percentage of available character spaces that are in use. Danchak (1976, p. 33) proposed that "display loading (the percentage of active screen area) should not exceed 25 percent." He went on to state that "an analysis of existing CRT displays that were qualitatively judged 'good' revealed a loading on the order of 15 percent" (p. 33). On the other hand, in a set of guidelines for the design of Spacelab displays, NASA (1980, p. 3-26) stated that "density generally should not exceed 60% of the available character spaces."

The screen size is generally fixed with character-mode screens (typically 80 characters wide by 25 lines high) and the designer simply decides how much of that space to use. An analysis of the character densities for 104 screens from commercial character-mode applications for the IBM PC lends credence to some of the guidelines, as shown in Figure 1. The mean density was 23.7%, while the distribution implies that a density higher than about 46% (two standard deviations above the mean) may be considered atypical and should perhaps be avoided.

With GUI screens, the designer is faced with two basic decisions: how large to make the window and how much information to put in it. An upper limit for the window size is given by the lowest resolution of the target display hardware (e.g., 640 x 480). But for windows and dialog boxes other than the main application window (which is usually sizable), the designer generally tries to take up less than the full physical screen. Figure 2 shows the distribution of window sizes for 171 fixed-size windows or dialog boxes from commercial Windows applications. The average total size of these windows was about 124,000 pixels, with an average width of 402 pixels and average height of 305 pixels. As one would expect, this ratio of width to

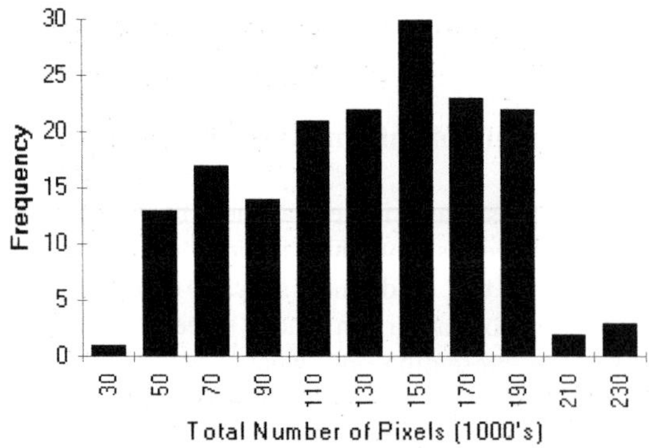

Figure 2. Distribution of window sizes for 171 fixed-size windows or dialog boxes from commercial Windows applications. Mean = 124,130 pixels (402 x 305), Standard deviation = 47,986 pixels.

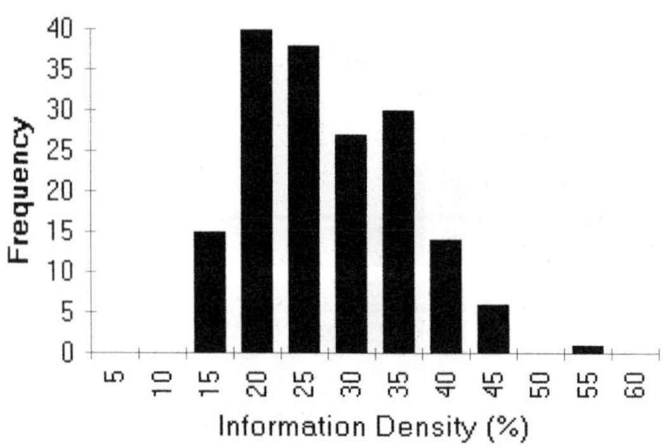

Figure 3. Distribution of information density (based on percentage of black pixels) for 171 fixed-size windows and dialog boxes from commercial Windows applications. Mean = 25.2%, Standard deviation = 8.2%

height (1.32) is very close to the ratio of typical screen width to height (640 x 480 or 1.33), since choosing an aspect ratio that conforms to the overall screen maximizes the usable space. Figure 2 also implies that a fixed-size window larger than about 220,000 pixels (e.g., 542 x 406), or two standard deviations above the mean, may certainly be considered atypical and should perhaps be avoided.

Calculating information density for GUI screens, analogous to character densities, is somewhat problematic. But an analysis of GUI screens reveals that the vast majority of textual elements are black. In addition, an analysis of the character set for a typical Windows font (MS Sans Serif, 8 point, non-bold) reveals that the average character takes up 57.6 total pixels, with 14.1 black pixels. These values can then be used to convert window sizes (in pixels) to equivalent character spaces available, and the number of black pixels to equivalent characters.

Figure 3 shows the resulting distribution of "presumed information density" for the same 171 windows and dialog boxes used in Figure 2. The resulting average (25.2%) is extremely close to the average density for character-mode screens (Figure 1). The distribution also implies that densities above about 42% (two standard deviations above the mean) may be considered atypical. The similarity of this distribution to the one for character screens seems to support the validity of these assumptions and implies that similar principles underlie the design of both types of screens.

Figure 4 shows sample GUI screens that are statistically sparse (< 12%), average (about 25%), and dense (> 40%).

Empirical Evidence

The empirical evidence addressing information density is generally consistent: as long as the information necessary to perform the task is present, human performance tends to deteriorate with increasing display density. A wide variety of studies have shown that time and errors in performing the task increase as the number of items on the display increases (e.g., Callan, Curran, and Lane, 1977; Dodson and Shields, 1978; Ringel and Hammer, 1964). For example, Figure 5 shows data from Experiment 1 of Tullis (1984) illustrating the effect of overall density of characters on search time. In this experiment, 52 different formats for displaying lists of airline or lodging information were shown to subjects who had to extract a single data item from each display (e.g., a flight's arrival time). The formats varied on many parameters, including overall density (10% to 58%). Search time generally increased with increasing density ($p < .02$), although the relatively low correlation ($r = .33$) indicates that other factors interacted with the effect of overall density.

This interaction of display density with other screen format variables is illustrated by Figure 6 and Figure 7, which are two of the lodging screens studied by Tullis (1984). While the two screens have approxi-

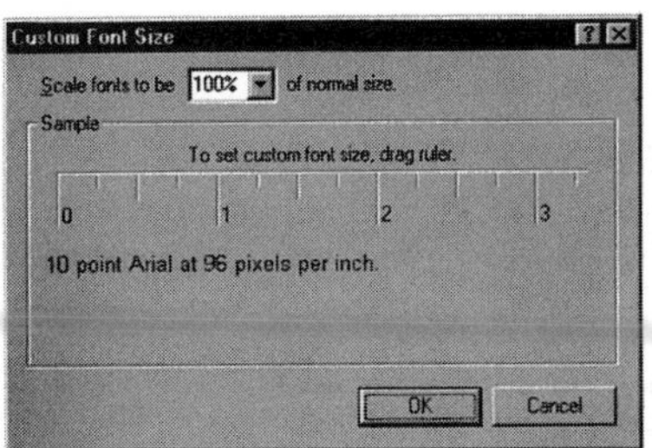

Statistically Sparse (<3% black, or <12% char's)

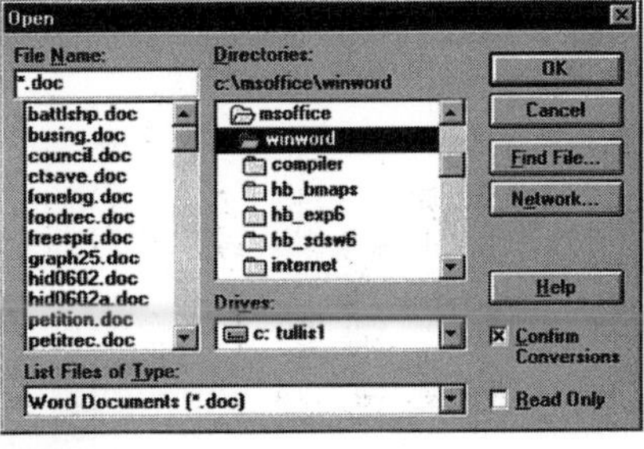

Statistically Dense (>10% black, or >40% char's)

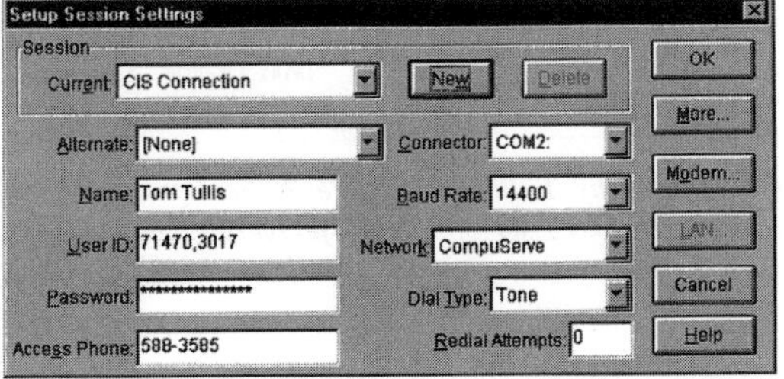

Statistically Average (~6% black, or ~25% char's)

Figure 4. Sample dialog boxes from commercial Windows applications that are statistically sparse, average, and dense.

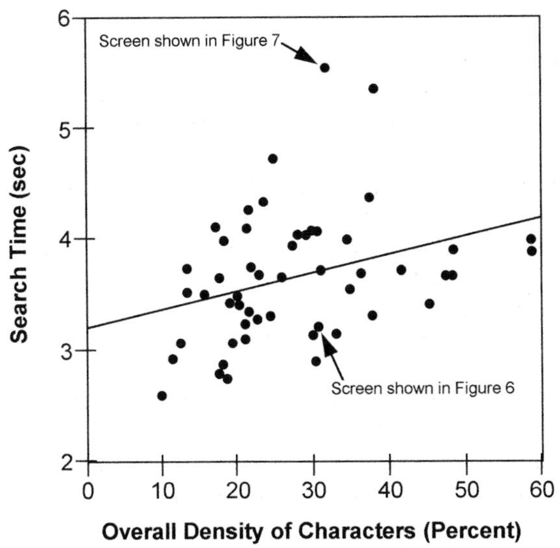

Figure 5. Effect of overall density of characters on the *screen on the average time users took to find a single item on the screen, from Tullis (1984) (r = .33).*

mately the same level of overall density (31% for Figure 6 and 32% for Figure 7), they yielded very different search times (3.2 seconds for Figure 6 vs 5.5 seconds for Figure 7). The shorter search time for Figure 4 was due primarily to the way the characters are grouped on the display (to be discussed in detail in Section 23.2.2). Thus, the tendency for higher densities to be associated with degraded human performance can be mediated by other screen format characteristics.

Even though the effectiveness of a particular screen might be enhanced by formatting the information differently, the fact remains that the optimum amount of information to present is that which is necessary for the task at hand-- no more and no less. At all points in the user's interaction with the system, the designer must determine what information the user needs from the system and, potentially, what information the system needs from the user. A particular screen should then be designed to display (or provide for the input of) all the information that is commonly needed at that point in the interaction. Information that is only rarely needed at that point should be available upon request.

Techniques for Reducing Density

Once the designer has determined what information needs to be displayed, several techniques can be used to ensure that the information is conveyed without overloading the screen. For example, Figure 8 and Figure 9 show two different screen formats studied by Tullis (1981) for presenting results of tests on a telephone line. With a few minor exceptions, the two examples contain essentially the same information. How-

South Carolina

City	Motel/Hotel	Area Code	Phone	Rates Single	Rates Double
Charleston	Best Western	803	747-0961	$26	$30
Charleston	Days Inn	803	881-1800	$18	$24
Charleston	Holiday Inn N	803	744-1621	$36	$46
Charleston	Holiday Inn SW	803	556-7100	$33	$47
Charleston	Howard Johnsons	803	524-4140	$31	$36
Charleston	Ramada Inn	803	774-8281	$33	$40
Charleston	Sheraton Inn	803	744-2401	$34	$42
Columbia	Best Western	803	796-9400	$29	$34
Columbia	Carolina Inn	803	799-8200	$42	$48
Columbia	Days Inn	803	736-0000	$23	$27
Columbia	Holiday Inn NW	803	794-9440	$32	$39
Columbia	Howard Johnsons	803	772-7200	$25	$27
Columbia	Quality Inn	803	772-0270	$34	$41
Columbia	Ramada Inn	803	796-2700	$36	$44
Columbia	Vagabond Inn	803	796-6240	$27	$30

Figure 6. Screen of lodging information studied by Tullis (1984). *Overall density = 31%, Average search time = 3.2 sec.*

```
Pennsylvania
Bedford  Motel/Hotel: Crinoline Courts
 (814) 623-9511  S: $18  D: $20
Bedford  Motel/Hotel: Holiday Inn
 (814) 623-9006  S: $29  D: $36
Bedford  Motel/Hotel: Midway
 (814) 623-8107  S: $21  D: $26
Bedford  Motel/Hotel: Penn Manor
 (814) 623-8177  S: $18  D: $25
Bedford  Motel/Hotel: Quality Inn
 (814) 623-5188  S: $23  D: $28
Bedford  Motel/Hotel: Terrace
 (814) 623-5111  S: $22  D: $24
Bradley  Motel/Hotel: De Soto
 (814) 362-3567  S: $20  D: $24
Bradley  Motel/Hotel: Holiday House
 (814) 362-4511  S: $22  D: $25
Bradley  Motel/Hotel: Holiday Inn
 (814) 362-4501  S: $32  D: $40
Breezewood  Motel/Hotel: Best Western Plaza
 (814) 735-4352  S: $20  D: $27
Breezewood  Motel/Hotel: Motel 70
 (814) 735-4385  S: $16  D: $18
```

Figure 7. Screen of lodging information studied by Tullis (1984). *Overall density = 32%, Average search time = 5.5 sec.*

```
TEST RESULTS   SUMMARY: GROUND

  GROUND, FAULT T-G
  3 TERMINAL DC RESISTANCE
    >  3500.00 K OHMS T-R
    =    14.21 K OHMS T-G
    >  3500.00 K OHMS R-G
  3 TERMINAL DC VOLTAGE
    =     0.00 VOLTS  T-G
    =     0.00 VOLTS  R-G
  VALID AC SIGNATURE
  3 TERMINAL AC RESISTANCE
    =     8.82 K OHMS T-R
    =    14.17 K OHMS T-G
    =   628.52 K OHMS R-G
  LONGITUDINAL BALANCE POOR
    =    39    DB
  COULD NOT COUNT RINGERS DUE TO
    LOW RESISTANCE
  VALID LINE CKT CONFIGURATION
  CAN DRAW AND BREAK DIAL TONE
```

Figure 8. Example of "narrative" format for presenting *results of tests on a telephone line, from Tullis (1981). Average time for experienced users to interpret display was 8.3 sec.*

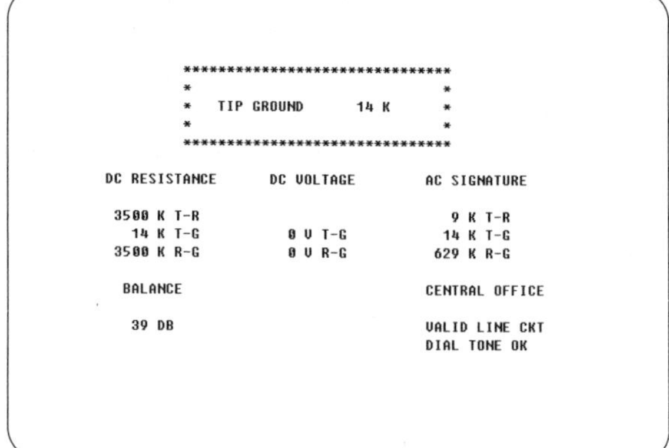

Figure 9. Example of "structured" format for presenting *results of tests on a telephone line, from Tullis (1981). Average time for experienced users to interpret display was 5.0 sec-- a 40% savings compared to the format shown in Figure 8.*

ever, the format shown in Figure 9 was the result of applying a variety of screen design principles to the information shown in Figure 8. The outcome was a 40% reduction in the time that it took users to interpret the display. Many of the redesign techniques involved ways of presenting the same information in less space on the screen. Some of these techniques are as follows:

- *Make appropriate use of abbreviations.* While many guidelines recommend using complete words in preference to abbreviations, they also commonly acknowledge that abbreviations are appropriate in cases where they save needed space and are well known to the users (e.g., Smith and Mosier, 1986, p. 103). When abbreviations are used, however, a consistent scheme should be adopted for developing them, and a dictionary of abbreviations should be available to the users. (See Ehrenreich and Porcu, 1982, for a thorough analysis of abbreviations.) One of the differences between the screen formats shown in Figure 8 and Figure 9 is a greater use of abbreviations in Figure 9 (e.g., "K" instead of "K OHMS", "V" instead of "VOLTS"). The us-ers of this system were highly experienced and not likely to be confused by any of the abbreviations used, most of which refer to electrical aspects of the telephone line.

- *Avoid unnecessary detail.* Figure 8 and Figure 9 also illustrate the point that the users should be given only as much detail as they actually need. The electrical measurements shown in Figure 8 were displayed to two decimal places, which was much

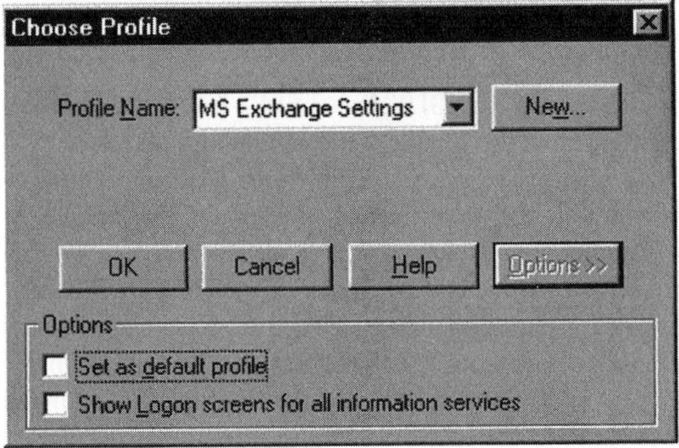

Figure 10. Example of an expanding dialog box. *In the initial presentation of the dialog box (top), rarely used options are not visible, but pressing the "Options >>" button causes the dialog box to expand and reveal the additional options (bottom).*

greater accuracy than the users needed or could make use of. Consequently, the version shown in Figure 9 displayed only whole numbers.

- *Use concise wording.* While this rule applies to most technical communication, it is particularly applicable to computer screens because of their limited space. As with abbreviations and the level of detail, the choice of wording must be made on the basis of what the users will understand. The screen shown in Figure 9 illustrates several uses of more concise wording than that used in Figure 8 (e.g., the elimination of "3 TERMINAL" in several places, which was largely irrelevant to the users).

- *Use familiar data formats.* Certain data items in certain contexts are so easily recognized that it may not be necessary to label each item individually. A classic example of this is a person's name, street address, city, state, and zip code, which, when shown together in their traditional format, are easily recognized. However, care must be taken to ensure that the proper context is always maintained (e.g., a zip code is not easily recognized as such when shown in the context of other numeric data).

- *Use tabular formats with column headings.* Tabular formats provide many advantages over other formats, one of which is that they allow for efficient labelling of related data items through the use of column headings. For example, one of the advantages of the lodging display shown in Figure 6 is that its tabular format allowed column headings to be used, unlike the format shown in Figure 7 where many of the labels were repeated for each record in the database (e.g., "Motel/Hotel:")

Several techniques are also available for making information readily available in a window without presenting it all at once:

- *Expanding dialog boxes.* In this approach, the dialog box has two sizes. The small version, which is shown by default, contains the most commonly needed items as well as a button for expanding to the larger version (e.g., "Options >>"). The larger version reveals additional options. (See Figure 10.)

- *Tab folders.* This technique makes use of the file folder metaphor for easily switching between different sets of data in the same window. A similar effect can be achieved using a bank of mutually exclusive buttons to determine the "state" of the window. (See Figure 11.)

- *Drop-down lists and other pop-ups.* This family of techniques provides easy access to additional information or options related to a specific control. In most cases, the user clicks on a button that temporarily reveals the additional options; in other cases, the pop-up automatically reveals itself when the user simply points to the associated control. (See Figure 11.)

Summary

A designer should ensure that each screen or window contains only the information that is actually needed by the users to perform the expected tasks at that point in the interaction. The temptation to provide additional data just because it is available should be avoided, since extra clutter clearly degrades the users' ability to extract the relevant information. With either character-mode or GUI screens, information densities of about 25% are average, while densities higher than about 40-45% are atypical. The tendency for higher densities to

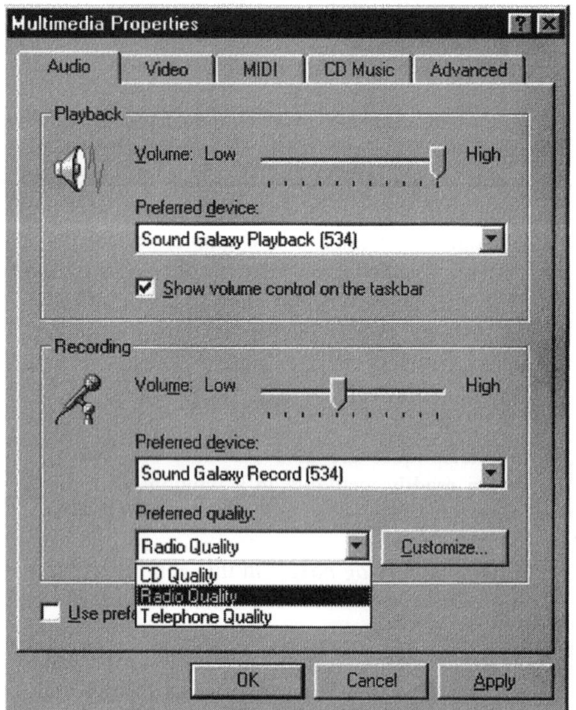

Figure 11. Example of dialog box that uses tab folders as a *way of easily switching between various sets of data and controls in the same window, and drop-down lists as a way of hiding selections until needed. In this example, the selections under "Preferred quality" were not visible until the down-arrow was clicked.*

be associated with degraded human performance can be mediated by other screen format characteristics, such as grouping. A variety of techniques can be used to minimize apparent information density.

23.2.2 Grouping of Information

Given a set of data items to display, there are many ways in which the elements can be visually grouped on the screen. The ways in which the elements are grouped plays an important role in both the ease with which the users can extract the information and the interpretations that they assign to it. This importance of grouping has been emphasized in most of the published guidelines. For example, "grouping similar items together in a display format improves their readibility and can highlight relationships between different groups of data" (Cakir, Hart, and Stewart, 1980, p. 114).

Two of the guidelines documents have taken this concept a step further and proposed in general terms how the grouping should be done. Both Cropper and Evans (1968) and Danchak (1976) state that the 5-degree visual angle to which the eye is most sensitive (approximately the foveal region of the retina) defines discrete areas on the screen and that the display should be structured with this in mind. For example, "the presentation of information in 'chunks'...which can be taken in at one fixation will help to overcome the limitations in the human input system in searching tasks" (Cropper and Evans, 1968, p. 96). Assuming an average viewing distance of 51 cm, 5 degrees corresponds to a circle about 4.4 cm in diameter on the screen. On a typical character-mode screen, that corresponds to an area about 13 characters wide and 6 lines high. On a typical GUI screen (14", 640 x 480), it corresponds to a circle about 105 pixels in diameter.

Unfortunately, the empirical evidence directly relevant to the grouping of elements on a display is somewhat sparse. Part of the problem is that a general technique for measuring grouping has not been widely used. Consequently, many of the studies that intended to address only the total amount of information on the screen (e.g., Dodson and Shields, 1978) confounded that variable with differences in grouping.

Measuring Spatial Grouping

Tullis (1983) proposed a general technique for measuring grouping on character-mode screens that was based upon the Gestalt law of proximity (Koffka, 1935). The basic technique was a modification to a proximity clustering algorithm described by Zahn (1971). In its simplest form, the technique involves treating as a group any set of characters that can be connected by linking together all pairs of characters separated by no more than one blank space horizontally and no blank lines vertically. This technique for detecting groups has been implemented in a computer program along with a variety of other techniques for analyzing screen formats (Tullis, 1986a). Figure 12 and Figure 13 show the results of the grouping analysis by this program for the lodging screens shown in Figure 6 and Figure 7. Obviously, the program detected many more groups for the screen shown in Figure 6. The program also measures the size of each group in terms of the visual angle (in degrees) subtended by the group at the viewer's eye.

Empirical Evidence

In using this program to analyze 52 different screen formats, Tullis (1984) found that the two best predictors of the time needed to find a single data item on the screens were the number of groups of characters and their average size (R = .65). Search time tended to in-

```
Grouping Analysis:
---------1---------2---------3---------4---------5---------6---------7---------8
11111 11111111

                                        2222              33333
4444            55555555555             2222  66666   333333  333333

7777777777  8888 8888888                999   ::::::::    ;;;     <<<
7777777777  8888 888                    999   ::::::::    ;;;     <<<
7777777777  8888888 888 8               999   ::::::::    ;;;     <<<
7777777777  8888888 888 88              999   ::::::::    ;;;     <<<
7777777777  888888 88888888             999   ::::::::    ;;;     <<<
7777777777  888888 888                  999   ::::::::    ;;;     <<<
7777777777  88888888 888                999   ::::::::    ;;;     <<<

========    >>>> >>>>>>>                ???   @@@@@@@@    AAA     BBB
========    >>>>>>>> >>>                ???   @@@@@@@@    AAA     BBB
========    >>>> >>>                    ???   @@@@@@@@    AAA     BBB
========    >>>>>>> >>> >>              ???   @@@@@@@@    AAA     BBB
========    >>>>>> >>>>>>>>             ???   @@@@@@@@    AAA     BBB
========    >>>>>>> >>>                 ???   @@@@@@@@    AAA     BBB
========    >>>>>> >>>                  ???   @@@@@@@@    AAA     BBB
========    >>>>>>>> >>>                ???   @@@@@@@@    AAA     BBB

---------1---------2---------3---------4---------5---------6---------7---------8
Group  # Characters  Visual Angle        Group  # Characters  Visual Angle
1            13           4.2            :            56           4.3
2             8           1.3            ;            21           3.7
3            17           4.2            <            21           3.7
4             4           1.2            =            64           5.1
5            11           3.0            >            85           5.6
6             5           1.2            ?            24           4.9
7            70           4.7            @            64           5.1
8            75           5.6            A            24           4.9
9            21           3.7            B            24           4.9

Number of groups =  18
Maximum size     =   5.6 degrees (Group 8)
Average size     =   4.8 degrees (weighted by # of characters in group)
```

Figure 12. Visual groups detected by a computer program for analyzing screen formats (Tullis, 1986a) for the lodging screen shown in Figure 6. *The program detected 18 groups, each of which is represented by a different character in the "map"; the groups subtend an average visual angle of 4.8 degrees.*

crease as either the number of groups or their average size increased. The effect of these two grouping measures on search time is illustrated in Figure 14, which plots search time vs. number of groups for the 52 screen formats and also indicates the size of the groups. The curve shown is a math model developed to fit the data (Tullis, 1986b). The sharp increase in search time on the left-hand side is due primarily to the increasing size of the fewer groups. The gradual increase in search time on the right-hand side is due primarily to the increasing number of smaller groups. In fact, for those screens with groups smaller than 5 degrees, search time is primarily a function of the number of groups (r = .64), while for those screens with groups larger than 5 degrees, search time is primarily a function of the size of the groups (r = .57).

These results indicate that some aspect of the user's processing of the screen changes when the average size of the groups gets larger than 5 degrees. It appears that a screen with groups no larger than 5 degrees can be scanned more efficiently than one with larger groups. Specifically, Tullis (1986b) proposed that groups smaller than 5 degrees can be fixated once and the necessary information extracted. On the other hand, groups larger than 5 degrees require more than one fixation per group, with the size of the group determining the number of additional fixations needed. Thus, the screen shown in Figure 6, whose groups are not much larger than 5 degrees, results in a more efficient pattern of eye movements than the one shown in Figure 7, whose one group is about 18 degrees.

On the other hand, consider the screen shown in Figure 15, which is another of the lodging formats studied by Tullis (1984). The grouping program detected 67 very small groups for this screen. (Essentially, each line contains six groups.) This screen also resulted in longer search times than the one shown in Figure 6, but because of the large number of groups, not their size. In essence, then, the optimum strategy for the screen designer is to minimize the number of

```
Grouping Analysis:
---------1---------2---------3---------4---------5---------6---------7---------8
111111111111
1111111  111111111111 111111111 111111
 11111 11111111  11 111  11 111
1111111  111111111111 1111111 111
 11111 11111111  11 111  11 111
1111111  111111111111 111111
 11111 11111111  11 111  11 111
1111111  111111111111 1111 11111
 11111 11111111  11 111  11 111
1111111  111111111111 1111111 111
 11111 11111111  11 111  11 111
1111111  111111111111 1111111
 11111 11111111  11 111  11 111
1111111  111111111111 11 1111
 11111 11111111  11 111  11 111
1111111  111111111111 1111111 11111
 11111 11111111  11 111  11 111
1111111  111111111111 1111111 111
 11111 11111111  11 111  11 111
1111111111  111111111111 1111 1111111 11111
 11111 11111111  11 111  11 111
1111111111  111111111111 11111 11
 11111 11111111  11 111  11 111

---------1---------2---------3---------4---------5---------6---------7---------8
Group  # Characters  Visual Angle
1          588           17.8

Number of groups =   1
Maximum size     =  17.8 degrees (Group 1)
Average size     =  17.8 degrees (weighted by # of characters in group)

The display contains large groups.
  The largest groups can be identified from the list above.  Consider
  breaking these groups into their logical components.  In general,
  each of these components can then be identified as a group by separating
  it from other characters by at least one blank line vertically and two
  blank spaces horizontally.  If you are using a color monitor, groups
  can also be designated by using different foreground or background
  colors.  Studies show that groups with a visual angle no greater than
  about 5 degrees can be scanned more effectively than larger groups.
```

Figure 13. Visual groups detected by a computer program for analyzing screen formats (Tullis, 1986a) for the lodging screen shown in Figure 7. *The program detected one large group of characters that subtends 17.8 degrees.*

groups by making each group as close to 5 degrees as is feasible. This conclusion, derived from empirical data, is virtually identical to the guidelines mentioned earlier that suggested, based upon what is known about human vision, that the screen be formatted into 5-degree “chunks” (e.g., Danchak, 1976).

While the research just described was based on these findings should generalize to GUI screens as well. The same proximity clustering technique that was used for character-mode screens can be adapted to GUI screens by operating at the pixel level rather than the character level. Using the same simplifying assumption that was used for calculating density (that informational elements on a GUI screen tend to be black), one can predict the visual groups for GUI screens. (See Figure 16 and Figure 17.) Basically, this technique involves “chaining” any black pixels that are within 20 pixels of each other to form groups. Figure 16 shows a window with 7 groups, all of which are relatively small, resulting in an average group size of 5.6 deg. On the other hand, Figure 17 shows a window with 6 groups, all of which are larger than 5 deg, resulting in an average group size of 10 deg.

Other Determinants of Grouping

So far this discussion has focused on spatial proximity, which is clearly a very powerful determinant of perceived grouping. However, there are other determinants of visual grouping besides spatial proximity, most of which are commonly used in current software products. These include the following:

- *Color*- Presenting different sets of display elements in contrasting colors clearly creates some degree of grouping within the elements in the same color. If they are also in close proximity, the visual asso-

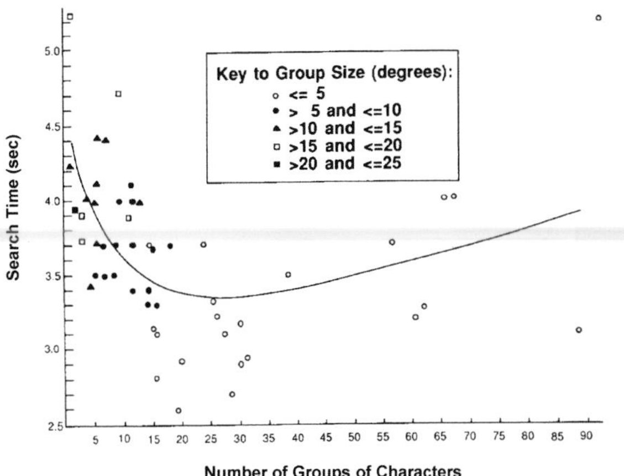

Figure 14. Scatterplot of groups of characters vs. search time for 52 screen formats studied by Tullis (1984), with the average size of the groups (in degrees of visual angle) indicated by the shape of the data points. The curve represents a math model developed to fit the data (Tullis, 1986b).

```
South Carolina
Charleston  Best Western  AC: 803  Ph: 747-0961  S: $26  D: $30
Charleston  Days Inn  AC: 803  Ph: 881-1800  S: $18  D: $24
Charleston  Holiday Inn N  AC: 803  Ph: 744-1621  S: $36  D: $46
Charleston  Holiday Inn SW  AC: 803  Ph: 556-7100  S: $33  D: $47
Charleston  Howard Johnsons  AC: 803  Ph: 524-4140  S: $31  D: $36
Charleston  Ramada Inn  AC: 803  Ph: 774-8281  S: $33  D: $40
Charleston  Sheraton Inn  AC: 803  Ph: 744-2401  S: $34  D: $42
Columbia  Best Western  AC: 803  Ph: 796-9400  S: $29  D: $34
Columbia  Carolina Inn  AC: 803  Ph: 799-8200  S: $42  D: $48
Columbia  Days Inn  AC: 803  Ph: 736-0000  S: $23  D: $27
Columbia  Holiday Inn NW  AC: 803  Ph: 794-9440  S: $32  D: $39
```

Figure 15. Screen of lodging information studied by Tullis (1984). *Number of visual groups = 67. Average size of groups = 2.9 degrees. Mean search time = 4.0 sec.*

ciation will be even stronger. Haubner and Neumann (1986) found, however, that setting off characters by spacing was more effective than setting them off by use of color.

- *Graphical boundaries-* Besides proximity, perhaps the most common technique used for conveying visual groupings is to draw graphical boundaries around the elements to be grouped. Most commonly, these groupings are accomplished by drawing rectangular boundaries, as in the screen shown in Figure 18. Compare that screen to the version shown in Figure 19, which contains the identical information but without the graphical boundaries. Although many of the groupings are still apparent, some are not. Thacker (1986) compared the effectiveness of groupings formed by spacing and the same groupings with graphical boundaries added. He found no significant effects of such "redundant" graphical boundaries on search time, but subjects clearly preferred them. In GUI screens, group boxes and 3D panels are commonly used to create these graphical boundaries.

- *Highlighting-* Another common technique for creating visual groups is the use of highlighting, such as increased brightness (boldness) or reverse video. A similar technique is the use of different background colors for regions that are to be visually grouped.

While this discussion has focused on the visual aspects of grouping, it should be clear that these visual groupings have a significant effect on the semantic interpretations that users assign to the information. Users should be able to assume that the elements contained in one visual group are somehow related to each other semantically. On the other hand, users are likely to be confused by a screen that contains visual groupings in which the elements of each group have little semantic association (e.g., the elements in the one large visual group of Figure 7).

Summary

Grouping is one of the most important determinants of how effectively a user can extract information from a screen. A screen containing many very small groups or only a few very large groups is harder to scan than one containing groups that tend to be about 5 degrees of visual angle (about 13 characters by 6 lines or about 105 pixels in diameter).

23.2.3 Highlighting of Information

A number of techniques can be used to draw the user's attention to certain elements on the screen. The most common highlighting techniques are described in the following sections.

Reverse Video

As mentioned in section 23.2.2, reverse video can be used quite effectively to create a visual grouping of

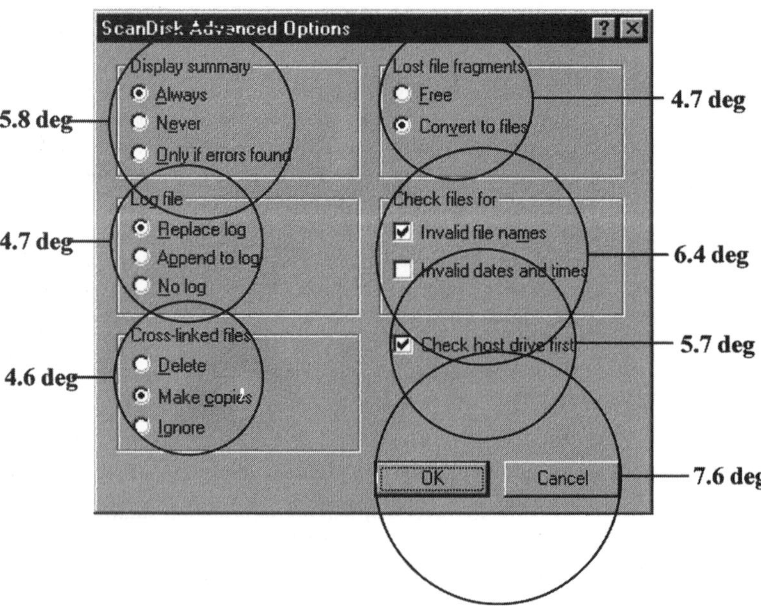

Figure 16. ***Sample GUI dialog box with visual groups indicated.*** *Number of groups = 7. Average visual angle = 5.6 degrees.*

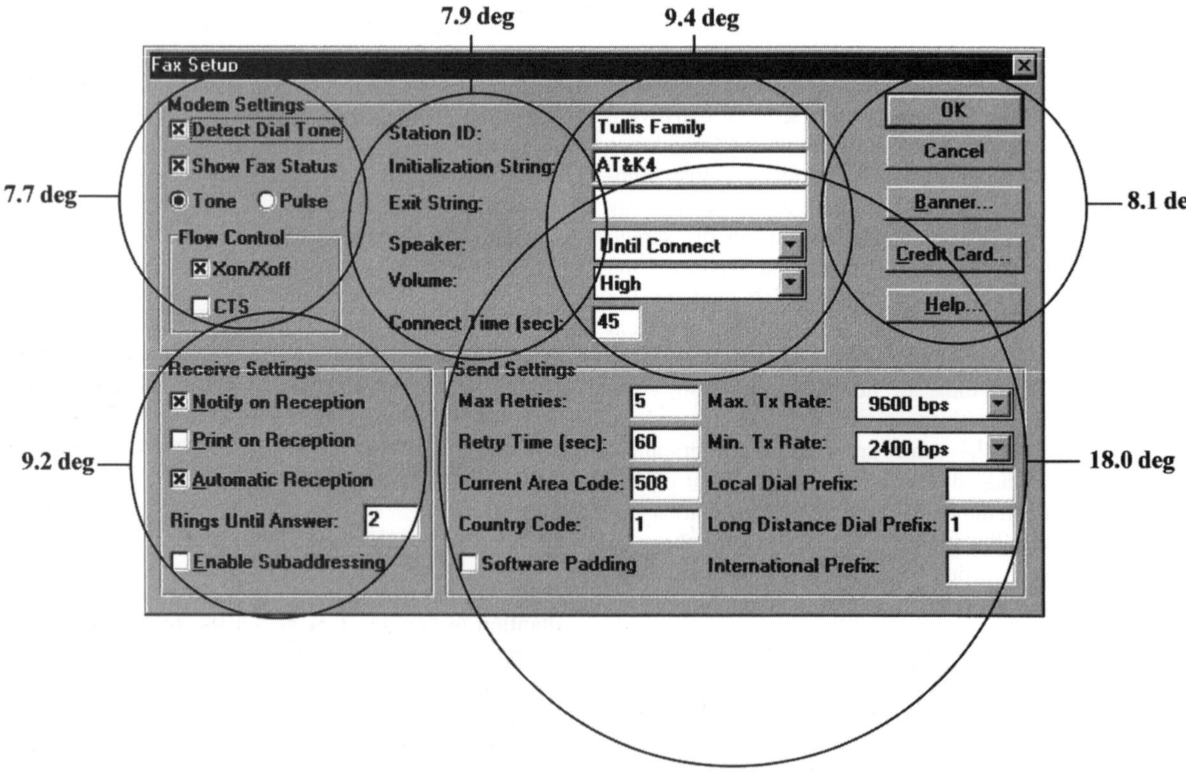

Figure 17. ***Sample GUI dialog box with visual groups indicated.*** *Number of groups = 6. Average visual angle = 10 degrees.*

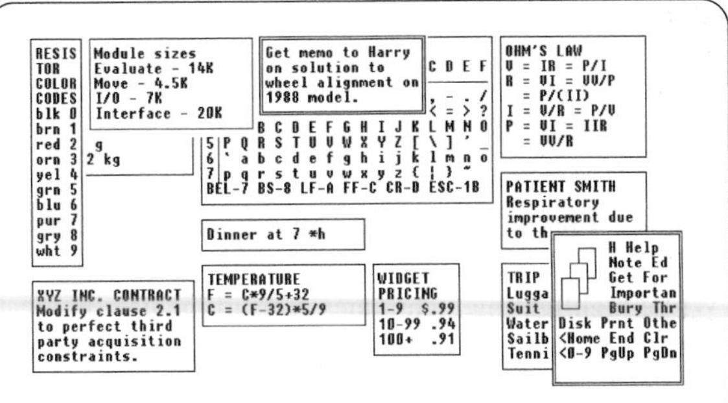

Figure 18. Screen that makes use of extensive graphical *boundaries to designate groupings.*

```
RESIS  Module sizes         Get memo to Harry            OHM'S LAW
TOR    Evaluate - 14K       on solution to      C D E F  V = IR = P/I
COLOR  Move - 4.5K          wheel alignment on           R = VI = VV/P
CODES  I/O - 7K             1988 model.         , - . /    = P/(II)
blk 0  Interface - 20K                          < = > ?  I = V/R = P/V
brn 1                     B C D E F G H I J K L M N O  P = VI = IIR
red 2  g               5 P Q R S T U V W X Y Z [ \ ] ' _    = VV/R
orn 3 2 kg             6 ` a b c d e f g h i j k l m n o
yel 4                  7 p q r s t u v w x y z { ¦ } ~
grn 5                  BEL-7 BS-8 LF-A FF-C CR-D ESC-1B  PATIENT SMITH
blu 6                                                    Respiratory
pur 7                                                    improvement due
gry 8                  Dinner at 7 *h                    to th
wht 9                                                          H Help
                                                               Note Ed
                       TEMPERATURE         WIDGET        TRIP  Get For
XYZ INC. CONTRACT      F = C*9/5+32        PRICING       Lugga Importan
Modify clause 2.1      C = (F-32)*5/9      1-9   $.99    Suit  Bury Thr
to perfect third                           10-99 .94     Water Disk Prnt Othe
party acquisition                          100+  .91     Sailb <Home End Clr
constraints.                                             Tenni <0-9 PgUp PgDn
```

Figure 19. Same screen as shown in figure 18, but without the graphical boundaries. *Note the loss of groupings in several cases, and the loss of a sense of "overlaying" of groups.*

those elements that share the reverse video background. But it can also be used to draw the user's attention to isolated elements on the screen. The most common use of this type is to indicate a screen element that is, in some sense, currently selected. This technique is used extensively in GUI systems, in which current selections from pull-down menus and list boxes are shown in reverse video. The basic idea of highlighting currently selected items is recommended by several of the guidelines documents (e.g., Smith and Mosier, 1986, p. 283) and has become so common that it is practically a standard.

Reverse video can be very effective in attracting the user's attention, but it should be used judiciously to avoid what Galitz (1993, p. 123) calls the "crossword puzzle effect": the haphazard arrangement of reverse-video elements in a way that creates an image resembling a crossword puzzle. For example, the screen shown in Figure 20 suffers from this effect due to its use of reverse video for several different purposes: to indicate data entry fields, window borders, headings,

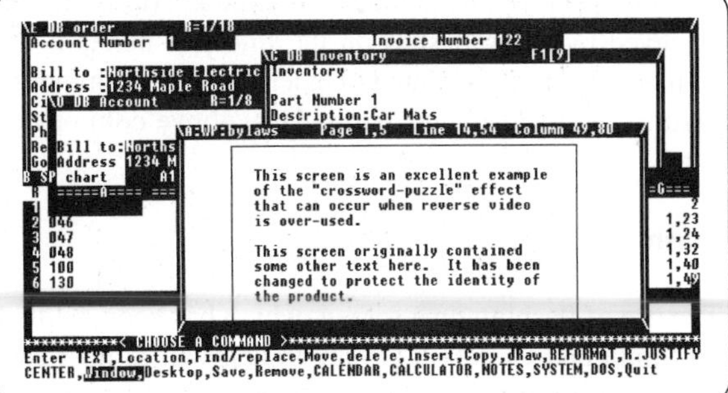

Figure 20. Screen that suffers from the "crossword-puzzle *effect" due to overuse of reverse video for highlighting*

and current selections. Another possible problem with reverse video is that, on some display systems, characters at the edge of a reverse-video area can be less legible than others because the edges of the characters may "bleed" into the background part of the display. This can be avoided by leaving a buffer zone of reverse-video blank spaces on either side of the characters.

Color

Another way of attracting attention to a particular screen element is to present it in a different foreground or background color than the other screen elements. The effectiveness of this highlighting technique tends to decrease as the number of different colors used on the screen increases. Also, be aware of legibility issues for various foreground/background color combinations. (See section 23.2.6)

Brightness (or Boldness)

Many display systems offer the capability of displaying text and graphics in different levels of brightness (or boldness, if the characters are dark on a light background). Smith and Mosier (1986, p. 180) suggest that brightness should be treated as being only a two-valued code, bright and dim, because of potential problems that may arise with user-adjustable brightness controls if more levels are used. A relatively common technique with data-entry screens is to present data labels in lower brightness and data items in higher brightness.

Underlining

Some display systems offer the ability to underline characters, but this should only be used if the underline does not interfere with the legibility of the characters.

If underlining is not practical, a similar effect can be achieved by using dashes on the line just beneath the element to be highlighted. Underlining is commonly used to set off headings, particularly above columns of data.

Flashing

The use of flashing on a screen, which has been studied by Smith and Goodwin (1971, 1972), will almost certainly get the user's attention. It will also almost certainly annoy the user if it is used excessively or cannot be turned off. At least three different techniques for creating a flashing message can be identified: (1) turning the message completely on and off, (2) alternating between lower and higher brightness, and (3) alternating between normal and reverse video. An obvious problem with the first technique is that it can reduce the legibility of the message. The latter two techniques alleviate this problem by leaving some form of the message on the screen at all times. For on/off flashing, the optimum blink rate appears to be 2 to 5 Hz, with a minimum "on" period of 50% (Smith and Mosier, 1986, p. 186). Several of the guidelines documents suggest that, if it is used at all, flashing should be reserved for items that must convey an urgent need for attention (e.g., Smith and Mosier, 1986, p. 185; Galitz, 1993, p. 123).

Comparison of Highlighting Techniques

The effectiveness of several of the above highlighting techniques has been compared in a series of empirical studies. Fisher and Tan (1989) compared color, reverse video, and flashing to a non-highlighted condition and found that color was the most effective. They also found that flashing was actually *less effective* than no highlighting, due to the increased difficulty in reading the flashing element. Likewise, Spoto and Babu (1989) found that reverse video was more effective than increased brightness.

Summary

While a variety of techniques exist for highlighting elements on a screen, there are several important points to remember about the use of highlighting. The first is that no matter which technique is used, it should be applied conservatively. Overuse of highlighting defeats its purpose. The second point is that color appears to be the most effective highlighting technique, followed by reverse video. The final point is that the elements to be highlighted should be chosen carefully, since they are likely to attract the user's attention. If the wrong elements are highlighted, the user will have more difficulty detecting the important information.

23.2.4 Placement and Sequence of Information

While highlighting techniques can aid the user in locating important information, it is not always possible to predict what may be important to the user at a given time. For this reason, every screen should be laid out in a manner that allows the user to easily find any of the information on it. One of the best ways of doing this is to adopt a consistent format for all the screens in an application or series of applications. This consistency allows the users to develop expectancies about where to find information on the screen, thus making it easier for them to learn how to use a new application that adheres to a format they already know. The benefits to be gained from consistent screen layouts have also been demonstrated empirically (e.g., Tullis, 1981; Teitelbaum and Granda, 1983).

Consistent Screen Formats

Most of the guidelines documents advocate the use of a consistent screen format. For example, Galitz (1993, p. 61) states that the designer should "reserve specific areas of the screen for certain kinds of information, such as commands, error messages, title, and data fields, and maintain these areas consistently on all screens." He goes on to recommend possible locations for common screen elements: screen title (upper center), screen identifier (upper right), command field or function key labels (bottom line), status or error messages (line above command field), and menu bar (top of the screen, just below the title). This is similar to the recommendations of Marcus and his associates (e.g., Marcus, 1992) that graphical screens be designed with a consistent layout using spatial grids.

Obviously there can be no one screen format that applies to all possible applications. Consequently, this is an area where designers must make the transition from guidelines, which are necessarily general, to specific design rules, or standards, for individual products and product families. (See Smith, 1986.) For example, both the Macintosh (Apple, 1992) and Windows (Microsoft, 1995) have adopted very detailed standards for the design of their windows and desktop (e.g., appearance and location of title bars, menu bars, buttons, etc).

Sequence of Data Elements

Since standard screen layouts must leave large parts of the screen's layout to the specific needs of the application, additional guidelines and design rules are needed to guide the developer in deciding where to place elements on the screen. Galitz (1993, p. 62) suggests that an obvious starting point should be provided in the upper-left corner of the screen: "This is near where visual scanning begins and will permit a left-to-right, top-to-bottom reading as is common in Western cultures." This scanning strategy is supported by the work of Streveler and Wasserman (1984), who manipulated the presence of a target item in the four quadrants of the screen and found that search times were shortest for targets in the upper left and longest for targets in the lower right. However, care should be taken in applying this principle, since it may only apply to predominantly textual screens, not the increasingly rich graphical screens common in GUI systems.

The optimum sequence for presenting data elements on the screen is determined by many different factors, including the following:

- *Sequence of Use-* If the data elements need to be used in a particular sequence, then they should be presented in that order. This is commonly the case when the user is entering information that is coming from an external source (e.g., a printed form or an interview with a client).

- *Conventional Usage-* There are many cases where generally accepted conventions have arisen for sequences of data elements. The most common example of this is name, street address, city, state, and zip code, but others exist in more specialized domains.

- *Importance-* In some cases, the developer can predict that certain data elements will be more important to the user than others (e.g., summary information, items that require quick response, etc). In those cases, the more important elements should be given a prominent location. For example, one of the differences between the two screen formats shown in Figure 8 and Figure 9 is that the key information has a more prominent location in Figure 9. Related to the idea of importance is the convention that required data entry fields should generally precede optional fields.

- *Frequency of Use-* In cases where some screen elements are used more frequently than others, the most frequently used elements should appear near the top of the screen. For example, in a menu of commands, the most frequently used commands might be presented first.

- *Generality/Specificity-* When certain data elements are more general than others, the more general elements should precede the more specific elements. This is particularly true when there is a hierarchical relationship among the data. More general data elements are usually those that establish a context for the subsequent data (e.g., the name of a file being edited).

- *Alphabetical or Chronological-* If none of the other rules for logically ordering the data elements apply, then some other technique should be adopted. For example, in the case of a listing of file names, an alphabetical list by name might be appropriate, or a chronological list by creation date, depending upon what the list is to be used for.

Summary

The main point to remember about the placement and sequence of elements on the screen is that the user should be able to develop very clear expectancies about what information will fall where. These expectancies might arise due to the adoption of a standard layout, or they might be due to the inherent structure of the information being presented.

23.2.5 Spatial Relationships among Elements

While the adoption of a standard layout and the proper sequencing of elements on the screen can make it easier for the user to find information, the spatial relationships among those elements are also important. Many spatial relationships, such as the use of alignment, can make it easier for the user to locate a particular element, and other spatial relationships, such as the use of indentation, can convey special meaning to the user.

Alignment of Lists

Almost all of the guidelines documents specify that a series of related data elements should be presented vertically in a list rather than horizontally in running text (e.g., Engel and Granda, 1975, p. 6; Smith and Mosier, 1986, p. 109). For example, Figure 21 and Figure 22 show two screen formats studied by Wolf (1986) for presenting the names of host computers

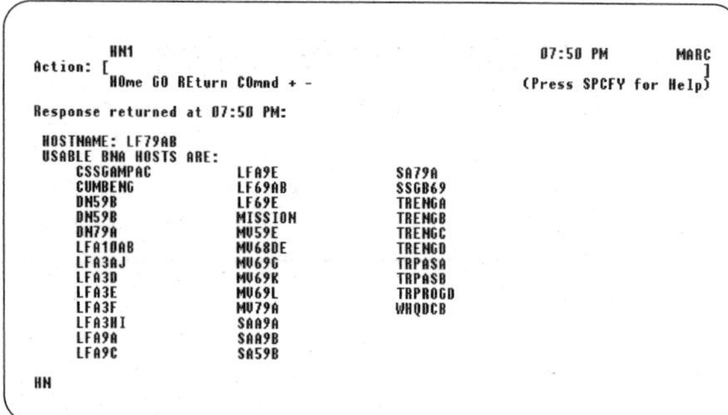

Figure 21. One of several screen formats studied by Wolf (1986) for presenting a list of host computers available in a network. In this version, the names were alphabetized within vertical lists.

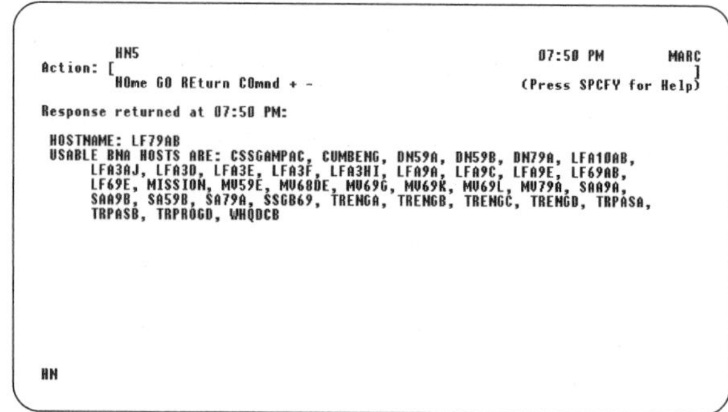

Figure 22. Another screen format studied by Wolf (1986) for presenting a list of host computers available in a network. This version, which alphabetized them in horizontal lists of running text, took 37% longer than the one in Figure 21 for users to find a specific name.

available in a network. She found that the format using vertical lists alphabetized within each column (Figure 21) resulted in 37% less time to locate a host name than did the format using horizontal lists in running text (Figure 22). Interestingly, the worst search times were for a format that was very similar to that of Figure 21, but the elements were alphabetized within the *rows* rather than the *columns*. This is a clear example of a case where the semantic aspects of a display (the alphabetical ordering by row) are in conflict with the spatial aspects (the grouping by column). Unfortunately, this type of alphabetized row format is very commonly used in many systems.

Most of the guidelines documents go on to suggest that the alignment technique used in vertical lists should differ depending upon the type of data being listed. Specifically, vertical lists of textual and alphanumeric data should be left-justified, and vertical lists of numeric data should be right-justified (or aligned on their decimal points) (e.g., Engel and Granda, 1975, p. 7; Smith and Mosier, 1986, p. 127). Left-justifying textual and alphanumeric items makes it easier to locate the beginning of each item, which is presumably where one would want to begin reading. Aligning numeric items on their decimal points makes it easier to compare the magnitudes of the items in the list.

Measuring Alignment

Tullis (1983) presented a general technique for quantifying this concept of how well-aligned the elements of a character-mode screen are with each other. The technique, which has been implemented in a computer program along with other screen format measures (Tullis, 1986a), is a modification of an algorithm proposed by Bonsiepe (1968). It involves counting the number of different rows or columns on the screen that are used as starting positions of alphanumeric data items (or as decimal-point positions for numeric data items). Information theory is then used to calculate the complexity (in bits) of this arrangement of starting positions. This value is minimized by aligning the data items with each other, because that results in fewer different starting rows or columns. For example, consider the alignments used in the lodging screens shown earlier in Figure 6, Figure 7, and Figure 15. Obviously, the format shown in Figure 6 most closely follows the alignment rules, while the format shown in Figure 15 appears to violate the rules the most. The layout complexity values for these screens correspond to that impression: 6.9, 7.6, and 8.6 bits for Figure 6, Figure 7, and Figure 15, respectively. While Tullis (1984) found that this layout complexity measure was not significantly related to users' search times, it was found to be the single best predictor of the users' subjective ratings of display formats. Higher values of layout complexity were associated with worse ease-of-use ratings.

Other Spatial Relationships

In addition to the use of alignments on a screen, several other spatial relationships among display elements should be considered:

- *Indentation*- Subordinate or hierarchical relationships among data elements can be conveyed quite effectively through the use of indentation. For example, consider Figure 23, which shows a screen from the Windows 95 Explorer, which makes use

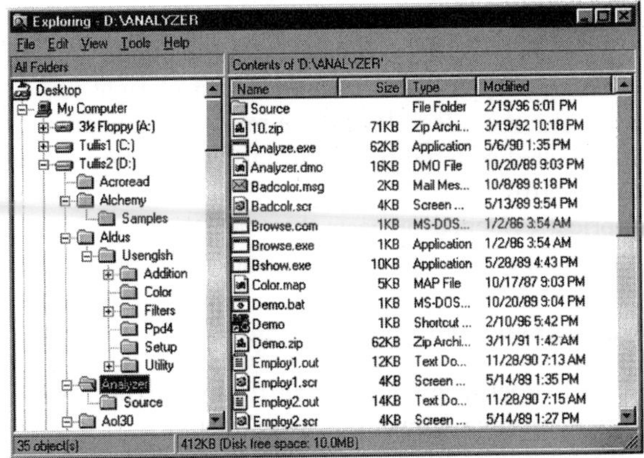

Figure 23. ***Sample window from the Windows 95 Explorer*** *illustrating the use of indentation to convey hierarchical relationships.*

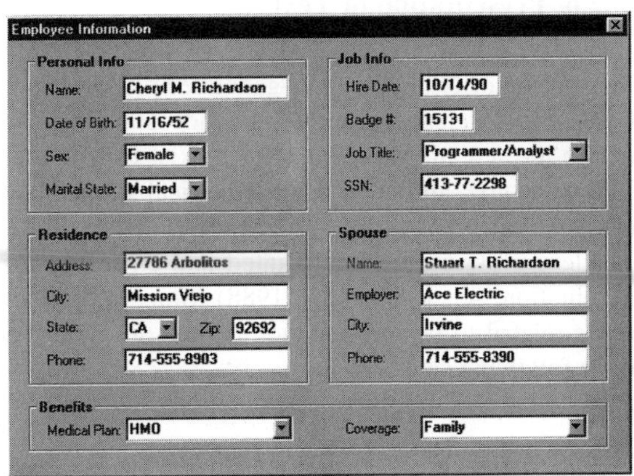

Figure 24. Sample window for a hypothetical employee information system. *Note the alignment of data labels with each other and data items with each other. Also note the use of bold text for data and non-bold for most labels, providing additional visual distinction between the types of items.*

of indentation (plus lines) to convey the hierarchical structure of the files listed in the left-hand portion.

- *Label/Data Relationships*- With few exceptions, every data item on a screen should be labelled in some way. There are two commonly accepted techniques for labelling: to the left of the data item and above the data item. Several guidelines recommend that the labels in a vertical list should be aligned with each other and the associated vertical list of data items should be aligned, as in the sample shown in Figure 24, which is from a hypothetical employee information system. However, this approach can result in too much space between some labels and associated data if the labels are quite variable in length. Two solutions to this problem have been used: right-justifying the labels instead of left-justifying them or using lines formed by dots to connect the labels and data.

- *Process Associations*- Computer-generated displays are becoming more common in situations that involve representing and controlling the status of some real-world process (e.g., nuclear power plants, telephone networks). Such displays commonly use graphical elements to represent actual elements of the process. The spatial relationships among the graphical elements should help convey to the user what the physical or functional relationships among the actual elements are.

- *Symmetry*- Several guidelines documents have proposed that the spatial relationships among the elements on a screen should provide some degree of symmetrical balance (e.g., Galitz, 1993, p. 64; Streveler and Harrison, 1985, p. 36) For example, Galitz proposed that symmetry should be achieved by centering the display itself and maintaining an equal weighting of elements on each side of the vertical axis. In addition, Streveler and Wasserman (1984) proposed a measure of "balance" as one of their objective techniques for assessing the spatial properties of screens. This balance was computed as the difference between the center of mass of the displayed elements and the physical center of the screen. However, they did not report any evidence to show that this measure actually helps predict the usability of the display.

Summary

The main point to remember about spatial relationships is that once the user has identified the locations of some elements on the screen, he or she should be able to use that information to find other elements on the screen. This kind of visual predictability can be achieved by aligning data elements with each other or by adopting other spatial relationships that are consistent with the semantic relationships among the data.

23.2.6 Presentation of Text

The vast majority of computer-generated displays, even those with extensive graphics, include some type of text on the screen. Many guidelines exist for the presentation of text, and quite a few empirical studies have addressed different aspects of text presentation. For an excellent overview of both printed and on-screen text presentation, see Rubinstein (1988). Some of the key issues related to the presentation of text are described in the following sections.

Letter Case

Perhaps the most common guideline related to text is that conventional upper and lower case should be used for presentation of most textual material (e.g., Smith and Mosier, 1986, p. 106; Engel and Granda, 1975, p. 17). AS THIS EXAMPLE ILLUSTRATES, ALL UPPER CASE TEXT TENDS TO BE UNIFORMLY RECTANGULAR AND LACKS THE DISTINCTIVE WORD SHAPES OF NORMAL UPPER AND LOWER CASE TEXT THAT FACILITATE READING. Several studies have shown that normal upper and lower case text is read about 13% faster than text in all uppercase (Tinker, 1955; Poulton and Brown, 1968; Moskel, Erno, and Shneiderman, 1984). At the same time, most of the guidelines recommend that all upper case be used for items that need to attract attention. This is supported by the work of Vartabedian (1971), who found that search time to locate a word on a CRT was about 13% shorter for uppercase words than for lowercase words.

Justification and Spacing between Words

Many designers use "fill justification" when presenting extended text because they believe even left and right margins create a neater appearance. However, with non-proportional (fixed-width) fonts, the extra spaces inserted between words to create the even right margin cause inconsistent spacing between the words. Contrary to this popular usage, several of the guidelines documents recommend that text be presented with consistent spacing between words, even if that means having ragged right margins (Smith and Mosier, 1986, p. 107; Marcus, 1992, p. 35; Galitz, 1993, p. 108). Several studies have shown that any detrimental effect of ragged right margins is outweighed by the detrimental effect of uneven spacing between words (Gregory and Poulton, 1970; Campbell, Marchetti, and Mewhort, 1981; Trollip and Sales, 1986). For example, Trollip and Sales (1986) found that fill-justified text took about 11% longer to read than unjustified text.

With proportional fonts, the effect of right justification is not as clear. By far the most common practice with printed material is to right justify, except possibly when narrow columns are used. However, the limited emprical evidence suggests that there is no difference in readability (Fabrizio, Kaplan, and Teal, 1967).

Spacing between Lines (Leading)

Several experiments have been done studying the effects of spacing between lines of text (which printers call "leading"). Ringel and Hammer (1964) manipulated the ratio of letter height to the total space between baselines in a table from 1:4 for low density to 1:2 for high density. (When measuring letter height, the typical approach is to measure the height of a lowercase 'x'.) They found that a density of 1:2 yielded slightly shorter search times. On the other hand, Kolers, Duchnicky, and Ferguson (1981) compared CRT text displays using line spacings of 1:1.3 and 1:2.7. They found that the very close line spacing (1:1.3) required more eye fixations per line and resulted in longer total reading time. Kruk and Muter (1984) compared CRT displays of single-spaced (1:1.3) and double-spaced (1:2.6) text. Mean reading speed was 11% slower for single spacing. In a survey of 50 published works (books and magazines), Rubinstein (1988, p. 170-174) found that the ratios in common use ranged from 1:2.1 to 1:2.7.

Taken together, these various studies suggest that a spacing on the order of 1:2 to 1:2.7 may be optimum. Basically, this means that the space between the bottom of one line and the top of the characters on the line below should be equal to, or slightly greater than, the height of the characters themselves.

Spacing between Paragraphs

Several guidelines documents recommend that a blank line be left between paragraphs of text (Smith and Mosier, 1986, p. 106; Galitz, 1993, p. 109). This approach is certainly consistent with the idea that large groups of alphanumeric items should be broken into smaller visual chunks (Section 23.2.2).

Line Length

Rehe (1974) and Marcus (1992, p. 34) both recommend that text lines should be no more than 40 to 60 characters long. Similarly, Lichty (1989) recommends that text lines should be no longer than 39 characters. These recommendations are based on the difficulty the reader has in scanning back to the beginning of longer lines. However, Bouma (1980) has pointed out that line length interacts with the spacing betweeen lines, with greater line spacing allowing for longer lines. Bouma suggested that the minimum acceptable ratio of inter-line spacing (measured from the bottom of one text line to the bottom of the next) to line length is about 1:30. Using relatively average dimensions for CRT text displays (0.2" inter-line spacing and 0.1" character width), Bouma's ratio implies that no more than 60 characters should be shown on each line.

Tinker (1963), in studying printed text, found that line lengths of 3-4 inches yielded the fastest reading speeds, while shorter or longer lines resulted in slower reading. With typical on-screen character sizes (10-11 characters per inch), that corresponds to about 30-44 characters per line. This finding was supported by Wiggins (1967), who found that a column width of 1.67 inches was read significantly slower than one of 2 inches. In a study of scrolling text, Duchnicky and Kolers (1983) found that reading rates did not significantly differ for line lengths of 78 and 52 characters, but both yielded faster reading than did lines of 26 characters.

Although the results are far from conclusive, these studies suggest that designers of textual displays should avoid very short lines (e.g., fewer than 26 characters per line) as well as very long lines (e.g., more than 78 characters). With longer lines, it would be wise to ensure that adequate inter-line spacing is provided.

Font Size and Style

In his classic studies of printed material, Tinker (1963) found no significant difference in the readability of text from 9 to 12 points. However, larger (14 point and higher) and smaller (6 point) type sizes were less legible and reduced reading speeds by 5% to 8%.

In studying on-screen presentation of text, Tullis, Boynton, and Hersh (1995) compared reading speed, accuracy, and subjective preference for four different font families in the Windows environment (MS Sans Serif, Arial, MS Serif, and Small Fonts) ranging from 6 point to 10 point. As one might expect, most measures improved with larger font sizes, although the differences from 8 to 10 points were small. At the larger sizes, the one serifed font (MS Serif) fared worse than did the sans serif fonts. This supports the conventional wisdom that serifed fonts should generally be avoided for on-screen use, possibly due to the inability of relatively low resolution screens to accurately represent the serifs. Giving equal weight to speed, accuracy, and subjective preference, Tullis *et al.* found that the two best fonts, of those they studied, were Arial and MS Sans Serif at 10 point. They found no difference in readability between bold and non-bold characters.

Gould, Alfaro, Finn, Haupt, and Minuto (1987) studied the effect of anti-aliasing of fonts (the use of grayscale to smooth the edges of black characters). Although they did not find a statistically significant difference in reading speed between normal and anti-aliased fonts, 14 of 15 users preferred the anti-aliased font.

Mono-spaced vs. Proportionally-spaced Fonts

The widespread use of GUI systems has brought with it a widespread use of proportionally spaced fonts, in contrast to the mono-spaced fonts used in character-mode systems. Of course, proportionally spaced fonts have been the norm in printed text since the earliest days of typesetting. Studies by Tinker (1963), Payne (1967), and Beldie, Pastoor, and Schwarz (1983) have shown that proportionally spaced fonts are generally read slightly faster (about 6%) than mono-spaced fonts.

Hyphenation

Nas (1988) found that reading is slower if words are divided (hyphenated) at the ends of the lines. However, a desire to avoid hyphenation needs to be traded off against a desire to minimize what are called "rivers" in justified text (areas of white space that can be followed from line to line) or very uneven righthand margins in unjustified text.

Image Polarity

Printed text is traditionally presented using dark characters on white paper. However, the vast majority of character-mode systems present text using light characters on a black background. Most GUI systems, perhaps due to a desire to mimic the printed page, commonly use dark characters on a light background. (Note that there is some confusion in the literature about whether this should be called positive or negative polarity.) Studies by Snyder, Decker, Lloyd, and Dye (1990) and Gould *et al* (1987) have supported the notion that dark characters on a light background are read faster than light characters on a dark background. There is also evidence that users prefer dark text on a light background (Radl, 1983). However, studies by Cushman (1986) and Kühne, Krueger, Graf, and Merz

Key: Best Worst

Foreground Color

Background Color

	Black	Blue	Green	Cyan	Red	Magenta	Brown	Lt Gray	Dk Gray	Lt Blue	Lt Green	Lt Cyan	Lt Red	Lt Magenta	Lt Brown	White
Black	0	15	75	90	38	53	113	192	128	29	150	179	76	105	226	255
Blue	15	0	60	75	23	38	98	177	113	14	135	164	61	90	211	240
Green	75	60	0	15	37	22	38	117	53	46	75	104	1	30	151	180
Cyan	90	75	15	0	52	37	23	102	38	61	60	89	14	15	136	165
Red	38	23	37	52	0	15	75	154	90	9	112	141	38	67	188	217
Magenta	53	38	22	37	15	0	60	139	75	24	97	126	23	52	173	202
Brown	113	98	38	23	75	60	0	79	15	84	37	66	37	8	113	142
Lt Gray	192	177	117	102	154	139	79	0	64	163	42	13	116	87	34	63
Dk Gray	128	113	53	38	90	75	15	64	0	99	22	51	52	23	98	127
Lt Blue	29	14	46	61	9	24	84	163	99	0	121	150	47	76	197	226
Lt Green	150	135	75	60	112	97	37	42	22	121	0	29	74	45	76	105
Lt Cyan	179	164	104	89	141	126	66	13	51	150	29	0	103	74	47	76
Lt Red	76	61	1	14	38	23	37	116	52	47	74	103	0	29	150	179
Lt Magenta	105	90	30	15	67	52	8	87	23	76	45	74	29	0	121	150
Yellow	226	211	151	136	188	173	113	34	98	197	76	47	150	121	0	29
White	255	240	180	165	217	202	142	63	127	226	105	76	179	150	29	0

Figure 25. Differences in gray values for all combinations of the sixteen standard colors available in the VGA palette for Windows. *This is a measure of the amount of contrast between the colors. Those in the top third (>170) (Most Legible) and bottom third (<85) (Least Legible) are highlighted. Note that there are far more that are bad than good.*

(1986) failed to find a statistically significant difference in performance between positive and negative polarity. Taken as a whole, the results appear to suggest that there may be a small difference in reading performance between the two polarities, but it is difficult to prove statistically. Rubinstein (1988, p. 191) points out that dark characters on a light background may be less fatiguing for users who must switch between the screen and paper.

In GUI systems, the most commonly used "light" background colors are white and light gray. (Light gray has become popular with the trend toward 3D interfaces.) Tullis *et al* (1995), using black text, found no difference in reading performance or preference between white and light gray backgrounds.

Color

Several studies have investigated performance and preference differences for various foreground/background color combinations for text (Lalomia and Happ, 1987; Pace, 1984; Pastoor, 1990), and several authors have presented guidelines for color combinations based on perceptual principles (e.g., Smith, 1986; Murch, 1985). White (1990, p. 73) and Fowler and Stanwick (1995, p. 331) have suggested that the main determinant of the legibility of a particular foreground/ background color combination is the amount of contrast between them. One technique for checking contrast is to create a bitmap showing the color combination to be tested and convert it to grayscale using an image manipulation program (such as PhotoShop). Then check the difference in gray values between the foreground and background. White (1990) and Fowler and Stanwick (1995) suggest that the difference in lightness should be at least 30% to be legible, or a difference in gray values of at least 77. (Gray values range from 0 for black to 255 for white.)

Figure 25 shows the differences in gray values for all combinations of the sixteen colors available in the standard VGA palette for Windows. Under ideal circumstances, it would seem reasonable to choose color combinations that are in the top third in terms of gray value difference, which would mean a difference of 170 or greater. For example, with the light gray background (gray = 192) commonly used in GUI windows, the best foreground colors to use would be black (difference = 192) or blue (difference = 177). On the other hand, the worst color combinations would be those in the bottom third, which would mean a difference of 85 or less. Again using light gray background as an example, the unacceptable foreground colors would be brown (79), dark gray (64), light green (42), light cyan (13), yellow (34), and white (63).

Summary

Ideally, text should be presented in mixed upper and lower case using an anti-aliased, proportionally spaced, sans serif font of at least 8 to 10 points in a high-contrast color combination using dark characters on a light background. Lines of running text should probably be at least 26 characters long, but not longer than about 78 characters, with as much space between the lines as the height of the lines themselves.

Figure 26. Sample window from an image manipulation application. (Photo by author.)

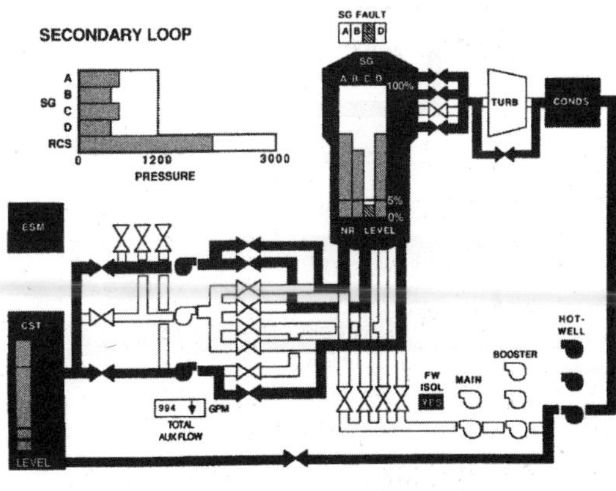

Figure 27. Sample screen from a hypothetical nuclear power plant control system, from EPRI (1984).

23.2.7 Uses of Graphics

There can be little doubt that, in some situations, a picture truly is worth a thousand words. But what are those situations? The following sections describe several situations where graphics have commonly been used or where graphics seem to be the most appropriate way of conveying the information. The list is by no means exhaustive, but is rather an attempt to identify some of the most common uses of graphics.

Representing Real-world (or Imaginary) Images

Consider the screen shown in Figure 26, which is from PhotoStyler for Windows. This program is an example of an application that involves building or representing images. It is obvious that graphical displays are required for representing such information. Imagine trying to convey to someone the precise appearance of this image using only alphanumeric descriptions.

Representing Complex, Real-world Systems

An increasingly common use of graphical displays is to represent the important characteristics of real-world systems and, in some cases, to control those systems. The most obvious applications are in the process-control arena (e.g., power plants, factories, refineries). For example, Figure 27. shows a sample screen proposed for a hypothetical nuclear power plant (EPRI, 1984). The actual screen used color to represent different features and states of the system (e.g., blue for water flowing through the pipes; green, yellow, and red for good, marginal, and bad states). The key distinction between displays like this and the PhotoStyler screen shown previously (Figure 26) is that these displays for complex systems rarely use literal images of actual objects, but rather stylized or symbolic graphics that attempt to represent functional relationships among the components of the system.

Techniques for designing process-monitoring displays have been described in a set of guidelines addressing nuclear power plant displays prepared for the Electric Power Research Institute (EPRI, 1984). Among the topics addressed are selecting picture elements, determining the picture content, and organizing the picture. An important issue in selecting picture elements for a process-control display is determining standard meanings for the graphic symbols (e.g., the pumps and valves shown in Figure 27) and then using them consistently in all the displays. One of the techniques for organizing these kinds of displays is to take advantage of the physical relationships among the elements in the real world.

While the benefits of using graphical displays to represent the status of a complex system seem apparent, they may also be useful in representing simpler systems. For example, Tullis (1981) compared the effectiveness of graphical and alphanumeric displays in representing a fairly simple real-world system: a single telephone line. The two alphanumeric formats studied were shown earlier in Figure 8 and Figure 9. One of the two graphical formats studied is shown in Figure 28. This format, which actually used color, was very similar to the other graphical format studied, which used monochromatic techniques to convey the color infor-

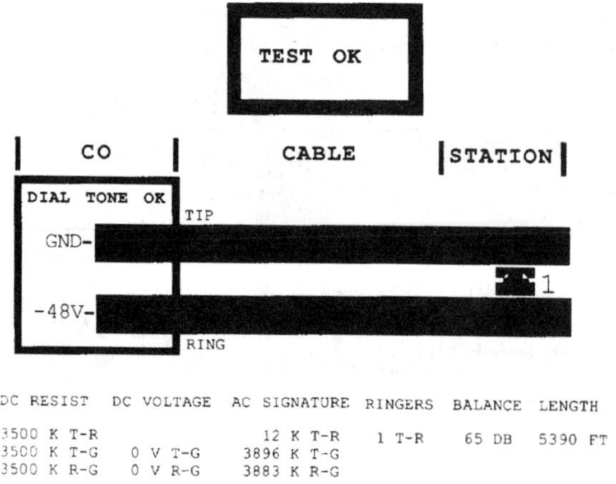

DC RESIST	DC VOLTAGE	AC SIGNATURE	RINGERS	BALANCE	LENGTH
3500 K T-R		12 K T-R	1 T-R	65 DB	5390 FT
3500 K T-G	0 V T-G	3896 K T-G			
3500 K R-G	0 V R-G	3883 K R-G			

Figure 28. ***Graphical screen format studied by Tullis*** *(1981) for conveying the electrical status of a telephone line. The two alphanumeric formats studied in this experiment were shown in Figure 8 and Figure 9.*

mation. The key result of the study was that the time to interpret both graphical formats was significantly shorter than that for the "narrative" format shown in Figure 8. However, after the subjects had practiced using all the formats, they could interpret the "structured" alphanumeric display shown in Figure 9 just as quickly as the graphical displays. The use of color did not have any effect on performance, but subjects did express a preference for it. These results were interpreted as indicating that while graphics may not be required for representing the status of relatively simple systems like this, they could be useful as training aids, or for use by relatively inexperienced or infrequent users.

Representing Numerical Data

Perhaps the most common use of graphics in computer systems is to represent numerical data, particularly data that is multi-dimensional or changing over time. Entire books have been devoted to this use of graphics (e.g, Tufte, 1983, 1990; Cleveland, 1985), so only some of the key points will be presented here.

Graphics are especially helpful when users must scan and compare related sets of data to detect differences or other trends (Smith and Mosier, 1986, p. 130). For example, consider the data shown in Figure 29. While the same data are represented in the spreadsheet and the graph, notice how much easier it is to make comparisons and detect trends using the graphical format in contrast to the tabular format. For example, try to determine at what weeks each district's sales reached their highest value, or at what week district A's sales first surpassed district B's.

Benbasat, Dexter, and Todd (1986) compared the effectiveness of line graphs and tabular presentations of the same data. Subjects were presented with a hypothetical marketing problem in which they had to make decisions about allocating promotional budgets among three sales territories, each with its own unique performance characteristics. After each trial, the subjects could request a history display that showed their expenditures and profit for all the trials up to that time. The history display was either a line graph or a table. They found that the number of subjects requesting the graphical history displays began to decline after the first several trials, while the number requesting the tabular displays stayed at a higher level. However, the results also indicated that those subjects who made consistent use of the graphical displays in the early trials completed the task in fewer trials. The results were interpreted as indicating that graphical displays are more useful when trying to determine promising directions to take, while tabular displays are more useful when the task requires precise computations. These results are generally consistent with those of Lalomia and Coovert (1987), who found that line graphs were more effective for problems that involved trend analysis and forecasting, while tabular displays were more effective for problems that involved locating a specific data value.

Obviously there are many other graphical techniques for presenting numerical data besides simple line graphs. For example, in their report on display guidelines for nuclear power plants, EPRI (1984) described eleven different types of picture elements suitable for representing process data. Several studies have been conducted to compare the effectiveness of some of these graphical techniques (e.g., Petersen, Banks, and Gertman, 1982) and, as one might expect, the results indicate that the effectiveness of each technique is highly dependent upon the nature of the task and data.

Representing Direct-Manipulation Objects and Actions

One very specific application of graphics, namely the use of icons, has become so popular that it warrants special treatment. Icons are small graphical images that are commonly used to represent objects that the system knows something about (e.g., documents, file folders, physical devices) or actions that can be performed (e.g., deleting or copying something, creating different kinds of graphics, turning a device on). Most commonly, icons are used in direct-manipulation interfaces in which the user conveys desired actions to the system

Week	District A	District B
1	250	700
2	300	600
3	340	530
4	500	450
5	610	400
6	700	380
7	600	420
8	550	350
9	480	330
10	350	280

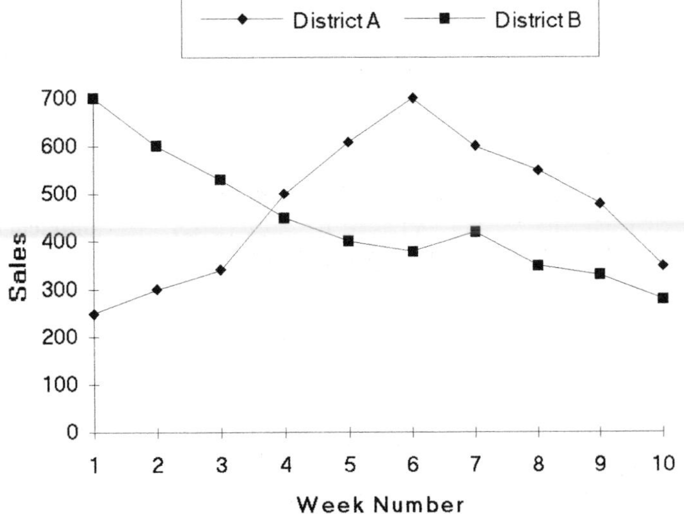

Figure 29. Tabular and graphical representations of the same hypothetical sales data over ten weeks for two districts. *Note the ease of detecting trends from the graphical display. For example, when did district A's sales first surpass district B's?*

by manipulating the icons. The manipulations usually involve pointing to the icon and then performing an action on it. A common example from several systems is that an object, such as a document, might be deleted by dragging its icon to a trash-can icon.

Direct-mainpulation interfaces are becoming more common in process-control systems, in which icons often represent real-world devices in the process being monitored (e.g., pumps, valves). Selecting one of those icons might cause a pop-up menu to appear that would allow the user to perform an action on the object, such as interrogating it for detailed status information or changing its state (e.g., closing a valve). For example, Williams, Seidenstein, and Goddard (1980) describe this use of direct manipulation to control electric-power transmission networks.

The use of icons to graphically represent real-world objects has obvious advantages over abstract representations since it capitalizes on the concrete nature of the objects and often mimics their appearance. However, icons have also become popular for representing more abstract objects and actions, such as computer files and computer-based drawing primitives. For example, the PhotoStyler screen shown earlier in Figure 26 makes extensive use of icons to provide very effective ways of allowing the user to select different drawing tools. In essence, icons often provide a more powerful way of conveying complex information in less space (e.g., Hemenway, 1982; Rohr and Keppel, 1984). Comprehensive reviews of the uses of icons, and guidelines for their design, have been presented by Gittins (1986), Galitz (1994, p. 405-418), Marcus (1992, p. 51-76), and Fowler and Stanwick (1995, p. 55-63).

Rogers (1986, 1993) evaluated the effectiveness of six different sets of twenty icons each designed to signify word-processing operations. Figure 30 shows examples of several icons from each set. The six sets were designed by using either abstract symbols, concrete objects, concrete analogies associated with the action, or some combination of these. Subjects were asked to match the icons to descriptions of the commands. Rogers found that the icon sets representing concrete objects being acted upon (sets 3 and 4 in Figure 30) resulted in the highest number of correct matches, with over 85% correct identifications. Abstract icons and more complex icons resulted in worse recognition.

Closely related to the use of icons is the use of different cursors, or pointers, to indicate different states of the system or modes of operation. This can be very effective because in many direct-manipulation interfaces the user's attention is often focused near the cursor. For example, Microsoft (1995, p. 30) specified fifteen different pointers for Windows 95, including an arrow (for most direct manipulations), an I-beam (for text selection), an hourglass (to indicate that an operation is in progress), and a magnifying glass (for zoom-

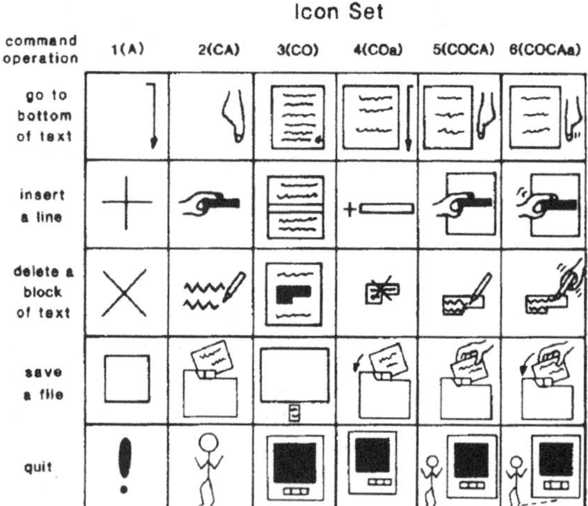

Figure 30. Examples of icons studied by Rogers (1986). *Six different sets of icons were developed (the six columns in this figure). The same twenty word-processing functions were represented by the icons in each set, of which five are shown in this figure.*

ing). Changing the shape of the pointer helps clarify to the user what the effects of a manipulation will be. A few points to keep in mind when designing cursors are the following: (1) Their appearance should help convey something about the state (e.g., the hourglass); (2) For maximum legibility, their design should be simple; and (3) If precise pointing is involved, the cursor should have an obvious "hot spot" (e.g., the point of an arrow). See Fowler and Stanwick (1995, p. 69-77) for a thorough discussion of pointer design.

Summary

Graphics are becoming an increasingly important part of the visual interface to computer systems. A wide variety of techniques exist for presenting information graphically, and more of these techniques are becoming viable for use in reasonably priced computer systems. There are certain situations where the necessary infomation can reasonably be conveyed only by using graphics, and many other situations where graphics appear to be a more effective method of conveying information than alphanumerics. Additional research is needed to define the types of graphical displays that are the most appropriate for various classes of tasks and data.

23.3 Screen Design Metrics, Models, And Systems

Since the mid-1980's there have been several attempts at developing models which could assist in designing or evaluating screen designs. Each has taken a somewhat different approach to the problem or focused on different types of screens.

23.3.1 Tullis' Screen Analyzer

Tullis (1984, 1986a, 1988) developed a program, called the Screen Analyzer, for measuring six layout metrics for character-mode screens: overall density, local density (a measure of the number of other characters near each character), number of visual groups, average size of the groups, alignment, and number of data elements. He then collected search times and subjective ratings for 520 screens that varied on these metrics. Multiple regression analyses were used to fit the performance and preference data with the screen layout metrics.

The best predictors of search time were overall density, local density, number of groups, and average size of the groups. Those four predictors accounted for 49% of the variance in search times. The two most significant predictors of search time were the two measures related to grouping. The best prediction system for subjective ratings included all six of the layout metrics and accounted for 80% of the variance in subjective ratings. The two most significant predictors of subjective ratings were the alignment and local density metrics.

Tullis validated the prediction system in a second experiment in which he collected data on a new set of 150 screens. He found that the four-predictor model for search times and the six-predictor model for subjective ratings both generalized quite well (r = .80 in both cases). In applying the prediction system to screens from six published studies (Streveler and Wasserman, 1984; Dodson and Shields, 1978; Ringel and Hammer, 1964; Callan *et al*, 1977; Burns *et al*, 1986; Wolf, 1986), he found that the correlations with their reported search time data ranged from r = .76 to r = .98 (Tullis, 1988).

Although Tullis' model demonstrated the potential of this approach for evaluating screen layouts, its major shortcomings included the fact that it was limited to character-mode screens, did not consider task characteristics, and ignored the semantics of the screen elements.

23.3.2 Streveler's Spatial Properties Measures

Streveler and his associates (Streveler and Wasserman, 1984; Streveler and Harrison, 1984, 1985) described three basic techniques for analyzing character-mode screen formats: "boxing" analysis, "hot-spot" analysis, and "alignment" analysis. "Boxing" is their method of detecting groups, "hot-spot" analysis is conceptually similar to Tullis' measure of local density, and their alignment analysis is similar to Tullis' measure of alignment. The similarity of these screen metrics is interesting, since they were developed totally independently. However, while Tullis focused on using screen metrics to predict empirical search times and subjective ratings, Streveler and his associates focused more on the measures themselves and subjective interpretations of their implications for screen design.

23.3.3 Perlman's Axiomatic Model

Perlman (1987) described an Axiomatic Model of Information Presentation in which the screen designer specified semantic relationships among the items to be presented. Unlike Tullis and Streveler, who focused on characteristics visible to the user, Perlman focused on the designer's intentions and desired relationships among screen elements. He also described a prototype system for using this information in designing and evaluating screen layouts. But, like the earlier systems, task characteristics were not incorporated.

23.3.4 Tanaka, Eberts, and Salvendy's Consistency Measures

Tanaka, Eberts, and Salvendy (1990) extended Tullis' work by using the same screen measures but adding the concept of consistency of those measures across multiple screens. They called this display consistency. Likewise, they used a GOMS analysis (Card, Moran, and Newell, 1983) to develop a measure of cognitive consistency. They found that both display inconsistency and cognitive inconsistency had detrimental effects on task performance. This work is particularly significant for its addition of task characteristics to the purely visual screen characteristics studied earlier.

23.3.5 Lohse's Model for Understanding Graphs

Lohse (1991) moved screen design models into the graphical world by developing a model for predicting the amount of time needed to extract information from a graph. Basically, he focused on the sequence of fixations that a user must make in the interpretation of a graph and the cognitive tasks required at each of those points. Although this model was limited to graphs, it introduced the concept of task sequencing within a given screen.

23.3.6 Sears' Layout Appropriateness

Sears (1993) extended the concept of task sequencing to any graphical interface containing multiple interface objects (e.g., GUI dialog boxes). He introduced a metric called Layout Appropriateness to measure how effectively a given window layout supports the required sequence of tasks. Conceptually, this is similar to link analysis, which human factors professionals have used for almost 40 years to identify optimum layouts of equipment (e.g., Chapanis, 1959, pp. 51-62). To compute Layout Effectiveness, the designer must identify the set of objects used in the interface, the sequence of actions users perform with those objects, and how frequently each sequence is used. Sears applied this metric to three layouts for a NASA screen and three layouts for the Macintosh "File Save As" dialog box. Overall, he found a high correlation ($r = .97$) between task completion times and Layout Appropriateness. More recently, Sears (1995) incorporated the Layout Effectiveness metric into a user interface development tool called AIDE which assists designers in iteratively creating and evaluating layouts a given set of interface objects.

23.3.7 Shneiderman and Associates' Consistency Checking Tools

Shneiderman and his associates at the University of Maryland have developed a family of tools for evaluating a set of related windows (Shneiderman, Chimera, Jog, Stimart, and White, 1995; Mahajan and Shneiderman, 1995). Like Tanaka *et al* (1990), they focused on consistency across an application as a key determinant of its usability. Their tools are designed to spot variations in color, font, font size and style, capitalization, abbreviations, button size and location, and terminology. Information about the screens is provided to the tools using a canonical file format for specifying characteristics of the interface objects.

23.3.8 Summary

A variety of metrics and several systems have been developed to help in developing effective screens. These systems have grown to encompass increasingly rich definitions of the visual characteristics of interfaces as well as the tasks they are used for. They show promise for eventually leading to a fully-featured "screen designer's workbench" in which a designer could iteratively refine screen designs automatically generated from basic interface requirements and task descriptions. While such a tool will never replace designer judgement and emprical usability testing, it could serve as a very valuable supplement.

23.4 References

Apple Computer Inc. (1992). Macintosh human interface guidelines. Reading, MA: Addison-Wesley.

Beldie, I. P., Pastoor, S., and Schwarz, E. (1983). Fixed versus variable letter width for televised text. *Human Factors, 25*, 273-277.

Benbasat, I., Dexter, A. S., and Todd, P. (1986). The influence of color and graphical information presentation in a managerial decision simulation. *Human-Computer Interaction, 2*, 65-92.

Bonsiepe, G. (1968). A method of quantifying order in typographic design. *Journal of Typographic Research, 2*, 203-220.

Bouma, H. (1980). Visual reading processes and the quality of text displays. In *Ergonomic Aspects of Visual Display Terminals*, E. Grandjean and E. Vigliani (Eds), 101-114. London: Taylor & Francis Ltd.

Burns, M. J., Warren, D. L., and Rudisill, M. (1986). Formatting space-related displays to optimize expert and nonexpert user performance. *Proceedings of CHI'86 Conference on Human Factors in Computing Systems*. New York: Association for Computing Machinery.

Cakir, A., Hart, D. J., and Stewart, T. F. M. (1980). *Visual display terminals: A manual covering ergonomics, workplace design, health and safety, task organization*. England: Wiley.

Callan, J. R., Curran, L. E., and Lane, J. L. (1977). Visual search times for Navy tactical information displays (Report # NPRDC-TR-77-32). San Diego, CA: Navy Personnel Research and Development Center. (NTIS No. AD A040543)

Campbell, A. J., Marchetti, F. M., and Mewhort, D. J. K. (1981). Reading speed and text production: A note on right-justification techniques. *Ergonomics, 24*, 633-640.

Card, S. K., Moran, T. P., and Newell, A. (1983). *The Psychology of Human-Computer Interaction*. Hillsdale, NJ: Erlbaum.

Chapanis, A. (1959). *Research techniques in human engineering*. Baltimore, MD: The Johns Hopkins Press.

Cleveland, W. S. (1985). *The elements of graphing data*. Monterey, CA: Wadsworth Advanced Books and Software.

Cropper, A. G., and Evans, S. J. W. (1968). Ergonomics and computer display design. *The Computer Bulletin, 12(3)*, 94-98.

Cushman, W. H. (1986). Reading for microfiche, a VDT, and the printed page: Subjective fatigue and performance. *Human Factors, 28*, 63-73.

Danchak, M. M. (1976). CRT displays for power plants. *Instrumentation Technology, 23(10)*, 29-36.

Dodson, D. W., and Shields, N. L., Jr. (1978). Development of user guidelines for ECAS display design (Vol. 1) (Report No. NASA-CR-150877). Huntsville, AL: Essex Corp.

Donner, K. A., McKay, T., O'Brien, K. M. and Rudisill, M. (1991). Display format and highlighting validity effects on search performance using complex visual displays. *Proceedings of the Human Factors Society 35th Annual Meeting*, 374-378. Santa Monica, CA: Human Factors Society. (Abstract: http://www.cis.ohio-state.edu/~perlman/hfeshci/Abstracts/91:374-378.html)

Duchnicky, R. L., and Kolers, P. A. (1983). Readability of text scrolled on visual display terminals as a function of window size. *Human Factors, 25*, 683-692.

Ehrenreich, S. L., and Porcu, T. A. (1982). Abbreviations for automated systems: Teaching operators the rules. In *Directions in Human-Computer Interaction*, A. Badre and B. Shneiderman (Eds.), 111-135. Norwood, NJ: Ablex Publishing.

Engel, S. E., and Granda, R. E. (1975). Guidelines for man/display interfaces (Technical Report TR 00.2720). Poughkeepsie, NY: IBM.

EPRI. (1984). Computer-generated display system guidelines. Volume 1: Display design. (NP-3701). Palo Alto, CA: Electric Power Research Institute.

Fabrizio, R., Kaplan, I., and Teal, G. (1967). Readability as a function of the straightness of right-hand margins. *Journal of Typographic Research, 1(1)*, Jan. 1967.

Fisher, D. L., and Tan, K. C. (1989). Visual displays: The highlighting paradox. *Human Factors, 31*, 17-30.

Fowler, S. L., and Stanwick, V. R. (1995). *The GUI style guide*. Cambridge, MA: AP Professional.

Galitz, W. O. (1993). *User-interface screen design*. Wellesley, MA: QED Information Sciences.

Galitz, W. O. (1994). *It's time to clean your windows:*

Designing GUIs that work. New York: John Wiley and Sons.

Gittins, D. (1986). Icon-based human-computer interaction. *International Journal of Man-Machine Studies, 24*, 519-543.

Gould, J. D., Alfaro, L., Finn, R., Haupt, B., and Minuto, A. (1987). Reading from CRT displays can be as fast as reading from paper. *Human Factors, 29*, 497-517.

Gregory, M., and Poulton, E. C. (1970). Even versus uneven right-hand margins and the rate of comprehension in reading. *Ergonomics, 13*, 427-434.

Haubner, P., and Neumann, F. (1986). Structuring alphanumerically coded information on visual display units. *Proceedings of the Conference on Work With Display Units*, Stockholm, Sweden, May 1986, 606-609.

Hemenway, K. (1982). Psychological issues in the use of icons in command menus. *Proceedings: Human Factors in Computer Systems* (Gaithersburg, MD), 20-25. New York: Association for Computing Machinery.

Keister, R. S., and Gallaway, G. R. (1983). Making software user friendly: An assessment of data entry performance. *Proceedings of the Human Factors Society 27th Annual Meeting*, 1031-1034. Santa Monica, CA: Human Factors Society.

Koffka, K. (1935). *Principles of Gestalt psychology.* New York: Harcourt, Brace, and World.

Kolers, P. A., Duchnicky, R. L., and Ferguson, D. C. (1981). Eye movement measurement of readability of CRT displays. *Human Factors, 23*, 517-527.

Kruk, R. S., and Muter, P. (1984). Reading of continuous text on video screens. *Human Factors, 26*, 339-345.

Kühne, A., Krueger, H., Graf, W., and Mers, L. (1986). Positive versus negative image polarity. *Proceedings: International Scientific Conference: Work with Display Units*, Stockholm, Sweden, May 12-15, 1986, 208-211.

Lalomia, M. J., and Coovert, M. D. (1987). A comparison of tabular and graphical displays in four problem solving domains. Unpublished technical report, Department of Psychology, University of South Florida, Tampa.

Lalomia, M. J., and Happ, A. J. (1987). The effective use of color for text on the IBM 5153 color display. *Proceedings of the Human Factors Society 31st Annual Meeting*, 1091-1095. Santa Monica, CA: Human Factors Society.

Lichty, T. (1989). *Design principles for desktop publishers*. Glenview, IL: Scott, Foresman and Co.

Lohse, J. (1991). A cognitive model for the perception and understanding of graphs. *Proceedings of CHI'91 Conference on Human Factors in Computing Systems*, 137-144. New York: Association for Computing Machinery.

Mahajan, R., and Shneiderman, B. (1995). A family of user interface consistency checking tools. University of Maryland Department of Computer Science Technical Report # CS-TR-3472.(Abstract: ftp://ftp.cs.umd.edu /pub/ papers/papers/3472/3472.bib)

Marcus, A. (1992). *Graphic design for electronic documents and user interfaces*. Reading, MA: Addison-Wesley. (Abstract: http://www.AMandA.com)

Marcus, A. (1995). Principles of effective visual communication for graphical user interface design. In R. Baecker *et al* (Eds), *Toward the year 2000: Readings in human-computer interaction*. San Francisco, CA: Morgan-Kaufman.

Marcus, A., Arent, M., and Browne, B. (1985). A visible language program for Perq's Accent operating system. *Proceedings of the 6th Annual Conference and Exposition of the National Computer Graphics Association*, 105-137.

Marcus, A., Smilonich, N., and Thompson, L. (1994). *The cross-GUI handbook for multiplatform user interface design*. Reading, MA: Addison-Wesley. (Abstract: http://www. AMandA.com)

Microsoft Corporation. (1995). *The Windows interface guidelines for software design*. Redmond, WA: Microsoft Press.

Moskel, S., Erno, J., and Shneiderman, B. (1984). Proofreading and comprehension of text on screens and paper. University of Maryland Computer Science Technical Report, June 1984.

Murch, G. M. (1985). Using color effectively: Designing to human specifications. *Technical Communication, 32(4)*, 14-20.

Nas, G. L. J. (1988). The effect on reading speed of word divisions at the end of a line. In G. C. van der Veer and G. Mulder (Eds), *Human-computer interaction: Psychonomic aspects*. Berlin: Springer-Verlag.

NASA. (1980). Spacelab display design and command usage guidelines (Report MSFC-PROC-711A). Huntsville, AL: George C. Marshall Space Flight Center.

Pace, B. J. (1984). Color combinations and contrast reversals on visual display units. *Proceedings of the 28th Annual Meeting of the Human Factors Society*, 326-330. Santa Monica, CA: Human Factors Society.

Pakin, S. E., and Wray, P. (1982). Designing screens for people to use easily. *Data Management*, July 1982, 36-41.

Pastoor, S. (1990). Legibility and subjective preferences for color combinations in text. *Human Factors, 32*, 157-171.

Payne, D. E. (1967). Readability of typewritten material: Proportional vs. standard spacing. *Journal of Typographic Research, 1(2)*, April 1967.

Perlman, G. (1987). An axiomatic model of information presentation. *Proceedings of the Human Factors Society 31st Annual Meeting*, 1229-1233. Santa Monica, CA: Human Factors Society. (Abstract: http://www. cis.ohio-state.edu/~perlman/hfeshci/ Abstracts/87:1229-1233.html)

Petersen, R., Banks, W. W., and Gertman, D. I. (1982). Performance-based evaluation of graphic displays for nuclear power plant control rooms. *Proceedings: Human Factors in Computer Systems* (Gaithersburg, MD), 182-189. New York: Association for Computing Machinery.

Poulton, E. C., and Brown, C. H. (1968). Rate of comprehension of an existing teleprinter output and of possible alternatives. *Journal of Applied Psychology, 52*, 16-21.

Radl, G. W. (1983). Experimental investigations for optimal presentation mode and colours of symbols on the CRT screen. In E. Grandjean and E. Vigliana (Eds), *Ergonomic aspects of visual display terminals*. London: Taylor & Francis.

Rehe, R. F. (1974). *Typography: How to make it more legible*. Carmel, Ind.: Design Research International.

Ringel, S., and Hammer, C. (1964). Information assimilation from alphanumeric displays: Amount and density of information presented (Tech Report TRN141). Washington, DC: US Army Personnel Research Office. (NTIS No. AD 601 973)

Rogers, Y. (1986). Evaluating the meaningfulness of icon sets to represent command operations. *Proceedings of HCI '86 Conference on People and Computers: Designing for Usability*, 586-603. London: British Computer Society.

Rogers, Y. (1993). Icons at the interface: Their usefulness. *Interacting with Computers: The Interdisciplinary Journal of Human-Computer Interaction, 1*, 105-117.

Rohr, G., and Keppel, E. (1984). Iconic interfaces: Where to use and how to construct. In *Human Factors in Organisational Design and Management*, 269-275. North Holland: Elsevier Science Publishers.

Rubinstein, R. (1988). *Digital Typography: An Introduction to Type and Composition for Computer System Design.* Reading, MA: Addison-Wesley.

Schwartz, D. R., and Howell, W. C. (1985). Optional stopping performance under graphic and numeric CRT formatting. *Human Factors, 27*, 433-444.

Sears, A. (1993). Layout appropriateness: A metric for evaluating user interface widget layout. *IEEE Transactions on Software Engineering, 19(7)*, 707-719. (Abstract: http://condor.depaul.edu/~asears/publications/la.html)

Sears, A. (1995). AIDE: A step toward metric-based interface development tools. *Proceedings of the ACM Symposium on User Interface Software and Technology (UIST'95)*, 101-110. New York: Association for Computing Machinery. (Abstract: http://condor.depaul. edu/~asears/publications/aide.html)

Shneiderman, B., Chimera, R., Jog, N., Stimart, R., and White, D. (1995). Evaluating spatial and textual style of displays. University of Maryland Department of Computer Science Technical Report # CS-TR-3451. (Abstract: ftp://ftp.cs.umd.edu/pub/papers/papers/3451 /3451.bib)

Smith, S. L. (1986). Standards versus guidelines for designing user interface software. *Behavior and Information Technology, 5*, 47-61.

Smith, S. L., and Goodwin, N. C. (1971). Blink coding for information display. *Human Factors, 13*, 283-290.

Smith, S. L., and Goodwin, N. C. (1972). Another look at blinking displays. *Human Factors, 14*, 345-347.

Smith, S. L., and Mosier, J. N. (1986). Guidelines for designing user interface software (Technical Report ESD-TR-86-278). Hanscom Air Force Base, MA: USAF Electronic Systems Division.

Smith, W. (1986). Computer color: Psychophysics, task application, and aesthetics. *Proceedings: International Scientific Conference: Work with Display Units*, Stockholm, Sweden, May 12-15, 1986, 561-564.

Snyder, H. L., Decker, J. J., Lloyd, C. J. C, and Dye, C. (1990). Effect of image polarity on VDT task performance. *Proceedings of the Human Factors Society 34th Annual Meeting,* 1447-1451. (Abstract: http://www.cis.ohio-state.edu/~perlman/hfeshci/Abstracts /90:1447-1451.html)

Spoto, C. G., and Babu, A. J. G. (1989). Highlighting in alphanumeric displays: The efficacy of monochrome methods. *Proceedings of the Human Factors Society 33rd Annual Meeting*, 370-374. Santa Monica, CA: Human Factors Society. (Abstract: http://www.cis.ohio-state.edu/~perlman/hfeshci/Abstracts/ 89:370-374.html)

Stewart, T. F. M. (1976). Displays and the software interface. Applied Ergonomics, 7.3, 137-146.

Streveler, D. J., and Wasserman, A. I. (1984). Quantitative measures of the spatial properties of screen designs. *Proceedings of INTERACT '84 Conference on Human-Computer Interaction*, London, England, Sept. 1984.

Streveler, D. J., and Harrison, P. B. (1984). Measuring the "goodness" of screen designs. *Proceedings of the Seventeenth Annual Hawaii International Conference on System Sciences, 1*, 423-430.

Streveler, D. J., and Harrison, P. B. (1985). Judging visual displays of medical information. *M.D. Computing, 2(2)*, 27-39.

Tanaka, T., Eberts, R. E., and Salvendy, G. (1990). Derivation and validation of a quantitative method for the analysis of consistency for interface design. *Proceedings of the Human Factors Society 34tht Annual Meeting*, 329-333. Santa Monica, CA: Human Factors Society.

Teitelbaum, R. C. and Granda, R. E. (1983). The effects of positional constancy on searching menus for information. *Proceedings of CHI '83 Conference on Human Factors in Computing Systems*, 150-153. New York: Association for Computing Machinery.

Thacker, P. (1986). *Tabular displays: A human factors study*. Doctoral dissertation, University of South Florida.

Tinker, M. A. (1955). Prolonged reading tasks in visual research. *Journal of Applied Psychology, 39*, 444-446.

Tinker, M. A. (1963). *Legibility of print*. Ames: Iowa State University Press.

Trollip, S. R., and Sales, G. (1986). Readability of computer-generated fill-justified text. *Human Factors, 28*, 159-163.

Tufte, E. R. (1983). *The visual display of quantitative information*. Cheshire, CT: Graphics Press.

Tufte, E. R. (1990). *Envisioning information*. Cheshire, CT: Graphics Press.

Tullis, T. S. (1981). An evaluation of alphanumeric, graphic, and color information displays. *Human Factors, 23*, 541-550.

Tullis, T. S. (1983). The formatting of alphanumeric displays: A review and analysis. *Human Factors, 25*, 657-682.

Tullis, T. S. (1984). *Predicting the Usability of Alphanumeric Displays*. Doctoral dissertation, Rice University, Houston, TX. 172 pages. Also summarized in Tullis, T. S. (1988).

Tullis, T. S. (1986a). *The Screen Analyzer*. Computer program.

Tullis, T. S. (1986b). Optimizing the usability of computer-generated displays. *Proceedings of HCI'86 Conference on People and Computers: Designing for Usability (York, England)*. London: British Computer Society.

Tullis, T. S. (1988). A system for evaluating screen formats: Research and application. In H. Hartson and D. Hix (Eds), *Advances in human-computer interaction, Vol. 2*, 214-286. Norwood, NJ: Ablex Publishing.

Tullis, T. S., Boynton, J. L., and Hersh, H. (1995). The readability of fonts in the Windows environment. Interactive poster session at the CHI '95 Conference on Human Factors in Computing Systems. New York: ACM. (http://www.acm.org/sigchi/chi95/ Electronic documnts/ intpost/tst_bdy.htm)

Vartabedian, A. G. (1971). The effects of letter size, case, and generation method on CRT display search time. *Human Factors, 13*, 363-368.

White, J. V. (1990). *Color for the electronic age*. New York: Watson-Guptill Publications.

Williams, A. R., Seidenstein, S., and Goddard, C. J. (1980). Human factors survey and analysis of electric power control centers. *Proceedings of the Human Factors Society 24th Annual Meeting*, 276-279. Santa Monica, CA: Human Factors Society.

Wiggins, R. H. (1967). Effects of three typographical variables on speed of reading. *Journal of Typographic Research, 1(1)*, 5-18.

Wolf, C. E. (1986). BNA "HN" command display: Results of user evaluation. Unpublished technical report, Unisys Corporation, Irvine, CA.

Yorchak, J. P., Allison, J. E., and Dodd, V. S. (1984). A new tilt on computer generated space situation displays. *Proceedings of the Human Factors Society 28th Annual Meeting*, 894-898. Santa Monica, CA: Human Factors Society.

Zahn, C. T. (1971). Graph-theoretical methods for detecting and describing Gestalt clusters. *IEEE Transactions on Computers, C-20*, 68-86.

Handbook of Human-Computer Interaction
Second, completely revised edition
M. Helander, T.K. Landauer, P. Prabhu (eds.)

Chapter 24

Design of Menus

Kenneth R. Paap and Nancy J. Cooke
Department of Psychology
New Mexico State University
Las Cruces, New Mexico, USA

24.1 Menu-Driven Interfaces

A precise, complete, and universally agreed upon definition of a menu is probably not needed in order to discuss the theoretical and applied research that is relevant to the design of menus. The distinction between menu-driven, command-based, and direct-manipulation interfaces can be a fuzzy one. The fuzziness comes about because menus have many characteristic features, but seem to lack defining features that are either necessary or sufficient. For our purposes, a menu will be defined as a set of options, displayed on the screen, where the selection and execution of one (or more) of the options results in a change in the state of the interface.

It is useful to consider the prototypical characteristics of a menu-driven interface. Menu panels usually consist of a list options. The options may consist of words or icons. The word or icon is not an arbitrary symbol, but conveys some information about the consequences of selecting that option. Sometimes the options are elaborated upon with verbal descriptors. When one of the options is selected and executed a system action occurs that usually results in a visual change on the screen. The total set of options is usually distributed over many different menu panels. This allows the system to prompt the user with options that are likely to be useful and to hide options that are unlikely or illegal. However, layering the options across many menu panels also requires that the user be able to navigate between panels in order to find options that are not available on the current panel. This brief description of a prototypical menu-driven interface highlights the fundamental issues of menu design that will be discussed in this chapter. That is, how can designers choose good names (icons or descriptors) for options, how should the options be organized within and between panels, and which selection technique should be implemented.

The relative importance of each of these characteristics may depend on the general purpose of the software. Two broad classes of software can be considered. The primary purpose of one class is to generate a product, e.g. a report from a spreadsheet or a document from a text editor. These applications tend to be highly interactive and selecting options from a menu or typing commands provide the means to create the product. In contrast, other programs are more passive and have as their primary purpose the retrieval of information. Information systems such as the British Prestel, Canadian Telidon, Dutch Viditel, and French Antiope are prototypes of this second class.

24.2 Designing a Single Menu Panel

Given a set of options that are to be presented on a specific menu panel, two important factors remain to be determined: the description of each option and the ordering or grouping of the options. The best design depends on the type of search and comparison operations that are likely to occur as users consider the contents of the menu panel: identity, equivalence, and class-inclusion.

24.2.1 Three Types of Comparison Operations

The first stage of interaction with any menu panel involves the user forming an intention (Norman, 1984) or a goal (Card, Moran, and Newell, 1983). For the present purpose, formulating a goal will be considered equivalent to defining a search target. The user directs his fixation to one of the options and evaluates the option in relation to the goal. If the option does not match the target, then attention must be redirected and search continues. Three types of comparison operations commonly occur when users are confronted with a menu panel.

The fastest and most simple type of search occurs when users have generated a specific target that is literally displayed as one of the options. When this situation exists, the user can engage in identity matching, i.e. the user compares each option to the specific target held in memory to see if they are identical. This type of matching is fast because a holistic comparison can be made on low-level visual codes. Posner (1982) provides a rich database and theoretical framework for evaluating the different types of matching operations. Identity matching is likely to occur when the user knows precisely how the target is presented on the menu. For example, when a user knows that the target *delete* will be listed as *delete* and not as *erase, drop, zap* or anything else.

The other two types of comparison operations require a semantic evaluation of the relationship between the target and an option. One of these, termed class-inclusion matching, is likely to occur at the root or other top-level panels of a hierarchical menu organization. The root or home panel frequently consists of a list of large and fairly abstract categories. Thus, users must make judgments about class inclusion, i.e. whether the target is an instance of the category specified by an option. For example, is *delete* an instance of the category *editing commands* ?

The other type of semantic search, termed equivalence search, is more likely to occur at the leaves or bottom levels of menu systems. Equivalence search occurs when the user knows what he wants, but doesn't know what it is called. Sometimes the target for an equivalence match will be formulated as a fairly abstract` intention. For example, the intention may be semantically equivalent to the phrase *a command that gets rid of a string*. In this case the equivalence search can be thought of as looking for an option whose name implies the actions specified by the phrase. On other occasions the fuzzy intention may lead to the generation of a candidate name, e.g. *erase*. When this happens the equivalence search can be thought of as a search for the candidate itself or for a synonym. Whether searching for the equivalent of a phrase or a name, the user can't rely on a fast holistic identity search, but must engage in a slower semantic analysis of the relationship between the target and each option.

Search time for any type of matching operation can be reduced by organizing the options so that the scope of the search can be limited. The best type of organization will depend upon the type of search that is likely to occur. If the user has a specific target in mind and engages in rapid identity matching, then an alphabetical ordering may be best. Alphabetical orders are very precise and people have a wealth of experience with this type of ordering. However, one can't effectively narrow the search for a word in the dictionary, a name in the telephone book, or an option on a menu unless you know precisely how the entry will be listed. Thus, when there is uncertainty about the precise form of the entry and users must engage in equivalence matching, a categorical organization may be better than an alphabetical ordering.

In summary, three types of search and comparison operations are common to menu interaction: (1) identity matching, (2) class-inclusion, and (3) equivalence. The best organization of the options on a menu panel is likely to depend on which type of comparison occurs most often. The next three subsections examine the experimental evidence for each of the three types of comparison operations.

Identity Matching

There are two circumstances under which a designer can be quite confident that users will be engaged in an identity search for a specific target that actually matches the menu option. The first is the case where the options correspond to a well known set of items that have conventional names, e.g. a list of the states, the months of years, etc. Users will also be able to search for specific targets if the menu panel will be used extensively and the users can quickly learn and remember the name of each option.

In other circumstances one should be very cautious before assuming that users will be able to successfully generate a specific target that matches the corresponding menu option. It is particularly easy to fall into the trap of believing that what strikes you as an obvious name for a menu option will be the same name that users think of when formulating their search target. Furnas, Landauer, Gomez, and Dumais (1984) asked people to name things in a variety of domains: commands for text editing, index words for cooking recipes, categories for want ads, and descriptions of common objects. The probability of any two people generating the same name or description ranged from 8% for the editing commands to 18% for the recipes. Experts were no better than others at generating names with high inter-subject agreement.

The scope of an identity search could be substantially reduced if the options are listed in alphabetical order and users capitalize on the first letter of the target in order to begin their search in the target area. Perlman (Experiment 1, 1984) reports that this advantage is not as substantial as one might expect. Subjects search through menus of 5, 10, 15, or 20 single-word options that were either randomly or alphabetically ordered. The words appearing on a list of *n* options were chosen so that there would be one word beginning with each of the first *n* letters of the alphabet. To the left of each item was either a '<' or a '>'. The task was to find a target that was displayed at the beginning of each trial and to indicate when it was found by pressing the corresponding arrow-key.

When the options were ordered randomly, search time was a linear increasing function of menu size. Each increment of five options resulted in about an additional half second of search time. As expected, search times were significantly faster when the words were in alphabetical order. For the small to medium size menus, alphabetizing cut the search rate by about one half.

The results confirm the expectation that the scope of the search can be significantly reduced when users formulate a specific target and conduct an identity search through an alphabetized list of options. However, the results also suggest that users are not very accurate in jumping to the target region, even under the best possible conditions. Recall that in the alphabetized list the options consisted of single words and there was one word starting with each of the first *n* letters of the alphabet. In real applications there will be key words starting with the same letter and many gaps where none of the key words start with the next letter of the alphabet. These uncertainties should make it even more difficult to jump directly to the target region. Even in Perlman's ideal alphabetical lists the advantage of the alphabetized list over the random list was nested primarily in those trials where the target was located near the top of the alphabetized list.

Card (1982) has investigated search times for an 18 item menu that was organized alphabetically, categorically, or randomly. The options were single word commands that were arranged vertically. Horizontal lines separated the list into groups of two to four options. In the categorized condition each group contained commands with related functions, e.g. insert, delete, replace. Specific targets were presented and subjects were required to find the target and select it with a mouse.

The mean total time after the first block of 43 trials was 0.8 seconds for the alphabetical order and 3.2 seconds for the random order. The average search time (1.3 seconds) for the categorical organization was about a half second slower than the alphabetical order, but nearly 2 seconds faster than the random order. Thus, Card's results support the conclusion that organized menus are much better than a random list of options and that alphabetical orders are somewhat better than functional groupings when users search for specific targets.

In a second experiment Card videotaped eye movements of subjects searching through the same 18-item menu lists. He then used an extension of the Kendall and Wodinsky (1960) search model to analyze differences in eye movement parameters associated with the different organizations and with practice. As expected, the parameter estimates show that more fixations are required to find the target on a random list than on an organized list. For the first block of trials users made 2.8, 4.5, and 11.3 fixations for the alphabetical, functional, and random conditions, respectively. After 20 blocks of practice (over 800 selections from the same menu) the differences due to organization have disappeared and the target is always found in the first fixation. If the user knows exactly what he is looking for and has extensive practice with a specific menu panel, he will know exactly where to look and the organization no longer matters. Practice effects, in general, are discussed under a separate heading later in the chapter.

Equivalence Matching

In our armchair analysis at the beginning of this section, it was hypothesized that uncertainty about the specific form of an entry usually induces a slow semantic search where the equivalence of each target and option is compared. Not only will equivalence matching take longer than identity matching, but also the optimal organization may be different. When uncertainty leads to equivalence matching the scope of the search can be restricted with categorical groupings, but not with alphabetical orders. Pushing this view to the limit, if the user carries out a pure semantic analysis of each option and has no specific candidates in mind, then an alphabetized list should be no better than a randomized list. However, if the options are grouped into visually and conceptually distinct categories, then a semantic search can be initiated in the appropriate group and appreciable time can be saved.

McDonald, Stone, and Liebelt (1983) were the first investigators to use both specific and fuzzy targets and, consequently, to compare identity searching to equivalence searching. All of their menu panels displayed 64-items arranged in four columns of 16. Items were instances drawn from the categories food, animals, minerals, and cities. Some groups of subjects received the specific name of the target while other groups received a fuzzy target consisting of a short definition.

Five organizations were tested. Two of the organizations treated all 64 items as a single list and either randomized or alphabetized them. The remaining three organizations grouped the 16 instances of each category into separate columns, but differed in how the items within a group were arranged. The instances within each group were either randomized, alphabetized, or arranged so that the items most related to one another were closer together. One might note that to take advantage of the categorized organization a user must first find a class-inclusion match between the target and the four categories and then initiate either identity or equivalence matching through the 16 options in the appropriate column.

Of interest are the results for the first block of 64 trials since McDonald et al, like Card, found that all effects of organization disappear with extensive practice with the same menu. Response times for the specific targets yield results similar to those reported by Card. Both categorical and alphabetical organization are much better (about 4 seconds) than a random order. However, when targets were fuzzy rather than explicit the categorical organization was significantly better than either alphabetized or random lists.

The implications of McDonald et al.'s results are important. If users are likely to know the name of what they are looking for, good performance is obtained with either an alphabetized or a categorized menu. However, if the user's are uncertain about the name of what they're looking for, categorized lists are likely to be more effective than alphabetized lists.

Class-Inclusion Matching

The root panel of a menu system usually consists of a set of options that specify large abstract categories and users must make class-inclusion judgments in order to access specific targets at lower levels (e.g. is a carrot an instance of the category flower?). Category decisions will be faulty if there is conceptual overlap between the categories and many targets might belong to two or more categories. Another problem arises if some targets don't seem to fit well into any of the available categories. A series of experiments by Somberg and Picardi (1983) show that it takes significantly longer to enter the correct category when the target is a less familiar exemplar of the category. Each trial began with the presentation of an instance from an unknown category. A short menu consisting of the names of five categories followed. The task was to decide, as rapidly as possible, which category the instance belonged to and to enter the corresponding identifier on a numeric keypad. The instance was either typical or atypical. For example, for the category bird the instance might be either robin or penguin. Accuracy was high, well over 90%, for both types of instances, but typical instances could be matched to the appropriate category 200 msec faster than atypical instances.

24.2.2 Aiding the Comparison Operator

Adding Descriptors

Most errors in menu-driven systems occur because the meaning of the options is not clear to the user. One method of increasing the clarity is to append an expanded descriptor to each key word or phrase. Lee,

Whalen, McEwen, and Latremouille (Experiment 6, 1984) report a direct comparison between the same set of options with and without descriptors.

In an investigation of the Videotex system, experts were asked to generate key words or phrases for the root index page. Three of these index pages were tested and compared to three other pages that contained identical key words, but also included a descriptor that consisted of a list of the options from the next level of the hierarchy. For example, one root index page listed the seven options: General Interest Guide, Business Guide, Canadian Government, Emergency, User's Guide, Telidon Explanation, and Telephone Numbers. The modified index page expanded the meaning of each option, e.g. General Interest Guide: News, Weather, Sport, Entertainment, Market Place, Employment, Travel, Leisure, Advice.

Subjects were given ten search questions for each menu and were also asked to rank order their preference for each index page. Although the options were selected by experts with great care, the overall error rate was 39%. However, the menus with descriptors were much preferred and had fewer errors. For each pair of pages, subjects made 82% fewer errors on pages with descriptors than on those without. The results clearly demonstrate that descriptors can be very effective when users have had limited experience with a menu panel that consists of options corresponding to fairly general and abstract categories. Thus, under these conditions descriptors may be a good idea. There are, of course, some costs associated with descriptors. Search times are probably somewhat longer and they take up space.

A similar experiment by Dumais and Landauer (1983) forces us to hedge our bets somewhat on the usefulness of descriptors for a set of general categories. In the first phase of this study a group of subjects sorted the names of the 307 largest sections of a Yellow Pages directory into five categories. A hierarchical clustering technique was used to partition the items into five supercategories. In the second phase a group of experts were asked to generate key words or phrases for the five supercategories that might serve as the top level of a menu access system. In the third and final phase of the study subjects were given 72 of the items from the original set and asked to select the category to which they belonged. If the item did not seem to fit in any category it could be placed in a miscellaneous category.

For different groups of subjects the categories were defined either on the basis of the name alone, the name plus example, or examples alone. The name alone condition (key phrases actually) was analogous to Lee et al.'s root index without descriptors while the name plus examples group was analogous to Lee et al.'s root index with descriptors. The overall error rate of 50% shows that the categories were somewhat more abstract and difficult than those used by Lee et al. Accordingly, one might expect even greater benefit from descriptors that provide a list of examples. Contrary to this expectation, the addition of three examples increased accuracy by only 6%. It is not the case that the examples are not informative. Three examples alone (whether chosen by experts or randomly) provide the same level of accuracy as the category label alone. Rather than a lack of information, it appears that the examples provide very little information beyond that which could be inferred from the category name alone.

There are two possible reasons for the discrepancy between the Dumais and Landauer study and the similar investigation by Lee et al. First, Lee et al.'s descriptors consisted of the options presented at the next level of the hierarchy. In contrast, the examples provided by Dumais and Landauer correspond to the leaves, rather than a middle level, of a hierarchical menu system. Second, Lee et al. listed as many as 11 items in their descriptors, whereas Dumais and Landauer systematically manipulated the number of examples across a range of only 0 to 3. Perhaps some categories need even more examples to provide the user with an understanding of the range of items contained in that category.

A study by Snowberry, Parkinson, and Sisson (1985) supports the view that errors can be significantly reduced by providing the options presented at the next level of hierarchy. The details of the procedure used by these investigators are discussed in a later section on the depth-breadth tradeoff. For present purposes, it should be noted that knowledge of the upcoming options was quite useful in making choices at the higher levels (e.g. errors reduced from about 14% to about 4%), but were not as helpful at the lower levels (e.g. errors reduced from about 8% to 3%). Kreigh, Pesot, and Halcomb (1990) also failed to find any systematic benefits for adding descriptors.

In a second experiment Dumais and Landauer used only two of the original conditions (one or three examples with no explicit category name) and eliminated the miscellaneous category. Performance improved by 45% when the miscellaneous category was omitted. The implication drawn by Dumais and Landauer from this comparison is straightforward, but good advise:

the presence of even one vague name can create a lot of confusion and entice navigators to the wrong path like a siren's song.

The degradation of performance produced by adding a vague category name like *miscellaneous* can be taken as a specific example of the powerful context effects that occur, i.e. the goodness of a name or phrase is very much determined by the other names appearing on the menu panel. It is useful to classify naming shortcomings into two categories. A name is too narrow if it implies fewer actions or objects than are actually controlled by the selection of that option. In contrast, a name is too imprecise if it implies more actions or objects than the option controls. However, imprecision does not become extremely costly until the bogus scope of one option encroaches on the legitimate territory of another option. Some progress has been made in the analysis of context effects for the names of commands (Carroll, 1982; Rosenberg, 1983), but more work needs to be done on contextual interactions between menu options.

Using Icons

Targets or categories can also be represented or supplemented with icons. Icons afford three possible advantages over verbal options. First, if icons replace words as target alternatives, then there are situations in which the display can be searched in parallel and there is no cost associated with having a large number of options on a single panel (Wolfe, 1994). Second, even if users are considering one option at a time and performing an equivalence match, categorizations of pictures can be faster than of words (Pellegrino, Rosinski, Chiesi, and Siegel, 1977). Third, icons, like verbal descriptors and examples, can provide additional information that increases the accuracy of selections. This makes icons sound too good to be true, and owing to some inherent tradeoffs it is, indeed, impossible to reap all of the above benefits at the same time.

Parallel search is likely to occur when the target possesses a global cue that is distinctive from all the alternatives. Arend, Muthig, and Wandmacher (1987) compared distinctive icons to both words and *representational* icons in a search task where the number of options was either six or twelve. Search time for the distinctive icons was independent of menu size and this produced a very large advantage for the menus with twelve options. Both words and *representational* icons showed a marked effect of menu size and did not differ from one another. Wandmacher and Muller also reported a speed advantage of icons over words, with no loss in accuracy.

There is a likely tradeoff in the design of distinctive icons. When the distinctiveness of an icon is enhanced by using simple figures that vary with respect to features like global shape, size, and orientation; it is likely that the simplification will make the icon more abstract and, thus, more error prone. On the other, more *representational* icons will be scanned sequentially, just like words.

One might speculate that you could have your cake and eat it too by adding distinctive icons to verbal labels. In an early study on the benefits of adding icons Muter and Mayson (1986) reported that appending a picture of a typical category member (e.g., an electric kettle) to a category label (e.g., appliances) reduced error rates from 5.6% to 2.8%. However, there was not a concomitant speed up in search time and a similar improvement in accuracy was achieved by adding a verbal example. MacGregor (1992) used menus similar to Muter and Mayson and replicated their result at both high and low levels of a menu hierarchy. The labels alone condition was far more difficult in the MacGregor study (32% errors), but both studies showed the adding more information reduced errors by about 40 to 50% and had no effect on search time. The results across these two experiments are consistent and simple: supplementing category labels with icons is equivalent to adding a one-word example.

A related study by Egido and Patterson (1988) investigated the use of videodisc pictures as options or as added information to verbal options. Subjects were required to navigate through a menu hierarchy until they found a target picture. The upper level options were either pictures, verbal labels or labels plus pictures. The bottom level always consisted of just pictures. The target domains were marine creatures, birds, and flowers.

Consider first the comparison between pictures only and labels only. Labels required significantly less search time compared to pictures! Despite the relatively poor performance obtained with pictures alone, adding a picture to a label should be as beneficial as adding an icon to a label. Experiment 2 confirms this expectation. Pictures plus labels required the fewest extra decisions and resulted in the most completed tasks. These gains in accuracy were somewhat offset by the fact that adding pictures to labels slowed search time compared to labels only. One should not assume that the gains in accuracy had anything to do with inherent differences between pictures and words. The picture was an example of the instances found under the labeled category. For example, a picture of a whale might be added to the category vertebrate. Thus, the benefit of adding a picture might be nothing more than the benefit that sometimes accrues from adding an example. The study would be more diagnostic if it included an option plus verbal example condition like that used by Muter and Mayson (1986) and MacGregor (1992).

The somewhat surprising recommendation is that icons or pictures should be used very selectively. They are not likely to support parallel search unless they stand alone without a verbal label. If they stand alone they should be easy to interpret and remember. Adding enough detail about both the object and action to make the icon highly representational and easily understood may eliminate its visual distinctiveness. Icons that visually dominate their verbal label are used in many applications, but have not been studied experimentally. Perhaps, these hybrids could support parallel search without sacrificing accuracy.

24.2.3 Search Strategies

The preceding section on types of comparison operations focuses on the type of judgment the user makes when an option is evaluated. This section examines a related, but different issue, viz., the strategies used to determine which options will be evaluated and the order of evaluation. Two questions need to be answered. First, are search-time functions logarithmic or linear? Second, how does a user decide to stop searching and execute a selection response? It is useful to consider a general framework for expressing the time it takes to search a single menu panel (ST) of b options and make a response:

$$ST = u(b) \tag{1}$$

Intuition provides an easy guide to the prediction that search time will monotonically increase as a function of the total number of options that must be considered, but what should be the shape of the function?

Logarithmic Models

Landauer and Nachbar (1985) predicted that the search time function will usually be logarithmic, particularly when the options enjoy some type of logical ordering, users have some familiarity with the menu system, and the comparison operation is not unusually complex and slow. The basis for the prediction is the assumption that the Hick-Hyman Law (Hick, 1952; Hyman, 1953) should apply to the cognitive operations that take place when users search through a menu and select an option:

$$RT = c + k \log_2 b \tag{2}$$

where RT is human reaction time, b is the number of response alternatives, and c and k are constants. Norman (1991) echoes this prediction when he states that ".... the results of choice reaction time studies suggest that decision and keypress time is best described by a log model (p. 199)."

Landauer and Nachbar (1985) investigated the search-time function in a study that required subjects to make a series of class-inclusion matches, but the classification task was, by design, very easy. Specifically, subjects were searching for a target number and each option was a range of numbers. Unlike the categories that appear on the root panel of most menus, there would be no uncertainty whether the target number belonged in a given category.

Details of the experimental procedure are as follows. Subjects were to navigate through a series of panels until they reached a target number. Each panel consisted of alternating blue and red stripes. Starting from the top, the number on each blue stripe increased by a fixed interval. Subjects were asked to choose the range that contained the target number by touching the red stripe between the two values closest to the target. The next panel sub-divided the selected range until finally a panel was reached that contained the target in a list of consecutive integers. The number of options per panel was manipulated by displaying either 2, 4, 8, or 16 red stripes per panel.

There were 4096 integers at the leaves of the tree. Accordingly, if there were 2 options per panel, then the options on the top panel would represent the ranges 1 to 2048 and 2049 to 4096. If the first range was selected the next panel would offer the ranges to 1 to 1024 and 1025 to 2048, etc. With only 2 ranges per panel, 12 selections were required to navigate to the lowest level. In contrast, only three selections were required when each panel listed 16 ranges. In a second block of trials subjects performed the same task, but 4096 words were used instead of digits. In this condition ranges were specified as segments of the alphabet.

Figure 1 shows response time as a function of the number of alternatives for the second session of the Landauer and Nachbar study and the study by Perlman (Experiment 1, 1984) that also manipulated list length. (Data points were estimated from the corresponding functions in the first figure of each report.) Inspection

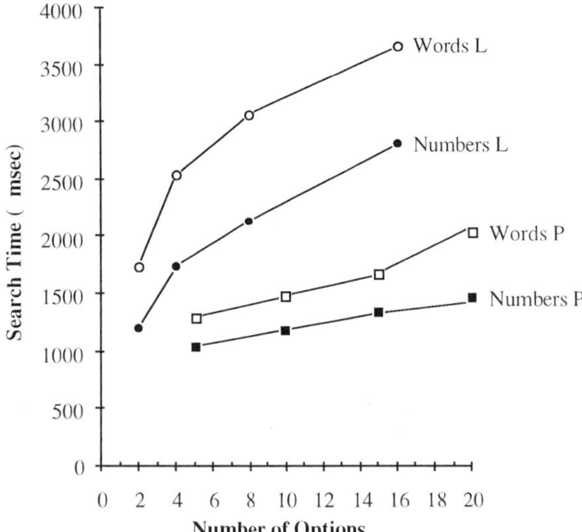

Figure 1. Response time on a single panel as a function of *the number of options (either sequential numbers or alphabetized words) on the panel. The two functions labeled L are from the second session of the Landauer and Nachbar (1985) study and the two labeled P are from the sorted conditions of Perlamn's 1984) Experiment 1. Values were estimated from the corresponding functions of figures presented in the original sources.*

of Figure 1 shows that Perlman's functions appear to be linear, whereas Landauer and Nachbar's functions appear to be log-linear. Are these log-linear relations typical of response-time functions for users selecting options from menu panels that consist of a single list of alphabetized or numbered options? The evidence is mixed at best.

The departure from linearity observed in Perlman's data with lists of 20 options is in the direction opposite from that predicted from a log-linear relation (cf. Figure 1). Why did Perlman find a linear (or near-linear) function? Because subjects usually failed to use the alphabetical order to reduce the scope of the search. Recall that Perlman reports that the advantage of the alphabetized list over the random list was nested primarily in those trials where the target was located near the beginning of the alphabet. This is consistent with Perlman's conclusion that subjects will use simple strategies, such as a self-terminating search begun at one end of the list or the other. It is entirely possible that Landauer and Nachbar's log-linear functions are limited to the highly artificial range-reduction task that was used in their study. Given that subjects could learn to predict the values and locations of the options on the upcoming panel and that there was a full second between response to one panel and the presentation of the next, one suspects that most of the cognitive components to the choice task were completed before the panel ever appeared. One might further suspect, as does Perlman (personal communication, January 10, 1989), that the sophisticated strategy was only adopted when there were only two choices per panel, as this is the only case where it is easy to perform the mental arithmetic. Perlman's suspicion is based on a careful examination of Figure 1. If one ignores the data points corresponding to two options per panel, then the function for Numbers appears perfectly linear and the function for Letters appears nearly linear. Thus, in contrast to Norman's belief that the preponderance of data favors the logarithmic model, Perlman is now reluctant to consider even Landauer and Nachbar's data as non-linear.

Assuming that Perlman is right and that little or no evidence exists for logarithmic functions in visual search, one might wonder why one of engineering psychology's few laws fails to apply when subjects search through a list of options for a target. With the benefit of hindsight, one can see that the visual search task falls within the fuzzy boundaries of known restrictions to the Hick-Hyman law. In his seminal book on cognitive psychology, Neisser (1967) observes that the Hick-Hyman law fails to apply when letters, numbers, or words are the stimuli, and their names are the responses; or when the stimuli and responses are otherwise highly compatible and well practiced. A user engaged in an identity search is, of course, doing nothing more than searching for a name.

Perhaps even more important is the fact that users scanning a panel of options are engaged in visual search not memory search. Demonstrations of the Hick-Hyman law usually involve the presentation of a single stimulus: a light in some position, a color, a symbol, a picture, or a face. With the exception of the alphanumeric material noted above, reaction time to a single stimulus is usually a logarithmic function of the number of stimuli in the experimental set. Thus, human decision time follows the Hick-Hyman law when subjects are answering the question: Which of n stimuli is this one? In contrast, searching through a list of options for a target is more likely to be a linear function of the number of options examined.

Linear Search: When to Stop?

Linear searches can also be characterized as exhaustive (a single pass through the entire list of b options) or self-terminating (search ends when an option exceeds a match criterion). Furthermore, self-terminating searches

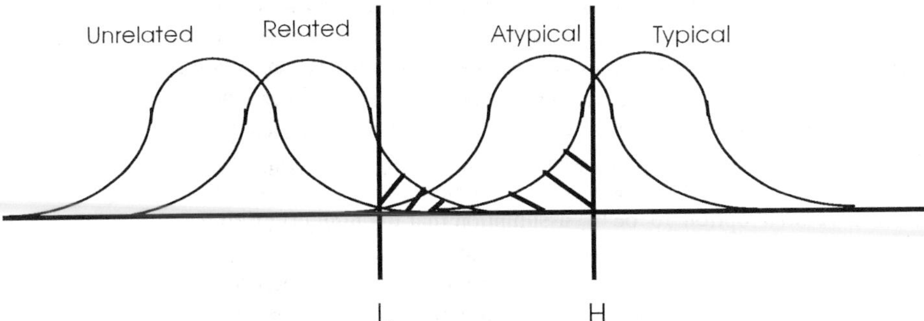

Figure 2. A dual-criterion model showing distributions of the likelihood that a target belongs to the category described by an option. *Exceeding the high-criterion (H) terminates the search and leads to the selection of the current option. Exceeding the low-criterion (L) places the option on a candidate list for later reconsideration. Falling below L eliminates the option from further consideration.*

may permit only one examination of an option or permit additional, redundant evaluations.

For the most simple case of exhaustive search, search time (ST) can be expressed as:

$$ST = (bt + k) \tag{3}$$

where b is the number of options, t is processing time per option, and k is human response time. If users adopt a self-terminating strategy and the options are examined in random order, then the target will be found, on average, midway through the list:

$$E(O) = (b + 1) / 2 \tag{4}$$

where E(O) is the expected number of options examined. Thus, a self-terminating strategy will cut the search rate in half:

$$ST = [\ (b + 1) / 2\ ]\ t + k \tag{5}$$

MacGregor, Lee, and Lam (1986) were the first to investigate factors that influence the choice of a search strategy. MacGregor et al. refer to their model as a criterion-based decision model since a key assumption is that the type of search will be determined by the outcome of comparisons between processed options and a criterion. The model owes an intellectual debt to a model of semantic verification proposed by Smith, Shoben, and Rips (1974) which, in turn, borrowed some machinery from a recognition-memory model first developed by Atkinson and Juola (1974). An adaptation of these models is shown in Figure 2.

The distributions lie along a continuum that represents the likelihood that the target might belong to the category specified by an option. Obviously, this model is concerned with the class-inclusion matches that occur above the bottom level of a menu hierarchy. Any comparison that yields a probability less than the low-criterion (L) will lead to the permanent rejection of that alternative and a continuation of the search. An option that exceeds the high criterion (H) will be immediately chosen and produce, by definition, a self-terminating search. (The existence of two criteria is implied by MacGregor et al, but not explicit.) Options that exceed L, but not H, are considered candidates. If after processing all the options, only one candidate has been nominated, then that option is selected and an exhaustive search has occurred. If multiple candidates exist, then some of the options may be examined again and the result is a partially redundant search in which the number of items processed actually exceeds the number of options on the panel. Although MacGregor et al. do not explicitly allow for it, it would also be reasonable to assume that when multiple candidates exist, users sometimes select the most likely candidate. This provides a second pathway to an exhaustive search and reduces the proportion of redundant searches.

The two distributions furthest to the right represent valid options that actually lead to the nested target. The distribution labeled *typical* represents probabilities associated with targets that are typical of the named category. For example, because robin is a typical instance of bird the subjective probability of finding robin under the option bird is higher than that for penguin and other atypical instances. More of the *typical* distribution lies to the right of H and, accordingly, there should be more self-terminating searches when targets appear typical than atypical.

The two distributions on the left represent invalid options that will not lead to the target. The distribution labeled *related* represents probabilities associated with targets that have some semantic relationship to the category, whereas the distribution labeled *unrelated* has no obvious relationship. When a category listed as an option appears related to the target it should be harder to reject and, indeed, Figure 1 shows a case where a non-trivial proportion of the right-hand tail lies to the right of L and causes a *related* option to be treated as a serious candidate. This will often lead to a redundant search when multiple candidates emerge. In a well-designed menu system the category names are highly distinctive from one another and there will be little overlap between the distributions for correct and incorrect options.

MacGregor et al. assume that the two criteria will be set higher for panels with few options. The rationale for this assumption is that the criterion probability should be higher than the a priori probability. Thus, for a panel with only two options a sensible criterion must be greater than .5. If the value of the criteria are inversely proportional to the number of options, then several predictions follows. For example, the percentage of self-terminating searches should start low (because there are few chances to exceed the high value of H) and increase with menu size. Conversely, the percentage of exhaustive searches should monotonically decrease because as b grows there will be more chances to exceed a lower value for L. These predictions are, in general, confirmed in an experiment where subjects can visibilize only one option at a time. This procedure makes it possible to determine which options have been examined and the order in which they are examined.

It is also interesting to note that for fairly complex videotex options (processing time per option = .88 s) and unfamiliar panels, the mean number of options processed in this experiment was 2.2, 5.1, 10.6, and 17.8 for the 2, 4, 8 and 16 option panels, respectively. Thus, a good estimate for E(O) under these conditions is 1.2 b. Self-terminating searches were rare in this environment, but they are likely to be more common if users can engage in identity matching, particularly on panels they are familiar with.

The criterion model has been extended in recent studies by Pierce, Parkinson, and Sisson (1992) and Pierce, Sisson, and Parkinson (1992). The first study is primarily an empirical report that investigates the effects of number of alternatives, omission probability, target-category typicality, and category distinctiveness. The second study uses the empirical data to estimate parameters for a dual-criterion model similar to the one shown in Figure 2. More specifically, the work by Pierce and his associates shows how characteristics of a menu design can influence the placement of the two criteria. In turn, the location of the criteria determine both the proportion of self-terminating, exhaustive, and redundant search and the quality of system performance.

The empirical study validated MacGregor et al.'s assumption that the high criterion becomes more lax as the number of options per page increases. When the number of options grows large there is a large cost associated with linear and exhaustive search. Accordingly, users should be more willing to reduce the H criterion as this will increase the probability that some comparison will exceed H and terminate the search. Indeed, the proportion of self-terminating searches increased as the number of options per page increased. In contrast, increasing the number of alternatives induces subjects to adopt a more strict low criterion. The post hoc rationale for this is that in the face of a large number of alternatives, of which one is correct and the rest are incorrect, you want to protect yourself from compiling a big list of viable candidates. Despite this adjustment toward a more strict value of L as the number of options increase, the results show a concomitant increase in the number of redundant searches and a decrease in the number of exhaustive searches. When users complete the scan of a long list of options they may no longer remember the details of their earlier evaluations and feel compelled to recheck the most likely candidates.

Pierce and his associates also manipulated the degree to which targets were typical of the correct category by pairing targets that appeared at Level 6 of a hierarchy initially developed by Miller (1981) to either a test page taken from the nearby Level 5 or the more distant and abstract Level 3. For example, the target *rose* would require the selection of *flower* in the typical condition, but the selection of *agriculture* in the atypical condition. The data showed that increasing typicality leads to an increase in the frequency of self-terminating search with concomitant reductions in the frequency of both exhaustive and redundant searches. The increase in the number of self-terminating searches is expected from the model shown in Figure 2 since typical cases will exceed the H criterion more often than atypical cases. The modeling exercise suggests that changes in typicality do not induce subjects to shift the H criterion.

Category distinctiveness was manipulated by selecting options that were either near or far from each other at higher levels in the hierarchy. A set of four nearby alternatives might be: *flower*, *vegetable*, *grain*, and *grazing*. A set of more distant alternatives might be: *flower*, *skeletal*, *eastern*, and *music*. Thus, if the target was *rose*, the three incorrect alternatives in the distant set would be completely unrelated and, as shown in Figure 2, these options should generate values less than L and lead to easy rejection. Consistent with this analysis, the data showed an increase on all measures of accuracy and a reduction in the number of redundant searches.

Another factor manipulated by Pierce's group was omission probability, the percentage of trials in which all the options were incorrect: 0%, 12.5%, 25%, and 37.5%. This is an interesting manipulation and has relevance for situations when users are likely to generate targets without certain knowledge that the system affords the target function or contains the target information. The results suggest that the frustration associated with frequent failures to find the target have deleterious side effects. Users become unwilling to reconsider possible candidates and this leads to a decrease in the hit rate when the target really is nested under one of the alternatives. In terms of the model's parameters this shift in search strategy occurs because users adopt a more strict L criterion.

The dual-criterion models holds a lot of promise with regard to increasing our understanding of what induces users to adopt different search strategies. However, all of the empirical determinations of search type that have been used to develop and test the model have relied on the sequential visibilization technique. This technique is, of course, artificial and may not reveal the same search strategies that occur when users can see all of the options on a page at the same time. To their credit, both groups of investigators have shown that the sequential visibilization format does not differ from the normal simultaneous format with regard to measures of accuracy. For example, the effect of number of options per page on the hit rate does not interact with display format.

Nonetheless, the planning and execution of eye movements is much faster than moving a cursor to the next desired option. Planning eye movements may also be more automatic in the sense of requiring less processing capacity and involve less conscious awareness. A study reported by Paap, Noel, McDonald, and Roske-Hofstrand (1987) strongly suggests that users may naturally search a display with their eyes in a more haphazard style than they do with their hand. In the Paap et al. experiment subjects searched for fuzzy targets through displays of 32 instances that were organized into either four or eight categories. Category labels appears above the instances in each category. Subjects rarely exhausted one category before peeking in another category. Furthermore, long saccades to the opposite side of the screen frequently landed on an instance in another category rather than a category label. Subjects evaluated the promise of this new category on the basis of the first example and either jumped to a new category or started an upward or downward scan within the current category. Another departure from patterns observed in sequential visibilization was that self-terminating searches often terminated one or two instances beyond the selected option. Perhaps the subject's eyes get ahead of their mind when they encounter a promising option.

24.2.4 Guidelines for Organizing and Naming the Options on a Single Panel

Organization

The empirical literature reviewed earlier compared random, alphabetical, and categorical organizations. The random organization should not be considered as a design option, but rather it served as a baseline to assess the benefits of the other two types of organization. Two other types of organization are viable alternatives, but have not been directly compared to alphabetical and categorical organizations. Some menus present a set of options that have a conventional order that is neither alphabetical nor categorical. For example, options may have a standard temporal order such as the days of the week or the months of the year. Other options may lie on an ordinal dimension of magnitude, e.g. small, medium, large.

Another potentially effective organization is to list the options in order of frequency of use. This would be particularly useful if there is a small subset of options that are selected much more often than the remaining options. This may occur quite often since a good rule of thumb, called Zipf's law (Zipf, 1949), is that the frequency with which words are used is a negative power function of their rank, i. e. a log-log plot of frequency of use as a function of rank order is a decreasing linear function with a slope of -1. Thus, in many communication environments it appears to be the case that the most frequent word occurs much more often than the second most, the second much more often than third, and so forth.

Figure 3 provides some guidelines for choosing between alphabetical, categorical, conventional, and frequency organizations. The upper portion of Figure 3

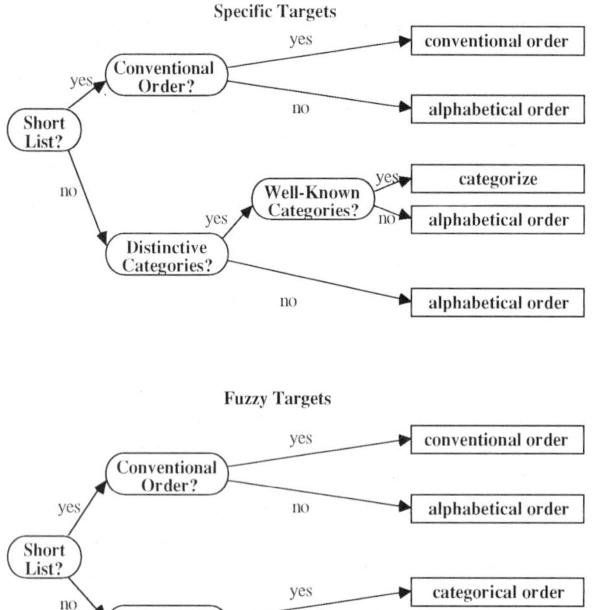

Figure 3. Guidelines for choosing an organization for the options on a single menu panel.

presupposes that most users will have a specific target in mind that is highly likely to match one of the menu options. Under these circumstances users can take advantage of an alphabetical order. As discussed previously designers can rarely assume that users will correctly anticipate the name of the desired option, but when it is appropriate the next question to ask is whether the list of options is long or short. Those sets of options that have conventional orders are likely to be short. Furthermore, conventional orders are likely to induce strong expectations for the options to be displayed in their familiar order. Under these circumstances it would be foolish to override the conventional order with an alphabetical order. If the list is long, then it is probably best to alphabetize the options unless the opportunity for using category information is great. If the options can be arranged in categories that are both distinct (having little conceptual overlap) and well-known to the end users, then grouping by category may be worthwhile.

The lower portion of Figure 3 offers guidelines for applications where it is likely that users will only have fuzzy targets in mind. Since it doesn't make sense to divide a short list into categories, the choice for short lists will usually be limited to conventional and alphabetical orders. One exception to this occurs if the short list consists of phrases or sentences that would be difficult to alphabetize since the initial word of the phrase may be fairly arbitrary or unimportant. Any type of semantic order or a frequency order may be better under these circumstances. For long lists, grouping by category will usually be the best strategy. One important exception to this case would be when a small subset of the options are selected much more frequently than the others. In this case, listing the options in decreasing order of frequency may be the better arrangement, particularly if the categories would not be distinctive or if the users may not be familiar with the proper instances of each category.

Naming

The name or phrase used to designate each option should be precise. The name should permit the user to infer precisely those actions or objects that are controlled by the selection of the option without missing anything that should be included or including anything that is extraneous. This is easier said than done. We know that adding a descriptor that consists of a list of examples or the options available on the next lower level of the hierarchy will help either a little or a lot, but the factors that dictate the magnitude of the benefit are poorly understood. For large menu-driven interfaces testing the names on each menu panel with a sample of end users is very costly, but it is the only technique guaranteed to remove all of the clinkers.

24.3 Choosing a Selection Technique

There are a number of different techniques for selecting items from menus. Some techniques like pull-down lists coupled with point-and-click selection using a mouse are more common than others. Other less conventional techniques like audio menus with phone-key press selection are tied to specific technologies. In this section we review the various techniques for menu selection and summarize research relevant to choosing a selection technique. Menu selection techniques all involve selection from a list of items that can be presented in a variety of visual or audio formats (e.g., pull-down, pop-up, pie). In addition, the techniques all involve the identification of a menu item using a selection device (e.g., pointing with a mouse, typing a letter or digit identifier). Therefore, this section is divided into those issues dealing with 1) menu layouts and 2) selection devices.

24.3.1 Types of Menu Layouts

Most commonly, menus contain lists of discrete items that are arranged either horizontally or vertically. In some cases, however, the options are not represented as a list, but in the form of prose, making the individual items difficult to scan (Norman, 1991). One instantiation of prose-based menus can be seen in "hot links" found in many hypertext documents. A hot link is a highlighted portion of the prose that can be selected for further information. In this case the menu items are not explicit in a list but embedded in the text. Embedded menus necessitate a discrimination between selectable and nonselectable text and therefore add to the potential difficulty of menu selection. See Chapter 38 for more information on selection in hypertext systems.

Given that the items are to be displayed in an explicit list, there are a number of possible layouts to explore. Horizontal list layouts are often found as a command line located at the top of the screen and always in view. In most other cases, however, menus items are arranged vertically and if not fixed (e.g., on the left hand side of the display) can be opened and closed using pull-down or pop-up menus. Pull-down menus are menus that are selected and displayed in the same location each time they are selected, whereas pop-up menus appear at the current cursor location.

Walker and Smelcer (1990) compared pull-down and pop-up menus in terms of movement time. They also investigated the concomitant effects of the presence of inpenetratable borders and "fittsizing" menu items. Inpenetratable borders are borders that back menu items and that cannot be penetrated. Their presence supposedly reduces overshooting of the target and the subsequent need for corrective sub-movements. "Fittsizing" refers to Fitts' law that relates selection time to target size and distance. Walker and Smelcer increased the selection area of items proportional to the distance that they were located from the starting point of the cursor, so that more distant selection areas were also larger. Results of the study indicated that inpenetratable borders and to a lesser extent, fittsizing targets, decreased movement time during menu selection and that overall access time was better for pull-down menus than for pop-up menus. This result is interesting, given that the distance from the cursor location to the bar at the top of the screen where the pull-down menus originated was often quite large. Walker and Smelcer attributed the relatively slow access time associated with pop-up menus to the typically narrow paths that the pointer must travel.

Another way of laying out menu items is in the form of a circle or pie. Items are placed around a circle at an equal radial distance. The starting point for the cursor is at the center of the circle such that each item is equidistant from this starting point. Each item is associated with a wedge of the pie which serves as the selection area. This configuration of items is purportedly advantageous because the distance from the center of the menu to the target is constant and short and because the selection area for each item is larger than what is typical for linear menus (Callahan, Hopkins, Weiser, and Shneiderman, 1988). Thus, Fitts' law would predict shorter selection time, compared to pull-down menus in which target distance typically increases as the selection area is made larger.

On the down side, pie menus take up more space on the screen than linear menus and are inappropriate for very long lists of menu items or for items that are linear in nature. For instance, a pie menu may be ideal for selecting hours of the day or compass positions, but not for linear information such as cost or weight. In their study, Callahan et al. (1988) compared pie menus to linear menus and found that subjects were significantly faster at identity matching using pie menus. In addition there was a marginally significant ($p=.075$) interaction between type of menu and type of materials suggesting that certain menu items are more appropriate for pie or linear menus than others.

The pie and linear menus that have been discussed thus far are appropriate for menu items that are presented visually. However, for audio interfaces such as those found in phone-based systems, it is necessary to display menu items auditorially. Due to the temp-oral nature of audio information, these interfaces necessitate a linear or serial layout of menu items. Specific issues pertaining to audio menus are discussed in more detail in a later section.

Other nonconventional layouts have also been proposed by Norman (1991), although there is little empirical research to back them. These layouts include a matrix layout (e.g., selecting elements from the periodic table) and a graphical layout (e.g., selecting locations on a map). Norman has more generally suggested that some sets of menu items may lend themselves to these nonlinear/spatial representations and that by capitalizing on this in the form of menu layout users' visual recognition and spatial memory capabilities will be facilitated, resulting in a more effective interface. In addition, the nonspatial arrangement of items may in some cases be more efficient than a linear arrangement.

Finally, it should be emphasized that the formatting of a list of menu items involves more than deciding on the geometric layout of those items. In particular, issues of item size, spacing, grouping, font-size and style, and color should be considered. These issues are the same as those involved in general screen design and will not be discussed in detail here (See Chapter on screen design).

24.3.2 Types of Selection Devices

Given a specific list format, the items in that list can be selected using a number of different techniques. The selection techniques generally fall into the categories of either pointing with a cursor or selecting items by entering specific identifiers. Devices and research associated with each category of selection are discussed in turn below.

Pointing

The growing popularity of direct manipulation interfaces has resulted in a trend away from menu selection via discrete identifiers and toward menu selection via pointing. More often, menu items are selected by moving a pointer to the location of the desired option and selecting that item. The location of an on-screen pointer or cursor can be manipulated with cursor keys, joysticks, trackballs, touch screens, pens, and mice.

Several early studies in human-computer interaction compared various subsets of these pointing devices. For instance, Card, English, and Burr (1978) found that the mouse was more efficient than a joystick or cursor keys. In their study they had subjects move the location of a pointer to targets of different size and at different distances with either a mouse, a pressure sensitive joystick, or cursor keys. The mouse was faster and more accurate than the other devices across all combinations of size and distance except for the nearest targets (1 cm away). The average total time to select a specified target was .7 seconds faster for the mouse than the best set of cursor keys.

Mice, unlike men, are not all created equal. Whiteside et al. (1985) reported that the mouse-driven cursor in two commercially available iconic systems is very susceptible to errors because the users' understanding about which segment of the cursor controlled selection did not correspond to the designers' implementation. Users frequently misselected objects when they mispositioned the cursor. Surprisingly, it was not easy to grow out of these errors as many users developed superstitious mouse-pressing behavior and formed a low opinion of the device's reliability.

In another study, Karat, McDonald, and Anderson (1984) compared the best of the on-screen pointer devices, the mouse, to both touch panels and keyboard entry of single-letter identifiers. The Karat et al. study is exemplary for the range of tasks that were used to investigate the three methods of selection. Three levels of task complexity were studied.

In a simple task designed to measure the demands of selection in isolation from any concomitant search and decision processes, each trial consisted of the presentation of a single screen containing a small box (14x13 mm) with a single letter inside. Subjects had to either touch the screen within the box, mouse the pointer within the box, or enter the letter appearing in the box. Subjects were much faster with the touch panel and keyboard (0.8 and 1.1 s) than with the mouse (2.7 s).

The selection operation was also embedded in two more complex and realistic tasks. A telephone task involved calling persons listed in various directories and modifying those directories by changing, deleting, or creating new entries. A calendar task included reviewing daily schedules and checking, scheduling, and modifying appointments. The two applications involved hierarchies of different breadth and depth with the telephone tasks requiring somewhat less depth (1 to 8 selections) than the calendar tasks (3 to 11 selections). In addition, half the tasks assigned to each application required the user to enter information in a specified field while the other half did not.

The average total time per task for the realistic applications was 112, 122, and 132 seconds for the touch panel, keyboard identifiers, and mouse, respectively. The type of selector did not interact with any combination of application (telephone aid or calendar) or task type (data entry or no data entry). Thus, over a wide range of tasks involving menus, selection was faster by touching than by entering an identifier which, in turn, was faster than using a mouse. Therefore, there are at least some cases in which selection by touch may be more efficient than by mouse. Additionally, the finding that selection by identifier entry can also be more efficient than pointing using a mouse suggests that this more traditional form of menu selection should not be discounted.

More recently Kurtenbach and colleagues (Kurtenbach and Buxton, 1993; Kurtenbach, Sellen, and Buxton, 1993) have investigated a new method of menu selection that has been tested with pie menu layouts and that lends itself particularly well to pen or stylus pointing devices. The method called "marking" involves item selection by marking from the center of the pie through the wedge associated with the to-be-selected menu item. In one study Kurtenbach, Sellen, and Buxton (1993) studied the effect of number of items, pointing device (mouse, pen or trackball), and whether the menus were in view at the time of selection or not. When they were not in view they were either completely hidden or they were hidden, but the mark left an "ink trail." In general, performance degraded for hidden menus as number of items increased, though not as much as expected for eight and twelve items. The authors suggest that performance with twelve items was so good because the positions of the items were reminiscent of a clock layout. The mouse and stylus were also found to be superior to the trackball.

In another study Kurtenbach and Buxton (1993) further explored the potential of marking menus. In particular they extended the method to selection from hierarchical menus by having users mark paths through wedges of multiple pies. They also investigated a "mark-ahead" feature in which users would not have to wait for the pie menu to pop-up, but could instead mark a path through the part of the screen where the pie would pop-up. Subjects in this study were capable of using these features, though more errors were made if the items to be selected were off the horizontal or vertical axes of the pie. Also, in this study, the pen was slightly more effective as a marking device than the mouse.

Identifiers

Another family of techniques for selecting menu items involves direct entry of an identifier associated with that menu item. The identifier is typically a letter or digit, but sometimes a letter string or abbreviation. Function keys can also serve as identifiers when the number of items is kept to a minimum, however the keys should be labeled meaningfully to best alleviate memory problems. Selection using identifiers involves two steps, the first of which is bypassed in pointing interfaces: 1) mapping from the target item to the identifier and 2) entry of the identifier. Often the response also requires a special character that precedes and/or follows the identifier (e.g., /, Alt-key, Control-key, Return).

Although identifier entry is becoming less common with the growing popularity of direct manipulation interfaces, there are several situations in which identifier entry may be the selection technique of choice. First, recall that Karat, et al. (1984) found that selection via keyboard entry was less efficient than pointing using a touch screen, but more efficient that pointing with a mouse, supporting the contention that selection by identifier may sometimes be warranted over other pointing methods. Second, in some cases, the technology enforces this choice. For instance, selection by pointing is not feasible in audio interfaces. Instead items are selected from the audio menu by entry of discrete identifiers via the phone key-pad. Third, in cases in which a set of menu items are repeatedly selected or similarly when users are highly experienced with a set of items, identifier entry may be more efficient than pointing. Some menu interfaces (e.g., Microsoft Word) offer the best of both worlds by allowing either pointing or identifier entry for many menu items. Fourth, in some applications like information retrieval in which the number of items is very large, it is often impractical to select by pointing. In these cases, entry of some type of identifier is more efficient. Finally, even when identifier entry is called for, it is not necessary to completely abandon the benefits of direct manipulation. Perlman (1988) suggests that increased compatibility between the selection hardware (keys in this case) and the menu layout can approximate direct manipulation. For instance, a vertical list should be selected using vertically arranged function or digit keys.

If identifiers are the selection device of choice, then one must decide whether to use letters or digits and how the identifiers are to be assigned to the options. Perlman (Experiment 2, 1984) provides the most complete investigation of identifiers. Subjects were required to find and select a specified target in a menu of eight computer terms. The terms were always presented in alphabetical order: assemble, buffer, compile, debug, edit, file, graph, and halt. Four arrangements of identifiers and options were tested by pairing two types of identifiers (the letters a through h or the numbers 1 through 8) so that the identifiers were either compatible or incompatible with the alphabetical ordering of the options. For example, in a compatible pairing the option compile might be paired with 3 or c .

In the analysis of selection times there was a significant interaction between identifier type and compatibility. When identifiers are compatibly mapped on the order of options, letter identifiers (1.1 s) are faster than digit identifiers (1.5 s). However, when the mapping is incompatible digits (1.9 s) are faster than letters (2.2 s).

Perlman makes several cogent recommendations based on these results. If the menu panel is used in an application where users make frequent selections and if the set of options do not change over time, then it may be worthwhile to use letter identifiers that can be compatibly paired to each option. Another advantage of compatible letter identifiers is that they will be easier to remember than number identifiers. This is particularly important if the primary method available to experienced users for taking shortcuts through a hierarchy is to chain the responses for a complete pathway on a single command line. The sequence QUF is easier to remember or reconstruct for the actions of quitting, updating, and filing than the numerical sequence 452 .

If the list of options is dynamic rather than static, the use of digits is a good compromise that costs only a third of a second per selection. Incompatible letter identifiers should be avoided. The costs for incompatible letters is over one second per selection relative to the optimal case of compatible letters and two-thirds of a second relative to the digit-identifier compromise. If should be noted that the best case, compatible letters, turns into the worse case if the menu options are translated into another language.

Prompts and Feedback

Providing default options and appropriate feedback is likely to be an important part of the design of any selection mechanism. Default options are particularly desirable when one option is selected much more often than any of the others. Under these circumstances search and selection operations can be made more efficient by highlighting the default option and preselecting it by having its identifier automatically displayed on the command line or having the pointer automatically located at the default option.

Regardless of the selection mechanism, the system should provide instructions regarding the context of the menu, how a response should be made and feedback indicating: (1) which options are selectable, (2) when an option is under the pointer and, therefore, can be selected (assuming a pointer is used), (3) which options have been selected so far, and (4) the end of the selection process. These feedback characteristics are particularly important in highly interactive applications where the options on pop-up or pull-down menus are likely to be lists of commands and/or arguments.

Two techniques are commonly used to prevent users from selecting inappropriate choices. One approach is to gray-out or otherwise mark those options that don't make sense in a given context. The unselectability of the faded option is reinforced when it is under the pointer since it will not become highlighted. The second approach is to dynamically alter the visibility of the options, i.e. inappropriate options simply disappear from the screen. It is difficult to offer guidelines with respect to these two techniques since their relative benefits and costs have not been explored empirically. Lieberman (1985) discusses this and several other issues concerning menu-based graphical interfaces. For example, he speculates that making commands disappear may distract the user, prevent him from associating a command with a physical screen location, and makes it more difficult to discover more about the system through browsing. Norman (1991) also advocates graying-out because it provides the user with stable cues regarding presence and location of items. In addition the inaccessible, though visible items, can help the user to achieve a more complete model of the items that are available and how they are related to other items.

Other more experimental techniques seem to be promising in terms of helping users make fast and error-free selections. These include the inpenetratable borders backing targets and the fittsizing procedure tested by Walker and Smelcer (1990). It is interesting that both of these techniques result in "larger" selection areas, a basic feature underlying the success of many menu selection techniques investigated in the lab.

24.3.3 Guidelines for Choosing a Selection Technique

In sum, although explicit linear pull-down and pop-up menus are most common, other list formats are possible and may be desirable given the items, task, and technology. Pie menus are best suited to shorter lists of items easily represented in a cyclical format and also work well with pen-based selection technologies and adequate screen space. The marking technique seems to offer a promising alternative to the traditional point-and-click interface when used in combination with pie menus and pen-based interfaces. If items lend themselves to dimensional or graphical representations then matrix or graphical layouts should be considered.

As far as selection devices go, the mouse tends to be favored over other pointing devices for most traditional menu interfaces. However, there is also support for identifier entry and touch screen input. Identifier entry seems most suitable for audio interfaces, familiar menu items, or very large databases of items. If single character identifiers are used as the method of selection, then the choice between letters and digits rests primarily on the stability of the options on the menu panel. If they are likely to remain static over time, then letter identifiers corresponding to the initial letter of each option provide a small advantage over digits. This may be an important consideration if selection processes make up a big proportion of the total task time. Mnemonic letter identifiers are also easier to remember and reconstruct than digit identifiers and this constitutes another advantage if the system permits response chaining as a way of taking shortcuts through the hierarchy. On the other hand, if the options dynamically change depending on the context, then it is difficult to maintain compatible letter assignments and digit identifiers are not a bad second choice. Incompatible letter identifiers should be avoided at all costs. Compatibility should also be maintained between selection hardware and layout of menu items.

When advanced technologies can be considered, it appears that touch screens may be ideally suited for menu-driven systems and that the mouse may be overrated, at least as an input device for dialogues that involve a lot of menu selecting. However, this technology is also associated with some problems. For example, the width of the finger and parallax problems can limit the precision of a touch screen. In addition, arm fatigue can be a problem over extended periods touch screen usage.

24.4 Organization and Navigation Between Menu Panels

This section examines the factors important to deciding how the total set of options (objects and/or actions) should be distributed across the individual menu panels. The distribution of options to panels will determine the navigation pathways, i.e. the sequence of selections that will be required to get from one menu panel to another.

24.4.1 Depth versus Breadth in a Hierarchical Menu Structure

Most menu systems are organized into a hierarchical tree, in which each node (menu panel) in the hierarchy can be reached only from a single superordinate node that lies directly above it in the hierarchy. Depth (d) is usually defined as the number of levels in the hierarchy. Breadth (b) is defined as the number of options per menu panel. When there are an equal number of options on every panel, the number of terminal nodes (N) is a function of breadth raised to the power of depth:

$$N = b^d \tag{6}$$

For example, 64 terminal nodes could be accessed by using 3 levels with 4 options on each panel:

$$64 = 4^3 \tag{7}$$

Or, alternatively the 64 nodes could be arranged in 6 levels with only 2 options per panel:

$$64 = 2^6 \tag{8}$$

Taking the logarithm of the power function and rearranging terms shows that for a fixed number of terminal nodes depth is inversely related to the logarithm of breadth:

$$d = \log_2 N / (\log_2 b) \tag{9}$$

For the two cases shown in Equations 2 and 3 this yields:

$$3 = \log_2 64 / (\log_2 4) = 6 / 2 \tag{10}$$

$$6 = \log_2 64 / (\log_2 2) = 6 / 1 \tag{11}$$

Note that a logarithmic transformation of both sides of Equation 6 preserves the equality regardless of the base of the logarithm. However, base 2 yields integer results for the examples considered and has other convenient properties.

Factors Favoring More Breadth

A hierarchical structure with several levels requires the user to either recall or discover how to get from where he is to where he wants to go. The navigation problem (i.e. getting lost or using an inefficient pathway to the goal) becomes more and more treacherous as the depth of the hierarchy increases. For example, Snowberry, Parkinson, and Sisson (1983) showed that error rates increased from 4.0% to 34.0% as depth increased from a single level to six levels. Despite the navigation problem there are three reasons for considering a system with greater depth: *crowding, insulation,* and *funneling*.

Crowding is the straightforward constraint imposed by the amount of available space on a panel. When the available space is exceeded, some depth must be introduced. Crowding many options onto a single panel should not be tolerated if it requires names or descriptors that are too short to be precise. *Insulation* refers to the opportunity for menu systems to prompt selections that are likely to be needed and hide those that are unlikely or illegal. The opportunity for insulation may be greatest when each population of users needs to learn only part of a complex system and the vast residual can be completely hidden.

Funneling is related to insulation, but emphasizes the efficiency gains that can accrue even when users are responsible for using the whole system. Funneling, as developed below, refers to a reduction in the total number of options processed that is achieved by designing a system with more depth and less breadth. When greater depth is traded for less breadth, funneling can generate efficiency gains, particularly when the processing time per option is long. Processing time includes the time it takes to encode the option, to compare the encoded representation with the target, and to decide whether to terminate the search or continue to examine more of the options. Processing time will be long when the user is engaged in a difficult semantic search that involves lengthy descriptors of each option and/or descriptors that are poorly understood.

For a simple example of the benefits of *funneling* consider a database of 64 items. If all items appear as options in a single master index page, an exhaustive search would lead to 64 options being processed. In contrast, if breadth is minimized and depth maximized (b = 2, d = 6, the case considered in Equation 8), an exhaustive search of both options on each of the six successive panels will accumulate to only 12 total options.

The benefits of funneling cannot be obtained without cost. As depth increases so does the number of panel transactions. A transaction is initiated by the user when a selection is made. Each additional panel requires one more response (e.g. key press, mouse selection) from the human and one more response (e.g. display) from the computer. Each transaction adds the response execution times for each component to the cumulative total. Thus, for the example given above, the organization with maximum depth would have six times the response-execution time compared with the single-panel case.

A General Framework for the Depth-Breadth Tradeoff

The tradeoff between funneling and response-execution time can be analyzed within the following framework for predicting Total Search Time (TST). In general TST will be some function of the total number of options examined, the time for each examination, the total number of computer responses, and the time for each response. One such general formulation is described by Kent Norman (1991) and presented below with minor notational modifications:

$$\text{TST} = \text{S}^{\,d} \{ u(b_i) + c(r_i) \}, \quad (12)$$

where $u(b_i)$ is the user response time to select from among b items at Level i, and $c(r_i)$ is the computer response time at Level i.

Equation 12 is very useful for highlighting several important distinctions that differentiate the competing specific models of the depth-breadth tradeoff. Most of the debate centers on $u(b_i)$, the time it takes for the user to select and execute a response from among the b options on a given menu panel. Recall that we concluded that there is little evidence or reason to believe that the search function for a single panel will follow the Hick-Hyman Law. Instead search is usually linear, but might be self-terminating, exhaustive, or redundant.

Distinctions between linear versus log-linear functions and self-terminating versus exhaustive searches only begin to characterize the variety of search strategies users may use. Simple models assume that search time per option is constant across all levels of the menu hierarchy, but more complex models allow the possibility that search may be faster for the more familiar root panels or the more concrete leaf panels. A further complication is that decision time may change during the examination of a single panel of options at some specific depth. For example, subjects might speed up as they reduce the scope of their search to the last few options on the menu panel. Most of the models described below make several simplifying assumptions.

Lee and MacGregor's Linear Model

Lee and MacGregor (1985) were the first to propose a quantitative model for TST. Their most simple case assumed a linear and exhaustive search of all options on every panel before a selection is made. Further assuming that breadth is invariant across levels, then total search time is:

$$\text{TST} = (bt + k + c)\, d \quad (13)$$

where b is breadth, t is processing time per option, k is human response time, c is computer response time, and d is depth.

The relationship between the specific model shown in Equation 13 and the general model shown in Equation 12 is evident to the mathematically sophisticated reader, but apparent to all with a bit of coaching. The time it takes a user to make a response on any given panel, $u(b_i)$, corresponds to the first two terms, (bt + k) of Equation 13. This is true because of the assumption that all b items will be examined in linear fashion for time t, before a single response is selected and executed for duration k. The time it takes for the computer to respond, $c(r_i)$, corresponds to the third term, c of the specific model shown in Equation 13. Because of the further assumption that all panels have the same breadth and that the time to examine an option is constant across breadth, the summation in Equation 12 is simply accomplished in Equation 13 by multiplying by the depth of the hierarchy. Because depth, as indicated in Equation 9, is the ratio of $\log_2 N$ to $\log_2 b$, this ratio can be substituted for d in Equation 13.

$$TST = (bt + k + c)\,[(\log_2 N / \log_2 b)] \qquad (14)$$

Although Equation 14 appears more complicated, it has the advantage of expressing TST in terms of breadth (b) and the total number of terminal nodes (N). Thus, given values for t, k, and c, the number of options per page (b) that minimizes search time can be computed by setting the derivative of Equation 14 with respect to b equal to zero. This yields:

$$b\,(\log_2 b - 1) = (k + c) / t \qquad (15)$$

When Lee and MacGregor iterated this procedure for several values of human response time (0.5 and 1.0 s), processing time per option (0.25, 0.50, 1.00, and 2.00 s), and computer response time (0.50, 0.60, 0.90, and 1.35 s), they found that optimal breadth ranged from three to eight alternatives per panel. The benefits of funneling were particularly apparent when response-execution times were fast and processing time per option was slow.

Using similar procedures, Lee and MacGregor show that the optimal breadth is in the range of 4 to 13 options if a self-terminating, rather than exhaustive, search is assumed. Self-terminating searches result in somewhat larger values for optimal breadth because they erode the funneling advantage that reduces the relative number of options that are examined. The 4 to 13 range was based on the assumption that search would terminate, on the average, halfway through the list, so that the expected number of options examined per panel, E(O), would be:

$$E(O) = (b + 1) / 2 \qquad (16)$$

where b is breadth, the number of options per page. In this case the derivative of the search time function is:

$$b\,(\log_2 b - 1) = 1 + 2\,(k + c) / t. \qquad (17)$$

The reduction in the funneling advantage caused by self-terminating search can be illustrated by reconsidering the example that assumes a database of 64 items. With exhaustive search, it was noted that an examination of 64 options was funneled to only 12 when breadth was decreased from all 64 options on one panel to only two options per panel. With self-terminating search, the total number of options processed would drop to 32.5 for the single-level hierarchy and to 9.0 for the six-level hierarchy. Thus, only 23.5 comparison operations (32.5 - 9.0) were saved with self-terminating search, as compared with 52 comparisons (64 - 12) with exhaustive search.

Paap and Roske-Hofstrand's Linear Model

Paap and Roske-Hofstrand (1986) extended Lee and MacGregor's analysis to cases where the user can restrict the scope of search either because of experience with the menu panel or because the options are organized into categories.

Experience with the same set of menu panels will shrink the scope of the search. Both McDonald et al. and Card found that all effects of organization disappear with practice. Card's eye movement analysis showed that after 800 selections from the same menu the target was always found in the first fixation. With experience, menu users move from a state of great uncertainty concerning the location of the target to one of complete certainty.

In order to handle the effects of experience, the constant of 2 in Equations 11 and 12 can be treated as a parameter f, that represents the average proportion of the list that is searched:

$$E(O) = (b + 1)/f \qquad (18)$$

$$b(\ln - 1) = 1 + f(k + c)/t. \qquad (19)$$

The parameter f should be thought of as an index of the degree to which the scope of the search can be restricted. When f = 2, the scope of the search is the whole list and, on average, the target will be found halfway through the list. When f = 3, the scope of the search is reduced to two-thirds of the list, and the target should be found after processing about one-third of all the options, and so forth. Thus, the reduction in the scope of the search with practice, and its consequences for optimal breadth, can be modeled by increasing the value of f in Equations 18 and 19. Optimal breadth, b, is very sensitive to f. For example, when response times are fairly long and processing time per item is fairly short, optimal breadth increases from 13 to 37 as f increases from 2 to 10 (cf. Paap and Roske-Hofstrand, 1986 for more details).

A similar reduction in the scope of search occurs when the menu options on each individual panel are arranged in descending frequency of use. If the most popular choice is always at the top and is selected most of the time, then search can be severely restricted most of the time even if there are a great many rarely used options that also appear on the panel.

Reducing the scope of the search by grouping the options into meaningful categories is an interesting special case. The results of McDonald et al. strongly suggest that users can restrict their search to an appropriate category. Recall that in this study 64 options were arranged in four columns of 16. In one condition each column consisted of the instances from one category and those were arranged in random order. If the four categories are also assumed to be arranged in random order, then Equation 16 for self-terminating search would predict that it would take 2.5 comparisons to find the correct category label and an additional 8.5 comparisons to find the target instance within the category. Thus, simply grouping the options into meaningful categories can reduce the number of options processed from 32.5 to just 11.0.

The preceding analysis of McDonald et al. shows appreciable savings by grouping 64 options into four categories, but even greater saving could be achieved. In general, the optimal number of groups, g, for a menu panel containing b total options is:

$$g = \sqrt{b}\,. \tag{20}$$

Assuming a random order of categories and a random order of instances within categories, the expected number of items (category labels plus instances) processed when b options are grouped into g categories is:

$$E(I) = (g + 1)/2 + ((b/g) + 1)/2. \tag{21}$$

The search time functions for grouped options becomes:

$$TST = ((E(I)t + k + c) / (\ln b))/(\ln n). \tag{22}$$

When the optimal value for g, given in Equation 20, is substituted into Equation 22, the derivative of Equation 22 can be set to zero and optimized in terms of b:

$$\sqrt{b}\ (\ln \sqrt{b-1}) = 1 + (k + c)/t. \tag{23}$$

Grouping is an extremely powerful factor in determining the depth-breadth trade-off. Without grouping, Lee and MacGregor conclude that under conditions of self-terminating search, optimal menu sizes will usually be between 4 and 8 and will sometimes be as high as 13. In contrast, when meaningful groups of options can be presented for each menu, the optimal breadth tends to be in the range of 16 to 36 and sometimes as high as 78.

One way of thinking about the benefits of an organized menu panel is that it accomplishes the same goal as funneling (i.e., both organization and funneling result in the user having to consider fewer options). Organization, unlike funneling, accomplishes this goal without the penalty of having to wait for the delays caused by human and computer response-execution times. Since there is no good reason for menu lists to be ordered randomly, Lee and MacGregor's analysis significantly underestimates the optimal number of alternatives per menu panel.

Varying Depth

Miller (1981) was the first to directly investigate the breadth-depth issue by manipulating the depth of search for a database of 64 items. Miller's task required subjects to find and select a target word that appeared as one of 64 options at the lowest level of each hierarchy. Four organizations were tested. The structure with the maximum breadth consisted of only a single level with all 64 words listed as options. The three hierarchical organizations varied depth, while holding breadth constant across the levels of any given hierarchy. Thus, the two level hierarchy had eight options per panel, the three level hierarchy had four options per panel, and the six level hierarchy had only two options per panel.

Both search time and error rate are in agreement and show that performance is best at the intermediate levels of depth. If other requirements permit it, Miller concludes that two levels with eight options per menu is the best organization. The results are consistent with the predictions based on Lee and MacGregor's analysis for self-terminating search. For short response times (k = 0.5, c = 0.5), the optimal breadth ranges from four to eight options per panel as reading speed varies. It is not surprising that Lee and MacGregor's analysis predicts Miller's results, since the options on each panel were not arranged in a task-relevant manner. Although the 64 words that appeared on the single-level organization were displayed in eight clusters, the eight words in any one cluster were typically drawn from four different categories.

Snowberry, et al. (1983) conducted an experiment that was very similar to Miller's. The materials, organization, and task were all the same. However, Snowberry et al. (1983) also included a single-word organization in which the 64 options were grouped according to category, as well as the unrelated grouping tested by Miller. The pattern of results obtained is the same for the conditions common to both experiments. However, the new single-level organization that presents the options in categories is best of all. The results are consistent with the grouping analysis reported by Paap and Roske-Hofstrand. Assuming that the 64 options were grouped into the optimal number of eight categories, then optimal breadth ranges from 16 to 78 options per page depending upon the estimates for response-execution times and processing time per item.

Kiger's (1984) study tested five types of hierarchical tree structures. Three of the organizations were identical to those tested by Miller and Snowberry et al. (1983): 2 levels with 8 options on each panel, 3 levels with 4 options on each panel, and 6 levels with 2 options on each panel. The other two organizations also had two levels. A top heavy organization had 16 options at the upper level and only 4 options at the lower level. The bottom heavy organization had the reverse arrangement. The results showed that performance (both time and accuracy) decreased as depth increased, confirming the trend across experiments that menu structures with a lot of depth present significant navigation problems to users.

The average retrieval times are much longer in Kiger's study compared to Miller's or Snowberry et al.'s. Furthermore, the range of retrieval time differences across depth levels is about 20 seconds in the former study compared to less than 6 seconds in the latter cases. The major contribution to this difference was that Kiger required his subjects to recover from their errors, whereas the other two studies aborted the trial once an error was made. Since recovery is a necessary procedure in the real world, Kiger's study probably provides a better estimate of the magnitude of the costs associated with deep hierarchical structures.

Varying Breadth Across Levels

Although Kiger's top- and bottom-heavy organizations constitute the first examples of varied breadth in the same hierarchy, the most systematic exploration of varied breadth was reported by Norman and Chin (1988). These investigators held depth constant at four levels and the number of terminal nodes constant at 64, but varied the way in which breadth was distributed across the four levels. The *constant* menu (4 x 4 x 4 x 4) served as a baseline. However, in view of the empirical findings reviewed in the previous section one might suspect that using four levels to reach 256 terminal nodes (in this case, gifts from a popular merchandising catalog) is a poor design compared to using less depth. In that light, one hopes that some pattern of varying breadth across levels might lead to considerable improvement over the baseline condition. The four patterns tested were the *decreasing* menu (8 x 8 x 2 x 2), the *increasing* menu (2 x 2 x 8 x 8), the *convex* menu (2 x 8 x 8 x 2), and the *concave* menu (8 x 2 x 2 x 8).

Like McDonald et al., Norman and Chin had subjects search for both specific and fuzzy targets. For example, one of the specific targets was *Sterling Silver Candlesticks* . The fuzzy version of the same target was described by the following scenario: "Your friends are about to celebrate their 25th wedding anniversary. You know that they are very romantic and love candlelight dinners. You also know that another friend is getting them a beautiful set of silverware. You would like to buy an appropriate gift." A trial ended when subjects selected the target gift. If they selected a nontarget they were told that the item was not in stock and that they had to search for another item. Thus, total response time and the total number of panels traversed include the steps required to recover from an error. At any point in their search, subjects were free to backup to the previous panel or to jump back to the top panel.

The pattern of depth that best funnels the user to the correct terminal panel should determine the best menu structure among those tested by Norman and Chin. Consider the breadth of the top panel and the desire to set off on the right pathway. If the user's goal is vague, then two options might be better than eight because there is at least a 50-50 chance of the first selection being correct. On the other hand, if the target is explicit, then greater breadth might be advantageous because eight options at the top are likely to be more specific and less ambiguous than only two very general options. In summary, the rule of thumb is as follows. If you have a clear idea of what you're looking for then its best to see all the cards laid out on the table in front of you as soon as possible. This is true because potential errors are not caused by your failure to know what you're looking for, but rather by your failure to understand the organization of the menu and, hence, how to get to your goal. In contrast, if you're not sure what will satisfy or optimize your needs, then playing a mini-version of twenty questions at the top levels may funnel you directly to a target that would otherwise be difficult to find.

The discussion above regarding the best organization for funneling users to the correct bottom panel is related to Norman and Chin's analysis in terms of information theory. Computing the total amount of uncertainty across the three top levels of each structure shows that the two menus with eight options on the bottom panels (*increasing* and *concave*) have the least amount of uncertainty, viz. 5, compared to 6 for the *constant* menu, and 7 for the *decreasing* and *convex* menus. Norman and Chin predict that performance should be inversely related to uncertainty, but the analysis based on information theory is most appropriate if the user is essentially guessing because they assume that the probability of selection is equal for all alternatives. For example, if the top panel has eight options, then three bits of information are gained if the user guesses the correct alternative. In contrast, only one bit is gained if the top panel has only two options. But what if the probability of selecting the correct option systematically varies with the number of alternatives? More specifically, assume that the correct selection will be more apparent when the choices consist of eight fairly specific and concrete categories compared to only two general and abstract categories. If these differences were great enough, there may actually be more uncertainty in the two alternative case than the one with eight. We believe that it more profitable, although more complicated, to expect that performance will involve an interaction between the degree of fuzziness of the target and the degree of ambiguity in the options and that, ambiguity tends to vary inversely with the number of specific alternatives. This belief remains that, and is open to further empirical confirmation or disconfirmation.

Turning to the results of the Norman and Chin experiment, when subjects were searching for specific targets the *increasing menu* was slightly superior to the other four structures. As the advantage was small and statistically nonsignfiicant, the remainder of the discussion will focus on the data obtained with fuzzy targets. For fuzzy targets both dependent measures (total search time and total number of panels traversed) yielded the same rank order of performance: (1) the *concave* menu, (2) the *increasing* menu, (3) the *constant* menu, (4) the *decreasing* menu, and (5) the *convex* menu.

What the two best structures have in common is more breadth on the bottom panels and, accordingly, the least amount of uncertainty across the top three levels. Because the mean number of panels traversed in the fuzzy target condition was about 14.5 and the optimal pathway is only 4.0 panels, the data suggest that either the targets were quite fuzzy and/or the higher-level options quite ambiguous. (The data are not reported by level, so the effects of these two factors can not be teased apart.) In any event, it is fair to say that there was a fair amount of uncertainty across the higher levels and that it is not surprising that structures that inherently reduce the amount of uncertainty showed some superiority over those that inherently tolerate more uncertainty.

Allocating many options to the bottom panels has a second and related consequence, viz. it reduces the total number of frames required to implement the system. As Norman and Chin point out the two most effective structures require only 57 (*concave* menu) and 39 (*increasing* menu) total panels, whereas the two worst require 201 (*decreasing* menu) and 147 (*convex* menu). Menu systems with fewer panels will enable users to become familar with their organization more quickly and further reduce the amount of navigational uncertainty.

Norman and Chin (1988) and Norman (1991) devote a fair amount of discussion to the superiority of the *concave* menu over the *increasing* menu, despite the fact that the advantage does not appear to be statistically significant. With that caveat aside, Norman (1991, p. 221) claims that "breadth is advantageous at the top *and* bottom of the menu." As mentioned earlier, a potential advantage for increased breadth on the top panel is that more specific and concrete alternatives may increase the likelihood that users will make the right first step. It would be interesting to know if that expectation was confirmed by the data obtained by Norman and Chin. Even if there was a substantial advantage in the structures with 8 options per top panel, it is evident that this is not sufficient to guarantee that the subject is accurately funneled to the correct bottom panel. This follows from the observation that subjects using the *decreasing* menu (8 x 8 x 2 x 2) visited an average of more than 16 panels per task.

Norman and Chin also report the frequency with which subjects use the *previous* and *top* commands in order to redirect search. The interesting finding is that subjects tend to select the option that will take them directly to a panel of eight options rather than two. Thus, the *top* command is frequently used for the *decreasing* or *concave* menus; but not for the *increasing* or *convex* structures. Why do user's prefer to redirect their search to a panel with more breadth? A likely, but untested answer is that they believe this is the most likely locus of their mistake and they need to retreat to this panel with eight options in order to get back on the right path. If this speculation is correct, then it implies that subjects did not perceive the eight option panels to be easier because the options were more specific and concrete than those encountered on the panels with only two options.

In summary, the results support the recommendation that for alternative designs of constant depth, allocate the most breadth to the bottom panels. There is weaker evidence to suggest that it is sometimes advantageous to also have greater breadth on the top panel. As usual, the recommendation can not be generalized to all cases. If users are searching for specific targets, rather than fuzzy targets, the menu structure may not matter very much, even if users often make navigation errors (e.g., Norman and Chin's specific target data).

Performance Changes Across Levels of the Hierarchy

Snowberry et al. (1983) report an interesting supplementary analysis of the error rate at each level of the six-level hierarchy. A higher proportion of errors occur at the top two levels than the bottom two levels despite the fact that every level involves a binary choice. The high error rates at the top follow from our earlier observation that the higher level nodes are more abstract and ambiguous than those at the bottom. Consistent with this view, a follow-up study (Snowberry, et. al, 1985) showed that a help field that looked ahead to the options at the next level of the hierarchy significantly reduced the error rates at the higher levels. Kiger presents the most extensive analysis of response times at each level of hierarchical structures. For the six-level hierarchy with only two options per panel response, times gradually become faster as the user gets closer to the goal. This is consistent with Snowberry et al.'s finding that fewer errors are made at lower levels.

Allen (1983) has also examined retrieval times at each level of a hierarchy. Subjects worked with only one four-level structure, but the targets (a company name, a telephone number, or an area code) were located at levels two through four. The hierarchy consisted of 60 different menus containing 260 unique labels. Consistent with the results reported above, Allen found that decisions were faster at level 4 than level 3 and these, in turn, were faster than the decisions at level 2. However, an inconsistent finding was that the top level decisions were as fast or faster than the decisions at the lower levels. As Allen points out, this may have occurred because users get more practice at the top than any place else in the hierarchy. Allen also required his subjects to recover from their mistakes. The cost of making an error was great: there was an average of 8.95 responses after an error until the subject was again on the correct path. This emphasizes our earlier conclusion that errors are very costly in multi-level structures, that the system must keep the user on the right track, and that experiments that magically relieve the subject of error recovery responsibility will severely underestimate the navigation problem.

Semantics and Syntax

As discussed earlier in the sections concerning the names for options and the benefits of adding descriptor lists, errors are usually caused by labels that are not natural or precise. The naming problem haunts and confounds all of the investigations of the depth-breadth tradeoff described above. When the same set of terminal options are divided into progressively smaller groups in order to accommodate the organizations with greater depth, there is no guarantee that a good name exist for each category at each level of the hierarchy. If the most natural subdivision of the set is into a small number of large categories, then naming considerations are likely to cause errors at lower levels. Conversely, when the most natural subdivision requires dividing the set into many small categories, then it will be difficult to find good names at the higher levels. More empirical work is needed to determine the optimal organization for a set of concepts, independent of category labels. It is, however, possible that a *good* organization which maximizes within category similarity while minimizing between category similarity may also yield categories that are the easiest to name. Our working hypothesis is that the semantics of a menu system (the quality of the names for categories and terminal options) are far more important than the syntax (the depth-breadth structure of the menu system).

Fisher, Yungkurth, and Moss (1990) have also stressed the need to use good semantics in order to minimize navigation errors and reasonably point out that good semantics may require a menu structure that varies in terms of breadth and depth. Given the nature of the domain, it may be the case the some panels at a given level might need to be broader than others. Similarly, some pathways might logically involve a number of meaningful subdivisions and have substantial depth, while other pathways might terminate quite quickly. Fisher et al. present a recursive algorithm that enables designers to select the most efficient structure from among those that are semantically well formed even when individual structures vary in terms of both breadth and depth. Designers wishing to use this algorithm need to consult the original article. Furthermore, the set of well-formed structures is sometimes so large that practical use will require requesting a C program directly from Donald Fisher at the University of Massachusetts.

Fisher et al. have added a valuable new tool for designing menus, but several restrictions still exist that will limit its general use. First, the algorithm needs to be seeded with a semantically well-formed hierarchy. A hierarchy is well formed if for each nonterminal panel all lower-level options that can be reached from an option, say *o*, in the nonterminal menu are members of the category represented by the option *o* and are not members of the categories represented by any other options in the nonterminal menu. Well formed hierarchies clearly exist for domains that have been organized with a formal taxonomy. Thus, animals may be subclassified as birds, reptiles, and mammals and it is easy to insure that all the options beneath birds are birds and not reptiles or mammals. But, even with an ideal case like the animal kingdom, what is semantically well-formed for a zoologist might be the tower of babel for a child or someone who has forgotten his freshman biology. Furthermore, it could be the case that, given the nature of the task, an organization based on the salient features that govern zoological taxonomy are not very useful. Imagine yourself the new owner of a large pet store and that you have computer access to information on the acquisition and care of a large number of animals. A useful distinction might exist between wild and domestic animals, but where are you going to find rabbits? Another useful distinction might exist between large and small animals, but where do you look for a goat? There are many meaningful and useful ways to organize the concepts in any domain and the salient attributes are likely to change from task to task. Functional organizations will rarely correspond to a pure hierarchy and, even when they do, they are not likely to be semantically well-formed. We return to this issue and offer some solutions in the section that looks at the role of user knowledge in menu design.

A second restriction on the use of the Fisher et al. algorithm is that one needs to estimate the probability that each option will be selected. In some applications this will amount to pure guesswork and, under that circumstance, the algorithm will not prove useful. Another problem, perhaps a bit more subtle, is that different users will be working on different types of tasks and with different levels of expertise. Thus, some options will be high frequency for some users and never used by others. A static menu structure based on frequencies averaged across all users may turn out to be quite inefficient for everyone!

24.4.2 Aids to Navigation

Iteration and Insulation

To this point the reader may have decided that depth should always be minimized. This conclusion is not justified since the potential benefits of insulation have yet to be examined. There are no experimental tests comparing systems that differ only with respect to the opportunity for insulation. However, the iterative testing of a menu-driven interface for the IBM System/34 by Savage and Habinek (1984) strongly suggests that greater depth can lead to better performance if the system reliably guides the user to those components that are task relevant and insulates him from those that are irrelevant.

The system/34 is a general purpose data processing system designed for a wide range of applications. A different set of ten experimental tasks were developed for three user groups: programmers, system operators, and work station operators. The hierarchical menu system provides the opportunity for the system to guide the user to only those functions relevant to his job.

The first phase identified several specific menu panels that were very confusing. For example, on the panel that specified ten of the system console operations, the correct option was selected by only 1 subject while the other 8 subjects spread their selections over five different options. Another problem was that subjects had a great deal of difficulty using their own job classification to get started down the appropriate path at the top of the hierarchy. Work station and system control operators wanted to make decisions based on the target function of the current task rather than their job classification. When four task-oriented options were substituted for these two job classifications in the second phase of the study users were much more likely to get started on the right track.

These examples illustrate the difficulty of writing and organizing option descriptions that will reliably guide a first-time user down the correct path. However, Savage and Habinek show that large improvements in performance can be achieved when the initial design is modified based on some careful human factors testing. Consider the average performance improvement between the first and second phase for the system and work station operators: time to complete each task improved 61%, the percentage of tasks that were never completed was reduced 75%, and the incidence of critical path errors in navigating through the system was reduced 93%! The gains achieved by iterative testing are enormous and can not be replaced by the finest set of guidelines.

Most of the modifications to the initial design involved breaking up larger menus into a set of smaller ones. The consequence of this was that the second version actually had a greater depth than the original. Thus, with proper insulation, user's preference and performance can be higher on a system with more levels.

Lee et al. have reported a series of experiments that further strengthen our conclusion that proper insulation requires careful attention to eliminating ambiguity on the upper level menu options and that iterative testing with end users is a valuable mechanism for removing major trouble spots. All of the experiments used a videotex system containing 900 to 1500 terminal nodes. The hierarchy had considerable depth, the average target appeared on the fifth level. Given the size and diversity of the database there is plenty of opportunity for the system to insulate the user from components irrelevant to his current task.

In their first experiment 10 naive users searched for 16 different documents. Each time a subject made the wrong choice he was asked to make another choice on the same menu panel until he chose the correct option. The overall error rate per menu panel was 21% and at least one error was made on half of the problems. More important was the distribution of errors. A whopping 80% of the errors occurred on just 6 (7.9%) of the 79 panels. Over 53% of the errors occurred at the two top levels of the hierarchy. The second phase provides another convincing demonstration of the value of iterative testing. A new group of videotex-naive people were asked to reclassify and/or to rename the six menus that were responsible for over 80% of the original errors. The first experiment was then replicated using the modified materials and another new group of subjects. Subjects made 40% fewer errors.

Another set of studies by Lee et al. demonstrate the dangers of design teams placing complete trust in their own judgments and the value of getting end users involved in the design process. Several videotex and information technology experts each designed a top index page they thought would be easy to use and compatible with the cognitive structures of novice users. Another group of experts rank ordered the set of menus for ease of use. The correlation between experts was virtually zero (r =.08). However, when the same set of menus were given to a representative sample of end users there was high agreement concerning which menus were best (r=.49). Furthermore, the end users preferences were highly correlated with their accuracy using the different menus (r=.72).

Traces, Maps and Fisheyes

Displaying a history of how the user arrived at the current panel may facilitate the navigation problem. The history should help the user consolidate a sequence of correct choices, enhancing the chances of being able to recall the correct pathway later. When an error is made, the history may help the user backtrack and find the correct path.

Apperley and Field (1984) have described a system that provides a history. Each menu panel includes an array of the choices leading to it, as well as the standard list of options that can be selected next. Previous actions can be canceled by selecting an item from the history rather than one of the new options. When an old item is selected (canceled) the menu immediately above the canceled action pops up and the user can make a fresh start from that point.

The database consisted of approximately a thousand panels of information relating to a hypothetical city. The subjects' task requires them to navigate through different regions in order to obtain and coordinate the information needed to satisfy the goal. For example, the goal may involve finding a theater where a particular film is showing, the most efficient method of traveling to the theater, a vegetarian restaurant which is open after the movie is over, and a means of getting home after the meal. Most of the target information is located at the fourth and fifth level of the hierarchy. Unlike the experiments on the depth-breadth trade-off that specify a single identifiable goal, this task involves some fairly complex problem solving. The task demands of the users processing resources are severe and the subjects are required to navigate through vast stretches of uncharted sea. If the special history and retreat functions had not helped in this context, they never would. The magnitude of the advantage was not reported.

One of the experimental conditions tested by Snowberry et al. (1985) provided a history of the selections that led to the current panel. There were no significant advantages in either search time or accuracy. However, the experimental design and procedure deprived the history of uses that would be quite common in real systems. First, Snowberry et al. (1985)

aborted a trial whenever the subject made a mistake in traversing the menu hierarchy. Histories should be particularly valuable when subjects must backup and recover from their mistakes. Also, information found in different locations did not have to be integrated in order to make a final decision. Integration may invite the revisitation of earlier panels and benefit greatly from a history that permits one to take a shortcut back to an earlier location.

In a well-designed study Billingsley (1982) demonstrated that previewing a map can facilitate the navigation task. A hierarchical menu structure was created from a set of 30 menu panels with familiar animals at the leaves. The upper level nodes were descriptors that categorized the animals in terms of their uses and habitats. Target animals were located at depths ranging from two to four selections. The subjects were all treated the same during the first block of nine trials. After the first block the subjects were divided into three groups and provided with different learning aids. One group was given a table that consisted of an alphabetized list of the animals that would appear as targets during the experiment. To the right of each animal was the sequence of menu options that led to the target. A second group was shown a map that displayed the hierarchical structure of the database, with all descriptors and target animals in the correct spatial and semantic relationship to each other. Subjects were given five minutes to study either the table or the map. The third group received no learning aid.

After the study period subjects continued with blocks two through five. In blocks two and three the same set of nine targets used in the first block were searched for again. A new set of nine animals served as targets in blocks four and five. It was hypothesized that the overall structure of the hierarchy could be understood and retained better with a pictorial map than an alphanumeric table and, accordingly, that the benefits of the map would be particularly apparent when subjects were forced to abandon their old well-known pathways (blocks 1-3) and hunt for new animals (block 4). The hypothesis was confirmed. In block 4 the mean search time for the nine new targets was only 19 seconds compared to 31 and 35 seconds for the table and control groups, respectively. The same pattern of results was obtained for the mean number of choices per trial: maps (4.7) and tables (8.3) produced more efficient searches than the control group (12.3).

One issue concerning maps is their level of detail and scope. Billingsley showed a map of the entire structure, but this will be impossible in large systems like that studied by Apperley and Field. Map size can be compressed either by reducing the scope and showing only the area of current interest or by reducing the detail by showing only the major highways. The former should be better for helping users who are stuck in a specific place, but the latter may be better for improving the users' overall mental model of the system and, hence, their long-term performance. Furnas (1986) has been developing a *fisheye view* that blends both local detail and important distant landmarks. The contents of the current panel are based on a degree of interest function that takes into account the distance of each node (option) in the system from the node currently in focus and the a priori importance of each node. Applied to a hierarchical menu structure, the fisheye view usually leads to the presentation of the sibling and parent options on the same branch because they are very near and grand^n parents on this direct ancestral line because they are the nearest nodes of high importance. Fisheye views based on the degree of interest are easy to compute and Furnas briefly describes a couple of test cases where their advantages have been demonstrated.

Networks versus Hierarchies

A network consists of a set of nodes and a set of links that connect the related nodes. Each node may have any number of incoming and outgoing links and the only requirement is that each node in a connected network must have at least one entry and one exit. (The entry and exit to a desolate node might be along the same link.) One potential advantage of networks is that they can provide redundant pathways to the same menu panel. In many applications a given panel naturally belongs to more than one general category. For example, if an information retrieval system contains a panel of information about a class in preventive medicine the panel could be linked in a network to panels relating to either education or medicine. A strict hierarchical tree structure would have to choose one or the other as the higher level superordinate. If the domain of the menu-driven interface does not fit into a hierarchical structure, a network organization should be considered.

Although hierarchical tree structures have been the dominant organization, a networking system called ZOG has been under development at Carnegie-Mellon University since 1972 (Robertson, McCracken, and Newell, 1981; McCracken and Akscyn, 1984). ZOG is designed for very large systems that might grow to networks of 50 to 100,00 panels. The ZOG system is based on a broad set of principles for the design of large-scale menu-driven interfaces. This section will describe only those portions of the ZOG philosophy that are relevant to the navigation problem.

If systems on the order of 10^1 or 10^2 panels can cause severe navigation problems one might expect very large systems with 10^3 or 10^4 panels to leave users hopelessly lost. However, McCracken and Akscyn report that the navigation problem is not as severe as they once believed. Part of the solution is organizing the overall network into functional groups, called subnets. Navigation within a subnet is aided with a set of tools similar to some of the traces and maps discussed earlier. Whenever a new panel is selected, the previous panel is saved on a back-up list. Specific panels can be marked on the back-up list as they are used. An orienting command allows the user to examine either the entire back-up list, the list of marked panels, or a list of panels that point to the panel currently displayed. A set of positioning commands allows the user to access these lists and bypass the normal mode of selecting options from a sequence of panels. Two of the positioning commands automatically retreat to either the last panel accessed or to the last marked panel. A go to command permits direct access by specifying the title of a target panel. A more general find command searches for a specified string. Search can be restricted to particular panel elements or sets of panels.

The ZOG rules permit any node in the network to be linked to any other node. However, a preference is expressed for tree structures for those portions of the database that have an inherent hierarchical structure. A distinction is also made between selections on a panel that point to lower levels of a tree versus selections that are *cross-references* to panels not within the tree structure. In ZOG this distinction is implemented by having the lower-level selections appear as the options on the main body and the *cross-references* appear as local pads in a right-hand column. In addition to the two sets of navigation options ZOG also has a row of global pads across the bottom of the panel that are used for general editing, browsing, and helping functions. Thus, ZOG effectively organizes the information on each panel by distinguishing global options from navigation options and vertical navigation from horizontal navigation. Selection can occur through either touch or keyboard entry. When selections are keyed, potential interference due to response competition has been minimized by using a different type of response for each of the three menus: vertical navigation is controlled by a digit identifier, horizontal navigation by a letter identifier, and the global functions by typing in the short name of the function.

24.4.3 Guidelines for Organizing the Entire Set of Menu Panels

The review of the empirical evidence suggests that the expression depth-breadth trade-off is somewhat of a misnomer. There is a structural trade-off in the sense that the inverse relationship requires that depth increase if breadth is decreased. However, there is no evidence to support the hypothesis of a performance trade-off between depth and breadth. Given that a large set of options can be meaningfully grouped on a single-level menu panel, performance is best when depth is avoided. Within the tested limit of 64 options, greater breadth is always better than the introduction of depth. The greatest weakness in the existing research evidence on menus is the absence of experiments exploring the potential benefit that depth can provide through insulation. The studies investigating the depth-breadth trade-off have not placed a premium on the prompting of appropriate options and the hiding of inappropriate options.

24.5 User-Generated Menu Organization

24.5.1 Advantages of User-Generated Organization

Given that a categorical or functional organization of items in a menu panel is warranted, how should that organization be determined? Further, how should menu panels be organized in relation to each other? In some cases, the categories are well-known and distinct (e.g., animals, minerals, cities) and the intuitions of the designer are "on-target" in relation to those of the user. However, in most cases the "appropriate" organizational scheme is not as clear cut. In these cases, software designers often generate their own organization, assuming that it is sufficiently like that of the typical user. However, this assumption is not always well-founded and thus, it is important to achieve some understanding of the user's perceived organization of the domain that is to be reflected in the menu organization. If items are categorized according to users' perceived organization, then users should be able to locate items more quickly and with fewer errors. In addition, it has been proposed that the organization of menu items affects not only menu search time and error rate, but also the formation of the conceptual model of the domain or system (e.g., McDonald, Stone, and Liebelt, 1983).

Thus in cases in which novice users do not possess a well-formed domain schema, the menu organization itself (generated from expert users) can help to reveal the "expert" schema to the novice, thereby easing the transition from novice to expert (Snyder, Happ, Malcus, Paap, and Lewis, 1985).

These advantages of user-generated menu organizations are supported by more than mere speculation. Several studies have indicated that menu organizations generated from user data are superior to those based on designers' intuitions. Hayhoe (1990) found that a pull-down menu structure of 48 items resulted in fewer errors, shorter selection times, and better recall, when it was based on the sortings of 48 subjects, rather than the sortings of four software designers. Similarly, Roske-Hofstrand and Paap (1986) found that pilots were able to complete their tasks faster when the panels of a Control-Display Unit were organized according to pilot judgments as opposed to judgments of a software design team. In these studies data collected from typical users guided the formation of the categories themselves. It is apparently insufficient to give users category labels identified by designers and have them assign individual items to these pre-formed categories. Fischoff, MacGregor, and Blackshaw (1987) found that this strategy actually produced menus which were associated with reduced ability of other subjects to locate items.

Two other caveats are critical here. First, it seems important that user-generated organizations are consensual in nature. They should not be based on the judgments of a single individual, even if that individual is the end user. McDonald, Dayton, and McDonald (1988) found that subjects who organized their own menus were actually slower on the first day of testing than subjects who used layouts that were organized on the basis of the judgments of a group of users. Also, Hayhoe (1990) found that individuals' personal categorizations were not superior to sorting-based categorizations of others. Hayhoe suggests that personal categories may be inferior to consensual categories due to poor reliability over time, as well as faulty category labels. The second caveat is that user-generated organizations will only be as successful as the users who generate them are typical of end users. For instance, Holland and Merikle (1987) found that menu organizations generated by expert users benefited other expert users more than novice users, especially in cases in which the task required an identity match. In sum, user-generated menu organizations should be based on data collected from multiple users who are representative of the target population. Of course, if the goal is to reveal to novice users the experts' schema, then the menu organization should be based on a representative group of experienced users.

Before describing some of the methods used to expose users' perceived organization of menu items, an alternative approach should be noted. This approach formalizes the procedure for basing menu organizations on the intuitions of the designer. For instance, Shurtleff (1992) uses a clustering method similar to that described below to organize menu items. However, instead of basing the distance data that is used as input to the clustering routine on user's judgments of relatedness, he based it on the number of shared properties of item pairs, according to the documentation. Similarly, Sachania (1985) reorganized UNIX commands using co-occurrence in the designer-based "see-also" references as estimates of distance. Shoval (1990) proposes a methodology for basing menu interfaces on data flow diagrams of system function. Whereas, this general approach to menu design eliminates the need for collecting user judgments, it is important to point out that none of these papers provide results concerning the validity of the approach compared to user-generated menus, or simply menus based less formally on designers' intuitions. On the other hand, there is evidence to suggest that designers' intuitions are not necessarily in agreement with one another (Lee et al., 1984) and can result in menu organizations inferior to those based on user data (Hayhoe, 1990; Roske-Hofstrand and Paap, 1986).

24.5.2 Exposing the User Model

There are a number of methods for eliciting knowledge from an end user or domain expert (Cooke, 1994). Psychological scaling techniques such as MDS (multidimensional scaling) and HCA (hierarchical cluster analysis) have been most often used to expose users' perceived organization of menu items. These techniques are best suited for eliciting the categorical and semantic knowledge relevant to menu organization. The output of these techniques ranges from a spatial map (i.e., MDS) to a hierarchical (i.e., HCA) or graphical representation (i.e., Pathfinder network scaling). These representations are conveniently mapped onto the grouping of items within a single menu panel, as well as the structure that interrelates multiple menu panels. The methodology employed with these techniques generally consists of data collection, followed by psychological scaling of the data. We will refer to the output of this process as a "user model."

Data Collection

In the data collection step estimates of proximity between menu items (or menu panels) are obtained from a representative user group. It is assumed that these estimates reflect the user's perceived organization of the items. Several different methods are available for obtaining these estimates (Cooke, 1994). Pairwise relatedness ratings, sorting and event records, three of the most common data collection methods, will be described in turn below.

Pairwise relatedness ratings. The collection of pairwise relatedness estimates involves having users judge the similarity or relatedness of all pairs (n(n-1)/2) of n items. If asymmetrical relations are considered (distance a-b ≠ distance b-a), then more judgments are required (n(n-1)). Thus, this technique is time consuming, impossibly so for large sets of items. Also, ratings are likely to be influenced by shifts in the dimensions used by judges in making ratings and the rating "frame" supplied by instructions or resulting from the composition of the set of items to be rated. This instability is not so much a defect of the methodology, as a reflection of a dynamic cognitive system (Barsalou, 1989). The pairwise rating procedure is also subject to considerable rating error since judges are required to rate all pairs of items even if they are not familiar with them. For this reason it is a good practice to collect familiarity ratings on each concept before pairwise estimates of relatedness are given. Ratings involving unfamiliar items can be later disregarded or given less weight in relation to familiar items.

Although these are the modal rating procedures, there are several variations (see Cooke, 1994), some of which reduce the number of ratings required (i.e., controlled association: Miyamoto, Oi, Osamu, Katsuya, and Nakayama, 1986). Ratings have most commonly been made on the basis of similarity (McDonald, Stone, Liebelt, and Karat, 1982; McDonald, Stone, and Liebelt, 1983; Roske-Hofstrand and Paap, 1986), McDonald, Dayton, and McDonald (1988) in their application of this methodology to the layout of items on a fast food keyboard, provide an excellent illustration of the situations in which it is more appropriate to use co-occurrence judgments than similarity judgments. In short, the nature of the end users' tasks should be considered when eliciting users' judgments that will impact menu design.

Sorting. Another common method for obtaining estimates of pairwise item proximity is to require judges to sort items into piles based on relationships (e.g., Hayhoe, 1990, Holland and Merikle, 1987; Fischhoff, MacGregor, and Blackshaw, 1987; Snyder et al., 1985; Tullis, 1985). As for pairwise ratings, the nature of the relationships can be specified (e.g., co-occurrence, functional similarity, physical similarity) and this decision should be based on the typical tasks that users will perform using the menu.

For each subject, a matrix is constructed in which pairs of items sorted together are assigned a 1 and those pairs not sorted together are assigned a 0. Other values can also be used if judges sort items into a hierarchy of groups and subgroups or if judges perform multiple sorts. However, without these variations the data obtained from a single judge is not as sensitive as obtained using pairwise ratings on a multi-value scale. To remedy this problem, individual's matrices of 0s and 1s are usually summed across subjects. Despite its lack of sensitivity, this technique is much more efficient than the method of paired comparisons, particularly for large sets of items (n > 30). Additionally, it is not as susceptible to frame distortions or shifts in the use of dimensions because all of the items must be sorted as a set. Finally, if judges are required to sort all items and items are not duplicated, the procedure produces data matrices which satisfy the triangle and ultrametric inequality (Miller, 1969). However, requiring judges to sort all items may introduce error into the data to the extent that judges are not familiar with the items to be sorted. Also, the use of duplicate cards allows non hierarchical structures which may be better representations of the underlying structures. Variations on this general sorting procedure can be found in Cooke (1994).

Event records. Proximities may also be obtained from event records including records of user-computer interactions, verbal think-aloud reports, or recall order (e.g., Cooke, Neville, and Rowe, in press; McDonald and Schvaneveldt, 1988). In these cases the sequential order of the events in the protocol is used to construct a matrix of pairwise proximities. Computing proximities can be done in a variety of ways. Most often, conditional probabilities (i.e., the probability that item b follows item a in the sequence) are computed from the raw transition frequencies (see Cooke, et al, in press, for details). One problem with this technique is that it does not guarantee a proximity estimate for each pair of items. Asymmetrical distance estimates are a natural consequence of this technique. One advantage to this technique is that it is indirect in that judges per se are not required. The data can be obtained automatically as a part of system monitoring functions.

Psychological Scaling Techniques

Once the pairwise proximity estimates have been collected, they can be submitted to a variety of multivariate scaling techniques. The general purpose of this step is to reduce the matrix of distance estimates to a form that is easier to visualize. The reduction is accomplished in different ways, by different techniques, but it is assumed that the output reveals the most important or salient aspects of the proximities. The three techniques that are used most frequently in menu design applications include MDS, HCA, and Pathfinder network scaling. Other quantitative techniques such as simulated annealing (McDonald, Molander, and Noel, 1988) and latent partition analysis (Hayhoe, 1990) have also been used. Each of the three commonly used methods is described below.

Multidimensional Scaling. MDS procedures (Shepard, 1962a, b; Kruskal, 1977; Kruskal and Wish, 1978) take the pairwise proximity estimates and generate a spatial layout of the items. There are various MDS routines, but the procedure common to them all involves identifying the best fit of the original data to distances in a d-dimensional spatial layout of the items. The dimensionality is determined by the analyst, although there are heuristics that facilitate this decision. For instance, the fit of the data to the original data is measured in terms of "stress." Stress decreases (i.e., improves) as d increases and optimal dimensionality can be identified as the dimensionality beyond which improvements in stress are minimal (i.e., the "elbow" in the curve relating dimensionality to stress). MDS routines can be metric or nonmetric. Factor analysis is closely related to metric MDS. Nonmetric routines assume only an ordinal relationship between proximities and MDS distances (Kruskal and Wish, 1978).

MDS routines typically assume that the data can be represented in terms of one or more continuous dimensions, that dimensions reflect features along which the concepts vary, and that metric distance between points in the space corresponds linearly or monitonically to conceptual proximity reflected in the judgments. Because of the first assumption, MDS is generally best suited for homogeneous sets of items that share many features, rather than heterogeneous ones that do not. The spatial information that MDS reveals is not always relevant to grouping of menu items or menu panel connections. It does, however, supply relevant information when spatial layout of items is required (e.g., McDonald, Dayton, and McDonald, 1988). It may also reveal discrete groups of items in the spatial layout (e.g., Holland and Merikle, 1987), however, HCA is probably better suited for this type of information.

Hierarchical Cluster Analysis. HCA routines (Lewis, 1991) reduce the proximities to a hierarchical set of clusters. It is assumed that each item is or is not a member of a cluster and that the proximity judgments reflect the extent of nested clustering or difference in levels of a hierarchy (Olson and Biolsi, 1991). The routine proceeds by first generating tight clusters from pairs of items that are the most highly related based on the proximities. Subsequent pairs of items are included in a cluster depending on the proximity between that item and items in the existing cluster. The various HCA routines differ in ways that distance between an item and a cluster of other items is computed (e.g., mean, maximum, or minimum).

The output of HCA represents each of the items and the point at which each item enters into a cluster. At one extreme, all items are in their own clusters, and at the other, all items are in the same cluster. In order to identify discrete clusters it is necessary to select a cutoff point beyond which clustered items are not considered to belong to the same group. HCA lends itself well to menu design because the output is in the form of discrete groups. Therefore, it may be used to organize items into groupings on a single menu panel (e.g., McDonald, Dayton, and McDonald, 1988; McDonald, Stone and Liebelt, 1983) or across multiple panels (e.g., Hayhoe, 1990; McDonald, Stone, Liebelt, and Karat, 1982; Tullis, 1985). There are a number of variations on this general procedure, most of which relax some of the constraints of strict nonoverlapping hierarchies (see Cooke, 1994).

Pathfinder network scaling. Pathfinder derives network structures (PFNETS) from the proximity estimates. The items are represented as nodes in the network and relations between items are represented as links. Links may indicate functional similarity, physical similarity, co-occurrence, or some other form of relationship depending on the nature of the original estimates. Conceptually the algorithm is quite simple. Links are assigned weights or strengths based on the associated proximity in the data matrix. Then for each pair of items, the proximity in the data matrix is compared with the distance of possible paths (a series of one or more links between two items) between those items in a network corresponding to the data matrix. A direct link between the two items is included in the derived PFNET unless a shorter indirect path is found. Two parameters, r and q determine the way that path distance is computed, and varying the values of these parameters allows for systematic variation in the complexity (number of links) of a network. The resulting network structure is not constrained to hierarchies as is HCA and is able to represent asymmetrical relations by virtue of directed links. This flexibility makes Pathfinder networks ideal representations for applications involving the interconnection of multiple menu panels (Roske-Hofstrand and Paap, 1986). Schvaneveldt (1990) provides additional details of the algorithm and example applications.

Multiple techniques. Each of the above scaling techniques is associated with slightly different assumptions concerning the relationship between the original proximities and the resulting output. For instance, MDS weighs all proximities equally, whereas Pathfinder network scaling tends to weigh close proximities most heavily. These different assumptions result in different ways of reducing and representing the data and these results may also differ in psychological meaningfulness (Cooke, 1992; Cooke, Durso, and Schvaneveldt, 1986). The technique that should be used may be dictated by the specifics of the application. For instance, whereas MDS may be most appropriate for a spatial layout , HCA may be best suited for discrete groupings, and Pathfinder for a network of menu panels. Similarly, the constraints of the application may dictate a particular data collection technique. The sheer number of items may rule out pairwise proximity ratings, whereas a lack of willing judges may dictate using event records. Where it is possible, it is best to use multiple methods (e.g., McDonald, Dayton, and McDonald, 1988). Each tends to provide a different view of the data. Furthermore, using the methods as converging operations can provide stronger support for design decisions.

24.5.3 Imposing the User Model on the Interface

Once the user's perceived organization of menu items or panels (i.e., the user model) has been exposed, this information needs to be reflected somehow in the menu organization. The output of the various scaling techniques mentioned above can be used to organize items within a single menu panel (e.g., McDonald, Dayton, and McDonald, 1988; McDonald, Molander, and Noel, 1988; McDonald, Dearholt, Paap, and Schvaneveldt, 1986; McDonald, Stone, Liebelt, and Karat, 1982) or to organize multiple menu panels (e.g., Hayhoe, 1990; Holland and Merikle, 1987; Roske-Hofstrand and Paap, 1986; Tullis, 1985). Note that the organization of items across multiple menu panels so that users can most easily find the items shares many of the same navigation problems and potential solutions as retrieval of information from large databases or hypertext documents. For example, as one aid to navigation the user model can be made explicit by actually displaying the model itself in the form of a map that the users can refer to as an aid to navigation (McDonald, et al. 1986). To better illustrate how user models are imposed on menu interfaces three examples of such application are discussed in detail below.

Example 1: Imposing the User Model on a Flexible Guide to UNIX Help Panels

The first example (McDonald, et al., 1986; McDonald and Schvaneveldt, 1988) illustrates how the user model associated with UNIX help panels can be imposed on the organization of those items within a single level guide. This example also illustrates how that organization can be made explicit to the user through a navigational map. In addition, this example illustrates how user models based on different organizational perspectives can be exposed and in turn imposed on the menu interface.

The goal of this project was to develop a menu for accessing help panels on UNIX commands (i.e., MAN panels), along with an interactive documentation guide (IDG) or map that reflects the organization of the panels. The organization of the menu is highly flexible in that it permits users to acquire help in a variety of ways. Part of the design task was to make several different organizations of the 219 MAN panels available to the user, each of which presented the system from a different perspective.

The organization or perspective that provides the best entry to the goal panel will depend on what the user knows about the information sought. Three perspectives are available: two at the level of specific command names and one at a higher, more conceptual level. Consider, as a first example, a user who knows how to remove files with the *rm* command, but doesn't remember the command for removing directories. Information is needed about a command that is functionally equivalent, but acts on a different type of object. Clearly, this user, on this occasion, would like to search the database of MAN panels from a perspective that shows the functional similarity between com-

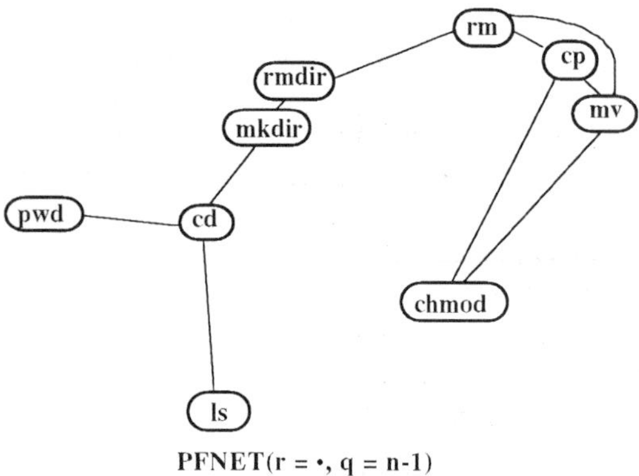

Figure 4. A functional perspective of a subnet corresponding to file and directory commands.

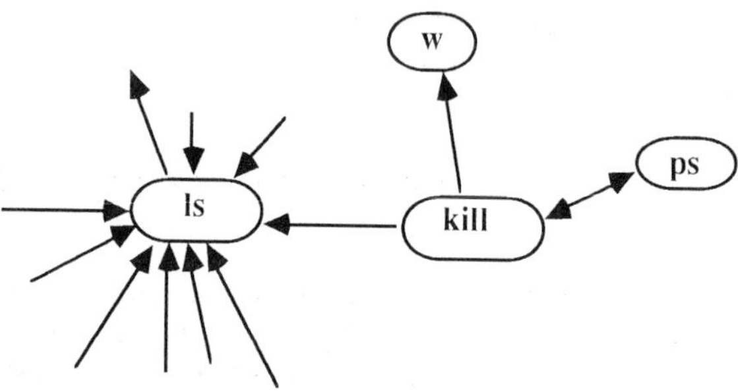

Figure 5. A subset showing a procedural perspective of that portion of the Pathfinder network derived from the history of expert UNIX users.

mands. Thus, the user should be able to ask for help on a command that is like *rm* and have displayed a map in the form of a subnet like the one shown in Figure 4. This subnet was derived from the Pathfinder solution that used functional similarity as the basis for the original sorting data. The direct link between *rm* and *rmdir* provides an immediate cue that the target command is *rmdir*. If the user needs additional help about the syntax or side effects of *rmdir*, the *rmdir* MAN panel can now be accessed directly.

On other occasions the user may not know a functionally related command that can be used to direct the interactive search for help. Under these conditions a procedural (rather than functional) perspective may be beneficial. Consider the following predicament. A user wants to kill a job, discovers that she must specify the ID of that job, but does not know the ID of the job that she wants to eradicate. A procedural subnet, similar to the one shown in Figure 5 will point the way to the solution. Procedural networks like the one illustrated were derived from event records, specifically the command protocols of expert UNIX users. A direct link between two commands in a procedural network indicates that the first command is often followed by the second. The procedural subnet shows that *kill* is frequently preceded by one command, *ps* (the program status command), which will provide the needed ID information. The solution to the problem should be discovered fairly quickly. Note that in this case the target command *ps* is not closely related to the *kill* command in the functional network and entering this network from the *kill* node would not have provided a solution to the problem.

The third perspective of the MAN database is a top-down view from a more conceptual level. A more abstract network of the UNIX operating system was derived from the category labels associated with the natural divisions of the command set and from other system concepts that transcend the function of individual commands (e.g., redirection, multi-tasking, filtering). This option permits the user to state goals in general terms and have displayed the system-specific instantiations that form the set of available alternatives. For example, a request for help on printing would return slices of subnets related to different devices, formats, etc. This third perspective adds an additional level to the MAN guide that is more abstract than the other two levels. In addition, this perspective was not user-derived like the other two levels.

In summary, the menu organization in this example is highly flexible. Users have the option of seeking help based on their functional knowledge of specific commands, procedural knowledge, or higher-level conceptual goals. These three ways of organizing the 210 MAN panels were determined by using a combination of the techniques described above (e.g., sorting, event records, Pathfinder) to expose the UNIX experts' user models. The basic mechanism for presenting help is to display portions of Pathfinder networks (i.e., subnets) based on the selected perspective. Detailed information about any displayed command is available (in the form of an existing MAN panel) to the user, by selecting a specific node from the displayed subnet.

Example 2: Imposing the User Model on the Organization of Flight Management Menu Panels

The second example illustrates how a user model can be applied to the menu design associated with the CDU (Control-Display Unit) of a flight management system for NASA's advanced concepts simulator. This problem, tackled by Roske-Hofstrand and Paap (1986), in-

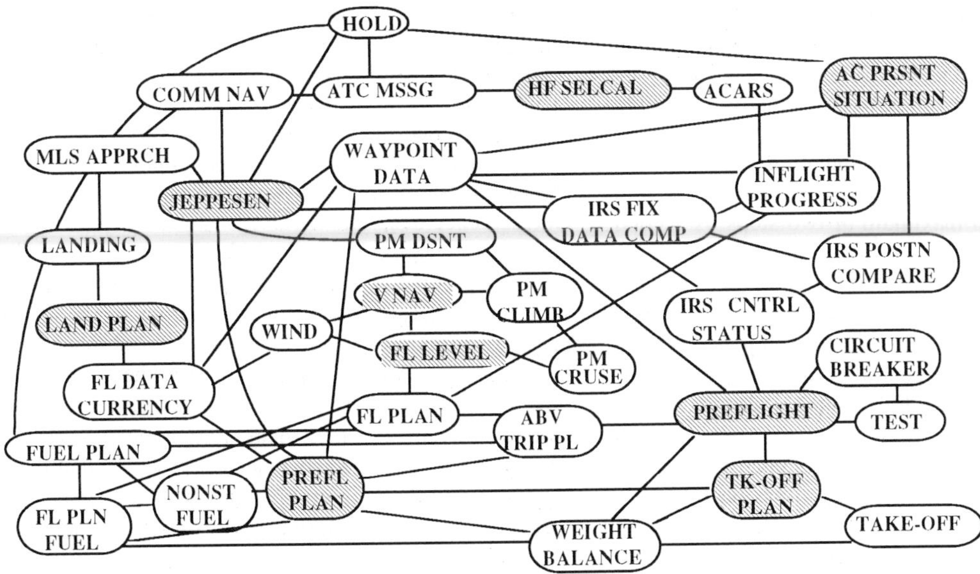

Figure 6. Pathfinder network for 34 panels of the control display unit in NASA's advanced concepts cimulator. *A set of dominating nodes is shown with the cross-hatching.*

volves the organization of multiple menu panels and thus, it also addresses the use of Pathfinder to represent levels of abstraction in a hierarchy.

The CDU is a fairly large menu-driven system that can be used to both acquire knowledge and take actions. In the prototypes that were evaluated in this project, the pilot sees a display which contains some text, sometimes a prompt for information that is to be entered, and a menu of selections. When the pilot selects an option by entering an identifier letter a new panel is displayed. Pilots with limited experience with the CDU can find it difficult to navigate from the current panel to a new target panel. The goal of the study was to compare menu organizations based on Pathfinder networks to an organization based on the specifications of the original design team.

A subset of 34 panels from the original specifications for the CDU were selected. The chunk of information controlled and/or displayed on each panel of the CDU was treated as a unitary concept. In an initial phase, four experienced pilots were familiarized with each of the 34 panels. In the next phase the pilots rated the similarity between each of the 561 pairs of panels on a scale of 0 to 9, with smaller numbers indicating closer distances, that is greater conceptual similarity.

Separate Pathfinder networks were derived from the similarity ratings for each pilot. Treating each of the 34 panels as a single node means that the algorithm starts with a network of 561 links. Four hundred of these links were eliminated in three of the four networks. This leaves the network of 70 links shown in Figure 6 in which the weight of each link can be assigned a value of 2, 3, or 4 on the basis of the number of individual networks that contained the link.

Although the local relationships between the panels will be very consistent with the pilot's expectations, the network alone does not provide a good model for a global organization of the CDU. A more coherent model could be communicated if the menu structure included a higher-level conceptual network that served as a top-down entryway to the lower-level panels. There are a number of ways to determine levels of abstraction in Pathfinder output (e.g., Branaghan, McDonald, and Schvaneveldt, 1991; Esposito, 1990), as well as a number of ways to represent levels of abstraction in the interface. Instead of imposing global structure with higher-level conceptual nodes Roske-Hofstrand and Paap simply instantiated high salience to a small set of the panels by placing them on a master index page that could be accessed with the touch of a special function key.

The panels that appeared on the master index were dominating nodes in the network. The set of dominating nodes is the smallest set of nodes that permit direct access to all other nodes in the network.

Starting from a set of dominating nodes, every node in the network can be reached by traversing a single link. For the network shown in Figure 6, the smallest set of dominating nodes consisted of nine concepts. One such set is indicated by crosshatching. One advantage of selecting dominating nodes for the index panels is that any panel that can be reached from any other panel in a maximum of two steps. A second advantage is that they are likely to be key nodes in the network. Many of them will have high degrees of centrality, i.e., several other panels will be directly linked to a dominating node. Those dominating nodes with more moderate levels of centrality are likely to be pivotal in the sense that they link remote nodes or subnets into the main network.

Sixteen experienced pilots participated in the validation test. The test was a training session that consisted of four blocks of 34 trials. On each trial the pilot read a scenario that described a set of current conditions, a general goal, and a specific question that could only be answered by accessing the appropriate CDU panel. The total task time for each trial was measured from the onset of the question to the pilot's response. Each of the 34 menu panels contained the target information for one trial in each block. Prototypes based on the cognitive networks, but differing in redundancy offered by the index items, were consistently easier to learn compared to the prototypes based on the original design specifications. For example, by the fourth and final block of training, the prototype based on Figure 6 was showing a 22 second advantage (84 versus 62 seconds) over that based on the original design. These results are consistent with our earlier conclusion that it is very difficult to devise an unambiguous organization without input from a group of typical end users. The results also support the view that the Pathfinder algorithm is a very effective tool for generating a representation of the end user's conceptual organization of the domain of interest.

Example 3: Imposing the User Model on Two Hierarchies of Multiple Panels

Tullis (1985) applied some of the methods described above to design a menu for the Menu Assisted Resource Control (MARC) interface for Burroughs mainframe systems. The system performs over 700 functions and is used to send messages, to access system news, and to access the functions for file maintenance, program execution, and system operation. This particular example not only demonstrates how sorting and hierarchical cluster analysis can be applied to the organization of multiple menu panels, but also illustrates how hierarchies of varying depth and breadth can be obtained by slicing the cluster analysis output at different levels.

Tullis based the menu structure on the user model rather than his own or other expert opinion. The user model of system functions was determined as follows. One sentence descriptions of each function were written on index cards. Five pilot subjects sorted the cards into groups on the basis of similarity. When all five subjects placed the same set of functions in the same group, one function was selected to represent that set in further testing. This procedure reduced the number of functions to 271. The next set of 15 subjects were instructed to sort the new deck into logically related groups and to assign a label to each group. When they were satisfied with the groups, they were then asked to sort these groups into larger groups called categories. For each subject, a matrix of perceived similarity between all pairs was determined by assigning a distance of 0 to all pairs in the same group, a 1 to all pairs in the same category (but different groups) and a 2 to all other pairs. All 15 individual matrices were then summed together and a hierarchical clustering analysis was performed on the overall distance matrix.

The hierarchical clustering resulted in 18 levels of clustering. Two different menu hierarchies were formed from this analysis by slicing the cluster analysis at two different levels and collapsing across the levels above the slice. One prototype with less breadth and more depth had a root index panel of 15 options. On the basis of the outcome of the clustering analysis, target functions could be accomplished by viewing two, three, or four panels. A second prototype with more breadth and less depth had a root index panel of 37 options. All functions could be accomplished by viewing only two menus.

A new group of 37 Burroughs' employees served as subjects in the next phase. About half were assigned to each of the two prototypes. Without guidance subjects were given 24 tasks to accomplish, e.g. printing a directory, sending a message, powering up a disk pack, and checking the status of a line printer. The two groups did not significantly differ on the total time required to complete all the tasks. However, the group using the system with less breadth and greater depth generated significantly more total steps (135 to 102) and more extra steps (55 to 32). Because of this Tullis concludes that the best menu hierarchy to use in the one that required fewer steps; the three column version with greater breadth and less depth.

Tullis' conclusion could be challenged. The lack of any significant differences in total time stands in marked contrast to the studies reviewed in the previous discussion of breadth versus depth. It appears that the advantage of breadth over depth may be one of diminishing returns at great levels of breadth. Additional comparisons between large and very large menus would be informative. It should also be noted that Tullis did not provide a different set of tasks for each type of subject despite the fact that subjects included system operators, programmers, and technical writers. If the subjects were required to access only those functions within the domain of their specific job and expertise, the insulating properties of menus with greater depth may have been more apparent.

24.5.4 Guidelines for Menu Design

The research and applications reviewed in this section suggest that when a categorical organization of menu items or panels is desired, but not obvious, user-generated menu organization should be considered. This organization is based on data collected from end users. Data should be collected from representative end users, or in cases in which the goal is to teach users an expert model, experienced end users. User models should be consensual rather than personal and categories themselves should be user-derived.

Although it is wise to use multiple data collection and scaling methods when possible, there are some cases in which one technique is favored over another. Pairwise relatedness ratings become unwieldy when the number of menu items exceeds 30 or so. Sorting, on the other hand, is more efficient, though less sensitive than pairwise ratings. In either case, when user judgments are elicited, care should be taken in dealing with unfamiliar items, effects of the context surrounding the judgments, and the nature of the relationship appropriate for the typical menu task. When users are unavailable for judgments or when a procedural perspective is desired event records are appropriate sources of data.

Once the data have been collected, one or more psychological scaling techniques can be applied to reduce the data to a form more easily imposed on the menu interface. MDS is most appropriate when spatial layout of items is important or when the items are homogenous and the nature of the underlying dimensions is questioned. HCA is useful for identifying discrete groups that may make up categories within a single menu panel or across menu panels, however it is restricted to a hierarchical structure. Pathfinder network scaling offers flexibility when the menu organization is not limited to a strict hierarchy. Pathfinder is also most appropriate to use when the data are in the form of event records, because it is capable of representing asymmetric relations.

24.6 Auditory Menus

It has become commonplace for telephone users to encounter auditory menus. Many of these users express complaints ranging from vague feelings of depersonalization to specific certitude that the system was designed to optimize profit for the company rather than convenience for the customer. A more benevolent view is that auditory menus have inherent limitations compared to visual menus and that well-intended designers need help in understanding and overcoming these limitations. A report by Richard Halstead-Nussloch (1989) provides a variety of recommendations for telephone-based interfaces and we have adopted many of his ideas in the following discussion.

The most important limitations for telephone menus accrue because audition is linear and vision is not. Speech arrives at a listener's ear one word at a time and the information normally contained in a single visual display must be distributed over time. The options are likely to be presented at a slower rate than silent reading and with less flexible control on the part of the user. The phrase *search-time* sounds inappropriate for most auditory menus. Users don't actively search for a target, rather they must wait and try to ambush it. The lack of flexible control can impose a greater load on working memory as unwanted interpolated material intervenes between candidate selections and the user's final choice.

One method of easing the limitations of auditory menus is to employ greater depth in the hierarchy and reap the benefits of funneling and insulation. Because spoken options will take longer to process than written options one should minimize the number of options the user must listen to. Recall from the example given early on the subsection of funneling that an exhaustive search of a flat list of 64 options can be reduced to an exhaustive search of only 12 options when the options are accessed from a 2^6 hierarchy. The efficiency gains of funneling will be augmented by insulating the user from options completely irrelevant to the current goal.

Increasing depth will bring about a concomitant reduction in breadth. Breadth, in the case of auditory menus, refers to the number of options on a given list.

Guidelines for organizing the options on a list are different for auditory menus than visual menus. The initial letter of a spoken word is not as salient as the initial letter of a printed word. Furthermore, in most auditory menus users can not easily jump to the end or the middle of a list. Accordingly, it is not surprising that Miller and Elias (1991) showed that alphabetical lists are no better than random lists. Because of the inherent difficulty in jumping to specific locations in a spoken list, categorical organizations are not likely to be effective. If options can be readily group into categories, then one might as well use the category labels in a higher-level list that increases the depth of the system. In contrast to the problems noted for either alphabetical or categorical lists, it makes great sense to present the list in decreasing order of frequency. On average, this will reduce the number of time-consuming unwanted options that users must wait for and listen to. Also, options should have the form "to do function X press identifier Y" rather than the opposite. This order permits the user to disregard the identifier if he or she is not interested in function X and to interrupt the message sooner.

Although we have persistently reminded the reader that auditory menus provide the user with less control than visual menus, there are features of auditory menus that improve the control problem. Users should be able to interrupt the presentation of an option or any other system message without having to listen to the whole thing. A small set of navigation commands should be available at all times, e.g., press * to go forward, press # to backup, press #1 to start over. The special navigation commands are similar in spirit, but not in detail, to the skip and scan menus developed and tested by Resnick and Virzi (1992). If single-digit numbers are always reserved as identifiers for each list, then experienced users can make a selection without listening to any of the options. In fact, a sequence of digits could be used to cut right through the hierarchy to the target option.

In summary and in contrast to visual menus, auditory menus should usually have more depth and less breadth, present the options in decreasing order of frequency of use, and provide a small set of commands that interrupt and redirect the flow of information. The greatest potential problem with the recommendation for more depth is the usual concern with navigation problems. It is more important than ever that the high-level options or prompts neatly cleave the domain into natural categories that the user will understand and anticipate. Some of the techniques and methods discussed in the earlier section on *User-Generated Menus* may be very helpful in this regard.

24.7 Menus and Practice

Some research has suggested that performance differences due to many of the factors discussed in this chapter dissipate with practice. For example, Card (1982) found that the benefits of alphabetical organization disappear after 800 selections of exact-match targets from an 18-item menu. Similarly, McDonald, Stone, and Liebelt (1983) found that reaction time advantages of exact-match target cues over definition target cues are virtually nonexistent after 64 selections from a 64-item menu In addition, Mehlenbacher, Duffy, and Palmer (1989) reported that for selections from a 22-item menu, performance differences due to type of target cue (identity match, synonym, iconic representation of the function) and menu organization (alphabetical or functional) were most pronounced in the first block of 14 trials and rapidly dissipated in the four remaining trials. Others (Hayhoe, 1990, Kreigh, Pesot, and Halcomb, 1990) indicate that effects of menu structure (depth vs. breadth) dissipate after many trials of exact-match target selection. Given that people seem to adapt to and learn even the poorest of menu interfaces, how important are issues such as target cue, menu organization, and menu structure? Are decisions about menu interfaces trivial beyond the first few hours of learning?

Other research suggests that this is not the case. For instance, Halgren and Cooke (1993) found that the same pattern results held for the first half and last half of a set of 24 problems that subjects had to solve using information accessible in a 64 item menu. In this study, problems varied in complexity, ranging from simple retrieval of information to more complex integration of information across different categories. Although it is possible that the pattern of results would change given practice beyond the 24 problems, other studies in which subjects have been given even more practice also find persistence of performance differences. In fact, Roske-Hofstrand and Paap (1986) found that the task time advantages of a well-organized menu only became apparent in the last two of four blocks (34 selections per block). In this experiment, experienced pilots selected menu items in order to display panels of a flight management system needed to answer specific questions. Also, McDonald, Dayton, and McDonald (1988) and McDonald, Molander, and Noel (1988) report that for a multiple-item selection task, differences due to factors such as menu layout persisted over 3 days (240 trials per day) and 156 trials, respectively. As the authors point out, the effects that persisted in this paradigm could be attributed to movement time from option to option on the touch screen keyboard. Regardless of the reason for the performance difference, these studies suggest that such differences can persist or even increase with extensive practice.

How can we reconcile the fact that performance differences attributed to menu interface design features dissipate with practice in some cases, but not others? One difference between the two sets of conflicting studies is the type of task that subjects are required to perform. The studies that demonstrate dissipation of performance differences with practice require subjects to simply select a menu item given a target cue. On the other hand, the studies resulting in persistence or increase in performance differences with practice, require subjects to perform more complex tasks such as selecting multiple menu items or answering questions that require problem solving or integration of information. These latter tasks may be more representative of actual menu use compared to the simple selection tasks. Furthermore, tasks that are more cognitively complex may require a well-developed conceptual model of the information available via the menu system. Factors such as menu organization may not only affect visual search time, but may also have even greater and longer lasting effects when it comes to facilitating the user's development of an appropriate conceptual model of the system (Halgren and Cooke, 1993, McDonald, Molander, and Noel, 1988). For instance, by noticing the categorical structure of menus, users may gain better insight into the scope and organization of the information that is available. Therefore, the benefits of specific menu features that can be attributed to conceptual model development may only be apparent for complex tasks and studies constrained to simple selection tasks may paint an overly optimistic picture of the benefits of practice.

Even if we ignore the evidence to the contrary, and accept the conclusion that with practice, some performance discrepancies due to menu features dissipate, we can still question the degree to which this occurs in actual use. That is, actual users seldom experience the extensive massed practice typical of lab studies (Mehlenbacher, Duffy, and Palmer, 1989). Instead of selecting items from the same menu hundreds of times in a sitting, with each item receiving an equivalent number of selections, actual users may select only one or two items from the same menu per session, and even when more selections are made, it is rare that each item is selected with equal frequency. Consequently, even users who are experienced with a system may have the occasion to search for a menu item that has not been practiced sufficiently to enjoy any benefits. On these occasions it is likely that factors such as menu structure and organization do make a difference.

24.8 References

Allen, R. B. (1983) Cognitive factors in the use of menus and trees: an experiment. *IEEE Journal on Selected Areas in Communication,* SAC-1(2), 333-336.

Arend, U., Muthig, K. P., and Wandmacher, J. (1987). Evidence for global feature superiority in menu selection by icons. *Behaviour and Information Technology, 6,* 411-426.

Apperley, M. D. and Field, G, E. (1984) A comparative evaluation of menu-based interactive human-computer dialogue techniques. *Proceedings of INTERACT '84* (pp. 103-107). London: IFIP.

Atkinson, R. C., and Juola, J. F. (1974). Search and decision processes in recognition memory (pp.242-293). In D. H. Krantz, R. C. Atkinson, R. D. Luce, and P. Suppes (Eds.) *Contemporary developments in mathematical psychology, Vol 1.* San Francisco, Freeman.

Barsalou, L. W. (1989). Intraconcept similarity and its implications for interconcept similarity. In S. Vosniadou and A. Ortony (Eds.), *Similarity and analogical reasoning,* (pp. 76-121). Cambridge: Cambridge University Press.

Billingsley, P. A. (1982) Navigation through hierarchical menu structures: Does it help to have a map? *Proceedings of the Human Factors Society 26th Annual Meeting* (pp. 103-107). Santa Monica: Human Factors Society.

Branaghan, R., McDonald, J. and Schvaneveldt, R. (1991). Identifying high-level UNIX tasks. *SIGCHI Bulletin, 23,* 73-74.

Callahan, J., Hopkins, D., Weiser, M., and Shneiderman, B. (1988). An empirical comparison of pie vs. linear menus. *CHI '88 Conference Proceedings on Human Factors in Computing Systems* (pp. 95-100). New York: Association for Computing Machinery.

Card, S. K. (1982) User perceptual mechanisms in the search of computer command menus. *Proceedings of Human Factors in Computer Systems* (pp. 190-196). Gaithersburg, MD: SIGCHI.

Reprint requests should be mailed to Kenneth R. Paap or Nancy Cooke, Box 3452, New Mexico State University, Las Cruces, NM 88003, U. S. A.

Card, S. K., English, W. K., and Burr, B. J. (1978) Evaluation of mouse, rate-controlled isometric joystick, step keys, and text keys for text selection on a CRT. *Ergonomics, 21,* 601-613.

Card, S. K., Moran, T. P., and Newell, A. (1983) *The psychology of human-computer interaction.* Hillsdale, NJ: Lawrence Erlbaum Associates.

Carroll, J. M. (1982) Learning, using and designing filenames and command paradigms. *Behaviour and Information Technology, 1* (4), 327-346.

Cooke, N. J. (1992). Eliciting semantic relations for empirically derived networks. *International Journal of Man-Machine Studies, 37,* 721-750.

Cooke, N. J. (1994). Varieties of knowledge elicitation techniques. *International Journal of Human-Computer Studies, 41,* 801-849.

Cooke, N. M., Durso, F. T., and Schvaneveldt, R. W. (1986) Measures of memory organization and recall. *Journal of Experimental Psychology: Learning, Memory, and Cognition, 12* (4).

Cooke, N. J., and Neville, K. J. , and Rowe, A. L. (in press) Procedural network representations of sequential data. *Human-Computer Interaction.*

Dumais, S. T. and Landauer, T. K. (1983) Using examples to describe categories. *Proceedings of CHI '83* (pp. 112-115). New York: ACM.

Egido, C., and Patterson, J. (1988). Pictures and category labels as navigational aids for catalog browsing. *CHI '88 Conference Proceedings on Human Factors in Computing Systems* (pp. 127-132). New York: Association for Computing Machinery.

Esposito, C. (1990). A graph-theoretic approach to concept clustering. In R. Schvaneveldt (Ed.), *Pathfinder Associative Networks: Studies in Knowledge Organization* (pp. 89-99). Norwood, NJ: Ablex.

Furnas, G. W. (1986) Generalized fisheye views. *Proceedings of CHI '86* (pp. 16-23). New York: ACM.

Furnas, G. W., Landauer, T. K., Gomez, L. M., and Dumais, S. T. (1984) Statistical semantics: Analysis of the potential performance of keyword information systems. In J. C. Thomas and M. L. Schneider (Eds.). *Human Factors in Computer Systems.* Norwood, New Jersey: Ablex.

Halstead-Nussloch, R. (1989). *CHI '89 Conference Proceedings on Human Factors in Computing Systems* (pp. 347-352). New York: Association for Computing Machinery.

Hayhoe, D. (1990). Sorting-based menu categories. *International Journal of Man-Machine Studies, 33,* 677-705.

Karat, J., McDonald, J. E., and Anderson, M. (1984) A comparison of selection techniques: Touch panel, mouse, and keyboard. *Proceedings of INTERACT '84* (pp. 149-153). London: IFIP.

Kendall, E. S., and Wodinsky, J. (1960). *Journal of the Optical Society of America, 50,* 562-568.

Kiger, J. I. (1984) The depth/breadth trade-off in the design of menu-driven user interfaces. *International Journal of Man-Machine Studies, 20,* 201-213.

Kreigh, R. J., Pesot, J. F., and Halcomb, C. G. (1990). An evaluation of look-ahead help fields on various types of menu hierarchies. *International Journal of Man-Machine Studies, 32,* 649-661.

Kruskal, J. B. (1977). Multidimensional scaling and other methods for discovering structure. In Enslein, Ralston, and Wilf (Eds.), *Statistical Methods for Digital Computers.* NY: Wiley.

Kruskal, J. B. and Wish, M. (1978). *Multidimensional Scaling.* Sage University. Paper Series on Quantitative Applications in the Social Sciences, #07-011. London: Sage Publications.

Kurtenbach, G., and Buxton, W. (1993). The limits of expert performance using hierarchic marking menus. *Human Factors in Computing Systems,* April 24-29, Amsterdam.

Kurtenbach, G., Sellen, A. J., and Buxton, W. A. S. (1993). An empirical evaluation of some articulatory and cognitive aspects of marking menus. *Human-Computer Interaction, 8,* 1-23.

Landauer, T. K., and Nachbar, D. W. (1985). Selection from alphabetic and numeric menu trees using a touch screen: Breadth, depth, and width. *CHI-85 Proceedings* (pp. 73-78). New York: Association for Computing Machinery.

Lee, E. and MacGregor, J. (1985) Minimizing user search time in menu retrieval systems. *Human Factors, 27* (2), 157-162.

Lee, E., MacGregor, J., Lam, N., and Chao, G. (1986) Keyword-menu retrieval: an effective alternative to menu indexes. *Ergonomics, 29*(1), 115-130.

Lee, E., Whalen, T., McEwen, S., and Latremouille, S. (1984) Optimizing the design of menu pages for information retrieval. *Ergonomics, 27* , 1051-1069.

Lewis, S. (1991). Cluster analysis as a technique to guide interface design. *International Journal of Man-Machine Studies, 35,* 251-265.

Lieberman, H. (1985) There's more to menu systems than meets the screen. *Proceedings of SIGRAPH '85* (pp. 181-189). New York: ACM.

MacGregor, J. N. (1992). A comparison of the effects of icons and descriptors in videotext menu retrieval. *International Journal of Man-Machine Studies, 37,* 767-777.

MacGregor, J., Lee, E., and Lam, N. (1986) Optimizing the structure of database menu indexes: A decision model of menu search. *Human Factors, 28*(4), 387-399.

McCracken, D. L. and Akscyn, R. M. (1984) Experience with the ZOG human-computer interface system. *International Journal of Man-Machine Studies, 21,* 293-310.

McDonald, J. E., Dayton, T., and McDonald, D. R. (1988). Adapting menu layout to tasks. *International Journal of Man-Machine Studies, 28,* 417-435.

McDonald, J. E., Dearholt, D. W., Paap, K. R., and Schvaneveldt, R. W. (1986) A formal interface design methodology based in user knowledge. *Proceedings of CHI '86* (pp. 285-290). New York: ACM.

McDonald, J. E., Molander, M. E., and Noel, R. W. (1988). Color-coding categories in menus. *CHI '88 Conference Proceedings on Human Factors in Computing Systems* (pp. 101-106). New York: Association for Computing Machinery.

McDonald, J. E., and Schvaneveldt, R. W. (1988). The application of user knowledge to interface design. In R. Guindon (Ed.), *Cognitive Science and its Applications for Human-Computer Interaction* (pp. 289-338). Hillsdale, NJ: Erlbaum.

McDonald, J. E., Stone, J. D., and Liebelt, L. S. (1983) Searching for items in menus: The effects of organization and type of target. *Proceedings of the Human Factors Society 27th Annual Meeting* (pp. 834-837). Santa Monica, CA: Human Factors Society.

McDonald, J.E., Stone, J. D., Liebelt, L. S., and Karat, J. (1982). Evaluating a method for structuring the user-system interface. *Proceedings of the Human Factors Society--26th Annual Meeting* (pp. 551-555). Santa Monica, CA: Human Factors Society.

Mehlenbacher, B., Duffy, T. M., and Palmer, J. (1989). Finding information on a menu: Linking menu organization to the user's goals. *Human-Computer Interaction, 4(3),* 231-251.

Miller, G. A. (1969). A psychological method to investigate verbal concepts. *Journal of Mathematical Psychology, 6,* 169-191.

Miller, D. P. (1981). The depth/breadth tradeoff in hierarchical computer menus. *Proceedings of the Human Factors Society 25th Annual Meeting* (pp. 296-300). Santa Monica, CA: Human Factors Society.

Miller, M. A., and Elias, J. W. (1991). Using menus to access computers via phone-based interfaces. *Proceedings of the Human Factors Society 35th Annual meeting* (pp. 235-237). Santa Monica, CA: Human Factors Society.

Miyamoto, S., Oi, K., Osamu, A., Katsuya, A. and Nakayama, K. (1986). Directed graph representations of association structures: A systematic approach. *IEEE Transactions on Systems, Man, and Cybernetics, 16,* 53-61.

Norman, D. A. (1984). Stages and levels in human-machine interaction. *International Journal of Man-Machine Studies, 21,* 365-375.

Norman, K. L. (1991). *The psychology of menu selection: Designing cognitive control at the human/computer interface.* Norwood, New Jersey: Ablex.

Olson, J. R., and Biolsi, K. J. (1991). Techniques for representing expert knowledge. In K. A. Ericsson and J. Smith (Eds.), *Toward a General Theory of Expertise* (pp. 240-285). Cambridge: Cambridge University Press.

Paap, K. R., Noel, R. W., McDonald, J. E., and Roske-Hofstrand, R. J. (1987). Optimal organizations guided by cognitive networks and verified by eye movement analyses. *Human-Computer Interaction - INTERACT '87.* In H. J. Bullinger and B. Shackel (eds.) Elsevier Science Publishers.

Paap, K. R. and Roske-Hofstrand, R. J. (1986) The optimal number of menu options per panel. *Human Factors, 28* (4).

Pellegrino, J. W., Rosinski, R. R., Chiesi, H. L., and Siegel, A. (1977). Picture-word differences in decision latency: An analysis of single and dual memory models. *Memory and Cognition, 5,* 383-396.

Perlman, G. (1984). Making the right choices with menus. *Proceedings of INTERACT '84* (pp. 291-295). London: IFIP.

Perlman, G., and Sherwin, L. C. (1988). Designing menu display format to match input device format. SIGCHI Bulletin, 20, 78-82.

Pierce, B. J., Parkinson, S. R., and Sisson, N. (1992). Effects of semantic similarity, omission probability and number of alternatives in computer menu search. *International Journal of Man-Machine Studies*, 37, 653-677.

Pierce, B. J., Sisson, N., and Parkinson, S. R. (1992). Menu search and selection processes: a quantitative performance model. *International Journal of Man-Machine Studies*, 37, 679-702.

Posner, M. I. (1978). *Chronometric explorations of mind.* Hillsdale, N.J.: Lawrence Erlbaum Associates.

Resnick, P., and Virzi, R. (1992). Skip and scan: cleaning up telephone interfaces. *CHI '92 Conference Proceedings on Human Factors in Computing Systems* (pp. 419-426). New York: Association for Computing Machinery.

Robertson, C. K., McCracken, D., and Newell, A. (1981). The ZOG approach to man-machine communication. *International Journal of Man-Machine Studies, 14*, 461-488.

Rosenberg, J. (1983) A featural approach to command names. *Proceedings of CHI'83* (pp. 116-119). New York: ACM.

Roske-Hofstrand, R. J. and Paap, K. R. (1986) Cognitive networks as a guide to menu organization: An application in the automated cockpit. *Ergonomics, 29*(11), 1301-1312.

Sachania, V. (1985). Link weighted networks and contextual navigation through a database. Unpublished M.S. thesis, New Mexico State University, Las Cruces, NM.

Savage, R. E. and Habinek, J. K. (1984) A multilevel menu-driven user interface: Design and evaluation through simulation. In J. C. Thomas and M. L. Schneider (Eds.) *Human factors in computer systems.* Norwood, N.J.: Ablex.

Schvaneveldt, R. W. (1990). *Pathfinder Associative Networks: Studies in Knowledge Organization.* Norwood, NJ: Ablex.

Shepard, R. N. (1962a). Analysis of proximities: Multidimensional scaling with an unknown distance function. I *Psychometrika, 27,* 125-140.

Shepard, R. N. (1962b). Analysis of proximities: Multidimensional scaling with an unknown distance function. II *Psychometrika, 27,* 219-246.

Shoval, P. (1990). Functional design of a menu-tree interface within structured system development. *International Journal of Man-Machine Studies, 33*, 537-556.

Shurtleff, M. S. (1992). Menu organization through block clustering. *International Journal of Man-Machine Studies, 37*, 779-792.

Smith, E. E., Shoben, E. J., and Rips, L. J. (1974). Structure and process in semantic memory: A featural model for semantic decisions. *Psychological Review, 81*, 214-241.

Snowberry, K., Parkinson, S. R., and Sisson, N. (1983) Computer display menus. *Ergonomics, 26* (7), 699-712.

Snowberry, K., Parkinson, S. and Sisson, N. (1985) Effects of help fields on navigating through hierarchical menu structures. *International Journal of Man-Machine Studies*, 22, 479-491.

Snyder, K. M., Happ, A,. J., Malcus, L., Paap, K. R., and Lewis, J. R. (1985). Using cognitive models to create menus. *Proceedings of the Human Factors Society 29th Annual Meeting (pp. 655-658).* Santa Monica, CA: Human Factors Society.

Somberg, B. L. and Picardi, M. C. (1983) Locus of information familiarity effect in the search of computer menus. *Proceedings of the Human Factors Society 27th Annual Meeting* (pp. 826-830). Santa Monica, CA: Human Factors Society.

Tullis, T. S. (1985) Designing a menu-based interface to an operating system. In *Proceedings of CHI '85*, (PP. 73-78). San Francisco, CA: SIGCHI.

Walker, N., and Smelcer, J. B. (1990). A comparison of selection times from walking and pull-down menus. *CHI ''90 Conference Proceedings on Human Factors in Computing Systems* (pp. 221-225). New York: Association for Computing Machinery.

Whiteside, J., Jones, S., Levy, P. S., and Wixon, D. (1985) User performance with command, menu, and iconic interfaces. *Proceedings of CHI '83* (PP. 144-148). New York: ACM.

Wolfe, J. M. (1994). Guided search 2.0: A revised model of visual search. *Psychonomic Bulletin and Review, 1(2)*, 202-238.

Zipf, G. K. (1949) *Human Behavior and the Principle of Least Effort.* Cambridge, Mass., Addison-Wesley.

Handbook of Human-Computer Interaction
Second, completely revised edition
M. Helander, T.K. Landauer, P. Prabhu (eds.)

Chapter 25

Color and Human-Computer Interaction

David L. Post
Armstrong Laboratory
Wright-Patterson Air Force Base
Ohio, USA

A decade or so ago, most of the displays used for human-computer interaction (HCI) were monochrome. Today, however, desktop computers come equipped routinely with color display systems offering 640 x 480 pixels or more, 256 or more colors, and non-interlaced refresh rates of 50 or 60 Hz or greater. Color printers and scanners are becoming increasingly common; they are available at prices many consumers can afford and offer levels of quality that a growing number of users find attractive. Furthermore, the price/performance ratios for these technologies continue to improve.

The software industry has taken advantage of the wide availability of color displays and increasing availability of color hardcopy equipment by using color in its products. To date, this use has been conservative for the most part, to assure compatibility with the large installed base of monochrome hardware. However, the general problem of using color in an effective and attractive manner to enhance HCI is no longer germane to only a few specialized applications—it is a problem faced by a substantial portion of the entire computing industry.

This chapter treats color-related topics that are relevant to HCI. The first section discusses the basics of color vision; the second and third sections introduce Commission Internationale de l'Éclairage (CIE) photometry and colorimetry, respectively, which are the bases for nearly all quantitative approaches to color; the fourth section covers alternatives to the CIE uniform color spaces that are especially relevant to computing; the fifth section describes equipment and procedures for measuring color; the sixth section treats a relatively new problem-area in human-computer interaction known as device-independent color transfer; the seventh section offers guidance for using color in computer systems; the eighth section discusses the use of computers to help solve color-related problems in HCI; the final section lists recommended sources for more detailed information.

25.1 Color Vision and Perception

A good way to approach the topic of color vision and perception is to start by defining *color:* from the psychophysical perspective, it is the aspect of visual perception by which an observer can distinguish among stimuli based on differences in the spectral composition of energy radiating from them. From the perceptual perspective, color is the attribute of vision consisting of chromatic and achromatic content in any combination, described by words such as red, white, etc.

25.1.1 Related versus Unrelated Color

An important dichotomy concerning color is whether it is *related* or *unrelated.* (*Surface* vs. *aperture* and *nonluminous* vs. *luminous* are closely related terms that are used instead, sometimes.) A related color is one that is perceived to belong to an area seen in relation to one or more other colors. An unrelated color is one that is perceived to belong to an area seen in isolation from other colors. Ordinarily, related colors are associated with reflecting and transmitting objects, whereas unrelated colors are associated with emissive sources, but in any event the visual system chooses an interpretation and perceives accordingly. For example, the greenness of grass appears to belong to the grass, whereas a green signal light at night appears to emit green light, even though the light entering the eye in these two cases may be the same. One of the interesting consequences of the distinction is that gray and brown can be perceived only as related colors; if they are viewed in isolation, gray will look white and brown will look like a dark orange or yellow.

25.1.2 Additive Versus Subtractive Color

Another important dichotomy concerning color is whether it is produced by an additive or subtractive process. Television is a familiar example of the additive-color process. A television screen consists of numerous tiny red, green, and blue dots (or stripes), each of which produces a variable amount of light. At normal viewing distances, the individual dots subtend very small visual angles at the eye, so the diffraction patterns they form on the retina overlap and mix. Thus, the tremendous range of colors we see on television is produced by adding only three primary colors together in varying proportions. Projection-CRT systems are another example: separate red, green, and blue images are projected and superimposed on a white screen, where they form a full-color image. The left side of Table 1 is a truth table that shows the eight colors that can be formed by mixing red, green, and blue primaries in an additive, all-or-nothing manner.

Most of the colors we encounter result from the subtractive-color process: light from the sun or some other source of radiant energy strikes objects; some of the wavelengths are absorbed to varying degrees by the objects, which subtracts them from the original light, and the remaining light is then reflected into our eyes. Thus, grass looks green because it tends to reflect wavelengths from the middle of the visible spectrum and absorb everything else. Similarly, the lens in a red traffic light transmits the longer visible wavelengths and absorbs others.

A color photograph works a bit differently because it would be impractical to use a different dye for every color in the picture. Instead, a photograph consists of three overlapping layers of transmissive cyan, magenta,

Table 1. Additive- and subtractive-color truth table.

Additive Primaries				Subtractive Primaries		
Red	Green	Blue	RESULT	Cyan	Magenta	Yellow
0	0	0	Black	1	1	1
1	0	0	Red	0	1	1
0	1	0	Green	1	0	1
0	0	1	Blue	1	1	0
0	1	1	Cyan	1	0	0
1	0	1	Magenta	0	1	0
1	1	0	Yellow	0	0	1
1	1	1	White	0	0	0
Note: 0 = "off" and 1 = "on." For subtractive primaries, "on" means filtering is active, so the associated wavelengths are being removed.						

and yellow dyes, applied in varying amounts on reflective white paper. The cyan layer absorbs red to varying degrees while leaving green and blue alone, the magenta layer controls green while leaving red and blue alone, and the yellow layer controls blue while leaving red and green alone. The right side of Table 1 is a truth table showing the eight colors that can be produced by mixing cyan, magenta, and yellow primaries in a subtractive all-or-none manner. It can be seen that the left and right sides of the table are logical "nots" of each other. This is because the cyan, magenta, and yellow subtractive primaries act basically as minus-red, minus-green, and minus-blue, respectively.

The ranges of colors that can be produced using the additive and subtractive processes differ and can lead to problems reproducing an image that was created using the additive process in a medium that uses the subtractive process (and vice versa). This issue is discussed in Section 25.6.2.

25.1.3 The Dimensions of Color Perception

Color perception can be decomposed into three fundamental attributes, or dimensions:

Hue. The main attribute of color stimuli by which observers distinguish among different portions of the spectrum, for example, blue versus green versus yellow, etc.

Brightness/Lightness. The former is associated with unrelated color and is the degree to which a stimulus appears to emit either more or less light, that is, appears "bright" or "dim"; the latter is associated with related color and is the degree to which a stimulus appears to reflect or transmit either more or less light, that is, appears "light" or "dark."

Saturation/Chroma. The former is the colorfulness of a stimulus, judged in proportion to its brightness. The latter is the colorfulness of a stimulus, judged as a proportion of the brightness of a similarly illuminated stimulus that appears white. Increasing (or decreasing) the brightness of a stimulus causes its chroma to increase (or decrease) but has no effect on its saturation, typically.

25.1.4 Photoreceptors

The three-dimensional character of color perception is reflected in visual physiology. For example, the normal human eye contains three types of color photoreceptors, called *cones* because of their shape, which have the spectral sensitivities illustrated in Figure 1. They are referred to as *long-, medium-,*and *short-wavelength sensitive (L, M,* and *S)* cones, according to their spectral sensitivities. The main physical difference among the three cone types is the photopigment each one contains; the sensitivity differences result from differences in the photopigments' absorption spectra. Notice that each cone type responds to a wide range of wavelengths and cannot discriminate among wavelengths within that range; therefore, the signal from a single cone carries no spectral information.

Figure 2 depicts photoreceptor densities in a normal right eye. The cones are concentrated in the central five degrees or so of the retina, in an area called the *fovea*, although they exist throughout the retina. Visual acuity is best in the central two degrees, where the cone concentrations are highest. Within the central eight degrees of the visual field, the ratio of L- to M-cones is roughly 2:1 (Nerger and Cicerone, 1992). S-

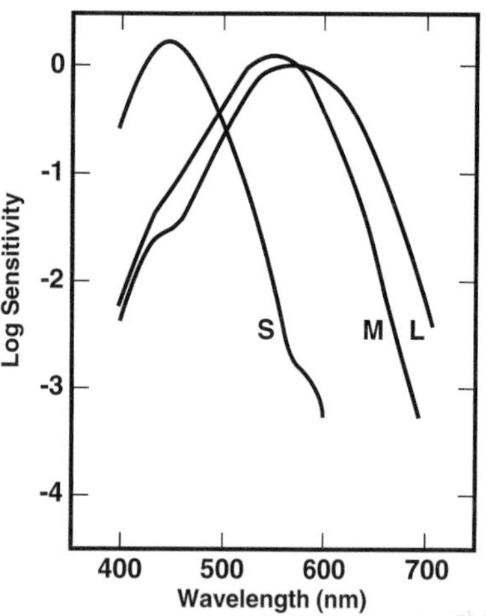

Figure 1. Spectral sensitivities of the cones, normalized for equal sensitivity to light having equal radiance at all visible wavelengths. *Figure provided by Jan Walraven, TNO Human Factors Institute, Soesterberg, The Netherlands*

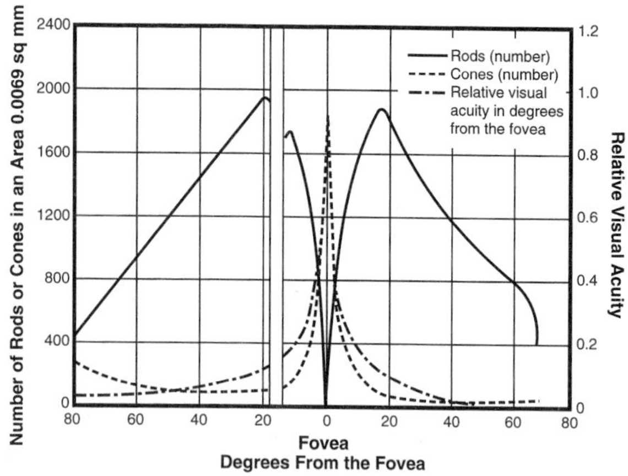

Figure 2. Distribution of cones and rods in the retina of a normal right eye. From Snyder, H.L. (1988). *Image quality. In M. Helander (Ed.), Handbook of human-computer interaction (pp. 437-474). Amsterdam: Elsevier*

cones are rare or absent altogether from the central 0.35 degrees of the retina; immediately outside this area, they constitute approximately 2% of the cones and become more common as eccentricity increases, rising to 7% at 3.5 degrees and beyond (Curcio et al., 1991).

Figure 2 also shows a second class of photoreceptors, called *rods* (again, because of their shape), which are responsible for night vision and are absent from the central fovea. Rods play only a minor role in color vision, so in introductory discussions such as this, they are treated usually as being inoperative at normal, daytime light levels (where color vision is fully operative) to avoid unnecessary complications. For present purposes, little is sacrificed by this simplification.

25.1.5 Color Channels

Figure 3 illustrates schematically how signals from the three types of cones are processed by the visual system: (1) signals from all three types are summed to produce an achromatic color channel that responds in proportion to the cone stimulation; (2) signals from L- and M-cones are differenced, yielding a red-green opponent color channel; and (3) signals from L- and M-cones are also summed to produce a signal that is differenced with S-cone output, yielding a yellow-blue opponent color channel. Thus, the three-dimensional character of color perception is evident at this level of the visual system also. The achromatic channel provides the basis for brightness and lightness perception, and the two opponent channels provide the basis for hue and chroma perception. Thus, the opponent-channel processing converts the spectrally ambiguous signals from the cones into ones that convey the chromatic aspects of light precisely.

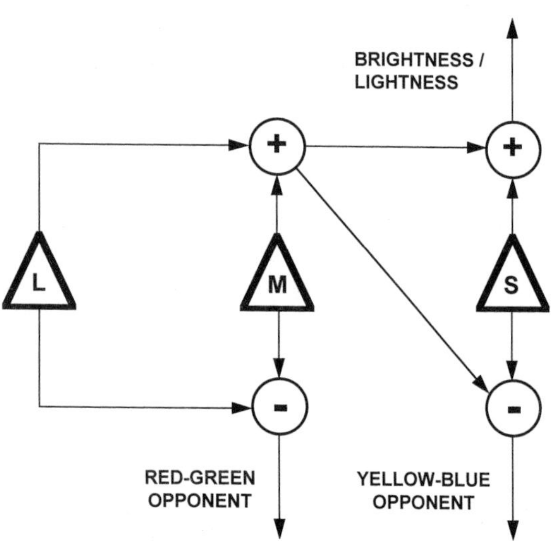

Figure 3. Color-channel schematic.

25.1.6 Metamerism

Figure 4 illustrates two spectral distributions of light that produce identical stimulation of the three cone types. Consequently, the cone signals produced in re-

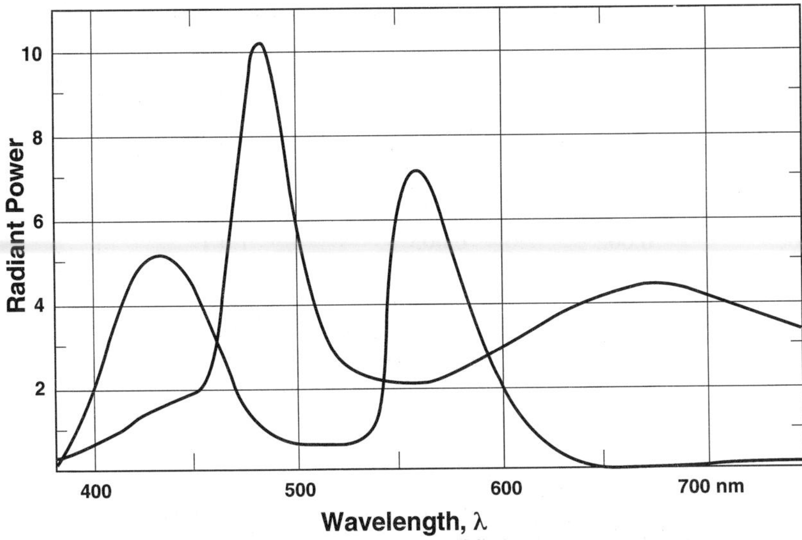

Figure 4. Metameric spectral distributions. From Wyszecki, G., and Stiles, W.S. (1982). Color science (2nd ed.). New York: Wiley. *Copyright © 1982 by John Wiley & Sons, Inc. Reprinted by permission of John Wiley & Sons, Inc.*

sponse to these lights are the same and the visual system cannot discriminate between them. Colors that have different spectral distributions but look the same are called *metamers*. Color television, which reproduces the colors of countless different spectral distributions by mixing only three color primaries in varying proportions, is a familiar example of metamerism. The fact that three primaries suffice to produce such a wide range of colors is a principle of color vision called *trichromacy* and is a direct consequence of the fact that there are only three types of cones.

25.1.7 Color Vision Deficiencies

Some people, called *dichromats,* can match all colors using only two primaries—at least, when they are viewing stimuli that subtend small visual angles (e.g., two degrees). They are classified as either *protanopes, deuteranopes*, or *tritanopes*, according to whether their L-, M-, or S-cones seem affected, respectively. Protanopes and deuteranopes are unable to discriminate among red, orange, yellow, and green. Tritanopes cannot distinguish blue from green, white from yellow, and red from purple. Interestingly, dichromats become trichromatic when larger stimuli are used, although their color vision is still abnormal in most cases.

A larger group of people has trichromatic vision even for small visual fields, but one of their cone types seems impaired to varying degrees. These people are called *anomalous trichromats* and are classified as either *protanomalous*, *deuteranomalous*, or *tritanomalous*. (Some people believe that tritanomalous observers are actually tritanopes whose rods partially replace the missing S-cone signals; see Pokorny, Smith, and Went, 1981.) Their color vision resembles that of the corresponding dichromats, in degrees that depend on the extent of their impairment.

A very small group of people can match all colors using only one primary. Some, called *cone monochromats*, behave as though they have only one cone type. Most commonly, they seem to have only S-cones and have poor (20/60 or worse) visual acuity. Another group, called *rod monochromats*, seem to have only rods. They have a blind spot in the center of their visual fields (i.e., at the fovea), especially poor (20/200) visual acuity, and are often unusually sensitive to light.

Many color-vision deficiencies are genetic in origin (they can result also from injury, illness, aging, and drugs) and their frequencies vary among the world's populations. Table 2, derived from Wyszecki and Stiles (1982, p. 464), shows the frequencies of occurrence for most types of deficiency in the US and Europe. In this population, the protan and deutan defects, which are sex-linked, are the most common. Ocular disorders and aging often preferentially reduce the amount of short-wavelength light reaching the retina, which tends to make blues look darker than they would otherwise. Other disorders cause a relatively greater loss of long-wavelength light, which tends to make reds look darker. The problem of designing displays for color-defective viewers is discussed in Section 25.7.8.

Table 2. Frequencies of Occurrence for Color-Vision Deficiencies in the US and Europe (Wyszecki and Stiles, 1982, p. 464)

Deficiency	Males (%)	Females (%)	Total (%)	Male/Female Ratio
Protanomalous	1.0	0.02	1.02	50:1
Deuteranomalous	4.9	0.38	5.28	13:1
Protanope	1.0	0.02	1.02	50:1
Deuteranope	1.1	0.01	1.11	91:1
Tritanope	0.002	0.001	0.003	2:1
Rod monochromat	0.003	0.002	0.005	1.5:1
TOTAL	8.005	0.433	8.438	18:1

25.1.8 Perceptual Phenomena

The processing that the visual system performs on the achromatic and opponent-color signals is complex and gives rise to numerous interesting perceptual phenomena. Space constraints prevent discussing them all in detail, but ones that are especially apt to be observed when designing HCI displays are summarized below.

Abney effect. If achromatic light is mixed progressively with monochromatic light (i.e., light consisting of only one wavelength), the hue of the resulting color changes gradually, in most cases. This means that, for most hues, lines of constant hue plot as curved lines on chromaticity diagrams (discussed below in Section 25.3). This, in turn, means it is difficult to write a computer program that allows a color's saturation to be changed without affecting its hue, or that generates colors having differing saturations but constant hue.

Assimilation. The color of a background may shift toward the color of a pattern placed on it, especially if the pattern is repetitive and consists largely of high spatial frequencies. This effect is the opposite of simultaneous contrast (described below). Figure 5 provides an example. When designing displays that may produce assimilation, one must be prepared to increase the colors' saturations or otherwise increase the color difference to restore the intended amount of color contrast.

Bezold-Brücke effect. For most hues, large changes in luminance (defined below in Section 25.2.1) cause the hue to shift. The main reason seems to be that the yellow-blue opponent signal changes with luminance more rapidly than the red-green signal. Like the Abney effect, the Bezold-Brücke effect is difficult to correct for automatically in software.

Chromostereopsis. If highly saturated colors having widely different hues are viewed simultaneously (e.g., red and blue characters on a black background), the colors may appear to lie in different depth planes. This effect is optical in origin, rather than a product of visual-system processing, and has two sources: (1) the optical and visual axes of the eyes are not aligned; and (2) the directional orientations of the cones vary. Figure 6 shows an example. The perception of chromostereopsis varies widely across observers, so it is better ordinarily to avoid color combinations and patterns that may create it, rather than trying to make use of it as a display feature.

Color afterimages *(known also as successive contrast).* Staring at a color may produce an afterimage having the opposite hue, particularly if the color is highly saturated. Figure 7 gives a demonstration. Most viewers dislike HCI displays that produce afterimages, so a common practice is to avoid the use of saturated colors for characters in text-processing programs and screen backgrounds in general.

Color constancy. In many cases, the colors reported by a person for reflecting objects—particularly ones in spatially complex scenes—are largely unaffected by changes in the spectral distribution of the illumination, although the viewer is usually aware that their appearances have changed. The viewer seems able to "discount" the illumination and determine the "true" colors. After a few minutes, the visual system adapts to the illumination and the appearance changes diminish. This effect is beneficial in HCI applications because it tends to reduce complaints about illuminant-induced color errors in hardcopy and screen displays

Simultaneous contrast. The color of a stimulus tends to shift away from the color of its background and toward the background's complementary color, providing enhanced contrast. Figure 7 gives several demonstrations. This effect can be beneficial in HCI applications.

Small-field* (or *threshold*) *tritanopia. As the visual angle subtended by a color is reduced below two degrees or so, its saturation tends to diminish, making its hue harder to discern. The effect's name reflects the

Figure 5. Demonstration of assimiliation. *The red is invariant across the figure, but appears lighter behind the yellow stripes.*

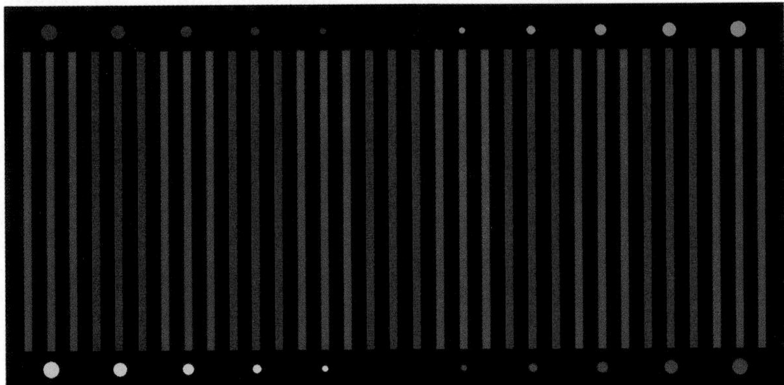

Figure 6. Two demonstrations. *Chromostereopsis: most viewers will see the blue stripes as being farther in depth than the red stripes, some will see the opposite, and a few will see no difference. Small-field tritanopia: the colors of the dots become harder to discern as they become smaller; the effect is most pronounced for the blue dots.*

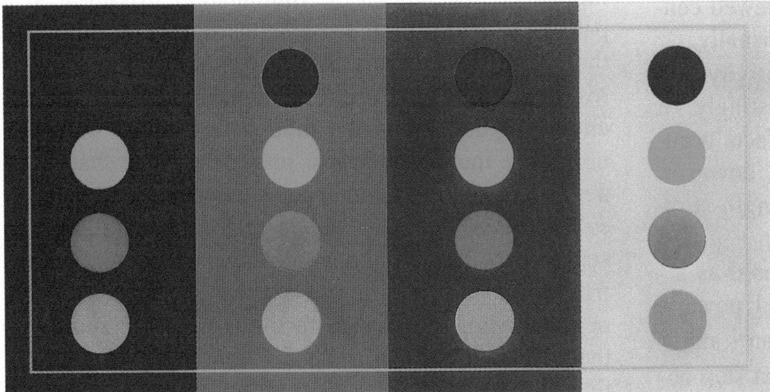

Figure 7. Two demonstrations. *Color afterimages: stare at the figure under bright light for 30 seconds, then look at a white surface; an afterimage containing opponent hues should appear. Simultaneous contrast: the colors of the circles and the stripe are the same in all four quadrants, but change appearance on the different backgrounds.*

fact that it is more pronounced for colors that stimulate S-cones preferentially and therefore tends to resemble a tritan defect. Figure 6 shows several examples. When designing displays containing small objects, one must be prepared to increase the objects' saturations, lightnesses, or brightnesses to counteract this effect.

25.2 CIE Photometry

Photometry is the science that is concerned with measuring the visual efficacy of light, that is, the ability of light to produce a visual sensation. It is used routinely in HCI design to quantify the visibility of electronic displays and hardcopy. Photometry has its origins in the desire of scientists to measure brightness. It was recognized long ago that the human visual system does not respond at all to most of the electromagnetic spectrum, and even within the relatively narrow range of wavelengths that it does respond to, sensitivity varies with wavelength. Therefore, brightness is not simply a function of radiant energy—measuring it requires knowledge of how the various wavelengths are weighted by the visual system.

25.2.1 CIE Photopic Luminous Efficiency Function

Early in this century, an international standardizing body for the measurement of light, known as the *Commission Internationale de l'Éclairage (CIE)*, combined data from several researchers to produce a human spectral sensitivity function that was accepted as the standard by international agreement in 1924. This standard is the *CIE 1924 photopic luminous efficiency function, $V(\lambda)$*, and is illustrated in Figure 8. The CIE recommends $V(\lambda)$ for stimuli that are viewed centrally and subtend from one to four degrees visually.

$V(\lambda)$ represents the overall spectral sensitivity of a normal, trichromatic visual system. Interestingly, it represents people with deutan and tritan defects accurately, as well. Persons with protan defects, however, have much lower sensitivity to long-wavelength stimuli.

To use $V(\lambda)$, a light's radiance is measured as a function of wavelength, yielding its spectral power distribution (SPD) in units of watts·steradian^{-1}· meter^{-2}·nanometer^{-1} (W·sr^{-1}·m^{-2}·nm^{-1})[1]. The next step is to cross-multiply the SPD by $V(\lambda)$ on a wavelength-by-wavelength basis and integrate the result with respect to wavelength, yielding total radiance weighted by human spectral sensitivity. Finally, the integration product is multiplied by a scaling constant to convert from watts, which are radiometric units, to lumens (lm), which are photometric units. The scaling constant is 683 which, by definition, is the number of lumens in 1 watt of energy having a wavelength of 555 nm (in normal air). The result is the light's *luminance*, having the units lm·sr^{-1}·m^{-2}. More succinctly,

$$L = k \int_{\lambda} L_{\lambda} V(\lambda)\, d\lambda \ , \tag{1}$$

where k = 683 lm·W^{-1}, L_{λ} is the SPD, and L is the resulting luminance. By definition, 1 lm·sr^{-1} = 1 candela (cd), so the units are reported more commonly (and conveniently) as cd·m^{-2}. So, for example, a light that consists solely of 1 W·sr^{-1}·m^{-2} at 555 nm has a luminance of 683 cd·m^{-2}. Luminance is used commonly (but incorrectly; see Section 25.2.6) as the psychophysical correlate of brightness and is measured using instruments that are discussed in Section 25.5.

The cd·m^{-2} is the internationally accepted Systéme Internationale (SI) unit for luminance. Some scientists still use the older and obsolete British unit for luminance, however, which is called the *footlambert (fL)*. The conversion is very simple: 1 fL = 3.43 cd·m^{-2}. This conversion is explained below in Section 25.2.5.

Sometimes, an object that reflects or transmits light, rather than emitting it (e.g., a liquid-crystal display or hardcopy), must be characterized. In these cases, the object has no inherent luminance; instead, its luminance depends on the illumination striking it. If a particular light source is used consistently to illuminate the object, it can make sense to measure the object's resulting SPD and use Equation 1 as if the object emitted light. Ordinarily, though, it is more useful to normalize the luminance to provide a value that is independent of the illuminance. This normalized value is called the object's *luminance factor* (also referred to sometimes as *luminous reflectance* or *luminous transmittance*, according to whether the object reflects or transmits). Luminance factor is used commonly as the psychophysical correlate of lightness (but see Section 25.2.6).

The luminance factor of a reflecting object is the ratio of its luminance to that of the *perfect reflecting diffuser* under identical illuminating and measuring

[1] The steradian is a unit of solid angle and is the three-dimensional analogue of the radian. It is defined as the solid angle subtended at the center of a sphere by an area on the surface equal to the square of the radius. There are 4π steradians in a sphere.

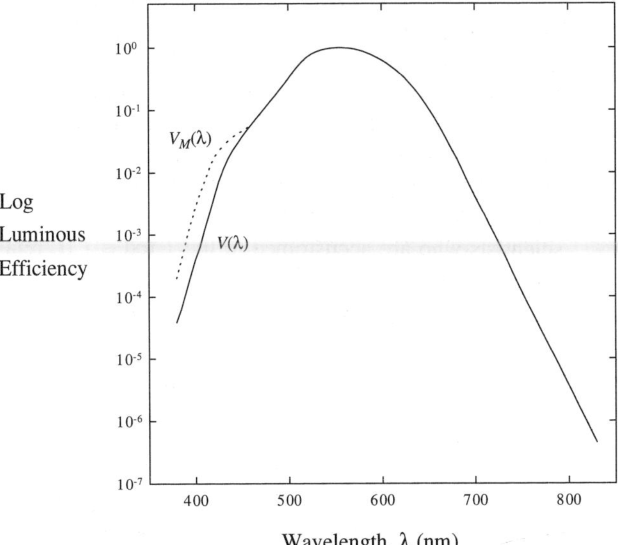

Figure 8. CIE photopic luminous efficiency function, V(λ), and CIE 1988 modified 2° spectral luminous efficiency function for photopic vision, $V_M(\lambda)$.

conditions.[2] A transmitting object's luminance factor is the ratio of the object's luminance to that of the *perfect transmitting diffuser* under identical illuminating and measuring conditions.[3] Thus, luminance factors always range from 0 to 1.

To compute an object's luminance factor using Equation 1, the first step is to measure its spectral reflectance distribution or spectral transmittance distribution (as appropriate). The spectral distribution is multiplied by the SPD of an assumed illuminant (CIE standard illuminants C or D_{65} are typical choices[4]) on a wavelength-by-wavelength basis to determine the object's SPD under the illuminant. This SPD becomes L_λ and, to accomplish the normalization described previously, k is set equal to 1 divided by the illuminant's luminance. (The necessary measurements and calculations can be performed automatically by a spectrophotometer, as described in Section 25.5.2.) To avoid ambiguity, the illuminant used in the calculation must be specified whenever the resulting luminance factor is reported.

A simpler method is to measure the object's luminance under a given illuminant, substitute a white reflectance (or transmittance) standard for the object and measure the standard's luminance, and then divide the former by the latter. Ideally, the standard's reflectance (or transmittance) under the illuminant should be known, so the measured luminance can be corrected to yield the value that would have been obtained for the perfect reflecting (or transmitting) diffuser. The luminance factor that results from this procedure is valid only for the illuminant that was used to make the measurements.

25.2.2 CIE Modified Photopic Luminous Efficiency Function

Shortly after $V(\lambda)$ was introduced, evidence began to accumulate that it underestimates spectral sensitivity to short wavelengths. Judd (1951) derived a correction that was refined slightly by Vos (1978) and has since been accepted (CIE, 1990) as a supplement to $V(\lambda)$. This supplemental function is known as the *CIE 1988 modified 2⁰ spectral luminous efficiency function for photopic vision,* $V_M(\lambda)$. Figure 8 compares $V(\lambda)$ with

[2] The perfect reflecting diffuser is an imaginary, idealized standard that has 100% reflectance and is an *isotropic diffuser*, i.e., when illuminated, its luminance does not vary with the viewing angle. This unique property results from the fact that the surface's luminous intensity, measured in candelas, and the angular area it subtends both vary with the cosine of the viewing angle and reach their maxima at zero viewing angle; therefore, changes in one compensate perfectly for the other as the viewing angle changes. Another term for an isotropic diffuser is *Lambert* (or *Lambertian*) *surface*.

[3] The perfect transmitting diffuser is an imaginary standard that has 100% transmittance and obeys the cosine law described in footnote 2.

[4] CIE standard illuminants represent phases of natural daylight and have SPDs that are defined officially in tables published by the CIE.

$V_M(\lambda)$, where it can be seen that the differences occur only at wavelengths below 460 nm. Therefore, $V(\lambda)$ and $V_M(\lambda)$ will yield significantly different results only for stimuli having a substantial proportion of their energy below 460 nm, in which case $V_M(\lambda)$ is arguably the appropriate choice. It remains to be seen whether $V_M(\lambda)$ will ultimately replace $V(\lambda)$ in general practice.

25.2.3 CIE Mesopic Photometry

CIE $V(\lambda)$ and $V_M(\lambda)$ are appropriate for luminances as low as 3 $cd \cdot m^{-2}$. Between this level and 0.001 $cd \cdot m^{-2}$ lies the *mesopic* range, in which color vision operates but degrades progressively as luminance decreases. Because the changes are continuous, no single function can characterize mesopic vision; therefore, the CIE has no officially recommended mesopic luminous efficiency function. CIE (1989) offers several experimental approaches, but they are too complex for general use and are intended mainly for research on the problem.

25.2.4 CIE Scotopic Luminous Efficiency Function

At luminances below 0.001 $cd \cdot m^{-2}$ or so, only rods are operative and vision is possible only with the peripheral retina. For such cases, the CIE recommends a function that represents the sensitivity of the rods, called the *CIE 1951 relative scotopic luminous efficiency function (for young eyes), $V'(\lambda)$*. To compute luminance using this function, $V'(\lambda)$ is substituted for $V(\lambda)$ in Equation 1, k is set equal to 1700 $lm \cdot W^{-1}$, and the result is referred to typically as *scotopic luminance* to distinguish it from the usual (photopic) case. Scotopic vision is necessarily colorless.

25.2.5 Illuminance

Luminance involves light leaving a surface, whereas illuminance involves light falling on a surface. The SI unit of illuminance is the $lm \cdot m^{-2}$ (called *lux* and abbreviated *lx*). The older and obsolete British unit, which is used sometimes, is the $lm \cdot ft^{-2}$ (called *footcandle* and abbreviated *fcd*). The conversion from one unit to the other is simple: since there are roughly 10.76 square feet in a square meter, 1 fcd = 10.76 lux.

An illuminance of 1 $lm \cdot m^{-2}$, arriving at the surface of the perfect reflecting (or transmitting) diffuser, produces a luminance of $1/\pi$ $cd \cdot m^{-2}$. It would be logical to suppose, therefore, that an illuminance of 1 fcd under the same circumstances produces a luminance of $1/\pi$ fL, but in fact the resulting luminance is 1 fL. This discrepancy results from the fact that the footlambert is defined as $1/\pi$ $cd \cdot ft^{-2}$—a convention that was adopted to simplify converting from illuminance to luminance. Since the introduction of the SI units, however, this convention has generated confusion and errors because scientists who are accustomed to the 1 fcd ≡ 1 fL relation forget sometimes why it holds and assume a 1 lux ≡ 1 $cd \cdot m^{-2}$ relation.

The preceding discussion explains why 1 fL = 3.43 $cd \cdot m^{-2}$. If not for the difference in the $1/\pi$ term, 1 fL would equal 10.76 $cd \cdot m^{-2}$ for the same reason that 1 fcd = 10.76 lux. Instead, however, 1 fL = $10.76/\pi$ $cd \cdot m^{-2}$ = 3.43 $cd \cdot m^{-2}$.

The luminance of an object obviously does not depend on the distance from which it is measured. Illuminance, however, is related to the distance and angle between the illuminant and the measuring device (or illuminated surface). For a point source of illumination,

$$E = I \cos \varepsilon / r^2 , \qquad (2)$$

where I is the source's luminous intensity in candelas, ε is the angle of incidence measured from the normal to the receiving surface, r is the distance in meters, and E is the resulting illuminance in $lm \cdot m^{-2}$. (These units are correct, although the result appears to be $cd \cdot m^{-2}$; see Wyszecki and Stiles, 1982, p. 266 for an explanation.) For extended sources, a commonly used rule is that Equation 2 produces an error less than 1% if the distance r is at least 10 times the largest maximum transverse dimensions of the source and receiving surface. Equation 2 is used frequently in such cases because the exact equations for extended sources are more complex and vary with the source's size and shape.

25.2.6 Luminance is not Brightness

Section 25.2 implied at the outset that $V(\lambda)$ provides a measure of brightness. The reader may have noticed, however, that the subsequent discussion has treated luminance and avoided further mention of brightness. The reason is that luminance and brightness are not the same, even when the more accurate $V_M(\lambda)$ function is used.

Brightness is a perception, which cannot be measured directly with instruments, whereas luminance is the psychophysical correlate, and the relationship be-

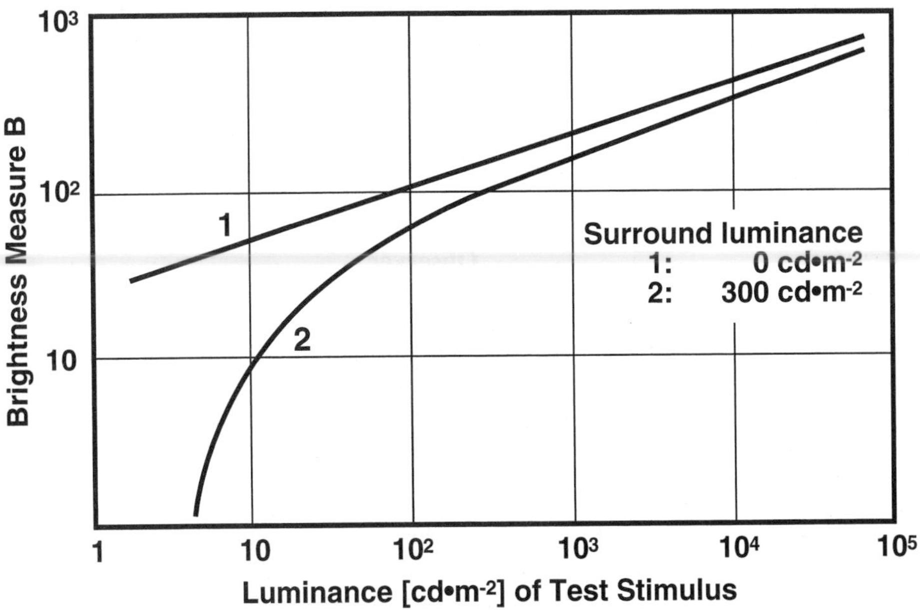

Figure 9. Brightness versus luminance of a stimulus viewed against two different surrounds. *From Wyszecki, G., and Stiles, W.S. (1982). Color science (2nd ed.). New York: Wiley. Copyright © 1982 by John Wiley & Sons, Inc. Reprinted by permission of John Wiley & Sons, Inc.*

tween the two tends to be nonlinear. Figure 9 shows brightnesses reported by observers as a function of luminance for a stimulus viewed against two different surrounds (note the use of log-log coordinates). It can be seen that the relation between the two is approximately a power function with an exponent of 1/3—at least, once the stimulus luminance surpasses the surround's. Therefore, doubling luminance, for example, produces less than a doubling of brightness, generally.

There is another way in which brightness and luminance differ. By definition, (photopic) luminance is a function of either $V(\lambda)$ or $V_M(\lambda)$, both of which were determined largely by a psychophysical method called *flicker photometry*. It is recognized now that this method eliminates contributions from the S-cones and, therefore, the resulting sensitivity functions reflect the L- and M-cones only. S-cones contribute significantly to the perception of brightness; hence, luminance cannot predict brightness accurately for stimuli having a substantial proportion of their energy at the shorter wavelengths of the visible spectrum (see Section 25.7.5 for a way to estimate luminances that will yield equal brightness for differing colors). On the other hand, S-cones contribute very little to visual acuity—probably because of their relative scarcity, as mentioned in Section 25.1.4—so luminance predicts visual acuity better than a more accurate psychophysical correlate of brightness would. Luminance predicts most other practical aspects of visual performance well also, so its use has continued and been widespread, even though it fails to meet its original purpose of correlating consistently with brightness.

There is one last point worth making: spectral sensitivity varies among observers, and $V(\lambda)$ and $V_M(\lambda)$ are averages; therefore, neither function predicts the spectral sensitivity of any specific person with complete accuracy. Ordinarily, though, it is impractical to determine and design for an individual's sensitivity, so it is necessary to rely on a reasonably accurate approximation. Experience has shown that $V(\lambda)$ and, particularly, $V_M(\lambda)$ serve this purpose adequately.

25.2.7 Practical Usage

Designers of display hardware often use the information that has been presented in Section 25.2 to make design predictions. For example, consider a hypothetical backlit transmissive display. It contains an illuminating system to which 5 watts of power can be delivered, has a luminous efficacy of 25 $lm \cdot W^{-1}$, measures 0.4 m^2, and delivers approximately uniform light to the display screen. The predicted illuminance on the screen is therefore (5 W · 25 $lm \cdot W^{-1}$ / 0.4 m^2 =) 313 $lm \cdot m^{-2}$. The screen measures 0.4 m^2, has a luminous transmittance of 0.5 relative to the illuminating system, and is

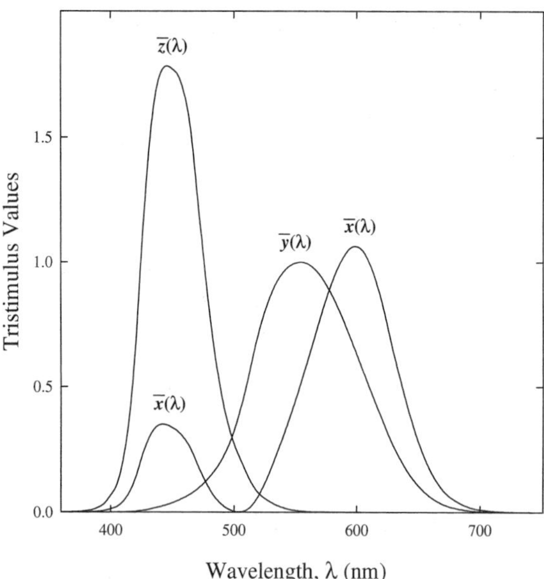

Figure 10. CIE 1931 $\bar{x}(\lambda)$, $\bar{y}(\lambda)$, and $\bar{z}(\lambda)$ color-matching functions.

treated as a Lambert surface (discussed in footnote 1), so its predicted luminance is (313 lm·m^{-2} · 0.5 / π =) 50 cd·m^{-2}. The same result is obtained for an emissive display having the same power, luminous efficacy, and area, if it is treated as an emitting Lambert surface with a non-diffusing faceplate that has 0.5 luminous transmittance.

As another example, consider a display under ambient illumination. The illuminant lies 2 m from the 20-cm display screen at an angle of 50 degrees, has a luminous intensity of 400 cd, and is treated as a point source. The screen is treated as a Lambert surface with a luminous reflectance of 0.1 relative to the illuminant. Using Equation 2, the predicted ambient illuminance on the screen (i.e., diffuse glare) is therefore (400 cd · cos 50° / (2 m)^2 =) 64 lm·m^{-2} and the resulting screen luminance is therefore (64 lm·m^{-2} · 0.1 / π =) 2 cd·m^{-2}. Section 25.3.7 shows how this result can be used to predict the illumination's impact on display color.

25.3 CIE Colorimetry and Color Spaces

Colorimetry is the science that is concerned with measuring the color-producing properties of light. Its development was motivated by the need in science and industry to have an objective, precise, and repeatable way to specify color. The most precise way of specifying a color is to show the spectral power distribution (SPD) of the light that produces it. This method is not very succinct, though, and it is inefficient because it overlooks metamerism; that is, it ignores the fact that different SPDs can produce identical colors.

25.3.1 CIE 1931 Standard Colorimetric Observer

In 1931, the CIE introduced a numerical method of color measurement and specification that takes advantage of the trichromacy of color vision and the metamerism that results. This method is based on color-matching experiments in which monochromatic lights were matched using mixtures of three monochromatic red, green, and blue primary lights. The CIE combined color-matching data from many different people and, for reasons that will be discussed momentarily, re-expressed them in terms of three imaginary primaries called ***X***, ***Y***, and ***Z***. The results, which are shown in Figure 10, are called the *CIE 1931 $\bar{x}(\lambda)$, $\bar{y}(\lambda)$,* and *$\bar{z}(\lambda)$ color-matching functions* (CMFs) and are referred to collectively as the *CIE 1931 standard colorimetric observer*. The CIE recommends its use for centrally fixated stimuli subtending one to four degrees visually.

The CIE 1931 $\bar{x}(\lambda)$, $\bar{y}(\lambda)$, and $\bar{z}(\lambda)$ CMFs show how much of the ***X***, ***Y***, and ***Z*** primaries are needed to match any monochromatic light having unit radiance. (For example, referring to Figure 10, it can be seen that 1.06 units of ***X***, 0.63 units of ***Y***, and 0.00 units of ***Z*** are needed to match a monochromatic light having one unit of radiance at a wavelength of 600 nm.) Because the choice of radiance units is arbitrary, the CMFs allow the amounts of ***X***, ***Y***, and ***Z*** that are needed to match any monochromatic light to be computed, regardless of its radiance. Furthermore, any non-monochromatic light can be treated mathematically as a mixture of monochromatic lights. Consequently, the CMFs allow calculation of the amounts of ***X***, ***Y***, and ***Z*** that are needed to match any light at all. These three quantities, which are called *CIE 1931 X-, Y-,* and *Z-tristimulus values*, specify any color uniquely and precisely.

The ***X***, ***Y***, and ***Z*** imaginary primaries have two advantages over any set of real primaries that might be used instead. First, they can be mixed in positive amounts to match any real color. Second, the ***Y*** primary is defined so that it represents luminance only, so calculating an SPD's *Y*-tristimulus value yields the SPD's luminance. This definition was accomplished by making the $\bar{y}(\lambda)$ CMF the same as $V(\lambda)$. Because all luminance is contained in the **Y** primary, the **X** and **Z** primaries have no luminance at all. This observation underscores the imaginary nature of the **X**, **Y**, and **Z** primaries. Real light cannot have luminance only and zero *X*- and *Z*-tristimulus values, as **Y** does, nor can real light have zero luminance, as **X** and **Z** do. Furthermore, no finite set of real lights can be mixed in positive amounts to match all real colors. The **X**, **Y**, and **Z** primaries exist as mathematical concepts only and cannot be reproduced physically.

The CIE 1931 standard colorimetric observer represents the behavior of an imaginary, idealized person who has normal color vision that is representative of the average person and who performs the color-matching task with perfect consistency. Of course, no real person is perfectly consistent, and there are differences in color vision, even among persons whose color vision is classified as normal. Therefore, no real person will match colors in exactly the same way as the CIE standard observer. However, the standard observer provides a satisfactory approximation in most cases, as attested by the fact that it has survived intact for more than six decades.

25.3.2 Calculating and Using CIE 1931 Tristimulus Values

The calculation of *X*-, *Y*-, and *Z*-tristimulus values is analogous to the calculation of luminance, that is,

$$X = k \int_\lambda L_\lambda \, \bar{x}(\lambda) d\lambda \ , \tag{3}$$
$$Y = k \int_\lambda L_\lambda \, \bar{y}(\lambda) d\lambda \ , \text{ and} \tag{4}$$
$$Z = k \int_\lambda L_\lambda \, \bar{z}(\lambda) d\lambda \ , \tag{5}$$

where, for emitting objects, k and L_λ are as defined in Section 25.2.1; thus the *Y*-tristimulus value is equal to the object's luminance. For reflecting and transmitting objects, k is set equal to 100 divided by the illuminant's luminance; thus, the *Y*-tristimulus value is equal to 100 times the object's luminance factor and ranges from 0 to 100.

Knowledge of a color's tristimulus values allows anyone to produce a color that will be judged by most people to match the original reasonably well, given similar viewing conditions. This can be accomplished merely by assuring that the colors have the same tristimulus values, which is the same as assuring that they are metamers. It is not necessary to assure that the SPDs are the same, nor is it necessary to know the original color's SPD; only the color's tristimulus values are needed.

It is important to realize that, although the tristimulus values specify the requirements for a color match, they do not specify the resulting color perception. That is, there is no one-to-one correspondence between tristimulus values and colors. This is because color perception is subject to many influences besides the tristimulus values—as discussed and demonstrated in Section 25.1.8—so the same tristimulus values can produce different color perceptions under different viewing conditions. The CIE did not intend its colorimetric system to be used to predict color perceptions. It is only a method for specifying color by showing how to reproduce it.

25.3.3 CIE 1931 Chromaticity Diagram

It is often useful to transform *X*-, *Y*-, and *Z*-tristimulus values into numbers representing proportions among the tristimulus values. Let us define

$$x = X/(X + Y + Z), \tag{6}$$
$$y = Y/(X + Y + Z), \text{ and} \tag{7}$$
$$z = Z/(X + Y + Z). \tag{8}$$

The values of x, y, and z for a given color specify the proportions among X, Y, and Z that are needed to obtain a chromatic color match. That is, x, y, and z represent the purely chromatic aspects of color matching, independent of luminance. Notice that the values of x, y, and z always sum to 1. Therefore, in a three-dimensional space having x, y, and z as axes, the range of possible values for x, y, and z (i.e., the range where $x + y + z = 1$) defines a plane containing all possible chromaticities, both real and imaginary. The values of x, y, and z for a given color specify its location on this chromaticity plane and are referred to therefore as the color's *chromaticity coordinates*.

It is useful to have a diagram that shows the domain of real chromaticities and against which chromaticity coordinates can be referred. A diagram of this type can be produced easily by plotting the coordinates of the visible wavelengths. Because all chromaticities lie in the plane defined above, this diagram can be drawn in only two dimensions, that is, only two coordinates are needed. For example, if the coordinates x and y are plotted for the visible wavelengths and the endpoints (i.e., the points representing 360 and 830 nm) are joined by a straight line, the diagram shown in Figure 11 is produced. This diagram projects the real portion of the chromaticity plane onto the z plane.

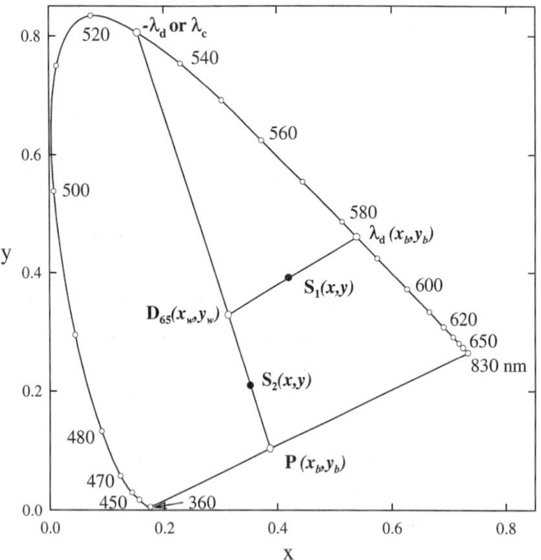

Figure 11. CIE 1931 (x,y)-chromaticity diagram.

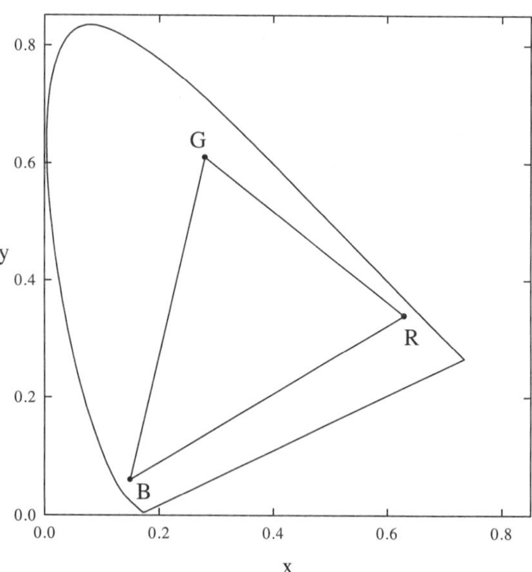

Figure 12. Typical color CRT monitor chromaticity gamut.

The diagram in Figure 11 is only one of an infinite number of projections that could be chosen, but it is convenient to choose one standard projection for universal use. The projection in Figure 11 has special significance because it is the standard that was chosen by the CIE. It is called the *CIE 1931 (x,y)-chromaticity diagram*. The curved line represents the visible wavelengths and is called the *spectrum locus* (because it is the locus of the spectrum). The straight line that closes the figure is called the *purple line*. All visible wavelengths lie on the spectrum locus, all pure purples (i.e., mixtures of 360 and 830 nm) lie on the purple line, and all other real colors lie somewhere in the interior.

A color can be specified completely by giving either its tristimulus values or its chromaticity coordinates and luminance. Since the chromaticity coordinates always sum to 1, only two need to be stated—by convention, x and y are used for this purpose. So, a color can be specified either in terms of X, Y, and Z or in terms of x, y, and Y.

The CIE 1931 (x,y)-chromaticity diagram has several useful properties. One is that all chromaticity coordinates that can be produced by mixing two primaries additively in positive amounts lie on a straight line between the coordinates of those two primaries. Similarly, all coordinates that can be produced by mixing three primaries lie on or within the triangle formed by the primaries on the diagram. (Figure 12, for example, shows the chromaticity gamut of a typical color CRT monitor. It was drawn by plotting the coordinates of the red, green, and blue channels and connecting them with straight lines.) This property generalizes to polygons formed by any number of primaries and is shared by all chromaticity diagrams.

The CIE 1931 (x,y)-chromaticity diagram can be used to define a quantity called *dominant wavelength* that correlates (imperfectly) with a color's hue. The dominant wavelength of a color is the wavelength of the monochromatic light that, when mixed in proper proportion with an achromatic light, matches the color. The achromatic light is defined typically as an equal energy source (this is usually the case if no explicit definition is stated) or CIE standard illuminant C or D_{65}.[5] Thus, in Figure 11, the dominant wavelength of S_1 is determined by drawing a straight line from the achromatic point (D_{65}, in this example) through S_1 to the spectrum locus at λ_d. The wavelength at λ_d is the dominant wavelength of S_1. Some colors, such as S_2 in Figure 11, have no dominant wavelength, but they can be mixed with a monochromatic light to match the achromatic light. The wavelength of this monochromatic light is the color's *complementary wavelength*. The complementary wavelength of S_2 in Figure 11 is the point at which a straight line, drawn from S_2 through the achromatic point, intersects the spectrum locus. This point can be denoted either $-\lambda_d$ or λ_c.

The chromaticity diagram can also be used to define a quantity called *excitation purity* that correlates

[5] An equal-energy source is one that has equal radiance at all wavelengths. Its (x,y)-chromaticity coordinates are both $=1/3$.

(imperfectly) with a color's saturation. The excitation purity of a color is the ratio of the color's distance from the achromatic point to the distance of the achromatic point from λ_d on the spectrum locus (or, for colors that have no dominant wavelength, the corresponding location on the purple line). This ratio is computed

$$p_e = (x - x_w) / (x_b - x_w) \text{ or, equivalently,} \quad (9)$$
$$= (y - y_w) / (y_b - y_w) \ , \quad (10)$$

where x and y are the color's chromaticity coordinates, x_w and y_w are the coordinates of the achromatic point, and x_b and y_b are the coordinates of the boundary point on the spectrum locus or purple line, as shown in Figure 11.

An alternative measure of saturation that is encountered sometimes is called *colorimetric purity*, which is defined

$$p_c = p_e \, y_b / y \ . \quad (11)$$

The preceding definition is the modern, officially sanctioned one (CIE, 1986). It can be useful to know that some of the literature on color vision and colorimetry uses an older definition for colors that have no dominant wavelength, however. In these cases,

$$p_c = (y_c / y) \, (x - x_w) / (x_c - x_w) \text{ or} \quad (12)$$
$$= (y_c / y) \, (y - y_w) / (y_c - y_w) \ , \quad (13)$$

where x_c and y_c are the chromaticity coordinates of the color's complementary wavelength.

25.3.4 CIE 1964 Supplementary Standard Colorimetric Observer and Chromaticity Diagram

For centrally fixated stimuli subtending four degrees visually or more, the CIE recommends the *CIE 1964 supplementary standard colorimetric observer*, often called either the *large-field* or *10-degree observer.* This observer consists of the $\bar{x}_{10}(\lambda)$, $\bar{y}_{10}(\lambda)$, and $\bar{z}_{10}(\lambda)$ CMFs, which are used to compute X_{10}-, Y_{10}-, and Z_{10}-tristimulus values just as X-, Y-, and Z-tristimulus values are computed using the 1931 observer. Figures 13 and 14 show the 1964 CMFs and associated *CIE 1964 (x_{10},y_{10})-chromaticity diagram.* The definitions of dominant wavelength, excitation purity, and colorimetric purity for the 1964 chromaticity diagram are the same as the 1931 diagram, but with x_{10} and y_{10} chromaticity coordinates substituted, as appropriate.

It can be seen that the differences between Figures 13 and 14 and their 1931 counterparts (Figures 10 and 11) are not very large. The differences are due mainly to the fact that the 1931 observer was derived from two-degree stimuli, whereas the 1964 observer was derived from ten-degree stimuli.

The CIE has approved the use of the $\bar{y}_{10}(\lambda)$ color-matching function as a provisional substitute for $V(\lambda)$ for stimuli subtending more than four degrees (CIE, 1978a). Researchers use this substitution sometimes for peripherally viewed stimuli also, when the observers are light-adapted. In fact, in such cases, the entire 1964 observer is probably more appropriate than the 1931 observer. The CIE has not recommended any practices for peripheral stimuli, though, or, for that matter, any generally useful practices for stimuli subtending less than one degree.[6]

In most display-design applications, the stimuli subtend two degrees or less and either are or will be fixated centrally once the viewer attends to them, so the 1931 observer is the more appropriate choice. For characterizing larger or peripheral stimuli, though, the 1964 observer is appropriate.

25.3.5 CIE 1976 Uniform Chromaticity-Scale Diagram

Figure 15 illustrates color-matching data obtained by MacAdam (1942), plotted on the 1931 chromaticity diagram. The ellipses show the standard deviations of color matching at various locations on the diagram, multiplied by 10 to improve the figure's visibility. The fact that the standard deviations plot as ellipses of varying size, rather than as circles of constant size, shows that the 1931 diagram is not uniform perceptually. Therefore, the distance between two points on the diagram does not predict their perceived chromatic difference in any consistent way.

For cases where a perceptually uniform chromaticity diagram is desired, the CIE recommends a projective transformation of the 1931 diagram, called the *CIE 1976 (u',v')-uniform chromaticity-scale (UCS) diagram.* Because the transformation is projective, straight lines on the 1931 diagram remain straight on the UCS

---

6 The CIE has recommended luminous efficiency functions for brightness matching of monochromatic point sources and monochromatic fields subtending two and ten degrees (CIE, 1988).

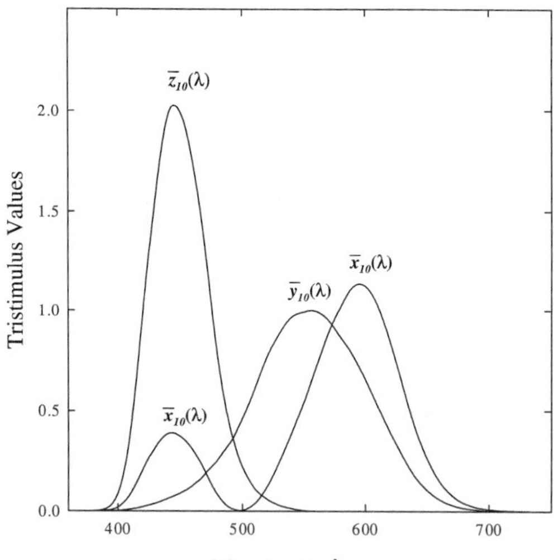

Figure 13. ***CIE*** $\bar{x}_{10}(\lambda)$, $\bar{y}_{10}(\lambda)$, ***and*** $\bar{z}_{10}(\lambda)$ ***color-matching functions.***

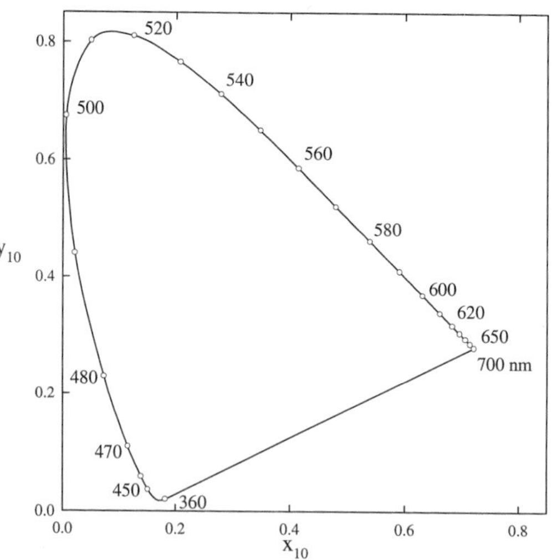

Figure 14. CIE 1964 (x_{10}, y_{10})***-chromaticity diagram.***

diagram. This property simplifies the production of graphical representations of additive color mixtures, such as chromaticity gamuts (e.g., Figure 12).

The UCS diagram is illustrated in Figure 16 with MacAdam's (1942) ellipses replotted. Comparison with Figure 15 shows that the UCS diagram provides a small but useful improvement in perceptual uniformity, both by increasing the circularity of the ellipses and by reducing the variability of their sizes. The chromaticity coordinates of the UCS diagram are

$$u' = 4x / (-2x + 12y + 3) \quad (14)$$

or, using 1931 tristimulus values,

$$= 4X / (X + 15Y + 3Z)\,, \quad (15)$$

$$v' = 9y / (-2x + 12y + 3) \quad (16)$$

or, using 1931 tristimulus values,

$$= 9Y / X + 15Y + 3Z)\,, \text{ and} \quad (17)$$

$$w' = 1 - u' - v' \quad (18)$$

Equations for performing the reverse transformations are

$$x = (27u'/4) / [(9u'/2) - 12v' + 9]\,, \text{ and} \quad (19)$$

$$y = 3v' / [(9u'/2) - 12v' + 9] \quad (20)$$

For stimuli subtending more than four degrees, the CIE recommends substituting X_{10}-, Y_{10}-, and Z_{10}-tristimulus values (or x_{10} and y_{10} chromaticity coordinates) for their counterparts in Equations 14-17, yielding coordinates denoted u'_{10}, v'_{10}, and w'_{10}.

The CIE recommends the UCS diagram for "comparisons of differences between object colors of the same size and shape, viewed in identical white to middle-gray surroundings, by an observer photopically adapted to a field of chromaticity not too different from that of average daylight" (CIE, 1986). An *object color* is one that is perceived as belonging to an object. The diagram is used routinely without regard to this restriction or the other guidance on observing conditions, though.

The 1976 UCS diagram replaces the older *CIE 1960 (u,v)-uniform chromaticity-scale (UCS) diagram.* The 1960 UCS diagram used the chromaticity coordinates $u = u'$ and $v = 2v' / 3$.

25.3.6 CIE Uniform Color Spaces

The CIE has adopted two systems that extend the notion of a perceptually uniform chromaticity diagram to the notion of a perceptually uniform three-dimensional color space; that is, one that includes an axis representing the luminance channel. The purpose is to provide color spaces based on the CIE 1931 system in which equal distance between colors produces equal color-difference perceptions.

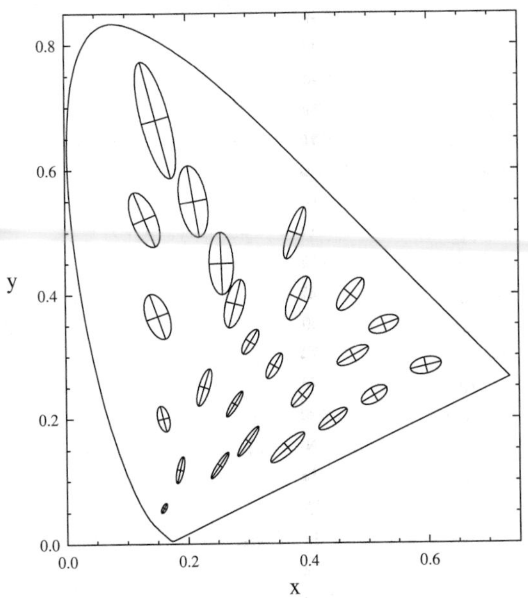

Figure 15. MacAdam's (1942) ellipses plotted on the CIE 1931 chromaticity diagram.

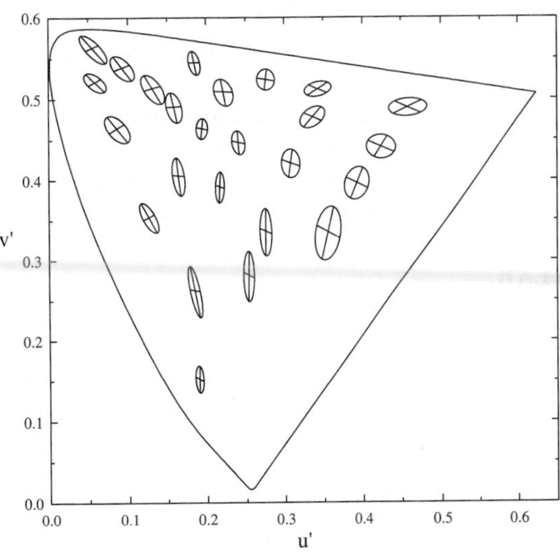

Figure 16. CIE 1976 (u',v')-uniform chromaticity-scale diagram with MacAdam's (1942) ellipses.

CIELUV

The first of the CIE uniform color spaces is a generalization of the 1976 UCS diagram, called the *CIE 1976 (L*u*v*) color space (CIELUV)*, having the axes

$$L^* = 116\,(Y/Y_n)^{1/3} - 16 \qquad (21)$$

for $Y/Y_n > 0.008856$,

$$= 903.3\,(Y/Y_n) \qquad (22)$$

for $Y/Y_n \leq 0.008856$,

$$u^* = 13L^*(u' - u'_n)\text{ , and} \qquad (23)$$

$$v^* = 13L^*(v' - v'_n)\text{ ,} \qquad (24)$$

where Y, u', and v' describe a given color, Y_n, u'_n, and v'_n describe a specified white object color (discussed at the end of this section), and the observing conditions are the same ones given above for the UCS diagram. The value of L^* is the color's *CIE 1976 lightness*. The measure of color difference between two colors is

$$\Delta E^*_{uv} = [(\Delta L^*)^2 + (\Delta u^*)^2 + (\Delta v^*)^2]^{1/2}\text{ ,} \qquad (25)$$

where ΔL^* is the difference between the colors' L^* values, etc. Guidance concerning the use of ΔE^*_{uv} to ensure the adequacy of color differences is given in Section 25.7.1.

The CIELUV system includes psychophysical correlates of saturation, chroma, hue, and hue difference, which are called *CIE 1976 u,v saturation, CIE 1976 u,v chroma, CIE 1976 u,v hue-angle,* and *CIE 1976 u,v hue-difference,* respectively, and are defined, respectively,

$$s_{uv} = 13[(u' - u'_n)^2 + (v' - v'_n)^2]^{1/2}\text{ ,} \qquad (26)$$

$$C^*_{uv} = (u^{*2} + v^{*2})^{1/2}\text{ ,} \qquad (27)$$

$$= L^* s_{uv} \qquad (28)$$

$$h_{uv} = \arctan\,[(v' - v'_n)/(u' - u'_n)]\text{ ,} \qquad (29)$$

$$= \arctan\,(v^*/u^*)\text{ , and} \qquad (30)$$

$$\Delta H^*_{uv} = [(\Delta E^*_{uv})^2 - (\Delta L^*)^2 - (\Delta C^*_{uv})^2]^{1/2}\text{ .} \qquad (31)$$

By convention, h_{uv} lies between 0^0 and 90^0 if u^* and v^* are positive, between 90^0 and 180^0 if u^* is negative and v^* is positive, between 180^0 and 270^0 if u^* and v^* are negative, and between 270^0 and 360^0 if u^* is positive and v^* is negative. Notice that increasing (or decreasing) a color's Y-tristimulus value while holding its chromaticity coordinates constant leaves the color's s_{uv} unchanged but causes its C^*_{uv} to increase (or decrease). These features model the distinction between saturation and chroma that was described in Section 25.1.3.

For constant L^*, CIELUV provides a (u^*,v^*)-diagram (which is *not* a chromaticity diagram) in which straight lines in the 1931 or UCS diagrams remain straight. The CIELUV system replaces an older color space, known as the *1964 CIE (U*V*W*) color space*, and associated color-difference equation, which were based on the (defunct) 1960 UCS diagram.

CIELAB

The second uniform color space recommended currently by the CIE is the *CIE 1976 (L*a*b*) color space (CIELAB)*, which uses the same L^* axis as CIELUV but otherwise has axes

$$a^* = 500\,[f(X/X_n) - f(Y/Y_n)] \text{ and} \quad (32)$$

$$b^* = 200\,[f(Y/Y_n) - f(Z/Z_n)]\ , \quad (33)$$

where

$$f(X/X_n) = (X/X_n)^{1/3} \quad (34)$$

for $X/X_n > 0.008856$,

$$= 7.787\,(X/X_n) + 16/11 \quad (35)$$

for $X/X_n \leq 0.008856$,

$$f(Y/Y_n) = (Y/Y_n)^{1/3} \quad (36)$$

for $Y/Y_n > 0.008856$,

$$= 7.787\,(Y/Y_n) + 16/116 \quad (37)$$

for $Y/Y_n \leq 0.008856$,

$$f(Z/Z_n) = (Z/Z_n)^{1/3} \quad (38)$$

for $Z/Z_n > 0.008856$, and

$$= 7.787\,(Z/Z_n) + 16/116 \quad (39)$$

for $Z/Z_n \leq 0.008856$,

where X, Y, and Z describe a given color, X_n, Y_n, and Z_n describe a specified white object color (discussed below), and the observing conditions are the ones given previously for the UCS diagram. The CIELAB measure of color difference is

$$\Delta E^*_{ab} = [(\Delta L^*)^2 + (\Delta a^*)^2 + (\Delta b^*)^2]^{1/2}\ , \quad (40)$$

where ΔL^* etc. have the same meanings as in CIELUV. *CIE 1976 a,b chroma, CIE 1976 a,b hue-angle*, and *CIE 1976 a,b hue-difference* are defined, respectively,

$$C^*_{ab} = (a^{*2} + b^{*2})\ , \quad (41)$$

$$h_{ab} = \arctan(b^*/a^*)\ \text{, and} \quad (42)$$

$$\Delta H^*_{ab} = [(\Delta E^*_{ab})^2 - (\Delta L^*)^2 - (\Delta C^*_{ab})^2]^{1/2}\ . \quad (43)$$

The conventions for h_{ab} are the same as for CIELUV's h_{uv}. CIELAB has no associated chromaticity diagram; therefore, CIELAB has no counterpart to CIELUV's s_{uv}. For constant L^*, CIELAB does provides an (a^*,b^*)-diagram, but straight lines on the (x,y)-, (u',v')-, and (u^*,v^*)-diagrams do not, in general, remain straight on (a^*,b^*)-diagrams.

CIE94

More recently, the CIE has recommended the *CIE 1994 ($\Delta L^* \Delta C^*_{ab} \Delta H^*_{ab}$) color-difference model (CIE94)* "when the size of the color difference can be considered small to moderate" (CIE, 1994). CIE94 uses

$$\Delta E^*_{94} = \left[\left(\frac{\Delta L^*}{k_L S_L}\right)^2 + \left(\frac{\Delta C^*_{ab}}{k_C S_C}\right)^2 + \left(\frac{\Delta H^*_{ab}}{k_H S_H}\right)^2\right]^{1/2} \quad (44)$$

as a replacement for Equations 25 and 40. For cases involving comparison against a color standard,

$$S_L = 1, \quad (45)$$

$$S_C = 1 + 0.045 C^*_{ab}\text{, and} \quad (46)$$

$$S_H = 1 + 0.015 C^*_{ab}\,, \quad (47)$$

where C^*_{ab} is the standard's CIE 1976 *a,b* chroma. Otherwise,

$$S_C = 1 + 0.045(C^*_{ab,1}\ C^*_{ab,2})^{1/2}\text{, and} \quad (48)$$

$$S_H = 1 + 0.015(C^*_{ab,1}\ C^*_{ab,2})^{1/2}, \quad (49)$$

(S_L is unchanged) where $C^*_{ab,1}$ is the first color's CIE 1976 *a,b* chroma, etc. The CIE assumes a specific set of viewing conditions, which includes 1000 lux of illumination from a source simulating standard illuminant D_{65}, a spatially uniform neutral background having $L^* = 50$, object-mode viewing, and spatially uniform colors that are immediately adjacent to each other, differ by 5 CIELAB units or less, and subtend a visual angle greater than four degrees. For these viewing conditions,

$$k_L = k_C = k_H = 1; \quad (50)$$

otherwise, different values may be needed, in which case these values should be shown (for example) as $\Delta E^*_{94}(2{:}1{:}1)$.

The CIE (1994) says "the CIE 1976 $L^*a^*b^*$ and CIE 1976 $L^*u^*v^*$ recommendations as color spaces, and the recommended use of CIELUV for users who require a uniform chromaticity diagram, remain in effect." Thus, the CIELUV and CIELAB color spaces, along with their measures of chroma, saturation, etc., remain valid; only Equations 25 and 40 have been replaced. Although Equation 44 presumably models color-difference perception more accurately than Equations 25 and 40 for the assumed viewing conditions, most HCI design involves notable deviations from those conditions. The CIE (1994) has provided no guidance for treating deviations, so it is uncertain at the moment whether the CIE94 color-difference model will prove to be more accurate than its simpler CIELUV and CIELAB counterparts in such cases and be accepted widely among HCI practitioners.

Object Size

For objects that subtend more than four degrees visually, the CIE recommends substituting the 1964 supplementary standard colorimetric observer for the 1931 system, yielding quantities that are denoted by the subscript *10*, for example, L^*_{10}, $\Delta E^*_{uv,10}$, etc. Figures 17 and 18 show the CIELUV and CIELAB spaces, respectively, plotted with respect to the CIE 1964 observer and using CIE standard illuminant D_{65} as the specified white object color, that is, to define Y_n, etc. The closed shape at each figure's center represents the range of coordinates that can be produced by reflecting objects under D_{65}, whereas the outer edges represent the spectrum locus and purple line. (The figures thus also illustrate the fact that, for a fixed illuminant, reflecting objects can reproduce only a limited range of the visual system's color gamut.)

CIELUV vs. CIELAB

CIELUV has been more popular than CIELAB among workers concerned with electronic displays, whereas CIELAB has been more popular for applications involving reflecting and transmitting objects. CIELUV provides a chromaticity diagram, on which colors can be plotted independently of their L^* values and additive light mixtures (which are produced by most electronic displays) can be shown easily using straight lines. Otherwise, there is little practical basis for preferring one space over the other because most comparisons (e.g., Alman, Berns, Snyder, and Larsen, 1989; Ikeda, Nakayama, and Obara, 1979; Lippert, 1986; Lippert, Farley, Post, and Snyder, 1983; Mahy, Van Eycken, and Oosterlinck, 1994; Moroney and Fairchild, 1993; Pointer, 1981; Post, Costanza, and Lippert, 1982; Post, Lippert, and Snyder, 1983; Robertson, 1977) have failed to demonstrate substantial and consistent differences in their accuracies for predicting color-difference perception.[7] A main reason for the difference in modeling habits seems to be the mistaken idea—which appears in various articles and even some textbooks—that CIELUV is intended for modeling luminous sources and CIELAB is intended for modeling reflecting objects. This idea may have originated from recognition that CIELAB was derived from attempts to model a set of reflective color samples that represent the *Munsell color system* (see Section 25.4.2), whereas the UCS diagram (on which CIELUV is based) was derived from efforts to model the full range of chromatic vision (Wyszecki and Stiles, 1982, pp. 501-502). Wyszecki (1986, p. 9-47) has made it clear, however, that the CIE intended CIELUV and CIELAB for modeling reflecting objects exclusively and, as of 1986, had not addressed extensions to luminous sources. Regrettably, the CIE94 recommendations do not address luminous sources, either.

Application to Self-luminous Displays

The problem posed by CIELUV and CIELAB for self-luminous displays (e.g., color CRT monitors, backlit liquid-crystal displays, projection displays, etc.) concerns the definition of the "specified white object color" and, in particular, the definition of Y_n. For reflecting objects, the usual practice has been to equate the reference white with the perfect reflecting diffuser, illuminated by a CIE standard illuminant, as approved

[7] It is generally conceded, though, that CIELAB's modeling of chromatic adaptation is in better agreement with the visual system's true behavior—this is most relevant for modeling reflecting objects, which may be viewed under varying illuminants. See Kim, Berns, and Fairchild (1993) and Lo, Luo, and Rhodes (1996) for evidence on this point.

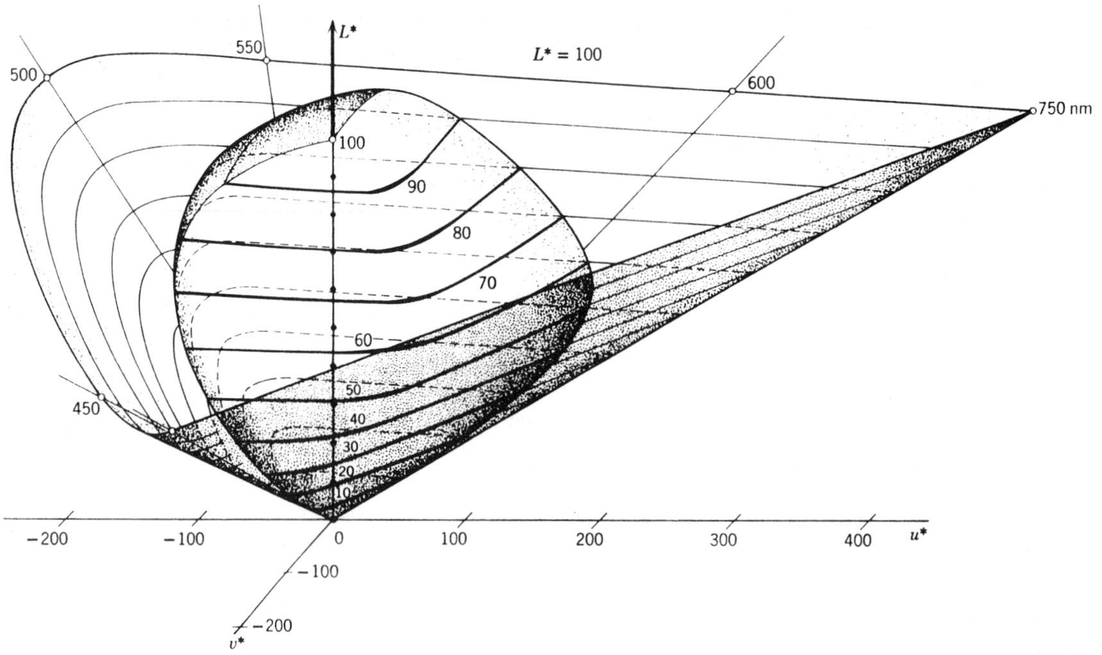

Figure 17. ***CIE 1976 (L*u*v*) color space.*** *From Judd, D.B., and Wyszecki, G. (1975). Color in business, science and industry (3rd ed.). New York: Wiley. Copyright © 1975 by John Wiley & Sons, Inc. Reprinted by permission of John Wiley & Sons, Inc.*

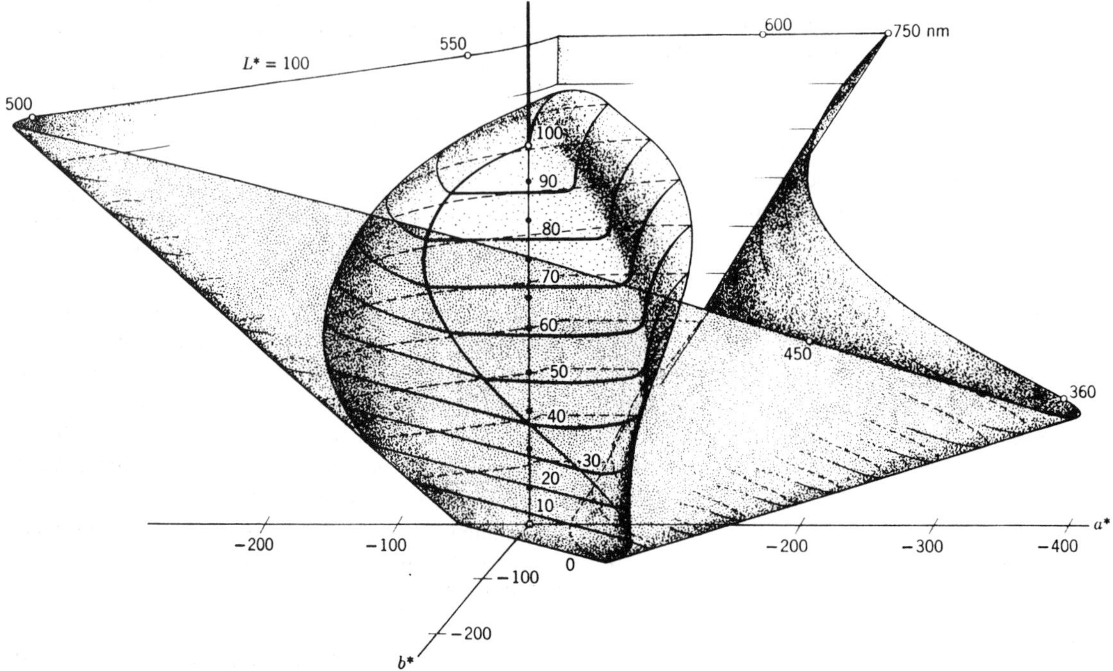

Figure 18. ***CIE 1976 (L*a*b*) color space.*** *From Judd, D.B., and Wyszecki, G. (1975). Color in business, science and industry (3rd ed.). New York: Wiley. Copyright © 1975 by John Wiley & Sons, Inc. Reprinted by permission of John Wiley & Sons, Inc.*

in CIE (1978b; superseded now by CIE, 1986). Some workers have used the actual illuminant or a white from the visual field, if a white was present, however. For self-luminous displays, the most popular convention has been the one suggested by Carter and Carter (1983), which equates Y_n with the luminance produced when the display's red, green, and blue channels are set to their maximum outputs and assigns the chromaticity coordinates of CIE standard illuminant D_{65} to the reference white. Some workers have used the coordinates produced by the display at its maximum output, which usually appear white, however.

Post (1984) noted, though, that the reference white is meant to represent the observer's state of adaptation, so the validity of equating it with a color that may not be visible is questionable. Furthermore, inconsistencies in displays' maximum luminances produce inconsistent CIELUV and CIELAB units under Carter and Carter's Y_n convention, which can lead to erroneous conclusions when attempts are made to generalize across displays. I argued that the issue is not whether the colors are truly luminous versus reflective, but whether they *appear* to be one or the other. Most vision researchers would agree, for example, that television images contain object colors typically. For modeling such cases, I recommended that a white be included in the visual field and used as the reference, regardless of whether the display is self-luminous or reflective. For modeling colors that appear luminous, I recommended dropping Y_n from the CIELUV and CIELAB equations and working in absolute units, as is conventional when dealing with colors that have luminance rather than lightness. More recently, CIE Technical Committee 1-27 has made recommendations for the object-color case that agree with mine (Alessi, 1994).

25.3.7 Practical Usage

The following relationships, which can be derived from Equations 6-8, are often useful when performing colorimetric calculations:

$$X = xY/y \;, \tag{51}$$
$$Z = zY/y \;, \text{and} \tag{52}$$
$$X/x = Y/y = Z/z = X + Y + Z \tag{53}$$

Two-color Mixtures

When computing additive color mixtures, the mixture's tristimulus values are equal to the sums of the constituent colors' tristimulus values. That is, if color A is an additive mixture of colors B and C, then

$$X_A = X_B + X_C \;, \tag{54}$$
$$Y_A = Y_B + Y_C \;, \text{and} \tag{55}$$
$$Z_A = Z_B + Z_C \;, \tag{56}$$

where X_A, Y_A, and Z_A are the tristimulus values of color A, etc. Equations 51-56 apply equally to computations involving the 1964 supplementary standard colorimetric observer.

Relationships equivalent with those in Equations 51-53 can be defined in terms of UCS chromaticity coordinates:

$$\overline{U} = u'Y/v' \;, \tag{57}$$
$$\overline{W} = w'Y/v' \;, \text{and} \tag{58}$$
$$\overline{U}/u' = Y/v' = \overline{W}/w' = \overline{U} + Y + \overline{W} \;, \tag{59}$$

where the quantities $\overline{U}$ and $\overline{W}$ are *not* UCS tristimulus values but are tristimulus values in a color space that uses Y to form one axis and has the UCS diagram as its chromaticity diagram. $\overline{U}$, Y, and $\overline{W}$ are a device that I find convenient when performing color-mixture calculations for colors given as u', v', and Y because they circumvent the need to transform into X, Y, and Z, do the sums, and then transform back into u', v', and Y. In the case of colors A, B, and C, for example, $\overline{U}_A = \overline{U}_B + \overline{U}_C$, etc. and $u'_A = \overline{U}_A/(\overline{U}_A + Y_A + \overline{W}_A)$, etc. Here too, the 1964 observer can be substituted.

Applying the preceding information to the example from Section 25.2.7 that involves a display under ambient illumination, assume that the UCS coordinates of the illumination are $u' = 0.2$ and $v' = 0.2$, the screen has uniform reflectance throughout the spectrum, and the display is producing $u' = 0.1$, $v' = 0.1$, and $Y = 10$. The u', v', and Y resulting on the screen from the mixture of the ambient illumination and display output are desired. Section 25.2.7 established that the illumination produces 2 cd·m^{-2} on the screen so, since the screen's reflectance is spectrally uniform (otherwise, the screen's tristimulus values relative to the illuminant would be needed), the values produced on the screen by the illumination are

$$\overline{U}_A = 0.2\,(2/0.2) = 2 \;, \tag{60}$$
$$Y_A = 2\ cd{\cdot}m^{-2} \;, \text{and} \tag{61}$$
$$\overline{W}_A = 0.6\,(2/0.2) = 6 \tag{62}$$

The values produced by the display are

$$\overline{U}_D = 0.1\,(10/0.1) = 10, \quad (63)$$
$$Y_D = 10\ cd{\cdot}m^{-2}\ \text{, and} \quad (64)$$
$$\overline{W}_D = 0.8\,(10/0.1) = 80 \quad (65)$$

The sums are

$$\overline{U}_T = 2 + 10 = 12\ , \quad (66)$$
$$Y_T = 2 + 10 = 12\ cd{\cdot}m^{-2}\text{, and} \quad (67)$$
$$\overline{W}_T = 6 + 80 = 86, \quad (68)$$

which yield the UCS chromaticity coordinates (the luminance is given in Equation 67)

$$u'_T = 12/(12 + 12 + 86) = 0.11\ , \quad (69)$$
$$v'_T = 12/(12 + 12 + 86) = 0.11\ . \quad (70)$$

Three-color Mixture

An example of color mixture that arises for self-luminous color displays is

$$\begin{bmatrix} X \\ Y \\ Z \end{bmatrix} = \begin{vmatrix} x_R/y_R & x_G/y_G & x_B/y_B \\ 1 & 1 & 1 \\ z_R/y_R & z_G/y_G & z_B/y_B \end{vmatrix} \begin{bmatrix} Y_R \\ Y_G \\ Y_B \end{bmatrix} \quad (71)$$

where x_R, x_G, x_B, etc. are the 1931 chromaticity coordinates of the display's red, green, and blue channels, respectively, Y_R, Y_G, and Y_B are the channels' luminances, and X, Y, and Z are the tristimulus values that result on the screen. If the 3 x 1 vector of luminances is denoted $\boldsymbol{L}$, the 3 x 3 matrix of chromaticity coordinates is denoted $\boldsymbol{C}$, and the 3 x 1 vector of tristimulus values is denoted $\boldsymbol{T}$, then Equation 71 implies

$$\boldsymbol{L} = \boldsymbol{C}^{-1}\boldsymbol{T}\ . \quad (72)$$

That is, the luminances needed from the red, green, and blue channels to produce a desired set of tristimulus values can be calculated by multiplying the desired tristimulus values by the inverse of **C**. The same calculation suffices to decompose a known color (i.e., a set of displayed tristimulus values) into the display luminances that constitute it.

Equations 71 and 72 can be combined to determine the luminances needed on one display to duplicate the color produced by a given set of luminances on another display (i.e., to match colors across displays), for example,

$$\boldsymbol{L}_2 = \boldsymbol{C}_2^{-1}\boldsymbol{C}_1\boldsymbol{L}_1\ . \quad (73)$$

It is convenient sometimes to normalize the channel luminances so they range from 0 to 1. In this case,

$$\begin{bmatrix} X \\ Y \\ Z \end{bmatrix} = \begin{vmatrix} X_{R,\,max} & X_{G,\,max} & X_{B,\,max} \\ Y_{R,\,max} & Y_{G,\,max} & Y_{B,\,max} \\ Z_{R,\,max} & Z_{G,\,max} & Z_{B,\,max} \end{vmatrix} \begin{bmatrix} \tilde{Y}_R \\ \tilde{Y}_G \\ \tilde{Y}_B \end{bmatrix} \quad (74)$$

where $X_{R,max}$ etc. are the tristimulus values of the red, green, and blue channels at their (individual) maximum outputs and $\tilde{Y}_R$ etc. are the normalized channel luminances, defined as $\tilde{Y}_R = Y/Y_{R,max}$, etc. Equations 72 and 73 hold for this case, given that the obvious substitutions are made. Equations 71-74 are valid also for computations made using the 1964 supplementary standard colorimetric observer and the $\overline{U}$, Y, $\overline{W}$ system.

25.4 Non-CIE Color Spaces and Systems

Alternatives to the CIE color spaces are so numerous that they cannot all be discussed in the space that is available for this chapter; therefore, attention is restricted to those that have the greatest current relevance to computer graphics. For this purpose, it is convenient to divide color spaces into two major categories: *device dependent* and *device independent.* The former use coordinates that relate to the specific hardware that implements them and have no consistent relationships with perception or coordinates in the CIE color spaces; the latter use coordinates that are intended to relate consistently with perception and often relate consistently with CIE coordinates.

25.4.1 Device-Dependent Color Spaces

RGB

The red, green, and blue luminances that appear on a display screen are determined by voltages that are applied to the display. On a computer-driven display, these voltages are related linearly to numbers that are stored in the graphics hardware. For convenience in general discussions, the numbers are often treated as

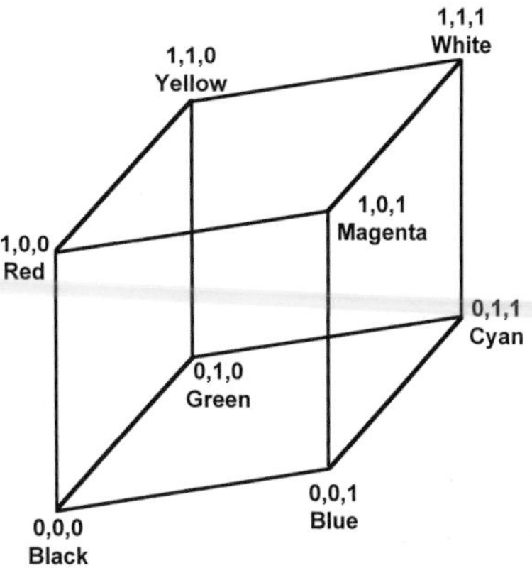

Figure 19. RGB additive-color space.

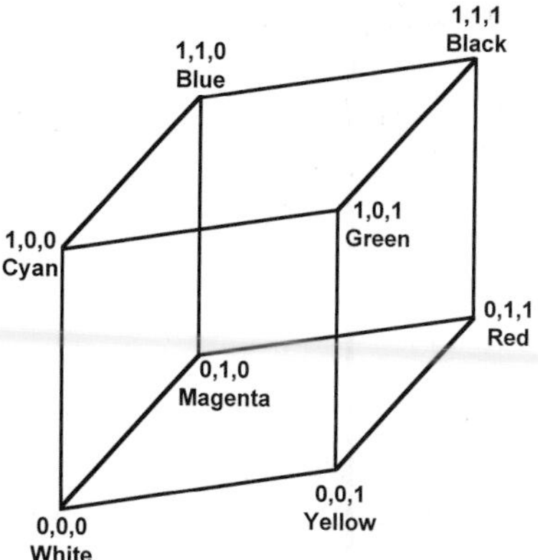

Figure 20. CMY subtractive-color space.

normalized values ranging from 0 to 1 and will be referred to here as *R, G,* and *B*. Color film recorders (which are used to produce photographic slides) also accept *RGB* inputs; scanners and high-end video cameras produce *RGB* outputs.

Figure 19, which depicts the left side of Table 1, illustrates the display color space defined by *R, G,* and *B*. If one views the colors associated with the corners of the figure on a display, they usually will match the appearances suggested by their labels, but the outcome depends on the display's state of adjustment and is not guaranteed. Further, if the colors are compared across different displays, their appearances are not apt to match because the displays will often respond differently to the voltages sent to them and the chromaticity coordinates of the displays' red, green, and blue primaries may differ.

CMY

Most color printing technologies use subtractive cyan, magenta, and yellow (*C, M,* and *Y*) primaries. If the numbers defining *C, M,* and *Y* are normalized to range from 0 to 1, the color space they form can be depicted as shown in Figure 20, which represents the right side of Table 1. Normalized *CMY* coordinates can be converted to normalized *RGB* coordinates and vice versa by the vector expressions

$$[R \;\; G \;\; B] = [1 \;\; 1 \;\; 1] - [C \;\; M \;\; Y] \text{ and} \tag{75}$$

$$[C \;\; M \;\; Y] = [1 \;\; 1 \;\; 1] - [R \;\; G \;\; B] \;. \tag{76}$$

The same sorts of limitations that were noted above concerning the appearance of colors defined in terms of *RGB* apply also to colors defined in terms of *CMY:* different printers may respond differently to the signals sent to them and may use different colorants and papers. Further, although Equations 75 and 76 convert between *CMY* and *RGB* coordinates, it is unlikely that the resulting colors will match.

CMYK

It can be difficult to achieve a good black by mixing *CMY* colorants, which tend to be more expensive than black ones. Therefore, some printing technologies use black as a fourth primary and conserve *CMY* by replacing them with black wherever possible by means of the expressions

$$K = min\,(C, M, Y), \tag{77}$$
$$C' = C - K, \tag{78}$$
$$M' = M - K \text{, and} \tag{79}$$
$$Y' = Y - K, \tag{80}$$

where *K* represents the normalized black coordinate and *C', M',* and *Y'* are the black-adjusted *CMY* coordinates.

HSV and HSL

The coordinates of the preceding color spaces are inconvenient for the adjustments people want to make ordinarily. For example, if a user wants to increase the saturation of a displayed yellow without affecting its color otherwise, examination of its *RGB* coordinates is not apt to make the required adjustments obvious. Two device-dependent color spaces are used commonly to address this problem: Hue, Saturation, and Value *(HSV)* and Hue, Saturation, and Lightness *(HSL),*

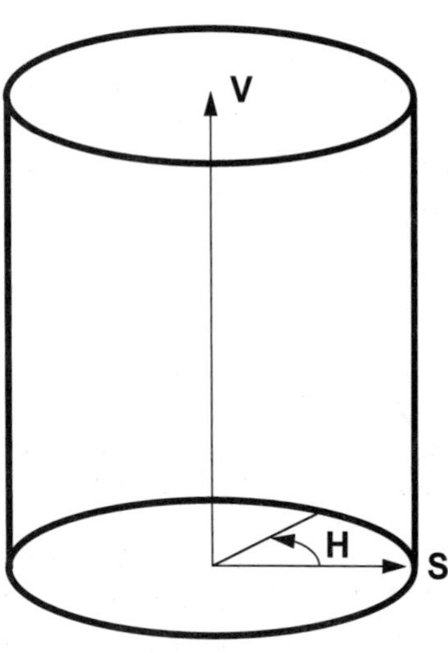

Figure 21. HSV color space.[8]

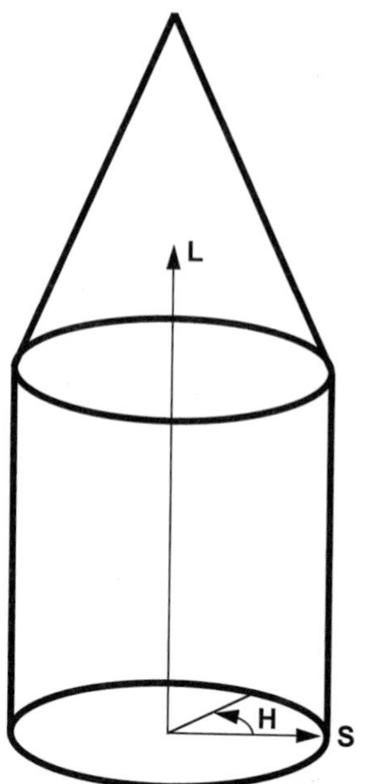

Figure 22. HSL color space.[8]

which are illustrated in Figures 21 and 22.[8] The *RGB* <—> *HSV* and *RGB* <—> *HSL* conversions are too lengthy to show here, but are given in Smith (1978) and Metrick (1979), respectively, as well as various texts (e.g., Foley, Van Dam, Feiner, and Hughes, 1990, pp. 590-595).

Both spaces use polar coordinates in which Hue is specified in degrees while Saturation and Value (or Lightness) range from 0 to 1. Grays lie along the central ($S = 0$) axis, with black at V or $L = 0$ and maximum white at V or $L = 1$. The main difference concerns the representation of Value versus Lightness: in *HSV*, $V = 1$ whenever R, G, or $B = 1$; in *HSL*, $L = 1$ only when $R = G = B = 1$. On most displays, $Y_G > Y_R > Y_B$ when $R = G = B$. Thus, each V plane in *HSV* contains the display's full chromatic gamut, but consists of colors having widely varying luminances. In *HSL*, luminance is inconsistent within each L plane, but the variance is smaller and, over the range $0.5 \geq L \geq 1$, the planes shrink to the display's maximum white.

Some people believe that *HSV* represents conventional thinking about color better than *HSL* and is therefore easier to use; others prefer *HSL* because it yields more consistent luminances and shows how the display's chromatic gamut shrinks at higher luminances. In neither case, however, do the axes correspond with constant hue, saturation, or lightness/brightness perception, so the objective of allowing one dimension to be adjusted while leaving the others unchanged is only approximated.

[8] *HSV* is referred to and illustrated usually as a hexcone, or sometimes a cone, but it is really a cylinder because $S = 1$ whenever R, G, or $B = 0$. Similarly, *HSL* is shown usually as a double hexcone or double cone, but is actually a cylinder at $L < 0.5$ because, in this case also, $S = 1$ whenever R, G, or $B = 0$. Both spaces have a discontinuity at $R = G = B = 0$, where they collapse to a single point representing black.

25.4.2 Device-Independent Color Spaces

Munsell

The Munsell color system is one of the oldest and most familiar device-independent color spaces. More specifically, it is a *color appearance system,* which means it was derived from perceptual scaling experiments and is meant to represent color in a perceptually uniform way. It uses a cylindrical arrangement, like *HSV*, with coordinates labeled Hue, Value, and Chroma and is exemplified by a physical standard called the *Munsell Book of Color.* Each page in the book is a constant Hue chart, with square color-sample chips arranged in rows and columns representing constant Value and Chroma, respectively. Each chip on a given row or column represents an equal perceptual step along its associated dimension and is identified by three numbers that identify its coordinates. For example, 5R 2/6 signifies a red having Hue 5R and lying 6 Chroma steps away from the central, neutral axis at Value 2. The perceptual spacing holds only for comparisons of chips against a middle-gray to white background under day-

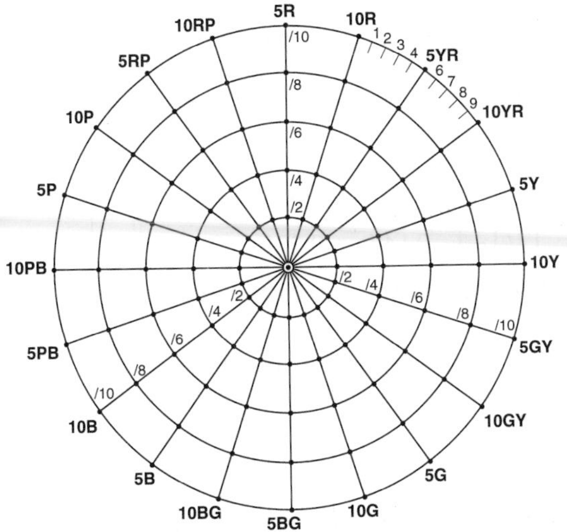

Figure 23. Munsell color space. *From Wyszecki, G., and Stiles, W.S. (1982). Color science (2nd ed.). New York: Wiley. Copyright © 1982 by John Wiley & Sons, Inc. Reprinted by permission of John Wiley & Sons, Inc.*

time illumination. Figure 23 illustrates a constant Value plane in the Munsell space.

Examination of Figure 23 shows that, although the Hue spacing is constant perceptually at a given Chroma, the spacing increases with Chroma. Thus, the perceived difference between 10R 2/6 and 5R 2/6 is much greater than the difference between 10R 2/2 and 5R 2/2. Inconsistent Hue spacing is an unavoidable consequence of the system's cylindrical arrangement. Another noteworthy point is that the Hue charts do not include chips representing all 100 possible combinations of Value and Chroma because they cannot all be realized physically. For example, there can be only one chip representing Value 10 (i.e., a white having Chroma = 0) because addition of pigment to produce Hue or other Chromas would cause absorption of light that would reduce the Value.

Newhall, Nickerson, and Judd (1943) published a revised spacing for the original Munsell colors, which is known as the Munsell Renotation System and has since become the standard Munsell system. Their paper provides CIE 1931 *x, y,* and *Y* relative to CIE standard illuminant C for all Munsell colors with Values ranging from 1 to 9. Most lines of constant Hue plot as curves on the 1931 chromaticity diagram, while loci of constant Chroma have varying degrees of curvature. Value is related to *Y* by a somewhat complicated polynomial (Wyszecki and Stiles, 1982, p. 508) that is approximated usually by using Equation 21 (i.e., L^*). A computer program is available that converts among the Munsell, CIE 1931, CIELUV, and CIELAB systems, as well as DIN and NCS (described below) and others (Smith, Whitfield, and Wiltshire, 1990).

DIN

The Deutsches Institut für Normung (DIN) system (Richter, 1955) is another color appearance system, which was developed by the German Standards Association and is the official German standard color space. It is arranged in a conical configuration having coordinates labeled DIN-Farbton (hue), DIN-Sättingung (saturation), and DIN-Dunkelstufe (relative lightness). The colors constituting this system are represented in the DIN Color Chart, which shows their CIE 1931 *x, y,* and *Y* relative to CIE standard illuminant C. Lines of constant DIN-Farbton have constant dominant or complementary wavelength relative to CIE standard illuminant C and therefore plot as straight lines on the 1931 chromaticity diagram. Loci of constant DIN-Sättingung plot as ovals, however. DIN-Dunkelstufe for a given color is a logarithmic function of Y/Y_0, where Y_0 is the greatest luminance factor that can be realized physically for that chromaticity.

NCS

The Swedish Natural Color System (NCS; Hård, Sivik, and Tonnquist, 1996a, 1996b) is a color appearance system that was produced by the Swedish Standards Institution and has been gaining popularity internationally since it was introduced in 1979. It is arranged in a double cone (i.e., two cones, joined at their bases) with the coordinates hue (Φ), blackness (s), and chromaticness (c). Black and white appear at the apices of the cones; red, blue, green, and yellow appear along the perimeter of the joined bases at 45-degree increments with red opposite green and blue opposite yellow. Planes of constant s resemble Figure 23 but shrink as they move away from the central plane, toward black or white. The NCS and Munsell color spaces seem closely related and transformations between the two are fairly simple (Nickerson and Judd, 1975).

CNS

The Color Naming System (CNS) (Berk, Brownstone, and Kaufmann, 1982) uses standardized English words to denote colors according to their hue, saturation, and lightness or brightness. It was developed for computer graphics use and was derived from a more complex naming system introduced by the U.S. National Bureau of Standards (known now as the National Institute of Standards and Technology) and the Inter-Society Color Council (Kelly and Judd, 1955). The CNS provides six basic hue names (red, orange, yellow, green, blue, and purple), plus brown, which can be substituted for orange. These names can be paired and used with "ish" as a suffix to denote 31 hues. Four levels of saturation (grayish, moderate, strong, and vivid) and five levels of lightness or brightness (very dark, dark, medium, light, and very light) are provided as modifiers, and there are seven achromatic hue names (black, very dark gray, dark gray, gray or medium gray, light gray, very light gray, and white), yielding (31 x 4 x 5 + 7 =) 627 possible color names. Of these, 480 are associated with specific Munsell chips and therefore defined colorimetrically, but the orange and brown names denote identical chips, so the number of unique chip correspondences is 340.

Pantone

The Pantone Matching System is used widely in commercial art for specifying colors by referencing physical standards. The main reference is the Pantone Color Selector: a book that shows 1012 colors that can be produced using the Pantone-licensed inks. Many more Pantone colors are available, however, and are documented in additional, special-purpose references that focus, for example, on metallic colors, pastels, and tints. All of the colors can be reproduced accurately by commercial printers, providing they use Pantone-licensed inks. Pantone has licensed a color management system (see Section 25.6) to several applications-software vendors, printer vendors, and a CRT monitor vendor, to allow the use of its system in integrated, color-calibrated computer graphics environments.

YIQ and *YUV*

Color television broadcasting in the US converts *RGB* signals from video cameras into a color space defined by the National Television Standards Committee (NTSC) standard, using the transformation

$$\begin{bmatrix} Y \\ I \\ Q \end{bmatrix} = \begin{vmatrix} 0.299 & 0.587 & 0.114 \\ 0.596 & -0.274 & -0.322 \\ 0.212 & -0.523 & 0.311 \end{vmatrix} \begin{bmatrix} R \\ G \\ B \end{bmatrix} \quad (81)$$

where Y is a luminance signal, I is a red-cyan opponent signal, and Q is a green-magenta opponent signal. Europe uses the Phase Alternate Line (PAL) and Sequential Couleur á Memoire (SECAM) standards, both of which use the transformation

$$\begin{bmatrix} Y \\ U \\ V \end{bmatrix} = \begin{vmatrix} 0.299 & 0.587 & 0.114 \\ -0.147 & -0.289 & 0.437 \\ 0.615 & -0.515 & -0.100 \end{vmatrix} \begin{bmatrix} R \\ G \\ B \end{bmatrix} \quad (82)$$

where U is a blue-yellow opponent signal and V is a red-cyan opponent signal (note that Y is the same as NTSC).

The strategy of separating the luminance and chrominance information has two advantages. First, monochrome displays need decode only the Y signal (this was important when color broadcasting was introduced because, otherwise, it would have been incompatible with the existing base of monochrome receivers). Second, transmission bandwidth can be conserved by allocating more to the luminance signal and less to the chrominance signals. Experience shows that, providing the bandwidths are adequate, most viewers do not notice the resulting relative loss of spatial chrominance modulation. One reason for this tolerance is the fact that chrominance modulation is accompanied by luminance modulation in most natural images.

One can debate whether *YIQ* and *YUV* are truly device-independent because they meet this criterion only if the displays and cameras have identical *RGB* primaries and white points.[9] This requirement implies matching the standards shown in Table 3, but many cameras and most displays deviate from these standards. (Contemporary television-phosphor standards for the US, Europe, and high-definition television are shown in Table 4; note the differences from the broadcast standards shown in Table 3. Many displays deviate from the Table 4 standards, too.) In such cases, conversions of the form shown in Equation 73 must be used to convert between the camera and display *RGB* primaries (after rescaling to account for the change in white point, if necessary) if accurate transformation is desired. Conversion from *YIQ* and *YUV* to *RGB* can be accomplished by inverting Equations 81 and 82, in the manner illustrated in Equation 72. Transformations to and from CIE *XYZ* can be made also, using the information in Tables 3 and 4.

---

[9] The white point of a display is the chromaticity produced when it receives equal *RGB* input voltages.

Table 3. NTSC, PAL, and SECAM Chromaticity Coordinates.

System	x	y	u'	v'
NTSC				
R	0.67	0.33	0.48	0.53
G	0.21	0.71	0.08	0.58
B	0.14	0.08	0.15	0.20
White (C)	0.3101	0.3162	0.2009	0.4609
PAL				
R	0.64	0.33	0.45	0.52
G	0.29	0.60	0.12	0.56
B	0.15	0.06	0.18	0.16
White (D_{65})	0.3127	0.3290	0.1978	0.4683
SECAM	Same as PAL with White = CIE std. illuminant C			

Table 4. Contemporary Standards for Television-Phosphor Chromaticity Coordinates

System	x	y	u'	v'
SMPTE C (US)				
R	0.63	0.34	0.43	0.53
G	0.31	0.60	0.13	0.56
B	0.16	0.07	0.18	0.18
EBU (Europe)				
Same as PAL—see Table 3				
CCIR 709 (High-Definition Television)				
R	0.64	0.33	0.45	0.52
G	0.30	0.60	0.13	0.56
B	0.15	0.06	0.18	0.16

YCbCr

The Joint Photographic Experts Group (JPEG) and Motion Picture Experts Group (MPEG) digital image-compression standards use a color space based on *YUV*. It uses the NTSC definition of *Y*, the PAL chromaticities, and defines the opponent-color signals as

$$C_b = (U/2) + 0.5 \text{, and} \tag{83}$$
$$C_r = (V/1.6) + 0.5 \,. \tag{84}$$

Here again, separation of luminance and chrominance information and emphasis on preserving the former is used to advantage. Due partly to this strategy, JPEG achieves compression ratios better than 2:1 (20:1 is not unusual) for color images in its lossy modes (i.e., modes in which the reproduction is allowed to degrade relative to the original), the exact ratio depending on the user's willingness to sacrifice fidelity. MPEG achieves roughly three times greater compression by taking advantage of spatial correlations among successive frames of typical moving images (Pennebaker and Mitchell, 1993, pp. 21 and 253-258).

25.5 Color Measurement Devices

Many commercial instruments that perform the measurements needed for CIE colorimetry are available.These instruments form three categories: spectroradiometers, spectrophotometers, and filter colorimeters. Colorimetric instruments also provide photometric measurements, of course. Instruments that are designed solely for photometry (e.g., photometers and illumination meters) are simplified versions of colorimetric instruments, basically. Color scanners resemble filter colorimeters but incorporate cost-saving design compromises that complicate efforts to obtain accurate CIE values.

25.5.1 Spectroradiometers

Spectroradiometers are used to measure spectral power distributions (SPDs). Light from the target to be measured is gathered by optics and dispersed into a spectrum by a prism or diffraction grating. In a *scanning spectroradiometer*, the spectrum is sampled by a slit, which allows only a narrow range of wavelengths (e.g., 1 or 5 nm) to pass through and illuminate a photosensor. An SPD is obtained by alternately recording the photosensor's signal and moving to sample the adjacent portion of the spectrum, starting at one end of the spectrum and ending at the other. Afterwards, the SPD is corrected by multiplying it by the instrument's spectral calibration function on a wavelength-by-wavelength basis, thereby compensating for imperfections in its spectral sensitivity and yielding the final, calibrated SPD.

A newer type of spectroradiometer is illustrated in Figure 24. The slit and photosensor are replaced by a multi-element photosensor, the elements of which are arranged in a row that is aligned with the spectrum. Thus, all the elements are illuminated simultaneously

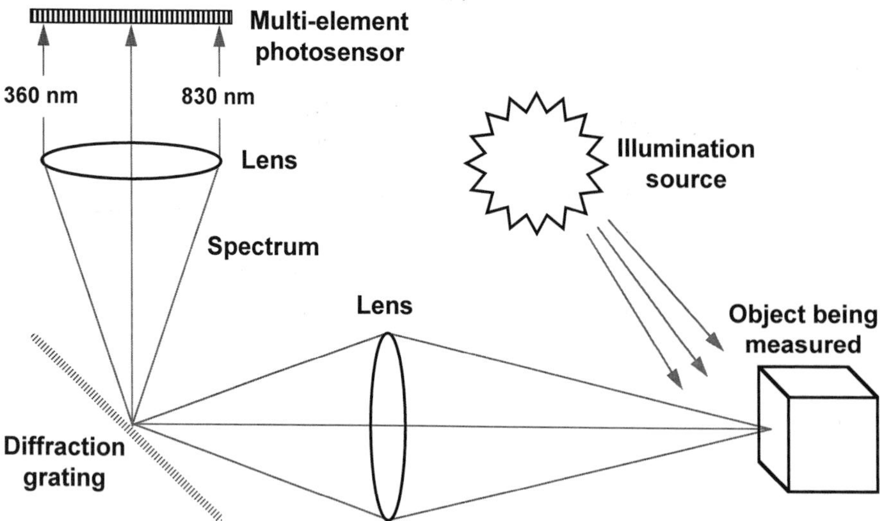

Figure 24. Simple schematic of a spectroradiometer that uses a multi-element photosensor.

and each element samples a narrow range of wavelengths, so the entire spectrum is measured at once without any moving parts. This arrangement tends to be faster than the scanning approach and eliminates wavelength errors caused by random variations in the positioning system.

Most modern spectroradiometers are automated and either include a computer and software or are designed to operate under the control of manufacturer provided software that executes on a user-provided computer. Thus, to obtain a measurement, the user needs only to assure that the light to be measured is being sampled correctly by the optics and issue the appropriate commands to the software. The instrument then performs the measurement, computes tristimulus values, etc., and displays the results. All commercial systems of which I am aware provide only the CIE 1931 color-matching functions (CMFs), though, and do not include the 1964 CMFs, $V_M(\lambda)$, or $V'(\lambda)$ as options; therefore, users who desire these alternatives must write custom software that reads the SPDs produced by the instrument and performs the necessary calculations.

The instrument's spectral calibration function is obtained by measuring a *standard light source*, which has a known SPD, and dividing the true SPD by the measured SPD on a wavelength-by-wavelength basis. For instruments that use a photomultiplier tube as the photosensor, the spectral calibration function must be redetermined every hour or so because the tube's spectral response tends to drift; instruments that use a solid-state photosensor are stable for months usually, but tend to be less sensitive.

Most users purchase a standard light source from a commercial vendor and rely on the vendor to provide the true SPD and perform occasional recalibration and maintenance. The true SPD is determined by comparison against a standard that is maintained by or traceable to a national standardizing body, such as the U.S. National Institute of Standards and Technology (NIST, known formerly as the National Bureau of Standards).

25.5.2 Spectrophotometers

Spectrophotometers are used to measure spectral reflectance distributions and spectral transmittance distributions; they can use either the sequential-scanning approach to measurement or the multi-element photosensor approach. The main differences between a spectroradiometer and a spectrophotometer are that the latter includes a chamber in which the target is placed, plus a lamp to illuminate the chamber. Light from the lamp illuminates the target and the target's SPD is measured with a photosensor. Next, the process is repeated while measuring a white comparison standard. Finally, the target's SPD is divided by the standard's SPD and multiplied by the standard's calibrated spectral reflectance (or transmittance) distribution on a wavelength-by-wavelength basis, yielding the target's spectral reflectance (or transmittance) distribution.

The lamp's SPD must be continuous, but need not be known to obtain a calibrated measurement because it cancels out when the target's SPD is divided by the standard's. The standard's spectral reflectance or transmittance distribution is needed, however. This in-

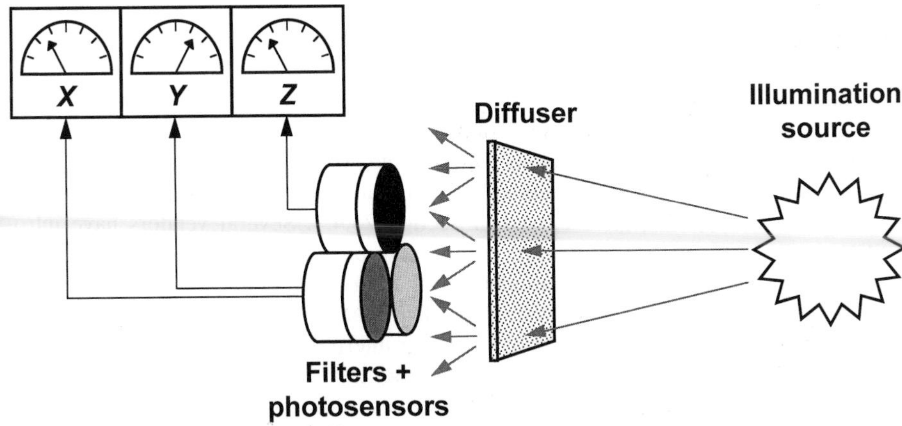

Figure 25. Simple schematic of a filter colorimeter that incorporates a diffuser.

formation is obtained by purchasing a standard that has a known spectral distribution and replacing it occasionally, to compensate for shifts in its spectral characteristics that occur unavoidably over time. Most modern spectrophotometers use solid-state multi-element photosensors, rather than photomultiplier tubes. The resulting loss of sensitivity is unimportant because the lamp's radiance can be increased to maintain a high measurement signal-to-noise ratio, when necessary.

25.5.3 Filter Colorimeters

Filter colorimeters yield CIE tristimulus values directly, without determining the target's SPD. The design illustrated in Figure 25 uses a set of three colored filters, each of which is paired with its own photosensor. Each filter/photosensor pair (FPP) has a spectral sensitivity that matches one of the CIE CMFs. Thus, the FPPs perform the spectral weightings and integrations called for in Equations 3-5 and, when the outputs are scaled properly, yield tristimulus values. A cheaper, alternative design uses only one photosensor. The filters are placed in a rotating wheel or some other moving system and the tristimulus values are obtained sequentially.

In most colorimeters, the FPPs are placed behind a diffuser, but other light-gathering methods can be used. (Photometers, for example—which are merely filter colorimeters containing only one FPP—typically include a lens that focuses an image of the target onto the FPP.) In colorimeters that are intended specifically for measuring self-luminous displays, the FPPs and diffuser are contained in a housing that is designed to be placed directly against the display's faceplate and positions the FPPs at a known, (fairly) consistent distance from the emitting surface. Thus, the luminance can be estimated from the measured illuminance.

Colorimeters that are designed for measuring reflecting or transmitting objects are similar to spectrophotometers. They include a lamp in the housing that contains the FPPs, to provide a constant set of illuminating tristimulus values that can be determined by measuring a white comparison standard. The housing assures a consistent measuring geometry and prevents external light from reaching the target. Thus, dividing the FPP outputs obtained for the target by the outputs obtained for the standard yields the target's tristimulus values under the built-in lamp. Some units attempt to convert these values to their equivalents under another illuminant (e.g., CIE standard illuminant C or D_{65}), but this yields inaccurate results because no mathematically valid conversion exists. A simple example proves this claim: the instrument will yield identical tristimulus values for two colors that are metamers under the colorimeter's built-in illuminant, both before and after conversion, even if they are not metamers under the target illuminant.

One important design issue for filter colorimeters concerns the CIE $\bar{x}(\lambda)$ CMF, which is difficult to duplicate with FPPs because it has two peaks: one at 442 and another at 599 nm (see Figure 10). Two different techniques are used to deal with this problem. The cheaper, but less desirable, technique takes advantage of the fact that the $\bar{z}(\lambda)$ CMF resembles the shorter-wavelength portion of the $\bar{x}(\lambda)$ CMF; therefore, if the output from the Z photosensor is scaled properly and added to the output from an FPP having spectral sensitivity that matches only the longer-wavelength portion of the $\bar{x}(\lambda)$ CMF, an approximation of X can be obtained. Thus, the Z FPP does double duty. The better design technique uses one FPP that matches the shorter-wavelength portion of the $\bar{x}(\lambda)$ CMF, plus another FPP that matches the longer-wavelength portion, and sums their outputs to obtain X. This approach is more expensive because four FPPs are needed.

Another design issue concerns the filters. One approach is to use single- or multi-layer filters; another is to build a mosaic filter from differently colored pieces of material that have the desired composite spectral transmittance. Accuracy can be increased by customizing each filter according to the spectral sensitivity of the specific photosensor it is paired with; this is easier to do with mosaic filters. Mosaic filters tend to yield the greatest accuracy and sensitivity but are more expensive to make, so single- and multi-layer filters are more common.

Each photosensor in a filter colorimeter samples a broad range of wavelengths at once, whereas the photosensors in spectroradiometers and spectrophotometers sample narrow ranges and therefore receive weaker signals for a given target. Hence, filter colorimeters often have greater sensitivity and yield measurements more quickly. Most filter colorimeters also have good repeatability, that is, yield the same measurement results for the same input. These qualities, plus their compactness and ruggedness, make filter colorimeters well-suited for purposes such as adjusting displays coming off a production line to the same white point. With the possible exception of well-built mosaic-filter designs, though, colorimeters tend to be significantly less accurate than spectroradiometers and spectrophotometers. Furthermore, it is impractical to adjust the spectral sensitivity of the FPPs after they are built, to compensate for errors in the original construction or changes in their spectral response that develop over time. At best, the processing of the FPP signals can be rebalanced to yield accurate measurements for a particular SPD.

25.6 Device-Independent Color Transfer

Readers who have scanned a color image into a computer and examined the result on a color display, or designed a color image on a display and printed a hardcopy, have probably found that the colors are inconsistent. The inconsistencies reflect a failure to achieve *device-independent color transfer* (DICT). Sometimes, this failure has no practical importance, but it is often displeasing aesthetically, and a growing number of people are using their computers for professional art and publishing purposes that demand accurate color transfer.

One obstacle to achieving DICT is the fact that every color scanner, display, film recorder, and printer has its own, unique color space and produces or interprets color coordinates in terms of that space, as discussed in Section 25.4.1. Several vendors have introduced proprietary *color management systems* (CMSs) that approach this problem by mapping color from one device-dependent space to another. Often, the mapping involves trilinear interpolation within a *rendering table* that describes color transfer across a given pair of input and output devices, although simpler transformations of the sort illustrated in Equation 71 are used instead, sometimes, to conserve computational resources.

The proprietary approach fails when files must be shared between application programs that use different, incompatible CMSs (or none at all) or when a needed rendering table is lacking. Platform vendors have begun addressing this problem at the system level: Apple has added a CMS extension called *ColorSync* to its Macintosh operating system, Microsoft has included a CMS module called *Image Color Matching* in its Windows '95 operating system, SUN Microsystems has announced plans to add a CMS to its Solaris operating system, and Silicon Graphics International plans apparently to do the same with its IRIS operating system; furthermore, Adobe Systems has included DICT features in the PostScript Level 2 page description language. Moves like these toward open-architecture system-level DICT support should help to eliminate the compatibility problems eventually.

Another important development has been the growing adoption of a standard profile format, created by a large group of computer hardware and software vendors that make up the International Color Consortium (ICC) to support cross-platform color transfer. A key feature of the ICC format is standardization on the use of CIE X-, Y-, and Z-tristimulus values (or, optionally, $L^*a^*b^*$ values) as base units for representing color, along with a standard output medium and set of viewing conditons to reference those values against. Scanner outputs are converted to X, Y, and Z (or L^*, a^*, and b^*) using a *device profile*. These values can then be converted to the data needed by an output device using that device's profile and knowledge of the actual viewing conditions. This two-step mapping technique eliminates the need for a rendering table for every possible pairing of input and output devices, thereby simplifying the addition of devices to a system. At the moment, the ICC profile format specification is being considered as a draft international standard by the International Standards Organization.

System-level support and the use of platform-independent device profiles promise to remove unnecessary barriers to achieving DICT, but more fundamental problems remain. These problems include device-profile error, gamut mismatch, inconsistencies in the viewing and scanning conditions, contrast limitations, and quantization error.

25.6.1 Device-Profile Error

Even if the manufacturer calibrates a unit accurately before it leaves the factory, there will be unit-to-unit variations that are not reflected in the device profile unless a custom profile is created for each unit. Furthermore, the user may adjust the device's color transfer functions afterwards, or those functions may shift as components age, optics become dirty, etc. Printers can exhibit sudden shifts due to a change in their inks, ribbons, or paper, and are sensitive to changes in temperature and humidity. Scanners are sensitive to temperature changes, too.

In principle, users can correct device-profile errors. For example, some CRT monitors come equipped with measuring devices that, in conjunction with built-in self-test functions, enable them to calibrate themselves. A custom profile can be produced for a scanner by scanning a test pattern having known tristimulus values under the scanner's built-in illuminant. A custom profile can be produced for a printer by printing a test pattern and scanning the result with an accurately profiled scanner. Users who are serious about DICT may be willing to exercise these remedies, but most people probably are not.

25.6.2 Gamut Mismatch

One problem that cannot be solved completely by a CMS concerns mismatches among the color gamuts of differing output devices. For example, a user working at a display may create an image containing a saturated blue that cannot be reproduced by the printer, or a user may scan a color photograph containing a saturated red that cannot be reproduced on either the display or the printer. Problems can occur in the lightness/brightness dimension, too. Photographic slides have contrast ratios (i.e., the ratio between the maximum and minimum luminances or luminance factors that can be achieved) as high as 1000:1. Under normal viewing conditions, typical color displays provide 100:1 or less (20:1 is a more common maximum, although a carefully adjusted CRT monitor, viewed in a dark room, can deliver 1000:1). Photographic prints and high quality offset and digital printers rarely achieve contrast ratios greater than 100:1, and many inkjet printers produce less. The CMS can detect problems like these when it consults the output device's profile, but the question of what to do about them remains.

The simplest compromise, which is used by some application programs, is to alert the user and offer a chance to correct the problems manually. Two automated fixes have been devised, also: *clipping,* which involves moving the colors inside the output device's gamut by desaturating and/or darkening them while trying to retain their original hues, and *compression,* which involves desaturating and/or darkening all colors in the image until the outliers are brought within the gamut. The optimality of these transformations is limited, of course, by the fact that no perceptually uniform color space having known lines of constant hue, saturation, and lightness/brightness exists to perform them in. Furthermore, both methods have weaknesses, and it can be difficult to decide which yields the better result. Clipping retains accurate rendering of most colors in the image, but it can eliminate differences among colors that are meant to differ. Compression is intended to retain the relative differences among the image's colors, but it reduces saturation and contrast and may spoil colors that need accurate rendering, such as flesh tones. Some people use methods (referred to sometimes as *soft clipping*) that combine clipping and compression in varying amounts in an attempt to obtain a satisfactory compromise.

25.6.3 Viewing and Scanning Inconsistencies

Suppose that a photograph is scanned and the resulting image file is displayed. If the scanner's accuracy is perfect and the display reproduces the scanner tristimulus values exactly, one might expect the displayed image's color appearance to match the photograph's. A match is unlikely, though, because the photograph and display reflect the room illumination differently and the images appear against different backgrounds. Color-appearance models have been developed to correct for such influences (Fairchild, 1994; Guth, 1995; Hunt, 1994, 1995; Luo, 1996; Nayatani, 1995; Nayatani, Sobagaki, Hashimoto, and Yano, 1995; Seim and Valberg, 1986), but they are complex and imperfect.

One of the problems described in Section 25.5.3 concerning filter colorimeters arises, too: the tristimulus values are obtained with the scanner's built-in illuminant, which probably does not match the illumination in the room. Therefore, the scanner values will not match those under the room illumination and a perfect match will result only if the original image is copied using the same colorants and paper, or if the scanner and room illumination match; exact reproduction of the scanner tristimulus values is appropriate in these cases. One potential solution to this problem would be the development of scanners that yield spectral reflectance distributions. Coupled with knowledge of the room illumination and an accurate color appearance model, this information would permit appropriate corrections to be computed. For the moment, however, the problems of developing such scanners and the likely cost of producing them prohibit this solution. A more feasible approach is to use assumptions about the spectral characteristics of the colorants used in the scanned materials to estimate the spectral reflectance distributions. Berns and Shyu (1995) have shown that fairly accurate estimates can be obtained, if the assumptions, predictive model, and scanner profile are accurate.

25.6.4 Quantization Error

A typical photocopy of a black and white photograph provides a familiar example of quantization error. The numerous shades of gray that are present in the photograph are reproduced with a smaller number of shades, causing contrast to be reduced in some areas and exaggerated in others. Some degree of contrast distortion would occur even if the photocopier had the same number of shades available, or even many more, because it is unlikely that a perfect match would exist for every shade in the photograph. Color images contain hue and saturation, for which additional distortions can occur. Readers who have examined color photographs on computer systems having a small color repertoire have seen examples of these distortions.

Quantization error is inherent in digitization and, hence, unavoidable in computer imaging. Errors that occur during the analog-to-digital sampling process can be corrected partially using image reconstruction methods. Errors that occur during the digital-to-analog output process can be compensated in several ways. One common method is *dithering*, which involves distributing the information from each pixel over adjacent pixels. For example, orange can be created on a printer that lacks it by printing a few red and yellow pixels close together and, thus, using the additive-color principle described in Section 25.1.2 in connection with television. Another output compensation method is *palette optimization,* which is used routinely on displays when the graphics card cannot produce the required number of colors simultaneously. Algorithms for palette optimization vary widely in sophistication, but their objective is to reduce the number of unique colors in a digital image while maintaining a color-appearance match.

The simplest, albeit expensive, way to reduce the visibility of the errors is to increase the number of bits per pixel and the number of simultaneously available colors. Most high-end color-graphics hardware today provides 24 bits/pixel (i.e., 8 bits each for R, G, and B—although special-purpose graphics cards providing up to 15 bits each are available for displays) and three (or more) 8-bit-deep image planes in the graphics card so that all ($2^{24} \approx$) 16.7 million colors are available at once. This level of performance appears adequate for most purposes if the system's color transfer functions are optimized. Theoretically, the optimum transfer functions are linear, but in practice nonlinear functions that are customized for each image often yield more pleasing results. That is, color transfer that is inaccurate in carefully chosen ways can look better than accurate transfer. This paradox has been known for years by artists, television engineers, printers, and photographers, but has been recognized only recently by the computer DICT community.

25.7 Color Usage

The main practical uses of color in computer images involve coding information and aiding visual search by making items in the image more discriminable from one another. For example, color can be used to indicate groupings or shared characteristics, to indicate state, to draw attention, or to communicate qualitative or quantitative differences or changes. The following subsections summarize information useful for these purposes.

25.7.1 Color Discrimination

If color is to assist visual search, the target's color must differ sufficiently from the color(s) of other, distracting objects on the display. One way to assess the magnitude of a color difference is to use the ΔE^*_{uv} formula given in Equation 25. This method is recommended by ANSI (1988, p. 21), along with a suggested minimum difference of 40 units that was derived by Carter and Carter (1982). However, on computer displays, the target and distracters are often smaller than the CIE 1931 standard observer's one-degree minimum (see Section

25.3.1). As explained in Section 25.1.8, small stimuli have reduced saturation so, for computer displays, Equation 25 tends to overestimate their perceived color differences. Silverstein and Merrifield (1985, pp. 149-154) therefore introduced the modification

$$\Delta E^*_{uv\text{-}sf} = [(K_L \Delta L^*)^2 + (K_u \Delta u^*)^2 + (K_v \Delta v^*)^2]^{.5}, \quad (85)$$

where $\Delta E^*_{uv\text{-}sf}$ is a small-field-corrected version of ΔE^*_{uv}; ΔL^*, Δu^*, and Δv^* are the target-distracter color differences along the corresponding CIELUV axes; and K_L, K_u, and K_v are correction factors that vary with the size of the stimuli.[10]

Carter (1989) subsequently developed equations for estimating the correction factors:

$$K_L = 1.0366 - e^{0.15263 - 0.05766A} \quad (86)$$

for $0 < A < 60$,

$$K_u = -0.0065 + 0.008991A \quad (87)$$

for $0 < A \leq 32$,

$$= -0.5403 + 0.0257A \quad (88)$$

for $32 < A < 60$,

$$K_v = -0.0420 + 0.005446A \quad (89)$$

for $0 < A \leq 32$, and

$$= -0.8594 + 0.0310A \quad (90)$$

for $32 < A < 60$,

where A is the visual angle subtended by the stimuli in arc-minutes. Negative solutions (which result, for example, from Equation 89 when A is less than 7.71 arc-minutes) should be rounded to zero. Carter (1989) also analyzed data on visual search for color-coded stimuli and revised the Carter and Carter (1982) finding by concluding that asymptotic performance occurs when the CIELUV color difference (corrected for size, if necessary) reaches 20 units. Therefore, the use of Equations 85-90 and a 20-unit minimum seems preferable to the ANSI (1988) recommendation.

[10] Nagy (1994) has presented evidence that applying stimulus-size corrections in a color space based on cone excitations would yield more accurate results, but a practical procedure for doing this has not been developed yet.

25.7.2 Symbol Legibility

To help assure the legibility of colored symbols, ANSI (1988, p. 21) recommends a minimum symbol-background color difference of 100 units, as assessed by an equation developed by Lippert (1986):

$$\Delta E_{Cu'v'} = [(155C)^2 + (367\Delta u')^2 + (167\Delta v')^2]^{.5}, \quad (91)$$

where C is the symbol-background luminance contrast (i.e., $[L_{max} - L_{min}]/L_{max}$, where L_{max} is the greater of the two luminances and L_{min} is the lesser).

More generally, ANSI (1988, p. 20) requires a symbol-background luminance contrast of 0.67 (which yields $\Delta E_{Cu'v'} = 103$ all by itself) and recommends a value of 0.86. ISO (1992) also requires a minimum of 0.67. Therefore, satisfying the ANSI- and ISO-recommended minimum for luminance contrast guarantees that the ANSI color-difference recommendation will be met and assures legibility on monochrome displays, also.

25.7.3 Color-Code Size

An important question that arises when designing color codes concerns the number of colors that can be used. The answer depends in part on the colors because, if they are not readily discriminable, user performance will be poor, even for a code containing only two colors. The answer depends also on the application. For pseudo- and false-colored images (i.e., images in which a variable, such as X-ray transmission or infrared reflectance, is mapped to differing colors), for example, the number can be very large because discrimination among adjacent, simultaneously presented colors is all that is required and most viewers can discriminate among millions of colors under these circumstances (Nickerson and Newhall, 1943). For situations where the colors must be recognized, the number is much smaller because recognition is more difficult than discrimination. The maximum number of colors that can be recognized on an absolute basis varies, depending on whether they differ in hue only or in brightness/lightness and saturation/chroma as well. In the former case, 11 is a reasonable upper limit (Smallman and Boynton, 1993). In the latter case, as many as 50 can be used if the viewers are given training (Hanes and Rhoades, 1959); otherwise, a limit of 24 to 30 colors is more realistic, (Derefeldt and Swartling, 1995). In all cases, though, it is best to minimize the number, because this tends to reduce errors and search time. See Post (1992a) for further discussion of these last points.

25.7.4 Color Selection

Given that the size of a color code has been decided, the problem of choosing the colors remains. Three approaches have been developed to assist in this task. One involves spacing colors in a perceptually uniform representation of the display's color gamut, another requires testing numerous colors to find a discriminable set, and the third makes use of population stereotypes.

Color-spacing Algorithms

Carter and Carter (1982) pioneered the development of algorithms that, given a desired color-code size *N* and a description of a display's color gamut, choose *N* colors within the gamut such that the perceptual difference between the two nearest colors is maximized. Thus, a set of *N* displayable and maximally discriminable colors is obtained. Others have improved on this idea; the most recent and mathematically sophisticated work is DeCorte's (1990). This approach to color selection has two weaknesses, though. First, a perceptually uniform color space is needed to gauge the color distances accurately, and no truly uniform space is available. Second, the algorithms have difficulty considering the colors' appearances; this poses problems if, for example, three maximally discriminable colors that look like red, yellow, and green are desired. Therefore, color sets produced by these algorithms should always be verified and, if necessary, modified empirically.

Discrimination Testing

McFadden (1992) performed a series of experiments to identify a set of colors that would remain discriminable and identifiable, even when members of the set were used as backgrounds for other members. The intended applications for the set include radar displays, medical images, and electronic maps and charts, where colors are often juxtaposed or superimposed and may therefore influence one another's color appearance. The test stimuli in the experiments consisted of solid circles subtending 0.5 degrees visually and having a luminance of 9 $cd{\cdot}m^{-2}$, centered within solid circles subtending 2 degrees and having a luminance of 10 $cd{\cdot}m^{-2}$. The resulting set of 11 colors is shown in Table 5; however, it must be noted that the set has never been tested in an actual color coding application, to the best of my knowledge.

Population Stereotypes

The third approach to color selection uses population stereotypes. Berlin and Kay (1969) and Boynton and Olson (1987) have presented evidence that there are only 11 (or so) color names for which stereotypical representatives can be established (the names are black, gray, white, red, pink, orange, yellow, green, blue, purple, and brown), so this technique works best for relatively small color codes. For such cases, though, it is preferable to the color-spacing technique described above, because Travis and Johns (1994) have found that visual search is less error-prone on displays coded using stereotypical colors than with non-stereotypical colors, even if the color differences (assessed using ΔE^*_{uv}) for the two cases are equal.

The first step in this method is to choose, by name, colors that are likely to convey the intended meanings without explanation. Table 6 (Bergum and Bergum, 1981), which provides data on typical color-meaning associations, can assist this process. (For cartography, there are special conventions, of course—see Olson, 1987 and Grossman, 1992 for useful reviews.) The second step is to choose specific chromaticity coordinates to represent the color names, also in accordance with population stereotypes. Post and Greene (1986), Post and Calhoun (1988, 1989), Kaufmann (1990), and Kaufmann and O'Neill (1993) have published chromaticity diagrams, showing the probabilities of obtaining common color names as a function of location on the diagram for various typical viewing conditions. These diagrams can be used to determine both the optimal chromaticity coordinates for representing colors and their colorimetric tolerances. Alternatively, if one's application allows for customization, the user can be asked to select optimal representatives for each color name, using a "color picker" interface. Smallman and Boynton (1993) have shown that this procedure yields good visual search performance on color-coded displays.

25.7.5 Heterochromatic Brightness Matching

It is desirable sometimes to equalize the brightnesses of two or more colors. One might suppose that an acceptable solution is to equalize their luminances, but this often fails to produce the expected result. The most obvious discrepancies involve blue stimuli frequently—for example, for a typical color CRT monitor, roughly twice as much luminance is needed from the green channel to produce a green having the same brightness as the blue produced by the blue channel—

Table 5. Eleven colors that remain discriminable and recognizable when juxtaposed or superimposed on one another (McFadden, 1992)

Name	x	y	u'	v'
Blue	.225	.216	.175	.378
Green	.298	.453	.152	.520
Red Purple	.317	.192	.271	.370
Orange Red	.520	.332	.350	.503
Yellow	.376	.398	.214	.510
Purple	.275	.213	.220	.383
Yellow Green	.349	.465	.177	.531
Red Orange	.437	.328	.288	.487
Red	.484	.283	.357	.469
Orange	.391	.354	.242	.493
Gray	.313	.328	.198	.468

Note: Color names are shown only to help distinguish the colors and suggest their appearances—you might not agree with the choices.

Table 6. Color-meaning associations for U.S. college students (Bergum and Bergum, 1981)

Meaning	Red	Orange	Yellow	Green	Blue	Purple
Stop	100.0	0.0	0.0	0.0	0.0	0.0
Go	0.0	0.0	0.0	99.2	0.8	0.0
Hot	94.5	2.4	0.8	0.0	2.4	0.0
Cold	0.8	0.8	0.8	0.8	96.1	0.8
Danger	89.8	5.5	4.7	0.0	0.0	0.0
Caution	11.0	7.1	81.1	0.0	0.8	0.0
Safe	0.0	2.4	16.5	61.4	18.1	1.6
Radiation	59.1	13.4	15.7	0.0	3.9	7.9
On	50.4	3.1	4.7	37.8	3.1	0.8
Off	29.9	6.3	4.7	15.0	31.5	12.6
Near	0.2	19.7	38.6	9.4	15.0	7.1
Far	2.4	15.0	11.0	6.2	30.7	34.6

Note: Tabled values are percentages.

but differences occur for many other pairings, too. Ware and Cowan (1983) analyzed most of the data relating to brightness-luminance relations as a function of color and produced the corrective equation

$$K = [alog (0.256 - 0.184y - 2.527xy + 4.656x^3y + 4.657xy^4]^{-1} \quad ,(92)$$

where x and y are a color's CIE 1931 chromaticity coordinates and K is a luminance weighting factor. For example, for a blue having the coordinates $x = 0.2$ and $y = 0.2$, Equation 92 yields $K = 0.746$. The equation is designed to yield approximately unity for CIE standard illuminant D_{65}; therefore, to make the blue's brightness match a D_{65} white having a luminance of 10 cd/m^2, the blue should be 7.46 cd/m^2. Calculations like this predict the luminances needed to equate the brightness of any color set, or to assure that some colors are brighter than others.

Ware and Cowan (1983) specified several restrictions on the equation's use: (1) the stimuli should subtend 30 arc-minutes or more; (2) their luminances should be 2 cd/m^2 or more; (3) their y-chromaticity coordinates must not be less than 0.02; and (4) they should have similar backgrounds. Calhoun and Post (1990) tested Equation 92 under conditions that met the preceding requirements and found that, in general, it provided better brightness matches than did equalizing luminance. A simpler alternative is to let users adjust the colors to produce equal brightness for their own eyes, if one's application can permit this.

25.7.6 Background Color

For a color stimulus, viewed against an achromatic background, increasing the background luminance increases the stimulus' saturation—at least, until the background luminance exceeds the stimulus luminance. Beyond this point, increases in background luminance reduce stimulus saturation until, finally, the stimulus appears black. Thus, an achromatic background tends to increase the perceived differences among stimulus colors and, for stimuli having equal luminance, the differences are maximized when the background and stimulus luminances are the same.[11]

[11] One should not conclude, however, that it is a good idea to equalize the stimulus and background luminances; this can tend to make the edges of the stimulus indistinct (Boynton, 1978) and may pose problems for color-defective viewers, as discussed in Section 28.7.8. Furthermore, motion detection for a stimulus that differs only in chromaticity from its background is poor (Anstis, 1986, p. 16-19).

For stimuli that differ in luminance, the maximizing background luminance will be the highest level that does not desaturate the lower-luminance stimuli too seriously. Carter and Carter (1988), for example, found that visual search on a color-coded display was enhanced by an achromatic background having a luminance that was intermediate to the stimulus luminances. Similarly, Jacobsen (1986) found that recognition of colors was better on an achromatic background than on a black background.

If the stimulus' background is colored, the stimulus' hue will shift away from the background hue and toward the background's complement ordinarily, as discussed in Section 25.1.8. Thus, colored backgrounds complicate efforts to produce specific color perceptions and control perceived color differences. There is another reason to prefer an achromatic background or, at least, a desaturated one if it must be colored for some reason: Pastoor (1990) assessed many symbol/background color pairs and found that the less saturated backgrounds were always preferred. Furthermore, for dark-on-light text (i.e., text luminance < background luminance), his subjects were largely indifferent to the text color when desaturated backgrounds were used. (For light-on-dark text, however, subjects preferred desaturated text colors, also.)

25.7.7 Peripheral Color Vision

Color vision can change in several important ways for stimuli that are not imaged on the fovea: their relative brightnesses may change, they tend to be less saturated, and their hues may change. For light-adapted viewers, the changes in brightness are due mainly to the *macular pigment:* a yellow pigment that produces significant filtering within the central ± 4 degrees or so of the retina (Stabell and Stabell, 1980), the effects of which are built into $V(\lambda)$. Luminance adjustments for peripheral{ XE "Color:peripheral" } stimuli can be computed by correcting $V(\lambda)$ for the pigment's spectral transmittance function. For most HCI practitioners, though, it is probably more useful to note simply that the effects are most apt to be noticeable for stimuli that have substantial radiance at wavelengths below 535 nm (and near 460 nm, particularly), such as typical blue and cyan stimuli on a CRT monitor.

Red/green discrimination tends to fail at eccentricities beyond 20 to 30 degrees (causing red and green stimuli to appear yellow) and complete color blindness sets in beyond 40 to 50 degrees (Kinney, 1979). To some extent, these effects can be offset by increasing the size or luminance of the stimulus. For

Table 7. Good and bad color pairings for color-defective viewers (Arditi and Knoblauch, 1994).

	Color 1	Color 2
Good	Any light color	Black
	Any dark color	White
	Light yellow	Dark blue
	Light green	Dark red
Bad	Light red	Dark green
	White	Yellow
	Light gray	Yellow
	Turquoise	Green
	Lavender	Pink

light-adapted viewers, minimum size recommendations for reliable color identification can be derived from Kuyk (1982): at 20, 30, and 45 degrees eccentricity, the angle subtended at the eye by the stimulus should be at least 2.2, 4.2, and 5.5 degrees, respectively.

Clearly, it is best to avoid requiring accurate color perception in the periphery. This is not a problem in most cases because, ordinarily, the viewer will fixate the stimulus after detecting it and peripheral detection can be triggered by making the stimulus bright or causing it to flash or move. If peripheral color perception is required, though, one should make the stimulus as large, bright, and saturated a possible, to maximize the chances that it will be perceived correctly.

25.7.8 Color-Defective Viewers

When designing color images for general use, it is important to avoid creating problems for color-defective viewers (see Section 25.1.7). Therefore, do not rely on color alone to identify or distinguish image content; instead, assure that color differences are redundant with shape or brightness/lightness differences. This design strategy is often mandatory anyway because applications must usually be compatible with monochrome displays.

One simple test of whether an image is problematic for color-defective viewers is to look at it, first with the display in monochrome mode and then with each of the display's color channels disabled (one at a time—alternatively, one can view the display through cyan, magenta, and yellow filters) and see whether the desired discriminations remain possible.[12] Here is a general guideline that helps assure success on these checks: when using colors from the spectral extremes, set their brightness/lightness low and pair them with colors from the spectral midrange, set at high brightness/lightness. Table 7, adapted from Arditi and Knoblauch (1994), may also be helpful. It gives some examples of color pairings that tend to yield good and bad contrast for the color-defective population. Another strategy that helps color-defective viewers is to design the application so the user can adjust the colors.

25.7.9 Psychological Effects of Color

Some of the published guidance on color usage presumes the validity of the common belief that "warm" colors such as red and orange have an arousing effect on humans, whereas "cool" colors such as green and blue are calming. This color-induced state of arousal is often supposed to influence such things as mood and productivity. Efforts to test these ideas using physiological measures have been reviewed by Kaiser (1985). He concluded that color can influence galvanic skin response and electroencephalograms, but the effects are inconsistent and may have more to do with color preferences and learned associations than with direct impact on physiology. Other physiologically based studies have been performed since Kaiser's (1985) review, but have not produced results that contradict the preceding summary.

Many other measures, such as muscle strength, motor performance, questionnaire-based assessments of mood, intelligence tests, and behavioral observation have also been used to assess effects of color on arousal. The most dramatic claims have concerned "Baker-Miller pink": an ill-defined color that is occasionally the subject of anecdotal reports, asserting that placing violent persons in a room painted with this color calms them. To date, however, no large or consistent effects of color on these alternative measures have been demonstrated in the scientific literature. With specific regard to Baker-Miller pink, perhaps the most telling observation is this: recently, I phoned the commanding officer at the U.S. Navy prison that reportedly obtained the original, near-miraculous results (Schauss, 1979). He was familiar with the claims concerning pink cells, but was unaware of his facility's early role in those claims and stated that, presently, pink is used only to help guards distinguish the female prisoners' areas from the male prisoners' (which are blue).

---

12 Do not suppose that exercises like these allow one to experience the perception of color-defective viewers. Usually, it is impossible to determine what these perceptions are, and in at least one case where determination was possible, the results were surprising. See Kaiser and Boynton (1996, pp. 452-455) for an interesting discussion of these points.

Most people have color preferences and preconceived notions about their significance (many of which are culturally dependent). It is plausible, therefore, that these psychological factors can cause color to influence behavior and mood. So far, however, no effects that would provide a sound basis for design recommendations have been demonstrated scientifically.

25.8 Computer Assistance

Perhaps the most interesting recent development in color and human-computer interaction is a trend toward using the computer as a color design aid. One of the simpler examples is an enhanced "color picker" that depicts the display screen's color gamut using a perceptually uniform, three-dimensional representation (Bauersfeld and Price, 1990). The user can select a color swatch from this space and move it about to see how it looks in the context of other colors that are on the screen already. Other improved color pickers have also been designed. For example, Beretta (1990, 1993, 1994) has developed one for working with colors of familiar objects and another for more general design. The former contains preset, colorimetrically calibrated palettes, such as skin tones or vegetation, and allows the user to mix them as an artist would mix paints. The latter allows the user to specify a base color and then automatically generates a palette of "harmonious" partner colors, based on geometric relationships in a perceptually uniform color space.

A logical extension of color pickers is the provision of expert assistance that applies color-design rules, derived from the sort of knowledge and guidelines contained in Section 25.7. Meier (1988) describes an early example: a program that recommends colors for objects on a desktop environment after the screen designer provides information about the objects and their inter-relationships. More recently, Hedin and Derefeldt (1990) have produced an aid that generates palettes according to different perceptual rules, depending on the user's intent. For example, given a background color specification, palettes that yield legible text per Equation 91 can be created automatically. Rogowitz, Gerth, and Rabenhorst (1995) have developed a similar but more complex interactive tool that gradually constrains the designer's choices of font and color as a screen design progresses to assure legibility. That is, the program "understands" spatial vision and the spatial characteristics of the fonts, as well as color vision, and decisions made early in the design process are analyzed in terms of perceptual rules to determine what remaining choices should be permitted.

Bergman, Rogowitz, and Treinish (1995) have created a program that generates colormaps for data visualization, based on data type (nominal, ordinal, interval, or ratio), spatial frequency content, and the representation task (isomorphic, segmentation, or highlighting).

Automated assistance has also been created for checking screens after they have been designed. Jiang, Murphy, Carter, Bailin, and Truszkowski (1993) describe a rule-based program that analyzes screen designs and determines whether they violate human factors guidance for color usage. If problems are found, the program suggests changes.

Sophisticated "color adjusters" have been designed for enhancing digital images. Kanamori and Kotera (1991) have developed an interactive color-correction system that uses fuzzy logic to help identify image areas that the user wishes to correct. In their demonstration, skin tone was adjusted globally without affecting other colors in the image, even though the pixels representing skin had varying *RGB* values. Sanger, Asada, Haneishi, and Miyake (1994) have created a program that analyzes images and identifies areas that correspond to human faces, to support color correction of skin tones. Katajamäki, Laihanen, and Saarelma (1996) have gone even further by developing an algorithm that analyzes images and corrects skin tones, overall color balance, and contrast automatically, without human intervention.

25.9 Additional Reading

Durrett (1987), Travis (1991), Widdel and Post (1992), and Jackson, MacDonald, and Freeman (1994) are fairly recent, overview-type texts that expand usefully on the material presented in this chapter, as well as covering additional, relevant topics. Readers desiring greater detail on specific sections of the present chapter may wish to consult the following:

Sections 25.1-25.3. For a good introductory text on color vision and CIE colorimetry, see Hurvich (1981). For more advanced treatments, see Judd and Wyszecki (1975), Wyszecki and Stiles (1982), MacAdam (1985), and Kaiser and Boynton (1996). Birch (1993) provides detailed coverage of defective color vision. Derefeldt, Menu, and Swartling (1995) offer a quick introduction to cognitive and physiological aspects of color and include many useful references.

Section 25.4. For information about color appearance systems, see Judd and Wyszecki (1975), Wyszecki and Stiles (1982), and Derefeldt (1991). Sproson's (1983) book is devoted entirely to television colorimetry; Hunt (1995) also provides good coverage of this subject. Pennebaker and Mitchell (1993) cover the JPEG standard in detail.

Section 25.5. Judd and Wyszecki (1975) and Wyszecki and Stiles (1982) discuss colorimetric equipment in general; Zwinkels (1996) provides more detail concerning use and calibration. Berns, Gorzynski, and Motta (1993) have presented a thorough study of several commercial devices.

Sections 25.6 and 25.8. Burger (1993) and MacDonald (1996) provide good introductions to color management systems. Post (1992b), Berns (1996), and Howard (1996) discuss issues relevant to color management on displays; Johnson (1996a, 1996b) does the same for scanners, digital cameras, and printers. Rhodes and Luo (1996) describe a state-of-the-art system for achieving device-independent color. Information about the ICC, including a copy of the latest profile format specification, can be obtained via the World-Wide Web at http://www.color.org/. The Society for Imaging Science and Technology (IS&T) has sponsored an annual *Non-Impact Printing Congress* since 1985. IS&T and the Society of Photo-Optical Instrumentation Engineers (SPIE) have jointly sponsored an annual *Color Hard Copy and the Graphic Arts* conference since 1992. These same two societies have also sponsored an annual *Device-Independent Color Imaging* conference since 1993. IS&T and the Society for Information Display (SID) have sponsored an annual *Color Imaging Conference* since 1993. There are published proceedings for all these conferences. It is best to obtain the most recent volumes of these proceedings and work backwards, because work on the topics discussed in Sections 25.6 and 25.8 is very active; any effort to capture the state of the art in a textbook is apt to be outdated quickly.

Section 25.7. Travis (1991), Post (1992a), and Jackson, MacDonald, and Freeman (1994) provide guidance on the use of color on displays. Also, IS&T and SPIE have jointly sponsored a *Human Vision, Visual Processing, and Digital Display* conference almost every year since 1989, plus an occasional *Human Vision and Electronic Imaging* conference since 1990, where relevant work is often presented.

25.10 Acknowledgments

I offer my sincere thanks to Alan Nagy (Wright State University) and Louis D. Silverstein (VCD Sciences, Inc.), who provided many helpful comments on an early draft of this chapter, and to Roy S. Berns (Munsell Color Science Laboratory), Gunilla Derefeldt (National Defense Research Establishment), and David S. Travis (System Concepts Ltd.), who did the same for a later version. I also thank Gary Beckler, Chris Calhoun and Gary Rankin (Logicon Technical Services, Inc.), who produced most of the figures.

25.11 References

Alessi, P. (1994). CIE guidelines for coordinated research on evaluation of colour appearance models for reflection print and self-luminous display image comparisons. *Color Research and Application, 19,* 48-58.

Alman, D. H., Berns, R. S., Snyder, G. D., and Larsen, W. A. (1989). Performance testing of color-difference metrics using a color tolerance dataset. *Color Research and Application, 14,* 139-151.

ANSI (1988). *American national standard for human factors engineering of visual display terminal workstations* (ANSI/HFS Standard No. 100-1988). Santa Monica, CA: Human Factors Society.

Anstis, S. (1986). Motion perception in the frontal plane. In K. R. Boff, L. Kaufman, and J. P. Thomas (Eds.), *Handbook of perception and human performance. Volume I: Sensory processes and perception* (pp. 16-1 thru 16-16-27). New York: Wiley.

Arditi, A., and Knoblauch, K. (1994). Choosing effective display colors for the partially sighted. *1994 Society for Information Display International Symposium Digest of Technical Papers, 25,* 32-35.

Bauersfeld, P. F., and Price, B. A. (1990). The 3D perceptual picker: Color selection in 3D. *1990 Society for Information Display International Symposium Digest of Technical Papers, 21,* 180-183.

Beretta, G. B. (1990). Color palette selection tools. *Conference Summaries of SPSE's 43rd Annual Conference,* 94-96.

Beretta, G. B. (1993). *Reference color selection system.* U.S. Patent #5,254,978.

Beretta, G. B. (1994). *Functional color selection system.* U.S. Patent #5,311,212.

Bergman, L. D., Rogowitz, B. E., and Treinish, L. A.

(1995). A rule-based tool for assisting colormap selection. *Proceedings of IEEE Visualization '95,* 118-125.

Bergum, B. O., and Bergum, J. E. (1981). Population stereotypes: An attempt to measure and define. *Proceedings of the Human Factors Society 25th Annual Meeting,* 662-665.

Berk, T., Brownstone, L., and Kaufmann, A. (1982). A new color naming system for computer graphics. *IEEE Computer Graphics and Applications, 3,* 37-44.

Berlin, B., and Kay, P. (1969). *Basic color terms.* Berkeley, CA: University of California Press.

Berns, R. S. (1996). Methods for characterizing CRT displays. *Displays, 16,* 173-182.

Berns, R. S., Gorzynski, M. E., and Motta, R. J. (1993). CRT colorimetry. Part II: Metrology. *Color Research and Application, 18,* 315-325.

Berns, R. S., and Shyu, M. J. (1995). Colorimetric characterization of a desktop drum scanner using a spectral model. *Journal of Electronic Imaging, 4,* 360-372.

Birch, J. (1993). *Diagnosis of defective colour vision.* Oxford: Oxford University Press.

Boynton, R. M. (1978). Ten years of research with the minimally distinct border. In J. C. Armington, J. Krauskopf, and B. R. Wooten (Eds.), *Visual psychophysics and physiology* (193-207). New York: Academic Press.

Boynton, R. M., and Olson, C. X. (1987). Locating basic colors in the OSA space. *Color Research and Application, 12,* 94-105.

Burger, R. E. (1993). *Color management systems.* San Francisco: The Color Resource.

Calhoun, C. S., and Post, D. L. (1990). Heterochromatic brightness matches via Ware and Cowan's luminance correction equation. *1990 Society for Information Display International Symposium Digest of Technical Papers, 21,* 261-264.

Carter, R. C. (1989). Calculate (don't guess) the effect of symbol size on usefulness of color. *Proceedings of the Human Factors Society 33rd Annual Meeting,* 1368-1372.

Carter, R. C., and Carter, E. C. (1982). High contrast sets of colors. *Applied Optics, 21,* 2936-2939.

Carter, R. C., and Carter, E. C. (1983). CIE L*u*v* color difference equations for self-luminous displays. *Color Research and Application, 8,* 252-253.

Carter, R. C., and Carter, E. C. (1988). Color coding for rapid location of small symbols. *Color Research and Application, 13,* 226-234.

CIE (1978a). *Light as a true visual quantity: Principles of measurement* (CIE Publication No. 41). Paris: Author.

CIE (1978b). *Recommendations on uniform color spaces - color-difference equations - psychometric color terms* (Supplement No. 2 to CIE Publication No. 15). Paris: Author.

CIE (1986). *Colorimetry* (2nd ed., CIE Publication No. 15.2). Vienna: Author.

CIE (1988). *Spectral luminous efficiency functions based upon brightness matching for monochromatic point sources* 2^0 *and* 10^0 *fields* (CIE Publication No. 75). Vienna: Author.

CIE (1989). *Mesopic Photometry: History, Special Problems, and Practical solutions* (CIE Publication No. 81). Vienna: Author.

CIE (1990). *CIE 1988* 2^0 *spectral luminous efficiency function for photopic vision.* (CIE Publication No. 86). Vienna: Author.

CIE (1994). *Industrial colour-difference evaluation.* (CIE Publication No. 116). Vienna: Author.

Curcio, C. A., Allen, K. A., Sloan, K. R., Lerea, C. L., Hurley, J. B., Klock, I. B., and Milam, A. H. (1991). Distribution and morphology of human cone photoreceptors stained with anti-blue opsin. *The Journal of Comparative Neurology, 312,* 610-624.

De Corte, W. (1990). Recent developments in the computation of ergonomically optimal contrast sets of CRT colours. *Displays, 11,* 123-128.

Derefeldt, G. (1991). Colour appearance systems. In P. Gouras (Ed.), *The Perception of Colour* (pp. 218-261). Volume 6 in J. R. Cronly-Dillon (Series Ed.), *Vision and visual dysfunction.* London: MacMillan.

Derefeldt, G., Menu, J.-P., and Swartling, T. (1995). Cognitive aspects of color. *Proceedings of the Society of Photo-Optical Instrumentation Engineers (SPIE): Human Vision, Visual Processing, and Digital Display VI, 2411,* 16-24.

Derefeldt, G., and Swartling, T. (1995). Colour concept retrieval by free colour naming. Identification of up to 30 colours without training. *Displays, 16,* 69-77.

Durrett, H. J. (Ed.). (1987). *Color and the Computer.* San Diego: Academic Press.

Fairchild, M. D. (1994). Visual evaluation and evolution of the RLAB color space. *The Second IS&T/SID*

Color Imaging Conference: Color Science, Systems and Applications, 9-13.

Foley, J. D., Van Dam, A., Feiner, S. K., and Hughes, J. F. (1990). *Computer Graphics Principles and Practice* (2nd ed.). Reading, MA: Addison-Wesley.

Grossman, J. D. (1992). Color conventions and application standards. In H. Widdel and D. L. Post (Eds.), *Color in electronic displays* (pp. 209-218). New York: Plenum.

Guth, S. L. (1995). Further applications of the ATD model for color vision. *Proceedings of the Society of Photo-Optical Instrumentation Engineers (SPIE): Device-Independent Color Imaging II, 2414,* 12-26.

Hård, A., Sivik, L., and Tonnquist, G. (1996a). NCS, natural color system—from concept to research and applications. Part II. *Color Research and Application, 21,* 206-220.

Hård, A., Sivik, L., and Tonnquist, G. (1996b). NCS, natural color system—from concept to research and applications. Part I. *Color Research and Application, 21,* 180-205.

Hanes, R. M., and Rhoades, M. V. (1959). Color identification as a function of extended practice. *Journal of the Optical Society of America, 49,* 1060-1064.

Hedin, C. E., and Derefeldt, G. (1990). Palette - A color selection aid for VDU images. *Proceedings of the Society of Photo-Optical Instrumentation Engineers (SPIE): Perceiving, Measuring, and Using Color, 1250,* 165-176.

Howard, C. M. (1996). Managing color appearance in self-luminous displays. *Proceedings of the Society of Photo-Optical Instrumentation Engineers (SPIE): Human Vision and Electronic Imaging, 2657,* 2-9.

Hunt, R. W. G. (1995). *The Reproduction of Colour* (5th ed.). Kingston-upon-Thames, England: Fountain Press.

Hunt, R. W. G. (1994). An improved predictor of colourfulness in a model of colour vision. *Color Research and Application, 19,* 23-26.

Hurvich, L. M. (1981). *Color Vision.* Sunderland, MA: Sinauer Associates, Inc.

Ikeda, K., Nakayama, M., and Obara, K. (1979). Comparison of perceived colour-differences of colour chips with their colorimetric ones in the CIE 1976 L*u*v* and the CIE L*a*b* uniform colour spaces. *CIE Proceedings, 19,* 83-89.

ISO (1992). *Ergonomic requirements for office work with visual display terminals (VDTs). Part 3. Visual display requirements* (ISO standard 9241-3). Geneva, Switzerland: Author.

Jackson, R., MacDonald, L., and Freeman, K. (1994). *Computer generated colour: A Practical Guide to Presentation and Display.* Chichester, West Sussex, England: Wiley.

Jacobsen, A. R. (1986). The effect of background luminance on color recognition. *Color Research and Application, 11,* 263-269.

Jiang, J., Murphy, E. D., Carter, L. E., Bailin, S. C., and Truszkowski, W. F. (1993). Knowledge-based evaluation of GUI color usage. *MOTIF '93 and COSE International User Conference Proceedings,* 78-87.

Johnson, T. (1996a). Methods for characterizing colour scanners and digital cameras. *Displays, 16,* 183-191.

Johnson, T. (1996b). Methods for characterizing colour printers. *Displays, 16,* 193-202.

Judd, D. B. (1951). Report of the U.S. secretariat committee on colorimetry and artificial daylight. In *CIE Proceedings, 1* (Part 7, p. 11). Paris: CIE.

Judd, D. B., and Nickerson, D. (1975). Relation between Munsell and Swedish Natural Color System scales. *Journal of the Optical Society of America, 65,* 85-90.

Judd, D. B., and Wyszecki, G. (1975). *Color in Business, Science and Industry* (3rd ed.). New York: Wiley.

Kaiser, P. K. (1985). Physiological response to color: A critical review. *Color Research and Application, 9,* 29-36.

Kaiser, P. K., and Boynton, R. M. (1996). *Human Color Vision* (2nd ed.). Washington, DC: Optical Society of America.

Kanamori, K., and Kotera, H. (1991). A method for selective color control in perceptual color space. *Journal of Imaging Science, 35,* 307-316.

Katajamäki, J. Laihanen, P., and Saarelma, H. (1996). Classification of images for automatic colour correction. *IS&T and SID's 3rd Color Imaging Conference: Color Science, Systems, and Applications,* 109-111.

Kaufmann, R. (1990). Effects of low-level red ambient lighting and stimulus size on classification of colours on displays. *Displays, 11,* 146-156.

Kaufmann, R., and O'Neill, M. C. (1993). Colour names and focal colours on displays. *Ergonomics, 36,* 881-890.

Kelly, K. L., and Judd, D. B. (1955). *The ISCC-NBS method of designating colors and a dictionary of color names* (NBS Circular 553). Washington, DC: U.S. Government Printing Office.

Kim, T. G., Berns, R. S., and Fairchild, M. D. (1993). Comparing appearance models using pictorial images. *The First IS&T and SID Color Imaging Conference: Transforms and Transportability of Color,* 72-77.

Kinney, J. A. S. (1979). The use of color in wide-angle displays. *Proceedings of the Society for Information Display, 20,* 33-40.

Kuyk, T. K. (1982). Spectral sensitivity of the peripheral retina to large and small stimuli. *Vision Research, 22,* 1293-1297.

Lippert, T. M. (1986). Color difference prediction of legibility performance for raster CRT imagery. *1986 Society for Information Display International Symposium Digest of Technical Papers, 17,* 86-89.

Lippert, T. M., Farley, W. W., Post, D. L., and Snyder, H. L. (1983). Color contrast effects on human performance. *1983 Society for Information Display International Symposium Digest of Technical Papers, 14,* 170-171.

Lo, M. C., Luo, M. R., and Rhodes, P. A. (1996). Evaluating colour models' performance between monitor and print images. *Color Research and Application, 21,* 277-291.

Luo, M. R. (1996). The LLAB model for colour appearance and colour difference evaluation. *Proceedings of the Society of Photo-Optical Instrumentation Engineers (SPIE): Color Imaging: Device-Independent Color Hard Copy and Graphic Arts, 2658,* 261-269.

MacAdam, D. L. (1942). Visual sensitivities to color differences in daylight. *Journal of the Optical Society of America, 32,* 247-274.

MacAdam, D. L. (1985). *Color measurement: Theme and variations* (2nd ed.). New York: Springer-Verlag.

MacDonald, L. W. (1996). Developments in colour management systems. *Displays, 16,* 203-211.

Mahy, M., Van Eycken, L., and Oosterlinck, A. (1994). Evaluation of uniform color spaces developed after the adoption of CIELAB and CIELUV. *Color Research and Application, 19,* 105-121.

McFadden, S. (1992). Discrimination of colours presented against different coloured backgrounds. *Color Research and Application, 17,* 339-351.

Meier, B. (1988). ACE: A color expert system for user interface design. *Proceedings of the SIGGRAPH Symposium on User Interface Software,* 117-128.

Metrick, L. (1978). Status report of the Graphic Standards Planning Committee. *Computer Graphics, 13(3),* III-6 & III-7; III-37 & III-38.

Moroney, N. M., and Fairchild, M. D. (1993). Color space selection for JPEG image compression. *The First IS&T and SID Color Imaging Conference: Transforms & Transportability of Color,* 157-159.

Nagy, A. (1994). Red/green color discrimination and stimulus size. *Color Research and Application, 19,* 99-104.

Nayatani, Y. (1995). Revision of the chroma and hue scales of a nonlinear color-appearance model. *Color Research and Application, 20,* 143-155.

Nayatani, Y., Sobagaki, H., Hashimoto, K., and Yano, T. (1995). Lightness dependency of chroma scales of a nonlinear color-appearance model and its latest formulation. *Color Research and Application, 20,* 156-167.

Nerger, J. L., and Cicerone, C. M. (1992). The ratio of L cones to M cones in the human parafoveal retina. *Vision Research, 32,* 879-888.

Newhall, S. M., Nickerson, D. M., and Judd, D. B. (1943). Final report of the O.S.A. subcommittee on the spacing of the Munsell colors. *Journal of the Optical Society of America, 33,* 385-418.

Nickerson, D., and Newhall, S. M. (1943). A psychological color solid. *Journal of the Optical Society of America, 33,* 419-422.

Olson, J. (1987). Color and the computer in cartography. In H. J. Durrett (Ed.), *Color and the computer* (pp. 205-219). San Diego, CA: Academic Press.

Pastoor, S. (1990). Legibility and subjective preference for color combinations in text. *Human Factors, 32,* 157-171.

Pennebaker, W. B., and Mitchell, J. L. (1993). *JPEG still image compression standard.* New York: Van Nostrand Reinhold.

Pointer, M. R. (1981). A comparison of the CIE 1976 colour spaces. *Color Research and Application, 6,* 108-118.

Pokorny, J., Smith, V. C., and Went, L. N. (1981). Color matching in autosomal dominant tritan defect. *Journal of the Optical Society of America, 71,* 1327-1334.

Post, D. L. (1984). CIELUV/CIELAB and self-luminous displays: Another perspective. *Color Research and Application, 9,* 244-245.

Post D. L. (1992a). Applied color vision research. In H. Widdel and D. L. Post (Eds.),*Color in electronic displays* (pp. 137-173). New York: Plenum.

Post, D. L. (1992b). Colorimetric measurement, calibration, and characterization of self-luminous displays.

In H. Widdel and D. L. Post (Eds.), *Color in Electronic Displays* (pp. 299-312). New York: Plenum.

Post, D. L., and Calhoun, C. S. (1988). Color-name boundaries for equally bright stimuli on a CRT: Phase II. *1988 Society for Information Display International Symposium Digest of Technical Papers, 19,* 65-68.

Post, D. L., and Calhoun, C. S. (1989). Color-name boundaries for equally bright stimuli on a CRT: Phase III. *1989 Society for Information Display International Symposium Digest of Technical Papers, 20,* 284-287.

Post, D. L., Costanza, E. B., and Lippert, T. M. (1982). Expressions of color contrast as equivalent achromatic contrast. *Proceedings of the Human Factors Society 26th Annual Meeting,* 581-585.

Post, D. L., and Greene, F. A. (1986). Color-name boundaries for equally bright stimuli on a CRT: Phase I. *1986 Society for Information Display International Symposium Digest of Technical Papers, 17,* 70-73.

Post, D. L., Lippert, T. M., and Snyder, H. L. (1983). Color contrast metrics for head-up displays. *Proceedings of the Human Factors Society 27th Annual Meeting, 2,* 933-937.

Rhodes, P., and Luo, M. R. (1996). A system for WYSIWIG colour communication. *Displays, 16,* 213-221.

Richter, M. (1955). The official German Standard Color Chart. *Journal of the Optical Society of America, 45,* 223-226.

Robertson, A. R. (1977). The CIE 1976 colour spaces. *Color Research and Application, 2,* 7-11.

Rogowitz, B. E., Gerth, J. A., and Rabenhorst, D. A. (1995). An intelligent tool for selecting colors and fonts for graphical user interfaces. *Proceedings of the Society of Photo-Optical Instrumentation Engineers (SPIE): Human Vision, Visual Processing, and Digital Display VI, 2411,* 35-43.

Sanger, D., Asada, T., Haneishi, H., and Miyake, Y. (1994). Facial pattern recognition and its preferred color reproduction. *IS&T and SID's 2nd Color Imaging Conference: Color Science, Systems, and Applications,* 149-153.

Schauss, A. G. (1979). Tranquilizing effect of color reduces aggressive behavior and potential violence. *Orthomolecular Psychiatry, 8,* 218-221.

Seim, T., and Valberg, A. (1986). Towards a uniform color space: A better formula to describe the Munsell and OSA color scales. *Color Research and Application, 11,* 11-24.

Silverstein, L. D., and Merrifield, R. M. (1985, July). *The Development and Evaluation of Color Systems for Airborne Applications* (Report No. DOT/FAA/PM-85-19). Washington, DC: U.S. Department of Transportation.

Smallman, H. S., and Boynton, R. M. (1993). On the usefulness of basic colour coding in an information display. *Displays, 14,* 158-165.

Smith, A. R. (1978). Color gamut transform pairs. *Computer Graphics, 12(3),* 12-19.

Smith, H. S., Whitfield, T. W. A., and Wiltshire, T. J. (1990). A colour notation conversion program. *Color Research and Application, 15,* 338-343.

Sproson, W. N. (1983). *Colour science in television and display systems.* Bristol, England: Adam Hilger.

Stabell, U., and Stabell, B. (1980). Variation in density of macular pigmentation and in short-wave cone sensitivity with eccentricity. *Journal of the Optical Society of America, 70,* 706-711.

Travis, D. S. (1991). *Effective color displays: Theory and practice.* San Diego: Academic Press.

Travis, D. S., and Johns, A. M. (1994). Back to basics. *1994 Society for Information Display International Symposium Digest of Technical Papers, 25,* 877-880.

Vos, J. J. (1978). Colorimetric and photometric properties of a 2 deg fundamental observer. *Color Research and Application, 3,* 125-128.

Ware, C., and Cowan, W. B. (1983). *Specification of heterochromatic brightness matches: A conversion factor for calculating luminances of stimuli that are equal in brightness* (Tech. Report 26055). Ottawa, Canada: National Research Council of Canada.

Widdel, H., and Post, D. L. (Eds.). (1992). *Color in Electronic Displays.* New York: Plenum.

Williams, D. R., MacLeod, D. I. A., and Hayhoe, M. M. (1980). Foveal tritanopia. *Vision Research, 21,* 1341-1356.

Wyszecki, G., and Stiles, W. S. (1982). *Color science* (2nd ed.). New York: Wiley.

Wyszecki, G. (1986). Color appearance. In K. R. Boff, L. Kaufman, and J. P. Thomas (Eds.), *Handbook of perception and human performance. Volume I: Sensory processes and perception* (pp. 9-1 thru 9-57). New York: Wiley.

Zwinkels, J. C. (1996). Colour-measuring instruments and their calibration. *Displays, 16,* 163-171.

Handbook of Human-Computer Interaction
Second, completely revised edition
M. Helander, T.K. Landauer, P. Prabhu (eds.)

Chapter 26

How Not to Have to Navigate Through Too Many Displays

David D. Woods and Jennifer C. Watts
The Ohio State University
Columbus, Ohio, USA

26.1 Introduction

26.1.1 Large Networks of Displays

The first and most basic response of system developers to the expanding power of the computer and its increasing penetration into application areas has been to collect and make available more and more raw data. The modular nature of the computer as a medium for representation has allowed system developers to accommodate the expanded set of data easily (at least from a technology point of view) by adding more and more displays to the set of potentially observable frames hidden behind the narrow keyhole of the computer screen. The combination of a large field of raw data and a narrow keyhole have created a variety of problems for practitioners, people engaged in the practice of a profession or occupation.

We have seen the emergence of three trends in information visualization which attempt to address the problems caused by large networks of displays of raw data:

- ***Information Animation.*** Instead of just displaying static values that capture current state, the computer medium also allows designers to emphasize change, activities, events, and contrasts that extend into the future as well as the past (Woods, Patterson and Corbin, 1996).

- ***Integrated Representations.*** (referred to by many labels such as object, configural, or emergent property displays; e.g., Bennett and Flach, 1992 and Vicente and Rasmussen, 1992). Instead of providing an independent display element for each piece of available data (one datum-one display), the computer medium supports development of more coherent views into some activity, process, or system.

- ***Coordination of Multiple Views*** to create a virtual perceptual field or a workspace in which practitioners carry out their work activity.

This third trend is the theme of this chapter. Because coherent domain activities must almost always require movement across displays, we are concerned with how the characteristics of computer-based networks of displays shape the cognition and performance of practitioners. We review common findings from field studies that have shown how large networks of displays, available through a limited keyhole, can place new mental burdens on users. We also provide an overview of some of the techniques that designers can use to break down the keyhole and help users focus on the relevant portion of the data field as activities unfold. Work in HCI that is concerned with this level of analysis of a computer based information system often goes under labels such as navigation, browsing, hypertext, dialogue design, or window management (e.g., Nielsen, 1990).

In this chapter, we discuss ways in which designers can coordinate different kinds of display frames within a virtual workspace (Woods, 1984; Henderson and Card, 1986). We refer to this level of analysis and design as workspace coordination--the integration of the set of displays and classes of views that can be seen together in parallel or in series as a function of context (Woods, 1996). At the level of workspace coordination one is concerned with support for knowing where to look next in a perceptual field given new events and changing priorities. This level interacts with another level of analysis and design where one is concerned with the kinds of views which the observer can select for display in a viewport (a view is a coherent unit of representation of a portion of the underlying process, device or system). From the perspective of workspace coordination, the critical challenges in designing large display networks revolve around how to help users:

- avoid getting lost in the large space of possibilities,
- find the right data at the right time as tasks change and activities unfold,
- integrate inter-related data that spreads across different kinds of display frames,
- avoid becoming focused on interface management itself (where is the data) in lieu of focusing on the task (what is the relevant data and what does it mean about system state and needed operator actions).

26.1.2 The Keyhole Property

When we look at a computer based display system, what do we actually see? We directly see one display or a few displays in separate windows on one or more CRTs (or more generally, visual display units, VDUs). What is not directly apparent is all of the other displays or views of the underlying system, process, or device that could be called up onto the viewports -- the data space hidden behind the narrow keyhole of the CRT. The relationships between different parts of this data space are not apparent. Glancing at what is directly visible usually does not reveal the paths or mechanisms or sequence of actions required to maneuver through the data space. There is a large difference between what is directly visible and what is behind the placid surface of the CRT screen (Figure 1). This is a description of one of the dominant characteristics of the computer as a medium for display--the keyhole property. The computer medium exhibits the keyhole property because the size of the available viewports (the windows/VDUs available) is very small relative to the size of the artificial data space or number of data displays that potentially could be examined. As a result, the proportion of the virtual perceptual field that can be seen at the same time, that is, physically in parallel, is very very small.

To technologists this property appears quite advantageous--a single physical device, the VDU, can be used to provide access in principle to any kind of view the designer, marketeer, or customer think relevant. Change or expansion is straightforward: the physical platform remains constant; one only has to modify or add more displays to the artificial space behind the physical viewports. One can respond to many different markets, niches and contexts simply by taking the union of all of the features, displays, options and functions that are needed in any of these settings and combining them on a single physical platform through software. The computer medium makes it easy to add new options to a menu structure or to add new displays

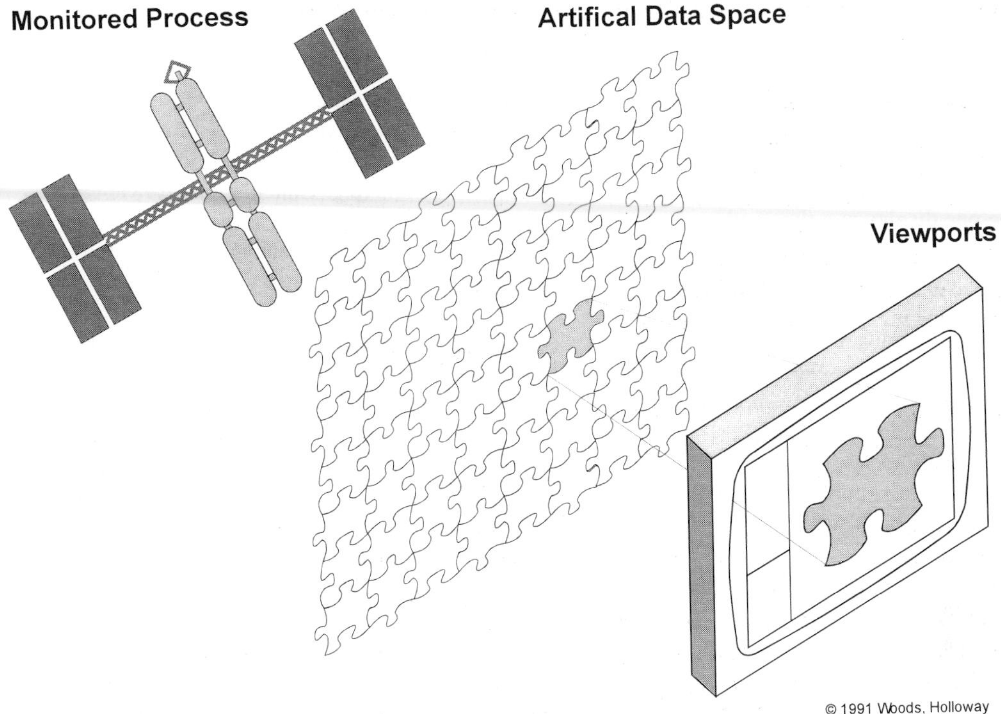

Figure 1. The keyhole property of computer-based display systems (from Woods, 1995a). *The computer medium consists of a large artificial data field behind a narrow viewport or viewports. The data field speaks to the state of affairs in some underlying process, device, system or field of activity--the monitored process. The keyhole property is that the number of potential views is much greater than the physical size of the available viewports. Coherent domain activities almost always involve extracting information across multiple views and knowing where to look next in the data space available behind the limited viewports*

which can be selected to appear on the same physical viewport if needed. The technologist only requires the HCI specialist to provide context free navigation mechanisms that make all of the options, functions and displays nominally accessible. Hence it is easy and common for developers to create large collections of data and possible displays hidden behind a narrow keyhole.[1]

26.1.3 Getting Lost

The practitioner's view is quite different than the technologist's. When developers create large networks of displays with little investment in supporting workspace coordination, practitioners bear the burden to navigate across all of these displays in order to carry out domain tasks and to meet domain goals. The danger is that users can become "disoriented" or "lost" in the space of possible displays. Three brief examples illustrate these dangers.

Example 1: A Computerized Control Room

One computerized control room for a nuclear power plant under development has evolved to include well over 16,000 possible displays that could be examined by operators. During development designers focused on individual displays and relied on a set of generic movement mechanisms and commands to support navigation across displays. Only after the control room was implemented for final testing in a high fidelity simulator did the developers realize that operators needed to focus a great deal of time and effort to find the appropriate displays for the current context (Easter, 1991). These difficulties were greatest when plant conditions were changing, the most critical times for operators to be focused on understanding and correctly responding to plant conditions.

Example 2: A Medical Infusion Device

A device for infusing small quantities of potent medi-

[1] What is large depends on user knowledge and experience with the material in question, task characteristics, e.g., self-paced or event-driven, and the consequences of misadventures.

cine is used to allow mothers with high risk pregnancies to control pre-term labor while remaining at home instead of in the hospital (the patient becomes the user and the nursing staff supervises). The device interface consists of about forty different displays nested at two levels (there are seven different "top level" displays; under each are one to seven more displays). Patient-users can only see one display at a time and must move across displays to carry out the tasks involved in control of pre-term labor and in coordinating with supervising nursing personnel. Patient-users easily become disoriented due to poor feedback about where they are in the space of possible displays and sequences of operation as well as other factors (Obradovich and Woods, 1996). Most commonly when lost, patient-users retreat to a default screen and attempt to begin the task over from the beginning although there are other potential consequences as well.

Example 3: A Hypertext Document

Students were asked to learn about a topic related to their (psychology) class by studying a hypertext document of 45 cards (McDonald and Stevenson, 1996). The hypertext document was organized either in a fixed linear sequence or in a non-linear structure where related cards were cross-referenced. No cues to structure or navigation aids were included except the variable of organization type--hierarchical or nonlinear. In the absence of any cues to structure (the non-linear condition) in this small but unfamiliar body of material, participants searched less, answered questions about the material more slowly and less accurately, and felt more disoriented.

These are examples of getting lost or disorientation effects which occurred when users worked with relatively large networks of displays (Elm and Woods, 1985; Conklin, 1987). Many forms of disorientation related problems have been observed. In some cases, the downside is literally a sense of disorientation--losing track of where they are relative to other locations in the space of possibilities. Another effect is cognitive--the limited support for workspace coordination increases mental workload or forces users to adopt deliberative mentally demanding strategies (e.g., Thuring, Hannemann and Haake, 1995). A third result is on performance: users may search less of the space of possibilities, miss "interesting" events, take longer to perform a task or perform with lower accuracy. One example of these effects has been called the "art museum effect" where observers who examine many items one or only a few at a time through the computer keyhole become overwhelmed and lose any larger coherent understanding of the individual pieces they have examined (e.g., Smith and Wilson, 1993). Another specific example occurs when users lose track of what portions of the space they have explored already because they can see only a small portion of the displays behind the keyhole (e.g., Shneiderman, 1987).

Disorientation and other problems like those exemplified above have led many to call for or to propose new techniques for spatially organizing networks of displays (Bolt, 1984; Woods, 1984; Smith and Wilson, 1993; Robertson, Card and Mackinlay, 1993; Kim and Hirtle, 1995). New concepts to make the structural and semantic properties of large networks of displays visible are emerging at a rapid pace driven by the challenge of managing ever larger collections of data and possible displays (e.g., Henderson and Card, 1986; Bernstein, 1988; Beard and Walker, 1990; Card, Mackinlay and Robertson, 1991; Mackinlay, Robertson and Card, 1991; Shneiderman, 1992; Pejterson, 1992; Robertson and Mackinlay, 1993; Mitta and Guning, 1993; Rao and Card, 1994; Lieberman, 1994; Zizi and Beaudouin-Lafon, 1995; Furnas and Bederson, 1995; Lamping, Rao and Pirolli, 1995; Card, Robertson and York, 1996; Mackinlay, Robertson and Deline, 1996; Kahn, 1996).

26.1.4 Avoiding Navigation Burdens

On some occasions investigators are able to observe users experience disorientation effects--in laboratory studies (e.g., McDonald and Stevenson, 1996) and during usability testing (e.g., Elm and Woods, 1985). However, when practitioners perform actual work in context, getting lost represents an egregious failure to accomplish their task goals. In effect, practitioners cannot afford to get lost in poorly designed networks of displays. Observational studies of users in context reveal that practitioners actively develop strategies and modify interfaces to avoid the danger of getting lost in poorly designed networks and to minimize any navigation activities during higher tempo or more critical aspects of job performance (e.g., Watts, 1994; Cook and Woods, 1996).

Example 4: Observing Extended Spreadsheet Users at Work

Watts (1994) observed users of extended spreadsheets (an interconnected set of data tables much larger than the available viewport) create paper maps of the spreadsheet structure. These users annotated portions of their hand-made maps with cues to spreadsheet structure by adding bold lines and spaces to denote meaningful groupings. They also added cues about spreadsheet semantics by labeling portions of the sheets with descriptions of the content of those portions. The annotated print outs served as maps available in parallel to the local views available on the CRT. The maps helped in many tasks such as correcting data base errors by reminding the user of the areas they needed to find and where these areas were located in the virtual workspace. In other words, the users created maps and tailored the extended spreadsheet to reduce navigation burdens.

When practitioners work around navigation burdens, they are sending designers a potent message: they are saying that the interface, at the level of workspace coordination, is poorly matched to the demands of their task world. Techniques users innovate to avoid navigation burdens are one potent source of more general concepts to design a coordinated virtual workspace.

This repeated observation of users actively working to avoid navigating has been noted in several different domains with several different kinds of users--anesthesiologists in the operating room, flight controllers in space mission control, financial analysts working with large extended spreadsheets. We believe this observation to be fundamental to understanding navigation problems and solutions. It is the basis for the title we chose for this chapter--how not to have to navigate through too many displays.

The consequences of the keyhole property are not immutable. They are the result of failing to design for across display transitions and how practitioners will coordinate a set of views as they perform meaningful tasks. We will discuss a set of techniques that focus on breaking down the keyhole inherent in computer-based display of data. Success is more than helping users travel in a space they cannot visualize. Success is creating a visible conceptual space meaningfully related to activities and constraints of a field of practice. Success lies in supporting practitioners to know where to look next in that conceptual space.

26.1.5 Our Stance

The work that drives our perspective on navigation issues comes, in large part, from studies of practitioners in event-driven worlds where pilots, space flight controllers, nuclear power plant operators, or physicians struggle to integrate computer-based display systems into the demands of their worlds. These worlds are event-driven because events in the world, such as faults, drive the pace of operations as opposed to self-paced tasks where users control when and how they will meet their task goals. In event-driven worlds, tempo varies and the demands of situations can escalate unpredictably. Interestingly, we find strong overlap between observations and techniques in complex domains and those derived from apparently simpler domains.

Our perspective is unabashedly context bound. We do not separate navigation issues from issues about the content and semantics of the underlying domain (Woods, 1995a). A context-bound view is concerned with helping practitioners find relevant information given the situation and state of the problem solving process (an issue related to task performance). A context-free view emphasizes efficiencies in moving from place to place in the artificial data space (an issue related to data availability). Context-free navigation techniques have wide appeal as potentially generic solutions. However, in our work we have seen little evidence that such techniques are sufficient by themselves to eliminate across-display processing difficulties. For a context bound approach the critical question is how to help practitioners find <u>the right data at the right time</u> in an evolving and changing situation.

This chapter is, in part, an update of the organizing heuristic of Visual Momentum (Woods, 1984; Hochberg, 1986). This concept was introduced

- to focus attention on across-display issues at a time when designers seemed focused largely on developing individual displays in isolation, and
- to introduce techniques from perception and cinematography that could aid the integration of information across successive display selections.

The Visual Momentum heuristic remains one useful way to organize many techniques that have been identified as potentially effective mechanisms (e.g., Furnas, 1986; Henderson and Card, 1986; Vicente and Williges, 1988; Aretz, 1991; Lamping, Rao and Pirolli, 1995).

Finally, as in the concept of Visual Momentum, our point of departure is derived from perception--how do we know where to look next in a complex perceptual field where new potentially informative events may occur at indeterminate times.

26.2 On Knowing Where to Look Next

26.2.1 Shifting Attentional Focus in a Changing Perceptual Field

A fundamental competency of human perceptual systems is the ability to orient focal attention to "interesting" parts of the natural perceptual field (Rabbitt 1984; Wolfe 1992).

> "The ability to look, listen, smell, taste, or feel requires an animal capable of orienting its body so that its eyes, ears, nose, mouth, or hands can be directed toward objects and relevant stimulation from objects. Lack of orientation to the ground or to the medium surrounding one, or to the earth below and the sky above, means inability to direct perceptual exploration in an adequate way (Reed, 1988, p. 227 on Gibson and perceptual exploration in Gibson, 1966)."

Both visual search studies and reading comprehension studies show that people are highly skilled at directing attention to aspects of the perceptual field that are of high potential relevance given the properties of the data field and the expectations and interests of the observer. Reviewing visual search studies, Woods (1984) commented, "When observers scan a visual scene or display, they tend to look at 'informative' areas . . . informativeness, defined as *some relation between the viewer and scene*, is an important determinant of eye movement patterns" (p. 231, italics in original). Reviewing reading comprehension studies, Bower and Morrow (1990) wrote, "The principle . . . is that readers direct their attention to places where significant events are likely to occur. The significant events . . . are usually those that facilitate or block the goals and plans of the protagonist."

How do we focus in on areas of high potential relevance when what is relevant depends on context? How do we shift attentional focus in a changing environment where new events may require a shift in attentional focus (or action) at indeterminate times? Basically, the ability to notice potentially interesting events and know where to look next (where to focus attention next) in natural perceptual fields depends on the coordination between orienting perceptual systems (i.e., the auditory system and peripheral vision) and focal perception and attention (e.g., foveal vision). The coordination between these mechanisms allows us to achieve a "balance between the rigidity necessary to ensure that potentially important environmental events do not go unprocessed and the flexibility to adapt to changing behavioral goals and circumstances" (Folk et al. 1992, p. 1043).

The orienting perceptual systems function to pick up changes or conditions that are potentially interesting and play a critical role in supporting how we know where to look next. To intuitively grasp the power of orienting perceptual functions, try this thought experiment (or better, actually do it!): put on goggles that block peripheral vision, allowing a view of only a few degrees of visual angle; now think of what it would be like to function and move about in your physical environment with this handicap. Perceptual scientists have tried this experimentally through a movable aperture that limits the observer's view of a scene (e.g., Hochberg, 1986). Although these experiments were done for other purposes, the difficulty in performing various visual tasks under these conditions is indicative of the power of the perceptual orienting mechanisms.

26.2.2 Virtual Perceptual Fields

We conceptualize navigation as the challenge of building representations in the computer medium that support rather than undermine the fundamental competency of knowing where to look next (Woods, 1984). The computer medium gives the designer control over the properties of the perceptual field the observer works within (Woods, 1996). This is in contrast to the usual state affairs where we study how perceptual systems function in a natural world that is given. The Gibsonian research agenda (e.g. Gibson, 1986) is concerned with identifying the structure in natural perceptual fields that our perceptual systems can pick up to carry out complex activities (e.g., the variable tau, time to contact, is a property of the perceptual world that supports complex activities from timing a jump to clear an obstacle to timing one's swing in baseball).

However, the virtuality of the computer medium inverts the situation. The designer now has control over the properties of the perceptual field, and there is nothing inherent in the computer medium that constrains the relationship between things represented and their representation (Woods, 1995a). For virtual perceptual worlds, the designer manipulates characteristics of across display activity and, as a result, influences the expression of the basic cognitive competency of knowing where to look next in a changing world. The designer creates what is perceivable by observers and controls how those attributes, objects, and views map onto the semantics of the domain. The designer decides what classes of views can be seen together in parallel or in series as a function of context. The designer decides what kinds of coherent views are available for the observer to select (where a kind of view is a coherent unit of representation of a portion of the underlying process or systems). The designer decides what kinds of supplementary views and landmarks are available to help observers orient to the larger data field while examining one portion in detail. The designer's choices affect the kind of cognitive processing that practitioners must bring to bear to perform their job successfully. For example, will deciding where to look next involve mentally effortful, serially bottlenecked, deliberative processes or will it be more a mentally economical, effectively parallel, perceptual process?

What then is the typical structure of the perceptual field created by developers of computer-based information systems? As Figure 1 illustrates the designer builds up a large artificial field of possible displays or views. However, the size of the viewports is very small so that users can see only one or very few of the potential displays at a time. But coherent domain activities almost always involve extracting information across multiple views and knowing where to look next in the data space available behind the limited viewports. Given such a large artificial data field behind a narrow set of viewports, shifting one's "gaze" is carried out by selecting another part of the artificial data space and moving it into the limited viewport. First, in this default or baseline design case, the previous view is replaced by the newly chosen view. This is an across-display transition of total replacement which minimizes any visual momentum as the observer reorients to the new display (analogous to a poor cut in film editing). Second, in this baseline case with the minimum support for across display transitions, the remainder of the field of possible views is invisible to the observer. The observer can see only one small portion of the total field at one time (i.e., physically in parallel). In other words, the default interface design leaves out orienting cues that indicate in mentally economical ways what else is in the virtual perceptual field, what is nearby on the local area, and whether something interesting may be going on in any other part of that field.

When some of the views contain menus or other selection mechanisms and other different views contain actual content about the topic, system or device in question, the total replacement of one view for another in the absence of any visible context creates an additional problem. Users may have to move through several layers of menus before one gets to examine even a small bit of content. What is surprising is how many computer-based information systems and how many hypertext systems (e.g., browse Web sites) have designs that come close to this default but extreme design of total replacement for across display transitions.

The default workspace structure of total replacement fragments data across different displays and forces the practitioner into a slow serial search to collect and then integrate related data. The observer must remember where the desired data is located and remember and execute the actions necessary to bring that portion of the field into the viewport, given he knows what data are potentially interesting to examine next. While the device may possess great flexibility for users to tailor their workspace by manipulating the number, size, and location of available windows and for users to call up different displays into these viewports, this flexibility creates new physical and cognitive tasks that can increase practitioner workload during high tempo periods. Practitioner attention shifts to the interface--where is the desired data located in the display space?--and to interface control--how do I navigate to that location in the display space?--at the very times where their attention needs to be devoted most to their job.

Note the contrast with a natural perceptual field where our orienting perceptual systems function to guide the movement of focal attention. In the baseline case of virtual perceptual fields, there are no cues to help orient the observer to the larger data field behind the keyhole. In other words, we create for users virtual perceptual fields that are the equivalent of trying to function in the natural perceptual world while wearing goggles and gear that eliminate our orienting perceptual systems (e.g., peripheral vision) as in our thought experiment. One can see the problems that can occur by imagining what it would be like to move about in a bustling physical environment with no peripheral vision or other orienting perceptual systems.

The search for solutions shifts when we reformulate the problem of navigation as supporting how one knows where to look next in a changing perceptual field. A context free view emphasizes efficiencies in moving from place to place in the virtual data space. But context free navigation aids, window managers and browsers in themselves may not be enough to solve the problems of clumsy workspace coordination. More efficient navigation within the interface is not the end; the goal is to help practitioners better focus on their job within their field of activity. A context bound view emphasizes helping practitioners find the relevant information given the changing state of the world and the state of their problem solving process. To accomplish this at the workspace coordination level we must think first about sequences of tasks, about what data needs to be seen in parallel in different contexts, and about how attention shifts to interrupt signals and new events.

In complex systems human activity ebbs and flows, with periods of lower activity and more self paced tasks interspersed with busy, high tempo, externally paced operations where task performance is more critical. These domains are characterized by multiple interleaved physical and cognitive activities where a shift from one activity to another may be triggered by knowledge or by new events in the world. Developing what kinds of views should be available, how to coordinate different views in parallel or serially in pace with the interleaved and changing tasks of the practitioner is critical to workspace coordination. Methods for modeling the ebb, flow and transitions in the field of activity using different kinds of scenarios will be needed to provide the information base for design of a coordinated virtual workspace.

If we adopt this context bound approach, we can begin to develop techniques that will help practitioners find the right data at the right time. These techniques then will guide the development of specific mechanisms or guide the application of technological advances in window managers, browsers, and other navigation aids.

26.2.3 The Shift from Physical Layout to Virtual Data Fields in Control Centers

To understand many of the issues involved in working with a virtual data field let us examine the evolution of control centers. Visualize a traditional hardwired control center and a fully computer based control center, and look carefully at the differences.[2] In the hardwired case much of the design work is directly visible in the layout of controls, displays, status panels and annunciators in the physically available space. But look closely at a picture of a proposed fully computerized control room. Yes, you can see the arrangement of the computer screens and workstations, but the real design action and potential complexity is behind the screens in the thousands of displays that an operator could call up (Example 1 described one computerized control room under development in the nuclear industry which has well over sixteen thousand computer displays and Case 2 in the next section describes one integrated patient monitoring system used during open heart surgery which has well over 150 menu screens to access various displays and capabilities).

The shift in technology means that control center design is no longer primarily the design of a physical workspace in terms of control and display layout. Instead, the designer develops a 'virtual' workspace that consists of the kinds of computer displays available to the operator and consists of the mechanisms for moving among these different views during actual operations and incidents.

Previously people navigated by a movement of their eyes, head or feet in a large spatially dedicated, physical array of data channels. Now they navigate by selecting commands in a virtual space of hundreds or thousands of computer displays. Each selection brings a display into a small, limited viewport provided by the VDUs and windows. This shift creates new HCI design challenges. The critical design bottleneck is shifted from individual displays to the system of displays. There are a variety of kinds of design errors that can occur at the level of the interaction across displays which will create new types of human performance problems. Examples include disorientation in the large network of display, users who are forced to access serially what are in fact highly inter-related data, users more easily trapped into a kind of tunnel vision onto only a narrow subset of displays, display thrashing where a user forced to move back and forth between displays that contain related data but can be seen only one at time, and new types of mental overhead related to managing the displays and interface rather than focusing on doing domain tasks (e.g., Henderson and Card, 1986; Cook and Woods, 1996).[3]

[2] It is very important to note that the cognitive functions in monitoring complex dynamic systems are not necessarily well supported by traditional control center designs. The support that does exist for these functions was not generally a deliberate or conscious act of individual design teams but a serendipitous property of the medium of representation -- physically parallel display, and the result of a historical process of human adaptation to the interacting constraints imposed by the representation and by the task demands.

However, the nature of the technological shift to a computer medium is a double edged sword. It both undermines the partially successful adaptations worked out for the previous medium and it provides new representational powers for supporting cognitive work. This means that we are capable of creating much worse and much better control centers than our previous baseline. The point of the comparison is that problems in the transition from traditional to computerized control centers give us clues about how to design virtual perceptual fields (e.g., the role of spatial dedication as an aid to navigation).

[3] The evolution of control centers has passed through or sometimes paused at an intermediate "hybrid" stage. Computer based information systems at first were simply backfitted into the larger context of the physically distributed control center. These computer based display systems generally contained only a limited number of displays. The computer system was viewed in the context of the physically parallel annunciator panels, status boards and panel displays which helped operators decide what was important to look at next. In high tempo operations, operators could abandon the computer-based displays and rely on the traditional physically parallel layout. In this context, the classic technique was to design a hierarchy of typically 3 levels to organize from 10 to as many as 30 or 40 individual computer displays. However, a system of thousands of displays without much of the traditional control center context is not a simple evolution from a 30 display page system organized in a simple hierarchy; it is a radical step change relative to information management.

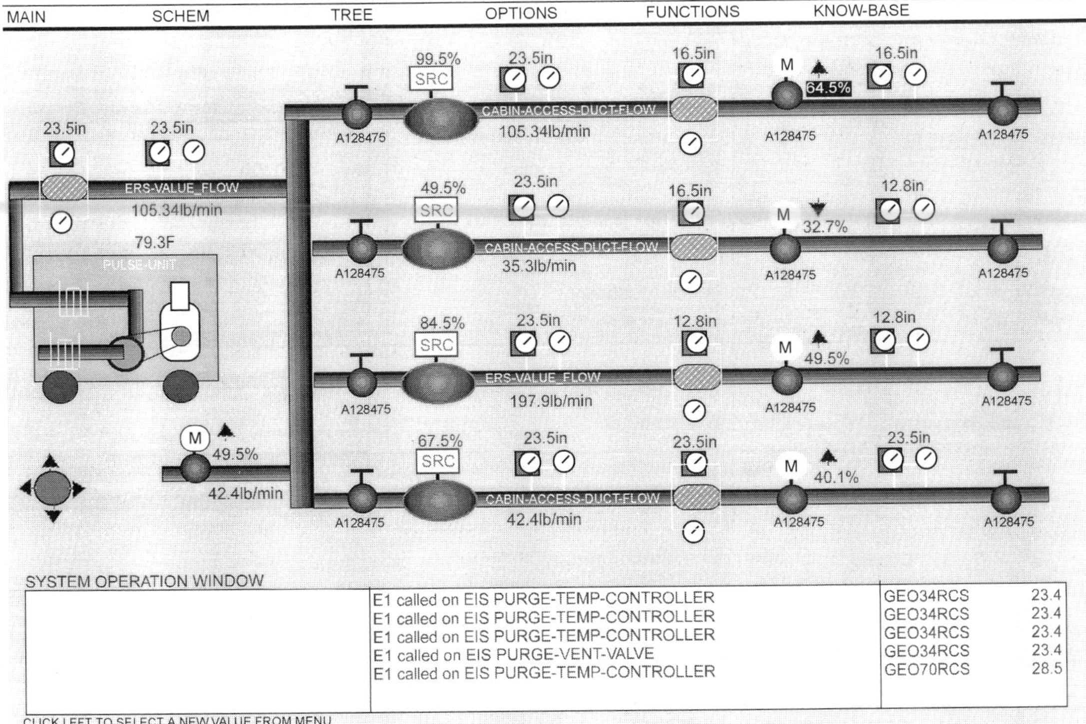

Figure 2. Clumsy workspace coordination in monitoring space systems, part 1 (adapted from Malin et al., 1991). *This illustrates a proposed interface design for an intelligent system. The practitioner will use this interface (the basic set of tiled windows on a single CRT) to monitor one system used in space shuttle missions. When the intelligent system identifies a problem, the relevant parameter changes hue (represented in the figure by the dark area behind one sensor value). From a workspace coordination point of view, the user is confronted with the decision: what other information is relevant to this event, where is it in the virtual field hidden behind the keyhole, and how do I get there?*

26.3 Typical Problems in Workspace Coordination

What are the cognitive consequences of providing large numbers of displays behind a narrow keyhole? Simply providing users with more techniques for navigating across displays may not be a solution to perceived 'navigation' problems. If these techniques attract attention to the interface itself, if they require additional knowledge, if they create new information to remember, or if the need to navigate goes up as task demands go up, then navigation 'aids' in practice may create new cognitive burdens and operational complexities. How will practitioners cope? They will attempt to re-design the virtual workspace themselves through system tailoring. They will develop stereotypical routes; they will throw away functionality to create a simpler device; they will adopt a fixed, spatially dedicated layout to avoid interactions at high tempo periods. They will also tailor their strategies in their field of activity to work around the complexities of the system. For example, they will escape from clumsy systems -- abandoning that device and its features in high tempo periods (Woods et al., 1994, chapter 5). This section presents several cases that illustrate typical problems in workspace coordination.

26.3.1 Case 1: Clumsy Workspace Coordination in Monitoring Space Systems

The following example illustrates some of the problems that can arise when the virtual perceptual field is poorly designed (when there is low visual momentum across displays). In particular, the example shows the extra workload and other burdens that can be imposed when the structure of the interface forces serial search for highly inter-related data. Consider a system that is designed in the following way and illustrated in Figures 2 and 3 (this description is based on a proposed system design and is taken from Malin, Schreckenghost, Woods, Potter, Johannesen, Holloway, and

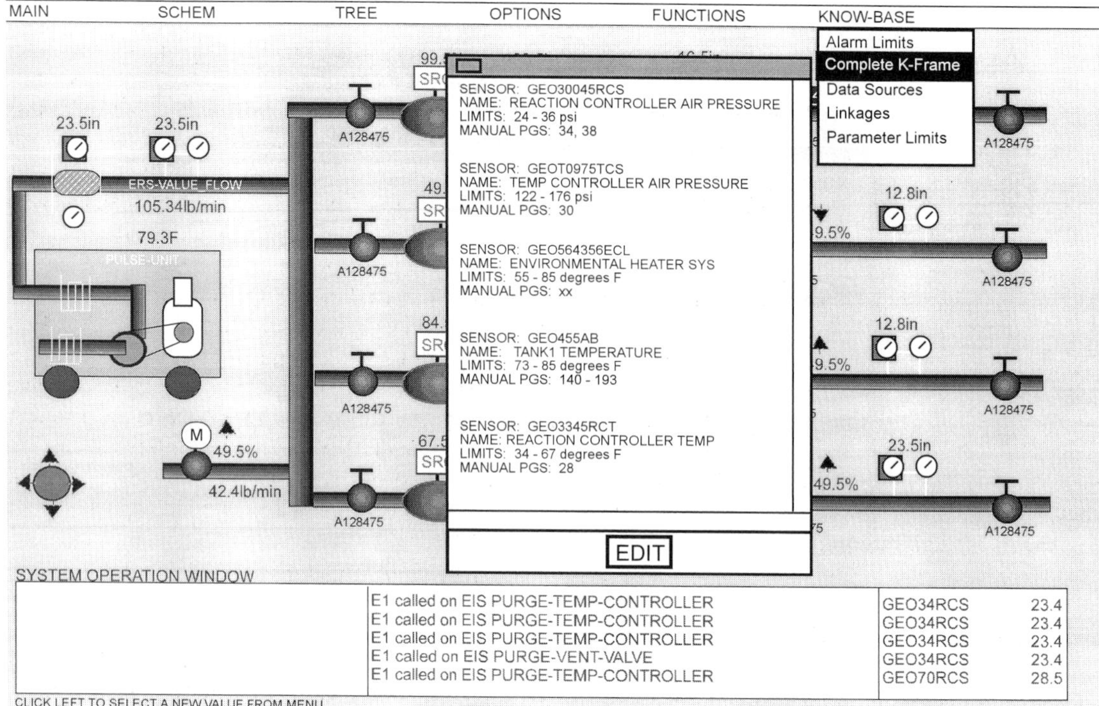

Figure 3. Clumsy workspace coordination in monitoring space systems, part 2 (adapted from Malin et al., 1991). *To follow up an event, the practitioner is forced into a serial search for related data. The practitioner has to decide what other information is relevant to this event, where is it in the virtual field (which pull down or pop up menu might lead me to relevant data), find the relevant item on the menu (the knowledge base frame for the affected sensor contains additional data such as limit values), open the relevant window, search for the desired data, and compare those values to the affected parameter which by now is obscured by the windows which have been opened.*

Forbus, 1991). Raw data is the basic unit of display, and the raw data states are represented as digital values. Several tiled windows provide viewports on a single CRT; users can call up a variety of displays including many different menus and many different displays that contain the sensor data on the state of the monitored process (note that the system includes intelligent capabilities for monitoring, diagnosis and action). The interface design in general places each piece of data in only one location within the virtual perceptual field (one "home"). Navigation mechanisms include pull down and pop up menus. Overall, the interface is close to the baseline case of minimum visual momentum across displays: calling up a new display replaces or partially covers up other displays and there are almost no visible cues to the structure or status of other views which are not currently displayed.

When an event occurs, the affected parameter values (a number or numbers) change hue from white (meaning -- 'normal') to red (meaning -- 'the component is being tested') or purple meaning -- 'a diagnosis has been performed and the component is in some sort of abnormal condition'). If the operators notice that an event has occurred (as indicated by a hue change), all they know is that this parameter is abnormal; they do not know in what way it is abnormal or why the intelligent system thinks this change is significant (Figure 2; the hue coding is represented by dark area behind the affected number).

The practitioners have to decide independent of the graphic and intelligent capabilities of the 'aiding' system what other data to examine to pursue this event and apparent anomaly further. The users have to decide where to look next in the virtual perceptual field beyond what is currently visible. The users have to decide whether this change is even important in the particular situation -- should other events be investigated first? is this change expected in the current context? does this signal warrant interrupting the ongoing lines of reasoning with regard to diagnosis or response selection?

To pursue what is the underlying event and its significance, practitioners need to think of the other related data that will support these evaluations. They have then to think of where these data reside in the virtual field (for the most part, each piece of data is in only one home within the virtual field available behind the keyhole) and how to call up these displays. Does the display contain reminders or prompts to the relevant data, displays, or navigation commands? Is the sequence direct or complicated, perhaps involving several layers of menu selections? For each menu or display called up, the practitioners must re-orient to the new view and search for the relevant item.

By the stage that the target data is found in the virtual space, practitioners will have gone through several steps and opened several windows (Figure 3). In this particular case the new windows obscure the abnormal data value and most of the primary display of the underlying system. Note how opening multiple windows to find the relevant, related data creates a new operator interface management task -- de-cluttering the workspace, where practitioners must remember to remove stale views/viewports. If de-cluttering is delayed, significant events in the monitored process may be missed since the stale views block access to much of the data on process state. Or practitioners may only realize the need to de-clutter their virtual workspace when a new event demands their attention. At this stage they must scramble to manipulate the interface when they should be focused on assessing the change in process state or on evaluating how to respond to the change.

This example is powerful especially because systems designed in this way have become so commonplace that we no longer notice how it limits practitioners (though beleaguered practitioners do). The structure of the computer information system forces practitioners into serial access to highly inter-related data. Users must search and assemble step by step and datum by datum the state of the process. Despite the graphic display capabilities of the system, the user must remember more not less (one example of what Norman, 1988 has called the conspiracy against human memory in the design of computerized devices). The representation of the monitored process in the computer medium is underutilized as an external memory. Practitioners must build and maintain their own mental model of the state of the monitored process and assessments and activities of the intelligent system. Practitioner attention is diverted to the computer system itself -- where is a datum located in the virtual space? which menu provides access? how do I navigate to that location? New interface management tasks are created such as de-cluttering. What makes this example particularly ironic is that advanced graphic and intelligent processing technologies were available in this prototype. However, these technological powers were used in a way that created new cognitive demands rather than support the practitioner's cognitive activities. Norman (1988) would refer to this design as having a wide gulf of evaluation (assessing the state of affairs) and a wide gulf of execution (translating intentions into actions that will achieve one's goals).

Increasing the efficiency of navigation within this type of workspace is a limited response -- one still is concerned with how to navigate in the interface. Users must know and remember how to navigate in the interface. In other words, even if they are more efficient with practice or aids, practitioners are still allocating their attention to the interface rather than to the task domain.

26.3.2 Case 2: Avoiding Navigation in the Operating Room

A study, in the context of operating room information systems, reveals how clumsy workspace coordination creates unintended complexities and provokes practitioner coping strategies (Cook and Woods, 1996). In this case a new operating room patient monitoring system was studied in the context of cardiac anesthesia. This and other similar systems are examples of a shift from older separated physically parallel devices to a single integrated computer based system. In this case the new patient monitoring system integrated what was previously a set of individual devices, each of which displayed and controlled a single sensor system, into a single CRT display with multiple windows and a large space of menu based options for maneuvering in the space of possible displays, options, and special features. The investigators observed how the physicians learned to use the new technology as it entered the workplace.

By integrating a diverse set of data and patient monitoring functions into one computer based information system, designers could offer users a great deal of customizability and options for the display of data (Figure 4). Several different windows could be called up depending on how the users preferred to see the data. However, these flexibilities all created the need for the physician to interact with the information system -- the physicians had to direct attention to the display and menu system and recall knowledge about the system. Furthermore, the computer keyhole created new interface management tasks by forcing serial access to highly inter-related data and by creating the need to periodically declutter displays to avoid obscur-

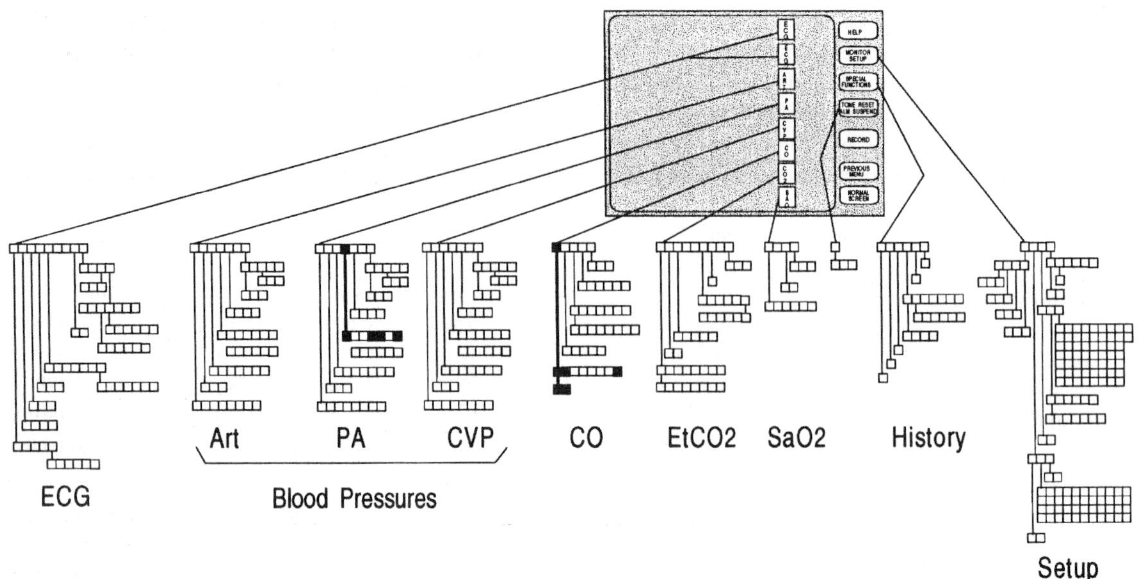

Figure 4. How users adapt to interface complexity (from Cook and Woods, 1996). *This figure shows a map of approximately one half of the menu selection space for a patient information system when used during open surgery. The highlighted areas represent the options actually invoked by the physician users during observations over a three month period. The small number of options utilized during this study show how physicians preferred to minimize interactions with the computer rather than exploit device flexibility and functions because using the interface created new cognitive demands that could interfere with patient care.*

ing data channels that should be monitored for possible new events.

Practitioners experienced problems because of a fundamental demand in event-driven worlds, the escalation principle (Woods et al., 1994): the greater the trouble in the underlying system or the higher the tempo of operations, the greater the information processing activities required to cope with the trouble or pace of activities. For example, demands for monitoring, attentional control, information, expertise, and communication among team members (including human-machine communication) all tend to increase with the tempo and criticality of operations. This means that the burden of interacting with the display system tends to be concentrated at the very times when the practitioner can least afford new tasks, new memory demands, or diversions of his or her attention away from patient state to the interface system per se.

The physicians tailored both the system and their own cognitive strategies to cope with this bottleneck. For example, Figure 4 shows a map of approximately one half of the menu selection space for the patient information system. The highlighted areas represent the options actually invoked by the physician users during observations over a three month period. Physicians coped with the complexity of the interface vis a vis the demands of their field of practice by simplifying the device. Physician users were observed to constrain the display of data into a fixed spatially dedicated default organization rather than exploit device flexibility. They forced scheduling of device interaction to low criticality self-paced periods in order to try to minimize any need for interaction at high workload periods. They developed stereotypical routines to avoid getting lost in the network of display possibilities and complex menu structures. Interestingly, when special circumstances arose that knocked users off of these common routes, they experienced significant problems since they now had to struggle through all of the complexity of the device and to focus on the device itself rather than medical functions.

26.3.3 Case 3: Flexible Data Availability is Not Enough

In Case 2, the computer provided great flexibility to call different data or displays into the viewports whenever the user wished. But the burden is on the user to decide what to examine when. In addition, the cognitive demands associated with:

- deciding what data to examine,
- remembering where it resides within the virtual space hidden behind the viewports, and
- recalling what series of navigation mechanisms will call up that display,

all fall unaided on the user. Designers frequently try to finesse the issue of workspace coordination by relying on the flexibility of computer based systems to provide the user with a number of navigation mechanisms to call desired data into the system's viewports. From one point of view, the designer's only responsibility is to make all of the data available and accessible (Woods, 1991); it is the domain practitioner's job to find the right data at the right time.

A case described by Moray (1986) illustrates how flexibility alone is not enough in the development of more automated information systems. In this case, a new fully computerized ship engine control room was developed. There were three CRT screens, and the operator could call up a variety of computer based displays and controls on whichever CRT he or she desired. A human factors review of the system predicted that, at some time in the life of this system, the operator would call up the computer display of the starboard engine controls on the port CRT and the computer display of the port engine controls on the starboard CRT -- a violation of stimulus-response compatibility guidelines. This could lead to an execution slip where the operator unintentionally manipulates the wrong ship engine.

Shortly thereafter, during simulated shiphandling with the new system, this situation arose and the predicted result followed. Alarms indicating starboard engine trouble occurred. The operator correctly diagnosed the situation and attempted to control the starboard engine. He manipulated the engine controls on the starboard CRT display which at that time displayed the port engine controls. If this had occurred at sea during a difficult navigation period, the ship could well have run aground.

As this case illustrates, simply relying on the flexibility of the computer is insufficient for effective workspace coordination. The designer decides implicitly or explicitly what are the different kinds of views available to practitioners, what can be seen in parallel and what can only be seen serially in different task contexts.

26.3.4 Case 4: Hierarchies of displays are not Necessarily the Means for Successful Workspace Coordination

Designers of computer based information systems often rely on a hierarchical organization of displays as a standard approach to workspace coordination ("users can always call up more information on desired topics"). At one level is some type of summary display. Users can select which part they want to "zoom" in on. The result is that the previous coarse grain view is replaced by a more fine grain view of just one part of the underlying system, process, or data base. Usually designers provide three or four levels of detail in the hierarchy. Users can shift among the levels in the hierarchy to obtain displays with a finer grain, but narrower field of view or displays with a wider field of view but coarser grain of detail.[4] Is this form of hierarchical organization successful as a method of workspace coordination?

Let us examine one example hierarchical organization of displays in some detail (a display system proposed as an interface to the thermal bus for the Space Station Freedom design; see Potter and Woods, 1994). Figures 5, 6, and 7 show the three levels of display available within the hierarchy for this system. At the highest level is a summary display of the complete system for transferring excess heat from the working portions of the station to condensors that radiate the excess into space (Figure 5). The user can select another level of detail by, for example, "zooming in" on the Transport section, the equipment hat support the movement of energy from source (evaporators) to sink (condensors; Figure 6). They can then select a third level of detail that focuses in on, for example, the Accumulators, two tanks in the transport section that act as a reservoirs for the ammonia that serves as the heat transport medium (Figure 7).

Note that all of the displays provide the same type of view. They all represent the monitored process in terms of the physical layout of the subsystems. Information about the status of the monitored process consists mainly of a small subset of raw sensor values that are represented numerically (digitally) and are located beside the physical subsystem or location from which

[4] The discussion of "zooming" in hierarchies of displays is related to pan and zoom techniques. Lieberman (1994) criticizes the traditional pan and zoom method on much the same cognitive grounds used in this case and goes on to propose an alternative technique to overcome some of these limitations by preserving the larger context of the overall space when one examines one locality in more detail.

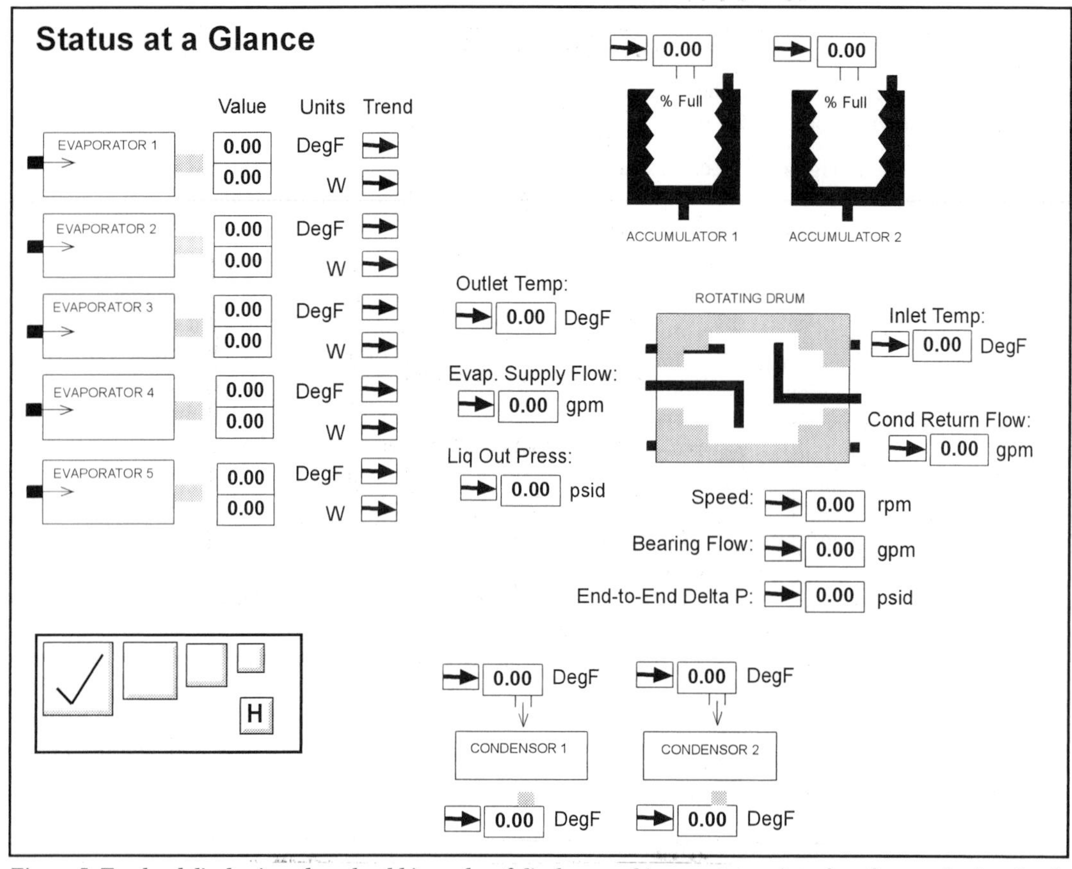

Figure 5. Top level display in a three level hierarchy of displays used in a prototype interface for monitoring the thermal bus in the Space Station Freedom design *(see Potter and Woods, 1994). This display is intended to provide an overview of the complete system for transferring excess heat from the working portions of the station to condensors that radiate the excess into space.*

they are taken. Look carefully at the information yield and loss as a user shifts from the summary (Figure 5) to the second level of schematics (Figure 6) and then to the third level of schematics (Figure 7). For this particular example of zooming in, the user goes from 2 sensors that indicate the status of accumulators subsystem, to 6 sensors at the second level of the hierarchy to 8 sensors on this topic at the most detailed level. As more sensors are visible on this portion of this subsystem, less sensors become visible on the status of other parts of the system. If users can see only a single display at a time, when they shift levels in the hierarchy, they lose sight of sensor data on other parts of the monitored process. In particular, they lose sight of the summary display which is supposed to provide a status at a glance.

Furthermore, there is no change in the type of view as they transition from one display to another. With each change (replacing a view at one level for a view at another level) their view remains the physical interconnections annotated with some number of sensors. It is only the density of sensors and the locations within the overall system that change with each display transition. The apparent "zooming in and out" is in fact trading sensor density with size of the field of view in this hierarchy.

It is also important to recognize that there are cognitive costs associated with shifts from one view to another -- across display transitions (Woods, 1984). For example, there are costs associated with deciding to change views, remembering how to change views, acting to call up new views, decluttering the set of views currently occupying the limited viewports, and reorienting to each new view.

Given the costs of display management in this type of virtual workspace, is there sufficient information gain from each across display transition to balance the costs of reorienting to the interface itself and to each new view? Will users frequently "zoom" in and out selecting displays from different levels of the hierar-

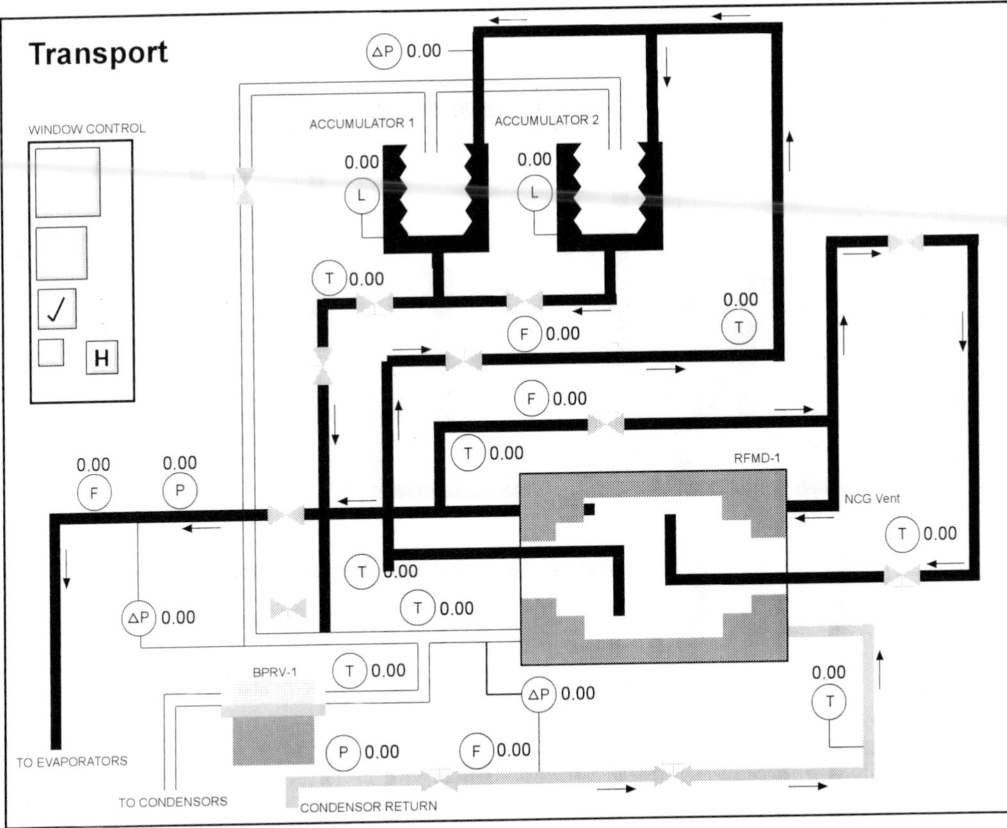

Figure 6. One middle level display in a three level hierarchy of displays used in a prototype interface for monitoring the thermal bus in the Space Station Freedom design *(see Potter and Woods, 1994). A display of the Transport section, the equipment that support the movement of energy from source (evaporators) to sink (condensors). The user can "zoom in" from the overview by selecting a display that covers a narrower field of view in greater detail.*

chy? If not, how will users cope with the burdens imposed by this type of system? Users in this case, like the physicians in Case 2, did not make use of the flexibilities in the display interface during task performance. They did not shift from views at one level of detail to views at another level very often; they did not use the system as designers imagined. The story used to justify a hierarchical organization of displays at different levels of detail did not fit the actual operational environment.

Instead, practitioners took advantage of the fact that this particular interface provided multiple windows and window management tools, which allowed simultaneous but overlapping display of different views from one or more of the levels in the hierarchy on the single CRT that was available. They developed their own customized, larger view of the monitored process by setting up a stable, spatially dedicated tableau of windows (Figure 8 illustrates one such tableau of windows). This collection of windows used together during some phase of the task is what Henderson and Card (1986) have called a 'room'. The practitioners set up this tableau prior to actual process operations (testing of an earthly working model of this space station system) during a low criticality low tempo period, and they tried not to interact with the interface during actual operations (ground testing). In other words, they tailored the system to conform to constraints of the task world in order to avoid congre-gating new cognitive burdens associated with the interface at high workload, high criticality or high tempo periods of the task.

Actual system use did not correspond to the designer's model of user-interface interaction in other ways as well. For example, the top level display did not function to provide a status at a glance, and the practitioners did not include this display as part of their custom tableau (see Reiersen, Marshall and Baker, 1988 for another case where the top level display 'summary' was abandoned in actual practice due to data sparseness).

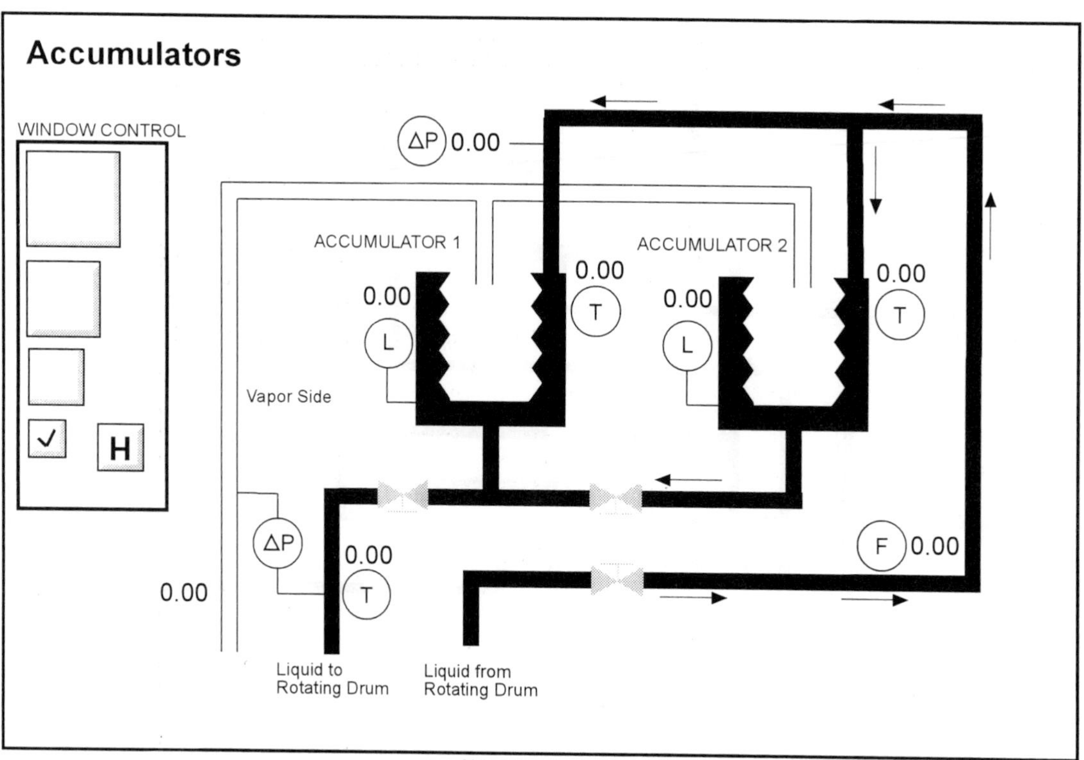

Figure 7. One lower level display in a three level hierarchy of displays used in a prototype interface for monitoring the thermal bus in the Space Station Freedom design (see Potter and Woods, 1994). *A display of the Accumulators, two tanks in the transport section that act as a reservoirs for the ammonia that serves as the heat transport medium. This display covers a very narrow portion of the system at the greatest level of detail in the proposed interface design. Note the change in coverage of the accumulators from Figure 5 to Figure 6 to Figure 7. In Figure 5 two sensors are displayed that provide data about the state of the accumulators (the reservoir levels). In Figure 6, four sensors are now visible that indicate the state of the accumulators (the levels plus ...). At the finest grain in Figure 7, eight sensors are now visible that indicate the state of the accumulators and the inflow/outflow balance.*

In this case, the flexibilities provided by multiple windows seem to have supported user tailoring of the system in ways that better matched their actual needs even if the way the users managed the technology surprised the designers. Unfortunately, the user tailoring in this case, as in Case 2, has limits (Woods et al., 1994). State data about parts of the system are obscured because the custom tableau does not make visible all of the sensor data given real estate limits and overlap across windows. Events can occur which force users to pay attention to and reconfigure the interface, and when such events occur it is likely to be during higher criticality higher tempo periods when practitioners can least afford to be diverted from their main tasks. The preferred tableau for a user or context must be reconfigured from scratch whenever a change occurs or is forced. There was no "rooms" construct in this case which would allow users to define, save, and manipulate a set of windows as a single entity. The kinds of views available are all of the same type (raw sensor data annotated to physical topology schematics) and are limited with respect to some user tasks. For example, the displays, especially the top level 'summary,' do not show directly how the system is functioning or malfunctioning (cf., Potter and Woods, 1994). Since the tailoring is ad hoc, there can be wide individual differences. Basically, the user tailoring can be brittle because the coordination between different views or different types of views has not been thought out in advance and over a far ranging set of possible scenarios.

26.3.5 Case 5: Annotate or Navigate

A basic tradeoff exists in the design of a computer-based information system between within-display search and across-display search. One can add more

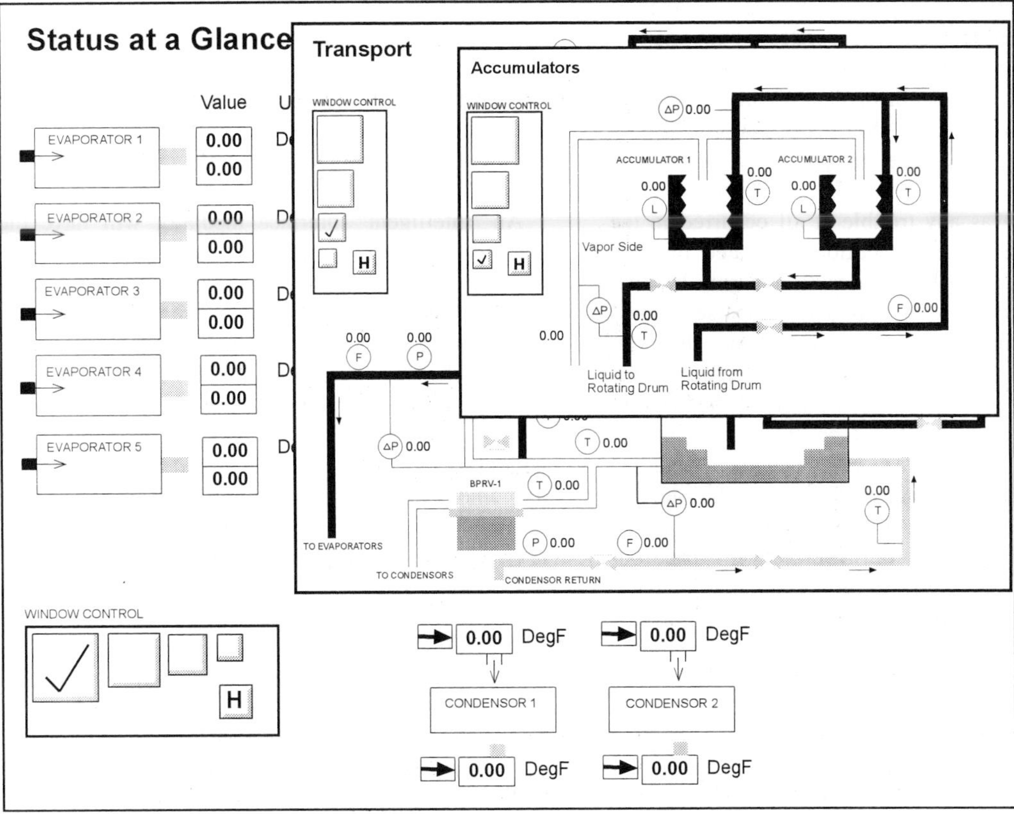

Figure 8. Example of the custom tableaus created by users to avoid navigation across the different levels of the display hierarchy during ground based testing of the thermal bus system *(see Potter and Woods, 1994).*

and more indications to a single display reducing the need to change displays. Or one can simplify (i.e., reduce the indications on) an individual display by distributing the data over multiple displays. Given that coherent tasks require integration of multiple pieces of base data, designers can lean one way to emphasize within-display search processes and reduce navigation across displays. Leaning the other way, designers simplify within-display search at the price of requiring the user to work more across multiple displays. We refer to this basic design tradeoff as "annotate or navigate." System developers seem to be more aware of the danger of cluttered ineffective individual displays than they are of the problems associated with poor workspace coordination across displays, preferring to reduce the data content of individual displays even though this means that users must work more across displays to accomplish coherent tasks. Users, at least in more event-driven worlds, seem to prefer data-rich displays, even if more complex, to reduce navigation burdens that distract them from their tasks. Nielsen (1996) may have found the same result in usability tests of Web sites where users preferred a single view condensed into one screen (visible all at once) over lengthy material that extended beyond the size of the viewport (i.e., that required scrolling). "Annotate or navigate" points out that there is a fundamental tradeoff that designers must confront. Effective workspace coordination uses a variety of techniques to support information extraction both within and across display units.

An example of the annotate or navigate tradeoff occurred when a new display system for nuclear power plants was tested in a simulation study (Reiersen, Marshall and Baker, 1988). The top level display was developed to give a very summarized and easy to understand overview of plant status through the exclusive use of hue coded icons.

Reiersen et al. found that operators of a simulated nuclear power plant did not use the display as the developers expected. For the most part they abandoned the hue coded icon display because it told them very little about the state of the plant (although what it did communicate was very clear especially for the inexperienced). They preferred to work with other displays that provided greater depth of data about the state of the plant in a single view. Since the hue coded icon display provided very little insight into a developing problem[5], operators were forced to switch to other displays as soon as any trouble at all occurred in the monitored process (i.e., practitioners treated the display as if it was a single master caution alarm). In other words for this context, it was a data sparse display forcing users into excessive navigation. User responded by trying to avoid the extra navigation burdens preferring to work with a single dedicated but more complex tableau. Based on the results of the study, a new overview was designed which provided practitioners with a better longshot of trouble--how it develops and the success of operator interventions.

Successful systems at the level of workspace coordination will find a balance in the annotate or navigate tradeoff by coordinating the choice of units of display, the kinds of views available, and the movement across displays for the demands of the operational context.

26.3.6 Case 6: Automated or 'Intelligent' Window Management

If too much interface flexibility or the wrong kind of flexibilities create burdens, then it seems that one solution path is to automate window management or provide for an intelligent interface that assists the user to decide what to look at when (e.g., Funke et al., 1993). Such an interface would be 'intelligent' in the sense that it functions as an autonomous, animate computer agent who mediates between process and practitioner.

However, such a capability also carries the danger of creating new complications for practitioners (Woods, 1993). To see one difficulty, imagine that you are monitoring a display when a change occurs automatically -- one display frame has been substituted for the page you were examining. You do not know why the display changed, or which pieces of data in the new display you should pay attention to, or why the machine thought that these data were important for the current situation. Following the automatic changes in what is displayed can raise the user's mental workload even though it appears that the computer is performing the work for him.

An 'intelligent' interface mediator will have the capability to change the interface, to change the representation of the monitored process, or to change allocation of functions autonomously without specific direction from the practitioner. But from the user's perspective, changes initiated by an intelligent mediator occur within a larger context of changes and events that they need to detect and understand. The intelligent mediator is but one of very many sources of change. Autonomous activities of the intelligent mediator will place new demands on the human practitioner's cognitive process, especially their attentional control processes. In data rich event-driven situations practitioners need support for the cognitive mechanisms that enable them to shift attention in a changing world and to focus in on the subset of data that is interesting in a particular context (Woods, 1995b). Flexibility, in the sense of autonomous changes by an interface mediator, creates uncertainty for the user and leads to new cognitive demands: monitoring -- did something change? situation assessment -- why did it do that or how did the system get into that state or configuration? anticipation or mental simulation -- what will it do next? coordination -- tracking and anticipating the partially autonomous mediator's assessments and activities (Sarter, Woods, and Billings, in press).

Multiple observations from the field suggest that adding clumsy intelligent mediators easily can result in creating new burdens and demands for the user they are supposed to assist and imposing these demands at the high tempo or high criticality parts of the task. Example 2 described at the outset of this chapter, the infusion device for control of pre-term labor at home (Obradovich and Woods, 1996), illustrates the problem. The user enters a sequence of commands. If these are illegal for the current device mode (this device has multiple poorly indicated modes), instead of obtaining the expected display, nothing happens for six to seven seconds and then the system automatically reverts to the baseline display. But the user receives no other feedback that the machine has judged her inputs to be illegal. The appearance of the baseline display comes as a surprise leaving the user confused and wondering how she got there; did she inadvertently enter a command to go to this surprising display or did the system

[5] The hue coded icons used in this display were essentially group alarms that once lit told the operator nothing more about the underlying contributors, the evolution of the trouble, or the process's response to their interventions. Human factors guidelines for control center design have long warned designers about the dangers of group alarms.

do something automatically. In this case, the autonomous machine capability in the context of poor feedback and multiple modes creates an "automation surprise."

In Case 2, the operating room patient monitoring information system, the designers developed features where the computer system autonomously changed the interface without direct instructions from the physician users. The patient monitoring system in the operating room automatically reorganized the display of data and the window configuration in order to offload some data management tasks. However, the results of field observations showed that these features created new uncertainties and new burdens that exacerbated interface complexity and also undermined the physicians' strategies (Cook and Woods, 1996). The physicians did not passively accept the uncertainty created by this kind of computer system flexibility, but resisted by trying to constrain the device to a fixed, spatially dedicated form.

Similarly, in studies of pilot interaction with flight deck automation (Sarter et al., in press), changes in the mode of flight control could occur without direct pilot command. Such indirect mode changes were commonly part of automation surprises (or more generally, coordination surprises) where pilots were unable to track or to anticipate how the automation's settings and targets would effect the course of the flight. The autonomy of these systems coupled with weak feedback led to frequent instances where pilots were left wondering -- did something change? why did it do that? what will it do next? how did the system get into that state or configuration?. Pilots, like the physicians confronting burdensome flexibilities, tried to escape from such highly autonomous modes of automatic flight control during high tempo and high criticality phases of flight.

On the other hand, Mitchell and Saisi (1987) used adaptive windows successfully in a simulated satellite control center. They developed a model of operator functions in the field of practice, in part, to define meaningful contexts. When the user expressed interest in a topic or activity through the selection of a particular display or control, the model shows what other kinds of information are relevant to that topic or activity. They grouped this related information and controls into windows which were displayed in parallel with the user-selected window. This and other aspects of the new design (e.g., integrated displays) enhanced user performance based on, in part, this model based and contextually sensitive display of related information and controls.

These kinds of results lead us to be cautious about the role of intelligent agents that manage the interface for the user unless they are designed to function as team players. The concern is not about the level of automation per se, but rather about the associated feedback and coordination mechanisms (Norman, 1990; Billings, 1996; and Roth, Malin and Schreckenghost, this volume). Unless such agents are developed in user and practice-centered ways, which will require good models of user functions in the field of practice, we expect to see more automation and coordination surprises.

26.3.7 Implications of Clumsy Workspace Coordination

The problems that arose in the above cases are typical of ineffective workspace coordination. These cases point to several generalizations about designing a computer-based information system to support workspace coordination:

- Across display transitions can be costly cognitively. These costs can include new knowledge demands, new memory demands, new tasks such as decluttering, and these new burdens can congregate at the wrong times.
- The balance between these costs and potential information gain affect how practitioners interact with a virtual data space available through a narrow keyhole.
- Connections between different views or types of views are important in workspace coordination. Designing these connections is based on what tasks need to be done in parallel versus serially and how one moves from one task to another.
- Effective workspace coordination is more than navigation efficiency. Coordination of views within the virtual workspace is tied to the content of a particular application. Cognitive task analysis, workload, timeline or other analyses sensitive to task transitions and incident evolution across different scenarios will be needed to provide the information base for the design of a coordinated virtual workspace.
- Effective workspace coordination helps practitioners focus on the underlying process not the interface management tools per se.

- Deciding what to call up, where to look next in the virtual data space is a cognitive task. Part of effective workspace coordination is aiding this process.

The example cases summarized above also point out some of the ways that practitioners learn to cope with the burdens of clumsy designs at the workspace coordination level.

- For experienced practitioners responsible in some field of activity, disorientation or getting lost represents an unacceptable and abrupt breakdown in their ability to meet their goals as responsible agents in that field of activity. Regardless of how cumbersome the virtual workspace and the navigation mechanisms, real practitioners cannot afford to get lost. Instead, they learn to tailor the system and their strategies in ways to try to cope with the clumsiness of the system. If there are too many possibilities, they drastically prune the ones they invoke. For example, Figure 4 from Case 2 (Cook and Woods, 1996) highlights how little of the space of options the system provided was actually invoked by users given the demands of the setting (open heart surgery) and the clumsiness of interface management.
- If the burdens of switching across displays or reconfiguring the windows are too great, the users try to develop their own fixed spatially dedicated tableau. They will put together a set of views that seem to balance observability of the underlying process or device with the need to avoid distracting interface management burdens that congregate at high criticality or high tempo periods.
- Ineffective designs at the level of workspace coordination force serial access to highly related data, add new interface management tasks that tend to congregate at high criticality and high tempo periods of the task, increase demands on user memory, undermine attentional control skills involved in knowing where to focus when, create the potential for getting lost or disoriented in the large space of options and displays. Given these kinds of potential problems, what do we need to know in order to design a coordinated virtual workspace?

26.4 Orienting In Virtual Perceptual Fields

We claim that designers of computer based information systems create a virtual perceptual field. It is easy for designers to create virtual perceptual fields where the observer must function without the assistance of orienting perceptual functions because of the keyhole property and because the computer affords designers freedom from the constraints acting on the referent real world objects (Woods, 1995a). When dealing with virtual perceptual fields in the computer medium, the burden is on the designer to explicitly build in mechanisms to support the operation of the orienting perceptual systems and the functions that they perform in a fully articulated cognitive system adapted to a changing environment. The designer of a virtual perceptual field develops the characteristics that allow or that undermine the role of orienting perceptual functions.

There are many techniques that can be used to support the coordination between orienting perceptual systems and focal attention in a virtual world (e.g., Woods, 1984). The remainder of this chapter describes several techniques organized by the heuristic of "visual momentum across displays." This is just one approach to aiding navigation. Some of the techniques suggested by this point of view are similar to or overlap techniques that have been developed by others (e.g., Furnas, 1986; Henderson and Card, 1986; Lamping, Rao and Pirolli, 1995; Kahn, 1995). In the case of other innovations, Visual Momentum may provide a more general and abstract basis to understand why these systems aid navigation.

26.4.1 Visual Momentum

Given that meaningful activities often involve moving across displays, designers should be able to aid the transition from one view into the artificial data field to another. The concept of Visual Momentum is borrowed from perception and cinematography (Hochberg, 1986) and refers to the impact of a transition from one view to another (a cut in cinematography) on the cognitive processes of the observer, in particular on the observer's ability to extract task-relevant information. As applied to HCI, "the amount of visual momentum supported by a display system is inversely proportional to the mental effort required to place a new display into the context of the total data base and the user's information needs. When visual momentum is high, there is an impetus or continuity across successive views that supports the rapid comprehension of data following the transition to a new display" (Woods, 1984, p. 231).

At one end of the dimension lies poor transitions which consist of (a) total replacement of one view for another and (b) the absence of any visible cues to the virtual field of possible views. When Visual Momentum is low, each "glance" into the artificial data field is independent of previous glances so that the observer must reorient from scratch to each new view as it is called into the limited viewport.

At the other end of the dimension the observer works within a conceptual space in which individual views are grounded. A conceptual space depicts relationships in a frame of reference (Woods, 1995a; 1996). In between lies a variety of techniques for building a sense of a conceptual space analogous to a physical space so that orienting and moving about the virtual perceptual field can employ the same perceptual and cognitive processes that allow us to fluently explore and reorient to new events and changing views in naturally occurring physical spaces. Some of the techniques to increase Visual Momentum are longshots, landmarks, content-laden cues to structure, spatial dedication, coordinating what can be seen in parallel and what in series as a function of task demands (Henderson and Card's "rooms"), center-surround, side effect views, cues to status. All of these techniques and many others (e.g., trails, bookmarks, 3D spatial metaphors) function as visible cues to the structure of the space of possibilities and cues to the status of those different parts of the domain represented by the artificial data field behind the keyhole. Designers can orchestrate these kinds of techniques to create what the user experiences as a tangible conceptual space to support effective workspace coordination.

26.4.2 The Longshot -- Showing the Big Picture

It is commonly accepted that an overview display will support coordination or navigation across the many views available within the virtual data space. In Cases 4 and 5 designers provided what they thought were summary displays, but these displays did not support practitioners and were rejected or little used. Case 4 illustrates that simply changing the relative density of data visible as the field of coverage of the underlying topology expands or contracts does not necessarily support effective across display transitions. Case 4 also shows that simply aggregating details into a display of generic status filters out too much information for it to support operators as an overview of system state and how state is changing relative to goals. What do designers need to do to create effective overviews?

Woods (1984) referred to summary displays that actually serve as effective orientation and navigation aids as longshot displays. In cinema, a longshot is an establishing view that shows relationships between characters and summarizes relevant information. It keeps the viewer involved in the flow of the plot by allowing him/her to step back from the details, discover why these details are important, how they relate to previous views and to establish a frame of reference to help the observer comprehend upcoming views.

The successful longshot in computer based information systems serves the same purposes. In essence it is a kind of global map (Billingsley, 1982; Kahn, 1995; Kahn, 1996). It helps practitioners step back from the details of the monitored process to assess overall system status. It helps them decide where to look next within the system. It helps them relate the view currently under examination to previous views and to integrate new views into their assessment of process state as they are called into a visible viewport.

Three functions contribute to the effectiveness of a longshot -- the status summary function (cues to status), the orienting function (cues to structure and mapping the structure to domain semantics), and the movement function (direct manipulation).

The Status Summary Function: Status at a Glance

Longshots containing status summary information allow users, in a mentally economical way, to step back and assess their overall situation with respect to the underlying process, device, or activity they are engaged in. By providing task relevant status information, longshots are content-laden. By showing the status of the process or activity behind the computer interface, longshots can help users decide where to look next in the virtual field. The concept of content-laden navigation aids which provide cues to status as well as to structure will echo throughout several of the techniques to enhance Visual Momentum across displays.

In a physically distributed control center (an open workspace), an experienced operator can stand at the back of the room and gain enough information to describe the status of the system, i.e., the current state, the current epoch or phase of operation, the direction things are headed in (e.g., deteriorating or recovering), the stance of actors towards the system (such as routine operations or a tense critical period). If a longshot includes the status summary function, it will externalize pertinent summary information found within the display structure, and thus allow an operator the opportunity to step back and assess the status of the monitored process and to quickly see how the system is behaving. The longshot provides cues to status across the entire system so that practitioners can remain in tune with changing conditions and the "big picture" while they are focused on a detailed task or part of the underlying process. Cues to status are an important technique to enable practitioners to easily "check read" or peripherally pick up what might be interesting changes in other parts of the underlying process that should guide a shift in attentional focus (Woods, 1995b).

Status summary information can also support tasks in domains that are more self-paced. Tasks in these domains often include updating and maintaining information within the display structure. For example, some spreadsheet users update lists of information or financial figures each month. A longshot could help spreadsheet users by providing status summary information about these updating activities (i.e., which areas of the sheet have been updated, and which ones have not; Watts, 1994).

For a longshot to support the status summary function, it must include the following attributes:

1. The summary information must be distilled.
The point of a summary is to distill the relevant information that characterizes the situation as whole in a concise, recognizable form. The relevant information must be represented in a way so that observers can size up the state of affairs at a glance. One indication of a concise distillation of relevant factors is that it is informative even if it is shrunk to a relatively small size. Summaries in which information is solely conveyed through the digital display of elemental data are rarely adequate for this function. Similarly, designers can easily over-summarize and provide too little data to be of value to experienced practitioners (e.g., group alarms).

2. Information in the summary must be abstracted.
To broaden the view of the system, information in the summary display should be abstracted to a higher level of information than that of raw data and other details about the system. It is important to note that abstracted information is not simply a lack of detail, but rather an integration of details that informs the observer about higher level questions (Vicente and Rasmussen, 1992). It involves collecting information from various areas of the system that speak to broader issues about routine and exceptional conditions. To do this, the designer may need to transform lower level data, integrate these data and contrast them to related values. Examples of abstracted information include answers to questions like: what mode is the system working in? is the system functioning normally, or is there a malfunction in one of the subsystems? what activities are taking place at this time?

3. The longshot must include information about change and sequence.
If practitioners are assessing the status of a system, they must be able to recognize patterns of change within that system. In addition to information about the current behaviors and states of the system, information about what has happened recently, and what kinds of trends may be developing often contributes to the overall assessment of the status of the system. For example, in event-driven worlds faults often result in a cascade of disturbances. A content-laden longshot will help the practitioners keep track of the big picture of disturbance evolution while they are pursuing diagnosis and response.

4. The longshot must show information that is relevant to the viewer's context.
The information in the longshot view should answer questions and provide information that makes sense to a practitioner in his or her task context. Examples of potentially relevant information include the activities that are currently ongoing and helping practitioners see if events are developing in accordance with their expectations. The longshot provides the larger context about the semantics of the field of practice in which one examines different and more focused views.

5. The longshot should support "check reading."
An abstracted and distilled overview should help users pick out what conditions or changes are potentially interesting quickly and in a mentally economical way given the current context and ongoing lines of reasoning.

One technique we have used for fulfilling the status summary function is to use a reduced scale version of a pattern-based or emergent property display as a longshot (e.g., Watson, Eastman, Woods, 1990; Ranson and Woods, 1996). The patterns in this type of integrated display are much larger (lower spatial frequency) than the elements from which they emerge. As a result, the patterns still stand out at a reduced scale while details become obscured (essentially the size reduction acts as a high spatial frequency filter). The patterns are effectively a dynamic summary of the status of the portion of the underlying process or device they cover. The patterns support the "check reading" activity that allows practitioners to peripherally pick up what might be interesting changes while they are engaged in other lines of reasoning (Woods, 1995b). Note that users have to be familiar with the fully detailed version of the pattern based display for the reduced scale version to work successfully as a longshot.

The Orienting Function

The orienting function of a longshot helps operators orient to where they are (the currently visible views) relative to the set of views that they could examine in this context. The orienting function helps them comprehend cuts from one view to another. Longshots contain map-like characteristics which show users where they are located in relation to the important parts or landmarks within the virtual perceptual field. The map can serve as a representational framework for capturing what options are relevant to the current situation, which options have been recently selected/inspected (a trail), and support user browsing through potentially relevant views. The latter raises the question of how a longshot can be developed to invite exploration (Norman, 1988).

The structure of the overview display should reflect the structure of the views within the workspace as they represent the semantics of the field of practice. This type of conceptual map makes movement in the large network of possible displays the equivalent of moving in the semantics of the domain from the point of view of a practitioner. When a summary supports both this function and provides information about significant status and change in the underlying process or device, (the system status function), the longshot helps the operators formulate relevant questions and helps them decide where to direct their attention next. Supporting the orienting function helps produce interface transparency where the practitioners can concentrate on their activities and goals in their field of practice instead of being focused on the interface control mechanisms themselves.

The following principles should be followed to support the orienting function of a longshot:

1. The longshot must be coordinated with other views.
The longshot needs to be coordinated with the other more local kinds of views available to users and the reverse as well. A longshot serves as a visual representation of the virtual data space otherwise hidden behind the narrow keyhole. This means the longshot must capture the structure of the virtual data space (cues to structure). When it fulfills this purpose, the longshot can serve as a reminder of what types of local views are available and which of these views are relevant to the user's task context. The goal of coordinating the different views is to enhance the user's ability to extract and integrate information across cuts or transitions from one view to another (the fundamental definition of high visual momentum).

2. The overview display should include relevant frames of reference.
Coordination between longshot and other views depends on choosing, coordinating or creating frames of reference related to the practitioner's tasks in the field of practice. A frame of reference specifies relationships between parts and part-whole relationships. Depicting these relationships for a field of practice creates the longshot. The longshot defines and makes apparent the frames of reference within which other views exist and can be integrated. The other views have a meaning as a portion, neighborhood or perspective of the larger frame of reference defined by the longshot. The portion currently visible becomes a place (where the user is "located") within the larger space defined by the longshot. However, system designers sometimes create "overview" displays that do not show the operators where they are in relation to where they could be. Problems range from showing a list of menu options without indicating where the operator is located within the display structure, to showing a broad view of the structure of the monitored process without indication of how the process is broken up into displayable chunks (Woods, 1991).

3. The overview display must always be available in parallel with other views.
Experience from several projects (Woods, 1984; Bolt, 1984; Case 4) all point out that a longshot is effective only if it is available physically in parallel with other types of views. The point of a longshot is to help the practitioner know where to look next in the virtual field. If the longshot is not constantly available, then the practitioner has to decide when it is appropriate to consult it with the associated cognitive burdens. If other constraints make it impossible to constantly show the longshot, relax those constraints. An effective longshot is one fundamental kind of view which should be available in parallel in a well coordinated workspace.

4. A longshot combines information about the state and behavior of the monitored process with indication of the different types of available views relevant to the context.
When the representation of the types of available views is combined with the information about the monitored process, the overview display shows where operators could shift their attention within the display structure by showing what is happening in other areas. Therefore, a longshot integrates abstracted information about the status of the system while indicating the set of options or other views that are of potential relevance

(Mitchell and Saisi, 1987). In effect, a longshot serves as a map of possibilities annotated with distilled data about the state of the process.

The Movement Function

In addition to showing overall system status and giving clues for where to look next within the system, the overview display should indicate how an operator can move to an area of interest within the display structure. The longshot functions as a map of other display possibilities in part. The map should make it apparent how one calls up or moves to or navigates to other views. Norman (1988) refers to this problem as the gulf of execution.

As a map of possibilities, a longshot provides a view of multiple options in parallel and shows the relationships between these options at multiple levels. This has led Billingsley (1982) and Woods (1984) to emphasize the need for maps or map-like structures to aid movement through a virtual space over a series of menu choices. Too often, systems of menus are designed in such a way as to force users through a long series of menu options which provide few options in parallel and which produce multiple across-display transitions without providing any content to the observer (see many Web sites). The longshot can support the movement function by allowing users to select from it the views for display in other viewports. Kahn (1995, 1996) shows a variety of ways that maps can be used to support movement within a Web site.

But a longshot can be more than a structured menu with multiple options in parallel. Since the longshot is a map that organizes parts and relationships between parts for the domain of interest, it is one of the prerequisites for providing a direct manipulation interaction (Hutchins, Hollan and Norman, 1986). Designers can use this map to allow users to directly specify where they want to go or how to instruct the system without thinking in detail about the interface mechanisms. Many of the interface and navigation problems in Example 2, the infusion device for home care of pre-term labor, discussed at the opening of this chapter disappear once a meaningful frame of reference for user activities is found (Obradovich and Woods, 1996). In this particular case, user activities are all about different rates of infusion over different time intervals and different bolus sizes at different points in time. In other words, what is informative in this field of practice are dose-time relationships. Since none of this is visible in the infusion device, the designers are forced to create awkward, arbitrary, and cognitively demanding sequences of displays and interaction to program the device. Not surprisingly, the result is classic HCI deficiencies in the device producing typical user problems and errors (Norman, 1988).

The solution to these problems is to provide a dose-time structure as the basic frame of reference. Users will be unable to see all of the relevant dose-time picture in detail at one time because of multiple therapy plans and because the relevant information may stretch out into the future or back into the past. But a longshot of the dose-time frame of reference can support navigation across more detailed views, and it can support direct manipulation mechanisms for instructing the system about desired therapy plans. This radical restructuring of the basic concept behind the interface, based on the semantics of the field of practice, would completely restructure the nature of the interaction. Users would no longer have to learn or remember the syntax of the interface; instead, the interface would match the semantics of their activity--setting up, modifying and monitoring dose-time relationships.

Longshots contain two kinds of information: information about the underlying process or field of practice (e.g., state information) and information about the virtual data space (e.g., what views are available). It is important to perceptually distinguish these two different categories of information. Case 1 is one example (Figures 2 and 3) where the visual indications of where one can click to open new views/windows are incomplete and ambiguous. Similar confusions about which visual marks are "clickable" and which are not have been found in usability tests of Web sites (Nielsen, 1996).

Status summary information, combined with the multiple parallel options and structured relationships between parts, then can act like a preview function to help the observer to quickly find and focus in on what is interesting given their context and goals.

Longshots allow practitioners to step back from the details of a part of the underlying process or one subtask to see important trends and activities about the process as a whole. This role means that longshots can be an important element in creating open workspaces that support cooperative activity if the longshot is available in common to the entire work team. Just because a display is available to all through a large screen display or other shared display mechanism is not sufficient for it to function as a longshot. The criteria in this section need to be met for the overview to contribute effectively to the shared workspace.

When an overview display provides the three functions discussed above--(1) status summary information, (2) visible cues to the semantic structure of the virtual field, and (3) allows practitioners direct mechanisms to shift their "gaze" within this space--then the overview functions as a longshot. The WWW is currently has many sites which lack effective longshots and demonstrate the cognitive and performance consequences as users are forced through multiple steps blindly trying to get to information relevant for their purposes. Because effective navigation is central for users to be able to take advantage of the Web's power, we have seen a wave of innovation in a number of techniques, most notably techniques for mapping web sites. Kahn (1995, 1996) provides many examples, principles and a method to help designers create effective longshots and increase visual momentum across displays for Web sites and other human-computer interfaces.

26.4.3 Landmarks

Another way to support navigation in the computer medium is to include landmarks in the artificial data field (Woods, 1984). Hochberg and Gellman (1977) define landmarks as "features that are visible at a distance that provide information about location and orientation." In the computer medium, landmarks are features in the interface that are visible at a glance and provide information about location and orientation.

Passini (1992) notes that landmarks play an important role in navigation in physical space. For example, the Space Needle, which can be seen from a distance from most areas of downtown Seattle, can be used to keep track of where people are in relation to where they are going. It provides information about both the relative distance they must travel to reach their destination, as well as the direction they must travel to get there. Once people become familiar with the area around the Space Needle, the structure can also serve as a reminder of the buildings and areas that surround it. In this case, the Space Needle serves as a summary of the surrounding area, as well as a frame of reference to help people establish their location relative to their destination.

Landmarks support repair processes for people who have become disoriented. If people lose their sense of where they are located, they can look for familiar landmarks to help them re-orient to their surroundings. For example, if people decide to take a new route to work, and the street takes unexpected turns, they can look for familiar landmarks in the distance to help them figure out where they are located, and which direction they are going. Landmarks also support repair processes in a virtual environment. If computer users attempt to choose a display from a menu, and mistakenly choose the wrong view, they can use the landmarks in that view to figure out where they are located within the virtual space.

Content free landmarks are structuring cues; content-laden landmarks provide perceptual cues to structure and signify something about the content of that area (e.g., the topic or the summary status). Both types play a role in building a virtual perceptual space.

Watts (1994) followed up her field work on the navigation strategies adopted by extended spreadsheet users (example 4 in the introduction to this chapter) with a simulation study that examined the role of landmarks and longshots as well as other cues to structure in supporting navigation. In this study, experienced users of large extended spreadsheets were given data related in a large set of interconnected data tables and asked to carry out various tasks modeled on the tasks user perform in actual organizations. She varied the cues to support navigation such as landmarks, longshots and others (e.g., spatial dedication). The results showed that landmarks are important cues for aiding navigation. Participants more directly targeted relevant data with landmarks than without. In fact, they considered landmarks so important that five of the seven participants when working with an extended spreadsheet without landmarks stopped performing the task and actually added landmarks to the extended spreadsheets before continuing with their tasks. Both content-laden and content-free were important to the participants in the study.

26.4.4 Spatial Dedication

Information is spatially dedicated when it appears in one fixed physical location. The classic exemplar is the physically distributed control center where each data channel occurs in a fixed location and, ideally, functionally related data channels are located in one region of the physical space.

The fixed spatial structure of data serves as a memory aid for users who are familiar with that structure. While the entire field of data is not visible in parallel, the fixed spatial structure allows users to travel directly to desired data channels or topics (e.g., the electrical portion of the plant is always just to the right of the steam portion or the feedwater pumps are below and to the right of the boiler). For example, if extended spreadsheet users always keep their raw data tables in the top left region of the extended spreadsheet, and their calculations in the bottom right area, they will always know where to find those kinds of information.

In a control center where data is physically distributed and spatially dedicated and operator engaged in one activity can still see or pick up changes in other parts of the control center. Since data channels are in fixed locations and groupings, if they notice a perceptually distinct change in one location or area, as experienced operators in that space, they know something about what has changed without directing focal attention to that specific data channel or set of data channels. Similarly, glancing at an area of the control center provides a quick check read of what is going on in that region of the monitored process.

The same issues apply to computer-based systems and virtual perceptual fields. We consistently observe users spontaneously try to introduce some degree of spatial dedication in many different kinds of settings (where they place the same kind of information in one consistent location) to help themselves overcome navigation burdens. For example, in Case 2 (anesthesiologists in cardio-thoracic surgery; Cook and Woods, 1996) and Case 4 (space mission operations) practitioners invested effort during low tempo periods to set up their computer-based workspace as a fixed tableau of views tailored as best they could to the demands of the tasks they perform at higher tempo, more critical periods. In other words, they invested effort to avoid or minimize the need to navigate and transition across displays during these potentially busy periods. Another source of information about navigation needs comes from cases where practitioner's attempts to avoid navigation break down. When circumstances conspire to force practitioners outside of their preferred configuration of views, they become caught up in the interface itself and recognize themselves that this activity is a diversion from their responsibilities.

These cases of practitioners expending effort to avoid navigation burdens come from event-driven, high consequence domains. However, even in apparently self-paced domains the pace of work varies and there are periods of relatively high demands. Watts (1994) also observed spreadsheet users invest effort to organize a dedicated information space to avoid navigation burdens. This kind of user tailoring was limited and brittle in this case as in the medical and space examples because the computer-based system was not explicitly designed to support this kind of user behavior.

These cases illustrate the repeated observation that users seem to prefer a spatially dedicated representation even if it is crude and deficient in other ways over keyholed computer systems despite apparent flexibility to call up many different features, displays, and options. Why? We think this phenomenon occurs because low visual momentum computer systems create new burdens for already loaded users. If practitioners used the computer-based system in the ways that designers envision, then they will be forced to interact with and devote limited attentional resources to the interface at times when their attention should be most focused on their job. Practitioners avoid this situation by throwing away flexibility and using characteristics of the computer to create their own spatially dedicated set of views of the underlying process or device.

26.4.5 "Rooms": What Can be Seen in Parallel and What in Series

The fragmentation of information into small chunks connected in large networks inevitably leads to the dissociation of related data. Data that must be seen together to support user tasks are often physically located in separate areas of the interface. One problem that can result is what Henderson and Card (1986) called "thrashing." If users must serially view each piece of information related to their task, they are forced to thrash back and forth between the displays to meet their task goals.

One way to reduce the problems caused by the dissociation of related data is by allowing users to see related views in parallel. This capability expands the narrow keyhole provided by the CRT to coordinate interrelated views. For example, the solution to many of the navigation problems in Case 2 (the operating room information system) is not to be found in more efficient navigation mechanisms. Rather the source of the problem is that practitioners using this interface cannot work in parallel on two kinds of activities (Cook and Woods, 1996). In this context there are two fundamental kinds of information and functions in a patient monitoring system: (a) monitoring patient vital signs which is always an important task and (b) various kinds of special asynchronous operations such as the sequence of tasks involved in measuring and computing the patient's cardiac output (a third category is interface manipulations). In the system studied, these two kinds of functions compete for the same limited real estate (opening up the window to support measuring and calculating cardiac output obscures a significant part of the patient's vital signs). But one kind of information (patient vital signs) needs to be continuously available, while the other is needed only on particular occasions. Thus, from a workspace coordination level of analysis, two parallel viewports are needed--one sufficient to show patient vital signs continuously and the other to handle the different kinds of asynchronous capabilities.

Another example comes from a hypertext system that was used to prototype an electronic version of the multiple paper volumes of emergency procedures used to guide operator actions in nuclear power plant accidents (Elm and Woods, 1985). The volume of procedural guidance is quite large, and the material is organized at multiple levels in a way designed to help operators apply the plans that best fit the actual problems in the plant. Because problems can evolve and change and because of the possibility of complicated diagnostic situations, the procedure system was designed with double checks and branches which were implemented in paper through foldout pages, cautions at the beginning of a task, and kick out steps to other parts of the procedure system. For example, while working through a particular procedure, various notes, cautions, and double checks would be relevant the entire time operators carried out this task (e.g., if a parameter exceeds a limit, stop doing this procedure and switch to another). This material was included in the paper system as a foldout page so that operators could see the double checks at the same time as they followed the specific steps in the procedure. The paper procedural system also contained background material about particular steps or sections of the procedure.

Converting the paper procedures to an electronic format appeared to offer a variety of advantages which could be obtained simply by converting the current paper system into the format of this hypertext system. The hypertext system was organized as a hierarchy of frames. The network consisted of two kinds of frames. Menu frames that contained a few options to select different parts of the procedure space (e.g., procedures for different kinds of faults and procedures to ensure that basic safety concerns were being addressed successfully). Content frames contained actual procedural guidance. Users could only see one frame at a time, either one content frame or one menu frame. Because of the small size of the frames, each contained only a few (one to three typically) statements from the paper procedure documents (e.g., steps, cautions, notes). As a result, finding task relevant procedural material could involve moving through as many as 4 menu frames before arriving at any procedural guidance about how to handle the evolving plant problems. Examining other material related to the current Content frame on view would involve calling up one to several menu frames before arriving at the related material. Each transition was an act of total replacement, and users could only look at one frame at a time.

Not surprisingly, usability tests in a simulator showed that different kinds of users (the procedure developers, experienced operators and experts in the hypertext system) all got lost in the network of displays in the sense that they could not follow the procedures in synchrony with the evolution of the incident in the power plant.

The navigation problems arose in part because users could not see related material in parallel (other problems existed as well, such as no longshot was available). Some of this was domain specific (e.g., seeing a procedure and the relevant foldout page in parallel) and other instances were generic (users were unable to see options and content in parallel). As in the operating room case, the navigation problems could only be addressed by changing the workspace coordination to allow users to see inter-related views in parallel. Figure 9 illustrates the workspace redesign.

Watt's 1994 field study of users of extended spreadsheets also showed that users will invest time and effort arranging their workspace to be able to see inter-related views in parallel. For example, study participants consolidated related information so they would not have to interrupt their tasks to attend to the interface management task of navigating between distant areas of the extended spreadsheet.

Designing a coordinated workspace is about deciding what kinds of views are available and which can be seen in parallel and which can be seen serially. This is a shift from simply building up a collection of single views to creating a "task-tunable" workspace of multiple views or perspectives (e.g., Card, Robertson and York, 1996).

1. Developers should study/analyze what views need to be seen in parallel (this is conditional on what kinds of views are being considered or designed, and it requires understanding user activities during coherent tasks). Henderson and Card (1986) suggest empirically tracking what views users call up together to identify sets of views that need to be coordinated. Methods for cognitive task analysis that analytically map meaningful domain contexts identify views that are inter-related and need to be seen in parallel (e.g., Mitchell and Saisi, 1987; Woods and Hollnagel, 1987).

2. Explicit representation of the workspace in terms of the kinds of views and their inter-relations is a prerequisite for the design of a coordinated workspace (Malin et al., 1991). Figures 4 and 9 are examples of explicit representations of the workspace (other examples include state-transition diagrams and innovative display ideas such as the document lens, Robertson and Mackinlay, 1993, or the information grid, Card et al., 1991). Developers very often leave this information out

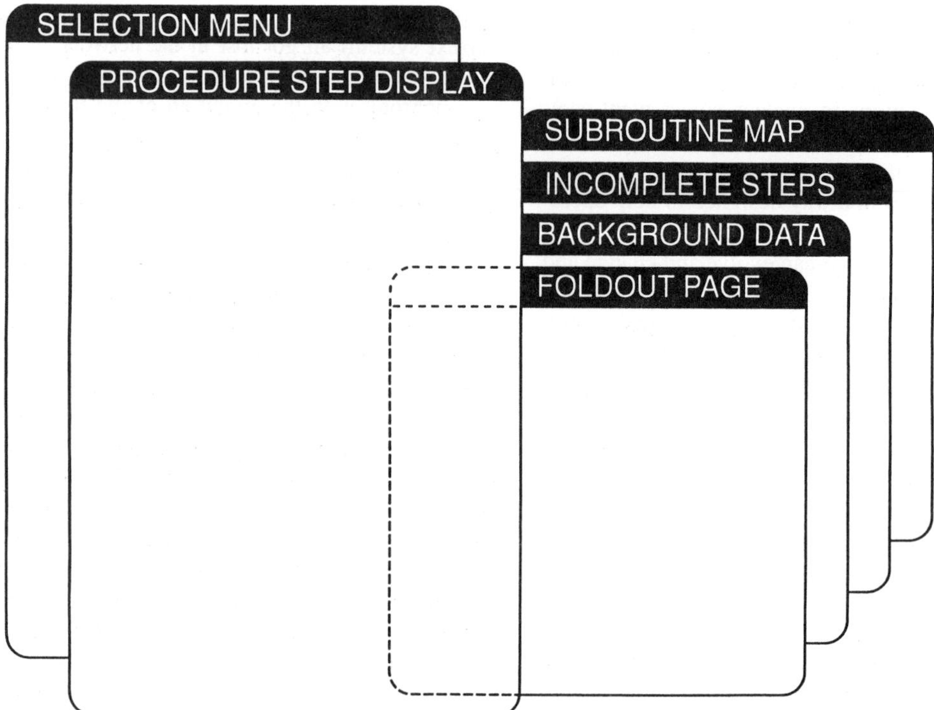

***Figure 9. The workspace redesign for a computer-based version of the emergency procedures in a nuclear power plant showing what kinds of views are available and which can be seen in parallel and which in series** (from Elm and Woods, 1985).*

and represent the design only in terms of the baseline views that appear by default in the standard viewports. When developing or evaluating a computer-based display system, we have found it necessary to characterize prototype systems in terms of a coordinated set of multiple views. Explicit, thoughtful design at this level of analysis of a computer-based display system cannot go forward without some way to represent the coordination of multiple views. The simple act of trying to represent the workspace often reveals many potential user problems, initiating rounds of design and evaluation that can lead to new innovations.

3. In general, users are likely to need to see specific kinds of views in parallel, e.g.,

- content and options need to be seen in parallel;
- longshot and local views need to be seen in parallel.

Other techniques are based in part on providing inter-related views in parallel (e.g., the center-surround technique and side effects views discussed in the next sections).

4. Designers should make provisions for users to be able to compose, save, and manipulate sets of views as a coherent unit, e.g., Henderson and Card's Rooms concept.

26.4.6 Center-Surround

In a natural perceptual field, people are able to switch attention and re-orient to interesting information in their environment (Rabbitt, 1984). The coordination of human focal attention and orienting perceptual functions such as peripheral vision supports the process of knowing where to look when. Orienting perceptual functions provide information about broad patterns in the surrounding environment and pick up changes that might warrant a shift of attention away from the current focus. Woods (1984) suggested that designers of virtual perceptual fields can model their systems on this characteristic of the human perceptual system--a center-surround technique. To support knowing where to look when, designers should surround a highly detailed central view coordinated with lower resolution, i.e., more distilled, views of physically or functionally related data. Lamping et al. (1995) have called this technique "focus plus context." Furnas (1986) proposed supporting navigation in a similar way by using an optical analogy, the fisheye lens.[6] All of these labels have in common the technique of balancing a high resolution detailed view with summary views of related parts of the virtual perceptual field.

The simplest way to develop a surround is to show nearby areas of the artificial data space in less detail. If the artificial data space is organized around discrete chunks, overlapping the chunks can help the viewer integrate the individual pieces into a complete picture of the overall space (as atlases show portions of adjacent regions around the region of interest). For example, the redesigned electronic procedure display system for nuclear power plants, instead of showing a few procedural steps in complete detail, showed one step in detail embedded in the context of previous steps and upcoming steps shown in less detail (Elm and Woods, 1985).

Another way to develop a surrounding context is to use locality maps, that is, a map of the neighborhood surrounding the current display of interest. One question becomes what criteria should be used to define nearby related material. In many designs, developers use the physical topology of the underlying device or process to define nearby material. Users can then pan and zoom to move the viewport across this large topology (or to move the topology relative to the viewport).

More powerful from the point of view of aiding practitioner information extraction and performance is representing functionally inter-related data in the surround. In this technique, the surround represents distant information and displays within the virtual space that are functionally related to the high-resolution view on the screen. This technique is model-based as it presupposes a model of relationships between different types of views and information about the domain in question.

For example, Woods and Hollnagel (1987) used one cognitive task analysis technique to map meaningful contexts for process control domains (see also Mitchell and Saisi, 1987). As a result, they were able to develop an information system concept where the computer system automatically displayed lower resolution views of contextualy related topics or areas (e.g., other related goals, mechanisms and requirements). When a practitioner selects a topic or area of interest for display in the high resolution viewport, he or she has defined a focus of attention. A functional model of the domain plus information on current status allows one to know what other topics are relevant to the primary view of interest. Based on this model, summaries about the status of these contextually relevant topics can appear in the surround automatically. These functionally related summaries in the surround can vary with context, i.e., the type and level of information displayed could depend on the state of the underlying system or on the state of the problem solving process.

The surround should cue the observer to related views within the display space and should provide status information as well. Just like the orienting function of peripheral vision, status information can help users decide when to change their focus of attention. The status summary function of the surround means that (as for longshots) the data displayed should be distilled and abstracted, reveal activities and change, and should support check reading.

Designers have to decide what kind of information at what level of summary and abstraction is appropriate for a surround. What is nearby needs to be thought of as a semantic property of the conceptual space if one is to use the center-surround technique to help observers know where to look when (linking domain semantics to the structure of the virtual perceptual field). In many domains this is complicated by the fact that there are multiple semantic relationships between topics, areas and data.

Recently, there have been a large number of innovations which are based, in part, on a center-surround concept (Mackinlay, Robertson and Card, 1991; Mitta and Grunning, 1993; Robertson and Mackinlay, 1993; Sarkar and Brown, 1994; Rao and Card, 1994; Bartram et al., 1995; Mackinlay, Robertson and Deline, 1996; Greenberg, 1996). These innovations go by varied names depending on their individual history of development but they all depend on the basic concept of providing a higher resolution focused view suurounded by contextually relevant information and views.

26.4.7 Side Effect Views

A specific kind of surround view is side effect views (Woods and Hollnagel, 1987). Side effect views provide users with information about distant areas of the information space that might be affected by actions they are taking or activities going on within their high-resolution central view. The goal is to give users a

[6] The fisheye lens, if taken literally, has the drawback that the surround area is optically distorted. The extant working model for a focus plus context technique is the center-surround organization of the visual field that supports the coordination between orienting perceptual functions and our focus of attention.

global picture of the state changes, both main effects as well as side effects, that occur as a result of actions taken.

Designers may want to consider side effect views whenever a domain has multiple interconnections between systems and functions so that actions can have multiple effects--the intended or main effects as well as other unintended "side" effects. In this kind of situation, it is relatively easy for practitioners to err by missing side effects of their plans and activities. Examples of domains with multiple interconnections are common in process control. For example, in nuclear power plants changing net water inflow to the reactor has multiple effects--coolant inventory changes, but reactivity (the nuclear reaction) can change as well because boron is dissolved into the coolant water to act as a moderator of the nuclear reaction. Increasing or decreasing net water inflow affects coolant level and boron concentration.

To reduce errors involving missed side effects, one nuclear control room computer-based display system included a specific side effects window (Woods and Hollnagel, 1987). If an operator is interested in one function (e.g., calls up displays on coolant inventory as the primary focus), the system also provides a summary of the status of other functions which could be influenced by changes in the primary area of interest in a side effects window (e.g., the reactivity/boron concentration function).

These kinds of complex interconnections happen in many other domains as well. For example, extended spreadsheets couple together multiple data tables. Values from one table may be used in calculations in other data tables. If a user of an extended spreadsheet changes the value of a cell on the screen, it may impact calculations and values in other data tables which are not visible because the extended spreadsheet is much larger than the available keyhole.

A side effect view can indicate whether a change in the table on a display causes numbers in distant areas of the extended spreadsheet to change in important ways (Watts, 1994). In this study, side effect views were proposed to explicitly represent the interconnections within and between spreadsheets, and to provide immediate feedback about how changes in one spreadsheet cell affects other cells and data tables. Side effect views can help users notice errors quickly, and can help users find the cause of errors by showing which cells contribute to an erroneous cell. Note that for a side effect view to provide immediate feedback about user actions, the view must be available in parallel with the active area of the spreadsheet. Also, the feedback must provide information that is relevant to user tasks and goals. For example, if users have the goal of keeping specific cells in their spreadsheet positive (i.e. if users do not want the cell representing a project budget total to be less than zero), a side effect view can aid this goal by showing when a formula result goes negative.

26.4.8 Cues to Status

Cues to status are an important technique to enable practitioners to easily "check read" or peripherally pick up what might be interesting changes in other parts of the underlying process that should guide a shift in attentional focus (Woods, 1995b). Many of the techniques discussed involve providing cues to status as well as to structure--content-laden landmarks, center-surround, side effects views.

For cues to status to be effective, users need to be able to "size up at a glance" the status or activities going on in that part of the artificial data space. This means that the cues should meet the criteria for the status summary function:

- a distillation of what is important about that aspect of the field of practice,
- an abstracted representation that goes beyond simply making raw data available,
- representations that support quick check reads and pattern recognition so that practitioners can pick up potentially interesting changes without disrupting their ongoing line of reasoning.

26.5 Conceptual Spaces and Workspace Coordination

Workspace coordination is as fundamental a part of the design of a computer-based information system or device as the design of individual displays. This level of analysis and design is important because users can easily get lost in a large network of displays and options hidden behind the narrow keyhole of the computer screen. But practitioners, as responsible agents in a field of practice, cannot afford the cost of getting lost in the interface. Instead, we observe practitioners adapt the system and their behavior to avoid being burdened by navigating in the interface itself when they should be focused on their job. They avoid navigating through too many displays when the job is resource-limited, fast paced, event-driven or critical to their goals.

Simply providing context free aids that increase the

efficiency of moving from one display to another is not enough to help practitioners perform coherent tasks across displays. While we are struck by the competency people exhibit in navigating physically distributed, spatially organized information spaces, simply reproducing the superficial properties of a physical space also is not enough to aid practitioners. We do not see all parts of a large physical space at once and in parallel. The competency we exhibit in physical spaces for focusing in on potentially relevant data comes from the coordination of orienting perceptual functions and focal attention. By supporting these mechanisms in a virtual perceptual field designers can break down the keyhole of the computer medium.

While the computer medium fundamentally presents the observer with a keyhole, the computer also provides designers with the power to develop new techniques to enhance practitioners ability to process data across displays as they perform coherent tasks. The problems associated with keyholed computer-based systems have spurred developers to use this power and innovate many different kinds of techniques for workspace coordination.

We think that techniques that contribute to breaking down the keyhole are based on a few basic concepts that should guide developers as they think about how to design a coordinated virtual workspace.

*1. **Build a conceptual space.*** Workspace coordination is about deciding what kinds of views should be available to practitioners and how to organize those views into a coherent conceptual space. A conceptual space depicts relationships in a frame of reference.

*2. **Link structure to semantics.*** Building a conceptual space is intimately concerned with understanding the nature of practice in some domain of activity:

- what are coherent activities and sequences,
- how are activities interleaved given resources and demands,
- how do activities ebb and flow regularly over different task epochs or irregularly driven by events,
- how do new events and changes require practitioners to shift focus,
- what data needs to be seen in parallel in different contexts?

This is the kind of information that is needed to develop what kinds of views should be available, how to coordinate different views in parallel or serially in pace with the interleaved and changing tasks of practitioners.

*3. **Provide visible cues to structure.*** Many of the techniques to aid navigation are methods for making the underlying structure visible to users. But the second principle points out that simply adopting a spatial metaphor may not be enough -- the representation may look like a physical space or we may adopt a fixed layout to pan and zoom across. The visible structure needs to capture the important semantics of the field of practice (e.g., Vora, Helander and Shalin, 1994).

*4. **Provide cues to status at a glance.*** A recurring theme in many of the techniques discussed specifically in this chapter is adding cues to status. In order to reorient attention the observer needs to be able to peripherally pick up some information about what is going on (activities, changes, inter-relationships) in other parts of the artificial data field. The goal is to allow observers who are focused on one view or activity to "check read" or to pick up what might be interesting changes in other parts of the virtual field that should guide a shift in attentional focus.

26.6 Acknowledgements

The ideas on workspace coordination in this paper have developed based on the support and cooperation of a number of people and projects -- Scott Potter, Matt Holloway, Emilie Roth, Bill Stubler, and Jane Malin. We especially want to thank the people at NASA who collaborated or shared their prototypes with us in the project How to make Intelligent Systems Team Players under Grant NAG9-390, Dr. Jane Malin technical monitor. We also thank Kim Vincente for his many insightful comments.

26.7 References

Aretz, A. (1991). The design of electronic map displays. *Human Factors*, 33(1), 85-101.

Bartram, L., Ho, A., Dill, J. and Henigman, F. (1995). The Continuous Zoom: A constrained fisheye technique for viewing and navigating large information spaces. In *UIST 95 ACM Symposium on User Interface Software and Technology*, (pp. 207-215). New York: ACM Press.

Beard, D. and Walker, J. (1990). Navigational techniques to improve the display of large two dimensional spaces. *Behavior and Information Technology*, 9(6), 451-466.

Bennett, K. B. and Flach, J. M. (1992). Graphical displays: Implications for divided attention, focused attention, and problem solving. *Human Factors, 34*(5), 513-533.

Bernstein, M. (1988). The bookmark and the compass: Orientation tools for hypertext users. *ACM SIGOIS Bulletin, 9*(4).

Billings, C. E. (1996). *Aviation Automation: The search for a human-centered approach.* Hillsdale, NJ: Erlbaum.

Billingsley, P. A. (1982). Navigation through hierarchical menu structures: Does it help to have a map? In *Proceedings of the 26th annual Meeting of the Human Factors Society*, .

Bolt, R. (1984). *The Human Interface: When People and Computers Meet.* Belmont, CA: Lifetime Learning Publications.

Bower, G. and Morrow, D. G. (1990). Mental models in narrative comprehension. *Science, 247*, 44-48.

Card, S. K., Mackinlay, J. D. and Robertson, G. G. (1991). The Information Visualizer: An information workspace. In *CHI 91 ACM Conference on Human Factors in Computing Systems*, New York: ACM Press.

Card, S. K., Robertson, G. R. and York, W. (1996). The WebBook and the Web Forager: An information workspace for the World Wide Web. In *CHI 96 ACM Conference on Human Factors in Computing Systems*, (pp. 111-117). New York: ACM Press.

Conklin, J. (1987). Hypertext: An introduction and survey. *IEEE Computer, 20*(9).

Cook, R. I. and Woods, D. D. (1996). Adapting to new technology in the operating room. *Human Factors, 38*(4), in press.

Easter, J. R. (1991). The role of the operator and control room design. In J. White and D. Lanning (Eds.), *European Nuclear Instrumentation and Controls* . World Technology Evaluation Center, Loyola college, Baltimore, MD (available from national information technology service, Springfield, VA, Report # PB92-100197): National Technical Information Service.

Elm, W. C. and Woods, D. D. (1985). Getting lost: A case study in interface design. In *Proceedings of the Human Factors Society, 29th Annual Meeting*, Santa Monica, CA: Human Factors Society (pp. 927 - 931).

Folk, C. L., Remington, R. W. and Johnston, J. J. (1992). Involuntary covert orienting is contingent on attentional control settings. *Journal of Experimental Psychology: Human Perception and Performance, 18*(4), 1030-1044.

Froehlich, E. and Quackenbush, J. (1996). Planning Diagrams: Visualize. *Navigate: The Online Magazine for Netscape*™ *Users*, October 31, 1996.

Funke, D. J., Neal, J. G. and Paul, R. D. (1993). An approach to intelligent automated window management. *International Journal of Man-Machine Studies, 38*, 891-1058.

Furnas, G. W. (1986). Generalized fisheye views. In *CHI '86 ACM Conference on Human Factors in Computing Systems*, (pp. 16-23) New York: ACM Press.

Furnas, G. W. and Bederson, B. B. (1995). Space-scale Diagrams: Understanding Multiscale Interfaces. In *CHI 95 ACM Conference on Human Factors in Computing Systems*, (pp. 234-241) New York: ACM Press.

Gibson, J. J. (1986). *The Ecological Approach to Perception.* Hillsdale, NJ: Erlbaum.

Greenberg, S. (1996). A fisheye text editor for relaxed-WYSIWIS groupware. In *CHI 96 ACM Conference on Human Factors in Computing Systems*, Volume 2 (pp. 212-213). New York: ACM Press.

Henderson, D. and Card, S. (1986). Rooms: The use of multiple virtual workspaces to reduce space contention in a window-based graphical user interface. *ACM Transactions on Graphics, 5*(3), 211-241.

Hochberg, J. (1986). Representation of motion and space in video and cinematic displays. In K. Boff, L. Kaufman, and J. Thomas (Eds.), *Handbook of Perception and Human Performance* (pp. 22-1 to 22-64). New York: John Wiley and Sons.

Hochberg, J. and Brooks, V. (1978). Film cutting and visual momentum. In J. Senders and D. Fisher (Eds.), *Eye Movements and the Higher Psychological Functions* Hillsdale, NJ: Erlbaum.

Hochberg, J. and Gellman, L. (1977). The effect of landmark features on mental rotation times. *Memory and Cognition, 5*, 23-26.

Hutchins, E., Hollan, J. and Norman, D. A. (1986). Direct Manipulation Interfaces. In D. A. Norman and S. Draper (Eds.), *User Centered System Design*, Hillsdale, NJ,: Erlbaum,.

Kahn, P. (1995). Visual cues for local and global coherence in the WWW. *Communications of the ACM, 38*(8), 67-69.

Kahn, P. (1996). Mapping Web Sites. Web Design and Development Conference 96. Washington, DC, Thursday, Oct. 31, 1996. URL http://www.DynamicDiagrams.com.

Kim, H. and Hirtle, S. C. (1995). Spatial metaphors and disorientation in hypertext browsing. *Behaviour and Information Technology*, *14*(4), 239-250.

Lamping, J., Rao, R. and Pirolli, P. (1995). A focus+context technique based on hyperbolic geometry for visualizing large hierarchies. In *CHI 95 ACM Conference on Human Factors in Computing Systems*, New York: ACM Press.

Lieberman, H. (1994). Powers of ten thousand: Navigating in large information spaces. In *UIST 94 ACM Symosium on User Interface Software and Technology*, (pp. 15-16). New York: ACM Press.

Mackinlay, J., Robertson, G. and Card, S. (1991). The perspective wall: Detail and context smoothly integrated. In *CHI 91 ACM Conference on Human Factors in Computing Systems*, New York: ACM Press.

Mackinlay, J. D., Robertson, G. G. and DeLine, R. (1996). Developing calendar visualizers for the Information Visualizer. In *UIST 94 ACM Symposium on User Interface Software and Technology*, (pp. 109-118). New York: ACM Press.

Malin, J., Schreckenghost, D., Woods, D., Potter, S., Johannesen, L., Holloway, M. and Forbus, K. (1991). Making Intelligent Systems Team Players. NASA Technical Report 104738, Houston TX: Johnson Space Center.

McDonald, S. and Stevenson, R. J. (1996). Disorientation in Hypertext: The Effects of Three Text Structures on Navigation Performance. *Applied Ergonomics*, *27*(1), 61-68.

Mitchell, C. M. and Saisi, D. L. (1987). Use of model-based qualitative icons and adaptive windows in workstations for supervisory control systems. *IEEE Transactions on Systems, Man and Cybernetics*, *17*(4), 573-593.

Mitta, D. and Grunning, D. (1993). Simplifying graphics-based data: Applying the fisheye lens viewing strategy. *Behavior and Information Technology*, *12*(1), 1-16.

Moray, N. (1986). Monitoring behavior and supervisory control. In K. R. Boff, L. Kaufman and J. P. Thomas (Eds.), *Handbook of Perception and Human Performance* (pp. 1-51). New York: Wiley.

Nielson, J. (1990). The art of navigating through hypertext. *Communications of the ACM*, *33*, 298-31.

Nielson, J. (1996). Interface design for SUN's WWW Site. Sun Microsystems, Inc., Mountain View, CA 94043, URL http://www.sun.com/sun-on-net/uidesign.

Norman, D. A. (1988). *The Psychology of Everyday Things*. New York: Basic Books.

Norman, D. A. (1990). The 'problem' of automation: Inappropriate feedback and interaction, not 'over-automation.' *Philosophical Transactions of the Royal Society of London, B327*, 585--593.

Obradovich, J. H. and Woods, D. D. (1996). Users as designers: How people cope with poor HCI design in computer-based medical devices. *Human Factors, 38*(4), in press.

Passini, R. (1992). *Wayfinding in Architecture*. New York: Van Nostrand Reinhold.

Pejterson, A. M. (1992). The Book House. An icon based database system for fiction retrieval in public libraries. In B. Cronin (Eds.), *The Marketing of Library and Information Services 2* (pp. 572-591). London: ASLIB.

Potter, S. S. and Woods, D. D. (1994). Breaking Down Barriers in Cooperative Fault Management: Temporal and Functional Information Displays. Cognitive Systems Engineering Laboratory Report, CSEL 94-TR-02, Columbus OH: The Ohio State University, March 1994.

Rabbitt, P. (1984). The control of attention in visual search. In R. Parasuraman and D. R. Davies (Eds.), *Varieties of Attention* . New York: Academic Press.

Ranson, D. S. and Woods, D. D. (1996). Animating computer agents. In *HICS 96, 3rd Annual Symposium on Human Interaction with Complex Systems*. New York: IEEE.

Rao, R. and Card, S. K. (1994). The Table Lens: Merging graphical and symbolic representations in an interactive focus+context visualization for tabular information. In *CHI 94 ACM Conference on Human Factors in Computing Systems*, (pp. 318-322). Boston MA: ACM Press.

Rao, R. Card, S. K., Jellinek, H. D., Mackinlay, J. D. and Robertson, G. G. (1992). The Information Grid. In *UIST 92 ACM Symosium on User Interface Software and Technology*, (pp. 23-32). Monterey CA: ACM Press.

Rasmussen, J., Pejtersen, A. M. and Goldstein, L. P. (1994). *Cognitive Systems Engineering*. New York: John Wiley and Sons, Inc.

Reed, E. S. (1988). *James J. Gibson and the psychology of perception*. New Haven, CT: Yale University Press.

Reiersen, C. S., Marshall, E. and Baker, S. M. (1988). An experimental evaluation of an advanced alarm system for nuclear power plants. In J. Patrick and K. Duncan (Eds.), *Training, Human Decision Making and Control* . North-Holland, New York: Elsevier .

Robertson, G. and Mackinlay, J. (1993). The document lens. In *ACM Symposium on User Interface Software an Technology*, New York: ACM Press.

Robertson, G., Mackinlay, J., and Card, S. (1991). Cone trees: Animated 3d visualizations of hierarchical information. In *CHI 91 ACM Conference on Human Factors in Computing Systems*, New York: ACM Press.

Robertson, G. G., Card, S. K., and Mackinlay, J. D. (1993). Information visualization using 3D interactive animation. *Communications of the ACM*, *36*(4), 57-71.

Robertson, G. G. and Mackinlay, J. D. (1993). The Document Lens. In *UIST 93 ACM Symposium on User Interface Software and Technology*, (pp. 101-108). New York: ACM Press.

Roth, E. M., Malin, J. and Schreckenghost, D. (this volume).

Sarkar, M. and Brown, M. (1994). Graphical fisheye views. *Communications of the ACM*, *37*(12).

Sarter, N. B., Woods, D. D. and Billings, C. (in press). Automation Surprises. In G. Salvendy (Ed.), *Handbook of Human Factors and Ergonomics*, second edition, New York: Wiley.

Shneiderman, B. (1987). *Designing the User Interface: Strategies for effective Human-Computer Interaction*. Addison-Wesley.

Shneiderman, B. (1992). Tree Visualization with Tree maps: A 2D space-filling approach. *ACM Transactions on Graphics*, *11*, 92-99.

Smith, P. A. and Wilson, J. R. (1993). Navigation in hypertext through virtual environments. *Applied Ergonomics*, *24*(4), 271-278.

Thuring, M., Hannemann, J. and Haake, J. M. (1995). Hypermedia and cognition: Designing for comprehension. *Communications of the ACM*, *38*(8), 57-66.

Vicente, K. J. and Rasmussen, J. (1992). Ecological interface design: Theoretical Foundations. *IEEE Transactions on Systems, Man, and Cybernetics*, *22*(4), 589-606.

Vicente, K. J. and Williges, R. C. (1988). Accommodating individual differences in searching a hierarchical file system. *International Journal of Man-Machine Studies*, *29*, 647-668.

Vora, P. R., Helander, M. G., and Shalin, V. L. (1994). Evaluating the influence of interface styles and multiple access paths in hypertext. In *CHI 94 ACM Conference on Human Factors in Computing Systems*, (pp. 323-329). New York: ACM Press.

Watson, C., Eastman, M. C. and Woods, D. D. (1990). Status tree monitoring and display system. Patent Number 4,902,469, Feb. 20, 1990.

Watts, J. C. (1994). Navigation in the computer medium: A cognitive analysis. In *Proceedings of the Human Factors and Ergonomics Society, 38th annual Meeting*, Santa Monica CA: Human Factors and Ergonomics Society.

Wolfe, J. (1992). The parallel guidance of visual attention. *Current Directions in Psychological Science*, *1*(4), 124-129.

Woods, D. D. (1984). Visual Momentum: A concept to improve the cognitive coupling of person and computer. *International Journal of Man-Machine Studies*, *21*, 229-244.

Woods, D. D. (1991). The Cognitive Engineering of Problem Representations. In G. R. S. Weir and J. L. Alty (Eds.), *Human-Computer Interaction and Complex Systems*, London: Academic Press.

Woods, D. D. (1993). The price of flexibility in intelligent interfaces. *Knowledge-Based Systems*, *6*, 1-8.

Woods, D. D. (1995a). Towards a Theoretical Base for Representation Design in the Computer Medium: Ecological Perception and Aiding Human Cognition. In J. Flach, P. Hancock, J. Caird, and K. Vicente (Eds.), *An Ecological Approach To Human Machine Systems I: A Global Perspective*, Hillsdale NJ: Erlbaum.

Woods, D.D. (1995b). The alarm problem and directed attention in dynamic fault management. *Ergonomics*, *38*(11), 2371-2393.

Woods, D. D. (1996). *Visualizing Function: The Theory and Practice of Representation Design in the Computer Medium*. Manuscript in preparation.

Woods, D. D. and Hollnagel, E. (1987). Mapping cognitive demands in complex problem solving worlds. *International Journal of Man-Machine Studies*, *26*, 257--275.

Woods, D. D., Johannesen, L., Cook, R. I. and Sarter, N. B. (1994). *Behind Human Error: Cognitive Systems, Computers and Hindsight.* Dayton OH: Crew Systems Ergonomic Information and Analysis Center, WPAFB.

Woods, D. D., Patterson, E. and Corbin, J. (1996). Apollo 13 Where's Waldo Game. Cognitive Systems Engineering Laboratory, Columbus OH: The Ohio State University, URL http://128.146.114.128/homepages/nasaproject/0.html.

Zizi, M. and Beaudouin-Lafon, M. (1995). Hypermedia exploration with interactive dynamic maps. *International Journal of Human-Computer Studies*, *43*(3), 441-464.

Part IV

Evaluation of HCI

Handbook of Human-Computer Interaction
Second, completely revised edition
M. Helander, T.K. Landauer, P. Prabhu (eds.)

Chapter 27

The Usability Engineering Framework for Product Design and Evaluation

Dennis Wixon
Digital Equipment Corporation
Nashua, New Hampshire, USA

Chauncey Wilson
FTP Software Inc.
North Andover, Massachusetts, USA

27.1 Overview

This chapter is organized for both the practitioner and the theorist. To accommodate these diverse audiences, we use a simple structure. We define usability engineering and then describe its origins. We then structure a discussion around each of the steps involved in doing usability engineering. For each step we provide:

- A definition of the step and an outline of how to complete that step
- Examples of what practitioners have done to complete that step based on the Computer-Human In-

teraction (CHI) literature, an informal survey, and our own experience
- A discussion of the issues and pitfalls involved in that step
- A summary

Practitioners can use the definitions and examples as a basis for their work. The issues and pitfalls identified at the end of each section provide background for establishing, marketing, and refining a usability engineering process in a development organization. Throughout this chapter, we provide notes for the theorist on the conceptual underpinnings of usability engineering and the interrelationships between usability engineering and other methods like Contextual Inquiry, inspections, and scenarios. The final part of this chapter lists ways in which other design models and methods complement the usability engineering framework.

27.2 What is Usability Engineering?

Usability engineering is a process for defining, measuring, and thereby improving, the usability of products. Usability engineering evolved because of a need to move usability from the realm of personal opinion to an attribute that is quantifiable like other engineering attributes. The basic usability engineering process has seven steps (Good, Spine, Whiteside, and George, 1986):

1. Define measurable usability attributes.
2. Set the quantitative levels of desired usability for each attribute. Together, an attribute and a desired level constitute a usability goal.
3. Test the product against the usability goals. If you meet your goals, no further design is needed.
4. If further design work is needed, analyze the problems that emerge.
5. Analyze the impact of possible design solutions.
6. Incorporate user-derived feedback in product design.
7. Return to Step 3 to repeat the test, analysis, and design cycle.

Usability engineering is flexible in both its application and methodology. It can be applied to new versions of existing products, new products which will be entering a market against established competitors, or to entirely new and innovative products. Usability engineering does not specify particular methods for defining goals, testing products, or incorporating user-derived feedback into the development process. Usability engineers can choose the methods that fit best into their development environments and budgets. The sine qua non of usability engineering is that it provides quantitative results that can be compared to explicit usability goals.

27.3 What are the Origins of Usability Engineering?

Usability engineering evolved from the experience of Digital Equipment Corporation's Software Usability Engineering team, collaboration with colleagues in the field and product engineering groups, and our study of the engineering and CHI literature (Butler, 1985, Deming, 1982; Gilb, 1981; Gilb, 1985; Good, 1985). In the early 1980's, we came to three major conclusions about usability.

1. A traditional experimental approach was inadequate for designing user interfaces.

In our early work on the design of text editors, we did many small experiments that focused on single, simplistic questions:

- Is overstrike effective?
- Should a cursor be free or bound to text?
- What is the best arrangement of cursor (arrow) keys on the keyboard?

These questions were oriented toward influencing the engineering of a new text editor. The results were convincing, and we met with some success in persuading engineers to incorporate these results into the EVE text editor (Good, 1985). However, we also experienced resistance to our experimental results. Software engineers questioned sample sizes ("How can you draw any conclusions from only 10 people?") even when the results attained conventional levels of statistical significance. Engineers were suspicious of anything they did not understand, like analyses of variance (ANOVAs) or *t* tests. The use of conventional statistical tests was denigrated by software engineers with comments such as "You can prove anything with statistics" or "Statistics can lie." These comments made us realize that the successful application of statistical methods did not guarantee that our results would be taken seriously. We also awakened to the fact that the mechanics of experimental testing and design were not well suited to handle multiple, interdependent questions like:

- How efficiently can an executive assistant use electronic publishing software to design pages for a complex report that is due tomorrow?
- How would a financial analyst learn to analyze complex financial data with a multidimensional spreadsheet and then roll up that data with data from other analysts?
- How does a wall street financier use analytic tools to make money for clients?
- What makes remote collaboration tools like electronic whiteboards effective?

Classical experimental designs focused on specific hypotheses (for example, "overstrike is more effective than insert"), required large samples, and stringent controls. An experimental study might conclude that "overstrike was more effective than insert" for editing a document, but not answer the myriad questions we faced daily in designing systems for complex environments.

2. To be treated seriously, usability efforts had to adopt the assumptions and language of engineering.

Over time we came to realize that engineering was based on different assumptions, used a different language, and answered different questions than the traditional experimental approach. Specifically, engineering is based on the translation of abstract qualities like reliability into empirical measures (mean time between failures) and specific thresholds (1000 hours between failures). This empirical framework provides a basis for analyzing trade-offs, for directing the work (what components should we cut and what should we keep?), and for evaluating the product (did it last for 1000 hours?). The engineering approach stood in stark contrast to the scientific approach we had been using. Bluntly stated, while science is concerned with uncovering truth, regardless of time or cost, engineering is concerned with the "art of the possible within constrained resources".

3. For usability to be taken seriously, we found that it had to be treated as part of engineering quality.

To be considered on a par with other engineering qualities, usability must be defined operationally with threshold levels for product acceptance. This operational approach is designed to bring usability into the engineering culture by elevating it to the level of other engineering qualities like reliability and performance. Creating operational definitions of usability also counters two destructive assertions. The first is: "usability is just a matter of opinion". By insisting on an operational definition of usability we overcame the software engineer's complaint that usability is just someone's opinion. The second destructive assertion is that particular implementation methods guarantee usability. Operational definitions separate the attribute of usability from the implementation methods used to achieve usability.

Early product specifications often included requirements that confused implementation methods and usability attributes. Here are some real examples that we have seen more than once.

- "The product will be usable because it contains on-line help and pull-down menus."
- "A direct manipulation user interface will make this product user-friendly."
- "The use of a toolbar and icons will ensure that this product is intuitive for new users."

Such statements equate usability attributes (ease of learning, ease of use) with the particular implementation methods (on-line help, toolbars, and pull-down menus). We found these statements destructive. The presence of on-line help, icons, and pull-down menus did not guarantee that an application would be usable. On the contrary, menus could be poorly labeled, awkwardly grouped, and require excessive navigation for simple operations. Toolbars often had mysterious icons that made users furrow their brows in bewilderment.

Modern GUI implementation methods do not automatically impart usability to a product. This is a lesson still being learned by many development groups.

As Digital's Software Usability Engineering Team realized the importance of operational definitions, two breakthroughs emerged for integrating usability into the engineering process. The first breakthrough was the concept that a "usability specification" could be created in the initial stage of the design process (Whiteside, Bennett, and Holtzblatt, 1988; Carroll and Rosson, 1985; Gould and Lewis, 1985). The second breakthrough was our realization that software engineering, like other forms of engineering, involves attributes which are fundamentally dichotomous, like available or unavailable features, and qualities which are continuous like response time (Gilb, 1988). Usability, like other engineering attributes, is a quality which can be specified and measured.

27.4 What is the Rationale for Usability Engineering?

There are five major advantages of usability engineering (Karat, 1991, 1994; Whiteside, Bennett, and Holtzblatt, 1988):

1. Developers can agree on a definition of usability.

Getting development teams to agree on the meaning of usability is essential (Chapanis and Budurka, 1990; Hix and Hartson, 1993; Smith and Siochi, 1995; Whiteside, Bennett, and Holtzblatt, 1988). For some developers, usability means ease of learning; to others it means long-run efficiency. Failure to get a consensus definition of usability leads to wasted development time and products without any systematic design focus.

2. Usability is quantified and not just personal opinion.

The phrases, "ease of learning" and "ease of use", are not sufficiently defined to play a role in any design process. Replacing statements like "our new Email product has to be really easy to learn" with the explicit goal that "new users should be able to send, read, address, forward, and print 3 Email messages in the first 30 minutes of use with no outside assistance", allows a development team to evaluate possible solutions and allocate resources in a rational way. The power of quantitative goals is well established in engineering practice (Arthur, 1993). For example, Gilb's Law of Quantitative Measurement (DeMarco and Lister, 1987, p. 59) highlights the importance of specific, quantitative goals:

> "Anything you need to quantify can be measured in some way that is superior to not measuring it at all."

DeMarco and Lister add that "Gilb's law doesn't promise you that measurement will be free or even cheap, and it may not be perfect -- just better than nothing."

3. Usability is put on an equal footing with other engineering attributes like reliability and performance.

Other software engineering goals like performance or reliability are quantitatively specified. Those goals which are clear and precise will command resources and mindshare. Vague and imprecise goals are often declared "met" when time and money have run out. One of the reasons attributes like "time to market" and "reliability" (eliminating bugs) play such a major role in the development process is that they have "metrics" that are clearly defined. Usability "bugs" can be just as severe as reliability bugs and should be treated with the same quantitative respect.

4. Usability problems can be prioritized as a function of their impact on usability goals.

Usability goals and metrics can serve as a basis for prioritizing usability issues from a user's perspective. If the goal is expressed as "time to complete a task", then usability problems can be prioritized in terms of the time that users spent making errors. Such a prioritization serves to balance the inevitable prioritization that will occur when resources are considered. By providing a user-based priority scheme, the design team can make meaningful tradeoffs and concentrate on high-impact problems that require the lowest effort.

5. Goals are clearly separated from the methods and implementation

The separation of goal from implementation is critical to both thoughtful design and meaningful evaluation. Any engineering effort is necessarily focused on **how** the system will be implemented. Any designer is focused on **what** the user will see and do with the system. Without a clearly stated goal or direction, these "hows" will overwhelm the "whats". Unfortunately, many design teams focus on the "how" by following a user interface style guide or copying the look and feel of a usable application. Choosing the implementation methods without a clear understanding of user goals is making a blind choice. Focusing on goals stated in users' terms establishes the appropriate grounding for the rest of the design work.

27.4.1 Survey of Usability Engineering

We conducted an informal survey of colleagues to get some concrete examples of usability engineering practices. We posted the survey to several Internet list servers and sent out mail surveys. We asked recipients about their usability engineering background, how often they set usability goals, and what usability engineering activities they practiced.

Table 1: Years of usability experience of our survey respondents

Years of Experience	% of Respondents (N = 25)
Over 10 Years	28
6-10 Years	16
4-6 years	24
1-3 years	16
7-12 months	12
No Answer	4

Table 2: Occupations of our survey respondents

Occupations	% of Respondents (N = 25)
Information Provider	20
Engineer	16
Manager	16
Usability Engineer	16
HF Consultant	12
HF Engineer	8
GUI Engineer	8
No Answer	4

Who Responded to Our Survey?

A total of 25 surveys were returned. The sample represented a cross section of experience levels and. occupations. Table 1 shows the distribution of our respondents' experience.

What Were the Occupations of Our Respondents?

The occupations of respondents are shown in Table 2. The most common occupation was information provider. This category included writers, editors, and graphic artists.

The respondents worked on a wide variety of applications including:

- Office applications
- Financial applications
- Networking applications
- Email or on-line services
- Manufacturing applications
- Operating systems
- Scientific applications
- Information retrieval
- Medical products
- On-line documentation

27.5 How do I do Usability Engineering?

Usability engineering is embodied by a general process and is highly flexible in its application. Figure 1 indicates the various inputs, steps, and decisions that occur during the usability engineering process.

Usability engineering may appear to be a highly structured and expensive process, but, in fact, it is a scaleable process that can range from very simple to quite elaborate. The simplest form of usability engineering involves the collection of questionnaire data on satisfaction attributes. An intermediate level of usability engineering requires a notebook, stopwatch, observational and interview skills, and the ability to analyze quantitative data. A more elaborate version involves a formal lab, extensive task analysis, video recording equipment, and data logging software.

27.5.1 Selling Usability Engineering

Before beginning a usability engineering effort, enlist the support of upper management (Erlich and Rohn, 1994; Mayhew and Bias, 1994). Since usability engineering often involves entire product teams, upper level support is critical, especially for the initial usability engineering cycle. Many usability engineers try to work bottom-up with developers; however, this is difficult given the competing demands on developers' time. Usability engineering is most successful when support is driven from both the top AND the bottom (Braun and Rohn, 1993). In most environments, you must sell usability engineering to different target audiences including corporate management, development managers, and individual developers.

To appeal to high level management, the people responsible for the profit and loss of a product, stress how the application of usability engineering can:

- Provide the basis for clearly stating the product's benefits. Usability data can be used to improve marketing literature, influence early adopters of new technology, and convince potential users that training costs will be low (Conklin, 1991).
- Reduce development costs and prevent errors which increase the costs of distribution and support (Mauro, 1994).
- Reduce risk by assessing how users will react to a product.

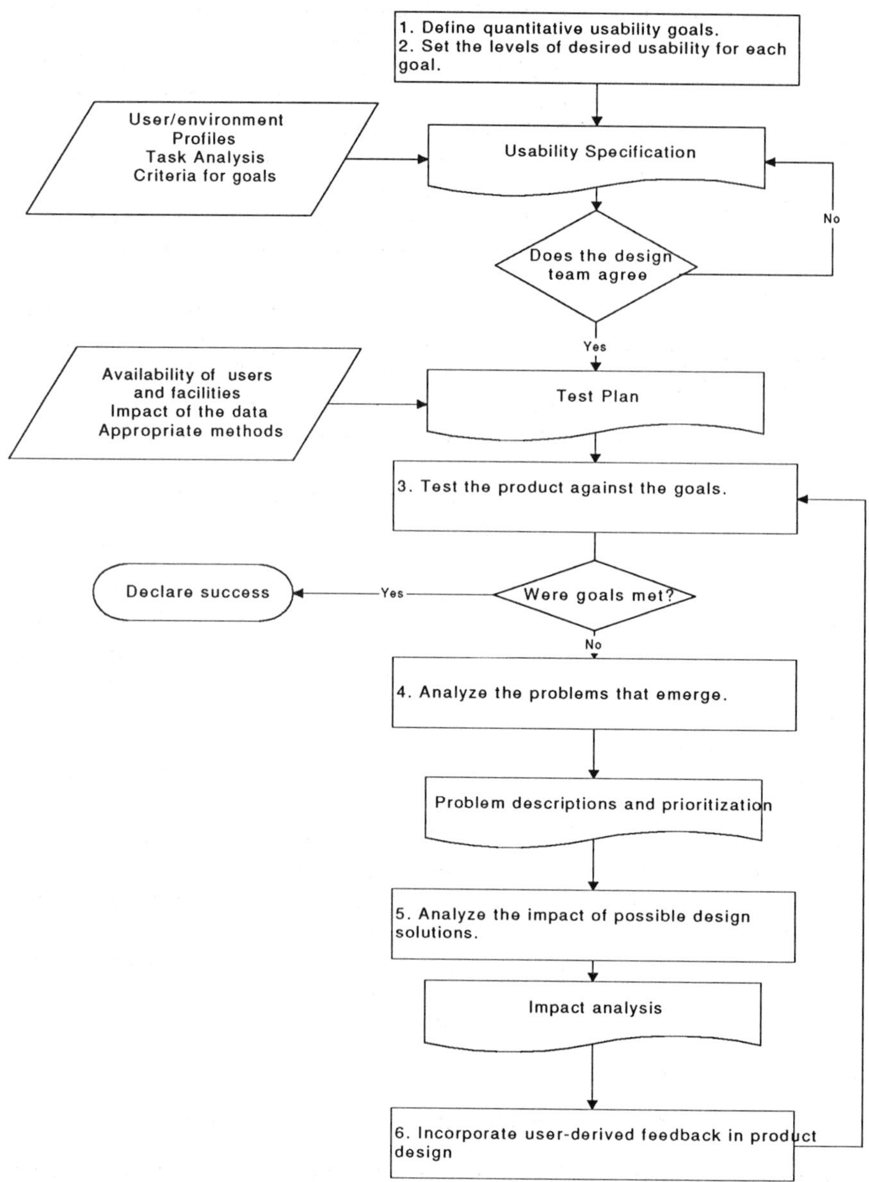

Figure 1. The usability engineering process.

- Reduce the potential for intellectual property or liability litigation (Mauro, 1994).
- Provide quantitative data on the usability of competitive products (Bachman, 1989).

To appeal to an engineering manager who is responsible for meeting a delivery schedule, stress how usability engineering can:

- Reduce time wasted in re-design due to unstated and unshared goals.
- Provide an objective way of prioritizing design problems (Ehrlich and Rohn, 1994).
- Lead a team to produce the interface early.

To the working level engineer, one should stress that usability engineering:

- Is objective and unbiased.
- Can be measured like other engineering attributes.
- Provides for creativity in the design process and a framework for a team to work quickly.

Cost-Justifying Usability Engineering

The selling of usability is becoming more focused on tangible benefits and cost-justifying usability engineering activities (Bias and Mayhew, 1994). Development managers are asking if the benefits of usability engineering outweigh the costs. Usability evangelists will argue that forgoing usability engineering is more costly than implementing it. The evangelists back up their claim with examples of usability problems found late in development that wreaked havoc on schedules, tempers, and budgets. Usability problems found in released products are likely to receive bad press and reduced sales. Nielsen (1993) notes that product usability is getting significant attention in the national media and usability is a strong focus of nearly all product reviews. The Wall Street Journal, for example, highlights usability problems in its technology columns and feature articles.

Usability testing can be costly, but the cost of testing must be balanced against the potential benefits of usability engineering. Usability is not something that can be left to chance. The costs of ignoring usability include (Bias and Mayhew, 1994):

- Inclusion of the "wrong" features or omission of the "right" features
- Time spent arguing on the basis of no data
- Time and money spent redesigning inconsistent or unusable user interfaces
- An increased number of support calls
- Negative impressions of the product and a loss of sales

Return on Investment (ROI)

One key to selling usability engineering is to show a tangible return on investment (ROI). ROI can be manifested in different ways. For an internal development project, the ROI for usability work might be measured in terms of reduced training, reduced support calls, and improved productivity. Hackos (1995), for example, found that usability engineering on an internal insurance product increased the probability of a successful sale by providing agents with more accurate data faster than the previous system. For commercial products, the ROI from usability engineering would come primarily from increased sales and reduced support calls. For example, Wixon and Jones (1996) describe an 80% increase in product revenues which was attributed in part to an improved user interface.

The ROI for usability engineering is relatively easy to assess for an internal corporate product where clear before-and-after studies can be conducted. Assessing the ROI of commercial products is more difficult since a direct link between usability engineering and sales is harder to establish (Nielsen, 1993). Karat (1994) provides a detailed example of how to calculate the expected return of usability engineering activities.

27.5.2 Planning the Usability Engineering Effort

A clear usability engineering plan represents a blueprint for work and thus serves to clarify definitions, roles and responsibilities before the project begins. The usability engineering plan answers the key questions:

- How much time and resources will be devoted to usability?
- How will usability engineering tasks be shared throughout the product team?
- How will the results be communicated to members who don't participate directly?
- What are the most opportune times for certain usability activities?
- How will each step complement the subsequent step?

What is a Usability Engineering Plan?

The usability engineering plan is a key document in the engineering process. The outline for a typical plan contains the following information:

1. Usability testing and design activities that will occur during the development process
2. The general goals for the product as a whole and for each test
3. The resources required for usability engineering activities
4. The types of tests that will be employed and when they will be completed
5. Who will be in the tests and who will conduct the tests

6. The kind of data you will collect
7. The methods of analysis and presentation of the data

The usability engineering plan is a deliverable that should be reviewed by the entire product team to ensure that the needs of everyone on the team are being met. Product managers can use the plan as input into the overall development schedule. Members of the development team can use the plan to schedule their work. The entire team can review and modify the usability engineering plan until a specific cut-off date.

The usability engineering plan should be integrated into the overall product development plan and agreed to by development managers. Usability engineers beginning work with new product teams may want to start with usability engineering plans that are not threatening to development managers in terms of time and other resources. Some practitioners of usability engineering recommend setting only a few usability goals that are generated and shared by the entire development team, and conducting simple usability tests that will generate quick results.

For each activity in the usability engineering plan, a more detailed test plan is required. This detailed test plan for each activity is reviewed and approved by the development team.

A successful usability engineering effort produces data when it is needed during the development process. In the most successful projects (Wixon and Jones, 1996), the usability work is tightly integrated into the development plan. Mayhew (1992) provides a detailed description of how usability engineering activities mesh with other development activities like the development of business plans, functional specifications, architectural design, coding, and customer delivery.

While Mayhew's description has heuristic value, she notes it does not readily indicate the iterative and recursive nature of the design process. Mayhew's comparison of the software development process and the user interface design process follows the waterfall model where each phase of product development follows from the previous phase in a one-way cascade. Product development is much more dynamic. Requirements, user profiles, and task descriptions change constantly in most development projects with major revelations often forcing substantial changes in product design.

Models that fit better with the dynamic nature of product development include the modified waterfall model where there are feedback loops between steps in the process and Boehm's (1988) spiral model. In the spiral model there is a continuous and iterative cycle of specification, goal setting, testing, analysis, and redesign. As the development process proceeds, the design iterations focus on smaller and smaller design issues. The spiral model meshes well with the iterative nature of usability engineering.

27.5.3 Issues and Pitfalls in Selling Usability Engineering and Developing a Usability Engineering Plan

Time and Budgets

New usability engineers should start with small, inexpensive studies that have a high probability of providing immediately useful data such as:

- Direct observation of usability problems
- Overall user performance
- Rank ordering of problems and difficulties

Smaller studies are easier to design and run, allow for more users to be tested, and provide the basis for more elaborate tests. In addition, simple reporting of results with an emphasis on providing direct access to user performance through descriptive statistics and anecdotes or videotape is often more desirable than lengthy complex reports (Hackos, 1995).

Ehrlich and Rohn (1994) suggest that usability engineers provide feedback within one day of test completion. This "quick feedback" should focus on obvious or frequent problems (the problems that everyone had in the test) and whether the usability goals were met. Development teams appreciate this quick feedback and rapid delivery of test results removes the common objection that "usability engineering takes too much time".

Usability engineers must follow through on their commitments to deliver the results by a specified date or lose credibility. A practical tip is to block out time (no meetings!) immediately after a usability test for analyzing and reporting test data.

What Can You Do To Make The Development Team Receptive To The Usability Engineering Process?

First, get the development team involved in setting the product goals, and reviewing the tasks used in usability tests. Second, ensure that all testing methods are empirical and open to observation and verification. Open, empirical methods can short circuit opinion wars. Finally, get members of the product team to observe testing sessions. Seeing users struggle while working on realistic tasks tends to orient teams toward real problems and reasonable solutions rather than endless debates about hypothetical problems.

Engineering management often has concerns about time and cost. These can be addressed by the scalability of usability engineering methods. Some usability engineers test 3 to 5 users in a few days, while other usability engineers may test large numbers of users in modern usability labs. In addition the testing can be conducted with a minimum impact on development time by the use of methods like one-day reports on major problems and whether usability goals were met, videotaped highlights of testing sessions, and summary analyses for team members who could not view testing sessions.

A major challenge for the usability engineer is getting the team to buy into the goal-setting process. Goal setting is more effective when done with a cross-functional team that includes product marketing, development, and potential customers and users. Like other aspects of usability engineering, the goal setting process is scaleable with the simplest method being that the usability engineer proposes a set of goals and metrics which are reviewed by the development team. A more complex approach to usability engineering involves benchmarking the major competitors to establish usability goals and metrics. The best approach is to go directly to users and to study their work using field methods (Whiteside, Bennett, and Holtzblatt, 1988; Wixon and Ramey, 1996). Field data provide task and goal information that can be used to design more realistic usability goals and testing scenarios.

What Does It Cost To Do Usability Engineering?

The cost of doing usability engineering can be divided into fixed costs which can be applied to a large number of usability studies and variable costs which are assessed for each usability study (Ehrlich and Rohn, 1994). The fixed costs generally deal with creating an infrastructure for usability testing and analysis. The infrastructure can include many elements. For example, formal usability labs with one-way mirrors, video and sound mixers, and sophisticated video editors, and a dedicated staff represent luxury usability testing. A fully equipped lab may cost several hundred thousand dollars. Formal labs may lack realism, but they have publicity value (lab tours for visiting customers are popular), allow multiple observers during testing, and serve as a hub for usability activities.

An inexpensive alternative is a portable usability lab. Portable usability labs can consist of a portable computer and a 8mm camcorder for about $5,000 or self-contained units for around $30,000 (Nielsen, 1993). Portable labs allow testing to occur almost anywhere and the more expensive portable units provide many of the capabilities of formal, permanent labs.

Major variable costs of usability engineering include:

- The loaded costs of usability engineers and consultants
- Administrative costs (locating and scheduling participants can consume many hours)
- Software engineers' time
- Software and hardware to support a specific test
- Supplies (for example, videotapes, transparencies, furniture for the lab)
- Travel to and from customer sites for task analysis or testing
- Compensation for participants

Bias and Mayhew (1994) provide detailed guidance for pricing usability engineering activities.

What Level Of Management Support Do I Have?

Some level of management support is required for effective usability engineering. Basically, management at some level must "buy into" a goal setting and testing process. Sources of resistance to usability engineering are often rooted in the inability or unwillingness to make decisions early in the development process. Or more accurately, the reluctance to make these decisions explicit. A product really cannot be developed without some notion of who the users are and how they will use the product. At the same time, the idea that such decisions must be explicit, recorded, and acted on, may encounter resistance. The failure to set any kind of usability goals at the outset of a product can be a useful warning sign that support for usability is not a development priority.

In addition to management support, there may be other resources that the usability engineer can draw on. These include members of the engineering team, writers, editors, customer support, and quality assurance specialists. Members of these groups are often omitted from the early stages of planning and welcome being included in a usability engineering effort. These "usability supporters" often have insights into usability issues through their attempts to describe complex procedures in product documentation, their interactions with customers, or their in-depth knowledge of the product.

How Much Must I Know About the Product?

At least two factors determine the level of knowledge about the product that the usability engineer must have to be effective. The first factor is the level of involvement of other members of the product team. If other members of the product team are highly involved, then the burden on the usability engineer may be reduced. The second factor is the process used in addressing the usability problems that are uncovered during testing. In some cases, the usability engineer may be intimately involved in developing solutions to usability problems. In these cases, an in-depth knowledge of the product and its underlying implementation may be essential. In other cases, the redesign is left to the other members of the development team and the knowledge required of the usability engineer is minimal.

The degree of knowledge may also be related to the number of products that a usability engineer is actively working on. When working on large numbers of products, the usability engineer must rely more heavily on others for product knowledge.

Some knowledge of the product is required to establish credibility and to set realistic usability goals. This can be done with the product team and often provides a good environment for learning about a product. Another method for gaining knowledge is to sit in on training classes for an earlier version of the product. The questions asked during training classes may provide some clues about usability issues and also the types of people who will use the product.

Determining what the product is supposed to do from the actual users is a good way to learn about the details of the product's features, workflow, and interface. The development of a task for testing requires not only understanding the general purpose of the product, but also a translation of those purposes into specific tasks, procedures, and results. It also requires knowing what kind of tasks the product will support at a given stage of development. Again this is best done in close cooperation with the development team. Finally, when suggesting solutions, the usability engineer needs to know something about what is possible.

A usability engineer's knowledge of the product domain is a key ingredient in establishing credibility with developers. Users and developers might provide the most important information about a product; however, there are other useful techniques for gathering product information. Reviewing the documentation, reading reviews in computer journals or internal memos, talking with support personnel, reviewing customer feedback in defect (bug) tracking databases, and using the product are other important techniques for understanding the product space. Reviews of commercial products are particularly helpful because they often highlight usability issues, discuss common user tasks, and sometimes even present the results of usability testing.

One danger of learning too much about a product or getting deep into the developer's thinking is that overlearning may make it hard to see new possibilities. Mayhew and Bias (1994) note that users who become integral members of a product team may suffer from a "hostage" effect where they slowly adopt the beliefs of the developers. The same thing can happen to usability engineers who are closely integrated with a development team. Usability engineers involved in design as well as evaluation need to periodically refresh their thinking and test their biases by interacting with users.

What Is My Role In Relation to the Development Team?

There are three basic roles that a usability engineer can play in the development of products: contributor from outside the engineering team, design collaborator, and technology transfer agent. The external contributor is called in to answer specific questions about a product and conduct independent investigations. Contributors from outside the development team may be corporate or external usability consultants. Usability engineers in this role often receive calls late in the development cycle from managers who are getting lambasted about their products' usability. The external consultant role often lacks the continuity needed for the iterative usability engineering process.

The design collaborator, unlike the external consultant, is a part of the development team and would be involved in most stages of development including:

- Defining requirements and usability attributes
- Developing and testing prototypes
- Providing design recommendations
- Conducting follow-up studies with users

This role provides continuity and greater possibilities for iterative design than the external consultant role.

Design collaborators face a conflict because they are asked to be integral members of the product team as well as user advocates. Design collaborators must be extremely good communicators since they will constantly be negotiating about what problems must be addressed and what the best solution is for each problem.

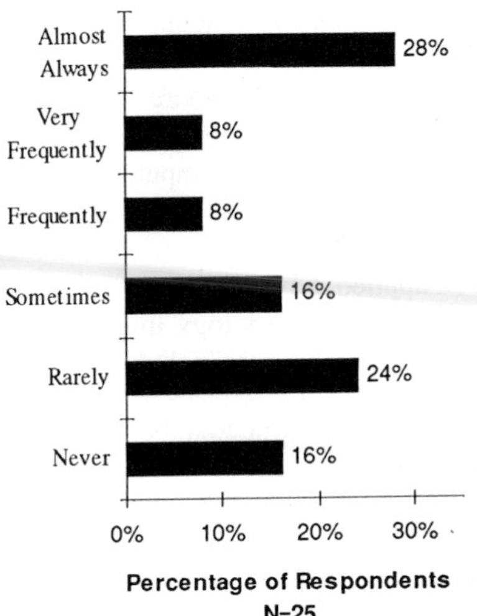

Figure 2: How often did our respondents work on projects with a user profile?

The last role is that of technology transfer agent. In this role, the usability engineer's goal is to teach the development team how to do usability engineering and then let them do it. This training may be in the form of seminars, classes, or an apprenticeship where the transfer agent shifts from collaborator to external consultant as the development team learns how to do usability engineering. For small usability groups in large corporations, the role of technology transfer is critical, since a small group may not be able to handle all the requests for work.

A technology transfer agent must make development teams aware of their biases about users and their work. One model of technology transfer is to have the usability group train usability evangelists in each product team. These evangelists (who could be software developers, quality assurance testers, or information designers) would promote, plan, and execute usability engineering activities. Since usability evangelists would have other duties, access to full-time usability engineers who can provide tips, up-to-date references, and help on specialized tasks like selecting a portable lab or determining what statistics, is important (Mrazek and Rafeld, 1992).

27.6 How Do I Set Usability Goals?

Usability goals are essential to a successful usability engineering effort. The definition of usability goals is a six step process:

1. Specify and categorize the users.
2. Conduct a task analysis.
3. Determine which usability attributes are relevant.
4. Decide on a measuring instrument.
5. Decide what measures will be taken from the measuring instrument.
6. Set performance levels for each usability attribute.

We will describe each step in detail.

27.6.1 Specifying Who the Users Are

The first step in defining usability goals is to identify the different categories of users. This categorization results in a user profile that describes classes of users and important user characteristics. Figure 2 shows how often our survey respondents worked on projects with an explicit user profile. Thirty-six percent of our sample "almost always" or "very frequently" worked on projects with a user profile. Twenty-four percent "sometimes" or "frequently" worked on projects with a user profile. Forty percent "rarely" or "never" worked on projects that had a user profile.

A common categorization for user profiles puts all users of a particular system into two categories - novice and expert. The goals for a novice user could be quite different than those for an expert user. Novices are curious, but afraid to make mistakes and reluctant to ask for help because they lack conceptual understanding of the products. On the other hand, experts or power users have a thorough grounding of product concepts, hate to waste time, and want shortcuts to make their work more efficient (Hackos, 1994).

A more useful categorization is suggested by Hackos (1994) who divides users into five categories:

- Novices
- Occasional users
- Transfer users (users who already know how to use one system, and are learning to use a new one)
- Experts
- Rote users (users who follow instructions, but do not understand the concepts underlying a computer system)

Many products must accommodate more than one of these categories so a usability specification could have multiple attributes (for example, ease of learning for novices, efficiency for experts, and number of errors for transfer users).

Beyond these fairly generic classifications, one needs to specify users for a particular market segment, for example, "Chemical Engineers with XXX level of experience". Such a definition is the basis for recruiting participants.

In some situations you must clearly distinguish users from customers. In corporate environments, customers of a product may be different from the users of that product. Although usability engineering is traditionally directed to understanding the needs of the user, in principle it could be extended to customers as well.

Where the market segment is well defined, one could begin with precise definitions like "chemical engineers" and then work "backward" to define important characteristics like amount of education or experience with similar products. Finally, you can proceed with fairly unrefined specifications of who the users are, but this increases the risk of the development effort.

Usability goals should reflect the characteristics of a representative sample of the different categories of users. User and workplace characteristics that can affect usability goals include:

- Frequency of use of a product
- Mandatory versus optional use of a product
- The type of product
- Educational background
- How many other similar products they have used
- Amount of training on the product and computers in general
- The number of interruptions in the environment
- The consequences of errors

A software product for making slide presentations might focus on ease of learning rather than efficiency since most users of presentation graphics tools are occasional users and seldom become experts. In contrast, users of air traffic control software receive months of training, use the software every day, and will become experts. Air traffic control software must be designed for maximum efficiency and errorless performance.

27.6.2 Conducting a Task Analysis

Once a user profile is defined, task analysis should be used to determine the major tasks and their frequency. Task analysis can also provide information on:

- The flow of work for an individual and the flow among different individuals
- Primary objects used in the work
- Workarounds in the current system
- Corporate and individual goals
- Exceptions from normal work flow (Nielsen, 1993)

This chapter won't go into depth about task analysis. There are significant discussions of task analysis elsewhere (Diaper, 1989; Drury, Paramore, Van Cott, Grey, and Corlett, 1987). We will adopt Landauer's (1995) precept that task analysis for computer systems is a "loose collection of formal and informal techniques for finding out what the job is to which the system is going to be applied, how it is done now, what role the current and planned technology might play." These formal and informal techniques include:

- Observing users in their environments
- Conducting Contextual Inquiry
- Reviewing existing business records
- Learning the job
- Conducting surveys
- Conducting time and motion studies
- Interviewing subject matter experts
- Leading focus groups

It is important to remember that at the early stages of product development a task analysis need not go into detail about the steps required to complete the task – a hierarchical decomposition is not needed. Rather what is needed is a set of high level scenarios that characterizes what users are trying to achieve. More detailed tasks analyses can be applied during the product development cycle. Theories and practical applications of scenarios are discussed by Carroll (1995).

27.6.3 Defining Usability Attributes

Usability attributes are characteristics of a product that can be measured in some quantitative way. General usability attributes include (Hix and Hartson, 1993; Nielsen, 1993; Rubin, 1994; Casaday and Rainis, 1996):

- Usefulness
- Learnability (initial performance)
- Efficiency (long-term performance)
- Error rates
- Memorability (ease of remembering after a period of disuse)
- First impressions
- Advanced feature usage
- Satisfaction or likability
- Flexibility (the extent to which the product can be applied to different kinds of tasks)
- Evolvability (how well does the system adapt to changes in user expertise)

Table 3. Usability Attributes Derived from Hypothetical User and Task Data

User Characteristics	User Environments:	User Tasks	Important Usability Attributes
• Manager in large health care product company • College educated; Significant computer experience • Highly motivated	• Superior technical support • High pay • High pressure, many people depend on you for quick response	• Supporting decisions • Accessing large databases	• Satisfaction • Error rates • Efficiency of use
• Clerk in a large financial corporation • High school education • Limited training	• Limited support • Low pay • Many interruptions during the day • Hierarchical organization	• Many different tasks including: typing memos, keeping calendars, electronic filing, out purchase requests...	• Satisfaction • Ease of learning
• Network manager of a mid-size corporation • Superior knowledge of computing system	• Many crises during the day • Many users on the system • Tight training budget	• Installs many products each week • Answers questions for many products	• Efficiency • Ease of installation • Satisfaction • Consistency among products

Usability attributes are part of the ISO Standard 9241. This standard, which is still undergoing revision, states that usability should be described and measured by the following attributes (Smith, 1996):

- System Effectiveness – To what extent can users achieve specified goals in a particular work setting?
- Efficiency – How much effort is required to meet usability goals?
- Satisfaction – How comfortable and acceptable do users find the system?

After important usability attributes are determined, they must be operationalized, be assigned quantitative performance levels, and be combined into a usability specification, the fundamental document for usability engineers.

27.6.4 Creating a Usability Specification

A usability specification is created by transforming general usability attributes like ease of learning into specific attributes that reflect the user's work context. Usability attributes relevant to a usability specification emerge from the task analysis and knowledge of the user.

Table 3 lists usability attributes that emerged from a hypothetical user profile and task analysis. Efficiency is an important usability attribute for high volume tasks like filling out invoices. Error rate is a critical attribute for data entry personnel, operators of process control systems or for police using bomb disposal equipment. Ease-of-initial-use would be critical for automated banking machines since they are used infrequently by a wide variety of users. Satisfaction would be an important usability attribute for many systems since it affects user morale, turnover rates, and training. Landauer (1995) notes that the introduction of a new computer system, especially in the guise of business re-engineering can have a disastrous effect on user morale and satisfaction

The setting of usability goals should be a collaborative effort. In our survey we asked respondents who was involved in setting usability goals. The results show that many stakeholders in the development process are involved. Table 4 shows that in our sample, the most frequently cited participants in goal setting were: developers, product managers, marketing, and customers or end users.

Once a set of usability attributes is defined, a measuring instrument is needed to provide values for each usability attribute. Hix and Hartson (1993) define measuring instrument as "... a description of the method for providing values for a particular usability attribute." A measuring instrument in usability engineering always provides quantitative values for a at-

Table 4. Who sets usability goals?

Participants	% of Respondents (N = 25)
Development	60
Product management	52
Marketing	36
Customers or end users	28
Customer support	20
Other	20
Information provider	16

tribute. The values can either be subjective (attitude or satisfaction data) or objective (time to complete a task or number of errors). Potential measuring instruments include:

- Benchmark tasks
- Questionnaires
- Data logs

More than one metric can be obtained from a measuring instrument (Hix and Hartson, 1993; Whiteside, Bennett, and Holtzblatt, 1988). For example, a benchmark task can yield all the following metrics:

- Time to complete a task
- Time to complete a task after a specified period of time away from a system (Nielsen, 1993, p. 32)
- Number of subtasks completed
- Number of errors per unit of time
- Time spent in errors versus time spent in productive work
- Number of steps required to complete a task
- Number of negative reactions to the system
- Number of times the user accesses the product's documentation or a simulated support line.
- Number of commands/icons remembered after task completion

Subjective measuring instruments like questionnaires can also provide more than a single metric. A questionnaire might have subsets of questions that relate to different usability attributes.

Once specific measuring instruments and metrics are chosen for each usability attribute, performance levels must be set. These levels define acceptable user performance with a product. These performance levels can be phrased in absolute terms like "a user should be able to complete task X with no more than 2 errors". They can also be put in relative terms like "a user of Product A should be able to complete task X with fewer errors than a person using Product B for an equivalent task".

Where do the values for performance levels come from? Some possible sources are:

- Previous usability testing
- Competitive usability testing or analysis
- Expert task times
- Data from corporate groups that have contact with customers (sales, marketing, technical support)
- Current business practices
- Field observation of users
- Informed opinion

Some samples of metrics and levels from our survey include:

- Time to find information for diagnosis (medical system)
- Time to complete a task
- Number of errors on a task
- Number of divergent paths chosen by experts
- Percentage of test participants who could use an interface object successfully
- Subjective rating of old and new system
- 30% improvement in the time required to install software over a previous usability test
- Product can be installed in 5 minutes without any outside help
- Small business owner is able to create a mailing list in 1/2 hour
- Biologist should be able to find an enzyme based reaction in under 1 hour

Whiteside, Bennett, and Holtzblatt (1988) suggest that four performance levels be set for each attribute. The current level is the performance of users with the product. If there is no current product, the current level might be the time required to complete a task manually or the number of errors that occur in the manual operation. If the proposed product is similar to competitive products, the current level might even be determined by competitive benchmarking.

After determining the current performance level on each usability attribute, the minimum performance level must be set. This is not the worst performance that might occur, it is the worst acceptable performance (Hix and Hartson, 1993). The minimum performance level should be greater than the current level since the new product should improve on the old one unless the new product is substantially cheaper to purchase and use (Dix, Finlay, Abowd, and Beale, 1993). If the minimum performance level is not met for each usability attribute, then the product would theoretically, not be ready to ship. Meeting the minimum acceptable value may satisfy the usability goal for an attribute, but it does not exclude further usability work to ensure product competitiveness.

The planned level of performance is considered to be the target for unquestioned usability success. If this value is attained, no further usability work is warranted. Where do you get the planned levels? These levels can be based on the existing product, primary competitors, or input from surveys, focus groups, and other data sources. In some cases, especially for customized systems, the goals may be specified by the customer. For example, the specification for a new system to enter invoices might call for users to complete 20% more invoices per week, than the old system. Requirements, marketing documents and request for proposals are worth perusing because they often have statements that relate to usability levels. For example, several years ago, one of the authors noticed that the marketing literature for a code management program claimed that people would be working error free within two hours after installing the software. This same author learned from others that a two day training course was a necessity.

The optimal level is a level of performance that could be theoretically achieved under ideal circumstances. These circumstances might include additional funding, well-trained designers, developers, and usability engineers, and early and continuous user involvement. Setting an optimal level is consistent with the usability engineering process since it provides a target for future design iterations. However, one has to be cautious in setting optimal goals since an unrealistic value may be unsettling to developers and misunderstood by management.

Once you have taken all the previous steps, you can integrate the individual usability goals into a simple table which constitutes a usability specification. Table 5 shows a usability specification from Compaq corporation, (Purvis, et., Figure 3, p. 119 in Wiklund: Usability in Practice, 1994, reprinted with permission of Academic Press).

There are six critical points about the elements of this table:

1. The usability attributes are qualities that are important to the user.
2. The attributes are translated into operational measures.
3. The operational statement of the attributes requires that the engineering team consider users, their environments, and tasks.
4. Different attributes are measured through the use of different techniques. Some attributes are assessed by rating scales; others by formal benchmarking.
5. The attributes tend to be holistic, they relate to overall performance of the system and not to performance of individual system components or minor subtasks.
6. The usability attribute and specification of levels of performance constitute a specific usability goal.

How Often are Usability Goals Set in Practice?

In our survey of usability engineering, about 25% of respondents set usability goals in the majority of their projects. Thirty-two percent set goals for between 21 to 60% of their projects, while another 32% rarely set usability goals.

27.6.5 Issues and Pitfalls in Setting Usability Goals

How Many Usability Goals Should I Have?

The number of usability goals contained in a usability specification should not overwhelm the product team. While some of our colleagues believe that the mere existence of a usability specification is worthwhile, the intent of usability engineering is to test against quantitative goals. We endorse the advice of Hix and Hartson (1993) that usability engineers introduce development teams to a small usability specification where there are 2-3 clear goals that can be tested within resource constraints. These goals should focus on important and frequent tasks. As development teams accept the value of usability goals, more complex specifications can be generated.

What Happens if I Don't Test All the Goals?

The greatest impacts of usability engineering are related to the initial stages of goal setting. Even if you do no test at all, designing with a clearly stated usability goal is preferable to designing toward a generic goal of "easy and intuitive". Our best advice is to set a reasonable number of goals and try to measure all of them.

What Type of Goals Should I Set?

Goals should be based on aspects of the product that are critical to success (Redmond-Pyle and Moore, 1995). For example, a high-volume data-entry system

Table 5. Usability specification

Attribute	Measuring Instrument			Measuring Method	Unacceptable Level	Minimum Level	Planned Level	Best Case Level
SOFTWARE INSTALLATION								
User's perception of install difficulty	Difficulty	1 2 3 4 5 6 7	Easy	Average Rating	<4.0	4.0 to 5.0	5.0 to 6..0	> 6.0
User's satisfaction with install	Frustrating	1 2 3 4 5 6 7	Satisfying	Average Rating	<4.0	4.0 to 5.0	5.0 to 6..0	> 6.0
Ease of locating information	Difficult	1 2 3 4 5 6 7	Easy	Average Rating	<4.0	4.0 to 5.0	5.0 to 6..0	> 6.0
Terminology	Unclear	1 2 3 4 5 6 7	Clear	Average Rating	<4.0	4.0 to 5.0	5.0 to 6..0	> 6.0
Detail of help provided	Not Helpful	1 2 3 4 5 6 7	Helpful	Average Rating	<4.0	4.0 to 5.0	5.0 to 6..0	> 6.0
DOCUMENTATION								
Documentation	Unclear	1 2 3 4 5 6 7	Clear	Average Rating	<4.0	4.0 to 5.0	5.0 to 6..0	> 6.0
Ease of locating information	Difficult	1 2 3 4 5 6 7	Easy	Average Rating	<4.0	4.0 to 5.0	5.0 to 6..0	> 6.0
Terminology used	Unclear	1 2 3 4 5 6 7	Clear	Average Rating	<4.0	4.0 to 5.0	5.0 to 6..0	> 6.0
OVERALL								
User's level of confidence to install and use utility	Not confident	1 2 3 4 5 6 7	Confident	Average Rating	<4.0	4.0 to 5.0	5.0 to 6..0	> 6.0
Time in errors/Total Time (%)		All tasks		Average Percentage	>30%	30% to 20%	20% to 10%	<10%
Number of experimenter Interventions		All tasks		Average number of interventions per subject	>3.0	3.0 to 2.0	2.0 to 1.0	> 1.0
Successfully install and use		All tasks		Percent of successes	N/A	N/A	100%	N/A

should have a goal that deals with the rate of performance like the number of documents entered per day. A system that will be used occasionally, like a once-a-year budgeting system, should have goals that focus on ease of learning since most users will have to relearn the system every year. Products where errors can lead to catastrophes like control systems in oil refineries or avionics for keeping planes aloft should focus on error rates and performance.

There are some non-functional goals like safety and system performance that are related to usability. These can be part of a usability specification. One

Table 6: What percentage of respondents set usability goals?

Were Goals Set?	% of Respondents (N=25)
Yes	68
No	28
No Answer	4

Table 7: Goal setting by experience

Experience Level	No Goals	Goals
7 months to 6 years	50%	50%
6 to 10 years	9%	91%

could, for example, have a safety goal of no injuries and a performance goal of a maximum response time of less than 3 seconds (Dix, Finlay, Abowd, and Beale, 1993).

How Do I Avoid Setting Incorrect Goals?

There are a number of pitfalls that lead to incorrect goals. First, the usability attribute may not be relevant to the particular user category. Ease of learning, for example, may not be a relevant goal for a complex system like an airplane or the Space Shuttle where the users will get months of formal training. Similarly, efficiency may not be important for the kiosk software that gives people information about museum exhibits. Ease of initial learning is a critical attribute for most kiosks since most people are likely to be first time users and will never become experts. Second, the measuring instrument may not be appropriate. A poor choice of a task scenario for measuring efficiency may lead to erroneous results. Interviews with users in the field can ensure that the measurement instruments are realistic. Third, the performance levels of the attribute may not be set appropriately. Development teams may, for example, set lenient performance levels to avoid looking bad.

While there is no absolute guarantee of setting correct goals, the usability engineer is well advised to solicit active participation of members of the product team and to allow sufficient time for the goals to be developed, reviewed, and modified. Getting consensus from the entire product design team is essential if the goals are to be taken seriously (Smith and Siochi, 1995).

How Often Do Usability Engineers Set Usability Goals?

Results from our survey shows that a majority of our respondents did set usability goals. Table 6 shows that over 2/3rd of those surveyed do set some usability goals.

Goal setting varied by experience. As Table 7 shows, we found that our more experienced respondents were more likely to set goals than our inexperienced respondents.

27.6.6 Summary of Goal Setting

Usability goals bring objectivity, rigor, and consensus to the design and development process. Choosing attributes that characterize the usability of a system requires an understanding of users and their work. Performance levels for each attribute must be set that reflect the user profile; task type, frequency and criticality. Multiple goals are usually recommended to encompass the product's capabilities. Usability goals are combined to create a usability specification that is part of product requirements. Multiple goals can be tested in a single session. Products must be tested against the usability goals and meet a minimum performance level for each goal. If the minimum performance level is not met, then the product must undergo iterative design and testing until the goals are met. Though usability goals have been recommended for at least a decade, their use is far from universal. This puts usability practitioners at a disadvantage because there are no metrics like the number of bugs and response time, to determine when a product should ship.

27.7 Testing for Usability

27.7.1 What Are Usability Tests and How Do I Create Them?

A usability test is a procedure for determining whether the quantitative goals defined in the usability specification have been achieved. The term "test" is a broad term that encompasses any method for assessing whether goals have been met. A test could be a formal laboratory test or the collection of satisfaction data through mail or phone surveys. This section provides an overview of the testing process and its relationship to usability engineering goals. Dumas and Redish (1994) and Rubin (1994) provide specific information on the actual practice of usability testing.

Our approach to usability engineering is that testing requires clearly defined goals and tasks based on those goals. The basic steps of a usability test are:

1. Define a task.
2. Choose the test method and define the procedure.
3. Construct the test materials and collect the needed equipment.

4. Conduct a pilot test.
5. Recruit the test participants.
6. At the start of each test session explain the goals of the test and brief the participants about their rights.
7. Conduct the test session.
8. Thank and debrief the participants.
9. Perform any initial analysis.

Each of these steps will be discussed in turn.

Defining Tasks for Usability Testing

The tasks for a usability test are developed from the usability specification and the task analysis. Like usability goals, tasks can differ in their specificity. Testing can be based on holistic tasks where participants are simply shown a result and asked to reproduce it. For example, we tested drawing packages by simply giving users a picture and asking them to reproduce the picture. Tests of this nature are called **results-based** tests. In other cases, we defined specific subtasks for the participants to complete in sequence. A test which specifies a sequential set of subtasks is called a **process-based** test. For example, in a general office procedures task, we gave users the following instructions:

1. Get a list of all the available documents.
2. Read through the sales and inventory figures.
3. Consolidate the sales and inventory figures into a report, named **report.txt**.
4. Check the report to be sure it contains all the data.
5. Send the data to Jones.

In a process-based task, the steps are outlined. The task description carefully avoids using names of commands, menu items, or other objects which are part of the system being tested to avoid cueing the participants.

The critical factor in task creation is that the tasks must match the usability specification. Other factors which need to be considered when constructing a task are:

- What tasks will the system support in its current state?
- Should the tasks be independent or interdependent?
- How long will the test session take?

In the early stages of development, the system may be a paper prototype that presents only a minimum of critical functionality. Tasks at the paper prototype level cannot be too detailed and must focus only on high level functions and navigation. Later versions of the system may be represented by a working prototype that can simulate much of the functionality. Tasks with working prototypes can be much more detailed.

What kinds of tests the system will support depends not only on the system itself, but also on the test procedure. If the procedure allows the tester to intervene when a problem occurs, then it is possible to test unreliable or incomplete parts of a system. In addition, it may be necessary to clearly indicate to the users when they have succeeded in a subtask. In the example task, Jones might call and thank the participant for the message. While test procedures that allow intervention are helpful in getting feedback from unreliable and incomplete systems, the effect of the intervention (time spent telling the user what to avoid, for example) must be factored out of the results – a time consuming process.

In setting up a test session, a usability engineer must decide whether the different tasks in the session will depend on each other. Independent tasks offer one major advantage: participants are able to move on to a new task if they don't succeed at the current task. If tasks are dependent on one another, failing to complete a subtask can create problems for the subsequent subtasks and may require intervention before the test can proceed. The drawback with the use of independent tasks is that they may not be mutually exclusive in actual work environments. Testers need to consider whether the ease of creating independent tasks outweighs their potential lack of realism.

Test sessions tend to be fatiguing for both users and testers. It is rarely productive to have sessions last over 2 hours, except in special cases, such as a monitoring system where the usability attribute might be continued vigilance for an 8-hour shift. If a study is going to last for several hours, a rest break can be scheduled into the session.

The Test Method and Procedure

Like the task, the test procedure and the methods used are determined by the usability specification. While many sources provide inventories of usability methods (for example, Nielsen, 1993), a few simple questions can be used to choose a particular method:

1. What are the goals of the test?
2. How important is it to capture the user's thinking?
3. How important is it to match the user's work environment?
4. What measures are needed?
5. What practical considerations like time, effort, and accessibility to equipment need to be considered?

If performance or efficiency goals have been set, then the tester should minimize interaction with the test participant. Testers may allow the participant to struggle and not complete the task or any part of it. Strict non-intervention, while unfortunate for the user, provides the designer with critical data about the seriousness of each problem. In contrast, there are situations where the tester should interrupt the participant. For example, if a goal is defined as the "number of errors per task", then the tester should interrupt once it is clear that the user has made an error. Interruptions will prevent users from spending all their time in a single error and thus provide the design team with a more complete understanding of the possible errors.

Capturing the user's thinking can provide important clues for redesign. Techniques such as thinking aloud or having two people co-participate in a test generate more insights into the user's thinking than testing a person alone with instructions like "complete these tests as quickly and accurately as possible". Testers can also sit with the participant and ask probing questions to uncover the participant's thoughts. However, the tester should avoid prompting users how to complete the task or how the system works.

In another approach, critical incident data can be collected in a test session (del Galdo, E. M., Williges, R. C., Williges, B. H., and Wixon, D. R., 1995) to provide the design team with insights about the participant's thinking. In all approaches where users reflect on their work, performance data can be collected by subtracting out the time spent in conversation and using the remainder as a rough performance indicator. While research psychologists may shudder, such "rough and ready" techniques work well in practice.

A powerful technique for gathering both performance data and clues for redesign is to videotape the test session and then review the test session with the participant. This "retrospective testing" provides for the clear collection of performance data during the initial videotaping. The follow-up review of the videotape provides an opportunity for user reflection about the test experience. There is evidence that participants can produce more insights by reviewing their taped performance than they can during the test. Retrospective testing, however, can be time consuming.

Similarity to the user's work environment is a final consideration in choosing methods and procedures. Again how one approaches this problem is derived from the usability goals. For example if one's goal is to be 20% better than a competitor or a previous version, then the test environment must match the original environment to evaluate the comparison system. If absolute goals, like completing five data-entry forms in an hour, have been specified, then the match to the work environment is more flexible. One approach that might mitigate the trade-off between realism and pristine data is to create a "field laboratory" where participants would hear office noise and be interrupted occasionally. This approach has been used to improve the ecological validity of psychology studies while still retaining an environment where performance data can be collected.

There are two general classes of measures that can be collected during usability testing: direct behavioral indicators and reflective responses. Examples of direct behavioral indicators are: time to complete a task, number of errors, and number of calls to a support line. Reflective responses are verbal responses provided spontaneously or in reaction to specific or general questions from the tester. They are often called subjective impressions. Reflective responses can be collected during or after the test. Sometimes reflective data can contradict behavioral data. Nielsen (1993) notes that users' subjective impressions of ease of use may be more influenced by peak difficulty rather than average difficulty. This peak difficulty bias may lead to discrepancies between actual performance and subjective ratings of performance. The use of both subjective and objective measures may provide deeper insights into a user's perception of a product's usability.

Usability methods can be mixed in a segmented test. For example, a performance test can be followed by a thinking out loud test using similar tasks. Multiple test procedures and various metrics can be mixed to assess a wide variety of usability goals and accommodate various practical concerns. In general, multiple procedures and assessments will make the overall test process more complex and difficult to administer. However, mixing of methods allows the tester to learn the maximum from each participant.

Test Materials and Equipment

This can be the most straightforward part of the testing process, but leaving it to the last minute can greatly increase the risk to the test. Develop the materials and tests several days or weeks before the test is conducted. Computer systems are notorious for failing to work in new environments, so they need to be thoroughly checked. Tests materials include not only the task descriptions and final questionnaires but also participant release forms, statements of informed consent, and non-disclosure forms that must be reviewed and signed. Testers should create a checklist of all the forms, supplies, and test materials and use the checklist for every test session.

Pilot Testing

An initial pilot test should be conducted with users and with members of the design team. The pilot test should ascertain that:

- Necessary data and applications are loaded on the computer
- All forms are ready
- All logging and observation systems are working
- The tasks can be accomplished within the allotted time
- The test system can be reset between test session
- Everyone on the observation team is aware of the testing procedures and rules for dealing with participants (for example, no laughing in the lab, don't turn the lights on in the observation room, don't wear white clothing behind a one-way mirror)

Sufficient time between the pilot test and the actual tests should be allowed to make changes in the test materials, tasks, or procedures. Our advice is to leave at least one day between the pilot testing and the beginning of the actual test.

Recruiting Test Participants

The usability plan defines who should participate. Usability engineers should plan adequate time and administrative support for finding appropriate users. Recruiting the appropriate users can be time consuming, taking from ½ to 6 hours for each external participant (Ehrlich and Rohn, 1994). The most significant questions for recruiting users are often logistical ones such as:

- Are the participants current or new customers?
- Are the participants available locally?
- Is there a large pool of participants (administrative support people) or a very select pool (nuclear engineers)?
- Do the participants have time available?
- Can you offer incentives?

The most difficult people to recruit are users who are not part of the existing customer base, who are distant, and who have limited time. There are a number of creative ways around this problem such as conducting remote usability tests, recruiting through the Internet, and providing large incentives (money, tickets to popular events, or free copies of software when that is possible). Fortunately the number of test participants can be relatively small. In general 5-10 users are often more than enough to establish a clear baseline of performance and to uncover many usability problems (Nielsen, 1993). In addition, external search firms can be hired solely for the purpose of recruiting participants at a premium price.

Explaining the Test Procedure

Some parts of the test procedure are invariant. Participants must always be informed of their rights as participants. This includes the right to leave at any time and the right to be informed of the purpose of the test. Often this is best accomplished with a Statement of Informed Consent which outlines these rights. This statement should also cover how the data will be used and who will see it. Any recording must be disclosed. If video or audio recording is used, the participant should sign a release form. Such a form should describe who will see or hear the data and how the data will be used. If recorded information is used in any way that is not described in the release form, then additional permission from the participant is required.

Non-disclosure forms may be used to prevent premature release of information about the software (and particularly its problems) by participants. These are a supplement to the release and consent forms, not a substitute for them.

The usability tester should make every possible effort to convince the participants that their performance reflects on the system and not them. Statements like, "this is an early version of the system and we are looking to improve it" and "don't worry if you don't complete all the tasks" are helpful. The participants should be aware of the general structure of the test, what they will be asked to do, how they will get their instructions, and how the tester or others will interact with them. The approximate duration of the test should be disclosed. Informed consent forms should be written in plain English and not in legalese. The absolute rule of testing is that the participants should leave the test session feeling no worse then when they arrived and better if possible.

Conducting the Test Sessions

Test sessions vary in their degree of formality. When user performance data (such as time to complete a task) is being collected the procedures tend to be more formal and the tester will interrupt less. Of course, there are some limits to a "hands off" approach. If the system fails in some way then the tester must intervene and fix the problem. If the participant is clearly upset, then the tester may need to ameliorate the distress. Such severe cases may result in a re-evaluation of the test approach and the product strategy.

Often development teams may wish to watch usability tests. This can be an effective method for establishing credibility and getting changes made. However, when team members watch testing they must refrain from coaching the participants, distracting them, or offering rationalizations of the existing design. The basic purpose of the test is to assess user reaction and performance. Implementation and design discussions are appropriate only after the data are analyzed.

If the tester has chosen a method like "think aloud" or "co-participation", it may be necessary to remind the participants of the procedure as they work. For example the tester may remind participants in a think aloud study to verbalize their thoughts with statements like (Dumas and Redish, 1994; Nielsen, 1993):

- "Could you tell us what you are thinking right now?"
- "Why did you just do that?"
- "Is that what you expected to happen?"

Nielsen (1993) provides some research results indicating that think aloud studies may actually improve the performance of participants and cautions that this effect may bias performance data.

Thanking and Debriefing the Participants

An appropriate debriefing can provide the design team with critical data and reduce the stress of the test. Some debriefings can be an extension of the data gathering. For example, participants may share their impressions with the design team during a short discussion after the testing. If a video tape was taken, then the participant may review it with the design team and reflect on the good and bad points of the product. When multiple participants are tested at the same time they may brought together and urged to share their impressions. Sufficient time should be provided at the conclusion of a test for the participants to say how they felt about the system. Any questions that the participants have about the use of the data should be answered. The tester should reaffirm that the data will be confidential or anonymous. If the testing was done in a formal usability lab, the tester should offer participants a short tour of the observation room. The observation team should be aware of such a possibility and a protocol worked out for making introductions and not overwhelming participants. Every effort should be made to make the experience a positive one for participant and observers.

27.7.2 Issues and Pitfalls in Usability Testing

There are several potential issues and pitfalls associated with usability testing in the usability engineering framework.

The Goals are too ambitious or there are too many Goals

It is easy to set many goals at the beginning of a project, but it may be very difficult to test all of them. Clearly each goal does not require a separate test. At the same time, more goals may result in more elaborate test procedures and more data to analyze. In practice, usability engineers often test a simple set of performance goals based on the time to complete a task, or number of errors, and a number of subjective goals which can be assessed at the end of a test.

Unworkable Test Procedure

The more complex the procedure the greater the risk it will fail. The test process itself could be too complex for users to understand. It could be too elaborate to carry out. In general our experience is that simple modular tests are best. Unworkable test procedures often emerge during pilot testing with representative users.

Unsupportive Team

Defining a test procedure without the active participation of the development team is a formula for disaster. When unexpected or disappointing results occur, it is important that questions about the validity of the task or testing method be minimized. Planning the tests with the team and keeping them informed of the results will increase the likelihood that results will be accepted and incorporated into a redesign. During iterations of testing on a product, make sure that positive feedback about the product is presented to the team. Too often usability engineers have a negativity bias and forget to highlight what is positive about a product.

The Test Cannot Cover The Whole System

Except for very simple systems it is impossible to test every aspect of the system. The choices involved in creating a test should be addressed when the goals are

Table 8: Activity matrix showing what tasks are performed by different categories of users.

User Groups	Task 1	Task 2	Task 3	Task 4	Task 5	...	Task N
Data entry clerk	x	x			x		x
Group manager	x	x	x	x	x	x	x
Division manager	x	x	x	x	x	x	
Auditor						x	
Support							x
Data analyst		x			x		x
.....							

set. The activity matrix described earlier represents one way to produce modular tests which can be customized. Representative parts of the system may be tested to gain insight about the overall system performance. In deciding on which parts of a system to test, ask the following questions:

- Are there parts of the system that everyone uses?
- Are there new features with high visibility?
- Are there features that are rarely used, but involve mission-critical outcomes?
- Are there old features being updated?
- Are there parts of the system about which the design team has reservations or concerns?
- Are there parts of the system that involve safety or liability concerns (for example, a feature for setting the intensity of X rays or the automatic dosage of drugs)?
- Are there features which are highlighted in the marketing literature?

Within the framework established by the goals of the system you can use a number of methods to choose specific tasks to maximize the value of the test session. One specific method for determining what tasks to include in a test is the **activity matrix** which lists user groups, tasks, and which group performs each task. Table 8 is an sample activity matrix. Use the activity matrix to determine what tasks are used across user groups and which tasks are specific to a particular user group.

The activity matrix allows testers to target tasks to specific classes of users and also to see what tasks are common across categories of users. Thus, a test could be set up that focuses on tasks that are done by almost everyone or on tasks that are only done by a few, but that have serious consequences.

Participants Do Not Show Up

The tester may plan to have one or two backup participants who can fill in for participants who fail to arrive at a session. A reminder the day before the scheduled test can reduce the likelihood of no-shows. If a group of participants are from one site, good word of mouth feedback about how much "fun" the test was can be helpful.

27.7.3 Summary of the Usability Testing Process

The design and conduct of usability tests are based on the usability goals set earlier. The choice of task and test method, and the approach to debriefing all follow from the goals. Task definition and test method are also affected by logistical concerns.. Recruiting participants is often a difficult logistical issue and requires careful planning. Throughout the test process the participants must be kept informed of their rights and every effort must be made to protect their self esteem and privacy.

27.8 Analyzing and Communicating the Results

Once the usability test has been completed, the next task is to analyze and communicate the results. The analysis and communication can take many forms. These forms vary in degree of sophistication, amount of work required, involvement of the development team, and level of quantification.

27.8.1 Simple Usability Engineering Analyses

Usability testing usually provides three types of data: quantitative data derived from observation of participants, qualitative data about usability problems, and survey data (scores on usability questionnaires). These data answer three general questions:

- Were the quantitative usability goals met?
- What are the usability problems with this product (or environment)?

- How important were these problems?

A simple analysis is the direct assessment of whether the usability goals were met. This often involves the straightforward collection of simple measures like subjective ratings, degree of task success, or overall time to complete a task. If the system has met the specified usability goals, no further analysis is required for this particular project.

A list of the usability problems associated with a product can be generated simply by reviewing the notes or recordings of a session and pulling out incidents where the user made an error, was inefficient in a task, had to look up information, or was unsure about what to do next. These problems can be grouped by frequency of occurrence, product component (dialog box, menu, window), criticality, or other category.

Perhaps the simplest and most direct form of analysis and communication involves immersing the development team in the collection of the results. For example, the usability round tables conducted at Lotus (Butler and Ehrlich, 1994) involved having the team watch the test, record and organize problems and design ideas, and proceed directly to redesign. This technique is fast and efficient and insures consensus about the understanding of problems and their prioritization. While just-in-time (JIT) analyses like usability round tables are appealing, they tend to be problem, rather than goal focused. The result of a JIT analysis is often a list of observed problems from a testing session arranged in some priority order rather than a set of values that can be compared to a goal in a usability specification. There is no formal impact analysis in a JIT study so the usability engineer cannot be certain how the problem affects the overall usability of the product. There are different techniques for categorizing qualitative data. A usability engineer could put each comment on a card and have members of the development team group the cards into conceptual categories. Another method that accomplishes the same purpose as the card sort is affinity diagramming. In affinity diagramming, each comment from a usability study is put on a Post-It® and stuck to a wall. Members of the development team then arrange the Post-Its into related groups and give a name to each group. If the cards or Post-its are coded by participant, it is possible to note how many people experienced a particular problem during a test and if one participant was contributing a noticeably larger number of comments than the others. One problem with qualitative analysis is establishing the unit of analysis. In a think aloud study, for example, where do you make the break between comments? The unit of analysis could be a particular theme, a sentence, a paragraph, or some other unit of utterance.

Once the usability problems are categorized, they must be prioritized. This prioritization can vary from a binary breakdown of "catastrophic" and "minor" problems to a continuous rating such as the time spent on a particular problem. Redmond-Pyle and Moore (1995) note that catastrophic problems fall into two categories: problems where the user fails to complete a task and problems where the user thinks that a task has been completed successfully, when in fact it was not. Minor problems are those that do not contribute to the task goal such as looking in the wrong menu for the necessary command. A common practice among usability professionals is to assign a priority of high, medium, or low based on a consensus of the observers. The consensus would be based on the number of times that users experienced the problem, the proportion of users who experience the problem, and the severity of the problem. A problem might be very common, but not have severe consequences (for example, a bad menu name draws users to choose the wrong menu, but the only consequence is some wasted time) or be uncommon and have severe consequences. With the limited number of participants usually available for usability tests, these judgments of problem severity are somewhat subjective.

27.8.2 Highlight Tapes

There are occasions where members of the development team are not always available to observe and categorize usability data as it is being collected. When this happens, videotape highlights of the problems encountered by users provide evidence to corroborate the usability engineer's list of problems and priorities. Highlight tapes are a powerful communication technique, however, the editing of tapes is time consuming – each hour of tape can take from 3 to 10 hours to analyze (Nielsen, 1993). Editing time can be reduced by keeping notes on a data logger about segments that should be considered for inclusion in a highlight tape. In addition, the usability engineer can produce a "rough cut" by simply noting when problems occur on the raw data tape and then showing those selected sections to a design team. A sense of balance and objectivity can be achieved by including some features of the product that drew positive reviews from users. The length of the highlight tape is a function of both the audience and the intended message. If the audience is senior management and the intended message is to convey a sense of the problems with the system, then a

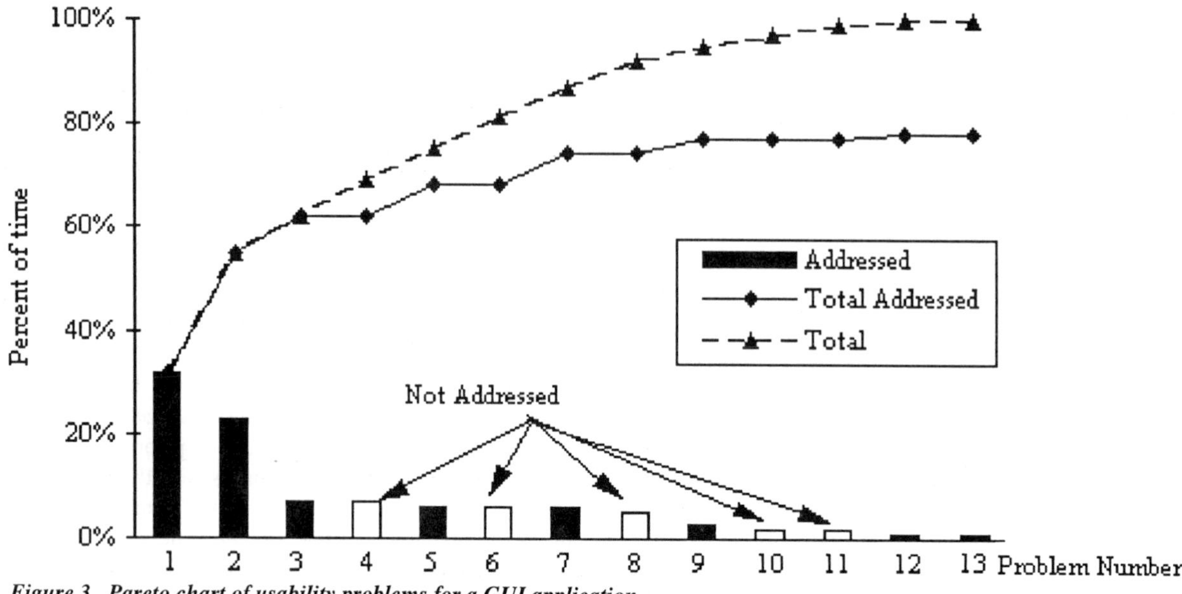

Figure 3. Pareto chart of usability problems for a GUI application

5 to 15 minute tape with key problem snippets would be appropriate. If the development team is invested in usability engineering, a 30 or 60 minute tape shown at a team meeting or lunchtime seminar is acceptable. If the intended result is to stimulate the design team to generate solutions then each snippet should be long enough to show how the user got into the problem and perhaps out of it. Videotape highlights, like usability roundtables, dramatize problems, but do not indicate in any quantitative way, the impact of the problem on the user's work.

If all the usability goals in a specification must be met, then the analysis becomes a pass-fail. More detailed analyses based on individual goals could include:

- A list of the frequency of each problem
- The amount of time spent in errors versus productive work
- The number of users who experienced a problem
- The number of steps required to complete each task
- The number of errors that occurred for each task
- Mean, median, or modal values and variability of questionnaire ratings

27.8.3 Pareto Charts and Impact Analysis

Perhaps the most powerful technique for making engineering trade-offs is the empirical impact analysis table combined with the Pareto chart (Deming, 1982). An impact analysis table shows the total effect of each usability problem on overall performance (Gilb, 1981). Within the impact analysis table, the number of instances (or time spent in) a particular problem occurs are summed to give a relative weighting for that problem. The Pareto chart is a visual extension of the impact analysis table. Arthur (1993) notes that Pareto analysis allows us to discern the 20% of problems that account for 80% of users' performance losses. Figure 3 is an example of a Pareto chart for a GUI application (Good, Spine, Whiteside, and George, 1986). The columns represent the percentage of time spent in a specific problem.

The chart is used to predict how much user performance would improve if certain interface problems are addressed. Pareto data provide an engineering team with the basis for trading off engineering resources required to fix a problem versus the predicted improvement in user performance.

In Figure 3, the engineering team chose to address 8 of 13 problems, including the top 3 (the problems chosen to be fixed are the black columns. On the basis of the data shown in the Pareto chart, a 22% improvement in user performance was predicted. This improvement would meet the minimal level of performance specified in the usability specification, and no further engineering resources would be spent.

The number of problems addressed by an engineering team depends on:

- How early the results are delivered
- How clear a solution is to the design team
- The interdependencies between the potential solutions and other product goals

Table 9. Problem solution table.

Rank	Problem	Impact on User Performance	Solutions	Chosen Solution	Estimated Engineering Cost	Resolution
1	User can't figure out how to modify the database	High	Move item to the main menu Provide a tip in the main window on startup	Move item to the main menu	30 minutes	Fix
2	Common error message is cryptic	High	Rewrite error message Change logic to prevent the error	Rewrite error message	30 minutes	Fix
3	Poor keyboard support in customer information entry window	Medium	Add keyboard shortcuts	Add keyboard shortcuts	1 hour	Fix
4	The search function is not powerful enough	Medium	Add fuzzy searching Allow wildcards	Allow wildcards	10 hours	Leave (fix in next version)

- The support of upper management for addressing usability goals
- The resources available

After deciding what problems to address, a problem solution table can be used to choose the best solution (Browne, 1994). Table 9 is a sample problem solution table. The usability problems are listed in rank order. Potential solutions are listed in Column 2 and the chosen solution in Column 3. The chosen solution is based on a trade-off between the severity of the usability problem and the engineering resources needed to implement the various potential solutions.

The inclusion of the resolution field provides the usability engineer with a simple metric - how many problems eventually get fixed. Some usability groups are tracking the percentage of problems that are "fixed" and use this as one metric of success.

After making design changes to the product based on the Pareto chart in Figure 3, we analyzed the actual improvement in performance with a second test. The result was a 34% improvement in overall user performance. Such results were fairly typical of our experience, in that our estimates were usually conservative with respect to predicted improvement. Improvements of about 30% in user performance were fairly typical when 70% to 80% of the interface issues were addressed.

27.8.4 Iterative Design and Testing

Iteration is a continuous process of design, implementation, and testing. Iterative design allows development teams to break large product designs into manageable stages and eliminate major problems early in design and lesser problems as development proceeds. One practical and political advantage of iterative design is that it allows the team to see successive improvements early. Evidence of a constantly improving product provides development managers with confidence that the complete product will be a success (Bauersfeld, 1994).

Iterative testing is an essential step in usability engineering, but often difficult to achieve in actual development.

Bauersfeld (1994) suggests the following practical tips for getting the most out of iterative design:

- In the beginning of iterative design, do not be too focused on details. Focus on larger issues like navigation and clear groupings.
- Devote significant time to the scheduling of iterative tests and tracking action items that emerge.
- Understand the constraints that the entire development team is working under. Keep in close contact with the team to track changes and unexpected roadblocks.
- Do not try to implement all the changes that emerge from a stage of iteration.

- Realize that the design concept may change substantially from one iteration to another.
- Prioritize problems based on user input, but keep in mind what can realistically be implemented.

Iterative design is not a panacea. Dix, Finlay, and Abowd and Beale (1993) highlight several problems with iterative design:

- Iterative design requires adequate prototyping tools, rapid testing methods, and a strong commitment to make substantial changes.
- Management may balk at building throwaway prototypes because this will be seen as taking time away from "real design".
- The ability to do rapid "throwaway prototypes" and quick usability tests is a counter argument.
- The planning and coordination of iterative design requires additional work by development managers and usability engineers.
- If the initial concept or early requirements are soundly flawed, iterative prototyping may yield a usable, but useless product. As Dix and his colleagues (1993) note "design inertia can be so great as never to overcome an initial bad design." Iterative design may yield symptoms of a larger problem. If care is not taken to probe more deeply, the symptom may be ameliorated enough to hide larger architectural problems. A solution to this problem is to employ usability methods that complement iterative testing.

27.8.5 Formal Reports

The value of formal written reports is often debated. Critics contend that long, detailed reports are time consuming to write and unlikely to be read by members of the design teams. While brevity is a reasonable goal, the usability of the report is paramount and sometimes a terse report may not provide the detail needed to truly understand the problem. Supporters argue that formal reports provide a design history and the detail needed to understand usability problems days or weeks after a test (not every problem can be fixed right after a test session). Formal reports allow the usability engineer some time to reflect on problems and see potential patterns that may not be clear from rapid analysis sessions. Formal reports may be more appropriate for development or product managers, who must allocate the resources for redesign efforts, than individual designers. A two or three page executive summary is appropriate for communicating results to senior management. A face-to-face walkthrough of the usability problems, the rationale behind the problems and possible solutions, is probably a better technique than a formal report for communicating the results of usability testing. However, the formal document can still serve as a memory aid after a walkthrough with a design team. This face-to-face walkthrough requires sensitivity on the part of the usability engineer who must sell the developer on the need for changes to the user interface.

Formal reports should minimally indicate whether the usability goals have been met, what aspects of the product were lauded by the users, and what problems emerged during testing. Since usability engineers are often problem focused, many reports fail to indicate what worked well during testing. The inclusion of a section on the positive things that emerged can be helpful in establishing a good relationship with the design team (Wilson, Loring, Conte, and Stanley, 1994). Problems can be organized by object (e.g., menu, window, dialog box), generality, severity, frequency, category (e.g., problems with text), or a combination of factors (for example. a measure that combines severity and generality) (Dumas and Redish, 1994). Rubin (1994) recommends that a report contain the following major sections: Executive summary, methods, results, and recommendations. Rubin also provides several different formats for presenting the information in these sections.

27.8.6 Issues and Pitfalls in Analyzing and Communicating Usability Test Results

Should I Use Inferential Statistics?

Inferential statistics can be appropriate in some testing, however their use presents several problems (Dumas and Redish, 1994). Many testers are not experts in choosing and interpreting the results of inferential statistics and few usability testers are familiar with appropriate statistics for small samples. Second, the computation of inferential statistics may not be appropriate because the assumptions for the statistic are not met (a random sample, a normal distribution). And third, decision makers are generally not well versed in the nuances of inferential statistics and may make mistakes in interpreting the results. Inferential statistics should be used with caution.

Allocating Time to Write

Testers should schedule time to write a document immediately after testing. Analyses like the Pareto chart are powerful, but time consuming to generate, so the writing time must include the time needed to finish analyses, interpret the results, and create data tables or figures. This analysis and writing time should be part of the agreement between the tester and the recipients of report. A goal for a usability report might be "finish the report within 3 working days of the completion of the test."

Presenting the Results

A short presentation of the results soon after a test can complement the written report and make the report easier to understand. The presentation can be enhanced by having videotaped highlights and screen shots to provide context for the development team.

Get Feedback on Your Usability Reports

Testers should gather feedback on the usability of their reports and iterate on the report content and format (Rubin, 1994). Feedback on the readability, level of detail, and organization is useful. Once you get a reasonable format, create a template and use it consistently.

Make Sure that the Document is Readable

Make the test report readable by using short sentences, parallel constructions, lists and tables, active voice, and illustrations. Many reports from usability tests have few graphics. A picture of a window where a user had a problem with some annotation about the issues involved can be a powerful way to convey usability concerns.

Optimize the Report Format for the People Who Will be Fixing Problems

Dumas and Redish (1994) suggest that usability test reports be designed for the people who will be fixing problems. The actual format may depend on how groups are organized. If a product has many components and different teams working on each component, the report might group problems by component. If you list problems in a large table and use a word processor that can sort by columns, you can create multiple versions of a report from the same file. One version could be sorted by component, another by severity, and yet another version would be sorted by whether particular usability goals were met.

Consider the Politics of Report Distribution

Testers should check with development managers about who should be on the report distribution list. Since reports focus primarily on problems, development managers may not want everyone in the company to see the report, especially early reports where long lists of problems might create unwarranted concern among senior managers. The mailing list for reports should be part of the testing agreement between the usability engineer and the development manager.

27.8.7 Summary of Analyzing and Communicating Usability Test Results

There are a variety of ways to analyze and communicate usability test data to development teams. These techniques range from having developers observe test sessions and categorize problems to quantitative analyses that reveal whether goals are met. The quickest forms of analysis often generate lists of problems and not the quantitative data needed to assess whether goals were met. We recommend that usability practitioners budget sufficient time in their testing plans for analyzing and reporting performance data. The most powerful form of analysis is the Pareto chart based on an impact analysis.

Time is a rare commodity for development teams. Test reports should be available soon after the completion of a test. The report should be readable and usable for the target audiences. Brevity is a good goal for a report, but the more important factor is the usability of the report. A terse report might be appropriate for a senior manager; a more detailed report would be needed by the actual implementers of design changes. A report should clearly indicate where redesign and additional testing is required.

27.9 Overall Discussion and Future Directions

So far, we have discussed the origins and techniques for usability engineering and have reported how usability engineering is actually practiced by the human factors community. In this section, we will place usability engineering in a broader framework including both overall methods for design and development of software and hardware products and relate usability engineering to other techniques for achieving usability in products.

27.9.1 Challenges and Pitfalls in Applying Usability Engineering

Like any process, usability engineering has its weaknesses and makes certain assumptions. While usability engineering represents a general framework for thinking about the design of usable systems, its application in some contexts requires creativity and finesse. In this section we will review some of the challenges and pitfalls in applying usability engineering. The discussion here is drawn from a number of reviews of usability engineering (Butler, 1996; Karat, 1994; Nielsen, 1993), our own experience, and our survey.

Usability Engineering Assumes That Usability Can And Should Be Operationalized

Assuming that one has defined the correct usability goals, one can still question operationalization in general. The full experience of the usability of a system is not captured in a set of metrics. In addition, usability is multifaceted and dependent on user, environment, and task characteristics. The more varied the users and environments, the more difficult it can be to arrive at a meaningful usability specification. Kukla, Clemens, Morse, and Cash (1992) note that design problems, like the operationalization of usability, become more difficult as they include more aspects of a user's life. One could maintain that a participatory design approach in which users are continuously involved in the design process would result in a usable system without resorting to the objective definition of work and the design and measurement of a system vis-à-vis that definition. Also certain perspectives (for example, Heidegger, 1962) appear to argue for a conception of tools that lies outside an operational approach. While we are sympathetic to the view that certain aspects of user experience and system design are not readily operationalized, experience shows that appropriate use of the operational definitions of usability engineering can contribute to positive user experiences, improved development processes, and more effective products.

Setting Quantitative Usability Goals Implies Laboratory Testing

In prior sections we pointed out that approaches to usability testing can be quite diverse. Certainly test location can be highly variable and test procedures can be flexible. In fact, quantitative data can be gathered in many settings. For example, one can give a survey at the end of an interview, a field observation, or beta test. Usability engineering does imply that a systematic approach is taken in the collection and analysis of observations. In addition, certain usability goals like performance measures imply that tasks be standardized and the influence of extraneous variables be minimized. However, we also pointed to test procedures such as review of videotapes which provide for high levels of interaction with participants and creative co-design.

Usability Testing May Be Unrealistic

Usability engineers can make both the task and the environment as realistic or as artificial as they choose. There may be a tradeoff between the ease of interpretation of the results and the realism of the test environment, but this tradeoff can be carefully considered when planning a usability engineering project. There are a number of possibilities for making a usability test more realistic. For example a number of practitioners have included a support line in lab or field test environments. This not only increases realism but can provide valuable data in terms of the number of support calls and the types of questions asked. Investigators have also used field observation and Contextual Inquiry to create testing scenarios that closely match users' work practices.

Usability Engineering Comes Too Late

Basically this argument is a variation of the one that says all evaluation comes too late. By the time the system is ready to be tested it can be shipped and there won't be time to make any changes. In addition, the argument goes "all the design decisions have already been made and it is too costly and difficult to reverse them".

This objection overlooks several critical aspects of usability engineering. First, the definition of usability attributes and goals should come as part of the requirements process. Goals are part of the product concept. Second, it overlooks the fact that specifying goals at the early stage of product design provides direction to the engineering and design effort; goal specification should precede any software design. Third, it overlooks the fact that the engineering cost of a design change has no necessary relation to usability impact. In some cases we have found that low cost changes provide large usability benefits (Whiteside, Good, Spine, and George,1985).

Usability Engineering Produces Relatively Small Improvements In Usability

By and large usability engineering results in a 30% improvement in the usability of products (Whiteside, Bennett, and Holtzblatt, 1988). There are relatively few methods which have such a consistent track record of effectiveness. In fact, most measures of the impact of usability techniques have looked at their ability to uncover problems rather than their impact on design (for example, Jefferies, et. al., 1991). In a larger sense, breakthroughs in product design and the reorganization of work are relatively rare. Some would argue that breakthrough systems such as Sketchpad (Sutherland, 1963), NLS (Englebart and English, 1968), and the spreadsheet, depend on visionaries rather than methods. In contrast, Card (1996) and Olson and Moran (1996) have grouped methods according to where they fit in the product conception, design, and evaluation cycle. Breakthroughs in design occur at the earliest or conception stage. The methods suggested at this stage are: design for yourself, use what you build, participatory design, field interviews, scenarios/use cases, naturalistic observation, metaphor brainstorming (Good, 1992), and task analysis. At these early stages of product design, methods which "immerse" the technologist in the work life of the user tend to be effective (Wixon, 1995) in creating new visions. These methods are also useful in providing a basis for establishing the metrics for a usability engineering project.

27.9.2 Relation of Usability Engineering to Other Methods and Approaches

In general, usability engineering fits well into a number of frameworks for product design and it complements a number of traditional and emerging usability methods. When considering usability engineering in relation to other methods it is important to have a overall framework to position usability methods. Such frameworks have been created for qualitative methods (Muller, Wildman, and White, 1993; Wixon 1995) and for methods in general (Card, 1996, and Moran 1996). Applying these frameworks to existing usability practice is made difficult by the fact that the actual practice of various individual methods varies widely. For example, Nielsen and Mack (1994) describe eight different methods of usability inspections. They also point out that methods in combination are more effective than any single method. However, as usability methods proliferate and existing methods are combined to form hybrids it will become increasingly important to place methods in a widely accepted framework rather than comparing them directly.

In the next section, we describe five conceptual dimensions that can be used to characterize usability methods and help determine their relevance to usability engineering and the product development process.

Dimensions of Usability Methods

There are several dimensions along which usability methods can be classified. These could be thought of as creating a multidimensional space. In theory, each dimension is logically independent, but in practice methods tend to cluster in certain areas defined by these dimensions. The dimensions are:

1. **Formative versus summative methods** Formative methods are used create a design. Metaphor brainstorming, scenarios, and storyboards are formative methods because they are used to create a design. Summative methods are used to evaluate a design. Benchmarking and satisfaction surveys are summative methods.

2. **Discovery methods versus decision methods** Discovery methods are aimed at discovering how users work, behave, or think and what problems they have. Discovery methods can also be oriented toward technology, competitive systems, or drawing design ideas from unrelated work or product domains. Decision methods are used to order or choose between elements of or entire interface designs. This distinction is sometimes called qualitative (discovery) versus quantitative (decision).

3. **Formalized methods versus informal methods** Many methods have been described formally. This chapter represents a "formal" description of usability engineering. Often the practice of methods is informal. Practitioners adapt the formalized methods to the needs of a situation. For example while there are formalized descriptions of cognitive walkthroughs (Wharton, 1994), there are also less formalized methods using roughly the same approach (e.g. the cognitive Jog-through (Rowley and Rhoades, 1992)

4. **Users are not involved versus users are involved** Methods differ in the extent to which users are involved in evaluation, analysis, and design. Some methods such as heuristic evaluation don't need users; professional designers are used. Other methods such as participatory design methods like CARD and PICTIVE involve users not just in data collection, but in evaluation and design.

5. **Complete methods versus component methods** Some methods cover all the steps needed to complete the usability design effort. Our description of usability engineering here is such a "complete" description. Other methods are component methods

they represent a part of a complete usability process. An example would be "thinking out loud". It represents a stylized way of interacting with users to uncover their thought processes. As such it needs to be supplemented by methods which would serve to address other needed steps in the design process (e.g. generating a task or reporting results).

Mapping Methods To Dimensions

Any particular method (as formally described or actually practiced) can be mapped onto each of these five dimensions. When doing such a mapping, one must consider the variety that may exist for any method. Thus a method may map along a range of each of these continua.

When usability engineering is mapped to these dimensions, we would see it as a summative, decision-oriented method. It ranges across the dimension from formal to informal. Usability engineering involves users, but primarily as sources of data rather than co-designers. It is also a complete method since it specifies the full range of activities within a design effort. However, like any other complete method it often works best when combined with other methods. For example, Contextual Inquiry provides a realistic set of user tasks which can serve as the basis for usability goals and metrics.

Some of the "oldest" usability testing methods involve "thinking aloud", interviewing users as they are tested, or testing users in pairs to encourage them to talk about their work (Comstock, 1995). These methods tend to be more formative and discovery-oriented. They seek to uncover the users' reactions to a given design to create a new design or an incremental improvement. However, they do require an existing design for users to react to.

Rather than wait for a design to be completed, practitioners may test an existing or competitive system or may generate a paper mock-up. These methods are often quite informal. Comstock (1995, reprinted from a 1983 article) treats testing users together as a practical suggestion, only later did it become "elevated" to the co-discovery method (Nielsen, 1993). Obviously in these methods the user is the critical component. Often there is limited and minimal data analysis; instead developers merely watch the tests and review the results. As such, these methods vary in terms of their completeness.

Usability inspection methods are difficult to classify since they constitute a "family" of techniques. Nielsen and Mack (1994) identify eight methods of usability inspection. These eight methods differ in terms of the dimensions suggested here. Heuristic evaluation is a summative method, the system design must exist for the inspection to take place. It is also a discovery method in that problems are uncovered; however when it is combined with a ranking of the relative importance of problems it becomes a decision method. It is quite formalized and has been extensively researched. Users are not involved and the method is complete.

The second method, guideline reviews, differ from heuristic reviews only in the number of rules (about 10 for heuristic reviews versus hundreds for guideline reviews); thus, from the perspective of this framework they are identical.

In pluralistic walkthroughs designers, users, developers and human factors experts step through a scenario and discuss usability issues as they go. A pluralistic walkthrough tends to be closer to the summative pole since a design must already exist. However, since the design must be in paper form the walkthrough could occur early in the process. It is a discovery method in that the main goal is to uncover user reactions without collecting empirical ratings. In some cases empirical ratings are added which makes it closer to a decision method. As described the pluralistic walkthrough is a fairly formal method with clearly specified procedure and roles. Users are directly involved and all participants are instructed to take a user's point of view (Bias, 1994). In addition the user's perspective is incorporated via a scenario that is used as the basis for the walkthrough of the interface. Finally it is a complete method which involves an entire team.

Consistency and standards inspections are summative evaluations which are oriented toward discovery. They are also formalized but a number of less formal versions exist. Users are not involved since the goal of the inspection is to conform with standards or guidelines. The method is complete in that is clearly specified (Wixon et. al 1994; Flanders, Sawyer, and Wixon, 1996). One of the oldest inspection methods (Lewis, et al. 1990), the cognitive walkthrough, has been extensively studied and compared with other methods (Wharton, Rieman, Lewis and Polson, 1994). The cognitive walkthough tends to be formative and discovery oriented methods which are highly formalized. Users are not directly involved and it is a complete method. Formal usability inspections (Kahn and Prail, 1994) are much like code inspections. They are summative, formal, and discovery oriented. They do not involve users and are complete in themselves.

Feature inspections involve looking at the function

of a system rather than its interface (see Kahn and Prail, 1994). As such they move to the formative side of an evaluation since they can take place early in the design process and evaluate early concepts like workflow. They are discovery oriented methods and are formalized. Users are involved and they are complete methods. For alternative formulations see Olson and Moran, 1996, Card, 1996).

From a practical perspective, the relevant question is how to combine this collection of methods into an effective overall approach given the constraints of the design problem and the development situation. Our bias is to treat usability engineering as a high-level process into which other methods can be integrated.

Practical Suggestions for Integrating Usability Engineering with Other Approaches and Methods?

Object-oriented Design. Using an object oriented approach combined with participatory design methods represents a straightforward way to incorporate the perspective of the user directly into the design of the system (Dayton and McFarland, 1995). A usability engineering approach can complement this method by providing user-based performance goals against which an evolving system can be evaluated. Since this participatory/object-oriented approach stresses continuous evaluation with the users of the system; usability goals would be applied in an informal way during design conversations. However, there is nothing in this approach that precludes the use of usability engineering to develop an acceptance test.

Cost Benefit Analysis. Cost benefit analysis rests on the measurement of the cost of developing a system in terms of dollars spent and the benefits in terms of dollars saved (Bias and Mayhew, 1994). Often the costs are clear, but the benefits are not. Defining benefits requires an objective definition of user work in terms of time, errors, lost sales, and support calls. Usability engineering requires not only an objective definition of work, but also the translation of that definition into metrics. As such, it can represent an essential part in a cost benefit analysis.

Contextual Inquiry/Design. Contextual Inquiry and Contextual Design (Whiteside, Bennett, and Holtzblatt, 1988; Wixon, Holtzblatt, and Knox, 1990; Holtzblatt and Beyer, 1995) are field-based observational approaches which provide an understanding of users in their own environments and a way to structure that input into a system design. The emergence of Contextual Inquiry began as a reaction to the artificiality of the usability laboratory. From a usability engineering perspective, the understanding of user work is the basis for defining usability metrics and setting usability goals. In addition, both Contextual Inquiry and Contextual Design provide a broad understanding of user work that balances and complements objectively specified measures. Such objective measures run the risk of being too narrow if not supplemented by an in-depth understanding of actual work. For example, a system could meet its specified usability goal in a test situation, but be unworkable in practice due to differences in system performance between the idealized test environment and the user's typical situation. Contextual Inquiry provides data on user environments, tasks, current usability problems, and large scale system issues.

Contextual Inquiry methods can complement formal usability testing in several ways:

1. Early analysis using Contextual Inquiry is useful in defining user profiles and important tasks. These tasks can be used to develop test scenarios that are realistic and rough conceptual models that can be translated into paper prototypes.

2. Field studies provide clues about critical aspects of the real work situation which can be used to increase the realism and relevance of a usability test. For example a system for entering and modifying invoices for a large corporation may have thousands of invoices in the current system. Doing a usability test on a prototype invoice system with only a few hundred invoices may lead to the erroneous conclusion that the prototype is fast, usable, and efficient. Making the context of the test realistic may be more important for generalizing the results than having a large sample size of users.

3. Contextual Inquiry can be helpful in setting usability goals for benchmarking tests. There are many systems where performance is a major goal and this is where the lab is powerful. We have often gotten good benchmarking data from field interviews that can be used to create usability goals.

Inspections and Design Reviews. There are a wide variety of techniques used in usability inspections and heuristic design reviews (Nielsen, 1993). However, in essence these methods represent systematic ways of applying expert opinion to interface designs. As such they are quick and effective. However, inspections do not involve direct assessment of user performance with a system. They do not even require that user tasks be specified; although many inspections begin from a proposed work flow. As such these methods cover a different, though possibly overlapping, set of design issues. For example inspections will most likely be more effective than usability engineering at identifying all the places that a system departs from a style guide. Thus, in assessing whether to apply usability engineering or inspections to a system the practitioner needs to be mindful of the purpose of each method.

Scenarios. The word scenario has many meanings (Carroll, 1995), but it generally involves a description of a task and the conditions under which the task is achieved. Scenarios are derived from some level of task analysis and are useful for developing realistic tasks for usability testing. Work scenarios can also help determine which usability attributes will be applied to the system (for example, ease of use and ease of learning).

User and Task Observation. User and task observation complement usability engineering in several ways:

- They provide data for developing user profiles and task descriptions. As we noted earlier, goals for different groups and task categories can differ.
- They provide data that can help in the redesign of problem areas.
- They provide hints on what levels should be set for usability attributes. For example, users may have quotas or time constraints for certain tasks (billing, entering transaction data, finding information in a corporate database). These constraints can be used in the development of usability testing.

Simplified Thinking Aloud. Simplified thinking aloud provides insight into users' thought processes and can yield ideas about how to redesign an interface to eliminate usability problems. Iterations of thinking aloud studies can be done quickly between the more formal sessions of quantitative measurement.

Metaphor Brainstorming. Metaphor brainstorming is a technique for generating user interface metaphors. These metaphors can serve as organizing concepts (e.g., an outline, a spreadsheet, a notebook) or as details in the user interface (icons, terminology, graphic layout). Metaphor brainstorming can be used to generate possible solutions for problem areas that arise during usability testing.

Questionnaires. Questionnaires can be used to assess satisfaction measures in the usability engineering process. We commonly ask users to fill out "Final Reactions" questionnaires at the end of usability testing. Many usability specifications include satisfaction goals that are assessed through questionnaires. Questionnaires can complement the usability engineering process providing the design team with information on:

- What usability goals are important to users
- Information on users
- Information on task frequency
- Common usability problems
- The perceptions and preferences of large number of users who cannot be involved in usability testing
- Product features that users like and dislike.

A practice becoming more common is to distribute early versions of products and on-line questionnaires. While performance data may be difficult to obtain over the Internet or on-line services, satisfaction data could easily be collected from large samples of users. Some products provide capabilities for polling which are then used to evaluate iterative designs.

Focus Groups. Focus groups are moderated discussion sessions where a group of 5-15 people are brought together to discuss product concepts, important work issues, and usage scenarios. Focus groups complement usability engineering by providing ideas about what usability attributes are important, what goal levels are possible, and what scenarios should be tested. Focus groups can also be used to get feedback on early prototypes that will evolve into the more robust prototypes used in usability tests.

User Feedback from Support Calls. User feedback from support databases, on-line feedback, and other sources can help determine the focus of usability testing and redesign efforts. Support calls are expensive and features that yield many support calls should be included in usability testing. A decrement in support calls could be a metric associated with an ease of learning.

27.10 Conclusions

In the mid-1980s, usability engineering evolved in an effort to place usability on a par with other factors that drive the product development process. The development of usability engineering was a conscious effort to structure our thinking about usability in engineering terms and to design an approach which could be plugged into the overall development process and yet remain flexible and adaptable to situations. We still believe that usability engineering represents a viable approach for incorporating the user's viewpoint into product development. In fact, usability engineering has been widely adopted and extensively documented. As an approach, it represents one of the few user interface design methods with an empirically documented record of success.

In this chapter, we chose to emphasize the practical aspects of usability engineering. We also chose not to discuss other methods at length. This approach contrasts with that taken in the original usability chapter where the philosophical foundations of usability engineering were established and Contextual Inquiry was introduced to a wide audience. We feel that usability engineering is a mature and established technique which merits consideration in any design effort.

In a sense, we see usability engineering as a way to bridge the gap between putting the user at the center of the design process and the interests of the other stakeholders in the design, development, and purchasing process. For the engineering community usability engineering provides an objective way to understand and address the user's viewpoint. For the financial community, which increasingly controls the development process, it represents a way to quantify the benefits of a system and thus serves to balance the inevitable consideration of the costs. For the marketing community, it represents a way to assess the benefits of a system in objective and holistic terms as compared to a fragmented and subjective approach. For buyers, it represents a way to evaluate a system in relation to their needs.

As a methodology, usability engineering addresses many of the traditional concerns of the interface design community. First, it provides a way to get involved in the design early through the setting of usability goals. Second, it represents a way to gain the respect of the engineering and management communities by speaking their language. Third, it represents a method for adding value to the overall design process while allowing room for others to make their contribution. Finally it represents a way to measure the effectiveness of the design effort and thus provide an opportunity for reflection and improvement.

We point out two pitfalls of the general approach. The first we discussed earlier; that is setting of goals which do not match the users' concerns or those of the market place. We urge the use of field oriented methods and a broad understanding of marketplace trends to minimize this risk. Second, the approach can be elaborate and time consuming. To avoid this pitfall, we urge flexibility and scaleability of the methods. However, we would urge the usability engineer not to ignore the importance of setting goals. One unfortunate trend has been the overemphasis on testing methodology (the how of testing) without corresponding emphasis on the process of setting usability goals (the why of testing). A detrimental result has been an increase in testing without objective usability goals.

Finally, at the most general level we see usability engineering as a way to establish the appropriate relationship between people and technology. In areas where new technology is emerging there is a tendency to place technology (object-oriented design, the World Wide Web, client/server architectures) in a pre-eminent position and assume that users should adopt the newest technology and adapt to it. Along with other perspectives such as participatory design and user-centered design, usability engineering represents a way to keep humans as the standard by which technology and products are assessed.

27.11 Acknowledgements

Dennis would like to thank John Whiteside, Sandy Jones, Karen Holtzblatt for shaping my view of how to understand users and incorporate their views in design. I also gratefully acknowledge my current colleagues at Digital especially Betsy Comstock and my supervisor Pat Baker. The opinions expressed in this chapter are mine and do not necessarily reflect those of Digital Equipment Corporation.

Chauncey would like to thank John Whiteside and Dennis Wixon for their support over 10 years of usability work. I would also like to acknowledge Mary Beth Raven for her review of this chapter and my wife, Penny Wilson, for her comments and loving support. The opinions expressed in this chapter are mine and do not necessarily reflect those of FTP Software, Inc.

27.12 References

Arthur, L. J. (1993). *Improving software quality: An insider's guide to TQM*. New York: Wiley.

Bachman, R. D. (1989). A methodology for comparing the software interfaces of competitive products. *In Proceedings of the Human Factors Society 33rd Annual Meeting* (pp. 1214-1217). Santa Monica, CA: Human Factors and Ergonomics Society.

Bauersfeld, P. (1994). *Software by design: Creating people friendly software*. New York: M&T Books.

Bennett, J. L. (1984). Managing to meet usability requirements: establishing and meeting software development goals. In J. Bennett, D. Case, J. Sandelin, and M. Smith (Eds.), *Usability issues and health concerns* (pp. 161-184). Englewood Cliffs, NJ: Prentice-Hall.

Bias, R. G. (1994). The pluralistic Walkthrouhg: Coordinated Empathies. In Nielsen. J. and Mack, R. *Usability Inspection Methods.* New York: John Wiley and Sons. 77-98.

Bias, R. G., and Mayhew (1994). *Cost-justifying usability*. Boston, MA: Academic Press.

Boehm, B. W. (1988). A spiral model of software development and enhancement. *IEEE Computer*, May, 61-72.

Braun, S. and Rohn, J. (1993). Structuring usability within an organization, Presented at UPA Conference. Redmond Washington.

Browne, D. (1994). *STUDIO: Structured User-interface design for interaction optimisation.* New York: Prentice Hall.

Butler, K. A. (1985). Connecting theory and practice: a case study of achieving usability goals. In *Proceedings of CHI '85 Human Factors in Computing Systems* (pp. 85-88). San Francisco, CA: ACM.

Butler, K. (1996) Usability Engineering Turns 10. *Interactions, January*. 59-75

Butler, M. B., and Ehrlich, K. (1994). Usability engineering for Lotus 1-2-3 Release 4. In M. Wiklund (Ed.). *Usability in practice: How companiés develop user friendly Products.* Cambridge, MA: AP Professional

Card, S. K. (1996). Pioneers and settlers: Methods used in successful user interface design. In M. Rudisell, C. Lewis, P. B. Polson, and T. D. McKay (Eds.), *Human-computer interface design: success stories, emerging methods, and real-world context* (pp. 122-169). San Francisco, CA: Morgan Kaufmann.

Carroll, J. M. (Ed.) (1995). *Scenario-based design: Envisioning work and technology in system development.* New York: Wiley.

Carroll, J. M. and Rosson, M. B. (1985). Usability specifications as tools in iterative development. In H. R. Hartson (Ed.*), Advances in human computer interaction. Vol. 1* (pp. 1-28). Norwood, NJ: Ablex.

Casaday, G., and Rainis, C. (1996) Requirements, Models and Prototypes. Tutorial Presented at ACM CHI'96. Vancouver, BC. April 13 - 18.

Chapanis, A. and Budurka, W. J. (1990). Specifying human-computer interface requirements. *Behaviour and Information Technology* 9(6), 479-492.

Comstock, B. (1995). *Human factors perspectives on human-computer interaction: Selections from proceedings of human factors and ergonomics society annual meetings 1983-1994* (pp. 29-33). Santa Monica, CA: Human Factors and Ergonomics Society.

Conklin, P. (1991). Bringing usability effectively into product development. In M. Rudisell, C. Lewis, P. B. Polson, and T. D. McKay (Eds.), *Human-computer interface design: success stories, emerging methods, and real-world context* (pp. 367-374). San Francisco, CA: Morgan Kaufmann.

Dayton, T. and McFarland, A. (1995). Testing task flows: A participatory object-oriented design approach. Tutorial presented at the Usability Professionals Association conference, Portland, ME, July 12-14.

del Galdo, E. M., Williges, R. C., Williges, B. H., and Wixon, D. (1995). An evaluation of critical incidents for software documentation design. *Human Factors Perspectives on Human-Computer Interaction: Selections from Proceedings of Human Factors and Ergonomics Society Annual Meetings 1983-1994* (pp. 29-33). Santa Monica, CA: Human Factors and Ergonomics Society.

DeMarco T., and Lister. T. (1987). *Peopleware.* New York: Dorset House.

Deming, W. E. (1982). *Quality, productivity, and competitive Position.* Cambridge, MA: MIT Center for Advanced Study.

Diaper, D. (Ed.) (1989). *Task analysis for human-computer interaction.* Chichester, U.K., Ellis Horwood.

Dix, A., Finlay, J., Abowd, G., Beale, R. (1993). *Human-computer interaction.* New York: Prentice Hall.

Drury, C., Paramore, B., Van Cott, H., Grey, S., and Corlett, E. (1987). Task analysis. In G. Salvendy (Ed.), *Handbook of human factors* (pp. 370-401). New York: Wiley.Dumas, J. S., and Redish, J. C. (1993). *A practical guide to usability testing*. Norwood, NJ: Ablex.

Englebart, D. C., and English, W. K. (1968). A research center for augmenting human intellect. In *AFIPS Proceedings of the Fall Joint Computer Conference* (Vol. 330), 395-410.

Erlich, K., and Rohn, J. A. (1994). Cost justification of usability engineering: A vendor's perspective. In D. J. Mayhew and R. G. Bias. (Eds.), *Cost-justifying usability* (pp. 73-110). New York: Wiley.

Flanders, A. Sawyer, P. and Wixon, D. (1996). Making a difference - the impact of inspections, *Proceedings of ACM CHI'96* (pp. 376-383). New York: ACM.

Gilb, T. (1981) System attribute specification: a cornerstone of software engineering. *ACM Software Engineering Notes*, July, 78-79.

Gilb, T. (1981). Design by objectives. Unpublished manuscript, Available from the author.

Gilb, T. (1985). The "Impact Analysis Table" applied to human factors design. In B. Shackel (Ed.), *Human-Computer Interaction -- INTERACT'84, Proceedings of the 1st IFIP Conference on Human-Computer Interaction* (pp. 655-659), Amsterdam: North-Holland..

Gilb, T. (1988). *Principles of software engineering management*. New York: Addison-Wesley.

Good, M. (1985). The iterative design of a new text editor. *In Proceeding of the Human Factors Society 29th Annual Meeting Vol. 1* (pp. 571-574). Santa Monica, CA: Human Factors and Ergonomics Society.

Good, M., Spine, T. M., Whiteside, J., and George, P. (1986). User-derived impact analysis as a tool for usability engineering. *In Proceedings of the ACM CHI'86 Conference* (pp. 241-246). New York: ACM.

Good, M. Participatory Deisgn of a Protable Torque-Feedback Device. *In Proceedings of the ACM CHI'92 Conference* (pp. 439-446). New York: ACM

Gould, J. D. (1988). How to design usable systems. In M. Helander (Ed.*), Handbook of human-computer interaction* (pp. 757-789). Amsterdam: North-Holland.

Gould, J. D. and Lewis, C. (1985). Designing for usability: Key principles and what designers think. *Communications of the ACM, 38* (3), 300-311.

Hackos, J. T. (1995). Personal communication.

Hackos, J. T. (1994). *Managing your documentation projects*. New York: Wiley.

Heidegger, M. (1962). *Being and time* (translated by J. Macquarrie and E. Robinson). New York: Harper and Row.

Hix, D., and Hartson, H. R. (1993). *Developing user interfaces: Ensuring usability through product and process*. New York: Wiley.

Holtzblatt, K. and Beyer, H. (1995). Making customer centered design work for teams. *Communications of the ACM, 36*, 92-103.

Jefferies, R., Miller, J.R., Wharton, C. and Uyeda, K.M. User Interface Evaluation in the Real World: A Comparison of 4 Techniques. *In Proceedings of the ACM CHI'91 Conference* (pp. 119-124).New York: ACM.

Kahn M.J. and Prail, A. (1994). Formal Usability Inspections. In J. Nielsen, and R. Mack (Eds.) *Usability inspection methods* (pp. 141-169). New York: Wiley..

Kan, S. H. (1995). *Metrics and models in software quality engineering*. Reading, MA: Addison Wesley.

Karat, C., (1991) Cost Bentefit and business case analysis of usability engineering. Human Factors of Computing Systems, ACM CHI'91 Tutorial Notes

Karat, C. (1994). A business case approach to usability cost justification. In R. G. Bias and D. J. Mayhew (Eds.*), Cost-justifying usability* (pp. 45-70). New York: Academic Press.

Karat, C. Campbell, R. and Fiegel, T. (1992) Comparison of Empirical Testing and Walkthrough Methods in User Interface Evaluation. *In Proceedings of the ACM CHI'92 Conference* (pp. 397 - 404). New York: ACM.

Kukla, Clemens, Morse, and Cash (1992). Designing effective systems: A tools approach. In Adler, P. S and Winograd, T. A. (Eds.), USABILITY: *Turning technologies into tools*. New York: Oxford University Press.

Landauer, T. K. (1995). *The trouble with computers*. Cambridge, MA: MIT Press.

Lewis C. Polson, P. Wharton, C. and Reiman. J. (1990).Testing the Cognitive Walktrough forms and Instructions,. *In Proceedings of the ACM CHI'90 Conference* (pp. 235 - 242). New York: ACM.

Mauro, C. L. (1994). Cost justifying usability in a contractor company. In R. G. Bias and D. J. Mayhew, (Eds.), *Cost-justifying usability* (pp. 123-142). New York: Academic Press.

Mayhew, D. J. (1992). *Principles and guidelines in software user interface design*. Englewood Cliffs, NJ: Prentice Hall.

Mayhew, D. J., and Bias, R. G. (Eds.) (1994). *Cost-justifying usability*. Boston, MA: Academic Press.

Mayhew, D. J., and Bias, R. G. (1994). Organizational inhibitors and facilitators. In R. G. Bias, and D. J. Mayhew (Eds.), *Cost- justifying usability* (pp. 287-318). New York: Academic Press.

Microsoft (1995). *The Windows interface guidelines for software design*. Redmond, WA: Microsoft Press.

Mrazek, D., and Rafeld, M. (1992). Integrating human factors on a large scale: "Product usabillity champions." *Human Factors Of Computing Systems, Proceedings of CHI'92 Conference* (pp. 565-570). New York, ACM.

Muller, M, Wildman, D. and White, D. Taxonomy of

PD Practices: A Brief Practioners Guide. *Communications of the ACM. 36* 26-28.

Nielsen, J. (199). *Usability engineering*, Boston, MA: AP Professional

Nielsen, J. and Mack, R. L. (Eds.) (1995). *Usability inspection methods.* New York, NY: Wiley,.

Olson, J. S., and Moran, T. P. (1996). Mapping the method muddle: Guidance in using methods for user interface design. In M. Rudisell,, C. Lewis, P. B. Polson, and T. D. McKay, (Eds.), *Human-computer interface design: success stories, emerging methods, and real-world context* (pp. 269-300). San Francisco, CA: Morgan Kaufmann.

Purvis, C. J., Czerwinski, M., and Weiler, P. (1994). The human factors group at Compaq computer corporation. In M. Wiklund (Ed.), *Usability in practice*, New York: Academic Press.

Redmond-Pyle, D., and Moore, A. (1995). *Graphic user interface design and Evaluation (GUIDE).* London: Prentice Hall.

Rowley D. E. and Rhoades, D.G. (1992). The Cogntive Jog Through: A Fast-paced User Interface Evaluation Procedure. *Proceedings of the ACM CHI'92.* New York: ACM. 381-395.

Rubin, J. (1994*). Handbook of usability testing: How to plan, design, and conduct effective tests.* New York: Wiley.

Smith, W. J. (1996). *ISO and ANSI ergonomic standards for computer products: A guide to implementation and compliance.* Upper Saddle River, NJ: Prentice Hall.

Smith, E., and Siochi, A. (1995). Software usability: requirements by evaluation. In G. Perlman, G. K. Green, and M. S. Wogalter, (Eds.), *Human factors perspectives on human-computer interaction: Selections from proceedings of Human Factors and Ergonomics Society annual meetings 1983-1994* (pp. 135-137). Santa Monica, CA: Human Factors and Ergonomics Society.

Sutherland, I. (1963). Sketchpad: A Man-Machine Graphical Communications System. Ph.D. Thesis, MIT.

Wharton, K., Reimann, J., Lewis, C., and Polson, P. (1994). The cognitive walkthrough: A practitioner's guide. In J. Nielsen, and R. Mack (Eds.) *Usability inspection methods* (pp. 105-141). New York: Wiley.

Whiteside, J., Bennett, J., and Holtzblatt, K. (1988). Usability engineering: Our experience and evolution. In M. Helander, (Ed.), *Handbook of human-computer interaction* (pp. 791-817). Amsterdam: North-Holland.

Wicklund, M. (Ed.) (1994). *Usability in practice: How companies develop user-friendly products.* Boston, MA: AP Professional.

Wilson, C. E., Loring, B. A., Conte, L. and Stanley, K. (1994). Usability engineering at Dun and Bradstreet Software. In M. Wicklund (Ed.), *Usability in practice: How companies develop user-friendly products.* Boston, MA: AP Professional.

Wixon, D. (1995). Qualitative research methods in design and development. *Interactions: New visions of human computer interaction, 2*(4), 19 -26.

Wixon, D., Holtzblatt, K., and Knox, S. (1990). Contextual design: An emergent view of system design. *Proceedings of the ACM CHI'90.* New York: ACM. 329-336.

Wixon, D. Jones, S. Tse, L. and Casaday, G. (1994) Inspections and Design Reviews: Framework, History and Reflection. In Nielsen. J. and Mack, R. *Usability Inspection Methods.* New York: John Wiley and Sons. 77-98.

Wixon, D., and Jones, S. (1996). Usability for fun and profit: A case study of the design of DEC Rally Version 2. In M. Rudisell,, C. Lewis, P. B. Polson, and T. D. McKay (Eds.), *Human-computer interface design: Success stories, emerging methods, and real-world context* (pp. 3-35). San Francisco, CA: Morgan Kaufmann.

Wixon, D. and Ramey, J. (Eds.) (1996). *Field methods casebook for software design.* New York: Wiley.

Handbook of Human-Computer Interaction
Second, completely revised edition
M. Helander, T.K. Landauer, P. Prabhu (eds.)

Chapter 28

User-Centered Software Evaluation Methodologies

John Karat
IBM T. J. Watson Research Center
Hawthorne, New York, USA

28.1 Introduction

I began formally evaluating software systems over 15 years ago. In those days, evaluations of software systems were generally a part of system tests late in the development cycle and generally followed good experimental design as practiced in academic behavioral science. Evaluations were not intended to inform design as much as they were intended to validate it (often by passing or failing it compared to some alternative). We spent most of our evaluation effort focused on measuring how good (or bad) something was and fairly little time trying to improve designs.

Gradually, the focus of what it means to evaluate software has been shifting. We have moved from the world of experimental design focused on hypothesis testing and statistical analysis to a view of evaluation as a means of gathering information to inform iterative design. While it is still important to ask about how to do an evaluation of a designed system, it seems more important to ask about the broader role of evaluation in the design of a system.

I will deal only briefly with the more traditional experimental methods of behavioral science evaluation in this chapter. While these remain important for some aspects of system development, there have been numerous account of why we need to shift focus to formative rather than summative evaluations (Landauer, 1995; Carroll, 1991). The methods and techniques for gathering design ideas are different than those which aim at measurement of the goodness of a system.

28.2 The Changing View of Evaluation

Let me start by setting a framework for discussing evaluations in general. All evaluations - even if I say I like seafood or the color blue - have some common features. In all cases there is an **object** being evaluated (e.g., musical recording, food, people) and a **process** through which one or more attributes are judged or given a value (e.g., tastes "good" for the taste attribute). Finally, we should consider that evaluations have a **purpose**. It is important to keep this in mind as we explore methods for evaluating systems - what you do to evaluate an object in a context depends very much on the reason for doing the evaluation in the first place. Consider the following statements:

- I give it a "78" Dick. It has a good beat and is easy to dance to.
- This dish needs a little more salt.
- That was a perfect 10.
- We give the movie two thumbs up.

- It took 3 minutes to dictate the document.
- This computer is easy to use.

The above are all evaluations - or more specifically, they are statements with evaluative content. In each, someone has had some experience with something and is reporting their evaluation of that experience. The evaluation was done in some setting (the grand total of which is the what makes up the context of the evaluation), and is focused on some aspect of the setting (the object) for the evaluation. The description of the context is very important, but is often not included in detail in an evaluation report. We generally try to include aspects of the setting that seem important in describing the context, but it is just not possible to completely describe all aspects of a setting that might impact it. For example, the moods of the people in the setting, weather conditions, or what you had for lunch, all might affect how you respond to a piece of music, but it would be impractical to try and list all such considerations.

Another thing to note about the evaluations above is that they can be **subjective** or **objective**. Subjective evaluations are those that result from someone's experience with something. Evaluations can also deal with attributes of the objects that we know how to measure independent of the human experience of the object (objective measures). For example, we can evaluate the amount of salt in a dish either subjectively (by asking people how it tastes), or objectively (by subjecting it to a chemical analysis). We know that there is a relationship between the properties of some objects and how people experience them. However, for many interesting objects the relationship between the properties of the object we can measure objectively and the human experience of the object are not known.

There can be a variety of reasons for offering the evaluation. That is, we can have different **objectives** (not to be confused with objective measures) for our evaluations. We can offer such evaluations simply to make conversation, but generally we do so in an effort to convey information to someone about the experience for some purpose. What I do when answering the question "How are you?" (the **process** or method I consciously or unconsciously carry out) depends on what I want to convey. How I would go about evaluating my condition to respond to my doctor may be different than how I would respond to someone passing in the hall.

Often, and certainly when we undertake to evaluate software or systems, we expect that evaluations will lead to actions. In an evaluation, we can indicate approval of an experience, and implicitly suggest that others would also approve. On the other hand, an evaluation can indicate disapproval ("I don't like it"), or make suggestions for improvement (e.g., "It's bland - needs more salt."). The output of the evaluation, whether a casual phrase or a formal report, can vary in effectiveness depending on how well it responds to the purpose of the evaluation. While we sometimes seek simple judgments (pass/fail) in an evaluation, more detail is usually called for in evaluating systems.

Evaluations are everywhere - which makes them both easy to recognize and produce, and difficult to understand (because we do so much evaluating without even thinking about it). For some things that we evaluate, we think about an evaluation as reflecting some fundamental attribute of the thing (e.g., "it is three feet long and two feet wide"). It is often easy to forget that most of the evaluations that we make and encounter are reflections of our experiences with things rather than measurements of attributes of objects.

28.2.1 Evaluation Processes

Some of the processes for producing evaluations can be made explicit in a way that enables them to be shared so that different people evaluating similar objects come up with similar evaluations. For example, we have the tools and vocabulary for evaluating attributes like weight, size, and color so that we expect agreement on evaluations of these attributes of various objects. We can specify tools for measuring (rulers, scales and color meters) and discuss rules for relating the measurements to our evaluation (over 6 feet in height is tall for an adult male, over 5 foot 7 is tall for an adult female, and so on).

But in many cases, the process by which we evaluate cannot be easily surfaced or shared (e.g., How do you decide if someone is "attractive"? Can we clearly identify the process that leads to evaluations of attractiveness?). In such cases we tend to accept disagreement in our evaluations - we don't expect everyone to agree with us - and can often engage in long reflections on why we made certain evaluations. For example, programs in which two critics discuss current movies often begin with a simple statement of the evaluation ("I like it" or "I didn't like it") and then delve into the details of the reasoning behind the evaluation. The reviewers have different explanations for how they produced their evaluations. While we might expect some broad agreement on "how to evaluate a movie", it does not seem likely that we would ever agree on the details.

Why can we agree on some evaluations and not on others? I think the difficulty arises whenever we are involved in an evaluation which depends on a human experience in a context. Consider the differences in deciding on someone's height versus deciding on whether or not they are tall or short. We might agree that height will simply be evaluated with a ruler. In a wide range of conditions (e.g., day of week, time of day, temperature) the method for evaluation could be thought of as context independent (though this might not be strictly true - as some elements, such as temperature, might have an impact on our measuring instrument). independent of context, but whether someone experiences someone else as tall or not depends on many factors in the experience (e.g., how tall they are, how tall the people are around them, personal relationships between the people). If we are discussing the process for evaluating a human experience, we need to be aware of the limits of our ability to develop context independent measurements of experiences. The best we can generally hope for are methods which produce measurements which correlate well with what we are really trying to measure.

Having set this framework for evaluations as the result of a **process** with a **purpose** in a context focused on an **object**, I will spend the rest of the chapter talking about evaluating the **usability** of software systems. The focus will be on the various processes (or **methods**) that might be employed for the purpose of judging how well software systems (objects) might be used to accomplish goals in some environment (context). Throughout this, I want to point out that selection of an evaluation method is not a context free activity. Discussing evaluation techniques without understanding the goals of the evaluation can be very misleading. It is important to understand that there are a variety of techniques available which serve different evaluation purposes. Techniques which are necessary for general theory building and hypothesis testing can be far too expensive and time consuming for resolving local issues (such as menu structure for a given application) in user interface design. Not every evaluation conducted needs to be of a style suitable for publication in a scientific journal. Usually it has to be tailored to communicate effectively to a development team rather than to a journal editor. To a large extent the time and effort expended on an evaluation should reflect the impact of the decision which will result from it.

28.3 Evaluating Software for Usability

Just as there are many different ways to evaluate a person (e.g., for attractiveness, for reliability), a food dish (e.g., for taste, for appearance), or a new car (e.g., for value, for styling), there are many different ways we could evaluate software systems. First, let me say that while I use "software" in the title of this chapter, most of what follows also applies to the evaluation of any other artifact. I focus on designing software mostly because there is a lot of software system construction going on at this time in history, and because though I have experience with construction of physical systems it is software that I work with mostly. Secondly, I will focus on evaluating the usability of such systems rather than trying to address all of the qualitative aspects of software that we might want to address. This does not mean that the following does not apply to attempts to measure "fun" or "motivational" aspects of software (Karat, 1994), only that the chapter is tuned to a consideration of an aspect called "usability."

Before we can talk about how to evaluating usability, we need to come to some agreement on what we mean by the term "usability." While there are many reasons why we might like a context independent definition of usability of a system (e.g., "A usable system is one that has a mouse, uses icons to represent objects, and utilizes direct manipulation for actions on objects"), agreement on such a definition would not be productive. There is no avoiding the fact that system usability is a product of someone's experience trying to do something with a system. Certainly the system influences the experience, but we cannot expect to evaluate usability without understanding context of use.

Borrowing from the work of the International Organization for Standardization (ISO) working group on human-system interaction, I think it makes most sense to begin with the following:

- **Usability** of a **product** is the extent to which the product can be used by specified **users** to achieve specified **goals** with **effectiveness**, **efficiency**, and **satisfaction** in a specified **context** of use.

This is a definition that has been years in development as a part of an effort to provide a standard (a guideline really) for statements about product usability. The use of the word "Product" in the definition can refer to a whole system or to a part of a system. That is, the object at the focus of the evaluation can be selected in many ways (in a very real sense, what is considered focus and what is context will be a fairly arbitrary distinction). We can talk about the "usability of the system menu icon" in an operating system, or we can talk about the usability of computer system with preloaded software for a specific domain. What is critical to point out is that if we are going to do any of these things, we need to specify the context of use relevant to the discussion. Building on this definition and adding the ideas from the framework for evaluations given above, I would emphasize the following:

- The usability of a product is not an attribute of the product alone it is an attribute of interaction with a product in a context of use.
- A **Usability Evaluation Method** is a process for producing a measurement of usability.

Given the definition above, what can we say about measuring usability? First of all the reader should have the sense that it is hard to do well. Measuring "effectiveness, efficiency and satisfaction" in real world contexts is often expensive and time consuming - not features that developers of interactive systems willingly accept. In practice such methods rarely measure the usability of a product directly - by the time it is possible to measure effectiveness, efficiency and satisfaction in a real context of use, those who are interested in measures of usability (often system developers) are off working on different products. While we can apply usability measures out of the context of real use, (generally cheaper and faster) the results of such evaluations may not reflect in context experience with a system. Controlled collection of objective measures (e.g., error rates or task completion times on laboratory tasks) is often treated as more valid than less well defined collection of information in a more realistic setting. While collecting such measures might be useful in some circumstances, both the requesting and evaluating parties should understand the limitations of such information.

Second, there needs to be an understanding about why one would want to go through the process of conducting an evaluation. Knowing what you hope to find helps you determine what tools to bring to bear on the task. Is information about task performance the main reason for collecting information? In cases where planning for use of an existing system rather than influencing the design of a new system is the information needed, this may be the case (e.g., deciding how many people will be required to process a certain volume of information). Is user preference information alone sufficient? When performance characteristics of alternative designs are known to be comparable, it may be. The key point is that since usability is a complex multidimensional concept, understanding the motives for examining it is not just a good thing to do. It is a necessary step in planning for evaluation.

28.3.1 Why Evaluate Usability?

We should consider some of the reasons that one might have for evaluating software. As a long time human-computer interaction researcher, I tend to think that the reasons are obvious. How else are you going to know if a system is good? How else can you understand how to design something better? Unfortunately (for me at least), most of the development world does not share this "because it's there" kind of enthusiasm. To a development project, usability evaluations are things that take time and cost money - impacting at least two parts of a world driven by "function, cost and schedule."

It is not just that people don't think usability is important. Usability evaluation activities are not yet structurally integrated into most development processes. On a recent project, I was in a position to develop a usability plan for a new system which was already under development. While "iterative evaluation with real users" made a lot of sense to everyone on the project management team, when it came to allocating resource to the required activities I was faced with a very interesting response. "What would we do with the information (which would likely include recommendations for changes in the system design)?" Budgets and schedules were tied to statements of work based on reasonably gathered requirements. There was no "slack" in the development schedule for such redesign. Does it make sense to spend resource on an evaluation, if there is no chance that the current project will make use of it? Maybe we should know better - but there are a number of structural forces in product development which will continue to make usability activities a hard sell at times.

Individuals involved in development of software products are interested in evaluations to assist in making design decisions and for determining whether or not the developed product achieves whatever quality measures must be met. While there is some similarity in the various kinds of evaluation methods which are employed in evaluating usability (all are looking to answer whether the system adequately meets the needs of the user), these interests are not served by a single evaluation methodology. A variety of techniques **will** be needed - not because we haven't discovered the correct method yet, but because usability is (and will remain) a complex attribute that we will be interested in looking at in a number of ways.

Consider some of the dimensions that can influence the choice of evaluation methods.

- **What is the purpose of the evaluation?** Do you simply want to make benchmark claims about a system or are you looking to provide information which will inform a design in progress?
- **Who will be doing the evaluation?** Is it better to have an "expert" review the system or to have "real users" do the evaluating?
- **What information to collect?** What are the measures that will be useful? Do you need a continuous measure or is Pass/Fail good enough? Do you want to collect "problems" or evaluate performance?
- **Who will be the audience?** Are you trying to influence developers or build a marketing case?
- **How much resource?** How much time and money is available for conducting the evaluation?

Of key interest in considering the nature of the evaluation will be the consideration of the nature of the criteria for evaluation. In the user-centered design view, evaluation of software involves evaluation of the total system in which the software is used. In this case characteristics of the user, the work environment (e.g. the availability of assistance), and the documentation or on-line assistance are all key factors in the evaluation of usability. One must carefully consider the importance of each of these factors before deciding on an evaluation plan. Throughout the process the most important thing to remember is that people use software systems to achieve goals. A system is successful if the user can easily achieve the goals using the system. The outcome of evaluating software should be to provide a picture of how easily users can carry out the desired tasks. The information of greatest value is that which will help you understand why users succeed or fail in carrying out their tasks - this is rarely a simple numeric measurement.

In many ways the task of specifying an evaluation technique would be simple and straight forward if it included a critical piece of associated information - how is the software to be judged as 'good' or 'bad'. What is missing is a specification of measurable behavioral objectives that must be met in order to pass judgment. With such objectives the evaluation process becomes relatively straight forward. Without them it becomes a very difficult and potentially useless exercise. The development of such objectives and their importance in measuring software user interface quality is key to a successful user-centered design process (see Whiteside, et al. (1988) for a more complete discussion of the role of measurable objectives).

28.4 Usability Information Sources

I described evaluations as involving a process that operated on information about a focal object. One way to classify usability evaluation methods is by the kind of data that they operate on. The kind of information that must be collected for an evaluation of any give type determines much of what the evaluation method is. That is, there are processes for gathering verbal reports or questionnaires from users of a system and for identifying problems or reaching conclusions from the specific kind of data.

The domain of usability evaluation methods is very broad. Rather than trying to be all encompassing, I would like to focus on a range of methods that I have used or seen used productively in **informing design** - that is in providing information to help in the design of software systems. In general the purpose to be served by such methods is to help in the identification of problems and their solutions rather than on identification of how good a system is. While there is a close relation between the two, the change from "how good is it" to "identify the problems and solutions" makes a big difference in choice of methods.

Strictly speaking such a survey should include methods for understanding user work outside of the context of the to-be-developed system. Such techniques include activities which are included in discussions of task analysis and contextual inquiry. Since understanding current work, and understanding new work can be expected to share some common methods, I will cover some techniques here also. However, most of the discussion below will focus on the general activity of how to evaluate incomplete design ideas or design prototypes at various stages in a development cycle.

The identification of usability problems in a prototype user interface (UI) is not the end goal of any evaluation. The end goal is a redesigned system that meets the usability objectives set for the system such that users are able to achieve their goals and are satisfied with the product.

The following sections describe some of the major information sources used in methods employed in user interface design evaluation, and sketches their relation to the software design process. Any evaluation method involves collecting source information. The information for usability evaluations can come directly from users (in the form of verbal reports, responses to questions, or through measurements of the use of a system or prototype). Alternatively it could come from potential users or from usability experts in the act of "inspecting" or "walking through" a system. Such re-

Table 1. Summary of information types and their use.

Method Source	Information Description	General Use
Verbal Reports	Record of cognitive processes of users in system usage	Any time in cycle when general information is desired. Best for problem identification.
Questionnaires	Subjective response of users to questions posed. Best with specific questions.	Any time in cycle when clear questions can be posed.
Use Data	Specific measures from actual or simulated use of a system	For specific tests of major alternatives and full coverage of the interface. Best for competitive evaluations, and performance data.
Design Walkthroughs	End user and development team feedback on general acceptability.	Early in design cycle to make early design decisions. Repeat several times.
Heuristic Reviews	Expert judgment from UI designers on general acceptability.	Early in design cycle to filter standard usability problems. Can be used to complement user-based information.
Theory-based Analysis	Predictions of expert user behavior.	Use in place of user testing for ease of use predictions.

views might be guided by general rules or by specific theory. Table 1 roughly summarizes the discussion of the techniques which will follow, and provides a very general indication of where each might be used in a software design project. By virtue of the type of information provided, some techniques are more useful in certain design procedures than in others. This should become apparent as the discussion progresses.

In general, the first three techniques in Table 1 rely on users as the source of information. In general, I will refer to these as "use based" sources of information and methods. This information can be collected in a realistic context or in some other setting. Such details are generally determined by a situational evaluation of some of the factors (such as time and resource constraints) mentioned earlier.

The remaining sources of information listed in Table 1 are primarily driven be inspections of a design by individuals who are not necessarily users of the target system. Design walkthroughs can be conducted in a variety of ways with a variety of participants (see Karat and Bennett, 1991). In general they are conducted out of the context of real use - sometimes by individuals and sometimes by teams that can include both users and developers. I distinguish design walkthroughs from heuristic evaluations (which are also generally out of context reviews of a design) by the specific guidelines provided in the heuristic procedures.

The final category in Table 1 is for theory-based analysis. I take these as differing from heuristic reviews (which can be motivated by psychological theory) in additional detailed specification of procedure. Techniques in this class (such as GOMS related modeling) have not yet proven sufficiently general to be of broad applicability in usability evaluations (though see Gray, John, and Atwood (1993) for a positive example and additional discussion below).

28.4.1 User-Centered Evaluations

Beyond the details of how to conduct an evaluation using potential users of the system, I cannot overestimate the value of doing so simply because the evaluator will be surprised by what people will do. There are invariably errors or misconceptions which will be discovered in any process of having users evaluate a system that even the most insightful of designers would miss. It is a necessary experience to become aware of the fact that none of us knows everything about how the human mind functions.

There are several techniques which can be used to gather information from users of systems. The type of evaluation which is appropriate depends on the time at which the evaluation is conducted and the use that is to be made of the information collected. Evaluations conducted during system development are generally aimed at providing information for improvements in the existing design. In these cases very specific information about interface details is of the greatest use. This kind of information can be obtained in verbal reports, walkthroughs and direct tests of interface alternatives. Evaluations conducted on completed systems are often less interested in information about specific details and seek information of a more general nature (such as which of several products is easier to learn to use or more productive in carrying out work tasks). Surveys, questionnaires, and general descriptive studies are often the evaluation of choice.

Space prohibits an extensive discussion of the various techniques, but I will briefly discuss them with emphasis on where each seems most appropriate. This should not be taken to mean that only selected techniques are appropriate in a given environment. Properly designed questionnaires can be useful in design cycles, and verbal reports useful in product assurance testing. The intention here is to point out some of the useful features and limitations of each technique.

At the most fundamental level, evaluations can be based on logging user behavior during interaction with a software system. After all, the purpose of any evaluation is to understand what goes on when someone uses the system, and logs of actual use is in many ways more desirable than tests or questionnaires involving subjects. Patterns of use collected by automatic logging programs have been found useful in any number of settings (e.g., Good, 1985). To the extent that such logging can provide sufficient data for a useful evaluation, there is little need to go farther. However, it is not always the case that questions concerning the quality of software can be answered through examination of such use data. A major problem is generally that it relies on the sort of extensive use only found with completed software. Very often the driving reason for conducting evaluations is to aid in design of systems yet to be built.

28.4.2 Verbal Reports/Think-Aloud Evaluations

Why not just have people tell you about their experience in using software? Professionals involved in software evaluation are generally trained in the formal techniques of experimental psychology. Part of the training and experience of obtaining this background is to develop a healthy distrust of what people say. Any individual's description of what they are doing or thinking is often viewed as merely an unverifiable single report, and given little attention until 'real' data are obtained. While there should indeed be much caution in basing far reaching decisions on verbal reports, with reasonable caution in their collection they can provide an excellent source of information.

It is easy to see how verbal reports are treated with such suspicion. Anyone can collect them without specific training, and they can be much more easily manipulated than other behavioral measures. Everyone is familiar with techniques such as 'leading questions' in which the observed can be manipulated into providing answers that the observer wants to hear. On top of this, even well intentioned careful researchers often have trouble knowing what to do with verbal reports once they are collected. Time to complete a task, number of correct or incorrect responses, and other such measures are relatively easy to classify and subject to statistical analysis. The analysis of verbal reports is far more difficult.

Useful results are possible. Careful consideration of the process of obtaining verbal reports, and an analysis of their origin leads to some practical considerations which removes some of the concerns about this type of data. In a very thorough treatment of the topic, Ericsson and Simon (1984) present some guidelines for collecting verbal reports which point out that such reports can be just as valid as other behavioral measures. A verbal report is considered as an excellent way to gain access to the contents of someone's short term memory. To insure the quality of the report (i.e., to insure that it accurately represents the cognitive activity associated with carrying out the primary task), Ericsson and Simon point out that it should be collected concurrently with task performance. Additionally there should be a minimum of intervention by the collector (by minimum of intervention We mean that prompting questions should be eliminated). The time is very important (i.e., concurrent with the task being studied), since it is the working memory contents that are desired. Retrospective reports are viewed as less useful. An individual's report of memory for what he or she must have been thinking some time in the past (i.e., the contents of a retrospective report), is extremely suspect, and while it may be occasionally useful to ask for such reports, they are far less reliable and detailed. The ideal situation would be one in which the observed is simply asked to 'think out loud' while performing the task, and they do so. A record of the report then is obtained for analysis much as a keystroke record would be used.

In practice one will rarely find a subject who gives a quality report with this little prompting. It is a fact that unlike pressing a key, thinking out loud is not something that all subjects do fairly easily. In fact thinking out loud is something that is not a well practiced activity for most of us, and providing a little practice with the task is something that helps considerably for a number of reasons. First of all it helps the subject understand what the observer would like to have done, and secondly it simply helps the subject feel comfortable 'talking to himself'.

A practice task that seems useful is to ask someone to think aloud as they tell you the number of windows there were in the house where they grew up. Often a subject will respond to this request by a moment or two of silence, and then an answer will be provided. At this point the subject can be asked to again go through the process, only this time to report the thoughts that led to the given answer. Unless someone has simply memorized this number, the typical response will be a sort of walk through the house, counting windows one by one. The subject can then be made aware that it is this 'mental walk' that is of interest. During the data collection in the task of interest, an occasional reminder to the subject to 'tell me what you are thinking'.

The procedure then is very simple. Provide the subject with a description of what you want done (i.e., think out loud), give a practice task or two, and then present the system to be evaluated. The report can be tape recorded, and someone should be present to remind the subject of the secondary task (thinking out loud). One must keep in mind not to expect a constant stream of insightful data from this technique. Some tasks do not produce rich reports. For example, asking someone to tell you the phone number of the house that they grew up in produces a much different response than the number of windows question. Questions that call for long term memory retrieval or that call on highly automated responses will not provide rich verbal reports.

Once the data are collected, one is faced with the task of deciding how to evaluate or score it. This can be done in either a formal fashion by classifying responses into defined categories (often more difficult than it sounds), or informally by simply looking at the contents of the responses for information. The formal approach is more appropriate for theory building or hypothesis testing, while the informal approach is typical of less well defined information gathering evaluations. It is precisely this information gathering approach that is the likely candidate for use of verbal reports in software evaluation. Many trade journals that report on software products actually utilize a rather unstructured verbal report technique in reporting their results.

There are some additional considerations in obtaining this type of data. First of all, care should be taken to avoid altering the normal thought process of the subject. To achieve this it is important to limit prompts to the subject to requests to keep talking (while the think aloud process does generally slow down performance on a task, it has not been found to substantially change behavior in other ways). Any other prompts (such as "are you thinking about x?") are likely to change behavior. Finally, it is unfortunately true that a significant number of subjects will simply not provide very useful verbal reports. It is generally the case that under half of the subjects drawn from a typical undergraduate subject pool will provide good protocols. While this might be troublesome for theory building in psychology, where one must be concerned with the reasons for the failure of significant numbers of subjects to provide data, it is of less concern if the goal of the evaluation is checking general features of a system design and looking for suggestions for future alternatives.

In practice, one sees few published reports of research conducted with collection of verbal reports as the primary data source. While formal theory development in psychology has made excellent use of the technique on occasion (Newell and Simon, 1972), it is rare to see applied reports detailing such success. This can be attributed to the nature of the results, and the fact that the technique is at its greatest usefulness in iterative design rather than formal evaluation. Difficulties in scoring and analysis make verbal reports extremely difficult to use in the more formal environment of comparative evaluations, theory testing, or research reports, and generally questionnaires can be constructed to provide information adequate to these purposes.

28.4.3 Surveys and Questionnaires

Once someone has experience with a system, it is fairly easy to ask them questions about the experience. The questions can be quite general, specific in details that the evaluation seeks to address, or very open requests for comments about the system. The responses solicited can be constrained (e.g. a check mark on some scale), or can be free form. The type of questionnaire used, and the questions asked should reflect the information sought by the evaluator.

Questionnaires have had a great deal of use in experimental and survey work in all types of evaluations. Questionnaires can be composed of any number of items in which the same response is given to each (such as indicating agreement or disagreement with some statement), or attitudes on a number of dimensions can be requested for a single item (such as ratings on scales such as consistent-inconsistent and friendly-hostile when evaluating how one found using the system). There is little to say overall to recommend one form of questionnaire over another, and such decisions are generally based on prior individual success or failure with a particular form.

In many respects questionnaires provide the easiest and least expensive method for obtaining measurement data on a system. Consider for example a situation in which one wanted to determine whether or not a system was 'easy to use'. While long and difficult theoretical discussions continue to take place on what it may mean for a system to be easy to use for an individual, it is possible through a questionnaire to simply ask someone the question directly. What the evaluator is doing in this case is trusting the user to create an internal definition of 'ease of use', and then to provide an answer to the evaluator. Different users may have quite different concepts, but if this is true of the population in general, there is no real problem in letting individuals provide their own definition. Alternatively, a definition could be provided in the question (or series of questions). One needs to keep in mind that what one gets from a questionnaire (or any evaluation) are simple data points. The usefulness of the evaluation will be in correct interpretation of the results.

There are a number of valuable discussions of the usefulness of questionnaire data in the evaluation of software. Root and Draper (1983) point out the need to keep questions specific rather than general, and the importance of asking questions about actual system experience rather that hypothetical questions about possible system changes or extensions. The task of answering the question should not be an adventure in creative thinking for the subject, but should rather request a report of experience. Coleman, Williges, and Wixon (1985) describe a methodology for developing an evaluation instrument that can be applied to user interfaces in general. They have found that the methodology can be applied to yield useful information in identifying trouble areas in an interface. Additional support is found in this work which suggests that questions should be concrete and specific if useful information is desired. For example, while it might be desirable to simply ask people to "tell me what was the hardest thing to learn about system x?", one is more likely to get usable information from more focused questions such as "can you tell me when to press the second mouse button?"

What are the shortcomings of the technique? While it is not necessary to constrain questionnaire answers to selections on a scale with a limited number of points (actually scales with only the extreme points labeled on which the subject can place a mark any place between the end marks are also useful), this is generally the technique used. This is primarily because such answers are much more easily quantified than open-ended answers to similar questions. Additionally, questionnaires usually are administered after an experience with a system rather than in the process of working with it. This creates a situation in which information about the experience is restricted (much information may be lost by the limited nature of the questions), and after the fact (recollections may be distorted). For many situations these concerns are not serious enough to outweigh the economy of collection, scoring and analysis. In other situations the additional detail available in more complete verbal reports describing system experience are called for.

28.4.4 Use Data Collection

I include this category for a couple of reasons. First of all, while both verbal reports and questionnaires can be collected from users in the course of system use, there are many other measures (such as errors, task completion times, requests for help, general logging data) which can be useful - often in combination with the above sources. Second, use data - which is generally more easily quantified than verbal report data - is often used in more formal quantitative analysis.

The distinction is obviously one of emphasis rather that a clear difference, since controlled experimental studies can also can use questionnaire or verbal report data as a source of information. There is a very long and detailed history of issues related to the collection and analysis of data in experiments designed to test the validity of some hypothesis (see for example Wiener, 1979), and we will not attempt to present the fine points associated with various experimental design decisions. It is sufficient to say that while someone with little formal training could develop a questionnaire or collect a verbal report, the design of a useful usability test requires fairly extensive training.

As with any evaluation, deciding what use data to collect and how to analyze it begins with the posing of a question to be answered. If one has developed a set of behavioral objectives for the evaluation, the nature of the questions to be answered is often obvious (while it is often difficult to determine the "right" question without them). If the goal is to "be better than the existing situation" (as it often is), one must determine on what behavioral measures. For example, what are the goals for training on the new system, and how quickly do you expect performance to become "better"? The question is commonly of a comparative nature (is system A better than system B on some measure), but can take many other forms (how much easier is it to learn a second word processing system once you already know how to use one). Objective measures are determined so that measures that can be collected in some test (such as time to complete a set of tasks), can be related to key elements of the question (such as ease of use). In general the techniques differ little from those in use in other areas of human factors (or in science in general). If a question can be clearly stated, an experimental evaluation to obtain empirical data can be designed an conducted to answer it.

With a clearly stated question in mind, and a plan for how the measures are to be collected, the next step is actually finding subjects for the test and collecting the data. Here again questions such as who should be tested are largely driven by an understanding of the particular system. The general guideline is 'test representative users'. The goal must be to have the evaluation data reflect as closely as possible the actual situation, and to do this the testing environment and population must be carefully selected.

Perhaps more so than with the other techniques, evaluations based on collecting use data rely on careful consideration of the exact nature of the question to be addressed. Certainly verbal reports, and to some extent questionnaire approaches, can be viewed as information gathering techniques which seek to help define interface questions as much as they seek to evaluate current states. In comparison, if the question is clearly defined, one can be much more confident of the answer produced by a well constructed experiment than that from less general verbal reports.

Usability testing can be completed in the field and in laboratory situations. See Karat (1989) for detailed discussion of usability testing in a field situation. Testing in the field can provide a cost-effective and timely means of collecting data from users and has the added benefit of providing the data on the user's environment of use that may shape the design of the system.

28.4.5 Design Walkthroughs

Design walkthroughs have been conducted for more than 20 years and are an excellent means of collecting feedback from users and engaging users in the design of the system. Design walkthroughs may be conducted in any environment using low-fidelity, paper and pencil or storyboard mockups of a system under development. The team that participates in a walkthrough is best composed of representative end users, as well as programmers, architects, usability engineers, and others who are part of the development team. It is critical to have a person with good facilitation skills guide the walkthrough process.

The team uses a prototype of the system to walk-through a series of typical end user tasks. At different points in the process, data can be collected in the form of expected problems or recommended design alternatives. The basic model is to have the team discuss the interface and explores design ideas, making sure that all aspects of the system are covered in the walk-through. When the walkthrough is supported by prototyping tools, possible redesigns of screens and navigation paths can be mocked up, and "walked through" with the same scenarios. For a more detailed example of such an approach see Bias (1994).

The key challenge of the design review is to consider all elements of the software system, and not just the ideal behavior. It should attempt to capture as much of typical actual use as is possible. This includes errors conditions and assistance seeking behavior. It is often the case that these error conditions are the most difficult for the design team to acknowledge (ego involvement can easily get in the way of objective evaluation). There is difficulty in evaluating potential error conditions without viewing them as a personal failure.

Design walkthroughs might be viewed as the common-sense approach to usability evaluation. In light of the fact that we do not have a detailed theory to guide evaluations, such reviews certainly should be carried out. As long as designers (like all humans) make mistakes which can easily be diagnosed on simple review, it will be useful to limit the number of design errors to be discovered in other evaluations.

Such informal reviews are more a part of the art of design than a solid science of the process. While a number of good principles can be suggested to make such reviews more productive, they are still largely dependent on the individuals involved for useful results. A design review involving individuals with a 'good feel' for software users and their problems will be successful. But simply asking a few bright individuals to walk through a design does not always work well.

28.4.6 Heuristic Reviews

The different heuristic reviews have substantive differences. They include pluralistic and usability walkthroughs, heuristic evaluations, cognitive walkthroughs, think-aloud evaluations, and scenario-based and guideline-based reviews (Bias, 1991, 1994; Desurvire, 1994; Desurvire, Lawrence, and Atwood, 1991; Desurvire, Kondziela, and Atwood, 1992; Jeffries, Miller, Wharton, and Uyeda, 1991; Jorgensen, 1990; Karat, 1994; Karat, Campbell, and Fiegel, 1992; Lewis, Polson, Wharton, and Rieman, 1990; Nielsen, 1989, 1992; Nielsen and Molich, 1990; Wharton, Bradford, Jeffries, and Franzke, 1992; Whitten, 1990; Wixon, Jones, Tse, and Casaday, 1994; and Wright and Monk, 1991). I will not try to summarize the differences in these techniques here, as they are covered in another chapter in this handbook.

28.4.7 Theory-based Reviews

There are a number of techniques which do not necessarily involve the testing or observation of potential users to obtain information. These are generally based on an analysis of what needs to be done by someone to use the system in question coupled with a theory-based representation of the user. To the extent that the theory is accurate, such reviews can substitute use based evaluations with analysis alone to provide insight into predicted use. In theory this replaces one form of evaluation which is viewed as costly with one that could be less costly.

This is not to suggest that the task based techniques consider examination of human cognition to be of no importance. The more formal techniques described actually contain simplified models of the human operator, and are thus theories of human performance. Also, models such as the keystroke-level model of Card, Moran, and Newell (1980) ultimately rely on experimentally derived measures of human performance for their predictions. These measures are general measures (such as cognitive cycle time or homing behavior in pointing), and their values can be obtained from other sources in many cases. The assumptions are that the limited elements contained in the models are sufficient to account for the interactions between the task complexity and the human performing the task. A key question to ask of the theory based techniques is whether or not they have been shown to be valid (i.e., whether or not the predictions of the models has been shown through experimentation to provide accurate descriptions of human behavior). For the techniques presented here, some effort has been made to provide this validation.

Considerable effort has been directed toward development of formal user interface analysis tools. Though perhaps for different reasons, attempts to 'harden' the science of human computer interface design have been called for from both the development (seeking to increase quality and lower development cost) and scientific (using computer systems to study human cognition) communities. There is both reason to believe that progress is being made and that we are still a long way from having really useful theoretical tools for system evaluation and design.

From the GOMS model of Card, Moran, and Newell (1983), to extensions of this work put forward by Kieras and Polson (1985), by Gray et al. (1993), and by John and Kieras (1994), we are seeing a number of techniques aimed at improving the design process for user interface development. There are similar attempts to develop useful design tools based on the programmable user model framework (Young, Green, and Simon, 1989) as well as other "cognitive architectures (see Barnard and May, 1993). In general, all of this work is relatively young, and more research with the techniques is needed before the work could transfer from academic settings to real systems design. These techniques claim to provide assistance that will enable accurate design decisions to be made, without necessitating costly user testing. They do not necessarily claim to eliminate the need for iterative testing of the design to fine tune the details, but they do hold a promise of a additional tools for the interface designer.

28.5 Some Comparisons - Use and Inspection Based Techniques

Human factors practitioners on development teams must make trade-offs regarding software-development schedule, human factors and cost-benefit issues in selecting a usability engineering method to use in a particular development situation (Karat, 1990). These decisions involve whether to use empirical usability testing or inspection methods or both, and the optimal points in the development process for them. Use of inspection methods has been encouraged by development cycle pressures and by the adoption of development goals of efficiency and user-centered design (Bias, 1991, 1994; Bellotti, 1988; Gould and Lewis, 1985; Jorgensen, 1990; Nielsen and Molich, 1990; Wright and Monk, 1991).

When development situations call for the collection of performance data (usually for making "goodness" decisions rather than for identifying problems), the case seems clear. In our experience in using both use data and inspection methods in software development cycles, we have found that it is not reliable to obtain user performance data such as time-on-task, error free task completion rates, and task completion rates with inspection as compared to testing methods. Karat, Campbell, and Fiegel (1992) collected task completion data from walkthrough evaluators in an unobtrusive manner; but we did not have a high degree of confidence in the validity of the data. Collection of time-on-task data and error free task completion rate data was not deemed possible. Given the wider use of usability performance objectives in development and the need for competitive data, the difficulty in collecting relevant data in these areas is a limitation of some inspection methods. Also, while theory-based techniques can be used for some performance predictions, they are considered more reliable for relative comparisons than for absolute predictions.

For problem identification evaluations intended to inform ongoing design, there are mixed results. The several published studies suggest that usability testing identifies more usability problems than inspection methods do. The Karat et al. (1992) study shows that the usability problems that an inspection method missed were relatively severe problems. The low commonality in problems found between methods in the Karat et al. (1992) and Jeffries et al. (1991) studies should caution human factors practitioners about the trade-offs they are making in employing one type of method rather than another or multiple methods. These methods can be viewed as complementary and likely to yield different results; they act as different types of filters in identifying usability problems. However, other recent work has suggested that inspection methods can identify more potential problems (e.g., Wharton et al., 1992). One difficulty with inspections though seems to be that it can identify problems that do not present themselves in a significant way in real use.

It has been our experience in working with developers that the key factor in their acceptance of data from usability walkthroughs or testing is whether or not they had an opportunity to observe or take part in the usability sessions. There is a "seeing is believing" component at work, as well as an issue of their involvement in and commitment to the usability evaluation process. When We conduct usability testing, I have developers join me in the test studio and watch the sessions. During breaks we discuss possible solutions to identified problems. We give them an opportunity to talk with the users during the debriefing sessions. We have seen programmers become so motivated that they work to improve the prototype between user testing sessions to see if particular usability problems can be eradicated.

During many usability walkthroughs in development, developers and designers participate in the walkthrough, listening to the end users and watching their reactions. The developers and designers provide their own comments and work with others as a team to determine solutions to problems. They experience ownership in the process. Developers have responded very well to leading the group walkthrough sessions as well. Usability inspection methods also further the goal of user-centered design by providing many different members of the development team opportunities to become more involved in the usability of the interface (Bias, 1991; Karat et al., 1992).

Table 2 summarizes briefly the strengths and weaknesses of usability testing and inspection methods as related to issues discussed in this section. For more detailed information, see Karat (1994).

Many different types of inspection methods exist, and usability practitioners need to understand the trade-offs involved in the different methods. Table 3 summarizes this section by outlining the key questions to answer when tailoring an inspection method for use in a development situation. Recommendations are made based on current research and case study data. For additional background, please see Karat et al. (1992).

28.6 Conclusions

Based on our knowledge of usability evaluation methods, we recommend that users of the methodologies carefully define and consider their project objectives in selecting which method to use in a particular situation. Users of these methods need to be able to select a method that meets their needs, or tailor a method to the requirements of their situation. The available data highlight the value of UI and domain expertise in conducting usability inspections. Involving more members of the development team and representative end users in the usability evaluation of a system can reap numerous rewards for an organization. Our experience in de-

Table 2. Strengths and weaknesses of usability testing and inspection methods

Issue	Usability Testing	Inspection Method
Ability to address evaluation objectives	Strong	Weak
Number and type of usability problems identified	Strong	Weak
Reliability of usability findings	Strong	Strong
Human factors involvement In conducting method	Weak	Strong
In data analysis	Strong	Weak
Ability to facilitate organizational acceptance of usability goals and activities	Strong	Strong
Appropriateness of method's use at different points in development cycle For numerous lower-level design trade-offs	Weak	Strong
For high-level design guidance, full coverage of interface	Strong	Weak
Effectiveness of method in generating recommendations for change	Strong	Weak
Cost-effectiveness of method	Strong	Strong

velopment suggests that team walkthroughs are an efficient and effective way to meet the objectives of identifying and resolving usability problems in complex interfaces. From experience we know that team walkthroughs require skilled group facilitators. We believe guidelines can be used to bring focus and consensus to the usability objectives for a project, while available research suggests they may be of limited added value to the effectiveness of the walkthroughs themselves. Use of prescribed scenarios or self-guided exploration may be determined based on characteristics of the evaluators and the project objectives. Consideration needs to be given to the way the data from the inspection methods will be collected, analyzed, and used in the development process.

Karat et al. (1992), Desurvire et al. (1991), and Whitten (1991) have suggested that usability inspection methods may be well suited for evaluation activities early in the development cycle and when deciding among competing design solutions. They are a method of choice when resource is very limited (Nielsen, 1989). Whitten (1991) states that an ideal positioning of usability walkthroughs in a project development cycle may include an initial walkthrough during high-level design stage, a second walkthrough after low-level design, and then two iterations of usability testing. A general plan for how one will position usability evaluations in a development project is helpful, but development cycles tend to include many unanticipated changes. Having the flexibility to choose among methods and knowledge of the trade-offs in the different methods should give practitioners a good opportunity for success. Finally, we think there are organizational issues that factor heavily in the success of usability activities on a project and practitioners are advised to communicate with the organization about the value of usability.

Further research can help improve the understanding of the trade-offs being made in using one usability evaluation method rather than another. The modest degree of overlap in the usability problems found by the walkthrough methods and usability testing by Karat et al. (1992), and the even smaller degree of overlap in the problems identified by the methods used by Jeffries et al. (1991) raise serious questions about the trade-offs made in selecting one method rather than another or both. Usability evaluation methods act as different types of filters of user interaction with a computer system, and this aspect of the methods needs to be better understood. It would be beneficial to better understand the added-value of components of the different techniques (e.g., prescribed scenarios versus self-guided exploration) through a more controlled analysis. Further study of team inspections is warranted. We do not understand all of the factors involved in evaluation

Table 3. Summary of issues and recommendations regarding inspection methods.

Issue	Recommendation
Individual Versus Teams	
• Complex judgment required?	Use a team
Evaluator Expertise	
• Expertise available?	Use UI and domain experts
• Development team involvement in user-centered design a goal?	Use representatives of development team and users
Prescribed Tasks Versus Self-exploration	
• Typical tasks known?	Use prescribed tasks
• Full coverage of interface needed?	Use self-exploration
Utility of Guidelines	
• Need to promote consensus about usability goals, bring along junior members on team?	Use guidelines
• Experienced developers only?	Little value in use of guidelines
Data Collection and Analysis	
• Who responsible for data collection?	Usability engineers or they coach development team to do it
• What data are collected?	Set a standard and communicate it
• All problems of equal severity?	Use severity classification scale to prioritize resource allocation
Generation of Recommendations	Include recommendations generation as part of inspection method
Role of Debriefing Session	Include debriefing session in inspection method, include relevant components
• Discuss recommendations for change?	
• Review identified problems?	
• Capture undocumented problems?	
• Collect recommendations for change?	
• Collect positive comments about the system?	
• Resolve interpretation issues?	

methods, nor how to maximize their effectiveness. Improvements can be made in how data are collected, analyzed, and incorporated into the development process. The available data can help practitioners be more effective in selecting or tailoring an appropriate usability evaluation method for a particular development situation, but many questions about usability evaluation methods remain to be addressed.

28.7 References

Barnard, P., and May, J. (1993). Cognitive modeling for user requirements. In P. Byerly, P. Barnard, and J. May (eds.) *Computers, Communication and Usability*, Amsterdam., Elsevier..

Bias, R.G. (1991). Walkthroughs: Efficient collaborative testing. *IEEE Software*, 8, 5, 1991, pp. 94-95.

Bellotti, V. (1988). Implications of current design practice for the use of HCI techniques. In Jones, D.M. and Winder, R., (Eds.), *People and Computers IV*. Cambridge University Press, Cambridge, pp. 13-34.

Carroll, J. M. (1991). *Designing Interaction*. Cambridge University Press, Cambridge, UK.

Coleman, W. D., Williges, R., and Wixon, D. R., (1985). Collecting detailed user evaluations of software interfaces. *Proceedings of the Human Factors Society 29th Annual Meeting*. Santa Monica, 240-244.

Desurvire, H., Kondziela, J., and Atwood, M. (1992). What is gained and lost when using evaluation methods other than empirical testing. Proceedings of HCI International 1992, Monk, A., Diaper, D., and Harrison, M.D. (Eds.) Cambridge University Press (University of York, U.K., September 15-18, 1992).

Desurvire, H., Lawrence, D., and Atwood, M. (1991). Empiricism versus judgment: Comparing user interface evaluation methods on a new telephone-based interface. *SIGCHI Bulletin* , 23, 4, 1991, pp. 58-59.

Ericsson, K. A., and Simon, H. A. (1984). *Protocol Analysis*. Cambridge, MA: The MIT Press.

Good, M. (1985). The use of logging data in the design of a text editor. Proceedings of the CHI 1985 Conference on Human Factors in Computing. Boston: ACM, 93-98.

Gould, J. D., and Lewis, C. (1985). Designing for usability: Key principles and what designers think. *Communications of the ACM*, 26, 295-308.

Gray, W. D., John, B. E., and Atwood, M. E. (1993). Project Ernestine: validating a GOMS analysis for predicting and explaining real-world task performance. *Human-Computer Interaction.*

Jeffries, R.J., Miller, J.R., Wharton, C., and Uyeda, K.M. (1991). User interface evaluation in the real world: A comparison of four techniques. In *Proceedings of CHI'91,* (New Orleans, LA, April 28-May 3, 1991), ACM, New York, pp. 119-124.

John, B. E., and Kieras, D. E. (1994). The GOMS family of analysis techniques: Tools for design and evaluation. *Carnegie Mellon University Technical Report CMU-CS-94-181*. Pittsburgh, PA.

Jorgensen, A.K. (1990). Thinking-aloud in user interface design: A method promoting cognitive ergonomics. *Ergonomics*, 33, 4, 1990, pp. 501-507.

Karat, C. (1994). A comparison of user interface evaluation methods. In Nielsen, J. and Mack, B. (Eds.), *Usability Inspection Methods*. NY, Wiley and Sons, pp. 203-234.

Karat, C. (1994). A business case approach to usability cost justification. In Bias, R. and Mayhew, D. (Eds.), *Cost-Justifying Usability*. Cambridge, MA: Academic Press, pp. 45-70.

Karat, C., Campbell, R., and Fiegel, T. (1992). Comparison of empirical testing and walkthrough methods in user interface evaluation. *ACM SIGCHI Conference on Human Factors in Computing Systems*, Monterey, CA, May 3-7, 1992, pp. 397-404.

Karat, J. (1982). A model of problem solving with incomplete constraint knowledge. *Cognitive Psychology*, 14, 538-559.

Karat, J., and Bennett, J. (1991). Using scenarios in design meetings— A case study example. In J. Karat (Ed.), *Taking Software Design Seriously: Practical Techniques for Human-Computer Interaction Design.* Boston: Academic Press.

Karat, J. (1994). Workplace applications: Tools for motivation and tools for control. In K. Duncan and K. Krueger (Eds.), *International Federation for Information Processing World Congress*. Amsterdam: North-Holland, pp. 382-388.

Landauer, T. K. (1995). The trouble with computers. Cambridge, MA: The MIT Press.

Lewis, C., Polson, P., Wharton, C., and Rieman, J. (1990). Testing a walkthrough methodology for theory-based design of walk-up-and-use interfaces. In *Proceedings of CHI'90* (Seattle, WA, April 1-5, 1990), ACM, New York, pp. 235-242.

Nielsen, J. (1994). Usability Inspection Methods, New York: Wiley and Sons

Nielsen, J. (1992). Finding usability problems through heuristic evaluation. In *Proceedings of CHI'92* (Monterey, CA, May 3-7, 1992), ACM, New York.

Nielsen, J. (1989). Usability engineering at a discount. In Salvendy, G., and Smith, M.J., (Eds.), *Designing and Using Human-Computer Interfaces and Knowledge-Based Systems.* Amsterdam: Elsevier Science Pulishers, pp. 394-401.

Nielsen, J. and Molich, R. (1990). Heuristic evaluation of user interfaces. In *Proceedings of CHI'90* , (Seattle, WA, April 1-5, 1990), ACM, New York, pp. 249-256.

Root, R. W., and Draper, S. (1985). Questionnaires as a software evaluation tool. *Proceedings of the CHI 1983 Conference on Human Factors in Computing.* Boston: ACM, 83-87.

Smith, S. L., and Mosier, J. N. (1984). *Design Guidelines for User-System Interface Software.* Report MTR-9420, Mitre Corporation, Bedford, MA.

Wharton, C., Bradford, J., Jeffries, R., and Franzke, M. (1992). Applying cognitive walkthroughs to more complex user interfaces: Experiences, issues, and recommendations. In *Proceedings of CHI'92* (Monterey, CA, May 3-7, 1992), ACM, New York.

Whiteside, J., Bennett, J. and Holtzblatt, K. (1988). Usability engineering: Our experience and evolution. In M. Helander (Ed.), *Handbook of Human-Computer Interaction* (pp. 791-818). Amsterdam: Elsevier Science Publishers.

Whitten, N. (1990). Managing Software Development Projects: Formula for Success . New York: Wiley & Sons, pp. 203-223.

Wixon, D., Jones, S., Tse, L., and Casaday, G. (1994). Inspections and design reviews: Framework, history, and reflection. In Nielsen, J. and Mack, R. (Eds.), Usability Inspection Methods, New York: Wiley and Sons.

Wright, P.C., and Monk, A.F. (1991). The use of think-aloud evaluation methods in design. *SIGCHI Bulletin* , 23, 1, 1991, pp. 55-57.

Young, R. M., Green, T. R. G., and Simon, T. (1989). Programmable user models for predictive evaluation of interface designs. In K. Bice and C. Lewis (Eds.*) Proceedings of CHI '89.* New York: ACM.

Ziegler, J. E., Hoppe, H. U., and Fahnrich, K. P. (1986). Learning and transfer for text editing with a direct manipulation interface. *Proceedings of the CHI 1986 Conference on Human Factors in Computing.* Boston:

Handbook of Human-Computer Interaction
Second, completely revised edition
M. Helander, T.K. Landauer, P. Prabhu (eds.)

Chapter 29

Usability Inspection Methods

Robert A. Virzi
GTE Laboratories Incorporated
Waltham, Massachusetts, USA

29.1 The Usability Inspection Methods

In this chapter, unlike other chapters in this book that focus on empirical methods for improving the usability of an interface, I will be describing the costs and benefits associated with a collection of non-empirical methods for evaluating user interfaces, collectively called *usability inspection methods*. These methods are considered non-empirical because rather than collecting data or observing users interacting with a system, they rely on the ability of judges who attempt to predict the kinds of problems users will experience with a user interface. While on the face of it this may seem to be pure folly, in practice variants of the technique have been demonstrated to be both cost-effective and reliable ways of evaluating usability in some cases. In this chapter, I first present the variety of techniques that fall under the umbrella term of *usability inspection*. Following this, research reports are reviewed. Section 29.3 presents considerations for practitioners considering using one of these techniques.

The term 'usability inspection' is a relatively new one. It was coined at a workshop in 1992 (Mack and Nielsen, 1993), some two years after the first papers on the topic emerged. Collected together under this general term are a broad variety of techniques that vary on three defining dimensions. All of the techniques presented in this chapter can be considered as a unique combination of settings on these dimensions shown below.

1. **The characteristics of the judges:** The level and kind of expertise of the judges performing the evaluations varies considerably in the reports found in the literature. The primary defining element is whether or not the judges have usability expertise or not. Other important factors include: application domain knowledge; prior design experience; and academic training of the judges. One class of the inspection techniques described in this chapter are designed for use by engineers or developers with no formal usability training. These evaluators have been called "non-experts" in the literature, which is a shorthand way of saying that they were not usability experts, although they may be quite expert in other domains. Another class of inspection techniques relies on usability experts to be the judges. Non-expert evaluators tend to be used when human factors specialists are either: (a) not available; or (b) judged to be too expensive for a given project's budget.

2. **Number of evaluators in a single session:** Some of the techniques rely on groups of people working together in a single evaluation, as when a design

team inspects an interface. Other methods rely on judges working alone, although the results of several judges may be combined to improve the quality of the information obtained. When choosing an inspection method, it is important to consider where on this dimension one wants to be. If, for example, code reviews are already part of the development process within a company, a group usability inspection may fit best within this culture. An organization based more on a consulting model might do best by soliciting individually conducted analyses. The literature does not speak to which of these approaches produces the best results. It appears to be better to match the approach to the situation in which it is embedded.

3. **The goals of the inspection:** While usability inspections are predominantly used to uncover general usability problems in an interface, this is not the only goal reported in the literature. One technique, the cognitive walkthrough, is specifically designed to evaluate problems associated with ease of learning. Other goals are also possible, though less common. For example, one could conduct a usability inspection to assess compliance with a set of standards. It is important to define the goals of an inspection and select a tool designed to meet those from what is available.

Other authors have suggested additional factors that differentiate the usability inspection methods. For example, Olson and Moran (1996) propose a two dimensional space that classifies these methods based on whether or not they employ guidelines and whether or not they use scenarios to guide the evaluation. Rather than pulling these factors out as separate dimensions, I have chosen to address these issues as minor variations within each of the techniques because there is no evidence that these factors influence the efficacy of the method.

When viewed in the structure provided by these three dimensions, the usability inspection techniques reported in the literature may be grouped into four loose categories or camps. Within each of these camps there is considerable variability and subtlety of practice. For example, some practitioners emphasize the use of guidelines by the evaluators (Nielsen and Molich, 1990; Muller, McClard, Bell, Dooley, Meiskey, Meskill, Sparks, and Tellam, 1996) whereas others do not (Virzi, Sorce, and Herbert, 1993). This variation in the technique is partially because this area is quite young and there is not much research to guide practice. Perhaps the more important contributor to this variability is the extreme malleability of the techniques themselves, and the need for practitioners to fit them into their specific situations. With this caveat in mind, the reader is invited to consider the four broad categories of usability inspection methods presented below.

29.1.1 Resource-Constrained Methods

One branch of usability inspection is devoted to finding ways for developers (people with little or no human factors training) to find usability problems in a system. These procedures are designed to work in highly resource-constrained situations when a human factors expert is not available or viewed as too costly. Evaluators work alone, and the power of the techniques come from combining the results over evaluators. One such technique, *heuristic analysis*, was described by Nielsen and Molich in 1990. Nielsen and Molich present a set of nine heuristics or design principles which they say can be used by people with little usability experience to evaluate a user interface. Individual developers compare the interface to the short list of heuristics, hence the name given the process. The intent of this original proposal was to provide a method for introducing some usability analysis to resource-limited projects when usability professionals were not available. A similar approach is taken by Wright and Monk (1991). They describe a process, called *cooperative evaluation*, which relies on non-expert evaluators working with a single user who thinks aloud. For both approaches, limited success (in terms of identifying usability problems in an interface) was demonstrated for each evaluator. The power of these approaches comes from combining the results of multiple evaluators to yield an acceptable level of problem detection sensitivity. For the purposes of this chapter, I will refer to this family of evaluation techniques as *resource-constrained methods*.

29.1.2 Usability-Expert Reviews

A second way to conduct a usability inspection is to employ usability experts as surrogates for the users. These usability experts are asked to critique a user interface with the goal of identifying usability problems. The reasoning behind this approach is that the experts, based on their prior experience with both systems and users, will be able to identify likely sources of difficulty in the interface. This technique is most similar to heuristic evaluation, with the exception that usability experts are used as the judges. The defining characteristic of this technique is that the experts are asked to work alone. The usability experts may be given a set of guidelines to apply (Desurvire, Lawrence, and Atwood, 1991; Karat, Campbell, and Fiegel, 1992) or not (Dumas, Sorce, and Virzi, 1995; Jeffries, Miller, Wharton, and Uyeda, 1991; Virzi, Sorce, and Herbert, 1993). Providing the experts with usage scenarios also varies in practice. Unfortunately, there are no studies examining whether or not these two procedural variations affect expert performance, leaving it to the practitioner to select the appropriate path. I will call this class of usability inspection techniques *usability-expert reviews*.

In the United States at least, usability-expert reviews appear to be more commonly used than the resource-constrained methods. This may be attributable to a higher penetration of human factors experts within U.S. companies than those in Europe and Asia, although it is still an open question.

For both the resource-constrained methods and usability-expert reviews, the ability to detect problems is greatly enhanced by the addition of judges. Although the judges work independently, aggregating the problems identified across judges leads to a higher proportion of usability problems identified (Dumas, Sorce, and Virzi, 1995; Nielsen and Molich, 1990; Wright and Monk, 1991). This is distinct from team-based review methods in which multiple evaluators work together. For this latter case, it is not clear that adding evaluators leads to better results (Kahn and Prail, 1994).

29.1.3 Group Design Reviews

In contrast to both the resource-constrained methods and usability-expert reviews, in which evaluators work independently, a separate class of usability inspection methods are *group design reviews*, in which multiple evaluators work together in a single session. The user interface to be evaluated is analyzed in a group setting, where the composition of the group can vary. Typically the group performing the evaluation has at least one human factors specialist and a variety of other disciplines, normally including the members of the development team and occasionally extended to include graphic artists, documentation or training specialists, marketing, user interface designers, and even users. Groups can be as small as two (Karat, Campbell, and Fiegel, 1992) or considerably larger as reported in Wixon, Jones, Tse, and Casaday (1994). The common goal of these evaluations is to identify potential usability problems in the interface under scrutiny. In the four studies reported in Wixon, et al (1994) human factors specialists were clearly involved in three of the evaluations. Bias (1994) reports a variant of the group design review process, called a *pluralistic usability walkthrough,* that defines a specific role for the human factors professional – as the process administrator and advocate for the user. Contrast this with Kahn and Prail (1994) who provide a group process specifically designed to work *without* a human factors specialist. This procedure was created so that their staff could impact a greater breadth of projects within their company.

The techniques described in this section can have considerable overlap with those presented in sections 29.1.1 and 29.1.2. For example, expert involvement and the use of guidelines varies equally widely in both. Group design reviews are bound together by the process of analyzing the interface in a single group. This distinguishes them from the individual inspection methods that rely on judges working alone.

29.1.4 Cognitive Walkthroughs

A *cognitive walkthrough* is a very specific type of usability inspection method that evaluates how easy an interface is to *learn*, while sacrificing other kinds of usability information (e.g., overall consistency). Thus it is distinguished from other usability inspection techniques primarily by its goal, rather than by the number of evaluators or their expertise. A detailed description of the technique is reported in chapter 30 of this handbook and also in Polson, Lewis, Rieman, and Wharton (1992). A cognitive walkthrough is compared to other usability inspection techniques in Jeffries, Miller, Wharton, and Uyeda (1991). The theory behind this methodology is that users learn how to use an interface by exploring its functionality, learning new aspects of the system only when they are needed for the task at hand. For example, a user of a word processor is presumed to learn how to italicize a word when he or she has a need to do so in a document, not by prior exposure to the function in a reference manual. The technique provides a formal framework that allows a designer to evaluate whether or not there is enough information present in the user interface to allow the user to learn how to accomplish the desired task. Specific scenarios are provided to the evaluators, who use a fixed set of rules or guidelines for evaluating the information present in the interface.

Like the other techniques, the cognitive walkthrough is being refined and adapted to the needs of designers at the time of this writing. At a high level, the user interface is evaluated in the following manner, as described in Wharton, Rieman, Lewis, and Polson (1994). The owner of the user interface design presents it to a group of his or her peers. It is then the job of the peers to evaluate the solutions proposed by the designer in light of the constraints placed on the design. Prior to presentation of the design, assumptions made about the users are made explicit, including who they are, their backgrounds, and the context in which the software will be used. The design itself may be presented in any number of ways, including sketches, low-fidelity mockups, or an interactive prototype. The designer would present a scenario under which the interface might be used, and step through each action the user would have to perform to complete the task. Each step is scrutinized by the peer-reviewers, who attempt to predict what the users' intentions would be, and look for supporting artifacts in the user interface. If there are affordances (Norman, 1988), attributes of the user interface that guide the user down the correct path, then the interface is judged to be acceptable. In this way, ease of learning is emphasized.

Cognitive walkthroughs are quite distinct from the other techniques in several respects. They are conducted in group settings, but the group is entirely made up of usability experts. This is rare in group design reviews, with an exception reported in one of the cases in Wixon, et al. (1994). Cognitive walkthroughs focus on how easy an interface is to learn, which is a much narrower focus than the typical inspection. Finally, it is quite formal as far as usability inspection methods go, prescribing usage scenarios to guide the evaluation and the use of specific evaluation criteria for the judges. It should be noted, however, that Wharton, et al. (1994) report an effort to relax the technique to make it more usable in practice.

29.1.5 Why GOMS (and other practices) Aren't Usability Inspection Techniques

Given the broad range of methods and procedures that seem to be employed in usability inspections, one might be tempted to ask, "What isn't a usability inspection?" GOMS (the Goals, Operators, Methods, Selection rules technique described theoretically in Card, Moran, and Newell, 1986, and practically in Gray, John, and Atwood, 1993) is not normally considered a usability inspection technique. Why not?

Consider what GOMS is. It is a method for predicting expert users' performance on specific tasks with a given interface. GOMS modelers do not run subjects, so it is not an empirical method. Typically the model is built by a small number of usability experts, although this was not the intent stated in Card, et al. (1986), who intended it to be used by non-experts. The outputs of a GOMS model are predicted task times, which are normally used to compare alternate designs.

I do not consider GOMS to be a usability inspection method for two reasons. First, GOMS is a resource intensive technique. Second, GOMS analysis does not lead directly to usability problem identification. The essence of the usability inspection techniques are that they (1) to conserve resources and (2) identify potential usability problems. Most do this by minimizing user involvement (Wright and Monk, 1991; Muller, et al., 1996) or eliminating it all together. This is the common link between all the inspection techniques, and what sets them apart from other usability methodologies. Gray and Salzman (1996) coined the broader term, *Usability Evaluation Method (UEM)*, which includes both GOMS and the variations on user testing.

29.2 Literature Review

29.2.1 History: Is there anything new here?

In an earlier edition of this handbook, Karat (1988) discusses the *informal design review* in his chapter on software evaluation methods. He describes it as "common sense testing" conducted by a group using a walkthrough methodology. From his discussion it is apparent that the technique had been in use for some time. Bias (1994) makes this same point humorously, while Bailey, Allan and Raiello (1992) make the claim explicitly: Usability inspection has been going on for years. Wixon, et al. (1994) state that an inspection process had been in place at Digital Equipment Corporation since 1987. So what change sparked the vast increase in interest in the technique?

Two reports of usability inspection techniques were presented at the Association for Computing Machinery Computer-Human Interaction Conference (ACM CHI) in 1990. Nielsen and Molich (1990) reported on the use of heuristic evaluation by computer scientists or other evaluators not trained in human factors. At the same conference, Lewis, Polson, Wharton, and Rieman (1990) reported a methodology for uncovering ease-of-learning issues by examining a user interface – what they called the cognitive walkthrough technique. The wide exposure these techniques received at the conference, coupled with a need to find less expensive but still effective ways to refine user interfaces, generated a revival of interest in what later came to be known as usability inspection techniques.

Since 1990, we have seen many papers that describe: refinements to procedures; quantitative studies comparing usability inspection to other techniques; and analyses of the kinds of problems uncovered. If nothing else, the human factors community was made more aware of usability inspection as an option, and the potential gains and drawbacks are becoming better understood. So, the answer to the question, "Is there anything new here?," is a qualified, "Yes." While the act of inspecting software for usability problems is not new, our breadth and depth of understanding how to conduct this process and what to expect from it is considerably greater.

29.2.2 Empirical Data on Non-Empirical Methods

A fair amount of research has been directed towards understanding the efficiencies and drawbacks of usability inspection techniques. In this section, studies quantifying the approaches are reviewed. A cautionary note is being prepared by Gray and Salzman (1996) at the time of this writing that questions the experimental soundness of several of the studies presented in this chapter. (Specifically, some or all of the claims made by Bailey, et al., 1992; Desurvire and Thomas, 1993; Desurvire, et al., 1991; Jeffries, et al., 1991; Karat et al., 1992; Nielsen, 1992; and Virzi, et al., 1993, among others, are questioned.) They take the position that flaws in the reporting and experimental procedures of these studies nullifies the utility of their results. While I acknowledge that Gray and Salzman have identified some serious problems in experimental methods, and that some authors may have overstated the claims of their work, I fear they have gone too far and thrown out the baby with the bath water, so to speak. While some of the experiments were indeed flawed, and statements made in the conclusion sections of the papers may be overstated, there is still some value in this work. I have tried to present these valuable lessons here.

Many articles in this literature discuss a problem detection rate (Karat, Campbell, and Fiegel, 1992; Nielsen and Molich, 1990; Virzi, Sorce, and Herbert, 1993; Wright and Monk, 1991; among others). This is a statistic used to compare the efficacy of various techniques within a given study. To calculate the rate, all of the unique usability problems found over all the analyses are tabulated. This occurs across both techniques and evaluators to form a union of all the problems identified in a user interface. Then, the detection rate for a given method, or for a typical evaluator within a method, is calculated as a percentage of the overall set. Techniques and evaluators that identify a greater percentage of the overall problem set are judged to be more effective. While this is a useful statistic for comparing results within a study, it is imprudent to make comparisons across studies because the statistic is sensitive to (a) how refined the user interface is when it is studied and (b) how thorough the analysis is that determines the union of all problems. This latter issue is compounded by different definitions being used by different researchers to determine what counts as a usability problem and what does not. While one researcher may aggregate several user behaviors into a higher-order usability problem, a different researcher may treat each of these behaviors as separate usability problems. All that said, there is considerable value in looking at the relative detection rates within a study, as these comparisons tend to be robust.

An interesting dilemma regarding problem detection is presented by both Bailey, et al. (1992) and Gray and Salzman (1996). Is it possible for usability inspection techniques to find 'problems' in a user interface that were not uncovered during user testing of that same interface? I believe the answer to this question is yes, for a variety of reasons. Consider that the user testing may not have been comprehensive or may not have had sufficient power to detect low-frequency problems. Also, if only one measure was taken in the usability testing, say task completion time, the inspection method may have uncovered a problem more closely related to another usability measure, perhaps error rates or preference. In any event, if the goal of the evaluation is to identify *potential* problems in a user interface for the designer to evaluate, both kinds of data are valid and should be considered in the redesign process.

Evaluating Resource-Constrained Methods

Nielsen and Molich (1990) proposed the use of heuristic evaluation by non-experts. They found that while any single developer is rather poor at finding problems in the user interface, aggregating results from a number of evaluators can lead to acceptable problem detection rates. For example, in Experiment 2 of Nielsen and Molich, individual evaluators found 38% of the total set of usability problems on average, where the total set was defined by the authors' evaluation of the interface. They report that aggregating results from five evaluators leads to approximately a 70% problem detection rate. Increasing the number of evaluators to ten leads to 83% of the usability problems being found, on average. The authors argue that this is quite acceptable, and that it is far better than the alternative of doing no evaluation at all.

Wright and Monk (1991) describe a technique also designed for use by developers which they call cooperative evaluation. This procedure requires the developer to conduct a think-aloud test with a single user. The developer, as evaluator, is expected to note any usability problems that occur in the session. In their test of the method (experiment 1) individual evaluators who were computer science undergraduates, detected about 30% of the total set of usability problems in a single testing session. Like Nielsen and Molich (1990), they show that aggregating results over evaluators improves the level or problem detection (see Lewis, 1994; and Virzi, 1992; for related discussions on the power of aggregating evaluators).

Based on Nielsen and Molich (1990) and Wright and Monk (1991) it would appear that resource-constrained methods can be valuable under some circumstances. In particular, it seems to be necessary to have fairly large numbers of non-trained evaluators to be confident that a majority of the usability problems will be found. Although these authors do not discuss it, it would appear to me that these methods benefit from a usability expert overseer, whose job is to coordinate the efforts of the multiple judges and collate the results into a single comprehensive report. Thus the technique might be best suited to the case where a small group of practitioners are trying to extend their reach to a relatively large number of usability projects within their company.

The Expert Advantage

Desurvire, Lawrence, and Atwood (1991) showed that human factors experts were better able to predict user performance than non-experts. They asked both usability experts and non-experts to predict user performance with an interactive telephone-based interface. The evaluations were performed using paper specifications of a system, not an interactive prototype or the actual system. Additionally, they had naive subjects interact with their system and the experimenters evaluated their performance. The experts' evaluations were significantly correlated with naive subjects' performance, whereas the non-experts' evaluations were not. This study demonstrated two important findings. First, part of the benefit of using expert evaluators is that they can better predict how users will use an interface. Second, an advantage of all usability inspection techniques is that they can be used very early in the design process, before any sort of prototype is prepared.

Desurvire, Kondziela, and Atwood (1992) evaluated the relative abilities of usability experts, system designers, and non-experts using two methods: group design reviews and cognitive walkthroughs. For both inspection methods, experts performed far better than the other two groups, reinforcing the fact that usability experts are better able to find problems in an interface than non-experts. This study also showed that group design reviews were more effective than cognitive walkthroughs in identifying usability problems. This result was attributed to the narrow focus of the latter. This advantage only obtained for the experts, most likely due to the low numbers of problems non-experts found in all conditions (i.e., a floor effect).

Jeffries, Miller, Wharton, and Uyeda (1991) compared three usability inspection techniques to empirical testing in an evaluation of a pre-release version of a graphical user interface. The four conditions in the experiment were: (1) a usability-expert review in which four usability experts independently evaluated the interface; (2) a resource-constrained review by three software developers who attempted to apply a set of 62 guidelines; (3) a cognitive walkthrough (the walkthrough, conducted by developers, was modified from the procedure given in Lewis at al., 1990, by adding a method for capturing assumptions about their non-naive users); and (4) an empirical usability study of six subjects. Jeffries, et al. reported that the usability-expert review was the most effective method. It identified the greatest number of problems, was successful in identifying serious usability problems, and because they did not include a charge for expert time, was lowest in cost. They note one drawback of the technique was that it also uncovered many low-priority problems which may not be cost effective to address. Both the resource-constrained method and the cognitive walkthrough missed some of the most severe problems. Usability testing, they concluded, was an effective means of identifying serious and recurring problems, and avoided identifying low-priority problems, but was the most expensive testing method.

What's a Cost and What's a Benefit?

While Jeffries, et al. (1991) provide an interesting analysis, the costs of the heuristic evaluation may have been under-represented. The time taken by the four expert reviewers was not measured and did not figure into the cost analysis. This may be a realistic assumption if you have usability experts on staff, but it certainly does not hold for all practitioners. Jeffries, et al. point to the identification of large numbers of usability problems as a benefit. Not all researchers view this as an advantage (Bailey, et al., 1992), suggesting that the shear number of problems experts identify make it hard to prioritize them.

Karat, Campbell, and Fiegel (1992) compared an empirical usability test to group design reviews and resource-constrained reviews. (Note: The participants were predominantly non-experts. Some small number of the participants were usability experts, but it is not clear how they were distributed across conditions. In this interpretation, I have treated all the evaluators as non-experts.) Both inspection methods employed a short set of guidelines that the evaluators were asked to use. Six users participated in the usability test, six individual inspectors conducted resource-constrained evaluations, and six pairs of inspectors participated in the non-empirical conditions for each of the two systems they evaluated. Contrary to the results reported by Jeffries, et al., they reported that the empirical test found significantly more problems than either of the two usability inspection methods, and that it was most successful at identifying the most severe problems. In this study, the usability inspection methods were less costly to conduct, but cost more on a per-problem basis than performance testing. The conflicting results could be attributed to differences in either evaluator expertise or to the amount of time allotted to the heuristic evaluators. Jeffries, et al. used heuristic evaluators that were both more experienced in human factors and who were allowed more time for their evaluations. Both of these would tend to yield more productive analyses than the procedures employed by Karat, et al.

Partially to address the questions raised by the Jeffries, et al. (1991) and Karat, et al. (1992) studies, Virzi, Sorce, and Herbert (1993) compared usability-expert reviews to think-aloud testing (see Lewis, 1982) and performance testing. They measured both the problem detection rates and the resources each of the techniques required on a per-evaluator basis. Six experts participated in the study, spending one hour each on the evaluation. Ten subjects were run in each of the empirical methods. These investigators reported that the usability-expert reviews (a) found the greatest number of problems; (b) did so in the shortest elapsed time; (c) at the lowest cost per problem if you do not have incremental costs for the experts. Realizing that laboratory costs, expert availability, and subject costs vary by project, they suggest considering all of these factors when choosing an evaluation methodology.

Virzi, et al. recommended a combination of usability-expert reviews and think-aloud testing for its ability to capture the broadest range of potential problems. This is based on the relatively meager unique contribution performance testing added to the set of usability problems they uncovered. This last recommendation can be compared to Bailey, Allan, and Raiello (1992) who argued that heuristic evaluation identifies many more problems than can be efficiently addressed, while giving no guidance as to which are the most severe. In general, this criticism has been directed towards all of the usability inspection methods because they rely on the inspectors' judgments of problem severity. Both Virzi, et al. and Jeffries, et al. argue that it is better to identify the problems and rely on other methods to resolve issues of prioritization (e.g., using consideration of what it would cost to fix a problem).

Improving the Methods

Dumas, Sorce, and Virzi (1995) start with the assumption that usability-expert reviews are effective. They address ways to improve the methodology. One question they asked was, "Is it better to have a smaller number of experts spend a greater amount of time evaluating an interface, or is it more effective to simply recruit more experts, holding expert-time on the project constant?" In their study, five experts evaluated an interactive voice response system in three one-hour blocks. They tracked the number of problems identified by the experts in each block. They stated that it appeared to be more effective to have a greater number of evaluators work for a shorter time, with the results aggregated. For example, an expert working for three hours produced an average problem detection rate of 60%. The results from three experts working for one hour each, when aggregated, produced a 70% problem detection rate, on average. Even though the total amount of expert time is preserved, a greater percentage of the usability problems are uncovered in the latter condition. A second methodological question they asked was, "Is there any benefit to bringing the usability experts together after they have completed their individual evaluations?" To examine this, they brought the expert reviewers together for a short time after the reviews to discuss what they had found. Dumas, et al. report this had the benefit of producing more integrated design solutions and higher-level problem descriptions than produced by the experts working in isolation, albeit at increased project costs. This last result is primarily anecdotal in nature, however.

An interesting amplification of the evidence that usability experts are the most effective at finding problems is given by Nielsen (1992). Double experts, those experts having both usability expertise and specific knowledge of the domain of the application were better at finding problems than professionals having only general usability expertise. So not only does it appear that using experts is advantageous, it appears to be productive to get experts with as much specific knowledge of your application area as possible.

There has been some recent work aimed at improving the effectiveness of evaluators in group design reviews. The results would apply equally to usability-expert or resource-constrained reviews. Desurvire and Thomas (1993) propose a technique called *Programmed Amplification of Valuable Experts* (PAVE). The approach taken in PAVE is to encourage evaluators to consider a broader array of perspectives in analyzing an interface. Evaluators were encouraged to assume roles in the hope that this would suggest a wider array of usability problems to them. For example, an evaluator might be invited to review the interface from the perspective of a "worried mother." By asking the evaluator to assume this perspective, it is hoped that they will view the interface in a new way, allowing them to see additional problems. This method, although still in need of refinement, did show some ability to improve the evaluations of non-experts. Expert performance was not affected.

Another attempt to bring to bear a broader perspective in conducting usability inspections is presented by Muller, et al. (1996). These authors suggest three or four new heuristics to add to the list presented by Nielsen and Molich (1990). Their work represents an attempt to shift the focus from the software to the work process supported by the software. The guidelines emphasize respecting the user's skills and privacy and the effect of the system on the employees environment. Initial evaluations of these new heuristics suggest they helped evaluators to find some unique usability problems related to these environmental factors. This method of improving evaluator performance is similar to Desurvire and Thomas (1993) in that both methods aim to increase the problem detection rate by asking inspectors to assume perspectives they might not normally assume. In effect, these techniques encourage the judge to cast his or her net wider, anticipating a greater catch.

29.3 Heuristics for Choosing a Usability Inspection Method

While it would be nice to conclude this chapter with a series of hard and fast rules for selecting a usability inspection method suitable for any project, it is simply not possible. In lieu of this, I have mapped out some of the questions one must consider first when deciding if a usability inspection is appropriate, and then how to go about choosing a specific methodology for those cases where it is.

29.3.1 Usability Inspection or Empirical Testing?

Usability inspection is not appropriate for every user interface testing situation. Karat (1988) presents usability inspection as a precursor to empirical testing, but not as a replacement. Nielsen and Molich (1990) proposed a specific resource-constrained inspection technique as a substitute for empirical testing when sufficient resources are not available to conduct user tests. The discipline appears to have moved from the former position towards the latter, viewing usability inspection as a valuable tool that can and should be used as a replacement for empirical tests under some circumstances, although individual practitioners seem to vary in their opinions regarding when it may prudently be used as a replacement. As a general rule-of-thumb, acceptance for the practice seems to be highest in earlier stages of an iterative design process, declining as a product comes closer to its final form.

Usability inspection is not intended as a replacement for empirical testing in cases where the level of user performance is critical. If one is attempting to refine task completion times to an absolute optimum, as when designing a system that will be used for millions of repetitions (e.g., a directory assistance operator interface), usability inspection techniques will fall short. They are not intended to provide the level of detail needed to make distinctions between alternatives that might vary by only a few seconds or tenths of seconds per task.

A practical consideration is, when confronted with a situation in which the choice is between conducting a usability inspection or doing nothing at all, what should one do? Some of the investigators who addressed this question in their discussion sections support the inspection option, most vocally Nielsen and Molich (1990), but also others with some reservations (Dumas, et al., 1995; Karat, et al., 1992; Virzi, et al., 1993). Wright and Monk (1991) describe cooperative evaluation as suitable only in early stages of development, and explicitly warn against using the technique for comparative purposes. Bailey, et al. (1992) appear to argue that user testing is, in the end, more cost effective because it focuses development effort on a small number of changes. The weight of the evidence suggests that, when the alternative is to do nothing at all, performing a usability inspection is a reasonable course of action.

29.3.2 Choosing a Specific Usability Inspection Method

There are many variations on the usability inspection theme presented in this chapter. To some extent, it goes beyond customization by individual practitioners to customization to fit the particular culture of a company and the needs of a given project. The techniques are highly flexible in how they can be applied, and it is advisable to exploit this to meet project goals. With this in mind, some practical considerations for selecting a method are considered next.

Forming an Inspection Team

Practically speaking, the judges selected for a project will be determined to a large extent by the company you work for or the resources you have available on the project. In large companies with a human factors department it is not uncommon to have access to ten or more usability experts. Similar situations can be found in medium sized human factors consulting organizations, where most of the staff will be trained human factors experts. In cases such as these, it is often very easy to recruit in-house colleagues to form a team of experts. If the project has enough budget, one can also hire a human factors consulting organization to create a similar group. The former case appears to have been used in Jeffries, et al. (1991) and in Virzi, et al. (1993). The latter scenario is reflected in Dumas, et al. (1995).

In many companies, even large ones, human factors expertise can be a scarce resource (Kahn and Prail, 1994; Wixon, et al., 1994). When there is only a single usability expert available for a project, one might tend towards using a group design review, led by this expert. The research results show that usability expert review by a single expert will be unlikely to find a large percentage of the usability problems in an interface (Desurvire, et al., 1992; Jeffries, et al., 1991; Nielsen, 1992; and Virzi, et al., 1993), even if the expert spends additional time on the evaluation (Dumas, et al., 1995). Group reviews can be quite effective, and the practitioner has many specific procedures to follow described in the literature (Bias, 1994; Desurvire and Thomas, 1994; Jeffries, et al., 1991; Kahn and Prail, 1994; Muller, et al., 1996; Wixon, et al., 1994). One word of caution, however. The relative inefficiency of non-expert judges should be taken into account, suggesting that the evaluation should employ a greater number of judges than if experts were used and these judges may benefit by added structure (e.g., providing them with typical usage scenarios).

Several researchers favor including development team members or representative users in the evaluation process because the increased sense of ownership will increase the likelihood that effective change will result (Bias, 1994; Kahn and Prail, 1994; and Muller, et al., 1996). This school of thought, combined with knowledge that usability expertise improves the inspection process, would tend to lead a practitioner towards forming a team with appropriate representation from selected groups, including usability experts as available.

Experts as Judges

All the findings point to usability experts being better able to find usability problems than non-experts (Desurvire, et al., 1991; Desurvire, et al., 1992; Jeffries, et al., 1991), with Nielsen (1992) showing that double-experts are even more effective at finding problems on a per evaluator basis. Therefore, it would seem to benefit the project to have human factors specialists as judges when available. If usability experts are not available, it is still possible to inspect the interface and find problems (Nielsen and Molich, 1990; Wright and Monk, 1991, among others). While each of the non-expert evaluators may be relatively inefficient at detecting usability problems, this inefficiency can be over come by adding additional inspectors. Indeed, whenever inspectors are working independently, it is beneficial to add inspectors, although this benefit declines as the number of inspectors increases (Nielsen, 1992; Virzi, et al., 1993; Wright and Monk, 1991). In designing a study such as this, the practitioner may want to employ between 3 and 12 evaluators. The lower end of the scale would be best for situations in which the judges have usability expertise and some domain knowledge, whereas the upper end of the scale might represent a case where non-experts were used for the evaluation. System complexity should also be considered, as more complex user interfaces may require more judges for effective coverage. Finally, consider whether this is to be the sole, or the first of several, usability evaluations the interface will be subjected to. In an iterative process, with further evaluations yet to come, it may be more important to conserve experts for later evaluations than to identify many problems in the current inspection.

Goals of the Inspection

When preparing for an inspection process of any kind, it is important to define the expected outcome. If the goal is to identify as many usability problems in an interface as possible, usability-expert review might be most appropriate. This procedure tends to be good at uncovering many usability problems. If experts are not available, one could take the tack of having a large number of non-expert evaluators. To assess how easy an interface is to learn, the cognitive walkthrough method, which addresses ease-of-learning at the expense of general problems, is called for (Wharton, et al., 1994). Alternatively, one could inspect an interface for conformance to standards (Wixon, et al., 1994) using a group review. In essence, it is possible to craft a review to meet most objectives. The planner has the ability to steer the inspection process through a variety of means, including: the usage scenarios chosen; the instructions given to inspectors; the point in the development cycle in which the inspection is performed; and the particular technique selected. What one must keep in mind, however, is that all of these are non-empirical techniques that involve some amount of risk relative to comprehensive user testing. Balancing this risk against cost is the key to choosing a successful evaluation plan.

29.4 Acknowledgments

I would like to publicly thank Demetrios Karis, Jeff Sokolov, David Fay, and Jim Sorce for their thoughtful and considerate reviews of drafts of this chapter. Thanks guys!

29.5 References

Bailey, R., Allan, R., and Raiello, P. (1992) Usability testing vs. heuristic evaluation: A head-to-head comparison. In *Proc. of the Human Factors Society 36th Annual Meeting,* pp. 409 - 412. Human Factors and Ergonomics Society: Santa Monica, CA.

Bias, R. G. (1994) The pluralistic usability walkthrough: Coordinated empathies. In J. Nielsen and R. Mack (Eds.), *Usability Inspection Methods,*. John Wiley and Sons: New York.

Card, S.K., Moran, T.P., and Newell, A. (1986) The model human processor: An engineering model of human performance. In K. Boff, L. Kaufman, and J. Thomas (Eds.), *The Handbook of Perception and Performance.* John Wiley & Sons: New York.

Desurvire, H., and Thomas, J. (1993) Enhancing the performance of interface evaluators using non-empirical usability methods. In *Proc. of the Human Factors Society 37th Annual Meeting,* pp. 1132 - 1136. Human Factors and Ergonomics Society: Santa Monica, CA.

Desurvire, H., Lawrence, D., and Atwood, M. (1991). Empiricism versus judgment: Comparing user interface evaluation methods on a new telephone-based interface. *SIGCHI Bulletin, 23,* pp. 58 - 59.

Desurvire, H., Kondziela, J., and Atwood, M. (1992). What is gained and what is lost when using methods other than empirical testing. In *Digest of short talks presented at CHI'92,* pp. 125 - 126, ACM: New York.

Dumas, J., Sorce, J., and Virzi, R. (1995). Expert reviews: How many experts is enough? In *Proc. of the Human Factors Society 39th Annual Meeting,* pp. 228 - 232. Human Factors and Ergonomics Society: Santa Monica, CA.

Gray, W.D., John, B.E., and Atwood, M.E. (1993). Project Ernestine: Validating a GOMS analysis for predicting and explaining real-world task performance. *Human-Computer Interaction, 8,* pp. 237-309.

Gray, W. D., and Salzman, M. C. (1996). Damaged merchandise? A review of experiments that compare usability evaluation methods. Manuscript submitted for publication.

Jeffries, R., Miller, J. R., Wharton, C., and Uyeda, K. M. (1991). User interface evaluation in the real world: a comparison of four techniques. In *Proc. of ACM CHI '91 Conference on Human Factors in Computing Systems,* pp. 119 -124, ACM: New York.

Kahn, M. and Prail, A. (1994) Formal usability inspections. In J. Nielsen and R. Mack (Eds.), *Usability Inspection Methods,*. John Wiley and Sons: New York.

Karat, C., Campbell, R., and Fiegel, T. (1992) Comparison of empirical testing and walkthrough methods in user interface evaluation. In *Proc. of ACM CHI'92 Conference on Human Factors in Computing Systems* pp. 397 - 404, ACM: New York.

Karat, J. (1988) Software evaluation methodologies. In M. Helander (Ed.), *The Handbook of Human Computer Interaction*, Elsevier Press: New York.

Landauer, T. K. (1988) Research Methods in Human Computer Interaction. In M. Helander (Ed.), *The Handbook of Human Computer Interaction,* Elsevier Press: New York.

Lewis, C. (1982) Using the "thinking- aloud" method in cognitive interface design. IBM Technical Report RC 9265 (#40713), 2/17/82.

Lewis, C., Polson, P. Wharton, C., and Rieman, J. Testing a walkthrough methodology for theory based design of walk-up-and-use interfaces. In *Proc. of ACM CHI'90 Conference on Human Factors in Computing Systems* pp. 235-242, ACM: New York.

Lewis, J.R. (1994) Sample sizes for usability studies: Additional considerations. *Human Factors, 36*, pp. 350 - 367.

Mack, R. and Nielsen, J. (1993) Usability inspection methods: report on a workshop held at CHI'92. *SIGCHI Bulletin, 25*, pp. 28 - 33.

Muller, M.J., McClard, A., Bell, B., Dooley, S., Meiskey, L., Meskill, J.A., Sparks, R., and Tellam, D. (1996) Participatory heuristic evaluation: Process-oriented approach to usability inspections. In Muller, M.J. (Ed.) *Participatory activities with users and others in the software lifecycle.* Tutorial at CHI 96. Available from the first author at muller.chi@xerox.com.

Nielsen, J. (1992) Finding usability problems through heuristic evaluation. In *Proc. of ACM CHI'92 Conference on Human Factors in Computing Systems* pp. 373-380, ACM: New York.

Nielsen, J. and Molich, R. (1990) Heuristic evaluation of user interfaces. In *Proc. of ACM CHI'90 Conference on Human Factors in Computing Systems*, pp. 249-256, ACM: New York.

Norman, D.A. (1988) The psychology of everyday things. Basic Books: New York.

Olson, J. and Moran, T. (1996) Mapping the method muddle: Guidance in using methods for user interface design. In M. Rudisill, C. Lewis, P. Polson, And T. MacKay (Eds.) *Human-Computer Interface Designs: Success Stories, Emerging Methods, and Real-world Context.* Morgan Kaufman Publishers: San Francisco.

Polson, P., Lewis, C., Reiman, J., and Wharton, C. (1992) Cognitive walkthroughs: A method for theory based evaluation of user interfaces. *International Journal of Man-Machine Studies, 36*, 741-773.

Virzi. R. (1992) Refining the test phase of usability evaluation: How many subjects is enough? *Human Factors, 34*, pp. 457 - 468.

Virzi, R. Sorce, J., and Herbert, L.B. (1993) A comparison of three usability evaluation methods: Heuristic, think-aloud, and performance testing. In *Proc. of the Human Factors Society 36th Annual Meeting,* pp. 309 - 313. Human Factors and Ergonomics Society: Santa Monica, CA.

Wharton, C., Rieman, J., Lewis, C., and Polson, P. (1994) The cognitive walkthrough method: A practitioner's guide. In J. Nielsen and R. Mack (Eds.), *Usability Inspection Methods*, John Wiley and Sons: New York.

Wixon, D., Jones, S., Tse, L., and Casaday, G. (1994) Inspections and design reviews: Framework, history, and reflection. In J. Nielsen and R. Mack (Eds.), *Usability Inspection Methods*, John Wiley and Sons: New York.

Wright, P. and Monk, A. (1991) A cost-effective evaluation method for use by designers. *Intl. J. of Man-Machine Studies, 35*, pp. 891 - 912.

Handbook of Human-Computer Interaction
Second, completely revised edition
M. Helander, T.K. Landauer, P. Prabhu (eds.)

Chapter 30

Cognitive Walkthroughs

Clayton Lewis
Department of Computer Science and
Institute of Cognitive Science
University of Colorado at Boulder
Boulder, Colorado, USA.

Cathleen Wharton
U S WEST Advanced Technologies
Boulder, Colorado, USA

30.1 Introduction

In this paper we present the Cognitive Walkthrough, a usability evaluation technique used to identify problems with a user interface and to suggest reasons for these problems. First we present a brief overview of the Cognitive Walkthrough and locate it in the space of interface evaluation methods. In the next section we present the Cognitive Walkthrough method in more complete detail, with practical instructions for its use. We then describe related methods that have been developed from the Cognitive Walkthrough idea. Following this we review published accounts of experience with these methods. Finally we present our considered advice on the method and its use, drawing on this review.

30.1.1 The Cognitive Walkthrough Method

The Cognitive Walkthrough (CW) is a method for evaluating user interfaces by analyzing the mental processes required of users. To perform a CW an analyst chooses a specific task from the suite of tasks that the interface is intended to support, and determines one or more correct sequences of actions for that task. The analyst then examines these sequences, in the context provided by the interface, and assesses whether a hypothetical user would be able to select an appropriate action at each point. If a difficulty is identified, a reason is assigned, for example, that a needed menu item will not seem related to the user's goals.

Five key features of the CW can be seen in this brief description. First, the method is performed by an analyst and reflects the analyst's judgments, rather than being based on data from test users. That is, the CW is not a user test. Second, the CW examines specific user tasks, rather than assessing the character of an interface as a whole (as is done for example in Heuristic Evaluation (Nielsen and Molich, 1990; Nielsen, 1992)). Third, the CW analyzes correct sequences of actions, asking if these correct sequences will actually be followed by users. It does not attempt to predict what users will do, beyond suggesting whether they will follow a correct path or depart from it. Fourth, the method aims not only to identify likely trouble spots in an interface but also to suggest reasons for the troubles. Fifth, the CW analyst identifies problems by tracing the likely mental processes of a hypothetical user, not by focusing on the interface itself. Thus the analysis considers matters like user background knowledge that influence mental processes but are not part of the interface.

These features are closely linked to the purposes of the CW method. CWs are intended to permit very early evaluation of designs, without requiring any implementation or even mock-up such as is needed for user testing. The design must only be mature enough to permit the analyst (who, in fact, might be the designer) to work out correct action sequences for one or more specific user tasks and to envision the cues and responses to be provided by the interface along those sequences. In practice an early design to be analyzed is usually represented on paper, but the CW method does not require this.

The focus of CWs on specific tasks is intended to help designers assess how the features of their design fit together to support users' work, or fail to do so. When used as intended, CWs are done using real or at least realistic tasks whose character and complexity represent things people actually want to do. The CW encourages concrete, detailed thinking about how these tasks would be performed and whether the interface adequately supports them.

The focus on critiquing correct action sequences rather than predicting user behavior is intended to provide the most useful feedback for the designer. Presuming that the interface is intended to support the task under review, the designer expects that users should be able to carry out some correct action sequence. The CW provides specific arguments about this expectation: users probably will do fine here and here but probably will have trouble there and there. This allows the designer to see just where his or her expectations are reasonable and where they are questionable.

This CW output differs from a behavioral prediction in two ways. First, the proposed correct action sequence is a required input to the CW, not an output from it. That is, the CW does not produce a predicted action sequence but rather critiques a sequence that is provided to it. Second, the CW makes no attempt to say what users will do if and when they depart from the correct sequence.

The emphasis on assigning reasons to troubles is intended to assist designers. Simply knowing that users have trouble at some point, as may be revealed in a user test, is not as useful as knowing why the trouble occurred when one is trying to fix the problem. For example, users may make an incorrect selection from a menu either because the menu labels are confusing or because they are trying to do something inappropriate. In the latter case, changing the menu labels will do no good and may do harm.

The focus on users' mental processes derives from the argument that a successful interface has to accommodate users' mental capabilities. Interfaces that require users to know things that they do not know or solve problems they cannot solve will not be usable.

30.1.2 The Cognitive Walkthrough Compared to Other Evaluation Methods

Table 1 locates the CW in the space of four other interface evaluation methods: Heuristic Evaluation (Nielsen and Molich, 1990; Nielsen, 1992), GOMS (Card, Moran, and Newell, 1983), user testing, and thinking aloud (Lewis, 1982). Of these, GOMS (Goals, Operators, Methods, and Selection rules) and related methods are discussed in this handbook (see the chapter on GOMS by Kieras). (Note that for the purposes of this discussion we have classified the approaches in the table according to traditional definition. These methods may vary in practice and consequently might be classified somewhat differently.)

Notice that the CW is similar to user testing, and especially to testing using thinking aloud, with the critical difference that user testing and thinking aloud supply actual data about how users respond to the interface, while the CW supplies only the analyst's judgments about how hypothetical users would respond. Of course, the point of bothering with an analyst's judgments is that they can be obtained very early in the design process and may, in fact, influence the initial design before it is finished and can be given to potential users.

The comparison with other evaluation approaches that rely on analysis rather than on user testing is also important. Heuristic Evaluation provides an overview of a complete design rather than a detailed examination of particular tasks. As such it can reveal some problems that would be missed in doing any reasonable number of CWs. For example, a heuristic evaluator might well critique wording of all screens and dialog boxes in a design, while a CW analyst would critique only those that figured in the specific tasks being studied. On the other hand, many problems in wording will not be apparent unless examined in the context of a particular task: wording is clear or not only with respect to what the user is trying to do

Table 1. The space of interface evaluation methods.

	Cognitive Walkthrough	Heuristic Evaluation	GOMS	User Testing	Thinking Aloud
Test users	No	No	No	Yes	Yes
Task specific	Yes	No	Yes	Yes	Yes
Traces correct paths	Yes	No	Yes	Maybe	Maybe
Assigns reasons for errors	Yes	Maybe	No	Maybe	Yes
Analyzes user mental processes	Yes	No	Yes	No	Maybe
Estimates learning time	Maybe	Maybe	Yes	Maybe	Maybe
Estimates performance time	No	No	Yes	Yes	Maybe

or find out in a particular situation. Thus the CW can detect some problems that an Heuristic Evaluation would not.

"Maybe" is entered in the table for Heuristic Evaluation for assigning reasons for errors because Heuristic Evaluation does not attempt to trace specific user behavior. Rather, it critiques the attributes of the interface itself. To the extent that this critique is specific and localized it may serve much the same role in guiding the designer as reasons for errors, but the critique will not always be specific and localized. We return to this point in Section 30.4.

Cognitive modeling approaches, exemplified in the table by GOMS analysis, can be seen in the table to be quite similar in attributes to CW. One difference visible in the table is the treatment of errors: current modeling approaches have mainly focused on correct performance, in fact often expert performance, and as such do not reveal much about when and whether to expect errors or how to eliminate them. This situation may change, however; as recent work by Kitajima and Polson (1995) incorporates error mechanisms.

Other differences relate to quantitative estimates of learning and performance times. GOMS models can provide these estimates, while CW provides no quantitative data. The "maybe" for learning time estimates entered in the table for CW reflects the fact that the CW can be used to judge whether an interface is likely to support "walk-up-and-use" usage, which corresponds to minimal learning time. But beyond that level the CW provides nothing but a crude inventory of material that users must know to operate the interface successfully.

A difference not shown in the table between the CW and cognitive modeling approaches is that the CW does not require learning of a modeling framework. The frameworks used in modeling approaches are in effect programming languages with syntax and semantics that must be learned. One of the goals in the development of the CW was to make available to designers and analysts some of the insights from cognitive modeling without the need for the depth of knowledge and technique needed to construct working models. But there is clearly a trade-off here: CW may be easier to do but it cannot match the precision of a well-crafted model such as Gray et al.'s Ernestine model (1992).

Another aspect of this trade-off is the incorporation of semantic judgments. In the CW the analyst decides whether the menu item "chart" will or will not look relevant to a user who is trying to make a "graph," or whether some change on the screen will suggest to the user that indeed progress is being made. Ideally a cognitive modeling framework would include knowledge and mechanisms to make these judgments, but in current practice they have to be coded into the model by hand based on the modeler's judgment. This means that behavioral predictions based on these judgments would have no firmer basis in the cognitive model than they do in the CW despite the added effort required to express them in a working model.

Advances in languages and environments for cognitive modeling are ongoing, pushing the trade-off against the CW and in favor of modeling. In the long run modeling frameworks capable of treating errors and representing semantic judgments in a principled way may exist, and may become sufficiently easy

Table 2. Outline of a cognitive walkthrough.

Preparation
• Define assumed user background • Choose sample task • Specify correct action sequence(s) for task • Determine interface states along the sequence(s)
Analysis
• For each correct action, Construct a success story that explains why a user would choose that action or Use a failure story to indicate why a user would not choose that action • Record problems, reasons, and assumptions • Consider and record design alternatives
Follow-up
• Modify the interface design to eliminate problems

to learn and use to make them the tool of choice in situations in which the CW might be preferred today. It is already possible that someone needing to analyze many interfaces could profitably amortize the investment in learning (say) the GOMS framework. Data and discussion from Gong, John, and Kieras (Gong and Kieras, 1994; John and Kieras in press-a and -b) also suggests that the actual effort required to build a model may not be excessive. Currently, however, it is not always practical to do detailed cognitive modeling from scratch in an industry setting, especially when quick turnaround is necessary such as is required in a product development environment.

Returning to the contrast between evaluation methods that use test users and those (like the CW) that do not, one can ask how any analysis method can help to detect usability problems, in the absence of any actual data on user behavior. Modeling approaches work by requiring user mental processes to be represented in a specified framework that distinguishes easy operations from difficult ones on some basis. Heuristic Evaluation directs the analyst's attention to particular aspects of a design that are associated with problems. The CW method works by directing the analyst's attention to the specifics of the design as revealed in the description of a detailed example.

This aspect of the logic of the CW is shared with some other design methods, in particular with "use case" analysis in systems design (Jacobson, 1992). The idea is that one can better evaluate a bunch of abstractions about a user interface or about an object-oriented design by considering in detail how some specific situation will be treated than by just reflecting on the abstractions themselves.

One application of this observation is common to the CW and object-oriented design. A system may offer a repertoire of functions that is logically adequate to support some set of tasks. But it may happen that the combination of functions needed to support a sample of actual user work is awkward. A CW of that sample of work, or a use case analysis, brings this awkwardness into focus.

More generally, it appears that designs of any complexity have to be examined by thinking through specific applications, not just by thinking about the design itself. The CW forces the transition from thinking about the design to thinking about particular applications.

30.2 How to Perform a Cognitive Walkthrough

Table 2 shows a summary of the main steps in performing a CW. Each is described in more detail below. A more extensive description, with more examples, can be found in Wharton et al. (1994).

30.2.1 Preparation

Define Assumed User Background

The success of an interface will depend on the knowledge users bring to it, so evaluating an interface requires some assumptions about knowledge users can be expected to have. For example, an interface might be intended for users familiar with Windows applications or Macintosh applications. Another interface might be intended for use by the general public without requiring any computer experience. Assumptions about task knowledge are also important. For a business graphics application, what prior knowledge of business graphics is assumed? Too, assumptions about anticipated environment of use will play a role. Different settings, for instance a kitchen vs. an airplane cockpit, have different affordances.

Before doing a CW these assumptions should be thought through and recorded, at least in general terms. Later, during the CW itself, the analyst can judge whether any particular knowledge that the interface requires is consistent with these assumptions.

Choose Sample Task

A CW examines a task the interface should support. Evaluating an interface will usually require several CWs, covering several tasks. Choosing the right tasks to examine is key, since aspects of the interface not involved in the tasks that are chosen will not be examined. We suggest two criteria to emphasize in choosing tasks: (1) tasks should be important, and (2) tasks should be realistic. (See also Wharton et al. 1992 for a more detailed discussion of task selection, coverage, and evaluation.)

Tasks should be important. Try to choose tasks that get to the heart of the value of the system, the tasks that show why one wants to use it. These are the tasks that have to be supported well. Important tasks, typically, are those that are most frequent or infrequent but critical tasks.

Tasks should be realistic. There are two aspects to this criterion. First, tasks should reflect as completely as possible the real nature of users' work. Contrived laboratory tasks can leave out critical details that can make or break a real system. Wixon and Jones (1996) report a telling example in which lab tasks used short sample filenames but real users systematically used filenames too long for the application to handle. It is worth the trouble to develop tasks based on observation of real user work and interviews with actual users.

Second, tasks should require completion of a realistic piece of work, not the exercise of different functions of the system in isolation. It is tempting to create a suite of tasks based on covering the separate functions that a system provides. But it can easily happen that a system that supports functions A and B adequately makes it very awkward to perform B based on the results from A, as may be needed in real work. Tasks that exercise the functions separately will not reveal this interdependence.

Except for very simple systems it will not be practical to examine tasks that cover all plausible uses of the system and all plausible sequences of operations. Aim to choose a few tasks that cover the most important uses with realistic complexity.

Specify Correct Action Sequence(s) for Task

For each task to be analyzed the CW starts with a correct way of performing the task, meaning a method that the designer would accept as the way he or she would be happy to see users proceed. If the designer is involved in the preparations this should not pose any problem, though this step may reveal that more work is needed on the design if the designer concludes that there is no satisfactory solution.

If the CW is being done without direct participation from the designer it may be necessary to consult the designer to ensure that the correct action sequence used is what the designer would envision. One does not want to bring "problems" to the designer based on a mistaken view of how the system will be used. Of course if the analysts could not figure out a reasonable way to perform the task there is a problem somewhere, but the time spent analyzing the incorrect path would be largely wasted.

Often there will be more than one acceptable way of performing a task. If these variations are important a CW can be done on more than one, but often it will be sensible to choose the most common, or perhaps the most problematic.

Note that the designer is ultimately responsible for determining the correct action sequence in a CW. The CW aims to critique the designer's assumptions about the design, not to predict what users will actually do. So the designer indicates the path he or she wants users to follow, and the CW indicates whether or not that is likely to happen, and if it is not likely, why not.

Determine Interface States Along the Sequence(s)

The final step in the preparation is to work out as fully as possible what the user will see at each step of the

Table 3. Questions to ask about each correct action

Will the user be trying to achieve the right effect?
Will the user notice that the correct action is available?
Will the user associate the correct action with the desired effect?
If the correct action is performed, will the user see that progress is being made?

sequence or sequences to be examined. If the design has been implemented there is no problem; the analyst can simply step through the implementation during the CW. But to use the CW early in design, before implementation, it will be necessary to create sketches of screen states or to document dialogue flows along the action sequence that include as much possibly relevant detail as possible. Doing this may force the designer to flesh out a partial design enough to indicate the key interface features along the path, a desirable side effect. This is an instance of the role of examples in CW in helping to evaluate general ideas: the designer is led to define how his or her general concept for the interface will play out in a specific situation.

30.2.2 Analysis

Now the CW itself begins. The analyst works through the sequence of correct actions, considering the state of the interface before and after each action, trying to determine how likely it is that users will follow that path. In making this determination the analyst considers the questions shown in Table 3.

For Each Correct Action, Construct a Success or Failure Story

The analyst tries to satisfy herself or himself that the answers to these questions are "yes," without requiring any knowledge on the user's part that is inconsistent with the assumptions about a user's background. In this case the answers to the questions, with an explanation of them, constitute a *success story*: they explain why the analyst expects that the user will take the correct action.

If the answer to one or more of these questions is "no" or "not always" the analyst has a *failure story*. The explanation of this answer will tell the designer why the analyst expects that some users will have trouble at this point.

The four questions in Table 3 form the skeleton of the CW analysis of an action, whether in a success story or a failure story. We consider each question in detail below.

Will the user be trying to achieve the right effect? The issue here is what the user is trying to do at this point in the interaction. If the user is not trying to do what the correct action will do, they are unlikely to choose the right action.

An example may clarify what is at stake. In an old office system it was necessary to clear a field on a form before typing new information into it. A key was provided that would do this, but users often did not use it, because they did not know they needed to clear the field. That is, they failed to take the correct action because they were not trying to achieve the effect that the interface required, clearing the field. However easy or difficult it is to clear the field, there will be trouble here if users do not know they need to clear the field.

This matter is least likely to cause trouble when the effect the user must work towards at each step in the interaction is clearly part of their task goal. But systems often impose other goals on users for implementation reasons. If the system provides a clear prompt that tells the user what is required all may be well. But if such a prompt is not present, the CW analyst will indicate a trouble spot unless there are some other grounds for claiming that the user will be able to see what is needed. For example, a design could rely on user training or experience to tell users what is needed (though a prudent designer will not trust this assumption too far and will be aware of the associated costs).

As we discuss in Section 30.4, experience with the CW indicates that this question is the most difficult to answer appropriately. We consider there how the difficulty may arise.

Will the user notice that the correct action is available? Users will not perform actions that they do not know they can do. Actions associated with obvious interface features like menus or buttons will not be problematic (if users have the necessary knowledge of interface conventions). But actions like double clicking a part of diagram that is not apparently a button may not be discovered (Franzke 1995). The CW analyst should note any required actions that are not clearly marked in a way that makes them obvious to users with the assumed background knowledge.

Will the user associate the correct action with the desired effect? If we suppose the user is trying to do the right thing and can see that the correct action is available, there will still be trouble if the correct action is not seen to be related to what the user is trying to do or if it is only one of a number of candidate actions that seem equally plausible. Examples of problems under this heading are menu labels that the user does not see as related to their intentions, multiple buttons with equally relevant labels ("call forward" and "send all calls" in one telephone interface), and commands that the user does not know and are not prompted. The analyst will not be satisfied on this question unless he or she can say clearly why the user can be expected to make the right choice.

If the Correct Action is Performed, will the User See that Progress is Being Made? If the user chooses the correct action trouble can still result if the user thinks something has gone wrong. The user may cancel the action, if possible, or undertake some inappropriate "corrective" action. The CW analyst will examine the feedback the interface provides for each action and determine whether such troubles are likely to arise.

Record Problems, Reasons, and Assumptions

In performing the CW the analyst is careful to follow the steps in the predetermined sequence of correct actions, since it is that sequence that defines the designer's expectations about the interface. Even if disastrous trouble is expected at an early stage of the interaction, the analysis should continue with subsequent correct actions: the designer may be able to fix the initial problem and will want to know whether the rest of the interaction is workable.

The analyst should record two kinds of information from this analysis. First, if an action was considered successful, but only on the assumption that users possess some particular knowledge, the assumption should be recorded if there is any doubt that users with the expected background would have the knowledge. For example, an analyst might note when an interface intended for Macintosh users uses an interaction technique that is standard but uncommon. The designer could then consider whether a more familiar technique could be substituted.

Second, the analyst should record all actions considered to be likely failures and the specific grounds for this determination. Just noting what CW question was answered negatively is not enough. For example, a user may fail to associate the correct action with its effect not because the label for that action is bad but because other labels seem equally good.

The analyst should also examine the trouble spots in the action sequence to see if apparent errors might in fact lead to alternative correct paths. Such cases should still be discussed with the designer (if the analyst is not the designer) to verify that the alternatives are satisfactory from the designer's point of view.

Consider and Record Design Alternatives

When a problem has been identified it may be natural to consider possible changes to the design that would help. If the analyst is the designer, such consideration will be inevitable and will be a direct outgrowth of the analysis. If the evaluator is not the analyst care must be taken to ensure that consideration of design alternatives does not substitute for clear identification of the problem and its assigned cause. The designer might well choose an entirely different way to deal with a problem and his or her freedom of action should be preserved. All relevant design alternatives should be recorded.

30.2.3 Follow-up

Modify the Interface Design to Eliminate Problems

The purpose of the CW is to suggest to the designer where his or her design is likely to fail, and why. The results of the analysis should provide quite specific guidance, indicating when problems may be fairly superficial (a poorly-chosen label) and when they may require more profound changes (eliminating a step that is unrelated to users' work as they conceive it). Further, since the analysis follows what the designer accepts as an appropriate action sequence for the task, the problems found will be directly related to the designer's view of the interface and hence of clear relevance to the designer.

30.3 Related Methods

There are many related user interface evaluation methods. Some are predecessors of the current version and some are direct off-shoots.

30.3.1 History of the Cognitive Walkthrough: The Predecessors

The CW, based on a theory of learning by exploration (Polson and Lewis, 1990), has been modified numerous times since its inception in 1990. The first version (Lewis et al., 1990) consisted of a single-page form that contained a set of questions designed to ask about a user's intentions and goals, actions, and system feedback. Although this form and the method were considered useful, people who were system developers with little or no training in the cognitive sciences found the method difficult to use: they did not have the requisite background.

One attempt to remedy this problem was to modify the CW by expanding the single-page form into a set of more detailed forms (Wharton, 1992; Lewis, Polson, and Rieman, 1991; Polson et al., 1992a). These new forms not only included the set of questions that were part of version one, but additional fine grained questions, illustrative examples, and detailed instructions. At this time, experimentation with richer forms of evaluator training occurred (Jeffries et al., 1991) and an automated version (i.e., computer prototype designed to get rid of the paper forms) was developed and trialed (Rieman et al., 1991). As a result of these modifications, use of the CW became even more formal. Instead of making the CW more accessible to those without formal cognitive science training, the CW became impractical in both evaluation time and tediousness (Wharton et al., 1992; Franzke, 1991). (Others that have discussed and used variants of this version of the CW include Bradford (1994), Desurvire, Kondziela, and Atwood (1992), Cuomo and Bowen (1992), Cockton and Lavery (1995), and Traynor (1995).)

Based on these experiences, we decided to modify the CW again (Lewis et al., 1992; Wharton et al., 1994; Polson et al., 1992b; Rieman, Franzke, and Redmiles, 1995). It is this third version of the CW that is presented in this chapter. The method was refined to address the criticisms, especially regarding practicality and requisite knowledge of cognitive science. Experiences with this new version have been very positive (John and Packer, 1995; Cassee, Ede, and Kemp, 1995; Marita Franzke, personal communication, July 1995, Bernhard Suhm, personal communication, May 1994). We believe that the method now is accessible to everyone regardless of their formal training and that the tediousness and lengthy evaluation time concerns have been remedied.

30.3.2 Other Approaches and Domain-specific Methods: Direct Off-shoots

During the course of its development, the CW has also led other researchers and practitioners to tailor the method to their own user interface development and evaluation environment or particular domain. Two example off-shoots are the Cognitive Jogthrough and the Programming Walkthrough.

Cognitive Jogthrough

The Cognitive Jogthrough (Rowley and Rhoades, 1992) is another approach for performing the structured method inherent to the first version of the CW. To make the CW less time-consuming and less of an ordeal for evaluators, Rowley and Rhoades introduced both participant roles and a new means for recording the evaluation session. They formally assigned participants to one or two of four roles: evaluator, presenter, moderator, and recorder. These participants would then meet as a group in a room to do the evaluation. To increase the pace of the evaluation session, the session itself was recorded on video tape. This recording made use of an in-house software package that could be used to log significant events, in real time, discussed during the evaluation. Event notes and a timestamp were thus associated with each event and the time was synchronized with the timer on the video camera.

Feedback was positive for the Cognitive Jogthrough. This is because of two factors: (1) all comments were recorded during the evaluation, not just the key decisions, and (2) the pace of the evaluation was significantly faster than the traditional CW resulting in about three times more problems being found in the same amount of evaluation time.

Programming Walkthrough

The Programming Walkthrough (Bell, Rieman, and Lewis 1991; Bell et al. 1994) is an adaptation of the CW tailored to the design of a programming language. The Programming Walkthrough, like the CW, is user task-centric: the purpose of the evaluation is to walk through a user's programming task and to evaluate the programming language accordingly. The language is evaluated with respect to both its facility (i.e., the ease with which a user can solve problems using the language) and expressiveness (i.e., the existence of attractive solutions in the language).

The main difference between the Programming Walkthrough and the CW is that programming lan-

Table 4. Summary of related studies and their conclusions.

Conclusions	Related Studies
CW finds about 40% percent (or more) of the problems revealed by user testing	Lewis et al. 1990 Jeffries et al. 1991 Mack and Montaniz 1994 Cuomo and Bowen 1994
CW takes substantially less effort than user testing	Jeffries et al. 1991 Karat, Campbell, and Fiegel 1992 Karat 1994
Considering problems found per unit effort, CW may not be much more cost effective that user testing	Karat, Campbell, and Fiegel 1992 Karat 1994
Heuristic Evaluation finds more problems than the CW and takes less effort	Jeffries et al. 1991 Dutt, Johnson, and Johnson 1994 Cuomo and Bowen 1994
CW can be tedious and too much concerned with low-level details	Jeffries et al. 1991 Wharton et al. 1992 Dutt, Johnson, and Johnson 1994
CW does not provide a high-level perspective on the interface	Jeffries et al. 1991 Wharton et al. 1992 John and Packer 1995 Cuomo and Bowen 1994
CWs performed by groups of analysts work better than those done by individuals	Karat, Campbell, and Fiegel 1992

guages and environments usually offer the user only very sparse cues: most problem-solving has to be controlled by the user with little support from the system interface. Thus, user knowledge of the language and how to employ it are even more important than is user knowledge of a typical end-user application. The Programming Walkthrough must try to evaluate long problem-solving processes largely on the basis of the knowledge apparently required to support them.

It is possible to envision a continuum of applications extending from typical end-user applications with heavily prompted interfaces, the territory of the CW, to sparsely-prompted systems like programming languages, passing through intermediate cases in which ideas from both walkthroughs are pertinent. An application like a spreadsheet may embody a largely unprompted macro facility; even basic operation of a spreadsheet involves dealing with a large collection of functions and operators, selections from which must largely be unprompted. A sophisticated editor/formatter may require largely unprompted decisions to use its style templates. The CW can provide insight into some superficial aspects of such systems, but the Programming Walkthrough would be needed to assess the difficulty of the problem-solving needed to use the unprompted features.

30.4 Experience With the Method

30.4.1 Interpreting Related Studies

The initial publication of the CW (Lewis et al. 1990) included an empirical evaluation comparing problems identified in a CW with problems observed in user tests. Since that time a number of similar evaluations have been done comparing CW results with those of other evaluation methods and in some cases recording and comparing the time required for different methods.

Table 4 summarizes the results of these studies by listing some broad conclusions together with citations of the studies supporting each conclusion. These findings need to be interpreted with care, for a number of reasons which we discuss below.

Early Versions of the Cognitive Walkthrough

First, all of the studies except John and Packer (1995) and Mack and Montaniz (1994) used early forms of the procedure, consisting of a highly-structured process guided by elaborate forms. The streamlined procedure described here and in other later presentations of the method would yield different, though of course not necessarily better, results.

Contributions to Redesign and Design Alternatives

Second, no study has compared the CW with any other method in a way that considers the contribution of the results to redesign. (Dutt, Johnson, and Johnson (1994) have indicated that the CW appears to provide a better basis for re-design over Heuristic Evaluation, but have not studied this issue in great detail.) It is a claim for CW, though unsubstantiated empirically, that CW analysis assigns reasons to problems in a way that would be useful in redesign.

Rowley and Rhoades (1992) include in their version of the CW the discussion of design alternatives during the analysis. They note that the original CW explicitly excluded such discussions and that this diminished the value of the method for designers (see also Wharton et al. 1992). We accept their modification as an improvement, as long as clear characterization of the problems is not displaced by consideration of alternatives.

Evaluations of Completed Systems

Third, partly because of the desire to obtain user test results for comparison, all of these studies evaluated completed systems, not designs in progress. Thus another claim for the CW, that it is applicable very early in the design process, is not tested in most of these studies. (One of us, Cathleen Wharton, has used the method early in the design process when only storyboards were available, and the CW performed quite well in this instance and led to a major redesign of the proposed system.)

Designers as Evaluators

Fourth, and related to the latter two points, most studies (Rowley and Rhoades (1992), and part of Wharton et al. (1992) are exceptions) have examined the use of the CW by evaluators who are not the designers. There has been a tradition in much usability work, an unfortunate one in our view, to accept a division of labor between designers and evaluators. One of the aims of the CW is to break through this wall and enable designers to do better usability evaluation of their own work.

We expect some advantages and disadvantages when designers do their own CW, relative to the results of the cited studies. On the positive side we think that designers would make better judgments about where to spend their time in analysis, thus making the method more efficient. We also think that redesign would be faster and more effective because of the designer's direct access to the specification of difficulties. On the negative side, there is the obvious possibility that the designer may have more difficulty seeing the defects in his or her design than someone more detached from it. It could also happen that a designer would accept success stories that an experienced usability specialist would recognize as implausible, for example stories that assume that users have memorized a large set of commands.

Though we may be too optimistic we see this last problem as being largely a consequence of the traditional division of labor. As long as designers are not expected to be knowledgeable about usability they will not be. We think that the direct participation by designers in usability evaluation, including user testing as well as analysis techniques like the CW, would rapidly increase their ability. This would leave the drawback of lack of detachment to be balanced against the greater efficiency of the analysis and more direct support of design.

Though as we have noted studies of CW have not focused on its connection to design, there has been some experience with the Programming Walkthrough by designers (Lewis, Rieman, and Bell 1991; Bell, Rieman, and Lewis 1991; Bell et al. 1994). The designers involved found the method to be extremely valuable. On the other hand, some found that the involvement of other people in the process was important, consistent with our caveat about lack of detachment.

Group Evaluations

A theme visible in many reports of the CW and its variants is the use of teams of analysts, as in the Cognitive Jogthrough (Rowley and Rhoades 1992). Comparisons suggest that group walkthroughs work better because of the pooling of problems detected by different individuals. Another factor, noted by Karat (1994) and others is the value of having people involved in a project cooperate in a joint evaluation.

A somewhat similar method to a group CW, with an independent origin, is Bias's Pluralistic Walkthrough (Bias 1994). A Pluralistic Walkthrough differs from a CW in that a group of evaluators work through a task without seeing a designated correct path. Evaluators indicate what action they would select at each juncture, with some evaluators charged with playing the roles of typical users (so that their choices should reflect these users' knowledge, not their own). The group is not constrained to focus on any particular criteria for evaluation, so that CW-style projections of user mental processes would be admissible but not promoted over other perspectives.

The group should include usability experts and developers, as well as user role-players, so that different perspectives and expertise are available to the group. A variety of participants makes it possible to blend evaluation with consideration of design alternatives, as is done in the Cognitive Jogthrough as well. As another perspective, one of us (Cathleen Wharton) also has experience in using this method in a group setting that included a project's designer, developer, marketer, project lead, and a CW method specialist (Cathleen Wharton). This evaluation proved successful and all parties involved in the evaluation felt that their viewpoints had been heard, their expertise was valued, and their design concerns were remedied to satisfaction.

30.4.2 Studies Comparing the Cognitive Walkthrough to Other Methods

Studies Comparing the Cognitive Walkthrough to User Testing

Another perspective on the evaluation studies that have been done is that the comparisons with user testing have to be considered in the light of the place of the CW in the overall development process. We would not advocate the CW being done instead of user testing. Yet, the CW is valuable due to its ability to detect usability problems early in the process, before full user testing is feasible. The relatively low yield of problems identified by the CW as compared with user testing is just what we would expect given the complexity of the interactions between design, user knowledge, task details, and chance occurrences that define the user's experience of a system. Brooks (1994) describes a number of limitations that all analysis methods have with respect to user testing. So, for us, a focus on the relative cost of the CW and user testing could be dangerously misleading in suggesting that if it were sufficiently cheap the CW (or some other analysis method) could replace user testing.

Studies Comparing the Cognitive Walkthrough to Heuristic Evaluation

The comparisons of the CW to Heuristic Evaluation have even more issues to consider. One might consider doing Heuristic Evaluation on more or less the same terms as the CW, using a preliminary design. The studies cited find the Heuristic Evaluation finds substantially more problems than the CW, with less effort (although Dutt, Johnson, and Johnson (1994) found about an equal number of problems). Do these findings mean that Heuristic Evaluation would be the early evaluation method of choice?

We don't think so. Rather, we see the methods as complementary, as suggested in Section 30.1 and as suggested by Dutt, Johnson, and Johnson (1994) and Cuomo and Bowen (1994). As a task-independent method Heuristic Evaluation offers a broad view of all aspects of an interface. But we think it is less effective than the CW in focusing on the details of how interface features interact to support specific user tasks, in part just because Heuristic Evaluation does not ask that evaluators examine any particular scenarios of use of a system (though scenarios can be suggested and are in some cases (Nielsen 1994)).

A second difference between the methods, already noted in Section 30.1, is that Heuristic Evaluation directs attention to the characteristics of the interface, while the CW asks the analyst to think about the mental processes of users. We think some important usability problems are more easily identified from this perspective than from the broader perspective of the Heuristic Evaluation. For example, a system can offer two clearly-presented alternatives in a dialog box that can't be faulted in its presentation, and thereby confront users with an intractable decision problem: which clearly-presented alternative is the one I want?

One of Brooks' examples (1994, p. 260) is interesting in this connection. Heuristic Evaluation failed to reveal that a design assumed a conceptual model of the task that was different from what users had. It is tempting to suppose that CW might have done better here. It is possible that CW analysts could buy into the same wrong assumption about the users' perspective that was implicit in the Heuristic Evaluation. But the CW at least invites the analyst to imagine what the user is thinking. A related advantage of the CW is its attention to required user knowledge. Heuristic Evaluation asks evaluators to flag situations in which the system does not "speak the user's language" or violates platform conventions. The CW goes farther in asking the analyst to identify what specific knowledge the inter-

Table 5. Summary of related studies with noted difficulties.

Difficulties	Related Studies
CW evaluators often do more of a user test on themselves than a CW	Mack and Montaniz 1994
Walkthrough Question 1 (about user intentions) is especially difficult	John and Packer 1995
Choosing good tasks is difficult	Wharton et al. 1992 John and Packer 1995

face requires that goes beyond the assumed background of users. Often such requirements can't be eliminated from the interface but must be addressed in documentation or tutorial. In this case it is helpful to know what they are.

Experience with the Programming Walkthrough has confirmed this point. The results of Programming Walkthroughs have been very useful in determining what points of knowledge must be stressed in the basic orientation to a novel language (Lewis, Rieman, and Bell 1991; Bell, Rieman, and Lewis 1991; Bell et al. 1994; Rosing et al. 1991; Weaver and Lewis 1990).

These arguments are not to recommend CW over Heuristic Evaluation. Rather, they are intended to clarify what can be expected from each approach. We think a practical usability process needs to include both task-independent evaluation, for which Heuristic Evaluation would be our choice, and task-specific analysis of key tasks, using a combination of CW (early) and user testing (later).

30.4.3 Difficulties in Using the Cognitive Walkthrough Method.

Table 5 lists difficulties in applying the method and cites the studies reporting them.

Critiquing the Designer's Intentions

The first issue in the table reflects a clash between the CW concept and a plausible, closely related, but importantly different idea. The CW assumes that an evaluation should critique the designer's intentions and hence should begin with a specification of them in the form of a correct (from the designer's perspective) sequence of actions for the task. Many analysts assume that they should undertake to choose the next action and then perhaps compare their choice with the correct one. In the CW the analysts construct a hypothetical account of the user's decision process; in the alternative the analyst tries to make a decision herself or himself and then makes a judgment about the adequacy of the interface based on that attempt.

The main argument for the CW approach is that the analyst's own attempts may have little resemblance to what a real user would do. It is easy to see how a step that is easy for the analyst could be difficult for a user, since very often users will have less knowledge of the concepts and conventions of the interface than typical analysts. But it can also happen that the typical user will know more than the analyst, especially about the task domain. In either case the CW analyst's responsibility is to envision the user's decision process, not his or her own.

On the other hand, as John and Packer (1995) note, it is plausible that the analyst's own experience in choosing actions could influence his or her understanding of the decision problem faced by users. Analysts in the Mack and Montaniz (1994) study, and others we have observed, may be implicitly assuming the value of this experience. There is an empirical question here: do people make better judgments about the probable mental processes of others in a task with or without their own experience of the task? In the absence of data it is tempting to suppose that as long as the analyst is clearly aware of the distinction between his or her own experience and the hypothetical experience of someone else with different background the analysis can only be improved by what is learned from his or her own efforts. From this point of view the right approach in the CW would be not to suppress the analyst's own problem-solving but to keep it separate from the user problem-solving the analyst is trying to envision. John and Packer (1995) suggest that the analyst should participate in constructing the correct action sequence as preparation for the analysis itself; this would seem to provide the desired separation.

What are the User's Intentions?

The second issue, the difficulty of dealing with questions of user intentions, has been noticed since the beginning of work on the CW. Early versions of the CW required elaborate representations of user goal structures, in an attempt to provide some discipline for the analyst. But the discipline was clumsy and time consuming and did not seem to help.

The heart of the problem seems to be the multiplicity of descriptions that are used interchange-ably for actions, and the fact that ordinary language blurs, rather than clarifying, the distinction between goals and actions. Alvin Goldman (1970) has provided a clear discussion of this matter.

Consider a situation in which someone comes into a room and flips the light switch, and the room is flooded with light. In describing their action, in answer to a question like "What did Pat do?," we could say any of "Pat flipped the switch," "Pat turned on the light," or "Pat flooded the room with light," shifting from a fairly concrete description of what Pat did physically to forms that really describe not what Pat did but what the result of Pat's action was. In describing Pat's goals we can similarly choose to say either something like "Pat wanted to flip the switch" or "Pat wanted to flood the room with light." So whether we are ostensibly describing Pat's action or Pat's intention we can choose to refer either to something close to the physical nature of Pat's action or to its outcome.

This flexibility in language causes trouble when we try to ask about users' goals in a CW. The interface for one of our telephones (Clayton Lewis' telephone) provides a clear example (presented more extensively in Wharton et al., 1994) for discussion. To forward calls it is necessary to cancel any earlier forwarding, rather than simply specifying a new number for forwarding. Canceling is done by pressing the two buttons # and 2 (to form the compound #2). Now suppose we are doing a CW on this interface and we arrive at the step where #2 is required. We want to know whether the user will have the right goal at this point, but what is the right goal? In ordinary language we could describe the goal that leads to pressing #2 as just "to press #2," staying close to the actual action required, or as "to cancel forwarding," pointing to the desired outcome of the action. But only the latter description is helpful: if we ask whether the user will have the specific goal "to press #2" the answer will almost surely be "no," or, equally unhelpfully, "yes, if the interface provides cues to link the user's actual goal to the action press #2." Now the question has to be asked again: what is the user's underlying goal that might lead to the subsidiary goal of pressing #2?

Everyday language provides no good way to make the needed distinction. If we try to ask, "Will the user be trying to do the right thing at this step?" this is multiply ambiguous. This question can be read as asking if the user's intentions are good, or whether the user will try the correct action, or (what we need to ask) whether the user is seeking the right result, canceling forwarding in this example. The CW designers have found no sure way around this difficulty. The wording suggested earlier, "Will the user be trying to achieve the right effect?," is an attempt to focus attention on the results the user is seeking rather than on the action, but may not be understood just because of the unfamiliarity of the discrimination it requires.

The telephone example helps to illustrate the discrimination. It is easy to see that the problem of users not knowing they need to cancel forwarding is separate from the problem of users perhaps not seeing how to cancel. But our experience in teaching the CW method, consistent with John and Packer's 1995 report, is that analogous problems in other situations remain difficult to spot.

Choosing Good Tasks is Difficult

The third difficulty in the table, choosing tasks, is a problem for all task-specific evaluation methods. There are at least three sources of difficulty. First, for many systems there is little reliable information about what user tasks will be most important, whether in frequency or in how vital the results are. This problem is made worse and more common by bad practice that isolates system development from the context of use, but even in full-fledged participatory design there can be uncertainty about how a new system will actually be used.

Second, for almost any system it takes many tasks to cover all of the features and functionality offered. Choosing any few tasks leaves much of the system unexamined.

Third, there is a temptation to improve the coverage of an evaluation by examining a number of small tasks that in combination exercise much of an interface, rather than examining a smaller number of bigger tasks. This practice often leads to the use of artificial tasks, with consequent lack of contact with what users really need to do, as well as to poor coverage of what happens when different functions must be combined.

We have no new remedies to suggest. We repeat our recommendation that tasks should reflect as much as possible the expected use of the system. There is no royal road to choosing such tasks, but the involvement with potential users that the effort requires is something that is critically important for many other reasons as well. There is no shortcut, but a shortcut would be a bad idea if there was one. Landauer (1995) gives a compelling discussion of the enormous waste stemming from the development of systems without sufficiently definite ideas about what they are for.

We also repeat our suggestion that the CW, and other task-specific evaluation methods, should be combined with Heuristic Evaluation or some other task-independent method to provide coverage of interface features that task-specific methods leave unexamined. (For a detailed discussion about task selection, coverage, and evaluation see also Wharton et al. (1992).)

30.5 Advice

Considering these findings, when and why should you consider the CW? What suggestions would we offer for making the best use of it?

The primary use we would recommend is early evaluation of design ideas. A CW can be done by a designer himself or herself, or as a group activity. A group CW will yield better results but requires more preparation and more person-hours than a CW done by an individual designer.

If you want to invest in a group process, consider Bias's Pluralistic Walkthrough rather than a CW. Bringing together designers, usability specialists, and users will provide a broader perspective than the more narrowly-focused CW. Also consider using video and a time stamping event logger to record your group session, as in the Cognitive Jogthrough.

Secondarily, a CW can be used later in design as a prelude to user testing. User testing is more effective if obvious problems have been eliminated beforehand and the CW can be an inexpensive way to detect some of these.

We would not generally recommend the use of the CW for evaluating finished systems, since user testing will provide much better results. But there are some situations in which user testing is logistically difficult, for example when user time is scarce and expensive. A CW can be useful in these situations but we urge that even here it be viewed as a preparation for or supplement to user testing or observation rather than as a substitute for it.

Supplement the CW with a task-independent method like Heuristic Evaluation. Use the CW to probe the most critical features of the design, not to cover everything.

The CW is not worthwhile if it is not done quickly. The results are not good enough to justify spending hours on a task. Strive for a pace in your analysis that moves quickly over the routine steps, with no or minimal recording, and dwells longer on steps where potential problems appear. Don't try to find problems on every step. On the other hand, if you are finding no problems go back and re-examine your assumptions. Do you really have good grounds for thinking that users will anticipate the necessity of each step, and will be able to understand all the cues? What are those grounds?

30.6 Acknowledgments

We thank George Engelbeck, Carolanne Fisher, Marita Franzke, Mike King, Monica Marics, Carrie Rudman, and our anonymous reviewers for their helpful comments on earlier versions of this chapter. We also thank our colleagues, Peter Polson and John Rieman, for their contributions to this work.

30.7 References

Bell, B., Citrin, W., Lewis, C., Rieman, J., Weaver, R., Wilde, N., and Zorn, B. (1994). Using the walkthrough to aid in programming language design, *Software Practice and Experience,* 24, 1, 1-25.

Bell, B., Rieman, J., and Lewis, C. (1991). Usability testing of a graphical programming system: Things we missed in a programming walkthrough. In *Proceedings of CHI 1991* (New Orleans, LA, April 28 - May 2 1991), ACM, New York, 7-12.

Bias, R. G. (1994). The pluralistic usability walkthrough: Coordinated empathies. In J. Nielsen and R. L. Mack (Eds.), *Usability Inspection Methods*, New York: John Wiley & Sons, 63-76.

Bradford, J. S. (1994). Evaluating high-level design. Synergistic use of inspection and usability methods for evaluating early software designs. In J. Nielsen and R. L. Mack (Eds.), *Usability Inspection Methods*, New York: John Wiley & Sons, 235-253.

Brooks, P. (1994). Adding value to usability testing. In J. Nielsen and R. L. Mack (Eds.), *Usability Inspection*

Methods, New York: John Wiley & Sons, 255-271.

Card, S. K., Moran, T. P., and Newell, A. (1983). The psychology of human-computer interaction. Hillsdale, NJ: Erlbaum.

Cassee, J., Ede, M. R., and Kemp, T. (1995). Growing simplicity: A task-based approach to containing complexity. In *Conference Companion of CHI '95* (Denver, Colorado, May 7-11 1995), ACM, New York, 139-140.

Cockton, G. and Lavery, D. (1995). Software Visualization: Challenges for Two HCI Approaches. In C. Johnson (Ed.), *Task centered approaches to interface design: Glasgow interactive systems group research review*, GIST Technical Report #G95.2, The Department of Computer Science at the University of Glasgow, Glasgow, G12 8QQ, 133-151.

Cuomo, D. L. and Bowen, C. D. (1992). Stages of user activity model as a basis for user-system interface evaluations. In *Proceedings of the Human Factors Society 36th Annual Meeting 1992* (Atlanta, GA, October 12-16 1992), Human Factors Society, Inc., Santa Monica, 1254-1258.

Cuomo, D. L. and Bowen, C. D. (1994). Understanding usability issues addressed by three user-system interface evaluation techniques, *Interacting with Computers*, 6, 1, 86-108.

Desurvire, H., Kondziela, J., and Atwood, M. (1992). What is gained and lost when using evaluation methods other that empirical testing. In A. Monk, D., Diaper, and M. D.. Harrison (Eds.), *Proceedings of HCI 1992* (University of York, U.K., September 15-18 1992), Cambridge University Press, 89-102.

Dutt, A., Johnson, H., and Johnson, P. (1994). Evaluating evaluation methods. In G. Cockton, S. W. Draper, and G. R. S. Weir (Eds.), *People and computers IX*, Cambridge, UK: Cambridge University Press, 109-121.

Franzke, M. (1991). Evaluation technique evaluated: Experience using the cognitive walkthrough. Bellcore Special Report SR-OPT-002130, November 4-6 1991. *Proceedings of Bellcore/BCC* Symposium on User Centered Design, 205-211.

Franzke, M. (1995). Turning research into practice: Characteristics of display-based interaction. In *Proceedings of CHI 1995* (Denver, CO, May 7-11 1995), ACM Press, New York, 421-428.

Goldman, A. I. (1970). A theory of human action. Englewood Cliffs, NJ: Prentice-Hall, Inc.

Gong, R. and Kieras, D. (1994). A validation of the GOMS model methodology in the development of a specialized, commercial software application. In *Proceedings of CHI 1994* (Boston, MA, April 24-28 1994), ACM, New York, 351-357.

Gray, W. D., John, B. E., and Atwood, M. E. (1992). The précis of project Ernestine or an overview of a validation of GOMS. In *Proceedings of CHI 1992* (Monterey, CA, May 3- May 7 1992), ACM, New York, 307-312.

Jacobson, I, M. Christerson, P. Jonsson, and G. Overgaard. (1992). *Object-oriented Software Engineering: A Use Case Driven Approach*. Reading, MA: Addison-Wesley Publishing Company.

Jeffries, R., Miller, J. R., Wharton, C., and Uyeda, K. M. (1991). User interface evaluation in the real world: A comparison of four techniques. In *Proceedings of CHI 1991* (New Orleans, LA, April 28 - May 2 1991), ACM, New York, 119-124.

John, B. E. and Kieras, D. E. (in press-a) Using GOMS for user interface design and evaluation: Which technique? *ACM Transactions on Computer-Human Interaction.*

John, B. E. and Kieras, D. E. (in press-b) The GOMS family of user interface analysis techniques: Comparison and Contrast. *ACM Transactions on Computer-Human Interaction.*

John, B. E. and Packer, H. (1995). Learning and using the cognitive walkthrough method: A case study approach. In *Proceedings of CHI 1995* (Denver, CO, May 7-11 1995), ACM, New York, 429-436.

Karat, C. (1994). A comparison of user interface evaluation methods. In J. Nielsen and R. L. Mack (Eds.), *Usability Inspection Methods,* New York: John Wiley & Sons, 203-234.

Karat, C., Campbell, R., and Fiegel, T. (1992). Comparison of empirical testing and walkthrough methods in user interface evaluation. In *Proceedings of CHI 1992* (Monterey, CA, May 3- May 7 1992), ACM, New York, 397-404.

Kitajima, M., and Polson, P. G. (1995). A comprehension-based model of correct performance and errors in skilled, display-based human-computer interaction. *International Journal of Human-Computer Systems*, 43, 65-99.

Landauer, T. L. (1995). *The trouble with computers: Usefulness, usability, and productivity.* Cambridge, MA: MIT Press.

Lewis, C. (1982). *Using the "thinking-aloud" method in cognitive interface design.* IBM Research Report

RC-9265, Yorktown Heights, NY.

Lewis, C., Polson, P. G., and Rieman, J. (1991). *Cognitive walkthrough forms and instructions.* Institute of Cognitive Science Technical Report #ICS 91-14. University of Colorado, Boulder, CO, 80309.

Lewis, C., Polson, P., Rieman, J., Wharton, C., and Wilde, N. (1992). Cognitive walkthroughs: A method for theory-based evaluation of user interfaces. Tutorial Notes for CHI 1992 (Monterey, CA, May 4 1992).

Lewis, C., Polson, P., Wharton, C., and Rieman, J. (1990). Testing a walkthrough methodology for theory-based design of walk-up-and-use interfaces. In *Proceedings of CHI 1990* (Seattle, WA, April 1-5 1990), ACM, New York, 235-242.

Lewis, C., Rieman, J., and Bell, B. (1991). Problem-centered design for expressiveness and facility in a graphical programming system. *Human-Computer Interaction*, 6, 3 & 4, 319-355.

Mack, R. and Montaniz, F. (1994). Observing, predicting, and analyzing usability problems. In J. Nielsen and R. L. Mack (Eds.), *Usability Inspection Methods*, New York: John Wiley & Sons, 295-339.

Nielsen, J. (1992). Finding usability problems through Heuristic Evaluation. In *Proceedings of CHI 1992* (Monterey, CA, May 3- May 7 1992), ACM, New York, 373-380.

Nielsen, J. (1994). Heuristic Evaluation. In J. Nielsen and R. L. Mack (Eds.), *Usability Inspection Methods,* New York: John Wiley & Sons, 25-62.

Nielsen, J. and Molich, R. (1990). Heuristic Evaluation of user interfaces. In *Proceedings of CHI 1990* (Seattle, WA, April 1-5 1990) ACM, New York, 249 - 256.

Polson, P. G. and Lewis, C. H. (1990). Theory-based design for easily learned interfaces. *Human-Computer Interaction*, 5, 191-220. Hillsdale, NJ: LEA, Publishers.

Polson, P., Lewis, C., Rieman, J., and Wharton, C. (1992a). Cognitive walkthroughs: A method for theory-based evaluation of user interfaces. *International Journal of Man-Machine Studies*, 36, 741-773.

Polson, P., Rieman, J., Wharton, C., and Olson, J. (1992b). Usability inspection methods: Rationale and examples. In *Proceedings of 8th Symposium on Human Interface* (Kawasaki, Japan, October 21-23 1992), 377-384.

Rieman, J., Davies, S., Hair, D. C., Esemplare, M., Polson, P. G., and Lewis, C. (1991).. An automated walkthrough. Demonstration presented for *Proceedings of CHI 1991* (New Orleans, LA, April 28 - May 2 1991), ACM, New York, 427–428.

Rieman, J., Franzke, M., and Redmiles, D. (1995).. *Usability evaluation with the cognitive walkthrough.* Tutorial Notes for CHI 1995 (Boston, MA, May 8 1995).

Rosing, M., Schnabel, R. and Weaver, R. P., (1991). The DINO parallel programming language, *Journal of Parallel and Distributed Computing*, 13, 30-42.

Rowley, D. E. and Rhoades, D. G. (1992). The Cognitive Jogthrough: A fast-paced user interface evaluation procedure. In *Proceedings of CHI 1992* (Monterey, CA, May 3- May 7 1992), ACM, New York, 389-395.

Traynor, C. (1995). *Analysis of GIS tasks using the cognitive walkthrough method.* Department of Computer Science Technical Report #96-01. University of Massachusetts at Lowell, Lowell, MA 01854.

Weaver, R. P. and Lewis, C. (1990). *Examining the usability of parallel language constructs from the programmer's perspective*, Department of Computer Science Technical Report #CU-CS-492-90, University of Colorado, Boulder, CO, 80309.

Wharton, C. (1992). *Cognitive walkthroughs: Instructions, forms, and examples.* Institute of Cognitive Science Technical Report #CU-ICS-92-17. University of Colorado, Boulder, CO, 80309.

Wharton, C., Bradford, J., Jeffries, R., and Franzke, M. (1992). Applying cognitive walkthroughs to more complex user interfaces: Experiences, issues, and recommendations. In *Proceedings of CHI 1992* (Monterey, CA, May 3- May 7 1992), ACM, New York, 381-388.

Wharton, C., Rieman, J., Polson, P., and Lewis, C. (1994). The cognitive walkthrough method: A practitioner's guide. In J. Nielsen and R. L. Mack (Eds.), *Usability Inspection Methods*, New York: John Wiley & Sons, 105-140.

Wixon, D. and Jones, S. (1996). Usability for fun and profit: A case study of the design of DEC Rally version 2. In Rudisill, M., Lewis, C., Polson, P., and McKay, T. (Eds.). *Human-Computer Interface Design: Success Stories, Emerging Methods, and Real-World Context*, San Francisco: Morgan-Kaufmann, 3-35.

Handbook of Human-Computer Interaction
Second, completely revised edition
M. Helander, T.K. Landauer, P. Prabhu (eds.)

Chapter 31

A Guide to GOMS Model Usability Evaluation using NGOMSL

David Kieras
University of Michigan
Michigan, USA

31.1 Introduction

31.1.1 Overview

Engineering Models for Usable Interface Design

The standard accepted technique for developing a usable system, empirical user testing, is based on iterative testing and design revision using actual users to test the system and help identify usability problems. It is widely agreed that this approach, inherited from Human Factors, does indeed work when carefully applied (Landauer, 1995). However, Card, Moran, and Newell (1983) have argued, and many HCI researchers have agreed (e.g., see Butler, Bennett, Polson, and Karat, 1989), that empirical user testing is too slow and expensive for modern software development practice, especially when difficult-to-get domain experts are the target user group. One response has been the development of "discount" or "inspection" methods for assessing the usability of an interface design quickly and at low cost (Nielsen and Mack, 1994). However, another response, which has been evolving since the seminal Card, Moran, and Newell work, is the concept of *engineering models* for usability. Analogously to the models used in other engineering disciplines, engineering models for usability produce quantitative predictions of how well humans will be able to perform tasks with a proposed design. Such predictions can be used as a surrogate for actual empirical user data, making it possible to iterate through design revisions and evaluations much more rapidly. Furthermore, unlike purely empirical assessments, an engineering model for an interface design can capture the essence of the design in an inspectable representation, making it easier to reuse successful design insights in the future.

The overall scheme for using engineering models in the user interface design process is as follows: Following an initial task analysis and proposed first interface design, the interface designer would then use an engineering model as applicable to find the usability problems in the interface. However, because there are other aspects of usability that are poorly understood, some form of user testing is still required to ensure a quality result. Only after dealing with design problems revealed by the engineering model would the designer then go on to user testing. If the user testing reveals a serious problem, the design might have to be fundamentally revised, but again the engineering models will help refine the redesign quickly. Thus the slow and expensive process of user testing is reserved for those aspects of usability that can only be addressed at this time by empirical trials. If engineering models can be fully developed and put into use, then the designer's creativity and development resources can be more fully devoted to more challenging design problems, such as devising entirely new interface concepts or approaches to the design problem at hand.

The GOMS Model

The major extant form of engineering model for interface design is the GOMS model, first proposed by Card, Moran, and Newell (1983). A GOMS model is a description of the knowledge that a user must have in order to carry out tasks on a device or system; it is a representation of the "how to do it" knowledge that is required by a system in order to get the intended tasks accomplished. The acronym GOMS stands for Goals, Operators, Methods, and Selection Rules. Briefly, a GOMS model consists of descriptions of the Methods needed to accomplish specified Goals. The Methods are a series of steps consisting of Operators that the user performs. A Method may call for sub-Goals to be accomplished, so the Methods have a hierarchical structure. If there is more than one Method to accomplish a Goal, then Selection Rules choose the appropriate Method depending on the context. Describing the Goals, Operators, Methods, and Selection Rules for a set of tasks in a formal way constitutes doing a GOMS analysis, or constructing a GOMS model.

John and Kieras (in press-a,b) describe the current family of GOMS models and the associated techniques for predicting usability, and list many successful applications of GOMS to practical design problems. The simplest form of GOMS model is the Keystroke-Level Model, first described by Card, Moran, and Newell (1980), in which task execution time is predicted by the total of the times for the elementary keystroke-level actions required to perform the task. The most complex is CPM-GOMS, developed by Gray, John, and Atwood (1993), in which the sequential dependencies between the user's perceptual, cognitive, and motor processes are mapped out in a schedule chart, whose critical path predicts the execution time.

In between these two methods is the method presented in this article, NGOMSL, in which learning time and execution time are predicted based on a program-like representation of the procedures that the user must learn and execute to perform tasks with the system. NGOMSL is an acronym for **N**atural **GOMS** **L**anguage, which is a structured natural language used to represent the user's methods and selection rules. NGOMSL models thus have an explicit representation of the user's methods, which are assumed to be strictly sequential and hierarchical in form. The execution time for a task is predicted by simulating the execution of the methods required to perform the task. Each NGOMSL statement is assumed to require a small fixed time to execute, and any operators in the statement, such as a keystroke, will then take additional time depending on the operator. The time to learn how to operate the interface can be predicted from the length of the methods, and the amount of transfer of training from the number of methods or method steps previously learned. Thus estimating times for learning and execution both require counting the number of NGOMSL statements involved; details on this process will be provided in this article.

One important feature of NGOMSL models is that the "how to do it" knowledge is described in a form that can actually be executed – the analyst, or an appropriately programmed computer, can go through the GOMS methods, executing the described actions, and actually carry out the task. A GOMS model is also a way to characterize a set of design decisions from the point of view of the user, which can make it useful during, as well as after, design. It is also a description of what the user must learn, and so can act as a basis for training and reference documentation.

NGOMSL is based on the cognitive modeling of human-computer interaction by Kieras and Polson (Kieras and Polson, 1985; Bovair, Kieras, and Polson, 1990). As summarized by John and Kieras (in press-a,b), NGOMSL is useful for many desktop computing situations in which the user's procedures are usefully approximated as being hierarchical and sequential.

Strengths and Limitations of GOMS Models

It is important to be clear on what GOMS models can and cannot do; see John and Kieras (in press-a,b) for more discussion.

GOMS Starts* After *a Task Analysis. In order to apply the GOMS technique, the designer (or interface analyst, hereafter just referred to as the designer) must conduct a task analysis to identify what goals the user will be trying to accomplish. The designer can then express in a GOMS model how the user can accomplish these goals with the system being designed. Thus, GOMS modeling does not replace the most critical process in designing a usable system, that of understanding the user's situation, working context, and goals. Approaches to this stage of interface design have been presented in sources such Gould (1988), Diaper (1989), Kirwan and Ainsworth (1992), and Kieras (in press).

GOMS Represents Only the Procedural Aspects of Usability. GOMS models can predict the *procedural* aspects of usability; these concern the amount, consistency, and efficiency of the procedures that users must follow. Since the usability of many systems depends heavily on the simplicity and efficiency of the procedures, the narrowly focused GOMS model has considerable value in guiding interface design. The reason why GOMS models can predict these aspects of usability is that the methods for accomplishing user goals tend to be tightly constrained by the design of the interface, making it possible to construct a GOMS model given just the interface design, prior to any prototyping or user testing.

Clearly, there are other important aspects of usability that are not related to the procedures entailed by the interface design. These concern both lowest-level perceptual issues like the legibility of typefaces on CRTs, and also very high-level issues such as the user's conceptual knowledge of the system, e.g., whether the user has an appropriate "mental model" (e.g. Kieras and Bovair, 1984), or the extent to which the system fits appropriately into an organization (see John and Kieras, in press-a,b). The lowest-level issues are dealt with well by standard human factors methodology, while understanding the higher-level concerns is currently a matter of practitioner wisdom and the higher-level task analysis techniques. Considerably more research is needed on the higher-level aspects of usability, and tools for dealing with the corresponding design issues are far off. For these reasons, great attention must still be given to the task analysis, and some user testing will still be required to ensure a high-quality user interface.

GOMS Models are Practical and Effective. There has been a widespread belief that constructing and using GOMS models is too time-consuming to be practical (e.g., Lewis and Rieman, 1994). However, the many cases surveyed by John and Kieras (in press-a,b) make clear that members of the GOMS family have been applied in many practical situations and were often very time- and cost-effective. A possible source of confusion is that the development of the GOMS modeling techniques has involved validating the analysis against empirical data. However, once the technique has been validated and the relevant parameters estimated, no empirical data collection or validation should be needed to apply a GOMS analysis during practical system design, enabling usability evaluations to be obtained much faster than user testing techniques. However, the calculations required to derive the predictions are tedious and mechanical; at the time of this writing, computer-based tools for developing and using GOMS models are under development (e.g, Byrne, Wood, Sukaviriya, Foley, and Kieras, 1994; Kieras, Wood, Abotel, and Hornof, 1995).

What is a GOMS Task Analysis?

Describing the Goals, Operators, Methods, and Selection Rules for a set of tasks in a relatively formal way constitutes doing a GOMS analysis. The person who is performing such an analysis is referred to as "the analyst" in this Guide.

Carrying out a GOMS analysis involves defining and then describing in a formal notation the user's Goals, Operators, Methods, and Selection Rules. Most of the work seems to be in defining the Goals and Methods. That is, the Operators are mostly determined by the hardware and lowest-level software of the system, such as whether it has a mouse, for example. Thus the Operators are fairly easy to define. The Selection Rules can be subtle, but usually they are involved only when there are clear multiple methods for the same goal. In a good design, it is clear when each method should be used, so defining the Selection Rules is (or should be) relatively easy as well.

Identifying and defining the user's goals is often difficult, because you must examine the task that the user is trying to accomplish in some detail, often going beyond just the specific system to the context in which the system is being used. This is especially important in designing a new system, because a good design is one that fits not just the task considered in isolation, but also how the system will be used in the user's job context. As mentioned above, GOMS modeling starts with the results of a task analysis that identifies the user's goals. For brevity, task analysis per se will not be discussed further here; excellent sources are Gould (1988), Diaper (1989), and Kirwan and Ainsworth (1992); see Kieras (in press) for an overview.

Once a Goal is defined, the corresponding method can be simple to define because it is simply the answer to the question "how do you do it on this system?" The system design itself largely determines what the methods are.

One critical process involved in doing a GOMS analysis is deciding what and what *not* to describe. The mental processes of the user can be of incredible complexity; trying to describe all of them would be hopeless. However, many of these complex processes have nothing to do with the design of the interface, and so do not need to be analyzed. For example, the process of reading is extraordinarily complex; but usually, design choices for a user interface can be made without any detailed consideration of how the reading process works. We can treat the user's reading mechanisms as a "black box" during the interface design. We may want to know *how much* reading has to be done, but rarely do we need to know *how* it is done. So, we will need to describe when something is read, and why it is read, but we will not need to describe the actual processes involved. A way to handle this in a GOMS analysis is to "bypass" the reading process by representing it with a "dummy" or "place holder" operator. This is discussed more below. But making the choices of what to bypass is an important, and sometimes difficult, part of the analysis.

31.1.2 Example of GOMS Analysis Results

Before presenting the details of the GOMS modeling methodology, it is useful to examine a sample GOMS analysis and see how it can capture an important aspect of interface "consistency." The tasks and systems are some file manipulation tasks in PC-DOS and Macintosh Finder. The set of user goals considered are:

- delete a file
- move a file
- delete a directory
- move a directory

The example consists of a list of methods for each system, expressed in the NGOMSL notation introduced in detail later in this Guide. One of the virtues of this notation is that it is pretty comprehensible without having studied its formal definition first. This example is intended just to give the overall flavor of what a GOMS model looks like, so no detail or explanation of the notation will be given at this time.

GOMS Model for Macintosh Finder

There is a specific method for accomplishing each one of the user goals under consideration. Notice how each method is simply an explicit step-by-step description of what the user has to do in order to accomplish the goal.

```
Method for goal: delete a file.
  Step 1. Accomplish goal: drag file to
  trash.
  Step 2. Return with goal accomplished.

Method for goal: move a file.
  Step 1. Accomplish goal: drag file to des-
  tination.
  Step 2. Return with goal accomplished.

Method for goal: delete a directory.
  Step 1. Accomplish goal: drag directory to
  trash.
  Step 2. Return with goal accomplished.

Method for goal: move a directory.
  Step 1. Accomplish goal: drag directory to
  destination.
  Step 2. Return with goal accomplished.
```

We can see from the above methods that they all have a simple pattern; it doesn't matter whether a directory or a file is being manipulated. So we can replace the above four methods with only two generalized methods, one for deleting and one for moving:

```
Method for goal: delete an object.
  Step 1. Accomplish goal: drag object to
  trash.
  Step 2. Return with goal accomplished.

Method for goal: move an object.
  Step 1. Accomplish goal: drag object to
  destination.
  Step 2. Return with goal accomplished.
```

In addition to the specific moving and deleting methods, there is a general submethod corresponding to the drag operation; this is the basic method used in most of the Macintosh Finder file manipulations. It is called like a subroutine by the above methods.

```
Method for goal: drag item to destination.
  Step 1. Locate icon for item on screen.
  Step 2. Move cursor to item icon location.
  Step 3. Hold mouse button down.
  Step 4. Locate destination icon on screen.
  Step 5. Move cursor to destination icon.
  Step 6. Verify that destination icon is re-
  verse-video.
  Step 7. Release mouse button.
  Step 8. Return with goal accomplished.
```

GOMS Model for PC-DOS

There are a large number of specific methods, and some of the user goals, such as moving a file, are accomplished by calling other methods. Notice also that there is no generalization over files and directories, because the PC-DOS command set forces us to use very different methods for these two types of objects. Each of these methods calls a general submethod for entering and executing a specified command.

```
Method for goal: delete a file.
  Step 1. Recall that command verb is
  "ERASE".
  Step 2. Think of directory name and file
  name and retain as first filespec.
  Step 4. Accomplish goal: enter and execute
  a command.
  Step 6. Return with goal accomplished.

Method for goal: move a file.
  Step 1. Accomplish goal: copy a file.
  Step 2. Accomplish goal: delete a file.
  Step 3. Return with goal accomplished.

Method for goal: copy a file.
  Step 1. Recall that command verb is "COPY".
  Step 2. Think of source directory name and
  file name and retain as first filespec.
  Step 3. Think of destination directory name
  and file name and retain as second
  filespec.
  Step 4. Accomplish goal: enter and execute
  a command.
  Step 5. Return with goal accomplished.

Method for goal: delete a directory.
  Step 1. Accomplish goal: delete all files
  in the directory.
  Step 2. Accomplish goal: remove a direc-
  tory.
  Step 3. Return with goal accomplished.

Method for goal: delete all files in a direc-
  tory.
  Step 1. Recall that command verb is
  "ERASE".
  Step 2. Think of directory name.
  Step 3. Retain directory name and "*.*" as
  first filespec.
  Step 4. Accomplish goal: enter and execute
  a command.
  Step 5. Return with goal accomplished.

Method for goal: remove a directory
  Step 1. Recall that command verb is
  "RMDIR".
  Step 2. Think of directory name and retain
  as first filespec.
  Step 3. Accomplish goal: enter and execute
  a command.
  Step 4. Return with goal accomplished.

Method for goal: move a directory.
  Step 1. Accomplish goal: copy a directory.
  Step 2. Accomplish goal: delete a direc-
  tory.
  Step 3. Return with goal accomplished.

Method for goal: copy a directory.
  Step 1. Accomplish goal: create a direc-
  tory.
  Step 2. Accomplish goal: copy all the files
  in a directory.
  Step 3. Return with goal accomplished.

Method for goal: create a directory.
  Step 1. Recall that command verb is
  "MKDIR".
  Step 2. Think of directory name and retain
  as first filespec.
  Step 3. Accomplish goal: enter and execute
  a command.
  Step 4. Return with goal accomplished.

Method for goal: copy all files in a direc-
  tory.
  Step 1. Recall that command verb is "COPY".
  Step 2. Think of directory name.
  Step 3. Retain directory name and "*.*" as
  first filespec.
  Step 4. Think of destination directory
  name.
  Step 5. Retain destination directory name
  and "*.*" as second filespec.
  Step 6. Accomplish goal: enter and execute
  a command.
  Step 7. Return with goal accomplished.
```

The following general submethods are called by the above methods. They reflect the basic consistency of the command structure, in which each command consists of a verb followed by one or two file specifications.

```
Method for goal: enter and execute a command.
Entered with strings for a command verb and
  one or two filespecs.
  Step 1. Type command verb.
  Step 2. Accomplish goal: enter first
  filespec.
  Step 3. Decide: If no second filespec, goto
  5.
  Step 4. Accomplish goal: enter second
  filespec.
  Step 5. Verify command.
  Step 6. Type "<CR>".
  Step 7. Return with goal accomplished.

Method for goal: enter a filespec.
Entered with directory name and file name
  strings.
  Step 1. Type space.
  Step 2. Decide: If no directory name, goto
  5.
  Step 3. Type "\".
  Step 4. Type directory name.
  Step 5. Decide: If no file name, return
  with goal accomplished.
  Step 6. Type file name.
  Step 7. Return with goal accomplished.
```

GOMS Comparison of Macintosh Finder and PC-DOS

Clearly there is a substantial difference in the number and length of methods between these two systems. The Macintosh Finder, in its generalized form requires only 3 methods to accomplish these user goals, involving a total of only 18 steps. To accomplish the same goals in PC-DOS requires 12 methods with a total of 68 steps. Thus we have a clear characterization of the extreme consistency of the Macintosh Finder compared to PC-DOS; only a few methods are required to accomplish a variety of file manipulation goals. A major value of a GOMS model is its ability to characterize, and even quantify, this property of *method consistency*.

The Guide describes below how these method descriptions can be used to derive predictions of learning and execution time. The user must learn these step-by-step methods in order to learn how to perform these tasks. According to research results, the learning time is linear with the number of steps. The execution time can be predicted as in the Keystroke-Level Model, as a total of the individual operator times.

31.1.3 Organization of This Guide

This presentation of the NGOMSL methodology supersedes earlier presentations (Kieras, 1988; 1994). The remainder of this Guide is organized as follows: Section 31.2 defines the parts of a GOMS model in terms of the NGOMSL notation. Section 31.3 discusses some of the general issues that underlie the approach. Section 31.4 presents the procedure for constructing a GOMS model, along with an extended example. Section 31.5 explains how to use a GOMS model evaluation of a design for predicting human performance, and how a revised design and documentation can be based on the model.

31.2 Definitions And a Notation for GOMS Models

This section defines each component of a GOMS model in more detail than Card, Moran, and Newell (1983). In addition, this section introduces a notation system, NGOMSL ("Natural GOMS Language"), which is an attempt to define a language that will allow GOMS models to be written down with a high degree of precision, but without the syntactic burden of ordinary formal languages, and that is also easy to read rather than cryptic and abbreviated. Despite the resulting verbosity and looseness, NGOMSL is close to a formal GOMS language that can be implemented as a running computer language. However, it is important to keep in mind that NGOMSL is not supposed to be an ordinary programming language for computers, but rather to have properties that are directly related to the underlying production rule models described by Kieras, Bovair, and Polson (Kieras and Polson, 1985; Polson, 1987; Kieras and Bovair, 1986; Bovair, Kieras, and Polson, 1990). So NGOMSL is supposed to represent something like "the programming language of the mind," as absurd as this sounds. The idea is that NGOMSL programs have properties that are related in straightforward ways to both data on human performance and theoretical ideas in cognitive psychology. If NGOMSL is clumsy and limited as a computer language, it is because humans have a different architecture than computers. Thus, for example, NGOMSL does not allow complicated conditional statements, because there is good reason to believe that humans cannot process complex conditionals in a single cognitive step. If it is hard for people to do, then it should be reflected in a long and complicated NGOMSL program.

In this document, NGOMSL expressions are shown in this typeface. In using this notation, you may well be tempted to abbreviate it; as long as the control structure and organization is not changed, this does not present a problem in interpreting the results.

31.2.1 Goals

A goal is something that the user tries to accomplish. The analyst attempts to identify and represent the goals that typical users will have. A set of goals usually will have a hierarchical arrangement in which accomplishing a goal may require first accomplishing one or more subgoals.

A goal description is an action-object pair in the form: <verb noun>, such as delete word, or move-by-find-function cursor. The verb can be complicated if necessary to distinguish between methods (see below on selection rules). Any parameters or modifiers, such as where a to-be-deleted word is located, are represented in the task description (see below).

31.2.2 Operators

Operators are actions that the user executes. There is an important difference between goals and operators. Both take an action-object form, such as the goal of revise document and the operator of press key. But in a GOMS model, a goal is something to be accomplished, while an operator is just executed. This distinction is intuitively-based, and is also relative; it depends on the level of analysis.

That is, an operator is an action that we choose not to analyze into finer detail, while we normally will want to provide information on how a goal is to be accomplished. For example, we would want to describe in a GOMS model how the user is supposed to get a document revised, but we would probably take pressing a key as a primitive action that it is not necessary to further describe.

A good heuristic for distinguishing operators and goals: if you interrupt the user, and ask "what are you trying to do?" you will get in response statements of goals, not operators. Thus, you are likely to get statements like "I'm cutting and pasting this," not "I'm pressing the return key."

Typical examples:

- goals - revise document, change word, select text to be deleted
- operators - press a key, find a specific menu item on the screen

The procedure presented below for doing a GOMS analysis is based on the idea of first describing methods using very high-level operators, and then replacing these operators with methods that accomplish the corresponding goal by executing a series of lower-level operators. This process is repeated until the operators are all *primitive external operators*, chosen by the analyst, that will not be further analyzed.

Kinds of Operators

External Operators. External operators are the observable actions through which the user exchanges information with the system or other objects in the environment. These include perceptual operators, which read text from a screen, scan the screen to locate the cursor and so forth, and motor operators, such as pressing a key, or moving a mouse. External operators also include interactions with other objects in the environment, such as turning a page in a marked-up manuscript, or finding the next markup on the manuscript. The analyst usually chooses or defines the external operators depending on the system or tasks. E.g., is there a mouse on the machine? Does the user work from a marked-up paper copy of the document?

Mental Operators. Mental operators are the internal actions performed by the user; they are non-observed and hypothetical, inferred by the theorist or analyst. In the notation system presented here, some mental operators are "built in;" these operators correspond to the basic mechanisms of the cognitive processor, the "cognitive architecture." These are based on the production rule models described by Bovair, Kieras, and Polson 1990). These operators include actions like making a basic decision, recalling an item in Working Memory (WM), retrieving information from Long-Term Memory (LTM), or setting up a goal.

Other mental operators are defined by the analyst to represent complex mental activities (see below). Typical examples of such *analyst-defined* mental operators are determining the string to use for a find command, and determining the editing change meant by a marking on a marked-up manuscript.

Primitive and High-level Operators. A particular task analysis assumes a particular level of analysis which is reflected in the "grain size" of the operators. If an operator will not be decomposed into finer level, then it is a primitive operator. But if an operator will be decomposed into a sequence of lower-level, or primitive, operators, then it is a high-level operator. Specifically which operators are primitives depends on the finest grain level of analysis desired by the analyst.

Some typical primitive operators are actions like pressing a button, or moving the hand. All built-in mental operators are primitive by definition. High-level operators would be gross actions, or stand-ins for more detailed analysis, such as `LOG-INTO-SYSTEM`. The analyst recognizes that these could be decomposed, but may choose not to do so, depending on the purpose of the analysis.

Standard Primitive External Operators

The analyst defines the primitive motor and perceptual operators based on the elementary actions needed by the system being analyzed. These correspond directly to the physical and some of the mental operators used in the Keystroke-Level Model. Some typical examples and their Keystroke-Level Model equivalents:

```
Home hand to mouse (H)
Press <key name> (K)
Type a string of characters <string> (T)
Press or release mouse button (B)
Click mouse button (BB)
Type <string of characters> (T(n))
Move cursor to <target coordinates>
  or Point to <target coordinates> (P)
Locate object on screen <object description>
  (M)
Verify that <description> (M)
Wait for <description> (W(t))
```

Standard Primitive Mental Operators

Below follows a brief description of the NGOMSL primitive mental operators; examples of their use appear later.

Flow of Control. A submethod is invoked by declaring its goal:

```
Accomplish goal: <goal description>
```

This is analogous to an ordinary CALL statement; control passes to the method for the goal, and returns here when the goal has been accomplished. The operator:

```
Return with goal accomplished
```

is analogous to an ordinary RETURN statement, and marks the end of a method.

A decision is represented by a `Decide` operator; a step may contain only one `Decide` operator, and all other operators in the step have to be contained inside this `Decide`. A `Decide` operator contains either one IF-THEN conditional with an optional ELSE, or any number of IF-THEN conditionals. Here are three examples:

```
1. Decide: If <operator...> Then <operator>

2. Decide: If <operator...> Then <operator>

3. Decide: If <operator...> Then <operator>
       If <operator...> Then <operator>
       If <operator...> Then <operator>
     ...
```

If there are multiple IF-THEN conditionals, as in the third example above, the conditions must be mutually exclusive, so that only one condition can match, and the order in which the If-Thens are listed is irrelevant. The `Decide` operator is for making a simple decision that governs the flow of control within a method. It is not supposed to be used within a selection rule set, which has its own structure (see below). The `IF` clause typically contains operators that test some state of the environment. Notice that the complexity of a `DECIDE` operator is strictly limited; only one simple `ELSE` clause is allowed, and multiple conditionals must be mutually exclusive and independent of order. More complex conditional situations must be handled by separate decision-making methods that have multiple steps, decisions, and branching.

There is a branching operator:

```
Goto Step <number>
```

As in structured programming, a `Goto` is used sparingly; normally it used only with `Decide` operators.

Memory Storage and Retrieval. The memory operators reflect the distinction between *long-term memory* (LTM) and *working memory* (WM) (often termed *short-term memory*) as they are typically used in computer operation tasks:

```
Recall that <WM-object-description>
Retain that <WM-object-description>
Forget that <WM-object-description>
Retrieve-from-LTM that <LTM-object-
  description>
```

The terminology is not ideal, but there are few choices in English. `Recall` means to fetch from working memory; `Retain` means to store in working memory, while `Forget` means that the information is no longer needed, and so can be dropped from working memory (although counter-intuitive, this is a real phenomenon; see Bjork, 1972). The methods presented here assume that information is not lost from working memory, so `Forget` refers only to the deliberate dropping of information. Any problems due to "memory overload" could be identified by looking at how much has been retained relative to forgotten (see below, on mental workload). There is only a `Retrieve` operator for LTM, because in the tasks typically modeled, long-term learning and forgetting are not involved. The WM operator execution time is always bundled into the time to execute the step. The `Retrieve-from-LTM` operator can take a **M** time or longer to execute if the user in inexperienced, but with practice, this operator time also becomes bundled into the step execution time.

Analyst-Defined Mental Operators

As discussed in some detail below, the analyst will often encounter psychological processes that are too complex to be practical to represent as methods in the GOMS model and that often have little to do with the specifics of the system design. The analyst can bypass these processes by defining operators that act as place holders for the mental activities that will not be further analyzed. Depending on the specific situation, such operators may correspond Keystroke-Level Model **M** operators, and so can be estimated to take 1.2 sec, but some, such as `Make up your mind` below, clearly will take much longer.

Some examples of analyst-defined mental operators:

> `Get-from-task <name>` represents the process of accessing or thinking of a task parameter designated by <name> and putting the information into working memory.
>
> `Get-next-edit-location` represents the process of scanning a marked up manuscript to determine the location of the next edit.
>
> `Think-of <description>` represents a process of thinking of a value for some parameter designated by `<description>` and putting the information into working memory.

`Read <name> value from screen` represents the process of interpreting characters on a screen that supply a value for some parameter designated by `<name>` and putting the information into working memory.

`Most-recent` represents determining the most recent of two time-stamped items

`Make up your mind <decision description>` represents a complicated decision making process designated by `<decision description>` that puts the final result into working memory.

31.2.3 Methods

A method is a sequence of steps that accomplishes a goal. A step in a method typically consists of an external operator, such a pressing a key, or a set of mental operators involved with setting up and accomplishing a subgoal. Much of the work in analyzing a user interface consists of specifying the actual steps that users carry out in order to accomplish goals, so describing the methods is the focus of the task analysis.

The form for a method is as follows:

```
Method for goal: <goal description>
  Step 1. <operator> ...
  Step 2. <operator> ...
  ...
  Step n. Return with goal accomplished.
```

Note that more than one `<operator>` can appear in a step (see guidelines below), and that the last step must contain only the operator `Return with goal accomplished.` Methods often call sub-methods to accomplish goals that are subgoals. This method hierarchy takes the following form:

```
Method for goal: <goal description>
  Step 1. <operator>
  Step 2. <operator>
  ...
  Step i. Accomplish goal: <subgoal descrip-
  tion>
  ...
  Step m. Return with goal accomplished.

Method for goal: <subgoal description>
  Step 1. <operator>
  Step 2. <operator>
  ...
  Step j. Accomplish goal: <sub-subgoal de-
  scription>
  ...
  Step n. Return with goal accomplished.
...
```

31.2.4 Selection Rules

The purpose of a *selection rule* is to route control to the appropriate method to accomplish a goal. Clearly, if there is more than one method for a goal, then a selection rule is logically required.

There are many possible ways to represent selection rules. In the approach presented here, a selection rule responds to the combination of a *general* goal and a specific context by setting up a *specific* goal of executing one of the methods that will accomplish the general goal. In other words, a selection rule specifies that for a particular general goal, and certain specific properties of the situation, then the general goal should be accomplished by accomplishing a situation-specific goal.

For example, in a text editor with a find function, if the general goal is to move to a certain place in the text, and the specific context is that the place is visible on the screen, then the general goal should be accomplished by accomplishing the specific goal of `move-with-cursor-keys`. But if the place is far away, then the general goal should be accomplished by the specific one of `move-with-find-function.`

If the analyst discovers that there is more than one method to accomplish a goal, then the general goal should be decomposed into a set of specific goals, one for each method. The analyst should then devise a set of mutually exclusive conditions that describe which method should be used in what contexts.

In the notation introduced here, selection rules are `If-Then` rules that are grouped into sets that are governed by a general goal. If the general goal is present, the conditions of the rules in the set are tested in parallel to choose the specific goal to be accomplished. The relationship with the underlying production rule models is very direct (see Bovair, Kieras, and Polson, 1990). The form for a selection rule set is:

```
Selection rule set for goal: <general goal
  description>
  If <condition> Then accomplish goal:
  <specific goal description>.
  If <condition> Then accomplish goal:
  <specific goal description>.
  ...
Return with goal accomplished.
```

Each `<condition>` consists of one or more operators that test working memory, test contents of the task description, or test the external perceptual situation; these operators cannot be motor operators such as pressing a key. All of the operators in a condition have to be true for the condition to be true. Notice that the

Decide operator is not used here. The order of the If-Then statements is not supposed to be significant; but they need to be written so that only one of the conditions can be true at a time. After the specific goal is accomplished by one of the If-Then statements, then the general goal is reported as accomplished.

A simple example for moving the cursor in a text editor:

```
Selection rule set for goal: move the cursor
If destination visible on screen Then
  accomplish goal: moving-with-arrow-keys.
If destination not visible on screen and dis-
  tance is short, Then
  accomplish goal: moving-with-scroll-keys.
If destination not visible on screen and dis-
  tance is long and
  the task description contains a find
  string, Then
  accomplish goal: moving-with-find-function.
Return with goal accomplished
```

The notation for a selection rule set resembles that for a method; it is like a method except for the property that the flow of control through the body of a selection rule set is not sequential, step-by-step, but instead follows whichever IF is true, and then continues with the final Return with goal accomplished operator. A common and natural confusion is when a Selection rule set should be used and when a Decide should be used. A Selection rule set is used exclusively to route control to the suitable method for a goal, and so can only have accomplish goal operators in the THEN clause, while a Decide operator controls flow of control within a method, and can have any type of operator in the THEN clause. Thus, if there is more than one method to accomplish a goal, use an Selection rule set to dispatch to the more specific method. If you want to control which operators in what sequence are executed within a method, use a Decide. Unfortunately, this distinction is still not entirely clear because a Decide with multiple If-Thens can masquerade as a Selection rule set; further experience will be needed to refine the distinction.

31.2.5 Task Descriptions and Task Instances

Task Description

A *task description* describes a generic task in terms of the goal to be accomplished, the situation information required to specify the goal, and the auxiliary information required to accomplish the goal that might be involved in bypassing descriptions of complex processes (see below). Thus, the task description is essentially the "parameter list" for the methods that perform the task.

Example: A sample task description for deleting text with a certain word processor contains the following items:

- the goal is to delete a piece of arbitrary text
- the starting location of the text
- the ending location of the text
- a find string for locating the beginning of the text

The goal associated with the task is described, along with the specifics of the task, namely what text is to be deleted. A piece of auxiliary information is the find string for locating the text.

The way to think of a task description is that it is a description of the data that the GOMS model needs in order to carry out the tasks. So the combination of the methods in the GOMS model, and the information in the task description, completely describes the knowledge that the user must have to accomplish the tasks. In the above example, including the find string in the task description means that we are assuming that accomplishing this task efficiently will involve using the find function. But by including the actual find string in the task description, we are making clear that our GOMS model methods are not responsible for computing the find string; we are assuming that users come up with it, but we are choosing not to describe how they do this.

Task Instance

A *task instance* is a description of a specific task. It consists of specific values for all of the "parameters" in a task description. For example, a task instance for the above task description would be:

- the goal is to delete a piece of arbitrary text
- the starting location of the text is line 10, column 1
- the ending location of the text is line 11 column 17
- a find string for locating the beginning of the text is "Now is the"

Notice that much of this example is essentially the same information in a mark-up on a paper manuscript.

If one has correctly specified a set of methods in a GOMS model, then one should be able to correctly execute a series of task instances by executing the steps in the methods using the specific values in the task instances.

31.2.6 NGOMSL Statements

Counting NGOMSL Statements

The estimation procedures used below involve counting the number of NGOMSL Statements. These are defined as follows:

• The step statement counts as one statement regardless of the number or kind of operators, including a `Return with goal accomplished` operator:
`Step n. <operator>...`

• The method statement must also be counted as one statement:
`Method for goal: <goal description>`

• The selection rule set statement counts as one statement:
`Selection rule set for goal: <general goal description>`

• The IF-THEN statement used in a selection rule counts as one statement:
`If <condition> Then accomplish goal: <specific goal description>.`

• The terminating statement of a selection rule set counts as one statement:
`Return with goal accomplished.`

• Steps containing a `Decide` operator involve a special case. As mentioned before, a step may contain only one `Decide` operator, and any other operators must be inside the `Decide` operator. Each IF-THEN or ELSE corresponds to a production rule, so to determine the number of statements that a `Decide` step should be counted as, count the number of If-Thens or Elses contained in the `Decide` operator; the result is the number of statements for the step. Thus, If the operator consists of a simple IF-THEN operator, such as:

```
Decide: If <operator...> Then <operator>
```

the step counts as one statement. However, if it contains IF-THEN-ELSE:

```
Decide: If <operator...> Then <operator>
Else <operator>
```

it counts as two statements. The following multiple-conditional `Decide` has three IF-THENS, and so counts at three statements:

```
Decide: If <operator...> Then <operator>
    If <operator...> Then <operator>
    If <operator...> Then <operator>
```

Execution of NGOMSL Statements

The NGOMSL expressions defined as "statements" above are actually executed, and so have to get counted in estimates of execution time. In particular, the `Method` statement that begins a method is counted as being executed. In terms of the underlying production rule model, the `Method` statement corresponds to a production rule that performs some housekeeping functions. (In most computer languages, the PROCEDURE statement actually compiles into some executed housekeeping code.)

Thus, the "overhead" time to call a method always consists of three NGOMSL statement execution times: one for the step in the calling method that contains the `Accomplish goal` operator that calls the method, one for the `Method` statement at the beginning of the called method, and one for the step in the called method that contains the `Return with goal accomplished` operator.

The statements in a selection rule set execute in a special way. The `Selection rule set` statement is executed first. Then, *only one* of the `If-Then` statements is executed, namely the one whose condition is met. In the production rule cognitive architecture, the conditions of all productions are tested simultaneously, in parallel, and only the one whose condition is satisfied is actually executed. Finally, the `Return with goal accomplished` statement is executed last. Thus, the time to execute a selection rule set is always 3 NGOMSL statement execution times; one for the `Selection rule set` statement, one for the `If-Then` that executes, and one for the `Return with goal accomplished`. This is the case regardless of how many `If-Thens` there are in the `Selection rule set`.

Likewise, in steps containing `Decide` operators, count toward execution time only one of the IF-THEN or ELSE clauses, no matter how many there are in the step.

31.3 General Issues in GOMS Task Analysis

31.3.1 Judgment Calls

In performing a GOMS task analysis, the analyst is repeatedly making decisions about:

- how users view the task in terms of their natural goals,

- how they decompose the task into subtasks,
- what the natural steps are in the user's methods.

It is possible to collect data on how users view and decompose tasks, but often it is not practical to do so. Thus, in order to do a useful task analysis, the analyst must make judgment calls on these issues. These are decisions based on the analyst's judgment, rather than on systematically collected behavioral data. In making judgment calls, the analyst is actually constructing a psychological theory or model for how people do the task, and so will have to make speculative, hypothetical claims and assumptions about how users think about the task. Because the analyst does not normally have the time or opportunities to collect the data required to test alternative models, these decisions may be wrong, but making them is better than not doing the analysis at all. By documenting these judgment calls, the analyst can explore more than one way of decomposing the task, and consider whether there are serious implications to how these decisions are made. If so, collecting behavioral data might then be required. But notice that once the basic decisions are made for a task, the methods are determined by the design of the system, and no longer by judgments on the part of the analyst.

For example, in the extended example below for moving text in MacWrite, the main judgment call is that due to the command structure, the user views moving text as first cutting, then pasting, rather than as a single unitary move operation. Given this judgment, the actual methods are determined by the possible sequences of actions that MacWrite permits to do cutting and pasting.

In contrast, on the IBM DisplayWriter, the design does not allow you to use the cut and paste operations embedded in the MOVE command separately. So here, the decomposition of moving into "cut then paste" would be a weak judgment call. The most reasonable guess is that a DisplayWriter user thinks of MOVE not in terms of cut and paste subgoals, but in terms of first selecting the text, then issuing Move command, and then designating the target location. So what is superficially the same text editing task may have different decompositions into subgoals, depending on how the system design encourages the user to think about it.

It could be argued that it is inappropriate for the analyst to be making *assumptions* about how humans view a system. However, notice that any designer of a system has in fact made many such assumptions. The usability problems in many software products are a result of the designer making assumptions, often unconsciously, with little or no thoughtful consideration of the implications for users. So, the analyst's assumptions, since they are based on a careful consideration from the user's point of view, can not do any more harm than that typically resulting from the designer's assumptions, and should lead to better results.

31.3.2 Pitfalls in Talking to Users

If the system already exists and has users, the analyst can learn a lot about how users view the task by talking to the users. You can get some ideas about how they decompose the task in to subtasks and what methods and selection rules they use.

However, remember that a basic lesson from the painful history of cognitive psychology is that people have only a very limited awareness of their own goals, strategies, and mental processes in general. Thus the analyst can not simply collect this information from interviews or having people "think out loud." What users *actually* do can differ a lot from what they *think* they do. The analyst will have to combine information from talking to users with considerations of how the task constrains the user's behavior, and most importantly, observations of actual user behavior. So, rather than ask people to describe verbally what they do, try to arrange a situation where they demonstrate on the system what they do, or better yet, you observe what they normally do in an unobtrusive way.

In addition, what users actually do with a system may not in fact be what they *should* be doing with it. As a result of poor design, bad documentation, or inadequate training, users may not in fact be taking advantage of features of the system that allow them to be more productive. The analyst should try to understand why this is happening, because a good design will only be good if it is used in the intended way. But for purposes of a GOMS analysis, the analyst will have to decide whether to assume a sub-optimal use of the system, or a fully informed one.

31.3.3 Bypassing Complex Processes

Many cognitive processes are too difficult to analyze in a practical context. Examples of such processes are reading, problem-solving, figuring out the best wording for a sentence, finding a bug in a computer program, and so forth. The approach presented here is to bypass the analysis of a complex process by simply representing it with a "dummy" or "placeholder" operator. In this way the analyst does not lose sight of the presence of the process, and can determine many things about what influence it might have on the user's performance with a design. Representing a bypassed process consists of using an analyst-defined operator together with information in the task description as place holders to document that the process is taking place and what its assumed results are.

For example, in MacWrite, the user may use tabs. How does the user know, or figure out, where to put them? The analyst might assume that the difficulties of doing this have nothing to do with the design of MacWrite (which may or not be true). The analyst can bypass the process of how the user figures out tab locations by assuming that user has figured them out already, and includes the tab settings as part of the task description supplied to the methods. The analyst defines a special operator that is used by the methods to access this information when it is needed (cf. the discussion in Bennett, Lorch, Kieras, and Polson, 1987).

As a second example, how does the user know that a particular scribble on the paper means "delete this word?" The analyst can bypass this problem by putting in the task description the information that the goal is to `Delete` and that the target text is at such-and-such a location (see example task descriptions above), and then using an analyst-defined operator that accesses the task description, such as `Look-at-document`. The methods will invoke this operator at the places where the user is assumed to have to look at the document to find out what to do. This way, the contents of the task description show the results of the complex reading process that was bypassed, and the places in the methods where the operator appears mark where the user is engaging in the complex reading process.

The analyst should only bypass processes for which a full analysis would be irrelevant to the design. But sometimes the complexity of the bypassed process is related to the design. For example, a text editor user must be able to read the paper marked-up form of a document, regardless of the design of the text editor, meaning that the reading process can be bypassed because it does not need to be analyzed in order to choose between two different text editor designs. On the other hand, the POET editor (see Card, Moran, and Newell, 1983) requires heavy use of find-strings which the user has to devise as needed. This process can still be bypassed with an analyst-defined operator, `think-up-find-string`, and the actual find strings specified in the task description. But suppose we are comparing POET to an editor that does not require such heavy use of find strings. Any conclusions about the difficulty of POET compared to the other editor will depend critically how hard the `think-up-find-string` operator is to execute. Thus, bypassing a process might produce seriously misleading results.

Representing Bypassed Processes

A bypassed process could be represented just by defining a complex mental operator and using it wherever it is needed in the methods. For example, we could define a `Most-Recent` operator that determines which of two time-stamped items (e.g. files) is the most recent. Exactly how the human cognitive process is done is irrelevant to the analysis. Once we have finished the analysis, we can, however, determine how often this operator is used, and thus see how important it is. Some designs may differ in how often complex processes are executed; if so, we can estimate or measure the time involved for the operators, and thus determine whether our design decisions are sensitive to these estimates.

But it seems to be better to put the results of a complex mental process into the task description, and then define a simple operator that just accesses this result when it is needed. This can be called the "yellow pad" heuristic; the concept is that the user has a complete description of the task written out on a yellow pad; all of the "thinking" unconnected with interacting with the system has already been done. The user's task is then only to interact with the system in order to carry out this completely described task, referring to the yellow pad as necessary to obtain the required information. Notice that this approach was followed in Card, Moran, and Newell's (1983, Ch.5) analysis of text-editing; their user is assumed to be working from a marked-up manuscript of the edited document, rather than composing the document or figuring out the desired changes while working at the computer. A similar approach was used in the Bennett, Lorch, Kieras, and Polson (1987) analysis of the task of entering a complex data table using different document preparation systems.

The reason why the yellow-pad approach is desirable is that the judgment calls on when and how much such complex processing is done seem to be relatively inconsistent, primarily because it is not very constrained by the design of the user interface. For example, one analyst might think that it takes 3 episodes of complex thinking to arrive at where to set a tab position in preparing a document, while another might think it would take 5, even though in both cases the methods involved in actually setting the location would be the same. Now, each such mental activity could be represented with a bypassing operator, which would normally be assigned a relatively large execution time estimate (e.g. at least 1.2 sec). But, since most other operators, like keystrokes, take a much shorter time, the uncertainty in the number of complex mental operators will cause the estimate of execution time to vary drastically, probably washing out the other differences between two similar designs. This weakening of the analysis is unnecessary, since these mental processes are often unrelated to the complexity of the methods entailed by the interface design.

The yellow-pad heuristic, by moving the complex mental processes "off-line" with just their results in the task description, eliminates these complex processes from the methods themselves. Thus the estimates of execution time depend much more heavily on the methods entailed by the actual interface design. In the meantime, the complex processes have not been ignored; their presence is documented in the task description. As discussed more below, at a later time, the analyst can consider whether these bypassed processes play an important role in the usability of the design, especially if two designs differ substantially in which processes are involved.

31.3.4 Analyze a General Set of Tasks, Not Specific Instances

Often, user interface designers will work with *task scenarios*, which are essentially descriptions in ordinary language of task instances and what the user would do in each one. The list of specific actions that the user would perform for a specific task can be called a *trace*, analogous to the specific sequence of results one obtains when "tracing" a computer program. Assembling a set of scenarios and traces is often useful as an informal way of characterizing a proposed user interface and its impact on the user.

If one has collected a set of task scenarios and traces, the natural temptation is to construct a description of the user's methods for executing these specific task instances. This temptation must be resisted; the goal of GOMS task analysis is a description of the *general* methods for accomplishing a set of tasks, not just the method for executing a specific instance of a task.

If you fall into the trap of writing methods for specific task instances, chances are that you will describe methods that are "flat," containing little in the way of method and submethod hierarchies, and which also may contain only specific keystroke operations. E.g., if the task scenario is that the user deletes the file FOOBAR, such a method will generate the keystroke sequence of "DELETE FOOBAR <CR>." But the fatal problem is that a tiny change in the task instance means that the method will not work. What if the task is to delete the file "FOO?" Sorry, you don't have a method for that! This corresponds to a user who has memorized by rote how to do an exact task, but who can't execute variations of the task.

On the other hand, a set of *general* methods will have the property that the information in a specific task instance acts like "parameters" for a general program, and the general methods will thus generate the specific actions required to carry out that task instance. Any task instance of the general type will be successfully executed by the general method. For example, a general method for deleting the file specified by <filename> will generate the keystroke sequence of "DELETE " followed by the string <filename> followed by <CR>. This corresponds to a user who knows how to use the system in the general way normally intended.

So, what should you do with a collection of task scenarios or traces? Study them to discover the range of things that the user has to do. Then set them aside and write a set of general methods, using the approach described below, that can correctly perform any specific task within the classes defined by your methods (e.g., delete any file whose name is specified in the task description). You can check to see if the methods will generate the correct trace for each task scenario, but they should also work for *any* scenario of the same type.

31.3.5 When Can a GOMS Analysis be Done?

After Implementation - Existing Systems

Constructing a GOMS model for a system that already exists is the easiest case for the analyst because much of the information needed for the GOMS analysis can be obtained from the system itself, its documentation, its designers, and the present users. The user's goals can be determined by considering the actual and intended use of the system; the methods are determined by what actual steps have to be carried out. The analyst's main problem will be to determine whether what users actually do is what the designers intended them to do, and then go on to decide what the users' actual goals and methods are. For example, the documentation for a sophisticated document preparation system gave no clue to the fact that most users dealt with the complex control language by keeping "template" files on hand which they just modified as needed for specific documents. Likewise, this mode of use was apparently not intended by the designers. So the first task for the analyst is to determine how an existing system is actually used in terms of the goals that actual users are trying to accomplish. Talking to, and observing, users can help the analyst with these basic decisions (but remember the pitfalls discussed above).

Since in this case the system exists, it is possible to collect data on the user's learning and performance with the system, so using a GOMS model to predict this data would only be of interest if the analyst wanted to verify that the model was accurate, perhaps in conjunction with evaluating the effect of proposed changes to the system. However, notice that collecting systematic learning and performance data for a complex piece of software can be an extremely expensive undertaking; if one is confident of the model, it could be used as a substitute for empirical data in activities such as comparing two competing existing products.

After Design Specification - Evaluation During Development

There is no need for the system to be already implemented or in use for a GOMS analysis to be carried out. It is only necessary that the analyst can specify the components of the GOMS model. If the design has been specified in adequate detail, then the analyst can identify the intended user's goals and describe the corresponding methods just as in the case of an existing system.

Of course, the analyst can not get the user's perspective since there are as yet no users to talk to. However, the analyst can talk to the designers to determine the designer's intentions and assumptions about the user's goals and methods, and then construct the corresponding GOMS model as a way to make these assumptions explicit and to explore their implications. Predictions can then be made of learning and performance characteristics, and then used to help correct and revise the design. The analyst thus plays the role of the future user's advocate, by systematically assessing how the design will affect future users. Since the analysis can be done before the system is implemented, it should be possible to identify and put into place an improved design without wasting coding effort.

However, the analyst can often be in a difficult position. Even fairly detailed design specifications often omit many specific details that directly affect the methods that users will have to learn. For example, the design specifications for a system may define the general pattern of interaction by specifying pop-up menus, but not the specific menu choices available, or which choices users will have to make to accomplish actual tasks. Often these detailed design decisions are left up to whoever happens to write the relevant code. The analyst may not be able to provide many predictions until the design is more fully fleshed out, and may have to urge the designers to do more complete specification than they normally would.

During Design - GOMS Analysis Guiding the Design

Rather than analyze an existing or specified design, the interface could be designed concurrently with describing the GOMS model. That is, by starting with listing the user's top-level goals, then defining the top-level methods for these goals, and then going on to the subgoals and submethods, one is in a position to make decisions about the design of the user interface directly in the context of what the impact is on the user. For example, bad design choices may be immediately revealed as spawning inconsistent, complex methods, leading the designer quickly into considering better alternatives. Clearly, this approach is possible only if the designer and analyst are closely cooperating, or are the same person.

Perhaps counter to intuition, there is little difference in the approach to GOMS analysis between doing it *during* the design process and doing it after. Doing the analysis during the design means that the analyst and designer are making design decisions about what the goals and methods *should be*, and then immediately describing them in the GOMS model. Doing the analysis *after* the system is designed means that the analyst is trying to determine the design decisions that were made *sometime in the past*, and then describing them in a GOMS model. For example, instead of determining and describing how the user does a cut-and-paste with an existing text editor, the designer-analyst *decides* and describes how the user *will* do it. It seems clear that the reliability of the analysis would be better if it is done during the design process, but the overall logic is the same in both cases.

31.4 A Procedure for Constructing a GOMS Model

The analysis of a task is done top-down from the most general user goal to more specific subgoals, with primitive operators finally at the bottom. All of the goals at each level are dealt with before going down to a lower level. The recipe presented here is based on this idea of thinking in terms of a top-down, breadth-first expansion of methods.

In overview, you start by describing a method for accomplishing a top-level goal in terms of high-level operators. Then you provide methods for performing the high-level operators in terms of lower-level operators. Then provide methods for these operators, and continue until you have arrived at enough detail to suit your needs, or until the methods are expressed in terms of primitive operators. So, as the analysis proceeds, high-level operators are replaced by goals to be accomplished by methods that involve lower-level operators. When you provide a method for a high-level operator, performing the operator becomes a goal, and so you provide a method for accomplishing that goal.

It is important to perform the analysis breadth-first, rather than depth-first. By considering all of the methods that are at the same level of the hierarchy before getting more specific, you are more likely to notice how the methods are similar to each other; such method similarities are critical to capturing the "consistency" of the user interface (see below).

You can choose to analyze in detail only selected portions of the user interface, and can leave at the level of high-level operators those portions where detail is not needed, or not possible. For example, suppose we aren't concerned with the specific keystrokes required to start a mail program that runs on different time-sharing systems, but are concerned with how to operate the mail program itself. We might describe the method to check for mail as follows:

```
Method for goal: check mail
  Step 1. LOG-INTO-SYSTEM
  Step 2. START-MAIL-PROGRAM
  Step 3. TYPE-IN "RETRIEVE<CR>"
  ... etc.
```

Logging in and starting the mail program are described with high-level operators, but we get down to specific keystrokes (the user types "RETRIEVE<CR>") once we are dealing with the mail program. If we are only concerned with the user interface of the mail program, we may choose to leave the high-level operators in Step 1 and Step 2 as unanalyzed. If so, we have chosen to bypass these processes, and are representing them with simple placeholders. We would then go on to describe in detail the methods involved in dealing with the mail program.

31.4.1 Summary of Procedure

Hint: since this is like writing and revising a computer program, use a text editor to allow fast writing and modification. An outline processor works especially well.

Step A: Choose the top-level user's goals

Step B: Do the following recursive procedure:

B1. Draft a method to accomplish each goal

B2. After completing the draft, check and rewrite as needed for consistency and conformance to guidelines.

B3. If needed, go to a lower level of analysis by changing the high-level operators to accomplish-goal operators, and then provide methods for the corresponding goals.

Step C: Document and check the analysis.

Step D: Check sensitivity to judgment calls and assumptions.

31.4.2 Detailed Description of Procedure

Step A: Choose the top-level user's goals

The top-level user's goals are the first goals that you will expand upon in the top-down analysis.

Advantages of Starting With High-level Goals. It is probably worthwhile to make the top-level goals very high-level, rather than lower-level, to capture any important relationships within the set of tasks that the system is supposed to address. An example for a text editor is that a high level goal would be `revise document`, while a lower-level one would be `delete text`. Starting with a set of goals at too low a level entails a risk of missing the methods involved in going from one type of task to another.

For example, many Macintosh applications combine deleting and inserting text in an especially convenient way. The goal of `change word` has a method of its own; i.e., double click on the word and then type the new word. If you start with `revise document` you might see that one kind of revision is changing one piece of text to another, and so you would consider the corresponding methods. If you start with goals like `insert text` and `delete text` you have already decided that this is the breakdown into subgoals, and so are more like to miss a case where the user has a natural goal that cuts across the usual functions.

As an example of very high-level goals, consider the goal of `produce document` in the sense of "publishing" - getting a document actually distributed to other people. This will involve first creating it, then revising it, and then getting the final printed version of it.

In an environment that includes a mixture of ordinary and desktop publishing facilities, there may be some important subtasks that have to be done in going from one to the other of the major tasks, such as taking a document out of an ordinary text editor and loading it into a page-layout editor, or combining the results of a text and a graphics editor. If you are designing just one of these packages, say the page-layout editor, and start only with goals that correspond to page-layout functions, you may miss what the user has to do to integrate the use of the page-layout editor in the rest of the environment.

Most Tasks Have a Unit-task Control Structure. Unless you have reason to believe otherwise, assume that the task you are analyzing has a unit-task type of control structure. This means that the user will accomplish the overall task by doing a series of smaller tasks one after the other. For a system such as a text editor, this means that the top-level goal of `edit document` will be accomplished by a unit-task method similar to that described by Card, Moran, and Newell, (1983). One way to describe this type of method in NGOMSL is as follows:

```
Method for goal: edit the document
  Step 1. Get next unit task information from
  marked-up manuscript.
  Step 2. Decide: If no more unit tasks, then
  return with goal accomplished.
  Step 3. Accomplish goal: move to the unit
  task location.
  Step 4. Accomplish goal: perform the unit
  task.
  Step 5. Goto 1.
```

The goal of performing the unit task typically is accomplished via a selection rule set, which dispatches control to the appropriate method for the unit task type, such as:

```
Selection rule set for goal: perform the unit
  task
  If the task is deletion, then
     accomplish goal: perform deletion proce-
  dure.
  If the task is copying, then
     accomplish goal: perform copy procedure.
  ... etc. ...
  Return with goal accomplished.
```

This type of control structure is common enough that the above method and selection rule set can be used as a template for getting the NGOMSL started. The remaining methods in the analysis will then consist of the specific methods for these subgoals, similar to those described in the extended example below.

Step B. Do the Following Recursive Procedure:

Step B1. Draft a Method to Accomplish Each Goal

Simply list the series of steps the user has to do. Each step should be a single natural unit of activity. Heuristically, this is just an answer to the question "how would a user describe how to do this?"

Make the steps as general and high-level as possible for the current level of analysis. A heuristic is to consider how a user would describe it in response to the instruction "don't tell me the details yet."

Use the principles for the Keystroke-Level Model for guidance on certain sequence of steps involving mental operators, such as locates before points.

Define new high-level operators, and bypass complex psychological processes as needed. Make a note of the new operators and task description information.

Make simplifying assumptions as needed, such as deferring the consideration of possible shortcuts that experienced users might use. Make a note of these assumptions in comments in the method.

If there is more than one method for accomplishing the goal, draft each method and then draft the selection rule set for the goal. My recommendation is to make the simplifying assumption that alternative methods are not used, and defer consideration of minor alternative methods until later. This is especially helpful for alternative "shortcut" methods.

Some Guidelines for Step B1

How Specific? As a rule of thumb, you should probably not be describing specific keystroke sequences until about four or so levels down, for typical top-level goals. For example:

```
goal of editing the document
 goal of copying text
   goal of selecting the text
    PRESS SELECT KEY
```

If the draft method involves keystroke sequences sooner, there is probably more structure to the user's goals than the draft method is capturing. Look for similarities between how different goals are accomplished; for example, many editors use a common selection method, suggesting that the user will have this as a subgoal, as in the above example. Really unusual or very poor designs may be exceptions.

How many steps in a method? As another rule of thumb, if there are more than 5 or so steps in the method, it may not be at right level of detail; the operators used in the steps may not be high-level enough. See if a sequence of steps can be made into a high-level operator, especially if the same sequence appears in other methods. Describing the methods breadth-first should help with noticing such shared sequences.

Example: Too many steps because level of detail is too fine:

```
Method for goal: start edit session
  Step 1. Type-in "edit"
  Step 2. Type-in filename
  Step 3. Press-key CR
  Step 4. If main menu present, Press-Key 1
  Step 5. Press-key CR
  etc.
```

Probably there should be higher-level operators:

```
Method for goal: start edit session
  Step 1. Enter editor with filename
  Step 2. Choose revise mode
  etc.
```

As in the above guideline, if there are too many steps, it may be due to a bad design, or there may be more structure to the user's knowledge than you are assuming.

How many Operators In a Step? How many operators can be done in a single cognitive step is an important question in the fundamental, and still developing, theory of cognitive skill (cf. Anderson's composition concept, Anderson, 1982). Based on Bovair, Kieras, and Polson (1990), these guidelines are reasonable:

- Use no more than one accomplish-goal operator to a step.
- Use no more than one high-level operator to a step.
- For ordinary or novice users, use no more than one external primitive operator to a step.
- For expert, very well practiced users, several external primitive operators can be used in a single step as follows: If there is a sequence of external primitive operators that is often performed without any decisions or subgoals involved, then this sequence of operators can appear in a single step.

Some standard mental operator sequences. Certain operators should be included in a procedure; these guidelines are similar to those associated with the Keystroke Level Model for the placement of mental operators (Card, Moran, and Newell, 1983). There should be a `Locate` operator executed prior to a `Point`, to reflect that before an object can be pointed to, its location must be known. If the system provides feedback to the user, then there should be a `Verify` operator in the method to represent how the user is expected to notice and make use of that feedback information. A `Verify` operator should normally be included at the point were the user must commit to an entry of information, such as prior to hitting the Return key in a command line interface. Finally, there should be a mental operator such as `Think-of` or `Get-from-task` for obtaining each item of task parameter information.

Developing the task description. A good way to keep from being overwhelmed by the details involved in describing a task is to develop the task description in parallel with the methods. That is, put in the task description only what is needed for the methods at the current level of the analysis. As the analysis deepens, add more detail and precision to the task description.

For example, early in the description of text editing methods, the type of edit (delete, move, etc.) may be needed by a method. But not until later, when you are describing the very detailed methods, will you need to specify information such as the exact position of the edit, what will be moved or deleted, and other detailed information.

Step B2. Check for Consistency and Conformance to Guidelines

- Check on the level of detail and length of each method.
- Check that you have made consistent assumptions about user's expertise with regard to the number of operators in a step.
- Identify the high-level operators you used; check that each high-level operator corresponds to a natural goal; redefine the operator or rewrite the method if not so.
- Maintain a list of operators used in the analysis, showing which methods each operator appears in.
- Check for consistency of terminology and usage with already defined operators. For example, we could end up with:

```
Look-for <manuscript markup information>
Look-at-manuscript-markup <information>
Look <markup-type>
```

when we probably should have just:

```
Look-at-manuscript-markup <type>
```

Redefine new or old operators to ensure consistency; and add new operators to the list.

- Examine any simplifying assumptions made, and elaborate the method if useful to do so.

Step B3. If Needed, Go to the Next Lower Level of Analysis

If all of the operators in a method are primitives, then this is the final level of analysis of the method, and nothing further needs to be done with this method. If some of the operators are high-level, non-primitive operators, examine each one and decide whether to provide a method for performing it. The basis for your decision is whether additional detail is needed for design purposes. For example, early in the design of a word processing system, it might not be decided whether the system will have a mouse or cursor keys. Thus it will not be possible to describe cursor movement and object selection below the level of high-level operators. In general, you should plan to expand as many high-level operators as possible into primitives at the level of keystrokes, because many important design problems, such as a lack of consistent methods, will show up mainly at this level of detail. Also, the time estimates are clearest and most meaningful at this level. If you choose to provide a method for an operator, rewrite that step in the method (and in all other methods using the operator). Replace the operator with an accomplish-goal operator for the corresponding goal. Update the operator list, and apply this recipe to describe the method for accomplishing the new goal.

For example, suppose the current method for copying text is:

```
Method for goal: copy text
  Step 1. Select the text.
  Step 2. Issue COPY command.
  Step 3. Return with goal accomplished.
```

and we choose to provide a method for the Step 1 operator `Select the text.` We rewrite the copying text method as:

```
Method for goal: copy text
> Step 1. Accomplish goal: select the text.
  Step 2. Issue COPY command.
  Step 3. Return with goal accomplished.
```

and then provide a method for the goal of selecting the text. To make the example clear, the changed line is shown in **Boldface** with a > in the left margin marking the changed line.

Step C. Documenting and Checking the Analysis

After you have completed writing out the NGOMSL model, list the following items of documentation:

- Primitive external operators used
- Analyst-defined operators used, along with a brief description of each one
- Assumptions and judgment calls that you made during the analysis
- The contents of the task description for each type of task

Then, choose some representative task instances, and check on the accuracy of the model by executing the methods as carefully as possible using hand simulation, and noting the actions generated by the model. This can be tedious. Verify that the sequences of actions are actually correct ways to execute the tasks (e.g. try them on the system). For a large project, you may want to consider implementing the methods as a computer program to automate this process. If the methods do not generate correct action sequences, make corrections so that the methods will correctly execute the task instances.

Step D. Check Sensitivity to Judgment Calls and Assumptions

Examine the judgment calls and assumptions made during the analysis to determine whether the conclusions about design quality and the performance estimates would change radically if the judgments or assumptions were made differently. This sensitivity analysis will be very important if two designs are being compared that involved different judgments or assumptions; less important if these were the same in the two designs. The analyst may want to develop alternate GOMS models to capture the effects of different judgment calls to systematically evaluate whether they have important impacts on the design.

31.4.3 Making WM Usage Explicit

Explicitly representing how the user must make use of Working Memory (WM) is a way to identify where the system is imposing a high memory load on the user. Probably, representing the WM usage can wait until the rest of analysis is complete; then the NGOMSL methods can be rewritten as needed to make WM usage explicit.

Notice that some kinds of memory are built-in to a GOMS model, such as the goal stack implied by the nesting of methods, and the pointer to the step in a method that is next to be executed. It is not clear theoretically whether this specialized control information is kept in the ordinary WM. In contrast, ordinary WM is definitely used to maintain temporary information that is not a fixed part of a method, such as the name of a file, the location of a piece of text, and so forth. It seems to be rare for ordinary methods on typical pieces of software to exceed WM capacity (cf. Bovair, Kieras, and Polson, 1990); if they did, they probably would have been changed! However, many computer system designs will strain WM in certain situations; often these are the ones where the user will be tempted to write something down on paper.

Representing WM usage requires making the methods explicit on when information is put into WM, accessed, and removed. To represent WM usage in the methods, identify the information that is needed from one step in a method to another, and describe each item of information in a consistent way. Ensure that when information is first acquired, a `Retain` operator is used, and that each step that needs the information `Recalls` it and when the information is no longer needed, then `Forget` it. . Because the underlying production rule models access to WM during condition matching and rule firing, the times for these basic WM operators are "bundled into the step execution time. Thus, WM operators would normally not occupy a step by themselves, but would always be included in a step that does other operators. For example:

```
Step 3. Find-menu-item "CUT" and retain item
  position.
Step 4. Recall item position and Move-mouse-
  to item-position.
Step 5. Forget item position, and press mouse
  button.
```

A more complete example appears in the extended example that follows.

31.4.4 An Example of Using the Procedure

This example shows the use of NGOMSL notation and illustrates how to construct a GOMS model using the top-down approach. The example system is MacWrite, and the example task is, of course, text editing. Only one type of text editing task, moving a piece of text from one place to another, is analyzed fully. The example consists of a series of passes over the methods, each pass corresponding to a deeper level of analysis. Four passes are shown in this example, but Pass 1 just consists of assuming that the unit task method is used for the topmost user's goal. After Pass 4, the operators, task description, and assumptions are listed.

In each pass, the complete GOMS model is shown. To make it easier to see what is new in each pass, the new material is shown in **boldface**, with the symbol > in the left margin on each new line. Following this example is an illustration of how some of the methods in the example would be modified to make WM use explicit.

Pass 1

Our topmost user's goal is editing the document. Taking the above recommendation, we simply start with the unit-task method and the selection rule set that dispatches control to the appropriate method:

```
>Method for goal:edit the document
> Step 1. Get next unit task information from
  marked-up manuscript.
> Step 2. Decide: If no more unit tasks, then
  return with goal accomplished.
> Step 3. Accomplish goal:move to the unit
  task location.
> Step 4. Accomplish goal:perform the unit
  task.
> Step 5. Goto 1.

>Selection rule set for goal:perform the unit
  task
> If the task is moving text, then
> accomplish goal:move text.
> If the task is deletion, then
> accomplish goal:delete text.
> If the task is copying, then
> accomplish goal:copy text.
> ... etc. ...
> Return with goal accomplished.
```

We also need a method for moving to the unit task location. In this example, we don't want to get into the gory details of how scrolling of the display is done. For this reason, the high-level operators in this method will not be further expanded. This method also provides an example of accessing the task description (the marked-up manuscript).

```
>Method for goal: move to the unit task loca-
  tion
> Step 1. Get location of unit task from
  manuscript.
> Step 2. Decide: If unit task location on
  screen, then
> return with goal accomplished.
> Step 3. Use scroll bar to advance text.
> Step 4. Goto 2.
```

In this example, we will next go on to provide a detailed method just for the goal of moving text.

Pass 2

Now, we begin the recursive procedure. Our current top-level goal is moving text. Our first judgment call is assuming that users view moving text as first cutting, then pasting. We write the new method accordingly:

```
Method for goal: edit the document
  Step 1. Get next unit task information from
  marked-up manuscript.
  Step 2. Decide: If no more unit tasks, then
  return with goal accomplished.
```

```
  Step 3. Accomplish goal: move to the unit
  task location.
  Step 4. Accomplish goal: perform the unit
  task.
  Step 5. Goto 1.

Selection rule set for goal: perform the unit
  task
  If the task is moving text, then
     accomplish goal: move text.
  If the task is deletion, then
     accomplish goal: delete text.
  If the task is copying, then
     accomplish goal: copy text.
  ... etc. ...
  Return with goal accomplished.

Method for goal: move to the unit task loca-
  tion
  Step 1. Get location of unit task from
  manuscript.
  Step 2. Decide: If unit task location on
  screen, return with goal accomplished.
  Step 3. Use scroll bar to advance text.
  Step 4. Goto 2.

>Method for goal: move text
> Step 1. Cut text
> Step 2. Paste text
> Step 3. Verify correct text moved.
> Step 4. Return with goal accomplished.
```

Step 1 and Step 2 of the new method are represented here *temporarily* with high-level operators. In the next pass, methods will be provided for them, and the high-level operators will be replaced with accomplish goal operators. Notice that in Step 3 we are assuming that the user will pause to verify that the desired results have been obtained. We will assume (perhaps wrongly) that a similar verification is *not* done within the cutting and pasting methods to be described below.

Pass 3

We now provide methods for cutting and pasting. Notice below how steps 2 and 3 of the moving text method have been changed from the previous pass. As an example, the first draft of the method for cutting is too long (see guidelines); in response to the guideline advice, this is fixed in the second draft.

```
Method for goal: edit the document
  Step 1. Get next unit task information from
  marked-up manuscript.
  Step 2. Decide: If no more unit tasks, then
  return with goal accomplished.
  Step 3. Accomplish goal: move to the unit
  task location.
  Step 4. Accomplish goal: perform the unit
  task.
  Step 5. Goto 1.

Selection rule set for goal: perform the unit
  task
  If the task is moving text, then
     accomplish goal: move text.
  If the task is deletion, then
     accomplish goal: delete text.
  If the task is copying, then
     accomplish goal: copy text.
  ... etc. ...
  Return with goal accomplished.

Method for goal: move to the unit task loca-
  tion
  Step 1. Get location of unit task from
  manuscript.
  Step 2. Decide: If unit task location on
  screen, return with goal accomplished.
  Step 3. Use scroll bar to advance text.
  Step 4. Goto 2.

Method for goal: move text
> Step 1. Accomplish goal: cut text
> Step 2. Accomplish goal: paste text
  Step 3. Verify correct text moved.
  Step 4. Return with goal accomplished.

>Method for goal: cut text - First Draft
> Step 1. Move cursor to beginning of text.
> Step 2. Hold down mouse button.
> Step 3. Move cursor to end of text.
> Step 4. Release mouse button.
> Step 5. Move cursor to EDIT menu bar item.
> Step 6. Hold down mouse button.
> Step 7. Move cursor to CUT item
> Step 8. Release cursor button.
> Step 9. Return with goal accomplished
```

Notice that this new method is correctly described, but it has too many steps. Also, this is only the second level of goals, and the method already has external primitive operators. Notice that Steps 1-4 correspond to a general method for how things are selected almost everywhere on the Macintosh, and Steps 5-8 are involved with issuing the CUT command. Perhaps the analysis has stumbled close to providing a trace-based method for executing a specific task rather than general methods that cover the tasks of interest, as discussed above. The second draft of the method corrects the problems with the judgment calls that (1) users know and take advantage of the general selecting function, and so they will have a "subroutine" method for selecting text, and that (2) similarly, they also have a general method for issuing commands. The corresponding sequences in the first draft can be collapsed into two high-level operators, as shown in second draft below of the cutting method. The pasting method is then written in a similar way.

```
>Method for goal: cut text - Second Draft
> Step 1. Select text.
> Step 2. Issue CUT command.
> Step 3. Return with goal accomplished.

>Method for goal: paste text
> Step 1. Select insertion point.
> Step 2. Issue PASTE command.
> Step 3. Return with goal accomplished.
```

Pass 4

We now provide some methods for selecting text and the corresponding selection rules, since MacWrite provides several ways of doing this. We also provide methods for selecting the insertion point and issuing CUT and PASTE commands. We make the simplifying assumption that our user does not make use of the command-key shortcuts.

```
Method for goal: edit the document
  Step 1. Get next unit task information from
  marked-up manuscript.
  Step 2. Decide: If no more unit tasks, then
  return with goal accomplished.
  Step 3. Accomplish goal: move to the unit
  task location.
  Step 4. Accomplish goal: perform the unit
  task.
  Step 5. Goto 1.

Selection rule set for goal: perform the unit
  task
  If the task is moving text, then
     accomplish goal: move text.
  ... etc. ...
  Return with goal accomplished.

Method for goal: move to the unit task loca-
  tion
  Step 1. Get location of unit task from
  manuscript.
  Step 2. Decide: If unit task location on
  screen, return with goal accomplished.
  Step 3. Use scroll bar to advance text.
  Step 4. Goto 2.

Method for goal: move text
  Step 1. Accomplish goal: cut text
  Step 2. Accomplish goal: paste text
  Step 3. Verify correct text moved.
  Step 4. Return with goal accomplished.

Method for goal: cut text
> Step 1. Accomplish goal: select text.
> Step 2. Accomplish goal: issue CUT command.
  Step 3. Return with goal accomplished.

Method for goal: paste text
> Step 1. Accomplish goal: select insertion
  point.
> Step 2. Accomplish goal: issue PASTE com-
  mand.
  Step 3. Return with goal accomplished.

>Selection rule set for goal: select text
> If text-is word, then
> accomplish goal: select word.
> If text-is arbitrary, then
> accomplish goal: select arbitrary text.
>Return with goal accomplished.

>Method for goal: select word
> Step 1. Locate middle of word.
> Step 2. Move cursor to middle of word.
> Step 3. Double-click mouse button.
> Step 4. Verify that correct text is se-
  lected
> Step 5. Return with goal accomplished.

>Method for goal: select arbitrary text
> Step 1. Locate beginning of text.
> Step 2. Move cursor to beginning of text.
> Step 3. Press mouse button down.
> Step 4. Locate end of text.
> Step 5. Move cursor to end of text.
> Step 6. Verify that correct text is se-
  lected.
> Step 7. Release mouse button.
> Step 8. Return with goal accomplished.
```

The last method above seems to be too long. This is the result of a judgment call that the user has to look at the marked-up manuscript to see where the text starts and then find this spot on the screen (Step 1), and then as a separate unit of activity, move the cursor there (Step 2). A similar situation appears in Steps 4 and 5. Some alternative judgment calls: Perhaps there is a `drag` operator and using it requires determining the end of the text before pressing down the mouse button. Alternately, perhaps the sequence appearing in Steps 1 and 2 and Steps 4 and 5 corresponds to a natural goal of `find a place and put the cursor there`, for which there should be a high-level operator and later a method. For brevity, these alternative judgment calls are not pursued in this example. The remaining methods are as follows:

```
>Method for goal: select insertion point
> Step 1. Locate insertion point.
> Step 2. Move cursor to insertion point.
> Step 3. Click mouse button.
> Step 4. Return with goal accomplished.

>Method for goal: issue CUT command
>(assuming that user does not use command-X
  shortcut)
> Step 1. Locate "Edit" on Menu Bar
> Step 2. Move cursor to "Edit" on Menu Bar
> Step 3. Press mouse button down.
> Step 4. Verify that menu appears.
> Step 5. Locate "CUT" in menu.
> Step 6. Move cursor to "CUT".
> Step 7. Verify that CUT is selected.
> Step 8. Release mouse button.
> Step 9. Return with goal accomplished.

>Method for goal: issue PASTE command
>(assuming that user does not use command-V
  shortcut)
> Step 1. Locate "Edit" on Menu Bar
> Step 2. Move cursor to "Edit" on Menu Bar
> Step 3. Press mouse button down.
> Step 4. Verify that menu appears.
> Step 5. Locate "PASTE" on menu
> Step 6. Move cursor to "PASTE".
> Step 7. Verify that PASTE is selected.
> Step 8. Release mouse button.
> Step 9. Return with goal accomplished.
```

Modifications to Show WM Usage

To illustrate how WM usage is made explicit, we will rewrite some of the methods to use a generic submethod for issuing a command that captures some of the consistency of the Macintosh menu-based command interface. This generic submethod uses WM to pass a "parameter" that is the name of the command to be issued. The use of working memory is explicitly represented in this method both informally and with variables.

Instead of separate methods for issuing a CUT and a PASTE command, there is now going to be just one method for issuing a command, whose name has been deposited previously in WM. First, the methods that called the previous command-issuing methods need to be modified to put the command name in WM, and to accomplish the generic goal of issuing a command.

```
Method for goal: cut text
  Step 1. Accomplish goal: select text.
> Step 2. Retain that the command is CUT, and
  accomplish goal: issue a command.
  Step 3. Return with goal accomplished.

Method for goal: paste text
  Step 1. Accomplish goal: select insertion
  point.
> Step 2. Retain that the command is PASTE,
  and accomplish goal: issue a command.
  Step 3. Return with goal accomplished.
```

The following method is the generic command-issuing method to replace the previous specialized methods for issuing a CUT and a PASTE command. The command name is like a subroutine parameter, and is passed in through WM. We assume that user must remember with a retrieval from LTM where in the menus the command is, and the user has to remember this menu name while executing the method.

```
Method for goal: issue a command
  Step 1. Recall command name and retrieve
  from LTM the menu name for it.
  Step 2. Recall menu name, and locate it on
  Menu Bar.
  Step 3. Move cursor to menu name location.
  Step 4. Press mouse button down.
  Step 5. Verify that menu appears.
  Step 6. Recall command name, and locate it
  in menu.
  Step 7. Move cursor to command name loca-
  tion.
  Step 8. Recall command name, and verify
  that it is selected.
  Step 9. Release mouse button.
  Step 10. Forget menu name, forget command
  name, and return with goal accomplished.
```

Notice how this analysis makes explicit that the user has to maintain two chunks in WM during this method; this might be a problem if the higher-level methods required keeping track of 3 - 5 more chunks.

Final GOMS Model

Below is the final version of the GOMS model, incorporating the WM usage version of the generic command entry method. The intermediate versions produced in the separate passes above are discarded.

```
Method for goal: edit the document.
  Step 1. Get next unit task information from
  marked-up manuscript.
  Step 2. Decide: If no more unit tasks, then
  return with goal accomplished.
  Step 3. Accomplish goal: move to the unit
  task location.
  Step 4. Accomplish goal: perform the unit
  task.
  Step 5. Goto 1.

Selection rule set for goal: perform the unit
  task.
  If the task is moving text, then accomplish
  goal: move text.
  If the task is deletion, then accomplish
  goal: delete text.
  If the task is copying, then accomplish
  goal: copy text.
  ... etc. ...
  Return with goal accomplished.

Method for goal: move to the unit task loca-
  tion.
  Step 1. Get location of unit task from
  manuscript.
  Step 2. Decide: If unit task location on
  screen, return with goal accomplished.
  Step 3. Use scroll bar to advance text.
  Step 4. Goto 2.

Method for goal: move text.
  Step 1. Accomplish goal: cut text
  Step 2. Accomplish goal: paste text
  Step 3. Verify correct text moved.
  Step 4. Return with goal accomplished.

Method for goal: cut text.
  Step 1. Accomplish goal: select text.
  Step 2. Retain that the command is CUT, and
  accomplish goal: issue a command.
  Step 3. Return with goal accomplished.

Method for goal: paste text.
  Step 1. Accomplish goal: select insertion
  point.
  Step 2. Retain that the command is PASTE,
  and accomplish goal: issue a command.
  Step 3. Return with goal accomplished.

Selection rule set for goal: select text.
  If text-is word, then accomplish goal: se-
  lect word.
  If text-is arbitrary, then accomplish goal:
  select arbitrary text.
  Return with goal accomplished.

Method for goal: select word.
  Step 1. Locate middle of word.
  Step 2. Move cursor to middle of word.
  Step 3. Double-click mouse button.
  Step 4. Verify that correct text is se-
  lected
  Step 5. Return with goal accomplished.
```

```
Method for goal: select arbitrary text.
  Step 1. Locate beginning of text.
  Step 2. Move cursor to beginning of text.
  Step 3. Press mouse button down.
  Step 4. Locate end of text.
  Step 5. Move cursor to end of text.
  Step 6. Verify that correct text is se-
  lected.
  Step 7. Release mouse button.
  Step 8. Return with goal accomplished.

Method for goal: select insertion point.
  Step 1. Locate insertion point.
  Step 2. Move cursor to insertion point.
  Step 3. Click mouse button.
  Step 4. Verify that insertion cursor is at
  correct place.
  Step 5. Return with goal accomplished.

Method for goal: issue a command.
  Assumes that user does not use command-key
  shortcuts
  Step 1. Recall command name and retrieve
  from LTM the menu name for it.
  Step 2. Recall menu name, and locate it on
  Menu Bar.
  Step 3. Move cursor to menu name location.
  Step 4. Press mouse button down.
  Step 5. Verify that menu appears.
  Step 6. Recall command name, and locate it
  in menu.
  Step 7. Move cursor to command name loca-
  tion.
  Step 8. Recall command name, and verify
  that it is selected.
  Step 9. Release mouse button.
  Step 10. Forget menu name, forget command
  name, and return with goal accomplished.
```

Step C: Documenting and Checking the Analysis

Table 1 shows the list of analyst-defined operators, and Table 2 shows the information contained in the task description for this GOMS model. The assumptions and judgment calls made are listed in Table 3.

As shown in Table 3 the methods assume that the user's hand is on the mouse and stays there throughout the editing tasks. If we identified which mouse moves had the property that the hand was on the keyboard, we could add the homing time to the time for that mouse move operator. We could do likewise for any keyboard keystroke times. A more elegant way would be to write a method for the move-cursor operator like this:

```
Method for goal: move the cursor to a speci-
  fied location
  Step 1. Decide: If hand not on mouse, then
  move hand to mouse.
      (.4 sec homing time)
  Step 2. Move cursor to specified location.
      (typically 1.1 sec)
  Step 3. Return with goal accomplished.
```

Then the move-cursor operators in the example methods would be replaced with accomplishing the goal of moving the cursor, which would invoke this method.

Table 1. Analyst-defined operators for the example.

`Get next unit task information from marked-up manuscript` - look at manuscript and scan for the next edit marking, and put some of the task description into working memory.
`No more unit tasks` - tells whether there was another edit marking.
`Task is ...` - tells whether task is of the specified type, such as move, copy, etc.
`Get location of unit task from manuscript` - look at edit marking on manuscript and determine its position.
`If unit task location on screen` - tells whether the material corresponding to the edit marking is on the screen.
`Use scroll bar to advance text` - a high-level operator that could be expanded into a set of methods.
`Locate` - get information from task description, and map to perceptual location on screen.
`Text-is` - tells whether text is a word, sentence, or arbitrary.
`Verify` - compare results to goal to check that desired result is achieved.
`Move cursor to` - move mouse until cursor at specified point.
`Click mouse button.`
`Double-click mouse button.`
`Press mouse button.`
`Release mouse button.`

Table 2. Example task description.

```
Task is to move specified piece of text
Piece of text is a word, or arbitrary
Position of beginning of text
Position of end of text, if it is arbi-
trary
Position of destination
```

Step D: Checking Sensitivity to Judgment Calls

The following are some examples of how the sensitivity of the analysis to the judgment calls can be checked.

Alternative view of the move task. Suppose the user does not decompose the move task into cut-then-paste as we did, but thinks of move as a single goal. Suppose you wrote out the methods according to this decomposition by providing a different move method that corresponds well to the user's decomposition. One

Table 3. Example assumptions and judgment calls.

The topmost goal in the analysis is editing a document; it was assumed that there are no critical interactions with other aspects of the user's task environment.
The unit-task control structure is assumed for the topmost method.
Users view moving text on this system as first cutting, then pasting.
Users know that selecting text is done the same way everywhere in the system, and take advantage of it by having a subgoal and a method for it, and likewise for invoking commands.
The analysis has been simplified by ignoring the command key shortcuts for CUT and PASTE.
When selecting an arbitrary piece of text, users view as two separate steps deciding what the beginning point is and putting the cursor there. Likewise, deciding where the end point is and putting the cursor there are two separate steps. There are plausible alternative judgment calls.
The user's hand is on the mouse and stays there throughout the editing tasks.

possibility is that the user could select the text, issue a move command, and then click the mouse where the text is to be moved to. A Macintosh-like system could actually execute the command by cutting the text and then pasting it, but the user would issue only a move command. Clearly, if users like to think of a move this way, they probably would think of a copy this way as well.

With methods tailored to this alternative judgment of how move and copy goals decompose, what you might see is that more methods would be needed overall because we couldn't share the cut and paste submethods with other editing methods. This means that the editor might be harder to learn overall, due to more methods to learn. So the quality of the design in terms of its learnability and consistency is probably sensitive to whether our judgment call is correct. We may want to explore these alternatives by actually working out an alternative set of methods and comparing the two analyses or designs in detail.

If we stick with the original judgment call, it would be a good idea to be sure that the user decomposes the task the same way, into the cut-then-paste form. We could find out if users actually do this, or since it seems to be a reasonably natural way to view the task, we could try to encourage the user to look at it this way, perhaps by pointing out the advantages of this view in the documentation. This way we would have some confidence that the methods actually adopted by the user are like those we based the design on (see the Documentation discussion below). So our check of sensitivity suggests that the original judgment call was satisfactory.

Effects of command shortcuts. As a second use of the analysis example, consider the simplifying assumption that the user would not use the command-key method of issuing commands on the Mac. Are our conclusions sensitive to this? Obviously both our learning time and execution time estimates will differ a lot depending on whether the user uses these shortcuts. If we are comparing two designs that differ in whether command-key shortcuts are available, this is actually not a question of a simplifying assumption, but of desirable features of the designs. But if we have simply assumed that the user will use the shortcuts in one of the designs, but not in the other, when they could be available in both, then the comparison of the designs will be seriously biased.

Consider the role of shortcuts in the above alternate analysis for move. We can conclude that the simplifying assumption that users would not use shortcuts would not influence the choice between the alternate designs for move. This is because the main differences between the designs will be how many commands have to be issued and how many methods have to be learned. Any differences will be reflected in the shortcuts the same as in the non-shortcuts, because the shortcuts have a one-to-one relationship with the full methods. So, for example, whichever design has the fewest methods to be learned, will also have the fewest shortcuts to be learned. So our check suggests that ignoring the shortcuts is not a bias on the particular choice of designs, but does produce much higher execution times.

31.5 Using a GOMS Task Analysis

Once the GOMS model analysis is completed (either for an existing system or one under design), it is time to make use of it to evaluate the quality of the design. Notice that if the model has been constructed during the design process itself, there is a good chance that some of the evaluation was in fact done on the fly; when a design choice ended up requiring a complex and difficult method, some change was probably made immediately.

The evaluation process described below will yield numbers and other indications of the quality of the design. As in any evaluation technique, these measures are easiest to make use of if there are at least two systems being compared. One of these systems might be an existing, competitive product. For example, IBM could have set the goal of making OS/2 for their PS line "as easy to learn and use as the Apple Macintosh." They could then have compared these measures for their new design with the measures from a GOMS model for the same tasks on a Macintosh to determine how close they were to this goal.

If heavy usage of a GOMS analysis is involved, consider implementing the methods as a computer program in order to automate checks for accuracy, and to generate counts of operators, steps, and so forth, used in the estimation procedures below.

31.5.1 Qualitative Evaluation of a Design

Several overall checks can be done that make use of qualitative properties of the GOMS model.

- Naturalness of the design - Are the goals and subgoals ones that would make sense to a new user of the system, or will the user have to learn a new way of thinking about the task in order to have the goals make sense?

- Completeness of the design - Construct the complete action/object table - are there any goals you missed? Check that there is a method for each goal and subgoal.

- Cleanliness of the design - If there is more than one method for accomplishing a goal, is there a clear and easily stated selection rule for choosing the appropriate method? If not, then some of these methods are probably unnecessary.

- Consistency of the design - By "consistency" is meant method consistency. Check to see that similar goals are accomplished by similar methods. Especially check to see that if there are similar subgoals, such as selection of various types of objects, then there are similar submethods, or better, a single submethod, for accomplishing the subgoals. The same idea applies for checking consistency between this and other systems - will methods that work on the other system also work on this one?

- Efficiency of the design - The most important and frequent goals should be accomplished by relatively short and fast-executing methods.

31.5.2 Predicting Human Performance

What is Learned Versus What is Executed

NGOMSL models can be used to predict the *learning time* that users will take to learn the procedures represented in the GOMS model, and the *execution time* users will take to execute specific task instances by following the procedures. It is critical to understand the difference between how these two usability measures are predicted from a GOMS model.

- *The total number and length of all methods determines the learning time.* The time to learn a set of methods is basically determined by the total length of the methods, which is given by the number of NGOMSL statements in the complete GOMS model for the interface. This is the amount of procedural knowledge that the user has to acquire in order to know how *to use the system for all of the possible tasks under consideration.*

- *The methods, steps, and operators required to perform a specific task determines the execution time.* The time required to accomplish a task instance is determined by the number and content of NGOMSL statements that have to be executed to get that specific task done. The time required by each statement is the sum of a small fixed time for the statement plus the time required by any external or mental operators executed in the statement.

There may be little relationship between the number of statements that have to be learned and the number of statements that have to be executed. The situation is exactly analogous to an ordinary computer program - the time to compile a program is basically determined by the program length, but the execution time in a particular situation can be unrelated to the length of the program; it depends on how many and which statements get executed.

Typically, performing a particular task involves only a subset of the methods in the GOMS model, meaning that the number of statements executed may be less than the number that must be learned. For example, you may know the methods for doing a lot of text editor commands, which might require a few hundred NGOMSL statements to describe. But to perform the task of deleting a character will only involve executing a few of those statements. On the other hand, performing a task might involve using a method repeatedly, or looping on a set of steps (e.g., the top-level unit task method, which loops, doing one unit task after another). In this case, the number of statements executed in order to perform a task might easily be much larger than the number of statements in the GOMS model.

So, in estimating learning time, count how many NGOMSL statements that the user has to learn in order to know how to use the system for all possible tasks of interest. In estimating execution time for a specific task, determine which and how many statements have to be passed through in order to perform the task.

Estimate Times at the Standard Primitive Operator Level of Detail

A useful feature of GOMS models is the they can represent an interface at different levels of detail. However, a GOMS model can predict learning and execution time sensibly only if the lowest-level operators used in the model are ones (1) that you can reasonably assume that the user already knows how to do, and (2) for which stable time estimates are available. A keystroke is a good example of an operator that a user is typically assumed to already know, and which is executed in a predictable amount of time. If a method involves only such standard primitive operators (see section 31.2.2), and the user already knows them, the time to learn a method depends just on how long it takes to learn the content and sequence of the method steps. Likewise, the time to execute the method can be predicted by adding up a standard execution time for each NGOMSL statement in the method plus the predicted execution time for each standard primitive operator executed in the method steps, plus the execution time assigned to any analyst-defined operators.

In contrast, if you have a GOMS model which is written just at the level of high-level operators that the user has to learn how to perform, then the learning time estimates have to be poor because the learning times for the operators will be relatively large and probably unknown. Typically, the execution time for operators at this level will also be fairly large and unknown. For example, consider the following GOMS model for the task of writing computer programs:

```
Method for goal: write computer program
  Step 1. Invent algorithm.
  Step 2. Code program.
  Step 3. Enter code into computer.
  Step 4. Debug program.
  Step 5. Return with goal accomplished.
```

Suppose our model stops with these very high-level operators, and we don't believe that users already know how to debug a program or invent algorithms. Estimating the learning time as a simple function of the length of this method is obviously absurd; it will take grossly different times to learn how to execute the operators in each of these steps, and these times will be very long. Likewise, these operators have grossly different, unknown, and relatively long execution times. In contrast, the typical primitive external operators such as pressing a key, or relatively simple mental operators such as looking at a manuscript, can be assumed to be already known to the user, and have relatively small, constant, and known execution times. Thus, if the methods have been represented at the standard primitive operator level, the calculations presented below for predicting learning and execution times will produce useful results.

Estimating Learning Time

Pure vs. Total Learning Time. In estimating learning time, we might be interested in the total time needed to complete some training process in which users learn the methods in the context of performing some tasks with the system, perhaps with some accompanying reading or other study. This total time consists of the time to *execute the training tasks* in addition to the time required to learn how to perform the methods themselves, which is the *pure learning time*. This pure learning time has two components, the *pure method learning time*, and the *LTM item learning time*, which is the time required to memorize items that will be retrieved from LTM during method execution. Once the methods and LTM items are learned, the same training situation could be executed much more quickly. Thus the pure learning time represents the excess time required to perform the training situation due to the need to learn the methods. This pure learning time can be estimated as shown below. If the procedures to be used in training are known, it may be useful to estimate the total learning time by adding the time required to execute the training procedures. Thus, in summary:

Total Learning Time =
Pure Method Learning Time +
LTM Item Learning Time + Training Procedure Execution Time.

Pure Method Learning Time. Kieras and Bovair (1986) and Bovair, Kieras, and Polson (1990) found that pure learning time was proportional to the number of production rules that had to be learned. NGOMSL was defined so that one NGOMSL statement corresponds to one production rule, and so the pure learning time can be estimated from NGOMSL statements as well. But the time required to learn a single NGOMSL statement depends of specifics of the learning situation, such as what the criterion for learning consists of. The Bovair, Kieras, and Polson work used a very rigorous training situation, while Gong (1993; see also Gong and Kieras, 1994) measured learning time in a much more realistic training situation.

The Bovair, Kieras, and Polson *rigorous* learning situation was as follows: The methods correspond to new or novice users, not experts. The methods are explicitly presented; the learner does not engage in problem-solving to discover them. Efficient presentation and feedback, as in computer-assisted instruction, are used, rather than "real-world" learning approaches. The methods are presented one at a time, and are practiced to a certain criterion, such as making a set of deletions perfectly, before proceeding to next method. The total training time was defined to be the total time required to complete the training on each method.

The Gong *typical* training situation was much more realistic: The users went through a demonstration task accompanied by a verbal explanation, and then performed a series of training task examples. The total training time was defined as the time sum of the time required for the demonstration and the training examples.

Thus, to estimate the pure method learning time, decide whether the rigorous or typical situation is relevant, and calculate:

Pure Method Learning Time =
Learning Time Parameter ×
Number of NGOMSL statements to be learned

Where:

Learning Time Parameter =
30 sec for rigorous procedure training
17 sec for a typical learning situation

Note that if the user already knows some of the methods, either from previous training or experience, or from having learned a different system which uses the same methods, then these methods should not be included in the count of NGOMSL statements to be learned.

LTM Item Learning Time. If many Retrieve-from-LTM operators are involved, then we would predict that learning will be slow due to the need to memorize the information that has to be retrieved when executing the methods. We can estimate how long it will take to store the information in LTM, using the Model Human Processor parameters (Card, Moran, and Newell, 1983, Ch.2), which is a value of about 10 sec/chunk for LTM storage time. Gong (1990) obtained results in a realistic training situation that suggest a value of 6 sec/chunk, which is the recommended value.

There is no established and verified technique for counting how many chunks are involved in to-be-memorized information, so the suggestions here should be treated as heuristic suggestions only. Count the number of chunks in an item with judgment calls as follows:

- one chunk for each familiar pattern in the retrieval cue
- one chunk for each familiar pattern in the retrieved information
- one chunk for the association between the retrieval cue and the retrieved information

For example, suppose the to-be-stored association for a command is *move cursor right by a word is ctrl-right arrow*. Then:

(move cursor right) (by a word) =
2 chunks for retrieval cue
(ctrl) (right-arrow) =
2 chunks for retrieved information
association between the two = 1 chunk

For a total of 5 chunks, or 50 sec minimum pure learning time. Add this estimated time to the total learning time.

Do not count LTM storage time if the item is already known. For example, the above example is a common convention on PCs, and so would probably be known to an experienced PC user.

Estimating Gains from Consistency. If the design is highly consistent in the methods, the new user will be able to learn how to use it more easily than if the methods are not consistent with each other. One sign of a highly consistent interface is that there are generic methods (see the Section 31.1.2 example, and the issue-command method in the above example) that are used everywhere they are appropriate, and few or no special case methods are required. So, if a GOMS model for a user interface can be described with a small number of generic methods, it means that the user interface is highly consistent in terms of the method knowledge. Thus, describing generic methods, where they exist, is a way to "automatically" take this form of interface consistency into account.

However, sometimes the methods can be similar, with only some small differences; the research suggests that this cruder form of consistency reduces learning time as well, due to the *transfer of training* from one method to another. Kieras, Bovair, and Polson suggested a theoretical model for the classic concept of common elements transfer of training (Kieras and Bovair, 1986; Polson, 1987; Bovair, Kieras, and Polson, 1990). These transfer gains can be estimated by identifying similar methods and similar NGOMSL statements in these methods, and then deducting the number of these similar statements from the above estimate.

The criterion for "similar" can be defined in a variety of ways. Here will be described a relatively simple definition based on the Kieras and Bovair (1986) model of transfer. In summary, consistency can be measured in terms of how many statements have to be modified to turn one method into another, related, method. Only a very simple modification is allowed. If two statements can be made identical with this modification, then the statements are classified as "similar." After learning the first of two similar statements, the user can learn the second one so easily that to a good first approximation, there is no learning time required for the second statement at all. The same procedure applies to both methods and selection rules.

More specifically, the procedure for estimating transfer is as follows:

1. Find candidates for transfer. Find the methods that might be similar to each other. You do this by finding two methods that have similar goals. Let's call them method A and method B. Normally the two methods will not be completely identical because the goals they accomplish will be different. If both the verb and the noun in the `<verb noun>` goal descriptions are different, the methods are not similar at all, and there will be no consistency gains between them. If they are different on only one of the terms (e.g. `MOVE TEXT` versus `COPY TEXT`) the methods are similar enough to proceed to determining how many statements are similar in the two methods.

2. Generalize Method Goals. To determine which statements in method A and method B are similar, generalize the goals of the two methods by identifying the single term in the goal specifications of the two methods that is different and change it to a "parameter." Make the corresponding change throughout both methods. What you have constructed is the closest generalization between the two methods. If they are identical at this point, it means you could have in fact defined a generic method for the two different goals; do so and go on look for other similar methods.

3. Count Similar Statements. If the two methods are not identical, start at the beginning of these two methods and go down through the method statements and the steps and count the number of NGOMSL statements that are identical in the two methods; stop counting when you encounter two statements that are non-identical. That is, once the flow of control diverges, there is no longer any additional transfer possible (according to the theoretical model). If the `Method` statement is the only one counted as identical, then there are no real similarities; the number of similar statements is zero, and there are no consistency savings between the two methods. But if there are some identical statements in addition to the `Method` statement, include the `Method` statement in the count.

4. Deduct Similar Statements from Learning Time. The identical statements counted this way are the ones classified as "similar." According to the model of transfer of training, only the first appearance of one of these similar statements requires full learning; the ones encountered later come "free of charge." Subtract the number of the similar statements from the total number of statements to be learned.

It is important to ensure that steps deemed identical actually contain or imply identical operators. The best way to ensure this is for the GOMS model to be worked out down to the level of primitive external operators such as keystrokes; the rigor at this level ensures that the higher-level methods will appear to be similar only if they invoke submethods that are in fact similar.

As an example of a transfer calculation, refer to the Final GOMS Model of the above example. Note that the two selection methods have some overlap and similarity:

```
Method for goal: select word.
  Step 1. Locate beginning of word.
  Step 2. Move cursor to beginning of word.
  Step 3. Double-click mouse button.
  Step 4. Verify that correct text is se-
  lected
  Step 5. Return with goal accomplished.
```

```
Method for goal: select arbitrary text.
  Step 1. Locate beginning of text.
  Step 2. Move cursor to beginning of text.
  Step 3. Press mouse button down.
  Step 4. Locate end of text.
  Step 5. Move cursor to end of text.
  Step 6. Verify that correct text is se-
  lected.
  Step 7. Release mouse button.
  Step 8. Return with goal accomplished.
```

The object in the goal specifications in the `Method` statements can be replaced with a parameter, `GOAL-OBJECT`, and the corresponding changes made throughout; these are our most generalized version of the two methods.

```
Method for goal: select GOAL-OBJECT.*
  Step 1. Locate beginning of GOAL-OBJECT.*
  Step 2. Move cursor to beginning of GOAL-
  OBJECT.*
  Step 3. Double-click mouse button.
  Step 4. Verify that correct text is se-
  lected
  Step 5. Return with goal accomplished.
```

```
Method for goal: select GOAL-OBJECT.*
  Step 1. Locate beginning of GOAL-OBJECT.*
  Step 2. Move cursor to beginning of GOAL-
  OBJECT.*
  Step 3. Press mouse button down.
  Step 4. Locate end of GOAL-OBJECT.
  Step 5. Move cursor to end of GOAL-OBJECT.
  Step 6. Verify that correct text is se-
  lected.
  Step 7. Release mouse button.
  Step 8. Return with goal accomplished.
```

We start counting identical statements from the beginning of the two methods. The `Method` statements, Step 1, and Step 2 are identical, but Step 3 is different, so we stop counting, giving a total of 3 similar statements (the `Method` statements, Step 1, and Step 2) for the two methods. The statements counted as similar are marked with an asterisk above.

The gain from consistency can now be estimated. Suppose the select-word method is learned first, requiring learning 6 NGOMSL statements, followed by learning the select-arbitrary-text method, which has a total of 9 statements. According to the transfer model, the user will have to work at learning the similar statements only the first time, while learning how to select words, and so will have to learn only Steps 3 through 8 of the select-arbitrary-text method. Thus, instead of a total learning time for the two methods of $(6 + 9) \times 30$ sec = 450 sec above the baseline, the estimated learning time will be only $(6 + 6) \times 30$ sec = 360 sec above the baseline, a substantial gain due to consistency.

As a negative example, consider the apparent similarity between the method for cutting text and the method for pasting text. Both seem to involve first selecting something, and then issuing a command based on the goal:

```
Method for goal: cut text
  Step 1. Accomplish goal: select text.
  Step 2. Accomplish goal: issue CUT command.
  Step 3. Return with goal accomplished.
```

```
Method for goal: paste text
  Step 1. Accomplish goal: select insertion
  point.
  Step 2. Accomplish goal: issue PASTE com-
  mand.
  Step 3. Return with goal accomplished.
```

The verb in the goal specifications in the method statements can be generalized with a parameter, `GOAL-VERB`, and the corresponding changes made:

```
Method for goal: GOAL-VERB text
  Step 1. Accomplish goal: select text.
  Step 2. Accomplish goal: issue GOAL-VERB
  command.
  Step 3. Return with goal accomplished.
```

```
Method for goal: GOAL-VERB text
  Step 1. Accomplish goal: select insertion
  point.
  Step 2. Accomplish goal: issue GOAL-VERB
  command.
  Step 3. Return with goal accomplished.
```

But, counting from the beginning, we see that the two methods diverge immediately at Step 1; selecting text is not identical with selecting the insertion point; generalizing the goal doesn't deal with this fundamental difference. So, according to the transfer model, there are no similar statements; the `Method` statements by themselves do not count. Accordingly, there is no transfer of learning between these two methods, and the user will have to pay the full cost of learning two separate methods.

Estimating Execution Time

Time Estimate Calculation. Estimating execution time is very similar to the Keystroke-Level Model approach (Card, Moran and Newell, 1983, Ch. 8). The time to execute a method depends on the time to execute the operators and on the number of cognitive steps, or production rules, involved. NGOMSL has been defined so that the NGOMSL statements defined above each correspond to a production rule that is executed. The execution time can only be estimated for specific task instances because only then will the number and sequence of steps and operators be determined.

To estimate the execution time for a task, choose one or more representative task instances. Execute the method (e.g. by hand) to accomplish each task instance, and record a trace of the NGOMSL statements and operators executed. Examine the trace and tabulate the statistics referred to below. The estimated execution time is given by:

Execution Time =
NGOMSL statement time +
Primitive External Operator Time+
Analyst-defined Mental Operator Time +
Waiting Time

NGOMSL Statement Time =
Number of statements executed ×
0.1 sec

Primitive External Operator Time =
Total of times for primitive external operators

Analyst-Defined Mental Operator Time =
Total of times for mental operators defined by the analyst

Waiting Time =
Total time when user is idle while waiting for the system

Thus, each NGOMSL statement takes 0.1 sec to execute, whatever operator times are involved is additional. Note that the time to execute the built-in primitive mental operators is bundled into the NGOMSL statement execution time. The time of 0.1 sec is based on the assumption that each NGOMSL statement is actually implemented as a single production rule, and on the results of modeling work which assumes that the cognitive processor has a production rule architecture. When such models are fitted to task execution time data, the resulting estimate of cycle time is 0.1 sec (see Bovair, Kieras, and Polson, 1990; Kieras, 1986). This value is consistent with, though somewhat slower than, the Card, Moran, and Newell (1983, Ch. 2) figure for cognitive processor cycle time.

The *primitive external operator time* can be estimated using the Keystroke-Level Model values from Card, Moran, and Newell (1983, Ch. 8). These times can be refined by using empirical results or more exact calculations, such as applying Fitts' Law to hand or mouse movement times.

Gong (1990; see also Gong and Kieras, 1994) found that many of the mouse moves in a Macintosh interface were much more accurately estimated with Fitts' Law than with the Keystroke Level Model time of 1.1 sec. For example, the time to move to select a window was only about 0.2 sec (a very large target) and moves within a dialog box were also very fast, e.g. 0.1 sec, (a short distance). The Keystroke Level Model estimate of 1.1 sec is actually based on large moves to small targets, as in document text editing. Instead, Gong used values calculated from Fitts' Law (see Card, Moran, and Newell, 1983; p. 242), and considerably increased the accuracy of the execution time prediction.

The *analyst-defined* mental operator time, in the lack of any other information, can be estimated as 1.2 sec for each analyst-defined mental operator (see Olson and Olson, 1989). Some of the operators normally represented as taking a mental operator time should be treated differently, depending on the whether the methods they appear in are assumed to be well-known to the user. With experienced Macintosh users learning a new Macintosh application, Gong (1990) found that certain operators in the standard Macintosh methods should be assigned zero execution time, apparently because an experienced use can overlap these operators with other activities. Thus, if an experienced user is assumed, estimate zero time for the following operators in well-practiced methods:

- a `Locate` that is followed by a `Point`
- a `Verify`
- a `Wait`

The *waiting time* is the time when the user is waiting, idle, for the system's response. This is typically negligible in echoing keyboard input, but can be substantial for other operations. You can omit this if you are concerned only with the user interface, and are willing to say that either the system will be fast enough, or it is somebody else's problem if it isn't! For an existing system, you can measure these times directly by executing the task instance on the system. For a system under design, you could estimate these times by measuring comparable operations on similar systems.

Mental Workload

Less is known about the relationship between GOMS models and mental workload than for the learning and execution times, so these suggestions are rather speculative. One aspect of mental workload is the user's having to keep track of where he or she is in the "mental program" of the method hierarchy. Using a specific task instance, one can count the depth of the goal stack as the task is executed. The interpretation is not clear, but greater peak and average depth is probably worse than less. Another aspect of mental workload is Working Memory load; quantifying this requires making WM usage in the methods explicit as described above. One could count the peak number of chunks that are `Retained` before a `Forget`; this is a measure of how much has to be remembered at the same time. It seems reasonable to expect trouble if more than 5 chunks have to be maintained in WM at once. Lerch, Mantei, and Olson (1989) reported results suggesting that errors are more likely to happen at peak memory loads as determined by a GOMS analysis.

A final aspect of mental workload is less quantifiable, but is probably of considerable importance in system design. This is whether the user has to perform complex mental processing that is not part of interacting with the system itself, but is required in order to do the task using the system. These processes would typically be those that were bypassed in the analysis. If there are many complex analyst-defined mental operators, and they seem difficult to execute, one could predict that the design will be difficult and error-prone to use. The evaluation problem comes if the two systems being compared differ substantially in the bypassing operators involved.

For example, consider the task of entering a table of numbers in a document preparation system using tabs to position the columns (cf. Bennett, Lorch, Kieras and Polson, 1987). A certain document preparation system is not a WYSIWYG ("what you see is what you get") system, and so to get tab settings in the correct positions, the user has to tediously figure out the actual column numbers for each tab position, and include them in a tab setting command. The analyst could represent this complex mental process with a bypassing operator like `Figure-out-tab-setting-column`. After executing this operator, the user simply types the resulting column number in the tab setting command. However, on a simple WYSIWYG system the user can arrive at the tab positions easily by trial and error, using operators like `Choose-new-setting` and `Does-setting-look-right`, which apparently would be considerably simpler to execute than `Figure-out-tab-setting-column`. But the trial and error method on the WYSIWYG involves more keystrokes, mouse moves, and so on, than simply typing in the tab column numbers. Which system will have the longer execution time? Clearly, this cannot be answered without getting estimates of the true difficulty and time required for these operators.

31.5.3 Suggestions for Revising the Design

After calculating performance estimates, the analyst can revise the design, and then recalculate the estimates to see if progress has been made. Some suggestions for revising the design are as follows (cf. Card, Moran, and Newell, 1983, Ch 12):

- Ensure that the most important and frequent goals can be accomplished by relatively easy to learn and fast-executing methods. Redesign if rarely accomplished tasks are simpler than frequent ones.

- Try to reduce learning time by eliminating, rewriting, or combining methods, especially to get consistency. Examine the action/object table for ideas - goals involving the same action should have similar methods.

- If a selection rule can not be stated clearly and easily, then consider eliminating one or more of the alternative methods. If there is not a clear occasion for using it, it is probably redundant.

- Eliminate the need for `Retrieve-from-LTM` operators, which indicate that the user has to memorize information, and which will result in slow performance until heavily practiced.

- If there are WM load problems, see if the design can be changed so the user needs to remember less, especially if the system can do the remembering, or if key information can be kept on the display until the user needs it.

- Modify the design to eliminate the need for the user to execute high-level complex mental operators, especially if they involve a slow and difficult cognitive process.

- The basic way to speed up execution time is to eliminate operators by shortening the methods. But notice that complex mental operators are usually much more time-consuming than simple motor actions, and so it can be more important to reduce the need for thinking than to save a few keystrokes. So do not reduce the number of keystrokes if an increase in mental operators is the result.

31.5.4 Using the Analysis in Documentation

The GOMS model is supposed to be a complete description of the procedural knowledge that the user has to know in order to perform tasks using the system. If the methods have been tested for completeness and accuracy, the procedural documentation can be checked against the methods in the GOMS model. Any omissions and inaccuracies should stand out. Alternatively, the first draft of the procedure documentation could be written from the GOMS model directly, as a way to ensure completeness and accuracy from the beginning. A similar argument can be made for the use of a GOMS model in specifying the content of On-line Help systems (see Elkerton, 1988).

Notice that if the documentation does not directly provide the required methods and selection rules to the user, the user is forced to deduce them. Sometimes this is reasonable; it should not be necessary to spell out every possible pathway through a menu system, for example. But it is often the case that even "good" training documentation presents methods that are seriously incomplete and even incorrect (cf. Kieras, 1990), and selection rules are rarely described.

While the GOMS analysis clearly should be useful in specifying the content of documentation, it offers little guidance concerning the form of the documentation, that is, the organization and presentation of procedures in the document. One suggestion that does stand out (cf. Elkerton, 1988) is to ensure that the index, table of contents, and headings are organized by user's goals, rather than function name, to allow the user to locate methods given that they often know their natural goals, but not the operators involved. Elkerton and his co-workers (Elkerton and Palmiter, 1991; Gong and Elkerton, 1990) provide more details and experimental demonstrations that GOMS-based documentation and help is markedly superior to conventional documentation and help.

31.6 Acknowledgments

Many helpful comments on earlier forms of this material have been contributed by Jay Elkerton, John Bennett, and several students. Thanks are especially due to the students in my Fall 1986 seminar on "The Theory of Documentation" who got me started on providing a procedure and clear notation for a GOMS analysis. Comments on this version of the procedure will be very much appreciated. The research that underlies this work was originally supported by IBM and the Office of Naval Research.

31.7 References

Anderson, J.R. (1982). Acquisition of cognitive skill. Psychological Review, 89, 369-406.

Bennett, J.L., Lorch, D.J., Kieras, D.E., and Polson, P.G. (1987). Developing a user interface technology for use in industry. In Bullinger, H.J., and Shackel, B. (Eds.), *Proceedings of the Second IFIP Conference on Human-Computer Interaction, Human-Computer Interaction - INTERACT '87.* (Stuttgart, Federal Republic of Germany, Sept. 1-4). Elsevier Science Publishers B.V., North-Holland, 21-26.

Bjork, R.A. (1972). Theoretical implications of directed forgetting. In A.W. Melton and E. Martin (Eds.), *Coding Processes in Human Memory.* Washington, D.C.: Winston, 217-236.

Bovair, S., Kieras, D.E., and Polson, P.G. (1990). The acquisition and performance of text editing skill: A cognitive complexity analysis. *Human-Computer Interaction, 5,* 1-48.

Butler, K. A., Bennett, J., Polson, P., and Karat, J. (1989). Report on the workshop on analytical models: Predicting the complexity of human-computer interaction. *SIGCHI Bulletin*, 20(4), pp. 63-79.

Byrne, M.D., Wood, S.D, Sukaviriya, P., Foley, J.D, and Kieras, D.E. (1994). Automating Interface Evaluation. In *Proceedings of CHI*, 1994, Boston, MA, USA, April 24-28, 1994). New York: ACM, pp. 232-237.

Card, S.K., Moran, T.P., and Newell, A. (1980a). The keystroke-level model for user performance time with interactive systems. *Communications of the ACM* , 23(7), 396-410.

Card, S., Moran, T. and Newell, A. (1983). *The Psychology of Human-Computer Interaction.* Hillsdale, New Jersey: Erlbaum.

Diaper, D. (Ed.) (1989). *Task analysis for human-computer interaction.* Chicester, U.K.: Ellis Horwood.

Elkerton, J. (1988). On-line Aiding for Human-Computer Interfaces. In M. Helander (Ed.), *Handbook of Human-Computer Interaction* (pp. 345-362). Amsterdam: North-Holland Elsevier.

Elkerton, J., and Palmiter, S. (1991). Designing help using the GOMS model: An information retrieval evaluation. *Human Factors, 33,* 185-204.

Gong, R. J. (1993). *Validating and refining the GOMS model methodology for software user interface design and evaluation.* Ph.D. Dissertation, University of Michigan.

Gong, R. and Elkerton, J. (1990). Designing minimal documentation using a GOMS model: A usability evaluation of an engineering approach. In *Proceedings of CHI'90, Human Factors in Computer Systems* (pp. 99-106). New York: ACM.

Gong, R., and Kieras, D. (1994). A Validation of the GOMS Model Methodology in the Development of a Specialized, Commercial Software Application. In *Proceedings of CHI*, 1994, Boston, MA, USA, April 24-28, 1994). New York: ACM, pp. 351-357.

Gould, J. D. (1988). How to design usable systems. In M. Helander (Ed.), *Handbook of human-computer interaction*. Amsterdam: North-Holland. 757-789.

Gray, W. D., John, B. E., and Atwood, M. E. (1993). Project Ernestine: A validation of GOMS for prediction and explanation of real-world task performance. *Human-Computer Interaction, 8*, 3, pp. 237-209.

John, B. E., and Kieras, D. E. (in press-a). Using GOMS for user interface design and evaluation: Which technique? *ACM Transactions on Computer-Human Interaction.*

John, B. E., and Kieras, D. E. (in press-b). The GOMS family of user interface analysis techniques: Comparison and contrast. *ACM Transactions on Computer-Human Interaction.*

Kieras, D.E. (1986). A mental model in user-device interaction: A production system analysis of a problem-solving task. Unpublished manuscript, University of Michigan.

Kieras, D.E. (1988). Making cognitive complexity practical. In *CHI'88 Workshop on Analytical Models,* Washington, May 15, 1988.

Kieras, D.E. (1988). Towards a practical GOMS model methodology for user interface design. In M. Helander (Ed.), *Handbook of Human-Computer Interaction* (pp. 135-158). Amsterdam: North-Holland Elsevier.

Kieras, D.E. (1990). The role of cognitive simulation models in the development of advanced training and testing systems. In N. Frederiksen, R. Glaser, A. Lesgold, and M. Shafto (Eds.), *Diagnostic Monitoring of Skill and Knowledge Acquisition*. Hillsdale, N.J.: Erlbaum.

Kieras, D. (1994). GOMS Modeling of User Interfaces using NGOMSL. Tutorial Notes, CHI'94 Conference on Human Factors in Computer Systems, Boston, MA, April 24-28, 1994.

Kieras, D. E. (in press). Task analysis and the design of functionality. In A. Tucker (Ed.) *CRC Handbook of Computer Science and Engineering*. Boca Raton, CRC Inc.

Kieras, D. E., and Bovair, S. (1984). The role of a mental model in learning to operate a device. *Cognitive Science*, 8, 255-273.

Kieras, D.E., and Bovair, S. (1986). The acquisition of procedures from text: A production-system analysis of transfer of training. *Journal of Memory and Language, 25*, 507-524.

Kieras, D.E. and Polson, P.G. (1985). An approach to the formal analysis of user complexity. *International Journal of Man-Machine Studies, 22*, 365-394.

Kieras, D.E., Wood, S.D., Abotel, K., and Hornof, A. (1995). GLEAN: A Computer-Based Tool for Rapid GOMS Model Usability Evaluation of User Interface Designs. In Proceeding of UIST, 1995, Pittsburgh, PA, USA, November 14-17, 1995. New York: ACM. pp. 91-100.

Kirwan, B., and Ainsworth, L. K. (1992). *A guide to task analysis*. London: Taylor and Francis.

Landauer, T. (1995). *The trouble with computers: Usefulness, usability, and productivity.* Cambridge, MA: MIT Press.

Lerch, F.J., Mantei, M.M., and Olson, J. R., (1989). Skilled financial planning: The cost of translating ideas into action. In *CHI'89 Conference Proceedings*, 121-126.

Lewis, C. and Rieman, J. (1994) *Task-centered user interface design: A practical introduction.* Shareware book available at ftp.cs.colorado.edu/pub/cs/distribs/clewis/HCI-Design-Book

Nielsen, J. and Mack, R.L. (Eds.). (1994). *Usability inspection methods*. New York: Wiley.

Olson, J. R., and Olson, G. M. (1989). The growth of cognitive modeling in human-computer interaction since GOMS. Technical Report No. 26, Cognitive Science and Machine Intelligence Laboratory, University of Michigan, November, 1989.

Polson, P.G. (1987). A quantitative model of human-computer interaction. In J.M. Carroll (Ed.), *Interfacing Thought: Cognitive Aspects of Human-Computer Interaction.* Cambridge, MA: Bradford, MIT Press.

Handbook of Human-Computer Interaction
Second, completely revised edition
M. Helander, T.K. Landauer, P. Prabhu (eds.)

Chapter 32

Cost-Justifying Usability Engineering in the Software Life Cycle

Clare-Marie Karat
IBM TJ Watson Research Center
Hawthorne, New York, USA

32.1 Introduction

Rapid paradigm shifts in computer technology in the last ten years, increased global competition, and a widespread business culture of reengineering and corporate downsizing have created a software development environment of shortened product cycles, pressure to get-to-market with products targeted at narrow windows of opportunity, and an ever-present focus on cutting costs. In the midst of this highly charged atmosphere, practitioners and researchers in the field of usability engineering have sought to educate, communicate, and influence corporate decision makers about the value of usability engineering in the software life cycle. Significant progress has been achieved. Much more work remains to be done for most companies to gain the competitive advantage that usability engineering can create.

Management has a heightened awareness of time, money, and resources allocated for projects. The focus on results has moved from relatively longterm goals to nearterm quarterly deliverables and profits. At the same time, customer service and satisfaction have become the lines for market differentiation (Jones and Sasser, 1995; Prokesch, 1995). Business leaders with sound judgment invest in usability engineering in order to reap the benefits and solve their pressing business problems. Usability engineering presents management with a vehicle for increased probability of success in the marketplace and reduced software development costs (Karat, 1994a).

This chapter summarizes the work that has been completed in the area of cost-justifying usability engineering in the software life cycle, and describes best practices in cost-justifying usability engineering. The chapter then focuses on current issues in incorporating usability engineering in the software life cycle, and speculates about the future of cost-justifying usability engineering.

32.2 A Review of Usability Cost-Benefit Analysis in the Software Life Cycle

32.2.1 The History of Cost-Benefit Analysis of Usability Engineering

The topic of cost-benefit analysis of usability engineering was introduced in the field with the 1988 paper by Marilyn Mantei and Toby Teorey (Mantei and Teorey, 1988) in which they discussed the costs of incorporating a wide range of usability engineering activities into the development cycle. In their analysis of the life cycle, the activities covered ranged from market analysis prior to requirements definition to product surveys as part of the maintenance phase. The analysis suggested that an investment of about $250,000 might be necessary to cover the usability work on a typical product.

I found this article compelling. As a practitioner in an industrial software development organization, I needed to be able to identify and communicate the value of the usability work I suggested to the product managers whose business goals I was supporting. The first product manager I was assigned to support told me he would encourage usability work on the product as long as I did not ask him for a significant amount of resource and did not lengthen the product development schedule. Product development was already underway and the programmers were working on the external design. I agreed to the conditions. As I was part of a centralized usability organization at that time, I did not need to ask him for financial resource to cover the usability engineering work. I did ask for a few hours of programming time from the developers during the course of the eight month development effort and that was a win-win for all involved in the work.

Given the constraints within which I needed to complete the usability work for the product assigned, I elected to employ low-fidelity prototyping of the user interface in order to field test the early design of the application user interface with representative end users. I asked that the lead developer accompany me to the first field test, and watched as she observed that the user interface was not "walk up and use" as the developers had intended. With the aid of a research assistant, we unobtrusively collected quantitative time-on-task data, task completion and error rate data from users, as well as qualitative data about the application and the users' suggested changes.

At the subsequent team meeting where I presented the summary data from the usability field test, the team agreed that there were usability problems with the user interface as designed. I redesigned the screens to resolve the identified usability problems and incorporate feedback received from the users, and then conducted another usability evaluation. This iteration of the design was much closer in reaching the usability objectives for the application. We fixed one last significant usability problem, and then the programmers coded that version of the user interface for the application. The application was rolled out on schedule and with high user satisfaction. The development team received bonuses for the high quality of the work. Usability engineering achieved significant acceptance from the whole development team as they could see the positive impact on their jobs. I had collected usability cost-benefit data during this project and communicated it first internally and then at the annual Human Factors Society conference (Karat, 1989) were it received significant attention from attendees. The initial conservative case study data showed a return of $2 for every dollar invested in usability on the project. This return on investment was achieved for the first three uses of the system by users. A more complete analysis of the same project showed a $10 return for every dollar invested in usability.

A group of usability engineers (Randolph Bias, Deborah Mayhew, Susan Dray, Page O'Neal, and myself) conducted a panel session the next year at the Human Factors Society conference to report and discuss further developments in the area of cost-benefit analysis (Karat, 1990a). I met and discussed the work with Marilyn Mantei at Interact '90 (Karat, 1990b) and we were both enriched by the dialogue on the topic. She was impressed with the level of results that could be achieved with minimal investment of time and resource in usability engineering.

I was encouraged by my peers to teach others in the usability field the cost-benefit methodology that I had developed, and I presented the first tutorial on the topic at the ACM SIGCHI CHI'91 conference (Karat, 1991a). I became a focal point for collecting and disseminating deidentified usability engineering cost-benefit data to the community, as those who had taken the tutorial or heard about it started using the methods and sending me their case study data and permission for it to be included in deidentified form in future versions of the course. I received and continue to receive requests from all over the world from usability engineers who need case study data and available facts to justify usability engineering resource allocation to management. The published data collected from the participants and my own experience have been used for this purpose many times worldwide and have been quoted in computer publications (e.g., ACM SIGCHI conference proceedings, Open Computing, IEEE Software, HFES Bulletin, HFES conference proceedings) as a key source for usability business case data.

I taught the cost-benefit of usability engineering tutorial several times, gave invited addresses (e.g., Karat, 1991b) and wrote invited articles (Karat, 1992, 1993b) on the topic. Susan Dray, who as one of her areas of expertise specializes in understanding organizational issues related to the introduction of usability engineering (Dray, 1995), and I had a number of conversations on this topic and analyzed together the human factors cost-justification of an internal development project (Dray and Karat, 1994). Randolph Bias and Deborah Mayhew edited a book on the topic of cost-justifying usability that brought together a large number of authors who were working in this area from a wide range of perspectives (Bias and Mayhew, 1994). This book includes a summary of the usability engineering cost-benefit methodology, case study data, and exercises that I had included in the final version of the tutorial (Karat, 1994a) as well as the work that Susan Dray and I completed together that is cited above.

During the same period of time, Jakob Nielsen was doing research on heuristic evaluation methods and discount usability methods. I was interested in research on usability walkthrough methods and how these might compare to usability testing in terms of the results achieved and the relative cost of use. We exchanged information and had conversations that influenced both of our research areas. Heather Desurvire and I also had research sessions on this topic and she completed several research studies in the area of the cost-effectiveness of different types of inspection methods and usability testing (Desurvire, 1994). Robert Virzi (1989, 1990) completed the first of several published research studies on the effectiveness of smaller sample sizes and low-fidelity prototyping methods that added to the field's knowledge. Dennis Wixon and his team were employing a contextual inquiry method and understanding its cost-benefit in the development cycle (Wixon, Jones, Tse, and Casaday, 1994). Jakob Nielsen held a workshop at the ACM SIGCHI CHI'92 conference on usability inspection methods that was attended by international representatives of the community interested in the topic of inspection methods and information related to the effectiveness and appropriateness of their use in different circumstances. Nielsen and Mack edited a book based on the discussions at the workshop and follow-on research activities by participants in the workshop (Nielsen and Mack, 1994). I wrote a chapter for the book on comparative methods research including cost-benefit data on the use of usability walkthroughs and testing methods (Karat, 1994b).

The members of the international usability engineering community continue to conduct research and communicate advances in the area of cost-benefit analysis of usability engineering. Consultants such as Randolph Bias, Susan Dray, and Deborah Mayhew work with Fortune 500 clients on engagements that focus on usability engineering cost-benefit analysis. Global workforce pressures make it imperative that usability engineers in a variety of organizational settings be able to measure and communicate the value of human factors work performed in development cycles for products. This handbook may serve as a key reference text in the performance of that work and the analysis and communication of the value of that work to the appropriate audiences for each practitioner or researcher in the field.

32.2.2 The Value of Usability Engineering in the Product Life Cycle

At the corporate level, including usability engineering in the development of a product presents management with a vehicle for increased probability of success in the marketplace and reduced software development costs (Karat, 1994a). Usability engineering can have significant direct and indirect positive effects for an organization (see Figure 1). Usability can contribute directly and positively to the definition of the product's goal and its external presentation through a focus on the end user's view of a product. The interaction modalities employed, the look and feel of the user interface, and the navigation through product functions to complete user tasks will reflect user preferences for comfort and effectiveness. A usability-engineered product will have higher user satisfaction and increased sales compared to a similar product without it, other variables remaining equal. Marketing will be able to use the results of usability engineering to target market the product to users and provide quantitative and qualitative data on the benefits of using the product to complete work.

When the usability work for a product covers information documentation and training, then the users have an easier time using the reference information for the system and answering their own questions. The organization achieves significant cost avoidance for their help desk, training, and information documentation groups through the incorporation of the results of usability work with the users. They are able to focus their efforts on areas identified by the users and reduce the number of iterations of deliverables due to early identification and resolution of usability problems. Regarding training costs for the customers who use these products, Karat (1993b) documents a case study of a usability engineered product that required a one-hour training session as compared to one week of training for similar systems built and used within the organization. The investment in usability saved the organization millions of dollars in training costs and in the opportunity costs of the employees' time in the first year alone.

If the organization employs a product in a dedicated manner to complete business tasks, the usability of the product can have the indirect positive result of

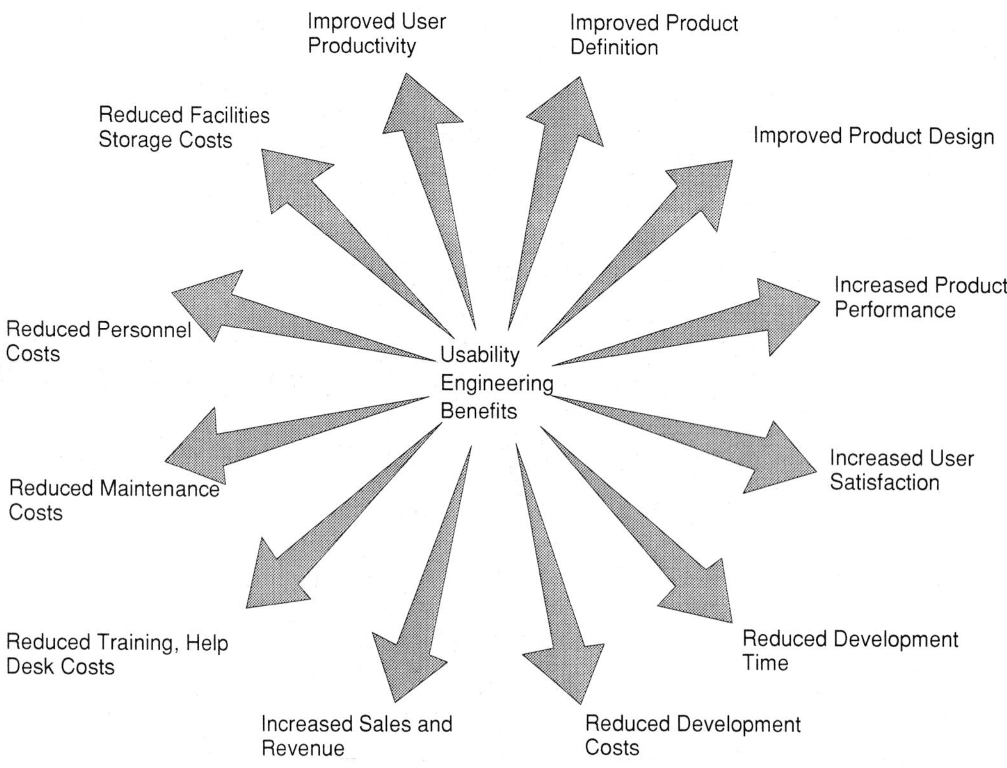

Figure 1. Business areas where usability engineering demonstrates significant direct and indirect positive effects for an organization

lowered personnel costs associated with the employees who have lower turnover rates and higher satisfaction with their work environment (Karat, 1994a). Other indirect benefits can include reduced costs for facility's storage, improved work process controls and audit trails, and lowered demand for equipment and consumables.

At the product development level of the organization, why would a product manager build a product without understanding the user, the work the user intends to complete with the product, and the environment in which the user will complete the work? Global competition has raised the standards on the base level of performance of products used by customers in the home, at work, and for entertainment purposes, and the usability of products is a key component of expected performance and purchase decisions (Jones and Sasser, 1995; Prokesch, 1995). Including usability engineering in the development of products is building quality into products to be used internally by organizations or offered in the marketplace to customers worldwide.

Usability is part of the critical path for development and, as mentioned above it may be leveraged by a number of associated groups such as marketing, education, and system maintenance (see Figure 1). As a critical path for development, it is key that usability objectives for a solution are objectively defined, as they define the performance level to be achieved by the product. Project managers and the associated development teams have many competing foci for their attention, and what gets measured, gets done (House and Price, 1991). And as customer service and satisfaction have become the lines of market differentiation in the '90's, organizations cannot afford to put products on the market that do not meet the base level of usability performance expected (March, 1994). There is essentially no second chance, no time to recover. And when an organization tries to recover from significant usability problems in a released product, the costs of post-release changes are unaffordable for most organizations. Even then, the loss of momentum and cus-

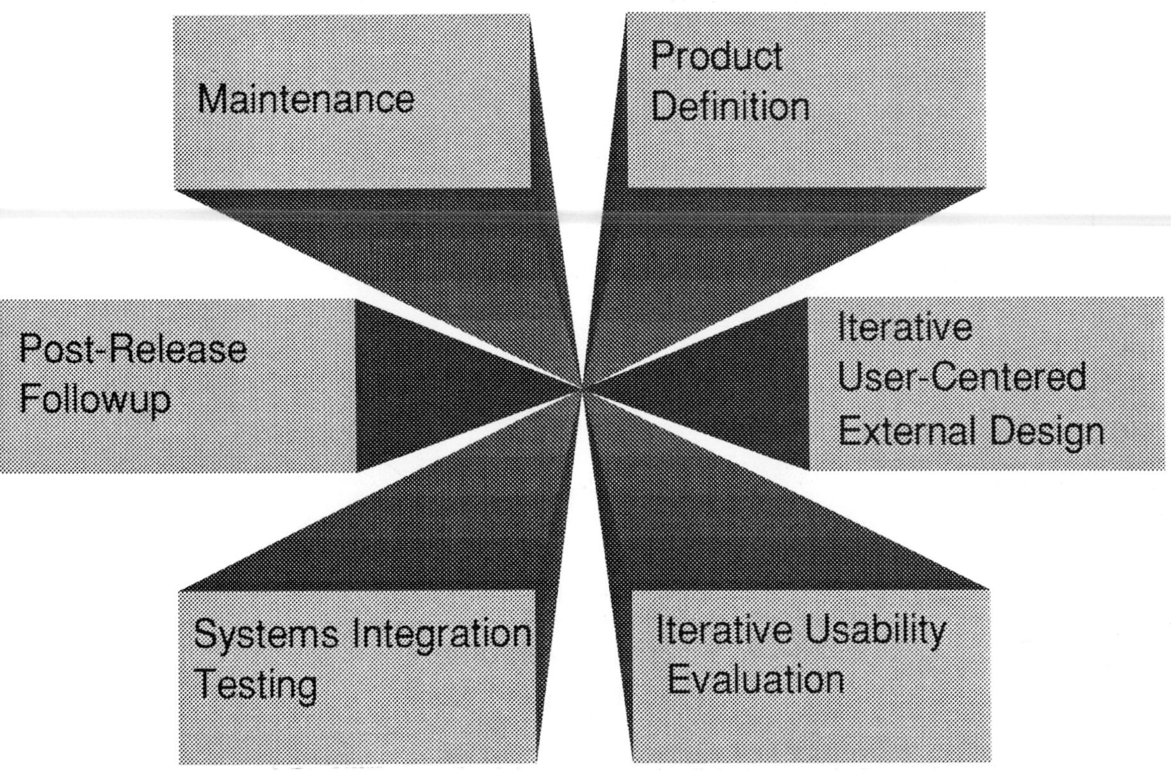

Figure 2. Contribution of usability engineering practices at various stages of the product life cycle.

tomer goodwill may make it very difficult or impossible to continue to be successful in the same market area.

In terms of usability engineering's ability to contribute to product development, these benefits can appear throughout the product life cycle, from product concept to post-release follow-up (see Figure 2). Recent data show that the user interface may account for up to 60% of the lines of code in an application and 40% or more of the development effort (Wixon et al., 1994; MacIntyre, Estep, and Sieburth, 1990). During software development, usability engineering can reduce the time and cost of development efforts through early definition of user goals and usability objectives, and by early identification and resolution of usability issues. This benefit can have a significant effect throughout the software life cycle due to the increasing cost of changes to the code (see Figure 3). A change may cost 1.5 units of project resource during conceptual design, grow to 6 units during early development, and then escalate to 60 units during systems testing, and 100 units during post-release maintenance (Pressman, 1992).

As mentioned above, usability engineering that has been completed during development can, after product release, result in increased sales and revenue, user satisfaction and productivity. It can also result in significant cost-avoidance in training and support, service, personnel, and maintenance (Karat, 1994a). The particular benefits that accrue due to usability engineering vary based on whether the product is created for internal use by the organization or for external sale in the marketplace.

Bringing a product to market earlier due to usability engineering can achieve huge benefits for a company. Speeding up market introduction can achieve 10% higher revenues due to increased volume or increased profit margins (Conklin, 1991). Wixon and Jones (1992) document a case study of a usability-engineered product that achieved revenues that were 80% higher than for the first release developed without usability engineering, and 60% above project projections. Interviews with customers showed that buying decisions were made based on usability. Alternatively, bringing a product to market six months late may cost companies 33% of after-tax profits (House and Price, 1991).

Eighty percent of the software life cycle costs are spent in the post-release maintenance phase (Pressman,

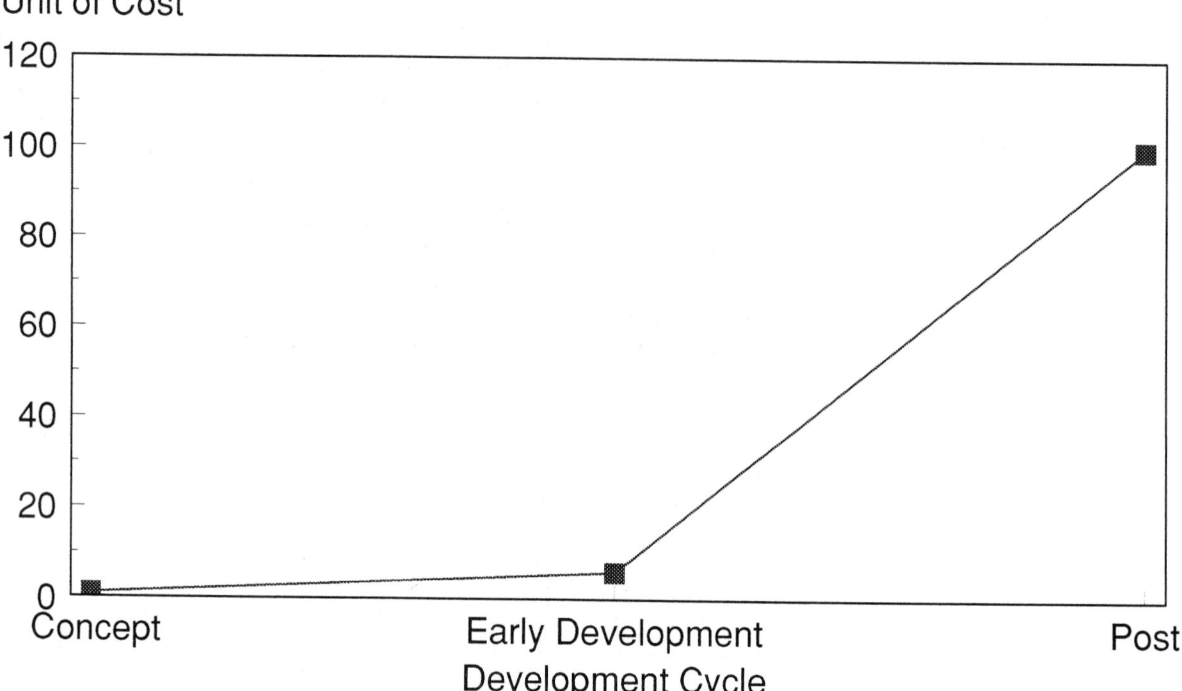

Figure 3. Cost of usability engineering at various stages of development cycle.

1992). Studies have shown that eighty percent of maintenance costs are spent on unmet or unforeseen user requirements, and only 20% are due to bugs. If usability engineering can identify and resolve the majority of these user requirements prior to product release, organizations will accrue substantial cost-avoidance.

32.3 Usability Cost-Benefit Analysis

32.3.1 Responsibility for Usability Cost-Benefit Analysis

I recommend that usability engineers proactively assume responsibility for collecting, preparing and communicating usability cost-benefit analysis data. Judgments about the cost-benefit of usability are being made with or without factual data. Usability engineers have a number of reasons to build skills and knowledge in this area. They can use the cost-benefit data to educate others in the organizations about the value of usability as it relates to their business goals and concerns. They can use the information to build business cases and provide management with better data on which to make decisions about which projects to allocate usability resource to and the number of usability engineers necessary to support the organization's work. Practitioners can use the cost-benefit data on different usability techniques to learn about how to make better tradeoffs in the use of usability methods in different situations.

32.3.2 Defining Usability Cost-Benefit Analysis

Cost-benefit analysis is a investment method for analyzing projects. There are three components to the analysis (Karat, 1994a). First, identify the financial value of the expected project cost and benefit variables. Second, analyze the relationship between expected costs and benefits using a type of selection technique. These techniques may be either simple or sophisticated. Finally, make the investment decision.

Organizations make investment decisions through business cases that include cost-benefit analysis data as well as a description of the project, market data, resource projections, timetables, and risks in implementing the project. Usability professionals who are stepping forward with usability cost-benefit data for inclusion in project business cases have leveled the playing field with the other groups involved in project development with whom usability engineers must compete for project resources and who traditionally have objective cost-benefit data available.

32.3.3 Calculating the Cost-Benefit of Usability Engineering

A usability cost-benefit analysis may be completed as part of a business case for a proposed project, or it may be completed at specific checkpoints during a product's lifecycle to document the value of usability engineering. A general approach to take in usability cost-benefit analysis is to compare a project's plan with and without usability engineering or to compare the cost-benefit to be achieved by investing usability engineering resource in one of several competing development project proposals. The goal of the analysis is to determine the cash value of the positive difference due to usability engineering. The analysis requires estimates of the expected costs (e.g., usability and programming resource, design and walkthrough sessions) and benefits (e.g., increased productivity, reduced training and development costs) of usability engineering.

A usability cost-benefit analysis will vary significantly based on the specifics of the proposed product. For example, is the product to be used internally by the organization or is it being built for external sale? What are the variables associated with the business workflow that the solution will address? What are the usability goals for the product? A recommended approach is to think about the key end user scenarios of use for the solution being proposed. Follow the scenarios through to identify all of the different groups who will use and be dependent on the product or its output. What other groups will come in contact with the solution? Who will pay for the solution and who will provide the support and maintenance for it? Collect benchmark information about current rates of productivity regarding the business workflow and also current error rates. This analysis will be helpful background for developing estimates of the costs to each of these groups of receiving incomplete or inaccurate data, correcting errors, misunderstanding information in the system, and storing information related to the business workflow. These cost areas will likely be targeted by usability engineering during product development and will be documented as areas of benefits, cost-avoidance or savings in a new solution. The resulting usability benefits may range, for example, from increased sales or revenues, to increased productivity, lower training and support costs, lower services and maintenance costs, cost-avoidance in reduced errors, lower employee turnover, and decreased storage, equipment and consumables costs.

The usability activities for a project and their associated costs need to be identified as well. The costs of usability engineering may cover work ranging from user profile definition, to focus groups, task analysis, benchmark studies, usability objectives specification, participatory design, design walkthroughs, prototype development, usability walkthroughs, usability tests, and customer surveys and questionnaires. In calculating these activity costs, remember to include all associated user, support and laboratory or facility costs. The latter costs may be allocated as part of overhead expenses that are included in fully burdened personnel costs.

The benefits to be derived from defined usability work must be categorized as tangible or intangible, and the cash value of the tangible benefits is estimated. Keep the list of intangible (e.g., improved image) benefits for future reference as you may determine a way to quantify their value and add them to an updated analysis later during the product's lifecycle. It is valuable to have the list of benefits reviewed by others with similar and different backgrounds so that no key variables are excluded from the analysis. For estimates of the cash value of the benefits, establish and nurture a network of domain experts who have knowledge and experience with the types of benefits to be realized. These domain experts may represent marketing, personnel, business planning, maintenance, financial analysis, training and support, and services groups. Contact customers and users for estimates for available data, and use past data for estimates where available.

Once the cost and benefit variables for a project have been identified, then the cost-benefit of the usability work can be calculated. Two types of analysis techniques exist for comparing costs and benefits for a project. The simple techniques include cost-benefit ratios, where financial benefit amounts are divided by cost amounts to determine the ratio of costs for $1(or other unit) of financial benefits. A variation on this is the calculation of the payback period which is a method for determining the amount of time required to generate benefits to recover the initial costs of a project. Sophisticated usability cost-benefit techniques include a calculation for the time value of money. These interest-based methods calculate the present value of future cash flows, and specify a rate of return and timeframe for the cash flows in order to facilitate better decision making. Each of the two techniques are appropriate in different situations. Examples are provided below of the use of the simple cost-benefit ratio in determining the value of usability engineering. For detailed information and hands-on calculation examples of the cost-benefit analysis of usability engineering, please see Karat (1994a).

Examples of Usability Engineering Cost-Benefit Calculation

In the first example, the benefit of including three iterations of usability design and testing in the development of an application (Application 1) is calculated. Application 1 is the project that is referred to at the beginning of the chapter where I was invited to incorporate usability engineering into the development project as long as I did not request resource or lengthen the development cycle. Application 1 was a security application that was used by 22,876 users about 12 times a day (Karat, 1990a). The application was built for internal use by the organization. The application would replace an existing outdated one. The usability objective for the system was that users would achieve peak performance on the system within the first three tasks completed using the new application. The development team had designed a user interface for the system which they intended to code as the final application interface. I used this user interface design as the iteration 1 user interface, and calculated the improvements in user productivity on the first three tasks from iteration 1 to iteration 3 as the value of the usability work. The three iterations of usability design and testing resulted in an increase in user productivity with the following benefit:

- Reduction in user time to complete first three tasks from initial to final version of Application 1 user interface:

  Total = 4.67 minutes

- Projected benefits in increased user productivity in completing first three tasks using Application 1:

  End user population = 22,876
  22,876 x 4.67 minutes = 1,781 hours
  1,781 hours x Productivity ratio x Personnel costs = $41,700

The computed savings of $41,700 do not include savings based on continued use of the system (users demonstrated productivity increases for many tasks past the first three uses of the application included in the analysis). Also, due to the "walk up and use" nature of the final version of the user interface, the cost of a help desk and projected maintenance costs were eliminated from the project budget.

The usability work for Application 1 included task analysis, development of a low-technology prototype, and three iterations of usability design and testing. The latter work was completed through a usability field prototype test, a laboratory prototype test, and a laboratory system integration test. Usability costs for the seven months of work were as follows:

- Usability resource = $18,800
- Participant travel = $700
- Test-related development work = $1,200
- Total cost for a year = $20,700

The cost-benefit of the usability work was $41,700/$20,700 or a cost-benefit ratio of 1:2 . This initial calculation was a very conservative estimate of the value of the usability work. When I included in the calculation the cost savings of the elimination of the help desk and reduced maintenance necessary for the product, the more complete cost-benefit analysis for the usability engineering work on the project resulted in a cost-benefit ratio of 1:10 .

In the second example, the value of the usability engineering completed for Application 2, an internal product built to replace a manual process, is calculated. For Application 2, three iterative usability tests were conducted on a system that is employed by users to complete 1,308,000 tasks a year (Karat, 1990a). The usability work resulted in an average reduction of 9.6 minutes per task. The first-year benefits in increased productivity due to usability were as follows:

- Reduction in time on task from first to final user interface design for Application 2:

  Average savings = 9.6 minutes

- Projected first-year benefits due to increased user productivity:

  Tasks per year = 1,308,000

  1,308,000 x 9.6 minutes = 209,208 hours
  209,280 hours x Productivity ratio x Personnel costs = $6,800,000

The usability work for Application 2 included a benchmark field test, development of a high-fidelity prototype, and three iterations of usability design and testing of the user interface for the application. The usability work was completed across 21 months.

- Usability resource = $23,300
- Participant travel = $ 9,750
- Test-related development work = $34,950
- Total cost for 21 months = $68,000

The cost-benefit ratio of usability work is $6,800,000/$68,000 or a cost-benefit ratio of 1:100 for the first year of application deployment.

Discussion of Usability Cost-Benefit Analysis

These two examples show the compelling evidence that usability cost-benefit analysis can provide in illustrating the financial value of the usability work in development projects. This type of an analysis may be completed for a proposed project's business case using conservative estimates of the positive contributions of usability engineering to the key variables of interest. Estimates might be employed based on data from similar past projects, relevant published data in the literature, or using estimates based on benchmarks or expert judgment. As the project moves through its lifecycle, the cost-benefit data can and should be updated based on documented achievements and changes that occur. The updated cost-benefit analysis and project business case is an excellent vehicle for communication about the project's status and the contribution of usability engineering to the project's success.

Usability practitioners can also use these cost-benefit techniques to collect objective data and make decisions on tradeoffs related to employing different usability methods in completing usability work on projects. For example, in Application 1, I developed a low-fidelity prototype to use in the field test with users and it was created in 20% of the time and at 10% of the cost of a high-fidelity prototype (Karat, 1989). The usability field test allowed me to collect the necessary quantitative and qualitative usability data in 25% of the time and cost of a laboratory usability test. Given the time and resource constraints within which I was working, these results were key to successful integration of usability in the project.

Robert Virzi has completed a series of research studies regarding the value and effectiveness of low-fidelity prototypes and smaller sample sizes in usability engineering work (Virzi, 1989, 1990). His research demonstrates the success of low-fidelity prototypes in evaluating user interfaces with representative users and documents the relative advantages in terms of quality of usability data gained from low versus high-fidelity prototypes, as well as their cost in terms of time and resources. He suggests that usability engineers may be able to employ sample sizes of between 4-6 users for an evaluation, depending on the specifics of the product and users. I advise practitioners to give themselves a sufficient probability of finding a low occurring but high-risk type of usability problem. This is an area where the correct balance depends on analysis of a number of variables specific to the situation, and a practitioner may identify new options overlooked previously. Tradeoffs regarding the type of evaluation need to be considered as well. Studies by Desurvire (1994) and Karat, Campbell and Fiegel (1992) identify tradeoffs in quality of evaluation data and cost of usability walkthrough, usability testing, and heuristic evaluation. These studies show that usability testing identifies more of the usability problems with a user interface, and more of the severe problems, than either usability walkthroughs or heuristic evaluation. The cost per usability problem found was not higher for usability testing as compared to the other methods. Nielsen (1994) demonstrates that heuristic evaluators who have both knowledge of usability and the user's task domain complete more valuable usability evaluations than other heuristic evaluators who do not have these background characteristics. Karat (1994b) provides a useful summary of performance and cost tradeoffs in selection of different usability methods during a project's lifecycle.

In each project, usability practitioners need to be able to make these types of tradeoffs and keep the "big picture" in mind about the relative value of usability work completed at any point in the development lifecycle for a product. Then there may be a larger question about where among competing projects to assign limited usability resource. I suggest that usability practitioners and their managers complete highlevel reviews to understand the potential projects' risks and rewards, and each project's possible contribution to the organization's goals.

Estimates of the relative positive impact that can be achieved through completion of usability work on each of the top-ranked projects will need to be completed. These estimates must be made with a highlevel understanding of the resource required to complete the priority usability work on each project. Usability practitioners and management will then be prepared to make the business cases for investment of usability resource in the priority situations. At the organizational level, I believe that a similar analysis of this kind can be successfully used to justify the number and type of usability experts hired and the facilities necessary to provide usability engineering support to development organizations.

32.4 The Future of Usability Cost-Benefit Analysis

As I look ahead to the future, I see a more pressing need for usability cost-benefit analysis than has existed to this point in time. Increased global competition and the widespread business culture of reengineering and corporate downsizing have created a software environment of shortened product cycles and pressure to get-to-market and capitalize on narrow windows of opportunity. There is increased pressure to be able to demonstrate the value of each job function related to software development, and then after release, the impact of that work on customer satisfaction and related customer service. Usability engineering is a competitive advantage during software development and is a market differentiator in terms of customer satisfaction after product release.

The pressure of global competition may increase further with advances in electronic communication and commerce. An effective way to compete is to collect cost-benefit information on different methods of usability engineering and software development, and to innovate and create new best practices based on the results. With globalization, there will be an increased number of international user interface issues to be identified and resolved. There will be a wider range of user characteristics for software products and solutions. The users will have a wider range of education, background, and cultural and work experience that they bring to the user interfaces of the future. The base level of usability performance demanded by users will continue to increase. With global competition providing a variety of choices in niche markets, users will be quick to leave products, services, and solutions that do not completely satisfy them. This is one of the messages of recent study reported in the Harvard Business Review regarding customer satisfaction (Jones and Sasser, 1995). Customers must be completely satisfied with a product or solution in order not to defect. And for those customers who are satisfied, the companies must continually look for new offerings to satisfy these customers' new business needs, or the companies will lose them to competitors. There is no room for complacency in the new global arena.

The move to more open systems and solutions adds an incentive to increase the use of usability engineering cost-benefit analyses as well. As the playing field for solution developers is leveled through open systems, then the avenues for market differentiation such as customer service and satisfaction demand that measurement of usability performance in these areas is incorporated in organizational strategies and operations. New technologies coming to market will enable a paradigm shift in user interface modalities and metaphors that are incorporated in solutions for users. Human-centric interfaces and advances in networking and communication technology will bring a dramatic change to the manner in which users complete their work. In this transition period, there will be a heightened need for usability engineering and its associated cost-benefit analysis to understand and guide the development of the new interaction modalities and to analyze where the investment in usability engineering is most profitable in this new paradigm.

I believe that usability engineering will become more closely tied to project management and organizational goals. In the last decade, customer value has been measured in terms of the proximity of a solution component to the customer, as the customer perceives the greatest value in the solution that he or she uses to complete work, rather than any underlying technology that enables it. The customer is willing to pay a premium price for an application solution that enables them to complete the work they do with higher quality and generate higher satisfaction in their customers.

There are currently some limitations to the use of usability engineering cost-benefit analysis. If usability practitioners and managers are going to reap the benefits of using the methodology, these will need to be overcome. First, effective use of this methodology takes some time, planning and forethought. I hear from my peers across a wide variety of industries and around the world, that the pressure they feel on the job has increased and they are working longer hours. Downsizing in many instances has not been accompanied by initiation of new business processes, so the remaining employees are expected to complete the work that many more had done previously. Without the time and energy to plan and institute new processes and measures, little change is possible. There also seems to be a short-term view in terms of the organizational measures. Across various industries, employees seem pressured to pursue quarter-to-quarter results, without a focus on the "big picture". Accompanied with this is a "heads down" pursuit of a project, without gaining knowledge and experience from synthesizing successful strategies across projects. Again, a lack of perspective is apparent regarding key organizational goals, and coordinated tactical and strategic plans for progress towards them. One result of this situation is a lack of organizational learning. Peter Senge has stated that an organization's inability to learn will be its downfall (Senge, 1990). A learning organization recognizes threats and opportunities and changes in order to thrive.

These issues need to be addressed within most organizations. One encouraging sign is the increasing awareness that an organization's most vital asset is the intellectual capital of the organization's employees. Given that a rebalancing occurs, the new communications technology may provide a means for employees to rapidly collect and analyze data to help organizations learn, grow and change. If this occurs, then organizations will be able to take advantage of the wealth of outcome analysis data their employees collect and synthesize, and create a productive and attractive future for the organizations and communities in which they exist. Usability engineering cost-benefit data will be one key data source for development organizations to collect and analyze, and to use as the basis for taking action to create their futures.

32.5 References

Conklin, P. (1991). Bringing usability effectively into product development. *Human-Computer Interface Design: Success Cases, Emerging Methods, and Real-World Context.* Boulder, Co., July, 24-36.

Desurvire, H. (1994). Faster, cheaper! Are Usability inspection methods as effective as empirical testing? In Nielsen, J., and Mack, R. (Eds.), *Usability Inspection Methods*. New York: John Wiley & Sons.

Dray, S. (1995). The importance of designing usable systems. *Interactions*, 2 (1), 17-20.

Dray, S. and Karat, C. (1994a). Human factors cost justification for an internal development project. In Bias, R. and Mayhew, D. (Eds.), *Cost-Justifying Usability*. New York: Academic Press.

House, C.H., and Price, R.L. (1991). The return map: Tracking product teams. *Harvard Business Review*, 69 (1), 92-100.

Jones, T.O., and Sasser, W.E. (1995). Why satisfied customers defect. *Harvard Business Review*, 6 (1), 88-99.

Karat, C. (1989). Iterative testing of a security application. *Proceedings of the Human Factors Society,* Denver, Colorado, 273-277.

Karat, C. (1990a). Cost-benefit analysis of usability engineering techniques. *Proceedings of the Human Factors Society*. Orlando, Florida, 839-843.

Karat, C. (1990b). Cost-benefit analysis of iterative usability testing. In D. Diaper et al. (Eds.), *Human Computer Interaction - Interact 90.* Amsterdam: Elsevier, 351-356.

Karat, C. (1991a). Cost-benefit and business case analysis of usability engineering. *Tutorial presented at the ACM SIGCHI Conference on Human Factors in Computing Systems.* New Orleans, LA, April 28-May 2.

Karat, C. (1991b). Measurable benefits of applied human-computer interaction. *Keynote address presented at the International Conference on Applied Human-Computer Interaction,* Toronto, June.

Karat, C. (1992). Cost-justifying human factors support on development projects. *Human Factors Society Bulletin*, 35 (11), 1-8.

Karat, C. (1993a). Usability engineering in dollars and cents. *IEEE Software*, 10 (3), 88-89.

Karat, C. (1993b). Cost-benefit and business case analysis of usability engineering. *Tutorial presented at the ACM SIGCHI Conference on Human Factors in Computing Systems*. Amsterdam, April 24-29.

Karat, C. (1994a). A business case approach to usability cost justification. In Bias, R. and Mayhew, D. (Eds.), *Cost-Justifying Usability*. New York: Academic Press.

Karat, C. (1994b). A comparison of user interface evaluation methods. In Nielsen, J. and Mack, R. (Eds.), *Usability Inspection Methods*. New York: John Wiley & Sons.

Karat, C., Campbell, R. and Fiegel, T. (1992). Comparison of empirical testing and walkthrough methods in user interface evaluation. In *Proceedings of CHI'92*, Monterey, CA, May 2-7, New York: ACM, 397-404.

MacIntyre, F., Estep, K.W., and Sieburth, J.M. (1990). Cost of user-friendly programming. Journal of Forth Application and Research, 6 (2), 103-115.

Mantei, M.M., and Teorey, T.J. (1988). Cost/benefit analysis for incorporating human factors in the software lifecycle. *Communications of the ACM*, 31 (4) 428-439.

March, A. (1994). Usability: The new dimension of product design. *Harvard Business Review*, 5(1), 144-149.

Nielsen, J. (1994). Heuristic evaluation. In Nielsen, J., and Mack, R., (Eds.), *Usability Inspection Methods.* New York: John Wiley & Sons.

Pressman, R.S. (1992). *Software Engineering: A Practitioner's Approach*. New York: McGraw Hill.

Prokesch, S.E. (1995). Competing on customer service. *Harvard Business Review*, 6(1), 101-112.

Senge, P. (1990). *The Fifth Discipline: The Art and Practice of the Learning Organization.* New York: Doubleday.

Virzi, R. (1989). What can you learn from a low-fidelity prototype? In *Proceedings of the Human Factors Society.* Orlando, Florida, 224-228.

Virzi, R. (1990). Streamlining the design process: Running fewer subjects. *In Proceedings of the Human Factors Society.* Orlando, Florida, 291-294.

Wixon, D. and Jones, S. (1992). *Usability for fun and profit: A case study of the design of DEC RALLY version* 2. Internal Report, Digital Equipment Corporation.

Wixon, D., Jones, S., Tse, L., and Casaday, G. (1994). Inspections and design reviews: Framework, history, and reflection. In Nielsen, J., and Mack, R. (Eds.), *Usability Inspection Methods.* New York: John Wiley & Sons.

Part V

Individual Differences and Training

Handbook of Human-Computer Interaction
Second, completely revised edition
M. Helander, T.K. Landauer, P. Prabhu (eds.)

Chapter 33

From Novice to Expert

Richard E. Mayer
University of California
Santa Barbara, California, USA

33.1 Introduction

What does an expert computer user know that a novice does not know? This is the question addressed in this chapter. When a novice begins in a new domain such as using a word processing system, a computerized data retrieval system, an operating system, or a general purpose programming language, the user makes many errors and requires a lot of time to solve problems. Eventually, over the course of tens or hundreds of hours of experience, the user becomes faster and more accurate. These changes in behavior prompt the deeper question of what cognitive changes occur as a novice becomes an expert. One potentially fruitful way of answering this question is to examine expert-novice differences, that is, to compare what an expert knows and what a novice knows about a particular human-computer interaction domain.

33.1.1 Types of Knowledge in Human-Computer Interaction

This chapter examines differences between how novices and experts interact with computers. Consistent with ongoing trends in software psychology involving a focus on the user (Card, Moran and Newell, 1983; Hoc, Cacciabue, and Hollnagel, 1995; Hoc, Green, Samurcay, and Gilmore, 1990; Shneiderman, 1980; Wender, Schmalhofer, and Bocker, 1995) and in cognitive science involving a focus on knowledge representation (Mayer, 1992a; Posner, 1989), this chapter examines differences in the knowledge that novice and expert computer users possess. Ehrlich and Soloway (1984, p. 113) have summarized the goal of expert-novice research as follows: "our goal is to identify specific knowledge which experts seem to have and use and which novices have not yet acquired." Kolodner (1983, p. 497) proposes a similar knowledge-based approach to describing expert-novice differences: "experts are knowledgeable about their domain" and they know "how to apply and use...knowledge more effectively."

Table 1 provides a framework for organizing the kinds of knowledge that may be relevant to problem solving, in general, and to human-computer interaction, in particular. The framework is modified from several analyses of the knowledge involved in programming, including Shneiderman and Mayer's (1979) distinction between syntactic and semantic knowledge, Pennington's (1987) distinction between knowledge of text structure and knowledge of plans, and Soloway and Ehrlich's (1984) discussion of tacit plan knowledge. As can be seen in Table 1, four types of knowledge in which experts and novices may differ are syntactic knowledge, semantic knowledge, schematic knowledge, and strategic

Table 1. Four kinds of programming knowledge.

Knowledge	Definition	Example	Common Tests
Syntactic	Language units and rules for combining language units	Distinction between X = Y + Z as acceptable and A + B = C as unacceptable	Recognizing whether or not line of code is correct
Semantic	Mental model of the major locations, objects, and actions in the system	Concepts of pipes and files in UNIX	Rating pairs of terms for relatedness; providing thinking aloud protocol
Schematic	Categories of routines based on function	Distinction among looping structures, DO-WHILE, DO-UNTIL, and IF-THEN-ELSE	Recalling program code or keywords; Sorting routines or problems; Recognizing and naming routines
Strategies	Techniques for devising and monitoring plans	Breadth-first, top- down search in debugging	Providing think aloud protocols; Answering comprehension questions

knowledge. Definitions, examples, and relevant research are presented for each of these kinds of knowledge in subsequent sections of this review.

33.1.2 Data Base

An extensive search of the research literature on expert-novice differences in human-computer interaction yielded a core data base of 33 published empir-ical research papers (Acton, Johnson, and Goldsmith, 1994; Adelson, 1981, 1984; Adelson and Soloway, 1985; Barfield, 1986; Bateson, Alexander and Murphy, 1987; Cooke and Schvaneveldt, 1988; Davies, 1989, 1990, 1991a, 1991b, 1994; Doane, Pellegrno, and Klatzky, 1990; Ehrlich and Soloway, 1984; Fleury, 1993; Goodwin and Sanati, 1986; Guerin and Matthews, 1990; Gugerty and Olson, 1986; Jeffries et at., 1981; Krems, 1995; McKeithen et at., 1981; Mobus, Schroder and Thole, 1995; Rist, 1990, 1991; Schank, Linn and Clancy, 1993; Schomann, 1995; Shneiderman, 1976; Soloway and Ehrlich, 1984; Vessey, 1985, 1986; Weiser and Shertz, 1983; Wiedenbeck, 1985; Wiedenbeck and Fix, 1993; Ye and Salvendy, 1994). In reviewing each study in this data base, I use the term "novice" to refer to the least experienced group of users, the term "expert" to refer to the most experienced group of users, and groups with intermediate levels of expertise generally are ignored. This data base does not include related research on novice programming, expert systems, learning computer programming, or measurement of programming.

33.2 Expert-Novice Differences in Problem Solving

Since human-computer interaction is a form of problem solving, it is instructive to begin by briefly considering expert-novice differences in problem solving (Chi, Glaser and Farr, 1988; Mayer, 1992a; Sternberg and Frensch, 1991). While an extensive review of this research is beyond the scope of this chapter, this section focuses on representative examples of three typically used research techniques: recall tasks, protocol analysis tasks, and sorting tasks.

Recall Tasks

In a classic recall study based on de Groot's (1965) original research, Chase and Simon (1973) compared a chess master and a beginning chess player on their memory for chess board configurations. Each person briefly viewed a board containing pieces from an actual game and a board containing the same pieces organized randomly on the board. As a recall test, the board was cleared and each person was asked to place the pieces where they had been on the board. The results indicated that the expert correctly remembered four times as many pieces as the novice for the real game boards, but did not differ from the novice in recalling randomly arranged boards. Chase and Simon concluded that experts do not have better overall memories than novices; rather, they are able to organize the individual chess players into meaningful chunks with each chunk containing several pieces. Thus, when an expert looks at a board containing 24 pieces he or she may be able to see several chunks, each containing several pieces and represented as a unit with an inherent meaning. Simon (1980) estimates that a chess master possesses approximately 50,000 chunks that is 50,000 different meaningful configurations of pieces on a chess board.

Protocol Tasks

In an exemplary protocol analysis study, Larkin et al. (1980) presented simple physics problems to novices, who were beginning college physics students, and experts, who were physics professors and advanced graduate students. Subjects were asked to "think aloud" as they solved the problems. As expected, experts were approximately four times faster than novices in solving the problems. However, a careful analysis of the thinking aloud protocols revealed that experts and novices differed in how they organized information and in their problem solving strategies. Experts tended to organize information in larger units containing several equations, whereas novice's knowledge was more fragmented; experts tended to approach the problem from the top by determining what was being asked and then finding a solution plan that corresponded to the problem, whereas novices tended to use a bottom-up, step-by-step procedure that lacked a more comprehensive plan.

Sorting Tasks

In a widely cited sorting study, Chi, Feltovich and Glaser (1981) presented a set of typical physics problems to novices, who were introductory physics students, and experts who were physics instructors. The task was to sort the problems into groups, putting similar problems in the same group. Novices tended to group problems that contained the same physical entities, such as "inclined planes," whereas experts tended to group problems that involved the same underlying principle, such as "Newton's Second Law." Apparently, novices are influenced by the surface characteristics of the problems but experts are able to relate the problems to higher-level categories that suggest plans for solution. Differences in sorting patterns seemed to be related to differences in student's knowledge of semantic concepts underlying physics, with experts more likely to use their conceptual knowledge of the physical world and novices less likely to do so.

Implications of Research on Expert-Novice Differences in Problem Solving

These three representative studies exemplify common research methods and findings concerning expert-novice differences. The methods focus on free recall, protocol analysis, and sorting of problems. The findings show that experts and novices differ with respect to their tendency to using chunking in free recall, to use comprehensive plans in solving problems, and to classify problems based on their underlying solution requirements. These studies in expert-novice differences in problem solving offer a context with which to examine the emerging research literature on expert-novice differences in human-computer interaction. In particular, each of the techniques described in this section have also been applied to the study of human-computer interaction and each of the results has been at least partially replicated in the human-computer interaction domain.

33.3 Expert-Novice Programmer Differences in Syntactic Knowledge

What is Syntactic Knowledge?

The first kind of knowledge listed in the introduction is knowledge of language syntax, or what Shneidernan and Mayer (1979) call "syntactic knowledge." As shown in the top portion of Table 1, syntactic knowledge refers to knowledge of the language units and the rules for combining the units. For example, in BASIC, the language units include keywords (such as LET, READ, IF, and PRINT), argument names (such as A1, B$, and XX), numbers (such as 10.20 and 101), symbols (such as + and =), and punctuation marks (such as commas, semi-colons, blank spaces and colons). Rules for combining language units may refer to ordering of units within a line of code (such as each line must begin with a line number separated by a blank space, or READ must be followed by a space and argument) or ordering of lines within a program (such as every FOR statement needs to be followed by a corresponding NEXT statement).

How can syntactic knowledge be evaluated in expert and novice programmers? One technique for measuring syntactic knowledge that has been applied to studying expert-novice programmer differences involves measuring the speed and accuracy of programmers for recognizing whether or not a line of code is syntactically correct. This technique is similar to lexical decision tasks used to evaluate English reading skill in which a reader must determine whether or not a set of letters is an English word, or a modified version in which a reader must determine whether a list of words is a syntactically correct sentence.

Research on Differences in Syntactic Knowledge

Recognizing syntactically correct code. Wiedenbeck (1985) provides an example of research on expert/novice differences in syntactic knowledge. The users were ten expert and ten novice FORTRAN programmers, with experts possessing 11,000 hours of experience and novices possessing 200 hours of experience. Each user was presented a series of lines of code, such as "X = Y + Z" or "A + B = C," on a computer screen. For each line of code, the user was asked to press a "yes" button if the line was syntactically correct and a "no" button if it was not. Results indicated that the experts were approximately 25% faster and had 40% lower error rates than the novices. Wiedenbeck (1985) concluded that experts have automated their lower level programming skills, such as recognition of syntactically correct code; therefore, they can devote their attentional capacity to higher level features of a program, such as its goal structure (as described below in the section on strategic knowledge). Wiedenbeck suggests that as less attention is required for recognizing syntactically correct code, more attention becomes available for comprehending the code's meaning. The finding that experts have automated basic program reading processes replicates results from research on expert-novice differences in reading English (LaBerge and Samuels, 1974; Samuels, 1979) and is consistent with Schmidt's (1986) finding that experts require less time to read lines of program code than do novices.

Implications of Research on Syntactic Knowledge

Research in cognitive psychology points to the extreme limits of attentional capacity in processing information. The main findings concerning syntactic knowledge suggest that experts have automated their syntactic processing of code so that they devote most of their attention to higher level processing, such as the meaning of the code and the goal of the program, whereas novices must devote more attention to syntactic rules while reading or generating code so they have less attentional resources to devote to higher level processing. As indicated in the top of Table 2, a preliminary conclusion is that experts have automated their syntactic knowledge to a higher degree than have novices. Another technique for evaluating syntactic knowledge involves measuring the speed and accuracy for generating syntactically correct lines of code (regardless of whether it accomplishes its goal); although this technique has not been extensively used to study expert-novice differences, Dyck and Mayer (1989) has used this technique to evaluate individual differences in learning BASIC.

33.4 Expert-Novice Programmer Differences in Semantic Knowledge

What is Semantic Knowledge?

The second kind of knowledge is knowledge of language meaning, or what Shneiderman and Mayer (1979) call "semantic knowledge." As shown in the second portion of Table 1, semantic knowledge refers to concepts that allow a user to represent what goes on inside the system when a line of code or command is executed. Some authors have used the term "mental model" (Gentner and Stevens, 1983) to refer to user's semantic knowledge of a system, and Mayer (1979) has analyzed this kind of knowledge into three parts: locations, such as memory spaces and input queues in BASIC; objects, such as numbers, strings, flags and pointers in BASIC; and actions, such as create, put, and erase in BASIC. For example, Mayer (1979, 1985, 1987) has shown that any BASIC statement can be analyzed into a list of transactions, with each transaction describing some action carried out on some object in some location of the computer.

How can semantic knowledge be evaluated in expert and novice programmers? Three techniques explored in this section are: asking experienced and inexperienced programmers to learn a new language either using conceptual models or not, asking experienced and inexperienced programmers to generate a diagram representation of a system, and asking expert and novice programmers to think aloud while generating a program.

Research on Differences in Semantic Knowledge

Learning programming with and without models. A study by Goodwin and Sanati (1986) provides an example of research on expert-novice's differences in semantic knowledge. Approximately 600 Pascal-naive

Table 2. Summary of expert-novice differences in computer programming.

EXPERTS	NOVICES
Have automated knowledge of language syntax • Recognize syntactically correct code more rapidly and accurately	**Lack automated knowledge of language syntax** • Recognize syntactically correct code more slowly and inaccurately
Have integrated conceptual model • Benefit less from conceptual model training • Represent parts of system in a coherent hierarchy • Describe simulated runs of mental models	**Have fragmented model of system of system** • Benefit more from conceptual model training • Represent parts of system as unrelated fragments • Do not describe simulated runs of mental models
Have functional categories for types of routines • Show more difference in recalling organized versus scrambled programs • Recall lines of code in larger chunksand based on routines • Group problems and routines by functional characteristics • Recognize and name routines more rapidly and accurately	**Lack functional categories for types of routines** • Show less difference in recalling organized versus scrambled programs • Recall lines of code in smaller chunks and based on surface characteristics • Group problems and routines by surface characteristics • Recognize and name routines more rapidly and accurately
Have hierarchical plans • Examine general goal of program and high-level program modules in debugging • Design overall structure of program from beginning to end • Decompose program into finer parts and explore alternative solutions • Perform better on answering abstract questions requiring specific details of how solution is implemented • Show more difference in comprehending plan-like versus unplan-like programs	**Have linear plans** • Focus on specific solutions and low-level program modules in debugging • Write program code in order before writing low-level code • Decompose program into fewer parts and explore fewer alternative solutions • Perform better on answering concrete questions requiring comprehension of program goal • Show less difference in comprehending plan-like versus unplan-like programs

students were taught Pascal in either a traditional course or in a course that allowed students to use a concrete model while learning. The model was a computerized display under the user's control that showed the internal states of the computer as each line of a program was executed. In the traditional course, the strongest predictor of success was amount of previous experience with non-Pascal programming and computers; in the model course, previous computing experience was not significantly related to success. The authors concluded that training in conceptual models can drastically reduce or eliminate the effects of expertise on learning a new language. An implication is that experienced programmers came to the learning environment with knowledge about how to construct a useful model, whereas novices did not. Providing concrete models brought the novices to the same level as the experts in terms of semantic knowledge, that is, knowledge of conceptual models. These results are similar to those reported by Mayer (1981, 1992) in which students with poorer backgrounds in computing learned a new language more effectively when instruction included emphasis on a conceptual model of the computer, whereas conceptual model training did not enhance the learning of more experienced students.

Generating a Conceptual Model. Several research teams have used a relatedness rating technique in which expert and novice programmers are asked to rate the relatedness of all possible pairs of a set of programming terms (Acton, Johnson and Goldsmith, 1994; Cooke and Schvaneveldt, 1988; Ye and Salvendy, 1994). For example, Cooke and Schvaneveldt (1988) asked 10 experts, who had 3 or more years of programming experience, and 10 novices, who had less than 1 year of experience, to make relatedness ratings among pairs of 16 computer terms (such as "parameter", "algorithm", and "subroutine") on a scale from 0 to 9. Acton, Johnson and Goldsmith (1994) asked 6 experts, who were graduate students and faculty in computer science, and 51 novices, who were taking an introductory Pascal course, to rate all possible pairs of 24 terms (such as "integer," "record, " and "array") for relatedness on a scale from 1 to 7. Ye and Salvendy (1994) asked 10 experts, who were graduate students in computer science, and 10 novices, who were undergraduates with one course in C programming, to rate the relatedness of all pairings of 23 terms (such as "default," "basic data type," and "loop control mechanism") on a scale from 0 to 6. Multivariate statistical techniques such as cluster analysis and Pathfinder analysis were used to represent the knowledge organization of experts and novices, based on their ratings. As expected, experts and novices produced qualitatively different organizations, with experts showing more agreement among themselves, being better able to define the relations among terms, and creating larger categories than did the novices.

Doane, Pellegrino and Klatzky (1990) used a graphing task to compare the mental models of expert and novice UNIX users, with experts averaging 1.5 to 2.0 years of programming experience and novices averaging less than .25 years of programming experience. Each user was given a stack of 58 cards, each containing an English description of a UNIX command or concept such as "delete a line in a file" or "shell scripts." Each user was asked to organize the cards into a graph that represented his/her conception of UNIX structure and to use string to connect the cards with string in a way that represented his/her conception of information flow. There were no differences in the "content-free" structure of the graphs generated by experts and novices, including no differences in the number of links or the number of nodes in each grouping. Experts and novices showed similarities in the lower level of their hierarchies, such as how they grouped the main function terms. However, experts and novices differed in the higher levels of their graphs, with experts showing a more detailed and consistent organization at the system and utility level. Doane, Pellegrino and Klatzky (1990) concluded that experts were able to build a higher level top-down organization based on the types of problems they solve in UNIX, whereas novices were tied to the lower level bottom-up organization based on the available functions and subutilities.

Providing a Thinking Aloud Protocol. Jeffries et al. (1981) asked four expert and five novice software designers to "think aloud" as they developed a page-keyed indexing system. Most of the expert-novice differences obtained in this study are reviewed in a subsequent section on strategic knowledge; however, one interesting finding concerning semantic knowledge was that experts performed better than novices in using computer concepts, such as flags, pointers, and data structures. Apparently, the mental models of novices did not yet include an accurate representation of several crucial conceptual objects.

Further evidence for the role of mental models in program creation comes from studies of programmers in their work environment. Adelson and Soloway (1985) videotaped three experts, who had 8 years of software design experience, and two novices, who had less than 2 years of experience, in their work environments as they generated software in response to design specifications. On average, the programmers took about two hours to work out a high-level design. The experts "form an internal working model" which is "capable of supporting mental simulations of the design in progress" (Adelson and Soloway, 1985, p. 1353). Furthermore, Adelson and Soloway (1985, p. 1354) "observed all of our subjects repeatedly conducting simulation runs of their mental models." In contrast, novices tended to work only at the level of pseudocode and did not build or run mental models.

Implications of Research on Semantic Knowledge

Cognitive analyses of the programming task have revealed that learning a programming language involves the acquisition of a mental model of the system. Research on expert-novice differences in programming provides consistent evidence that experts have a more coherent model than novices, benefit less from' conceptual model instruction than novices, and conceive of the conceptual objects of system (such as pointers and flags) more accurately than do novices. These expert-novice differences in semantic' knowledge are summarized in the second portion of Table 2. Some additional ways of measuring semantic knowledge that could be applied to expert-novice differences include asking users to predict the output of programs--a technique used by Bayman and Mayer (1984) to determine users' mental models of electronic calculators--and asking users to draw a diagram of the internal state of the system before and after executing a statement--a technique used by Bayman and Mayer (1988) to evaluate learning of BASIC.

33.5 Expert-Novice Programmer Differences in Schematic Knowledge

What is Schematic Knowledge?

The third kind of knowledge is knowledge of common subroutine structures or functional units of code--which have been called "chunks" (Mayer, 1979; Norcio and Kerst, 1983) and "plans" (Gilmore and Green, 1988; Rist, 1989; Spohrer, Soloway and Pope, 1985). These chunks or plans are "program fragments that represent stereotypical action sequences in programming" (Gilmore and Green, 1988, p. 423). As shown in the third portion of Table 1, schematic knowledge refers to a repertoire of types of subroutines categorized by function. For example, some typical chunks or plans for BASIC programming include various types of looping configurations, sorting configurations, and randomization configurations. A programmer who possesses schematic knowledge is able to search his or her memory for subroutine constructions that match functional requirements in a program rather than having to generate the code from scratch.

Several techniques have been used to measure schematic knowledge of expert and novice programmers. These include asking expert and novice users to recall programs, to recall keywords, to sort problems, and to recognize program chunks.

Research on Differences in Schematic Knowledge

Chunking in Free Recall of Programs. Several studies have used a recall procedure to study differences in how experts and novices organize computer programs. For example, McKeithen et al. (1981) compared 24 novices. who had no experience in ALGOL with six experts who had over 400 hours of ALGOL programming experience and 2000 hours of general programming experience. On each of five trials, users viewed a 31-line ALGOL program presented in either normal or scrambled order for two minutes and then were given three minutes to recall the program. For the normal programs, experts recalled approximately three times as many lines as the novices; for the scrambled programs, the expert-novice differences were largely erased. These results replicate previous results involving chess (Chase and Simon, 1973; de Groot, 1965), and suggest that experts are able to chunk several lines of code into meaningful units.

Similar results were obtained by Shneiderman (1976) and by Bateson, Alexander and Murphy (1987) using FORTRAN code, by Barfield (1986) using BASIC code, and by Guerin and Matthews (1990) with COBOL code. In Shneiderman's study, 16 novices and 16 experts studied a 74-line FORTRAN program that was presented in either normal or scrambled order. For novices, scrambling did not significantly affect amount recalled but for experts scrambling significantly reduced amount recalled. Bateson, Alexander and Murphy (1987) obtained the same pattern of results in comparing how 20 novice and 30 expert recalled a 20-line FORTRAN program that was presented in normal or scrambled order. Similarly, in Barfield's study, a group of 26 experts recalled less from a scrambled than a normal BASIC program whereas the recall performance of a group of 80 novices was much less affected by scrambling. Finally, Guerin and Matthews (1990) obtained the same pattern in comparing how 52 experts and 52 novices recalled a 110-line COBOL program that was presented in normal order and in scrambled order.

Taking a slightly different approach, Adelson (1981) compared five novices who were undergraduate students in a programming course with five experts who were teaching assistants (TAs) for the course. On each of nine trials users saw 16 individually presented lines of PPL code and were asked to recall as much as possible. Although the lines came from three coherent programs, they were presented in random order. As might be expected, the experts recalled more lines than did the novices; however, experts and novices also organized their recall differently. Experts tended to organize the lines of code as executable routines, whereas novices tended to organize lines of code based on syntax with similar kinds of statements recalled together. Compared to novices, experts tended to generate larger chunks, to order their recall more consistently from trial to trial, and to be more similar to one another in their recall order. Apparently, experts recalled more because they were better able to chunk the statements based on typical routines or program configurations.

A more direct way to examine this hypothesis is to ask experts and novices to describe their encoding processes for memorizing a program. Schomann (1995) presented LISP programs, one line at a time, to experts who were advanced programmers, and novices who had no programming experience, and then asked them to recall the programs. As expected, experts recalled more than novices. In a subsequent interview, most of the experts reported they memorized the program by evaluating how it would run whereas most of the novices reported they memorized the program by rehearsing the lines in order. Schomann (1995, p. 202) concluded that "most of the novices proceeded using list learning strategies and tried to rehearse a program" whereas "advanced programmers focused on relevant programming schemata."

Chunking in Free Recall of Keywords. In a related study, McKeithen et al. (1981) asked eight novices and eight experts to study 21 ALGOL reserved words until they could correctly recall them all twice in a row. Then, the users were asked to freely recall the words 25 more times. Consistent with the foregoing recall data, novices tended to chunk the words by surface characteristics such as letters in the word whereas experts tended to chunk by function, putting together words required to carry out a meaningful function such as IF, THEN, and ELSE. Apparently, the experts possessed knowledge of common code configurations.

Chunking in Sorting of Problems and Subroutines. In a sorting study, Weiser and Shertz (1983) compared six novices who were undergraduates just beginning to take a programming course and nine experts who were computer science graduate students. Each user was given a set of 27 problems stated in English and was asked to sort the problems into groups based on "similarities in how you would solve them." Novices tended to group problems based on the surface characteristics of the problems such as putting all business applications in one pile, all operating systems applications in another pile, and string manipulation problems in another pile. In contrast, experts sorted based on type of algorithm required such as sorting, searching, or statistical. These results replicate similar findings involving arithmetic word problems (Silver, 1979) and physics problems (Larkin et al., 1980), and suggest that experts have a useful repertoire of types of solution routines.

In a somewhat similar study, Schank, Linn and Clancy (1993) asked 2 novices, who were taking a Pascal course, and 2 experts, who had taken at least three semesters of programming courses, to sort and describe a stack of 15 to 20 subroutines. Experts created fewer but larger categories than did novices, and experts were better able to describe the categories than were novices. Consistent with previous research, experts tended to sort based on structural or functional features (e.g., clustering all subroutines using a given looping structure) whereas novices sorted based on surface or syntactic features (e.g., clustering all subroutines that involved arrays).

Recognizing Program Chunks. Wiedenbeck (1985) provides additional support for the idea that experts recognize meaningful chunks of program code more efficiently than novices. Ten experts who had logged over 11000 hours of programming experience and 10 novices who had programming experience of about 200 hours were given a series of matching problems presented on a terminal screen. The user saw a label such as "DO LOOP" followed by some FORTRAN code such as,

```
DO 5 I= 1,, 7
IM(I) = 0
5 continue
```

and were asked to press a "yes" button if the label matched the code and a "no" button if it did not. Experts produced less than half as many errors and responded in almost half as much time as novices. Wiedenbeck (1985) concludes the experts have automatized their recognition of familiar chunks of programming code so each chunk can be recognized as a unit.

In a follow-up study, Wiedenbeck and Fix (1993), asked 20 experts, who averaged 8 years of programming experience, and 20 novices, who had taken one Pascal course, to study a 135-line Pascal program for 15 minutes and then answer questions about it. Experts outperformed novices on matching procedure names to the procedures they call, writing descriptions of the goals of selected procedures, and matching variable names to the procedures in which they occur. Consistent with previous research, these results suggest that experts are more likely than novices to represent programs as meaningful plan-based chunks of code.

Not only do experts possess stereotypical program segments, they also know how to access them. Davies (1994) asked 12 experts, who were Pascal instructors or professional programmers, and 12 novices, who were first year undergraduate students who passed a short introductory Pascal course, to study a 24-line Pascal program for 10 minutes. On a recognition test, for each of 40 items, a line of code was presented on the screen and the participant was asked to indicate whether or not the line had been in the program they studied. Some of the items were "focal lines"--lines central to a plan such as a running total loop or a counter variable plan--and some were "non-focal lines"--lines that were not central to a plan. Experts were more accurate and faster than novices, especially on focal rather than non-focal lines. Davies (1994; p. 712) concluded that experts "access abstract schema-based structures which represent stereotypical programming knowledge." In short, "experts may possess a greater number of program-specific schemata than novices" and can access them quickly (Davies, 1994, p. 706).

In a related study, 15 experts and 15 novices, were given a partial Pascal program along with three fragments, and asked to choose the best fragment for completing the program (Davies, 1990). Experts were more successful than novices in completing a program with a fragment that corresponded to the plan of the program, and experts were much faster than novices in making their choice. Also, novices were more likely than experts to choose fragments that violated basic discourse rules such as, only test for a condition if the condition has the potential for being true or do not include statements in a program that will not be used. The results suggest that experts possess a collection of plan-based program segments which they can access in an automated manner.

Implications of Research on Schematic Knowledge

The role of schemas and chunking has been a dominant theme in the cognitive psychology of knowledge representation (Chi, Glaser and Rees, 1982; Mayer, 1992a). Research on expert-novice differences in programmers' schematic knowledge indicates that, compared to novices, experts generate a greater differences in recalling organized and scrambled programs, experts recall programs by building larger chunks based on routines, experts sort problems based on the type of solution/routine required, and recognize common program routines more rapidly and accurately. These findings are summarized in the third portion of Table 2.

Apparently, becoming an expert user of a computer system includes acquiring a vast repertoire of commonly used subroutine structures organized by function. In an analysis of musical expertise, Hayes (1985) estimated that an expert possesses 50000 chunks of knowledge--equivalent to a subroutine structure in programming--and that ten years of experience are required to acquire this amount of knowledge. For human-computer interaction, an expert is likely to know the kinds of subproblems generally involved in programming and to know several kinds of subroutine structures that are suitable for solving each subproblem.

33.6 Expert-Novice Programmer Differences in Strategic Knowledge

What is Strategic Knowledge?

The final kind of knowledge reviewed in this chapter is knowledge of how to devise and monitor solution plans--what can be called "strategic knowledge." As summarized in the bottom portion of Table 1, strategic knowledge involves planning how to use the available information in order to achieve a goal. For example, one typical planning strategy is stepwise refinement in which the user breaks a programming problem into to separate subproblems, breaks each sub-problem into smaller subproblems, and so on. Rist (1989) has described a strategy in which programmers generate "focal lines" corresponding to the major modules of the program, and then in successive cycles flesh out the modules through a process of "focal expansion." Ehrlich and Soloway (1984) have observed that this kind of planning knowledge is often tacit, that is, the user may not be consciously aware of his or her planning strategies.

Three methods of evaluating strategic knowledge in expert and novice programmers are explored in this review: asking users to think aloud as they generate or debug a program, observing users as they generate or debug a program, and asking users to answer comprehension questions that either do or do not depend on understanding the plan of a program solution.

Research on Differences in Strategic Knowledge

Providing a thinking aloud protocol of planning strategies. In an exemplary study, Vessey (1985, 1986) compared eight novices and eight experts in COBOL programming within the same organization. Each user was given a program to debug and asked to think aloud. An analysis of the resulting protocols indicated several interesting differences in the debugging strategies used by experts and novices: experts' were more likely to examine high level modules in the program and to initially familiarize themselves with the program before trying to solve the problem whereas novices examined more modules and produced more phases in their solutions. Vessey summarized the findings by saying that experts prefer to work at a high level, use a breadth-first search, and take a system view of the problem whereas novices focus on getting a solution rather than understanding the program. Vessey also points out that the ability to use effective chunking strategies, as described in the foregoing section, is directly related to the use of expert solution strategies. Vessey's analysis of planning strategies in programming is consistent with Hayes and Flower's (1980) analysis of strategic processing in writing English compositions.

In another protocol analysis study, Jeffries et at. (1981) asked four experience software designers (e.g., including a professional designer with 10 years of experience) and five novice software designers (e.g., undergraduates who had taken four to eight computer science courses) to design a page-keyed indexing system. Each designer was asked to think aloud while wording on the project. An analysis of the thinking aloud protocols revealed differences in the solution processes used by experts and novices: experts decomposed the problem into finer subparts than novices, and experts considered several alternative ways of solving a subpart whereas novices tended to use the first method they thought of.

Rist (1990, 1991) asked 10 experts, who had 200 hours of programming experience, and 10 novices, who were taking an introductory Pascal course, to think aloud as they wrote programs to solve specific problems. In addition to being slower and more variable than experts, novices tended to work in linear order whereas experts developed a hierarchy of plan structures before writing a line of code. Rist (1991, p. 8) postulates that the "development of expertise is...defined as a shift from plan creation to plan retrieval."

Providing a Behavior-based Protocol of Planning Strategies. Davies (1989, 1991a, 1991b) has reported a well-controlled series of studies aimed at a microanalysis of the strategies that experts and novices use in generating programs. For example, Davies (1991a) asked 20 experts, who were instructors and professional programmers with an average of 6 years of Pascal programming experience, and 20 novices, who were undergraduate students who had taken a course in Pascal, to create a program to solve a problem, such as calculating the average for a series of input values. The programs were generated on line, without the use of any paper and pencil, and usually required about one hour to complete. In analyzing the programmers' strategies, each new line of code was classified as "focal" if it implemented the current goal and as "non-focal" if not. During the first half of the session experts generated more focal lines and fewer non-lines than did novices, whereas during the second half of the session novices generated more focal lines and fewer non-focal lines than did experts. Also, during the first half of the session experts produced more between-hierarchy jumps (e.g., moving from a focal line to a non-focal line) and fewer within-hierarchy jumps (e.g., moving from a non-focal line to another non-focal line) than did novices, whereas the reverse trend occurred during the second half of the session. According to Davies (1991a, p. 183) experts take a hierarchical approach in which "the abstract structure of the program, represented as the instantiation of focal lines, is mapped out at an early stage in the evolution of the design." Davies (1991a) concluded that at the early stages of program generation "expert programmers adopt a broadly top-down approach to the programming task" (p. 186) and "make many jumps between structures at the same level of abstraction" (p. 183), but as the "task progresses...strategy is seen to be more opportunistically oriented" (p. 184). In contrast, novices tend to write code from beginning to end while also displaying "opportunistic behavior throughout the course of the program design activity."

In a similar set of studies (Davies, 1989; Davies, 1991b), experts made more inter-plan jumps (e.g., moving cursor to a different plan structure) and fewer intra-plan jumps (e.g., moving cursor to a new place within the same plan structure) than did novices when writing a program. Even in a recall task, experts made more inter-plan jumps and fewer intra-plan jumps in reconstructing the program than did novices (Davies, 1989). The picture that emerges is that novices are more likely to use a linear strategy whereas experts are more hierarchical in writing a program. For example, unlike the linear approach of novices, experts take a broad approach, laying out the beginning of each plan structure and later fleshing them out via stepwise refinement. Davies also points out that programmers--rather than being purely linear or purely hierarchical--are also opportunistic in their coding.

Answering Comprehension Questions. In a series of comprehension studies, Adelson (1984) compared 42 novices who were undergraduates in an introductory computer programming course and 42 experts who were teaching fellows for the course. For each of eight PPL programs, each user was given a concrete or abstract flowchart followed by the program and by concrete or abstract comprehension questions. Abstract questions focused on the underlying plan of the program such as "Is the field wider than it is long?" whereas concrete questions focused on surface details of how the program earned out the plan such as "Which border of the field is filled in first?" Experts performed better on abstract questions whereas novices performed better on concrete questions. Adelson concludes that experts represent programs abstractly because they focus on a general solution strategy rather than specific details. These findings complement reading comprehension results in which expert readers perform better on remembering conceptually important information and making inferences whereas less skilled readers perform better on verbatim memory (Mayer, 1984).

In a set of related studies, Soloway and Ehrlich (1984) and Ehrlich and Soloway (1984) asked novices, who had taken one Pascal programming course, and experts, who had taken several Pascal programming courses, to fill in a missing line form a "plan-like" or an "unplan-like" Pascal program. The plan-like program had a clear solution goal and subgoals whereas the unplan-like program did not. For plan-like programs, experts clearly outperformed novices; however, for unplan-like programs there was no significant difference between expert and novice performance. Apparently, experts can make use of their tacit knowledge of programming plans in comprehending a program whereas novices are less able to use plan knowledge.

Krems (1995) asked 8 experts, who had at least 3 years of LISP programming experience, and 8 novices, who had passed a LISP course, to pretend that they were hot-line advisors. They were given a 12-line LISP program that did not work and asked to debug it. They could edit and run the program, and they could ask questions to the user via the CRT. As expected, experts were much more successful than novices in debugging the program, and experts used more goal-guided strategies than did novices. Experts were more likely to ask questions about the user's goal and the nature of the error message that the user received whereas novices' questions were more diverse. Krems (1995, p. 246) concluded that "the advantage of the experts is based on their ability to generate well-structured hypotheses."

Additional research suggests that experts are better able to comprehend programs than are novices, because they are more sensitive to the hierarchical organization of complex programs. For example, Fluery (1993) asked four experts, who had at least two years of programming experience, and 23 novices, who were taking an introductory programming course, to rate the readability of various programs. Experts considered a program more readable if it used parameters to avoid duplicate code, but novices praised repeating a procedure. Experts considered a program to be more readable if consisted of well-defined modules whereas novices preferred short programs to hierarchical ones. These results are consistent with findings by Gugerty and Olson (1986, p. 25) in which experts outperform novices on debugging programs because of "the ease with which they understand what the program does."

Implications of Research on Strategic Knowledge

Strategic planning is a high level activity on which experts and novices differ greatly. The bottom portion of Table 2 summarizes the differences by noting that experts are more likely than novices' to examine the goal of the program, to decompose the program into finer parts, to explore more solution alternatives, to comprehend the abstract goals of a program, and to benefit more from modifying well-planned programs than from programs that lack plans. These studies suggest that experts are far more efficient than novices at generating and monitoring plans for programming. Research on writing English compositions shows that planning activity takes more time than any other activity including actually putting words on the paper or reviewing what was written (Gould, 1980; Hayes and Flower, 1980). Similarly, the results of protocol analyses of programmers indicates that planning--i.e., either devising plans for a new program or determining the author's plan for an existing program--requires a great deal of attention and effort.

33.7 Conclusion

The study of expert-novice differences between computer users is scarcely two decades old. The growing data base that has emerged during this short period is beginning to provide some answers to the question of what an expert computer user knows that a novice does not know. Some surprisingly consistent trends have begun to emerge concerning differences between experts and novices in syntactic, semantic, schematic, and strategic knowledge. While early research focused mainly on expert-novice differences in speed and accuracy on tasks such as sorting and recall, more recent research has examined the strategies that experts and novices use in creating and debugging programs. Although additional research is needed, the preliminary findings are summarized in Table 2. In this conclusion section, implications of these findings are examined for theory, research, and practice.

Theoretical Implications

The results of expert-novice difference studies of computer users are remarkably consistent with corresponding research in other problem solving domains. The theme of this work is that expert problem solving in a domain depends on the expert's possession of an extremely rich knowledge base that must be acquired through extensive experience. The knowledge-based approach to assessing expert-novice differences appears to offer a fruitful theoretical. framework that requires additional refinement. The list of four types of knowledge summarized in Table 1 offers a starting point, but future theoretical work is needed to specific the nature of what experts and novices know. The logical goal of this theoretical work is the development of precise models corresponding to expert and novice computer users.

Research Implications

It is clear from the foregoing review that researchers have not reached a consensus on standard research methods. The most commonly used methods appear to borrow techniques from earlier research on expert-novice differences in problem solving in non-programming domains: recall tasks, protocol tasks, and sorting tasks. Other techniques include Wiedenbeck's modified version of a lexical decision or verification task and Soloway and Ehrlich's (1984) modified version of a cloze task. Some consensus needs to be reached on the appropriate level of analysis for protocols; although the qualitative summaries presented by some protocol researchers are a useful preliminary step, there is also a need for more fine-grained, quantitative analyses of programming such as those of Davies (1991a, 1991b). There does not, however, seem to be strong justification for any more replications of expert-novice differences in the recall of scrambled and normal programs.

Another set of methodological problem arises from differences among researchers in how they define expert and novice status. In some studies, the criteria for determining expertise were vague such as counting undergraduates as novices and graduate students as experts. In other studies, more exact criteria were used to evaluate expertise such as number of programming courses taken or number of hours of programming experience; however, even when more exact criteria were used, the definitions of amount of experience needed to be an expert was inconsistent among researchers.

In summary, future expert-novice comparisons should use a wider battery of effective measures aimed at each kind of knowledge. The analyses should be as fine grained as possible and the definitions of expert and novice should be standardized. Longitudinal studies would also offer an excellent complement to expert-novice designs.

Practical Implications

Research on expert-novice differences in computer users also suggests some tentative practical implications, all of which require additional study. First, to the degree that experts and novices differ with respect to the knowledge they possess, there is a role for training and education. To become an expert requires the acquisition of a body of knowledge, much of which presumably can be taught. Thus, while there is no shortcut to acquiring knowledge and while differences in the ability to learn programming cannot be ignored, the road to expertise appears to be paved with hours of experience.

Second, this line of research offers some suggestions concerning how programming should be taught. As the differences between what experts and novices know become more clearly specified, training of novices can focus more specifically on reducing these differences. In particular, the present state of the research literature suggests that far more attention needs to be paid to teaching semantic, schematic, and strategic knowledge in addition to the current emphasis on syntactic knowledge (Mayer, 1987).

In summary, twenty years ago, this review could not have been written. Ten years ago researchers had just begun to address the question, "What do expert computer users know that novices don't know?" Today, these is a growing research base on expert-novice differences that yields some insights into the nature of human-computer interaction. If this review, in any way, stimulates fruitful research and practice in the years to come, it will have served its purpose.

33.8 Acknowledgment

Preparation of this chapter was supported by grant MDR-8470248 from the National Science Foundation.
The author's address is: Richard E. Mayer, Department

of Psychology, University of California, Santa Barbara, CA 93106. The author's email address is mayer@psych.ucsb.edu

33.9 References

Acton, W.H., Johnson, P.J., and Goldsmith, T.E. (1994). Structural knowledge assessment: Comparison of referent structures. *Journal of Educational Psychology, 86,* 303-311.

Adelson, B. (1981). Problem solving and the development of abstract categories in programming language. *Memory and Cognition, 9,* 422-433.

Adelson, B. (1984). When novices surpass experts: The difficulty of a task may increase with expertise. *Journal of Experimental Psychology: Learning, Memory, and Cognition, 10,* 483-495.

Adelson, B. and Soloway, E. (1985). The role of domain experience in software design. *IEEE Transactions on Software Engineering, 11,* 1351-1360.

Barfield, W. (1986). Expert-novice differences for software: Implications for problem-solving and knowledge acquisition. *Behaviour and Information Technology, 5,* 15-29.

Bateson, A.G., Alexander, R.A., and Murphy, M.D. (1987). Cognitive processing differences between novice and expert computer programmers. *International Journal of Man-Machine Studies, 26,* 649-660.

Bayman, P. and Mayer, R. E. (1984). Instructional manipulation of users' mental models for electronic calculators. *International Journal of Man-Machine Studies, 20,* 189-199.

Bayman, P. and Mayer, R. E. (1988). Using conceptual models to teach BASIC computer programming. *Journal of Educational Psychology, 80,* 291-298.

Card, S. K., Moran, T. P. and Newell, A. (1983). The psychology of human-computer interaction. Hillsdale, NJ: Erlbaum.

Chase, W. G. and Simon, H. A. (1973). Perception in chess. *Cognitive Psychology, 4,* 55-81.

Chi, M. T. H., Feltovich, P. J. and Glaser, R. (1981). Categorization and representation of physics problems by experts and novices. *Cognitive Science, 5,* 121-152.

Chi, M.T.H., Glaser, R. and Farr, M.J. (Eds.). (1988). *The nature of expertise.* Hillsdale, NJ: Erlbaum.

Chi, M. T. H., Glaser, R. and Rees, E. (1982). Expertise in problem solving. In R. J. Steinberg (Ed.), *Advances in the psychology of human intelligence.* Hillsdale, NJ: Erlbaum.

Cooke, N.J. and Schvaneveldt, R.W. (1988). Effects of computer programming experience on network representations of abstract programming concepts. *International Journal of Man-Machine Studies, 29,* 407-427.

Davies, S.P. (1989). Skill levels and strategic differences in plan comprehension of computer programs. In A. Sutcliffe and L. Macaulay (Eds.), *People and computers V* (pp. 487-502). Cambridge: Cambridge University Press.

Davies, S.P. (1990). Plans, goals and selection rules in the comprehension of computer programs. *Behavior and Information Technology, 9,* 201-214.

Davies, S.P. (1991). Characterizing the program design activity: neither strictly top down nor globally opportunistic. *Behaviour and Information Technology, 10,* 173-190.

Davies, S.P. (1991). The role of notation and knowledge representation in the determination of programming strategy: A framework for integrating models of programming behavior. *Cognitive Science, 15,* 547-572.

Davies, S.P. (1994). Knowledge restructuring and the acquisition of programming expertise. *International Journal of Human-Computer Studies, 40,* 703-726.

de Groot, A.D. (1965). *Thought and choice in chess.* The Hague: Mouton. [Original work published in 1946.]

Doane, S.M., Pellegrino, J.W. and Klatzky, R.L. (1990). Expertise in a computer operating system: Conceptualization and performance. *Human-Computer Interaction, 5,* 267-304.

Dyck, J. L. and Mayer, R.E. (1989). Teaching for transfer of computer program comprehension skill. *Journal of Educational Psychology, 81,* 16-24.

Ehrlich, K. and Soloway, E. (1984). An empirical investigation of the tacit plan knowledge in programming. In J. C. Thomas and M. L. Schneider (Eds.), *Human Factors in Computer Systems* (,pp. 113-133). Norwood, NJ: ABLEX.

Fleury, A.E. (1993). Student beliefs about Pascal programming. *Journal of Educational Computing Research, 9,* 355-371.

Gentner, D. and Stevens, A. L. (Eds.). (1983). *Mental models.* Hillsdale, NJ: Erlbaum.

Gilmore, D.J. and Green, T.R.G. (1988). Programming plans and programming expertise. Quarterly Journal of Experimental Psychology, 40A, 423-442.

Goodwin, L. and Sanati, M. (1986). Learning computer programming through dynamic representation of computer functioning: Evaluation of a new learning package for Pascal. *International Journal of Man-Machine Studies, 25,* 327-341.

Gould, J. D. (1980). Experiments on composing letters: Some facts, some myths, and some observations. In L. W. Gregg and E. R. Steinberg (Eds.), *Cognitive processes in writing.* Hillsdale, NJ: Erlbaum.

Guerin, B. and Matthews, A. (1990). The effects of semantic complexity on expert and novice computer program recall and comprehension. *Journal of General Psychology, 117,* 379-389.

Gugerty, L. and Olson, G.M. (1986). Comprehension differences in debugging by skilled and novice programmers. In E. Soloway and S. Iyengar (Eds.), *Empirical studies of programmers* (pp. 13-27). Norwood, NJ: Ablex.

Hayes, J. R. (1985). Three problems in teaching general skills. In S. F Chipman, J. W. Segal and R. Glaser *(Eds.), Thinking and learning skills: Volume 2, Research and open questions.* Hillsdale, NJ: Erlbaum.

Hayes, J. R. and Flower, L. S. (1980). Identifying the organization of writing processes. In L. W. Gregg and E. R. Steinberg (lids.), *Cognitive processes in writing.* Hillsdale, NJ: Erlbaum.

Hoc, J.M., Green, T.R.G., Samurcay, R., and Gilmore, D.J. (Eds.). (1990). *Psychology of programming.* London: Academic Press.

Hoc, J., Cacciabue, P.C. and Hollnagel, E. (Eds.). (1995). *Expertise and technology.* Hillsdale, NJ: Erlbaum.

Jeffries, R., Turner, A., Polson, P. and Atwood, M. (1981). The processes involved in designing software. In J. Anderson (Ed.), *Cognitive skills and their acquisition* (pp. 255-283). Hillsdale, NJ: Erlbaum.

Kolodner, J. L. (1983). Towards an understanding of the role of experience in the evolution from novice to expert. *International Journal of Man-Machine Studies, 19,* 497-518.

Krems, J.F. (1995). Expert strategies in debugging: Experimental results and a computational model. In K.F. Wender, F. Schmalhofer, and H-D. Bocker, (Eds.). *Cognition and computer programming* (pp. 241-285). Norwood, NJ: Ablex.

LaBarge, D. and Samuels, S. J. (1974). Toward a theory of automatic information processing in reading. *Cognitive Psychology, 6,* 293-323.

Larkin, J. H., McDermott, D., Simon, D. P. and Simon, H. A. (1980). Expert and novice performance in solving physics problems. *Science, 208,* 1335-1342.

Mayer, R. E. (1979). A psychology of learning BASIC computer programming: Transactions, prestatements, and chunks. *Communications of the ACM, 22,589-593.*

Mayer, R. E. (1981). The psychology of how novices learn computer programming. *Computing Surveys, 13,* 121-141.

Mayer, R. E. (1984). Aids to prose comprehension. *Educational Psychologist, 19,* 30-42.

Mayer, R. E. (1985). Learning in complex domains: A cognitive analysis of computer programming. In G. Bower (Ed.), *Psychology of learning and motivation,*

Vol. 19 (pp. 89-130). Orlando, FL: Academic Press.

Mayer, R. E. (1987). Cognitive aspects of learning and using a programming language. In J. M. Carroll (Ed.), *Interfacing thought: Cognitive aspects of human-computer interaction* (pp. 61-79). Cambridge, MA: MIT Press.

Mayer, R. E. (1992a). *Thinking, problem solving, cognition (2nd ed.).* New York: Freeman.

Mayer, R.E. (1992b). Teaching for transfer of problem-solving skills to computer programming. In E. De Corte, M.C. Linn, H. Mandl and L. Verschaffel (Eds.). *Computer-based learning environments and problem solving* (pp. 193-206). Berlin: Springer-Verlag.

McKeithen, K. B., Reitman, J. S., Rueter, H. H. and Hirtle, S.C. (1981). Knowledge organization and skill differences in computer programmers. *Cognitive Psychology, 13,* 307-325.

Mobus, C., Schroder, O., and Thole, H-J. (1995). Online modeling: the novice-expert shift in programming skills on a rule-schema-case partial ordering. In K.F. Wender, F. Schmalhofer, and H-D. Bocker, (Eds.). *Cognition and computer programming* (pp. 63-105). Norwood, NJ: Ablex.

Norcio, A. F. and Kerst, S. M. (1983). Human memory organization for computer programs. *Journal of American Society for Information Science, 34,* 109-114.

Pennington, N. (1987). Stimulus structures and mental representations in expert comprehension of computer programs. *Cognitive Psychology, 19,* 295-341.

Posner, M.I. (Ed.). (1989). *Foundations of cognitive science.* Cambridge, MA: MIT Press.

Rist, R.S. (1989). Schema creation in programming. *Cognitive Science, 13,* 389-414.

Rist, R.S. (1990). Variability in program design: the interaction of process with knowledge. *International Journal of Man-Machine Studies, 33*, 305-322.

Rist, R.S. (1991). Knowledge creation and retrieval in program design: A comparison of novice and intermediate student programmers. *Human-Computer Interaction, 6,* 1-46.

Samuels, S. J. (1979). The method of repeated readings. *Reading Teacher, 32,*403-408.

Schank, P.K., Linn, M.C. and Clancy, M.J. (1993). Supporting Pascal programming with an on-line template library and case studies. *International Journal of Man-Machine Studies, 38*, 1031-1048.

Schmidt, A.L. (1986). Effects of experience and comprehension on reading time and memory for computer programs. *International Journal of Man-Machine Studies, 25*, 399-409.

Schomann, M. (1995). Knowledge organization of novices and advanced programmers: Effect of previous knowledge on recall and recognition of LISP-procedures. In K.F. Wender, F. Schmalhofer, and H-D. Bocker, (Eds.). *Cognition and computer programming* (pp. 193-217). Norwood, NJ: Ablex.

Shneidennan, B. (1980). Software psychology. Cambridge, M.A: Winthrop.

Shneiderman, B. (1976). Exploratory experiments in programmer behavior. *International Journal of Computer and Information Sciences, 5,* 123-143.

Shneiderman, B. and Mayer, R. E. (1979). Syntactic-tic/semantic interactions in programmer behavior: A model and experimental results. *International Journal of Computer and Information Science, 8,* 219-238.

Silver, E. A. (1979). Student perceptions of relatedness among mathematical verbal problems. *Journal of Research in Mathematics Education, 10,* 195-210.

Simon, H. A. (1980). Problem solving and education. In D. T. Tuma and F. Reif (Eds.), *Problem solving and education: Issues in teaching and research. Hillsdale,* NJ: Erlbaum.

Soloway, E. and Ehrlich, K. (1984). Empirical studies of programming knowledge. *IEEE Transactions on Software Engineering, 10,* 595-609.

Spohrer, J.C., Soloway, E. and Pope, E. (1985). A goal/plan analysis of buggy Pascal programs. *Human-Computer Interaction, 1,* 163-207.

Sternberg, R.J. and Frensch, P.A. (Eds.). (1991). *Complex problem solving.* Hillsdale, NJ.: Erlbaum.

Vessey, I. (1986). Expertise in debugging computer programs: An analysis of the content of verbal protocols. *IEEE Transactions on Systems, Man, and Cybernetics, 16,* 621-637.

Vessey, I. (1985). Expertise in debugging computer programs: A process analysis. *International Journal of Man-Machine Studies, 23,* 459-494.

Weiser, M. and Shertz, J. (1983). Programming problem representation in novice and expert programmers. *International Journal of Man-Machine Studies, 19,* 391-398.

Wender, K.F., Schmalhofer, F., and Bocker, H-D. (Eds.). (1995). *Cognition and computer programming.* Norwood, NJ: Ablex.

Wiedenbeck, S. (1985). Novice/expert differences in programming skills. *International Journal of Man-Machine Studies, 23,* 383-390.

Wiedenbeck, S. and Fix, V. (1993). Characteristics of the mental representations of novice and expert programmers: An empirical study. I*nternational Journal of Man-Machine Studies, 39*, 793-812.

Ye, N. and Salvendy, G. (1994). Quantitative and qualitative differences between experts and novices in chunking computer software knowledge. I*nternational Journal of Human-Computer Interaction, 6*, 105-118.

Handbook of Human-Computer Interaction
Second, completely revised edition
M. Helander, T.K. Landauer, P. Prabhu (eds.)

Chapter 34

Computer Technology and the Older Adult

Sara J. Czaja
Department of Industrial Engineering
University of Miami
Miami, Florida, USA

34.1 Introduction

The number of older people in the population has been growing and will continue to increase in the next decade. Forecasts project that by the year 2030 people aged 65+ will represent 22% of the people living in the United States, an increase of almost 10% since 1990 (United States Senate, 1991). At the same time that the population is aging, technology is rapidly being integrated into most aspects of life and changing the nature of work, the form and scope of personal communication, education, and health care delivery. Some form of computer technology is commonplace in most environments including the home. Many routine activities such as banking, information retrieval, bill paying, and shopping increasingly involve the use of computers. For example, most people interact with automatic teller machines or computerized voice mail systems on a regular basis. In other words it is highly likely that older people will need to interact with some form of computer technology to carry out routine activities. Further, computer technology holds the promise of enhancing the quality of life and independence of older people as it may augment their ability to perform a variety of tasks. This is especially true for elderly who are frail or homebound. Many older people have problems with mobility and require assistance with routine activities. Computer applications, such as electronic mail, may allow this population to perform tasks they were previously unable to perform.

Given that older people represent an increasing large proportion of the population and are likely to be active users of technology, issues surrounding aging and computer use are of critical importance within the domain of human-computer interaction. Essentially, we need to understand the implications of age-related changes in functional abilities for the design and implementation of computer systems. Although this topic has received increased attention by researchers since the last edition of this handbook, there are still many unanswered questions. This chapter will attempt to summarize the current state of knowledge regarding computer technology and older adults as well as identify areas of needed research. Topics which will be discussed include: acceptance of technology by the elderly, training, and hardware and software design. A detailed discussion of the aging process will not be provided as an overview was provided in the last chapter (in the first edition of this handbook) and there are many excellent sources of this material (e.g. Charness, 1985). It is hoped that this chapter will serve to motivate researchers and system designers to consider older adults as an important component of the community of computer users.

34.2 Older Adults and the Use of Computer Technology

There are a number of settings where older people are likely to use computers including the workplace, and their own homes. This section will present an overview of the potential use of technology by older people within these settings. The intent is to demonstrate the importance of including the needs of older adults in the design of technology. For a more complete discussion of this issue, see Czaja (in press).

34.2.1 Workplace

One setting where older people are likely to encounter computer technology is the workplace. The rapid introduction of computer and other forms of automated technology into occupational settings implies that most workers need to interact with computers simply to perform their jobs. Computer-interactive tasks are becoming prevalent within the service sector, office environments, and manufacturing industries. For example, office personnel need to use word processing, e-mail, and database management packages to perform routine office tasks. Cashiers, sales and bank clerks also use computers on a routine basis and computer tasks are becoming more prevalent within manufacturing and process control industries. Given that the workforce is aging the implications, of the explosion of technology in the workplace, for older workers needs to be carefully evaluated. For example, issues such as worker retraining and skill obsolescence are especially important for older workers as they are unlikely to had have experience with computers. Further although computers reduce the physical demands of tasks they generally increase the mental demands. These changes in job demands need to be carefully evaluated for older workers as there are age-related changes in cognition. It may be that computer tasks are more stressing inducing for older people or that some types of computer tasks are more appropriate for older adults than other types of tasks. In essence we need to understand if there are age differences in the performance of computer based tasks and if so, the nature of these performance differences. This type of information is needed so that design interventions can be developed which help insure that older people are not at a disadvantage in today's work environments.

34.2.2 Home Environments

There are a number of ways older people can use computers within their home to enhance their independence and quality of life. Home computers can provide access to information and services and can be used to facilitate the performance of tasks such as banking and grocery shopping. Many older people have problems performing these tasks because of restricted mobility, lack of transportation, inconvenience, and fear of crime (Nair, 1989). Data from the National Health Interview Survey (Dawson, Hendershot, and Fulton, 1987) indicate that about 27% of people aged 65+ yrs. require help with activities such as shopping. Home computers can also be used to expand educational, recreational, and communication opportunities. Several studies (e.g. Furlong, 1989; Eilers, 1989; Czaja, Guerrier, Nair, and Landauer, 1993) have shown that older adults are receptive to using e-mail as a form of communication and that e-mail is effective in increasing social interaction among the elderly. Computers may also be used to augment the memory of older people by providing reminders of appointments, important dates, and medication schedules. Chute and Bliss (1994) have shown that computers can be used for cognitive rehabilitation and for the training and retraining of cognitive skills such as memory and attention. Schwartz and Plude (1995) found that compact disc-interactive systems are an effective medium for memory training with the elderly.

Computers can also enhance the safety and security of older people living at home. The percentage of older people, especially older women, living alone in the community is increasing (U.S. Bureau of the Census, 1980). Systems can also be programmed to monitor home appliances, electrical, and ventilation systems, and can be linked to emergency services.

34.2.3 Healthcare

Computer technology also holds the promise of improving health care for older people. Electronic links can be established between health care professionals and older clients, providing care givers with easy access to their clients and allowing them to conduct daily status checks or to remind patients of home health care regimes. For example, Leirer, Morrow, Tanke, and Parienate (1991) demonstrated that voice mail was effective in reducing medication noncompliance among a sample of elderly people. Similarly, Tanke and Leirer (1994) found that voice mail increased the compliance of a sample of elderly patients to tuberculosis medication appointments. Conversely, the elderly patient may use the computer to communicate with their care givers. They may ask health related questions or indicate that they are experiencing some type of problems.

Computers may also be used for health care assessment and monitoring. Ellis, Joo, and Gross (1991) demonstrated that older people can successfully use a microcomputer-based health risk assessment. In the future computers may be used to monitor a patient's physical functioning such as measuring blood pressure, pulse rate, temperature, etc. The use of computers in health care management offers the potential of allowing many people who are at risk for institutionalization to remain at home. There are vast opportunities for research within this area.

Clearly, there are many arenas where older people are likely to encounter computer technology. It is not a question of whether older people will need to interact with computers but *if and how* they will use this technology (Garfein, Schaie, and Willis, 1988). The following section will examine the acceptance of computer technology by older people.

34.3 Attitudes Towards Computer Technology

One issue which needs to be considered when discussing aging and computers is the willingness of older people to use computer technology. Clearly the success of this technology in improving the lives of the elderly is highly dependent on the degree to which older people are willing to interact with computer systems. A number of studies, examining the impact of technology and automation within work organizations, have shown that the success of the technological innovation is largely influenced by the extent to which the technology is accepted by the user population.

A commonly held belief is that older people are resistant to change and unwilling to interact with high tech products. However, the data which are available largely disputes this stereotype. A number of studies have examined the attitudes of older people towards computer technology and while the findings from these studies are somewhat mixed, overall the results indicate that older people are receptive to using computers. In fact, a recent study (Dyck and Smithers, 1994) which examined the relationship among computer anxiety, computer experience, gender, and education, found that older adults had more positive attitudes towards computers than younger adults. However, the older people expressed less computer confidence than the younger people. The results also indicated that people who had experience with computers had more positive attitudes and greater computer confidence. Jay and Willis (1992) also found that experience with computers has an influence on computer attitudes. They examined the attitudes towards computers of a sample of older adults pre and post participation in a two week computer training course. They found that the attitudes of the training participants became more positive following training. Specifically, the participants expressed greater computer comfort and computer efficacy.

Charness, Schumann and Boritz (1992) did not find any age differences in computer anxiety in a study examining the effects of age, training technique and computer anxiety on learning to use a word processor. They did, however, find that computer experience had an impact on computer anxiety such that the computer-related anxiety was reduced for all participants following computer training. In our studies of word processing, we also found that experience with computers had an impact on computer attitudes. We (Czaja, Hammond, Blascovich, and Swede, 1989) measured attitudes towards computers pre and post word processing training, among a sample of adults ranging in age from 25 to 70 years. Study results showed that post training attitudes were related to the training experience such that people who rated the training experience and their own performance positively also had more positive post training attitudes towards computers. We failed to find any age effects for either pre or post training computer attitudes. Danowski and Saks (1980) also found that a positive experience with computer-mediated communication resulted in positive attitudes towards computers among a sample of older people.

Generally, user satisfaction with a system, which is determined by how pleasant the system is to use, is considered an important aspect of usability. User satisfaction is an especially important usability aspect for systems that are used on a discretionary basis such as home computers (Nielsen, 1983). Given that home computers offer enormous potential for older adults, it would appear that this aspect of usability is especially important for this population. Brickfield (1984) surveyed 750 adults ranging in age from 45 to 65+ years and found that the older people had less positive attitudes towards technologies and were less willing to use them. In a recent study, Rodgers, Cabera, Johnson, and Rousseau (1995) found that older adults were less likely to use automatic teller machines than younger adults. However, the majority of the older people in their sample indicated they would be willing to use ATMs if trained to do so. In this regard the investigators found that an on-line tutorial was a more effective with respect to training older people to use ATMs than was providing them with a description of the system.

Gomez, Egan, and Bower (1986), in their study of text-editing, found a slightly negative relationship between computer attitudes and age. However, computer attitudes were not related to performance. Krause and Hoyer (1984) did not find any relationship between age and attitudes towards computers and Collins, Bhatti, Dexter, and Rabbit (1993) found that current use of technology was a stronger predictor of the perceived usefulness of future technology than was gender or age. Edwards and Engelhart (1989) examined survey data from a sample of older adults who has visited AARP's Technology Center. They found that the majority of respondents were willing to use a computer to perform routine tasks such as banking. In our study of e-mail (Czaja et al.., 1993), all participants found it valuable to have a computer in their home. However, the perceived usefulness of the technology was an important factor with respect to use of the technology. When the participants were asked what type of computer applications they would like available, the most common requests included: emergency response, continuing education, health information, and banking/shopping.

Further evidence that older people are receptive to learning to use computers comes from examination of the data regarding the enrollment of older people in computer education courses. For example, the computer education program at a senior center, Little House , has been extremely successful. In 1981 when the program began, there were four participants whereas in 1988 there were 200 elders enrolled in the program. The average age of the students is 73 yrs. (Eilers, 1989). SeniorNet, which is a computer network for older adults, currently has over 17,000 members and over 70 learning sites. About 33,000 seniors have been introduced to computer technology through SeniorNet (SeniorNet, 1995).

The available data suggests that older people are not technophobic and are willing to use computers. However, the nature of their experience with computers and the available computer applications are important determinants of attitudes. Gitlin (1995) concurs and indicates that the decision to accept or reject computers or other forms of technology is a complex one and determined by an interaction of factors such as perceived need, sociocultural influences, and the design of the technology. It does not appear that age per se is a strong predictor of a person s willingness to interact with computers.

34.4 Learning And Training

Given that the majority of older adults will need to interact with some form of computer technology, a critical issue is whether they will be able to acquire the skills necessary to interact with computer hardware and software. In general, the literature on aging and skill acquisition indicates that older people have more difficulty acquiring new skills than younger people and that they achieve lower levels of performance. Further, there is substantial evidence that there are age-related declines in most component processes of cognition including: attentional processes, working memory, information processing speed, inference formation and interpretation, encoding and retrieval processes in memory, and discourse comprehension (Park, 1992). Since computer tasks are primarily characterized by their mental demands, decrements in these component processes could place older adults at a disadvantage with respect to performing computer-interactive tasks.

As shown in Table 1 there have been a number of studies which have examined the ability of older people to learn computer skills. A number of these studies were concerned with identifying training strategies which are effective for older adults. In general, the results of this research indicate that older people are able to learn to interact with computers but they have more difficulty learning computer skills than do younger people and generally achieve lower levels of performance. This section will review the literature examining the ability of older people to learn computer tasks. This will be followed by a discussion of the studies examining aging and computer training. The section will conclude with recommendations for the design of training programs for older people.

34.4.1 Age as a Predictor of Computer Task Performance

In a series of experiments concerned with identifying individual characteristics which predict ability to learn text-editing, Egan and Gomez (1985) found that age and spatial memory were significant predictors of learning difficulty. Both of these variables contributed to the prediction of first try errors and execution time per successful text change. With increased age the number of first try errors increased as did execution time. Specifically, age was associated with difficulty producing the correct sequence of symbols and patterns to accomplish the desired editing change. Spatial memory was related to finding a target and generating the correct command sequence.

Elias, Elias, Robbins, and Gage (1987) conducted a study to determine if age had an impact on learning to use a basic word processing program and if so, to identify the possible sources of the age differences.

Table 1. Computer training and older adults.

Study	Age Range	Application	Findings
Caplan and Schooler, 1990	18 - 60	Drawing software	Conceptual model detrimental for older adults; older adults had lower performance
Charness, Schuman, and Boritz, 1989	25 - 81	Word-processing	Older adults took longer to complete training and required more help
Czaja, Hammond, Blascovich and Swede, 1989	25 -70	Word-processing	Older adults took longer to complete task problems and made more errors
Czaja, Hammond, and Joyce, 1989	25 - 70	Word-processing	Older adults took longer to complete task problems and made more errors; goal-oriented training improved performance
Egan and Gomez, 1985	28 - 62	Word-processing	Age and spatial memory were significant predictors of performance
Elias, Elias, Robbins, and Gage, 1987	18 - 67	Word-processing	Older adults had longer learning times and required more help
Garfein, Schaie, and Willis, 1988	49 - 67	Spreadsheet	No age differences
Gist, Rosen, and Schwoerer, 1988	Mean = 40	Spreadsheet	Older adults performed more poorly on a post training test; modeling improved performance
Hartley and Hartley, 1984	18 - 75	Line-editor	No age differences in performance efficiency; older adults took longer to complete training and required more help
Morell, Park, Mayhorn, and Echt, 1995	young- old (X = 68.6) old- old (X = 79.9)	Electronic bulletin board	Procedural training superior to conceptual; age effects
Zandri and Charness, 1989	20 - 84	Calender and Notepad	Advanced organizer not beneficial; age effects for training time and needed more help

The training program consisted of an audiotape and a training manual. They found that all participants were able to master the fundamentals of word processing, however, the older people took longer to complete the training program and required more help. The older participants also performed more poorly on a review examination.

Garfein, Schaie, and Willis (1988) found that older adults were able to learn the fundamentals of a spread sheet package. Further, they found that practice improved performance. They did not find any age differences in learning, however, the age range in their sample was restricted. The age of the participants ranged from 49 yrs. to 67 yrs. All of the participants were able to operate the computer with some degree of proficiency after only two brief training sessions indicating that older people are capable of learning to operate new technologies. In terms of other factors affecting computer proficiency, the authors found that two measures of fluid intelligence, Space and Letter Series subscales of the Primary Mental Abilities Test (Thurstone, 1958), were related to proficiency.

Hartley, Hartley, and Johnson (1984), in their study of word processing, found no differences between younger and older adults in recall of information about the program or in the correctness with which the computer operations were performed. The older adults did require more time to carry out the procedures and also needed more assistance during training. The participants received twelve hours of instruction over six training sessions. The instruction was computer-assisted and included presentations of concepts. It was structure such that learners received practice on simple tasks before proceeding to more complex editing functions. Ogozalek and Praag (1986) also found no age performance differences among a sample of younger and older adults carrying out computer-based composition tasks. Further, the older adults were more enthusiastic about computers than the younger people. The participants used a keyboard and a simulated listening typewriter to compose letters. The sample size was relatively small (n=12) and all participants had at least 6 months of computer experience.

We (Czaja and Sharit, 1993a, 1993b) completed a study which examined the impact of age on the performance of three computer tasks, commonly performed in work settings (data entry, file modification, and inventory management), and found that older people performed at a lower level than younger people. For all three tasks, the older adults took longer to complete task problems and committed more errors. They also found the tasks to be more stress inducing and difficult.

As discussed by Kelley and Charness (1995) age differences in spatial memory might explain some of the age differences in computer performance. Several researchers (Egan and Gomez, 1985, Czaja et al., 1989) have found a relationship between spatial abilities and the ability to perform computer tasks. In fact, Egan and Gomez (1985) found that the effect of age on performance was reduced when holding spatial memory constant. In our studies of text-editing, we found that spatial memory was significantly related to performance however, age effects were still evident even when controlling for differences in spatial memory. Understanding the impact of component abilities on performance is important as it identifies potential areas for design intervention. For example, software could be designed to reduce the demands on spatial memory or training could be provided to enhance spatial skills. We designed a goal oriented training method for teaching people text editing and as one component of this method we attempted to reduce the spatial demands associated with the text editing tasks. This involved drawing attention to screen location cues during training and providing highlighted illustrations of various keyboard and menu elements in the training manual.

In addition to examining cognitive abilities, other individual differences such as familiarity with computers need to be evaluated with respect to explaining age performance differences. In our study (Czaja and Sharit, 1993b) examining the influence of age on the performance of computer tasks, we found that prior experience with computers was a significant predictor of performance. As anticipated, the older adults had significantly less computer experience. However, we still found age performance differences when controlling for these differences. Some researchers have suggested that attitudes towards computers may have an impact on a person s ability to learn to use computers. However, as discussed there is little evidence suggesting that older people have more negative attitudes than younger people so therefore it is highly unlikely that this variable is contributing to age performance differences. Other abilities such as typing skill (Czaja et al., 1989) and reading skill (Egan and Gomez, 1985) have also been shown to be related to performance of computer tasks.

34.4.2 Computer Training and Older Adults

A number of studies have been concerned with identifying training strategies which enhance the ability of older people to learn to use computers. We (Czaja, Hammond, Blascovich, and Swede, 1989) evaluated the ability of older adults, with no prior computer experience, to learn a word processing program using three training strategies: instructor-based, manual-based, and on-line. All of the techniques were based on the training material which accompanied the software package. The study participants ranged in age from 25 yrs. to 70 yrs. We found that for all participants, the manual and instructor-based training were superior to the on-line training. We also found age differences in performance on the post training tasks. The older participants took longer to complete the tasks and made more errors.

In a follow-up study, we (Czaja, Hammond, Blascovich, and Joyce, 1989) attempted to identify a training strategy which would minimize age differences in learning. We designed a goal oriented training program and compared it with a more traditional approach - use of a manual and lecture. The goal oriented approach was based on the active discovery approach developed by Belbin (Belbin and Belbin, 1972) which proved to be an effective training strategy for older adults. Our approach involved introducing the elements of text-editing in an incremental fashion, moving from the simple to the more complex, e.g. opening a file vs. moving text. We also structured the training into a series of problem solving tasks where the learner had to discover and achieve the goal of completing the task. We tailored the training manual so that it was written as a series of goal -oriented units and streamlined the content, minimizing the amount of necessary reading. In addition, we attempted to draw analogies between computer concepts and familiar concepts. The results of our study indicated that the goal-oriented training was superior for all participants. The participants in this training condition performed the post training tasks more successfully - they completed the tasks more quickly and made fewer errors. However, there were no age by training interactions and there were age effects. Despite the training manipulation, the older people still performed at a lower level than the younger people. They took longer to complete the word processing tasks, completed fewer successful editing changes, and made more errors. However, the results demonstrate that the learning performance of older people can be improved by manipulation of training techniques. As noted we also found spatial memory to be a significant predictor of performance. Further, there were age differences in spatial memory with the younger people exhibiting better spatial memory than the older people.

Valasek (1988) (as reported in Sterns and Doverspike, 1989) developed a program of instruction for the use of a computer terminal on the basis of a task analysis. The program was self-paced, provided practice on each task component, and gradually introduced new components when the old ones were mastered. The task analysis program proved to be beneficial for both younger and older adults. However, there were still age differences in performance. The older adults took longer to complete the training and got fewer items correct on the post training test. Rodgers et al. (1995) also found that providing practice on individual task components was beneficial for older adults attempting to learn to use an ATM machine.

Zandri and Charness (1989) investigated the influence of training method on the ability of older people to use a calendar and notepad system. Specifically, they examined if providing an advanced organizer would impact on the acquisition of computer skills for younger and older adults. They also examined if learning with a partner would have an influence on learning. Study participants ranged in age form 20 to 84 years and were assigned to one of two training groups, individual or with a partner, half of each group received the advanced organizer before training. The results indicated an age by training method (learning alone or with a peer) by organizer (with or without preliminary information) interaction for only one dependent variable, performance on a final test. For the older adults who received training without a partner, the advance organizer resulted in better performance. For the other group of older people, there was no performance effect. For the younger subjects, having the advanced organizer resulted in worse performance if they learned alone but it made no difference if they learned in partners. These results suggest that provision of an advanced organizer may be differentially effective for older people under some learning conditions. The authors indicate that the interaction must be interpreted with caution given the small number of participants (n = 46). There were no interactions for the other variables, time to complete the task and amount of help required. The investigators concluded that the advanced organizer did not facilitate performance. Irrespective of training method, they also found age differences in performance. The older people were about 2.5 times slower than the younger people in the tutorials or test sessions and they required about three times as much help.

In a follow-up study Charness et al. (1992) investigated how training techniques and computer anxiety affected the acquisition of computer skills for both younger and older adults. In the initial experiment, novice computers users, ranging in age from 25 to 81, were taught basic word processing skills via a self-paced training program. Half of the participants received an advanced organizer prior to training. Provision of the advance organizer did not improve performance. The older people took longer to complete the training, required more help, and performed more poorly on a review test. In a second experiment, the investigators attempted to control the nature of the training session. A group of naive computer users ranging in age from 24 to 24 yrs. were assigned to a either a self-paced learning condition where they were actively involved in the tutorial or a fixed paced condition where they passively observed a pre-determined tutorial sequence of activities. The self-paced training resulted in significantly better performance for both the younger and older adults. As in the first study, the older people took longer to complete the tutorial and required more help. The investigators point out that, although they failed to find an age by training interaction, the results should be viewed in a positive light as they imply that employers need not design specialized training programs for older learners. They also discuss the importance of providing adequate training time for older people. Finally, the investigators suggest that one factor that could have contributed to the poorer performance of the older people was the quality of the screen. The majority of the older participants reported some difficulty reading the screen. The system used in the study provided a fairly low resolution display.

Gist, Schwoerer, and Rosen (1988) investigated whether behavioral modeling would have an impact on training performance for two groups of people, those under age 40 and those over age 40. The computer application was a spreadsheet program. The modeling approach involved watching a videotape of a middle-aged male demonstrating the use of the software and then practicing the procedure. The other training approach, the tutorial condition, involved a computer-based step-by-step interactive instructional package. They found the modeling approach to be superior for both groups of participants. Consistent with other investigators, they also found that the older people exhibited lower levels of performance on the post training tasks.

The results of the above studies indicate that older people are able to acquire computer skills and that the method of training has an impact on skill acquisition for both younger and older people. However, none of the researchers have identified a training technique which eliminates age differences in performance. It may be that if older people were provided with more time and/or more practice, age differences in learning and performance would be reduced. The results of the majority of studies indicated that the older people required more training time. Also, most of the studies only provided a limited amount of training over a rather limited time period. For example, in our initial study the training was approximately four hours. Gist et al. (1988) provided three hours of training and Charness et al. (1992) provided about 90 minutes of training per day over a two day period. In the Hartley et al. study (1984), participants received 12 hours of training over 6 sessions and, as discussed, no major age performance differences were found.

Morell and Echt (in press) suggest that instead of focusing on training technique, researchers should investigate the instructional material. They suggest that instructional materials that reduce cognitive demands on the part of learners are likely to enhance performance of older adults. They identify four cognitive processes which are influenced by age and are likely to be important to the performance of computer tasks: text comprehension, working memory, spatial visualization ability, and perceptual speed. Instructional materials should be designed to accommodate age-related changes in these cognitive components. For example, writing instructions in simple language and adding illustrations to text might be beneficial for older people. Further, these types of improvements are likely to be beneficial for all users. Morrell, Park, and Poon (1989) compared memory and comprehension of medication instructions for a sample of younger and older adults using two formats, the original instructions as presented on a prescription from a pharmacy and a revised version where the instructions were explicitly stated in a standard format. They found that the revised format resulted in better comprehension and memory performance for both younger and older people.

Morell and colleagues at the Center for Cognitive Aging Research are currently evaluating how age-related changes in cognition and instructional formats affect performance on the ELDERCOM bulletin board system. They are also examining the mediating effects of verbal and spatial working memory, text comprehension ability, verbal ability, and perceptual speed on the performance of older adults. With respect to instructional format, they are examining conceptual and procedural training vs. procedural training alone. Results from sixty subjects (30 young-old and 30 old-old) indicate that procedural instructions presented in a written and illustrated manual format are more beneficial for older adults than conceptual instructions. The conceptual instructions were designed to present an overall conceptual model of the bulletin board system. The procedural instructions were clear, concise and in an illustrated step-by-step format. The investigators also found that young-old subjects performed at a higher level than the old-old subjects and that all cognitive variables had some relationship to performance. However, consistent with the findings of other investigators, spatial working memory was found to be the strongest predictor of performance (Morell, Park, Mayhorn, and Echt, 1995). More research of this type is needed as it is important to understand the source of the age performance differences. We (Czaja and Sharit) are currently conducting a study examining the relationship among component cognitive abilities and the performance of three computer-interactive tasks: a data entry task, a database query task, and an accounts balancing task.

Caplan and Schooler (1990) investigated whether providing trainees with a conceptual model of the software would facilitate learning. They provided half of their subjects, aged 18-60, with an analogical model of a painting software program prior to training. They found an age by training interaction such that the model was beneficial to younger learners but detrimental to older learners. Other investigators have also shown that providing a conceptual model of a computer system is beneficial for younger adults. However, as discussed by Morell et al. (1995) provision of a conceptual model may not be beneficial for older people because the need to translate the model into actions may increase working memory demands. Clearly this is an area where more research is needed. It would appear that some knowledge of how a system works would prove beneficial to older people as it would allow them to formulate cognitive schemata which would provide contextual support for procedural information. It is generally recognized that age differences in learning and recall are more pronounced if the learning problem exists in an unfamiliar cognitive domain where there is little contextual support (Welford, 1985). It may be that older people need more time to integrate the conceptual information or that it should be presented in a more simplistic manner emphasizing analogies to familiar concepts. In this regard, while the use of analogies may be beneficial it must be approached with caution, taking care must be taken to point out differences between old and new concepts.

Elias et al. (1987) found that some of the difficulties encountered by older adults attempting to learn text-editing may have been attributable to difficulty suppressing knowledge that was inappropriate for text-editing such as knowledge related to the operation of a typewriter. In our study of text-editing (Czaja et al., 1989), we found that older participants had difficulty using the enter key and understanding the wrap around feature of the software. The participants in our e-mail study (Czaja et al., 1993) also had problems using the enter (return) key to input commands (such as an addressee s name) into the computer. Interestingly, this was especially problematic for people who had better typing skills. Generally, older people have more difficulty than younger people modifying existing concepts (Rodgers and Fisk, 1991).

Although none of the studies examining training technique conducted to date have identified a training method which is especially beneficial for older adults, the results do suggest ways in which the learning performance of older people may be improved for computer tasks. Table 2 summarizes these recommendations. In general, the recommendations will be beneficial to learners of all ages.

While consideration of how to best train older people to use computers is an extremely important issue, an equally if not more important consideration is the design of the interface. It may be that some of the difficulties encountered by older people during the learning process would be eliminated or reduced if the interface was designed so that it was easier to use. Nielsen (1993) underscores the importance of learnability and indicates that it is one of the most fundamental attributes of usability. Systems must be designed so that they are easy to learn, especially since a person's initial encounter with a system is learning to use it. The next sections will discuss how the design of the system interface may impact the performance of older adults.

34.5 Design Of the User Interface

34.5.1 Hardware Considerations

There are number of age-related changes in visual functioning which have implications for the design of computer systems. Aging is associated with reductions in light sensitivity, color perceptions, resistance to glare, dynamic and static acuity, contrast sensitivity, visual search, and pattern recognition (Kosnik, Winslow, Kline, Rasinski, and Sekuler, 1988). These changes generally impact the ability of older people to perform everyday tasks. For example, survey data, collected from a sample of community dwelling adults ranging in age from 18 to 100 yrs., indicated that the older adults had more difficulty than the younger peo-

Table 2. Summary of training recommendations for older adults.

1. Allow extra time for training; self-paced learning schedules appear to be optimal.
2. Ensure that help is available and easy to access; create a supportive learning environment.
3. Ensure that the training environment is free from distractions.
4. Training materials should be well organized and important information should be highlighted.
5. Make use of illustrations in training manuals where possible.
6. Training manuals should be designed so that they are concise and easy to read. How to information should be presented in a procedural step-by-step format.
7. Allow the learner to make errors but provide immediate feedback regarding how to correct mistakes.
8. Provide sufficient practice on task components.
9. Provide an active learning situation; allow the learner to discover ways of accomplishing tasks.
10. Structure the learning situation so that the learner proceeds from the simple to the more complex.
11. Minimize demands on spatial abilities and working memory.
12. Familiarize the learner with basic concepts regarding hardware and software and use of the equipment; address any concerns the learner has about use of the equipment (e.g. Will I break the computer if I do this?)
13. Emphasize distinctions between computers and typewriters.

ple performing a variety of everyday visual activities. Specifically, they had more trouble with glare, low levels of illumination, and near visual tasks (e.g. reading small print). They also reported more problems locating targets amidst visual clutter, tracking and processing moving targets and needed more time to perform visual tasks (Kosnik et al., 1988). These findings suggest that the visual demands of computer-interactive tasks may be problematic for older people.

Although the implications of age-related changes in vision for the performance of computer tasks has not received a great deal of research attention, the available data suggest that visual problems may contribute to age performance differences. For example, Charness et al. (1992) reported that the majority of older participants, in their study of word processing, experienced some difficulty reading the screen and that these difficulties may have contributed to the lower performance of older people. Hedman and Briem (1984) found a slightly higher incidence of eyestrain among a sample of older telephone operators who used computer terminals. Camisa and Schmidt (1984) found that older people took longer than younger people to process information presented on a computer screen. A recent study by Charness (Charness et al., 1995) indicated that target size affected the ability of older people to perform transactions such as clicking and dragging using a mouse and light pen.

Consideration of character size and contrast are especially important for older computer users. Generally larger characters and high contrast displays should be beneficial for older people. This is not a major problem with most computers used in the home or the workplace as it is relatively easy to enlarge screen characters. However, it may be an issue for computers in public places such as information kiosks and ATM machines. In addition to character size and contrast it is also important to minimize the presence of screen glare.

The organization and amount of information on a screen is also important as there are declines in visual search skills and selective attention with age. Older adults have difficulty processing complex or confusing information and are more likely to experience interference from irrelevant information (Plude and Hoyer, 1985). Therefore only necessary information should be presented on a screen and important information should be highlighted. Further principles of perceptual organization, such as grouping, should be applied. However, caution must be exercised with respect to the use of color coding as there is some decline in color discrimination abilities with age. This is particularly evident in the shorter wavelengths, the blues and greens.

Design and labeling of the keyboard also needs special consideration. In our study of e-mail (Czaja et al., 1993) people commonly confused the send and the cancel keys. Even though these keys were labeled, they were identical in size and shape and close in proximity. The labeling may not have been sufficient for people with vision problems. In fact, we found a significant relationship between visual acuity and these types of errors. People with poorer acuity tended to confuse these keys more often. These findings underscore the importance of clearly differentiating keys so that labeling is easy to read and keys are easily identified.

Level of illumination also affects visual performance. In general older people require higher levels of illumination than do younger people to compensate for visual declines. The placement of the light sources also needs to be considered as older adults are more susceptible to problems with glare. Finally, the layout of the computer workplace is especially important for older people. Presbyopia, a loss of near visual acuity, is very common among the elderly and many older people wear bifocals to compensate for this condition. Thus it is important to position the computer screen so that older adults are able to clearly view the screen contents while maintaining a comfortable posture.

34.5.2 Input Devices

Although there is a growing body of research examining the relative merits and disadvantages of various input devices, there are only a few studies which have examined age effects. Middle-aged and older people are much more likely to suffer from disabling conditions such as arthritis which may make devices such as keyboards or light pens less than optimal for this group of users. Declines is spatial abilities may also impact on an older s persons ability to successfully use input devices such as a mouse.

Charness et al. (1995) found that older people learning a graphic user interface committed a greater number of mouse errors than younger people and that they had particular difficulty with smaller targets. Analysis of videotape data indicated that some of the difficulties may have involved learning to control the find positioning aspects of movement. In a follow-up study they compared the light pen and a mouse. They found that older people exhibited longer response times with the mouse for both clicking and dragging tasks. They also found that they had difficulty with small targets and they required more practice than younger people. The authors suggest that a light pen may be easy to use because it is a direct addressing device, eliminating the need translate the target selection device onto the display. However, devices such as light pens may be difficult to use for people with arthritis or tremors as it may be hard for them to grasp and point the pen. Charness did not investigate the impact of these types of disabilities on use of the light pen.

Ellis et al. (1991) found that older users made more effective use of a computerized health care appraisal system when the user interface was a keyboard rather than a mouse. They noted that individuals with hand trouble had particular difficulty using the mouse. The authors concluded that a touchscreen version of the appraisal system may have eliminate the interface problems experienced by older users. Casali (1992) evaluated the ability of persons with impaired hand and arm function (age unknown) and nondisabled persons to perform a target acquisition task with five cursor control devices: a mouse, trackball, cursor keys, joystick, and tablet. She found that even persons with profound disabilities were able to operated each device by using minor modifications and unique operating strategies. The mouse, trackball, and tablet resulted in better performance than the joystick and trackball for all participants. Consistent with Charness, she found that small targets were problematic for the physically impaired users as was the task of dragging. In a follow-up study (Casali and Chase, 1993) with a sample of persons with arm and hand disabilities, the data indicated that while the mouse, trackball, and tablet tended to result in quicker performance, these devices were more error prone than the keyboard and joystick. In addition, performance improved with practice.

Clearly much work needs to be done to evaluate which types of input devices are optimal for older people, especially for those who have restrictions in hand function. It appears that devices such as mice and trackballs might not be appropriate for older adults or at least that they will require more practice to effectively use these types of devices. It may be that speech recognition devices will eliminate many of the problems (visual and movement) associated with manual input devices. In this regard Ogozalek and Praag (1986) found that although using a simulated listening typewriter as compared to a keyboard editor made no difference in performance of a composition task for both younger and older people, the voice input was strongly preferred by all participants.

34.5.3 Software Considerations

There has been very little research examining the impact of the design of the software interface on the performance of older computer users. Given that there are age-related changes in cognitive processes, such as working memory and selective attention, it is highly likely that interface style (e.g. function keys vs. menus) will have a significant influence on the performance of older adults. The limited data which are available support this conclusion.

Joyce (1990) evaluated the ability of older people to learn a word-processing program as a function of interface style. The participants interacted with the program using one of three interface styles: on-screen menu, functions keys, and pull-down menus. She found that people using the pull-down menus performed better on the word processing tasks. Specifically, they performed the tasks more quickly and made fewer errors. They also executed a greater number of successful editorial changes. Joyce hypothesized that the pull down-menu reduced the memory demands of the task as the users did not have to remember editing procedures. Although the on-screen menu provided memory cues, the names of the menu items were not reflective of menu contents, thus requiring the user to remember which items were contained in which menu. The names of the pull-down menus were indicative of menu contents.

Egan and Gomez (1985) found that a display editor was less difficult for older adults that a line editor. The line editor was command based and required the user to remember command language and produce complicated command syntax. Using the display editor, changes were made by positioning a cursor at the location of change and using labeled function keys rather than a command language. Thus there were fewer memory demands associated with the display editor. Further, the display editor was less complex than the line editor and in accordance with age-complexity hypothesis we would anticipate smaller age effects (Cerella, Poon, and Williams, 1980).

In our study of e-mail, we found that study participants sometimes had difficulty remembering the address name required to access a particular application. We also had to provide on-screen reminders of basic commands (e.g. Press enter after entering the address) even though the system was simple and there were no complex command procedures. Similarly, in our research on text-editing, we found that the older participants had more difficulty remembering editing procedures than younger adults.

Charness et al. (1992) examined the differential effect of a keystroke-based command, menu, and menu+icon interface on word processing skill acquisition among a sample of younger and older adults. They found that the menu and the menu+icon interface yielded better performance for all participants. The menu conditions provided more environmental support and was associated with fewer memory demands.

Consistent with the cognitive aging literatures, these results suggest that systems which place minimal demands on working memory would be suitable for older people. In addition, the should be minimal demands placed on spatial abilities. In this regard, interface styles such as windows should prove beneficial. However, while windowing systems and icons may reduce the demands on memory they may still be problematic for older adults as window systems are spatially organized and it is sometimes easy to get lost within a windows environment. Also, windows may initially increase cognitive demands as users are required to learn window operations. Further, it may be hard for older people to clearly distinguish among icons as they are typically small in size, and unless they are labeled and unambiguous they will not serve to memory demands.

There are a number of interface issues which need to be investigated. At the present time we can only offer general guidelines with respect to designing interfaces to accommodate the needs of older users. Table 3 presents a summary of these guidelines. Clearly, there is an abundance of research which needs to be carried out within this area. For a overview of general ergonomic guidelines for older adults see Charness and Bosman (1990).

Table 3. Summary of interface design guidelines for older adults.

1. Maximize the contrast between characters and screen background.
2. Minimize screen glare.
3. Avoid small targets and characters which are small in size (fonts <12).
4. Minimize irrelevant screen information.
5. Present screen information in consistent locations (e.g. error messages).
6. Adhere to principles of perceptual organization (e.g. grouping).
7. Highlight important screen information.
8. Avoid color discriminations among colors of the same hue or in the blue-green range.
9. Clearly label keys.
10. Maximize size of icons.
11. Use icons which are easily discriminated, meaningful and label icons if possible.
12. Provide sufficient practice on the use of input devices such as a mouse or trackball.
13. Provide sufficient practice on window operations.
14. Minimize demands on spatial memory.
15. Provide information on screen location.
16. Minimize demands on working memory.
17. Avoid complex command languages.
18. Use operating procedures which are consistent within and across applications.
19. Provide easy to use on-line aiding and support documentation.

34.6 Conclusions

There are many areas where older people are likely to interact with computer technology including the workplace, the home, service and health care settings. The current data indicate that older adults are generally receptive to using this type of technology but often have more difficulty than younger people acquiring computer skills and using current computer systems. This presents a challenge for human factors engineers and system designers. We need to understand the source of age performance differences so that we can design systems which are usable by this population.

Although research in this area has grown, there are many unanswered questions. Currently, we are unable to generate design guidelines which accommodate the needs of older adults. For example, issues of screen design, input devices, and interface style, are largely unexplored and our knowledge within these areas is limited. In order to maximize the potential benefits of computer technology for the older population and optimize the interactions of older people with these types of systems, older people must be perceived as active users of technology and included in system design and evaluation efforts. They will not only serve to benefit older adults but all potential users of computer systems.

34.7 References

Belbin, E., and Belbin, R.M. (1972). *Problems in adult retraining*. London: Heinman Pub. Co.

Brickfield, C.F. (1984). Attitudes and perceptions of older people toward technology. In P.K. Robinson and J.E. Birren (Eds.), *Aging and Technological Advances* (pp, 31-38). New York: Plenum Press.

Camisa, J.M. and Schmidt, M.J. (1984). Performance fatigue and stress for older VDT users. In E. Grandjean (Ed.), *Ergonomics and Health in Modern Offices* (pp. 270-275). London: Taylor and Francis.

Caplan, L.J., and Schooler, C. (1990). The effects of analogical training models and age on problem-solving in a new domain. *Experimental Aging Research, 16*, 151-154.

Casali, S.P. (1992). Cursor control use by persons with physical disabilities: implications for hardware and software design. Proceedings of the 36th Annual Meeting of the Human Factors Society, Atlanta, GA., pp. 311-315.

Casali, S.P., and Chase, J. (1993). The effects of physical attributes of computer interface design on novice and experienced performance of users with physical disabilities. Proceedings of the 37th Annual Meeting of Human Factors and Ergonomics Society, Seattle, WA., 849-853.

Charness, N. (1989). Age and expertise: Responding to Talland's challenge. In L.W. Poon, D.C. Rubin, and B.A. Wilson (Eds.) *Everyday cognition in adulthood and later life* (pp.437-456). Cambridge: Cambridge University Press.

Charness, N., and Bosman, E. (1990). Human factors and design for older adults. In J.E. Birren and K. W. Schaie (Eds.) *Handbook of the Psychology of Aging (3rd Ed.)* (pp. 446-464). New York: Academic Press.

Charness, N., Schumann, C.E., and Boritz, G.A. (1992). Training older adults in word processing: Effects of age, training technique and computer anxiety. *International Journal of Aging and Technology*, *5*, 79-106.

Charness, N., Bosman, E.A., and Elliot, R.G. (1995). Senior friendly input devices: Is the pen mightier than the mouse? Paper presented at the 103 Annual Convention of the American Psychological Association. New York, New York, August.

Charness, N., Kelley, C., and Bosman, E. (In press). Cognitive theory and word processing training: When prediction fails. In W.A. Rodgers, A.D. Fisk, and N. Walker (Eds.), *Aging and skilled performance: Advances in theory and applications*, Hillsdale, N.J.: Erlbaum.

Chute, D.L., and Bliss, M.E. (1994). ProsthesisWare: Concepts and caveats for microcomputer-based aids to everyday living. *Experimental Aging Research, 20*, 229-238.

Collins, S.C., Bhatti, J.Z., Dexter, S.L., and Rabbit, P.M.A. (1993). Elderly people in a new world: Attitudes to advanced communication technologies. In H. Bouma and J.A.M. Graafmans (Eds.), *Gerontechnology, Amsterdam*, ISO Press, pp, 277-282.

Craik, F.I.M. and Simon, E. (1980). Age differences in memory: The roles of attention and depth of processing. In L.W. Poon, J. L. Fozard, L.S. Cermack, D. Arenberg, and L.W. Thompson (Eds.), *New directions in memory and aging: Proceedings of the George a. Talland Memorial Conference*. Hillsdale New Jersey: Lawrence Erlbaum.

Czaja, S.J., Hammond, K., and Joyce, J.B. (1989). word processing training for older adults. Final report submitted to the National Institute on Aging (Grant # 5 R4 AGO4647-03).

Czaja, S. J., Hammond, K., Blascovich, J.J., and Swede, H. (1989). Age related differences in learning to use a text-editing system. *Behavior and Information Technology*, *8*, 309-319.

Czaja, S.J., Guerrier, J., Nair, S.N., Landauer, T.K. (1993). Computer communication as an aid to independence for older adults. *Behavior and Information Technology*, *12*, 197-207.

Czaja, S.J., and Sharit, J. (1993a). Stress reactions to computer-interactive tasks as a function of task structure and individual differences. *International Journal of Human-Computer Interaction*, *5*, 1-22.

Czaja, S.J., and Sharit, J. (1993b). Age differences in the performance of computer-based work. *Psychology and Aging*, *1*, 1-9.

Czaja, S.J. (in press). The implications of computer technology for older adults. In W.A. Rodgers, A.D. Fisk, and N. Walker (Eds.), *Aging and skilled performance: Advances in theory and applications*, Hillsdale, N.J.: Erlbaum.

Danowski, J.A., and Sacks, W. (1980). Computer communication and the elderly. *Experimental Aging Research*, *6*, 125-135.

Dawson, J.A., Hendershot, G., and Fulton, J., (1987). Aging in the eighties: Functional limitations of individuals aged 65 years and older. National Center for Health Statistics Advance Data 1987; 133: 1-11.

Dyck, J.L., and Smither, J.A. (1994). Age differences in computer anxiety: the role of computer experience, gender and education. *Journal of Educational Computing Research, 10*, 239-248.

Edwards and Engelhart, K.G. (1989). Microprocessor-based innovations and older individuals: AARP survey results and their implications for service robotics. *International Journal of Technology and Aging, 2*, 6-41.

Egan, D.E., and Gomez, L.M. (1985). Assaying, isolating, and accommodating individual differences in learning a complex skill. *Individual Differences in Cognition, 2*, 174-217.

Eilers, M.L. (1989). Older adults and computer education: Not to have the world a closed door. *International Journal of Technology and Aging, 2*, 56-76.

Elias, P.K., Elias, M.F., Robbins, M.A., and Gage, P. (1987). Acquisition of word-processing skills by younger, middle-aged, and older adults. *Psychology and Aging, 2*, 340-348.

Ellis, L.B.M., Joo, H., and Gross, C.R. (1991). Use of a computer-based health risk appraisal by older adults. *Journal of Family Practice, 33*, 390-394.

Furlong, M.S. (1989). An electronic community for older adults: The SeniorNet network. *Journal of Communication, 39*, 145-153.

Garfein, A.J., Schaie, K.W., and Willis, S.L. (1988). Microcomputer proficiency in later-middle-aged adults and older adults: Teaching old dogs new tricks. *Social Behavior, 3*, 131-148.

Gitlin, L.N. (1995). Why older people accept or reject assistive technology. *Generations, 19*, 41-46.

Gist, M., Rosen, B., and Schwoerer, C. (1988). The influence of training method and trainee age on the acquisition of computer skills. *Personnel Psychology, 41*, 255-265.

Hartley, A.A., Hartley, J.T., and Johnson, S.A. (1984). The older adult as a computer user. In P.K. Robinson, J. Livingston, and J.E. Birren (Eds.), *Aging and Technological Advances*, New York: Plenum Press, 347-348.

Hedman, L. and Briem, V. (1984). Focusing accuracy of VDT operators as a function of age and task. In E. GRANDJEAN (Ed.), *Ergonomics and Health in Modern Offices* (pp. 280-284). London: Taylor and Francis.

Hockey, G.R., Briner, R.B., Tattersell, A.J., and Wietoff, M. (1989). Assessing the impact of computer workload on operator stress: The role of system controllability. *Ergonomics, 32,*, 1401-1418.

Jay, G.M., and Willis, S.L. (1992). Influence of direct computer experience on older adults attitudes towards computers. *Journal of Gerontology: Psychological Sciences, 47*, 250-257.

Joyce, B.J. (1989). Identifying differences in learning to use a text-editor: the role of menu structure and learner characteristics. Master's thesis submitted to the State University of New York at Buffalo.

Kelley, C.L. and Charness, N. (1995). Issues in training older adults to use computers. *Behavior and Information Technology, 14*, 107-120.

Kosnik, W., Winslow,L., Kline, D., Rasinski, K., and Sekuler, R. (1988). Visual changes in daily life throughout adulthood. *Journal of Gerontology: Psychological Sciences, 43*, 63-70.

Krauss, I.K., and Hoyer, W.J. (1985). Technology and the older person: Age, sex, and experience as moderators of attitudes towards computers. In P.K. Robinson, J. Livingston and J.E., Birren (Eds.), *Aging and technological advances* (pp. 349-350). New York: Plenum.

Leirer, V.O., Morrow, D.G., Tanke, E.D., and Pariante, G.M. (1991). Elder's nonadherence: Its assessment and medication reminding by voice mail. *The Gerontologist, 31,* 515-520.

Morell, R.W., Park, D.C., and Poon, L.W. (1989). Quality of instructions on prescription drug labels: Effects on memory and comprehension in young and old adults. *The Gerontologist, 29*, 345-354.

Morell, R.W., Park, D.C., Mayhorn, C.B., and Echt, K.V. (1995). Older adults and electronic communication networks: Learning to use ELDERCOMM. Paper presented at the 103 Annual Convention of the American Psychological Association. New York, New York, August.

Morell, R.W. and Echt, K.V. (In press). Instructional design for older computer users. In W.A. Rodgers, A.D. Fisk, and N. Walker, (Eds.), *Aging and skilled performance: Advances in theory and application*, Hillsdale, N.J.: Erlbaum.

Nair, S. (1989). A capability-demand analysis of grocery shopping problems encountered by older adults. a thesis submitted to the Department of Industrial Engineering, State University of New York at Buffalo in partial fulfillment for the requirement for master of Science.

Neilsen, J. (1993). *Useability engineering*. New York: Academic Press.

Neilsen, J., and Schafer, L. (1993). Sound effects as an interface element for older users. *Behavior and Information Technology, 12*, 208-216.

Ogozalek, V.Z., and Praag, J.V. (1986). Comparison of elderly and younger users on keyboard and voice input computer-based composition tasks. *Proc. CHI 86 Human Factors in Computing Systems* (Boston, April, 1986). New York: ACM, pp. 205-211.

Park, D.C. (1992). Applied cognitive aging research. In F.I.M. Craik and T.A. Salthouse (Eds.), *The handbook of aging and cognition* (pp. 449-494). Hillsdale NJ: Lawrence Erlbaum Associates.

Plude, D.J. and Hoyer, W.J. (1985). Attention and performance: identifying and localizing age deficits. In N. Charness (Ed.), *Aging and human performance* (pp. 47-99). New York: John Wiley.

Rabbit, P.A. (1965). An age decrement in the ability to ignore irrelevant information. *Journal of Gerontology, 20*, 233-238.

Rogers, W.A., and Fisk, D. (1991). Age-related differences in the maintenance and modification of automatic processes: Arithmetic stroop interference. *Human Factors, 33*, 45-56.

Rodgers, W.A., Cabrera, E.F., Jamieson, B.A., and Rousseau, G.K. (1995) Automatic teller machines and older adults: Usage patterns and training needs. Paper presented at the 103 Annual Convention of the American Psychological Association. New York, New York, August.

Salthouse, T.A. (1984). Effects of age and skill in typing. *Journal of Experimental Aging Psychology: General, 113*, 345-371.

Salthouse, T.A. (1985). Speed of behavior and its implication for cognition. In J.E. Birren and K.W. Schaie (Eds.), *Handbook of psychology of aging* (pp. 400-426). New York: Van Nostrand Reinhold.

Salthouse, T.A. (1993). Speed and knowledge as determinants of adult age differences in verbal tasks. *Journal of Gerontology, 48*, 29-36.

SeniorNet (1995). Welcome to SeniorNet. Introductory brochure.

Smither, J.A. (1993). Short term memory demands in processing synthetic speech by old and young adults. *Behavior and Information Technology, 12*, 330-335.

Sterns, H.L., and Doverspike, D. (1989) Aging and the training and learning process. In I. Goldstein and associates (Eds.), *Training and development in organizations* (pp. 299 -332). San Francisco: Jossey-Bass Publishers.

Schwartz, L.K., and Plude, D., (1995). Compact disk-interactive memory training with the elderly. Paper presented at the 103 Annual Convention of the American Psychological Association. New York, New York, August.

Tanke, E.D. and Leirer, V.O. (1993). Use of automated telephone reminders to increase elderly patients adherence to tuberculosis medication appointments. Proceedings of the Human Factors and Ergonomics Society 37th Annual Meeting, Seattle, WA., pp. 193-196.

United States Senate (1991), *Aging America: Trends and Projections*, U.S. Senate Subcommittee on Aging, American Association of Retired Persons, Federal Council on Aging, and U.S. Administration on Aging, DHHS Publ. No. (FcoA)91-28001, U.S. Department of Health and Human Services.

Welford, A.T. (1985). Changes of performance with age: An overview. In N. Charness (Ed.), *Aging and Human Performance* (pp. 333-365). New York: John Wiley and Sons.

Willis, S.L. (1987). Cognitive training and everyday competence. In K.W. Schaie and C. Eisdorfer (Eds.), *Annual review of gerontology and geriatrics* (pp. 159-188). New York: Springer Pub. Co.

Willis, S.L. (1989). Improvement with cognitive training: Which old dogs learn what tricks? In L.W. Poon, D.C. Rubin, B.A. Wilson (Eds.) *Everyday cognition in adulthood and late life* (pp. 545- 572). Cambridge, Mass.: Cambridge University Press.

Witte, K.L. (1975). Paired-associate learning in young and elderly adults as related to presentation. *Psychological Bulletin, 82*, 975-985.

Zandri E., and Charness, a. (1989). Training older and younger adults to use software. *Educational Gerontology, 15*, 615-631.

Handbook of Human-Computer Interaction
Second, completely revised edition
M. Helander, T.K. Landauer, P. Prabhu (eds.)

Chapter 35

Human Computer Interfaces for People with Disabilities

Alan F. Newell and Peter Gregor
University of Dundee
Dundee, Scotland

35.1 Summary

This chapter is concerned with the design of human computer interfaces for people with disabilities, but, before any reader decides whether or not to investigate this chapter further, we would like them to contemplate why they have decided to turn to this particular chapter, or why they have stopped at it during their browse through the book. The main purpose of this chapter is not to tell the reader exactly how to cope with the peculiar demands of people with disabilities, but to examine the question of why human computer interface engineers should seriously consider the problems posed by people with disabilities. We believe that this will lead to a more widespread understanding of the true nature and scope of human computer interface engineering in general. This will be followed by some pointers which we hope will assist the readers to improve their methodologies and to gain more understanding of the particular problems presented by people with disabilities.

We wish to consider a number of questions:

- Why should a book on HCI contain one chapter concerned with people with disabilities ?
- Why do HCI engineers consider people with disabilities and are these appropriate and valid reasons ?
- What are the particular advantages for researchers, teachers and industrialists to considering interfaces for people with disabilities ?
- What are the important research and development methodologies and criteria which should be used when designing for people with disabilities ?

35.2 Why Should a Book on HCI Contain One Chapter Concerned with People with Disabilities ?

Readers may consider that it is perfectly in order for a book on HCI to contain one chapter concerned with people with disabilities; the underlying point of this particular question, however, is: "Why should a book on HCI contain *one (and only one)* chapter concerned with people with disabilities?" It is important to ask this question because this particular statistic could be a reflection of the overall importance with which practitioner within this field view people with disabilities. The number of books on HCI is very large indeed, but very few are concerned with people with disabilities. Also, within text books on HCI, it is very unusual to find references to the problems posed by people with disabilities. This characteristic of the field can be seen in HCI conferences over a number of years. In the 1986 CHI, Shneiderman, commented that " we should be aware of subtle design decisions that make usage more difficult for people with physical and mental difficulties ... and not create a situation where the disadvantaged become more disadvantaged". There was little evidence in future conferences, however, that his message had been taken seriously, and HCI conferences continued to contain very few, if any, papers which concerned this issue. CHI has very marginally improved since Newell gave his keynote address "CHI for everyone" in 1993, In 1995 Interact (Lillehammer, Norway - June 25-29, 1995) the position had changed in an interesting way. Some papers in the scientific section may have been relevant to users with disabilities, but in only two cases (one being the last paper on the last day) had the authors actually mentioned such users in their titles. There were, however, two workshops "Human Computer Interaction and Disability" and "Usability in assistive enabling and rehabilitation technologies" and a Tutorial Session "Access to Graphical User Interface for Blind Users". Thus on the basis of this single sample, efforts are being made to offer HCI developers educational opportunities to learn about the problems of people with disabilities; this subject, however, does not yet make any significant impact on the general scientific focus of HCI research.

If we examine population statistics, this lack of interest in issues of this nature is somewhat surprising. It is not easy to obtain an exact definition of disabilities, (this problem will be addressed later in the chapter), but commonly accepted figures are that, in the "developed world", between 10% and 20% of the population have disabilities.

More detailed estimates include:

- 1 in 10 of the population have a significant hearing impairment and 1 in 125 are deaf.
- 1 in 100 of the population have visual disabilities, 1 in 475 are legally blind and 1 in 2000 totally blind.
- 1 in 250 people are wheelchair users with over 300,000 in the USA being under 44 years old (there are 10,000 serious spinal injuries per year in the USA alone).
- There are 6 million mentally retarded people in the USA with 2 million in institutions.
- It has been estimated that 20% of the population have difficulty in performing one or more basic physical activities with 7.5% being unable to walk, lift, hear, or read, alone or only with help. 14% of these are aged between 16 and 64 years of age.
- In the UK 800,000 are unable to express their needs in a way that their nearest and dearest can understand , and 1.7 Million struggle to communicate

There is, however, an even wider population which is affected by disabilities. As a rule of thumb, every person has at least three other important people in their lives with whom they interact regularly. Thus the population affected directly by disability is at least a factor of three greater than the numbers quoted above. There is also a direct effect on the working economy, with disability affecting the working lives of some 12% of the population and 5% being prevented from working entirely, due to their disabilities.

It is a sobering thought that, within the next year, almost one in 500 of the readers of this chapter will suffer a stroke which will render them partially paralysed, and a third of those will experience some degree of speech, language or cognitive impairment caused by that stroke.

What is even more concerning is demographic trends. Medical science may be curing more people of disease, but it is also ensuring that many more people stay alive with greater and greater levels of disability and for longer and longer periods. By the year 2000, 10% of the population of the developed world will be over the age of 80 (Figure 1).

Ageing brings with it multiple physical and sensory disabilities, and an even more worrying and distressing statistic is that one in four of those over 80 suffer from dementia, the typical symptoms of which include confusion, disorientation, forgetfulness and can include profound personality changes. The incidence of dementia amongst younger groups is also growing.

Fortunately, society seems to be more aware of the problems of people with disabilities than the HCI community, and, for example the Americans with Disabilities Act of July 1992 has two "Titles":

Title One stated that employers must reasonably accommodate the disabilities of employees and applicants, and it became illegal for companies employing more than twenty four workers to discriminate against employees with disabilities.

Figure 1. "By the year 2000, 10% of the population of the developed world will be over 80"

Title Two stated that all government facilities, services and communications should be accessible to individuals with disabilities.

Many other countries have, or are developing, similar legislation; there is some evidence that the research funding organisations are beginning to respond to this understanding. For example, within the European Union, a specially funded research program into the use to Technology for the Elderly and Disabled (TIDE) was instituted in 1993, and the 1995 UK Technology Foresight programme commented that "the ageing populations in the developed world and the consequent increase in chronic disease and disability will have a major impact on health care needs" and that an important growth area was "technologies for sustaining reasonable quality of life for the elderly and infirm, and the use of "information and communication systems ... to support ... medical practice."

Thus people who have to interact with machines in the future will include

- A rapidly growing number of aged people, and
- A growing number of people with disabilities, some of whom will have multiple disabilities.
- These people with have increasing expectations of quality of life, and
- They will have to be cared for in a cost-effective way as society will have to cope with fewer economically active people.
- The increasing perception in some countries that people should be cared for in the community, rather than in special institutions, will increase the need for effective and efficient support systems.
- The problems of providing for people with disabilities is likely to be exacerbated by Government regulations which respond to the increased voting power of this group of people and their immediate carers.

These figures would seem to show that human computer interfaces which are designed for, or at least accommodate, people with disabilities are of substantially greater importance than the field itself seems to realise, and that practitioners in the field should be generating more and more serious education, research and development with this particular focus.

Figure 2. "Very few engineers show an interest in disability, even though they themselves are growing older".

35.3 Why do HCI Engineers Consider People with Disabilities and are these Appropriate and Valid Reasons ? Is HCI for People with Disabilities a Social Service or an Engineering Discipline ?

Having been in the field for a number of the years, the authors have observed that there are a range of reasons why engineers show an interest in people with disabilities. Our perception, however, is that this group tend to be mainstream engineers, some of whom formally move the focus of their research and/or development activity to rehabilitation engineering. Very few main-stream human computer interaction researchers and designers have made this transition even though they themselves are growing older (Figure 2).

A major problem of this lack of interest may be the perceptions of the field. It is clear that Human Computer Interface Engineering is:

- Of high theoretical and practical value
- Obviously "high tech" and contains leading edge research,
- Is important and an academically respectable discipline.

In contrast, designing systems to be used by people with disabilities is often perceived as:

- Having little or no intellectual challenge,
- Being a charitable rather than a professional activity,
- Being, at the most, of a fringe interest to researchers,
- Requiring individualised designs, thus
- Involving small unprofitable markets,
- Needing simple, low cost solutions (usually made of wood!), and
- Being dominated by home-made systems.

The contrast could not be greater, and although many University Departments and Research Laboratories have small scale projects which address these issues, they rarely form a significant or important part of the portfolio of the group. Again there are exceptions such as our own MicroCentre group in Dundee, Rick Foulds' group in Delaware, the Hugh Macmillan Centre/University of Toronto Group and the TRACE Centre at the University of Wisconsin.

The tendency thus seems to be that people with disabilities are included in research portfolios because of a randomly generated interest (one of the authors of this paper became interested this field for exactly such a reason in 1968). Other factors include conscience, a feeling of duty, or often a chance life event, a friend or relative who acquires a disability, or a chance encounter with a therapist who has an unresolved problem with a patient. Rarely is the motivation the same as those for joining main-stream science, which include academic curiosity, career prospects, prestige, and money.

The danger of work in this area being considered a fringe interest are many: these include lack of quality control and commitment, disappointed users, and a deleterious effect on the commercial sector.

Firstly such activity often does not have the same quality control as mainstream work. It is not unusual to listen to conference presentations on systems developed for people with disabilities where the author has only a very skimpy knowledge of the actual problem he or she is tackling and no idea of the prior art in the field. Also the department or company often has much less long term commitment to such projects and this not only affects their quality but also their viability (a company may invest in a product because the MD has a relative who has a disability, but such a product may not survive a change in MD).

Such work also generates an ethical problem, particularly in the education sector, which can be underestimated. Often such projects are generated by a link with a member of staff and a therapist who has a problem with a particular client. The University lecturer thus sets this as a student project (again with little background knowledge to support the students). In the early period of the project, the client has his or her hopes raised by the enthusiastic student, and cannot understand why the student suddenly loses interest (this coincides with examinations) and there is no subsequent contact. There are many therapists and their clients who have been sadly disappointed by the "help" they have been offered in this way.

A further problem caused by such activity is the effect on the commercial market. The therapist seems to be getting the equipment very cheaply, which gives the impression that such equipment can be manufactured at a very low cost. This puts the commercial sector at risk, and the commercial sector has a much greater chance of providing a usable and supported system in the long term.

The lack of interest in this field, might appear odd when we examine the statistics given in the first section of this chapter, and certain "disability" markets have proved very lucrative - spectacles and hearing aids being the most obvious. Also the companies who market, for example, wheelchairs or prosthetic devices such as artificial limbs, do not perform noticeably worse than firms in other market sectors.

In terms of the intellectual challenge posed by the field, one would have thought it likely to be more difficult to design an effective interface for a user with an impairment than one for a completely able-bodied user. This is clearly the case for physical and sensory difficulties, and the problems posed by users with intellectual and language dysfunction are even more challenging. Later sections of this chapter will illustrate how important these considerations can be to the general field of human computer interface design.

Designing for people with disabilities is not only intellectually challenging, and provides scope for a greater range of inventiveness than many other areas of human computer interaction; it is also very rewarding, as the achievements can be much greater and are obviously worthwhile. In addition the market is not small: it is significant and rapidly growing market, where leading-edge technology has an important part to play.

35.4 What are the Particular Advantages for Researchers, Teachers and Industrialists of Considering Interfaces for People with Disabilities ?

The actual size of the market segment provided by people with disabilities is reason enough for researchers, teachers and industrialists to become involved in the development of equipment for them. The other major justification, however, is that such an involvement will be beneficial to the field in general.

The designers of human machine interfaces have to be far more inventive and original when they are trying to cope in an effective and efficient manner with the problems presented by the interfaces for people with disabilities. Indeed this has led to the phenomenon of a number of very successful designs, initially targeted at people with disabilities, providing major advantages for everyone. This has appeared in American literature as the "curb-cut" phenomenon. The increasing awareness of the problems presented by people in wheelchairs encouraged the insertion of curb-cuts in the sidewalks of American cities, but it soon became clear that these curb-cuts were of great benefit to a much wider range of people including people with prams, carts, or even those with luggage on wheels.

There are other examples of where this has happened. The cassette tape recorder was originally designed because blind people could not cope with the reel-to-reel tape recorders on which they had to play their talking books. Many engineers at the time believed this design could only be targeted at blind users, because the sound quality was inferior and thus able-bodied people would not be attracted by the system. This was an early example of engineers not realising that a good human interface can outweigh other disadvantages. However, it is possible that, were it not for an inventive designer having to tackle the problem of providing talking books for the blind, we might still be threading reel-to-reel tape recorders! There are many other examples of ubiquitous inventions having been first designed for people with disabilities: these include the remote control on televisions (originally developed for those with mobility impairment), the carpenter's mitre block (for the blind), the ball point pen (for people with dysfunctioning hands) and there is even a story, which the authors have not been able to substantiate, that the first typewriter was designed for a blind Countess. Thus it can be seen that there are many examples from history where a very successful and widely used product has started life as what was apparently a very specialised device for what was perceived to be a very limited market.

Not only are human computer interface designers in danger of ignoring a substantial market segment, but also the designs which we produce for that market segment can be much more widely useful than the inventors originally may have intended.

35.5 Who and What at are "People with Disabilities" Anyway ?

In the foregoing sections of this chapter, the assumption has been made that there are two quite distinct groups of people, those with disabilities and those without. This binary division of society was useful as an introduction and for the purposes of the arguments presented in those sections, but, in general, it is deeply flawed.

35.5.1 The Average User Myth

The vast majority of human interfaces seem to have been designed on the basis of an "average user" with little or no account being taken of the range of abilities which are presented by the human race. Some of the more extreme examples (the UNIX operating system for computers being one, most video tapes recorders another) are clearly designed on the assumption that the user is a 25 year old white Anglo-Saxon male computer science major who is besotted by technology, and much more interested in what the system can do than what he actually needs the system for. The clothing analogy would be for clothing manufactures to make only tee shirts for a 42 inch chest with outrageous sexist motifs and jeans which fit a six foot tall man with a 34 inch waist.

Such manufacturers would also provide a range of 256 fastenings to the fly, but the customer would have to read page 227 of a 300 page booklet to find out how to close the arrangement which was usually provided, and another 60 page booklet if he wanted to open it again! It is clear that such a manufacturer would be targeting a very specialised audience, but many software houses and human computer interaction laboratories do not appreciate the narrowness of the vision they have of the human race.

Not only does the human race include females, people from different cultural backgrounds, but also young children and elderly people and, as has been explained above, many of these people will have permanent disabilities. In addition most, if not all will have temporary disabilities from time to time. Rather than considering the "average" human being, and deviations from this, the authors prefer to consider human beings as represented on a multi-dimensional space, each axis of which represents a particular characteristic. Thus there will be many axes devoted to physical characteristics (size, shape, strength, dexterity of vari-

ous limbs) axes devoted to sensory abilities (resolution, field of view, colour perception, auditory abilities) and axes devoted to intellectual and emotional functionality. Clearly this space is a highly dimensional one, and each individual at any point in time can be plotted as a particular point in such a space. If we view human beings in this light, it is clear that there is a continuum along the vast majority of these dimensions which ranges from the weakest to the strongest, the cleverest to the most intellectually challenged. Where the division between able-bodied and disabled is on any particular dimension is clearly arbitrary - how much more arbitrary is the classification of the whole person. Some well known athletes may be at an intellectual disadvantage but, unless this is severe, we do not classify them as disabled, nor do we describe the university professor who walks with a stick and has poor eyesight as a disabled person. But someone who combined these two dysfunctional characteristics may have difficulty in not being so classified. If we want our human computer interfaces to be as useful as possible, they should be appropriate for as large a hypervolume as possible within this space, and, in order to increase that hypervolume, the designers ought to be aware of the effects of being in different parts of the many different axes which exist in the hyperspace of human abilities.
Each individual person can thus be thought to be in a particular point in such a space at a particular moment in time. It is also important to realise, however, that people move about this space. It is obvious that people's abilities undergo gross changes as they proceed from being children through adult-hood and old age, but there can be just as major changes over a much shorter timescale. Not only can people be temporarily disabled by accident or illness, but also stress, work load, lack of sleep, the types of food recently ingested, or hypoglycaemia due to not having eaten recently, can all cause major and rapid change in abilities. Cognitive ability particularly can change very rapidly and may not be too noticeable even to the person themselves. Each individual thus moves around the hyperspace which represents their abilities from hour to hour if not from minute to minute, as well as the more gradual changes with time scales of many years.

A further characteristic which affects the interaction of human beings with the outside world is the effect of environment. Many systems have been designed on the basis that they will only be used by human beings within an office environment. In contrast, a typical day of many possible users will include a significant time spent in bed, eating, walking, relaxing, indulging in sporting activities, and, if we are lucky, lounging on a beach or in a swimming pool. If we are to provide systems that are more generally useful, designers should take this factor into account.

A recent example of how many designers did not anticipate the effects of an increasing range of environments is the evolution of the "lap-top" computer. The name even implies that they should be usable on a person's lap, but the early versions were marketed with a standard mouse, which required a desk top to use.

"Using the Internet to find the next black run!"

These systems may have been portable, but they were not usable on the lap. It is interesting that the need for a true "lap top" has led to the re-invention and refinement of the roller ball, which had been superseded by the mouse. The roller ball however, has some significant advantages compared with mouse, not the least being that people with manipulative skills found roller balls easier to use. In this case increased environmental constraints arguably have provided improved the human computer interface design, or, at the very least, a wider range of available human computer interfaces. There is also little evidence that "palm tops" have been designed to be used in the palm, although they will quite happily sit there!

Just as peoples' abilities change with time, so do environmental conditions. Most computer systems now operate in a greater range of environmental situations

Figure 3. "The soldier in the battlefield is severely disabled by the environment".

than the first mainframes, which required much better conditions than the humans who operated them. Human interface design, however, still tends to assume that environmental conditions will always be good, and they persist in this view even in those situations where it is vital that the human machine communication should continue to operate despite the environment becoming hostile. For example, in an emergency caused by fire or malfunction of plant, the room in which the interface has to be operated may have become full of smoke, very noisy and may provide substantially increasing stress on the operator. The interface, however, may not have been designed to be operated by a deaf, visually impaired operator whose intellectual functions have been severely reduced.

Some of the most extreme examples of people being disabled by their environment are soldiers on a battlefield, (Figure 3) and underwater divers. Soldiers can be blinded by gunsmoke, deafened by the noises of battle, have impaired dexterity due to safety suits, will probably have impaired mobility because of the terrain, and will be in fear of their lives, leading to some reduction in cognitive ability. Divers will be even more seriously visually and auditory impaired. Their mobility and manual dexterity will be restricted by their diving suits, they will often be disorientated by being in such a hostile environment, as well as being under stress leading to cognitive impairment. Should such people exhibit these handicaps in a normal office environment, they would probably be considered not fit for work. Designers, however, tend to assume that they are designing for fit human beings. The authors recently gave a workshop to designers within a space research organisation and asked for a description of their users. Initially we were told that the people who worked in space were excellent specimens of the human race and were all in the peak of physical and mental condition. After some questioning, particularly about the effects of being in space suits, both in terms of the restrictions they applied, and also the fatiguing effects of operating in such an environment for even relatively short periods of time, however, the designers realised that the human being for whom they were designing equipment had very serious disabilities, with very little visual and auditory abilities, poor dexterity and mobility, almost no strength, and rather stressed!

The effects of the operating environment on users are often underestimated by people who design and test human interfaces for equipment. It is little short of scandalous if the equipment is intended to be used in situations which are very different from the offices and laboratories in which the designers sit. Designers, however, ought also to take into account those environmental conditions which may arise due to the circumstances outside the users' control. Good design ought to be robust to changes of environment, as it should be to changes in the characteristics of the user. This chapter argues that both goals can be achieved by the same methodology. That is consideration of the effects of impairment on the human computer interface.

The parallel between able bodied people and the people with disabilities stretches further than just the effect of the environment. Every human being is constrained by their abilities: there are sounds nobody can hear, there is a maximum rate at which human beings can perform physical functions, there is a limit to the amount of visual information anyone can process. Thus all human computer interaction is subject to bandwidth limitations. People with disabilities are often disadvantaged solely by a decreased bandwidth between themselves and the machine. The problem posed to designers of equipment for people with disabilities is simply a more extreme one than that posed when designing for able-bodied users. The importance of this proposition is that addressing the problems of extremes can provide the impetus for better designs overall. We have already mentioned the cassette tape recorder, but this philosophy also applies when able-bodied users are working at the limits of their abilities. For example fighter pilots do not have sufficient input bandwidth to monitor as much about their planes, their position in space and their enemies as designers would like. Equally they do not have sufficient hands and operational speed to input data as quickly as would be desired. In this sense they are in the same position as person with a visual disability who can only see very large print and thus cannot see as much of the text as is desirable when using a word processor, or the person with a physical disability whose rate of production of text is slow because they cannot operate the keyboard very rapidly. It is thus appropriate to investigate methodologies which have been used successfully to improve the performance of a person with disabilities (or extra-ordinary person) in an ordinary environment, to see whether they can be utilised when an ordinary person operates in a high work load or high stress environment (or extra-ordinary environment).

The authors and their colleagues have been examining such parallels within particular situations: the flight deck of an aircraft, an air traffic control system, and a non-speaking secretary with a physical disability. They have been approaching the problems in two ways

(a) using prediction to improve the effectiveness of signals which are transmitted across the interface and

(b) using multi-modal interaction to increase the bandwidth of the interface.

There is a long and successful history of developing predictive systems to improve the efficiency with which people with physical disabilities can interact with computer systems, particularly word processors. Such techniques also have a place in high work load situations such as air traffic control and the flight deck.. Multi-modal interaction is a relatively novel technique in human computer interfaces, and is an attempt to take fuller advantage of the capabilities of human beings. Much traditional human machine interaction has involved rather more modes than are used in interaction with conventional computer systems. For example the motor car requires not only the use of the eyes and the hands, but also the feet; useful information is also provided (in particular of error states of the equipment) via the users' ears and nose. Some musical instruments, such as the pipe organ and the piano, are also examples of using more communication channels than simply the hands.

The conventional computer system actually implicitly assumes that the operator has multiple disabilities.

"The conventional computer system assumes that the operator has multiple disabilities".

Users of computer systems could be very successful despite having tunnel, and probably monochrome vision, being paralysed from the neck downwards (with no neck movement) and only having +/- 3 inches of horizontal movement in the lower arms. Such a user could also be gender free with no emotional responses and stone deaf for sounds other than a audible click. Some of the more exotic interfaces which are being marketed disable the operator even more than a traditional keyboards. Current speech interfaces may provide more individual entry codes than a standard keyboard, but they are also significantly less precise than a keyboard. An able bodied person using a speech interface is equivalent to a keyboard user having such severe disabilities that they are no longer able to accurately target each key. Equally the rate at which command words can be spoken is often closer to the keyboarding speed of people with physical disabilities than that of a competent typist. It is not without significance that the Dragon Dictate speech recognition system is provided with a predictive interface which has a very similar look and feel to the predictive word processor which was developed at the authors' laboratories to cope with the problems of keyboard users with physical disabilities.

In practice, speech recognition has been promised as the major breakthrough in interface technology which will occur "within the next five years" since 1960, but even now a substantial portion of the major users of speech recognition systems are people with disabilities. The only speech recognition/synthesis technology which has consistently reached its market projections has been speech synthesis systems for use with people with disabilities. These have been particularly successful in reading systems for the blind and for conversational systems for the speech impaired. The penetration of conventional markets, however, has been very patchy and has never lived up to the expectations of researchers and futurologists. In contrast more simple interface systems have been used very successfully by people with disabilities but have not transferred to conventional markets. People with disabilities have used their feet for input (in fact almost any part of their anatomy which is controllable) whereas even the simple foot-mouse has never been successfully marketed. Also monitoring and control by head position and eye gaze have been utilised successfully by rehabilitation engineers for many years, but have hitherto engendered little enthusiasm from mainstream designers.

Picture based and iconic interfaces have been more successful in mainstream applications, but they appeared in systems designed for people with disabilities many years before they became fashionable for standard systems. Because of the greater range of user characteristics, and also the greater fluctuation with time of the severity of the consequences of disabilities, rehabilitation engineers have also been very aware of the need to customise interfaces, and to provide adaptive interfaces for their clients. The research into customised and adaptable interfaces for users with disabilities again tended to precede that in more mainstream human computer interface engineering. In an attempt to reduce the handicaps caused by the disabilities of users, rehabilitation engineers have developed a much wider range of successful interface techniques than mainstream designers. Such technology, however, has rarely been transferred to the mainstream and when it has (such as the cassette tape recorder), the origins of the development within the community of people with disabilities have been forgotten.

There are some encouraging signs that the needs of people with disabilities are being taken into account in the mainstream. For example, the Internet, or World Wide Web, is yet another technology which is currently only accessible by a relatively narrowly defined group of users. This limitation in user coverage has been recognised, however, and the Computer Science and Telecommunication Board of the National Research Council in the USA has set up a workshop of experts in the field to consider research and development needed "Towards an Every-Citizen Interface to the National Information Infrastructure" (Washington D.C., August 1996). The report from this meeting will be used to advise government and the private sector in making decisions and on future funding and major initiatives. This will be one of the first occasions when a group has specifically come together to consider how everyone can have access to computer based information, and the report should be of great relevance to all human computer interface designers.

35.6 The Parallels and Advantages of Considering Users with Disabilities as Part of the Population of Users of Human Computer Interfaces

There is some moral obligation for engineers to try wherever possible to assist people who are less fortunate than themselves, but in addition the world of mainstream human computer interface engineering is losing out significantly by not considering users with disabilities as part of the population of users of human computer interfaces, for a number of reasons:

- Considering users with disabilities will increase market share,

- Demographic trends will increase the size of the specialised market of equipment for people with permanent disabilities,
- Extra-ordinary needs are only exaggerated ordinary needs,
- Most people have a mix of ordinary and extra-ordinary needs ,
- Many "able bodied" users will acquire temporary disabilities, either due to injury or illness, and would still wish to operate their equipment whilst they are in this condition,
- Environmental considerations handicap users in the same way as personal disability does,
- There is a direct parallel between the bandwidth limitations caused by disability and the need for more information transfer than the normal human computer bandwidth can carry.
- Similar techniques can often solve both problems alluded to above, and
- Rehabilitation engineers have developed a wider range of interfaces, and developed them much earlier than mainstream human computer interface designers. Lack of knowledge of these techniques is inhibiting innovation within mainstream HCI.
- Rehabilitation engineers have a much longer history of the practical use of customised design and adaptable and "intelligent" interfaces than main stream designers.

There is one final, but very important educational and/or procedural advantage of requiring human computer interface students and designers to consider the problems of users with disabilities. As we have said previously, it is difficult to persuade designers that the user population differs very much from themselves, and this leads to the interfaces which were described above as being designed by and for a twenty-five year old male computer scientist with an obsession with playing with software. If such a designer was told that his user population contained people with disabilities he would know that they were different from himself, and thus would be more inclined to actually consider what were the characteristics of the real user population. Thus, including users with "obvious disabilities" within the potential population may not lead to a system which can be operated by them, but at the very least it will ensure that the designer follows user-centred design principles by first considering the actual characteristics of the real users, and the real environments in which they will have to operate the equipment.

The research and development is also more challenging because it demands an even wider range of disciplines than mainstream human computer interface design. It needs input, not only from medicine and the therapeutic professions (speech and language, occupational therapy, mental health), but users are also much more likely to be affected by education, training and life experience than would be expected of the population who do not have significant disabilities. Human Computer Interface Engineering can suffer from poor communication between the various disciplines which it needs and the different motivation and mores of, for example, Engineering and Psychology. Bringing the "caring professions" into this group is essential if one is to consider design for people with disabilities, but this has to be done with great care if there is to be effective and efficient communication between the different disciplines. Again the lessons learned from communicating with the paramedical professions and from users with communication dysfunction will be invaluable to the mainstream designer.

35.7 Conclusions

Consideration of all users, including those with obvious disabilities, is central to good human interface engineering. It improves the practice of human interface research and development, and encourages a wider range of solutions to human interface problems. A consideration of users with greater needs also increases the scientific and technical challenge of providing effective and efficient user interfaces. Last, but not least, it adds to the excitement of the work, and makes one's work clearly worthwhile and socially valuable.

We strongly recommend this discipline to all mainstream human computer interface designers, and look forward to an increasing awareness within the human computer interaction literature of the needs and wants of all users.

35.8 Bibliography

35.8.1 Further reading

"Extra-Ordinary Human-Computer Interaction", edited by Alistair Edwards (Cambridge, 1995) is an excellent source of material and further references in the areas covered by this chapter.

35.8.2 Associated World Wide Web Sites

There are now a number of World Wide Web sites which deal with accessibility and disability HCI issues and research. Among these are:

MicroCentre, University of Dundee
`http://alpha.mic.dundee.ac.uk/acsd/research/`

TRACE Centre, University of Wisconsin:
`http://trace.wisc.edu`

CALL Centre, University of Edinburgh:

`http://call-centre.cogsci.ed.ac.uk/CallHome`

IRV, Netherlands:
`http://www.tno.nl/expert/inst/irv.html`

ASEL, University of Delaware:
`http://www.asel.udel.edu/`

35.8.3 Work Associated with the Authors

Newell A. F. (1986). Speech Communication Technology - Lessons from the Disabled, *Electronics & Power*, Sept.1986, pp.661-664. Reprinted *Journal of The British Society of Hearing Therapists*, No.8, Oct. 1987, pp.12-15.

Newell A F. (1987). How Can We Develop Better Communication Aids?. *Augmentative and Alternative Comm,* Vol.3, No.1, March 1987, pp.36-40.

Alm, N. Newell, A. F. and Arnott J. L. (1989). Revolutionary communication system to aid non-speakers. *Speech Therapy In Practice*, 4(7), Mar. 1989, pp. vii-viii.

Newell A. F. (1989). PAL and CHAT: human interfaces for extraordinary situations. In Computing *Technologies, New Directions and Applications* by P. Salenieks (Ed.) (Ellis Horwood, Chichester, 1989 pp. 103-127.

Newell, A. F. and Booth L. (1990). The development of the predictive adaptive lexicon and its use by dyslexics. In *Proc. of the British Dyslexia Association Conf. Advances in Computer Applications for Dyslexics*, Hull, Aug.1990.

Wright, A. G. and Newell A. F. (1991). Computer help for poor spellers. *British Journal of Educational Technology*, 22(2), May 1991, pp. 146-148.

Waller, A. Broumley, L. Newell A. F. and Alm N. (1991). Predictive retrieval of conversational narratives in an augmentative communication system. In *Proc. of the 14th Annual Conference of the Rehabilitation Engineers Society of North America (*RESNA), Kansas City, MO, USA, 1991.

Murray, I. R. Arnott, J. L. Alm N. and Newell A. F. (1991). Emotional synthetic speech in an integrated communication prosthesis. In *Proc. of the 14th Annual Conference of the Rehabilitation Engineers Society of North America.*

Newell, A. F. Booth, L. Arnott, J. L. and Beattie, W. (1992). Increasing literacy levels through the use of linguistic prediction. *Child Language Teaching and Therapy*, 8(2), pp. 138-187.

Alm, N. Arnott, J. L. and Newell, A. F. Prediction and conversational momentum in an augmentative communication system. *Comms. of the ACM*, 35(5). Association for Computing Machinery: New York) pp. 46-57.

Alm, N. Murray I.R., Arnott, J.L. and.Newell, A.F. (1993). Pragmatics and affect in a communication system for non speakers. *J. of the American Voice I/O Society* 13, 1-16

Newell, A.F. (1993). Interfaces for the ordinary and beyond. *IEEE Software*, 10(5), pp 76-78

Newell, A.F.and Cairns A.Y. (1993).Designing for extra-ordinary users. *Ergonomics in Design*, 1993, pp 10-16

Newell, A. F. (1995). Extra-ordinary Human Computer Operation. In *Extra-ordinary Human-Computer Interaction*, A. D. N. Edwards (Ed.), Cambridge University Press

Alm, N. Arnott, J.L.and Newell A.F. (1994). Techniques for improving computer-assisted communication for physically impaired non-vocal people through using prestored texts. *In Proc. IEEE Systems, Man, Cybernetics Conference,* San Antonio, Texas, pp 1446-1451.

Newell, A. F. Arnott, J. L. Booth, L. Beattie, W. Brophy B. and Ricketts I. W. (1992). The effect of the PAL word prediction system on the quality and quantity of text generation. *Augmentative and Alternative Communication*,8 ,Decker Periodicals Inc., Ontario, Canada, pp.1-8.

Newell, A.F.(1987). Technical considerations when developing a communication aid. In *Assistive Communication Aids for the Speech Impaired*, P. Enderby (ed.) Churchill-Livingstone pp.56-66.

Newell, A. F. Booth, L. and Beattie W. (1991). Predictive text entry with PAL and children with learning difficulties. *Brit. J. of Ed. Tech*., 22(1), 1991, pp.23-40.

Newell, A.F. (1992).Today's dreams - tomorrow's reality Phonic Ear Distinguished Lecture, *Augmentative and Alternative Communication*, 8,Decker Periodicals Inc., Ontario, Canada, pp. 1-8.

Newell, A.F. (1996).Technology and the Disabled., Technology, Innovation and Society. *Journal of the Foundation for Science and Technology.* Vol. 12, No. 1.

Handbook of Human-Computer Interaction
Second, completely revised edition
M. Helander, T.K. Landauer, P. Prabhu (eds.)

Chapter 36

Computer-Based Instruction

Ray E. Eberts
Purdue University
West Lafayette, Indiana, USA

36.1 Introduction

Before the topic of human-computer interaction was recognized as an important area to be researched in its own right, extensive research was already being carried out on how students interact with computerized instructional systems. Although difficult to pinpoint the date of the emergence of the area of human-computer interaction, it probably did not occur until the mid to late 1970s when people started interacting directly with the computer instead of using cards to input information. At the beginning of this time period, however, researchers using a computer-based instruction (CBI) system, PLATO, at the University of Illinois, had already been investigating students using computers for about a decade. Little interaction between the areas of CBI and human-computer interaction has occurred despite the common interests and the head start that CBI work had on the field. The purpose of this chapter is to try to bridge this gap and point out how much of the research done in CBI has relevance to the general area of human-computer interaction. The focus will not be on surveying the general area of CBI; these surveys would be most appropriate for educational handbooks. Rather, the focus will be on looking at the methods used in CBI and the research issues which could be applied to other human-computer interaction tasks.

One of the advantages of looking at CBI research and its implications for general human-computer interaction tasks is that extensive research records have been kept of important parameters of humans interacting with computers. As an example, consider the data in Table 1. When preparing a computerized lesson, the user (called the author in this area) must write the program which controls the interaction between the student and the computer. Usually, the lesson author is a subject-matter expert and a novice on the computer. An important metric which has been measured in this area is the number of hours of programming time needed per hour of instruction provided. Over the years, the instructional techniques have not changed too much—this remains a constant—but the efficiency of the methods to interact with a computer has changed. So,

Table 1. Advances in interaction efficiency

Language	Dates Available	Hours per hour	Reference
FORTRAN	Before July, 1967	2286	Avner, 1979
Authoring in batch mode	Before October, 1968	615	Avner, 1979
Authoring on-line	After 1968	151	Avner, 1979
Authoring with menus and prompts	1990	18	Towne and Munro, 1991
Presentation software	1994	4-6	Personal experience

by looking at this metric over the years across many different kinds of interaction milestones, the increases in efficiency can be plotted. Example times for this interaction and the milestones have been summarized in Table 1.

The interaction efficiency was very low when a general-purpose programming language in batch mode was used in the early years. A large advance of almost 400% occurred when a special-purpose programming language was developed so that the authors did not have to program the same kinds of features over and over again. Another 400% increase in efficiency occurred when the authoring language was used in an interactive on-line mode. An 1800% increase in efficiency occurred when the authoring was performed with menus and prompts (this time of 16 hours was reported by the software designers based upon an expert doing the programming). The final entry is for using presentation software for instructional purposes. Presentation software, often conceptualized as computerized slide shows, are used in lectures and other instructional environments to present the information in textual or graphics form. These specialized software packages often incorporate templates, drawing capabilities, and text-editing capabilities to make the preparation of the materials efficient. Personal experience indicates that each hour of instruction requires four to eight hours of programming using the software package. These data are very important to understand the increases in human-computer interaction efficiency because they show human-computer interaction has become more efficient over the years.

The first section of this chapter surveys the techniques that are used in computer-based instruction. These techniques demonstrate that the computer can be used to assist instruction at different levels. Several kinds of computer-based instruction will be considered: Computer-managed instruction (CMI), computer-assisted instruction (CAI), intelligent computer-assisted instruction (ICAI), presentation software, multimedia, and distance learning.

The last section will investigate some of the themes which have occurred in CBI research. These themes transcend the application areas of the previous section. The themes can be used to formulate principles and rules for designing the instruction and how students interact with the computer.

36.2 Computer-Managed Instruction

Most current instructional environments use some kind of CMI as the bookkeeper or housekeeper in an instructional program. In CMI, the computer performs many of the administrative tasks of instruction such as record keeping, updating of grades, registration, and grading of tests in which computer forms were used. CMI could range from an individual instructor using a spreadsheet to record and tally grades to a more complete computerized system which does all the bookkeeping tasks and will additionally specify an individual program of study based upon the student's performance on the computer-based lessons.

In a CMI system, the goal is to have computers perform the tasks they perform best and the instructors perform the tasks for which they are best. The computer excels at manipulating, storing, and retrieving large amounts of information. Therefore, the computer is often utilized for the routine record keeping, monitoring progress of the students, calculating grades from the raw scores, and comparing students with some kind of measure of average performance. For more complicated CMI systems, the computer can take on more tasks such as individualizing the lessons based upon past performance and scheduling time on the computers so that the resources are used efficiently.

Without having to perform the mundane tasks, the instructors should have more time to do what they do best which is to provide individual help to the students and to prepare the lessons. Instructors are required to write CAI lessons and to provide live instruction. Because much of the clerical work is automated, instructors should be free to spend more time interacting with the students and more time preparing quality lessons. CMI utilizes live instruction to a great degree, and this could be a good consequence. Live instruction is a time-tested procedure.

Most large-scale instructional environments are computerized currently to varying degrees. The degree of CMI implementation will vary from site to site, however. School systems and universities have computerized record keeping but have difficulty implementing large-scale CMI because the school years are divided into semesters or quarters. Having students proceed at their own pace would require massive structural changes. The military and some businesses, not locked into the semester or quarter system, have had more success at large-scale CMI. The use of CMI in military settings has demonstrated millions of dollars in savings when compared to traditional instructional techniques.

36.3 Computer-Assisted Instruction

In computer-assisted instruction (CAI), the computer takes over many of the roles of the traditional instructor. Whole sections of the material can be presented on the computer while other sections of the material can still be presented by an instructor. The amount of computer control over the complete instructional process varies with the application. CAI can be used as an ancillary part of an instructor's lesson, providing instruction on a small subset of the total material. At the other end of the spectrum, ICAI can be used to control all aspects of the pedagogical interactions with little or no assistance from an instructor.

36.3.1 Courseware

Actual CAI instructional material, called courseware, can take many forms. Courseware is the special-purpose software that is authored by a subject-matter expert or a computer programmer to provide the instructional interactions. Bunderson (1981) makes a distinction between authoring system courseware and delivery system software. The authoring system courseware controls the interaction between an author of instruction and the computer. It provides a system whereby the courseware can be created and later edited (such as changing the material or inserting new text). The authoring system is an important component of a CAI package. The author/computer interaction is made as simple as possible so that subject-matter experts will be able to author the courseware with little software training. The delivery system software, on the other hand, controls the interaction between the student and the computer. It takes care of providing the text, evaluating student answers, and recording the correctness of the responses.

Several courseware systems have existed over the years. The goal of these systems has been to make it easy for a subject-matter expert, not necessarily a computer programmer, to design the instructional material. These systems have differed in how the instructional lesson is implemented. Generally, the kinds of instructional lessons can be classified into four groups: drill and practice, tutorials, simulations, and games. For drill and practice, questions or problems are presented to the student. The student answers the questions, the computer tracks the answers, and will continue to the next lesson or level only when material is mastered. For tutorials, the computer carries on a dialogue with the student and may specify the required actions to solve a problem. In many cases, the computer will proceed to the next step only when the actions are performed by the student. In simulations, physical tasks are represented on the computer screen. These programs often incorporate graphics and animation to illustrate how something works. Finally, games incorporate animation, graphics, and sometimes sound to make the lesson entertaining. In most cases, the performance of the student will be scored so that the students will compete against themselves or others. Many CAI lessons will transcend several of the categorizes with a primary emphasis in one of the areas.

PLATO (Programmed Logic for Automated Teaching Operations), the result of a collaborative effort at the University of Illinois between engineers, physicists, psychologists, and educators, was one of the first CAI systems developed. PLATO was completed in 1960 and was funded through various military, industrial, and educational sources for about $1 billion (Lyman, 1981).

For PLATO, the emphasis had been placed on creating a courseware language that is easy to use yet highly flexible; objectives that are not always compatible with one another. PLATO remained flexible by not being geared to any particular strategy. The strategy used depended on what the individual authors thought would be the most effective instructional technique. To allow more structure and make programming easier, however, lesson drivers—such as tutorials, drills, and simulations—were built upon a specific model of student instruction. Each less-on driver came with a customized editor.

Other courseware systems have been developed based upon particular lesson strategies. As an example, TICCIT was based on a rule/example/practice model instead of the more flexible structure of PLATO (Reigeluth, 1979). As a slightly different approach, other courseware packages allow the courseware authors to use pseudo-code, similar in structure to computer programs, to program the lessons. One courseware package, called PLANIT, divided the program into four frames: decision (D), programming (P), multiple choice (M), or question (Q). The M and Q frames were used to present text. The D frame is similar to the if-then statements in computer program-ming and could branch control to different parts of the program. A P frame operates similarly to a subroutine in a computer program and could be called from different places in the courseware. This kind of system provided PLANIT with the flexibility similar to a computer program with the code specific to presenting instructional materials.

36.3.2 Trends

In the early years of CAI, the trend was for large integrated hardware and software systems which could not be decoupled. The PLATO system consisted of a video display terminal, a keyboard, a touch panel display, and the courseware authoring system. After its development at the University of Illinois, Control Data Corporation (CDC) bought the license for the system and had extensive plans for marketing it. CDC was one of the largest and most successful computer companies during the 1970s. Their marketing plans failed and soon this highly successful company was having financial problems and was eventually dismantled. They were plagued by other problems besetting the large mainframe manufacturing computer companies at the time, but the failure in selling a combined hardware/software CAI system contributed to their failure.

The trend in CAI then moved away from requiring specific hardware to support the software and moved toward designing software authoring systems and stand-alone games which could be supported by the popular operating systems independent of the machine manufacturer. With an increase in access to computers both in homes and at the schools, software companies started to offer commercial packages in the 1980s. To analyze the trends in educational software during the years 1981-1988, Sales, Tsai, and McLeod (1991) contacted the leading educational software companies and asked them to indicate what they thought were their most successful and innovative products. Twenty-five products were received and the trends were analyzed in several ways. CAI software seemed to be most successful in problem areas where facts had to be learned such as in math and science. In terms of instruction technique, most used games (11 out of 25) or simulations (9 out of 25) instead of drills (4 out of 25) or tutorials (1 out of 25). Animation was used in a majority of the programs (20 out of 25) as was color (23 out of 25). Only five out of the 25 used adaptive instruction. Many of these trends, especially the trends to animation and color, are present in current CAI software. Multimedia, incorporating animation, graphics, and sound on CD-ROM is becoming more and more popular.

In recent years, a marriage has occurred between CAI lessons and software packages. The trend has been for well-supported software packages, such as Microsoft Word or Corel's WordPerfect, to incorporate CAI lessons on how to use the package. For Microsoft Word and other Microsoft packages such as Excel and PowerPoint, a tutorial is included under the Help menu. Through textual instructions, the user is asked to perform the button presses or the commands to perform the functions needed for using the software. These tutorials incorporate some animation (the cursor is seen moving to the appropriate command) and some simulations (tasks are simulated during the lessons). The Corel tutorials are very similar with many of the same features. Other packages, such as CorelDraw (a popular drawing program), have less extensive tut-orials. In these tutorials, the Help text is displayed and the user goes through these Help pages under a single topic at a self pace. To stay competitive, other soft-ware packages will have to incorporate tutorials on the level of Microsoft and Novell.

36.3.3 Advantages of CAI

Measuring the effectiveness of CAI as compared to other instructional techniques is difficult because many examples exist where CAI is better, in terms of material learned, and examples exist where the other techniques are better. Generalizations may not be appropriate because a good CAI lesson is better than a poor conventional lesson and a good conventional lesson is better than a poor CAI; determining whether a failure of a CAI lesson is due to the lesson itself or the general computerized technique is difficult. Kulik, Kulik, and Cohen (1980), however, review several studies which have compared computerized instruction to conventional instruction on the same material. Of the 54

Table 2. Reduction in instruction time due to individualization.

Percent Reduction in Time to Complete	Description	Reference
66	Training at United Airlines	Conkwright, 1982
64	Average from evaluation of military systems	Orlansky and String, 1977
63	Technical maintenance training at American Airlines	Conkwright, 1982
50-67	CAI courses in school districts	Morgan, 1978
40	College courses	Avner, Moore, and Smith, 1980
33	Course at Federal Aviation Administration	Buck, 1982
28	Course at automobile company on the fundamentals of pneumatic devices	Maul and Spotts, 1993
15-27	Navy advanced maintenance course	Montague, Wulfeck, and Ellis, 1983b
15-25	Navy apprentice training	Montague, Wulfeck, and Ellis, 1983b

studies examined, 37 found that students using CAI scored better on exams; 17 studies found that conventional instruction was better. Eleven of the 54 studies measured attitudes towards the instruction and found that the ratings were higher for CAI lessons in eight of the studies. The overall increase in achieve-ment in all 54 studies combined, however, was very low, only one-quarter of a standard deviation.

The main advantage of CAI is in terms of the reduction in instructional time due to individualization. In a classic classroom situation, instruction time for the whole group is driven by the slowest learners. For computerized instruction, the instruction time is driven by the individual student's capabilities and motivations. Individualized instruction can reduce the instruction time which, in turn, reduces costs. Also, the fast learners may not be as bored if they do not have to proceed at such a slow pace. Table 2 lists several references that have evaluated the percent reduction in time to complete a computerized course when compared to a traditional course. The reduction in instruct-ion time due to individualization ranges from 14% to 67%. The savings can be particularly high when students as well as instructors must be paid, as occurs in military and industrial environments.

36.3.4 Disadvantages of CAI

The major disadvantage of CAI is the length of time required to author one hour of instruction (see Table 3). As can be seen from the table, this time is dependent on several factors including the kind of lesson produced and the experience level of the author. The estimates range from over 2,000 hours to just a few hours per hour of instruction. Another disadvantage is that the modes of communication between the student and the computer are limited. Presently the communication is done through a keyboard, mouse, or joystick. Natural language and voice input, as in conventional classroom instruction, could be beneficial, but they are still in the experimental stages. A third disadvantage is that the responses must be in the range anticipated by the author; CAI courseware cannot handle unexpected or unique answers. A fourth problem is that CAI has limited application in some areas; it is probably best applied where the content to be learned is factual, with specific goals and objectives. The Kulik et al. (1991) review showed that most commercial CAI is limited to math and science applications. CAI is less applicable in areas where the knowledge to be learned is less explicit. This limitation of conventional CAI has led the push for intelligent CAI which will be discussed next.

36.4 Intelligent Computer-Assisted Instruction

Intelligent computer-assisted instruction (ICAI) uses artificial intelligence (AI) techniques to enhance training and instruction for computer-based systems. AI techniques, using human intelligence as both a model and a source of data, instruct students by interacting with the student naturally, answering questions, and

Table 3. Authoring time.

Hours per Hour of Instruction	Method of Estimation	Range or Type of Instruction	Experience of Author	Reference
2286	Averaged	Full	Not specified	Avner, 1979
615	Averaged	Full	Not specified	Avner, 1979
300	Averaged	Sophisticated	Inexperienced	Avner, 1979
295.1	Experiment averaged	Full	Inexperienced	Avner, 1979
250	Estimate	Simulation	Variable	Dallman et al., 1983
200-500	Estimate	Sophisticated	Not specified	Fairweather and O'Neal, 1984
196	Averaged	Full	Variable	Hofstetter, 1983
165-610	Experiment range	New lesson	Low	Avner, 1979
151	Averaged	Full	Not specified	Avner, 1979
100-150	Estimate	Comprehensive	Variable	Brackett, 1979
82	Experiment	Moderate	High	Hillelsohn, 1984
80	Estimate	Full	High	Avner, 1979
72	Experiment	Moderate	High	Hillelsohn, 1984
54	Experiment	Moderate	High	Hillelsohn, 1984
49.7	Averaged	Moderate	High	Brackett, 1979
32	Averaged	Full	Experienced	Avner, 1979
30-70	Estimate	Variable	Not specified	Brackett, 1979
27-180	Experiment	New lesson	High	Brackett, 1979
26.4	Experiment	Full	Experienced	Avner, 1979
25-50	Estimate	Simple	Not specified	Avner, 1979
21	Estimate	Full	High	Avner, 1979
17	Experiment	Full	High	Avner, 1979
8-63	Experiment	Full	Low	Avner, 1979
8	Estimate	Not specified	High	Fairweather and O'Neal, 1984
6.9	Experiment	Simple	Not specified	Avner, 1979
6-39	Estimate	Simple	High	Avner, Smith, and Tenczar, 1984
3-6	Estimate	Presentation software	High	Personal experience

providing a data structure so that facts can be acquired and retrieved efficiently. ICAI pro-gramming is generative; it can be run repeatedly by the same student although his or her learning situation is different each time. Thus, ICAI is not completely dependent on programming that attempts to account for every possible interaction future students may require.

ICAI is targeted towards complex learning domains and provides several benefits over the types of computer-based systems that have been discussed previously. First, the computer instruction can be very flexible. With an intelligent system, the courseware author does not have to anticipate every instructional situation; the program can use its own intelligence to handle an unforeseen situation. Second, instruction is tailored to the individual student; most ICAI programs try to understand the individual student by deriving a model of what the student does and does not know. Third, the student is allowed to play a more active experimental role in the learning process. Like any good instructor, ICAI programs are designed to direct, not lead. An emphasis is placed on providing situations in which the student can query the computer to try to discover the correct answers. Finally, many of the instructional strategies used in the program are based on modeling expert instructors. If the best instructors can be modeled, then their effective teaching strategies can be distributed to many students all over the world on an individualized basis.

Several ICAI programs have been developed and have been successful on a research level. Examples include SOPHIE (Burton and Brown, 1979) which allowed students to problem solve in electronic troubleshooting; WUSOR (Goldstein, 1978) which taught students about simple logic and probability in a game setting; GUIDON (Clancey, 1983) which taught medical diagnostic problem solving; and STEAMER (Hollan, 1984; Williams, Hollan and Stevens, 1981) which was a graphics-based simulation to teach Navy personnel about steam propulsion systems.

36.4.1 Characteristics of ICAI

The ICAI program that have been developed are the results of intensive research and development efforts in the late 1970s and early 1980s. None have really proved a commercial success or have had wide implementation. The value of these programs is still in the methods that have been developed and researched for making computerized instruction more intelligent.

Three components are present in most ICAI systems: The representation of the subject material, the student model, and the instructional strategy used. A discussion of each of these components follows.

When representing knowledge in an ICAI system, the information must be organized so that acquisition, retrieval, and reasoning can be done efficiently. For a computer-based system, the machine must be able to acquire knowledge easily in the sense that the author can quickly enter facts into an organized database. An ultimate goal has been for an ICAI system to acquire knowledge automatically by making analogies from old knowledge and applying it to new knowledge. After knowledge is acquired, it must be retrievable by the system. Knowing the information that is relevant to a particular problem and being able to retrieve it is an especially important issue when the problems are complex. Instead of having facts stored for every problem, a feature of an intelligent system would be to have the system infer information and reason from the fixed facts. The form of the data structure often determines how inferences and reasoning can be done.

The use of a student model is a second feature of ICAI systems which distinguishes them from CAI systems. A student model infers from the student's behavior what the student knows. By presenting only information that the student does not know already and by correcting the student's misconceptions, instruction can be more individualized than that available on traditional CAI systems. ICAI systems can incorporate student models in several ways such as tracking the information with which the student has been presented, tracking the dialogue and questions that the student asks, comparing the student's knowledge with experts' knowledge, tracking the misconceptions demonstrated by the student, and characterizing student knowledge according to the plans used to solve a particular problem. Because of ambiguities in student performance and in classifying errors and learning, some student models have incorporated fuzzy logic to make them more tractable (Katz, Lesgold, Eggan, and Gordin, 1992).

Finally, the instructional strategies used by ICAI systems differ from CAI systems. One of the characteristics of an intelligent system is that it can fulfill many of the roles of traditional instructors. The traditional instructor must interact with the student, format the educational session or manage the dialogue, choose topics, select problems, evaluate answers, provide feedback and evaluate and modify instructional techniques. Most of these duties have been incorporated into ICAI programs.

36.4.2 Evaluation

Many of the same issues can be raised for ICAI evaluations as were raised when evaluating the CAI programs. Generalizations are difficult because the quality of the programs differ. ICAI programs are even more individualized than CAI programs so that cost savings due to individualization can be expected similar to that shown in Table 2 for CAI programs. Showing improvements in actual exam scores is more problematic.

Anderson, Boyle, Corbett, and Lewis (1990) reviewed the research they performed on two intelligent tutors based and developed on the ACT model of learning. For a LISP programming tutor used for college students, time on task was reduced especially for difficulty tasks using the intelligent tutor when compared to a control group taught using traditional methods. For a high school geometry class, students using an intelligent tutor scored significantly better than a control group of students taught without the intelligent tutor.

Legree and Gillis (1991) reviewed the literature which evaluated the effectiveness of ICAI programs. About half the research papers showed some advantage for intelligent tutoring systems when compared to human tutoring. As an example, students using a LISP tutor developed by Anderson, Boyle, and Reiser (1985) performed 43% better on exams than those in traditional instructional groups although the ICAI lessons required more time to learn the material. The ICAI program MACH III also was shown to increase student performance on exams (Kurland, Granville, and MacLaughlin, 1990). The ICAI program Smithtown also reduced learning time when compared to traditional learning (Katz and Raghavan, 1989). Research on the ICAI programs West and Proust, however, showed no differences in exam scores for those using the ICAI programs and those not using the programs (Center for the Study of Evaluation, 1986).

36.5 Presentation Software

A software package that allows a person to present a computerized slide show during a lecture or conference talk is called presentation software. Several different packages, with different capabilities, are commercially available such as Microsoft PowerPoint, Aldus Persuasion, and Corel Presentations. Most of these share certain capabilities.

The purpose of these packages is to assist an instructor during a lecture with professional looking text and graphics. Although each package is slightly different, most have common features. Packets of information are contained on separate slides and the presenter will push a button (either on the keyboard or on the mouse) to move from one slide to the next. Most packages have some authoring capability for text and drawing. The slides can contain text, pictures (clip art), graphics, sound, and charts, or combinations of these on one slide. Some presentation packages also have capabilities for animation, video, and morphing (gradually changing one picture into another picture). The packages are available for personal computers and require a connection to a separate LCD display to project the slides on a screen. Some laptop and notebook computers come with a detachable screen which can be overlaid on top of an overhead projector for displaying the slides on the screen.

The purpose of presentation software is different from the other computer-based instruction applications reviewed previously. For CAI and ICAI, the purpose was to individualize instruction and do the presentations on the computer. For presentation soft-ware, the purpose is to assist lecturing. The instructor is still needed to fill in information through the lecture and control the rate of the presentation. Since presentation software is not designed necessarily for student self learning, no capability is present for asking questions or testing students on the material from the slides.

This special software can save authoring time when compared to doing the presentations with word processors or drawing programs. Large time savings occur because templates are used for constructing the material. The author has several possibilities for colorful and professionally drawn slide backgrounds, slide layouts (where the text and graphics will be located on the slide), and color possibilities. Most packages will automatically choose color combinations for the background and text which are compatible and offer high contrasts. The author saves time because he or she does not have to draw the backgrounds, choose the color combinations, or spend time choosing locations for the different elements on the slide.

Time savings also can occur due to savings in the preparation of accompanying material. Most software packages have the capability to change easily from slides to outlines and notes. The author can specify that the same material be presented in slide form or in outline form. Preparing the outline notes for the audience from the slides is often just a matter of a few button presses.

Another advantage and potential time savings for presentation software is that information from other software packages can be exported to the presentation software and placed in the slides. Calculations and charts from spreadsheets, graphics from drawing programs, text from word processors, scanned images from photo-paint programs, equations from equation editors, and animation from multimedia packages are all examples of items which do not have to be created again and can be merely placed on a slide.

The authoring time for presentation software should be less than that seen for other computer-based instructional techniques because less of the instruction is computer controlled. Personal experience indicates that a lecture including only text would take about two hours per hour of instruction for an experienced user. A lecture which includes text and graphics requires about four to six hours of preparation time per hour of instruction for an experienced user. Including animation and morphing can increase the authoring time to 10 to 20 hours per hour of presentation.

36.6 Multimedia

Many commercial computer-based instruction material is now in the form of multimedia and is placed on CD-ROM. Multimedia is characterized by animation, graphics, and sound. Multimedia is considered elsewhere in this handbook (see Chapter 39) and will not be discussed in detail in this chapter.

One interesting trend for computer-based instruction is the growing practice of including software with textbooks. As an example, one of the most popular textbooks for Physics classes, Halliday and Resnick's *Fundamentals of Physics* published by Wiley, has a CD-ROM which can be purchased separately to accompany the text. The target audience for this CD-ROM is those students who may need more problems to solve and help in visualizing the problems. Instead of replacing the textbook, the purpose of the CD-ROM is to supplement the material.

An alternative to purchasing the software separately, some books contain a disk or CD-ROM with computerized lessons. A question is how often do buyers of the book utilize this software. Vernon (1993) performed a survey to determine how many professors used the software that accompanied a psychology textbook. He found that 28/105 (26.7%) used the software in some capacity. For the others not using the software, he asked the respondents to explain why they did not. Twenty people (19%) reported that they were not inclined to use this kind of software. Ten indicated that the nature of the course or previously adopted software precluded its use. Twenty-six indicated that they did not have the resources available to use the software.

36.7 Distance Learning

Distance learning is a term applied to a teaching environment in which the instructor is in a different physical location from the students. Students can be distributed at different sites such as companies or colleges and universities. Distance learning occurs in three general ways ranging from the simple to the more complex: videotaped lectures delivered to students at remote sites; live video and audio lectures sent over satellite systems to sites which have a satellite hookup; and instruction through the World Wide Web (hereafter referred to as the "Web").

Videotaped lectures and material transmitted live over satellite systems do not require that students interact with computer systems and, thus, falls outside the scope of this handbook. In these situations, how-ever, computer programs are used for some demonstrations, word processors are used for preparing assignments, spreadsheets are used for homework assignments (such as statistical analyses), and e-mail is used for communication between instructor and student. E-mail is being used increasingly to enhance the communication between instructor and student. Personal experience indicates that in a distance learning environment, students, on a whole, will use e-mail to communicate with the instructor about half of the time; the phone is used for the other half of the communications. The use of e-mail has increased dramatically in the last couple of years, from about 20% of the communications in 1994 and 1995 as companies have made e-mail available to their employees. Most companies lagged behind universities in the use of e-mail because of security concerns of allowing network access to their computer systems.

Of the three distance learning technologies, the use of the Web is most directly related to human-computer interaction issues. Most interaction with the Web occurs through http (hypertext transfer protocol) sites using the hypertext mark-up language (html). Html uses hypertext to interact with the user. Hypertext can allow students to click on keywords during a lesson to reference past material, elaborate on a concept, or reference a definition for a term. Graphics and animation can also be used. As an example for animation, Macromedia's Director, which uses a movie script metaphor, has a plug-in that can be downloaded from Macromedia's Web site to convert standard Director software into software that can be accessed through the Web. In terms of graphics, most graphics packages come with conversion programs which can be used to convert graphics files into formats which can be read through the Web. The Web can also make use of chat rooms and FAQs (frequently asked questions). FAQs allow the students some of the learning opportunities of a live lecture hall where all students have access to the question and the answer from the instructor.

The main advantage of distance learning using the Web is its accessibility. Anybody with a computer, a modem, and access to an Internet browser is a potential student. For students taking courses from industry, this kind of accessibility is especially useful for those who must travel due to job demands. Another advantage is that hypertext and graphics capabilities are built into html directly and these capabilities can be utilized easily in the lesson plan.

Another advantage is the potential for easier interactivity between the instructor and the student (Bourne Brodersen, Campbell, Dawant, and Shiavi, 1996). E-mail access, chat rooms, and FAQs can make interaction easy for the students.

The main disadvantage of Web distance learning is the relatively long time needed to display some kinds of information. Time to display depends on the complexity of the images, the speed of the computer, and the speed of the modem. Text and graphics can be displayed relatively quickly. Animation, using the specialized packages, can also be displayed quickly. Video and digitized pictures can take much longer to display (more than a minute and many times up to five minutes). Research at Purdue has indicated that users will not wait to access images that take over 30 seconds to display. Because of the long time needed to display video and pictures, traditional lectures cannot be used.

Offerings currently range from some engineering courses at Purdue University and Vanderbilt University and English courses at the University of Missouri and Indiana University, to name only a few. Courses which rely on student interactions and discussions can be converted fairly easily to Internet format. Courses which require more development time with graphics, animation, and hypertext, require longer amounts of time to develop. Since many engineering courses currently utilize computer simulations for laboratories, these can be converted easily to Web offerings. Because of the amount of time needed to develop a comprehensive set of courses, though, offering a degree entirely through Internet courses is difficult.

Vanderbilt University developed and evaluated a beginning engineering course. The course used Web pages to stimulate discussion in the time periods devoted to lectures and laboratory simulations were conducted over the Web. Results showed that 85% of the students thought the course objectives were accomplished, 50% liked the modality of learning through the Internet better than other features, 91% liked having the course materials on-line, and 90% felt comfortable using computers after the course was finished compared to 47% comfort when queried at the beginning of the semester.

36.8 Issues and Themes

Some themes have transcended the usual classifications of CAI, CMI, or ICAI. These themes are also important to human-computer interaction in general. The themes which will be examined in the next sections are: individual differences, knowledge of results, amount of practice, augmented feedback, part-whole tasks, adaptive instruction, conceptual rep-resentations, motivation, attention, and virtual reality. Individual differences are important in the development of user profiles so that the displayed information can be tailored to individuals or groups of individuals. Knowledge of results is important when considering the kinds of feedback to give the users; an emphasis has been placed on making the feedback as specific as possible. The amount of practice variable is important when considering that the users will be using the system as they develop their expertise so they should be given the opportunity to improve and become more skilled. Augmented feedback has implications for the design of graphics and the highlighting of information on the screen. Adaptive instruction is important when the interaction must be designed for both experts and novices. The section on conceptual representations emphasizes the cognitive approach to design of the interaction. Motivation is an important variable in the design of the interaction so that the information is interesting to the user and as game-like as possible. Some research is reported that examines how skills such as controlling attentional resources can be learned from game-like environments. Finally, research in training has addressed the amount of realism in virtual environments. The following summarizes some of the research done in these areas; references are provided for further reading.

36.8.1 Individual Differences

Traditionally, individual differences have been studied with the goal of selecting the right personnel for the appropriate job. The premise is that instruction time can be reduced by selecting people who have certain measurable characteristics and training only them. This approach is primarily concerned with matching instruction to a student. In many cases, however, matching the person to the job may not be possible. Researchers must learn to be able to choose the correct learning strategy for the person based upon a quick evaluation of the student's abilities. Only then will truly individualized instruction be achieved.

Instruction must be neither too difficult nor too easy for the student. If too difficult, the student may give up on the task altogether; if too easy, the student will become bored, losing interest or motivation. Individual differences must be evaluated and difficulty levels must be set appropriately.

Although this has been the goal, this has been rarely achieved (Steinberg, 1977). This lack of success could be due to either choosing inappropriate individual characteristics or choosing inappropriate instructional design based on the individual differences. Table 4 targets some of the important individual differences and provides examples of how the individual differences have been used to individualize CAI courses.

36.8.2 Knowledge of Results (KR)

Knowledge of results (KR) is defined as the feedback or reinforcement that is given to students to tell them how well they performed on the task. The form of KR

Table 4. Individual differences.

Individual Difference	Description	Implication	Reference
Time-sharing ability	People vary in their natural ability to time-share, to carry on more than one task at a time	Adjust the task difficulty to take into account this ability	Ackerman, Wickens, and Schneider, 1984; North and Gopher, 1976
Holistic vs. analytic processors	Evidence indicates that holistic processors process information as a whole and analytic processors process information feature by feature	Present information differently depending on processor type	Cooper, 1976
Learning strategies	Good students in physics analyze problems abstractly and poor students analyze problems literally	Indicate abstractions to the student	Larkin, 1981, 1982
Field dependent vs. field independent	Used to structure CAI for foreign language learning; no evaluation of program done	Possible variable to use for other applications	Raschio and Lange, 1984
Measured from pretest	CAI lesson that was structured individually depending on the score of the pretest; no performance differences were found when this group was compared to a control group	The individual differences may not have been important to performance; lesson structuring may not have been optimal	Tatsuoka and Birenbaum, 1981
Student's major	Individualized group was only slightly better than non-individualized group	Student's major may not provide individual difference information	Ross, 1984
General	Potential exists for structuring lessons according to individual differences	Potential, but little or no data to indicate this will work	Cronbach, 1967; Farley, 1983; Glaser, 1982
General	In reviews of CAI lessons structured according to individual differences, concluded that lesson authors have not been able to acquire and use enough information about the learner to provide ideally individualized instruction	More research needs to be done; do not know how to use individual differences in CAI at this time	Berliner and Cohen, 1973; Bracht, 1970; Bracht and Glass, 1972; Cronbach and Snow, 1977; DiVesta, 1973; Glaser, 1970; Hall, 1983; McCann, 1983; Tobias, 1976

Table 5. Knowledge of results.

Issue	Discussion	Reference
Performance improvement in knowledge acquisition depends on knowledge of results (KR). The rate of improvement depends on the precision of KR	In a very early experiment on skill training, a group given qualitative KR performed best, a group given quantitative KR (Yes or no) performed next best, and groups given no KR or irrelevant KR were worst	Trowbridge and Cason, 1932
Feedback should be immediate	Anything over two seconds and the student may be thinking about something else; immediate feedback has been a guiding principle in intelligent tutors	Anderson, Boyle, Corbett, and Lewis, 1990; Miller, 1978
Delay of feedback may have detrimental effect on retention of material	A delay of 30 seconds had a detrimental effect on retention of math material	Gaynor, 1979
Feedback on correct responses may not be useful or could be detrimental to performance	In a review of studies, 9 studies found no difference or a decrement in performance for feedback given on correct responses	Anderson, Kulhavy, and Andre, 1971
CAI offers good opportunity for giving immediate feedback	Hypothesized that reason CAI group in a music course was better than a control group was because the CAI group knew precisely how they were doing on each drill and the control group only received feedback when the homework was returned	Arenson, 1982
CAI Feedback should be used to target misconceptions	In the ICAI program SOPHIE, feedback is used to target misconceptions and to offer alternative ways to conceptualize the problem	Burton and Brown, 1979

can range from a simple "yes" or "no" to a more detailed "the shot was off target to the right by 22mm." KR was one of the earliest variables manipulated in the study of the acquisition of skills and has a long history of research behind it. Table 5 summarizes some of the important basic and applied research findings on feedback and knowledge of results.

36.8.3 Amount of Practice

One of the best determinants of the amount of skill students obtain is the amount of practice they have performing the task to be learned. Experts are usually distinguished from novices in that they have had more practice performing a particular task. As an example, it is estimated that expert radiologists have analyzed nearly half a million radiographs (Lesgold, Feltovich, Glaser, and Wang, 1981).

In discussing the amount of practice, several issues will be considered: What causes practice to increase performance? How can practice be made more efficient? How can instruction be achieved in less time? These questions are summarized in Table 6.

36.8.4 Augmented Feedback

Lintern (1980) defines augmented feedback as experimentally or system-provided perceptual cues that enhance the intrinsic task-related feedback. As an example, in a tracking task, Gordon and Gottlieb (1967) turned on a yellow light that further illuminated the tracking display when subjects were tracking off target. In a simulated landing task, Lintern (1980) provided subjects with augmenting visual cues that indicated the correct flight path. Augmented feedback has been used in simulation and for the training of perceptual skills. Table 7 summarizes some of the results.

Table 6. Amount of practice.

Issue	Discussion	References
Performance during practice seems to follow a power law	Reviewed several areas of research; developed a lawful relationship between performance and practice; performance improves with practice	Newell and Rosenbloom, 1981
Practice can be made more efficient if consistent practice is given	Several experiments look at the acquisition of perceptual skills through computer-based training; research shows that the students must be able to see the consistent relationships between the input and the output	Eberts and Schneider, 1986; Schneider and Fisk, 1981; Schneider and Shiffrin, 1977; Shiffrin and Schneider, 1977
Time compression can be used to present information in a shorter time period	Training on perceptual tasks that look at slowly occurring trajectories, such as radar operation and air traffic control, can be made more efficient by time-compressing the paths	Bloomfield and Little, 1985; Scanlan, 1975; Schneider, 1981
In a simulation, processes that take a long time with providing little information can be shortened	In STEAMER, long processes like filling up a tank with water can be shortened so that more trials of practice can be given	Hollan, Stevens, and Williams, 1980
Practice can be speeded up by increasing the presentation rate	Presentation rate was increased from 10 characters per second (cps) to 30 cps with no drop in performance	Dennis, 1979
Drill and practice	Important function of drill and practice method is to bring learner to level of "automaticity" on lower level subskills so that learner can more readily perform some higher level complex skill	Merrill and Salisbury, 1984
For effective transfer of training to occur, difficult practice situations should be provided which forces students to process the information	Random practice, reduced feedback, and variable practice make knowledge acquisition more difficult but result in better transfer performance	Schmidt and Bjork, 1992

36.8.5 Part-Whole Training

Part-whole training is concerned with the issue of whether it is more beneficial to break down a task and train component parts (part training) or whether it is more beneficial to train the whole task all at once (whole training). This issue has important implications for computer-aided training because part training is typically less expensive to do on a computer system than is whole training (Wheaton, Rose, Fingerman, Korotkin, and Holding, 1976). Certain parts of the task can be simulated on a small personal computer whereas the whole task might require a larger system where the many complex interactions of a particular system are simulated. If part training is more beneficial than whole training, then instruction could be done less expensively. If whole training is more beneficial, the amount of benefit must be determined before the increased cost can be justified. Whaley and Fisk (1993) showed that the patterns of learning for part-task and whole-task training were very similar. Table 8 summarizes some of the research results addressing part-whole training.

Table 7. Augmented feedback.

Issue	Discussion	Reference
Provide augmenting cues only when students are not performing accurately	Using this method, the difficulty of the task will automatically adapt itself to the level of the student (i.e., more help in the beginning and less help once experienced)	Gordon, 1968; Lintern, 1980; Lintern, Roscoe, Koonce, and Segal, 1990
Augmenting cues can be effective	In a flight simulation, highway-in-the-sky augmenting cues were used to increase performance	Lintern, 1980
Augmenting cues should make the consistencies in the task more salient	In a computer-aided tracking task, augmenting cues were only effective if they made the consistencies in the task more salient	Eberts and Schneider, 1985
Students must not form a dependency on the augmenting cues	Augmenting cues should be presented on only some of the trials so that students are forced to do some trials without the augmentation	Wheaton, et al., 1976
Augmenting cues such as graphics can make the task too easy	In a CBI lesson incorporating graphics and animation, students complained that the graphics did too much of the work for them	Gould and Finzer, 1982
Training using augmenting cues is effective when the cues pinpoint the invariant properties in the task.	An invariant property is one which remains unchanged as other properties irrelevant to the task change.	Lintern, 1991

36.8.6 Adaptive Training

Lintern and Roscoe (1980) define adaptive training as a "method of individualized instruction in which task characteristics are automatically changed from an easy or simple form to the difficult or complex criterion version." The reasons to use adaptive training were discussed for augmented feedback and part-whole training. All of these methods are used to decrease or increase the difficulty of the task; the distinctions between them sometimes get hazy. One of the important issues in CBI is whether the sequencing of instruction should be program- or student-controlled. Control can be done by the computer depending on the pattern of errors made by the student. This and other issues of adaptive instruction are summarized in Table 9.

36.8.7 Conceptual Representations

Determining people's conceptual representations of information is important for instruction because the material to be learned must fit in with how a person eventually comes to conceptualize the problem; the material must fit into the person's memory structures. Ausubel (1968) articulates this concept by stating that the learning of new material depends on its interaction with the cognitive structures held by the student. The cognitive structures of the student provide a kind of "ideational scaffolding" that can be used as an anchor for the new material. The following issues should be considered with regard to instruction and conceptual representations. What special capabilities do humans have for internally representing the outside world? How do experts internally represent complex concepts? How can computers be used to present information that will be compatible with the conceptual representations? Table 10 summarizes some of the research which has been done on conceptual representations.

36.8.8 Motivation

Much work has been done on motivation and learning. In the presentation of relevant research on motivation in Table 11, the discussion is limited to the special

Table 8. Part-Whole training.

Issue	Discussion	Reference
Part-whole training depends on the organization of the task	If the task is highly organized, whole-task training should be used. If the task is not highly organized, part-task training should be used.	Stammers, 1982
Should dual-task performance (doing two tasks at one time) be trained by training the two tasks separately or by training the two tasks together?	If the two tasks are sufficiently different, dual task training is better than training on the two separate tasks.	Detweiler and Lundy, 1995
Students should be exposed to the target task early during part-task training.	Training purely on the part-tasks was not effective. When students were exposed to the whole-task during part-task training, performance improved.	Carlson, Khoo, and Elliott, 1990
Some tasks are so difficult that the student cannot approach the required skill level to perform the task	May have to break the task into components so that the students can build towards this more complex task; finding in basic skill instruction	Gaines, 1972
Part learning is necessary when the amount of learning is large	Conclusion from review of several studies	Wheaton et al., 1976
Whole learning is slightly better if the sequence is long and complex	Conclusion from review of several studies	Wheaton et al., 1976
CAI lessons must address one specific objective at a time	The goal must be stated clearly and be obtainable; may have to break overall task down into parts to achieve this	Jay, 1983
CAI can be used for part-task simulation rather than for whole course	Principle used in the Navy beginning in the mid-1970s based upon successes and failures in CAI	Montague, Wulfeck, and Ellis, 1983a
Choice of part-task training method depends on whether trainees will perform in a single- or dual-task situation	Integrated part-task training, in which subjects were exposed to the whole game, transferred better to dual-task situations than did hierarchical part-task training, in which subjects practiced on subtasks. Both part-task training situations were better than whole training	Fabiani, Buckley, Gratton, Coles, and Donchin, 1989

features of computers which can be used to increase motivation.

36.8.9 Attention

Computer games can teach attentional skills that transfer to real-world tasks. Gopher, Weil, and Bareket (1994) showed that practice on a computer game trained skills on how to control and allocate attention to tasks in high-workload situations. They showed that playing a video game allowed subjects to practice several strategies to allocate attention to tasks. These

Table 9. Adaptive instruction.

Issue	Discussion	Reference
Students with little subject matter expertise do not perform very well when they are allowed to control the material and lessons presented by the computer.	Learner control is intuitively plausible to increase students' motivation, but the experimental literature does not support the idea that learner control is better than computer control.	Steinberg, 1989
The variable that is adaptively manipulated must not significantly change the nature of the task	In teaching tasks, variables such as the order of control and the gain of the system were adaptively manipulated; no benefit was found for this manipulation	Gopher, Williges, and Damos, 1975
Analyze student's on-task error patterns to adaptively control CAI material presented	Effective method for adaptively presenting material to students; shown to be better than nonadaptive or learner controlled	Park and Tennyson, 1980; Ross, 1984; Tennyson, Tennyson, and Rothen, 1990
Can adaptively manipulate several different variables	Concluded that the following variables can be adaptively manipulated: 1) amount of instruction; 2) sequence of instruction; 3) instructional display time; 4) control strategy with advisement information	Tennyson, Christenson, and Park, 1984
Hint explisiveness is adapted to quality of decisions	Using an avionics troubleshooting tutor, the program automatically adjusts the feedback provided to students	Lajoie and Lesgold, 1992
Software-based student evaluation is often wrong or totally inaccurate	Software may be inadequate for adapting instruction, human teachers are needed in evaluation and decision-making for adapting instruction	Hativa and Lesgold, 1991

strategies transferred to flying aircraft under workload conditions where all tasks could not be attended to at once and the subject had to make optimal decisions about how to allocate attention. The attentional demands of a task can also be reduced, or automatized, through specialized computer training for tasks such as reading (see Resnick and Johnson, 1988, for an overview).

36.8.10 Virtual Reality

Virtual reality has received much interest recently as a method to present training materials to students through simulations. In a virtual environment, the user has the experience of moving around within a digital environment. Most systems include goggles to present the images to the eyes and a sensor for head movements. As the head is moved, the computer-generated scene displayed over the goggles changes. As an example, when a person looks to the right, the scene will change to display the part of the environment to the right. The goggles also incorporate some method to present three-dimensional images by slightly changing or offsetting the images presented to the two eyes. Most virtual reality systems also include data gloves which sense the position of movements of the hands. The user interacts with the environment by pointing to objects displayed through the goggles.

Virtual reality holds promise as a training technique because it allows the user to actively explore the environment. Most users indicate that they experience a feeling of actually being present in the virtual world.

Table 10. Conceptual representations.

Issue	Discussion	Reference
Knowledge can be acquired by experts and put into a structure for training novices.	Subject matter experts will often leave out information that is automatized. Procedures, such as conceptual graph analysis, can be adapted to many situations to fill in incomplete or unclear structures from knowledge acquisition procedures.	Gordon, Schmierer, and Gill, 1993
Analogies can make acquisition of a task easier.	In experiments, analogies improved performance; Anderson et al.'s ACT model of learning incorporates analogies	Anderson, Boyle, Corbett, and Lewis, 1990; Webb and Kramer, 1990
The cognitive structures of the student provide an "ideational scaffolding" for new material	The material presented must fit into the student's memory structures	Ausubel, 1968; Hartley and Davies, 1976
Compatibility must exist for training operators of complex systems	Should be a compatibility between the physical system, the internal representation that the operator has of the system, and the interface (the display) between the two	Wickens, 1984
Spatial representation of information	Computer graphics can be used to help the student visualize concepts; has been used especially in engineering, math, and music	DuBoulay and Howe, 1982; Forchieri, Lemut, and Molfino, 1983; Gould and Finzer, 1982; Harding, 1983; Lamb, 1982; Pohlman and Edwards, 1983; Rogers, 1981; Stevens and Roberts, 1983
Programming used to structure information	Understand complex subjects, such as math, by writing a program; helps to specify steps	DuBoulay and Howe, 1982
Pictorial and graphics movement on instructional displays are only effective under some conditions	Review showed six conditions are important: demonstrating sequential actions; simulating causal models; making the invisible visible; illustrating tasks difficult to describe verbally; providing visual analogies; and focusing attention on specific tasks	Park and Hopkins, 1993

One training technique has the user follow the hand movements on the display, such as hitting a tennis ball with a tennis racket, and the training system signals the user if the movement deviates from the correct path or form (Fritz, 1991). New techniques for human-computer interaction are also being studied. The data glove can be used to move a slider inside a cube to navigate within the environment and three-dimensional maps are used to show the user's location within the space (MacDowall, 1994).

A list of some of the applications of virtual reality is included in Table 12. Virtual reality has several advantages over other graphics presentation computer systems.

Table 11. Motivation.

Issue	Discussion	Reference
Effectiveness of CAI may be dependent on students' computer anxiety and alienation.	Scales have been developed to determine computer anxiety and alienation. Results show that performance is not dependent on gender, but people who have much experience with computers and those who own computers exhibit less anxiety and alienation.	Morrow, Prell, and McElroy, 1986; Ray and Minch, 1990
Computer animation actually had a negative effect on motivation because students claimed that it took too long.	Students were given animated problems to teach Newtonian physics concepts. The animated group did not perform any better than a control condition. The subjects complained that the animation took too long to occur and became boring.	Rieber, Boyce, and Assad, 1990
To make computer learning intrinsically motivating, CAI can utilize challenge, fantasy, and curiosity	In a study of computer games, these features were incorporated; the same features could be used in CAI	Malone, 1980
Can use graphics to express new ideas and thoughts	Children used LOGO to creatively and actively manipulate images	Vaidya, 1983
Competition has different motivating effects on students	For a CAI program in an elementary school, boys were more competitive than girls and increased competitive behavior of high achievers but not low achievers	Hativa, Lesgold, and Swissa, 1993

Table 12. Virtual reality

Issue	Discussion	Reference
Applications give users a feeling of experiencing the training environment	Applications include: flight training; astronaut training; customers walking around a virtual environment of a proposed building design; simulated golf games on virtually any course in the world	Carr, 1992; Fritz, 1991
Can be used for "telecollaboration"	Two people separated by distances can collaborate through a shared virtual environment.	Fritz, 1991
Navigation within a three-dimensional space enhanced through virtual reality	Virtual reality was compared to a two-dimensional navigational training program	Regian and Shebilske (1992)
Virtual reality training did not transfer to the real-world environment	Transfer of training was compared for no training, virtual reality (VR) training, and real-world training; VR training was similar to no training and both were worse than real-world training	Kozak, Hancock, Arthur, and Chrysler (1993)

36.9 References

Ackerman, P. H., Wickens, C. D., and Schneider, W. (1984). Deciding the existence of a time-sharing ability: A combined methodological and theoretical approach. *Human Factors*, 26, 71-82.

Anderson, J., Boyle, C., Corbett, A., and Lewis, M. (1990). Cognitive modeling and intelligent tutoring. *Artificial Intelligence*, 42, 7-49.

Anderson, J. R., Boyle, C. F., and Reiser, B. J. (1985). Intelligent tutoring systems. *Science, 228,* 456-462.

Anderson, J. R., Kulhavy, R. W., and Andre, T. (1971).Feedback procedures in programmed instruction. *Journal of Educational Psychology, 62,* 148-156.

Arenson, M. (1982). The effect of a competency-based computer program of the learning of fundamental skills in a music theory course for non-majors. *Journal of Computer-Based Instruction, 9,* 55-58.

Ausubel, D. P. (1968). *Educational psychology: A cognitive view.* New York: Holt, Rinehart, and Winston.

Avner, A. R. (1979). Production of computer-based instructional materials. In H. F. O'Neil, Jr. (Ed.), *Issues in instructional systems development.* New York: Academic Press.

Avner, A., Moore, C., and Smith, S. (1980) Active external control: A basis for superiority of CBI. *Journal of Computer-Based Instruction, 6,* 115-118.

Avner, A., Smith, S., and Tenczar, P. (1984). CBI authoring tools: Effects on productivity and quality. *Journal of Computer-Based Instruction, 11,* 85-89.

Berliner, D. C., and Cohen, L. S. (1973). Trait-treatment interaction and learning. *Review of Research in Education, 1,* 58-94.

Bloomfield, J. R., and Little, R. K. (1985). Operator tracking performance with time-compressed and time integrated moving target indicator (MTI) radar imagery. In R. E. Eberts and C. G. Eberts (Eds.), *Trends in ergonomics/Human factors, Vol. II* (pp. 219-223. Amsterdam: North-Holland.

Bourne, J. R., Brodersen, A. J., Campbell, J. O., Dawant, M. M., and Shiavi, R. G. (1996, July). A model for on-line learning networks in engineering education. Journal of Engineering Education, 253-262.

Bracht, G. H. (1970). Experimental factors related to attribute-treatment interactions. *Review of Educational Research, 40,* 627-645.

Bracht, G. H., and Glass, G. V. (1972). Interaction of personological variables and treatment. In L. Sperry (Ed.), *Learning variables and treatment.* In L. Sperry (Ed.), Learning performance and individual differences: Essays and readings. Glenview, IL: Scott, Foresman.

Brackett, J. W. (1979). Traidex: A proposed system to minimize training duplication. In H. F. O'Neil, Jr. (Ed.), *Issues in instructional systems development.* New York: Academic Press.

Bunderson, C. B. (1981). Courseware. In H. F. O'Neil, Jr. (Ed.), *Computer-based instruction: A state-of-the-art assessment.* New York: Academic Press.

Burton, R. R., and Brown, J. S. (1979). Toward a natural-language capability for computer-assisted instruction. In H. F. O'Neil, Jr. (Ed.), *Procedures for instructional system development* (pp. 273-3313). New York: Academic Press.

Carlson, R. A., Khoo, B. H., Elliott, R. G. (1990). Component practice and exposure to a problem-solving context. *Human Factors, 32,* 267-286.

Carr, C. (1992, October). Is virtual reality virtually here? *Training and Development,* 37-41.

Center for the Study of Evaluation. (1986). *Intelligent computer aided instruction (ICAI): Formative evaluation of two systems* (ARI Research Note 86-29). Alexandria, VA: U.S. Army Research Institute (DTIC No. AD-A167 910).

Clancey, W. B. (1983). Guidon. *Journal of Computer-Based Instruction, 10,* 8-15.

Conkwright, T. D. (1982).PLATO applications in the airline industry. *Journal of Computer-Based Instruction, 8,* 49-52.

Cooper, L. A. (1976).Individual differences in visual comparison processes. *Perception and Psychophysics, 12,* 43-444.

Cronbach, L. J. (1967). How can instruction be adapted to individual differences? In R. M. Gagne (Ed.), Learning and individual differences (pp. 23-39). Columbus, OH: Merrill.

Cronbach, L., and Snow, R. (1977).Aptitudes and instructional methods: *A handbook for research on interactions.* New York: Irvington.

Dallman, B. E., Pieper, W. J., and Richardson, J. J. (1983). A graphics simulation system—Task emulation not equipment modeling. *Journal of Computer-Based Instruction, 10,* 70-72.

Dennis, V. E. (1979). The effect of display rate and

memory support on correct responses, trials, total instructional time and response latency in a computer-based learning environment. *Journal of Computer-Based Instruction, 6,* 50-54.

Detweiler, M. C., and Lundy, D. H. (1995). Effects of single- and dual-task practice on acquiring dual-task skill. *Human Factors, 37,* 193-211.

DiVesta, F. J. (1973). Theory and measures of individual differences in studies of trait by treatment interaction. *Educational Psychologist, 10,* 67-75.

DuBoulay, J. B. H., and Howe, J. A. M. (1982). LOGO building blocks: Student teachers using computer-based mathematics apparatus. *Computers and Education, 6,* 93-96.

Eberts, R. E., and Schneider, W. (1985). Internalizing the system dynamics for a second-order system. *Human Factors, 27,* 371-393.

Eberts, R. E., and Schneider, W. (1986). Effects of perceptual training of sequenced line movements. *Perception and Psychophysics, 39,* 236-247.

Fabiani, Monica, Buckley, J, Gratton, G., Coles, M. G. H., and Donchin, E. (1989). The training of complex task performance. *Acta Psychologica, 71,* 259-299.

Fairweather, P. G., and O'Neal, A. F. (1984).The impact of advanced authoring systems on CAI productivity. *Journal of Computer-Based Instruction, 11,* 90-94.

Farley, F. H. (1983). Basic process individual differences: A biologically based theory of individualization for cognitive, affective, and creative outcomes. In F. H. Farley and N. J. Gordon (Eds.), *Psychology and education: The state of the union.* (pp. 9-29). Berkeley, CA: McCutchan.

Forchieri, P., Lemut, E., and Molfino, M. T. (1983). The GRAF system: An interactive graphic systems for teaching mathematics. *Computers and Education, 7,* 177-182.

Fritz, M. (1991, February). The world of virtual reality. *Training,* 45-50.

Gaines, B. R. (1972). The learning of perceptual-motor skills by man and machines and its relationship to training. *Instructional Science, 1,* 263-312.

Gaynor, P. (1979). The effect of feedback delay on retention of computer-based mathematical material. *Journal of Computer-Based Instruction, 8,* 28-34.

Glaser, R. (1970). Psychological questions in the development of computer-assisted instruction. In W. H. Holtzman (Ed.), *Computer-assisted instructed, testing and guidance* (pp. 74-93). New York: Harper and Row.

Glaser, R. (1982). Instructional psychology: Past, present and future. *American Psychologist, 37,* 292-305.

Gopher, D., Weil, M., and Bareket, T. (1994). Transfer of skill from a computer game trainer to flight. *Human Factors, 36,* 387-405.

Gopher, D., Williges, R. C., and Damos, D. L. (1975).Manipulating the number and type of adaptive variables in training. *Journal of Motor Behavior, 7,* 159-170.

Goldstein, I. (1978). Developing a computational representation for problem solving skills. In *Proceedings of the Carnegie-Mellon Conference on Problem Solving and Education: Issues in Teaching and Research.* Pittsburgh: CMU Press.

Gordon, N. B. (1968). Guidance versus augmented feedback and motor skill. *Journal of Experimental Psychology, 77,* 24-30.

Gordon, N. B., and Gottlieb, M. J. (1967). Effects of supplemental visual cues on rotary pursuit. *Journal of Experimental Psychology, 77,* 24-30.

Gordon, S. E., Schmierer, K. A., and Gill, R. T. (1993). Conceptual graph analysis: Knowledge acquisition for instructional system design. *Human Factors, 35,* 459-481.

Gould, L., and Finzer, W. (1982). A study of TRIP: A computer system for animating time-rate-distance problems. *International Journal of Man-Machine Studies, 17,* 109-126.

Hall, K. B. (1983). Content structuring and question asking for computer-based education. *Journal of Computer-Based Instruction, 10,* 1-7.

Harding, R. D. (1983). A structured approach to computer graphics for mathematical uses. *Computers and Education, 7,* 1-19.

Hartley, J., and Davies, I. K. (1976). Pre-instructional strategies: The role of pre-test, behavioral objectives, overviews, and advanced organizers. *Review of Educational Research, 46,* 339-265.

Hativa, N., and Lesgold, A. (1993). The computer as tutor--Can it adapt to the individual learner? *Instructional Science, 20,* 49-78.

Hativa, N., Lesgold, A., and Swissa, S. (1993). Competition in individualized CAI. *Instructional Science, 21,* 365-400.

Hillelsohn, J. J. (1984). Benchmarking authoring systems. *Journal of Computer-Based Instruction, 11,* 95-97.

Hofstetter, F. T. (1983). The cost of PLATO in a university environment. *Journal of Computer-Based Instruction, 10,* 248-255.

Hollan, J. (1984). Intelligent object-based graphical interfaces. In G. Salvendy (Ed.), *Human-computer interaction* (pp. 2933-296). Amsterdam: North-Holland.

Hollan, J., Stevens, A., and Williams, N. (1980). *STEAMER: An advanced computer-assisted instruction system for propulsion engineering,* Paper presented at the Summer Simulation Conference, Seattle.

Jay, T. B. (1983). The cognitive approach to computer courseware design and evaluation. *Educational Technology, 23* (1), 22-26.

Katz, S., Lesgold, A., Eggan, G., and Gordin, M. (1992). *Journal of Artificial Intelligence in Education, 3,* 495-518.

Kozak, J. J., Hancock, P. A., Arthur, E. J., and Chrysler, S. T. (1993). *Ergonomics, 36,* 777-784.

Kurland, L. C., Granville, R. A., and MacLaughlin, D. M. (1990). *Design, development, and implementation of an intelligent tutoring system (ITS) for training radar mechanics to troubleshoot.* Unpublished manuscript, Bolt, Baranek, and Newman, Systems and Technologies Corporation, Cambridge, MA.

Lajoie, S. P., and Lesgold, A. M. (1992). Dynamic assessment of proficiency for solving procedural knowledge tasks. *Educational Psychologist, 27,* 365-384.

Lamb, M. (1982). An interactive graphical modeling game for teaching musical concepts. *Journal of Computer-Based Instruction, 9,* 59-63.

Larkin, J. H. (1981). Enriching formal knowledge: A model for learning to solve problems in physics. In J. R. Anderson (Ed.), *Cognitive skills and their acquisition.* Hillsdale, NJ: Erlbaum.

Larkin, J. H. (1982). Understanding problem representations and skill in physics. In S. Chipman, J. Segal, and R. Glaser (Eds)., *Thinking and learning skills: Current research and open questions.* Hillsdale, NJ: Erlbaum.

Lesgold, A. M., Feltovich, P. J., Glaser, R., and Wang, Y. (1981). *The acquisition of perceptual diagnostic skill in radiology* (Office of Naval Research Technical Report No. PDS-1). Pittsburgh, PA: University of Pittsburgh, Learning Research and Development Center.

Lintern, G. (1980). Transfer of landing skill after training with supplementary visual cues. *Human Factors, 22,* 81-88.

Lintern, G. (1991). An informational perspective on skill transfer in human-machine systems. *Human Factors, 33,* 251-266.

Lintern, G., and Roscoe, S. N. (1980). Visual cue augmentation in contact flight simulation. In S. N. Roscoe (Ed.), *Aviation Psychology.* Ames, IA: Iowa State University Press.

Lintern, G., Roscoe, S., Koonce, J. M., and Segal, L. D. (1990). Transfer of landing skills in beginning flight training. *Human Factors, 32,* 319-327.

Lyman, E. R. (1981). *PLATO highlights.* Urbana, IL: University of Illinois Computer-Based Education Research Laboratory.

MacDowall, I. (1994, May). 3D stereoscopic data for immersive displays. *AI Expert,* 18-21.

Malone, T. W. (1980). What makes things fun to learn? A study of intrinsically motivating computer games (Report CIOS-7 [SSL-80-11]). Palo Alto, CA: Xerox PaRC.

Maul, G. P., and Spotts, D. S. (1993). A comparison of computer-based training and classroom instruction. *Industrial Engineering Magazine, 25*(2), 25-27.

McCann, R. H. (1983). Learning strategies and computer-based instruction. *Computers and Education, 5,* 133-140.

McDonald, B. A., and Crawford, A. M. (1983). Remote site training using microprocessors. *Journal of Computer-Based Instruction, 10,* 83086.

Merrill, P. F., and Salisbury, D. (1984). Research on drill and practice strategies. *Journal of Computer-Based Instruction, 10,* 19-21.

Miller, R. B. (1978). Response time in man-computer conversational transactions. In *AFIPS Conference Proceedings.* Washington: Thompson Book Co.

Montague, W. E., Wulfeck, W. H., and Ellis, J. A. (1983a). Computer-based instructional research and development in the Navy: An overview. *Journal of Computer-Based Instruction, 10,* 83.

Montague, W. E., Wulfeck, W. H., and Ellis, J. A. (1983b). Quality CBI depends on quality instructional design and quality implementation. *Journal of Computer-Based Instruction, 10,* 90-93.

Morgan, C. E. (1978). CAI and basic skills information. *Educational Technology, 18* (4), 37-39.

Morrow, P. C., Prell, E. R., and McElroy, J.C. (1986). Attitudinal and behavioral correlates of computer anxiety. *Psychological Reports, 59,* 1199-1204.

Newell, A., and Rosenbloom, P. S. (1981). Mechanisms of skill acquisition and the law of practice. In J.

R. Anderson (Ed.), *Cognitive skills and* their acquisition (pp. 1-55). Hillsdale, NJ: Erlbaum.

North, R. A., and Gopher, D. (1976). Measures of attention as predictors of flight performance. Human Factors, 18, 1-14.

Orlansky, J., and String, J. (1977). *Cost-effectiveness of computer-based instruction in military training* (IDA Paper P-13375). Arlington, VA: Institute for Defense Analyses.

Park, O and Hopkins, R. (1993). Instructional conditions for using dynamic visual displays: A review. *Instructional Science, 21,* 427-449.

Park, O., and Tennyson, R. D. (1980). Adaptive design strategies for selecting number and presentation order of examples in coordinate concept acquisition. *Journal of Educational Psychology, 72,* 362-370.

Pohlman, D. L., and Edwards, B. J. (1983). Desk top trainer: Transfer of training of an aircrew procedural task. *Journal of Computer-Based Instruction, 10,* 62-65.

Raghavan, K., and Katz, A. (1989). Smithtown: An intelligent tutoring system. *Technological Horizons in Education Journal, 17,* 50-54.

Raschio, R., and Lange, D. L. (1984). A discussion of the attributes, roles and use of CAI material in foreign languages. *Journal of Computer-Based Instruction, 11,* 22-27.

Ray, N. M., and Minch, R. P. (1990). Computer anxiety and alienation: Toward a definitive and parsimonious measure. *Human Factors, 32,* 477-491.

Regian, J. W., and Shebilske, W. L. (1992). Virtual reality: An instructional medium for visual-spatial tasks. *Journal of Communication, 42,* 136-149.

Reigeluth, C. M. (1979). TICCIT to the future: Advance in instructional theory for CAI. *Journal of Computer-Based Instruction, 11,* 22-27.

Resnick, L. B., and Johnson, A. (1988). Intelligent machines for intelligent people: Cognitive theory and the future of computer-assisted learning. In R. S. Nickerson and P. P. Zodhiates (Eds.), *Technology in education: Looking toward 2020* (pp. 139-168). Hillsdale, NJ: Erlbaum.

Rieber, L. P., Boyce, M. J., and Assad, C. (1990). The effect of computer animation on adult learning and retrieval tasks. *Journal of Computer-Based Instruction, 17,* 46-52.

Rogers, D. F. (1981). Computer graphics at the U.S. Naval Academy. *Computers and Education, 5,* 165-182.

Ross, S. M. (1984). Matching the lesson to the student: Alternative adaptive designs for individualized learning systems. *Journal of Computer-Based Instruction, 11,* 42-48.

Sales, G. C., and Tsai, B., and McLeod, R. (1991). The evaluation of K-12 instructional software: An analysis of leading microcomputer-based programs from 1981-1988. *Journal of Computer-Based Instruction, 18,* 41-47.

Scanlan, L. A. (1975). Visual time compression: Spatial and temporal cues. *Human Factors, 17,* 84-90.

Schmidt, R. A., and Bjork, R. A. (1992). New conceptualizations of practice: Common principles in three paradigms suggest new concepts for training. *Psychological Science, 3,* 207-217.

Schneider, W. (1981). Automatic control processing concepts and their implications for the training of skills (Technical Report HARL ONR-8101). Champaign, IL: University of Illinois, Human Attention Research Laboratory.

Schneider, W., and Fisk, A. D. (1981). Degree of consistent training: Improvements in search performance and automatic process development. *Perception and Psychophysics,* 31, 160-168.

Schneider, W., and Shiffrin, R. M. (1977). Controlled and automatic human information processing: I. Detection, search, and attention. *Psychological Review, 84,* 1-66.

Shiffrin, R. M., and Schneider, W. (1977). Controlled and automatic human information processing: II. Perceptual learning, automatic attending, and a general theory. *Psychological Review, 84,* 127-190.

Stammers, R. B. (1982). Part and whole practice in training for procedural tasks. *Human Learning, 1,* 185-207.

Steinberg, E. R. (1977). Review of student control in computer-assisted instruction. *Journal of Computer-Based Instruction, 3,* 84-90.

Steinberg, E. R. (1989). Cognition and learner control: A literature review, 1977-1988. *Journal of Computer-Based Instruction, 16,* 117-121.

Stevens, A., and Roberts, B. (1983). Quantitative and qualitative simulation in computer based training. *Journal of Computer-Based Instruction, 10,* 16-19.

Tatsuoka, K., and Birenbaum, M. (1981). Effects of instructional backgrounds on test performance. *Journal of Computer-Based Instruction, 8,* 1-9.

Tennyson, R. D., Christenson, D. L., and Park, S. I.

(1984). The Minnesota adaptive instructional system: An intelligent CBI system. *Journal of Computer-Based Instruction, 11,* 2-13.

Tennyson, C. L., Tennyson, R. D., and Rothen, W. (1980). Content structure and management strategy as design variables in concept acquisition. *Journal of Educational Psychology, 72,* 491-505.

Tobias, S. (1976). Achievement treatment interactions. *Review of Educational Research, 46,* 671-674.

Towne, D. M., and Munro, A. (1991). Simulation-based instruction of technical skills. *Human Factors, 33,* 325-341.

Trowbridge, M. H., and Cason, H. (1932). An experimental study of Thorndike's theory of learning. *Journal of General Psychology, 7,* 245-258.

Vaidya, S. (1983). Using LOGO to stimulate children's fantasy. *Educational Technology, 23* (12), 25-26.

Vernon, R. F. (1993). What really happens to complimentary textbook software? A case study in software utilization. *Journal of Computer-Based Instruction, 20,* 35-38.

Webb, J. M., and Kramer, A. F. (1990). Maps or analogies? A comparison of instructional aids for menu navigation. *Human Factors, 32,* 251-266.

Whaley, C. J., and Fisk, A. D. (1993). Effects of part-task training on memory set unitization and retention of memory-dependent skilled search. *Human Factors, 35,* 639-652.

Wheaton, G. R., Rose, A. M., Fingerman, P. W., Korotkin, A. L., and Holding, D. H. (1976). *Evaluation of the effectiveness of training devices: Literature review and preliminary model* (Research Memorandum 76-6). Alexandria, VA: U.S. Army Research Institute for the Behavioral and Social Sciences.

Wickens, C. D. (1984). Engineering psychology and human performance. Columbus, OH: Merrill.

Williams, M., Holland, J., and Stevens, A. (1981). An overview of STEAMER: An advanced computer-assisted instruction system for propulsion engineering. Behavior Research Methods and Instrumentation, 13, *85-90.*

Handbook of Human-Computer Interaction
Second, completely revised edition
M. Helander, T.K. Landauer, P. Prabhu (eds.)

Chapter 37

Intelligent Tutoring Systems

Albert T. Corbett and Kenneth R. Koedinger
Human Computer Interaction Institute
Carnegie Mellon University
Pittsburgh, Pennsylvania, USA

John R. Anderson
Department of Psychology and Computer Science
Carnegie Mellon University
Pittsburgh, Pennsylvania, USA

37.1 Introduction

Computers have been employed to achieve a variety of educational goals since the early 1960s. Some of these goals include automated testing and routine drill and practice tasks that had been mechanized with earlier technologies, as far back as the thirties. Other computer assisted instructional programs engage the students in challenging and entertaining reasoning tasks and capitalize on multimedia capabilities to present information (cf. Larkin and Chabay, 1992). Computer-based instruction has successfully penetrated all education and training markets: home, schools, universities, business, and government, but remains far from the modal educational experience.

In the early 1970s a few researchers defined a new and ambitious goal for computer-based instruction. They adopted the human tutor as their educational model and sought to apply artificial intelligence techniques to realize this model in "intelligent" computer-based instruction. Personal human tutors provide a highly efficient learning environment (Cohen, Kulik and Kulik, 1982) and have been estimated to increase mean achievement outcomes by as much as two standard deviations (Bloom, 1984)[1]. The goal of intelligent tutoring systems (ITSs) would be to engage the students in sustained reasoning activity and to interact with the student based on a deep understanding of the students behavior. If such systems realize even half the impact of human tutors, the payoff for society promised to be substantial.

Seminal intelligent tutoring efforts are well documented in two classic books, Sleeman and Brown (1982) and Wenger (1987), and research efforts over the ensuing twenty-five years have yielded some notable successes in achieving the promise of intelligent tutoring (Lesgold, Eggan, Katz and Rao, 1992; Koedinger, Anderson, Hadley and Mark, 1995). In this chapter we abstract a set of design recommendations

[1]Evaluations of instructional effectiveness employ a variety of learning time and achievement measures. The conventional method for comparing educational manipulations is to convert effect sizes into standard deviation units, that is, to subtract the mean of a control group from the mean of the experimental group and divide by the standard deviation of the control group. An effect of 2 standard deviations indicates that 98% of the experimental group performed as well as the top 50% of the control group. This is not a perfect measure, since apparent effect sizes depend on sample variability.

from this extended research effort. The chapter contains three main sections. The first provides an overview of intelligent tutoring systems. The second section provides a prescription for ITS design and development methods. The third section addresses several issues concerning ITS design principles.

37.2 Overview of Intelligent Tutoring Systems

This section provides an overview of intelligent tutoring systems. We begin with a comment on competing research goals in the field, followed by descriptions of two successful systems: (1) our own PUMP Algebra Tutor Project and (2) the SHERLOCK project (Lesgold, Eggan, Katz and Rao, 1992). These two systems are being deployed in real-world educational environments with substantial success. We briefly describe the underlying theory and implementation of each, to motivate later discussions. We follow with a description of the standard components in an intelligent tutoring system and conclude with a discussion of HCI assessment issues unique to educational software. Readers who are well-versed in the field may wish to skip over this overview to the following sections on design methods and principles.

37.2.1 Research Goals: AI vs. Education

While there has been a sustained research effort in the application of artificial intelligence to education over the past twenty-five years with some notable success stories, intelligent tutoring has had relatively little impact on education and training in the real world. There are several reasons for this lack of penetration. Intelligent tutoring systems are expensive to develop and until relatively recently, the necessary computing power was expensive to deploy. However, we believe that an even more important reason can be traced to the ontogeny of the field and *the consequences for software evaluation.* The creative vision of intelligent computer tutors has largely arisen among artificial intelligence researchers rather than education specialists. Researchers recognized that intelligent tutoring systems are a rich and important natural environment in which to deploy and improve AI algorithms. We have outlined elsewhere a variety of consequences that derive from this history in AI, (Anderson and Corbett, 1993) but the bottom line is that intelligent tutoring systems are generally evaluated according to artificial intelligence criteria - the coverage of the systems in interpreting and responding to student behaviors - rather than with respect to a cost/benefit analysis of educational effectiveness.

The first intelligent tutoring program, SCHOLAR (Carbonell, 1970) merits special recognition and serves to exemplify this pattern. This program attempted to engage the student in a *mixed-initiative* dialogue on South American geography. The program and student communicated through a sequence of natural language questions and answers. The tutor could both ask and answer questions and keep track of the ongoing dialogue structure. This tutor was constructed around a semantic network model of domain knowledge. Such network models of conceptual knowledge were revolutionizing our understanding of question answering and inferential reasoning in cognitive science (cf. Anderson and Bower, 1973; Collins and Loftus, 1975) and remain the modal model of conceptual knowledge today (cf. Anderson, 1983). However, the effort to sustain a dialogue revealed the importance of unexplored issues in dialogue structure and pragmatic reasoning. This fed into an interesting research program and successive dialogue tutors (Stevens and Collins, 1977; Collins and Steven, 1991; Woolf and McDonald, 1984), but in the end the fascinating and challenging issues in natural language comprehension took precedence over research in how to deploy dialogue tutors effectively.

While there has been a rich intellectual history in intelligent tutoring, we believe that for intelligent tutors to seriously penetrate the educational/training system, the evaluative focus must begin to shift to educational impact and away from artificial intelligence sufficiency. This has begun to happen, but at each of the two most recent International Conferences on Intelligent Tutoring Systems (Frasson, Gauthier and McCalla, 1992; Frasson, Gauthier and Lesgold, 1996), only 25% of non-invited papers included empirical evaluations of any sort. Among these empirical studies only about one in ten (i.e., 2.5% of all papers) assessed the effectiveness of a computer-based learning environment by comparing student performance to other learning environments. We believe the emphasis on educational impact must permeate all stages of ITS development, deployment and assessment. After twenty five years we can frame many important questions in effective intelligent tutoring, but can provide only preliminary answers.

37.2.2 The PUMP Algebra Tutor (PAT) Project

We have been developing and using intelligent tutoring systems for mathematics and programming for a little over a decade (Anderson, Corbett, Koedinger and Pelletier, 1995). Four years ago we partnered with the Pittsburgh School District to develop an intelligent tutoring system for introductory algebra. Events in mathematics education at the national level coalesced with the situation in the Pittsburgh schools to make this an opportune target. The recent National Council of Teachers of Mathematics (1989) curriculum standards advocates mathematics for all students. These standards recommend an algebra curriculum that is relevant for students bound for college or directly for the workplace. They de-emphasize symbol manipulation and emphasize reasoning about authentic problem situations with multiple representations, including symbolic expressions, natural language, graphs and tables. In emphasizing relevance, the standards also advocate reasoning about mathematics in the context of modern computational tools, e.g., graphics calculators and spreadsheets. These recommendations directly speak to mathematics education in Pittsburgh, which is typical of a city its size. Only about two-thirds of high school freshmen take algebra I and among students who enter the academic mathematics track (algebra I, geometry, algebra II, precalculus), about 40% drop out each year. Mathematics achievement levels are appreciably below the national average.

A number of mathematics teachers and curriculum supervisors in the school district are active in mathematics curriculum reform at the national level and contributed to the National Council of Teachers of Mathematics standards that emphasized academic mathematics for all students. These local mathematics educators formed the Pittsburgh Urban Math Project (PUMP) to develop a new algebra curriculum consistent with the new standards. This curriculum became the starting point for the PUMP Algebra Tutor (PAT). PAT is an algebraic problem solving environment. Each task presents a problem solving situation that describes the relationships among two or three quantities and presents from three to six specific questions to answer. The students are asked to represent the quantities as spreadsheet columns, answer the questions in the spreadsheet rows, induce an algebraic description of the relationships and graph these relationships.

Figure 1 displays the algebra word problem tutor screen in the middle of an exercise. The exercise description appears in a window at the upper left. In this exercise the student is solving an exercise that calls for a system of two equations. In the lower left, the student has constructed the table that exemplifies the relationships among the quantities in the exercise. This table is characteristic of a typical computer spreadsheet application. The columns represent the quantities and the rows represent different example values. In this exercise, the first column represents distance traveled and the second and third columns represent the cost of renting a car from two different agencies. The student has labeled the quantities at the top of each column and indicated the units in the first row. The student also enters a mathematical variable, e.g., x, into the second row of the first column to formalize this quantity. The student has constructed mathematical expressions for deriving each of the other two quantities with this variable (0.21x + 525 and 0.13x + 585) and entered them into the second and third columns. Finally, the student enters example values into the remaining rows in response to specific queries in the exercise description. Having constructed this table, the student also graphs the equations in the upper right. The student generates an appropriate scale and label for each axis, and identifies the intersection of the two lines. Thus, the student gains experience with alternative representations: the table, the symbolized expression and the graphical representation.

PAT's first classroom piloting came in 1992-1993 in Pittsburgh's Langley High School. Students worked with the tutor in about 25 algebra I class periods (out of almost 180) that first year. In 1993-1994 all incoming freshman in Langley high school entered the academic mathematics track via the PUMP algebra course and the PAT project expanded to two other Pittsburgh high schools. In this second year, students spent about 40 class periods with the tutor. By 1995-1996, approximately 750 students in six area high schools worked through the PUMP algebra course and tutor. In 1993-1994 and 1994-1995 year-end assessments, PUMP algebra students performed 100% better than comparable traditional algebra I students on assessments of reasoning among multiple representations in authentic problem solving situations (a one-standard deviation improvement). PUMP algebra students also performed 10-15% better on standardized mathematics tasks, e.g., Math SAT exercises, that are de-emphasized in the PUMP/PAT curriculum.

Note that we cannot separate the impact of the intelligent tutoring system from the impact of the reformed curriculum. In the past we have achieved similar one-standard deviation effects of intelligent tutoring with a constant curriculum (Anderson, Boyle, Corbett and Lewis, 1990; Corbett and Anderson, 1991; Koedinger and Anderson, 1993a). However, the more important point is that this project that began with an assessment of educational needs rather than concern with artificial intelligence innovation and resulted in an integrated package that yielded a one-standard deviation benefit compared to traditional practice.

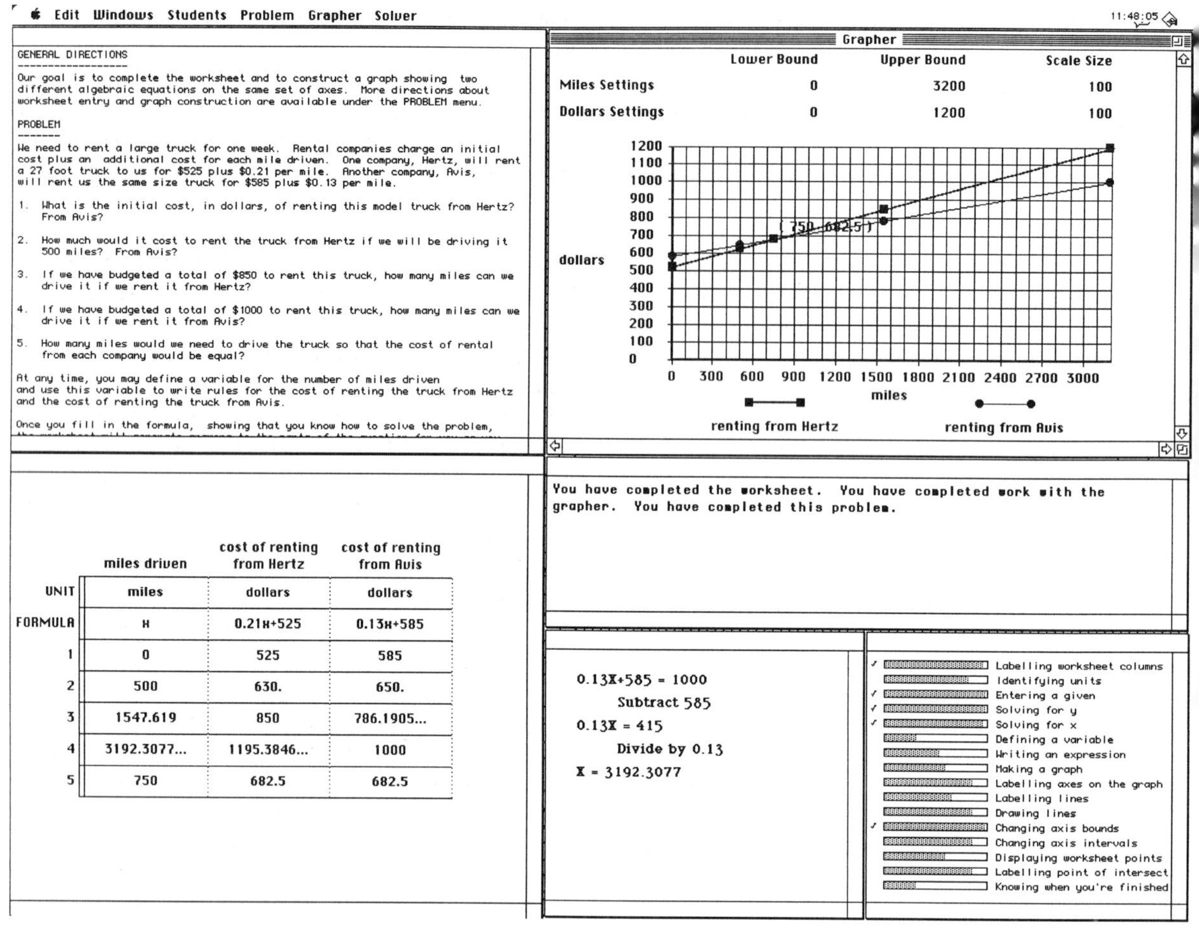

Figure 1. The PUMP algebra tutor.

37.2.3 Cognitive Theory

The tutors reflect the ACT-R theory of skill knowledge (Anderson, 1993). This theory assumes a fundamental distinction between declarative knowledge and procedural knowledge. Declarative knowledge is factual or experiential. For example, the following sentence and example on equation solving in an algebra text would be encoded declaratively:

> When the quantities on both sides of an equation are divided by the same value, the resulting quantities are equal.
>
> For example, if we assume 2X = 12, then we can divided both sides of the equation by 2, and the two resulting expressions will be equal, X = 6.

ACT-R assumes that skill knowledge is encoded initially in declarative form through experiences such as reading. While such declarative knowledge is a prerequisite of domain expertise, efficient problem solving requires the encoding of goal-oriented procedural knowledge. ACT-R assumes that early in practice the student solves problems by applying general procedural rules to the domain-specific knowledge. As a consequence of this early activity, domain-specific procedural knowledge is acquired. With subsequent practice, both declarative and procedural knowledge are strengthened so that performance grows more rapid and reliable. Like many cognitive theories (cf. Kieras and Bovair, 1986; Newell, 1990; Reed, Dempster and Ettinger, 1985) ACT-R assumes that procedural knowledge can be represented as a set of independent production rules that associate problem states and problem-solving goals with actions and consequent state changes. The following goal-oriented production can be derived from the declarative example above through practice in solving equations:

> IF the goal is to solve an equation for variable X and the equation is of the form aX = b,
> THEN divide both sides of the equation by a to isolate X.

PAT contains many rules, for labeling table columns, entering problem givens and computing results, inducing algebraic expressions from examples, solving equations, labeling and scaling graphs and placing points. We call the set of programming rules built into the tutor the *ideal student model*, because it embodies the knowledge that the student is trying to acquire. The ideal model plays two roles in our tutors, as described below. First, it allows the tutor to solve exercises step-by-step along with the student in a process we call *model tracing*. Second, it is used to trace each student's growing knowledge in a process we call *knowledge tracing*.

Model-Tracing Tutors. A model-tracing tutor solves each problem step-by-step along with the student, providing assistance as needed. The goal is to follow each student's individual solution path (sequence of problem solving actions) through a problem space that may contain thousands of solution paths. In each problem solving cycle the student selects an interface element to work on, (e.g., a spreadsheet cell), and performs a problem solving action, (e.g., typing a numeric value). Each of these interface elements is linked to an internal representation of a problem solving goal with links to relevant information in the current problem solving state. The tutor applies its production rules to the goal the student implicitly selects and generates a set of one or more applicable rules that satisfy the goal. The student's action is compared to the actions this set of applicable rules would generate. If the student action matches a production rule action it is assumed that the student has fired the same cognitive rule and the actions are carried out. If not, the tutor reports that it does not recognize the student's action.

Tracing the student's step-by-step solution enables the tutor to provide individualized instruction in the problem solving context. Prototypically our tutors provide immediate feedback on each problem solving action: recognizably correct actions are accepted and unrecognized actions are rejected. Our tutors do not try to diagnose student misconceptions and do not automatically give problem solving advice. Instead, they allow the student maximum opportunity to reason about the current problem state. The tutors do provide a feedback message if the student appears confused about the nature of the current problem state or a problem solving action. For example, the tutor will point out if the student has entered the right answer for one cell in the wrong cell of a table. The tutors provide goal-directed problem solving advice upon request. We recognize three general levels of advice: a reminder of the current goal, a general description of how to achieve the goal, and a description of exactly what problem solving action to take. Each of these three levels may be represented by multiple messages.

The ideal student model is also used to trace the student's growing knowledge state and to implement a variation of mastery learning. Each curriculum section introduces a set of rules in the ideal model. The tutor estimates the probability that the student knows each production based on the student's action at each opportunity to apply the rule in a process we call *knowledge tracing*. This process employs a simple Bayesian decision process described elsewhere (Corbett and Anderson, 1995b). In mastery learning, students continue solving problems in a section until the probability that the student knows each rule has reached near certainty.

37.2.4 The SHERLOCK Project

SHERLOCK is a practice environment for electronics troubleshooting commissioned by the Air Force (Lesgold, LaJoie, Bunzo and Eggan, 1992; Katz and Lesgold, 1993). Where PAT represents one of the mainstreams in intelligent tutoring, mathematics problem solving (Sleeman, Kelly, Martinak, Ward and Moore, 1989;) SHERLOCK represents a second mainstream, diagnosis (Brown, Burton and Zdybel, 1973; Clancey 1982; Gitomer, Steinberg and Mislevy, 1995; Tenney and Kurland, 1988). SHERLOCK is designed to give technicians practice in troubleshooting the F-15 Avionics Test Station. The test station is itself an electronic system for diagnosing failures in F-15 electronic equipment. However, the test station may malfunction and this poses an interesting problem. While there are detailed procedures for using the test station to diagnose electronic failures in the F-15, there are no fixed procedures for troubleshooting the test station. Since the test station breaks down infrequently, there is limited opportunity for technicians to learn troubleshooting heuristics on the job. Many of the technicians are in the relevant maintenance position for a limited time, so there is scant opportunity to build up expertise. SHERLOCK addresses this problem by providing ample troubleshooting opportunities.

In a characteristic simple problem solving scenario the trainee is informed that the test station was used to measure an F15 electronic component and the meter reading indicated component malfunction. However, when the suspect F15 component was replaced the meter reading still indicated component malfunction, suggesting that the test station itself is malfunctioning. The problem solving goal is to track down the source of the test station malfunction. SHERLOCK presents a visually realistic simulation of the external control panel of the avionics test station as shown in Figure 2A and the student can manipulate the controls with the mouse. The internals of the test station are represented by schematic diagrams. Figure 2B displays the schematic for one test station component. The student can take measurements by indicating the points on the schematic to 'attach' leads and the student can manipulate components , e.g., tightening connections to or 'swapping-in' a replacement for suspect components in the schematic diagram. The student communicates an intended action category and test station component through a set of hierarchical menus.

Unlike PAT, SHERLOCK generally does not provide immediate feedback on problem solving actions. Like PAT, SHERLOCK provides advice on problem solving steps upon student request. Four types of feedback are available: (1) advice on the what test action to carry out and how, (2) advice on how to read the outcome of the test, (3) advice on what conclusion can be drawn from the test and (4) advice on what option to pursue next.

The cognitive theory underlying SHERLOCK is compatible with ACT-R, but the tutor's internal representation of domain knowledge is quite different. Any problem solving task can be characterized as a problem solving "space" containing problem solving states that are linked by problem solving actions. PAT dynamically generates this problem space as rules in the cognitive model are applied in problem solving. In SHERLOCK, this problem solving space is stored as an explicit data structure. Only abstract problem states and problem solving actions are explicitly represented. Details concerning the device and concrete actions are embedded in executable code. Students navigate through this problem solving space with the set of hierarchical menus mentioned above. Student actions are interpreted with respect to information stored in each state.

Independent field tests of SHERLOCK were conducted by the Air Force, comparing three groups: (1) an experimental group of relative novices who completed 20-25 hours of coached practice with SHERLOCK, (2) a control group of similar novices who continued with usual work activities, and (3) a group of experienced technicians. The two novice groups completed pretests and posttests of their diagnostic skills while the expert group completed a single test. The two novice groups performed equivalently on the pretest, while the expert technicians scored about 40% higher. On the posttest the experimental group scores rose about 35%, essentially overtaking the expert technicians, while the control scores did not rise significantly. A regression analysis indicates that the 20-25 hours of practice with SHERLOCK had an equivalent impact to 4 years of on-the-job experience. SHERLOCK achieves this stunning result in two ways, by affording the opportunity for extensive practice and by creating educationally effective instructional conditions.

Despite these impressive results, this field test was essentially a formative evaluation, designed to examine and redesign the system where necessary (Lesgold, Eggan, Katz and Rao, 1992). This analysis led to a series of changes embodied in the SHERLOCK II system. The schematic representations of the test station internal components were replaced by faithful visual representations. In SHERLOCK I measurement readings were stored in tables rather than computed dynamically and students could only take measurements that were judged to be reasonably related to the problem situation. In SHERLOCK II measurement readings are generated dynamically and students can perform unexpected measurements. An analysis of problem solving procedures across SHERLOCK's problem situations led to a hierarchical model of progressively more abstract methods. This representation is used in SHERLOCK II to provide advice at more abstract levels to mediate feedback. Finally, a "reflective follow-up" was added to each problem solving task in which students can replay their problem solving actions, explore the problem state at each step and obtain advice on optimal strategy.

37.2.5 Intelligent Tutoring Architecture

While the seminal intelligent tutoring project SCHOLAR employed a conversational dialogue, the overwhelming majority of intelligent tutoring systems employ a different tutoring model as exemplified in

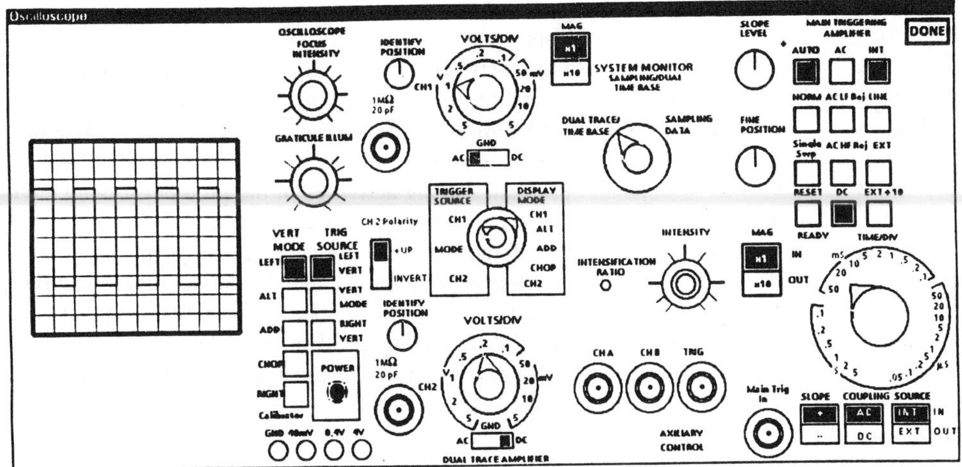

Figure 2A. An external control panel of the F15 Avionics test station. *From A.Lesgold, S. Lajoie, M. Bunzo and G. Eggan, 1992. Reprinted by permission.*

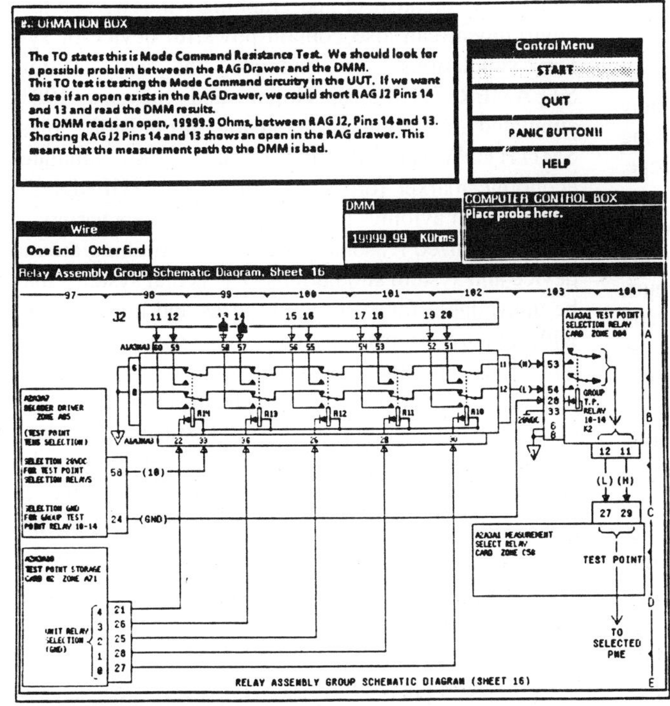

Figure 2B. The SHERLOCK interface displaying a schematic representation of an internal component of the F15 avionics test station. *From A.Lesgold, S. Lajoie, M. Bunzo and G. Eggan, 1992. Copyright 1992 by Lawrence Erlbaum Associates. Reprinted by permission.*

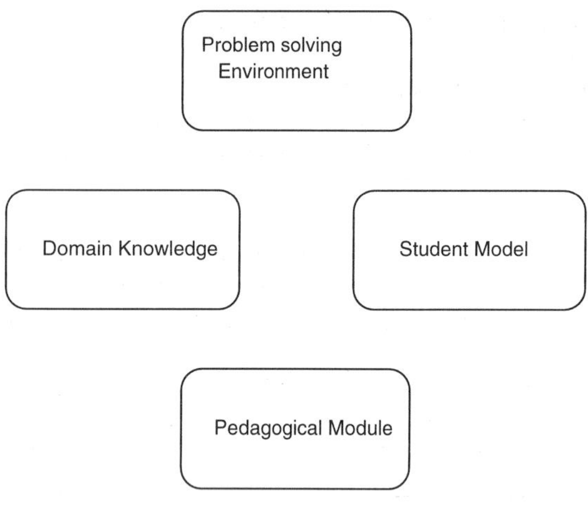

Figure 3. Components of an intelligent tutor architecture.

PAT and SHERLOCK: coached practice. In these environments instruction is delivered in the context of students engaged in problem solving tasks. There are pedagogical reasons for the dominance of this paradigm: It embodies the "learning-by-doing" model of cognitive skill acquisition. There are also computational advantages associated with this paradigm. Many problem solving domains provide a problem solving formalism that is easier to parse than natural language. As might be expected, the earliest problem solving tutors focused on such formal domains as mathematics (Brown, 1983; Burton and Brown, 1982), programming (Johnson and Soloway, 1984; Miller, 1979; Westcourt, Beard and Gould, 1977; cf. Brusilovsky, 1995) and electronics (Brown, Burton and Zdybel, 1973). As recently as the 1992 International Conference on Intelligent Tutoring Systems (Frasson, Gauthier and McCalla, 1992) 50% of the presentations were drawn from these three areas, although the proportion of presentations in these areas dropped substantially by the 1996 conference (Frasson, Gauthier and Lesgold, 1996). In addition, a problem solving task constrains the reasoning space for both the student and tutor. In a dialogue if the tutor does not understand a question or know the answer, the dialogue flounders. Pragmatically, in problem solving, the tutor can always give advice even if it cannot interpret the student's action. Moreover, there is less of a premium on a "natural" interaction style in coached practice than in a dialogue. Our discussion of intelligent tutoring systems will focus on coached practice systems.

The classic intelligent tutoring architecture consists of four components, as displayed in Figure 3: (1) a task environment, (2) a domain knowledge module, (3) a student model and (4) a pedagogical module. An extended discussion of these components can be found in Polson and Richardson (1988). Students engage in problem solving activities in the problem solving environment. These actions are evaluated with respect to the domain knowledge component, typically expert problem solving knowledge. Based on this evaluation a model of each student's knowledge state is maintained. Finally, the pedagogical module delivers instructional actions based on the evaluation of student actions and on the student model.

The Problem-Solving Environment. This component of the tutor defines the problem solving activities in which the student is engaged. At minimum it consists of an editor that accepts and represents student actions. For example, in the case of programming tutors, the interface may be a text editor (Johnson and Soloway, 1984), structure editor (Anderson and Reiser, 1985) or graphical editor (Reiser, Kimberg, Lovett and Ranney, 1992). As can be seen in Figure 1, the PAT interface contains a spreadsheet and graphing window. The task environment can also contain powerful device or system simulations. For example, the early system STEAMER (Williams, Hollan and Stevens, 1981) simulated a shipboard steam propulsion plan. SMITHTOWN (Shute and Glaser, 1990) simulates economic market forces and, of course, SHERLOCK simulates an avionics test station. There are a variety of well-recognized reasons for structuring training around device and system simulations. The actual systems may be unavailable for training purposes and novice errors with actual systems may cause expensive damage or dangerous situations. A simulation's response to student actions provides a form of feedback, independent of tutorial advice, that enables the student to reason about the problem solving situation. Finally, simulations can yield substantial savings in learning time. In the case of SHERLOCK for example, students do not have to spend time physically connecting lead wires to take measurements.

There is a strong consensus on two principles of problem solving interface design.

(1) The ITS problem solving environment should approximate the real world problem solving environment.

(2) The ITS problem solving environment should facilitate the learning process.

The first principle is implicit in the NCTM recommendations that students use real world computational tools in learning mathematics. When we began developing intelligent tutors over a decade ago we thought of the problem solving interface primarily as a vehicle for learning an abstract skill. We have come to recognize that at least at first, skill acquisition is closely tied to overt problem solving actions, and that even the expression of abstract knowledge requires the learning of many concrete interface activities. Consequently, similarity of learning environments and real world environments affords greater transfer of learning. This recognition has led to a strand of research in which we are building tutors for commercially available mathematical software applications (Ritter and Koedinger, 1995). This research is in an early stage but it may lead to a shift in the deployment of intelligent tutoring technology. Instead of acquiring a tutor to learn a skill, the user will acquire a software application with "lightweight tutoring agents" that can be engaged to support learning in the environment.

On the surface the second principle is in conflict with the first; it recommends deviating from the workplace problem solving environment to increase learning rate. There are several ways in which the interface can be modified to support learning. First, it is possible to abstract away irrelevant aspects of the problem solving task. In the case of device simulations this means eliminating potentially time consuming physical actions such as attaching electronic leads (Lesgold, Eggan, Katz and Rao, 1992). A second modification is to provide augmented feedback on device states or problem solving states. This can include reifying (explicitly displaying) the problem solving goal structure (Singley, Carroll and Alpert, 1993), or displaying implicit machine states in program execution (Eisenstadt, Price and Domingue, 1993; Ramadhan and du Boulay, 1993). Finally, the student may be asked to complete activities that are not required in the real-world problem-solving process. This can include requiring the student to specify a problem solving plan (Bonar and Cunningham, 1988; Bhuiyan, Greer and McCalla, 1992), or to specify implicit problem states (Reiser, Kimberg, Lovett and Ranney, 1992; Corbett and Anderson, 1995a). Finally, cognitive task analyses may recommend entirely reconfiguring the standard problem solving interface (Koedinger and Anderson, 1993b; Singley, 1987). We will consider these issues further in the final section on design principles.

The Domain Expert. As its name suggests, the domain expert module represents the content knowledge that the student is acquiring. This module is at the heart of an intelligent tutoring system and provides the basis for interpreting student actions. Classically, the domain module takes the form of an expert system that can generate solutions to the same problems the student is solving.[2]

One of the very important early results in intelligent tutoring research is the importance of the cognitive fidelity of domain knowledge module: It is important for the tutor to reason about the problem in the same way that humans do. Such cognitively valid models can be contrasted with "black box" and "glass box" models (Anderson, 1988). A black box model is one that fundamentally describes problem states differently than the student. The classic example of such a system is SOPHIE I (Brown, Burton and Zdybel, 1973). It was a tutor for electronic troubleshooting that used its expert system to evaluate the measurements students were making in troubleshooting a circuit. The expert system did not apply causal human reasoning, but based its decisions by solving sets of equations. As a consequence the tutor can recommend optimal actions in each problem solving context, but it was entirely up to the student to construct a description of that problem solving context and the rationale for the appropriate action.

A glass box model is an intermediate model that reasons in terms of the same domain constructs as a human experts, but with a different control structure. The classic example of such a system is Clancey's (1982) GUIDON system that tutored medical diagnosis. This system was constructed around the expert diagnostic system MYCIN. MYCIN consists of several hundred if-then rules that probabilistically relate disease states to diagnoses. These rules reference the same symptoms and states doctors employ in reasoning, but with a radically different control structure. MYCIN reaches a diagnosis by an exhaustive backward search. Although the expert system and doctor would agree on the description of any problem solving state, Clancey pointed out that it is difficult to tutor a doctor on what to do next when the expert system and student are following a different trajectory into and out of the state.

These studies revealed early on the likely futility of building an intelligent tutor around an off-the-shelf ex-

---

[2]This applies to coaching tutors. In dialogue tutors domain knowledge consists primarily of declarative knowledge. Other approaches are possible in coaching tutors; the domain knowledge module may be constructed to evaluate student solutions rather than generate solutions.

pert system. Instead, it is necessary to develop a true cognitive model of the domain knowledge that solves exercises in the same way students solve them. We refer to this domain expert as an ideal student model, since it is a computational model of the ideal knowledge the student is acquiring. As a result, one of the crucial steps in intelligent tutor development is a careful analysis of how humans, both expert and novice approach the problem solving task.

The Student Model. The student model is a record of the student's knowledge state. There are classically two components in a student model: an overlay of the domain expert knowledge and a bug catalog.

The first component is essentially a copy of the domain expertise model in which each knowledge unit is tagged with an estimate of how well the student has learned it. PAT, for example, assumes a simple two state learning model in which each production rule is either learned or not. As students work PAT estimates the probability that each rule is in the learned state. SHERLOCK II assumes five learning states: no knowledge, limited knowledge, unautomated knowledge, partially automated knowledge and fully developed knowledge. SHERLOCK II estimates the probabilities that each knowledge unit is in each of the five states.

The bug catalog is set of misconceptions or incorrect rules, each carrying an indication of whether the student has acquired the misconception. Much of the early interest in intelligent tutoring systems was motivated by the promise of diagnosing and remediating student misconceptions, but this early enthusiasm has faded for two reasons. First, enduring misconceptions are less frequent than assumed (VanLehn, 1990; Sleeman, Ward, Kelly, Martinak and Moore, 1991). VanLehn argues that many actions consistent with misconceptions are simply "patches" for problem solving impasses. While the impasse may be enduring, the student may try a different patch the next time around. Second, an influential paper by Sleeman, Kelly, Martinak, Ward and Moore (1989) indicated that providing remedial feedback tuned to bugs is no more effective than instruction that simply reteaches the correct approach. McKendree (1990) has demonstrated that carefully hand-tuned bug messages can be instructionally effective, but in general, the cost benefit analysis on bug modeling is questionable.

Statistical methods for estimating a student's knowledge state from response data has been a fundamental challenge in psychology (cf. Green and Swets, 1973) and psychometrics (cf. Crocker and Algina, 1986). Student modeling in intelligent tutoring adds two complications. First, the student's knowledge state is not fixed, but is assumed to be increasing. We have successfully incorporated a simple Bayesian statistical model into our model tracing tutors to solve this problem (Corbett and Anderson, 1995b). This approach draws on early computer assisted learning methods (Atkinson, 1972), is employed to guide problem selection to implement mastery learning (Anderson, Conrad and Corbett, 1989; Corbett and Anderson, 1995) and is quite accurate in predicting students' posttest performance outside the tutoring environment (Corbett and Anderson, 1995b). The SHERLOCK II student model requires a more complex updating scheme (Lesgold, Eggan, Katz and Rao, 1992) and is used to guide problem selection and to modulate hint messages.

The second complex issue concerns grain size. Traditional psychological learning theories could assume that each response corresponds to an atomic cognitive chunk. However, student actions in complex problem solving may reflect knowledge components that can themselves be decomposed into hypothetical components. Bayesian belief nets have been introduced in intelligent tutoring systems to draw inferences about component knowledge from behavioral atoms (Gitomer, Steinberg and Mislevy, 1995; Mislevy, 1995; Martin and VanLehn, 1995).

The Pedagogical Module. The pedagogical module is responsible for structuring the instructional interventions. This module may operate at two levels (Pirolli and Greeno, 1998). At the curriculum level it can sequence topics to ensure an appropriate prerequisite structure is observed (Capell and Dannenberg, 1993) and individualize the amount of practice at each level to ensure the students master the material (Corbett and Anderson, 1995b). At the problem-solving support level, it can intervene to advise the student on problem solving activities. Towne and Munro (1992) outline five types of instructional interventions:

(1) Performance demonstration - The program demonstrates a successful sequence of actions in a problem solving task.

(2) Directed step-by-step performance- The program provides a sequence of actions for the student to follow in a problem solving task.

(3) Monitored performance - The student solves a problem set by the program. The program intervenes if the student makes mistakes or gets stuck.

(4) Goal seeking - The student solves a problem set by the program. The program monitors the level of abstract problem states rather than individual actions.

(5) Free Exploration - The learner freely manipulates the problem solving environment.

A sixth condition may be included, one in which the program sets a problem solving task but does not provide support. Our model tracing tutors exemplify the third type of support, although as we shall see there are several variations on this category. SHERLOCK exemplifies the fourth category. The appropriate mix of problem solving interventions is perhaps the most contested topic in intelligent tutoring systems, in part because of the many types of learning goals that can be set. It should be noted that the educational context must be considered in making such pedagogical decisions. Optimal instructional interactions can depend on whether the intelligent tutor is working in conjunction with a classroom teacher or in isolation. We shall consider this topic further in the third section.

37.2.6 HCI Evaluation Issues

The essential measure of educational effectiveness is learning rate (as a function of cost). This can be expressed in two ways: Educational software environments are effective to the extent that they enable students to reach higher achievement levels in the same amount of learning time or to reach the same achievement levels with less learning time. This raises some unique issues in software evaluation. The general metric for comparing software environments is output produced divided by effort expended. In intelligent tutoring systems the observable product is problem solutions. As in any software environment, the efficiency with which the student can solve problems is an important consideration. However, the ultimate and unobservable product is knowledge. As a result, the assessment of educational software ultimately involves a transfer task: how well the students can solve problems working on their own outside the tutoring environment.

The evaluation issue is further complicated since there are multiple aspects to learning:

(1) The student needs to learn basic declarative facts in a domain, e.g., dividing the quantities on both sides of an equation maintains the equality.

(2) The student has to learn to associate these facts with problem solving goal structures. For example,

If the goal is to isolate variable X in an equation of the form X*expression1 = expression2, Then divide both sides of the equation by expression 1.

(3) Transfer of knowledge to other environments, notably the non-tutor environment is essential.

(4) Retention (or inversely, forgetting) is an important knowledge parameter.

(5) Ideally students will acquire 'metacognitive' skills in learning (Bielaczyc, Pirolli and Brown, 1995; Chi, Bassok, Lewis, Reimann and Glaser, 1989; Pirolli and Recker, 1994; Schoenfeld, 1987) to gauge their own state of knowledge and learning processes. Educational software is most successful if it supports not just learning of the specified curriculum, but helps prepare the student to acquire subsequent knowledge.

(6) Student satisfaction or motivation or feeling of competence is also important. The student's achievement level is meaningless if the student chooses not to exercise the skill after acquiring it.

In short, the evaluation process is somewhat more complex than for most software environments. One measure of success for PAT is that the first class of PAT Algebra I students (1992-1993) were twice as likely as comparable students in traditional Algebra I to be enrolled in academic mathematics two years later. This key piece of evaluation could only be obtained two years after students had completed Algebra I.

A final complication is that students may not be the only users. When tutors are deployed in the classroom, teachers are also users. Teachers may place many direct demands on the software: (1) entering new problems, (2) structuring the curriculum, (3) intervening in the students' current state in the system and (4) requesting summary reports. Of equal importance, a tutoring system changes the teacher's interaction with students (Schofield and Evans-Rhodes, 1990). It is important to maximize the teacher's effectiveness in these capacities.

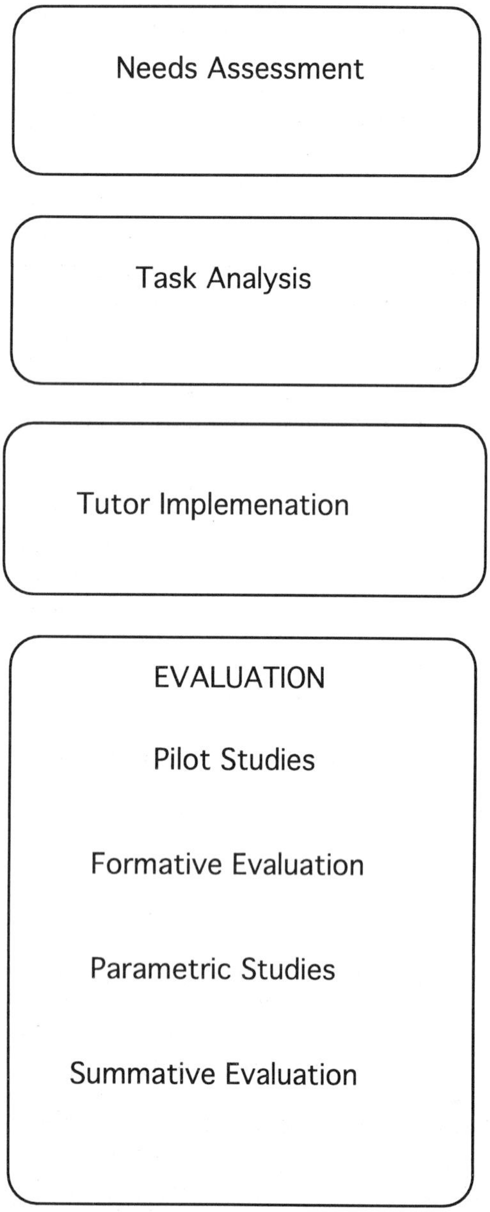

Needs Assessment

Task Analysis

Tutor Implemenation

EVALUATION

Pilot Studies

Formative Evaluation

Parametric Studies

Summative Evaluation

Figure 4. Intelligent tutoring design and development signs.

37.3 Design and Development Methods

Figure 4 displays the major activities in tutor development: (1) needs assessment, (2) cognitive task analysis, (3) tutor implementation and (4) evaluation. The first step is common to all software design. In the case of ITS design, this involves specifying educational goals and curriculum. The second stage is common to expert systems programming, although the target is defined more narrowly here: a cognitively valid model of problem solving performance. The third phase consists of initial tutor implementation, which is followed by a series of evaluation activities: (1) pilot studies to confirm basic usability and educational impact; (2) formative evaluations of the system under development, including (3) parametric studies that examine the effectiveness of system features and finally, (4) summative evaluations of the final tutor's effect: learning rate and asymptotic achievement levels.

37.3.1 Needs Assessment

As in any software development project, the initial step is to assess user needs. This is primarily the task of the domain expert, either the expert practitioner or the teacher. As a result, educational software development is necessarily an interdisciplinary task. In the PUMP algebra project, the domain experts, both curriculum specialists and mathematics teachers identified convergent needs at the local and national levels: To include all students in academic mathematics with a reasonable chance of success, to embed academic mathematics knowledge in authentic problem solving situations so that it is relevant to both the college bound and non-college bound, and to embed it in the framework of modern computational tools. It was obvious that the goal was not to computerize traditional algebra I, but develop a new curriculum structure. It should be observed that there is a second, pragmatic, reason to work closely with domain authorities in addition to drawing on their expertise: They share a common framework and typically common experiences with domain instructors and can play a major role in getting over the hurdle of classroom adoptions.

Having set these abstract goals, it is necessary to define the problem solving tasks and the role of the tutor in the curriculum (cf. Reusser, 1993). For example, in PUMP algebra students spend three class periods a week in collaborative problem solving activities and two days on individual problem solving with PAT. At CMU, on the other hand, our ACT Programming Tutor is used to teach a self-paced programming course in which students read on-line text and complete programming exercises on their own. It is an equally important step to decide what will count as success. We strongly believe that this should be defined in terms of student, and to a lesser extent teacher behavior, and should be defined before tutor development begins.

The critical measure is not the coverage of the tutor in interpreting student behavior. It is also not an abstract sense of what the student knows, but rather an objective measure of what the student can do. There are perhaps three crucial dimensions: (1) the probability a student is able to solve problems; (2) the time it takes to reach this performance level and (3) the probability the student will actively use this knowledge in the future. Secondarily, it should be noted that educational software will only be successful to the extent that vendors are willing to sell it, administrators to buy it and teachers to use it.

This focus on an operational definition of knowledge goes along way to defining a curriculum, since the best way to acquire a skill is to practice performing the skill. In the case of the PUMP algebra project, the skill of manipulating symbolic expressions was deemphasized and the skill of modeling authentic problem situations in various formalisms was emphasized. This led directly to a curriculum specification and classroom activities. The tutor in turn was integrated in the overall structure of the course from its inception.

Along with curriculum goals, the technology base must be assessed. A limiting factor historically in the penetration of intelligent tutors into the real world has been the cost of artificial intelligence workstations. When we first piloted the Geometry Proof Tutor (GPT) in a city high school ten years ago, each workstation cost $20,000. Technology costs have declined more than 8-fold since then and a workstation in our PUMP algebra labs costs under $2500. The cost of providing a workstation to every student in a classroom, about $60000, is well within reach of most institutions, but is not a discretionary spending amount. Funding for high school labs has been the greatest barrier to widespread dissemination.

Student entry characteristics must also be assessed. For example, many students entering PUMP algebra have not mastered middle school mathematics. Consequently learning experiences with the earliest versions of PAT did not generalize in the expected way. Although in principle students have acquired the unifying concept of rational number in middle school, students who successfully manipulate expressions with positive integer coefficients and terms in PAT often struggle with negative integer and fractional components. While entry characteristics may be predicted by experts, in the end they must be determined empirically. There are two important points to make here. First, while needs assessment is logically prerequisite to software design, it is an iterative process. We only recognized students' entry characteristics after they started working with the system. Second, the mismatch between student entry characteristics and the tutoring system was not revealed by breakdowns in our AI representation of domain knowledge. The tutor was perfectly capable of coping with each student action irrespective of the students' various entry characteristics. Instead, it was revealed by detailed monitoring of transfer of student performance across contexts.

Finally, teacher entry characteristics must be assessed. It should be noted that teachers as well as students are system users when tutors are deployed in conventional educational settings and the technology itself can be a challenge for teachers. It is important to provide sufficient in-service training for teachers to feel comfortable with the technology. Currently, new teachers in the PUMP project engage in a week of full-time in-service training just before the school year starts.

In summary, for any educational technology to succeed it must be used. To be used it must be integrated with the other classroom activities and must be accepted by the teachers and it must be appropriate for students. These are among the goals of the initial needs assessment.

37.3.2 Cognitive Task Analysis

Following the needs assessment, the cognitive scientist enters the picture. The goal of the cognitive task analysis is to develop a psychologically valid computational model of the problem solving knowledge the student is acquiring. There are three chief methods for developing a cognitive model: (1) interviewing domain experts, (2) conducting "think aloud" protocol studies with domain experts and (3) conducting "think aloud" studies with novices. The first approach is the most common and easiest approach. It includes a common situation in which the cognitive scientist is familiar with the field in question and simply generates the cognitive model. However, it is generally recognized that interviewing experts, including the cognitive scientist, is not a sufficient method to develop a pedagogically optimal model. An important goal of the task analysis is to recognize the expert's implicit goal structure (Koedinger and Anderson, 1993b), heuristics and mental models (Means and Gott, 1988; Kurland and Tenney, 1988), and experts often prove incapable of reporting these cognitive components. The preferred method to obtain cognitive model evidence is the think aloud study (Ericsson and Simon, 1984) in which the expert is asked to report aloud what she is thinking about in solving typical problems.

For example, think aloud protocols of geometry

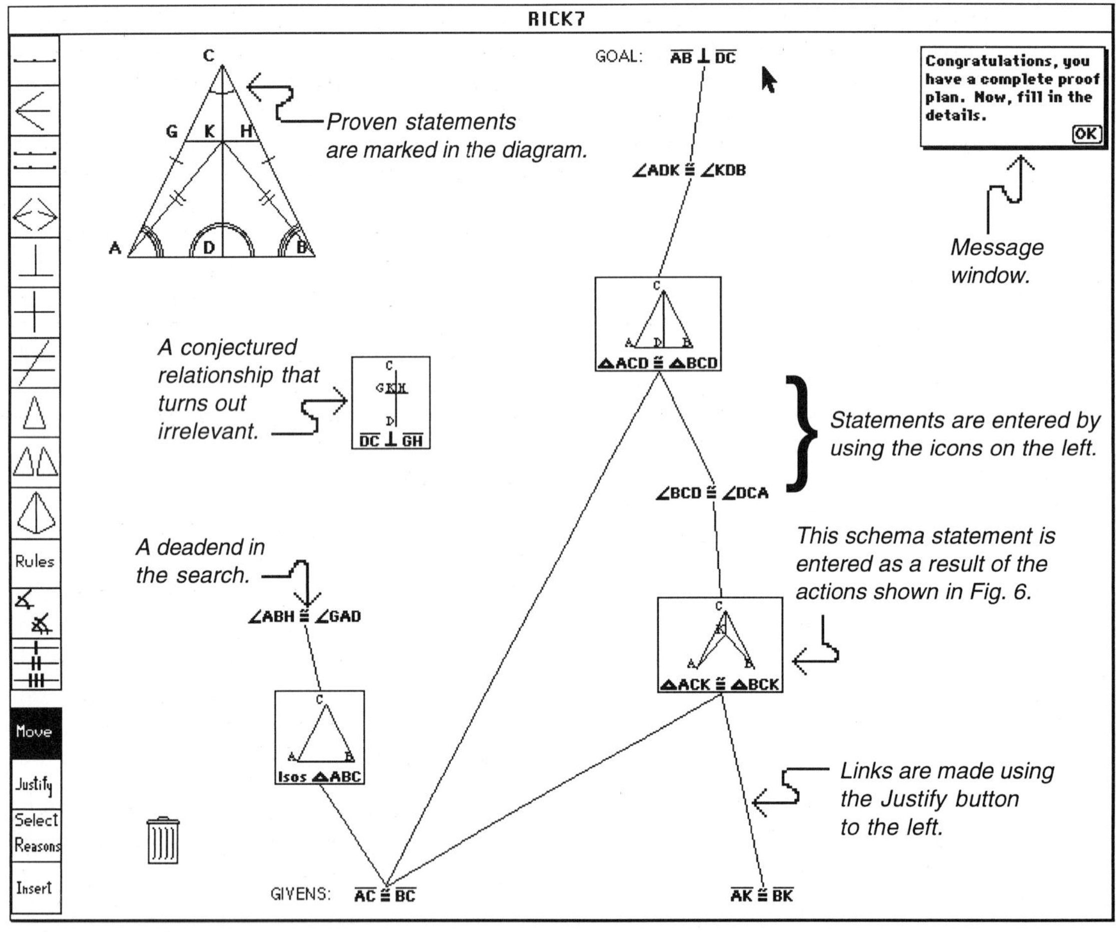

Figure 5. The ANGLE geometry tour.

teachers working proofs (Koedinger and Anderson, 1990) revealed that these experts departed substantially from the expected mechanisms of step-by-step forward chaining from problem givens and backward chaining from the goal statement to be proved. Instead, these experts begin by inspecting the problem diagram, recognizing familiar visual patterns and reasoning about the conclusions that can be proved independent of the problem solving goal. Only then do they consider the goal itself. The second major difference is that these experts reason through their proof by setting major subgoals and then go back and fill in details. This led to a geometry proof tutor ANGLE that (a) employs visual icons that correspond to the experts' perceptual processing of diagrams and that (b) allows students to post subgoals. Figure 5 displays the ANGLE interface. In this problem solving environment students build a proof graph (Anderson, Boyle and Reiser, 1985) rather than a two column proof. Students construct each statement in the proof by selecting an icon from the set of icons on the left side of the screen that reify the types of visual patterns the experts detect. As can be seen in the figure, students can post free floating subgoals in this interface, as well as working directly forward from the givens or backward from the goal.

Finally, observation of novice problem solvers is desirable to identify aspects of problem solving that students find difficult (Anderson, Farrell and Sauers, 1984; Means and Gott, 1988; Kurland and Tenney, 1988). At minimum such observations will reveal unwarranted assumptions. A few issues emerged from the PUMP curriculum. For example, in labeling spreadsheet columns and in labeling graph axes it turned out that students blurred the distinction between the quantity being measured, e.g., time, and the unit of measurement, e.g., hours. This led us to revise not just the cognitive model for PAT, but to alter the problem solving task and interface to incorporate labeling activities that we took for granted. It should be noted that if novice problem solving studies are not conducted in this phase, they are necessarily completed in subsequent tutor evaluation phases.

37.3.3 Tutor Implementation

Following the cognitive task analysis, we are ready to implement the tutor. As described earlier, the goal is to set up a problem solving environment that enables authentic problem solving and that helps support the problem solving process. The cognitive analysis yields an expert system that can reason about the problems, but may also yield interface modifications as in the case of ANGLE. We will postpone a consideration of tutor design principles to the third section of this chapter. Two points are worth noting. First, we estimate that 200 hours of intelligent tutor development are required to deliver a full hour of instruction. Second, evaluation should begin as early as possible in the development process.

37.3.4 Evaluation

The phases in educational software evaluation are similar to that in any software evaluation. Pilot studies follow quickly on the heals of tutor development as a rapid check on the usability and effectiveness of the tutor. Formative evaluation and revision iterate through the development of the system. The development process is capped by summative evaluations of the educational impact of the tutor, ideally in the form of field testing.

Piloting. Initial pilot studies are intended to reveal serious misjudgments concerning the problem solving environment and to establish that the tutor supports a minimally acceptable degree of learning. In a typical study, students complete a pretest, work through problems with the tutor and complete a post-test. Pilot studies with PAT revealed an unexpected difficulty in graphing. While the cognitive model focuses on issues in point and line plotting, it emerged that students did not have good heuristics for setting the axis scales and bounds dependent on the size of the values being plotted in each problem. Students performed these activities in the interface, but we did not model them in the domain expert. Consequently the tutor was unable to help as students floundered in setting up their graphs. We subsequently expanded the cognitive model to support this activity.

Formative Evaluations. Formative evaluations can focus on any of the four intelligent tutor components. In our lab, our analyses primarily focus on the validity of the cognitive model with respect to educational outcomes. In particular, we seek evidence that the students are not learning the ideal rules in the cognitive model, as revealed in failure of the knowledge to generalize across expected contexts. For example, if we trace out successive opportunities to apply production rules, we typically find regular learning curves. That is, error rate and response time in applying a cognitive rule tend to decline systematically across opportunities to apply the rule, as shown in Figure 6.

Figure 7 in contrast, displays the learning curve for one rule in the original cognitive model of the APT Lisp Programming Tutor:

> In writing a Lisp program, declare one parameter variable for each argument (input value) that will be passed when the program is executed.

This rule is expected to fire each time a variable is declared in a function definition. As can be seen, error rate for this rule decreases monotonically over the first four applications, but then jumps for the fifth and sixth applications. The first four points are drawn from the first four programming exercises, in which a single variable is declared. The fifth and sixth points represent the fifth programming exercise and the first definition in which two parameter variables are declared. The seventh and eighth points represent two more function definitions with a single parameter and the ninth and tenth points represent the next exercise that requires multiple parameters. The 55% error rate at goal six in this figure suggests that just under half the students had encoded the ideal rule initially and were able to apply it in the new situation. The other students initially encoded a non-ideal rule that was sufficient to complete the first four exercises but failed to generalize. There are several possible non-ideal rules:

> Always code one variable to stand for the whole list of arguments (too general).
>
> Code one variable when there is one argument (too specific - no thought of more arguments).
>
> Code one variable because that's what the example has (no functional understanding).

Similar patterns were observed for a variety of ideal rules in the model.

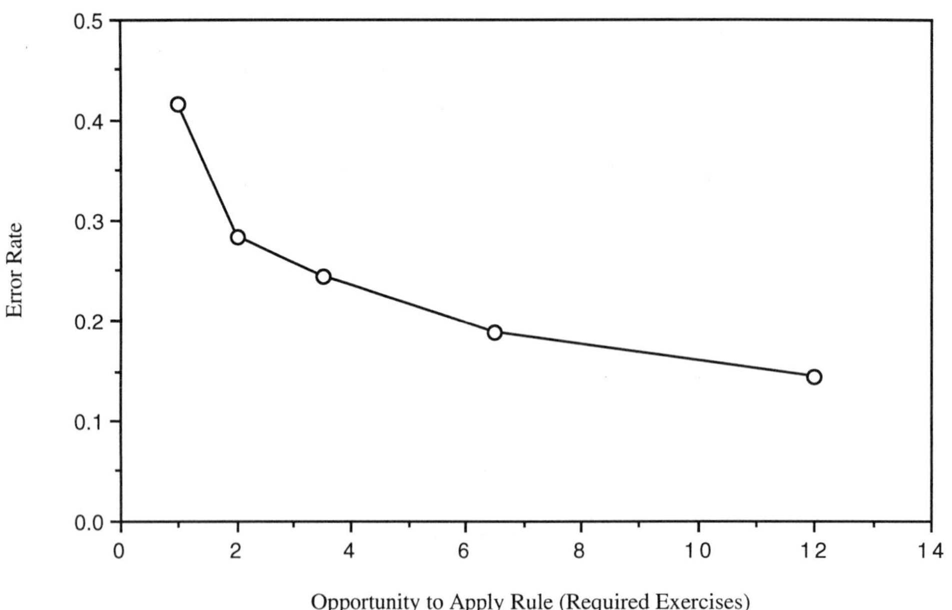

Figure 6. The mean learning curve for coding rules introduced in the first lesson of the Lisp tutor curriculum. *Mean error rate is plotted for successive opportunities to apply the rules. From A. Corbett and J. Anderson 1995b. Copyright 1995 by Kluwer Academic Publishers. Reprinted by permission.*

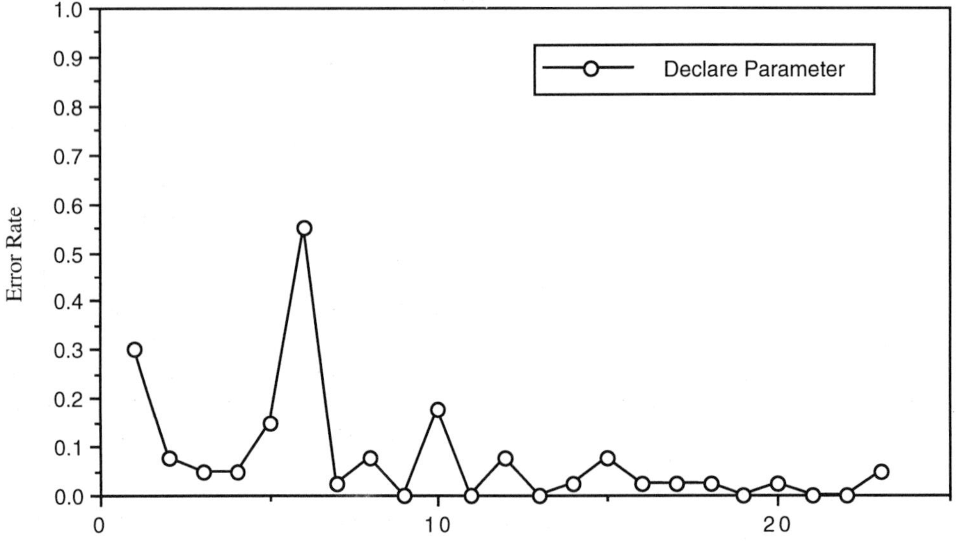

Figure 7. The learning curve for a hypothetical rule that declares a variable in a function definition. *Error rate is plotted for successive opportunities to apply the rule. From A. Corbett and J. Anderson 1995b. Copyright 1995 by Kluwer Academic Publishers. Reprinted by permission.*

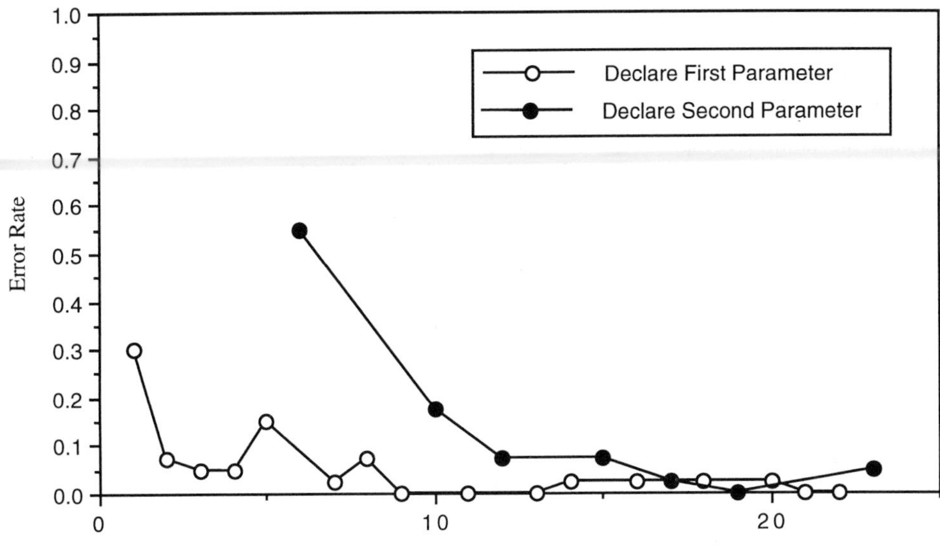

Figure 8. A partitioning of the single learning curve for variable declarations in Figure 7 into separate learning curves for two distinct variable declaration rules. *From A. Corbett and J. Anderson 1995b. Copyright 1995 by Kluwer Academic Publishers. Reprinted by permission.*

We revised the Lisp Tutor cognitive model in response to this problem so that procedural knowledge for variable declarations is represented as two rules:

> In defining a Lisp function, declare one variable for the first argument that will be passed.
>
> In defining a Lisp function, declare one additional variable for each additional argument that will be passed.

Figure 8 re-plots the data points for declaring variables. The points from the original learning curve in Figure 7 are plotted as two separate learning curves for these rules. Under this analysis the sixth, tenth, twelfth, fifteenth, seventeenth, nineteenth and twenty-third opportunities to declare a variable are really the first through seventh opportunities to apply the second rule.

In the course of successive refinements of this part of the Lisp Tutor curriculum the cognitive rule set more than doubled. While there is a natural tendency to write general rules in the ideal student model that apply in multiple contexts, there are two reasons to accurately represent the actual though perhaps less-general rules students are encoding. One is to accurately represent the student's knowledge state for purposes of judging mastery as knowledge tracing does. The second is to provide context-specific help messages in the psychologically distinct contexts.

Parametric Evaluations. In addition to naturalistic observations of students and teachers working with the tutor, formative evaluations can include experimental manipulations of tutor components. In intelligent tutoring systems these parametric evaluations have tended to focus on pedagogical issues, notably feedback content and control, as described in the third section on design issues (Corbett and Anderson, 1991; Corbett, Anderson and Patterson, 1990; Koedinger and Anderson, in press; Reiser, Copen, Ranney, Hamid and Kimberg 1995; Shute, 1993). These studies focus on the impact of the manipulation on learning time, asymptotic achievement levels, affective measures and individual differences.

Summative Evaluation. Summative evaluations examine the overall educational impact of the tutoring system. Such evaluations compare the intelligent tutoring environment to standard educational conditions. Ideally, such summative evaluations take the form of field tests in which the tutor is deployed in an authentic educational environment. Necessarily such studies compare learning outcomes — assessing students' problem solving success in post tests following learning. Pretests of problem solving ability are not strictly necessary in such comparison across learning environments, although they are important if students are assigned non-randomly to condition. A difficult issue in such summative evaluations is that the natural comparison conditions may have different educational goals. For example, the educational goals of traditional algebra I differ from the goals of PUMP algebra. Our solution to this problem is to present posttests appropriate to each learning environment to all students (Koedinger, Anderson, Hadley and Mark, 1993). In the case of our tutoring project, students in the PUMP algebra classes were 100% better at reasoning among multiple representations in problem solving, but also 10-15% better on standardized algebra tests targeted by traditional algebra classes.

Learning time is the second principal assessment measure in summative evaluations. Intelligent tutors make an important contribution to education when they speed learning substantially. This can happen in two ways. First, they can increase the rate at which practice opportunities are presented. For example, SHERLOCK offers what would ordinarily be several years' worth of troubleshooting opportunities in the space of several days of practice. Second, tutors can increase the rate at which students learn from practice opportunities. For example, Corbett and Anderson (1991) found that students working with the APT LISP Tutor completed a fixed set of programming exercises in one third the time required by students working in the same editing interface without tutorial support and performed reliably better on a posttest.

37.4 Design and Development Principles

In this section we consider a set of general principles for intelligent tutor design and conclude with a discussion of pedagogical guidelines concerning help messages. In 1987 we published a set of eight principles for intelligent tutor design (Anderson, Boyle, Farrell and Reiser, 1987). Recently we revisited those principles and found them generally sound (Anderson, Corbett, Koedinger and Pelletier, 1995). However, we have come to believe that a single overarching principle governs intelligent tutor design:

> Principle 0: Enable the student to work to the successful conclusion of problem solving.

While there are many variations on intelligent tutoring environments, we believe that the major factor in their success comes from enabling the student to reach a solution to each problem. (cf. Lesgold, Eggan, Katz and Rao, 1992). Our strongest evidence for this principle comes from a study with the APT Lisp Tutor. The Lisp Tutor is a model tracing tutor that assists students is completing short Lisp programming problems. We employed this tutor in a study of feedback timing and control (Corbett and Anderson, 1991) with four feedback conditions. One was a standard immediate feedback condition in which the tutor provides feedback on each symbol. A second, error flagging condition, flagged errors immediately, but did not require correction. Students could correct errors when they chose. The tutor also checked code by testing so it was possible for students to succeed with a program definition the tutor did not recognize. In a third condition, feedback-on-demand, the tutor provided no assistance until requested by the student. When asked for assistance in this condition, the tutor traces through the student's code symbol-by-symbol, and reports the first error it finds. In the fourth condition, students completed programming exercises in the same problem solving environment, but without any tutorial assistance. Students in the three feedback conditions were required to reach a correct solution to each problem, since the environment provided sufficient feedback to guarantee success. In the control condition, students could work on an exercise for as long as they desired, but in the end were allowed to give up, in which case the tutor displayed a correct solution. There were substantial differences in the time taken to complete the fixed set of exercises, but more importantly, here, students in the baseline control failed to solve approximately 25% of the exercises. Students completed posttest in three different environments, both on-line and paper-and-pencil. There were no reliable accuracy differences across the three posttest environments among the three feedback groups, but the feedback groups performed reliably better than the control group in all posttest environments.

37.4.1 Eight Design Principles

As indicated above, we believe the following eight design principles have stood the test of time:

(1) Represent student competence as a production set. This represents a theoretical stance on a more general principle: represent problem solving knowledge is a psychologically valid way. A substantial body of

empirical evidence supports the validity of a production rule decomposition of procedural knowledge (Anderson, Conrad and Corbett, 1989), but it should be noted that alternative representations have been employed in intelligent tutoring systems, including plan based representations (Johnson and Soloway, 1984) and case-based representations (Riesbeck and Schank, 1991; Weber, 1993, in press).

(2) Communicate the goal structure underlying the problem solving. Successful problem solving involves the decomposition of the initial problem state into subgoals and bringing domain knowledge to bear on those subgoals. This is a universally accepted principle. SHERLOCK is a strong embodiment of the principle; it explicitly models problem solving goal states, but not specific action sequences to achieve the goals. Again, there are two general methods for communicating the goal structure. First, it can be reified in the problem solving environment. For example, the problem solving goal tree can be explicitly represented on the computer screen (Singley, Carroll and Alpert, 1993) or the problem solving formalism can be modified to reflect the problem subgoal structure, as it is in the ANGLE's proof tree representation (Koedinger and Anderson, 1993a). Second, the goal structure can be communicated through help messages. For example, when a student asks for help in our model tracing tutors, the first level of help at each problem solving step is a reminder of the current goal in the context of the overall problem (the current state of the problem and the desired subgoal state). Subsequent help messages advise on how to accomplish the goal.

(3) Provide instruction in the problem solving context. As suggested earlier, this is an almost universally accepted principle that cuts across disparate educational philosophies ranging from behaviorism to constructivism.

(4) Promote an abstract understanding of the problem-solving knowledge. Again, this is a well-accepted principle. Means and Gott (1988) state: "The most powerful aspect of expertise, and at the same time, the hardest aspect to capture is what Sleeman and Brown (1982) called its 'abstracted' character." The goal is to help students to encode problem solving states, actions and consequences in the most general form consistent with the problem solving goal in order to foster transfer across contexts. Following the formative evaluation of SHERLOCK, the design team began analyzing 'families' of tasks over which transfer was expected (Lesgold, Eggan, Katz and Rao, 1992). A hierarchy of general methods and task-specific specialization was defined that enabled SHERLOCK II to provide feedback at an appropriate level of abstraction. Hint messages in our model tracing tutors are also constructed to provide an abstract description of how to achieve the current problem solving goals. A concrete action is described only as a last resort when there is no expectation that a teacher will be present in the environment to interact with the student.

(5) Minimize working memory load. Sweller (1988) demonstrated that a high working memory load can interfere with problem solving. There are multiple tactics to reduce working memory load in an intelligent tutoring system. Efforts described earlier to reify problem solving states and device states in the problem solving interface serve to reduce working memory load as well as to foster comprehension. The interface may also simplify problem solving actions to reduce the load on working memory as well as allowing students to focus on a more abstract problem solving level. For example, our programming tutors employ structure editors that remove much of the burden of remembering surface syntax. SHERLOCK simplifies the task of taking measurements to mouse clicks. Littman (1991) observes behavior by human tutors that is consistent with this principle; they do not interrupt students (and their current working memory state) to point out relatively minor errors that have little consequence for the student's overall goal structure. As Lesgold, Eggan, Katz and Rao (1992) observe there can be a conflict between principles (3) and (5), since setting a problem solving goal imposes a working memory load that can interfere with full processing of the problem solving state. The authors propose a reflective review at the conclusion of problem solving as a solution to this conflict In this reflective review process students replay there solutions step-by-step. They can examine the device state and problem solving state at each step and also get advice on how an expert would solve the problem.

(6) Provide immediate feedback on errors. This has been our most controversial principle. The chief benefit of immediate feedback is to reduce learning time substantially (Anderson, Corbett, Koedinger and Pelletier, 1995). However, others point out that immediate feedback can interfere with aspects of learning. We discuss this issue in more detail under pedagogical guidelines below.

(7) Adjust the grain size of instruction with learning. As students practice and become familiar with

standard goal decompositions in problem solving tasks, they should be able to reason in terms of relatively high level goals and instruction should be targeted at these high level goals. For example, consider the equation 2X + 4 = 8. Early in equation solving practice, instruction may focus on the individual steps of collecting constant terms and dividing by 2 (or vice versa). Once these tactics have been mastered, it should no longer be necessary to interact pedagogically on the individual steps in achieving these goals. Similarly in programming, once a student has learned well-defined algorithms such as reading and totaling a sequence of inputs, it may be necessary in later to instruction to advise that the algorithm is called for, but it should not be necessary to support the student in writing the appropriate code. Little empirical work has been directed at this principle.

(8) Facilitate successive approximations to the target skill. This principle suggests that a student's problem solving performance should gradually come to reflect real-world problem solving performance. In one sense this happens automatically; as the students practices and becomes more skilled the tutor is called upon to provide less assistance. A second important implication of this principle is that scaffolding in the problem solving environment should fade as the student continues practicing.

37.4.2 Pedagogical Guidelines

In this section we consider guidelines for providing help in intelligent tutoring systems. When to present advice and in what form has been an enduring issue in the field, in large part because of the complexity of the learning process. At one end of the continuum, some environments based on device or system simulations emphasize student exploration and discovery learning (Shute and Glaser, 1990). At the other end, some environments provide immediate feedback on each student action (Anderson, Corbett, Koedinger and Pelletier, 1995). Other environments provide assistance only when asked by the student or when the student seems to be in serious trouble (Corbett, Anderson and Patterson, 1990; Lesgold, Eggan, Katz and Rao, 1992). Meta-analyses of feedback timing reveal little consistent impact on the acquisition of target skills (Bangert-Drowns, Kulik, Kulik and Morgan, 1991; Kulhavy, 1977; Kulik and Kulik, 1988). However, feedback timing can have indirect effects on the acquisition of a complex skill. Immediate feedback can effectively speed the acquisition of a target skill, by reducing floundering. However, immediate feedback can interfere with the acquisition of associated skills.

One approach to this issue has been to examine what human tutors do (Merrill, Reiser, Ranney and Trafton, 1992). In general, human tutors do provide immediate feedback, if only on "important" errors (Littman, 1991). Two studies (Lepper, Aspinwall, Mumme and Chabay, 1990; Fox 1991) indicate that human tutors effectively provide feedback on each action, perhaps just by saying "ok." They signal errors subtly, perhaps by pausing before saying 'ok', allowing students ample opportunity to correct errors on their own and giving students a sense of control. We have converged on this type of feedback in our model tracing tutors, particularly in view of Sleeman et. al.'s (1989) results on the ineffectiveness of diagnostic feedback. In our early tutors we provided immediate diagnostic feedback on errors, when possible (about 80% of the time). Our current generation of mathematics and programming tutors still conventionally provides immediate feedback on each problem solving action, but does not provide advice on the nature of the error or how to arrive at a correct action. This prevents the student from wasting time going down the wrong path, but allows the student to rethink the problem solving situation, much as a human tutor does.

There is a second important point to make here: While intelligent tutoring systems are modeled on human tutors, it is not clear that the analogy should be taken too literally. Indeed, we have moved away from the human tutor analogy for two reasons. First, it is too high a standard to live up to; if you set the standard of a human tutor, the user is going to be sorely disappointed. Second, we want students and teachers to view these tutors as learning tools. That is, we want students to think of the tutors as tools they are employing, rather than as taskmasters. Similarly, we want teachers to think of the tutors as tools that can free their time to interact individually with students. Schofield, Evans-Rhodes and Huber (1990) studied the impact of our original geometry tutor GPT in the classroom and found two relevant results, First, although it provided immediate feedback it was highly motivating for students and teachers. Second, students came to perceive their teacher as a collaborator in learning rather than as a remote expert. In short, the overall effect of the tutor in the classroom was to give students a greater sense of control.

We propose the following guidelines for feedback timing:

(1) feedback should be provided at a time when the relevant information (problem state

and action consequences) can be communicated effectively to the student,

(2) feedback should not change the requirements of the task,

(3) feedback should not disrupt performance of the task,

(4) to optimize learning of the target skill, as measured in elapsed time rather than in elapsed problem solving exercises, feedback should be presented as early as possible.

Results of a variety of past studies on feedback timing in skill acquisition have been consistent with these principles. For example, Schmidt, Young, Swinnen and Shapiro (1989) examined the acquisition of a motor task requiring a small set of precise movements with no environmental feedback. While students in an immediate feedback condition appeared to acquire the task more quickly than students in a blocked feedback condition, they performed worse in no-feedback posttests. In this case, immediate feedback after each movement substantially changes the task, however. Performance in a no-feedback environment requires a long-term internal model of the motion. Students in the immediate feedback condition, in contrast, may succeed by making adjustments in a transient trace of the immediately preceding performance. Munro, Fehling and Towne (1985) found immediate feedback to be detrimental in a radar monitoring task, but the feedback interfered with the real-time demands of the task. Lewis and Anderson (1985) found that immediate feedback was superior to delayed feedback, but this was in an adventure task in which it was difficult to reinstate past problem states. Corbett and Anderson (1991; Corbett, Anderson and Patterson, 1990) found it took students substantially longer to complete a fixed set of programming exercises with delayed feedback than with immediate feedback, although there were no differences in posttest accuracy levels across groups.

As suggested above, immediate feedback on a target skill can interfere with acquisition of other problem solving skills. Classically, in the case of programming, immediate feedback on program generation blocks practice on program debugging. In general, immediate feedback on solution generation interferes with the development of meta-cognitive self monitoring skills and error recovery skills. For example, Reiser, Copen, Ranney, Hamid, and Kimberg (1995) found that students who learned to write programs in an exploratory environment developed greater debugging skills than students who learned to write programs with immediate feedback. This effect interacted with student background however. Students with strong mathematics and programming backgrounds acquired greater debugging skills in the discovery environment, while students with weak backgrounds did not. We believe that this result highlights the fact that this is a curriculum issue as much as, or more than a pedagogical issue. Ideally, an intelligent tutoring environment should be based on a cognitive task analysis of all aspects of problem solving, including solution generation, error recovery and self-monitoring, and should support the student in all aspects of problem solving.

A general consensus seems to be emerging on the content of advice messages, along the following lines. When error feedback is presented, it should generally just signal the error without commenting. This enables the student maximum opportunity to analyze the correct the situation. When advice is given, the most cost effective content focuses on "reteaching" a correct analysis of the situation rather than debugging misconceptions. This correct analysis should be administered in at least three or four stages: (1) a reminder of the problem solving goal, (2) a description of relevant features of the current problem state and the desired goal state, (3) a description of the rule for moving from the current state to the desired state, and (4) a description of a concrete action to take.

Shute (1993) provides evidence of a second "aptitude-treatment" interaction with implications for the content of help messages. In this study students were learning some basic laws of electricity in an intelligent tutoring system. Students received feedback on their solution to each problem and Shute developed two variations on the tutoring environment with respect to this feedback. In the *rule application* version, the tutor described an applicable rule, i.e., the key relationship among a set of variables. In the *rule induction* version, the tutor pointed out the relevant variables but left it up to the student to induce the relevant relationship. Shute measured students exploratory behavior and found that high-exploratory students were more successful in the induction environment, while low exploratory students were more successful in the more directive application environment. This suggests that student learning style as well as current knowledge state should govern the content of tutor advice. Notice, however, that the graduated advice framework described in the preceding paragraph may accomplish the same goal without the need for student modeling. Shute's high-exploratory students benefit most from level (2) advice while the low-exploratory students benefit most from level (3) advice. It would be an interesting study in meta-cognitive skills to see if students zero in on the level of help they find most useful in such an environment.

37.5 Conclusion

Intelligent tutoring systems have provided a fertile ground for artificial intelligence research over the past twenty-five years. Some of these systems have been demonstrated to have a very large impact on educational outcomes in field tests, including effective learning rate, asymptotic learning levels and motivation. We are just entering a time when intelligent tutoring systems can have a real impact in the educational marketplace as technology costs decline, but we believe this will happen only if ITS research focuses on educational outcomes as well as AI issues. In this paper we describe a process model for developing effective intelligent tutoring systems that includes a needs assessment, cognitive task analysis and early and extensive evaluation. We also describe what we view as an emerging consensus on principles and guidelines for ITS design, but recognize that more formative evaluation is required to assess and refine these prescriptions. New issues continue to emerge in the area, including ITS authoring environments, collaborative learning, world wide web deployment and virtual reality environments. However, it is important for the field to remain focused on valid pedagogical principles and educational outcomes in exploring these areas.

37.6 References

Anderson, J.R. and Bower, G.H. (1973). *Human associative memory. Washington,* DC: V.H. Winston and Sons.

Anderson, J.R. (1983). *The architecture of cognition.* Cambridge, MA: Harvard University Press.

Anderson, J.R. (1988). The expert module. In M. Polson and J. Richardson (Eds.) *Foundations of intelligent tutoring systems.* Hillsdale, NJ: Lawrence Erlbaum Associates.

Anderson, J.R. (1993). *Rules of the mind.* Hillsdale, NJ: Lawrence Erlbaum Associates.

Anderson, J.R., Boyle, C.F., Corbett, A.T. and Lewis, M.W. (1990). Cognitive modeling and intelligent tutoring. *Artificial Intelligence*, 42, 7-49.

Anderson, J.R., Boyle, C.F. and Reiser, B.J. (1985). Intelligent tutoring systems. *Science*, 228, 456-462.

Anderson, J.R., Conrad, F.G. and Corbett, A.T. (1989). Skill acquisition and the LISP Tutor. *Cognitive Science,* 13, 467-505.

Anderson, J.R. and Corbett, A.T. (1993). Tutoring of cognitive skill. In J. Anderson (Ed.) *Rules of the mind.* Hillsdale, NJ: Lawrence Erlbaum Associates.

Anderson, J.R., Corbett, A.T., Koedinger, K.R. and Pelletier, R. (1995). Cognitive tutors: Lessons learned. *The Journal of the Learning Sciences*, 4, 167-207.

Anderson, J.R., Farrell, R. and Sauers, R. (1984). Learning to program in LISP. *Cognitive Science*, 8, 87-129.

Anderson, J.R. and Reiser, B.J. (1985) The LISP Tutor. *Byte, 10,* 159-175.

Atkinson, R.C. (1972). Optimizing the learning of a second-language vocabulary. *Journal of Experimental Psychology*, 96, 124-129.

Bangert-Drowns, R.L., Kulik, C.C., Kulik, J.A and Morgan, M. (1991). The instructional effect of feedback in test-like events. *Review of Educational Research*, 61,213-238.

Bielaczyc, K., Pirolli, P.L. and Brown, A.L. (1995). Training in self-explanation and self-regulation strategies: Investigating the effects of knowledge acquisition activities on problem solving. In *Cognition and Instruction,* 13, 221-252.

Bhuiyan, S., Greer, J.E. and McCalla, G.I. (1992). Learning recursion through the use of a mental model-based programming environment. In C. Frasson, G. Gauthier, G. and G. McCalla, (Eds.) *Intelligent tutoring systems: Second International Conference, ITS'92.* New York: Springer-Verlag.

Bloom, B.S. (1984). The 2 sigma problem: The search for methods of group instruction as effective as one-to-one tutoring. *Educational Researcher*, 13, 4-16.

Bonar, J.G. and Cunningham, R. (1988). Bridge: Tutoring the programming process. In J. Psotka, L. Massey and S. Mutter (Eds.) *Intelligent Tutoring Systems: Lessons learned.* Hillsdale, NJ: Lawrence Erlbaum Associates.

Brown, J.S., Burton, R. and Zdybel, F. (1973). A model-driven question-answering system for mixed-initiative computer-assisted instruction. *IEEE Transactions on Systems, Man and Cybernetics*. SMC-3, 248-257.

Brusilovsky, P. (1995). Intelligent learning environments for programming: The case for integration and adaptation. *Proceedings of the 7th World Conference on Artificial Intelligence in Education.*

Burton, R.R. and Brown, J.S. (1982). An investigation of computer coaching for information learning activities. In D. Sleeman and J. Brown (Eds.) *Intelligent tutoring systems.* New York: Academic Press.

Capell, P. and Dannenberg, R.B. (1993). Instructional design and intelligent tutoring: Theory and the precision of design. *Journal of Artificial Intelligence in Education*, 4, 95-121.

Carbonell (1970). AI in CAI: An artificial intelligence approach to computer-assisted instruction. *IEEE Transactions on Man-Machine Systems*, 11,190-202.

Chi, M.T.H., Bassok, M., Lewis, M.W., Reimann, P. and Glaser, R. (1989). Self-explanations: How students study and use examples in learning to solve problems. *Cognitive Science*, 13, 145-182.

Clancey, W.J. (1982). Tutoring rules for guiding a case method dialogue. In D. Sleeman and J. Brown (Eds.) *Intelligent tutoring systems.* New York: Academic Press.

Cohen, P.A., Kulik, J.A. and Kulik, C.C. (1982). Educational outcomes of tutoring: A meta-analysis of findings. *American Educational Research Journal*, 19, 237-248.

Collins, A.M. and Loftus, E.F. (1975). A spreading-activation theory of semantic processing. *Psychological Review*, 82, 407-428.

Collins, A.M. and Stevens, A.L. (1991). A cognitive theory of inquiry teaching. In P. Goodyear (Ed.) *Teaching knowledge and intelligent tutoring.* Norwood, NJ: Ablex Publishing.

Corbett, A.T. and Anderson, J.R. (1991). Feedback control and learning to program with the CMU Lisp Tutor. Paper presented at the annual meeting of the American Educational Research Association, Chicago, IL.

Corbett, A.T. and Anderson, J.R. (1995a). Knowledge decomposition and subgoal reification in the ACT Programming Tutor. *Proceedings of the 7th World Conference on Artificial Intelligence in Education..*

Corbett, A.T. and Anderson, J.R. (1995b). Knowledge tracing: Modeling the acquisition of procedural knowledge. *User modeling and user-adapted interaction*, 4, 253-278.

Corbett, A.T., Anderson, J.R. and Patterson, E.G. (1990). Student modeling and tutoring flexibility in the Lisp Intelligent Tutoring System. In C. Frasson and G. Gauthier (Eds.) *Intelligent tutoring systems: At the crossroads of artificial intelligence and education.* Norwood, NJ; Ablex Publishing.

Crocker, L. and Algina, J. (1986). *Introduction to classical and modern test theory.* New York: Harcourt Brace Jovanovich College Publishers.

Eisenstadt, M., Price, B.A. and Domingue, J. (1993). Redressing ITS fallacies via software visualization. In E. Lemut, B. du Boulay and G. Dettori (Eds.) *Cognitive models and intelligent environments for learning programming.* New York: Springer-Verlag.

Ericsson, K.A. and Simon, H.A. (1984). *Protocol analysis: Verbal reports as data.* Cambridge, MA: The MIT Press.

Fox, B. (1991). Cognitive and interactional aspects of correction in tutoring. In P. Goodyear (Ed.) *Teaching Knowledge and Intelligent Tutoring.* Norwood, NJ: Ablex Publishing.

Frasson, C., Gauthier, G. and McCalla, G.I. (1992). *Intelligent tutoring systems: Second International Conference, ITS'92.* New York: Springer-Verlag.

Frasson, C., Gauthier, G. and Lesgold, A. (1996). *Intelligent tutoring systems: Third International Conference, ITS'96.* New York: Springer-Verlag.

Gitomer, D.H., Steinberg, L.S. and Mislevy, R.J. (1995). Diagnostic assessment of troubleshooting skill in an intelligent tutoring system. In P. Nichols, S. Chipman and R. Brennan (Eds.) *Cognitively Diagnostic Assessment.* Hillsdale, NJ: Lawrence Erlbaum Associates.

Green, D.M. and Swets, J.A. (1973). *Signal Detection theory and Psychophysics.* Huntington, NY: Robert E. Krieger Publishing.

Johnson, W.L. and Soloway, E.M. (1984). PROUST: Knowledge-based program debugging. *Proceedings of the Seventh International Software Engineering Conference*, Orlando, FL.

Katz, S. and Lesgold, A. (1993). The role of the tutor in computer-based collaborative learning situations. In S. Lajoie and S. Derry (Eds.) *Computers and Cognitive Tools.* Hillsdale, NJ: Lawrence Erlbaum Associates.

Kieras, D.E. and Bovair, S. (1986). The acquisition of procedures from text: A production system analysis of transfer of training. *Journal of Memory and Language*, 25, 507-524.

Koedinger, K.R. and Anderson, J.R. (1990). Abstract planning and perceptual chunks: Elements of expertise in geometry. *Cognitive Science*, 14, 511-550.

Koedinger, K.R. and Anderson, J.R. (1993a). Effective use of intelligent software in high school math classrooms. In P. Brna, S. Ohlsson and H. Pain (Eds.) *Proceedings of AIED 93 World Conference on Artificial Intelligence in Education.*

Koedinger, K.R. and Anderson, J.R. (1993b). Reifying implicit planning in geometry: Guidelines for model-based intelligent tutoring system design. In S. Lajoie and S. Derry (Eds.) *Computers and Cognitive Tools.* Hillsdale, NJ: Lawrence Erlbaum Associates.

Koedinger, K.R. and Anderson, J. R. (in press). Illustrating principled design: The early evolution of a cognitive tutor for algebra symbolization. *Interactive Learning Environments.*

Koedinger, K.R., Anderson, J.R., Hadley, W.H. and Mark, M.A. (1995). Intelligent tutoring goes to school in the big city. *Proceedings of the 7th World Conference on Artificial Intelligence in Education.*

Kulhavy, R.W. (1977). Feedback in written instruction. *Review of Educational Research*, 47, 211-232.

Kulik, J.A. and Kulik, C.C. (1988). Timing of feedback and verbal learning. *Review of Educational Research*, 58, 79-97.

Larkin, J. H. and Chabay, R.W. (1992). *Computer-Assisted Instruction and Intelligent Tutoring Systems: Shared Goals and Complementary Approaches.* Hillsdale, NJ: Lawrence Erlbaum Associates.

Lepper, M.R., Aspinwall, L., Mumme, D. and Chabay, R.W. (1990). Self-perception and social perception processes in tutoring: Subtle social control strategies of expert tutors. In J. Olson and M. Zanna (Eds.) *Self inference processes: The sixth Ontario symposium in social psychology.* Hillsdale, NJ: Lawrence Erlbaum Associates.

Lesgold, A., Eggan, G., Katz, S. and Rao, G. (1992). Possibilities for assessment using computer-based apprenticeship environments. In J. Regian and V. Shute (Eds.) *Cognitive Approaches to Automated Instruction.* Hillsdale, NJ: Lawrence Erlbaum Associates.

Lesgold, A., Lajoie, S. Bunzo, M and Eggan, G. (1992). SHERLOCK: A coached practice environment for an electronics troubleshooting job. In *J. Larkin and R. Chabay (Eds.) Computer-assisted instruction and intelligent tutoring systems: Shared goals and complementary approaches.* Hillsdale, NJ: Lawrence Erlbaum Associates.

Lewis, M.W. and Anderson, J.R. (1985). Discrimination of operator schemata in problem solving: Learning from examples. *Cognitive Psychology*, 17, 26-65.

Littman, D. (1991). Tutorial planning schemas. In P. Goodyear (Ed.) *Teaching Knowledge and Intelligent Tutoring.* Norwood, NJ: Ablex Publishing.

Martin, J. and VanLehn, K. (1995). A Bayesian approach to cognitive assessment. In P. Nichols, S. Chipman and R. Brennan (Eds.) *Cognitively Diagnostic assessment.* Hillsdale, NJ: Lawrence Erlbaum Associates.

Means, B. and Gott, S.P. (1988). Cognitive task analysis as a basis for tutor development: Articulating abstract knowledge representations. In J. Psotka, L. Massey and S. Mutter (Eds.) *Intelligent tutoring systems: Lessons learned.* Hillsdale, NJ: Lawrence Erlbaum Associates.

Merrill, D.C., Reiser, B.J., Ranney, M. and Trafton, G.J. (1992). Effective tutoring techniques: A comparison of human tutors and intelligent tutoring systems. *The Journal of the Learning Sciences*, 1,

Miller, M.L. (1979). A structured planning and debugging environment for elementary programming. *International Journal of Man-Machine Studies*, 11, 79-95

Mislevy, R.J. (1995). Probability-based inference in cognitive diagnosis. In P. Nichols, S. Chipman and R. Brennan (Eds.) *Cognitively diagnostic assessment.* Hillsdale, NJ: Lawrence Erlbaum Associates.

Munro, A., Fehling, M.R. and Towne, D.M. (1985). Instruction intrusiveness in dynamic simulation training. *Journal of Computer-Based Instruction*, 12, 50-53.

National Council of Teachers of Mathematics (1989). *Curriculum and Evaluation Standards for School Mathematics.* Reston, VA: The Council.

Newell, A. (1990). *Unified theories of cognition.* Cambridge, MA: Harvard University Press.

Pirolli, P.L. and Greeno, J.G. (1988). The problem space of instructional design. In J. Psotka, L. Massey and S. Mutter (Eds.) *Intelligent tutoring systems: Lesson learned.* Hillsdale, NJ: Lawrence Erlbaum Associates.

Pirolli, P.L. and Recker, M. (1994). Learning strategies and transfer in the domain of programming. *Cognition and Instruction*, 12, 235-275.

Polson, M.C. and Richardson, J.J. (1988). *Foundations of Intelligent Tutoring Systems.* Hillsdale, NJ: Lawrence Erlbaum Associates.

Ramadhan, H. and du Boulay, B. (1993). Programming environments for novices. In E. Lemut, B. du Boulay and G. Dettori (Eds.) *Cognitive models and intelligent environments for learning programming.* New York: Springer-Verlag.

Reed, S.K., Dempster, A. and Ettinger, M. (1985). Usefulness of analogous solutions for solving algebra word problems. *Journal of Experimental Psychology: Learning, Memory and Cognition*, 11, 106-125.

Reiser, B.J., Copen, W.A., Ranney, M., Hamid, A. and Kimberg, D.Y. (1995). Cognitive and motivational consequences of tutoring and discovery learning. Unpublished manuscript.

Reiser, B.J., Kimberg, D.Y., Lovett, M.C. and Ranney, M. (1992). Knowledge representation and explanation in GIL, An intelligent tutor for programming. In J. Larkin and R. Chabay (Eds.) *Computer-assisted instruction and intelligent tutoring systems: Shared goals and complementary approaches*. Hillsdale, NJ: Lawrence Erlbaum Associates.

Reusser, K. (1993). Tutoring systems and pedagogical theory: Representational tools for understanding, planning, and reflection in problem solving. In S. Lajoie and S. Derry (Eds.) *Computers and Cognitive Tools*. Hillsdale, NJ: Lawrence Erlbaum Associates.

Riesbeck, C.K. and Schank, R.C. (1991). From training to teaching: Techniques for case-based ITS. In H. Burns, J. Parlett and C. Redfield (Eds.) *Intelligent tutoring systems: Evolutions in design*. Hillsdale, NJ: Lawrence Erlbaum Associates.

Ritter, S. and Koedinger, K.R. (1995). Towards lightweight tutoring agents. *Proceedings of the 7th World Conference on Artificial Intelligence in Education.*

Schmidt, R.A., Young, D.E., Swinnen, S. and Shapiro, D.C. (1989). Summary knowledge results for skill acquisition: Support for the guidance hypothesis. *Journal of Experimental Psychology: Learning, Memory and Cognition,* 15, 352-359.

Schoenfeld, A.H. (1987). What's all the fuss abo*ut metacognition? In A. Schoenfeld (Ed.) Cognitive Science and Mathematics Education*. Hillsdale, NJ: Lawrence Erlbaum Associates.

Schofield, J.W. Evans-Rhodes, D. and Huber, B.R. (1990). Artificial intelligence in the classroom: The impact of a computer-based tutor on teachers and students. *Social Science Computer Review*, 8, 24-41.

Self, J.A. (1990). Bypassing the intractable problem of student modeling. In C. Frasson and G. Gauthier (Eds.) *Intelligent tutoring systems: At the Crossroads of Artificial Intelligence and Education*. Norwood, NJ; Ablex Publishing.

Singley, M.K. (1987). The effect of goal posting on operator selection. *Proceedings of the Third International Conference on Artificial Intelligence and Education*. Pittsburgh, PA.

Singley, M.K., Carroll, J.M. and Alpert, S.R. (1993). Incidental reification of goals in an intelligent tutor for Smalltalk. In E. Lemut, B. du Boulay and G. Dettori (Eds.) *Cognitive Models and Intelligent Environments for Learning Programming*. New York: Springer-Verlag.

Shute, V.J. (1993). A comparison of learning environments: All that glitters.... In S. Lajoie and S. Derry (Eds.) *Computers and Cognitive Tools*. Hillsdale, NJ: Lawrence Erlbaum Associates.

Shute, V.J. and Glaser, R. (1990). A large-scale evaluation of an intelligent discovery world: Smithtown. *Interactive Learning Environments*, 1, 51-76.

Sleeman, D. and Brown, J.S. (1982). *Intelligent Tutoring Systems*. New York: Academic Press.

Sleeman, D., Kelly, A.E., Martinak, R., Ward, R.D. and Moore, J.L. (1989). Studies of diagnosis and remediation with high school algebra students. *Cognitive Science*, 13, 551-568.

Sleeman, D., Ward, R.D., Kelly, A.E., Martinak, R. and Moore, J.L. (1991). An overview of recent studies in PIXIE. In P. Goodyear (Ed.) *Teaching knowledge and Intelligent Tutoring*. Norwood, NJ: Ablex Publishing.

Stevens, A.L. and Collins, A.M. (1977) The goal structure of a Socratic tutor. *Proceedings of the ACM Conference*. New York: Association for Computing Machinery.

Sweller, J. (1988). Cognitive load during problem solving: Effects on learning. *Cognitive Science*, 12, 257-285.

Tenney, Y.J and Kurland, L.C. (1988). The development of troubleshooting expertise in radar mechanics. In J. Psotka, L. Massey and S. Mutter (Eds.) *Intelligent Tutoring Systems: Lessons learned.* Hillsdale, NJ: Lawrence Erlbaum Associates.

Towne, D.M. and Munro, A. (1992). Supporting diverse instructional strategies in a simulation-oriented training environment. In J. Regian and V. Shute (Eds.) *Cognitive Approaches to Automated Instruction*. Hillsdale, NJ: Lawrence Erlbaum Associates.

VanLehn, K. (1990). *Mind bugs: The origins of procedural misconceptions*. Cambridge, MA: The MIT Press.

Weber, G. (1993). Analogies in an intelligent programming environment for learning LISP. In E. Lemut, B. du Boulay and G. Dettori (Eds.) *Cognitive Models and Intelligent Environments for Learning Programming*. New York: Springer-Verlag.

Weber, G. (in press). Episodic learner modeling. *Cognitive Science*.

Wenger, E. (1987). *Artificial Intelligence and Tutoring Systems: Computational and Cognitive Approaches to the Communication of Knowledge*. Los Altos, CA: Morgan Kaufmann Publishers.

Westcourt, K., Beard, M and Gould, L. (1977). Knowledge-based adaptive curriculum sequencing for CAI: Application of a network representation. *Proceedings of 1977 Annual Conference, Association for Computing Machinery*.

Williams, M.D., Hollan, J.D. and Stevens, A.L. (1981). An overview of STEAMER: An advanced computer-assisted instruction system for propulsion engineering. *Behavior Research Methods and Instrumentation*, 13, 85-90.

Woolf, B.P. and McDonald, D.D. (1984). Building a computer tutor: Design issues. *IEEE Computer*, 17, 61-73.

Part VI

Multimedia, Video and Voice

Handbook of Human-Computer Interaction
Second, completely revised edition
M. Helander, T.K. Landauer, P. Prabhu (eds.)

Chapter 38

Hypertext and its Implications for the Internet

Pawan R. Vora
U S WEST Communications
Denver, Colorado, USA

Martin G. Helander
Linköping Institute of Technology
Linköping, Sweden

38.1 Introduction

Vannevar Bush (1945) pointed out the inefficiency and artificiality of the index-based methods of storing and retrieving information, which required that "having found one item... [one must] emerge from the system and re-enter a new path" (p. 106). Bush claimed that "[t]he human mind does not work that way. It operates by association. With one item in its grasp, it snaps instantly to the next that is suggested by the association of thoughts..." (Bush, 1945, p. 106).

Hypertext is intended to overcome the artificiality of index-based systems of storage and retrieval by providing computer-supported links between related pieces of information. Put simply, in hypertext, the information is divided over several pieces of text (referred to as nodes) and the related pieces are connected by links; see Figure 1. By doing so, hypertext permits non-sequential (or non-linear) associative mode of information access, and provides a method of accessing information that is both more direct and more immediate than possible in a conventional paper-based system of information storage (Jones, 1987).

Hypermedia is essentially multimedia hypertext. That is, the nodes are not limited to textual information, but can have graphics, sound, animation, and video. Through a variety of media hypermedia has the potential of "enriching the flow of information across the interface between computers and their users" (Waterworth, 1992; p.11).

Hypertext and hypermedia are often distinguished, with hypertext referring to text-only systems and hypermedia referring to systems that support multiple media. This distinction is not made in this chapter, however; the term 'hypertext' is used generically to refer to both text-only and multimedia systems.

38.1.1 What is Hypertext

To date, there are no clear definitions of hypertext. In fact, hypertext may refer to one or several of the following:

- ***Information creation***. Nelson (1967) described hypertext as "non-sequential writing"—a *liberating* medium. In hypertext, the information creation is no longer only in the realm of the authors. Readers can also annotate and make their own links making different paths through the text.
- ***Information storage and management***. Smith and Weiss (1988) defined hypertext as an approach to information management in which data is stored in a network of nodes connected by links. Conklin (1987) defined hypertext as "windows on a screen," which are associated with objects in a database. Links are provided between these objects both graphically as labeled icons and in the database as pointers. There are no constraints on the types of data or information in a node; nodes may have text, graphics, sound, audio, video, or a combination of them.

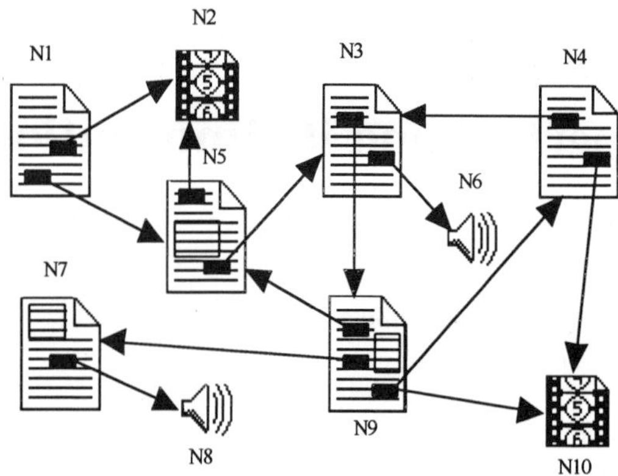

Figure 1. A simplified version of hypertext. N1 to N10 represent nodes and the arrows between them represent links.

- ***Information presentation and access***. Nielsen (1990a; 1995a) emphasized that hypertext is characterized more by its "look and feel" rather than the technology. Hypertext should make users *feel* that they can move freely through the information according to their own needs (Nielsen, 1990a). Hypertext is an 'interactive' technology, where users point (either directly or indirectly) to reactive objects that are displayed on the screen. The user is given several options and controls sequencing of information. This ability to navigate (non-linearly) in the database using links is an important characteristic of hypertext .

38.2 A Brief History of Hypertext

The concept of hypertext has been around for about 50 years. Vannevar Bush, Ted Nelson, and Doug Engelbart are considered visionaries and pioneers in the field of hypertext. Their visions were quite different, however. Bush (1945) envisioned supporting intellectual work using the complex interlinkage of accumulated knowledge. "Docuverse" envisioned by Nelson (1981) would contain all the world's literature, accessible and interlinked from any point in the global network. Engelbart, on the other hand, emphasized the cooperative work environments through shared electronic spaces where groups of workers could manage and exchange concepts and ideas in the form of linked structures (Engelbart and English, 1968). Ted Nelson (1995) also emphasized these differences: "Doug [Douglas Engelbart] and I started from completely opposite premises: he to empower work groups and make them smarter, I to free the individual from group obtuseness and impediment."

Despite the differences, they described hypertext as a means for enhancing the following primary categories of idea processing (Carlson, 1989):

- Reading: goal-oriented (information seeking) navigation through a large, unstructured library of information or casual browsing through a pool of text and graphics in a non-linear fashion.
- Annotating: recording ideas dynamically generated while reading text (including critiquing); explicating difficult passages; storing user-produced mnemonic aids; communicating with other users.
- Collaborating: electronic conferencing and/or multiple authoring of complex documents.
- Learning: accommodating varying learning styles, varying speeds of ingesting materials, and personalized structuring of bodies of information.

38.3 Why Hypertext?

The main justification for hypertext is the claim that useful information retrieval is much easier through associations, rather than through indexing. The ensuing freedom to browse is the single most important advantage of hypertext technology.

Hypertext also permits us to assemble large collections of discrete materials composed in various media, and to *link* them in a variety of ways, without destroying the integrity of the individual components (Slatin, 1988). Nielsen (1995a) considered managing and retrieving information from multimedia databases one of the important advantages of hypertext. Further, the information is accessible from multiple perspectives and through different search strategies. For example, a telephone list could have parallel alphabetic, geographic, and social organizations, with readers free to exploit whichever structure they find most convenient (Wright and Lickorish, 1989).

Hypertext is a potential solution to problems that involve voluminous, densely cross-referenced databases that must be searched by many different people attempting to retrieve highly divergent type of information (Berk and Devlin, 1991). Hypertext systems also offer the ability to its users to add their own links and annotations.

The flexibility in linking information has made hypertext useful in educational applications as well. One of the main reasons for growing interest in hypermedia in education is because it supports the currently popular 'constructivist' theory of learning (Cunningham *et al.*, 1993; Merrill, 1991): the view that students should construct knowledge rather than simply consume. Furthermore, a rich learning experience can be achieved by integrating a variety of media more effectively than simply text and graphics.

Hypertext also allows a writer to "Write now, organize later" (Seyer, 1991), which makes it easier for the writer to capture "inspirational" thoughts without leaving the current work space. Hypertext allows writers to keep their organization fluid and view and organize information in multiple ways without rewriting before committing it, if necessary, to a linear format.

Finally, hypertext can avoid the high costs associated with paper. For example, the documentation for an F-18 fighter aircraft is 300,000 pages (Ventura, 1988) and requires 68 cubic feet of storage space when printed on paper. The same information in a CD-ROM format would occupy about 0.04 cubic feet of space. Not only does hypertext save on storage space, it also saves on the cost of updating the information (Nielsen, 1995a).

In sum, hypertext has not only the benefits of 'liberation' (Nelson, 1974) and 'intellectual augmentation' (Engelbart, 1962), but also the potential for improved information access, education, writing, and ease in presenting and maintaining the information. Hypertext has become popular as it provides the authors and publishers the necessary freedom to associate and the readers the freedom to explore (Streitz, 1995).

38.4 Why not Hypertext?

There are also arguments against hypertext. First, the several claims in favor of hypertext that hypertext resembles the brain; hypertext resembles the structure of memory; and hypertext, like mind, "operates by association" are unfounded (see Nyce and Kahn, 1991; McKendree *et al.*, 1995). In fact, there are several competing theories for how the mind and memory works (see Anderson, 1983; Newell, 1990; Rumelhart *et al.*, 1986). McKendree *et al.* (1995) called these the "homeopathic fallacies" about hypertext "in an analogy to the notion from Medieval and Renaissance times that assumed the effects or appearance of a medicine must resemble the symptoms of the disease which it is meant to treat." Therefore, claiming effectiveness or usefulness of hypertext based on the structural similarity does not hold.

Second, the claimed advantage of hypertext, that users are in control of how information is sequenced and can take an active role in sequencing decisions, needs to be revisited. When a hypertext system does not offer any support to navigate in information space and any help in decision-making, the freedom and flexibility often becomes a burden. The ensuing problems are cognitive overhead and disorientation (Conklin, 1987):

Cognitive overhead. Conklin (1987) defined cognitive overhead as the additional effort and concentration necessary to maintain several tasks or trails at a time. It is the additional mental overhead on authors to create, and keep track of nodes and links. For readers, it is the overhead due to making decisions as to which links to follow and which to abandon, given a large number of choices. The process of pausing (either to jot down required information or to decide which way to go) can be very distracting. It can become a serious problem if there are a large number of nodes and links.

Disorientation. Disorientation is the tendency to lose one's sense of location and direction in a non-linear document (Conklin, 1987). Foss (1989) described two phenomena related to disorientation: *The Embedded Digression Problem* and *The Art Museum Phenomenon*. In the former, the user keeps following chains of thought until the original goal is lost; a common problem in using an encyclopedia with cross-referencing. The Art Museum Phenomenon is the situation where, after spending a long period browsing through several items of information, there is a loss of distinction between the individual items and an inability to abstract the general characteristics from the particular.

One of the reasons for disorientation is that hypertext does not offer any spatial cues for one's location in the information space (Carlson, 1989). The problem of disorientation or "getting lost in space" arises from the need to know where one is in the network, where one came from, and how to get to another place in the network (Elm and Woods, 1985). In traditional text, it is not easy to get lost. There is the table of contents, an index, page numbers, and bookmarks. According to Jones (1987), "hypertext allows us to create a rich network of associations but it does not give us the process to interpret this network... If the appropriate connections are not made, this information may be effectively rendered irretrievable in hypertext."

Another reason is that hypertext encourages fragmentation and proliferation of nodes (Carlson, 1989). Some consider that hypertext breaks down the notions of coherence and cohesion, so important for comprehension of linear text (Whalley, 1993).

Despite these shortcomings, hypertext has a conceptual appeal due to the ease of associations and user interactivity. And, if the above problems can be solved, then hypertext has an unmatched potential for improved ways of storing, accessing, and presenting information.

In sum, the freedom to navigate is both a benefit and a cost. To mitigate the problems, users should be provided with navigation support features. Simply stated, navigation support is needed in hypertexts to help answer readers' questions such as: Where am I? Where to go next? How do I get there? How do I return? (Elm and Woods, 1985).

38.5 Navigation Support Systems

Before discussing navigation support systems, we distinguish between two forms of information seeking: navigation and browsing. Information retrieval (IR), yet another form of information seeking, is discussed in Section 38.6. The main distinction between navigation and browsing is based on user goals. In browsing, users explore the available hypertext to get a general idea about one or several topics. Whereas, in navigation, users have a specific goal in mind.

Navigation or browsing is often difficult. In a complex hypertext system, the structural complexity may be overwhelming for effective navigation. Users can quickly become disoriented and navigation and visualization tools are often needed (Glenn and Chignell, 1992). Below, we discuss some of the common ways designers try to help users navigate in hypertext.

38.5.1 Paths, Guided Tours, and Tabletops

One way of supporting navigation in unfamiliar hypertext and overcoming disorientation is to provide preauthored linear paths through the document—referred to as *guided tours* (Trigg, 1988) and/or *paths* (Zellweger, 1989). These are comparable to the notion of 'trails' suggested by Bush (1945), where the authors ('trailblazers') suggest a useful path through the information. Zellweger (1989) defined three path models: (1) a *sequential path*, which is an ordered sequence of

Table 1. Implementation of backtrack models (from Nielsen, 1995a).

Backtrack Model	Original Navigation Sequence	Backtrack Sequence
Chronological	A » B » C » D » C » E	E » C » D » C » B » A
Single-revisit	A » B » C » D » C » E	E » C » D » B » A
First-visit	A » B » C » D » C » E	E » D » C » B » A
Detour-removing	A » B » C » D » C » E	E » B » A

nodes, (2) a *branching path*, which suggests branches from which the reader must choose, and (3) a *conditional path*, which recommends different branches for different conditions.

The "ordered sequence of nodes" does not restrict the presentation to only one node at a time. Trigg (1988) suggested use of tour stops where a screenful of nodes are presented. He called them "table tops." A tabletop is essentially a snapshot of several nodes and as the reader moves from one stop to another, the current tabletop is automatically closed and next one is brought up.

Usually the designer will provide several optional guided tours or paths from which a user can select the one that is most appropriate. This tour can be initiated either by the user or by the system (Zellweger, 1989).

Note that paths and guided tours violate the basic notion of non-linearity and browsing freedom in hypertext. None the less, they may facilitate navigation particularly for novice users. A hypertext system may, therefore, utilize a combination of associative non-linear links and guided-tour based sequential links.

38.5.2 Backtrack

According to Nielsen (1995a), the most important navigation facility in hypertext is backtracking to previous nodes. Backtracking is comparable to multiple "undo" operations and improves user control. Nielsen (1995a) recommended two features for implementing backtrack function:

1. Backtrack should always be available and should always be activated in the same way.
2. User should be able to backtrack all the way to the introduction node. This is important to re-establish the context (Fairchild *et al.*, 1988).

Backtracking can be implemented in several ways (Nielsen, 1995a; Bieber and Wan, 1994; Garzotto *et al.*, 1995) (see Table 1.):

- Chronological backtrack: This is the most basic model, where nodes are presented in strictly a reverse order. But, it may be inefficient if the user has visited the same nodes several times, since they will have to be revisited.
- Single-revisit backtrack: This model removes the redundancy in chronological backtracking.
- First-visit backtrack: This model also removes the redundancy while backtracking. However, it considers the first visit to a node and not the last visit as in the single-revisit model.
- Detour-removing backtrack (Bieber and Wan, 1994): This model suggests that the user should not revisit nodes that were visited by mistake. Such nodes are identified by analyzing repetitions in the navigation sequences.
- Parameterized backtrack (Garzotto *et al.*, 1995): This model allows the user to backtrack to nodes of certain type in a hypertext that has typed nodes (e.g., gIBIS).

38.5.3 History

Unlike backtrack, history lists allow the users to directly jump to any of the previously visited nodes. It can also be used by the reader to check "Where have I been?" History lists may be presented graphically by showing visited nodes in an iconic form (e.g., Apple's HyperCard™), textually by listing the node names (e.g., Hypertext '87 Trip Report [Nielsen, 1990b]), or by a combination of both the icons and the node name (e.g., My First Incredible, Amazing Dictionary [Kindersley, 1994]). The choice of method would, of course, depend on the content of nodes. For example, in a strictly textual hypertext system, the list should be textual rather than graphical. History lists may not be in a strict chronological or reverse chronological order as the term 'history' may imply. Several hypertext have used the backtracking models discussed in the previous section in their implementation of history lists.

Nielsen (1990a) suggested an interesting design alternative to history lists, called 'visual cache,' which keeps recently visited nodes visible on the screen. This design was based on the belief that users are more likely to return to recently visited nodes. Another interesting implementation is in SemNet (Fairchild *et al.*, 1988), where both nodes and links are shown in a list.

38.5.4 Bookmarks

Some hypertext systems allow users to bookmark nodes so that they can return to them later. Bookmarks are particularly useful for browsing large hypertext systems such as World-Wide Web, where users stumble across interesting information that they may wish to peruse later. To efficiently manage bookmarks, some hypertext systems allow the users to group them and create hierarchical lists (e.g., Netscape Navigator and Internet Explorer browsers for the World-Wide Web). Recently some implementations of bookmark functionality have used proximity or neighbor-based organizations; for example, Web Squirrel from Eastgate systems (www.eastgate.com/ squirrel/) helps organize Web addresses and other Internet resources into neighborhoods (groups of items clustered around a large label) and lists (items stacked together). It also supports agents that scan the collection of bookmarks, referred to as *information farm*, for items that meet user-defined criteria. Eastgate systems refers to WebSquirrel™ as an *information farming* tool — a program that helps users keep track of information they cultivate, organize, and harvest every day.

Bookmarks typically mark the entire page. However, there may be a need to bookmark only a chunk of the information on a page. We believe that such an implementation will be useful for large documents to facilitate search for the desired information. It may help the user answer the question: "Now, what was in this node that prompted me to place a bookmark?"

38.5.5 Landmarks

Landmarks, both natural and man-made, often help to identify the current position and help in orientation (Fairchild *et al.,* 1988). According to Glenn and Chignell (1992), one of the difficulties in browsing hypertext is the occurrence of two different types of navigation. First, there is navigation through the structure of hypertext as designed by the author. Second, there is the inherent structure of information and relationships between topics that is in the user's mind. However, this semantic structure in the users' mind is rarely identical to the author-designed structure of hypertext. One way to help the user to negotiate the structure of hypertext is to define cognitive landmarks within the network with visual cues that emphasize them. These landmarks can represent features on a mental map, and help users navigate through conceptual structures. One approach to identifying cognitive landmarks is connectivity (Valdez, Chignell, and Glenn, 1988; Chignell and Valdez, 1989). The basic idea is that important topics tend to be connected either to many other topics directly or to topics that are in turn well connected.

38.5.6 Overview Diagrams or Maps

The approaches to support navigation discussed so far were devised with the assumption that most users try to locate pertinent information. These techniques are of limited benefit for users who set out to understand the overall structure of hyperdocument (Noik, 1993). One obvious solution is to use overview diagrams or maps, similar to the way table of contents in linear texts provide an overview of their scope and organization.

Overview diagrams or maps are among the most widely researched areas in hypertext navigation. They provide a visual representation of the node-link structure of the hypertext, and are also referred to as "browsers." In addition to providing information about the hypertext organization in a general sense, Overview diagrams provide visual cues that inform users (Glenn and Chignell, 1992):

1. Where they are relative to other information, and
2. Where they can move to, from their present location.

In linear text, overviews help readers comprehend the organization of information, which in turn help in navigation (Pohl, 1982). Similarly, overview diagrams are beneficial in non-linear hypertext environments. Parton *et al.* (1985) found that a tree diagram of the entire menu structure led to better performance, better comprehension, and greater satisfaction among novice users. Dee-Lucas and Larkin (1991) showed that users presented with an overview diagram (a content map) explored more items. Hammond and Allinson (1989) found that users performed better in both exploratory and directed tasks when they used overview maps. Use of overview diagrams also helps authors to present multiple viewpoints of the content (see Landow and Kahn, 1992).

However, spatial representation of non-hierarchical conceptual structures is, often problematic (Fillenbaum and Rapaport, 1973; Tversky and Hutchinson, 1986) and tree representations are often used to reduce complexity within a hypertext network — for example, NoteCards browser (Halasz, 1988). Furnas and Zacks (1994) also proposed reducing directed acyclic graphs

(DAGs) to hierarchies to improve both comprehension and navigation.

The advantage of overview diagrams is that they make explicit to users the information about relationships within the data space and provide a familiar visualization of information structure. However, their major weakness is that they raise expectations that one can navigate around hypermedia as if one were using a map of a two dimensional surface. In many situations, the question is not whether to build such a map, but rather how to build one that it is usable and minimizes violations between the actual hypermedia structure and its representation (Glenn and Chignell, 1992). A common practice is to provide a graphical representation of the hypertext structure. These overview diagrams are typically two-dimensional representations of node-link structures. However, even for a medium-sized hypertext with moderate connectivity, the node-link structure may appear to be a 'visual spaghetti.' (see Conklin, 1987; Noik, 1993). Therefore, it may be necessary to reduce the size of the displayed network. Alternatively, if users are allowed to zoom into a part of the hypertext network and to pan to other parts, it is possible to display local details with a sacrifice in global context. Researchers have observed that browsing a large layout by scrolling and link traversing tends to obscure the global structure of a hypertext network (Hollands *et al.*, 1989). The problem faced by the designers is then how to represent the structure so users can both comprehend and efficiently navigate. Solutions proposed to solve this problem include: (1) fisheye views; (2) 3-D representation of the hyperspace; (3) multi-level overviews; and (4) filtered hypertext. Most of these techniques allow users to examine local detail while still maintaining a global perspective.

Fisheye Views

Furnas (1986) suggested *fisheye browsers* to provide a balance of local detail and global context. A fisheye view (FEV) of a graph displays details of the area of interest while other areas are presented successively in less detail. Fisheye views are implemented by computing a degree-of-interest (DOI) value for every node, then displaying only those nodes that have a DOI value greater than a certain threshold value. The DOI value for a node increases with its a priori importance (API) and decreases with its distance from the node that is currently in focus. Fisheye views have been found to significantly improve user performance when compared with the traditional zooming on a hierarchically clustered network (Schaffer *et al.*, 1993).

Sarkar and Brown (1994) argued that in Furnas's (1986) formulation a node is either present in the fisheye view in full detail or is completely absent from the view. This causes both space and time discontinuity in the information space as nodes appear and disappear from the view during browsing. These discontinuities may disturb the orientation of the viewer and make navigation more difficult (Mackinlay *et al.*, 1991). Therefore, unlike Furnas (1986), who defined the distance function as an arbitrary function between two nodes in a structure, they suggested use of Euclidean distance separating two nodes in a network. Each node in the network is then specified by its coordinates, and a size, which is represented by the length of a side of the bounding box for that node. Each node is also given a number to represent its global API (*a priori importance*). Finally, each node is assigned a *visual worth* (VW), based on its distance from the focus (in normal co-ordinates) and its API. The size of each node and its distance from other nodes is displayed according its visual worth. In the final fisheye representation nodes are presented with sizes and distances according to their visual worth values.

Thus, fisheye views are loosely grouped into two categories: filtering FEVs and distorting FEVs (Noik, 1993; Leung and Apperley, 1994). Filtering FEV approaches, like Furnas's (1986), use thresholding to constrain the display of information (e.g., Mitta, 1990; Godin *et al.*, 1989). Whereas, distorting FEV approaches geometrically distort visualizations to obtain visual fisheye effects (e.g., Misue and Sugiyama, 1991; Sarkar and Brown, 1994).

Noik (1993) argued that the main problem with the current approaches is their reliance on a geometric interpretation of distance. The resulting FEV depends completely on the original drawing of the graph: elements positioned near a focal point receive a higher DOI rating. Such approaches are effective only in cases where the semantic distance between nodes corresponds to their proximity in the drawing (e.g., transportation networks where nodes are positioned according to cartographic data).

Three-Dimensional (3D) Representations

One of the problems in representing large structures in a two dimensions is that crossing points between links may be confused with nodes. Fairchild *et al.* (1988) proposed SemNet, which represents information as directed graphs in a three-dimensional space. When users interact with the structure by direct manipulation of the nodes and links, the view-point moves and the users can perceive a three-dimensional space where arcs no longer intersect.

Other 3D visualization techniques, developed under the Information Visualizer project at Xerox PARC, include Cone Trees for visualizing hierarchies and perspective walls for visualizing linear structures (Rao *et al.*, 1995; Robertson *et al.*, 1993). Most of these 3D representation techniques are variations of "focus+context" techniques (Rao *et al.*, 1995). They attempt to reveal structure by showing nodes and links, while details are de-emphasized (Fairchild *et al.*, 1988).

Cone trees are hierarchies laid out uniformly in three dimensions, either vertically or horizontally. An obvious disadvantage of a vertical cone trees is that the display of text does not fit the aspect ratio of the representation of the nodes (3 X 5-inch index card). Consequently, text can be shown only for selected paths. Cone Trees have been used to visualize an entire UNIX directory hierarchy with 600 directories and 10,000 files (from Card, 1996).

Perspective walls represent linear structures having wide aspect ratios that are difficult to accommodate in a single view. With a large amount of information and extreme aspect ratio, it is difficult to see the details while maintaining the global context. To solve this problem, the Perspective Wall folds a 2D layout into a 3D wall that provides the details in the central region and smoothly integrates two perspective regions on each side for viewing context.

An interesting 3D representation is *File System Navigator* (FSN) by Silicon Graphics (see Fairchild, 1993). The file system hierarchy is laid out on a "landscape," with each directory represented by a pedestal with individual files as boxes on top of it. The 3D space is augmented with other visual cues such as box size to represent the file size and color to represent their age.

Usability of the 3D representations is enhanced by using color, lighting, shadow, transparency, hidden surface occlusion, continuous transformation, and motion cues to induce object constancy and 3D perspective. Smooth interactive animation is used to shift the navigation from a cognitive to a perceptual task, freeing cognitive resources for doing the tasks (Robertson *et al.,* 1993). An important usability problem with 3D representations is the choice of input device for manipulation. This problem may be solved when three-dimensional control and display devices become available (Fairchild *et al.,* 1988).

Multi-level Overviews

Another solution to the problem of representing large information spaces may be to abstract information at several levels to provide overviews either to support orientation within the hypertext network or to provide progressive disclosure of the content. These overviews are often presented as hierarchical structures with various levels of detail. This approach can be useful not only for navigation, but also for improving comprehension.

Nielsen (1990b) used two levels of overview diagrams for a hypertext system. The global diagram provided a coarse-grained sense of location in the global information space and the local overview map provided more fine-grained information on the local neighborhood of the current node. Two levels of overview were possibly sufficient for Nielsen's (1990b) system which only had 95 nodes. For larger hypertexts, it may be necessary to have multiple levels of overview diagrams with varying details. With several levels of overview diagrams, however, it may become necessary to support "meta-navigation" — that is, navigation to move within the overview diagrams (Nielsen, 1995a).

Filtering Hypertext Network

Several browsers used for argumentation applications such as gIBIS (Conklin and Begeman, 1987) and Aquanet (Marshall *et al.*, 1991) provide capability to filter the hypertext network based on user queries. Filtered views of hypertext network are possible because these systems classify both nodes and links. Users can specify their interest in terms of node and link types and the system can then generate a filtered hypertext and present it graphically.

Some hypertext systems, because of the web-like structure of connectivity, lend themselves to "structure search." In these systems, both nodes and links are classified, and a user could ask for a diagram of all subnetworks that match a given pattern of node and link types.

38.5.7 Improving Hypertext Comprehension

An implicit assumption in the interaction model of hypertext is that the readers are capable of creating coherent virtual structures by selective browsing through nodes in hypertext (Samarapungavan and Beishuizen, 1992). Reality, however, is that hypertext allows us to create a multitude of networks of association, but does not help us in their interpretation (Jones, 1987). Unless the structure of hypertext is made comprehensible to the user, the user will find hypertext fragmented and incoherent. Many researchers believe that it is incomprehensibility of hypertext that causes disorientation, not nonlinearity per se (Thüring *et al.*, 1995; 1991; Vora, 1994; Charney, 1987; Spyridakis and Isakson, 1991)

There are two ways of improving comprehensibility of hypertext: (1) by using appropriate metaphors and (2) by improved design to create coherent hypertext structures.

Use of Metaphors

One obvious way of improving comprehension of hypertext is through the use of metaphors. There is evidence that a clear metaphorical model improves both efficiency and memorability (Borgman, 1986). Metaphors have several advantages:

1. The structure of hypertext is made intuitively recognizable. A familiar organization helps users to understand the organization of nodes and links (McLean, 1989).

2. The advantage of using metaphors lies in the 'cognitive transfer' associated with their use. Users can transfer knowledge and skills from a familiar domain to another less familiar area (Barker, 1993; Carroll *et al.,* 1988). The need for learning is minimized since the behavior of objects can be predicted (Waterworth, 1992).

Several types of metaphors have been used in hypertext systems: Cards, books, encyclopedias, libraries, cities, and maps. The analogies are often tenuous. Systems usually have functionality beyond that embodied in real world metaphors. Smith (1987) called them 'magic' aspects of the system. Hammond and Allinson (1987) specifically examined the use of metaphorical versus magical features in their hypermedia tuition system built around a travel metaphor. Surprisingly, magic features did not present problems of recognition or use. It seems that a metaphor can enhance the usability of a system if there is a natural match between that metaphor and the application focus (Waterworth, 1992). But a single metaphor can be restrictive and cumbersome — unless the intent is to restrict the flexibility with which users may interact with a system (Benest *et al.*, 1987). The use of multiple metaphors may often be desirable (Weyer and Borning, 1985).

Metaphors should be selected carefully, however. Badly chosen metaphors are counter-productive. A non-metaphorical interface, with well-designed features, often works better.

Design of Coherent Hypertext Structures

Comprehension is often characterized as the construction of a mental model that represents the objects and their semantic relations (Johnson-Laird, 1983). In linear text, a coherent representation is necessary not only for comprehension but also for navigation. A coherent linear text facilitates *forward navigation,* that is, making predictions of what will come (Pohl, 1982; Perrig and Kintsch, 1982), and *backward navigation,* that is, finding previously encountered information. Since forward and backward navigation are relevant for information access in hypertext as well, it is important to understand what makes a linear text coherent and consider them in hypertext design (see Charney, 1987; Smith, Weiss, and Ferguson, 1987; Thüring *et al.*, 1991; Dillon, 1991b; Spyridakis and Isakson, 1991, Vora, 1994).

Cohesion or Local Coherence. An important factor in determining coherency of text is cohesion or connectivity or *local coherence.* Local coherence refers to "the way in which linguistic conventions allow one part of the text to be linked to another at sentence level" (Colley, 1987). In text, the most common forms of linkages are by the use of conjunction (e.g., It is raining outside today *and* I do not have a raincoat.) or by anaphoric referencing, where objects and events are common to two or more sentences (e.g., Carol didn't go to work today. *She* was feeling ill).

Global Coherence. Coherence at the local level is not sufficient for comprehension. Global coherence is also important; a text must have a consistent theme and be organized in a sensible sequence (Colley, 1987). There are two levels of Global coherence: *macrostructure* level and *superstructure* level. The macrostructure level characterizes the theme of the discourse and is built during the course of reading the text , and is therefore bottom-up (Kintsch and van Dijk, 1978). Superstructures are familiar rhetorical structures that facilitate the macroprocesses in comprehension (Kintsch and Yarbrough, 1982). Superstructures make it possible to predict the likely ordering and grouping of constituent elements of a body of text; a text is considered coherent if it is organized according to such superstructures (Kintsch and Yarbrough, 1982). In sum, a superstructure is a schematic form that organizes the global meaning of a text. Such a superstructure consists of functional categories and rules that specify which categories may follow or combine with what other categories (van Dijk and Kintsch, 1983). For example, a scientific article may have the superstructure: Introduction, Method, Results, and Discussion (Dillon, 1991b).

In sum, there are *levels of comprehension*: "One may comprehend the words, but not the meaning of a sentence, or one can understand sentences and still be confused by the overall organization of the text" (Kintsch and Yarbrough, 1982; p. 828).

In applying these principles to hypertext, one should provide cues at both the *node level* and at the *net level* (Thüring *et al.*, 1995). To improve coherence within the node, one can use the traditional reading models as discussed above to improve local and global coherence. At the net level, however, to increase coherence, the designers of hypertext should attempt to limit the "fragmentation" so users can understand how the text is distributed over several nodes and what they have to do with each other.

Local coherence at the net level can be achieved by the following measures (Thüring *et al.*, 1995; Vora, 1994):

1. **Labeling the links.** The semantic relationships between the nodes can be made explicit by labels. Labels enable readers to identify the links of interest at any particular time and makes hypertext more clear and easier to read (Parunak, 1991).

   In an empirical investigation, Vora (1994) observed that by labeling the links, the users were able to search faster, navigate more efficiently, and construct more complete maps of information structure, compared to the system where links were not labeled.

2. **Providing context.** Context can be preserved by showing the actual node together with its predecessor. This conveys a sense of continuity across nodes that is important for comprehension by forming semantic relationships between nodes.

Cues at the global level are important so that users can identify the major components of hypertext. To increase global coherence the hypertext designers can do the following (Thüring *et al.*, 1995; 1991):

1. **Aggregate the information into higher order units.** "Composite nodes" proposed by Halasz (1988) help users to identify important themes (or functional categories) of hypertext.

2. **Provide a comprehensive overview.** Graphical representation or maps can convey the structure to the user. Vora (1994) found that graphical representation of information with labeled links helped in comprehension and improved navigation and search performance. An interesting design question is whether providing multiple overview diagrams or access paths would affect the coherence of the presented material. Though Edwards and Hardman (1989) and Mohageg (1992) did not find any benefits of multiple structures, Vora *et al.* (1994) showed that multiple access paths are beneficial for navigation if the paths are coherent and indicate the semantic relationship between the nodes.

38.5.8 Virtual Reality type Navigation Tools

Wilkins and Weal (1993) described two applications which use virtual space as a metaphor to aid in navigation.

1. Bath - An English City. A joint project with the Architecture Department of Bath University led to the development of a virtual space model of the city of Bath. A three dimensional model of Bath was constructed so that users could walk through the model selecting objects of interest. For example, clicking on Bath Abey produced historical text and photographs of the building.

2. Pirelli - A cable manufacturing machine. Several thousand documents contained within a manual makes traditional navigation tools difficult to use. In this systems, users may simply point at a particular part of a machine in order to obtain more information about it.

38.5.9 Adaptive/Intelligent Navigation

All intelligent filters or navigation support mechanisms share a common purpose: *to help the users select a path through the textbase that is tailored for a particular application or a purpose* (Carlson, 1989). Kibby and Mayes (1989) described an interesting aspect of 'intelligent support.' They discussed ways of automatically computing the degree of relatedness between member nodes of a hypertext system. They believed that the use of explicitly hard coded links in hypertext and hypermedia would limit the construction and use of large systems. Consequently, in their StrathTutor system they did not emphasize fixed links, although the system did contain some. Instead, they preferred to use dynamic links calculated from similarity measures while a user was navigating in the system.

Most adaptive hypertext system take into consideration either the user goals or user characteristics to provide intelligent navigation support. For example,

Table 2. Comparison of IR and IF (Belkin and Croft, 1992).

Information Retrieval	Information Filtering
• typically concerned with single uses with a one-time goal and one-time query	• repeated use by user(s) with long-term goals and interests
• recognizes inherent problems in query formulation	• assumes that profiles can correctly specify information interests
• concerned with collection and organization of text	• concerned with distribution of text to user(s)
• selection of text from a relatively static database	• selection or elimination of text from a dynamic data stream
• timeliness is not a typical concern	• timeliness of text is often of overriding significance
• assumes highly motivated users	• motivation or user attention cannot always be assumed
• privacy is not an issue... or is not addressed	• privacy may be important

the Hyperflex system takes into account user goals and advises users of relevant nodes (Kaplan, Fenwick, and Chen, 1993). The system captures user goals based on the user's navigation in the hypertext. Based on a predetermined set of user goals, the links in Hyperflex has a set of values associated with them. As the user navigates in Hyperflex — that is, traverses links — the system determines the goals of the user and recommends an ordered list of nodes. Another example is MetaDoc, an on-line reference manual that attempts to match the degree of explanation based on user profile (Boyle and Encarnacion, 1994). Usandisaga *et al.* (1996) is working on an educational system, HyperTutor, that integrates an intelligent tutoring system with hypertext so as to adapt the system behavior to the student characteristics such as orientation skills and cognitive abilities.

38.6 Information Retrieval and Information Filtering

Finding information in hypertext simply by traversing links, especially in large hypertexts, can become cumbersome and compromise usability. As asserted by Inaba (1990; p. 175): "The more energy required to obtain information, the less likelihood the information will be used." Therefore, most reasonably-sized hypertexts provide ways of accessing information other than static links.

There are two major ways to facilitate access of information in hypertext: Information Retrieval (IR) and Information Filtering (IF). As summarized by Lashkari (1995): "**Information filtering** refers to the filtering of a *continuously changing* stream of documents to select only those documents relevant to a user's interests. **Information retrieval**, on the other hand, refers to the process of retrieving all documents matching a user's current information need from a (normally relatively static) database of documents. Information filtering is a long term process, while information retrieval is normally a short term process limited to the duration of the current query session." For example, information retrieval might be to find the name of the companies that make cellular phones; information filtering might be used to inform a user every time a new wireless communication device is introduced in the market.

A caveat is in order. Neither IR nor IF guarantee increase in hypertext usability. A good user interface is important to ensure that information is used effectively and that the users can quickly get to the relevant information (Nielsen, 1995a).

Although IR and IF may be two sides of the same coin; there are several differences between these two methods (Belkin and Croft, 1992); see Table 2.

38.6.1 Information Retrieval

Information Retrieval begins when the user identifies a need for information—what Belkin and Croft (1987) refer to as Anomalous State of Knowledge (ASK). Due to the inherent difficulty of representing ASKs, the query is always considered to be approximate and imperfect.

Information Retrieval Models

There are three major models for the information retrieval engine to match a query: Boolean, vector space, and probabilistic retrieval (Belkin and Croft, 1992). The first of these is based on the "exact match" principle and the other two are based on the concept of "best match." The term "Boolean" is used because a query is expressed as words or phrases, combined using the Boolean operators such as AND, OR, NOT, XOR, etc. The result of Boolean retrieval is a partition of the database into a set of retrieved documents and a set of non-retrieved documents. The Boolean exact-match retrieval model is the standard model for current large-scale retrieval systems. A major problem with this model is there is no relevance ranking of the retrieved document set. Best-match retrieval models have been proposed to solve this problem. In the *vector space model* (Salton and McGill, 1983), the terms of a query can be *weighted* to consider their importance. These weights are computed using statistical distributions of the terms in the database, and in the texts. *Probabilistic information retrieval models* rank the texts in the database in the order of their probability of relevance to the query, given all the evidence available. This model considers that representation of both information need and text is uncertain, and the relevance relationship between them is also uncertain. To estimate the probability of relevance of a text to a query, the most typical source of evidence is the statistical distribution of terms in the database, and in relevant and non-relevant texts. More recent IR models have suggested use of *relevance feedback*, where the query is modified through user evaluation (Salton and McGill, 1983). In such systems, the user selects one or more of the items returned by the system to the initial query. The subsequent search then attempts to identify items similar to those selected by the user.

Another promising method is *Latent Semantic Indexing* (LSI) (Furnas *et al.*, 1988; Berry, Dumais, and Letsche, 1995). Traditional lexical matching (keyword-based) methods described so far are prone to errors as there exist many words having the same meaning (*synonymy*) and same words having many meanings (*polysemy*). LSI retrieves information on the basis of concepts rather than words and thereby alleviates the problems of polysemy and synonymy. LSI assumes an underlying latent structure in word usage that is, at least partially, hidden in the variability in word selections. It uses singular value decomposition (SVD) to estimate the structure in word usage across several documents. Retrieval is then based on using the database of words and clusters of associated words — or vectors — obtained from the SVD. In a study by Furnas *et al.* (1988), the average precision using LSI ranged from comparable to 30% better than that obtained using keyword-based methods.

Graphical Querying

Traditionally, information retrieval or querying is text-based. Golovchinsky and Chignell (1993) proposed a graphical query-based browsing system called "Queries-R-Links" (QRL).

QRL uses a graphical notation for expressing boolean to a full text retrieval enginein an interactive (point-and-click) fashion. Keywords are selected as they appear in the test.An AND relationship is specified between selected keywords by connecting them with a line; otherwise, an OR relationship is assumed. Thus, a graph can be constructed on top of the displayed text; see Figure 2.

This graphical query approach allows users to navigate within text when they do not have a clear search target in mind, or are not fully aware of the domain vocabulary. Golovchinsky and Chignell (1993) found a tendency for inexperienced users to do better with the graphical notation than when formulating Boolean queries as text strings. Graphical queries may also be easier to edit because components can be selected independently with a pointing device. Additionally, the language of the query can be reused for output, encouraging an incremental query refinement.

TileBars interface for Presenting Query Results

The results of a query are usually displayed as a list of items with their titles, and sometimes descriptions, ordered according to some function of the number of hits for each query term. Often the rationale behind the order of the items is not clear to the users. To address this problem, Hearst (1995) proposed the TileBars interface, which allows the users to simultaneously view the relative length of the documents and the frequency of the query terms. The TileBars interface displays a document as a rectangle in front of each retrieved document. Each text segment is shown as a square "tile" within the rectangle—referred to as TextTile. The darker the tile, the more frequent the term (white indicates 0, black indicates 8 or more instances). The bars for each set of query terms are shown next to each other. The TileBars display exploits the natural pattern-recognition capabilities of human perceptual system. This interface helps conceptualizes relative document

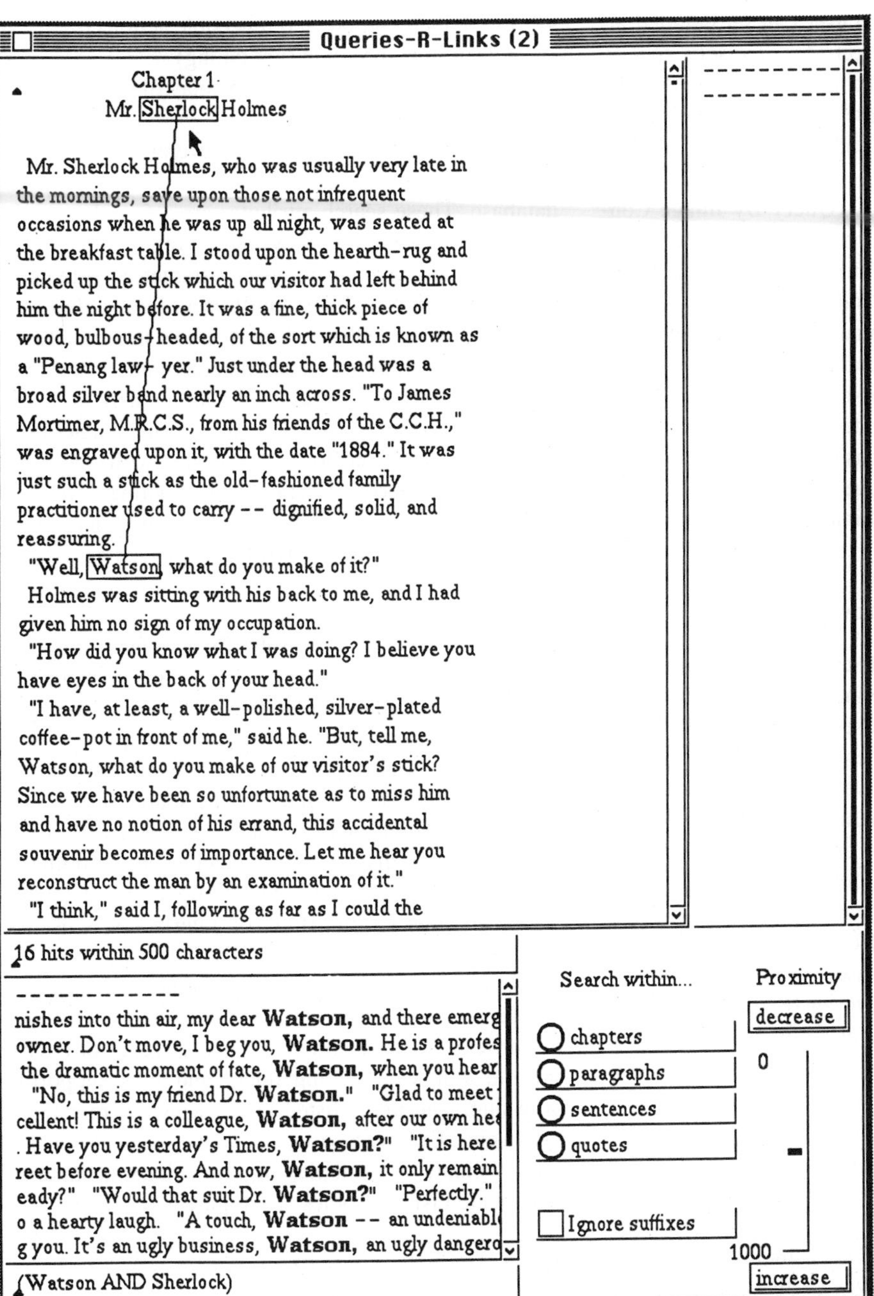

Figure 2. Queries-R-Links (from Charoenkitkarn et al., 1993).

length, query term frequency, and query term distribution. The users can thus easily and visually identify the most relevant documents.

Querying Images

More and more hypertext systems make generous use of images either on their own or to complement text. In these systems, though it is possible to see the data in a graphic form, searches for images are usually based on their textual or numeric attributes. Nishiyama *et al.* (1994) proposed a visual interface to retrieve images from Image Databases Systems (IDBSs). The user can specify their searches using icons and colors (instead of a text field). Moreover, the user can set detailed attributes for representing objects to precisely specify their image query reduce the number of candidates. Thus, the user can specify the feature of a picture at three levels, areas, objects, and attributes, to retrieve images from a database.

Another example is QBIC (Query By Image Content) developed by IBM which allows construction of queries based on image content such as color percentages, color layout, textures, and shapes of images and their objects (wwwqbic.almaden.ibm.com/~qbic/qbic.html). In future we should see more integration of textual and visual query mechanisms. An evidence is work on MAVIS (Microcosm Architecture for Video, Image, and Sound) to create extensions to Microcosm architecture to support not only image-based retrieval but retrieval of other types of multimedia content (Lewis *et al.*, 1996)

Integrated Querying and Browsing

Lately, considerable research effort is being spent to combine querying and browsing to facilitate information access from large databases. Traditional IR interfaces require the user to switch between querying and reading modes with cognitive overheads associated with each mode switch (Wright, 1991). Golovchinsky and Chignell (1996) describe an information exploration interface for "hiding" information retrieval engine in hypertext interface. In their electronic newspaper prototype, when the user selects a hypertext link, the words around the link are used to form a *context-specific* query and submitted to an IR engine. The results of the query are returned as a ranked collection of articles and displayed on the screen. The user also sees hypertext-like links, which are created dynamically using the terms of the query. Though the user is given an impression of a hypertext-like interface through link-anchors, there are no pre-authored links and both link-following and display of link-anchors is dynamic based on the surrounding context of the link. Other two examples are: *Starfield displays* (Ahlberg and Shneiderman, 1994) and the *Butterfly interface* (Mackinlay *et al.*, 1995).

Starfield displays. Ahlberg and Shneiderman (1994) proposed a Visual Information Seeking (VIS) approach which combined browsing and querying using the following direct manipulation principles:

- visual representation of the world of action including both objects and actions
- rapid, incremental, and reversible actions
- selection by pointing (not typing)
- immediate and continuous display of results

Users control the search using several sliders on the screen that represent the attributes of the objects in the database. These search attributes are referred to as dynamic query filters as they allow "rapid, incremental and reversible changes to query parameters, often simply by dragging a slider, [and] users [are] able to explore and gain feedback from displays in a few tenths of a second" (Ahlberg and Shneiderman, 1994). The results of queries are presented continuously on a spatial display—the "starfield" display. The starfield display is a two-dimensional scatterplot with additional features to support selection and zooming. The user can progressively refine the query using sliders or select any object in the scatterplot (displayed as a dot or a "star"); See Figure 3.

Butterfly interface. The Butterfly interface integrates search and browsing using a 3D interface in shape of a pyramid (Mackinlay *et al.*, 1995). The top of the pyramid is used to visualize the results of the queries. Each query result is portrayed as a horizontal layer in the pyramid and colored to indicate the source of the database. The current query result is described with a butterfly, which is displayed in the center. For simultaneously exploring three DIALOG bibliographic databases across the Internet, the Butterfly interface was used as follows: the head of the butterfly listed the source of the article, the left wing listed references given in the article, and the right wing listed the authors who cited this article. A user could click on a reference or citer to execute a link-generating query and thus supporting browsing. The items listed in the wings were referred to as veins. Color was used in butterfly veins for access management; for example, the vein color was darkened to indicate visited articles; see Figure 4.

38.6.2 Information Filtering

In information filtering, an incoming stream of objects is compared to many profiles (user interests) at the same time, rather than submitting a single query to a large, relatively static database. This means that, for every incoming object O_j, the probabilities associated with all profile nodes P_1 through P_n are computed. Based on the computation, the object O_j is either retained or removed (Belkin and Croft, 1992). In general, then, filtering could be defined as the process of de-

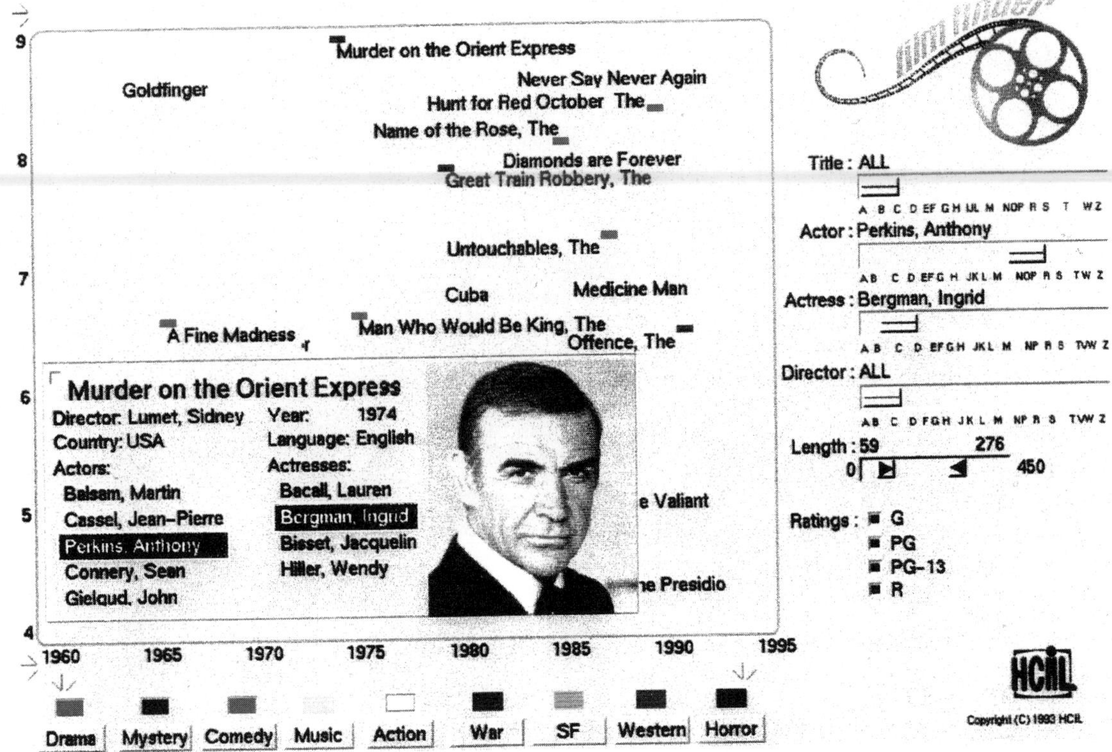

Figure 3. A "Starfield" display (Ahlberg and Shneiderman, 1994)

termining which profiles have a high probability of being satisfied by a particular object from the incoming stream.

Information Filtering models

A common information filtering technique is *content-based filtering*. Content-based filtering is an attempt to form a representation of pertinent documents based on its extracted features. Correlations are then calculated between the content of documents and the user profile (preferences set by the user). For textual documents, this normally takes the form of a vector-like representation of the keywords found in the document along with other features such as the author, the source, etc. A content-based filtering system needs to run every document against each user's profile to determine whether it will interest this user. For very large number of users, such as the World-Wide Web, this could require considerable resources and time. Content-based filtering systems have following limitations (Shardanand and Maes, 1995; Lashkari, 1995):

1. The items must be either in machine-parsable form (e.g., text) or attributes must be pre-assigned manually. Content-based analysis can not effectively deal with non-textual documents such as images and sound, the content of which cannot be parsed automatically — at least not currently.
2. Content-based filtering techniques have no inherent method for exploring potentially new areas of interest; the system recommends more of what the user has seen before.
3. Content-based filtering methods cannot judge a document's quality - something that is actually very important for the World-Wide Web, which contains documents of widely fluctuating quality.

Shardanand and Maes (1995) described *social information filtering technique* that automates the process of "word of mouth" recommendations by suggesting items based on the values assigned by other people with similar taste. In essence, these techniques exploit the similarities between the tastes of different users to recommend or advise against items. Note that user's

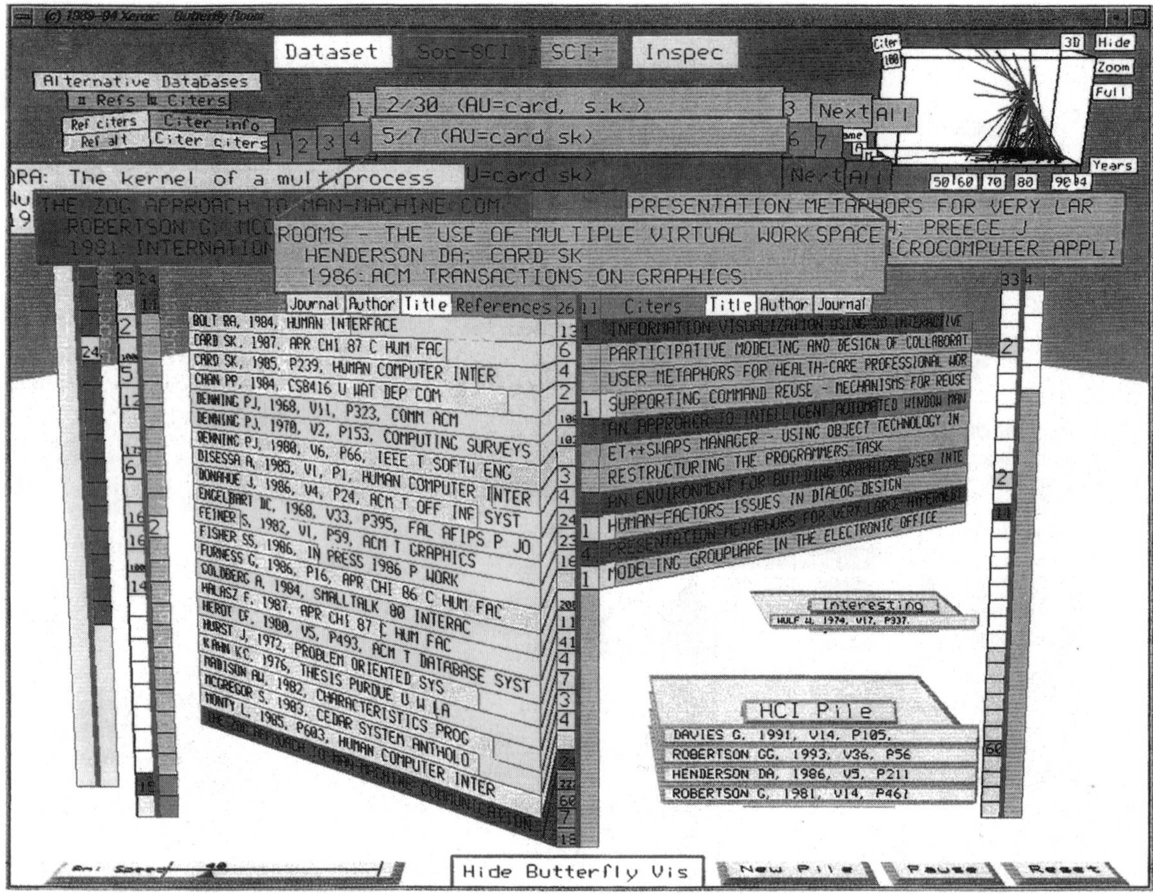

Figure 4. Butterfly Interface. (Mackinlay et al., 1995)

profile is not static; it changes over time as the user rates (indicates) more interests/disinterests. Social information filtering techniques have the following benefits over content-based filtering:

- Items being filtered need not be parsable.
- The system may recommend items which have very different content from what the user has indicated before. Serendipitous finding is, therefore, possible.
- Recommendations are based on the quality of the items, rather than their objective properties.

As the error in recommendation relates to the number of people profiles consulted to make the recommendation, the social information filtering system becomes more competent as the number of users in the system increases. One limitation, however, is that social information filtering requires a community of active users to regularly update their profile — that is, provide interest or relevance ratings to the content of the items they have recently accessed.

Shardanand and Maes (1995) described the development of a social information filtering system called Ringo, which recommends music to people on the Web (webhound.www.media.mit.edu/ringo/ringo.html; recently Ringo was renamed to HOMR [Helpful Online Music Recommendation Service]).

38.6.3 Evaluation of IR and IF systems

A number of measures have been developed to evaluate IR systems. The best-known are *recall* and *precision*. Precision is the proportion of a retrieved set of documents that is actually relevant. Recall is the proportion of all relevant documents that are actually retrieved. Performance of an IR system can then be based on average precision across several levels of recall. These measures are useful for evaluating the effectiveness of information filtering (IF) systems as well.

38.7 Hypertext Usability

38.7.1 Usability Dimensions for Evaluating Hypertext

Nielsen (1990a; 1995a) identified following usability dimensions: *Learnability*, *Efficiency*, *Memorability*, *Errors*, and *satisfaction*. Other important usability dimensions, especially relevant for hypertext, are *disorientation* and *hypertext comprehension*. Below, we will discuss each of these usability dimensions.

Learnability. Nielsen (1993) considered learnability as the most fundamental usability attribute, since the first experience most people have with a new system is learning to use it. Ease of learning refers to the novice user's experience during the initial stages of interaction with the system. Highly learnable systems allow rapid improvements in performance within a short period of time.

Efficiency. Efficiency refers to the steady-state level of performance after the system has been learned (Nielsen, 1990a). Efficiency is often measured in terms of expert performance. Finding information in hypertext requires subjects to "navigate" in hypertext — that is, traversing links to get to the desired node. Therefore, navigation measures are very useful efficiency measures (Canter *et al.*, 1985, McKnight *et al.*, 1989). An efficient hypertext system should allow users to quickly find the desired piece of information. Task completion time (time to navigate in hypertext and answer a given search question) and time spent per node (a combined effects of reading time, search time, and thinking time) are common efficiency measures.

Canter *et al.* (1985) suggested several indices to characterize navigation: pathiness, ringiness, loopiness, spikiness. A *path* is a route through the data which does not cross any node twice, a *ring* is a route which returns to the node at which it starts and may include other rings, a *loop* is a ring which contains no other structures and typically stands alone, and a *spike* is a route which on return journey retraces exactly the path taken on the outward journey. Spikiness in the data may characterize a feeling of disorientation (Canter *et al.*, 1985). Other navigation measures are: number of node visits (NV) and number of unique nodes visited (NU) (Canter *et al.*, 1985). These measures suggest the extent of exploration of the hypertext system.

Memorability. This measure is relevant for casual users., a memorable system enables users to remember how to use and navigate in hypertext after some period of not having used it (Nielsen, 1990a).

Errors. There are two types of errors in hypertext: *failure to complete the task* (navigation or search task) and *deviations from the ideal path*. The usability measure that is often selected is the inverse of errors — *accuracy*. Since there are several paths to arrive at a particular node of information, deviations from the ideal path may be the more relevant measure. However, the navigation measures, discussed before, such as number of nodes visited, may provide an indirect measure of such errors.

Satisfaction. An important measure of success of any human-computer interface is user satisfaction. Questionnaires and interviews are often used to capture users' satisfaction, attitudes, and possible anxieties, which are difficult to measure objectively.

Disorientation. A common difficulty experienced by hypertext users is *disorientation*, often referred to as "getting lost in hyper space" (Conklin, 1987). For example, Nielsen and Lyngbæk (1990) observed that users were often confused about 'where they were,' felt that 'if they did not read something when stumbled across it, they would not be able to find it later,' or were confused about 'how to get back to where they came from.'

Four kinds of disorientation are particularly relevant when evaluating the usability of hypertext systems (cf. Edwards and Hardman, 1989): not knowing where to go next; not knowing where one is in the display network; not knowing how one arrived at a particular node; knowing where the information is, but not knowing how to get there. Elm and Woods (1985) recommended considering only objective measures of getting lost rather than subjective feelings of being lost. Simpson and McKnight (1990), however, argued that if readers are frequently lost while using a hypertext system, they will become frustrated and cease to use it. Therefore, both objective and subjective measures are necessary. The navigation measures discussed previously such as spikiness and ringiness can provide useful objective measures of disorientation. Whereas, to obtain subjective measures of disorientation, users may be asked to provide ratings to the statements on different kinds of disorientation such as not knowing where to go next, not knowing where one is in the display network, etc. (see Edwards and Hardman, 1989).

Another measure of hypertext usability and disorientation is determining user perceptions of the size of hypertext. Linear text is usually available in paper books and presents clear boundaries, so readers know the scope of the information. In hypertext, no such cues are available (Shneiderman, 1989). Gray's (1990) study revealed that the "getting lost" problems get compounded since users don't have a sense of database size and consequently are never sure whether they have explored the entire information space. McKnight, Dillon, and Richardson (1990) found that subjects in most cases tended to overestimate size of a hypertext document.

Hypertext Comprehension. As mentioned earlier, an important consideration for hypertext users is understanding of the underlying structure of the information database. The overall structure of the hypertext must make sense so that users can form a mental image of the hyperspace (Shneiderman, 1989).

We suggest that hypertext comprehension be defined as the understanding of relationships among the nodes in hypertext and not necessarily the content of each node. Therefore, useful indicators of comprehension are users' mental models of the information organization in hypertext. The following methods have been employed to capture users' mental model of the information organization of hypertext.

Construction of hypertext maps. Cognitive maps are created through a process of psychological transformations by which an individual acquires, codes, recalls, and decodes information about the relative locations and attributes of items in a spatial environment (Downs and Stea, 1973). Thus, the users' ability to construct the maps of information in hypertext may provide pointers to their ability to navigate within a hypertext document (Vora, 1994). Simpson and McKnight (1990) observed that the maps produced by subjects provided with a hierarchical contents list were more accurate than those produced by subjects using an alphabetical index.

Verbal protocols. Often users' mental model can be captured by knowing what they are thinking. Verbal protocol methods are widely used for this purpose (Ericsson and Simon, 1984). They require participants to think aloud about what they are doing, how they are doing it, and why they are doing it. Two general classes of protocol analysis techniques involve asking an individual to verbalize about his/her system interaction (concurrent think-aloud) or having two users thinking aloud together (co-discovery method). Vora and Helander (1995) used a teaching method to capture participants' mental models. In the teaching method, a user first learns the system. Subsequently, he/she is asked to teach another user how the system is organized and how to use it for tasks such as finding information. Unlike concurrent think-aloud method, teaching method does not interfere with task performance and is more natural to the participants; it is easier to instruct someone than just to think-aloud.

38.7.2 Linear Text vs. Hypertext

Since hypertext (non-linear text) is claimed to free the users of the constraints of linear text, the foremost issue may be whether hypertext provides any benefits over conventional text. There are several comparative studies.

Shneiderman (1987) compared paper and hypertext versions of historical articles. Although the results favored paper-based text, hypertext was helpful when users had to "jump around" in the information. McKnight, Dillon, and Richardson (1989) presented the same text in four formats: two hypertext and two linear. There were no differences in task completion time. However, users answered questions faster and more accurately with linear formats. Users spent surprisingly little time following hypertext links, but a great deal of time jumping back and forth between text and indices. These two studies favored linear presentation of information. Experiments with SuperBook, however, showed that hypertext combined with text search capabilities was superior to conventional paper documentation (Egan *et al.*, 1989). It is important to note that in Egan *et al.*'s (1989) comparative study, it was the third revision of SuperBook, designed iteratively based on formative evaluation with the users, showed improvement in performance and user satisfaction. This study clearly demonstrated the impact of understanding the nature of user tasks and user involvement on the usability of hypertext.

In addition to understanding of user tasks, the effectiveness of hypertext also depends on its user interface. This importance of user interface design is evident in the work by Instone *et al.* (1993) and Mynatt *et al.* (1992). In the design of HyperHolmes, the user interface was revised based on usability testing. The changes included the following: (1) tiled windows instead of overlapping windows, (2) removing "outgoing links," (3) simplifying search features, and (4) providing direct access to an overview page. These seemingly minor changes led to substantial improvement in subjects' search performance and emphasized the importance of user interface in success of hypertext systems.

Hypertext, however, is not always a good choice. As suggested by Whalley (1993), hypertext is "fundamentally flawed" for expository text, where the main concern for the reader is coherence and cohesion. Hypertext format would fragment the presentation.

38.7.3 Design Issues Related to Hypertext Usability

In this section, we summarize two important design issues related to hypertext usability: hypertext structure and authored links versus directed searches.

Hypertext Structure

In "reading" hypertext, one has to choose the order in which to obtain information. This places the responsibility on users to be aware of the structure (Waterworth and Chignell, 1989). The design of hypertext structure is, therefore, an important usability issue. Glenn and Chignell (1992) asserted that it is the complexity of the information structure rather than nonlinearity that causes disorientation.

Most research has showed beneficial effects of hierarchical structures. Simpson and McKnight (1989) observed that users navigated more efficiently and produced more accurate maps of the hypertext structure with a hierarchical table of contents than an alphabetical index. Dee-Lucas and Larkin (1990) compared a "hierarchical" hypertext using a spatially structured content map with a "list" hypertext using an index of items. The "list" hypertext resulted in longer task times than the hierarchical hypertext. Users of the "list" hypertext tended not to integrate and evaluate information, unless this was an explicit part of the task. Dee-Lucas and Larkin (1990) concluded that the extent to which readers take advantage of the flexibility of hypertext to explore new content depends on the ease of use of the content map.

Another important question is whether users should be provided with one or several organizational structures. For information search (fact-finding) tasks, the use of multiple information structures could hinder the formation of cognitive maps (Edwards and Hardman, 1989) and may not provide any benefits over single hierarchical structures (Edwards and Hardman, 1989; Mohageg, 1992) . However, Salomon (1990) observed that for users of InfoBooth (an interactive kiosk at the CHI'89 conference), it was beneficial to have several ways of accessing information. She observed that 18% of the users chose the Time Table sorting method, 21% chose the Author list, 7% chose the Title list, and 17% chose the topic checklist. Vora *et al.* (1994) found that alternative organization structures based on user tasks, improve both comprehension and navigation.

Vora (1994) further distinguished between a semantic organization and a syntactic structure in that the former defines the relation among the constituent elements ('nodes') whereas the latter does not make this relationship explicit. In essence, a semantic organization is an arrangement of information based on the content of the nodes. A syntactic structure on the other hand, is an arrangement of the constituent elements based on some arbitrary rules. For example, list structures in an alphabetical or a numerical order. Designing hypertext links based on presence of keywords also results in an arbitrary network structure. Both the index and key-word based structures are artificial and while they may be able to suggest location of an information element by itself, they do not clearly define its relation with other elements. For example, an alphabetical list of automobiles (index structure) does not indicate a *size_subcompact* relation between, say, Honda Civic and Toyota Corolla. Same is true for a key-word based relational structure, which is opportunistic since the links are established based on the presence of keywords in the node. Consequently, it fails to provide navigational predictability. In the studies by Edwards and Hardman (1989) and Mohageg (1992), the hierarchical structures served as a semantic organization as it helped the readers understand how the nodes were inter-related and why they were related and provided the necessary navigational predictability. Therefore, the results in favor of a hierarchical structure, a semantic organization over a syntactic structure, were obvious and expected.

In sum, the issue is not just using single or multiple structures preferentially, but identifying a structure or structures that meet user expectations and needs. It is interesting to note that Mantei (1982) created two similar structures using the same data set; one of the structure invoked disorientation, whereas the other did not.

Authored Links versus Directed Searches

Directed or computed searches seem to facilitate navigation compared to authored or static links. Directed searches do not, however, provide a final solution. Browsing is more natural but it is less efficient than a query which gets straight to the relevant information. However, successful queries are rare. Most people cannot express search concepts as Boolean strings (e.g., Borgman, 1986). Furthermore, users may not have a clear idea of what information they want. Like art, people sometimes know what they are looking for when they see it, but they can't describe it adequately a priori (Glenn and Chignell, 1992).

According to Murray (1993), a combination of directed search and authored links is the ideal solution.

Unfortunately, creating useful authored links requires an understanding of the semantics of the task and is time consuming. Full-text search is much easier to implement, and has therefore become relatively more attractive. Though authored hypertext links, consistently conceived and properly implemented, provide substantial value that searches cannot (Murray, 1993), directed searches and "computed links" remain essential since it is almost impossible to anticipate all user requirements.

As demonstrated by Campagnoni and Ehrlich (1989), novice users prefer simple browsing strategies over analytical strategies and that browsing is an important component of the search technique of users unfamiliar with an information retrieval system (Marchionini *et al.*, 1993). Browsing involves generation of broad query terms and scanning much larger sets of information in a relatively unstructured fashion traversing links. Whereas, analytical searches require formulation of specific, well-structured queries, and a systematic, iterative search for information. The following reasons were suggested for a preference for browsing strategies by Marchionini (1995):

- Many users, especially novices, are unwilling or unable to cogently formulate their search objective.
- Browsing replaces less cognitive load on the user. In browsing, a user only has to recognize a term related to the search objective, whereas in analytical search the user has to recall and/or formulate the search query. The conditions for matching are thus far less stringent for browsing.
- As the time to retrieve a topic is nearly instantaneous in most current systems, users could safely explore the system knowing that it would be quick and easy to return to the previous topic.

38.7.4 Heuristics or Guidelines for Hypertext Evaluation

Heuristics are well-recognized usability principles that are intended to improve usability independent of the specific application area, user profile(s), and user task(s). Garzotto *et al.* (1995) offered the following heuristics for evaluating hypertext systems.

- *Richness* — expresses the abundance of information items and ways to reach them.
- *Ease* — measures information accessibility and how easy to grasp operations are.
- *Consistency* — measures application regularity, and can be summed up by a simple rule: Treat conceptually similar elements in a similar fashion and conceptually different elements differently.
- *Self evidence* — expresses how well users guess the meaning and the purpose of whatever (content or navigational element) is being represented.
- *Predictability* — expresses how well users anticipate an operation's outcome.
- *Readability* — expresses the overall "feeling" about an application's validity; readability depends upon all factors mentioned.
- *Reuse* — considers using objects and operations in different context and for different purposes; reuse promotes consistency (and therefore predictability); also, presenting the same material under different perspectives and viewpoints enhances an application's richness; reuse greatly expands an application's apparent size while minimally increasing its physical size.

Considering the heuristics offered by Nielsen (1994) for user interfaces in general, Garzotto *et al.*'s heuristics do not address heuristics related to *error prevention and recovery*. This may be because their focus was on read-only hypertext systems.

Currently, there do not exist a set of guidelines for designing hypertext systems. Most hypertext designs are still based on the designer's intuitions and past experience. Therefore, it is important for a hypertext designer not only to apply the hypertext design heuristics mentioned here, but Also conduct iterative usability evaluations (see Instone *et al.*, 1993; Mynatt *et al.*, 1992).

38.8 Applications of Hypertext

As traditional texts, there are many types of applications of hypertext. Nielsen (1995a; 1990a) categorized hypertext applications into computer, business, intellectual, educational, and entertainment and leisure applications.

38.8.1 Computer Applications

In most computer applications, hypertext is used to manage and access on-line documentation. For example, during software development , hypertext can be used to link a large number of specification and implementation documents. The Dynamic Design project at Tektronix is an example where hypertext was integrated with the CASE (Computer Aided Software Engineering) environment to support software development (Bigelow, 1988). Hypertext can integrate several forms of user assistance, including a manual, introductory tutorial, help system, and even error messages. Examples are: Symbolics Document Examiner (Walker, 1987) and Sun*386i* workstation's help (Campagnoni and Ehrlich, 1989).

Hypertext is also useful for documenting design decisions or design rationale—issues, positions, and arguments, used to support design decisions. Hypertext-based tools that support design rationale include gIBIS (Conklin and Begeman, 1987), Aquanet (Marshall *et al.*, 1991), and QOC (Maclean *et al.*, 1993).

38.8.2 Business Applications

Hypertext is useful for trade shows, product catalogs, and advertising. It is possible to access large amount of information, but display to users only the most pertinent information. This property of hypertext has been used in SoftAd for Buick, Ford Simulator hypertext, and several World-Wide Web sites.

For specific business applications, hypertext has been used in the legal field to support document creation and management. For example, the Contract Drafting System by NYNEX produces tailored contracts for large purchase contracts (France, 1994). This system has reduced costs and time in producing contracts. Price Waterhouse Technology Center in Menlo Park (De Young, 1989) used hypertext for auditing. Here, hypertext is helpful to link documents that substantiate the accuracy of information.

Other obvious business applications include use of dictionaries and reference books (e.g., Manual of Medical Therapeutics (Frisse, 1988), the Oxford English Dictionary (Raymond and Tompa, 1988); and repair and other manuals (e.g., The MIT Movie Manual, The IGD (Interactive Graphical Documents) system [Feiner *et al.*, 1982]).

38.8.3 Intellectual Applications

Hypertext has been useful in supporting idea generation and brainstorming by co-ordinating and linking disparate pieces of text created by several users. Examples of such cooperative systems include gIBIS (graphical Issue Based Information System), NoteCards from Xerox PARC (Halasz *et al.*, 1987), and the cooperative SEPIA system developed at the German Research Institute GMD-IPSI (Streitz *et al.*, 1992).

The basic principle of computer conferences and most electronic mail is that several participants write messages which comment on previous messages. The HyperNews system from the Technical University of Denmark is such a hypertext interface for a conferencing environment on the Internet (Andersen *et al.*, 1989). Hypertext links connect relevant message both forward and backward in time.

Other applications of hypertext are research and journalism, where support is required for gathering and organizing information. To allow its anchor Peter Jennings fast access to relevant information ABC (American Broadcasting Corporation) produced a hypertext with about 10,000 nodes for its coverage of the U.S. Presidential election in 1988.

38.8.4 Educational Applications

There are two distinctly contrasting views about usefulness of hypertext in education. Whalley (1993) considered hypertext as a fragmented text form and therefore fundamentally flawed as an expository medium and more suitable for encyclopedic (or fragmented) forms of knowledge. Whalley (1993) argued that because of its fragmented nature, hypertext does not provide a true cohesive reference. In contrast, Duffy and Knuth (1990) suggested that hypertext is ideally suited for supporting constructivist learning environments, where students construct interpretations, appreciate multiple perspectives, and develop and defend their own positions while recognizing other views. According to Barrett (1988), there are many ways to read the material, and each reader can have a different experience with the same material and learn different things from it. Hutchings *et al.* (1992) claimed that hypertext provides greater learner control, improves access to multimedia learning materials; and provides a variety of new modalities of interaction for use with learning materials.

One application of hypertext in education is in learning of foreign languages. The IRIS InterLex server adds dictionary and thesaurus support to Intermedia; the Video Linguist is a hypermedia system that teaches a language by showing clips of television broadcasts from a country speaking that language. Á la Recontre de Philippe from MIT's Project Athena teaches French by a role-playing simulation where the student must help a Parisian named Philippe find a new apartment (Hodges *et al.*, 1989).

38.8.5 Entertainment and Leisure Applications

One important application of hypertext is in design of Public Access Systems. According to Kearsley (1994), they encompass three main functions: providing services, information, and/or entertainment. Most kiosk-type hypertext applications are designed for informal, short-term interactions and are oriented towards ease of use as opposed to great functionality (Salomon, 1990). As in InfoBooth at CHI'89, it is a good practice to avoid text menus or type-in areas. This approach strives to reduce cognitive load on the users.

We believe that hypertext categories should be based at a higher abstraction level such as descriptions of user tasks so that useful design principles will be identified and suggested for user interface and navigation support. These principles can then be consistently applied to improve efficient and effective utilization of hypertext systems. For example, for a word processor, a spreadsheet, a database application, or a paint program, we clearly have expectations what the interface may look like and how it will behave. Dillon and McKnight's (1990) work on identifying text-types may be a step in the right direction.

38.8.6 World-Wide Web (WWW): A "Killer App"

Probably the most important application of hypertext is the World-Wide Web (or W3 or the Web). Since its introduction at Hypertext'91 conference, the growth of the Web has been astronomical. In just past few years the number of Web servers has risen from 130 in December 1993 (Gray, 1996) to about 600,000 in December 1996 according to a recent Netcraft survey (www.netcraft.com).

Before disucssing the World-Wide Web, it is important to know the history and evolution of the Internet. This will help make clear the reasons for Web's impact on the Internet community.

38.9 The Internet and the World-Wide Web

38.9.1 The Internet

Simply described, the Internet is a "network of networks" that spans almost the entire world and provides access to a tremendous amount of information and services. The Internet grew out of an initiative of the U.S. Department of Defense in the late 1960s to design a network that could withstand disasters such as a nuclear war. The use of standard protocol – TCP/IP (Transmission Control Protocol/ Internet Protocol) – ensured such reliable communication by treating each computer on the network as an equal, without depending on a particular machine or portion of the network for its operation. Another primary motivation for the creation of the network (named ARPAnet after the government's Advanced Research Projects Agency) was to help scientists and researchers share precious computing resources and information.

38.9.2 Internet Applications

Several applications were developed by the Internet community to help users to communicate and collaborate with each other, to find information, and to share resources on the Internet. Some of these common Internet applications – e-mail, FTP, telnet, Archie, Usenet (or Newsgroups), Gopher, and Veronica – are briefly described below.

Among the Internet applications, the most commonly used application is e-mail. Although interpersonal communication was not a primary reason for creating the network, the use of electronic mail became common among the Internet users quite early. In addition to e-mail, two other applications are quite common on the Internet: *Telnet* and *FTP*. Telnet is the protocol for remotely logging on to another computer over the Internet. FTP (File Transfer Protocol), on the other hand, allows users to move files from one computer to another as long as both the computers are on the Internet and can communicate with each other using FTP. FTP does not depend upon the operating systems used by those computers. FTP does, however, require that the user be able to log on to both the computers – that is, the user have a UserID and Password on those computers. To make sharing of resources convenient, services like anonymous FTP, which allowed anyone to gain access to and transfer files without obtaining prior permission (as long as one knew exactly where the file was located), became widespread.

In parallel to the development of the Internet, a system called Usenet was developed in the late 1970s for communication between computers at different universities. By the early 1980s, Usenet was being used for discussion about a wide variety of topics. As the Internet developed, it became a prime method of transport for Usenet news, and the use of the network for information transfer began to grow rapidly.

Even though the Internet use was not as mainstream during 1980s – it was used mainly by Universities and research institutes – a vast amount of information was available to the users. Several tools were created to help organize and manage the information on the Internet to help users find information. For example, *Archie* was developed at McGill University to catalog files available via anonymous FTP services. Archie made it easier to find information on the Internet by searching through many different file libraries for text strings that users specified. Similarly *Hytelnet*, developed at the University of Saskatchewan, provided a catalog of publicly available telnet services, and allowed users to search through this catalog of sites.

Although services such as Archie and Hytelnet made it easier to access the Internet information, users still needed a working understanding of UNIX – the most common operating system on the Internet. They also were required to understand how to use the basic FTP and telnet services. Gopher, developed in 1991 and named after the mascot of the University of Minnesota, was one of the first applications to make the Internet a little more usable. Gopher provided a text menu interface to a variety of Internet services so that users could access information without having to worry about UNIX commands, where the information was located, or the underlying protocols that were used to transfer the information. Applications like Veronica and Jughead followed the development of Gopher to further aid users in finding information in Gopherspace.

38.9.3 Usability of Internet Applications

Although graphical user interfaces were being developed to access the Internet, and the Internet was growing rapidly with the advent of Gopher, several usability problems remained with using the Internet. First, users needed to know and understand several Internet protocols and to learn several applications to access the Internet resources. Second, Internet users could not see the content before downloading a file to their local computer and viewing it. Finally, there was no simple way to get to the resources related to the current piece of information. The World-Wide Web (WWW), a hypertext-based application, provided solutions to all of these problems – this made it a "killer app" for the Internet. On the WWW, any part of a document can be linked to any part of any other document conforming to the hypertext protocol. In addition, WWW documents can include multiple media – graphics, sound, and video. As a result, users could seamlessly jump around the Internet in quest for all types of information. In addition, many WWW applications – referred to as Web browsers – provide interfaces to Archie, FTP, Gopher, and telnet, shielding the user from the lower-level protocols. For Internet users, this new generation of interfaces eliminated the need to understand several protocols and applications. Instead, they could concentrate on doing useful tasks: communicating, collaborating, researching, and sharing information. It would be fair to state that the Internet has surpassed the critical mass largely because of the WWW, which has made the Internet usable for casual and novice users (Krol and Ferguson, 1995).

38.9.4 The World-Wide Web

Work on the Web began in March 1989, when Tim Berners-Lee of CERN proposed the project to be used as a means of transporting research and ideas throughout the organization; the WWW project is now shared by CERN and MIT. The initial goal was to provide a single unified means of accessing hypermedia documents anywhere on the Internet (Berners-Lee *et al.*, 1994).

It is a common misconception that the Internet and the Web are the same. The Internet is the physical medium used to transport the data. Whereas, the Web is a collection of protocols and standards used to access the information available on the Internet. The Web defines and unifies the "languages" used to retrieve the data available on the Internet (Richard, 1995).

The Web is defined mainly by three standards: URIs (Uniform Resource Identifiers), HTTP (Hypertext Transfer Protocol), and HTML (HyperText Markup Language). These standards provide a simple mechanism for locating, accessing, and displaying information.

URI. Universal Resource Identifiers (URIs), also called URLs (Uniform/Universal Resource Locators), are a convention to specify the location of an Internet server. They are essentially addresses of objects such as documents, images, sound, movies (Berners-Lee *et al.*, 1994). The Web pages use URIs to create a hypertext link to other pages on the Web.

Three pieces of information are specified in a URI: the protocol to be used, the server and the port to which to connect, and the file path to retrieve. That is: protocol://server-name:port/path. An example of the URI is:

```
http://info.cern.ch/ hypertext/WWW/
TheProject.html
```

The prefix "http" in this example stands for HyperText Transfer Protocol and indicates the type of network protocol to be used. Other common network protocols that can be used are File Transfer Protocol (FTP), Network News Transfer Protocol (NNTP), Gopher, and Wide Area Information System (WAIS). info.cern.ch is the address of the server to be contacted. The remaining information after "/" indicates the directory-file hierarchy. In the above example, the request is made to get the file TheProject.html that is located on the server info.cern.ch in the directory hypertext and subdirectory WWW. The port information is not provided in the above example, as it uses the standard port on that server.

HyperText Transfer Protocol (HTTP). The HyperText Transfer Protocol, or HTTP, is a client-server based Internet protocol. It is not a protocol for transferring hypertext, but a protocol for transferring information with the efficiency necessary for making hypertext jumps (Berners-Lee *et al.*, 1994). HTTP can transmit multimedia documents such as graphics, audio, and video files as well. This versatility in transmitting data of any format is the most significant advantage of HTTP and the Web.

HyperText Markup Language (HTML). HyperText Markup Language is a language of interchange for hypertext on the Web; it is the language (or format) that every Web client (commonly referred to as the Web browser) understands. HTML is an instance (document-type definition [DTD]) of Standard Generalized Markup Language (SGML) and describes the logical structure of the document and leaves the presentation aspects to the Web browser. That is, it provides functional and not visual information. Currently widely supported version of HTML (HTML 2.0) is limited in its presentation and layout capabilities. This problem will be solved to a certain extent by the new standard, HTML 3.2, which provides mechanisms to flow text around images, display tables, create client-side imagemaps, and allow use of Java-based applets and applications (discussed later). Web browsers such as Netscape and Internet Explorer currently provide capability to interpret several of the HTML 3.2 tags and many more as HTML extensions.

Navigating the Web

Web Browsers

Documents on the Web, referred to as Web pages (text, images, sound, etc.) reside on a server and are accessed by client programs (i.e., Web browsers). The Web browsers request documents from a server as specified in the URI and interpret hypertext documents written in HTML to present them to the readers.

Browsers are either *text-based* or *graphical*. There are several differences between the text-based and graphical browsers. One difference is the user's mode of interaction. In text-based browsers, selection of hypertext links is accomplished using a keyboard. In graphical browsers, selection and request are accomplished using a pointing device such as a mouse. Another difference is the absence of multimedia capabilities in text-based browsers. However, they are fast and efficient way for getting text-based information on the Web. Perhaps the most commonly used text-based browser is Lynx, developed by Lou Montulli at The University of Kansas. Other text-based browsers include Emacs W3-mode, and Line Mode browser (from CERN).

There are several graphical browsers available in the market today such as Netscape Navigator, Mosaic, and Internet Explorer. Navigating the Web with graphical browsers is much simpler. The hypertext link anchors are made salient on source Web pages with cues such as underlining, color, or bounding rectangles, and the user simply clicks on them using a pointing device such as a mouse to access the destination Web page. Most graphical browsers have multimedia capabilities; however, users often have to pay a penalty in terms of response time.

Though Mosaic was the browser of choice and made World-Wide Web usable, the two most commonly used browsers, at the time of this writing, were Netscape Navigator and Internet Explorer.

Mosaic was developed at the National Center for Supercomputing Applications (NCSA) at the University of Illinois at Urbana-Champaign. It is available free for academic, research, and internal commercial use.

Netscape Navigator is developed by Netscape Communications Corporation and is currently the browser of choice. At the time of this writing, an estimated 70-80% of the users used Netscape Navigator. In addition to providing access to Web-based resources, Netscape also provides support for integrated email and newsgroup readers.

Finally, Netscape Navigator also offers dynamism and interactivity in the Web pages through Javascript and Java. Netscape JavaScript makes cross-platform scripting of events, objects, and actions easier and allows a Web page designer to access events such as user mouse clicks or Web page entry and exit. Java is an object-oriented C++ like language. Sun Microsystems built Java to provide an easy-to-use, powerful adjunct to the standard Hypertext Markup Language (HTML). Java is platform-independent, allowing for easy portability across environments. Java's main attraction lies in creation of "applets" — small programs that can be sent across the Web to run on the viewer's system. Java applets bring animation, real-time interaction, and live updating to static Web pages. Java lets Web servers send applets to browsers that are Java-enabled such as Sun's HotJava and Netscape Navigator (version 2.0 and above) from Netscape Communications Corp. HotJava acts as an interpreter to let interactive Java-based programs run on the users' workstations regardless of platform. (for more information on Java, see java.sun.com). Other software companies are also developing similar object-based technology on the Web, including Microsoft, Apple, and General Magic.

An interesting application of Java is by Syracuse University's used of the National Library of Medicine (www.npac.syr.edu/projects/vishuman/). Here you can use Java to get a unique look at a human cadaver.

Although HTML is the language of choice on the Web, a growing number of users use browsers that support VRML (Virtual-Reality Modeling Language). VRML, a 3D equivalent for HTML, is a language for describing 3D scenes and objects. Using VRML, one can construct Web worlds within which a user can move around in a three-dimensional space. To view VRML Web worlds, the users need VRML browsers. Some of the popular VRML browsers are:

Fountain (www.caligari.com/ws/fount.html),

Liquid Reality (www.dimensionx.com),

VRealm (www.ids-net.com/ids/instruct.html),

WebFX (www.paperinc.com),

WebSpace (www.sgi.com/Products/WebFORCE/WebSpace/), and WorldView (www.intervista. com).

The first released version of VRML, VRML 1.0, was limited in that it did not support movies, sounds, or other multimedia elements and it did not allow interactivity with objects and with other online users. Recently released specifications of VRML (VRML 2.0) based on Moving Worlds specification from Silicon Graphics Inc. (SGI) addresses these limitations. VRML 2.0 allows creation of static and animated objects, which can have hyperlinks to other media such as sound, movies, and images (vag.vrml.org/VRML2.0/FINAL/Overview.html). The users can, therefore, have a richer and more interactive experience and accomplish tasks such as manipulate the object, rotate it along various axes, or just explore the 3D virtual world from different viewpoints. VRML 2.0 also supports *scripting*, which allows the VRML author to create effects by means of events in the virtual world. The next version, VRML 3.0, will cover multi-user or avatar behaviors and capabilites.

Indexes and Search Engines

Like the Internet, the Web has a chaotic organization. Furthermore, because of its exponential growth, finding information on the Web is neither easy nor effective by simply browsing the pre-authored hypertext links. Several Web sites now maintain indexes that categorize and organize information is by subject; for example, Yahoo! (www.yahoo.com/) and the EINet Galaxy (www.einet.net). Popularity of indexes is evident in the fact that Yahoo! is visited by almost 800,000 people a day; Yahoo! lists more than 200,00 Web sites under 20,000 different categories (Steinberg, 1996).

Indexes are helpful, but they are not very efficient considering the volume of data that is made available daily on the Web, especially when the categorization is done by humans. Search engines that allow topic or keyword searches of the Web content may be better. A few of the popular search engines on the Web are: Alta Vista (www.altavista.digital.com), Lycos (www. lycos. com), InfoSeek (www.infoseek.com) and WebCrawler (webcrawler.com). The results of searches are usually returned immediately as an HTML document containing links to the matched documents. Most search engines allow searching the documents published on the Web. Alta Vista offers additional capability in that it can query both the Web and Usenet newsgroups. A new group of search engines, called *metasearches*, which search more than one search engines and resport the results will very likely become popular in future. One such metasearch engine is Symantec's Internet FastFind (www.symantec.com). WebFind – a component of FastFind – runs user search queries through seven Web search engines: AltaVista, Magellan, Excite, Infoseek, Lycos, WebCrawler, and Yahoo. The search results are presented to the users after removes the redundancies in and ranking the results in a descending scoring order. FastFind, through its suite of utilities, also allows the users to search FTP sites (NetFileFind) and notifies users when there has been a change to the Web site or the FTP site.

Search engines are not a panacea, however. The recall and precision problems associated with searches are very severe on the Web because of the size of the Web and absence of a consistent way to provide or extract information about the content of the documents published on the Web. Also, the searches do not solve the polysemy and synonymy problems common with information retrieval. Architext Software's Excite system (www.excite.com) attempts to solve this problem by indexing the Web pages based on concepts rather than on keywords. Another optimistic attempt is currently underway at Oracle with the development of a system called ConText. ConText attempts to understand English based on its knowledge from grammar and a detailed hierarchy of concepts; for example, it "knows" that Paris is a city in France, which is a country in Europe (see Steinberg, 1996). However, it is still unclear how it will scale up to the Web pages that are not written in English and how much effort it would take to build a knowledge-base for different languages and cultures. And, as Steinberg (1996) points out: "No matter how good the technology, it can only work when the meaning of document is directly correlated with the words it contains. Fiction — or anything that relies on metaphor or allegory, that evokes instead of tells — can't be usefully classified or indexed (p. 182)."

To aid in gathering information about Web pages, indexes and search engines use what is commonly referred to as Web Robots, Wanderers, and Spiders to gather information about the Web sites. A Web robot is a program that traverses the Web's hypertext structure by retrieving a document, and then recursively retrieving all documents that are linked by that document (Koster, 1996).

We hope that as the Web evolves more facilities becomes available to efficiently associate meta data about the content of the documents that will help more effective indexing of information and facilitate information access.

Agent-based Systems

With the rapid growth in the number of Web sites it is almost impossible to keep up-to-date with the new information. Therefore, the emphasis has to shift to software agents, which can find information based on the interests specified by the users and eliminating the need for intermediaries!

Mercury Center's NewsHound service is an example of such an agent, which searches stories, news wires, and advertisements for articles matching user profiles; see www.sjmercury.com. The NewsHound profile searches every hour from various sources, sending the most relevant to the users. The agent, therefore, delivers the appropriate news to the user, rather than forcing the user to search it. A user may change profiles at any time depending on current interests or needs.

Another interesting service is WEBHOUND from MIT Media Lab (webhound.www.media.mit.edu/projects/webhound/doc/Webhound.html). WEBHOUND is a personalized WWW document filtering agent that allows users to rate a Web page on a scale from 1 through 7, as well as to provide written annotations. WEBHOUND then uses a technique known as "Automated Collaborative Gathering" to automate the process of "word of mouth" amongst system users. WEBHOUND determines which users have similar opinions and makes recommendations for Web sites accordingly.

The role of software agents in future may become more important. As Negroponte (1996) foresees: "By 2000, we can expect a billion users on the Net... we're likely to find those billion human users joined by a much larger number of software agents, Web crawlers, and other computer programs that will do the browsing for us. The Net will be roamed mostly by programs, not people. When people do use the Net, it will be for more suitable purposes: communicating, learning, and experiencing [and not browsing] (p. 200)."

Reasons for the Web's Success

- Open Architecture: One important reason for the success of the web is its open architecture that is easily extensible and can accept advances in technology, including new networks, protocols, object types and data formats.
- Consistent interface: All documents, whether real, virtual or indexes, look similar to the reader and are contained within the same addressing scheme. The World-Wide Web provides users a consistent means to access a variety of media in a simplified fashion.
- Universal readership: Information on the Web is accessible from any type of computer, anywhere, and using any of the client browsers.
- Universal authorship: Because of the client-server based nature of the Web, any person with some knowledge of HTML can publish on the Web.

Usability of the Web

A commendable aspect of the Web is that one doesn't need extensive resources to publish on the Web. This is a limitation as well. Because of the uncontrolled growth of the Web, and the absence (or disregard) of good Web interface design guidelines, thousands of mediocre Web pages crowd the Web. There are several important usability issues: poor, outdated, and incomplete content on the Web; unnecessary and gratuitous use of graphics; poor response time; lengthy textual information requiring extensive scrolling; poor navigation support; dangling links; and so forth. The central problems are the lack of any specification of user interface and the perceived rush to have a Web presence. Below, we discuss two of these problems: navigation and dangling links.

Navigation Problem. Though the link-based navigational model of the Web is easy to understand, accessing information on it has become increasingly difficult. Georgia Tech's Graphic, Visualization, and Usability Center's (GVU) 6th WWW User Survey reported that after speed (response time), the next big problem was "finding known information" (34.09%) and being able to find Web pages already visited (13.41%).

The links provided on the Web are often cumbersome, irrelevant, or trivial. This problem is compounded by inconsistencies in indicating link anchors: what aspects of a word, phrase, should be marked as a link has not been addressed. There are several occasions, where instead of linking the words describing the destination Web page, hypertext links are made to the action of clicking (e.g., "Click here for Research on Hypertext" instead of "Research on Hypertext." Another common problem is links from graphic images, which do not afford the action of clicking and is often difficult for the readers to know which graphics are linked on a web page. Nielsen and Sano (1995) suggested creating a 3D button-like look for linked graphics to provide necessary affordances and alleviate this problem.

Another navigation problem is due to the single-window design of the Web browsers. This precludes the preservation of visual context that could be achieved is both anchor and destination were displayed (Kahn, 1995). This lack of support for local context makes the need for supporting global context even more acute. To support local and global navigation, Kahn (1995) designed a graphical table of contents in the form of highway signs. Each highway sign represented a link or destination in global structure of the collection. Recently Netscape 2.0 has provided the ability to use "Frames" which may provide a partial solution to this problem. Frames permit laying-out the Web browser window into sections, which users can view and interact with individually. In some cases, frames may be a more effective way to view information; for example, Web designers can provide navigational controls in one frame that always stay visible, even if the contents of another frame change.

HyperLINK, developed at Los Alamos National Lab, provides another approach to support navigation in the Web (Keahy and Rivenburgh, 1996); it provides contextual information by creating a graphical visualization of the Web navigation. HyperLINK represents a user's traversal in the Web as links between nodes of a directed graph, which is constructed in a separate window as the user navigates in the Web. The user can then interact with this graphical representation of the graph to navigate among nodes. Furthermore, the graphical representation helps in navigation as it helps preserve the context while providing important history information. An interesting functionality in HyperLINK is that it provides the user with several non-linear magnification techniques to create fisheye and perspective views.

To summarize, rapid growth of information on the Web has left the reader asking questions such as "What Web site am I in?," "What part of Web site does this page represent?," "How do I return to the Web site I recently visited?," and so forth. To minimize these navigation problems, it is important that Web page designer pay attention to the principles of good interface design and documentation design; see for example, Sano (1996) and Horton *et al.* (1995).

Dangling links problem. Davis (1995) attributed this problem to the embedded links in the Web: The Web embeds links (as HTML markup). The advantage is that the document and its links form a self-contained object that may be moved and edited without damaging any of the links the document contains. However, moving (or deleting) a document involves checking all references to this document within all other documents. For the Web this would involve checking all other documents in the world. Failing to check results in dangling links.

Response time problem. GVU's (1996) 6th WWW User Survey found that, like previous surveys, response time (or speed) was the number one problem for Web users (GVU, 1996). Though several factors affect response time, the most important reason is the trend for designing graphic-rich and multimedia-heavy Web sites. The GVU (1996) survey also reported that the most common connection speed reported was 28.8 Kbps (51.40%) followed by 14.4 Kbps (19.69%). Considering the rule-of-thumb that 1Kb of data requires 1 second to download, graphic-rich site that require download of 60-70 Kb of data require at least 60 seconds of response time (Weinman, 1996). With increasing number of users accessing the Web using slow-speed modems (and not high-speed ISDN or T1 lines), designing graphic rich sites seriously affect usability not only of those Web sites, but also of the Web in general because of increase in traffic over the Internet.

Opaqueness of technology. Finally, no longer is the Web technology transparent to the users. The users now need to understand the terms such as plug-ins, helper applications, Shockwave, PDF, Java, JavaScript, ActiveX, etc. to take full advantage of the Web.

Usability of Web Browsers

Though graphical Web browsers have made the Web more accessible and usable, several usability issues still need to be addressed in their design. Two important problems are inconsistent implementation of HTML standard in Web browsers and inadequate user interface.

1. Implementation of HTML standard. With the Web browsers competing for the market share, very little attention has been paid to HTML standards. Though all Web browsers support HTML 2.0 standard, browsers like Netscape Navigator and Internet Explorer support several of the new HTML 3.2 standard and beyond. And, since 70-80% of the users are claimed to use Netscape Navigator, a majority of Web pages are designed using Netscape extensions. The presentation of these Web pages is unpredictable on other browsers and is often unusable to users with non-Netscape browsers. Also, it forces the Web page authors to spend more time designing their Web pages either for more than one type of browser or designing for the lowest common denominator (HTML 2.0) compromising the presentation effectiveness of the Web pages.
2. Web browser interface. Though there are several usability problems related to the browser interfaces, very few empirical studies have been conducted to identify them and explore the alternatives. One such study evaluated the "history" facility provided in Netscape Navigator and Mosaic (Jones and Cockburn, 1996; Tauscher and Greenberg, 1996). The navigation model for "history" in these browsers is stack-based and is not based on chronological or reverse chronological order. The study clearly indicated that most users could not explain how the "history" worked and what model was used to include or remove the Web pages visited by them.

38.9.5 Intranets

The use of the Web is extending from the Internet to corporate Web environments called *intranets* to facilitate information sharing and communications as extensions or replacements to groupware types of applications. The growth of the Web technology on the intranet may exceed that on the Internet. According to International Data Corporation (IDC), intranet servers will outsell Internet servers 4.6 million to 440,000 by the turn of the century. For corporations, intranets promise several payoffs: universal information distribution through a standard client (the Web browser); guaranteed access through a common network protocol (IP) and access methods; and the replacement of the complexity of existing systems with a few standard technologies such as CGI, HTTP, and HTML (and, possibly Java and/or ActiveX technologies in future). One particularly appealing feature that has caused the proliferation of intranets is that the Web provides a consistent interface to both information resources and internal databases. These intranet servers typically reside on a private network, with firewalls limiting access to and from the larger, public Internet.

Intranets are also likely to extend to *extranets*, which are networks based on the Internet protocol through which companies run Web applications for external use by customers. With advances in extranets, electronic commerce on the Internet may become commonplace.

38.9.6 The growth of the Internet and its implications

To a large degree, the Internet has become a victim of its own success. In past few years, the Internet has grown to astronomical proportions. According to the Network Wizards survey conducted in July 1996 (www.nw.com), the Internet has nearly doubled in size from 6.6 million hosts in mid-1995 to 12.8 million hosts in mid-1996. During the same period, the number of domains have multiplied four-fold from 120,000 to 488,000, with WWW (referring to a World-Wide Web host) being the most popular host name with 212,155 host names; note that a host name may not begin with WWW to be on the Web. Also, Hoffman, Kalsbeek, and Novak (1996) estimated that in August 1995 there were at least 28.8 million users just in the U.S. who are 16 years and older have access to the Internet.

This growth in Internet use, combined with advances in multimedia technologies on the Internet and increasing use of automated browsing or searching technologies – which browse the Web for the users, obtain customized information, and index the Web for search engines – is pushing the bandwidth capacity of the Internet to its limits.

Both the use and the activity on the Internet has led to severe degradation in response time. During peak hours, accessing the Internet is so poor, that many people refer to the World-Wide Web as "Word-Wide Wait." The strain on the Internet is also evident in the recent "brownouts" experienced by the Internet users. For example, in November, within 10 days, users of the AT&T Worldnet service on the Internet experienced 3 "brownout" sessions: 31 hours on November 7 and 8, 1996; 5 hours on November 13, 1996; and 2-1/2 hours on November 14, 1996.

Another problem faced by the Internet community is the exhaustion of Internet address space as each host on the Internet requires a unique IP address. Many analysts claim that, possibly by the turn of the century, there may not be more addresses to give out on the Internet.

The original Internet was not designed for the current rate of growth.The solutions involve not only upgrading hardware and software of the Internet backbone, switches, and routers, but also improvement of protocols to supplement TCP/IP.

To support the current growth on the Internet, the Internet Engineering Task Force is working a new system of protocols. Currently taking shape is IPng – Internet Protocol Next Generation or IPv6 (current version of the Internet Protocol is version 4). IPv6 is designed to run well on high performance networks and at the same time is still efficient for low bandwidth networks (e.g., wireless). It will also support *nomadic personal computing devices* – that is, this protocol can work seamlessly over a variety of physical networks with auto-configuration capability and will have built-in authentication and confidentiality. Of the several improvements in IPv6 over the current protocols, the most important is the extension of the available address space from 32 bits to 128 bits, making multi-billion node Internet both possible and practical. For more information on IPv6 specification, see ftp://ds.internic.net/rfc/rfc1883.txt and http://playground.sun.com/pub/ipng/html/INET-IPng-Paper.html.

Another proposal is RSVP (Resource ReSerVation Protocol). This protocol enables bandwidth-on-demand. For example, it would enable developers to reserve bandwidth on the Internet for the transmission of multimedia data streams. For more information on RSVP, see Resource ReSerVation Protocol (RSVP) Version 1 Functional Specification, Internet Draft, ftp://ietf.org/internet-drafts/draft-ietf-rsvp-spec-14.txt.

38.10 Converting Text to Hypertext

In recent years, there has been a great amount of enthusiasm in converting printed documents into a hypertext format. The main reasons are the following limitations of hard-copy, linear documents (Cook, 1988):

1. Storage: Often the physical size of the printed manuals is very large and some run into several volumes.
2. Search: Searching through such large volumes of printed materials is cumbersome using table of contents and indices.
3. Update and distribution: Printed materials cannot be updated as easily as "soft" materials and distribution is time-consuming and expensive.
4. Arrangement: Information cannot be dynamically re-arranged to suit the needs of individuals.

In contrast, hypertext offers the following benefits (Raymond and Tompa, 1988; Cook, 1988):

1. Storage: Several volumes of information can be conveniently stored on a few CD-ROMs or other magnetic or optical media.
2. Search: Hypertext supports browsing and offers both lexical and associative search facilities. Queries can be supported as well.
3. Update and distribution: Updating is relatively easy and the changes can be distributed in electronic form.
4. Arrangement: Information can be arranged dynamically to suit the needs of individuals.

Given these seductive qualities, there has been a rush to convert printed documents to hypertext. However, before converting, one must consider if the material is suitable for hypertext. Shneiderman (1989) proposed three **golden rules** to qualify a document for hypertext:

1. A large body of information organized into numerous fragments.
2. The fragments relate to each other.
3. The user needs only a small fraction at any time.

Nielsen (1995a) added another rule: Do not use hypertext if the application requires the user to be away from the computer.

Whalley (1993) suggested characterizing text along a continuum from Reader Control to Author Control to determine its suitability as a hypertext. This continuum referred to a dimension of text types ranging from *text as database*, where the reader has complete control, to *text as argument*, where the author guides the reader's study. This dimension is also characterized by the length of cohesive reference within the text: the longer the referential links, the more the author's argument controls the reader. It can then be suggested that text with reader control is more suitable for hypertext conversion.

38.10.1 Approaches to Conversion

There are two approaches to conversion: manual and automated. Manual conversion involves using a hypertext authoring tool (such as KMS, Guide, HyperCard, HyperTIES, etc.) to create nodes and links manually. The quality of resulting hypertext depends on how well the author has understood the users' needs for information organization and how well the interface is designed. Because of the effort and time and cost resources involved in dividing the information into nodes, linking them, and debugging the network — ensuring that dangling links do not exist, link anchors are correctly marked, links point to the right information nodes, and so forth — manual conversion is more suitable for small-sized hypertexts. Also, the manual construction of hypertext could lead to any of the following types of errors (Johnson, 1995): missing nodes, nodes of the wrong type, and nodes with incorrect object properties, links to the wrong destination, dangling links, and too many links to the same node.

Another problem with manual conversion is that currently there is no well-defined scheme of linking. Manual linking may be acceptable if the objective is simply to convert a linear document into a hypertext-like online document, where links are provided from table to contents to each individual section and index to specific sections. Otherwise, humans are very inconsistent in assigning hypertext links in a document. Ellis *et al.* (1994) observed that the similarities between hypertext versions of the same document (PhD theses and journal articles) were very low and variable, indicating that inter-linker consistency was low. Though Green (1996) found inter-linker consistency improve for short newspaper articles, it was still very low to automate the linking process.

Automated conversion, on the other hand, is based on the recognition of structural elements from a piece of text and identifying nodes and links from these structural elements (or tags) based on a pre-defined criteria (Riner, 1991). Note that the links should capture both referential and organizational links from the structural elements.

Rada (1992) suggested converting text into hypertext using two stages: first-order hypertext and second-order hypertext. First-order hypertexts reflect the document markup; using a document markup languages such as troff, TeX, SGML, and so forth. First-order hypertext is then generated automatically and includes only links from the markup of the text. Second-order hypertext then adds links computed from word patterns (Frisse, 1988) and/or lexical chains (Green, 1996).

Manual intervention is often necessary in hypertext conversion. For example, to convert the reference work *Inside Macintosh*, document markup was exploited, but to fit the small, low-resolution computer screen, some text was manually reorganized (Bechtel, 1990).

38.10.2 Task Orientation

"Just as the best films are not made by putting a camera in the front row of a theater, the best hypertexts are not made from the text that were originally written for a linear medium." (Nielsen, 1990a; p. 173).
Before converting a piece of text into hypertext one must understand the user's tasks. Several examples clearly illustrate the need for understanding user tasks in converting text to hypertext. Dillon (1991a), based on his study of usage of technical manuals, asserted that "an electronic text that merely replicated paper manuals would be relatively useless. It would share all the disadvantages of paper version... Since usage is so goal-oriented, large sections of manual's contents are irrelevant for much of the time...". Sjöberg *et al.* (1992) observed that medical-clinical documents use diseases as the only entry point. However, to help diagnosis by General Practitioners or nurses, it was found important to enter the information through symptoms as well as diseases.

To summarize, in converting text to hypertext, one should consider the tasks that will be performed (Glushko, 1989) and how a particular hypertext representation will serve that task (Rada, 1991).

38.11 Future of Hypertext

Predicting the future of any technology is difficult — especially hypertext. This is obvious from the unexpected astronomical success of the World-Wide Web. Presently, research and development both on- and off-the-Web suggest the following trends.

38.11.1 Personal Hyperspaces

The rate at which new information is made available on the Web, is accompanied by the evolution of intelligent software agents that seek and retrieve. In fact, additional services are announced every day. Some of these services, as previously discussed, include personalized news service agents such as NewsHound from Mercury center (www.sjmercury.com), PointCast Network (www.pointcast.com); music recommendation service HOMR; Web site recommendation agent WEBHOUND. We agree with Nicholas Negroponte (1996) that:

> "By 2000, we can expect a billion users on the Net... At the turn of the millennium, we're likely to find those billion users joined by a much larger number of software agents, Web Crawlers, and other computer programs that will do the browsing for us."

These agents will not only gather information in its raw form, but also interpret information to create personalized hyperspaces, and finally personalize to fit user tasks and needs. This development will be possible as the information objects will be richer and carry extensive metadata. Nielsen (1995b) predicted "attribute rich" objects suggesting alternative interpretations and principles of aggregation.

We trust that this will happen. Bush's (1945) vision of integration of hypertext trails by combining trails created by different people is finally coming true — but on a much greater scale than Bush could have imagined.

38.11.2 Collaborative Hyperspaces

Future hypertext systems will also create collaborative hyperspaces through improved methods of collaboration and by improving the medium of communication (Engelbart, 1995; Streitz, 1996; Simpson *et al.*, 1996). Collaboration will be possible both asynchronously and synchronously, between remote locations (Streitz, 1995), and it will also support "nomadic" environments (mobile participants) (Schnase *et al.*, 1995). This will create what Streitz (1996) called "Ubiquitous Collaboration" which supports *polyphasic activities*. In other words, incompatibilities due to differences in presentation format and media will disappear. Evidence of such collaborative work can be seen in Cooperative SEPIA and DOLPHIN systems from GMD-IPSI (Streitz, 1996; Streitz *et al.*, 1992; Streitz *et al.*, 1994).

Streitz (1996) also envisioned *virtual organizations*: temporary networks of co-operative but physically distributed organizations. Such virtual organizations will: (1) enable accessing and pooling distributed competencies, (2) minimize organizational structures, and (3) allow flexibility and adaptability.

The Web offers an obvious opportunity for collaboration because of its inherent distributed and decentralized form. However, to make collaboration successful it is necessary to develop underlying shared rules and protocols (Berners-Lee in Simpson *et al.*, 1996). The idea of collaborative hyperspaces on the Web is of course not new. In fact, Tim Berners-Lee, designed the Web for collaboration in the first place by providing interactive editing and creation of links.

38.11.3 Open Hypermedia Systems

To enable creation of personal and collaborative hyperspaces, availability of open hypermedia systems (OHS) will become necessary. Traditional multimedia tools have often used private formats to store both links and data. This limits interaction. With open hypertext systems, authors may link information from a variety of third-party applications to create new applications.

End-users will have increased power, too. They may create hypertext links and add their own hypertext as a separate layer beyond the original hypertext. Adaptive Electronic Document Viewer (AEDV) from NASA Ames is a good example that we predict will become common-place in future hypertext systems. Using AEDV, users assign subjective indexing information, called *topics*, to portions of documents marked by annotations; subsequent retrieval of topics can then be done by searching these annotations. Furthermore, AEDV also supports collaborative work as the users can publish their topics and annotations and simultaneously subscribe to topics and annotations from other users.

Engelbart (1995) considered open hyperdocument system a technological cornerstone and encouraged creation of "an integrated, seamless multi-vendor architecture in which knowledge workers share hyperdocuments on shared screens. Hyperdocuments are multimedia files supporting linking and multiple object types. The hyperdocuments system should enable flexible, on-line collaboration development, integration, application, study and reuse of CoDIAK [Concurrent Development, Integration and Application of Knowledge] (p. 30)."

38.11.4 Content-based Linking and Retrieval and Integration of Virtual Reality

In the future, linking and retrieval of information will be based not only on text or simple graphics, but will also use images, sound, and video. Even images may be retrieved by using a "query image." The users will also be able to control each attribute through direct manipulation interfaces similar to the "starfield" display (Ahlberg and Shneiderman, 1994). The Infomedia project at Carnegie Mellon University supports this development. This is an intelligent multimedia database retrieval system that combines natural language processing with image processing and retrieval. Probably the biggest advances will be made in linking among temporal media such as sound and video. A glimpse of such a system can be observed in HyperCafe (Sawhney *et al.*, 1996), where links are not just present on a page, but they become spatial and temporal opportunities with the progression on video narrative.

Future hypertexts will also merge with virtual reality to create not just virtual worlds, but with the inclusion of temporal media and interactivity, will create hyperworlds. This integration of temporal media and virtual reality will create richer hypertext environments, providing not just interactive, but immersive experience as well. These hyperworlds will be more expressive and will offer richer affordances to its users.

To summarize, future hypertexts will be based on an open architecture and will allow content-based linking and retrieval to enhance personal information spaces and support ubiquitous access and collaboration. In addition, as copyright and intellectual property rights laws are debated and implemented, there will be new ways of including other published material on the Web — possibly a refinement of Nelson's (1995) idea of *transclusions* : "reuse with original context available, through shared instancing (rather than duplicate bytes) (Nelson, 1995; p. 32)." According to Nelson (1995), transclusion provides a copyright method that makes republication fair as "[e]ach user buys each quotation from its own publisher, assuring proper payment (and encouraging exploration of the original)."

Finally, we believe that hypertext as a separate technology will cease to exist. Hypertext will become so integrated with other technologies — may be other way round — that "hypertext" will become *the way* to interact with information on computers. And, we may find that hypertext was not the most important legacy of Vannevar Bush, but rather the implications of hypertext which make it possible to achieve human collaboration.

38.12 References

Ahlberg, C. and Shneiderman, B. (1994). Visual information seeking: Tight coupling of dynamic query filters with starfield displays. *CHI'94 Conference Proceedings,* 313-317.

Andersen, M. H., Nielsen, J., and Rasmussen, H. (1989). A similarity-based hypertext browser for reading Unix network news. *Hypermedia, 1,* 255-265.

Anderson, J. R. (1983). *The Architecture of Cognition.* Cambridge, MA: Harvard University Press.

Barker, P. G. (1993*). Exploring Hypermedia.* London: Kogan Page.

Barrett, E. (Ed.) (1988). *Text, Context, and Hypertext: Writing with and for the Computer.* Cambridge, MA: The MIT Press.

Bechtel, B. (1990). Inside Macintosh as hypertext. *ECHT'90 Conference Proceedings,* 312-323.

Belkin, N. J. and Croft, W. B. (1987). Retrieval techniques. In M. E. Williams (ed.), *Annual Review of Information Science and Technology.* Chapter 4, p. 109-145. [2]

Belkin, N. J. and Croft, W. B. (1992). Information filtering and information retrieval: Two sides of the same coin. *Communications of the ACM, 35* (12), 29-38.

Berk, E. and Devlin, J. (1991). *Hypertext/Hypermedia Handbook.* New York: McGraw-Hill.

Berners-Lee, T., Cailliau, R., Luotonen, A., Nielsen, H. F., and Secret, A. (1994). The World-Wide Web. *Communications of the ACM, 37(8),* 76-82.

Berry, M. W., Dumais, S. T., and Letsche, T. A. (1995). Computational methods for intelligent information access. *Proceedings of Supercomputing'95,* San Diego, CA, December 1995.http://scxy.tc.cornell.edu /sc95/proceedings/473_MBER/SC95.HTM

Bieber, M. and Wan, J. (1994). Backtracking in a multiple-window hypertext environment. *ECHT'94 Conference Proceedings,* 158-166.

Bigelow, J. (1988). Hypertext and CASE. *IEEE Software, 5* (2), 23-27.

Borgman, C. (1986). The user's mental model of an information retrieval system: An experiment on a prototype online catalog. *International Journal of Man-Machine Studies, 24,* 27-64.

Boyle, C. and Encarnacion, A. O. (1994). MetaDoc: An adaptive hypertext reading system. *User Modeling and User-Adapted Interaction, 4,* 1-19.

Bush, V. (1945). As we may think. *Atlantic Monthly, 176,* 101-108.

Campagnoni and Ehrlich (1989). Information retrieval using a hypertext-based help system. *ACM Transactions on Information Systems, 7,* 271-191.

Canter, D., Rivers, R., and Storrs, G. (1985). Characterizing user navigation through complex data structures. *Behaviors and Information Technology, 4,* 93-102.

Card, S. (1996). Visualizing retrieved information: A Survey. *IEEE Computer Graphics and Applications,* 63-67.

Carlson, P. A. (1989). Hypertext and intelligent interfaces for text retrieval. In E. Barrett (Ed.), *The Society of Text: Hypertext, Hypermedia, and the Social Construction of Information.* Cambridge, MA: The MIT Press.

Carroll, J. M., Mack, R. L., and Kellogg, W. A. (1988). Interface metaphors and user interface design. In M. Helander (Ed.), *Handbook of Human-Computer Interaction.* New York, NY: Elsevier Science Publishers.

Charney, D. A. (1987). Comprehending linear text: The role of discourse cues and reading strategies. *Hypertext'87 Proceedings,* 269-289.

Colley, A. M. (1987). Text comprehension. In J. Beech and A. Colley (Eds.), *Cognitive Approaches to Reading.* New York: Wiley.

Conklin, J. (1987). Hypertext: An introduction and survey. *IEEE Computer, 20,* 17-41.

Conklin, J. and Begeman, M. L. (1987). gIBIS: A hypertext tool for team design deliberation. *Hypertext'87 Proceedings*, 247-251.

Cook, P. (1988). Multimedia technology: An encyclopedia publisher's perspective. In S. Ambron, S. And K. Hooper (Eds.), *Interactive Multiemdia: Visions of Multimedia Developers, Educators, & Information Providers.* 217-240.

Cunningham, D. J., Duffy, T. M., and Knuth, R. A. (1993). The textbook of the future. In C. McKnight, A. Dillon, and J. Richardson (Eds.), *Hypertext: A Psychological Perspective.* New York: Ellis Horwood.

Davis, H. (1995). To embed or not to embed.... *Communications of the ACM, 38 (8)*, 108-109.

De Young, L. (1989). Hypertext challenges in the auditing domain. *Hypertext'89 Conference Proceedings*, 169-180.

Dee-Lucas, D. and Larkin, J. H. (1991). Content map design and knowledge structures with hypertext and traditional text. Poster presented at the ACM Conference on Hypertext, *Hypertext'91*, San Antonio, Texas, USA.

Dillon A. and McKnight, C. (1990). Towards a classification of text types: a repertory grid approach. *International Journal of Man-Machine Studies, 33,* 323-336.

Dillon, A. (1991a). Requirements for hypertext applications: the why, what, and how approach. *Applied Ergonomics, 22,* 258-262.

Dillon, A. (1991b). Readers' models of text structures: The case of academic articles. *International Journal of Man-Machine Studies, 35,* 913-925.

Downs, R. M. and Stea, D. (Eds.) (1973). *Cognitive Maps and Spatial Behavior: Process and Products.* Chicago, IL: Aldline Publishing Co.

Duffy, T. M. and Knuth, R. A. (1990). Hypermedia and instruction: Where is the match? In D. Jonnassen and H. Mandl (Eds.), *Designing Hypermedia for Learning.* New York: Springer-Verlag.

Edwards, D. and Hardman, L. (1989). 'Lost in hyperspace': Cognitive mapping and navigation in hypertext environment. In R. McAleese (Ed.), *Hypertext: Theory into Practice.* Oxford: Intellect.

Egan, D. E., Remde, J. R., Gomnez, L. M., Landauer, T. K., Eberhardt, J., and Lochbaum, C. C. (1989). Formative design-evaluation of 'SuperBook.' *ACM Transactions on Information Systems, 7,* 30-57.

Ellis, D., Furner-Hines, and Willett, P. (1994). On the creation of hypertext links in full-text documents: Measurement of inter-linker consistency. *The Journal of Documentation, 50,* 67-98.

Elm, W. C. and Woods, D. D. (1985). Getting lost: A case study in interface design. *Proceedings of the Human Factors Society 29th Annual Meeting* (pp. 927-931). Santa Monica, CA: Human Factors Society.

Engelbart, D. (1995). Toward augmenting the human intellect and boosting our collective IQ. *Communications of the ACM, 38(8),* 30-33.

Engelbart, D. A. (1963). A conceptual framework for the augmentation of man's intellect. In P. W. Howerton and D. C. Weeks (Eds.), *Vistas in Information Handling*, 163-174.

Engelbart, D. C. and English, W. K. (1968). A research center for augmenting human intellect. *AFIPS Conference Proceedings,* 395-410.

Ericsson, K. A. and Simon, H. A. (1984). *Protocol Analysis: Verbal Report as Data.* Cambridge, MA: MIT Press.

Fairchild, K. M. (1993). Information management using virtual reality-based visualizations. In A. Wexelblat (Ed.), *Virtual Reality: Applications and Explorations.* New York: Academic Press.

Fairchild, K., Poltrock, S., E., and Furnas, G. W. (1988). SemNet: Three-dimensional graphic representations of large knowledge bases. In R. Guindon (Ed.),

Cognitive Science and its Applications for Human-Computer Interaction. Hillsdale, NJ: Lawrence Erlbaum Associates.

Feiner, S., Nagy, S., and van Dam, A. (1982). An experimental system for creating and presenting interactive graphical documents. *ACM Transaction on Graphics, 1*, 59-77.

Fillenbaum, S. and Rapaport, D. (1973). *Structures in Semantic Lexicon.* New York: Academic Press.

Foss, C. L. (1989). Tools for reading and browsing hypertext. *Information Processing Management, 25*(4), 407-418.

France, M. (1994). Smart contracts. *Forbes ASAP, August 29*, 117-118.

Frisse, M. E. (1988). Searching for information in a hypertext medical handbook. *Communications of the ACM, 31*, 880-886.

Furnas, G. W. (1986). Generalized fish-eye views. *Proceedings of CHI'86.* ACM, New York. 16-23.

Furnas, G. W. And Zacks, J. (1994). Multitrees: Enriching and reusing hierarchical structures. *CHI'94 Conference Proceedings*, 330-336.

Furnas, G. W., Deerwester, S., Dumais, S. T., Landauer, T. K., Harshman, R. A., Streeter, L. A., Lochbaum, K. E. (1988). Information retrieval using a singular value decomposition model of latent semantic structure. *SIGIR Conference Proceedings*, 465-480.

Garzotto, F., Mainetti, L., and Paolini, P. (1995). Hypermedia design, analysis, and evaluation issues. *Communications of the ACM, 38 (8),* 74-86

Glenn, B. T. and Chignell, M. H. (1992). Hypermedia: Design for browsing. In H. Rex Hartson and D. Hix (Eds.), *Advances in Human-Computer Interaction, Vol. 3.* (p. 143-183). Norwood, NJ: Ablex Publishing Corp.

Glushko, R. J. (1989). Design issues for multi-document hypertexts. *Hypertext'89 Conference Proceedings,* 51-60.

Godin, R., Gecsei, J., and Pichet, C. (1989). Design of a browsing interface for information retrieval. *SIGIR'89 Conference Proceedings,* 32-39.

Golovchinsky, G. and Chignell, M. (1996). Merging hypertext and information retrieval in the interface. Demonstration at *Hypertext'96*, ACM Conference on Hypertext. Washington, DC.

Golovchinsky, G. and Chignell, M. H. (1993). Queries-R-Links: Graphical Markup for Text Navigation. *Proceedings of INTERCHI'93*, 454-460.

Gray, S. H. (1990). Using protocol analysis and drawings to study mental model construction during hypertext navigation. *International Journal of Human-Computer Interaction, 2,* 359-377.

Gray, M. (1996). *Internet statistics: Growth and usage of the Web and the Internet.* http://www.mit.edu/people/mkgray/net/

Green, J. (1996). Using lexical chains to build hypertext links in newspaper articles. Poster presented at *Hypertext'96,* ACM Conference on Hypertext. Washington, DC.

GVU (1996). GVU's 6th WWW User Survey. http://www.cc.gatech.edu/gvu/user_surveys/survey-10-1996/

Halasz, F. G. (1988). Reflections on NoteCards: Seven issues for next generations of hypermedia systems. *Communications of the ACM, 31*, 836-852.

Halasz, F. G., Moran, T. P., and Trigg, R. H. (1987). NoteCards in a nutshell. *CHI+GI 1987*, 45-52.

Hammond, N. and Allinson, L. (1987). Extending hypertext for learning: An investigation of access and guidance tools. In Sutcliffe, A., Macaulay, L. (Eds.), *People and Computers V,* 293-304.

Hammond, N. and Allinson, L. (1987). The travel metaphor as a design principle and traveling aid for navigating around complex systems. In D. Diaper and R. Winder (Eds.*), People and Computers III.* Cambridge: Cambridge University Press.

Hearst, M. A. (1995). TileBars: Visualization of term distribution information in full text information access. *CHI'95 Conference Proceedings,* 59-66.

Hodges, M. E., Sasnett, R. M., and Ackerman, M. S. (1989). A construction set for multimedia applications. *IEEE Software, 6*, 37-43.

Hoffman, D. L., Kalsbeek, W. D., and Novak, T. P. (1996). Internet and Web use in the U.S. *Communications of the ACM, 39* (12), 36-46.

Hollands, J. G., Carey, T. T., Matthews, M. L., and McCann, C. A. (1989). Presenting a graphical network: A comparison of performance using fisheye and scrolling views. *Proceedings of 3rd International Conference in Human-Computer Interaction*, 313-320.

Horton, W., Taylor, L., Ignacio, A., and Hoft, N. L. (1995). *The Web Page Design Cookbook: All the Ingredients You Need to Create 5-Star Web Pages.* New York: John Wiley & Sons.

Hutchings, G. A, Hall, W., Hammond, N. V., Kibby, M. R., McKnight, C., and Riley, D. (1992). Authoring and evaluation of hypermedia for education. *Computers and Education, 18,* 171-177.

Inaba, K. (1990). Converting technical publications into maintenance performance aids. *Proceedings of International Conference Human Machine Interaction and Artificial Intelligence in Aeronautics and Space,* Toulouse-Blagnac, France, 43-57.

Instone, K. Teasley, B. M., and Leventhal, L. M. (1993). Empirically-based re-design of a hypertext encyclopedia. *CHI'93 Conference Proceedings,* 500-506.

Johnson, S. (1995). Control for hypertext construction. *Communications of the ACM, 38 (8),* 87.

Johnson-Laird, P. (1983). *Mental Models.* Cambridge, MA: Cambridge University Press.

Jones, S. and Cockburn, A. (1996). A study of navigational support provided by two World Wide Web browsing applications. *Hypertext'96 Conference Proceedings,* 161-169.

Jones. W. P. (1987). How do we distinguish the hyper from hype in non-linear text? In H-J. Bullinger and B. Shackel (Eds.), *INTERACT'87.* New York: North-Holland.

Kahn, P. (1995). Visual cues for local and global coherence in the WWW. *Communications of the ACM, 38 (8),* 67-69.

Kaplan, C., Fenwick, J., and Chen, J. (1993). Adaptive hypertext navigation based on user goals and context. *User Modeling and User-Adapted Interaction, 3,* 193-220.

Keahey, T. A. and Rivenburgh, R. (1996). HyperLINK: Visualization of WWW navigation. Demonstration *at Hypertext'96,* ACM Conference on Hypertext. Washington, DC.

Kearsley, G. (1994). *Public Access Systems: Bringing Computer Power to the People.* Norwood, NJ: Ablex Publishing Corp.

Kibby, M. R. and Mayes, J. T. (1989). Towards intelligent hypertext. In R. McAleese (Ed.), *Hypertext: Theory into Practice,* 164-172.

Kindersley, D. (1994). *My First Incredible, Amazing Dictionary.* CD-ROM for PC. Dorling Kindersley Publishing. Sunnyvale, CA: MediaMart.

Kintsch, W. and van Dijk, T. A. (1978). Towards a model of text comprehension and production. *Psychological Review, 85,* 363-394.

Kintsch, W. and Yarbrough, J. C. (1982). Role of rhetorical structure in text comprehension. *Journal of Educational Psychology, 74,* 828-834.

Koster, M. (1996). *WWW Robot Frequently Asked Questions.*http://info.webcrawler.com/mak/projects/robots/faq.html

Krol, E. and Ferguson, P. (1995). *The Whole Internet for Windows 95: User's Guide and Catalog.* Sebastopol, CA: O'Reilly & Associates.

Landow, G. P. and Kahn, P. (1992). Where's the hypertext? The Dickens Web as a system-independent hypertext. *ECHT'92 Conference Proceedings,* 149-160.

Lashkari, Y. (1995). *A lay-person's overview of information filtering and retrieval.* http://webhound.www.media.mit.edu/projects/webhound/doc/ Server.html

Marshall, C. C., Halasz, F. G., Rogers, R. A., and Janssen, W. C., Jr. (1991). Aquanet: a hypertext tool to hold your knowledge in place. *Hypertext'91 Conference Proceedings,* 261-275.

Mackinlay, J. D., Rao, R., and Card, S. K. (1995). An organic user interface for searching citation links. *CHI'95 Conference Proceedings,* 67-73.

Mackinlay, J. D., Robertson, G. G., and Card, S. K. (1991). The perspective wall: Detail and context smoothly integrated. *CHI'91 Conference Proceedings,* 173-179.

Maclean, A., Bellotti, V., and Shum, S. (1993). Developing the design space with design space analysis. In P. F. Byerley, P. J. Barnard, and J. May (Eds.), *Computers, Communications, and Usability: Design Issues, Research and Methods for Integrated Services.* Amsterdam: Elsevier.

McKnight, C. Dillon, A. and Richardson, J. (1989). Problems in hyperland? A human factors perspective. *Hypermedia, 1,* 167-178.

McKnight, C., Dillon, A., and Richardson, J. (1991). *Hypertext in Context.* England: Cambridge University Press.

McKnight, C., Richardson, J., and Dillon, A. (1989). The authoring of hypertext documents. In R. McAleese (Ed.*), Hypertext: Theory into Practice.* Norwood, NJ: Ablex.

McLean, R. S. (1989). Hypermedia "usability" has lessons for us all. *CALM Development Newsletter, 5*(9), 1-2.

Merrill, M. D. (1991). Constructivism and instructional design. *Education Technology, 31* (5), 45-54.

Misue, K. and Sugiyama, K. (1991). Multi-viewpoint perspective display methods: Foundation and application to compound graphs. *Fourth International Conference on Human-Computer Interaction,* 834-838.

Mitta, D. A. (1990). A fisheye presentation strategy: Aircraft maintenance data. *INTERACT'90,* 875-880.

Mohageg, M. (1992). The influence of hypertext linking structures on the efficiency of information retrieval. *Human Factors, 34,* 351-367.

Murray, P. C. (1993). Tyrannical links, loose associations, and other difficulties of hypertext. *ACM SIGLINK Newsletter, 2,* 10-12.

Mynatt, B. T., Leventhal, L. M., Instone, K., Farhat, J., and Rohlman, D. S. (1992). Hypertext of book: Which is better for answering questions? *CHI'92 Conference Proceedings,* 19-25.

Negroponte, N. (1996). Caught browsing again. *Wired, 4.05,* 200.

Nelson, T. H. (1967). Getting it out of our system. In G. Schecter (Ed.), *Information Retrieval: A Critical Review.* Washington, DC: Thompson Books.

Nelson, T. H. (1981). *Literary machines.* T. H. Nelson, Swarthmore, Pennsylvania.

Nelson, T. H. (1995). The heart of connection: Hypermedia unified by transclusion. *Communications of the ACM, 38*(8), 31-33.

Newell, A. (1990). *Unified Theories of Cognition.* Cambridge, MA: Harvard University Press.

Nielsen, J. (1990a). *Hypertext and Hypermedia.* New York: Academic Press.

Nielsen, J. (1990b). The art of navigating through hypertext. *Communications of the ACM, 33*(3), 296-310

Nielsen, J. (1993). *Usability Engineering.* New York: Academic Press.

Nielsen, J. (1994). Enhancing the explanatory power of usability heuristics. *CHI'94 Conference Proceedings,* 152-158.

Nielsen, J. (1995a). *Multimedia and Hypertext: The Internet and Beyond.* New York: Academic Press.

Nielsen, J. (1995b). The future of hypermedia. *Interactions, 2,* 66-78.

Nielsen, J. and Lyngbæk, U. (1990). Two field studies of hypermedia usability. In R. McAleese and C. Greene (Eds.*), Hypertext: State of the Art.* Oxford: Intellect.

Nielsen, J. and Sano, D. (1995). *SunWeb: User Interface Design for Sun Microsystem's Internal Web.* http://www.sun.com/sun-on-net/uidesign/sunweb/

Nishiyama, H., Kin, S., Yokoyama, T., and Matsushita, Y. (1994). An image retrieval system considering subjective perception. *CHI'94 Conference Proceedings,* 30-36.

Noik, E. G. (1993). Exploring large hyperdocuments: Fisheye views of nested networks. *Hypertext'93 Conference Proceedings,* 192-199.

Nyce, J. M. and Kahn, P. (1991*). From Memex to Hypertext: Vannevar Bush and the Mind's Machine.* Boston, MA: Academic Press.

Parton, D.. Huffman, K., Prodgen, P., Norman, K., and Shneiderman, B. (1985). Learning a menu selection tree. *Behaviour and Information Technology, 4*(2), 81-91.

Parunak, H. V. D. (1991). Ordering the information graph. In E. Berk and J. Devlin (Eds.), *Hypertext/Hypermedia Handbook.* New York: McGraw-Hill.

Perrig, W. and Kintsch, W. (1982). Propositional and situational representation of text. *Journal of Memory and Language, 24,* 503-518.

Pohl, R. F. (1982). Acceptability of story continuation. In A. Flammer and W. Kintsch (Eds.), *Discourse Processing.* Amsterdam: North-Holland.

Rada, R. (1992). Converting a textbook to hypertext. *ACM Transactions on Information Systems, 10*(3), 294-315.

Rao, R., Pedersen, J. O., Hearst, M. A., Mackinlay, J. D., Card, S. K., Masinter, L., Halvorsen, P.-K., and Robertson, G. G. (1995). Rich interaction in the digital library. *Communications of the ACM, 38 (4),* 29-39.

Raymond, D. R. and Tompa, F. W. (1988). Hypertext and the Oxford English Dictionary. *Communications of the ACM, 31* (7), 871-879.

Rearick, T. C. (1991). Automating conversion of text into hypertext. In E. Berk and J. Devlin (Eds.), *Hypertext/Hypermedia Handbook.* New York: McGraw-Hill.

Richard, E. (1995),. Anatomy of the World-Wide Web. *Internet World, April* , 28-30

Riner,R. (1991) Automated conversion. In E. Berk and J. Devlin (Eds.), *Hypertext/Hypermedia Handbook.* New York: McGraw-Hill.

Robertson, G. G., Card, S. K., and Mackinlay, J. D. (1993). Information visualization using 3D interactive animation. *Communications of the ACM, 36 (4),* 57-71.

Robertson, G. G., Mackinlay, J. D., and Card, S. K. (1991). Cone trees: Animated 3D visualizations of hierarchical information. *CHI'91 Conference Proceedings,* 189-194.

Rumelhart, D. E., McClelland, J. L., and the PDP Research Group. (1986). *Parallel Distributed Processing: Explorations in the Microstructure of Cognition, Vol. 1, Foundations*. Cambridge, MA: The MIT Press.

Salomon, G. (1990). Designing casual-use hypertext: The CHI'89 InfoBooth. *CHI'90 Conference Proceedings*, 451-458

Salton, G. and McGill, M. J. (1983). *Introduction to Modern Information Retrieval.* New York: McGraw-Hill. [22]

Samarapungavan, A. and Beishuizen, J. (1992). Hypermedia and knowledge acquisition from non-linear expository text. In B. V. Hout-Wolters and W. Schnotz (Eds.), *Text Comprehension and Learning from Text.* Berwyn, PA: Swets and Zeitlinger.

Sano, D. (1996). *Designing Large Scale Web Sites: A Visual Design Methodology*. New York: John Wiley.

Sarkar, M. and Brown, M. H. (1994). Graphical fisheye views. *Communications of the ACM, 37* (12), 73-84.

Sawhney, N., Balcom, D., and Smith, I. (1996). HyperCafe: Narrative and aesthetic properties of hypertext. *Hypertext'96 Conference Proceedings*, 1-10.

Schaffer *et al.* (1993). Comparing fisheye and full zoom techniques for navigation of hierarchically clustered networks. In *Proceedings of Graphics Interface*.

Schnase, J. L., Cunnius, E. L., and Dowton, S. B. (1995). The StudSpace project: Collaborative hypermedia in nomadic computing environments. *Communications of the ACM, 38(8)*, 72-73.

Seyer, P. (1991). *Understanding Hypertext: Concepts and Applications.* Blue Ridge Summit, PA: Windcrest Books.

Shardanand, U. and Maes, P. (1995). Social information filtering: Algorithms for automating "Word of Mouth." *CHI'95 Conference Proceedings*, 210-217

Shneiderman, B. (1987). User interface design for the HyperTIES electronic encyclopedia. *Hypertext'87 Conference Proceedings,* 189-194.

Shneiderman, B. (1989). Reflections on authoring, editing, and managing hypertext. In E. Barrett (Ed.), *The Society of Text: Hypertext, Hypermedia, and the Social Construction of Information*. Cambridge, MA: The MIT Press.

Simpson, A. and McKnight, C. (1989). Navigation in hypertext. *Proceedings of Hypertext II*, University of York, June 29-30.

Simpson, A. and McKnight, C. (1990). Navigation in hypertext: Structural cues and mental maps. In R. McAleese and C. Greene (Eds.), *Hypertext: State of the Art.* Oxford: Intellect.

Simpson, R., Renear, A., Mylonas, E., and Van Dam, A. (1996). 50 years after "As We May Think": The Brown/MIT Vannevar Bush symposium. *Interactions, 3 (2)*, 47-67.

Sjöberg, C., Timpka, T., Nyce, J. M., Peolsson, M., and Klercker, T. af. (1992). *From clinical literature to medical hypermedia: Procedures and experiences.* Department of Computer and Information Science. Linköping University, Linköping, Sweden, LiTH-IDA-R-92-25, ISSN-0281-4250.

Slatin, J. (1988). Hypertext and the teaching of writing. In E. Barrett (Ed.), *Text, ConText, and HyperText: Writing with and for the Computer.* Cambridge, MA: The MIT Press.

Smith, J. B. and Weiss, S. F. (1988). Hypertext. *Communications of the ACM, 31(7),* 816-819.

Smith, J. B., Weiss, S. F., and Ferguson, G. J. (1987). A hypertext environment and its cognitive basis. *Hypertext'87 Conference Proceedings*, 195-214.

Smith, R. B. (1987). Experiences with the Alternate Reality Kit: An example of the tension between literalism and magic. *CHI+GI'87 (Conference on Human Factors in Computing Systems and Graphics Interface) Conference Proceedings*, 61-67.

Spyridakis, J. H. and Isakson, C. S. (1991). Hypertext: A new tool and its effect on audience comprehension. *IPCC 91 Conference Proceedings*, 37-44.

Steinberg, S. G. (1996). Seek and ye shall find (may be). *Wired, 4.05*, 108-114 and172-182.

Streitz, N. A. (1996). Plenary Session, Opening Keynote: *Ubiquitous Collabo-ration and Polyphasic Activities: From Desktops and Meeting Rooms to Cooperative Buildings and Virtual Organizations.* Hypertext'96, ACM Conference on Hypertext, Washington D.C., USA.

Streitz, N. A. (1995). Designing hypermedia: A collaborative activity. *Communications of the ACM, 38(8)*, 70-71.

Streitz, N., Geißler, J., Haake, J., Hol, J. (1994). DOLPHIN: Integrated meeting support across LiveBoards, local, and remote desktop environments. *Proceedings of the ACM 1994 Conference on Computer Supported Co-operative Work (CSCW'94).* Chapel Hill, NC, 345-348.

Streitz, N., Haake, J., Hanneman, J., Lemke, A.,

Schuler, W., Schütt, H., Thüring, M. (1992). SEPIA: A cooperative hypermedia authoring environment. *Proceedings of the ACM Conference on Hypertext (ECHT'92),* Milan, 11-22.

Tauscher, L. and Greenberg, S. (1996). Design guidelines for effective WWW history mechanisms. Presented at *Designing for the Web: Empirical Studies,* Microsoft Corp., Redmond, WA. October 30, 1996.

Thüring, M., Häake, J. M., and Hanneman, J. (1991). What's Eliza doing in the Chinese Room? Incoherent hyperdocuments — and how to avoid them. *Hypertext'91 Conference Proceedings*, 161-177.

Thüring, M., Hannemann, J., and Haake, J. M. (1995). Hypermedia and cognition: Designing for comprehension. *Communications of ACM, 38*(8), 57-66.

Trigg, R. H. (1988). Guided tours and tabletops: Tools for communicating in a hypertext environment. *ACM Transactions of Office Information Systems, 6,* 398-414.

Tversky, A. and Hutchinson, J. W. (1986). Nearest neighbor analysis of psychological spaces. *Psychological Review, 93,* 3-22.

Usandizaga, I., Lopisteguy, P., Perez, T. A., and Gutierrez, J. (1996). Hypermedia and education: A new approach. Poster presented at *Hypertext'96*, ACM Conference on Hypertext. Washington, DC.

Valdez, F., Chignell, M., and Glenn, B. (1988). Browsing models for hypermedia databases. *Proceedings of Human Factors Society 32nd Annual Meeting,* 318-322.

van Dijk, T. A. and Kintsch, W. (1983). *Strategies of Discourse Comprehension*. London: Academic Press.

Ventura, C. A. (1988). Why switch from paper to electronic manuals? *Document Processing Systems Conference Proceedings,* 111-116.

Vora, P. R. (1994). *Evaluating Interface Styles and Multiple Access Paths in Hypertext.* Unpublished Ph.D. Dissertation, Department of Industrial Engineering, State University of New York at Buffalo.

Vora, P. R. and Helander, M. (1995). A teaching method as an alternative to the concurrent think-aloud method for usability testing. In Y. Anzai, K. Ogawa, and H. Mori (Eds.), *HCI International'95: Symbiosis and Human Artifact, 375-380.*

Vora, P. R., Helander, M. G., and Shalin, V. L. (1994). Evaluating the influence of interface styles and multiple access paths in hypertext. *CHI'94 Conference Proceedings,* 323-329.

Walker, J. H. (1987). Document Examiner: Delivery interface for hypertext documents. *Hypertext'87 Conference Proceedings*. 307-323.

Waterworth, J. A. (1992). *Multimedia Interaction with Computers: Human Factors Issues.* New York: Ellis Horwood.

Waterworth, J. A. and Chignell, M. H. (1989). A manifesto for hypermedia usability research. *Hypermedia, 1,* 205-234.

Weinman, L. (1996). *<designing web graphics>: How to Prepare Images and Media for the Web.* Indianapolis, IN: New Riders Publishing.

Weyer, S. A. and Borning, A. H. (1985). A prototype electronic encyclopedia. *ACM Transactions of Office Information Systems, 3*, 63-88.

Whalley, P. (1993). An alternative rhetoric for hypertext. In C. McKnight, A. Dillon, and J. Richardson (Eds.), *Hypertext: A Psychological Perspective.* New York: Ellis Horwood.

Wilkins, R. J. and Weal, M. J. (1993). VirtualMedia: Virtual reality as a hypermedia navigation tool. A poster presentation at *Hypertext'93*, ACM Conference on Hypertext, Seattle, Washington, USA.

Wright, P. (1991). Cognitive overheads and prostheses: Some issues in evaluating hypertexts. *Hypertext'91 Proceedings,* 1-12.

Wright, P. and Lickorish, A. (1989). The influence of discourse structure on display and navigation in hypertexts. In N. Williams and P. Holt (Eds.), *Computers and Writing: Models and Tools*. Oxford: Intellect.

Zellweger, P. T. (1989). Scripted documents: A hypermedia path mechanism. *Hypertext'89 Conference Proceedings,* 1-14.

Handbook of Human-Computer Interaction
Second, completely revised edition
M. Helander, T.K. Landauer, P. Prabhu (eds.)

Chapter 39

Multimedia Interaction

John A. Waterworth
Department of Informatics
Umeå University, Sweden

Mark H. Chignell
Dept. of Industrial Engineering
University of Toronto, Canada

39.1 Introduction

Increasingly, sensory information is being provided through computers and digital media. The boundary between the real and the artificial is blurring as recordings of real events are merged with computer-generated sounds and images to create dynamic composites and interactive virtual worlds. The computer is becoming an interactive device for generating perceptual experience. This is a natural evolution of technology in response to the impressive array of senses that humans have, and their extraordinary ability to integrate sensory information into powerful perceptual models of their environment.

The word "multimedia" has been used as a catch-all term to cover the potentially vast domain of computer-based interactive information presentation. In the final decade of the twentieth century we are witnessing the birth of multimedia technology. It is as if the parchment and pen had just been invented and now we have to figure out how to write, format, and publish. In time, no doubt, we will be able to create the multimedia equivalents of great novels and encyclopaedias, but right now it is as if we are just learning to write using multimedia technology.

There are many questions about what multimedia is, and when and how it should be used. There is, for example, a dichotomy between a performance model of multimedia and a document model of multimedia. In the performance model, multimedia is a kind of theatrical presentation, with different media elements (actors) making their presentations according to a sequence and timing that is jointly defined by the orchestration imposed by the multimedia author, and the actions of the user/reader. In contrast, the document model inherits many of the features of traditional documents, including page (screen) layouts, the use of textual commentary and description to organise media elements, and embedded linear structures with associated navigational tools (next, previous, table of contents, index, etc.). In the long run, we expect multimedia to take on a unique identity of its own, comprising both and neither the performance model and/nor the document model.

39.1.1 Roadmap of the Chapter

This chapter provides a broad overview of multimedia, including discussions of multimedia development, interface design, usage, and specific issues such as the use of hyperlinks within multimedia. After this introduction, the chapter continues with a brief history of multimedia.

Multimedia technologies are then reviewed, with particular reference to the ways in which improvements in computational speed, storage capacity, and communications bandwidth are likely to influence future developments. The role of multimedia standards is discussed, including the use of Hypertext Mark-up Language (HTML) for creating general representations of multimedia documents.

User interface and interaction design for multimedia is considered in detail. After considering the technology and the user interface, we focus on the tasks of authoring and publishing multimedia, before finally outlining emerging trends in multimedia interaction.

The remainder of this introduction is concerned with characterising what is meant by the overused word "multimedia" and about what new implications it has for human-computer interaction.

39.1.2 What is Multimedia?

There are many different perspectives on multimedia. First, there are the various digital media-handling functionalities that make multimedia presentations on computers possible. These include digital media storage and playback and various enhancements to computers and their software to meet the heavy demands that multimedia makes on storage capacity, communication bandwidth, and computation generally. Collectively, digital media functionalities form the basis of multimedia technology.

Our focus in this chapter is on the user interface design strategies and interaction techniques that underlie effective multimedia interaction. We will briefly cover some of the major technological issues only insofar as they provide a necessary background and foundation for understanding issues in multimedia application design and use. Our simple definition of multimedia is that it involves computer-assisted interactive presentations in more than one sensory modality. Notice that this definition does not specify the type of interaction, and thus subsumes performance, document and other models of multimedia.

Since multimedia involves computers, it generally involves digital media, and software programmes that can execute logic at various levels of complexity in controlling and co-ordinating the presentation of information. For instance, the programmability of multimedia presentations makes it possible to render animations on the fly and integrate them into a presentation of stored video clips, or to build a link dynamically to the corresponding map file in a database whenever the name of a country is mentioned.

The interactive nature of multimedia means that the way in which information is presented to the user depends to a significant extent on inputs from the user. Media presentations in which the user has only a passive role as purely a recipient of information, such as broadcast television, the cinema, or recorded music and video CDs, do not qualify as multimedia no matter how many different media are involved.

The simple definition of multimedia given above does not necessarily require the use of digital video. For instance, computer control of slide projectors and laser disks could also be (and has been) used to construct significantly interactive multimedia presentations. However, rapid advances in digital media technology have made digital media dominant in multimedia authoring and presentation, and this dominance will increase in the future.

In practice, the term "multimedia" is now applied almost synonymously with the term "hypermedia" which was originally an amalgam of the terms hypertext and multimedia, implying some degree of non-linearity in the way information entities ("nodes") are connected (by "links"). Although it was possible, just a few years ago, to characterise information systems as either hypermedia or multimedia, it is now unusual to find a multimedia system that does not support some degree of non-linearity. We follow the current usage and use "multimedia" to cover any interactive system supporting the presentation of several media, including hypermedia systems. We use the term "hypermedia" only when our focus is specifically on the non-linear aspects of multimedia interaction.

39.1.3 The Impact of Multimedia

Multimedia is often linear to some degree, but it is the nonlinearity and interactivity of multimedia that makes it fundamentally different from printed text. Multimedia includes not only the non-linearity of hypertext, but may also have sound, video action, 3D graphics and animation; all of which might be expected to support the idea that the senses, rather than the intellectual faculties, are the main beneficiaries of this new technology. Multimedia may thus favour the immediate gratification of "mediacy" rather than the deferred and effortful fruits of traditionally educated literacy (Waterworth, 1992; p183-184). The perceived danger, with multimedia, is that it tends to encourage sensory experience at the expense of thoughtful reflection (Norman, 1993).

While the psychological impact of multimedia is still a matter of research and debate, the commercial impact is indisputable. The first major developer conference on multimedia was sponsored by Apple Computer in 1988. Since then multimedia has become a driving force in the computer industry. The major academic conference on multimedia was introduced by the Association for Computing Machinery (ACM) in 1993, and has occurred annually since that first meeting.

The initial impact of multimedia has been on the sales of computer hardware and peripherals, including sound and video cards. Since the storage and processing of digital media is comparatively expensive, this has required people to upgrade their computers to keep up with the "multimedia revolution". This has led to the joke that multimedia is "anything that requires the computer salesman to take more than one trip to the car to get". However, one of the motivations for the rapid development of multimedia has been migration of computers into schools and homes. With the near saturation of the business market in the early 1990s, hardware and software companies were looking for new markets for their products. Multimedia, with its potential for education and entertainment became a vehicle for attracting a large new segment of the population to computing.

One obvious impact of multimedia technology is that information now exists in an increased variety of forms. These include graphics, electronic mail, voice annotations, video clips, snapshots of handwritten notes, and, more importantly, combinations of many such forms. These are all accessed by technology that was standardised before some of these media were available - that is, via multiple-window systems based around some variety of graphical user interface commonly referred to as a WIMP interface (Windows, Icons, Menus, and Pointer). These WIMP environments worked well for text and graphics. Now they are being stretched to breaking point (or, rather, their users are) by the addition of multimedia capabilities.

If, as Marshall McLuhan put it, the medium is the message (which is debatable), then new forms imply new content. Whether the slogan is true or not, more forms of information give rise to the possibility of communicating different content. For instance, text plus graphics is inherently static, and cannot convey the information content of a video clip of a drop falling into a pool of milk, captured at high speed and shown dramatically slowly. Similarly, a video of time-lapse satellite photography depicting the development of a storm formation conveys something new about the phenomenon - something that simply could not be communicated adequately in other ways. These two examples illustrate the fundamentally new characteristic of multimedia, the capability to communicate dynamic information directly, in time and with super-realistic impact.

Another radically new characteristic of multimedia, in the broadest use of the term, is that information can be organised in new, flexible ways. New ways of information organisation promote new forms of knowledge. In the past, text and associated graphics were arranged in essentially chronological order, like a novel. To make sense of the 'story' being told (by the report, technical paper, or whatever) the reader was expected to start at the beginning and work through to the end. With the advent of hypermedia, non-linear structures can be created, allowing information to be explored through a variety of routes. The routes can then be tailored to the needs of individual readers. Multimedia, usually including some degree of non-linearity, is now being applied to a wide range of application areas, including medicine, business, documentation, education, and entertainment (particularly these last two).

39.1.4 Weaving the Multimedia Tapestry

Ultimately, multimedia is concerned with the creation of computer-assisted experience. As such it is closely related to virtual reality, but without necessarily involving the three-dimensional spatial aspects of that technology. Current approaches to multimedia assume that multimedia presentations are situated in the physical world and experienced through a desktop computer, usually with one person controlling the presentation at a time. Comprehensive models of collaborative multimedia and multimedia embedded within virtual environments have yet to be developed.

Multimedia can be thought of as a tapestry in space and time, with various textual and media elements embroidered into the tapestry at different spatial and/or temporal locations. Before the computer, tapestries hung on walls and often documented important events. For instance, the Bayeux tapestry describing the Norman conquest of England contains many scenes which the reader/observer can read through. At one point, Duke William is shown lifting the helm of his helmet to show his troops that he is still alive. At another point King Harold is shown pulling out the arrow that struck him in the eye. The tapestry forms a vivid and compelling presentation, but the reader has to use her knowledge and imagination to enrich the presentation and bring it to life.

Comic books serve as latter day tapestries of a kind. In a comic book, a sequence of events is broken down into panels. Various annotations and pictorial clichés are used to enrich the reader's understanding of the events being portrayed. As an example of this, we will briefly describe "King Ottokar's Sceptre" (Hergé, 1962), one of the stories from the well known comic series "The Adventures of Tintin". In the English translation, the book runs to 62 pages. The first two pages consist of 23 cartoon panels. The first 22 of these can be summarised as follows:

panels 1-2 Tintin walking in the park
panels 3-6 Tintin discovers a briefcase on a bench
panels 7-8 Tintin walks back to the owner's residence
panels 9-10 Tintin enters the residence and climbs the stairs
panels 11-22 Tintin returns the briefcase and has a discussion with its owner

Panel 14 is particularly interesting because it is actually a split panel that shows Tintin and Professor Alembick (the owner of the briefcase) in the top half, and two men electronically eavesdropping on them from another room in the lower half of the panel.

In this example, the cartoonist has managed to portray movements through space and time, and the occurrence of simultaneous events in different locations. Split panels are used to handle simultaneity in nearby locations, while textual annotation of panels (e.g., "meanwhile in Klow", on page 33) are used to imply simultaneity over a distance. The reader naturally assumes sequencing of events unless simultaneity is explicitly indicated. Non-speech sound is also vividly portrayed in the cartoon series. For instance, "TING-TING-TING" is used to portray the sound of a knife hitting a wine glass on page 5, while "RRRRING-RRRRING- RRRRING" is used to portray the sound of a telephone ringing on page 7. "RRRING", accompanied by some subtly different pictorial cues, is used to portray the sound of a doorbell a few panels later on the same page.

The cartoonist also uses a number of graphical and textual devices to signify emotional and cognitive states which cannot be directly inferred from what is spoken by the characters in the cartoon. For instance, the sequence of having a mental query followed by a flash of inspiration is indicated by a large exclamation mark followed by a question mark, a lightning bolt symbol, and finally a jagged exclamation mark (page 44). Similarly, unconsciousness, or the grogginess caused by a blow to the head (which seems to happen a lot in Tintin cartoons!) is indicated by a series of stars around the head of the afflicted person.

As cartoon books like the Tintin and Asterix series demonstrate, a good cartoonist provides a coherent textual and pictorial narrative that conveys a compelling series of events, the sights and sounds that go with them, and even some insight into the cognitive and emotional states of the people involved in those events.

McCloud (1993) discussed the major elements of the comic. He defined comics (p. 9) as "juxtaposed pictorial and other images in deliberate sequence". One of the issues he addressed was why the simplified images of comics are so engaging. He argued that while we see other people's faces in realistic detail, we usually have only a sketchy awareness of our own faces. Thus we are able to identify more easily with a cartoon-like face (e.g., Tintin) than with a more realistically drawn face. As McCloud (p. 36) put it: "The cartoon is a vacuum into which our identity and awareness are pulled...an empty shell that we inhabit which enables us to travel in another realm".

The relationship between pictures and words is a challenge facing multimedia that has already been addressed by comics. McCloud (1993, p. 49) argued that pictures and words have to adjust to each other in order to develop a unified language of comics "where words and pictures are like two sides of one coin". For pictures (according to McCloud) this adjustment involves making them more abstracted from "reality" so that, like words, they require "greater levels of perception". Words on the other hand have to move in the opposite direction in comics, requiring lower levels of perception by being bolder and more direct.

The last point made by McCloud that we shall note here is the principle of closure that is used in comics. He defines closure as the phenomenon of observing the parts but perceiving the whole. In comics: "...the audience is a willing and conscious collaborator, and closure is the agent of change, time, and motion" (McCloud, 1993, p. 65).

The principles of abstraction, word-picture integration, and closure, should, in principle, be applicable to multimedia as well as to comics and other media. In MYST, for instance, the computer-generated world of the game uses a considerable amount of abstraction. MYST also requires mental closure to infer continuous space and movement from the discrete snapshots that are actually displayed on the screen.

In our view, there has generally been little, if any, word-picture integration in multimedia. It is possible that the current distinction between document and presentation multimedia (as noted above) reflects a failure to integrate words and pictures successfully in multimedia, with words being dominant in document multimedia and pictures (images, animations, etc.) being dominant in presentation multimedia.

Tapestries and comic books can teach us about how to organise and enrich multimedia content. Other relevant forms of communication include film, theatre, books, photography, and business presentations.

Multimedia, as currently defined, is a diverse concept that incorporates a set of technologies that can be applied to almost all conceivable types of content and domain. Our earlier definition of multimedia as involving computer-assisted interactive presentations can be more formally expressed as:

> The process and technology of handling and presenting digitised information using a variety of perceptual and display channels within an interactive human-computer interface.

This definition sounds fairly straightforward, but the design of appropriate interactive human-computer interfaces turns out to be challenging. In particular, the co-ordination of linear and nonlinear navigation in multimedia and hypertext was identified in the late 1980s as a particularly difficult problem.

The growing use of hypermedia in the 1980s, as a prelude to full-scale multimedia, brought about a kind of crisis, a re-examination of what human-computer interaction is all about (Waterworth and Chignell, 1989). Initially, the non-linear (and hence, perhaps, non-rational) nature of hypertext was accounted for by suggesting that the loose linking of fragments of information in hypermedia in some way mirrors how information is really organised in the human mind. Since we can use this mind to do cognitive work, hypermedia, with its associative structure, was assumed to help us do well-structured, information processing and problem solving. However, research on navigation in hypertext demonstrated that the associative networks of hypertext were difficult to navigate (e.g., Nielsen, 1990a), indicating that any advantages of associative chunking of information in multimedia and hypertext cannot be attributed to some structural isomorphism with human cognition.

In hindsight, after thousands of years of developing the linear presentation technology of books and associated print media, it seems surprising that nonlinear presentation should have been thought of as replacing linearity. The segmentation and de-linearisation of chunks of information in hypermedia/multimedia tends to de-contextualise knowledge. The more we use hypermedia, and even word processors, the stronger the temptation roughly to cobble together "mindbites" - nuggets of information or argumentation - into something that looks like a coherent document, but which often lacks linear structure and some of the lexical cohesion that is often found in printed text. The idea that using non-linear information structures in some way mirrors how information is stored in the human mind, and therefore will make communication between author and reader more accurate (e.g. Ginige et al, 1995), does not stand serious examination (Waterworth, 1996c). Linearity and non-linearity are both important in multimedia; non-linear organisation of materials must be used judiciously.

39.2 Historical Trends In Multimedia

Multimedia has captured people's imaginations, because it enables a new style of interactivity that transcends the earlier models of presentation possible with slide projectors, film projectors, and the like. The enthusiasm for multimedia cuts across both the private and public sectors. For instance, many school districts in the 1990s were committing large portions of their capital budgets, and sections of their curricula, to multimedia hardware and software, at a time when there was relatively little evidence of the educational impact of multimedia (whether good or bad).

The current enthusiasm for multimedia can best be understood within an historical perspective. We need to think back to a time when computers could only handle text and numbers and analogue media were dominant; back to a time when computing rooms contained more refrigerant than people.

There is a standard history of hypertext and it has been presented in a number of places (e.g., Parsaye et al, 1989, chapter 5). In contrast, there is no standard version of the history of multimedia. In part, this may be because multimedia is a diverse topic that spans several technical and artistic (compositional) domains.

In the 1960's simple computer graphics pioneered by Ivan Sutherland and Doug Engelbart (among others) were revolutionary. At that time, there was no VCR or videotape, and computers had neither the power, storage, nor peripherals to handle different media. As processing and storage capacity increased, there was a corresponding relaxation of constraints on what computers could do, redefining computing. The invention of bit-mapped graphics fundamentally changed the nature of the computer. When first developed, they were horrendously expensive in terms of computer power and storage. A screenful of information, for instance, might require a megabyte or more of storage, more than the amount of random access memory (RAM) typically available at that time. However, computing technology caught up with the demands of bit-mapped graphics in the 1970s and 1980s, enabling the graphical user interface, driving the microcomputer revolution, and leading to painting and drawing tools, sophisticated animation, rendering and computer graphics, desktop publishing, and, in the 1980s, to digital video on computers.

Bit-mapped graphics, along with sound generation and playback facilities, turned the computer screen into a theatre. Associated advances in digital media and mass storage devices enabled the computer to become a multimedia device. By the late 1980s, all the elements of the multimedia computer were in place, beginning with the Macintosh and Amiga and then moving to other platforms. Although some of the essential technological problems of multimedia had been solved, the issue remained of how to use the new multimedia capabilities effectively. Two key issues were how to build effective multimedia presentations, and how to create appropriate user interfaces and navigation tools for those presentations.

A multimedia presentation is unlike a traditional presentation not simply because it uses multiple media, but because the actual presentation that is made in a particular user interaction is jointly defined by the author(s) of the multimedia and the user/reader. This creates a somewhat novel situation where authors must create not one organization of information but many, with associated navigational tools that allow different users to interact with the information in different ways. Building on the ideas of Bush (1945), multimedia applications were frequently structured as networks of information, with users being able to choose different combinations of links (paths or trails) through the information. Thus hypertext (the organization of information in node and link structures) became closely associated with multimedia. The mixture of hypertext and multimedia was sometimes referred to as hypermedia, although by the mid-1990s multimedia had largely absorbed the hypertext idea, with hyperlinking being one of the main ways in which multimedia was organised and browsed.

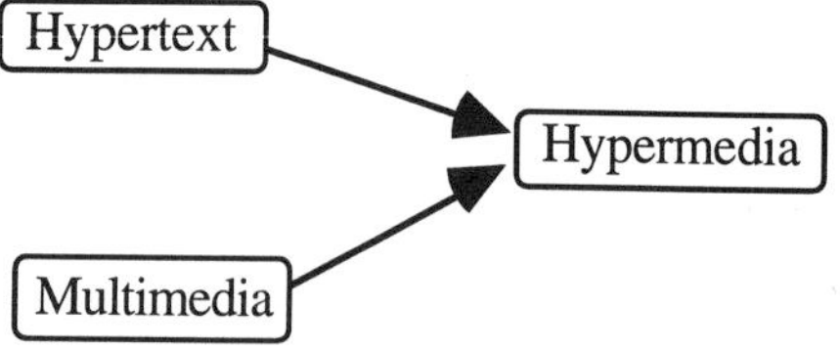

Figure 1. The relationship between hypermedia and multimedia in 1987.

Hyperlinking in multimedia shares the same strengths and weaknesses that apply to hypertext in general. A series of studies (e.g., Gordon et al, 1988, Monk et al, 1988) showed that in some situations it was easier to assimilate information in the form of linear text than in hypertext format. Informal observations in our own laboratories at that time suggested that subjects overestimated the size and complexity of information (in terms of the number of nodes and the amount of text used) when presented in hypertext, relative to the amount of text that was actually used. More recently (Marsh, 1996) carried out a study where subjects misjudged the relative size of four Web sites. In her experiment, a site with 1,277 nodes was judged to be significant smaller than a site with only 353 nodes, and to be of approximately the same size as a node with 109 nodes. In this case, the sites that appeared to be larger than they really were also had a higher degree of connectivity between node. The increase in the apparent size of sites with high connectivity suggests that hypertext and the associated nonlinearity might sometimes increase the complexity of the reader's task, rather than decrease it. Thus, the nonlinearity of hyperlinking is probably best seen as a potentially useful optional feature that can sometimes supplement traditional methods of linear information presentation and navigation (e.g., McKnight, Dillon, and Richardson, 1991), rather than as an end unto itself.

The relationship between multimedia, hypertext, and related technologies is evolving. Figure 1 shows how the conceptualisation of the relationship between

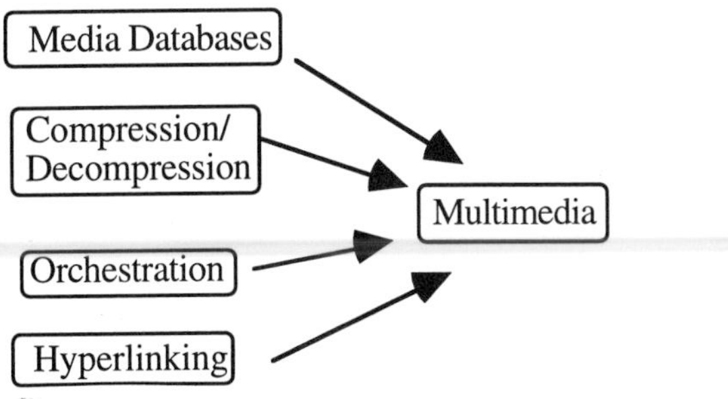

Figure 2. The view of multimedia in 1990.

hypermedia and multimedia changed in the critical period of 1987-1990. In 1987, there was a great deal of excitement about nonlinearity and hypertext. Multimedia, at that time, was seen as a way of enriching hypertext documents to create hypermedia.

However, there was a growing realisation that multimedia was a much broader concept than simply playing different media, as shown in Figure 2. By 1990, multimedia was seen as an umbrella term that included media integration and hyperlinking as components. The concept of multimedia, with its wide range of technical and compositional issues, seemed to be richer than the basic issue of hyperlinking that underlay hypertext. Thus, hyperlinking is now subsumed under the rubric of multimedia, rather than vice versa.

The process of learning when and how to use multimedia continues. The 1990s became a time of gadgetry as people experimented with the new media. One of the ongoing experiments involved the form and the role of the video camera. In the 1980s, the video camera and the video recorder merged to form the camcorder. Then the camcorder and the television merged in the Viewcam from Sharp. This was followed by experiments (e.g., by Sony) in putting the viewfinder back on the Viewcam. Meanwhile, companies like Connectix were creating inexpensive digital cameras that could be connected to computers, enabling applications such as videoconferencing (multi-party picture telephony), turning the computer into a media capture (as well as media playback) device.

Other forms of gadgetry have emphasized portability and convenience. For instance, Casio brought out a watch based remote control. Portability also affected the television, driven by the emerging technology of LCD displays. In 1993 a more radical version of the portable TV became available from Virtual Vision, where a TV was mounted in a set of goggles (wraparound sunglasses) using technology similar to that used in head-mounted displays for virtual reality. Using LCD displays and mirrors, the TV appeared like a normal sized television placed ten feet in front of the person. Meanwhile the sound was piped through earphones. One promising application of this technology was its use in the dentist's office, where small children could be distracted from the discomfort of dental procedures by watching the TV.

Change was also occurring in the way that film and video were produced, particularly in the domain of animation. For instance, the early 1990s saw a trend towards computer generated animation. Once again, synergy and integration were the order of the day. Movements of human actors were sometimes used to control the movement of a computer generated animated character. The resulting animation was then integrated with a soundtrack and animated backgrounds to create an animated film or video.

Multimedia is transforming the way we communicate and learn. As multimedia publishing evolves, it is changing the relative roles of authors and readers and it is also putting the power of publishing in the hands of the masses. Like the printing press, multimedia is a socially-transforming technology. The printing press greatly increased the quantity of books available and decreased their price. This made it possible for people to buy books and put them in their homes, leading to dissemination of information on a much larger scale than ever before. It has been suggested that the Reformation was stimulated by the invention of the printing press and the cheap bibles that it produced. People could read the bible for themselves and decide what it meant, thus weakening the power of the established church which had previously had a near monopoly in bibles and their interpretation. The printing press increased the number of books and the number of readers. However the cost of the printing press, the expertise required, and the costs of marketing and distributing books meant that publication on a large scale was restricted to an elite set of publishing houses.

It was the development of the Internet and the World Wide Web (Web) that made really cheap mass publication viable. The Web created an environment where a document could be simultaneously published and available around the world. By 1996, there were twenty million documents published on the Web with millions more being added each year. For the first time since the printing press, a mainstream publishing medium was available where there were roughly as many authors as there were readers. While the quality of many of the Web documents is debatable (to put it charitably), there can be no doubting the impact that

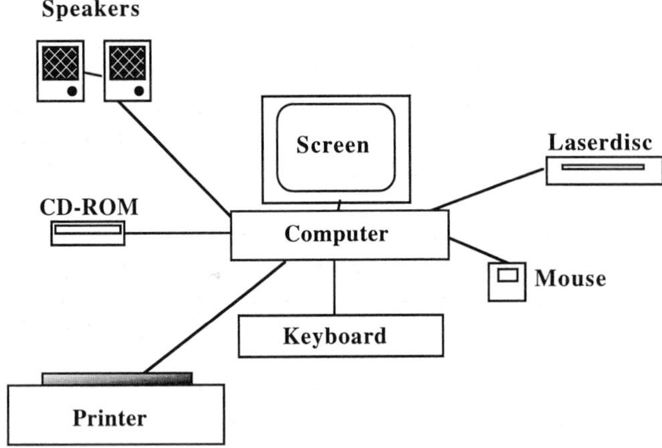

Figure 3. Early model of Multimedia Architecture

multimedia and the Internet are having in bringing the power of publishing (as distinct from reading) to the masses.

As electronic publication of documents becomes the norm (beginning with the widespread creation of Web pages in HTML on the Internet), multimedia authoring is likely to become more of a mainstream activity. This should lead to an increase in the variety of software tools that are available for creating multimedia, which should in turn increase the amount of multimedia publishing activity. This trend was already visible in the early 1990s with the proliferation of CD-ROM authoring tools and video editing, graphics, and animation tools, all of which are finding niches as part of the overall multimedia authoring process.

39.3 Multimedia Technology and Standards

Figure 3 shows an early model of multimedia architecture, focusing on the hardware aspects. The basic components of this model are the computer, the CD-ROM drive, and the laser disc player. This model (as of 1988), assumed that multimedia would be developed using a tool such as HyperCard, with its HyperTalk scripting language, to control and present the digital media. Since the early days of multimedia, there has been a growing awareness of the importance of developing flexible architectures for multimedia that include the interlinking of different databases at run-time, rather than the development of a monolithic structure, and inherently less flexible presentations. Multimedia architectures that rely on database technology provide access to diverse media and documents interactively.

The demands of multimedia data handling have stimulated considerable research into multimedia server and database technologies (e.g., Keeton and Katz, 1995; Tierney et al, 1994). There is also considerable research interest on topics such as distributed multimedia (Guha et al, 1995) and on multimedia databases that can handle still and moving images (e.g., Chua, Lim, and Pung, 1994).

39.3.1 Storage and Compression

Multimedia requires digital media which have to be stored, compressed and played back. Digital media have much higher storage requirements than text. For instance, a page of double spaced printed text (around 250 words) might require approximately 2K (2 kilobytes) of storage. In contrast, a single image might require several hundred kilobytes, while a relatively short video clip might require many megabytes, with the actual size varying according to the size and quality of the video (e.g., resolution and frame rate) and the compression method used.

The first widely available technology for handling time-based media in a general way was QuickTime. QuickTime is a system extension developed by Apple Computer that made it possible for users to view video, animation, music, text, and other dynamic information on a variety of platforms. QuickTime enabled developers to create multimedia content once, then distribute that content across multiple platforms easily. Later versions of QuickTime supported MPEG-compressed video, a standard that enabled smoother, higher-quality video playback using hardware decompression.

Compressed time-based data has to be decompressed for playback. A codec (compressor/ decompressor) handles storage and retrieval of multimedia data using compression technology that removes redundant data. Compression ratios tend to vary between 5:1 and 50:1 with good codecs providing reasonable quality results at about 20:1 for typical video data.

Different codecs have been developed that differ according to which properties of an image are used to achieve compression. The most popular of the QuickTime codecs as of 1996 was Cinepak. The Cinepak codec is highly asymmetrical, taking significantly longer to compress a frame than it does to decompress it. For instance, compressing a 24-bit 640 x 480 image on a Macintosh Quadra class (68040) computer could take 150 times longer than decompressing it using Cinepak.

The storage requirements of video are especially important with CD-ROM, which has a limited bandwidth (data transfer rate) for playing back information. This was of particular concern with the first generation (single speed) CD-ROMs where the sustainable data transfer rate was in the order of 100-150K per second. Later CD-ROM drives provided much higher data transfer rates. For instance, a quadruple speed (4X) drive could play video back at from 500-600K per second. By 1996, 8X CD-ROM drives were available, with higher speed drives soon to be available, making it possible to present video at full frame rate (i.e., at the North American standard of 30 frames per second). At the same time, the storage size of CD-ROM was expanding from the initial 600 megabytes or so to multiple gigabytes in the DVD (digital video) standard. As full screen, broadcast quality video became the norm on desktop computers, and storage technologies (e.g., DVD) improved, the computer subsumed the role of the VCR as a video storage and playback device. It seems likely that the evolution of the computer as a multimedia appliance will continue in the future.

Multimedia has been, and is likely to continue to be, on the cutting edge of personal computing technology. Humans actively seek rich perceptual environments and multimedia is the vehicle through which new forms of computer-mediated perceptual experience are expressed. For instance, desktop video allows new forms of interaction with images and video and is a central component of multimedia. However, multimedia is not just concerned with media playback, but with the manipulation and exploration of perceptual worlds created through various combinations of media playback and computer animation.

One early and compelling example of exploration of a perceptual world was QuickTime VR. QuickTime VR is a technology for assembling a collection of images into a panoramic scene, or a three-dimensional view of an object. The images used to construct the object or scene are either photographed or rendered using computer graphics. The images are then composited (stitched together) to create the object or scene. The object or scene can then be played back with a QuickTime VR player. For instance, one early QuickTime VR scene showed the interior of the Winter Palace in St. Petersburg. Viewers can move through the palace. As they point with the mouse to the left of the screen, the view pans around to that portion of the scene, and so on.

The Winter Palace scene, and other QuickTime VR scenes are panoramic photographs representing the view that one would see by standing in a single spot called a node, and turning full circle. QuickTime VR also allow interactive objects to be embedded within scenes, and labelled by hot spots. Hot spots can trigger various actions such as playing a video or audio clip, or displaying text.

39.3.2 Standards and Formats

As of 1996, methods for representing the structure and content of multimedia were still evolving. The Dexter Reference Model (See Gronbaek and Trigg, 1994) grew out of work carried out in the hypertext and hypermedia communities. HyTime is an alternative approach that emphasized the time-based nature of multimedia elements.

Hypermedia/Time-based Structuring Language (HyTime) is an International Standard (ISO/IEC CD 10744). HyTime addressed the problem of hypertext linking, time scheduling, and synchronisation by providing basic identification and addressing mechanisms. However, HyTime failed to address higher level issues such as object content, link types, processing and presentation functions, and semantics. HyTime allowed for all elements of time-dependent documents to be synchronised. It focused on the timing and duration of digital media in hyperdocuments (multimedia). It avoided higher level issues such as semantics, and the layout or formatting of multimedia documents. HyTime is an SGML (Standard Generalized Mark-up Language) application conforming to the SGML International Standard (ISO 8879).

HTML (the HyperText Mark-up Language) is another SGML application. It describes multimedia documents in ASCII text. Media elements are stored in files and either connected to a particular document by links, or else embedded in the document (e.g., as an inline image) with references back to the file location where the original of the media element is stored. People who want to publish multimedia on the Web have to prepare their documents in HTML.

A survey of several thousand Web users carried out in April 1995 (GVU, 1995) found that most respondents claimed that it took them between one and six hours to learn HTML. Graham (1995) provides a good overview of HTML. There is also considerable information about HTML available on the Web itself. For instance, Torkington (1995) provides an introduction to the HyperText Mark-up Language (HTML). Other materials on HTML are also available on the Web and are referenced by Torkington (1995) and others. An equivalent standard for the definition of three-dimensional spatial representations on the Web, Virtual Reality Mark-up Language (VRML) is becoming increasingly widely used.

HTML provides a way of encoding document structure with a minimum of presentation information. HTML is a DTD (document type definition) of SGML. The DTD for HTML is also available on the Web (CERN, 1993). HTML consists of plain text with tags attached. As with other SGML document types, the tags are enclosed in angle brackets (<...>) and the names of the tags reflect the structure of the document. Some tags enclose headings (e.g., <H1>This is a heading at level 1</H1>), others delineate the title of the document (<TITLE>The Title</TITLE>), etc.

One of the trickiest operations in HTML editing is authoring multimedia links. The authoring of each link requires the following operations:

- choosing what information to link
- finding out where the information is located
- writing the link to that information as an HTML tag

Choosing what information to link is an information seeking and exploration task (Waterworth and Chignell, 1991; Marchionini, 1995). One may either have a reasonably firm target concept in mind and then search for it with queries, or else browse through information structures until interesting material is found. There are a number of tools for searching on the Web. These include the Webcrawler, and index servers such as Lycos (physically located at Carnegie-Mellon University) Harvest (physically located at the University of Colorado) and the Open Text index run by Open Text Corporation of Waterloo (Ontario, Canada). With millions of HTML documents available on the Web these search tools are under continuous development. Browsing on the Web for information to link to is also possible, but with the huge amount of information available it can be very time consuming. We have observed that people tend to use search tools more frequently as they get more experienced in "surfing" the Web.

The path to a document located elsewhere on the Internet is specified by a URL (Uniform Resource Locator). The URL is a text string that indicates the server protocol (HTTP, FTP, WAIS, etc.) to be used in accessing the resource, the Internet Domain Name of the server, and the location and name of the document being referenced on that server (Graham, 1995). Partial URLs may also be used to specify the location of the link document relative to the current document. Typing URLs into HTML hyperlinks is often frustrating, since typing errors, or forgetting about the full path information in the URL will produce an incorrect or "broken" link. In our experience, specifying hyperlinks is the most time consuming activity in HTML authoring. This has led to the development of drag and drop HTML editors that take much of the effort and frustration out of linking media elements and other documents to an HTML document. An example of such a tool is SGI's authoring tool, Web Magic.

Drag and drop link authoring greatly simplifies the task of writing hyperlinks in HTML documents. However, other tools are also needed to help people figure out what kind of information is available for linking to. Tools for visualising Web and file structure (Hasan et al, 1995) and concept structures may be particularly helpful for this task.

Standards and formats for representing multimedia are still evolving. As of 1996, the three main methods were the Dexter Reference Model, HyTime, and HTML. Of these, HTML appears to have the most momentum, because of its widespread use on the Web. It seems likely that HTML will evolve into a general representation model for document based multimedia. However, there is also clearly a need for a standard like HyTime which focuses on the synchronisation issues that arise in the stage (performance) model of multimedia.

39.4 User Interfaces And Interaction Issues

A multimedia user interface must provide a wide variety of easily understood and usable media control tools. In addition, informational views need to be integrated with structural views, since the viewing of information will often alternate with moving through the structure by one means or another.

There are a variety of different input devices and methods that can be used with multimedia. Input methods can also be combined in various ways to create dialogues or communication styles. For instance, one form of interaction in a graphical user interface is the dialogue box. Here the user selects from a number of different options (which may themselves generate nested dialogue boxes) until the parameters have been set appropriately and the "OK" button is pressed, or else the operation is aborted. Another form of interaction is the selection of items of choices from a menu structure. At a higher level of description, these detailed interaction methods may be incorporated within an interaction metaphor (e.g., the desktop metaphor).

Different methods of interaction are appropriate for different types of multimedia. One cannot expect a single interaction method, or even set of methods incorporated within a metaphor, to cover a range of different tasks and domains. Requesting information from a system, perhaps by means of a textual query in standard information retrieval style, is very different from exploring a visually presented 3- D scene, and requires different interaction methods and metaphors.

Navigation by the user is not easy, even using direct manipulation techniques, partly because of the number of dimensions that may be involved. For instance, one would provide controls to move up, down, left, right, in, out, show more detail, show less detail, and so on. The facility to browse around a knowledge base in a general way, collecting items of possible interest, is often desirable, especially for more creative activities such as putting together a promotional presentation. Usually, this type of browsing is provided as direct manipulation navigation by the user. Users follow pathways, open folders, choose from menu items, all in a direct manipulation manner. If the database is large, just tracking down the right general area to explore can be a time- and manipulation-intensive activity.

39.4.1 Multimedia Information Retrieval

With multimedia, we are often dealing with non-textual media. Even so, most approaches to retrieval are based on searching textual descriptions attached to the video, image or sound sample. The obvious way to request information from such a system is by textual description. But increasingly, multimedia systems will be developed with the aim of allowing non-textual information to be used directly, in a demonstrational manner. Even when text is present other media provide different, additional information. Also, when dealing with multimedia, users are naturally disposed to interact in ways other than those developed for text.

A first step to giving the user the impression that he is dealing directly with non-textual material allows database search on the basis of identifying images that best suit the user's purposes. An initial query that turns up a large number of images can be refined by allowing the user to point to a few images out of the set that contain items of interest. The system can then use the text descriptions attached to the chosen images to form a new query and offer a further set of possibly more relevant images. Although nothing much has changed from the perspective of the system, since text-based search is still being used, from the user's perspective he is interacting directly with images - he does not even have to think about how he would describe what he wants in words. Garber and Grunes (1992) present an example of this applied to the task of art directors selecting material for advertisements. The Picture Archival group at the Institute of Systems Science in Singapore has also developed similar capabilities (Ang et al, 1991).

A more directly demonstrational approach is also possible. Kato et al (1991) described a system that allows users to provide a sketch of a graphical item; essentially, this is a non-textual description. This is then used to locate similar figures stored in the database.

While the development of nontextual feature representations of video, image, and non-speech sound content is a current challenge, once the indexing problem is solved standard methods of information retrieval can be used (e.g., Salton and McGill, 1983). Many of the mathematical models for query matching apply to feature representations as well as text. Thus the technological problems associated with multimedia information retrieval are largely concerned with how to index multimedia objects appropriately. There are also significant issues concerning what user interfaces should be used for multimedia information retrieval.

One obvious strategy is to use direct manipulation to select objects that are similar to the ones of interest from menus (as described above). However, although such systems have been developed, there is little evidence about how well they work, or how well accepted they are by typical users. In using such systems, we have found the lack of explicit feedback about the current query a little unnerving. When a search goes well, one gets to the images or objects one wants and it almost seems like magic. When a search goes poorly, one seems to be going round in circles and it is unclear what search concepts are being inferred by the system based on the selections made.

39.4.2 Hyperlinking

In this section we focus on the non-linear aspects of

multimedia systems, from which arises the notorious "lost in hyperspace" problem (e.g.. Nielsen, 1990b). While non-linearity can be seen as liberating and powerful, it also places great demands on users to find their way around complex information spaces. How to alleviate these demands is the main issue in designing the HCI aspects of multimedia systems.

Multimedia interface designers have typically used a navigation/map metaphor, a menu/hierarchy metaphor, or a journal (sequence) metaphor. An example of the first strategy is the Virtual Museum, produced by Apple Computer. Here the user (visitor) accesses the multimedia information by navigating through the (virtual) museum, moving from room to room by selecting directions of movement. Examples of the second strategy include on-line encyclopaedias and electronic books where a table of contents is used to organise the material. An example of the third strategy is the CD-ROM "From Alice to Ocean". That multimedia document is organized as a journey from Alice Springs to the coast of Western Australia, with a map also being used to organise the material into a journey.

The power of multimedia resides in the rich linking of heterogeneous information sources. It enables authors to assemble, and readers to access, in one application, material that would otherwise only be available through consultation with physically or conceptually discrete information sources. Suitable applications for multimedia tend to integrate information that does not have a single common thread. In other words, simple unifying concepts to aid design may be hard to find. The challenge for the interface designer is to provide rich linking between heterogeneous information without confusing the user. Ideally, when users traverse a link they should have a good sense of where they have moved to and where they have come from. In practice, this means that regions within the multimedia or information space should be distinctive and recognisable. For instance, if one has links between rooms in a virtual museum, when users traverse one of those links they should know right away that they are in a different room, and they should have some idea of what the nature of that room is.

Because the material in a multimedia application will often be heterogeneous and therefore linked in a complex way, both authors and readers are required to take an active role in navigating the resultant structures; hence the need for sophisticated information tools. In a sense, multimedia interfaces place users directly within the informational structure they are creating or exploring. The need for this intimate involvement with structure complicates the issue of how interfaces for multimedia should be realised (see Evenson et al, 1989).

Unfortunately, people are not used to navigating around information spaces. The closest analogues are the book and the library, but neither of these traditional repositories of information allow rich linking between heterogeneous sources of information. However, books do provide powerful forms of navigation (McKnight, Dillon, and Richardson, 1991), and available evidence suggests that book-like styles of navigation may be preferred in multimedia, when they are available (Valdez and Chignell, 1992). Thus attempts have been made to develop electronic books that capture many of the aspects of traditional books (e.g., Benest et al, 1987). However, the book metaphor is often considerably enriched, as in the SuperBook project (Egan et al, 1989) where the features of book, hypertext, and information retrieval system are combined.

Multimedia interfaces attempt to create a model that is intelligible to users without unduly limiting the functionality of the tools provided. The search for adequate metaphors has been much less successful for multimedia than for other types of interface. The danger is that designing for ease of use may result in applications which no longer exhibit the power of multimedia to engage users actively in documents that are rich in both diversity of contents and complexity of structure.

The major problems of multimedia that have been alluded to in the literature (e.g., disorientation, lack of a suitable user interface metaphor, lack of an authoring paradigm, lack of a data model or standard linking typology) result from the fluid and virtual nature of multimedia documents. In contrast to earlier definitions of hypertext/multimedia as collections of nodes and links, multimedia is more profitably seen as heterogeneous information presented in the form of a virtual document. Understanding what a virtual document is will help greatly in future development of usable and effective multimedia.

One of the major innovations of multimedia is that it effectively unifies and integrates the document and the information system, at least conceptually. Links and pointers may be stored in a separate relational database but, functionally, moving through a multimedia document is equivalent to navigation in an information system. Much of the difficulty in devising suitable user interfaces for multimedia (cf. Waterworth and Chignell, 1989) arises from an unresolved mismatch between multimedia as document and multimedia as information system.

There are relatively few instances of successful

multimedia documents that exploit the full power of the technology currently available. Where multimedia has appeared to succeed it has been well-structured, carefully crafted (authored), and comparatively limited in extent (as for instance in "From Alice to Ocean", see the section on Authoring and Publishing, below). In other words, the successful instances of multimedia have tended to be multimedia documents, not multimedia information systems.

The notion of nonlinearity in hypertext is sometimes confused with the general responsiveness of electronic text. People have compared hypertext vs. hard copy but this really confounds two issues: linear vs. nonlinear, and hard copy vs. electronic. Linear features are functions that can be found in linearly-designed documents (whether in electronic or paper form). Examples of linear functions are: going to the table of contents, going to the index, flipping to the next or previous page, etc. Nonlinear functions have a different use: e.g., the users can "jump" to a different page in the document where more information on some topic of interest is presented to him.

Valdez (1992) developed methods for testing the usage of linear and nonlinear functions in books and hypertexts. His research showed that nonlinear functions (jumping between sections and chapters) are sometimes used just as frequently in printed documentation as they are in hypertext documentation. He also found individual differences, with some people tending to rely more on nonlinear functions, while others relied on linear functions. These results suggest that the intuitive idea that hypertexts are nonlinear and books are linear is incorrect. Linearity vs. nonlinearity is a function of the strategy a person uses in reading a material as much as it results from the particular structure or presentation of the material in the document.

The idea that people impose their navigational style on a document using whatever tools are available is also supported by the finding that with some linear texts, such as scientific journal articles, people frequently read the articles in a different order from the one in which they are written (Dillon, Richardson, and McKnight, 1988).

Since people tend to have different navigational styles, and they use whatever tools or cognitive prosthetics (Wright, 1991) are available, in most applications a judicious mixture of linear and non-linear structuring will work best (Parsaye and Chignell, 1993). For instance, a table of contents is extremely useful in a hypertext document and it seems counterproductive to deliberately exclude useful linear structures and tools from hypertext systems.

39.4.3 Handling Dynamic Media

In the days preceding writing (and this time period consumed the vast majority of the "life span" of our species, homo sapiens, up to this point), media were predominantly dynamic and ephemeral. Words were spoken and then lost to history. The only databases existed in human memory. Where words were preserved for any length of time, it was done so through the use of oral traditions where words were memorised and passed down from one person to another.

Multimedia is returning us to the dynamic media and oral tradition of thousands of years ago but with the major difference that the dynamic media can now be stored electronically. Dynamic media, such as speech, music, motion video, animations are arrayed in time (and in the case of the latter two, also in space). The temporal characteristics of dynamic media presentation are coming under the user's control. The reader/listener can play backwards as well as forwards, at varying speeds, through the dynamic media.

With sound data, we have the added difficulty that, not only may there be no text description (or a very inadequate one), but the sound itself is essentially invisible. Speech and sound are particularly difficult because they cannot be 'frozen' in time. A video can be held stationary while the viewer scans the contents of the display, but static speech or music has no meaning. Until we convert sound into some kind of graphical representation our methods of direct manipulation are wholly inapplicable to sound. We do not naturally 'look for sounds', we listen for and to them. When we want to describe a sound to others, we use sound to provide an example. If I want to ask you the title of a melody I am trying to identify, I am most likely to sing a few bars to you. This method can be used to locate sounds from a multimedia knowledge base. The user hums a tune, or even imitates a non-musical sound, and the system finds the nearest match. This kind of scenario is becoming more realistic as methods for automated pitch extraction and sound processing become more generally available (e.g., Arons, 1994).

A general issue with dynamic information is that of how we represent content in a way that makes sense to the user, that can be displayed in graphical form, and can be of utility in facilitating machine searches as part of the process whereby a user locates information of interest. What, for example, are the perceived dimensions of non-speech sound? Or of voices? If we can establish a mapping between user perception, graphical representation, and the way these items are stored in the knowledge base then this provides the basis for the system learning the way in which a particular user or set of users perceive and classify, say, human voices.

Motion video, with its captivating combination of action, realism and drama is inevitably going to play a significant role in a range of application areas, from games to computer-based learning to group work systems to sales promotions and real-time communications. At the moment, video is an optional addition to many systems. In the future, video may well become the primary medium of communication, with text and graphics serving as extra forms to support points made as a video presentation.

Integrated tools for dealing with information items in a variety of media - including video, sounds and still images - are already available. Built around a multimedia database system they allow items to be previewed, edited, and copied to form multimedia documents. Finding items from the database is achieved via text descriptions, and this is the major limitation to such applications. Another is the failure to provide adequate means for selecting and editing motion video segments.

New ways of handling video are needed to realise the full potential of the medium. A video sequence is generally a 'closed book' as far as computer applications are concerned; all that is known is its title, length and perhaps a few topic keywords that may have been added if someone has viewed the sequence in its entirety. Taking relatively long video sequences, editing into meaningful components, and cataloguing for later access are done manually and are labour intensive.

New tools began to appear from research labs in the early 1990s. Ueda et al (1993), for example, presented a system that integrated several new developments, such as automatic cut detection, object detection and tracking (to aid partitioning and cataloguing), and the use of micons (moving icons) and other visualisation techniques (to support browsing and manipulation of detected sequences).

The true integration of video into office and home computing systems will change the style of communication, in the same way that television and the 'sound bite' have changed the style of electioneering for government. While we may be saying essentially the same thing, using digital video will encourage us to argue for it in a different way - less logically, less on the basis of argument and debate, more dramatically, and emotionally, for immediate impact. This tendency is revealed in a recent emphasis on the commonalities between HCI design and theatre (Laurel, 1991; Tognazzini, 1993)

39.4.4 Input From User to System

The availability of a wide variety of media has so far tended to focus on the path from the computer system to the user. From the perspective of human computer interaction (HCI) the process is becoming rather lopsided. The user can view videos, hear sound files, listen to a synthesiser reading electronic mail, watch animations, read text and graphic displays; this is the output side of multimedia. On the input side (from user to computer), there is a distinction between input directly from the user, and input that is captured from external sources such as scanners, cameras, and microphones. While high bandwidth information can be captured from external sources, communication from human to computer is generally limited to typing and pointing with the mouse. Few multimedia systems yet incorporate multimodal input such as speech commands, gesture recognition, or eye movement detection. Thus current methods of detecting input directly from users severely limit the bandwidth of human expression, turning gestures into button presses; and speech, with all its inflections and subtleties, into keystrokes.

Requesting information from a system, perhaps by means of a textual query in standard information retrieval style, is very different from exploring a visually presented 3D scene. We need to expand the available repertoire of input technologies and learn which match particular purposes best. There are a variety of input methods which vary in terms of the number of dimensions of input they provide and the type of response mapping (e.g., Buxton, 1987). Other aspects of 3D controllers may have a significant effect on performance for different types of interactive task (Zhai, 1995).

Current input devices in general use tend to be 2D controllers (e.g., the mouse and the trackball). However, as 3D scenes become more widely used in multimedia, 3D controllers will become more prominent. While 3D controllers should be useful, it is still possible to define 3D input actions with inherently 2D controllers. One method is to augment a 2D controller such as a mouse with a secondary control (e.g., a thumbwheel). For instance, the mouse could control the X and Y dimensions, while the thumbwheel controls the Z dimension. The problem with this type of controller is that the thumbwheel is poorly integrated with the other controller actions.

An alternative approach (Venolia, 1993) is to redefine the behaviour of the mouse for a particular application. Imagine that a three-dimensional image or view is a spherical object. The user can then roll the sphere to the right by clicking on the right of the sphere, to the left by clicking on the left. The sphere can also be rolled backwards (away from the viewer) by clicking towards the top of it, or forwards (towards the viewer) by clicking near the bottom of it. Combinations of rolling can then be used to manipulate the scene or image into a desired position. Furthermore other actions such as zoom can be added with additional mouse buttons or as menu or toolbar options.

39.4.5 Visual Menus and Hotspots

Menus and hierarchies are powerful and popular tools for improving navigability of hypermedia by adding structure. The use of menu alternatives can provide a limited navigation facility even in the absence of visualisation. Menu alternatives may be displayed in a number of different ways. In the HyperTies system (Shneiderman and Kearsley, 1989), for instance, menus are embedded in text and menu items are indicated as bold-faced items. Replacement buttons in Guide (Brown, 1987) also serve as embedded menu items. In other approaches, visual menus are used where menu icons are embedded within a visual scene, much as menu items may be embedded as words or phrases within text.

The SuperBook project (Remde, Gomez, and Landauer, 1987) showed how navigation can be achieved through non-spatial structures. In this case the book metaphor includes selecting information through index and table of contents. As Remde et al point out, this approach has the advantage that SuperBook is able to access existing documents while most hypermedia systems require authoring of new information structures.

In other systems, trees (hierarchies) are often used to convey the overall structure of a portion of hypermedia. Trees are used, for instance, in the NoteCards browser (Halasz, Moran, and Trigg, 1987). Trees allow nodes to be organising into categories that are nested at different levels of abstraction. Nodes can then be directly selected from the browser, i.e., the map of the tree structure. Selectable tree systems (browsers) are a good method of visualising hypermedia. Browse trees are an explicit representation of the hierarchical representation that is otherwise available in a table of contents. However, recent evidence suggests that presentation of three-dimensional visualisations of trees may actually impair learning of information structure in some circumstances (Poblete, 1995).

Webs (but not "The Web"!) are a refinement of the tree or network visualising techniques, where links may be filtered according to context or interests. Intermedia webs (Yankelovich, Haan, and Meyrowitz, 1988) are an implementation of this concept. Webs are an example of a general principle that users should only have to view the subset of links and nodes that are of interest to them. Methods for using inference to dynamically construct or reconfigure hypermedia based on criteria such as the purpose of browsing or user interests are discussed elsewhere (Parsaye, Chignell, Khoshafian, and Wong, 1989, Sections 5.6 and 7.2.6).

39.4.6 Information Visualisation and Information Structure

One of the major impacts of advances in computer graphics (Foley et al, 1990) has been an increase in the use of visualizations in simulation, modelling, and a wide variety of other applications. Scientific visualizations help researchers envision large data sets using various graphs and models (Brooks, 1988). They also accommodate the human preference for viewing and manipulating information in a visual format, including highly automatised processes such as visual pattern recognition and feature extraction and integration (Lindsay and Norman, 1977). Visualisations can also enhance user interfaces and highlight important information. The fisheye lens model (Furnas, 1986), for instance, is motivated by the observation that humans often represent their own neighbourhood in great detail, yet only indicate major landmarks for more distant regions. This phenomenon can be demonstrated both within a city and across larger geographic regions. It also reflects the functioning of the human eye, where closer objects are seen in more detail.

Visualizations are becoming an important method for displaying information associated with a range of domains including; scientific models, business data, and information structure. Research suggests that the representation used can influence how people perceive information structure and navigate through that structure (e.g., Woods, 1984). If an information presentation is very cluttered and disorganised, then the user has a difficult time understanding the system. This is especially true if the presentation does not resemble the system it is representing. If users do not already have a strong mental model of the system, then they will generally base their cognitive representation on the layout or the type of information used in the presentation. The general rule of thumb is that the representation used to present information should be compatible with structures and metaphors already familiar to the user (Staples, 1993).

One common way of representing information structure is the hierarchy. The familiar table of con-

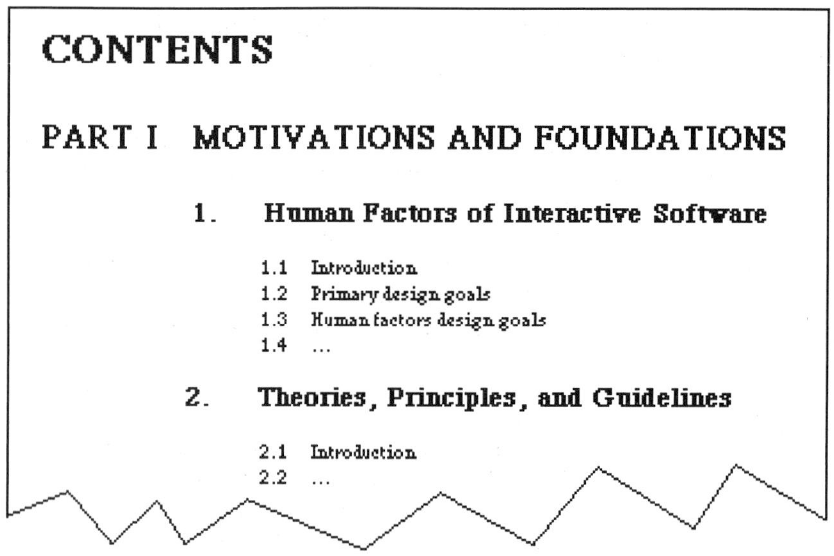

Figure 4. A table of contents hierarchy. *(after Poblete, 1995, Figure 2.1)*

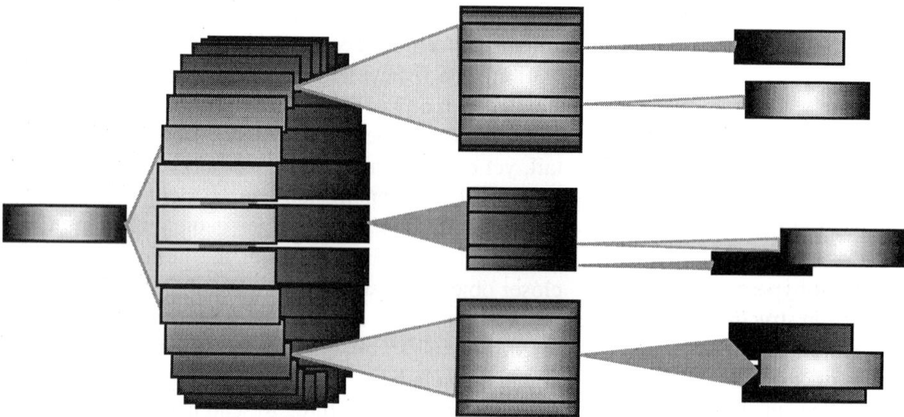

Figure 5 . Cone tree. *(this figure originally appeared as Figure 2.3 in Poblete, 1995)*

tents in a book, for instance, is a hierarchy. A hierarchical display of information can be thought of as a map of that information, showing points of interest and connecting paths. Hierarchies allow for quick browsing of information using a visual search (e.g., Neisser, 1967). They are used in multimedia to show the organization of information, and to allow users to select topics. Thus hierarchies serve as both information overviews and as access points for exploration.

Figure 4 shows a standard table of contents layout (taken from the table of contents of Shneiderman, 1987). Indentation is used to indicate the different levels of the hierarchy.

Hierarchies can also be represented in a tree format. With three-dimensional graphics, hierarchies can now be presented as three-dimensional objects. Figure 5 shows a schematic representation of a three-dimensional hierarchical model as a cone tree.

Another presentation of hierarchical structure is the two dimensional display TreeMap (Johnson, 1993; Shneiderman, 1992), where the parent-child relationships are shown as rectangles nested within rectangles. In addition, the size of the rectangles can be used to indicate a feature of the information (e.g., the amount of disk space occupied by the corresponding file directory).

According to Anderson (1985), it is the manner in which information is processed, rather than the motivation of the subject, that determines how much is learned. In information visualisation and exploration, incidental (or unintentional) learning could greatly facilitate navigation by allowing the subject to learn about the structure and organization of the information while they are consciously doing another task.

Poblete (1995) studied the extent to which watching versus manipulation of hierarchical structure promotes learning of information structure in a question answering task. He tested learning of information structure by asking subjects to sort the information into a hierarchical structure after the question answering task was completed. Any such learning was presumably unintentional or incidental, since subjects were not told that they would be required to do the sorting task.

In one experiment Poblete compared the effectiveness of two conditions for presenting three-dimensional drum-shaped hierarchies on the computer. The two conditions varied in terms of the interaction methods used, with one condition using animation and the other using direct manipulation of the tree via rotation. In addition, the learning effect for both of these conditions was compared with a control condition where there was no opportunity for learning. In a second experiment he contrasted interaction with a physical model of the 3D hierarchy that the subjects could touch and manipulate with a menuing style of interaction using a 2D hierarchy. In this latter condition, only one branch of the hierarchy was visible at a time. To see a different branch, the subjects had to back up to the appropriate node and then work their way down the new branch (at which point the branch that they were previously on was no longer shown).

Poblete (1995) found no evidence of learning of information structure in the conditions that used drum-shaped 3D hierarchies (either computer generated or on a physical drum) to present the information. In contrast, the 2D menuing interaction did produce a significant amount of learning. These results suggest the need for a cautious approach in implementing new information visualisation techniques. In particular, we cannot expect incidental learning of information structure to occur simply because that structure is displayed as a realistic and manipulable three-dimensional object. It seems likely that the interaction methods used, and the associated cognitive processing that is required, may be key determinants of what is learned about information structures as people manipulate visualizations of them in performing different tasks.

39.5 Authoring And Publishing Multimedia

The usability and functionality of multimedia is determined to some extent by the user interface, but also by a number of other factors including the quality of the content material and the quality of the authoring process. Since they have a major impact on usability, methods of multimedia authoring and development are also of concern to the discipline of human-computer interaction.

The task of creating multimedia presentations is poorly understood, and is referred to as "authoring". It is not at all clear what multimedia authoring involves. The term is somewhat confusing, since authors write books, but multimedia authoring involves very little writing, at least in the traditional sense of authoring text. Multimedia authoring seems to be more a process of selecting material and stitching it together into an aesthetically pleasing whole.

There is a useful distinction to be made between 'multimedia in the large' and 'multimedia in the small'. It is difficult to say exactly what the boundaries of multimedia in the small are, but one provisional definition is that small scale multimedia contains no more than 10,000 significant pieces of information (e.g., not including figure captions), where each piece of information may be a picture, text, video, sound, animation, etc. 10,000 pieces of information may sound like a lot, but limiting multimedia to just a few thousand information fragments is like limiting the amount of RAM in an operating system to 640K. Sooner or later the need for more capacity will become obvious.

On a small scale, it is quite possible to create exquisite multimedia presentations with content material specially created from scratch. One good example of this is the CD "From Alice to Ocean" created after a trek through the Australian outback that was sponsored by the National Geographic Society. "From Alice to Ocean" contains original photos, maps, video, and text within a carefully crafted presentation. Even within the scope of a 600 MB CD, "From Alice to Ocean" must have required considerable authoring effort.

How are we going to make the jump from multimedia in the small to multimedia in the large, where the handcrafting approach to multimedia authoring is no longer feasible? This transition can only be made with a new set of support tools for authoring, and possibly a redefinition of what the authoring process involves.

Designing multimedia within a consistent framework (e.g., using standard templates and style guides), and increase usability of the multimedia, since a consistent presentation format will generally make the content material easier to browse and assimilate.

Links and overview and search tools can also be used to make navigation easy and effective. Visualizing a multimedia document or application is particularly important for multimedia developers, and this problem is receiving attention, with particular respect to the Web. For instance, there are a number of products for visualizing and modifying Web sites, including WebAnalyzer, from InContext Corporation. Thus implementation may include the addition of special maps, overviews, tables of contents, etc.

The usablity of multimedia should be evaluated just like any other software application. Evaluation of usability should be done early and often in the development process. However, as the size of multimedia applications grows it is becoming increasingly difficult to assess their usability. With particularly large multimedia documents the concept of overall usability tends to break down, since there is usually sufficient heterogeneity of content and format within the document that it makes more sense to talk about the usability of portions of the document rather than the whole.

The advent of multimedia complicates the informational structures to which users have access. Different media are often associated with each other in relation to a particular topic, and will tend to be cross-connected over several different topics. Research into the usability of hypermedia points out the difficulties users can experience when trying to navigate their way through richly interlinked information in a variety of forms. It is hard to get a feel for the overall structure, hard to know which links to profitably traverse, hard to find a given item of information a second time, and hard to know if all relevant items have been located.

A clear, explicit representation of structure is needed to overcome these problems, particularly with voluminous sources of information. The user needs to have an impression of the knowledge base as a whole (what is where?) and locally, in relation to this whole (where am I?). With multimedia, understanding and navigating the structure of information is intimately related to monitoring, finding and collecting information.

39.5.1 Multimedia Authoring Tools

Multimedia development began as a highly crafted activity. Early examples of multimedia were often insubstantial and flashy, requiring a great deal of effort to develop, or else were well produced, but extremely costly to make. As multimedia development evolved into a more mature activity, there was considerable pressure to reduce costs of development and to improve the quality of the resulting product.

General purpose multimedia development started with programming environments that were "media-aware". Special functions were available for playing back video and audio from disk or from a peripheral device, and for creating hyperlinks. The first of the media-aware environments was HyperCard, launched by Apple in 1987. HyperCard was really a collection of tools, including paint tools, user interface development tools (menus, buttons, etc.), and a scripting language (HyperTalk). While multimedia applications could be built, HyperCard had no inherent model of multimedia or hypertext. HyperCard was followed a couple of years later by ToolBook, a similar product that ran on the Windows platform. Other more traditional programming languages were also extended with various tools to facilitate multimedia development. A good example of this trend was Visual Basic, which in the early 1990s became a tool for both interface prototyping and multimedia development.

Authorware and Director are more specialised tools for multimedia development. Authorware was intended for development of computer based training materials using flowcharting structures. In contrast, Director used a stage metaphor and emphasized the orchestra of different multimedia events as "actors" on the "stage".

The period from 1987 to 1993 may be regarded as the formative years of multimedia. Around 1993, two things happened which had a major impact on how multimedia is created and used. First, there was the penetration of the CD-ROM into the consumer market. Although Microsoft had organized a major CD-ROM developer conference back in 1986, it took several years for the obvious potential of CD-ROM to start paying off on a large scale. By 1993, prices of CD-ROM readers had fallen to a few hundred dollars and healthy sales meant that there was now a large installed base of drives, providing the critical mass needed for large scale CD-ROM publishing. The age of multimedia was also signalled by the growing practice of selling computers with built-in CD-ROM drives. While Macintosh computers had to some extent always been "multimedia ready", PC hardware and software manufacturers now rushed to provide multimedia capability for the Windows computing market.

In contrast to the coming of age of CD-ROM which had long been anticipated, the second event in

1993 was totally unexpected, at least by most people. In one of those surprising twists that seem to be characteristic of the history of computing, one of the major revolutions in multimedia was initiated at CERN, the European high energy particle physics laboratory located in Switzerland. This revolution was called the "World Wide Web" (the Web) and was facilitated by the HTML mark-up language and the HTTP protocol as methods for publishing multimedia documents, interlinking them around the world, and making them available over the Internet (see the earlier section on Standards and Formats for more details of HTML and HTTP). The Web and HTML emphasise a document-oriented approach to multimedia that contrasts sharply with the stage and orchestration metaphor that was dominant in the early years of multimedia.

Recently, there has been a growing emphasis on the development of specialised computing languages that can generate different types of multimedia authoring tools and environments. An example of this type of language is ScriptX, a product of Kaleida labs. Apple and IBM formed Kaleida Labs in 1992. Version 1.0 of ScriptX was released across a variety of platforms, including Macintosh and Windows, in 1995. Kaleida's multimedia authoring platform consisted of three elements: the Kaleida Media Player, the ScriptX Language and Class Library and ScriptX application development and authoring tools.

The Kaleida Media Player (KMP) provided a complete programming interface for presenting media, creating user interface elements, storing and retrieving data and managing memory. The programming interface for the KMP was both hardware and operating system independent. The Kaleida Media Player enabled multimedia developers to write one version of an application targeted at the KMP, instead of many versions targeted at various operating systems. The ScriptX Language and Class Library (ScriptX) provided object-oriented development tools for multimedia. Using ScriptX, applications could be developed for KMP.

ScriptX was a platform for creating multimedia authoring tools. As software moves from monolithic applications to componentware, we can expect multimedia development to involve the co-ordination of a variety of software tools and packages. This could already be seen in the early 1990s with a typical multimedia development project requiring tools such as Premiere, PhotoShop, Word, SoundEditor, and Director, among others.

Although it is hard to predict exactly how multimedia development tools will progress in the future, we can make some reasonable assumptions about the tools that will be required based on earlier experience with hypertext and other technologies. Tasks in authoring hypertexts that benefit from the use of tools include; outlining, indexing, listing or visualisation of links and nodes, and retrieval on information from a pool of content material. Tools for performing such tasks are also useful in multimedia development, along with tools for media capture, editing, and organization.

39.5.2 Free Form Multimedia

As we noted earlier, hypermedia is the hyperlinking, or non-linear aspect of multimedia. One of the unresolved problems for multimedia/hypermedia is what sorts of linking models and typologies should be used. For instance, should there be one set of standard link types, or should developers be free to "roll their own" as required"? Perhaps the best solution may be to have a common set of standard link types which can be supplemented with non-standard link types that are created as needed to meet the requirements of particular tasks and application domains.

There is a continuum of hyperlinking strategies, from situations where all links are left untyped, to situations where some links are typed as needed, to situations where all links must have types selected from a standard set of link types. Recently, "free-form" multimedia has been defined where links are untyped from the system's point of view, but are treated by users as if they are typed, by inferring semantics on the basis of visual anchors attached to the links.

Free-form multimedia (Brown, 1993; Brown and Chignell, 1995) is a style of multimedia where nodes and links can be "typed" according to the shared intentions of authors and readers. This typing is carried out by attaching visual labels (icons) to links, rather than by using a software language construct for typing. The "behaviour" of the multimedia is then determined by the particular combination of nodes and links that are used, and the way in which link labels are interpreted by the readers/users. Developers and authors are then free to find the form of information structure (or lack thereof) that best suits the application (or family of applications) being developed.

Early hypertext and multimedia systems provided some, but by no means all of the functionality of free-form multimedia. For instance, Intermedia (Smith, 1988) provided a prodigious number of link types and documents types that made it essentially unrestricted in scope. However, it relied on the classical division of different application software distinguishing different document types, thereby reinforcing the division be-

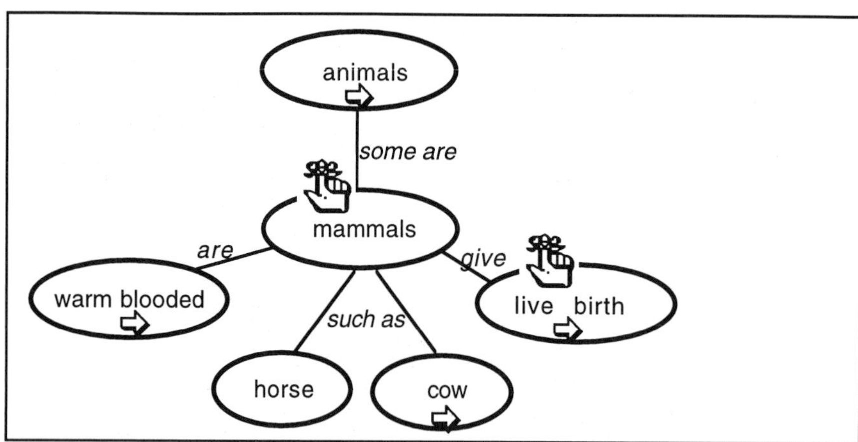

This anchor links to notes on the concept

This anchor links to the part of the network centered on that concept

Figure 6. Use of free form multimedia to create semantic structures. *(after Figure 4 in Brown and Chignell, 1995).*

tween information content and information structure. The notion of a Box in the BOXER program (diSessa, 1985) also provided some free form functionality. The box is a generalised container, that may hold different kinds of entities, from pictures to program script fragments.

Free-form multimedia (Brown, 1993) depends primarily on three operational characteristics:

1. An unrestricted node model. A node can represent anything - a document, a concept, a physical entity, a diagram, an index, etc.
2. An open-ended linking facility. Links have unrestricted semantics that allow users to develop specific links for different situations, or use them as undistinguished link types.
3. An easy-to-use linking mechanism, without any additional overhead for specifying link semantics.

Brown developed the Anchors Aweigh system to demonstrate some of the principles of free form multimedia. To construct a link in Anchors Aweigh, the user selects from a palette of anchors and then clicks the mouse at the two desired locations (start point and end point) for the link anchors. The link anchor palette allows quick access to alternative anchor icons during link creation. Selecting an anchor symbol from the palette invokes the "stamp tool" and the cursor changes from a hand (signifying browse mode) to a stamp (signifying link authoring mode).

Once the link has been constructed (i.e., the start and end points have been selected) the user returns to browse mode with the cursor changing back from the stamp tool to the hand browser. To browse a link, the user then clicks at an existing anchor and the node of the other associated anchor (i.e., the other end of the link) appears. The basic link operations use only point-and-click mouse operations. No keyboarding or menus are involved. Sound, highlighting, and cursor shape provide feedback regarding what operation the user is performing, and help the user locate anchors and nodes. Brown's (1993) experience indicated that users found this mechanism simple and obvious.

Providing too much structure for authors may inhibit their own interpretation and understanding of the material. Free-form multimedia environments allow users to generate information structures themselves. An example of how this capability is realised is shown by a node depicted in Figure 6. The node shown there is part of a concept network in which each node or frame shows one central concept and a number of attached concepts.

Attached concepts have similar frames which can be accessed by following the appropriate link. For example, in the case of Figure 6, we can activate a link to bring us to the part of the network centred on the "animals" concept. Thus, the arrow-shape anchor becomes integrated into this specific semantic form, and becomes a navigation tool for traversing the concept-net. Link labels can be combined with images in nodes to create the appearance of specialised data structures. Figure 6 shows how Anchors Aweigh can be used to construct a semantic network without the semantics.

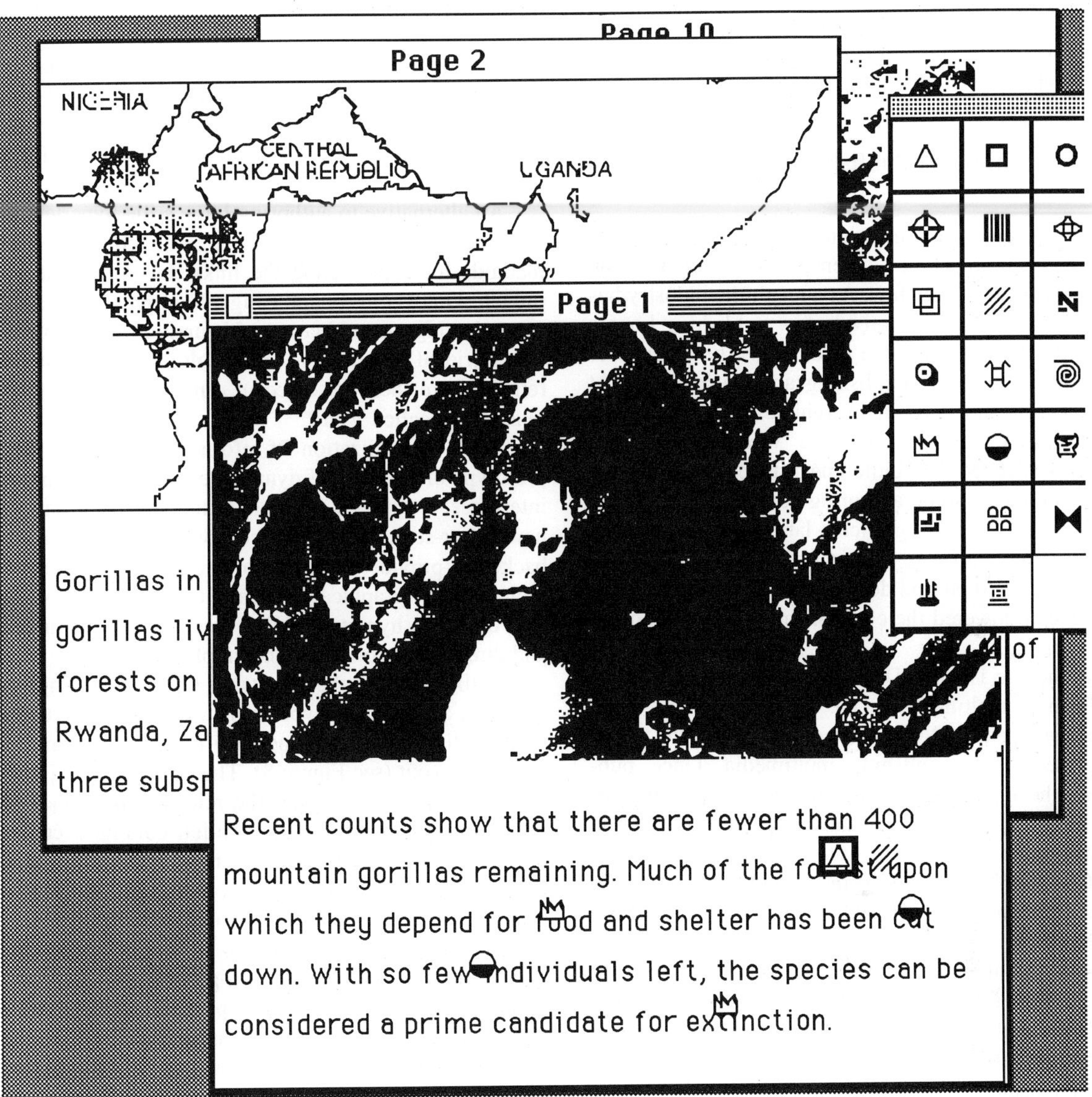

Figure 7. A Screen shot from Anchors Aweigh showing labeling of links with abstract symbols. *(Figure 3 in Brown and Chignell, 1995).*

In some experiments with Anchors Aweigh, Brown (Brown and Chignell, 1993) used meaningless abstract symbols to study naive use of linking. Figure 7 shows a screen shot of an application where Anchors Aweigh is used in this fashion. Use of abstract symbols makes it possible to investigate what meanings subjects generate spontaneously. For the data shown in Figure 7, the triangle symbol was denoted by the subject to mean "location".

Authors can extend free form multimedia by adding new types of links and nodes, or by adding commentaries or notations not previously available. A user can also develop a new kind of navigation tool in free-form multimedia, rather than being constrained to the particular fixed tools provided by the software.

Free-form multimedia appears to work well in certain kinds of (constructivist) educational settings and in areas where simple application development by end users is appropriate. However, there are other situations where more formal models of multimedia may be appropriate.

39.5.3 Multimedia Publishing

Traditional publishing has significant barriers to entry. Printing equipment is expensive, and distribution channels are relatively few. As a result the industry has been dominated by a relatively few publishing houses that publish books in large quantities. The barriers to entry for multimedia publishing are much lower. At present there are two main vehicles for multimedia publishing: CD-ROMs, and the World Wide Web (Web). CD-ROMs are quite cheap to produce, requiring a computer, some authoring software, and a CD-writing drive. While significant labour is required, the hardware and software is fairly cheap, costing in the order of a few thousand dollars. Publishing multimedia on the Web lowered the costs of multimedia authoring even further.

In the late 1980s, CD-ROM emerged as a preferred platform for multimedia. In the early 1990s, this "write once, read many" (WORM) medium became the dominant method of publishing multimedia. Once published, the multimedia was available as read-only information. Thus early multimedia did not encourage annotation, extension, or customisation by the user.

One problem with multimedia publishing on CD-ROM was distribution. How do you get the CD-ROM to the people who want it? In some cases this may not be a concern. For instance, if one is producing a corporate training manual on CD-ROM, then one probably knows who the target audience is. In other cases, e.g., publishing an interactive novel, distribution can be a real concern. Publishing multimedia on the Internet reduced the transportation and distribution problem. People could simply come to someone's site and read the multimedia document as part of their browsing (surfing). The problem now was one of getting noticed, so that people would come to one's site in the first place.

While there are still problems to be solved in multimedia publishing, there will be many more people publishing multimedia than there will be publishing books. One can already see this on the Web. There are millions of documents on the Web, and their number is rising rapidly. With all this multimedia publishing activity going on, an efficient process for creating multimedia is needed, along with a set of tools to facilitate that process.

39.5.4 Dynamic Hypertext

The world-wide Web is one solution to the problem of creating a large scale multimedia document. In the case of the Web, the hundreds of thousands of authors have made a chaotic network of documents with little if any global coherence.

An alternative to authoring large scale hypertext or multimedia by many authors is to create computational methods for constructing the links. In one recent approach (Golovchinsky and Chignell, in press), links are created using a combination of heuristics and information retrieval algorithms. The resulting nodes that are retrieved are then presented in a newspaper interface, in a system called VOIR.

VOIR (Visualization Of Information Retrieval) is a prototype of a family of dynamic electronic newspaper interfaces. It supports multiple article presentation in a newspaper-style interface, incorporates graphical feedback, and provides a variety of browsing mechanisms, including two graphical Boolean query notations, static and dynamic hypertext links, free-format text input, and direct interaction with the graphical displays.

VOIR displays the results of users' browsing requests in a newspaper-type format. Up to eight articles may be displayed simultaneously in a four column by two row layout (see Figure 8). The position and size of each column correlate with the relative importance of the corresponding article: the top-left column occupies the most space and displays the most important article (as determined through relevance ranking). Article importance decreases from left to right and from top to bottom. When more than eight articles must be displayed, articles are divided into groups of eight. Each group is displayed on a separate page, and the user may flip among the pages by using a slider or the next/previous buttons. The slider and the buttons are disabled when only one page is available.

Users can specify search topics by typing a phrase or set of keywords into the query input field, or by selecting an arbitrary passage in an article. The system retrieves a collection of relevant articles and displays the first eight articles (i.e., those ranked one through eight) on the screen. It then identifies anchor candidates among the keywords provided by the user, and highlights these anchors in the text. Terms are selected based on their ability to discriminate among articles (e.g., using the inverse document frequency, Salton and McGill, 1983). It selects terms that occur frequently in a few documents, thereby establishing statistically-likely connections among documents.

Context-specific links are used to create the dy-

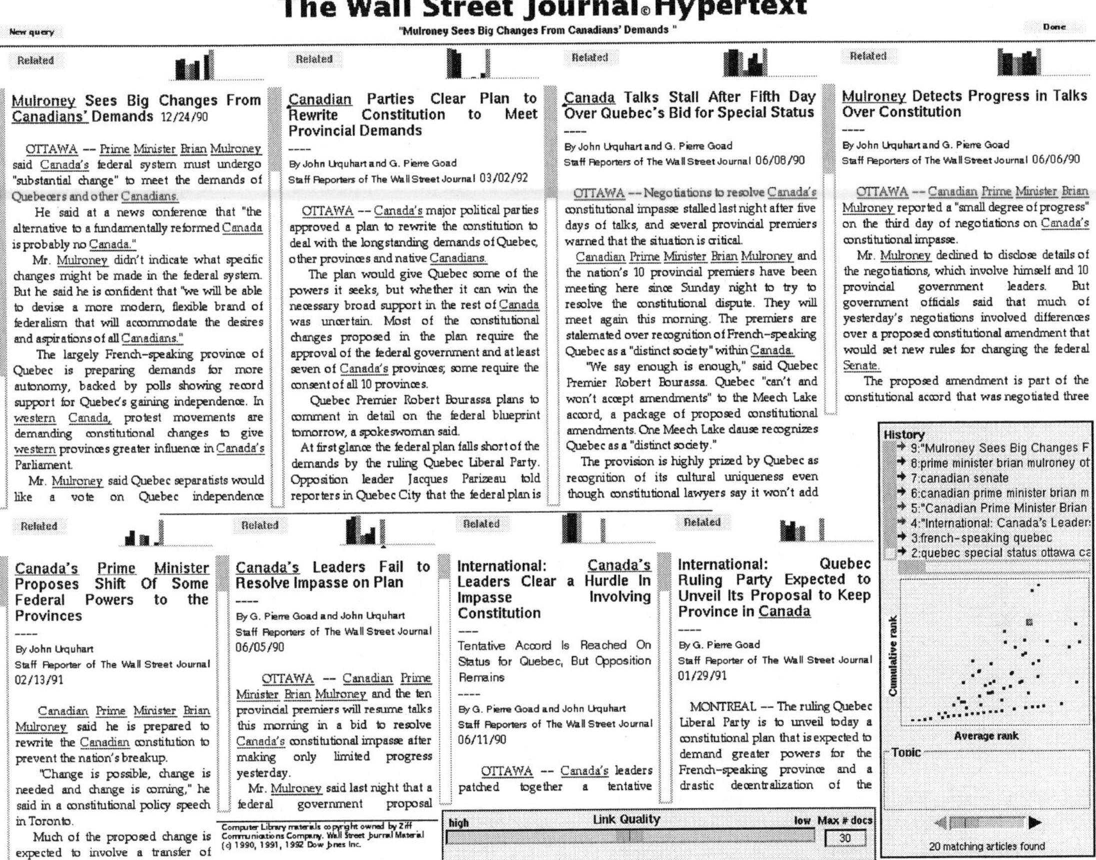

The Wall Street Journal© Hypertext

New query — "Mulroney Sees Big Changes From Canadians' Demands" — Done

Related

Mulroney Sees Big Changes From Canadians' Demands 12/24/90

OTTAWA -- Prime Minister Brian Mulroney said Canada's federal system must undergo "substantial change" to meet the demands of Quebecers and other Canadians.

He said at a news conference that "the alternative to a fundamentally reformed Canada is probably no Canada."

Mr. Mulroney didn't indicate what specific changes might be made in the federal system. But he said he is confident that "we will be able to devise a more modern, flexible brand of federalism that will accommodate the desires and aspirations of all Canadians."

The largely French-speaking province of Quebec is preparing demands for more autonomy, backed by polls showing record support for Quebec's gaining independence. In western Canada, protest movements are demanding constitutional changes to give western provinces greater influence in Canada's Parliament.

Mr. Mulroney said Quebec separatists would like a vote on Quebec independence

Related

Canadian Parties Clear Plan to Rewrite Constitution to Meet Provincial Demands

----

By John Urquhart and G. Pierre Goad
Staff Reporters of The Wall Street Journal 03/02/92

OTTAWA -- Canada's major political parties approved a plan to rewrite the constitution to deal with the longstanding demands of Quebec, other provinces and native Canadians.

The plan would give Quebec some of the powers it seeks, but whether it can win the necessary broad support in the rest of Canada was uncertain. Most of the constitutional changes proposed in the plan require the approval of the federal government and at least seven of Canada's provinces; some require the consent of all 10 provinces.

Quebec Premier Robert Bourassa plans to comment in detail on the federal blueprint tomorrow, a spokeswoman said.

At first glance the federal plan falls short of the demands by the ruling Quebec Liberal Party. Opposition leader Jacques Parizeau told reporters in Quebec City that the federal plan is

Related

Canada Talks Stall After Fifth Day Over Quebec's Bid for Special Status

----

By John Urquhart and G. Pierre Goad
Staff Reporters of The Wall Street Journal 06/08/90

OTTAWA -- Negotiations to resolve Canada's constitutional impasse stalled last night after five days of talks, and several provincial premiers warned that the situation is critical.

Canadian Prime Minister Brian Mulroney and the nation's 10 provincial premiers have been meeting here since Sunday night to try to resolve the constitutional dispute. They will meet again this morning. The premiers are stalemated over recognition of French-speaking Quebec as a "distinct society" within Canada.

"We say enough is enough," said Quebec Premier Robert Bourassa. Quebec "can't and won't accept amendments" to the Meech Lake accord, a package of proposed constitutional amendments. One Meech Lake clause recognizes Quebec as a "distinct society."

The provision is highly prized by Quebec as recognition of its cultural uniqueness even though constitutional lawyers say it won't add

Related

Mulroney Detects Progress in Talks Over Constitution

By John Urquhart and G. Pierre Goad
Staff Reporters of The Wall Street Journal 06/06/90

OTTAWA -- Canadian Prime Minister Brian Mulroney reported a "small degree of progress" on the third day of negotiations on Canada's constitutional impasse.

Mr. Mulroney declined to disclose details of the negotiations, which involve himself and 10 provincial government leaders. But government officials said that much of yesterday's negotiations involved differences over a proposed constitutional amendment that would set new rules for changing the federal Senate.

The proposed amendment is part of the constitutional accord that was negotiated three

History
9:"Mulroney Sees Big Changes F
8:prime minister brian mulroney ot
7:canadian senate
6:canadian prime minister brian m
5:"Canadian Prime Minister Brian
4:"International: Canada's Leader:
3:french-speaking quebec
2:quebec special status ottawa ca

Related

Canada's Prime Minister Proposes Shift Of Some Federal Powers to the Provinces

----

By John Urquhart
Staff Reporter of The Wall Street Journal 02/13/91

Canadian Prime Minister Brian Mulroney said he is prepared to rewrite the Canadian constitution to prevent the nation's breakup.

"Change is possible, change is needed and change is coming," he said in a constitutional policy speech in Toronto.

Much of the proposed change is expected to involve a transfer of

Related

Canada's Leaders Fail to Resolve Impasse on Plan

By G. Pierre Goad and John Urquhart
Staff Reporters of The Wall Street Journal 06/05/90

OTTAWA -- Canadian Prime Minister Brian Mulroney and the ten provincial premiers will resume talks this morning in a bid to resolve Canada's constitutional impasse after making only limited progress yesterday.

Mr. Mulroney said last night that a federal government proposal

Computer Library materials copyright owned by Ziff Communications Company. Wall Street Journal Material (c) 1990, 1991, 1992 Dow Jones Inc.

Related

International: Canada's Leaders Clear a Hurdle In Impasse Involving Constitution

----

Tentative Accord Is Reached On Status for Quebec, But Opposition Remains

----

By G. Pierre Goad and John Urquhart
Staff Reporters of The Wall Street Journal 06/11/90

OTTAWA -- Canada's leaders patched together a tentative

Related

International: Quebec Ruling Party Expected to Unveil Its Proposal to Keep Province in Canada

----

By G. Pierre Goad
Staff Reporter of The Wall Street Journal 01/29/91

MONTREAL -- The ruling Quebec Liberal Party is to unveil today a constitutional plan that is expected to demand greater powers for the French-speaking province and a drastic decentralization of the

Figure 8. A screenshot showing the newspaper interface in the VOIR system

namic hypertext. When the user selects an imbedded anchor by clicking on it, the system constructs a weighted-term query based on the selected anchor, its immediate context and the prior history of the user's browsing. VOIR uses the sentence as the unit of context. The terms comprising the selected anchor are given the highest weight. The rest of the anchors in the sentence and anchor candidates (see below) are given the next highest weight, followed by the rest of the terms in the sentence, followed by the global context. The global context consists of all anchors of the past three links. It provides additional stability to the query, controlling the effect of ambiguous sentences. The context is limited to three links to allow the user to evolve the topic of interest over time.

When an anchor is selected, all capitalized words in that sentence become candidates for anchors. This heuristic is based on the assumption that capitalized words represent proper names and thus may be used to identify related articles.

The current version of VOIR works with a database of 75,000 articles (about 250 megabytes of text). In principle a system can be scaled up to databases of arbitrary size, limited mainly by the capacity of the underlying information retrieval engine to carry out searches quickly enough. We expect that systems like VOIR may also be used in the future to construct large dynamic multimedia documents.

39.6 Emerging Trends in Multimedia Interaction

In this section we highlight three dominant trends that are emerging in the development of systems for multimedia interaction: (i) the use of visualisation techniques, especially those based on three-dimensional spatial representation, to convey structural information about a multimedia collection; (ii) the increasing tendency for multimedia systems to provide the flexibility to allow the same information to be experienced in different media, and thus through different sensory channels, which has been referred to as the development of 'synaesthetic media'; and finally (iii) 'cybermedia', the result of the trend for multimedia information spaces increasingly to be shared by many users, and used for purposes of social interaction as well as for information publishing and access.

39.6.1 Promoting Familiarity and Memorability with Visualisation and Space

When reading a book, we often go through an orientation process where the book starts off seeming strange and unfamiliar, and then becomes more familiar to us as we read through it and absorb the narrative structure. By the end of the book the characters often seem both familiar and memorable. Multimedia often doesn't have the same degree of linearity and narrative structure as a book.

Although the problem of visualising multimedia structures is a new one, visualisation itself is a topic with a long history. Disciplines such as geography, statistics, maths modelling, architecture, and anthropology have explored and used visualising formalisms successfully. Techniques for visualisation have been described by Tufte (1983, 1990) and others. Brooks (1988) has reviewed some of the work on visualisation in scientific modelling and methods for navigating around spatial representations of information have also been discussed (e.g., Hammond and Allinson, 1988; Fairchild, Poltrock, and Furnas, 1988).

In spite of this history of visual representation in other scientific disciplines, the visualisation of multimedia poses some unique problems due to the need for the user to navigate within a complex and often unfamiliar structure (unless we are dealing with very restricted set of items). Perhaps the most difficult problem is that of mapping the conceptual space of information onto some 'physical' (i.e. three-dimensional) and visualisable representation. One of the most intuitively appealing methods of visual representation is to represent a hypermedia network as a three-dimensional structure. The user may then move around inside this structure much as they would inside a physical space, but using the mouse to navigate in a way that is analogous to driving or flying in physical space.

The use of a three-dimensional network for visualisation was explored in the SemNet project at MCC (Fairchild, Poltrock, and Furnas, 1988). The goals of this project were to allow users to navigate around knowledge bases. Techniques were explored such as using motion parallax to induce a feeling of three-dimensionality from a viewing point and using scaling, clustering, and annealing methods to create and simplify the three-dimensional configurations. The SemNet method appeared to work quite well for relatively small numbers of nodes (53 in one case) and with the well structured type of information that exists in knowledge bases, but it remains to be seen whether three-dimensional networks will be feasible with messier information structures consisting of larger numbers of nodes. Anecdotal evidence suggests that such visualisations are not particularly helpful when dealing with large and complex structures.

More recently, there has been a trend towards the use of realistic three-dimensional spatial structures, such as buildings, cities (e.g. Dieberger and Tromp, 1993), and even archipelagos of islands (e.g. Waterworth, 1996a) to represent the organisation of sets of multimedia information. This is only possible if either the organisation of information is constrained to fit the physical structure used (by, for example being confined to simple hierarchies) or the physical structure provides only a partial representation of the organisation of information (though several different views may be provided in this way). Waterworth (1996b) provides more detail on these points. It has become fashionable to try to apply the principles of visual recognition in city navigation to the problems of information navigation in multimedia, often drawing heavily on the pioneering work on the imageability of cities by Lynch (1960). It remains unclear how successful such strategies are in practice, compared to other ways of providing a structural overview of a collection of multimedia information.

The idea of using physical spaces to represent informational spaces is far from new. From pre-literary times, mental visualisations of three-dimensional space have been used to enhance memory (Yates, 1984). Such systems generally work by associating to-be-remembered items with various locations within a three-dimensional world such as a set of linked rooms in a building, a complicated theatre set, a well-known city structure, and so on. Spatial organisation is the key to the success of such systems; a large list of items can be recalled easily if each is mentally associated with a particular location in a real or imaginary three-dimensional structure. These mnemotechnic systems are known as 'artificial memory'. It seems plausible that multimedia systems can themselves serve as artificial memory for their users. Because multimedia systems are artificial but not merely imaginary, users can capitalise on both imagery and motor memory in the recollection of the location of items of information. We might thus expect that once users have explored the 3D objects in a spatial multimedia interface, and seen which items are associated with what location in that structure, they would experience little difficulty in recalling where to find a particular item the next time it was needed (assuming this is not offset by experiencing inconsistent views of the objects).

Some of the arguments in favour of the use of three-dimensional structures include the fact that people are very familiar with three-dimensional spaces and with the visual cues associated with them. These arguments at first glance seem so overwhelming and obvious that it is not surprising that they have generally been accepted without much question. However, the enthusiasm for using three-dimensional structures for visualising hypermedia should be tempered by the following concerns.

1. Although people live in a three-dimensional world, they tend to navigate on two-dimensional planes parallel to the surface of the earth. The tendency to navigate in two-dimensions was used as a plot device in one of the Star Trek movies when an intelligent, but novice pilot who was still thinking two-dimensionally was out-manoeuvred by an experienced starship pilot who had been trained to think three-dimensionally. Thus, while people are highly skilled at viewing a three-dimensional world, they may require some training in learning to navigate effectively in three dimensions.

2. It is probably unreasonable to expect a large number of information concepts to fit into a three- (or even four-) dimensional structure. Spatial structures generally impose metric constraints (e.g., Shepard, 1974) that may be too severe. Associative links can potentially link almost anything to anything else based on criteria that can hardly be predicted from a spatial structure. Spatial structures that represent relatively small (less than 60, say) numbers of nodes or objects may not effectively "scale up" to represent larger numbers of objects.

3. The creation of a three-dimensional structure raises the question of how that structure will be used in browsing. While users may be able to view the structure without difficulty, how will they navigate around the structure? The effectiveness of browsing may well depend on what techniques are available for viewing the structure from different vantage points. Other navigation features that are likely to have a strong effect on browsing performance include the ways in which the relative salience or importance of different objects, and the different types of links, are represented.

4. Should different subtopics reside in separate spatial representations, or should they be linked within a single monolithic representation? If separate representations are used, how is the user going to switch between them during browsing?

39.6.2 Synaesthetic Media

Synaesthesia is a naturally-occurring condition whereby certain individuals experience information that is usually experienced in one modality (say, a sound) in a different modality (as a visual pattern, for example). It has been known throughout history, it is relatively rare (especially in adults), and it is often associated with creativity. While at times the experience of synaesthesia can be problematic for the individuals concerned, it is generally seen by them as life-enhancing. People with this condition (or ability) seem to have a richer experience of reality than the rest of us (Cytowic, 1995). They experience sounds as visual phenomena (colours, graphics, patterns), visual stimulation as sounds, have colour associations of rooms or letters, tactile experiences of sounds, and so on. Naturally-occurring synaesthesia in people is, however, not under their control to any great extent, and it tends to fade with age.

From the multimedia perspective, the key lesson of synaesthesia is that reality (information) has no intrinsic form. To hear the sound of an alarm bell ringing is no more accurate an experience of that event than to experience it as a painful red visual glare (Marks, 1978). Reality has content which may be experienced in a variety of ways. To understand reality (information) as fully as we can, we need to experience it in as many forms as possible.

From the perspective of synaesthesia in people, recent developments in multimedia and virtual reality are a promising start in attempting to enhance sensory (and hence perceptual) experience, to broaden the experience of reality of users of these systems. These new technologies are evolving towards artifacts that can mimic synaesthesia but that are under the control of their users. Waterworth (1995, 1996c) referred to such technologies as 'synaesthetic media'. They change how the world of information is perceived, by altering users' sensory experiences of that world. A new research agenda is emerging, concerned with the best way to offer choice of sensory modality as a function of the nature of the information and the user's task, preferences and characteristics. This is the art and science of 'sensory ergonomics', although research that leads the way towards such media translation is by no means entirely novel. Indeed, one can see the history of human-computer interaction design as preparatory stages in developing the field of sensory ergonomics.

There are many examples of work to develop the capability to take information in one medium, and present it to the users in one or more other media. A relevant case is the pianoFORTE project (Smoliar, Waterworth and Kellock, 1995), which developed a computer system that recorded electric piano performances as MIDI (Musical Instrument Digital Interface) data. The obvious way to display these data would be as sound, to be experienced as a repeat of the acoustic events that were produced during a performance. But pianoFORTE was designed to be a medium of communication between the piano student and his teacher. It does this by allowing piano performances to be displayed visually, as graphical annotations to the score that was played. The annotations can be chosen to reflect different aspects of the performance, such as dynamics, tempo and articulation. The displays comprise a synaesthetic medium of communication between teacher and student that, unlike the original performance, is not ephemeral. It is significant that the visual displays were found to enhance listening ability; both students and teachers learned to hear things in performances, after experience of viewing the displays, that they would otherwise not have detected. Their musical perception was enhanced.

Other relevant work includes graphical displays of dynamic database queries (e.g. Ahlberg and Shneiderman, 1994), the 'auralisation' of information (e.g. Brewster et al, 1994), the visual and/or auditory display of motor performance in sports coaching and movement rehabilitation (e.g. Krichevets et al, 1995), the use of gestures for musical composition (e.g. Buxton et al, 1979), associating information with colour and/or spatial location (e.g. Roth et al, 1994) and, most obviously, the large body of work in the field of scientific visualisation (e.g. McCormick et al, 1987). These can all be seen as attempts to support new perceptual experiences by mimicking synaesthesia with multimedia technology. There are also a few examples in the literature of "designing synaesthesia" (Smets at al, 1994), by which is meant the art of creating visual and tactile forms that (to some extent) represent information in other modalities, such as smells, tastes and sounds (e.g. Smets and Overbeeke, 1989). Virtual reality systems can be seen as dramatic examples of the power of artificial synaesthesia although, like almost all existing applications, they have generally not been designed with an emphasis on user selection of display media. There is now an interesting trend to apply virtual reality techniques to scientific visualisation (see Bryson, 1996).

Key directions for designing synaesthetic media are: perceptually large-scale, selectable and transmutable displays of information (which can also be preserved and recalled as needed) and rich synchronous and asynchronous communications. Synchronous communications are vital for real-time collaboration involving a shared (real or virtual) space (see Hutchins, 1990; Heath and Luff, 1992). Asynchronous communications are important not only for delayed collaboration (across several time zones, for example) but also for communicating with oneself over time, a vital aspect of which is self-reminding.

39.6.3 Cybermedia

'Cybermedia' is the result of the burgeoning trend for multimedia information spaces to be shared by many users, and used for social as well as purely informational purposes. At the moment, this predominantly means the multimedia component of the Internet, the World Wide Web, which is by far the most popular and used multimedia environment that exists.

The technologically-mediated world of shared computer-generated information spaces (and experiences) is generally referred to as cyberspace. It is a world that was introduced to many people in William Gibson's science fiction novel, "Neuromancer". Gibson's version of cyberspace is vivid and immersive. A more mundane example of cyberspace is the space that we occupy and imagine when we are involved in an engaging telephone conversation. When two people talk on a telephone they enter a shared psychological space that is at neither of the locations that they physically occupy. The current general conception of cyberspace is somewhere between the two and is based on experiences with the Internet and the Web. At our present level of development, this conception includes the idea that there are public 'places' in cyberspace that anyone can visit, the idea that most people have a home (page) which is itself a public place where we can encounter information selected by the individual concerned, and the idea that we can send electronic messages to anyone else who uses the system (if we know their address).

Multimedia is often considered separately from virtual reality and cyberspace, but it is becoming increasingly clear that this is an unsustainable distinction. In fact, there is considerable potential for synergistic combinations of the three technologies. One such combination is virtual multimedia. Virtual multimedia refers to the inclusion of multimedia documents within virtual reality applications. For instance, say that we have an existing multimedia document on how to maintain a complex aircraft. How should this be integrated within a virtual reality implementation of that aircraft, which includes full flight simulation capability as well as the ability to move within and around the aircraft? Adding to the conceptual confusion of those who like to compartmentalise these technologies, small-scale virtual realities are beginning to proliferate on the Web, based on the use of VRML (virtual reality mark-up language).

The Web is an early form of cyberspace, implemented as a global collection of interconnected documents. It is actually a combination of cyberspace and multimedia, hence our use of the term cybermedia. But the Web is an extremely limited implementation of the potential of cybermedia. The problem is that the vast number of idiosyncratically formatted documents on the Web create an inharmonious set of boundaries that the user has to traverse repeatedly during exploration. As communication bandwidth in global networks improves, and as consistent authoring styles and shared spatial metaphors develop, cybermedia could become a powerful alternative both to virtual reality, and to more conventional on-line information exploration. But since no-one is actually designing the Web, there seems little hope for its current evolutionary path to lead to a single organisational structure.

In the future, the social aspects of cybermedia will become much more significant. At present, when we visit a public place on the Web, we generally do not know if anyone else is currently visiting that site. Hence, the potential for social interaction on the Net (mostly through e-mail) is not integrated with access to multimedia information on the Web. Even if we do not want to be personally identifiable on the Web, we currently don't even have presence as anonymous people in cyberspace. All we can tell, sometimes, is how many people have visited a site before us (or rather, how many visits have been made to the site). For cyberspace to become truly social and realise the full potential of cybermedia, we need a sense of people's presence (and absence), with suitable protection for privacy if that is possible. This trend will lead to research exploring how best to represent the people in cyberspace, not just the information contained there, once again combining cyberspace, multimedia and virtual reality.

A limited sense of what shared presence in the Web would bring is provided by experiences in 'multi-user dungeons' (MUDs) and the Internet Relay Chat services. The recent book by Turkle (1995) gives a good insight into those worlds, although the MUD and Chat users are probably not typical of Web users. Specifically, they are self-selected for their interest in role-playing and/or a need to alleviate real life loneliness. Turkle points to the ease of adopting multiple personae in cyberspace, to present the face we choose to present rather than the real-life person we have become over the years. This can be seen as partial or selective presence in cyberspace.

We can think of degrees of presence, from totally concealed (invisible), through anonymous (featureless) but visible, to articulated personae one of which might be a representation of our real world personality. Should we be able to choose how we appear to others? Should we be able to appear present when we are not, and not present when we are? False presence arises when we appear to be in one place but are actually (or also) elsewhere. Multiple personae multiply the scope for interpersonal deception. But the converse of this is that, if we know which people, or even just how many people, are in the same vicinity as we are in cyberspace, we can behave as the essentially social animals we are. Our shared sense of presence may return some human context to the tangle of dislocated multimedia information that is the current Web.

39.7 Conclusions

Evolution in computing technology is typically measured in terms of processor architectures, or programming paradigms. However, it can also be measured in the number of processing cycles or operations per unit time, or the amount and type of primary and secondary storage capacity. Capacity as measured in these latter quantities, particularly if referenced to the cost of computing power, has been increasing continuously and exponentially over the past few decades.

Interactivity and integration are costly in computing terms because they require the storage and playback of digital media in primary and secondary memory. This has led to an emphasis on storage, compression, and decompression technologies in the fledgling multimedia industry. These concerns are being met in a variety of ways, from the development of CD-ROM drives with faster throughput and higher capacity, to the availability of multiple gigabyte optical drives, and to new video encoding formats.

As the technology roadblocks are being dismantled, it is becoming clearer that interactivity and integration are also costly in terms of human labour. This should not be surprising, since information presentations of any complexity or sophistication require some artistic and aesthetic input. Simply providing the user with a collage of different media is not the same as providing users with an integrated and interactive presentation. Good interactive multimedia presentations have to include appropriate information content and media clips, suitable sequencing, linking, and orchestration of the media content, and a good set of navigation tools within a well-crafted user interface.

Multimedia is, without doubt, a technology that allows us to broaden our channels of sensation and communication and so experience reality more fully within computer-mediated applications. Thus it provides a challenge for HCI researchers and practitioners to develop suitable theoretical and practical frameworks for incorporating and exploiting sensory ergonomics within software user interfaces, and for dealing with the increasingly social nature of human interaction with multimedia systems.

This chapter does not provide definitive guidelines on how to construct multimedia user interfaces, largely because of the relative immaturity of the field. However it is clear that multimedia is, and will increasingly be, a major part of computing, and that user interface design is especially important for multimedia because of its highly sensory and dynamic nature. In addition, while multimedia can benefit from including the principles and practice of human-computer interaction and user interface design, HCI as a discipline will also benefit from the new challenges that multimedia as an application area poses to its methodologies and assumptions.

Other sources of information on multimedia and related issues include the series of Hypertext conferences organized by the Association for Computer Machinery (Hypertext'87, '89, '91, '93, etc.) and equivalent conferences held in Europe, along with the annual ACM conferences on multimedia (beginning in 1993), and various scientific journals on hypermedia and multimedia (e.g., IEEE Multimedia). The reader may also wish to refer to a related chapter on multimedia (Chignell and Waterworth, 1997), where the ergonomic aspects of multimedia are discussed, and some tentative design recommendations are provided.

39.8 Acknowledgements

We would like to acknowledge the contribution of research colleagues such as Felix Valdez, Luis Serra, and Ferdinand Poblete to our understanding of multimedia. Angie Wong assisted in editing and revising the chapter. Support for some of the research described was provided to the second author through operating grants from the National Science and Engineering Research Council of Canada, and through research grants from the Information Technology Research Centre of Excellence of Ontario.

39.9 Bibliography

Ahlberg, C. and Shneiderman, B. (1994). Visual Information Seeking: Tight Coupling of Dynamic Query Filters with Starfield Displays. In *Proceedings of CHI'94: Conference on Human Factors in Computing Systems (*Boston, April 1994). New York: ACM.

Anderson, J.R. (1985). *Cognitive Psychology and its Implications*, Second Edition. San Francisco: Freeman.

Ang, Y.H., Ng, P.S. and Loke, H.C. (1991). Image Retrieval through Fast Browsing and Visual Query. *Proceedings of International Conference on Multimedia Information Systems* '91, Singapore, 161-174. New York: McGraw-Hill.

Apple Computer (1995). *Using the QuickTime VR authoring tools suite*. Cupertino, CA: Apple Computer.

Arons, B.M. (1994). *Interactively skimming recorded speech.* Unpublished Ph.D. dissertation, Program in Media Arts and Sciences, Massachusetts Institute of Technology.

Benest, I.D., Morgan, G. and Smithurst, M.D. (1987). A Humanised Interface to an Electronic Library. In *Proceedings of Interact '87*, Bullinger, H. J. and Shackel, B. (eds). Amsterdam: Elsevier Science.

Brewster, S.A, Wright, P.C. and Edwards, A.D.N. (1994). The Design and Evaluation of an Auditory-Enhanced ScrollBar. In *Proceedings of CHI'94: Conference on Human Factors in Computing Systems* (Boston, April 1994). New York: ACM.

Brooks, F.P. (1988). Grasping reality through illusion - Interaction graphics service science. *Proceedings of CHI'88,* 1-11. N.Y.: ACM Press.

Brown, E. (1993). Unpublished Ph.D. Dissertation. Ontario Institute for Studies in Education, Toronto, Canada.

Brown, P.J. (1987). Turning ideas into documents: The Guide system. *Proceedings of Hypertext'87.* Chapel Hill: North Carolina.

Brown. E. and Chignell, M.H. (1993). Learning by linking: Pedagogical environments for hypermedia authoring. *Journal of Computing in Higher Education*, 5(1), 27-50.

Brown, E. and Chignell, M.H. (1995) Free-form Multimedia for Learning and Design. To appear in E. Barrett and M. Redmond (Eds.), *Culture, Technology, Interpretation: The Challenge of Multimedia*. Cambridge, Massachussetts: MIT Press.

Bryson, S. (1996). Virtual Reality in Scientific Visualization. *Communications of the ACM*, 39 (5), 63-71.

Bush, V. (1945). *As We May Think. Atlantic Monthly*, July 1945. See also Bush, V (1967) Memex Revisited. In V Bush (Ed), Science is not Enough. William Morrow and Co.

Buxton, W.A.S. (1987). The haptic channel. In R.M. Baecker and W.A.S. Buxton (Eds.), *Readings in Human Computer Interaction* (pp. 357-365). Los Altos, CA: Morgan Kaufmann.

Buxton, W.A.S. (1993). HCI and the inadequacies of direct manipulation systems. *ACM SIGCHI Bulletin*, 25 (1), 21- 22.

Buxton, W.A.S., Sneiderman, R., Reeves, W., Patel, S. and Baeker, R. (1979). The evolution of spss score-editing tools. *Computer Music Journal*, 3, 14-25.

CERN (1993). The HTML Document Type Definition. Available on the Web at http://info.cern.ch/hypertext/WWW/MarkUp/HTML.dtd.html.

Chignell, M. H. and Waterworth, J. A. (1997). Multimedia. In Salvendy, G. (Ed.) *Handbook of Human Factors and Ergonomics:* 2nd edition. New York: Wiley.

Chua, T.-S., Lim, S.-W., and Pung, H.-K. (1994). Content-based retrieval of segmented images. *Proceedings of ACM Multimedia* 1994, 211-218. San Francisco, October 1994.

Cytowic, R E (1995). Synesthesia: Phenomenology and Neuropsychology. Psyche, 2-10-syn_phenomenology-1. [http://psyche.cs.monash.edu.au/]

Dieberger, A. and Tromp, J.G. (1993). The Information City Project - a virtual reality user interface for navigation in information spaces. In *Proceedings of the Virtual Reality Symposium* Vienna, December 1-3, 1993.

Dillon, A., Richardson, J., and McKnight, C. (1988). Reading from paper versus reading from screens. *The Computer Journal*, 31(5), 457-464.

diSessa, A. (1985). A principled design for an integrated computational environment. Journal of Human-Computer Interaction, 1(1), 1-47.

Egan, D., Remde, J., Landauer, T., Lochbaum, C. and Gomez, L. (1989). Behavioral evaluation and analysis of a hypertext browser. In *Proceedings of CHI'89*, 205-210. NY: ACM Press.

Evenson, S., Rheinfrank, J., and Wulff, W. (1989). Towards a Design Language for Representing Hypermedia Cues. *Hypertext'89 Proceedings*. New York: ACM.

Fairchild, K.F., Poltrock, S.E., and Furnas, G.W. (1988). SemNet: Three-dimensional Graphic Representations of Large Knowledge Bases. In R. Guindon (Ed.), *Cognitive Science and its Applications for Human-Computer Interaction*. Hillsdale, NJ: Lawrence Erlbaum Associates

Foley, J.D., van Dam, A., Feiner, S.K., and Hughes, J.F. (1990). *Computer Graphics, Principles and Practice, second edition*. Reading, Massachusetts: Addison-Wesley Publishing Company.

Furnas, G.W. (1986). Generalized fisheye views. *Proceedings of ACM CHI'86* Conference, 16-23, New York: ACM.

Garber, S.R. and Grunes, M.B. (1992). The Art of Search: A Study of Art Directors. Proceedings of ACM CHI'92 Conference, 157-164, New York: ACM.

Ginige, A., Lowe, D.R. and Robertson, J. (1995). Hypermedia Authoring. *IEEE Multimedia*, 2 (4), 24- 35.

Golovchinsky, G. and Chignell, M.H. (in press). The newspaper as an information exploration metaphor. *Information Processing and Management.*

Gordon, S., Gustavel, J., Moore, J., and Hankey, J. (1988). The effects of hypertext on reader knowledge representation. *Proceedings of the Human Factors Society* 32nd Annual Meeting, 296-300.

Graham, I.S. (1995). HTML Sourcebook: A complete guide to HTML. N.Y. Wiley.

Gronbaek, K. and Trigg, R.H. (1994). Special Section on Hypermedia. *Communications of the ACM*, 37(2), 26-86.

Guha, A., Pavan, A., Liu, J.C.L., and Roberts, B.A. (1995). Controlling the process with distributed multimedia. *IEEE Multimedia* 2(2), 20-29.

Halasz, F. G., Moran, T..P., and Trigg, R.H. (1987). NoteCards in a Nutshell. *Proceedings of CHI+GI 1987*.

Hammond, N. and Allinson, L. (1988). Travels around a learning support environment: Rambling, orienteering or touring. *Proceedings of CHI'88 Conference*, 269-273. New York: ACM.

Hasan, M., Mendelzon, A., and Vista, D. (1995). Visual Web surfing with Hy+. *Proceedings of CASCON'95*. Toronto, Canada, November 7-9, 1995.

Heath, C. and Luff P. (1992). Collaboration and Control: Crisis management and multimedia technology in London Underground line control rooms. *Computer Supported Cooperative Work*, 1, 69-94.

Hergé (1962). *The Adventures of Tintin: King Ottokar's Sceptre.* London: Reed International Books (English edition translated from French original published by Éditions Casterman).

Hutchins, E. (1990). The Technology of Team Navigation. In *Intellectual Teamwork: the Social and Technological Foundations of Cooperative Work,* Galagher, J, Kraut, R E and Egido, C (Eds). Hillsdale, NJ: Lawrence Erlbaum.

ISO (1991). *"HyTime" Hypermedia Time-based Structuring Language*. ISO/IEC 10744. Edited by Charles F. Goldfarb.

Johnson, B.S. (1993). *Treemaps: Visualizing hierarchical and categorical data.* Unpublished Ph.D dissertation, Department of Computer Science, University of Maryland, UMI-94-25057.

Kato, T., Kurita, T., Shimogaki, H., Mizutori, T. and Fujimura, K. (1991). A Cognitive Approach to Visual Interaction. *Proceedings of International Conference on Multimedia Information Systems'91,* Singapore, 109-120. New York: McGraw-Hill.

Keeton, K. and Katz, R.H. (1995). Evaluating video layout strategies for a high-performance storage server. *Multimedia Systems*, 3, 43-52.

Krichevets, A.N, Sirotkina, E.B, Yevsevicheva, I.V and Zeldin, L.M (1995). Computer Games as a Means of Movement Rehabilitation. Disability and Rehabilitation, 17 (2), 100-105.

Laurel, B. (1991). *Computers as Theater.* Reading, Mass.: Addison-Wesley.

Lindsay, P.H and Norman, D.A. (1977). Human Information Processing: *An Introduction to Psychology*, 2nd Edition. N.Y.: Academic Press.

Lynch, K. (1960). *The Image of the City.* Cambridge, Mass: MIT Press.

Marchionini, G. (1995). *Information seeking in electronic environments.* Cambridge: Cambridge University Press.

Marks, L (1978). *The Unity of the Senses: Interrelations among the Modalities'.* New York: Academic Press.

Marsh, A.V.C. (1996). *Structure and memorability of Web sites*. Unpublished Master's thesis, Department of Mechanical and Industrial Engineering, University of Toronto.

McCloud, S. (1993). *Understanding Comics : the Invisible Art.* Northampton, MA: Kitchen Sink Press, 1993.

McCormick, B., DeFanti, T.A. and Brown, M.D. (Eds.) (1987). Visualization in Scientific Computing. *Computer Graphics*, 21 (6).

McKnight, C., Dillon, A. and Richardson, J. (1991). *Hypertext in Context.* Cambridge, England: Cambridge University Press.

Monk, A.F., Walsh, P. and Dix, A.J. (1988). A comparison of hypertext, scrolling, and folding. In R. Winder (ed.). People and Computers IV, *Proceedings of HCI'88.* Cambridge: Cambridge University Press.

Neisser (1967). *Cognitive Psychology.* N.Y.: Appleton Century-Crofts.

Nielsen, J. (1990a). The Art of Navigating through Hypertext. *Communications of the ACM*, 33, 297-310.

Nielsen, J. (1990b). *Hypertext and Hypermedia.* New York: Academic Press.

Norman, D.A. (1993). *Things That Make Us Smart.* Reading, Mass.: Addison-Wesley.

Parsaye, K. and Chignell, M.H. (1993). Intelligent Database Tools and Applications. Chapter 6, Hyperinformation and Hyperdata. N.Y.: Wiley

Parsaye, K., Chignell, M.H., Khoshafian, S., and Wong, H.K.T. (1989). *Intelligent Databases: Object-Oriented, Deductive Hypermedia Technologies.* N.Y.: Wiley.

Poblete, F. (1995). *The Use of Information Visualization to Enhance Awareness of Hierarchical Structure.* Unpublished M.S. thesis. Department of Industrial Engineering, University of Toronto.

Remde, J.R., Gomez, L.M., and Landauer, T.K. (1987). SuperBook: An automatic tool for information exploration-hypertext? *Proceedings of Hypertext'87.* Chapel Hill, North Carolina.

Roth, S.F., Kolojejchick, J., Mattis, J. and Goldstein, J. (1994). Interactive Graphic Design Using Automatic Presentation Knowledge. In *Proceedings of CHI'94: Conference on Human Factors in Computing Systems* (Boston, April 1994). New York: ACM.

Salton, G. and McGill, M.J. (1983). *Introduction to modern information retrieval.* New York: McGraw-Hill.

Shepard, R.N. (1974). Representation of structure in similarity data: Problems and prospects. *Psychometrika*, 39, 373-421.

Shneiderman, B. (1987). *Designing the User Interface*. Reading, Mass.: Addison-Wesley.

Shneiderman, B. (1992). Tree visualization with tree-maps. A 2-D space-filling approach. *ACM Transactions on Graphics*. 11(1) , 92-99.

Shneiderman, B. and Kearsley, G. (1989). *Hypertext Hands-On! An Introduction to a New Way of Organizing and Accessing Information*. Reading,MA: Addison-Wesley.

Smets, G. and Overbeeke, C. (1989). Scent and Sound of Vision: Expressing Scent or Sound as Visual Forms. Perceptual and Motor Skills, 69, 227-233.

Smets, G., Overbeeke, K. and Gaver, W. (1994). Form-Giving: Expressing the Non-Obvious. In *Proceedings of CHI'94 Conference on Human Factors in Information Systems* (Boston, April 1994), 79-84. New York: ACM.

Smith, K.E. (1988). Hypertext - linking to the future. *Online*, 12(2), 32-40.

Smoliar, S.W., Waterworth, J.A. and Kellock, P.R. (1995). pianoFORTE: a System for Piano Education beyond Notation Literacy. *Proceedings of ACM Multimedia'95* Conference, San Francisco, November 1995.

Staples, L. (1993). Representation in virtual space: Visual convention in the graphical user interface. *Proceedings of INTERCHI'93*, 348-354. NY: ACM Press.

Tierney, B., Johnston, W.E., Herzog, H., Hoo, G., Jin, G., Lee, J., Chen, L.T., and Rotem, D. (1994). Distributed parallel data storage systems: A scalable approach to high speed image servers. *Proceedings of ACM Multimedia* 94. San Francisco, October 1994, 399-405.

Tognazzini, B.(1993). Principles, Techniques, and Ethics of Stage Magic and their Application to Human Interface Design. *Proceedings of INTERCHI'93* Conference, 355-362, New York: ACM.

Torkington, N. (1995). *An Information Provider's Guide to HTML*. Victoria University of Wellington, New Zealand. Published on the World Wide Web at http://www.vuw.ac.nz/non-local/gnat/www-html.html.

Tufte, E.R. (1983). *The Visual Display of Quantitative Information*. Cheshire, Conn: Graphics Press.

Tufte, E.R. (1990). *Envisioning Information*. Cheshire, Conn: Graphics Press.

Turkle, S. (1995). *Life on the Screen*. New York: Simon and Schuster.

Ueda, H., Miyatake, T., Sumino, S. and Nagasaka, A. (1993). Automatic Structure Visualisation for Video Editing. *Proceedings of INTERCHI'93*, 137-141 New York: ACM.

Valdez, J.F. (1992). *Navigational strategies in using documentation*. Unpublished Ph.D. dissertation. Department of Industrial and Systems Engineering, University of Southern California.

Valdez, J.F. and Chignell, M.H. (1992). Methods for assessing the usage and usability of documentation. *Proceedings of the Third Conference on Quality in Documentation*. Waterloo, Ontario, November 1992.

Venolia, D. (1993). Facile 3D direct manipulation. *Proceedings of INTERCHI'93*, 31-42. NY: ACM Press.

Waterworth, J.A. (1992). *Multimedia Interaction: human factors aspects*. Chichester, England: Ellis Horwood. Simon and Schuster International.

Waterworth, J.A. (1995). HCI Design as Sensory Ergonomics: Designing Synaesthetic Media. *Proceedings of IRIS 18 Conference*, Denmark, August 1995. D Dahlbom, F Kämmerer, F Ljungberg, J Stage and C Sorensen (eds), Gothenburg Studies in Informatics, Report 7, 1995, 744-753

Waterworth, J.A. (1996a). A pattern of islands: exploring public information space in a private vehicle. In: P. Brusilovsky, P. Kommers and N. Streitz (eds.): *Multimedia, Hypermedia and Virtual Reality: Models, Systems, and Applications*. Lecture Notes in Computer Science, Berlin: Springer-Verlag, pp. 266-279. 1996.

Waterworth, J.A. (1996b). Personal Spaces: 3D Spatial Worlds for Information Exploration, Organisation and Communication. *Proceedings of BCS Conference on 3D and Multimedia on the Internet, WWW and Networks*, 17-18 April 1996, UK.

Waterworth, J.A. (1996c). Creativity and Sensation: The Case for Synaesthetic Media. *Proceedings of Creativity and Cognition 96*. LUTCHI Research Centre, Loughborough University, 29-30th April, 1996.

Waterworth, J.A. and Chignell, M.H. (1989). A Manifesto for Hypermedia Usability Research. *Hypermedia*, , 1(3), 205-234.

Waterworth, J.A. and Chignell, M.H. (1991). A Model of Information Exploration. *Hypermedia*, 3(1), 35-58.

Woods, D. (1984). Visual momentum: A concept to improve the cognitive coupling of person and computer. *International Journal of Man-Machine Studies*, 21, 229-244.

Wright, P. (1991). Cognitive overheads and prostheses: Some issues in evaluating hypertexts. *Proceedings of Hypertext'91,* 1-12.

Yankelovich, N., Hann, B., and Meyrowitz, N. (1988). Intermedia: The Concept and the Construction of a Seamless Information Environment. *IEEE Computer,* January 1988.

Yates, F. A. (1984). *The Art of Memory.* London: Routledge and Kegan Paul. First published in 1966.

Zhai, S. (1995). *Human Performance in Six Degree-of-Freedom Input Control.* Unpublished Ph.D. dissertation. Department of Industrial Engineering, University of Toronto.

Handbook of Human-Computer Interaction
Second, completely revised edition
M. Helander, T.K. Landauer, P. Prabhu (eds.)

Chapter 40

A Practical Guide to Working with Edited Video

Wendy A. Kellogg
IBM T.J. Watson Research Center
Yorktown Heights, New York USA

Rachel K.E. Bellamy
Apple Computer, Inc.
Cupertino, California USA

Mary Van Deusen
InterMedia Enterprises
Wrentham, Massachusetts, USA

40.1 Introduction

We are at an exciting time in the development of video as a medium. Never before has it been as easy for the HCI practitioner to integrate the use of video into practice. Video cameras are coming down in price. Simple analog editing is now possible with consumer VCRs as manufacturers produce lower-cost equipment with the kinds of controls such as shuttle/jog, previously available only on professional equipment. Video is also moving from the analog to the digital. Although digital cameras are still beyond the financial reach of most of us, for many HCI practitioners computer technologies for digitizing analog video and software programs for manipulating the digitized video are both financially accessible – as technology comes down in price — and technically accessible — with the introduction of easy-to-use software applications for digital video. So what exciting opportunities does video create for HCI practitioners?

In HCI work, video has typically been seen as a medium for communicating finished work to others. This mirrors the everyday use of video where it is typically used as a medium for mass communication. Although this is an excellent use of video, it is just one of the many excellent uses to which video can be put by the HCI practitioner. Some of the other uses that will be discussed in this chapter are: video as an interface element in multimedia applications, video prototyping, and data collection and data analysis. If your exposure to video in your workplace has been primarily observation video (e.g., in usability studies), then you perhaps haven't had the opportunity to see the power that tightly editing only the significant parts of your video can have to bring forward only the points you want to make.

Video offers new opportunities because it is a medium that supports activities that cannot be done using alternative static, non-time-based media such as paper, photographs, or (until recently) Web pages. For example, video offers a record of an event that can be referred to later. Video is concrete; it provides a detailed record of the context and of situational factors that are normally backgrounded. Such a detailed record of events is not usually captured by other media. For example, a video of a cookery demonstration captures far more than the abstract record of a recipe. As a tool for learning, such a video allows the novice cook to see details such as where to place a spoon, how to drop an egg into a pan. Such details could never be as conveniently portrayed in a textual description.

In addition to the unique time-based properties offered by video and the capture of rich contextual detail, with the increased accessibility of digital video, video also offers interactive properties that extend it's use in HCI. Interactive video can be used to express multiple viewpoints, to clarify process, to provide a rich description of a user study through the combination of video-as-data with other data such as graphical views of numerical data, pictures of artifacts made by subjects, audio of interviews, etc. Finally, video is rich in the sense of its ability to engage viewers; its sights and sounds seem unusually compelling, appealing as they do to the dominant senses by which we perceive the world. As such, video carries the potential for high emotional impact that is often harder to achieve through alternative media.

This chapter describes simple techniques that can be used to give you acceptable results for either analog or digital video. We discuss how to get good (raw) material, prioritizing and partitioning work among yourself and professional support people, and factors to consider in the post production process as you edit your raw material into a final product. We have also included some tricks of the trade that will help you make decisions about how to allocate a limited budget and work with limited professional help for the best end result. Given a minimum level of equipment, and the enthusiasm to acquire the necessary skills, video can be a one-person job.

An important point about video is that it must be good quality. Viewers will respond negatively to your material and possibly to your entire system if the video is poorly done. As a culture, we are bombarded by high-quality video, and as professionals using video we must give people the quality they expect from professionals. This does not mean that we must throw a massive budget at every project involving video. Good video can, and has been, produced on a limited budget. However, this only happens when the people involved in making the video understand the technology and the process, and know where they can cut corners without losing production value.

This chapter starts by discussing video as a medium and defining particular genres of video that are useful to HCI work. A brief primer on video follows. The primer discusses general terms and technology. This leads into a section on the process of making a video. Finally, there is detailed discussion covering practicalities relevant to production of video for each of the genres we have highlighted as important ones for HCI.

If you're interested in doing a certain kind of video, read both the Primer in Video (section 3) and the specific section dealing with that type of video (in section 5). Technical terms can be found in a brief glossary at the end of the chapter.

40.2 Video as a Medium

The key characteristics of video are that it is time-based, provides a detailed visual and audio record of context, is a permanent record, and has a narrative structure. These characteristics lend themselves to particular uses, for example, the time-based and narrative structure of video allow you to tell a story. But just as with software, video as a medium must be viewed broadly — beyond the technology. The nature and culture of the "user" of video — the viewers — interacts with how video needs to be structured to accomplish various goals. The key characteristics of viewers are that:

- their attention fluctuates moment to moment,
- they typically bring a wealth of past experience in viewing video, and
- their retention for material after one viewing is limited.

How do videographers take these characteristics into account when they design a video?

First, in order to keep people's attention along with

effectively conveying information, a video should be interesting, even entertaining. There is no problem with entertaining people while you inform them; if your video loses the viewer to boredom or lack of attention, even the most carefully chosen and best-structured material will fail to inform.

Secondly, people have implicit standards from being exposed to massive amounts of video in TV and movies. TV has become such a pervasive part of our lives that we have developed a vast fund of knowledge for experiencing and interpreting moving pictures, a kind of unconscious expertise. We understand when a character is seen in a long-distance "establishing" shot (i.e., one that sets the scene), and begins to sit down that the person in the following close-up is the same person, and has already become seated. Originally, filmmakers would repeat the sitting down action in both shots so that viewers would know for certain what they were seeing. What we do today with a camera is a form of shorthand, one that succeeds because we can count on shared assumptions with the audience. In the US, MTV's music videos have championed a style of fast cuts and an impressionistic succession of images rather than narrative, that is now observable in television commercials and elsewhere. All of this constitutes a background against which *your* video will be interpreted, quite unconsciously, by your audience (whether they watch TV or not).

Thirdly, video is a more difficult medium than print for people to access and to remember. Video flies by, and it isn't easy for the viewer to go back and find a particular image, sentence, or sequence (even if the viewer has control over the rewind button). Knowing this has implications for how quickly your program goes by (e.g., how fast a technical explanation can go by). Video can incorporate motion to support understanding — e.g., a diagram can become "alive" and be more accessible. But if the concept is not well-explained or if it is explained too quickly, the live diagram can fly by and mean nothing. So viewers must be given (visual and auditory) anchors and a foundation carefully constructed to unfold through time lest they be lost. Video thus has to be created in a different way than print, with a keen understanding of its unique strengths and weaknesses. One cannot merely translate print into video, or apply the standards of communicating in print, or even live oral presentations, to video. An explanation of reasonable complexity and depth in print may be far too complex for a video narration; an explanation that seems personable and to the point when given live, may be far too expansive and unfocused for video.

40.2.1 Genres of Video for HCI

There are a variety of ways that video is currently used in HCI, but each purpose to which video is put affects characteristics such as the length, structure, amount of viewer control, and the viewer expectations at play — in other words, purposes foster distinct genres of HCI video. We distinguish the following genres: Interactive Video, Technical Presentation Video, Video Prototypes, and Video as HCI Data. These genres differ in final form, and also lay different requirements on each phase of video making. However, each genre is basically a variation on a theme — the common elements in making any video. Before describing these genres in more detail, it is necessary to understand video as a technology and practice in more detail. In the following two sections, sections 3 (A Primer in Video) and 4 (Creating a Video), we present the common thematic elements in understanding video and making an edited video. Then in the last section, section 5, we return to discuss in more detail each genre to clarify, and give examples of, the most significant uses of video in HCI.

40.3 A Primer in Video

In this section we provide an introduction to the general aspects of video. In particular we discuss the technical aspects of video. If you are new to professional video production, it is a good idea to scan this section, since later sections will rely on some of the information here. If you skip ahead and become confused, check back here. If you want to learn more, see the References section.

40.3.1 The Way of Video

Video is not only a unique medium, as discussed in the last section, but making a video is an experience like no other. Each basic phase of videomaking, pre-production, production, and post production, calls on a variety of skills that run the gamut from creative vision to the ability to carry out finely detailed work and manage complex logistics. In pre-production, "proper prior planning" is highlighted to ensure that all the needed elements will be obtained during production. Production is focused on the logistics of getting all these elements on tape at minimal cost, while remaining flexible enough to capitalize on chance and to exploit unforseeable aspects of shooting — for example, aspects of the location on the particular day on which shooting occurs. Post production in a real sense is "where it's at" in creating edited video, where the power of creativity and technical editing skill are brought to bear on the available raw material to craft a coherent result.

Creating video has aspects that are unlike many other creative activities with which we are familiar. First, the parts of the final production, even those that will appear together, are almost always created in separate pieces (for example, narration is produced in a separate "shoot" from the visual material that will accompany it), and only come together during post production. Sometimes, the individual pieces may not be balanced when they are placed together. For example, narration intended for voice over that sounds appropriate during recording may turn out to be too emphatic or too weak when paired with its video. This is one of the reasons that a Director with a strong vision of the final production is critical to creating a good result.

Second, good post production editing really comes down to the single frame level, for a variety of reasons. Inadvertent camera movement during a shot, the subject's expression, a movement in the background, off-camera noise, among many other things, constrain which frames of video are usable in the final production. In addition, the composition and timing or flow of the video and audio are crucial to its quality, comparable to composing and scoring music, or choreographing a dance. Learning to recognize and work within the constraints of the raw material, and becoming sensitive to the relationship between particular edits and the overall effect in the composition, are skills that can only develop over time and with experience.

Third, professional videographers typically display a passion for quality that can be unfathomable to the uninitiated, in part because the differences in final result often rely on perceptual sensitivities that only develop after much experience working with video. If you work with experienced videographers, you may notice an almost fanatic attitude about quality issues. For example, experts will object to "dropping generations of tape" during post production unless it is absolutely necessary. By this they mean that they do not want to edit from duplications of tape rather than the original (i.e., the original footage is "first generation," and each subsequent duplication of the footage "drops" a generation). In other words, professional videographers will want to edit the final production from original tapes, not from copies of the original footage, except under extreme, almost unimaginable, situations. Experts are also prone to be particular about other quality issues, such as the quality of the audio, the advisability and kind of special effects to use (opinions vary on this, but are bound to disagree with your own intuitions), the usability of video footage (e.g., the professional says, "it's too dark, remove it" and you say "but that's the best thing he says!"), etc. In general, quality issues have a distressing tendency to trade off against content issues (i.e., choosing or creating and best content may entail compromises in quality, or, alternatively, creating the best quality may entail compromises in content).

Aside from the significant effort it will take to meet such demanding standards, you may wonder whether viewers can really tell the difference. Our answer is that perceptible differences in the final product will exist, but it may take a trained ear and eye to detect them, at least consciously. But greater quality *will* positively influence your viewers, just as flaws that viewers may not be able to articulate or put their fingers on will detract from the impression your video makes. As your appreciation for quality in video, and what it takes to produce it, grows, you partake of a professional ethic that is similar to the more familiar situation of application and interface design, where the details matter, whether or not they are noticeable to the casual observer. As it is with great software design, so it is with great video.

40.3.2 Roles in Creating Video

Even the shortest video production incorporates a diverse set of considerations and activities. Each of the roles described in Table 1 has an impact on the final production, and depending on each situation, may be played by separate team members, or mostly by one person.

A reasonable minimum crew for producing a video is three people: Director, Cameraperson, and Audio Engineer. Hiring a professional cameraperson for the most critical shots is highly recommended. Audio is a highly technical specialty, so professional assistance during the shoot is also recommended. All the rest of the tasks described above can be performed by one person. If you can't afford two people with these skills to assist you, it's easier to lose the cameraperson than the audio engineer.

40.3.3 Videomaking Equipment

In the world of photography, we are familiar with wide ranges of quality and sophistication in equipment, from "disposable" cameras in a box handed out to partygoers, through "instamatic" cameras, automatic and manual 35mm SLRs (Single-Lens Reflex), to the elaborate cameras, lenses, tripods, lighting kits, and light meters

Table 1. Roles and responsibilities in a video production.

ROLE	RESPONSIBILITIES
Producer	This person has administrative responsibility for the project (e.g., obtains funding, approves hiring of staff, monitors and makes decisions about incurring budget overruns, etc.)
Director	This person has creative responsibility for the video; s/he envisions the final result, and defines the staffing needed to achieve that result. The Director is also responsible for deciding how to obtain all the needed material for the final production (e.g., what shots are needed, the order of production of visual and audio parts, etc.).
Scriptwriter / Storyboard Creator	This person scripts the video, including visuals needed and where they will go, narrative and/or dialog, etc. This person may also assist the Director in creating a storyboard of the video during pre-production.
Props	This person has responsibility for obtaining the props called for in the script, and for assisting the Director with set decoration in preparation for the shoot.
Director of Photography / Cameraperson	This person lights the scene and captures the video.
Audio Engineer	This person is responsible for making decisions about how audio will be captured, and for executing the audio capture during shoots and/ or narration capture.
Editor	This person edits the raw footage into a final result in accord with the Director's direction.
Production Assistant	This person takes notes during the shoot to facilitate finding particular footage during editing. For example, s/he might note that the second take of a particular speech was considered the best take by the Director, or note the location of ambient sound recordings.
Transcriber	This person listens to the raw footage (e.g., in the case of an interview) and produces a written transcript.
Editor's Assistant	This person logs the raw footage, noting the timecode of significant visual and/or auditory events.

used by professional photographers. Equipment to support the capture and editing of video covers at least the same range of choices, and probably more, given that both the medium and the process of working with it are more complex than taking still photographs. Our goal in this section is to provide a brief overview of the range of options, and to describe the minimal level of equipment that you will need to make your own edited video.

Designing Your Studio

A "studio" for editing video can be as small and simple as having a couple of video machines and a desktop editing system in your home or office (Figures 1 and 2), to an elaborate studio encompassing sophisticated post-production editing capabilities (Figure 3).

As long as your system supports frame-accurate

Figure 1. A home video studio with computer-controlled analog equipment (Van Deusen/Kosinski studio).

Figure 2. Digital desktop equipment. *The set-up uses a Power Macintosh 8100, a RasterOps Video Vision digitizing card and 230 megabyte optical drive for storage. The two monitors each show millions of colors. On the shelf above the monitors is a Sony Hi-8 VTR (video tape recorder) that can be controlled from the computer. This kind of set-up can be used for producing short clips to be output to VHS tape. Not shown here, but with the ability to produce even higher quality digital footage are professional digital video equipment and software systems, such as AVID.*

editing, you will be surprised how much you can produce with a minimum of equipment. One of us (Van Deusen) has produced professional-quality video on the S-VHS system shown in Figure 1 for several years, including video for broadcast on cable television.

What You Need During Production

During the production (shooting) phase, the minimum you will need is a camera (with battery capability if you're shooting on location), a video deck (this can be a camcorder, where the camera and video deck are combined), microphones, an audio mixer (great help), and a lighting kit.

What You Need During Post Production

For post production editing, the minimum you will need is an editing setup that includes two VCR's with insert audio/video capability. For the best results, be sure that your equipment supports audio-only and video-only edits. Equipment requirements for analog vs. digital editing differ, as discussed below.

Using Outside Facilities (e.g., Edit Suites)

An editing studio usually has various editing rooms,

Figure 3. A professional-quality studio (IBM T.J. Watson Research Center).

with equipment that can produce more complex results. When you need to create special effects (for example, creating the illusion of a live computer system by editing video into a shot of a blank monitor) that are beyond your (or your equipment's) ability, you may want to utilize a professional studio. You pay by the hour, which normally includes staff to operate the equipment. You need to know the most complicated thing that you will have to do, so that you don't pay for more than you need. Because hourly rates are so high, it is important to be thoroughly prepared before going to the studio, with what elements from the raw footage you want to work with, and in what order. This is not the time or place for decision-making.

40.3.4 Technical Aspects of Video

Within the US, there is a standard for video, called NTSC (for National Television Standards Committee; also sometimes referred to as "Never The Same Color"). Whether your tape format is VHS, U-matic, or Beta, the signal on the tape is still NTSC. Therefore, if you can hook the machines together, you can copy footage from one format to another. In Europe, other standards, such as PAL and SECAM, are used. Translating among *standards* involves more than copying the footage; rather, the video signal must be read and converted.

You can think of a videotape as having three parts: a video track, audio tracks, and control information (often called timecode). Within the video track, NTSC captures a frame of video 30 times a second. A frame is captured in a two-pass process by "scanning" across the camera image 525 times. Imagine going from left to right first on line 0, then skipping to line 2, then to line 4, etc. When we have scanned to the bottom of the image, we have scanned a field. Now the scanner returns from the bottom right of the image to the top left, and begins the scan again, this time on line one, three, five, etc., thus picking up all the lines that were skipped in the first pass. This produces field two. A frame of video is then composed by interlacing fields 1 and 2 (Figure 4). One difference between video standards — PAL, NTSC and SECAM — is in the frames/sec and number of scanlines (Table 2). NTSC captures 30 frames per second with 525 scanlines. PAL captures 25 frames per second with 625 scanlines. In other words, objects in the PAL format are of higher resolution, but move with more jerk. SECAM, used primarily in France, combines the best of both words: it captures 30 frames per second with 625 scanlines.

Now let's talk about tape formats, remembering that within a standard, such as NTSC, you can copy between any two formats. Within a standard, the resolution derives primarily from the material of which the

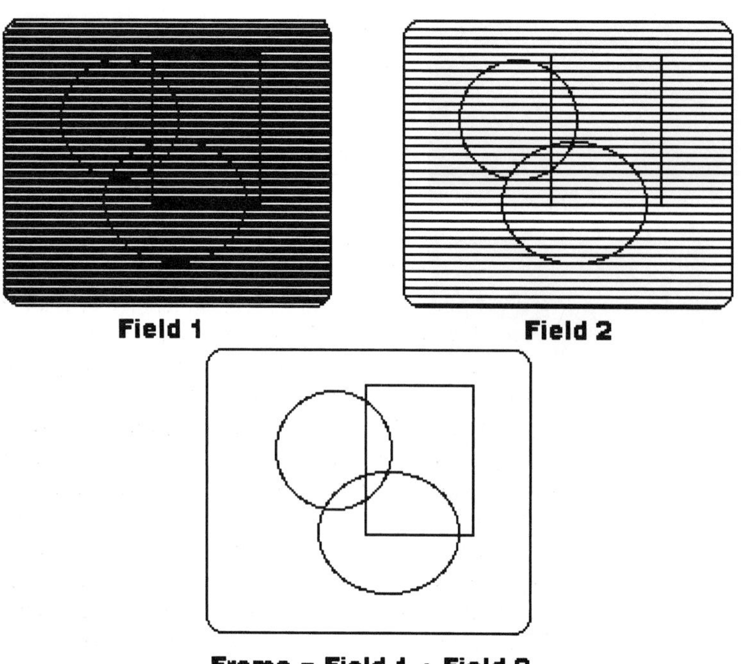

Figure 4. A frame of video is made from two fields. *The first field is composed of every other line starting from 0 to 524 shown by the lines in the figure on the left above. The second field is composed from every other line starting from 1 to 525, shown by the lines in the figure on the right above. The frame is then produced by interlacing the two fields, as shown immediately above.*

Table 2. Frames/sec and scanlines for different video standards.

Video standard	Frames/Sec	Scanlines
NTSC	30	525
PAL	25	625
SECAM	30	625

tape is composed, and by what method the signal is encoded on the tape, not only from the width of the tape. Figure 5 shows a list of tape formats ordered by increasing clarity of image.

Tapes are often referred by their width, for example, 1/2", but the width of a videotape is only partly responsible for its resolution. For instance, VHS and Betamax are both 1/2" formats, and so are Betacam and M-2. However, as you can see in Figure 5, Betacam and M-2 are higher resolution formats than VHS or Betamax. The upshot is that if you have a choice of formats with which to work, you should work with the highest clarity format available to you.

Timecode

For the best results during the editing phase, timecode should be as accurate as possible. The information in this section will help you to understand the range of options in getting timecode, and how they differ in accuracy and will affect your editing process. For example, most consumer camcorders record no timecode at all. Instead, they use something called "Control Track," which is a series of pulses, each specifying, in effect, "here lies a frame." Because the timing information is not recorded on the tape itself and seeing the timecode relies on a mechanical device (i.e. the counter) in the playback machine, there is no certain relationship between the counter number and, for example, a frame on the tape -- frames being the objects of interest during editing. Instead, Control Track yields a "relative" address for each frame, the absolute number of which can vary over successive playbacks.

When you record on a VHS tape, information about the speed at which you're recording is laid down

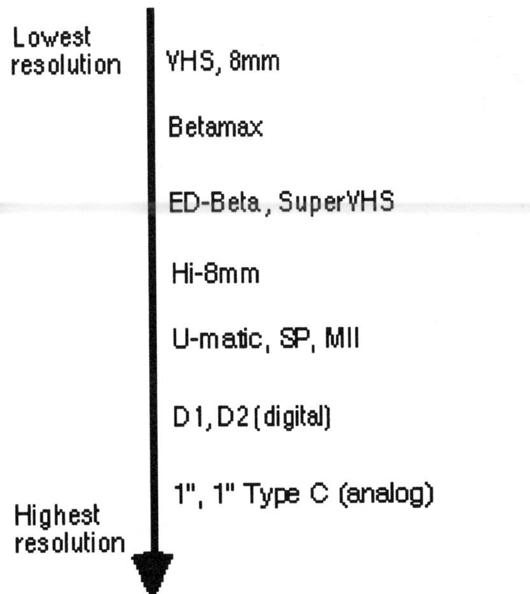

Figure 5. The clarity of images possible on videotape, ordered from least to best quality.

on the tape. Where you are on the tape is identified by a counter, which ticks as the tape rolls. But if you play forward and backward many times, the counter becomes inaccurate. Accurate editing is dependent on reproducibility, so there is a way to put actual position information into the tape. This information is called timecode.

There are two basic types of timecode: linear timecode (LTC) and vertical interval timecode (VITC) (and a Hi-8mm variant called RCTC, for Rewriteable Consumer Timecode). These timecodes provide a time stamp of each frame consisting of hours, minutes, seconds, and frames (e.g., 00:05:00:15 to indicate the 0th hour, 5th minute, 0th second, and 15th frame out of 30). VITC is kept in the part of the tape that holds the video signal. Depending on the tape format (e.g., VHS vs. Betacam), LTC timecode is either placed on one of the two audio tracks, or is given a separate track of its own. It's possible to record both LTC and VITC on a tape, and editing machines are capable of displaying both. Several years ago, LTC was the prevalent standard in the field; thus many professionals work exclusively with LTC (and many camcorders today still record only in LTC).

However, this standard is changing, for the following reason: when you pause LTC to look at a single frame, there is no guarantee that the machine can display the correct timecode (within an accuracy of a few frames). The reason has to do with where the LTC signal is recorded: just as when you pause a tape you can no longer "hear" its audio, when you pause a tape to see its LTC, as the tape slows down, the information in the audio track can't be read, forcing the machine to approximate the LTC with a counter. That counter is only accurate with some probability, usually within a frame or two. In addition, when playing back at speeds other than 1x (i.e., normal speed), LTC is rendered meaningless. This makes the editing process more difficult.

When a videotape is paused, however, the picture is still visible. In the same way, VITC, recorded on the video portion of the tape, is accurately read even when the tape is paused. Thus, only VITC can support frame-accurate editing. In the field, there is no guarantee that you can record VITC on your source tapes. If you can do it, you should, and you should record them such that they display consistent numbering for the tape — i.e., they both show the same timecode for a given frame. Because editing decks are more sophisticated than recorders in the field, it is often possible to get VITC in the edit suite even when the source tapes do not have it, if you are willing to work from a copy of the original footage. This way, you would have frame accuracy in your master tape, which facilitates editing. The bottom line is: get the best you can. If all you can get is LTC, take it! If you can get VITC also, take them both, and make sure they're consistent.

One additional thing to make sure of during production is the camera's setting with respect to timecode. Having described the basics, we must now tell you that timecode is not quite as simple as 30 frames per second. When color television came into being, nobody foresaw much future for it (!). So the simple method for calculating frames per second traditionally used for black and white pictures was retained. The slight difference in color pictures, which are actually recorded at 29.(something) frames per second, means that over some period of time a "frame-sized" discrepancy in the timecode will develop. When you're making an industrial video, or a movie in Hollywood, these discrepancies don't really matter, and so you use a timecode setting called "non-drop frame" (NDF), which is simple to read and understand. The bottom line here is that when you record in "non-drop" mode, the length of your program as indicated by the timecode will be somewhat different from elapsed clock time (the real time length of the program). You do not need to worry about this, should you notice it.

The place where this difference does matter is in television, where commercials pay by the second and it's important to know precisely how long the program material is. For these cases, "drop frame" (DF) timecode is used, and a calculation, similar to leap year calculations on calendars, drops frames when necessary until the last frame of the program is equivalent to the elapsed time of the program as measured by the standard 30 frames per second translation. The only reason for you to know this, is to make sure that when you use a professional cameraperson, they set the camera to "non-drop" frame mode, and that when you're editing, the editing decks are set to "non-drop" mode. This will insure not only easy-to-read timecode values, but also that what you see (on your source tape monitors) is what you see (on your edited tape monitor) and that you will always get the frames you think you are getting during the editing process.

Audio

Audio is complex physically as well as psychologically, and represents a technical specialty. As basic a goal as creating a final production with even audio levels (i.e., a sound track that doesn't keep increasing and decreasing on playback at a consistent setting) can be a challenging piece of work. Common video effects — such as a voice over a natural scene (with its own sounds) — are difficult edits to produce, at a minimum requiring mixing audio from two separate sources (hence each requiring their own levels and adjustments for best quality) onto the Edit Master in a way that matches the existing audio on the master tape. Maintaining even "ambient" sound across your production can also be difficult — especially if for some edits you have had to boost the signal level of a source tape for which the audio was inadequately captured. To a first approximation, the video you capture during production is the video you work with in the studio, modulo calibrating to the color bars at the beginning of each source tape. Editing audio, on the other hand, only *begins* with calibrating to the tone at the beginning of the source tape. From there, seemingly endless adjustments are possible — sometimes essential — for getting a good result. It is for these reasons that next to the Director, the Audio Engineer is the least dispensable member of the production team. Caruso and Arthur (1992) and Hausman and Palombo (1993) provide good descriptions of the basics of audio and its post production.

Editing

Insert vs. Assembly Editing. When you record a TV program at home, you know that when you play back your tape, it starts out and ends with some static. The only way to get a "clean" edit between the first recorded material and a new piece, is to play the tape, and pause it near the end of the recorded material, set the machine for "Record+Pause," and then release the Pause to begin recording. The transition from the old to new material in this case will be seamless (i.e., if you look at the transition frame by frame , there will be no frames containing black or static). But the end of the newly recorded material will end in static. This method of editing a videotape is known as "Assembly" editing, assembling the finished tape from accreting pieces of recording.

The only way to guarantee no static at the beginning or end of recorded material is to use a type of recording called "Insert" editing. Insertion editing depends upon the fact that a videotape has been previously recorded. Typically, we prepare a tape for insert editing by recording black and silence onto the tape. Of course, it would work just as well to insert into Star Wars, but creating and previewing your edits out of the chaos of another recorded program would be difficult, to say the least. You can insert audio, video, or both in a given edit, and the result is to replace whatever was formerly on the master tape with the source audio and/or video. This separation of edit functions is useful for crafting exactly the result you want: for example, to "center " narrative audio "under" a visual scene. Or, for example, to provide a "lead" into the next scene by starting the audio from that scene before cutting to it visually (known as an "audio advance"). As with other technical aspects of edited video, there is a tradeoff in quality and effort to use these different editing methods.

Linear vs. Nonlinear. By its very nature, creating a video means copying audio and video from a source tape to a master tape, piece by piece, in order, until the final production is finished. If you then discover an error in the middle of the production, and the fix requires a longer or shorter piece of video to replace what's there, you're in trouble. In such a case, you either have to fix the mistake and re-record everything that follows it, or you're going to have to "drop" a generation by copying the production up to the mistake, insert the correction, and then copying the rest of the original production. This calamity obviously results from the linear nature of videotape, and is a description of linear editing.

In the world of film, it's much easier. You find the mistake in the middle of your production, grab your scissors, cut it out, splice in the new scene, and you have a corrected production. For years, filmmakers eschewed video as a medium largely for this reason. As a result, effort was invested in making video editing simulate film editing. Nonlinear editors have been the result (see Rubin, 1991, for a well-written account of the evolution of film editing from traditional methods to nonlinear editing).

A nonlinear editor keeps an internal representation of the video program, and requires that all source material be available through random access. Before it was practical to do this with digital storage, random access was achieved by replicating the source footage needed for a particular section of the final production onto multiple videotapes or laserdiscs that were then made simultaneously accessible (e.g., by a bank of camcorders or machines). There was no recorder in the nonlinear editing process; its only result was a list -- the edit decision list, that specifies exactly which bits of source video and audio to put where in the final production.

From the system's point of view, then, nothing more than a set of instructions is being created. From the editor's (or filmmaker's) point of view, however, "running" the edits was indistinguishable from viewing an actual edited tape. Once the list of edit decisions is made, the final production tape can be made automatically. In fact, in many ways, a nonlinear editing system makes it easier for the Director and Editor to produce a variety of rough cuts.

From the earliest (and very expensive) systems, to the desktop systems of today, nonlinear systems are steadily improving their interfaces and their cost/space tradeoffs. Many television and movie projects are now carried out with nonlinear editing systems, that are workstation-based. Today these systems usually cost in the tens of thousands of dollars, but the power gained in quality and convenience of work is enormous. This is the future.

Digital video places huge demands on your computer in terms of hard disk space and processing speed. A 15 min. movie, 320X240 pixels (1/2 screen size), with 15 frames per second (fps) could easily fill 300MBs. The same movie at 30 fps (full motion as in USA TV) and full screen (640X480 pixels) could take up 2GB. To obtain decent results with any size or frame-rate you need at least a 68040 or 486 processor (or even better, a 604 or Pentium processor). Benford (1995) and Soderberg and Hudson (1995) provide good introductory overviews of digital desktop editing.

Tape Types

You'll be surprised by the number of tapes that you will have by the end of a project. Just remember that all new tapes should be prepared in advance of their use. It is best to put bars and tone on all tapes.

The following is a summary of the kinds of tapes that will make up your work.

Source tape(s). A 30-minute source tape is much better than a 2-hour tape, since it reduces the amount you have to shuttle back and forth on tape during editing to find the piece of video you want. Compared to shuttling on the tape, putting in a different tape saves wear and tear on both the human editor and the editing equipment. Set your timecode to separately identify each tape. For example, start your first source tape at 01:00:00:00, your second source tape at 02:00:00:00, etc., noting that if you have more than 12 source tapes (6 hours of footage), the number will repeat on a 12-hour clock. This enables quick identification of the tape during editing. For a 30-minute tape, you can get away with 30 seconds to 1 minute of bars and tone.

Collection Tapes. If you have many source tapes, and the tapes you will be editing onto are of high enough quality to tolerate duplication well (e.g., U-matic or better quality; see Figure 5), it is often simpler to copy those pieces of source material that you know you will use onto a single intermediate location -- a collection tape. This enables easier access to related material, the goal being to edit the final production from only a single or multiple collection tapes. Collection tapes can also facilitate grouping related material when the source tapes contain that material in a widely dispersed manner (for example, when editing from multiple interviews, where answers to the same question by different interviewees will be dispersed across the set of source tapes). We will have more to say about strategies for working with material in section 40.4.3.

Rough Cut Edit Master. This is a draft version of your program. Unless you have unlimited access to a high-end edit suite, you will probably want to create a draft of your final program in a less expensive environment. There are other reasons to create a rough cut as well. A rough cut allows you to work out the detailed decisions about your edits in a prototype of the final piece.

Throughout production, you will have what feels like an unassembled jigsaw puzzle in your mind of all the pieces, the possible elements of audio and video for your final result. These need to be blended together to create the final, polished production, and doing so involves a cascade of detailed decisions about what material to include, in what order, and what exactly to include on each edit. In post-production, these elements are meticulously laid down on tape to create the final result. If at that point you or your customer finds the result unacceptable or unsuitable, there will be a lot of work involved in redoing it.

Prototyping the elements of the final program in a rough cut allows you to put your initial effort and attention on content selection and composition rather than the creation of perfect edits. The rough cut allows you to get a sense of whether the program will be successful. Do a rough cut rough, dirty and fast, expending the least amount of effort possible to get the result. Don't worry about color. Don't worry about audio volume, or the exact coordination of audio and video. Don't be compulsive about "flash" frames (one or two empty frames between edits). Let them be, and then show it to everybody and anybody who will watch (just ask the security guards at IBM, who over the years have become astute video critics). What you are trying to do is to make decisions about what you want, what works, and, to a fairly precise degree, what you want to create on the final tape. Another reason to do this is that your customer may not know what they really want until they see a program that really isn't what they want.

So the main goal of creating a rough cut is to come to a concrete understanding of the final production. Once that is achieved, the challenge is to produce the edits in a final tape, the Edit Master. If you are working exclusively in a high-end edit suite, the information recorded in the edit decision list (EDL) during the creation of the rough cut will provide the information needed to create the final Edit Master. For most of us, however, a less extravagant approach is necessary. An approach that helps is to make all of the edits onto the rough cut tape using the "window dub" technique, wherein the resulting recorded video image has timecode visibly "burned" into it. This means that later, when viewing the rough cut, you can manually assemble an edit list to guide the creation of the final Edit Master. For audio from a source other than the video footage used in an edit (e.g., a narration source), a manual list of edits will be helpful.

Edit Master. This is the tape on which you create your production from source tape material. It *is* the final video production, composed of numerous video, audio, video + audio, and/or special effect edits, as well as titles, etc. The Edit Master may also be a 30-minute tape or it may be a two-hour tape; the general rule is to use one edit master per production, whether your production is ten minutes or an hour long. This can mean "wasting" some tape that might be used for a future production, but guaranteeing the safety of finished work is more important than using every bit of available tape. Your work is much more valuable than the tape, and it is still far too easy to inadvertently overwrite a finished piece of work (e.g., by incorrectly specifying the location of an edit). A single Edit Master supports a practice of storing the Edit Master as soon as a production is finished. Single tapes for archival storage also lend themselves to more flexibility in how they are categorized (and hence how easily they may be retrieved in the future).

Typically, to prepare an Edit Master, you will record black and silence on the entire tape, set your timecode to 00:00:00:00 at the beginning of the tape, record bars and tone for 30 seconds, followed by 15 seconds of bars only, then 15 seconds of black and silence, followed by a countdown from 10. You are then ready to record the edits in your final program. A variation that we often use is to record bars and tone for two minutes, followed by 30 seconds of black and silence, and then the program, which begins at 00:02:30:00.

Duplication Master. As long as your tape format is of sufficiently high quality that it can tolerate copying, it is always better to copy your Edit Master onto a fresh tape, called the Duplication Master, which is then used for mass reproduction of your program (which is often outsourced). Sometimes providing a Duplication Master will be required. If you are making a laserdisc, for example, you will send a Duplication Master rather than an Edit Master tape, because the laserdisc production process is more reliable with single-edit tapes (i.e., the Duplication Master has a single edit created by the act of copying the entire Edit Master tape). Now we can appreciate one of the practical reasons that professionals are so reluctant to work with duplicated raw footage during the editing process: final reproductions made from a Duplication Master (which is *at best* a second generation tape -- one generation for the Edit Master and a second generation for the Duplication or "Dupe" Master), will be, at best, *third* generation video.

40.3.5 Ethical and Legal Issues

The only video you can put into your production is that to which you have legal rights. Even if you videotape someone yourself, unless you have their permission, you do not have legal tape. The best recommendation for shooting on a street corner or other public place, is that if you offer any direction to the subjects (e.g., "Could you walk closer to the wall?"), you must obtain a signed release from that person. But for a crowd walking by, to whom you give no direction , the video may be used. This statement is not intended to constitute legal advice, and you should get legal counsel to be sure what you are doing is legal.

Most companies have standard copyright release forms covering spoken or written words recorded from individuals in the course of company work. Most professional societies also have standard release forms (e.g., ACM). Obviously it is advisable to use any forms standard to your organization before creating your own. An old adage says that contracts are not binding that do not include an exchange of value. If your copyright form says that you pay your subject nothing, the release may not be legal. By convention, the release form often calls for a payment of "one mil" in order to meet the requirement of a valid release.

Ethical issues raised by video and audio recording can be complex (Mackay, 1995), but at the least, the setting, the purpose of making a recording, and how it will be used should be part of any informed consent obtained from people or organizations being taped. In addition, videographers have an obligation to show "talent" or interviewees in as straightforward and honest a manner as possible. The potential for introducing bias during the editing process is great; for example, editors are taught how to "handle" debates. If a person hesitates before answering a question, a viewer will tend to see that person as uncertain of themselves, or perhaps lying. A person who responds immediately, on the other hand, may be perceived as confident and truthful. This places a lot of power, and hence responsibility, in the hands of the editor who can decide whether or not the hesitation is included in a final edit, and/or whether different actors are deliberately edited differently for effect. Another example is to take care to light the subject appropriately. Video has great power to make a person look more or less attractive. Taking the time to literally show each person you film in their best light shows respect for them.

40.3.6 Using Professional Support

It isn't always obvious to know when or how much professional support you may need on a particular project, and we can't give you a definite answer without knowing what you are trying to do and your personal knowledge and skills . As stated previously, a 3-person crew for production is the recommended minimum. But this crew assumes that you will assume all of the other roles (i.e., producer, director, scriptwriter, etc.). If you are unable or unwilling to assume all of these roles, there are professionals who can be used in a collaborative manner to achieve your goals.

For post production, most people can learn how to edit, but not all edit production houses will allow access to their equipment. If you have access to your own post production equipment, the advantages of being able to take your time, and to indulge a greater degree of experimentation, may pay off in a better result. If you have worked collaboratively during production with a person experienced in making video, they may also be a great asset during post production, both because they know the material that you have to work with, and for their experience in composing material. The operator of a hired edit suite, on the other hand, expects you to come in with a plan.

40.4 Creating an Edited Video

Now that we have laid out some of the fundamental aspects of video, we turn our attention to the actual process of creating an edited video. An overview of this process is shown in Figure 6, placing the main activities of videomaking within the Pre-Production, Production, and Post Production stages. This scheme constitutes a generic plan for making a video. In this section, we discuss each of the activities, beginning with a consideration of what makes a video good and continuing with how each of the activities supports the creation of a successful video. For further information, Hedgecoe (1992, 1989) provides a thorough introductory treatment of the process of creating a video.

40.4.1 Pre-Production Phase

The style and amount of pre-planning depends largely on what you are recording and for what end-purpose. Although it is quite possible to do the wrong sort of planning, in our experience it is hard to do too much of the *right* sort of planning, with the general case being that "proper prior planning prevents poor performance." Planning of the unproductive sort can waste time or even cause failure during production, for example, if it is too general or too specific about the shots to be obtained, or if it makes assumptions incompatible with the shooting situation (e.g., assuming a degree of control, coordination with actors/interviewees, schedule, or direction that is not possible under the circumstances). Planning of the better sort creates a solid sense of purpose and a focus on what needs to be accomplished during production, and documents in advance resources that may need to be called upon due to unforeseen circumstances on site. Such plans may well contain detail (e.g., the order of questions to be asked

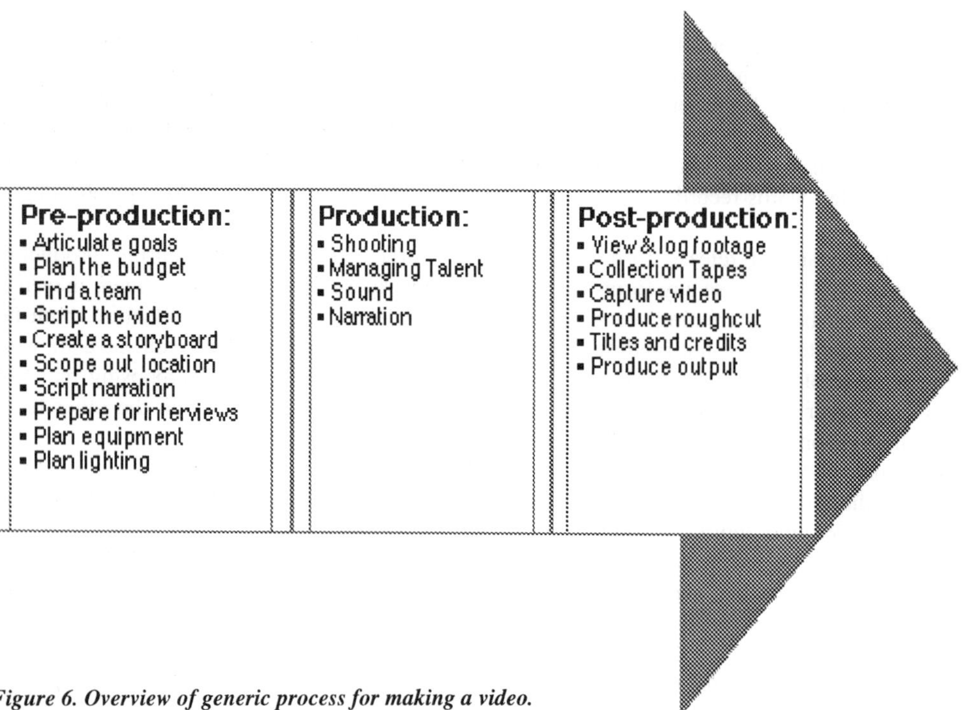

Figure 6. Overview of generic process for making a video.

of an interviewee), but they also should prepare the Director and other crew members to feel that they will be able to adapt to the circumstances at hand without jeopardizing their goals (e.g., to skip questions, expand on questions, and/or to return to questions later in the interview, depending on the interviewee's responses).

Articulate Goals

A good video is one that fulfills its purpose. It is *always* important to know who the audience is for the video, and at the end of watching it, what they will know that they didn't know before viewing it. If you cannot answer these questions after watching your video, or worse, if you never asked these questions while making your video, the final result will suffer, along with your viewers.

How a video will be used, and the context in which it occurs is important, too. Video has some properties that must be kept in mind when planning how to present information: for example, that the information passes by quickly and there is no guarantee (even if there is opportunity) that missed material will be replayed. If viewers will have no control over seeing it again, then you have to pace your presentation to make sure that the information will penetrate. This can mean that you make an explicit organization very obvious, so that viewers can put information into context easily. It can mean that you repeat information. It can mean that you summarize at the end of the video what has been presented. A style that is desirable (and perhaps familiar from other contexts) is: tell your audience what you're going to say, say it, and then tell them what you said. This method may sound needlessly redundant, but for an audience unfamiliar with your material, it can make a tremendous difference in how much of your message gets through. With video, such blatant organizational cues can be even more important than in other contexts.

If your goal is to have someone learn, it is essential not to bore them. If a person's mind wanders while the video is playing, they can miss crucial information that cannot easily be picked up later. Judging pace is difficult, and requires a solid knowledge of the audience and sensitivity to the material you are trying to convey. Unless the viewer happens to be your Mom or a dedicated friend, a viewer's attention can be expected to naturally fluctuate in any case while viewing your material, so construct your video to provide structural cues to attract and direct the viewer's attention. Lessons from filmmaking may be useful here to give you an idea of how different aspects of a shot (for example, setting, camera angle, framing, how tight a shot, camera movement such as push or pull during the shot, etc.) can be used to create specific reactions in the viewer (e.g., Preston, 1994; Rabiger, 1989).

Even when viewers do have control over the video, so they can back it up and replay it (as, for example, in an interactive software system), video is not the same as a paper reference, such as a book. If someone is speaking, it is hard to find in the video the part that you want to hear again. Books can be searched in a variety of ways by content; searching video can be far more frustrating. No matter what the intended use, it usually benefits viewers when the Director creates structure in the video that can be exploited later for finding material by its content.

If your purpose is to sell an idea or concept, to convince someone of the truth of what is being said, then including detailed information, which viewers may not remember specifically, can still support an impression that the argument is well-supported. What *is* remembered is the overall points that the detail supported. If, on the other hand, the goal is to be informative, or to convey the details themselves, then it will be important to use the "preview-present-summarize" technique described above. Videos aren't really ideally suited for giving extremely detailed presentations -- for example, showing the mathematics of physical principles -- but what they *do* do well is to show motion. So while watching a series of equations being written on a chalkboard may be tedious on video, an illustration of how a mathematical formula works could be exciting. Taking a mathematical concept and demonstrating the relationship captured by an equation -- for example, inverse proportionality -- through video takes much better advantage of the strengths of video. Video might not be that great for showing the derivation of a formula, but for gaining insight into what the formula captures, it may be great.

Plan the Budget

Money and access to the best equipment is not enough to ensure a good production. A person, using minimal resources, using creativity in the design and the types of visual shots used, can create a video with very high impact. Sometimes having a large budget can backfire, if the Director is sucked in by fancy, but unmotivated "bells and whistles" (e.g., fancy transitions). The only time a transition should be used is to make some statement. This is comparable to the use of multiple fonts in a desktop publishing-created newsletter.

On the other hand, what you have to work with in terms of resources should be considered and planned for carefully for the best result. Think of the design of your video as a great interior decorator might think about creating a magnificent and dramatic interior design on the slimmest of budgets: you might use one elaborate piece that draws attention, build a focal point, and then make sure the rest of the room adds to it, giving it a rich context. In the same way, video can have a lot of "cheap" elements to add richness (e.g., stills to fill out an interactive software system), but you want to make sure it has some elements that shine, as well. For example, if you're using a narrator, don't have them sitting down the whole time. Rather, have them go to the lab and look at the people working. Do something different, and that becomes an exciting element. Every part of the video does not have to be dramatic and different, but a few elements done this way can go a long way.

Where do you want to invest your available money? Good audio is essential. If you can't understand what speakers are saying, you're going to lose your audience. Audio mixers and microphones are very cheap to rent, and can enhance the quality of your results dramatically. If your people are green, on the other hand, viewers will probably just think they are a little nervous on-screen or adjust the controls on their monitor.

Lighting is important. The typical lighting kit involves 3 lights: a main light to light from the front, a backlight to separate the subject from the background, and a fill light to get rid of shadows. Lighting kit rentals are pretty cheap. If your budget can't afford that, you can go to the hardware store and buy 3 aluminum reflectors and hang some netting in front of it (avoiding fire hazards). This breaks up the light and smoothes it out, since the light out of lamps is usually too harsh. This is why photographers often shine the light at a reflective surface (such as white cardboard) instead of directly at the subject. Most directors of photography keep a "junk" box with scraps of black velvet, clothes pins to hold colored filters or gauze-like entities, and other odds and ends that may be helpful in lighting a scene. What's essential in lighting is to be creative, try various things, and watch the result on the monitor.

The tape format you work with is a place that's worth spending money. Work in the highest-quality format you can afford. This investment will pay itself back in multiple ways: making textual shots more readable, holding up better under the inevitable degradation that results from copying during the editing process, and overall better-looking pictures due to better resolution. Even when your end-product is a VHS tape, your production will benefit from shooting and editing in a better-quality format. You do *not* have to shoot and edit in the same format as the final delivery format.

"Renting" people is fun too. Frequently collaborate with other members of a production team. If you can find a cameraperson, they will often have an audio engineer that they like to work with, and vice versa. Capitalize on such relationships; it will save time and hassle during production. Although the cameraperson will probably also have a grip to recommend, a member of your project can usually be drafted to carry heavy equipment, and will enjoy being part of movie-making. It's also another way to get another person who understands the goals of the video on site for second opinions.

Your cameraperson will often be able to provide good advice on whether you have all the equipment you need on the day of the shoot, etc., if you discuss with them what you plan to do. They may help you with opinions on set decoration, framing of your shots, etc., and they really like being considered part of the creative team. If the Director merely gives them orders, they will tend to follow them and shut up. If the Director solicits their advice, they will usually test to see if you really mean it, and once they're convinced, can be an invaluable asset. Use extra paid-for time to have them teach you!

Find a Team

It is always hard to find a good team the first time. The best approach is word-of-mouth. Talk to people who have used video professionals in your geographic area, and find out who they like to work with and why. Don't, however follow such advice blindly. Regardless of how you find the names of potential people to work with always ask for and contact references, and listen carefully to what these people say. Ask to see a portfolio of their previous work. When studying previous work from a cameraperson, look carefully for how s/he shoots. What is the composition of the shot? Be sure to assess what kind of work a cameraperson has done previously; shooting live television sports coverage, movies, interviews, or weddings, for example, requires different skills that may be more or less appropriate to your situation. Try to find someone whose strengths and experience complement what you are trying to achieve.

Professional video crews will often work together, so once you've found one person, you can always ask them for the names of other people they like working with. But again, follow-up references and ask for examples of their previous work.

One of the decisions you will have to make is whether to use paid or unpaid actors (in video jargon these people are referred to as 'talent,' as is anyone you film to whom you provide direction). In choosing between paid and unpaid talent, there are tradeoffs. Unpaid talent tends to be more believable in technical areas — they know how to pronounce technical terms, and on screen often seem more comfortable with the material. Their weakness is that they will not know how to work with the camera, they may feel uncomfortable looking into the camera, or they may lose their composure when the camera is rolling. There is no way to predict this: sometimes an introverted person will blossom when the camera turns on; they will work to a camera better than to another person. Other times, a strong, personable individual will turn to mush when the camera rolls. A mistake you sometimes see in video is that a person who is used to live public presentations will go into a shoot situation with a lot of confidence. But in fact, presenting to a camera is very different. A speaker who fidgets, fumbles, hems and haws may be fine in a live presentation, but will be horrible in video, where instead of relief and pacing, the viewer is likely simply to be irritated. A general guideline is that a presentation that might take an hour to present live, may be only 10 minutes when the material is carefully edited in a video.

Paid talent may be used to the camera, but may be less convincing in the end. One of the advantages of paid talent is that they usually have control over their voice. Unpaid talent tends to "punch" the beginning of their sentences, and trail off at the end. This makes editing very difficult. An experienced speaker knows to keep voice tone within recording boundaries, and can adjust their "energy" level in what they are saying as the Director requires. Paid talent is guaranteed to be comfortable in front of a camera.

Another thing not to forget when considering talent, whether paid or not, is to make sure that you obtain the necessary release forms to use them on video that you will freely distribute.

Script the video

Creating a script for a video — laying out in text the order of shots, the narration, the visuals needed, and sometimes the structure of the video — is always a good idea. Most of the time you will script before you shoot, but for some kinds of video the scripting is essentially done after footage is shot and the content of the footage is therefore known. For example, documentaries, or composing material for an interactive system from interviews, require that any detailed scripting wait until the material has been shot.

You need to decide how long to make your video.

An average-length video that people tolerate is about 10 minutes. If your video is particularly exciting, you can hold them for longer, but you really don't want to go over 20 minutes (remember, 20 minutes of "video" time can be roughly comparable to 2 hours of lecture material). To make a longer video, see it in shorter pieces, where the breaks between pieces are obvious enough that a viewer knows when to take a break. For example, the American news magazine program "*60 Minutes*" is really four 15-minute programs, and each 15-minute program is typically broken down into three 5-minute segments.

A simple but effective format for a script has three parts to a page (Figure 7). The topmost part is an (optional) diagram that shows the graphic you're going to use (or a picture or sketch of the video image or animation sequence). The middle part of the script page is the list of visuals and, optionally, a list of the main audio elements. Every time the scene changes, it gets a different number. The third part of the script page is the narration, with the location of visuals and audio changes marked in the narrative (by inserting the list number at the exact location of the change).

Create a Storyboard

It is also a good idea to storyboard your video. A storyboard (Figure 8) consists of a sketch of the main frames of the video. You can use the storyboard as a framework for taking notes about lighting and how you will get particular shots when visiting the location before the shoot. This kind of visual record of your intentions is also useful for discussions with other members of the team in preparing for the shoot.

Scope Out the Location

If you are interested in shooting at a particular location, you will need to visit it first to determine whether it is available for shooting, and under what conditions. If you are shooting in a public location, you must consider the impact of other people and activity on your production: Will crowds of people milling nearby destroy your audio? The people who own these locations should buy into your project and also feel part of the team. This is facilitated by advance planning and getting people synchronized before challenges arise.

When visiting a location, you must work out the camera positions, and check for lighting conditions at different times of day. If you're going to shoot inside, then you should check the availability and positions of electrical outlets. Be sure to find out what constraints exist on moving furniture or other items that you may want to adjust to create a better set.

Another area of logistics is to plan for equipment failure. Few people take a backup camera on site because it's just too expensive. But if something bizarre happens, it is helpful to know whether and where backup equipment can be obtained quickly. If you cannot replace equipment, the considerable expense involved in mounting a shoot can be wasted. If you have hired a crew local to the location of the shoot, they will often know the resources of the area intimately.

Script Narration

The purpose of the narration script is to support the production of narration. The script is used both by the Director, to see what the narrator is supposed to say, and by the narrator to say it. A narration script should use short sentences, should be printed in short lines with an easy to read font, and marked with prosody (i.e., marking the text with visual cues to intonation, such as words to emphasize). Some narrators prefer to begin with an unmarked script and mark it up themselves during shooting as it becomes clear what works best. Including the list of the visuals and indexing them to the narration script can assist the narrator in understanding what the video is trying to convey.

Prepare for Interviews

Interviews can be conducted either with the interviewer on camera or off camera. In videos for HCI, it will probably be more common for the interviewer to be off camera, so we will concentrate on this situation, although the kinds of questions are generally similar. However, interviewing a subject while you are off camera creates some unusual features you need to be aware of, compared to normal conversation. As for the questions themselves, general, open-ended questions tend to produce more interesting answers and keep the interviewee more relaxed than a specific question that may cause your talent to panic if they can't think of anything immediately. We recommend that you always begin an interview with concrete, easy-to-answer questions, to give the interviewee time to accommodate to being on camera.

The physical setup for an interview is as follows. The interviewer sits slightly behind the camera, and next to it (the subject looks slightly off camera). As interviewer, you should concentrate completely on the interviewee: make eye contact and hold it, listen intently,

The Global Desktop of the Future

(1) (2) (3)

Part 1: Overview

(1) fade from black to David at MIDI keyboard
(2) dissolve to "The Global Desktop of the Future"
(3) David at the computer terminal
(4) CU of transposer change
(5) David pulling apart component cables
(6) David at computer terminal
... (etc.)

(A1) Fade up introductory music (David playing in studio)
(A2) Fade down introductory music
(A3) David playing duet with remote colleague

(1) (A1) Meet David. David makes his living composing music for the movies. Up until a few years ago, David had nothing more to do with a computer than using the MIDI interface to his keyboards and his synthesizers. But in this world of tomorrow, David's life has changed.

What's different? Computing is different. And because of that, the art of composing has changed as well. (2) (A2)

Figure 7. Part of a script, used by the authors in 1992 in making a usage scenario video entitled "The Global Desktop of the Future."

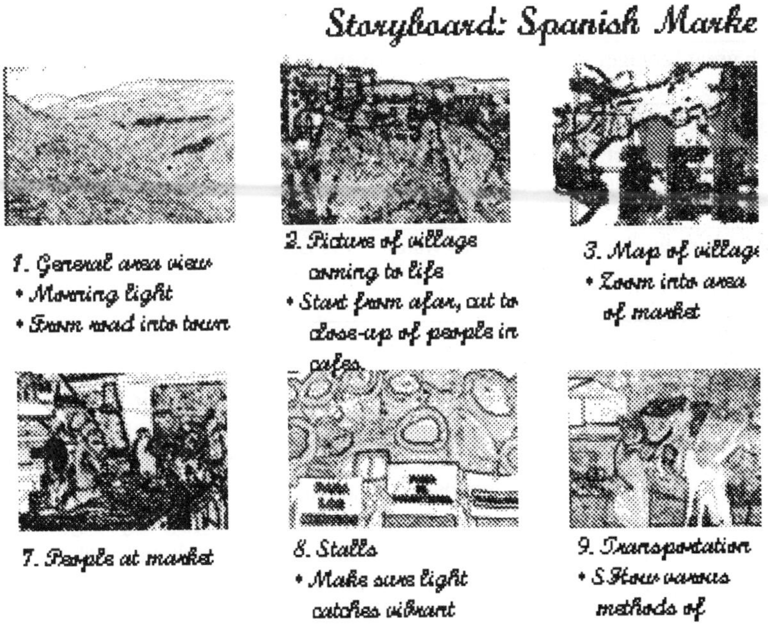

Storyboard: Spanish Marke

1. General area view
• Morning light
• From road into town

2. Picture of village coming to life
• Start from afar, out to close-up of people in cafes.

3. Map of village
• Zoom into area of market

7. People at market

8. Stalls
• Make sure light catches vibrant

9. Transportation
• Show various methods of

Figure 8. A fragment of a storyboard for a video. *Storyboards create a visual record of the video, which can be used to make notes and for discussion with other members of the team.*

react to what you hear strongly but silently, be aware that your face can hold a lot of excitement and intensity to get up and keep up the excitement of the interviewee. Nod your head in agreement, encourage them. Tell them beforehand that you will not be able to make any sound in response to them, but you will let them know how they're doing by your facial expression. The interviewer can NOT talk: saying 'yes' or 'no' or 'I'll say,' etc. The hardest thing for an interviewer is to be quiet!

Before the interview, you should take a reasonable amount of time (perhaps up to 30 minutes), to talk to the interviewee to make them comfortable and to build a bond. This conversation preferably takes place well away from the hustle and bustle of preparing the scene for shooting. The interviewee needs to trust you, for best results. Encourage the interviewee not to make reference to you, to things they've already said, or to answer a question without repeating it first, and warn them that this can seem awkward at first, but they will get used to it. Give them a chance to practice repeating a question before answering it. If possible, sit on the same type of chair, to keep eyes at the same level. You don't want the interviewee looking up or down. The camera eye should look straight on into the interviewees eyes. If they flub a question, remember it yourself, and don't make a big deal of it, but towards the end of the interview, come back to that topic and ask again. If you're outside, expect that you will have to pause for airplanes, ambulances, etc. ("it's a jungle out there!"). If an interviewee does refer to you, or make other mistakes, don't worry about it, and don't keep correcting them, which will only make them nervous and perhaps ruin the whole interview. Praise them continuously; most people are nervous on camera, and they need feedback to know how they're doing and how they're coming across -- and not just at the beginning. So tell them they're doing a good job (white lies can be handy here), and do so throughout the shoot.

Plan Equipment and Lighting

Before going out on the shoot, you should check all the equipment. Make sure that it is all functioning appro-

Table 3. A summary of tips for shooting

• Great movies start with great footage. Videotape is cheap, so shoot lots of it.
• Use a variety of shots -- take close-ups as well as panoramas. Shoot the same scene from several angles. Remember to shoot long (30-60 seconds) shots — good for establishing shots and backdrops for titles.
• Use a tripod-- bouncy camera work is impossible to watch. This is especially true for digital movies.

priately and you have the necessary batteries, lenses, tripods, lighting gear (with spare bulbs, etc.). The day before the shoot you should charge all the batteries. You must also check all your tape stock. You can never be over-prepared for a shoot! It may seem like a lot of set-up effort, but remember that you often have only one chance to get the footage, so you want to make sure that everything you need is there and in good working order. Do not scrimp on supplies because you plan a shoot of only a certain duration. Production time is the time to follow the old adage of "Be Prepared."

40.4.2 Production Phase

Shooting

Inevitably, the day or days of major shooting come to pass. Capturing the original footage you need for your video is one of the most exciting and nerve-racking aspects of working with video (Table 3). So much depends on the quality of the footage you are able to shoot. In addition, conducting a shoot is (relatively) expensive, so there is pressure not to waste time or resources, but at the same time not to forget any piece of video that will be needed in post production and hard to replace if it is not shot. It's good to remember that while the people involved in your shoot may be expensive, videotape is not, and a shoot is your big chance, so shoot early and shoot often, and err on the side of getting too much rather than too little.

As the Director, it is important to know whether what you shot is what you need. To determine that, you can't rely on your cameraperson telling you that you have the shot. You need to make sure that there is a monitor connected to the camera during the shoot, and that you are watching the monitor (not the talent) during the shoot. Very few camerapeople, when the shoot has been going for a while, are willing to tell you of a slight camera motion (or other mistake) that is made during a good take of your talent. Since it is often impossible to tell whether you can live with such mistakes while on site, you will need to detect them and decide whether to retake the shot immediately.

Tape can have blemishes. The only way to guarantee you have a good take is to go back and look at the take you want to keep while on site. So as the take is being shot, the Director watches the monitor to make sure the action is right, the talent is good, etc. Afterwards, watching the take meant to be used again, the Director watches for the quality of the shot. On reviewing, any problems with the tape will show up. In other words, first watch for content, then review for mechanical or other quality glitches.

An experienced cameraperson will naturally tend to frame shots in a way that seems appropriate to him or her, and will push, pull, or pan the shot as appropriate to the action. Nevertheless, as the Director, you may want to retake shots with a different framing than the cameraperson adopts spontaneously. It is your responsibility to make sure you get a variety of shots at different distances and angles, to get establishing shots of long duration, to record ambient audio (shooting "silence" with everything and everybody in place; see the section on Sound below) at regular intervals along the tape, etc. As you watch the monitor during shooting, keep in mind what you may want to do with the footage you are looking at during post production. For example, if a subject is being interviewed and saying great stuff, but hemming and hawing at the beginning of each sentence, be sure to get ambient immediately after the interview (or even during it if you expect it to be very long) so that you will have appropriate "silence" to clean up the interviewee's speech in post production.

Finally, if you have an assistant available during the shoot, you can attempt to have them generate a rough log of each tape being shot. Having this can save time during post production in locating particular footage, and in remembering which takes you considered best, and why. At the very least, assistant or not, note the location (camera timecode) of ambient sound recordings, and what is on the tape, if not specific takes. Making a record can also help you to assess whether you are getting what you need at each shooting location.

Managing Talent

Talent refers to anyone you shoot to whom you provide direction. This includes a wide range of people, from experts or laypeople being interviewed on tape, to people being shot in a "natural" setting, to professional actors and narrators. Be prepared to address a range of personal and sometimes delicate issues as Director. In our experience, a matter-of-fact and early approach to such issues will resolve them most effectively.

The somewhat chaotic business of setting up a shoot, culminating in an array of hot lights, people, and a camera lens — all focused on a single spot — can make a person nervous, particularly if they are unaccustomed to being on camera. When people get nervous, some of them sweat. The camera sees that perspiration, and it either makes you wonder about the speaker, or it annoys. You want to find some way of cleaning them up. You can bring powder to use, but be sure it is hypo-allergenic if you use it. A dry person with hives is no better than a wet person without them. Keeping a supply of wet and dry paper towels to wipe the talent down between takes, is helpful. Keeping the talent away from the hubbub of the setup can be useful as well; if you can spare a sympathetic person, have them sit down in a quiet place with the talent and chat.

People are often sensitive about their appearance, and part of the Director's responsibility, particularly when people are presenting themselves, is to make the talent look their best on tape. A person with thin hair, for example, doesn't like to be reminded of it. But they can forget the fact that you powdered their head more easily than seeing it shine every time they watch your video. It might be a little embarrassing to talk to the talent about such topics, but it's better to do it once, and forever have a better result when they (or others in their presence) watch the video. This is also why it is often advisable to limit the shoot to the people directly involved.

Sound

When you have a person speaking, you'll naturally record and use the sound of the person's voice. However, when you are shooting "cutaways" (footage that will "cover" a person speaking — e.g., as in showing a playground while a parent being interviewed is talking about dangers), it is important to record and use the sound that is natural to the cutaway scene (e.g., the sound of the children in the playground). This adds richness your production, and without it, the video feels flat and the absence of sound from what is being seen distracts the viewer. A door slams and there is no sound. That would be considered weird in real life, so don't do it in your video either if the effect you are after is realism.

Music adds a whole dimension of richness to video, and is used for a wide variety of purposes, including to add drama, to evoke a mood or establish a context, to attract the viewer's attention, to convey emotional aspects of the visual scene, to help structure the video, to signal the appearance of characters, transitions, etc. The use of music should be as deliberate as any other aspect of your video production, which is to say that it should be motivated by how it contributes to your overall goals, and then planned and integrated with the other elements of the production.

Though we are not often aware of it, not all "silence" is equal. The sound of silence, the "ambient" background noise, varies with each location at which you shoot. *Recording ambient sound from every shoot location is essential*; it is absolutely required. It is what the Editor uses to make otherwise unusable audio usable, and to compose audio that is unsuitable in its timing to the video. For example, the Director wishes to use one sentence of narration after another sentence, but the last word of the first sentence, and the first word of the second sentence are too close together. "Ambient" allows the Editor to build a natural-sounding separation that will lengthen the amount of time between the two sentences. When recording ambient, it is important to mark the location of ambient on the source tape visually by focusing on the same thing each time a recording is made, or waving one's hand in front of the camera, etc. The visual signal later makes it easier for the Editor to locate a source of ambient when needed. If the tape is long, recording ambient at multiple sites on the tape is useful; a guideline is to record ambient once every 15-30 minutes on each source tape. You can later pick up needed ambient without navigating the entire tape. Ambient should be recorded under *exactly* the same circumstances as the shoot: with everyone in the same place, the talent still miked, etc. Everyone freezes for 30 seconds on the Director's cue while the camera rolls. It sounds easy, but try it before you decide. 30 seconds can seem like a long time,

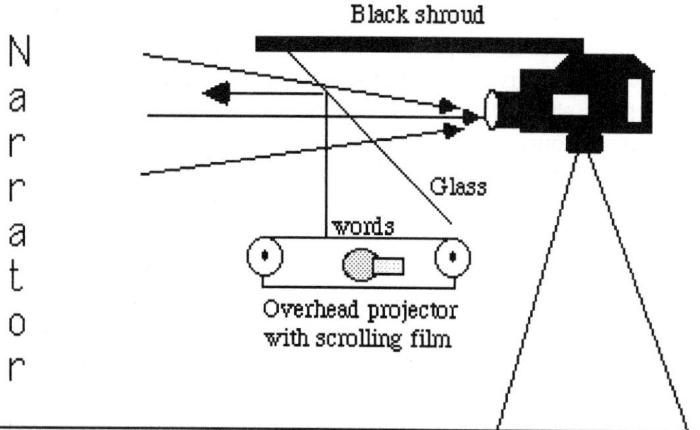

Figure 9. How to make a teleprompter. *(Kelley, personal communication)*

especially if you're trying not to move or make noise. Worse, waiting for the Director to signal the end of an ambient recording can produce irresistible urges to giggle; if this happens, the Director may use discretion in dealing with transgressors.

Narration

Narration is used to inform. An entire video can be composed with an unseen narrator or we can see the narrator at some times and cover him or her with other footage at other times. We can structure the video so that one voice conveys general principles, and a second voice teaches specifics. The person narrating needs to be moved far away from the whir of onsite machines, such as the recording machine, or a computer. Usually you'll attach a directional mike to the person's clothing, making sure that it doesn't brush against their clothes as they move and talk. If you're using a boom (overhead) microphone, you will need to apply constant vigilance to the monitor to prevent the boom from appearing in the shot.

On television, news commentators are reading from a rolling script placed directly in front of the camera (i.e., the TelePrompTer). This uses a reflecting glass which behaves so that the camera in effect sees through it. In the olden days, the cues were on the side of the camera, and you could see the narrator looking slightly off camera. (In modern days, that is now, you can still observe most weather newscasters in front of a weather map staring straight *ahead* as they gesture blindly to their *side* at the map. This is because in the studio there is nothing but a blank screen where the television viewer sees the "map." The newscaster is actually looking at a monitor displaying the map in front of them). The sentences on a TelePrompTer are very short; if not, you can see eye movements as the narrator reads. It is possible to create a prompter yourself if it is important to have the narrator speaking directly to the camera, see Figure 9. If you're going to have your narrator speak directly to the camera from a "memorized" script, remember that they only have to look at the camera for the length of time that it is intended that they be on camera and not covered with other footage. This can be one of the advantages of scripting in advance, as it can prevent having to do many retakes to get the narrator to look exactly right.

If you find that you've designed a section of narration that is too long for your talent to memorize in one take to the camera, there are several ways to get around the problem. All have to do with changing the camera. Find out what part they can say smoothly and let them say that plus a little more. Then you stop them and change the camera angle or the camera distance enough to avoid a jump cut (i.e., the subject moving from one pose to another with a change of less than 30 degrees of camera arc), and have them begin again, starting with the last sentence of the first section. This gives you the sound of a continuing speech in the part you will actually want to use during editing. Another thing you can do is have the narrator move in their chair, turn and cross their legs, etc. The change in motion can enhance and make more natural the camera move needed to get the whole piece of narration done. Always do this as many times as need be to get what you need. The only alternative is to redesign the plan for the video (e.g., devising an additional cutaway) to change the narration needs. The name of the game for success here is flexibility.

The script is a plan, which hopefully will be executed flawlessly. But the ideal outcome of being able to simply shoot the script is never guaranteed. A good Director will be prepared with the knowledge and the wherewithal to cope with change when it is needed. Directing is not for the faint of heart!

40.4.3 Post Production Phase

Having survived production, you may feel the hard part is over, but in many ways with the start of post production the moment of truth arrives, and you begin to see what you can make out of what you have. Depending on your post production facilities, you will edit either analog tape offline, or digitized video on a computer. Much of what we have to say about post production applies to both kinds of editing, however some tasks (notably converting raw footage to a digital representation) do not enter into analog editing, and some information is specific to one type of editing or another.

View and Log Your Footage

As you begin the post production process, you will need to get well-acquainted with the footage you have available. The best way to do this, that will benefit you time and again through the post production process, is to produce a log of each tape as you view and review each tape. Logging is most easily done with a VTR (Video Tape Recorder) equipped with a "shuttle/jog" control that will enable you to move back and forth through the footage more rapidly and easily. (The shuttle control allows you to traverse large sections of tape rapidly, and to see what is on the tape as you shuttle back and forth. Jog is used to roll the tape efficiently from frame to frame once you're in the general neighborhood of the frame you want). If you are planning to edit with a digital system, logging your footage before digitizing can save time by allowing you to easily locate clips for capturing to the computer.

At a minimum, your log should show the starting and ending timecode of usable shots, a transcript of what is being said, if someone is speaking, a description of the place and action in the shot (what is happening, who is in it, where is it taken), and any evaluative comments you have (e.g., subject looks relaxed, or seems tense, etc.). If you have several takes and are not yet sure which one you will use, try to mark each tape with a comment that will help you differentiate and remember the different takes.

Viewing and logging your footage might arguably be viewed as grunt work, but it is the kind of grunt work that will pay handsomely as you create your final production. First, it is absolutely necessary for the Director to get a feel for all of the footage that is available. Second, a good log will repay the cost of creating it many times during the heat of editing when you hit a creative block or come to an editing impasse where something else, but you're not sure just what, is needed. The video, audio, narration, and music available to you form a vocabulary from which you will express what your video has to say; the better you know those words, so to speak, the more you can concentrate on singing the song.

Using Collection Tapes

If your footage was of the nature that scripting needed to wait until shooting was complete, now is the time to create a script to guide creation of the final result. Depending on the nature of your material and your situation, you may want to use collection tapes at this point to explore your material, or to ease the actual editing process by putting material you will want to use in the final production onto a single tape (as discussed previously, this requires that you are working with a format that can tolerate duplication well). However, creating collection tapes can be a useful technique whether or not you intend to edit from them.

For example, in one project worked on by two of the authors (the IBM-New England Medical Center project), parents of children being treated for leukemia were interviewed. The interview questions were similar for the seven families and eleven parents interviewed, but the answers were dispersed across twelve hours of raw footage. Some of the interview "questions" we experimented with during the shoot were actually open-ended, "complete the sentence with the first thing that comes to mind" probes, such as "What I've learned is that ...". We had no idea what these probes would evoke during the shoot, and had little idea even after the shoot. Not until each person's response had been placed back to back with all the others' responses did we see a powerful message conveyed by the juxtaposition of different people's responses; as each responds differently to the probe, so does each person respond in their own way to the stress of a seriously ill child.

Collecting the responses together on separate tapes for these questions, as well as interviewees' comments on different topics and themes that arose during the interviews, made the necessary selection from a wealth of excellent material easier during the editing process. In this case, the collection was done on about 20 VHS

Table 4. Compression standards for still images and video.

JPEG (Joint Photographic Experts Group) is a still image compression standard.
M-JPEG produces a stream of individual frames compressed with JPEG.
MPEG (Moving Pictures Experts Group) is a relatively new compression standard that achieves 30 fps playback at just under VHS quality. It requires specialized hardware.

tapes from VHS window dubs (copies with timecode overwritten on the video) of the raw footage. This allowed promising material to be identified and edited roughly into sequences. It also allowed desirable sequences to be easily reconstructed later during final editing (because the visible timecode from each segment of a sequence specified which original tape, and where on that tape the raw footage was located). Thus, the collection tapes themselves were never meant to support production of the Edit Master, but rather to support the Director in finding the gold and scripting the material for the final production.

Capturing Video for Digital (Nonlinear) Editing

If you are going to be using a nonlinear editing system for your video editing then the next stage of the process is to digitize your raw footage. The following discussion is based on the assumption that you are working with a desktop system similar to the one shown previously in Figure 2.

The first step in video capture is to transfer the video from your analog source to the computer. Analog source may be a live feed through a camera, or prerecorded tape played in a camera or in a VTR (Video Tape Recorder). This requires your computer to have both audio and video digitizing capabilities, which usually demands specialized hardware and software.

There are a variety of ways to physically connect your analog source to the computer, depending on the kind of source with which you are working and what cables and connectors you have on hand. Most often you will use either a cable with standard RCA-style (composite) connectors or one with an S-Video connector. Use S-Video if your analog source is Hi-8 or S-VHS. S-Video splits the chrominance (the color dimension of a video signal) and luminance (the brightness of the video) signals of the video into separate sources. Preserving this separation, if it is present in your source, in the digitizing process will result in a better-quality digitization.

You will need to adjust the settings of your video capture software to get the best digital quality. This will probably mean spending some time experimenting with the settings of your particular software on your particular hardware, and reading the manuals carefully. The factors that determine the final quality are: movie size, frame rate, color bit-depth and compression.

The movie size refers to the size of the video window you will display on the screen. Frame rate is the number of frames per second at which the captured movie will be displayed. The color bit depth is the number of bits used to encode each pixel. The higher the bit depth, the more colors in the image. This results in a higher quality the image, and a bigger file size. Compression is the algorithm used to reduce the size of the movie for more efficient storage in the computer.

Because video takes up so much space, compression is essential. There are a variety of different methods currently being used for compression, which are either time-based or image-based. Table 4 shows a summary of the current standards.

Once you have settled on the settings for your capture software, and your source is connected to the computer, you can begin digitizing. Table 5 presents some tips for making this process go more smoothly.

Editing

Editing is where the proverbial rubber meets the road, where the Director's dreams and imaginings of how the video might be are turned into reality, or WYSIWYG (What You See Is What You Get), to use the HCI term. Going from vision to reality is typically a mixed blessing, both painful and exhilarating (see Rosenblum and Karen, 1979, for a description of editing from the

Table 5. Tips for digitizing source video.

- Optimize your hard disk to get optimal recording speeds.
- Devote maximum processing power to video capture — turn off any background processes, or any extensions or other pieces of running code apart from those necessary when digitizing.
- Capture video in small snippets — it's easier to open and manipulate small clips than to work with large ones that contain many scenes. A reasonable goal might be up to 30 seconds per clip.
- Check each clip after it has been digitized. Glitches during the conversion process can sometimes introduce frames of garbage.
- Capture your video at the specification of your final movie.
- Choose the correct frame rate. Video captured at 30fps won't necessarily look smoother than video captured at 15 fps. If the flow of data at higher frame rates overwhelms your hardware, the digitizing process will drop frames in order to keep up, resulting in very poor quality video. In some cases high frame rates can result in a movie that looks worse than one output to a lower frame rate.
- Capture movies in 16 bit color. Movie captured at 16 bit look almost as good as those captured at 24 bit, but they play twice as smoothly.

perspective of filmmaking). Editing requires patience! But the result will be worth it. Proportionately, post production will take the lion's share of the time you spend making your video; no matter how you edit, it just plain takes a lot of time and effort. When you are done, you may feel perfectly content with what you have wrought, but be forewarned that another likely possibility is that you will stop editing only because you have to, or because you absolutely can't stand to see it any more. This is normal, and we advise you to allow yourself to "abandon" your production in its "imperfect" state (try assessing the video through other people's eyes) and to begin to think about a new project.

To briefly review the process discussed previously, in post production you will create a series of edits that will lay end to end to form your final product -- an Edit Master. We recommended previously that you create one or more rough cuts of the video before attempting to produce a video of Edit Master quality. Finally, if you are working in analog video, once the Edit Master has been cut, you will most likely prepare a Duplication Master to support reproduction of your program or transfer to its final form. Whether analog or digital, Edit Masters should be protected vigorously starting with the moment they are finished. Duplicate the Edit Master immediately, and then hide it away in a safe place. If you are working with digital video, back it up, back it up, and then back it up once more. Once you have been through the editing process, this advice will be superfluous; you will not want to lose any of your work if there is anything you can do to help it.

If you are heeding the advice of this chapter, by the time you are ready to begin editing, you will be familiar with all of your footage, no doubt somewhat opinionated about what the best footage is, and you will be in possession of a detailed log of that footage, if not a complete transcript. If you are editing in digital format, you will have the raw footage captured in digital format, and you are ready to start the process of choosing the clips you want to compose into the final movie. You will have a script to guide you in sequencing the Edit Master, and, even better, you will have acquired all of the elements you need to implement the script in the final product. So where should you start

Produce a Rough Cut

Although most videos begin with a title and credits, you do not necessarily want to start at the very beginning and work straight through. If you are going to produce a rough cut, you do not need to worry about quality. That means you can assemble parts and sequences of the script independently on a collection tape, and then create a rough cut that simulates the final product from the collection tapes. The only caveat to doing things this way, especially if you are working in analog, is that you will want to keep track of an exact description of the pieces of video and audio you are using (i.e., timecode starts and stops), and where they came from (i.e., location on source footage) so that the edits can be more easily recreated when it comes time to make the final Edit Master. So start with the first scene, or start with the scenes for which you have the clearest mental image, and go on from there. Don't start with a sequence requiring fancy editing techniques or special effects. Just pick something straightforward, perhaps something centered around one of your most effective pieces of video, and get going.

One useful technique for knowing how to edit a particular scene or sequence is to consider what aspect of the video — either visual or auditory — dominates the scene. Then, lay down the dominant source first, and match the secondary source to it. Imagine that you are making a music video, for example. In such a video the audio dominates; the music under most circumstances does not want to be altered. So the audio is laid down first, and then video-only edits are created to match the audio. On the other hand, suppose you are trying to teach a procedure, such as how to make a burrito, or how to give CPR (cardio-pulmonary resuscitation). In these cases, the visual information probably dominates: the procedure has to look natural, has a natural rhythm, flow, or timing, and could be misleading if altered to fit the narration. So the Editor lays down a coherent visual sequence, and then adjusts the narration to flow "under" the visuals (this is where those ambient recordings come in handy again). Of course, it helps to have a visual sequence that is not wildly unmatched with the length of the narration. If the material is too disparate, then you may be unable to stretch or compress one or the other enough to make the sequence work.

If you have had a successful shoot, you may at times find yourself with more than one candidate piece of video for a particular purpose. Each candidate will no doubt have its strengths, and it can be hard to decide which piece to use: this one makes the point you are trying to convey exactly, but this other one is so much more persuasive! We can't give you a procedure for deciding among different video pieces, but we can tell you to pay attention to your own reactions as you view the piece repeatedly. If you find yourself becoming annoyed, bored, or impatient, it may be a sign that the video is not as strong as you think it is, no matter what the subject is saying. Really great video tends to hold up on repeated viewing; you like it as much or better with each time you see it -- it engages you. That's the video to look for and use; the more of it, the better. At least try to resist the temptation to include poor video because it's all you have; look for another way to make the point if possible. This is another reason to not scrimp on videotape, takes, or shooting during production. Production exists not only to fulfill the script, but to create resource for addressing issues that will only surface during post production.

Once the rough cut has been produced and approved by your customer, you should produce a full Edit Master, including all titles and credits (see next section), and reproducing the edits with careful attention to quality and the adjustment of color, sound, and timing. This is the time to clean up all of the things you deliberately let slide by in an effort to rough out the final program. Special effects should be completed at this time if they weren't before. If you are doing desktop editing, special software is available for creating the final edited movie. Many of these programs also support creation of special effects, spiffy transitions, titles and credits, the addition of multiple audio tracks, and audio effects. It is worth getting to know your software well in order to take advantage of these facilities. Do consider using special effects to help structure your video, as discussed previously. But don't succumb to the temptation to use special effects to the point where they begin detracting from your content. Simple cuts, wipes and dissolves can be effective.

Add Titles and Credits. If you are creating titles and credits for analog video, special equipment is usually needed. Most post production facilities will have a standard way of doing titles, and you will have to learn what is required to prepare your titles and transfer them onto the tape. Sometimes that will mean no more than having the titles and credits you want prepared to input through titling software. More traditionally, adding titles required a special edit where a titling machine produces a source containing the title on a transparent background (which lets the underlying video show through). Carrying out an edit with the underlying video (and/or audio, as desired) and the title as sources produces the desired effect.

Produce the Output: There are many options for the delivery medium for your video. If it is in digital form, you can dump the final movie to videotape, or view it on the computer, include it on a CD, or put it on the Web. Don't overlook new software that is becoming available for the creation of interactive video, such as QuicktimeVR. If your Edit Master is in analog form, you can digitize the final production, or create a Duplication Master to support mass reproduction or a laserdisc of your video. It is important to remember that even within analog video, you do not need to edit in the same format as your final output medium. Work with the best quality tape or digitized representation you can afford, even if VHS is your delivery medium. Your video will still look better than if production and post production were all done with VHS from the start.

40.5 Creating Particular Genres of Edited Video in HCI

In this final section, we describe how to apply the techniques discussed throughout this chapter to particular kinds of video in which HCI researchers and practitioners are likely to be interested. We can only offer a brief discussion of each of these, but the information and processes described in sections 3 and 4 combined with the pointers we are able to offer here should enable you to complete any of these projects.

40.5.1 Interactive Video: Creating Video for Interactive Applications

The advent of digital video formats such as Quicktime and QuicktimeVR has allowed video to become an integral part of software applications. This means that as HCI professionals we need to consider video as an interface element — what role can it play? How can it be integrated smoothly into an interface? The most common use today of video in the interface is in multimedia titles. Many of the titles available today in entertainment and educational applications include some video, for example, MYST™, the Grolier Multimedia Encyclopedia™, the Star Trek Interactive Technical Manual™, From Alice to Ocean™, The Visual Almanac™, and VizAbility™, to name a few.

Different titles use video in different ways. For example, adding a human dimension and affective content is one use of video in interactive applications intended to inform. In an interactive CD-ROM project called VizAbility (1996), the authors, Woolsey, Kim, and Curtis, present a course in visual thinking, using video to augment the material being presented with the personal reflections of different visual thinkers. In Vizability several people who use visual thinking as part of their daily activity — among them a designer, a teacher, a scientist, and a student -- appear throughout the CD commenting on the exercises and giving their views and feelings about the subjects being presented.

The use of video to convey personal stories was also central in two research projects carried out at IBM. *John Cocke: A Retrospective by Friends* (1990) was an interactive tribute to a distinguished scientist, based on several important technical contributions of IBM Research in which Cocke played a pivotal role. The story unfolds through a large set of cross-referenced anecdotes from friends and coworkers about what John Cocke was like, how he worked, and their memories of the trials and tribulations faced by the various projects, and through interviews with Cocke himself. The excitement of the ideas driving the work, the experience of being part of a crack team, as well as the thrill of hearing the "inside story" from people who were there is palpable to users of the system.

A second IBM project, the IBM/New England Medical Center research project (1991), was an interactive system centered on video of children with leukemia and their parents. The system was intended to support the parents of newly-diagnosed children during their initial period of adjustment. Interviews with families at different stages of treatment were used to help address emotional and informational issues faced by new families, and interactive video was used to guide parents through reasoning about their child's condition and performing medical procedures while at home.[1] The latter use demonstrated how video can be used to convey procedures. Parents who chose to perform routine medical procedures at home could use a voice-controlled video of the procedure as a step-by-step guide during a procedure, or could simply review the procedure in its entirety before performing the procedure. The video of the procedures was enhanced by the stories experienced parents told about learning to do the procedures themselves, and the practical tips they had discovered for getting through the procedures without mishap. These personal stories seemed especially meaningful to new families, perhaps because they came from people facing the same situation.

Another use of video in multimedia titles is to convey a sense of place — either a real place, as in From Alice to Ocean™ (1993), or an imaginary place, as in MYST™ (1994) or the Star Trek Interactive Technical Manual™ (1994). QuicktimeVR is particularly useful for conveying a sense of place, because it allows the viewer to grow from a passive recipient of information shown in a video clip, to an active viewer who can move around in a room, open drawers, go outside, etc.

Video has also been used in media titles to convey process. For example, The Visual Alamanac™ (1991) uses a video of a merry-go-round to portray the concept of velocity and centrifugal force. The video is synchronized with a graphic program that draws a graph while the video plays, allowing viewers to see two linked representations of the forces at work. For example, one part of the video shows children clustered at the center of the merry-go-round and then they move to the outer edge. The corresponding graph of velocity against time is plotted as the video plays. The user can stop the video at any time and replay the action of both graph and pictures.

Many interactive applications use video effectively

---

[1] The video based on parent interviews was created at the IBM T.J. Watson Research Center by Wendy Kellogg and Mary Van Deusen; the video of procedures and tips from experienced parents was created by Linda Tetzlaff and Mary Van Deusen.

to engage the user and add emotional tone, but sometimes video is used more as a gimmick than as real value added to the title. It is best to think carefully about when to use video in a multimedia title, if for no other reason than because video takes a lot of disk space and reduces the space available for information that may be more readily communicated using text or pictures. Video should only be used when it is absolutely necessary for conveying the information contained in the title, or for carrying the required entertainment effect.

40.5.2 Presentation Video: Creating Video for Technical Presentations

Video will become increasingly important in interactive software systems, but it is also valuable for other things. If you've ever built a successful piece of software, or had a significant point to make, you've had the experience of being asked to present that software, or make that point to a succession of audiences. While this can be a productive use of one's time, there are also times when it is not possible or not productive to keep demoing, etc. Video can provide a way to relieve some of the burden of repeating yourself, and in some cases may serve as a legitimate substitute for making a personal presentation. It can also, of course, convey to an audience the look and feel of your software, and/or the users' context.

Familiar examples of this kind of video are the technical video programs of the SIGCHI conference, videos used in conference presentations, seminars, and other technical talks, and/or videos used to teach new users how to use a system. Technical videos typically have a narrative structure, and range from a couple of minutes to up to perhaps ten or fifteen minutes in duration. For talks, a video may instead be a collection of short vignettes, that are intended to be interspersed with the verbal presentation. In either case, for these videos to be persuasive, understandable, and successful, they must be carefully structured and well-executed. This is not always the case when authors of the technical work who are unfamiliar with videomaking attempt to produce the video themselves. We have observed situations where authors attempt to shoot a "demonstration" of their software without a script, ad libbing as they go, and editing with the camera. Such a technique is guaranteed to produce a poor result.

Increasingly, video is becoming a standard prop for technical presentations. Video clips may be integrated into a "live" talk, or into a demo of a system. In such circumstances, it is an important part of planning the video to find out about the video equipment that will be provided for the presentation. Lighting controls should also be accessible to the presenter, so that lights can be dimmed for showing the video. Issues such as accessibility to controls for the video system relative to the position of the podium, or other props, such as overhead projector, may determine how interleaved the playback of the video can be within the presentation. If the video controls are non-trivial, it is best to avoid video, or at least save it for the end of the presentation.

Sometimes a video presentation can be used in place of a "live" presentation to relieve some of the burden of having to give the same talk over and over again to different audiences. If a video is to be used in place of a "live" presentation, and there will not be a presenter to introduce the video and answer questions, then the video must be designed to be standalone. One quick and easy way to make a video presentation is to record a "live" presentation to video, and then edit it to include closeups of demos or other props (e.g., slides).

When planning a video of a technical presentation that includes a demo of a system, beware of the problems of getting computer screens to video. Video resolution is not as great as standard computer monitor resolution, thus any picture of a computer screen degrades, and anything less than 18 point font is almost illegible to all but the first row of the audience. This is the least of your problems, however. One of the hardest problems is getting the monitor scan rate to synchronize with the video scan rate. If you just point a video camera at a computer screen and start recording, the resulting video will have black lines flickering up and down over the screen due to the different scan rates of video and computer monitors. What you need to do to get rid of this is either use software that will change the monitor scan rate to sync with the standard NTSC video scan rate, or a camera that has the ability to sync to a computer screen, either built-in or via connection through a scan converter. Once you've solved this problem, there are two additional potential problems to be aware of. The first is caused by the interlacing of the fields of video making up a frame. The problem here is that any horizontal line that is only one pixel high on your computer screen will flicker on and off as the different fields are displayed. This is easily resolved by making sure that all horizontal lines on your demo are at least two pixels high. The second problems is that the NTSC color palette is unlikely to match that of your application. This means that if color is an important part of the application in the video, you will need to do some very careful testing to make sure that the colors do not change in a way that is unacceptable.

40.5.3 Video Prototypes: Creating Visions and Usage Scenarios in Software Design

A further, perhaps less common, use of video is as a means for prototyping ideas about future software systems. Frequently, a software prototype can demonstrate some aspects of the final system, but does not necessarily have the end look and feel that is so crucial to conveying the user experience. A video can highlight the purpose and look and feel of a system without getting bogged down in an implementation. This is often useful for promoting a project in search of backing. In our experience as HCI professionals, we have also found this type of video to be useful in encouraging software developers to think beyond the architecture of the implementation to the user experience; even to realize that the way users would interact with the function being designed had not yet been considered.

There are several examples of "vision" videos in HCI, beginning with Apple's "Knowledge Navigator," created for the 1989 Apple Developer's Conference to share a vision of the future of computing. Other videos in this genre include Microsoft's "Information at your Fingertips," Sun's "Starfire," Hewlett-Packard's "Magellan," the authors' own "Global Desktop," and "Collaborations" videos (done at IBM Research), and even the 1995 batch of "AT&T of the future" television commercials in the US. These videos make a valuable contribution by making new ideas and ways of interacting with technology look and feel plausible to viewers, in a way that verbal description or static media such as slide presentations cannot. They show rather than tell what the future might be like.

A good vision or usage scenario video need not be elaborate to convey its message effectively. The "Collaborations"video mentioned above was scripted, shot, and minimally edited within a few days on a simple Hi-8mm deck. Because we wanted both to produce something quickly to convey the ideas, and we wanted an interface with a realistic look and feel -- for example, one with actual windows and window controls -- rather than one that looked like it was drawn, we used an novel technique to produce the video.[2] The interface elements were created in an interface prototyping tool, and the scenario was implemented in the tool step-by-step beginning with the final screen and last interaction to the first screen and interaction for a given scene. Then the camera (focused on the screen) was turned on, and one of the authors used the "Undo" function to (re)create the action of the scenario from start to finish. The narration and action among actors in the scenario was shot live. Although this approach is crude, and certainly not appropriate for material intended for public presentation, for our purpose of communicating internally, it was sufficient.

Video prototyping is not only useful for prototyping the look and feel of the interface, but also for prototyping uses of technology. Such prototypes can be used to drive the design of new technology, the redesign of existing technology, or to demonstrate novel uses for technology. For example, "Cloudforest Classroom" is a video made by Apple Computer to explore the use of wireless technology within an educational context. Working with the engineers, end users and usability specialists, a scenario of use was developed. Wireless portable computers would be used by students on a field trip to study rainforest ecology in the Costa Rican Cloudforest. Students working in different elevations in the forest would share the information they collected, and their analysis of the information using the wireless communication system. The video was shot by a professional cameraperson on-location, as a documentary. Being part of a team making a video about the use of the technology they were developing forced the designers to rethink their design from this use perspective. In addition, the resulting video also provided a vehicle for communicating about the use for wireless technology to others, such as Government officials legislating use of wireless bandwidth for computer communications.

40.5.4 Video as Data: Creating Edited Ethnographic or Usability Records

The use of video for collecting usability data has been common HCI practice for a number of years. More recently, video has been used to capture aspects of users' workplaces in order to analyze and communicate the context in which software to be designed will be used. Often these types of video are not edited, but analysis takes place on the raw footage. However, there are some very good reasons for using edited footage of video data. Often there are huge amounts of video data from a particular study. Managing these data, both during analysis and as reference material for later referral is very difficult.

The first, and perhaps still the most common, use of video in HCI was to create records of usability tests. Such records have been used to supplement the notes or logging a usability professional created while facilitating a test session, and to support later analysis of

---

[2] The method described here was created by John Vlissides of IBM T.J. Watson Research and co-author of the Collaborations video.

what happened, why it happened, and what test subjects said. We will have relatively little to say about this genre, both because it is common practice in our field, and because such video is typically never edited, unless to prepare a summary presentation for the development organization or a conference, which often does not go beyond a collection of clips.

Creating a video record of users and their context presents similar challenges to usability data: it typically generates a large amount of raw footage that can be a challenge to organize to analyze and convey important aspects of the users' situation. However, the technique of creating collection tapes, if you are going to edit on analog equipment, or of digitizing episodes and cataloging them, can help not only to discover the messages in the footage, but also to help organize and manage the editing process.

Edited video can be a useful way to tell the abbreviated story of a long-term user study. Here, the final edited video consists of edited clips of video from the original video data tapes. This is just like writing a paper to summarize your results, only the final medium for the report is a video. This technique was used in the video "Rolling Up Your Sleeves," made by Apple Computer. This video summarizes a multi-year study of the introduction of technology into a K-8 school. The video consists of video data of classroom use of technology, and video interviews with the staff at the school. It should be noted that if video data is to be used in this manner, everything stated previously about quality holds, the footage must be good quality, and the audio must be clear.

40.6 Conclusions

Producing good video takes a variety of skills, and learning those skills, or learning to coordinate and manage a team with those skills will take time and effort. One suggestion that we can offer is to become an avid video critic -- evaluate the video you see, and find and analyze compelling examples of the genres in which you are most interested. Much can be learned by watching the work of other professionals with an analytical eye.

Start small, and progress to more ambitious projects as your energies and skills allow. Making a music video, for example, can be an excellent way to acquire and practice basic editing skills, and when you're done, you have something short that you can show all your friends without fear of reprisal.

Use consultants if you possibly can, especially while you are still learning. Not only can judiciously applied professional assistance save you time and effort, you will learn an amazing amount by just being around people who know the ropes. There's really no substitute for an apprenticeship, even if it's only a couple of days in duration.

Even before your skills have developed to a professional level, set high standards and put in the time needed to meet them. Developing good habits early in working with edited video will put you in very good stead for the long run, helping you to avoid common flaws and costly errors. This chapter should give you a good start in understanding what it means to produce high-quality work.

Finally, have fun! We're convinced you will find working with video as compelling and exciting as we do, along with many other videographers, both professional and amateur. The road to producing excellent video is clear into the foreseeable future, with rapidly improving tools and capabilities, and more help than ever for people who want to learn to work with edited video. It's a great time to be a videomaker. Good luck!

40.7 Acknowledgments

We thank Paul Kosinski for technical assistance in many video projects over the years, and for painstaking (sometimes just painful) tutelage in the technical aspects of video, particularly audio engineering. We thank Katie Candland, Eileen Genevro, Tom Hewett, and Geoff Wheeler for comments on earlier drafts of this chapter.

40.8 Glossary of Video Terms

We can only include a small subset of terms here. See Singleton (1990) for an extensive glossary of terms from the filmmaking industry.

ambient: The surrounding sound of a scene on production when everyone is silent, including breathing, natural sounds in the scene, sounds made by equipment on site, etc. Capturing frequent ambient recordings during shooting makes it easier for the Director and Editor to "fix" otherwise unusable video, or to adjust an edit to better fit the sequence of which it is a part (e.g., to "stretch" a piece of narration to span the visual it describes).

chroma key: A particular chrominance (color), usually pink or blue, that is treated as a transparency in a video. For example, if a video shot of a blank computer monitor is to be filled with an animation of the monitor's contents, a chroma key rectangle would be fitted to the outline of the monitor in the source video, and then the source video and the animation would be edited together such that the animation fills the chroma keyed area. The result is the illusion that the monitor is displaying the animation.

CU (close up): An abbreviation used in scripts.

dropping generations of tape: Each time an analog tape is copied, it "drops" a generation. Raw footage shot in the camera is first generation. A copy of that footage is second generation, etc. Only the highest quality formats (roughly U-matic and higher quality; see Figure 5) tolerate duplication well. In the best possible world of analog productions, final delivery tape will be at least fourth generation (from camera to Edit Master to Duplication Master to delivery vehicle). Working with duplicated tape in the edit process further degrades the quality of the final product.

dub: A double, or copy of a tape.

Duplication Master: A high-quality copy of the Edit Master that is used to support replication of the video program or its transfer to other delivery mechanisms, such as laserdisc. A Duplication Master consists of a single edit -- the one used to copy the entire Edit Master. Also referred to as a "Dupe" Master.

Edit Master: The final video program that is the result of post production. The Edit Master consists of multiple video, audio, video + audio, and special effects edits to produce the full program.

establishing shot: A full-view shot of a scene that "establishes" where the action to follow takes place. For example, many television situation comedies start with an establishing shot of the house or school where much of the action takes place, before cutting to an interior scene.

flash frame: A single frame of black (or static) that typically is introduced during the editing process by mis-specifying the beginning timecode on the recorder for a new edit. Flash frames are detectable with practice while a tape plays at speed.

(videotape) format: The way a video signal is physically recorded on a tape, including the mechanism for producing a magnetized representation that can be read by a videotape recorder. Common formats include VHS, Super-VHS, 8mm, Hi-8mm, Betacam, U-matic, D1 and D2. Contrast this with video standards such as NTSC, PAL, and SECAM.

narration script: The script that the narrator uses to record the narration for a video.

post production: The phase of videomaking in which the pieces are finally put together under the direction of the Director and with the technical expertise of one or more Editors.

pre-production: The phase of videomaking that involves initial conceptualization, budget, staffing, research, logistics planning, and scheduling and coordinating the production process.

production: The phase of videomaking involving shooting and acquiring other raw footage (such as narration) necessary for creating the final product.

rough cut: A prototype of the final production (the Edit Master), produced with minimal regard for the quality of individual edits. The purpose of the rough cut is to assist the Director in defining precisely what s/he is trying to accomplish, and for communicating with the customer who has commissioned a video.

shuttle/jog control: A control on an edit deck, or sometimes on a VCR (Video Cassette Recorder) or VTR (Video Tape Recorder) that allows the user to "play" the videotape forward and backward at up to 50 times normal speed, or down to a single frame at a time. At all but the highest speeds, the video is visible, thus facilitating locating particular pieces of video visually.

script: A written plan for a video, usually consisting of a sketch or other representation of visuals to be used, a numbered list of significant visual and auditor events, and the textual narrative, with imbedded references to the list of events.

(video) standard: One of the common schemes for recording a video signal on tape, such as NTSC, PAL, or SECAM. Video standards vary in the number of lines scanned per field, and in the resolution of the signal. Contrast this with (videotape) formats, such as VHS, U-matic, Hi-8, or Betacam.

talent: Anyone shot in a videotape production who receives direction from the Director or crew.

timecode: The part of a videotape that identifies each frame of the tape, in a four-part representation such as 01:00:02:15, which stands for 1 hour, 0 minutes, 2 seconds and 15 frames.

VCR: Video Cassette Recorder.

VTR: Video Tape Recorder.

window dub: A copy of an original footage tape that adds timecode over the video image so that it can be easily seen during editing.

40.9 References to Videos

Cloudforest Classroom, Apple Computer Inc., 1993.

Collaborations, IBM T.J. Watson Research Center, 1993.

Global Desktop of the Future, IBM T.J. Watson Research Center, 1992.

Information at Your Fingertips, Microsoft Corporation, 1993.

Knowledge Navigator, Apple Computer Inc., 1989.

Magellan, Hewlett-Packard, 1995.

Rolling Up Your Sleeves, Apple Computer Inc., 1995.

Starfire: A Vision of Future Computing, Sun Microsystems, 1995.

40.10 References to Interactive Systems and CD-ROM's

From Alice to Ocean™: A Fascinating Multimedia Journey Across the Australian Outback, Claris Clear Choice™, 1993.

IBM/NEMC Research Project, IBM T.J. Watson Research Center, 1991.

John Cocke: A Retrospective by Friends, IBM T.J. Watson Research Center, 1990.

Groliers Multimedia Encyclopedia™, Grolier Electronic Publishing, Inc., 1995.

MYST™, Broderbun Software, Inc. and Cyan, Inc., 1994.

Star Trek: The Next Generation®, Interactive Technical Manual™. Simon and Schuster Interactive, 1994.

Visual Almanac™, Apple Computer Inc., 1991.

VizAbility™, Woolsey, K., Kim, S., and Curtis, G., PWS Publishing Company, 1996.

40.11 References

Benford, T. (1995). *Introducing desktop video.* New York, NY: MIS Press.

Caruso, J.R. and Arthur, M.E. (1992). *Video editing and post production.* Englewood Cliffs, NJ: PTR Prentice Hall.

Drucker, D.L. and Murie, M.D. (1992). *Quicktime handbook: The complete guide to Mac movie making.* Hayden.

Hausman, C. and Palombo, P.J. (1993). *Modern video production: Tools, techniques, applications.* New York, NY: HarpersCollins College Publishers.

Hedgecoe, J. (1992). *John Hedgecoe's complete guide to video.* New York, NY: Sterling Publishing Co.

Hedgecoe, J. (1989). *John Hedgecoe's complete video course.* New York, NY: Simon and Schuster, Inc.

Mackay, W. (1995). Ethics, lies, and videotape. In C. Lewis and P. Polson (Eds.), *Human Factors in Computing Systems*, CHI'95 (May 1-7, 1995, Denver, Colorado), pp. 138-145.

Preston, W. (1994). *What an art director does: An introduction to motion picture and production design.* Los Angeles, CA: Silman-James Press.

Rabiger, M. (1989). *Directing: Film techniques and aesthetics.* Boston, MA: Focal Press.

Rosenblum, R. and Karen, R. (1979). *When the shooting stops ... the cutting begins: A film editor's story.* New York, NY: Da Capo Press (A subsidiary of Plenum Publishing Corporation).

Rubin, M. (1991). *Nonlinear: A guide to electronic film and video editing.* Gainesville, Florida: Triad Publishing Co.

Schorr, J. (1995). 5 easy steps to perfect videos. *MacUser Magazine*, September 1995, pp. 68-75.

Singleton, R.S. (1990). *Filmmaker's dictionary.* Los Angeles, CA: Lone Eagle Publishing Co.

Soderberg, A. and Hudson, T. (1995). *Desktop video studio.* New York, NY: Random House/NewMedia Series.

Squires, M. (1992). *The Camcorder Handbook.* London, UK: Headline.

Handbook of Human-Computer Interaction
Second, completely revised edition
M. Helander, T.K. Landauer, P. Prabhu (eds.)

Chapter 41

Desktop Video Conferencing: A Systems Approach

Jonathan K. Kies, Robert C. Williges, and
Beverly H. Williges
Department of Industrial and Systems Engineering
Virginia Tech
Blacksburg, Virginia, USA

41.1 Introduction

Video-mediated communication has existed in one format or another for the better part of the twentieth century. Since the commercial introduction of the videophone in 1964, the success of video systems for personal communication has frequently been less than what forecasters had promised (Angiolillo, Blanchard, and Israelski, 1993). Recently, a number of social and technical factors have combined to generate a resurgence in the implementation of desktop video conferencing systems with considerable attention being paid by human-computer interaction (HCI) professionals. Due to increased computer networking and higher bandwidth networks in our offices, the advancement of better compression algorithms, and the availability of faster computer processors, the ability to transfer multimedia information between sites is becoming feasible. The advantages of video communication in the current environment of distributed, interdisciplinary work groups are clear: save money, save time, avoid travel, and enrich interpersonal communication.

One problem, however, is that the diversity of technologies and system requirements can be overwhelming to the system administrator or office ergonomist who is placed in charge of recommending or installing systems and equipment (Koushik, 1994). Many human factors considerations make the study and implementation of video-mediated communication systems challenging. The purpose of this chapter is to provide a systems approach to the discussion of human factors issues related to the use of desktop video con-

Figure 1. Screen shot of a typical desktop video conferencing system.

ferencing systems. An example interface is depicted in Figure 1. Each component of the system—communication technology, conferencing technology, physical environment, social environment and task environment—is discussed separately from a human factors point of view. The overall goal of this chapter is to present guidelines, methods, and issues to consider when designing video conferencing systems that promote effective communication.

41.1.1 The Electronic Office

Current technology supports many computer-based applications that facilitate information work in modern offices. The work place is becoming an electronic office centered around ubiquitous computing devices. Individual workstations can be networked to tie together workers within the same building and with workers located anywhere around the world. In addition to the networking of these workstations, current communication technology allows computers to be integrated with voice and video conferencing. Together these technologies are used in electronic offices for the management and communication of information. Traditional communication channels have been extended from telephones and fax machines to include email, the world-wide-web, and desktop video conferencing.

Of these technologies, video has the greatest potential to simulate a face-to-face meeting between remotely located participants. Along with the promise of better communication, these technologies—desktop video conferencing in particular—can complicate office work and create opportunities for misapplication, abuse, and severe usability concerns. For better or worse, desktop video conferencing, like many other new forms of computer-mediated communication, is fundamentally altering the structure of white-collar tasks, changing traditional worker relationships, and challenging the organizational structure of today's work environments.

41.1.2 Historical Perspective

The study of video-mediated collaborative work dates back to the early 1970's when Chapanis (1971) set out to determine how humans would communicate with computers in the future. Although interaction modalities have remained largely limited to the keyboard 25 years later, a research program was conducted for nearly a decade, contributing much to our knowledge of human-human communication (Ochsman and Chapanis, 1974; Chapanis, 1975; and Weeks and Chapanis, 1976). One of the most significant and consistent findings across these studies was that the audio channel is most critical to the majority of tasks examined.

At roughly the same time, researchers in Great Britain were examining the human factors of communication media (Short, Williams, and Christie, 1976). These researchers developed the Theory of Social Presence which described the ability of various communication media to simulate the sense of being colocated with a remote participant. This research determined that certain tasks were, in fact, aided by a video channel (Williams, 1977). These tasks were considered to be interpersonal tasks that required the transmission of non-verbal cues for activities such as negotiation or persuasion. Researchers at Carnegie-Mellon University (Kiesler, Siegel, and McQuire, 1984) and New Jersey Institute of Technology (Hiltz, Johnson, and Turoff, 1987) also conducted valuable research on electronic communication media.

Study of the role of communications media gained more attention in the early 1990's as desktop video conferencing systems became viable products due to advanced computing power and networking of computer workstations. Studies often examined prototype video systems, known as "media spaces" which consisted of expensive combinations of high bandwidth networks, analog video, and large displays.

Various research groups at Rank Xerox EuroPARC (Borning and Travers, 1991; Heath and Luff, 1991; Gaver, 1992; Gaver, Moran, MacLean, Lövstrand, Dourish, Carter, and Buxton, 1992; Heath and Luff,

1992; Gaver, Sellen, Heath, and Luff, 1993; Dourish, 1993; Dourish, Adler, Bellotti, and Henderson, 1994) evaluated the use of several different systems used at their site, including the prototypical RAVE, Polyscope, and VROOMS. Some of the issues examined through the study of their systems include the importance of gesture and eye contact in video conferencing sessions, the affordances of video communication from an ecological point of view, privacy concerns, and the use of multiple views of a remote site.

Several researchers at the University of Toronto (Mantei, 1991; Mantei, Baecker, Sellen, Buxton, Milligan, and Wellman; 1991; Buxton, 1992, Sellen, 1992) have implemented different systems in their research facilities for the study of group communication, telepresence, gaze, and conversation fluidity, among other issues. These researchers built systems published as "Hydra", "Picture in a Picture", and "CAVECAT" that were designed to understand the theoretical foundations of video communication.

The groups at Bellcore (Fish, Kraut, and Chalfonte, 1990; Cool, Fish, Kraut, and Lowry, 1992; Fish, Kraut, Root, and Rice, 1992; Hollan and Stornetta, 1992) also studied video-mediated communication using systems known as "VideoWindow" and "CRUISER". These systems were developed and studied to understand evaluation techniques, social artifacts, the design of video conferencing systems, and the theories behind making video a better medium than face-to-face contact.

Researchers in Japan (Ishii and Kobayashi, 1992; Ishii and Miyke, 1994) developed video conferencing systems that attempt to overcome the common eye contact problems using impressive technical solutions such as drawing on an angled video monitor displaying a remote participant. These systems, known as "Team Workstation" and "ClearBoard" provide future designers with notions of how traditional desktop video conferencing paradigms can be altered so that distributed meetings can minimize adverse video communication side effects. Researchers in Germany conducted extensive research using sophisticated video conferencing systems that permitted the study of features such as stereoscopy, resolution, and eye contact (Mühlbach, Böcker, and Prussog, 1995).

In general, this corpus of research has expanded our understanding of video-mediated communication in several ways. First, the technical feasibility associated with implementing high-end video networks and display systems has been presented for future designers to learn from the mistakes and accomplishments of early prototypes. Second, social scientists working at these institutions have elaborated on theories of communication and interaction between participants remotely located. Finally, guidelines for the configuration of video-mediated communication systems have been established, providing insightful suggestions for issues such as eye contact, audio localization, contextual cues, and the conveyance of gesture.

Additional studies were conducted using systems available on today's computers. For example, Green and Williges (1995) examined the benefits of different communication media in a shared word processing application. Tang and Isaacs (1993) and Isaacs and Tang (1994) studied desktop video systems and determined what aspects of video communication were seen as enhancements by the users in realistic working environments. Results from these studies support the conclusion that desktop video conferencing can provide a viable communication alternative if properly configured in electronic offices.

Important findings regarding the usability and usefulness of video-mediated communication have come from this extensive body of research. This chapter seeks to summarize the valuable discoveries made over the past twenty-five years and parlay the relevant literature in a format that is intended to encompass all aspects of a desktop video conferencing system.

41.1.3 Video Conferencing System

A video conferencing system is an excellent example of a complex human-computer interface, and a systems perspective offers the most appropriate framework for discussing all issues relevant to the HCI practitioner. The system can be subdivided into five inter-related components as shown in Figure 2. Each of these components must be considered to achieve successful human-human collaboration and communication when using computer-mediated video conferencing. The communication and conferencing technologies embody more than the computer interface. They include hardware, software, networks, displays, cameras, speakers, and microphones. The physical environment requires special consideration due to the sensitive nature of networked multimedia communications. The social environment involves the work group, which is a more complex set of users than HCI practitioners are accustomed due to their range of computer abilities, motivations, and the social context inherent in real-time collaborative group activities. Finally, the task environment represents a wide spectrum of activities for which video can serve as an effective medium.

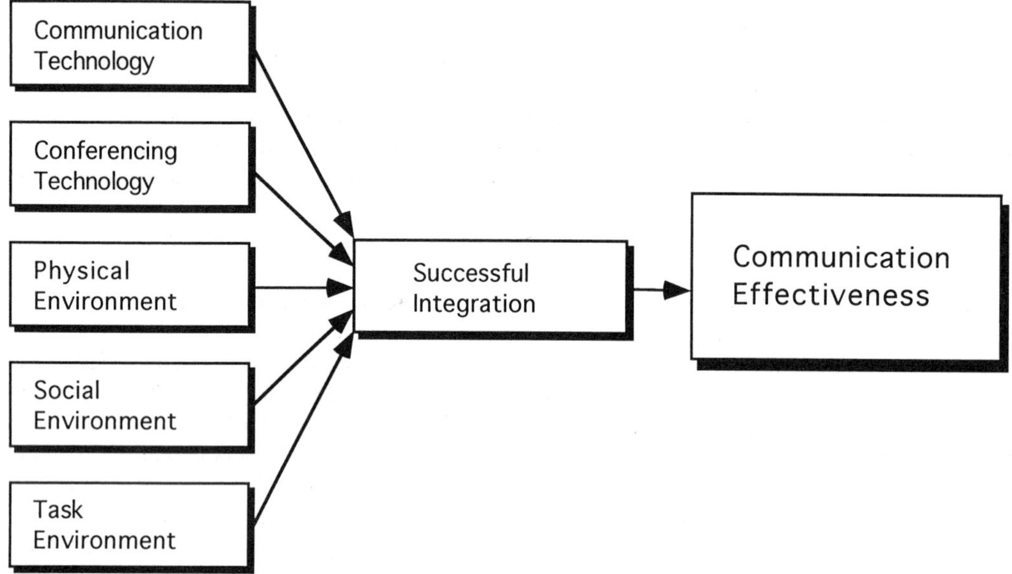

Figure 2. Desktop video conferencing system components.

41.2 Understanding the Communication Technology

The technical aspects of video-mediated communication systems deal with communication networks, computer platforms, auditory functionality, video functionality, collaboration tools, transmission and compression standards, and conferencing configuration. The HCI practitioner must understand the various alternatives in these fundamental technologies in order to make appropriate design considerations that will facilitate human communication.

41.2.1 Communication Networks

Most video conferencing systems operate over one or more of the following networks: traditional analog telephone service, digital circuit switching, or a packet-switched local area network. Each technology uses different transmission techniques and has different bandwidth limitations. These differences have performance implications for the video conferencing system.

Plain Old Telephone Service (POTS). Traditional voice service using analog narrowband lines is often referred to as "Plain old Telephone Service", or POTS. Private Branch Exchange networks (PBX) which are common in large corporations and organizations have many of the same characteristics as the POTS lines commonly found in residences and can be treated the same as POTS for purposes of this discussion. Of all the network options, POTS represents the lowest bandwidth, and therefore, the poorest video communication performance. However, due to its ubiquity and low cost, this network option should not be ignored by HCI practitioners. Most POTS lines have an effective bandwidth between 2.4 Kbps and 28.8 Kbps depending upon the modem baud rate. Advances are being made to increase these levels.

Integrated Services Digital Network (ISDN). ISDN technology establishes a digital network connection through which a number of media, including video, can pass. There are several varieties of ISDN. ISDN-BRI, the Basic Rate Interface, provides the user with two 64 Kbps B (bearer) channels and one 16 Kbps D (delta) switching channel. A multiplexer can increase bandwidth by allowing the use of several basic lines. ISDN-PRI, the Primary Rate Interface (T1), provides twenty-three 64 Kbps B channels (30 in Europe) and one 64 Kbps B channel used for synchronization and switching. Using ISDN requires the service, an adapter card, and a network termination unit that allows the two-line ISDN connection to interface with the four-line computer connection. ISDN connections have much higher bandwidth than POTS, affording higher performance video and audio. ISDN is offered currently throughout 75% of the United States, but availability is expected to increase and prices are expected to drop as the demand for networked multimedia applications rises.

Local Area Network (LAN). The current trend in networked computing distributes computing power between *servers* and a multitude of less powerful *clients*. Such networks are typically interconnected via a local area network (LAN). LAN connections can be configured in a variety of ways, but all are intended for packet-switched data not circuit switched data. POTS and ISDN embody a connection technique by which the line is dedicated to the two parties for the duration of the session and is therefore circuit-switched. LAN technologies, by contrast, are generally configured to make use of the network on a need basis and consequently send addressed packets of data to the appropriate destination whenever needed.

Ethernet, a common LAN technology was designed over 20 years ago for "bursty" data to connect laser printers at Xerox PARC. It was not intended for the type of data that video conferencing sessions require: continuous streams of synchronized audio and video. Using ethernet often results in jerky video due to loss of frames as well as audio that is not synchronized with a speaker's lips. The advantage, however, is increased bandwidth. The most common type of ethernet currently operates at 10 Mbps (although maximum throughputs reach only approximately 7 Mbps).

A number of solutions have been proposed to solve the drawbacks of transmitting video data over packet switched networks, including microsegmentation, switched ethernet which allows for temporary high-speed links between computers, and 100 Mbps ethernet (Trowt-Baynard, 1994). Other LAN-based solutions include synchronous optical network (SONET), the asynchronous transfer mode (ATM), and fiber distributed data interface (FDDI) that will continue to expand in the coming years. LAN-based networks are considered the fastest means for transmitting video data, despite potentially deleterious effects on video quality and audio/video synchronization.

41.2.2 Computer Platforms

One of the leading technical advances bringing desktop video conferencing systems into affordable reach is the exponential growth of computer processor speed. Processing digital video requires tremendous computing power, and only recently have personal computers been able to handle the task affordably. Video conferencing systems are currently available for PC, Macintosh, and UNIX machines, and usually require a video board designed specifically to handle video data or a "codec". Codec stands for "code/decode" or "compress/ decompress" and is used to compress the large amount of data required to represent digital video prior to transmission and subsequently decompress the data for display following transmission. Many new processors are now powerful enough to handle video signals without a separate code. Although the compression schemes used by most vendors are not currently compatible with each other, more vendors are promoting cross-platform compatibility.

41.2.3 Communication Standards

The most common standard for video conferencing known as H.320 (or Px64) was established by the International Telecommunications Union (ITU) and was intended for room-based video conferences. Currently, some vendors offer compliance with this standard in their desktop systems, but it has been argued that the standard was not designed for desktop PCs or local area networks. For these reasons, many vendors have been complicating issues by offering their own proprietary standards until a new standard is proposed by the ITU. System administrators must be sensitive to the compatibility issue and understand the platforms and growth potential of their users' needs prior to committing to a particular standard.

Desktop video conferencing sessions require the transmission of several data types: voice, image, video, and data. These data types reflect different service requirements as listed in Table 1. Of special interest is the reliability and sensitivity of video data. Delay sensitivity is the degree to which the communication medium can withstand lags in data delivery without adversely affecting the communication process. Reliability sensitivity is the degree to which the communication medium can withstand data transmission losses without adversely affecting the communication process. Uncompressed video data are not sensitive to reliability failures due to the immediate replacement of another frame. However, compressed video, which is used in many desktop video conferencing systems, is sensitive to reliability because the redundancy inherent in the data has been removed allowing data loss to propagate (Rettinger, 1995).

41.2.4 Conferencing Configuration

Desktop video conferencing systems can take one of two configurations: point-to-point or multi-point (multi-cast). A point-to-point arrangement involves the simple connection of two sites and requires only two video windows to be open at each site (one for the remote participant and one for the local participant). A

Table 1. Service requirements for various data types (From Rettinger, 1995).

Service Requirements	Data Types			
	Data	**Voice**	**Image**	**Video**
Delay Sensitivity	No	Yes	No	Yes
Reliability Sensitivity	Yes	No	Yes	Yes/No

multi-point arrangement can have any number of sites. The disadvantage of the multi-point arrangement is that considerably more bandwidth is required to send and receive numerous audio and video streams, and not all document conferencing software can handle multi-point connections. Some systems, such as CU-SeeMe developed by Cornell University, make use of a reflector site which "bounces back" all the input video and audio streams to the participants. Other systems use a single video window that switches to whichever site is talking. Still others use multicast protocols which conserve bandwidth by sending a single video "stream" which multiple users can access. The MBONE or Multicast Backbone leverages this technique over the internet for audio and video broadcast (Macedonia and Brutzman, 1994).

41.3 Understanding the Conferencing Technology

Computer-based conferencing technology involves hardware and software consideration. Issues related to both the audio and video channels of communication must be addressed. In addition, special purpose collaboration software is needed to support effective desktop conferencing.

41.3.1 Audio Functionality

One of the most critical features of any communication session is the quality of the audio link. The two broad classes of audio are full duplex and half duplex. Half duplex allows only one voice to carry across the connection at a time. Full duplex, however, allows both speakers to converse simultaneously. The issue generally becomes apparent when using inexpensive, analog speaker phones. When possible, full-duplex audio should be used to ensure fluid conversation irrespective of the video link.

Ochsman and Chapanis (1974) measured the effects of several communication modes on team problem solving, and deemed the auditory component most important. For this reason, HCI practitioners should not compromise audio. Kies, Kelso, and Williges (1995) found that degraded audio using a LAN-based system was so disruptive as to require a separate, dedicated phone link to conduct a series of video conferences.

Although the audio channel is most critical to successful communication, the video channel presents the most human factors challenges to configuring desktop video conferencing systems. For this reason, the bulk of this section will focus on video functionality issues.

41.3.2 Video Functionality

The degree to which a video conferencing session replicates the communication efficiency of a face-to-face conference hinges upon the value added by the visual component. Much research has been conducted questioning the importance of the visual channel in communication (Chapanis, 1975; Gale, 1990). However, other researchers argue that visual cues enhance the process of communication (Tang and Isaacs, 1993; Fussell and Benimoff, 1995). In either case, the video channel is central to desktop video conferencing. Table 2 lists the important issues to be considered in designing and implementing desktop video conferencing systems.

Visual Cues. Harrison (1974) discusses several factors which are critical to influencing how the head and face are involved in the communication process. First, the face provides general appearance cues such as demographic information, status and occupation, facial expressions, and emotions. Subtle changes in facial expression and head nods can evoke significant reactions from meeting participants and fundamentally alter the communication process. Likewise, the behavior of the eyes has the ability to influence conversation fluidity and perceptions of the other participant, as discussed in the previous section.

The importance of gaze in human communication should not be underestimated. Argyle (1975) and Ar-

Table 2. Video functionality issues.

Component	Issues	References
Visual Cues	Conveyance of gaze, facial expressions, gesture, and body positions; effect on speaker transitions; differences between video and face-to-face communication	Argyle (1975); Argyle and Cook (1976); Harrison (1974); Rutter and Stephenson (1977); Duncan and Niederehe (1974); Duncan (1972); Cook and Lalljee (1972); Gaver (1992); Heath and Luff (1991; 1992)
Audio/Video Synchrony	Conversation fluidity; dissatisfaction with the system	Kies, Kelso, and Williges (1995); Tang and Isaacs (1993); Cooper (1988)
Color versus Grayscale	Effect on bandwidth and cost; user preferences; realistic depiction of participants	Shneiderman (1992)
Compression	Effect on bandwidth; effect on image quality	Gale (1992); Angiolillo, Blanchard, and Israelski (1993)
Video Frame Rate	Performance/preference difference; velocity and detail dependent; effect on transmission of visual cues	Masoodian, Apperley, and Fredrickson (1995); Tang and Isaacs (1993); Pappas and Hinds (1995); Apteker, Fisher, Kisimov, and Neishols (1994); Chuang and Hinds (1993); Kies, Williges, and Rosson (1996)
Image Resolution	Performance/preference difference; velocity and detail dependent; effect on transmission of visual cues	Westerink and Roufs (1989); Lund (1993); Böcker and Mühlbach (1993); Kies, Williges, and Rosson (1996)
Aspect Ratio and Image Size	Effect on sense of presence; tradeoff between gesture and facial expressions; influence on participant relationships	Mantei, Baecker, Sellen, Buxton, Milligan, and Wellman (1991); Prussog, Mühlbach, and Böcker (1994); Fussell and Benimoff (1995)
Camera Angles and Views	Eye contact problems; tradeoff between contextual cues and communicative cues; self-view; privacy concerns	Kies, Williges, and Rosson (1996); Mühlbach, Böcker, and Prossog (1995); Ishii and Kobayashi (1992); Fussell and Benimoff (1995); Gaver, Sellen, Heath, and Luff (1993); Duncanson and Williams (1973); Angiolillo, Blanchard, and Israelski (1993); Prossog, Mühlbach, and Böcker (1994); Borning and Travers (1991); Olson and Bly (1991)

gyle and Cook (1976) claim that the face is the most important area for non-verbal signaling. They estimate that gaze is used 75% of the time for listening tasks and 40% of the time for speaking tasks. Speakers spend less time making eye contact and only occasionally glance at the audience to discern whether or not they are receiving gaze. Listeners tend to spend more time making eye contact with a speaker. In terms of conversation fluidity, gaze is a useful mechanism for passing control of the floor and reducing cognitive loads while formulating new comments (Fussell and Benimoff, 1995).

Harrison (1974) also discusses the importance of the hands and body in the communication process and postulated several key factors. The appearance of the body can project the overt characteristics of participants such as age and gender, as well as more subtle information, such as personality. Similarly, the posture of an individual can reveal confidence, interest, and the tension level of a participant. Harrison also argues that hand movements can play a tenuous role in the communication process. For example, the hands can be used for illustration, the regulation of conversation, affect, and emblems (icon-like gestures such as forming a "V" with the fingers to signify "victory").

It is important to understand that visual cues can aid the communication process in several ways. Understanding their role will enable one to understand how a video conferencing session may degrade communication due to poorly transmitted visual cues. For one, visual cues promote smooth transitions between speakers (Rutter and Stephenson, 1977). Some of the signals that are used to take the floor include paralinguistic cues such as audible inhalation and body motion cues such as head shifts and the initiation of gesticulation (Duncan and Niederehe, 1974). Duncan (1972) found that body motions play a critical part in coordinating turn-yielding. However, there is some controversy in the literature in that some studies found no communication difference between audio-only and visual-audio media (Cook and Lalljee, 1972) perhaps due to the redundant nature of human communication. Indeed, the Chapanis (1975) research confirmed that the most critical component of human communication is the auditory channel.

The importance of visual cues in a video conferencing environment can also be understood within the context of the ecological affordances offered by the medium. Gaver (1992) emphasizes this approach, and outlines three primary affordances for video communication.

First, video offers a restricted field-of-view on remote sites which limits the normal ability to perceive scenery in the periphery. This limitation can include obstruction of a shared workspace, other participants, or simply contextual information about the remote location. These restrictions require the user to become accustomed to limited field-of-view, but could also create advantages not found in face-to-face settings, such as the ability to do multiple tasks or hold side conversations without appearing impolite. The use of large monitors and a wide angle lens can help alleviate some field-of-view problems.

Second, video has resolution artifacts not encountered in real life. For example, a closer examination of the video display does not yield more detail, rather, it reveals the grainy structure of the image on the display. This characteristic prohibits a user from viewing details in the remote scene and may restrict the type of collaborative tasks which are performed. Compared to face-to-face meetings, this may enhance communication by minimizing visual distractions of the participants and focusing their attention on a small window of impoverished detail.

Finally, video fails to reproduce the three-dimensional structure of a scene. While not a devastating limitation, users may have difficulty detecting motion and positioning of remote participants faithfully. Some researchers (Prussog, Mühlbach, and Böcker, 1994) have attempted to correct this phenomenon with shutter glasses but found few benefits to stereoscopy in terms of subjective satisfaction.

In light of these video-based limitations, it is helpful to understand how visual cues are transmitted and received through a video-mediated technology. Conversational communication between individuals relies to a large extent on visual modalities, subtle and otherwise. A primary advantage of video conferencing systems over traditional voice-only communication is that it attempts to transmit gestures and facial expressions to create a richer communication session.

Heath and Luff (1991; 1992) examined the differences between video-mediated gesture and face-to-face gesture. One example of altered gesture behaviors occurs when participants attempt to garner the attention of other participants. Typically, in a face-to-face situation, one attempts to make eye contact by glancing at the other participant prior to speaking. In a video-mediated system, such fine gestures are often not adequately transmitted, necessitating more drastic measures such as waving the hands or arms. Once a session is established and conversation is initiated, gesture plays other roles. When gesture is needed to illustrate a point, communication effectiveness may break down. Similarly, when gesture is used to gauge the attentiveness of the other participant, conversation may become stilted or abandoned when acknowledgment cues are not returned.

Gesture in face-to-face settings tends to occur in the visual periphery, not the direct line of sight (Heath and Luff, 1991). Video-mediated gesture, however, is much smaller in the field of view, and thus, only gross motor movements can be transmitted effectively. The technology may alter the size, shape, and pace of the gesture. It is here where the factor of frame rate is most important. By slowing the frame rate, gross motor movements can be exaggerated or distorted to affect communication adversely and minor gesturing can be lost completely. As such, it is critical that the minimal gesture cues capable of being transmitted be displayed as faithfully as possible.

Audio/Video Synchrony. The delay inherent in the video coder/decoder processor can last up to 590 ms due to the time required to compress and decompress (Taylor and Tolly, 1995). Many compression schemes delay the audio for the sake of maintaining audio/video synchrony which can result in undesirable communication side effects. For example, delays may disrupt the flow of conversation by causing participants to speak during imposed pauses and inadvertently interrupt the other speaker (Angiolillo, Blanchard, and Israelski, 1993). These researchers also claim that inexperienced users do not attribute stilted conversation flow to the limitations of the technology; rather, they tend to blame the other participant.

However, not all systems synchronize the audio and video. Some researchers (Kies, Kelso, and Williges, 1995; Tang and Isaacs, 1993) separated the video and audio streams into two channels in an effort to preserve the high audio quality users are accustomed to from the public telephone network. Kies, Kelso, and Williges (1995) for example, used an internet video conferencing system in conjunction with a separate telephone link to maintain a superior audio quality level. The drawback to this configuration is that the video stream may lag considerably behind the audio portion. However, Tang and Isaacs (1993) suggest that users prefer desynchronized audio and video to the less desirable situation of degraded audio.

The audio/video synchronization problem may be more serious than we know, even in closely coupled high-bandwidth systems. Cooper (1988), for example, notes that experience has finely tuned our perceptual systems to expect a brief (roughly 18 ms) lag of speech behind the visual sensation of moving lips and gestures. Television systems, however, pass the video component of the signal through a series of processing devices which have the effect of serving the audio slightly ahead of the video. Cooper proceeds to claim that fatigue and lowered enjoyment of the subject material can result as a side effect of these synchronization errors. Although such effects have not been proven empirically, the appropriate synchronization between the audio and video component should be considered in the design of video conferencing systems as well as future research, especially considering the tendency of packet-switched networks to loose data or cause audio and video streams to loose synchrony.

Color versus Grayscale. Video conferencing sessions can be conducted using either grayscale or color displays. Grayscale systems offer the advantage of cheaper cameras and monitors as well as a reduced bandwidth requirement. Because black and white images require less information for accurate digital representation, higher frame rates can be achieved compared to color systems, given all other factors are equal. Color, however, is often preferred by users, and should be used when realistic portrayal of imagery is vital (Shneiderman, 1992).

Compression. Unfortunately, many vendors use proprietary compression schemes instead of ITU standard H.320, forcing users to interact only with those who have the same system. A common theme among the compression schemes is to transmit only the changes in the imagery. In this manner, a scene with considerable detail and motion will have significantly reduced frame rates from a comparatively still scene. Another technique is the use of tiling of similarly colored pixels. This method groups like pixels and transmits them together, reducing the data load, as well as the resolution and the number of colors displayed. As a result, the quality of the video may suffer when compressed (Gale, 1992; Angiolillo, Blanchard, and Israelski, 1993).

Video Frame Rate. Another important variable affecting the image quality in a video conferencing system is the frame rate. To provide the illusion of movement, many frames must be scanned by the display each second. The National Television Standards Committee (NTSC) which governs the television standards in North America has set broadcast television at approximately 30 frames per second (fps). However, the human eye's critical flicker fusion threshold is near 60 Hz. To overcome the perception of annoying flicker, NTSC requires that broadcast television use interlacing. Interlaced displays employ two separate scans, each operating on every other line thirty times per second. Each scan is called a field, and two fields are necessary for the creation of a complete frame. In this manner, displays can be refreshed effectively at a rate of 60 Hz. Motion picture standards dictate a 24 frame per second rate and use special interrupting shutter blades to overcome the critical flicker fusion characteristics of the human visual system.

Because network configurations are not capable of transmitting all of the data required for full motion video, frames may be lost or omitted resulting in significantly reduced frame rates. The frame rate in digital video communications is a function of the software, network bandwidth, and hardware and varies between less than 1 fps and nearly full motion rates.

Several studies have examined the relationship between frame rate and task performance or subjective assessment of the video conferencing session. Masoodian, Apperley, and Fredrikson (1995) conducted an experiment in the spirit of the communication studies of the 1970's (Ochsman and Chapanis, 1974; Chapanis, 1975) and concluded that for an intellectual task, the reduced frame rate video condition had no impact on task performance. However, they failed to detect any difference between the various communication media on their choice of task

It has been argued by Tang and Isaacs (1993) that the 1970's studies focused on the end *product* of the communication session and failed to touch upon the *process* of communication. Additionally, Isaacs and Tang (1994) argued that these studies concentrated on contrived tasks performed by participants unfamiliar with each other. Thus, they were unable to gauge the effects of the many complex social interactions which comprise realistic work group situations. Reduced frame rate may in fact have more serious consequences after extended use.

Although Tang and Isaacs (1993) did not vary frame rate in their studies of video conferencing in collaborative activities, they did use a reduced video frame rate (5 fps). They learned that although the reduced frame rate was clearly noticeable, it did not adversely affect the users' opinions of the system. Few other studies have directly examined user performance or preference in reduced video frame rate conferencing applications.

Pappas and Hinds (1995) examined the tradeoff between frame rate and level of grayscale. They found that when frame rates dropped below 5 fps, subjects were willing to make tremendous compromises such as choosing binary gray level to full gray scale in order to avoid these low frame rates. They concluded that 5 fps is the critical level at which video quality becomes highly objectionable.

Another study, conducted by Apteker, Fisher, Kisimov, and Neishols (1994) attempted to assess the watchability of various types of video imagery under different frame rate degradations. They manipulated the temporal nature of the video and the importance of the video and audio information to understanding the message. Compared to a benchmark 100% watchability for 30 fps, video clips high in visual importance dropped to a range of 43% to 64% watchability when displayed at 5 fps, depending upon the audio importance and temporal nature of the scene. Overall, subject assessments of the video clips dropped significantly with each 5 fps decrease in frame rate (5, 10, 15 fps). These data suggest that although the video will certainly degrade in subjective watchability over decreased frame rates, the ratings are highly contingent upon factors such as the importance of the audio or video information to message comprehension as well as the temporal nature of the imagery.

Due to potentially limited bandwidth availability, Chuang and Haines (1993) were interested in finding the slowest acceptable frame rate for video monitoring of laboratory rats in a proposed space station project. The frame rate (5, 2, and 1 fps) was manipulated for two types of scenes (slow action and fast action) over descending and ascending directional changes. The method of limits was used by exposing subjects either to decreasing frame rates or increasing frame rates. The results, based on a sample size of nine subjects, showed that the highest frame rate that yielded an unacceptable image quality rating for the slow scene was 6.2 fps. For the fast scene the highest frame rate yielding an unacceptable rating was 4.8 fps. Therefore, as expected, fast motion scenes require faster frame rates than slow action scenes.

Their research also supports the tendency for subjects experienced with this task were able to tolerate slower frame rates and obtain the needed information from the video. In other words, considerable individual differences are present and may be explained by the prior experience the subject has had with the task domain. Although these data may not extrapolate well to electronic office task domains, frame rates of approximately 6 fps are considered acceptable. These data agree with Tang and Isaacs (1993) and suggest that video conferencing sessions could also be conducted at rates well below the 30 fps NTSC standard.

Finally, the Chuang and Haines (1993) research supports the study of video frame rate acceptability through the application of rigorous psychophysical measurement techniques which may be appropriate for future research on the subjective quality of sub-optimal video. It is apparent that research is needed to investigate a potential task performance-frame rate relationship, as well as how reduced frame rates may affect the work process for a variety of tasks over extended time.

A recent study by Kies, Williges, and Rosson (1996) employed laboratory and field research to study the effects of reduced bandwidth on image quality in a distance learning application. In a simulated college course, frame rate was manipulated and dependent measures were taken in terms of quiz performance and subjective assessments. The results indicated that performance does not suffer under reduced image quality conditions, but subjective satisfaction plummets. A field study was then conducted to validate these findings in a shared lecture series using desktop video conferencing over the internet. Quiz performance was relatively unchanged, but again user satisfaction of low frame rates was unacceptably low for continued use of the system.

The constraints of limited bandwidth are of concern and have been studied in other domains such as undersea telerobotics (Deghuee, 1980), interactive educational multimedia (Christel, 1991), and unmanned aerial vehicles (Swartz, Wallace, and Tkacz, 1992). These studies may provide some clues regarding how users will be able to communicate successfully via sub-optimal frame rates. Factors such as the velocity of the scenery and the amount of detail may influence the effect of low frame rates. For desktop video conferencing, more research is needed to address both task performance degradations and subjective assessments under reduced frame rate conditions.

Image Resolution. One of the primary factors influencing subjective assessments of video image quality is the degree of resolution (Moon, 1992). Image resolution is the ability of the display to reproduce fine detail in a given scene and is commonly discussed in terms of horizontal and vertical resolution. Horizontal resolution is the maximum number of vertical bars that can be represented on the display. Vertical resolution is the maximum number of horizontal lines that can be presented within the vertical height of the display.

Little research has been conducted on the effects of reduced resolution on video conferencing communication effectiveness. Research in this area is hampered by differing standards and methods for measuring spatial resolution. Westerink and Roufs (1989) investigated the effect of different resolutions in terms of periods per degree on subjective image quality for static images. Subjective image quality was found to increase with resolution up to approximately 25 periods per degree at which point the judgments reached asymptote. Lund (1993) examined the effects of image resolution on viewing distances for NTSC television (525 scan lines) and high definition television (HDTV–1125 scan lines) and found that the HDTV resolution was not a strong predictor of viewing distance. In other words, the increased resolution did not compel participants to sit closer to the screen as was predicted by the literature, indicating the higher resolution was not beneficial.

Böcker and Mühlbach (1993) also varied spatial resolution in a study investigating the effects of various video conferencing configurations on communicative presence. The normal resolution setting was based upon the European PAL standard of 626 scan lines, while the reduced resolution condition was half that setting. During the study, two people at each end of a point-to-point session participated in a conflictive task and a cooperative task. The reduced resolution condition prevented the detection of eye movements and decreased the recognizability of gestures directed toward a particular participant, thereby creating confusion as to which participant was being addressed. This study makes clear the importance of spatial resolution which supports non-verbal communication among participants.

Kies, Williges, and Rosson (1996) manipulated resolution (160x120 versus 320x240) and collected task performance measures for a simulated class lecture. In contrast to other studies, these results indicated that reduced resolution did not adversely impact task performance (knowledge comprehension) for verbally or visually presented information. While this finding is encouraging news for low bandwidth desktop video conferencing, the subjective satisfaction measures indicated strong dislike for the reduced resolution condition. As is the case with low frame rates, the reduced resolution effect may be influenced by the velocity of the scenery and the level of detail. More research needs to address the impact of resolution on task performance for a variety of office tasks as well as the long term subjective satisfaction of its use.

Aspect Ratio and Image Size. The aspect ratio of a display is the proportion of horizontal scan line length to the vertical distance covered by the scan lines. Current television, for example, has an aspect ratio of 4:3. Image size is the size of the object of interest on the display used for the video conferencing session. This size of the video image is determined by four factors: screen size of the monitor, distance of the viewer from the monitor, distance of the remote participant from the camera, and zoom setting of the camera (Mantei, Baecker, Sellen, Buxton, Milligan, and Wellman, 1991).

The size of the image on the display has been shown to have a number of influences on the video conferencing session. First, Lund (1993) has shown that the size of the image can affect the viewer's sense of presence (see Section 41.4.3) with larger images increasing participants' feeling of presence. In a related vein, Prussog, Mühlbach, and Böcker (1994) investigated the tradeoff between image size and the display of contextual cues. Their research showed that when a remote participant was displayed on the screen as the natural size of a co-present participant as indicated by the visual angle, the sense of presence was increased, the visibility of facial expressions increased, and the general acceptance of the technology as a communication medium increased. Because Prussog, Mühlbach, and Böcker (1994) found no effect of contextual cues on telepresence, they recommend that the contextual cues be de-emphasized in favor of natural size of a participant when a tradeoff must be made.

Another tradeoff related to the size of the image is between gesture, facial expressions, and work context. A close-up view of a participant enhances the transmission of facial cues, but limits the representation of the work surroundings. Similarly, a contextual view may reveal a participant's gestures and surroundings, but fail to convey the subtle expressions of the face and eyes (Fussell and Benimoff, 1995). Users or system designers must confront the inevitable tradeoff between the display of facial information (and gaze) and gesture information based on the requirements of the task and the communication style to be supported.

The size of the image is also theorized to affect the personal impact a participant has during a session. For example, during a multi-point session, Mantei, Baecker, Sellen, Buxton, Milligan, and Wellman (1991) found that larger images made individuals have more impact on the session than those depicted in smaller windows.

Camera Angles and Views. The placement and angle of cameras and the views they create are critical in the design of a well-configured video conferencing system. Camera angles depend upon several factors, including the object of interest, the number of participants and cameras, the lighting, and the task. When configuring the cameras for a simple point-to-point video conference, the best camera placement is directly above the display unit to minimize the traditional eye contact problem associated with such systems. It is important to place the camera in a manner such that the user need not turn his/her head to gaze between the camera and the display screen. Another possibility is the use of self-focus cameras for scenes involving motion and tracking. However, self-focus can cause motion sickness for other viewers when the subject is coming in and out of focus.

When manipulating the camera during the session, care should be taken not to make extremely jerky movements or fast pans. When operating under low frame rate conditions, such actions will prevent the viewer from understanding the context of the object of interest, as well as degrade the participant's subjective impression of the conference. The findings presented in Kies, Williges, and Rosson (1996) suggest that contextual shots of a classroom in a distance learning application are more useful than the image of the lecturer. Many students in this study felt the close-up view of the lecturer was distracting, especially considering the reduced image quality characteristics of the configuration. However, in office task scenarios involving two users, the best scenery depends upon the situation.

Camera angles play a large role in the transmission of small facial cues and eye contact. Eye contact in video communications is often hampered by the discrepancy between the camera and the video window of the remote participant. For example, a 20 cm difference between the camera and the video window can result in significant eye-contact problems. Mühlbach, Böcker, and Prussog (1995) examined the effects of horizontal and vertical viewing angles on conversation flow and subjective parameters such as the sense of being addressed. The eye contact angles (8 degrees horizontal and 10 degrees vertical) hindered conversation flow and the sense of being addressed and looked at, but had no impact on the satisfaction or acceptance of the system.

To overcome eye contact problems, participants may be instructed to look at the camera when speaking, although this precludes looking directly at the remote participant on the display. Alternatively, sophisticated technical solutions that involve the use of half-silvered mirrors to present a shared drawing space overlaid on a video window have been proposed. These systems seek to make eye contact with a remote participant a seamless experience from the shared work activity (Ishii and Kobayashi, 1992). Unfortunately, such solutions are not feasible for most current systems and may not be practical in light of the inconclusive effects of eye contact angles on communication success found by Mühlbach, Böcker, and Prussog (1995). Often there is a tradeoff between technical factors such as field-of-view and resolution in displaying information in a video window (Fussell and Benimoff, 1995).

An issue raised by many detractors of video communication systems is that seeing a small "talking head" does not add sufficient value to the communication process. Providing alternative views with multiple camera positions is one solution to this criticism. Gaver, Sellen, Heath, and Luff (1993) propose using several cameras in each office so that a shared workspace can be maintained, allowing the focus of communication to revolve around a common artifact. Despite problems with additional complexity, providing multiple views was found to be a desirable configuration due to the heavy use of the task-centered view as opposed to the face-to-face view. The data from an early study by Duncanson and Williams (1973) also reflect the advantage of supplying the conference participants with multiple views. In the Duncanson and

Williams (1973) experiment, users were asked which views would be most desirable when different people were speaking. The overhead view of the other room was considered most desired when either the respondent was speaking or when the speaker was another in the same room. This view was actually preferred slightly more than the view of the person being addressed by the respondent. These studies reveal that the "talking head" is not the most critical view when speaking.

The issue of a "self-view" is critical to user satisfaction and acceptance of video conferencing systems. Angiolillo, Blanchard, and Israelski (1993) describe four related subfunctions of the self view:

(1) *Local View:* The capacity to view the local video source, whether it be of the participant or some other object of interest.

(2) *Self-View:* The capacity to view the image of oneself that is being transmitted to the remote participant.

(3) *Monitor:* The ability to view whatever is being transmitted to the remote participant.

(4) *Preview:* The ability to view a video signal prior to transmission.

In addition to being able to view oneself during a conference, it is also advantageous to have the ability to view the mirror image of oneself. This is the perspective we are accustomed to through daily life, and it requires no relearning of eye-body coordination (Angiolillo, Blanchard, and Israelski, 1993). As video conferencing technologies and video telephony products become more advanced and ubiquitous, they will incorporate more of these viewing features.

Although it seems that the inclusion of contextual cues such as a worker's office setting in the video window of a remote participant could contribute to the sense of presence or overall satisfaction, Prussog, Mühlbach, and Böcker (1994) found no evidence of contextually enhanced views aiding subjective impressions of the session, including the sense of presence. They claim that given a restricted view, the camera should close in on the remote participant and forgo the contextual cues surrounding the person. Still, it seems that contextual cues such as office decor, remote site configuration, and the general appearance of the remote site can contribute important social cues to the communication process. For example, viewing a remote office in disarray can influence the perspective or first impression of participants much the way such opinions can be formed in face-to-face situations.

Besides the contextual cues mentioned above, perceptually based characteristics of the physical environment can also facilitate understanding the surroundings of a remote participant. For example, depth cues associated with stereoscopy can establish a better sense of proportion, distance, and the size of remote objects through video mediated communication systems (Mühlbach, Böcker, and Prussog, 1995). In this study, shutter glasses were used to establish binocular depth cues. The results showed that stereoscopy enhances spatial presence, but does not increase overall user satisfaction. Because the technique necessary to create stereoscopic representations is expensive and technically sophisticated, such a solution is not a reasonable method for enhancing the sense of presence or overall effectiveness of a communication session.

Concerns over the issue of privacy have arisen in continuous-use video conferencing projects (Borning and Travers, 1991; Olson and Bly, 1991) as well as discussions of contemporary video telephony (Angiolillo, Blanchard, and Israelski, 1993). The overriding concern of the designers of the media space discussed by Olson and Bly (1991) was to avoid implementing privacy controls which could be accomplished through social means. Technologies such as video conferencing ought not to impose novel control structures or privacy violations not grounded in our everyday experiences. To avoid these concerns, the media space used by Olson and Bly (1991) allowed a person to know if someone was looking at them and provided them with the ability to see that person. The later feature was coined "ethical video" and is related to the concept implemented by Borning and Travers (1991) known as symmetry. Borning and Travers also used the concept of "control" – the ability to determine whether or not others can see you.

The camera angle affects the ability to make eye contact, the view affects the tradeoff between contextual cues and facial cues, and the camera itself provides the capability to permit privacy. In addition to these factors, cameras must be selected on the basis of color, focal length, and the amount of scenery encompassed in one view. Certain applications require a wider angle of view than others. For example, distance learning applications in which an entire class is to be included in one view require a special wide angle lens. The characteristics and use of the camera in desktop video conferencing is crucial to the success of any meeting.

41.3.3 Collaboration Tools

In addition to the enhanced auditory and visual communication environment provided by desktop video

Table 3. Collaboration tools for desktop video conferencing.

Collaboration Tool	Example
Shared Workspaces	
Electronic Whiteboard	ShowMe™
Group Text Editor	Aspects™
Application Sharing	ShowMe™
File Sharing and Transfer	Visit™
Group Decision Support	
Voting	Ventana™
Consensus Building	OptionFinder™
Remotely Controlled Software	Timbuktu Pro™
Communication Support Tools	
Chat Window	CU-SeeMe
Video Mail	Simplicity™
E-Mail	Eudora™
Organization-wide Tools	
General-Purpose Groupware	Lotus Notes™
Intranets	Netscape Navigator™

conferencing systems, many packages are shipped with collaboration tools that take advantage of the processing power of the desktop computer. It is here that the true collaborative advantage of video conferencing systems will be realized and will propel video conferencing into the mainstream work environment. The recent widespread implementation of organization-wide programs such as Lotus Notes™ and intranets is an indication of the trend toward computer-based collaboration environments.

A wide range of collaboration tools exists and many can be incorporated into either a video conferencing system or used alone. Table 3 presents collaboration tools which can be used as part of an integrated desktop video conferencing package or in conjunction with a system. These ancillary applications are often called shared workspaces, but they can take a wide range of forms. One example of a shared workspace is the electronic whiteboard. An electronic whiteboard provides a window that can be accessed by both parties. Either party can draw on the whiteboard, making the application useful for a variety of office tasks. Some applications can be shared much the same as an electronic whiteboard, as in Sun's ShowMe™ product. Another shared workspace is the group editor such as Aspects™ that allows participants to work simultaneously on a common text document (Green and Williges, 1995).

Group decision support applications that attempt to improve the decision-making process through the use of computer technology may also be available with video conferencing systems (Ellis, Gibbs, and Rein, 1991). Applications such as Ventana™ often provide mechanisms to allow participants to vote on issues or to facilitate discussion or debate on an issue in the context of a business meeting tool.

An interesting technique for sharing a workspace involves the use of remotely controlled software. Products such as Timbuktu Pro™ allow a user to control the software on another computer remotely. Kies, Kelso, and Williges (1995) demonstrated that distance learning applications can be enhanced through the remote control of presentation software over computer networks. Other collaboration support mechanisms include sharing files and communication enhancements such as real-time chat windows, video mail, and traditional email.

41.4 Understanding the Physical Environment

When designing human-computer interfaces, the physical environment is often not a central consideration. Video conferencing systems, however, represent a much more complex integration of ambient noise, lighting, and the social context.

41.4.1 Ambient Noise

Successful communication is dependent on the transmission and amplification of audio signal, which require appropriate ambient noise control. A critical environmental influence on effective communication is that of ambient audio levels. According to the American National Standard for Human Factors Engineering of Visual Display Terminal Workstations (ANSI/HFS 100-1988), ambient noise levels should not exceed 55 dbA. Again, with video-teleconferencing systems, care must be taken to maintain minimum noise levels so as not to impede vocal communication.

Mantei, Baecker, Sellen, Buxton, Milligan, and Wellman (1991) report difficulties reducing ambient noise levels so as not to disrupt vocal communications in trials of prototype video conferencing systems. Office doors may have to be closed, the movement of furniture minimized, and other conversations avoided. Some systems have audio controls which allow the user to manipulate the microphone level according to the type of room, but these systems are not a perfect solution to the problem of ambient noise.

41.4.2 Lighting

Communication relies heavily on the robust transmission and display of visual imagery, necessitating proper lighting conditions. Lighting problems can have a profound impact on the perceived image quality of the system (Angiolillo, Blanchard, and Israelski, 1993). ANSI/HFS 100-1988 recommends that for most displays and in most situations ambient illuminance should be in the range of 200-500 lux.

When capturing video images of workers in an office environment, care must be taken to achieve the correct illuminance levels such that the subject's image is not washed out or bathed in shadow (Mantei, Baecker, Sellen, Buxton, Milligan, and Wellman 1991). Studio lighting used in high-end video conferencing rooms may be impractical or too expensive, necessitating make-shift solutions. One technique found useful is the placement of a small lamp atop or behind a CRT display to luminate the subject's face adequately. Another solution is to employ cameras with automatic light adjustments, but such devices may prove expensive or ineffective (Mantei, Baecker, Sellen, Buxton, and Milligan, 1991).

41.4.3 Degree of Presence

One goal of video conferencing systems is to establish a sense of "presence" akin to that of a face-to-face meeting. Several theories have been suggested to account for different behavior observed under various communication modalities.

The Theory of Social Presence (Short, Williams, and Christie, 1976) makes the case that higher bandwidth communications induce a more robust sense of being co-located with remotely located participants. Social presence is defined as a quality of a communication medium that depends upon its capacity to transmit verbal and nonverbal cues as well as aspects such as the apparent distance or realness of the participants. *Telepresence*, a related concept defined by Böcker and Mühlbach (1993), is the transferability of cues that allow one to get the impression of sharing space with a remote site. They also defined *communicative presence* as the capacity of a system to transfer the verbal and non-verbal communicative signals of participants. These concepts define a general impression affecting the degree to which participants feel as if they are sharing space with a remote site. It appears as if the quality and robustness of a system in terms of frame rate, resolution, image size, and audio/video synchrony will have a positive effect on the sense of presence participants feel in a video conferencing system.

A similar theory which has been suggested is called the Media Richness Theory (Daft and Lengel, 1986). The ability of a group to resolve uncertainty and convey information between its members is said to be influenced by the richness of a communication medium. More rich media include video conferencing and telephony, while less rich media include email and other text-based technologies. Rich media, in general, allow important communicative tools such as feedback and personalization to be transmitted.

These theories contribute to our understanding of human behavior in complex distributed group working environments and are helpful in predicting the usage of emerging communication technologies such as desktop video conferencing. However, they have difficulty explaining certain phenomena. For example, the finding that video is more similar to audio-only than face-to-face communication is not well-explained by these theories.

More research is needed to allow system designers to predict the success of a new technology based on its communicative affordances. Also, a fuller understanding of the need to simulate a face-to-face meeting should be pursued so that the goal of increasing the sense of presence is validated. Some researchers have discussed the philosophy of trying to make electronic communication better than co-presence (Hollan and

Figure 3. Single-user configuration.

Figure 4. Several-users configuration.

Stornetta, 1992). Understanding the means by which desktop video conferencing systems act as a communication filter, creating an environment different from face-to-face meetings will permit researchers and designers to create the most effective communication settings.

41.5 Understanding the Social Environment

The study of users in a video conferencing setting is significantly more complex than the human-computer interaction of a single user. A large number of social and personal factors can come into play.

41.5.1 Work Group

User Background. The background of the users is a key variable in studying any human-machine interface. In the context of human communication, Tubbs (1992) points out that factors such as personality, sex, age, experience, attitudes, and values all serve as critical influences. In addition to these individual variables several group factors, like the type of group, group norms, conflict, leadership, and status, must be considered. Together, all these factors can impact the success of a video conferencing session.

Group Configuration. Kies, Kelso, and Williges (1995) conducted a preliminary study investigating the differences between various group configurations on the effectiveness of video conferencing communication. They considered point-to-point communications which involve only one hardware configuration at each end of the connection. At each point, however, the participants can consist of one user, several users, or a large group of users. Certain considerations must be made with respect to the equipment required and task suitability for each configuration. The most common, and perhaps the most appropriate configuration for desktop applications is the one-to-one arrangement. Figure 3 depicts this type of group configuration. Due to the relatively small size of most current computer displays, and the even smaller size of the windows containing the video, more than one person on each end becomes cumbersome, and multiple parties can clog a LAN. In terms of technical issues such as image size, contextual cues, and required resolution, one-to-one sessions offer the most realistic settings. In regard to social issues such as communication fluidity and speaker control, this setup best supports optimal group communication.

Most desktop video conferencing sessions also support several participants at each site as depicted in Figure 4. By including several users at each site, the problem of coordinating conversation becomes more cumbersome because both computer-mediated and face-to-face communication are present. The problems associated with eye contact become difficult to overcome. For instance, when attempting to overcome the eye contact problem by looking into the camera, participants at the remote site are given no non-verbal cues indicating which participant is being addressed. The transmission of visual cues is also hindered by the reduced size of the participants in a particular video window.

Applications such as distance learning through remote lectures often require dealing with groups as large as the size of a standard classroom. For the large group, the problems of seeing and hearing the lecturer are not so prominent, assuming adequate display size and loudspeaker placement. However, the lecturer may have difficulty discerning the remote group and scanning for details such as raised hands or inattentive participants. Prior to the implementation of desktop video conferencing technology, system designers should carefully consider the group size and the ability of the technology to support the communication needs of the group.

41.5.2 Social Context

Another key component of the systems approach to understanding a video conferencing system is the social/organizational context in which the work is being conducted. A number of factors such as corporate culture, reward structures, and time constraints, (Olson, Kuwana, McGuffin, and Olson, 1993) as well as competition, and conflicting interests combine to establish a unique context in which to work. Additionally, differences between cultures and countries may contribute to strained collaboration.

The acceptance of various communication media among white-collar workers is influenced by the prior experiences of a group and the social dynamics among group members (Fulk, Steinfeld, Schmitz, and Power, 1987). This theory, known as the Social Information Processing Theory, was put forth to explain communication media usage from the perspective of the social interaction of the users, as opposed to the richness of the media itself.

From a similar point of view, the Theory of Symbolic Interactionism suggested by Trevino, Lengel, and Daft (1987) claims that the richness of the media combines with the symbolic messages perceived from the use of a particular medium. For example, high status technologies may come into vogue not due to their utility or ability to simulate a face-to-face meeting adequately, but because an influential group member championed its use.

Because desktop video conferencing is an emerging communication technology, its use may be explained by the social context of the work group in light of these theoretical explanations. It is important to understand the differences and intricacies of the organizational context before implementing a video-based working environment.

41.6 Understanding the Task

Desktop video conferencing, by definition, involves communication tasks. There are a variety of communication tasks which may be appropriate for video conferencing. These tasks usually involve the sharing of workspaces and require accommodations for users with special needs.

41.6.1 Task Taxonomies

One relevant and frequently cited framework for studying and analyzing tasks for communication research is the office worker taxonomy outlined by McGrath (1984). This taxonomy describes eight categories of tasks, including planning, creativity tasks, intellectual tasks, decision-making, cognitive conflict tasks, mixed motive tasks, competitive tasks, and performances. Each quadrant (generating alternatives, choosing alternatives, negotiating among alternatives, and execution) describes the tasks within the taxonomy. Other task perspectives could be developed to reflect application areas such as education (distance learning), military, and healthcare scenarios.

For purposes of understanding communication media benefits and drawbacks, tasks are often divided into information exchange tasks and interpersonal tasks (Williams, 1977; Angiolillo, Blanchard, and Israelski, 1993). Studies on the use of video have often indicated that the video channel facilitates communication and improves task performance for interpersonal activities (e.g. Weeks and Chapanis, 1976) but offers little benefit to tasks involving information exchange activities (e.g. Chapanis, 1975; Gale, 1991) Unfortunately, many of the tasks studied in the literature do not fit easily into these classifications, and the complex, mercurial goals of realistic communication scenarios are difficult to deconstruct into an artificially-imposed distinction. For example, many discussion tasks involve negotiation, which is highly interpersonal, but also require parties to incorporate aspects of information exchange tasks.

Williges and Williges (1995) proposed a preliminary taxonomy of information tasks and task activities performed in an electronic office. Their scheme subdivides the tasks into two major categories: information management and information communication and is listed in Table 4. Although this is not a validated classification scheme, it is a helpful tool for understanding the kinds of tasks which are performed in contemporary electronic offices.

Understanding tasks and devising useful classification schemes is critical to the future development of computer-supported work applications (Olson, Card, Landauer, Olson, Malone, and Leggett, 1993). Research is needed to study these tasks to determine whether video will support successful performance and what aspects of the tasks are influenced by video communications. A more sophisticated understanding of how the video medium acts as a filter to alter task performance and the work process is needed.

Table 4. Information management and communication tasks (From Willigies and Willigies, 1995).

I. Information Management

1. Planning

a. Notetaking/Reminders
b. Appointments/Meetings
c. Work Scheduling
d. Budgeting
e. Decision Support

2. Control

a. Environmental Control
b. Security/Priority
c. Purchasing/Billing
d. Payroll/Personnel Appointments

3. Search and Retrieval

a. Bibliographic Databases
b. Equipment Inventory
c. Personnel Records
d. Document Filing

4. Analysis

a. Spreadsheet Layout
b. Statistical Data
c. Financial/ Accounting

5. Design

a. Drafting
b. Computer-Aided Design
c. Computer-Aided Engineering
d. Architectural Design
e. Simulation/Modeling
f. Software Development

6. Document Preparation

a. Outlining
b. Word Processing
c. Graphics/Charting
d. Drawing/Painting
e. Scanning
f. Page Layout
g. Copying
h. Printing
i. Mailing

II. Information Communication

1. Presentation

a. Slide/Overhead Preparation
b. Lecture Presentation
c. Multimedia Preparation

2. Conference

a. Audio Conferencing
b. Video Conferencing
c. Computer Conferencing

Forming taxonomies of tasks such as McGrath (1984) or the related classification outlined in Table 4 provides researchers with a starting point for understanding the differences between activities in computer-supported cooperative work (CSCW) applications and how different communication media can be beneficial. These task taxonomies also highlight areas in which research needs to be conducted.

41.6.2 Shared Workspaces

Shared workspace applications suffer from a variety of interface and coordination problems not known to single user domains. Due to the tremendous demands on coordination in using a groupware application, the need for communication and a common protocol between users is especially critical (Ellis, Gibbs, and Rein, 1991). Gale (1990) discusses the imbedding of social protocols that are found in face-to-face interactions into the software itself. While this notion shows promise, many questions concerning effective implementation of social protocols remain to be investigated. The implementation of video conferencing technology can serve either to hinder or enhance the group protocol. It has been argued by Ellis, Gibbs, and Rein (1991) that a groupware user can become distracted easily when other users make changes (as in a co-authoring environment). Video may serve to aggravate this distraction problem, unless its integration and usage are carefully considered.

Another problem cited by Ellis, Gibbs, and Rein (1991) is that of responsiveness. The success of some computer-supported group activities such as brainstorming and decision-making are contingent upon the responsiveness of the system. Because of their high processing overhead and tendency to clog networks, video connections may serve to create detrimental lags in activities requiring a high degree of synchrony. As mentioned earlier, lags caused by data compression can result in stilted conversation or negative perceptions of other participants. Taken together, the issues involved with the implementation of video communications in groupware applications should be considered carefully to ensure the coordination and smooth interaction of the users and the system.

41.6.3 Designing for Special Populations

Desktop video conferencing offers specific advantages for users with special needs. For example, individuals with mobility impairments often have difficulty traveling to meetings and conferences. By using computer conferencing these individuals can travel electronically rather than physically.

Williges and Williges (1995) describe a portable hardware/software configuration that can be used as a surrogate electronic traveler (SET). This equipment is shipped to the meeting in lieu of travel by the mobility impaired worker. The SET must be transportable, low cost, support a variety of computer platforms and conferencing media, and must be accessible. Additionally, desktop video conferencing can allow individuals to work from their home office and participate in distance learning activities while they are permanently, or temporarily, disabled.

If computer-based video conferencing is used in this way, careful attention must be given to accommodate the special needs of individuals who may have visual, auditory, cognitive, and motor impairments so that they can be full participants in conferencing activities. Casali and Williges, (1990) describe a selection model for choosing appropriate computer accommodations and reference some available databases of assistive technology. When appropriate electronic connectivity is not provided, users with special needs may not be able to use desktop video conferencing.

From a human factors point of view, an iterative, three-phase methodology should be used to facilitate accessible interface design. The three design phases are: (1) identify accessibility barriers; (2) select cost-effective design alternatives; and (3) evaluate empirically the efficacy of the design solution. Lin, Williges, and Beaudet (1995) demonstrated the effectiveness of this methodology to design and evaluate remote controls for older users with mild visual impairments.

41.7 Research and Evaluation Methods

Since many usability, organizational, and technical issues surround the use of desktop video conferencing systems, a good deal of research remains to be conducted. In addition, evaluations of alternative conferencing parameters need to made in order to improve the design of desktop video conferencing systems.

Research Methods. McGrath (1984) outlines the advantages and disadvantages to a host of methods ranging from psychophysical to field studies with regard to generalizability, realism, and precision when conducting research in multi-user applications.

Traditional human factors studies have often involved controlled experimental conditions in which users interact with an interface, and performance is measured in terms of time to complete a task, number of errors, and quality of performance. A considerable amount of research in video communications has involved two people working together on a task under differing communication conditions. This approach has been criticized in the CSCW community for measuring a contrived situation, unrealistic task, and group members who have no significant past or future (Tang and Isaacs, 1993). This lack of realism and generalizability must be balanced against control over sample size, independent and dependent variables, and extraneous variables.

An effort to circumvent the criticisms of controlled laboratory studies is often made by CSCW researchers who advocate the use of ethnographic methods. Methods of social psychology, sociology, and anthropology are being used to study multi-user applications and electronic communication. Often videotape analyses are made of interactions. Subsequent conversation analysis procedures, detailed task analyses, and trend analyses are performed. These methods can create enormous amounts of data which must be painstakingly analyzed. However, even though ethnographic methods lack precision, they offer the promise of learning from behavior in highly realistic settings.

Evaluation Methods. Apteker, Fisher, Kisimov, and Neishols (1994) suggest that alternative desktop video conferencing systems can be evaluated in terms of Quality of Service (QoS). Traditional human factors approaches have concentrated on the *usability* of a computer system. In addition to this important quality, the *communication effectiveness* of the system needs to be gauged. Both human performance and user satisfaction metrics can be used to evaluate QoS. Together, these can serve as a means by which the subjective component of the desktop video conferencing system can be evaluated across the diversity of conferencing tasks.

A family of empirical models which predict QoS as a function of communication technology, conferencing technology, physical environment, and social environment factors needs to be developed. Williges, Williges,

Table 5. Guidelines for designing desktop video conferencing systems.

Communication Technology

- Consider transmission speed requirements when choosing communication networks.
- Maintain high audio quality (i.e., full duplex, telephone-quality).

Conferencing Technology

- Provide a variety of visual cues of participants (e.g., facial expression, eye, hand, and body movement, etc.).
- Allow both task-centered and face-to-face views.
- Maintain a minimum video frame rate 5 frames per second (fps).
- Expect lip synchronization and delay problems.
- Look into the camera when possible to make eye contact.
- Make no rapid movements when video frame rate is low.
- Do not use rapid camera movements with low video frame rates or resolutions.
- Use low resolution rather than a highly degraded video frame rate of under 5 fps if such a tradeoff is possible.
- Retain natural image size of remote participant when possible.
- Use color rather than grayscale, grayscale rather than binary black and white.
- Locate camera adjacent to video window.
- Minimize horizontal and vertical visual angle.
- Allow self-view to be mirror-image.
- Provide a privacy feature for a continuous or long term video conference.
- Use a close view rather than a contextual view.
- Provide a variety of collaboration software tools (electronic whiteboard, shared text editor, group decision support, remote computer control, etc.).

Physical Environment

- Ensure proper lighting levels of 200-500 lux to illuminate the subject.
- Reduce ambient noise to less than 55 dbA.
- Maximize a psychological sense of presence.

Social Environment

- Accommodate both one-to-one and one-to-many conferencing configurations.
- Maximize communication fluidity and speaker control.
- Represent the organizational context and work group dynamics.

Task Environment

- Support both information exchange and interpersonal communication tasks.
- Establish communication protocols for shared workspaces.
- Maximize system responsiveness to support collaborative work.
- Allow alternative communication channels for users with sensory deficits.
- Provide adjustment of video, audio, and text for users with sensory dysfunction.

and Han (1992; 1993) describe sequential experimentation procedures that can be used to collect the necessary and sufficient data to generate polynomial regression empirical models, the use of these models to build an integrated database of design parameters, and the development of design guidelines based on these prediction models.

41.8 Human Factors Design Guidelines

The human factors specialist should provide technical guidance based on empirical research for the proper systems design of desktop video conferencing systems. For example, Table 5 summarizes several human factors design guidelines which can be inferred from the current scientific literature summarized in this chapter. Since communication technology and desktop video conferencing systems are developing rapidly, these design guidelines are quite limited and most of them concentrate on characteristics of the conferencing technology. As desktop video conferencing research continues, the design guidelines shown in Table 5 need to be updated, expanded, and validated.

41.9 Conclusions

The implementation of desktop video conferencing systems in the workplace appears to be increasing rapidly. Human factors practitioners will be called upon to determine that the proper fit between humans and computers is made to ensure successful human-human communication in computer-mediated conferencing. Designing usable desktop video conferencing systems will be particularly challenging due to the diversity of hardware and software, a broad application domain, and a diverse user group. More research will be needed to provide a better understanding of the influences of video-mediated communication in long-term work groups performing a variety of tasks. To enhance communication, systems designers and human factors practitioners need to consider the state-of-the-art of communication and conferencing technology, the physical and social environment, as well as the task environment when implementing desktop video conferencing systems.

41.10 Acknowledgments

Preparation of this chapter was supported, in part, by funds provided by the National Science Foundation and the Southeastern University and College Coalition for Engineering Education (SUCCEED). The authors acknowledge this financial support.

41.11 References

Angiolillo, J. S., Blanchard, H. E., and Israelski, E. W. (May/June, 1993). Video telephony. *AT&T Technical Journal*, 7-20.

ANSI/HFS 100-1988 (1988). *American National Standard for Human Factors Engineering of Visual Display Terminal Workstations.* Santa Monica, CA: The Human Factors Society.

Apteker, R. T., Fisher, J. A., Kisimov, V. S., and Neishols, H. (1994). Distributed multimedia: user perception and dynamic QoS. In *Proceedings of SPIE,* 2188, 226-234. Bellingham, WA: The International Society for Optical Engineering.

Argyle, M. (1975). *Bodily communication.* New York, NY: International Universities Press.

Argyle, M. and Cook, M. (1976). *Gaze and mutual gaze.* Cambridge, U. K.: Cambridge University Press.

Böcker, M. and Mühlbach, L. (1993). Communicative presence in video communications. In *Proceedings of the Human Factors and Ergonomics Society 37th Annual Meeting*, (pp. 249-253). Santa Monica, CA: Human Factors and Ergonomics Society.

Borning, A. and Travers, M. (1991). Two Approaches to Casual Interaction over Computer and Video Networks. In *CHI'91: Human Factors in Computing Systems* (pp. 13-19). New York, NY: Association for Computing Machinery.

Buxton, W. A. S. (1992) Telepresence: Integrating shared task and person spaces. In *Proceedings of Graphic Interface'92* (pp. 123-129) San Francisco, CA: Morgan Kaufman Publishers.

Casali, S., and Williges, R. (1990). Databases of accommodative aids for computer users with disabilities. *Human Factors,* 32(4), 407–422.

Chapanis, A. (1971) Prelude to 2001: Explorations in human communication. *American Psychologist*, 26, 949-961.

Chapanis, A. (1975). Interactive human communication. *Scientific American*, 232(3), 36-42.

Christel, M. G. (1991) *A comparative evaluation of digital video interactive interfaces in the delivery of a code inspection course.* Unpublished doctoral dissertation, Atlanta, GA: Georgia Institute of Technology.

Chuang, S. L. and Haines, R. F. (1993). A study of video frame rate on the perception of compressed dynamic imagery. In *Society for Information Display'93 Digest*. (pp. 524-527). Santa Ana, CA: Society for Information Display.

Cook, M. and Lalljee, M. G. (1972). Verbal substitutes for visual signals in interaction. *Semiotics*, 3, 221-221.

Cool, C., Fish, R. S., Kraut, R. E., and Lowery, C. M. (1992) Iterative design of video communication systems. In *CSCW'92: Computer-Supported Cooperative Work*. (pp. 25-32) New York, NY: Association for Computing Machinery.

Cooper, C. B. (1988). Viewer stress from audio/visual sync problems. *SMPTE Journal*, Feb., 140-142.

Daft, R. L., Lengel, R. H. (1986) Organizational information requirements, media richness, and structural design. *Management Science*, 32(5), 554-571.

Deghuee, B. J. (1980) *Operator-adjustable frame rate, resolution, and gray scale tradeoff in fixed-bandwidth remote manipulator control*. Unpublished master's thesis. Cambridge, MA: Massachusetts Institute of Technology.

Dourish, P. (1993) Culture and control in a media space. In *Proceedings of the European Conference on CSCW*. New York, NY: Association for Computing Machinery.

Dourish, P., Adler, A., Bellotti, V., and Henderson, A. (1994) *Your place or mine? Learning from long-term use of video communication*. Technical Report EPC-94-105. Cambridge, UK: Rank Xerox EuroPARC.

Duncan, S. (1972). Some signals and rules for taking speaking turns in conversations. *Journal of Personality and Social Psychology*, 23(2), 283-292.

Duncan, S. and Niederehe, G. (1974). On signaling that it's your turn to speak. *Journal of Experimental Social Psychology*, 10, 234-247.

Duncanson, J. P. and Williams, A. D. (1973). Video conferencing: reactions of users. *Human Factors*, 15(5), 471-485.

Ellis, C. A., Gibbs, S. J., and Rein, G. L. (1991). Groupware: some issues and experiences. *Communications of the ACM*, 34(1), 39-58.

Fish, R. S., Kraut, R. E., and Chalfonte, B. L. (1990) The videowindow system in informal communications. In *Proceedings of CSCW'90: Computer-Supported Cooperative Work*. (pp. 1-11). New York, NY: Association for Computing Machinery.

Fish, R. S., Kraut, R. E., Root, R. W. and Rice, R. E. (1992). Evaluating Video as a Technology for Informal Communication. In *CHI'92: Human Factors in Computing Systems* (pp. 37-48). New York, NY: Association for Computing Machinery.

Fulk, J., Steinfeld, C. W., Schmitz, J., and Power, J. G. (1987) A social information processing model of media use in organizations. *Communication Research*, 14(5), 529-552.

Fussell, S. R. and Benimoff, N. I. (1995). Social and cognitive processes in interpersonal communication: implications for advanced telecommunications technologies. *Human Factors*, 37(2), 228-250.

Gale (1990) Human aspects of interactive multimedia communication. *Interacting with Computers*, 2(2), 175-189.

Gale, S. (1991) *Adding audio and video to an office environment*. In Bowers, J. M. and Benford, S. D. (Eds.) Studies in Computer Supported Cooperative Work. New York, NY: Elsevier Science Publishing Company, Inc.

Gale, S. (1992) Desktop video conferencing: Technical advances and evaluation issues. *Computer Communications*, 15(8), 517-526.

Gaver, W. W. (1992). The affordances of media spaces for collaboration. In *CSCW'92: Computer Supported Cooperative Work*. New York, NY: Association for Computing Machinery.

Gaver, W., Moran, T., MacLean, A., Lövstrand, L., Dourish, P., Carter, K. and Buxton, W. (1992). Realizing a Video Environment: Europarc's RAVE System. In *Proceedings of CHI'92: Human Factors in Computing Systems* (pp. 27-35). New York, NY: Association for Computing Machinery.

Gaver, W., Sellen, A., Heath, C. and Luff, P. (1993). One is not Enough: Multiple Views in a Media Space. In *INTERCHI'93* (pp. 335-341). New York, NY: Association for Computing Machinery.

Green, C. and Williges, R. C. (1995). Evaluation of alternative media used with a groupware editor in a simulated telecommunications environment. *Human Factors*, 37(2), 283-289.

Harrison, R. P. (1974). *Beyond words: an introduction to nonverbal communication*. Englewood Cliffs, NJ: Prentice-Hall.

Heath, C. and Luff, P. (1991). Disembodied conduct: communication through video in a multi-media office environment. In *CHI'91: Human Factors in Computing*

Systems (pp. 99-103) New York, NY: Association for Computing Machinery.

Heath, C. and Luff, P. (1992) Media space and communicative asymmetries: preliminary observations of video-mediated interaction. *Human-Computer Interaction*, 7, 315-346.

Hiltz, S. R., Johnson, K., and Turoff, M. (1987) Experiments in group decision making: communication process and outcome in face-to-face versus computerized conferences. *Human Communication Research,* 13(2), 225-252.

Hollan, J. and Stornetta, S. (1992) Beyond being there. In *Proceedings of CHI'92: Human Factors in Computing Systems* (pp. 119-125) New York, NY: Association for Computing Machinery.

Isaacs, E. A. and Tang, J. C. (1994). What video can and cannot do for collaboration: a case study. *Multimedia Systems*, 2, 63-73.

Ishii, H. and Kobayashi, M. (1992). Clearboard: a seamless medium for shared drawing and conversation with eye contact. In *CHI'92: Human Factors in Computing Systems* (pp. 525-532) New York, NY: Association for Computing Machinery.

Ishii, H., and Miyake, N. (1994) *Multimedia groupware: Computer and video fusion approach to open shared workspace.* In Buford, J. F. K. (Ed.) Multimedia Systems. New York, NY: ACM Press.

Kies, J. K., Kelso, J., and Williges, R. C. (1995). The use of scenarios to evaluate the effects of group configuration and task on video-teleconferencing communication effectiveness. In *Proceedings of the Third Annual Mid-Atlantic Human Factors Conference.* (pp. 22-28) Blacksburg, VA.

Kies, J. K. Williges, R. C., and Rosson, M. B. (1996) *Controlled laboratory experimentation and field study evaluation of video conferencing for distance learning applications.* (Available at URL: http://hci.ise.vt.edu/~hcil/HTR.html) Human-Computer Interface Laboratory, Blacksburg, VA. HCIL-96-01.

Kiesler, S., Siegel, J., and McQuire, T. W. (1984) Social psychological aspects of computer-mediated communication. *American Psychologist,* 39(*10*), 1123-1134.

Koushik, G. (1994). *The Specifications of an Expert System for Configuring Teleconferencing Systems.* Unpublished master's project report, Blacksburg, VA: Virginia Polytechnic Institute and State University.

Lin, J., Williges, R. C., and Beaudet, D. (1995) Accessible remote controls for older adults with mildly impaired vision. In *Proceedings of the Human Factors and Ergonomics Society 39th Annual Meeting.* (pp. 148-152) Santa Monica, CA: Human Factors and Ergonomics Society.

Lund, A. M. (1993). The influence of video image size and resolution on viewing-distance preferences. *SMPTE Journal*, May, 1993, 406-415.

McGrath, J. E. (1984). *Groups: interaction and performance.* Englewood, NJ: Prentice-Hall.

Macedonia, M. R. and Brutzman, D. P. (1994) MBone provides audio and video across the internet. *IEEE Computer,* April, 30-36.

Mantei, M. M. (1991) Adoption patterns for media space technology in a university research environment. In *Friend 21*, Tokyo, Japan.

Mantei, M. M., Baecker, R. M., Sellen, A. J., Buxton, W. A. S., Milligan, T., and Wellman, (1991). Experiences in the Use of a Media Space. In *CHI'94: Human Factors in Computing Systems* (pp. 203-208). New York, NY: Association for Computing Machinery.

Masoodian, M, Apperley, M., and Fredrickson, L. (1995) Video support for shared work-space interaction: an empirical study. *Interacting with Computers*, 7(3), 237-253.

Moon, D. L. (1992). Electro-optic displays–the system perspective. In Karim, M. A. (Ed.) *Electro-Optical Displays*. New York, NY: Marcel Dekker.

Mühlbach, L., Böcker, M., and Prussog, A. (1995). Telepresence in videocommunications: a study on stereoscopy and individual eye contact. *Human Factors*, 37(2), 290-305.

Ochsman, R. B. and Chapanis, A. (1974). The effects of 10 communication modes on the behavior of teams during co-operative problem-solving. *International Journal of Man-Machine Studies,* 6, 579-619.

Olson, M. H. and Bly, S. A. (1991). The Portland experience: a report on a distributed research group. *International Journal of Man-Machine Studies,* 34, 211-228.

Olson, G. M., Kuwana, E., McGuffin, L. J., and Olson, J. S. (1993). Designing software for a group's needs: a functional analysis of synchronous groupware. In Bass and Dewan (Ed.) *User Interface Software*. New York, NY: Wiley.

Olson, J. S., Card, S. K., Landauer, T. K., Olson, G. M., Malone, T., and Leggett, J. (1993). Computer-supported co-operative work: research issues for the 90s. *Behaviour and Information Technology*, 12(2), 115-129.

Pappas, T. N. and Hinds, R. O. (1995). On video and audio integration for conferencing. In *Proceedings of SPIE*, 2411. Bellingham, WA: The International Society for Optical Engineering.

Prussog, A., Mühlbach, L. and Böcker, M. (1994). Telepresence in Video communications. In *Proceedings of the Human Factors and Ergonomics Society 38th Annual Meeting* (pp. 180-184). Santa Monica, CA: Human Factors and Ergonomics Society.

Rettinger, L. A. (1995). *Desktop Videoconferencing: technology and use for remote seminar delivery*. Unpublished master's thesis. Raleigh, NC: North Carolina State University.

Rutter, D. R. and Stephenson, G. M. (1977). The role of visual communication in synchronizing conversation. *European Journal of Social Psychology*, 7(*1*), 29-37.

Sellen, A. J. (1992). Speech patterns in video-mediated conversations. In *CHI'92: Human Factors in Computing Systems* (pp. 49-59). New York, NY: The Association for Computing Machinery.

Short, J., Williams, E., and Christie, B. (1976). *The social psychology of telecommunications*. London: Wiley.

Swartz, M., Wallace, D., and Tkacz, S. (1992). The influence of frame rate and resolution reduction on human performance. In *Proceedings of the Human Factors and Ergonomics Society 36th Annual Meeting* (pp. 1440-1444). Santa Monica, CA: Human Factors and Ergonomics Society.

Taylor, K. and Tolly, K. (1995) Desktop videoconferencing: Not ready for prime time. *Data Communications*, April, 1995.

Tang, J. C. and Isaacs, E. (1993).Why do users like video? studies of multimedia-supported collaboration. *Computer Supported Cooperative Work (CSCW)*, 1, 163-193.

Trevino, Lengel, and Daft (1987) Media symbolism, media richness, and media choice in organizations. *Communications Research*, 14(*5*), 553-574.

Trowt-Baynard, T. (1994). *Videoconferencing: the whole picture*. Chelsea, MI: Flatiron Publishing.

Tubbs, S. L. (1992). *A systems approach to small group interaction*. New York, NY: McGraw-Hill.

Weeks, G. D. and Chapanis, A. (1976) Cooperative versus conflictive problem solving in three telecommunication modes. *Perceptual and Motor Skills*, 42, 879-917.

Westerink, J. H. D. M. and Roufs, J. A. J. (1989). Subjective image quality as a function of viewing distance, resolution, and picture size. *SMPTE Journal*,. Feb., 113-119.

Williams, E. (1977) Experimental comparisons of face-to-face and mediated communication: a review. *Psychological Bulletin*, 84(*5*), 963-976.

Williges, R. C. and Williges, B. H. (1995). Travel alternatives for the mobility impaired: the surrogate electronic traveler (set). In Edwards, A. D. N. (Ed.) *Extra-ordinary Human-Computer Interaction*. Cambridge, England: Cambridge University Press.

Williges, R. C., Williges, B. H., and Han, S. H. (1993). Sequential experimentation in human-computer interface design. In Hartson, H. R. and Hix, D. (Eds.), *Volume IV, Advances in human-computer interaction*. (pp. 1-30) New York: Ablex.

Williges, R. C., Williges, B. H., and Han, S. H. (1992). Developing quantitative guidelines using integrated data from sequential experiments. *Human Factors*, 34, 399-408.

Handbook of Human-Computer Interaction
Second, completely revised edition
M. Helander, T.K. Landauer, P. Prabhu (eds.)

Chapter 42

Auditory Interfaces

William W. Gaver
Royal College of Art
Kensington Gore
London, UK

42.1 Introduction

Our lives are filled with sound, though we may not be aware of it very often. As I write this, I hear a fan whirring to my right, pushing air through my living room. My stereo is playing quiet music to motivate me and drown out distractions. I hear a breeze rustle through a tree in the garden, shaking a random arpeggio from my windchimes. My cat meows at me, asking me to pet her, an airliner passes overhead, occasional traffic noises filter through from the street, and I hear my upstairs neighbor walking up the steps. None of this bothers me; on the contrary, it immerses me in my surroundings, providing the texture of my environment.

My computer, on the other hand, is conspicuously silent. I hear my fingers tapping on the keyboard, and it might beep at me to warn me of some problem, but that's about all. I don't hear anything as I select icons, move them around, copy them, or delete them. Occasionally, I might hear the hard disk spin up as it accesses data, but other than this my computer doesn't tell me anything about its internal state, its processes, or its modes, without using a visual display. I don't hear other people on the network, nor other events about which I might want information. My computer is seen but not heard, and its reticence maintains a distance between me and the world it represents.

This is unfortunate, because there are a myriad of opportunities for using sound in computers. Many of the most obvious involve using speech as input or output. In this chapter, however, I focus on ways to use *nonspeech* audio in the interface—uses for sound that may be less obvious but as powerful as those involving speech (speech interfaces are the topic of another chapter in this volume).

Nonspeech audio can be used in computers as we use it in the everyday world, and new ways to use it are also emerging. I start with three examples of experimental auditory interfaces in order to ground the discussion and give an idea of the space of audio interface design. Then I discuss why sound is a valuable resource for interaction design, and speculate about why it hasn't been used more extensively. In the following section, I describe a variety of ways to think about and manipulate sound. Finally, I devote the majority of this chapter to a more thorough review of systems that have used nonspeech audio to convey information, ending with a discussion of new opportunities for auditory interface design.

42.1.1 Three Orienting Examples

Sound is a relatively unexploited medium in current computers, but researchers have explored a variety of ways that sound might be used. Their examples define an implicit space for auditory interface design—one which is constantly expanding as new research is done. This space of design is defined by decisions made about three primary issues: First, what information an auditory interface is to provide; second, the kinds of sounds used; and third, the kind of mapping used to establish sound as a representational system. In this section, I briefly describe three examples of auditory interfaces as introductory landmarks for exploring this space.

Data Auralisation

One of the earliest applications of sound in computer interfaces addressed the goal of representing multivariate data. Graphical depiction is strained when faced with more than three data dimensions, but sound offers many dimensions to which data might be mapped. For instance, Bly (1982a, 1982b) demonstrated that sound could be used to discriminate between three different species of iris flowers. Each flower is characterized by four variables: sepal length and width, and petal length and width. These variables are generally sufficient to classify a given flower as belonging to one of three species, but it is difficult to read numerical data in making such a classification. Bly showed that these classifications are easy to make if the data are mapped to variables of sound. By mapping sepal length to pitch, sepal width to volume, petal length to duration, and petal width to waveform, she represented each flower with its own simple sound. She presented experimental participants with examples of tones representing flowers from each of the species, and then asked them to classify new tones as belonging to one of the three groups. People were able to use the sounds to classify flowers as accurately as they could using most graphical methods (most of the listeners could accurately classify all but one or two of the flowers).

Bly's work is an example of *data auralisation*, in which parameters of sound are used to represent multidimensional data. It exploits sound's ability to form patterns that we can hear at a higher level than they are explicitly represented by the computer.

Alarms and Musical Messages

Another common use for sound is to alert people about some event. Alarm clocks exhort us to get up in the morning, ambulance sirens warn us to pull over, and foghorns alert sailors to dangerous rocks. The interrupt beep used by computers is an example of such sounds, but the information it provides is so generic that it can easily be customised (from bells to cartoon samples) without confusing its users. In contrast, many other situations require that alerts sounds are not only noticed, but that they are identified and discriminated from other alarms. For instance, as many as 60 alarms may have sounded during the Three Mile Island accident (Sanders and McCormick, 1987).

Roy Patterson and his colleagues (e.g., Patterson et al., 1986; Patterson, 1982) have designed a system for generating multiple alarms that work together. First, the ambient noise level in the target environment is analysed, and used to design basic sounds that are neither too quiet to be heard, nor so loud as to be disruptive. These sounds are combined to form short tunes, or motives, that serve as the alarms. The motives can be seen as very simple pieces of music; incomparable in complexity or aesthetics to conventional music, but exploiting many of music's basic attributes. Rhythm and pitch are used to give each alarm a distinct identity, to convey the appropriate sense of urgency, and to mimic the alarms meaning (e.g., a motive with an increasing tempo is used to indicate that the speed of an aircraft is too high). The alarms themselves are repeated every few seconds while the situation applies, providing gaps during which operators may discuss the situation and take remedial action; but if the situation persists the alarm is played again, more urgently, to remind them to address the problem. This basic strategy has been tested with target users, and employed in airlines, intensive care wards, and railways.

Patterson's alarms are an example of using simple *musical messages* in interaction design, one that exploits sound's potential to create distinctive figures that we can associate with events.

The ARKola Simulation

A third use for sound in the interface is to convey information from computer systems about objects, events, and other people. For instance, Gaver et al. (1991) used a collection of everyday sounds to support people collaborating on a process control task. Pairs of people ran a simulated softdrink bottling plant, consisting of eight interconnected processes, that was too large to fit on the computer screen. Sounds were designed to indicate when machines were running, how fast they ran, and when supplies were being wasted—a total of about a dozen sounds playing at once. Users operated the plant to produce as many bottles of softdrink as possible, refilling supplies as they were used and dealing with programmed breakdowns of the machines. Comparing people's performance with and without sound, it became clear that sounds were useful in helping people monitor individual processes, allowed the higher-level activity of the plant as a whole to be perceived, encouraged collaboration without necessitating a shared visual focus, and motivated users by increasing the tangibility of the simulation.

The ARKola simulation is an example of using sound to provide feedback about user actions, to indicate ongoing processes, to support collaboration and to support peripheral awareness of events. In particular, the use of *auditory icons*—environmental sounds designed to be appropriate for the virtual environment of the interface—allows people to listen to events in the computer as they do to those in the everyday world. These three examples indicate some of the possible strategies for using sound in interaction design, and some of the applications for auditory interfaces. Each depends on using a set of sound attributes and dimensions to stand for categorical and continuous information, through a mapping that can vary in the degree to which it is arbitrary or constrained.

Note that none of these examples come from the wide range of games and multimedia products that use sound. This is because, in general, the focus of sound design in such applications is on its emotional and aesthetic impact, rather than its ability to systematically convey useful information. In addition, games and multimedia designers have rarely discussed their designs and techniques in a research context. This is unfortunate. As I will suggest in concluding this chapter, there is much we can learn from the sound effects used in games and multimedia. In the body of this discussion, however, I will focus on relatively academic research on auditory interfaces.

42.1.2 Why use Sound? Sound as a Medium

The success of auditory interfaces depends on an understanding of the structure of sound that can be used in design as well as real problems that might benefit from sound. More deeply, they depend on an appreciation of the qualities of sound that make it a valuable medium for some tasks. Implicitly, auditory interfaces all offer answers to the question: Why use sound?

Vision and hearing are our two primary distance senses, allowing us to gather information about the world without physical contact. For most people, vision seems far more important than sound, to the point that what something looks like is almost inextricably tangled with what it is. Sounds seem secondary. Noises might tell us something about an object, but they seldom really define it. Seeing is believing; hearing only tells us where to look. Vision seems richer, more detailed, and more exact than sound, and thus better used in designing, creating, and communicating new interface worlds.

What this perspective ignores, however, is that sound is a different sort of medium from vision, one that provides information that vision cannot. What we see about an object is not what we hear about it. What we *see* is patterned variations of light frequencies, usually reflected from the surfaces of objects in the environment around us. These patterns and their variations can tell us about the size of objects, their corners and curves, their textures and materials. But what we *hear* is patterns of moving air, often emitted from objects as they vibrate due to some event. Sound usually conveys information about the substances and dynamics of objects, rather than their surfaces. Sound tells us about the size of objects, their internal makeup, their parts and their hollows, their textures and consistency. Sound tells us about events, about the contacts and scrapes, bounces and breaks as things move and interact around us. And sound tells us about our environment, interacting with the spaces and surfaces around us before reaching our ears amplified, echoed, and filtered. Sound has different affordances as a medium than vision does; it offers different sorts information in the everyday world, and therefore different opportunities for providing information from designed systems.

The affordances offered by the media differ also because the sensory systems with which we gather information from light and sound have different characteristics. Our eyes can register detailed differences in light patterns only over a few visual degrees, and even peripheral vision only extends over about a third of the potentially spherical field of view that surrounds us. Thus we move our eyes, our heads, and our bodies to see what is around us. Visual objects tend to persist in a given spatial location, and we can turn to scrutinise them, or turn away to obliterate them from sight. Our ears, in contrast, register vibrations from all around us (and even from within our own bodies). We need not turn to hear something; in fact we cannot turn away or close our ears.

The different spatial characteristics of our visual and auditory systems interact with temporal characteristics of the media. Sound-producing events tend to have finite duration, and to change in complex ways over time, while visual objects tend to be more stable. So, just as spatial arrangements mean we cannot see everything at once, so do temporal dynamics mean we cannot hear everything at the same time. Visual objects exist in space but over time, while sound exists in time, but over space (Gaver, 1989).

Finally, the ways we structure the world visually and sonically in building cultural artifacts are also different. Music is a language—using the term broadly—developed from sound that has no clear counterpart in vision. On the one hand, music relies on proportional relations of pitch and rhythm that make it analogous to visual graphs and charts. On the other hand, music can convey mood, emotion, and narrative tension and resolution while remaining abstract from particular content, in ways similar to, but perhaps more developed than, the abstract visual arts. Music certainly seems more universal than either charts or abstract art, and tonal musical structure in particular is recognised very widely, even by cultures in which it is not indigenous. The ability to harness musical power is an important opportunity for interface design.

In sum, sound is a powerful medium for conveying information. Sound complements vision, providing information about distant objects and events, their internal configurations, timing, and dynamics. Sound can reveal patterns in data, give feedback about user actions or allow monitoring of system processes. Sound can provide peripheral awareness about other people and their activities, support an immersive presence in artificial or remote environments, and can be used to create mood, drama, and narrative flow. Because we need not orient our bodies in any particular direction to hear these things, we can look at one thing while hearing another. Moreover, when combined with speech, sound can be used to make computers accessible without any need for vision or visual displays at all.

42.1.3 Why Sound Isn't Used

Given the potential of sound as a resource for interface design, it is worth exploring why it has not been used more extensively in interface design. The first reason is that it has not been clear what sound might offer; in fact, the term "bells and whistles" is sometimes used colloquially to refer to unnecessary extravagance in design. But sound can go beyond being a mere fillip to being an integral and essential part of the interface. This may be clearest where text and graphics have no role, as in interfaces for the visually impaired, or phone-based systems. In graphical systems, too, sounds may present information more clearly or more effectively than graphics. This will be shown over and over again by the research I discuss in this chapter.

Another pervasive objection to sound, of course, is that it can be annoying. Sounds permeate environments, and many people are disturbed by the idea of increasing noise levels. There are several answers to this objection. First is to note that, by definition, "noise" is unwanted sound. To a great degree, if sounds are useful and meaningful, they will not be annoying. Second, while there is some truth in saying that sound is inherently distracting—after all, we have no "earlids"—we are nonetheless surrounded by sound at all times, and in many cases can simply relegate it to the background of our attention. Thus auditory interfaces that seem irritating when we concentrate on them can fade to the background as we use them, if they are well designed, and provide their information relatively unobtrusively. Finally, sounds' annoyance can be controlled. Research by Patterson et al., (1986), Edworthy et al. (1991), and Swift et al. (1989) has considered how attributes of simple sounds contribute to their perceived urgency, which may be seen as a correlate of their potential to distract or annoy us. They have found that easily controllable factors such as attack time, spectral type, and rhythmic regularity all contribute to urgency. Matching urgency to the information to be conveyed can help auditory interfaces become an unobtrusive, helpful part of the auditory ambience. There is no reason that sounds need to be annoying to be effective.

A final reason that sound has been underdeveloped in current interfaces is that hardware and software resources for using sound have been limited. It has only been relatively recently that commercially available computers have made it easy to control sound production beyond the ability to trigger a simple beep. The history of auditory interface design is the story of applications that push the boundaries of currently available systems, to make them useful for interface work. And, indeed, there has been phenomenal development of support for sound in current computers, and with it increasing sophistication in auditory interfaces. However, while new sound-making possibilities do encourage the wider use of auditory interfaces, it is important to recognise that the constraints they place may shape research in undesirable ways. The largest impetus for the development of sound-processing software and hardware comes from the music and entertainment industries. Auditory interfaces often require control over

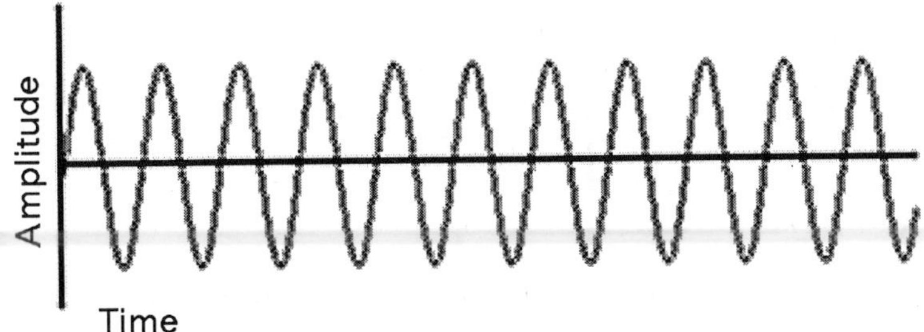

Figure 1. A simple sine waveform.

different attributes of sound, so there are still serious limitations in the resources available for design. In the next section, I describe a number of frameworks for understanding sound, to give an idea of the resources that could potentially be useful.

42.2 Parameters of Sound and Hearing

Designing with sound involves, at the most fundamental level, manipulating sound along various dimensions to produce different effects. This can involve mapping dimensions of sound to dimensions of data to produce the sonic equivalent of graphs (data auralisation), the creation of a discriminable set of musical motives to be used as labels for events (musical messages), or mapping perceptible attributes of source events to those we want to convey (auditory icons). In any case, it is necessary to identify relevant dimensions of sound that can be used in design. Building this common vocabulary is the purpose of this section.

Sound is a rich and many-layered medium, and different frameworks may be used to describe its structure. Here I discuss six. I start with acoustics and psychoacoustics, the basic sciences of sound and hearing that serve as a foundation for any strategy of using sound. Then I discuss everyday listening, which seeks to describe sound and hearing in terms of the perception of events in the world. I focus next on our ability to localise sounds, a topic which overlaps psychoacoustics and everyday listening, and explain systems which allow sounds to be located perceptually in a three-dimensional, virtual auditory space. After that, I turn to musical structures, and propose that the higher levels of organisation they offer might be applied to auditory interfaces more than they have been so far. Related to this are genre sounds, which may be musical or everyday sounds, but are linked to their meanings by long cultural history. Finally I briefly discuss the effects that sound processing technologies have on how we think about and use sound, suggesting particularly that they offer a large number of separate, overlapping ways to think about timbre, the quality of sounds.

These are broad topics, and I can only summarise some of the relevant issues and research here. For more complete coverage interested readers should consult the references cited in each section as well as more general texts such as those by Bregman, (1990), Handel (1989), or Pierce (1983).

42.2.1 Acoustics and Psychoacoustics

Many of the dimensions used in designing auditory interfaces—e.g., physical dimensions such as frequency, amplitude, or spectrum, or perceptual ones such as pitch, loudness, or timbre—are described by acoustics and psychoacoustics. Acoustics describes the structure of sound itself, while psychoacoustics concerns the mapping between dimensions of sound and dimensions of our perception. This mapping is not linear, and thus it is important to distinguish the two. A design which naively assumes a straightforward correspondence between physical manipulations of sound and perceived differences may be ineffective or misleading.

Acoustics: Frequency, Amplitude, Waveforms and Spectra

Sounds are pressure variations that propagate through an elastic medium (usually the air, but also any other substance, such as walls, water, or bone). A simple description of sound can be created by graphing its *waveform*, which shows pressure variations over time (Figure 1). The wave shown here is periodic, repeating itself with a *frequency* described in units of cycles per second, or Hertz (Hz). The *amplitude* of the wave refers to the degree of departure from the mean pressure level, and relates to the *intensity*, or force per unit area, of a sound. Since people are sensitive to a vast range of intensity—the most intense sound tolerable is about 10^{12} times as intense as the weakest that can be detected–amplitude is commonly expressed using the logarithmic *decibel* (dB) scale.

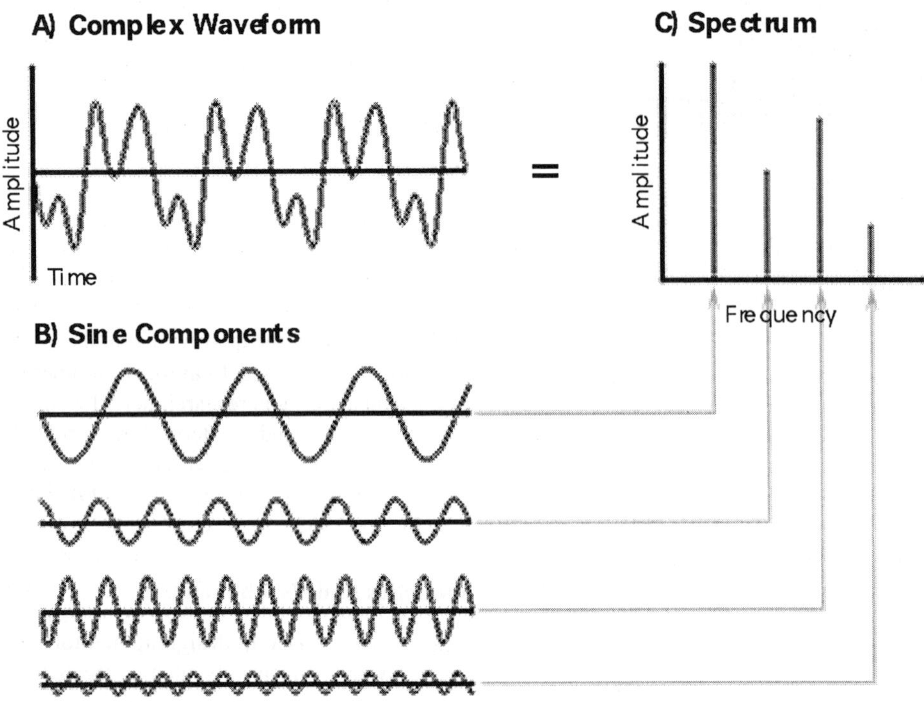

Figure 2. A complex waveform created by adding four sine waves. *In A, the waveform is shown; B shows the four component sine waves, and C shows the equivalent spectrum.*

The waveform shown in Figure 1 is a *sine wave*. Though rare in nature, sine waves are often considered the simplest sort of sound because virtually any complex wave can be described as the sum of a number of sine waves with different frequencies, amplitudes, and phases (phase refers to the how the waveform is shifted in time). Figure 2A shows a complex wave, and Figure 2B the simpler sine waves from which it is made. *Fourier analysis* is an important analysis technique for analysing waves in terms of their component (sine wave) frequencies, called *partials*. When a wave is Fourier analysed, the results may be shown in a *spectral plot* that shows a wave's partials as energy plotted by amplitude and frequency (Figure 2C). Conversely, *additive synthesis* is a technique for synthesising sounds by adding together sine waves of different frequencies and amplitudes.

Complex waves may be categorised according to the frequency patterns of their partials. Musical sounds tend to be *harmonic*: the frequencies of their partials (also called *harmonics* for such sounds) are integer multiples of the lowest, *fundamental* frequency (e.g., a wave with partials at 100, 200, 300_ Hz. is harmonic, with a fundamental frequency of 100Hz.). Harmonic waveforms are repetitive at the frequency of their fundamental and are heard with a distinct pitch.

Many natural sounds are *inharmonic*: the frequencies of their partials are not integral multiples of their fundamental frequency. Such sounds tend not to be repetitive, and if they are heard with a clear pitch—often they sound like a combination of different pitches—it depends on their average frequency, weighted by amplitude, rather than on their fundamental. Finally, *noises* are made up of energy at many different frequencies, with continuous spectra, rather than the peaked spectrum shown in Figure 2C. White noise has a spectrum that is flat, while other noises may be *bandlimited*; that is, they may contain energy within a range of frequencies characterised by their *bandwidth*. Such sounds, like inharmonic sounds, may be heard with a rough pitch corresponding to their average, amplitude-weighted frequency.

The categories of harmonic, inharmonic, and noise sounds provide useful landmarks in considering the

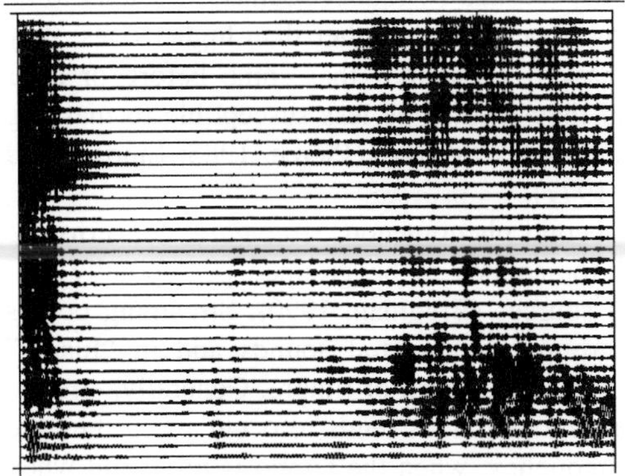

Figure 3. A spectrogram showing amplitude (darkness) by frequency (vertical axis) by time (horizontal).

structure of sounds, and in considering the kinds of sound that might be used for design. In practice, however, the boundaries are not entirely distinct. For instance, most acoustic musical instruments produce sounds that are only approximately harmonic, and their slight inharmonicities produce a richness that is important for their perception (Pierce, 1983). Similarly, the sounds made by some instruments, such as violins, tend to be so complex that hundreds of sine waves would be necessary to recreate their waveforms. A more efficient approach to synthesising such sounds is to use filters to shape a continuous noise spectrum, a process known as *subtractive synthesis*.

Sounds tend to evolve over time, as their partials rise and fall in amplitude, and vary in frequency. Thus a series of spectral plots, showing a sound's frequency components at a given moment of its evolution, tend to be joined to form a *spectrogram* showing the amplitude by frequency over time. Often spectrograms are shown with amplitude plotted as the darkness of a point plotted against time and frequency (Figure 3); alternatively, three dimensional graphs can be used to show all three dimensions.

Waveforms (Figures 1, 2A and B) and spectrograms (Figures 2C and 3) show sounds using different coordinate systems, and tend to be useful for different tasks. Waveforms can show the temporal evolution of sounds' amplitudes more clearly than spectrograms, and thus are often used in sound editing programs (the fact that they are much less computationally expensive also plays a role). Spectrograms can show the detailed frequency makeup of a sound much better than waveforms, however, and tend to be the more powerful of the two. This is due, in part, to the fact that phase relations among sounds' partials are not usually represented in spectral plots, but are very salient in waveform plots. Since phase relations tend not to be heard (Cabot et al., 1976), waveforms that look very different may sound identical. Thus systems that depend on manipulations of the waveform can be misleading.

Psychoacoustics: Pitch, Loudness, Timbre, Masking, and Streaming

The acoustic dimensions discussed have correlates in our perception of sound. For instance, the frequency of a sound corresponds roughly to its *pitch*, that is, whether it sounds high or low. Its amplitude correlates to *loudness*. Its time-varying spectrum correlates to its *timbre*, or tone-colour. But the mappings between acoustic and psychoacoustic dimensions tend to be nonlinear, so that equal changes along an acoustical dimension do not necessarily produce equal changes of perception. These mappings are also not orthogonal, but often interact. Changing the amplitude of a tone, for instance, can change its perceived pitch as well as its loudness. The combination of nonlinearity and lack of orthogonality makes it very difficult to design sounds so that their perceptions may be exactly predicted.

Pitch does not relate linearly to frequency, but logarithmically: In general, doubling frequency raises the pitch by an octave, so that doubling a 220Hz tone to 440Hz raises the pitch by one octave, but to raise it by two octaves one must increase it four-fold to 880Hz. In addition, pitch is affected by loudness: As sine waves get louder, their pitch goes down if they are under 1000Hz, and up if they are over. Moreover, pitch is not a single perceptual dimension (Shepard, 1964). Pitch *height*, how high or low a note sounds, interacts with pitch *chroma*, which note is being played. For instance, two notes an octave apart may sound more similar than two that are only a semitone (one twelfth of an octave) apart, because they share the same chroma even if they are more dissimilar in pitch height.

Loudness does not relate linearly to amplitude, either. Roughly speaking, loudness (L) relates to amplitude (I) according to a power law: $L = kI^{0.3}$. This means that a 10dB increase of amplitude only doubles loudness. But loudness depends on frequency, as well, with tones between 1000 and 5000Hz perceived as louder than those that are higher or lower (more exact functions of loudness with frequency can be found in the form of *equal-loudness* curves; Fletcher and Munson, 1933). Loudness is also affected by bandwidth, the spread between the highest and lowest frequency components of a sound, with high bandwidth sounds seeming louder than equal-energy low-bandwidth ones.

Loudness also depends on duration, with sounds shorter than about a second increasing in loudness with duration (Scharf and Houtsma, 1986), while sounds longer than a second remain constant in loudness.

Timbre is a single term used to describe the most meaningful variations in sound, including those that make raindrops sound different from bells, roosters from train whistles, and flutes from ocean waves—assuming they have the same pitch and loudness. In fact, it is defined as "...that attribute of auditory sensation in terms of which a listener can judge that two sounds similarly presented and having the same loudness and pitch are dissimilar" (American National Standards Institute, 1973). This negative definition means that timbre is "the psychoacoustician's multidimensional wastebasket category" (McAdams and Bregman, 1979).

Despite timbre's fundamental role in sound perception, remarkably little is known about its structure or dimensions. As Helmholtz (1885/1954) showed, timbre is influenced by the spectrum of a sound, so that changing a sound's partials will generally change its timbre. But it is also critically dependent on spectral dynamics, to the point that the perception of brass tones, for instance, depends more on low partials building up faster than high ones than it does on the exact spectral makeup of the sounds (Risset and Wessel, 1982).

Though research has tried to uncover meaningful perceptual dimensions of timbre and their acoustic correlates (see, e.g., Grey, 1977; Wessel, 1979), no encompassing system has yet been established. Recently, many computer musicians have been turning away from the goal of determining abstract timbral dimensions. Instead, there is an increasing interest in using physical models of acoustic instruments to understand and control sound (e.g., Borin et al., 1993; McIntyre et al., 1983). These are related to attempts to recast timbre in terms of auditory event perception (as described in the section on Everyday Listening later in this chapter; see also the discussion of Device Models later in this section).

Apart from understanding the perceptual correlates of acoustic dimensions such as frequency and loudness, psychoacoustics also studies other effects of the auditory system on how we hear sound. Here I only touch on two issues that are salient for auditory interface design. Both concern the perception of multiple sounds.

The first, *masking*, concerns the ability for one sound to make another inaudible (as when you can't hear what somebody is saying in a noisy room). Sounds are typically masked by louder sounds, they tend to be masked by lower sounds rather than higher ones, they can be masked by sounds that come before or after them, and they tend to be less susceptible to masking the more complex they are (Pierce, 1983; Lindsay and Norman, 1977).

The second phenomenon, *streaming*, concerns the tendency for sounds to be grouped perceptually into perceived sources (Bregman, 1990). Streaming occurs both in grouping sequential sounds and in "fusing" partials in the perception of timbre. Generally, streaming of sequential sounds tends to occur when they are close in frequency, when the tempo is high, and when they share a common timbre. Fusing of partials tends to be encouraged when they share a "common fate," undergoing similar changes in frequency or amplitude; thus vibrato is often applied to fuse inharmonic sounds (Pierce, 1983). Clearly, controlling both masking and streaming has great practical importance for auditory interface design.

Acoustics and psychoacoustics are the most fundamental sciences of sound and hearing, and a basic understanding of their terms and issues is crucial for all auditory interface design. My description here is far longer than the following descriptions of other frameworks for understanding sound, but it is still woefully short to do the subject justice. Nonetheless, I hope to have introduced the topic well enough to allow readers new to the field to understand the following discussion.

42.2.2 Everyday Listening

A second approach to sound and hearing stresses *everyday listening*. Where psychoacoustics is concerned with hearing sounds per se, everyday listening is concerned with the experience of hearing sounds in terms of their *sources* (e.g., Gaver 1993a, 1993b, 1988). For instance, if one drops a crystal vase while carrying it in a darkened room, one is less likely to attend to the pattern of pitched impulses it produces than one is to try to ascertain what it landed on and whether it broke. The experience of listening to the attributes of the sound – its pitch, loudness, duration, or timbre—is an example of *musical listening*. The experience of listening to determine the source itself—whether it involves a hard or soft surface, a bouncing or breaking object, a threatening or harmless event— is an example of *everyday listening*.

The approach to audition captured by everyday listening is suggested by Gibson's (1979) ecological perspective on perception. The ecological approach emphasises that perception should be understood in

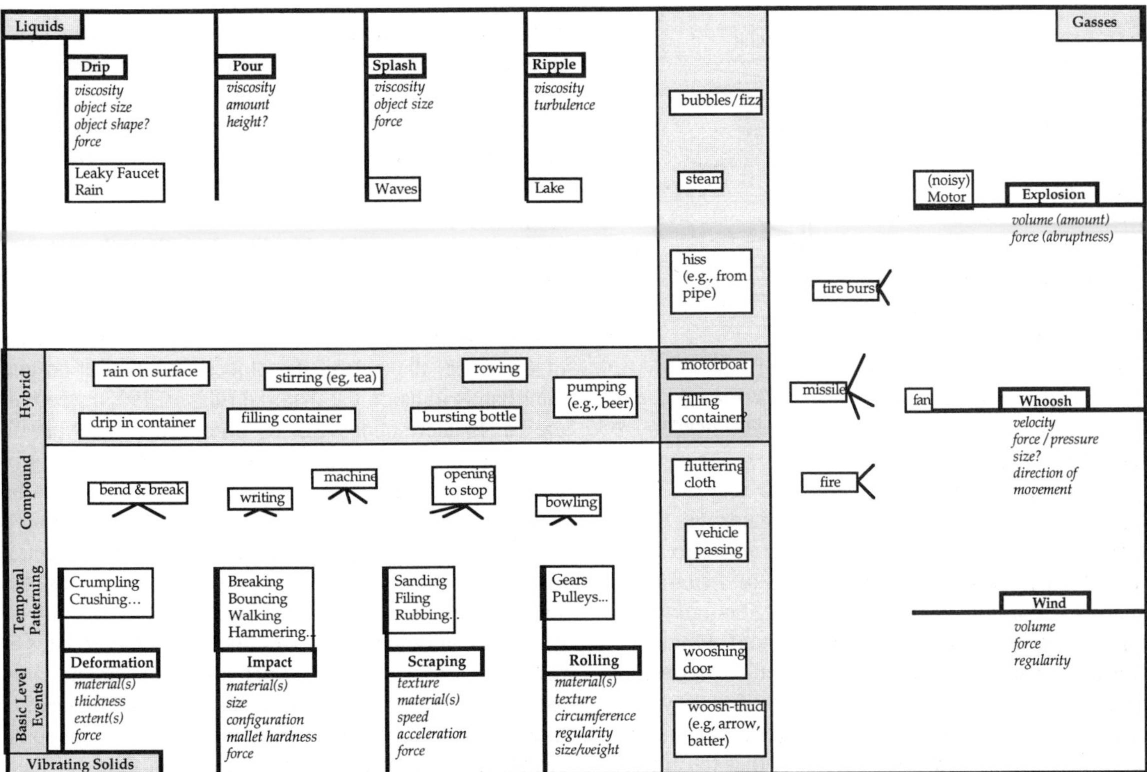

Figure 4. A framework for understanding everyday listening. *Basic level events and attributes from three categories—solids, liquids, and gasses—are shown on the edges, with more complex events towards the centre (from Gaver, 1993b).*

terms of the fit between the organism and a structured environment. For audition, one implication is a new framework for describing sound and hearing, one which complements more traditional approaches (see Gaver, 1993). The vast variety of sounds we hear in the world may be characterised in terms of their sources, their attributes in terms of source attributes. Instead of talking about pulses and buzzes, pitches and timbres, we can talk about impacts and scrapes, size and material. Instead of relating sensations to simple acoustic attributes, as psychoacoustics does, we can relate source perception to more complex acoustic patterns. Most importantly (at least for the purposes of this chapter), we can build auditory interfaces using this framework. Instead of mapping information to *sounds*, we can map information to *events*.

Two questions are important in orienting to the new framework suggested by everyday listening. The first is what do we hear? If traditional terms for describing sound and hearing are to be replaced by those referring to source events, what objects, attributes, and dimensions are appropriate? A possible framework is shown in Figure 4, based on a mixture of protocol studies and physical analyses (Gaver, 1993b, 1988). All sound producing events involve an interaction of objects. Basic level events—the simplest combinations of objects and interactions—are grouped according to three basic material categories of solids, liquids, and gasses, and shown on the outside of the figure with the attributes that might be conveyed by sound. More complex events, which can be classed as temporal patterns, compound events, and hybrid events (involving materials from more than one category) are shown towards the centre of the figure. Complex events inherit the attributes of their basic components, so that any sound involving a struck solid, for instance, conveys information about size, material and so on. In addition, complex events convey higher-level information, such as the speed of a machine or space left in a container being filled with liquid. This is a tentative and simple framework, but it is useful in capturing ideas about everyday listening, guiding future research, and serving as a palette for the design of auditory icons.

Of course, listeners are not always accurate in their identification of sound-producing events, or in evaluating the dimensions (e.g. size) of sources they do identify. Ballas (1994a, 1994b) has done extensive research on factors underlying the accuracy and speed with

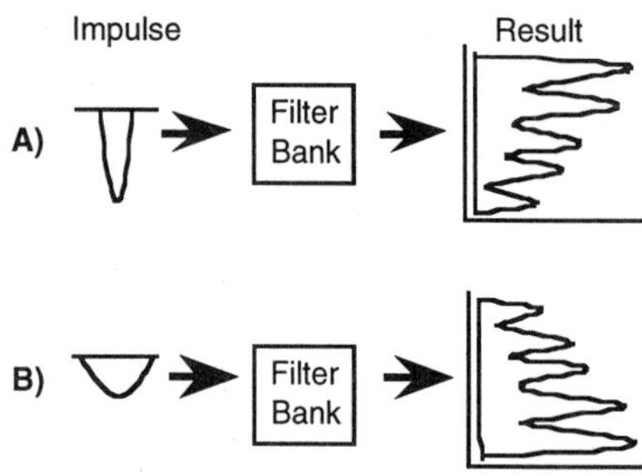

***Figure 5. Objects can be modeled as filter banks, and** impact hardness by impulses with varying degrees of sharpness (from Gaver, 1993a).*

which listeners can identify everyday sounds. He found that simple acoustic variables were not related to accuracy and speed, but that the continuity of spectral information in continuous and discrete sounds was. Identification was also related to sound typicality. When primed with the name of an event, experimental participants were quicker to confirm that a typical sound could have been produced by the event than an atypical one, even if they would agree that the untypical one could have been too. Causal uncertainty, derived by asking participants to estimate the number of sources that could have produced a given sound (the more sources, the higher the uncertainty), is also related to speed and accuracy. Finally, Ballas and Mullin (1991) found context effects for identification of sounds. They embedded target sounds in sequences that could be consistent, inconsistent, or random, and found that while an inconsistent context had large negative effects on both free and forced choice identification, a consistent one made only small positive effects. All these experiments were performed on relatively short sounds (less than .6 seconds), but they are valuable in indicating that people are best at identifying sounds that are typical, unambiguous with regards to source, and embedded in a congruent auditory ambience.

The second question for everyday listening is how do we hear it? What are the acoustic correlates to perceptual attributes of sources? If frequency is the major acoustic correlate of pitch perception, for example, what are the acoustic correlates to the perception of size, for instance, or texture? These questions can be addressed by comparing acoustic analyses of recorded sounds with experimental data about their perception. For instance, Freed (1988; Freed and Martins, 1986) has shown that people can perceive the hardness of a mallet used to strike a solid object, and that this may be conveyed by the ratio of high- to low-frequency energy in the resulting sound. Physical analyses of sound producing events are also useful in this endeavor. Wildes and Richards (1988), for example, showed analytically that the internal friction characterising different materials determines both the damping and definition of frequency peaks, and thus the material of a struck object may be perceptible. Finally, algorithms that attempt to synthesise sounds directly in terms of events and their attributes can also be useful. For instance, a given object may be modeled as a filter bank, where the frequencies of the filters depend on the object's configuration and their bandwidths on the material (Gaver, 1993a; see Figure 5). Impact sounds can be produced by passing an acoustic impulse through these filters, where the sharpness of the impulse depends on the hardness of the striking object, while scraping sounds can be produced by passing a longer, noisy signal, where noise's spectral makeup depends on surface texture. Insofar as the sounds resemble those made by the actual events, the algorithms can be said to capture the acoustic correlates to perceived source attributes. Such algorithms are not only useful for understanding the acoustic bases of everyday listening, but are useful in allowing auditory icons to be synthesised and parameterised directly in terms of their source attributes.

Everyday listening represents a new approach to sound and hearing, one that is relatively unexplored as yet. We know little about how best to summarise perceptible events and their attributes in a general system that goes beyond focused descriptions of individual event classes. We know even less about how to characterise the acoustic information for events, the physical variables that underlie our perception of sound-producing events. Nonetheless, the perspective suggested by everyday listening has already proved valuable for design, helping to guide the creation of parameterised auditory icons that convey information as it is conveyed in the everyday world.

42.2.3 Localisation

Our ability to hear the *location* of sound sources, both in terms of their distance and their direction, provides a meeting ground for research on psychoacoustics and everyday listening. On the one hand, localisation is a perceptual problem that has been well studied by traditional psychoacousticians. On the other hand, our ability to hear the location of a sound source, and even something about the environment in which it is played, is clearly related to everyday listening. Moreover, the ability to provide location information artificially for

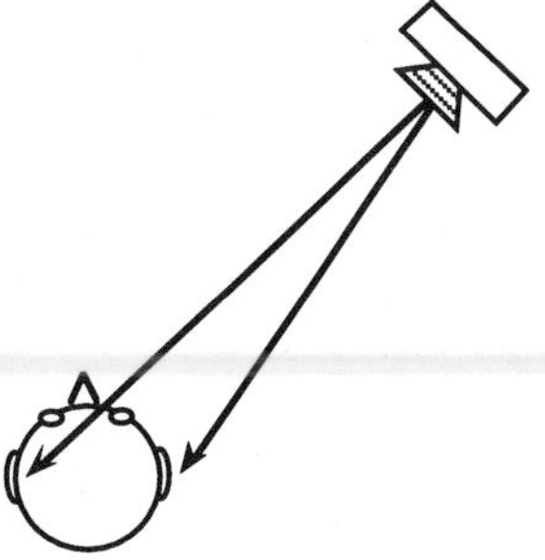

Figure 6. Sound travels along different paths to reach our ears.

sounds has great potential for auditory interfaces, and especially for virtual reality systems. In this section, I briefly summarise the acoustics and psychoacoustics of distance and direction perception, and explain the principle behind systems which allow sounds to be located artificially. For more information, see Begault (1994), on which much of this discussion is based.

Distance

There are several cues for the distance of a source. To some degree, the amplitude of a sound will determine its perceived distance. Physically, the amplitude of a sound made by a point source (which radiates sound equally in all directions), decreases with the square of the distance, so that doubling distance corresponds to a change of 6dB, while line sources (for instance, a river or a road) decrease in amplitude at a rate of only 3dB for every doubling of distance. Perceptually, however, loudness, not amplitude, may be the important variable, such that slightly higher amplitude differences are needed to give the impression of distance doubling.

Amplitude manipulations alone do not always give a compelling sense of distance, however. First, the effects of amplitude are stronger for unfamiliar sounds than they are for familiar ones (otherwise we might think a car passing ten feet away was closer than a watch held next to our ear). Second, most research on loudness has been done in anechoic environments, where echoes and reverberations are kept to a minimum. In a normally reverberant environment, the effects of sounds reflecting from nearby surfaces can drastically change the way that amplitude fades with distance.

Reverberation itself provides information for distance (as well as for other aspects of the environment). In a normal environment, sounds not only reach our ears directly from the source, but also after reflecting from various surfaces. These later reverberations, by definition, travel a longer path than the direct sound, and thus have a lower amplitude. But as a listener moves further from the direct source, the total amplitude of reflected sounds increases compared to that of the direct source. Thus increasing the R/D ratio, the ratio of reverberant to direct sound, can give a convincing impression of increasing depth up to the auditory horizon, at which point further increases in reverberation will not have an effect. Reverberation is a very effective way to produce depth impressions, one that is becoming increasingly easy to achieve with new technologies.

A final cue for distance is in the spectral content of a sound. There are two aspects to this. First, as sound travels through air it tends to lose high frequency energy to a degree that depends on factors like humidity and temperature. Second, the spherical waveform produced by a point source emphasises low frequencies to a degree depending on the waveform's radius, up to about 6 feet when the wavefront becomes effectively planar. There is little experimental evidence that either of these cues produce strong effects on distance perception. Nonetheless, experience suggests that low-pass filtering of a sound to diminish high frequencies can be used (especially with changes of loudness and reverberation) to make sounds seem more distant.

Direction

Direction is expressed with respect to the listener's frame of reference, with the azimuth and elevation of a sound's direction measured in angles horizontally and vertically from a point directly in front of the listener. The cues for distance described above need only one ear to work; they are *monaural* cues. In contrast, cues for direction are largely *binaural*, depending on differences in the sounds that strike our two ears. Sound waves produced by a given source travel different paths to each ear (Figure 6), producing two cues for direction on the azimuth. The first is the *interaural time delay* (ITD): The sound reaching the further ear will be slightly delayed with respect to that reaching the nearer (about .00065 seconds maximum). The second is the *interaural intensity difference* (IID): The sound reaching the further ear is shadowed by the head, and thus of lower amplitude than that reaching the nearer ear (this is basically the principle used in stereo systems). There has been a great deal of research on the details of both these sources of distance information (see Begault, 1994), but each can be an effective cue for direction.

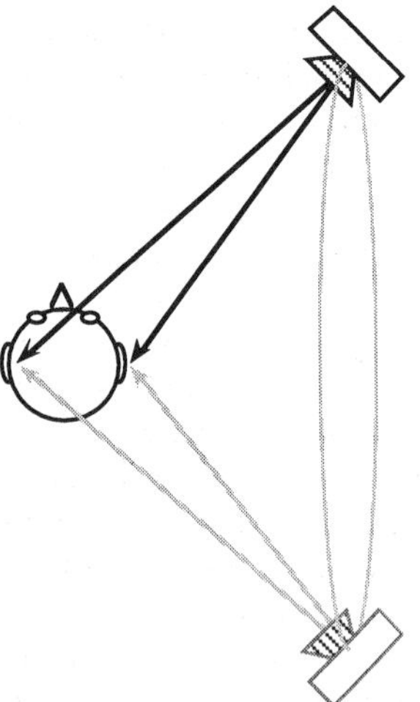

Figure 7. The cone of confusion.

The difference in sounds reaching the two ears is not sufficient to specify direction, however. In Figure 7, it is easy to see that the sound source could be behind the listener's head, with the sound waves travelling the same distance to each ear. In fact, the sound could be anywhere along the *cone of confusion* shown in Figure 7; each location on the surface of the cone would involve the same ITD and IID. Because of this, using time and intensity differences alone can give rise to both front-back and up-down errors.

One source of information for disambiguating direction along the cone of confusion is movement. Imagine that the listener in Figure 7 turned her head towards the source of sound, in front of her and to her right. As she oriented towards the source, both the ITD and IID would be reduced. If the source were actually behind her, turning towards the right would *increase* both differences. Not surprisingly, it has been shown experimentally that allowing listeners to move improves their ability to judge direction.

We need not move to hear the direction of a sound, however. It turns out that this is possible because our outer ears, or pinnae, filter incoming sounds before they reach our eardrums. As the sound waves pass over the curved, convoluted surfaces of our ears, energy at various frequencies is delayed by different amounts, and the pattern of these changes depends on which direction the sound is coming from. These spectral changes—which also depend on reflections and shadowing from the torso, shoulders, and ear canal—are referred to as *head-related transfer functions* (HRTFs). They can be measured by inserting a microphone deep into the ear canal, playing a known sound (e.g., a click) from many different directions, and recording the sound that actually reaches the microphone. The results can be used to capture the spectral changes produced by the pinnae and body, as well as ITD and IID information.

Head-related transfer functions can be used to build systems that artificially locate sounds in virtual space. The Convolvotron (e.g., Wenzel et al., 1988) is a seminal example of such a system. Designed by Scott Foster and Beth Wenzel for NASA in the late eighties, it filters sounds (produced elsewhere) using HRTF data collected by Wightman and Kistler (e.g., Wightman and Kistler, 1989). When the resulting sounds are played over headphones, they produce an impressive illusion of a sound source at a location exterior to the listener (in contrast, stereo recordings played over headphones always sound like they are coming from inside the head). Moreover, the Convolvotron uses a head-tracking device so that listeners may move their heads, while the virtual sound source will seem stable. New versions of the system even allow the specification of localised early reflections from surfaces in the environment, giving a still more realistic impression of being immersed in a virtual sound space.

The Convolvotron was an impressive technical achievement for its time, and thus very expensive. But newer systems are appearing which make artificial localisation more approachable. For instance, the Focal Point system developed by Bo Gehring uses specialised audio cards on either Macintosh or PCs, while Burgess (1992) managed to implement a HRTF based localisation system in software for use on Sun workstations. Though not as sophisticated as the Convolvotron family of systems, both produce reasonably realistic spatial impressions, and we may expect that more, better, and less expensive systems for localisation will appear over the next few years.

42.2.4 Music

Psychoacoustics, everyday listening, and localisation are all frameworks in which sounds are *analysed*. Music, in contrast, involves ways that sounds can be *combined*. Music has given rise to what are by far the most sophisticated systems for thinking about and manipulating groups of sound. It is structured at many different levels, from details of individual notes that can be understood in terms of acoustics and psychoacoustics, to overarching thematic and harmonic movements that give relatively simple shape to compositions that may last hours. These overlapping structures could be exploited by auditory interfaces to convey multileveled information. Moreover, music has profound expressive possibilities which are, at least to some degree, accessible to analysis and manipulation.

Auditory interfaces have so far drawn relatively little on the possibilities suggested by music (though see the section later on Musical Messages). One reason may be that the control needed for research on auditory interfaces implies a level of explicit articulation which the complexity of music resists. This situation contrasts with designers of multimedia or games environments, who happily exploit music's potential to create mood without needing to articulate exactly how they are doing so. In addition, it may be that many researchers on auditory interfaces are not themselves musicians (including myself, for instance), and that musicians have not been involved in the design process early enough to deeply influence the approaches taken (a striking counter example is Cohen's 1994b OutToLunch system, described later). Nonetheless, it seems useful to speculate here about some of the possibilities for exploiting higher-level musical structures in auditory interfaces.

Rhythm offers a great deal of inherent structure that could be mapped to the structure of data or events that designers want to convey. Different rhythms are often used to distinguish musical messages, as Patterson did in creating the auditory alarms described earlier (Patterson et al., 1986; Patterson, 1982). But rhythm offers other possibilities beyond allowing us to tell one sequence of sounds from another. For instance, tempo, the overall repetition rate of a rhythm, might be used to convey a sense of activity, excitement, or even alarm. The number of divisions applied to a basic repetition rate (i.e., the use of quarter, eighth, sixteenth_ notes) provides one way to build a sense of rhythmic complexity, as does the degree of syncopation used. These might be used to convey any quantity, and particularly those that are semantically related to complexity (e.g., the relative timing of related processes, as in the ARKola simulation described above). Finally, rhythm may be varied from measure to measure, building levels of repetition and change over increasingly long periods of time. This might be used to convey a sense of the overall flow of complex processes with many subordinate parts.

Melodic or harmonic structures also offer a rich resource for auditory interface design. The overall shape of simple tunes may suggest semantic interpretations, a fact exploited in creating musical messages. But musical relationships offer meanings that have yet to be exploited. Major and minor keys often seem to sound happy and sad respectively, at least within western cultures. This sort of effect works at many different levels simultaneously. Individual notes set up varying patterns of tension and resolve within their harmonic contexts. The same is true for chords. At an even higher level, modulating from key to key sets up the same shifting patterns of extending and returning. Like rhythm, then, harmony might be used at a number of different organisational scales simultaneously.

A speculative example may help explain the uses of high-level musical structure I am suggesting here. Each time I read email from home, a complex and repetitive set of processes are set off. Imagine each one was linked to a melodic movement. A drone at the fundamental note might indicate that my reader is watching for mail on the server. When new mail comes, a melodic sequence building in tension and rhythmic complexity might play as each message is read into memory, then a related one, resolving the last both harmonically and rhythmically, might indicate that the message has successfully been written to disk. The chords from which these sequences were chosen could be varied for each new message, building and resolving tension at a larger level as all the mail was read. Finally, the overall key could be changed as I switched to my actual mail reader, first increasing tension as it accesses my spool file and reads the new messages, then resolving it again, by shifting keys once again, as I actually start to read my mail.

This scenario might not work in practice (it is a bit melodramatic), but it captures the possibility of multilevel structure that music might offer interface design. Currently, auditory interfaces tend to work only at the lowest level, associating sounds with events defined at a single level. Using the hierarchical structure of music, we might be able to give equally meaningful information about multiple levels of events, so that sound could inform us, not only about a single email message being received, but about the entire process of reading email. In any case, it should be clear that musical structure is described along dimensions going well beyond pitch, loudness, timbre, and the other simple attributes of individual sounds described by acoustics and psychoacoustics.

42.2.5 Genre Sounds

Genre sounds are musical or everyday sound that are strongly associated with a given event, not because the event causes them, but because they have been linked with that event regularly over a long time. Telephone ringing sounds are a good example of such sound stereotypes. Although they are sometimes used mistakenly as examples of everyday listening, there is no necessary physical mapping between the sound and the fact that somebody is on the line waiting to be answered. Instead, particular ringing sounds are the result of design, particularly product design, and cultural standardisation. They have been remarkably stable within cultures, and so serve as almost irresistible symbols for telephone calls. But they differ substantially between countries, so that US phone bells may not be recognised by Europeans. In addition, telephone rings are becoming more diverse with new phone designs, so that the classic ringing sound may become a kind of dead metaphor, reified by a culture that doesn't use it anymore.

Cohen (1993) pointed out the huge number of genre sounds with which people are familiar, and suggested their use in interface design. He used sounds from a cult science fiction television show for an interface, and found that most people had no problem recognising the sounds. Genre sounds can be drawn from a wide variety of sources—television and movies, cartoons, popular music, appliance, and so forth. In most cases, genre sounds themselves are particularly successful, or at least well-known, examples of auditory interface design. Telephone bells, the theme from Jaws, the "boing" sound indicating an impact in cartoon-worlds, are all examples of sounds that have been designed to convey certain meanings. In their historical success, they have the advantage of being recognisable, and thus potentially applicable to new designs.

Note, however, that recognising the sounds is not the same as recognising their meanings within a given interface. Genre sounds serve as a vocabulary for auditory interface design, which still must be mapped to the meanings to be conveyed. There are several potential drawbacks to using genre sounds. First, most genre sounds are culturally specific. Just as telephone bells vary between cultures, so do science-fiction shows, cartoons, and movies. Second, genre sounds are usually not easy to parameterise. They tend to serve as labels for events, with no ready-made system for indicating variations of the basic message. Finally, genre sounds are mapped closely to their cultural meaning, and this may make them resistant to new mappings. Imagine, for instance, that the motive usually used to indicate an approaching shark is newly mapped to a reminder that you are to meet your boss. Even if this new mapping is remembered when the sound is heard, it is fairly certain that the old one will be too. This may interfere with hearing the intended message, and may well add an undesirable (at least to your boss) emotional tone to the interface.

Despite these problems, however, genre sounds are potentially a powerful resource for auditory interface designers. Well-known genre sounds are powerful indications of their messages, and can be a strong foundation for building new meanings. They are relatively easy to find, and to appropriate for new uses. Finally, they can be fun and expressive, enlivening auditory interfaces.

42.2.6 Idiosyncratic Device Models

The frameworks I have discussed so far are all relatively explicit. The devices we use to record, manipulate, and synthesise sounds, however, implicitly convey their own frameworks for thinking about sound and hearing. To some degree, the controls of such devices reflect dimensions described by acoustics and psychoacoustics, and, at a higher level, dimensions used in creating music. At the same time, however, many of their controls are much more idiosyncratic to particular devices. These controls embody their own models of sound, and in particular of timbre, the little understood but vital "quality" of sounds. The device models they embody are important because they are the ones that auditory interface designers actually use to create informative sounds.

The degree to which device controls are standardised not surprisingly reflects accepted theories about psychoacoustics and music. Almost all sound-producing systems allow control over pitch, loudness, and duration. In addition, many devices allow pitch bending, a continuous change in frequency, which can be used to create glides between notes or microtonal variations of traditional scales. They also support vibrato and tremolo, repetitive microvariations of frequency and loudness similar to those produced by violin players. Finally, some parameters of timbre control are also reasonably standard. Many devices allow the "onset velocity" of sounds to be varied, which usually varies attack times and brightness (bandwidth), by analogy with the way that the sharpness and brightness of piano notes depends on the force with which keys are struck. It is also common to provide some control over sounds' amplitude envelopes, which determine how amplitude grows and decays within the course of the note duration, though the degree of control can vary considerably.

The standardisation of basic parameters offered by most sound-producing systems has both caused and been encouraged by the Musical Instruments Digital Interface (MIDI; Loy, 1985; IMA, 1983), a standard protocol created for communicating among computers and commercial signal processing devices (samplers, synthesisers, effects units, etc.). Typically, notes are triggered at designated pitches and "key velocities," varied as they play via devices like pitch benders and foot pedals, and stopped on command. MIDI has been extremely successful in allowing the integration of sound systems, but it is limited in a number of ways. Perhaps most important is its adherence to a keyboard-centred view of control, which leads to a focus on triggering and stopping discrete notes. More continuous control parameters are not standardised, and the ways that sounds vary in response to continuous controllers must be defined using the devices themselves. For instance, it is easy to use MIDI to create simple motives, such as those used by Patterson (Patterson et al., 1986; Patterson, 1982) and Blattner (e.g., Blattner et al., 1989; see below). It is more difficult to use MIDI to make continuous variations to the timbres used in a motive, beyond selecting from a variety of device-dependent presets.

In dealing with timbre, devices vary widely, and MIDI does not offer a standard set of parameters for controlling them. Instead, timbres and control parameters are usually specified separately on each sound-producing device to be used. Devices differ in the ways they actually create sound, with the most basic distinction between samplers and synthesisers. These two classes of device tend to have different sounds, though some systems share characteristics of both. Samplers allow any sound to be recorded, and often manipulated to change its pitch, loudness, duration, attack rate, decay, and so forth. Synthesisers, in contrast, create sounds algorithmically. This means that, in principle, they allow almost complete specification of any sound. In practice, however, the sounds synthesisers can create are limited by the algorithms they use. For instance, in realistic instrumental sounds, the amplitude of every component frequency varies independently and continuously. Early synthesisers, however, typically allowed only the specification of a simple amplitude envelope to be applied to a repetitive waveform; even in many current systems, independent control over each partial is not generally available.

The algorithms used to synthesise or manipulate sounds mean that some sounds are easier to create than others, and that some manipulations are easier to make than others. In effect, each technique carves up the "wastebasket category" of timbre differently, representing different ways to understand its underlying dimensions and attributes. Additive synthesis, for instance, involves adding together time-varying sine waves to create more complex sounds, in a sort of inverse to the Fourier analysis described earlier. For this sort of technique, the focus is on controlling parameters of these component sine waves. In contrast, frequency modulation (FM) synthesis, another powerful technique, involves controlling the frequency of a carrier waveform by the amplitude of another waveform. When this is done at audio rates, modulation gives rise to many "side-band" frequencies, thus providing an efficient way to generate rich sounds. For this sort of technique, the emphasis is on controlling groups of component frequencies, their density and frequency relations, rather than individual components themselves. Finally, synthesis based on physical modeling is becoming more prevalent. This allows control parameters to be expressed in terms of virtual sound sources, such as the hardness of a drum head, or where a string is plucked.

Different techniques embody different frameworks for thinking about timbre, and these are not always comparable. Moreover, because creating complex sounds is computationally expensive, many synthesisers exploit nonlinear synthesis techniques. For instance, continuous changes of the carrier or modulator frequencies in FM synthesis produce categorical changes in the sounds that are produced, because only small integer ratios of carrier and modulating frequencies create harmonic sounds. This may mean that the control parameters offered by some devices are more closely related to their implementation than to perception, which is clearly a problem for their use. More often, though, these techniques simply offer different ways to think about sounds. It is difficult to control the amplitude and evolution of individual harmonics using FM synthesis, for instance, but likewise, it is difficult (and computationally expensive) to set up large numbers of hierarchically related partials using additive synthesis. Each technique affords its own style of sound creation and manipulation., its own way of thinking about sound.

The idiosyncratic control parameters offered by commercial equipment reflect the difficulty of establishing a common vocabulary for sound manipulations beyond the obvious ones of pitch, loudness, etc. Rushing to form a standard description of timbre would clearly be a serious mistake. Given the rich variations of sound lumped under the term, any such system would almost certainly be contrived and incomplete. But the sheer range of techniques available in commercial equipment may paradoxically have the effect of constraining the possibilities that researchers explore in creating auditory interfaces. It is difficult to report new interfaces, or to transfer them to new equipment, if they depend deeply on specialised techniques. There may be a tendency to use preset voices instead of using the ability to create and control timbre along the many dimensions that are available. Clearly, this is unfortunate, given that timbre's underlying dimensions are very powerful resources for auditory interface design. The best tactic to take, it seems, is to understand the frameworks being used as well as possible, to exploit them fully in design, and to translate the effects employed into standard psychoacoustic terms in reporting the results. This will allow us to take full advantage of the resources offered by current equipment, without losing the ability to communicate about our designs.

42.3 Auditory Interfaces

In this section, I review examples of working interfaces that use sound to convey information from computers. Three dimensions are useful in characterising these systems. The first has to do with the choice of sounds to be used—from simple multidimensional tones, to musical streams, to everyday sounds. This further implies a choice of frameworks for manipulating sound, as described in the last section. The second dimension has to do with the way sounds are mapped to information, from completely arbitrary mappings on the one hand to metaphorical and literal ones on the other. Finally, the third dimension concerns the kinds of functionality that sounds have provided, from allowing exploration of multidimensional data to coordinating distributed work groups. Together, these three dimensions define a design space that encompasses existing auditory interfaces.

In the following section, I discuss the space of auditory interfaces in more detail. Here it is important to note, however, that sounds, mappings, and functions are not independent dimensions. Instead, systems have tended to cluster in certain areas of the space. In this section, I describe the three most well-developed groups: data auralisation, musical messages, and auditory icons. In the next, I point to ways that the design space can be filled out and extended.

42.3.1 Data Auralisation

One of the earliest and most recurrent form of auditory interface uses sound to support perception of complex, often multidimensional, data. The basic strategy is simple: data parameters are mapped to parameters of sound, forming individual tones or continuous streams of sound that change with variations in the data. By analogy to graphs or scatter plots, the perceptible variations in the sounds thus formed may be used to form an impression of patterns, groups, or variations in the represented data. These techniques, then, serve as an auditory analogue to data visualisation.

Patterns in Multidimensional Data

The essence of a good auralisation is to allow multidimensional data points to be perceived as integral wholes, so that high-level patterns become perceptually available. To accomplish this, a good knowledge of psychoacoustics is necessary to avoid pitfalls such as mapping data linearly to sound dimensions that are heard logarithmically. In addition, systems should offer a wide variety of sound dimensions and manipulations, and allow users to explore their data sonically once these mappings have been established. Ideally, the auralisation should present data so that people can perceive structures at a higher level of organisation than they are represented by the computer.

Consider the iris data described at the beginning of this section, for example. The length and width of the petals and sepals (the four parameters used for classification) are integral aspects of every iris, so that it is possible to discriminate species just by looking at them. Measuring these variables abstracts them from their original context, requiring that they be approached analytically if patterns are to be found. The goal of auralisation is to reunite the variables in a single presentation. Thus when Bly (1982a, 1982b) mapped the iris data to sounds, the integration of the four variables could be heard in much the same way that a flower is seen.

Traditional graphing techniques also have the goal of bringing multidimensional data together into a single presentation. The location of each point in a scatter plot, for instance, conveys information about two dimensions simultaneously. Beyond using the three spatial dimensions, however, graphical techniques become problematic. Although other attributes, such as colour, shape, or size, can also be used, it is surprisingly difficult to come up with many good candidates. Mapping dimensions to more literal pictorial representations can be effective (e.g., Holmes, 1993), but pictures can be misleading when data dimensions only map approximately to pictorial ones (Tufte, 1990, 1983). In any case, the results of such mappings can be cluttered, and patterns difficult to see. Sound has the advantage that it is naturally multidimensional, perceived integrally, yet abstract enough not to mislead listeners.

Auralisations can complement visualisations in presenting complex data. Bly showed this in another example, in which she mapped sounds to six-

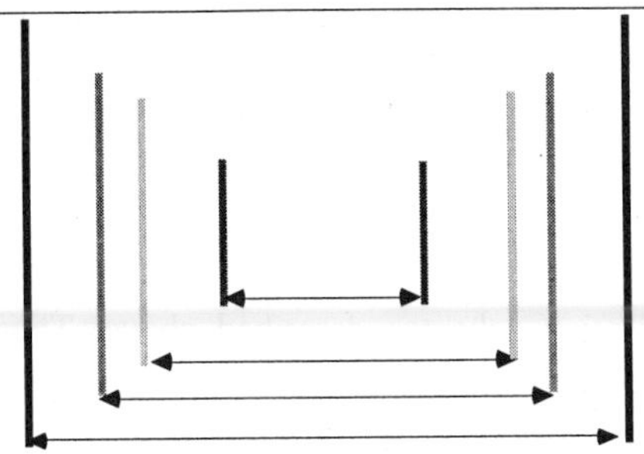

Figure 8. ***Frysinger and Slivjanovski (1984) mapped time-****varying data to mirrored, vertical lines which appeared to move in and out as data changed over time.*

dimensional data sets that overlapped in any five dimensions, and asked people to classify sounds based on examples from each set. The technique was again effective, with subjects scoring as well using the auditory display alone as they did using visual scatterplots. Moreover, they performed even better with a mixed auditory and visual display. This suggests that the sounds and graphics can work together in allowing the perception of high level patterns.

Auralisation is also clearly relevant for the visually-impaired. Lunney and Morrison (1990; 1981; Lunney et al., 1983) use sound to present the results of infrared spectronomy, an important tool for identifying inorganic compounds. They preprocess a continuous infrared spectrum, replacing absorption peaks with single vertical lines. The frequency of these peaks are then mapped to notes from several octaves of a chromatic scale. The sets of notes thus produced is presented in three ways. In the first, notes representing peaks are played in a descending scale, with the absorption intensity mapped to the duration of the corresponding note. Second, notes are played in order of decreasing peak intensities, with all notes of equal intensity. Finally, the notes for the six strongest peaks are played in a chord (this is the most concise but least memorable representation). Informal testing has shown that these representations allow reliable matches to be made between test and sample spectrograms. The ability to listen to explore the data in three different forms seems particularly useful, with each representation allowing the data to integrate in new ways.

Time-Varying Data

Because sound is an inherently temporal medium, it is well suited for representing streams of data that vary with time. Bly (1982a, 1982b) demonstrated this possibility by representing simulated battles between two opposing armies. Each army was mapped to a distinctive timbre. The number of troops at the front was indicated by pitch, while intensity was used to encode the number approaching the front. The resulting "battle songs" enabled observers to distinguish the evolution of battles with the same outcome, though listeners could not always track the individual streams of sound.

Similarly, Mezrich, Frysinger and Slivjanovski (1984) used a visual and auditory display to track changes in four dimensional economic data over time, and tested the ability for people to perceive correlation among the dimensions. The visual display was created by mapping each data dimension to a pair of vertical lines that grew and shrank symmetrically around the middle of the display (Figure 8). The auditory display was created by mapping the four parameters to notes over three octaves of a major scale. Thus each data dimension was associated with a pattern of moving lines, and with a stream of sound over time, with the four dimensions together creating a polyphonous "tune" which rose and fell with the changes of data. When people used this system, they could perceive much smaller correlations than they could using either overlaid or stacked graphs. Although they did not assess the utility of the auditory display alone, Frysinger and Slivjanowski's (1984) results again indicate the effectiveness of this sort of technique, and particularly that of integrated dynamic auditory and visual displays.

Interactive Auralisation

While most auralisation strategies have focused on presenting data to listeners, Grinstein, Smith and their colleagues (Smith et al., 1990; Grinstein and Smith, 1990; Smith et al., 1994). have developed a system that allows interactive control over auralised data. The system involves creating visual and auditory "textures" from large amounts of data, from which higher-order variations and patterns may be detected. Visual textures are created by mapping each multidimensional data point to a simple multi-limbed stick figure called an "icon" with the length, intensity, and angles determined by individual data dimensions. Two data dimensions are typically used to specify the horizontal and vertical placement of each icon, creating a texture field when many are used. Each icon is also associated with a sound (usually short tones or noise bursts), which may be determined by the same or different data dimensions. Sounds are played as the user moves the mouse over the icons, so that an aural texture may grow and change as multiple icons are swept. This aural texture can be used to identify and explore different regions of the data space, and allows discrimination even of data structures that may be invisible. The significant development of this system is that it allows people to explore and probe the data space quickly and interactively, which may be expected to help them better understand its structure.

Towards General Auralisation Tools

Recently there has been a move away from designing specific auralisation techniques towards designing more general hardware and software systems that allow experimentation with many different sorts of auralisation for a variety of application domains. A good example of this is the Kyma system, designed by Scalletti and her colleagues (Scalletti, 1994, Scalletti and Craig, 1991). Kyma is an object-oriented, stream-based system which allows direct manipulation of data sources, sound streams, and a variety of manipulators. In particular, it offers a suite of prototype tools which exemplify some of the most useful techniques for turning data into sound:

- *Shifter* interprets a data stream as an acoustic waveform, potentially shifted from the sub or ultra sonic range to be audible, allowing it to be heard "directly" . Shifters can also—and are usually—used to produce data streams that control other parameters.

- *Mappers* implement the basic auralisation strategy of allowing data streams to control sound parameters such as frequency, deviations from a base frequency, amplitude, low pass filters, event density, and stereo panning.

- *Combiners* arithmetically combine two or more sound streams, via sums, differences, or products. Using amplitude modulation, for instance, in which the two streams are multiplied, frequencies are produced that correspond to the magnitude of their differences, as well as to one of the original streams.

- *Comparator* is a variation of a combiners that plays two sound signals simultaneously to the right and left stereo channels respectively, allowing the signals to be compared for the timing and degree of any differences.

- *Markers* allow sounds to be triggered when specific conditions are met—for instance, when a signal exceeds a threshold.

- *Histogram* represents classes of data by single frequencies, and their magnitude by the corresponding amplitude. The result can sound like a single time-varying timbre, a chord, or a collection of voices.

These tools, in combination with standard arithmetic operators, allow the construction of any of the specific auralisation schemes described above. Thus they are useful in abstracting away from specific case studies to a more general range of techniques. For instance, though the Shifter allows data to be heard directly, which would appear the simplest form of data auralisation, Scalletti (1994) reports that it is useful only for quasi-periodic and slowly changing data, such as tide movements, frequency measurements, and the like. The Mapper, on the other hand, is a generally powerful tool that captures the essence of most auralisation strategies, including, for instance, Bly's (1982a, 1982b), Frysinger and Mezrich's (1984), and Grinstein and Smith's (1990). Finally, the sonic histogram seems functionally equivalent to the chord mapping used by Lunney and Morrisson (1990) to represent infrared spectra; it has also been found useful in exploring other sorts of data such as the effects of fire prevention on forest aging (Scalletti, 1994). The system suggests other strategies as well, such as amplitude modulation to compare streams, or markers to signal significant events. In general, tools such as Kyma may be expected to encourage many new and different applications of data auralisation.

Auralisation: Discussion

The basic strategy of mapping data parameters to dimensions of sound appears to be simple, powerful, and easy enough that systems using this strategy have appeared with regularity over the last number of years, most applying variations of the sort of strategies discussed above to specific application areas. The advent of systems like Kyma, and the increasing power of PC-based signal processing in general, is likely to increase this trend, and to make auralisation increasingly available to non-expert users. This is encouraging insofar as the work described here indicates that sound can be a useful way to represent data for exploration. Nonetheless, auralisation remains a less mature endeavour than visualisation. A number of issues may be responsible for this.

First, progress has been slowed by hardware and software limitations on sound synthesis and processing. Much of seminal work described here was accomplished with much difficulty: for instance, Bly (1982a) had to build special hardware and a custom computer interface in order to undertake her work. The practical difficulties of using sounds has tended to seriously constrain the ability to experiment with novel sound parameters and mapping techniques. Recently, sophisticated digital signal processing has moved from being the exclusive province of academic computer science departments to being more widely available on PC's and off-the-shelf synthesisers, effects units, etc. Even so, these new tools offer only partial support for auralisation; as Smith et al. (1994) have pointed out, MIDI equipment—and most software as well—is designed for making popular music, and thus does not always allow the appropriate controls for auralising data.

In part because of these limitations, widespread publication of sound, especially in academic contexts, is much rarer than publications of graphics. It is common to receive academic journals with a variety of printed graphs, charts, and visualisations, but rare to receive an audio CD or cassette. In addition, graphics can be seen on the page, while sound examples require playback systems extrinsic to the publication. This barrier, too, may fall as interactive CDs and the Internet become more popular outlets for publication, allowing the seamless incorporation of auralisations into research reports.

A more fundamental issue for using sound to explore data involves it being a temporal medium, rather than one that is spatial and relatively static, like vision. The ability to scan a visualisation, to focus on particular regions, to quickly look back and forth between different parts all combine to help visualisations support the perception of data patterns. The equivalent of these abilities seems difficult to define for sound, much less to provide. The ability to interact with an auralisation, as demonstrated by Smith et al.'s work (1990), is a significant step in towards providing similar capabilities, but they may not come naturally to this medium.

With the serial nature of sound comes other difficulties. By their nature, data visualisations and auralisations tend to involve many arbitrary mappings between the semantics of data dimensions and values and their representations. For visualisations, tools such as keys, scales, and indices have developed to represent those mappings directly. For auralisations, such tools have not been well developed, and there are practical difficulties for doing so. For instance, reference tones might be played to indicate the extremes of a given dimension, but if many dimensions need to be indicated it is impossible to play them all at once, and playing them sequentially raises memory problems. Again, a high degree of interactivity may provide a solution to this problem, but these issues have only begun to be addressed.

Perhaps most importantly, though there are many examples of auralisation, there are few or none in which auditory representations have been shown clearly to lead to new insights about real data (Scalletti, 1994). This may be equivalent to saying that there has been no "killer app" for auralisation, and asking or a single convincing example of its effectiveness (rather than a host of lesser examples) may be unfair. Nonetheless, most work so far has focused on techniques and implementations of auralisation rather than on specific insights about real content areas. It may be only when it is natural to report the content of data first, and the auralisation techniques used to discover it second, that these techniques will have come of age.

42.3.2 Musical Messages

Auralisations focus on using sound to understand data, a domain in which the computer is a tool used to accomplish some task. Most other auditory interfaces are concerned with supporting interaction with the computer itself, by providing information about events, objects, and processes within it.

One strategy for conveying information about events using sound is to create auditory messages from a musical vocabulary. Patterson's alarm sequences, described at the beginning of this chapter, are an example of this strategy (Patterson et al., 1986; Patterson, 1982). Different alarms are created by varying their rhythms, melodies, and timbres to create short, distinctive tunes. These map to the messages they are meant to convey in a variety of ways. Sometimes the mapping is simply arbitrary, and must be memorised by listeners. Other times the tunes are modeled on the intonation and rhythm of the equivalent spoken message, or on a sort of analogy to the message to be conveyed.

The motives used by Patterson and his colleagues (Patterson et al., 1986; Patterson, 1982) are the culmination of work focused primarily on the basic psychoacoustical requirements for effective musical messages. His work is exemplary in showing how sounds can be shaped to fit the auditory environment in which they will be heard, using acoustic analyses in the design of sounds that will be loud enough to be heard, while not so loud as to interfere with communication or concentration (a real problem for commercial aircraft alarms, for which existing alarms have often used mechanisms originally designed for World War II bomber cockpits). In addition, he and his colleagues (Patterson et al., 1986; Edworthy et al., 1991; Swift et al., 1989) have

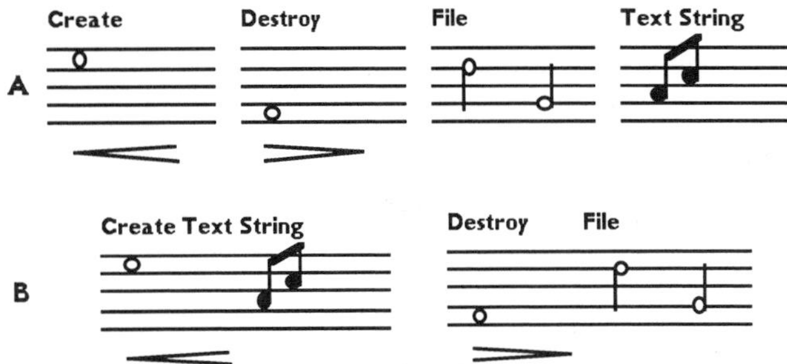

Figure 9. Simple earcons A, can be concatenated to form combined earcons B (after Blattner 1989).

pioneered work on the acoustic factors that make sounds more or less urgent, showing that high frequencies, abrupt onsets, inharmonic timbres, and changes in frequency and amplitude all contribute to urgency. Finally, his use of short alarm bursts punctuated by silence is a good example of the restraint desirable in creating auditory cues, especially those that are meant to provide information over protracted periods of time.

Earcons: Creating Families of Musical Messages

Blattner and her colleagues have developed a similar approach, applying it to the domain of computer interfaces (e.g., Blattner et al., 1989; Blattner et al., 1994, Stevens et al., 1994; Brewster et al., 1994). The idea is that such messages could be used to indicate a wide variety of events in the interface, such as error conditions or feedback about user operations. However, where Patterson focuses on psychoacoustical factors, Blattner has been concerned with developing a systematic methodology for designing families of musical messages in which related messages sound similar. The system she has developed uses simple motives as building blocks, which are used to construct more complex cues called *earcons*—a bad pun first used by Bill Buxton—through combinations, modifications, and hierarchy.

Motives are essentially very short melodies used as individual, recognisable entities (Blattner et al., 1989). For example, Peter and the Wolf uses motives to stand for the various characters; similarly, the familiar pulsing sound used to indicate the shark's presence in *Jaws* is also a motive. Blattner et al. (1989) identify rhythm and pitch as the *fixed parameters* of a motive, those which are used to give each its individual identity. Families of motives are created using *variable parameters* of sound, such as timbre, register, and dynamics. According to Blattner et al. (1989), these parameters may be varied fairly widely, while leaving the basic identity of the motive unchanged.

Some of the basic recommendations for earcon construction suggested in Blattner et al. (1989) have been modified with experience and experimental work. For instance, early examples of motives used very simple waveforms (e.g., sine, square, and triangle waves) as variations of timbre. However, experimental work by Brewster et al (1994) has shown that such waveforms are often confused, so more recent work has tended to use instrumental timbres as found on MIDI controlled synthesisers. Similarly, Blattner et al. (1989) recommended using pitches from a musical scale within a single octave to avoid octave confusions, but again, Brewster et al. (1994) found that this makes motives relatively indistinguishable from one another and recommend that a wider range of pitches be used.

More complex earcons, and families of earcons, can be constructed from simple motives in several different ways. *Combined* earcons are created by playing two or more basic ones in succession. For instance, Figure 9A shows simple earcons denoting two operations (create and destroy) and two entities (file and text string). Figure 9B shows combined earcons made by concatenating these simpler elements, representing "create text string," and "destroy file;" other combinations can obviously be made in a similar way.

Families of earcons can also be made by constructing hierarchies in which earcons at each subordinate level are differentiating using a new musical parameter. For example, a class of error messages (Figure 10) can be defined by a rhythmic pattern of unpitched sounds (i.e., clicks). Different classes of error messages—in this case, operating system vs. execution errors—can be given different melodies, while specific messages (e.g., "file unknown" or "underflow") can be distinguished by using different timbres.

Blattner et al. (1989) suggest playing the earcon corresponding to each level of a hierarchy in series, so

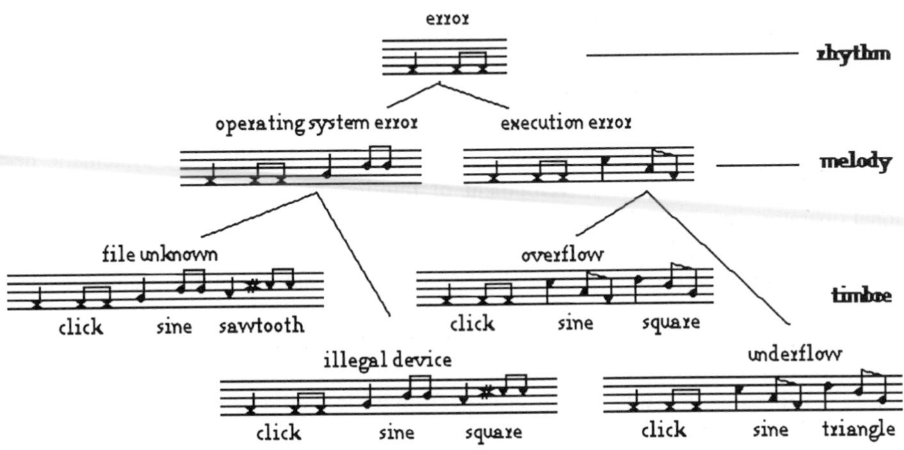

Figure 10. A family of error messages can be built as a hierarchy in which each subordinate level is distinguished by a new musical parameter. *In this example, the earcon corresponding to each level is played sequentially. Combining all cues into a single rendition of the motive (the last in each example) is also possible. (After Blattner et al., 1989).*

that, for instance, the earcon for "overflow" would consist of first the rhythmic pattern indicating "error," then the melody indicating "execution error," and finally the melody using a square wave timbre that indicates "overflow." This strategy has the advantage of being very clear for beginners, but produces earcons that may be unacceptably long—especially considering that hierarchies of five or more levels are possible according to their scheme. A more succinct version of these earcons would use only the earcon associated with the final nodes of the hierarchy, so that "underflow" could be indicated simply by the square-wave version of the basic melody. These are called *transformed* earcons by Blattner et al. (1989), because the family of earcons in this case is created using musical transformations of an implied prototypical earcon, rather than by explicitly traversing the branches of a hierarchy.

Using Earcons to Create an Auditory Map

Blattner et al. (1994) report on the design on an auditory map, in which earcons were added to an interactive, digital aerial view of Lawrence Livermore National Laboratory. Sounds played as the cursor was moved over various buildings on the map, indicating access privileges, administrative units, and computers. The earcons were associated to these entities by way of two sets of analogies. First, entities were mapped to actions that could be visualised: knocking for access privileges, a schematic tree diagram for administrative units, and a visual icon of a computer for computers. Then musical analogues were found for each of these visual images: a uniform tom tom drum sound for knocking, three notes on a saxophone to stand for walking up a tree, and a "whirring noise sounded out by four notes on a flute" to indicate computers. Animated versions of the visual analogues were presented when the map was opened to help users learn the meaning of the sounds.

The earcons were combined, transformed, and used inheritance to indicate more than the mere existence of an entity at a particular location. The level of access privileges was mapped to frequency, so that higher required privileges sounded like higher, faster knocking. Summary data about the number of administrative units and computers in a given area was indicated by varying the amplitudes of their respective sounds. In addition, very short versions of each earcon—consisting only of a short tone of the appropriate timbre—were played as the user moved the cursor over a region, to avoid having to play the entire messages.

Algebra Earcons: Summarising Equations for the Visually-Impaired

Stevens et al. (1994) developed an innovative system that used earcons to represent algebraic equations. The system was targeted at visually-impaired users, and was meant to give the sort of high-level information about an equation's structure that readers get at a glance—information about an equation's length, complexity, the presence of fractions, and so on. The intent was to provide the sort of information used by sighted readers to plan their reading of an equation, and to form an idea of the structure into which various terms should fit. Moreover, Stevens' system allowed users to explore mathematical structures in more detail, by navigating in and out of different levels of auditory information.

Sounds were designed to reflect the syntax of algebra equations. Different syntactic types (base level operands, binary operators, relational operators, superscripts, fractions, and subexpressions) were mapped to different musical timbres (e.g., pianos, pan pipes). The timing, pitch, and amplitude of each sound was then varied according to rules based on prosodic cues. For instance, each new term in an equation started at middle C, except the last one which was played at A4 to mimic the way people's voices drop as they finish reading an equation. In addition, some of the sounds were designed to map intuitively to their referents. For instance, superscripts and subscripts were at high and low pitches, respectively, matching their graphical appearance.

The strategy was tested using a forced choice test in which subjects heard a target equation, and then picked its written version from three distracters. Since the distracters were designed to differ from the original equations in only one respect, the data could be used not only to assess the strategy's overall effectiveness, but particular problems as well. The system was accordingly redesigned, and retested using the previous subjects. Most of the subjects showed marked improvement and, moreover, most scores increased on the previously problematic equations. Though the experiments did not directly address the question of whether the system will give visually impaired users the same sort of information that sighted people obtain by glancing at equations, they do indicate that people can recover syntactic information about equations using these sounds.

This system is an excellent example of the potential for tailoring earcon design to specific tasks. In general, the rules used to generate these "algebra earcons" do not reflect the general principles for designing earcons suggested by (Blattner et al., 1989), though they can be seen as examples of combined earcons. Instead, the system builds on the original principles, basing its mappings on more specific considerations of the syntax of equations, and on analogies to prosody and typographic layout. This approach allows an appropriate mapping between algebraic and sound structures to be realised, one which matches relatively abstract sounds to the abstractions of mathematics.

Earcons: Discussion

There are relatively few examples of systems that use earcons, and many of the ideas from the original proposal—most notably, that of creating rich hierarchical families of earcons—have yet to be demonstrated in working prototypes. Nonetheless, the strategy is an interesting one for creating auditory cues. The appeal is in creating a system which allows the systematic development of families of auditory cues from simple, readily-created musical sounds. It makes use of people's ability to make symbolic mappings between essentially arbitrary combinations of representations and referents, as when using a ballpoint pen to stand for a bus in a story about motorcycling home.

In addition, the idea of creating hierarchical families of cues from basic motives is a powerful one, particularly when all the variations are incorporated in one sound (c.f. parameterised auditory icons, described in the next section). This strategy makes use of people's ability to listen to sounds at different levels of detail, perhaps obtaining information at a high level ("that's an error sound") even if they cannot distinguish lower levels (e.g., confusing overflow and underflow errors). An everyday analogy to this ability is our differing sensitivities to automobile noises: I may take my car to a mechanic because "it's making an awful rattling noise," while to her it may sound clearly like a faulty carburetor. Even the high-level information can be useful, and with experience and motivation we may learn to understand the details as well.

There are several potential problems with earcons, however. Perhaps most important, they tend to be arbitrarily mapped to their referents, which means that they must be learned without benefit of past experience. I will address this issue at greater length in the next section. In addition, the tendency to use musical sounds, as well as arbitrary mappings, suggests that there will be difficulty in designing them to integrate with graphical interfaces. Musical phrases may not mesh well with working environments, as well, especially as people tend to find repetitions of simple tunes annoying (Gaver and Mandler, 1987). Finally, earcons tend to have relatively long durations. While this may be necessary to achieve good recognition (especially in experimental trials with limited training), the designs are often less subtle and more intrusive than might be possible.

These problems do not seem fatal for the basic approach, however. It is easy to imagine systems which use earcons designed carefully to be short, subtle, and recognisable. In fact, we already have good examples of what such systems might sound like: The melodic chirping sounds made by many of the devices in Star Trek seem recognisable as future cousins to the earcons that have so far been demonstrated.

42.3.3 Auditory Icons

Another way to use sound as an integral part of the interface involves creating auditory icons, everyday sounds mapped to computer events by analogy with everyday sound-producing events (e.g., Gaver 1993b, 1986). Auditory icons are like sound-effects for computers: For instance, selecting a file icon in a graphical user interface might make the sound of a notebook being tapped, with the type of file indicated by the material of the object, and the file size by the size of the struck object. In contrast to earcons, which rely on essentially arbitrary mappings between sounds and interface entities, auditory icons are similar to visual icons in that both rely on an analogy between the everyday world and the model world of the computer.

Like earcons, auditory icons can be varied to produce "families" of related sounds. Unlike earcons, this is done by *parameterising* auditory icons along dimensions relevant for events that make sound. Thus auditory icons can reflect not only categories of events and objects, but can also reflect their relevant dimensions as well. For instance, the material involved in some sound-producing event might be used to represent the type of interface entity involved in a computer interaction. In this case, all auditory icons concerning that type of object would involve sounds made by that kind of material. So text files might always sound wooden, but selecting them might make a tapping sound, moving them might make a scraping sound, and deleting them might make a splintering sound. The result is a system that maps the attributes that are perceptually relevant for a given sound-producing event to those relevant for the event to be represented. In this way, a rich system of auditory icons may be created that relies on relatively few underlying metaphors.

When the same analogy underlies both auditory and visual icons, the increased redundancy of the interface may help users learn and remember the system. For instance, one novice user reportedly didn't realise that icons stood for files until hearing the sounds made when they were selected. In addition, using auditory icons may allow more consistent model worlds to be developed, because some computer events may map more readily to sound-producing events than to visual ones. The timing and nature of difficult to visualise events like disk accesses may be one example of this. Finally, making the model world of the computer consistent in its visual and auditory aspects seems to increase users' feelings of *direct engagement* (Hutchins et al., 1986) with that world—the feeling of working in the world of the task, not the computer.

A number of systems have been created which illustrate the potential for auditory icons to convey useful information about computer events. These systems suggest that sound is well suited for providing information:

- about previous and possible interactions,
- indicating ongoing processes and modes,
- useful for navigation, and
- to support collaboration.

In the following sections, I describe a variety of systems that have used auditory icons.

The SonicFinder: Extending a Graphical User Interface

The SonicFinder (Gaver, 1989) was the first system to incorporate auditory icons. Developed for Apple, it was an extension to the Finder, the application used to organise, manipulate, create and delete files on the Macintosh.

The SonicFinder extended the underlying code for the Finder to play sampled sounds modified according to attributes of the relevant events. This allowed auditory icons to accompany a variety of interface events (see Table 1). Most of the sounds were parameterized, although the ability to modify sounds on the Mac was limited at the time the SonicFinder was developed. So, for instance, sounds which involved objects such as files or folders not only indicated basic events such as selection or copying, but also the object's types and sizes via the material and size of the virtual sound-producing objects. In addition, the SonicFinder incorporated an early example of an *auditory process monitor* in the form of a pouring sound that accompanied copying and that indicated, via changes of pitch, the percentage of copying that had been completed (auditory process monitors have been explored more extensively by Cohen, 1994a, as described later).

The SonicFinder was never released commercially by Apple, largely because the size of the sampled sounds was deemed too large (at the time, Macintosh system releases could be distributed on single 800K floppies). However, it was distributed quite widely in an informal fashion, with users in North America, Europe, Australia, and Asia. No formal user testing or evaluation studies were ever carried out on its reception, but anecdotal evidence suggests that while some people stopped using it after a short time, others found it valuable, or at least appealing, and when it finally

Table 1. Events, sounds, and parameters used in the SonicFinder. *(after Gaver, 1989)*

Events	Auditory icons
Icons	
• Selection type (file, application, folder, disk, trash) size	• Hitting sound source material (wood, metal, etc.) source size (frequency)
• Opening size	• Whooshing sound size (frequency)
• Dragging size where (windows or desk) possible drop in	• Scraping sound size (frequency) texture (bandwidth) selection sound of container
• Drop-in destination size	• Noise of object landing size (frequency)
• Copying amount copied	• Pouring sound frequency
Windows	
• Selection	• Clink
• Dragging	• Scrapping
• Growing size	• Clink on release size (frequency)
• Scrolling revealed area	• Tick sound size (frequency)
Trashcan	
• Drop-in	• Crash
• Empty	• Crunch

became obsolete due to new system releases, lobbied for its return. Because the Macintosh is a single-processing machine with a fairly simple interface, the sounds used in the SonicFinder basically provided feedback and information about possible interactions (as well as more general information about file size and type, dragging location, and the like). Nonetheless, the fact that it was a popular extension of a widely-used interface meant that it provided a valuable example of the potential of auditory icons, showing that sounds such as these can be incorporated in graphical user interfaces in intuitive and informative ways.

SoundShark: Multiple Sounds, Navigation, and Collaboration

The SonicFinder was useful in incorporating auditory icons into a well-known and often-used interface, but the simplicity of the Macintosh's operating system and the finish of its interface limited the possibility of exploring novel functions for auditory icons. For this reason, Gaver and Smith (1990) demonstrated their use in a large-scale, multiprocessing, collaborative system called SharedARK, and dubbed the resulting auditory interface SoundShark.

SharedARK was a collaborative version of ARK, the Alternate Reality Kit. Developed by Smith (1989), ARK was designed as a virtual physics laboratory for distance education. The "world" appeared as a huge flat plane over which the screen could be moved, on which a number of 2.5D objects could be found. These objects could be picked up, carried, and thrown using a mouse-controlled "hand." They could be linked to one another, messages could be passed to them using "buttons," and, because SharedARK used a multiprocessing system, their associated processes could run simultaneously. In addition, SharedARK allowed the same world to be seen by a number of different people on their own computer screens (and was usually used in conjunction with audio and video links that allowed users to see and talk to one another). They could see each other's "hands", manipulate objects together, and thus collaborate within this virtual world. The result of all this was a large and complicated world, with pockets of activity separated by blank spaces: navigation and orientation were problematic in this environment.

This interface was extended by adding auditory icons to indicate user interactions, ongoing processes and modes, to help with navigation, and to provide information about other users. Sounds were used to provide feedback as they were in the SonicFinder: Many user actions were accompanied by auditory icons which were parameterized to indicate attributes such as the size of relevant objects. Collaborators could hear each other even if they couldn't see each other, which seemed to aid in coordination. In addition, ongoing processes made sounds that indicated their nature and continuing activity even if they were not visible on the screen. Modes of the system, such as the activation of self-perpetuated "motion," were indicated by low-volume, smooth background sounds. Finally, distance between a given user's hand and the source of the sound was indicated by the sounds' amplitude and by low-pass filtering, aiding with navigation. The apparent success of this manipulation led to the development of "auditory landmarks," objects whose sole function was to play a repetitive sound that could aid orientation.

ARKola: Sound Ecologies and Peripheral Awareness

Experience with SoundShark suggested that auditory icons could provide useful information about user-initiated events, processes and modes, and about location within a complex environment. This work led to the development of the ARKola study (Gaver et al., 1991) described at the beginning of this chapter. The ARKola study allowed exploration of issues concerning the design of many sounds that could be played continuously and simultaneously, the possibility of using sound to integrate perception of complex processes, and the use of sound in supporting collaboration.

With as many as 12 sound playing simultaneously, designing the sounds so that all could be heard and identified was a challenge. In general, temporally complex sounds were used to maximise discriminability, and the sounds were designed to be semantically related to the events they represented. Two strategies were found to be useful in avoiding masking. First, sounds were spread fairly evenly in frequency, so that some were high-pitched and others lower. Second, continuous sounds were avoided, and instead repetitive streams of sounds were used to maximise the chance for other sounds to be heard in the gaps between repetitions (cf. Patterson's use of intermittent alarms).

As expected, the sounds helped people keep track of the many ongoing processes, allowing them to track the activity, rate, functioning, and problems with individual machines. More surprisingly, the auditory icons merged together in an auditory texture that encouraged people to hear the plant as an integrated complex process. Sounds were also used as an important resource for collaboration. Without sound, participants had to rely on their partner's reports to tell what was happening in the offscreen part of the plant. With sound, each could hear events and processes they could not see. This shared audio context seemed to lead to greater collaboration between partners, with each pointing out problems to the other, discussing activities, and so forth. The ability to provide foreground information visually and background information using sound was essential in allowing people to concentrate on their own tasks, while coordinating with their partners about theirs.

Finally, sound also seemed to add to the tangibility of the plant and increased participants' engagement with the task. This became most evident when one of a pair of participants who had completed an hour with sound and were working an hour without remarked "we could always make the noises ourselves..." In sum, the ARKola study indicated that auditory icons could be useful in helping people collaborate on a difficult task involving a large-scale complex system, and that the addition of sounds increased their engagement as well.

EAR: Environmental Audio Reminders

Where SoundShark and ARKola explored the use of auditory icons to support collaboration in software systems, another system, called EAR (for Environmental Audio Reminders), demonstrated that auditory icons are also helpful for supporting collaboration in the office environment itself (Gaver 1991). This system distributed a variety of nonspeech audio cues to offices and common areas to keep people informed about a variety of events around their workplace.

A wide variety of sounds were used to remind people about a range of events managed by the Khronika system (Lövstrand, 1991). For instance, when new email arrived, the sound of a stack of papers falling on the floor was played. When somebody connected to a video camera in our media space, the sound of an opening door was heard a few seconds before the connection was made, and the sound of a closing door just after the connection was broken. Ten minutes before a meeting, the sound of murmuring voices slowly increasing in number and volume was played to subscribers' offices, then the sound of a gavel. And finally, when somebody decided to call it a day, they might send their friends the "pub call," the sound of laughing, chatting voices in the background with a beer being pulled in the foreground, to suggest the evenings arrival.

Although the sounds used in EAR were somewhat frivolous, they were easily learned and recognised. In addition, they were designed to be unobtrusive, following the findings of Patterson and his colleagues (Patterson et al., 1986; Edworthy et al., 1991; Swift et al., 1989). Most were short; those that were longer had a slow attack so that they could subtly enter the auditory ambience. The sounds had relatively little high-frequency energy, and noisy or abrupt sounds were avoided. In sum, the sounds fit into the existing office ambience, rather than intruding upon it. Most telling, though the sounds were designed rather quickly and informally, they were used intensively over a long time, with hundreds of sounds being played each day over several years.

ShareMon: Monitoring Background Activities

Experience with SoundShark, ARKola, and EAR suggests that sound is useful for monitoring peripheral events without disrupting foreground activity (Gaver, 1991). Cohen (1994a) focused on this possibility in producing ShareMon, a system that allows users to monitor network file sharing activity using a number of auditory icons. In addition, he used an iterative strategy to develop sounds that were useful, learnable, and unobtrusive.

ShareMon monitored file sharing activity on networked Macintosh computers. Auditory icons were designed to indicate a variety of the events associated with file sharing. In an initial version, knocking was used to indicate logging in, a slamming door to indicate logging out, an "ahem" sound to remind of an idle user's continued presence, and varying speeds of walking, jogging, and running to indicate CPU usage. Several alternatives for the CPU sounds were also designed: continuous humming or pink noise sounds, pulsed humming sounds, and ocean waves. The continuous sounds raised in pitch with greater CPU usage, while the pulses and waves increased in repetition frequency. Text-to-speech and visual notifications (text messages that moved across the screen autonomously, unless users "trapped" them by holding down the mouse button) were also used as comparisons to non-speech feedback.

User feedback was obtained from people who tried the system while ostensibly working on an independent "foreground" task. File sharing events were automatically generated with high frequency during the sessions, and users were asked periodically to report on file-sharing activity. The results of this study, and more informal comments made during development, indicated mixed success for the sounds. One problem was that several of the sounds were annoying to users. This was a particular problem for sounds indicating CPU usage, which seemed to convey little information but were played quite frequently (though the ocean wave sounds were reported to be pleasant in this context). Another problem was in mapping the sounds to the events. Most users could not initially guess what the sounds meant, though they seemed to remember their meanings after being told. Some users seemed to build elaborate narratives from the sounds (e.g., of somebody knocking on a door, not being answered, and then pacing outside) which were not intended. Others found it difficult to distinguish the system's sounds from those occurring in the space around them, and vice versa.

On the basis of these results, the sounds were changed in several ways. In the final system, CPU usage was not indicated, to avoid the problem of frequently notifying users of a relatively unimportant event (though Cohen opines that such sounds are probably useful, and that new CPU sounds might be designed). Instead, the sound of a file drawer opening and closing was used to indicate files being opened and closed. The misleading connotation of knocking indicating a request to log in, rather than an actual connection, was corrected by adding the sound of a door creaking open; in addition, registered users were distinguished by using the sounds of keys jingling and turning a lock rather than knocking. Finally, the connection reminder was changed from the annoying "ahem" sound to the sound of a creaking chair. A new round of user testing showed these sounds were more successful than the initial ones. People enjoyed the sounds more, and were better able to correctly guess what the sounds meant. There were still problems with interpretation, however, as well as with the affective connotations of some of the sounds (most notably the use of a slamming door to indicate log off, which sounded angry to some participants).

ShareMon provides a useful example of auditory interface design, for several reasons. Perhaps most importantly, it illustrates the difficulty of designing auditory icons which succeed at a number of levels, from being unobtrusive to meaningful. The domain addressed by ShareMon was particularly challenging, because there was no complementary visual interface to aid interpretation of the sounds, the sounds played autonomously rather than in response to user activity, and they were heard quite frequently. In this context, the utility of testing such systems was well illustrated. Cohen's (1994a) strategy of testing mapping by asking people to guess the sounds' meanings may have been overly severe, and perhaps a more realistic criterion would have been whether people could remember the meanings once they are introduced. Nonetheless, the studies were not only useful in guiding the design of new sounds, but in emphasising the affective and narrative power of everyday sounds. Finally, a major success of the ShareMon system is that it was used beyond the studies by a number of "faithful adherents" in their working lives. This sort of long-term experience, and the insights it brings, is difficult to simulate in experimental settings.

Mercator: Giving Access to the Visually Impaired

Possibly the most ambitious use of auditory icons is in the Mercator system, which provides access to X Windows applications for visually impaired users (Mynatt, 1994a, 1994b). The system addresses a problem that is clearly significant: while direct manipulation interfaces may provide significant advantages to sighted users, they are more difficult to translate into other modalities than are language-based systems, and thus represent a step backwards for the visually impaired (Boyd et al., 1990; Buxton, 1986).

Completely mapping the spatial layout of a graphical interface to the temporal medium of sound seems difficult in principle, since the ability to play and hear simultaneous sounds is far more limited than the ability to display and scan multiple graphical entities. Moreover, as Mynatt (1994a, 1994b) notes, many elements in graphical interfaces are artifacts of a limited screen size (e.g., scrollbars) and may be unnecessary or distracting in auditory versions. For this reason, the Mercator system doesn't map the visual interface per se to sound, but instead uses sound to convey the semantics of interaction components. It does this by translating the hierarchy of widgets used to implement an interface into a hierarchy of "auditory interface components" corresponding, for example, to buttons, menus, and windows. This is not a simple mapping, since some widgets are idiosyncratic to visual interfaces, and each component may consist of many different widgets (e.g., a menu is typically created using widgets such as lists, shells, and buttons). Thus the components presented to users of Mercator are an abstracted version of those used to actually build the corresponding graphical interfaces; the attempt is to make the mapping at the level of units that are semantically meaningful to users.

Users navigate Mercator by using the keyboard to traverse the component tree structure, moving up, down, and sideways from superordinate to subordinate nodes. This eliminates the problem of dealing with the empty spaces between meaningful items in graphical interfaces, which are essential for spatial layout but lead to useless and frustrating "dead space" in auditory translations. Moreover, as users move from component to component, they can hear where they are, but must select the component explicitly if they want to interact with it. This allows users to "scan" the interface without actually causing any unintended actions (a lesson learned from Stevens et al., 1994).

Though speech output can be requested as needed (and is a necessary and integral part of interactions with entities such as text fields), by default Mercator uses auditory icons to provide feedback. A variety of sounds are used, such as the sound of tapping on a glass pane when a window is reached, various push button sounds for the various types of interface buttons, and a typewriter sound when a text field is reached. Auditory icons are parameterised as well, so that location in lists and menus is indicated by pitch, the complexity of containers by reverberation, etc. This strategy was suggested by Ludwig et al's (1991) work on *filtears*, simple manipulations (such as pitch-shifting, filtering, and reverberation) that can be made on any sound to convey information.

The design of auditory icons for such a system is challenging, because sounds must be found for every interface component, and they must work without corresponding graphical displays. User feedback was employed in finding the sounds for Mercator: people were presented interface entities and asked to choose the best sound from several alternatives, or conversely were presented a sound and asked to choose the interface entity that corresponded best. These studies were useful in guiding the sounds used in Mercator, but in the end their results depend fundamentally on the sounds offered as alternatives. For instance, early versions used short, heavily edited sampled sounds for these icons, but these were lengthened somewhat to improve recognition (Mynatt, 1994b).

Using Mercator is surprisingly simple, given the lack of visual feedback, the model of traversing a hierarchy of interface components, and the reliance on nonspeech audio cues. More formal user testing, with both sighted and visually impaired users, also suggests that the system does a good job of making X Windows applications accessible. However, it is difficult to avoid the feeling that something is lost in translating the spatial layout of a graphical interface to a hierarchy that is examined node by node. Space is an important resource for graphical displays, affording grouping, scanning, focusing, and overviewing multiple entities; these affordances are lost in Mercator's hierarchical system. Future work should focus on regaining these affordances, perhaps through the use of multiple sounds, shifting focus, and novel input techniques. To do this will probably require deeper investigations about how visually impaired people use and represent space. For now, however, Mercator represents a significant milestone in translating visual interfaces to nonvisual form.

Auditory Icons: Discussion

Auditory icons and earcons represent different strategies for using sound to convey information from interfaces. Auditory icons use everyday sounds, earcons use musical ones. Auditory icons stress the importance of metaphorical or iconic mappings between sound-producing events and the things they are to represent, exploiting our existing skills of listening to the everyday world. Earcons use arbitrary mappings, relying on people's abilities to learn such associations. Auditory icons use the natural structure of events and their attributes to parameterise sounds, creating families of sounds that map to interface events. Earcons use invented hierarchies of sound attributes to do the same thing. Auditory icons are designed to be easy to understand, but this may require exacting sound design. Earcons must be learned, but they are easy to create and manipulate, especially using MIDI equipment. In many ways, auditory icons and earcons take diametrically opposed approaches to providing much of the same functionality.

Attempts have been made to experimentally compare auditory icons and earcons (e.g., Sikora et al.,1995; Lucas, 1994). Sets of auditory icons and earcons are designed for a selection of interface entities, and participants asked to rate how well the sounds communicate as well as how attractive they are. Auditory icons tend to be judged as mapping better (more clearly, more memorably) to interface events, but earcons tend to be judged as more pleasant.

These experiments may seem useful in examining the differences between auditory icons and earcons, but they are actually quite limited. Such studies depend on the design of the sounds meant to represent auditory icons and earcons. If a well designed set of auditory icons were compared with a poorly designed set of earcons, for instance, it is easy to suppose that auditory icons would be rated as better mapped and more likeable. The generalisability of such results, however, would be suspect at best. In addition, ratings of mapping may not correspond well to long term memorability. Similarly, preference judgments made after brief exposure in laboratory settings may not relate well to preference after long term exposure in a work setting. In general, the results of experiments meant to compare these different approaches must be taken with some skepticism.

Because of their differences, there has traditionally been a kind of implicit rivalry between auditory icons and earcons. The two approaches may turn out to complement one another, however. Auditory icons map more closely to interface entities than earcons when metaphorical or iconic mappings are used, but such mappings may be impossible to develop for some interface events. In these cases, the arbitrary but systematic mappings offered by the earcon approach may be more suitable than inappropriate or misleading everyday sounds. Similarly, parameterising auditory icons along dimensions of sound-producing events is an ideal that is sometimes only approximately implemented (e.g., changing the pitch of a sampled sound to indicate size is only an approximation of the actual acoustic correlates of size). When this is the case, the acoustic dimensions used to parameterise auditory icons are not much different from those used to build hierarchical earcons. Similarly, recent examples of earcons have moved towards varying sounds by analogy with everyday sound-producing events (e.g., the auditory map and algebra earcons described earlier) This represents a move away from the development of arbitrary languages for sound, and towards the metaphoric and iconic mappings of auditory icons. In practice, then, the differences between these approaches may not be as great as the theories would suggest.

Systems have also developed recently which merge auditory icons with techniques used for auralisation. In Alber's (1994) Varèse system, for example, auditory icons were designed to indicate the operational states of six satellite subsystems. The proximity of each subsystem to its next operational state was mapped to the speed with which its auditory icon was played and repeated. This may be seen as an example of parameterising auditory icons, but it also draws on auralisation techniques that set thresholds between operational states rather than merely reflecting their basic parameters (see, e.g., the Kyma system described earlier). Similarly, Fitch and Kramer (1994) developed a number of auditory icons representing various physical variables (e.g., heart rate, temperature, blood pressure) of a simulated patient in an anaesthesiology task, and modified them using more abstract parameters such as pitch, timbre, and filtering. They found this hybrid technique to be very successful: Participants in their experiment actually performed better using the sounds than with visual displays.

Despite the number of systems that have used auditory icons, the strategy has only begun to be developed. One issue that deserves more emphasis is the design of unobtrusive sounds than still convey adequate information. The work by Patterson et al., (1986), Edworthy et al. (1991), and Swift et al. (1989) on perceived urgency and annoyance could be a useful guide for this. Nonetheless, the design of truly subtle auditory icons—sounds as subtle as that made by moving a sheet of paper across a desk—will require careful attention to design. Such attention can be found in the design of some of the auditory icons beginning to appear in commercial systems: the whoosh as a window is compressed, for instance, or the click of a software button. But these sounds seem designed in an ad hoc fashion, without taking advantage of parameterisation or the creation of ecologies of sound. We may be beginning to see the emergence of auditory icons as a standard interaction technique, but there are still many possibilities that have yet to be explored or developed in commercial products.

42.4 New Directions In the Design Space

Though it is a cliché to say that auditory interface design is a new field, it should be clear at this point that this is not really the case. The earliest work I describe here, by Bly (1982a, 1982b), is already 15 years old, an extraordinarily long time in interface-years. The precursors to this research are even more ancient: With anecdotal reports of computer scientists tuning radios to their computers or wiring speakers to shift registers, it is likely that people have been trying to listen to computers from their very inception.

Nonetheless, it is fair to say that research on auditory interfaces is not mature. A number of disparate strategies for creating auditory interfaces have been explored over the last fifteen years or so, but they can be differentiated along relatively few dimensions. First, the kinds of sounds employed vary at a number of levels. Second, the kinds of mappings created between sounds and the meanings they are to convey also vary, along a dimension from completely arbitrary mappings to very literal, iconic ones. Finally, the kinds of functionality auditory interfaces are to provide vary as well, from allowing people to perceive patterns in data, to providing information about events and processes that are useful for social coordination.

Though research has ranged over a broad space of sounds, mappings, and functions, this space has been relatively sparsely populated by working systems and rigorous research. Moreover, the area is still relatively restricted. In part, this is because the dimensions of sound, mapping, and functionality are not really independent: a choice on one dimension constrains the possible choices along the others. In this section, then, I discuss the space of interfaces that has developed, and suggest several ways that it might be better filled by new research. I end by discussing the need to expand the field, to help research on auditory interfaces merge with new developments in interaction design.

42.4.1 Sound: The Sonic Palette

The most obvious distinguishing characteristics of auditory interfaces is in the auditory vocabulary they employ. A primary distinction can be made between those systems that use musical sounds and those which use everyday sounds. Within these categories, however, the sonic structures used vary in complexity, and simpler systems have typically been explored more thoroughly than more complex ones The choice of a framework for understanding sounds, and the level of complexity explored within that framework, together have strong implications for the sorts of mappings that can be achieved between sounds and their meanings, and ultimately for the kinds of functionality that can be addressed.

Musical sound is a very broad category, encompassing everything from the discrete tones used by Bly (1982a, 1982b), the simple motives used by Patterson (Patterson et al., 1986; Patterson, 1982), Blattner et al. (1989) and their colleagues, to more complex, expressive music. Each of these subgroups offers its own parameters for control or encoding, from the basic psychoacoustic parameters used to describe simple tones, to the simple musical attributes used in motives, to the higher level musical structures that might allow even more complex information to be integrated. In addition, there is the potential for controlling—and the impossibility of avoiding—the expressive dimensions that characterise music, and which are used, for instance, in the design of films, games, or multimedia products. The sorts of dimensions we might use to describe musical sounds at this level—mood, atmosphere, texture—are not well understood from a scientific point of view, but could be a powerful addition to auditory interface design.

Similarly, everyday sounds range from simple sound effects used without variation, to parameterised auditory icons, to ecologies of everyday sounds meant to be played together. Opportunities for control here range from simply choosing a representative sound from the infinite variety of possibilities, to determining the source-specific attributes that might be used to parameterise auditory icons, to controlling aspects of a virtual auditory environment such as localisation and room acoustics. Beyond this, entire auditory environments might be defined, similar to that demonstrated by the ARKola system (Gaver et al., 1991), in which numerous everyday sounds combine to form an integrated whole. This sort of potential, which mirrors the possibility of using more sophisticated musical structures, is not very well understood, though psychoacoustical factors concerning masking, for instance, are clearly important, as well as higher-level ones concerning congruency, place, and narrative.

In sum, there are many ways to use musical and everyday sounds, and this is one of the primary dimensions of the space of design for auditory interfaces. Not surprisingly, most systems have tended to use relatively simple sounds—whether musical or everyday—rather than the more complex structures that are possible. One way in which auditory interface design may be expected to expand, then, is towards more complex vocabularies of sound, whether musical or everyday. This will allow more complex mappings to be made from sound to meaning, and permit new functionality for auditory interfaces as well.

42.4.2 Mapping Sound to Meaning

The mappings between sounds and information is the second dimension along which auditory interfaces may be distinguished. Mappings vary in how systematic or determined they are. On one extreme, many mappings are completely arbitrary, as when pitch is used to stand for some data dimension which has nothing to do with pitch, or frequency. On the other hand, they may be very literal, or iconic, as when the sound of crumpling paper is used to indicate that a text file has been deleted in an appropriate model world (see Gaver, 1989, 1986).

Arbitrary mappings are used in many auditory interfaces. Most auralisations set up arbitrary mappings between data and sound, just as most graphing techniques arbitrarily assign data to vertical and horizontal dimensions, symbols, colour, and so forth. This works reasonably well for auralisation. In many cases, the mappings are specified by their users, and they are almost always introduced shortly before the auralisation is actually played. Arbitrary mappings are more problematic for alarms, especially in environments such as aircraft cockpits or intensive care units where many alarms are used. A similar problem faces systems that use motives: the more mappings required in a particular interface, the more careful design is needed to make them clear and unambiguous. Earcons often use arbitrary mappings, (in fact, the ease of establishing such mappings is one of the appeals of the strategy). For this reason, rules for generating families of motives are important because basic motives may be arbitrary, but their variations are rule-based. Finally, even everyday sounds may be arbitrarily mapped to their referents (e.g., Brown et al., 1989), though the results do not really fit the definition of auditory icons. In general, arbitrary mappings are seductive to designers because they are easy to establish. They are problematic for users, however, because they are often difficult to learn and remember.

The clearest mappings are those that are iconic, that is, those formed when the relation between a sound and event is causal. This is possible to achieve in computer interfaces when a deep metaphor is used to establish a model world, and the sounds created by particular entities in that world are those that would be created by their physical counterparts (Gaver, 1989). Iconic mappings, along with the use of everyday sounds, are the defining features of auditory icons. Such mappings have seldom been used in other sorts of auditory interfaces, though they have appeared occasionally in auralisations. Iconic mappings are obviously desirable when they can be found. Even if they are not immediately guessable, they are often learned and remembered after a single explanation. However, sounds that map iconically to a given event or message may be difficult to find, not least because not all events make sound. In addition, the psychoacoustical requirements for sounds that are clearly meaningful may conflict with those that make sounds unobtrusive.

Taken together, these properties gives iconic mappings contrasting strengths compared to arbitrary mappings. On the one hand, iconic mappings may not be very useful for auralisations, because their memorability is relatively unimportant for temporary mappings, and they might constrain designers or confuse listeners. For instance, if voices were used to represent population variables, how would occupation be represented? Would it matter what the voices were saying? On the other hand, iconic mappings may be more useful for alarms, because memorability becomes an important issue. Many different alarms may need to be interpreted, and yet they are sounded fairly rarely (one hopes). However, the sheer naturalness of iconic mappings to everyday sounds may undercut alarms' functions by failing to convey the essential fact that the alarm sound is an intentional message with a human author. Finally, iconic mappings, in the form of auditory icons, have proved to be very useful for more general interfaces, not only because they tend to be easily learned and remembered, but also because they tend to integrate well with graphical interfaces and the overall context of use.

Between arbitrary and iconic mappings are a large variety of mappings that are more systematic than purely arbitrary mappings, yet less literal than iconic ones. These are commonly glossed as "metaphorical" mappings, though this single term tends to mask the various kinds of analogy that are used. For instance, the use of high pitches to stand for something near the top of the screen, and low pitches for things near the bottom, relies on a cross-modal sensory correspondence which, though powerful, is little understood (see Marks, 1978). The use of walking, jogging, and running sounds to stand for CPU usage in ShareMon (Cohen, 1994a), on the other hand, relies on a higher-level semantic analogy between speed and effort of walking and the processing load. Finally, the use of a whooshing sound to indicate opening and closing windows in the SonicFinder (1989) is a sound effect, a sound that is iconically mapped to a nonexisting event.

Metaphorical mappings are both flexible and powerful. The traditional conflict between difficult-to-learn arbitrary mappings and difficult-to-develop iconic ones increasingly seems to imply an unreasonable choice between two extremes. Suitable metaphors may be very difficult to find or develop, and poorly designed ones may be misleading. Nonetheless, metaphors share the best features of arbitrary and iconic mappings, being more flexible than literal mappings, yet more easily learned and remembered than arbitrary ones. Because of this, it seems likely (and desirable) that the use of metaphorical sounds will increase, ideally accompanied by better analyses of how they work, and by heuristics for their design. This development, in turn, should allow new functionality to be addressed, as the tools for mapping sound to meaning become simultaneously more powerful and more intuitive.

42.4.3 Functions for Auditory Interfaces

A final perspective for distinguishing auditory interfaces focuses on the functions they are meant to perform. As the systems I have discussed suggest, there are many uses for auditory interfaces: from alarms indicating some event, to auralisations allowing data patterns to be discerned, to motives that summarise equations, to auditory icons that support collaboration. The range of uses to which sounds may be put do not themselves define a dimension, of course, but there are dimensions along which they may be considered.

One way to think about the functions that sounds perform is in terms of the complexity of information that is conveyed. This is not the same thing as the complexity of the sounds themselves. Even complex sounds often signal only a single bit of information; namely, that some event has occurred. For example, most interrupt beeps—whether simple tones or complex samples—indicate only that a condition has been reached in which somebody decided that an interrupt beep should be played. A step up from this are sounds that basically serve as labels, such as Patterson's (1982) alarms, simple versions of Blattner et al.'s (1989) earcons, or unparameterised auditory icons. Finally, some sounds convey rich systems of information, such as multidimensional auralisations, hierarchical earcons, or parameterised auditory icons. In general, the amount of information conveyed by a given sound is a trade-off between simplicity and ease of learning on the one hand, and efficiency on the other. Simple systems are easy to learn, while multi-layered systems can provide large amounts of information. Strategies such as parameterisation of everyday sounds seek to gain the benefits of very efficient, rich messages, while making them as easy to learn as simpler cues.

Another perspective to take on the functions served by auditory interfaces concerns their use over time. How an interface is to function over time affects how well various mappings will work. At one extreme, many auralisations are extremely ephemeral, with a given mapping between sound and data established only for a few exploratory trials. At the other extreme, genre sounds such as telephone rings, ambulance sirens, and cuckoo clocks have such a long history that the mappings between sound and meaning they use seem almost necessary (Cohen, 1993). In between the extremes of fleeting use and historical stability, most alarms, earcons, and auditory icons are designed for relatively long use, without having the benefits of a preexisting history. It is for this reason that metaphorical or iconic mappings are valuable, in allowing the benefits of a related history to be applied to new sounds.

The functions performed by auditory interfaces can also be considered in terms of the prospective audience for the sounds. Data auralisations again represent an extreme, this time one in which the designer and audience are often the same, at least until some interesting pattern is determined. Even when auralisations are played for third parties, they are buttressed by their designer's explanations. On the other hand, most other auditory interfaces are at least nominally designed for use by an audience who has never met the designer. Some of these interfaces, such as most alarms, must be designed for a non-specialised audience with little desire to learn new mappings, and thus must be immediately distinctive, communicative, and motivating. Others, such as those using earcons and auditory icons, may be designed initially for audiences more likely to learn novel mappings. It is dangerous to overestimate this kind of tolerance, however, and again techniques for improving mappings are probably appropriate for any general audience. Finally, at the opposite extreme from auralisations are systems meant to support collaboration. To mediate social interaction flexibly and subtly, such systems should ideally use auditory mappings as rich as those used for earcons and auditory icons, but their meaning should not rely on learning or the presence and authority of the designer. In fact, the meaning of given sounds may change as their role in social interaction is negotiated by their users.

42.4.4 Expanding the Space

There are many possibilities for new work on auditory interfaces. Here it is useful consider the space in reverse order from the previous discussion. After all, the extension of existing strategies to new domains has characterised the field, and we can expect auditory interfaces to follow wherever digital technologies may go (and in some cases to lead the way). In doing this, new kinds of mappings become possible and desirable. These mappings, in turn, lead to new possibilities for thinking about and designing sounds. So while sounds may be the most obvious attributes of existing interfaces, it is their functionality that drives development. As new functionality is explored, the boundaries of existing research—the distinctions among auralisations, musical messages, and auditory icons—become blurred. In the end, new dimensions may appear as well, as aesthetic and design sensibilities are included in work on auditory interfaces. This is a move that could dramatically expand the space of auditory interfaces.

For instance, there has been a great deal of research on the spatialisation of sound, but little work on the systematic design of sounds for virtual reality systems. As I described earlier, basic research on localisation has led to powerful enabling technologies and techniques for creating virtual auditory realities. This has been used to spatialise overlapping streams of speech, improving comprehension in aircraft cockpits (Begault, 1994). In addition, Wenzel and her colleagues (Wenzel et al., 1988) explored a system of nonspeech cues that helped replace tactile cues in a virtual reality manipulation task. Finally, many virtual reality systems have included sound, sometimes to striking effect (e.g., Laurel et al., 1994). Nonetheless, more systematic work addressing the new functions sound could perform in these environments would be helpful. This is a major opportunity for new research.

Similarly, auditory interfaces have not really kept up with the emergence of portable hand-held devices. Stifelman (e.g., Stifelman et al., 1993) has pursued innovative research on auditory-only PDAs, but though her designs have included auditory icons, her systems rely mainly on speech recognition and output. An alternative would be to focus on using nonspeech audio to convey information about events and colleagues, allowing such a devices to be used as a portable awareness server (see Hindus et al., 1995). More generally, collaborative systems offer a rich domain for exploring auditory interfaces, and may be especially suited to the use of sound to maintain group awareness while allowing individual activity (Gaver, 1991). Finally, the explosion of the World Wide Web offers scope for interface design of all sorts. Albers and Bergman (1995) designed a system that produced a variety of auditory icons to provide feedback about the state of a web browser. This is a start in the right direction, but more work could be done on the use of sound to orient oneself in the strangely homogenous space offered by the web.

Approaching new functionality will encourage explorations of new forms of mapping. An integral part of expanding the range of mappings that can be used—and, by implication, the range of acceptable sounds and approachable functionality—is the provision of tailorable and interactive interfaces to users. This is not a trivial problem: Customisation must be constrained to ensure that appropriate sonic attributes and dimensions are used, to guard against psychoacoustical problems like masking and interactions, and (not least) to avoid aesthetically horrifying results. Nonetheless, interactivity may enable greatly expanded uses of sound. It is one of the key elements of systems like Kyma (Scalletti, 1994) that allow users to quickly set up their own data auralisations. Tailorability is also likely to help systems using earcons and auditory icons avoid confusions in mappings, and moreover would allow users to tune auditory interfaces to fit their working environments.

Finally, work in new domains, and the use of more flexible mappings, has implications for the sounds that are used as well. There is a vast array of sounds, for instance, that defy easy categorisation as either musical or everyday. Some are familiar, such as the whistling of wind, the drone of an engine, or the melody of running water. Others may be constructed, either by synthesis or manipulated recordings (e.g., Eno, 1982). The potential of such sounds is to combine the iconic possibilities of everyday sounds with the ease of manipulation of musical ones; an added value is greater freedom in aesthetically controlling the results.

Overall, there are many ways to extend the possibilities of auditory interfaces; to use a greater and more structured lexicon of sounds, to apply sounds to new functional domains, and to explore new and more responsive mappings among sounds and information. There are also rich opportunities for research meant to consolidate existing strategies. Each of the three major strategies for using sounds—auralisation, musical messages, and auditory icons—need more and better examples of real world applications. For each, the appearance of projects focused around their applications to real problems, which report the difficulties, failures and successes of the process, and the benefits of the resulting system, would be extremely valuable. From this perspective, the best way to improve the space of auditory interfaces would be to help colonise it.

42.4.5 Blurring the Boundaries

As auditory interfaces have been used in new domains, the boundaries that have traditionally defined the research are beginning to blur, so that the design space is beginning to be more evenly filled. Several examples help illustrate how newer systems have started to merge strategies for creating auditory interfaces.

OutToLunch

An excellent example of new developments in sound design comes from a system called OutToLunch (Cohen, 1994b). OutToLunch was designed to recreate the aural experience of working in a shared space, in which sounds naturally provide awareness of group activity. The system counted each user's keystrokes, mouse clicks, and total mouse movement, and then represented this information to users using recordings of real keystrokes, mouse clicks, and mouse rolling noise. Unfortunately, the original prototype proved too annoying for continuous daily use. Cohen (1994b) speculates that this was because the sounds conveyed relatively little information (no information about who was active, or where), and that they were not aesthetically well designed (the sounds were too loud and had low resolution). Thus in the second iteration, OutToLunch was redesigned to simply indicate whether or not each member's machine was being used. This gave people a sense of who was around and what they were doing, without distracting them with detailed mechanical activity.

What moved the new version onto new ground, however, was the sound design it employed. The new version used sounds designed by Michael Brook, a professional musician and producer (e.g., Brook, 1992). Brook started by creating a continuous drone by looping a low-pitched, quiet guitar sound that faded in and out when activity started or stopped and played continuously during any group activity. Then he fashioned a set of concordant musical themes from short guitar or synthesiser melodies which had slow attacks, long decays, and a great deal of reverberation and echo, allowing them to merge with the underlying themes. Group members chose their own themes to represent them in the resulting display. In the final system, the drone would fade up as the group became active, and each theme would be added to the mix at random offsets within a thirty second period: The overall effect was of a very atmospheric, non-repeating musical texture much like the sort of "ambient" music pioneered by Brian Eno (1975).

The iterated OutToLunch was not used very long by the group (which disbanded—for unrelated reasons—soon after it was deployed). Nonetheless, the new sounds represent a qualitative step forward in sound design for auditory interfaces. This reflects the contribution of a professional musician to the crafting of a set of expressive, aesthetically focused sounds. In part, this meant that Cohen and Brook were unconstrained by the strategies for using sounds discussed earlier. The focus on peripheral monitoring is typical of work on auditory icons (e.g., Gaver, 1991), but the musical themes are suggestive of the earcon approach, and the use of sounds to represent essentially numerical data is strongly reminiscent of auralisation work. OutToLunch mixed aspects of auralisations, musical messages, and auditory icons in an eclectic way, drawing on each to support unobtrusive group awareness. It is a cliché in auditory interface design to recommend that a sound designer be used in creating auditory interfaces, but OutToLunch represents one of the few, and best, examples of how this should be done.

Audio Debugging

Recently several systems have been developed to help programmers debug sequential and parallel programs. These systems resemble auditory icons and earcons in that their overall purpose is to allow programmers to monitor events in the computer, but they employ strategies more reminiscent of auralisation in producing their sounds.

For instant, Sonnet (Jameson, 1994) is a visual programming interface that allows sounds and sound modifications to be "attached" to lines of code in a sequential program. Typically sounds are triggered after some line of code, and stopped sometime later. In addition, parameters of the sounds may be modified to indicate, for instance, the number of times the sound has been triggered, or the value of some variable. These sounds and modifications are then played in realtime as the program is run. Jameson (1994) describes several examples of how Sonnet might be used. For instance, a note might be triggered just before, and stopped just after, an iterative loop is declared. If the note doesn't stop when the program is run, then the loop is not exiting, either because it is endless or because some subroutine is defective. More information can be obtained by modifying the volume of the note (usually in a triangle form, so over time a tremolo effect is produced) just before the first statement within the loop is reached. If the resulting sound doesn't change in volume, then there is probably a bad subroutine; if the volume changes but doesn't end, then the exit condition is probably wrong. Similarly, note parameters can be used to track the values of variables, or to indicate access to variables. Simply by "labelling" various lines of code with sounds, the details of code execution may be listened to, and problems identified by unexpected sounds.

A similar strategy has been developed by Jackson and Francioni (1994) for debugging parallel program behaviour. Like Jameson (1994), their system starts and stops notes to indicate various events within a program. But it is much more difficult to debug and optimise parallel programs than sequential ones, because overall system behaviour depends crucially on the interactions among a number of processors as well as the sequential behaviour of each of them. Thus Jackson and Francioni (1994) focus on using sound to track the communications and timing among processors. For instance, each processor may be assigned a different pitch, and notes triggered to indicate that it has sent or received a message. Sustained notes may be used to indicate when processors are idle or busy, or started when a message is sent and stopped when it is received. Finally, notes may be used to indicate specific events within each processor.

Using these sorts of mappings, patterns of behaviour can be heard emerging from a group of processors running in parallel. Jackson and Francioni (1994) suggest that the sounds are useful in helping to focus attention on relevant aspects of visual representations, or on details of timing that are difficult to perceive from visual representations. For instance, lost messages–those that are sent but not received–can be heard if a note triggered by a send is not stopped by a receive. The relative activity of processors can be heard by assigning different pitches to each, or by playing sounds while processors are idle. Finally, the sounds that result are often strikingly musical in nature, creating a variety of auditory textures, melodies, or harmonies.

Sound is an appealing medium for debugging, as these systems have shown. Perhaps most importantly, sounds can be played as a program is running, without interfering with it. There is no need to step through a program, nor to set breakpoints at which variables can be examined. Of course, in many cases the same kinds of information could be printed out as text, but sounds have the same sort of advantage over text that graphs do: by integrating data, they allow the perception of patterns that would be more difficult to apprehend using lists or tables—particularly information about timing, as Jackson and Francioni (1994) point out. Sound allows processes to be monitored while visual attention is directed elsewhere, for instance at screen behaviour. Finally, triggering or modifying sounds for debugging is relatively lightweight. Many systems offer at least basic functionality for playing and modifying sounds, and MIDI equipment can be used to play a greater range of sounds at much less cost to the processor.

The tactic used by both Jackson and Francioni (1994) and Jameson (1994) of playing sounds that depend on events in the computer is similar to the strategies used in creating auditory icons and earcons, and the resulting ability to monitor several simultaneous dynamic processes is also similar. But there are striking similarities to auralisation work as well. Because these debugging tools are meant to be used by programmers themselves, rather than distributed to a large audience, relatively little importance is placed on making the sounds map to events in intuitive or memorable ways. Instead, the emphasis is on allowing programmers to set up highly discriminable and flexible sound mappings to be played soon afterwards. In addition, both debugging systems tend to rely on triggering simple notes which are then modified to indicate various parameters (such as processor number or the value of a variable), just as many auralisations trigger sounds for each new data point, then vary them to indicate values along several dimensions. In the end, this work is not only valuable in its own right, but also because it emphasises the potential of merging the various techniques and strategies that have already been developed.

42.4.6 Throwing Open the Gates: Multimedia and Games

While traditional interfaces have yet to incorporate sound as a standard element of interaction, multimedia and games systems routinely employ very sophisticated music and sounds. Unfortunately, there has been little conversation between the research community and the ever-growing community of content developers. At the least, a survey of how sounds are used in a wide variety of multimedia products would be a valuable addition to the literature. It is clearly time for research on auditory interfaces to look to the established practices of these fields for inspiration and new ideas. Conversely, it should be realised that research on auditory interfaces has a great deal to offer games and multimedia work in return.

What multimedia and games have to offer auditory interface designers is a routine adherence to standards of sound design, the aesthetic crafting of sounds, that have seldom been met in auditory interface research (barring Cohen and Brook's OutToLunch system). It is difficult to overstate the importance of good sound design to auditory interfaces. Bad sound design can make information-rich interfaces seem distracting, irritating, and trivial. Good sound design can reinforce a sound's message, allow it to fit into its environment of use, help avoid auditory fatigue, and allow and interface to be accepted and enjoyed. In general, research on auditory interfaces could learn a great deal about effective sound design from multimedia and games work.

Sound's expressive capabilities are often more important to games and multimedia designers than the drier goal of systematically transmitting information. This reflects the traditions of sound design for radio, television and movies. In such fields, sound's ability to provide information is almost tangential to its ability to produce tension, convey mood, and communicate and evoke emotion. As with these fields, so with multimedia and games: Sounds are used to engage users, to heighten the excitement and pace of games, to create an atmosphere appropriate to a given topic in multimedia treatments.

The aesthetic and expressive dimensions of sound have largely been overlooked in auditory interface research. Occasionally an auralisation will make appropriate emotional mappings between sound and data (e.g., Scalletti 1994 mapped pollution levels to coughing sounds). Work on urgency (Patterson et al., 1986; Edworthy et al., 1991) can be seen as an example of trying to study a simple parameter of mood using psychoacoustical methodologies. Finally, work on auditory icons has been concerned with crafting sounds for their environments, and with sound's ability to engage users with systems (see, e.g., Gaver et al., 1991). Nonetheless, crafting sounds for their aesthetic qualities, and designing them to create mood and emotion, has seldom been anything but incidental to more functional goals. A greater concern for these issues could lead to auditory interfaces that better reflect the importance and implications of various events, not just their dry informational values.

On the other hand, there is much that auditory interface research can offer multimedia and games designers. The ability to systematically map sounds and their dimensions to information, to create families of related musical messages, and to vary everyday sounds along source dimensions could complement the sophisticated aesthetic and expressive sound design already employed, making multimedia and games more engaging, easier to use, and more challenging as well. As it is, it is not clear that most examples use sound to convey important information. Though Buxton (1989) speculated that turning off the sound on a video game would lead to lower scores, I am skeptical that this is generally true (the relevant data has never been collected). If multimedia and games designers drew more on auditory interface work, we would be much more likely to see sound's influence reflected in the scores.

42.5 Conclusion

There are three major lines of endeavour that should help the field truly become mature. First, we need to generate more examples of systems that fulfill real user needs, whether these be to analyse complex data, comprehend complex messages, orient to real and virtual events, or simply to have fun. Second, we need to understand and explore the richer structural possibilities of sound, whether these be musical, metaphorical, or environmental. Finally, we need to focus our attention on sounds that are aesthetically controlled, as subtle and beautiful as those we hear in the orchestra hall, or on a walk through the woods.

42.6 Acknowledgments

I am very grateful to Beth Mynatt, Anne Schlottmann, Jayne Roderick, and Sara Bly for their comments on earlier drafts of this chapter.

42.7 References

Albers, M. C. (1994). The Varese system, hybrid auditory interfaces, and satellite-ground control: Using auditory icons and sonification in a complex, supervisory control system. In G. Kramer and S. Smith (eds.), Proceedings of the Second International Conference on Auditory Display (Santa Fe, N.M, 7-9 November, 1994), 3 - 14.

Albers, M. C., and Bergman, E. (1995). The audible web: Auditory enhancements for Mosaic. *CHI'95 conference companion*, ACM Conference on Human Factors in Computing Systems, 318-319.

Ballas, J. A. (1994a). Common factors in the identification of an assortment of brief everyday sound. *Journal of Experimental Psychology: Human Perception and Performance*. 19: 250 - 267.

Ballas, J. A. (1994b). Delivery of information through sound. In Kramer, G. (ed.), *Auditory Display*. New York: Addison-Wesley, 79 - 94.

Ballas, J. A., and Mullin, T. (1991). Effects of context on the identification of everyday sounds. *Human Performance*. 4: 199 - 219.

Begault, D. R. (1994). *3-D sound for virtual reality*. New York: Academic Press.

Blattner, M. M., Papp, A. L. III, and Glinert, E. P. (1994). Sonic enhancement of two-dimensional graphic displays. In Kramer, G. (ed.), *Auditory Display*. New York: Addison-Wesley, 447 - 470.

Blattner, M., Sumikawa, D. and Greenberg, R. (1989). Earcons and icons: Their structure and common design principles. *Human-Computer Interaction* 4(1), Spring 1989.

Bly, S. (1982a). *Sound and computer information presentation*. Unpublished doctoral thesis (UCRL-53282), Lawrence Livermore National Laboratory and University of California, Davis, CA.

Bly, S. (1982b). Presenting information in sound, *Proceedings of the CHI '82 Conference on Human Factors in Computer Systems*, 371-375. New York: ACM.

Borin, G., De Poli, G., and Sarti, A. (1993). Algorithms and structures for synthesis using physical models. *Computer Music Journal*, 16(4), 30 - 42.

Boyd, L. H., Boyd, W. L., and Vanderheiden, G. C. (1990). The graphical user interface: Crisis, danger, and opportunity. *Journal Visual Impair. and Blind.* 496 - 502.

Bregman, A. S. (1990). *Auditory scene analysis: The perceptual organization of sound.* Cambridge, MA.: MIT Press.

Brewster, S.A., Wright, P. C, and Edwards, A. D. N. (1994). A detailed investigation into the effectiveness of earcons. In Kramer, G. (ed.), *Auditory Display*. New York: Addison-Wesley, 471 - 498.

Brook, M. (1992). *Cobalt blue*. CAD 2007 CD, 4AD.

Brown, M., Newsome, S. and Glinert, E. (1989). An experiment into the use of auditory cues to reduce visual workload. *Proceedings of the CHI '89*. New York: ACM, 339-346.

Burgess, D. A. (1992). Real-time audio spatialization with inexpensive hardware. (Report No. GIT-GVU-92-20). Graphics Visualization and Usability Center, Georgia Institute of Technology.

Buxton, W. (1986). Human interface design and the handicapped user. *Proceedings of CHI'86*, 291 - 297.

Buxton, W. (1989). Introduction to this special issue on non-speech audio. *Human-Computer Interaction* 4(1), Spring 1989.

Cabot, R.C., Mino, M.G., Dorans, D.A., Tackel, I.S. and Breed, H.E. (1976). Detection of phase shifts in harmonically related tones. *Journal of the Audio Engineering Society*, 24, 568-571.

Cohen, J. (1993). "Kirk here:" Using genre sounds to monitor background activity. *INTERCHI'93 Adjunct Proceedings* (Amsterdam, April 24 - 29, 1993), 63 - 64.

Cohen, J. (1994a). Monitoring background activities. In Kramer, G. (ed.), *Auditory Display*. New York: Addison-Wesley, 499 - 531.

Cohen, J. (1994b). Out to lunch: Further adventures monitoring background activity. In G. Kramer and S. Smith (eds.), *Proceedings of the Second International Conference on Auditory Display* (Santa Fe, N.M, 7-9 November, 1994), 15 - 20.

Edworthy, J., Loxley, S., and Dennis, I. (1991). Improving auditory warning design: Relationship between warning sound parameters and perceived urgency. Human Factors. 33(2), 205-231.

Eno, B. (1975). *Discreet music*. EEGCD 23, E.G. Records Ltd.

Eno, B. (1982). *Ambient 4 / On land.* EEGCD 20, E.G. Records Ltd.

Fitch, W. T. , and Kramer, G. (1994). Sonifying the body electric: Superiority of an auditory display over a visual display in a complex, multivariate system. In Kramer, G. (ed.), Auditory Display. New York: Addison-Wesley, 307 - 326.

Fletcher, H.F. and Munson, W.A. (1933). Loudness, its definition measurement and calculation. *Journal of the Acoustic Society of America,* 5, 82-108.

Freed, D. J. (1988). *Perceptual control over timbre in musical applications using psychophysical functions.* Unpublished Masters Thesis, Northwestern University.

Freed, D. J., and Martins, W. L. (1986). Deriving psychophysical relations for timbre. *Proceedings of the International Computer Music Conference*, Oct. 20-24, 1986, The Hague, The Netherlands, 393-405.

Gaver, W. W. and Smith, R. (1990). Auditory icons in large-scale collaborative environments. In D. Diaper et al. (Eds.), *Human-Computer Interaction - INTERACT '90,* Elsevier Science Publishers B.V. (North-Holland), 735-740.

Gaver, W. W. (1986). Auditory icons: Using sound in computer interfaces. *Human-Computer Interaction.* 2, 167-177.

Gaver, W. W. (1988). *Everyday listening and auditory icons.* Doctoral Dissertation, University of California, San Diego.

Gaver, W. W. (1991). Sound support for collaboration. *Proceedings of ECSCW'91* (Amsterdam, September 24 - 27, 1991). Kluwer, Dordrecht. Reprinted in Baecker, R. (ed.), *Readings in groupware and CSCW: Assisting human-human collaboration.* Morgan Kaufmann, San Mateo, CA, 1993.

Gaver, W. W. (1993a). How do we hear in the world? Explorations of ecological acoustics. *Ecological Psychology,* 5(4): 285 - 313.

Gaver, W. W. (1993b). What in the world do we hear? An ecological approach to auditory source perception. *Ecological Psychology,* 5 (1): 1-29.

Gaver, W. W., and Mandler, G. (1987). Play it again, Sam: On liking music. *Cognition and Emotion, 1* (3) 259-282.

Gaver, W. W., (1989). The SonicFinder, a prototype interface that uses auditory icons. *Human Computer Interaction,* 4, 67 - 94.

Gaver, W. W., Smith, R. and O'Shea, T. (1991). Effective sounds in complex systems: the ARKola simulation. *Proceedings of CHI '91,* ACM Conference on Human Factors in Software, 85-90.

Gibson, J. J. (1979). *The ecological approach to visual perception.* New York: Houghton Mifflin. (Also published by Lawrence Erlbaum Associates, Hillsdale, New Jersey, 1986).

Grey, J. M. (1977). Multidimensional perceptual scaling of musical timbres. *Journal of the Acoustical Society of America.* 61, 1270-1277.

Grinstein, G. and Smith, S. (1990). The perceptualization of scientific data. In E. Farrell (Ed.). *Extracting meaning from complex data: processing, display, interaction.* Proceedings of the SPIE, Vol. 1259, 190-199.

Handel, S. (1989). *Listening: An introduction to the perception of auditory events.* Cambridge, MA: The MIT Press.

Helmholtz, H. L. F. (1885/1954). *On the sensations of tone as a physiological basis for the theory of music.* New York: Dover.

Hindus, D., Arons, B., Stifelman, L., Gaver, W., Mynatt, E., and Beck, M. (1995). Designing auditory interactions for PDAs. *Proceedings of the ACM Symposium on User Interface Software and Technology,* 143-146

Holmes, N. (1993). *The Best in Diagrammatic Graphics.*

IMA (1983). *MIDI musical instrument digital interface specification 1.0.* North Hollywood, CA: IMA. (Available from IMA, 11857 Hartsook Street, North Hollywood, CA, 91607, USA.)

Jackson, J. A., and Francioni, J. M. (1994). Synchronization of visual and aural parallel performance data. In Kramer, G. (ed.), *Auditory Display.* New York: Addison-Wesley, 291 - 306.

Jameson, D. H. (1994). Sonnet: Audio-enhanced monitoring and debugging. In Kramer, G. (ed.), *Auditory Display.* New York: Addison-Wesley, 253 - 266.

Laurel, B., Strickland, R., and Tow, R. (1994). Placeholder: Landscape and narrative in virtual environments. *ACM Computer Graphics Quarterly,* 28(2).

Lövstrand, L. (1991). Being selectively aware with the Khronika system. *Proceedings of ECSCW'91* (Amsterdam, September 24 - 27, 1991). Kluwer, Dordrecht. Reprinted in Baecker, R. (ed.), *Readings in groupware and CSCW: Assisting human-human collaboration.* Morgan Kaufmann, San Mateo, CA, 1993.

Loy, G. (1985). Musicians make a standard: The MIDI phenomenon. *Computer Music Journal,* 9(4), 8-26.

Lucas, P. (1994). An evaluation of the communicative ability of auditory icons and earcons. *Proceedings of the Second International Conference on Auditory Display* (Santa Fe, N.M, 7-9 November, 1994).

Paul A. L., Ludwig, L. F., and Cohen, M. (1991). Multi-dimensional audio window management. *International Journal of Man-Machine Studies*, 34(3): 319 - 336.

Lunney, D. and Morrison, R.C. (1990). Auditory presentation of experimental data. In E. Farrell (Ed.). *Extracting meaning from complex data: processing, display, interaction.* Proceedings of the SPIE, Vol 1259, 140-146.

Lunney, D., and Morrison, R. C. (1981). High technology laboratory aids for visually Handicapped chemistry Students. *Journal of Chemical Education*, 58, 3, 228-231.

Lunney, D., Morrison, R.C., Cetera, M.M., Hartness, R.V., Mills, R.T., Salt, A.D. and Sowell, D.C. (1983). A microcomputer-based laboratory aid for visually impaired students. *IEEE Micro*, 3(4), 19-31.

Marks, L. E. (1978). *The unity of the senses: Interrelations among the modalities.* New York: Academic Press.

McAdams, S. and Bregman, A. (1979). Hearing musical streams. *Computer Music Journal*, 3 (4), 26-43, 60, 63. Also appear in Roads, C. and Strawn, J. (1985). *Foundations of Computer Music.* Cambridge MA: MIT Press, 658-698.

McIntyre, M. E. , Schumacher, R. T., and Woodhouse, J. (1983). On the oscillations of instruments. *Journal of the Acoustical Society of America*, 74 S52.

Mezrich, J. J., Frysinger, S., and Slivjanovski, R. (1984). Dynamic representation of multivariate time series data. *Journal of the American Statistical Association.* 79, 34-40.

Mynatt, E. D. (1994a). Auditory presentation of graphical user interfaces. In Kramer, G. (ed.), *Auditory Display.* New York: Addison-Wesley, 533 - 555.

Mynatt, E. D. (1994b). Designing with auditory icons. In G. Kramer and S. Smith (eds.), *Proceedings of the Second International Conference on Auditory Display* (Santa Fe, N.M, 7-9 November, 1994), 21 - 30.

Patterson, R. D., Edworthy, J., Shailer, M. J., Lower, M. C., and Wheeler, P. D. (1986). Alarm sounds for medical equipment in intensive care areas and operating theatres. *Report AC598.* University of Southhampton Auditory Communication and Hearing Unit.

Patterson, R.D. (1982). Guidelines for auditory warning systems on civil aircraft. *CAA Paper 82017.* London: Civil Aviation Authority.

Pierce, John R. (1983). *The science of musical sounds.* New York: W. H. Freeman and Company.

Risset, J. C, and Wessel, D. (1982). Exploring timbre by analysis and synthesis. In D. Deutsch (Ed.), *The psychology of music.* New York: Academic Press.

Sanders, M. S. and McCormick, E. J. (1987). *Human factors in engineering and design* (6th ed.). New York: McGraw-Hill.

Scaletti, C. and Craig, A. (1991). Using sound to extract meaning from complex data. *Proceedings of the 1991 SPIE/SPSE Symposium on Electronic Imaging Science and Technology.*

Scalletti, C. (1994). Sound synthesis algorithms for auditory data representations. In Kramer, G. (ed.), *Auditory Display.* New York: Addison-Wesley, 79 - 94.

Scharf, B., and Houtsma, A. J. M. (1986). Audition II: Loudness, pitch, localization, aural distortion, p pathology, In K. R. Boff, L., Kaufman, and J. P. Thomas (Eds.), *Handbook of perception and human performance.* New York: Wiley, Vol. I, 15.1-15.60.

Shepard, R.N. (1964). Circularity in judgements of relative pitch. *Journal of the Acoustical Society of America*, 36, 2346-2353.

Sikora, C., Roberts, L., and Murray, L. T. (1995). Musical vs. real world feedback signals. *CHI'95 Conference Companion*, New York: ACM, 220 - 221.

Smith, S., Bergeron, R.D. and Grinstein, G.G. (1990). Stereoscopic and surface sound generation for exploratory data analysis. *Proceedings of CHI'90, ACM Conference on Human Factors of Computing Systems,* 125-132.

Smith, S., Pickett, R. M., and Williams, M. G. (1994). Environments for exploring auditory representations of multidimensional data. In Kramer, G. (ed.), *Auditory Display.* New York: Addison-Wesley, 79 - 94.

Stevens, R., Brewster, S., Wright, P., and Edwards, A. (1994). Design and evaluation of an auditory glance at algebra for blind readers. In G. Kramer and S. Smith (eds.), *Proceedings of the Second International Conference on Auditory Display* (Santa Fe, N.M, 7-9 November, 1994), 21 - 30.

Stifelman, L., Arons, B., Schmandt, C., and Hulteen, E. (1993). VoiceNotes: A speech interface for a hand-held voice notetaker. In Proceedings of INTERCHI'93, pp.179-186.

Swift, C. G., Flindell, I. H., and Rice, C. G. (1989). Annoyance and implusivity judgments of environmental noises. Proceedings of the Institute of Acoustics 1989 Spring Conference. Vol. 11, Part 5, 551 - 555.

Tufte, E. (1983). *The visual display of quantitative information.* Cheshire, CT: Graphics Press.

Tufte, E. (1990). *Envisioning information.* Cheshire, CT: Graphics Press.

Wenzel, E. M. (1994). Spatial sound and sonification. In Kramer, G. (ed.), *Auditory Display.* New York: Addison-Wesley, 127 - 150.

Wenzel, E. M., Wightman, F.L. and Foster, S.H. (1988). A virtual display for conveying three-dimensional acoustic information. *Proceedings of the Human-Factors Society,* 32, 86-90.

Wenzel, E.M., Wightman, F.L. and Kistler, D.J. (1991). Localization with non-individualized virtual acoustic display cues. *Proceedings of CHI '91*, ACM Conference on Human Factors in Software, 351-359.

Wessel, D. (1979). Timbre space as a musical control structure. *Computer Music Journal*, 3(2), 45-52. Also appear in Roads, C. and Strawn, J. (1985). *Foundations of Computer Music.* Cambridge MA: MIT Press.

Wightman F. L., and Kistler, D. J. (1989). Headphone simulation of free-field listening. I: Stimulus synthesis. *Journal of the Acoustical Society of America*, 85, 858 - 867.

Wildes, R., and Richards, W. (1988). Recovering material properties from sound. Richards, W. (ed.), *Natural computation.* Cambridge, MA: MIT Press.

Handbook of Human-Computer Interaction
Second, completely revised edition
M. Helander, T.K. Landauer, P. Prabhu (eds.)

Chapter 43

Design Issues for Interfaces using Voice Input

Candace Kamm
Applied Speech Research Department
AT&T Bell Laboratories
Murray Hill, New Jersey, USA

Martin Helander
Division of Industrial Ergonomics
Linköping Institute of Technology
Linköping, Sweden

43.1 Introduction

Automatic speech recognition (ASR) is a technology for communicating with a computer using spoken words or phrases. Speech interfaces provide an additional input modality for human-computer interaction, either as a component of a multi-modal system combined with manual input or when other input modalities are occupied, unavailable, or not usable. Speech interfaces are often characterized as being "more natural" than other types of input devices (e.g., keyboard, mouse, touch screen), because they provide more human-like communication. Several studies (Chapanis et al., 1972, 1977; Kelly and Chapanis, 1977; Michaelis et al., 1977; Ochsman and Chapanis, 1974; Cohen, 1984; Oviatt and Cohen, 1991) have demonstrated the improved efficiency of speech over other modalities for human-human communication. An underlying assumption for the desirability of human-computer speech interfaces is that the skills and expectations that users have developed through everyday communication (speaking to other humans) will result in speech being more efficient and effective than alternative methods for transferring information between human and machine (Leiser, 1989). There are additional benefits for tasks that require focused attention on the screen. In this situation manual input may be distracting and speech is preferred.

An ideal voice interface would be one that performed flawlessly for spontaneously spoken input on any topic - not only transcribing the spoken words correctly, also understanding their meaning and generating appropriate responses or actions as a consequence. This is referred to as spoken language understanding (SLU). Although we encounter this ideal interface frequently in science fiction, current technology does not support completely unrestricted spoken input. However, over the past decade, there have been significant incremental improvements in the technology, along with substantial human factors efforts in applying the technology in ways that overcome its remaining limitations. As a result, speech recognition interfaces have been useful and successful in limited applications, in-

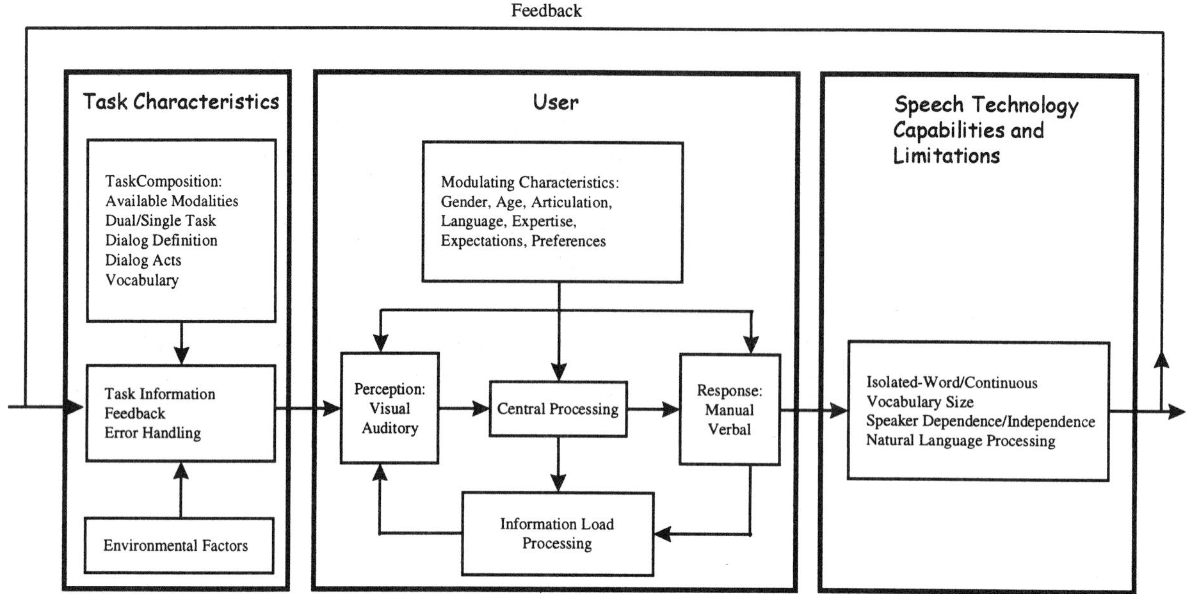

Figure 1. A systems view of user interfaces for voice application.

cluding command and control, information retrieval, dictation, computer-aided design, and transaction processing in limited domains. Figure 1 shows a system level overview of the issues that must be considered in developing a speech interface.

As shown in Figure 1, the task, the user, and the speech recognition system form a control system with error feedback. To optimize the performance of this system and to create successful applications, the user interface designer must consider not only the capabilities of the technology, but also the effects of the task requirements and environment, as well as user's expectations, expertise, and capabilities. As with every other computer interface, it is important to analyze the task characteristics and design a computer dialogue that is consistent and in agreement with user expectations.

This analysis is critical when speech is the only available input modality, and becomes even more complex for systems where ASR is used simultaneously with manual input through keyboards and other devices. Such tasks usually involve several task components that are allocated between auditory and visual displays and where the input may be via voice or manually. To design such a system, the characteristics of human information processing, and particularly the capacity for handling multi-modal tasks, must also be considered.

This chapter reviews human factors issues in ASR interfaces. First, a brief overview of automatic speech recognition is presented, along with a discussion of current capabilities and limitations of the technology. Then we discuss user and task characteristics and describe several speech interface design strategies that have been used to create successful applications despite mismatches between user expectations and technological capabilities. A final section identifies several research areas that are critical for advancing toward truly "natural" speech-based computer-human interfaces that provide optimal efficiency, effectiveness, and usability.

43.2 Automatic Speech Recognition

43.2.1 ASR Technology Overview

Speech recognition is fundamentally a pattern matching task. A speaker talks into a microphone and the computer system digitizes the speech signal, analyzes various characteristics of the incoming speech, and finds the "best" match of the incoming speech to models of speech sequences the system was trained on. Automatic speech recognition is a difficult task because the speech signal is highly variable - across speakers (e.g., gender, age, accent), speaking rate, context, and acoustic conditions (e.g., back ground

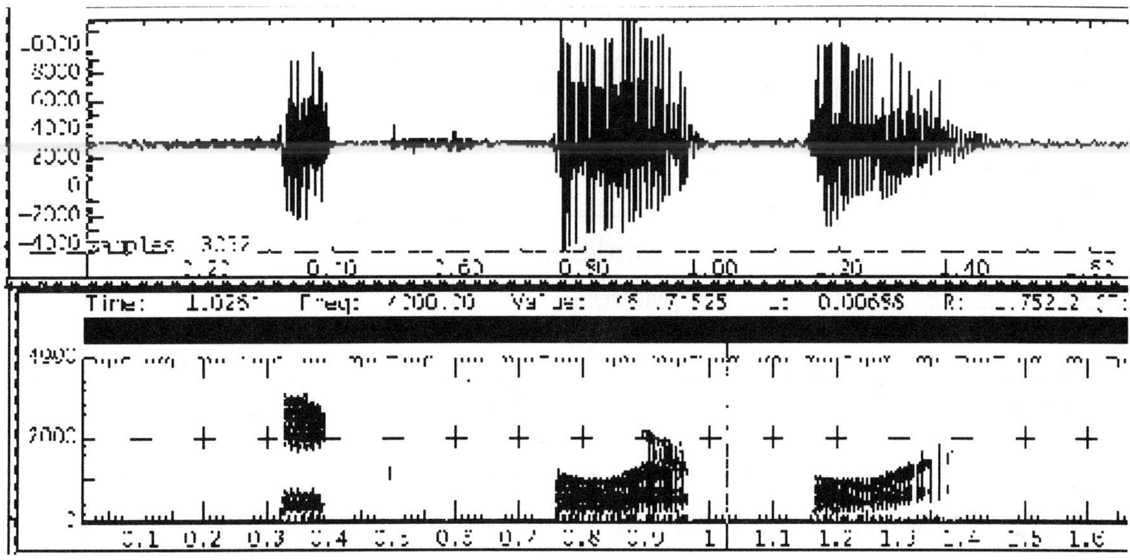

Figure 2. Speech waveform (upper panel) and speech spectrogram (lower panel) of the utterance "six, four, four" spoken by a female talker. *The speech waveform displays amplitude of the speech signal over time. The spectrogram is a 3-dimensional display showing frequency on the ordinate, time on the abscissa, and relative intensity of the various frequency components in the utterance indicated by the gray scale.*

noise, transmission characteristics of the microphone). The task in speech recognition is to determine which of the variations are salient for discriminating among the words in the recognizer's vocabulary. Speech is a dynamic signal, varying in frequency composition and amplitude over time. The upper panel in Figure 2 shows a speech waveform of the phrase "six-four-four", plotting signal amplitude on the ordinate and time on the abscissa. A speech spectrogram of the same utterance is shown in the lower panel of Figure 2. A spectrogram is a three-dimensional spectro-temporal representation of the speech signal, with time on the abscissa, frequency plotted on the ordinate, and the intensity of speech energy plotted as the gray scale, where darker bands show regions of higher energy. Research on human perception of speech has demonstrated that, for many of the sounds in a language, the most salient cues are the locations in time and frequency of the major concentrations of energy in the speech signal (called formants). (Notice the similarity in the formants of the vowel portion of the two repetitions of "four", from 0.64 to 0.94 seconds and 1.16 to 1.55 seconds.)

In contrast, a word's identity is generally unaffected by the absolute durations of its component sounds, which can vary considerably depending on the position of the word within a sentence, the degree of emphasis or stress that is placed on the word, and overall speaking rate. (Note the longer duration of the second utterance of the word "four" in the lower portion of Figure 2).

Most speech recognition systems make use of this acoustic-phonetic knowledge, representing the speech signal spectrally to extract frequency information, and incorporating algorithms that ensure that non-salient duration differences do not affect recognition decisions. Figure 3 shows the basic components of a speech recognition system. The feature extraction component performs an acoustic analysis of successive short duration segments (typically 10-30 msec) of the incoming speech to extract a set of spectral features. Among the most widely-used spectral representations are spectral amplitudes derived from fast Fourier transform (FFT) or filter bank outputs (sometimes scaled to reflect the frequency selectivity characteristics of the human auditory system), Linear Predictive Coding (LPC) coefficients (based on the source/filter model of the human vocal tract), and cepstrum coefficients (For a review of feature representations and analysis techniques, see Rabiner and Juang, 1993).

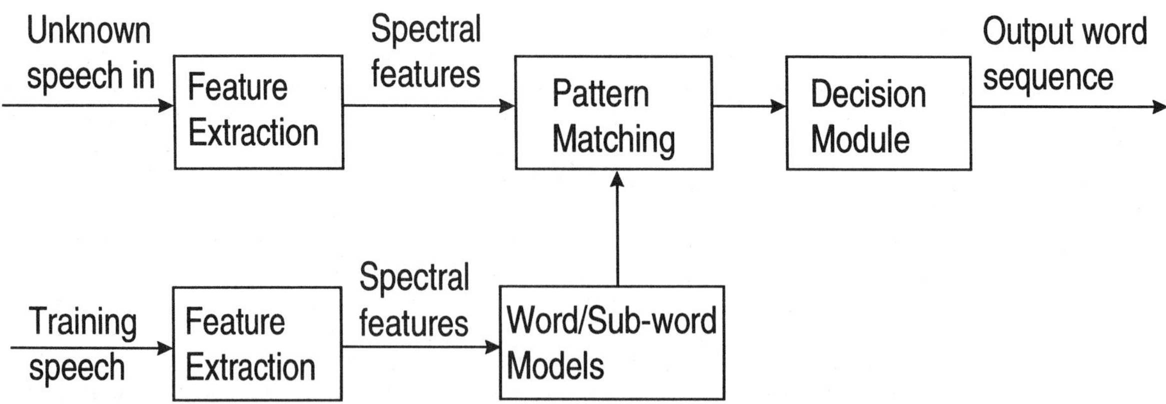

Figure 3. Basic components of a speech recognition system.

The second component in Figure 3 is a pattern matching component. The purpose is to align a sequence of spoken feature vectors against a set of stored reference units or models obtained which have been obtained earlier during the training process. The pattern matching component determines which model (or sequence of models) optimally represents the input speech. The basic set of reference units may consist of complete words in the recognition vocabulary (whole-word recognition) or may model sub-word units (for example, the speech sounds or phones in a language), which can be concatenated into sequences to represent any word in the language.

A major advantage of using phone-based units is the ability to add to or modify the recognition vocabulary without collecting new training sets for new vocabulary items. The disadvantage of sub-word systems is that their performance may not be as robust as that of comparable whole-word systems, which can more accurately model the acoustic variability that occurs within a word due to coarticulation effects of neighboring phones. The performance of sub-word systems improves substantially when the sub-word model set is expanded to include separate models for the same phone in different phonemic contexts (c.f. Huang, Lee, Hon, and Hwang, 1991).

Four basic classes of pattern matchers have been used for speech recognition: template matchers, rule-based systems, neural networks, and Hidden Markov Models (HMMs). Roe and Wilpon (1993) and Mariani (1989) provide a more detailed discussion of these methods. Currently, Hidden Markov Model (HMMs) are the most successful speech recognition algorithms and are used in most applications (Roe and Wilpon, 1993). The use of HMMs involve stochastic modeling to decode a sequence of symbols. This provides a powerful representation of speech as a two-stage probabilistic process. (See Rabiner (1989), for a tutorial on the use of HMMs for speech recognition.). Speech is modeled as a sequence of transitions through states. For example, an HMM can be used to represent a word, with internal states representing characteristic acoustic segments (e.g., phones). Associated with each state are two sets of probabilities: state probabilities, defining the probability of observing one of a set of symbols or features while in a particular state, and transition probabilities, specifying the probabilities for moving from one state to another. These two sets of probabilities are assumed to be independent. Each word in the vocabulary is associated with an HMM, and the state and transition probabilities for each word HMM are estimated from the statistics obtained by processing a large corpus of training speech containing numerous examples of the words in the vocabulary. During recognition, the pattern classification is accomplished by determining which of the HMMs has the highest statistical likelihood of having produced the observed sequence of acoustic vectors in the input speech.

Part of the power and flexibility of the HMM approach is the ability to represent different levels of the speech recognition task in the HMM framework. For example, an HMM can represent a sub-word unit (e.g., a context-dependent phone), with its internal states representing an arbitrary partitioning of the phone into initial, medial, and final portions. Or, an HMM can represent a phrase or sentence, with the internal states representing words, and the transition probabilities for moving from state to state based on the frequency of occurrence of word sequences observed in the training data. Thus, a recognition system can be composed of a structural hierarchy of HMMs, with sentence HMMs composed of word HMMs, which are in turn composed of sub-word HMMs (Levinson, 1985). The output of the pattern classification component of a recognizer is the "best" hypothesis (or the top-N hypotheses) for the word or word sequence in the input utterance. The decision component may apply additional criteria for choosing among alternatives with similar likelihood scores or to determine whether the best choice is "good enough" to be reliable. Most recognition systems apply a "rejection" criterion, so that no recognition decision is made if even the best match to the input speech is not very good. (If the input speech is not in the recognizer's vocabulary, for example, "rejection" is the correct decision for the recognizer to return.)

The decision component may consider only the acoustic likelihoods computed during the pattern classification stage, or it can also incorporate language processing (Roe and Wilpon, 1993). Currently, most ASR systems fold rudimentary "language processing" back into the pattern classification component by including language models based on the probabilities of observing particular word sequences in the training data or by explicitly defining a grammar (i.e., specifying the entire set of legal word sequences used in the application). This technique improves performance by constraining the recognizer's task, but it can be relatively brittle, since it cannot deal well with input utterances that stray from the expected word sequences, even when the meaning of the input sentence may be identical to that of a valid word sequence. This reliance on a rigid grammar demonstrates a fundamental difference between most currently-deployed speech recognition systems and research systems for spoken language understanding that attempt to use higher-level linguistic knowledge from syntactic and semantic analysis to allow unconstrained spontaneous speech input. (Spoken language understanding systems will be described further later in this chapter, in the section on Research Trends).

43.2.2 ASR Dimensions

ASR systems are generally differentiated along several dimensions that reflect the kinds of speech input that they can handle. Speaker-dependent systems require training using examples of the speech of each person who uses the system. Speaker-independent systems are trained on a large corpus of utterances spoken by many different people, in an attempt to capture the range of characteristics of the expected user population. As a result, speaker-independent systems may be used by people who do not have prior experience with or exposure to the system.

Obviously, for applications where the identity of the user is unknown or where training is impossible, speaker independent systems are required. Current performance of speaker-independent systems approaches that of speaker-dependent systems for some applications. Some systems use speaker-independent sub-word models to build user-specific vocabularies, such as personal dialing lists for voice dialing applications (Wilpon, 1994).

Speaker-adaptive systems are speaker-independent systems that have the additional feature of updating the system during an interaction with a user, based on small amounts of user speech. Thereby the match between the models in the system and the user's speech is improved. Most large vocabulary dictation systems use speaker adaptation techniques.

A second factor influencing ASR performance is the fluency of the input speech. Unlike written input, where the separation of the input into words is reliably detectable as white space between words, normal conversation does not have predictable silences between words - in fact, some of the "silences" in a speech signal occur within a single speech sound (for example, the silent gap from 0.35-0.39 sec in the lower panel of Figure 2 is part of the stop consonant /k/ in the word "six"). As a consequence, segmenting a speech signal into individual words is a difficult problem.

Some speech recognizers require that the input be spoken as isolated words or phrases. Most of the commercially-available products for automatic dictation require slight pauses, although there are research prototypes for dictation that use continuous recognition. These more advanced systems permit users to speak more normally, but generally at the cost of slightly poorer performance. "Word spotting" technology, which can recognize a vocabulary word embedded in a continuous speech stream, has been extremely successful in dealing with minor disfluencies and hesitations in user speech, relaxing the strict requirement for isolated word input. Performance of "word spotting" technology deteriorates as vocabulary size increases, so systems that use "word spotting" typically deal with relatively small vocabularies (<100 words).

Vocabulary size also influences recognizer performance. In general, as vocabulary size increases, the acoustic confusability among the words in the vocabulary also increases. To achieve adequate recognition accuracy (and therefore usable applications) with very large vocabularies, (e.g. 100,000 word dictation systems), it is necessary to use additional information beyond the word pronunciation models - most importantly, knowledge of the probabilities of word sequences in the language or for the particular task domain. This language modeling technique constrains the set of words the recognizer may consider at any point in decoding a word sequence, and improves overall recognition performance.

Variability in the transmission channel that transmits the speech from the user to the recognizer is another dimension that influences recognizer performance. Speech signals that are corrupted by distortions introduced by the transmission channel (e.g., limited bandwidth such as telephone transmission, coding noise, distorting introduced by wireless transmission) or background acoustic conditions (high environmental noise or extraneous speech by the speaker or other talkers) are more difficult for speech recognizers to handle successfully than high-quality speech. In addition, user characteristics such as accent (regional or foreign), speaking-rate, and involuntary changes in speech production due to psychological stress (such as induced in an air plane cockpit by information overload or high noise G-forces) affect the user's speech pattern and thereby hamper ASR performance.

The most common method of dealing with differences in speech pattern is to train the speech recognizer using samples of speech of real users collected under the same environmental/acoustic conditions that are likely to be encountered when the ASR system is used.

43.2.3 System Capabilities

Several system capabilities not directly related to speech technology per se also affect the success of voice interfaces. Some systems are incapable of "listening" to speech input while they simultaneously produce speech. The user must then wait until the speech prompt is completed before responding. The user interface for these systems must be designed to detect and discourage violations of this protocol by the user. Much more natural are systems that detect human speech during prompts and interrupt the prompt. These types of systems electronically cancel echoes from the outbound prompt so that the signal reaching the recognizer includes only speech from the user, and when user speech is detected, stop playing the remainder of the outbound prompt. Some systems implement this "barge-in" capability as soon as any incoming speech or speech-like signal is detected, while others wait until there is evidence that the incoming speech is likely to be a valid word or phrase in the recognition vocabulary. The former strategy produces a quick reaction to user interruptions of the system, but also has a high probability of triggering falsely on unintended speech or noises from the user or the user's environment. The recognition-based strategy will have fewer false alarms, but the "reaction" time of the system in stopping a prompt in response to user input will be slower. "Barge-in" may also slightly reduce overall ASR performance, because of distortions introduced by the echo cancellation process. In addition, allowing barge-in may increase ambiguity regarding which prompt the user's input was intended to address. As a result, the user interface for a system with barge in may need a more complex strategy for determining whether responses that interrupt prompts are delayed responses to prior prompts or anticipatory responses to the interrupted prompt. Despite these potential drawbacks, "barge-in" capability is an advance that has improved the "naturalness" of speech interfaces significantly, particularly for applications where the system prompts are lengthy.

Long system response times and lack of feedback create user dissatisfaction (Shriberg, Wade and Price, 1992). To provide feedback to users systems with slow response times for speech and language processing can play interim messages (e.g., "Please wait, your request is being processed."). This reduces perceived response time and increases user acceptance. With continuing advances in processor speed and in the efficiency of recognition search and language processing algorithms, near real-time system response is becoming feasible even for complex speech understanding tasks, so system response time may soon cease to be a significant interface issue.

In most applications, the speech system is only a small component of a larger system, and constraints on system architecture or resources may have a major impact on the user interface. For example, in telephone network applications, resource limitations may require in order to access the recognizer, the customer must dial a special access code rather than having the ASR system immediately "on line" whenever the customer picks up the telephone. Other system constraints that can influence the design of the user interface include whether a human agent is available in the event of recognition failure and whether relevant information and databases are available throughout the interaction or only during fixed portions of the interaction.

43.2.4 Characterizing ASR Performance

All speech recognition systems, whether computer or human, make errors. In characterizing ASR performance on an application, it is important to consider how the system performs not only when it is presented with

Table 1. Input speech categories and corresponding outcomes in speech recognition.

Input Speech Categories	**Speech Recognition Outcomes**			
	Recognition Hypothesis Matches Input	Recognition Hypothesis Does Not Match Input	No Recognition Decision	No Speech Detected
Target Vocabulary Only	correct recognition	substitution error	rejection error	deletion error
Embedded Target	correct recognition	substitution error	rejection error	deletion error
Out of Vocabulary - Relevant	impossible outcome	false acceptance	correct rejection	detection error
Out of Vocabulary - Irrelevant	impossible outcome	false acceptance	correct rejection	detection error
Non-speech	impossible outcome	false acceptance	correct rejection	correct outcome

speech conforming to the vocabulary it expects, but more generally how it performs over the set of all the acoustic input that it "hears" during the interaction. To describe recognition performance, it is useful to consider the relationships between the different possible outcomes of a speech recognition event and the different speech inputs that trigger those outcomes. Table 1 shows a matrix relating speech recognition outcomes to different categories of input speech. The set of inputs to the speech recognizer includes: a) utterances containing words and phrases that are within the "target" vocabulary of the recognizer, b) utterances containing words within the vocabulary, but in the presence words that are not in the vocabulary ("embedded target"), c) words that are outside the vocabulary, but that express the same intent from the user ("out of vocabulary - relevant"), d) speech that are irrelevant to the task ("out of vocabulary - irrelevant"), and e) non-speech events and noises. So, for example, if the vocabulary for the recognizer consisted of the two words "yes" and "no", the utterance "yes, I will" would be considered an "embedded target", the utterance "sure" could be considered "out of vocabulary - relevant", and the utterance "what time is it?" would be considered "out of vocabulary - irrelevant".

There are four types of recognizer outcomes: a) a recognition decision is made and the recognized word matches the actual word spoken, b) a recognition decision is made, but the recognized word does not match the input word, c) no recognition decision is made because the recognizer failed to detect spoken words, and d) no recognition decision is acted on because the best hypothesis was not good enough relative to a rejection criterion set by the system designer.

Recognition errors result when the following combinations of speech input and recognizer outcome co-occur. Substitution errors occur when an utterance in the target vocabulary is misrecognized as another vocabulary item, and false acceptances occur when a non-vocabulary item is recognized as a vocabulary item. Deletion errors occur when a target vocabulary item is not detected. Insertion errors occur when a non-target utterance is recognized as a target item. Rejection errors occur when a target item is detected but not recognized. When out of vocabulary inputs are detected but not recognized, the system is correctly rejecting the input.

There is a trade-off between false acceptance errors and rejection errors that depends on the preset threshold for rejection. Because the importance and cost of different kinds of errors differs widely depending on the task and the reliability of error correction strategies, optimal rejection thresholds are necessarily task-dependent.

In describing performance of speech recognition systems it is important to describe performance in terms of the range of inputs that the system encounters in a real task. Limiting the performance statistics to only the "target vocabulary" inputs may not reflect actual task completion rates or user's perceptions of system performance. For example, in a task where most of the utterances do not contain target vocabulary, having a low false acceptance rate may require tolerating a higher rejection rate, because, a rejection error that leads to a reprompting of the user for additional input may not be as detrimental to task completion as a false acceptance error that initiates an inappropriate action. In addition, from the user's viewpoint, "target", "embedded target" and "out of vocabulary -relevant" inputs may all seem legitimate, so rejection of an input utterance that is "out of vocabulary -relevant" may appear to the user as a system error, even though it is the "correct" response for the recognizer.

43.2.5 Current ASR Applications

Current speech applications incorporate tasks that range from very simple ones to those that are very complex. An example of a simple application is when the tasks requires the system to recognize single words, such as binary-choice response to a single question (e.g., "Say yes if you will accept this collect call; say no if you won't"). A complex task is when the user speaks in sentences or phrases conforming to a restricted grammar. An even more complex task scenario is the recognition of a complex query addressing a limited domain (e.g., "What times are the flights between Dallas and Boston on Monday?").

The interfaces to these applications can be highly structured, with either the computer or the user primarily responsible for controlling and directing the interaction, or more conversational, with mixed initiative - that is, the computer and the user frequently switching between the directive and passive participant roles during the course of the dialog. These applications differ in the amount and type of information that needs to be exchanged during the interaction and also in the size and composition of the application vocabulary. In addition, applications may vary in the input and output modalities available to the user, as well as in the costs of interaction failures.

Current applications demonstrate a wide range of capabilities and performance. Although spoken-language understanding systems (SLUs) are not yet commercially available, prototype SLUs for completing interactions in limited domains handle vocabularies of 300 to 1000 words and can accept spontaneous speech without user training (Appelt and Jackson, 1992; Pallett, 1992). Examples of these systems include travel planning and providing directions. Currently, they achieve an understanding rate of about 70% (Cole, Hirschman, et al., 1992).

Several commercially-available voice dictation systems incorporate speaker-dependent or speaker-adaptive isolated word recognition technology for 5000 to 100,000 word vocabularies (Makhoul and Schwartz, 1993). In contrast, most current telephone applications area restricted to small vocabularies, limited grammars, and word-spotting technology in order to maintain acceptable recognition accuracy in the more adverse and variable electro-acoustic environment of the public switched telephone network. Rudnicky, Hauptmann and Lee (1994) surveyed error rates for different ASR tasks and reported word error rates ranging from 0.4% per word for speaker-independent continuous speech recognition of digits, to 4% for speaker-independent isolated word recognition for the letters of the English alphabet, to 5-13% error rates for speaker-independent continuous speech dictation systems.

43.3 Interactions with User Abilities, Behaviors, and Expectations

Speech input is often portrayed as a "natural" interface modality because people are familiar with using speech to communicate. This extensive prior experience actually brings about some drawbacks for the still imperfect ASR technology. Because users have so much experience with human-human speech interactions many things are taken for granted. New users may expect a human-computer voice interface to allow the same conversational speech style that is used between humans. When the system cannot perform accurately with normal conversational speech input, the user is typically instructed to speak in the manner that the recognition system has been designed to accept, such as making distinct pauses between words. However, many speech behaviors are over-learned, and it is difficult for users to overcome these habits. This may be particularly true if the system has limited grammar capability, because the user may erroneously conclude that the system understands "natural speech". Three common behaviors are: a) speaking in a continuous manner; that is without pausing between words, b) anticipating responses and speaking at the same time as the other talker, and c) interpreting pauses by the other talker as implicit exchange of turn and permission to speak.

The use of pauses between words is unnatural, and the tendency to speak continuously is difficult to correct, particularly when the user's is focused on completing a task. In an early telephone application that used isolated-word speech recognition technology, users were required to recite a seven-digit telephone number and pause briefly after each digit. In one study, 35% of the customers who spoke seven-digit numbers did not speak the digits in an isolated manner. This demonstrates the difficulty people have in overcoming the natural behavior of speaking without inter-word pauses, even when they are instructed to do so (Wilpon, 1985). In another telephone study only 37% of the customers responded with appropriate inter-word pauses (Yashchin et al., 1989).

In spontaneous speech, people often produce extraneous speech and hesitation sounds (like "uh" or "um"), particularly when restarting or repairing. The inability to reliably coax humans to speak in isolation, without any non-vocabulary words or sounds, has been a driving force for the development of word-spotting and continuous speech recognition algorithms. Word-spotting allows accurate recognition of a small vocabulary in the presence of non-vocabulary utterances, even when they are modified by the co-articulatory effects introduced by continuous speech.

In conversational settings, participants often begin to respond as soon as they understand the speaker's request. In an analysis of fifty conversations between telephone service representatives and customers, Karis and Dobroth (1991) observed that overlapping speech occurred on 12.1% of the utterances of service representatives and 14.4% of the customer's utterances. This simultaneity rarely impairs the information flow in human-human dialogs and, as a result, most users expect that their speech will be heard and understood even if the other person is still talking. This behavior has been a primary driver for the development of "barge in" capability in ASR systems.

In a human-human dialog subtle cues in the speech signal are used by the participants to indicate that they want to take or release control of the speaking role or to confirm that they understand or have been understood by the other party. Violating these cues can cause difficulties in user interfaces. Turn-taking permission is often conveyed by prosodic pauses. In an early implementation of an automated billing service for collect calls, customers were responding consistently at a particular phrase break (i.e., brief pause) during the system's prompt (Bossemeyer and Schwab, 1990) but before the system was ready to accept speech input. These customers interpreted the pause at the phrase break as an invitation to take the floor and respond to the prompt. After the pause duration in the prompt was shortened, users were much more likely to wait until the appropriate response window to respond, and the user interface was more successful. Balentine and Scott (1992) described an interface that takes advantage of the predictability of the turn-taking that is likely to occur during pauses. In their system, the recognizer is activated during pauses between items, so that the user can respond immediately after hearing the menu item he/she wants. If the recognized word matches the menu item, the system proceeds to that selection. If the recognized word is ambiguous, the system asks for confirmation about whether the menu item presented before the interruption is the desired selection.

Users also have different expectations and needs depending on their experience with a particular system. First-time or infrequent users are likely to require instructions and/or guidance through a system to allow them to build a cognitive model of how the system works and how to interact with it. In contrast, experienced users who interact frequently with the system want ways to bypass the instructions and move through the interaction more efficiently. Similarly in human-human collaborative dialogs, users increase the efficiency of the interaction as they gain experience and abbreviate portions of the dialog to the minimum sufficient information necessary to accomplish the task (Leiser, 1989). For example, confirmation utterances become shorter or occur less frequently, and unnecessary function words may be omitted (e.g., "There are 48 pages in volume I, 42 in volume II, 36 in III"). Successful user interfaces for automated systems should accommodate both the needs of novices and the preferences of expert users.

43.4 Task Composition and Analysis: When is Voice Input Useful?

The rapidly advancing state of ASR technology offers a myriad of choices to interface designers. It is currently feasible to design a system that uses speaker-independent, continuous speech recognition for transaction tasks, as long as the task is constrained by a restricted grammar so that the recognition problem is relatively trivial. With a well-designed dialog, these systems can work quite well for cooperative users in benign environments. At the other extreme, however, are applications where unsuspecting or less motivated users encounter an ASR system under more adverse conditions. These applications generally rely on technology with more limited capabilities and require a more structured interaction to maintain adequate task performance.

For some applications, the decision to use speech input is based on necessity. Speech has been identified as a potentially advantageous input modality when the user's hands or eyes are busy, when keyboard input or screen output is limited or not available (e.g., telephone applications), or for disabled users (Cohen and Oviatt, 1994). For other applications, speech input is just one of several possibilities. The main criteria for evaluating the success of ASR is productivity or effectiveness of the interface for the task. Several studies have compared voice entry to other types of input devices. There seems to be no clear trend in their results - sometimes manual entry is faster and sometimes voice entry is the most efficient - not surprisingly, it depends on the task. Skriver (1987) compared the time to enter text and data using keyboard and speech recognition. He found that keyboard entry was 11% faster than voice recognition and that the time for error correction was about three times greater for voice input than for manual input. Reising and Curry (1987) compared the efficiency of voice recognition to manual control for a menu-selection task in a cockpit environment. In the manual task, command names were chosen by touch control from menu selections in a multi-layered menu. Subjects performed a simultaneous loading task which consisted of manual tracking in a video game. Voice entry was superior to manual entry, with lower error rate and task completion times for voice input. In a second experiment, the manual entry was modified so that the most commonly used functions were immediately available on the first level of the menu. In this case, task completion times for voice recognition and manual control were similar, but voice recognition induced more errors. The authors concluded that the advantage of either voice recognition or manual entry depends upon task characteristics. Both the manual and the voice systems must first be optimized so that fair comparisons of both task efficiency and user preference can be made.

In a multi-modal condition, speech input can not be viewed solely as an alternative to other modalities, but rather as working in coordination with other modalities. The availability of several modalities allows the user to select the most efficient modality for entering input. It also allows the system to request an alternative input modality if it determines that the present modal-ity being used is not productive. For example, in a telephone application where disturbances from background noise is consistently resulting in incorrect recognition, the system may ask the user to switch to the telephone keypad so that the task can be completed successfully.

Interfaces that make use of multiple modalities may exploit the strengths and the weaknesses of the different modalities. From a cognitive processing standpoint, Sandry and Wickens (1982) pointed out that a task with both visual/manual and auditory/speech components is ideal for time sharing, because there is little competition for information processing resources. A task with such dual features results in better performance than if the components are performed with either mode individually. Certain tasks may be better suited for visual presentation and manual control than for auditory presentation and speech control. For example, a tracking task performed in the cockpit is better suited for manual control than for speech, since the tracking task is continuous in nature while speech input is discrete. Wickens, Vidulich, and Sandry-Garza (1984) presented the results of a dual task experiment where they concluded that verbal tasks are best served by auditory input and speech responses, whereas spatial tasks are best served by visual input and manual responses. Oviatt and Olsen (1994) examined how people integrate spoken and written input during multi-modal computer-human interaction, and observed that task content, presentation format (unconstrained versus form-filling), and contrastive functionality determined users' selection of either speech or writing. Subjects tended to use speech and writing in contrastive ways to designate a shift in content or functionality (for example, to indicate original versus corrected text, data versus command, digits versus text). Multi-modal input was preferred over unimodal speech or writing.

Whether a speech interface is used in unimodal or multi-modal applications, the success of the application as a whole depends on a careful design of the interfaces (voice, screen, type of feedback, etc.). This requires an understanding of the principles for interface design for each modality and the cognitive implications of using single or multiple modalities. Figure 4 illustrates how a task analysis could be performed (Helander, Moody, Joost, 1988).

In Figure 4 the various subtasks are identified first. In the case of multi-modal interfaces, this includes determining which subtasks might be combined into dual task entities that could be performed simultaneously using voice and manual input. Dialogues are designed for each modality, along with adjunct presentation features (e.g., screen layout for visual modalities, vocabularies and grammars for speech input). The systems are then evaluated during user tests and improved in an iterative design procedure.

43.5 User Interface Strategies

Guided by the initial analysis of task, user characteristics, and technological factors, the user interface de-

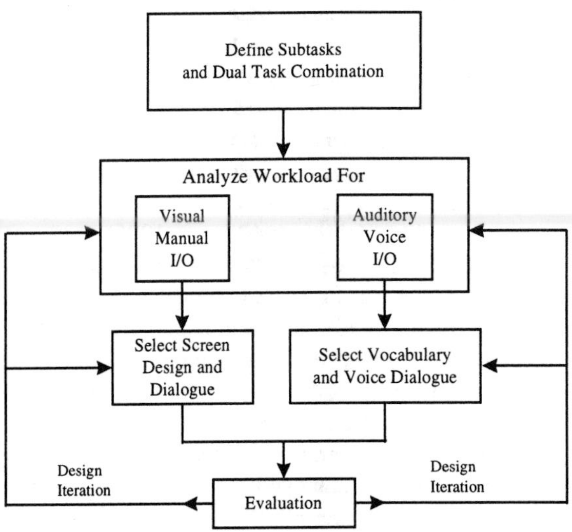

Figure 4. Task analysis for dual task manual and voice interface.

signer can use strategies that take advantage of the technological capabilities while simultaneously side-step technological limitations. These include dialog flow strategies using appropriately directive and informative prompts and the use of sub-dialog modules to provide access to instructions, to confirm that the user's input has been correctly recognized, and to detect errors and recover from them. Theses issues will be addressed in the following sections.

43.5.1 Dialog Design

Underlying every user interface is a plan for obtaining the (Mazor, Zeigler, and Braun, 1992) necessary to complete the task. Speech interfaces currently in use range in complexity from simple command and control applications, generally requiring only a single information element to initiate an action, to transaction processing, where the number of information elements required to complete the task is obtained through multiple queries and in variable order, requiring a protracted dialog between the system and the user.

The information requirements of the task are central to the development of any user interface. For applications that would otherwise occur as human-human dialogs, it is essential to understand how the dialog typically progresses between humans. This can help identify the information that must be elicited from the user in order to accomplish the task. Analysis of human-human interaction can also identify information that is unnecessary and not critical to task completion. The user interface designer can use this knowledge to determine a natural order for eliciting the information elements, and to determine how much effort should be expended in eliciting each element (Mazor, Zeigler, and Braun, 1992). The observation that users interact quite differently with machines than with humans, argues against models of human-human dialog. However, analysis of the human-human interaction may help define task vocabulary, suggest appropriate wording for prompts, and identify the probable syntax of frequent responses.

Some applications never had a human-human analog, but were originally designed as automated systems with keyboard input. Although analysis of such systems can provide useful insights of voice interfaces, they may sometimes be misleading. For example, an automated bank-by-phone application using input from the telephone keypad may use an audio menu to direct the user: "For checking (account balance), press 1, for savings, press 2". Early implementations of voice interfaces for such systems directly translated this request into "For checking, say 1; for savings, say 2", rather than: "Do you want the your account balance for checking or savings?" For the key-based interface, the non-semantically-related vocabulary (press 1 or press 2) is necessary because of the limitations inherent in the design of numerical keyboards. For ASR the use of meaningful vocabulary can make the task easier.

In highly structured interactions, the order of acquiring information elements may be explicitly defined, whereas in more conversational interfaces, the order in which the information is gathered may be controlled more by the user. Yankelovich (1994) defined the primary design principles for a conversational interface as a) maintaining conversational flow by including barge-in technology and allowing mixed initiative, b) maintaining context, and c) providing sufficient feedback to handle recognition errors. Zeigler and Mazor (1995) described an automated system for generating telephone-service-disconnect orders that uses a highly structured transaction, but with carefully chosen natural queries to elicit responses consistent with the ASR vocabulary requirements. In both structured and mixed initiative systems, however, vocabulary design and prompt wording are critical to success.

43.5.2 Vocabulary Design

The selection of vocabulary words for ASR is a crucial component in system design. From the user's perspective, the vocabulary must be memorable and meaningfully associated with the task. At the same time, from the system designer's viewpoint, the vocabulary words must be selected to minimize the likelihood that the speech recognizer will confuse words.

The memorability of vocabulary words might be enhanced if users could select the vocabulary words that are meaningful and natural to them for a particular task. The primary disadvantage to this strategy is that users may choose words that are acoustically similar. For example, the words "on" and "off" may be very natural commands for a user, but spoken over the reduced bandwidth of the telephone network, most of the acoustic distinctions between these two words are lost, and they are not ideal vocabulary candidates for that reason.)

Some recognition systems calculate a confusion index (MacAuley, 1984) that provides information regarding the probability of correct recognition for each vocabulary item and identifies any likely confusion of two or more vocabulary items, thereby allowing vocabulary items to be changed. Roe and Riley (1994) described a tool for detecting phonetically similar words based on pronunciations generated by a text-to-speech synthesis system and phonetic confusions exhibited by a phone-based recognizer. These systems do not completely predict the errors of a recognition system, but they show general agreement with the recognizer's errors and may be useful for improving speech recognition performance by flagging word pairs that are likely to be highly confusable.

Another way to increase the flexibility of the vocabulary, and thus make it "memorable" for more users, is to use "multiple mappings". Several alternative command words or phrases hare then given the same interpretation (compare the problem in the Yellow pages of finding an attorney or a lawyer). In this case, a user is free to say any one of the command synonyms (presumably the one that is most natural and memorable to the user) rather than having to learn a specific command.

All other factors being equal, polysyllabic words are generally easier to recognize than monosyllabic words. For example, the letters of the American English alphabet constitute a particularly difficult vocabulary: Almost all are monosyllables, and they differ by a single phoneme (such as for the letters b, c, d, e, v, t, p, z, g). Similarly, polysyllabic words pairs with overlapping subparts, such as "repair" and "despair" are frequently confused by recognition systems.

43.5.3 Prompts

Prompts are used to elicit spoken user responses. They are critical to the success of a speech interface. When visual screen output is available, it may be possible to display the legal vocabulary for the user, but when only speech output is available, it is generally impractical, slow, and unacceptable to the user to list all the vocabulary options at every point in a dialog. A careful construction of prompts to emphasize brevity and to provide semantic and prosodic cues can result in a productive interaction (Zeigler and Mazor, 1995).

Prompts that include words in the recognition vocabulary can increase user compliance to system restrictions. Kamm (1994) described a study of customer responses to alternate billing prompts. She demonstrated that the percentage of acceptable inputs to a word recognition system with a two word vocabulary ("yes" and "no") increased from about 55% to 81% when the prompt was changed from "Will you accept the charges (for a collect call)?" to "Say yes if you will accept the call; otherwise, say no". Other studies of the similar applications have demonstrated similar effects (Bossemeyer and Schwab, 1990; Spitz et al., 1991).

Prompts can also be used after ambiguous input or error conditions to tell the user how to modify the next input to improve the chances of recognition. For example, in a study of voice-activated dialing Yashchin et al. (1994) noted that if the system detected high energy at the beginning of the input to the recognizer and simultaneously had low certainty about the accuracy of the recognized word or phrase, it was assumed that the user spoke too early. The user was re-prompted to "please speak after the beep" (with stress on the word "after").

43.5.4 Instructions

In order to use a system efficiently and effectively, the user must know what is expected and how the system can provide instructions. For simple tasks, the instructions may consist of a single prompt. For more complicated interactions with a variety of options, the instructions may be quite lengthy and detailed. To support mixed initiative interactions, users should have the option of accessing instructions. The system should also offer instructions if the user's behavior suggests that they are needed.

A stock quotation application developed at Bell Northern Research (Lennig et al., 1992) includes extensive instructions describing the capabilities of the system. The brief welcoming prompt to this service tells the user to say the name of the stock, or "Instructions" to hear the instructions. Thus, the expert user can bypass the instructions and progress directly to the primary task. New users, however, are provided with the opportunity to access the instructions. At the beginning of the instructions, the user is told how to exit, so the user knows how to regain control of the interaction.

43.5.5 Confirmation and Error Detection

Errors inevitably occur in human-computer interactions, just as they do in interactions between humans. Such communication failures in ASR may result from the human providing unexpected or inappropriate input, the system misrecognizing or misinterpreting the user's speech, or a combination of the two. One way to limit erroneous actions by the system is to give the user feedback about the application's state and to request confirmation that the system's interpretation of the input or impending action on that input is what the user intended. However, feedback and confirmation on each piece of information results in a lengthy, tedious, inefficient, and dissatisfying interaction.

In determining its responses to ambiguous or incomplete input, the system can be designed to consider the cost and probability of errors. For example, in an information retrieval system, an incorrect answer from the system may provide sufficient information for the user to determine that the original query was misunderstood. The cost of an error is then the time the user spent in making the query and listening to the incorrect answer. If a confirmatory dialog has a similar time cost, it may be more efficient to let the user reformulate the question. In this case, we assume that the user can distinguish between inappropriate responses and correct responses, and to either inform the system of its error or reconstruct the query. On the other hand, if an incorrect action has a high cost or greatly impedes task performance, the system should either request explicit confirmation of the user's input prior to performing that action or provide feedback about the impending action in order to permit the user to cancel the action.

For applications where the cost of errors is very high, systems should be designed to redirect the user to a non-speech input modality or to a human agent in the event that it becomes apparent that repeated interchanges between the user and the system have not resulted in progress toward task completion.

Many applications ask for confirmation only when the input is ambiguous, such as when the most likely recognition candidate has relatively low likelihood, or when an input utterance to a spoken-language system cannot be parsed. In these cases the system should not request a repetition of the input utterance, since chances are that utterance has a history of not being handled successfully. One strategy is to request confirmation by phrasing the request as a yes/no or forced choice question between alternative candidates for recognition. Katai et al. (1991) observed that even when the yes/no confirmation strategy is used, users often respond with a repetition of the command, suggesting that it might be useful to include the command word in the response set for confirmation.

Cues for confirmation or signaling of potential errors are often provided by repeating the information to be confirmed, along with specific intonation patterns. For example, falling intonation can imply acknowledgment, while rising intonation of the confirmatory phrase signals uncertainty and potential error (Karis and Dobroth, 1991). Currently, such intonational cues are not recognized reliably by automated systems, but advances in understanding the contribution of intonation patterns to dialog flow will provide a powerful enhancement to user interfaces, not only for confirmation and error recovery, but also for detecting user hesitations and repairs (i.e., self-corrections a user makes within an utterance). A better understanding of how intonation is used to convey intent would also be useful in constructing prosodically appropriate messages for voice output (Karis and Dobroth, 1991).

43.5.6 Error Recovery

Error recovery strategies may be initiated by either the system or the user. In the stock quotation application described above, the user initiates error correction by saying "Incorrect Stock" (Lennig et al., 1992). The system then provides the stock information for the next best match to the original input, and asks the user if that is the correct stock. The system will propose a few alternate candidates, and if the user disconfirms, the user is asked to repeat the stock name. If no new candidates are highly likely, the system suggests that the user check to be sure the requested stock is really offered on that stock exchange.

In other applications, the system flags the error or uncertainty and initiates error recovery. For example, in voice dictation the system signals recognition uncertainty by presenting a screen display of possible alternatives for the user to confirm. To increase the likelihood of correct recognition of the user's corrective response, the error recovery display uses a much more restricted vocabulary than the general dictation task.

When provided with error feedback users do modify their subsequent behavior. Hunnicutt et al. (1992) observed that users of a travel planning system were able to make use of the system's error messages to rephrase their queries and reliably recovered from errors about 80% of the time. Additional studies by the same authors showed that, in a fully-automated system that occasionally hypothesized incorrect utterances, users were generally able to identify misleading system responses and successfully recover from them, even when system error messages were not very specific.

These results suggest that if a system can make a reasonable assumption about the probable cause of the error, directive error messages (e.g., "I didn't hear your response. Please speak louder" after a system time-out) are useful. In addition, even if the system's assumption is wrong (e.g., the user didn't speak too softly, but rather not at all), the user generally has sufficient information to be able to disregard inappropriate messages arising from the system's incorrect hypotheses.

Finally, some voice interactions will not succeed, no matter how clever the error detection and recovery strategies. In these cases, the user interface should inform of the problem, its probable cause, and direct the user to an alternative solution - for example, a human agent, or an alternate input modality that may be more reliable. As a general principle, user interfaces should also allow a graceful exit from the application at any stage in the interaction.

43.6 Research Trends

43.6.1 Spoken Language Understanding

Work on spoken language understanding (SLS) systems is in its infancy, although research in the two underlying technologies (automatic speech recognition and natural language processing) has been going on for over 40 years. Over the past decade, there have been several projects aimed at developing spoken language understanding systems capable of dealing with spontaneous speech in limited domain transaction-based applications. One notable example is the Air Travel Information Service (ATIS) application, sponsored by the Advanced Research Project's Agency (ARPA) (Price, 1990). SLS developed for the ATIS application have used a combination of syntactic parsing and semantic analysis to find meaning-bearing phrases in the speech input and construct a meaning representation from them, in order to generate responses to spoken queries about airline flight and scheduling information. Among the major enhancements over conventional speech recognition systems were: a) the ability to extract meaning based on partial analysis (Ward et al., 1992; Jackson et al, 1991, Seneff, 1992), and b) integrating the speech recognition and language-understanding components by providing multiple hypothesis from the recognizer to improve both understanding and recognition (Kubala et. al, 1992; Zue et. al., 1992; Hirschman et al., 1991) .

These systems show promise, but several major problems remain to be resolved, including : a) dealing with repairs in spontaneous speech, b) developing systems that can detect when the input speech is not relevant to the task domain ("knowing when you don't know"), c) making more use of discourse and dialog theory to create more conversational interfaces automatically, and d) learning how to adapt the language understanding component to new task domains more automatically (Cole, Hirschman, et al., 1992).

43.6.2 Dialog Theory

Recently, research has begun to focus on modeling task-oriented dialogs in order to identify the structure of dialog and to use expectation to predict user input (and intent) and in turn to drive the system's response (Smith and Hipp, 1994; Bennacef, Neel, and Maynard, 1995; Kumamoto and Ito, 1992, Litman and Allen, 1990). Dialogues are described as goal-directed interactions that are composed of sub-dialogs, each with a specific sub-goal. Sub-goals may involve task-specific information exchanges, non-informational goals (e.g., confirmation, correction, pause, and restart), and exchanges about the structure of the dialog itself. Dialog modeling should improve spoken language interfaces because a) the expectations of each sub-dialog are highly predictive of the subsequent input and can be used as constraints for decoding of the acoustic input, and b) the structure of the dialog model permits mixed initiative, where either party can take control of the dialog - a feature that is important for efficient error detection and correction.

43.6.3 Multi-modal Interactive Systems

Multi-modal systems in which speech is one component may provide more flexible and robust interfaces for new applications, particularly for portable systems that may not have full-sized keyboard capabilities and may rely on other modalities like speech, handwriting recognition or pointing devices (Cole, Hirshman et al., 1992.) Multi-modal interfaces provide more options of error avoidance and error correction by allowing users to switch to a different modality when errors occur (Cohen and Oviatt, 1994). Since the hardware and software capabilities that support multi-modal systems are relatively new, user interface issues for creating successful multi-modal applications are still being defined. Some of the research issues that must be addressed include understanding the characteristics of and interactions among communication modalities, defining methods of evaluating the performance of multimodal interfaces, dealing with coordination, synchronization, and integration issues that arise when multimodal input is permitted, and developing a general theory of communicative interaction that takes into account the possibility of multiple modalities (Cole, Hirschman et al., 1992).

43.7 Summary

The state of the art in applying speech recognition technology to real applications is advancing rapidly. Current applications range from simple menu-driven command and control small vocabulary applications to transaction-based applications that mimic conversational flow, even though the legal speech input is limited to restricted vocabularies and grammars.

Research prototype speech understanding systems demonstrate the feasibility of handling unrestricted speech input for solving limited domain problems. Further research is needed to improve the robustness of the speech technology, to incorporate higher level linguistic knowledge, and to develop and apply the principles of dialog theory, in order to create robust, usable speech interfaces and to determine how best to integrate speech into efficient, successful multi-modal interactive systems.

43.8 References

Appelt, D. and Jackson, E. (1992). SRI International February 1992 ATIS Benchmark test results. *DARPA Workshop on Speech and Natural Language Processing.*

Balentine, B. E. and Scott, B. L. (1992). Goal orientation and adaptivity in a spoken human interface. *Journal of the American Voice I/O Society, 11*, 46-60.

Bennacef, S. K., Neel, F., and Maynard, H. B. (1995). An oral dialogue model based on speech acts categorization. *ESCA Workshop on Spoken Dialogue Systems,* 237-240.

Bossemeyer, R. W. and Schwab, E. C. (1990). Automated alternate billing services at Ameritech. *Journal of the American Voice I/O Society, 7,* 47-53.

Chapanis, A., Ochsman, R. B., Parrish, R. N., and Weeks, G. D. (1972). Studies in interactive communication: I. The effects of four communication modes on the behavior of teams during cooperative problem solving. *Human Factors*, 14, 487-509.

Chapanis, A., Parrish, R. N., Ochsman, R. B., and Weeks, G. D. (1977). Studies in interactive communication: II. The effects of four communication modes on the linguistic performance of teams during cooperative problem solving. *Human Factors*, 19, 101-125.

Cohen, P. R. (1984). The pragmatics of referring and the modality of communication. *Computational Linguistics*, 10, 97-146.

Cohen, P. R. and Oviatt, S. L. (1994). *The role of voice in human-machine communication.* In Roe, D. and Wilpon, J. (eds.) Voice Communication between Humans and Machines, Washington, D. C.: National Academy Press, 34-75.

Cole, R., Hirschman, L., Atlas, L., Beckman, M., Bierman, A., Bush, M., Cohen, J., Garcia, O., Hanson, B., Hermansky, H., Levinson, S., McKeown, K., Morgan, N., Novick, D., Ostendorf, M., Oviatt, S., Price, P., Silverman, H., Spitz, J., Waibel, A., Weinstein, C., Zahorain, S., and Zue, V. (1992). The challenge of spoken language systems: research directions for the nineties. NSF Workshop on Spoken Language Understanding. Technical Report CS/E 92-014, Oregon Graduate Institute.

Helander, M.G. , Moody, T.S. and Joost, M.G. (1988). *Systems Design for Automated Speech Recognition.* In Helander, M.G. (Ed.). Handbook of Human-Computer Interaction,. Amsterdam, The Netherlands: North-Holland.

Hirschman, L., Seneff, S., Goodine, D., and Phillips, M. (1991). *Integrating syntax and semantics into spoken language understanding.* Proceedings of the DARPA Speech and Natural Language Workshop, P. Price (ed.), San Mateo, CA: Morgan Kaufman, 366-371.

Huang, X. D., Lee, K. F., Hon, H. W., and Hwang, M.-Y. Improved acoustic modeling with the SPHINX speech recognition system. *Proceedings of ICASSP 91,* 345-347.

Hunnicutt, S., Hirschman, L., Polifroni, J., and Seneff, S. (1992). Analysis of the effectiveness of system error messages in a human-machine travel planning task. *Proceedings of ICSLP 92,* 196-200.

Jackson, E., Appelt, D., Bear, J., Moore, R., and Podlozny, A. (1991). A template matcher for robust NL interpretation. *Proc. Fourth DARPA Speech and Natural Language Workshop.* San Mateo, CA: Morgan Kaufman.

Kamm, C. A. (1994). *User interfaces for voice applications.* In Roe, D. and Wilpon, J. (eds.) Voice Communication between Humans and Machines, Washington, D. C.: National Academy Press, 422-442.

Karis, D. and Dobroth, K. M. (1991). Automating services with speech recognition over the public switched telephone network: Human factors considerations. *IEEE Journal on Selected Areas in Communications, 9,* 574-585.

Katai, M., Imamura, A., and Suzuki, Y. (1991). Voice activated interaction system based on HMM-based speaker-independent word-spotting. Paper presented at *American Voice I/O Society 91,* Atlanta, GA.

Kelly, M. J. and Chapanis, A. (1977). Limited vocabulary natural language dialogue. *International Journal of Man-Machine Studies, 9,* 479-501.

Kubala, F. et al. (1992). *BBN Byblos and HARC February 1992 ATIS Benchmark Results.* In Proc. of the Speech and Natural Language Workshop, San Mateo, CA: Morgan Kaufman, 72-77.

Kumamoto, T. and Ito, A. (1992). Recognizing user communicative intention in a consultant system with a natural language interface. *IEEE International Workshop on Robot and Human Communication,* 311-316.

Lennig, M., Sharp, D., Kenny, P., Gupta, V., and Precoda, K. (1992). Flexible vocabulary recognition of speech. *Proc. ICSLP,* 93-96.

Leiser, R. G. (1989). Improving natural language and speech interfaces by the use of metalinguistic phenomena. *Applied Ergonomics, 20,* 168-173.

Levinson, S. E. (1985). Structural methods in automatic speech recognition. *Proc. IEEE, 73,* 1625-1650.

Litman, D. J., and Allen, J. F. (1987). A plan recognition model for sub dialogues in conversations. *Cognitive Science, 11,* 163-200.

MacAuley, M. E. (1984). Human factors in voice technology. *Human Factors Review,* 1984, 131-166.

Makhoul, J. and Schwartz, R. (1994). *State of the art in continuous speech recognition.* In Roe, D. and Wilpon, J. (eds.) Voice Communication between Humans and Machines, Washington, D. C.: National Academy Press, 165-198.

Mariani, J. (1989). Recent advances in speech processing. *Proceedings of ICASSP 89,* 429-440.

Mazor, B., Zeigler, B. and Braun, J. (1992). Automation of conversational interfaces. *Proceedings of American Voice I/O Society,* San Jose, CA.

Michaelis, P. R., Chapanis, A., Weeks, G. D., and Kelly, M. J. (1977). Word usage in interactive dialogue with restricted and unrestricted vocabularies. *IEEE Transactions on Professional Communication,* PC-20.

Ochsman, R. B. and Chapanis, A. (1974). The effect of 10 communication modes on the behaviour of teams during cooperative problem solving. *International Journal of Man-Machine Studies, 6,* 579-620.

Oviatt, S. and Cohen, P. R. (1991). *The contributing influence of speech and interaction on human discourse patterns.* In J. W. Sullivan and S. W. Tyler (eds.), Intelligent User Interfaces, ACM Press Frontier Series. New York: Addison-Wesley, 69-83.

Oviatt, S. and Olsen, E. (1994). Integration themes in multi-modal human-computer interaction. *Proceedings of ICSLP 94,* 551-554.

Pallett, D. (1992). ATIS Benchmarks. *DARPA Workshop on Speech and Natural Language Processing,* February, 1992.

Price, P. (1990). Evaluation of spoken language systems: the ATIS domain. In R. Stern (ed.), *Proceedings of the Third DARPA Speech and Language Workshop.* New York: Morgan Kaufman.

Rabiner, L. R. (1989). A tutorial on hidden Markov models and selected applications in speech recognition. *Proc. IEEE, 77,* 257-286.

Rabiner, L. R. and Juang, B. H. (1993). Fundamentals of Speech Recognition. New York: Prentice-Hall.

Reising, J. M. and Curry, D. G. (1987). A comparison of voice and multifunction controls: logic design is the key. *Ergonomics, 30,* 1063-1078.

Roe, D. B. and Riley, M. D. (1994). Prediction of word confusabilities for speech recognition. *Proceedings of. ICSLP 94,* 227-230.

Roe, D. B. and Wilpon, J. G. (1993). Wither speech recognition: the next 25 years. *IEEE Communications Magazine,* November 1993, 54-62.

Rudnicky, A. I., Hauptmann, A. G., and Lee, K.-F. (1994). Survey of current speech technology. *Communications of the ACM, 37,* 52-57.

Sandry, D. L., and Wickens, C. D. (1982). The effect of stimulus-control processing-response compatibility and resource competition on pilot performance. Technical Report EPL-82-1. Urbana-Champaign, IL: University of Illinois.

Schmandt, C. (1994). *Voice Communication with Computers: Conversational Systems.* New York: Van Nostrand Reinhold.

Seneff, S. (1992). Robust parsing for spoken language systems. *Proceedings of. ICASSP 92*, 189-192.

Shriberg, E., Wade, E., and Price, P. (1992). Human-machine problem solving using Spoken Language Systems (SLS): Factors affecting performance and user satisfaction. *Proceedings of the DARPA Speech and Natural Language Workshop,* M. Marcus (ed.), San Mateo: Morgan Kaufman.

Skriver, C. P. (1987). Airborne message entry by voice recognition. *Proceedings of. of the 31st Annual Meeting of the Human Factors Society*. Santa Monica, CA: Human Factors Society.

Spitz, J. and the Artificial Intelligence Speech Technology Group. (1991) Collection and analysis of data from read users: Implications for speech recognition/understanding systems. *Proc. DARPA Speech and Natural Language Workshop,* P. Price (ed.), San Mateo, CA: Morgan Kaufman.

Smith, R. W. (1994). Spoken variable initiative dialog: an adaptable natural-language interface. *IEEE Expert*, February 1994, 45-50.

Smith, R. W., and Hipp, D. R. (1994). Spoken Natural Language Dialog Systems: A Practical Approach. New York: Oxford University Press.

Ward, W., Issar, S., Huang, X., Hon, H.-W., Hwang, M.-W., Young, S., Matessa, M., Liu, F.-H., and Stern, R. (1992). Speech understanding in open tasks. *Proceedings of. 5th DARPA Speech and Natural Language Workshop*. M. Marcus (ed.), San Mateo, CA: Morgan Kaufman.

Wickens, C. D., Vidulich, M. and Sandry-Garza, D. (1984). Principles of S-C-R compatibility with spatial and verbal tasks: the role of display control interfacing. *Human Factors, 26*, 533-534.

Wilpon, J. G. (1985). A study on the ability to automatically recognize telephone-quality speech from large customer populations. *AT&T Technical Journal,* 64, 423-451.

Wilpon, J. G. (1994). *Voice-processing technology in telecommunications.* In Roe, D. and Wilpon, J. (eds.) Voice Communication between Humans and Machines, Washington, D. C.: National Academy Press, 280-310.

Yankelovich, N. (1994). SpeechActs and the design of speech interfaces. Paper presented at the *CHI 94 Workshop on the Future of Speech and Audio in the Interface.* 1994 ACM Conference on Human Factors in Computing Systems, Boston, MA, April 24-28, 1994.

Yashchin, D., Basson, S., Lauritzen, N., Levas, S., Loring, A., and Rubin-Spitz, J. (1989). Performance of speech recognition devices: Evaluation speech produced over the telephone network. *Proceedings of. ICASSP 89*, 552-555.

Zeigler, B. L., and Mazor, B. (1995). Query-response relationships in the OASIS speech-recognition system. *Proceedings of the 4th European Conference on Speech Communication and Technology*, Madrid, Spain (in press).

Zue, V., Glass, J., Goddeau, D., Goodine, D., Hirschman, L., Phillips, M., Polifroni, J., and Seneff, S. (1992). The MIT ATIS System: February 1992 Progress Report. *Proceedings of. 5th DARPA Speech and Natural Language Workshop,* M. Marcus (ed.), San Mateo, CA: Morgan Kaufman.

Handbook of Human-Computer Interaction
Second, completely revised edition
M. Helander, T.K. Landauer, P. Prabhu (eds.)

Chapter 44

Applying Speech Synthesis to User Interfaces

Murray F Spiegel
Bellcore
Morristown, New Jersey, USA

Lynn Streeter
US West Advanced Technologies
Boulder, Colorado, USA

44.1 Introduction

Today's state-of-the-art user interface is multimodal, making effective use of multimedia content, such as text, graphics, and audio. Many believe that people will soon converse with machines as naturally and as effortlessly as they converse with one another face-to-face, since they believe that underlying technological problems, such as natural language understanding and speech recognition are close to being "solved" for all practical purposes. While advances in natural language understanding and speech recognition have been impressive, neither approaches the maturity of speech synthesis technology. Optimistically, it is possible to interact using typed input and voice output with limited vocabularies and simple syntax. While spoken language recognition in interfaces is becoming more common, usability results are very variable, depending on factors such as speakers, training, vocabulary, environmental effects, and dialog complexity. However, the ability to produce acceptable, intelligible speech from unrestricted text is a reality. This is not to say that there is no room for improvement. No one would mistake the best synthetic speech for a human being, nor would one choose to listen to a synthesizer read a novel or poem in preference to a skilled human reader. Yet, among the aforementioned components of a truly intelligent interface, spoken output is the one that can best be done today.

44.1.1 Chapter Overview

Speech interfaces are described in terms of the enhancing properties of the acoustic medium, such as the ability to perform tasks requiring divided attention; they are also described in terms of shortcomings of speech, such as its disruptive, invasive nature. Several applications that push that state-of-the-art in speech interfaces are surveyed with particular attention to performance and interface problems that emerge. Many of these applications use speech recognition as input and speech synthesis as output. When such interfaces are deployed to the general public, speech recognition front ends pose significant dialog design problems and the observed recognition performance is not as high as is needed.

The second half of the chapter takes the practitioner's perspective on how to construct applications that use speech as output and begins with a consideration of when to use natural speech and when to use synthetic speech. When the output is relatively unpredictable and unbounded, synthetic speech is the only practical choice. However, hurdles to correct pronunciation arise in most realistic applications. The most frequent hurdle is that most applications that require synthesis also access databases that were never intended to have spoken language output. Second, most synthesizers are limited and tuned to everyday speech, not to specialized vocabularies, proper names, acronyms, etc. Since the majority of applications need to interface with preexisting databases, the most prevalent features that derail synthesizers are presented along with potential fixes, which usually take the form of software filters.

While speech synthesis can be purchased as a commodity and as a black box technology, it is important to have some overall understanding of the underlying technologies and how synthesis is actually done. To this end phonetic representation and production issues are outlined, including how a sound inventory is produced.

There are several choices in how to represent what is to be pronounced; letter-to-sound rules, pronouncing dictionaries or some hybrid approach. Considerations of each approach are outlined and evaluated against technological trends, such as increased processor speeds and decreased storage costs.

Additional linguistic machinery is needed when moving from synthesizing individual words to synthesizing sentences, such as how intonation should be modeled phonetically and how to realize this acoustically. The major consideration is syntactic structure, but other factors must be considered, such as how a person's affective state, age, personality, etc. should be communicated (paralinguistic information). At present, we have a better handle on producing intelligible speech than we have on producing sentences with realistic intonation.

44.2 Characteristics of the Speech Channel

44.2.1 Multimodal Processing

People can process information in several modalities simultaneously, as demonstrated by the experience of driving while listening to the radio or talking on a hands-free cellular phone. Although there is a limit of how much competing information users can cope with, in a well-designed application two or more modalities can supplement each other nicely. Thus, a person can listen to speech providing instructions and guidance while simultaneously operating a terminal, automobile, or crane. When riding in an automobile or flying an aircraft, one does not want the driver or pilot to alternate between reading and driving. Indeed, the desirability of using vocal instructions for real-life navigation tasks has been clearly shown (Robinson, 1985; Streeter, Vitello, and Wonsiewicz, 1985).

Since speech output is intrusive, there is more likelihood that the message will often be attended to. By comparison, written instructions are much easier to skim or ignore.

44.2.2 Multimodal Interfaces

There are circumstances in which having multiple ways to interact with an application is better than one. This includes situations which on the surface seem quite natural for a speech-only interface, such as interacting with map displays in automobiles. However, car environments are noisy and make it difficult for speech recognizers to perform adequately. Also, people have trouble talking about spatial information correctly, leading to production errors, such as saying "north", when meaning "south" or to disfluencies. In general, when speech input will be: (1) degraded by noise, or (2) difficult to formulate into the correct spoken input or (3) highly variability in terms of what can be said, it makes sense to design an interface with multiple input modes, such as handwriting, direct manipulation, gestures, etc.

The above conclusions follow from the work of Sharon Oviatt and coworkers. Oviatt (1996) has convincingly shown performance advantages of multimodal inputs, in her case pen-based and speech, over speech input alone when interacting with a complex visual interface - a dynamic map. She has found that when the dialogue is unstructured, resulting in a great number of things the user can say, users exhibit greater disfluencies. These disfluences are difficult for any speech recognition system to cope with. While better interface design can reduce the speaker's linguistic input variability by impressive factors of 2-to-8 (Oviatt, Coehn, and Wang, 1994; Oviatt, 1995), when error conditions do arise, such as the system "not understanding", it is prudent to have alternative input modes for error recovery, such as direct manipulation of the interface or writing the response. Speech recognition errors are positively correlated with one another, i.e. one error is likely to lead to another error. Everyone is familiar with a speech recognizer failing to understand a word and asking the user to repeat the input. The typical user normally repeats the word louder, which actually reduces the probability of recognition! In addition, some things are just plain difficult to talk about, such as spatial information – communicating location or direction. For example, in attempting to articulate a location one subject said:

> "Add an open space on the north lake to b-
> include the north lake part of the road and north."

In contrast, the same task was achieved multimodally simply by circling an area and saying, "Open space." (Oviatt, 1996).

There is power in multimodal interfaces, particularly for the growing portable computing environment. However, incorporating multiple modalities into interfaces adds problems not encountered in the single mode, such as synchronizing and coordinating inputs and outputs; selecting the best modes and technology to best support the input, e.g. which pen-based computer; structuring the dialogue, which is now more complex, etc. (For a more complete discussion, see Cole et al. (1995)). While the interface designer's job may be made more difficult, data indicate that complex visual display applications or applications which must operate in adverse environmental conditions are better accomplished with multimodal inputs; speech alone may be ineffective, leading to more errors, longer task completion times, and greater user frustration.

44.2.3 Friendliness and Versatility

Speech is one of the oldest forms of human communication; humans have evolved to process speech effectively and efficiently. Good interfaces that use speech will be considered more natural than those without it. For instance, speech can more easily convey emotion and tone than does text. However, there have been cases in which use of speech has been misapplied. Take for instance the talking automobiles of the 1980s. Drivers quickly found the speech annoying and requested a simple auditory warning in its place.

44.2.4 Best Modality for Impaired Users

Speech provides the primary modality for communication for the visually impaired; for the deaf and speech impaired, speech technology provides a communication channel with considerable capability.

44.2.5 Faster Comprehension of Written than Spoken Language

A typical speaking rate is about 120-150 words/minute[1], whereas a typical reading rate is about 200-300 words/minute, and it is possible to scan text usefully at a rate of 1000 words/minute. Although people can understand speech at rates higher than average speaking rates, the limit of comprehension is of the order of 200 to 300 words (Fairbanks, Guttman, and Miron, 1957; Foulke 1971; deHaan, 1977).

However, understanding speech rates this high requires much concentration and motivation, and is not the type of task people would do voluntarily for long periods of time. While compression at higher rates cannot be comprehended well, it can be used to scan text to find a topic of interest, especially by listeners experienced with compressed speech.

44.2.6 Transitory nature of Speech

Because speech is ephemeral, it cannot be easily scanned or replayed. Also, since the signal travels through the airwaves it is subject to environmental noise effects and degradation. Thus, in some of situations in which speech would be most effective are the most aversive, e.g., in vehicles or battlefields. How-

[1] According to the Guinness Book of World Records, John Moschitta (who appeared in Fed-Ex commercials) has been clocked speaking at a rate of 586 wpm.

ever, the increased demand for hands-free communication is stimulating research in the areas of noise suppression and speech enhancement techniques in these harsh environments.

44.3 Applications Of Speech

Not surprisingly, most interfaces that use speech are telecommunications applications. The telephone is the most ubiquitous and frequently used information appliance in the world. Part of the telephone's long-standing popularity is attributable to the stability and standardization of the interface, which were byproducts of a regulated environment. Currently, around 95% of residences in industrialized countries have telephones. This is in sharp contrast to the proportion of homes in America that have PCs, which was between 30 and 40% as of the writing of this chapter. However, a fertile area for speech interface technology is interfacing with one's workstation environment using a telephone.

It has become relatively common place to construct and deploy simple Interactive Voice Response (IVR) interfaces, using voice menus that operate with touchtones (see Marics and Englebeck's chapter on Voice Menu Applications in this volume). However, as speech recognition continues to improve steadily, it is becoming a more popular way to input information to voice-based services. Correspondingly, as the quality and general public's acceptance of synthetic speech increases, using synthesis as the output for voice services will become more prevalent.

Voice-based telecommunications applications have proliferated world-wide. In the United States certain numbers are reserved for audiotex services. Their growth rate peaked in the early 1990s and actually declined there after, because of some rapacious pay-for-use scams that gave these services a bad name. In France, where videotex had its largest success with over 20,000 services on the Teletel network. Even though audiotex appeared as a service alternative only recently, the growth of audiotex services has surpassed videotex. As of 1993, approximately 3,700 audiotex services were available to the general public. Most of these services provide information, such as transportation schedules, stock quotes, etc. Others can process customer orders or give customer specific information, such as account balances.

In what follows, exemplary applications in a few key areas are described:

- Information Access
- Customer Ordering
- Information for Drivers
- Interfaces for the Disabled

44.3.1 Information Access

Information access constitutes the largest category of voice applications and for the use of speech synthesis, in particular. Several examples sampling the information access domain are given below. Applications were selected with a bias towards those that were not only state-of-the-art, but had either been deployed and/or had undergone some sort of user evaluation.

News Service (Gavignet et. al, 1993).

The French Press Agency provides a news service over the telephone network. Customers speak one of about 40 prespecified keywords corresponding to a particular scientific domain. After the topic keyword has been recognized by the system, the customer is given a list of titles and abstracts, which is delivered by speech synthesis. If so desired, the complete text can be ordered and transmitted via fax. This system is one of the AUDIOTEL services, the French audiotex service.

Reverse Directory Service (Yuschik, et al., 1994; Spiegel, 1996).

In a normal directory assistance call, the user supplies the operator with a name and receives a telephone number in return. In a reverse directory service, the customer gives the operator a number, and receives the name associated with that number as the response. In two regions of the United States, where this service has been deployed, the customer name and address are synthesized using the ORATOR system with its customized rules for surname pronunciation (Spiegel and Macchi, 1990). Pronouncing customer name and address is a particularly apt, yet challenging use of speech synthesis: the number of lexical items is very large, and as yet errorless pronunciation is impossible to achieve in all cases. However, acceptable accuracy has been achieved and these services are the most heavily used services involving speech synthesis anywhere. It is used in several large areas of the United States and, at this writing, across Italy.

Railway Timetables (Temem and Gitton, 1993).

The customer's goal is to determine time and place information about a particular train. However, the dialogue structure required to accomplish this seemingly modest goal is quite complex. In particular, the information needed includes the departure and arrival stations, times, and dates. Once these items have been retrieved from the database, the system must be equipped to supply questions about next and previous trains as well as plan a return trip. The French Railway (SCNF) manages about 4700 railway stations, and processes approximately 40 million calls using live operators each year. With the IVR, the customer can either input the information using touch tones or use voice recognition. The station name and time information are delivered to the user using a combination of speech synthesis and concatenated prerecorded speech. The problems encountered in using this service included: (1) synthesis problems due to incorrect pronunciation of place names; (2) tediousness of the touch tone interface; and (3) speech recognition errors. Although no precise figures were given on recognition rates, appearance of a flexible user-system dialogue encourages users to ask freer form questions than the system can handle. Another lesson learned from this service was the difference between laboratory and field testing, in that convergence on the best system-user dialogue cannot be done without extensive testing in the public arena. The service is currently experimentally available to the German public and is the focus of two European (EU) projects.

Voice Access to Electronic Mail (Yankelovich, Levow, and Marx, 1995).

"Road warriors" want timely access to electronic mail and often a laptop is not as practical a telephony solution. "SpeechActs" (and a similar model developed at the MIT Media Lab called "Mail Call") is a research prototype that allows users to access their electronic mail, calendar, and other utilities with a "conversational" interface over the telephone. SpeechActs presents information using synthetic speech. The major challenges of this application were implementing a usable conversational interface and dealing with the numerous errors that speech recognizers produce. Given the project's focus on getting the dialogue structure right, an example interaction is given:

SpeechActs: You have 14 new messages and 47 old messages. The first new message is from Eric Baatz regarding "report completed."

User: Let me hear it.

SpeechActs: "The first draft is ready for your comments. Eric."

User: Reply and include the current message.

SpeechActs: Preparing message to Eric Baatz. Begin recording after the tone. When finished, pause for several seconds.

User: Eric, I'll get those to you this afternoon.

SpeechActs: Say cancel, send, or review.

User: Send.
SpeechActs. Message sent. What now?

User: Next message.

SpeechActs: New message two from Stuart Adams, subject "Can we meet at 3:00 today?"

User: Switch to calendar...

44.3.2 Customer Ordering

Catalogue Sales (Gagnoulet and Sorin, 1993)

The largest French catalogue merchant, CAMIF has had an IVR ordering system running since 1992. The user inputs information using touch tones and the system responds with confirmation of customer name and address and product information using speech synthesis. While there is a 7% pronunciation error rate on customer surnames and place names, customers tolerate these errors, since it is familiar personal information, and the feedback is only for verification.

France Telecom Sales Agent (Gagnoulet and Sorin, 1993)

France Telecom installed a service for customers to order products and services after hours using a speech recognition front-end. This automated sales agent has used in two France Telecom offices since 1991 with positive results.

44.3.3 Information for Drivers

Perhaps the greatest potential for all speech interfaces is for people traveling in automobiles. Drivers are engaged in their primary task and have one unloaded channel for receiving information, the auditory channel. Similarly for input, the preferred mode of response is vocal. However, the significant noise challenges due to the vehicle itself and to road noise in this environment make anything but limited speech recognition difficult.

The Traveler's Dream - a Perfect Backseat Driver.

Davis' *Backseat Driver* prototype gave a driver spoken directions in Boston (Davis, 1989, also described in Schmandt, 1994). The driver input the destination either using a keyboard or a telephone keypad. The car was equipped with a high-end workstation, a map database of the Boston area on CD-ROM, and a speech synthesizer which were appropriately housed in the backseat. As additional equipment, an inertial navigation system kept track of the vehicle's position, speed and direction, which was synchronized by software with the map database. *Backseat Driver's* task was to get the driver to his or her destination by giving timely directions while compensating for the user's driving errors and for the driver's reaction to road obstructions. *Backseat Driver* attempted to give directions precisely when they were needed, e.g. such as telling the driver to take a right turn at a traffic light, just before entering an intersection. In addition, the directions incorporated helpful hints, such as, "Get into the left-hand lane because you are going to take a left at the next set of lights."

While *Backseat Driver* was never subjected to formal usability testing, it was a functioning demonstration system that piqued people's interest and imagination in such services.

Recent Driver Information Systems

Davis' full-blown idea has not been commercialized as yet. However, with pressures to better use the existing road system to improve traffic flow, there has been an increase in activity to access information from the car environment. One system that has been piloted and undergone some field testing gives traffic information to drivers using speech recognition as input and speech synthesis as output (Granström et al., 1993). Another pilot system in Berlin gave drivers oral instructions through the electronically signposted major road system. Interestingly, drivers using this system were sometimes unduly startled by the vocal directions as they were delivered in an overly terse and authoritative fashion. More recently, Hertz has equipped rental cars with its "Never Lost" system that combines a Global Positioning Satellite, inertial guidance, a map database, and an in-car display and spoken voice directions (New York Times, August 9, 1995). The Never Lost system is quite close in functionality to Back Seat Driver.

44.3.4 Interfaces for the Disabled

There are two primary uses of speech synthesis for the disabled: as an artificial mouth for those with speech impairments, and as artificial eyes that read printed or computer information for the vision impaired. For those unable to speak clearly, synthesizers allow them to communicate with others. The world-famous cosmologist Steven Hawkings has lectured for many years using synthesizers, once ALS (Lou Gherig's disease) impaired his ability to speak. The primary problem with this use of the technology is impatience with the difficulty of input; no one can type fast enough to maintain natural conversational rhythms. Predictive typing, semantic compaction[2] (Baker and Nyberg, 1989; Chang et al., 1993), and dynamic displays (Blackstone, 1993) reduce excess keystrokes for those who can type. However, many users are multiply disabled, eliminating entirely the use of typing. Primative use of alphabet boards has been replaced by sensors driven by head pointers, eye gaze, etc. \- virtually any muscle under stable voluntary control is harnessed to develop or select text for a synthesizer. Equally important to the disabled person is that the synthesizer's voice rarely matches the vocal model users want to convey. While early users had to cope with mismatches as basic as gender, current complaints are subtler (accent, pitch range, age, and personality). The listener's comprehension of synthesized speech is also still a problem, especially for less expensive systems. As stated by Vitale (1991) "We live in an age of electronics. The image of a child with a headpointer and communication board watching a movie on a sophisticated electronic device such as a VCR is a strange juxtaposition. ... As long as technical individuals are the sole users of high technology such as speech I/O, then we ... will have failed."

Speech synthesizers also read books and computer text for the visually impaired. Many major libraries contain Optical Character Reading (OCR) systems connected to speech synthesizers; patrons place a book on a reader to hear its pages read. Many commercial products perform screenreading functions for individual computer users. For instance, many aspects of DEC's synthesizer were expanded (wider range of speaking rates, wider selection of punctuation and citation formats) to accommodate this population's special needs (Vitale, 1993). At first, these seem to be less demanding uses of the speech technology, as the lis-

[2] See http://kaddath.mt.cs.cmu.edu:80/scs.

teners are dedicated and take the time to learn a synthesizer's foibles (mispronunciations, poor intelligibility, and unnaturalness). However, these users often try to scan large sections of text by pushing speaking rates above 400 words per minute - the result is less than optimal. The visually impaired also have problems associated with selecting the text on a terminal to be spoken. Finally, visual aspects of the text (e.g.: indenting, columns, tables) are not easily conveyed in an audio modality, yet are often critical to parsing information. Unfortunately, the movement toward modern window-oriented and graphical interfaces have made auditory navigation through computer interfaces especially problematic.

Another major aid for the disabled is the automation of Dual Party Relay, described in section 44.9.

44.4 Speech Interface Challenges

44.4.1 Dialogue Design Challenges

The usefulness of applications such as SpeechActs is obvious. However, usability data show that there are substantial design challenges to be overcome in such interfaces. The first, simulating conversation could be abandoned altogether in favor of the more common explicit prompt interface. However, the goal of determining principles for natural dialogues is laudable, so some of the problems Yankelovich et al. (1995) encountered in doing so are worthy of mention. First, if explicit prompting is eliminated, participants have trouble knowing what to say, particularly after a sub-dialogue has been completed. In a graphical user interface, the interface can pop the dialogue stack to the previous level by simply presenting a new menu. In conversation, there needs to be something comparable, such as "What now?", which was helpful in this study. Second, conversations rely on prosody, yet most speech synthesizers do a poor job of conveying human intonation contours. Achieving more natural sounding interactions requires knowledge of prosodics as well as how to tweak the particular synthesizer, and even then the naturalness is lacking. Third, normal listener expectations concerning conversational rhythm or pacing are violated in these interfaces, due to delays introduced by the speech recognition process. Fourth, people want to interrupt the synthesizer with their voice as they would another human. Normally, the architecture does not allow this and it should. Lastly, experienced users want to control the speaking rate of the synthesizer in some natural way.

44.4.2 Speech Recognition as a Front-end

Many of the more ambitious applications relied on speaker independent recognition for input. While not all referenced applications supplied usability data, there are enough data as well as revealing comments to indicate that speech recognition is still the Achilles' heel in such interfaces. As Yankelovich et al. (1995) state:

> "Not only are the recognition errors frustrating, but so are the recognizer's inconsistent responses. It is common for the user to say something once and have it recognized, then say it again and have it misrecognized. This lack of predictability is insidious. It not only makes the recognizer seem less cooperative than a non-native speaker, but, more importantly, the unpredictability makes it difficult for the user to construct and maintain a useful conceptual model of the application's behaviors. When the user says something and the computer performs the correct action, the user makes many assumptions about cause and effect. When the users say the same thing and some random action occurs due to a misrecognition, all the valuable assumptions are now called into question. Not only are users frustrated by the recognition errors, but they are frustrated by their inability to figure out how the applications work." (p. 374)

The Yankelovich et. al (1995) study found that recognition rates on a per utterance basis varied from 52% for females, 68.5% for males, and interestingly 75.3% for developers of the system. The lower recognition rates also contributed to fewer tasks completed: 17 out of 22 for females, 20 out of 22 for males, and 22 out of 22 for the developers. However, this interface was probably the most complex presented. Athimon et al. (1994) give field results for the general public using two information services - Les Baladins, which gives cinema information, and a French Telecom sales agent system. Their data are shown in Table 1.

A few things to note about these data. First, the two services are used differentially - Les Baladins is used frequently by the same people, whereas the Sales Agency data consist of primarily of first-time users. However, the 78% correct recognition rate for the cinema service is not out of line with other reported data, e.g., 80% and less correct recognition rates for Xspeak, a system to control the X Window system by voice (Schmandt et al., 1990); 55.5% correct recognition with a vocabulary size of 21 words a public informa-

Table 1. Field evaluations for two services. *(From Athimon et al., 1994)*

	Les Baladins	Sales Agency
Vocabulary size	26 words	6 words
Input Distribution		
Detected utterances	30,000	20,500
- correct	78.5%	34%
- incorrect	21.5%	66%
Error Distribution		
Substitution errors	0.9%	0.1%
False rejections	8.2%	5.8%
False acceptances	2.3%	0.6%
Global error rate	11.4%	6.5%
Major error rate	**3.2%**	**0.7%**

tion service (Gagnoulet et al., 1991); 75.4% correct recognition for a 12 word vocabulary for a Horoscope service used by the general public (Mathan and Morin (1991)). Collectively, these data indicate that we are still on the verge of successful application of speaker independent recognition for the general public for small vocabularies (less than 30 words). Speaker dependent recognition works reasonably well for large vocabularies now. However, when other input mechanisms are available, they are often preferred to speech. The design of the interface is made much more complex when speech is to be input, and calls into play issues such as vocabulary selection, dialogue structure, talk-over facilities, rejection of extraneous input, and error correction strategies to a much greater extent than with any other input mechanism.

44.5 Vocabulary Demands Affect Speech Output Technology Selection

44.5.1 Fixed Message vs. Unrestricted Text

Applications using speech output can be divided roughly into the following three types, based on statistical characteristics of their speech:

1. Small numbers of predictable words, phrases, or sentences.
2. Small numbers of carrier phrases, with a generally predictable set of variable items within the carrier messages.
3. Unrestricted text, not predictable prior to service.

Small Numbers of Predictable Words

For the first category, the technology usually used involves encoded pre-recorded words and phrases. Although technically not "speech synthesis," a term usually reserved for *synthetic speech* or full text-to-speech synthesis, the pre-recorded speech technology is sometimes referred to as speech synthesis. For a relatively small investment (inexpensive disk space and virtually no CPU drain), one can obtain very high quality speech output. Thus, when applications can be designed to employ a limited, predictable set of words or phrases, pre-recorded speech is generally preferred because of its high quality. (Earlier concerns about disk storage space have largely been obviated by declining storage costs.)

Carrier Phrases with Variable Items

Other applications bridge the gap between a very small set of words and unrestricted vocabularies. These can sometimes be structured as carrier phrases with "slots," where variable text is pasted in. This form of mixing single words and phrases is used in banking ("Check number ___, written for ____ dollars and ___ cents, was posted on ____") and telephony applications ("You have a collect call from ____"). The dropped-in speech can either be pre-recorded words (often digits), speech captured from a caller, or synthetic speech.

The best applications are those in which the transition between the carrier phrase and the inserted vocabulary items are as seamless as possible. When there are large speech quality differences or speaker characteristics between the carrier and the speech in the variable "slots," more cognitive load is placed upon listeners.

For seamless transitions between the carrier phrases and the variable words, care must be taken to make pitch, intensity and inflection as appropriate as possible. For example, if the final application requires that a vocabulary item fit in a phrase, such as, "The next flight to San Francisco leaves at 1 am," the vocabulary item, such as "San Francisco," should be recorded in a carrier phrase with the same inflection as the destination phrase. If the destination phrases differ in inflection, the same vocabulary item should be recorded with several inflections. Recorded items are digitized and then edited using digital waveform editing programs to excise the vocabulary item and to remove silent portions between phrases. Items may need to be adjusted to insure proper amplitude levels among vocabulary words and carrier phrases. The edited vocabulary items are then stored in separate speech files. On output the waveforms of the appropriate carrier phrase(s) and word(s) are concatenated and converted from digital to analog form.

When the speaker that a synthetic speech synthesis system is based on is available to also record an application's carrier phrases, a high-quality hybrid system can be developed. A listener would hear carrier phrases provided via high-quality, pre-recorded, speech, and variable text via synthetic speech that was as close to the carrier phrases as possible. An early use of this technique (Dobler, et al., 1993) was encouraging; some listeners thought the degradation due to synthetic speech was caused by "telephone disturbances." This hybrid technique is not possible in most applications, as the speakers used as models for synthesis systems are not widely available for recording every application's prompts and phrases. However, the day may arrive when a high quality synthesis system can be rapidly and automatically developed based on any given speaker's speech. Then, one could select a speaker for prompts and carrier phrases, and generate a synthesis system to match that voice.

Unrestricted Text

The last category of applications, those involving unrestricted text input, requires a full text-to-speech system. As the messages are not predictable in advance, no speaker can pre-record the phrases. Text-to-speech synthesis also must be used whenever the potential phrases are too numerous to pre-record, as would be the case for all the telephone listings in a large state. .

Yet another feature of applications using text-to-speech are that they are based on text databases that change rapidly, as occurs with news, advertising, or (again) telephone directories. (By the time all telephone directory listings were recorded, many would be out of date.)

Most potential applications require text-to-speech technology, since many computer databases that can form the basis of desirable services, happen to share one or more of the features of unrestricted vocabulary, motility, or massive size. The main obstacles for their use is either the technology (the speech quality was not yet at a level of naturalness acceptable to the general public) or the database (information in a format not appropriate for synthesis). As the speech technology continues to improve, along with techniques for automatically coping with large databases originally intended for other purposes, we will see much larger, profitable use of text-to-speech technology.

44.6 Hurdles For Successful Applications

In spite of the enormous potential for desirable customer services, relatively few public services using synthesized speech have actually been offered. A major barrier is that current synthesis technology is *not* mature enough to withstand being mindlessly dropped into an application \- close attention to a myriad of details is still necessary to create a successful public service using speech synthesis. Nevertheless, there are some significant success stories. These successful services were carefully designed in terms of proper selection of synthesizer, answering a true need for information, but, especially, adequately handling problematic situations inherent to the service. This chapter will highlight some of the preparations necessary for successful implementation of speech synthesis.

Hurdles arise for many reasons. Primary among them is that the databases that services are based on were probably designed for other purposes, such as visual display (Bachenko and Fitzpatrick, 1990), and not for use by speech synthesis. Another reason is limitations in the capabilities of synthesizers. Some services are based on text with a preponderance of acronyms, mixtures of names and words (Spiegel and Macchi, 1990), other specialized vocabularies, or complex syntactic structures. Any of these factors can overwhelm the capacity for most synthesizers to achieve excellent translation accuracy and enable high comprehension. A final problem finds its source in the listener. Some people might be highly motivated, experienced or even daily users of speech synthesis (such as part of the disabled population), but most users tend to be customers who unexpectedly hear a synthetic voice when requesting an automated service (Levinson, et al., 1993).

It must be emphasized that these hurdles can be and have been overcome, even in trying situations. The manner in which these hurdles are handled can make the difference between a belligerent user and a cooperative one. The existence of successful implementations using text-to-speech synthesis, in spite of user opinions regarding unnatural speech quality, confirms the value of efforts that overcome these hurdles.

44.6.1 Pronunciation Accuracy

Names and Other Specialized Vocabularies

The first challenge presented by many synthesis applications is proper pronunciation of specialized vocabularies. Many of the first specialized applications of speech synthesis required good pronunciation of proper names (names of people, locations, businesses), in applications such as providing stock information and reverse telephone directory services (also called Automated Customer Name and Address or ACNA). Another need for proper names arises in applications that provide driving directions or traffic information, because accurate pronunciation of geographic data (towns and streets) is crucial. Other services require correct pronunciation of specialized vocabularies, as contained in technical manuals, medical literature, or even the names of wines or plants. In applications where the specialized language component comprises a large proportion of the database text, poor pronunciation leads to poor comprehension; user satisfaction is predicated on high pronunciation accuracy whenever language context does not help the user.

As mentioned in the technology overview, names are a particularly difficult sub-language, because of their sheer number and derivation from many different languages. Although many efforts are underway to improve the name pronunciation accuracy of English and European systems (Spiegel, 1985, 1990; Coker, et al., 1990; Coile, et al., 1992; Belhoula, 1993; Schmidt, et al., 1993), some deployed systems still have poor accuracies. How can this be corrected? One approach has been to use a very large dictionary of names and their pronunciations, either via an external preprocessor (Patterson, 1986), or within a system, such as AT&T's FlexTalk (Coker, et al., 1990), while a more classical approach has been to develop name pronunciation rules (Spiegel, 1985; Spiegel and Macchi, 1990; Vitale, 1991). The first approach was taken in the first trial of a reverse telephone directory service, because the synthesizer used had very poor name pronunciation accuracy (Patterson, 1986). Systems now are available that achieve more than adequate pronunciation accuracy (Golding and Rosenbloom, 1993; Golding and Rosenbloom, 1993; Yuschik, et al., 1994).

Mixed Text: Names and Words

Although high name pronunciation accuracy suffices for some applications, such as identifying the senders or recipients of voice mail, faxes, or telephone calls, the text for many other services have names intermixed with English text. Newspaper stories, electronic mail, and telephone business listings are examples where names may occur within text, and often there are few reliable syntactic or lexical (e.g., capitalization) cues signaling proper nouns. In fact, business listings may be the most widely used database in which names and words are mixed so thoroughly.

Although using separate rule/dictionary sets have been considered for telephone business listings (English rules for business listings, name rules for residence listings), there will be significant error rates for business listings, because 2/3 of the items are names[3]. Thus, a unified approach to pronouncing names and general text, which is being taken by the best systems, will have the most utility.

Lacking these capabilities in a general text-to-speech system, preprocessors would have to be employed to assure high accuracy. These programs could also analyze input to determine proper pronunciations for name/word homographs, such as in "*Reading County Reading Center*" or "*Joe Fried's Fried Clams.*" Preprocessors can also select field-dependent or domain-specific vocabularies when required.

As mentioned earlier, correctly pronouncing town and street names is critical for direction or traffic services. Where the underlying general-purpose synthesizer does not have high accuracy, preprocessors in the form of specialized rules or lists (or entries in a user dictionary, which usually provides nearly identical functionality) can be used for correction (e.g., Dobler, et al., 1993).

Acronyms

Acronyms, or words conventionally written in upper-case characters, are problematic for automated services for two major reasons:

(a) Their pronunciation style is not easily predictable. Some acronyms are pronounced as a word (UNICEF), some are spelled out (IBM), and some use a combination of both (CMOS, EPROM).

(b) Their detection within all-upper-case databases is very difficult. "BEK SYSTEMS" might be pronounced "Bek Systems" when referring to the family of Bek (of which there are 77 in the U.S.), or might be pronounced "B E K Systems" if it's a reference to an acronym BEK.

The first problem, pronunciation of acronyms, is best addressed via the development of sensible pronunciation rules for acronyms integrated into a synthesis system. Early generations of text-to-speech systems

[3] Using a good dictionary look-up scheme that splits off plurals and other inflectional affixes, roughly 66% of the items (types) in business listings are not found (i.e., they only occur as names). A similar analysis of residence listings, which are expected to consist mostly of names, finds that 99% of the items are not found with dictionary look-up. By contrast, only 1% of the items in a typical issue of the New York Times are not found.

were abysmally poor at pronouncing acronyms, choosing either to spell out all upper-case text, or to pronounce every acronym that contains a vowel. Some high-end synthesizers now address this problem accurately, such as Bellcore's Orator, AT&T's FlexTalk and newer versions of DECTalk. In time, other synthesizers will also provide improved capabilities.

The second problem, detecting acronyms embedded in all-upper-case text, is assisted by domain- and application-specific knowledge such as, in the case of telephone directories, whether the input is a residence or business listing. However, this assistance is meager; it does not disambiguate the majority of cases. Identification of a domain is not decisive for the acronym in the text "US SENATE" vs. "TOYS R US," or UPS in "UPS SERVICE" vs. "PICK UPS," because these strings are often found in similar domains. The problem is more difficult than that of locating abbreviations not signaled by a period within text, although methods used to solve each problem are similar. The current state-of-the-art is achieved by searches through databases to produce lists of acronyms that are a) unambiguously acronyms, b) acronyms when found in certain rule-defined contexts, and c) acronyms when in certain lexical contexts (Kalyanswamy and Silverman, 1991). Because this ad-hoc procedure is labor intensive, it is very helpful to use automated assistance based on phonotactic constraints (Spiegel, 1993). More accurate statistical methods and training systems are needed.

Abbreviations

A pervasive problem for speech synthesis is the accurate detection and translation of abbreviations in text. One does not want to hear *Dr* pronounced as "drr," nor will customers be happy with a wrong context-dependent translation to the word "drive." All high-end synthesizers contain facilities for translating some abbreviations. Since this is an open-ended problem, no synthesizer will handle all idiosyncratic abbreviations that exist in every database, although some will perform better than others on common abbreviations. In many cases, context-dependencies, domain-specific or even semantic disambiguation and inferences regarding pragmatics are necessary to resolve the correct translation of abbreviations, such as those that occur at the end of a sentence - consider "Send me the report on Jan." (Jan or January), "Wizard of Oz." (Oz, not ounces), and "Say hi to Oh." (the surname Oh or Ohio). Knowing the appropriate context is hard for a program: sometimes users will want character-by-character readout of non-ascii marks ("one slash two," "apostrophe nine six") but most other times they want to read "profits were up in the first 1/2 of '96."

In directing effort to accurately translate abbreviations, especially non-standard entries for which there are no established lists, the first problem is again proper detection. Just as was the case for acronyms, searches based on the absence of vowels and violations of phonotactic constraints is only a helpful first step. The mechanism for proper translation can be ordered lists of contexts, bigram or trigram statistics, or more sophisticated techniques.

44.6.2 Preparation of Input Text

Most information in databases was not stored with the expectation that it would be spoken. Either it was stored in a format appropriate for programmatic query or, if accessible by humans, for visual display. These formats are usually inappropriate for synthesis because they contain inconsistent abbreviations, truncations, visually indicated hierarchies and relationships, inconsistent field separations, and virtually scrambled word ordering. Any of these distortions of the text, if left uncorrected, renders direct synthesis of the information incomprehensible. This section highlights some of the problems that were solved with domain-specific preprocessing in viable services (Kalyanswamy and Silverman, 1991; Cotto, 1993; Spiegel, 1993).

- *Character Length Restrictions.* Field length restrictions often severely limit text. Those *seeing* "Jonathan Rosenb" or "Best Secrtrl Crp" might reconstruct some of the missing information; however, *synthesis* of truncated text with idiosyncratic abbreviations will be confusing to everyone.

- *Ambiguous or Inconsistent Abbreviations.* Since abbreviations ease data entry, inconsistently applied or gratuitous abbreviations are found even in databases without field length restrictions. The results include highly ambiguous abbreviations: "Comm" can stand for Communications, Commercial, Committee, Common, Commission, Commonwealth, Commerce, and many other words.

- *Field Information Lost Between Database Translations.* One database is often a derivative of other database. Important information such as delimiters or field identification is lost during conversion from one database format to another, which often creates ambiguities difficult to resolve during a preprocessing stage.

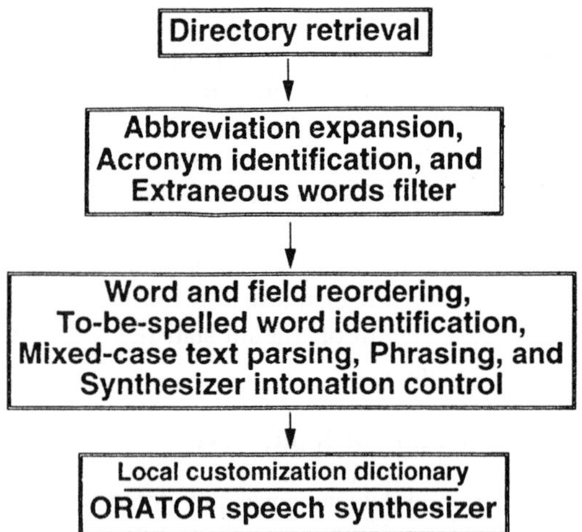

Figure 1. Information flow through a popular synthesis service.

- *'Scrambled' Word Ordering*. Text may be stored in an order designed for rapid retrieval in an existing service, with the most important words placed first. Often the text order is completely inappropriate for synthesis. If sent unaltered, text like "Embassy House The Apartments," "Adults Sexually Abused As Children The Center For," and "Bingham Carleton Dr and Carol, Rev," will simply not be understood.

- *Inconsistent Information Ordering*. Text entered according to rules not strictly adhered to can be problematic for a processing stage responsible for word reordering. A postal code may be found within a locality field rather than in its own field, or the locality name may be placed within a street name field.

- *Extraneous Information*. Often extraneous information is embedded in the text. For example, in fields intended only for addresses, all of these were found: "Call after 5 pm," "Touchtone phone only," "See also [company_name]," or "[location] telephone number." In some cases, the extraneous information cannot be easily removed by preprocessors, due to similarity in other contexts with desired information.

- *Unmarked Fields*. Some databases lack indication, for instance, of which portion of an entry is a stock code and which is the name, or which portion of a listing is the name vs. the address. This creates problems when phrasing for good intonation and for applying field-dependent processing.

- *Visually Encoded Information*. A text's formatting is often implicit in its visual layout, as in business presentations, faxes, even some aspects of E-mail. These aspects are difficult to recover when translated to straight characters.

Potential Solutions.

There are two common approaches for solving these hurdles. In the first, the database is permanently altered to minimize its problems for synthesis (or switched with another database that is more benign). To reduce the effort associated with correcting relatively large databases, automatic real-time techniques (as described below) can produce a first-pass correction; this can be fine-tuned manually to increase its accuracy. All subsequent entries can also undergo an automated procedure. In the second option, a customized preprocessor converts the "dirty" database in real time to one appropriate for a speech-based service. This was the approach followed in the first two U.S. telephone company reverse directory services, and have been described elsewhere (Spiegel and Winslow, 1995). Figure 1 shows the information flow through the preprocessors.

Automatic preprocessors for large, dynamic, databases can require significant development time, but may closely approach 100% accuracy. For instance, the task of locating massive numbers of idiosyncratic abbreviations in a database can be assisted via lexical analysis to list possible abbreviations (Spiegel and Winslow, 1995). Statistical techniques can help determine likely translations. One hundred percent accurate recovery may not be achievable for large databases that are updated frequently with no monitoring of data entry, since new ad-hoc abbreviations appear daily.

44.7 Unrestricted Text-To-Speech Synthesis

Full text-to-speech synthesis is a most challenging and interesting technology, which requires successfully integrating knowledge from the fields of text analysis, phonetics, phonology, syntax, and acoustic phonetics as well as signal processing.

44.7.1 Technology Overview: Text-To-Speech Synthesis

There are two main stages in converting text to speech:

1. Converting the input text to a phonetic representation.
2. Producing sound from that phonetic representation.

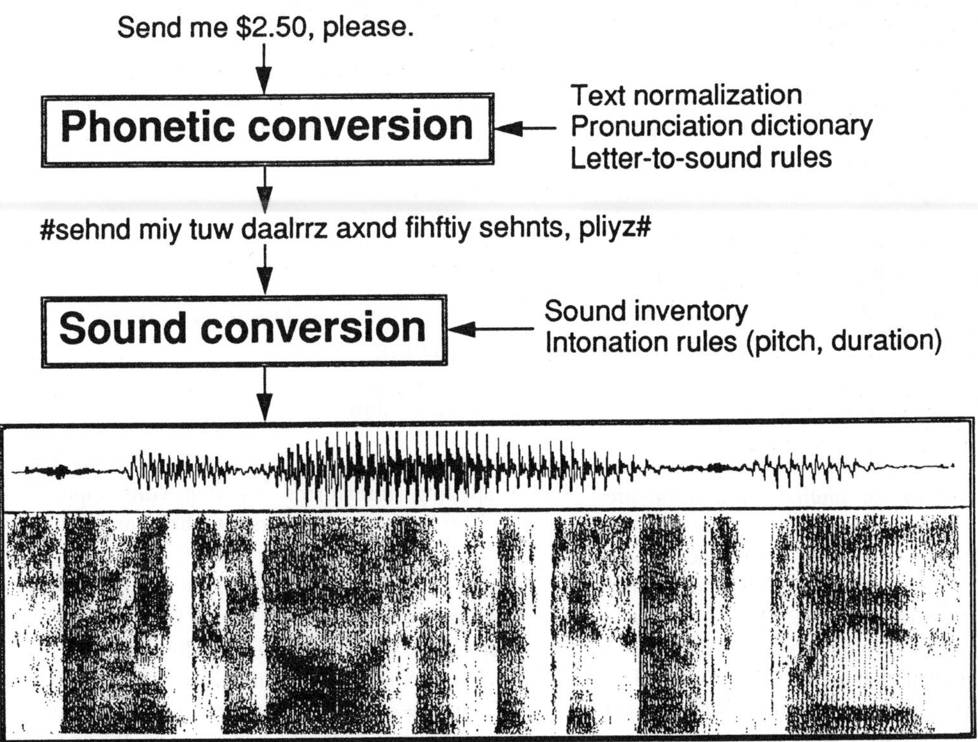

Figure 2. Steps involved in text-to-speech synthesis. (To show appropriate detail in spectrogram and waveform, time scales do not match.)

Figure 2 depicts the stages typically associated with text-to-speech synthesis, for the example sentence, "Send me $2.50, please."

Phonetic Representation

In order to produce a phonetic representation, or pronunciation, the text first undergoes a step that translates into words all numbers, symbols, and abbreviations, as would be required by the artificial sentence "I rcvd your check for $5 million for 100 lbs of diamonds, rubies, etc, at 5:05 a.m. on 11/3/97."

The next major step along the way towards a phonetic representation of the input checks each word in pronunciation dictionaries and letter-to-sound (or letter-to-phoneme) pronunciation rules. Although Spanish contains simple pronunciation rules without any exceptions for its native vocabulary, the pronunciation rules for most languages do not characterize how all their words are pronounced. For instance, the pronunciation rules for English are not only complex, many English words are exceptionally pronounced. The result of accessing both the pronunciation dictionaries and pronunciation rules in a synthesis system is a phonetic representation for each word to be spoken. As shown in Figure 2, the production of the phonetic representation completes the first stage of processing.

Producing Speech

The second stage produces speech conforming to the pronunciation obtained from the first stage. Many different techniques are used for this second stage in synthesizers, but they all reflect the need to specify specific speech parameters (duration, pitch, overall amplitude, spectrum, etc.) for each segment of the speech output. All synthesizers contain rules that create or select a fundamental frequency (loosely, pitch) contour for each phrase and sentence. Similarly, rules affect the duration of vowels and consonants in the output. These parameters (pitch and duration) primarily express the *intonation* for each sentence. As shown in Figure 2, intonation rules are only part of the second stage's processing. As might be expected in converting a pronunciation into sound, a key role is played by an inventory of speech sounds.

Features of a Sound Inventory

The largest difference in this second stage between

various synthesizers is the manner in which speech sounds are actually produced. This difference is characterized in a description of the features of a synthesizer's *sound inventory*. The first important feature describes how the inventory is encoded, which determines how the synthesizer makes its intonational (pitch, duration, etc) adjustments. In some synthesizers (eg: DECTalk), the sound inventory consists of models for individual phonemes. In these synthesizers, sometimes referred to by the phrase "analysis-by-synthesis," rules adjust the parameters of the phoneme models. In so-called concatenative synthesizers (eg: Orator and FlexTalk), the sound inventory consists of spectral parameters obtained from recordings of a specific human speaker. In the last class of synthesizers, the sound inventory is also based on recordings of specific humans. However, the adjustments of pitch and duration are performed directly on the original waveform (eg: synthesizers from CNET), using a technique called PSOLA (Pitch-Synchronous Overlap and Add), rather than to spectral parameters of the recordings.

Another important feature of a synthesizer's sound inventory is the length and number of its units. The smallest synthesizers employ sound inventories based on the phoneme. This provides great economy of storage (English contains about 40 phonemes, although most phoneme-based synthesizers contain over 100 allophones - phonemes as they vary in linguistic context). Larger synthesizers are based on longer sound units (diphones [pairs of phonemes], demisyllables [half-syllables]), and units of varying length. Soon we will see commercial systems based on the syllable or word. Some laboratory systems are based on units of varying length; smaller units are used when their acoustic representation is not affected much by neighboring environments and larger units are used when this is not the case. Synthesizers based on longer units aim for higher naturalness and intelligibility, as their units naturally embody complex phonetic interactions between phonemes that need phoneme-based systems need to simulate by rule. Early synthesizers were entirely based on the phoneme. Increased storage and CPU power has made practical systems based on longer units; these systems will predominate in the future.

In current systems, the techniques for encoding covaries with unit size, although there is no reason that a particular encoding technique need be associated with particular unit length for the sound inventory. Most analysis-by-synthesis systems are based on single phonemes. Concatenative synthesizers typically use inventories based on segments longer than the single phonemes (eg: half-syllables in Orator, diads in FlexTalk, diphones in Lernout and Houspie), and all PSOLA-based synthesizers currently operate on diphone sound inventories.

We will now go into more detail on the methods used to produce a phonetic representation. Later, we explain some of the difficulties associated with modeling intonation, which is important to give naturalness to a synthesizer's speaking of sentences.

44.7.2 Transforming Text to a Phonetic Spelling

Text Normalization

As mentioned above, the first step in obtaining a phonetic spelling transforms all non-word input into words. This includes numbers, symbols, and abbreviations.

Some symbols and abbreviations can be dealt with via a straightforward lookup table (@→ at, +→ plus, etc→ et cetera, bldg → building). However, many difficult cases exist. For example, 1 *ft* should trigger "foot," whereas 2 ft should be "feet," but does your favorite synthesizer properly handle "one ft" and "two thousand ft"? Is the *no* in "no one" the word "no" or "number"? Clearly, in the context *Hwy no one*," the abbreviation stands for the word "number." Similar context sensitivity plagues translations of many numbers and symbols. Aside from the oft-quoted *Dr. King Dr.* and *St. Martin St.*, correct translation often requires world knowledge, as would be needed to correctly distinguish *Jill St Wright* from *Market St Mission*. The textual representation for abbreviations vary; some abbreviations occur without their characteristic periods, while others are not spelled consistently the same way. There are also preferences for how numbers are spoken - telephone numbers, street addresses, and zip-codes are phrased differently by different people - systems need customizability at this (rule) level to be able to model this variability.

Letter-to-Sound Rules

The core module responsible for word pronunciation for most systems is their letter-to-sound rules. Each input word is first checked in an exception dictionary (see below); if not contained there, its pronunciation is developed by a set of rules embodying the pronunciation rules of the language. Consider the translation of the phrase "Two cats." The pronunciation for the word "cats" will likely be obtained using pronunciation rules well-known to any 1st-grader: when followed by the vowels a, o, or u, the letter *c* is nearly universally pronounced as /k/ (when followed by the other vowels, the letter *c* is pronounced as /s/). The letter *t* is always pronounced /t/ except in environments like "thin" "nation" and "future." The letter *a* in simple, monosyllabic words is usually pronounced with the vowel /@/ in, well, the word "cat." The number of pronunciation rules depend upon language. Spanish has very few pronunciation rules, whereas English requires many (most English synthesizers claim to have on the order of 1000 pronunciation rules). The number of rules also depends on the complexity and scope of the synthesizer's goals. Systems that were designed to pronounce well both names and words (eg: Orator) contain more rules (and more complex rules) than do systems designed only for words.

Using a Pronunciation Dictionary

Consider again the translation of "Two cats." Whereas quite simple pronunciation rules govern the pronunciation of "cats," no regular rules predict how the word "two" is pronounced. In no other English word is the "w" silent in a "tw" combination, and in no other word is a single "o" pronounced /u/. To obtain the pronunciation for the word "two" (and other many other common words like none, one, of, and sugar), a pronunciation dictionary is used. This dictionary is sometimes called an *exception* dictionary, because common words that are exceptions to a system's pronunciation rules are placed there. English is a difficult language to pronounce, as many words are not pronounced in a regular way. For example, consider the words "tough," "bough," "though" and "through." All end in "ough," yet they are pronounced in radically different ways. Some systems rely on pronunciation dictionaries more than others - where the dictionary is very large, or dictionary extension techniques particularly clever, the pronunciation rules are hardly used at all, even for words like "cat" (e.g., AT&T's FlexTalk). As is the case with its influence on large sound inventories, decreasing costs and size for computer memory will make large-dictionary systems even more practical in the near future.

All major systems also contain a user-customizable dictionary in addition to the system pronunciation dictionary. No system will ever perfectly anticipate all pronunciations, especially for specialized vocabularies (eg, the fields of pharmacology or technology). Even a synthesizer doing a spectacular job of modeling one person's pronunciations would not suffice, for different people, and people in different areas of the country, pronounce words differently. For example, the word "pecan" has strongly regionalized pronunciations, and the same may apply to bayou, buoy, and rodeo. User dictionaries help application designers customize a synthesizer's pronunciations according to local custom and preference.

Dictionaries also provide important information necessary for intonation. One of the most important is identification of part-of-speech. The fact that given words are prepositions, for instance, helps identify the phrasing of a sentence. Also, part-of-speech information (contained in a dictionary) for neighboring words can be a pronunciation aid. When a word is a homonym (has different pronunciations when a noun and when a verb, as in CONvict vs conVICT, REcord vs reCORD, and excuses with final /s/ vs. final /z/), it's pronunciation can largely be determined by the sequence of part-of-speech types of neighboring words.

However, it will be long time before pronunciation rules become passe\z\(aa. Well written pronunciation rules produce more understandable output when dealing with typographical errors; dictionaries require a perfect match with the input. In other words, letter-to-sound rules allow for "soft" failures in a system. Also, where there is interest in modeling different dialects, pronunciation rules are more easily modified to represent pronunciations appropriate for various dialects. But most importantly, pronunciation rules are necessary to handle, in unrestricted text, neologisms and proper nouns (names of people, businesses, and products). We'll cover this topic in greater detail below.

Before leaving the topic of dictionaries, we must explain the function of one more specialized dictionary often used in synthesizers - a dictionary of morphemes (or morphs). Entries in a morph dictionary help a system analyze words into their constituent word roots, prefixes, and suffixes. A word such as "clearinghouses" would be analyzed as clear + ing + house + s, simplifying the job of pronunciation. Morph dictionaries help prevent laughable pronunciations (some early synthesizers said vie-YOU-gruf for the word "viewgraph"). When analyzed as containing the morph "holder," a word like "cupholder" won't be pronounced with an /f/ sound (from the combination of p and h), and in words like "stakeholder" or "officeholder," the silent e will be treated as such.

Thus, through the combination of user dictionaries, pronunciation dictionaries, morphological dictionaries and their combination rules, analysis of part-of-speech sequences, and letter-to-sound rules, current synthesis systems develop quite accurate pronunciations for running text.

Table 2. Surnames in metro areas in order of frequency.

Rank	Boston	Manhattan	Philadelphia	Columbus, OH	Shreveport	Chicago	Seattle
1	SMITH	SMITH	SMITH	SMITH	SMITH	JOHNSON	JOHNSON
2	SULLIVAN	RODRIGUEZ	WILLIAMS	MILLER	JOHNSON	SMITH	SMITH
3	MURPHY	BROWN	JOHNSON	JOHNSON	WILLIAMS	WILLIAMS	ANDERSON
4	JOHNSON	WILLIAMS	BROWN	BROWN	JONES	BROWN	MILLER
5	BROWN	LEE	JONES	WILLIAMS	BROUSSARD	JONES	BROWN
6	WILLIAMS	JOHNSON	MILLER	JONES	BROWN	MILLER	WILLIAMS
7	WHITE	COHEN	DAVIS	DAVIS	FONTENOT	ANDERSON	JONES
8	OBRIEN	MILLER	ROBINSON	MOORE	DAVIS	DAVIS	NELSON
9	WALSH	JONES	JACKSON	WILSON	HEBERT	JACKSON	DAVIS
10	MCCARTHY	DAVIS	THOMAS	THOMPSON	MILLER	THOMAS	WILSON
11	MILLER	RIVERA	WILSON	TAYLOR	THOMAS	HARRIS	LEE
12	JONES	PEREZ	HARRIS	THOMAS	JACKSON	WILSON	PETERSON
13	DAVIS	GONZALEZ	COHEN	MARTIN	GUIDRY	TAYLOR	THOMPSON
14	KELLY	GARCIA	WHITE	CLARK	TAYLOR	MOORE	TAYLOR
15	ANDERSON	SCHWARTZ	TAYLOR	WHITE	MOORE	WHITE	MARTIN
16	LEE	MARTINEZ	MOORE	ANDERSON	RICHARD	LEE	CLARK
17	COHEN	HARRIS	GREEN	HARRIS	MARTIN	MARTIN	OLSON
18	MARTIN	LOPEZ	KELLY	BAKER	LANDRY	GARCIA	THOMAS
19	BURKE	LEWIS	LEE	HALL	WHITE	RODRIGUEZ	WHITE
20	COLLINS	WONG	THOMPSON	JACKSON	LEBLANC	NELSON	MOORE
21	WILSON	MARTIN	SCOTT	LEWIS	WILSON	ROBINSON	LEWIS
22	RYAN	TORRES	LEWIS	YOUNG	LEWIS	THOMPSON	YOUNG
23	MACDONALD	FRIEDMAN	ANDERSON	WRIGHT	WALKER	MARTINEZ	JACKSON
24	KING	GREEN	MARTIN	EVANS	GUILLORY	WALKER	HANSEN
25	TAYLOR	THOMAS	CLARK	KING	THIBODEAUX	CLARK	HARRIS

Pronouncing Proper Names

Pronouncing proper names correctly is difficult for text-to-speech synthesis and continues to be an active research area. Indeed, pronouncing surnames is something that trips up otherwise fluent speakers. Consider the probability of correctly pronouncing all the names on a typical university class roster. Names come from different linguistic origins, with each language requiring somewhat different letter-to-sound rules to pronounce them in an Anglicized fashion. If one selected a telephone book for one city as representative of the country as a whole, and made sure that the rules correctly pronounced every name in the selected phone book, there still would be many names that would not be included in the sample. Table 2 shows the most frequent surnames for 7 American cities. This table demonstrates the diversity of language sources of American surnames, and hints at the vast number of surnames.

How many different names exist? US government records (Social Security Administration, 1985) indicate that there are over 1.5 million uniquely spelled surnames in America; from telephone directories one of the authors has collected 180,000 first names. (Comments relating to names refer to U.S. data; however, generalizations to other nations and languages are appropriate. For statistics regarding the problems associated with non-native names in Europe, see Carlson, et al., 1992)

Because storage costs are continually decreasing, it is tempting to rely on large databases for many aspects of speech technology. This is as true for pronunciation systems (Coker, et al., 1990; Schmidt, et al., 1993) as it is for synthesis inventories (Sagasaka, et al., 1992; Hauptmann, 1993), and training corpora for part of speech statistics (Coker, et al., 1990). However, surname dictionary databases of quite extensive size still won't be comprehensive - see Figure 3. A small dictionary is somewhat useful: 2000 surnames (.13% of the 1.5 million surnames in the U.S.) covers 50% of the population. This implies even a rule-based system with very poor accuracy can be bootstrapped to provide moderate accuracy quite easily by relying on a small

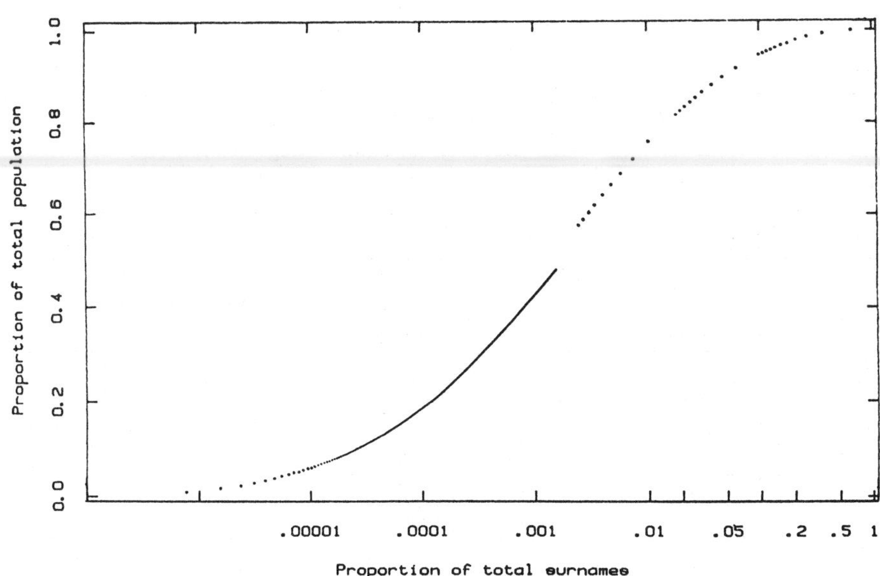

Figure 3. Cumulative distribution of surnames in the U.S.

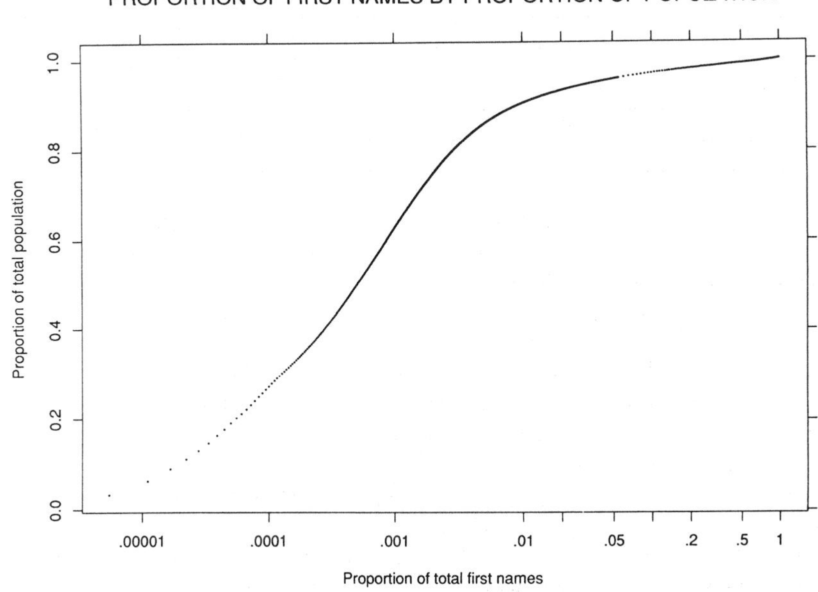

Figure 4. Cumulative distribution of first names in the U.S.

dictionary. But, attempting comprehensive coverage and high accuracy via a surname dictionary is nearly prohibitive. Because the tail of the distribution of names is very long, encountering *rare* family names is in fact a very *common* occurrence. A 50,000-name database would not cover the bottom 20% of the population. Even a database with one million names will completely miss about one person in every 500.

Contrast this with the distribution of first, or given, names, derived from a database of 180k first names in the U.S. The set of first names that cover any given proportion of the general population constitutes a much smaller fraction of all first names (see Figure 4). For instance, only 92 names (about .05% of all first names) covers 50% of the population, and only 518 names (.3% of all first names) covers 80% of the population.

Developing a very large surnames database of high accuracy is very labor intensive, and for all practical purposes, the set is unbounded, for new names continually enter the lexicon via immigration, name changes, and the creativity of parents. The same factors apply to business names: there are many of them, and new names are created daily in the business world.

The fundamental problem for proper-name pronunciation is that no reliable name pronunciation dictionary exists. In contrast the words of a language, where dictionaries can guide pronunciation rule development (or where the dictionary itself can be used), the lack of an authoritative name pronunciation source means rule and dictionary development for proper names relies on guesswork, intuition, and polling. The European speech community currently sponsors ONOMASTICA (Schmidt, et al., 1993), a project coordinated in Edinburgh that has the goal of developing phonetic translations (with appropriate alternate pronunciations) for up to one million proper names (first names, surnames, place names, business names) in 11 European languages. Unfortunately, no corresponding project is considered at the present time for North American names.

Until that time, one must rely on name-pronunciation programs developed by a minority of synthesizers (eg: DecVoice, FlexTalk, Orator). The approaches embodied within them broadly parallel the techniques used by synthesizers to pronounce general English: letter-to-sound rules are used for names not contained in a dictionary of names not following the system's pronunciation rules. However, names differ from English in two important ways. First, there are many more names than words. As mentioned above, there are over 1.5 million last names, several hundred thousand first names. In addition, there are over 2 million trademarked product names, and many more business names, with new ones of each created daily. While one could hope to use a dictionary file providing pronunciations for English words, because of names' constant dynamic creativity, no comprehensive dictionary can be hoped for.

Second, some name sets (first names and surnames) are of various ethnic origins. Many names found to be common in North America have their basis in dozens of different languages. Thus, "standard" name pronunciation rules (if such animals really existed) would not be appropriate for these names. One approach (Church, 1986) used techniques to derives probabilities that a name is from various etymologies (eg: Yanagisako is Japanese with .98 likelihood, French with .00 likelihood, etc), and selects the letter-to-sound rules for the language with the highest likelihood. However, the pronunciations of North American names derived from foreign languages do not strictly follow the pronunciation rules of their original language. Thus, the best systems "flavor" the pronunciation based on an ethnic categorization to better model how names are actually pronounced, rather than rigidly follow foreign-language rules.

State-of-the-art pronunciation systems pronounce names as well as humans (Spiegel, 1990; Golding and Rosenbloom, 1993), and continue to improve. The goal of automatically developing rule sets with minimal human intervention is attractive, either by analogy or psychological principles (Sullivan and Damper, 1990; Dedina and Nusbaum, 1991; Golding and Rosenbloom, 1993), but have yet to come close to the accuracies found in the best commercial systems. Systems that rely mainly on pronunciation rules also offer the opportunity for systematized adjustment for differences in dialect or automatic generation of alternate pronunciations. Such changes can be applied to large pronunciation databases, but only with more difficulty.

Even more confounding is that alternate pronunciations abound. Although there is only one pronunciation of Smith, there are two common U.S. pronunciations for Smythe and Epstein, and several for names like Caughron, Fournier, Koch, and Meagher. Some alternate pronunciations are rare and may be confined to small geographic regions. Unfortunately for application developers, usually when alternate pronunciations occur, they are widespread. Unless an application permits the citation of several alternative pronunciations (using a system that has that capability), or customizations down to the level of individual customer record are possible, at best users may hear a sensible *mis* pronunciation of a name. There is evidence that customers can accept this where the service provides enough utility (Sorin, 1990). Nevertheless, many people are surprised to discover their own pronunciation of their name is not the only one possible or even the commonest (Yuschik, 1994).

44.8 Intonation

General purpose synthesizers strive for an ambitious goal: to pronounce any text well enough for anyone to understand it. Although adequate for some services, current synthesizers need much better prosodic rules. When natural prosody is imposed on an otherwise synthetic utterance, the naturalness is significantly improved (Levinson, et al., 1993). Synthesizers try to produce the prosody directly from text input. In order perform well, synthesizers must mimic an understanding of what's being said. Current semantic models fall far short of providing the minimum amount of needed control.

However, most application domains limit semantic variability. This means that utilizing domain-specific information and assumptions accomplishes a substantial improvement in a synthesizer's prosody. This in turn will lead to higher user comprehension and perceptions of naturalness. A wide variety of intonation patterns need not be used for catalog entries or stock quotes.

A significant amount of prosodic work has been directed to names and addresses for reverse directory services (Bladon, 1992; Silverman, 1993; Spiegel, 1993). Most of these efforts have been directed toward a) enunciating the name as clearly as possible, b) correctly deaccenting items in compounds ("auxiliary line"), with special attention to c) phrasing different classes of prefixed titles (Mr, Dr) and accentable suffixes (Inc, Ltd), and d) appropriate pauses and phrasing needed for complex information. The overall intention is to make the listing easy for transcription, should that be needed, without making the speech so slow or deliberate that users who are only verifying information become annoyed. Some of these adjustment schemes are much more successful than others (Silverman, 1993; Silverman, et al., 1993, see also House, et al., 1993).

44.8.1 Dialog

Automation of a Telephone Relay (or Dual Party Relay) Service is another service that is the product of significant research. This service enables the deaf community to communicate with the general population. Deaf or hearing-impaired users type their side of the conversation; communication is facilitated by an operator who speaks the text for the other party, and types what the other party says. To reduce the costs of this service, in a partially automated version of the service, a synthesizer speaks the text typed by the hearing-impaired customer, and the operator types only what the non-impaired customer says. Among other technological hurdles, the typed input contains few punctuation marks (including sentence-final periods) and varying influences of the syntax and grammar of American Sign Language. This makes it difficult to determine phrase and sentence boundaries.

For an automated telephone relay service, a special parser was written and tested (Bachenko and Fitzpatrick, 1990; Tsao, 1991), so that a stream of text without punctuation could be delivered to the hearing users, one phrase at a time. This manner of presentation was much more successful than synthesizing the input one word at a time or buffered until the typing was completed. The normal linguistic processing of the text stream was augmented with an analysis of the timing of the input. Pauses in typing often indicated phrase or sentence boundaries, and were a good cue in determining when to start speaking the buffered text (Lincoln, 1993).

The automated Dual Party Relay Service involves a conversation between two people, with one speaking through a synthesizer. The dialog is completely under human control. Some of its challenges are based on limitations in typing speed on the part of the sender, and in comprehension and patience on the part of the listener. In other services, where a customer tries to obtain information, such as flight information, or to purchase a product from a catalog, the synthesized dialog is controlled programmatically. Usually the focus of research is to direct users through transactions governed by speech recognition. This involves dialog issues such as guiding a user toward giving the kind of information and using language the system knows how to deal with. Often the default prosody of a synthesizer must be improved to successfully guide a dialog. Adjusted prosodic control of the discourse is seen as making an important contribution, although prosody's contribution is sometimes difficult to measure and sometimes has contradictory effects (House, et al., 1993).

In novel circumstances, a one-way "dialog" can be developed between a synthesizer in response to an inanimate object. In (Davis and Hirschberg, 1988), a program generated driving directions for a car moving through Cambridge, Mass. Since the program had access to the car's changing position, the discourse program was in effect responding to the car actions - the program gave broad preview statements to the driver whenever no specific directional information was necessary, preparatory statements when the car approached difficult intersections, and gave corrective directions when the driver did not follow the spoken directions (accidentally or purposefully). The intonation preprocessor for controlling the synthesized discourse was integral to the system, and was crucial to its success.

As text-to-speech synthesizers get better, the role of preprocessors will shrink. Early speech synthesizers contained rudimentary text normalization routines and did not translate decimal numbers correctly. Thus, to supplement the deficiencies in such early synthesizers, an application preprocessor needed to incorporate number pronunciation rules, such as those needed to translate *3.455* to the words "three point four five five." Few current high-end synthesizers have similar elementary problems, thus obviating the need for such corrections. In similar manner, the current state-of-the-art in synthesis produces rudimentary intonation by default, so as to be a compromise between the often conflicting needs of different text domains. Preprocessors, with their access to domain-specific knowledge, can often dramatically improve comprehension of a synthesizer within a service context (Silverman, 1993). One can hope that large future systems will successfully cope with many different application domains, just as current systems cope with different numerical formats. But, useful service interfaces can be established with present-day technology by a judicious marriage of adequate preprocessing to a good synthesizer.

44.8.2 Role of Paralanguage in Synthetic Speech

Until now we have concentrated on the linguistic information-bearing aspect of speech. However, human speech provides listeners with paralinguistic information as well, conveyed by variations in pitch, speech rate, loudness, and the like. For instance, information about the speaker's affective state is communicated by paralanguage. An early study by Allport and Cantril (1934) demonstrated that people could judge (better than chance) the age of a speaker and some personality characteristics from voice alone.

Certain voices appear (correctly or not) to belong to salient personality types. In other words, there are vocal stereotypes. For example, more rapid speech is perceived as more persuasive. Hesitant or disfluent speakers are perceived to have undesirable personality traits, such as having low credibility. It is difficult, however, to use natural speech to establish putative relationships among vocal parameters and personality attributes, since these parameters (e.g., amplitude, pitch, and rate), tend to covary in natural speech. To overcome this problem, Apple, Streeter, and Krauss (1979) factorially varied speech rate (slow, normal, fast) and average fundamental frequency (low, normal, and high) using alterations introduced by resynthesizing naturally elicited speech from a large number of speakers. All speech was coded using linear predictive coding, so that rate and pitch could be manipulated without changing other vocal parameters. They found these two variables affected people's ratings of personality attributes. Decreasing speech rate had deleterious effects on the perceived persuasiveness, fluency, and nervousness of speakers. Increased average pitch lowered ratings of persuasiveness, and increased the impressions of nervousness and deceptiveness. Thus, to pick a voice type that possesses the most socially desirable traits, one should select a voice with a lower than average pitch and one with a faster than normal speech rate.

It is important to know the degree to which the communication context interacts with vocal qualities in selecting the most appropriate voice. To this end, Rosson and Cecala (1986) varied voice qualities ("head size," pitch, richness, and smoothness) using the modifiable voice dimensions on a commercial synthesizer. A standard phrase was interpreted by listeners in one of a number of communication contexts appropriate for synthetic speech, such as, a financial advice system, the voice in a video game, a body-function monitor, etc. Two derived dimensions, fullness and clarity, described the perceptual space of the generated test voices, whereas three dimensions described the communication contexts; information providing, entertainment, and giving feedback. For contexts that provided information, listeners preferred "full," "clear" voices. (Full voices were those that were "rich" and had "low pitch.") For entertainment contexts listeners preferred medium or low pitched voices emanating from large heads. In contexts for which feedback was required, listeners preferred some degree of harshness.

Studies such as the above are important in showing that the communication context affects the vocal parameters that are deemed most appropriate. Also, the same vocal parameters will be interpreted differently depending on the context. For instance, talking slowly about a simple topic is perceived as more undesirable than talking slowly about something complex (Apple, et al, 1979). Similarly, talking quickly is not always persuasive, since talking quickly about something simple is not rated as persuasive as talking normally. In normal speech, rate and cognitive complexity are negatively related (Goldman-Eisler, 1968). In normal speech, stress tends to increase average pitch. Listeners may implicitly know relationships such as these and use them in making judgments of appropriateness. Thus, listeners take more into account than simply the acoustic data, and consequently a better understanding of these intervening factors would increase our ability to produce more "appropriate sounding" synthetic speech.

44.9 Mixing Synthesized And Natural Speech

Synthesis research has made tangible progress in the quality (naturalness and intelligibility) of synthetic speech. Yet, there remain many challenges on the frontiers of research to improve the naturalness of synthetic speech. While we await their future conquest, we presently have a useful technology for diverse applications. When first confronted with a "robot" voice, those users unaccustomed to synthetic speech may need more than a little convincing of its utility. Often new users can be given some help to adjust to synthetic speech by clever use of speech technology, either through judicious use of stored voice or by switching voices. An application's predictable phrases or prompts provide opportunities to guide the user successfully toward acceptance. This section will describe the effects of various options available for mixing synthetic speech with stored prompts.

The most attractive option is using the *same* speaker for the predictable phrases, carrier phrases, and/or prompts as is used for the synthesis. This option is not (yet) possible for parametric synthesizers, for they do not have spectral characteristics similar enough to any individual to have the potential for merging a stored and synthesized representation seamlessly and imperceptibly. However, concatenative synthesizers, which have sound inventories based on an individual's speech, have the potential of using the same speaker for prompts and for the synthesizer. In a speech recognition interface to a service providing information on new postal codes (Dobler, et al., 1993), sound inventory units encoded for synthesis via the PSOLA technique were extracted from the same speaker as that used for prompts and carrier phrases. The researchers were encouraged that in a demonstration system (heard via a handset in a partially open telephone booth at a fair), only some listeners commented there was some "disturbance" on the telephone line, e.g., they did not appear to notice the transition between stored voice and synthesis. This is a pleasing result, even though the total duration of synthesis was small (a town name). As the effort necessary to develop a high-quality synthesizer from a person's stored recordings decreases in the future, we expect to see more services that mix same-speaker synthesis and prerecorded speech. In addition, with the use of polyphones, extra long units, and reliance on larger inventories of stored speech (Sagasaka, et al., 1992; Hauptmann, 1993; Lamel, et al., 1993), the line between stored voice and synthesis becomes blurred.

For most current applications, using the same speaker for the prompts and the synthesizer is not possible. Thus, the most commonly used mixtures of prompts and database retrieval portions are either a) use of a recorded voice for the prompts and a synthesizer for the rest, or b) use of the same synthesizer for the entire service (prompts, carrier phrases, as well as database retrieval). Each option has *prima facie* merits. Use of pre-stored voice for the prompts and carrier phrases insures that the highest quality speech is used at all times, and might be expected to elicit the highest ratings of overall satisfaction and intelligibility. On the other hand, perception of synthetic speech improves with practice (Schwab, et al., 1985); switching voices in a message may be disruptive to practice effects. Also, the contrast between natural speech and synthetic speech in the same service may cause the synthetic speech to sound more unnatural than if it were the only speech heard. Thus, use of synthesis throughout might be expected to yield higher naturalness ratings for the synthetic speech.

Two studies closely mimic service conditions (Yuschik, et al., 1994; Spiegel and Winslow, 1995). In Yuschik, et al, listeners heard one phonetically balanced telephone listing that was synthesized. Some listeners heard the synthesized listing introduced by a greeting and carrier phrase that was also synthesized, some heard a natural-speech initial greeting and synthesized carrier phrase, and some heard both the greeting and carrier phrase conveyed with pre-stored speech.

In Spiegel and Winslow, listeners retrieved either of two sets of nine listings selected from the NJ directories as representative of the directory's ethnic variety and listing complexity. Listeners heard either the combination of natural speech greeting and synthetic speech carrier phrases prior to the listings, or heard natural speech greeting and carrier phrases. Both natural female and natural male speech were tested. (In both studies, the synthetic speech was a male voice.) .P
In both studies, transcription of the synthesized telephone listing and its spelling were more accurate when the carrier phrases was synthesized, with lower accuracies for the synthesized listing as more and more introductory natural speech was used. This supports proposals for using synthesized speech for the entire interaction because it allows users to adapt to synthetic speech. In Spiegel and Winslow, subjective ratings were also obtained. Mixing female speech with the (male-voice) synthesis was clearly not preferred, receiving the worst ratings for Listing Enunciation, Spelling Clarity, and Overall Service rating. The natural male speech alone, without synthetic-speech transitions to the listing, generally obtained the highest set of ratings.

Because the literature contains contradictory results (see Zeigler and Dobroth, 1988), one should conclude results depend on more than just which speech mode is used. Taking likely endpoints as benchmarks, speech synthesis should *not* be used for the entire interaction if the synthesizer has less than state-of-the-art intelligibility, or the messages are somewhat unpredictable or contain long instructions. Speech synthesis should perhaps be used for the entire interaction if the prompts are short; the user population includes occasional customers; and the synthesizer is first-rate. The most cogent advice must be this: Be sure to test different options for your particular application with representative samples of users. Successful applications have been installed with both options (Sorin, 1994; Yuschik, et al., 1994).

One final option, mixing synthesized voices, has been proposed. This now becomes possible with the advent of synthesizers capable of multiple synthesized voices. As suggested in (Granström and Nord, 1991), messages of different types or different urgencies could be synthesized using different voices. This potentially compounds the problem of accommodating to synthetic speech by using more voices that one must adapt to. Thus, until speech synthesis quality further improves this suggestion is probably best applied in environments where users are highly familiar with each voice, or where the message set and context is somewhat predictable. In the future, one can expect to hear more use of multiple synthetic voices as naturalness continue to improve.

44.10 Summary

The challenges are daunting, but the prospects are great: Anywhere, any time, access to any database, with comprehension and full utility. Of course, this oft-quoted vision of the future of information retrieval likely overstates future reality, for technological dreams rarely play out as expected. It *is* safe to say however that speech technology will continually improve and will find wider acceptance with expanding utility. However, the seamless interface in good applications between technology and user does not happen by accident. Much careful design and selection goes into successful application, and as shown by this chapter, much customization of the underlying technology is often required for the service. This compendium of issues, problems and solutions was not intended to be comprehensive, merely representative. To all those who employ synthesis in applications: in spite of imperfect technology and flawed input to that technology, users can be happy with the results of your efforts.

44.11 References

Allport, G. W., and Cantril, H. (1934). Judging personality from voice. *Journal of Social Psychology*, 5,37-55.

Apple, W., Streeter, L. A., and Krauss, R. M. (1979). The effects of pitch and speech rate on personal attributions. *Journal of Personality and Social Psychology,* 37, 715.

Athimon, C., Bigorgne, D., Cherbonnel, B., Dubois, D., Gagnoulet, C., Jouvet, D., Marzio, H., Monne, J. Py, S., Sorin, C., and Toularnoat, M. (1994). Operational and experimental french telecommunication services using CNET speech recognition and text-to-speech synthesis. In *Second IEEE Workshop on Interactive Voice Technology for Telecommunications Applications,* Kyoto, Japan, September 25-27, 1994, 1-6.

Bachenko, J. and Fitzpatrick, E. (1990). A computational grammar for discourse-neutral prosodic phrasing in English. *Comp. Ling.*, 16, 155-170.

Baker, B. and Nyberg, E. (1989). Semantic compaction: A basic technology for artificial intelligence in AAC. *Proc. of the 4th Ann. Minspeak Conf,* Nov 15-16, St Louis, MO, 1-5.

Belhoula, K. (1993). Rule-based grapheme-to-phoneme conversion of names. *Proc. of Eurospeech,* 881-884.

Blackstone, S. (1994). Augmentative Communication News, March, 7 (2).

Bladon, A. (1992). Synthesis of names using careful speech style. *JASA, 92(4),* 2477.

Carlson, R., Granström, B., and Lindström, A. (1989). Predicting name pronunciation for a reverse directory service. *Proc. of Eurospeech*, 113-116.

Chang, S.K., Orefice, S., Polese, G., and Baker, B. (1993). Deriving the meaning of iconic sentences for augmentative communication. *Proc. of Visual Lang. Conf,* Bergen, Norway.

Church, K.W. (1986). Stress assignment in letter-to-sound rules for speech synthesis. *Proc. of the IEEE International Conf. on Acoustics, Speech and Signal Processing*, 4, 2423-2426.

Coker, C.H., Church, K.W., and Liberman, M.Y. (1990). Morphology and rhyming: Two powerful alternatives to letter-to-sound rules for speech synthesis. *Proc. ESCA synthesis workshop*, Autrans, France, 83-86.

Coile, B.V., Leys, S., and Mortier, L. (1992). On the development of a name pronunciation system. *Proc. of ICSLP*, 487-490.

Cole, R., Hirschman, L, Atlas, L., Beckman, M., Biermann, A.,Bush, M., Clements, M., Cohen, J., Garcia, O., Hanson, B., Hermansky, H., Levinson, S., McKeown, K., Morgan, N., Novick, D. G., Ostendorf, M., Oviatt, S., Price, P., Silverman, H., Spitz, J., Waibel, A., Weinstein, C., Zahorian, S., and Zue, V.

(1995).The challenge of spoken language systems: Research directions for the nineties. *IEEE Transactions on Speech and Audio Processing, (3:1),* 1-21.

Cotto, D. (1993). Improvement of unrestricted text synthesis by the linguistic preprocessing tool: Texor. *ESCA workshop Applications of Speech Technology,* Lautrach, Germany, 199-202.

Davis, J.R., and Hirschberg, J. (1988). Assigning intonational features in synthesized spoken directions. *Proc. of Assoc for Comp. Ling.*, 187-193.

Davis, J. R. (1989). Back Seat Driver: Voice assisted automobile navigation. Ph.D. thesis, MIT Media Arts and Sciences Section.

Dedina, M. and Nusbaum, N.C. (1991). Pronounce: A program for pronunciation by analogy. *Comp. Speech and Lang.* 5, 55-64.

deHaan, H. J. (1977). Speech-rate intelligibility / comprehensibility threshold for speeded and time-compressed connected speech. *Perception and Psychophysics*, 22, 366-37

Dobler, S., Meyer, P., and Ruhl, H.W. (1993). Voice-controlled assistance for the new German mail area codes. *ESCA workshop Applic. of Speech Technol.*, Lautrach, Germany, 23-26.

Fairbanks, G., Futtman, N. and Miron, M. (1957). Effects of time compression upon the comprehension of connected speech. *Journal of Speech and Hearing Disorders, 22*, 10-19.

Foulke, E. (1971). The perception of time-compressed speech. In D. Horton and J. Jenkins (eds.), *The Perception of Language.* Columbus, Ohio: Merrill.

Gagnoulet, C., Jouvet, D., and Damey, J. (1991). MAIRIEVOX, a voice-activated information system. *Speech Communication 10*, 23-31.

Gagnoulet, C. and Sorin, C. (1993). CNET speech recognition and text-to-speech for telecommunications applications. In *Applications of Speech Technology.* September, Bavaria, Germany, 31-33.

Gavignet, F., Charpentier, F., Merle, M., Toen, J., and

Mitha, A. (1993). Voice access to the AFP Scientific News Service through the telephone network. *In Applications of Speech Technology.* September, Bavaria, Germany, 15-18.

Golding, A.R. and Rosenbloom, P.S. (1993). A comparison of Anapron with seven other name-pronunciation systems. *Journal of AVIOS, 14*, 1-21.

Granström, B., and Nord, L. (1991). Ways of exploring speaker characteristics and speaker styles. *Proc. of XIth ICPhsS*, Aix-en-Provence, *4*, 278-281.

Granström, B., Blomberg, M., Elenius, K. Roström, A., Nordholm, S., Nordebo, S., Claesson, I, Waernulf, B., and Eke, K. (1993). An experimental voice-based traffic information provider for vehicle drivers. *Applications of Speech Technology*. September 16-17, Bavaria, Germany, 79-82.

Hauptmann, A.G. (1993). SpeakEZ: A first experiment in concatenation synthesis from a large corpus. *Proc. of Eurospeech*, 1701-1704.

House, J., MacDermid, C., McGlashan, S., Simpson, A. and Youd, N. (1993). Evaluating synthesised prosody in simulations of an automated telephone enquiry service. *Proc. of Eurospeech*, 901-904.

Kalyanswamy, A. and Silverman, K. (1991). Say What? Problems in preprocessing names and addresses for text-to-speech conversion. *Proc. of AVIOS*, Atlanta, GA.

Lamel, L.F., Gauvain, J.L., Prouts, B., Bouhier, C., and Boesch, R. (1993). Generation and synthesis of broadcast messages. *ESCA workshop Applic. of Speech Technol.*, Lautrach, Germany, 207-210.

Levinson, S.E., Olive, J.P., and Tschirgi, J.S. (1993). Speech synthesis in telecommunications. *IEEE Comm. Mag.*, 46-53.

Lincoln, C.E. (1993). AT & T's synthesis applications, personal communication.

New York Times. (1995). Business Travel, Paul Burnham Finney, August 9, p. C4.

Oviatt, S. L., Cohen, P. R., and Wang, M. Q. (1994). Toward interface design for human language technology: Modality and structure as determinants of linguistic complexity. *Speech Communication, 15*, 283-300.

Oviatt, Sharon. (1995). Predicting spoken disfluencies during human-computer interaction. *Computer Speech and Language, 9*, 19-35.

Oviatt, Sharon. (1996). Multimodal interfaces for dynamic interactive maps. *Proc. of CHI '96 Conf.*, Vancouver, British Columbia, Canada, April 13-18, 95-102.

Patterson, B.R. (1986). Development evolution of automated customer-name-and-address (ACNA). Bellcore publication, TM-NPL-008219.

Pierrehumbert, J. (1981). Synthesizing intonation. *Journal of the Acoustical Society of America 70, 985-995.*

Robinson, C. P. (1985). Eyes/ears/spatial/verbal: How should a cockpit talk to a pilot? In R. E. Eberts and C. G. Eberts (Eds.), *Trends in Ergonomics/Human Factors II.*

Elsevier Science Publishing, B. V., North-Holland.

Rosson, M. B. and Cecala, A. J. (1986). Designing a quality voice: An analysis of listeners' reactions to synthetic voices. *Human Factors in Computing Systems*, Proc. of Chi '86 Conf.

Sagasaka, Y., Kaiki, N., Iwahashi, N., and Mimura, K. (1992). ATR ν-talk speech synthesis system. *Proc. of ICSLP*, 483-486.

Schmandt, C., Hindus, D., Ackerman, M., and Manandhar, S. (1990). Observations on Using Speech Input for Window Navigation. Proc. of the IFIP TC 13 *Third International Conference on Human-Computer Interaction*, 787-793.

Schmandt, C. (1994). *Voice Communication with Computers*. New York, Van Nostrand Reinhold, 1994

Schmidt, M., Fitt, S., Scott, C., and Jack, M. (1993). Phonetic transcription standards for European names (Onomastica). *Proc. of Eurospeech*, 279-282.

Schwab, E.C., Nusbaum, N.C., and Pisoni, D.B. (1985). Some effects of training on the perception of synthetic speech. *Human Factors*, 27, 395-408.

Silverman, K.E.A. (1993). On customizing prosody in speech synthesis: Names and addresses as a case in point. *Proc. of ARPA workshop Human Lang. Technol.,* 317-322.

Silverman, K., Kalyanswamy, A., Silverman, J., Basson, S., and Yaschin, D. (1993). Synthesiser intelligibility in the context of a name-and-address information service. *Proc. of Eurospeech*, 2169-2172.

Social Security Administration: Report of distribution of surnames in the social security number file, Sept 1, 1984, SSA Pub No. 42-004, April 1985.

Sorin, C. (1990). Text-to-speech synthesis and telephone network experiments in France. *ESCA Tutorial Day on Speech Synthesis*, Autrans, France.

Sorin, C. (1994). CNET's synthesis applications, personal communication.

Spiegel, M.F. (1985). Pronouncing names automatically. *Proc. of AVIOS*, 107-132.

Spiegel, M.F. (1990). Speech synthesis for network applications. Proc. of Speech Tech, 347-351.

Spiegel, M.F. and Macchi, M.J. (1990). Development of the ORATOR synthesizer for network applications: Name pronunciation accuracy, morphological analysis, customization for business listings, and acronym pronunciation. *Proc. of AVIOS*, Bethesda, MD.

Spiegel, M.F. (1993). Coping with telephone directories that were never intended for synthesis applications. *Proc. of ESCA workshop Applic. of Speech Technol.,* Lautrach, Germany.

Spiegel, M.F. (1996). Advances in Human-Interface Engineering for Reverse Directory Assistance (ACNA) Services. *Int. J. of Sp. Tech.,* 1, in press.

Spiegel, M.F. and Winslow, E. (1995). Advances in the Implementation of Effective Reverse Directory (ACNA) Services. *Proc. of AVIOS Conf.*, San Jose, CA, Sep 12-14.

Streeter, L. A., Vitello, D., and Wonsiewicz, S. A. (1985). How to tell people where to go: Comparing navigational aids.*International Journal of Man-Machine Studies 22*, 549-562.

Sullivan, K.P.H. and Damper, R.I. (1990). A psychologically-governed approach to novel-word pronunciation within a text-to-speech system. *ICASSP*, 341-344.

Temem, J., and Gitton, S. (1993). An experience with speech technologies applied to SNCF's Telephone Information Centres. In *Applications of Speech Technology*. September, Bavaria, Germany, 39-42.

Tsao, Y.-C. (1991). Text-to-speech technology for dual party relay services. *Proc. of Human Factors Soc*, 213-216.

Vitale, A.J. (1991). An algorithm for high accuracy name pronunciation by parametric speech synthesizer. *Comp. Ling.*, 17, 257-276.

Vitale, A.J. (1991). Assistive speech I/O in the 1990's: Current priorities and future trends. Keynote Speech at the Cal. State Univ. Northridge Conference at Palm Springs, Voice Input/Output and Persons with Disabilities, Palm Springs, CA.

Vitale, A.J. (1993). Hardware and software aspects of a speech synthesizer developed for persons with disabilities. *Journal of AVIOS*, 13, 27-40.

Yankelovich, N., Levow, G., and Marx, M. (1995). Designing SpeechActs: Issues in speech user interfaces. In *Human Factors in Computing Systems, Proc. of CHI '95 Conf.*, May 7-11, Denver, CO., 369-376.

Yuschik, M. (1994). Ameritech's ACNA application, personal communication.

Yuschik, M., Schwab, E.C., and Griffith, L. (1994). ACNA - The Ameritech customer name and address service. *Journal of AVIOS, 15*, 21-33.

Zeigler, B.L. and Dobroth, K.M. (1988). Pairing text-to-speech and natural speech in a single speech message. *Proc. of AVIOS.*

Handbook of Human-Computer Interaction
Second, completely revised edition
M. Helander, T.K. Landauer, P. Prabhu (eds.)

Chapter 45

Designing Voice Menu Applications for Telephones

Monica A. Marics and George Engelbeck
U S WEST Advanced Technologies,
Boulder, Colorado, USA

45.1 Introduction

Millions of people use Phone-Based Interfaces (PBIs) every day. Because of its vast coverage, the touchtone telephone has become the primary terminal used by many software applications. Example applications include: automated banking, data base querying, order entry, remote self-help, directory assistance, audiotext, automated call routing, voice mail, and call screening. PBIs are popular primarily because they are readily available to many users. In 1993, over 70.5 percent of Americans owned a touchtone telephone (Yankee Group, 1994).

45.1.1 Purpose

This chapter is intended as a "how to" guide for designing PBIs. We concentrate on how to create usable applications rather than explaining how and why certain designs work. Our experiences include developing PBIs, doing research on PBIs, and participating in domestic and international standard bodies. Both of us have practiced at regional telephone companies within the United States. Although we have little experience developing PBIs for markets outside the United States, we believe much of our design experience is applicable to international settings.

45.1.2 Scope of this Chapter

Our focus is narrow. We discuss how to design voice menu applications for mass market consumers. These PBIs use the telephone's keypad and mouthpiece as an input devices and the telephone's earpiece as the output device. Mass market products can be divided into single use and repeated use applications. Single use applications include those where users unexpectedly encounter the application, or use the application infrequently. In repeated use applications, users gain enough experience with the application to begin memorizing menu choices and interrupting prompts. Design guidelines for both application types are covered.

Traditionally, application user interface development consists of five areas: requirements, functional specification, design, development, and test. This chapter discusses issues mainly in the design phase–interaction components, guidelines and standards for voice menu applications. We assume that the application has been appropriately scoped, users have been identified and profiled, and a user task analysis has been performed.

For other voice menu design guideline documents, refer to the Voice Messaging User Interface Forum (Information Industry Association, 1990), User Interface to Telephone-based Services-Voice Messaging Applications (ISO, 1995), Increasing the Usability of Interactive Voice Response Systems: Research and Guidelines for Phone-based Interfaces (Schumacher, Hardzinski, Schwarts, 1995), Designing Phone-based Interfaces (Halstead-Nussloch, DiAngelo, Thomas, 1989), User Friendly Recommendations for Voice Services Designers (France Telecom, 1991), U S WEST Touch Tone Standards for Voice Prompted User Interfaces (Bain, 1990), and Ameritech Phone-based User Interface Standards and Design Guidelines (Schwartz, Hardzinski, 1993). We do not discuss how to design for telephone interfaces using speech recognition (see Dobroth, Karis, Ziegler, 1990; Waterworth, 1982), or designs for screen-based telephony (see Davies, 1995).

45.1.3 PBI User Interfaces

PBIs are appropriate when:

- potential users have access to a touchtone telephone,
- information needs to be accessible from many locations,
- users' tasks are constrained and goal directed,
- interactions are relatively short, and
- modest amounts of information are transferred.

Human conversational speech averages from 175 to 225 words per minute, which translates to approximately 300 baud (Schmandt, 1994). In addition, audio output is transitory so users have to remember more information than they would with a comparable visual display. Poorly designed PBIs can tax the working memories of their users to the point where users cannot successfully use the application (Kidd, 1982).

There are three primary styles for PBIs: voice menus, command driven, and skip and scan.

Voice Menu

Voice menus are the most frequently used interface style for phone-based applications. Applications using this style typically present a title, ask a question, or present a menu of instructions to users. Users choose the action they want by pressing the action's corresponding key.

The voice menu style is frequently chosen for phone-based applications because it is easy to use and requires little training. These characteristics are important since many phone-based applications are intended for use by populations that do not receive training. The success of these applications depends on users being able to dial up "cold" and use them effectively.

Command Driven

Command driven interfaces have key sequences (e.g., ∗72 or ∗h) that correspond to application operations. Example applications of this type include Call Forwarding and Call Trace. Compared to voice menu interfaces, command driven interfaces tend to be difficult to learn and difficult to remember how to use. One disadvantage is that users must remember, rather than recognize, command names and entry syntax. This situation is exacerbated by the 12-button keypad which leads to cryptic command strings. However, they may be more efficient for applications where users are willing to take the time and effort needed to become proficient.

Skip and Scan

Resnick and Virzi (1992) describe a PBI interaction

style called skip and scan. A skip and scan application maps navigation commands to the keypad. During playback of information, pressing 7 takes users to the previous item, pressing 9 takes users to the next item, and 1 selects the item. Skip and scan is good for information retrieval applications where long audio files can be easily skipped. With a skip and scan application, users can skip ahead to information of interest without listening to all of a current message.

However, the advantages of skip and scan are also its limitations. There is an initial time cost while users learn the navigational commands. Skip and scan does not allow experienced users to choose an item directly. Additionally, as Resnick and Virzi report (p. 424), the voice menu style is becoming a *de facto* standard. Skip and scan is seen by users as being a non-standard way to interact with a phone-based application.

45.1.4 Structure of this Chapter

Section 45.2 discusses the structure of applications and voice menus. Section 45.3 discusses prompts and prompt recording. Section 45.4 discusses data input and common data elements. Section 45.5 discusses general application issues such as timeouts, prompt interrupt and error recovery. Finally, Section 45.6 contains a summary of guidelines and recommendations.

45.2 Menu Structure

Voice menu applications present prompts, menus and messages to users. Specifically, a *prompt* is an application request for input–for example, “Please enter your password.” A *menu* is a collection of prompts. For example, “To erase, press 1. To send, press 2. To exit, press star,” is a menu consisting of three prompts. There are also application *messages* which merely convey information without requesting action–for example, “Loan amounts are updated on the first of each month.”

Schmandt (1994) wrote, “The awareness that speech takes time (and acceptance that time is a commodity of which we never have enough) should permeate the design process for building any speech application.” This is the essence of a successful voice menu application design. To make users’ interaction with the application most efficient, the auditory information should short and concise. Encourage users to interrupt menus by making selections. This highlights the importance of the wording and structure of the menus.

45.2.1 General Structure

Voice menu applications take the form of a branching tree structure. Typically, there is a Main Menu which users hear upon entering the application. The options on the Main Menu lead to sub-menus containing more choices, or to task paths. The standard factors concerning the depth versus breadth of menus apply (see Lee and MacGregor, 1985). Users progress forward and backwards through the tree by making selections. At each node in the tree structure, context sensitive help may be provided. A global command to back-up through or exit the tree structure may also be provided.

45.2.2 Titles

The Main Menu and all other important menus should have titles. It is easy for users to become lost in an interactive telephone application. Given the auditory nature of voice menus, users can forget where they are within the application, and how to return to a previous point in the application's flow. To help users understand the structure and where they are within the application, important menus should be titled. To be effective sign-posts, titles should be task related.

45.2.3 Items per Menu

The majority opinion is that four items per menu is about right. If more than four menu items are offered, users can forget which items were offered, and which one they wanted (Engelbeck and Roberts, 1990). Although menus should be limited to four items, global commands such as Help and Exit need not be included in this count. Also, menus may have additional items that are not stated in the menu for expert users.

45.2.4 Order of Items

Menu items should be ordered according to frequency of use, natural order, functionality or consistency.

Frequency of Use

Frequency of use is the preferred way to order menus. The most frequent menu choice should be the first item on a menu. If frequent choices are listed first, users do not have to listen to and remember the entire menu. This saves users' time and application connect time. Users will feel that the application is well designed because they do not have to wade through lengthy prompts to find the item of interest.

The frequency of use guideline can be overridden if the menu choices have a natural or functional order. If the same menu is offered in several places, consistency of menu choices should take precedence over frequency of use.

Natural Order

Some menu choices have a natural order. For example, you have to *add* things to a list before you can *delete* them. Preserving the natural order of items can help users remember the choices.

Functionality

Related menu items should be mentioned together to help users keep track of the choices. For example, suppose you have the following menu items for a telephone banking application: savings account information, pay bills, transfer funds, and checking account information. You might place the savings and checking account information items next to one another in the menu since they are functionally similar, although user testing should confirm such design decisions.

Consistency

If the same menu choices are offered several times in an application, then those choices should be ordered consistently, and consistently assigned to the same key. Confirmation of data should be placed on the 1 key, and negation on the 2 key consistently throughout the entire application. For example, "If you own a car, press 1. If you don't, press 2." In many cases, you can even rephrase the question so that confirmation is the most frequent answer in addition to being consistently offered first. Consistency between menus can help users quickly learn an application's structure.

45.2.5 Numbering Menus

Menu choices should be numbered consecutively starting at 1. Users expect that the first menu choice they hear will be on the 1 key. Likewise, they expect the second choice to be on the 2 key and the third choice to be on the 3 key. Numbering choices consecutively helps users keep track of the choices. It also allows them to guess which key is next once they hear the beginning of a prompt.

Avoid skipping numbers or presenting numbers out of order. In some cases, this may be difficult. For example, some users may not have access to all the features, or you may be reserving a number in a menu for a future feature.

Menu items should be stated before the key corresponding to the action, e.g. "To do action, press 1". With this wording, if users are not interested in the action, they do not have to actively remember the associated key. Authors such as Halstead-Nussloch (1989) and Engelbeck and Roberts (1989) recommend an action-key ordering.

45.2.6 Mnemonics

Mnemonics should not be used to specify menu choices. For example, it may seem natural to specify, "For yes, press y. For no, press n." However, there are several reasons why mnemonics are not desirable:

- It takes longer for users to locate a letter on the telephone, such as "y," rather than a number, such as "9." (Try dialing "1-800-Rentals" rather than "1-800-736-8257.")
- There are often several terms for the same command. For example, "erase," "delete" and "remove" do approximately the same thing. Users have to remember which form of the command is being used in order to remember which letter to press.
- Not all phones have letters on the keypad.
- The position of Q and Z is not consistent across telephones, if they even appear at all.
- If commands begin with different letters and those letters are on the same telephone key, there is a conflict. If commands begin with the same letter, there is also conflict. For example, P, R, and S all appear on the 7 key. In voice messaging, which command would you put on the 7 key: Pause, Play, Rewind, Reply, or Repeat?
- Mnemonics won't work if the application is expanded to international markets. Not only are words spelled differently, but languages which do not use the Roman alphabet, such as Russian, Japanese, Chinese and Arabic, will not be able to use the interface.

45.2.7 Active Menu Options

If a menu option is currently not available to users, don't speak that option in the menu. For example, users should not be prompted to "delete" unless something has already been "created". Likewise, don't prompt users to turn a feature off if the feature is already off. (Note: this may create a hole in the order of menu items.)

45.2.8 Global Commands

The keys 0, * and #, are typically mapped to the global commands help, cancel, and delimit input. Global commands should always perform the same action throughout an interface (with the exception of 0 in data entry). In addition, the keys should be active in all parts of the application. If the keys only work in some parts of the application, users may be unable to discriminate when the keys are active, and when they are inactive. Since these keys perform the same functions throughout an application, they need not be counted as menu items.

45.2.9 Vocabulary

The wording of the menu choice should clearly represent the functionality accessed by that choice, and should be used consistently across the application. Words mean different things to different users. Succinctness (e.g., "Turn on, press 1.") and clarity (e.g., "To turn on toll blocking which disallows all outgoing toll calls, press 1.") should be balanced (e.g., "To block toll calls, press 1.") If the words are ambiguous, even users who know what they want to do will be confused about which menu option to select.

We have found that the verb *enter* works well when asking users to enter a sequence of touchtone keystrokes; *dial* works well when specifically asking users to enter a telephone number; *press* works well for single keystrokes, and *speak* works well for asking users to record or input speech. (The verb *dial* also works well for interfaces that accept both touchtone and rotary input, although this should be balanced against the proportion of expected touchtone and rotary users.) In phrasing menu options, use *for* when referring to an object, and *to* when referring to an action. Examples include "For schedules, press 1. To change your itinerary, press 2." It is not necessary to add the word *key* or *button* after each menu item (e.g., "To listen, press the 1 key."). From context, users understand that 1 refers to the keypad. In addition, it lengthens the prompt and sounds repetitive across several menu items.

If users are sure about which menu item maps to their goal, they do not have to remember other menu items, and can choose that item immediately after it is spoken. Decreased ambiguity can allow the presentation of a greater number of menu items without degrading performance. When users are unsure of which menu item they want, they may listen to the entire menu and try to remember every menu choice offered. Additionally, users may have to listen to the menu several times before choosing a menu item. This greatly decreases users' satisfaction with the application's interface.

45.3 Application Prompts and Recordings

Recording prompts and messages can be a very costly and time intensive process. Selecting a voice for the application is important. In addition, for each individual recording attention must be paid to the speech rate, inflection, intonation, volume, and phrasing of the voice.

45.3.1 Talent Selection

Voice preference is very subjective. We often get user input on different voices prior to making a talent decision. If the application is one of a family of applications, then making a mistake with the original voice can have long lasting ramifications. Users are sensitive to voice changes once an application is in the field. When we changed the voice talent for a voice messaging product, we received numerous user comments like "is she sick" or "was she fired." Keep in mind that the voice is the major affective element of your application, and becomes a trademark of your service.

It is well worth the expense to hire a professional voice talent to record application prompts. The voice talent will need to understand the application in order to record prompts with the correct intonation. If a prototype of the application is available, letting the talent go through the prototype will help him or her get a feel for the interface. If larger messages are created from smaller pieces, the talent must be able to inflect each phrase so that it sounds natural when strung together. A trained voice and ear are invaluable for this process.

When selecting an application voice, the specific characteristics of the voice seem to be far more important than the gender of the voice. In our experience, users prefer a good voice over an unpleasant voice regardless of the gender. Traditionally, female voices have been used for instructions and information in the telephone network. Empirical data (Cox and Cooper, 1981) show that male and female voices are both appropriate depending on the degree of "agreeableness" and "assertiveness" in the specific voice.

Use only one voice for your application's prompts, menus and messages. Using different voices disrupts the application's flow. Introducing a new voice focuses attention on the voice, rather than on what is being said. There is one exception to this rule. A different voice may be used to differentiate or emphasize an example from the rest of the prompts. For example, if you offer a sample greeting to voice messaging users, the sample greeting might be recorded in a voice different from the application's voice.

Synthesized speech (computer-generated, rule-based speech) is useful for speaking information that continually changes, or can't be predicted. For example, synthesized speech might be used to read out inventory information to delivery people, or to pronounce customer names and addresses. This type of information is so varied that it would be nearly impossible to pre-record. However, the unnaturalness of synthesized speech limits it applicability. Because the pronunciation software does not understand the meaning of what it is saying, it cannot provide natural phrasing, correct word accents, inflection or emotion. In addition, synthesized speech has lower intelligibility and imparts a higher cognitive load on the listener (see Luce, Feustel and Pisoni, 1983; or Chapter 44 of this volume).

45.3.2 Voice Characteristics

The voice for an application should be selected to match the context and purpose of the interactive application. (Marics, 1989; Rosson and Cecala, 1986) While the words in a prompt give users information, the tone and cadence of the speech prompts give users affect and atmosphere. Different voices have different affect. For example, Oksenberg and Cannell (1988) review how the vocal characteristics of telephone survey administrators significantly affected their customer response rate. A regional accent may be appropriate for a local calendar of events, but not for a world news broadcast. An excited tone is appropriate for lottery or sports results, but not when calling in for a bank balance. The right voice makes a large difference in users' perception of the application.

45.3.3 Prompt Files

Human voices change from day to day and hour to hour. Record all the prompts for an application in a single session if at all possible. Prompts recorded at different times will have obvious differences in volume, tone, pitch, and inflection. After recording, play back the prompt files over a speakerphone to see whether any of the prompts are misinterpreted by the application as touchtone input. This phenomenon, commonly called "talk off," occurs more frequently with female voices. If any of the prompts are "talking-off" the application, those prompts will need to be re-recorded, filtered, or a new voice talent selected.

While it is tempting to reuse prompt files within different parts of an application, this is a risky approach. If you later decide to change the wording in one area of the application, you will need to cross check all the other instances where that prompt is used before understanding the effects of the desired change on the application. The complexity of reusing prompts between applications is even greater since it is difficult to track how every prompt is used in each application.

Some applications will attempt to save memory by recording prompt segments and concatenating them into longer prompts as needed. Although a necessity for prompts with variable information such as times, dates, and telephone numbers, this approach makes the prompts sound choppy and artificial. Playback time is usually increased since the application has to locate and play multiple files rather than a single file. Recording is more difficult since each fragment requires intonation suitable for several contexts rather than a single context. Finally, maintenance of the prompts is also more difficult since fragments are reused in multiple instances. In general, this approach is not recommended.

45.3.4 Phrasing

Rate of Speech

In many applications, prompts are spoken at a slow, constant rate so that users can catch every word. Unfortunately, this also has the effect of making the prompts tedious and boring. We recommend a fairly rapid speaking rate for prompts. DeGroot and Schwab (1993) report that time compression of prompts did not degrade task performance or users' ratings of the application. However, the time compression did not lead to shorter task times due to a slower response to menus. Mulligan, Whitten and Tsao (1988) found that compression of natural speech up to 275 words per minute had no effect on retention, however the speech was rated less favorably by participants. It is our belief that prompts spoken in an energetic and brisk manner contribute to users' perception that the application is quick paced, even if the overall task duration times do not bear this out.

Intonation

The intonation of prompts and prompt phrases is critical to perceived application quality. Users seem to be particularly sensitive to the intonation used when recording error messages. For example, in two different applications the authors have worked on, users have complained that the application scolds them for not taking the correct action. Re-recording the same prompt with a softer intonation ended the complaints.

Intonation is also important when combining prompt segments into a longer prompt. For example, when recording digits which will be combined and played back as a local telephone number, it will sound most natural if each digit is recorded three times using three different intonations (France Telecom, 1991). A neutral intonation is used for digits when they occur within a sequence. A "mid tonal" intonation is used for digits prior to a pause in the digit string, and a "final descending" intonation is used for digits at the end of the string. If a single intonation is used for all positions, the telephone number playback sounds awkward and seems to end suddenly since there is no lowering of the tone for the final digit. Intonation is also important for other prompt strings such as times, dates, spelled letters, or monetary amounts.

Silence and Pauses

Pauses during speech can convey several meanings to users. For example, a pause might indicate a change of topic, or that the information to follow is very important. Pauses are also used to group related pieces of information. In the example below, the pauses are inappropriately placed. Users might become confused as to whether "press 2" refers to "hotel reservations" or to "car reservations."

Incorrect: "For airline reservations ....press 1. For car reservations .... press 2. For hotel reservations .... press 3. To exit .... press star."

Correct: "For airline reservations, press 1. .... For car reservations, press 2 .... For hotel reservations, press 3. .... To exit, press star."

45.3.5 Content

Repetitiveness

Early phone-based interfaces made liberal use of "please" and "thank you" in the application prompts. However, over time users have found continual (and artificial, since it is a computer) politeness annoying. While politeness is useful to soften the tone of some prompts, such as error and help messages, use it sparingly to avoid annoying users.

Similarly, early applications appended the word "now" at the end of each menu phrase (e.g., "For checking, press 1 now. For savings, press 2 now. For money market, press 3 now...") Stuart, Desurvier and Dews (1991) recommend against this practice for two reasons. First, it implies that users should wait for the prompt to finish before entering the appropriate keystroke. Second, it implies that the only time users can enter the keystroke is after the prompt. (Use of "now" may be appropriate if the application can, in fact, only accept input after a prompt. Also, see Section 45.5.5 for information on uninterruptible prompts.)

Sometimes "thank you" can be used to acknowledge user input. However, removing excessive repetition from prompts allows users to complete their tasks more quickly and with less annoyance.

Brevity

Prompts should be as brief as possible while still conveying the intended meaning to users. Although some applications allow users to toggle between verbose "novice" prompts and succinct "expert" prompts, we do not recommend this practice. First, it doubles the amount of prompts to write, record and maintain. Second, if prompts are concisely phrased to begin with, there is little gain in adding more verbiage. Remember that users hear the prompts in the context of the larger application. This contextual knowledge can be used to eliminate redundancy in the prompts. Samples are shown in Table 1.

While making prompts concise, care should be taken not to be abrupt. Recording these prompts with a softened intonation is important.

Vocabulary

Prompts for interactive applications should use language common to users. State things in the simplest way possible. Make sure users understand terms that are specific to your application. For example, users might not know their "geographic location number," but they do know their "postal code / zip code."

Conversational Style

An application should not refer to itself using a pronoun, nor over-naturalize the interaction to the point of pretending to be a person. For example, users of a particular voice mail application disliked prompts where the application pretended to apologize (e.g., "Sorry you are having trouble.") and prompts where the application pretended to converse with users (e.g., "Are you still there?"). While error messages are necessary, these prompts offer no information or assistance to users, they simply waste time.

Table 1. Prompt brevity.

Original	Revised
"For a listing of all hotels within your local area, press 1. For a listing of all vacation cottages in the area, press 2. For listings of rental homes and condos in the area, press 3."	"For local hotels, press 1. For cottages, press 2. For rental homes and condos, press 3."
"If you would like to add a name to the list, press 1. To remove a name from the list, press 2. To hear all the names on the list, press 3."	"To add a name, press 1. To remove a name, press 2. To hear the list, press 3."
"You have entered 555-1234. If this telephone number is correct, press 1. To change it to a different telephone number, press 2."	"555-1234. If this is correct, press 1. To change it, press 2."

45.4 Data Elements

This section describes user interface practices for the input and manipulation of common data elements such as times, dates, and alphabetic characters.

45.4.1 Sequence of Data Entry

Data entry usually includes the following sequence: prompt for input, receive input ending with a delimiter, and confirm input.

Prompting for Input

Tell users how to enter their input, and what format their input should take. With applications that mix voice recording and key input, users might need to be reminded when to use the keypad and when to speak. For example, "Using the telephone keypad, enter ...," "After the tone, please speak your ..." Whenever the mode of input changes, remind users of the change. Be as specific as possible when asking users for input. This will reduce input errors and make the application more friendly to users. For example, "Enter your *four digit* password," "Enter the *hour and minutes* you want your message delivered," "Enter your *area code and telephone number*."

Input Delimiters

The purpose of an input delimiter is to let the application know users are finished with their input. For fixed length input strings, delimiters are not necessary. For variable length strings, the # key or a timeout are typical delimiters.

There are several tradeoffs to consider between requiring users to enter a specific keystroke delimiter, such as the # key, and using a timeout to delimit the data entry. Studies have shown (Aucella and Ehrlich, 1986; Davis, 1988; Halstead-Nussloch, Logan, Campbell, and Roberts, 1989; Marics, 1990; Stuart, Desurvier, Dews, 1991) that users often forget to enter keystroke delimiters. In addition, sometimes it takes as long to prompt for the delimiting keystroke, as it takes to merely timeout (Stuart, et. al., 1991). sing a timeout to delimit input requires the same amount of time for users who do not interrupt prompts, but is much easier since users do not have to remember anything or take any additional steps.

In applications designed for repeat users, delimiting keystrokes are desirable since they allow users to avoid waiting for the timeouts to expire. Even when delimiting keystrokes are accepted in an application, if users forget to enter the delimiter, a timeout should also delimit the data entry.

Our recommendation is as follows. If # is entered after a menu choice, fixed, or variable length data string, always accept it as a delimiter. If # is not entered by users, assume the data is delimited after an application timeout. (For timeout length, see Section 45.5.1.) Applications intended for repeat users should prompt for the # key. This prompt helps users learn the keystroke delimiter, and saves them time since repeat users can be expected to interrupt prompts as their familiarity with the application grows. Applications intended for one-time or infrequent users should not prompt for the

Table 2. Confirming Input.

Original	**Revised**
"One two dollars and zero six cents."	"Twelve dollars and six cents."
"Eight two three am."	"Eight twenty-three am."
"March two three, one nine nine nine."	"March twenty-third, nineteen ninety-nine."

key (but accept it if entered), and use a timeout to delimit data entry. This reduces the complexity of the prompts for infrequent users and does not increase the time penalty of application use.

Confirmation

During the confirmation step, the application should repeat the data input and ask users to confirm the information (e.g., "June 22 at 2:00 pm. If this is ok, press 1. To change it, press 2. To cancel and exit, press *.") The confirmation step tells users what the application recognized, and gives them a chance to change or cancel the entry.

When the application confirms data input, the data should be spoken using common language. If users enter a product code or account number, avoid reading back the number entered. Instead, give the product name (e.g., blue cotton sweater) or the account title (e.g., checking account). If users enter a dollar amount, time or date, speak the information using its natural form. Examples are shown in Table 2.

45.4.2 Time

A standard sequence for time entry is: request time, request if am or pm , confirm entry. If only 24 hour time is accepted, the request for am/pm can be eliminated. An example is shown below.

Service:	"Enter the hour and minutes you want the message delivered."
User:	8 3 0
Service:	"For am, press 1. For pm, press 2."
User:	2
Service:	"Eight-thirty pm. If this is correct, press 1. If not, press 2."

An application should accept time entry of 1, 2, 3 or 4 digits. If the entry is one or two keystrokes, assume that the user has entered an hour. If the entry is three or four keystrokes, assume that the last two digits entered are the minutes and the initial digit(s) are the hour. Do not require leading zeros.

After the time has been entered, ask if it is am or pm. If the time entered was 12:00, rather than asking for am/pm ask if the time was noon or midnight since these terms are more commonly used.

The application should accept 24 hour time, but not require it unless it is commonly used in the environment of the application (e.g., non-U.S. or military). If the application can determine that an entry is in 24 hour time, the am/pm step can be eliminated. However, you should still ask users to confirm the time entered.

45.4.3 Days of the Week

Days of the week can be entered as a digit between 1 (Monday) and 7 (Sunday). Assume that all times are in the future. For example, if today is Friday and a user specifies a 2 for Tuesday, assume that the user means next Tuesday rather then the one that has already past. As shown in the example below, users will need to be prompted for this convention.

Service:	"Days are numbered from 1 to 7 starting with Monday as 1. Please enter the day."

45.4.4 Dates

Dates should be entered in two steps–enter month, and enter day. The order of the steps is dependent upon local convention. Do not require a leading zero. If necessary, ask for the year. Finally, confirm the entry. An example of date entry is shown below.

Service:	"Please enter a number from 1 to 12 for the month."
User:	3
Service:	"Enter the day."
User:	21
Service:	"Enter the year."
User:	98
Service:	"March twenty-first, ninteen ninty eight. If this is correct, press 1....."

45.4.5 Monetary Amounts

The format for dollar amounts depends on whether users need to enter whole dollars or both dollars and cents. If only whole dollars are needed, ask users to enter "the whole dollar amount." If dollars and cents are required, either break the request into two separate parts, prompt users to enter the decimal point, or have the application insert the decimal point automatically.

Prior experience (Goodwin, 1988) has shown that if the latter is implemented, the prompt should explicitly state that users have to include cents, and that the decimal point will be included automatically. The application studied by Goodwin assumed that users were automated bank teller machine users. Asking for dollars and cents with a single prompt was chosen, in part, because it was similar to the format required by most automated bank teller machines. This style of entering dollar amount may not be the best style for other domains. An example is shown below.

Service: "Enter the dollars and cents, a decimal point will be inserted automatically."

User: 3 7 5 2

Service: "Thirty-seven dollars and fifty-two cents. If this is correct, press 1. If not, press 2."

45.4.6 Telephone Numbers

Telephone numbers vary in length depending on the local network. In the input prompt, specify the expected length of the telephone number, and whether or not special prefixes are required for long distance calls. Sample input prompts are shown below:

Service: "Please enter the 4 digit extension."

Service: "Enter your area code and phone number, then press pound."

Service: "Dial the forwarding number as you would if you were placing a call."

Service: "Dial the 7 digit phone number. For long distance calls, include 1 plus the area code."

45.4.7 Spelling

Spelling information in English is accomplished using the letters on the touchtone keypad. The letters Q, Z and punctuation are typically not printed on the touchtone keypad (Figure 1). However, the ISO/IEC inter

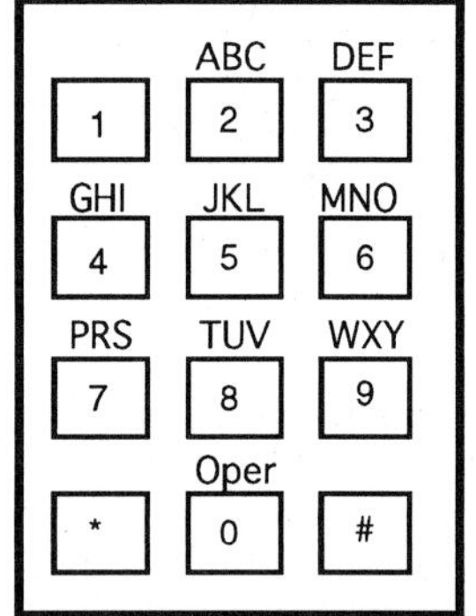

Figure 1. Alphabet assignments to a 12-key numeric pad.

national standard (ISO/IEC 9995 Part 8, 1994) places the letter Q on the 7 key, and Z on the 9 key (see also Blanchard, Lewis, Ross and Cataldo, 1993; Davis, 1991; and Marics, 1990). In most applications, users can skip over punctuation when entering information. If the punctuation is essential, such as in an inventory or stock number, then users need to be given instructions on how to enter the punctuation.

There are two styles of alphabet entry in use: unique letter entry, and *ambiguous* letter entry. Ambiguous entry uses one keypress per letter. A person using this method to enter the name "Pat" would press the 7 key for P, the 2 key for A, and the 8 key for T. There are 27 possible letter combinations formed by the keys 7-2-8. A database look-up or statistical algorithm can be used to guess which word was entered. If several matches are found, the user is presented with a menu of the possible choices and is asked to choose which item was intended. In unique entry, each For example in the repeat key method, users press a key 1, 2 or 3 times depending on whether the first, second, or third letter on the key is desired. For example, to enter the name "Kim," a user would press the 5 key twice, the 4 key three times, and the 6 key once. Although each letter is entered, there may be problems distinguishing between adjacent letters if both letters fall on the same key. Additionally, users may forget to account for the Q and Z when entering letters using the 7 and 9 keys. For a description of the various unique entry methods, see Kramer (1970) or Detweiler, Schumaker, and Gattuso (1990).

45.4.8 User Recordings

User recordings are a form of data input. Examples of user recordings include greetings, messages, and names. User recordings should be preceded by a record tone, which indicates to users that they can begin speaking. In telephone answering applications after an outgoing greeting has been played, the record tone can also be detected by other automated applications to indicate that a machine, not a human, has answered a call. The ISO standard on voice messaging user interfaces (ISO, 1995) specifies a record tone sequence of 150 ms of a 500 Hz pure sine wave, a pause of 75 ms, and 150 ms of 620 Hz sine wave. The frequencies and durations should be accurate to plus or minus 2% to be standard compliant.

User recordings can be delimited by either a keypress, typically #, or by a silence timeout. This timeout is calculated by measuring the duration of silence in the recorded string. If the silence is longer than, for example, 4 seconds, the application assumes the user is finished recording and asks for confirmation. This silence time should then be removed from the end of the original voice recording prior to processing.

45.4.9 Lists

Lists occur in many phone-based interfaces. For example, users might have message distribution lists, dialing lists, or lists of calls to screen. List elements generally require many different actions - adding, removing, skipping, selecting, reviewing, and changing the contents of an element or an entire list. These actions can be direct or implied.

Implied Action: In this situation, only two actions, add and remove, are allowed. Users enter an item and if the item is not on the list it is added; however, if the item is already on the list it is removed. While conceptually elegant, this paradigm is somewhat awkward for users. Since users cannot see the actual list, they must remember the status of a given element in order to infer that the appropriate action that will take place.

Direct Action: In direct action, users request the specific action to be taken (e.g., add, remove, change, review, etc.). Users can specify the object of the action either before or after specifying the action itself. This method seems less confusing to users since the action is specified and not implied. In addition, it allows for a greater variety of actions such as reviewing or changing a portion of the data element.

In many cases, lists and list elements can be "tagged" with recorded names to aid in identifiying the object of the list actions. For example in voice messaging group distribution lists, it is easier for a user to identify group list "management action committee" rather than group list "number 5."

45.4.10 Schedules

Schedules can be difficult to implement in phone-based interfaces because of memory constraints and the imperfect mapping of two dimensional calendars onto a single auditory dimension. There are several different types of schedules which vary in complexity: a single, one-time event; a simple repetitive event; complementary schedules which flip between two alternatives; schedules which vary by day-of-week and time-of-day; and complex repetitive events. Little has been published about scheduling in PBI applications. See Plaisant and Shneiderman (1992) for a brief discussion of scheduling issues for graphical user interfaces.

For single events, users generally enter the day and time of the event. The day can either be a date, or a day of the week where Monday = 1 and Sunday = 7. For simple ongoing events, users generally enter the day of week and time of the event. An example of a single event might be scheduling a birthday reminder, while a simple, ongoing event might be remembering to take the trash out each Wednesday. These events are fairly straightforward and have been successfully implemented in a variety of phone-based interfaces. This type of schedule can be used successfully by first time users.

The following schedule types should be used with caution. They are most appropriate for infrequently changed schedules and motivated users. In some cases, successful usage will require training, written documentation, or memory aids.

- Complementary schedules occur when either of two schedules is active. Examples might include separate schedules for weekdays versus weekends, or school nights versus weekend nights. These schedules require entry of separate event times for each schedule, and knowledge of when the different schedules take effect. These schedules are complex and there is a high probability of confusion surrounding events which occur across a schedule boundary (e.g., between the weekday / weekend boundary).

- Time-of-Day/Day-of-Week schedules offer more flexibility and are likewise more complex. For each day, users enter one to several time intervals. The intervals can be copied across days if necessary. For example, a small business might be open Tuesday through Saturday, with early closing on Saturday and extended hours on Thursday night.

- Complex, repetitive events require entry of the start date and time, and of the repetition parameter.

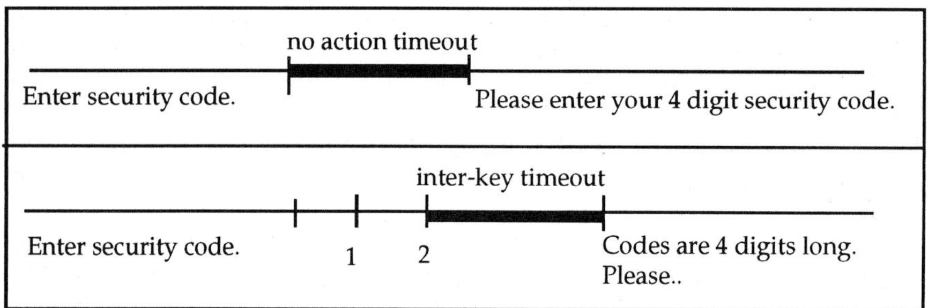

Figure 2. Timeouts.

For example, someone might have class every other Tuesday, or meet the first Wednesday of every month. These schedules are extremely difficult to implement in a phone-based interface because of the large variety of repetition parameters to select from, and because feedback about the schedule setting is auditory rather than visual.

For all schedules, care must be taken when events cross day boundaries. For example, suppose a business owner wants to forward calls when the business is closed. The business closes at 5 pm and reopens at 8 am each morning. However, poorly designed applications might not allow schedules to cross the day boundaries. In that case, the owner would have to translate the closed hours to a 24 hour day (e.g., each 24 hour day, the store is closed from midnight to 8 am and then from 5 pm to midnight). In addition, if the store is closed on the weekend, a second schedule would have to cover Saturday and Sunday. Error checking should alert users to overlaps in schedules or unscheduled blocks. Holidays and other temporary suspensions of schedules merely increase the complexity.

45.5 General Application Issues

45.5.1 Timeouts

Voice menu applications have timeouts for user input. There are two reasons for this. First, each user of a PBI application ties up a telephone line dedicated to the application. Users who are not interacting with the application may be denying access to other users. The second reason is that if users do not respond to an input prompt, they may be having a problem. They may not have understood the prompt; They may have understood the prompt, but not know what to enter; They may not want to be at this spot in the application and they are trying to figure out how to exit; Or, they might just need more time to look up an account number of phone number. Timeouts can occur in two contexts: When users do not take action after an application prompt (*no action timeouts*), and when users stop interacting within a sequence of actions (*inter-key timeouts*). Figure 2 gives an example of a no action and an inter-key timeout.

No Action

A no action timeout occurs when the application has prompted users for input but has not received any. In most cases, a no action timeout of about 5 seconds works well.

If users need to refer to external materials for information, such as a credit card from their wallet, the timeout should be extended. Users may require different amounts of time to enter different pieces of information. For example, users will be able to enter their own telephone number fairly quickly. However, it may take users much longer to enter their social security number. It will take users longer to spell alphabetic information into the interactive application than it will take them to enter numeric information. Elderly and differently abled users may take longer to enter information. Additionally, applications where users use telephones with the keypad built into the handset may need to allow extra time for users to access the keypad.

When a no action timeout occurs, the application should repeat the prompt or menu, and may include additional information about how to cancel a task or access help. If users timeout repeatedly, the application might return users to the nearest titled sub-menu, or disconnect them from the application.

Inter-key Timeout

An inter-key timeout occurs when the application is receiving a string of touchtone inputs from users. Again, a timeout of about 5 seconds works well. This time may need to be adjusted according to the situation. For example, it may be shortened for security codes, or lengthened for credit card numbers.

When an inter-key timeout occurs, the application should do one of two things. If a timeout occurs and the input is a valid, the application should use the timeout as a delimiter (see section 45.4.1). If a timeout occurs and the input is not valid, the application should present an error message and ask users to reenter the data.

Timeout During Record

Timeouts during recordings should be treated as though the users had entered the delimiter. If nothing was recorded prior to the timeout, this can be treated as a recording error condition.

45.5.2 Hang-ups

Frequently, users will implicitly exit a voice menu application by hanging-up the telephone. Unfortunately, users will also hang-up the telephone when they get confused or wish to cancel a task. To avoid premature hang-ups, applications should confirm the completion of tasks (see also section 45.5.7).

When the completion of tasks is confirmed, frequent users will listen for the start of the confirmation before hanging up. First time users who listen to the confirmation, will know that the task has been performed. However, users who make a menu selection, change their mind, and then hang-up will not hear the confirmation, nor know that their action had been completed. The application will fail to meet the expectations of these users. However, users who have heard prior confirmations for tasks tend to listen for the confirmations.

Tasks should be designed around users' goals. Information central to the users' goals should be gathered last so as not to give users a false sense of task completion. For example, when leaving a message in a messaging application, expect users to hang-up after speaking the message. This means that the application should ask for the telephone number needed to deliver the message, before asking users to record the message.

Optional parameters can be set after the goal central information is gathered (Polson, Lewis, Rieman, and Wharton, 1992). Again, in a messaging application it might make sense to prompt for delivery options after users have recorded the message. Those users who wish to change delivery options are unlikely to hang-up after recording the message. Those users who are comfortable with the defaults for the delivery options are free to hang-up.

45.5.3 Error Conditions

Error messages should help users determine what went wrong. These messages should not blame users, nor should they scold them. Messages should suggest how to fix the problem. For example, "Invalid stock number. Stock numbers are 6 digits long. Please enter a stock number." After several consecutive errors, the application may offer context sensitive help, return users to a titled sub-menu, or disconnect.

45.5.4 Prompt Interrupt

The ability to interrupt a long menu with a keystroke is critical. If users know or hear the choice they want, they should be able to select it immediately. Once users have entered a command, users should be taken to the requested place in the application. This will speed a user's path through the application, increase user satisfaction and decrease call connect time.

Non-interruptable prompts should be avoided. If necessary, divide a prompt into non-interruptable and interruptable segments. The non-interruptable segment should be as brief as possible. Users should not be forced to listen to any part of an application. They should control the application, not vice versa. Consider the situation where an incorrect password has been entered. Often users will realize that they made a mistake before they have even finished entering the number. Why force users to listen to an error message when they may already know the problem? Simply let users interrupt the error message and re-enter their correct password.

Non-interruptable messages should contain only exceptionally important information. Input entered during a non-interruptable message should be ignored by the application. Only input during regular interruptable messages and prompts should be stored and acted upon.

45.5.5 Dial Ahead

Dial ahead is the ability to enter touchtone input before the application has requested it. If the application is one that users use frequently, they quickly will become familiar with the menu choices and keystrokes. Repeat users will be able to traverse the menu structure without listening to intervening prompts. For example, in a banking application, repeat users may enter 3-1-2 at the Main Menu to quickly learn their account balance. If repeat users want to skip menus without listening to them, that capability should be available.

If an entry error occurs when users are typing-ahead, the stacked input should be discarded and an error message played where the entry error occurred. For example, suppose a user wants to log onto voice mail and listen to the third message in the mailbox. Users enter "9-9-9-9" for their four digit security code, a "1" to listen to messages, and two "#'s" to skip to the third message. Users' stacked input is "9-9-9-9-1-#-#". If users make a mistake entering the security code, then the stacked input should be discarded (i.e. 1-#-#) and the error message, "Invalid security code. Please re-enter..." should be played.

45.5.6 Help

Help generally takes two forms, either transfer of the call to a human attendant, or playback of a help prompt containing additional, context sensitive information. Help prompts should be interruptible so that any input during the prompt has the same effect as if that input had been entered from the application menu where help was accessed.

Service:	"For gift ideas, press 1. For mail order, press 2. For help, press 0."
User:	0 (wants bridal registry, but did not hear that option)
Service:	"Gift ideas include suggestions for birthday gifts, wedding gifts, and bridal registry. Mail order...."
User:	1
Service:	"For birthday gifts, press 1. For wedding gifts, press 2. For bridal registry, press 3."
User:	3

Most PBIs place the help functionality on the 0 key. During data entry, an isolated 0 followed by a timeout may be interpreted as a request for help. Otherwise, the 0 key is interpreted as a digit. During data input, users have to cancel or finish the input (either by a timeout, by pressing * or by pressing #) before being able to request help.

Brevity of prompts also applies to help messages. Elaborate explanations are easily tuned-out or forgotten by users. Help messages of over two minutes are generally too long for users to remember. In addition, users like to refer to information while performing tasks. Placing detailed help within the application, such as the steps needed to set up a schedule, prevents its effective use while users are actually performing the task. Finally, help messages can be softened by recording in an appropriate tone of voice and using "please" judiciously.

45.5.7 Feedback

After users have made a selection, the application should begin playing the next prompt within three seconds of receiving the input 90 percent of the time. If users interrupted a prompt with their selection, the prompt should stop playing within 0.5 seconds 90 percent of the time (ISO, 1995).

When an application performs an action, users should hear feedback telling them what has happened. Confirmation reassures users that the intended action has occurred, and provides a sense of task closure before continuing with the application. For example,

Service:	"Transfer three hundred pounds from savings to checking. If this is ok, press 1. If not, press 2."
User:	1
Service:	"Money has been transferred. Main menu..."

The application should also confirm cancellation of input. In this situation, the application should state exactly what *did not* happen. For example,

Service:	"Transfer three hundred pounds from savings to checking. If this is ok, press 1. If not, press 2."
User:	* (implicit cancel)
Service:	"Transfer canceled. Main menu..."

45.5.8 Terminology

PBIs should use terminology common to users. In our experience, the users are not necessarily familiar with the names for the * and # keys, the differences between "rotary" and "pushbutton" telephones, and the differences between "pulse" and "tone" dialing.

- * - We recommend you refer to this as the "star" key. Another common name for this key is the "asterisk" key.
- # - In the United States, we recommend you refer to this as the "pound" key. American users

are not always familiar with the name of this key. It may help to prompt users, upon timeout, that the "pound key is located under the 9 key." Other common names for this key vary by country and include: number sign, tic-tac-toe, box, square, hash, or sharp.

- Rotary and Pushbutton - Rotary phones are phones with a circular dial rather than a button keypad. Rotary phones do not have * and # on their dial, and use pulse (loop) signaling to the switch. Pushbutton phones typically have a 12 key keypad with * and #, and use tone or pulse signaling, see below.
- Pulse and Tone Signaling - In pulse signaling, the telephone emits a series of clicks for each digit dialed. All rotary phones use pulse signaling, and all telephone lines accommodate it. In tone signaling, the telephone emits a DTMF (dual tone multifrequency) signal for each digit dialed. Unlike pulse signaling, users' telephone lines have to be configured for DTMF signaling.

Most PBIs require access to pushbutton phones that emit DTMF. However, some applications are able to accommodate both DTMF and pulse input.

45.5.9 Service Set-up

Many PBIs guide users in setting up a service the first time they call in. These set-up sequences prompt users through a procedure, and explain the various elements in the service. For example, in a voice messaging service, an introductory set-up sequence might include having users set a security code, record a greeting, and explain how to retrieve messages. Some set-up sequences are only available the first time users call the service, others allow users to save the tutorial to share with all household members, and others are reached by a toll free number and are always available. Set-up sequences are highly effective, and are recommended for complex applications that need to be set-up before they can be used.

45.5.10 Rotary Callers

In every application, there will be callers who try to access the application from a rotary dial telephone, or from a push-button telephone with pulse dialing. Application designers must be prepared for this situation and give such callers a graceful exit from the application.

There are several ways to address this situation. The first prompt might tell callers that a touchtone telephone is required and give alternate instructions for rotary callers. Or, callers might be asked to input a touchtone digit. If they don't respond, the application can assume they are rotary callers and transfer them to a live attendant. A slightly more elegant approach is to first assume that callers do have touchtone phones. If they don't respond to the first request for actual input, transfer the call to a live attendant, or play a help message which gives them an alternate number to call. In considering the alternatives, evaluate what percentage of users can be expected to call with a rotary telephone, and how long they will have to wait before being given additional instructions.

45.5.11 Modifying Existing Applications

As with most software applications, changing requirements often dictate the need to add to, or less frequently, remove functionality from an application. PBI's are more similar to main-frame applications than they are to desktop software. Since PBI users call into a central application, whenever the central application is changed, all users are affected. Because users have not purchased or installed updated software, they might not be aware that an application has changed.

The degree to which application changes affect users depends upon the change and the user population. Sometimes significant changes in menu structure are required to add functionality. The trade-off between accommodating existing users and optimizing for the new design depends on the size of the current user base, usage patterns, and expected growth. For repeated use applications, such as voice mail, it can be expected that many users have memorized functionality/keystroke bindings and possibly programmed common sequences into a memory string. If users are interrupting prompts and navigating through an application by rote, they might not hear the newly worded prompts prior to entering keystrokes. Users can end up in an unexpected place in the interface because their old keystroke sequence has a new meaning under the revised interface.

For repeated use applications, we recommend the following. (Note that these recommendations may conflict with guidelines in Section 45.2.) When revising applications, avoid renumbering existing menu items. If possible, new items should be added to the end of the menu. Removed items should leave menu gaps so that users do not have to learn new key bindings. Do not move destructive functions to a previously assigned key. For example, if "repeat message" was on the 3 key, do not replace this function with "erase message" so as to avoid having users erase messages when they intend to merely repeat them. Avoid inserting steps, lengthening prompts, or making the interaction appear longer to users. Finally, because experienced users may not listen to prompts, alert users to a change in application functionality up front. For example, place a brief, non-interruptable, alerting message prior to login or directly before the Main Menu.

For single use applications, application changes are less problematic. Users of these applications are unlikely to have memorized keystroke bindings, and they are more likely to listen to application prompts. In these situations, application changes can be fairly extensive without significantly impacting users.

45.6 Summary

The following summarizes user interface design recommendations for voice menu applications for telephones.

Menu Structure

1. Title all important menus.
2. Limit each menu to 4 or fewer items.
3. Order menu items according to frequency of use, natural order, functionality and consistency.
4. Number menu choices starting at 1.
5. Number menu choices consecutively.
6. Word prompts for actions "To do action, press Y."
7. Word prompts for attributes "For attribute, press Y."
8. Use numbers, not letters or other mnemonic prompts, for menu choices.
9. Don't speak that option in the menu, if an option is not available.
10. Provide global command keys for Help, Cancel, Back-up and Skip.
11. Use global commands consistently.
12. Word menu choices so they clearly represent the functionality of that choice.
13. Keep menus as brief as possible.
14. Carefully choose menu vocabulary.

Application Prompts and Recordings

15. Use a professional voice.
16. Use a single application voice.
17. Choose a voice to match your application's personality.
18. Use synthesized speech for speaking information that continually changes and can't be assembled from prompt segments.
19. Record all prompts, menus and messages during a single session.
20. Don't design prompts just to facilitate reuse of prompt files.
21. Check to make sure your prompts don't "talk off" the application.
22. Record prompts at a fairly rapid rate.
23. Prompts should be spoken with energy.
24. Make sure the intonation of prompts does not mislead or annoy users.
25. Use pauses between phases to convey meaning.
26. Use "please" and "thank you" conservatively.
27. Keep prompts simple and concise.
28. Use language that is familiar to users.
29. Don't have the application refer to itself using pronouns, nor over-naturalize the interaction.

Data Elements

30. Tell users how to enter their input.
31. Tell users what format their input should take.
32. Give users enough time to enter the input.
33. Always accept #, if entered, as a delimiter.
34. Repeat data back to users using common terms.
35. Let users actively confirm input.
36. Applications should not require input delimiters.
37. Design for Q, Z and punctuation during alphabetic entry.
38. Precede user recordings with a record tone.
39. After an activity is completed, return users to a familiar place.
40. Tell users how to exit.
41. Match tasks to a user's goal structure.

General Application Issues

42. Give users more information if users do not enter anything.
43. Confirm the completion of application tasks.
44. Error messages should state the problem and how to correct it.
45. Let users interrupt the application with keystrokes.
46. Avoid non-interruptable messages.
47. Make non-interruptable messages as short as possible.

48. Let users type-ahead through several menus.
49. Discard input entered during a non-interruptable message.
50. Let user interrupt help prompts.
51. Tell users what action the application has taken.
52. Confirm the cancellation of input.
53. Use a set-up sequence for applications that need user data to function.
54. Give rotary callers a way out.
55. Tell users when applications have changed.
56. Avoid renumbering exiting menus.

45.7 References

Aucella, A.F. and Ehrlich, S.F. (1986). Voice messaging- enhancing the user interface based on field performance. *Proceedings CHI-86 Human Factors in Computing Systems*. New York: ACM. 156-161.

Bain, L. (1990). U S WEST Touch Tone Standards for Voice Prompted User Interfaces. U S WEST Technical Report.

Blanchard, H.E., Lewis, S.H., Ross, D. and Cataldo, G. (1993). User performance and preference for alphabetic entry from 10-key pads: Where to put Q and Z. *Proceedings of Human Factors Society 37th Annual Meeting,* 225-229.

Cox, A.C. and Cooper, M.B. (1981). Selecting a voice for a specified task: The example of telephone announcements. *Language and Speech*. 24(3), 233-243.

David, J.R. (1991) Let your fingers do the spelling: Implicit disambiguation of words spelled with the telephone keypad. *Journal of the American Voice I/O Society*. March 1991, 57-66.

Davies, S. (1995). Lessons learned in screenphone user interface design: A human factors perspective. *Proceedings of the 2nd Advanced Screen Telephony Business Issues Forum.* April 18-19, 1995. Atlanta, Georgia.

Davis, J. R. (1988). When things go wrong: An analysis of user errors with Direction Assistance. *Proceedings of Speech Tech '88.* American Voice Input/Output Society, New York, NY. 304-306.

DeGroot, J. and Schwab, E.C. (1993). Understanding time-compressed speech: the effects of age and native language on the perception of audiotext and menus. *Proceedings of the Human Factors Society 37th Annual Meeting,* 244-248.

Detweiler, M.C., Schumacher, R. M., and Gattuso, N. L. (1990) Alphabetic Input on a Telephone Keypad. *Proceedings of the Human Factors Society 34th Annual Meeting,* 212-216.

Dobroth, K.M., Karis, D., and Zeigler, B.L. (1990). The design of conversationally capable automated systems. *International Symposium on Human Factors in Telecommunications.*, 389-396.

Engelbeck, G. and Roberts, T. (1990). The effects of several voice-menu characteristics on menu-selection performance. *Proceedings of the Bellcore Symposium on User Centered Design.* Bellcore Special Report SR-STS-001658. Red Bank, NJ. 50-63.

France Telecom (1991). User -friendly recommendations for voice services designers. Ref: NT/LAA/TSS/426-TARIF:150 F HT (177, 90 TTC).

Goodwin, Pat (1988). Interface usability evaluation of project Aries. U S WEST Advanced Technologies Technical Report. PS-08-05-00003-001.

Halstead-Nussloch, R. (1989). The design of phone-based interfaces for consumers. *Proceedings CHI-89 Human Factors in Computing Systems.* New York: ACM. 347-352.

Halstead-Nussloch, R., DiAngelo, M., and Thomas, J. (1989) Designing Phone-Based Interfaces. Workshop presented at the Human Factors Society Meeting, Denver, Colorado. October 16-20, 1989.

Halstead-Nussloch, R., Logan, R., Campbell, R., Roberts, J. (1989). Usability test of the self help phone interface. *IBM Technical Report TR 00.3534.*. Watson Research Center, Yorktown Heights, NY.

Information Industry Association. (1990). Voice Messaging User Interface Forum Specification Document. Information Industry Association, 555 New Jersey Ave. NW, Washington, D.C. 20001

International Standards Organization. (1994). Information Technology - Keyboard Layouts for Text and Office Systems - Part 8: Allocation of letters to the keys of a numeric keyboard. ISO/IEC 9995-8. Geneva, Switzerland.

International Standards Organization. (1995). Information Technology - Document Processing and Related Communication - User Interface to Telephone-based Services - Voice Messaging Applications. ISO/IEC 13714:1995(E). Geneva, Switzerland.

Kidd, A.L. (September, 1982). Problems in man-machine dialog design. *Paper presented at the Sixth International Conference on Computer Communication* (531-536), London.

Kramer, J.J. (1970). Human factors problems in the use

of push-button telephones for data entry. *Proceedings of Symposium on Human Factors in Telephony.* Berlin. 241-258.

Lee, E. and MacGregor, J. (1985). Minimizing users search time in menu-retrieval systems. *Human Factors,* 27(2), 157-162.

Luce, P.A., Feustel, T.C., Pisoni, D.B. (1983). Capacity demands in short-term memory for synthetic and natural speech. *Human Factors,* 25, 17-32.

Marics, M.A. (1989). Voice Characteristics for Auditory Interfaces. Poster session at *The Human Factors Society 33th Annual Meeting.* Denver.

Marics, M.A. (1990). How do you enter D'Anzi-Quist using the telephone keypad? *Proceedings of the Human Factors Society 34th Annual Meeting.* Orlando, FL. 208-211.

Mulligan, R.M., Whitten II, W.B. and Tsao, Y-C. (1988). Parameters of information-rich auditory announcements. *Proceedings of the Human Factors Society 32th Annual Meeting,* 242-246.

Oksenberg, L. and Cannell, C. (1988). Effects of interviewer vocal characteristics on non response. Chapter in *Telephone Survey Methodology.* 257-269.

Plaisant, C. Shneiderman, B. (1992) Scheduling home control devices: design issues and usability evaluation of four touchscreen interfaces. *International Journal of Man-Machine Studies.* 36, 375-393.

Polson, P., Lewis, C., Rieman, J., and Wharton, C. (1992). Cognitive walkthroughs: A method for theory-based evaluation of user interfaces. *International Journal of Man-Machine Studies,* 36, 741-773.

Resnick, P and Virzi, R.A. (92) Skip and scan: Cleaning up telephone interfaces. *Proceedings CHI'92, Human Factors in Computer Systems.* New York: ACM. 419-426.

Rosson, M. B. and Cecala, A. J. (1986). Designing a quality voice: an analysis of listeners' reactions to synthetic voices. *Proceedings CHI '86 Human Factors in Computer Systems.* New York: ACM. 192-197.

Schmandt, C. (1994). *Voice Communication with Computers - Conversational Systems.* Van Nostrand Reinhold, New York.

Schumacher, R.M., Hardzinski, M.L., and Schwartz, A. (1995). Increasing the usability of interactive voice response systems: research and guidelines for phone-based interfaces. *Human Factors. 37* (2), 251-264.

Schwartz, A. and Hardzinski, M.L. (1993). *Ameritech phone-based user interface standards and design guidelines,* Rel 1.0. Ameritech Services. Hoffman Estates, IL.

Stuart, R., Desurvier, H. and Dews, S. (1991). The truncation of prompts in phone based interfaces: Using TOTT in evaluations. *Proceedings of the Human Factors Society 35th Annual Meeting.* 230-234.

Waterworth, J.A. (1982). Man-machine dialog acts. *Applied Ergonomics, 13,* 203-207.

Yankee Group (1994). White paper on consumer communications. *YankeeVision,* 11 (7), May 1994.

Part VII

Programming, Intelligent Interface Design, and Knowledge-Based Systems

Handbook of Human-Computer Interaction
Second, completely revised edition
M. Helander, T.K. Landauer, P. Prabhu (eds.)

Chapter 46

Expertise and Instruction in Software Development

Mary Beth Rosson and John M. Carroll
Department of Computer Science
Virginia Polytechnic Institute and State University
Virginia, USA

46.1 Introduction

Programming, and software development more broadly, was the first focus of research in human-computer interaction (e.g., Shneiderman, 1980). These pioneering investigations, carried out under the banner of "software psychology," focused on problems of professional programmers. The scope of this research was quite broad, encompassing topics like team organization and management, individual differences, and design problem-solving. Teaching and learning were only a small part of this project. Thus, Shneiderman (1980: 54) briefly contrasted syntactic-oriented drill-and-practice with language-independent problem-solving as paradigms for programming education, but no research presented in his book addressed this or any other teaching and learning issue.

After 1980, learning emerged as a central topic in software psychology. This development was fueled by the same forces that propelled HCI more generally: many people were encountering programming and interactive applications for the first time, creating an interest that was both pervasive and intense, as well as a significant training challenge. A measure of the intensity of interest in programming at that time is the claim of Papert (1980) that programming should become the cornerstone of elementary education (cf. Dalbey and Linn, 1985).

Progress was initially disappointing for two reasons. First, many of the earliest studies were quite atheoretical. They tended to pursue extremely narrow and concrete research questions, instantiating the schema "Does the feature X facilitate/impair learning?" An example is Mayer's (1975) finding that flowcharts facilitate program composition, but can slow down comprehension. It is difficult to generalize such results across programming languages and environments without a theoretical framework. These isolated results were difficult to apply in the design of new languages and environments. Indeed, a second limitation of the early work was that it was not effectively coupled to software technology development and work design. It often focused on issues pertaining to software technologies and practices that were declining rather than emerging, and ignored issues related to the applications being supported by software technologies.

In this chapter we survey the research of the late 1980s and early 1990s on the nature of software development expertise and approaches to teaching software development skills. We see in this literature several

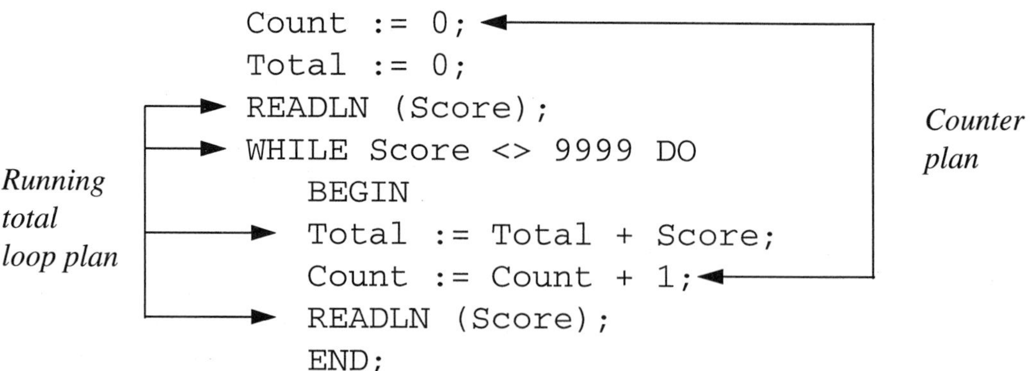

Figure 1. Two interleaved plan structures in a segment of a Pascal program. *(adapted from the sample programs used by Soloway and Ehrlich, 1984)*

complementary developments addressing the limitations of the early work. First, we review how a cognitive science perspective was employed to develop a theoretical framework for interpreting and refining the empirical studies. Instead of focusing on the efficacy of particular features, research began to characterize the knowledge and skill of programmers, and how that knowledge and skill is acquired and developed. Second, we review how studies of software expertise have raised the level of analysis from individual lines of code to the design of software systems and to the teamwork involved in such activities. Finally we examine research and development of programming and design instruction that incorporates these new perspectives on software development expertise.

46.2 Cognitive Analyses of Programming

The first researchers to make detailed analyses of the nature of expertise in programming were cognitive scientists interested in the structure and application of mental representations. The emergence of cognitive science in the early 1980s focused research attention on the computational "architecture" of cognition (Anderson, 1983; Newell, 1980; Newell and Simon, 1972; Pylyshyn, 1984; Schank and Abelson, 1977). Complex problem solving became the touchstone task for this research, which typically integrated studies of human performance and computational modeling. Programming was a particularly attractive domain for investigation: it was obviously complex, at least partially closed with respect to knowledge of the world, and most of the investigators already knew how to program and so could supplement their empirical work with introspection. The nature, acquisition and use of mental representations in programming quickly became a standard cognitive science research area (e.g., Brooks, 1977; Anderson, Farrell and Sauers, 1984; Soloway and Ehrlich, 1984).

46.2.1 Schematic Knowledge

Cognitive architectures define general types of mental structures that mediate learning, comprehension and action. These structures are theories about the nature of knowledge and the ways knowledge can be acquired and used. A structure adopted and developed extensively in the domain of programming is the *plan* (Schank and Abelson, 1977). A plan is a schematic structure describing stereotypical concepts and events in a type of situation.

In programming, a plan is considered to be an abstract representation of the goals and subgoals necessary to achieve the function of a program or program segment; the most detailed level of a plan contains links between subgoals and specific computational structures that implement them. Most discussions of plans refer to fairly low-level structures, for example a plan that creates a running total loop or a counter (see Figure 1). However in principle a plan may encompass an entire program or subroutine and be composed of other plans, for example a routine that sorts a set of scores. In actual program code, plans are interleaved to meet the problem specifications.

A number of early studies arguing for the psychological validity of the programming plans were carried out by Elliot Soloway and his colleagues (e.g., Ehrlich and Soloway, 1984; Soloway and Ehrlich, 1984; Soloway, 1986). For example, as evidence for the existence of plans in experts, Soloway and Ehrlich (1984) demonstrated that the program comprehension of experts was more disrupted by deviations from plan-like structures than that of novices. Rist (1986) reported that experts in a code-sorting task used plan structure in grouping code segments while novices relied more on control structure and syntactic features. Letovsky and Soloway (1986) showed that experienced programmers found programs with delocalized plans (i.e., the elements were distributed across the physical program code) difficult to understand. For languages in which the plan structure is clear (e.g., block-structured languages), experts tend to generate code one plan at a time (Détienne, 1995; Rist, 1990; 1991). Scholtz and Wiedenbeck (1992) reported that experienced programmers applied programming plan knowledge from a known language when faced with an unfamiliar language, even when the familiar plans led to suboptimal solutions.

More recent analyses of programming expertise have elaborated the original notion of a programming plan as a "chunk" of expert knowledge. Rist (1990) proposed that plans have a nonlinear structure in which one line is central or "focal." For example in a counter plan the main "result" line in which the counter is incremented has a focal role because it implements the plan goal.

Davies (1994) discussed nonlinearity in plan structures in considering programming plan acquisition. He argued that the individual elements of a plan are not learned simply through steady accretion and tuning as the programmer moves from novice to expert. Rather a restructuring process takes place, yielding plans that have a hierarchical structure organized around focal elements. When Davies (1994) asked programmers varying in expertise were asked to recognize plan elements, he found that performance of experts was significantly better for focal vs. non-focal elements, but that novice and intermediate programmers did not respond differentially to focal elements. He cited this as evidence for a hierarchical restructuring of plan knowledge during the evolution from intermediate to expert programmer.

Earlier work by Brooks (1983) on program comprehension also assumed a more articulated view of expert programmers' knowledge structures. He proposed that expert program comprehension involves a hypothesis generation and testing procedure. Experts browse a program to develop initial hypotheses, then search for evidence that would confirm or disconfirm these hypotheses. The hypotheses are associated with stored knowledge of typical programming structures (or plans) and Brooks argued that experts search for plan "beacons" to test or refine their hypotheses. So for example, a programmer may recognize a line of code implementing a stereotypical exchange of values in an array as a cue for a sort routine. A variety of studies of expert programming comprehension have confirmed the role of beacons in plan recognition (e.g., Koenemann-Belliveau and Robertson, 1991; Gellenbeck and Cook; Wiedenbeck, 1986).

Although most work on programming plans has described knowledge structures at the code level (e.g., counters, loops, guards), it seems clear that experts also possess higher-level schematic knowledge that guides their planning of an overall solution structure. For example, Jeffries, Turner, Polson and Atwood (1981) proposed the existence of design schemas that are independent of particular problems, but that organize experienced programmers' problem-solving; an example might be a high-level plan to organize a solution into components that can handle input, processing, and output. Guindon (1990) observed experts relying on schematic knowledge that may have been learned through experience on related problems, for example the knowledge of alternatives and tradeoffs that should be considered in managing race conditions in distributed control systems.

46.2.2 Strategic Knowledge

Knowledge of programming plans is recruited and applied through the course of various programming activities. A programmer could know the appropriate plan structure for a given problem, but fail to apply it correctly. It is therefore useful to separate knowledge about programming plans from knowledge about how and when to engage programming plans while comprehending or generating code. The latter is often called strategic knowledge.

An early proposal by Rist (1989) argued that because expert programmers possess well-formed programming plans, they should be able to retrieve and "read out" these plans in a linear fashion. They simply must activate the appropriate plan, expand the plan to its most detailed level, and output the lines of code that correspond to the leaf nodes of the plan. In contrast, novices should exhibit a problem-solving programming style, in which they first seize upon a salient (i.e., focal) element of a solution approach and then gradually expand the plan from there. Rist reported programming protocols in which novices did in fact generate lines of code in a nonlinear fashion (i.e., not corresponding to the final text order of the program). In contrast, experts seemed to write lines of code in final plan order. This early model reflected a classic plan-based view of code generation attributing little strategic control to experts—they simply rely on their schematic knowledge to generate and output code in an orderly fashion.

However, in other work at about the same time, Green, Bellamy and Parker (1987) observed significant code generation *nonlinearities* for experienced programmers working on Pascal and Basic programs. These researchers noted that the programmers would often return to earlier sections of their code to insert new material. They proposed the "parsing-gnisrap model" to account for these nonlinearities in code production: a programmer generates and partially implements a plan; later the partial code structures are expanded through a process of re-comprehension to retrieve the original plan (parsing), followed by the inverse process of code generation (gnisrap). Green et al. further observed that the incomplete code structures usually contained the more important (in Rist's terms focal) elements of the plan. Thus they confirmed Rist's notion of focal lines, but demonstrated that experienced programmers do not always write code in complete and orderly plan chunks. They argued that this is especially likely to occur when memory capacity is stressed, as this is when the programmer will externalize the contents of working memory by writing down salient features of plans in progress.

The study of Green et al. did not contrast novices and experts, but Davies (1993) used their general findings to argue that experts should be more likely than novices to generate and later expand focal lines, because these plan features are relatively more salient in the experts' (hierarchical) internal representations. Although at first glance this proposal appears to contradict Rist's (1989) earlier observations of greater plan orderliness in expert versus novice programmers, it seems quite likely that the degree of nonlinearity in production will be a function of both expertise and task characteristics: experts with sufficient cognitive processing capacity may expand a plan internally before writing down any code and thus output lines in plan order. Novices still struggling to learn plans will exhibit less orderliness and in particular may seize on particularly salient elements of the solution they are developing. However, if the problem is difficult and the plans complex, or if the language or environment impose additional processing demands, even an expert may not be able to fully expand a piece of knowledge before writing down his or her solution. In such a case, experts too will exhibit nonlinearities in code generation.

Rist (1995, p. 537-538) has offered an integrative account of several sorts of nonlinearity in the use of programming plans. He proposes that different aspects of a plan should have more or less cognitive saliency in different situations. In particular, he distinguishes among the "basic" object, action and result of a plan, as well as its beacon. According to Rist, the basic object and action are the operation and datum that implement the plan goal. For example in a bubble sort, the basic action is < (a magnitude comparison) and the basic object is next (the next element in the array); he argues that when an expert is generating this plan, the focal line would be `if this > next`. However, once the bubble sort plan had been retrieved and elaborated, the focus shifts to the basic *result* of the comparison, in this case the code in which the elements are swapped (e.g., `next := this`). Rist argues that plan beacons serve yet another function—plan recognition during program comprehension—and thus should correspond to the characteristics of a plan that best discriminate it from other "near neighbors." These discriminability features may or may not be the same characteristics that guide application of the plan in program composition.

Of course expert programming strategies include more than how schematic knowledge is activated and applied (Gilmore, 1990). Indeed a study of expert Cobol debugging by Vessey (1985; 1987) reported that adoption of a systematic testing strategy was more important to successful debugging than knowledge of particular programming plans. Widowski (1987) demonstrated that a distinguishing characteristic of expertise is an ability to switch among multiple comprehension strategies (e.g., structure-oriented and variable-oriented) as necessary, when faced with complex code.

Pennington (1987) suggests that the ability to coordinate problem information with program constructs may be an important characteristic of programming expertise: she compared the behavior of high- and low-performing programmers, using a pretest to identify the top and bottom quartiles in a group of professional programmers. When she examined verbal protocols from a program comprehension task, she found that the most successful programmers exhibited a cross-referencing strategy, explicitly mentioning the relations between program elements and entities from the problem domain. Good programmers make an effort to understand *why* a particular feature of a solution exists; in Eisenstadt's (1993) study of debugging anecdotes, the most common account of what makes a bug "hard" was a large distance between the cause and the effect of the bug.

Petre and Winder (1988; Petre, 1990) have examined expertise from the perspective of programming language knowledge. They asked expert programmers to program a variety of non-trivial problems in several languages; the target languages were chosen by the experts themselves. The researchers were interested in determining if different languages were seen as more or less suitable for the various problems. The problem-solving protocols and subsequent interviews with the experts suggested that the experts first devised their solutions in a private pseudo-language, then translated the abstract plan into the target language. These pseudo-languages appeared to be an amalgam of multiple language paradigms which permitted the experts to apply different but appropriate approaches to various aspects of a problem. These observations suggest that experts possess a highly refined repertoire of programming constructs which they recruit and apply eclectically as required by a problem.

46.3 From Programming to Design

Most cognitive science studies of programming expertise have analyzed the production or comprehension of small, self-contained programs or modules. In such studies "design" refers to the code-level planning needed to implement a function or subroutine. But the generation of lines of code is only a small part of the development of software systems and applications; it affords a very limited view of software design. Before particular modules can be designed, the larger application problem must be described, understood, and decomposed into pieces that will become modules.

These "upstream" phases of problem analysis and design in software development are ill-structured, complex and difficult to study empirically, relative to module-level design and implementation (Krasner, Curtis and Iscoe, 1987). But these upstream activities are also more important to the ultimate success of a software development project: a superior sorting algorithm cannot save a poor overall design. There is an increasing sense of urgency for cognitive scientists and educators to characterize and teach design skills (Shaw, 1990).

46.3.1 Opportunism in Design

Simon (1973) characterized design in general as an ill-structured problem, and suggested the application of systematic hierarchical decomposition as a means of simplifying and managing a complex design space. For the case of software problems, this classical view of design encouraged the development of top-down, hierarchically-organized "structured" methods, such as Jackson System Development (Jackson, 1983). In these structured methods, a software design problem is decomposed into increasingly more detailed levels of goals and sub-goals in a top-down and breadth-first fashion. The assumption is that a carefully controlled and systematic approach will permit designers to delay commitment to low-level (potentially constraining) design decisions until a complete and coherent high-level plan is developed, and that it will lead to well-organized and modular design substructures.

Early empirical studies of design reported behavior consistent with these structured approaches to design problem-solving. Jeffries et al. (1981) observed a top-down decomposition strategy for both novice and experienced designers, with subparts of the solution developed through progressively more detailed levels until its elements could be implemented by actual program code. A distinguishing feature of experts appeared to be the extent to which a *breadth-first* approach was also applied: experts were likely to develop a coherent structure at one level before proceeding to the next, in contrast to novices who showed a tendency to solve one subproblem completely before moving on to the next. Adelson and Soloway (1985; Adelson, 1984) reported similar results, observing in general a top-down and breadth-first strategy for experts solving both familiar and unfamiliar design problems.

However, not all of the expert design behavior documented by these early studies was top-down and breadth-first. Carroll, Thomas and Malhotra (1979) observed considerable switching among levels in a case study of a complex system design project. Even in the more constrained laboratory programming studies described above, experts would sometimes deviate from a systematic breadth-first approach to pursue a particular subproblem depth-first. These deviations seemed to occur most often when a subproblem was seen as critical to success of the overall design, was especially unfamiliar or difficult, or had a well-known solution. Thus researchers speculated that one aspect of design expertise might be knowing when to *depart* from a systematic top-down and breadth-first decomposition process.

More recent studies of expert designers have developed this point, suggesting that much of expert design problem-solving is not systematic or structured at all, but rather is quite *opportunistic* in character (Guindon and Curtis, 1988; Guindon, 1990; Ullman,

Stauffer and Dietterich, 1986; Visser, 1987; 1990). These studies build on the concept of opportunism originally described by Hayes-Roth and Hayes-Roth (1979), who observed individuals planning a solution to a problem at several levels simultaneously and interactively reinterpreting the problem statement as the problem situation changed.

Visser reported considerable deviation from top-down decomposition in experts working on design of a program (Visser, 1987) and on the functional specifications for a program (Visser, 1990). She characterized the expert behavior as opportunistic because it reflected frequent interruptions in planned or ongoing decomposition activities to address issues at other levels. She proposed that expert design problem-solving—whether reflecting systematic decomposition or opportunism—is guided by a specific design activity's perceived *cognitive cost* (i.e., how easily it can be executed) and *importance* (i.e., its significance to the overall problem).

In contrast to the earlier studies by Jeffries et al. and by Adleson and Soloway, Visser did not provide her experts with well-structured artificial problems to be solved in a laboratory setting; rather she simply observed the normal activities of individual designers over an extended period of time, intruding only to ask for verbalizations concerning their activities. It may be that this naturalistic setting was an important contributing factor in the degree of opportunistic behavior she observed, decreasing the well-structuredness of the problem being analyzed, thus increasing the overall complexity of the problem-solving process (Visser, 1990).

Guindon and her colleagues (Guindon and Curtis, 1988; Guindon et al., 1987; Guindon, 1990) also have observed experts using opportunistic design strategies when solving the Lift Control Problem, a standard problem in software specification and software requirements research. These researchers coded their experts' behavior into a number of categories at different levels of analysis—problem scenarios, requirements, and three levels of solution development—and reported a significant degree of switching among levels, often as the result of a sudden discovery of a partial solution or a new requirement. They have argued that in realistic design situations, it is not surprising to observe experts exhibiting a rather heterarchical style of problem-solving, as they work to better understand ill-defined specifications or take advantage of insights that occur at unexpected times.

The body of work characterizing expert design as highly opportunistic in nature has recently been examined critically by Ball and Ormerod (1995). These researchers suggest that the term opportunism is poorly chosen, as it tends to connote "unsystematic" or even "unprincipled" activity, and that in fact, many of the deviations from classic top-down design can still be seen as part of a structured problem-solving process. According to Ball and Ormerod, expert designers use a flexible mixture of breadth-first and depth-first processing modes, with a preference for breadth-first. Thus while experts do on occasion engage in depth-first excursions, these researchers have argued that such excursions are usually made in a principled fashion, based on a sophisticated assessment of *cognitive effectiveness*. Their notion of cognitive effectiveness is intended to capture a broad-based prioritization of possible design activities that will optimize the overall process; they contrast this to Visser's (1990) notion of cognitive cost which captures the immediate ease of executing a particular activity at some point in time.

Regardless of the terminology used, it seems clear that an important characteristic of design expertise is the ability to shift among different problem decomposition strategies as a function of problem familiarity, memory demands, perceived criticality of subgoals and so on. These observations stand in direct contrast to conventional instruction and methodologies for software design which emphasize a tightly controlled and systematic hierarchical decomposition (Dahl, Dykstra and Hoare, 1972; Wirth, 1971).

46.3.2 Object-Oriented Design

The emergence of the object-oriented (OO) paradigm has also contributed to the increased interest in design problem-solving. In the development of object-oriented systems, design concerns are paramount: the most important questions concern what object abstractions to define, what responsibilities to give them, and how to specify their lines of collaboration (Wirfs-Brock, Wilkerson and Wiener , 1990). A partial design for an object-oriented electronic town hall (Rosson and Carroll, 1996c) appears in Figure 2; it conveys the nature of collaboration among objects required even for a single scenario within an object-oriented application. Of course programmers also write code for object-oriented programs just as they do for other systems, but they often are able to reuse a good deal of code through the specialization of rich class libraries.

Rosson and Alpert (1990) discussed the implications of object-oriented design (OOD) for the cognitive processes involved in design problem-solving. For example, they described how OOD might reduce the cognitive distance between a design problem and the

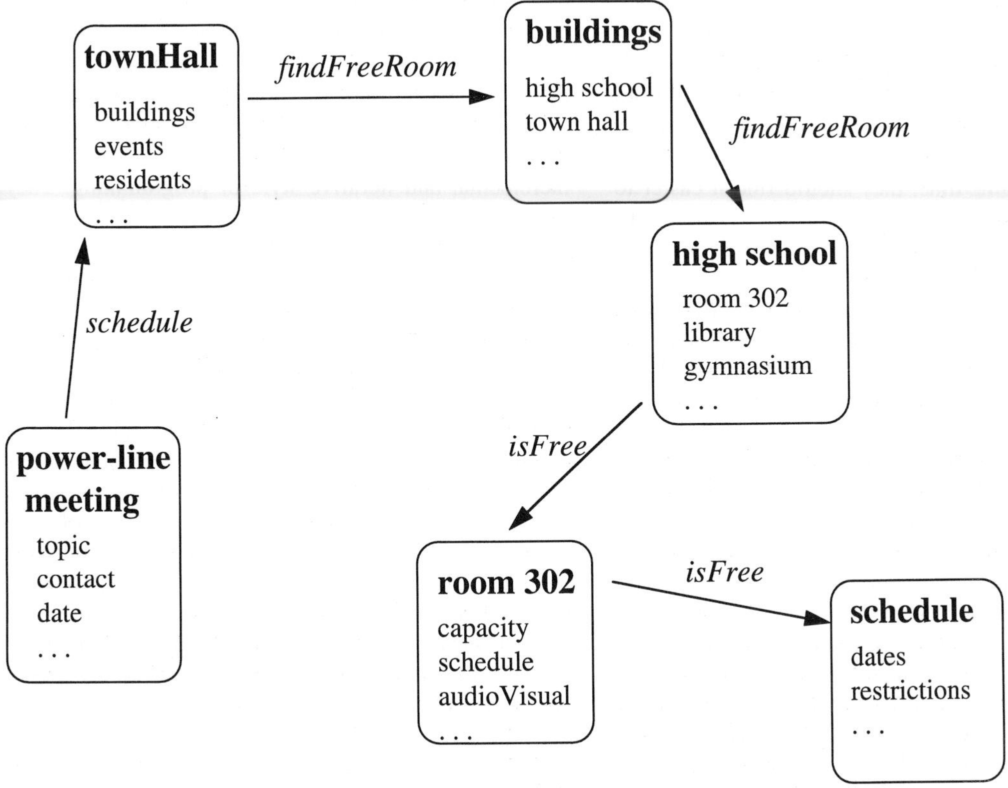

Figure 2. An object collaboration graph depicting some of the objects that would contribute to a scenario setting up a meeting to discuss a powerline proposal in a virtual town hall *(Rosson and Carroll, 1996c). The nodes represent objects; each is named and contains private data. The named links represent messages sent from one object to another and convey the delegation of responsibilities typical of OOD problems.*

software constructs needed to solve it. In the traditional procedural design paradigm, programmers first decompose the problem situation to develop detailed functional requirements, then go through a translation process to map these requirements onto data structures and procedures. In contrast, OOD seems to support a more direct mapping between functional requirements and software implementation, in that many of the software elements are computational versions of problem entities (e.g., a document, its paragraphs, etc.).

Initial support for this mapping claim was provided by Rosson and Gold (1989): experts in either procedural or object-oriented design (OOD) were asked to develop a conceptual design for a gourmet shopping store. The OOD experts' analyses tended to focus on problem objects and how they would be rendered as software objects (e.g., a recipe, a shopping cart), whereas the procedural experts first developed a list of requirements, then moved to discussion of generic facilities (e.g., a database, a display manager) that could be used to achieve these requirements.

A study by Pennington, Lee and Rehder (1995) offered a more detailed analysis of OOD expertise. These researchers assessed the time spent by OOD experts, procedural design experts and OOD novices on analysis of a problem situation (a swim meet competition problem adapted from an OOD textbook) prior to developing their solution plans. They found that relative to procedural experts and OOD novices, OOD experts spent little time in situation analysis, but considerably more time in defining data and procedural abstractions (objects and methods in OOD terminology). Although the OOD experts tended to take more time overall in producing their solutions, they produced more complete solutions, accomplishing more per unit of time spent on the problem. Thus the researchers suggested that closely integrating situation analysis with solution development might increase the efficiency of the design process.

Rosson and Alpert (1990) also argued that the encapsulation of objects should aid management of a complex solution structure as it evolves: because of the increased modularity, designers are less likely to need information from other subproblems and will be better able to develop an in-depth solution for a given component. At the same time, they should find it easier to shift among subproblems, because object abstractions serve as coherent chunks in working memory (or in their external notes or diagrams).

Again, the study of Pennington et al. provided an intriguing glimpse of such effects: OOD experts moved quickly into detailed design (i.e., almost immediately beginning to specify object characteristics and behavior); this is consistent with the observation that these experts analyzed the problem through creation of an object space. However, the experts' overall design activity appeared to be relatively top-down, orderly and balanced, with few excursions "back up" to more abstract concerns. Thus we might speculate that OOD encourages opportunistic behavior of the depth-first sort (i.e., early detailed design of particularly interesting or important objects), but at the same time may promote a balanced approach overall (e.g., identifying a relatively complete set of candidate objects early in the process).

Another much-discussed feature of OOD is its supposed potential for increasing software reuse (see, e.g., Cox, 1986; Meyer, 1988). From the perspective of design problem-solving, the impact of reuse should appear in experts' recruitment of specific pre-existing abstractions (e.g., existing object classes or frameworks) while solving new problems. Pennington et al. (1995) did observe that the OOD experts reused standard object classes (e.g., lists, sets) in their solutions, while the expert procedural designers showed no such tendency; similar findings were reported by Rosson and Gold (1989). This highlights another aspect of OOD expertise, the acquisition of detailed declarative knowledge of complex class hierarchies. Of course, the need for learning library routines is present for any language supplemented by library functions, but the emphasis on reuse is much greater for object-oriented languages (Meyer, 1988).

Learning a large object-oriented library is challenging to novices (Rosson and Carroll, 1990), and in many situations, even an expert cannot be familiar with all possible reusable components. Thus OOD experts must possess skills for locating and applying *unfamiliar* but appropriate components (Helm and Maarek, 1991; Fischer, 1987). Little is known about these skills, but a recent study by Rosson and Carroll (1993; 1996b) explored the strategies employed by four expert Smalltalk programmers while they attempted to reuse an unfamiliar user interface widget. The experts recruited a variety of information resources available in the environment—code from other applications already using the target class, feedback from interactive tools suggesting how to refine their emerging solution—as fuel for an incremental and iterative style of programming. They resisted learning about the unfamiliar class in detail and instead learned facets of its functionality and behavior in an as-needed fashion to support their programming activities. This programming approach is reminiscent of the opportunistic design activities documented by other researchers, and reinforces the conclusion that one hallmark of programming and design expertise seems to be the ability to move flexibly among different levels and sources of problem information.

Another design skill needed in support of software reuse is an ability to produce high-quality reusable software. We know of no empirical work examining the development of expertise in carrying out this specialized design task. Johnson and Foote (1988) have suggested heuristics that designers might follow to design more reusable classes; Gamma, Helm, Johnson, and Vlissides (1995) have proposed that a feature of OOD expertise is knowledge of reusable "design patterns," stereotypical collaborations among functionally-related objects. However these proposals have been formulated from analyses of existing software artifacts rather than on the problem-solving activities of reuse designers. Given the practical implications of high-quality reuse repositories, an analysis of expert design-for-reuse strategies seems long overdue.

46.4 Domain Knowledge and Teamwork

Cognitive science analyses of expertise in programming and design have focused almost exclusively on individual programmers, yet programming in the real world typically involves teams of programmers working within organizations of varying complexity. The performance of an organization is a collective result of individuals working together, but it is not merely the sum of the individual contributions. Understanding and supporting individual-level programming efforts may or my not effectively support programming organizations.

Flor and Hutchins (1991) have described team programming activities as a case of *distributed cognition*, wherein a project result is seen as the result of a complex system of programmers, their internal mental activities, and their shared externalized task representations. Their analysis was based on a study of programming pairs working together on a maintenance task. They observed that the programmers often exhibited a highly condensed form of communication that implied a shared understanding of the problem specification and of the programming plans that were relevant. At the same time, they sometimes voiced different plans for a subproblem, leading them to analyze more alternatives than either would have done alone.

Analysis of the skills and knowledge that software developers bring to group collaborations is challenging and labor-intensive. The investigators must leave the controlled simplifying context of the experimental laboratory and move into the field, observing and interviewing team members as they work. Although it is difficult to construct detailed analyses of these naturalistic situations, important themes are beginning to emerge concerning knowledge distribution and the importance of communication skills.

46.4.1 Application Knowledge

Curtis, Krasner and Iscoe (1988; Krasner, Curtis and Iscoe, 1987) described a field study of 17 projects in nine companies. Based on their observations, the researchers formulated a layered behavioral model of software development in which issues are identified and analyzed at multiple levels, from psychological factors influencing the individual team member, to group dynamics influencing team and project work, to organizational variables influencing the company and business milieu. One of the variables the researchers analyzed within this framework was the important role played by team members possessing application expertise.

At the level of individual group members, Curtis et al. observed that deep application knowledge was critical to the team's success but not always available. The fortunate teams contained one or more exceptional designers or project gurus. These individuals were not necessarily high-performing programmers but rather tended to be interdisciplinary and able to integrate overlapping bodies of knowledge to create and maintain an overall vision for the project. The presence of application experts on a team influenced team dynamics, as they contributed a great amount to group discussions, and quickly formed small but powerful coalitions that helped to control the direction of the team. These are extremely important finding, as they challenge the expectation that more and better programming skills are a path to success in software development organizations. Instead an exceptional designer appears to be one who is able to integrate and coordinate multiple sources of knowledge.

46.4.2 Communication and Coordination

Although having gifted personnel—particularly those with deep knowledge of the application domain—is critical to the success of software development projects, it is not enough. Even when a team is fortunate enough to contain one or more project gurus, the vision created and maintained by these individuals must still be communicated to others on the team and to other teams in the project. Curtis et al. observed that the project gurus did more than control team direction; they also expended substantial personal effort on communicating their application knowledge and their design vision within and across team boundaries. Thus the researchers argued that communication skills and coordination mechanisms will also be key determinants of a project's ultimate success.

Several of the projects analyzed by Curtis et al. involved fluctuating and conflicting requirements. Communication and coordination processes were crucial in managing these software development situations. Even in cases where the overall business requirements were stable, specifications sometimes fluctuated because teams applied different interpretations to interdependent sets of requirements, and did not sufficiently coordinate their design efforts. At the individual level, instability was sometimes introduced by programmers who went beyond the official requirements to add system features in response to their own programming or design aesthetics. Paradoxically, it may be that extremely high programming expertise on an individual level may work against team success if it is not balanced by equally good skills at communicating and coordinating plans and progress.

The Curtis et al. field study also provided several interesting observations concerning the effectiveness of different communication mechanisms. Documentation and formal communication processes seemed to be relatively ineffective as communication media, especially as the size and complexity of a project increased. Instead project members relied on informal verbal communication, and in particular on the development and maintenance of appropriate communication networks. A key ingredient for large projects was the emergence of *boundary spanners*, project members who could translate the concerns and proposals of one team into language understood by another. These observations suggest that intensive training in formal communication and documentation skills will be much less effective than giving software developers exposure to a broad range of disciplines and problem-solving approaches.

Researchers have also carried out more detailed analyses of group collaboration, videotaping and analyzing in detail the activities of group design meetings. For example, Curtis and Walz (1990) analyzed a series of design meetings over a period of several months. Each utterance was categorized according to its role in the group discussions They found an interesting pattern with respect to utterances representing agreement among participants. In contrast to a simplistic model which would predict gradually increasing agreement as the team developed and refined a solution, the researchers report an inverted U-shaped curve: agreement gradually increased until the point at which a specification document was released, then began to decrease after that. The researchers acknowledged that many factors may have produced this pattern—for example, it may be necessary to reach consensus to produce the specifications, but then the team can relax and reopen conflicts raised earlier; or it may have been that the initial consensus process addressed a different, perhaps more abstract, level of analysis. Clearly these are very preliminary analyses, but they represent some initial steps at characterizing the structure of collaboration in software development contexts.

Olson and his colleagues (Olson, Olson, Carter and Storrøsten, 1992; Herbsleb, Klein, Olson, Brunner and Olson, 1995; Olson, Olson, Storrøsten, Carter, Herbsleb and Reuter, 1996) have also analyzed the structure of discussions in design meetings; they analyzed videotaped records of meetings conducted for several projects in different organizations. Like Curtis and Walz, these researchers defined categories (e.g., issue, alternative, clarification) for encoding utterances; they then examined the frequency of utterance types as well as the transitions from one type of utterance to another. Their analyses have confirmed the importance of communication and coordination skills—in one study, approximately one third of discussion time was spent in clarifying the content of questions raised. The implication is that if participants had been better trained on communication skills, significant time might have been saved.

Berlin (1993) examined the communication patterns associated with a specific type of collaboration, that between experts mentoring apprentices about a complex project. She reported an informal conversational style, where the topics and threads are implicitly negotiated by both the expert and the apprentice. The experts volunteered information that they thought was key to understanding a system issue, but also were quite willing to follow tangents generated by the apprentice's problem-solving or by external artifacts (e.g., details of a piece of code). As a result, the successful mentors were not simply those who possessed software expertise, but also responsive conversational skills. Berlin also observed that one characteristic distinguishing experts from apprentices was that they more quickly sought advice from other experts when relevant. This suggests that another important skill for team members is knowing *when* to interact with colleagues on a problem.

46.5 Teaching Software Development

Teaching software development skills is one of the most important applications of theories and analyses of software development expertise. It addresses a critical need for more and better-qualified software developers. But new approaches to teaching software skills do more than this: by refining what is taught and how it is taught, they ultimately alter what is known and how that knowledge is used in software development work. A great variety of educational settings have been investigated, and many approaches and techniques have been employed. Some researchers have built directly from the cognitive analyses of programming expertise, developing instruction that specifically targets recognized elements of this expertise, attempting to render the development of programming expertise more efficient and predictable. Other work has pursued the broader goal of embodying general theories of learning and skill acquisition in intelligent tutoring systems, and treating programming as one of potentially many application domains. Still other work has focused on higher-level design skills, that is, in contrast to programming language skills. Relatively little explicit attention has been given to instruction in collaboration skills needed for real world software development work. However, current trends in university curricula reflect a move in this direction, with an increasing emphasis on team projects and cumulation across courses.

46.5.1 Instruction on Plans

One outgrowth of research pointing to the involvement of plan knowledge in expert programming has been work aimed at direct instruction on plans (Soloway, 1986). Non-programmers have a great deal of knowledge potentially relevant to programming, for example, knowledge about how to take an average over a set of bowling scores, or how to find the largest number in a bank statement. They may not recognize the relevance of this knowledge, and they almost certainly do not know how to specify such informal "plans" as programming language plans. But learners do often try to engage their prior knowledge: attempts apply informal understandings are a common source of misconceptions and errors in novice programming (Bonar and Soloway, 1989).

The BridgeTalk environment (Bonar and Cunningham, 1988; Bonar and Liffick, 1990) introduces novices to plans they can use to build small programs in Pascal. The environment represents a set of Pascal plans (e.g., a counter, a running total) graphically, assigning each plan a unique icon with smaller icons used to represent the variables or constants needed by the plans. The icons are designed to look like puzzle pieces, and students build a program by joining plan elements together. The intent is to teach novices the vocabulary of plans, to help them make the translation from their informal plans to Pascal-specific plans, and to support program writing through plan composition. The emphasis is on program construction out of the plan elements; students are allowed to connect elements together in a flexible fashion. The argument is that providing a language built of plans while hiding the details of plan implementation focuses initial learning on an appropriate intermediate level of analysis.

The Goalposter component of MoleHill (an intelligent tutor for Smalltalk; Singley, Carroll and Alpert, 1991) also attempts to teach novices about programming plans, but in a less direct fashion. Rather than assuming that novices should learn and apply a specific plan vocabulary, the Goalposter tries to infer from a learner's actions what goals he or she might be pursuing, then offers an interpretation and suggestions for further actions via a hierarchical goal decomposition tree. As the student fulfills a goal, that goal listing takes on a different color in the tree to indicate completion; inferences concerning "buggy" goals are highlighted in red to better attract the learner's attention. These researchers argue that a goal tree should be seen as just one possible representation of a learner's activity and may or may not be useful at any given point in time. Because the goal tree is provided as information only (i.e., not forcing the novice to interact with it to create programs), the learner can refer to it when confused or unsure but is not forced to work in its terms.

A recent paper by Rist (1996) describes his efforts to integrate the long history of work on programming plans with instruction on modern object-oriented languages. He asserts that objects and plans are orthogonal: an object may participate in a multitude of plans and any given plan will rely on multiple objects. According to Rist, novices to OOD solve problems by first developing a concrete plan for a solution, then applying design rules to add object structure and transform the procedural solution into an object-oriented one.

Rist and his colleagues (Rist and Terwilliger, 1995) are exploring the usefulness of several representations that will help students make the transition from procedural plans to object-oriented designs, when used in conjunction with a small set of design guidelines. They suggest the use of *system structure charts* in reasoning about how to encapsulate problem data into objects (see Figure 3); they claim this encapsulation analysis is the fundamental first step in moving from a procedural to an object-oriented model. The structure charts integrate plan knowledge (in the form of named goals) with object abstractions (in the form of named classes with their associated data). After a student has identified the object abstractions relevant to a goal, he or she then elaborates each goal into a plan that exercises the object abstractions.

Another approach to teaching novices programming language constructs involves the use of structured editors. Structured editors are not designed to teach plans; rather they introduce more generic aspects of program structure (e.g., the type of components allowed, what the ordering should be, syntactic rules for combining components). So for example, the Struedi editor conveys knowledge about LISP programs (e.g., templates of LISP language constructs, Köhne and Weber, 1987). It assists learners by managing some of the details of implementing these elements (e.g., appropriate keywords and ordering of parameters), while at the same time implicitly communicating information about the acceptable structure of program components. A problem with these editors is that because they express program design knowledge that is unknown to novices, they must be carefully designed to minimize confusion (Goldenson and Wang, 1991). Such editors also tend to impose a top-down order of development on the learner; Green (1990) raises this as a general concern given the modern view of programming as containing a great degree of opportunism and iteration.

46.5.2 Intelligent Tutors

Intelligent tutoring systems constitute perhaps the most explicit use of cognitive science theory in support of teaching and learning. In this approach, a computer system monitors students' activity, guiding problem-solving at a fairly fine level of resolution. The tutor has

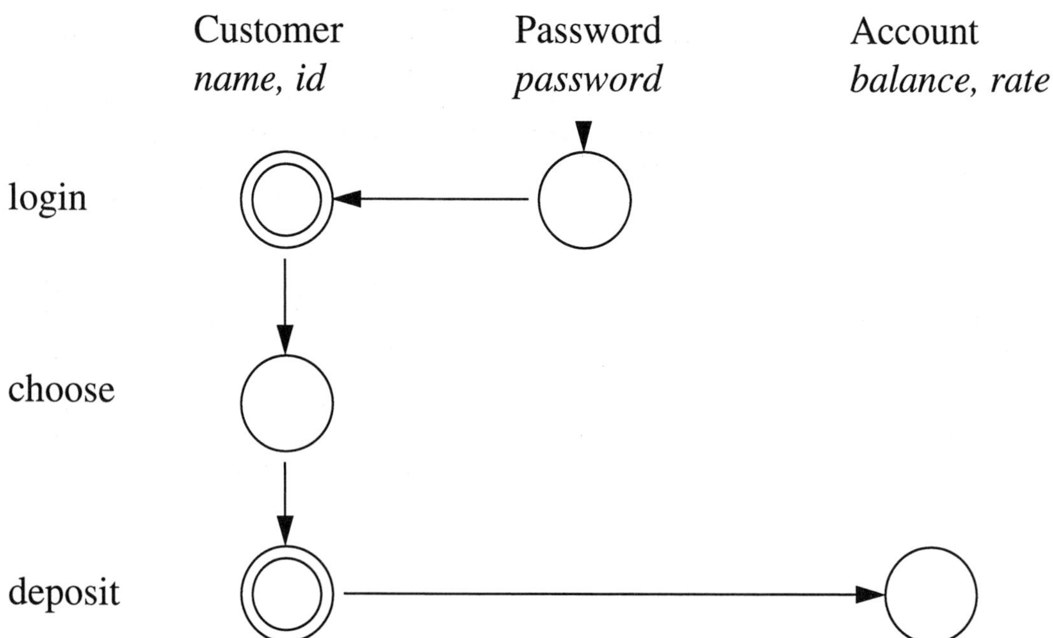

Figure 3. A system structure chart for the goal to deposit money in an ATM; *adapted from Rist (1996, p. 31). The empty circles depict nodes in the structure chart, each reflecting a contribution by an object to the goal; the double circles represent a goal selection; and the lines indicate control flow within or between classes. The arrowheads reflect data flow, either input from the user (top), a result from a procedure (right) or an argument into a procedure (left).*

a knowledge base for the instructional domain, capabilities for comparing student performance against a standard of correct performance to build a model of what the student knows, and rules for providing helpful coaching interventions. The representations of domain knowledge and the rules for pedagogical intervention are typically derived from cognitive science theories, and tutors are often regarded as testbeds for cognitive theories. The goal of most tutoring systems is to be as domain-independent as possible. That is, ideally only the knowledge base should be domain-specific. Programming has been a popular example of an open-ended design problem in which to exercise these theoretical frameworks.

A good example of a cognitive science theory-based intelligent tutor is the LISP Tutor developed by John Anderson and his colleagues (Anderson, Conrad and Corbett, 1989; Anderson and Reiser, 1985, Pirolli, 1986). The LISP Tutor uses a technique known as *model-tracing*, in which a rule-based domain expert (the tutor with programming language knowledge encoded as a production system) tracks a student's progress with sample problems in a step-by-step fashion, matching student actions with its predicted actions and thereby identifying errors. In addition to recognizing mismatches in steps, the tutor reasons about the programming plans relevant to the current problem, making inferences about the student's likely plan as well as comparing it to other possible plans for the current problem (Anderson, Boyle and Reiser, 1985). This reasoning capability allows the intelligent tutor to provide ongoing and immediate feedback to the student, for example suggesting a substitute action that would move the learner toward successful completion of an inferred plan. Immediate feedback of this sort has obvious benefits for the learner and has been documented in many situations studying successful human tutors (Merrill, Reiser, Ranney and Trafton, 1992; Merrill, Reiser, Merrill and Landes, 1995).

Empirical assessments of intelligent tutors such as the LISP Tutor have attempted to distinguish between the merits of the model-tracing methodology and the characteristics of the interactive tool-based environment in which these feedback mechanisms are typically embedded (Merrill et al., 1992). Thus Reiser, Copen, Ranney, Hamid, and Kimberg (1995) contrasted students learning to program using the GIL tutor with model tracing to students using an exploration-based version of GIL with no model-tracing feedback (GIL is an intelligent tutor for LISP that also offers a graphical programming interface; Reiser, Beekelaar, Tyle and Merrill, 1991). The exploration-based system provided the same graphical representation of the programming problem and the same set of tools for editing and correcting programs, but it did not intervene to make suggestions or to comment on the student's inferred strategy. The researchers found that although students using the exploration-based environment took almost twice as long to complete the problem set, they subsequently performed better on a debugging task, perhaps because they had been forced to detect and correct their own errors during learning. However, the two groups demonstrated an equal ability to write programs and predict program behavior.

Corbett and Anderson (1991) reported similar findings for the LISP Tutor: students using the model-tracing environment mastered LISP programming more quickly than students using the tutor's structured editing interface but no model-based feedback. The combination of these findings suggests that at the least an intelligent tutor using model-tracing can produce more efficient learning of correct programming plans.

Reiser et al. (1995) also suggested that the model-tracing environment may have motivational consequences for some learners. In their experiment the lower-ability students in the model-tracing condition reported more positive opinions about their programming abilities than did their low-ability counterparts in the exploratory environment. These findings may indicate that the guidance provided by intelligent tutors can have a positive impact on novices' (especially low ability novices) motivation, in that it helps them to avoid prolonged error episodes in which they struggle to develop or implement a programming plan.

A key issue for intelligent tutors is choosing when to offer assistance. Merrill et al. (1995) emphasized that expert human tutors do not simply offer encouragement of good strategies and correction of poor; rather they carefully coordinate their interventions so as to allow students to perform as much work as possible on their own. This allows students to actively construct their understanding of the problem instead of simply following the directions of a tutor. Unfortunately it is difficult to build this level of intervention strategy into a computer tutor; the tutor must be able to predict when a student's difficulty is about to lead to unrewarding and demotivating floundering versus when the student is likely to be able to detect, correct and learn from an error or misconception.

One response to this problem of knowing when to intervene is to back off from the intelligent tutoring system vision, and give more control to the learner. The MoleHill tutor (Singley et al., 1991) described earlier takes this approach, offering various kinds of help and advice for the learner to choose among. The Goalposter component uses model tracing to infer the Smalltalk programming plans that might be useful at any given point. However this goal knowledge is provided simply as one resource in the programming environment. The learner can also browse problem-relevant code in the Smalltalk library, access commentary about this code at arbitrary levels of detail, and call up a Smalltalk "guru" (a videotaped segment of an expert providing programming advice) when specific confusions arise. The intention is to let the learner choose the form of support that is useful at any given point, as well as to encourage active reasoning about the multiple related resources.

46.5.3 Teaching Design through Active Learning

As the educational focus in software development has broadened from relatively constrained programming problems to include relatively open-ended design problems, researchers have begun to explore the teaching of software design by active learning. Active learning shifts emphasis from *modeling* the student's learning processes to *supporting* the student's learning activities. More control and more responsibility is reserved for the student. Implicit in this work is the assumption that learning how to design is complex and unpredictable and is likely to involve both systematic and opportunistic learning episodes.

The Minimalist Tutorial and Tools for Smalltalk (MiTTS; Rosson, Carroll and Bellamy, 1990) applied the minimalist instruction model to the domain of Smalltalk programming and design. MiTTS provides tools to help learners analyze a paradigmatic example Smalltalk application. MiTTS includes an application browser that presents a filtered view of the sometimes-overwhelming Smalltalk class hierarchy, to guide the learner's analysis of the application's design. It provides a View Matcher tool that coordinates multiple views of running application code (the user interface, a filtered view of the class hierarchy, active objects, message-passing, and design-level documentation; see Figure 4).

Learners analyze the design and the run-time structure of the application, and design and implement enhancements to it. The example application (a card game) was crafted to be engaging, simple enough to be accessible to Smalltalk novices (it has fewer than a dozen major objects), yet complex enough to realisti-

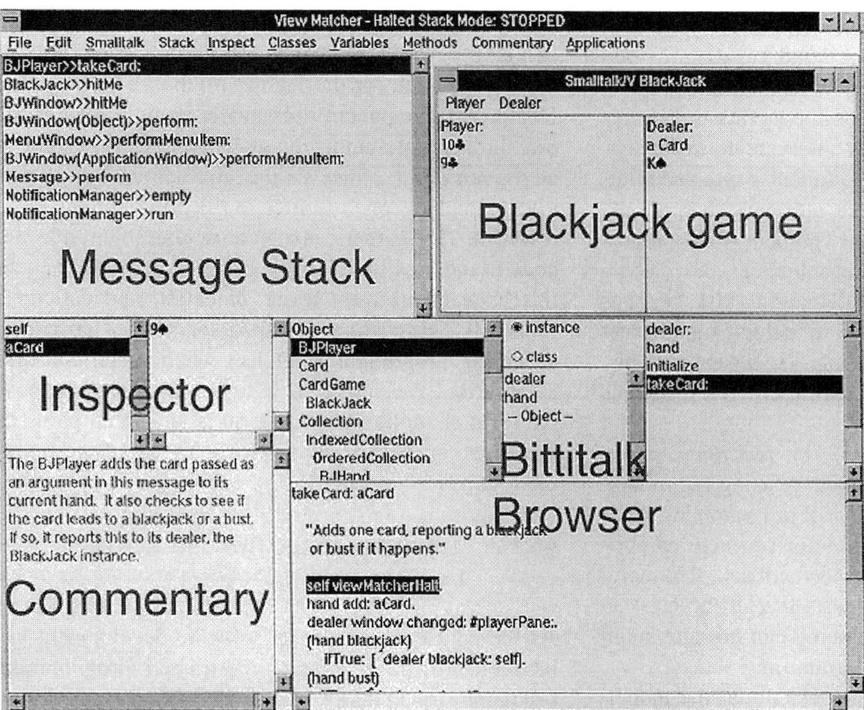

Figure 4. The View Matcher coordinates multiple views on a running paradigmatic object-oriented Smalltalk application, in this case an interactive blackjack game. *The views convey complementary analyses—the blackjack game, its program code, a stack of messages currently being processed, an inspector on the active objects, and an integrative commentary—intended to provoke active reasoning about how the application works.*

cally illustrate the OOD paradigm of collaborating objects with well-defined responsibilities, and the Smalltalk model-view-controller application design framework. The learners also get experience with the major system tools of the Smalltalk environment through using these capabilities in the well-integrated context of the View Matcher.

Novices must also learn to use a sophisticated programming environment and to integrate their programming with an extensive hierarchy of reusable classes (Rosson and Carroll, 1990). MiTTS helps learners manage this complex learning process by exposing the example application through a spiral curriculum that begins with a simplified version of the example and gradually adds more levels of complexity.

The MiTTS curriculum involves a scaffolded (Bruner, 1960) series of four successively more comprehensive analyses and enhancements of the example application. This sequence of experience helps the coordinated views of the example cumulate to promote reasoning and inference, as well as introducing standard representations (i.e., the class hierarchy, the message execution stack) that are central to programming in Smalltalk.

The MiTTS system coupled teaching Smalltalk programming with teaching OOD; it introduced OOD constructs implicitly as characteristics of the example (e.g., the division of responsibilities between application and user interface objects). A subsequent system—the Scenario Browser (Rosson and Carroll, 1995; 1996c)—focuses directly on OOD. Instead of guiding learners in analysis of a running application, it provides multiple views of an application's design specification. As with MiTTS, the learning experience is organized into a series of application scenarios. As learners explore these scenarios, they discover that each scenario can be elaborated into an object model. These object models emerge through the creation and elaboration of individual object's "points of view," object-specific versions of the scenario focusing only on a particular object's responsibilities and collaborations with other objects. The final design of the entire application is then seen as a synthesis and generalization of the object models generated for individual scenarios.

MiTTS and the Scenario Browser teach software skills through the use of scaffolded examples (Rosson and Carroll, 1996a). They rely on learners' incremental and cumulative analysis of a paradigmatic example to discover design and programming constructs. However, they guide learners' exploration in a way that also introduces and reinforces a *method* that learners can follow to produce software artifacts on their own. The multiple representations that the learners encounter, and the order in which they encounter them, communicate not only the content of the learning example but also a set of general techniques and tools for building object-oriented applications.

Another learning environment aimed at active learning is the Object Design Exploratorium (ODE; Robertson, Carroll, Mack, Rosson and Alpert, 1994). ODE also supports learning with an example design, but rather than offering the example for direct exploration, the example is used to give learners feedback on their own efforts at doing OOD: Learners are guided to identify candidate objects for a design problem. When they identify objects that match the (hidden) example design solution, they are "rewarded" by gaining access to additional information about these objects—videotaped animations in which the objects describe their responsibilities and collaborations with each other. These animations support further analysis of the proposed objects, including the identification of other design elements not yet realized. Because the elaborations only become available when a student-proposed object matches an element of the example design, they provide implicit feedback that students are "on the right track."

46.5.4 Learning in the Classroom

Much programming instruction focuses on conveying the syntactic features of a particular programming language and on specifying and implementing small, well-defined algorithms or data structures. Low-level knowledge such as this is relatively easy to describe and can be exercised and evaluated by relatively small student programs in a relatively small period of time. However, researchers studying computer science education are now investigating the much more difficult problem of educating undergraduates on design skills that will support the analysis, construction and development of software systems of realistic size (Linn and Clancy, 1992a; Shaw, 1990). These efforts are addressing issues at the level of both techniques for classroom instruction and curriculum structure.

Modeling the Design Process

Linn and Clancy (1992a; 1992b) have argued that one way to teach design skills to students is through the provision of expert case studies. Their proposal is rooted in the observation that successful educators will often model the design process for their students, including considerations and decisions concerning alternative designs, and perhaps even the intentional commission and recovery from errors or misconceptions (see also Lalonde, 1993). Linn and Clancy have suggested that a well-constructed set of expert case studies might provide such a model in a more systematic fashion, and in a way that makes the model accessible to a range of learners working in varied educational settings.

The case studies explored by Linn and Clancy (1992a) consist of a series of documented problem-solution examples that cumulated to demonstrate reuse of design approaches. Each case study in the series includes a statement of the problem, a narrative description of an expert's solution written in terms that a student can understand, the actual worked-out solution associated with this narrative, study questions that guided students' analysis of the case, and test questions that assessed students' final understanding. The case studies illustrate generally useful design heuristics such as divide and conquer, or the use of multiple representations. The researchers demonstrated that by providing the expert commentary along with the other problem information, students developed a more integrated understanding of software development, and learned to attend to aspects of the design process normally ignored or avoided by novices—for example the consideration of design alternatives and the development of design rationale.

Experts are clearly an important source of insight for students learning software skills. However, a study by Riecken, Koenemann-Belliveau and Robertson (1991) offers a cautionary note. According to these researchers, expert and novice programmers may not always share a common view of what ought to be communicated: experts believe that novices should be guided to understand the function and behavior of a program, whereas novices expect to receive assistance in understanding syntactic details. This difference in emphasis is consistent with the knowledge level of the two populations: experts have moved beyond syntactic details, whereas novices are often struggling simply to parse the written code. Clearly if expert commentary is to be gathered, care must be taken that the content of the example developed serves the needs of the learners it is intended to help. This is especially critical when the expert is not "live" and thus cannot respond and adjust to the learner's needs.

Implicit in the work on experts as models is a recognition that teaching the *process* of software design is more important than a focus on software products (i.e., the code; see Soloway, Spoher and Littman, 1988). Lalonde (1993) addresses this goal in his efforts to produce "canDo" students, students who pay attention to process information instead of simply memorizing facts about a programming language. Such students may not do well on conventional measures—exams that assess declarative knowledge—but Lalonde argues that they will be more prepared to succeed in software development beyond the university environment. Lalonde tries to convey process information by carrying out a large number of live demonstrations of program design, including planned errors and error recovery strategies. Although this approach is very demanding of the instructor, it is based on live expert commentary, and thus can be delivered in a more flexible format than the prepared case studies studied by Linn and Clancy.

Design-Oriented Curricula

The ACM/IEEE Computing Curricula '91 report (Tucker et al., 1991) highlights design as one of three fundamental processes in which students should receive training; it also advocates an early emphasis on software engineering methods and concerns. This is in contrast to many traditional computer science programs which have targeted initial instruction more narrowly on low-level programming skills, on programming-in-the-small rather than programming-in-the-large (Shaw, 1990).

Many educators have taken these new recommendations as a call for curriculum reform and have begun exploring the impact of new courses, especially at the introductory level. For some, the call for an early emphasis on software engineering concerns has prompted efforts to "turn the curriculum upside-down" (Rosson and Heliotis, 1993), incorporating team projects and considerations of social and ethical issues in software development into the first two years of instruction, rather than waiting until the third and fourth years (Epstein and Tucker, 1993; Tewari and Friedman, 1993). Others advocate an even more radical approach, introducing students early on (e.g., in their second semester) to relatively large-scale application-development projects that rely on code libraries and high-level programming environments (Lalonde, 1993). Such an approach allows students to confront from the beginning the problems of understanding problem requirements and of developing and considering design alternatives. McKim (1993) also points out that larger and more demanding projects may be more interesting for students, and that students will learn more effectively if they have fun.

The appearance and general acceptance of the object-oriented paradigm has been a major enabling factor in the evolution toward a broader and more design-centered computer science curriculum (Osborne, 1993). Object-oriented languages typically provide rich libraries of reusable components which can serve both as "expert" examples of well-conceived abstractions and as the building blocks for larger application-oriented class projects. The object-oriented paradigm also emphasizes the software design concerns of abstraction and reuse, which were among the themes highlighted by Computing Curricula'91.

Universities are just beginning to tackle the problem of training students to design and use reusable software—companies now expect such skills but often find that their new programmers have not been trained to expect a reuse culture (Cameron, Berman, Gossain, Henderson-Sellers, Hill and Smith, 1996). To some extent, assigning large projects that require use of code libraries forces students to develop the skills needed to locate, assess and apply reusable software modules. Hüni and Metz (1993) describe a more active ap-proach, in which students work on increasingly more complex projects, reusing their own work as they proceed. An even more demanding approach would require students to contribute to the ongoing development of reuse libraries, developing components for use by peers in other projects. The Computer Science Department at Ohio State is developing a 3-semester course sequence that will do just this, teaching students first to be clients of off-the-shelf reusable components, then moving on to implement their own components, and to carry out a large system design project using these student-built components (Tim Long, personal communication).

It is unclear how the need for communication and coordination skills in software development will be met by computer science curriculum efforts—computer science professors are trained in programming and design techniques, not in group dynamics! Simply assigning group project work forces some attention to such skills on the part of the student; to the extent that the instructor defines roles and provides appropriate coaching, the experience can be even more beneficial. A more comprehensive approach might be to develop computer science curricula that are explicitly interdisciplinary, including exposure to the methods and findings in social and organizational psychology concerning group communication and coordination.

Educators are beginning to examine some of these possibilities: for instance, a Ph.D. project at Virginia Tech is examining the relationship of variations in team member roles on software project outcome (Todd Stevens, personal communication). Kautz (1996) described a graduate course he taught at the Technical

Instructional Approach	Pedagogical Features
BridgeTalk (Bonar and Cunningham, 1988)	iconic plan language, programming by composition
System structure charts (Rist, 1996)	integration of procedural plans with object analysis
Struedi (Köhne and Weber, 1987)	fill-in templates conveying program structure
Molehill (Singley et al., 1991)	goal tree guiding programming activities
LISP Tutor (Anderson and Reiser); GIL	model-tracing supporting immediate feedback
MiTTS (Rosson et al., 1990)	coordinated multiple views of paradigmatic example
Scenario Browser (Rosson and Carroll, 1996c)	successive elaboration from scenarios to design
ODE (Robertson et al., 1994)	example design offered as feedback on progress
Expert case studies (Linn and Clancey, 1992a;b)	consideration of alternatives, design rationale
Live programming demonstrations (Lalonde, 1993)	focus on process, on producing "canDo" attitude
Cumulative design and reuse projects (Hüni and Metz, 1993; Ohio State, personal communication)	attention to maintenance and longterm usefulness of design products
Role-playing in design projects (Kautz, 1996)	practice on social and communication skills

Figure 5. A summary of instructional approaches surveyed in section 46.5.

University of Berlin. In the course, group projects were organized in which groups of 6-9 students developed prototypes for an interactive information system. Students were assigned roles: two or three were "users," two to four were "developers," and two were prototyping and method consultants. Students maintained project diaries throughout the eight weeks they worked on these projects, and a written report on the development process was required along with the typical documentation and the prototype itself. Kautz found that the students were amenable to the role-playing and that very sincere conflicts emerged, and served as grist for discussions about how such conflicts can be addressed.

46.6 Future Directions

We have surveyed a variety of approaches to teaching software development skills, many based directly on the evolving theoretical frameworks applied to the analysis of these skills (see the summary in Figure 5). However many challenges remain. Software development expertise is multifaceted, incorporating complex knowledge structures, strategies and skills—programming plans and strategies, flexible design problem-solving heuristics, an understanding of application semantics and pragmatics, and collaboration and communication abilities. It should not come as a surprise that teaching and learning software development skills is a major and open-ended technical challenge. It is continuously tempting to surrender in the face of this challenge, and to take the advice of Brooks (1987) who concluded that it would be more effective to focus effort on identifying designers with natural talent, than to try to make software design accessible to all through education and training.

The past decade of research and development on teaching and learning software development skills has been very promising. The application of cognitive science theory to the analysis of knowledge structures and strategies of programming and software design have created a scientific foundation to guide the development of more effective pedagogy including support tools and environments. This work is now generally well-coupled to areas of current technological concern, such as object-oriented design, in a way that was not always true in the past.

Three issues in particular seem ripe for advances in the near term. One of these is integrated design instruction. The tension between top-down, systematic design and interactive, rapid prototyping is largely unresolved both in design practice and in design pedagogy. We need well-structured software systems that are easy to understand and maintain. But we need to support flexible and creative design problem-solving as well. The best designers implicitly know how to integrate the two—we need to characterize and teach this strategic knowledge. This should involve cognitive science studies of design knowledge, and the development of experimental curricula and tools to convey and support mixed design strategies. For example, one might integrate rapid prototyping tools with an intelligent tutoring system for design or some other critiquing capability.

A second issue that seems ripe for near term advance is realistic learning. The need of students for experience with projects of realistic size and complexity is well-understood; increasingly it is acknowledged that communication, teamwork, and the management of application knowledge must also be taught. Many universities already have "cooperative education" programs in which students work in industry for one or two semesters during their education. However, these programs are not themselves coordinated with academic pro-grams, and may not produce as much insight and learning as they could. Perhaps cooperative education programs could be improved merely by asking students to create "lessons learned" portfolios. A more ambitious alternative would be to organize significant software development projects within the university and the community, spanning several semesters and involving many students in various roles.

A third issue is lifelong learning. Teaching and learning in software development has often been seen as technical education (for example, learning to program or learning about software engineering in Computer Science university courses) or as technical training (for example, a tutorial or short course on Smalltalk for Pascal programmers). In both cases, it has been seen as short-term. There are indications that a third paradigm is emerging in which software organizations more broadly reconceive themselves as learning communities in which education goes on all the time. Currently there is interest in the creation and sharing of design rationale as a routine work activity (Moran and Carroll, 1996). This points to a need for tools supporting the recording, integration and cumulation of shared knowledge (see, e.g., Carroll, Rosson, Cohill and Schorger, 1995).

Teaching and learning software development skills is an open-ended challenge. In the past decade, as in the decade that went before it, software technology became more diverse and more complex, it elaborated its basic concepts and practices, it expanded the range of its application, and it attracted ever more people in need of various sorts of training and education. In the next decade, we must expect that this pattern will continue.

46.7 Acknowledgments

We are grateful to comments on an earlier version of the chapter by Rachel Bellamy and Jürgen Koenmann.

46.8 References

Adelson, B. (1984). When novices surpass experts: The difficulty of a task may increase with expertise. *JEP: Learning, Memory and Cognition, 10*, 483-495.

Adelson, B. and Soloway, E. (1985). The role of domain experience in software design. *IEEE Transactions on Software Engineering, SE-11*, 233-242.

Anderson, J. R. (1983). *The Architecture of Cognition.* Cambridge, MA, Harvard University Press.

Anderson, J. R., Boyle, C. F., and Reiser, B. (1985). Intelligent tutoring systems. *Science, 228*, 456-462.

Anderson, J. R., Conrad, F. G., and Corbett, A. T. (1989). Skill acquisition and the LISP tutor. *Cognitive Science, 13*, 467-505.

Anderson, J. R., Farrell, R., and Sauers, R. (1984). Learning to program in LISP. *Cognitive Science, 8*(2), 413-487.

Anderson, J. R. and Reiser, B. (1985). The LISP tutor. *Byte, 10*, 159-175.

Ball, L. J. and Ormerod, T. C. (1995). Structured and opportunistic processing in design: A critical discussion. *International Journal of Human-Computer Studies, 43*(1), 131-151.

Berlin, L. (1993). Beyond program understanding: A look at programming expertise in industry. In C. R. Cook, J. C. Scholtz, and J. C. Spoher (Eds.), *Empirical Studies of Programming: Fifth Workshop.* Norwood, NJ, Ablex, pages 6-25..

Bonar, J. and Cunningham, R. (1988). Bridge: Tutoring the programming process. In J. Psotka, L. D. Massey and S. A. Mutter (Eds.), *Intelligent Tutoring Systems: Lessons Learned* . Hillsdale, NJ, Lawrence Erlbaum, pages 409-434.

Bonar, J. and Liffick, B. W. (1990). A visual programming language for novices. In S.-K. Chang (Ed.), *Principles of Visual Systems.* Englewood, CA, Prentice-Hall.

Bonar, J. and Soloway, E. (1989). Preprogramming knowledge: A major source of misconceptions in novice programmers. In E. Soloway and J. C. Spoher (Eds.), *Studying the Novice Programmer.* Hillsdale, NJ, Lawrence Erlbaum, pages 325-353.

Brooks, F. (1987). No silver bullet: Essence and accidents of software engineering. *IEEE Computer, 20*(4), 10-19.

Brooks, R. (1977). Towards a theory of cognitive processes in computer programming. *International Journal of Man-Machine Studies, 9,* 737-751.

Brooks, R. (1983). Toward a theory of the comprehension of computer programs. *International Journal of Man-Machine Studies, 18,* 543-554.

Bruner, J. S. (1960). *The Process of Education.* Cambridge, MA: MIT Press.

Cameron, L., Berman, C., Gossain, S., Henderson-Sellers, B., Hill, L., and Smith, Randall. (1996). Perspectives on reuse. Panel discussion at *OOPSLA'96: Object-oriented Programming Systems, Languages and Applications.* (6-10 October, 1996, San Jose, CA).

Carroll, J. M., Rosson, M. B., Cohill, A.M., and Schorger, J. (1995). Building a history of the Blacksburg Electronic Village. In *Proceedings of the ACM Symposium on Designing Interactive Systems: DIS'95.* New York: ACM, pages 1-6.

Carroll, J. M., Singer, J., Bellamy, R. K. E., and Alpert, S. R. (1990). A View Matcher for learning Smalltalk. In J. C. Chew and J. Whiteside (Eds.), *Human Factors in Computing Systems: Proceedings of CHI'90* , New York, ACM, pages 431-437.

Carroll, J. M., Thomas, J. C. and Malhotra, A. (1979). Clinical-experimental analysis of design problem solving. *Design Studies, 1,* 84-92.

Corbett, A. and Anderson, J. R. (1991). *Feedback control and learning to program with the CMU LISP Tutor.* Paper presented at the Annual Meeting of the American Educational Research Association, Chicago, IL.

Cox, B. J. (1986). *Object Oriented Programming: An Evolutionary Approach.* Addison-Wesley, Reading, MA.

Curtis, B. (1987). Five paradigms in the psychology of programming. In M. Helander (Ed.), *Handbook of Human-Computer Interaction* , Amsterdam, Elsevier, pages 87-105.

Curtis, B., Krasner, H. and Iscoe, N. (1988). A field study of the software design process for large systems. *Communications of the ACM, 31*(11), 1268-1287.

Curtis, B. and Walz, D. (1990). The psychology of programming in the large: Team and organizational behavior. In J.-M. Hoc, T. R. G. Green, R. Samurçay, and D. J. Gilmore (Eds.), *Psychology of Programming.* London, Academic Press, pages 253-270.

Dahl, O-J., Dykstra, E. W. and Hoare, C. A. R. (1971). *Structured Programming.* London: Academic Press.

Dahlby, J. and Linn, M. C. (1985). The demands and requirements of computer programming: A literature review. *Journal of Educational Computing Research, 1,* 253-274.

Davies, S. P. (1993). Models and theories of programming strategy. *International Journal of Man-Machine Studies, 39*(2), 269-304.

Davies, S. P. (1994). Knowledge restructuring and the acquisition of programming expertise. *International Journal of Human-Computer Studies, 40*(4), 703-726.

Détienne, F. (1995). Design strategies and knowledge in object-oriented programming: Effects of expertise. *Human-Computer Interaction, 10,* 129-170.

Ehrlich, K. and Soloway, E. (1984). An empirical investigation of the tacit plan knowledge in programming. In J. C. Thomas and M. L. Schneider, (Eds.) *Human Factors and Computer Systems.* Norwood, NJ, Ablex, pages 113-133.

Eisenstadt, M. Tales of debugging from the front lines. In C. R. Cook, J. C. Scholtz, and J. C. Spoher (Eds.) *Empirical Studies of Programmers: Fifth Workshop.* Norwood, NJ, Ablex, pages 86-112.

Epstein, R. G. and Tucker, A. B. (1993). Introducing object-orientedness into a breadth-first introductory curriculum. *Computer Science Education, 4*(1), 35-44.

Fischer, G. (1987). Cognitive view of reuse and redesign. *IEEE Software 4*(3), 60-72.

Flor, N. V. and Hutchins, E. L. (1991). Analyzing distributed cognition in software teams: A case study of team programming during perfective software maintenance. In J. Koenemann-Belliveau, T. G. Moher, and S. P. Robertson (Eds.),*Empirical Studies of Programmers: Fourth Workshop* . Norwood, NJ, Ablex, pages 36-64.

Gamma, E., Helm, R., Johnson, R., and Vlissides, J. (1995). *Design Patterns: Elements of Reusable Object-Oriented Software.* Addison-Wesley, New York, NY.

Gellenbeck, E. M. and Cook, C. R. (1991). An investigation of procedure and variable names as beacons during program comprehension. In J. Koenemann-Belliveau, T. G. Moher and S. P. Robertson (Eds.), *Empirical Studies of Programmers: Fourth Workshop* . Norwood, NJ, Ablex, pages 82-98.

Gilmore, D. J. (1990). Expert programming knowledge: A strategic approach. In J. -M. Hoc, T. R. G. Green, R. Samurçay, and D. J. Gilmore (Eds.), *Psychology of Programming.* London, Academic Press, pages 223-234.

Goldenson, D. R. and Wang, B. J. (1991). Use of

structure editing tools by novice programmers. In J. Koenemann-Belliveau, T. G. Moher and S. P. Robertson (Eds.), *Empirical Studies of Programmers: Fourth Workshop* . Norwood, NJ, Ablex, pages 99-120.

Green, T. R. G. (1990). Programming languages as information structures. In J.-M. Hoc, T. R. G. Green, R. Samurçay, and D. J. Gilmore (Eds.), *Psychology of Programming* . London, Academic Press, pages 117-138.

Green, T. R. G., Bellamy, R. K. E. and Parker, J. (1987). Parsing and Gnisrap: A model of device use. In G. Olson, S. Sheppard and E. Soloway (Eds.), *Empirical Studies of Programmers, Second Workshop.* Hillsdale, NJ, Ablex, pages 132-146.

Guindon, R. (1990). Designing the design process: Exploiting opportunistic thoughts. *Human-Computer Interaction, 5*, 305-344.

Guindon, R. and Curtis, B. (1988). Controll of cognitive processes during software design: What tools would support software designers? In *Human Factors in Computing Systems: Proceedings of CHI'88.* New York, ACM, pages 263-286.

Guindon, G., Krasner, H., and Curtis, B. (1987). Breakdowns and processes during the early activities of software design by professionals. In G. M. Olson, S. Sheppard and E. Soloway (Eds.), *Empirical Studies of Programmers: Second Workshop.* Norwood, NJ, Ablex, pages 65-82.

Hayes-Roth, B. and Hayes-Roth, F. (1979). A cognitive model of planning. *Cognitive Science, 3*, 275-310.

Helm, R. and Maarek, Y. S. (1991). Integrating information retrieval and domain specific approaches for browsing and retrieval in object-oriented class libraries. In *Object-Oriented Programming, Systems and Applications: Proceedings of OOPSLA'91.* New York, ACM, pages 47-61.

Herbsleb, J. D., Klein, H., Olson, G. M., Olson, Brunner, H., Olson, J. S., and Harding, J. (1995). Object-oriented analysis and design in software project teams. *Human-Computer Interaction, 10*(2,3), 249-292.

Hüni, H. and Metz, I. (1993). Teaching OO software engineering by example: The games factory. *Computer Science Education, 4*(1), 111-122.

Jackson, M. A. (1983). *System Development.* Englewood Cliffs, NJ: Prentice-Hall.

Jeffries, R., Turner, A. S., Polson, P., and Atwood, M. E. (1981). The processes involved in designing software. In *Cognitive Skills and their Acquisition*, ed. J. R. Anderson. Hillsdale, NJ, Erlbaum, pages 225-283.

Johnson, R. and Foote, B. (1988). Designing reusable classes. *J. of Object-Oriented Programming, 1*(2),22-35.

Kautz, K. (1996). User participation and and participatory design: Topics in computing education. Human-Computer Interaction, *11*, 267-284.

Koenemann, J. and Robertson, S. P. (1991). Expert problem solving strategies for program comprehension. In *Human Factors in Computing Systems: CHI'91 Conference Proceedings,* ed. S. P. Robertson, J. S. Olson, and G. M. Olson. ACM, New York, NY, pages 125-130.

Köhne, A. and Weber, G. (1987). Struedi: A Lisp-structure editor for novice programmers. In H. -J. Bullinger and B. Shackel (Eds.), *Human-Computer Interaction—INTERACT'87.* New York: Elsevier, pages 125-130.

Krasner, H., Curtis, B. and Iscoe, N. (1987). Communication breakdowns and boundary spanning activities on large programming projects. In In G. M. Olson, S. Sheppard and E. Soloway (Eds.), *Empirical Studies of Programmers: Second Workshop* . Norwood, NJ: Ablex, pages 47-64.

Lalonde, W. (1993). Making object-oriented concepts play a central role in academic curricula. *Computer Science Education, 4*(1), 13-24.

Letovsky, S. and Soloway, E. (1986). Delocalized plans and progoram comprehension. *IEEE Software, 3*, 41-49.

Linn, M. C. and Clancey, M. J. (1992a). Can experts' explanations help students develop program design skills? *International Journal of Man-Machine Studies, 36*(4), 511-552.

Linn, M. C. and Clancey, M. J. (1992b). The case for case studies of programming problems. *Communications of the ACM, 35*(3), 121-132.

Mayer, R. E. (1975). Different problem-solving competencies established in learning computer programming with and without meaningful models. *Journal of Educational Psychology, 67,* 725-734.

McKim, J. (1993). Teaching object-oriented programming and design. *Journal of Object-Oriented Programming, 6*(1), March/April, 32-39.

Merrill, D. C., Reiser, B. J., Ranney, M., and Trafton, J. G. (1992). Effective tutoring techniques: A comparison of human tutors and intelligent tutoring systems. *Journal of the Learning Sciences, 2*, 277-306.

Merrill, D. C., Reiser, B. J., Merrill, S. K., and Landes, S. (1995). Tutoring: Guided learning by doing. *Cognition and Instruction, 13*(3), 315-372.

Meyer, B. (1988). *Object-Oriented Software Con-*

struction. Prentice Hall, New York, New York.

Moran, T. P. and Carroll, J. M. (1996). Overview of design rationale. In T. P. Moran and J. M. Carroll (Eds.), *Design Rationale: Concepts, Techniques and Use.* Mahwah, NJ, Erlbaum, pages 1-20.

Newell , A. (1980). Reasoning, problem-solving and decision processes: The problem space as a fundamental category. In R. Nickerson (Ed.), *Attention and Performance VIII.* Hillsdale, NJ, Erlbaum.

Newell, A., and Simon, H. A. (1972). *Huan problem solving.* Englewood Cliffs, NJ, Prentice-Hall.

Olson, G. M., Olson, J. S., Carter, M. R., and Storrøsen, M. (1992). Small group design meetings: An analysis of collaboration. *Human-Computer Interaction, 7*, 347-374.

Olson, G. M., Olson, J. S., Storrøsen, M., Carter, M., Herbsleb, J., and Reuter, H. (1996). The structure of activity during design meetings. In T. P. Moran and J. M. Carroll (Eds.), *Design Rationale: Concepts, Techniques, and Use* . Hillsdale, NJ, Erlbaum, pages 217-240.

Osborne, M. (1993). Computing Curricula 1991 and the case for object-oriented methodology. *Computer Science Education, 4*(1), 25-34.

Papert, S. (1980). *Mindstorms. Children, computers, and powerful ideas.* New York, Basic Books.

Pennington, N. (1987). Comprehension strategies in programming. In *Empirical Studies of Programming: Second Workshop*, ed. by G. M. Olson, S. Sheppard, and E. Soloway. Norwood, NJ, Ablex, pages 100-113.

Pennington, N., Lee, A. Y., and Rehder, B. (1995). Cognitive activities and levels of abstraction in procedural and object-oriented design. *Human-Computer Interaction, 10*(2,3), 171-226.

Petre, M. (1990). Expert programmers and programming languages. In *Psychology of Programming*, ed. J.-M. Hoc, T. R. G. Green, R. Samurçay, and D. J. Gilmore. London, Academic Press, pages 103-115.

Petre, M. and Winder, R. L. (1988). Issues governing the suitability of programming languages for programming tasks. *People and Computers IV: Procceedings of HCI'88.* Cambridge, Cambridge University Press.

Pirolli, P. (1986). A cognitive model and computer tutor for programming recursion. *Human-Computer Interaction, 2*, 319-355.

Pylyshyn, Z W. (1984). *Computation and cognition.* Cambridge, MA, MIT Press.

Reiser, B. J., Beekelaar, R., Tyle, A., and Merrill, D. C. (1991). GIL: Scaffolding learning to program with reasoning-congruent representations. In *The International Conference of the Learning Sciences: Proceedings of the 1991.* Evanston, IL, Association for the Advancement of Computing in Education, pages 382-388.

Reiser, B. J., Copen, W. A, Ranney, M., Hamid, A., and Kimberg, D. Y. (1995). Cognitive and motivational consequences of tutoring and discovery learning. *Cognition and Instruction.*

Riecken, R. D., Koenemann-Belliveau, J., and Robertson, S. P. (1991). What do expert programmers communicate by means of descriptive commenting? In T. G. Moher, and S. P. Robertson (Eds.), *Empirical Studies of Progorammers: Fourth Workshop.* Norwood, NJ, Ablex, pages 177-195.

Rist, R. S. (1986). Plans in programming: Definition, demonstration, and development. In E. Soloway and R. Iyengar (Eds.), *Empirical Studies of Programmers.* Norwood, NJ, Ablex, pages 28-47.

Rist, R. S. (1989). Schema creation in programming. *Cognitive Science, 13*, 389-414.

Rist, R. S. (1990). Variability in program design: The interaction of process with knowledge. *International Journal of Man-Machine Studies, 33*(2), 305-322.

Rist, R. S. (1991). Knowledge creation and retrieval in program design: A comparison of novice and experienced programmers. *Human-Computer Interaction, 6,* 1-46.

Rist, R. S. (1995). Program structure and design. *Cognitive Science., 19*(4), 507-562.

Rist, R. S. (1996). Teaching Eiffel as a first language. *Journal of Object-oriented Programming, 9(1)*, 30-41.

Rist, R. S. and Terwilliger, R. (1995). *Object-oriented Programming in Eiffel.* Syndey: Prentice-Hall.

Robertson, S. P., Carroll, J. M., Mack, R. L., Rosson, M. B., and Alpert, S. R. (1994). ODE—An Object Design Exploratorium. In *Proceedings of OOPSLA'94.* New York, ACM, pages 51-64.

Rosson, M. B. and Alpert, S. R. (1990). The cognitive consequences of object-oriented design. *Human-Computer Interaction, 5*, 345-379.

Rosson, M. B. and Carroll, J. M. (1990). Climbing the Smalltalk mountain. *SIGCHI Bulletin, 21*(3), 76-79.

Rosson, M. B. and Carroll, J. M. (1993). Active programming strategies in reuse. In *Proceedings of ECOOP'93 — Object-Oriented Programming.* Berlin, Springer-Verlag, pages 4-18.

Rosson, M. B., and Carroll, J. M. (1995). Narrowing the gap between specification and implementation in object-oriented development. In J. M. Carroll (Ed.), *Scenario-Based Design: Envisioning Work and Technology in System Development* . New York, John Wiley, pages 247-278.

Rosson, M. B. and Carroll, J. M. (1996a). Scaffolded examples for learning object-oriented design. *Communications of the ACM, 39*(4), 46-47.

Rosson, M. B. and Carroll, J. M. (1996b). The reuse of uses in Smalltalk programming. *ACM Transactions on Computer-Human Interaction, 3*(3), 219-253.

Rosson, M. B. and Carroll, J. M. (1996c). Object-oriented design from user scenarios (Tutorial). In *Human Factors in Computing Systems: CHI 96 Conference Companion*. New York, ACM, pages 361-362.

Rosson, M. B., Carroll, J. M., and Bellamy, R. K. E. (1990). Smalltalk scaffolding: A case study in Minimalist instruction. In J. C. Chew and J. Whiteside (Eds.), *Human Factors in Computing Systems: Proceedings oi CHI*. New York, ACM, pages 423-429.

Rosson, M. B. and Gold, E. (1989). Problem-solution mapping in object-oriented design. In *Proceedings of OOPSLA'89*. New York, ACM, pages 7-10.

Rosson, M. B. and Heliotis, J. E. (1993). The OOPSLA'92 Educators' Sympsium (guest editors' introduction). *Computer Science Education, 4*(1), 1-4.

Schank, R. and Abelson, R. (1977). *Scripts, Plans, Goals and Understanding*. Hillsdale, NJ, Lawrence Erlbaum.

Scholtz, J. and Wiedenbeck, S. (1992). The role of planning in learning a new language. *International Journal of Man-Machine Studies, 37*(2), 191-214.

Shaw, M. (1990). Prospects for an engineering discipline of software. *IEEE Software, 7*(6), 9-12.

Shneiderman, B. (1980). *Software Psychology*. Cambridge, MA, Winthrop Publishers, Inc..

Simon, H. A. (1973). The structure of ill-structured problems. *Artificial Intelligence, 4,* 181-201.

Singley, M. K., Carroll, J. M., and Alpert, S. R. (1991). Psychological design rationale for an intelligent tutoring system for Smalltalk. In J. Koenemann-Belliveau, T. G. Moher and S. P. Robertson (Eds.), *Empirical Studies of Programmers: Fourth Workshop* . Norwood, NJ, Ablex, pages 196-209.

Soloway, E. (1986). Learning to program = learning to construct mechanisms and explanations. *Communications of the ACM, 29*(9), 850-858.

Soloway, E. and Ehrlich, K. (1984). Empirical studies of programming knowledge. *IEEE Transactions on Software Engineering, SE-10*, 595-609.

Soloway, E. , Spohrer, J., and Littman, D. (1988). E Unum Puribus: Generating alternative designs. In R. E. Mayer (Ed.), *Teaching and learning computer programming*. Hillsdale, NJ, Erlbaum, pages 137-152.

Tewari, R. and Friedman, F. L. (1993). A framework for incorporating object-oriented software engineering in the undergraduate curriculum. *Computer Science Education, 4*(1), 45-62.

Tucker, A., Barnes, B., Aiken, R., Barker, K., Bruce, K., Cain, S., Conry, S., Engel, G., Epstein, R., Lidtke, D., Mulder, M., Rogers, J., Spafford, E., and Turner, A. (1991). *Report of the ACM/IEEE CS Joint Curriculum Task Force: Computing Curricula 1991.* New York, ACM and IEEE Press,.

Ullman, D. G., Stauffer, L A., and Dietterich, T. G. (1986). *Preliminary results of an experimental study on the mechanical design process.* Technical Report 86-30-9, Corvallis, OR, Oregon State University.

Vessey, I. (1985). Expertise in debugging computer programs: A process analysis. *International Journal of Man-Machine Studies, 23*, 459-494.

Vessey, I. (1987). On matching programmers' chunks with program structures: An empirical investigation. *International Journal of Man-Machine Studies, 27*, 65-89.

Visser, W. (1987). Strategies in programming programmable controllers: A field study on a professional programming. In G. M. Olson, S. Sheppard and E. Soloway (Eds.),*Empirical Studies of Programmers: Second Workshop* . Norwood, NJ, Ablex, pages 217-130.

Visser, W. (1990). More or less following a plan during design: Opportunistic deviations in specification. *International Journal of Man-Machine Studies, 33*, 247-278.

Widowski, D. (1987). Reading, comprehending and recalling computer programs as a function of expertise. *Proceedings of CERCLE Workshop on Complex Learning*. Grange-over-Sands, UK, CERCLE.

Wiedenbeck, S. (1986). Beacons in computer program comprehension. *International Journal of Man-Machine* Studies, *25*, 697-709.

Wirfs-Brock, R., Wilkerson, B. and Wiener, L. (1990). *Designing Object-Oriented Software.* Englewood Cliffs, NJ, Prentice-Hall.

Wirth, N. (1971). Program development by stepwise refinement. *Communications of the ACM, 14*, 221-226.

Handbook of Human-Computer Interaction
Second, completely revised edition
M. Helander, T.K. Landauer, P. Prabhu (eds.)

Chapter 47

End-User Programming

Michael Eisenberg
Department of Computer Science, Institute of Cognitive Science, and Center for Lifelong Learning and Design
University of Colorado
Boulder, Colorado, USA

47.1 Introduction

It is standard practice to begin an essay such as this one with a definition of terms: what exactly, then, is "end-user programming"? A plausible first stab at a definition would be that end-user programming is the use of a programming language by someone not trained as a professional computer scientist or programmer. Typically, the "end user" in question will be a professional—an architect, scientist, artist, business-person—whose programming activities center around the use of selected commercial applications related to his or her field. Thus, a scientist might develop mathematical models in a system such as Mathematica [S5] or Maple[S4]; an architect might program in the Lisp dialect provided with AutoCAD [S1], or some similar design tool; an advertiser might create a presentation using the Lingo language provided with the Director [S2] application; and so forth.

A closer look at this informal definition, however, reveals some underlying questions. First, what precisely is a programming language? Many application designers—perhaps fearing that the term "programming" sounds too daunting to their customers—prefer to describe their systems' language components with alternative terms, such as "scripting." Is there any meaningful distinction between a "scripting language" and a "programming language"? And going further, should other variants of formal notation—such as the formula languages provided with most spreadsheet applications—be viewed as programming media? When an accountant writes a sum notation into a cell of a spreadsheet, is he doing programming?

Then again, how should we characterize "end users"? Are mathematicians and scientists—people with extensive technical training—what we have in mind when we refer to "typical" end users? Or are we thinking instead of people in "nontechnical" fields (whatever those might be)? And what about the use of programming languages (such as Logo) in K-12 education: are children—as nonprofessional programmers— "end users" in the sense of our definition?

These questions might seem to be matters of academic hair-splitting were it not for the fact that they frame ongoing, highly unresolved, and increasingly contentious questions about how software applications should be written. Should we, as designers of software, include programming languages in our applications; and if so, what should those languages look like? Should we avoid or embrace end-user programming? If end-user programming is deemed necessary or desirable in application design, how should it be introduced in educational settings?

This essay will not attempt to provide hard and fast answers to these questions—indeed, in design domains (such as the creation of software applications), such answers are generally not to be found. In compensation, though, this essay will try to illuminate these questions in the light of current research and practice in end-user programming, and to point toward interesting (and in some cases insufficiently explored) pathways for future work. The following section will initiate the discussion by delineating the arguments over whether end-user programming is a goal worth pursuing at all—i.e., whether end users should (or should be expected to) write programs. That discussion will introduce the most salient "pro" and "con" arguments about end-user programming in terms that will recur throughout this essay. The subsequent (third) section will focus on whether "end-user" programming is in fact distinct from what might be called "professional" programming: are "end users" a special breed of programmers, and if so, how? This is followed by a brief discussion, in the fourth section, of children's programming as a particular instance of "end-user" programming; and finally, the fifth section describes some of the important research issues facing proponents of end-user programming in the near future.

47.2 End-User Programming: Pro and Con

One can certainly make a plausible—and historically grounded—case against the desirability of end-user programming. The first users of personal computers in the late 1970's and early 1980's were primarily hobbyists and computer professionals; for these individuals, programming was, if not a pleasure, hardly a burden. In contrast, the past decade has seen an explosive growth of software applications aimed at people who have never programmed (and may never want to). This sea change in system design was signaled in the academic realm by the ascendance of "direct manipulation" as a paradigm for application design. Originally the notion of "direct manipulation" implied a mapping between visible user actions on the screen and operations performed in some visibly-represented model or computational system (cf. the seminal papers of Shneiderman (1983) and Hutchins, Hollan, and Norman (1986)). Over time, however, the term has been employed more loosely to indicate any "point-and-click" graphical interface whose style of interaction is dominated by the use of icons, menus, palettes, dialog boxes, and the like; and since this style of interface design has come to be viewed as the norm for application design, one can easily interpret the growth of direct manipulation as a historical repudiation of the need for end-user programming.

We will return to the issue of "direct manipulation versus programming" a bit later in this chapter; but for now, we can employ the observation that most popular applications do not include programming languages as a springboard for the central question surrounding end-user programming—namely, whether it is desirable at all. After all, if end-user programming is such a marvelous idea, why do so few major applications make use of it?[1]

The arguments, both con and pro, maybe summarized as follows:

47.2.1 Arguments Against End-User Programming

(Con 1) The Learnability Argument. Programming is hard—too hard for most non-computer-scientists to master. From the economic standpoint, then, any application that includes an extensive programming environment is liable to be found intimidating by ordinary users and will lose in the marketplace to its more

[1] It should be mentioned here that, in the opinion of some observers, direct manipulation interfaces do in fact present a type of programming environment to the user. On this account, "programming" is defined as "issuing commands that are implemented by a computational system", and users of direct manipulation interfaces are engaged in programming when they (e.g.) select a font from a menu of choices. My own belief is that this represents an overly inclusive notion of programming—on this account, users of pocket calculators, calendar watches, and telephones might likewise be said to engage in programming. For the purposes of this essay, then, "programming" will be defined as the explicit use of a symbolic notation (a programming language) characterized by the presence of features such as control constructs, compound data objects, and means of procedural abstraction; on this definition, the typical direct manipulation interface, while presenting the user with the capacity to perform actions that have computational consequences, nonetheless does not provide the user with a full-fledged language. We will return to the complex question of what constitutes a "programming language" in the fifth section of this essay.

learnable competitors. Moreover, since programming takes a long time to learn, and since application users generally are engaged in tasks accompanied by deadlines, language-based applications place their users under unworkable time constraints.

(Con 2) ***The Who-Needs-Programming Argument.*** Programming is unnecessary. Virtually anything that one can do with a language one can accomplish via nonlinguistic means. The richness and functionality of the best language-free applications is a testament to the versatility of direct manipulation as a paradigm for application design.

47.2.2 Arguments for End-User Programming

(Pro 1) The Customizability Argument. Non-programmable applications, lacking a language, consequently lack any straightforward means for user-created extensions. Programming provides a mechanism for the customization or elaboration of otherwise insufficiently powerful software.

(Pro 2) The Medium of Expression Argument. Programming languages provide expressive media in which users may reconceptualize domains. As such, they permit the expression of ideas that otherwise would go undiscovered in the absence of linguistic media.

(Pro 3) The Medium of Communication Argument. Programming languages provide a medium of communication of ideas between users. Once a user has developed her own program for some particular purpose, that program may be shared and extended by other users. Written languages—in particular, textual languages—thus act as what some researchers have termed a "grapholect" (Ong, 1982): a medium through which entire communities of users develop and store a collective memory of previous work. Languages thus become the representative medium of a "user culture."

These arguments, telegraphically expressed, form the core of the debate over the utility of end-user programming. The astute reader will note that there is actually very little in the way of direct or inevitable contradiction among these arguments. Consider, for instance, the responses to the two "anti-programming" positions. Proponents of end-user programming do not really deny that programming is difficult (or at least non-trivial) to learn; but they respond that the power or expressiveness gained by programming is worth the effort. Similarly, the "who-needs-programming" argument is perhaps true in principle—that is, any *particular* task that one can accomplish via programming may be accomplished by some "point-and-click" tool—but in practice, the plasticity and fecundity of a programming language may well provide users with an elegant and compact medium whose utility could be matched only by a huge or unbounded collection of individual direct-manipulation elements.

This last sentence is, in fact, an elaboration of the "customizability" argument, the argument most often encountered among proponents of end-user programming. Nardi (1993) puts the matter with special eloquence:[2]

> "We have only scratched the surface of what would be possible if end users could freely program their own applications.... In fact, such an ability would itself constitute a new paradigm.... As has been shown time and again, no matter how much designers and programmers try to anticipate and provide for what users will need, the effort always falls short because it is impossible to know in advance what may be needed. Customizations, extensions, and new applications become necessary. End users should have the ability to create these customizations, extensions, and applications...." [p. 3]

The point, then, is not that direct manipulation cannot in principle match the power of language for any individual task (the who-needs-programming position). Rather, it is whether non-programmable media are in practice ever truly rich enough: after all, life is lived in practice and not in principle. Moreover, by avoiding the use of languages, nonprogrammable applications commit themselves to a path of continual "upgrades" characterized by an ever-more-unwieldy proliferation of features and extensions. The net result is that what began as a nod to learnability—i.e., the decision not to burden the user with a programming language—becomes over time a commitment to greater and greater complexity as users struggle to master huge collections of new *ad hoc* features within applications. (Eisenberg and Fischer, 1994).

While the "customizability" argument focuses on the accomplishment of particular tasks, the "medium of expression" argument portrays programming languages less as a means of achieving certain specific ends than as a means of rethinking an entire domain. The notion is suggested by this passage from Papert's influential

2 For similar arguments, see the opening paragraphs of both Tazelaar, 1990 and Ryan, 1990.

book *Mindstorms*, here focusing on the educational use of a Logo turtle "specialized" for the subject matter of physics (Papert, 1980):

> "How can students who know Turtle geometry (and can thus recognize its restatement in Turtle laws of motion) now look at Newton's laws? They are in a position to formulate in a qualitative and intuitive form the substance of Newton's first two laws by comparing them with something they already know.... These contrasts lead students to a qualitative understanding of Newton. Although there remains a gap between the Turtle laws and the Newtonian laws of motion, children can appreciate the second through an understanding of the first." [p. 127]

Abelson (1991) makes a similar case for the role of programming in engineering education, describing computer science generally as "an activity that formalizes ideas about methodology by constructing appropriate languages"; while Kynigos (1995) presents several case studies of students (at a range of age levels) employing programming as "a means of expressing and exploring domain-specific ideas." [p. 399]

The implication in these arguments is that, by expressing ideas within a programming language, we come to a new and potentially richer understanding of these ideas: the formalism becomes a tool to think with. Similar observations are common in the history of mathematical notations: one might say, for instance, of Arabic numerals that they lend themselves more readily to certain types of operations (such as multiplication and division) than Roman numerals. Thus, an individual working with Arabic numerals is more likely to understand (or for that matter, invent) the notion of division than someone working with Roman numerals. In an analogous manner—according to this argument—certain ideas are facilitated by the use of programming languages.

An example may help to make this argument more concrete. Consider the following representations of a circle; the first is the standard representation from high school analytical geometry, the second is a turtle-graphics representation similar to that of the Logo programming language:

$$(x-a)^2 + (y-b)^2 = r^2$$

```
repeat 360 [forward 1 right 1]
```

The first notation for the circle highlights certain features of the shape—for instance, that it has a center (in this case, the point (a, b)) and a radius r. Likewise, the second notation highlights alternative features: that the circle may be regarded as an approximation to a closed regular polygon with a large number of sides. Each notation in turn suggests its own style of variation: in the first case, by changing the terms on the left to

$$((x-a)/d)^2 + ((y-b)/f)^2$$

we derive the equation for an ellipse. Likewise, by changing the turtle graphics representation so that the turtle-step increases by a fixed ratio at each step (rather than remaining constant at 1), we get an approximation to a logarithmic spiral. (Abelson and diSessa, 1981).

The point of this example is not that one notation is superior, but rather that each representation of a circle highlights certain features and operations while suppressing others. Where spirals are almost never encountered in high school analytical geometry (they are typically represented by parametric curves), they appear as a natural variation of the turtle-graphics circle; conversely, while it is rather difficult to create an ellipse in the turtle-graphics formalism, that shape appears as a straightforward variation of the circle as rendered by analytical geometry. Thus, by presenting concepts such as the circle in the light of a programming language, we can achieve a new understanding—not a *total* understanding, but a new one—of those concepts. The benefits of end-user programming, in the light of this argument, appear in the way in which they enrich our own vocabulary about certain domains, much as the turtle-graphics notation enriches our understanding of the geometry of the circle.

It is important that this argument not be misconstrued as a debate over whether the activity of programming has more general cognitive benefits—e.g., whether programming leads to more disciplined or planful "top-down" reasoning. This "pro" argument might be added to the list above as

(Pro 4) The Improved Mind Argument. Programming is an activity whose cognitive benefits transfer or extend to domains other than the particular subject matter of the programs themselves. People (especially children) who engage in programming may thereby become better problem-solvers, learning general techniques or cognitive skills (such as logical reasoning, top-down design, and so forth) that are applicable to a wide variety of domains.

The "improved mind" argument is contentious; we'll return to it later in this essay, in the discussion of children's programming. For now, we wish merely to distinguish this argument from the (less ambitious) "means of expression" argument, which downplays the role of transfer and focuses instead on the expressive range that programming affords within particular domains. In effect, the means of expression argument casts programming languages in the role of domain-specific "cognitive artifact", in much the same spirit described by Norman (1993):

> "The powers of cognition come from abstraction and representation: the ability to represent perceptions, experiences, and thoughts in some medium other than that in which they have occurred, abstracted away from irrelevant details.... The important point is that we can make marks or symbols that represent something else and then do our reasoning by using those marks." [p. 47]

The third argument for end-user programming—namely, the "means of communication argument"—is the one least often encountered in debates on the subject; but in this writer's opinion, it is at least as important as the first two. This argument shifts the focus away from programming as a means of communicating ideas between user and machine, and instead looks at programming as a way of communicating ideas between people. An example of this idea, as realized within a "culture" of end users, may be seen within the Mathematica community: several textbooks have appeared in which Mathematica code is an essential means of presenting mathematical material (e.g., (Gray and Glynn, 1991; Gray, 1993)), and a quarterly journal has appeared in which (among other features) users present or swap new procedures in the Mathematica language.

It may be replied at this point that nonprogrammable applications similarly develop "user cultures" in which novel techniques are exchanged; for instance, a user of a nonprogrammable paint program might explain to others the steps for creating (say) a drawing that looks like a tree. But there are important differences between this scenario and one mediated by a programming language. First, the language (especially if it is a textual as opposed to visual or iconic language) affords an exceptionally convenient medium in which to communicate new ideas: it does not, in the general case, require full screen shots to convey the idea. Secondly, the communication of ideas through the programming language often does not require the presence of the computer; to an experienced Mathematica user, one might learn much about (say) Fourier transforms by reading a procedural representation of the transform algorithm, without necessarily running it. (In contrast, a new nonprogrammable paint program technique would be harder to communicate or employ in the absence of the program itself.) And finally, the structure of a programming language lends itself naturally to the development of layers of abstraction: thus, if a Mathematica user obtains a new Fourier transform procedure, that procedure may be incorporated as a "primitive" element in some still more complex procedure, which may itself be incorporated as a primitive element in yet another procedure, and so forth. The presence of a programming medium thus lends itself, by the accretion of vocabulary, to what Abelson, Sussman, and Sussman (1981) refer to as "metalinguistic abstraction": the building of new languages within older ones.

The arguments for and against end-user programming are unlikely to be settled by academic debate: rather, they are currently being waged—and will continue to be waged—in the software marketplace. But, as we will see throughout the remainder of this chapter, both the "pro" and "con" arguments color the history and likely future of the field. And while it is true that most current applications are designed to be nonprogrammable (on the assumption that this is the decision least likely to intimidate users), it is also interesting to note that in some cases (the Director, AutoCAD, and Word [S7] programs are cases in point), a nonprogrammable application has evolved over time into a more powerful programmable version. This suggests that the need for end-user programming, and the expressiveness it provides, may well be a byproduct of the steady growth of expert user communities for particular applications.[3] While novice application-users may prefer relatively "lean" and simple systems, experts may derive more power from programming languages than from burgeoning point-and-click feature sets.

47.3 End-User Programming vs. Professional Programming

The very term "end-user programming" implies that this is a different beast from the notion of "professional programming" that most computer scientists employ. This section will examine those aspects both of programming language design and program construction that distinguish end-user programming from its professional cousin. (See also Guzdial *et al.*, 1992) for thoughtful discussion of these questions.) In some in-

[3] See McNurlin (1981a, 1981b) for an early, and intriguingly optimistic, account of the value of end-user programming in business communities.

stances, we argue that the differences between end-user and professional programming reflect mild shifts of emphasis rather than fundamental qualitative distinctions.

47.3.1 Designing End-User Languages I: The New Language-vs.-Traditional Language Issue

The design of an end-user programming language can reflect a variety of concerns: indeed, these concerns may be mapped to the arguments of the previous section. To the extent that a designer of an end-user programming language focuses on responding to the "Learnability" argument, she will attempt to create a more easily-learned language; to the extent that she focuses on the "Extensibility" and "Means of Expression" arguments, her language will attempt to incorporate the largest and most powerful possible vocabulary (with special attention, perhaps, to the subject domain for which the language is intended); to the extent that she focuses on the "Means of Communication" argument, her language may be structured so that it is more easily read (perhaps incorporating optional natural-language keywords, as in the HyperTalk language (Goodman, 1990), acknowledging some possible sacrifice in the ease of writing (as opposed to reading) programs.

The first crucial choice facing the designer of an end-user language is whether to start from scratch—i.e., whether to create a brand new, application- or domain-specific language, or to expand upon some already-existing general purpose language. Examples of the first alternative include Director's Lingo language, HyperCard's [S3] HyperTalk language, and the Mathematica language; examples of the second include AutoCAD's dialect of Lisp and Word's dialect of Basic (Cobb Group, 1994). There are undoubtedly good arguments to be made in favor of either alternative. A new, application-specific language may be designed with special attention to learnability or readability (at least the latter is arguably true of HyperTalk); the language may take special advantage of the surrounding application structure (e.g., most spreadsheet formula languages incorporate an effective "dataflow" notion of control that would be tricky to realize in the standard general-purpose languages (cf. (Nardi, 1993), pp. 41-50); or the language may incorporate visual or iconic elements. On the other hand, there are advantages to using an application-enhanced general purpose language as well. First, the same underlying language substrate may be used in multiple applications: for instance, both the Emacs editor (Stallman, 1986) and AutoCAD make use of a Lisp dialect. Thus, a user who picks up the rudiments of Lisp may employ that knowledge to master more than one application (rather than having to learn a new application-specific language for each new domain). Thinking again of the "means of communication" argument, it should be noted that an AutoCAD programmer may—with some hope of success—present her ideas to a community of Lisp programmers who are not necessarily AutoCAD users; in contrast, programs written in application-specific languages will be difficult to understand outside the community of users for that specific application. Finally, it must be acknowledged that some "classical" interpreted languages such as Lisp and Basic have an extensive history of study, resulting in the development of a well-understood semantics for the language, as well as tools such as compilers and debuggers; the designer who elects to create a brand new language cannot easily capitalize on the "lore" that has accumulated around general-purpose languages (cf. the discussions of these questions in (Cook, 1990) and (Eisenberg, 1991).

47.3.2 Designing End-User Languages II: The Learnability Issue

The preceding paragraph touched indirectly upon the question with which we opened this section—namely, the difference (if any) between end-user programming and professional programming. In this case, the question focuses on language design: are end-user languages necessarily different from professional languages? If an AutoCAD user employs the application's Lisp dialect, is he facing radically different programming tasks than a professional Lisp programmer?

This general question—of what, precisely, distinguishes end users from professionals—pervades all aspects of end-user language design. In this light, perhaps the most fundamental difference between professional and non-professional programmers lies in the extent of their assumed interest in learning the craft of programming itself (and any given language). End users of applications are, by this argument, more interested in simply getting their work done: they thus have little time to learn the fine points of programming (such as the design of modular programs, the use of black-box abstraction, and other staples of elementary software engineering courses). Moreover, end users wish to devote the least possible time to learning a formal language, as they take little aesthetic delight in the subject matter of programming. In short, then, end users are content (again, according to this argument) to write sloppy programs in hastily learned media.4

The logical extension of this argument is that in providing end users with programming languages, learnability of the language becomes a paramount issue. This concern for learnability is expressed in practice in two major ways: first, in the attempt to design easier-to-learn languages; second, in the attempt to design end-user programming environments that include improved tools with which to learn the application's language. (Note that in this second case, the application language may not itself be designed for learnability.) We will examine each of these methods in turn.

47.3.3 The Quest for the Learnable Language

As discussed in the previous section, the creation of an end-user programming environment begins with a choice of language. An extensive body of research has lent support to the notion that programming (at least as embodied in traditional general-purpose languages) is a difficult skill to learn. Indeed, one paper by du Boulay (1986) begins with the observation, "Learning to program is not easy." Du Boulay's paper goes on to discuss the difficulties that novices encounter in understanding concepts such as assignment of a value to a variable, flow of control, and the use of compound data objects (the examples are drawn from Basic and Pascal). Numerous excellent studies and summaries echo these sentiments; a small but representative selection are mentioned here:[5]

- Rogalski and Samurçay (1990) summarize a variety of difficulties encountered by novice programmers in a wide range of languages (these include misconceptions about iteration, recursion, the use of variables, and more general errors such as implicitly endowing the computer with interpretive abilities derived from natural rules of communication);

- Kurland and Pea (1985) describe the difficulties that children encounter in understanding recursion (particularly embedded recursion) in Logo procedures;

- Spohrer and Soloway (1986) present an interesting and influential account of the difficulties that students have in writing Pascal programs, attributing the origins of many bugs not to misunderstanding of individual language constructs (such as the "repeat" form) but to problems in understanding and combining program fragments ("plans") that embody stereotyped actions such as reading in and processing a sequence of values until some special "sentinel" value is encountered (see also Rist (1986), Spohrer *et al.* (1985));

- Gugerty and Olson (1986) and Carver (1988) discuss difficulties in debugging (the former study employed undergraduates and graduate students working in Logo and Pascal; the latter focused on the development of an effective "debugging curriculum" for elementary school students using Logo).

The overall portrait painted by this body of research indicates that learning to programming is a difficult, time-consuming, and often unmotivating task, fraught with error and misconception. In all fairness, it should be noted that this portrait may be a little *too* pessimistic: after all, for all of its purported difficulty, programming is nonetheless a skill that is acquired (if imperfectly) over the course of a semester or so by thousands of students every year. Nonetheless, in the judgment of many application designers, the traditional general-purpose languages (C, Fortran, Basic, Lisp) are seen as too difficult or unmotivating to learn for end users: hence the need to create newer and more learnable languages.

Of course, any effort to create a learnable language must (at least implicitly) involve a judgment as to what makes programming difficult in the first place. Several major approaches to creating learnable languages can be identified, each associated with its own assumptions about the important sources of difficulty in programming:

Visual/Iconic Languages. The history of visual programming languages has a long and extensive his-

[4] There are echoes of this discussion in Green's (1990) division of programming languages (and environments) into the "neat" and "scruffy" variety; the former type of language, to Green, emphasizes program correctness and avoidance of ambiguity, while the latter type of language places greater emphasis on fluidity and use-in-context ("their [scruffy languages'] interpretation very frequently depends on how the system has been tailored for local purposes" [p. 22]).

[5] There are several valuable books in which much of the best of this work has been collected over time: Coombs and Alty (1981), Mayer (1988), Soloway and Spohrer (1989), and Hoc *et al.* (1990) are good compendia. The series of Empirical Studies of Programmers Workshop proceedings (Soloway and Iyengar (1986), Olson *et al.* (1987), Koenemann-Belliveau *et al.* (1991), and Cook *et al.* (1993)) are also extremely worthwhile.

tory—and indeed, the subject is too vast to survey here. For the purposes of this discussion, we should note that there are many varieties of "visual" languages. Some languages work almost exclusively through graphical elements (i.e., virtually every aspect of the language, including numeric operations, has been replaced by some sort of graphical representation); some mix textual and iconic elements; some use the visual element to affect program layout, using flow diagrams or nested boxes to lend structure to basically textual programs.

The question of whether any of these styles of language design do, in fact, make for more learnable programming languages is unresolved. There is, in fact, some evidence that presenting a program's structure through diagrammatic means—i.e., the last of the several techniques mentioned in the previous sentence—increases the understandability of that program relative to a purely textual presentation (Cunniff and Taylor, 1987). Smith (1993) makes the argument that visual (or "analogical") representations, being closer to our mental representations of objects, require less translation than textual/symbolic ("Fregean") representations[6]; this argument would presumably apply to the first two techniques mentioned. On the other hand, Green *et al.* (1991) compared the comprehensibility (for experienced programmers) of a commercial visual dataflow language to a textual language; among their subjects, the textual language proved easier to understand. Petre (1995) makes an interesting argument that the inclusion of graphical elements in formal languages is a technique often more suited to domain experts than to novices: the interpretation of visual representations (such as icons or diagrams) is itself, according to this argument, a sophisticated skill requiring time to learn.

In disentangling these arguments, it is worth distinguishing between the "Learnability" and "Means of Communication" arguments. Graphical or visual elements have undoubted communicative advantages over text for some purposes: one can include a huge range of structural information in a picture (e.g., of a landscape) that can be directly "read off" the picture in a way that would be far more unwieldy to convey in text. In the same vein, designers of visual languages—programming languages that include visual or iconic elements—have often made the claim that such languages can be far more richly communicative than purely textual languages. This is, in essence, an extension of the "Means of Communication" argument: here, the rationale for visual languages is that they are capable of representing ideas that would be effectively inexpressible in text alone. By extension, one might argue that for certain tasks—tasks that are difficult to express by any other means—visual languages should be more learnable than their textual cousins. This does not necessarily mean, however, that visual languages will be more easily learned by novices (whether those novices are new to programming or to the domain of the visual language), at least for those tasks that may be reasonably well expressed both by textual and visual means.

"Implicit" or "Hidden" Languages. A different technique for easing the language-learning process for users is to dispense with language syntax altogether, allowing users to create programs without actually writing code. The notion here is that programs may be created by allowing the user to specify examples of how the program should work; the programming environment then creates an operational program consistent with the examples that the user has presented. A number of working "programming-by-demonstration" systems have been created, including Myers' (1993a) Peridot system for creating user interfaces; Maulsby and Witten's (1993) Metamouse system (in which a Logo-style turtle "infers" procedures for drawing and manipulating graphical objects from a user-provided example); and Cypher's (1993) Eager system, which infers iterative procedures from two to three repeated examples.

For most efforts in programming-by-demonstration, the goal is expressly to shield the user from the need to learn such programming concepts as variables, loops, and conditionals (cf. Cypher (1993), pp. 4-5): in essence, then, users can delegate the actual writing of programs to the computational system without the need for learning programming syntax. A programming-by-demonstration system can thus finesse the learnability issue, since (in principle) users need to learn at most very little beyond the informal operations that they already know how to perform with software.

In practice, the goal of programming by demonstration has yet to be realized for large and complex tasks beyond those illustrated in research systems. Nardi (1993) points out some of the practical problems with the idea: it is often difficult for users to provide unambiguous examples of a more general procedure—examples may include minor "slips", or may be generalized in any number of plausible ways. These arguments focus on pragmatic questions of achievability—whether programming-by-demonstration is feasible in rich and complex applications. Undoubtedly, the cur-

[6]The references to "analogical" and "Fregean" representations are derived in turn from Sloman (1971).

rent work in the area is both fascinating and promising; and more elaborate systems are surely on the way. Still another question worth raising about programming-by-demonstration, however, involves its relation to the arguments for end-user programming raised earlier. In effect, the notion of programming-by-demonstration appears most relevant to the "customizability" argument: in principle, users could eventually extend applications by demonstrating the extensions that they wish to create. On the other hand, the other arguments for end-user programming—the "means of expression" and "means of communication" arguments—seem less relevant to programming by demonstration techniques. One might argue that it is by virtue of having an explicit, readable, and formal representation of an idea that one is able to extend, reflect upon, or communicate that idea. The notion of demonstrating a procedural idea not only avoids the drawbacks of having to represent that idea formally for the computer; it also avoids the potential advantages of being able to represent that idea communicably and unambiguously to other users. To the extent, then, that one accepts these additional arguments for end-user programming, programming-by-demonstration may only highlight some of the benefits of end-user languages while de-emphasizing others.

Domain- or Interface-Specific Languages. For many end-user languages, the emphasis is less on devising a radically new programming syntax and more on integrating the language elements with a particular application, interface, or domain. Spreadsheet formula languages (Jolly, 1994) have something of this flavor, inasmuch as they are expressly devised to work with the contents of spreadsheet cells as archetypal data objects. The HyperTalk language is likewise tailored around the HyperCard interface (and the essential "card" data element) (Goodman, 1990); and the typical introductory HyperTalk procedure (structured as a response to some user action) reflects the system's focus on the construction of interactive interfaces.

The interface-specific language strategy reflects a blending of the "learnability" and "means of expression" arguments. Thus, while HyperTalk may present the user with some challenges in learning—like any other language, it includes its own particular formal syntax—it is extremely expressive within the domain (of interface construction) and the application with which it is associated. (Conversely, one would be less likely to employ HyperTalk as, e.g., a language for scientific modeling and computation.) It is plausible that the learnability of such a language, rather than being an abstract function of the language's syntax, is in fact strongly influenced by the application and interface context for which the language was constructed. Thus, it would be unfair to compare, for example the learnability of HyperTalk and Mathematica in the abstract: rather, their learnability must be assessed in the presence of the application-specific interfaces and domains for which these languages were designed.

Tools and Environments Supporting Language Learning

The previous discussion illustrated several means by which the designers of end-user languages attempt to address the learnability issue through the creation of more learnable languages. Another technique, often employed in concert with the strategies above, is to design additional tools or features within an application to support users in learning the language. Mathematica's "function browser" is one such feature: this permits users to explore the (very large) set of Mathematica primitives by perusing a hierarchical "index" ordered by topic areas. Director's interface likewise permits the user to browse through Lingo primitive names in a scrolling box. Most end-user programmable systems include both editable sample programs and standard help facilities of some form or other to at least provide the user with an introduction to the language vocabulary and/or basic control constructs.

Various research systems have employed still other means to facilitate the learning of an end-user language. Lieberman's Mondrian system for graphical editing (1993), and Myers' (1993b) Garnet system for interface construction, for example, both intermingle programming by demonstration with textual program construction (i.e., it is feasible to begin creating a program by presenting an example of the program in operation; the system then generates textual code—Lisp, in both systems—which may be edited directly by the user). Although neither system was expressly intended as a means of teaching Lisp programming constructs to a novice user, such techniques could eventually prove extremely powerful as the basis for language-tutoring systems. In a similar vein, DiGiano's Chart 'n' Art system (DiGiano and Eisenberg, 1995), a chart design application based upon Lisp, introduces the notion of a "self-disclosing" language component that unobtrusively and gradually reveals more tutorial information to the user as she works with the direct manipulation portion of the application.

47.3.4 End-User vs. Professional Programming: Where are the Differences?

The discussion in this section thus far has centered upon strategies for developing more learnable programming languages and environments for end users. It should be noted, however, that—with the exception of some efforts in programming-by-demonstration—virtually all of this discussion could easily be applied, with at most small modification, to professional programming environments. After all, professional programmers might well want to incorporate graphical or visual elements in their languages; they might well appreciate domain- or interface-specific extensions for their own professional system-building projects; they would undoubtedly appreciate tools for learning or extending their knowledge of their own favorite language. So we might once more return to the question of where the differences really lie between end-user and professional programming.

It is in fact my own feeling—as mentioned earlier—that the distinctions between end users and professional programmers (and by extension, the distinctions between the languages, tools, and environments for these two communities) are generally overestimated. Before elaborating on this opinion, however, it is worth presenting the most salient differences of emphasis between end users and professionals:

- End users, unlike professional programmers, typically write short and relatively simple programs. Thus, whereas professional programmers are often engaged in the creation of system-level projects with many thousands of lines of code, end users may typically find themselves writing programs of perhaps a few pages at most.

- Professional programmers—working as they do on large projects—often are employed to work as members of large teams, whereas end users most typically create programs on their own or in very small teams.

- Professional programmers (at least in academia) tend to analyze languages using the conceptual tools of denotational semantics: thus, they will debate the merits of languages according to (e.g.) the order of evaluation of arguments, whether the language employs lexical or dynamic scoping, whether the language is strongly typed or not, whether the language includes functions as first class objects, and so forth. These notions in turn reflect an ongoing concern with whether programs may in some cases be proven correct; whether programs may be easily altered, tested, and maintained by large teams; whether elements of written programs are available for reuse; and so forth. Thus, professional programmers tend to view programming languages as abstract formalisms, to be analyzed as much as possible in isolation from particular implementations. In contrast, the analysis of end user languages is almost inseparable from their particular application context: we do not generally expect to see "language standards" defined for end-user languages as we do for professional languages. Similarly, end-user languages—as discussed just a bit earlier—are judged more often for their appropriateness to a particular domain or interface, or for their learnability than for (say) the manner in which they lend themselves to the construction of provably correct code.

All these distinctions are real and visible in the comparison of end-user programming and professional programming. But they are better regarded as tendencies—matters of degree—rather than hard and fast laws of programming practice. Certainly, most end users write short and simple programs, but not all: there are plenty of moderate-to-large Mathematica and HyperTalk programs in existence. For these larger projects, the question of debuggability and maintainability looms as prominently as it would for a large C or Lisp program. Likewise, end users of programmable systems might not work in huge teams; but as has been recorded in some cases, they do form communities in which certain individuals take on the role of a "local developer", creating programs for a group of colleagues. (Gantt and Nardi (1992) refer to a person in this role as a "gardener"; Zink (1984) describes such a person as a "champion.") For such local developers, then, the question of whether programs may be readily communicated and understood by others might well become meaningful, just as it would in a professional programming team. And finally, the question of program analyzability and correctness is beginning to be recognized in the end-user programming field as well. One well-known study, for instance, showed that over 40 percent of the (relatively simple) test spreadsheets created by experienced spreadsheet users contained programming errors; according to the experimenters, these users spent relatively little time in systematic debugging (Brown and Gould, 1987).

In short, then, we should not assume that end users are "nonprogrammers"—some irretrievably lost species of being. Rather, end users are *potential* programmers whose typical concerns are somewhat (but not entirely) different from those of professional programmer—much as the concerns of a person writing a friendly letter (felicity of expression, clarity, economy) are often not too much different from those of a professional novelist. And as end users become, over time, increasingly expert in the use of their own programming media, they are likely to experience, acutely and at first hand, the issues of program correctness, debuggability, recoverability, and communicability that are putatively the sole province of professional software engineers.[7]

47.4 Children as Programmers

Thus far, this chapter has for the most part focused on end-user programming as an instance of adult professional activity. Nonetheless, almost identical issues and arguments arise when the "end users" in question are children, and when the programming in question is done in educational settings. In fact, the two realms—of adult end-user programming and children's programming—are inextricable. Certainly, if end-user programming becomes sufficiently widespread in professional adult communities, then the question of whether, and at what educational stage, children should be introduced to programming is unavoidable. Moreover, designers of educational applications and simulations are faced with the very same questions about the role of programming as are their counterparts in the world of professional or business applications.

Nonetheless there is one unique aspect, historically, to the arguments surrounding end-user programming in educational settings. Whereas in the adult realm, the arguments for end-user programming typically focus on productivity—getting one's work done—children's programming is generally debated according to the purported merits of programming as an activity in its own right. Thus, in addition to the "pro" arguments mentioned earlier, there might be additional arguments such as the "improved mind" position mentioned earlier (and whose discussion we postponed):

(Pro 4) The Improved Mind Argument. Programming is an activity whose cognitive benefits transfer or extend to domains other than the particular subject matter of the programs themselves. People (especially children) who engage in programming may thereby become better problem-solvers, learning general techniques (such as logical reasoning, top-down design, and so forth) that are applicable to a wide variety of domains.

A more pragmatic style of argument, focusing on economic rather than cognitive benefits, might run as follows:

(Pro 5) The Computer Literacy Argument. Programming is a valuable skill in the adult world, much like the skills of reading and writing. Children should thus be introduced to programming as a form of "technological literacy", if for no other reason than that acquiring this skill will eventually make them more employable adults.

The "improved mind" argument has, in fact, long been implicit in much of writing about children's programming. One can hear echoes of the argument in Papert's *Mindstorms* (1980):

"Stated most simply, my conjecture is that the computer can concretize (and personalize) the formal. Seen in this light, it is not just another powerful educational tool. It is unique in providing us with the means for addressing what Piaget and many others see as the obstacle which is overcome in the passage from child to adult thinking. I believe that it can allow us to shift the boundary separating concrete and formal."

and in these passages from one of the co-inventors of the Basic language, John Kemeny (1983):

> "In sum, learning computer programming has a beneficial effect on human thinking, because it teaches skills that are fundamental to most professions." [p. 223]

> "We have a unique opportunity to improve human thinking. If we recognized the areas of hu-

---

[7] Much of this discussion echoes the argument in Cowan *et al.* (1992), who point out the importance of features such as type safety and software reuse in end-user programming languages and environments. Still, those authors reach a very different conclusion, arguing that the requirements of end-user languages are (or should be) distinct from those of other languages. Cowan *et al.* write, "End-users will be 'amateur' programmers; we can not expect end-users to use a formal design cycle or programming concepts, such as encapsulation or inheritance, since their exposure to substantive training in programming may be minimal." [p. 57] While I agree with many of Cowan *et al.*'s points, my own feeling is that end users and professional programmers share many of the same basic concerns (e.g., program correctness), albeit with differing degrees of emphasis. As Nardi (1993) observes, "In our spreadsheet study we found that communities of users span a *continuum* of programming skill ranging from end users to local developers to programmers" [p. 104; emphasis in the original].

man knowledge where ordinary languages are inappropriate, and if computer literacy is routinely achieved in our schools, we can aspire to human thought of a clarity and precision rare today." [p. 230]

While such claims may be intuitively compelling, supporting evidence for the "improved mind" argument has been difficult to come by. One well-known (and much-debated) study by Pea and Kurland (Pea, Kurland, and Hawkins, 1987); for general discussion see (Pea and Kurland, 1987), aimed at investigating transfer between Logo programming experience and planning skills among elementary school children in a task involving cleaning the classroom, demonstrated no effect of programming experience. Soloway and his colleagues performed several studies aimed at demonstrating transfer between programming and algebra; in perhaps the most extensive of these (Olson, Catrambone, and Soloway, 1987), they compared the performance (on algebra problems) of undergraduates taking psychology, programming, and statistics courses, and found no evidence of specific transfer (i.e., improvement in problem-solving) from programming as compared to the control students. Mayer, Dyck, and Vilberg (1986) found only modest improvement in some programming-related tasks in college students following a course in Basic. In contrast, Clements and Gullo (1984) did show a measurable positive effect of Logo experience in young children (in comparison to a control group that worked with computer-presented tutorial programs in reading and arithmetic) on psychological tests of reflectivity and divergent thinking; while Lee and Pennington (1993) report that experienced programmers do show transfer of specific debugging and diagnostic skills to an unfamiliar domain (in this case, electronics). One of the most interesting studies of the "transfer question" for Logo, done by Lehrer *et al.* (1988), resulted in a complex mixture of both positive and negative results: to give a brief and partial summary, children working in Logo classrooms showed no improvement in general problem solving tasks (such as the Tower of Hanoi problem) relative to children working with (nonprogrammable) software. On the other hand, children in the Logo classroom did show improvement in their understanding of geometry (a domain closely related to their work with turtle graphics), and in fact performed better than the control students on a "planning" task not unlike that in the Pea, Kurland, and Hawkins study. Lehrer *et al.* also report, in describing an earlier study, that children learning Logo in a "mediated inquiry" context (involving instruction in topics such as variables and problem decomposition) did better at detecting ambiguity in the procedural directions for a map-reading task than did students in a "less intensive, discovery-oriented" Logo classroom; as the authors write, "these results suggest that the quality and duration of instruction in LOGO significantly influences its transferability." [p. 92] Finally—to mention one other view—Salomon and Perkins (1987), in their interpretation of earlier research, distinguish between what they call "high-road" transfer (resulting from reflection and "mindful generalization") as opposed to "low-road" transfer (resulting from "extensive practice and automatization). In particular, they attribute the Clements and Gullo's positive results to the likely presence of the former sort of transfer.

On the basis of these studies, it is fair to say that proponents of children's programming can point to *some* encouraging evidence of across-domain transfer of particular skills related to programming; and at the same time, it should be noted that the level of programming skill that would be needed to witness this sort of transfer is not often attained by children. As Linn and Dalbey (1985) write, "It is certainly unreasonable to expect progress in general problem solving from a first course in programming."[8] Still, the overall case for programming as a "mind-building" activity seems not much stronger than that of (say) mathematics or Latin as similar carriers of mental discipline. And the "computer literacy" argument is, if anything, shakier than the mind-building argument. First, even if many adults are now compelled to use computers professionally, programming itself has yet to achieve anything remotely like the importance of literacy in adult life. And since a relatively small number of adults need to learn programming, it is hard to argue for the inclusion of programming (as opposed to general experience with applications) within a school curriculum. Moreover, even if we accept the argument that programming is a valuable skill for adult employment, the landscape of professional languages is so volatile as to make it questionable whether children should invest the time in learning the skill until they are older. Children educated in the mid 1980's with a view to employability might (for that purpose) have been taught Cobol or Pascal as a first language; such an education would be of far less value for those same

[8] In a similar vein, Mendelsohn *et al.* (1990) write, "It is unrealistic to think that one hour a week of programming over a one-year period will allow transfer of such a specialized competence as planning." (p. 181)

children upon graduating high school today, when C and C++ are the main languages of professional practice (and these language may likewise be obsolete in another decade or so). Thus, the analogy between programming and literacy fails on two counts: unlike literacy, programming is not crucial to adult life, and unlike literacy, programming is a highly unstable and changeable skill. (Cf. the discussion in Snyder (1986), pp. 96-98.)

It is in fact fair to say that through most of the past decade—indeed, until quite recently—interest in children's programming has been in steady decline (perhaps reflecting a lack of conviction in the "improved mind" and "literacy" arguments). This represents a noticeable shift: in the early 1980's, children's programming was at the center of many debates within educational computing (e.g., the question of whether Logo or Basic was preferable as a child's first language was hotly contested—cf. the discussion (Solomon, 1986), pp. 90-102). The past decade, however, has seen children's programming substantially supplanted in classrooms by a variety of educational tools, games, and simulations. While the best of these are indeed quite beautiful, and allow children to engage in exploratory learning, they are almost universally nonprogrammable. It may be, however, that the same arguments that have led some professional applications toward programmability—namely, the "extensibility", "means of expression", and "means of communication" arguments—will over time be applied to the realm of educational tools and applications as well. Thus, rather than simply manipulate simulation parameters (as in the popular SimCity [S6] game), children might—through the use of some sort of programming language—actively construct simulation objects and algorithms for themselves. (Eisenberg, 1995).

There have also been a number of efforts in the field of children's programming aimed at making children's languages more learnable through the incorporation of visual elements. The Boxer language (diSessa and Abelson, 1986), one of the more venerable of these efforts, augments a basically textual language with two-dimensional "boxes": the box acts both as a fundamental data object in the language, and as a syntactic means for grouping regions into expandable and shrinkable units. Boxer's rules for interpretation also involve a "visual" or spatial metaphor in which arguments to procedures may be thought of as being copied into the appropriate regions of the screen before being evaluated. A somewhat more recent system, Function Machines (based on an idea of Paul Goldenberg, and developed at BBN Labs under the direction of Wallace Feurzeig (Feurzeig, 1993; Cuoco 1995), presents functions as constructible animated "machines" on the computer screen, equipped with input hoppers and output spouts (function composition is achieved by connecting the spout of one machine to the input hopper of another). Still more recent efforts include the ToonTalk (Kahn, 1995) system (in which a variety of animated figures are integrated with the creation and evaluation of programs), Agentsheets (Repenning and Sumner, 1995), and KidSim (Smith *et al.*, 1994) (these last two systems are essentially based on a programming paradigm of creating graphical rewrite rules that operate on a two-dimensional plane). Yet another effort worth mentioning in this context is the *Logo language (Resnick, 1994)—this system does not incorporate visual programming, but does extend the basic Logo paradigm of one (or several) programmable "turtles" into massively parallel programming with hundreds or even thousands of turtles.

47.5 Whither End-User Programming?

The debates surrounding end-user programming are unlikely to disappear for a long time, in large part because all the "pro" and "con" arguments outlined in the second section have substantial elements of truth. The benefits of programming—in personalization of tools, in expressiveness and communicability of ideas—are manifest; the barriers to programming—in learnability and in the need to invest substantial time—are equally manifest. Application designers will thus continue in their creative attempts to overcome the barriers while realizing the benefits. This section will outline some of the theoretical directions that are likely to arise over the next decade in the design of end-user languages.

47.5.1 A Taxonomy of Languages and Environments

As noted at the outset of this chapter, the terminology surrounding end-user programming is so imprecise as to be counterproductive. One popular application denotes the ability to name recorded sequences of operations as "creating a script"; other applications refer to "scripting languages"; still another refers to a "formula language" in which arithmetic expressions (but not much more) can be written. When an application says that it includes a "language", then, what should we expect?

At the very least, some coarse-grained distinctions need to be made. My own feeling is that "scripting" and "programming" mean—or at least *should* mean—

Table 1. Taxonomy of application-based language types.

	Language properties present	*Some or all language properties absent*
Objects/Operations derived entirely from interface	Scripting Language	Partial Scripting Language
Objects/Operations beyond those available within interface	Programming Language	Partial Programming Language

different things (i.e., "scripting" should not simply be the advertiser's less-threatening term for "programming"). In particular, a reasonable working definition of a "scripting language" is that it is a means of textual representation, within an application, of operations that could be performed (if tediously) via direct manipulation in the application's interface. In other words, the data objects in a scripting language should correspond only to visible objects within the application; the primitive operations should correspond to user actions. Thus, "scripting"—suggesting as it does a recipe for human performance—should mean writing out a sequence of steps that a user could then follow within the application. To take an example, suppose we have a paint application in which we can select a pen color (say, red); select a pen-width (say, 5x5 pixels); and then draw a square on the screen. If the application allows us to give the name "Red5Square" to this sequence of operations, then it should qualify (at least) as a scripting language; if, on the other hand, the language allows us to create new colors, pen-styles, gradients, or basic shapes that could not be selected via the paint program's interface, then it has gone beyond the power of a "scripting" language alone.

In the same context, it is reasonable to stipulate at least several properties of anything that calls itself a "language" (whether this is a "scripting" or full-fledged "programming" language). First, a language ought to exhibit at least some nontrivial control structures beyond simple sequencing (e.g., the ability to respond to conditions, to repeat operations, to call procedures recursively, to perform several operations in parallel, and so forth). Not all of these techniques need be present in a programming language; but at least some should. Second, a language ought to permit the user to create and name some form of compound data structure (e.g. sets, lists, trees, arrays). Third, and perhaps most important, a language ought to provide users with a means of abstraction: most typically, a means of naming and parametrizing operations as procedures with variable arguments. Whether these procedures (and arguments) are written in text, pictures, or a mixture of the two is immaterial to this definition: it is the ability to build vocabulary items for oneself, and to use those new items in the very same manner as one uses the language primitives, that constitutes the heart of the programming enterprise.

Note that this description of what constitutes a "language" is not derived from considerations of computational complexity, but is rather intended to address those elements of a language that present themselves to the user. Thus, it is possible to devise a system that is equivalent to a Turing machine, and is consequently capable of performing (in principle) any effective computation, but that is not a "language" in our sense (since, for instance, it may not give the user any capability for naming compound data structures and procedures). Moreover, there are many other pragmatic concerns for language-building—e.g., whether anything worth the name of "language" must have means for editing, saving, and debugging programs—that should perhaps be added to the skeletal set of properties given in the preceding paragraph.

In any event, we now have the beginnings of a basic taxonomy of application-based language types, depending on (a) whether the language's objects and operations are derived entirely from a description of user actions within the interface, and (b) whether the language includes all three aforementioned "crucial" properties. We can summarize this taxonomy as in table 1: This table is of course only a very sketchy attempt at what should eventually be a much finer-grained taxonomy. The larger issue, in any case, is that the "classical" categories of programming language (e.g., functional, imperative, logic-based) are insufficient to deal with the welter of application-based languages and partial languages that characterize the current spectrum of end-user programmable systems.

47.5.2 Integration of Programming Languages and Direct Manipulation Interfaces

Early in this chapter, the debates surrounding the value of end-user programming were framed in terms of the contrast between programming languages and direct manipulation interfaces. Historically, direct manipulation and programming have been characterized as representing distinct strategies for the creation of applications (Shneiderman's , 1983) influential article, for instance, characterized direct manipulation as a "step beyond programming languages".) In practice, however, there are numerous ways of integrating end-user programming with direct manipulation interface constructs. (Eisenberg, 1991) Users may write simple programs to tailor the operation of, for example, sliders or radio buttons in an interface; or the user might employ, for example, direct manipulation drawing tools to create a graphical object that will be used as an argument to a written procedure; or the user might write a program which, in the course of running, prompts her for some sequence of direct manipulation actions.

The strengths of direct manipulation interfaces and programming languages may, in fact, be seen as complementary. Direct manipulation constructs are ideal for those tasks that place an emphasis on human judgment and/or hand-eye coordination—tasks such as choosing a pleasing color combination, recognizing a face, or steering a cursor around an obstacle. In contrast, programming constructs are suited to those tasks most economically expressed in formal terms: simulating a scientific model, drawing a random walk or fractal or tiling pattern, searching a large database for a pattern expressed by a complex conjunction of properties.

Just as we need, then, a taxonomy of end-user languages in terms of the types of constructs that they provide—such as the presence of conditionals or compound data objects, as mentioned above—so do we also require a taxonomy of strategies for integrating programming and direct manipulation constructs. For instance, we might wish to characterize direct manipulation operations in terms of the information that they might provide to a programming language: thus, selection (of an icon, a radio button, etc.) would designate a discrete data object, whereas other types of direct manipulation operations might be intended as illustrations of procedural ideas (as in programming-by-demonstration systems). Similarly, we might wish to distinguish various types of strategies by their "directionality": whether a programming language construct "tailors" an element of the interface (as in setting the operation of a button), or whether an interface action provides input to (or an illustration of) some language construct.

Again, these are rather loose suggestions for what could, over time, develop into an extremely fine-grained taxonomy of techniques; but such a taxonomy might have value well beyond providing some precision to discussions of end-user programming. As new interface technology—virtual reality interfaces, 3D viewing devices, gestural and speech input, etc.—become more commonplace, application designers will increasingly wish to integrate these techniques with end-user languages. We might, for instance, wish to adjust the parameters of a running program via spoken commands; or we may wish to write programs that later prompt us for gestural input; or we may wish to tailor the resolution of a 3D viewing device according to some conditional rule (e.g., depending on the direction of gaze). For such projects, having a taxonomy of language-interface integration techniques could serve both to structure our discourse and to stimulate our imaginations about the ways in which new interface hardware and new programming languages might eventually interact.

47.5.3 The Tower of Babel Problem in End-User Programming

We have already noted that many of the issues once thought to be unique to professional software engineering—such as the problem of proving programs correct—likewise arise in the realm of end-user programming. In the same spirit, the continually expanding variety of end-user languages presents many of the same opportunities and problems as the existence of numerous programming languages in the professional realm. On the positive side, distinct end-user languages have different strengths (e.g., for creating interactive interfaces, for searching databases, for graphing mathematical functions); and there is a benefit to the entire end-user programming community to maintaining a certain creative pluralism in the styles of languages available and new languages being developed. On the other hand, the fact that there are many end-user languages effectively means that few end users have a realistic hope of becoming expert in more than a couple of applications: each new and interesting application will likely present its own language, with its own syntax and vocabulary, and with its own learning curve. (Cook, 1990) makes similar observations.) Moreover, the efforts expended within one language community will have difficulty transferring to any other: if a Mathematica programmer, for instance, writes a set of procedures for viewing and manipulating three-dimensional solids, he will have to expend a nontrivial amount of effort to port that work into some other system.

The problem of "the benefits of standards versus the benefits of choice" is one of the ultimate dilemmas of human existence. In principle, an all-purpose (but highly extensible) extremely learnable language would make for an ideal standard: indeed, much of the attention in a recent workshop report (Myers *et al.*, 1992) was devoted to a thoughtful discussion of what such an idealized language might look like. Still, in the real world of end-user languages, there is little hope that any one language will achieve dominance over the field—if anything, the widely varying domains and interfaces with which end-user languages are coupled will enforce a multiplicity of approaches. A research direction well worth pursuing, then, would be to find means of alleviating the disadvantages of pluralism in the world of end-user programming.

One possibility along these lines would be to pursue the creation of "language modules"—in essence, fragments of end-user languages—which could be written in such a way as to be loadable within multiple target end-user languages. Thus, if (say) a Mathematica programmer creates a collection of procedures for working with Fourier transforms, she could—according to this idea—create a transferable language module (perhaps best conceived as a self-contained "package" for the domain of Fourier transforms) that could then be loaded into other end-user language systems. In principle, this idea is not too different from the popular idea of "modular applications", except employed for end-user languages; realizing such an idea would require extensive technical efforts (e.g., in devising means for allowing users to access, browse, and test public collections of such language modules). Still, this might be one workable approach to a (partial) resolution of the Tower of Babel problem in end-user languages by exploiting the ability of programming languages to accommodate embedded "sublanguages" (cf. Abelson and Sussman with Sussman, 1985).

47.5.4 End-User Programming: The Social Dimension

The traditional portrait of the end-user-as-programmer is a solitary worker, making occasional small extensions to her favorite application. While such a stereotype undoubtedly holds in some cases, it ignores an important social dimension to end-user programming. For instance, Gantt and Nardi (1992) and Mackay (1991) have studied the sorts of "user cultures" that evolve around programmable applications (the former presenting a fairly optimistic picture of cooperative user cultures, the latter a more cautionary picture of unused application functionality). Quite probably, the success or failure of many a programmable system will depend on the social structures—in classrooms, in corporations, in on-line newsgroups—that exist to support a growing culture of end-user programmers. This in turn implies the importance of research to study the formation and survivability of such cultures, and how language design itself can assist or obstruct the growth of such cultures. (This is related to the "means of communication" argument in favor of end-user programming: i.e., that languages can act as cultural artifacts binding together communities of end users.)

Going beyond questions of how particular applications are assimilated into particular communities, there are broader social questions surrounding end-user programming—questions that implicitly and often unconsciously color the debates surrounding the subject. It is often argued, for instance, that programming languages take too long to learn—that most end users are more concerned with completing some momentary (and presumably urgent) task than they are with investing time in learning a language, no matter how empowering that language may be. Such an argument makes strong (and arguably grim) assumptions about the inevitable nature and pace of human work. Suppose—just suppose—that people were permitted and even encouraged to take the time needed to develop a high level of expertise and craftsmanship in their tools; in such a culture, end-user programming might be a much less controversial notion, and the individual creativity permitted by programming might be pleasurably widespread. Similarly, if every elementary school student were to have access to programmable applications designed for children, then working with programming languages might seem a far less daunting (and indeed, far more pleasurable) prospect for those children when they eventually reached adulthood. In such a world, the populace would not be divided into gurus and "nonprogrammers", but rather would be composed of myriad "programmers" of different styles, areas of expertise, and levels of dedication. If we need an analogy to this utopian portrait, we might think of (say) musical or writing abilities: rather than divide people into sharply distinguished categories of musical "experts" and "nonmusicians", we instead are comfortable acknowledging the talents of the concert pianist, the rock star, the folk singer, the chamber music hobbyist, or the person singing in the shower. In any event—whether one is sympathetic to this sort of analogy or not, whether or not programming can ever be as democratically widespread and casual as the humming of a tune—researchers in the social dimension of end-user programming need occasionally to take a proactive stance, and to ask what sort of world we would like to promote rather than what sort of world we are prepared, reluctantly, to accept.

47.6 Acknowledgments

The ideas and outlook expressed in this chapter were heavily influenced by the work of Hal Abelson and Gerald Jay Sussman. Thanks also to Gerhard Fischer, Clayton Lewis, and the members of the Center for LifeLong Learning and Design at the University of Colorado for comments and conversation. The author's work is supported in part by a National Science Foundation Young Investigator Award IRI-9258684; by the Advanced Research Projects Agency (Award DOD-N66001-94-C-6038); and by NSF and ARPA under Cooperative Agreement No. CDA-9408607.

47.7 References

Abelson, H. (1991). Computation as a Framework for Engineering Education. In *Research Directions in Computer Science: An MIT Perspective*, A. Meyer, J. Guttag, R. Rivest, and P. Szolovits (eds.). Cambridge, MA: MIT Press, pp., 191-213.

Abelson, H. and Sussman, G. with Sussman, J. (1985). *Structure and Interpretation of Computer Programs.* Cambridge, MA: MIT Press.

Abelson, H. and diSessa, A. (1981). *Turtle Geometry.* Cambridge, MA: MIT Press.

Carver, S. A. (1988). Learning and Transfer of Debugging Skills: Applying Task Analysis to Curriculum Design and Assessment. In R. E. Mayer, ed. Teaching and Learning Computer Programming. Hillsdale, NJ: Lawrence Erlbaum, pp. 259-297.

Brown, P. and Gould, J. (1987). An Experimental Study of People Creating Spreadsheets. *ACM Transactions on Office Information Systems*, 5:3, pp. 258-272.

Clements, D. and Gullo, D. (1984). Effects of Computer Programming on Young Children's Cognition. *Journal of Educational Psychology*, 76:6, pp. 1051-1058.

Cobb Group, with M. Stone, A. Poor, and M. Crane. (1994). *Word 6 for Windows Companion.* Redmond, WA: Microsoft Press.

Cook, C.; Scholtz, J.; and Spohrer, J. (eds.) (1993). *Empirical Studies of Programmers: Fifth Workshop.* Norwood, NJ: Ablex.

Cook, R. (1990). Full Circle. *Byte*, 15:8, pp. 211-214.

Coombs, M. J. and Alty, J. L., eds. (1981). *Computing Skills and the User Interface.* London: Academic Press.

Cowan, D. D.; Ierusalimschy, R.; and Stepien, T. M. (1992). Programming Environments for End Users. In F. H. Vogt (ed.), *Personal Computers and Intelligent Systems, Information Processing 92, Volume III.* Amsterdam: North-Holland, pp. 54-60.

Cuoco, A. (1995). Computational Media to Support the Learning and Use of Functions. In A. diSessa, C. Hoyles, and R. Noss with L. Edwards (eds.), *The Design of Computational Media to Support Exploratory Learning.* Heidelberg: Springer-Verlag, pp. 79-107.

Cunniff, N. and Taylor, R. (1987). Graphical vs. Textual Representation: An Empirical Study of Novices' Program Comprehension. In Olson, G.; Sheppard, S.; and Soloway, E. (eds.) *Empirical Studies of Programmers: Second Workshop.* Norwood, NJ: Ablex, pp. 114-131.

Cypher, A. (1993). Introduction: Bringing Programming to End Users. In A. Cypher (ed.), *Watch What I Do.* Cambridge, MA: MIT Press, pp. 1-11.

Cypher, A. (1993). Eager: Programming Repetitive Tasks by Demonstration. In A. Cypher (ed.), *Watch What I Do.* Cambridge, MA: MIT Press, pp. 204-217.

DiGiano, C. and Eisenberg, M. (1995). Self-Disclosing Design Tools: A Gentle Introduction to End-User Programming. *Proceedings of DIS'95: Symposium on Designing Interactive Systems.* Ann Arbor, MI, pp. 123-130.

diSessa, A. and Abelson, H. (1986). Boxer: A Reconstructible Computational Medium. *Commun-ications of the ACM*, 29:9, pp. 859-868.

Du Boulay, B. (1986). Some Difficulties of Learning to Program. Reprinted in E. Soloway and J. Spohrer, eds. *Studying the Novice Programmer.* Hillsdale, NJ: Lawrence Erlbaum, 1989, pp. 283-299.

Eisenberg, M. and Fischer, G. (1994). Programmable Design Environments. *Proceedings of CHI'94*, Boston, pp. 431-437.

Eisenberg, M. (1995). Creating Software Applications for Children: Some Thoughts About Design. In A. diSessa, C. Hoyles, and R. Noss with L. Edwards (eds.), *The Design of Computational Media to Support Exploratory Learning.* Heidelberg: Springer-Verlag, pp. 175-196.

Eisenberg, M. (1991). Programmable Applications: Interpreter Meets Interface. MIT AI Lab Memo 1325.

Feurzeig, W. (1993). Explaining Function Machines. *Intelligent Tutoring Media*, 4:3/4, pp. 97-108.

Gantt, M. and Nardi, B. (1992). "Gardeners and Gurus: Patterns of Cooperation among CAD Users," *Proceedings of CHI'92*, pp. 107-117.

Goodman, D. (1990). *The Complete HyperCard 2.0 Handbook*. Toronto: Bantam Books.

Gray, A. (1993). *Modern Differential Geometry of Curves and Surfaces*. Boca Raton, FL: CRC Press.

Gray, T. and Glynn, J. (1991). *Exploring Mathematics with Mathematica*. Redwood City, CA: Addison-Wesley.

Green, T. R. G. (1990). The Nature of Programming. In J.-M. Hoc, T. R. G. Green, R. Samurçay, and D. J. Gilmore (eds.), *Psychology of Programming*. London: Academic Press, pp. 21-44.

Green, T. R. G.; Petre, M.; and Bellamy, R.K.E. (1991). Comprehensibility of Visual and Textual Programs: A Test of Superlativism Against the 'Match-Mismatch' Conjecture. In *Empirical Studies of Programmers: Fourth Workshop*, J. Koenemann-Belliveau, T. Moher, and S. Robertson, eds. Norwood, NJ: Ablex, pp. 121-146.

Gugerty, L. and Olson, G. (1986). Comprehension Differences in Debugging by Skilled and Novice Programmers. In E. Soloway and S. Iyengar, *Empirical Studies of Programmers*. Norwood, NJ: Ablex, pp. 13-27.

Guzdial, M.; Reppy, J.; and Smith, R. (1992). Report of the "User/Programmer Distinction" Working Group. In B. Myers (ed.), *Languages for Developing User Interfaces*. Boston: Jones and Bartlett, pp. 367-383.

Hoc, J.-M.; Green, T. R. G.; Samurçay, R.; and Gilmore, D. J., eds. (1990). *Psychology of Programming*. London: Academic Press.

Hutchins, E.L., Hollan, J. D. and Norman, D. A. (1986). Direct Manipulation Interfaces. In D.A. Norman, S.W. Draper (eds.), *User Centered System Design, New Perspectives on Human-Computer Interaction*, Lawrence Erlbaum Associates, Hillsdale, NJ, pp. 87-124.

Jolly, K. (1994). *Excel for the Macintosh*. Wilsonville, OR: Franklin, Beedle, and Associates Inc.

Kahn, K. (1995). ToonTalk—An Animated Programming Environment for Children. *Proceedings of National Educatonal Computing Conference*, Baltimore, June, pp. 243-249.

Kemeny, J. (1983). The Case for Computer Literacy. *Daedalus*, 112:2, pp. 211-230.

Koenemann-Belliveau, J.; Moher, T.; and Robertson, S. (eds.) (1991). *Empirical Studies of Programmers: Fourth Workshop*. Norwood, NJ: Ablex.

Kurland, M. and Pea, R. (1985). Children's Mental Models of Recursive Logo Programs. Reprinted in E. Soloway and J. Spohrer, eds. *Studying the Novice Programmer*. Hillsdale, NJ: Lawrence Erlbaum, 1989, pp. 315-323.

Kynigos, C. (1995). Programming as a Means of Expressing and Exploring Ideas: Three Case Studies Situated in a Directive Educational System. In A. diSessa, C. Hoyles, and R. Noss with L. Edwards (eds.), *The Design of Computational Media to Support Exploratory Learning*. Heidelberg: Springer-Verlag, pp. 399-419.

Lee, A. and Pennington, N. (1993). Learning Computer Programming: A Route to General Reasoning Skills? In *Empirical Studies of Programmers: Fifth Workshop*. C. Cook, J. Scholtz, and J. Spohrer, eds. Norwood, NJ: Ablex, pp. 113-136.

Lehrer, R.; Guckenberg, T.; and Sancilio, L. (1988). Influences of LOGO on Children's Intellectual Development. In R. Mayer (ed.), *Teaching and Learning Computer Programming*. Hillsdale, NJ: Lawrence Erlbaum, pp. 75-110.

Lieberman, H. (1993). Mondrian: A Teachable Graphical Editor. In A. Cypher (ed.), *Watch What I Do*. Cambridge, MA: MIT Press, pp. 340-358.

Linn, M. and Dalbey, J. (1985). Cognitive Consequences of Programming Instruction. Reprinted in E. Soloway and J. Spohrer (eds.), *Studying the Novice Programmer*. Hillsdale, NJ: Lawrence Erlbaum, pp. 57-81, 1989.

Mackay, W. E. (1991). "Triggers and Barriers to Customizing Software," *CHI'91 Conference Proceedings*, pp. 153-160.

Maulsby, D. and Witten, I. (1993). Metamouse: An Instructible Agent for Programming by Demonstration. In A. Cypher (ed.), *Watch What I Do*. Cambridge, MA: MIT Press, pp. 154-181.

Mayer, R. E., ed. (1988). *Teaching and Learning Computer Programming*. Hillsdale, NJ: Lawrence Erlbaum.

Mayer, R. E.; Dyck, J. L.; and Vilberg, W. (1986). Learning to Program and Learning to Think: What's the Connection? Reprinted in E. Soloway and J. Spohrer (eds.), *Studying the Novice Programmer*. Hillsdale, NJ: Lawrence Erlbaum, pp. 113-124, 1989.

McNurlin, B. (1981a). 'Programming' by End Users. *EDP Analyzer*, 19:5, pp. 1-12.

McNurlin, B. (1981b). Supporting End User Programming. *EDP Analyzer*, 19:6, pp. 1-12.

Mendelsohn, P.; Green, T. R. G.; and Brna (1990). P. Programming Languages in Education: The Search for an Easy Start. In J.-M. Hoc, T. R. G. Green, R. Samurçay, and D. J. Gilmore (eds.), *Psychology of Programming*. London: Academic Press, pp. 175-200.

Myers, B. (1993a). Peridot: Creating User Interfaces by Demonstration. In A. Cypher (ed.), *Watch What I Do*. Cambridge, MA: MIT Press, pp. 124-153.

Myers, B. (1993b). Garnet: Uses of Demonstrational Techniques. In A. Cypher (ed.), *Watch What I Do*. Cambridge, MA: MIT Press, pp. 218-236.

Myers, B.; Smith, D. C.; and Horn, B. (1992). Report of the "End-User Programming" Working Group. In B. Myers (ed.), *Languages for Developing User Interfaces*. Boston: Jones and Bartlett, pp. 343-366.

Nardi, B. (1993). *A Small Matter of Programming*. Cambridge, MA: MIT Press.

Norman, D. (1993). *Things that Make Us Smart*. Reading, MA: Addison-Wesley.

Olson, G.; Catrambone, R.; and Soloway, E. (1987). Programming and Algebra Word Problems: A Failure to Transfer. In Olson, G.; Sheppard, S.; and Soloway, E. (eds.) *Empirical Studies of Programmers: Second Workshop*. Norwood, NJ: Ablex, pp. 1-13.

Olson, G.; Sheppard, S.; and Soloway, E. (eds.) (1987). *Empirical Studies of Programmers: Second Workshop*. Norwood, NJ: Ablex.

Ong, W. (1982). *Orality and Literacy*. London: Routledge.

Papert, S. (1980). *Mindstorms*. New York: Basic Books.

Pea, R. and Kurland, D. (1987). On the Cognitive Effects of Learning Computer Programming. In *Mirrors of Minds*, R. Pea and K. Sheingold (eds.). Norwood, NJ: Ablex, pp. 147-177.

Pea, R., Kurland, D. and Hawkins, J. (1987). Logo and the Development of Thinking Skills. In *Mirrors of Minds*, R. Pea and K. Sheingold (eds.). Norwood, NJ: Ablex, pp. 178-197.

Petre, M. (1995). Why Looking Isn't Always Seeing: Readership Skills and Graphical Programming. *Communications of the ACM*, 38:6, pp. 33-44.

Repenning, A. and T. Sumner (1995).. "Agentsheets: A Medium for Creating Domain-Oriented Visual Languages," *IEEE Computer*, 28:3, pp. 17-25.

Resnick, M. (1994). *Turtles, Termites, and Traffic Jams*. Cambridge, MA: MIT Press.

Rist, R. (1986). Plans in Programming: Definition, Demonstration, and Development. In E. Soloway and S. Iyengar, *Empirical Studies of Programmers*. Norwood, NJ: Ablex, pp. 28-48.

Rogalski, J. and Samurçay, R. (1990). Acquisition of Programming Knowledge and Skills. In J.-M. Hoc, T. R. G. Green, R. Samurçay, and D. J. Gilmore (eds.), *Psychology of Programming*. London: Academic Press, pp. 157-174.

Ryan, B. (1990). Scripts Unbounded. *Byte*, 15:8, pp. 235-240.

Salomon, G. and Perkins, D. (1987). Transfer of Cognitive Skills from Programming: When and How? *Journal of Educational Computing Research*, 3:2, pp. 149-169.

Shneiderman, B. (1983). Direct Manipulation: A Step Beyond Programming Languages. *IEEE Computer*, 16:8, pp. 57-69.

Sloman, A. (1971). "Interactions Between Philosophy and Artificial Intelligence: The Role of Intuition and Non-Logical Reasoning in Intelligence." *Proceeding of the Second International Joint Conference on Artificial Intelligence*. IJCAI, London, August 1971, pp. 270-278.

Smith, D. C.; Cypher, A.; and Spohrer, J. (1994). KidSim: Programming Agents Without a Programming Language. *Communications of the ACM*, 37:7, pp. 55-67.

Smith, D. C. (1993). Pygmalion: An Executable Electronic Blackboard. In A. Cypher (ed.), *Watch What I Do*. Cambridge, MA: MIT Press, pp. 19-47.

Snyder, T. and Palmer, J. (1986). *In Search of the Most Amazing Thing*. Reading, MA: Addison-Wesley.

Solomon, C. (1986). *Computer Environments for Children*. Cambridge, MA: MIT Press.

Spohrer, J. and Soloway, E. (1986). Novice Mistakes: Are the Folk Wisdoms Correct? Reprinted in E. Soloway and J. Spohrer (eds.), *Studying the Novice Programmer*. Hillsdale, NJ: Lawrence Erlbaum, pp. 401-416, 1989.

Spohrer, J.; Soloway, E.; and Pope, E. (1985). A Goal/Plan Analysis of Buggy Pascal Programs. Reprinted in E. Soloway and J. Spohrer (eds.), *Studying the Novice Programmer*. Hillsdale, NJ: Lawrence Erlbaum, pp. 355-399, 1989.

Stallman, R. (1986). *GNU Emacs Manual* (Fifth Edition, Version 18). Cambridge, MA: Free Software Foundation.

Tazelaar, J. M. (1990). End-User Programming. *Byte*, 15:8, p. 208.

Wolfram, S. (1988). *Mathematica: A System for Doing Mathematics by Computer*. Redwood City, CA: Addison-Wesley.

Zink, R. (1984). The tilt to end-user programming. *ComputerWorld*, July 23, pp. 5-14.

Software

[S1] *AutoCAD*. AutoDesk, Inc. Sausalito, CA.

[S2] *Director*. MacroMedia, Inc. San Francisco, CA.

[S3] *HyperCard*. Apple Computer, Inc. Cupertino, CA.

[S4] *Maple*. Waterloo Maple Software, Waterloo, Ontario, Canada.

[S5] *Mathematica*. Wolfram Research, Inc. Champaign, IL.

[S6] *SimCity*. Maxis, Inc. Orinda, CA.

[S7] *Word*. Microsoft, Inc. Redmond, WA.

Handbook of Human-Computer Interaction
Second, completely revised edition
M. Helander, T.K. Landauer, P. Prabhu (eds.)

Chapter 48

Interactive Software Architecture

Dan R. Olsen Jr.
Computer Science Department
Brigham Young University
Provo, Utah, USA

48.1 Introduction

The issues that arise in creating interactive software are quite diverse. In an article such as this it is impossible to provide details. This overview will cover the central issues that must be addressed. An overall architecture of an interactive program will be presented which lays out the basic parts. This will be followed by a discussion of each of the architectural components.

48.2 Overall Software Architecture

In its simplest form an interactive program can be viewed as a process that accepts a stream of inputs from interactive devices, interprets those inputs and then draws images on the workstation display screen. In practice, however, this is complicated by the fact that more than one application may be active at a time. On modern workstations the interactive devices and display screen space must be multiplexed among multiple applications. This function is performed by the windowing system.

A windowing system allows applications to allocate rectangular (and on some systems arbitrary shaped) windows. Each application can treat a window like an independent display screen of its own. When the user manipulates the interactive devices, input events are generated. It is up to the windowing system to determine which of the windows should receive each event. Such an input event is forwarded to the application which owns the selected window and the application will then process it. From the application's point of view, each window has it own display space and input event stream. The existence of other windows and programs can, for the most part, be ignored.

Within an interactive application, each window is managed by three primary components: the model, the view and the controller. This model-view-controller paradigm (MVC) was developed by the SmallTalk group at Xerox as part of their development of object-oriented interactive environments. In many systems one or more of these components are combined but it is still instructive to consider the issues of each individually.

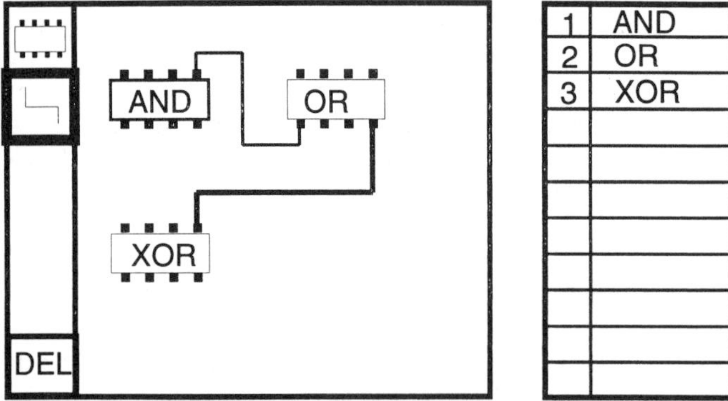

Figure 1. A schematic layout application.

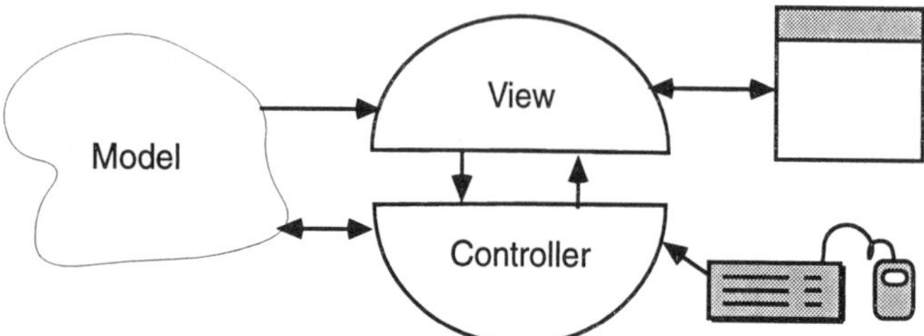

Figure 2. Model-view-controller.

To better understand these issues, consider the simple schematic layout application shown in Figure 1. This application consists of two windows, one for laying out schematics and the other which displays a parts list. The relationships among the model, view and controller components are shown in Figure 2.

The Model component stores and manages the information that is functionally important to the application. In our schematic example, the model would manage the data structures which represent the schematic. The Controller component receives the input event stream from the interactive devices through the windowing system. It must interpret this stream to determine the user's intentions. The propose of the View is to visually present the data in the Model on the screen. In our example the View is responsible for drawing the circuit layout and parts list on the screen.

As the schematic layout example shows, a given model may have multiple views and controllers. In many systems the View and Controller functions are implemented together as a single window handler. In our example application the layout window would have one View-Controller pair while the parts list window would have another. Both windows would share the same model.

The three components must communicate with each other to make the entire process work. The Controller must invoke commands in the Model to get information updated or actions performed. The Controller may also request the View to modify the display in some way such as scrolling a window or closing a window. Such requests do not involve changing the underlying data and therefore they are not sent through the Model. The Controller also needs information from the View to interpret many inputs. For example a mouse button event which occurs inside of the layout window may signal that the user is selecting a chip or a wire. Only the View has the geometric information as to where the chips and wires are located on the display. The View must ask for this information. The Model must communicate with the View each time data is modified so that the View can appropriately update the display. The View must request data from the Model if it is to correctly draw the parts list or the schematic layout.

In most applications, much of the interactive functionality is drawn from a tool kit of interactive parts rather than being reimplemented. This provides for

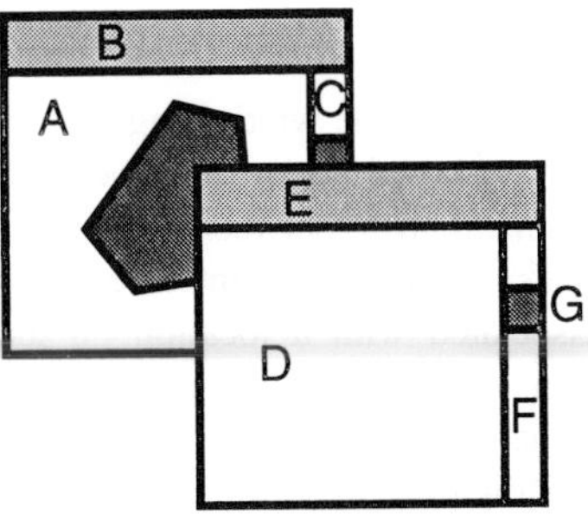

Figure 3. A collection of windows.

more uniform interfaces and greatly simplifies the creation of new programs. Such preprogrammed parts are called controls or widgets. They implement push buttons, scroll bars, menus, text type in boxes and a variety of other interactive parts that are frequently used. Each of these widgets can be viewed as a small MVC system of its own. Take for example a scroll bar. It has a small rectangular view area. Its model consists of three integers: Max, Min and CurrentValue. If the application changes any of the three model values, the scroll-bar's view will update the display. If the user drags the scroll-bar thumb, the scroll-bar's controller will modify CurrentValue in the Model which will cause the View to update the display.

In a widget, the model is usually quite simple. The most complex widget models would be lists of items for a menu or other selection technique. Each widget is programmed to generate a set of higher level events in response to their models being changed. For example, whenever a scroll-bar is moved causing CurrentValue to be changed, a higher level event is generated indicating the change. This higher level event can then be directed to the Controller components of higher level processes to perform such functions as scrolling a window to match the new scroll-bar position. So, for example, the controller for the schematic layout window may respond to not only interactive input events but also events generated by the scroll bar widget which is to control the scrolling of the window.

In almost all modern interactive systems, the control flow of the application is as follows. There is a main loop which continuously retrieves input events from the windowing system's event queue. Based on the window to which each event is directed, a controller is selected and is notified of the event. The controller then processes the event and at appropriate times invokes its model, its view or generates some higher level event which is placed in the event queue and communicated to some other part of the system. Because this main event loop is so standardized, in many systems it is completely hidden from the programmer. This is very disconcerting to new programmers of interactive systems because they cannot find the main program from which to begin. Programmers of interactive applications do not control the flow of execution in the application, the user does. They program MVC units which respond to the events that they receive from whatever source may produce them.

48.3 Windowing Systems

The purpose of a windowing system is to preserve for the application, the illusion that each window is a complete display of its own with its own input event stream. In order to do this it must manage the allocation of screen space among multiple windows and also manage the dispatching of input events to the appropriate windows. In systems where overlapping windows are allowed, the windowing system must also resolve the problems where multiple windows believe that they own the same screen space. In the case of some windowing systems such as X and NeWS, the user is not working on the same computer as the application is running. This means that the windowing system is also responsible for the network traffic which allows the application to be unaware of where on the internet the user is actually located.

There are four primary problems which the windowing system must solve.

- Managing the window structure
- Allocation of screen space
- Dispatching of events to windows
- Managing the drawing activity of applications

The collection of windows in Figure 3 will illustrate these problems.

48.3.1 Managing the Window Structure

There are two primary ways in which a windowing system will manage its windows: in a flat structure, or as a tree. The Apple Macintosh uses a flat structure where only the main windows are managed by the windowing system. In Figure 3, there would only be two windows with all of the other areas being managed within those windows by widgets or by the application. In most windowing systems, however, the space is managed as a hierarchy of windows, as shown in Figure 4.

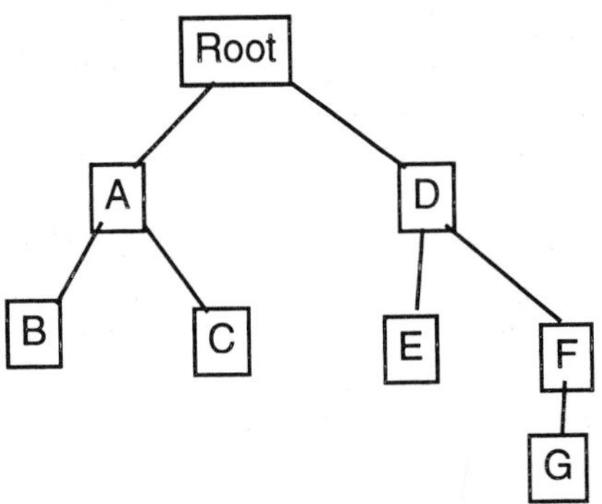

Figure 4. Window hierarchy.

In the window hierarchy each sub-piece can have its own window and manage its own events. Windowing systems which support hierarchies differ on how the geometry of a sub-window relates to its parent. In many systems a sub-window moves with its parent and must reside entirely within the space allocated to the parent. In other systems the sub-window can reside outside of its parent's space but still moves with the parent. This allows for palettes and other service windows to be clustered around a main window. In other systems the position of a sub-window can be completely free from that of its parent.

48.3.2 Allocating Screen Space

The allocation of screen space to a window is the prerogative of the windowing system rather than the individual applications. Most windowing systems allow the application to request a particular location and size for a window, but the windowing system is not obligated to honor such a request. The most common organization for windows is the overlapping window model shown in Figure 3 where the user is given control over the placement and sizing of windows. Putting the user in control requires that there be interactive techniques which interpret user events so as to perform the window sizing and placement. This function is performed by the *window manager.* These windowing functions are typically performed in a frame around the application window. This window frame has its own MVC structure which is implemented by the window manager. When a window is moved or resized by the window manager the application must be notified. To do this the window manager generates higher level events which are sent to the window controller provided by the application.

48.3.3 Dispatching of Events

When an input event is received, the windowing system must decide which window should receive the event. In dispatching events we distinguish between geometric and non-geometric events. Geometric events are those which are naturally associated with a location on the screen. Mouse movement events, for example, have a clear screen location. The buttons on the mouse don't have a geometry of their own but they are naturally associated with the position of the mouse. Keyboard events, for example, are non-geometric events. There is no natural position associated with a keyboard event.

When a geometric event is received, the windowing system determines the front-most window that geometrically contains the event's position. This technique is almost universally used by commercial windowing systems. In a hierarchic windowing system, however, there is still some ambiguity. In Figure 3, a mouse event inside of window G is also inside of windows F and D. The question then arises as to which of these should receive the event. In systems such as X, the lowest window in the tree receives the event (G in this case). If that window rejects the event, then it is promoted up the tree for processing. This is *bottom-up* event handling. In other systems such as MS-Windows the event is passed to the highest window (D in this case) which can then forward the event on. In such *top-down* event handling, higher level windows can watch and/or filter the events sent to lower level windows. Using standard components the normal strategy is to forward events on to the lowest level window, which produces an effect like that of the bottom-up strategy. The top-down strategy, however, provides much more flexibility.

48.3.4 Managing Drawing Activity

In a windowing system, the interactive application wants to treat a window as if the application owned it completely. In Figure 3, however, window A is partially obscured by another window. The application for window A cannot be allowed to draw over the top of window D. Unfortunately the application controlling window A knows nothing about window D. The windowing system handles this by managing a *visible region* for each window which takes into account all of the other windows which may overlap. Any drawing done into window A will be clipped to this region so as to prevent damage to window D.

A problem also arises when window D moves or window A is brought to the front. In these cases, part of window A, which was previously obscured, now becomes visible. Again an application knows nothing about the other windows which might cause this to occur. The windowing system detects these conditions and creates higher level events which notify an application about which window display regions need to be updated. The mechanisms to accomplish this will be discussed in the section on views.

48.4 View Presentation

The purpose of the view component is to handle all geometry and drawing for the MVC unit that it is part of. There are actually three aspects to this activity:

- drawing the model on the screen,
- determining what portion of the screen needs to be changed as a result of some change to the model data,
- determining which, if any, model objects are selected by a given input position.

48.4.1 Drawing

An important characteristic of modern 2D windowed graphics is that all drawing for an object is collected together in a single routine or module. In most object-oriented systems each view object has a Redraw method that has the responsibility for drawing the object on the screen. This Redraw method is generally invoked in response to a Redraw event generated by the windowing system and being directed to the particular window for which the view object is defined. This redraw event can be generated in response to window movement or changes or may be triggered by the application itself as will be shown later.

The process of drawing an object is relatively straightforward. Most graphics texts contain the general knowledge required and most windowing systems provide manuals for the particular calls which will cause lines, circles, text and other graphical objects to be drawn on the screen. When the view's Redraw method is called it is generally not the case that the entire view needs to be redrawn, but rather only selected portions such as the part of a window that has been uncovered or a single circuit part that needs to be redrawn because it has moved. To accommodate this, windowing systems maintain an *update region* which is the region of the screen which needs repair.

This update region is both passed to the method and is used as the clipping region. Clipping is the process of discarding all drawing requests or portions of those requests which lie outside of a specified region. Using the clipping region a simple Redraw method can draw the entire view and let the windowing system's graphics package trim away any unneeded drawing fragments. A more efficient approach can test the update region against the model/view geometry to determine which fragments need attention. For example the bounding box of each wire and chip in our circuit example can be tested against the update region. Any parts which do not intersect the update region can be ignored. In some cases this can greatly speed the drawing process.

48.4.2 Updating a Drawing

Information in a model can changed for a variety of reasons and in a variety of ways. When such a change occurs the model will then send events or object-oriented messages to all views that are registered with the model. If in our example, a chip is deleted, both the chip list view and the chip layout view must be notified. In response to this notification, each view must update it portion of the display.

Figure 5 shows a simple drawing where a white polygon is to be moved. The model (consisting of a list of drawing objects) is changed and then notifies the view that the white polygon has new coordinates. What must be done is to erase the polygon in its old position and draw it in its new position. Figure 6 shows what might happen if a simple-minded erase mechanism is used. Note that the other drawing elements are incorrectly damaged by the erasure of the white polygon in its old position.

This simple-minded erase / draw strategy cannot account for all of the possible overlapping of objects. This is particularly problematic in the presence of other windows which are completely unknown to this view.

All 2D windowing systems use a damage/redraw architecture for updating the screen. All windowing systems provide methods to be called which inform the windowing system that certain regions of a window are no longer valid. The windowing system collects all of these damaged regions and generates the appropriate redraw events which will get the damaged regions restored. This is the same mechanism used to handle areas of a window being uncovered or new windows being opened.

When moving the white polygon, the view would "damage" the rectangles shown in Figure 7 which cover both the old and new locations of the white polygon. The windowing system would generate redraw events which would cover these areas. Since the model has been changed to represent the new location, the

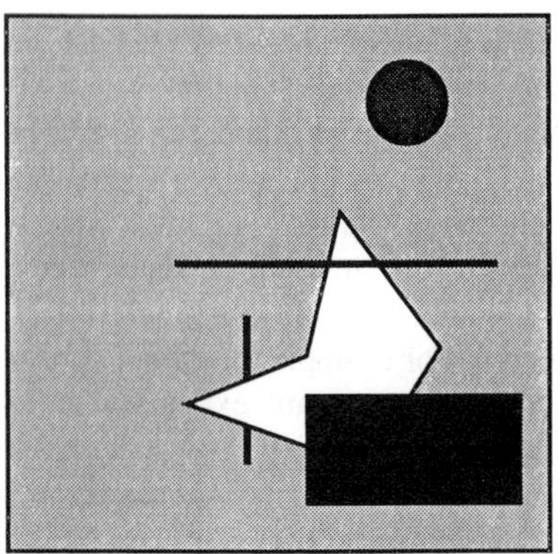

Figure 5. Before dragging the white polygon.

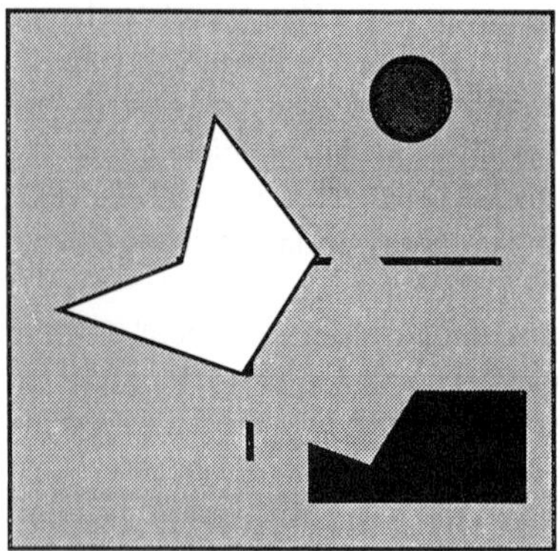

Figure 6. Simple erase of the white polygon.

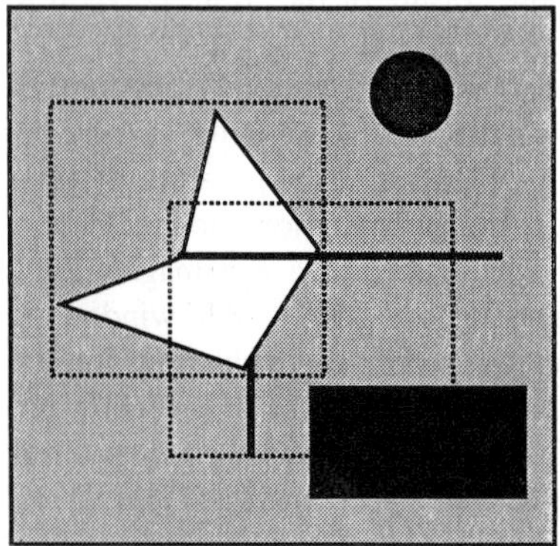

Figure 7. Damage regions.

view will draw background or other objects in the old area and will draw the white polygon in its new area. The result is a correct drawing of the new state of the model. By using this damage / redraw architecture all of the changing of raster displays can correctly be handled.

There are some cases where continuous movement is required. In many such cases the damage / redraw mechanism is fast enough to update the screen in less than 1/5 of a second, which is necessary for good interaction. In other cases, it is not sufficient and specially optimized techniques are required.

48.4.3 Selection Geometry

The last task which must be performed by the view is processing of selection requests from the controller. Only the view has the actual geometry information to determine which items, if any, are selected by a given mouse input point. This is essentially a problem of determining whether a point is close to or inside of a particular geometric shape. For these problems the reader is referred to any good analytic geometry text.

48.4.4 Layout Design Tools

The view determines the visual presentation of the user interface. In cases such as the chip layout view, the presentation is generally hand-coded by the programmer. In cases such as the buttons on the left of the chip layout or menus, palettes, and scroll bars, a visual layout tool can be used. Many of commercial tool kits provide a layout tool which has a palette of widgets. The designer selects tools from this palette and lays them out on a 2D surface. This process generally assigns a rectangular area to each widget which is stored. Based on this rectangular area, each widget, behaving as its own MVC unit, can manage itself.

A problem arises, however, when a window is resizable. When a window is resized, its label wants to stay in the center. The buttons want to stay attached to the sides,. The chip layout area for example wants to grow to fill the entire window. This behavior cannot be handled by fixed rectangles assigned to each widget.

48.4.5 Constraint Systems

A more general mechanism for handling visual layouts is the use of constraint systems. A constraint is an equation which relates two or more values. A simple constraint might be of the form ScrollBar.Bottom = Window.Bottom. A constraint to center an object in a proportional position might be Button.Left = (Window.Left + Window.Right)/2.

Constraint systems are quite general and can express a variety of geometric relationships. Whenever the window size changes, the constraints are reevaluated to determine new positions for all of the objects.

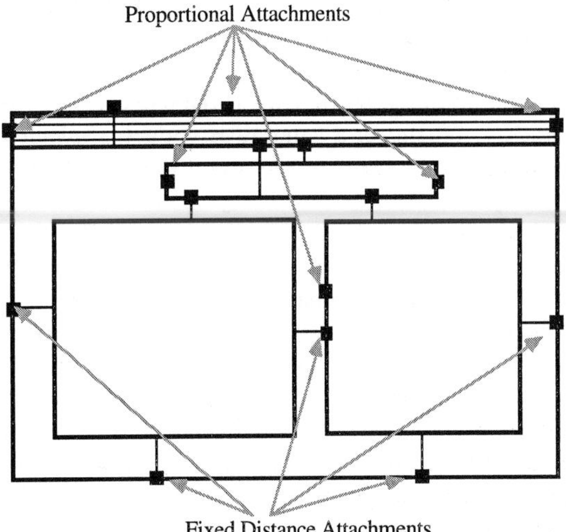

Figure 8. Constraint creation by attachments.

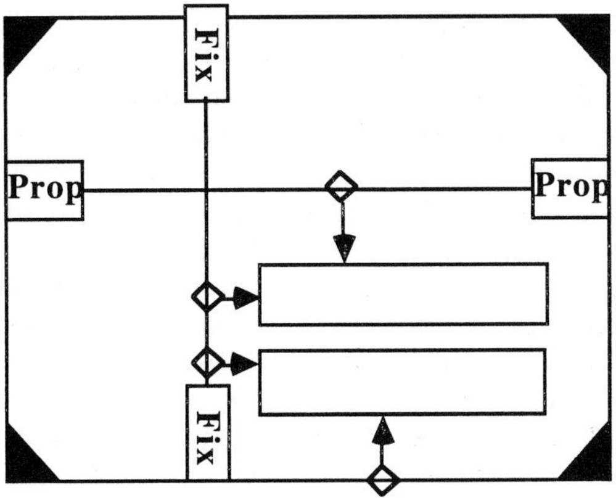

Figure 9. Apogee alignment constraints.

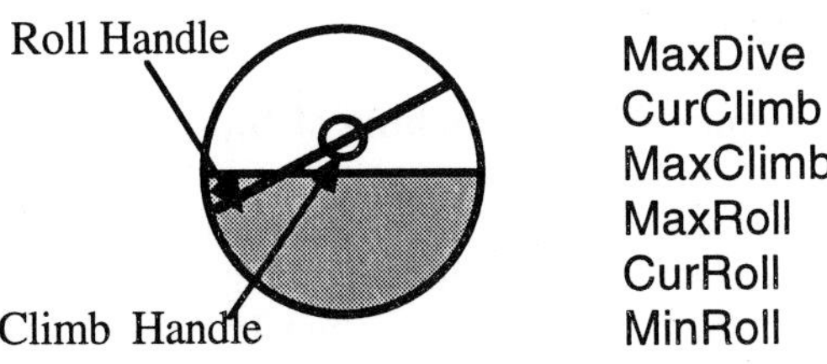

Figure 10. Artificial horizon widget.

A central problem is to find efficient algorithms for solving such systems of constraints. This is usually achieved by restricting the set of constraints in some way. For a complete bibliography of constraint systems and their solution algorithms see (Vander Zanden and Myers et al., 1994).

A major problem with constraints is that interface designers generally lack the mathematical sophistication to use them correctly. What is required is a graphical user interface to the constraint system which hides the mathematics. Cardelli (Cardelli, 1988) devised the graphical attachments model shown in Figure 8. A more complex and flexible approach is provided by Hudson's Apogee system (Hudson, 1989) which uses reference lines to create complex alignments, as shown in Figure 9.

These systems of constraints are essentially top-down in that the window size is determined and then from that each subcomponent has its location determined and so forth down the window tree. An alternative model is the "boxes and glue" model used in InterViews (Linton and Vlissides et al., 1989). In this model every object reports to its parent how big it wants to be and how much it can squish and stretch. Based on this bottom-up information the parent window can more intelligently partition the available space among the sub-components and then propagate the position constraint information downward.

48.4.6 Model / View Mapping Tools

Tools have also been developed which aid in developing the mapping between the visual display and the model information. This is an essential component of any view implementation. The Browse / Edit model for user interfaces (Olsen, 1988) views the view/controller unit as an editor of some semantic object (the model). The interface design problem is then to tie the semantics of the editor to some model. This effectively hides most of this complexity in predefined components. This has been incorporated into a workspace model (Olsen and McNeill et al., 1992) which forms an editing framework for an entire application.

One of the most challenging problems is relating values from the model to geometric positions of visual objects. Constraint systems are the appropriate mechanism, but the specification of the constraints is a problem. Figure 10 shows a complex model for aircraft attitude and its geometric view.

The GITS system (Olsen and Allan, 1990) provides an editor which allows uses to graphically specify constraints between the view geometry and the model. The Peridot (Myers and Buxton, 1986) system develops such constraints by demonstration. The system guesses at appropriate constraints and then requests user confirmation. The Lemming (Olsen and Ahlstrom et al., 1995) system infers arbitrary mappings between geometry and the model using multiple examples.

48.5 Controller Issues

The role of the controller is to process the input events and handle them in some meaningful way. The key problem is that there are many more actions that can be taken than there are events generated by input devices. A primary role of the controller is to multiplex the meaning of the input events in some way. This task is performed in conjunction with the windowing system. There are two primary methods for assigning meaning to input events: temporal and spatial multiplexing. Spatial multiplexing assigns meaning to an input event depending on where on the screen the event occurs. For example, a mouse click means something different over the delete button than it does over a wire in the chip layout window. This is problematic if the event has no associated position, such as a keyboard event. Temporal multiplexing assigns meaning based on the sequence of inputs. For example a mouse move event may mean something different if it occurs after a mouse down event and before the next mouse up event than it does if the mouse button has not been depressed at all.

48.5.1 Spatial Dispatching of Input Events

Spatial multiplexing is by far the most obvious to the user because of the correspondence to visual objects on the screen. This is also true because most event sequences are highly stylized with a very few standard sequences being used in a variety of situations. Spatial multiplexing is the primary mechanism used by the windowing system. There are, however, two fundamental problems in spatial multiplexing of input events. They are: non-positional events and interaction outside of a window.

Events such as the keyboard or function buttons have no position and thus cannot be spatially multiplexed. All windowing systems have a convention for how such events should be handled. This issue has two great religions: mouse position and key focus. In the mouse position approach, non positional events are dispatched according to the current position of the mouse. This is easy to implement but has some problems. The first is the fact that if the mouse gets moved accidentally the keyboard events may get redirected to a different window. The second problem is forms. When people are filling in forms they want some "tab" function on the keyboard which will move the keyboard events to the next blank space in the form. This prevents device swapping by the user. Such "tabing" operations are completely independent of the mouse position.

A solution to these problems is the use of a key focus strategy. Whenever a window or widget is selected by the mouse or by "tab" processing it requests the *key focus*. Keyboard events are always sent to the window/widget that has the key focus. A controller then requests the key focus whenever its input event sequence indicates that keyboard events are desired.

The key focus model is complicated by the fact that the widget which is losing the focus must be informed. There is also the problem of "Which widget is the next widget in the "tab" sequence?" This is all handled by the windowing system sending events to the widgets involved and processing their responses. Any new controller development must deal with these additional events. In many tool kits these issues are hidden inside the implementation of text typing widgets and the programmer can ignore them.

It is frequently the case that a widget or window may want to deal with interaction occurring outside of its own bounds. Take for example the Macintosh Finder which transfers files between directories by dragging them from one window to another. While the file is being dragged it will at some point not be in any window associated with the Finder, but the Finder must still be able to process the input events. A similar problem occurs in input dialogs to resize or move a window. A related problem occurs in some widgets such as scroll bars where one is dragging the thumb and the mouse leaves the area of the scroll bar. It is most helpful if the scroll bar continues to receive mouse events as long as the user has not released the mouse button. All of these problems are handled using the concept of a *mouse focus*. A window/widget can capture and release the mouse focus by requesting it from the windowing system. The mouse focus overrides the normal spatial multiplexing of inputs and directs them all to the window/widget that has the focus.

48.5.2 Sequential Dispatching of Input Events

Even with spatial multiplexing of input events there is still not enough power to extract meaning from the input event stream. Consider the simple example of dragging out a rectangle. This involves a mouse-down, zero or more mouse-moves and a mouse-up. There are specific actions involved with each of these events. A mouse-move that occurs outside of the mouse-down, mouse-up pair has very different meaning. This sequence is further complicated by the location where the mouse-down occurs. In our chip layout window, if the mouse-down occurs over a chip, then the mouse-moves involve dragging the chip and the mouse-up at the end indicates a message to the model which changes the chip location. If the mouse-down event occurred in empty space then the mouse-moves involve dragging out a selection rectangle and the mouse-up indicates that the view should be interrogated to determine which objects are selected. Each of these sequences is further complicated by the mouse moving outside of the window before mouse-up occurs. If the mouse moves back in again, while the button is still down, what should happen?

In our example dragging scenarios, the meaning associated with the input events was determined by the sequence of events and semantic conditions (i.e. selection of a chip) that occurred in the immediate past. As indicated by the mouse leaving and reentering the window, these sequences can become quite complex. Most windowing systems and user interface tool kits have buried most of these issues in the widgets and left the remaining input sequencing issues to be programmed by hand.

There have been several models proposed for dealing with input sequencing. The earliest models used finite state machines (Newman, 1968; Jacob, 1982) or grammars (Hanau and Lenorovitz, 1980; Olsen and Dempsey, 1983) to represent the event ordering. Such models were derived from language processing and are suited for highly ordered streams of inputs. In interaction, the user inputs are generally not highly ordered. Take for example the problem of entering N inputs, each exactly once, in any order. State machine approaches require an exponential number of states and transitions to model the N-input problem.

In order to model the sequential aspects of the input stream and provide the programmers with some aid in developing such systems. Specifications based on production systems (Hill, 1986; Olsen, 1990) have been proposed. These approaches independently model such issues as {mouse-up, mouse-down}, currently selected object and the set of actions that can be performed. A similar attack on the same problems is based on Petri nets (Bastide and Palanque, 1990) and temporal logic (Johnson and Harrison, 1992).

A major advantage of using some specification of the input sequence is that it can be analyzed automatically to ensure that certain properties hold. The most important of these is that the controller will correctly respond to events that it was not expecting at all. Error handling is a particular problem in hand-written controllers because programmers are focused on what should happen rather than all of the weird things that might happen. All of these more formal representations handle erroneous inputs automatically without crashing. Some work has been done on automatic analysis of such dialog specifications (Bleser and Foley, 1982; Monk and Olsen et al., 1995) to determine a variety of other dialog properties.

48.5.3 Object Oriented Implementation

By far the most popular model for implementing controllers is to combine the controller and the view into a single object class which is associated with some area of some window. This view/controller class has methods for each of the various events that can be received, including the redraw events, input events, focus negotiation events, and window sizing events. These methods are frequently defined in an abstract class from which the programmer can create subclasses. Each new subclass overrides the appropriate methods to provide the appropriate implementation. When the windowing system wants to dispatch an event to one of these view/controller objects it invokes the method corresponding to that event. The message/method binding of the object-oriented language then handles the actual dispatching of the message to the appropriate code.

There are two major problems with this approach. The first is that the sequential multiplexing of the events is left entirely up to the programmer. The second is the connection of such view/controller objects to the models that they are presenting and manipulating. In the case of widget design, it is desirable to write general widgets which can then be attached to a variety of models in a variety of ways.

48.6 Models

The implementation of the model defines exactly what an interactive application can do. In general the design of the model is driven by the task analysis of the goals to be accomplished. From this a set of objects with their data and methods are designed which serve the functional needs of the user. In our chip layout example, the model would consist of classes for a Circuit which would contain Chips and Wires. Each of these classes would have information about their contents and methods for creating, modifying and deleting such objects. These methods are invoked by the controller to perform the model changes. Methods are also needed for the view to obtain information about the model to support its redraw function.

On top of this functional design of what the application must do, there are a series of issues relative to the user interface which must be addressed in the model's implementation. They are:

- Notification of all relevant views whenever the model changes
- Defining the connection between the model and the controller/view
- Cut, Copy and Paste
- Undo and Redo

48.6.1 View Notification

In the MVC architecture, the controller or some application code will make modifications to the information in the model. When this happens all relevant views must be informed so that the display can be updated to reflect the change. In our chip layout example there are two different views of the same model: the layout and the parts list. What is required is a mechanism by which views can register with models and models can inform all views of their changes.

A rather straight forward register/notify mechanism is a single abstract Model class which defines the methods RegisterView, UnregisterView and NotifyViews. There must also be an abstract View class which is the parent of all views and has a RegisterModel method and the virtual method ModelChangeNotify. Whenever a new view object is created a pointer to its model is passed to the RegisterModel method which saves the pointer in the view and invokes the RegisterView method to inform the model of its new view. Whenever a view object is destroyed, it first invokes its model's UnregisterView to remove itself from the list.

Any time the model has any of its data changed it will invoke NotifyViews on itself which will then run through the list of views and invoke ModelChangeNotify on each of them. When a new view class is created, the ModelChangeNotify method is reimplemented so as to perform the necessary damage operations to get the screen updated using the damage/ mechanism described earlier.

This model / view communication and registration architecture is fairly straightforward. The problem lies in exactly how the model informs the view as to what has changed. In our chip layout example, suppose a new Wire object was created. If NotifyViews has no parameters then no information can be passed to ModelChangeNotify. In such a case the view does not know what part of the model has changed and has no choice but to damage the entire layout display to make sure that everything is drawn correctly. What is needed is to communicate to the view exactly what part of the model has changed, so that the view need only update the appropriate parts of the display. Providing this information in a general way is still problematic in most user interface tool kits.

48.6.2 View/Controller Interface

A key problem in designing interfaces is the connection between the general user interface tools provided for implementing views and controllers and the wide variety of application models that must be served. Early systems such as Motif allowed designers to attach the addresses of C procedures to all of the places in the view / controller for which the application model might have an interest. This does work but it is somewhat clumsy. Some systems have been proposed which generate this interface automatically from a description of the classes which make up the model. The Mickey (Olsen, 1989) and Sushi (Olsen, 1992) systems adopt this approach. Microsoft's Visual C++ uses its Class Wizard to make these connections from inside of its interface layout tools.

48.6.3 Cut, Copy and Paste

A key component in any modern user interface is the ability to copy or cut information in one part of an application and then paste it into a different part of the same or a different application. Some windowing systems do this in a limited way for textual and sometimes pixel mapped information with minimal involvement from the application. The problem is, in general, more complex than that.

All modern windowing systems support the concept of a *paste buffer*. In some systems more than one such buffer is supplied. There are two major problems that must be addressed in dealing with paste buffers. The first is that when moving information from one application to another there are a variety of formats in which the information can be passed and the second is that the information may be very large and thus should not be duplicated needlessly.

A example of the formatting issue arises when a user copies a section of a Microsoft Excel spreadsheet. If this information is pasted into another Excel spreadsheet or into Microsoft Word (which understands Excel's format) then all of the Excel information should be passed. If, however, the information is pasted into a simple text editor, then a textual form of the information should be passed. If the spreadsheet section is pasted into a paint program then perhaps a PICT image of the section should be passed. The point is that when the original copy was performed it was not known how it would be used. Generating all versions of the different formats at the time of the copy is unacceptable.

When performing a copy the model must register, with the windowing system, a pointer to the information that should go in the paste buffer. In addition the model should register identifiers for the various formats of information that it can generate. When a paste is performed, the model at the paste's destination must select a format and request the information transfer. The source model then generates the information in the requested format which the destination model converts into modifications of its own data and then notifies its own views of the changes. In some cases the information being pasted is too large for one message and a protocol which gets the information a piece at a time is required. The details of this process vary widely among windowing systems but the basic architecture is the same.

48.6.4 Undo / Redo

One of the key features of direct manipulation systems is to make exploration safe for new users so that they will try things without fear of permanently loosing information. A key feature of this is an Undo mechanism which can restore the state of the model to what it was before the action was taken. A related facility is the ability to redo the last action that was undone. This is an Undo of the Undo.

There are various levels of Undo which each require more resources than lesser forms. The simplest is an undo of the last action performed. A more complex model maintains a history of the last N actions which can be successively undone to back up to any point in the last N steps. This requires significantly more resources. An even more complex scheme will display a representation of the last N steps and allow any one of them to be selectively undone (Berlage, 1994). In all of these cases, sufficient information must be saved so that the model can be restored to its previous state. The problem is that Undo is a general feature of all good user interfaces but the information and processing needs of an Undo operation varies widely.

The dominant undo strategy uses a set of *command objects* (Meyer, 1988) as the controller / model interface. An abstract class Command is defined with two methods: Do and Undo. Every action which the controller can perform on the model is represented as a separate subclass of Command. When the controller, for example, wants to move a chip from one location to another it creates a new MoveChip object and gives it the model pointer and the new location. It then invokes the Do method on the MoveChip object. The MoveChip class has its own versions of the Do and Undo methods. When Do is performed on a Command object it will first save in itself any information required by the Undo method in order to restore the state of the model. The Command object will then modify the model and then place itself in the Undo history. The model can then notify the view to get the screen updated. In our example the Do method on MoveChip would save the old location of the chip in the MoveChip object and then set the model's location to the new locations. If the Undo method is invoked on this same MoveChip object, it can restore the chip location to the saved values.

Each of the Undo styles described above vary in how they store the Command objects to be undone and how users can select which object can be undone. In general, however, when a user requests Undo, a Command object is selected from the history and its Undo method is invoked. Since each command is a separate class with its own Undo method and each object has all of the information it needs stored inside of itself, the Undo method can restore the model to its original state. The model then informs the view of the changes and the display is updated.

This undo architecture is quite general. Its only problem, however, is that a very large number of Command subclasses need to be defined. This can make the design and implementation of new interactive models very tedious.

48.7 Summary

User interface software can be conceptually partitioned into a model, view and controller MVC. In many cases such structures are composed of smaller scale MVC units which provide interaction with smaller fragments of the interface. The model implements the functional semantics of the application and is responsible for Undo/Redo as well as notification of all views when changes to the data occurs. A view is responsible for all display and geometry issues. The controller then interprets the stream of user inputs, associates meaning with those inputs and invokes commands on the model to perform the user's desires. All of this activity occurs through a windowing system which manages interactive resources such as input devices and screen space.

48.8 References

Bastide, R. and P. Palanque (1990). *Petri net objects for the design, validation and prototyping of user-driven interfaces.* Human-Computer Interaction -- Interact '90, Elsevier Science Publications, North Holland, Netherlands.

Berlage, T. (1994). "A Selective Undo Mechanism for Graphical User Interfaces Based on Command Objects." *ACM Transactions on Computer-Human Interaction* 1(3): 269-294.

Bleser, T. and J. D. Foley (1982). *Towards Specifying and Evaluating the Human Factors of User-Computer Interfaces.* Human Factors in Computer Systems,

Cardelli, L. (1988). *Building User Interfaces by Direct Manipulation.* ACM SIGGRAPH Symposium on User Interface Software, Banff, Canada, ACM.

Hanau, P. R. and D. R. Lenorovitz (1980). Prototyping and Simulation Tools for User/Computer Dialogue Design.*Computer Graphics* 14(3): 1980.

Hill, R. D. (1986). "Supporting Concurrency, Communication, and Synchronization in Human-Computer Interaction -- The Sassafras UIMS." *ACM Transactions on Graphics* 5(3): 179-210.

Hudson, S. E. (1989). *Graphical Specification of Flexible User Interface Displays.* ACM SIGGRAPH Symposium on User Interface Software and Technology, ACM.

Jacob, R. (1982). *Using Formal Specifications in the Design of Human-Computer Interaction.* Proceedings of Human Factors in Computer Systems,

Johnson, C. W. and M. D. Harrison (1992). "Using temporal logic to support the specification and prototyping of interactive control systems." *International Journal of Man-Machine Studies* (36): 357-385.

Linton, M. A., J. M. Vlissides, et al. (1989). "Composing User Interfaces with InterViews." *IEEE Computer* 22(2): 8-22.

Meyer, B. (1988). *Object-Oriented Software Construction.* Englewood Cliff, N.J., Prentice-Hall.

Monk, A. F., D. R. Olsen, et al. (1995). "Algorithms for automatic dialogue analysis using propositional production systems." *Human Computer Interaction* 10(1): 39-78.

Myers, B. A. and W. Buxton (1986). "Creating Highly Interactive and Graphical User Interface by Demonstration." *Computer Graphics* 20(4): 249-258.

Newman, W. (1968). *A System for Interactive Graphical Programming.* Spring Joint Computer Conference, Thompson Books.

Olsen, D. R. (1988). *A Browse / Edit Model for User Interface Management.* Graphics Interface'88, Edmonton, Alberta, Canada,

Olsen, D. R. (1989). *A Programming Language Basis for User Interface Management.* Human Factors in Computing Systems (CHI'89), ACM.

Olsen, D. R. (1990). *Propositional Production Systems for Dialog Description.* Human Factors in Computing Systems (CHIí90),

Olsen, D. R. (1992). Editing Dialog Models. *User Interface Management Systems: Models and Algorithms.* San Mateo, California, Morgan Kaufmann Publishers. 183-202.

Olsen, D. R., B. Ahlstrom, et al. (1995). *Building Geometry-based Widgets by Example.* CHI '95, ACM.

Olsen, D. R. and K. Allan (1990). *Creating Interactive Techniques by Symbolically Solving Geometric Constraints.* Third Annual Symposium on User Interface Software and Technlogy, ACM.

Olsen, D. R. and E. P. Dempsey (1983). "SYNGRAPH: A Graphical User Interface Generator." *Computer Graphics* 17(3):

Olsen, D. R., T. G. McNeill, et al. (1992). *Workspaces: An Architecture for Editing Collections of Objects.* CHI '92, Monterey, California, ACM Press.

Vander Zanden, B., B. A. Myers, et al. (1994). "Integrating Pointer Variables into One-Way Constraint Models." *ACM Transactions on Computer-Human Interaction* 1(2): 161-211.

Handbook of Human-Computer Interaction
Second, completely revised edition
M. Helander, T.K. Landauer, P. Prabhu (eds.)

Chapter 49

User Aspects Of Knowledge-Based Systems

Yvonne Wærn
Department of Communication Studies
Linköping University
Linköping, Sweden

Sture Hägglund
Department of Computer and Information Science
Linköping University
Linköping, Sweden

49.1 Characteristics of Knowledge-based Systems

Knowledge-based expert systems emerged originally as an attempt to build software that could compete with humans in solving problems at an expert level in a given domain of application. A typical definition of the term "expert system" emphasizes its character as an intelligent computer program which otherwise uses knowledge and logical inference to solve problems which demand significant human expertise for their solution. Such software systems attempt not only to formalize information from the application domain and the procedures for computing with such representations, but also to allow reasoning about informal and experience-based qualities of decision making. The key to success in this endeavour seems to be the ability to represent and use within the computer system a wide variety of knowledge from the application domain.

We follow common practices in the area and refrain from trying to give an exact definition of the term "knowledge-based". It will thus be used here as a generic term denoting various kinds of insights which can serve as the basis for intellectual processes in humans. The instrumental character of knowledge is thus emphasized, which means that when we refer to knowledge of the kind that can be symbolically represented in a computing system, we also assume that some generalized procedures are provided for reasoning with that knowledge.

It would be difficult to find any practical procedure for deciding whether a computer program is 'knowledge-based' or 'just an ordinary program'. Obviously, all programs are knowledge-based in the sense that they were designed on the basis of an understanding of the problem to be solved. However, the term "knowledge-based" is usually utilized to refer to software which contains an explicit representation of knowledge from the application domain. This representation should allow the knowledge to be inspected, understood and verified by domain experts. Further, it is usually assumed that the system is able to produce explanations of its reasoning or computations and argumentation justifying its results, using this knowledge. Normally these qualities are provided by the software architecture, with an independent knowledge base that provides a parameter structure for an interpreter (or compiler) which controls the processing called for by the user of the system. In this way the characteristics of the functions provided by the system can be directly related to aspects of domain knowledge, as understood by domain experts and, presumably, also end users.

With this general definition, a knowledge-based system is thus characterized by its explicit representation of knowledge from the application domain. The term "expert system" is used almost synonymously with knowledge-based system, but often emphasizes problem solving, or expert-level consultative advice in a given domain of application.

Knowledge-based systems are thus generally viewed as exhibiting the following characteristics:

- They provide expert-level problem solving or decision support for some suitably restricted domain of application.
- Domain knowledge is explicitly represented within the system and changes in the implemented functions can be accomplished in terms of the domain knowledge.
- Stored knowledge can be used for inferring facts and solutions to problems in a multitude of ways.
- Explanations and motivations can be provided in order to elucidate the reasoning of the system and justify its results.
- The development process and supporting tools tend to promote an improved understanding of problem solving in the given domain and the nature of the knowledge involved.

Typical applications for knowledge-based expert systems are tasks which involve monitoring, interpretation, diagnosis, design, planning, and so forth. In many cases the problem to be solved is reformulated as a classification problem (distinguishing between possible categories on the basis of a set of observations) or a configuration problem (finding a combination of components which realizes a required function under given constraints).

Knowledge-based systems can at present be used to represent expertise in small but presumably complex domains. They are useful as a means of conveying specialist knowledge to a less experienced user. Examples of typical applications include: technical equipment trouble shooting, intelligent front-ends to databases, financial advisors, medical diagnosis and therapy selection, design aids and various kinds of decision support systems.

One important mechanism for knowledge representation provided by most systems is the use of rules. Rules are conditional structures which can be used to define logical necessity, causal relationships, situation-action pairs and production rules for substitution patterns. It is assumed that there is a well-defined mechanism for reasoning with the rules and facts in the system. This mechanism, or inference procedure, can then establish various conclusions from available facts by identifying and evaluating relevant rules from the knowledge base. However, pure rule-based approaches do not always allow control of the reasoning process to be expressed in a straight-forward way. In particular, the need for a system to exhibit a natural dialogue behaviour may call for additional means of controlling the flow during consultation. Thus, most of the existing tools and shells for building expert systems now available support hybrid mechanisms for knowledge representation, for instance by combining rules with object-oriented approaches.

Case-Based Reasoning (Kolodner, 1993) presents another paradigm, which allows users to relate a decision problem to previous cases by analogical reasoning and at the same time provides a framework for the interaction with the user. Other popular technologies for capturing and modelling intelligent behaviour, such as neural networks and genetic algorithms, play an important role in present day systems, but these can also be seen as black-box implementations which do not greatly affect human factors aspect of knowledge-based systems.

From a technical perspective, knowledge-based systems should be distinguished from systems based purely on technologies such as hypermedia, database management, information retrieval, object orientation and procedural processing. Of course, all these technologies can be utilized in the context of a knowledge-based system, but the explicit representation of knowledge is essential for the class of systems discussed in this chapter. It may also be noted that from a user point of view the underlying techniques are not always visible.

As to communication, knowledge-based systems may present results and interact with their users in various ways, ranging from standard GUIs to quasi-natural language. In addition the underlying flow of dialogue control and the division of initiative between the user and the system is of particular interest. Interfaces which build on natural language involve interesting research problems per se, and these are presented elsewhere in the handbook.

49.2 A Short History of "Intelligent" Processes

49.2.1 Artificial Intelligence

The term "artificial intelligence" dates as far back as 1956, when a group of researchers met at a summer conference in Dartmouth and discussed the prospects for the scientific study of mechanized intelligence inspired by the emerging computing technology. Already at that time there were a few "intelligent" systems available, in the sense that they could perform tasks which require intelligence when performed by human beings. One such system, dealing with logic proofs (The Logic Theorist) was implemented by Herbert Simon and Allan Newell (Newell and Simon, 1956). It was based upon the formalism of production systems and incorporated some ideas as to solving intellectual tasks in the so called "General Problem Solver". The system was, in fact, very successful in performing the well-defined tasks of logical proofs. It had, however, little in common with human intelligence, neither in terms of modelling human thinking, nor in terms of interacting with human beings.

49.2.2 Modelling Human Reasoning

Later, Herbert Simon, Allan Newell as well as Marvin Minsky and Roger Schank embarked on the task of modelling human reasoning, problem solving and text processing, fields which were considered to require human intelligence. A fair amount of success was achieved by "intelligent" programs. Herbert Simon and Allan Newell were able to simulate traces of detailed human reasoning processes using a production system model (Newell and Simon, 1972). It was soon found that a more elaborated model of human representation of knowledge was necessary. Such models were proposed by Marvin Minsky, who formulated the concept of "frames" (Minsky, 1975) and Roger Schank and his collaborators, who formalized the concept of "script" for modelling human comprehension (Schank and Abelson, 1977). Both these concepts aimed at modelling general human knowledge, which could be "instant-iated" by specific situational characteristics.

However these systems had one major weakness: they were based applications containing very little domain knowledge. They worked quite well with well constrained microworlds (one illuminating example is the cyryptoarithmetic problem, analyzed by Newell and Simon (1972)), but they did not seem well equipped to manage problems where extensive human knowledge was involved.

49.2.3 Early Expert Systems

The step from the laboratory to the real world was taken in the seventies. Edward Feigenbaum suggested that the knowledge possessed by human beings could be represented in a computer program (Feigenbaum, 1980). This was the first step towards representing one person's knowledge in computers for use by another person. Such systems were called "expert systems", since it was considered that they incorporated the knowledge of "experts". The implications were, for instance, that expertise might be made supplied through computers in situations where experts were scarce or unavailable. Knowledge bases were also seen as an opportunity to preserve knowledge which was in danger of being lost, such as knowledge of trouble-shooting of steam-engines.

The expert systems soon migrated from the laboratory to real world settings. As early as 1988, Feigenbaum, McCorduck and Nii (1988) listed 139 expert systems in use by the commercial sector in various areas as agriculture, computers, construction, utilities, finance, manufacturing, mining, geology, medicine, science and transportation.

49.3 Current Knowledge-based Systems

Knowledge-based systems vary in the distribution of tasks between human beings and the systems themselves, as well as the type of human-computer communication used

A high level of automatization implies that the system more or less takes over the task. The human user is a "servant" to the system, feeding the system with information. The human user has the responsibility of checking and interpreting the result provided by the system.

A medium level of automatization implies that human beings and computer systems both contribute to the solving of the problem. Computer systems may be regarded as intelligent agents which might solve parts of the task independently and which might offer advice or criticism related to the human problem-solving effort. A low level of automatization requires that the system serve as a tool at the request of the user. Knowledge-based systems at this level may serve as intelligent help or intelligent information seekers.

A typical task for knowledge-based systems is to give consultative advice, comparable to what an expert would provide if called by telephone. Traditionally, such systems have been realized as goal-driven, rule-based systems, where the dialogue with the end user is generated during the process of collecting enough information to allow a conclusion to be drawn from relevant rules in the knowledge base. With this approach, the system has the initiative and the user is asked to provide additional information whenever needed (c.f. Hayes-Roth, Waterman and Lenat, 1983).

In many situations it is undesirable to allocate a passive role to the user. Nor is it always a good solution to have the recommendation for a decision produced by the system, while the responsibility is left with the user. Users may all too easily accept the system's recommendation without considering the reliability of the expert advice. Such a dependence would lead to errors in decision, because it is difficult for both the system and the user to keep track of the limits and applicability of the system knowledge.

Recent developments have been oriented more towards supporting the user's own decisions than towards directly suggesting a recommendation. Thus it is assumed in expert critiquing systems (Miller, 1986; Fischer, 1991; Silverman, 1992c; Hägglund, 1993), that the user initially proposes a decision or course of action. The system then reviews this suggestion and produces comments regarding the appropriateness of the proposal, necessary prerequisites, reasonable alternatives and their merits, and so forth.

Several different paradigms for providing consultative advice in a cooperative computer system may be identified, namely *transaction systems, consultation systems* and *critiquing systems:*

Transaction Systems

These represent the classical data processing approach where specific tasks correspond to specific transactions in the system. Each transaction is associated with a fixed set of input data, which are to be provided by the user. Data is usually entered in a prescribed format, without the possibility to interact with the application program or the background database during the transaction. Such systems tend to be rather rigid. They assume that tasks have to be solved in a predominate way, require fixed-form data where the user must learn syntactical and technical details. Still, transaction systems equipped with good direct-manipulation interfaces allow the user to take the initiative and feel in control of the system.

Expert Consultation Systems

A typical approach is the use of rule-based systems, where the system tries to solve a task by reasoning from its knowledge base. When additional information is needed, the user is queried. The final result is often accompanied by an argumentation for the proposed decision, including how the result was derived from the input data and what knowledge was used. Explanations are usually hand-crafted and stored in advance, or produced from a trace of the computation carried out in the system. Although considerably more flexible and powerful than traditional transaction systems, the initiative in the problem-solving and dialogue process is basically allocated to the system, and this might sometimes frustrate the users.

Expert Critiquing Systems

Typically one or maybe several alternative solutions are submitted to the system by the user in order to have them commented upon. In this way, the user can control when, during the decision-making process, the advice from the computer is called for. The overall approach to problem solving is primarily controlled by the user's preferences, as expressed in the proposed decision to be critiqued by the system.

These three paradigms represent increasing degrees of complexity in the computational processes and the knowledge representation needed for their implementation. The discussion in this chapter will focus on the experience of traditional advice-giving expert consultation systems, which is the approach most widely used and documented in the literature. The general trend is, however, in the direction of joint cognitive systems, where the human and the computer cooperate in problem solving and decision making (Woods, 1988).

49.3.1 Classical Expert Consultation Systems

Many expert systems are characterized by a high level of automatization and by rather limited communication with the user. One early example is R1/XCON, designed to configure computer systems at Digital Equipment. (Bachant and McDermott, 1984). This system did not primarily aim at modeling human reasoning, nor did it rely on interaction with human beings. Still, it is presumably the most successful example of a commercial expert system. Its knowledge-based approach demonstrates how the immense complexity of the task can be effectively managed, and how the knowledge base can be modified in order to cope with changing requirements. One interesting observation from XCON's long history is the importance of attending not only to the technical problem, but also to the particular attitudes of the individuals that the system was developed to assist - namely their attitudes toward work, computer assistance, process explicitness, and so forth. Thus the experience with R1/XCON points to the importance of research in workplace analysis. (Bachant and McDermott, 1984).

More typical of knowledge-based expert systems is that a consultation is carried out in dialogue with the user and that the system supports user decision making. In fact, the break-through for expert systems in the 1970s can be partly attributed to the convincing demonstrations of qualified advice combined with useful justifications and explanations, as exhibited by MYCIN and other systems developed in the Heuristic Programming Project at Stanford (Buchanan and Shortliffe, 1984). It was shown that comparatively small rule bases, such as the 500 rules in MYCIN, could capture significant expertise in an important and difficult application domain. At the same time explanations and justifications of results and recommendations were provided with little extra effort as a side effect of the rule-based approach.

The dialogue with the user in expert systems belonging to this class of rule-based systems is generated from information requirements in the antecedent part of rules involving inferences leading towards a specified goal. When information is needed which is not known or deducible from facts in the system, a question to the user is generated. The reasoning in the system chains backwards from a given goal (the sought solution) until facts known to the user can be entered. With this way of querying the user, there is no need for an elaborate mechanism for processing natural language input. Output to the user may be stated in natural language generated by simple templates and canned text. This applies to results produced by the system as well as to the automated translation of rules stored in the knowledge base.

The main weaknesses of this approach are the inability to handle more complex input which cannot be stated as simple facts, and the lack of initiative on the part of the user, who has to wait for the system to be queried for information. Of course, it would be possible to design a more elaborated and programmer controlled user dialogue, but then much of the simplicity and elegance of the rule-based approach would be lost.

An important result of the MYCIN experience, was the EMYCIN shell (van Melle, 1981). A number of commercial products followed very closely the solutions employed in MYCIN/EMYCIN. Such tools, or *shells*, have been successfully used to build effective expert consultation systems for many applications.

A related rule-based approach was taken in the Prospector system (Duda, 1980), although the dialogue management was much more ambitious. The user was here offered the opportunity to volunteer information by entering observations in (a subset of) natural language. This possibility not only presupposes the system's ability to parse and analyze English input, but also requires a semantic network and a taxonomy of concepts which can be used to relate general rules to specific instances. For instance, when the user enters the observation "I have found a rhyolite plug", the system must be able to decide whether rules mentioning volcanic rocks apply. The Prospector system demonstrated convincingly the ability to model and reason with expert knowledge in the complex domain of geological exploration. However, it was never possible to construct an easy-to-use shell for building similar systems in other domains, and thus the more advanced dialogue management style in Prospector did not inspire many followers.

In addition to the potential for automated explanations and transparency of knowledge offered by pure rule-based systems, Clancey (1986) demonstrated that such knowledge-based systems can be turned into intelligent tutoring systems. However, this style of explanation and tutoring has severe limitations. Explanatory information and specific knowledge related to tutoring must be added in order to improve the situation.

Managing the user interface presents a special challenge in the context of knowledge systems, where the system as well as the user generate communicative actions. The reason is that expert system architectures typically de-emphasize the dialogue structure in favour of the reasoning required to solve the domain problem. One possibility is to use a UIMS (user-interface management system) which can manage the discourse and mediate between the reasoning and the dialogue processes.

Researchers have long argued about the benefits of separating the implementation of user interfaces from the underlying software functionality. Numerous tools and architectures have been developed to support such separation. An example of a system for user-interface management of expert systems is the expert system UIMS Ignatius (Löwgren, 1992). This combines a surface interaction manager, responsible for the interaction techniques of the user-interface, and a plan-based session dialogue manager which addresses the dialogue structure (in the sense discussed above).

49.3.2 Critiquing Systems

Expert critiquing systems provide feedback to users on their decision proposals. The user initially proposes a decision or course of action. The system then reviews this suggestion in the context of known circumstances, tries to evaluate the proposed solution, provides suggestions for improvements, draws attention to possible risks, indicates alternatives and evaluates their merits, and so forth. A critiquing system is characterized both by its approach to problem solving and by its style of interaction with the user, as will be detailed below.

Miller (1986) who worked with medical applications introduced the concept of expert critiquing to a wider audience. Related issues were also investigated in the context of the MYCIN tradition, where the need for resolving conflicts between users and an advice-giving program were recognized (Clancey, 1977; Langlotz and Shortliffe, 1983). An interesting alternative, albeit not conceived of explicitly as critiquing, was employed in the HELP system, where medical treatment decisions were scrutinized and alerts generated whenever contraindications were detected (Pryor, 1983). The feasibility of generating critique based solely on medical records was investigated in a series of studies by Van der Lei (1991). These studies demonstrated that existing documentation of patient data was sufficient for generating useful critique.

Early studies of similar ideas were also performed in the area of engineering design. This is an example of a domain, where it is very difficult to automate or even mechanize decision making, due to the complexity of design. An example of early work is the CRITTER system, which evaluates and comments upon digital circuit designs (Kelly, 1984). Important contributions in the area of design critiquing have also been made by Fischer and colleagues, starting with a LISP critic (Fischer, 1987) and leading up to general work on human-computer collaborative design support (Fischer, 1993).

A theory of expert errors and critiquing formed the basis for work by Silverman, and resulted in the COPE system which can be viewed as a generic critic shell (Silverman, 1987). An extensive presentation of methodological and practical issues in critic engineering is given in (Silverman, 1992b). Aspects of usability of expert critiquing have also been discussed by, for instance, Hägglund and Rankin (1988).

Numerous applications today use the expert critiquing approach (for a recent overview see Silverman, 1992a). There are several arguments for the use of expert critiquing systems. In general, expert critiquing systems exhibit several interesting features:

- They can be based upon heuristic domain expertise or upon formal decision theories. This distinction applies to expert systems in general. Practical experience indicates, however, that the heuristic approach provides a more convenient foundation for the development of working systems, and the critiquing paradigm is well suited for coping with the lack of formal theories underlying the decision making.
- They can be either knowledge-based or algorithmic. An example of the latter are spelling checkers.
- They might take either an analytical or a differential approach to critiquing. The analytical approach means that aspects of the user's proposal for a decision are evaluated and commented upon, while the differential approach is based on a comparison of the proposed solution against some "correct" or standard solution. Depending on the application, either of these solutions may be preferred.
- They may focus upon the generation of a critique of the user's preferred solution but also upon a justification of the system's own proposals. In general we may conceptualize expert critiquing systems as systems capable of engaging in an argumentative discussion with the user.
- They may use an ad hoc or linguistic approach to text generation. Especially important is the content and underlying structure of a critique, and the rhetorical means used for the discourse (Rankin, 1993).

The utility of a critiquing system or a more conventional approach to knowledge engineering depends on several factors:

- It is typically more complicated to build an expert critiquing system than a conventional system. This is because a critiquing system must have both the knowledge to derive a preferred solution, and the power to critique a broad variety of alternative approaches to solving a given problem.

- The scope of applications is greater with a critiquing approach, since one can build systems even for applications where the system is not proficient enough to generate complete solutions on its own. It may still be possible to provide useful comments on various proposals suggested by the user.
- A critiquing system may be preferred over a conventional expert system in cases where the user appreciate to be in control of the decision making. By providing the first solution proposal, the user becomes engaged and user satisfaction is improved.
- A critiquing system can conveniently handle conflicting expertise in a domain. The system does not have to produce one specific recommended solution, but it can maintain a knowledge base with alternative approaches for handling a given problem. If an analytical approach to critiquing is employed, a user proposal can easily be compared with different solution alternatives.
- A critiquing system is useful also with partial domain knowledge. When only certain aspects of a problem can be handled by the system, or when knowledge of a given situation lacks depth, the system can inform the user about the quality and reliability of the generated comments and critique.
- The expert critiquing approach may offer transitional support for developing a proficient expert system from a critiquing system with a limited knowledge base. Thus a conventional expert system cannot be used in practice before the knowledge base is reasonably complete and validated. Here the critiquing approach offers a opportunity to gain practical experience from using the system at an early stage of construction with a partial knowledge base, as discussed before. Once the knowledge base is sufficiently complete, it can be used as a problem-solving aid in the style of traditional expert systems.

One may also distinguish between several types of critique:

- Critique used as mechanism for reasoning and problem solving. In this case the purpose is to organize the knowledge and inference needed to handle a problem. The knowledge base is typically organized as a set of critics that apply in different situations and these critics may, for instance, be used in a generate-and-test approach to problem solving. An application example is for critiquing software specifications (Fickas, 1988).
- Critique used to provide non-intrusive advice to a computer user. In this case the main purpose is to make sure that the user is in control of the decision making. The system restricts itself to commenting upon the user's suggestions, even if it would be possible for the system to propose an alternative solution. The main focus is to monitor the interaction between the system and the user, see for example Fischer (1993).
- Critique presenting understandable arguments and explanations to the user. In this case the main focus is on the semantics of the critique, its extent, components and rhetorical structure. Work on text generation relates to this aspect of critiquing (Rankin, 1993).

One interesting challenge is the current development to apply expert critiquing to the design of truly collaborative, user-friendly knowledge-based systems.

49.4 Discussions of Expert Systems

The utility of expert systems method has been discussed extensively. Several issues have been raised, one being the highly speculative and presumptuous claims made for expert system technology by the pioneers. Another is related to the simplification of "knowledge" as implied in expert systems. Knowledge as a topic has been extensively studied by researchers in the humanities for thousands of years, and it is premature to disregard all the accumulated reasoning, such as for instance the social and constructive nature of knowledge, and the human meaning of "meaning" (cf. Dreyfus and Dreyfus, 1986; Searle, 1984).

Further, expert systems may challenge crucial human values. If expert systems can perform "intelligent" tasks, what then will distinguish people from automata? The main differentiating characteristic may then be emotional and motivational aspects, which in the current Zeitgeist are not valued as highly as intellectual feats.

Let us examine some concerns, as well as benefits, of knowledge-based systems.

49.4.1 Criticism of "Intelligent" Systems

The most cogent argument against "intelligent" systems came from philosophers. Human knowledge is intentional, that is to say that reasoning is meaningful as well as purposeful. Mechanical systems, however sophisticated, can never reason about or reflect upon their own knowledge (cf. Searle, 1984).

This criticism is mainly relevant to the early artificial intelligence movement, such as the heuristic[1] problem solvers proposed by Newell and Simon, which aim at simulating human reasoning (Newell and Simon, 1972). The criticism has no bearing upon algorithmic or mathematical models.

Usually, however, knowledge-based systems are used for situations where algorithms have not yet been developed. Their problem-solving capacity relies upon heuristics derived from expert reasoning. When such heuristics are used in stand-alone systems, the critique is valid. However, when heuristics are used for situations where human and computer "collaborate" in problem-solving, the situation is quite different. Such collaborative processes are envisioned in current attempts at designing critiquing systems, intelligent agents and collaborative learning systems, as described above.

Another kind of criticism concerns the explicit formulation of expert knowledge required by most knowledge-based systems. Winograd and Flores (1990) argued that knowledge is not reflected upon until it breaks down. Thus, knowledge cannot be explicitly represented but should rather be regarded as an emergent property, derived from subsymbolic processes. For communicative purposes in "break-down" situations, some explicit formulation of knowledge would appear to be necessary.

Lucy Suchman (1987) argued that people do not make up plans to be strictly followed, they rather develop plans in accordance to the demands of the current situation. As an example, she showed how breakdowns in people's understanding and handling of a copier machine with advanced help facilities could be attributed to failures in understanding the nature of human plans. The help system was based upon a simple, sequential model of users' plans in copying documents. When something went wrong, people abandoned the plan, and the system became confusing rather than helpful. Her reasoning was backed by philosophical arguments, holding that human knowledge is not "represented" *within* heads, but rather that it is enacted in a social context.

These arguments have applicability beyond knowledge-based systems. Simply to condone knowledge-based systems in general is, however, as unwarranted as would be a general skepticism against algebra. For example, people do not think in algebraic terms, though algebraic methods are useful for those who know to apply them in a relevant context.

It is important to investigate when and how knowledge-based heuristics can be developed, used and communicated in various contexts.

49.4.2 Concerns with Expert Systems

Despite the philosophical and theoretical criticism, knowledge-based systems are continuously used. There are remaining concerns related to their practical use. These deal with responsibility, the "withering" of human knowledge and user acceptability.

Who is Responsible?

Let us assume the scenario where the system proposes a misleading or wrong decision or advice. Who is responsible?

By law, the user is generally held responsible for final action taken, whether or not an expert system is consulted. However, the system is usually consulted because its user may not have all the knowledge necessary to solve the problem and make the optimal decision. How can the user then be blamed? Should the expert be held responsible? The problem of representing and acquisition of knowledge is well documented in the literature. Could then the knowledge engineer be held responsible? Probably not. A knowledge engineer may represent uncertainties and hesitations of which the expert is aware. However, unconscious situational assumptions which limit the use of the system are not known to the knowledge engineer; they belong to the expert's "tacit knowledge".

A system may propose a wrong or irrelevant solution since it is used in a non-relevant situation. Users of the system must be made aware of all limitations. A possible way of supporting the user in deciding whether or not to rely upon the expert advice is to indicate in what contexts the system is supposed to be used (and not used).

[1] "Heuristic" methods refer to non-algorithmic problem solving methods, for instance consisting of "shortcuts". They often lead to correct solutions, although they are not guaranteed to do so.

The "Withering" of Human Knowledge

The fear of losing knowledge with the introduction of new tools is not new. Even Socrates wrote about the god, Thamos, who argued against the invention of writing by the god Theus as follows: "this will encourage forgetfulness in the minds of your pupils, because they will not exercise their memories, relying on the external, written symbols rather than on the process of reminiscence within themselves".

Knowledge is embodied in many ways. Artifacts as well as individual minds can hold knowledge and knowledge may be distributed over situations and individuals and does not reside only within individual minds.

With the conception of knowledge as being tied to individual minds, it may be the case that expert knowledge "withers" away with the development and use of knowledge-based systems. When the expert has disappeared, the expert system gives but a pale image of her knowledge. The use of the expert system may not encourage further skill training or knowledge development, just as the use of pocket calculators makes mental arithmetic unnecessary and the use of word-processors to some extent makes handwriting obsolete. Knowledge required and developed will change as soon as a new thinking tool is used.

This insight leads to a second view of knowledge which proposes that human knowledge as a whole is always evolving, and that the development of any artifact will change knowledge as well as the circumstances. Knowledge is embodied in the artifact as well as in its use. The situation cannot be reversed to the scenario without the artifact.

Let us take an example from aircraft automation. Here it has been suggested that if users forget that they are working together with a system and not alone, they might start overestimating their own skills. At worst they will recognize that these skills are insufficient when it is too late. This cause has been attributed to an accident in an Airbus A320, where the pilot disabled the automated flight system and apparently thought he would be able to handle the aircraft better alone (Lenorowitz, 1988). The solution proposed is to train pilots not only *with* the system but also *without* it. Individuals will have to develop new skills and new knowledge, this time related to the use of the artifact and the appreciation of the situation which requires different uses of the artifact according to the circumstances. Another accident with the same type of aircraft showed how an inadequate use of a system could not be counteracted within the available time (Airbus, 1990). Although these examples apply to aviation and not to expert systems, similar human reactions may happen in all cases where a human-system performance is increased by means of automation.

The new artifact of knowledge-based systems does not mean that people do not have to reflect, rather their reflection will have to change. Their reflection will be mediated by the artifact. New analyses may be required (not supported but sometimes caused by the artifact) and new judgments will be demanded (for instance checking the validity of the outcome or relating the use of the artifact to the present scenario).

Acceptance of Expert Systems

There are several reasons why expert systems may be resisted rather than accepted. First, the experts themselves may consider the danger of being replaced by the systems. Secondly, the users may consider the work situation with an expert system as tedious. Thirdly, the users may not trust the expert system and find that their situation has been made more difficult rather than improved.

If systems are intended to replace experts the experts face unemployment. However, expert systems may be used to expand expertise, which is usually in short supply, and experts may still find their place because expert systems will cover only a limited area of the problem domain. Experts will also be needed for unexplored parts of the domain and will also be necessary to explain in what circumstances the system is useful.

The tedious aspect of early expert systems was due to the practice where users "served" the system. The system requested input at different stages of the problem-solving process, and users had to comply. If the users wanted to know anything, they could perhaps ask why the system needed the information (cf. Hayes-Roth, Waterman and Lenat, 1983). Critiquing systems which "keep the users in the loop", give users a more active role.

Some studies have investigated how users perceive computer advice. If computers are perceived as "partners" in a problem solving process, it is possible that people will attribute characteristics to them just as people attribute characteristics to other people in a social setting. It seems to be the case that people judge computers more negatively when they are asked to only imagine computers as advice givers than when they have actually experienced an interaction with them

(Wærn and Ramberg, 1996). The trust in computer advice is related to the familiarity with the system (Wærn and Ramberg, 1996). It also seems that the form of the advice affects people's trust; a more human (verbose) form is less trusted than a more mechanistic one (cf. Quintanar, Crowell and Pryor, 1982; Nass, Steele, Henriksen and Dryer, 1994),

One important issue is related to incorrect advice and operator distrust. Some general principles seem to bias human beings towards first believing what they comprehend, and only later reject or distrust presented information (Gilbert, Krull and Malone, 1990). In interpersonal communication it has repeatedly been found that people believe what they are told (cf. Zuckerman, DePaulo and Rosenthal, 1981). Rejecting a proposal (with good reasons) requires more knowledge than uncritically accepting it. Thus novices in a domain tend to give more credence to advice than experts (Ramberg, 1996, Will, 1992). Wærn and Ramberg (1996) showed that people became less confident and trusted the system more when they were themselves wrong and the system gave incorrect advice.

These findings suggest that people who have not enough knowledge will tend to accept false advice.

The acceptance and usability of expert systems probably depends on the extent to which users can judge their reliability. Such opportunities are offered by systems which "explain" their reasoning. Acceptability also depends on the opportunities for users to check the applicability of the system's advice to their current problem. This may be far more difficult, given the tendency of human beings to believe rather than disbelieve.

49.5 Empirical Studies of Expert Systems

The types of systems most commonly used are the more automated and less communicative ones, such as expert consultation systems. Most of the empirical research has been performed on these types of systems.

Reported experience from the use of expert systems differs radically, depending upon who does the reporting. From developers, mainly success stories are described, and few hesitations are voiced. A description of the development and use of intelligent systems in business (Richardson and DeFries, 1990) is a good illustration of the developers' standpoint. Methods are developed, problems are solved, systems are accepted, and the remaining problems will easily be fixed. Reports from long term use are, however, much more sparse and cautious. An overview by Sviokla (1990) shows that there has been surprisingly little research on the practical usage of expert systems, or on their consequences.

To reflect the users' point of view, it may be most relevant to look at studies performed by people outside of the expert system development community.

49.5.1 Case Studies

One of the most apparent consequences of expert systems is the effect on the organization of work. Most empirical studies are case studies. This is expected, since it would be difficult to find generalizations over systems, domains and users. Thus, each case study has to be interpreted with respect to the particular circumstances prevailing.

One family of systems, which has been extensively investigated, is the XCON (Mumford and MacDonald, 1989). One study shows the effect of organizational culture (cf. Metselaar, 1994). XCON was used with great success, whereas a marketing system, XCEL, aimed at supporting the sales staff only succeeded in the US. The European sales managers wanted XCEL to be used by specialists and not by the sales people. The specialists did not feel any need to use the system, however, and it therefore fell into disuse.

Other case studies have been performed by Bradley and Holm (Holm, 1993). One study concerned the introduction of an expert system into the process for investment advice. Another concerned the diagnosis of malfunctions in aircraft motors. These studies illustrated both advantages and disadvantages. Advantages are related to increases in efficiency and the possibility of using the knowledge base for education and documentation. The disadvantages concerned the demand for enough competence on part of the user. Another effect relates to the decrease of social contacts. In both studies, the users did not have to get in touch with expert people as often as before, since some of the knowledge was available in the system. This was experienced both as an advantage (not having to disturb other people) and a disadvantage (less social contact with important people).

In the case of giving investment advice, it was found that the users changed focus and thereby competence from judging investment risks and benefits to talking to the customers. The bank case study also indicated that the system worked best with complex problems. At low levels of complexity, the advisers could as easily make judgments based on the data available without having to insert this into the expert system.

As to the change in organizational roles, both case studies indicated that the knowledge engineer had a central role, both in terms of system design and updating the system. It was considered important that the knowledge engineer was also a domain expert. At the same time, however, the project could not do without computer experts to solve software related problems of knowledge representation and system-user interactions.

49.5.2 Experimental Studies

In order to understand factors affecting the use of knowledge-based systems there are several variables that could be varied experimentally: the domain covered, the model of knowledge used and the kind of interaction with the users. Unfortunately, there is not yet enough knowledge on the effects of these variables to allow any predictions to be tested. Further, the problems of setting up experiments with realistic expert systems, where users are busy performing their real life tasks, makes it difficult to draw wide-ranging conclusions.

Will (1992) reported a study of engineers who used an expert system for analysing the build up of pressure in oil wells. This study was performed in a real world situation, and the experimental variation concerned the use or non-use of the expert system. It was found that users had more confidence in their solutions when they had used the system as compared to when they had not used the system. However, the quality of decisions was similar in both cases. Experts were much less in favour of the system than novices.

A study reported by Nass, Steuer, Henriksen and Dryer (1994) varied the type of interaction between a computerized tutor and the users. In particular, the variation covered the extent to which the tutor praised or blamed itself or another computerized tutor. It was found that performances that received self-praise were more highly valued by the users than performances that received self-criticism. It was also found that a system which offered criticism was regarded as smarter than a system which offered praise. Thus the confidence the tutor had in itself was reflected in the influence it had on the users.

Conclusion

The experimental studies show that the form of system advice affects user's trust of the system. The content of the advice interacts with users' knowledge of the domain. It is difficult to define "expertise" in a domain satisfactorily, however. Both the experts providing the knowledge and the knowledge system users cover parts of the available knowledge, a certain perspective of the knowledge or certain strategies of solving problems in the domain. Therefore, the studies of "experts" and "novices" have to be interpreted relatively, i.e. as possessing "high" or "low" levels of knowledge. With this caution, we may summarize the relationships between system characteristics and users' reactions to the system in Figure 1.

Figure 1 aims at an overview of results from studies showing interactions between system knowledge, system form and user knowledge. First, user knowledge is important for user trust. It is often the case that users with low domain knowledge unconditionally trust the system (if they have had experience with the system, i.e., not shown here). Users with higher domain knowledge may judge the knowledge of the system and only trust it if the system has shown good records of high knowledge. If the knowledge of the system is doubted, users' self-confidence is important. High self-confidence may lead to distrust in the system, as was exemplified above by the aircraft accidents. Users with low self-confidence may be more dependent on system form for trusting it. A mechanical form was found to be more trusted than a humanistic form in one study (Quintanar, Crowell and Pryor, 1982). However, the study did not distinguish between users, so the conclusion suggested here is still tentative.

49.6 Strategies of Intelligent Intervention

Let us turn to issues related to other types of knowledge support, where the end user has to take control over the problem-solving process and the knowledge base serves as a support. An important issue is whether a system of joint human and computer intelligence can outperform either one of human and computer. Other issues relate to how tasks could be distributed between human and computer intelligence, how to arrange the communication between computers and humans, how the knowledge of both should be made available to the other party, and when the system should interrupt the user and vice versa.

49.6.1 Issues Related to Joint Cognitive Systems

The task of problem solving, planning, or decision making is problematic both for a designer of a computer system and for a human being immersed in the task situation. The designer will have to design for

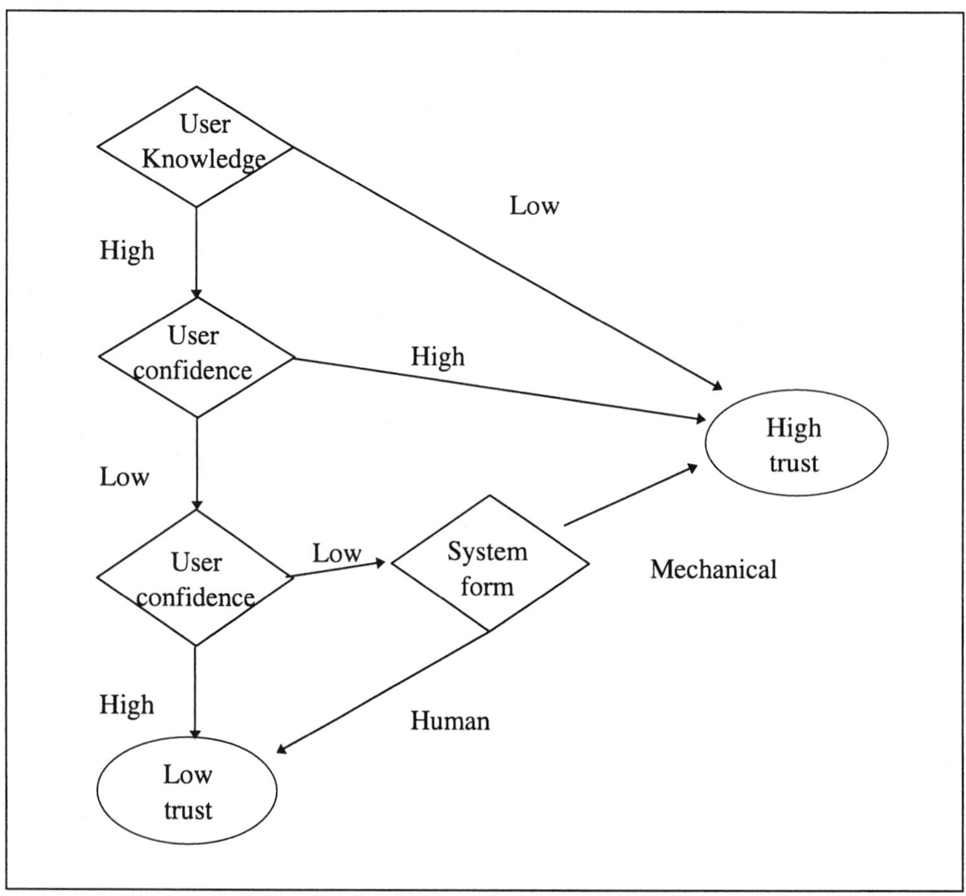

Figure 1. Characteristics of knowledge-based systems and users affecting user trust.

predictable situations, and will therefore neglect unplanned and unpredictable situations. The user, however, has to cope with predictable as well as unplanned situations. It is far too simple to believe that human beings can "fill in" the gaps which not are covered by the computer system, when unplanned situations occur. The introduction of a computer system may further cause new problems, since the user must interpret and validate the computer expertise. These two difficulties are referred to as the "ironies of automation" (Bainbridge, 1987).

How may a satisfactory solution of a joint cognitive system be achieved? One approach is to consider that computers should do what computers are good at and humans should do what humans are good at. This proposal is, however, superficial since it does not acknowledge differences in environmental requirements, the nature of the task, the competence and form of the computer support as well as individual differences. Studies indicate that all these factors have important effects on the efficiency of the performance of the joint cognitive system.

In a study of three different ways of supporting pilots in en-route flight route replanning tasks, Layton (1994) found that pilots selected a poor plan to a greater extent in a more automated situation. This finding suggests that users cannot reliably judge the quality of a plan in complex situations.

Dalal (1994) compared the cognitive task requirements to the cognitive "style" of the user and the computer support . The question asked was whether the computer system should be similar in cognitive style to the person or whether it should complement the person in order to jointly produce a good performance. The results indicated that, depending upon the situation, both similarity and complementarity were important. Thus, further analysis of the aids and the tasks must be performed in order to draw general conclusions.

The research on human factors in joint cognitive systems shows a lack of a theory governing the search for relevant factors. Neither similarity nor complementarity, neither task allocation nor task negotiation, seem to work as general principles. Rather the principles may have to based upon the circumstances in which the joint cognitive system has to operate. Complexity of task and time pressure may be important dimensions, as may also be whether solutions are convergent or divergent, thus making the task oriented more towards decision making or producing creative solutions. Other important factors concern the uncertainty in the environment, the incompleteness of the system, and the dynamic nature of the task. Thus it is difficult to propose definite guidelines.

49.6.2 Deep Knowledge and Cognitive Biases

Whereas the concept of joint cognitive systems concentrates upon the task to be performed and how the computer and the user may collaborate to achieve this task, another approach focuses upon the deep knowledge required to handle the task and the possible cognitive human biases that must be countered by a computer system (Silverman, 1992a).

Research in cognitive psychology has identified several biases in human cognitive reasoning. For instance, humans are prone to disregard negative information. This tendency induces them to accept rather than reject hypotheses and also to formulate hypotheses for acceptance rather than for rejection (Wason, 1968). This type of reasoning may have a detrimental effect since users can not evaluate the advice given by a computer system.

Humans also have a tendency to disregard the base rate of events. This makes them overestimate the likelihood of an event when the base rate is small or underestimate it when the base rate is high (Kahnemann, Slovic and Tversky, 1982).

Knowledge-based systems may support users in avoiding such biases by making them attentive to the information they would usually neglect. Silverman (1992a) has developed experimental systems to prevent or critique user errors. He reported that more complex problems seem to require preventive help or decision support. This means that users should not only be alerted to their possible biases but they should also be given the adequate means to overcome the bias. One example could be a formula used for probability calculations.

In another study Silverman (1992b) investigated the style of interaction between the system and the user. The question was how factors as cognitive orientation, deep knowledge, intention sharing, control plasticity, adaptivity and experience affect the performance with and the perception of the system. It was found that novices in a domain were helped more (and were satisfied more) by a system which was more to the point, gave more domain principles, initiated more control and offered fixed information rather than dynamic inferences. Experts in the domain, on the other hand, preferred subtle reminders, were satisfied with shallow maxims, preferred flexible control and wanted dynamic information. Silverman thus concludes that a critique should be tailored differently for different users, not only with respect to the domain knowledge or the handling of biases but also with respect to the interaction style.

49.6.3 Explanations in Knowledge-based Systems

In joint cognitive systems, parties must communicate about the tasks. Computer explanations are therefore important - particularly for critiquing systems, collaborative learning systems or other kinds of intelligent support.

The design of explanations has been one of the stumbling-blocks to knowledge-based systems. Research indicates that the earliest practice of only giving a trace of the system' s reasoning is insufficient (Clancey, 1983; Clancey, 1986; Southwick, 1991; Swartout, 1983). The reason is that the trace not always is very relevant for system end users. A trace of the reasoning is not intended to link familiar concepts to unfamiliar ones, but to support inference. Thus, the trace may contain points which are unfamiliar and which have to be explained further, or it may contain inference steps which are trivial.

To be able to meet the psychological requirements, an explanation must be relevant to the knowledge of the recipient. Thus a user model is necessary (cf. Kass and Finin, 1988; Wærn, Hägglund and Rankin, 1988). Second, for transfer of learning, problem-specific rules are not sufficient. What is needed is a model of the domain relevant relationships. These considerations lead to further inquiry into the problem of "deep explanations" (Southwick, 1991). A "deep model" of the domain explicitly represents relations that are only implicitly represented in the rules of a knowledge base. The deep model may be used for both modeling user knowledge and identifying the knowledge to be used for explanations.

Thirdly, a reliable method for handling communication requirements has to be identified (cf. Kidd and Cooper, 1985; Wærn, Hägglund, Löwgren, Rankin, Sokolnicki and Steinemann, 1992). Merely using an inference model is not sufficient for the intended communication.

The communicative aspect of explanations has been addressed by several researchers (Maybury, 1992; Wærn, Hägglund, Ramberg, Rankin and Harrius, 1995; Wærn, Ramberg, Österlund, 1996). Rankin (1993) covers still another issue, namely the formulation of the argumentative support needed for the negotiation that takes place between the system and the user in a critiquing context. The paper shows how argumentation theory (Toulmin, 1958) can be used as a framework for critiquing and justificatory texts, and it also extends the discussion to dialogue situations by introducing a language game metaphor for critiquing. He reviewed techniques for text generation and demonstrated that the real challenge is the deep generation of a critique, i.e. deciding on what information to include, which argumentative structure to apply and how to adapt the presentation to a particular user. These challenges have still not been met, although surface generation of text is feasible.

It is obvious that some information beyond the rules in the knowledge base is required to provide explanations. Explanations may be classified into classes of description, narration, exposition and argument, each of which may be further subdivided. Each of these require additional information, most of which cannot be produced automatically. An investigation by Wærn, Hägglund, Ramberg, Rankin and Harrius (1995) indicated that the acquisition of information for explanations can be regarded as a new knowledge solicitation event, which demanded a lot of extra effort from the expert who provided the knowledge.

As to the comprehension and usefulness of explanations in the context of performance and learning, a study by Ramberg (1996) indicated that different kinds of explanations were useful for novices and experts respectively. Domain novices preferred extensive explanations with both naive and expert knowledge, including both specific and general principles. Domain experts on the other hand preferred explanations which were short and to the point.

To offer relevant and useful information, individual differences have to be considered. We have seen above that a "user model" may contain several types of information, from hypotheses concerning domain knowledge via task relevant issues to surface structure issues. User modeling is a vital issue, which is dealt with in other chapters, concerning design of advice, help, instruction as well as user interface design.

49.7 Discussion and Conclusion

From the user's perspective, design of knowledge-based systems have many challenges which are different from computer systems used for routine tasks. They are intended to be used in complex situations where there are no algorithms for solving problems. Usability aspects are still sparsely covered in the literature and empirical studies are as yet rather inconclusive. New systems are continuously developed, and empirical studies follow a moving target. Therefore, the contribution of research should be related to the development of theories related to knowledge-based work, as well as to guidelines that will promote development of such support.

At present there is not much research that can be used as a theoretical basis for knowledge-based work. The currently dominant theories focus on limited aspects of the problem area, primarily dealing with individual decision making or problem solving. The work context requires additional aspects to be covered. Recent developments in the area of "distributed cognition" may be relevant, however this research is just in its wake (cf. Hutchins, 1995).

Human factors guidelines for developing expert systems have only recently been formulated. Suh and Suh (1993) proposed the following guidelines, to be explained below:

- Ensure user cooperation
- Ensure that tasks are appropriate
- Ensure compatibility
- Ensure diversity of perspectives
- Find compromises for contradictory maxims.

User Cooperation

Despite the wide acknowledgment of the need for user-centered design in system development, this practice has not seem spread to the design of knowledge-based systems. Berry (1994) suggested that the development methodology of knowledge-based systems should be similar to other computer support. These techniques are discussed in several chapters of the handbook.

Appropriate Tasks

Knowledge-based systems cannot be designed or used for all kinds of tasks. In particular, the following qualifications should be posed upon tasks to be considered for a knowledge-based support. (Keyes, 1989) :

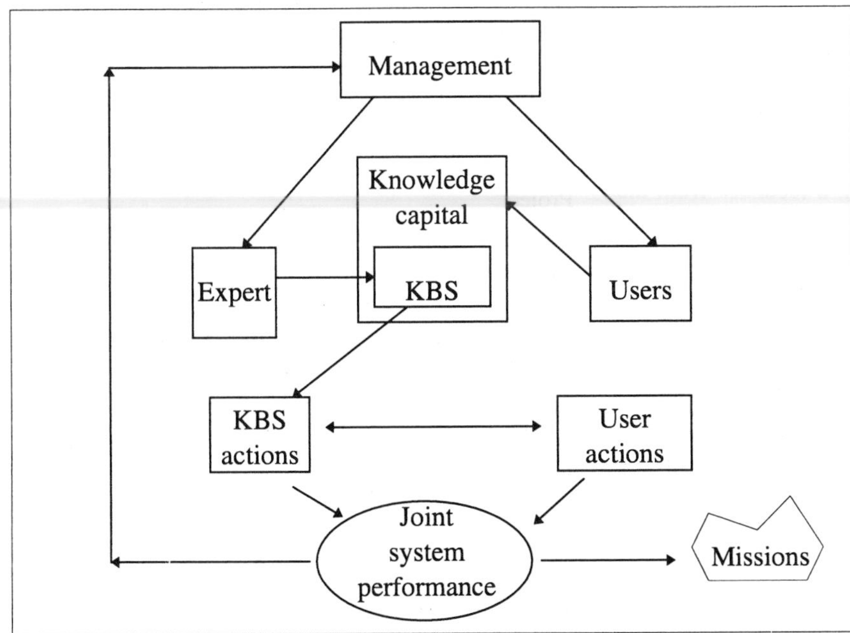

Figure 2. Knowledge-based systems may develop through feedback.

- An answer is possible
- An answer can be obtained in a short period of time
- The answer is not based simply on common sense
- There is a readily accessible expert who can explain how to solve the problem.
- Depth rather than breadth is important
- The information does not change continually
- The system must be able to demonstrate its worth through results, such as increased productivity or lower costs.

Compatibility

It is important that knowledge-based systems, as well as any other computer support, be compatible with existing tasks. If users have to change work routines and if new routines are incompatible with old practices, they will resent the new system, and they will have difficulty learning the new routines required.

Diversity of Perspectives

The demand for diversity of perspectives is a challenging one. It relates to the diversity both of experts and of users. At present, most knowledge-based systems rely on a single perspective. However, experts may have complementary knowledge as well as complementary strategies in solving problems. Some of these may be incompatible with some views and knowledge of the users. At the same time, diversity of perspectives may expand knowledge not only of the users but also of the experts.

Compromises Between Contradictory Maxims

Finally, the compromises to be found concern *inter alia* the ideas of the formal work organization held by managers and the actual work performed by the knowledge workers. This means that the knowledge of a task to be performed may appear quite different from the management point of view and the knowledge workers' perspective. The latter may "override" rules which to them seem unnecessary or find shortcuts which do not comply with the prescribed procedures. Management should have good reasons for sticking to "unnecessary" procedures.

Final Words

In Figure 2 we summarize the concerns from the management's point of view.

An organization has a need to develop its "knowledge capital". Knowledge-based systems offer one technique for doing so. The organization has to be careful with both its experts and the users of the knowledge-based system so that knowledge does not "wither" or get misused. Although all factors mentioned above may be considered, a feedback from the actual joint system performance should be enabled. Thus, the knowledge capital should be considered as evolving, with inputs from users as well as experts, from experience of use as well as from prior domain knowledge. The figure suggests that management is responsible for this development. Other kinds of allocation of responsibilities are, of course, also possible.

The ultimate challenge is to design systems which may solve problems by a combination of human and computer intelligence and then find the right combination of these according to the circumstances. For this endeavor creative cooperation between human factors and technical experts will be necessary.

49.8 References

Airbus may add to A320 safeguards, act to counter crew "over-confidence". (1990). *Aviation Week and Space Technology*, April 30, 59.

Bachant, J.J. and MCDermott, J. (1984). R1 revisited: Four years in the trenches. *AI Magazine,* 5, 21-32.

Bainbridge, L. (1987). The ironies of automation. In. J. Rasmussen, K. Duncan and J. Leplat (Eds.) *New Technology and Human Error*. London: Wiley.

Berry, D. (1994). Involving users in expert system development. *Expert Systems*, 11, 23-28.

Buchanan, B. G., and Shortliffe, E.H. (1984). *Rule-Based Expert Systems*. Addison-Wesley.

Clancey, W. J. (1977). An Antibiotic Therapy Advisor which Provides for Explanations. *Proceedings of 5th International Joint Conference on Artificial Intelligence*, Cambridge, Mass, 858.

Clancey, W.J. (1986). From GUIDON to NEOMYCIN and HERACLES in *Twenty Short Lessons: ORN Final Report* 1979-1985, the AI Magazine, 40-60.

Dalal, N.P. (1994). The design of joint cognitive systems: the effect of cognitive copuling on performance. *International Journal of Human-Computer Studies*, 40, 677-702.

Duda, R.O. and Gaschnig, J.G., (1981). Knowledge-based expert systems coming of age. *Byte* 6 (9), 238-281.

Dreyfus, H.L. and Dreyfus, S.E. (1986). *Mind over Machine. The Power of Human Intuition and Expertise in the Era of the Computer*. New York: The Free Press.

Feigenbaum, E.A. (1980). *Knowledge Engineering: The Applied Side of Artificial Intelligence*. Stanford, Ca: Stanford University: The Heuristic Programming Project.

Feigenbaum, E.A., McCorduck, O. and Nii, P. (1988). *The Rise of the Expert Company*. New York: Times Books.

Fickas, S., and Nagrajan, P. (1988) Critiquing Software Specifications. *IEEE Software*, 5 (6), 37-47.

Fischer, G. (1987). A Critic for LISP. *Proceedings 10th International Joint Conference on Artificial Intelligence,* Milan, 177-184.

Fischer, G., Lemke, A.C., McCall, R., and Morch, A. (1991). The role of critiquing in cooperative problem solving. *ACM Transactions on Information Systems*, 9 (2), 123-151.

Fischer, G., Nakakoji, K., Ostwald, J., Stahl, G., and Summer, T. (1993). Embedding Critics in Integrated Design Environments. *The Knowledge Engineering Review,* 8 (4), 285-307.

Gilbert, D.T., Krull, D.S. and Malone, P.S. (1990). Unbelieving the unbelievable: some problems in the rejection of false information. *Journal of Personality and Social Psychology*, 59 (4), 601-613.

Hägglund, S., and Rankin, I. (1988). Investigating the Usability of Expert Critiquing in Knowledge-Based Consultation Systems. *Proceedings of the ECAI'88 Conference*, Munich, 152-154.

Hägglund, S. (1993). Introducing expert critiquing systems. Guest editor's introduction. The Knowledge Engineering Review, 8(4). 281-284.

Hayes-Roth, F., Waterman, D.A. and Lenat, D.B. (Eds.) (1984). *Building Expert Systems*. Reading, MA: Addison-Wesley.

Holm, P. (1993). A Social and Organisational Perspective on Computerisation, Competence, and Standardisation. Licentiate Thesis, The Department of Computer and Systems Sciences, Stockholm University.

Hutchins, E. (1995). *Cognition in the Wild*. Cambridge: MIT Press.

Kahnemann, D., Slovic, P. and Tversky, A. (1982). *Judgement under Uncertainty: Heuristics and Biases*. London: Cambridge University Press.

Kass, T. and Finin, T. (1988). The Need for User Models in Generating Expert System Explanations. In *International Journal of Expert Systems Research and Applications*, 1, 345-375.

Kelly, V. E. (1984). The CRITTER system: Automated critiquing of digital circuits design. *Proc of the 21st Design Automation Conf*, 419-425.

Keyes, J. (1989). Why expert systems fail. AI Expert, 4, 50-53.

Kidd, A.L. and Cooper, M.B. (1985). Man-machine interface issues in the construction and use of an expert system. International Journal of Man-Machine Studies, 22, 91-102.

Kolodner, J.L. (1993). *Case-Based Reasoning*. Morgan Kaufmann Publishers, Inc.

Langlotz, C. P., and Shortliffe, E. H. (1983). Adapting a consultation system to critique user plans. *International Journal of Man-Machine Studies,* 19, 479-496.

Layton, C., Smith, P.J. and McCoy, C.E. (1994). Design of a cooperative problem-solving system for en-route flight planning: an empirical evaluation. *Human Factors,* 36, 94-119.

Lenorowitz, J.M. (1988). A320 crash investigation centers on crew's judgment during flyby. *Aviation Week and Space Technology*, July 4, 28-29.

Löwgren, J. (1992) The Ignatius Environment. Supporting the Design and Development of Expert System User Interfaces. *IEEE Expert*, 7 (4), 49-57.

Maybury, M. (1992). Communicative acts for explanation generation. *International Journal of Man-Machine Studies,* 37, 135-172.

Metselaar, C. (1994). Matching knowledge-based systems with organizations through user-producer interaction. In: G.E. Bradley and H.W, Hendrick (Eds.) *Human Factors in Organizational Design and Management - IV*. Amsterdam: Elsevier.

Miller, P. (1986). *Expert Critiquing Systems*, Springer Verlag.

Minsky, M. (1975). A Framework for representing knowledge. In. P.H. Winston (Ed.) *The Psychology of Computer Vision.* New York: McGraw-Hill.

Mumford, E. and MacDonald, W,B, (1989). *XSEL's Progress, The Continuing Journey of an Expert System.* Chichester: Wiley.

Nass, C., Steuer, J., Henriksen, L and Dryer, D.C. (1994). Machines, social attributions, and ethopoeia: performance, assessments of computers subsequent to "self" or "other" evaluation. *International Journal of Human-Computer Studies*, 40, 543-559.

Newell, A. and Simon, H.A. (1956). The Logic Theory Machine: a complex information processing system. *IRE Transactions on Information Theory*, IT-2, 61-79.

Newell, A. and Simon, H. (1972). *Human Problem Solving*. Englewood Cliffs, NJ: Prentice-Hall

Pryor, T. A., Gardner, R. M., Clayton, P. D., and Warner, H. R. (1983). The HELP system. *Journal of Medical Systems* 7 (2), 87-102.

Quintanar, L.R., Crowell, C.R., and Pryor, J.B. (1982). Human-Computer interaction: A preliminary social psychological analysis. *Behavior Research Methods and Instrumentation,* 14, 210-220.

Ramberg, R. (1996). Construing and testing explanations in a complex domain. *Computers in Human Behavior*, 12, 1, 29-49.

Rankin, I. (1993). Natural language generation in critiquing. *Knowledge Engineering Review,* 8(4), 329-347.

Richardson, J.J. and DeFries, M.J. (Eds.) (1990). *Intelligent Systems in Business: Integrating the Technology.* Norwood, New Jersey: Ablex.

Schank, R.C. and Abelson, R. (1977). *Plans, Goals, and Understanding*. Hillsdale, NJ: Lawrence Erlbaum Associates

Searle, J. (1984). *Minds, Brains and Science.* Cambridge, Mass: Harvard University Press.

Silverman, B. G. et al., (1987). COPE: A Case Oriented Processing Environment. Proceedings, *European Computing Conference*, Avignon.

Silverman, B. G. (1992a). Survey of Expert Critiquing Systems: Practical and Theoretical Frontiers. Comm. of the ACM, 35 (4), 106-127.

Silverman, B. (1992b). Human-Computer Collaboration. *Human-Computer Interaction,* 7, 165-196.

Silverman, B. (1992c). *Critiquing Human Error.* London: Academic Press.

Southwick, R.W. (1991). Explaining reasoning: an overview of explanation in knowledge-based systems. *The Knowledge Engineering Review*, 1-19.

Suchman, L. A. (1987). *Plans and Situated Action.* Cambridge, Ma: Cambridge University Press.

Sviokla, J.J. 1990. An examination of the impact of expert systems on the firm: the case of XCON, *MIS Quarterly*, 14, 126-140.

Suh, C-K. and Suh, E-H. Using human factor guidelines for developing expert systems. (1993), *Expert Systems*, 10, 151-156.

Swartout, W.R. (1983). XPLAIN: a system for creating and explaining expert consulting programs. *Artificial Intelligence,* 21, 285-325.

Toulmin, S. (1958) *The Uses of Argument.* Cambridge University Press.

Van der Lei, J. (1991). Critiquing based on computer-stored medical records. PhD dissertation, Erasmus University, Rotterdam.

Van Melle, W., Shortliffe, E.H. and Buchanan, B.G. (1981). EMYCIN: a domain-independent system that aids in constructing knowledge-based consultation programs. *Machine Intelligence, Infotech State of the Art Report 9*, no. 3. Pergamon Infotech Ltd.

Wærn, Y., Hägglund, S. and Rankin, I. (1988) Expert Critiquing Systems - Psychological and Computational Aspects of Generating Comments, preprints *4th European Conference on Cognitive Ergonomics*, Cambridge.

Wærn, Y., Hägglund, S., Löwgren, J., Rankin, I., Sokolnicki, T. and Steinemann, A. (1992). Communication Knowledge for Knowledge Communication. *International Journal of Man-Machine Studies*, 37, 215-239.

Wærn, Y. Ramberg, R. and Österlund, B. (1996). On the role of explanations in understanding a complex domain. *Zeitschrift für Psychologie*, in press

Wærn, Y., Hägglund, S., Ramberg, R., Rankin, I., and Harrius, J. (1995). Computational advice and explanations - behavioural and computational aspects. In: K. Nordby, P.H. Helmersen, D.J. Gilmore and S.A. Arnesen (Eds.) *Human-Computer Interaction, Interact '95.* 203-207. London: Chapman & Hall.

Wærn, Y. and Ramberg, R. (1996). People's perception of human and computer advice. *Computers in Human Behavior* 12, 1, 17-27.

Wason, P.C. (1968). On the failure to eliminate hypotheses ... a second look. In P. N. Johnson-Laird and P.C. Wason, (1977). Thinking. *Reading in Cognitive Science.* Cambridge: Cambridge University Press, 241-242.

Will, R.P. (1992). Individual differences in the performance and use of an expert system. *International Journal of Man-Machine Studies*, 37, 173-190.

Winograd, T., Flores, F. (1990) *Understanding Computers and Cognition.* Addison & Wesley Publishing Company, Inc.: Reading, MA.

Woods, D and Roth, E. (1988). Cognitive systems engineering. In M. Helander (Ed.) *Handbook of Human-Computer Interaction,* Elsevier, 3-43.

Zuckerman, M., DePaulo, B.M. and Rosenthal, R. (1981). Verbal and nonverbal communication of deception. In L. Berkowitz (Ed.) *Advances in Experimental Social Psychology,* 14, 1-59. New York: Academic Press.

Handbook of Human-Computer Interaction
Second, completely revised edition
M. Helander, T.K. Landauer, P. Prabhu (eds.)

Chapter 50

Paradigms for Intelligent Interface Design

Emilie M. Roth
Westinghouse Science and Technology Center
Pittsburgh, Pennsylvania, USA

Jane T. Malin
NASA Johnson Space Center
Houston, Texas, USA

Debra L. Schreckenghost
Metrica Inc.
Houston, Texas, USA

50.1 Introduction

With the increased availability of computational power and the technical advances in artificial intelligence there has been a growing interest in applying machine intelligence to higher-level cognitive tasks, such as monitoring, situation assessment, diagnosis, and planning. Early attempts to utilize machine intelligence focused on developing autonomous problem-solving agents (Clancey and Shortliffe, 1984; Miller, 1994). The paradigm was to build "expert systems" to which users would present their problems to be solved.

Over time the conception of how machine intelligence could be deployed has changed and broadened. There has been a growing shift from attempts to develop stand-alone problem-solving systems to attempts to use machine intelligence to create 'intelligent interfaces' that support human cognitive activity (Chignell and Hancock, 1988; Malin, Schreckenghost, Woods, Potter, Johannesen, Holloway and Forbus, 1991; Terveen, 1995). The term 'intelligent interface' has grown to be an umbrella term that covers a wide and diverse range of topics including dialogue understanding, user modeling, adaptive interfaces, cooperative person-machine approaches to problem-solving and decision making, and use of machine intelligence to create more effective explanations and visualizations. An overview of some of the artificial intelligence approaches to design of intelligent interfaces and emerging issues can be found in Terveen (1995). Collections of papers representative of the variety of approaches to the design of intelligent interfaces can be found in Sullivan and Tyler (1991), Gray, Hefley and Murray (1993), and Maybury, (1993a). The common thread among these diverse areas is the use of machine intelligence in the service of human cognitive activities.

In this chapter we use the term 'intelligent interface' to refer both to the design of user interfaces for intelligent systems and the design of user interfaces that utilize knowledge-based approaches. We examine three broad paradigms for development of intelligent interfaces:

- intelligent interfaces as *cognitive tools* that can be utilized by practitioners in solving their problems;
- intelligent interfaces as *members of cooperative person-machine systems* that jointly work on problems and share task responsibility;

intelligent interfaces as *representational aids* that dynamically structure the presentation of information to make key information perceptually salient.

Although each paradigm emphasizes a different use of intelligence to support the user, all paradigms subscribe to human-centered design that yields much commonality in design approach.

The chapter begins with a review of some of the limitations associated with the stand-alone machine problem-solver paradigm that stimulated exploration of alternative paradigms for deployment of machine intelligence. This is followed by a description of each of the three paradigms for intelligent interface design. In each case we present examples of systems that represent that paradigm, and some of the key design principles that derive from that paradigm. While, for expository purposes, the three paradigms are presented as if they were distinct, contrasting, approaches, in fact, as will be seen, these approaches are not mutually exclusive, but rather complementary metaphors that provide converging insights.

50.2 The 'Greek Oracle' Approach to Machine Intelligence: Characteristics and Limitations

Early attempts to utilize machine intelligence focused on developing autonomous problem-solving agents that were intended to make decisions, assessments or selections for the user (Clancey and Shortliffe, 1984; Miller, 1994). Miller and Masarie (1990) coined the term 'Greek Oracle' to describe this approach to decision-aiding. In this paradigm the user is presumed to have limitations in knowledge or processing that cause him or her to be unable to solve a problem. The user turns to the machine expert for help, transferring all relevant information to it. The machine expert then utilizes "superhuman" reasoning to solve the user's problem. Once it is done, the machine expert outputs its answer, and provides an explanation based on "black box" reasoning that is often cryptic to the user. This paradigm has also been referred to as the *prostheses* approach to decision-aiding (Woods, 1986) in that the intelligent system is intended to serve as a replacement or remedy for a presumed deficiency in the user. Figure 1 provides a graphic representation of the relation between the user and the machine expert presumed by the 'Greek Oracle' model. The user is assigned two roles. First, the user serves as a *data gatherer* for the machine expert, providing it with the information it needs to solve the problem. Second, the user serves as a *solution filter*. Because it was recognized that the solution provided by the machine expert would be wrong some percentage of the time, it was assumed that

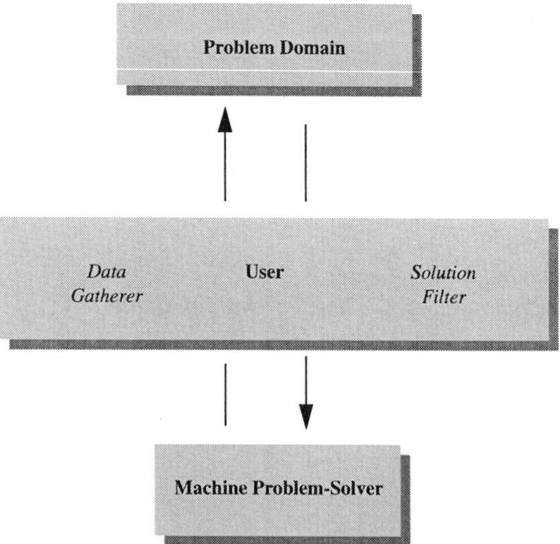

Figure 1. The 'Greek Oracle' or 'prostheses' paradigm assigns the machine the role of autonomous problem solver. *The user is assigned the passive role of data gatherer and solution filter.*

the user would have the responsibility of evaluating the appropriateness of the solution to the situation.

As systems that exemplified the 'Greek Oracle' paradigm began to be fielded, serious limitations with this approach to decision aiding quickly became apparent. Reports of problems with decision-aids built within this paradigm were observed in domains as diverse as medical diagnosis (e.g., Shortliffe, 1982; Miller and Masarie, 1990; Heathfield and Kirkham, 1992), aircraft pilot aids (e.g., Layton, Smith and McCoy, 1994), decision-aids for troubleshooting malfunctioning equipment (e.g., Roth, Bennett and Woods, 1987), and real-time fault management in aerospace domains (e.g., Malin et al., 1991).

Problems observed include:

- *Lack of user acceptance.* Some of the earliest problems noted were reluctance of users to use the systems because of the "data gathering" demands it placed on them. Miller and Masarie (1990) report that physicians could not afford the 30 to 90 minutes of time required to complete a diagnostic consultation with the INTERNIST-I expert system for internal medicine. Langlotz and Shortliffe (1983), developers of ONCOCIN, an expert system designed to assist with the treatment of cancer patients, report similar complaints with the "solution filtering" role assigned to the user. They report that "The most frequent complaint raised by physicians who used ONCOCIN is that they became annoyed with changing or 'overriding' ONCOCIN's treatment suggestion".

- *Brittleness in the face of unanticipated variability.* A more serious limitation of the 'Greek Oracle' approach is that the performance of the systems tended to be *brittle* . The machine experts performed well for the set of cases for which they were designed, but performance broke down when confronted with situations that had not been anticipated by system designers (Guerlain, 1995; Roth, Bennett and Woods, 1987). Unanticipated novelty and variability in situations is a recurrent challenge for design of fully automated systems (Woods and Roth, 1988a; Norman, 1990). Brittleness in the face of unanticipated situations was illustrated in a study by Roth et al. (1987) that examined the performance of technicians diagnosing faults in electro-mechanical devices with the aid of an expert system modeled after the 'Greek Oracle' paradigm. Roth et al. observed 18 cases. In 78% of the cases deviations from the "expected" solution path arose. Sources of unanticipated variability included novel situations beyond the machine's competence, situations where adaptation to special conditions were required, and situations where recovery from human or machine errors was demanded. Contrary to the assumptions of the 'Greek Oracle' model, the technicians did not behave as passive data gatherers for the machine expert. Troubleshooters actively and substantially contributed to the diagnostic process. In cases where the human complied with the passive data gathering role, the joint system performance was degraded.

- *Deskilling/irony of automation.* A related concern with the 'Greek Oracle' paradigm is that having the machine expert solve problems for the user reduces the opportunity for users to utilize and sharpen their skills. This raises a concern of deskilling -- that reliance on the machine expert will reduce user's level of competence. Paradoxically, the 'Greek Oracle' paradigm assigns the user the role of *solution filter.* The users are expected to detect and deal with the cases that are beyond the capability of the machine expert, which are presumably the most difficult cases, even though they don't have the opportunity to work through the simpler cases. Bainbridge (1983) coined the term "irony of automation" to describe a parallel dilemma that she observed in the early introduction of automation.

- *Biasing human decision process.* A final concern with the 'Greek Oracle' paradigm is that the introduction of a machine expert can alter users' cognitive and decision processes in ways that decrease their effectiveness as solution filters. There have been several empirical studies that have compared the performance of individuals performing cognitive tasks with and without the aid of an expert system or other decision-aid that generated a problem solution. A consistent finding is that the availability of such an expert system alters people's information gathering activities, and narrows the set of hypotheses that they consider, increasing the likelihood that they will miss critical information or fail to generate the correct solution in cases where the expert system's recommendation is wrong (Endestad, Holmstroem and Volden, 1992; Guerlain, 1993; Layton, Smith and McCoy, 1994; Mosier, Palmer and Degani, 1992; Parasuraman, Molloy and Singh, 1993). As example a recent study of airline pilots and dispatchers showed that in a scenario where the computer's recommendation was poor, the generation of a suggestion by the computer early in the person's own problem solving produced a 30% increase in inappropriate plan selection over users of a version of the system that provided no recommendation (Layton et al., 1994).

Experience with decision-aids built on the 'Greek Oracle' paradigm highlighted the importance of considering the performance of the joint person-machine system in designing and evaluating intelligent aids (Woods, 1986). Performance is a function of the contributions of both the human and machine components of the joint or distributed cognitive system (Hutchins, 1995; Roth, Bennet and Woods, 1987; Sorkin and Woods, 1985; Woods and Roth, 1988a; Woods, 1996). The people on the scene have access to real-time information and common-sense knowledge not available to the machine. Their contribution to successful joint system performance, particularly in unanticipated situations, is substantial. At the same time, it is important to consider how the introduction of the intelligent machine affects the human's cognitive processes, and what new cognitive demands are introduced.

The shift in focus to the performance of joint cognitive systems in turn has led to a shift in emphasis from building stand-alone problem-solvers to developing intelligent interfaces that facilitate human cognitive performance. The shift in emphasis has changed the questions asked from how to compute better solutions to how to determine what assistance is useful, and how

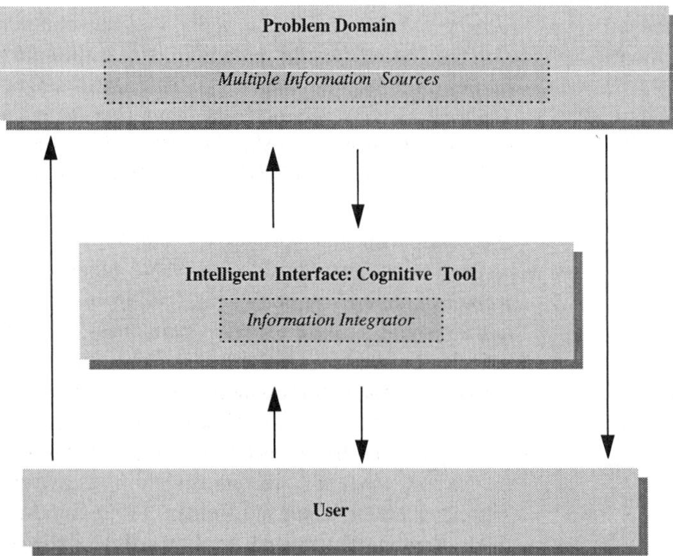

Figure 2. The 'Cognitive Tool' paradigm for intelligent interface design. *This paradigm emphasizes the use of machine intelligence to create new integrated sources of information for the human problem-solver who has the responsibility to produce an overall solution, and has access to additional sources of information not available to the intelligent machine.*

to situate it and deliver it in the interface (Fischer and Reeves, 1992; Terveen, 1993).

In the next sections we describe three paradigms for intelligent interfaces that have emerged:

- cognitive tools that can be wielded in support of human decision-making;
- elements of cooperative person-machine systems for accomplishing cognitive tasks;
- dynamic representational aids that support problem solution by making key information perceptually salient.

These three paradigms should not be viewed as mutually distinct approaches. They represent alternative metaphors that provide converging insights into the features required for intelligent support of human problem-solving and decision-making tasks.

50.3 Intelligent Interfaces as Cognitive Tools

One intelligent interface paradigm that has emerged is the use of machine intelligence to develop *cognitive tools* (Woods, 1986; Woods and Roth, 1988a). The cognitive tool approach emphasizes the active role of the person in the system. The metaphor is one of competent practitioners wielding intelligent tools to respond adaptively to the many different circumstances and problems that can arise (Woods, 1996).

Figure 2 illustrates the relation of the person and intelligent interface in the cognitive tool paradigm. The intelligent interface is viewed as a source of information for the person who has the responsibility to produce an overall solution, with the explicit recognition that the person has access to other sources of knowledge and information not available to the machine.

Instead of thinking of the intelligent system's output as an "answer" to the problem, the cognitive tool metaphor emphasizes the use of machine intelligence to create new integrated sources of information for the human problem-solver. Machine intelligence is deployed to produce better (e.g., processed) information (data synthesis), to support information management, and to help the person overcome data overload. Responsibility for problem solution resides with the person, who serves as a manager of knowledge resources that can vary in the kind and amount of "intelligence" (Malin et al., 1991).

A recent review of intelligent fault management systems in the aerospace domain supports the cognitive tool perspective (Malin et al., 1991; Malin, Schreckenghost and Rhoads, 1993). Intelligent systems that attempted to improve on human capabilities by providing an omniscient advisor inevitably drew wrong conclusion on occasion, since it is impossible to predict all possible circumstances that might occur in this complex, highly dynamic domain. Such inconsistent systems were quickly deemed unreliable by users. Further, when the systems were introduced as stand-alone aids that were independent of other sources of fault management data, they exacerbated the existing data overload problem, by creating yet another information channel that needed to be tracked. In contrast, the more successful aerospace intelligent system applications functioned more as cognitive tools in the hands of expert practitioners (Malin et al., 1991). Machine intelligence was deployed to provide better visualization of the monitored process, better information handling capabilities that avoided data overload problems, and conceptualization aids that allowed the user to search for and discover patterns in the data.

A trend toward utilizing machine intelligence to create cognitive tools has also been observed in medical applications (Heathfield and Kirkham, 1992; Miller, 1994; Miller, McNeil, Challinor, Masarie and Myers, 1986). Miller and Masarie (1990) have argued that tools "which are malleable under the physician's guidance to suit the complex needs of a specific problem" are more likely to be accepted. They have proposed an aiding paradigm based on development of intelligent tools for providing and managing diagnostic information (Miller and Masarie, 1990; Miller, et al., 1986).

An example of this approach is the Quick Medical Reference (QMR), a successor to the INTERNIST-I expert system for internal medicine (Miller, et al., 1986). QMR is an example of a cognitive tool that is intended to improve diagnostic accuracy and efficiency by providing easy access to information and tools for managing diagnostic information. It can be used as an electronic textbook, an information retrieval tool, or a sophisticated analytic tool. For example it can be used to retrieve disease profile summaries that would take a week or two to produce from primary sources. It can also be used to support particular steps in a physician's diagnosis. Examples include connecting seemingly unrelated findings; having the user assert one or more diagnoses as being present in a patient and then processing the residual unexplained findings; and providing critiques of user-entered hypotheses.

50.4 Intelligent Interfaces as Elements of Cooperative Systems

A second paradigm for deployment of machine intelligence is based on the metaphor of cooperative teams. The focus is on developing intelligent, semi-autonomous, machine agents that participate as cooperative members of distributed person-machine systems for accomplishing cognitive tasks (Hutchins, 1995; Malin et al., 1991). Within this paradigm the machine agent alternatively takes the role of a subordinate to whom specific cognitive activities are delegated (e.g., Sheridan, 1988); a colleague who provides a consulting or critiquing role (Fischer, Lemke, Mastaglio and Morch, 1991); or a member of a team of individuals with different skills and responsibilities all working toward a common goal (Malin, et al., 1991; Jones and Mitchell, 1995).

The principles for design of cooperative systems have drawn on analyses of human-human consulting situations (e.g., Alty and Coombs, 1980; Fischer and Reeves, 1992; Gadd, 1995; Pollack, Hirschberg and Webber, 1982), naturalistic studies examining the behavior of human teams (e.g., Hutchins, 1990; Roth, Mumaw and Lewis, 1994; Roth, in press; ; Johannesen, Cook and Woods, 1994), and psycholinguistic theory, including conversational analysis (Clark and Brennan, 1991; Grice, 1975). A recurrent finding in studies of human-human interaction is the importance of participants having a common understanding of the situation and of each other's intentions and actions. This is referred to as a *common ground* or a *shared frame of reference*. Communication breakdowns occur when participants engaged in problem solving do not have access to the same information about situation state or to the response strategy of other participants (Roth et al., 1987).

A central tenet of the cooperative system paradigm is the need to provide team members with shared knowledge of the current situation and the goals and actions of participants, both human and machine. General ways to create a shared frame of reference are to use external representations, available to all participants, to make assessments and behavior evident, and to present advice in the context of these situation representations. This function is most often achieved through the use of graphic interfaces that provide a shared external representation of the problem state and a means for communicating the goals and activities of team members. Figure 3 illustrates the role of a shared external representation in supporting communication and coordination among human and intelligent machine agents in the cooperative system paradigm.

Below we review two approaches to providing systems that cooperate with humans. One approach has been to develop critiquing systems that take on the role that a "colleague" or "mentor" might play by critiquing human-generated solutions. The second approach draws on the concept of multi-person teams and focuses on developing intelligent systems that act as good team players.

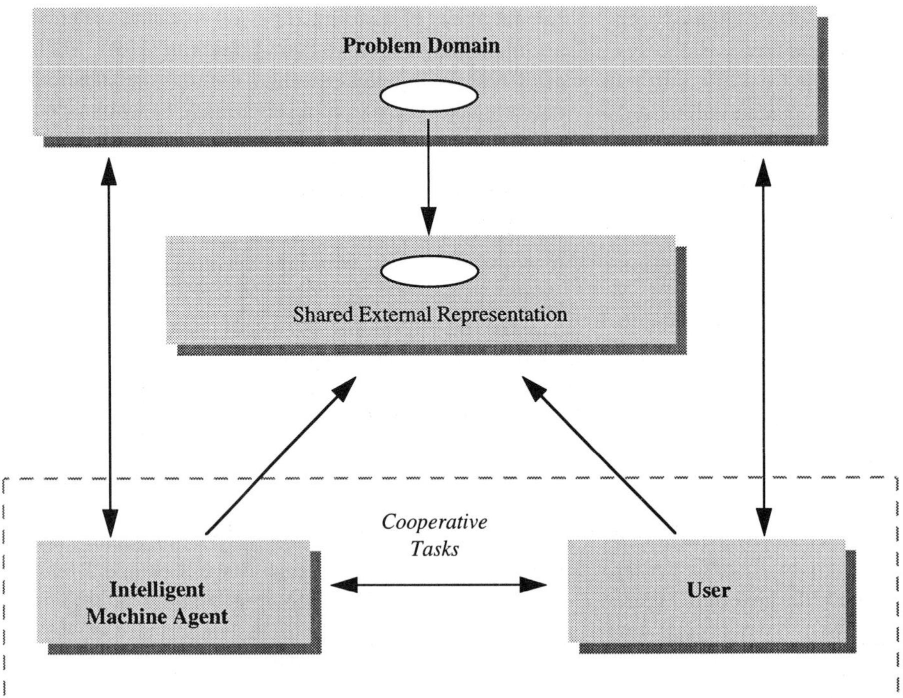

Figure 3. The 'Cooperative System' paradigm for intelligent interface design. *In this paradigm, semiautonomous intelligent agents participate as cooperative members of distributed person-machine problem-solving systems. A common feature of cooperative systems is the use graphic interfaces that provide shared external representations to support communication and coordination among team members, both human and machine.*

50.4.1 Critiquing Systems

Critiquing systems are computer programs that examine a human generated solution and offer advice if the solution is deemed incomplete or incorrect (Fischer, Lemke, Mastaglio and Morch, 1990; Fischer, 1994; Fischer, Nakakoji and Ostwald, 1995; Guerlain and Smith, 1996; Miller, 1986; Silverman, 1992). Such a system is analogous to a human "colleague" or "mentor" who might look over the shoulder of the user and offer occasional advice (Fischer et al., 1990). Types of advice offered might include alerting the person to errors or oversights, suggesting relevant issues to consider, and filling in details that were not fully specified.

A critiquing system is an example of a cooperative system in that the person and intelligent machine work jointly on problem solving , applying their expertise in context. The critiquing system structures its analysis and feedback around the proposed solution generated by the person. This contrasts with the 'Greek Oracle' model where the computer outputs a solution, without regard to the person's current state of problem-solving.

Critics can be passive, coming into play only when invoked by a user, or they can be active, continuously monitoring user performance and interjecting critiques when they notice a problem or have suggestion. They can work in batch mode, processing the entire solution after the user has finished, or they can work incrementally. Spelling and grammar checkers that the user invokes in batch mode are examples of simple, passive critics. Context-sensitive help messages in word processor and CAD packages are examples of simple active critics; as are automatic correcting features that are beginning to appear in word processors that flag spelling errors and correct capitalization as the user types.

The critiquing approach was pioneered by Perry Miller (1986) who developed medical applications. Early examples of critiquing systems utilized a passive, batch mode, critiquing approach. ATTENDING, a critiquing system developed by Perry Miller for anesthesiology problems, had physicians enter patient data as well as their proposed diagnoses and treatment. The computer then generated a critique of the proposed solution. A similar critiquing approach was used by Langlotz and Shortliffe (1983) who adapted their diag-

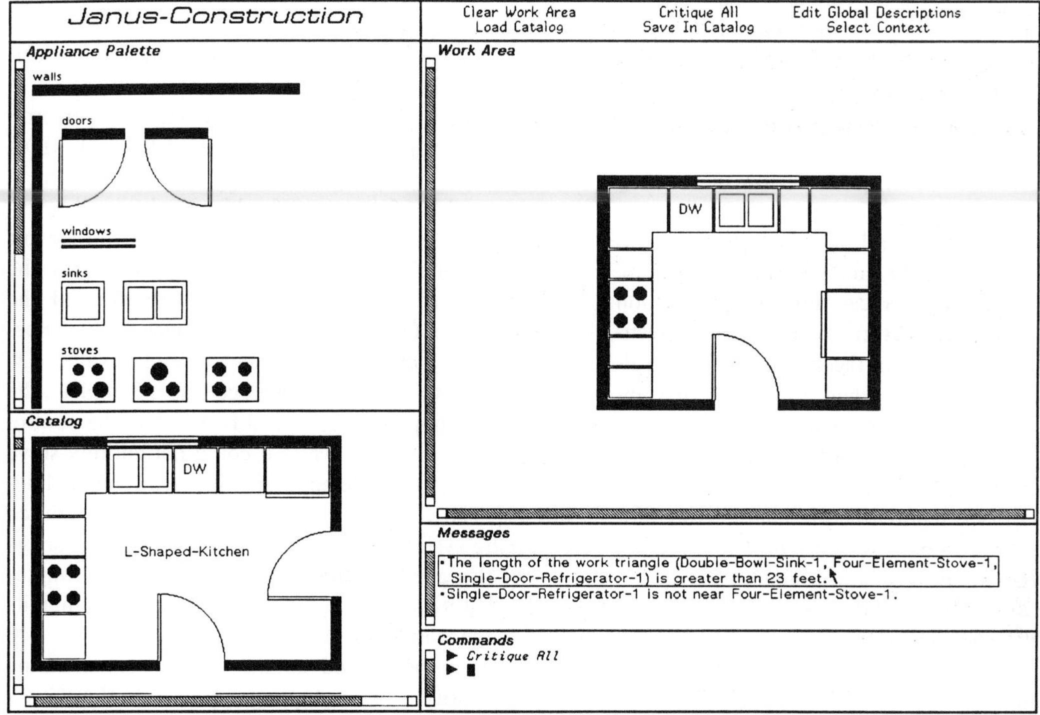

Figure 4. ***An illustration of the JANUS graphic interface*** *(Fischer, 1994). Building blocks (design units) are selected from the Palette and moved to desired locations inside the Work Area. Designers can also use complete floor plans from the Catalog. The Messages pane displays critic messages automatically after each design change that triggers a critic. Clicking with the mouse on a message displays the argumentation related to that message.*

nostic expert system for cancer treatment, ONCOCIN, to be a critiquing system.

More recent approaches to critiquing employ active critics that monitor users during the problem-solving process, offering critiques and suggestions as appropriate (Fischer et al., 1990; Guerlain, Smith, Obradovish, Smith, Rudmann, and Strohm, 1995; Terveen, 1993). Typically these systems include graphic interfaces that provide a workspace within which users construct their solutions. The workspace provides an environment that is inspectable by both the human and machine agents. It serves as a shared external representation that enables person-computer cooperation to take place through the manipulation of graphic objects. Machine critics are able to identify the need for intervention based on the state of objects in the external representation. In turn, they deliver their advice by manipulating the display of objects in the workspace. Terveen (1993) has coined the term 'collaborative manipulation' to describe this style of cooperative system.

An example of collaborative manipulation is the JANUS system that supports the design of residential kitchens (Fischer et al., 1990; Fischer, 1994). JANUS provides an integrated graphic environment in which users construct kitchen designs. During the design session, JANUS uses knowledge of building codes, safety standards, and functional preferences as triggering events to critique a user's design as it evolves. Critics detect suboptimal designs, provide explanations for their "opinion" and suggest alternative solutions. Figure 4 provides an illustration of the JANUS graphic user interface.

A second example of collaborative manipulation is a tool for building knowledge bases called the HITS Knowledge Editor (HKE) that was developed at the MCC Human Interface Laboratory (Terveen, 1993). Users build knowledge structures using a sketch tool that provides a shared external representation of the state of the task. By inspecting partial knowledge structures, HKE is able to infer missing information based on the usage of objects in the sketch and the information in the knowledge base; catch inconsistencies between the sketch and the knowledge base; and suggest additional issues for users to consider. When HKE identifies potential advice, it annotates the relevant object in the sketch with a resource that explains the situation, and suggests ways to deal with it. If the user agrees, HKE updates the display of objects in the sketch to reflect the accepted suggestion.

A noteworthy feature of the HKE system is that users are not forced to interrupt their flow of thinking to make an immediate decision about accepting the suggestion of a critic. Since all information is continuously visible in the display, and objects that require attention are flagged, users can turn their attention away from an issue, and return to it at their convenience. Embedding critiques in the graphic interface allows advice to be delivered when a problem first appears and is fresh in the user's mind, while not forcing an interruption that might disrupt the ongoing train of thought and run the risk of the user losing track of an issue. Terveen (1993) reports that an alternative editor that used sequential menus or query-based dialogues, increased rather than decreased user cognitive load because they forced users to shift from their main concern to consider issues of lesser importance.

A third critiquing system that exemplifies cooperative problem solving is the Antibody Identification Assistant (AIDA) that aids medical technologists in solving antibody identification cases (Guerlain et al., 1995). AIDA is particularly noteworthy because it was the subject of a series of elegant controlled laboratory studies that empirically examined the effect of critiquing systems on human problem-solving performance (Geurlain, 1993; Guerlain, 1995; Guerlain and Smith, 1996). The studies provide some of the first empirical evidence that critiquing is potentially a more effective approach to aiding human decision making and design than the 'Greek Oracle' model.

AIDA provides a graphic interface that allows practitioners to solve antibody identification cases on the computer in a way similar to how they currently perform the task with paper forms. Through use of the interface, the person provides the information the critiquer needs to detect problems and provide feedback. The AIDA graphic user interface provides another example of collaborative manipulation, in that communication between the person and machine is a natural byproduct of task performance.

Guerlain and her colleagues (Guerlain, 1993; Guerlain, 1995; Guerlain and Smith, 1996) performed two empirical studies examining the effect of AIDA on the ability of practitioners to solve antibody identification cases. An important feature of the studies is that they included cases that the machine expert was able to solve (i.e., cases within its competence) and cases for which its strategies were inappropriate (i.e., cases beyond its competence). This enabled the studies to examine the effect of the aiding system on human decision making in both types of situations.

One study (Guerlain, 1995), compared performance of a group of subjects who used the full AIDA system with critiquing features turned on (treatment group), to that of a group of subjects who used a version of AIDA with the critiquing features turned off (control group). The treatment group, that had the benefit of critiquing, significantly outperformed the control group. On cases where AIDA was fully competent, outcome errors were completely eliminated. On the case where AIDA's knowledge was incomplete, the treatment group still performed better than the control group because AIDA, while it could not entirely solve the problem, could detect errors in user-generated solutions. The results highlight that a carefully crafted critiquing system can be effective in eliminating errors it was designed to catch, and perhaps more importantly, that it can be helpful even on cases for which its knowledge is incomplete.

Guerlain performed another study demonstrating the superiority of the critiquing approach to the 'Greek Oracle' model of decision support (Guerlain, 1993). The study compared the performance of subjects solving antibody identification problems with the aid of, in one case, a system that critiqued user solutions, and in the other case, a partially automated system that generated solutions for the user. There was no statistical difference in performance between the two aiding approaches for cases for which the system's knowledge was competent; however, in the case where the system's knowledge was incomplete, performance was significantly better with the critiquing system.

More detailed examination of performance on the case that was beyond the system's competence revealed that users of the partially automated system were unable to detect when the strategy used by the computer was inappropriate to the situation. This was variously due to inability to follow the computer's line of reasoning (because of a lack of knowledge or inaccurate mental models of the aiding system), and over-reliance on the computer resulting in failures to critically evaluate the system's solution. In contrast, when the computer was assigned the role of critiquer, the critiquing interactions provided an opportunity for the user to learn the system's knowledge and strategies and how they differed from those of the user. This enabled users to recognize situations where the computer's strategy was inappropriate and ignore its advice, relying instead on their own strategies to solve the problem.

Silverman (1992) has expanded the concept of a critiquing system to include features intended to prevent errors, in addition to critics intended to catch and correct errors. He has developed a taxonomy of critiquing approaches, and conducted empirical studies examining the impact of different types of critics on human performance. Silverman has argued that critiquing systems should include a library of functions intended to prevent and correct errors. These include *influencers,* that provide guidance before or during a task to help prevent reasoning errors; *debiasers,* that alert users to errors and suggest corrective action after the error occurs; and *directors,* that walk users through task steps, in cases where they are unable to perform the task on their own. He has proposed that critiquing systems should include a "decision network" of functions in which redundant strategies interrupt the user only if earlier strategies fail to remove an error. Silverman has developed and empirically tested critiquing systems embodying these concepts.

Silverman's studies (1992) suggest value in including influencers as well as debiasers in critiquing systems. He compared performance on two versions of a critiquing system designed to help people avoid common biases when interpreting word problems that involved multiplicative probability. One version included only debiasers. The second version included influencers as well as debiasers. The results showed substantial benefit from the inclusion of influencers in addition to debiasers.

Some general principles can be drawn from review of critiquing systems. First, there is substantial evidence that critiquing is more effective in supporting human decision-making than the 'Greek Oracle' model. Second, a factor that appears to be instrumental to the success of critiquing systems is the availability of an external representation of problem state that is inspectable by both the person and machine agents. Successful critiquing systems include a graphic workspace within which users construct their solutions, and critics provide their advice. Third, developing critiquing systems shifts the questions asked from how to compute advice to what are the situations where advice may be needed, and what form should that advice take. Answering these questions requires careful analysis of how practitioners go about their work, including assessment of what strategies they use; what types of errors are commonly made and what factors contribute to those errors; and what techniques can be used to prevent or correct errors (Jordan and Henderson, 1995; Roth and Woods, 1989).

Some of the advantages of the critiquing approach include:

- It preserves the user's accustomed role;
- It is less likely to cause loss of skill, and may even result in learning from the critiques;
- It has the potential to provide effective support even when there is less than perfect knowledge of the domain and/or of the person's solution;
- It is less likely to make performance worse in cases beyond its competence.

50.4.2 Intelligent Systems as Team Players

A second approach to development of cooperative systems draws on the analogy of multi-person teams. The goal is to understand the factors that contribute to successful team performance and develop systems that enable person and machine agents to work as effective teams. In contrast to the critiquing approach, where the person is allocated the entire cognitive task, and the machine expert serves as critiquer, in the cooperative team approach, the machine agent is allocated a portion of the cognitive tasks, and the human and machine agents work as a team, coordinating their activities toward a common goal. This paradigm has been particularly influential in complex dynamic system management domains (e.g., space flight control; aircraft digital auto pilot; military command and control centers; medical operating rooms; power plant control rooms).

The nature of complex, dynamic domain situations makes human-computer teamwork essential. The human team member provides necessary expertise and judgment that cannot be compensated for with automation. The software team member is necessary to reduce human workload and to provide the human with a view of the "inaccessible" aspects of system and situation. Domains requiring human-computer teamwork have the following characteristics:

- *Domain Inaccessibility and Response Criticality*: Domain inaccessibility can result from remotely located processes, hazardous conditions, "black box" or proprietary design, and scales disproportionate to human manipulation. Such domains can be difficult to observe and control, due to data noise or dropout, and design limitations on sensing, effecting and communications bandwidth. These factors exacerbate situations where safety concerns increase risk. An intelligent software team member can complement human skills by performing tasks not suited to human intervention (e.g., automating time-critical tasks (Jones and Mitchell, 1995)).

- *Operational Complexity*: Human workload often increases during critical phases of domain operation (e.g., anomaly response, high risk operations like aircraft take-off and landing) due to additional tasks, time-constraints on task completion, and greater task difficulty (Tenney, Rogers and Pew, 1995). During such phases, multiple continuous situations must be managed in parallel (e.g., respond to an anomaly while maintaining basic operating capability (Woods, 1994)). Additionally, the domain system often moves through a series of complex configurations of human and machine operations and services in response to the critical situation. Human teamwork is an effective way for operators to manage workload during high-activity, critical operations (Roth, Mumaw and Lewis, 1994). These teamwork concepts can be extended to human-computer cooperation.
- *Variability of Situation:* The intelligent software will sometimes draw wrong or irrelevant conclusions because it reflects standard operating procedures in response to typical domain behavior. But situations outside of such typical behavior occur in complex domains. A human supervisor must be able to override or take over from intelligent software that has failed in situations outside of its designed function (Tenney, Rogers and Pew, 1995).

Effective intelligent interface software for complex dynamic system management domains supports collaborative human-computer teamwork and cooperative human-computer problem-solving (Malin et al, 1991; Jones and Mitchell, 1995; Johannesen, Cook and Woods, 1994). Systems developed within this paradigm are human-centered, highly interactive, and share responsibility for task performance with human team members, under the assumption that the human and machine agent provide essential but overlapping expertise (Johannesen, Cook and Woods, 1994).

In the cooperative team approach, intelligent software may accomplish some portion of the human cognitive tasks or assist the human in reasoning about or evaluating the performance of these tasks. Examples of tasks allocated to the intelligent software team member include system configuration, monitoring and situation assessment (what Jones and Mitchell (1995) refer to as "bookkeeping" or vigilance tasks), decision support for the human during critical operational phases (problem isolation and testing, response planning), and performance of time-critical safing operations. Thus, team player automation changes the nature of the task but does not exclude the human from task performance. The result is a joint human-machine cognitive system (Woods, Roth and Bennett, 1990).

This concept of an intelligent software team member is a departure from earlier typical "expert" systems that were designed to know more than the human and be super-humanly able to take over when the human could not cope. Instead, the intelligent software is designed for *group interaction* during task performance. Such software coordinates with human plans and tasks without being able to accomplish them alone (c.f., the Shared Plan of Lochbaum, Grosz and Sidner, 1990). It is "cognizant" of other activities in a flexible task context, and is able to pick up tasks from the human when asked, or may volunteer help when appropriate (what Johannesen et al., 1994, call providing "unprompted information"; note the relationship to the critiquing systems in section 50.4.1). The software team member can handle interruption and supports the strategy of "divide and conquer" to make complex tasks tractable (Roth, Mumaw and Lewis, 1994). Such human-computer collaboration requires frequent, synchronized interaction and flexible allocation of roles among team members. In such a team, the human and the intelligent software share responsibility for *task performance*, but the human team leader remains responsible for achieving *task goals* (Tenney, Rogers and Pew, 1995).

This team-player paradigm changes interface requirements, affecting both the information presented to the human and the interaction with the underlying software functionality. In this section we describe design principles for building intelligent software that is a *team player* (that effectively supports the human-computer team concept, Malin and Schreckenghost, 1992). These design principles address four required characteristics of team player systems:

- *Support for the human as the team leader.* The intelligent software should "defer" to human authority by responding to human control. This can include asking for advice and taking correction from the human, and providing informative assessments of its own state and activities.
- *Reliable and consistent performance.* The intelligent software should take predictable actions, and provide consistent and clear assessments of situation. It should avoid potentially harmful actions in unusual or unexpected situations.
- *Coordination and dynamic task sharing.* Intelligent interaction requires supporting flexible team member roles and task allocations. To enable effective communication during shared or coordinated ac-

tivity, it is important to maintain shared knowledge (common ground) and make intelligent software functioning apparent (software intelligibility).

- *Cooperative communication.* The interface is a communication medium for new information for both the human and the intelligent system. By representing domain knowledge in a situation context, the intelligent software supports developing a shared understanding of a situation and its relevance. Team members no longer need to maintain all possible relevant knowledge, because the interface supports efficient communication of relevant knowledge in context.

We discuss design principles for each of these team player characteristics in the remainder of this section. This discussion includes design guidance and illustrations of this guidance. For more information see related work by Malin et al., 1991; Jones and Mitchell, 1995; Johannesen, Cook and Woods, 1994; and Terveen, 1993.

Principles for Effective Design

The role of intelligent systems as team players provides a constraining framework for design of both the intelligent system and its user interface. We discuss principles that support each of four defining characteristics of team-player intelligent systems.

- A team player is a good follower: directable, supervisable, supportive;
- A team player is reliable: predictable, dependable and correctable;
- A team player is a good coordinator: directable, timely and non-interfering;
- A team player is a good communicator: relevant and efficient.

The design principles focus on using the intelligence of the system to achieve these team player characteristics while keeping the primary domain tasks in the foreground and not increasing human workload or distraction. Sources for these design principles include theoretical arguments (e.g., Suchman, 1987; Woods and Roth, 1988a; Norman, 1990; Terveen, 1993), studies of interaction with intelligent systems (e.g., Roth, Bennett, and Woods, 1988; Jones and Mitchell, 1995), studies of human teams (Johannesen, Cook and Woods, 1994; Roth, Mumaw and Lewis, 1994; Roth, in press), surveys of users (Tenney, Rogers and Pew, 1995), and studies of successful intelligent system designs (Malin et al., 1991). There is striking common agreement on these characteristics and design principles in several relevant domains, including process control, medicine and aviation.

A Team Player is a Good Follower. A common theme in the design of team-player intelligent systems is human-centered automation, in which the intelligent system is subordinate to the human. Humans perform dual roles, both as team members responsible to perform tasks and as supervisors or leaders who manage the activities and performance of the team. This role definition reflects the risk and task difficulty in complex environments that has led to the formation of human teams with designated leaders (see Roth and Woods, 1988; Miller and Masarie, 1990; Roth, Mumaw and Lewis, 1994). In such environments, operators have experienced problems with intelligent systems designed for more dominant roles (see Roth and Woods, 1989; Billings, 1991; Diamond et al., 1995). Since humans and computers have many different and compensating strengths, it is often more effective for intelligent systems in complex domains to assume roles that complement human capabilities rather than replace human capabilities (which can be a difficult technical challenge).

There are a number of ways that intelligent systems manifest "good follower" characteristics. In the medical field, such an intelligent system would provide useful, "catalyzing" information to help a physician complete a difficult step in the diagnostic process, rather than solve the whole problem while the physician passively observes (Miller and Masarie, 1990). In dynamic fault management applications, the intelligent system is guided by the human team leader (Malin and Schreckenghost, 1992) who retains authority and responsibility for achieving task goals (Jones and Mitchell, 1995). In aviation, human-centered automation (Billings, 1991; Tenney, Rogers and Pew, 1995) complements human strengths and weaknesses while the pilot retains task responsibility and command authority.

There are three main tenets for designing intelligent systems supporting human authority. First, the human team member has command authority, including the authority to delegate tasks either exclusively to the intelligent system or supporting a mixed initiative for certain types of aiding. Second, the human has responsibility for supervision and correction of the intelligent system. Finally, the subordinate intelligent system fulfills an aiding role, providing information to assist the responsible human in developing an understanding of the big picture or situation (Tenney, Rogers and Pew, 1995).

The design of a system that is a good follower in a human-centered automation team is a by-product of de-

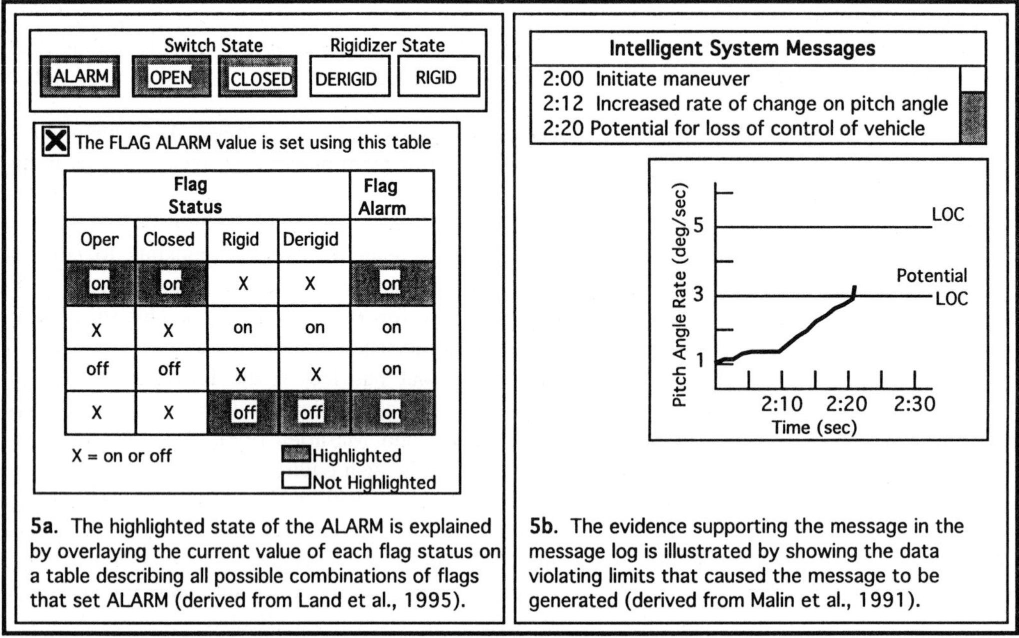

5a. The highlighted state of the ALARM is explained by overlaying the current value of each flag status on a table describing all possible combinations of flags that set ALARM (derived from Land et al., 1995).

5b. The evidence supporting the message in the message log is illustrated by showing the data violating limits that caused the message to be generated (derived from Malin et al., 1991).

Figure 5. An open system provides evidence underlying its conclusions.

veloping a system that has the three remaining characteristics of a team player system. Support for supervision and correction results from building *reliable* systems. Support for task sharing and delegation is addressed by designing for team *coordination*. Support for providing information to assist human domain and supervisory tasks, including situation assessment, results from designing for effective *communication*. Each of these topics is discussed in the remainder of this section.

A Team Player is Reliable. In uncertain, complex and risky environments, a reliable team member can be trusted to do what is expected consistently and, in the worst case, to degrade gracefully by supporting correction to avoid harmful or interfering effects, or by easing hand-over of tasks to other team members. We discuss two major approaches to achieving such reliability. First, openness (Jones and Mitchell, 1995) and observability of functioning can make the system predictable. Second, robustness to difficulties can make the system dependable.

Openness and observability of system functioning helps humans in establishing clear expectations of system behavior, and avoids building "chatty" systems that distract the user and add to workload. Suchman (1987), Terveen (1993) and Johannesen et al (1994) propose that understanding of a tool or system can be achieved implicitly by making functioning apparent or easily discoverable. One way to accomplish this is by providing an external representation that is inspectable by both the human and machine agent as was discussed in Section 50.4.1. A related approach is to make the intelligent system's reasoning apparent by informing the user of the evidence supporting its conclusions, as shown in Figure 5.

Designing for openness encourages the development of systems that are easier to understand and predict (essential characteristics of useful automation, according to airline pilots, Tenney, Rogers and Pew, 1995). Such openness helps the human operator understand what the intelligent system is capable of doing, what it is doing at any given time (and why), and how its activities affect other members of the team. It is easier to detect when an open system is in a situation outside its boundaries of competence. A representation shared between the human and the intelligent system can assist the human in understanding and advising the intelligent system. Methods for designing open systems are discussed further in the sections on good team-player Coordination and Communication.

Robustness can be achieved either by compensating for intelligent system anomalies or correcting them. Unexpected process behavior or environmental conditions may lead the intelligent system to behave in an anomalous manner (e.g., failing to detect an important event), or the human operator to alter accepted procedures (e.g., executing a contingency procedure unknown to the intelligent system). In such situations, the first strategy for robustness is to alert the team of uncertainty in conclusions and to provide redundant capabilities, so that the degraded situation can be detected and handled gracefully (with minimum impact to the team). For example, the DESSY system, used for Space Shuttle flight control, marks conclusions as provisional when related data are inconsistent (Land et al., 1995). This type of robustness can pose challenging design problems, and impose additional requirements on the system's reasoning and representation.

If the situation cannot be handled gracefully, a reliable intelligent system will either support alternate ways of accomplishing its tasks or assist human repair of the intelligent system for continued operations. To ensure that the intelligent system doesn't obstruct operations in such situations, the human should at least be able to disable the intelligent system and perform its tasks (i.e., reallocate intelligent system tasks to the human). Providing for task reallocation is the most common approach to robustness today. Task reallocation can range from a partial reallocation (e.g., disable a portion of a rule base) to a complete override of all task responsibilities (e.g., turn off the intelligent system).

An intelligent system embedded in a larger support system should permit access to information and provide support for a human to take over intelligent system tasks when the intelligent system is disabled. The disabled state of the intelligent system should also be clearly identified on the display. For example, when higher level processing is "disabled" in the DESSY system (Land et al., 1995), it continues to provide basic sensor data, but a gray shade is used to de-emphasize the portions of the display showing the high level situation assessments of the intelligent system.

The second approach, repair of the intelligent system, can be performed by the human or the intelligent system (i.e., self repair). Repairs may include modifying or correcting intelligent system activities, reasoning, or the information it uses. The characteristics of system openness and subordinate systems support the human in repairing the intelligent system. Openness of functioning assists the human in understanding intelligent system activities leading up to the error (why the error occurred). Designing a system that is a "good follower" helps the human in monitoring the effectiveness of the repair.

Although real-time repair of intelligent systems is beyond the capability of most systems today, a limited form of repair can be achieved by designing for the human to correct "bad" data used by the intelligent system (e.g., override noisy data values causing the intelligent system to make wrong conclusions). The intelligent system may also perform some type of self repair, such as designating conclusions as provisional until confirming evidence is observed, or retracting conclusions based on data later deemed to be bad. This type of self repair can sometimes be accomplished without complex self assessment by the intelligent system. Future capabilities for repair include providing more sophisticated self assessment, and support for the human to alter the knowledge and reasoning of the intelligent system in real time, permitting a form of on-the-job training of the intelligent system by the human. Providing these capabilities is likely be a significant challenge to the developers of intelligent systems.

A Team Player is a Good Coordinator. A team provides the opportunity to simultaneously perform multiple tasks and pursue multiple objectives. Such teamwork is often essential in coping with time-critical problems in complex environments (cf. Roth, Mumaw and Lewis, 1994; Roth, in press). Division of effort among team members requires coordination to synchronize activities and avoid conflicts, and to hand over tasks effectively. There have been significant problems in hand-over from automation systems in the past (Woods, 1994; Tenney, Rogers and Pew, 1995), related to maintaining situational awareness in the team members assuming task responsibility from other team members.

It is also necessary to support the human team leader in supervision and task delegation, as well as task sharing and mixed initiatives. The human monitors the effects of team activities to ensure they proceed as expected. The human coordinates and re-plans team activities when these effects are not as expected, when goals are altered, or to compensate for an overworked or anomalous team member.

Teamwork may require representing and integrating multiple task perspectives (Jones and Mitchell, 1995), because the basic knowledge and new situation information possessed by team members differs as a result of differing roles or tasks (Cannon-Bowers, Salas and Converse, 1993). Supporting multiple perspectives may require representing information at multiple levels of abstraction (Rasmussen, 1986). For example the DESSY system simultaneously shows state conclusions organized around a system-subsystem hierarchy, which supports situational awareness at multiple levels of abstraction (Land et al., 1995).

For system design, the issue is how to use intelligent interface capabilities to meet coordination needs without increasing workload, and to keep coordination

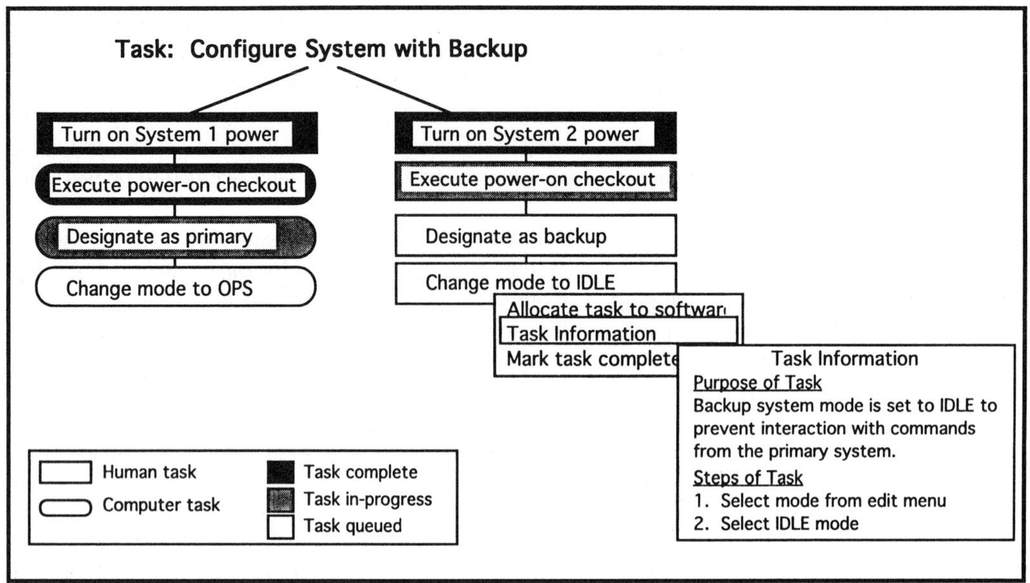

Figure 6. Configuration of monitored system by a joint human-computer team. *This blackboard display illustrates the use of graphics to provide a shared context for coordination of person and machine tasks. Tasks are annotated with information on allocation (to person or computer) and completion status to support coordination and delegation of tasks (Malin, Ryan, and Schreckenghost, 1994; Jones and Mitchell, 1995).*

in the background so that task accomplishment can remain in the foreground. Team members should be able to back each other up (e.g., the human should be able to perform intelligent system tasks as a contingency). Team members should be able to maintain awareness of each others' activities, but focus their attention and efforts on their current job assignment. As with reliable systems, a key method is designing the intelligent system to be open and to share its understanding of situation (what we call an *open shared context*). An open shared context makes coordination information implicitly available.

The Georgia Tech Mission Operations Cooperative Assistant (GT-MOCA) system is a prototype operator's associate for satellite ground control that exemplifies attributes of a cooperative team player (Jones and Mitchell, 1995). It provides a good example of a system that exploits external graphic representations to achieve an open shared context and support person-machine coordination. The GT-MOCA interface includes an interactive visualization of current activities, organized message lists of important events, and graphics depicting the current state of the controlled system. The user can manipulate this activity representation to allocate tasks. Figure 6, derived from systems like GT-MOCA and the engineering analysis tool SPRAT (Malin, Ryan, and Schreckenghost, 1994), illustrates the use of graphics to provide a shared context for coordination of person and machine tasks. This blackboard display provides a hierarchical view of the team action plan at several levels of abstraction. Tasks are annotated with information on allocation (to person or computer) and completion status, providing simple and clear support for coordination and delegation of tasks.

The GT-MOCA system has been empirically tested in use by satellite ground control personnel in a controlled laboratory setting (Jones and Mitchell, 1995). Performance of ground controllers was compared with and without the aid of the GT-MOCA system. The study showed that GT-MOCA significantly improved performance of ground controllers. Operators perceived GT-MOCA to be a useful aid, liked the capability to allocate activities to the machine, and relied on the blackboard display to keep track of task allocation and status.

In the future, shared human-intelligent system tasks may require that the human and the intelligent system coordinate even more closely, monitoring each others' activities and exchanging information about the task (e.g., activities, goals, plans, beliefs, intentions). This information exchange depends on a common understanding among team members of what is relevant to the current situation. Ways to represent such information to achieve a common understanding of a situation are discussed in the next section.

A Team Player is a Good Communicator. The primary goal of cooperative communication is to transfer relevant information between team members to support task accomplishment. There are three classes of design issues that arise from this goal. First, what principles help design the system for mutual intelligibility (Jones and Mitchell, 1995) or a shared context in which the relevance of information is evident (Johannesen, Cook and Woods, 1994)? Second, how should the designer handle discourse issues in the communicative give and take that includes managing interruptions and communication breakdowns (Jones and Mitchell, 1995) and managing explanatory dialogue (Terveen, 1995)? Third, what information presentation or representational aiding principles (Vicente and Rasmussen, 1992) lead to efficient and effective communication of situation information and advice in an information-rich environment?

These issues are especially important in complex dynamic environments, where intelligent system communications may interrupt or distract the human from higher priority tasks. The human operator may already be overloaded with information. The problem of information overload becomes especially important in real-time environments where complex, high risk tasks are performed, and where human errors can represent serious risk.

There is evidence that establishing a common grounding in domain and situation information among team members supports mutual intelligibility and openness (Johannesen, Cook and Woods, 1994). Common ground limits the need for team members to search for relevant and related information once a situation requiring action develops, and provides a shared context for human-computer communication resulting in briefer, more effective "conversations". It improves the readiness of team members to take over tasks from other team members. Maintaining common ground requires sharing a variety of types of information, described by Johannesen, et al. (1994), as the following *shared contexts*:

- *domain knowledge:* knowledge about system design and operation, and common practice in the domain
- *local knowledge:* knowledge about specific team protocols and practice
- *temporal context:* knowledge about the history of the process in a particular situation
- *physical context:* knowledge of the task environment, and the availability of situation information in that environment

Providing a common workspace for integrated information presentation is a strategy that supports common grounding. Several examples of systems that include a common workspace are given in Section 50.4.1 on critiquing systems. The GT-MOCA blackboard display provides another example of a common workspace used by a human-computer team (See Figure 6).

Effective human-computer discourse during team activities resembles similar human-human discourse in many respects:

- it is embedded in a context of shared information obtained through on-going conversation and shared activity;
- it is most effective when brief and focused;
- it may require repair during the course of the conversation (cf. correcting intelligent system information in the discussion of team-player reliability);
- it presumes openness and honesty.

An important aspect of effective discourse is that distracting interruptions are minimized, because all participants share considerable "common" knowledge (don't ask pointless or redundant questions) and have a clear understanding of roles and protocols (is this an appropriate time for an interruption?) and task assignments (am I the appropriate participant to make this interruption?). When distractions do occur, the human should be able to manage them quickly by overriding or repairing the interrupting agent, or by delaying response when the information/situation is not time-critical (cf. Terveen, 1993).

It is important to recognize that not all interruptions are "bad". Providing unprompted information can be an important way of developing shared context (Johannesen, Cook and Woods, 1994). An effective interruption is one that is relevant to the developing situation and that contributes to the resolution of that situation. This is a technique utilized by critiquing systems (See Section 50.4.1).

Explanation systems can be a source of distracting interruption. The instructional style of these systems requires the human to focus attention on the system and away from the domain situation (contributing to increased workload and information overload). Most explanation systems operate retrospectively, requiring the operator to wait until after a situation has stabilized (and the intelligent system has reached a conclusion) before attempting to describe what happened. This further dissociates the explanation system from the ongoing situation. In real-time support environments, the operator may not be able to wait until system behavior stabilizes, if the safety impacts are too great. Retrospective situation descriptions are also not sufficient for team coordination during joint activities (see the discussion of team-player coordination).

Even if a human operator has time to hold a conversation with the intelligent system, a problem remains with traditional approaches to explanation. Affecting the behavior of a human operator requires that the human both understand the meaning and consequences of the explanation, and accept them as correct. Most explanation systems assume that failure to influence human behavior occurs because the human failed to understand the explanation, and continue to provide more detailed justification directed at improving understanding. But, contrary to this assumption, acceptance does not necessarily result from understanding. The human may understand the intended meaning but choose not to believe it, due to information unknown to the intelligent system or not considered by it. Or the human may believe the information but be unwilling to alter behavior, due to awareness of adverse side-effects that may result from altering behavior or to the judgment that the consequences of altering behavior are of no significance.

Researchers in explanatory discourse have worked to improve explanatory dialogues with intelligent advisory systems. This work has focused on intelligent interface systems with sophisticated understanding of their own explanations and explanatory goals and of the user's knowledge (Moore and Swartout, 1990; Cawsey, 1991; Lemaire and Moore, 1994). For intelligent systems being designed for real-time tasks, the use of such retrospective explanatory dialogues should probably be avoided. Systems that are open and that share their understanding of situation can minimize the need for explanation. A shared external representation can enable a person to follow operational situations as they unfold and develop assessments consistent with intelligent system assessments (a *shared view*; what Johannesen, Cook and Woods (1994) call a mutually held interpretation) as part of normal monitoring and control operations. An important task in designing for communication via shared representations is identifying the information needed to develop such a shared view.

Researchers in collaborative discourse have developed a similar concept, the SharedPlan, which represents the understanding collaborators develop of unfolding team plans to accomplish goals (Lochbaum, Grosz and Sidner, 1990; Grosz and Kraus, 1993; Sidner, 1994). This SharedPlan is formed out of team dialogue, to keep track of the current beliefs and intentions of the collaborators concerning the team plan, activities and status. Systems such as GT-MOCA may support maintaining SharedPlans for human-computer teams without interactive dialogue, in cases where the plan changes are limited to pre-defined alternative allocations of activities to team members.

Developing a shared view of a situation requires showing how it develops, including the important event sequences that characterize the situation. These events include not only failures, but important state transitions and configuration changes in the monitored process. To share the intelligent system view of a situation, the operator must also understand the bases of intelligent system conclusions about that situation (see Figure 5). One method for clarifying intelligent system conclusions is to present evidence supporting these conclusions (e.g., plots or tables of data annotated with expected behavior; see Figure 5b and Horvitz et al., 1992). The design goal is to provide intelligent system conclusions that are so well integrated with other representational aids that the conclusions are self-evident within the context of the situation. In effect, such an intelligent system becomes *self-explanatory*.

Common presentation approaches and representation strategies for intelligent system conclusions are message lists and annotated schematics. Both message lists and schematics can obscure intelligent system information important to the human operator (Woods et al., 1991). As shown in Figure 7, situations develop as patterns of events indicated by changing state and status. Schematics normally are used to present only the latest event (i.e., the current system configuration or states of subsystems). Also, if events are not related to physical structure (e.g., functional status), they can be difficult to present clearly using a schematic. Mes-sage lists do capture some event history, but do not illustrate the relationships between events (e.g., events occurring in parallel, the temporal distance between events) necessary to reveal behavior patterns. Since chronology is the means of sorting messages, related information can become dissociated. Potter and Woods (1991) have investigated timelines as an alternative to message lists. Woods et al. (1991) recommend considering alternatives to the physical schematics as well. If schematics are deemed appropriate, they recommend approaches for emphasizing the information important to the task. Potter et al. (1992) have investigated representation aiding to identify the important functional changes in situation and to focus operator attention on those changes.

Some general principles can be drawn from this review of cooperative intelligent system. These prin-

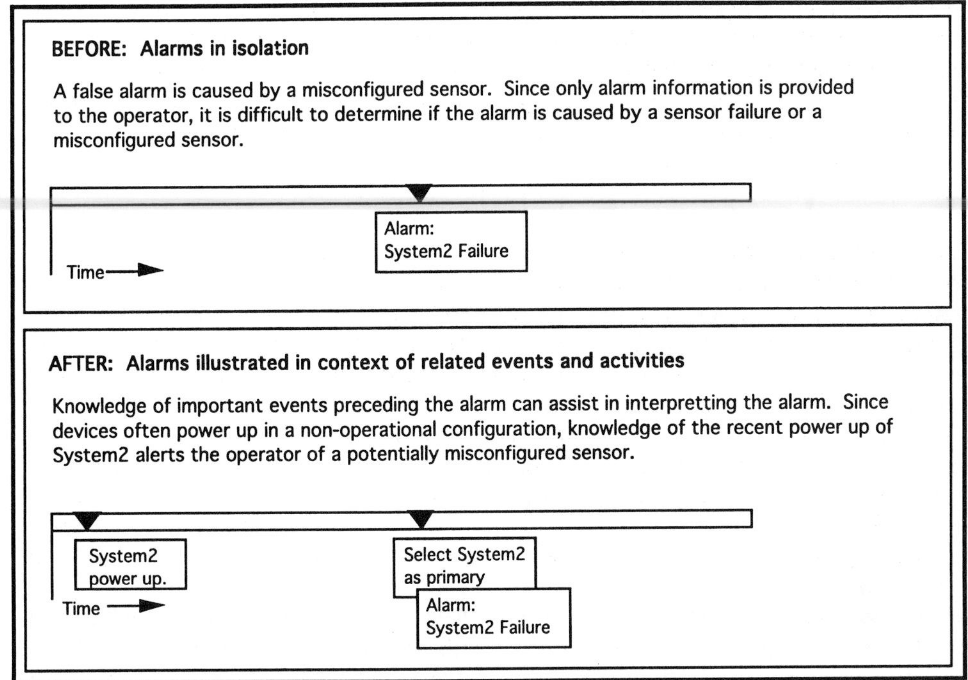

Figure 7. Use of timelines to display situations as they develop. *(Derived from Malin et al., 1991).*

ciples encourage use of the intelligence of the software to achieve four key characteristics of team player systems. First, designing for system openness and robustness results in system reliability (predictability and dependability) that is needed for human supervision and correction. Second, shared situation context improves task coordination and supports task sharing and delegation without increasing workload. Third, embedding communications in a common understanding of situation enables brief, relevant and self-explanatory communication that effectively supports human supervision in complex domains. Finally, support for human authority is a by-product of designing for the other objectives. The unifying theme of these design principles is use of software intelligence to achieve open access to shared information about an unfolding situation.

50.5 Intelligent Interfaces as Representational Aids

A common theme that emerges from both the intelligent interface as cognitive tool paradigm and the intelligent interface as an element of cooperative systems paradigm is the value of external representations in providing shared context and enhancing task performance. A third paradigm for deployment of machine intelligence explicitly focuses on the design of external representations that support human performance, in particular the design of computer-generated presentations. The term 'presentation' is used to cover a variety of computer outputs that include text, graphics, video, natural language, and speech and non-speech audio.
A well established finding in cognitive science is that people's ability to reason about and solve problems is highly influenced by the way information about the problem is presented to them. The goal of this approach to decision-aiding is to capitalize on advances in graphics and knowledge-based techniques to create computer-generated presentations that facilitate human problem-solving and decision-making. Woods (1991; 1995) has coined the term *representational aiding* to describe this approach to decision-aiding. Vicente and Rasmussen (1992) use the term *ecological interface* design to describe a similar approach.

Figure 8 depicts the 'representational aiding' approach to intelligent interface design. In this paradigm, machine intelligence is used to automate the design of computer-generated presentations. The emphasis is on supporting human problem-solving and decision-making by making key information perceptually salient.

One strand of research within this paradigm has concentrated on developing theoretical and empirical

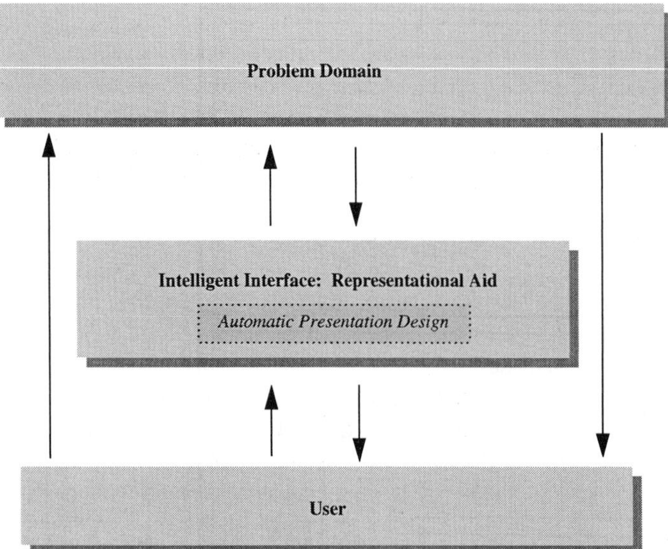

Figure 8. The 'representational aiding' paradigm for intelligent interface design. *In this paradigm, machine intelligence is used to automate the design of computer-generated presentations. The emphasis is on supporting human problem-solving and decision-making by making key information perceptually salient.*

foundations for presentation design. This literature attempts to articulate how computer-generated representations can influence human performance, and to identify principles and techniques for effective representation design (Hill, Hollan, Wroblewski and McCandless, 1992; Kosslyn, 1989; Vicente and Rasmussen, 1992; Woods, 1995).

Woods (1995) discusses ways that external representations can impact the cognitive activities of human problem-solvers. These include:

- *Problem structuring* -- external representations can affect people's (internal) problem representations and the strategies that are used to solve a problem (Larkin and Simon, 1987);
- *Exploiting mentally economic forms of processing* -- effective representations enable critical task-relevant information to be perceptually apparent. The goal is to minimize the need for deliberate, serial, cognitive processing and problem-solving for situation awareness, and to capitalize on more parallel perceptual processes instead (e.g., substituting judgments of distance and size in a display for mental arithmetic or numerical comparisons);
- *Reducing memory load* -- effective representations can provide external memory aids that off-load internal memory requirements (Hutchins, 1991);
- *Directing attention* -- good representations support management of attention, including pre-attentive reference or peripheral processing, cues for attention switching, and guidance for where to look next.

A guiding principle of representation aiding is the importance of establishing an effective mapping between task-relevant information and perceptually salient features of the representation (Vicente and Rasmussen, 1992; Woods, 1995). This involves two aspects. First, effective mapping depends on uncovering the task-meaningful domain semantics to be mapped into the structure and behavior of the representation (i.e., establishing what is informative to communicate). This requires an analysis of the domain to identify the practitioners' goals and task context, and the critical data relationships, constraints, and meaningful changes that need to be communicated in light of those goals (Jordan and Henderson, 1995; Roth and Woods, 1989; Rasmussen, Pejtersen and Goodstein, 1994; Vicente and Rasmussen, 1992; Woods and Roth, 1988b).

A second requirement for effective mapping is to establish mapping rules for assigning domain-relevant information to properties of the representation that enable task-relevant information, and meaningful changes, to be perceptually apparent and easily extracted under conditions of actual task performance. This requires a better understanding of the factors that influence people's ability to extract and utilize information from different types of media (e.g., natural language, text, graphics, video), and different presentation forms within a given media (e.g., different types of graphics such as tables, charts, configural displays). There is a growing body of literature addressing these issues (e.g., Cleveland, 1985; Kosslyn, 1989; Roth and Mattis, 1990; Bennett, Toms and Woods, 1993; Sanderson, Haskell and Flach, 1992) but there is need for more empirical research on the psychology of display comprehension.

A second, related strand of research has focused on using knowledge-based techniques to automate the process of presentation design. Research has focused on the development of prototype systems that illustrate automated presentation design.

Early systems focused on automated design of graphic displays such as charts, tables, and network diagrams (e.g., Mackinlay, 1986; Roth and Mattis, 1990). More recent systems have focused on generating presentations that involve multiple, coordinated, media (e.g., combinations of graphics, text, natural language, gestural pointing and/or non-speech audio). Maybury (1993a) provides in-depth descriptions of some of the current approaches to the design of intelligent multimedia interfaces. Representative examples of intelligent multimedia interface systems include:

- systems that combine graphics and natural language text for business applications such as project management (e.g., Roth, Mattis and Mesnard, 1991);
- systems that provide procedural instructions through a combination of natural language and realistic graphics or maps. One example is a system that explains the operation and maintenance of an Army field radio and guides test performance (Feiner and McKeown, 1993). Another example is a system that provides narrated animations of route plans on map displays (Maybury, 1993b);
- systems that generate multimedia output to support military situation monitoring and planning (e.g., Burger and Marshall, 1993).

Current research in automated presentation focuses on uncovering the knowledge that underlies effective display design, and more generally effective communication, and extending artificial intelligence formalisms to capture and utilize that knowledge to automatically generate presentations. Roth and Hefley (1993) provide a thorough discussion of technical issues and research questions currently confronting the design of knowledge-based multi-media systems. Research questions addressed by this literature include:

- identifying and representing the characteristics of data relevant to creating presentations;
- establishing and representing the communicative intent or purpose of the presentation;
- establishing criteria for apportionment of different types of information to different media (e.g., what is most effectively communicated through natural language? through graphics?);
- establishing and representing design knowledge for selecting and assembling presentation forms within a media (e.g., the rules by which to create an effective bar chart or a configural display);
- establishing and representing knowledge for coordinating different media (e.g., how to coordinate graphics and accompanying text?);
- applying models of discourse and focus of attention in guiding the design and updating of presentations in response to user queries or evolution of events.

One of the areas where significant strides have been made is in developing a vocabulary for characterizing communicative goals and data characteristics that support appropriate mapping between data and graphics (e.g., Roth and Mattis, 1990; Goldstein, Roth, Kolojejchick and Mattis, 1994). One of the most successful examples of systems built on this approach is the SAGE system (Roth and Mattis, 1990; Roth, Kolojejchick, Mattis and Goldstein, 1994). SAGE automatically generates integrated information graphics (e.g., charts, tables, network diagrams) based on (1) a characterization of the properties of the data that are relevant to graphic design (e.g., scale of measurement; domain of membership such as time or temperature) and (2) a characterization of the tasks that the graphics are intended to support (e.g., looking up accurate values; comparing two or more values; judging correlations; performing approximate computations.)

The SAGE system has proved to be a highly productive vehicle for uncovering and articulating (1) a vocabulary for describing the elements of graphics; (2) knowledge about their appropriateness for different types of data and tasks; and (3) design principles for how to combine the elements to create integrated graphics (Goldstein, Roth, Kolojejchick and Mattis, 1994).

One recent extension of the SAGE system has been to add natural language generation capabilities to create explanatory captions to accompany the information graphics (Mittal, Roth, Moore, Mattis and Carenini, 1995). The resulting system produces sophisticated information graphics that integrate multiple types of information, and use natural language captions to help us-

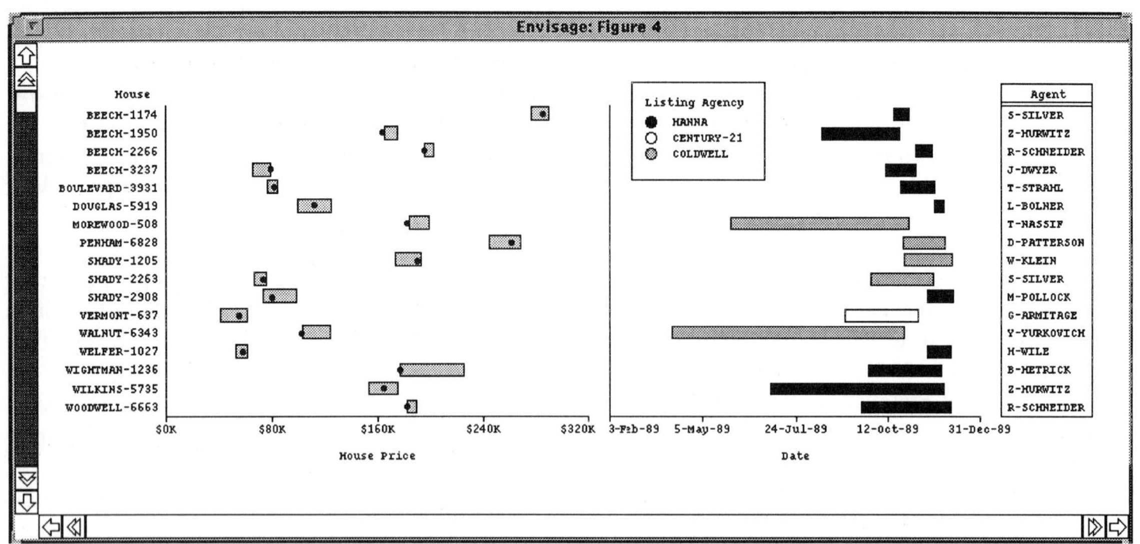

These three spaces show infomation about house-sales from data-set HOUSE-SALES-1. In the three spaces, the Y-axis shows the houses. In the first chart, the house's selling price is shown by the left edge of the horizontal interval bar, whereas the house's asking price is shown by the right edge of the bar. The agency estimate of the house price is shown by the horizontal position of the mark. For example, the selling price of 1236 Wightman Street is 177,000 dollars, its asking price is 225,000 dollars, and its agency estimate is 176,000 dollars. In the second chart, the left edge of the horizontal interval bar shows the house's date on the market, whereas the right edge of the bar shows the house's date sold. The color of the bar shows the house's listing agency. The table shows the house's listing agent.

***Figure 9. An example of a graphic display and associated caption that is automatically generated by SAGE** (Mittal et al., 1995).*

ers understand the information being depicted. Figure 9 provides an example of a graphic display and associated caption produced by SAGE to describe real estate transactions.

A second interesting extension has been to embed SAGE in an interactive data exploration system called SageTools that assigns the user a more active role in specifying and creating graphic displays (Roth, Kolojejchick, Mattis, and Goldstein, 1994; Goldstein, Roth, Kolojejchick and Mattis, 1994; Chuah, Roth, Kolojejchick, Mattis, and Juarez, 1995). SageTools takes a user-directed approach to graphics designs. It starts from the premise that graphic design involves two interrelated processes: (1) constructing designs from graphic elements, and (2) finding and customizing previously stored graphics. SageTools contains three components:

- SageBrush, which provides sketch tools that allow users to create designs or partial design specifications;
- SageBook, which supports browsing and retrieval of previously created data graphics to use as a starting point for designing new displays; and
- SAGE, which utilizes knowledge-based design techniques to complete partial design specifications.

The progression from SAGE, which is an automated graphics generator, to SageTools, which takes a user-directed approach, is particularly noteworthy in that it mirrors the progression from stand-alone automated problem-solvers (i.e., the 'Greek Oracle' model) to 'cognitive tools' or 'members of cooperative systems' that has been seen in other decision-aiding contexts (See Sections 50.3 and 50.4). A similar evolution has been observed in the development of intelligent support systems for design, where there has been a shift toward developing coordinated suites of intelligent tools intended to support different cognitive aspects of the design process (Fischer, 1994; Fischer,

Nakakoji and Ostwald, 1995). An example is the KID design environment for kitchen design that has evolved from the JANUS system described in Section 50.4.1 (Fischer et al., 1995). The KID system includes a specification component that supports users in specifying and keeping track of design goals, criteria and constraints; a catalog of previous design examples that the user can draw upon; a construction component that supports the actual floor plan layout process; and a critiquing system that alerts users to design problems and suggest solutions.

The evolutions of the SAGE and KID systems illustrate the significant overlap and convergence in insights and principles that have emerged from the three paradigms presented above. Both systems provide suites of coordinated intelligent tools intended to augment human task performance that is reminiscent of the 'cognitive tool' paradigm. At the same time the two systems embody elements of cooperative systems in that they include intelligent machine agents that collaborate with the user on task performance. Finally both systems have as a central feature an external representation that provides a shared context for communication and task performance.

50.6 Summary

In this chapter we defined 'intelligent interface' as an umbrella term that covers user interfaces for intelligent systems as well as user interfaces that utilize knowledge-based approaches. We considered three broad paradigms for development of intelligent interfaces:

- intelligent interfaces as *cognitive tools* that can be utilized by practitioners in solving problems and accomplishing tasks;
- intelligent interfaces as *members of cooperative person-machine systems* that jointly accomplish cognitive tasks; and
- intelligent interfaces as *representational aids* that dynamically structure the presentation of information to make key information perceptually salient.

In each case we described examples of systems that represent the paradigm, and some of the key design insights to be derived from research within that paradigm. For expository purposes, we presented the three paradigms as if they were distinct, contrasting, approaches. In fact they are better thought of as alternative metaphors that provide mutually-reinforcing insights for guiding intelligent interface design. What they fundamentally have in common is a commitment to viewing the user as the central actor, and the intelligent interface as a means for supporting the user's cognitive processes.

Among the common themes that emerge from the three paradigms are:

- the idea that machine intelligence should be deployed in service of human cognitive activity;
- the importance of understanding the demands of the domain, and identifying what aspects of human cognitive performance require support as input to the design of the system architecture and user displays;
- the importance of providing an external representation that supports human performance and facilitates human and machine cooperative activity by providing a shared frame of reference.

50.7 References

Alty, J. L. and Coombs, M. J. (1980). Face-to-face guidance of university computer users-I: A study of advisory services. *International Journal of Man-Machine Studies*, *12*, 390-406.

Bennett, K. B., Toms, M. L., and Woods, D. D. (1993). Emergent features and graphical elements: Designing more effective configural displays. *Human Factors*, *35*, 71-97.

Bainbridge, L. (1983). Ironies of automation. *Automatica*, *19*, 775-779.

Burger, J. D. and Marshall, R. J. (1993). The application of natural language models to intelligent multimedia. In M. T. Maybury (Ed.), *Intelligent multimedia interfaces* (pp. 174-196). Cambridge, MA: The MIT Press.

Billings, C. E. (1991). *Human-centered aircraft automation: A concept and guidelines* (NASA Technical Memorandum 103885). Moffett Field, CA: Ames Research Center.

Cannon-Bowers, J. A., Salas, E., and Converse, S. A. (1993). Shared mental models in expert team decision-making. In N. J. Castellan, Jr. (Ed.), *Current issues in individual and group decision making* (pp. 355-377). Hillsdale, NJ: Erlbaum.

Cawsey, A. (1991). Generating interactive explanations. In *Proceedings of the Ninth National Conference on Artificial Intelligence, AAAI-91* (pp. 86-91). Menlo Park: AAI Press/MIT Press.

Chignell, M. H. and Hancock, P. A. (1988). Intelligent Interface Design. In M. Helander (Ed.), *Handbook of human-computer interaction* (pp. 969-995). Amsterdam, The Netherlands: Elsevier Science Publishers B. V. (North-Holland). .

Chuah, M. C., Roth, S. F. Kolojejchick, J., Mattis, J. and Juarez, O. (1995). SageBook: searching datagraphics by content. In *Human Factors in Computing Systems CHI'95 Proceedings* (pp. 338-345). New York, NY: Association for Computing Machinery, Inc.

Clancey, W. J. and Shortliffe, E. (1984). *Readings in medical artificial intelligence: The first decade*. Reading, MA: Addison-Wesley.

Clark, H. H. and Brennan, S. (1991). Grounding in communication. In L. B. Resnick, J. M. Levine, and S. D. Teasley (Eds.) *Perspectives on socially shared cognition* (pp. 127-149). Washington DC.: American Psychological Association.

Diamond, L. W., Mishka, V. G., Seal, A. H., and Nguyen, D. T. (1995). Are normative expert systems appropriate for diagnostic pathology? *J. Am. Medical Informatics Assoc.*, 2 (2), 85-93.

Cleveland, W. S. (1985). *The elements of graphing data*. Monterey, CA: Wadsworth Advanced Books and Software.

Endestad, T. Holmstroem, B. O. and Volden, F. S. (1992). Effects on operators' problem solving behavior when using a diagnostic rule-based expert system developed for the nuclear industry. In *Proceedings of the 1992 IEEE Fifth Conference on Human Factors and Power Plants* (pp. 266-272). New York, NY: Institute of Electrical and Electronics Engineers.

Feiner, S. K. and McKeown, K. R. (1993). Automating the generation of coordinated multimedia explanations. In M. T. Maybury (Ed.), *Intelligent multimedia interfaces* (pp. 117-138). Cambridge, MA: The MIT Press.

Fischer, G. (1994). Domain-Oriented Design Environments. *Automated software engineering, 1*, 177-203.

Fischer, G., Lemke, A. C., Mastaglio, T., and Morch, A. I. (1991). The role of critiquing in cooperative problem solving. *ACM Transactions on Information Systems, 9*, 123-151.

Fischer, G., Lemke, A., Mastaglio, T. and Morch, A. (1990). Using critics to empower users. In *CHI90 Human Factors in Computing Systems Conference Proceedings* (pp. 337-347). New York, NY: Association for Computing Machinery.

Fischer, G., Nakakoji, K. and Ostwald, J. (1995). Supporting the evolution of design artifacts with representations of context and intent. In *Proceedings of DIS'95, Symposium on Designing Interactive Systems* (pp. 7-15). New York, NY: Association for Computing Machinery.

Fischer, G. and Reeves, B. (1992). Beyond intelligent interfaces: exploring, analyzing, and creating success models of cooperative problem solving. *Journal of Applied Intelligence, 1*, 311-332.

Gadd, C. S. (1995). A theory of the multiple roles of diagnosis in collaborative problem solving discourse. In *Proceedings of the Seventeenth Annual Conference of the Cognitive Science Society* (pp. 352-357). New Jersey: LEA Publishers.

Goldstein, J., Roth, S. F., Kolojejchick, J. and Mattis, J. (1994). A framework for knowledge-based interactive data exploration. *Journal of Visual Languages and Computing, 5*, 339-363.

Gray, W. D., Hefley, W. E. and Murray, D. (Eds). (1993). *Proceedings of the 1993 International Workshop on Intelligent User Interfaces.* New York: ACM Press.

Grice, H. P. (1975). Logic and conversation. In P. Cole and J. L. Morgan (Eds.), *Syntax and semantics, Vol. 3: Speech acts* (pp. 41-58). New York: Academic Press.

Grosz, B. and Kraus, S. (1993). Collaborative plans for group activities. In *Proceedings of the International Joint Conference on Artificial intelligence, IJCAI '93* (pp. 367-373). San Mateo, CA: International Joint Conferences on Artificial Intelligence, Inc.

Guerlain, S. A. (1993). Factors influencing the cooperative problem-solving of people and computers. In *Proceedings of the Human Factors and Ergonomics Society 37th Annual Meeting* (pp. 387-391). Santa Monica, CA: Human Factors Society.

Guerlain, S. A. (1995). Using the critiquing approach to cope with brittle expert systems. In *Proceedings of Human Factors and Ergonomics Society 39th Annual Meeting* (pp. 233-237). Santa Monica, CA: Human Factors Society.

Guerlain, S. A, Smith, P. J., Obradovich, J., Smith, J., Rudmann, S., and Strohm, P. (1995). The antibody identification assistant (AIDA), an example of a cooperative computer support system. In *Proceedings of the 1995 IEEE International Conference on Systems, Man, and Cybernetics* (pp. 1909-1914). Piscataway, NJ: IEEE Press.

Guerlain S. and Smith, P. (1996). Decision support in medical systems. In R. Parasuraman and M. Mouloua (Eds.), *Automation and human performance: theory and application* (pp. 385-406). Mahwah, NJ: Lawrence Erlbaum Associates.

Heathfield, H. and Kirkham, N. (1992). A cooperative approach to decision support in the differential diagnosis of breast disease. *Medical Informatics*, *17*, 21-33.

Hill, W. C., Hollan, J. D., Wroblewski, D. and McCandless, T. (1992). Edit wear and read wear. In *Human Factors in Computing Systems CHI'92 Conference Proceedings* (pp. 3-9). New York, NY: Association for Computing Machinery, Inc.

Horvitz, E., Ruokangas, C., Srinivas, S., and Barry, M. (1992). A decision-theoretic approach to the display of information for time-critical decisions: The Vista project. In *Proceedings of the 6th Annual Workshop on Space Operations Applications and Research* (pp. 407-417). NASA Conference Pub. 3187.

Hutchins, E. (1990). The technology of team navigation. In J. Galegher, R. Kraut, and C. Egido (Eds.), *Intellectual teamwork: the social and technological bases of cooperative work* (pp. 191-220). Hillsdale, NJ: LEA.

Hutchins, E. (1991). *How a cockpit remembers its speed.* (Distributed Cognition Laboratory Technical Report). La Jolla: University of California, San Diego.

Hutchins, E. (1995). *Cognition in the wild.* Cambridge, MA: The MIT Press.

Johannesen, L. J., Cook, R. I., and Woods, D. D. (1994). *Grounding explanations in evolving diagnostic situations.* (Cognitive Systems Engineering Lab Report 1994-TR-03). Columbus, OH: The Ohio State University.

Jones, P. M., and Mitchell, C. M. (1995). Human-computer cooperative problem solving: Theory, design and evaluation of an intelligent associate system. *IEEE Transactions on Systems, Man, and Cybernetics*, *25*, 1039-1053.

Jordan, B. and Henderson, A. (1995) Interaction Analysis: Foundations and Practice. *The Journal of the Learning Sciences*, *4*, 39-103.

Kosslyn, S. M. (1989). Understanding charts and graphs. *Applied Cognitive Psychology*, *3*, 185-226.

Larkin, J. H., and Simon, H. A. (1987). Why a diagram is (sometimes) worth ten thousand words. *Cognitive Science* , *11*, 65-99.

Land, S. A., Malin, J. T., Thronesbery, C., and Schreckenghost, D. L. (1995). *Making Intelligent Systems Team Players: A Guide to Developing Intelligent Monitoring Systems.* (NASA Technical Memorandum 104807). Houston, TX: NASA Johnson Space Center.

Langlotz, C. P., and Shortliffe, E. H. (1983). Adapting a consultation system to critique user plans. *International Journal of Man-Machine Studies*, *19*, 479-496.

Layton, C. Smith, P. J. and McCoy, E. (1994). Design of a cooperative problem-solving system for en-route flight planning: An empirical evaluation. *Human Factors*, *36*, 94-119.

Lemaire, B. and Moore, J. D. (1994). An improved interface for tutorial dialogues: Browsing a visual dialogue history. In *Human Factors in Computing Systems, CHI '94 Conference Proceedings* (pp. 16-22). New York: Association for Computing Machinery.

Lochbaum, K. E., Grosz, B. J., and Sidner, C. L. (1990). Models of plans to support communication: An initial report. In *Proceedings of the Eighth National Conference on Artificial Intelligence, AAAI-90* (pp. 485-490). Menlo Park: AAI Press/MIT Press.

Mackinlay, J. D. (1986). Automating the design of graphical presentations of relational information. *ACM Transactions on Graphics*, *5*, 110-141.

Malin, J. T., and Schreckenghost, D. L. (1992). *Making Intelligent Systems Team Players: Overview for Designers.* (NASA Technical Memorandum 104751). Houston, TX: NASA Johnson Space Center.

Malin, J. T., Ryan, D., and Schreckenghost, D. (1994). Modeling actions and operations to support mission preparation. In *Proceedings of the 3rd International Symposium on Artificial Intelligence, Robotics, and Automation for Space (i-SAIRAS)* (pp. 385-388). Pasadena, CA: Jet Propulsion Laboratory Publication 94-23.

Malin, J. T., Schreckenghost, D. L., Woods, D. D., Potter, S. S., Johannesen, L., Holloway, M., and Forbus. K. D. (1991). *Making Intelligent Systems Team Players: Case Studies and Design Issues. Vol 1: Human-computer Interaction Design; Vol 2: Fault Management System cases.* (NASA Technical Memorandum 104738). Houston, TX: NASA Johnson Space Center.

Malin, J. T., Schreckenghost, D. L., and Rhoads, R. W. (1993). *Making Intelligent Systems Team Players: Additional Case Studies.* (NASA Technical Memorandum 104786). Houston, TX: NASA Johnson Space Center.

Maybury, M. T. (1993a). *Intelligent multimedia interfaces.* Cambridge, MA: The MIT Press.

Maybury, M. T. (1993b). Planning multimedia explanations using communicative acts. In M. T. Maybury (Ed.), *Intelligent multimedia interfaces* (pp. 59-74). Cambridge, MA: The MIT Press.

Miller, P. (1986). *Expert critiquing systems: Practice-*

based medical consultation by computer. New York: Springer-Verlag.

Miller, R. A. (1984). Internist-I/CADUCEUS: Problems facing expert consultant programs. *Methods of Information in Medicine, 23*, 9-14.

Miller, R. A. (1994). Medical diagnostic decision support systems -- Past, present, and future: A Threaded bibliography and brief commentary. *Journal of the American Medical Informatics Association, 1*, 8-27.

Miller, R. A., and Masarie, F. E. Jr. (1990). The demise of the "Greek oracle" model for medical diagnostic systems. *Methods of Information in Medicine, 29*, 1-2.

Miller, R. A., McNeil M. A., Challinor, S. M, Masarie, M. D. and Myers, J. D. (1986). The INTERNIST-1/QUICK MEDICAL REFERENCE Project -- Status report. *Western Journal of Medicine, 145*, 816-822.

Mittal, V., Roth, S., Moore, J., Mattis, J. and Carenini, G. (1995). Generating explanatory captions for information graphics. In *Proceedings of the Fourteenth International Joint Conference on Artificial Intelligence, IJCAI '95* (pp. 1276-1283). San Mateo: Morgan Kaufmann.

Moore, J. D. and Swartout, W. R. (1990). Pointing: A way toward explanation dialogues. In *Proceedings of the Eighth National Conference on Artificial Intelligence, AAAI-90* (pp. 457-464). Menlo Park: AAAI Press/MIT Press.

Mosier, K. L., Palmer, E. A. and Degan, A. (1992) Electronic Checklists: Implications for Decision Making. In *Proceedings of the Human Factors Society 36th Annual Meeting* (pp. 7-11). Santa Monica, CA: Human Factors Society.

Norman, D. A. (1990). The 'problem' of automation: Inappropriate feedback and interaction, not 'over-automation.' *Philosophical Trans. Royal Society of London, B 327*, 585-593.

Parasuraman, R., Molloy, R. and Singh, I. (1993). Performance consequences of automation-induced "complacency". *International Journal of Aviation Psychology, 3*, 1-23.

Pollack, M. E., Hirschberg, J. and Webber, B. (1982). User participation in the reasoning processes of expert systems. In *Proceedings of the National Conference on Artificial Intelligence, AAI-82* (pp. 358-361). Los Altos, CA: William Kaufmann.

Potter, S. and Woods, D. (1991). Event-driven timeline displays: Beyond message lists in human-intelligent system interaction. In *Proceedings of the 1991 IEEE International Conference on System, Man and Cybernetics* (pp. 1283-1288). New York, NY: Institute of Electrical and Electronics Engineers, Inc.

Potter, S. S., Woods, D. D., Hill, T., Boyer, R. L., and Morris, W. S. (1992). Visualization of dynamic processes: Function-based displays for human-intelligent system interaction. In *Proceedings of the 1992 IEEE International Conference on Systems, Man, and Cybernetics* (pp. 1504-1509). New York, NY: Institute of Electrical and Electronics Engineers, Inc.

Rasmussen, J. (1986). *Information processing and human-machine interaction: An approach to cognitive engineering*. New York, NY: Elsevier.

Rasmussen, J. , Pejtersen, A. M. and Goodstein, L. P. (1994). *Cognitive systems engineering*. New York, N. Y.: John Wiley and Sons, Inc.

Roth, E. M. (in press). Analysis of decision making in nuclear power plant emergencies: An investigation of aided decision making. In C. Zsambok and G. Klein (Eds.), *Naturalistic decision making*. Mahwah, NJ: Lawrence Erlbaum Associates.

Roth, E. M., Bennett, K. B., and Woods, D. D. (1987). Human interaction with an "intelligent" machine. *International Journal of Man-Machine Studies, 27*, 479-525.

Roth, E. M., Mumaw, R. J. and Lewis, P.M. (1994). *An empirical investigation of operator performance in cognitively demanding simulated emergencies*. (NUREG/CR-6208). Washington D. C.: U. S. Nuclear Regulatory Commission.

Roth, E. M., and Woods, D. D. (1988). Aiding human performance: I. Cognitive analysis. *Le Travail Humain, 51*, 39-64.

Roth, E. M., and Woods, D. D. (1989). Cognitive task analysis: An approach to knowledge acquisition for intelligent system design. In G. Guida and C. Tasso (Eds.). *Topics in expert system design (pp. 233-264)*. New York, NY: Elsevier.

Roth, S. F. and Hefley, W. E. (1993). Intelligent multimedia presentation systems: research and principles. In M. T. Maybury (Ed.), *Intelligent multimedia interfaces (pp. 13-58)*. Cambridge, MA: The MIT Press.

Roth, S. F., Kolojejchick, J., Mattis, J. and Goldstein, J. (1994). Interactive graphic design using automatic presentation knowledge. In *Human Factors in Computing Systems CHI'94 Conference Proceedings* (pp. 112-117). New York, NY: ACM/SIGCHI.

Roth, S. F. and Mattis, J. (1990). Data characterization for intelligent graphics presentation. In *Human Factors in Computing Systems CHI '90 Conference Proceedings* (pp. 193-200). New York, NY: ACM/SIGCHI.

Roth, S. F., Mattis, J. and Mernard, X. (1991). Graphics and natural language as components of automatic explanation. In J. W. Sullivan and S. W. Tyler (Eds.), *Intelligent user interfaces* (pp. 207-239). New York, N Y: ACM Press (Addison-Wesley Publishing Company).

Sanderson, P. M., Haskell, I., and Flach, J. M. (1992). The complex role of perceptual organization in visual display design theory. *Ergonomics, 35*, 1199-1219.

Sheridan, T. (1988). Task allocation and supervisory control. In M. Helander (Ed.), *Handbook of human-computer interaction* (pp. 159-173). New York, NY: Elsevier.

Shortliffe, E. J. (1982). The computer and medical decision-making: Good advice is not enough. *IEEE Engineering in Medicine and Biology Magazine, 1*, 16-18.

Sidner, C. L. (1994). An artificial discourse language for collaborative negotiation. In *Proceedings of the Twelfth National Conference on Artificial Intelligence, AAAI-94* (pp. 814-819). Menlo Park: AAAI Press/MIT.

Silverman, B. (1992). Building a better critic. Recent empirical results, *IEEE Expert*, April, 18-25.

Sorkin, R. D. and Woods, D. D. (1985) Systems with human monitors: A signal detection analysis. *Human-Computer Interaction, 1*, 49-75.

Suchman, L. (1987). *Plans and situated actions: the problem of human-machine communication*. Cambridge, England: Cambridge Univ. Press.

Sullivan, J. W. and Tyler, S. W. (Eds.) (1991). *Intelligent User Interfaces*. New York: ACM Press.

Tenney, Y. J., Rogers, W. H., and Pew, R. W. (1995). *Pilot Opinions on High Level Flight Deck Automation Issues: Toward the Development of a Design Philosophy*. (NASA Contractor Report 4669). Huntington, VA: NASA Langley Research Center.

Terveen, L. G. (1993). Intelligent systems as cooperative systems. *Journal of Intelligent Systems, 3* , 217-249.

Terveen, L. G. (1995). An overview of human-computer collaboration. *Knowledge-Based Systems*, 8, 67-81.

Vicente, K. J. and Rasmussen J. (1992). Ecological interface design: theoretical foundations. *IEEE Transactions of SMC, 22,* 589-607.

Woods, D. D. (1986). Cognitive Technologies: the design of joint human machine cognitive systems. *AI Magazine, 6*, 86-92.

Woods, D. D. (1991). Representation aiding: A ten year retrospective. In *Proceedings of the 1991 IEEE International Conference on Systems, Man, and Cybernetics* (pp. 1173-1176). New York, NY: Institute of Electrical and Electronics Engineers, Inc.

Woods, D. D. (1994). Cognitive demands and activities in dynamic fault management: Abductive reasoning and disturbance management. In N. Stanton (Ed.), *Human factors of alarm design* (pp. 63-92). London: Taylor & Francis.

Woods, D. D. (1995). Toward a theoretical base for representation design in the computer medium: Ecological perception and aiding human cognition. In Flack J. M., Hancock, P. A., Caird, J. K., and Vicente, K. J. (Eds.), *An Ecological Approach to Human Machine Systems, Vol. I: A Global Perspective* (pp. 157-188). Hillsdale NJ: Erlbaum.

Woods, D. D. (1996). Decomposing Automation: Apparent Simplicity, Real Complexity. In R. Parasuraman and M. Mouloua (Eds.), *Automation and human performance: theory and application* (pp. 3-17). Mahwah, NJ: Lawrence Erlbaum Associates.

Woods, D. D., Johannesen, L. J. Cook, R. I., and Sarter, N. B. (1994). *Behind Human Error: Cognitive Systems, Computers, and Hindsight*. (Technical Report SOAR 94-01). Dayton, OH: CSERIAC Publication.

Woods, D. D., Potter, S. S., Johannesen, L., and Holloway, M. (1991). *Human Interaction with Intelligent Systems. Vol. 1. Trends, Problems and New Directions.* (Cognitive Systems Engineering Lab Report, 1991-001). Columbus, OH: The Ohio State University.

Woods, D. D. and Roth, E. M. (1988a). Cognitive Systems Engineering. In M. Helander (Ed) *Handbook of human-computer interaction* (pp. 3-43). Amsterdam, The Netherlands: Elsevier Science Publishers B. V. (North-Holland).

Woods, D. D and Roth, E. M. (1988b). Aiding human performance: II. From Cognitive Analysis to Support Systems. *Le Travail Humain, 51*, 139-171.

Woods, D. D., Roth, E. M., and Bennett, K B. (1990). Explorations in joint human-machine cognitive systems. In S. Robertson, W. Zachary, and J. Black (Eds.), *Cognition, computing, and cooperation (pp. 123-158).* Norwood, NJ: Ablex.

Handbook of Human-Computer Interaction
Second, completely revised edition
M. Helander, T.K. Landauer, P. Prabhu (eds.)

Chapter 51

Knowledge Elicitation for the Design of Software Agents

Guy A. Boy
European Institute of Cognitive Sciences and Engineering (EURISCO)
Toulouse, France

51.1 Abstract

For many years, the theory and practice of knowledge acquisition for knowledge-based systems tended to focus on how to elicit and represent knowledge in a context-free way. More recently, the evolution of the design of software agents has forced the focus to shift so that the context of the interaction between human and software agents has become the unit of analysis. In terms of empirical research, the initial goal was to establish a unified model that would guide knowledge elicitation for the design of software agents. The SRAR (Situation Recognition and Analytical Reasoning) model has been developed over the last ten years to serve this goal. Subsequently the knowledge block representation has been elaborated as a mediating representation to help formalize elicited knowledge from experts or, more generally, end-users. Hence, human-centered automation studies have more recently started to focus on the requirements for the design and evaluation of "human-like" systems that are currently called software agents. In this chapter, we introduce the cognitive function analysis method that helps elicit task/activity models from experts.

51.2 Introduction

For many years, the theory and practice of knowledge acquisition for knowledge-based systems (expert systems) tended to focus on how to elicit and represent knowledge in a context-free way. This reflected a position which was dominant both in cognitive psychology and artificial intelligence (AI) in the 1970s and 1980s, where cognition was seen as a product of isolated *information processors* (Newell and Simon, 1972), and where the notion of context was not a central issue. Even worse, AI research mainly focused on decontextualization of knowledge. In the late 1980s, several research efforts began to highlight the importance of context from a social perspective.

> "A major weakness of the conventional approach to knowledge elicitation (and the epistemology that underpins it) is that it ignores the social character of knowledge ‹ that is, the possibly unpalatable (to AI), but none-the-less inescapable fact that knowledge is part-and-parcel of the social world (Collins, 1987)... Sociologists of science argue that much of knowledge is held in a tacit basis forming part of our inter-subjectively shared commonsense understanding of the world... the rules contained in an expert system are meaningless; their meaning arises from the social or cultural contexts within which expertise is usually embedded and rests on an immense foundation of tacit knowledge." (Bloomfield, 1988, page 20)

Dreyfus's (1981) critique of AI microworlds, and AI in general, was based on the fact that "a world is an organized body of objects, purposes, skills, and practices in terms of which human activities have meaning or make sense." In this chapter, we will assume that software agents are computer programs that are designed and developed within/for a social context to respond to specific needs such as enhancing human productivity, comfort and safety. From this perspective, the design of software agents such as intelligent assistant systems (Boy, 1991) requires the use of knowledge elicitation techniques in order to gather requirements from various viewpoints that can be either technical, economical, psychological, or sociological. Typically, such software agents are designed to be used for *decision support*, i.e., systems that support the decision of people who already know quite a lot about a given domain (Bloomfield, 1988).

> "As a further consequence of the over-emphasis on knowledge which can be articulated, knowledge engineering largely ignores the visual/ostensive component of expertise. For instance, experts — like most other humans — tend to employ pictures or images as part of their thinking processes and indeed such elements have been an integral part of scientific and technological development. It turns out that the visual component of expertise also has a tacit dimension rooted in our learning experiences within the social world around us." (Bloomfield, 1988, page 23)

An expert system emulates what a human expert can do. In the context of human-computer interaction, such an expert system is a specialized application at the disposal of the user. In this chapter, a *software agent* is defined as a specialized application with an appearance that is the visual dimension of its purpose.

> "There has been some debate concerning whether intelligent interfaces should be structured as agents or whether it is better to think of them as tools with intelligently organized direct-manipulation options available to the user. In the interface-as-agent view, the interface is seen as a separate entity that mediates between the user and the machine." (Chin, 1991).

Obviously, the user needs to know what to do with the agent, i.e., possible actions on it, messages that can be sent to and from the agent, the agent's behavior, its possible reactions, etc. Conversely, the agent view requires that the interface has a well-defined model of the dialogue between the user and the interface. Our agent approach differs from conventional natural language dialogues in the sense that it is more constrained. Our goal is, however, to keep a natural interaction mode and its relative flexibility. Sometimes, the interface has greater knowledge than the user. Thus it may automatically correct user's mistakes, suggest an alternative course of action, and provide appropriate information to help the user to interact with it. In other words, interface agents assist the user to perform a particular task.

> "Human interface designers are struggling to generate more effective illusions for purposes of communicating to their users the design model of their applications. At the same time, they are confronting serious issues of ethics: when does an attempt to create an empowering illusion become trickery, when does an attempt at anthropomorphism become cheap fraud?" (Tognazzini, 1993).

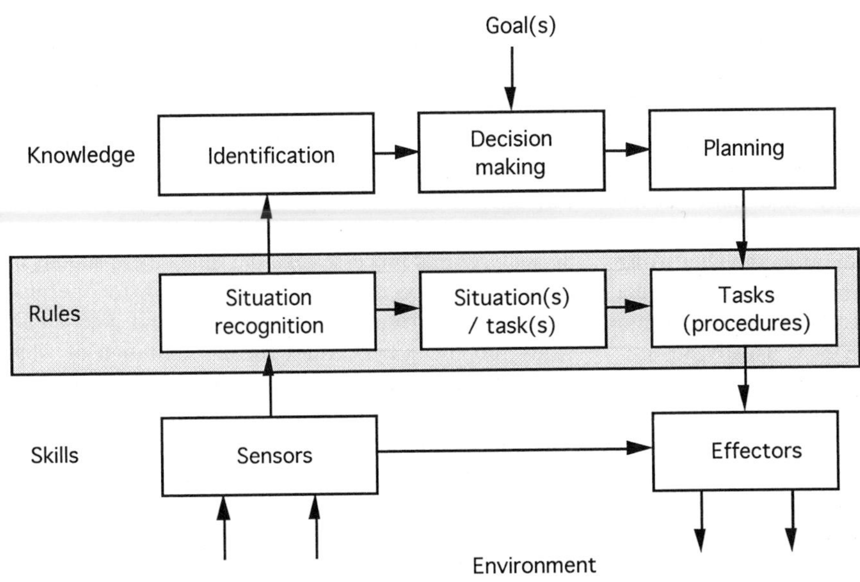

Figure 1. The intermediate level of Rasmussen's performance model as a major source of knowledge from expert explanations.

Thus, the products of knowledge elicitation for the design of software agents are not only rules and facts that would be used by an information processor, but also pictures, graphics and sound. That is, a software agent is not only a "crunching" mechanism, but also a visible and audible entity.

51.2.1 Knowledge Elicitation

Knowledge elicitation is an inherently co-operative activity (Addis, Gooding and Townsend, 1993). For this reason, the design of software agents is an incremental process that should enable the design and refinement of artifacts approximating expert views. The computer screen is then a mediating tool that enables collaborative design of such artifacts. A software agent can be constructed using a diagrammatic representation (knowledge blocks) associated with an appearance design tool. Experts and cognitive engineers cooperate through the current block base and its corresponding appearances. The more appearances are familiar to the expert, the more visual design is improved.

Leplat gave six general traits characterizing an expert (Leplat, 1986):

- the expert knows how to solve problems in his/her field, even those occurring for the first time;
- the expert knows how to restate badly formulated problems clearly and to represent the problem in such a way as to allow it to be solved;
- the expert knows how to evaluate the consequences of a deviation from optimal conditions in the solving of a problem;
- the expert builds up his/her knowledge through practice and may periodically reorganize this knowledge;
- the expert can make decisions with incomplete or temporarily missing information (Lenat, 1983); in certain cases, the expert is also the person who knows how to combine different types of knowledge that are available concerning a particular phenomenon in order to predict its properties or behavior (Hawkins, 1983).

Expert knowledge is inherently *compiled* by analogy with a compiled computer program. Once it is compiled, it is extremely difficult and often impossible to decompile it. The only way to approximate such knowledge is to observe the result of its processing, and rely on a relevant model. Rasmussen (1983) has already proposed a categorization of human behavior (Figure 1).

The acquisition of *skill-based behavior*, both sensory-motor and cognitive, is the result of long and intensive training. Skill-based behavior permits rapid stimulus-response type operations. The level of *rule-based behavior* is also an operative level, with manipulation of specific plans, procedures (e.g. a checklist or a cooking recipe) or rules (know-how). *Knowledge-based behavior* is the "true" level of intelligence. Current expert systems are mostly still at the level of procedures, because it is difficult (and often impossible) to elicit the compiled expert knowledge which exists at the skill-based behavior level (Dreyfus, 1982). Expert explanations usually come from the intermediate level. Like a professor teaching, the expert must "decompile" his knowledge to explain the "why" and "how" of his behavior. The result of such decompilation is easily transferable to a declarative form on a computer using for example the IF...THEN... format (generally called a rule). Unfortunately, the result of the decompilation through the observation of behavior is usually not sufficient to elicit the internal cognitive processes that generated this behavior. Furthermore, the analytical process of decompilation usually performed by a cognitive engineer or psychologist does not necessarily capture the knowledge and the expert behavior used at the skill-based level without a good cognitive model.

> "It is simplistic and misleading to assume that the process that leads to the emulation of human expertise in a computer program is one of transferring knowledge—'expertise transfer' is an attractive metaphor but it leaves open questions of what is expertise and how it may be transferred. A better metaphor might be one of modeling, that the emulation involves building a model of expertise, where a 'model' is according to Webster's dictionary: a representation, generally in miniature, to show the construction or serve as a copy of something." (Gaines, 1993).

Gaines's remark of the shift from expertise transfer to expertise modeling is essential, and deserves further analysis. We claim that expertise transfer (from human to machine) leads to clumsy automation (Wiener, 1989) when it is not controlled using a socially-recognized model and incrementally assessed through experimental protocols. Knowledge cannot be dissociated from its related inference mechanisms. Furthermore, knowledge elicitation is guided by specific intentions that influence the knowledge acquired, e.g., human-centered automation where one of the major objectives is to master the balance of control and monitoring between the human and the machine being automated (Billings, 1991). Finally, we need to consider that expertise evolves. We cannot trust a snapshot of it. This is why context is important to capture in order to properly index expertise.

51.2.2 User-Centered Design: A Problem Statement

Over the years, we have developed the paradigm of *integrated human-machine intelligence* (IHMI) (Boy and Nuss, 1988; Shalin and Boy, 1989; Boy and Gruber, 1991) to provide a framework for acquiring knowledge useful for the implementation of a software agent. This paradigm is presented in Figure 2. Arrows represent information flows. In this model, a software agent has three modules: a proposer that displays appropriate information to the human operator; a supervisory observer that captures relevant actions of the human operator; and an analyzer that processes and interprets these actions in order to produce *appropriate information* for the proposer module. Human-factors research and practice already propose generic rules for the definition of what *relevant actions* and *appropriate information* means in specific context and domains. However, there is no universal model available for the specification of such entities in general. The proposer, the supervisory observer and the analyser use two knowledge bases: the technical knowledge base and the operational knowledge base. The technical knowledge base is the theory (syntax and semantics) of the domain that the agent should know. It represents how its environment works. The operational knowledge base is the pragmatism that the agent should possess to act on the environment effectively. This model includes two loops:

- a short-term supervisory control loop that represents interactions between the human operator and the software agent; it involves mutual control between the human operator and the software agent; and
- a long-term evaluation loop that represents the knowledge acquisition process; it involves a designer and a knowledge acquisition method.

In the past, software design that leads to advanced automation has been essentially constructed and applied by engineers. Human factors people had very little impact on the design of complex systems. Marc Pélegrin, a well-recognized scientist in control theory, advocated in his introductory talk at the French Academy of Sciences that "the future of automation is semi-automation," apologizing for the fact that automation specialists have gone too far without taking into account end users. We would like to add that end users are only one concern. Software design needs to be considered in a broader sense for the whole of humanity including social, ecological, economical as well as psychological repercussions. Thus, software design needs to be human-centered because it should be done for the benefit of the largest range of end users. This benefit is related to a massive use and self-customization of the information technology, e.g., the Internet.

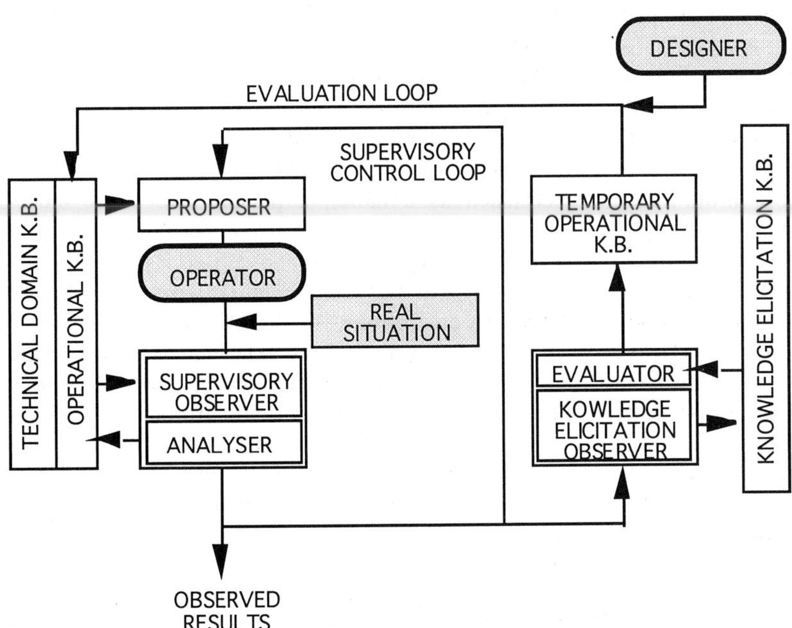

Figure 2. An integrated human-machine intelligence model.

The aeronautical industry used to be a good example of human-centered design. In the early days, airplanes (we might say flying machines) were built by the people who flew them. Thus, they adjusted the controls and other important devices according to their needs and knowledge. Today there is a chain of jobs between design and routine use. The main problem is to bridge the gap between design and routine use. This issue is about viewpoint management. The more we broaden the spectrum of viewpoints during design, the more complex the design process (it is difficult to manage too many creative people!). Efficiency is at stake here. A designer alone in his/her office or laboratory can be very efficient but not necessarily open to other viewpoints (not because his/her mind is not open, but because he/she does not have access to other people's experience). Introducing end users in the design loop is not trivial for many reasons such as cooperation, complexity and the difficulty of gathering the right people at the right time. This can be extremely inefficient, and there is a price to pay in terms of adaptation to a new way of doing things, but the price may decrease as we better understand how various participants in the design phase can communicate, share context, negotiate, etc. Cooperative work in design is therefore an important issue that is developed in other chapters of this handbook.

An important issue is to make the constraints explicit enough to guide the decisions during the design process. Some constraints are economical, others might be safety-oriented or ecological. People in charge of a project are responsible for the decisions they make and need to know explicitly what they are doing! If deciders know about potential risks or potential problems that a new design induces, they will reconsider this design. Design should be human-centered for the designers themselves. Human-centered design tools are extremely important in the perspective of an efficient use of a corporate memory. The concept of corporate memory has become important for several reasons (Boy, 1995). One of them is the visualization (conceptualization aid) of the concepts/artifacts being designed. In particular, explicit visualization of designed artifacts facilitates usability tests.

51.2.3 Context Categories

The concept of context is not easy to define. We will take the reflexive-deliberative viewpoint to define the context, in contrast with an environment-driven viewpoint (Suchman, 1987). Context can be related to the persistence of a situation (see section 51.3.1 for the definition of a situation), i.e., the more a situation persists, the more it is contextual. For instance, if you stay in the same room everyday in the morning for three hours, this pattern becomes contextual. We *contextual-*

ize by incrementally constructing increasingly complex but meaningful contextual patterns. For instance, words are defined by incrementally using them in various specific situations. Even if you do not know what the word *wishbone* means, the following sentences will contribute to its definition:

He used the best *wishbone* available in the race... This very short *wishbone* allowed him to turn shorter than the others at the marker buoy... Another reason is that such a *wishbone* is attached very high on the mast... In fact, all windsurf boards having such a *wishbone* should be used by real professionals...

After the first sentence, we learn that a *wishbone* can be used in a race. Even if we do not know what kind of race, this eliminates the possibility of an animal bone. In the second sentence, we learn that the *wishbone* is used on the water because of the marker buoy. After hearing the third sentence, we know that the *wishbone* is on a boat or some floating device. Finally, in the last sentence, we learn that a *wishbone* is part of a windsurf board (we assume that we know what a windsurf board is, otherwise we will continue to identify this new word in following conversations).

Thus, by adding situations (context) in which a word is used, this word can be incrementally defined. Such a context is called verbal context. This means that a word defined in a *verbal context* is defined by the other words around it. In information retrieval, the keyword in (verbal) context (KWIC) has been used as visual correlation during the selection (Luhn, 1959). This technique has been automated by Zimmerman (1988) and is used in CID (Boy, 1991c).

There is another form of context, that is *physical* and *social*. If you are presented with a windsurf board for instance, its owner may explain to you how to use it. In the conversation, he may say, "If you take the *wishbone* that way, the wind will push the sail in that direction". You suddenly discover that this piece of light metal supporting the sail laterally is called the wishbone. You learn this in a physical context. It may even happen that you will remember this word in this context forever, i.e., each time you think about your friend demonstrating his windsurf board, you will remember the anecdote of the wishbone, and conversely when you think about the wishbone. This is to say that context is very important for remembering things. In particular, in information retrieval, we claim that if context is used appropriately, it will enhance the search in memory. Hayakawa (1990) says that:

The "definitions" given by little children in school show clearly how they associate words with situations. They almost always define in terms of physical and social contexts: "Punishment is when you have been bad and you have to sit on the stairs for a time out." "Newspapers are what the paperboy brings."

In more formal terms, context can be defined by relationships between objects. An object can be a word or phrase, a picture, a movie sequence, a physical object (such as a table), a person, etc. These attribute/value pairs may be descriptions of verbal context (what is around the object and defines it in some situations), physical and social context (what one can point out in the environment of the object to concretize its definition), or historical context (what happened before and is causally related to the object being described). For instance the context of an information retrieval search could be described by a user profile (user model), e.g., the type of user, the type of task he/she is currently doing, the time, etc. The main problem with formal definition of context is that it can lead to a very large set of attribute/value pairs. From a computational point of view, consequent pattern matching may become practically impossible. This leads to the idea that context is usually defined by default for the most frequently used attribute/value pairs structure. This structure may have some exceptions. For instance, when we use the word "chair", it denotes a physical device that is used to sit on. However, in the context of a conference, the "chair" is usually the person who is in charge of the conference.

As Hayakawa (1990) pointed out, words have *extensional* and *intensional* meaning. If a word can be described by a real object that you can see in the environment, its meaning is extensional. For instance, if you point at a cow in a field, you denote the cow. If a word is described by other words to suggest its presence, then its meaning is intensional. For example, you may describe a cow by saying that it is an animal, it has horns, it lives on a farm, etc. Each object can be associated to a particular intensional description according to who is giving the description, when the description is given, etc. Again, context is a key issue when objects have to be described. It is a fallacy to claim that each object could be associated with a single word. Anyone who has tried to retrieve documents in a library using keywords equations knows this. It is almost impossible to retrieve the desired information because the description one gives for the query seldom matches the descriptions that librarians have developed. However, if you ask the librarian, he/she may help you better by acquiring more context from you. In the best case, if the librarian is a good friend and knows your work and needs, then he/she will be very helpful. If the librarian does not know you, he/she can capture physical context by simply looking at you. He/she may consider facts such as: you are young; you wear a lab coat; etc. He/she will also capture context from what you say (verbal context). Hayakawa says that "an examination of the verbal context of an utterance, as well as an examination of the utterance itself, directs us to its intensional meanings; an examination of the physical context directs us to the extensional meanings."

Context includes a temporal aspect, i.e., context summarizes a time period. Furthermore, persistence of some events reinforces context. For instance, a user told the librarian that he/she is looking for some information on geometry, he/she is currently involved in a computer class, he/she has a problem of drawing curves using a set of points, he/she needs to obtain a continuous drawing on the screen, and later he/she finally requested a reference on splines. The librarian usually integrates historical context, and, in this specific example, will not be confused between mathematical spline functions (what the requester needs) and the physical splines that draughtsmen used in "ancient" times. In this example, the words "computer" and "screen" help to decide that the requested "splines" will be used in the last quarter of the 20th century.

51.2.4 The Agent Perspective

The agent-orientation of human-machine interaction is not new. Autopilots have been commonly used since the 1930's. Such agents perform tasks that human pilots usually perform, such as following a flight track or maintaining an altitude. Transferring such tasks to the machine modifies the original task of the human operator. The job of the human operator evolves from a manipulation task (usually involving sensory-motor skills) to a supervisory task (involving more cognitive processing and new situation-awareness skills) (Sheridan, 1992). Creating *software agents* involves new cooperation and coordination processes that were not explicit before. Software agents involve active behavior of the users. They enable users to center their interactions at the content level (semantics) partially removing syntactical difficulties. They also enable the indexing (contextualization) of content to specific situations that they understand better (pragmatics).

Software agent technology is consistent with the design and development of component software architectures such as OpenDoc, OLE 2.0 or CORBA. These architectures support collaboration, integration and customization of applications. They provide software interoperability by enabling the design and refinement of distributed, cross-platform component software. They enable cooperative design. The nature of component programming leads to the notion of component assembly to fit the targeted task. Software agents are components that must be kept simple to understand and use. We claim that knowledge elicitation is easier and more efficient when it is possible to create and "immediately" assess software images of knowledge chunks. A chunk is defined as a parcel of knowledge that can be treated as an independent variable. In addition, this constructive process improves with experience. For instance, the six letters "A", "T", "L", "E", "B", and "S" can be treated independently, as the word "TABLES" can also be treated independently and results from assembly of the previous six letters.

Knowledge elicitation becomes a design process enhanced by the interactive and component-based software technology. However, this technology-rich approach should not overshadow the awareness of the representational model that is used in such a knowledge design process. Ferber (1989) differentiated three different representational models: analytical, structural and interactionist.

- The *analytical* approach considers knowledge as a set of assertions in a particular domain. These assertions may be first principles (e.g. physical laws), transcriptions of system behavior in the form of statements (e.g. "the thermostat regulates the temperature of the room") or facts based on experience (e.g. "generally when it gets too cold, it is because the thermostat is broken"). Logic has been used as a basic representation in this kind of approach. The analytical approach is linguistic (no knowledge without language), logical and reductionist (inference is made from primitive elements). This approach fails when temporal entities have to be considered, when statements describe dynamic processes, when different statements are contradictory (resulting from different points of view), and when ambiguities are present.
- The *structuralist* approach considers knowledge as a network of interrelated concepts. Semantic networks and frames have been used to understand deep structures in natural languages. In particular, generic (classes) and individual (instances) concepts and inheritance mechanisms have been studied in this approach. Knowledge processing is considered to be a form of general pattern recognition. The main limitation of this approach is its lack of definition and formalization. The structuralist approach is well developed in Europe, especially with Piaget's work (1967) on the development of intelligence.

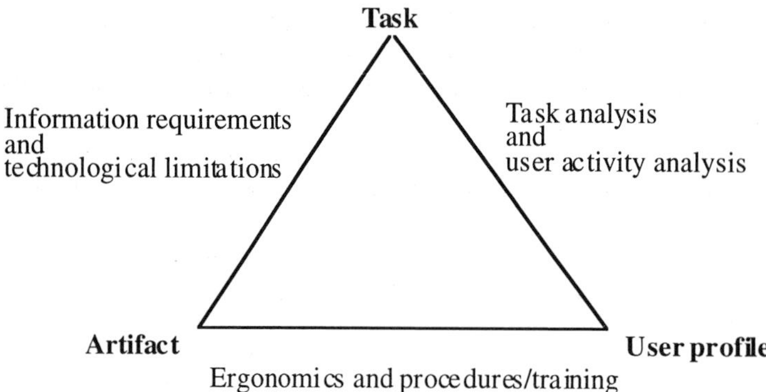

Figure 3. The artifact-task-user triangle.

- The *interactionist* approach is very recent. It is based on the principle that knowledge is acquired and structured incrementally through interactions with other actors or *autonomous agents*. Interaction and auto-organization are the key factors for the construction of general concepts. There are two main currents: automata networks (von Neumann, 1966; McCulloch and Pitts, 1943; Rosenblatt, 1958) and connectionism (Rumelhart et al., 1986; McClelland et al., 1986); and distributed AI (Minsky, 1985; Hewitt, 1977; Lesser and Corkill, 1983).

The knowledge elicitation approach developed in this chapter is essentially interactionist. It is based on the design/refinement of a model of the human-machine system being developed. Following Gaines, expertise should be modeled to better understand what should be automated (transferred to the machine) and what should be kept by the human to process. Knowledge elicitation is then enhanced through the mediating role of computer media. On this perspective, the term "Sociomedia" has been introduced to emphasize the social construction of knowledge (Barrett, 1992). The main issue is not so much to validate assumptions as to find appropriate assumptions to test (abduction process). Thus the usual hypothetical-deductive approach mainly based on a (one shot) batch process is replaced by a multi-abduction approach relying on interaction.

51.2.5 Designing Agents by Incremental Knowledge Elicitation

We have advocated the position that knowledge elicitation should be situated. Software agents both help knowledge elicitation in context, and are designed and refined from this knowledge elicitation. An artifact is a physical or conceptual human-designed entity useful for a given class of users to perform specific tasks. Carroll and Rosson (1991) described transactions between tasks and artifacts. It is sometimes difficult to know if the task defines the artifact or if the artifact defines the task. In reality, users' profiles, tasks and artifacts are incrementally defined. The classical engineering tradition is centered on the construction of the artifact. The task and the user are usually taken into account implicitly. Tasks can be modeled from a *task analysis* or a model of the process that the artifact will help to perform. A specified task leads to a set *of information requirements* for the artifact. Conversely, the artifact sends back its own *technological limitations* according to the current availability of technology. Users can be incrementally taken into account in the design loop either through the development of syntaxo-semantic user models or through the adaptation of analogous user models. User modeling can be implicit or explicit, and leads to the definition of appropriate *user profiles*. When a version of the artifact and the task are available, the user can use the artifact to perform the task. An *analysis of the user activity* is then possible, and contributes to modifying both the task and the artifact. The use of the artifact provides data to adapt both the artifact to the user (*ergonomics*), and the user to the artifact (*procedures and training*). The *artifact-task-user triangle* is described in Figure 3. It implicitly defines an incremental approach to design that is elsewhere described as a spiral model for software development (Boehm, 1988). It is based on the design of representative components that are incrementally validated with respect to functional requirements, hardware and software constraints, and strategic and economic issues of the organization. Design rationale is attached to each component.

A similar analysis was provided by Woods and Roth (1988) with their cognitive systems triad. They outlined the factors that contribute to the complexity and difficulty of problem solving by describing: the world in terms of dynamism, many interacting parts, uncertainty and risk; the representation that can be fixed, adaptive, computational or analogical; and the agent in terms of multiple agents and joint cognitive systems. In our approach, these dimensions are taken as independent variables useful for incremental definition of the task, the artifact and the user.

In the next section, an agent model is proposed. The process of incremental knowledge elicitation is supported by the *SRAR* model that is described at length in section 51.4. This model leads to the *knowledge block* representation presented in section 51.5. Knowledge blocks support the representation of cognitive functions that are useful for modeling user-centered designs. This new method, called *cognitive function analysis* (CFA) is presented, and a global approach to design is provided in section 51.6. Section 51.7 is devoted to conclusions and perspectives.

51.3 An Agent Model

Various definitions have already been proposed for an agent. Commenting the on-line Random House Dictionary definition of an agent, Minsky said:

> "When you use the word 'agent'... there is no implication that what the agent does is simple... the agent is seen as having some specialized purpose. If you need help with making investments, you call a financial agent. If you're looking for a job you call an employment agent. In the present-day jargon of computer interface agents, the word is used for a system that can serve as a go-between, because of possessing some specialized skill." (Minsky and Riecken, 1994)

The function of an agent can be defined in several ways. In an aircraft for example, a human copilot shares the work with the pilot — but not the ultimate responsibility. The pilot can consult the copilot on any point concerning the flight but will make ultimate decisions. If the pilot delegates a part of his responsibilities to the copilot, the copilot will take this delegation as a task to execute. The same principle applies to the pilot who is mandated by his company to transport safely and comfortably the passengers from one airport to another. The pilot can stop the execution of a copilot task at any time, if it is necessary. However, a copilot may have personal initiatives, e.g., testing parameters, constructing his/her own awareness of the actual situation, predicting deducible failures, etc. A copilot may process the information included in an operation manual at the request of the pilot. He should be able to explain, at an appropriate level of detail, the result of his processing.

A substantial increase in the presence of software agents in work situations causes a job shift from a control activity to a supervisory control activity (Sheridan, 1984). For instance, software agents such as flight modes in modern aircraft cockpits tend to change the nature of pilots' jobs. The choice of a model for the description of an agent is rather difficult since we need to represent information gathering, processing and control, as well as to provide conceptual tools for taking into account factors such as cooperation or delegation. We have adopted a mixed approach to modeling agents that is both structuralist and interactionist. Our agent model is based on Newell and Simon's classical model (1972). It was first developed during the MESSAGE project of analysis and evaluation of aircraft cockpits (Boy, 1983; Boy and Tessier, 1985).

Following Minsky's definition of an agent, an agent is itself a society of agents (Minsky, 1985). Thus, the agent model includes a *supervisor* sub-agent managing three other types of sub-agents called *channels*, that are receptors, effectors and cognition (Figure 4). Each sub-agent may act autonomously accomplishing tasks that were required by the supervisor agent or wait for new requirements from the supervisor. The internal function of an agent is based on a cognitive architecture usually called a blackboard (Nii, 1986). Each channel exchanges information with the supervisor. The supervisor may sequence tasks for the channels, or leave them to work independently as active demons. It may use a performance model such as Rasmussen's (1983). The notions of automatic and controlled processes, introduced and experimentally observed by Schneider and Shiffrin (1977), have been implemented in the supervisor of the generic agent of the MESSAGE system (Tessier, 1984). This allows the generation and execution of tasks either in parallel (automatisms), or in sequence (controlled acts). In our agent model, automatic processes involve specific knowledge modeled by a *situational representation*. In contrast, controlled processes involve knowledge represented by an *analytical representation* (see section 51.3.2).

51.3.1 Situational Representation

The term situation is used here to characterize the state of affairs of the agent's local environment. A situation is described by a set of components called facts. Facts are causal entities that can be events, circumstances,

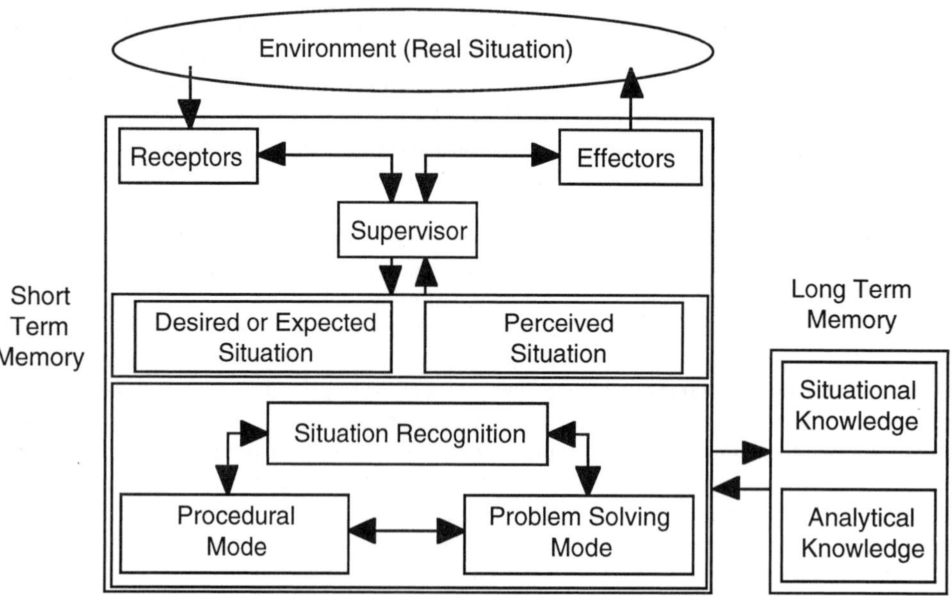

Figure 4. Agent model.

stories or conditions. Formal notations are introduced here to show the reader both the complexity of the concept of situation and the extreme difficulty to elicit situation rationally. A generic fact will be noted f_i (meaning fact number i). At a given time, three basic types of situation will be distinguished (Boy, 1983):

(1) The *real situation* characterizes the "true" world. It is only partially accessible to the operator and must be interpreted as: "The real situation at a given time t is the fact set, which may be restricted to the local environment". The set is a priori infinite. It is noted:

$$SR(t) = \{ f_i / i = 1, \infty \}.$$

(2) The *perceived situation* is a particular image of the local environment. It is the part of the environment accessible to the operator. It is characterized by incomplete, uncertain and imprecise components. It will be noted:

$$SP(t) = \{ \pi_i / i = 1, n \},$$

which must be interpreted as: "The perceived situation at a given time t is the set of facts perceived by the operator." This set is assumed to be finite. Each perceived fact π_i is the result of the mapping of operator P_i on a subset of the fact set:

$$\pi_i = P_i(\{ f_j / j = 1, p \}).$$

In general, operator P_i is "fuzzy" in Zadeh's sense (1965). All the subsets of the fact set characterizing each perceived fact are also assumed to be finite.

(3) The *desired situation* characterizes the set of operator's goals. It will be noted:

$$S_D(t) = \{ \partial_i / i = 1, m \},$$

which must be interpreted as: "The desired situation at a given time t is the set of the goals which the operator intends to reach." This set is assumed to be finite. Each goal ∂_i is the result of the mapping of the operator Di on a subset of the fact set:

$$\partial_i = D_i(\{ f_j / j = 1, q \}).$$

In general, operator D_i is "fuzzy". All the sub-sets of the fact set characterizing each goal are also assumed to be finite.

The real situation characterizes the local environment. Perceived and desired situations characterize the operator's short term memory. In the expert system terminology, the perceived situation is called the fact base (i.e., "perceived facts") and the desired situation is called the goal (and sub-goal) base.

Situation Patterns

The concept of a *situation pattern* is fundamental. A situation pattern characterizes the operator's *expected situation* at a given time. We will say that a situation pattern is activated if it belongs to the short term memory. It will be noted:

$$S_E(t) = \{ \mu_i / i = 1, l \},$$

which must be interpreted as: "The expected situation at a given time t is the set of the situation patterns which are activated in the short term memory". This set is assumed to be finite. Each situation pattern μ_i is the result of the mapping of operator Π_i on a sub-set of the fact set:

$$\mu_i = \Pi_i (\{ f_j / j = 1, r \}).$$

In general, operator Π_i is "fuzzy". All the sub-sets of the fact set characterizing each situation pattern are also assumed to be finite. In practice each fact f_j is represented by a (numerical or logical) variable v_j, and its tolerance functions { $TF_{i,j}$ } in the situation pattern μ_i. A *tolerance function* (TF) is an application of a set V into the segment [0,1]. The elements of V are called "values", e.g. the values indicated by a numerical variable. V is divided into three sub-sets: preferred values {TF(v)=1}, allowed values {0<TF(v)<1}, and unacceptable values {TF(v)=0}. This model of a tolerance function is able to take into account logical variables, e.g. position of a valve or truth of a statement, and numerical variables, e.g. temperature or pressure. An ordinal scale has been defined in accordance with the above definition of the three sub-sets. This definition is appropriate where natural language concepts must be modeled and manipulated. In fact, a tolerance function is a membership function related to the concept tolerance. The major attraction of this representation is its ability to handle the vagueness inherent in categories of language, e.g. "the pressure P1 is close to the maximum."

A situation pattern is an element of the operator's long-term memory. It is the result of a long period of learning. At each time interval, the operator's vigilance will be characterized by the number and relevance of the situation patterns "activated" in the short-term memory. For instance, in a monitoring process, the operator matches perceived facts with activated situation patterns. Reason (1987) calls this process: "similarity matching". At a given instant, if several patterns are candidate for a perceived situation, Reason's results show that the most frequent pattern is selected first. He calls this process: "frequency gambling." We also call this process "conflict resolution." We have defined the total process as *situation recognition* (Boy, 1987).

It seems reasonable to envisage that situation patterns (i.e. situational knowledge) are *compiled* because they are the result of training, which is a type of learning. The situational knowledge of an expert results mainly from the compilation, over time, of the analytical knowledge he relied on as a beginner (see section 51.4.3). This situational knowledge is the essence of expertise. It corresponds to skill-based behavior in Rasmussen's terminology. "Decompilation", i.e. explanation of the intrinsic basic knowledge in each situation pattern, is a very difficult task and is sometimes impossible. Such knowledge can be elicited only by an incremental observation process.

51.3.2 Analytical Representation

When a situation is recognized, problem solving generally follows. A problem is initiated by an event (i.e., perceived or desired situation) which necessitates that the operator allocate intellectual resources. These intellectual resources can be represented by structured objects and inference rules, such as: IF <Conditions> THEN <Hypothesis> AND <Actions>. Note that if several situation patterns have been matched and kept as "interesting to be considered", then several hypotheses are suggested. Thus, problem solving can be multi-hypotheses. Generally, each hypothesis defines an "extension" ("world" or "viewpoint"). Consistency maintenance in each extension and between generated extensions is a central mechanism. Such a mechanism has been formally described and developed by De Kleer (1986). De Kleer called this mechanism an "Assumption-Based Truth Maintenance System". Thus, generally, analytical reasoning involves a problem solver and a consistency-maintenance mechanism.

The problem solver provides inference. Inference can be performed in forward chaining (from data to conclusions) or in backward chaining (from goals to elementary actions). Human problem solving has been defined as "opportunistic" by Hayes-Roth and Hayes-Roth (1978), i.e., either forward or backward chaining is possible at any given time. Moreover, the human being tends to reason using knowledge already structured in *knowledge chunks*. Each chunk is connected to one (or several) situation pattern(s) and defines a context. In multi-hypotheses problem solving, each extension is said to be working in its *context*. The corresponding representation will be called *analytical representation*. This notion will be further developed in section 51.4. Analytical knowledge can be decomposed into two types: procedures or know-how, and theoretical knowledge.

Procedural knowledge can be represented in the form of *instantiated* plans. It can generally be translated into production rules and propositional logic. Thus, it is also the result of instantiation of more general knowledge. We here use interchangeably the terms instantiated knowledge, surface knowledge and procedural knowledge. The knowledge in operation manuals is almost exclusively of this type. Rasmussen (1983) relates rule-based behavior to this level of knowledge. Procedural knowledge is the easiest to acquire. It may be more or less easy to formalize.

Another type of processing, called *knowledge exploration*, is based on so-called *deep knowledge* (Van der Velde, 1986). From a formalization viewpoint, this kind of knowledge is not always available in all disciplines and corresponds to the theoretical basis of the domain in which one is working. Several models (and sometimes theories) may be used to describe or reason about an engineered system. In fault diagnosis, for example, one might develop a structural model of the system to be diagnosed and then decompose it into its basic components and the relationships among those components. Sometimes, a graphical model is necessary. A functional model will permit simulation of the behavior of the various components. A causal diagram may then be drawn to establish the various connections between the properties of the components. The associated type of reasoning will call on a mechanism for instantiation of general knowledge. This knowledge is organized according to the structure of the field of the problem to be solved: its topology, its functionality, its causality, and other aspects such as the hierarchy of objects and the autonomy and *heteronomy* of various parts of the system. Deep knowledge is the basis of Rasmussen's knowledge-based behavior.

51.4 The SRAR Model

Using software agents is a situated activity. We proposed a model called the *situation recognition and analytic reasoning* model (SRAR). This model has been applied to various dynamic situations and problems.

51.4.1 The HORSES Experiment

In this section, we describe a knowledge elicitation experiment that was carried out at NASA Ames Research Center (Boy, 1987). The Orbital Refueling System (ORS) used in the space shuttle to refuel satellites was chosen as an example of a system to be controlled. Three software agents were used to implement knowledge elicitation experiments: an ORS simulator, a malfunction generator, and a fault diagnosis expert system, called HORSES (Human—ORS—Expert System). These software agents were concurrent processes, communicating through a shared memory. The malfunction generator generated simulated malfunctions for the ORS, and introduced them at the appropriate times into the ORS simulation. HORSES was composed of a set of software agents having a graphical appearance on IRIS 1200 graphic system. HORSES has been incrementally improved through an incremental knowledge elicitation process.

Two groups of four pilots participated in the experiment. The first group was naive in the ORS operations whereas the second was knowledgeable in that domain. Sessions were videotaped for subsequent analysis. Pilots were asked to oversee the transfer of fuel from one container to another and were given simulated display and controls as they were currently implemented in the ORS. Each pilot was involved in five sessions of 3 hours, performed on 5 days. The first session was training only. Fifteen runs were proposed to pilots during the three following sessions. For each run there was a probability of encountering a failure. Faults were leaks, sensor biases, and avionics failures. During these experiments, two types of operator assistance were tested. The first type corresponds to the use of a classical paper operation manual. The second type corresponds to the use of HORSES connected to the system being controlled. It helped by determining possible situations (contexts) that the operator then selected. HORSES was able to start a process of analytical reasoning, interacting with the operator. It asked the same questions, requested the application of the same procedures, and gave the same diagnoses as the operation manual. The operator answered the questions, applied the procedures or not, and could stop the reasoning at any time. The last session was a debriefing during which individual interviews were performed. Experiments involved subjects being asked to think aloud while interacting with the ORS. Protocols (the chronological history of all the pilot's actions and system responses) were transcribed for later analysis. Verbal reports were very useful to understand what variables and processes were used when pilots performed diagnosis tasks, i.e., the analytic reasoning. But, as the situation recognition process is very interconnected with the diagnosis inference, verbal information from the pilots during the process control task was also very useful for identifying situation patterns. Verbalizing information is shown to affect cognitive processes only if the instructions require verbalization of information that would not otherwise be attended to (Ericsson and Simon, 1980). Thus, the experimenter did not ask any question during operations. The results are based primarily on protocol analysis. They rely on the use of three criteria: the importance of an event during the run, its frequency, and the number of pilots dealing with it (Robert, 1985). In the analysis, the following three topics were considered: operation manual versus software agent; beginners versus experienced operators; and the derivation of SRAR model (see below) for fault identification.

51.4.2 Derivation Of the SRAR Model

Operation Manual Versus Software Agent

Pilots using the operation manual could be separated into two groups. The first group used the *procedure-following mode*: "Pressure P1 is not normal according to what it should be on the graph, therefore I take the procedure to diagnose the fault." They recognized critical situations by matching observations to situation patterns included in the operation manual. They used the operation manual very carefully and diagnosed faults according to the knowledge available in the operation manual. Detection and subsequent reasoning were very straightforward. The second group used an *intuition-based* mode: "Losing pressure P1, I have a leak in tank 1, close immediately valve 4." They recognized situations not necessarily included in the operation manual. The first group was slower than the second in diagnosing faults when the fault was easy to detect. The second group failed more often. The first group always applied procedures, whereas the second was generally problem-solving-driven.

Pilots using the software agent as an intelligent assistant could be divided into two groups: situation *recognizers* and *diagnosis processors*. In the former group, pilots used the software agent as an assistant in situation recognition. They tended to rely on the advice of the software agent about the situation. However, they also used the explanation facility very often. They generally used the software agent in a forward-chaining mode. In the latter group, pilots used the situation recognition agent after having detected a problem by themselves. They acknowledge the results given by the situation recognition agent, and started the corresponding analytical processing. These pilots generally guessed a diagnosis and asked the software agent to verify it in a backward-chaining mode. It was observed typically that the situation recognizers are inclined to use a procedure-following mode, whereas the diagnosis processors correspond to an intuition-based mode.

Beginners Versus Experienced Operators

Experienced people monitored the system being controlled with more sophisticated situation patterns than the beginners. Once they recognized a situation, experts implemented short sequences of tests. The analytical reasoning they employed at this stage was minimal, by comparison with beginners. Thus, experts and beginners recognize differently situations and subsequently implement associated analytical reasoning differently.

The situation patterns of beginners are simple, precise and static, e.g. "The pressure P1 is less than 50 psia". Subsequent analytical reasoning is generally major and timeconsuming. When a beginner uses an operation manual to make a diagnosis, his behavior is based on the *precompile, engineering logic* he has previously learned. In contrast, when he tries to solve the problem directly, the approach is declarative and uses the first principles of the domain. Beginner subjects were observed to develop, with practice, a personal procedural logic (operator logic), either from the precompiled engineering logic or from a direct problemsolving approach. This process is called *knowledge compilation.* Conversely, the situation patterns of experts are sophisticated, fuzzy and dynamic, e.g. "During fuel transfer, one of the fuel pressures is close to the isothermal limit and this pressure is decreasing". This situation pattern includes many implicit variables defined in another *context*, e.g. "during fuel transfer" means "in launch configuration, valves *V1* and *V2* closed, and *V3, V4, V7* open." Also, "a fuel pressure" is a more general statement than "the pressure P1." The statement "isothermal limit" includes a dynamic mathematical model, i.e. at each instant, actual values of fuel pressure are compared *fuzzily* ("close to") to a timevarying limit [P_{isoth} = f(Quantity, Time)]. Moreover, experts take this situation pattern into account only if "the pressure is decreasing," which is another dynamic and fuzzy pattern. It is obvious that experts have transferred part of analytical reasoning into situation patterns. This part seems to be concerned with dynamic aspects.

Thus, with learning, dynamic models are introduced into situation patterns. It is also clear that experts detect broader sets of situations. First, experts seem to fuzzify and generalize their patterns. Second, they have been observed to build patterns more related to the task than to the functional logic of the system. Third, during the analytical phase, they disturb the system being controlled to get more familiar situation patterns which are usually static: for example, in the ORS experiment, pilots were observed to stop fuel transfer after recognizing a critical situation.

By definition, a pair {S_i, A_i} is called a SRAR chunk (Figure 5). Beginners have small, static and crisp situation patterns associated with large analytical knowledge chunks. Experts have larger, dynamic and

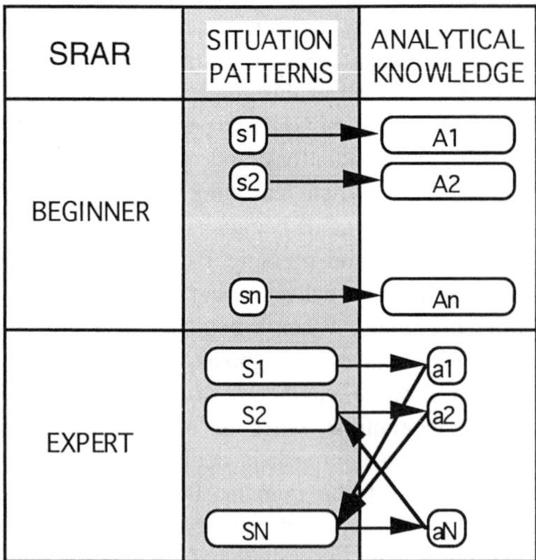

Figure 5. The situation recognition / analytical reasoning model.

fuzzy situation patterns associated with small analytical knowledge chunks. The number of beginner chunks is much smaller than the number of expert chunks.

51.4.3 SRAR Chunks as Interface Components

The following generalizations can be drawn from the HORSES experiments. First, by analyzing the human-machine interactions in the simulated system, it was possible to design a display that presented more polysemic information to the expert (e.g. a monitor showing the relevant isothermal bands). *Polysemic* displays include several types of related information presented simultaneously and are readily understandable to experts because the presentation is derived from their situation patterns. This improved user and system performance. Second, the HORSES agent achieved a balance in the sharing of autonomy. The original system designer did not anticipate the way that the operators would use the system, but letting them have indirect control over the assistant allowed them to utilize what they had learned to do well.

SRAR can be used to design interface agents that would help human operators to anticipate the evolution of dynamic systems. It is intended to provide help to find the best compromise in the design of interface and procedures. Taking the example developed in section 51.4.1 above, experts were observed using a diagram displaying two curves to follow the evolution of the pressures with respect to the quantity of fuel transferred. These curves were graphical representations of two ideal models, namely isotherm and adiabatic (Figure 6). Experts followed the evolution of the point (Q, P) represented by the quantity transferred Q and the corresponding pressure P within the domain defined by these two curves.

Paper-based technology makes it possible to use easily complex patterns such as the one displayed by the indicator (Q, P). Operations are rather difficult—and most of the time impossible‹due to the fact that the human operator needs to use several sheets and manuals at the same time. In books, situation patterns are very simple and crisp conditions that can be written as titles to index pages of analytical reasoning. Expert situation patterns are constructed by experience. They cannot be stored in books because they are far too complex and, even if this storage was possible, human operators would have immense difficulty in retrieving them. When integrated in the user interface, they are easy to use because they are used as monitoring displays. The next section proposes a methodology to approximate expert situation patterns and subsequent user-centered interface components.

51.4.4 Constructing Situation Patterns: the LSS Model

The construction of situation patterns is a learning mechanism. Learning can be viewed as a bi-directional transformation: specialization and generalization. Most research efforts in automatic symbolic learning (Kodratoff and Tecuci, 1987; Michalski et al., 1986) have focused on generalization. In expertise, however, specialization plays a major role. An expert is not necessarily "intelligent", in the sense of possessing highly sophisticated and general knowledge, but possesses specialized situation patterns for his domain of expertise. These patterns have been built with experience. Generalization consists in building disjunctive chunks, while specialization consists in building conjunctive chunks.

The LSS (learning by specialization/structuring) model is one of a class of symbolic learning processes which are based on explanation (Boy and Delail, 1988). The explanations come from experts in the domain under consideration, or from external observers. At the beginning of the learning process, the input is procedural knowledge. The learning process can be decomposed into three phases:

- acquisition of procedural knowledge (explanations) and construction of a suboptimal knowledge base (analytical and situational);
- transfer (specialization) of certain elements of the

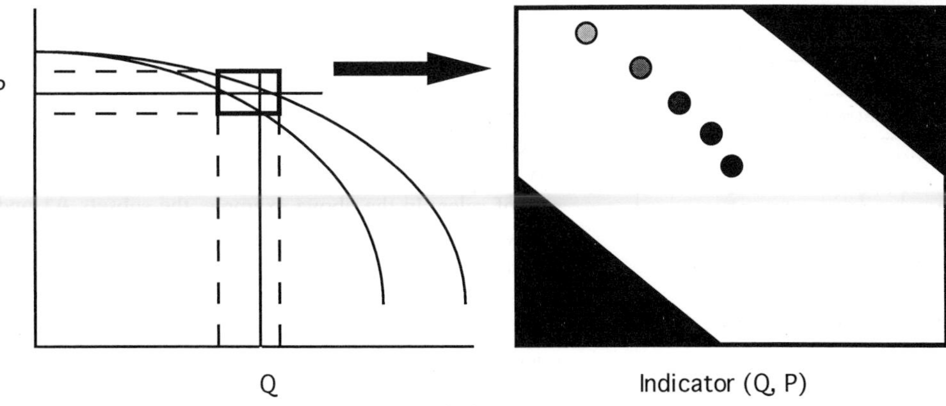

Figure 6. Construction of the indicator (Q, P) as an expert situation pattern.

analytical knowledge into situation patterns, as the result of experimentation;

- restructuring of the analytical knowledge as a function of the new patterns, i.e. new "chunks" are created.

In some ways, this method is similar to the chunking method developed in the SOAR system (Laird et al., 1987). The difference is that here, the process of chunking works explicitly on two types of knowledge, i.e. analytical and situational. In addition, chunks based on the concept of situation patterns open the possibility of parallel processing of knowledge. This parallelism is concerned not only with asynchronous processing of situational knowledge, but also with the processing of several analytical reasoning processes simultaneously. As in SOAR, the specialization process reduces the search.

Initial Suboptimal Knowledge Base

The first phase of the process consists in building a suboptimal knowledge base (KB) which will be refined by experimentation. The situation patterns in the suboptimal KB are small and crude. These are the Demons which suggest subsequent analytical reasoning. The initial analytical KB describes the functioning of the system to be controlled. It is divided into several subsets of rules, each of which contains a large number of rules (SRAR beginner in figure 4). We have taken the following example from an operator assistance (Boy and Delail, 1988; Mathé, 1990) project in space telemanipulation. The situation patterns and the analytical rules are written here in the form:

```
IF      <premise(s)>
THEN    <hypothesis>
AND     <action(s)>
```

Under these conditions, an example from the initial suboptimal knowledge base is:

Situation Pattern:

```
IF      { TETA1 > 60 }
THEN    suggest subset-of-rules(A)
AND     start-the-analytical-reasoning
```

Analytical knowledge:

```
IF      user-acknowledgment
THEN    subset-of-rules(A)
AND     reset user-cross-check
```

The first analytical rule functions in backward-chaining mode if its consequence (hypothesis) is suggested by a situation pattern, as is the case in the above example. For simplicity, we will restrict discussion to this case. If, however, a situation pattern leads to a new set of values for a set of facts, then a forward-chaining mechanism would be used. As the analytical reasoning progresses, the corresponding knowledge is instantiated and thus may be represented in tree form. The instantiated knowledge from the above example is summarized in the following graph (Figure 7).

Specialization

We have already shown (Boy, 1987b) that as operators gain experience in using the system with which they are charged, their situation patterns become more complex, more dynamic and more numerous (SRAR

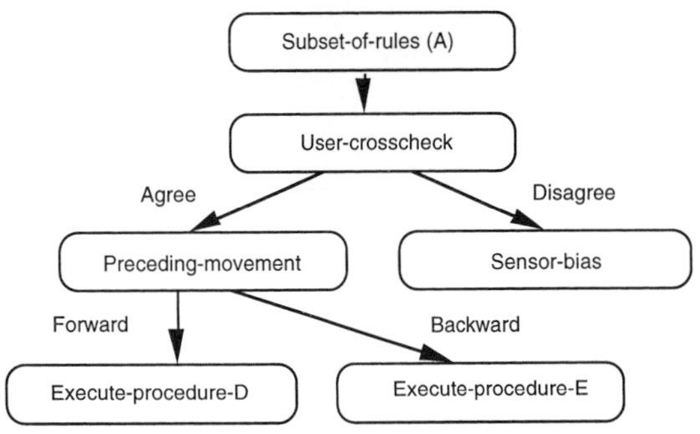

Figure 7. Analytical search tree.

expert in Figure 4). In the above example, we found that all the experts considered the node Preceding-movement very early in the process of situation detection. This element of knowledge can thus be transferred into the situational part of the knowledge base. Thus, specialization of the knowledge base proceeds as follows. (1) Detection of the values or instances of the node to be transferred. Here, the fact Preceding-movement can take the values Forward or Backward.

(2) Identification of the initial situation pattern from which the node was deduced, and construction of n new patterns corresponding respectively to n values or instances of the transferred node. Each new situation pattern is a conjunction of the contents of the initial pattern and a particular instance of the transferred node. In the above example, the new situation pattern is:

```
IF      { TETA1 > 60
AND      Preceding-movement (Forward ) }
THEN    suggest subset-of-rules(A1)
AND     start-the-analytical-reasoning

IF      { TETA1 > 60
AND     Preceding-movement (Backward ) }
THEN    suggest subset-of-rules(A2)
AND     start-the-analytical-reasoning.
```

(3) Restructuring of the analytical knowledge base. As n situation patterns have just been created in step 2 of the learning process, the analytical KB can be redivided into n corresponding subsets. This transformation results in the duplication (n times) of the part of the analytical KB which was initially upstream to the transferred node. In a more schematic form, let T be the node transferred, and I1 and I2 the values or particular (relevant) instances of T. S is the initial situation pattern, and A, B, C, D, E are other nodes (Figure 8).

Structuring

Step 3 of the specialization process requires restructuring of the part of the graph upstream from the transferred node. The concept of structuring of the analytical KB introduces the concept of hierarchy among the subsets of rules. In the above example, the subsets A1 and A2 were constructed from the initial subset A. A1 and A2 contain the same subset of nodes (B and C). Thus, these nodes are common to the disjunctive subset (A1 v A2). The process of restructuring thus leads to the extraction of the intersection of the disjunctive subsets of rules elaborated by the specialization process, and to the contextual connecting of this intersection to "specialized" disjunctive subsets (Figure 9).

Implementation of this technique in the form of rules leads to the first rule of the analytical reasoning (A1, for example):

```
IF      user-cross-check
AND     Preceding-movement (Forward ) }
THEN    suggest subset-of-rules (A1)
AND     reset user-cross-check
AND     suggest
        subset-of-rules (A1 v A2)
```

and the subset (A1 v A2) starts with the same type of rule in backward chaining. If this first rule does not contain an action of the type suggest subset-of-rules(...), then the corresponding subset of rules is called a terminal subset. In all other cases, there will be a common subset. Each subset of rules has a priority corresponding to its degree of commonalty. Thus, various degrees of commonality exist. This concept (degree of commonalty) introduces the notion of recursiveness on several common subsets of rules (Figure 10). It should be noted that a common subset of rules may be activated directly by its own situation pattern, if such a pattern exists.

51.4.5 Problem Statement and Problem Solving

The situational/analytical distinction induces another distinction: the *statement of a problem and its solution*. We have seen that problem solving may be of two kinds: using know-how and exploring theoretical knowledge. Until now, most research in AI has addressed problem solving. We consider here the well-known maxim "a problem well-stated is a problem already half-solved." In effect, an expert problem-solving method has a refined and sophisticated problem statement, and an easy-to-implement problem solution.

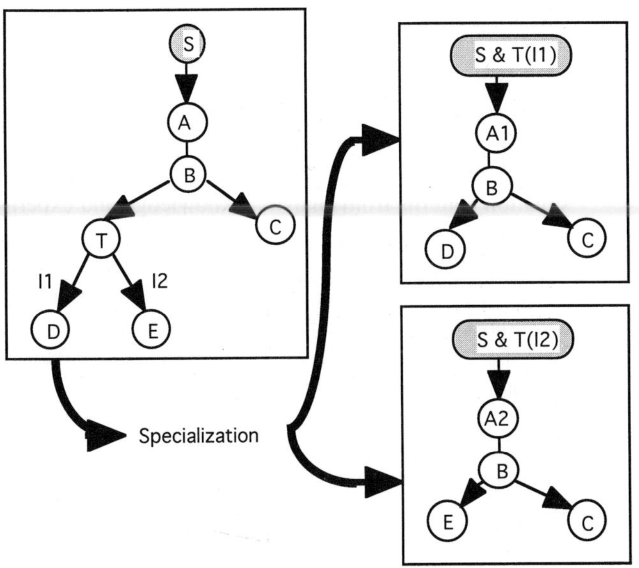

Figure 8. The specialization process.

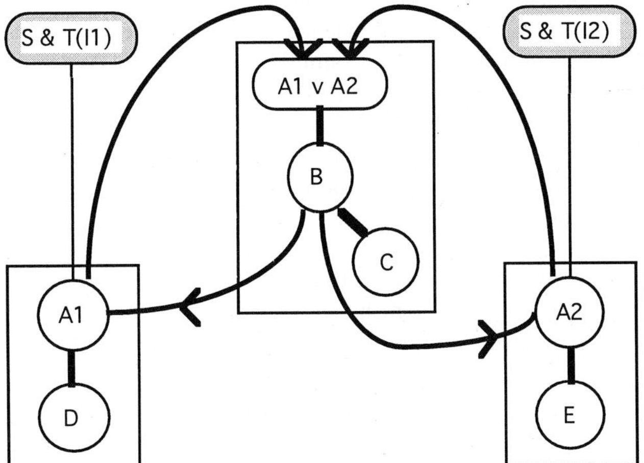

Figure 9. The structuring process.

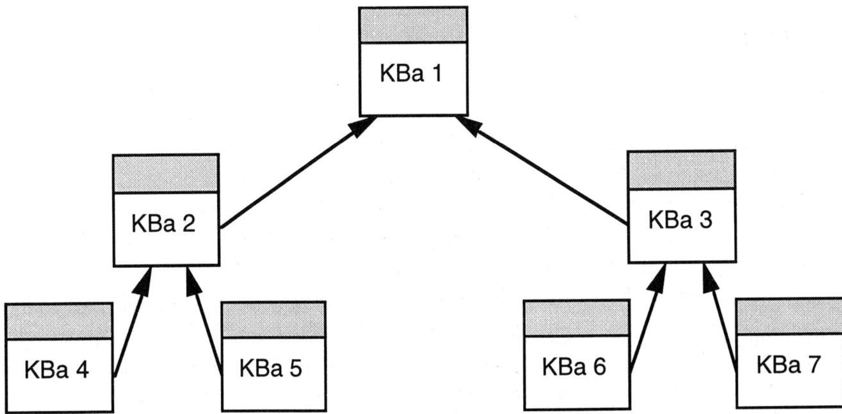

Figure 10. Commonality among the subsets {Kbai}. For example, KBa2 is common to KBa4 and KBa5.

However, the problems that we propose to study in this work are poorly defined and cannot be expressed in algorithms. It should be noted that a problem may be badly stated a *priori* but its statement may be refined by experience.

We have seen that it is very difficult, and sometimes impossible, to elicit expert knowledge. In contrast, it is easy to ask an expert to give a tutorial. If this tutorial is taken as analytical knowledge, this knowledge can be tested incrementally and used to generate situational knowledge progressively by experimentation. In the same way, the statement of a problem may evolve with experience, and asymptotically approach a genuine skill. Certain experts, when faced with a problem, function by stimulus response with virtually no reasoning remaining. Because it corresponds to the mechanisms used by human operators, the situational/analytical distinction can be used to implement intelligent assistant systems which improve the overall performance of man-machine systems. In particular, an expert system built using this model enables the developer to design an initial knowledge base which is essentially analytical and, by using a complementary simulation tool, to construct the situational knowledge base incrementally by experimentation.

We have already defined a situation pattern as a set of constraints bearing on a finite set of facts. We know that a person's behavior becomes more and more rapid as he accumulates such "patterned" knowledge. For example, consider the task of driving a car. The more a driver encounters cases of a particular type of situation, the more he will develop situation patterns which thereafter will be activated by reflex when a real situation of that type is perceived. In other words, he will not have to think for a long time to make a "right" decision. The corresponding learning process could be described as the compilation of patterns, i.e. this process creates automatisms.

If we try to explain the observed behavior of the driver by a computerized model separating out analytical and situational reasoning and the process of learning by specialization and structuring, it quickly becomes apparent that as the number and complexity of patterns increases, the calculation time also increases. This is exactly the opposite of what is observed in human behavior. This phenomenon has been explained in (Tambe and Newell, 1988).This phenomenon can only be explained by the parallel processing in human mechanisms of cognition and perception, as opposed to the essentially sequential functioning of computers, up to the present.

51.5 The Block Representation

This section presents the *knowledge block* representation that was developed to support the SRAR model and consequently the LSS model. Such a representation was designed to support the incremental construction of situation patterns from analytical knowledge and experience. Consequently, the knowledge block representation is commonly used as a *mediating representation* to help design teams eliciting operative models from users. In addition, knowledge blocks are declarative entities that can be linked whenever necessary to simulate (operational) procedural knowledge (Boy, 1989).

When beginners start to operate a particular system, they start learning formal procedures which they will improve incrementally over time. The procedural knowledge improves by augmentation of the knowledge base, and by transformation of the various entities of available procedures into more contextual procedures that are better suited for routine use (see section 51.4). Results of this transfer lead incrementally to more operational knowledge. Such a knowledge compilation mechanism is similar to those of Anderson (1983) and Rosenbloom (1983). The main claim of our approach is that contextual knowledge can be gained through experimentation. Thus, computers can provide experimental support for an incremental contextualization of knowledge.

In this section, we present a new approach to knowledge elicitation that utilizes existing procedures and modifies them by introducing the concept of abnormal conditions. It is based on a *block* representation. Its advantage in eliciting knowledge is its naturalness to humans. The resulting knowledge bases are similar in form to technical and operation manuals. Furthermore, the block representation is very convenient for incrementally building operational knowledge. The resulting system uses on-line user requirements and suggestions either to reinforce current procedures in cases of success or to generate new recovery procedures in cases of failure. This allows the system to provide helpful responses, even when no robust user model is available.

51.5.1 Knowledge Block Definition

A *block* can be described as a set of goals, a set of conditions, and a set of actions to achieve the goals. Conditions are decomposed into triggering preconditions, abnormal conditions and contextual conditions (Figure 11).

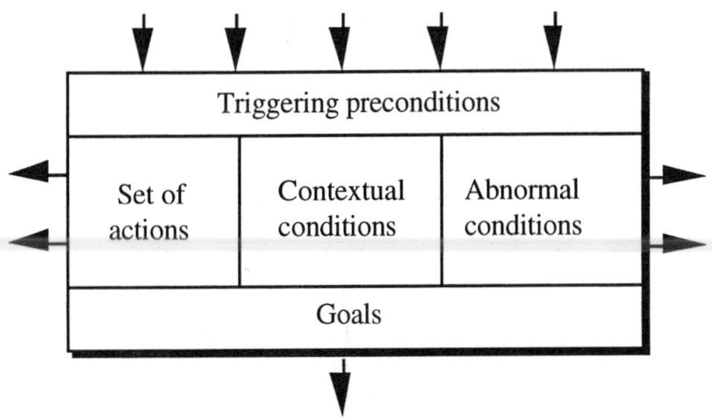

Figure 11. Block representation.

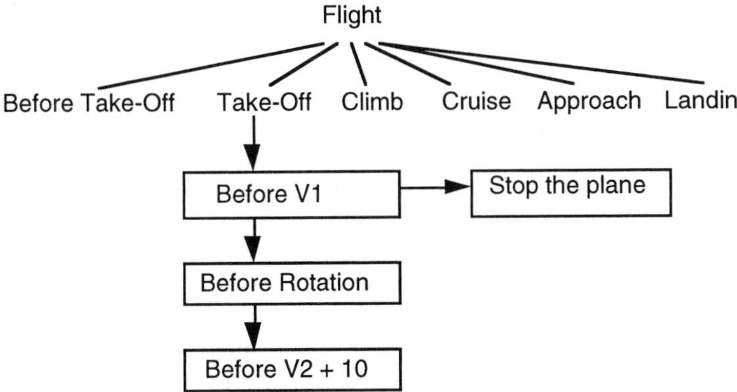

Figure 12. Simple hierarchy of contexts.

51.5.2 Context Versus Triggering Preconditions

As we have already seen in the previous section, situation patterns are constructed incrementally by experimentation. In a situation pattern, we distinguish between contextual conditions and triggering conditions. In section 51.2.3, context has been already described as a set of persistent conditions that remain valid for a certain period of time. Thus, when such conditions are persistent, it is not necessary to trigger them at any time. We will say that contextual conditions are contributing factors to the activation of a situation pattern. In contrast, there are other preconditions that need to be triggered to actually start analytical reasoning.

For instance, if somebody is solving a problem in a given environment, there are a lot of tacit preconditions which are "obvious" (e.g. constant) in that environment. These preconditions are included in the contextual conditions. Given this definition, if a system is in a context, reasoning can be done on the set of blocks belonging to that context. Thus, triggering preconditions can be made much simpler, leading to faster pattern matching.

Contexts are organized in hierarchies. This facilitates the organization of the block knowledge base. For example, in aviation, a flight is generally organized into phases, which are decomposed into subphases and finally each subphase is described in the form of knowledge blocks or procedures (Figure 12).

In the context of a flight, there are several subcontexts (such as before take-off and take-off). In each terminal context (e.g. take-off), a set of blocks has to be performed. The corresponding block representation of the take-off context of blocks is given in figure 13. If everything is normal, the pilot accelerates the plane up to a decision speed (called V1) after which he will not be able to stop the plane in case of a major incident. He executes the first block *Before* V1 (block A in figure 13). The block *Before* V1 is valid in the context *take-off.* It is triggered when the precondition *Brake release* and *Maximum power* are satisfied. The goal of this block is to reach the speed V1. A variety of actions

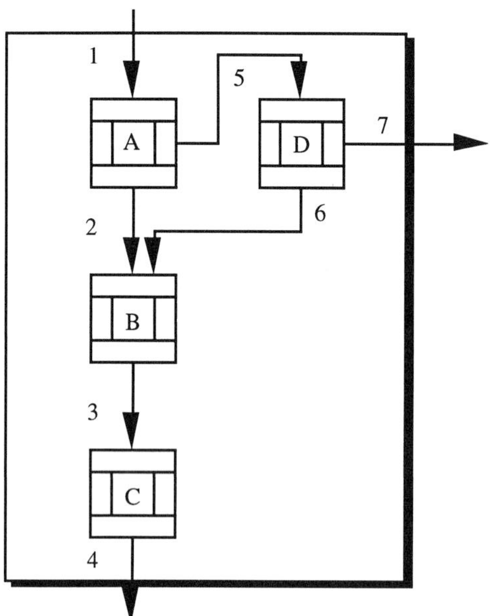

Figure 13. Context of knowledge blocks.

can be offered by the block. Some actions can be designed as resources to reach the goal. Some other actions are only loosely connected to the goal. If no abnormal condition occurs, he executes the blocks *Before rotation* (block B) and *Before* V2+10 (block C). If an abnormal condition is satisfied during the execution of the block Before V1, then he can decide to execute the block *Stop the plane* (block D). The notion of context of blocks is mutually inclusive, i.e., a block is included in a context that itself is included in a more general context, and so on. For instance, Figure 13 presents a context of blocks that is a block with the following characteristics:

- triggering condition: the triggering condition of block A;
- goal: goal of block C;
- abnormal condition: abnormal condition of block D.

51.5.3 Abnormal Conditions and Non-monotonic Reasoning

The abnormal conditions of a block can be satisfied or not satisfied. When a set of actions is no longer applicable to the current situation, the situation is said to be abnormal for this block and an abnormal condition corresponding to this situation must be attached to the block. Abnormal conditions can be associated with the entire block or with a specific set of actions. For instance, during the execution of a navigation procedure in an aircraft, a cabin depressurization in flight is an abnormal condition which leads to the application of a recovery procedure.

The execution of a block consists in performing its actions and controlling the satisfaction of the corresponding abnormal conditions. Abnormal conditions can be of two types: weak abnormal conditions that, if they occur, will cause an exit from the current block towards another block in the same context; and strong abnormal conditions that, if they occur, will cause an exit from the current block towards another context of blocks.

For instance, a blown bulb in an aircraft cockpit may be a weak abnormal condition that does not necessitate changing the context of the flight. Conversely, an engine shut-down will cause a radical change of context, i.e. the pilot will adopt a different strategy (fly to the closest airport, for example) and apply the appropriate recovery procedures.

An example of a context of blocks is represented in Figure 13 in the form of a flow diagram. Let {A, B, C, D} be a set of blocks having the same contextual conditions. Arrows represent links. Links between blocks are identified by numbers, from 1 to 7 in Figure 13. For example, A and D are connected by link 5 when a specific abnormal condition of block A is satisfied. Block A is called the "root" of the context of blocks. Notice that a context of blocks is a block itself. In our example, triggering preconditions of the context block are the triggering preconditions of block A, its abnormal conditions are those of block D, and its goal is the goal of block C.

In the previous aviation example, blocks A, B, and C stand for procedures *Before* V1, *Before Rotation* and *Before* V2+10. In normal situations, blocks are organized and processed in a tree sequence, i.e. A->B->C. We will call the resulting process *linear browsing* of a set of blocks. Abnormal situations interrupt this linear sequence to branch onto other blocks (generally called recovery procedures). In our aviation example, let us assume that, when applying the procedure *Before* V1, the speed indicator shows an unacceptable value (weak abnormal condition 5). The pilot has to use procedure D, that is, to monitor the thrust, except if the speed is lower than a given threshold (strong abnormal condition 7). In this case, the pilot has to change the context and *Stop the plane*. If the speed is within an appropriate range, then procedure D succeeds and the pilot can apply procedure B (link 6). We will call the resulting process *nonlinear browsing*, i.e. A->D->B->C.

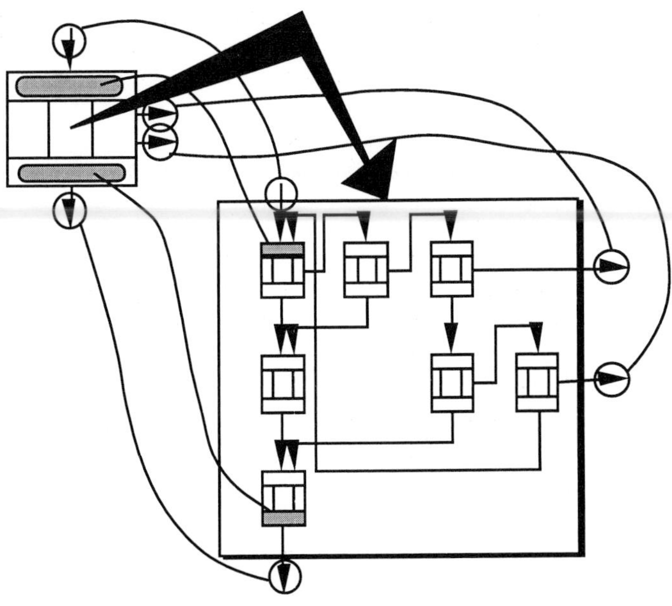

Figure 14. Decomposing a block.

51.5.4 Incremental Construction of Blocks

This representation is very convenient for representing knowledge that is needed to perform tasks which have to be performed to accomplish given operations on an engineered system. Usually, task analysis is performed by operations engineers who design and develop operation manuals that have to be revised often. This representation allows for declarative programming by incremental decomposition.

Knowledge design starts from raw blocks described from a high-level (macroscopic) point of view. A block can be decomposed into a network of blocks which will inherit the context of the initial block (Figure 14). This will create layers of contexts of blocks which can be browsed easily. Furthermore, as a context of blocks is a block itself, the lowest granularity of knowledge is being represented in the same way as the highest. This property is very interesting from a knowledge acquisition point of view because the level of description of some parts of a domain, a task or a function may be different according to current available expertise and knowledge.

A situation pattern is a problem statement that leads to analytical reasoning on a context of blocks. The situation pattern of a context of blocks is composed of the minimal set of preconditions of the blocks characterizing the context. "Minimal" expresses the fact that, if a precondition is expressed in two different blocks of the same context, it will be taken only once in the situation pattern. Blocks are then explored and executed to solve the problem stated by the situation pattern.

A knowledge block represents a cognitive function that is used by a human operator to perform a task. It enables the representation of how a human operator performs the task. In the first place, the block is instantiated with the knowledge corresponding to the prescribed task (what the operator should do). Once a first prototype is built, it can be used and assessed. The corresponding block representation can be modified according to the information elicited from the observation of the operator activity. In particular, contextual and abnormal conditions are generated by experimentation.

51.6 Cognitive Function Analysis (CFA)

51.6.1 Cognitive Function: Definition

According to the French tradition in ergonomics (Laville, 1976), a distinction is made between *task* (prescribed task) and *activity* (effective task). When a job needs to be performed, it can be decomposed into tasks. Thus, tasks (at any level) are the requirements of the job. When someone performs a task, he/she produces an activity. This activity may differ from the original requirements, i.e., the effective task differs

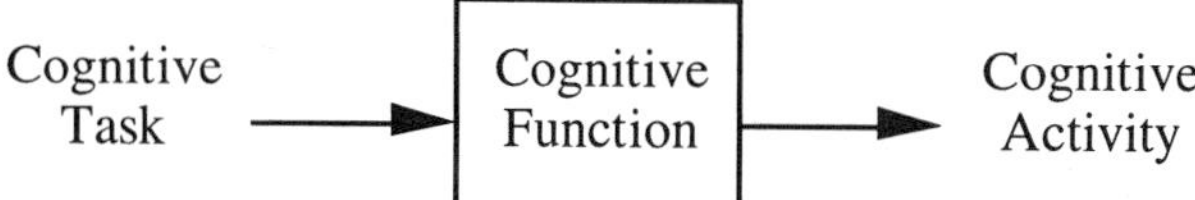

Figure 15. A cognitive function (CF) transform a task (what is prescribed) into an activity (what is effectively done).

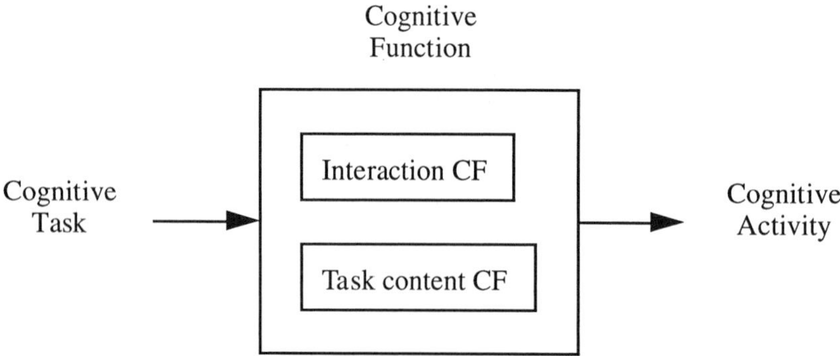

Figure 16. Interaction and task content components of a cognitive function.

from the prescribed task. This is due to the fact that all situations are very difficult to anticipate when tasks are designed. A human operator facing a situation produces a specific activity according to the requirements, but may need to *adapt* the task to this situation. *Cognitive functions* are the representation of the mechanisms that produce activities (Figure 15).

In the sense described above, cognitive functions are agents. From a purely pragmatic viewpoint, the term cognitive function is better suited to describe human cognitive agents (processes). The term agent denotes humans or machines. Cognitive functions denote the processes that they use to perform the tasks that are assigned to them.

At design time, these cognitive functions can only be speculated upon according to past experience, accumulated knowledge and know-how. When a new device is being designed, it is extremely difficult to anticipate how it will be used. The designer has a use in mind, but cannot imagine all the possible uses of this device. At evaluation time, these users can be inferred from the observation of real activities. In both cases, they enable the simulation of cognitive processes. We call *cognitive simulation* the simulation of the appropriate cognitive functions. Examples of cognitive functions in aeronautics include:

- clearance transmission;
- frequency change;
- rolling authorization;
- parking space allocation; and
- flight level allocation.

A cognitive function (CF) can be decomposed into smaller grain cognitive functions. In particular, a CF invoked for performing a specific task can be decomposed into two main CFs (Figure 16):

- the CF devoted to the interaction: it is related to the syntax used to perform the task;
- the CF devoted to the content of task itself; which is related to the semantics of the task.

An easy-to-use user interface usually results in simple CF interaction components. For instance, if the task is to program a flight plan using the current interface called the multifunction command and display unit (MCDU). Most pilots do not like to use the MCDU, e.g., they do not like its lateral location, its alphanumeric keyboard, its overloaded screen, its complex menu system, etc. We carried out a study to improve the current concept of MCDU (Boy, 1995). The pilot needs to push keys (e.g., a first interaction sub-CF is devoted to locating the right key and checking what the computer response is), browse menus that can be more or less complicated due to the depth or recursion of these menus, etc. The interaction component (I-CF) of the overall CF can be complicated. CFs devoted to the content of the task are concerned with

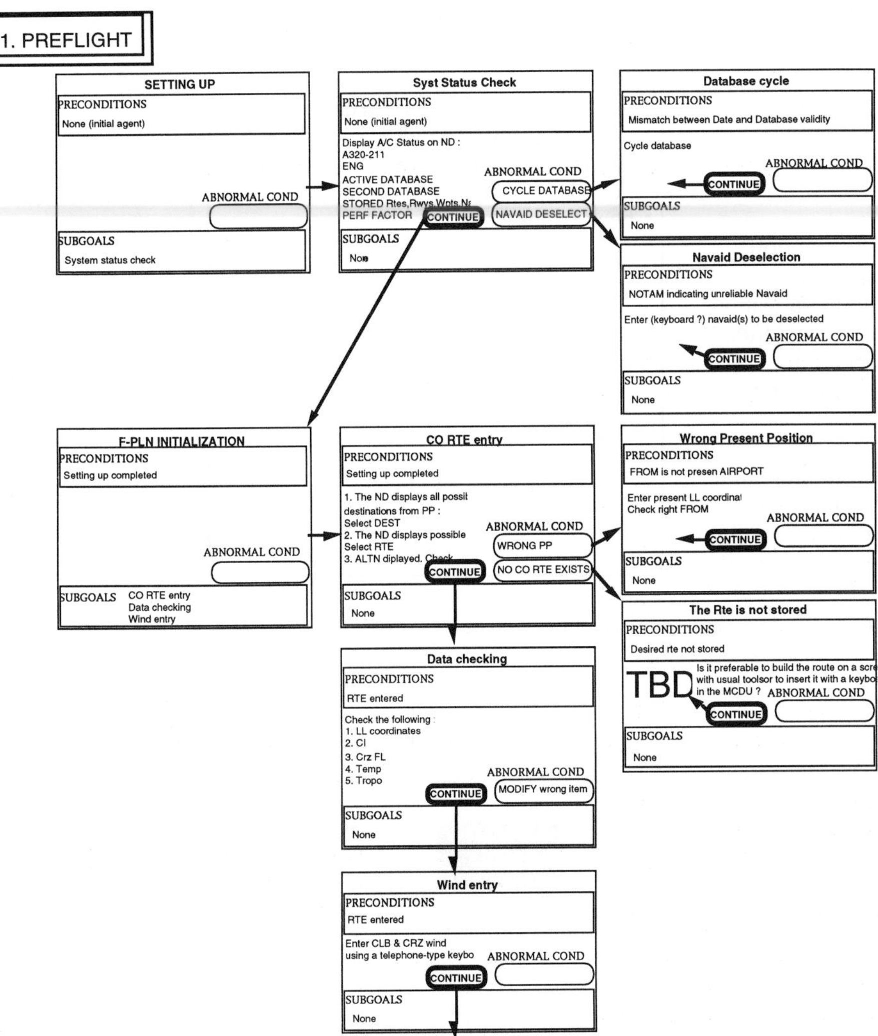

Figure 17. Example of a network of blocks for the Preflight cognitive function in the MCDU example.

processes such as minimizing the distance between two points, satisfying a constraint imposed by Air Traffic Control (ATC), etc.

A complex cognitive function such as programming a flight plan using a MCDU can usually be decomposed into a graph of knowledge blocks. The first layer of blocks mainly represents TC-CFs such as presented in Figure 17. For instance, the *Preflight* TC-CF is decomposed into three TC-CFs *Setting up*, *Flight plan preparation*, and *Performance* (Figure 18). The *Setting up* TC-CF is then decomposed into two TC-CFs *System status check*, and *Navaids deselection*. The *System status check* TC-CF is conditionally (If A/C *Status page is not displayed*) decomposed into four I-CFs Depress 'DATA' key, Select 'A/C STATUS', *Check Database period of validity*, and *Check Clock/Date*.

A cognitive function analysis of the flight programming task enabled the elicitation of eight primitive cognitive functions: *browse, check, depress, enter, insert, modify, select* and *set*. Each more complex cognitive function is a composition of these primitives.

51.6.2 Automation as Cognitive Function Transfer

The development of new tools can facilitate the execution of such cognitive functions by taking over part of the job currently performed by humans. The cognitive functions that are purely devoted to interaction itself (I-CFs) could be usually directed towards the machine

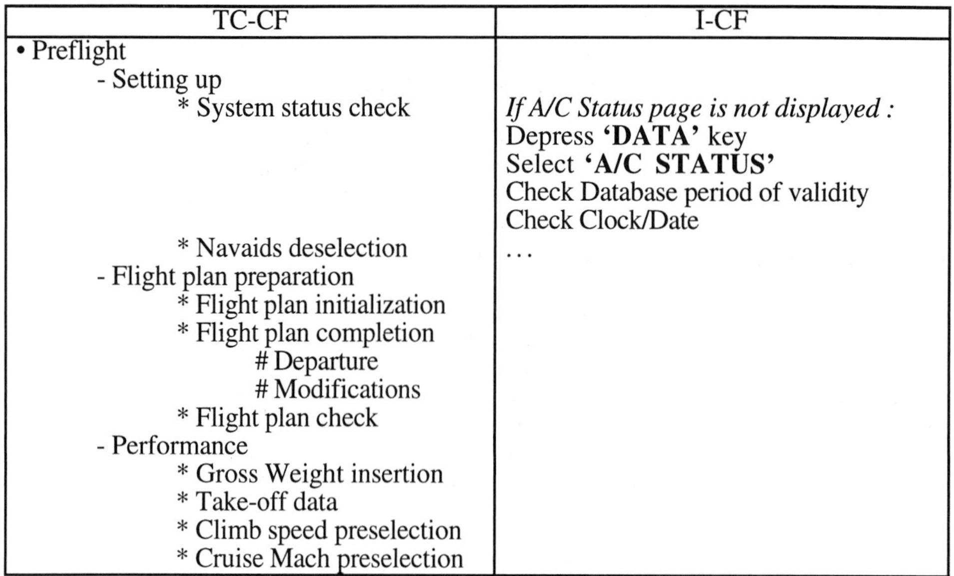

TC-CF	I-CF
• Preflight	
- Setting up	
* System status check	*If A/C Status page is not displayed :* Depress **'DATA'** key Select **'A/C STATUS'** Check Database period of validity Check Clock/Date
* Navaids deselection	...
- Flight plan preparation	
* Flight plan initialization	
* Flight plan completion	
# Departure	
# Modifications	
* Flight plan check	
- Performance	
* Gross Weight insertion	
* Take-off data	
* Climb speed preselection	
* Cruise Mach preselection	

Figure 18. Decomposition of the Preflight programming cognitive function.

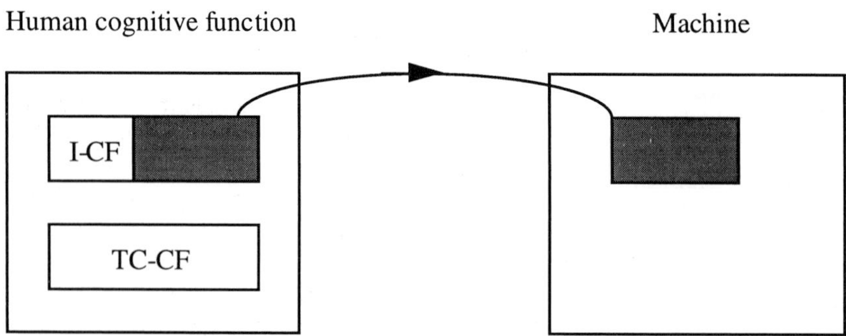

Figure 19. Transfer of part of an interaction cognitive function (I-CF) to the machine.

(Figure 19), and the cognitive functions that are purely devoted to the content of the task are directed towards the human. *Transferring cognitive functions from humans to machines is also called automation.* For instance, technology-mediated human-human communication can be greatly enhanced by directing tedious and time-consuming I-CFs towards the machine.

Note that TC-CF also can be transferred to the machine. I-CF transfer defines an automation that transforms a physical interaction into a more cognitive interaction. TC-CF transfer defines an automation that distributes the responsibility of the task between the human and the machine. The way TC-CF are understood by designers is crucial because a transferred TC-CF necessarily has limited autonomy. The way this autonomy is perceived by end-users is an important issue. Sometimes users may not anticipate this limited autonomy because the system (using the transferred TC-CF) functions well most of the time.

There are several goals that motivate automation. These goals can be classified according to the following list of goals adapted from the list proposed by Billings for the air transportation system (Billings, 1991, page 68):

• *accountable*; it must inform the human operator of its actions and be able to explain them on request;	• *subordinate*; except in pre-defined situations, it should never assume command. In those situations, it must be able to be countermanded easily;
• *predictable*; it should be able to be foretold on the basis of observation or experience;	• *adaptive*; it should be configurable within a wide range of human operator preferences and needs;
• *comprehensible*; it should be intelligible;	• *flexible*; it should be tractable, characterized by a ready ability to adapt to new, different, or changing requirements;
• *dependable*; it should do, dependably, what it is ordered to do; it should never do what it is ordered not to do; it must never make the situation worse;	• *informative*; it must keep the human operator informed; what is the system doing; what is the automation doing; have I any problems; where am I now; where do I go next; where do I do it;
• *error-resistant*; it must keep human operators from committing errors wherever that is possible;	• *error-tolerant*; some errors will occur, even in a highly error-resistant system; automation must detect and mitigate the effect of these errors.

Figure 20. Attributes of automation. *(Billings, 1991)*

- *safety*: to conduct all operations, from start to end, without harm to persons or property;
- *reliability*: to provide reliable operations without interference from environmental variables;
- *economy*: to conduct all operations as economically as possible; and
- *comfort*: to conduct all operations in a manner that maximizes users' and related persons' health and comfort.

Formalizing the transfer of cognitive functions is a means to better understanding and controlling automation according to a list of automation goals such as safety, reliability, economy or comfort.

In the MCDU experiment, it was decided to remove the alphanumeric keyboard and to introduce a larger navigation display (ND) screen and a direct manipulation facility such as a trackball to manage information on this screen. This is an alternative to the current one. We consequently developed a set of cognitive functions that are used by the pilots to program flight plans. The efficiency of these functions was assessed using a keystroke level model analysis (Card et al., 1983), performed with the help of operational people. It showed that the alternative to the current setup is much better, i.e., it takes much less time to access any planning function when one uses this alternative design.

51.6.3 Human Factors Criteria

Our objective is to make this automation human-centered. What is human-centered automation (HCA) from a cognitive function viewpoint? As stated earlier, CFA involves eliciting, constructing and chaining cognitive functions that are involved in a specific task. HCA is a step further as it involves a set of principles and guidelines that guide CF transfer from an agent to another, and help understand the repercussions of this transfer. These repercussions can be expressed in terms of new CFs created and new relations between agents. HCA principles and guidelines are supported by design rationale criteria expressed in terms of attributes of automation (Billings, 1991); see Figure 20.

Billings' attributes of automation can be reinterpreted as ranges of dimensions that enable the designer to direct CF transfer towards I-CF and TC-CF as shown in Figure 21.

Billings provided a framework for analyzing human-centered automation that is based on the analysis of *monitoring functions* and *control functions*. The more a machine is automated, the more users can be subject to boredom, complacency and competence erosion. The more users need to perform the work manually, the more they can be subject to fatigue and high workload. Billings's analysis showed that CF transfer influences psychological factors such as bore-

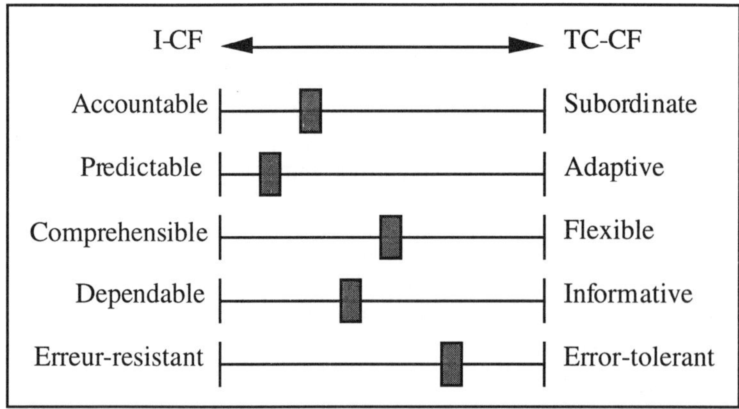

Figure 21. Transferred CFs in terms of attribute of automation.

dom, complacency, competence erosion, fatigue or workload. These factors can be used to assess the relevance of CF transfer. Billings provides a list of principles for HCA (Billings, 1991):

- the human operator must be in command;
- to command effectively, the human operator must be involved;
- to be involved, the human operator must be informed;
- the human operator must be able to monitor the automated systems;
- automated systems must be predictable;
- automated systems must also be able to monitor the human operator;
- each element of the system must have knowledge of the others' intent;
- functions should be automated only if there is a good reason for doing so; and
- automation should be designed to be simple to train, to learn, and to operate.

51.6.4 Elicitation Method Using a Cognitive Simulation

Cognitive functions are difficult to capture. The main idea of the method is to *incrementally refine elicited cognitive functions* in order to simulate cognitive interactions, in the use of the tool or system being designed. Cognitive simulations make it possible to *test design alternatives*. Cognitive function analysis (CFA) involves a cognitive simulation based on the block representation (cognitive designer part) and explicit interface artifacts (user part) (Figure 22).

The cognitive simulation is started using the block representation by specifying a starting context and satisfying (one or several) triggering condition(s) (Figure 17). There is a direct correspondence between the formal knowledge block and its interface artifact, i.e., an appropriate metaphor of its meaning. For instance, if a block represents the various actions to take in the *before* V1 context, its *interface artifact* will be all the relevant instruments and procedures to follow in this context. This interface artifact can be static or dynamic according to the level of detail that we would like to investigate. Standard hypermedia tools can be used to develop such external faces.

This simulation enables *domain experts to assess the relevance and correctness of the cognitive function analysis*. In particular, the level of *granularity* of the representation is essential in order to capture relevant and necessary cognitive functions useful in air-ground communications. The CFA method consists of the following steps:

- define a first sub optimal set of contexts using classical elicitation methods such as interviews, brainstorming, terrain observation;
- develop the knowledge blocks that describe processes responsible for both pilots' and controllers' activities within these contexts;
- run a cognitive simulation and assess its relevance and correctness;
- refine current contexts and knowledge blocks; and
- run a new cognitive simulation and assess its relevance and correctness.

We claim that the cognitive simulation method enables the study of human-machine interactions. Other authors agree with this view (Woods and Roth, 1995).

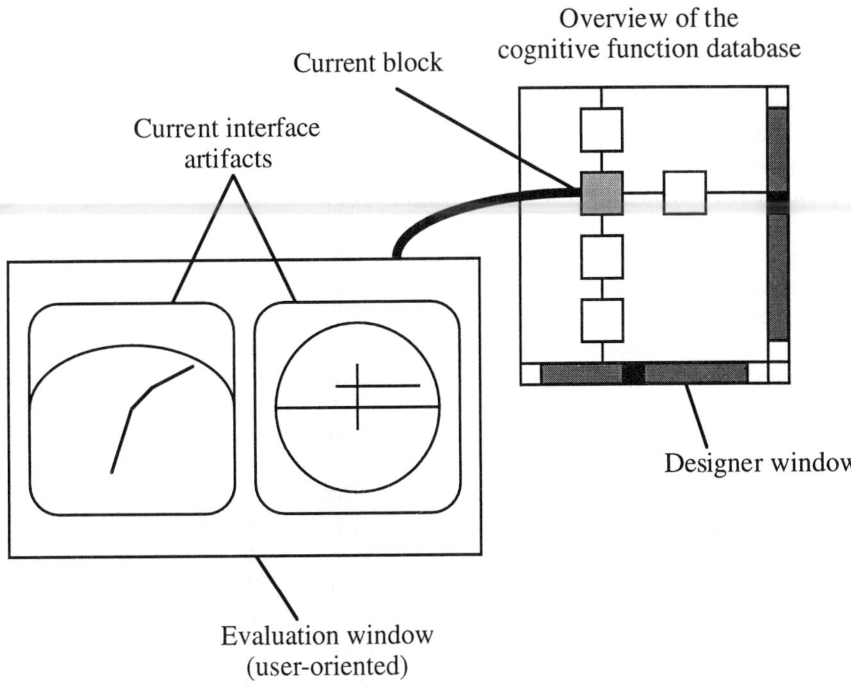

Figure 22. A view of a cognitive simulation using the CFA approach.

This is due to the fact that it has been intrinsically based on the concept of agent. The main difficulty is to determine the level of granularity that we would like to study. This involves tradeoffs and compromises. In the MCDU example, each cognitive function interface artifact was designed on a Hypercard card that gave to the user the illusion of a "real" navigation display screen. Using such a hypermedia tool enables the generation of active documents that can both simulate a real-world behavior and provide on-demand explanations.

This example has demonstrated that the use of such a cognitive simulation to rationalize design decisions can be extremely useful to explain why a part of a device has been specifically designed (Boy, 1995). This approach can be understood by designers and end users. Cognitive functions represented as knowledge blocks provide a powerful tool for mediating interaction between these practitioners. Furthermore, blocks enable incremental storage of design rationale in context, and easy retrieval and better interpretation of design rationale in context.

51.6.5 CFA Improves the Task Analysis Concept

CFA can be used to design procedures that are usually designed to improve performance, workload, safety, recovery from errors and failures in complex systems control tasks. A task analysis breaks down a task into sequences of « elementary » actions and control decisions. Since the role of the operator has evolved from direct control of a physical process (doing) to supervision and decision making of an automated system controlled by computers (thinking), task analysis has also evolved from physical to cognitive tasks. GOMS (Goals, Operators, Methods and Selection Rules) is a good model for analyzing the way goals and actions are organized for the accomplishment of a task (Card et al., 1983). A GOMS analysis is basically *goal-driven*, and one of the main difficulties of GOMS is to describe the goal structure. In addition, GOMS was developed to analyze and predict the total time for user task performance in human-computer interaction. The types of tasks that are usually analyzed using GOMS do not involve process control. In flying tasks, context and abnormal situations are important issues. GOMS does not enable the analyst to take into account context and abnormal conditions easily. In contrast, the block representation was originally designed to take into account these two types of attributes. Context and abnormal conditions enable the development of *event-driven* analyses. In addition, pilots have difficulties to explain their activity by decomposing their goals-subgoals. They usually prefer to tell stories in an event-driven way.

Another important problem with traditional task analyses is that they provide a theoretical (analytical) model that can be very far from the real world interface/procedures to be designed. CFA associates the block descriptions with the current interface artifacts incrementally designed. Thus, users can be directly associated within the design cycle and contribute to design decisions through usability tests of incrementally developed interface artifacts. CFA offers a mediating representation accessible both to designers and users. Such a mediating representation enables the users to improve their ability to generate hypotheses and immediately test them. In this sense, CFA is a good tool that facilitates *abduction*, i.e., heuristic generation of relevant hypotheses.

Sheridan's recommendations for computer functions to aid supervisory control of physical processes are based on generic tasks (Sheridan, 1988). Abilities and limits of human operators and also the flow of information guide the development of such functions. CFA is very consistent with Sheridan's approach to supervisory control functions. In addition, CFA proposes a function allocation framework based on usability assessments of discrete event simulations of an incrementally upgraded prototype. CFA enables designers to better anticipate the distribution of cognitive functions between humans and machines. They can test how various configurations affect cognitive attributes such those defined in section 51.6.3. NASA's project MIDAS is another approach that develops and validates simulations of cockpit design tests the same kind of configurations by assessing workload and goal completion (Corker and Pisanich, 1995).

51.7 Conclusion and Perspectives

The research that went into developing the block representation for the design of software agents produced several contributions to the study of knowledge elicitation.

MESSAGE, first developed as a cognitive simulation to study the usability and safety of aircraft cockpits (Boy, 1983; Boy and Tessier, 1985), motivated an early attempt at the design of human agents and associated software agents. Subsequently, HORSES was developed to carry out a study of (human-machine) cooperative fault diagnosis, and the SRAR model was derived (Boy, 1987). The LSS model was derived to represent the incremental construction of situation patterns (Boy and Delail, 1988). It highlighted the need for a knowledge representation that makes it possible to model situated learning. The block representation was developed and first tested on a space telerobotic application. Considerably more information about the block representation can be found in Nathalie Mathé's doctoral dissertation (Mathé, 1990). More details are available in the proceedings of various knowledge acquisition workshops (Boy and Caminel, 1989; Boy, 1990; Boy, 1991b), and a NASA Technical Memorandum (Boy, 1991d).

Computer Integrated Documentation (CID) has been designed and developed according to the principles and methods that were presented in this chapter (Boy, 1991c, 1992). CID is now a fully developed system that enables its users to index and retrieve documents in context. Several software agents have been developed that help users customize documents. In the beginning, agents are "inexperienced" and must rely on broad analytical knowledge—that is, nominal models of tasks and procedures that may be incomplete and incorrect. These models may be constructed through analytical knowledge elicitation methods (LaFrance, 1986; Wielinga et al., 1992). Learning mechanisms incorporated in CID software agents rely on the reinforcement of successful actions, the discovery of abnormal conditions, and the generation of recovery knowledge blocks to improve performance.

This chapter introduced a knowledge elicitation methodology for the design of software agents that is based on the incremental construction and refinement of cognitive functions. From a cognitive viewpoint, software agents can be defined as the result of the transfer of a cognitive function to the computer, and as a knowledge block with an interface artifact. Cognitive function analyses based on appropriate human factors criteria can be developed and simulated to help analyze, design and evaluate emerging software agents.

A decade of experience in the domain of knowledge elicitation for the design of automated systems has led us to believe that the software agent technology enhances human-centered design. In addition, people use computers for more and more complex tasks, often involving multiple programs and a variety of media. We need simple solutions to handle this increasing complexity. Object-oriented programming has become a real practice in industry. From a software development viewpoint, software agents can be programmed as an object augmented with an attitude (Bradshaw, 1994). Component programming is becoming a reality with new interoperable software architectures. In this perspective, software agents are components that can be exchanged between people to enhance knowledge elicitation.

51.8 Acknowledgments

Many ideas described here benefited from discussions with Nathalie Mathé, Rachel Israel, Erik Hollnagel, Jeff Bradshaw, Laurent Karsenty, Mark Hicks, David Novick and Alain Rappaport. I would like to specially thank Helen Wilson for her comments on several drafts of this paper.

51.9 References

Addis, T.R., Gooding, D.C. and Townsend, J.J. (1993). Knowledge acquisition with visual functional programming. Knowledge Acquisition for Knowledge-Based Systems. *Proceedings of the 7th European Workshop, EKAW'93.* Lecture Notes in Artificial Intelligence 723, Springer-Verlag, Berlin, 379-406.

Anderson, J.R. (1983). Knowledge compilation: the general learning mechanism. *Proceedings of the International Machine Learning Workshop,* Monticello, Illinois, June, 203-212.

Barrett, E. (1992). Sociomedia: An introduction. In E. Barrett (Ed.), *Sociomedia: Multimedia, hypermedia, and the social construction of knowledge.* Cambridge, MA: MIT Press, 1-10.

Billings, C.E. (1991). Human-centered aircraft automation: A concept and guidelines. *NASA Technical Memorandum* 103885. Moffett Field, CA.

Boehm, B.W. (1988). A spiral model of software development and enhancement. *IEEE Computer,* 21 (5), May, 61-72.

Boy, G.A. (1983). Le système MESSAGE: Un Premier Pas vers l'Analyse Assistée par Ordinateur des Interactions Homme-Machine, *Le Travail Humain,* 46 (2), 271-286.

Boy, G.A. (1987). Operator assistant systems. In E. Hollnagel, G. Mancini and D.D. Woods (Eds.) *Cognitive engineering in complex dynamic worls, Computer and People Series,* London: Academic Press, 85-98. Also in International Journal of Man-Machine Studies, 27, 541-554.

Boy, G.A. (1989). The Block representation in knowledge acquisition for computer integrated documentation. *Proceedings of the Fourth AAAI-Sponsored Knowledge Acquisition for Knowledge-Based Systems Workshop,* Banff, Canada, October 1-6.

Boy, G.A. (1990). Acquiring and Refining Indices According to Context. Proceedings of the Fifth AAAI-Sponsored Knowledge *Acquisition for Knowledge-Based Systems Workshop*, Banff, Canada, Nov. 4-9.

Boy, G.A. (1991a). *Intelligent Assistant Systems.* Academic Press, London.

Boy, G.A. (1991b). Some Theoretical Issues on the Computer Integrated Documentation Project. *Proceedings of the Sixth AAAI-Sponsored Knowledge Acquisition for Knowledge-Based Systems Workshop,* Banff, Canada, October 6-11.

Boy, G.A. (1991c). Indexing Hypertext Documents in Context. *Proceedings of the Hypertext'91 Conference,* San Antonio, Texas, December.

Boy, G.A. (1991d). *Computer Integrated Documentation. Technical Memorandum,* NASA Ames Research Center, Moffett Field, CA.

Boy, G.A. (1992). Computer integrated documentation In E. Barrett (Ed.), *Sociomedia: Multimedia, hypermedia, and the social construction of knowledge.* Cambridge, MA: MIT Press, 507-531.

Boy, G.A. (1993). Knowledge acquisition in dynamic systems: How can logicism and situatedness go together? Knowledge Acquisition for Knowledge-Based Systems. *Proceedings of the 7th European Workshop, EKAW'93.* Lecture Notes in Artificial Intelligence 723, Springer-Verlag, Berlin, 23-44.

Boy, G.A. (1995). Supportability-Based Design Rationale. Proceeding of the IFAC/IFOIP/IFORS/IEA *Symposium on Analysis, Design and Evaluation of Man-Machine Systems*, Boston, MA, pp. 541-548.

Boy, G.A. and Caminel, T. (1989). Situation Patterns Acquisition improves the Control of Complex Dynamic Systems. *Proceedings of the Third European Knowledge Acquisition Workshop,* Paris.

Boy, G.A. and Delail, M. (1988). Knowledge acquisition by specialization/structuring: a space telemanipulation application. *Proceedings of the AAAI Workshop on Knowledge Acquisition*, Saint Paul, Minnesota, USA.

Boy, G.A. and Gruber, T. (1990). Intelligent assistant systems: support for integrated human-machine systems. *Proceedings of the AAAI Spring Symposium on*

Knowledge-Based Human Computer Communication, Stanford, March 27-29.

Boy, G.A. and Nuss, N. (1988). Knowledge acquisition by observation: application to intelligent tutoring systems. *Proceedings of the 2nd European Knowledge Acquisition Workshop*, Bonn, Germany.

Boy, G.A., and Tessier, C., (1985). Cockpit Analysis and Assessment by the MESSAGE Methodology, in Analysis, Design and Evaluation of Man-Machine Systems, Edited by G. Mancini, G. Johannsen and L. Martensson, *Proceedings of the and IFAC/IFIP/IFORS /IEA Conference,* Varese, Italy, September 10-12.

Bloomfield, B. P. (1988). Expert systems and human knowledge: A view from the sociology of science. *AI and Society*, 2 (1), 17-29.

Bradshaw, J.M. (1994). Brief summary of software agent technology. Emerging technology, *Aviation Industry Computer-Based Training Committee* (AICC).

Brazier, F.M.T., Treur, J., and Wijngaards, N.J.E. (1995). Modeling interaction with experts: The role of a shared task model. *Technical Report* IR-382, Vrije Universiteit Amsterdam, The Netherlands.

Cacciabue, P.C. and Hollnagel, E. (1995). Simulation of Cognition: Applications. In *Expertise and Technology: Cognition and Human-Computer Cooperation* (J-M. Hoc, P.C. Cacciabue and E. Hollnagel, eds.), Lawrence Erlbaum Associates, Pub., Hillsdale, New Jersey, pp. 55-73.

Card, S.K., Moran, T.P. and Newell, A. (1983). *The psychology of human-computer interaction*. Lawrence Erlbaum Associates, Hillsdale, NJ.

Chin, D.N. (1991). *Intelligent interfaces as agents. In Intelligent User Interfaces*, Edited by Joseph W. Sullivan and Sherman W. Tyler, ACM Press, New York, Addison-Wesley Publishing Company, Reading, MA.

Collins, H.M. (1987). Expert systems and the science of knowledge. In Bijker, Hughes and Pinch (Eds.) *New directions in the sociology of technology*. MIT Press, Cambridge, MA.

Corker, K.M. and Pisanich, G.M. (1995). Analysis and modeling of flight crew performance in automated air traffic management systems. Proceeding of the IFAC/IFOIP/IFORS/IEA *Symposium on Analysis, Design and Evaluation of Man-Machine Systems,* Boston, MA, pp. 629-634.

Carroll, J.M. and Rosson, M.B. (1991). Deliberated Evolution: Stalking the View Matcher in Design Space. *Human-Computer Interaction*, Lawrence Erlbaum Associate, Inc., 6, 281-318.

De Kleer, J., (1986). An Assumption-based TMS. *Artificial Intelligence*, 28, 127-162.

Dreyfus, H.L. (1981). From micro-worlds to knowledge representation: AI at an impasse. In Haugeland (Ed.) *Mind design*. Bradford Books, Montgomery, Vermont.

Ericsson, K.A., and Simon, H.A. (1980). Verbal Report Data. *Psychological Review*, 87, May.

Ferber, J. (1989). Objects and Agents: A Study of Representation and Communication Structures in Artificial Intelligence. Doctoral Thesis. Université Pierre et Marie Curie, Paris 6, June (in French).

Gaines, B.R. (1993). Modeling and extending expertise. Knowledge Acquisition for Knowledge-Based Systems. *Proceedings of the 7th European Workshop, EKAW'93*. Lecture Notes in Artificial Intelligence 723, Springer-Verlag, Berlin, 1-22.

Hawkins, D. (1983). An analysis of expert thinking. *International Journal of Man-Machine Studies*, 18, 1-48.

Hayakawa, S.I. (1990). *Language in Thought and Action.* Fifth Edition. Harcourt, Brace & Jovanovich, New York.

Hewitt, C. (1977). Viewing control structures as patterns of message passing. *Artificial Intelligence*, 8 (3).

Kodratoff, Y. and Tecuci, G. (1987). DISCIPLE-1: interactive apprentice system in weak theory fields. *Proceedings IJCAI*, Vol. 1. Morgan Kaufmann Publishers, San Mateo, CA.

Lafrance, M. (1986). The knowledge acquisition grid : a method for training knowledge Engineers. *Proceedings of Knowledge Acquisition for Knowledge-Based Systems Workshop*, Banff, November.

Laird, J.E., Newell, A. and Rosenbloom, P.S. (1987). Soar: an architecture for general intelligence. *Artificial Intelligence,* 33, 1-64.

Laville, A. (1976). *L'ergonomie. Que sais-je ?* Presses Universitaires de France, Paris.

Lenat, D.B. (1983). Theory formation by heuristic search. The nature of heuristics II: Background and examples. *Artificial Intelligence*, 21, 31-60.

Leplat, J. (1986). The elicitation of expert knowledge. In E. Hollnagel et al. (Eds.). *Intelligent Decision Support in Process Environments.* NATO ASI Series, 21, Springer-Verlag, Berlin.

Lesser, V. and Corkill, D. (1983). The distributed vehicle monitoring testbed: a tool for investigating distributed solving networks. *AI Magazine*, 4 (3).

Luhn, H.P. (1959). Keyword-in-Context for Technical Literature (KWIC Index), *American Documentation*, 11, pp. 288-295.

Mathé, M. (1990). Intelligent Assistance to Process Control: A Space Telemanipulation Application (In French). PhD Thesis Dissertation. ENSAE, Toulouse, France.

McCulloch, W. and Pitts, W. (1943). A logical calculus of the ideas imminent in nervous activity. *Bulletin of Mathematical Biophysics*, 5.

Michalski, R.S., Carbonell, J.B. and Mitchell, T. (1986). *Machine learning: an AI Approach Volume 2,* Morgan Kaufmann Publishers, San Mateo, CA.

Minsky, M. (1985). *The Society of Mind.* Touchstone Simon and Schuster.

Minsky, M., and Riecken, D. (1994). A conversation with Marvin Minsky about agents. *Communications of the ACM,* July, 37 (7), 23-29.

Newell, A. and Simon, H.A. (1972). *Human Problem Solving*, Englewood Cliffs, N.J., Prentice Hall.

Nii, P. (1986). Blackboard Systems, *AI Magazine*, 7 (2 and 3).

Piaget, J. (1967). *Biologie et Connaissance.* Gallimard, Paris.

Rappaport, A.R. (1987). Cognitive Primitives. *Proceedings of the Second AAAI-Sponsored Knowledge Acquisition for Knowledge-Based Systems Workshop*, Banff, Canada, October, 15.0-15.13.

Rasmussen, J. (1983). Skills, rules and knowledge; signals, signs, and symbols, and other distinctions in human performance models. *IEEE Transactions on Systems, Man, and Cybernetics*, 3, 257-266.

Reason, J (1986). Cognitive aids in process environments: Prostheses or tools ?, In E. Hollnagel, G. Mancini and D.D. Woods (Eds.) *Cognitive engineering in complex dynamic worlds, Computer and People Series*, London: Academic Press, 7-14.

Rosenblatt, F. (1958). The perceptron: a probabilistic model for information storage and organization in the Brain. *Psychological Review*, 65.

Rosenbloom, P.S. (1983). The Chunking of Goal Hierarchies: A Model of Practice and Stimulus-Response Compatibility. Doctoral Dissertation, Carnegie Mellon University.

Rumelhart, D.E., and McClelland, J.L. The PDP Research Group (1986). *Parallel Distributed Processing. Exploration in the Microstructure of Cognition. Volume 1: Foundations*, The MIT Press, Cambridge, Massachusetts.

Rumelhart, D.E., Smolensky, P., McClelland, J.L. and Hinton, G.E. (1986). Schemata and sequential thought, processes in PDP models, pp. 7-57 in *Parallel Distributed Processing, Vol. 2,* McClelland, J.L., Rumelhart, D.E. and the PDP Research Group (Eds.). MIT Press, Cambridge, MA.

Schneider, W. and Shiffrin, R.M. (1977). Controlled and Automatic Human Information Processing: I. Detection, Search, and Attention - II. Perceptual Learning, Automated Attending, and A General Theory, *Psychological Review,* 84 (1 and 2).

Shalin, V. and Boy, G.A. (1989). Integrated Human-Machine Intelligence. *IJCAI'89*, Detroit, MI.

Sheridan, T.B. (1984). Supervisory Control of Remote Manipulators, Vehicle and Dynamic Processes: Experiments in Command and Display Aiding, in *Advanced in Man-Machine Systems Research*, J.A.I. Press Inc., 1, 49-137.

Sheridan, T. (1988). Task allocation and supervisory control. In: *Handbook of Human Computer Interaction* (M. Helander, ed.), Elsevier Science, pp. 159-173.

Sheridan. T.B. (1992). *Telerobotics, Automation, and Human Supervisory Control.* MIT Press, Cambridge.

Suchman, L. (1987). *Plans and situated actions: The problem of human-machine communication.* Cambridge, England: Cambridge University Press.

Tambe, M. and Newell, A. (1988). *Why Some Chunks are Expensive.* CMU-CS-88-103, Department of Computer Science, Carnegie Mellon University, Pittsburgh.

Tessier, C. (1984). MESSAGE : Un Outil d'Analyse Ergonomique de la Gestion d'un Vol, Doctorate Dissertation ENSAE, France.

Toggnazzini, B. (1993). Principles, techniques, and ethics of stage magic and their application to human interface design. *Interchi'93 Conference Proceedings.* ACM, pp. 355-362.

Van der Velde, W. (1986). Learning Heuristics in Second Generation Expert Systems, *Int. Conference - Expert Systems and their Applications*, Avignon, France.

von Neumann, J. (1966). *The Theory of Self-Reproducing Automata.* Urbana, University of Illinois Press.

Wiener, E. (1989). Human factors of advanced technology ("Glass cockpit") transport aircraft. *Technical report 117528*. Moffett Field, CA: NASA Ames Research Center.

Wielinga, B., Van de Velde, W., Schreiber, G. and Akkermans, H. (1992). The CommonKADS Framework for Knowledge Modelling. *Proceedings of the Seventh Knowledge Acquisition for Knowledge-Based Systems AAAI Workshop*, Banff, Canada, October.

Woods, D.D. and Roth, E.M. (1988). Cognitive Systems Engineering. *Handbook of Human-Computer Interaction,* M. Helander (ed.), Elsevier Science Publishers B.V., North Holland.

Woods, D.D. and Roth, E.M. (1995). Symbolic AI Computer Simulations as Tools for Investigating the Dynamics of Joint Cognitive Systems. In *Expertise and Technology: Cognition & Human-Computer Cooperation* (J-M. Hoc, P.C. Cacciabue and E. Hollnagel, eds.), Lawrence Erlbaum Associates, Pub., Hilldale, New Jersey, pp. 75-90.

Zadeh, L.A. (1965). Fuzzy Sets, *Information and Control,* 8, 338-353.

Zimmerman, M. (1988). TEX version 0.5. *Technical report*, Silver Spring, MD.

Handbook of Human-Computer Interaction
Second, completely revised edition
M. Helander, T.K. Landauer, P. Prabhu (eds.)

Chapter 52

Decision Support Systems: Integrating Decision Aiding And Decision Training

Wayne W. Zachary and Joan M. Ryder
CHI Systems Incorporated
Lower Gwynedd, Pennsylvania, USA

52.1 Introduction

This chapter concerns the design of decision support systems. It represents a substantial revision of this chapter from the previous edition of this Handbook, but maintains the same overall approach — that of integrating current decision theory and computational technology into a general design methodology. This design methodology is, consistent with the concept of a Handbook, intended to give practitioners a framework with which to think about decision support applications, and to give them a set of tools with which to analyze, design, and develop decision support systems. The chapter begins with a review of recent developments in decision theory, in the context of the broader trends in the field. From the perspective of current theory, a framework for classifying decision problems and decision support solutions is developed. An important feature of this analytical framework is that it provides a way of integrating two aspects of decision support — training and aiding — that have historically been considered as quite separate. Based on this analytical framework, the second half of the paper presents a methodology for analysis and design of decision support applications.

52.2 From Pure Rationality to Naturalistic Decision Theory

Since the publication of the first edition of this Handbook, the underlying psychological theory of decision making has undergone a revolution of sorts. Until recently, human decision making has been consistently viewed as inherently flawed and in need of help. Beginning with the publication of Von Neuman and Morgenstern's (1947) *Theory of Games and Economic Behavior* and for nearly two decades thereafter, the standard of ideal decision making was pure rationality, as represented by mathematics and mathematical logic. In this pure rationality framework, decision problems were normalized into well-defined mathematical relationships. Typically, the decision was formalized as having a distinct outcome, and this outcome was expressed as a measurable quantity to be maximized (or minimized, as the case may be). The decision problem was then formalized as a series of constraints on that maximization. It was proven formally that when decision making was defined in this way, optimal decisions could be precisely determined by application of symbolic and numerical techniques. Moreover, given this definition of decision, human decision making clearly fared poorly in comparisons with mathematically-based optimal processes. People were seen as inherently poor decision makers, unable to maintain and manipulate the underlying relationships mentally. External decision support was offered to compensate for this deficiency, first in terms of mathematical algorithms and later in terms of computer implementations of those algorithms. Such tools can be considered the first generation of decision support.

Before long however, economists such as Simon (1955, 1972) and March (1976), began to point out that defining rationality as pure optimization was inappropriate. When viewed in the context of the behavioral situation in which decisions were made, they pointed out that often people only had to be 'good enough'. Formally optimal decisions had little or no actual benefit over other sub-optimal decisions that achieved the desired end; such decisions came to be called 'satisfying' solutions, in contrast to the optimized solutions derived from a pure rationality approach. For such situations, the notion of bounded (rather than pure) rationality was developed. The key issue in decision making under bounded rationality was that of the knowledge required. In addition to the knowledge about the problem and its constraints that were needed for purely rational decision making, a decision maker acting under bounded rationality needed knowledge about the behavioral context of the decision, i.e., about the boundaries to formal rationality.

The idea of bounded rationality slightly softened the notion of human as flawed decision maker, by pointing out that the reasoning processes implied by a pure rationality theory were inappropriate to bounded contexts. This led to more interest in the processes by which people actually did make decisions, and led to two separate lines of research and theory. One line concerned the process by which people acquired and applied the knowledge required to make decisions under either pure or bounded rationality. Researchers such as Raiffa (1968); Edwards, Phillips, Hays, and Goodman (1968); Leal and Pearle (1977); and Keeney (1982) developed models of the processes by which people should acquire, formalize, and apply knowledge about decisions problems and their contexts. This research was heavily driven by the notion of decision support, often in a business context. It emphasized an analytical approach to decision making, in which problems were systematically analyzed and broken into components and steps, typically specifying what knowledge (in the form of judgments) or problem-specific data needed to be elicited and applied along the way. These methods, and their computer implementations, came to be the second generation of decision support.

The other line of research that began in the wake of the theory of bounded rationality was behavioral decision theory. This framework attempted to develop a theory of decision making not from analyzing what formal logic seemed to require (as did the pure rationality theory), but from the basis of how people really made decisions. During much of the 1970s and 1980s, behavioral decision theory researchers tried to map out the characteristics of human decision processes. Again, the result was less than complimentary of human abilities. Empirical behavioral research showed that people used heuristics of various sorts in making decisions, and that, more importantly, the most commonly used heuristics led to what appeared to be systematic biases and errors in judgments (see Kahneman, Slovic, and Tversky, 1982, for an excellent summary of this research; also see Slovic, Fischhoff, and Lichtenstein, 1977, and Wason and Johnson-Laird, 1972). Once again, the conclusion from decision theory was that people were structurally flawed, and needed decision support.

Throughout the 1980's, however, this view began to come under attack. L. J. Cohen (1981) was one of the first to note two flaws in the 'heuristics and biases' framework of behavioral decision theory. The first was that most researchers were using formal rationality as the model against which to measure the biasing effect of various heuristics. Second, he argued that the decisions that Kahneman and Tversky found as biased could in fact be observed only in highly artificial problems that were unlikely to occur in everyday behavior. In fact, an even broader implication can be made from Cohen's arguments. Like the much earlier work on decision making under pure rationality, and even much of the work on decision making under bounded rationality, the behavioral decision theorists had sought to study human decision making out of natural behavioral context (i.e., in artificial laboratory settings), and with contrived (i.e., 'toy') problems that had quantifiable and optimizable solutions. They were making implicit assumptions that:

- the behaviors observed out of natural context would be the same as those observed in the 'real world', and
- decision making in the 'real world' would have the same characteristics as the well-defined and quantifiable problems studied in the laboratory.

As has been shown in recent years, both assumptions proved faulty.

While Cohen had reacted to the direction of behavioral research theory, an even more powerful but ultimately converging wave of research was beginning to build from another direction. H. L. Dreyfus and colleagues, most notably Klein, began to react to what they saw as the overformalization of decision making (see Dreyfus, 1979). As early as 1980, Klein (1980) had pointed out that expert decision making seemed different from novice decision making not merely in degree but in kind. In driving, for example, novice drivers approached many elementary actions as decisions (e.g., how to turn in traffic, when to use the clutch) and seemed to use something akin to formal decision processes. Expert drivers achieved higher performance, but not by merely performing the same processes faster. However, they did not completely abandon them either. Something other than process had to be at work, but it took another decade to develop a theory about it.

Over the decade of the 1980's, Klein and other researchers began to do empirical studies of human decision making in field settings. Unlike the laboratory studies on which the earlier behavioral decision theory was based, there were uncontrolled conditions in these studies, and comparable data were difficult to collect. In fact, the decision problems themselves appear to defy the long-held definitions of decision dating back to the era of pure rationality. The decisions studied in the field, such as fire-fighting, tactical command and control, medical diagnosis, etc. — seemed to share characteristics such as competing goals and objectives, little structure, and uncertain and dynamic environments. At the same time, these were all situations where the stakes were high, and the outcomes of the situation really mattered to the decision makers (characteristics hard to duplicate in laboratory settings). This complex of characteristics[1] was used to define decision making as it occurs in natural (i.e., socially and organizationally situated) settings or naturalistic decision making (Klein, 1989).

A new naturalistic decision theory has arisen from this definition and the field studies on which it is derived (see Klein, Orasanu, Calderwood, and Zsambok, 1993). In naturalistic settings, decision making loses the crispness that the classical rationality theories imposed on it. There is no decision event, but rather a larger dynamic task in which decision makers take actions. Often, it is only after the fact that some of these actions are seen (especially by outside observers) as having required decisions. Importantly, decision makers in naturalistic settings (as defined above) are expert in the domain — they have extensive knowledge in the domain and substantial experience performing the tasks in which the decisions are embedded. Because of their expertise, decision makers are able to rapidly identify a primary action alternative and customize it to the situation, typically without the intermediate analytical steps suggested by more traditional decision theory. Despite the fact that the problems are too ill-defined to be subject to formally rational (or even boundedly rational) decision methods, human experts handle these situations with speed, clarity, and usually excellent outcomes. A third generation of decision support has arisen in the last decade, emphasizing capturing and automating the expertise of highly proficient decision makers.

Naturalistic decision theory has come to a very different view of human capabilities than previous forms of decision theory. It suggests that human decision processes are non-analytical, that people succeed in situations in which classical models would fail, and ultimately that people are inherently good decision makers, given appropriate expertise. By the mid 1990's, naturalistic decision theory had grown from a critique of classical theories to become the dominant theory about decision making. As is often the case, though, in making some long-deserved criticisms of classical theory, the movement may have begun to throw away the baby with the bath water.

52.3 The Underlying Theory of Decision Situations

Naturalistic decision theory has several main tenets:

- human decision making is different in its social/behavioral context than it is in the laboratory, and should therefore be studied in its naturalistic context;
- the underlying task in which a decision is embedded, and the situation in which a specific problem instance occurs, are critically important to a human expert in framing his or her approach to it;
- action and decision are highly interrelated, to the extent that decisions are only evident *a posteriori* in the actions that are taken;

[1]Orasanu and Connolly (1993) define a list of eight characteristics of naturalistic decision making.

- human experts do not make decisions in an analytical manner, indeed or even in a conscious manner, but rather apply their accumulated experience and knowledge (collectively called their expertise) to identify and effect the most appropriate action. They "know what to do" rather than deliberately "figure out how to decide."

In making these points, the proponents of naturalistic decision theory raised fundamental questions about the value of the more classical approaches, which emphasize analysis and formalization. However in pointing out the limits in classical theories, the proponents of this new body of theory may have obscured the fact that there are still many areas where the two theories are complementary, not contradictory.

The first point of complementarity lies in the kinds of decision situations on which the various theories focus. Ignoring the methodological conflict over controlled data collection in the laboratory versus naturalistic observation in the field, it is clear that naturalistic decision theory has focused on a very different class of decision situations than traditional theories. The naturalistic school has studied decision situations which, although they may be poorly defined individually, are nonetheless well situated in the domain where the decision maker has expertise. This means that they are defined in the terms and principles of that domain, that the space of actions is established by the domain, and that past experience is a useful guide for future decision instances. Thus, within the context of the decision maker's expertise, the problems are interpretable, if not recurring. The classical studies of pure and bounded rationality, on the other hand, were developed from problems in economics. In decisions to introduce a new product, for example, or to invest in a certain way, the actual implementation of the decision would not only resolve the decision problem, it would also change the domain — the competitors would change, the marketplace would change, etc. Thus, once the decision has been made, no future decision would be similarly situated in the domain. In this type of decision, although the analytical approach might be reusable, the domain is sufficiently dynamic that it is unpredictable how much past expertise in the domain could be useful in making future decisions.[2] Decision making in such one-of-a-kind situations in fact benefits from a careful formalization of the problem and a systematic, analytical decision process. Thus, there are types of situations for which naturalistic theories apply better, and types of situations for which classical theories apply better.

A second area of complementarity concerns the degree of expertise of the decision maker. The naturalistic decision making school has focused strongly on the behavior of expert decision makers, people with substantial experience in the task in which the decision is embedded and with substantial knowledge of the domain in which the task is situated. It should be clear that the opportunity to gain expertise occurs only in certain classes of domains. Decisions that are inherently one-of-a-kind, or even infrequent, do not afford anyone enough instances of decision making to develop what can be called expertise. For example, fire captains face fire-fighting decisions literally every day, over a period of years, whereas nuclear plant operators may only face one instance of a serious event (e.g., loss of coolant) in a lifetime (if that). Thus, naturalistic decision theorists have, in focusing on expert decision making, implicitly limited themselves to classes of problems and/or domains where the opportunity to develop expertise exists. However, even in those domains, not all decision makers are experts. Clearly, the experts began as novices and slowly developed experience and knowledge, improving their decision making along the way. It is useful to note that the novice decision maker in a stable domain (who may grow to be an expert over time), and a decision maker facing a one-of-a-kind decision are in much the same situation. They both lack the base of experience and knowledge of relevant domain principles. This suggests that the same delivery formalization that can aid the latter, could also support the former. This observation is discussed in more detail below.

The world is not divided into two cases — stable domains with recurring, similar problems, and evolving domains with unique, one-of-a-kind problems. There is in fact a continuum between these two extremes, which can be used to create a more meaningful categorization of the space of decision making (and therefore the space of opportunities for decision support). At one end of this continuum are unique problem contexts which do not allow an individual decision maker to gain expertise. At this end of the continuum, everyone is by definition a novice decision maker. At the other end are problem contexts which present problems with recurring characteristics, and which afford a persistent individual the opportunity to develop meaningful expertise. At this end of the continuum there are various sorts of decision makers — experts, those with inter-

[2]This idea of *domain* instability should not be confused with the idea of *problem* instability, which is often cited as a characteristic of naturalistic decisions.

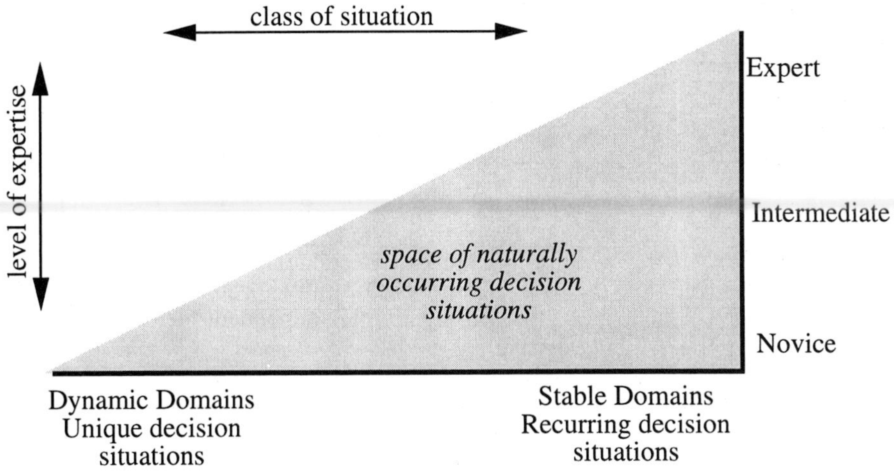

Figure 1. Space in which decision making occurs.

mediate skills, and varying degrees of novice. This structure is pictured in Figure 1.

The asymmetrical nature of the space in Figure 1 has further implications for decision theory and decision support. For domains further along right side of Figure 1, naturalistic decision theory argues that experts don't make deliberative (i.e., classically analytical) decisions, but rather "know what to do" based on prior experience and domain knowledge. Another way to put this, however, is that the expert decision maker has "learned" what to do. A clear, although less frequently discussed corollary of naturalistic decision theory is that decision making is a domain-based skill that is learned, and that experts are therefore made not born.[3] This suggests that there is a relationship between decision making and decision learning, and with it, a relationship between decision support and decision training.

On the right side of the continuum in Figure 1, less-than-expert decision makers need to acquire expertise (i.e., to learn) to improve their decision making skill and perform at more expert levels. This implies that they would benefit from decision training to support their development of expertise. However, to the degree that they must perform in an actual decision making role, they would also benefit from decision aiding to support them doing the best that they can when they have to make real decisions.

The same is not true, however, for the left side of the continuum. Because those domains do not pose decision situations with recurring structure, there is little value in decision training, at least in the naturalistic decision theory sense of acquiring knowledge about domain principles and relationships. However, decision support, particularly in the form of analytical process aiding, may help people make the best possible decisions, given the novelty of the situation. By adding the concept of decision making skill acquisition to the decision support, some important new questions immediately arise:

How does decision making skill evolve as individuals move from novice to expert?

Can "one size fit all", or are different kinds of support (either training or performance aiding) needed for novices, intermediate levels of skill, and experts?

Can there be a common design methodology for both aiding and training forms of decision support?

The remainder of this paper addresses these questions, in the order listed above.

52.4 The Evolution from Novice to Expert

In recent years, a consensus has begun to emerge on the way in which individual decision making expertise evolves through learning and experience. Numerous studies of novice-expert differences and decision skill learning (see especially Chi, Glaser, and Farr, 1988; Logicon, 1989; Brecke and Young, 1990; Ryder, Zachary, Zaklad, and Purcell, 1994a; or VanLehn, 1996)

[3]There is likely some underlying ability factor in determining which persons have the capacity to become expert, but there are few research results of substance in this area.

Novice	Expert
Domain Knowledge Facts, basic concepts	Domain Knowledge Interrelationship between concepts Causal relationships Abstract and/or general principles
Problem Solving Characteristics Sequential subgoals, local focus Analytical problem solving Weak, general methods	Problem Solving Characteristics Chunking of subgoals, global focus Case-based/intuitive problem solving Strong, domain dependent methods

Figure 2. Characteristics of the novice-expert continuum.

have led to common conclusions. At the most general level, this work has demonstrated clear differences between novices and expert decision makers, as shown in Figure 2, particularly along two major dimensions — domain knowledge and decision making strategy.

From an individual development/learning perspective, the changes that occur in domain knowledge and problem solving strategy are highly interdependent (e.g., increases in and restructuring of knowledge allow more expert strategies to emerge since the mechanisms of the strategies depend on more sophisticated connections between domain concepts). Two aspects of knowledge can be said to change as a person becomes more expert in the domain:

1) Quantity of domain knowledge. As a person moves from novice to expert, that person, of course, acquires more knowledge about the domain.

2) Quality of domain knowledge. Knowledge of the domain for the novice is composed largely of facts and basic concepts. Procedural or rote knowledge of actions and reactions in relation to entities follows. At the highest level of understanding, the person grasps the relations between concepts in the domain, (e.g., causal relationships) as well as abstract and more general understanding. Concepts, facts, and relations are organized within semantic categories; hierarchical relations are understood in terms of whole-part relations, objects are organized into functional categories rather than physical characteristics, etc.

As a person gains expertise, a mental model of the domain is developed and evolved in content and quality in the above ways. The qualitatively different mental model supports the changes in decision making strategy.

In general, decision strategy is qualitative in nature, although the changes that take place as novices become expert decision makers lead to quantitative increases in task efficiency.[4] These changes depend on at least the following four aspects of problem solving capability:

(1) Ability to compile subgoals, strategies within the problem space. Increased expertise is evidenced by the consolidation of steps or subgoals that advance one towards the solution of a given problem or resolution of a decision point or step. This process is called chunking. It is analogous to the qualitative changes that occur in the development of domain knowledge discussed above.

(2) Replacement of analytical by more intuitive or case-based approaches to navigating the problem space. Novices will tend to analyze or parse problems in terms of assessing multiple variables that define the state of the problem and the possible range of solutions. As the person becomes more adept, the consolidated knowledge and problem solving approaches

[4]Working in symbolic computation models of human decision-making, Amarel (1969; 1982) has actually mapped out this process for a single domain. His work has demonstrated how changes in decision-making strategy go hand-in-hand with changing problem representation as the decision moves from novice to expert levels of performance.

support the use of seemingly more "intuitive," "holistic," or case-based approaches. Klein (1989) has termed this process "recognition primed". Whatever it is called, this approach allows the decision maker to capitalize on the more highly organized knowledge and goal structures that experience supplies.

(3) Replacement of weak, more general methods of problem solving by strong, domain dependent methods. The novice employs domain independent strategies such as trial and error and exhaustive brute force methods when exploring problems. As knowledge of the domain increases, these techniques are abandoned in favor of methods tailored to the idiosyncrasies of the domain; recognition of patterns or other key diagnostic clues feed more expert, direct paths to solutions.

(4) Evolution from local focus to a global focus. The novice responds to individual data about the problem, acting in response to small portions of the overall conditions posed by the problem. The expert, in contrast, will set goals or subgoals that enable him or her to solve either portions of the problem or the complete problem.

These distinctions can be used to develop a somewhat more refined model of the stages in decision skill development, based on the changes in problem representation and decision strategy. There is a general consensus that there are three central stages in decision skill development which can be termed *novice*, *intermediate*, and *expert*.

"Novice" is defined as one possessing relatively complete descriptive or baseline knowledge of the domain, but without any high-level organization or chunking of that knowledge, and without the development of any domain-specific decision strategies. The novice is distinguished from an individual who is completely foreign to the domain. This latter level of development is termed a 'neophyte', and is excluded from inclusion in the model here, because that individual must have substantial domain training before becoming even a novice. At the other end of the continuum, an "expert" is defined as an individual who has evolved a complex set of integrated declarative and procedural knowledge both about the domain (e.g., a set of patterns which can prime decisions), and about the decision tasks to be performed in the domain (e.g., a set of skills that allow multiple and conflicting task goals to be used, understood, and traded off in the context of a specific decision/task instance). In addition, an expert is defined as one who has evolved detailed procedures for solving partial problems, specific problems, and (ultimately) problem classes in the domain and who has further chunked these into retrievable units, perhaps on the recognition of specific patterns or decision types. Novices exhibit an analytical and piecemeal approach to decision making and problem-solving. On the other hand, experts exhibit what has variously been called a holistic, intuitive, and/or recognition-based approach to decision making and problem solving.

However, it is also clear that individuals do not move from novice to expert representations directly. Rather, they go through stages in which they build domain knowledge, learn and chunk situationally-effective procedures or partial-solution procedures, and emphasize analysis of problem conditions as a way of paring down the space of possible problem solutions or decisions. An individual who is in this stage of development is defined to be at the "intermediate" level. The literature suggests (see the various sources cited above) that highly expert representations share many features regardless of domain, as do novice representations. This can be interpreted as meaning that experts tend to discover, or learn from each other, a common set of domain-dependent representations and strategies. Therefore, in a given domain it is possible that as expertise grows, individuals converge on a single, general expert representation (or more properly, a single meta-representation). The same appears to be true for novices; there is probably a single novice meta-representation, probably because novices tend to acquire the same general facts about the domain. It is unclear from the current empirical or theoretical literature, however, whether there is one general intermediate problem meta-representation, a finite number of them, or a broad range of intermediate representations which are all domain specific. Thus, a given intermediate decision maker's problem/domain representation can be described only as being somewhere between the typical expert and the typical novice meta-structures, without specific reference to where precisely it sits on the various continua of expertise. These distinctions among the three stages are summarized in Figure 3.

Figure 3 states that novices lack domain-specific decision-strategies, and therefore rely on more general, albeit weaker, analytical methods. This is as would be predicted, or at least recommended, by classical decision theory. As the individual gains expertise by learning richer representations of the domain such as causal relationships and domain principles, some do-

	REPRESENTATION	DECISION-MAKING STRATEGY
EXPERT	Highly elaborated conceptual structure or mental model based on underlying principles	Highly developed domain-specific procedures Case-based recognitional problem solving methods
INTERMEDIATE	Increased amount of conceptual knowledge Partial knowledge of domain principles and causal relationships; some links among concepts	Partial chunking of subgoals Procedural skill for selected problem subgoals
NOVICE	Basic facts and concepts of the domain in declarative form	Weak, general analytical methods Step-by-step procedures

Figure 3. Three-stage model of decision skill acquisition.

main-specific strategies are developed. Typically, these are evidenced in a person who can solve some situations, or parts of situations, with domain-specific expert-like solutions, but falls back onto more general purpose novice-like strategies elsewhere. As true expertise develops, the individual has a very rich conceptual model of the domain, and has learned highly elaborated domain-based solutions to many classes of problems in it. With this structure, the expert can simply recognize the case into which a specific decision situation fits, from that recognition retrieve the appropriate solution strategy, and directly apply it with little or no intermediate analysis or reasoning.[5] This is as would be predicted by naturalistic decision theory.

52.5 Does One Size Fit All?

The analysis of decision making domains (Figure 1) showed that there are some domains in which people can never be anything but novice decision makers, and others where there are varying opportunities to develop decision making expertise specific to the domain. The analysis of the evolution of expertise showed that in this latter type of domain, decision makers will go through different stages of development, each associated with a different problem-domain representation and decision-strategy. And it has been noted that there are two distinctly different ways to think about supporting a human decision maker — by aiding the actual decision performance in a specific problem instance, and by training the decision maker so that she or he can move along the progression toward expertise. This makes the problem of decision support system design potentially quite complex. It is also reasonable to wonder whether these distinctions matter — might it not be possible to provide one form of support that works as well for both training and aiding? or to provide aiding (or training) that works equally well with novices, intermediates and experts?

Unfortunately, the answer seems to be no, on all counts. Numerous empirical studies have shown the difficulties in applying expert-oriented aiding (or training) to novices and vice versa. One example of

[5]A few researchers, e.g., Dreyfus and Dreyfus (1980), add two more stages, one at the mastery level above the level of expert, and another at the neophyte level, below the level of what is called a novice here.

this can be taken from experience with a decision aid called PANDA, which helped aerial searchers develop patterns for ocean-based searches. PANDA used an expert-oriented problem representation, generating suggested patterns based on different assumptions about the underlying case into which the problem-at-hand fit. It also included a numerical rule for scoring the candidate search plans. During experimental evaluation, PANDA was used by a combination of expert and novice users, with very different results (Glenn and Harrington, 1989). The novice users typically reviewed PANDA's suggestions, and then picked the pattern with the highest overall score because they had no basis to analyze or interpret the suggestions any further. Such an interpretation really required an expert level of representation that these novices lacked. However, the aid's suggestions were only based on heuristics, not on a formal optimization (the problem, in fact, is not amenable to a formal optimization solution). Experts using the aid were able to interpret the suggestions more knowledgeably. They typically determined which heuristic should be used to generate a solution, and if they found a PANDA-generated solution that fit that case, they accepted it. When they felt the situation was subtly different, however, they generated a solution of their own, typically as an improvement on one made by PANDA. The results, in simulated searches, was much higher performance by the experts, and a greater improvement between unaided and aided conditions, than by novices.

Still, it might be argued, the novices did benefit from the aid. This was not always the case. One novice, for example, ventured to generate a pattern of his own, and found that it yielded a slightly higher combined score in that problem than any of the solutions suggested by the aid. This led the novice to overestimate his own ability, and he then proceeded to generate his own solution to each successive problem. In no case did his solution approach the overall score PANDA's suggestions, and in each of these cases he relented and accepted an aid-generated solution after a long analysis and review process. But in each of these cases, a much longer period of time was required to generate the solution, even though time to generate a pattern was presented to the subjects as a primary evaluation criterion. The lesson from PANDA evaluation is that the expert subjects, because they understood the (expert-level) representation and approach of PANDA, knew when to trust and accept the aid's advice, and when to modify or reject it. Novices, lacking an expert level understanding were unable to do this, and either over-trusted or under-trusted the aid. This led to poorer solutions, longer decision times, and no greater understanding of the decision environment.

Woods, Roth and Bennett (1990) provides some other examples of problems that arise when novices use expert-level aids. They reviewed experiences with a diagnosis/trouble-shooting aid intended to help electronics repair technicians. The decision aid used standard expert system techniques, and directly incorporated reasoning rules used by experts in the domain, and thus was built around an expert representation and solution strategy for the domain. Many difficulties in use of the aid by non-experts were reported, the net effect of which was to dramatically decrease the frequency with which the proper diagnosis and repair was completed in an aided situation. Some of the cases are particularly illustrative here. A major difficulty was with a boundary condition on many of the rules contained in the expert decision aid. Each rule implicitly assumed that only one problem was present in the device at a time. This is clearly how experts represent diagnostic knowledge, but they also know that sometimes this assumption is invalid. A typical expert will follow this assumption originally, but if initial attempts at diagnosis prove confusing or fail, then the expert will conditionally hypothesize multiple failures and try to isolate one or more components so that different diagnostic methods can be followed. Novices lacked this conditioning knowledge, and in several real-world cases, multiple problems were present. The novices, in these cases, followed the aid's advice, and when it failed to lead to a diagnosis, they simply 'gave up' on the problem and left it for a more expert technician (and probably learned nothing in the process either).

Another, and even more subtle problem reported in Woods et al. (1990), was the linkage between behavioral skills and expert knowledge. Expert knowledge, as it turned out, implicitly assumed an expert level of skill with the motor and psycho-motor aspects of the job. Thus, it was assumed that the person had the necessary skills to successfully apply all the diagnostic instruments involved. However some instruments are more difficult to use or interpret than others. Novices, in many cases, were not sufficiently skilled in these instruments to apply or interpret them correctly, and hence gave faulty readings back to the decision aid, which then propagated this faulty information forward and led to incorrect decisions/suggestions. This again led to 'dead ends,' in which the novice simply gave up and left the problem for a more skilled technician.

The case of experts using novice-oriented aids is simpler. Novice-oriented representations involve highly-analytical processes targeted at a 'disaggregate' or novice level of understanding. The experts, in such cases, typically reject or refuse to use such aids because the aids do not permit the experts to utilize their highly evolved, experience-based and recognitional decision strategies. This issue is discussed in more detail in Zachary (1985).

52.6 Principles for Decision Support

Early in the development of decision support, little attention was given to factors such as the expertise level of the decision maker versus the expertise level of the aid, or to the differences between training benefits and aiding benefits. The main thrust of this paper to this point has been to identify such factors and to document their importance. It would be easy, at this point, to over generalize and argue that each decision support application is unique, and that there can be no common design methods or tools. In fact, a number of principles for how and where to apply decision support can be distilled from the preceding analyses of decision problems, expertise, and decision support.[6] They are as follows:

- Maximally effective decision aiding requires the problem representation in the decision aid to reflect the problem representation and cognitive processes of the decision maker using the aid.
- Decision making training must be based on the current mental representation and knowledge structure of the student or trainee, as well as on the specific details of the domain or system which is the subject of the training.
- The training development method must integrate behavioral considerations within a cognitive approach.
- Decision making skill can be decomposed into three knowledge/skill components:
    - conceptual knowledge/skill — domain facts and concepts,
    - procedural knowledge/skill — rules and procedures for how to accomplish job tasks and ability to perform them, and
    - relational knowledge/skill — domain-specific decision making skill based on integrated conceptual and procedural knowledge.
- Skill development involves a progression from conceptual to procedural to relational knowledge/skill, in addition to a progression in problem representations (schemes, mental models) of increasing complexity.

These principles have some implications for the development of a design methodology that can be applied to decision support in a general way. Four particularly important implications are given below.

The first is that decision support must be tailored (or perhaps 'targeted') to a specific position or region of the expertise continuum shown in Figure 2. Decision aiding must focus on the user population or populations, and provide different aiding regimens based on population expertise level. There can be no useful 'one size fits all' decision aid, no matter how economically attractive such a concept might be. In fact, the three-level hierarchy in Figure 3 implies that there should be three levels of decision aiding, targeted to novice, intermediate, and expert decision makers.

The second implication is that decision aid design must involve analysis of the cognitive processes and problem representation of the user(s) as well as analysis of the external domain and physical systems involved. (A corollary of this is that decision aid designs which fail to take into account user cognitive processes are much more likely to be rejected, or fail to provide meaningful support for the targeted user). An initial step in the design of decision aiding components of a decision support system must therefore include a process of cognitive description and cognitive modeling of the system's user(s). This modeling must then be followed by a cognitive analysis that generates specific requirements for a decision aid for that user or user population expertise level. Since the decision aid is to have users at three levels of expertise, separate cognitive models and analyses must be undertaken for the three levels to generate appropriate aiding requirements for each user population.

The third implication is that a large part of the training component design within the decision support system could be developed from the same cognitive modeling and analysis used for decision aid design, provided that the (cognitive) method incorporates appropriate components.

The fourth implication is that training can take two forms. One type of training can be characterized as within-level training, and the other as cross-level training. The first kind of training is called *Incremental*

[6]More details on the derivation of these principles can be found in Ryder et al., (1994a).

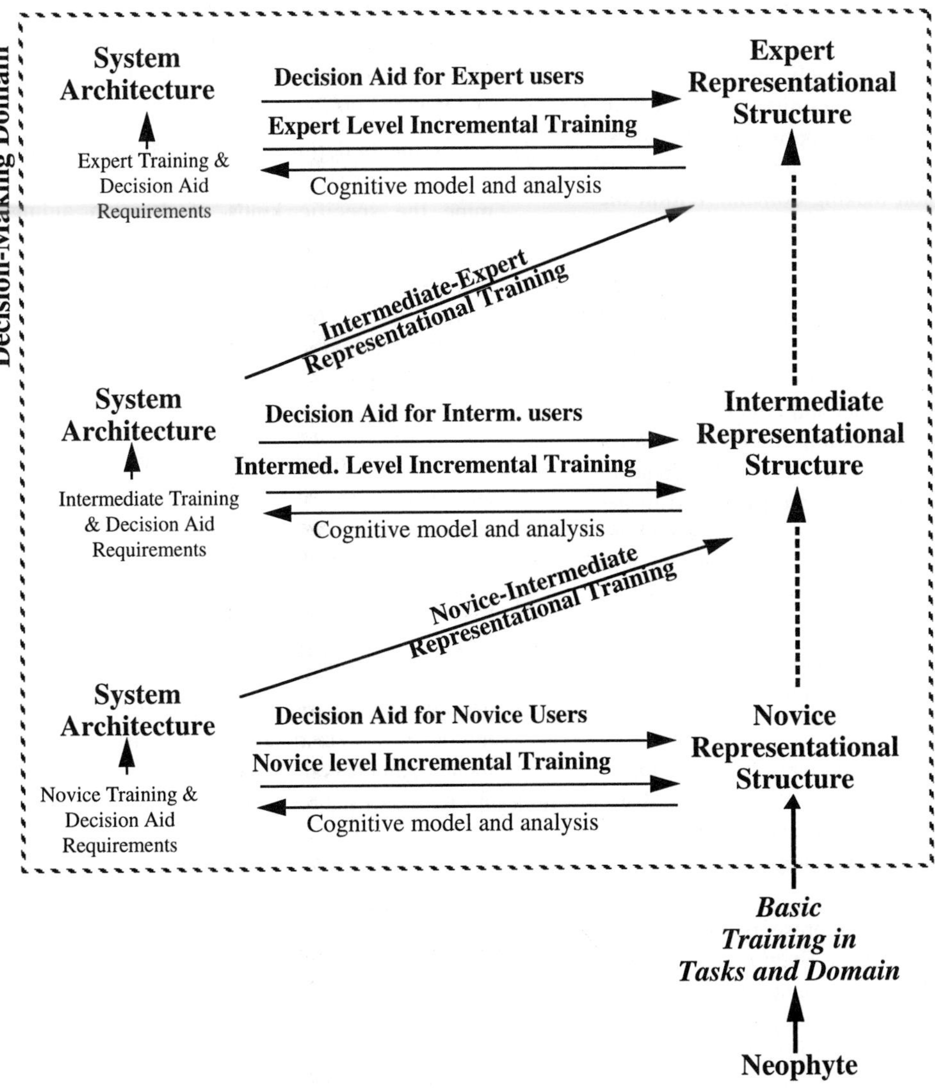

Figure 4. A decision support framework integrating training and aiding.

Training. Incremental or within-level training has the goal of providing small but clear improvements in decision performance based on additions or modifications of selective pieces of knowledge. Incremental Training can be designed by analyzing a given cognitive representation, using some sort of metric to identify local deficiencies or inefficiencies, and applying a training approach designed to remove these limits or deficiencies. The second kind of training is called *Representational Training*. Its goal is to lead the student to make major revisions in his/her problem representation. Representational training can be designed by analyzing a given cognitive representation, selecting a target representation that is more expert-like, and applying a cross-level training method (discussed in Ryder et al., 1994a) to help elicit the change in representation.

A perhaps surprising conclusion of this discussion is that while a decision support system should clearly reflect the differing levels of expertise of its users, the design of its training and aiding components can and should proceed from a common cognitive analysis of the user. Figure 4 integrates the various principles and their implications into a general model for fully integrated decision support systems.

The right side of Figure 4 shows the progression of the decision maker from neophyte to expert. As noted above, certain basic training is needed to give the neophyte enough knowledge about the domain and decision tasks even to begin to apply general purpose decision strategies. This basic training is not considered as any kind of decision support, and so is excluded from the dashed box which represents the range of options in the decision making domain. Within the box, the left side of the figure represents different support system architectures, each focusing on a representational structure of a given level of user expertise. At each one of these levels, a cognitive modeling and analysis process is first undertaken to capture the representational structure and decision strategies of individuals at that level. This model and cognitive analysis is used to create training and aiding requirements for a support system focusing on that level. The requirements, together with the analysis, are then used to define a support system architecture that meets those requirements. At each level, the support system will provide two primary types of support to its users:

- performance aiding, which helps users at a given level improve their performance in actual decision tasks, and which focuses on the needs of individuals at that level; and
- incremental training, which helps users at that level incrementally improve their knowledge of the domain and decision task, and to build and apply better decision strategies, given their level of expertise.

The incremental training represents evolutionary training and applies to all levels. Even experts can incrementally improve their performance by sharpening their situation analysis skills and improving their understanding of underlying domain principles. For novice and intermediate decision makers, however, their problem representations must at some point undergo a more revolutionary transformation. They must learn to represent the domain and their decision tasks at a more sophisticated level indicative of the next higher level on the development hierarchy (Figure 3). This is representational training, and again will probably be different for the novice than for the intermediate.

52.7 Integrated Design Method for Decision Training and Decision Aiding

An overall process of decision support system design can be identified from Figure 4. This design process falls into five general phases:

1) <u>cognitive decomposition and modeling</u>, in which the representation and decision strategy of the user (classes) to be supported are studied and mapped out;

2) <u>requirements definition</u>, in which the decision maker cognitive model is analyzed to determine the specific kinds of decision aiding and/or decision training that are required;

3) <u>functional design</u>, in which the identified requirements are used to define specific aiding/training functions for:

   - decision aiding,
   - incremental decision training, and
   - representational decision training,

   and each set of desired functionality is matched with component technologies to provide the functionality;

4) <u>architecture specification</u>, in which component technologies are assembled into a decision support system architecture; and

5) <u>detailed design and implementation</u>, in which low-level system details are specified, implemented, and tested.

It should be noted that step 3) could be only partially completed to create a decision support system that provided only one or two of the forms of support listed.

An ideal design methodology should follow an

- explicit and systematic approach, using a series of tools or databases to:
- identify functional requirements for decision aiding (DA) and decision training (DT) subsystems,
- define the full range of computational technologies that could fulfill these requirements,
- select specific technologies based on cost/benefit factors specific to the application, and
- use the selections to define specific architectural modules and architectural arrangements that can support both DA and DT operation.

Figure 5 presents the general flow of a DSS design process with these properties that is based on the design framework in Figure 4.

The overall methodology decomposes the analysis and design process into well-defined steps and supports each step with:

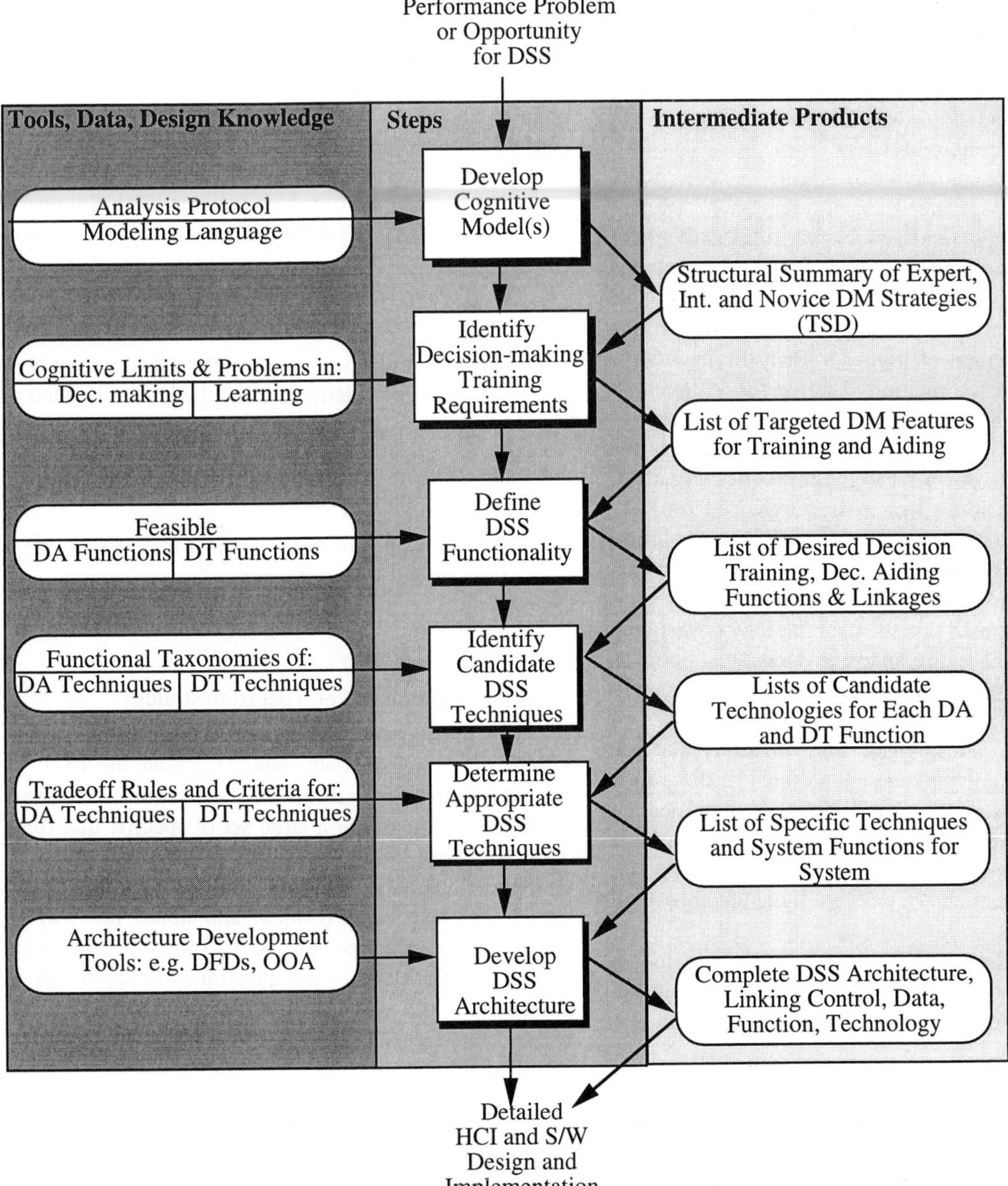

Figure 5. Decision support system design methodology.

- data and/or knowledge bases of relevant <u>general</u> design information,
- rules/guidelines for applying the general data/knowledge to aspects of the specific application case at hand,
- a specific format for documenting/capturing the results of applying the rule/guidelines at each step, and
- a means of using problem-specific information derived from the previous step as a basis for completing the current design step.

Thus, each step gives the designer general information to work with, general rules or techniques to apply the general information to the domain-specific information and the decision support application at hand, and a 'target' for what the resulting analysis (at that step) is supposed to look like.

This structure, as shown in Figure 5, also yields several ways of viewing the methodology. If one just looks at the steps (and associated rules/guidelines) down the center column of Figure 5, then the methodology is very procedural — a cookbook for design. If one looks just at the general data/knowledge bases down the left column of Figure 5, then the methodology looks like an information resource for designers, a compendium of information relevant to DSS design at all stages. And if one looks only at the sequence of intermediate results down the right column of Figure 5, the methodology looks like a well-organized progression of design documentation, in which the evolution of each individual feature can be traced clearly to earlier design decisions and analytical steps.

It should be noted that the methodology is designed to work across the entire space of decision support as depicted in Figure 1. For unique decision situations in dynamic domains, there is only one type or class of user to focus on — novices. For situations that are more recurring and in more stable domains, there may be multiple classes of users — novices, intermediate users, and experts. Each class of user may require a separate analysis and 'pass' through the methodology, but the overall methodology is equally applicable in all these cases.

In the remainder of this paper, each step in the methodology as shown in Figure 5 is described in additional detail. Additional details can be found in Ryder et al. (1994b).[7]

52.7.1 Cognitive Decomposition and Modeling

This first step in the methodology produces the cognitive/behavioral task analysis that is required to drive the major aspects of system design. It is supported by two interrelated tools for gathering and analyzing data on user problem representation and decision strategy. The first tool is a data collection protocol for collecting data on user cognitive structures, and the second is a more detailed modeling language for representing cognitive and behavioral processes. These tools are described in more detail shortly below.

The first step in the methodology produces an intermediate result, a structured decision Task Summary Description (TSD). The format for the TSD is shown in Figure 6.

The TSD is a structured description that covers elements of:

- the domain/environment, such as a summary of information elements available and their physical presentation;
- the task, in terms of its main goal, dynamics, and underlying process;
- the decision processes, such as main value criteria used to make choices;
- the decision maker's domain representation; and
- the decision maker's decision strategy.

The tools used in the cognitive analysis are designed to provide the data needed to create the TSD.

The first tool — the behavioral/cognitive analysis protocol — consists of a large set of specific questions (see Zachary, 1986: Appendix) about the task to be aided/trained, about the environment and domain in which the task is performed, and about the way in which novice, intermediate, and expert operators perform the task. Many of the questions are applicable in all cases, while others are applicable in only special cases. Others depend on the answers to prior questions. Most of the questions are open ended and point to aspects of the domain or task that simply need to be described in narrative or summary fashion. The DSS designer must review the protocol against the design problem at hand, and determine which questions are applicable and in what sequence. Then the designer must manage the data generated by the responses. The protocol and the narrative responses should be maintained in a data recording journal. After application of the protocol is complete, the analyst then uses the information in the data journal to fill in the first five sections of the TSD, as shown above. Importantly, these task/behavioral data (and the first five levels of the TSD) are generally those which do NOT vary with user levels of expertise, because they are dictated by the external environment or organization in which the task

[7]This methodology is adapted from the one detailed in the previous edition of this Handbook (Zachary, 1988), and represents a substantial elaboration of the original methodology. The full discussion of the version of the design methodology presented here can be found in Ryder et al. (1994b). At the same time, many of the details in the original remain applicable today. Therefore, the reader is encouraged to use Zachary (1988) as well as Zachary (1986) as a background and supplement to the discussion here, and not as having been superseded entirely by the present paper.

DECISION TASK: (Name or title of decision task)

TASK GOAL: (Highest level goal that defines the situation, ideally expressed in terms of the "goal event" — physical or observable events(s) that the decision maker is trying to achieve or accomplish)

TASK DYNAMICS: (Characteristics of task development, timing, repetition occurring; e.g., closed-loop iterative, unfolding, or single-instance)

UNDERLYING PROCESS: (A brief description of the observable process in which this decision task is embedded)

VALUE CRITERIA: (listing of the individual criteria by which a candidate decision is compared against the goal event; this list specifies the attributes on which the quality of a decision is measured by the decision maker)

PHYSICAL INFORMATION ENVIRONMENT:

Inputs	**Outputs**	**Parameters**
(list of external information items that are available to the decision maker and that may change in value during an instance of the situation)	(list of individual information items that are created during the task; some or all of these may be aspects of the task results but may change from instance to instance)	(list of external information items that are available for the decision process but which do not change in value during a given instance of the task)

DOMAIN REPRESENTATION:
(A representation of the domain knowledge of the decision maker organized as a blackboard structure with independent aspects of the domain in the form of separate panels. Each panel is divided into levels of information, which are organized according to panel-specific criteria, such as hierarchy, importance, or temporal information flow. The domain representation includes both dynamic and static aspects of the decision situation.)

TASK MODEL:
(Decomposition of the decision task goal into subgoals and steps. The task model consists of a set of subgoals, each of which can be further decomposed into actions or operators. The actions include both behavioral actions and cognitive actions that are undertaken to achieve the goal. Cognitive actions include operations to update the dynamic aspects of the domain representation. The task model also includes a trigger that is a set of conditions under which the task should be initiated.)

REQUIRED JUDGMENTS:
(A listing of the heuristic judgments that must be made during some or all instances of this task; the list should focus on those judgments that involve prior expertise, or processing of uncertain information.)

Figure 6. Generic TSD format.

is performed. The opposite is the case with the last three levels.

The last three sections of the TSD are concerned with problem representation, task/reasoning strategies, and heuristic judgments. As noted earlier, these items (particularly the first two of these), are the basis for distinguishing between the three identified levels of expertise. Thus, in completing these portions of the analysis, a more detailed approach is needed, one which can be separately applied to novice, intermediate, and expert operators. These are the portions of the TSD which are based on a more detailed cognitive description language called COGNET.

COGNET, the second tool, is a cognitive modeling technique and description language that was designed to focus on complex decision problems in dynamic situations. The methodology is fully described in Zachary et al. (1992) and Zachary (1989).[8] COGNET produces a model of the decision maker with three separate levels of detail:

- A multi-panel blackboard model captures the decision maker's mental model or cognitive representation of the problem; the blackboard's structure and internal organization varies with the level of decision maker expertise.
- A set of reasoning steps or cognitive tasks defines chunks of problem-solving activity that the operator has acquired through training or experience; the context under which each chunk can/should be undertaken is also represented within it, in terms of patterns of information on the blackboard. Here again, the number and richness of the tasks vary with expertise, as does the complexity of the triggering conditions.
- A detailed description, expressed in a GOMS-like[9] language, which characterizes the decision strategy contained in each cognitive task. The number and complexity of these varies (and tends to increase) with increasing operator expertise.

These three portions of the COGNET analysis are summarized to fill in the last three portions of the TSD, separately for each level of operator expertise (novice, intermediate, and expert).

The ability to create a complete summary task description is an indication that there is sufficient data to proceed with the design/analysis process. Conversely, when the user is unable to complete certain sections of the summary, this indicates that more data or analysis of the existing data is needed.

52.7.2 Functional Requirements Definition

Once the DSS designer has constructed a complete set of TSDs and is satisfied with them, the methodology proceeds to the next step in Figure 5. Together, the second step "Identify Aiding/Training Requirements" and the third step "Define DSS Functionality" result in the generation of a set of functional requirements for the DSS application being built. They are therefore treated together here. In these steps, the system designer:

1) analyzes the TSDs produced by the first step to identify specific knowledge and/or cognitive and knowledge limitations that constrain the operator's decision making performance, and/or affect the decision maker's skill acquisition process, and then
2) translates each decision making and/or learning limitation into functional requirements for decision aiding, decision training, or both.

The methodology provides tools, in the form of background knowledge and data, that support these analyses. First, it provides breakouts of the cognitive limitations and knowledge limitations that affect decision performance and skill acquisition. These are shown in Figure 7. The decision making column represents cognitive limits that can ultimately be extended or removed through decision aiding technology; the list of cognitive limits is taken directly from Zachary (1988). The training/skill acquisition column represents analogous limits in the development of individual competence (see Ryder et al., 1994b and Zachary and Hicinbothom, 1993).

There is a general correspondence between these six categories (the rows of Figure 7) and the last six portions of the TSD format. Specifically:

- Underlying processes of the problem environment are the source of both *process prediction* problems (being able to predict the outcome of a potential course of action in the environment) and *process understanding and practice* needs. In decision performance, the person must sometimes predict the outcome or trajectory of some external process. In decision training, the person may need practice in interacting with the process in order to develop understanding of the process and knowledge about how to predict and reason about it.

  Value criteria that are complex give rise to both problems in *combining decision-option attributes* and in *learning situational cues and case attributes* which are used to partition the decision problem into cases. In decision performance, the person may know in general what cues and attributes are important, but may

[8] Examples of its previous application can be found in Zachary and Zubritzky (1989); Zachary, Zaklad, Hicinbothom, Ryder, and Purcell (1993); Seamster et al. (1993); validation data are presented in Ryder and Zachary (1991).

[9] GOMS stands for Goals, Operators, Methods and Selection rules, and is shorthand for a seminal cognitive description language created by Card Moran and Newell (1983).

Decision Making Difficulties and Problems	Training/Skill Acquisition Difficulties and Problems
process prediction	process understanding and practice
combining decision attributes	learning situations cues and case attributes
information organizing, access, monitoring	distinguishing important from irrelevant information
limits in visualizing/representing	testing/evolving representation
applying reasoning methods	acquiring and chunking reasoning strategies
attention management, identification of appropriate heuristic/domain-based knowledge	acquiring attentional strategy; developing metacognitive knowledge; mapping situational cues and case attributes to case-based heuristics and knowledge

Figure 7. Summary of main limitations in skill acquisition and decision making.

have difficulty in combining them, particularly when they are temporal, spatial, and/or quantitative. In decision training, the person may have difficulty in learning to recognize the attributes and cues that are used by experts to partition the problem space into meaningful cases.

- Complex information environments lead to difficulties in *organizing, accessing, and monitoring task/problem information* as well as to the need to *learn to separate important information from irrelevant information.* In decision performance, even the expert individuals may have problems in dealing with high data volume and/or poor data organization/quality. In decision training, the more novice individual must first learn which data are relevant and how they are relevant.
- Complex and abstract mental representations of (complex) problem environments can lead to limited ability to *maintain and visualize these representations*, and to the need to *question and evolve representational structures* across levels of expertise. In decision performance, the person may have difficulty in applying a problem representation to the situation at hand; in decision training, the person may have difficulties learning 'how to think' about the problem domain.
- Complex reasoning strategies, at all levels of expertise, can exceed the ability of operators to *apply them effectively and efficiently* in decision performance. In decision training, an individual can also experience difficulties in *acquiring them*, as well as *chunking them* into higher level and more sophisticated reasoning tasks.
- Limits in judgmental and recognitional processes can lead to problems in *attention management and in identifying appropriate heuristic/domain-based knowledge* in decision practice, particularly in fast-paced and/or high workload decision situations. In decision training, the person can experience difficulties in *acquiring an attentional strategy; developing metacognitive knowledge; or mapping situational cues and case attributes to case-based heuristics and knowledge.*

Within the overall design process, the DSS designer must determine whether and to what extent the factors in Figure 7 are present in the decision making tasks to be supported with the DSS application. This is done by systematically reviewing the information in a given level of all the TSDs, for instances of the types of decision making and/or training needs indicated in the corresponding row of Figure 7. The designer then makes design decisions about which effects are actually present, and how they are to be described. This latter element is recorded as the output of step 2 in

Decision Aiding Functions	Decision Training Functions
process prediction	environment for practice/exploration
choice modeling	performance feedback and assessment
information management	problem query/data scaffolding
representational support	conceptual training
automated reasoning/interpretation	performance advice/tutoring/scaffolding
attention cueing/partitioning of problem space	metacognitive training/cognitive diagnosis

Figure 8. Summary of feasible DSS functionality.

Figure 5 (i.e., a list of decision making and skill acquisition problems targeted for training and aiding).

Next, the user must translate these targeted features into the DSS functional requirements. The methodology supports this step by providing a typology of "feasible" decision aiding and decision training functions. A *feasible* function, in this sense, is one that has been successfully implemented and fielded. This is summarized in Figure 8. The decision aiding column represents aiding functions that have been successfully provided in past decision aiding applications, based on the categories provided in Zachary (1988). The decision training column represents training functions that have been successfully achieved in the fielded decision training systems, or demonstrated in intelligent tutoring or decision training research.

Each row of this table corresponds to a row of Figure 7 and, roughly, to a section of Figure 5 (the TSD). Specifically:

- Models of real-world processes can extend the persons' abilities to predict processes, as well as provide an environment for practice in the domain and for exploration-based learning.
- Mathematical and/or computer choice models alleviate problems in combining choice attributes; these same types of models can also support provision of dynamic feedback on student performance, as well as evaluative performance assessment.
- Information management assistance can relieve difficulties in managing information during decision making; it can also provide trainees with the ability to query for specific data in interactive learning environments, and/or with automated support or 'scaffolding' for trainee problem solving.
- Representational technologies can be used to extend the decision maker's ability to maintain and visualize the problem using their own mental representation, and these methods can also support the kind of representational training required for movement between levels of expertise.
- Automation of all or parts of reasoning and interpretation strategies can extend decision makers' abilities to apply their own strategies effectively, and can also provide advice and tutoring on performance as a way to support chunking of reasoning steps and acquisition of more sophisticated ones. In this latter sense, automation of reasoning strategies can provide dynamic scaffolding analogous to the static data scaffolding mentioned above.
- Automated cueing of decision maker attention can remove cognitive and vigilance biases in unaided tasks, and can help the decision maker partition the problem space into relevant cases. In decision training, this same functionality can be used to train the person to perform these tasks (i.e., attentional scaffolding), or can be used to dynamically diagnose and assess the trainee's unsupported performance in attention management and recognition of specific problem-domain cases.

In the third step of Figure 5, the DSS designer must use the generic functionality in Figure 8 together with the data generated in the preceding steps to define the desired functionality of the decision support system.

This is done by systematically reviewing the list of targeted decision training and decision aiding features (resulting from the previous step) together with the data in the TSDs. The designer must identify problem-specific decision aiding and decision training functions that could address each of the targeted issues in the list. Each of these is then expressed as a functional requirement for the DSS application, and forms the results of the third step in the methodology.

This product (a functional requirement specification) is actually more than a simple listing, because it identifies both the cognitive/knowledge limitations that the application is addressing, and the specific functional requirement(s) that arise from each identified limitation. The limitations are, of course, identified from focused analysis of the TSD and its supporting breakdowns. This provides for traceability of the functional analysis, which is very important to the systems engineers who must build actual components to meet those functional requirements.

52.7.3 Functional Design

Once the designer has developed a set of functional requirements, the process proceeds from the analysis phase to a functional design phase. This includes the next two steps in Figure 5, labeled "Identify Candidate DSS Techniques" and "Determine Appropriate DSS Techniques". The goal of this portion of the DSS design process is to determine the range of decision aiding and embedded training techniques that should be used to meet the specified functional requirements. The same pattern as in the preceding steps is seen here. The methodology incorporates a taxonomy of component computational techniques that can be applied in both decision aiding and decision training.[10] The taxonomy is organized and indexed by the (increasingly specific) type of function each technique can perform. The taxonomy is shown in Figure 9.

The taxonomy is organized around the same lines as the TSDs and Figure 7 and 8. That is, at the top level it contains branches that correspond to the six rows in Figures 7 and 8 and to the last six sections of the TSD. Each of these branches represents a set of underlying technologies, any of which could be used to provide the corresponding type of function in Figure 8, as follows:

- Process Modeling technology can provide process prediction, problem practice, and exploration-based learning environments.
- Choice Modeling technologies can provide computational models of attribute combination in decision processes, and dynamic student performance evaluation. In addition, these same techniques can be used to provide feedback during training
- Information Control technologies provide access, organization, and monitoring of information for control of problem data in decision making. They can also support data-oriented scaffolding for decision training, and can provide for organization of and access to instructional data in automated training.
- Representational Technologies provide support for visualization and maintenance of integrative problem representations during decision making, and for presenting new representational alternatives to operators during representational training.
- Automated Reasoning and Analysis Methods include a large set of computational techniques that can provide automation of some portions of a decision maker's reasoning strategy as a way of improving the accuracy, efficiency, or quality of a decision process. These same methods can provide interactive advice on task performance and embedded tutoring to support acquisition of more complex reasoning strategies during decision training. In interactive training environments, these types of techniques can also be used to create more dynamic scaffolding for trainees.
- Attention management and Judgment Augmenting methods provide varying ways of augmenting vigilance and attention processes in complex decision environments, and evaluating and providing feedback on human judgmental processes to improve metacognitive skill. These methods can also be used to provide dynamic assessment of trainee's attention and problem space partitioning skills. Methods in this class can also be used to provide cognitive diagnosis, by comparing the

[10]The taxonomy is based on a taxonomy originally presented in Zachary (1986). However, it has been revised and updated to reflect technology developments since the original publication, as well as to extend the original structure to deal with the dual scope of decision aiding and decision training.

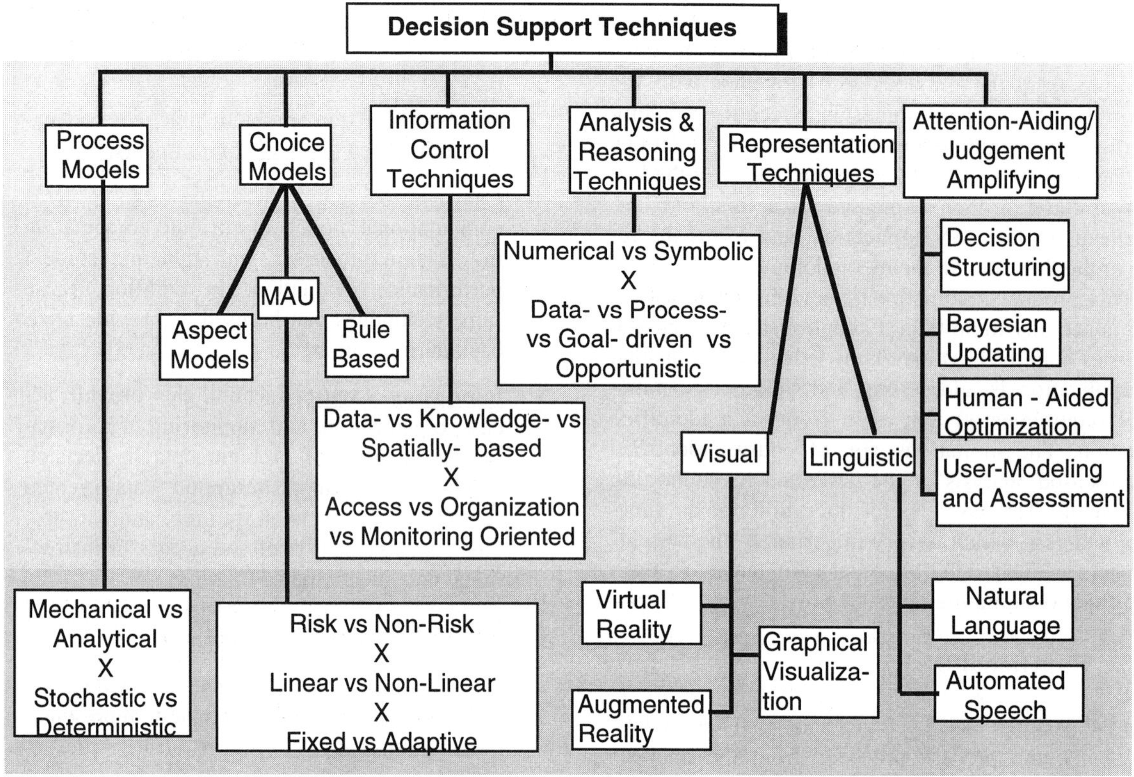

Figure 9. Taxonomy of decision support component technology.

trainee's partitioning of the problem space with an automated expert-level partitioning.

Each type of functional requirement is mapped into a corresponding part of this technology taxonomy. The designer must determine the mapping between the taxonomy of decision aiding and decision techniques and the DSS functional requirements. This determination is supported by the prior information generated in the design process (e.g., the details of the functional requirements, the decision making and skill acquisition limits it addresses, and the basic cognitive/task analysis data in the TSD on which the limit analysis was based). Zachary (1986, 1988) provides detailed comparisons of the relative capabilities and advantages of most of the techniques in the taxonomy. It should be noted here that the emphasis in this step of the methodology is on applicability of a technique, not on its appropriateness. Thus, several techniques might be identified as applicable to a given functional requirement at this point. The question of appropriateness is addressed in the next step in the methodology.

The intermediate product that is produced by the tool from this design step is a set of tables that:

- match the DSS application's functional requirements with the various decision aiding and decision training techniques that could be used to meet that requirement; and
- state the basis for each of these "matches."

This is simply a hierarchical table that indicates, for each functional requirement, the set of applicable techniques that have been identified as able to meet this requirement in the decision support system under design. The result of this step can present a critical point in the design process. The designer must assess whether each of the requirements can be matched with at least one candidate "off the shelf" technique. If this is the case, then the design process can proceed to the next stage. If not, however, the designer must determine whether to:

1. revise or relax the functional requirements to eliminate or loosen the unmet requirement(s),

   or

2. review and revise the task analyses so that a broader or looser set of functional requirements could be (re-) generated.

A third alternative, of course, is to stimulate technology research and development in order to create a technique or technology that could fulfill the "offending" functional requirement. In certain large system contexts (e.g., building a space station, launching a new telecommunications system) this may be a viable path. In most cases, however, it is too slow, expensive, and uncertain a path to generate an immediate solution. Thus, reconsideration of the requirements and/or underlying analysis are the more likely paths.

When the designer is able to identify at least one candidate approach to meet each functional requirement for the DSS system under design, the analysis proceeds to the next step, labeled "Determine Appropriate DSS Techniques." The purpose of this step is to refine the list of candidate techniques for the DSS application to a single list of techniques/technologies that will be incorporated into the DSS system being designed.

The design methodology intends that a problem-specific cost/benefit analysis be undertaken at this point in the process. This analysis compares techniques that were selected as capable of meeting the same functional requirement. In general, the criteria at this (early) stage of design should focus on very general development and implementation costs and benefits, such as:

- relative cost of implementation,
- relative speed of implementation,
- computational requirements, and
- likely speed/efficiency in the DSS application.

The specific criteria and tradeoff values, of course, vary by individual technique, and by the details of the application domain. After defining the cost/benefit analysis structure, the designer must determine and specify the relevant constraints, such as the time and costs available for development, or the computational host anticipated for the DSS application.

This information must then be applied to making the individual tradeoff decisions, based on the sets of comparisons created by the previous design step. The user must choose a single technique for each point where, in the preceding step, more than one technique may have been found to be feasible. This process identifies the final selected technique for each functional requirement of the system under design. This listing is used to develop a DSS architecture.

This point constitutes another potentially critical place in the design process. The designer must emerge from this cost/benefit analysis process with at least one approach that meets the cost/benefit constraints of the current application for each functional requirement in the DSS application design. It is possible that none of the technological alternatives for a given functional requirement can meet the constraints as entered. When this is the case, the designer must again consider several choices:

- first, attempt to reconsider the cost/benefit constraints of the application, either finding some way to relax them or to state them more precisely in hope that some technique may now pass;
- second (i.e., if the first fails), to revisit the matching process by which candidate techniques were identified to see if any other techniques could have been included that would meet the constraints; or
- third (i.e., if the second fails), to reconsider the functional requirements themselves and/or the task analyses that gave rise to them.

52.7.4 Architecture Design, Detailed Design, and Implementation

In the final step of the methodology, the various functions and techniques selected to fulfill them are integrated to create a software functional architecture. The dynamics of the human decision maker's task and decision processes play a major role in organizing the control scheme for this architecture, because the DSS must fit into the dynamics of the task environment of the decision maker. The task dynamics, as identified in the very top of the TSD, come back into play here, establishing the general control flow. For example, an iterative task will require a closed loop control flow, while an unfolding sequence of decisions will require a more hierarchical control flow. Next, the individual functional components (each representing one technique selected in the preceding step) are situated in the control structure. Finally, the data flow requirements are determined. This involves defining which components must provide data to or receive data from which other components, and which must provide data to send to or receive from the human decision maker/system user. Ideally, these architectural relationships are captured in some formal specification technique, such as data flow diagrams (De Marco, 1978), object-oriented specification (e.g., Booch, 1994), etc. Finally, from this level of formal specification of the DSS, the detailed engineering of the software, the human-computer interface, and the data environment of the DSS are undertaken. These steps, like the architecture specification, are more standard software and systems engineering issues, and are not discussed in further detail here.

52.8 Conclusions

This paper has tried to build a bridge between competing theories for decision support, particularly the current naturalistic decision theory and the more classical normative theories focusing on pure and/or bounded rationality. In doing so, it has reconsidered the basic definitions and characteristics of decision making, mapping out a space for decision support that is neither simple, nor symmetrical. The decision support space, it has been argued, should be defined by two dimensions — the characteristics of the problem domain in which decision making is occurring, and the degree of expertise of the decision maker being supported. The space is asymmetrical because the first of these dimensions gives rise to some problems where there is no opportunity for decision makers to gain expertise, and to others where there is such an opportunity. It is only on this latter side of the first dimension that the distinctions between expert, intermediate, and novice decision can be applied. However in domains where this second dimension is applicable, it has been argued that decision support must make clear assumptions about the expertise level of the person or class of person to be aided. This dimension of expertise, largely motivated by naturalistic decision theory, also shows that it is necessary to view decision support as consisting of two complementary aspects — decision aiding, which supports decision making performance, and decision training, which supports the acquisition of decision making expertise. This theoretical analysis, it is hoped, can provide some unification to a decision support field that has fragmented seriously in recent years, and appears in danger of losing its identity completely.

The paper has gone beyond theory, however, to address issues of practice. It has presented a detailed methodology for designing decision support systems that is at the same time oriented toward the practitioner, and yet consistent with and based on the theoretical arguments made at the beginning of the paper. This methodology, like the theory on which it rests, shows how the design of decision aiding and decision training systems, traditionally addressed in very separate ways, can be undertaken in an integrated manner. The integrated DSS design method shows how these two functions can be designed from a common cognitive analysis approach, a common technology base, and a common set of analytical techniques. This methodological analysis, it is hoped, can simplify the tasks of designing decision aids, decision trainers, and integrated decision support systems for the future.

52.9 Acknowledgments

The development of the ideas in this paper was supported, in part, under contracts N61339-90-C-0082 and N61339-92-C-0050 from the Naval Training Systems Center (now the Naval Air Warfare Center, Training Systems Division), and by CHI Systems Internal Research and Development. This paper, however, does not reflect an official position of any of these organizations; the ideas and opinions, as well as any errors contained herein are solely the responsibility of the authors. The contributions of Robert Ahlers, James Hicinbothom, Nina Chatham, Floyd Glenn, and Janine Purcell are gratefully acknowledged.

52.10 Bibliography

Amarel, S. (1969). On the representation of problems and goal-directed procedures for computers. Communications of the American Society for Cybernetics, 1.

Amarel, S. (1982). *Expert behavior and problem representations* (Tech report CBM-TR-126), Laboratory for Computer Science Research, Rutgers Univ.

Booch, G. (1994). *Object-oriented analysis and design.* Redwood City, CA: Benjamin/Cummings.

Brecke, F.H., and Young, M.J. (1990). *Training tactical decision-making skills: An emerging technology* (AFHRL-TR-90-36). Wright-Patterson Air Force Base, OH: AFHRL/LRG.

Card, S., Moran, T., and Newell, A. (1984). *Psychology of human-computer interaction.* Hillsdale, NJ: Lawrence Erlbaum Associates.

Chi, M.T.H., Glaser, R., and Farr, M.J. (1988). *The nature of expertise.* Hillsdale, NJ: Lawrence Erlbaum Associates.

Cohen, L.J. (1981). Can human irrationality be experimentally demonstrated? *The Behavioral and Brain Sciences, 4,* 317-370.

DeMarco, T., (1978). *Structured analysis and system specification,* New York: Yourdon Press.

Requests for reprints or other communications with the authors should be directed via electronic mail to Wayne_Zachary@chiinc.com or Joan_Ryder@chiinc.com.

Dreyfus, H.L. (1979). *What computers can't do: A critique of artificial reason.* New York: Harper.

Dreyfus, H.L., and Dreyfus, S.E. (1980). *A five-stage model of the mental activities involved in directed skill acquisition* (Technical Report under Air Force Contract F49620-79-C-0063). Berkeley, CA: University of California, Berkeley.

Edwards, W., Phillips, L.D., Hays, W.A.L., and Goodman, B. (1968). Probabilistic information processing systems: Design and evaluation. *IEEE Transactions on Systems Science and Cybernetics, SSC-4*, pp. 248-265.

Glenn, F., and Harrington, N. (1984). Evaluation of the Sonobuoy Pattern Planning Decision Aid. In *Proceedings of the 7th MIT/ONR Workshop on C3 Systems.* Cambridge, MA: Massachusetts Institute of Technology.

Kahneman, D., Slovic, P., and Tversky, A. (Eds). (1982). *Judgment under uncertainty: Heuristics and biases.* Cambridge, UK: Cambridge University Press.

Keeney (1982). Decision analysis: An overview. *Operations Research, 30*, 803-838.

Klein, G. (1980). Automated aids for the proficient decision-maker. In *Proceedings of 1980 IEEE Conference on Cybernetics and Society*, pp. 301-304.

Klein, G. (1989). Recognition-primed decisions. In W. Rouse (Ed.), *Advances in man-machine systems research, 5*, 47-92. Greenwich, CT: JAI Press, Inc.

Klein, G., Orasanu, J, Calderwood, R., and Zsambok, C. (Eds.). (1993). *Decision making in action: Models and methods.* Norwood, NJ.: Ablex.

Leal, A., and Pearl, J. (1977). An interactive program for conversational elicitation of decision structures. *IEEE Transactions on Systems, Man, and Cybernetics, SMC-7,* pp. 368-376.

Logicon, Inc. (1989). *A model for the acquisition of complex cognitive skills.* (Technical Report, Logicon Project 1150). San Diego, CA: Logicon, Inc.

March, J. (1978). Ambiguity, bounded rationality, and the engineering of choice. *Bell Journal of Economics, 6*, 587-608.

Orasanu, J., and Connolly, T. (1993) The reinvention of decision making. In G. Klein, J. Orasanu, R. Calderwood, and C. Zsambok (Eds.) *Decision making in action: Models and methods* (pp. 3-20). Norwood, N.J.: Ablex.

Raiffa, H. (1968). *Decision analysis.* Reading, MA: Addison Wesley.

Ryder, J.M., and Zachary, W.W. (1991). Experimental validation of the attention switching component of the COGNET framework. In *Proceedings of Human Factors Society 35th Annual Meeting.*, Santa Monica, CA: Human Factors Society.

Ryder, J.M., Zachary, W.W., Zaklad, A.L., and Purcell, J.A. (1994a). *A cognitive model for Integrated Decision Aiding/Training Embedded Systems (IDATES)* (Technical Report NTSC-92-010). Orlando, FL: Naval Training Systems Center.

Ryder, J.M., Zachary, W.W., Zaklad, A.L., and Purcell, J.A. (1994b). *A design methodology for Integrated Decision Aiding/Training Embedded Systems (IDATES)* (Technical Report NTSC-92-011). Orlando, FL: Naval Training Systems Center.

Seamster, T.L., Redding, R. E., Cannon, J.R., Ryder, J.M., and Purcell, J.A. (1993). Cognitive task analysis of expertise in air traffic control. *International Journal of Aviation Psychology, 3(4)*, 257-283.

Simon, H.A. (1955). A behavioral model of rational choice. *Quarterly Journal of Economics, 69*, 99-118.

Simon, H. A. (1972). Theories of bounded rationality. In C.B. Radner and R. Radner (Eds.) *Decision and organization* (pp. 161-176). Amsterdam: North Holland.

Slovic, P., Fischhoff, B., and Lichtenstein, S. (1977). Behavioral decision theory. *Annual Review of Psychology, 28*, 9-30.

VanLehn, K. (1996). Cognitive skill acquisition. *Annual Review of Psychology, 47*, 513-539.

Von Neumann, J., and Morgenstern, O. (1947). *Theory of games and economic behavior.* Princeton, NJ. Princeton University Press.

Wason, P.C., and Johnson-Laird, P.N. (1972). *Psychology of reasoning: structure and content..* Cambridge, MA: Harvard University Press.

Woods, D., Roth, E., and Bennett, K. (1990). Explorations in joint human-machine cognitive systems. In S.P. Robertson, W. Zachary, and J.B. Black (Eds.), *Cognition, computing and cooperation* (pp. 123-158). Norwood, NJ: Ablex Publishing Company.

Zachary, W. (1985). Beyond user-friendly: Building decision-aid interfaces for expert end users. In *IEEE 1985 Proceedings of the International_Conference on Cybernetics and Society*, pp. 641-647.

Zachary, W. (1986). A cognitive based funtional taxonomy of decision support techniques. *Human-Computer Interaction, 2*, 25-63.

Zachary, W. (1988). Decision support systems: Designing to extend the cognitive limits. In M. Helander (Ed.), *Handbook of human-computer interaction* (pp. 997-1030). Amsterdam: North-Holland.

Zachary, W. (1989). A context-based model of attention switching in computer-human interaction domains. In *Proceedings of the Human Factors Society - 33rd Annual Meeting* (pp. 286-290). Santa Monica, CA: Human Factors Society.

Zachary, W. W., and Hicinbothom, J. (1994). *A design tool for Integrated Decision Aiding/Training Embedded Systems (IDATES)* (Technical Report 93-010). Orlando, FL: Naval Air Warfare Center, Training Systems Division.

Zachary, W., Ryder, J., Ross, L., and Weiland, M. (1992). Intelligent computer-human interaction in real-time, multi-tasking process control and monitoring systems. In M. Helander, and M. Nagamachi (Eds.), *Design for Manufacturability* (pp. 377-401). New York: Taylor and Francis.

Zachary, W.W., Zaklad, A.L., Hicinbothom, J.H., Ryder, J.M., and Purcell, J.A. (1993). COGNET representation of tactical decision-making in anti-air warfare. In *Proceedings of the Human Factors and Ergonomics Society - 37th Annual Meeting.* Santa Monica, CA: Human Factors and Ergonomics Society.

Zachary, W.W., and Zubritzky, M. (1989). A cognitive model of real-time data fusion in Naval air ASW. In *Proceedings of the Third Tri-Service Data Fusion Symposium.* Laurel, MD: Johns Hopkins University.

Handbook of Human-Computer Interaction
Second, completely revised edition
M. Helander, T.K. Landauer, P. Prabhu (eds.)

Chapter 53

Human Computer Interaction Applications for Intelligent Transportation Systems

Thomas A. Dingus and Andrew W. Gellatly
Virginia Polytechnic Institute and State University
Virginia, USA

Stephen J. Reinach
The University of Iowa
Iowa, USA

53.1 Introduction

The use of micro-electronics inside vehicles has increased dramatically over the past two decades. This increase in the use of electronics has transformed the motor vehicle and the driving task in numerous ways. Advanced electronics have been applied to many diverse elements of the automobile, including engine control, transmissions, instrumentation, and in-vehicle comfort, convenience, and entertainment systems. Inexpensive and miniaturized application-specific integrated circuits perform multiple system functions, including sensing, intelligent processing, and communications. Another wave of changes to the vehicle and to driving will come as this technology, along with new driver interface designs and vehicle control systems, are applied to Intelligent Transportation Systems (ITS). Applications for such areas as advanced traveler information systems (ATIS), collision avoidance and warning systems (CAWS), automated highway systems (AHS), vision enhancement systems (VES), advanced traffic management systems (ATMS), and commercial vehicle operations (CVO) are available and potentially affordable. Moreover, the programmable nature of integrated circuits means that functionality of such systems can be refined and adapted to specific circumstances or needs, such as specific vehicle types, environmental conditions, or driver performance capabilities.

This deluge of electronic devices inside the automobile has challenged traditional approaches to human-computer interaction (HCI). Traditionally, HCI research has examined how people interact with computers in a home or work environment. In these environments, interacting with the computer is typically the user's primary task. People may use their computers to accomplish such primary tasks as word processing, database management, electronic mail communication, and interactive entertainment. The approach has been to evaluate specific interactions while performing tasks to determine how a particular interface design affects overall task performance and user acceptance. Interactions which negatively affect task performance are redesigned until acceptable levels of performance and satisfaction are achieved.

The driver of an automobile, however, operates in a dual-task environment. The primary task in the automobile environment is driving. Attending to the forward road scene and obtaining visual information to maintain the vehicle on the road and avoid collisions with other objects is a driver's primary task (Wierwille, 1993). Interacting with in-vehicle computers becomes a secondary task which drivers perform only when they feel it is safe to do so. Attentional resources must be shared between the environment outside the vehicle and the environment inside the vehicle. Attentional demand and time-sharing become primary issues in the development of usable interfaces for intelligent transportation systems and change the approach of HCI design and evaluation to some degree. Task performance while interacting with an in-vehicle computer is no longer of primary importance. Instead, the effect that human-computer interaction may have on driving performance and behavior will determine whether a computer-interface design is appropriate or not. Tradeoffs must be made between computer-interface designs which optimizes secondary-task performance and user acceptance but degrade driving performance and interface designs which are less than optimal for secondary-task performance but produce no negative affects on driving performance.

The traditional approach of HCI is still useful for the design of intelligent transportation system interfaces, but the emphasis on task performance and user acceptance has changed from just the computer interaction alone to the computer interaction while concurrently driving. Now, the approach to designing usable interfaces for ITS must include the impact such interfaces not only have on performing interactions with the system, but also on driving performance and behavior. The following chapter outlines the role of HCI in intelligent transportation systems. The chapter first describes the various classes of intelligent transportation systems. Specifically, the chapter discusses advanced traveler information systems, collision warning and avoidance systems, automated highways, vision enhancement systems, advanced traffic management systems, and commercial vehicle systems. Next, specific human-computer interaction issues are addressed. Finally, the future of human-computer interaction in ITS is discussed.

53.2 Classifications of Intelligent Transportation Systems

The primary goals of ITS are (1) to alleviate urban congestion by utilizing existing transportation resources more effectively; (2) to improve transportation safety by implementing technology which alerts drivers to hazardous or dangerous situations and acts to prevent accidents when the driver is unable to respond in a reasonable manner; and (3) to reduce environmental impact by improving the fuel efficiency and reducing the air pollution associated with current transportation conditions. To accomplish these goals, an international effort is being placed on integrating knowledge on driver behavior and decision making into the design of systems that comprise ITS. Techniques to reduce urban congestion, improve transportation safety, and reduce environmental impact have typically focused on capital intensive strategies such as the development of new roads or light rail to increase system capacity, the implementation of new legislation governing crash safety of vehicles, and the development of alternative fuel source vehicles. However, an alternative strategy, which is less capital intensive, is to design an information system that is based specifically on the traffic information needs of private and commercial drivers.

Intelligent transportation systems are only one of many possible approaches to reducing traffic congestion, improving transportation safety, and reducing environmental impact. It is highly unlikely that any single solution will produce a quick fix given the tremendous increase in the amount of traffic on our major roadways and given the complexity of the problems associated with the movement of people and material from one location to another. For example, it is well known that urban travel patterns are intrinsically related to developments in city structure, the location of workplaces, the activities of the drivers, their residences, and the characteristics of the driving population (Barfield, Haselkorn, Spyridakis, and Conquest, 1989).

There are, however, a number of attractive features of information-based solutions to transportation problems. They are relatively inexpensive compared to other solutions to transportation problems (e.g., the building of new roads); they have low social and environmental impact; and in addition to their primary goals, they can produce a number of secondary benefits by carrying public relations and educational messages. Furthermore, the importance of an ITS is clear when one considers the specific benefits which are expected to occur from its usage. For example, an ITS is expected to reduce traffic congestion, improve navigational performance, decrease the likelihood of an accident, reduce fuel costs and air pollution, and improve driver efficiency. The following is a brief overview of the various intelligent transportation systems that are being proposed.

53.2.1 Advanced Traveler Information Systems (ATIS)

In-vehicle advanced traveler information systems are viewed as the foundation for the development of an intelligent transportation system (Hulse, Dingus, and Barfield, in press). The purpose of an advanced traveler information system is to regulate the flow of vehicles along roads and highways by using emerging sensor, computer, communication, and control technologies. The safety aspects of such systems are expected to occur because they will provide additional, more timely, and more accessible information regarding regulation, guidance, and hazardous situations. Another benefit associated with an advanced traveler information system is that this system will provide safety advisory and warning messages to the motorist. This information will be especially beneficial in decreased visibility situations due to poor weather or congestion (Mobility 2000, 1989).

To accomplish the overall advanced traveler information system goal of safer and more efficient travel, several classes of systems have been identified under the ATIS concept. Lee, Morgan, Wheeler, Hulse and Dingus (1993) have outlined the following proposed functional capabilities for each of these systems. A brief description of the various traveler information subsystems is provided below.

In-vehicle routing and navigation systems (IRANS). A routing and navigation system provides drivers with information about how to get from one place to another, as well as information on traffic operations and recurrent and non-recurrent urban traffic congestion. At this time, seven functional components have been identified. The first functional component, trip planning, considers the route planning of long, multiple destination journeys. Trip planning may include coordinating overnight accommodations, restaurant, and vehicle service information, as well as identifying scenic routes and historical sites.

The multi-mode travel coordination and planning component provides coordination information to the driver on different modes of transportation (e.g., buses, trains, and subways) in conjunction with driving a vehicle. This information may include real-time updates of actual arrival and departure times for the different transportation modes as well as anticipated travel times.

A third functional component, pre-drive route and destination selection, allows the driver to select any destination and/or route while the vehicle is parked. The characteristics for the pre-drive selections include inputting and selecting the destination and selecting a departure time and a route to the destination. System information may include real-time or historical congestion information, estimated travel time, and routes that optimize a variety of parameters.

A related component, dynamic route selection, allows the driver to select any route to a destination while the vehicle is in motion. This capability includes the presentation of updated traffic and incident information that may affect the driver's route selection. In addition, the system would alert the driver if he or she makes an incorrect turn and leaves the planned route. Dynamic route selection could generate a new route based on the drivers new location.

A route guidance function provides the driver turn-by-turn and/or directional information to a selected destination. This information can be in the form of a highlighted route on an electronic map display, icons indicating turn directions on a head-up display (HUD), or a voice commanding turns.

A route navigation function provides information to help the driver arrive at a selected destination. However, it does not include route guidance information. A route navigation system may include presenting an in-vehicle electronic map with streets, direction orientation, current location of vehicle, destination location, and services or attractions locations. A route navigation system would provide the same information typically found on paper maps.

The last functional component of in-vehicle routing and navigation systems, automated toll collection, would allow a vehicle to travel through a toll roadway without the need to stop and pay tolls. Tolls would be deducted automatically from the driver's account as the vehicle is driven past toll collection areas.

In-vehicle motorist service information systems (IMSIS). A motorist service information system provides the driver with a broad range of information services and capabilities. These services and capabilities include the following. (1) Broadcast information on services and attractions which provides travelers with information that might otherwise have been found on roadside signs. It would be very similar to the services and attractions directory; however, the driver does not need to look for this information. The information is presented as the vehicle travels down the road. (2) A services and attractions directory provides the driver with information about overnight lodging; automobile fuel and services; and entertainment, recreational, and emergency medical services. The driver would be able to access information concerning businesses or attractions that satisfy his or her current driving needs when using this system. (3) The destination coordination function enables the driver to communicate and make arrangements with various destinations. This may include making restaurant and/or hotel reservations from the road. And finally, (4) the message transfer capability would allow the driver to communicate with others. Currently, this function implemented by cellular telephone and two-way radio communication (e.g., CB radios). In the future, systems may improve upon this technology by automatically generating preset messages at the touch of a button and by receiving messages for future use. Message transfer may involve both text and voice messages.

In-vehicle signing information systems (ISIS). A signing information system provides the driver with information which is currently depicted on external roadway signs inside the vehicle. This may include non-commercial routing, warning, regulatory, and advisory signing information. The following three major categories of sign information will be displayed by an in-vehicle signing information system: (1) roadway sign guidance information which includes street signs, interchange graphics, route markers, and mile posts; (2) roadway sign notification information which includes roadside signs that currently notify drivers of potential hazards or changes in the roadway such as merge signs, advisory speed limits, chevrons, and curve arrows; and (3) roadway sign regulatory information which includes speed-limit sign, stop sign, yield sign, turn prohibition, and lane use. Again, this sign information would be presented to the driver from inside the vehicle.

In-vehicle safety and warning systems (IVSAWS). A safety and warning system provides the driver with warning information on immediate hazards, road conditions, or situations affecting the roadway ahead. It provides sufficient advanced warning to permit the driver to take remedial action (e.g., to slow down). However, this system does not encompass in-vehicle safety warning devices that provide warnings of imminent danger requiring immediate action (e.g., lane-change or blind-spot warning devices, imminent-collision warning devices, etc.). An in-vehicle safety and warning system may provide immediate hazard-proximity information to the driver by indicating the relative location of the hazard, the type of hazard, and the status of emergency vehicles in the area. Specifically, this may include notifying the driver of an approaching emergency vehicle or warning the driver of an accident immediately ahead. Road condition information may also be provided by these systems. This function may provide information on traction, congestion, construction, etc., within some pre-defined proximity to the vehicle or the driver's route.

In addition, in-vehicle safety and warning systems provide for the capability of both automatic and manual aid requests. The automatic aid request function provides a "may day" signal in circumstances requiring emergency response where a manual aid request is not feasible and where immediate response is essential (e.g., severe accidents). The signal will provide location information and potential severity information to the emergency response personnel. The manual aid request function encompasses those services which are needed in an emergency (police, ambulance, towing, and fire department). It will allow the driver to have access from the vehicle without the need to locate a phone, know the appropriate phone number, or even know the current location. This function may also include feedback to notify the driver of the status of the response, such as the expected arrival time of service.

Thus far in the evolution of advanced traveler information systems, the vast majority of developed systems and empirical research has centered around routing and navigation system applications. Motorist service information system functions are empirically represented in a few instances, and signing information systems and safety and warning systems are greatly under-represented in early system development. A summary of the functions of recent advanced traveler information system projects provided by Rillings and Betsold (1991) illustrates the emphasis on routing and navigation systems to date. It is apparent that a major reason for the development activity centered around route guidance and navigation applications is the number of potential benefits and the perceived marketability of such systems. Navigation to an unknown destination, particularly in instances where one is driving without passengers, is a difficult task, and in most cases is performed inefficiently or unsuccessfully. Outram and Thompson (1977), as cited in a paper by Lunenfeld (1990), estimate that between 6% to 15% of all highway mileage is wasted due to inadequate navigation techniques. This results in a monetary loss of at least 45 billion dollars per year (King, 1986).

An additional cost that can potentially be reduced by widespread use of navigation systems is traffic delay. Several systems under development are designed to interface with advanced traffic management systems (described below) that will eventually be based in metropolitan areas. Once such systems are in place, real-time traffic delays can be broadcast to in-vehicle systems. These systems can then be utilized to continuously calculate the fastest route to a destination during travel. Such a capability, if widely used, has the potential for increasing efficiency for an entire infrastructure network.

While the majority of effort to date has been expended on in-vehicle routing and navigation system development, the other traveler information subsystems hold promise for improving driving efficiency and safety. A paper by Green, Serafin, Williams and Paelke (1991) rated the relative costs and benefits of advanced traveler information system features. Based on ratings by four human-factors transportation experts regarding the costs and benefits associated with accidents, traffic operations and driver needs and wants, several in-vehicle safety and warning system features were found to be most desirable in future systems. Several in-car signing features were also highly ranked. In contrast, some routing and navigation system features were ranked relatively low, primarily due to the potential safety cost of using such systems (Green et al., 1991).

In summary, this section laid a foundation for further discussion of human-computer interaction issues relevant to advance traveler information systems by providing a description of current systems under development. As will be discussed later, for advanced traveler information system benefits to be realized designers of traffic information systems must implement HCI knowledge and design principles into the design of such systems.

53.2.2 Collision Avoidance and Warning Systems (CAWS)

In 1990 there were an estimated 16 million motor vehicle crashes (police-reported plus non-police-reported) resulting in nearly 45,000 fatalities, 5.4 million non-fatal injuries, and 28 million damaged vehicles (derivations based on 1990 General Estimates System crashes and vehicles' involvement). The estimated economic cost of motor vehicle crashes in 1990 was $137.5 billion, greater than 2% of the U.S. Gross National Product. Included in these losses were lost productivity, medical costs, legal costs, emergency service costs, insurance administration costs, travel delay, property damage, and workplace productivity losses. The average cost per crash was about $8,600.

The electronics revolution has resulted in order-of-magnitude decreases in cost and improvements in capabilities of electronic sensors and processors that might be applied to crash avoidance and/or collision warning. An electronics "budget" of $1,800 per vehicle could achieve a 25% reduction in crashes (Dingus, Jahns, Horowitz and Knipling, in press). The apparent attractiveness of this investment from a purely economic standpoint is helping to drive the current intense interest of industry and researchers in high-technology crash prevention devices. Moreover, this monetary cost-benefit perspective is conservative since it does not encompass the humanitarian benefits (and the resulting marketing benefits) that may be achieved through a lessening of the current toll of pain and suffering from motor vehicle crashes.

Crash causes. One of the most extensive studies of crash causes was the Indiana Tri-Level Study (Treat, Tumbas, McDonald, Shinar, and Hume, 1979). In that study, driver errors were determined to be a definite or probable cause, or a severity-increasing factor, in 93% of crashes. In contrast, environmental factors were cited as "certain" or "probable" for 34% of the in-depth cases; vehicle factors were cited in 13%. These percentages add to more than 100 since more than one causal or severity-increasing factor could be cited. However, the Tri-Level study found that human factors were the only cause of 57% of crashes.

The human errors which cause crashes include recognition, decision, and performance errors. Of course, many crashes involve multiple interacting causal factors including driver errors, environmental factors, and vehicle factors. Recognition errors include situations where a conscious driver does not properly perceive, comprehend, and/or react to a situation requiring a driver response. It includes inattention, distraction, and "improper lookout" (i.e., the driver "looked but did not see"). Recognition errors were a definite or probable causal factor in 56% of the in-depth Tri-Level crashes.

Decision errors are those in which a driver selects an improper course of action (or takes no action) to avoid a crash. This includes misjudgment, false assumption, improper maneuver or driving technique, inadequate defensive driving, excessive speed, tailgating, and inadequate use of lighting or signaling. Decision errors were a definite or probable causal factor in 52% of the Tri-Level crashes.

Performance errors are those in which the driver properly comprehends a crash threat and selects an appropriate action, but simply errs in executing that action. Performance errors include overcompensation (e.g., over-steering), panic or freezing, and inadequate directional control. Less common than recognition or decision errors, they were apparent in 11% of the Tri-Level crashes.

A general conclusion from the Tri-Level study and most other studies of crash causation is that most crashes are caused by the errors of "well-intentioned" drivers rather than by overt unsafe driving acts such as tailgating, weaving through traffic, or even alcohol and/or excessive speed (GES, 1993; Evans, 1991). Unsafe driving acts obviously increase the probability and likely severity of crashes, and thus must be contravened by whatever means are available to society. But unsafe driving acts do not account for a majority of crashes. The majority of motor vehicle crashes are caused by the same kinds of "innocent" human errors that cause most industrial and other transportation mishaps.

The Tri-Level study was a landmark contribution to crash avoidance research. More recent studies of crash causation (e.g., Knipling, Wang, and Yin, 1993b) have generally corroborated these findings. Nevertheless, the Tri-Level findings may be misleading if they are not understood from a human factors perspective. Attribution of crashes to human error as a category apart from vehicle and environmental causes may lead to a mistaken inference that these human errors are unrelated to vehicle or highway design characteristics. From a prevention standpoint, attribution of crashes to driver error may obscure the fact that safety enhancements to the vehicle (e.g., collision warning systems) and/or the environment (e.g., intelligent signing) may make crashes due to "driver error" less likely to occur.

Crash types. There are several different categories of crash types. They include backing, rear-end, lane-change or lane-merge, single vehicle roadway departure, head-on, and intersections or crossing paths. Crashes involving backing include those where a vehicle is backing up and hits a stationary or slow moving object (encroachment) and those where another vehicle or object crosses the path of the vehicle backing up. Encroachment backing crashes are almost always due to the backing driver's lack of awareness of the presence of the struck person, vehicle, or object in their travel path (Tijerina, Hendricks, Pierowicz, Everson, and Kiger, 1993). Rear-mounted sensors (e.g., ultrasound, radar, laser) may be used to detect objects in the backing vehicle's path. The likely effectiveness of rear-obstacle warning systems depends on many different variables; for example, system range, vehicle rearward speed and/or acceleration, initial distance between sensor and target, driver reaction-time, and braking efficiency. Rear-end crashes account for 23% of police-reported crashes and an even larger percentage of non-police-reported crashes and crash-caused delay (Knipling et al., 1993b). Analysis of rear-end crashes has revealed two major subtypes (Knipling, Mironer, Hendricks, Tijerina, Everson, Allen, and Wilson, 1993a). About 70% involve a stationary lead (struck) vehicle at the time of impact, whereas about 30% involve a moving lead-vehicle. Typically, the lead vehicle is stopped waiting to turn and/or at a traffic signal. The most common causal factor associated with rear-end crashes is driver inattention to the driving task. A second, and overlapping, causal factor is following too closely. One or both of these factors are present in approximately 90% of rear-end crashes (Knipling et al., 1993a). Based on this causal factor assessment, one applicable countermeasure concept appears to be headway detection. Headway detection systems would monitor the separation and closing rate between equipped vehicles and other vehicles (or objects) in their forward paths of travel.

About 4% of all crashes involve a lane change or merge vehicle-maneuver. Causal factor assessments (e.g., Chovan, Tijerina, Alexander, and Hendricks, 1994; Treat et al., 1979) indicate that approximately three-quarters (or more) of lane-change or lane-merge crashes involve a recognition failure by the lane changing or merging driver. In other words, the driver "did not see" the other vehicle until the crash was unavoidable. Thus, a potential vehicle-based countermeasure to these crashes is a proximity or "lateral encroachment" warning system (or, possibly, automatic control system) that would detect vehicles adjacent to the equipped vehicle, especially in the area of the driver's lateral blind zone. The technology options for lateral proximity detection are substantially the same as for backing crashes. However, the required driver interfaces may be different. The nature of the driver interface for lane-change or lane-merge crash warning systems is more problematic since the driver's steering maneuver to avoid the lane change crash is likely to be less reliable (and thus more hazardous) than a braking response in a backing situation.

Single vehicle roadway departure (SVRD) crashes, which include crashes into parked vehicles, account for 29% of crashes and 46% of fatal crashes. A review of 100 SVRD crashes by Hendricks et al. (1993) revealed a "mixed bag" of causal factors and scenarios:

- 20% Slippery road (snow or ice)
- 20% Excessive speed / reckless maneuver
- 15% Driver inattentive / distracted (including evasive maneuver to avoid rear-end crash)
- 14% Evasive maneuver to external crash threat (e.g., animal, other vehicle encroaching in lane)

- 12% Drowsy driver (fell asleep at wheel)
- 10% Gross driver intoxication (often including excessive speed, reckless maneuver, etc.)
- 8% Other (e.g., vehicle failure, driver illness).

With so many diverse crash causes, no single countermeasure concept emerges for these crashes. One potential countermeasure concept is road edge detection. Such a system would monitor the vehicle's lateral position within the travel lane and detect imminent roadway departures. The system could activate a warning to the driver or automatic vehicle control (i.e., corrective steering).

Other countermeasure concepts are applicable to portions of the single vehicle roadway departure problem. For example, the headway detection concept discussed under rear-end crashes would be applicable to such crashes resulting from an evasive maneuver to avoid a rear-end crash. Drowsy driver countermeasures are applicable to a subset of these types of crashes. Infrastructure-based warning or advisory systems may be applicable to crashes on slippery roads and/or involving excessive speeds, especially at hazardous locations such as curves.

The "classical" head-on crash occurs on a two-lane rural roadway during an attempted passing maneuver. The passing vehicle is unable to complete the maneuver in time and collides head-on with an oncoming vehicle, perhaps on a curve or at a hill crest where visibility is limited. This scenario may be "classical," but it represents less than two percent of head-on crashes. Only about 1 vehicle in 5,000 will ever be involved in a passing-related head-on crash during its operational life. Instead, most head-on crashes result from unintended lane departures associated with negotiating curves, loss-of-control, an evasive maneuver (e.g., to avoid a rear-end crash), or simple driver inattention. In addition, a large number are associated with a left-turn-across-path maneuver.

Thus, the countermeasures to head-on crashes may principally be countermeasures to other crash types that have the ancillary benefit of preventing head-on crashes. For example, a headway detection system that prevents rear-end crashes will also prevent head-on crashes occurring as a result of panic evasive maneuvers to avoid rear-end crashes.

About 44% of all crashes occur at or near intersections (1991 GES). Of interest here are those crashes that involve crossing vehicle paths--especially crossing straight paths at 90° angles or a left turn of one vehicle across the travel path of another. Crossing path configurations represent about 22% of all crashes. In addition to crash configuration, a major factor influencing intersection crash causation and prospects for mitigation is the presence or absence of traffic control signals. At controlled intersections there is a salient physical indicator of right-of-way privilege, whereas at signed intersections this is determined solely by driver judgment and decision-making. Perhaps more importantly, signalized intersections are already equipped with an infrastructure for advanced electronics systems that might be employed as crash countermeasures.

Intersection crashes include several distinct causal scenarios and, thus, potential mechanisms for crash prevention. For example, a causal factor analysis of 50 signalized intersection straight crossing path crashes by Tijerina, Chovan, Pierowicz, and Hendricks (1994) indicates the following percentage breakdown of principal causes:

- 39% Deliberately ran signal
- 23% ran red light
- 16% tried to beat signal change
- 36% Inattentive driver (e.g., "did not see" signal)
- 13% Driver intoxicated
- 12% Other

These causal factor data have implications for countermeasure applicability. A "red light warning system" might be highly applicable to the inattentive driver cases, partially applicable to the intoxicated driver and "tried to beat signal change" cases, but not applicable at all to the "deliberately ran red light" cases.

Similarly, left-turn-across-path crashes may involve a number of possible driver errors, including a recognition failure (e.g., the left-turning driver "looked but didn't see" the oncoming vehicle), an incorrect gap decision by the left-turning driver, a false assumption about the other vehicle's planned action, a failure to execute the left turn maneuver in a timely manner. Available data (e.g., Treat et al., 1979) indicate that recognition failure is probably the most common category of driver error for these crashes. Thus, a countermeasure that works by assisting drivers with the gap decision would be applicable to only a portion of left-turn-across-path crashes.

It is the goal of crash avoidance and warning display designers to increase the situation awareness level of the typical driver to a level where common performance errors will be reduced, thereby reducing the overall crash rate of vehicles. To accomplish this care will have to be taken that the systems in fact orient attention to the hazard and not merely to the display. Long term use of the systems and their effect on driving behavior will have to be closely monitored. It is possible that a false sense of security could be instilled that will have tragic effects if a warning or avoidance system fails. Technology has given system designers an opportunity to make great strides in accident reduction and increases in transportation safety. One must never forget that technology is a double edged sword, and must be wielded with care.

53.2.3 Automated Highway Systems (AHS)

An automated highway system is defined as a system that combines vehicle and roadway instrumentation to provide some level of automated driving (Levitan and Bloomfield, in press). The proposed benefits for implementing such a system include improved safety for vehicles traveling in the automated lanes; increased travel efficiency (e.g., vehicles will travel at higher speeds and at closer following distances); predictable travel times to exit destinations from the automated road; reduced environmental pollution due to decreases in fossil fuel consumption and emissions; and reduced driver-stress while traveling in automated lanes compared with manual driving (National Automated Highway System Consortium, 1995).

Vehicles that are capable of operating on an automated highway must be dual-mode in nature. These vehicles must capable of operating on both normal and automated roads. It is proposed that automated lanes will either occupy part of the current highway structure or that additional "automated-only" driving lanes will be built on to the current highway structure. For a driving lane to be considered automated, it must allow for some level of controlled velocity and steering of appropriately instrumented vehicles.

The design of an automated highway system may vary along several dimensions. The first dimension along which an automated highway may vary is the degree of automation offered by the system. At one end of the continuum, full control over vehicles in the automated lanes is expected. Full control includes both steering and speed maintenance, as well as coordination of all vehicle movement within the automated lane (e.g., lane keeping, vehicle spacing, collision avoidance, and lane changing into or out of the automated lane). The driver of the vehicle would only need to input an exit destination from the automated highway and the highway system will drive the vehicle to that destination. At the other end of the automation continuum, only partial control of the vehicle would be provided. A current example of a partial automation in vehicles is the simple cruise control. Cruise control allows the driver to select the speed he or she wishes to travel at and the vehicle automatically attempts to maintain that speed.

A second dimension along which automated highway systems may vary is the type of infrastructure and vehicle equipment required. At one end, a fully automated system would consist of sophisticated roadside systems that would communicate control and coordination functions to instrumented vehicles on the automated roadway. Every vehicle would be fitted with equipment to communicate with the roadside system, sensors to detect other vehicles on the road, and controllers to execute steering, braking, and accelerating commands given by the roadside system. A well designed interface would be required to allow this information to be transferred between the driver and the automated highway system. On the other end, the vehicle itself will contain the majority of the intelligence to perform all control and coordination functions independent of a roadside system. In-vehicle systems would perform automated lane-tracking and speed maintenance as well as maintain safe travel distances from lead vehicles and perform collision avoidance. Lane changes, however, would not be automated and must be performed manually by the driver.

A third dimension of an automated highway is the degree of separation between automated and manual-controlled traffic. Some proposed systems have the automated lanes physically separated from normal driving lanes. Separate entrance and exit points would exist for the automated highway. Other systems have automated lanes separated from normal driving lanes by barriers; however gaps exist between the barrier allowing vehicles to move between automated and manual travel lanes. Still other proposed systems have no barriers existing between automated and normal driving lanes. Whichever level of separation is selected, the roadside system would coordinate and control movement between manual driving lanes and an automated lane to minimize traffic flow disruption and prevent accidents.

The final dimension of proposed automated highway systems is the vehicle control rules. A fully automated system may either control individual vehicles on the road or groups of vehicles (e.g., a string or platoon of vehicles). A string of vehicles would consist of several closely spaced vehicles traveling at relatively high speeds.

Numerous HCI issues need to be addressed despite whichever automated highway system dimensions are selected for implementation. Issues such as transfer of control between the driver and the automated system or vice versa; the effect of automated travel on subsequent manual driving behavior (e.g., reaction to unexpected events, following distance, speed maintenance, etc.), and the presentation of system failure information and the role a driver can be expected to play when a failure occurs must be evaluated. Interaction with a computer controlled automated highway will most certainly fall beyond the realm of traditional human-computer interaction approaches. New approaches for interfacing the driver with an automated vehicle will need to be developed to ensure that implementation of an automated highway system is successful.

53.2.4 Vision Enhancement Systems (VES)

Vision enhancement systems are being proposed to improve driver vision under nighttime or limited visibility (e.g., fog) conditions. A well designed VES has the potential for increasing driver performance, comfort, mobility, and overall traffic safety (Kiefer, 1995). Various technologies are being considered for use on vehicles such as infrared sensors and Doppler radar. The use of infrared imaging technology in vehicles will allow the driver to see beyond what is normally illuminated by the headlights under nighttime driving conditions. The use of Doppler radar technology will allow the driver to see objects normally obscured by inclement weather (e.g., fog, rain, or snow) or by vehicle design (e.g., "blind-spots" around the vehicle produced by hood-line and roof-pillar location). Regardless of the technology employed, a vision enhancement system consists of two primary components--the sensor and the display.

The major HCI issue for a vision enhancement system is how best to display the sensor information to the driver. System information can be displayed as either a primary or secondary source of visual information to the driver (Kiefer, 1995). Using a head-up display (HUD), VES information can be presented to the driver outside the vehicle as a virtual image. This virtual image can be overlaid on actual objects detected by the vision enhancement system (e.g., in a contact analog fashion) or the image can show the general location of detected objects (e.g., a pedestrian along the right side of the road). Contact analog presentation of VES information would seem the logical choice if the purpose of the system is to help the driver detect objects that cannot be seen using normal vision. However, current technological limitations of HUD design (i.e., limited field-of-view; binocular disparity between the virtual image and the forward scene object; and misalignment between the virtual image and a detected object caused by driver head movements) make non-contact analog methods for displaying VES information more reasonable.

Displaying VES information as a secondary source of visual information to the driver can be achieved by using either an in-vehicle display or a non-contact analog HUD. Detected objects are displayed offset from their true location in the forward scene. A limitation with this method is the driver must interpret the displayed information to gain knowledge about a detected object's actual location with respect to the vehicle so that appropriate action can be taken.

The major concern with vision enhancement systems is how driver performance and behavior will be affected when using such systems. Display design parameters (e.g., field-of-view, magnification, location, display format, etc.) will most certainly affect driver performance and behavior. A fear designers have is that drivers may attempt to drive a vehicle using a vision enhancement system as the primary source of visual information about the forward road scene under conditions which they would not normally drive if such a system was not available. Issues of information displayed, location, and format must be addressed if a vision enhancement system is to be safely and successfully implemented in ground-based vehicles.

53.2.5 Advanced Traffic Management Systems (ATMS)

The primary goal of a traffic management system is to facilitate the movement of people, goods, and vehicles through a roadway system while minimizing delays. Advanced traffic management systems will be capable of accomplishing this goal through its operators' interpretation of information from a multitude of sensors capable of monitoring traffic flow and roadway conditions. A traffic management system allows operators to control traffic signals and ramp meters, to remotely control closed-circuit television cameras and monitor their images, to identify roadway incidents and coordinate emergency response, to interact with complex computer-based support systems, and to transmit commands via various in-vehicle, roadside, and broadcast devices to control traffic and influence driver behavior (Kelly and Folds, in press).

Kelly and Folds (in press) have developed a set of system objectives that must be met by the advanced traffic management system if it is to be successful. The first objective of a traffic management system is to maximize the effective capacity of the existing roads monitored by the system. This is accomplished by distributing traffic load over the roadways to minimize congestion and delays. The second objective is to minimize the impact of accidents and incidents by reducing the probability of occurrence and minimizing the delay caused by such conditions. The third objective is to facilitate the response and movement of emergency services over roadways serviced by the system. A fourth objective is to contribute to the regulation of roadway demand. Maintenance activities or special events may create conditions in which roadway demand exceeds available capacity. An advanced traffic management system can serve to regulate this demand by persuading drivers to reschedule trips, reroute trips, or take alternative modes of transportation. The final objective is for the system to create and maintain public confidence in the information and services provided.

The HCI issues concerning an advanced traffic management system are analogous to those found in control room operations (e.g., a nuclear power plant control room; a manufacturing process control room; etc.). Operators of a traffic management system will be bombarded with information from sensors and video cameras about traffic flow and roadway conditions serviced by the system. The operators, seated at workstations, will be responsible for interpreting some or all of the information and make appropriate decisions about controlling traffic signals, variable message signs, etc. to maintain peak throughput for the roadways. Workstation design, information display layout and design, methods for inputting commands, and automation of some system functions become important issues that must be addressed before an advanced traffic management system can be successfully implemented.

53.2.6 Commercial Vehicle Operations (CVO)

A commercial vehicle operation encompasses those vehicles with physical characteristics or operational uses that differentiate them from vehicles normally used by the private driver. A commercial vehicle operation will have different needs for ITS technology than the general public. These needs are the result of both physical and operational differences that exist between commercial vehicle drivers and the general driving population. Drivers of commercial vehicles differ from the general public in the amount of training they have received in operating their vehicles and the stringent health, knowledge, and experience requirements they must possess to operate these vehicles. Special licensing is required for most operators of commercial vehicles. Wheeler, Campbell, and Kinghorn (in press) have classified three different types of commercial vehicle operations. They are: (1) commerce which includes all operations that involve the movement of goods and materials from one location to another. (2) Personal transport which includes such services as taxis, buses, and limousines. And (3) emergency response operations which include police, fire, ambulance as well as public utilities and tow trucks. Tasks associated with these commercial vehicle operations are briefly discussed below.

Intelligent transportation system technology may improve commercial vehicle operation task performance. These tasks may include route planning, dispatching, in-vehicle tasks performed by the driver, and regulatory compliance. Traveler information system technology adapted to commercial vehicle operations would offer improved methods for determining how best to get from a present location to a single or multiple destinations. This route planning may be performed for long-distance journeys, special cargo operations (e.g., hazardous materials, wide loads, etc.), or local deliveries to minimize distance traveled and maximize scheduling of trips. Advanced traveler information system and advanced traffic management system technology would offer improved dispatching of emergency response vehicles and improved service. Traveler information system, collision avoidance and warning system, and automated highway system technology would aid commercial vehicle drivers in performing in-vehicle tasks such as navigation, driving, data logging and information retrieval, and communication / coordination with shipping and receiving sites. Additional ITS technology is being developed to improve commercial vehicle operations. This technology includes advanced communications systems and advanced regulation systems. These systems would improve the interaction between commercial vehicle operators and their customers and commercial vehicle operations and state/national regulatory agencies.

Human-computer interaction issues surrounding commercial vehicle operations are similar to those of other proposed ITS systems (e.g., ATIS, CAWS, AHS, ATMS, etc.). The major differences are the user population for a commercial vehicle and the nature of the tasks performed by the driver. These differences must be considered when designing intelligent transportation systems that are specific to commercial vehicle operations.

53.3 Human-Computer Interaction Issues In Intelligent Transportation Systems

New technologies will be implemented inside vehicles as part of the Intelligent Transportation Systems revolution. These new technologies will generate a whole new set of human-computer interaction issues for drivers and automobiles. Designing intelligent transportation systems that drivers can use safely and efficiently is a difficult undertaking. The difficulty is derived from a number of causes: (1) the inherent complexity of systems being planned or produced, (2) the widely ranging knowledge, skills, and abilities of the driving population, (3) the limited opportunities for training and instruction with regard to ITS technology and, (4) the requirement that system use under all circumstances minimally interferes with the primary task of driving. To meet these challenges a number of HCI issues must be successfully addressed. Many of these issues are discussed in this chapter. The potential for compromising safety can be minimized with a proper understanding of the HCI issues in ITS driving.

53.3.1 Sensory Modality Allocation

Correctly choosing the appropriate sensory modality (e.g., auditory, visual, or tactile) to use for the delivery of in-vehicle information is an important task to consider when designing ITS systems. Sensory modality allocation, that is, whether to present information to the visual, auditory, or haptic modalities, can greatly affect both the safety and usability of intelligent transportation systems. For example, excessive amounts of visual information delivered through an in-vehicle system can overload the modality that already provides roughly 90% of a motorist's driving information (Rockwell, 1972). In addition, if in-vehicle auditory information is not designed based on human factors guidelines, the use of auditory information can lead to a system that is unusable, frustrating, annoying, and even dangerous. In order to make design decisions relating to the allocation of information to the various sensory modalities, designers must carefully consider the user, the system, and the environment as well as the specific capabilities of the particular sensory modality.

Visual and auditory information presentation. There is significant research being conducted on the use of visual presentation of information and appropriate formats for that information. As previously discussed, displayed information should be limited to only that which is absolutely necessary. For example, when following a prespecified route, Streeter (1985) recommends that the necessary information consists of the next turn, how far away the turn is, which street to turn on, and which direction to turn. Streeter found that people who are familiar with an area prefer to be given the cross street of the next turn, whereas people who are unfamiliar with an area prefer to be given distance information.

In addition to proximal (i.e., next turn) route following information, notice of upcoming obstacles or traffic congestion would also be of great potential benefit. Such information could conceivably make the composite task of driving safer, given that it can be displayed without requiring substantial driver resources (Dingus and Hulse, 1993).

There is significant evidence to support the use of auditory displays in vehicles. Many authors (e.g., Means, Carpenter, Szczublewski, Fleischman, Dingus and Means, 1992; Dingus and Hulse, 1993; Dingus, McGehee, Hulse, Jahns, Natarajan, Mollenhauer and Fleischman, 1995) have found that giving turn-by-turn directions via the auditory channel leads to quicker travel times, fewer wrong turns, and lower workload. Furthermore, when considering the delivery of route information, the use of auditory information allows the driver to give more attention to the primary task of driving, than when route information is displayed on a visual map (Labiale, 1990; Parkes, Ashby, and Fairclough, 1991; Streeter, Vitello and Wonsiewicz, 1985; McKnight and McKnight, 1992).

To support the idea that auditory information should be used as an in-vehicle display, there is additional evidence to support the notion that driving performance suffers when drivers are simultaneously looking at various in-vehicle displays. In this case, drivers tend not to react to situations on the road (McKnight and McKnight, 1992), deviate from their course (Zwahlen and DeBald, 1986), and reduce their average driving speed (Walker, Alicandri, Sedney and Roberts, 1991). Additional research assesses the workload differences associated with presenting information either visually or aurally. An example of this line of research can be found in Labiale (1990), who showed that workload during guided route-following is lower when navigation information is presented aurally than when it is presented visually. Also noteworthy is that this study showed that drivers preferred auditory route guidance information. The drivers explained that they felt it provided a safer system.

Despite the inherent advantage of efficient sharing of processing resources with the use of auditory displays while driving, there is also research support for the use of simple visual displays in navigational tasks. For example, Aretz (1991) makes the case that without some sort of map representation, drivers cannot construct an internal cognitive map of their routes. Therefore, a driver might arrive at a destination with no navigational problems, yet have no idea of the destination's location relative to the driver's starting point or to other landmarks. Along these lines Streeter, et al. (1985) noted that drivers preferred navigation systems that kept them informed of their current location.

Dingus and Hulse (1993) cite some potentially negative aspects of using speech presentation in lieu of visual presentation for advanced traveler information systems. These include: (1) improper prioritization and instinctive reaction to voice commands, even cases where they conflict with regulatory information, (2) the lack of intelligibility of low-cost speech synthesis devices, and (3) the inability of low-cost digitized speech devices to provide a vocabulary that provides all desired information. However, the reader should note that great technological advances are being made in speech technology which will impact points (2) and (3) above. In addition, much of the information that will be provided by advanced traveler information system is too complex to effectively display aurally. Another point to consider for traveler information system design, according to Williges, Williges, and Elkerton (1987) and Robinson and Eberts (1987), is that for a spatial task like navigating, performance is optimal when using visual stimuli coupled with manual responses. If the task is a verbal one, an auditory stimulus should be coupled with a verbal response from the person, such as a verbal verification for the acceptance of a new route. These articles suggest that for a navigation task, a visually displayed arrow indicating the direction of travel would help more than would verbal information (e.g., an auditory speech display).

Information provided to the driver must be timely and must be prioritized appropriately. ITS information varies greatly in its required response time from immediate reaction to avoid a crash, to several seconds for an upcoming turn, to purely discretionary. Sufficient time must be allowed for the driver to respond to any information. The driver needs time to hear and/or see the information, decide whether it is relevant, and act upon it. An above average human response time is required--most (i.e., 95% or 99%) of the drivers should have ample time to respond under most driving circumstances. The time required by the driver to process information and respond is dependent upon a number of factors, including the task and the type of display format selected, and is beyond the scope of this chapter. A discussion of driver response time requirements can be found in several sources, including the National Highway Traffic and Safety Administration Driver Performance Data Book (Henderson, 1986).

Haptic information in-vehicle. Haptic information has historically been rarely used as the primary channel to transmit information while driving, but is gaining more and more acceptance, particularly in Europe. Haptic feedback constitutes information gained via the "touch senses" including both tactile and proprioceptive information. The most common use of haptic information thus far is in the design of manual controls to provide feedback. Godthelp (1991) used an active gas pedal to provide feedback to the driver about automobile following distances. When the following distance between two cars was too close, the force needed to maintain a given speed with the accelerator was increased. They concluded that a gas pedal that offers more resistance when the following distance is too short can increase following distances. This demonstrates that haptic information is a viable method of providing selected information to drivers.

In addition, preliminary testing has shown that haptic warning information can have a higher degree of driver acceptance than auditory warning information. Anecdotal observations indicate that drivers may be embarrassed by the activation of an auditory alert with passengers in the car (Williams, 1995). Unfortunately, no specific guidelines for haptic displays have been developed for driving. However, tactile display guidelines have been developed for rehabilitation medicine (Kaczmarek and Bach-Y-Rita, 1995). In terms of tactile sensitivity, sensitivity in the hand increases from the palm to the fingertips. However, tactile sensitivity is degraded by low temperatures, a situation which occurs when drivers live in areas where severe winter weather is frequent. The most frequent type of stimuli for tactile displays has been mechanical vibration or electrical stimulation. Information can be transmitted through mechanical vibrators based on location of the vibrators, and their frequency, intensity, or duration. Electric impulses can be encoded in terms of electrode location, pulse rate, duration, intensity, or phase. In terms of display design, displays can be designed as a function of size, shape and texture. For shape design, controls that vary by 1/2 inch in diameter and by 3/8 inch in thickness can be identified by touch very accurately.

The tactile channel is rarely used as the primary channel to transmit information, but is used instead as a redundant form of information. The most common use of the tactile channel is in the design of manual controls to provide feedback. On a computer keyboard, the "F" and "J" keys often have a raised surface to indicate the position of the index fingers on the home row. Many aircraft have a "stick shaker" tactile display connected to the control column. Whenever the plane is in danger of stalling, the control column will vibrate to alert the pilot to take corrective measures (Kantowitz and Sorkin, 1983). Tactile displays are also used on highways. Reflective strips placed on the white line of the emergency lane or on the yellow dividing lines not only enhance the road contours, but will make the car vibrate if one crosses over them.

Based on the above, it can only be stated that an effort should be made to encode manual controls with tactile information, this will enhance feedback and enable drivers to manipulate controls without taking their eyes off the road. Designers of in-vehicle systems should seriously consider the use of tactile feedback displays. There is a great need to perform research relevant to the use of tactile displays, in order to further define their value.

Sensory modality allocation summary. The following sensory modality selection guidelines can be gleaned from the literature as outlined above. (1) Auditory only information provides a good allocation of information processing resources when combined with driving. However, for many ITS applications, some visually displayed information is necessary. (2) Visual information should be as simple as possible while conveying necessary information. Complex displays, such as moving maps, should be avoided if possible, or used in conjunction with auditory displays to alleviate attention demand. An exception would be to display complex visual information only when the vehicle is not moving; for example, when the vehicle is parked or the vehicle is stopped at a light or sign. (3) Intelligibility of auditory speech information is of concern in the automotive environment. Auditory messages should be simple, with volume adjustments and a repeat capability. Care in message selection is suggested as there is some evidence that voice commands may be followed in lieu of conflicting warning or regulatory information. (4) Auditory information should be used to supplement visual information to alert the driver of a change in visual display status or to provide speech-based instructions. Speech instructions have been shown to be a beneficial supplement for both simple and complex displays. (5) Tactile information displays are potentially useful for advanced traveler information system designs either as a means to provide redundant coding of information or as a means to gain driver attention or help avoid visual modality overload.

53.3.2 Display Format for Route Selection and Navigation

Display formats, the general way that information is presented, can greatly affect a system's safety and usability. When directions are communicated from one person to another, the message generally uses one of two presentation formats, either a map or a verbal list of instructions. A person either uses a map to show how to get to a destination, or a person informs the other person with a verbal list of instructions. What must be determined is which option is better for an in-vehicle navigation information system? The answer appears to be task specific. Bartram (1980) tested subjects' ability to plan a bus route using either a list or a map. The subjects who used a map made their decisions more quickly than those who used a list. In another study, Wetherell (1979) found that subjects who studied a map of a driving route made more errors when actually driving the route than did subjects who studied a textual list of turns. Wetherell concluded that two factors could have caused these findings: (1) the spatial processing demands of driving, seeing, and orienting interfere with maintaining a mental map in working memory, and (2) subjects had a harder time maintaining a mental model of a map learned in a north-up orientation when they approached an intersection from any direction but North. In a study conducted by Streeter, et al. (1985), subjects who used a route list (a series of verbal directions) to drive a route through neighborhoods drove the route faster and more accurately than subjects who used a customized map with the route highlighted. In terms of attentional resources required by a visual display, a well-designed turn-by-turn format will require less attentional resources than will a full route format. A turn-by-turn format displays to the driver specific information for each individual turn, and it requires very little information- only the direction of turn, distance to turn, and turn street name. This information is easy to display in a legible format that imposes a low attention demand.

McGranaghan, Mark and Gould (1987) have characterized route-following as a series of view-action pairs. The following is an example of a view-action pair. Information is required for an upcoming event (e.g., a turn), the event is executed, the information for the next event is displayed, the event is executed, etc. McGranaghan and his associates believe that for route following, only the information for the next view-action pair should be displayed. In their view, any additional information is extraneous and potentially disruptive to the route-following task.

However, there are advantages, such as route preview, to displaying an entire route. When the driving task requires relatively little attention, the driver can plan upcoming maneuvers. For complex routes, preplanning could alleviate much of the need for in-transit preview. Drivers may prefer to recall information and review it at their own pace. A second advantage to providing route information arises during maneuvers that happen one right after another, as when two (or more) quick turns are required. The information for the second turn may come up too soon for the driver to comfortably execute the second maneuver, and under it maybe circumstances where attention is needed for driving. If the route map is displayed, such an event can be planned for in advance.

When selecting a turn-by-turn or route map visual display format, designers must ensure that the information is displayed in a usable and safe manner. If they choose a turn-by-turn configuration, designers must consider close proximity and preview in general. If a route map is used, it is essential that the designer minimize the information present so that drivers' attention resources are not overloaded. Even when full route map information is minimized, it is not clear from the literature that driver resources will not become overloaded in circumstances of high required driving attention.

Dingus, et al. (1995) showed that providing turn-by-turn information in either a well designed textual or graphical format resulted in effective navigation performance and attention demand level. Some of the studies described above indicate that textual lists are easier to use than full maps when drivers are navigating to unknown destinations. Note, however, that graphical depictions can provide additional information such as special relationships to other streets, parking, hospitals, and other landmarks that textual lists can not. Therefore, the choice of a map or a list must depend on the desired task and required information. Depending on the requirements of the system under design, the inclusion of both display formats (displayed in different situations) may provide the most usable overall system.

Most of the results on navigation systems seem to support the recommendations outlined by Streeter (1985), that drivers should be presented with information that is most proximal to their location. However, previous research also suggests that studying paper maps of a given route either substitutes for a cognitive map, or aids in developing one. This cognitive map provides an orienting schema, which helps people organize information about an unfamiliar area (Antin, Dingus, Hulse, and Wierwille, 1990). Therefore, presenting drivers with full-route information might aid in the overall navigational task by helping them develop a cognitive map and survey knowledge of the area surrounding their route.

53.3.3 Visual Display Considerations

A major concern with the design of a visual display in the automobile is legibility of information, regardless of whether that information is text or graphic. A delineation of all appropriate display parameter options (e.g., resolution, luminance, contrast, color, glare protection) is a complex topic that is beyond the scope of this chapter. Actual guidelines for determining the proper color, contrast, and luminance levels to be used in cathode ray tube (CRT) displays within vehicles can be found in Kimura, Sugira, Shinkia, and Nagai (1988). In addition, a number of legibility standards are in existence for visual displays, including those developed for aircraft applications (Boff and Lincoln, 1988). Since the automobile is fraught with many of the same difficulties as the aircraft environment, many of these standards apply as well with respect to display legibility. However, note that the selection of a display in the automotive domain will be much more highly constrained by cost and perhaps have limitations well below the state of the art.

Legibility parameters have minimum acceptable standards below which the display is unusable. It is therefore critical to ensure that these minimum standards have been met in spite of the constraints for a given application. In addition, the problem of selecting display parameters is compounded since viewing distance is limited due to the configuration constraints present for an automotive instrument panel. Adding to the difficulties found in the automobile are those introduced by the user population. Older drivers with poorer visual acuity and/or bi-focal lenses must be carefully considered during the specification of the display parameters. To overcome this combination of limitations, the display parameters must be optimized within practical limits. For example, Carpenter, Fleischman, Dingus, Szczublewski, Krage, and Means (1991) used a "special high-legibility font" in a color CRT application to ensure that drivers could glance at the display and grasp the required information as quickly as possible. Other design aspects that aid in legibility include always presenting text information in an upright orientation (even in map applications), maximizing luminance and/or color contrast under all circumstances, maximizing line widths (particularly on map displays) to increase luminance, and minimizing the amount of displayed information in general to reduce search time (Dingus and Hulse, 1993).

Additional legibility design considerations include contrast, brightness, and character size. The greater the degree of contrast the quicker the detection and identification time for any target (up to a point). The brightness of the instrumentation panel has been shown to have an effect on reading performance when character size is relatively small (1.5 and 2.5 mm) (Imbeau, Wierwille, Wolf, and Chun, 1989). Character size also plays an important role in response time. Imbeau et al. found that smaller character sizes yielded significant performance decrements for older drivers.

The use of color. Another basic visual display concern stems from the presence of color deficiency and color blindness in the population. Approximately 8% of the male population and 4-5 % of the female population have some degree of color deficiency or color blindness. It is therefore important in consumer product applications to avoid reliance on color coding of critical information. Additional color issues include avoiding selected color combinations (Boff and Lincoln, 1988). For example, blue lines on a white background, since this combination causes the line to appear to "swim." Boff and Lincoln also recommend using color coding of information sparingly, since too many colors create more information density and an increase in search time.

Brown (1991) found that highlighting techniques using color resulted in quicker and more accurate recognition of targets on a visual display. Although instrument panel color has been shown to have no significant effect on reading and driving performance (Imbeau et al., 1989), Brockman (1991) found that color on a computer display screen can be distracting if used improperly. Brockman recommends several guidelines to avoid confusion when using color to code information. First, color codes should be used consistently. Colors from extreme ends of the color spectrum (i.e., red and blue) should not be put next to each other, since doing so makes it difficult for the reader's eye to perceive a straight line. Second, familiar color coding, such as red for hot should be used. Third, color alone should not be relied on to discriminate between items. Brockman recommends designing applications first in black and white, then adding color to provide additional information.

Visual display location. A major component of the driving task is scanning the environment and responding appropriately to unexpected events. Fortunately, humans are very sensitive to peripheral movement. An object moving in the periphery often instantly gains attention. In fact, some human factors professionals believe that peripheral vision is as important as foveal vision for the task of driving (Dingus and Hulse, 1993).

Given the above considerations, the placement of an information display becomes critical. The information contained on even a well-designed display system will require a relatively large amount of visual attention. Therefore, if the display is placed far from the normal driving forward-field-of-view, none of the driver's peripheral vision can be effectively utilized to detect unexpected movement forward of the vehicle. Another disadvantage of placing a display far away from the forward-field-of-view is increased switching time. Typical driver visual monitoring behavior involves switching back-and-forth between the roadway and the display in question. Dingus, Antin, Hulse, and Wierwille (1989) found that while performing most automotive tasks, switching occurs every 1.0 to 1.5 seconds. The farther away the display is from the roadway, the longer the switching time. Therefore, less time can be devoted to the roadway or the display (Weintraub, Haines, and Randle, 1985).

The position of an in-vehicle visual display was also studied by Popp and Farber (1991). It was found that a display positioned directly in front of the driver resulted in better driving performance, including lane tracking and obstacle detection, than one mounted in a peripheral location. However, performance on a symbolic navigation presentation format was hardly affected due to the change in position, and the results for peripheral location were still quite good. Tarrière, Hartemann, Sfez, Chaput, and Petit-Poilvert (1988) review some ergonomic principles of designing the in-vehicle environment and echo the opinion that a CRT display to be used while driving should be near the center of the dashboard and not too far below horizontal. The paper suggests that the screen be mounted 15° below horizontal, but should not exceed 30° for optimal driver comfort.

According to the discussion above, the display should be placed as close to the forward field of view as is practical. High on the instrument panel and near the area directly in front of the driver are desirable display locations. There is, however, another automotive option that is currently just beginning to be explored, a head-up display (HUD). Briziarelli and Allen (1989) tested the effect of a HUD speedometer on speeding behavior. Although no significant difference was found between a conventional speedometer and the HUD speedometer, most subjects (70%) felt that the HUD speedometer was easier to use and was more comfortable to read than a conventional speedometer. Subjects also reported being more aware of their speed when using the HUD speedometer. Campbell and Hershberger (1988) conducted HUD/conventional display comparisons in a simulator under differing levels of workload. Under both low and high workload conditions, steering variability was less for drivers using a HUD than for those using a conventional display. Also, steering variability was minimized when the HUD was low and centered in the driver's horizontal field of view. In another simulator study, Green and Williams (1992) found that drivers had faster recognition times between a navigation display and the 'true environment' outside the vehicle when the display was a HUD compared to a dash mounted CRT.

Given the above arguments, a HUD providing ITS information on the windshield could be a good choice since it is "in" the forward field of view. Besides the arguments described above, another advantage of most HUD designs is that they are focused at (or near) optical infinity, thus reducing the time required for the driver's eyes to accommodate between the display and the roadway. A number of concerns have been raised by Dingus and Hulse (1993) about the use of HUDs. The luminance may be a severely limiting factor in the automobile due to the presence of glare and stringent cost constraints. Certainly, a HUD that was too dim and hard to read could be much worse than an in-dash display. Issues regarding display information density and distraction must also be carefully addressed for HUDs and could result in their own set of problems. Also, an issue exists regarding the division of cognitive attention with HUDs. The fact that a driver is looking forward does not mean that roadway/traffic information is being processed. The importance of this division of attention to driving task performance has yet to be determined.

Human factors design principles applicable to display location. From the discussion above some general human factors guidelines can be given. (1) For optimal driving performance, the in-vehicle displays should be located as close to the center of the front windshield field-of-view as practical. Note that the center of the windshield field-of-view, or central viewing axis, is defined from the driver's eye point and is the center of the lane of travel near, but just below, the horizon. (2) Good display location does not alleviate requirements for minimization of visual display complexity. That is, displays must be simple, and displays which can not be made simple should be accessible only while the vehicle is not in motion. (3) A display should not placed too far below the horizontal. The optimal position for mounting the display screen is 15 degrees below horizontal, and should not exceed 30 degrees. (4) The maximum horizontal angles of comfort range is between 15 and 30 degrees left or right to the central viewing axis.

For head-up displays, the display should be located in the center of driver's horizontal field of view. The location of a holographic combiner can be located in one of two places. One is located on the periphery of driver's field of view. The other is also in the lower part of the windshield in the middle between the driver and the passenger. An instantaneous field of view with dimensions of about 6 degrees vertically by 10 degrees horizontally provides a comfortably large field of view. An ideal HUD focus range is considered to be a little more than 2 meters from the driver. Because truck windshields are nearly vertical, a HUD image cannot be placed directly on them. Therefore, the combiner should be a separate part of the HUD package. This makes the HUD a completely self-contained unit that can be located in any usable and convenient position in the vehicle.

53.3.4 Response Modality Research

Many control related technological advancements are available for use with computers, and therefore are available for potential use as part of intelligent transportation systems. The trade-off between "hard" buttons and "soft" CRT touch-screen push buttons has become a concern of the ITS human factors community (Dingus and Hulse, 1993). With the use of CRTs and flat panel displays in the automobile, there has been a strong temptation to use touch screen overlays for control activation. While this can be a very good method of control in the automobile for pre-drive or zero speed cases, research has shown that this is not true for in-transit circumstances. Zwahlen, Adams, and DeBald (1987) looked at safety aspects of CRT touch panel controls in automobiles as a function of lateral displacement from the centerline. This study found an unacceptable increase in lateral lane deviation with the use of touch panel controls. The study found the touch screen control panels were visually demanding, as demonstrated by the relatively high probabilities of lane deviations. Zwahlen et al. (1987) suggest that use of touch panel controls in automobiles should be reconsidered and delayed until more research with regard to driver information acquisition, information processing, eye-hand-finger coordination, touch accuracy, control actions, and safety aspects has been conducted and the designs and applications have been improved to allow safe operation during driving.

Monty (1984) found that the use of touch screen keys while driving required greater visual glance time and resulted in greater driving and system task errors than conventional "hard" buttons. The reasons for this performance decrement are twofold: (1) the controls are non-dedicated (i.e., they change depending on the screen), and (2) soft keys do not provide tactual feedback. For a "hard" button, the driver must (depending on the control and its proximity) glance briefly at the control and then find the control using tactile information to accomplish location "fine-tuning." For the soft keys, the driver must glance once to determine the location, and glance again to perform the location "fine-tuning" (Dingus and Hulse, 1993).

Clearly, one way to minimize control use while in-transit is to severely limit control access. Therefore, as with the display information previously discussed, it is important to assess the necessity of every control in terms of both in-transit requirements and frequency of in-transit use to minimize driver control access. Those controls that are not absolutely necessary for the in-transit environment can then be allocated to predrive or zero-speed circumstances (Dingus and Hulse, 1993).

Control location has been shown to be important in automotive research. The farther a control is located from the driver, the greater the resources needed to activate the control. This has been demonstrated by Bhise, Forbes, and Farber (1986) and Mourant, Herman, and Moussa-Hamouda (1980) who found that the probability of looking at a control increased with increased distance. Therefore, controls present on the steering wheel, or otherwise in close proximity to the driver, are easier to use. Complexity of the control activation and the potential for steering interference have also been shown to be important issues. Monty (1984) has shown that continuous controls or controls requiring multiple activations are significantly more difficult to operate. Therefore, limiting controls to single, discrete activations will provide fewer resource requirements.

Automatic speech recognition (ASR) systems may prove useful in situations where the eyes and hands are occupied with control and monitoring functions (Baber, 1991; Bennett, Greenspan, Syrdal, Tschirgi, and Wisowaty, 1989; Cochran, Riley, and Stewart, 1980; Cohen and Mandel, 1982; Cohen and Oviatt, 1994; Jones, Frankish, and Hapeshi, 1992; Markowitz, 1995; Poock, 1986, Quinnell, 1995), when low light or dark levels exist (Poock, 1986), or where speech can provide an additional channel for input to reduce operator workload (Jones et al., 1992; Peckham, 1984). However, ASR systems will only be useful for certain types of functions in complex systems.

Jones, Hapeshi, and Frankish (1989) provide a limited set of qualitative speech recognition interface guidelines which can be used for the allocation of functions in complex systems. (1) Speech should only be used when input is required infrequently. (2) The assignment of function to modality should preserve the coherence of the task components. Speech should be assigned in a consistent way to one component of the task; for example, use speech for commands only versus commands and data entry. (3) The care with which tasks are assigned to the speech modality should also be extended to functions within the task. For example, speech input is not useful for performing continuous input functions such as positioning a cursor on a display (Murray, Van Praag, and Gilfoil, 1983) or adjusting mirror positions in an automobile (Vail, 1986).

Speech recognition technology may allow the driver of a vehicle to concurrently perform certain in-vehicle secondary tasks without adversely affecting performance of the primary driving task. Currently, all in-vehicle secondary tasks are accomplished through manual input from the driver. Automotive systems that are designed to be controlled via manual input may affect driving performance by forcing the driver to look away from the forward road scene and remove one hand from the steering wheel to complete the task. The fact that the driver must divert visual, manual, and/or cognitive attention away from the primary driving task to successfully perform an in-vehicle task raises concern over how these in-vehicle systems should be designed and what modality of input should be used to control these systems.

53.3.5 Older Drivers

Many abilities, including cognitive and visual abilities decrease with age. In fact, one of the most prevalent issues with regard to user demographics is that of the aging driver. Parviainen, Atkinson, and Young (1991) take an extensive look at both the aging population and the handicapped with regard to in-vehicle systems development. Parviainen et al. (1991) stated that the number of aging drivers will double by the year 2030, and that systems must be designed to accommodate these special populations. According to Franzen and Ilhage (1990) the population of drivers who are over 65 will soon make up one out of every seven drivers on the road. However, there continues to be problems associated with design for an aging driver population, including age discrimination and lack of highway traffic engineering. Discrimination is present due to licensure. Waller (1991) states that the basic information that is necessary to evaluate driving ability has not been developed by the research community. When highways were first designed, the engineers did not take into account the older driver. Highways are usually designed based on measurements derived from young, male drivers (Waller, 1991).

Regarding driver age, research has shown that older drivers spend significantly more time looking at navigation displays than younger drivers. Several experiments which compared the visual glance frequencies of both elderly and young drivers directed toward a CRT screen displaying navigation information have been conducted (Pauzie, Martin-Lamellet and Trauchessec, 1991; Dingus, Antin, Hulse, and Wierwille, 1989). In summary, it was found that younger drivers spent 3.5% of the driving time looking at the display, while elderly drivers spent 6.3%. Consequently, when navigation systems are involved, this group devotes less time directed toward the roadway. This dictates that special consideration must be given to this segment of the population, and that minimization of glance time in design of a navigation information display is critically important.

The perception of risk by older drivers is another important consideration for ITS (Winter, 1988). Winter suggests that more older drivers are "running scared," frightened away from traffic situations they can probably handle as well as from those they cannot. Psychologically, some of them experience fear and anxiety about their vulnerability in a fast, complex traffic world, especially in relation to citations, insurance, and licensing examinations. Winter suggests that older drivers may develop compensatory attitudes and behaviors, some of which are positive and contribute to safety and some of which are negative and promote unsafe practices. On the positive side, they become more responsible and law-abiding. However, older drivers may deny that their skills are decreasing and continue to drive under conditions highly unsafe for them. Winter reasons that a prime factor in the immoderate attitudes of the elderly toward driving is the fear of an accident or a violation that would lead to reexamination for licensure and end in a possible loss of both the license and of the independence it affords. Another threat is the cancellation of insurance or the rise in premiums that would make driving too costly.

Research has shown that older drivers' visual performance improves through the use of specific display characteristics. Babbitt-Kline, Ghali, and Kline (1990) report that the use of icons improves user visibility in both distance and lighting conditions (daylight versus dusk). Hayes, Kurokawa, and Wierwille (1989) report that many performance decrements in viewing visual displays can be countermeasured by increasing the character size of textual labels. Yanik (1989) observed that for color displays, drivers had better visual responses to yellows, oranges, yellow-greens, and whites on contrasting backgrounds. Yanik also found that analog displays (moving pointer) were preferred over digital or numerical displays. Other studies involving the visual abilities of older drivers are reported by Mortimer (1989), Ranney and Simmons (1992), and Staplin and Lyles (1991).

Obviously, designers of transportation systems will have to consider the needs of the older driver. Mast (1991) stresses a greater need for research and development in transportation systems for older drivers in areas of traffic control devices, changeable message signs, symbol signing, hazard markers, night driving, sign visibility, intersection design, traffic maneuvers, left turns against traffic, and merging/weaving maneuvers. Lerner and Ratté (1991) reported that focus groups identified the following needs and generated ideas and countermeasures for the safer use of freeways by older drivers. (1) Lane restrictions, time restrictions, separate truck road-ways, and other methods are needed to reduce interaction with heavy trucks. (2) Greater police enforcement, new enforcement technologies such as photo radar, new traffic-control technologies, and other methods are needed to reduce speed variability in the traffic stream. (3) Better graphics, greater use of sign panels listing several upcoming exits, and other methods to improve advance signing are required so that it better meets the visual and information needs of the elderly. (4) Wide, high-quality shoulders, increased patrol, brightly lit roadside emergency phones, promotion of citizens band radio use, better night lighting, more frequent path confirmation, and other methods are needed to overcome the frequently expressed concerns about personal security. (5) More legible maps, map-use training in older-driver education courses, in-vehicle guidance systems, and other pre-trip planning aids that are designed to be used by older drivers need to be provided. (6) Appreciation for the safety benefits, on-road "refresher" training for those who have not used high-speed roads recently, training in recovery from navigational errors, and other older-driver education specific to freeway use are necessary. (7) Eliminating short merge areas and other methods are needed to improve the interchange geometries that the focus groups identified as contributing to anxiety.

53.4 Driver Acceptance and Behavior

When developing components of ITS it is important to consider the attitudes of the users of the system. Is the system acceptable, usable, and affordable? A good review of the issues associated with ITS acceptance is presented in a literature review by Sheridan (1991). A survey by Marans and Yoakam (1991) found that most commuters felt that ITS was a plausible solution to traffic congestion. The highest approval of ITS (48%) came from commuters whose work commute was from suburban to suburban localities. The survey also reported that 86% of the commuters drove their own car to work.

A University of Michigan Transportation Research Institute (UMTRI) focus group study (Green and Brand, 1992) elicited attitudes on in-vehicle electronics. Areas discussed were general driver attitudes toward and use of sophisticated, in-vehicle display systems, how people learn to use these systems, automotive gauges and warning systems, entertainment systems, CRT touch screens, trip computers, head-up displays, cellular phones, navigation systems, and road hazard monitoring systems. The navigation systems were regarded with caution by drivers. Most indicated that they were good for someone else to use, in specific situations. It was noted that men prefer maps and women prefer directions. Turning directions were preferred as left/right rather than compass north/south. In a survey by Barfield, Haselkorn, Spyridakis, and Conquest (1989), commuters rated commercial radio as the most useful and preferred medium from which to receive traffic information both before and while driving, as compared to variable message signs, highway advisory radio, commercial TV, and telephone hotline systems. Departure time and route choice were the most flexible commuter decisions. Few commuters indicated that they would be influenced to change their transportation mode.

Driver acceptance of technology was assessed by McGehee, Dingus, and Horowitz (1992) while studying a front-to-rear-end collision warning system. They report that drivers often follow at distances that are closer than the brake-reaction time permits for accident avoidance. This close driving behavior may result from the rarity of consequences from previous experiences. A front-to-rear-end collision warning system (whether it is visual, aural, or a combination of both) has the potential to provide added driver safety and situation awareness and was generally accepted as a worthwhile device by subjects tested. Preference for text and voice warning message systems was demonstrated in a study on safety advisory and warning system design by Erlichman (1992). The results of these studies have applicability to in-vehicle safety and warning systems.

53.5 Summary and Conclusions

The previous sections have discussed many of the important issues for the design of intelligent transportation systems. It is not however, inclusive of all issues of interest, nor should it be utilized as more than one of many sources of ITS design information. Two reasons for this caveat are: (1) adequate treatment of this complex topic is beyond the scope of this chapter, and (2) there are a number of research issues which must be addressed in order to develop a comprehensive set of human-computer interaction guidelines for ITS. A preliminary and partial listing of some of these research needs appears below.

The ITS research to date has tended to be system description-oriented, with details of the organization of research that is being conducted or needs to be conducted. A number of research issues have been resolved for ITS and need not be re-addressed. It is apparent that as the development of hardware progresses, the next few years will see a marked growth in the literature available from both U.S. demonstration projects and foreign sources. It is anticipated that the data from initial U.S. operational tests and additional European and Japanese projects will serve to fill some of the largest gaps in the current human factors knowledge base. In order to develop comprehensive and generalizable guidelines that will be usable and useful for years to come, models of driver performance while using intelligent transportation systems must be developed. This model development research will likely include application and/or modification of existing models, as well as creation of new models or model parameters associated with ITS specific applications.

A key knowledge gap requiring both application of existing guidelines and the creation of new guidelines is driver capacity. The human factors community is currently divided on the issue of what is safe and what is unsafe in the driving environment. The primary cause of this debate has centered around in-vehicle routing and navigation system applications and will require additional research to resolve. Carefully planned and executed experiments that provide generalizable principles instead of system-specific "do's and don'ts" are needed. In addition, a careful understanding of potential safety benefits and costs of utilizing ITS are needed for meaningful guideline development. It is easy to dismiss a display that provides complex information as requiring too many driver resources. However, until a comparison is made with current techniques for retrieving necessary information, and an assessment is performed to determine the benefit of having the information, a proper assessment cannot be made.

A final general area of necessary research involves driver acceptance of ITS technology. Even a very safe and efficient system design will not achieve the goals of ITS if the needs and desires of the user are not met. Poor market penetration will result. Although a number of surveys have been conducted that describe desirable ITS features, ongoing research will be necessary to establish the information and control requirements for system (and product) success. Once information requirements have been established, the process of establishing human-computer interaction design guidelines can progress.

53.6 References

Antin, J.F., Dingus, T.A., Hulse, M.C., and Wierwille, W.W. (1990). An evaluation of the effectiveness and efficiency of an automobile moving-map navigational display. *International Journal of Man-Machine Studies, 33*, 581-594.

Aretz, A.J. (1991). The design of electronic map displays. *Human Factors, 33*(1), 85-101.

Babbitt-Kline, T.J., Ghali, L.M., and Kline, D.W. (1990). Visibility distance of highway signs among young, middle-aged, and older observers: Icons are better than text. *Human Factors, 32*(5), 609-619.

Baber, C. (1991). *Speech technology in control room systems: A human factors perspective*. New York: Ellis Horwood.

Barfield, W. Haselkorn, M., Spyridakis, J., and Conquest, L. (1989). Commuter behavior and decision making: Designing motorist information system. In *Proceedings of the Human Factors Society 33rd Annual Meeting* (pp. 611-614). Santa Monica, CA: Human Factors Society.

Bartram, D.J. (1980). Comprehending spatial information: The relative efficiency of different methods of presenting information about bus routes. *Journal of Applied Psychology, 65*, 103-110.

Bennett, R.W., Greenspan, S.L., Syrdal, A.K., Tschirgi, J.E., and Wisowaty, J.J. (1989). Speaking to, from, and through computers: Speech technologies and user-interface design. *AT&T Technical Journal, 68*(5), 17-30.

Bhise, V.D., Forbes, L.M., and Farber, E.I. (1986). *Driver behavioral data and considerations in evaluating in-vehicle controls and displays*. Presented at the Transportation Research Board 65th Annual Meeting, Washington, D.C.

Boff, K.R., and Lincoln, J.E., (1988). Guidelines for alerting signals. *Engineering Data Compendium: Human Perception and Performance, 3*, 2388-2389.

Briziarelli, G., and Allen, R.W. (1989). The effect of a head-up speedometer on speeding behavior. *Perceptual and Motor Skills, 69*, 1171-1176.

Brockman, R.J. (1991). The unbearable distraction of color. *IEEE Transactions of Professional Communication, 34*(3), 153-159.

Brown, T.J., (1991). Visual display highlighting and information extraction. In *Proceedings of the Human Factors Society 35th Annual Meeting* (pp. 1427-1431). Santa Monica, CA: Human Factors Society.

Campbell, and Hershberger (1988). *Automobile head-up display simulation study: Effects of image location and display density on driving performance*. Hughes Aircraft Company, unpublished manuscript.

Carpenter, J.T., Fleischman, R.N., Dingus, T.A., Szczublewski, F.E., Krage, M.K., and Means, L.G. (1991). Human factors engineering the TravTek driver interface. In *Vehicle Navigation and Information Systems Conference Proceedings* (pp. 749-756). Warrendale, PA: Society of Automotive Engineers.

Chovan, J.D., Tijerina, L., Alexander, G., and Hendricks, D.L. (1994). *Examination of Lane Change Crashes and Potential IVHS Countermeasures*. National Highway Traffic Safety Administration Technical Report # DOT-VNTSC-NHTSA-93-2.

Cochran, D.J., Riley, M.W., and Stewart, L.A. (1980). An evaluation of the strengths, weaknesses, and uses of voice input devices. In *Proceedings of the Human Factors Society 24th Annual Meeting* (pp. 190-194). Santa Monica, CA: Human Factors Society.

Cohen, A., and Mandel, A.F. (1982). Considerations for integrating speech I/O technology into factory automation systems. In *Wescon/82 Conference Record* (pp. 29-1/1-8). El Segundo, CA: Electron.

Cohen, P.R., and Oviatt, S.L. (1994). The role of voice in human-machine communication. In D.B. Roe and J.G. Wilpon (Eds.), *Voice Communication Between Humans and Machines* (pp. 34-75). Washington, D.C.: National Academy Press.

Dingus, T.A., Antin, J.F., Hulse, M.C., and Wierwille, W.W. (1989). Attentional demand requirements of an automobile moving-map navigation system. *Transportation Research, 23A*(4), 301-315.

Dingus, T.A. and Hulse, M.C. (1993). Some human factors design issues and recommendations for automobile navigation information systems. *Transportation Research, 1C*(2), 119-131.

Dingus, T., Jahns, S., Horowitz, A., and Knipling, R. (In press). Collision avoidance systems. In W. Barfield and T. Dingus (Eds.), *Human Factors in Intelligent Transportation Systems.* Lawrence Erlbaum Associates: Hillsdale, NJ..

Dingus, T., McGehee, D., Hulse, M., Jahns, S., Natarajan, M., Mollenhauer, M., and Fleischman, R. (1995). *TravTek evaluation task C3–camera car study.* Federal Highway Administration Technical Report # FHWA-RD-94-076.

Erlichman, J. (1992). A pilot study of the in-vehicle safety advisory and warning system (IVSAWS) driver-alert warning system design (DAWS). In *Proceedings of the Human Factors Society 36th Annual Meeting* (pp. 480-484). Santa Monica, CA: Human Factors Society.

Evans, L. (1991). *Traffic safety and the driver.* New York: Van Nostrand Reinhold.

Franzen, S., and Ilhage, B. (1990). Active safety research on intelligent driver support systems. In *Proceedings from 12th International Technical Conference on Experimental Safety Vehicles (ESV)* (pp. 1-15).

Godthelp, H. (1991). Driving with GIDS: Behavioral interaction with the GIDS architecture. In Commission of the European Communities (Eds.), *Advanced telemantics in road transport.* (pp 351-370). Amsterdam: Elsevier.

Green, P. and Brand, J. (1992). Future in-car information systems: Input from focus groups. In *SAE Technical Paper Series.* SAE No. 920614 (pp.1-9). Warrendale, PA: Society of Automotive Engineers.

Green, P., Serafin, C., Williams, M., and Paelke, G. (1991). What functions and features should be in the driver information systems of the year 2000? In *Vehicle Navigation and Information Systems Conference Proceedings.* SAE No. 912792, (pp. 483-498). Warrendale, PA: Society of Automotive Engineers.

Green, P. and Williams, M., (1992). Perspective in orientation / navigation displays: A human factors test. In *Vehicle Navigation and Information Systems Conference Proceedings* (pp. 221-226). Warrendale, PA: Society of Automotive Engineers.

Hayes, B.C., Kurokawa, K., and Wierwille, W.W. (1989). Age-related decrements in automobile instrument panel task performance. In *Proceedings of the Human Factors Society 33rd Annual Meeting* (pp. 159-163). Santa Monica, CA: Human Factors Society.

Henderson, R. (Ed.). (1986). *Driver performance data book.* Washington, DC: National Highway Traffic and Safety Administration.

Hulse, M. C., Dingus, T. A. and Barfield, W. (In press). Advanced traveler information systems. In W. Barfield and T. Dingus (Eds.), *Human Factors in Intelligent Transportation Systems.* Lawrence Erlbaum Associates: Hillsdale, NJ.

Imbeau, D., Wierwille, W.W., Wolf, L.D., and Chun, G.A. (1989). Effects of instrument panel luminance and chromaticity on reading performance and preference in simulated driving. *Human Factors, 31*(2), 147-160.

Jones, D.M., Frankish, C.R., and Hapeshi, K. (1992). Automatic speech recognition in practice. *Behaviour and Information Technology, 11*, 109-122.

Jones, D., Hapeshi, K., and Frankish, C. (1989). Design guidelines for speech recognition interfaces. *Applied Ergonomics, 20*, 47-52.

Kantowitz, B.H. and Sorkin, R.D. (1983). *Human Factors.* New York: John Wiley & Sons.

Kelly and Folds (In press). Advanced Traffic Management Systems. In Barfield, W. and Dingus, T.A. (In press) *Human Factors in Intelligent Transportation Systems.* Lawrence Erlbaum Associates: Hillsdale, New Jersey.

Kiefer, R.J. (1995). Human factors issues surrounding an automotive vision enhancement system. In *Proceedings of the Human Factors and Ergonomics Society 39th Annual Meeting* (pp. 1097-1101). Santa Monica, CA: Human Factors and Ergonomics Society.

Kimura, K., Sugiura, S., Shinkai, H., and Nagai, Y. (1988). Visibility requirements for automobile CRT displays - color, contrast, and luminance. In *SAE Technical Paper Series*. SAE No. 880218 (pp. 25-31). Warrendale, PA: Society of Automotive Engineers.

King, G.F. (1986). Driver attitudes concerning aspects of highway navigation. *Transportation Research Record, 1093*, 11-21.

Knipling, R., Mironer, M., Hendricks, D., Tijerina, L., Everson, J., Allen, J., and Wilson, C. (1993a). *Assessment of IVHS countermeasures for collision avoidance: Rear-end crashes*. NHTSA Technical Report Number DOT-HS-807995.

Knipling, R., Wang, J., and Yin, H., (1993b). *Rear-end crashes: Problem size assessment and statistical description*. NHTSA Office of Crash Avoidance Research. Technical Report Number DOT–HS–807994.

Labiale, G. (1990). In-car road information: Comparison of auditory and visual presentation. In *Proceedings of the Human Factors Society 34th Annual Meeting* (pp. 623-627). Santa Monica, CA: Human Factors Society.

Lee, J.D., Morgan, J., Wheeler, W.A., Hulse, M.C., and Dingus T.A. (1993). *Development of human factors guidelines for ATIS and CVO: Description of ATIS/CVO functions*. Federal Highway Administration Report.

Lerner, N.D., and Ratté, D.J. (1991). Problems in freeway use as seen by older drivers. *Transportation Research Record, 1325*, 3-7.

Levitan, L., and Bloomfield, J.R., (in press). Human factors design of automated highway systems. In W. Barfield and T. Dingus (Eds.), *Human Factors in Intelligent Transportation Systems*. Lawrence Erlbaum Associates: Hillsdale, N.J.

Lunenfeld, H. (1990). Human factor considerations of motorist navigation and information systems. In *Vehicle Navigation & Information Systems Conference Proceedings* (pp. 35-42). Warrendale, PA: Society of Automotive Engineers.

Marans, R.W., and Yoakam, C. (1991). Assessing the acceptability of IVHS: Some preliminary results. In *SAE Technical Paper Series*. SAE No. 912811 (pp. 657-668). Warrendale, PA: Society of Automotive Engineers.

Markowitz, J.A. (1995). Talking. *Journal of Systems Management, 46*(3), 9-13.

Mast, T. (1991). Designing and operating safer highways for older drivers: Present and future research issues. In *Proceedings of the Human Factors Society 35th Annual Meeting* (pp. 167-171). Santa Monica, CA: Human Factors Society.

McGehee, D.V., Dingus, T.A., and Horowitz, A.D. (1992). The potential value of a front-to-rear-end collision warning system based on factors of driver behavior, visual perception and brake reaction time. In *Proceedings of the Human Factors Society 36th Annual Meeting* (pp. 1011-1013). Santa Monica, CA: Human Factors Society.

McGranaghan, M., Mark, D.M., and Gould, M.D. (1987). Automated provision of navigation assistance to drivers. *The American Cartographer, 14*(2), 121-138.

McKnight, J.A. and McKnight, S.A. (1992). *The effect of in-vehicle navigation information systems upon driver attention*. Landover, MD: National Public Services Research, 1-15.

Means, L.G., Carpenter, J.T., Szczublewski, F.E., Fleishman, R.N., Dingus, T.A., and Krage, M.K. (1992). Design of the TravTek auditory interface (Tech. Report GMR-7664). Warren, MI: General Motors Research and Environmental Staff.

Mobility 2000 (1989). Proceedings of the workshop on intelligent vehicle highway systems. *Texas Transportation Institute*. Texas A & M.

Monty, R.W. (1984). *Eye movements and driver performance with electronic navigation displays*. Unpublished master's thesis, Virginia Polytechnic Institute and State University, Blacksburg, VA.

Mortimer, R.G. (1989). Older drivers' visibility and comfort in night driving: Vehicle design factors. In *Proceedings of the Human Factors Society 33rd Annual Meeting* (pp. 154-158). Santa Monica, CA: Human Factors Society.

Mourant, R.R., Herman, M., and Moussa-Hamouda, E. (1980). Direct looks and control location in automobiles. *Human Factors, 22*(4), 417-425.

Murray, J.T., and Van Praag, J., and Gilfoil, D. (1983). Voice versus keyboard control of cursor motion. In *Proceedings of the Human Factors Society 27th Annual Meeting* (pp. 103). Santa Monica, CA: Human Factors Society.

National Automated Highway System Consortium (1995). *Automated Highway System (AHS) System Objectives and Characteristics Draft*. Troy, MI.

Outram, V.E. and Thompson, E. (1977). Driver route choice. *Proceedings of the PTRC Summer Annual Meeting*, University of Warwick, UK. Cited in Lunenfeld, H. (1990). Human factor considerations of motorist navigation and information systems. In *Vehicle Navigation & Information Systems Conference Proceedings*. Society of Automotive Engineers, 35-42.

Parkes, A.M., Ashby, M.C., and Fairclough, S.H. (1991). The effect of different in-vehicle route information displays on driver behavior. In *Vehicle Navigation and Information Systems Conference Proceedings* (pp. 61-70). Warrendale, PA: Society of Automotive Engineering.

Parviainen, J.A., Atkinson, W. A.G., and Young M.L. (1991) *Application of micro-electronic technology to assist elderly and disabled travelers*. (Tech. Report TP-10890E). Montreal, Quebec, Canada: Transportation Development Centre.

Pauzie A., Marin-Lamellet C., and Trauchessec, R. (1991). Analysis of aging drivers behaviors navigating with in-vehicle visual display systems. In *Vehicle Navigation and Information Systems Conference Proceedings* (pp. 61-67), Warrendale, PA: Society of Automotive Engineering.

Peckham, J.B. (1984). Automatic speech recognition -- a solution in search of a problem? *Behavior and Information Technology, 3*, 145-152.

Poock, G.K. (1986). Speech recognition research, applications, and international efforts. In *Proceedings of the Human Factors Society 30th Annual Meeting* (pp. 1278-1283). Santa Monica, CA: Human Factors Society.

Popp, M.M. and Farber, B. (1991). Advanced display technologies, route guidance systems and the position of displays in cars. In Gale, A.G. (Ed.). *Vision in Vehicles-III* (pp. 219-225). North-Holland: Elsevier Science Publishers.

Quinnell, R.A. (1995). Speech recognition: no longer a dream but still a challenge. *EDN*, *40*(2), 41-46.

Ranney, R.A. and Simmons, L.A.S. (1992). The effects of age and target location uncertainty on decision making in a simulated driving task. In *Proceedings of the Human Factors 36th Annual Meeting* (pp. 166-170). Santa Monica, CA: Human Factors Society.

Rillings, J., and Betsold, R.J. (1991). Advanced driver information systems. *IEEE Transactions on Vehicular Technology*, *40*(1), 31-40.

Robinson, C.P. and Eberts, R.E. (1987). Comparison of speech and pictorial displays in a cockpit environment. *Human Factors*, *29*(1), 31-44.

Rockwell, T. (1972). Skills, judgment, and information acquisition in driving. In T. Forbes (Ed.), *Human Factors in Highway Traffic Safety Research* (pp. 133-164). New York: Wiley.

Sheridan, T.B. (1991). Human factors of driver-vehicle interaction in the IVHS environment (Tech. Report DOT-HS-807-837). Washington, DC: National Highway Traffic Safety Administration.

Staplin, L. and Lyles, R.W. (1991). Age differences in motion perception and specific traffic maneuver problems. *Transportation Research Record, 1325*, 23-33.

Streeter, L.A. (1985). Interface considerations in the design of an electronic navigator. *Auto Carta*.

Streeter, L.A., Vitello, D., and Wonsiewicz, S.A. (1985). How to tell people where to go: Comparing navigational aids. *International Journal of Man-Machine Studies*, *22*, 549-562.

Tarrière, C., Hartemann, F., Sfez, E., Chaput, D., and Petit-Poilvert, C. (1988). Some ergonomic features of the driver-vehicle-environment interface. In *SAE Technical Paper Series*. SAE No. 885051 (pp. 405-427). Warrendale, PA: Society of Automotive Engineers.

Tijerina, L., Chovan, J.D., Pierowicz, J., and Hendricks, D.L. (1994). *Examination of Signalized Intersection, Straight Crossing Path Crashes and Potential IVHS Countermeasures*. National Highway Traffic Safety Administration Technical Report # DOT-VNTSC-NHTSA-94-1.

Tijerina, L., Hendricks, D., Pierowicz, J., Everson, J., and Kiger, S. (1993). *Examination of Backing Crashes and Potential IVHS Countermeasures*. National Highway Traffic Safety Administration Technical Report # DOT-VNTSC-NHTSA-93-1.

Treat, J.R., Tumbas, N.S., McDonald, S.T., Shinar, D., and Hume, R.D. (1979). *Tri-Level Study of the Causes of Traffic Accidents*. Bloomington, IN: Institute for Research and Public Safety. Report # DOT-HS-034-3-535-79.

U.S. Department of Transportation, National Highway Traffic Safety Administration. (1990). *National accident sampling system general estimates system (GES)*. Washington, D.C.: National Center for Statistics and Analysis.

U.S. Department of Transportation, National Highway Traffic Safety Administration. (1991). *National accident sampling system general estimates system (GES)*. Washington, D.C.: National Center for Statistics and Analysis.

U.S. Department of Transportation, National Highway Traffic Safety Administration. (1993). *National accident sampling system general estimates system (GES).* Washington, D.C.: National Center for Statistics and Analysis.

Vail, R.E. (1986). Suitability of voice-activated hand controls for the physically handicapped driver. In *Proceedings of the Human Factors Society 30th Annual Meeting* (pp. 662-666). Santa Monica, CA: Human Factors Society.

Walker, J., Alicandri, E., Sedney, C., and Roberts, K. (1991). *In-vehicle navigation devices: Effects on the safety of driver performance.* Tech. Report FHWA-RD-90-053. Washington, DC: Federal Highway Administration.

Waller, P.F. (1991). The older driver. *Human Factors, 33*(5), 499-505.

Weintraub, D.J., Haines, R.F., and Randle, R.J. (1985). Head-up display (HUD) utility. II. Runway to HUD transition monitoring eye focus and decision times. In *Proceedings of the of the Human Factors Society 29th Annual Meeting* (pp. 615-619). Santa Monica, CA: Human Factors Society.

Wetherell, A. (1979). Short term memory for verbal and graphic route information. In *Proceedings of the Human Factors Society 23rd Annual Meeting* (pp. 464-469). Santa Monica, CA: Human Factors Society.

Wheeler, Campbell and Kinghorn (In press). Commercial Vehicle Operations. In Barfield, W. and Dingus, T.A. (Eds.) *Human Factors in Intelligent Transportation Systems.* Lawrence Erlbaum Associates: Hillsdale, New Jersey.

Wierwille, W.W. (1993). Visual and manual demands of in-car controls and displays. In B. Peacock and V. Karwowski (Eds.), *Automotive Ergonomics* (pp. 299-320). London: Taylor and Francis.

Williges, R.C., Williges, B.H., and Elkerton, J. (1987). Software interface design. In G. Salvendy (Ed.), *Handbook of Human Factors.* (pp. 1416-1448). New York: J. Wiley & Sons.

Winter, D.J. (1988). Older drivers: Their perception of risk. *The Engineering Society for Advancing Mobility Land Sea Air and Space*, 19-29.

Yanik, A.J. (1989). Factors to consider when designing vehicles for older drivers. In *Proceedings of the Human Factors Society 33rd Annual Meeting* (pp. 164-168). Santa Monica, CA: Human Factors Society.

Zwahlen, H.T., Adams, C.C., and DeBald, D.P. (1987). *Safety aspects of CRT touch panel controls in automobiles.* Presented at the Second International Conference on Vision in Vehicles, Nottingham, England.

Zwahlen, H.T. and DeBald, D.P. (1986). Safety aspects of sophisticated in-vehicle information displays and controls. In *Proceedings of the Human Factors Society 30th Annual Meeting* (pp. 256-260). Santa Monica, CA: Human Factors Society.

Part VIII

Input Devices and Design of Work Stations

Handbook of Human-Computer Interaction
Second, completely revised edition
M. Helander, T.K. Landauer, P. Prabhu (eds.)

Chapter 54

Keys and Keyboards

James R. Lewis
International Business Machines Corp.
Boca Raton, Florida, USA

Kathleen M. Potosnak
Independent Consultant
Kingston, Washington, USA

Regis L. Magyar
Magyar and Associates
Chapel Hill, North Carolina, USA

54.1 Introduction

Keyboards have been around for over 100 years and are in widespread use both on typewriters and as input devices to computers. Early refinements of the typewriter keyboard aimed at improving its mechanical action so that it would operate more smoothly with fewer malfunctions. Later work focused on improving typing speed and accuracy.

This chapter describes keyboard design factors that affect skilled typing and data entry. The information presented should apply equally well to typewriter and computer keyboards. Some data also apply to telephones and other specialized keypads used for data entry tasks.

54.2 Keyboard Layouts

The locations of letters and numbers on keys has been a matter of research, theory, debate, contests and patent applications since the appearance of the first conventional typewriter keyboard. Although other typewriters existed previously, the design patented in 1868 by Sholes, Glidden, and Soule was the first to include many of the characteristics of modern typewriters (Yamada, 1980). The letters originally had an alphabetic arrangement.

54.2.1 The Standard (QWERTY) Layout

Fast typists ran into trouble with the early design of the Sholes keyboard because the typebars of successive keystrokes would interfere with each other. The current QWERTY layout (named for the top left-most row of letters) increased the spacing between common pairs of letters to reduce the frequency of jamming sequentially struck typebars[1]. Touch typing on the Sholes keyboard was not common until around 1900 (Yamada, 1980). The first patent showing the QWERTY layout appeared in 1878 (Cooper, 1983; Noyes, 1983b). There have been several attempts to improve the keyboard layout by developing non-QWERTY arrangements.

54.2.2 The Dvorak Simplified Keyboard Layout

The most well known of these attempts was the Dvorak Simplified Keyboard (known as DSK). August Dvorak received a U.S. patent for his design in 1936. Dvorak designed his layout using principles of time-and-motion study and scientific measurement of efficiency (Dvorak, 1943). Dvorak assumed for his analyses ten-fingered touch typing.

The principles underlying Dvorak's layout included assumptions such as simple motions are easier to learn and perform rapidly than more complex motions, and rhythmic motions are less fatiguing than erratic ones. With the DSK layout, typists use the right hand more than the left, with fingers assigned proportionate amounts of work. Almost 70% of the typing is on the home row. The placement of vowels and frequently-used consonants on opposite halves of the keyboard increases the frequency of two-handed typing sequences[2].

Many experiments, field trials and analytical studies have compared the DSK with the QWERTY arrangement. Dvorak conducted some of his own tests with reportedly positive results. Five other studies comparing DSK and QWERTY keyboards appear below.

[1] There are other theories about how QWERTY came into existence. For a summary, see Noyes (1983). Alleviation of typebar jamming problems was the explanation appearing most frequently in the literature.

[2] The Dvorak measurements assume English text. For recent applications of Dvorak-like principles to the design of non-English keyboards, see Kan, Sumei, and Huiling, 1993; Lin, Lee, and Chou, 1993; and Marmaras and Lyritzis, 1993.

The Navy Department Study

In the 1940s, the Navy Department compared two groups of typists who received on-the-job training (U.S. Navy Department, 1944a, 1944b). The first group consisted of QWERTY-trained typists who learned the DSK layout. The second group of QWERTY typists received additional training on the standard keyboard.

Increases in typing speeds and decreases in error rates were higher for the DSK group. However, the gain in net words per minute (nwpm) was not statistically significant. Also, there were pre-existing differences between the two groups because the DSK typists initially were faster on QWERTY than the other group.

The Navy Department report did not focus on the final nwpm, but instead described differences between the groups in terms of *percentage gain in nwpm as a function of the number of hours of additional training*. In measuring this learning rate, the researchers used zero as the baseline for the DSK group because they had never used DSK before. The QWERTY group baseline was their typing rate before additional training. The use of different baselines affected the calculation of learning rate. Also, the initial learning rate for the DSK group could have been quite high because some previously learned typing skills (such as finger movements) would be relevant for learning DSK. Later performance might not show such a rapid rate of learning.

Navy Department researchers also calculated the costs and benefits of retraining compared to additional QWERTY training. However, the cost figure was "corrected" by subtracting the value of increased production during the latter part of the retraining period *for the DSK group only*. That is, once typists in the DSK group exceeded their original QWERTY typing rates, the increase in production received a dollar value. The correction factor was the number of hours each typist worked at greater than 100% of QWERTY typing speed multiplied by the individual's hourly wage. Without this correction factor, the average cost of retraining was actually cheaper per hour for additional QWERTY training ($1.27/hour DSK and $0.90/hour QWERTY).

The Navy Department report concluded with highly favorable statements about DSK retraining and recommendations for implementing such retraining. The following facts invalidate this conclusion: a) differences in final typing performance were not statistically significant; b) measures of learning rates unfairly favored the DSK group; and c) calculations of costs and benefits unfairly favored the DSK.

The Strong Study

Strong (1956) conducted his study for the U.S. General Services Administration. Strong trained QWERTY typists on DSK keyboards until they reached their previous QWERTY typing performance levels. This took an average of about 28 days. In the second part of the experiment, the DSK group received additional instruction time to increase their speed and accuracy on DSK. A comparable group of QWERTY typists began the experiment in the second half and received only this additional training (but on QWERTY). After training, the QWERTY group performed better on typing tests than the DSK group (Alden, Daniels, and Kanarick, 1972; Noyes, 1983b). Strong concluded that there were no advantages to the DSK and that "brush up" training on QWERTY was more effective (Yamada, 1980).

Other researchers have questioned the Strong report. Some tried to obtain the original experimental data for re-evaluation, but learned that all the data had been destroyed. There has been speculation that the study unfairly favored QWERTY (Noyes, 1983b) and that Strong himself was "hardly an unbiased investigator" (Yamada, 1980, p. 188). Regardless of whatever motivated Strong to write such a report, it clearly was a major blow to public acceptance of DSK and the adoption of DSK by the U.S. government (Cassingham, 1986; Yamada, 1980).

Kinkead's Simulation

It is difficult to conduct a fair experiment to compare DSK and QWERTY due to QWERTY's widespread use. Previous experience could affect both DSK retraining and additional QWERTY training in unknown ways. To circumvent the methodological difficulties of training and retraining typists on each keyboard, Kinkead (1975) collected data on the times required for the fingers to type each possible sequence of two letters (called a "digram" or "digraph") on the QWERTY keyboard. The second part of the analysis was to obtain the frequency with which each digraph occurs in English.

Kinkead (1975) assumed that the time to make a particular finger motion ("keystroke time") would be the same for both DSK and QWERTY. That is, the keys and rows have the same arrangement on both keyboards, so they require the same finger motions. The only difference between layouts was the assignment of letters to the key locations and thus the frequency of use for each finger motion. Kinkead used the sum of all "digraph frequency x keystroke time" values to estimate the typing speed for each keyboard layout.

The results of this analysis indicated that, at best, DSK is 2.3% faster than QWERTY. (This value of 2.3% appears below his table of calculations; in the text, the number is 2.6%.) There are some minor discrepancies between these values and calculations based on the numbers in Kinkead's (1975) report. For example, using the same numbers as Kinkead, the advantage of DSK over QWERTY could be either 3.1% or 3.2%, depending on the use of Kinkead's first (155 msec/keystroke) or second (151 msec/keystroke) estimate of average keystroke time.

Another difficulty in interpreting the Kinkead (1975) data stems from the effect of context on typing speed and the "leveling effect". The context surrounding a character affects the speed of typing that character. If the size of the affecting context is larger than a digraph, then Kinkead's estimates might not be accurate. Gentner (1983) reported that the size of the effective context is two letters before and one character after the currently typed character. Calculations for trigraphs (three-letter sequences) show that when a particularly slow keystroke occurs, other keying sequences surrounding it also slow down. Fast keying sequences tend to speed up surrounding keystrokes (Hiraga, Ono, and Yamada, 1980). This tendency to maintain a constant typing speed from one keystroke to the next is the leveling effect. The context and leveling effects could explain why Kinkead obtained such a low estimate for DSK's advantage over QWERTY, because the analysis used digraphs only.

A Computer Simulation

Norman and Fisher (1982) performed another comparison of DSK and QWERTY using "a computer simulation of the hand and finger movements of a skilled typist" (p. 154). Their model accounted for the context effect because it "allows for the simultaneous movement of the fingers and hands toward different letters of the word being typed, thus capturing the parallel, overlapping movements seen in high-speed films of expert typists" (p. 515). They calculated that DSK provides about a 5.4% advantage in typing speed over QWERTY. Application of the model resulted in a typing rate of about 58 words per minute (wpm) for DSK compared to about 56 wpm for QWERTY.

This study addressed some of the criticisms of the Kinkead (1975) report. The computer model took into account more than just digraph frequencies in determining speed of finger motions. Note, however, that both simulations (Kinkead, 1975; Norman and Fisher, 1982) address only typing speed of expert typists.

An Automated Search for the Best Key Layout

Noel and McDonald (1989) used an artificial intelligence search procedure to discover the best possible key layout for the standard keyboard configuration. Their algorithm used the typing model developed by Norman and Fisher (1982) to direct the search. Their program considered 50,000 keyboard layouts from the first to the final iteration of the search. The results indicated that the DSK was about 10% better than QWERTY, and that the best possible layout was 1.2% better than DSK.

Conclusions

Most studies have confirmed that DSK is faster than QWERTY. However, there is disagreement about the size of the difference between the two keyboard layouts. Earlier accounts claimed that DSK was from 15% to 50% faster than QWERTY (Yamada, 1980). More recent calculations give much smaller numbers, ranging from 2.3% to 17% (Kinkead, 1975; Norman and Fisher, 1982; Yamada, 1980). Because the best design their search procedure could turn up was only 1.2% better than the DSK, the results of Noel and McDonald (1989) suggest that it would be fruitless to attempt to develop a layout in the standard keyboard configuration significantly superior to the DSK.

Because there are so many unknowns (such as how long it will take a particular typist to retrain), a switch to DSK would probably not provide a practical improvement in productivity. With an estimated 5 to 10% increase in output over QWERTY (Noel and McDonald, 1989; Norman and Fisher, 1982), the switch might be cost effective for some typists, but essentially worthless for most. For example, a typist with an average speed of 50 wpm would, after complete retraining, produce 52.5 to 55 wpm. At roughly 800 words per single-spaced page, this hypothetical retrained typist, typing nonstop for eight hours per day, would increase production from about 30 pages per day up to 31.5 to 33 pages per day. Also, a typist trained on QWERTY can easily transfer his or her skill to any other standard keyboard, but a typist trained on DSK could not.

54.2.3 Alphabetical Keyboards

Another method of designing a keyboard is to place letters on the keys in alphabetical order. Such a layout has appeared on some children's toys, on a stockbroker's quotation terminal, on some portable data devices, and sometimes appears as the default on-screen keyboard for some touchscreen applications.

Research Comparing QWERTY and Alphabetical Keyboards

Hirsch (1970) tested one group of non-typists on QWERTY and another group on an alphabetically arranged keyboard. After seven hours of practice, the QWERTY group improved their typing speed from 1.47 to 1.99 keystrokes per second. The alphabetical group, however, did not even reach their pre-experimental QWERTY typing rates (1.47 keystrokes per second for QWERTY compared to 1.11 for alphabetical).

Michaels (1971) expanded on the work of Hirsch by including people with a broader range of typing skills, ages and backgrounds. Results showed that both the high- and medium-skill groups were significantly faster on QWERTY, while the low-skill group showed no significant difference in typing speed on the two keyboards. Also, skilled typists were faster at keying numerical sequences on QWERTY than on the alphabetical keyboard even though the number keys were exactly the same on both typewriters, a result that might have been due to a leveling effect.

Norman and Fisher (1982) tested non-typists on four different keyboards: QWERTY, Alphabetical-Horizontal (letters A through Z arranged from left to right starting with the letter keys at the upper left of the keyboard), Alphabetical-Diagonal (with letters arranged from top to bottom and then from left to right starting at the upper left of the keyboard), and a Random keyboard (letters assigned to letter keys at random). Typing was more than 65% faster on QWERTY than on any of the other layouts. Statistical tests revealed that the first three keyboards were all significantly better than the random arrangement, and that QWERTY was better than both alphabetical layouts (which were not significantly different).

A study of small keypads for an enhanced telephone application compared QWERTY and alphabetical layouts (Francas, Brown, and Goodman, 1983). The size of the keypads limited typing to a one- or two-finger strategy. The 20 participants in the study had keyboard experience ranging from those who had not used a keyboard in the previous year to those who used a keyboard daily. The average time for entering sentences was 54.4 seconds for QWERTY and 97.5 seconds for the alphabetical layout. The typists in the study strongly preferred the QWERTY to the alphabetical layout. The advantage for QWERTY did not appear to be a function of the typists' experience.

Recent interest in portable data devices and on-screen keyboards for touch screens have led to additional research in the evaluation of nonstandard alphabetic arrangements. Lewis, Kennedy, and LaLomia (1992) used a cost function based on Fitts' Law[3] and English digraph frequencies to evaluate (1) the alphabetical arrangement created by replacing the QWERTY letters with alphabetically-sequenced letters and (2) the alphabetical arrangement created by placing the letters in a roughly 5 x 5 key matrix (with "Z" placed just outside the square matrix, and (3) the standard QWERTY arrangement given expert (completely learned) typing with a stylus or a single finger (hereafter referred to as stylus-typing). (Note that the problems associated with Kinkead's (1975) use of digraphs are primarily a consequence of typing with ten fingers, and do not apply to typing with a stylus or one finger.) For expert stylus-typing, the cost function predicted that the conventional alphabetic arrangement would be 3% slower than QWERTY, but that the roughly square alphabetic arrangement would be about 13% better than QWERTY.

Because one assumption of the cost function was expert performance, Lewis (1992) studied initial user preference and performance with the layouts. Although predicted expert performance is important in selecting a typing-key layout, it is also important to evaluate users' initial performance with and preference for competing layouts. This is especially true if it is unlikely that users will work with a device enough to develop an expert level of performance. In the study, 12 participants used a stylus to tap keys on paper models of the layouts to type four sentences. All the participants had previous experience with the QWERTY layout, and had self-reported typing speeds ranging from 10 to 65 wpm. The participants (who were at this point, non-expert stylus-typists) performed better with and preferred the QWERTY layout. Thus, initial performance differed from predicted expert performance, with initial performance favoring the QWERTY layout. Even though this study evaluated only initial performance, stylus typing with the square alphabetic arrangement was significantly faster than that for the conventional alphabetic arrangement, as predicted by the user model. There are no data on how long a person would have to practice with these nonstandard layouts to achieve expert performance.

Coleman, Loring, and Wiklund (1991) also found an advantage for a touch-screen QWERTY arrangement over an alphabetical arrangement using a matrix seven keys across and four keys high. Their experiment, however, had a confounded variable because only the alphabetical layout had an embedded numeric pad, making it slower for typing numbers. MacKenzie et al. (1994) compared a touch-screen QWERTY arrangement with an alphabetical arrangement 13 keys across and 2 keys high. Fifteen participants with prior QWERTY experience typed sentences (lower case only, no punctuation) significantly faster with the QWERTY layout and significantly preferred the QWERTY. Quill and Biers (1993) had 24 participants (both touch and non-touch typists) use a mouse and cursor keys to select characters from an on-screen QWERTY layout, a 3-row (QWERTY-like) alphabetical arrangement, and a 1-row alphabetical arrangement to type a mixture of words and nonwords, presented one at a time. The participants significantly preferred the QWERTY layout to both alphabetical arrangements, with no significant difference between the alphabetical layouts. Input with the mouse was always faster than with the cursor keys. Using the mouse, the typing speed results were the same as the preference results. For the cursor keys, typing speeds with the QWERTY and 1-row alphabetical arrangements were not significantly different, but both were significantly faster than the 3-row, standard alphabetical arrangement.

Conclusions

Alphabetically arranged keyboards (apparently regardless of specific arrangement) provide no advantages over QWERTY, even for unskilled typists using a reduced-size keypad (Francas et al., 1983), or for typists restricted to using a stylus or mouse (Lewis, 1992; MacKenzie et al., 1994; Quill and Biers, 1993). Performance on QWERTY might be better than alphabetical keyboards because the QWERTY arrangement is not random, reducing the difficulty of search. Another possible explanation is that most people, even inexperienced typists, have some experience using a QWERTY keyboard. Overall, the evidence suggests that in most situations designers should provide a QWERTY rather than an alphabetical layout.

54.2.4 Other Keyboard Layouts

A few researchers have developed nonstandard layouts in nonstandard arrangements for special purposes. Getschow, Rosen, and Goodenough-Trepagnier (1986) used an artificial intelligence search procedure (the "greedy"

---

[3] Fitts' Law (Fitts, 1954) is a model of human performance that describes the time required to touch a target accurately. Specifically, Fitts' Law states $\underline{MT} = \underline{a} + \underline{b}\log_2(2\underline{A}/\underline{W})$, where $\underline{MT}$ is movement time, $\underline{A}$ is the amplitude (distance to the target), $\underline{W}$ is the size (width) of the target, and $\underline{a}$ and $\underline{b}$ are empirically determined constants. The law essentially states that increasing $\underline{A}$ or decreasing $\underline{W}$ increases movement time in a specific and definable way. See Welford (1976) for a detailed description of this and other versions of Fitts' Law.

algorithm) to develop a layout that minimized the weighted average distance between English digraphs (with keys occupying a roughly 5 x 5 key square matrix). Theoretically, this should be the best layout for an expert typing with a stylus or a single finger, but Getschow et al. did not perform any user testing with the layout.

Lewis et al. (1992) used a path-analysis program to design a minimum-distance layout similar to that developed by Getschow et al. (1986). Using a cost function based on the frequency of English digraphs and Fitts' Law, Lewis et al. estimated that, for stylus typing by a highly practiced expert, this minimum-distance layout would be 27% faster than a QWERTY layout. Using the same assumptions (highly practiced stylus typing with the layout), Lewis (1992) estimated that a layout based on that developed by Getschow et al. would be 31% better than QWERTY.

The cost function of Lewis et al. (1992) predicts expert stylus typing performance, but is not applicable to initial, nonexpert typing. Because a designer might consider a nonstandard arrangement for situations in which typists might not acquire an expert level of skill, it is important to understand initial user performance with such layouts. In an assessment of initial user preference and performance with the layouts (Lewis, 1992), however, 12 typists using paper models of the layouts significantly preferred and performed better with the QWERTY layout (and had their second-best performance with a 5 x 5 alphabetical arrangement). There was no performance difference between the Lewis et al. and Getschow et al. layouts, but participants significantly preferred the layout by Lewis et al.

Matias, MacKenzie, and Buxton (1993) developed a one-handed keyboard called the Half QWERTY, designed to take advantage of a typist's existing skill with the QWERTY layout. Taking advantage of cross-hand skill transfer, the Half QWERTY has two character functions on each key from the left half of the QWERTY layout, with a mirror image of the right half placed on the left half. For example, the Q key is also the P key; the T key is also the Y key; the B key is also the N key. Typists press a key as usual to get the normal letter associated with the key, but press and hold the space bar to get the alternate, mirror-image letter. Ten participants learned to use the Half QWERTY as they typed sentences presented by a computer program for ten sessions, with each session lasting about an hour. The average typing speed at the end of the first session was 13.2 wpm with 16% errors. The average speed after the tenth session was 34.7 wpm with 7.4% errors. Subjects reached 50% of their two-handed typing speed after about eight hours.

Montgomery (1982) proposed a wipe-activated capacitive keyboard. The "keyboard" is a flat tablet that the fingers glide across or wipe to create characters. To take advantage of the wiping motion, Montgomery also developed a new character layout to enable the input of many small words with a single wiping motion. An alternative method of operation is to use a stylus to interact with the keyboard. Because it has no moving parts, this device can be almost any size. This keyboard has undergone no tests other than analyses comparing number of wipes to number of keystrokes required on standard keyboards.

Conclusions

The concepts discussed in this section are interesting, and might have application under certain unusual circumstances. However, designers should always assess an alternative layout against a QWERTY layout designed to fit in the same physical dimensions as the alternative before committing to an alternative design, especially if it is not reasonable to expect users of the keyboard to become expert.

54.2.5 Keyboard Layouts: Conclusions

Given the structure of the standard keyboard (three rows of letters with an upper row of numbers), there are many ways to arrange the alphabetic keys. By starting from an alphabetically ordered arrangement, then rearranging keys to reduce type bar jamming, the inventors of the standard keyboard created the QWERTY layout. Even if their intention was to reduce typing speed as well as reduce jamming, separating commonly co-occurring letters increases the frequency with which a typist strikes characters with fingers between hands (from hand to hand). Analysis of skilled typists has shown that typing with fingers on alternate hands is faster than typing with fingers on a single hand (which is faster than typing with a single finger) (Cooper, 1983). Thus, the inventors of the standard keyboard seem to have accidentally created a layout that allows skilled touch typists to type with about 90% of the speed theoretically attainable with the best possible layout for touch typing (Noel and MacDonald, 1989).

Most recent estimates suggest that Dvorak's design closed the gap to about 95 to 99% of the maximum possible touch-typing speed. To date, no other keyboard layout has received more attention than DSK as an alternative to QWERTY, but it appears that most typists do not believe that the relatively minor benefit of learning the DSK would overcome the costs. Other than as an academic exercise, any further redesign of the QWERTY layout for touch typing appears to be a fruitless effort, a conclusion consistent with the ANSI/HFS 100-1988 standard's recommendation to use the QWERTY layout for typing keyboards (Human Factors Society, 1988).

A remarkable finding from the more recent evaluations that have compared the QWERTY layout with other layouts for reduced-size devices and on-screen keyboards (both alphabetically ordered and digraph ordered) is the consistent superiority of the QWERTY layout, at least in the short term. Clearly, the first choice for designers providing a keyboard or typing layout for almost any purpose is the QWERTY layout.

54.3 Data-Entry Keypads

In addition to the main alphanumeric section, most computer keyboards have a separate numeric keypad for data entry. Also, use of push-button telephones as remote terminals to computers continues to rise (a phenomenon originally reported by Bayer and Thompson, 1983; Hagelbarger and Thompson, 1983). This section considers the design of keypads for telephone and other applications.

54.3.1 Layout of Numbers and Letters

Lutz and Chapanis (1955) tested six key configurations to determine where people expected each letter and number to appear on ten-button keysets for use by long-distance telephone operators. The key arrangements were two horizontal rows of five keys, two vertical rows of five keys, or three rows of three keys with a single key placed at the top, bottom, left or right of the block of nine keys. In general, people placed letters and numbers on keys in the same order as they read text (that is, from left to right and from top to bottom) regardless of the key configuration. When numbers were already on the keys: a) people consistently placed letters on the keys from left to right and from top to bottom when the numbers had that arrangement; and b) if the arrangement of numbers was not from left to right and top to bottom, about half of the people placed the letters to be consistent with the ordering of the numbers, and the other half persisted in arranging the letters from left to right and from top to bottom. The most frequent number arrangement was that found on the majority of modern U. S. telephones.

Detweiler, Schumaker and Gattuso (1990) asked telephone company employees to assign by memory the alphabetic letters of the telephone keypad (which does not list "Q" or "Z") on a blank representation of the keypad. Only 18% of these subjects were able to correctly place the letters on the keys with 100% accuracy on the first trial. After subsequent training, however, 72% of the participants achieved 100% accuracy. Detweiler et al. concluded that despite the thousands of interactions that people have with the telephone keypad, few people really have learned the mappings between the letters and keys.

Other studies have compared performance with the telephone layout (1, 2, 3 across the top with 0 at the bottom) and the common calculator layout (7, 8, 9 across the top). Conrad and Hull (1968) asked housewives to enter numeric codes and found the telephone layout was superior in both speed and accuracy. Paul, Sarlanis, and Buckley (1985) tested air traffic controllers and found that the telephone layout was better for entry of letters and mixed (letter and number) data, but that performance was the same for entry of numbers only.

A related study (Goodman, Dickinson, and Francas, 1983) used a simulation methodology to determine the best layout of keys for Telidon (Canadas Videotex system) keypads. They tested both a horizontal (1 through 0 in a single row) and a telephone arrangement. Speed and accuracy were slightly better on the telephone layout in a reaction-time task. However, differences in more realistic performance were not statistically significant. Preferences were strongly in favor of the telephone arrangement for a problem-solving task that simulated expected use of the Telidon system, but were slightly in favor of the horizontal arrangement for the reaction-time task.

Magyar (1986a) compared numeric entry throughput and error rate by typists performing an extended numeric entry task (5-digit numbers) using either the keyboard's horizontal top row of numbers or the separate 10-key calculator keypad. Half of the test participants had experience using a 10-key numeric keypad. The typists worked as they normally would with the two configurations, using both hands to enter numbers from the top row and one hand to enter numbers with the calculator keypad. Although the participants tended to commit fewer keying errors with the 10-key keypad, there were no significant differences between overall speed and accuracy with the two methods. Reanalysis of the data to evaluate performance differences attributed to user experience revealed that keying time for experienced keypad users was significantly faster on the keypad than with the top row. Keypad entry speed for experienced participants was faster than that by the inexperienced operators. Although keying speed for inexperienced users was faster with the top-row keys than with the numeric keypad, overall speed and accuracy for the top-row keys were equivalent for both groups. Similar to the findings of Goodman et al. (1983), the participants strongly preferred using a calculator keypad for the numeric entry task rather than the top row keys, citing increased speed and accuracy as the primary reasons for their preference.

Conclusions

The design and use of data-entry keypads depends to a great extent on the keying task required. For numeric and mixed input, the telephone layout is slightly superior to the calculator layout, especially for people who are not familiar with calculators or adding machines. Experienced keypad users who need to perform extensive numeric entry tasks appear to benefit from having a separate numeric-entry keypad on their keyboards. These data and conclusions are consistent with the ANSI/HFS 100-1988 standard's recommendation to provide a numeric keypad when the primary task includes the entry of numeric data, and to consider the application when choosing the calculator or telephone layout (Human Factors Society, 1988).

54.3.2 Alphanumeric Entry with Telephone Keypads

Because telephone keypads contain more than one letter on each key, their use for alphanumeric data entry requires a strategy for designating which letter goes with each keypress (or sequence of keypresses). Procedures for differentiating letters located on the same key are "disambiguation" techniques. Davidson (1966) suggested using the two extra keys on push-button telephones as control keys. The left (*) button would indicate the first letter, the right (#) button would indicate the third letter, and a keypress without a control key would indicate the middle letter. Francas, Brown, and Goodman (1983) compared Davidson's suggested method with both a miniature QWERTY keypad and an alphabetically arranged one. For entering alphabetic data, the telephone keypad with left and right control keys was significantly slower than either the QWERTY or alphabetical keysets, but accuracy was the same for all entry methods. The authors concluded that the telephone keypad was not suitable for entering letters in their application. However, for tasks that primarily require accuracy and have severe space limitations (or simply require the use of a standard telephone), the telephone keypad with control keys might be acceptable.

A particular problem with using the standard telephone keypad for alphabetic data is the absence of the letters "Q" and "Z" as well as other punctuation marks such as hyphens or apostrophes. Marics (1990) examined the ways that users would attempt to enter special names (e.g. O'Brien or Razzler) using the traditional telephone keypad. Results did not indicate a clearly preferred method of entering the Q, Z, and Hyphen. About one third of the subjects chose a non-alphabetic character key (such as "*") for these letters while another third chose the key where the letter should have been (for example, by pressing "7" (PRS) for "Q"). Eighty percent of the participants ignored (did not enter) characters such as apostrophes. Thus, there is no clearly superior method for assigning missing alphabetic and punctuation characters to the numeric and non-numeric keys of the standard telephone keypad, and a standard has yet to emerge.

A study of data entry for aircraft cockpits compared three keypads designed for one-handed keying (Butterbaugh and Rockwell, 1982). Task performance was fastest and most accurate with a keyboard having separate keys for each letter and number. However, further analyses showed that this difference was mainly due to the fact that the two other multifunction keypads required more keystrokes to enter each letter. Raw keypressing speed (but not letter input) was fastest with a telephone layout with letters assigned horizontally to the number keys. Butterbaugh and Rockwell recommended using a full keyboard if at all possible. If a space requirement forced the use of a smaller keypad, they suggested a telephone layout with letters assigned from left to right and from top to bottom. They also recommended using three control keys (for left, middle, and right characters) located in the top row of keys.

Brown and Goodman (1983) compared several methods of entering alphabetic text through a telephone keypad by employing various arrangements of control keys located above the telephone keypad. In one condition, subjects entered letters by pressing a single control key, then pressing the telephone key with the desired letter on it the number of times corresponding to the position of the letter in its group of three. In the two-control key arrangement, participants pressed either the "left control" key (for the first of the triplet letter per key) or the "right control" key (for the third letter) or both control keys (for the second letter) before each letter, then pressed the key with the selected letter. In the three-control key condition, letters were selected by pressing the "left", "center", or "right" control key, then the number key with the given letter. Alphabetic data entry using the two-control key arrangement was significantly faster and showed significantly greater improvement with practice than either the single-key or the three-control key arrangements, which did not differ in entry speed. Accuracy across all three conditions was comparable, however, and there were no significant differences in error rates. Although the two-control key method appeared superior to the three-key method recommended by Butterbaugh and Rockwell (1982), the authors concluded that the slow speeds of less than 10 wpm for all three of the arrangements were clearly impractical for tasks requiring extended text entry.

Detweiler, Schumacher, and Gatusso (1990) evaluated five different strategies for entering alphabetic letters (but not mixed alphanumeric data) from a telephone keypad. Because some methods (such as the "Repeat-Key" method) specified a purely cognitive strategy of entering alphabetic data (to press the key containing the letter the number of times corresponding to its ordinal position on the key), but others (such as the "Modal-Position" method) specified the use of "control" keys (to press the *, 0, or # key to designate the first, second or third letter on the next numeric key pressed), it is difficult to compare or generalize these performance findings to other studies that employed separate or additional control keys to allow for mixed alphanumeric entry on the same telephone keypad. Although there were few statistically significant differences in performance among the methods investigated, Detweiler et al. recommended (with qualifications) the Repeat-Key method. As they pointed out, however, the Repeat-Key method does not provide a clear way to enter the letters or other special characters not represented on the telephone keypad and requires users to pause for a detectable period of time between the entry of letters that appear on the same key.

Alternative approaches to disambiguation have investigated methods that do not require the user to learn a particular cognitive strategy or to use separate control keys on the keypad. Instead, a computer system incorporates statistical techniques to "predict" the word or name that a user is entering by examining unique key combinations, consulting an internal dictionary, and using trigram-based transistional probabilities to generate the most likely word for a combination of keystrokes (Minneman, 1985). Current models using statistical disambiguation techniques can achieve 90% correct prediction rates, but the extent to which the errors affect overall performance is unknown (Foulds, Soede, Balkom, and Boves, 1987). Because statistical disambiguation is not perfect, telephone keypads with statistical disambiguation systems need either (1) a key to allow users to signal disambiguation errors or (2) voice prompts to guide users through structured transactions, including the identification of disambiguation errors[4].

Conclusions

For the entry of letters or mixed alphanumeric data, telephone (and other small multifunction) keypads are no match for even reduced-size QWERTY or alphabetic keyboards. If speed is not important, but accuracy and space are critical, then a telephone keypad might be acceptable for limited data entry. The telephone keypad appears to be acceptable (but not optimal) for use as a remote terminal. Using a telephone keypad for limited alphanumeric entry will require adequate labeling of keys (or user instruction) to allow the entry of all the letters of the alphabet and a means for performing character disambiguation.

54.4 Physical Features of Keys and Keyboards

This section summarizes experimental and rational investigations of physical aspects of keys and keyboards. Because research has not provided comprehensive data on how the features might interact in affecting typing performance, each aspect receives separate discussion.

54.4.1 Keyboard Height and Slope

Scales and Chapanis (1954) conducted an experiment to determine the best slope for keysets used by long-distance telephone operators. People who had no previous experience with this keyset entered sequences of letters and numbers with the keyset sloped at either 0, 5, 10, 15, 20, 25, 30 or 40 degrees for each session. There were no differences in speed or errors among the eight slope conditions. All participants preferred some slope over a flat (zero degree) keyset; half of them preferred an angle between 15 and 25 degrees.

Galitz (1965) tested a computer keyboard at 9, 21, and 33 degrees. Although there were no performance differences due to keyboard slope, typists preferred the 21-degree angle. This slope was closest to the 16- to 17-degree angle on equipment the typists normally used. Galitz recommended that computer keyboards

[4] It is also possible to apply disambiguation techniques to the design of special-purpose keyboards that do not conform to the layout restrictions of a telephone keyset. For an example, see Kreifeldt, Levine, and Iyengar (1989).

have a slope adjustable between 10 and 35 degrees to satisfy individual preferences.

Emmons and Hirsch (1982) compared three slopes for an IBM 30 mm keyboard. Because a change in angle also resulted in a different home-row height, their height (angle) settings were 30 mm (5 degrees), 38 mm (12 degrees), and 45 mm (18 degrees). They also used a non-IBM 30 mm (5 degrees) keyboard. Tests of 12 experienced typists revealed no differences in error rates among the three angles/heights. With regard to typing speed, the 38-mm and 45-mm keyboards resulted in faster rates than either of the 30-mm keyboards. Typists preferred the 45-mm keyboard most and the 38-mm keyboard second-most. When asked about discomfort, five participants found everything uncomfortable, five said the 30-mm keyboard caused discomfort, one reported the 45-mm keyboard as uncomfortable, and one person had no discomfort with any of the keyboards.

Miller and Suther (1981; 1983) examined preferences for keyboard slope and height. U.S. and Japanese participants from the 5th, 50th, and 95th percentiles in height (compared to their respective populations) adjusted a workstation to their preferred settings and then transcribed some text from a written document into a computer terminal. Keyboard slope settings ranged from 14 to 25 degrees with an average of 18 degrees. Preferred slope significantly correlated with seat height (r=.71) and with individual stature (r=.43). Short people or people who preferred lower seat heights also liked to have a keyboard with a steeper slope. Because stature correlates with hand length, a steeper slope makes it easier for short-handed people to reach all of the keys. They recommended that keyboard slope be adjustable up to at least 20 degrees (with 25 degrees being better) to suit individual preferences. The keyboard used in the study was 77 mm high. Preferred home-row height was 637 to 802 mm above the floor, with an average of 707 mm. Keyboard height significantly correlated with stature (r=.71), preferred seat height (r=.74), and preferred CRT height (r=.57). They recommended that keyboards be as thin as possible to satisfy table-height requirements and that users be able to independently raise and lower the keyboard-support surface relative to the display.

In Suther and McTyre (1982), experienced typists used a thin-profile (30 mm) keyboard at 5, 10, and 25 degrees and a thick-profile keyboard at 15 degrees. There were no differences in typing performance for the four angles. None of the typists preferred the 5-degree keyboard. One person liked 25 degrees best, and the rest of the typists rated the 10- and 15-degree keyboards as preferable. This study also found preferences related to stature and hand length. Taller people and those with long hands tended to like the lower slope, but short people and those with short hands liked the steeper slope. Suther and McTyre recommended that keyboards have an adjustable slope between 10 and 25 degrees.

Abernethy (1984) and Abernethy and Akagi (1984) compared a 30-mm (8 degrees) keyboard with a 66-mm (12 degrees) keyboard. They reported that typists' hands tended to "curl" more with the 30-mm keyboard. That is, "the fingers curved around more as though they were forming a [loose] fist . . . for the lower keyboard" (C. N. Abernethy, personal communication, September 12, 1985).

A comparison of the same 30-mm keyboard with a 44.5-mm (8 degrees) keyboard showed that the wrist angle "pronated" more with the lower keyboard. Pronation describes the motion of the hand turning inward about the axis of the wrist, such that "the wrist angle flattened out, becoming more parallel to the floor, from the higher to the lower keyboard height" (C. N. Abernethy, personal communication, September 12, 1985). Pronation was greater when the keyboards were on a lower typing stand than when they were at desk height (8 degrees pronation compared to 5 degrees pronation). In another test, a modified 30-mm keyboard allowed adjustment of the slope from 8 to over 30 degrees. The average angle chosen by participants was 16.1 degrees at desk height and 14.4 degrees at typing stand height.

Najjar, Stanton, and Bowen (1988) examined typing performance and preference for standing typists using three keyboard home row heights (74, 99, and 125 cm) and three keyboard angles (O-, negative 15- and positive 15- degree slopes). At the lowest home row height, performance with 0- and negative 15-degree slopes was significantly better than with the positive 15 degree slope. Participants preferred typing on the 0-degree and positively sloped keyboards at the medium and highest home row. Using a positively sloped keyboard at the lowest home row height appeared to result in significant wrist dorsiflection (hands bent upward at the wrist), producing discomfort for the standing operators.

In an experiment designed to simulate dual-task conditions in aircraft cockpits, Hansen (1983) tested three slopes for a small keypad. There were no performance differences between 0-, 15- and 35-degree slopes, but 75 percent of the pilots tested preferred the 15-degree slope.

Burke, Muto, and Gutmann (1984) tested a keyboard with a fixed 11-degree slope at four heights (35,

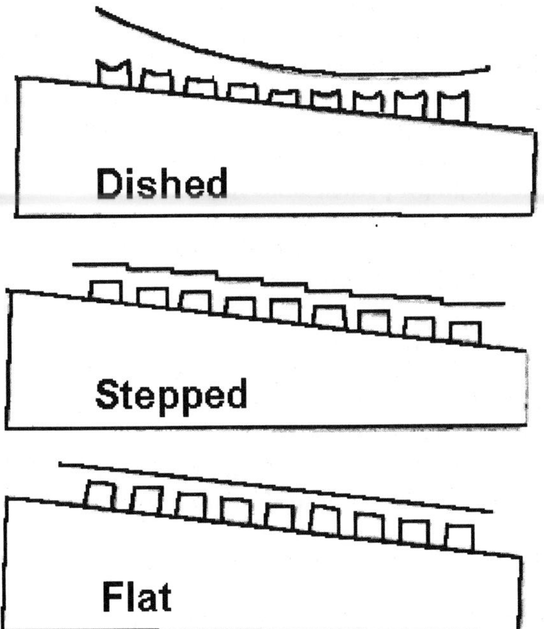

Figure 1. Keyboard profiles.

64, 84, and 104 mm). Again, there were no significant differences in either speed or accuracy of performance. The participants expressed the least preference for the height of 35 mm and the greatest preference for the height of 84 mm. The 64-mm keyboard also received high ratings.

Conclusions

The results of this research show that a wide range of keyboard heights and slopes do not appear to affect typing performance. Typists appear to prefer some slope in a keyboard. The angle of slope should be adjustable to at least 15 degrees, and perhaps even steeper to accommodate individual preferences. These conclusions are consistent with the ANSI/HFS 100-1988 standard's recommendation to provide a keyboard slope between 0 and 25 degrees (preferably limited to the range of 0 to 15 degrees) (Human Factors Society, 1988).

The height and slope of keyboards became a matter of debate when the West Germans announced their requirement for low-profile (30 mm) keyboards having a slope of no more than 15 degrees, enforcing this since January 1, 1985. Long-term comfort and avoidance of muscular strain appear to be the primary considerations behind the law. Although the 30-mm requirement caused quite a stir when first proposed, keyboard designers, manufacturers, researchers and users have come to accept low-profile keyboards (Paci and Gabbrielli, 1984).

54.4.2 Detachable Keyboards

There is no research available on the need for keyboards that are detachable from the display housing. The purpose of detachable keyboards is to satisfy individual sizes, preferences and task needs for locating the keyboard on the work surface.

The advantage of a detachable keyboard might be limited by the selection of work surfaces. Although a separate keyboard-support surface increases flexibility for height of the keyboard, it can reduce flexibility for placing the keyboard to one side of the workstation. Locating the keyboard support at the center of a workstation might interfere with tasks that do not require the use of a keyboard.

Another important point is that it is not always necessary to have a detachable keyboard. For office tasks that are brief or infrequent, users might not need a detachable keyboard. Laptop computers might be more difficult to use if the keyboards were separate. For public access terminals, a detachable keyboard might even be a liability.

Keyboard Profile

The relative angles and placement for different rows of keys on the keyboard create the keyboard profile. Most keyboard profiles conform to either a flat (on which keytops are parallel to keyboard slope), dished, or stepped design (see Figure 1).

Only two studies to date have tested different keyboard profiles. Paci and Gabbrielli (1984) evaluated performance by three typists using either a stepped or a dished profile keyboard. The angle at which the typists' fingers touched the keys ranged from 2 to 13 degrees on the stepped keyboard and from 8 to 11 degrees on the dished keyboard. Performance was reportedly better with the dished profile, and the typists expressed a preference for this keyboard. However, these effects might be the result of a difference in slopes because the stepped keyboard had a 9-degree slope and the dished keyboard had a 12- degree slope. Paci and Gabbrielli recommended the dished profile for the alphanumeric keys, the stepped profile for the numeric keypad (because this is common for calculators), and a flat profile for function keys because visual requirements (such as labeling and readability) are more important for these keys.

Magyar (1985) compared performance and preference of twelve typists using a flat, a dished, or a stepped keyboard profile. Each operator performed twenty timed typing trials per day with each of the three keyboard profiles. The typists received feedback on throughput and error rates after each trial, and completed a questionnaire daily after using each keyboard. Throughput performance with the flat keyboard was significantly lower than that for either the dished or stepped keyboards, which were not significantly different. Although detected error rates were comparable across all three profiles, undetected errors with the flat keyboard were significantly higher. Deficits inherent in the configuration of the keyboard used for the test prevented the detection of a clear-cut preference for any particular keyboard profile. Typists complained that the size and placement of the backspace, enter, and shift keys made typing difficult independent of the differences in the specific keyboard profile. Nevertheless, it appeared that the stepped and dished keyboard profiles were superior to the flat profile.

Conclusions

Although there might be subtle performance differences between flat, stepped, and dished keyboards, recommendations generally agree that the stepped and dished profiles are acceptable. There is insufficient data, however, to warrant a firm conclusion regarding the purported superiority of the dished and stepped designs over the flat profile. The data suggest that the influence of keyboard profile on user performance and preference might be minimal relative to the influence of other keyboard parameters.

54.4.3 Key Size and Shape

With the proliferation of portable devices, keyboard designers have a great desire to reduce the size of their keyboards by reducing the size of keys, but need to understand the impact of reduced key size on typing performance. Because the keytops are the point of immediate contact between a user and a keyboard, the size and shape of the key might have a lot to do with typing performance. However, relatively little research has addressed this hypothesis (with less for shape than size). Alden et al. (1972) stated that the design of individual keys depended more on "design convention rather than empirical data" (p. 280).

Clare's Proposals

Clare (1976) proposed four goals for the design of key shapes:

1. The operator should be able to see the key label.
2. The finger should be able to locate the key without hitting other keys or fingers.
3. The distribution of pressure on the finger should indicate the location of the finger on the key.
4. The force of pressing the key should be distributed to the proper portion of the finger.

Clare recommended that key tops should be 12.7 mm square and have a distance of 19 mm between keytop centers. Smaller keytops (such 9.5 mm) were "less satisfactory" (p. 102).

Calculator Key Size

Deininger (1960) tested different key sizes and shapes for a ten-key numeric keypad. Keying times and accuracy improved when key size increased from 9.5 to 12.7 mm. To provide guidance for the development of numeric keypads for portable computers, Loricchio and Lewis (1991) had 15 participants use three commercial calculators with different key spacing and key size. There were no significant accuracy differences, but user preference and speed improved as the key size increased from 10 mm square to a key measuring 14 x 10 mm.

Alphanumeric Keyboards

PC Magazine (Rosch, 1984) reported the results of a typing test to evaluate various computer keyboards. Typing performance was much poorer with keyboards having small keys. When typists used these same key mechanisms with larger keys, performance was among the best for the eleven keyboards tested. Loricchio and Kennedy (1987) investigated the effect of reducing vertical key spacing from 19 to 15 mm. They found no difference in keying rates or errors after 2.5 hours practice, but there was a strong user preference for the standard 19 mm key spacing. Wiklund, Dumas, and Hoffman (1987) conducted a walk-up-and-use (no practice) evaluation of four commercially available keyboards for both two- and one-handed use. Key spacing ranged from 19 x 19 mm to 13 x 12 mm. Although Wiklund et al. conducted no statistical analyses, the reported mean typing rate was greater for the largest keys, regardless of whether participants used one or two hands. For all keys except the smallest, two-handed typing was faster than one-handed typing.

Some guidelines cite round keys as acceptable, but square keys might be better because they provide more surface area within the same amount of space between keytop centers (Cakir, Hart, and Stewart, 1980). In an evaluation that included keycap differences, typists preferred keycaps that "resemble the somewhat rounded, dished keycaps of earlier model Selectric typewriters" (Texas Instruments, 1983, p. 26). The next most preferred keys were those with large, square touch surfaces with a cylindrical indentation from front to back. The keyboard with round keytops received the worst ranking.

Conclusions

The center-to-center spacing of keys on standard alphanumeric keyboards is generally 19 mm. Use of smaller center-to-center spacing will result in slower typing. There are no data available on upper limits for key size, but there is little incentive to explore the upper limit. Designers usually seek to minimize rather than maximize the size of their keyboards (especially in the development of portable devices). Clearly, designers should strive to provide full-size (19 mm spacing) keys for the major typing areas of their keyboards (certainly the alphanumeric area and, if possible, the numeric keypad). This conclusion is consistent with the recommendation provided in ANSI/HFS 100-1988 (Human Factors Society, 1988) that horizontal spacing should be between 18 and 19 mm and vertical spacing should be between 18 and 21 mm. The ANSI-HFS 100-1988 recommendation for the minimum striking surface width is 12 mm.

With regard to the shape of keys, there is some evidence that they should fit the shape of the finger tip for ease of location and finger placement. Preferences appear to lean toward keys that have spherical indentation as opposed to those having a cylindrical indentation. The ANSI/HFS 100-1988 standard (Human Factors Society, 1988) makes no recommendation regarding indentation, and states that any keytop shape (square, round, or rectangular) is acceptable as long as the keys conform to the recommended key spacing.

54.4.4 Key Force, Travel and Tactile Feedback

The "force/displacement" function of a key describes the force with which a finger must press the key to actuate it and the distance the key travels before, during and after actuation. A generalized force/ displacement function appears in Figure 2, which shows:

- on the horizontal axis, the distance the key travels
- on the vertical axis, the force applied to the key
- separate curves for the downstroke and upstroke of the key (arrows show the direction of travel)
- the key's actuation point ("switch closed")

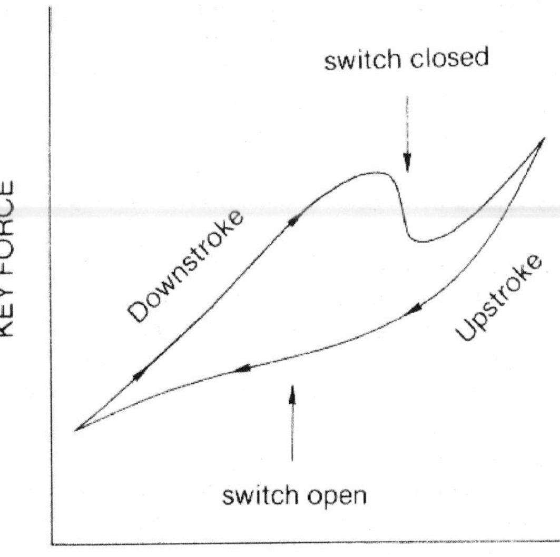

Figure 2. A generalized force-travel function.

- the "switch open" point at which pressing the key creates another character
- changes in the slope of the function corresponding to the "feel" of the key at different points along its travel
- tactile feedback caused by a rapid drop in force before the "switch closed" point and a subsequent increase in force beyond this point
- hysteresis, that the "switch open" and "switch closed" points occur at different places along the key's travel

Studies on the effects of different force/ displacement functions have not been systematic, so it is difficult to create a model of how a particular aspect of the function will affect keying performance or preference. Research has uncovered ranges within which neither the amount of key force nor the distance of travel affects performance. Other investigations have compared keyboards for which the entire force/travel function varied.

Studies on Key Force and Displacement

A study of telephone usage and occasional data entry (Deininger, 1960) found no performance differences due to either a decrease in maximum force from 14.1 to 3.5 ounces (400 to 100 grams) or a decrease in maximum travel from 0.19 to 0.03 inches (4.8 to 0.8 mm).

Kinkead and Gonzalez (1969) found key pressing performance was best at low levels of force and travel. They recommended values between 5.3 and 0.9 ounces (150.3 and 25.5 grams) for force and between 0.25 and 0.05 inches (6.4 and 1.3 mm) for key travel.

In a similar study, Loricchio (1992) compared text entry typing on keyboards having identical key travel (2.7 mm) but different operating-point key forces (58 grams vs. 74 grams). Although there was no difference in error rates between the two keyboards, throughput speed was significantly faster on the 58 gram keyboard. Test participants also highly preferred the lighter force keyboard over the heavier touch keyboard. Because Loricchio compared only two forces, however, the data in this study did not indicate if further decrements in force would continue to improve or degrade performance (but see Akagi, 1992, below).

Switch Technology or Key Force?

Brunner and Richardson (1984) compared three switch technologies: a snap-spring keyboard that had a very slight drop-off in force before the point of actuation and a gradual increase in force after this point; a linear-spring keyboard that had no change in the force/displacement function to indicate tactile feedback; and an elastomer switch that provided distinct tactile feedback. Considering both speed and errors, the elastomer keyboard was about 2% to 6% better than the other keyboards. Incorrect insertions of characters occurred more often on the linear-spring keyboard. Ratings by typists indicated that the elastomer keyboard was acceptable relative to the other keyboards tested. It is not possible, however, to determine exactly which keyboard features caused the performance differences reported in this study.

A factor that might have influenced the results of this study was the different key force for each type of keyboard. A snap-spring keyboard key force is typically about 70 grams, an elastomer-dome keyboard key force is about 60 grams, and a linear-spring key force is about 30 grams (Akagi, 1992). Using this reasoning, Akagi compared preference and performance of four keyboards having different key forces and travel characteristics. He had participants type with two linear-spring keyboards, one with low force (42.5 grams) and one with high force (70.9 grams), and with two snap (tactile) action keyboards, one with low force (35.5 grams), and one with high force (70.9 grams). While a majority of the test participants typed faster on the linear-spring keyboards, typing speed was not significantly different between the tactile and linear-spring action keyboards. Error rates, however, were significantly higher on the low force keyboards than on high force keyboards for both the tactile and linear-spring action keyboards. The typists distributed their preferences evenly among the four keyboards tested. Akagi suggested that an optimally designed keyboard should be a tactile-spring keyboard having a key force midway between the values he used in his test (approximately 57 grams). This recommendation is consistent with the results provided by Loricchio (1992, see above), who reported that a tactile action keyboard having a key force of 58 grams produced superior performance over a similar keyboard with heavier key force (74 grams).

Key Movement

In another study, typists rated smooth key movement as a highly important facet of keyboard quality (Monty, Snyder, and Birdwell, 1983; Texas Instruments, 1983). Comparing six keyboards, the factors that seemed to be most important to users were:

1. key switches that do not have noisy key bottoming
2. tactile-snap feedback caused by an abrupt change in the force required to actuate the key
3. a force/displacement curve shaped like a "roller coaster"
4. a smooth force/displacement curve undisturbed by jitter
5. keycaps with minimal lateral wobble

Because the performance data showed a speed-accuracy tradeoff, it was impossible to determine the specific effects of different force/travel curves on performance.

Experiments with Capacitance and Membrane Technologies

Touch keys that lack key travel (such as capacitance and membrane technologies) appear to cause slower keying performance than conventional mechanical keys (Cohen, 1982; Pollard and Cooper, 1979). Although the disadvantage of these switches decreases as users adapt to the absence of tactile feedback, the addition of cues such as embossed edges, metal domes, and tones or clicks on actuation can reduce the early negative effects (Roe, Muto, and Blake, 1984).

Barrett and Krueger (1994) compared performance and acceptance by touch typists or casual users using either a tactile keyboard having full travel and kinesthetic feedback or a flat piezo-electric keyboard without any tactile or kinesthetic feedback. Throughput performance and accuracy by both subject groups were significantly higher on the conventional keyboard, and the flat keyboard had a more adverse effect on touch typists' than casual users' performance. In contrast to previous reports, however, performance on the flat keyboard did not improve with practice, and the authors concluded that touch typists were unable to adapt to the absence of tactile feedback. Analysis of the subjects' video data suggested that the reason for the subjects' failure to adapt was that the removal of kinesthetic feedback effectively reduced their level of skill (from touch typist to casual user) by increasing their dependence on visual feedback from the flat keyboard. Adding peripheral cues to a non-tactile keyboard (via audio feedback, embossed edges on keys, etc.) should consequently enhance performance by reducing the need for typists to look at the keyboard. Indeed, there is mounting evidence that auditory feedback in part may influence or interact with the degree of tactile feedback reported by typists (Brunner and Richardson, 1984; Magyar, 1986d; Pollard and Cooper, 1979; Roe, Muto, and Blake, 1984).

Key Force and Finger Force

Clare (1984) recommended that force/ displacement curves should differ for different fingers and key locations. According to Clare, upper keys should have shorter travel and lower keys should have longer travel to produce the same feel for the fingers.

Actual measurement of the finger force that typists exert on the keys indicates that the force-displacement characteristics of the keyboard can affect the degree of fingertip forces applied during typing performance. Rempel and Gerson (1991) collected peak fingertip forces for each keystroke using strain gauge load cells while subjects typed on three keyboards that differed in terms of key force and travel characteristics. While the results showed that the average peak fingertip forces applied by subjects were more than three times greater than the force required for key activation, keyboards requiring less activation force and shorter key travel actually resulted in reducing the subjects' peak fingertip force by as much as 18%.

A subsequent study (Armstrong, Foulke, Martin, Gerson, and Rempel, 1994) replicated the previous results, and found that average peak keystroke forces were lowest on keyboards requiring the least amount of activation force. This study also found that peak forces corresponding to each keystroke were 2.5 to 3.9 times the required activation force, indicating that subjects consistently displaced the keys to their mechanical limits. Although it is not clear whether the subjects failed to respond to the key breakaway force or whether the range of motion following the key activation point was of insufficient distance for the finger to stop, the authors concluded that key force exerted by typists is largely related to the design and stiffness of the keys.

Conclusions

The literature on actuation force and travel indicates minimal effect on performance within a wide range of these parameters. Recommended values range from about 1 to 5 ounces (about 28 to 142 grams) of force and about 0.05 to 0.25 inches (about 1.3 to 6.4 mm) of travel. The increased error rates for Akagi's (1992) light touch keyboards combined with Loricchio's (1992) results suggest that about 55 to 60 grams is a good design point for key force, but 35 grams is too light. These data and conclusions are consistent with the ANSI/HFS 100-1988 standard's recommendation to provide a key travel between 1.5 and 6.0 mm (preferred 2.0 to 4.0 mm) and key force[5] between 25 and 153 grams (preferred 50 to 60 grams) (Human Factors Society, 1988), particularly with respect to the preferred key force.

More important than the amount of force and travel is the tactile feedback caused by a gradual increase in force followed by a sharp decrease in force required to actuate the key (the breakaway force) and a subsequent increase in force beyond this point for cushioning. The result is a curve shaped like a roller coaster. From the data available, keyboards should provide tactile feedback because it improves keying performance and typists prefer it. Capacitive and membrane keys that require only a minimal touch and little or no travel are inferior to conventional keys in terms of typing performance. Because a number of factors appear to affect the perception of tactile feedback, and because many factors could have influenced the results of the relevant studies, more research in this area would clearly be useful.

54.4.5 Auditory Feedback

Auditory clicks, beeps and tones for typewriter keyboards are unnecessary for skilled typists in high speed data entry tasks (Alden et al., 1972). The sound gener-

[5] The ANSI/HFS 100-1988 standard expresses key force in Newtons, with an acceptable force between .25 and 1.5 N, and a preferred key force between .5 and .6 N.

ated by the typewriter's print hammer striking the paper platen provides a sufficiently loud and correlated auditory feedback signal following each key press. However, the advent of personal computers eliminated the auditory feedback provided by impact printers and introduced newer keyboard technology (such as elastomer, capacitive, and membrane switches) that allowed designers to create truly silent key action. These keyboards can have auditory feedback as an add-on feature to turn on and off. Some also allow adjustment of the volume of the click. Performance data with such keyboards indicate that typing is significantly faster and more accurate with auditory feedback on than with it off (Monty, Snyder, and Birdwell, 1983; Roe, Muto, and Blake, 1984). Moreover, most typists prefer auditory feedback, but they also want the ability to turn it off depending on its physical characteristics and the environment in which they use the keyboard.

For telephone keypads there is some evidence that adding a single tone allows faster keying than a click or a visual signal (Pollard and Cooper, 1979). When the user cannot see the keys for dialing telephone numbers, speech feedback reduces keying errors (Nakatani and O'Connor, 1980).

The Timing of Auditory Feedback

The amount of time lag between a key press and the auditory feedback from the print hammer or keyboard is an important variable. If the lag is too long, it can interfere with typing performance (Clare, 1976; Texas Instruments, 1983). Long (1976) showed that when the print mechanism of a teletype was delayed or irregular in relation to typing on the keyboard, speed of typing slowed for both unskilled and experienced typists. The effect disappeared with practice, but only for skilled typists.

Magyar (1982) noted a similar disruption in typing performance for an electronic typewriter that substituted an ink-jet printing mechanism for the standard mechanical impact printer and a relatively silent membrane keyboard instead of a mechanical keyboard. As in Long's (1976) study, the irregular and delayed auditory feedback of the ink-jet printhead following keystrokes resulted in decreased typing speed and increased error rates. Modifying the keyboard to generate a distinct acoustic click after each keypress resulted in significant performance improvements. In trials with the clicker turned "On," typing speed immediately increased and the error rate decreased. Turning the clicker "Off" resulted in immediate decrements in typing speed with simultaneous increases in error rate. Magyar speculated that the quality of the auditory feedback appeared to be important. Operators preferred keyboards providing short duration, low frequency (less than 1000 Hz) auditory feedback sounds such as "clicks" and showed less preference for high frequency (greater than 2500 Hz) "beeps" or tones.

The Interaction of Auditory and Tactile Feedback

Although it is generally accepted that tactile feedback is more important for keying speed than is auditory feedback, there is mounting evidence suggesting that the two variables may exert significant interactions influencing both performance and preference (Roe et al., 1984; Magyar, 1986d; Walker, 1989).

Brunner and Richardson (1984) evaluated performance and preference for experienced and occasional typists across several keyboards having different levels of tactile feel and auditory feedback. They reported that auditory feedback was the most important determinant of a user's initial reaction to a keyboard. The importance of auditory feedback, however, diminished over time. Although there was no difference in typing performance across keyboards for either group, the occasional typists rated their performance as better on keyboards having auditory feedback.

Schuck (1994) examined the effect of auditory feedback on the performance of operators typing on a touch-screen keyboard having no key travel. Results revealed that the feedback did not affect error rates, but the addition of auditory feedback to a typing task did improve typing speed under all tested conditions. These results might not generalize to a more skilled typing population. The actual experience level of the typists was not clear because operators rated their own level of typing skill. It seems likely that the typists were not highly skilled because throughput speeds during the test appeared to be rather slow (12-25 wpm).

In a test comparing a buckling-spring keyboard having tactile feel against a much quieter membrane keyboard with little tactile feel, Magyar (1986d) initially reported an even split of the preferences of experienced typists across the two keyboards. The typists who preferred the buckling-spring keyboard cited its superior touch and feel, while those who preferred the membrane keyboard liked its quietness. In a replication of the study (using the same keyboards), typists listened to "white noise" played through headphones to mask differences in auditory feedback between the two keyboards. Results of the second study revealed a shift in preference to the buckling-spring keyboard, with the majority of typists citing superior touch and feel as the basis for their preference. Magyar concluded that, in the absence of auditory feedback, users appeared to base their preference primarily on the tactile characteristics of the keyboards.

Conclusions

Auditory feedback appears to have a positive effect on typing performance and user preference, especially for keyboards having little or no tactile feedback. While there is some evidence indicating a possible interaction between auditory and tactile feedback, the exact relationship between these two variables is unclear. If designers add auditory feedback to a keyboard, they should also provide operators with a way to control the presence or absence of the sound (preferably with a volume control for maximum user flexibility). Although auditory feedback appears to be an important determinant of keyboard usability, the physical values defining its "optimum" characteristics (such as the ideal amplitude, frequency, and timbre) still require investigation.

54.4.6 Visual Feedback

Common sense suggests that it might be helpful to have a visual display of a telephone number to reduce errors when dialing the phone. However, E. T. Klemmer (personal communication, December 10, 1981) found such a display to be "of no value for ordinary dialing of telephone numbers." Visual displays for telephones appear to offer no advantage because "telephone users can easily operate with an acceptably low error rate without the display and the effort involved in checking the display is not worthwhile. Moreover, if the user suspects that an error was made (more than half of all errors are self-detected) it is more efficient to simply re-key the number than to read the display, check for accuracy, and then re-key the number" (E. T. Klemmer, personal communication, December 10, 1981). (For very long numbers, such as those used when sending faxes internationally, a visual display might be helpful. We know of no research in this area.)

For touch typists on regular keyboards, visual feedback does not appear to provide any advantage for speed of typing, but it does affect the typist's ability to catch and correct errors (Alden et al., 1972; Rosinski, Chiesi, and Debons, 1980). With fewer than 9 characters displayed at a time, typists were less likely to correct their own errors (Rosinski et al., 1980) than with a larger number of letters displayed. Visual feedback also might be useful when first learning to type (Alden et al., 1972).

As with auditory feedback, timing of visual feedback is important. When the print mechanism of a teletype was delayed and irregular in relation to typing on the keyboard, speed of typing slowed for both unskilled and experienced typists (Long, 1976). The effect disappeared with practice, but only for skilled typists. Delay of visual feedback on a computer display also affects typist behavior and satisfaction (Williges and Williges, 1981; 1982). Boyle and Lanzetta (1984) found that the perceptual threshold of delay for subjects typing at a computer was 165 ms for single keystrokes, and 100 ms for multiple keystrokes.

54.4.7 Error-Avoidance Features

Variables such as rollover, buffer length, hysteresis and repeat functions can affect the rate of typing errors, but have not received experimental investigation.

Rollover

Rollover is the ability of the keyboard to store each keystroke in proper sequence. Without rollover, typists must release each key before pressing the next. High-speed typing without rollover results in some character loss or generation of erroneous codes. Two-key rollover will generate two keystrokes accurately when a typist presses the second key before releasing the first. With n-key rollover, any number of keystrokes can overlap without disturbing the proper sequence of characters.

Another aspect of rollover is shadow rolling, which refers to the sequence of keystrokes in which the typist presses and releases the second key before releasing the first. Shadow rolling with two-key rollover does not generate the second character. With n-key rollover, the sequence will be correct. Thus, n-key rollover is better than two-key rollover (Cakir, Hart, and Stewart, 1980; Davis, 1973).

Hysteresis

Actuation occurs at the "switch closed" point on the downstroke (see Figure 2). Upon release, the switch remains closed until the key travels past the "switch open" point. If the closed and open points occur at the same place, it is possible to experience extra, unwanted keystrokes when the typing finger hesitates or is not smooth on the upstroke (key bounce). Hysteresis (the travel distance between the "switch close" and "switch open" points) eliminates this problem. With hysteresis, the switch remains closed on the upstroke past the actuation point on the downstroke.

Interlocks

If the key does not have mechanical hysteresis, an electronic interlock can provide the same benefit. On most modern keyboards, an electronic polling scheme imposes a minimum time between keystrokes. The system assumes short inter-key times are due to key bounce or unintended keystrokes. The effect of the interlock is to transmit keystrokes at a controlled rate, ignoring these short inter-key times.

The optimal transmission rate depends on maximum keying rates, which usually occur in fast bursts of typing. If the interlock period is too short, it will not be effective at screening out unintended keystrokes. Recommendations for interlock systems vary, but in general should account for a typing rate of at least 100 gross words per minute. This value represents an interlock period of about 100 msec. Because typing burst rates can be much faster than 100 msec per keystroke (as low as 4 msec for skilled typing of certain digrams), shorter interlock intervals might be necessary. Alden et al. (1972) proposed a lower limit of 50 msec. A firmer recommendation will require further research.

Buffer Size

Many computer keyboards allow the user to type ahead of the display. This feature is particularly useful when the display depends on the response of the system. If the user knows ahead of time what input to enter next, he or she can store keystrokes in a buffer until the system is ready to receive them.

In a comparison of buffers storing 1, 2, 4, 6 and 7 characters, buffer size interacted with the speed of visual feedback in determining typing speed (Williges and Williges, 1981; 1982). With a fast visual display, smaller buffers did not affect typing speed. A display delay of as much as 1.5 seconds required a larger buffer. Buffer size was less important than speed of visual display: long delays in visual feedback resulted in slower performance regardless of the size of the buffer. Because computer response times often result in delayed visual feedback, the recommended buffer size is at least seven characters.

Repeat Features

Although there are no experimental data to support the need for key-repeat features, experience shows that "typamatic" keys are handy for many purposes, such as underlining and other graphic symbols used to make tables. On many computer keyboards, all keys are typamatic. The delay before creating repeated characters after pressing and holding the key should be neither too long nor too short, but the literature does not contain any specific recommendations for the optimal delay length. A common default value for the delay is 0.5 seconds between the first and second productions of the key on a single press, and with 0.1 seconds between subsequent key productions.

54.4.8 Color and Labeling

Recommendations for the color and labeling of keys and keyboards typically rely on the requirement for visibility and for coding purposes, rather than experimental investigations. Neither the keys themselves, nor the entire keyboard should be so shiny as to create a glare source. The usual recommendation is a matte to silky matte finish. The names of keys should be legible and understandable to the user. A slightly rough (matte) finish on the keytops aids finger positioning but should not reduce the legibility of the key label. Grouping and coloring keys by function assist visual search. This is particularly helpful on computer keyboards, because they usually act as more than typing devices for text entry (Cakir, Hart, and Stewart, 1980).

Lewis (1984) conducted a study on different designs of an Alternate key to determine if, because the primary purpose of an Alternate key is to place other keys into an alternate state, the color and position of the word "Alternate" on the Alternate key should look like a primary function or, for ease of association, if the word "Alternate" should look like an alternate function. The three variables examined were position (the word "Alternate" appeared at the position of the primary or the alternate function for the non-alternate keys), color (the word "Alternate" was either the color of the primary or the alternate functions), and background (the Alternate key's background either matched or failed to match the color of the alternate functions). He found that the subjects made the fewest selection errors (primary versus alternate functions) when the color and position of the word "Alternate" matched that of the alternate functions on the other keys.

54.4.9 Special Purpose Keys

The special purpose keys are the keys that are not part of the standard alphanumeric typing area or the numeric keypad, such as the Backspace key, the Enter key, the cursor control keys, and the function keys. Some relatively recent research has addressed the design of these keys.

The Enter and Backspace Keys

The Enter key has assumed a variety of shapes on modern keyboards, including the vertical Enter key (taller than wide), the horizontal Enter key (wider than tall), and the backwards-L shaped "dogleg" Enter key, which occupies the combined space of the vertical and horizontal Enter keys. In a series of studies, Magyar (1984; 1986b; Magyar and Robertson, 1986) determined the order of typists' preference and performance with the three types of Enter keys is dogleg first, horizontal second, and vertical third. Typists weakly preferred the dogleg Enter to the horizontal Enter, and significantly preferred both the dogleg and horizontal Enter keys to the vertical Enter key. The speed of acquiring all three types of Enter keys appeared to be equal, but the magnitude of acquisition errors for the vertical Enter key was roughly twice that of the dogleg and horizontal Enter keys.

Backspace keys typically occupy either the space of one (single-wide Backspace) or two (double-wide Backspace) normal keys, and are usually located in the upper right corner of the standard typing area. Magyar (1984, 1986b) conducted studies to evaluate user preference for and performance with the two types of Backspace keys, and found that people prefer and perform better with the double-wide Backspace. The error rates for the horizontal and dogleg Enter keys were about equal, but the ratio of errors for the single-wide relative to the double-wide Backspace key was 24.0 for simple text (typing restricted to the QWERTY area) and 9.0 for complex text (input text included non-alphanumeric characters).

Kennedy and Lewis (1985) conducted a small field study to determine the relative rates of acquisition of the Backspace and Enter keys when people used both word processing and spreadsheet programs. The results showed that the ratio of Enters to Backspaces was 2.2 for word processing and 5.3 for spreadsheets.

Considerations of these findings suggest that the best keyboard design (disregarding keyboard real estate limitations) would include both the dogleg Enter key and the double-wide Backspace key. If keyboard real estate limitations lead to a tradeoff in the space allocated to the Enter and Backspace keys, the best tradeoff would result in a horizontal Enter key and a double-wide backspace key. Although typists typically acquire the Enter key more often than the Backspace key (Kennedy and Lewis, 1985), the increase in typing errors due to reducing the size of the Backspace key is enough greater than the increase in errors due to reducing the Enter key to a horizontal shape to justify a keyboard design with a double-wide Backspace key and a horizontal Enter key.

Cursor Control Key Arrangements

The cursor control keys are the arrow keys used to move the cursor (the on-screen symbol that indicates the focus of typing -- where any typed input will appear on the screen). A number of different layouts for these four keys have appeared in various keyboard designs. The most common arrangements are the box, cross, and inverted-T. The box arrangement has the left and right arrow keys located directly under the up and down arrow keys in a 2 by 2 key matrix. Thus, the box arrangement has appropriate control-response compatibility for left and right, but not for up and down. The cross arrangement has the arrow keys arranged around an empty key space, with the left and right arrow keys on the left and right of the empty space, and the up and down keys located above and below the empty space. This arrangement creates correct control-response compatibility for all four keys, but is somewhat awkward to use. The inverted-T arrangement is similar to the cross, but the down arrow key occupies the empty space of the cross arrangement. This results in an inverted-T shape, with the left and right arrows located to the left and right of the down arrow, and the up arrow immediately above the down arrow.

Emmons (1984) demonstrated the superiority of the cross layout over the box layout, especially for inexperienced users. In a following study, Emmons (1987) found no performance difference between the cross and inverted-T arrangements, but reported that 13 of 18 participants preferred the inverted-T. Magyar (1986c) reported similar results.

Function Keys

Function keys are keys that operate as defined by software. There is no published research on different function key arrangement. Although this seemed to be a promising area of research when this chapter first appeared (Potosnak, 1990), recent developments in graphical user interfaces (specifically, the use of mice and on-screen buttons) have reduced the importance of such research, making future research in this area unlikely.

54.5 Alternative Keyboard Designs

A number of investigators have studied physical reconstruction of the keyboard and modifications in the means of operating a keyboard. The two major areas of

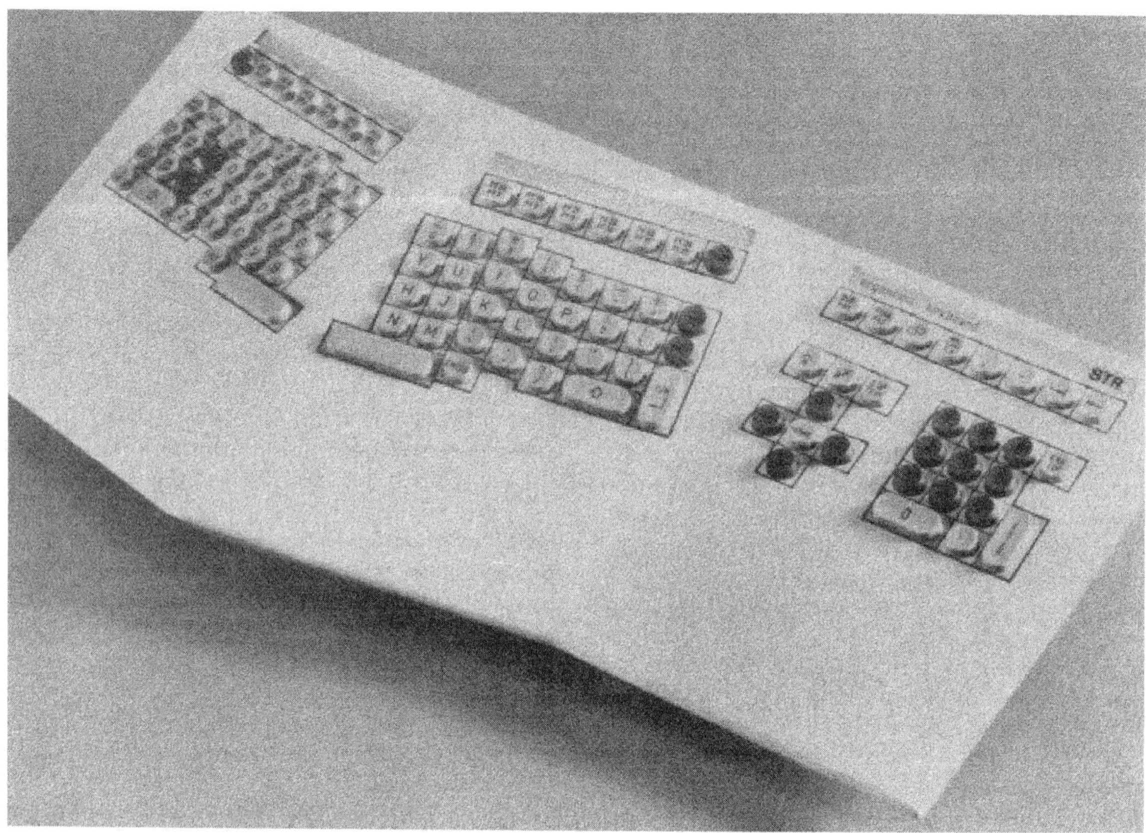

Figure 3. The STR split keyboard of Nakeseko et al.

research in such alternative keyboards are split keyboards and chord keyboards.

54.5.1 Split Keyboards

Studies of how people naturally hold their hands and arms compared to their postures at conventional typewriters have led some researchers to hypothesize that there might be components of fatigue inherent in the design of conventional keyboards (Kroemer, 1972; Nakaseko, Grandjean, Hunting, and Gierer, 1985; Zipp, Haider, Halpern, and Rohmert, 1983). Consistent with these observations, several ergonomists and inventors have developed or contributed to the development of "ergonomic" split keyboards. These keyboards have at least two sections, angled apart in the horizontal plane (producing non-parallel key rows). Some also angle the keyboard sections down from the horizontal plane. Some split keyboards have fixed angles, while others allow a range of adjustment. See Figure 3 for an example of a split keyboard.

The split keyboard literature is too large to review comprehensively in this chapter, but see Lewis (1994; 1995a) for recent literature reviews and Lewis (1995b) for a meta-analysis of preference for split keyboards. This section contains a review of the research conducted with two older split keyboards (the K-keyboard and the STR™ keyboard) and two newer split keyboards (the Kinesis™ keyboard and the Health Comfort Keyboard™).

The K-Keyboard

Kroemer (1972) named his K-keyboard for Klockenberg, an early proponent of split keyboards who published a critique of the standard typewriter in 1926. The K-Keyboard's 30 keys were in straight columns, with curved rows to attempt to fit different finger lengths. The space bars (one for each hand) curved to fit the reach of the thumb, and the keyboard provided a generous area for palm supports. Because the keyboard was experimental, Kroemer did not completely determine the assignment of characters to keys, but assigned characters to 16 of the 30 keys so the participants in his experiments could type the same sentence repeatedly.

Experiments with the K-keyboard indicated that the degree of lateral tilt of the two halves did not affect key tapping frequency or errors (Kroemer, 1972). Of the angles tested (0, 30, 60 and 90 degrees from horizontal), the data presented suggested that typists preferred an angle of 60 degrees over no tilt. (These data, however, are difficult to interpret due to discrepancies between the description of the assignment of participants to conditions and subtotals for the associated table of results.) In another test, typists made significantly more errors (about 5% more) on a standard keyboard than on the K-keyboard with a 45-degree tilt. Kroemer (1965) attributed this difference in errors to differences between the keyboards' key arrangements rather than to effects of keyboard geometry. In particular, the standard keyboard contained extra keys (relative to the K-keyboard) in its top two rows that seemed to be responsible for a number of the errors made with the standard keyboard. There were no differences either in typing speed or the number of heart beats (used as a measure of circulatory strain). Kroemer reported that participants terminated the task for different reasons. Users of the standard keyboard more often complained of "aches and pains," while K-keyboard typists were more likely to report that they could not concentrate any longer (although this group also reported some aches and pains). Kroemer did not treat these results with any statistical test. A clear comparison of the two keyboard geometries was not possible in these experiments because the K-keyboard had built-in palm supports, but the standard keyboard did not.

The STR Keyboard

Nakaseko and his colleagues (Nakaseko, Grandjean, Hunting, and Gierer, 1985) conducted experiments to test different opening angles between halves, the angle of tilt, and the size of the forearm-wrist support surface of an experimental split keyboard. Later work with this keyboard led to the development of a final product by Standard Telephon and Radio (STR) AG (Buesen, 1984), which won a design award at Ergodesign in 1984.

In an initial experiment, Nakaseko et al. (1985) reported that typists found the split keyboard acceptable and favored the design with lateral tilt of 10 degrees and an opening angle of 25 degrees. In a second experiment, 31 participants typed for 30 minutes with each of three keyboards. One keyboard was a traditional keyboard with a large forearm-wrist support, one was an experimental split keyboard (using the design favored by typists in the preceding experiment) with a large forearm-wrist support, and one was the same experimental split keyboard with a small forearm-wrist support. Participants used the keyboards in randomized orders, and after use completed a questionnaire to indicate if they felt pain in different parts of their upper limbs and shoulders. The experimenters recorded the amount of pressure the participants placed against the forearm-wrist supports and made a number of body posture measurements. They reported their feelings after each trial, using a seven-point scale with the end points of *very relaxed* and *very tense*, and ranked the keyboards according to their preference.

There were no statistically significant differences among the keyboards for reported pains in the neck-shoulder and arm-hand areas. For the relaxed-tense ratings, the keyboards did differ for the arms and hands and the back, with the experimental keyboard with the large forearm-wrist support having the most favorable ratings. None of the average ratings, however, exceeded the center point of the seven-point scale (Neither-Nor). On the basis of the preference ranks, the authors stated, "The traditional keyboard was preferred by a scarce 30%, whereas more than two thirds prefer one of the two experimental keyboards" (p. 185). The authors did not perform an overall statistical test on the preference ranks, nor did they report any performance data.

Examination of the row totals shows that the preference ranks reported in Nakaseko et al. (1985) must be incorrect (Lewis, 1994). With 31 participants, each rank row total should be 31. However, the row total for the ranks of 1 is 32, and that for the ranks of 2 is 30. Therefore, there are one too many first-place ranks and one too few second-place ranks, and no way to tell which column is incorrect. After adjusting the columns in all three possible ways (by subtracting 1 from a first-place rank total and adding it to the corresponding second-place rank total), Friedman tests on all three versions showed that, overall, the preference ranks among the keyboards were not significantly different (p ranged from .3 to .4). Accepting the data as given, a binomial test comparing the first-place ranks for the split (16 first-place ranks) and standard (9 first-place ranks) keyboards with large forearm-wrist supports was not significant (two-tailed p=.22).

In addition to these analytical problems, the experimental design for this study has a fundamental flaw. The authors manipulated two independent variables, each of which had two levels (experimental versus traditional keyboard, small versus large forearm-wrist support). Therefore, the complete design for this experiment would have had four rather than three conditions. From an experimental design perspective, the condition with a traditional keyboard and a small forearm-wrist support is missing. Nakaseko et al. (1985) chose to emphasize the experimental keyboard when they claimed that two-thirds of their participants preferred the experimental keyboard. However, because the experimental design is a fractional (rather than a complete) factorial, an alternative interpretation is that the data show that more than three-quarters of the participants preferred a large forearm-wrist support to a smaller one. Given this experimental design, it is impossible to separate the effects of keyboard type and forearm-wrist support size.

Brigham and Clark (1986) conducted an experiment to compare the STR keyboard to a standard keyboard. Twenty experienced typists practiced with the keyboards for 20 minutes, then typed for seven 20-minute sessions separated by 5-minute rest periods. Brigham and Clark reported that performance on the standard keyboard was superior to that on the STR for all sessions. Their participants also indicated that they found the standard keyboard more comfortable to use and preferred it.

The Kinesis Keyboard

The Kinesis keyboard is a sculptured, nonadjustable split keyboard, featuring a large forearm-wrist support that extends 14 cm from the home row to the edge. Jahns, Litewka, Lunde, Farrand, and Hargreaves (1991) reported a pilot experiment in which eight healthy typists used the Kinesis keyboard for about eight hours over three experimental sessions. Six of eight participants stated that they preferred the Kinesis overall. This finding, however, was not statistically significant (binomial test two-tailed $\underline{p}$=.28) (Lewis, 1994). With about eight hours experience with the Kinesis keyboard, the participants still typed, on the average, slower (about 95% of their baseline speed) and with more errors than on the standard keyboard.

Smith and Cronin (1993) reported an experiment in which 25 participants used both a standard and a Kinesis keyboard to type normal and random text. Unlike the Kinesis, the standard keyboard did not have a built-in forearm-wrist support. All participants practiced with the Kinesis for seven hours the day before using it in the experiment. During the comparative part of the study, half the participants used the standard keyboard first and half used the Kinesis first. The researchers also collected electromyographic (EMG) measurements from 11 of the participants. The EMG results showed significantly lower muscle load for the hand and wrist, but not for the arm or shoulder muscles. Participants typed significantly faster with the standard keyboard, but there were no significant differences in errors. Participants stated they preferred the Kinesis keyboard for comfort, but preferred the standard keyboard for performance.

As part of her dissertation, Lopez (1993) had 36 female touch typists use four keyboard designs over a two-day period: a standard keyboard, a standard keyboard with a contoured wrist rest, the Kinesis keyboard and the Health Comfort Keyboard (HCK^{TM}). Twenty of the typists had carpal tunnel syndrome (CTS), and the remaining 16 typists made up a normal control group. On the first day, the participants became familiar with the HCK and Kinesis keyboards, performed two three-minute typing tests with the standard keyboard to establish a performance baseline, then practiced with the Comfort and Kinesis keyboards for 50 minutes each (with order of presentation randomized). Typists took three-minute typing tests at the 30-, 40-, and 50-minute points within each practice session. On the second day, the participants performed typing tasks with the four keyboards. After each typing session, Lopez made various physiologic measurements and participants completed various questionnaires, including ranking the keyboards from least to most preferred. Most of the physiologic measurements (nerve conduction velocity, vibrometry, hand strength, hand and distal forearm volume change) were significantly different between the participant groups (CTS and control), but the keyboard used had no effect on these measures. The type of keyboard used affected participants' wrist position when typing. The CTS group rated the Kinesis keyboard as the most comfortable for the upper arm, forearm and wrist. The control group rated the Kinesis keyboard as the most comfortable for the forearm and wrist, but felt the standard keyboard was more comfortable for the upper arm. (The average comfort ratings, however, for both the Kinesis and standard keyboards fell between the scale points of None and Minimal, indicating little discomfort with these keyboards.) Although the differences were not statistically significant, the fastest reported typing speeds were those for the standard keyboards. Typing speed with the Kinesis was the slowest of the four keyboards. The analysis of ranks showed that both groups significantly preferred the traditional keyboards to the Kinesis.

Gerard, Jones, Smith, Thomas, and Wang (1994) measured initial learning rates and EMG activity while six participants typed with the Kinesis and standard keyboards. Participants practiced with each keyboard for two hours (which included 24 five-minute trials with a one-minute break between each trial and a five-minute break every three trials). On a separate day, the participants used the keyboards again while the experimenters recorded EMG levels. The average typing speed for these participants on the standard keyboard was 73 wpm. After the 115 minutes of practice, the typists' speed with the Kinesis was 53 wpm, 72% of their speed with the standard. Their peak accuracy with the Kinesis was 97% of their accuracy with the standard. Gerard et al. did not report any statistical tests for differences in typing speed or accuracy. The EMG analysis showed that the muscle load (percent of maximum voluntary contraction) was consistently less with the Kinesis keyboard (an average difference of 2.0% across the four measured muscle groups, a statistically significant result).

The HCK Keyboard

The Health Comfort Keyboard is an adjustable (variable geometry) split keyboard. The only experimental data currently available for the HCK are those reported by Lopez (1993). (See the preceding section on the Kinesis keyboard for a description of this study.) For both the CTS and control groups, the HCK was the least comfortable keyboard for the upper arm, forearm, and wrist (with average comfort ratings for the HCK falling between the scale points of Minimal and Moderate). Although the differences were not statistically significant, the fastest reported typing speeds were those for the standard keyboards. Typing speed with the HCK was faster (but not statistically significantly faster) than that with the Kinesis. The analysis of ranks showed that both participant groups significantly preferred the traditional keyboards to the HCK.

Conclusions

The literature indicates two fairly clear effects of typing with split keyboards. First, typing speed is generally slower on split compared to standard keyboards. Second, EMG measurements typically show reduced muscle load in the wrist-forearm area for split relative to standard keyboards. Meta-analysis of the combined preference outcomes of the split keyboard experiments conducted from 1972 to 1993 has demonstrated that user preference across the studies is in favor of standard rather than split keyboards (Lewis, 1995b). Thus, it is difficult to interpret the typically lower EMG measurements for split keyboards. Part of the effect might be due to the difference in keyboard geometry resulting in lower static muscle contraction, but the effect might also be due in part to slower typing with split keyboards. Furthermore, the EMG evidence from Gerard et al. (1994) suggests that the EMG differences between split and standard keyboards, although consistent enough to produce statistical significance, might be too small to be of practical consequence (an average difference of about 2.0% of maximum voluntary contraction). The data from Lopez (1993) show a similar pattern for comfort ratings. Even though the Kinesis keyboard received better comfort ratings than the standard keyboard in Lopez's study, the average ratings for both the Kinesis and standard keyboards fell between rating points of None to Minimal discomfort. That alterations from standard keyboard geometry produce, at best, minimal impact on error rate, comfort, or fatigue, but typically cause an initial drop in typing speed, is consistent with preliminary results of a study of split keyboards recently conducted by the National Institute of Safety & Occupational Health (Naomi Swanson, personal communication, February 16, 1995).

Given certain environments and workstation configurations, split keyboards might enhance typing comfort, but with a probable reduction in typing speed for some unknown period of time. Rather than introducing a split keyboard into a workstation as an initial intervention for improving the comfort of a given typist, it might be simpler and more effective to enhance other environmental and physical features of the workstation. In any specific case of operator discomfort, an ergonomics specialist should evaluate the job and the total work setting.

54.5.2 Chord Keyboards

With traditional keyboards, typists press keys one at a time to create characters in sequence. Chord keyboards require the typist to press several keys simultaneously to input data (as in striking a chord on a piano). Because key combinations define the input, a chord keyboard requires fewer keys than a standard keyboard. For example, a five-key chord keyboard with binary switches could produce up to 31 (2^5 - 1) key combinations. A five-key chord keyboard with ternary (three-position) switches could produce up to 242 (3^5 - 1) key combinations. Two-handed chord keyboards allow for even more combinations. Some chord keyboards translate chords into phonemes and syllables; others translate the chords into single characters and numbers.

The most widely used chord keyboards are the Stenograph (patented in 1930) and the Palantype (patented in 1941). Typists who use these keyboards learn to associate chords with phonemes to produce syllables. This method of typing allows stenographers to develop very rapid input rates (fast enough to keep up with most talkers) with high speeds of around 250 to 300 words per minute (wpm), faster than a fast typist's speed of a little more than 100 wpm, but requires about three years for the acquisition of the skill (Beddoes and Hu, 1994). Beddoes and Hu reported work to develop a new chord stenograph keyboard (the minimum chord stenograph, or MCS), designed to be easier to learn. With the MCS, chords represent pairs of phonemes. Five people who learned the MCS typed, after 50 hours practice, from about 38 to 52 wpm. These typists needed from 2.5 to 11 hours to learn the MCS code. No data is yet available on how long typists must practice with the MCS to approach the speeds acquired by traditional stenographers.

Gopher and his colleagues have reported experiments with a two-handed chord keyboard designed for computer text entry (for example, Gopher, Hilsernath, and Raij, 1985; Gopher and Raij, 1988). The two halves of the keyboard were mirror images, connected in a lateral tilt arrangement. The chords for creating letters were the same on each half, and corresponded to the same fingers of each hand. Gopher and Raij conducted tests with people typing Hebrew text with a QWERTY-like keyboard (four participants), the chord keyboard with one hand (five participants), and the chord keyboard with two hands (six participants). They reported that participants learning the chord keyboard memorized the 23 character codes in about 30-45 minutes. Initial input rates for all conditions were about 7 to 8 wpm. After 25 hours of training, the reported typing rate for the chord keyboards was 32 wpm, while that for the QWERTY-like keyboard was 20 wpm. With extended practice (more than 25 hours), the participants using the two-handed keyboard produced faster keying than the other participants. One participant using the two-handed chord keyboard continued practicing for 60 hours and reached a rate of 59 wpm.

Most chord keyboards use two-position keys (resting or pressed). A number of researchers have recently studied a chord keyboard with three-position keys (resting, pushed away from the typist, or pulled toward the typist). The ternary chord keyboard (TCK) has eight keys, one for each finger. Callaghan (1991) studied the ease of activation of the 64 "simple" chords produced by the simultaneous movement of one finger from each hand. McMulkin and Kroemer (1994) had five people use a one-handed TCK to input 18 symbols (the ten digits and eight numeric functions) using 18 of the possible 24 two-finger chords. The participants needed an average of 34 minutes to learn the 18 chords with 97% accuracy. Their average initial typing rate was about 34.5 cpm (7 wpm). After 60 hours of practice, the average of each participant's fastest trial was 170 characters per minute (cpm), which roughly corresponds to 34 wpm. (The translation to wpm is imperfect because the stimuli were numbers rather than sentences and the participants typed using only 18 chords.) McMulkin and Kroemer reported that the function $\underline{CPM} = 34.5*(\underline{Trial}^{0.244})$ provided a good fit to the learning curve observed in their experiment.

In a similar study, Kroemer (1992) had two groups of people use two TCK prototypes (12 participants with TCK #2 and 10 with TCK #3). (Kroemer makes no mention of a TCK #1. TCK #3 was similar to TCK #2 for key type and placement, but had both keysets in one housing and provided fixed wrist rests for each hand.) The TCK #2 participants learned 58 of the 64 simple chords; the TCK #3 participants learned 59 of the simple chords. Participants needed from two to ten hours to memorize the chords. Experimental trials consisted of having participants type letters of the alphabet, numbers and punctuation. Initial typing rates with TCK #2 were about 30 cpm (6 wpm) and with TCK #3 were about 35 cpm (7 wpm). After 40 trials (about 10 hours), participants averaged about 75 cpm (15 wpm) with 97% accuracy. Despite the difference in number of chords learned (58 and 59 versus 18), this is comparable with the results reported by McMulkin and Kroemer. The function that McMulkin and Kroemer used to model their learning curve indicates that their typists produced an average of 85 cpm (17 wpm) at the 40th trial.

Lu and Aghazadeh (1992) reported a preliminary evaluation of the Infogrip Chordic Keyboard™ (ICK). The ICK is a two-handed binary chord keyboard consisting of a pair of 7-key keyboards, one for each hand. The fingers of a hand control four keys, and the thumb controls the remaining three. Four college students practiced typing 28 characters plus "space" and "return" for two hours with one hand. The participants needed an average of 108 minutes to learn the chords. The average initial typing rate was about 40 cpm (8 wpm). After two hours of typing the same sentence repeatedly, the average input rate was 49 cpm (10 wpm). This, too, is comparable to the results reported by McMulkin and Kroemer (1994), even though the keyboards and tasks were substantially different. Estimating from Kroemer (1992) and McMulkin and Kroemer, two hours of practice should correspond to about eight trials. The learning function provided by McMulkin and Kroemer indicates that their typists produced an average of 11.5 wpm at the eighth trial.

Conclusions

To draw reasonable conclusions from the experimental outcomes for chord keyboards, it would be valuable to have comparable data for the acquisition of skill with a standard keyboard, preferably collected using a large number of participants over a broad range of tasks, measuring speed and errors at least once per hour. Unfortunately, no such characterization seems to exist in the literature. The closest applicable data are those reported by Gopher and Raij (1988), but the sample size for their "standard" keyboard condition was only four participants typing Hebrew text. To compare typing acquisition gained with the sight method versus touch-typing, Book (1908, reported in Book, 1925) carefully studied the acquisition of typing skill by four participants (two participants per method). Problems with this study, however, are that the sample size was small, the minimum time period for analysis was the day rather than the hour, and the primary goal of the study was introspection about performance rather than quantification of performance. West (1956) evaluated the effectiveness of four types of practice as 345 airmen learned to type. After two hours of practice, their average typing rate ranged from 30 to 35 cpm (6 to 7 wpm). In a more recent study (Glencross and Bluhm, 1986), 241 participants learning to type with computer keyboards had an initial typing speed (after 90 minutes of training) of 35 cpm (7 wpm), increasing to about 70 cpm (14 wpm) after seven additional 45-minute practice sessions (a total amount of about 5 hours practice). This result for learning a standard keyboard is also comparable to the results reported by McMulkin and Kroemer (1994) for learning a chord keyboard. Estimating from Kroemer (1992) and McMulkin and Kroemer, five hours of practice should correspond to about 20 trials. The learning function provided by McMulkin and Kroemer indicates that their chording typists produced an average of 71 cpm (14 wpm) at the 20th trial. Certainly, there is a need for more research on both early and long-term typing with both chord and standard keyboards.

The information that is available indicates that beginning typists, both standard and chord, start with a typing speed of about 7 wpm. The learning curve reported by McMulkin and Kroemer (1994) seems to provide a reasonable characterization across the literature for the acquisition of chord typing (despite important differences between chord keyboards, number of chords, and material typed), with the exception of Gopher and Raij (1988). The one participant in Gopher and Raij's experiment who practiced for 60 hours attained a typing speed of 295 cpm (59 wpm). This was a particularly impressive performance given that the fastest participant in McMulkin and Kroemer (1994) achieved, during a comparable 60 hour practice period, a maximum speed of 186.3 cpm (37 wpm), only 63% of the maximum speed reported in Gopher and Raij. This variance in outcomes suggests that the human factors literature would benefit from an independent replication of Gopher and Raij, using both Hebrew and English text and using both binary and ternary chord keyboards.

The tasks in most chord keyboard evaluations have required participants to learn far fewer chords (in most cases, fewer than 30 chords) than keys typically present on a computer keyboard (about 90 to 100). Kroemer (1992) came the closest to a realistic assessment when requiring participants to learn 59 chords. Chord keyboard researchers typically do not assess chord retention or the use of chords for infrequently-used characters or functions. Because they allow such a rapid entry of data (given appropriate training), chord keyboards will continue to be the input device used by stenographers. Otherwise, chord keyboards are likely to see only limited application. For example, workers at the U. S. Post Office have used chord keyboards for mail sorting (Noyes, 1983a). (But see research by Richardson et al., 1988, showing a substantial advantage in training times for a calculator relative to a chord keyboard for entering zip codes. They did not report long-term performance data.)

As a final note on the topic, standard computer keyboards do require some simple chording with keys such as Shift, Alt, and Ctrl (for example, in the production of capital letters in lowercase mode). There are seven possible chording patterns with these three keys (2^3 - 1) which, combined with the remaining keys on a standard keyboard, allow the production of well over 500 characters and functions.

54.6 Conclusions

Although the modern standard keyboard reflects some design decisions initially made over 100 years ago, it also incorporates almost a century of subsequent research in typing and keying behavior. Proponents of the best-publicized alternatives to the standard keyboard (the Dvorak layout, split keyboards, and chord keyboards) have generally failed to provide convincing empirical cases for their wholesale replacement of the standard, although they might see reasonable application in certain special settings. A well-designed standard keyboard is an extremely effective data-entry device, and will probably remain a key component in human-computer interaction for the foreseeable future.

54.7 Acknowledgments and Trademarks

54.7.1 Acknowledgments

This chapter is a revision of the chapter published in the first edition of this handbook, which was itself a condensation and revision of the Office Systems Ergonomic Report, Vol. 5, Num. 2, March/April 1986, published by the Koffler Group, Santa Monica, California. The authors gratefully acknowledge permission to use this material.

54.7.2 Trademarks

The following are trademarks of the indicated companies: STR (Standard Telephon and Radio), Kinesis (Kinesis Corporation), Health Comfort and HCK (Health Care Keyboard Company, Inc.), and Infogrip Chordic Keyboard (Infogrip, Inc.).

54.8 References

Abernethy, C. N. (1984). Behavioural data in the design of ergonomic computer terminals and workstations -- a case study. *Behaviour and Information Technology, 3*, 399-403.

Abernethy, C. N., and Akagi, K. (1984). Experimental results do not support some ergonomic standards for computer video terminal design. *Computers & Standards, 3*, 133-141.

Akagi, K. (1992). A computer keyboard key feel study in performance and preference. In *Proceedings of the Human Factors Society 36th Annual Meeting* (pp. 523-527). Santa Monica, CA: Human Factors Society.

Alden, D. G., Daniels, R. W., and Kanarick, A. F. (1972). Keyboard design and operation: A review of the major issues. *Human Factors, 14*, 275-293.

Armstrong, T. J., Foulke, J. A., Martin, B. J., Gerson, J., and Rempel, D. M. (1994). Investigation of applied forces in alphanumeric keyboard work. *American Industrial Hygiene Association Journal, 55*, 30-35.

Barrat, J., and Krueger, H. (1994). Performance effects of reduced proprioceptive feedback on touch typists and casual users in a typing task. *Behaviour & Information Technology, 13*, 373-381.

Bayer, D. L., and Thompson, R. A. (1983). An experimental teleterminal -- the software strategy. *Bell System Technical Journal*, January 1983, 121-144.

Beddoes, M. P., and Hu, Z. (1994). A chord stenograph keyboard: A possible solution to the learning problem in stenography. *IEEE Transactions on Systems, Man, and Cybernetics, 24*, 953-960.

Book, W. F. (1925). *The psychology of skill with special reference to its acquisition in typewriting*. New York, NY: Gregg.

Boyle, J. M., and Lanzetta, T. M. (1984). The perception of display delays during single and multiple keystroking. In *Proceedings of the Human Factors Society 28th Annual Meeting* (pp. 263-266). Santa Monica, CA: Human Factors Society.

Brigham, F. R., and Clark, N. (1986). *Comparison of initial learning and acceptance: STR ergonomic keyboard vs. standard keyboard* (653-ITT-00894). Essex, England: ITT Europe.

Brown, S. L., and Goodman, D. (1983). A mathematical model for predicting speed of alphanumeric data entry on small keypads. In *Proceedings of the Human Factors Society 27th Annual Meeting* (pp. 506-510). Santa Monica, CA: Human Factors Society.

Brunner, H., and Richardson, R. M. (1984). Effects of keyboard design and typing skill on user keyboard preferences and throughput performance. In *Proceedings of the Human Factors Society 28th Annual Meeting* (pp. 267-271). Santa Monica, CA: Human Factors Society.

Buesen, J. (1984). Product development of an ergonomic keyboard. *Behaviour and Information Technology, 3*, 387-390.

Burke, T. M., Muto, W. H., and Gutmann, J. C. (1984). Effects of keyboard height on typist performance and preference. In *Proceedings of the Human Factors Society 28th Annual Meeting* (pp. 272-276). Santa Monica, CA: Human Factors Society.

Butterbaugh, L., and Rockwell, T. (1982). Evaluation of alternative alphanumeric keying logics. *Human Factors, 24*, 521-533.

Cakir, A., Hart, D. J., and Stewart, T. F. M. (1980). *Visual display terminals*. New York, NY: John Wiley.

Callaghan, T. F. (1991). Differences in execution times of chords on the ternary chord keyboard. In *Proceedings of the Human Factors Society* (pp. 857-861). Santa Monica, CA: Human Factors Society.

Cassingham, R. C. (1986). *The Dvorak keyboard*. Arcata, CA: Freelance Communications.

Clare, C. R. (1976). Human factors: A most important ingredient in keyboard designs. *EDN Magazine (Electrical Design News), 21(8)*, 99-102.

Cohen, K. M. (1982). Membrane keyboards and human performance. In *Proceedings of the Human Factors Society 26th Annual Meeting* (p. 424). Santa Monica, CA: Human Factors Society.

Coleman, M. F., Loring, B. A., and Wiklund, M. E. (1991). User performance on typing tasks involving reduced-size, touch screen keyboards. In *Proceedings - Society of Automotive Engineers* (pp. 543-549). Warrendale, PA: SAE.

Conrad, R., and Hull, A. J. (1968). The preferred layout for numerical data entry keysets. *Ergonomics, 11*, 165-173.

Cooper, W. E. (1983). *Cognitive aspects of skilled typewriting*. New York, NY: Springer-Verlag.

Davidson, L. (1966). A pushbutton telephone for alphanumeric input -- two extra buttons. *Datamation*, April 1966, 27-30.

Davis, S. (1973). Keyswitch and keyboard selection for computer peripherals. *Computer Design, 12(3)*, 67-79.

Deininger, R. L. (1960). Human factors engineering studies of the design and use of pushbutton telephone sets. *Bell Systems Technical Journal, 39*, 995-1012.

Detweiler, M. C., Schumacher, R. M., Jr., and Gattuso, N. L., Jr. (1990). Alphabetic input on a telephone keypad. In *Proceedings of the Human Factors Society 34th Annual Meeting* (pp. 212-216). Santa Monica, CA: Human Factors Society.

Dvorak, A. (1943). There is a better typewriter keyboard. *National Business Education Quarterly*, December 1943, XII-2, 51-58 and 66.

Emmons, W. H. (1984). A comparison of cursor-key arrangements (box versus cross) for VDUs. In E. Grandjean (Ed.), *Ergonomics and Health in Modern Offices* (pp. 214-219). London, UK: Taylor and Frances.

Emmons, W. H., and Hirsch, R. S. (1982). Thirty millimeter keyboards: How good are they? In *Proceedings of the Human Factors Society 26th Annual Meeting* (pp. 425-429). Santa Monica, CA: Human Factors Society.

Emmons, W. H., and Schonka, S. (1987). *A comparison of three cursor key arrangements: Dedicated cross, imbedded cross, and inverted-T* (Tech. Report HFC-66). Santa Teresa, CA: International Business Machines Corp.

Fitts, P. M. (1954). The information capacity of the human motor system in controlling the amplitude of movement. *Journal of Experimental Psychology, 47*, 381-391.

Francas, M., Brown, S., and Goodman, D. (1983). Alphabetic entry procedure with small keypads: Key layout does matter. In *Proceedings of the Human Factors Society 27th Annual Meeting* (pp. 187-190). Santa Monica, CA: Human Factors Society.

Foulds, R., Soede, M., van Balkom, H., and Boves, L. (1987). Lexical prediction techniques applied to reduce motor requirements for augmentative communication. In *RESNA 10th Annual Conference* (pp. 115-117). San Jose, CA: RESNA.

Galitz, W. O. (1966). *CRT keyboard human factors evaluation: Study II*. Univac, Systems Application Engineering, Roseville DOD, February 1966.

Gentner, D. R. (1983). Keystroke timing in transcription typing. In W. E. Cooper (Ed.), *Cognitive Aspects of Skilled Typewriting* (pp. 95-120). New York, NY: Springer-Verlag.

Gerard, M. J., Jones, S. K., Smith, L. A., Thomas, R. E., and Wang, T. (1994). An ergonomic evaluation of the Kinesis ergonomic computer keyboard. *Ergonomics, 37*, 1661-1668.

Getschow, C. O., Rosen, M. J., and Goodenough-Trepagnier, C. (1986). A systematic approach to design of a minimum distance alphabetical keyboard. In *RESNA 9th Annual Conference* (pp. 396-398). Minneapolis, MN: RESNA.

Glencross, D., and Bluhm, N. (1986). Intensive computer keyboard training programmes. *Applied Ergonomics*, 17, 191-194.

Goodman, D., Dickinson, J., and Francas, M. (1983). Human factors in keypad design. In *Proceedings of the Human Factors Society 27th Annual Meeting* (pp. 191-195). Santa Monica, CA: Human Factors Society.

Gopher, D., Hilsernath, H., and Raij, D. (1985). Steps in the development of a new data entry device based upon two hand chord keyboard. In *Proceedings of the Human Factors Society 29th Annual Meeting* (pp. 132-136). Santa Monica, CA: Human Factors Society.

Gopher, D., and Raij, D. (1988). Typing with a two-hand chord keyboard: Will the QWERTY become obselete? *IEEE Transactions on Systems, Man, and Cybernetics, 18*, 601-609.

Hagelbarger, W., and Thompson, R. A. (1983). Experiments in teleterminal design. *IEEE Spectrum, 20(10)*, 40-45.

Hiraga, Y., Ono, Y., and Yamada, H. (1980). *An analysis of the standard English keyboard* (Tech. Report 80-11). Department of Information Science,

Faculty of Science, University of Tokyo, 7-3-1 Hongo, Bunkyoku Tokyo, 113 Japan.

Hirsch, R. S. (1970). Effects of standard versus alphabetical keyboard formats on typing performance. *Journal of Applied Psychology, 54*, 484-490.

Hufford, L. E., and Coburn, R. (1961). *Operator performance on miniaturized decimal entry keysets* (NEL/Report 1083). San Diego, CA: US Naval Electronics Laboratory.

Human Factors Society. (1988). *American national standard for human factors engineering of visual display terminal workstations* (ANSI/HFS Standard No. 100-1988). Santa Monica, CA: Author.

Jahns, D. W., Litewka, J., Lunde, S. A., Farrand, W. P., and Hargreaves, W. R. (1991). Learning curve and performance analysis for the Kinesis™ ergonomic keyboard -- a pilot study. Presented as a poster at the HFS 35th Annual Meeting (San Francisco, CA, September 2-6, 1991). Copies available from Kinesis.

Kan, Z., Sumei, G., and Huiling, Z. (1993). Toward a cognitive ergonomics evalution system of typing Chinese characters into computers. In M. J. Smith and G. Salvendy (Eds.), *Human-Computer Interaction: Applications and Case Studies* (pp. 380-385). Amsterdam, Netherlands: Elsevier.

Kennedy, P. J., and Lewis, J. R. (1985). A method of analyzing personal computer use in an application environment. In *Proceedings of the Human Factors Society 29th Annual Meeting* (pp. 1057-1060). Santa Monica, CA: Human Factors Society.

Kinkead, R. (1975). Typing speed, keying rates, and optimal keyboard layouts. In *Proceedings of the Human Factors Society 19th Annual Meeting* (pp. 159-161). Santa Monica, CA: Human Factors Society.

Kinkead, R. D., and Gonzalez, B. K. (1969). *Human factors design recommendations for touch-operated keyboards -- final report* (Document 12091-FR). Minneapolis, MN: Honeywell, Inc.

Kreifeldt, J. G., Levine, S. L., and Iyengar, C. (1989). Reduced keyboard designs using disambiguation. In *Proceedings of the Human Factors Society 33rd Annual Meeting* (pp. 441-444). Santa Monica, CA: Human Factors Society.

Kroemer, K. H. E. (1965). Vergleich einer normalen Schreibmaschinen-Tastatur mit einer "K-Tastatur" (Comparison of a keyboard of a normal typewriter with a "K-Keyboard"). *Internationale Zeitschrift angewandt Physiologie, 20*, 453-464.

Kroemer, K. H. E. (1972). Human engineering the keyboard. *Human Factors, 14*, 51-63.

Kroemer, K. H. E. (1992). Use and research issues of a new computer keyboard. In *Proceedings of the Human Factors Society* (pp. 272-275). Santa Monica, CA: Human Factors Society.

Lewis, J. R. (1984). Association of visually coded functions with an alternate key. In *Proceedings of the Human Factors Society 28th Annual Meeting* (pp. 973-977). Santa Monica, CA: Human Factors Society.

Lewis, J. R. (1992). *Typing-key layouts for single-finger or stylus input: Initial user preference and performance* (Tech. Report 54.729). Boca Raton, FL: International Business Machines Corp.

Lewis, J. R. (1994). *A critical literature review of human factors studies of split keyboards from 1926 to 1993* (Tech. Report 54.853). Boca Raton, FL: International Business Machines Corp.

Lewis, J. R. (1995a). *The effects of standard typing experience and split keyboard experience on split keyboard experimental outcomes: Evidence from the split keyboard literature* (Tech. Report 54.898). Boca Raton, FL: International Business Machines Corp.

Lewis, J. R. (1995b). *Meta-analysis of preference for split versus standard keyboards: Findings from 1972 to 1993* (Tech. Report 54.899). Boca Raton, FL: International Business Machines Corp.

Lewis, J. R., Kennedy, P. J., and LaLomia, M. J. (1992). *Improved typing-key layouts for single-finger or stylus input* (Tech. Report 54.692). Boca Raton, FL: International Business Machines Corp.

Lin, C. C., Lee, T. Z., and Chou, F. S. (1993). Intelligent keyboard layout process. In M. J. Smith and G. Salvendy (Eds.), *Human-Computer Interaction: Software and Hardware Interfaces* (pp. 1070-1074). Amsterdam, Netherlands: Elsevier.

Long, J. (1976). Effects of delayed irregular feedback on unskilled and skilled keying performance. *Ergonomics, 19*, 183-202.

Lopez, M. S. (1993). *An ergonomic evaluation of the design and performance of four keyboard models and their relevance to carpal tunnel syndrome*. Unpublished doctoral dissertation, Texas A&M University, College Station, TX.

Loricchio, D. (1992b). Key force and typing performance. In *Proceedings of the Human Factors Society 36th Annual Meeting* (pp. 281-282). Santa Monica, CA: Human Factors Society.

Loricchio, D. F., and Kennedy, P. J. (1987). Keyspace and user productivity. In *Abridged Proceedings of Poster Sessions of the Third International Conference on Human-Computer Interaction* (p. 48). New York, NY: Elsevier.

Loricchio, D. F., and Lewis, J. R. (1991). User assessment of standard and reduced-size numeric keypads. In *Proceedings of the Human Factors Society 35th Annual Meeting* (pp. 251-252). Santa Monica, CA: Human Factors Society.

Lu, H., and Aghazadeh, F. (1992). Infogrip Chordic Keyboard evaluation. In *Proceedings of the Human Factors Society 36th Annual Meeting* (pp. 268-271). Santa Monica, CA: Human Factors Society.

Lutz, M. C., and Chapanis, A. (1955). Expected locations of digits and letters on ten-button keysets. *Journal of Applied Psychology, 39*, 314-317.

MacKenzie, I. S., Nonnecke, R. B., McQueen, C., Riddersma, S., and Meltz, M. (1994). A comparison of three methods of character entry on pen-based computers. In *Proceedings of the Human Factors and Ergonomics Society 38th Annual Meeting* (pp. 330-334). Santa Monica, CA: Human Factors and Ergonomics Society.

Magyar, R. L. (1982). Effects of auditory feedback on typing performance for the Domino-1 electronic typewriter. Internal IBM report.

Magyar, R. L. (1984). An evaluation of size and placement of the backspace and enter keys in keyboard design. Paper presented at IBM internal conference.

Magyar, R. L (1985). Effects of curved, flat and stepped keybutton configurations on keyboard preference and throughput performance. Internal IBM report.

Magyar, R. L (1986a). *A comparison of keyboard numeric entry using top-row keys or a 10-key number pad* (Tech. Memorandum 08.173). Lexington, KY: International Business Machines Corp.

Magyar, R. L. (1986b). *Comparison of text-entry performance on keyboards employing a horizontal or vertical enter key* (Tech. Report 08.183). Lexington, KY: International Business Machines Corporation.

Magyar, R. L. (1986c). *Comparison of user performance and preference for cursor keypad configuration and numeric keypad position* (Tech. Memorandum 08.162). Lexington, KY: International Business Machines Corp.

Magyar, R. L. (1986d). *Tactile feedback and keyboard design* (Tech. Memorandum 08.164). Lexington, KY: International Business Machines Corp.

Magyar, R. L., and Robertson, P. (1986). *Comparison of typists' performance and preference for the U.S. domestic and worldtrade "G" keyboard* (Tech. Report 08.243). Lexington, KY: International Business Machines Corp.

Marics, M. A. (1990). How do you enter "D' Anzi-Quist" using a telephone keypad? In *Proceedings of the Human Factors Society 34th Annual Meeting* (pp. 208-211). Santa Monica, CA: Human Factors Society.

Marmaras, N., and Lyritzis, K. (1993). Design of an alternative keyboard layout for the Greek language. *International Journal of Human-Computer Interaction, 5*, 289-310.

Matias, E., MacKenzie, I. S., and Buxton, W. (1993). Half-QWERTY: A one-handed keyboard facilitating skill transfer from QWERTY. In *Conf. Proc. on Human Factors in Computing Systems -- CHI '93* (pp. 88-94). New York, NY: Association for Computing Machinery.

McMulkin, M. L., and Kroemer, K. H. E. (1994). Usability of a one-hand ternary chord keyboard. *Applied Ergonomics, 25*, 177-181.

Michaels, S. E. (1971). Qwerty versus alphabetic keyboards as a function of typing skill. *Human Factors, 13*, 419-426.

Miller, I., and Suther, T. W. (1981). Preferred height and angle settings of CRT and keyboard for a display station input task. In *Proceedings of the Human Factors Society 25th Annual Meeting* (pp. 492-496). Santa Monica, CA: Human Factors Society.

Miller, I., and Suther, T. W. (1983). Display station anthropometrics: Preferred height and angle settings of CRT and keyboard. *Human Factors, 25*, 401-408.

Minneman, S. L. (1986). Keyboard optimization technique to improve output rate of disabled individuals. In *RESNA 9th Annual Conference* (pp. 402-404). Minneapolis, MN: RESNA.

Montgomery, E. B. (1982). Bringing manual input into the 20th century: New keyboard concepts. *Computer*, March 1982, 11-18.

Monty, R. W., Snyder, H. L., and Birdwell, G. G. (1983). Keyboard design: An investigation of user preference and performance. In *Proceedings of the Human Factors Society 27th Annual Meeting* (pp. 201-205). Santa Monica, CA: Human Factors Society.

Najjar, L. J., Stanton, B. C., and Bowen, C. D. (1988). *Keyboard heights and slopes for standing typists* (Tech. Report 85-0081). Rockville, MD: International Business Machines Corp.

Nakaseko, M., Grandjean, E., Hunting, W., and Gierer, R. (1985). Studies on ergonomically designed alphanumeric keyboards. *Human Factors, 27*, 175-187.

Nakatani, L. H., and O'Connor, K. D. (1980). Speech feedback for touch-keying. *Ergonomics, 23*, 643-654.

Noel, R. W., and McDonald, J. E. (1989). Automating the search for good designs: About the use of simulated annealing and user models. In *Proceedings of Interface 89* (pp. 241-245). Santa Monica, CA: Human Factors Society.

Norman, D. A., and Fisher, D. (1982). Why alphabetic keyboards are not easy to use: Keyboard layout doesn't much matter. *Human Factors, 24*, 509-519.

Noyes, J. (1983a). Chord keyboards. *Applied Ergonomics, 14*, 55-59.

Noyes, J. (1983b). The QWERTY keyboard: A review. *International Journal of Man-Machine Studies, 18*, 265-281.

Paci, A. M., and Gabbrielli, L. (1984). Some experiences in the field of design of VDU work stations. In E. Grandjean (Ed.), *Ergonomics and Health in Modern Offices* (pp. 391-399). Philadelphia, PA: Taylor & Francis.

Paul, F., Sarlanis, K., and Buckley, E. P. (1985). A human factors comparison of two data entry keyboards. In *Institute of Electrical and Electronics Engineers Symposium on Human Factors in Electronics*.

Pollard, D., and Cooper, M. B. (1979). The effect of feedback on keying performance. *Applied Ergonomics, 10*, 194-200.

Potosnak, K. M. (1990). Keys and keyboards. In M. Helander (Ed.), *Handbook of Human-Computer Interaction* (pp. 475-494). Amsterdam: North-Holland.

Quill, L. L., and Biers, D. W. (1993). On-screen keyboards: Which arrangements should be used? In *Proceedings of the Human Factors and Ergonomics Society 37th Annual Meeting* (pp. 1142-1146). Santa Monica, CA: Human Factors and Ergonomics Society.

Rempel, D., Gerson, J., Armstrong, T., Foulke, J., and Martin, B. (1991). Fingertip forces while using three different keyboards. In *Proceedings of the Human Factors Society 35th Annual Meeting* (pp. 253-255). Santa Monica, CA: Human Factors Society.

Richardson, R. M., Telson, R. U., Koch, C. G., and Chrysler, S. T. (1987). Evaluation of conventional, serial, and chord keyboard options for mail encoding. In *Proceedings of the Human Factors Society 31st Annual Meeting* (pp. 911-915). Santa Monica, CA: Human Factors Society.

Roe, C. J., Muto, W. H., and Blake, T. (1984). Feedback and key discrimination on membrane keypads. In *Proceedings of the Human Factors Society 28th Annual Meeting* (pp. 277-281). Santa Monica, CA: Human Factors Society.

Rosch, W. L. (1984). Keyboard ergonomics for IBMs. *PC Magazine*, 3(19), 110-122.

Rosinski, R. R., Chiesi, H., and Debons, A. (1980). Effects of amount of visual feedback on typing performance. In *Proceedings of the Human Factors Society 24th Annual Meeting* (pp. 195-199). Santa Monica, CA: Human Factors Society.

Scales, E. M., and Chapanis, A. (1954). The effect on performance of tilting the toll-operator's keyset. *Journal of Applied Psychology, 38*, 452-456.

Schuck, M. M. (1994). The use of auditory feedback in the design of touch-input devices. *Applied Ergonomics, 25*, 59-62.

Schumacher, Jr., R. M., Hardzinski, M. L., and Schwartz, A. L. (1995). Increasing the usability of interactive voice response systems: Research and guidelines for phone-based interfaces. *Human Factors, 37*, 251-264.

Smith, W. J. and Cronin, D. T. (1993). Ergonomic test of the Kinesis keyboard. In *Proceedings of the Human Factors and Ergonomics Society 37th Annual Meeting* (pp. 318-322). Santa Monica, CA: Human Factors and Ergonomics Society.

Strong, E. P. (1956). *A comparative experiment in simplified keyboard retraining and standard keyboard supplementary training*. Washington, DC: General Services Administration.

Suther, T. W., and McTyre, J. H. (1982). Effect on operator performance at thin profile keyboard slopes of 5, 10, 15, and 25 degrees. In *Proceedings of the Human Factors Society 26th Annual Meeting* (pp. 430-434). Santa Monica, CA: Human Factors Society.

Texas Instruments, Inc. (1983). *VPI keyboard study*. Dallas, TX: Design Development Center.

U.S. Navy Department (1944a). *A practical experiment in Simplified Keyboard retraining: A report on the retraining of fourteen Standard Keyboard typists on the Simplified Keyboard*. Training Section, Departmental Services, Division of Shore Establishments and Civilian Personnel, Navy Department, Washington, DC, July 1944.

U.S. Navy Department (1944b). *A comparison of typist improvement from training on the Standard Keyboard and retraining on the Simplified Keyboard: A supplement to 'A practical experiment in Simplified Keyboard retraining'.* Training Section, Departmental Services, Division of Shore Establishments and Civilian Personnel, Navy Department, Washington, DC, October 1944.

Walker, H. W. (1989). *Designing a usable keyboard: Five commonly asked questions (and answers)* (Tech. Memorandum 51-0821). Austin, TX: International Business Machines Corp.

Welford, A. T. (1976). *Skilled performance.* Glenview, CA: Scott, Foresman, and Co.

West, L. J. (1956). An experimental comparison of nonsense, word, and sentence materials in early typing training. *Journal of Educational Psychology, 47,* 481-489.

Wiklund, M. E., Dumas, J. S., and Hoffman, L. R. (1987). Optimizing a portable terminal keyboard for combined one-handed and two-handed use. In *Proceedings of the Human Factors Society 31st Annual Meeting* (pp. 585-589). Santa Monica, CA: Human Factors Society.

Williges, R. C., and Williges, B. H. (1981). Univariate and multivariate evaluation of computer-based data entry. In *Proceedings of the Human Factors Society 25th Annual Meeting* (pp. 741-745). Santa Monica, CA: Human Factors Society.

Williges, R. C., and Williges, B. H. (1982). Modeling the human operator in computer-based data entry. *Human Factors, 24,* 285-299.

Yamada, H. (1980). *A historical study of typewriters and typing methods: From the position of planning Japanese parallels* (Tech. Report 80-05). Department of Information Science, Faculty of Science, University of Tokyo, 7-3-1 Hongo, Bunkyoku Tokyo, 113 Japan.

Zipp, P., Haider, E., Halpern, N., and Rohmert, W. (1983). Keyboard design through physiological strain measurements. *Applied Ergonomics, 14,* 117-122.

Handbook of Human-Computer Interaction
Second, completely revised edition
M. Helander, T.K. Landauer, P. Prabhu (eds.)

Chapter 55

Pointing Devices

Joel S. Greenstein
Clemson University
Clemson, South Carolina, USA

55.1 Introduction

This chapter focuses upon input devices which designate locations and movements in two-dimensional space, including touch screen devices, light pens, graphic tablets, mice, trackballs, and joysticks. These devices are all reasonably well suited to pointing or selection among items on a display as well as to the input of graphical information. They are not well suited to alphanumeric data entry, for which keys and keyboards, addressed in Chapter 54 of this handbook, remain the devices of choice. Human factors considerations affecting the design and selection of the different pointing devices will be considered first. Compara-

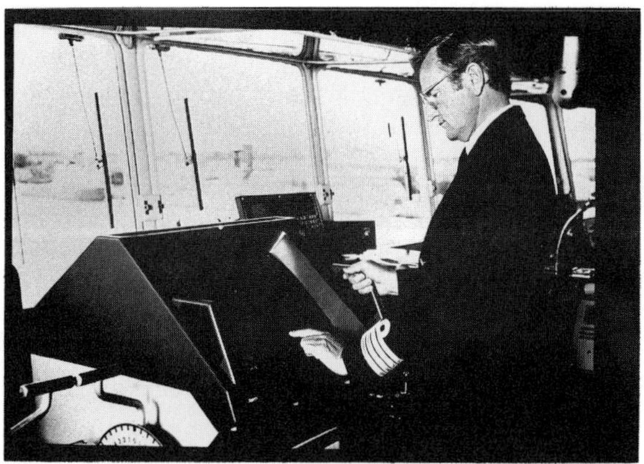

Figure 1. A capacitive touch screen. *(Courtesy of MicroTouch Systems, Inc., Methuen, MA.)*

tive human performance and preference data are then presented to aid in the selection of an appropriate device for a particular application. While brief descriptions of the technologies underlying each device type are provided in this chapter, Sherr (1988) addresses input device technologies in much greater detail.

55.2 Touch Screens

55.2.1 Technologies

A touch screen device produces an input signal in response to a touch or movement of the finger on the display. Figure 1 depicts the use of a touch screen in a ship navigation radar system. There are two fundamental principles of touch screen operation; either an overlay is contacted or signals projected over the screen are interrupted.

In the first category are resistive, capacitive, piezo-electric, and cross-wire devices. The resistive touch screen has two layers, one resistive and one conductive. When pressure is applied, the two surfaces touch and a circuit is completed. The capacitive touch screen has a conductive film deposited on the back of a glass overlay. The body's capacitance causes an electrical signal to be generated when an individual touches the overlay. The piezo-electric touch screen employs a glass overlay with a force transducer at each corner of the overlay. When a touch is applied at a particular location on the overlay, the forces transmitted to the transducers are used to determine the initial location of the touch. Movement of the finger following the initial touch is not reliably detected with this technology. The cross-wire device uses a grid of horizontal and vertical wires set in transparent sheets placed on the display. A voltage is applied to either the vertical or horizontal wires and a signal is produced when a touch forces a vertical and horizontal wire together at their intersecion.

Surface acoustic wave and infrared touch screens are activated when the finger interrupts a signal. In a surface acoustic wave touch screen, a glass plate is placed over the screen and ultrasonic waves are generated on the glass by transducers placed along the edges. When a waveform is interrupted, the reflected horizontal and vertical waves are detected by the transducers. On an infrared touch screen, light emitting diodes are paired with light detectors and placed along opposite edges of the display. When the user touches a finger to the screen, light beams are interrupted.

Touch Resolution

Resistive screens tend to have the highest touch resolution, with from 1000 x 1000 to 4000 x 4000 discrete touch points. The resolution of capacitive screens is relatively high, while that of surface acoustic wave screens is generally lower. Infrared screens may have as few as 25 x 40 touch points due to limitations on the number of light emitters and detectors that can be placed around the screen (Logan, 1985). For applications requiring high touch resolution, infrared devices may be unsuitable. Even if high touch resolution is not required, the greater the number of touch points, the easier it is to map them to targets on the display; screen design may thus become more flexible. If a target is not placed directly under a touch point, errors in selection may occur (Beringer and Peterson, 1985).

Parallax

Parallax occurs when the touch surface or detectors are separated from the targets. For all touch screen technologies, the touch surface will always be at least slightly above the target due to the glass surface of the display. An overlay separates the finger and the target even more. This problem can be alleviated by requiring the user to be directly in front of the target and to place the finger perpendicular to the screen. Unfortunately, such a requirement somewhat offsets the advantage of the naturalness of the required input, especially for targets at the sides of the display.

When infrared touch screens are used with curved CRT displays, the parallax problem is more severe. Because light beams travel in a straight line, the beams must be positioned to pass above the curved display surface. When the user touches the screen, the beam may be broken at a point that is not directly above the

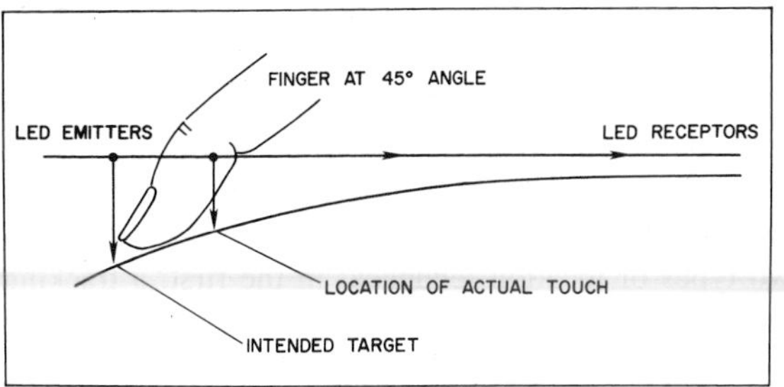

Figure 2. Parallax due to the removal of the infrared light beams from the display surface. *(From Logan, 1985. Copyright 1985, by Hearst Business Communications, Inc. and reproduced by permission.)*

target, especially if the touch is at the edges of the CRT (see Figure 2).

Durability

Touch screen durability is primarily a problem in dirty environments and in cases of continual use. The resistive touch screen uses a plastic sheet that may be scratched fairly readily. The glass surface on a surface acoustic wave touch screen may also be scratched; besides potentially obscuring the screen, dirt or scratches may falsely activate this device. Capacitive piezo-electric, and infrared screens tend to be resistant to damage.

Optical Clarity

Optical clarity is of primary importance when an individual uses a touch screen for extended periods of time, since a decrease in display quality can lead to operator strain and fatigue. Infrared touch screens best preserve optical clarity because there is no overlay to obscure the display (Schulze and Snyder, 1983). Surface acoustic wave touch screens have a clear glass overlay, and thus they may not reduce display clarity as much as resistive, capacitive, and cross-wire devices. The overlays on the latter devices tend to reduce the amount of light transmitted from the display.

Environmental Limitations.

Dirt and static electricity (which attracts dust) can be a problem for some touch screens. The surface acoustic wave device may be activated by dirt or scratches on the glass; infrared beams can also be broken by dirt or smoke. Since the capacitive screen uses the capacitance of the human body, it typically must be activated by a finger or a conductive stylus; therefore, "clean room" and other environments in which users wear gloves dictate against the use of the capacitive touch screen, although some designs are available that enable the use of thin latex gloves. In general, targets will probably not become obscured with any of the devices through regular use. Fingerprints may become apparent on the display surface, but the screen or overlays can be easily cleaned.

Ease of Use

Perhaps the most important yet least well-defined touch screen characteristic is ease of learning and operation. Although touch screens require a natural pointing gesture, and thus require minimal training in the basic concept, they may respond in unexpected ways. For example, because the LED beams for an infrared device are above the screen, the user does not need to touch the display to activate the device; if the user does not understand this, there may be problems with inadvertent activations and incorrect target selections due to parallax. Another factor is the pressure required to activate an overlay. If too much pressure is required, activation may take longer and lead to user discomfort. Finally, touch screens with low resolution may be frustrating if touch points are not centered over the targets.

Empirical Results

Schulze and Snyder (1983) compared five touch screens: acoustic, capacitive, resistive, cross-wire, and infrared. The infrared device permitted the highest display resolution because there was no overlay. The capacitive device resulted in the least display noise in terms of display luminance variation and CRT raster modulation. On the basis of errors and total time to complete three tasks, the authors reported that the infrared and cross-wire devices provided the best performance. Overall, the cross-wire device was preferred by the participants.

55.2.2 Implementation Issues

Touch Key Design

Valk (1985) compared the 10 touch screen "buttons" or keys shown in Figure 3 when identifying design guidelines for an industrial process control application. Keys with adjacent color-coded squares with a label in each square (i.e., Keys 1 and 10) led to more confusion than those with both labels in one square. Keys that indicated motions incompatible with the necessary direct press required (such as the sliding switch in Key 5)

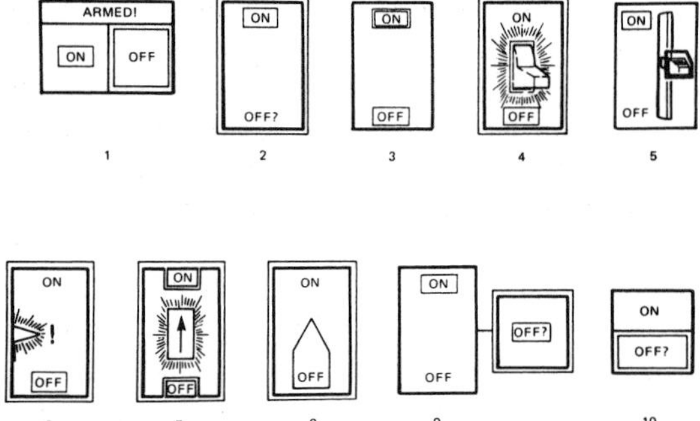

Figure 3. The 10 touch screen key designs tested by Valk (1985). *(From Proceedings of the Human Factors Society 29th Annual Meeting, 1985, Vol. 1, p. 131. Copyright (1985), by the Human Factors and Ergonomics Society, Inc. and reproduced by permission.)*

also led to a decrease in performance. Keys that could be activated in any area rather than a single part tended to decrease confusion, as did the presence of recognizable designs (such as the light switch and pointer in Keys 4 and 8). Participants also tended to touch the on and off labels in each key even if a press was permitted elsewhere. Key 10 led to the most errors.

Key Size

Hall, Cunningham, Roache, and Cox (1988) investigated the effects of a number of factors on the accuracy of users' target selections with a piezo-electric touch screen. Participants used the system at both seated and standing workstations. For seated users, analysis showed no further significant benefits to accuracy of increasing target size once the target width reached 28 mm (at which the likelihood of touching within this width was 99.6%) and the target height reached 22 mm (the likelihood of touching within this target height was 99.5%), or when the target width and height both reached 26 mm (the likelihood of touching within this target was 99.2%). For standing users, somewhat larger target sizes were required to reach equivalent accuracy levels. There were no further significant benefits to accuracy once the target width reached 30 mm (likelihood of touching within this width: 99.7%) and the target height reached 32 mm (likelihood of touching within this height: 99.5%), or when the target width and height both reached 30 mm (likelihood of touching within this target: 99.0%).

Feedback and Acceptance of Input

Feedback of both the current cursor location and the correctness of a user's actions can be provided. Software can also be designed to act on only certain portions of the input stream of position coordinates generated by the user's touch. Weiman, Beaton, Knox, and Glasser (1985) studied both of these design parameters using an infrared touch screen. They provided two types of location feedback: in the first, a tracking cursor echoed finger movement in the active touch area, while the second generated the tracking cursor as well as highlighting the key containing the cursor. Two touch input sampling strategies designed to reduce the selection error rate were also tested. The first, "last touch," accepted the touch coordinates registered as the user's finger exited the active touch area, rather than those registered when the finger initially entered the area. The second algorithm, "last key," accepted coordinates from the last valid key site touched prior to the finger's exit from the active touch area; this algorithm tended to ignore inadvertent movements beyond key boundaries that occurred as the finger was removed from the display. The results showed that either type of feedback plus the last-touch algorithm reduced selection error rates relative to a baseline group with neither of these modifications, and feedback plus the last-key algorithm reduced the error rate even more.

Beringer and Peterson (1985) studied response biases inherent in touch screen use and the effects of feedback and software compensation on these errors. The top of the screen on which targets were displayed was progressively tilted away from the participants to achieve screen angles to line of sight from 90 to 45 deg. Results indicated that users tended to touch slightly below the target, especially for targets near the top of the display and for the larger amounts of screen tilt. The authors state that these errors were probably due to parallax and a need to extend the arm farther for the top targets.

In a second experiment, Beringer and Peterson tested two methods of decreasing this response bias: providing feedback to train the users and incorporating software to compensate for the bias. The task was to touch a square target on a blank field. User training was accomplished by providing feedback in the form of a square around the touch point. Software models based on the performance of individual users were developed to provide the automatic response bias compensation. Both methods reduced the response errors.

Beringer (1989) also investigated the effect of several touch sampling strategies on selection accuracy with small (3.2 mm x 3.2 mm square) targets. Performance with resistive and infrared touch screens was investigated. Five touch sampling strategies were considered: use of the first point in the input stream;

the last point; a lagged sampling strategy in which the first several samples in the input stream were disregarded and contact position was registered after this settling period; a back sampling strategy in which the last several samples in the input stream were disregarded and contact position was registered prior to this withdrawal period; and a windowing strategy in which the contact point was based on the samples falling within a window beginning and ending at specified proportions of the way through the entire input stream. The results showed that the magnitude of the selection error (the straight-line distance between the target and the calculated touch panel contact point) was minimized for the resistive screen using back sampling in which the sample taken 50 ms prior to release determined the "intended" contact point. Error magnitude for the infrared screen was minimized using windowing and basing the contact point on the samples falling within a window beginning 43% of the way through the input stream and ending 75% through the stream.

Potter, Weldon, and Shneiderman (1988) studied the effects of three touch screen input strategies on the selection of relatively small, densely packed items. The first strategy, "land-on," used only the position of the first touch on the screen for selection. If a selectable item was under the initial touch, then it was selected; otherwise nothing was selected. All further contact with the screen was ignored until the finger was removed. The second strategy, "first-contact," was not limited to the initial touch on the screen. All position data generated by the finger on the screen was analyzed until the finger first contacted a selectable item. The third strategy, "take-off," analyzed position data generated by the finger until the finger was removed from the screen. Because selection was deferred until finger removal, users could adjust their finger location following their initial touch. To assist adjustment in this strategy, feedback was provided by placing the cursor indicating the selected coordinates about 1/2 inch (12.7 mm) above the finger's location. The take-off strategy also included two additional enhancements: the display cursor was stabilized to enable users to better keep the cursor in one place while deciding if its placement was appropriate and selectable items were highlighted when the cursor appeared on top of them. Users selected two-letter postal service abbreviations of the fifty U.S. states from a 10-row by 5-column array. Each abbreviation was approximately 1/4 in x 1/4 in (6.4 mm x 6.4 mm) in size. The results showed that the first-contact strategy was significantly faster than the take-off strategy. However, there were significantly fewer errors with the take-off strategy than with either the land-on or the first-contact strategies. The take-off strategy also received a significantly higher satisfaction rating from subjects than the land-on strategy. These results suggest that in applications that require selection of relatively small, densely packed items, the take-off strategy can be used to reduce error rates, albeit with some increase in selection times. Where speed is a more important consideration than errors and targets are predefined, the first-contact strategy seems appropriate. (If the user is selecting a location on the screen to create an item at that location (for example, a starting or ending point for a line), there is no predefined target to contact and the first-contact strategy cannot be applied.)

Sears and Shneiderman (1991) investigated the ability of users to select small targets using touch screens. A capacitive touch screen was used with and without stabilization software. This software filtered and smoothed the user's touch inputs to enhance the user's ability to stabilize the cursor's location on the display. The take-off strategy was used to input target selections. Four rectangular target sizes were tested: 1, 4, 16, and 32 pixels per side (0.4 x 0.6, 1.7 x 2.2, 6.9 x 9.0, and 13.8 x 17.9 mm, respectively). The four pixel per side target had approximately one-quarter the area of a character of text. Users preferred the stabilized touch screen over the non-stabilized screen. There were no significant differences in performance with the two touch screens for the three larger target sizes. However, the stabilized touch screen resulted in significantly faster selections with significantly fewer errors for the single pixel target. The mean selection time and number of selection errors with the stabilized touch screen increased from 1.9 s and 0.01 errors/target for the 16 pixel per side target to 4.1 s and 0.15 errors/target for the 4 pixel per side target and to 11.4 s and 0.73 errors/target for the 1 pixel per side target. Thus, appropriate touch-entry and cursor stabilization strategies can enable the selection of even very small targets with a touch screen, although selection times and error rates can be expected to increase sharply as the targets become very small.

55.2.3 Advantages and Disadvantages of Touch Screens

The most obvious advantage of touch screen devices is that the input device is also the output device. Thus, they require no additional space and they enable direct eye-hand coordination and a direct relationship be-

Figure 4. A light pen. *(Courtesy of FTG Data Systems, Stanton, CA.)*

tween the user's input and the displayed output. A second advantage is that all valid inputs are displayed on the screen; thus, no memorization of commands is required. Since the only input typically required by a touch screen device is a natural pointing gesture, training is minimized, as is the need for operator selection procedures. Individuals can become quite skilled at target selection in a short period of time. A particular advantage of capacitive, piezo-electric, and infrared touch screens is that they have no moving parts. These technologies have proven to be very durable in public access applications.

Touch screens have several disadvantages. Because the output surface is also the input medium, parallax effects are introduced. Also, the user must sit within arm's reach of the display. These characteristics of touch screens may constrain both workplace design and operator mobility. The need to repeatedly lift a hand to the display may also produce arm fatigue. Additionally, the user's finger or arm may block the screen. Another disadvantage is that the size of the user's finger tends to limit target resolution. The take-off touch entry strategy or a stylus can be used to address this problem, but the pointing gesture then becomes somewhat less natural. Finally, since the touch screen must be fitted onto a display, there can be a problem with retrofit if the display has already been purchased.

55.2.4 Applications

Touch screen devices are best used to work with data already displayed on the screen; they are inefficient for inputting new graphic information or for freehand drawing. Touch screen devices are quite useful in menu selection tasks. Although slower, touch screen keyboards can be used for limited alphanumeric data entry when the use of a conventional keyboard is not practical (Gould, Greene, Boies, Meluson, and Rasamny, 1990; Plaisant and Sears, 1992; Sears, 1991; Sears, Revis, Swatski, Crittenden, and Shneiderman, 1993). Touch screens are useful in applications where it is time consuming or dangerous to divert attention from the display, such as air traffic control tasks (Gaertner and Holzhausen, 1980; Stammers and Bird, 1980), and tactical display workstations (Davis and Badger, 1982). Touch screens are also beneficial in other high workload or high stress situations where the possible inputs are limited and well defined, as in airplane cockpits for navigation purposes (Beringer, 1979). Finally, touch screens are effective when it is impractical to provide training in the use of a system; touch screen devices have been used effectively, for example, to provide information in shopping malls, banks, and hotels.

55.3 Light Pens

55.3.1 Technologies

The light pen, depicted in Figure 4, is a stylus that generates position information when it is pointed at the display screen. The light pen contains a light detector or photocell. When the electron beam of a CRT display passes over and refreshes the phosphor at the spot where the light pen is pointing, the detector senses the increase in brightness and generates a signal. Based on the timing of this signal, the coordinates of the spot on the display are calculated. Light pens typically include a switch that can disable them to prevent inadvertent activation. Light pens are typically used with CRT displays, although, with a more complex interface, they may also be used with other display technologies.

55.3.2 Implementation Issues

Modes of Operation

The light pen may be used in either of two modes. In *pointing* mode, a character or figure may be selected by pointing to a spot on the display and enabling the light pen. In *tracking* mode, the operator aims the light pen at a display cursor and then moves the pen. As long as the cursor remains in the light pen's field of view, a line will be traced where the pen is moved. The light pen must be moved at a steady rate or the cursor will be lost and tracking will be interrupted.

Figure 5. ***A stylus-operated graphic tablet.*** *(Courtesy of Wacom Technology Corp., Vancouver, WA.)*

Target Size

The appropriate size and spacing of the displayed targets depends to some extent upon the field of view of the light pen. A large field of view may make it easier to select a small target, but it also requires that targets be widely spaced to permit discrimination between adjacent targets. The resolution obtainable with a light pen is typically approximately 5 pixels. Hatamian and Brown (1985), however, report the development of a light pen accurate to 1/4 of a pixel on a screen with 1000 x 1000 resolution. Such a resolving capability enables the light pen to select one target from a group of small, closely spaced targets. As the resolution capabilities of the light pen increase, the lower bounds on target size are dictated more by operator capabilities than by technological limitations. For example, Avons, Beveridge, Hickman, and Hitch (1983) report that children using a light pen for target selection had from 1.7 to 3 mm mean placement error.

55.3.3 Advantages and Disadvantages of Light Pens

Like the touch screen, the light pen uses the output display as the input interface. This provides a direct relationship between output and input and allows natural pointing and drawing gestures to be used to input data. The light pen does not require extra desk space.

Use of a light pen imposes the additional actions of picking up and putting down the input device. Because input takes place at the display surface, the light pen operator must sit within arm's reach of the display. In addition, holding the light pen to the screen can be fatiguing. Avons et al. (1983) report that young children were unable to rest their elbow while using a light pen, and as a result they encountered more fatigue than did older children. The light pen and the operator's arm may also obscure parts of the display.

Light pens typically lack high resolution capabilities. Parallax may be a problem, especially when pointing to objects at the sides of the display. Using only the center of the screen to display targets may alleviate this problem; however, this solution limits the usefulness of the device. A more satisfactory solution might be to make targets at the sides of the screen large enough to minimize the effects of incorrect placement. Operator training may also be useful.

55.3.4 Applications

Because the light pen is used with a natural pointing gesture, this device is well suited for menu selection. While a light pen may be used for drawing, it is not suitable for precise sketching. The constant rate of movement necessary in tracking mode creates additional difficulties in drawing tasks. The light pen is not capable of tracing from paper copy. Parrish, Gates, Munger, Grimma, and Smith (1982) suggest that light pens are most useful in locating and moving symbols on a display.

55.4 Graphic Tablets

55.4.1 Technologies

Graphic tablets consist of a flat panel placed on a table in front of or near the display. The tablet surface represents the display, and movement of a finger or a stylus on the tablet provides cursor location information. Figure 5 shows a stylus-operated graphic tablet.

With matrix-encoded tablets, a special stylus or puck detects electrical or magnetic signals produced by a grid of conductors in the tablet. Voltage-gradient tablets have a conductive sheet as the surface of the tablet. A potential is applied to a stylus, and a decrease in potential on the plate at the stylus position is measured.

Acoustic tablets have a stylus that generates a spark at its tip. The sound is detected by microphones mounted on adjacent sides of the tablet. An alternative acoustic technique, the electroacoustic method, generates electrical pulses on the tablet that are detected by a stylus. Electroacoustic tablets are quieter than acoustic tablets and are less sensitive to noise in the environment.

Touch-sensitive tablets work without a special stylus. In a touch-sensitive acoustic tablet technology, high frequency waves are transmitted across a glass surface. When these waves are interrupted by a finger or pen they are reflected back to the tablet edge. The delay between wave generation and reception is used to calculate position coordinates. Resistive touch-sensitive tablets use layers of conductive and resistive material at the tablet surface. When the layers are pressed together, an electrical potential is generated. Capacitive touch-sensitive tablets use the body's capacitance to generate an electrical signal when the user's finger contacts the tablet's surface. A disadvantage of touch-sensitive tablets is that inadvertent touches can activate them. The tablets may be designed to minimize this possibility.

55.4.2 Implementation Issues

Method of Cursor Control

When an individual places a finger on the tablet, the display cursor can be programmed to move from its current position and appear at a position that corresponds to the location of the finger on the tablet. Movement of the finger on the tablet generates new cursor locations that are always referenced to the current coordinates of the finger on the tablet. This is referred to as an *absolute* mode of cursor control. A second approach is to maintain the display cursor at its current position when the finger is initially placed on the tablet. Movement of the finger produces a corresponding cursor movement that is always relative to this initial cursor location; thus, this is referred to as a *relative* mode of cursor control. In absolute mode, cursor position information is provided, while cursor movement information is specified in relative mode.

The nature of the task may dictate which method should be used. Arnaut and Greenstein (1986) found that absolute mode resulted in faster target acquisition rates than did relative mode, as did Epps, Snyder, and Muto (1986). Ellingstad, Parng, Gehlen, Swierenga, and Auflick (1985) reported that there was less error on a compensatory tracking task with absolute mode. However, when circumstances dictate that the tablet be small in comparison to the display, absolute mode requires that small movements on the tablet be made to move the cursor a large amount on the display. Relative mode might then be preferred since the amount of movement of the display cursor resulting from a movement on the tablet is not dictated by the tablet size.

Display-Control Relationship

The amount of movement of the display cursor in response to a unit of movement on the tablet is referred to as *display/control gain.* Arnaut and Greenstein (1986) found that gains between 0.8 and 1.0 resulted in better performance on a target acquisition task than did higher or lower gains for both relative and absolute modes. This range of gains appeared to be optimal because while gross movements to the vicinity of the target are faster with higher gains, fine positioning movements into the target area are more difficult. With lower gains, any improvements in fine positioning performance are outweighed by the additional time required for gross movement.

Tablet gain can interact with the cursor control method. When a tablet is used in absolute mode, the gain dictates the tablet size because the location of the finger on the tablet is directly translated into a corresponding position on the display. For example, a gain of 1.0 requires that the tablet be the same size as the display, while a gain of 2.0 requires that the tablet be half the size of the display. With relative mode the finger can be anywhere on the tablet, since the display cursor is driven by finger movement, not finger location. Thus, the size of the tablet is independent of the tablet gain. However, if the size of a tablet used with relative mode and a given gain is such that a movement across the entire tablet surface does not move the cursor across the entire display, then the user will have to make several sweeping movements with his or her finger to move the cursor across an appreciable part of the display. This situation arises when a small relative-mode tablet is used with a low gain.

It is possible to program a tablet in relative mode to include a gain component that is proportional to finger velocity in addition to the position gain just discussed. A rapid finger movement of a given displacement will move the cursor a greater distance than a gradual movement with the same displacement. Because human control inputs tend to be rapid during gross movement and slower during fine positioning, adding a velocity-gain component provides higher overall gain during gross movement, that diminishes to a lower gain during fine positioning. Becker and Greenstein (1986) compared a pure position-gain system with a position- and velocity-gain touch tablet (referred to as a lead-lag compensation system). Target acquisition was faster for the lead-lag system, although there was a slight increase in the error rate compared to a pure position-gain system.

While gain is an important feature of some interfaces, it should be noted that in cases where more than the overall display size and the amount of movement allowed on the input device are changed, gain is an inadequate specification for performance. Arnaut and Greenstein (1990) found that when target size is also changed, gain does not account sufficiently for performance since it only considers two of these three important display/control components.

Tablet Configuration

Because graphic tablets are separate from the display, they are more flexible than touch screens. The tablet size is free to vary from one that fits in a keyboard to an entire digitizing table. The low profile of the tablet in comparison to a joystick or trackball makes inadvertent activation less likely. An additional advantage of the tablet's flat surface is that it may be configured in many ways. A template may be placed over the tablet to correspond with positions on the display in a menu selection task. Alternatively, an overlay may indicate operations that are not directly referenced to the display. For example, a software package designed to teach music basics might include a tablet overlay imprinted with a piano keyboard.

Brown, Buxton, and Murtagh (1985) suggest that the tablet surface may be divided into separate regions analogous to display windows, with each region configured as a different virtual input device. For example, one window may have areas that can be treated like buttons, while another window may be in relative mode and be used like a trackball. This capability can be useful in system prototyping to aid in making hardware selections for the system.

Feedback and Confirmation

Due to the indirect nature of the graphic tablet, Swezey and Davis (1983) suggest that it is important to include a feedback and/or confirmation mechanism. An audible click or tone and/or a visual indication can signal that an entry has been recognized. Visual and auditory feedback are especially helpful with graphic tablets since no useful tactile feedback occurs when pressing the tablet.

A problem related to confirmation is "fall-out" or "jitter" (Buxton, Hill, and Rowley, 1985; Whitfield, Ball, and Bird, 1983). As the finger is removed from the tablet, the centroid of finger pressure shifts, and the display cursor moves in response. Fall-out may be avoided in at least three ways. First, a stylus may be used to focus the area over which pressure is applied. Second, the last few data samples may be discarded after lift-off so that the cursor remains in the position it was in just prior to removal of the finger from the tablet. Finally, the user could leave his or her finger on the tablet and press a confirmation button with the other hand.

Ellingstad et al. (1985) studied the following methods of confirming an entry for several tasks: 1) lifting the finger off the tablet; 2) lifting the finger off the tablet and pressing a separate area on the tablet; 3) lifting the finger off the tablet and pressing a key located off the tablet; and 4) keeping the finger on the tablet and pressing a separate key off the tablet. Lift-off-only tended to be the fastest method, but it led to more errors than the other methods (possibly due to fallout). Lift-off with a separate enter key produced good performance in terms of errors and response time across all tasks. The authors suggest that this method is to be preferred when error correction is not readily available. If error correction procedures are available, or if the targets provided are large enough that fall-out error is minimal, lift-off only may be a better choice. It should be noted that when subjects were required to lift their finger and press a separate area on the tablet, the same hand was used for cursor positioning and confirmation. In the methods in which a key was pressed, the opposite hand was used for confirmation. This may have caused the liftoff with confirmation on the tablet to take somewhat longer; this method may be useful in place of the lift-off with separate enter key if two hands are used.

Finger, Stylus, and Puck Control

A touch-sensitive tablet can typically be used with either a finger or a stylus. The advantage of using a finger is that there is no stylus to lose or break. A stylus, however, can provide greater resolution since the area over which it applies pressure is smaller than that of a finger, and it also allows an operator to make small movements by moving the stylus with the fingers without requiring the entire hand or arm to move. Ellingstad et al. (1985) reported that for cursor positioning, compensatory tracking, data entry, and function selection tasks, the use of a stylus resulted in faster and more accurate responses than did use of a finger.

Rosenberg and Martin (1988) examined the effect of using a 2.5-power magnifier on users' positioning of a digitizer puck over specified points in documents placed on a matrix-encoded tablet. They found that use of the magnifier in place of the puck's non-magnifying optical sight reduced the average range of the users' target selections from 0.16 mm to 0.13 mm. Thus, in digitizing applications, where the accurate input of the spatial coordinates of points is of primary importance, the use of a puck and magnifying optical sight can

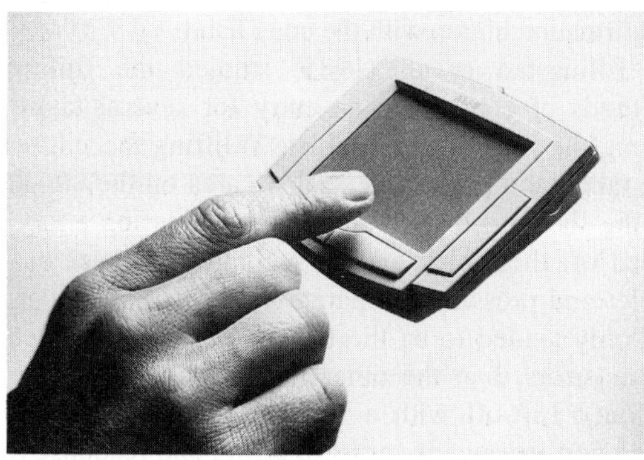

Figure 6. ***A compact touch tablet.*** *(Courtesy of Alps Electric USA, Inc., San Jose, CA.)*

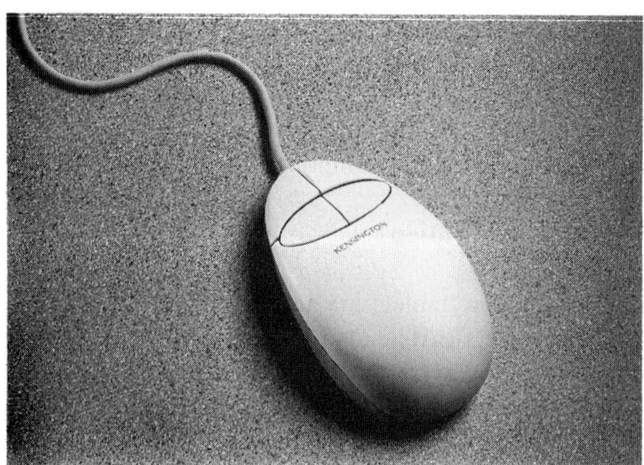

Figure 7. ***A mechanical mouse.*** *(Courtesy of Kensington Technology Group, San Mateo, CA.)*

achieve relatively high levels of positioning accuracy with very small targets.

Input Dimensionality

Touch tablets can transmit information in more than two dimensions. For example, pressure-sensitive tablets have been developed that respond differentially to varying amounts of pressure in the same location. Thus, a light touch may be used for cursor positioning, while a heavy touch might indicate a target selection. For graphics applications, different degrees of pressure can be used to generate different widths of lines.

55.4.3 Advantages and Disadvantages of Graphic Tablets

The movement required by a tablet and the display-control relationship are natural to many users. Since the tablet surface is constructed of one piece with no moving parts, tablets are suited for "hostile" environments in which other devices may be damaged, and they can be easily cleaned.

In comparison with touch screens, Whitfield et al. (1983) identify four advantages of the tablet. First, the display and the tablet may be positioned separately according to user preference. Second, the user's hand does not cover any part of the display. Third, there are no parallax problems. Fourth, drift in the display will not affect the input. In addition, the user is not likely to experience fatigue associated with continually lifting a hand to the screen.

Graphic tablets have several disadvantages. Some technologies may not provide high positioning accuracy, although matrix-encoded and voltage-gradient tablets typically provide very high resolution. Graphic tablets do not allow direct eye-hand coordination, since they are removed from the display. The tablets can take up a good deal of space on the work surface; however, as Figure 6 illustrates, light, small touch tablets are available that are well-suited to portable computing applications. Because operation using the finger requires the user to press and slide the fingertip on the tablet, soreness and fatigue may be a problem over extended use periods. It is important to select and adjust the tablet so that the pressure required does not fatigue the operator. Fatigue may also occur if users must hold their arms and hands away from the tablet surface to avoid inadvertent tablet activation.

55.4.4 Applications

A graphic tablet is better suited to drafting and free-hand sketching than virtually any other input device. Parrish et al. (1982), in an attempt to standardize military usage of input devices, recommend that graphic tablets be used for all drawing purposes. Graphic tablets are also appropriate to select an item from an array or menu, especially when a template is used. While tablets are increasingly becoming more efficient for recognition of printed and handwritten characters, alphanumeric data entry is slow when performed by selecting characters from a menu.

55.5 Mice

55.5.1 Technologies

A mouse is a small hand-held box that fits under the palm and fingertips (see Figure 7). Movement of the mouse on a flat surface generates cursor movement. Mice typically have one or more buttons that are pressed to perform such functions as changing menus, drawing lines, or confirming inputs.

Movement of the mouse is detected mechanically or optically. The mechanical technique typically involves mounting a small ball in the bottom of the mouse. Rotation of the ball is sensed by potentiometers or optical encoders and used to determine orientation information. Mechanical mice may produce some noise during movement, and dust from the table surface may become lodged inside the mouse. However, mechanical mice can operate on almost any surface. Optical mice use optical sensors in place of the rolling ball and track the passage of the mouse across a grid of horizontal and vertical lines printed on an accompanying pad. These mice have no moving parts; thus, they make no noise and do not pick up debris from the work surface. However, their operation is confined to the special pad. Resolution may also be lower than that of mechanical mice.

55.5.2 Implementation Issues

Display/Control Gain

As with graphic tablets, the gain of the mouse may be changed. Thus, movement of the mouse may result in either more, less, or the same amount of movement of the cursor on the screen. However, unlike the graphic tablet, the mouse works only in relative mode.

Jellinek and Card (1990) investigated the effect of various display/control gain functions on target acquisition times using an optical mouse. In their first experiment, they studied the effect of six gain settings (1,2, 4, 8, 16, and 32) on target acquisition times with a "constant-gain" mouse. They found that changing the gain of the mouse from its original value of 2 either made no difference or slowed performance. (The original gain of 2 had been set based on a study of user preferences by William English more than 20 years earlier.) The authors believe that performance slowed for the higher gains due to quantization effects: at these gains the 200 spot/in (78 spot/cm) resolution of the mouse spuriously magnified display cursor movements in response to small movements of the mouse, causing accuracy to suffer. For the lowest gain of 1, moving the cursor even halfway across the screen typically required the user to lift and reposition the mouse several times, slowing performance.

Jellinek and Card also studied whether using a "variable-gain" mouse (one in which the mouse's initial gain changed to a higher value when the mouse's velocity exceeded a specified threshold) enhanced target acquisition times relative to a constant-gain mouse. They found no evidence that it did. They suggest that rather than speeding cursor movement, the primary effect of a variable-gain mouse is that it enables the user to move the mouse less to achieve a specified cursor movement than a constant-gain mouse with the same initial gain. If the area on the desk in which the mouse may be moved is limited, the variable-gain mouse will reduce the number of situations in which the user runs out of room to complete a mouse movement and must lift and reposition the mouse to complete an action. Jellinek and Card recommend employing a higher initial gain with a constant-gain mouse as a better means to reduce the desktop area required for efficient mouse operation, so long as the mouse's resolution is sufficient to minimize quantization effects at that gain.

Jellinek and Card's findings are supported by the results of a study by Tränkle and Deutschmann (1991) using a mechanical mouse. They found no significant differences in target selection times using constant gains of 1 and 2. They also found that a variable gain (in which the mouse's gain gradually increased from 1 to 2 after the mouse's velocity exceeded a threshold value) increased target selection times. In general, they found that target selection times were reduced by increasing practice, decreasing the distance the mouse must be moved to acquire a target, increasing the size of the target, and, to a lesser extent, increasing the size of the display.

Use of Mouse Buttons

Price and Cordova (1983) compared two methods of using mouse buttons to indicate whether a mathematical problem was correct or incorrect. In all cases, "correct" was indicated by a single click of one mouse button. For one condition, "incorrect" was entered by a single click of a different button on the mouse, while in the other condition "incorrect" was entered by two rapid clicks of the same mouse button. Performance was consistent for all responses which required a single button click, but was not as good when a double click was required. Thus, when there are two equally likely responses, it may be better to associate the responses with single clicks of different buttons than with different numbers of clicks of the same button.

Hill, Gunn, Martin, and Schwartz (1991) studied the relative difficulty perceived by right-handed users performing various tasks with a three-button mouse. A single click action was judged easier than a double click action. Both of these actions were judged to be easier than the other actions studied: press/hold, press/drag, triple click, click/press/hold, and click/press/drag. Click/press/hold and click/press/drag were perceived to be among the most difficult actions. The left mouse button was judged easier to use than the center mouse button. Both of these buttons were judged easier to use than the right mouse button. In fact, the chorded combination requiring simultaneous pressing of the left and center mouse buttons was perceived to be easier than the use of the right mouse button alone. Chorded combinations that included the right mouse button were ranked among the most difficult tasks. The authors recommend that the right mouse button not be used as a default setting for frequently used functions.

Mouse Configuration

Hodes and Akagi (1986) conducted a series of studies with users to optimize the mouse from anthropometric and biomechanical perspectives, accommodating the way users hold, move, and actuate the device. This involved creating a shape that allows a relaxed hand posture for movement and button activation, maintains a straight wrist orientation to minimize wrist fatigue, and provides strong tactile cues so the fingers can be correctly positioned on the buttons without requiring the user to take his or her eyes from the screen. The studies indicated that users preferred designs possessing the following features:

1. a rounded peak close to the center of the mouse case, rather than a flat top surface, to allow freer finger movement and a natural palm support.
2. a rounded rather than an angular back.
3. button positions on the front surface rather than the top of the mouse.
4. buttons stiff enough to support resting fingers without activation.
5. button switches that provide good tactile and auditory feedback of their actuation.
6. a top front surface as wide or wider than the back of the mouse so fingers can spread naturally.
7. a matte top surface texture to prevent glare.
8. a highly textured gripping surface on the sides.
9. a rolling (or sliding) mechanism designed to assure steadiness of the mouse when pushing the buttons.

This research led to the design and implementation of a mouse that incorporated these features, illustrated in Figure 8.

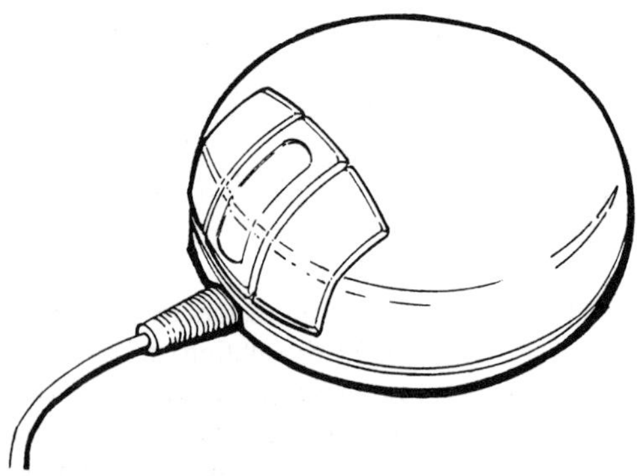

Figure 8. The mouse design developed by Hodes and Akagi (1986). *(From Proceedings of the Human Factors Society 30th Annual Meeting, 1986, Vol. 2, p. 900. Copyright (1986), by the Human Factors and Ergonomics Society, Inc. and reproduced by permission.)*

Pekelney and Chu (1995) developed a set of design criteria for a mouse directed toward reducing the user's exposure to risk factors for upper extremity musculoskeletal disorders. The design team sought to minimize the forces the user would have to apply to the sides and buttons of the mouse; to minimize awkward, static, and constrained postures of the user's hand; and to minimize repetitive movement of the mouse, minimize repetitive use of the mouse buttons, and encourage rest breaks.

The following features were incorporated into the mouse design to minimize the forces applied to the mouse:

1. a software-driven drag-lock feature that enables the user to "drag" the cursor without sustained depression of a mouse button. Additional buttons are also provided to allow easy access to the drag-lock feature without conflicting with the normal uses of the standard buttons.
2. mouse sides that are wider at the top and narrower at the base to reduce the pinch forces needed to hold the mouse. To further reduce the required pinch forces, the sides of the mouse are also covered with a firm, high-friction, textured styrenic material.
3. a front end lower than the rear end of the mouse to promote a curled finger posture when activating the buttons, based on evidence that the finger produces force more efficiently when operating in a slightly curled posture than when in a straight posture. A low force switch and button combina-

tion (activated by approximately 60 grams of applied mass) is also used.

The following features were incorporated to minimize awkward, static, and constrained postures of the user's hand:

4. curved sides and a tapered front to mimic the natural architecture of the hand during grasping.
5. a button layout with two buttons forward and two to the rear to enable both the little and ring fingers to oppose the thumb during grasping. This layout also enables a narrow width profile, reducing the space between the fingers and the range of motion required to operate the buttons.
6. buttons in close proximity to one another with the front buttons tapered, to enable the buttons to be easily activated by the index finger alone, or in conjunction with the middle finger, reducing the need to use the little and ring fingers to activate the buttons.
7. a symmetrical, sculpted shape that allows several grip postures, to reduce the opportunity for static loading.
8. a tapered shape from back to front to accommodate larger hands further back and smaller hands further forward. The button layout, along with reprogrammable buttons, allows small-handed users to use the rear buttons as the "standard" buttons.

The following features were incorporated to minimize repetitive movement of the mouse, minimize repetitive use of the mouse buttons, and encourage rest breaks:

9. adjustable cursor acceleration with a slow cursor feature to permit the use of large arm movements to achieve fine cursor control, thus minimizing repetitive cursor corrections. Software also permits automatic positioning of the cursor on the default selection when a dialog is opened and the definition of and jumping to "hotspots" on the screen near high frequency targets.
10. programmable mouse buttons to permit the user to send multiple clicks with a single click of a mouse button.
11. software that can be used to prompt the user to rest after a user-specified interval of keyboard or mouse use has been exceeded.

The product with these features that was developed is illustrated in Figure 7.

Feedback and Confirmation

Akamatsu and Sato (1994) modified a standard two-button mechanical mouse to provide tactile and force feedback. Tactile information was provided to the user by a small pin that projected slightly above the left mouse button when a solenoid was actuated. Force feedback was produced by adding resistance during mouse movement. This was generated by a small electromagnet attached to the bottom of the mouse. When the mouse was operated on an iron surface, the resistance to movement could be increased by applying current to the electromagnet. Akamatsu and Sato studied target acquisition performance using this "multi-modal" mouse and a standard mouse. When the display cursor was within the target area, both tactile and force feedback were provided by the multi-modal mouse. No feedback other than the location of the display cursor and the target was provided with the standard mouse. The authors found that the presentation of tactile and force information reduced target acquisition times approximately 7 to 10 percent. They also found that users tended to confirm their target selections with the standard mouse when the display cursor was close to the center of the target area. When users were provided tactile and force feedback, however, their confirmations occurred over much more of the full target area. Thus, the addition of the tactile and force feedback appears to increase the "effective" area of the target.

Akamatsu, MacKenzie, and Hasbroucq (1995) used the multi-modal mouse to study the effect of five different feedback conditions on target selection: (1) *no feedback* other than the location of the display cursor and target, (2) an *auditory* tone while the cursor was inside the target, (3) *tactile* feedback by the solenoid-driven pin to the finger when the cursor was inside the target, (4) *visual* feedback by highlighting the target when the cursor was inside it, and (5) auditory, tactile, and visual feedback in *combination* when the cursor was inside the target. (The force feedback capability of the multi-modal mouse was not used in this study.) There were no significant differences in the overall target selection times across the five feedback conditions. However, analysis of the time to confirm a selection once the cursor entered the target (the component of the selection time that followed the onset of feedback) revealed that this time was shortest for the tactile feedback condition (237 ms) and longest for the no feedback condition (298 ms), with the means for the combined, the auditory, and the visual feedback conditions falling in between (246, 262, and 265 ms, respectively). It was again observed that users in the feedback

Figure 9. A trackball. (Courtesy of Kensington Technology Group, San Mateo, CA.)

conditions tended to confirm their target selections over a wider area of the target than in the no feedback condition. Interestingly, when participants were asked to indicate their preferences among the different feedback conditions, visual feedback was ranked most preferred, tactile feedback second, auditory and combined feedback third, and no feedback least preferred.

55.5.3 Advantages and Disadvantages of Mice

Mice have become very popular as computer peripheral devices. They can work in small spaces because the mouse can be picked up and repositioned. The operator can usually locate and move a mouse while looking at the display. Cordless mice which use infrared beams are available, so that a cord will not interfere with the use of the device.

While the mouse may only require a small surface, it does require some space in addition to that allotted to a keyboard; thus, it is not compatible with many mobile or laptop computer applications. Because the confirmation button is on the device, the mouse may move during confirmation, leading to difficulty in selecting small targets, particularly for novice users. A mouse can only operate in relative mode; this limits its usefulness for graphic applications. Additionally, drawing with a mouse is not as natural as is drawing with a pen or pencil; some experience is necessary to effectively use the mouse for graphic tasks.

55.5.4 Applications

The mouse is best suited for pointing and selection tasks. It is capable of performing drawing and design tasks, but the graphic tablet provides a better interface for such applications.

55.6 Trackballs

55.6.1 Technologies

A trackball is composed of a fixed housing holding a ball that can be rotated freely in any direction by the fingertips, as shown in Figure 9. Movement of a trackball is detected by optical or shaft encoders. This in turn generates output which is used to determine the movement of the display cursor.

55.6.2 Implementation Issues

The diameter, rotational inertia, and frictional drag forces of the trackball may all be adjusted. Display/control gain must also be specified. Like the mouse, the trackball is solely a relative mode device. In a manner similar to those discussed for the graphic tablet and mouse, the display/control gain of the trackball may be made a function of its rotational velocity. Rapid movements of the ball will then result in larger cursor movements per unit of ball rotation than gradual movements. The trackball's gain function may then be adjusted so that both gross movement speed (for which high gain appears to be appropriate) and fine positioning accuracy (which appears to be easier with lower gain) are possible.

Engel, Goossens, and Haakma (1994) modified a standard trackball to provide force feedback by mounting servo motors on the shafts of its optical position sensors. They studied the effect of this feedback in a target acquisition task by positioning a "force field" around the border of the displayed target. When the display cursor entered this field, the servo motors exerted forces on the trackball to assist entry of the cursor into the target or to resist exit of the cursor from the target. Participants in the study were able to acquire targets more quickly and with fewer errors when this feedback was provided by the trackball.

55.6.3 Advantages and Disadvantages of Trackballs

A large trackball on a supportive work surface can be comfortable to use for extended periods of time because users can rest the forearm, keep the hand in one place, and spin and stop the trackball with the fingers. The trackball provides direct tactile feedback from the

Figure 10. ***A displacement joystick.*** *(Courtesy of CH Products, Vista, CA.)*

ball's rotation and speed. It requires a small, fixed amount of space, can be integrated with a keyboard, and can be located and operated without taking the eyes off the display. Unlike mice, trackballs cannot be inadvertently run off the edge of the work surface.

Disadvantages include the fact that the trackball is a rotational device that operates only in relative mode, which limits its usefulness for drawing tasks. It cannot be used to trace drawings or to input hand-printed characters. It is also difficult to operate buttons associated with the trackball using the thumb while using the fingers of the same hand to roll the ball or hold it stationary, due to the interaction of the muscles and limbs used to effect these separate control actions (MacKenzie, Sellen, and Buxton, 1991).

55.6.4 Applications

The trackball is best suited for pointing and selection tasks. While trackballs may be used to draw lines and sketch, Parrish et al. (1982) suggest that they should only be used for these applications when requirements for drawing speed and accuracy are not very stringent.

55.7 Joysticks

55.7.1 Technologies

A joystick consists of a lever mounted vertically in a fixed base. Displacement joysticks use potentiometers to sense movements of the lever. There is a continuous relationship between the magnitude of lever displacement and the output signal generated. Both on-and off-axis movements may be made. The lever may be spring-loaded so that it returns to center when released. A displacement joystick is illustrated in Figure 10.

With a switch-activated or *binary* joystick, movement of the lever generates output by closing one or more switches positioned around the base of the lever. The output signal generated by the device is either "on" in a particular direction or "off," and it is not proportional to the magnitude of the lever displacement. An "on" signal in a given direction results in cursor movement at a constant rate in that direction. When the spring-loaded lever is released it returns to center and the cursor stops moving.

A force or *isometric* joystick has a rigid lever that does not move noticeably in any direction. Strain gauges are used to determine the direction and magnitude of the force applied to the joystick. The cursor moves in proportion to the amount of force applied. When the lever is released the output drops to zero.

55.7.2 Implementation Issues

Display-Control Relationship.

As with touch tablets, mice, and trackballs, the gain of the joystick may be changed. Jenkins and Karr (1954) found that the optimal joystick gain for movement of a pointer was approximately 0.4 (in terms of pointer displacement relative to the linear displacement of the tip of the joystick). The dimensions of the joystick levers and display screens used in graphics applications, however, typically constrain displacement joystick gain to a range of 5 to 10 for absolute mode, making fine positioning of a cursor difficult. Accordingly, Foley and van Dam (1982) suggest that the joystick is better used for graphics tasks as a *rate control,* in which constant displacement of a displacement joystick (or constant force applied to a force joystick) results in a constant rate of cursor movement, than as a *position control,* in which constant displacement of a displacement joystick (or constant force applied to a force joystick) results in a specific cursor displacement. With rate control, a larger displacement of the displacement joystick (or force applied to the force joystick) results in a higher cursor velocity, while reducing the displacement (or force) to zero halts the movement of the cursor. Foley and van Dam note the importance of incorporating a small *dead zone* of zero velocity around the center position of a rate-control joystick so that nulling the joystick input is not difficult. Gain remains

Figure 11. A keyboard-integrated, rate-control, force-operated joystick. *(Courtesy of IBM PC Co., Somers, NY.)*

an issue in the design of rate-control joysticks. In this case, the gain specifies the cursor speed that results from a unit displacement of the displacement joystick or a unit force applied to the force joystick.

Figure 11 illustrates an implementation of a rate-control force joystick in a laptop computer. The joystick is located between the "G," "H," and "B" keys within the computer's keyboard and protrudes slightly over the typing keys. It has a soft tip that accommodates single-finger operation by the index finger of either hand. The stick does not move. The direction of the display cursor's movement is determined by the direction of the tangential force applied by the finger to the stick's tip. The cursor's speed corresponds to the amount of force applied. When tangential force is discontinued, the cursor stops. Thumb-operated buttons positioned below the space bar on the keyboard provide the joystick with functionality equivalent to that of a mouse.

Force-Displacement Relationship

The force-displacement relationship of a joystick specifies the displacement of the joystick that results from the application of a specific force to the joystick. The force joystick is characterized by its extreme force-displacement relationship: displacement of the joystick is negligible regardless of the force applied. At the other extreme, it is possible to design a joystick that offers negligible resistance to displacement. Most displacement joysticks, however, offer at least some resistance to displacement and in this case there are two common relationships between the force applied to the joystick and its resulting displacement: elastic and viscous resistance.

A spring-loaded joystick displays elastic resistance. The application of a constant force to the joystick results in a constant joystick displacement. Increasing the force applied to the joystick increases its displacement. This direct relationship between applied force and resulting displacement can be used by the operator to enhance positioning accuracy. Spring-loading is also beneficial when it is desirable to automatically return the joystick to its center position upon release. Finally, in tracking tasks requiring sudden reversals of cursor movements, spring loading enhances the operator's ability to execute these reversals.

When a joystick has viscous resistance, the application of a constant force to the joystick results in a constant rate of joystick movement. Increasing the force applied to the joystick increases the rate of displacement. Viscous damping helps in the execution of smooth control movements and is appropriate if maintaining a constant rate of cursor movement or acquiring a cursor location at a particular time are important aspects of the cursor positioning task.

55.7.3 Advantages and Disadvantages of Joysticks

The advantages of the joystick include the fact that it requires only a small fixed amount of space, and it can be made small enough to fit into a keyboard. If a palm or hand rest is provided, the joystick may be used for extended periods of time with little fatigue. However, the modest size of most joysticks leads to gains too high for accurate positioning in absolute mode. This limits their usefulness for drawing tasks. Joysticks cannot be used to trace or digitize drawings.

Mithal and Douglas (1996) compared the movement characteristics of a hand-held mechanical mouse and a fingertip-operated rate-control force joystick. They found that, in general, cursor movements in the acquisition of a target using the mouse consisted of a large primary submovement toward the target, followed by a few smaller submovements to finally acquire the target. Each of these submovements was characterized by a smooth increase and decrease in the speed of the cursor. The velocity of the cursor during target acquisition using the joystick, in contrast, displayed a great deal of random-appearing jitter, or jerkiness. Mithal and Douglas conclude that the finger-operated force joystick is particularly sensitive to physiological tremor, the random variations in force exerted by the muscles of the finger (and the rest of the body). They suggest that the inherently force-sensitive force joystick, operated by an unsupported finger, provides very little inertial or frictional damping of the finger tremor transmitted to it. This tremor thus causes involuntary changes in the velocity at which the display cursor moves, making it more difficult for users of the finger-operated force joystick to achieve fine control of the cursor.

55.7.4 Applications

Joysticks tend to be best suited to continuous tracking tasks and to pointing tasks that do not require a great deal of precision. Their small size and the ease with which they can be integrated with a keyboard have made them a popular choice for mobile computing applications.

55.8 Devices on the Horizon

The input devices discussed thus far can all be described as ubiquitous. They are available commercially in a variety of implementations and their modest cost justifies their consideration in a wide range of applications. There are a number of input devices under active development that, while currently useful in specialized applications, may be expected to find wider application as their underlying technologies and interaction techniques mature. Two of these device types are briefly described in this section. More information about applications of these devices may be found in chapters 8 and 35 of this handbook, on virtual environments, and interfaces for people with disabilities, respectively.

55.8.1 Eye-controlled Input

Several groups of researchers have begun to investigate the use of eye movements as a method of computer input (Calhoun, Janson, and Arbak, 1986; Glenn, Iavecchia, Ross, Stokes, Weiland, Ross, and Zakland, 1986; Jacob, 1991; Starker and Bolt, 1990; Ware and Mikaelian, 1987). Jacob (1991), for example, investigated the use of an eye tracking technology that tracks the corneal reflection (from an infrared light shining on the eye) and the outline of the pupil (illuminated by the same light). Visual line of gaze is computed from the relationship between the two tracked points. This eye tracker sits several feet from the user and does not touch the user in any way. The action of its servo-controlled motor, however, which enables the light to follow the motions of the user's head, does tend to convey the feeling of being watched.

Implementation issues for eye-controlled input include the provision of locational feedback, the method of confirming selections, and target size. Feedback can be either continuous, such that the computed point of attention is always shown on the display, or discrete, in which a target is highlighted only when the gaze is near or on the target. Glenn et al. (1986) compared these methods and found no significant differences between them in either speed or accuracy of target acquisition. Work by Calhoun et al. (1986) and Ware and Mikaelian (1987) suggests that a conveniently located physical button should be used to designate the selection of an item on which the eye has fixated. Additional work by Ware and Mikaelian (1987) indicates that target sizes should subtend at least one degree (0.02 rad) of visual angle.

Eye-controlled input is attractive for item selection and target tracking tasks because it uses eye movements inherent in these tasks as the control input. Eye-controlled input can reduce workload, free the hands to perform other tasks, and eliminate the time-consuming operations of locating, grasping, and moving manual input devices. This form of input is not well suited to tasks involving very small targets, however. Because a number of involuntary eye movements take place even while the eye is attempting to fixate on a point, at times the eye's line of sight only approximates the true point of visual attention. Currently available eye-tracking technologies are also at least somewhat intrusive.The technological complexity and cost of current eye-tracking technologies make eye-controlled input appropriate primarily for applications in which rapid hands-off input of target locations is of paramount importance.

55.8.2 Gestural and Spatial Input

Another set of technologies uses operator gestures as a basis for input. Just as touch screens are used for small screens, a gesture-based system may be used to point with a large screen display. Bolt (1984) describes a technique in which both a small "transmitter" cube and a large "sensor" cube are surrounded by magnetic fields. The sensor is placed several feet away from the transmitter. Movement of the transmitter by the user is sensed by the large cube based upon changes in the magnetic fields and is used to calculate spatial coordinates.

Zimmerman, Lanier, Blanchard, Bryson, and Harvill (1987) report the development of an instrumented glove that tracks the position, orientation, and gestures of the hand. Flex sensors on the glove measure finger bending. Hand positioning and orientation are measured either by ultrasonics or magnetic flex sensors. Piezo-ceramic benders, mounted underneath each finger, provide tactile feedback to the user when a computer-generated image of the fingers "touches" the surface of a displayed object. The glove allows users to interact with displayed objects as they do with real objects: displayed objects can be picked up, twisted, squeezed, thrown, and set down.

In tracking hand position, orientation, and movement of the hand, gesture-based input offers a natural and unobtrusive means for input of object designation and manipulation actions typically performed by the hand directly. The capability of the hand to simultaneously move, rotate, and grab can thus be exploited to flexibly and efficiently accomplish tasks requiring the manipulation of displayed objects.

55.9 Empirical Comparisons

The advantages and disadvantages of each input device can aid in initial decisions as to which devices are appropriate for a given user population, task, environment, or hardware configuration. However, often more than one device can satisfy these constraints. To determine which devices lead to better performance under given conditions, controlled experiments comparing several input devices have been performed. While not all studies can be easily categorized, several task types have been a focus of study: target acquisition, item selection, dragging, and continuous tracking. Research on the use of input devices in graphical windowing environments and for drawing is currently relatively sparse.

The majority of experimental comparisons of input devices have involved target acquisition or item selection tasks. That is, a stationary object is displayed and the participant must position the display cursor at or inside the object's position. In target acquisition, the designated object is the only one presented; in item selection, the designated object is one of several selectable items presented on the display at one time. For either task, a confirmation action may or may not be required. In the following subsection, target acquisition studies are reviewed; item selection tasks are considered in the second subsection. Continuous tracking tasks are addressed in the third subsection and studies which investigated more than one type of task are reviewed in the concluding subsection.

55.9.1 Target Acquisition Tasks

Albert (1982) compared the performance of seven input devices on a target acquisition task. The devices were: touch screen, light pen, graphic tablet with puck, trackball, spring-loaded displacement joystick used as a rate control, force joystick used as a rate control, and cursor positioning keys. A footswitch was used with each device to confirm acquisitions; however, the light pen and the touch screen were also tested without an accompanying confirmation action. The task was to position the cursor at the center of a 1.25 in (3.18 cm) square target and then confirm task completion. The positioning accuracy of the different devices did not vary greatly when the footswitch was used. The accuracy of the two devices tested with and without footswitch confirmation (the touch screen and light pen) was significantly higher when the footswitch was used. The touch screen and light pen, with or without footswitches, resulted in the fastest positioning speeds, while the cursor positioning keys, the joysticks, and the trackball were slowest. Albert attributes this to the direct eye-hand coordination present with the touch screen and the light pen. He also suggests that requiring input confirmation leads to a tradeoff; while the response becomes more accurate, it also takes more time. Participants preferred the touch screen, light pen, and graphic tablet to the trackball, joysticks, and cursor positioning keys.

Gomez, Wolfe, Davenport, and Calder (1982) compared a trackball to a touch-sensitive tablet in absolute mode for a task in which participants superimposed a cursor over a target appearing at a pseudorandom location on the screen. A confirmation area was provided on the tablet, and a confirmation switch was placed next to the trackball. Response times across groups were not significantly different for the two devices. However, the trackball resulted in significantly less error than the tablet. The authors attribute the latter result to the higher precision characteristics of the trackball, in particular to the fact that the hand was stabilized with trackball operation and not with the tablet.

Mehr and Mehr (1972) optimized five input devices on a target acquisition task and then compared their performance. The devices were: 1) a center-return displacement joystick used as a rate control; 2) a remain-in-position displacement joystick in absolute mode; 3) a thumb-operated force joystick mounted in a hand-held grip used as a rate control; 4) a finger-operated force joystick used as a rate control; and 5) a trackball. Participants positioned a cursor within a circle presented in the middle of a CRT, and then pressed a stop button. The trackball resulted in the shortest positioning times, followed closely by the finger-operated force joystick, while the two displacement joysticks resulted in the longest positioning times. The trackball and the finger-operated force joystick also provided the most accurate performance.

Epps, Snyder, and Muto (1986) optimized six input devices on a target acquisition task and then compared their performance. The task included square targets that varied in size from 0.13 to 2.14 cm and in distance from the initial cursor position (2, 4, 8, and 16 cm). The devices were: an absolute-mode touch tablet, a relative-mode touch tablet, a trackball, a force joystick used as a rate control, a displacement joystick used as a rate control, and an optical mouse. A separate confirmation key that was operated with the opposite hand was used for all devices except the mouse, which had its own confirmation button. For the smallest target size, the mouse and the trackball led to the shortest target acquisition times. The times for the absolute-mode tablet were longer than those for the mouse and trackball, but significantly shorter than those for the relative-mode tablet. The two joysticks led to the worst performance for small targets. As the target size increased, the differences between the devices were less apparent. For the shortest cursor-to-target distance, the mouse and the trackball led to the shortest acquisition times. The mouse, trackball, and absolute-mode tablet achieved the shortest times at longer distances. The two joysticks led to the worst performance at all target distances.

Sears and Shneiderman (1991) compared speed of performance, error rate, and user preference for an optical mouse and a stabilized capacitive touch screen. The stabilization software used with the touch screen filtered and smoothed the user's touch inputs to enhance the user's ability to stabilize the cursor's position on the display. The *take-off* strategy was used with the touch screen to input target selections. In this strategy the user placed a finger on the screen, dragged the finger until the cursor acquired the target, and then lifted the finger from the screen to select the target. The cursor was placed about 8 mm above where the user's finger touched the screen to allow the user to view both the cursor and the target. When using the mouse, participants began an acquisition task by clicking any of the mouse's buttons. Selections with the mouse were made by positioning the display cursor on the target and clicking any of the mouse buttons. Four rectangular target sizes were tested: 1, 4, 16, and 32 pixels per side (0.4 x 0.6, 1.7 x 2.2, 6.9 x 9.0, and 13.8 x 17.9 mm, respectively). The four pixel per side target had approximately one-quarter the area of a character of text. There were no significant differences in performance with the two devices for the three larger target sizes. However, the mouse resulted in significantly faster selections and significantly fewer errors with the single pixel target. Users preferred the mouse over the touch screen.

Strommen, Revelle, Medoff, and Razavi (1996) studied the target acquisition performance of 64 three-year-old children using a binary joystick, mouse, and trackball. Equal numbers of boys and girls served as participants. To acquire a target, the children had to move the display cursor into the target and then press the button on the device they were using. Children used the same device in one six-minute session per day for five consecutive days. By the fifth day of testing, joystick users were fastest in making first contact with the target. Joystick and mouse users acquired the most targets, while trackball users acquired the least. The joystick, however, resulted in significantly more overshooting of the target than either the mouse or trackball. This aspect of its performance did not improve over the five days of testing. Joystick users also consistently spent more time with their display cursors stuck on the screen borders than did users of either the trackball or mouse. Trackball users spent the least time on the screen borders.

Strommen et al. suggest two reasons the performance problems associated with the joystick did not prevent it from achieving, with the mouse, the highest number of target acquisitions on the final day of testing. First, the fast movement of the cursor with the joystick compensated for the time required to correct overshoots of the target. Second, several of the children discovered that keeping the joystick button depressed while the joystick was in motion would result in the acquisition of the target the moment the cursor intersected it. This strategy was effective in this target acquisition task, but would not be useful in tasks such as item selection, which present more than one potential target on the screen at the same time.

Where children's cursor movement using the joystick was fast, but error-prone, their cursor movement with the mouse and trackball was slower, but more accurate. Children using either device took approximately twice as long as joystick users to first contact the target with the cursor. The trackball was the least difficult device for the children to control. Those using the trackball had the lowest number of target overshoots and spent the smallest amount of time with the cursor stuck on the screen borders. The relative superiority of the trackball on these measures persisted across all five days of the study. Strommen et al. suggest that the trackball may be easiest for children to control because their use of the device produces cursor movement that is not continuous, but broken up into short, discrete movements. Children roll the trackball by drawing their fingers across it in a repetitive series of approximately equal-length strokes. At the end of each stroke, the cursor is stationary and its position can be evaluated. The next stroke can then be modified as needed to produce steady movement toward the on-screen target.

55.9.2 Item Selection Tasks

In one of the earliest computer input device comparisons reported, English, Engelbart, and Berman (1967) compared a light pen, a knee control, a Grafacon arm (an extendible pivoted rod, originally intended for curve-tracing), position- and rate-control joysticks, and a mouse. Two item selection tasks in which a cursor was positioned at one of several targets on the display were performed. Some method of confirmation (such as pressing a switch) was required for all devices. Experienced subjects had the shortest selection times with the mouse and the longest times with the the position-control joystick. Inexperienced users performed best in terms of selection time with the knee control and the light pen, and worst with the two joysticks. All subjects made the fewest errors with the mouse. The light pen and the position-control joystick resulted in the highest error rates for experienced users, and the light pen and rate joystick resulted in the highest error rates for the inexperienced users.

Card, English, and Burr (1978) compared four input devices on a text selection task. The input devices were: a mouse, a rate-control force joystick, step keys (a set of four keys that move the cursor up, down, left, and right one line or character at a time), and text keys (function keys that position the cursor at the previous or next character, word, line, or paragraph). Participants positioned the cursor at a target in text displayed on a CRT and then pressed a button to confirm the selection. For all devices except the mouse the opposite hand was used to press a button that was separate from the device. Total response time was divided into homing time (time from task initiation to cursor movement) and positioning time (time from initial cursor movement to selection). The mouse was superior to the other devices in terms of total response time, positioning time, and error rate. The continuous devices (the mouse and joystick) were faster than the key-operated devices (the step and text keys). The mouse achieved shorter positioning times than any other device for all target sizes (1, 2, 4, and 10 characters) and at all target distances greater than 1 cm (distances of 1, 2, 4, 8, and 16 cm were tested), its advantage increasing as target distance increased. The authors attribute the superiority of the mouse to the continuous nature of the movement it allows. They also suggest that the mouse requires less mental translation to map desired movement of the cursor into motor movement of the hands than the other devices.

Karat, McDonald, and Anderson (1986) compared a touch screen, a mouse, and a keyboard for target selection, menu selection, and menu selection with typing tasks. With the keyboard, participants simply typed the letter associated with the target or menu item. Selections with the mouse were confirmed by a press of a mouse button, and no confirmation action was required for the touch screen or keyboard. Target selection was faster with the touch screen and the keyboard than with the mouse. Menu selection (with and without a typing subtask) was faster with the touch screen than with the mouse. Menu selection performance with the keyboard fell between the touch screen and the mouse and was not significantly different from either. Participants preferred the touch screen and the keyboard to the mouse for all tasks.

Given Card et al.'s (1978) results, Karat, et al. were surprised by the relatively poor showing of the mouse. They conducted a second experiment to test possible explanations of the inferior mouse performance. Participants in the first study had been skilled typists, so the second study tested both skilled and non-skilled typists. Even unskilled typists may be more familiar with the keyboard than with the mouse; thus, practice with each device was extended, since Card et al. focused upon performance in long-term use. The display/control gain of the mouse was also increased from 1.0 to 2.0 (i.e., the display cursor now moved 2 cm for each centimeter of mouse movement) to match Card et al.'s study.

Using the same tasks as the first study, both target and menu selection were faster with the touch screen than with the keyboard or mouse. Menu selection performance with the mouse improved from the first study, but was still not significantly different from performance obtained with the keyboard. There were no significant differences in preference for the three input devices for target selection, but as in the first study, users preferred the touch screen and keyboard to the mouse for menu selection. The authors suggest that since touch selection is a highly practiced skill, the pointing action required with the touch screen may involve less cognitive processing than the actions required with the keyboard and mouse.

While the mouse proved superior in the study reported by Card et al. (1978) and inferior in the studies of Karat et al. (1986), the results are not in conflict. Card et al. compared the mouse to a joystick, step keys, and text keys, while Karat et al. compared it to a touch screen and typing an alphanumeric key. In addition, Card et al. required a confirmation action with all the devices, but only the mouse offered an integrated confirmation button. In the Karat et al. study, the mouse was the only input device tested that required a confirmation action. Thus, the different results of the two studies may reflect in part the overhead introduced by a confirmation action. This overhead was observed quite clearly in Albert's (1982) target acquisition study.

Ahlström and Lenman (1987) evaluated the effectiveness of a touch screen, cursor positioning keys, and a mechanical mouse for selecting a word from a set of 16 words presented in a 4 x 4 matrix, with and without a subsequent typing task. The size of the selectable area around the designated word was also tested at two levels: small (1 line by 6 columns on a 25 line by 80 column display) and large (3 lines by 12 columns). Selections were confirmed by pressing a mouse button with the mouse and pressing the "return" key with the cursor positioning keys. No confirmation action was required following a touch on the touch screen. The time to select a word was generally shortest with the touch screen. The times for the cursor positioning keys and the mouse were similar, with the cursor positioning keys appearing to achieve slightly faster selection times. The number of selection errors was relatively high for the touch screen when the selectable area was small. In general, selection accuracy appeared to be lowest with the touch screen and highest with the mouse. Participants preferred the touch screen for minimizing cursor positioning times, but preferred the cursor positioning keys for precision and convenience.

Ewing, Mehrabanzad, Sheck, Ostroff, and Shneiderman (1986) compared the use of a mouse and arrow-jump keys to select highlighted words in text presented by an interactive encyclopedia system. Arrow-jump keys are a set of four keys that advance the cursor up, down, left, and right to highlighted words. These keys differ from step keys in that a single press of a step key moves the cursor one line or one character at a time while arrow-jump keys can move the cursor to a highlighted word far from the current cursor position with one keystroke if no other highlighted words are on the designated path. Both short and long distances between targets were tested. The study focused on short-term use; thus, users did not have much practice with the devices prior to testing: The arrow-jump keys were quicker than the mouse for both short and long target distances, and users preferred the arrow-jump keys.

Whitfield, Ball, and Bird (1983) compared touch screens and touch-sensitive tablets in three experiments with menu selection tasks. The touch screen did not require a confirmation action. When using the tablet users either pressed a confirmation key or simply removed their finger from the tablet to confirm an entry. Total response time was a combination of both target selection and confirmation time. For all tasks the touch tablet without the confirmation key resulted in the longest response times while the touch screen led to the shortest times. This result was attributed to the longer tablet confirmation time due to a need to reverse finger pressure to confirm an entry. The touch tablet was especially slow for selection of small targets, a result which the authors attribute to the direct eye-hand coordination present with the touch screen but not with the tablet. With respect to errors, the two input devices were comparable. A trackball was also included in the third study. The trackball resulted in somewhat slower response times than either the touch screen or tablet. However, the trackball resulted in a lower error rate than the two touch input devices at all levels of resolution. The authors suggest that touch input devices in general should not be used with high resolution targets or when the task is paced. However, they feel that the touch screen and tablet provide comparable performance.

Haller, Mutschler, and Voss (1984) compared a light pen, matrix-encoded graphic tablet, mouse, trackball, cursor positioning keys, and voice recognizer for a task requiring the location and correction of 18 erroneous characters in a page of text. Location was performed using one of the six devices, and correction was performed using either keyboard or voice. Positioning time, excluding correction, was shortest for the light pen and longest for voice input. The average times for the graphic tablet, mouse, trackball, and cursor keys fell between the light pen and voice input and did not differ significantly from each other. The average positioning errors were: light pen and cursor keys, 0%; voice input, 0.9%; graphic tablet, 1.4%; mouse, 4.2%, and trackball, 5.6%. Both correction methods, keyboard and voice input, resulted in equivalent performance. The authors suggest that the light pen is well suited for cursor positioning, as are the mouse and trackball if their gain is sufficiently low.

Struckman-Johnson, Swierenga, and Shieh (1984) compared cursor keys, a position-control displacement joystick, a trackball, and a light pen for a text-editing task. Fifty words were displayed on the screen, ten of which contained an extra highlighted letter. Participants positioned the cursor at the extra letter and, for all devices but the light pen, pressed an associated enter key, thereby deleting the letter. The light pen did not require a separate confirmation action. In terms of task completion time, significant differences were found between all devices. The light pen was the fastest, followed by the trackball, joystick, and keyboard, respectively. With respect to errors, the keyboard and trackball resulted in the best performance, with the joystick worst (a measure of errors was not obtained for the light pen). The trackball and light pen were preferred over the keyboard and the joystick.

Revelle and Strommen (1990) investigated the effects of practice on children's ability to use a binary joystick, mouse, and trackball. Three-year old children used the devices to perform an item selection task over five consecutive days. The results indicated that while task completion times for all three devices declined substantially over the five sessions, the joystick had the longest task completion time both before and after practice. Completion times for the mouse and trackball were not significantly different from each other. On both days 1 and 5, boys were faster than girls using the joystick, while girls were faster than boys using the trackball. There was no gender difference in the speed of mouse use. On the first day of use, the mouse resulted in more selection errors than the joystick or trackball, which were not significantly different from each other. In the fifth session, however, there were no significant differences in error rates across the three devices. Of all the devices, the children appeared to have the most difficulty controlling the joystick. They were relatively quick with the mouse on the first day, but were the most inaccurate in using it. By the fifth day, however, they gained in both speed and accuracy, using the mouse quickly and with many fewer errors. The high initial error rate seemed to be due to the mouse's requirement that the cursor be moved and the confirmation button be pressed using the same hand. Children inadvertently moved the mouse as they pressed a button to select an item. With practice, they gained enough control over their movements to overcome this difficulty. The trackball seemed to allow children tighter initial control of the cursor than either the joystick or the mouse. With the trackball fixed in a stable base, pressing the confirmation button (with the opposite hand) did not result in movement of the trackball.

55.9.3 Continuous Tracking Tasks

In a continuous tracking task, the operator uses an input device to try to match a cursor's position at all times with that of a moving target. Although there is a rich history of research on human performance in continuous tracking tasks (see, for example, Poulton, 1974), only a few recent studies compare computer input devices in continuous tracking tasks.

Swierenga and Struckman-Johnson (1984) compared a trackball, a position-control displacement joystick that was not spring loaded, and a mouse in a compensatory tracking task (that is, one in which only the direction and magnitude of the error between the target and the tracking cursor is displayed). Tracking error was lower for the trackball and joystick than for the mouse. The trackball and joystick did not differ significantly. Participants preferred the joystick to either the trackball or the mouse for this task. Reinhart and Marken (1985) compared a mouse and a rate-control force joystick on a pursuit tracking task (that is, both the target and the tracking cursor were displayed). In terms of root-mean-square error and stability, the mouse led to better performance than the joystick.

55.9.4 Multiple Tasks

Epps (1987) compared performance with six devices (absolute touch tablet, relative touch tablet, optical mouse, trackball, rate-control displacement joystick, and rate-control force joystick) on several tasks related to graphics editing: adjusting the aspect ratio and size of a rectangle; aligning a cursor with horizontal, vertical, and oblique lines; acquiring a square target; and drawing short horizontal and vertical lines between two points. Prior to conducting the study the display/control gain functions for the mouse, trackball, relative tablet, displacement joystick, and force joystick were optimized based on the results of a series of independent experiments. Two buttons were operated by the participant's nondominant hand with all devices except the mouse, which had its own buttons. Across the different tasks, participants consistently completed the tasks most quickly with the trackball and the mouse. The trackball and mouse were preferred by participants over the other devices. Differences among the remaining four devices were less obvious. The absolute touch tablet was about as quick as the trackball and mouse for tasks requiring only moderate cursor positioning accuracy (adjusting the aspect ratio and size of a rectangle and acquiring a square target), but was slower for tasks requiring greater positioning accuracy (aligning the cursor with lines and drawing short lines between two points).

Sperling and Tullis (1988) compared the performance of a mechanical mouse and a trackball on target acquisition, dragging, and tracing tasks. In the target acquisition task, participants moved the display cursor into a 1 cm x 1 cm square target and confirmed the acquisition by clicking the mouse or trackball button. In the dragging task, participants selected a designated menu heading, dragged the display cursor through the menu's items to a designated item, keeping the button on the input device held down, and selected the menu item by releasing the device button. In the tracing task, participants traced the display cursor along a thick zigzag line composed of horizontal and vertical segments while holding the device button down. In their first study, involving only the target acquisition task, there was no significant difference in the number of acquisition errors made with the mouse and trackball (errors were made on about 2% of the trials). There was a significant difference in the target acquisition times: The mouse resulted in times about 15% shorter than those with the trackball. Both the participants who reported normally using the trackball in their work and those who reported normally using the mouse acquired targets faster with the mouse in this study. In their second study, involving the target acquisition, dragging, and tracing tasks, Sperling and Tullis found no significant difference in the number of errors made with the mouse and trackball on the acquisition and dragging tasks (errors were made on about 3% of the trials with these tasks). The tracing task, however, was performed with significantly fewer errors using the mouse than with the trackball. The mouse was faster than the trackball on all three of the tasks.

Han, Jorna, Miller, and Tan (1990) compared the performance of a mechanical mouse, position-control displacement joystick, touch tablet, and trackball on a target acquisition task in one experiment and on a target acquisition task, a file and icon manipulation task (opening and closing windows, menu selection, and dragging files and folders), a text selection and editing task, and a drawing task in a second experiment. In the first study, the participants acquired targets fastest with the mouse and joystick, which had task completion times not significantly different from each other. The touch tablet was slower and the trackball was slowest. In the second study, participants from the first experiment were classified as experienced users. Another group of participants had prior experience with the mouse, but not with the other devices. These users were classified as novice users. For the target acquisition task, the experienced users were faster with the joystick than with the touch tablet, with the times for the mouse and trackball falling in between. The "novice" users were faster with the mouse than with the touch tablet, with the times for the joystick and trackball falling in between. Time measures were not taken for the object manipulation, text entering and editing, and drawing tasks. Users expressed the greatest preference for the mouse, in terms of speed, accuracy, ease-of-use, comfort, and overall performance. The position-control displacement joystick placed second in terms of user preference, followed by the trackball, with the touch tablet least preferred.

Mack and Montaniz (1991) compared the use of a mechanical mouse and a capacitive touch screen on several tasks performed within a graphical windowing environment designed for use with a mouse and keyboard. Users controlled how touch screen interactions were interpreted by tapping an icon at the bottom of the screen. The icon cycled through three states: In state 1, a single tap on the touch screen was interpreted as a single button click with a mouse. In state 2, a single tap was interpreted as a double-click with a mouse. In state 3, a tap, touch, and drag was interpreted as a dragging action with a mouse (i.e., moving the mouse with the mouse button depressed). The tasks included opening one or more document files in windows, editing document content, arranging windows, and copying and pasting data from one document to another. Two display orientations were tested with the touch screen: vertical, as with the mouse, and with the top of the screen tilted back 30 degrees (0.52 rad) from vertical. The touch screen was also tested using both a finger and a stylus. The results indicated that task completion times were comparable for the mouse and the tilted touch screen used with a stylus. Task completion times with the mouse were, however, faster than those for the vertical touch screen with stylus, and the vertical and tilted touch screens with finger. The results were similar with respect to errors: The mouse and touch screen did not differ significantly when the touch screen was tilted and operated using a stylus. These two interaction techniques were significantly less errorful than any of the other techniques, which did not differ significantly from each other. Mack and Montaniz suggest that for tasks performed within graphical windowing environments, the finger is an awkward instrument compared with the mouse and the stylus, and should be used only when such an interaction technique has some significant added value that trades against the performance difficulties imposed by its implementation.

Casali (1992) compared performance of cursor positioning keys, a trackball, a mechanical mouse, a stylus-operated graphic tablet in absolute mode, and a displacement joystick in a target acquisition task. Two selection modes were tested: point and click (i.e., move to the target and click a button down to select the target) and drag (click a button down, move to the target, and release the button to select the target). Three groups of individuals were tested: a group of nondisabled users, a group of users with impaired hand and arm function (as a result of a spinal cord injury) who scored relatively high on an upper extremity motor skills assessment test, and another group of users with impaired hand and arm function who scored relatively low on this test. Regardless of the physical skill level of the user, the rank ordering of the five devices with respect to target acquisition speed was the same: The mouse, trackball, and tablet provided faster performance than the cursor positioning keys, which provided faster performance than the joystick. Hence, the "better" devices for individuals with limited hand and arm motor skills were the same as for those without such limitations, provided the individuals had the physical skill to operate the device (either in its standard configuration or with the addition of an aid or modification). Performance with the trackball, mouse, and tablet was not affected by the selection mode; however, dragging resulted in slower performance than pointing and clicking for the joystick and the cursor positioning keys.

MacKenzie, Sellen, and Buxton (1991) compared three devices (a mechanical mouse, a trackball, and a stylus-operated graphic tablet) in the performance of pointing and dragging target acquisition tasks. In both tasks targets appeared on each side of the screen. In the pointing task participants moved the cursor back and forth between the two targets with the mouse or trackball button up (or with little downward pressure on the graphic tablet stylus). A down-up action on the mouse button, trackball button, or graphic tablet stylus selected a target once it had been acquired by the cursor and initiated the next target acquisition task. In the dragging task movement occurred with the mouse or trackball button down (or with heavier downward pressure on the graphic tablet stylus). An up-down action on the mouse button, trackball button, or tablet stylus selected a target once it had been acquired and initiated the next acquisition task.

Mean movement times for the mouse, tablet, and trackball were 674, 665, and 1101 ms, respectively, for the pointing task and 916, 802, and 1284 ms, respectively, for the dragging task. Performance was generally faster for the pointing task than for the dragging task. The movement times for the mouse and tablet were comparable for the pointing task, but performance degraded more for the mouse than for the tablet or trackball when the task was changed to dragging. As a result, the tablet was faster than the mouse for the dragging task. The trackball was the slowest device for both the pointing and dragging tasks. Error rates for the pointing task were 3.5% for the mouse, 4.0% for the tablet, and 3.9% for the trackball. Error rates for the dragging task were higher, with means of 10.8% for the mouse, 13.6% for the tablet, and 17.3% for the trackball. The differences in error rates for the three devices were not significant for the pointing task. They were significant for the dragging task, with the mouse yielding the fewest errors and the trackball the most. The authors explain the trackball's slow movement times for both tasks and its high error rate during dragging by noting the extent of muscle and limb interaction required to maintain the "button down" action during dragging and to change the button position while holding the trackball stationary. The button on the trackball was operated with the thumb while the ball was rolled with the fingers of the same hand. It was particularly difficult to hold the ball stationary with the fingers while releasing or depressing the button with the thumb. The mouse and tablet separated the means to effect these actions to a greater extent: Motion was realized through the wrist or forearm, while mode transitions were executed by the index finger for the mouse or by applying different degrees of downward pressure for the tablet.

Kabbash, MacKenzie, and Buxton (1993) ran a follow-up experiment to that reported by MacKenzie et al. (1991). The study was essentially identical, except in one respect: In this study the participants (all right-handed) used their left (nondominant) hand to perform the tasks. Overall, for each hand the slowest device was the trackball, with performance on the mechanical mouse somewhat slower than on the stylus-operated tablet. Movement times for the mouse and tablet were about 27% longer with the left hand than with the right. However, there was no difference in movement times between hands for the trackball. The effect of task was reflected in slower movement times for dragging than pointing. Although the right-handed movement times showed greater degradation for the mouse than for either the tablet or the trackball when going from pointing to dragging, the left hand showed equal degradation for the mouse and the tablet, with less degradation for the trackball. Error rates for left-handed operation were approximately equal to those reported for the right-handed users by MacKenzie et al. (1991), with two exceptions: Right-handed operation was superior to left-handed when the mouse was used to perform the dragging task and left-handed operation was superior to right-handed when the trackball was used to perform the dragging task. Thus, the use of the thumb to operate the trackball button while using the fingers of the same hand to roll the trackball, seemed to be difficult when users did this with their right (dominant) hand (MacKenzie et al., 1991), but did not seem to present difficulty when users did this with their left (nondominant) hand. The authors conclude from the results of their study (including the results of some finer-grained analyses of movement time not presented here) that for rough pointing or motion, the non-dominant hand can be as effective as the dominant hand. While there was the least change between hands with the trackball, non-dominant hand performance with the tablet and mouse was still superior to performance with the trackball. The authors caution that this does not imply that a mouse for each hand is the best choice if one is to use both hands to perform tasks: for some tasks, the ease of acquiring a fixed position device (such as the touch tablet, trackball, or joystick) may more than compensate for slower task performance once the device is acquired.

Rutledge and Selker (1990) compared the performance of a mechanical mouse located adjacent to a computer keyboard on the user's preferred side and a 2 mm diameter by 2 cm long index-finger-operated rate-control force joystick located between the "G" and "H" keys within the keyboard. Two tasks were employed: an item selection task that required a sequence of target acquisitions with no keyboard involvement and a target acquisition task in which the target acquisition started and ended with the hands placed on the keyboard in the touch typing home position. The second task was intended to be representative of those in which a touch typist is engaged in a typing task interspersed with single pointing actions: in such situations a pointing action would begin and end with the typist's hands on the keyboard in the home position. In both tasks, targets were acquired by moving the display cursor to the area within the target and clicking a button: a mouse button for the mouse or a button below the space bar of the keyboard for the joystick. For the task involving the keyboard, each target acquisition started and ended with the user pressing the "J" key (or the "F" key with left-handed users) on the keyboard. The participants in the study were experienced mouse users, but aside from video game experience, relatively inexperienced with the joystick. The results indicated that for the item selection task with no keyboard involvement, the mouse was faster than the joystick. However, for the target acquisition task in which each acquisition started and ended with the hands on the keyboard, the keyboard-integrated joystick was faster than the mouse.

Yamada and Tsuchiya (1994) followed up on Rutledge and Selker's studies with two experiments that compared performance and preference for a commercially available version of the rate-control force joystick studied by Rutledge and Selker, a mechanical mouse, and a small trackball. The new version of the joystick, called the Trackpoint II, was positioned between the "G," "H," and "B" keys within the keyboard. It protruded slightly above the typing keys. An associated pair of click buttons were centered below the keyboard's space bar. The trackball was mounted at the upper right corner of the keyboard. Their first study compared performance of the three devices on Rutledge and Selker's target acquisition task in which the task started and ended with the hands on the keyboard. The participants in the study had never used the Trackpoint II device before. The results of this study differed from those of Rutledge and Selker's study of the same task: the total task completion time was fastest for the mouse, the joystick placed second in speed, and the trackball was slowest. Yamada and Tsuchiya's second study compared participants' preferences for the three devices on Rutledge and Selker's item selection task, which required a sequence of target acquisitions with no keyboard involvement, as well as on their target acquisition task, in which each acquisition started and ended with the hands on the keyboard. The results showed that for the item selection task with no keyboard involvement, the mouse was the most preferred device, the joystick placed second, and the trackball was least preferred. For the target acquisition task in which each acquisition started and ended with the keys on the keyboard, the mouse was again the most preferred device. There was no significant difference in overall preference for the joystick and the trackball.

Douglas and Mithal (1994) compared the performance of a mechanical mouse located adjacent to a computer keyboard and a right-index-finger-operated rate-control force joystick located within the "J" key of the keyboard. There was no visible difference between the appearance of the key joystick keyboard and a standard keyboard apart from cues such as additional legends on the "J" key. To move the display cursor, a user pressed down on the "J" key. After the key was held down for a prespecified interval of time, the keyboard switched to pointing mode. At typical typing speeds, pressing and releasing the "J" key produced a character on the screen. But in pointing mode, the speed and direction of cursor movement was controlled by the magnitude and direction, respectively, of the tangential force applied by the finger to the "J" key. The "F" key was operated by the index finger of the left hand and provided functionality equivalent to a button on a mouse. Releasing the "J" key while in pointing mode returned the keyboard to typing mode. Two tasks were employed: In the first, a target acquisition task, a trial started when a participant clicked to initiate the acquisition and ended when the participant clicked inside the target. The second task was similar to the first, with one addition:

After the participant clicked inside the target, a dialog box appeared asking the participant to type in a specified word. Thus, two additional actions were required to complete this task: after target acquisition the participant had to switch from pointing to positioning the hands appropriately on the keyboard to type, and then the participant had to type a word. The participants in the study had no prior experience with either a mouse or a joystick. The results from the pure target acquisition task showed that participants acquired targets faster with the mouse than with the key joystick. The results from the target acquisition with typing task showed that they took less time to acquire the target with the mouse, less time to switch from the target acquisition subtask to the typing subtask with the key joystick, and about the same amount of time to type the word after using either device to acquire the target. Despite the smaller time to switch from the target acquisition subtask to the typing subtask with the key joystick, participants completed the entire target acquisition with typing task faster with the mouse than with the key joystick. With the overall task time averaging about 2600 ms, the 229 ms saved by the key joystick relative to the mouse when switching subtasks was not enough to compensate for the 588 ms saved by the mouse relative to the joystick in the target acquisition subtask. One aspect of this particular joystick implementation that perhaps limited the time savings possible with it was the constraint imposed by using the "J" key to serve both a typing and a pointing function. This required that the "J" key be pressed down for an interval of time before the keyboard switched to pointing mode so that such a keypress could be differentiated from one in which the user was simply attempting to type the letter "j." In contrast, the keyboard-integrated joystick studied by Rutledge and Selker (1990) and Yamada and Tsuchiya (1994) was a separate device from the typing keys in the keyboard, located between keys in the keyboard. Because it functioned only as a pointing device, no waiting time was imposed by the device before beginning a pointing action.

55.10 Conclusion

There is risk in drawing generalizations about the optimality of a specific input device for a given task or environment based on the empirical research just presented. First, most studies compare a limited number of devices and the devices used vary across studies, making it difficult to compare all of the devices with each other. Second, these studies were published over a period spanning three decades. Improvements in the design of the input devices, as well as the software and hardware with which they were interfaced also make it difficult to draw generalizations. Third, when the same device was used in different experiments, the respective researchers may not have optimized the device for their particular interface. The latter two factors may partially account for discrepancies in results for the same input devices used in different experiments. Additionally, differences in tasks, training, and users result in performance differences with the same device.

Nonetheless, the results of the studies performed to date seem to support a few generalizations reasonably well, particularly for tasks that focus primarily on pointing at or selecting among stationary targets. These tasks include target acquisition and item selection. The direct pointing devices (the touch screen and the light pen) are the fastest at these tasks. Several studies support this conclusion, including those by Ahlström and Lenman (1987), Albert (1982), Haller et al. (1984), Karat et al. (1986), Struckman-Johnson et al. (1984), and Whitfield et al. (1983). The advantage of the direct devices is likely due to their high degree of eye-hand coordination and the familiarity of the pointing actions they employ. The studies by Ahlström and Lenman (1987) and Sears and Shneiderman (1991) suggest that the touch screen is less accurate for positioning a cursor within small targets than the indirect devices (graphic tablet, mouse, trackball, and joystick). The accuracy advantage of the indirect devices is perhaps a result of their freedom from parallax problems, their permitting an unobstructed view of the target and cursor during acquisition, and their use of a separate confirmation action following acquisition of a target. There is little data available on which to base conclusions regarding the accuracy of the light pen. Relative to the indirect devices, it seems likely it would be less accurate: like the indirect devices, it is possible to use a separate confirmation action following acquisition of a target by the light pen; but the light pen introduces parallax problems and it also obstructs the view of the target and the cursor during target acquisition.

Introducing a separate confirmation action following cursor positioning increases response accuracy, but decreases response speed. Albert's (1982) study demonstrates this most clearly with its comparison of a touch screen and light pen with and without a confirmation action. The mouse and the puck-operated graphic tablet offer an efficient configuration for tasks in which a confirmation action is appropriate. A confirmation button can be located underneath the fingertips resting atop the mouse or the puck so that little additional movement is required to execute the confirmation action.

The studies reported by Card et al. (1978), Casali (1992), Douglas and Mithal (1994), Epps (1987), Epps et al. (1986), Rutledge and Selker (1991), and Yamada and Tsuchiya (1994) suggest that among the indirect input devices, the mouse is faster than the joystick. Most of the studies that have compared the speed of the graphic tablet or the trackball with that of the joystick have found the tablet and trackball to be faster than the joystick as well (Albert, 1982; Casali, 1992; Epps, 1987; Epps et al., 1986; and Struckman-Johnson et al., 1984). The studies by MacKenzie et al. (1991), Sperling and Tullis (1988), and Yamada and Tsuchiya (1994) suggest the mouse is also faster than the trackball. However, other studies (Casali, 1992; Epps, 1987; Epps et al., 1986; and Haller et al., 1984) did not find them significantly different in terms of speed. It is difficult to draw a conclusion about the speed of the mouse relative to the graphic tablet: Epps (1987) found the mouse to be faster than the tablet for tasks requiring high levels of positioning accuracy. Most studies that have compared these two devices have not found them to be significantly different in speed (Casali, 1992; Epps et al., 1986; Haller et al., 1984; and MacKenzie et al., 1991). The results are also inconclusive about the speed of the graphic tablet relative to the trackball: Epps (1987) found the trackball to be faster than the tablet for tasks requiring high levels of positioning accuracy. Albert (1982), MacKenzie et al. (1991), and Whitfield et al. (1983) found the tablet to be slower. Other studies that have compared the tablet and the trackball have not found them to be significantly different in speed (Casali, 1992; Epps et al., 1986; Gomez et al., 1982; and Haller et al., 1984).

With respect to the relative accuracy of the indirect input devices, the studies that have been conducted thus far do not provide sufficient data on accuracy to support any general conclusions. It is likely that the overall fit of the device's capabilities to the task and environment, and the quality of the design and implementation of the particular device selected for implementation are more important concerns than any differences in accuracy among the indirect input devices that have not been revealed by the relative speed capabilities of these devices. It appears that users are capable of accurate performance with all of the indirect devices; but the speed data summarized above suggests that it takes longer to complete acquisition and selection tasks accurately with some of the devices than with others, particularly for small target sizes.

It is difficult to draw firm conclusions on the basis of the small amount of work investigating input device performance in continuous tracking tasks. It seems likely that the conclusions drawn for the acquisition of stationary targets are applicable to the tracking of slowly moving targets as well, with one caveat: because operation of the direct pointing devices (the touch screen and light pen) may obscure the operator's view of target movement, these devices may be less appropriate for tracking, especially if the target is small. This leaves the mouse, trackball, and graphic tablet as the devices of choice for the tracking of small, slowly moving targets.

If targets move rapidly and change direction frequently, speed of response to changes in the target location is critical. In such circumstances the trackball and joystick may enhance the operator's ability to respond quickly because they require redirection of finger and hand movement only. A spring-loaded or force-operated joystick may enhance the user's ability to respond to reverses in target direction. The force-operated joystick may also speed response by eliminating the need to move the hand, fingers, and device.

With respect to user preference for the different input devices, the studies that have been conducted suggest that over the range of tasks and situations investigated, the mouse is most frequently the device for which users express the strongest preference. This may in part reflect the versatility of the mouse across tasks and environments. It may also reflect the maturity of the mouse, in terms of its design and refinement relative to the other devices, as well as the greater amount of experience many users have had with this device. Certainly, however, there are a variety of situations (e.g., public access systems that may be used by people unfamiliar with computers and computer input devices) or applications (e.g., handheld, laptop, and mobile computing) in which touch screens, tablets, trackballs, or joysticks are preferred. Further, these devices may be more strongly preferred as their designs and supporting software mature.

The selection of an input device for a specific application should involve the following considerations. First, the characteristics of the task, users, use environment, and existing hardware should be determined. Both present and future demands of the application should be considered. Next, the characteristics of the candidate input devices should be compared with the requirements of the application to narrow the list of candidate devices. Table 1 summarizes the characteristics and relative capabilities of the input devices discussed in this chapter. Previous research and experience concerning the input devices under consideration should be reviewed at this point. User preferences should also be considered. While subjective preferences do not always correspond to ob-

Table 1. Strengths and weaknesses of the standard pointing devices.

	Touch Screen	Light Pen	Touch Tablet with Stylus or Puck	Graphic Tablet	Mouse	Track-ball	Joy-stick
Eye-hand coordination	+	+	0	0	0	0	0
Unobstructed view of display	-	-	+	+	+	+	+
Ability to attend to display	+	0	+	0	0	+	+
Freedom from parallax problems	-	-	+	+	+	+	+
Flexibility of placement within workspace	-	-	+	0	0	+	+
Minimal space requirements	+	+	0	-	-	+	+
Minimal training requirements	+	0	0	0	0	0	0
Comfort in extended use	-	-	0	0	0	0	0
Absolute mode capability	+	+	+	+	-	-	-
Relative mode capability	-	-	+	+	+	+	0
Capability to emulate other devices	-	-	+	+	-	-	-
Suitability for:							
rapid pointing	+	+	0	0	+	0	-
accurate pointing	-	-	0	+	+	+	0
pointing with confirmation	-	0	0	+	+	0	0
drawing	-	0	-	+	0	-	-
tracing	-	-	-	+	-	-	-
continuous tracking, slow targets	0	0	+	+	+	+	0
continuous tracking, fast targets	-	-	0	0	0	0	+
alphanumeric data entry	0	-	-	0	-	-	-

Legend: + Strong 0 Neutral - Weak

jective performance capabilities, it is important to provide the user with a tool she or he will use.

Once a tentative selection has been made on the basis of human performance, user preference, engineering, and cost considerations, the input device should be tested in the working environment (or a simulation of this environment) with representatives of the intended user population. The implementation of the device should then be optimized to suit the users and the environment. A systematic approach to implementation should ultimately provide a tool that is accepted by its users and well matched to its tasks and environments.

55.11 References

Ahlström, B., and Lenman, S. (1987). Touch screen, cursor keys, and mouse interaction. In B. Knave and P.-G. Widebäck (Eds.), Work with Display Units 86 (pp. 831-837). Amsterdam: Elsevier.

Akamatsu, M., MacKenzie, I. S., and Hasbroucq, T. (1995). A comparison of tactile, auditory, and visual feedback in a pointing task using a mouse-type device. *Ergonomics, 38,* 816-827.

Akamatsu, M., and Sato, S. (1994). A multi-modal mouse with tactile and force feedback. *International Journal of Human-Computer Studies, 40,* 443-453.

Albert, A. E. (1982). The effect of graphic input devices on performance in a cursor positioning task. In *Proceedings of the Human Factors Society 26th Annual Meeting* (pp. 54-58). Santa Monica, CA: Human Factors and Ergonomics Society.

Arnaut, L. Y., and Greenstein, J. S. (1986). Optimizing the touch tablet: The effects of control-display gain and method of cursor control. *Human Factors, 28,* 717-726.

Arnaut, L. Y., and Greenstein, J. S. (1990). Is display/control gain a useful metric for optimizing an interface? *Human Factors, 32,* 651-663.

Avons, S. E., Beveridge, M. C., Hickman, A. T., and Hitch, G. J. (1983). Considerations on using a lightpen-interactive system with young children. *Behavior Research Methods & Instrumentation, 15,* 75-78.

Becker, J. A., and Greenstein, J. S. (1986). A lead-lag compensation approach to display/control gain for touch tablets. In *Proceedings of the Human Factors Society 30th Annual Meeting* (pp. 332-336). Santa Monica, CA: Human Factors and Ergonomics Society.

Beringer, D. B. (1979). The design and evaluation of complex systems: Application to a man-machine interface for aerial navigation. In *Proceedings of the Human Factors Society 23rd Annual Meeting* (pp. 75-79). Santa Monica, CA: Human Factors and Ergonomics Society.

Beringer, D. B. (1989). Touch panel sampling strategies and keypad performance comparisons. In *Proceedings of the Human Factors Society 33rd Annual Meeting* (pp. 71-75). Santa Monica, CA: Human Factors and Ergonomics Society.

Beringer, D. B., and Peterson, J. G. (1985). Underlying behavioral parameters of the operation of touch-input devices: biases, models and feedback. *Human Factors, 21,* 445-458.

Bolt, R. A. (1984). *The human interface: Where people and computers meet.* Belmont, CA: Lifetime Learning Publications.

Brown, E., Buxton, W., and Murtagh, K. (1985). Windows on tablets as a means of achieving virtual input devices.*Computer Graphics, 19,* 225-230.

Buxton, W., Hill, R., and Rowley, P. (1985). Issues and techniques in touch-sensitive tablet input. *Computer Graphics, 19,* 69-85.

Calhoun, G. L., Janson, W. P., and Arbak, C. J. (1986). Use of eye control to select switches. In *Proceedings of the Human Factors Society 30th Annual Meeting* (pp. 154-158). Santa Monica, CA: Human Factors and Ergonomics Society.

Card, S. K., English, W. K., and Burr, B. J. (1978). Evaluation of mouse, rate-controlled isometric joystick, step keys, and text keys for text selection on a CRT. *Ergonomics, 21,* 601-613.

Casali, S. P. (1992). Cursor control device use by persons with physical disabilities: Implications for hardware and software design. In *Proceedings of the Human Factors Society 36th Annual Meeting* (pp. 311-315). Santa Monica, CA: Human Factors and Ergonomics Society.

Davis, G. I., and Badger, S. (1982). User-computer interface design of a complex tactical display terminal. In *Proceedings of the Human Factors Society 26th Annual Meeting* (pp. 768-771). Santa Monica, CA: Human Factors and Ergonomics Society.

Douglas, S. A., and Mithal, A. K. (1994). The effect of reducing homing time on the speed of a finger-controlled isometric pointing device. In *Proceedings of the CHI '94 Conference on Human Factors in Computing Systems* (pp. 474-481). New York: ACM.

Ellingstad, V. S., Parng, A., Gehlen, G. R., Swierenga, S. J., and Auflick, J. (1985, March). *An evaluation of the touch tablet as a command and control input device* (Tech. Report). Vermillion: University of South Dakota, Dept. of Psychology.

Engel, F. L., Goossens, P., and Haakma, R. (1994). Improved efficiency through I- and E-feedback: A trackball with contextual force feedback. *International Journal of Human-Computer Studies, 41,* 949-974.

English, W. K., Engelbart, D. C., and Berman, M. L. (1967). Display-selection techniques for text manipulation. *IEEE Transactions on Human Factors in Electronics, HFE-8,* 5-15.

Epps, B. W. (1987). A comparison of cursor control devices on a graphics editing task. In *Proceedings of the Human Factors Society 31st Annual Meeting* (pp. 442-446). Santa Monica, CA: Human Factors and Ergonomics Society.

Epps, B. W., Snyder, H. L., and Muto, W. H. (1986). Comparison of six cursor devices on a target acquisition task. In *1986 SID Digest of Technical Papers* (pp. 302-305). Los Angeles, CA: Society for Information Display.

Ewing, J., Mehrabanzad, S., Sheck, S., Ostroff, D., and Shneiderman, B. (1986). An experimental comparison of a mouse and arrow-jump keys for an interactive encyclopedia. *International Journal of Man-Machine Studies, 24,* 29-45.

Foley, J. D., and van Dam, A. (1982). *Fundamentals of interactive computer graphics.* Reading, MA: Addison-Wesley.

Gaertner, K.-P., and Holzhausen, K.-P. (1980). Controlling air traffic with a touch sensitive screen. *Applied Ergonomics, 11,* 17-22.

Glenn, F. A., Iavecchia, H. P., Ross, L. V., Stokes, J. M., Weiland, W. J., Weiss, D., and Zaklad, A. L. (1986). Eye-voice-controlled interface. In *Proceedings of the Human Factors Society 30th Annual Meeting* (pp. 322-326). Santa Monica, CA: Human Factors and Ergonomics Society.

Gomez, A. D., Wolfe, S. W., Davenport, E. W., and Calder, B. D. (1982, February). *LMDS: Lightweight modular display system* (NOSC Tech. Report 767). San Diego, CA: Naval Ocean Systems Center.

Gould, J. D., Greene, S. L., Boies, S. J., Meluson, A., and Rasamny, M. (1990). Using a touchscreen for simple tasks. *Interacting with Computers, 2,* 59-74.

Hall, A. D., Cunningham, J. B., Roache, R. P., and Cox, J. W. (1988). Factors affecting performance using touch-entry systems: Tactual recognition fields and system accuracy. *Journal of Applied Psychology, 73,* 711-720.

Haller, R., Mutschler, H., and Voss, M. (1984). Comparison of input devices for correction of typing errors in office systems. In *Proceedings of the Interact '84 Conference, First IFIP Conference on 'Human-Computer Interaction'* (Vol. 2, pp. 218-223).

Han, S. H., Jorna, G. C., Miller, R. H., and Tan, K. C. (1990). A comparison of four input devices for the Macintosh interface. In *Proceedings of the Human Factors Society 34th Annual Meeting* (pp. 267-271). Santa Monica, CA: Human Factors and Ergonomics Society.

Hatamian, M., and Brown, E. F. (1985). A new light pen with subpixel accuracy. *AT&T Technical Journal, 64,* 1065-1075.

Hill, G. W., Gunn, W. A., Martin, S. L., and Schwartz, D. R. (1991). Perceived difficulty and user control in mouse usage. In *Proceedings of the Human Factors Society 35th Annual Meeting* (pp. 295-299). Santa Monica, CA: Human Factors and Ergonomics Society.

Hodes, D., and Akagi, K. (1986). Study, development, and design of a mouse. In *Proceedings of the Human Factors Society 30th Annual Meeting* (pp. 900-904). Santa Monica, CA: Human Factors and Ergonomics Society.

Jacob, R. J. K. (1991). The use of eye movements in human-computer interaction techniques: What you look at is what you get. *ACM Transactions on Information Systems, 9,* 152-169.

Jellinek, H. D., and Card, S. K. (1990). Powermice and user performance. In *Proceedings of the CHI'90 Conference on Human Factors in Computing Systems* (pp. 213-220). New York: ACM.

Jenkins, W. L., and Karr, A. C. (1954). The use of a joystick in making settings on a simulated scope face. *Journal of Applied Psychology, 38,* 457-461.

Kabbash, P., MacKenzie, I. S., and Buxton, W. (1993). Human performance using computer input devices in the preferred and non-preferred hands. In *Proceedings of the INTERCHI '93 Conference on Human Factors in Computing Systems* (pp. 474-481). New York: ACM.

Karat, J., McDonald, J. E., and Anderson, M. (1986). A comparison of menu selection techniques: Touch panel, mouse, and keyboard. *International Journal of Man-Machine Studies, 25,* 73-88.

Logan, J. D. (1985). Touch screens diversify. *Electronic Products,* Nov. 1, 61-67.

Mack, R., and Montaniz, F. (1991). A comparison of touch and mouse interaction techniques for a graphical windowing software environment. In *Proceedings of the Human Factors Society 35th Annual Meeting* (pp. 286-289). Santa Monica, CA: Human Factors and Ergonomics Society.

MacKenzie, I. S., Sellen, A., and Buxton, W. (1991). A comparison of input devices in elemental pointing and dragging tasks. In *Proceedings of the CHI'91 Conference on Human Factors in Computing Systems* (pp. 161-166). New York: ACM.

Mehr, M. H., and Mehr, E. (1972). Manual digital positioning in 2 axes: A comparison of joystick and trackball controls. In *Proceedings of the Human Factors Society 16th Annual Meeting* (pp. 110-116). Santa Monica, CA: Human Factors and Ergonomics Society.

Mithal, A. K., and Douglas, S. A. (1996). Differences in movement microstructure of the mouse and the finger-controlled isometric joystick. In *Proceedings of the CHI '96 Conference on Human Factors in Computing Systems* (pp. 300-307). New York: ACM.

Parrish, R. N., Gates, J. L., Munger, S. J., Grimma, P. R., and Smith, L. T. (1982, February). *Development of design guidelines and criteria for user/operator transactions with battlefield automated systems. Phase II Final Report: Volume II. Prototype handbook for combat and materiel developers* (Tech. Report). Alexandria, VA: U.S. Army Research Institute for the Behavioral and Social Sciences.

Pekelney, R., and Chu, R. (1995). Design criteria of an ergonomic mouse computer input device. In *Proceedings of the Human Factors and Ergonomics Society 39th Annual Meeting* (pp. 369-373). Santa Monica, CA: Human Factors and Ergonomics Society.

Plaisant, C., and Sears, A. (1992). Touchscreen interfaces for alphanumeric data entry. In *Proceedings of the Human Factors Society 36th Annual Meeting* (pp. 293-297). Santa Monica, CA: Human Factors and Ergonomics Society.

Potter, R. L., Weldon, L. J., and Shneiderman, B. (1988). Improving the accuracy of touch screens: An experimental evaluation of three strategies. In *Proceedings of the CHI'88 Conference on Human Factors in Computing Systems* (pp. 27-32). New York: ACM.

Poulton, E.C. (1974). *Tracking skill and manual control.* New York: Academic.

Price, L. A., and Cordova, C.A. (1983). Use of mouse buttons. In *Proceedings of the CHI '83 Conference on Human Factors in Computing Systems* (pp. 262-266). New York: ACM.

Reinhart, W., and Marken, R. (1985). Control systems analysis of computer pointing devices. In *Proceedings of the Human Factors Society 29th Annual Meeting* (pp. 119-121). Santa Monica, CA: Human Factors and Ergonomics Society.

Revelle, G. L., and Strommen, E. F. (1990). The effects of practice and input device used on young children's computer control. *Journal of Computing in Childhood Education, 2,* 33-41.

Rosenberg, D. J., and Martin, G. (1988). Human performance evaluation of digitizer pucks for computer input of spatial information. *Human Factors, 30,* 231-235.

Rutledge, J. D., and Selker, T. (1990). Force-to-motion functions for pointing. In D. Diaper, et al. (Eds.), *Human-Computer Interaction-INTERACT '90* (pp. 701-706). Amsterdam: Elsevier.

Schulze, L. J. H., and Snyder, H. L. (1983, October). *A comparative evaluation of five touch entry devices* (Tech. Report HFL-83-6). Blacksburg: Virginia Polytechnic Institute and State University, Department of Industrial Engineering and Operations Research.

Sears, A. (1991). Improving touchscreen keyboards: Design issues and a comparison with other devices. *Interacting with Computers, 3,* 253-269.

Sears, A., Revis, D., Swatski, J., Crittenden, R., and Shneiderman, B. (1993). Investigating touchscreen typing: The effect of keyboard size on typing speed. *Behaviour & Information Technology, 12,* 17-22.

Sears, A., and Shneiderman, B. (1991). High precision touchscreens: Design strategies and comparisons with a mouse. *International Journal of Man-Machine Studies, 34,* 593-613.

Sherr, S. (Ed.). (1988). *Input devices.* San Diego: Academic.

Sperling, B. B., and Tullis, T. S. (1988). Are you a better "mouser" or "trackballer?" A comparison of cursor-positioning performance. *SIGCHI Bulletin, 19* (3), 77-81.

Stammers, R. C., and Bird, J. M. (1980). Controller evaluation of a touch input air traffic data system: An "indelicate" experiment. *Human Factors, 22,* 581-589.

Starker, I., and Bolt, R. A. (1990). A gaze-responsive self-disclosing display. In *Proceedings of the CHI'90 Conference on Human Factors In Computing Systems* (pp. 3-9). New York: ACM.

Strommen, E. F., Revelle, G. L., Medoff, L. M., and Razavi, S. (1996). Slow and steady wins the race? Three-year-old children and pointing device use. *Behaviour & Information Technology, 15,* 57-64.

Struckman-Johnson, D. L., Swierenga, S. J., and Shieh, K. (1984, January). *Alternative cursor control devices: An empirical comparison using a text editing task* (Final Report: Task 11.2). Vermillion: University of South Dakota, Human Factors Laboratory.

Swezey, R.W., and Davis, E.G. (1983). A case study of human factors guidelines in computer graphics. *IEEE Computer Graphics and Applications, 3* (8), 21-30.

Swierenga, S. J., and Struckman-Johnson, D. L. (1984, January). *Alternative cursor control devices: An empirical comparison using a tracking task* (Final Report: Task 11.3). Vermillion, SD: University of South Dakota, Human Factors Laboratory.

Tränkle, U., and Deutschmann, D. (1991). Factors influencing speed and precision of cursor positioning using a mouse. *Ergonomics, 34,* 161-174.

Valk, M. A. (1985). An experiment to study touchscreen "button" design. In *Proceedings of the Human Factors Society 29th Annual Meeting* (pp. 127-131). Santa Monica, CA: Human Factors and Ergonomics Society.

Ware, C., and Mikaelian, H. H. (1987). An evaluation of an eye tracker as a device for computer input. In *Proceedings of the CHI+GI 1987 Conference on Human Factors in Computing Systems and Graphics Interface* (pp. 183-188). New York: ACM.

Weiman, N., Beaton, R. J., Knox, S. T., and Glasser, P. C. (1985, September). *Effects of key layout, visual feedback. and encoding algorithm on menu selection with LED-based touch panels* (Tech. Report HFL 604-02). Beaverton, OR: Tektronix, Human Factors Research Laboratory.

Whitfield, D., Ball, R. G., and Bird, J. M. (1983). Some comparisons of on-display and off-display touch input devices for interaction with computer generated displays. *Ergonomics, 26,* 1033-1053.

Yamada, S., and Tsuchiya, K. (1994). A study of coordination of typing and mouse pointer control in computer operation. In *Proceedings of the 22nd Seminar on Science and Technology, Symposium for the Application of Ergonomics in Design and Engineering* (pp. 29-43). Tokyo: Interchange Association, Japan.

Zimmerman, T. G., Lanier, J., Blanchard, C., Bryson, S., and Harvill, Y. (1987). A hand gesture interface device. In *Proceedings of the CHI+GI 1987 Conference on Human Factors in Computing Systems and Graphics Interface* (pp. 189-192). New York: ACM.

Handbook of Human-Computer Interaction
Second, completely revised edition
M. Helander, T.K. Landauer, P. Prabhu (eds.)

Chapter 56

Ergonomics of CAD Systems

Holger Luczak and Johannes Springer
Inst. of Ind. Engineering and Ergonomics
Aachen University of Technology
Germany

56.1 Introduction

Today's design departments are usually equipped with highly sophisticated CAD systems. Their application should increase the design efficiency to rationalize the product-development-process. But, more and more experiences of CAD users show a gap between the goals and reality of CAD implementation (e.g. Abeln, 1990). Also, experiments in different design departments verify deficiencies in the use of advantages of the functional capacities of CAD systems (Luczak, et al. 1991). This is one reason for the poor performance in producing technical drawings.

In a design department there is neither a question of the rationalization goal nor the implementation of CAD systems. Today the characteristics of a CAD system which are important to improve are the adequacy to task requirements and the adaptation to different user qualifications. But if ergonomic design rules are ignored the consequence will be a low design efficiency and a higher strain level.

56.1.1 Characteristics of Design Work and CAD Systems

Any ergonomics approach to solve an ergonomic design problem begins with an analytical procedure to identify and systematize the features and characteristics of the respective work or task. So, if it is the objective of the paper to describe and order the facts, regularities, and laws, how CAD-systems interfere in design work, it is necessary to introduce something like a task separation or sequence of actions, by which the essentials of this (design) work become obvious.

Technically speaking, in the generation of a product, design is the functional unit in a company, where customer orders specified as customer demands or technical requirements are transformed into a mostly graphical model of the product, which means parts lists, parts drawings, and composition drawings (see figure 1) as work results on the basis of the application of natural science and engineering knowledge about the product domain. The purpose of the CAD-system in this context

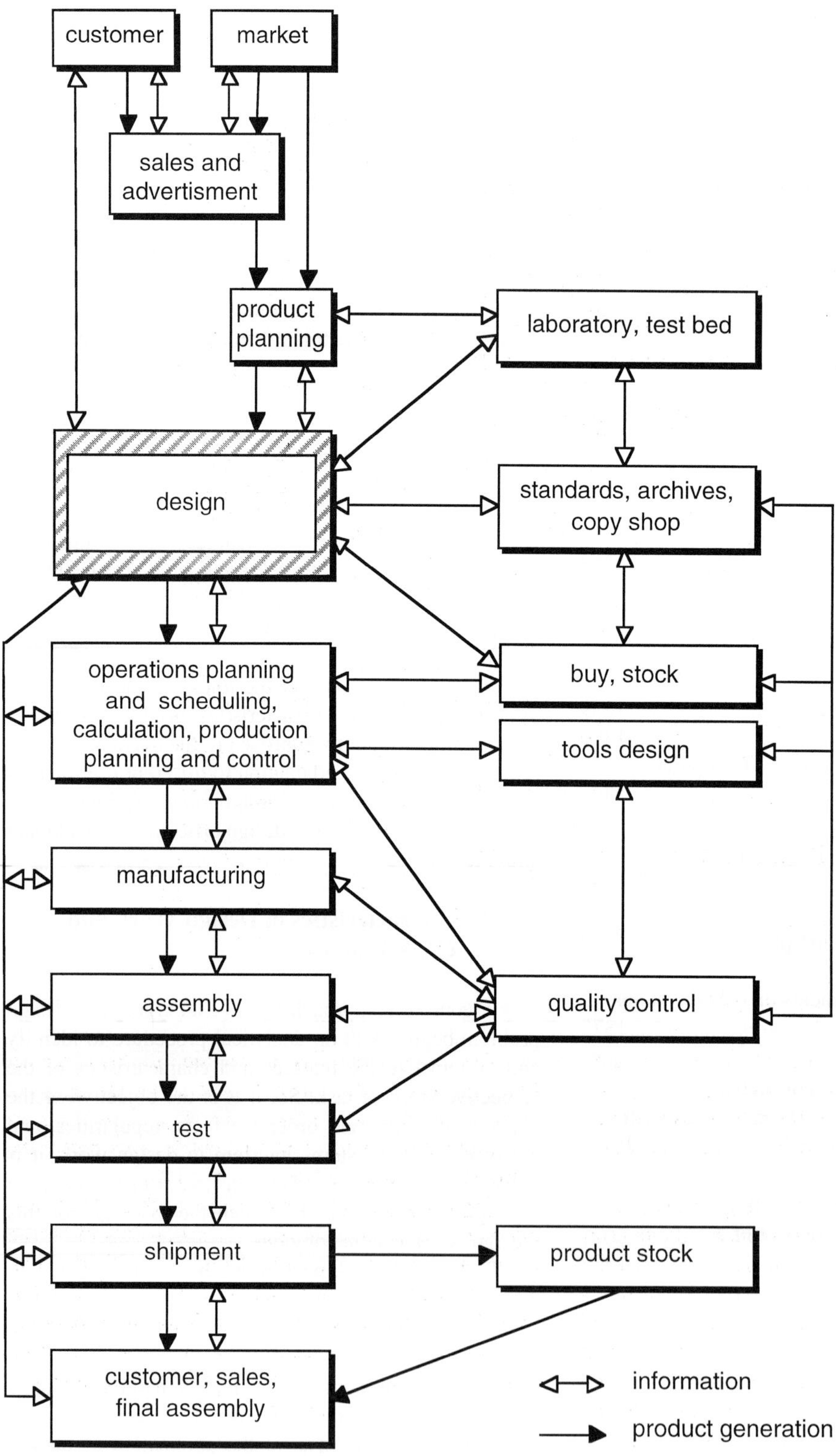

Figure 1. The design department in the companies context. *(Beitz and Ehrlenspiel, 1984).*

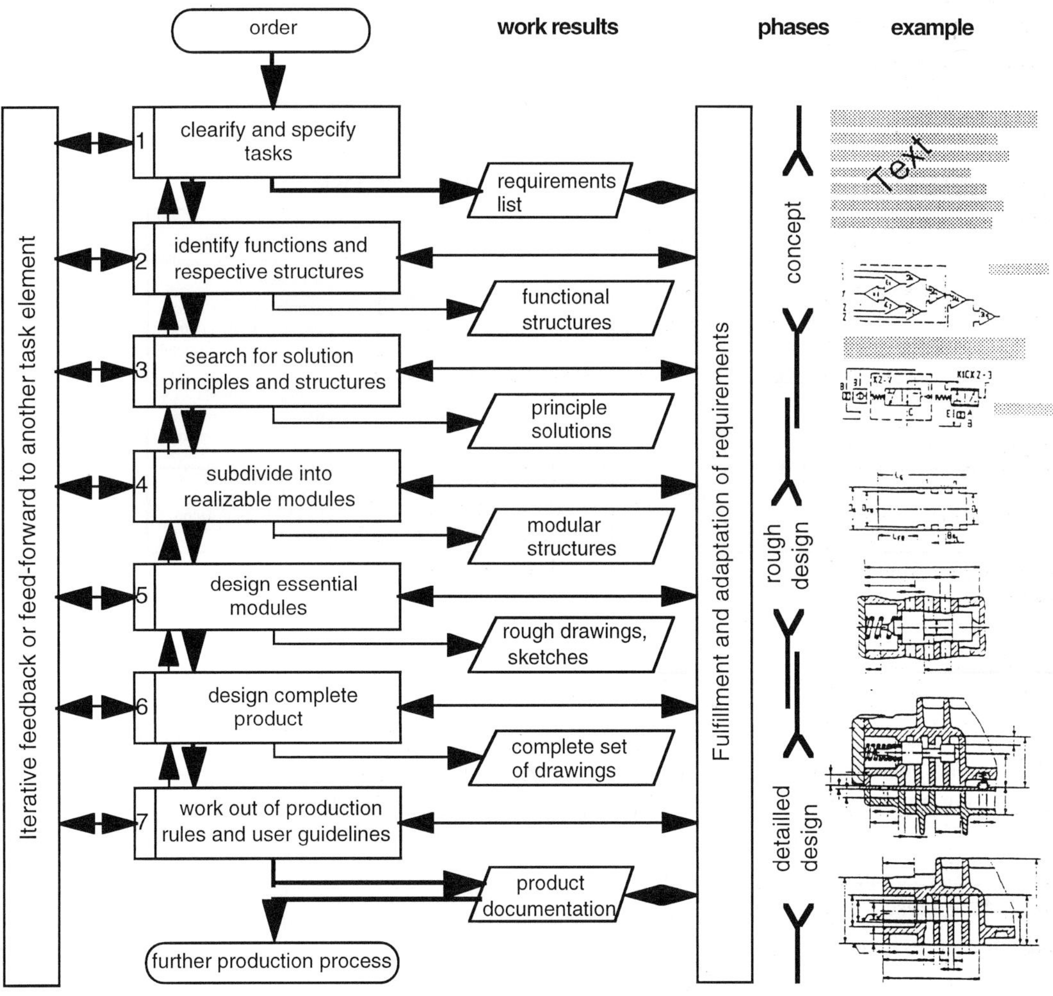

Figure 2. Steps and work results in the design process. *(VDI, 1993)*

is to have the work result coded in a computer-compatible form, which means, that the engineering data produced in the design department can be used via an access to the respective data repository by all functional units in the whole company.

Organizationally speaking, the design process consists of phases, in which an order is subdivided into tasks and sub tasks with a specified intermediate or final work result (see figure 2). Beneath this phase-oriented sequential labour partition according to the approaches of design methodology, a hierarchical labour partition from the academically qualified design engineer in a wide range down to the draftsman can be found, as well as a competency-oriented labour partition into mechanical, electrical, hydraulic etc. problem solving and integration procedures.

The CAD-system has the function in this organizational context to rationalize the operations management of information handling and of the integration of different information chunks into a complete work result, the completely documented technical product.

Ergonomically speaking design work is "informatory work" in the pure sense of consisting only of human information processing procedures, but with different levels of cognitive control and of the possibility to influence the working process by identifying and supporting algorithmic tasks execution through software components. With respect to these continua four principle components can be identified, namely:

- creative informatory components, like defining objectives of a product, setting goals for development

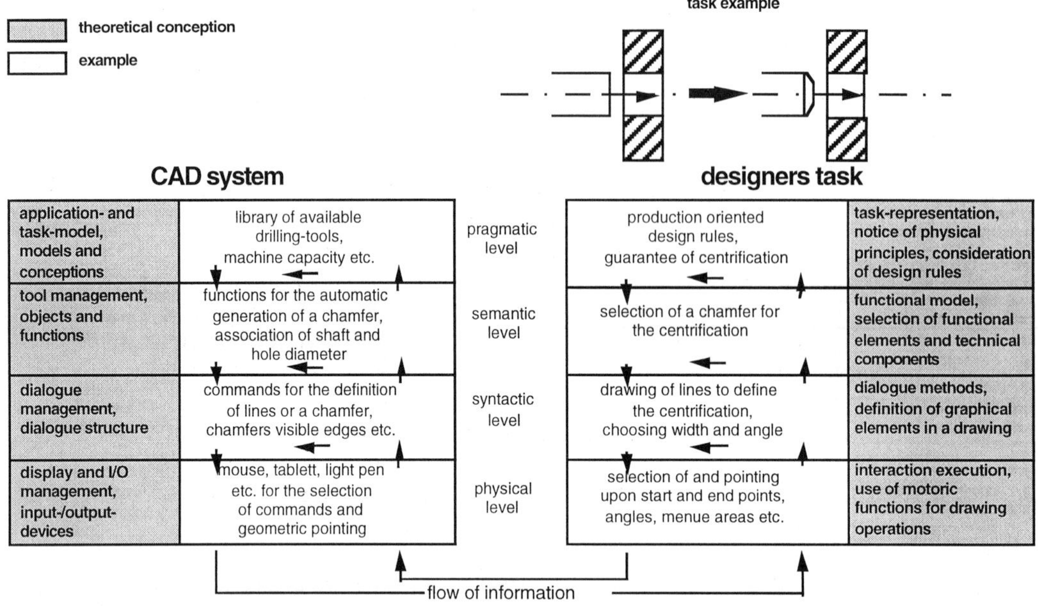

Figure 3. Design procedures in the semiotic model of Human-Computer interaction (example). *(Springer, 1993).*

procedures, identifying problem domains and initiating problem solving, where methods are unknown, or even developing problem solving methods themselves,

- strategic informatory components, like problem and task solving along prescribed methods/ procedures with algorithmic and perhaps iterative character, such as the application of iterative optimization tools or simulation procedures to test functional components of the product, mathematical model formulation and calculation,
- routine informatory components, like the application of more simple algorithms, assigning and coding tasks, such as creation of parts lists, creation of dimensions, transforming sketches into drawings etc.,
- automated informatory components, like data entry, data transfer, data recall without loading conscious processes in the brain.

This ergonomic differentiation in forms of work or types of tasks has to do a lot with a semiotic model - as firstly described by Morris (1946) -, that was applied frequently to human-computer-interaction. It is capable to bridge the gap in between a person/human work centred view and a tools/means and measurements of support centred view and thus may be used to describe the interaction in between a design engineer and his CAD-system (figure 3) as well. By this description the tool-character of the CAD system for the individual work of the design engineer is emphasized.

As outlined before, the design engineer and his CAD-system are bound to an organizational context by responsibilities for certain types of orders: This may be "manufacturing and assembly oriented design of layer", as shown in figure 3. These orders are redefined as tasks or task elements on a pragmatic level: In a cyclic and/or stepwise process of order processing task elements are assigned to the human designer and/or to the respective tool in the CAD-system: Taking the example shown the designer has to consider the physical principles of layer functioning and production, but in his task execution the task-representation and modelling in the CAD-system leads to a provision and support with a "library of available drilling tools", a survey on "machine capacities" in surface quality, a.o.

On the semantic level functions of the CAD-system are used to specify and generate functional elements/technical components of the artefact to be designed: The selection of a chamfer for the centrification of the layer - for example - is supported by tools in the CAD-system for object generation or manipulation in the sense, that the chamfer is generated according to shaft diameter automatically, and that shaft and hole diameter are associated with a certain fit.

On the syntactic level the definition of graphical

elements in the drawing comes into focus, which means, that the user disposes over dialogue methods, with which he easily can define and arrange lines and other standardized graphical components of the drawing (lines of centrification, visible edges etc.), dialogues with a defined structure and coding are initiated.

Last not least the physical level concerns input-output-devices as shown in figure 3 as well, which take care, that any of the dialogue steps are executed by physical operations and represented by perceivable representations on displays. This forms a technical information aspect, the signs must be interchanged by a physical way, e.g. visual, auditive, or kinesthetic information (Rasmussen, 1983).

The semiotic model is not only useful for the overview and the example shown, it may serve as a structuring guideline to a specification of features of CAD-systems, as found today in use in industry (see Table 1).

56.1.2 Model of Human Work and Design Activities

To penetrate in more detail into the use of ergonomics knowledge for the design of designer's work with CAD-systems in a systematic manner, it is necessary to have an idea about a systematic consideration of the problem field (Luczak and Volpert, 1987).

Theories, methods and design principles depend upon the context, they are built in. To systematize this broad, cross-section oriented context, a paradigm is needed, that guarantees, that the whole problem field is covered and that the separate problems can be seen in their coherence (table 2). The paradigm divides working processes and working structures into seven levels, the highest level representing work related to its societal impacts (level 7), the lowest (level 1) representing elementary physiological processes. The three lower levels distinguish between a subject-oriented (human) approach and an object-oriented (work-environment, workplace, work means related) approach.

Interests of the lowest level (1) are anatomical and physiological basics, like biomechanics of the workplace, metabolism and effects of the working environment, rhythmic functions related to working hours etc.

Interests of the second level (2) are the elementary human functions in physical and psychical terms: Anthropometric workplace design, the investigation of movements, and movement control and the physical design of displays and controls are dominating.

Object of level 3 are those psychical processes on the one hand, which allow and steer a sensible sequence of operations; on the other hand the system analysis and system evaluation of workplaces, in other words the functional and time-line oriented cooperation of humans and technical means to fulfill a purpose (that is for instance production of a good or delivery of a service).

On the central level 4 the worker, the human being as individual working person, is focused; the typical approach on this level is a holistic view of human work as an entity of motivational, voluntary, qualification-based and social elements. On this level and all higher levels a distinction between a subject-oriented and object-oriented approach is no longer necessary.

The level 5 brings into focus the working groups and group work, which means the cooperation of individual working persons with their specific tasks. This implies work/labour partition, hierarchical aspects, behaviour of crew-leaders, participation as well as questions of communication and information transfer, with respect to human relations.

Level 6 describes industrial relations of employers and employees' representatives. Questions of codetermination with respect to new information technologies, questions of organization of work in enterprises and other strategic decisions with respect to human work in computer integrated systems are brought up.

According to this scheme level 7 is oriented to comprehensive socio-political and societal contexts of work. Typical questions on this level deal with work regulation and standardization, work in the national economy, structural and economical components of employment, working market and activities of employers and unions in socio-politics.

A special advantage of this paradigm is, that it brings together the different disciplinary approaches with respect to the analysis and design of "work", here designers work. So it seems to be a good basis for the structuring of approaches for the human side in HCI. The other advantage is, that the scheme especially refers to an object-oriented side, which means working equipment and so comprises especially computer-systems, here CAD-systems, and all the scientific problems of analysis and design, that lie in or behind CAD-technology.

As can be seen in table 2 a segmentation of the problem structure with respect to the "Ergonomics of CAD-systems" can be easily derived from the paradigm. Thus this path of bringing an order into the views and aspects to be covered here will be followed further in this report.

***Table 1. Features of CAD systems related to the levels of the semiotic interaction model (only those criteria differing between** existing CAD products on the market are specified, e.g. the generation of geometrical objects (semantical level) is only differentiated by sufficient/unsufficient functionality, because most of the systems nearly using the same generating functions)*

Technical features on the physical level

Computer Hardware

technical features of the computing machinery

- computer architecture (32/64 bit)
- scalable working memory
- performance (resp. time), numerical operations
- performance (resp. time), graphical operations

storing capabilities

- type (disk devices (hard/floppy), tape devices, CD ROM)
- availability at the work place
- duration of storing/receiving procedures
- interfaces
- local area networks
    - availability
    - performance (bandwidth)
    - stability
    - load (amount of users)
- wide area networks
    - availability at the workplace
    - availability for cooperation partners
    - performance (ISDN, ATM, etc.)
    - stability
    - costs (fix and variable)

Input Devices (technical features)

keyboards

- consistent writing keyboard (QWERTY or QWERTZ)
- function keyboards
    - user defined keys (definition procedure, transparency of actual status etc.)
    - location of function keys (integrated into writing keyboard, separate device etc.)

tablets

- menu fields
    - area of menu fields sufficient
    - drawing area sufficient
    - changability of menus
    - user defined menus
    - information coding of menus
- positioning device
    - pen / reticular lens
    - keys at the device (location, number)
- functions of the tablet
    - identification of objects
    - selection of commands
    - selection of parameters
    - hand sketch drawings
    - gesture input
    - digitizer
- hardware characteristics
    - area of the digitizer
    - performance of the digitalization process
    - precision
- local intelligence
    - availability of different coordinate systems
    - user defined neutral points
    - measurement of difference lengths
- additional information input
    - user defined digitization scales
    - user definition of precision
- automatic digitizer

mouse

- number of keys
- adjustment of acceleration, precision etc.
- cord or cordless
- cleaning abilities

trackball

- number of keys
- adjustment of acceleration, precision etc.
- cord or cordless
- cleaning abilities

other input devices

- joystick (number of keys, adjustment of accel eration, precision etc.)
- dials (number, location, change of precision)
- 3D input devices
    - space mouse (precision, ability to differen tiate between the degrees of freedom)
    - space ball (precision, ability to differentiate between the degrees of freedom)
    - data glove (precision, weight, effort to wear on and of, feedback)
- light pen
- microphone (headset, positioning, adjustability etc.)

Output Devices

graphic output device

- technical features
    - display area

Table 1 (continued). Features of CAD systems related to the levels of the semiotic interaction model ....

frequency
resolution

- presentation features
  number of colours
  adjustability of colour, brightness, contrast
- hardware aids for graphic performance
  zoom and pan functions
  layer maps
  translation, rotation
  polygons (wire frame and shaded)
  surface templates

alphanumerical out device

- integrated into graphics monitor/separate device
- using same / different keyboard
  plotter and printer
- type (pen based, electrostatic, ink jet, thermo, laser, micro film etc.)
- plotter area
- output characteristics
  number of pens, colours
  speed of the plotter / printer
  types of printing materials (paper, foils etc.), use of different. material at the same device
- network characteristics
  cache memory
  management of produced drawings

<u>Technical features on the syntactical level</u>

<u>Media of information input (availability)</u>

alphanumeric information

- conventional keyboard
- function keyboard
- gestures
- hand sketch
- natural language
  selection and positioning
- cursor keys
- mouse / trackball
- joystick
- tablet (pen or reticule lens)
- dials
- 3D input devices

<u>Methods of dialogue</u>

command input (language, command description (users / programmers language))

hot keys / abbreviations (structure of hot keys / abbreviations, relation to commands)

parameter input

- transparency of parameter effects
  perceivable in a relation to an object
  adjustable in amount of description
- standard parameters
  user accept (from field to field, all parameters with a single button)
  adjustability
- conventions in parameter input sequence (consistent to existing tables etc.)

menus

- static menus
  location on the screen
  information coding and presentation (verbal, symbolic, colour)
  status coding and presentation (verbal, symbolic, colour)
  user definition of location, information content etc.
- dynamic menus
  type (pop up, pull down, pull out)
  location on the screen
  information coding and presentation (verbal, symbolic, colour)
  status coding and presentation (verbal, symbolic, colour)
  reaching of menus (directly, through menus trees, cross menu jumps etc.)
  user definition of location, information content etc.

<u>Response time and system messages</u>

Response time

- adjustability of response time
- constancy of response time
- transparency of expected response time (percent process done indicators)

system messages

- transparency of messages
- adjustability of amount of information
- display of system states
  working states (continuos actualization of display)
  parameter states (layers, colours, pens, scale etc.)
- transparency how to reach another system state
- feedback when changing a system state

Table 1 (continued). Features of CAD systems related to the levels of the semiotic interaction model ....

<u>Help system and error management</u>
help system
- presentation
    - on line
    - situation dependent
    - location (always the same location, related to the help requesting event)
- information detail
    - adjustable by the user dependent on the situation
    - pre-adjustments (e.g. qualification dependent)
- content of the help information
    - application oriented
    - dialogue oriented
    - hypertext based links between content elements
- transparency and understanding of help information
- connectivity to learning aids

error management
- display of errors
    - modality (visual, auditive, other)
    - status information or error location
- error tolerance
    - automatic recovery of typing errors
    - display of error recovery
- error correction
    - proposal of error recovery by the user
    - undo / redo function (one step, more steps, history function)
    - correction type (deletion / new input, correction by editing)
- error prevention
    - critical functions are saved by user request (user defined)
    - automatic data storing (user defined)
    - automatic protocol files with user activities for error recovery (user defined)

<u>Technical features on the semantic level</u>
<u>Operating system / network characteristics</u>
multitasking / multi-user system characteristics
management of individual user / task profiles
- storage of layers, colours, pens, scales, etc.)
- storage of user interface characteristics
    - availability of applications nearly location independent

data management
- data management on the basis of the operating system
- conventional data bases
- specialized (engineering) data bases
- data operations (generate, copy, transfer, rename, delete, recovery, relate, etc.)

<u>CAD visualization aids</u>
coordinate systems
- definition (object related / screen related, temporary / static)
- type of coordinate system (cartesian, polar, cylindrical, ball coordinates)
- relation of coordinates (absolute, relative, incremental)

drawing grids
- type of visualization (on / off, static / dynamic, points / lines)
- geometrical manipulations (rotation, translation of the grid)
- user defined grid characteristics (distances, increments)
- snap function (user defined, end-, middle-, cross-, grid-, tangent-points, dist. dependent)

visualization functions
- zooming (zoom by scale, by window, etc.)
- translation / rotation
- scrolling (geometric scrolling, layer scrolling, etc.)
- clipping (user defined directions, selectable clipping distances)
- user defined views (no. of viewpoints, definition procedure naming, management, etc.)
- scale definition (predefined scales, user defined, viewing of several scales)
- viewing types (wire frame, hidden elements, shaded volumes)
- snap shot functions (bit map or vector graphics)

layer technique
- number of layers
- visualization of layers
- references between elements on different layers
- user determined effects on objects by various functions

explosion visualization
- 2D / 3D explosion
- automatic generation of explosion

Table 1 (continued). Features of CAD systems related to the levels of the semiotic interaction model ....

CAD functions
manipulation functions
- rotation (absolute / relative, free positioning / quantification by data input)
- translation (absolute / relative, free positioning / quantification by data input)
- mirroring (projection at a point / at a line)
- duplication
- change of parameters
  - geometric dimensions (scaling)
  - colour / pen type / line type etc.
- stretching
  - direction symmetric / one direction
  - freehand / quantification by data input
- bending (only 3D)
- trimming (cut / enlarge, end / middle / border elements / virtual cross sections, 2D / 3D)

generation aids
- construction elements (centre lines, tangent lines etc.)
- operations for element generation (lines, circles, surfaces, volume primitives, etc.) sufficient
  - generation with various limits (existing elements, quantification etc.)
  - flexible combination of limits as well as generation functions
- grouping
  - contour selection
  - window selection
  - identification by name
  - flexible selection and unselection
- calculation (cross sections, circumference, area, angle, pocket computer functions)
- fillets and chamfer
  - radius / angle / distance definition
  - variable radius
- cross sections / cross surfaces
  - definition (real / virtual)
  - visualization

programming
- user defined macros (complexity of macro language)
- variant programs
  - graphical definition / programming
  - debugging procedures
  - integration of other programming languages
  - interfaces to other data bases (interoperability)

hand sketches / digitization
- automatic element recognition (no. of different elements, recognition safety etc.)
- geometrical reconstruction

2D basic objects (characteristics)
standard elements (point, line, circle, arc)
special elements (ellipse, parabolic curve, hyperbolic curve)
splines (cubic, B-, Bezier)

3D basic objects
wire frame models (characteristics of boundary curves)
- standard elements (point, line, circle, arc)
- special elements (ellipse, parabolic curve, hyperbolic curve)
- splines (cubic, B-, Bezier)
- generation of a 3D model
  - rotation of a curve
  - translation (along a line / along a curve)
  - connection of elements (by straight lines)

surface model (boundary representation -B-rep-, characteristics of boundary surfaces)
- basic surfaces (planes, cylinders, parabolic / hyperbolic surfaces)
- pyramidal surfaces
- torus
- profiles (by rotation, by translation along a line / along a curve)
- ruled surface
- sculptured (freeform) surface (cubic splines, Bezier surfaces, B-spline surfaces)
- fillet surfaces

volumetric model (constructive solid geometry -CSG-, characteristics of basic volumes)
- generation meth. (rotation, translation, mirroring, bending, pressing, Boolean operations)
- basic elements (cube, prism, pyramid, cylinder)
- cone (circular, ellipse, parabolic, hyperbolic basic surface)
- profile volume (by rotation, by translation - along a line / along a curve)
- ruled volume
- sculptured (freeform) volume (cubic splines, Bezier surfaces, B-spline surfaces)
- fillet volume

Drawing documentation
dimensions and text
- types of dimensions (horizontal, vertical, parallel, thickness, angle, radius, diameter)

Table 1 (continued). Features of CAD systems related to the levels of the semiotic interaction model ....

- types of dimensioning (real objects, cross sec tions, reference objects, dimension chains)
- constraints between geometry and dimensions
- dimensioning lines (help lines, symbols, place ment of dimension text)
- dimensioning text
    - orientation (horizontal, vertical, user de fined, parallel to curve, parallel to line)
    - generation (user defined, automatic)
    - type of dimension (metric, imperial, both simultaneously)
    - font
    - symbols (diameter, surface description, tol erances)
- cross hatchings
    - generation meth. (automatic area identifica tion, user selection of (vitual) elements)
    - type of hatchings (pre-defined, user defined, company defined)
    - constraints between hatchings and geometry
    - layout of the paper based documentation
    - formats (pre-defined, user defined, company defined
    - scales (user defined scales, several scales in one drawing)
    - description of the drawing (automatic num bering / description, user controlled)

Engineering data bases

product information (characteristics of the data base, availability, structuring method etc.)

- structuring of design elements and assembly parts
- features (geometrical, technological, economic, life cycle features)
- material information
- differing elements and products (macros, vari ants, standard parts, buying parts, etc.)

process information (characteristics of the data base, availability, structuring method etc.)

- guidelines for specific design problems
- order characteristics, capacities
- project management information

interfaces (IGES, VDA-FS, STEP)

Technical features on the pragmatic level

Integration of calculations

type of calculation (geometrical, thermal, mechanical, rheological)

calculation methods (Finite Element Methods, specialized methods)

data exchange between CAD and calculation

presentation of the calc. results (alphanum., graphical integrated / separated from CAD)

simulation (movement, collision, product functionality, manufacturing, life cycle)

Integration into the company information infrastructure (CIM)

connection to order characteristics (deadlines, milestones, cooperations, etc.)

connection to cost calculation (different types of costs, methods of calculation)

connection to manufacturing planing (available tools, capacities, etc.)

NC-coupling

connection to quality control functions

connection to marketing demands / integration of the customer

Organization of CAD

consideration of the hierarchical structure of the design department (control loops)

information sharing, personal data, corporate data

user support (centralized, decentralized)

Table 2. Use of ergonomic knowledge for CAD work related to the structural and procedural levels of the work process.

Levels of the work process	Procedural Levels of the Work Progress	Aspects of Human(s) & Human Work	Examples of Ergonomic Design Parameters for CAD work
Braodest Context / Production and Traffic Conditions	Work Related Political Action	(7) Society & Social and Work Policy	Political Restrictions of CAD Use (Working Hours, Data Security, etc.)
Medium Context / Structure of the Company	Interaction of the Working Actors	(6) Company & Companywide Organizational Measurements	Telecooperative CAD ("Interhouse" CSC(D)W), Engineering Data Management
Narrowest Context / Structure of the Work Group	Cooperative Group Work	(5) Work Group & Cooperative Processes	Design Project Management and "Inhouse" - CSC(D)W
Subject System / Task of a Person (System of Activities)	Motive Related Activity	(4) Qualification, Motivation & Types of Work	CAD - Application and Task Oriented CAD Tools
Functional Means of a Person / Purpose Oriented Subsystems (Single Activities)	Goal Oriented Conciously Regulated Action	(3) Activities & Work Place	CAD - Dialogue Structures and Functions
Upper Level of Physical Means / Productive Subsystems (Sensomotorics)	Sensumotoric Automatisms (Operations)	(2) Consciously Controlled Organic Systems & Tools	CAD - Input- and Output Devices (Screens, Tablets, Keyboards, Mouse/Pen/ Track Balls etc.)
Lower Level of Physical Means / Reproductive Sub-systems of the Body		(1) Autonomous Organic Systems & Work Environment	Environmental (Lighting, Noise, Climate, Radiation) and Situational Factors (e.g. Strain of CAD Users)

56.2 Environmental Factors and Sensory-Motor Operations

56.2.1 Environmental Factors

The environmental factors in the CAD office are basically the same as in the normal office (lighting, noise, climate, radiation, substances in the air, Frieling et al., 1987).

Special environmental factors in the CAD office are:

- Usually, the technical drawings used during the design process (and produced by the designer) are of large size, like DIN-A0 and even larger, e.g. 1:1 scale drawings in automobile design. Furthermore, different existing (paper based) drawings are necessary during the design to take into account all necessary boundary conditions. That means space must be existing sufficiently in the design office and in the surrounding of the CAD work place.
- Especially lighting conditions are difficult to adjust because of the different tools and information material used in the CAD office. Figure 4 shows an example of positioning different light sources in the CAD workplace.
- Especially in the case of complex geometrical objects the designer uses physical models (e.g.

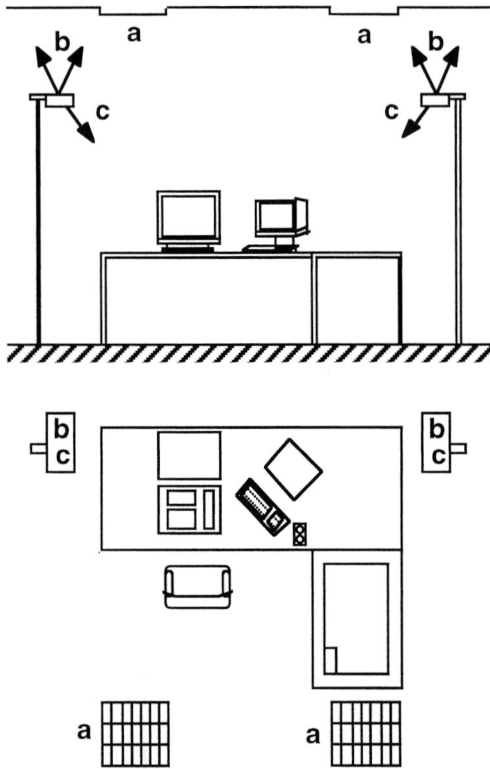

Figure 4. ***Positioning of lighting at the CAD workplace:*** *a: room lighting (limiting beam angle is fitted to the CAD workplace), b: indirect lighting by a standing light, c: direct lighting by standing light, components are adjustable individually*

prototypes, clay models etc.) during the design process. The model is used for orientation in the complex topology or as a discussion medium for communication with other persons. Dependent on the dimensions of the products to be designed sufficient space and special equipment (desk, boards) is required.

- The handling of large drawings or models on a 20"-monitor is one of the main hardware problems in using CAD systems (e.g. in architecture the construction of buildings). Moreover, if more than one drawing or model is used in parallel, the monitor area is too small. Therefore, most CAD systems can be equipped with two (ore more) graphic monitors to expand the drawing area and to reduce efforts to organize windows etc.

- Furthermore, the designer uses an heterogeneous mix of applications (CAD, CAE, office applications, etc.) which are based on different platforms (today normally workstation and PC-based). This is the main reason why very often the designer's workplaces are equipped with different computers, one for workstation based CAD, an other one for office application like word processing, spread sheets, project management, telephone if integrated into PC (CTI-Computer Telephony Integration) a.o. Therefore, the designer´s workplace should provide enough space to place the different equipment (figure 5). Additional ergonomic aspects are the interchange between sitting and staying/walking to reduce stress (low back pain etc.) and the adjustability of the furniture in height and angle of desk plates.

- Using 3D CAD models, future CAD applications will be equipped with 3D Input-/Output devices. Because of their special characteristics (stereo shutter, electromagnetic field sensors etc.) special efforts must be made to adapt the office environment (lighting, electromagnetic fields emitted from monitors, etc.) to these equipment.

56.2.2 Sensory-Motor Operations

On the sensory-motor level the input-/output devices used at CAD systems are relevant for an ergonomically system design. Typical input operations are typing, positioning and selection. Widely used devices and special problems in the CAD domain are:

Keyboards are used as standard QWERTY keyboards, in addition sometimes as special function keyboards. Because of the functional complexity of the CAD system, function keys are used as hot keys to shorten the time for the execution of special commands. These function keyboards are normally customized. Ergonomic criteria are the transparency for the user of the key functions which can be changed by the user in relation to task requirements. Solutions are templates which must be put over the keyboard (and must be changed when switching from one function block to another) or soft keys on an additional (LCD) screen (figure 6) controlled by light pen or touch screen.

If more than one computer system is used at the CAD workplace (s. above), normally two and more QWERTY keyboards are used. Consistency between the keyboards (key placement, key description) is the main ergonomic problem in these cases.

Tablets with a pen or a "reticule lens" are used for the selection of menus and as a reference surface to the monitor. Because of the limited screen space, static tablet menus reduce the required space on the screen. On

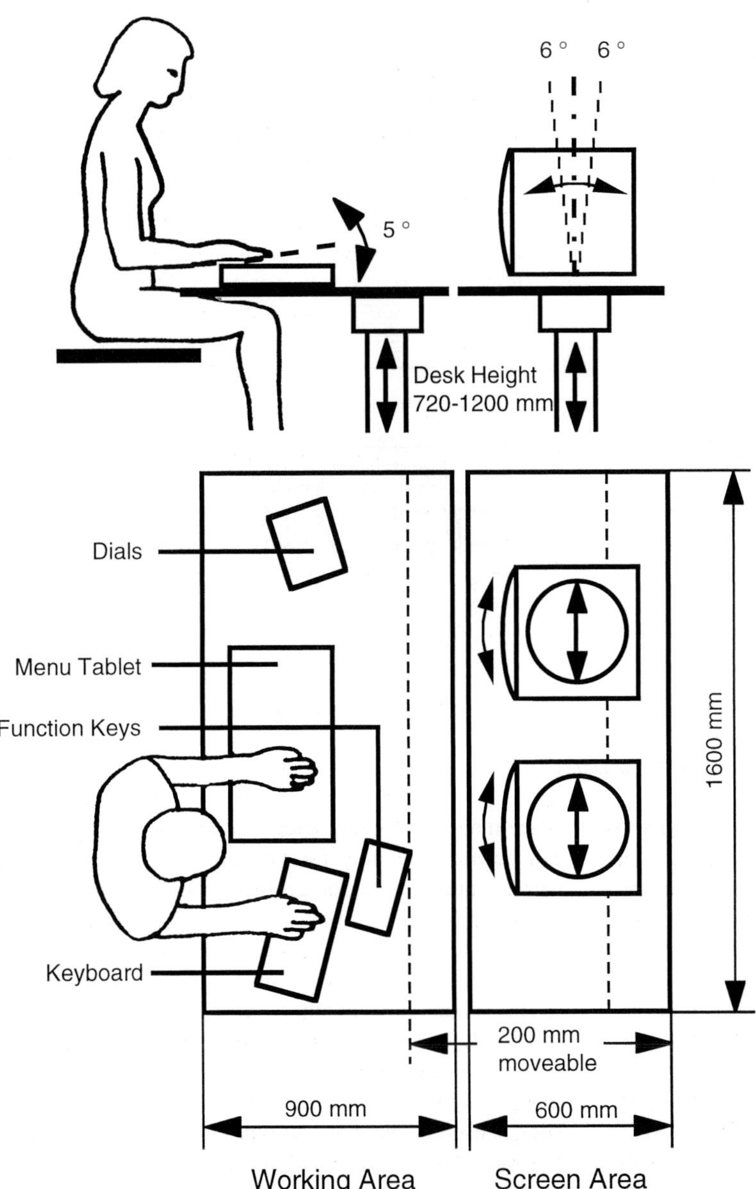

Figure 5. Typical arrangement of interaction devices at the CAD workplace.

the other hand, the user has to change his focus (and light/dark adaptation) between screen and tablet, which induces a higher strain to the visual system. Ergonomic criteria are the structure and design of the tablet menus (Frieling and Pfitzmann, 1987). If CAD systems allow the input of hand sketches and handwriting, e.g. for dimensioning and text, an electronic pen is strictly necessary for effective input. The most important advantage in these cases is the consistency of tools used by the designer in conventional workplaces.

Mouse or trackball are used as pointing devices in most CAD applications. Because the mouse is more precise and faster to use, the trackball is normally used only in mobile applications, like in detail construction directly at the building site (assembly of complex plants, buildings

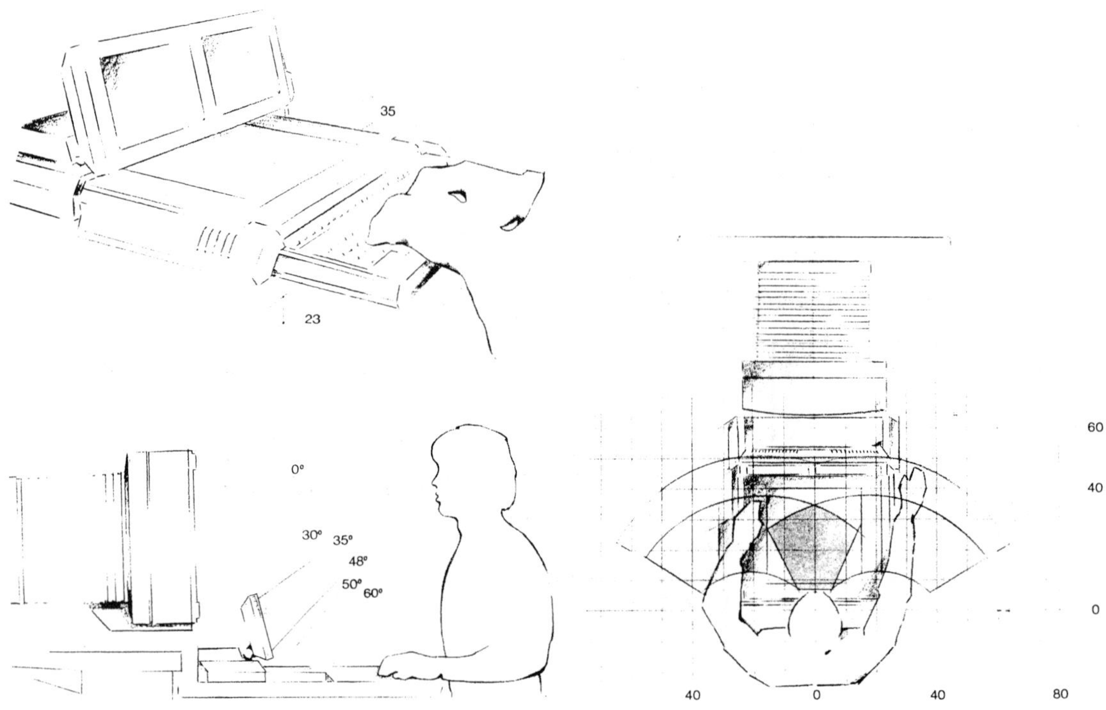

Figure 6. ***LCD Screens as soft keyboards.*** *(courtesy of Norsk Data).*

etc.). Ergonomic criteria are the design of the device itself, the compatibility and consistency in relation to the CAD application, e.g. 2- or 3-button mouse. The software parameters like speed, acceleration factors etc. should be customizable by the user. If the mouse (or trackball) is used in a CAD application, menus, buttons, the drawing or modelling area, status information, and others are placed on the screen. Based on the space problems the user has to control precisely his sensory-motor movements (figure 7) which increase visual strain. Because of the eye-hand coordination the user needs to control every positioning as well as selection process visually, which is inconsistent to the use of real objects.

Dials are widely used in 3D CAD systems for viewing functions such as zooming, translation or rotation of geometric objects. Because of the 6-degrees of freedom and the additional zooming function, 7 (or 8) dials are implemented in an extra dial board located near the keyboard. The iterative operation of each single dial is one of the main ergonomic problems (inconsistency to natural 6-degree of freedom manipulations) using dials.

The spaceball or "virtual balls" operated by a conventional mouse are reducing the sensory-motor effort because more than one degree of freedom can be manipulated simultaneously. Other input devices are the space mouse or the data glove. Especially the data glove can be used not only for viewing operations but as a natural input device for geometric manipulation. Ergonomic problems are the insufficient precision and, especially for geometric manipulation tasks, the missing haptic feedback of the resulting manipulation (touch sensitivity and force feedback during manipulation).

Joysticks are sometimes implemented into a CAD system. Because a joystick is an acceleration controlled input device, only in acceleration control tasks the joystick is useful. These are all types of tracking tasks such as simulation, walkthroughs etc.

Speech input has reached a stage of development which allows the use of such systems in many different areas. Traditionally, these are applications for disabled persons, e.g. the control of home environments and personal computers. Other applications are used for persons, whose eyes and hands are busy, as an alternative input device instead of keyboard, mouse or others, for example during an assembly job. Recent developments use speech as an input for word processing systems. Such systems use a microphone instead of a keyboard. Ergonomic requirements using a speech input system are mainly determined by recognition safety (figure 8).

Because of the high complexity of CAD systems

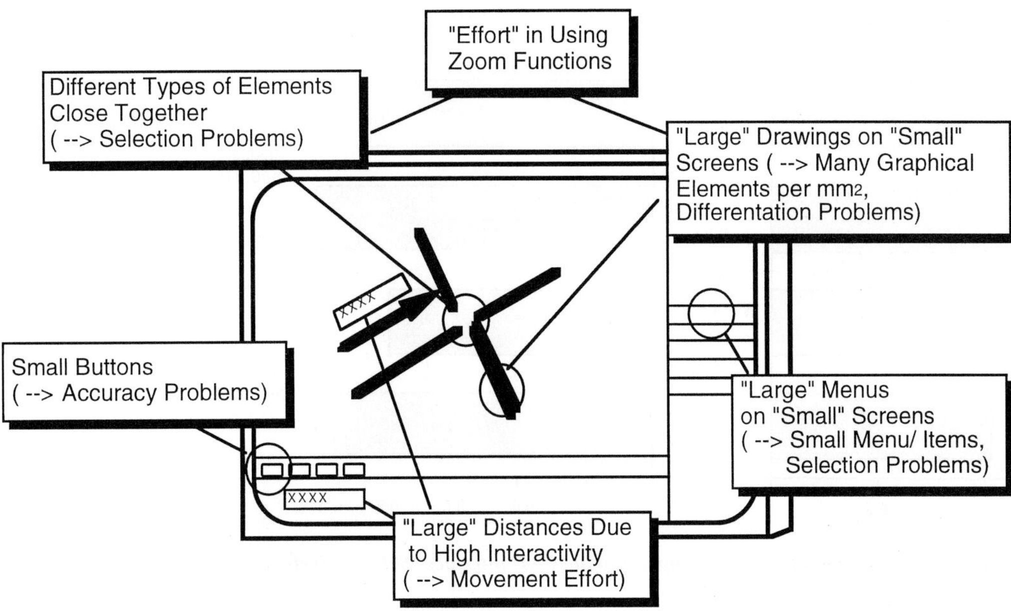

Figure 7. Sensory-motor problems using CAD systems.

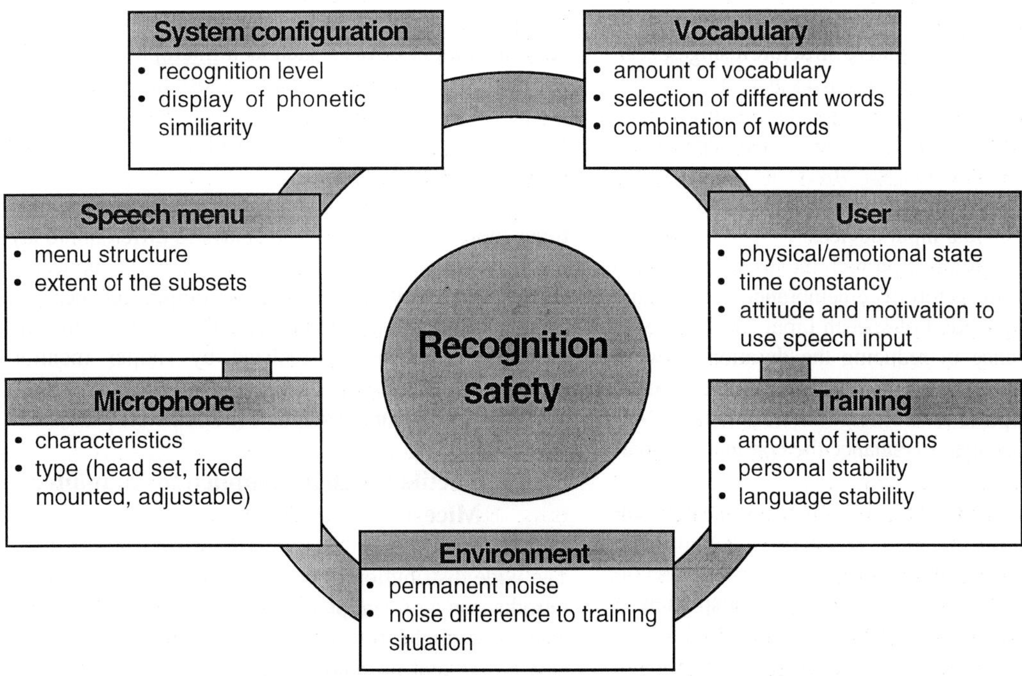

Figure 8. Influences on recognition safety at speech input systems .

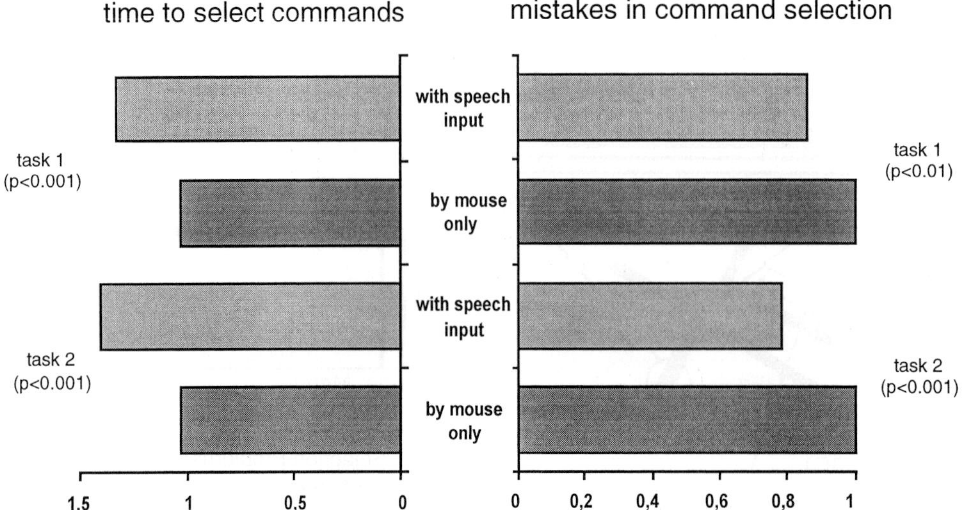

Figure 9. Performance results of integrating speech input into the CAD interface (Scherff, Springer, 1994).

(normally more than 300 different commands are implemented into standard systems) speech input offers the possibility to navigate in the command network by shortcuts as well as by using natural language as a cognitively consistent navigation method.

An experimental investigation with CAD systems (Scherff, Springer, 1994) proved that a spoken word or a notion is easier to remember than an abstract keyboard command (figure 9). Obviously there are more entries to the semantic net in the cognitive structure using speech in addition to keyboard, which makes it possible to remember the required command faster and with less mistakes. Thus the execution of commands by speech requires less transformation activities in the cognitive structure than by keyboard only. This effect can be used to optimize multimodal input devices.

Moreover, in combination with menus which should originally reduce the effort of remembrance in command structures, an application of speech input for "hot keys" provides the chance of reducing the duration of work flow interruption. For example, often used command sets like cut and paste or zooming functions within CAD systems are predestined to enhance the continuity of performing a task.

The possibility to use self-defined commands enables the user to select command names which are well-known to the subject and therefore allow a faster recollection with less mistakes. In this way the adaptation of the man-machine interface to the user is possible and leads to strain reduction as well as to a more efficient way of learning to work with a software product.

Gestures can be used as a dialogue metaphor in combination with input devices like tablet or mouse. Because gesture recognition needs computer performance (and therefore time) only commands which are used in-between the normal operations (like zoom, undo, etc.) are useful to be performed by the users gestures. In combination with hand sketch input it is obvious that gesture input is a powerful dialogue method and input device.

In cooperative CAD systems the designer needs additional input devices such as a microphone for voice mailing and/or audio conferencing with his CAD system, and a video camera for transmission of his own picture as well as pictures (or movies) of physically existing parts, work operations etc.

Necessary output devices are large screens, sometimes more than one, colour displays to differentiate layers, pens, parts, status information etc. In 3D application (Burdea and Coiffet, 1994) stereo output enhances the capabilities of the user to perceive the three-dimensional topology. This can be realized by shutter monitors (active shutter displays), shutter glasses (Foley et al., 1990) or head mounted displays (McAllister, 1993).

56.2.3 Tactile Feedback Applied to Computer Mice

The wide distribution of computer-mice started with the introduction of graphical-user-displays and menu-controlled application programs. Commands no longer have to be kept in mind and the user has only to select the desired function by moving the mouse cursor to the corresponding position. In CAD programs most of the

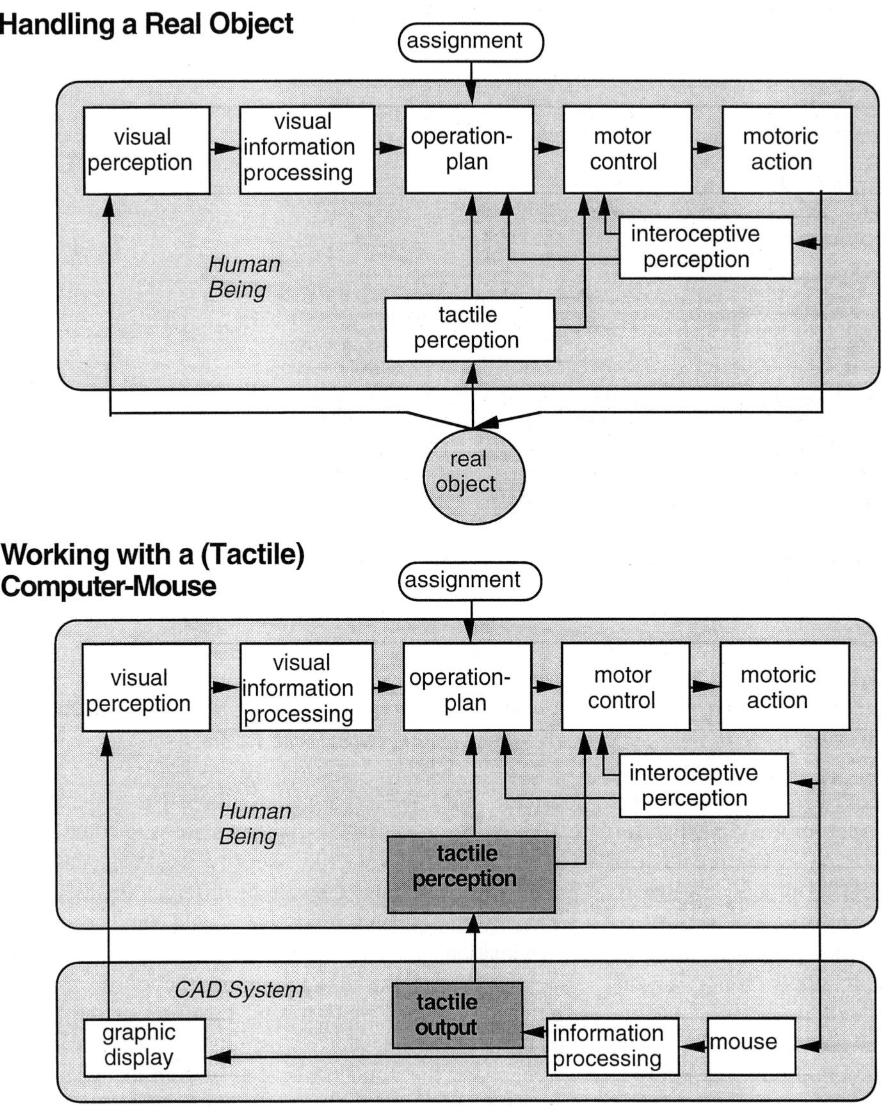

***Figure 10. Information flow for man-machine interaction: comparison of handling real objects and working with a (tactile) computer mouse** (Göbel et al., 1995a).*

output is graphical information. Therefore, the mouse is used predominantly as graphical input device for selection and pointing on graphical objects. In addition, an increasing number of commands are implemented by direct manipulation techniques such as stretching, moving etc. Such functionality also requires a graphical input device. Consequently, cognitive load using the CAD system is reduced (command remembrance etc.), but on the other hand motoric and sensory load is increased due to the dynamic movement character.

The comparison of information flow while using a computer-mouse and while handling real objects points out an essential difference (Göbel et al. 1995a): For the movement of a computer-mouse, subjects have two senses available, that are visual information and interoceptive information (muscle tension and joint angles). To handle a real object, one more important sense is used: tactile and kinesthetic senses give information about touching an object and about the exerted or back driven forces. All three senses can be processed in parallel, since they make use of different human resources (figure 10).

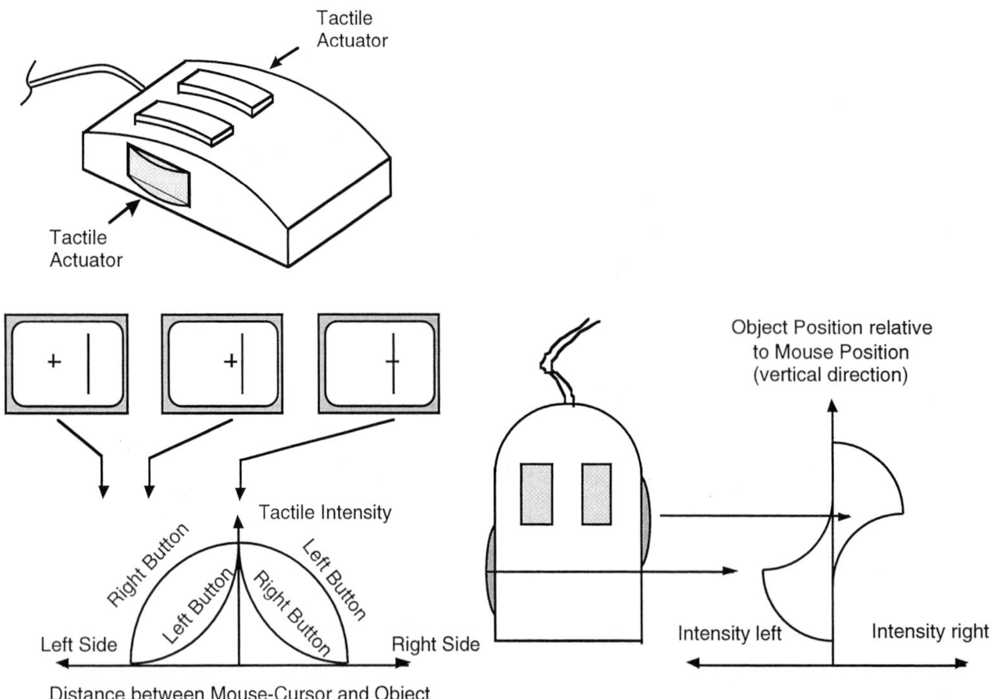

Figure 11. Realization of tactile feedback for horizontal and vertical positioning tasks (Göbel et al. 1995b).

The absence of tactile and kinesthetic information leads to a concentration on visual information. Further, the construction of movement strategies is more difficult than in real environment, since the processing time is longer and visual information processing is already required for other system operations (Taghavi and Penning, 1970; Tekano and Student, 1989). This is a well-known problem of VDT-works.

It can hypothesized, that an additional tactile or kinesthetic feedback, which transmits redundant information about object handling on the screen will allow a more intuitive handling of screen objects and therefore increase task performances and decrease human strain.

With regard to the regular functions of cutaneous sensory information and their influences in a real environment (Blume and Boelke, 1990), tactile information should be primarily used to enhance object usability. Even as a kinesthethic feedback seems to be more important for the handling of real objects, it is quite difficult to accomplish for a computer-mouse design. A vibrotactile feedback could be used as a virtual energy-field which would seem to be radiated by the screen objects and indicates the approximation of the mouse-cursor to an object on the screen (Craig, 1963; Hill, 1967).

The horizontal positioning of the mouse-cursor to a specified object would be supported by vibrotactile stimuli on the side-planes of the mouse-body (Gescheider et al., 1978). As the cursor is to come closer to the object, vibrotactile intensity would increase. To allow the distinction between the different directions, the intensity of left and right side would vary during approximation.

For the vertical direction either the left or the right actuator is placed more toward the front of the mouse than the other (and thus to use these actuators for both vertical and horizontal direction) or both mouse buttons are used for tactile signal transmission. This kind of representation would generate a redundant feeling of the display while moving the mouse, just as the display-content would be additionally engraved into the table-plate. The size of the vibrotactile detection area would determine whether the approximation or the exact positioning is predominantly indicated (figure 11).

An experimental investigation of an additional tactile feedback shows that even with a very simple tactile-feedback-device significant changes in movement behaviour result. The changes in reaction strategies imply a more direct and intuitive reaction if tactile feedback is available. Therefore, aside from the measured increase in total performance, a considerable decrease in human strain is indicated (figure 12). Further, it becomes visible, that the adaptation of tactile feedback to the user is

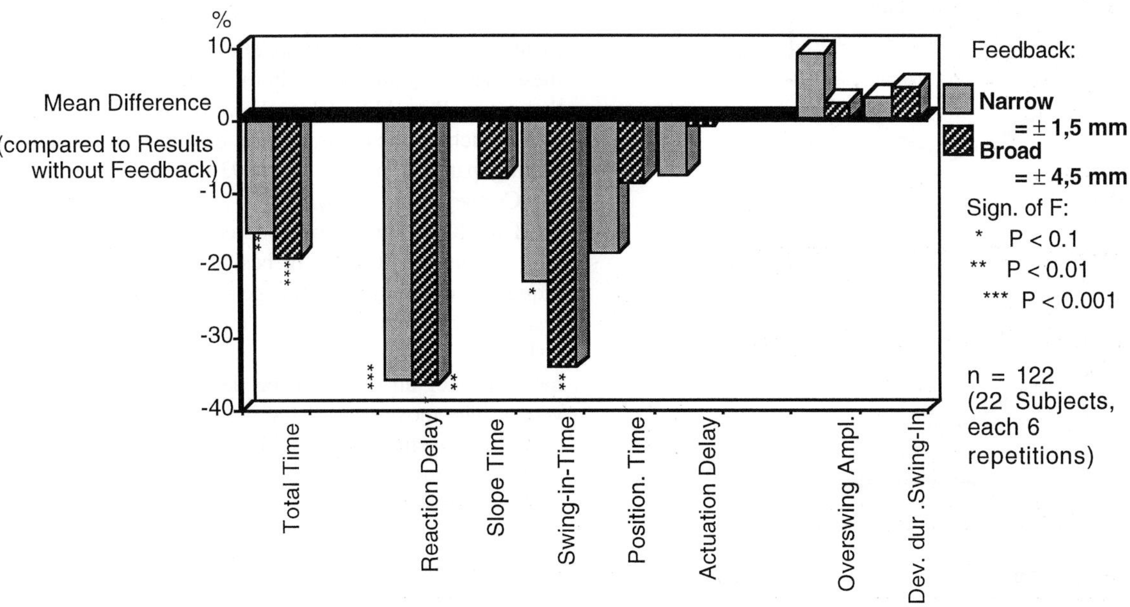

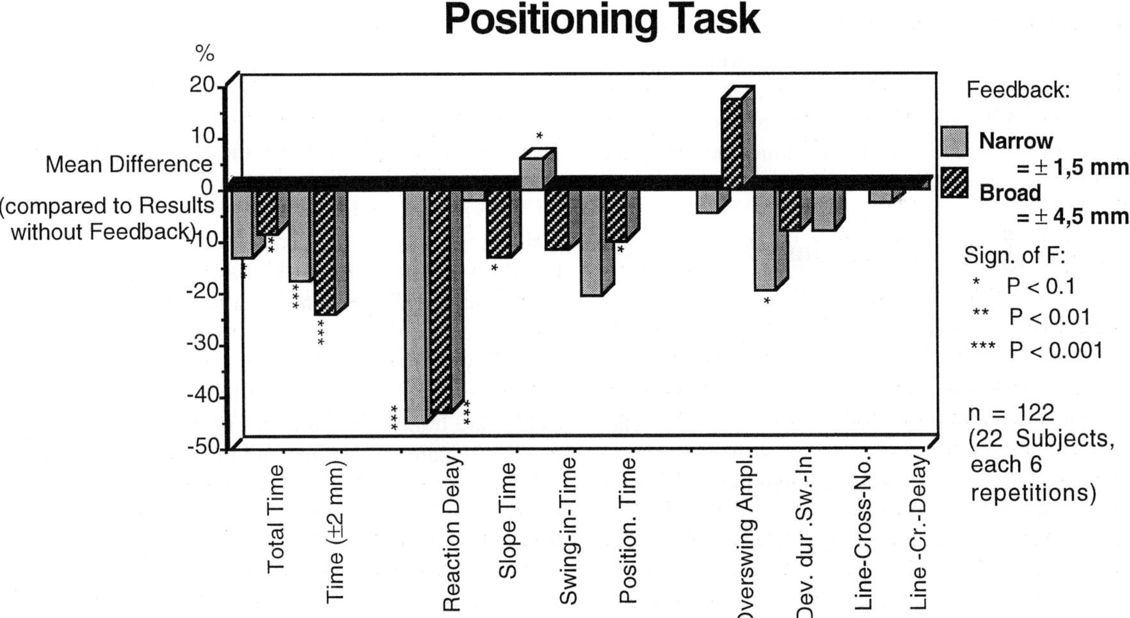

***Figure 12. Changes in performance characteristics by an additional tactile feedback during the execution of a selection and a positioning task** (Göbel et al. 1995a).*

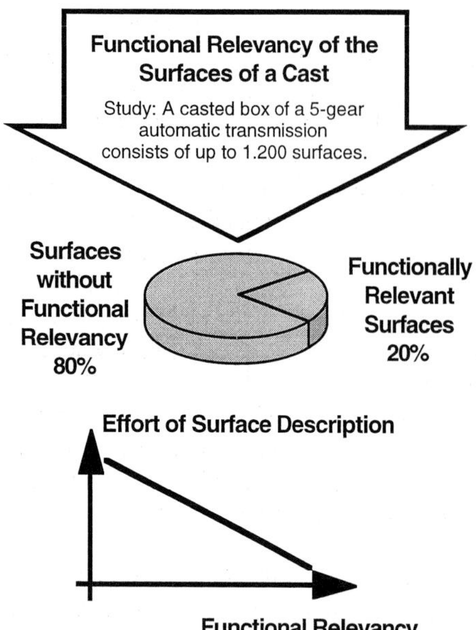

***Figure 13. Qualitative vs. quantitative description of sculptured surfaces** (source: a study of a casted box of a 5 gear automatic transmission, which consists of up to 1200 surfaces).*

not yet optimized. Especially during the swing-in-phase of ballistic movements, subjects tend to overestimate their control-performances. For future applications not only a static characteristic, but a dynamic one may lead to further improvements.

56.3 Task Oriented Actions - Examples of Sculptured Surface Manipulation

The manipulation of sculptured surfaces in a CAD system requires normally a high effort for the designer. The most important knowledge consists in mathematical understanding of surface definition and manipulation. This is for example linear algebra or B-spline approximation. Studies in sculptured surface design indicate that only 20% of the surfaces are of functional relevancy. In contradiction those surfaces of high relevancy for the functionality of the product are those with less effort for surface description whereas surfaces with less functional relevancy (qualitative requirements such as fillings, connection surfaces, etc.) need a large effort (figure 13).

The consequence in practise is to describe only those surfaces relevant for functionality. A task appropriate way would be the use of qualitative description method for "qualitative" surfaces.

Because of the broad application of sculptured surface systems within domains where the manual abilities of the worker plays an important role for task fulfillment, sculptured surface modellers should contribute to these manual qualification. In this context manual means that normally additional tools were used, e.g. cutting tools. Such applications are for example the design of casting parts (Jones et al., 1993), or wooden models (McCartney et al., 1993).

Direct Manipulation of objects in a CAD system which is used instead of or beside other dialogue techniques (like command language or menu selection) corresponds very closely to the "tool idea" within design tasks. For example, it is no longer necessary for the movement of an object to be defined by a movement vector. The movement of the input device directly controls the movement of the object. Nevertheless, in most CAD systems one must first select the command "movement of an object". It is not possible to activate this function just by a selection of the desired element and doing the manipulation interactively like in most graphic software.

CAD functions controlled by Direct Manipulation use, for example, rubber banding methods for the manipulation or generation of geometrical elements to control the consequences of an input parameter. Due to the efforts to achieve high computer performance, the more often direct Manipulation controlled functions are implemented in 2D applications, the less they occur in 3D systems.

One idea of using Direct Manipulation as a realistic dialogue technique for geometric design problems is based on tools which, on the basis of a flexible rough geometrical topology, generate a new volume by distortion of the part or cutting or adding material to a new volume. By this idea, processes of manual geometric modelling, used for example in model-design in cast industry, are transformed directly to software technology. Application areas for a free and manual modelling process are, for example, industrial design or the design of casts, where (i.e. a radius) has in most cases cast-technological and not functional objectives. Therefore, a more qualitative description of a radius would be sufficient in such cases.

Systems of that kind do not need any more special functions in a menu or command language because different tools are implemented in the system to be selected by the user. But, an essential barrier in the handling of such a system is the missing feedback of the object's characteristics (tactile and for kinesthetic information) when the user manipulates the object. This feedback should be integrated into the input device because of the

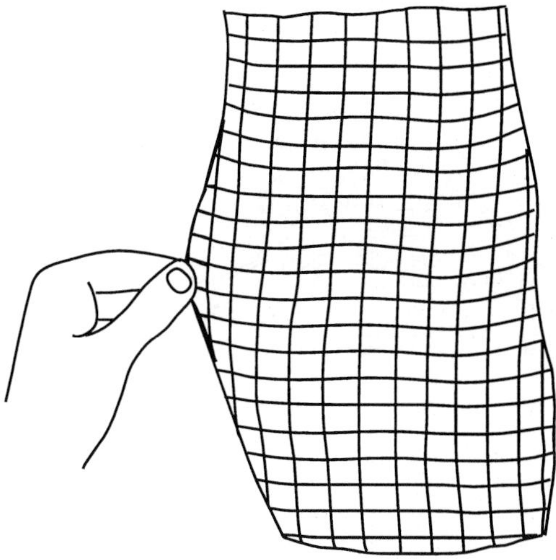

Figure 14. Scheme of the virtual clay metaphor.

necessary information content for the preparation of the task. The general metaphor of such a system is a virtual clay model (Burdea and Coiffet, 1994) (figure 14).

Requirements on haptic feedback devices incorporated into an input device are:

- they should be low weight devices because of energetic effort for the user,
- they should produce relatively high forces, in general nearly the same forces as they can be generated by the user himself,
- they should not be restricting in movement characteristics neither of the hand nor of single fingers,
- their feedback characteristics should be realistic in space as well as time resolution,
- they should be as simple as possible to wear on, to adjust, and to calibrate onto specific characteristics of the user.

To improve the tasks of qualitative topology description by a CAD-system and therefore to use the advantages of software-control, (i.e. possibility of easy manipulation, possibility of memorizing the data material etc.) a concept was developed combining the by hand abilities and the tactile-kinesthetic experience of the designer with the Direct Manipulation characteristics of the CAD-system.

The dialogue structure of a normal command-driven CAD-system with mouse control requires a lot of iterative steps (Chen et al., 1988, Foley et al., 1990) which implies a high planning effort in each step to estimate the influence of one parameter upon the total result of surface manipulation. In contrast to the Mouse Version, the Glove Version of the system combines the advantages of Direct Manipulation - "put the function into the action" - with a three dimensional input medium (Miwa et al., 1993). Such a device is able to control three directions simultaneously and is therefore avoiding iterative steps for each direction. To control the surface model visually, the model should be rotated and zoomed in all directions. The glove is also used for that function. After making a gesture, the glove switches to an input device, which controls the zooming and rotation of the CAD model. Making another gesture, the device has already manipulation function.

The properties of the modelling material are characterized by a set of parameters. They define the simultaneous movements of neighbouring points on the manipulated surface and, with that, the extent of area manipulation.

The necessary feedback, which is controlled by the surface model, was realized by a tactile feedback in the glove (EXOS - Exoskeleton HandMaster™ , figure 15, (Speeter, 1992) as an information source for the user when he modifies the surface.

Today kinesthetic feedback devices (Iwata, 1993) are realized and tested, at present normally consisting of different pneumatically driven cylinders (Burdea and Zhuang, 1991; Burdea et al. 1992). The main problem of the device is to transmit fairly high forces into the fingers which requires energy. Energy means normally a high amount of mass and therefore it increases the weight of the device. The pneumatic cylinders are of the advantage to produce high forces with a low weight because of an external pressure generator (figure 16).

Such a device will give the designer the possibility to simulate material characteristics for getting a more realistic impression while using Direct Manipulation techniques in the design and manipulation of sculptured surfaces.

56.4 Activities at the CAD Workplace

CAD as an activity oriented tool of the designer - this objective requires the structuring of the CAD system, which is oriented to the requirements of the working task and to the users demands that is the development of the product, the designers and the engineering draughtsmen. The design of the user interface dependent on semantic and pragmatic aspects (functions/objects and application modules) becomes one of the essential factors of success when an efficient and accepted use of a CAD system is concerned.

Using CAD software the designers normally have a considerable scope of action, which can be used in dif-

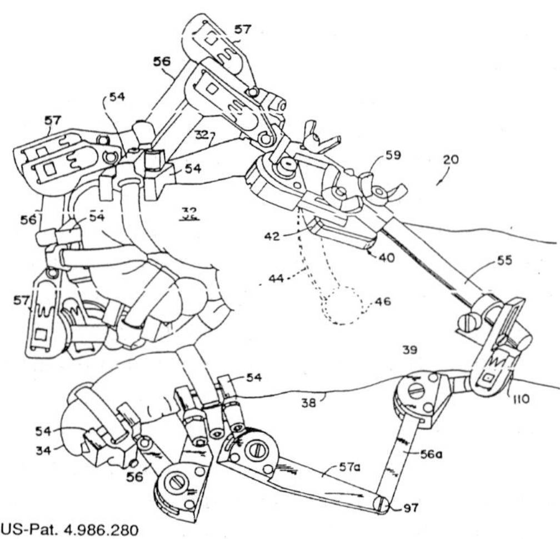

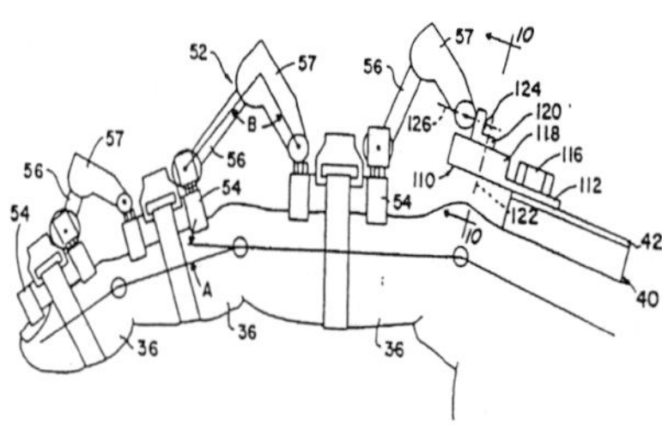

Figure 15. ***Dextrous HandMaster™, US Pat. 4.986.280.***

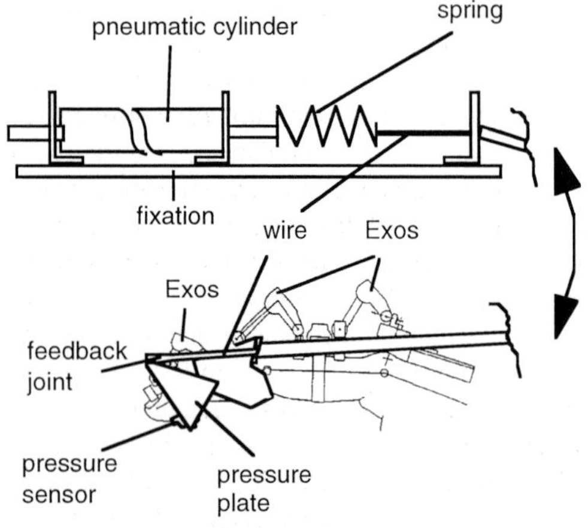

Figure 16. External pneumatically driven cylinders for force feedback of the Data Glove

ferent ways so that deficits of the software are compensated:

- Instead of a function, of which the design of the CAD system shows deficits, the designer uses other functions which also meet the requirements of the task. But normally this increases, however, the complexity of the necessary activities, and the consequence is longer lasting processing times of the task as well as an increased strain.
- The designers create, even under the almost always existing deadlines, a solution, which meets the requirements of the task, but of which, however, the quality could be even better if the CAD tool would be in an optimal condition.
- The designers use conventional methods although they are able to estimate which increase the efficiency of a computer aided design could have. Using conventional methods can be absolutely positive in the sense of a flexible application of different tools and design methods, but a permanently forced alternation between conventional and computer aided methods leads to insufficiency and unnecessary strain. This is because interruptions in the work process, media brakes, and interchanges between the different concepts in the methods.
- The task of a designer can be divided into sub tasks which implies activities and operations. A task oriented systematically based analysis of a realistic design process opens the possibility to identify bottle necks and system deficiencies and to build a basis for concrete system improvements. System deficiencies are interpreted by operational characteristics and identified strain situations. One problem of such methods are the design tasks themselves: they are complex and mostly the operations are not determinable. That is the reason why ergonomic requirements were scarcely formulated to CAD system design rules. Furthermore, in existing requirements only some are based on experimental data and the most include mainly performance aspects to the work with CAD systems (Heinecke, 1991). Neither stress and strain aspects nor the characteristics of necessary design activities and operations were taken into consideration.

56.4.1 Methodological Problems in Analyzing Design Work: Strain Induced Video-Self Confrontation

Several studies which are part of a larger research efforts should shed light upon problems in engineering and design with respect to the increasing CAD-use (Springer et al., 1990, Springer et al., 1991). One of the major objectives was to develop principles and guidelines for effective CAD. Mainly three different studies were carried out:

1. A laboratory study compared design work on a conventional drawing board to a low cost CAD system;
2. field studies in 11 design departments, each with another CAD system, were performed with 43 qualified designers and draughtsmen.
3. In a laboratory study working on a design-task with conventional tools and a computer-based design-management-system was compared. The design-management-system (DMS) used in this study consists of a geometric modeller (CATIA), expert-system-components for principal functional problems, a module for the structuring of functional capabilities of the to-be-designed product and a generator for requirements lists. It should provide the user with a computer-aid in every design phase.

Working with the CAD system was analyzed with the criteria stress and strain as well as with activity related and performance measurements. During the experiments the following variables were measured (on-line) to evaluate stress and strain:

- the heart- and respiration-rate that increase under most forms of stress,
- the heart-rate-variability, which decreases in case of informational or physical stress,
- the heart-rate power spectrum, which indicates stress on the short-term memory.

Every experiment was videotaped to identify stress factors directly after the experiments. Because the possible stressor can result from many different sources (task, design activities, CAD system, disturbances, etc.) an interpretation of the stressor related to a strain reaction can be made only with the help of the subject.

Therefore, after the identification of sequences with significant parameters for strain, these were combined with the corresponding sequences from the videotape. The subjects were then confronted with the videotaped sequences that indicated exceptional strain. During the confrontation the subjects were asked to comment the scene in order to gain insight into the causes of strain. The interviews were recorded and transcribed later on.

The interviews were evaluated using content analyses. Whereas psycho-physiological indicators are common to the analyses of stress and strain, content analyses is not normally used in this context. This method which is used mainly in the social sciences for the analyses of written material allows to analyse text by coding and structuring. This two-step-procedure (measurement of psycho-physiological indicators and the content analyses of the interviews) is thought to lead to a significant reduction in the amount of data and at the same time allow for a deeper insight into the strategies and problems of the subjects.

Each sequence was then categorized into phases using a normative model of problem-solving. Accordingly the process of problem-solving can be subdivided in phases of orientation, goal-setting, planning, decision, execution, and control. Inside each sequence the various statements of the subject were attached to different classes of items: activity (draw, do), task (work, succeed), heuristics (tactics, methods), self-management ("get rid of"), machine-elements (wedge, piston), technical terms (scale, ...) and knowledge (know, believe). These classes were defined along the transcripts in an open-coding manner. The subdivision in problem-solving-phases and items enabled us to compare the subjects relative to the quantity of strain-sequences. The succession of phases gives an illustration of the overall strategy of problem-solving chosen by the different subjects. With the help of the different phases of problem-solving and the attached items it was possible to create a qualitative matrix for each subject, presenting various kinds of problems - causes of strain - in the various phases of the design process.

In general the following results could be obtained from the various studies (Rückert, Springer, 1994):

- Most of the strain results from handling operations at the CAD system due to ergonomic deficiencies of the systems.
- Stress can be minimized if the CAD system is designed as task appropriate as possible.
- The evaluation of the elaborated solutions shows that the chosen strategy of problem-solving is in the most cases more or less far from being a linear progression through the various phases. Individual problem solving strategies must be supported.
- Organizational factors like user qualification and

training, support structures, data exchange with other applications, etc. are the most important factors for an efficient (and economic) CAD application.

56.4.2 Ergonomic Requirements on CAD Systems Based on Empirical Analyses

Requirements on the personal activity level of the work system are related to the pragmatic (application models and concepts) and the semantic (functions and objects) levels of the HCI model (Springer, 1992).

Related to models and concepts used in the design process the following requirements are important:

- The designer should have information about the characteristics of models (products, parts etc.) everytime and everyplace (e.g. in a meeting with the customer).
- The designer should use a CAD internal model whose characteristics are compatible to the mental model of the designer, thus decreasing necessary coding and decoding effort.
- The CAD system has to have an easy to use functionality to change characteristics of models.
- The designer should be able to describe characteristics by fuzzy data, especially in the early phases of the development process.
- The designer should be able to generate task and/or individual specific models by combination of different predescribed models, e.g. geometry and function of the product and costs.
- Different models and different views on a model (e.g. functional vs. cost view) should be managed simultaneously and the designer should have the ability to switch efficiently between those models, e.g. switching between
- global and detail problems (analysis/ synthesis),
- concrete and abstract definition of model characteristics (abstraction level)
- different alternatives for problem solution
- Models should be coupled to link interdependent characteristics.

Activities directly related to the design task should be aided by the following conceptional characteristics of a CAD system:

- At solutions which have not reached their final state the designer should be able to indicate by special application functions that further adaptation of the geometry is necessary or that better solutions might exist, e.g. like in conventional design work by "perfect" drawn graphical elements vs. hand sketch drawn elements.
- Because the designer is using various abstraction levels for the description of the solution, all descriptions must be related to each other. Hand sketch drawings (of functional structures as well as of geometrical layouts) play an important role.As indicated in figure 17 the path of a designer through the "solution space" is characterized by a large number of iterations between the various information resources. This requires the parallel handling of the different resources as well as the connectivity between the representation modes.
- The designer should be able to switch between different views on a design, e.g. symbolized functionality, 2- or 3-D views, scaled or non-scaled views, isometric or perspective views etc.
- Different concepts for problem solving or optimizing solutions should be incorporated (e.g. simulation, application programs like solution data bases, advanced calculation methods like FEM - Finite Element Method, etc.)
- Different concepts for evaluation (e.g. use value analysis) should be integrated, the designer should be able to use task or individual specific evaluation parameters and he should be able to prove the evaluation results.

Effective information management is necessary for an effective design process:

- The designer should be able to get and to use different information sources based on alphanumeric as well as on graphical information like standards, company standards, supplier information, similar designs once performed, handbooks, guidelines, legal regulations etc.
- Information should be given in a consistent way to the designer, e.g. by using the same parameter descriptions in a supplier's database and a calculation procedure in a guideline.
- Functions for the navigation, for activation and deactivation of constraints, for visualization and for the control of consistency should be integrated (figure 18).
- Functions for searching information by different

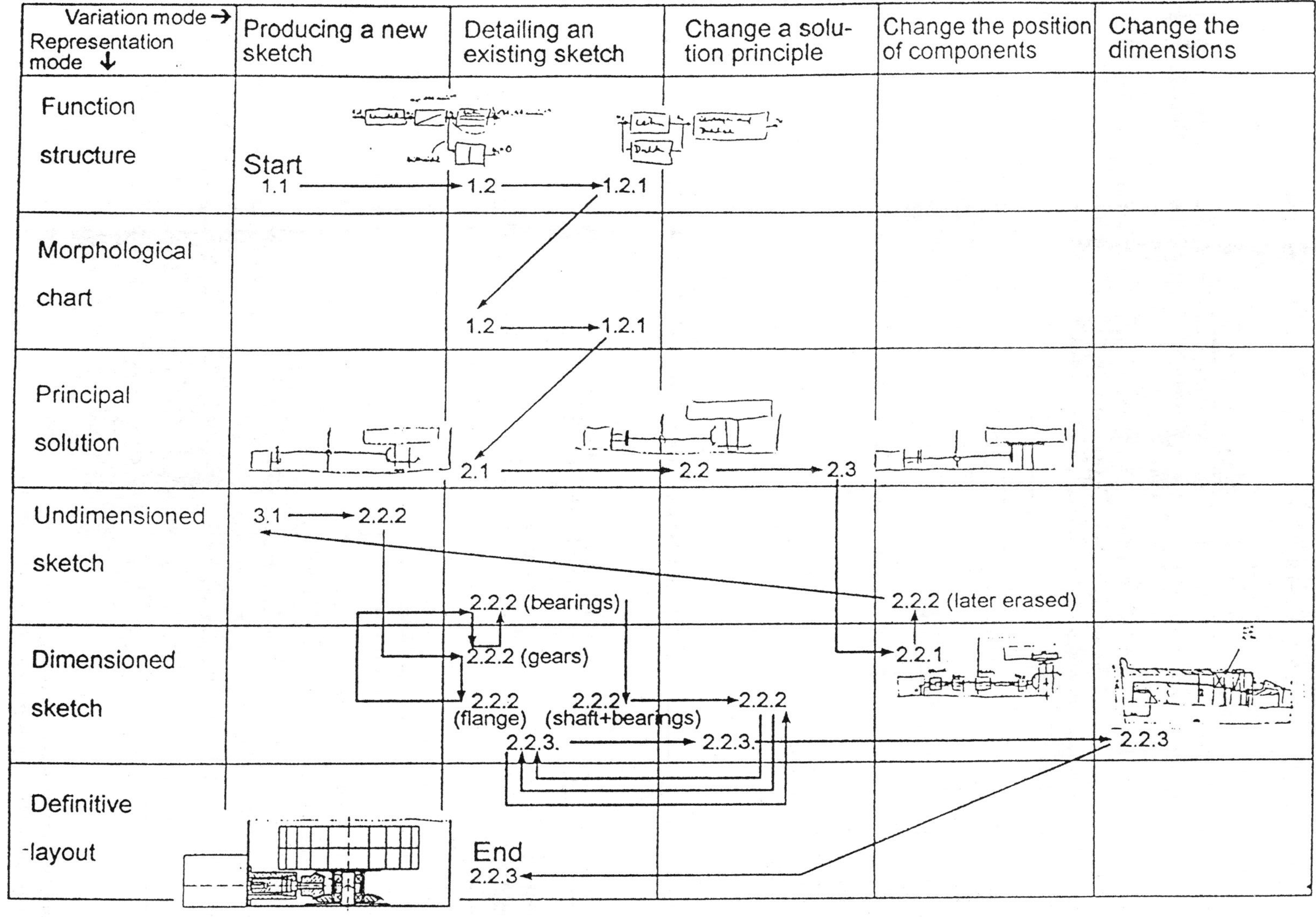

Figure 17. ***Activities of a designer through different representation modes.*** *(from Rückert and Springer, 1994). Example of a designer who is proceeding his design steps nearly according to the methodological design process (see chapter 1).*

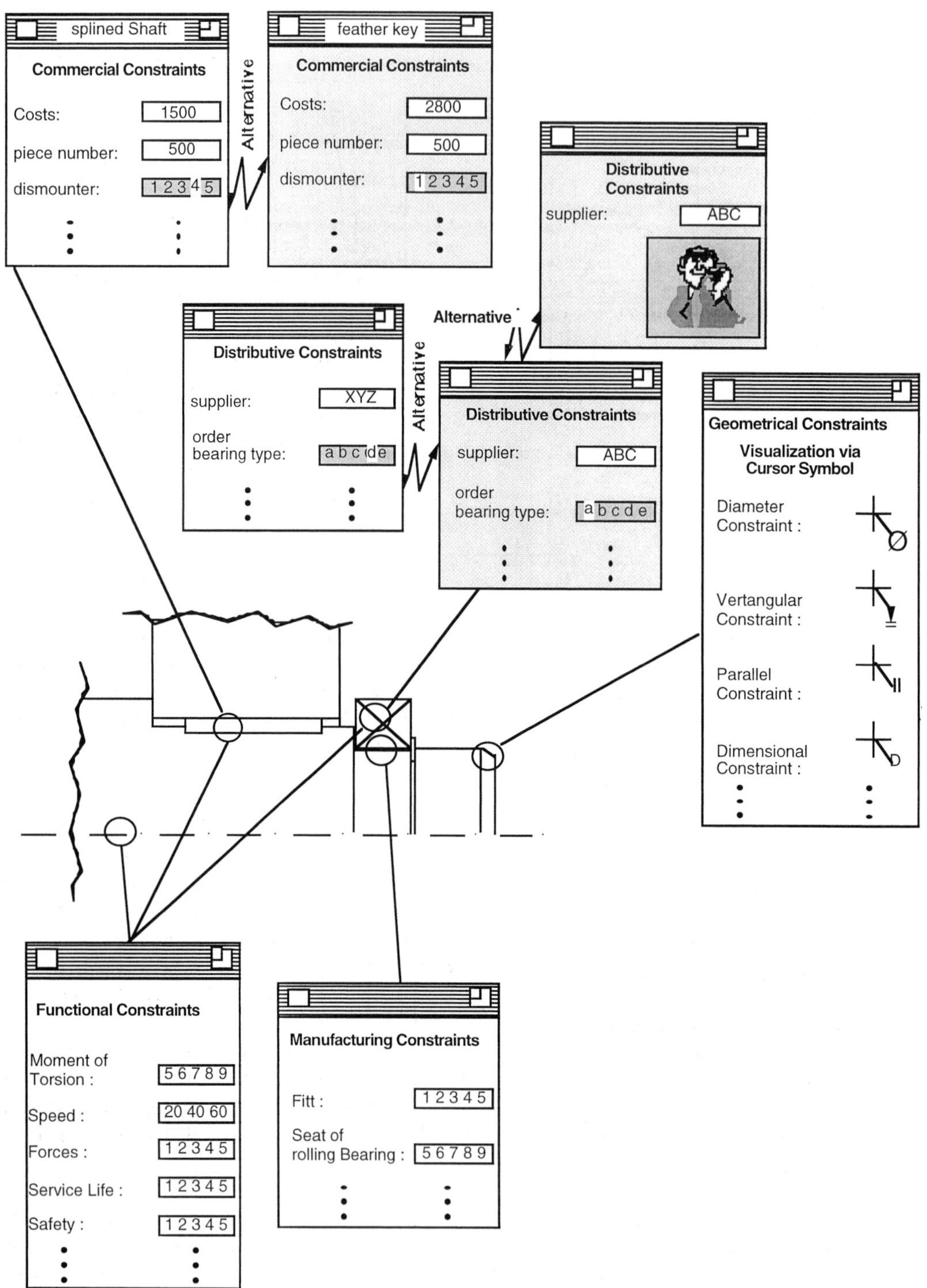

Figure 18. Example of presentation and management of information networks (constraints between different data and models, e.g. geometrical, functional, technological, economic etc.) in design.

criteria and using information in different ways, e.g. cut and paste, manipulation etc., should be integrated.

- The designer should be able to manage different information resources simultaneously.

- Information must be actualized permanently.

The activities of the designer are highly dependent of the availability and design of functions to operate on the various objects in design. Therefore, the characteristics of functions and objects of the CAD system are important for effective design. Requirements on functions based on the designer's activities are:

- Direct manipulation should be used as much as possible due to the interactive tool metaphor behind this interaction technique (transparency of the result). Direct manipulation supports the generation of objects (rubber bendings to visualize the effects of generation), the geometrical manipulations like stretching, bending, pressing, moving, rotating etc., as well as the deletion of complex objects by simply using virtual erasers (Drisis, 1996) like they are used in conventional drawing. Therefore, functionality must be integrated into the objects themselves, and must be visualized by dialogue metaphors as parts of the objects.

- Because most of the geometrical definitions must contain exact dimensions, numerical feedback must be given continuously during the design process. It can be realized through written dimensions like in technical drawings, through numerical displays, software rulers, or snap modi based on user defined grids. The user should be able to switch between consistent visualization of geometry and dimensions (scaled drawings) and unscaled visualization as often used in hand sketch drawings (figure 19), e.g. to make transparent a special functionality (tolerances, functional measures like eccentricity etc.).

- Hand sketch functionality should be integrated into the CAD systems (Jansen and Krause, 1984, figure 20). But the CAD system should provide the user with the decision whether the hand sketch should be changed into the final geometry (CAD elements), or the hand sketch is used to visualize the unfinished character of a solution. Furthermore, hand sketches and handwriting can be used also for dimensioning the geometry and thus for a fast and consistent data input into the CAD system (Jansen and Krause, 1984).

  An UNDO-function should exist to recover anytime from an error and to aid an iterative design process. Mechanisms for storing a design history are also required, that means copies of different design states must be stored in a user defined (and documented) way for the documentation of the decision processes as well as for going back to previous design steps.

- The whole functionality of the CAD system must be adaptable dependent on the requirements of the task as well as the individual strategies of problem solving. Reduction can be made either by modular software design (reduction on the function level) as well as reduction on the dialogue level (reduction on the interface level).

Objects of the CAD system are data which are operated on by the functions of the CAD system. Because of the various demands on the product to be designed, a large number of different objects must be handled by the designer. Therefore, the type and the structure of objects managed by a CAD system are important for an ergonomic system design.

- All types of geometric information should be integrated into a homogenous and consistent data structure, that is surface characteristics, tolerances, movement spaces etc. Constraints between geometry and related geometric objects like dimensions, crosshatches, etc. should be defined when the designer creates this related objects, and they should be managed by the CAD system automatically.

- Knowledge based systems should be integrated into the design process. This requires interfaces between the CAD system and the knowledge based system and the interchange of data between these applications.

- The user needs anytime information about the characteristics of defined objects and its relations to other objects outside the CAD system (costs, technological data, etc., see above).

Requirements on the syntactical and physical level can taken from the criteria list (table 1) as well as from ISO standards (ISO 9241) for CAD non-specific requirements.

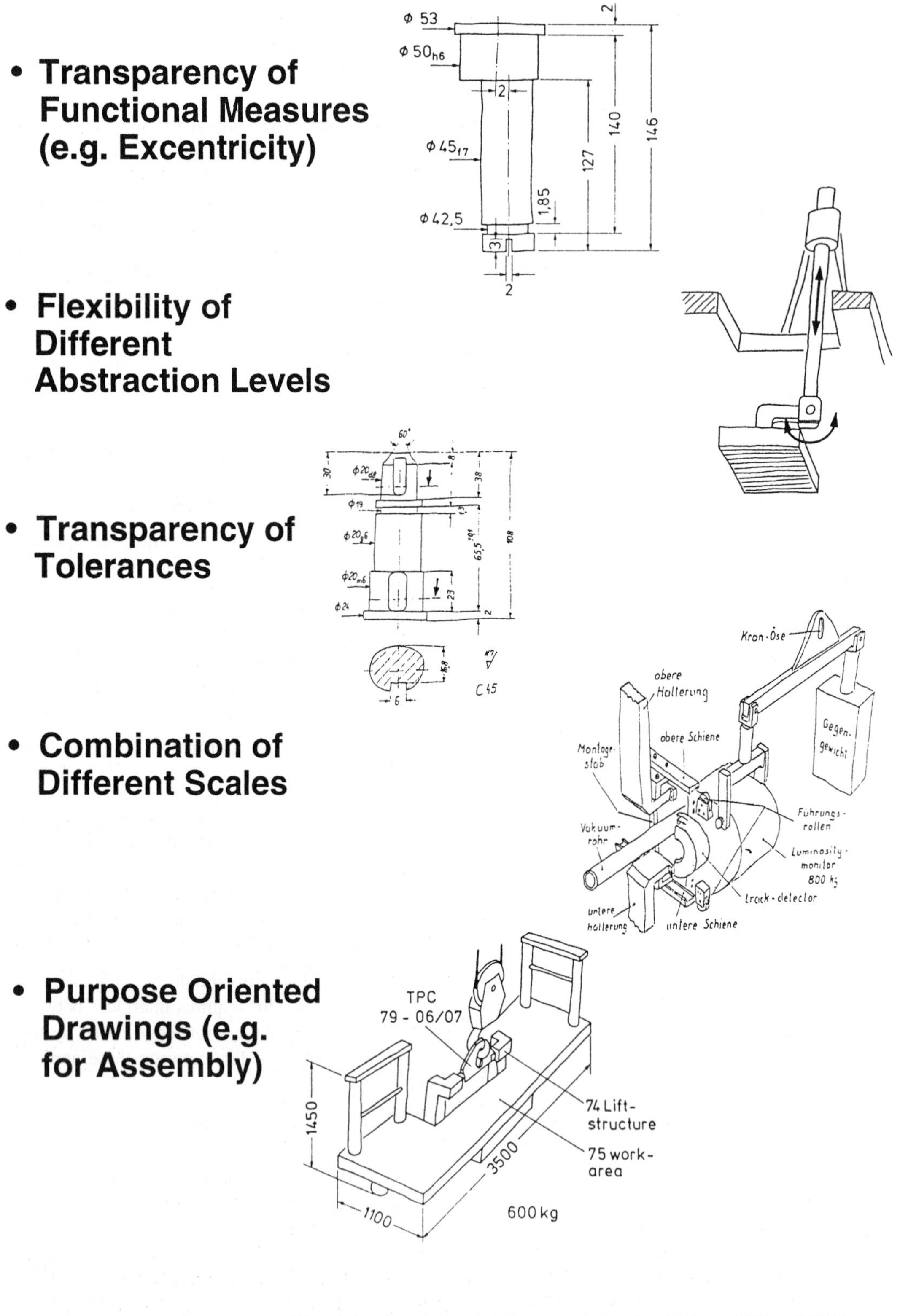

- **Transparency of Functional Measures (e.g. Excentricity)**
- **Flexibility of Different Abstraction Levels**
- **Transparency of Tolerances**
- **Combination of Different Scales**
- **Purpose Oriented Drawings (e.g. for Assembly)**

Figure 19. Functional advantages of hand sketch and unscaled drawings *(related to Richter, 1987 and 1990).*

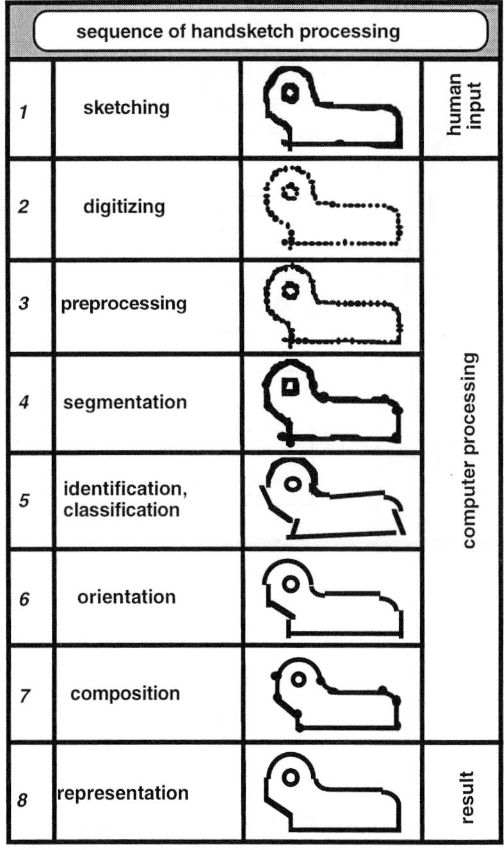

Figure 20. Sketching functionality, automatic recognition of hand sketch drawings. *(Jansen and Krause, 1984)*

56.5 Group Cooperation Related Focus: Reorganization Of Design Departments With CAD

With the introduction of CAD-systems into design departments the question arises, how work and labour partition is effected by this "new technology" in the sense, that the structures of group work and the features of the working group are changed. In principle this is a problem of "work structuring" superimposed by a new allocation of functions between "work force" and "CAD-functionality" and a shift in labour-partition between persons with very heterogeneous qualifications and competencies - the creative design engineer with all academic degrees to the draftsman -. Another difficulty in this context of determining the effects of CAD-systems on the group work process may be the heterogeneity of incoming orders, their profile and priority, which have to be redefined as individual tasks in a social environment, in which a "free" disposition over preferred tasks to be executed by an individual gives a scope of action for creative work. Thus it is no wonder, that empirical studies about the effects of CAD-systems on group work are missing. Whenever organizational experiments in a real environment seem to be impossible, simulation may be applied; however a classical "work-station queuing model" for simulation in this context cannot be the "right" approach for "creative informatory work", because tasks executed are not determined directly by incoming orders in the design department, but by the individual preferences of creative designers and their "troops" / assigned crews. Thus, as reported by Steidel et al. (1990), Luczak et al. (1992), and Steidel (1994)

- a model has been developed to design task execution with labour partition,
- the model has been transferred into a simulation software that was specifically developed as a person-centred simulation approach for freely structured, creative working processes,
- the model was tested with empirical data from three analysed design departments, and
- design variants were generated by systematic variation of parametres of organization and evaluation of these variants through simulated system behaviour.

The model is based upon an analysis of design methodology and empirical investigations in real design processes under two aspects: the process of problem solving of individual designers and design as a process of cooperative efforts. Formal tasks like the documentation of intermediate results influence the process of design. Thus in co-operative design a phase-oriented modelling of design operations by rules and algorithms is possible. The number of phases and tasks/work contents of the process mostly depend on the type of orders that are input in the department.

Beneath the process-oriented modelling, the whole model implies a person-model, which characterizes persons with respect to performance and qualification criteria. Other elements of the complete model represent performance criteria of the means of technical work, such as CAD-systems, and the rules of work organization in terms of competencies and responsibilities, possibilities of co-operation, etc.

The transformation of the model into a simulation software on the basis of standardized software packages failed because of the task-driven and process-oriented concept of these tools. Persons are treated as resources

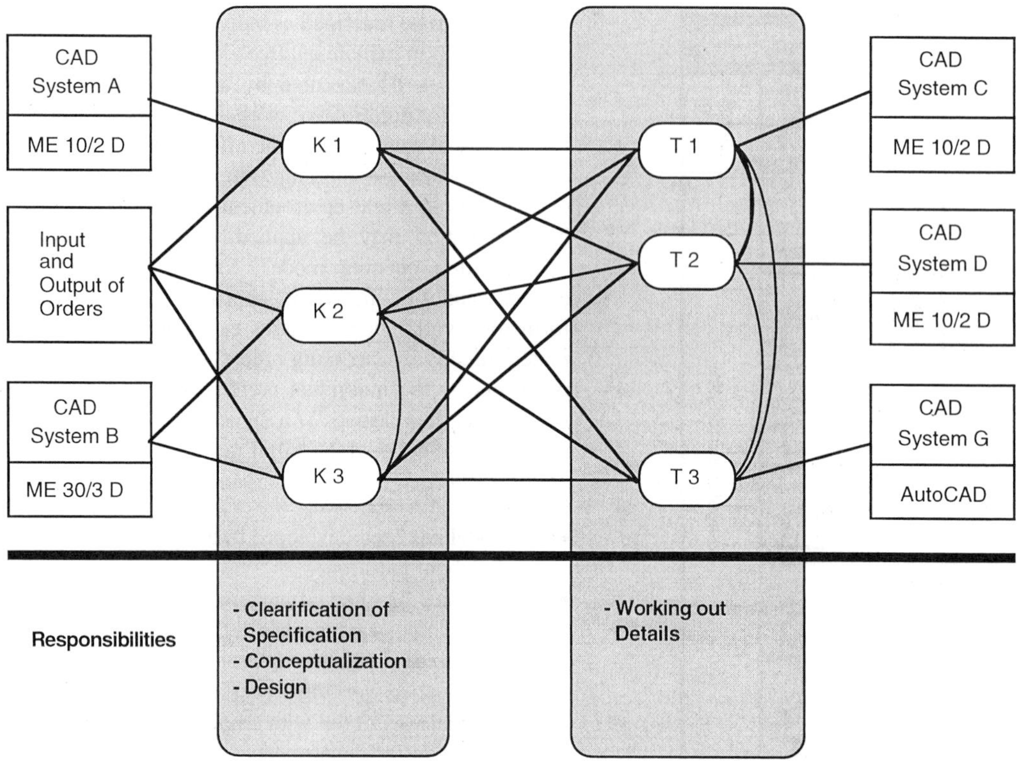

Figure 21. System analysis of a design department with 3 design engineers (K) and 3 draughtsmen (T) using 3 different CAD systems (Steidel, 1994).

in these tools, and can be disposed of freely. With this treatment the only index of organizational connection of a person is his/her responsibility for singular tasks. Other organizational restrictions of the use of personnel cannot be mapped such as individual capacity, priority of performing orders, etc.

In order to simulate co-operative group work a new person-centred simulation approach was developed. In such a simulation persons are mapped as actors with decision competence as in real work processes, with labour partition among highly qualified people. The development of a new software tool was necessary to realize the approach. With the person-oriented simulation tool, the model for the description of persons (qualification, competence, performance, etc.) and work-means/tools, and for the organizational rules as combination guidelines, a mapping of any work system with variable work organization becomes possible.

The concept and the model were validated by empirical data sets that were documented in three design departments for several weeks. For example a case study of a design department (Luczak et al., 1989) with six persons and three different CAD-systems (figure 21) showed minor deviations of simulation from reality (figure 22).

Thus the simulation model of work organization in design departments could be used for prospective organizational design. Typical forms of organization were generated, as can be found in industry, and are discussed in the context of "simultaneous engineering" to cut short design times. When varying as independent variables the number of group members, the task-oriented scope of qualification and responsibility of persons, the power of the CAD-tool, and the synchronization of operations at different partial orders (Simultaneous-Engineering-Concept), characteristic effects on, for example, lead time of orders, can be diagnosed.

To summarize the qualitative results of these simulation experiments: design conditions can be optimized in relation to human-oriented criteria as well as in relation to output and performance of the system. These identified design conditions are characterized by a broader qualification and responsibility of persons along the design process with smaller group size (approx. 12)

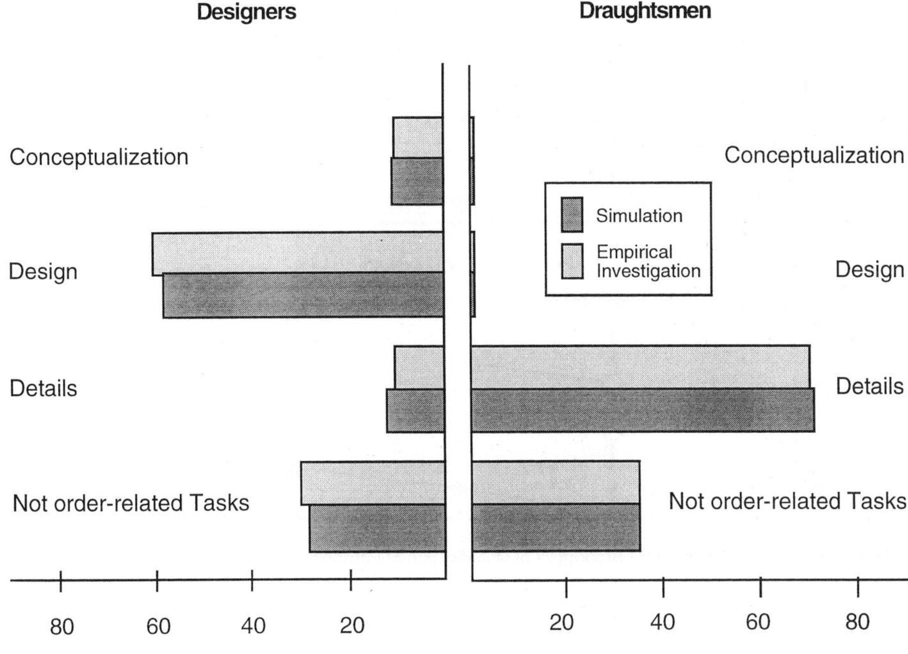

Figure 22. Comparison of simulation results with empirical data for time spent on different design tasks by designers and draughtsmen (Steidel, 1994).

and a work partition according to order types, that are assigned to groups as a complete set of tasks - all in comparison with traditional work organization of design departments, as empirically documented.

The use of CAD-systems cuts short lead time only if bottlenecks in the capacity of certain qualification groups occur. The potential set free by CAD use can hardly cause a diminution of lead times in cases of optimal organizational design. Thus the conclusion can be drawn that in design departments organizational measures have a higher efficiency of the intervention than the use of sophisticated technology, for example, the most advanced CAD-systems (figure 23).

56.6 CAD Integration into the Information and Communication Infrastructure Of a Company

The designers work and CAD is related to several functions and applications in a company (figure 24). In general the designer has to manage two different categories of information and documents: formal documents provide those information which is strictly required for the full description of the product and its related processes. Secondly informal information like notices, e- and voice-mails etc. are strongly relevant for the transparency of decision processes in the design. Thus informal as well as formal information must be managed by the designer. Today's data management conceptions discriminate between EDM (Engineering Data Management) systems for the formal data and work flow management systems for informal information.

Empirical investigations on the efficiency of design departments showed the importance of using project management methods (Klaus, 1992, Dorner, 1993). The more transparency in used capacities, the proceeding of the tasks, allocated costs concerning the elaborated solutions etc., the more economic factors are fulfilled: proceeding time is reduced, the quality of the design is improved, and the product meets the predetermined costs. Thus the integration of project management methods into the CAD process is strongly requested. From an ergonomic point of view it has diverse influences on the designer, i.e.:

- The use of the CAD applications is controlled by the project management.
- Administrative tasks performed with the help of data and process management systems (formal as well as informal) become more important.
- The designer has to perform his tasks "process ori-

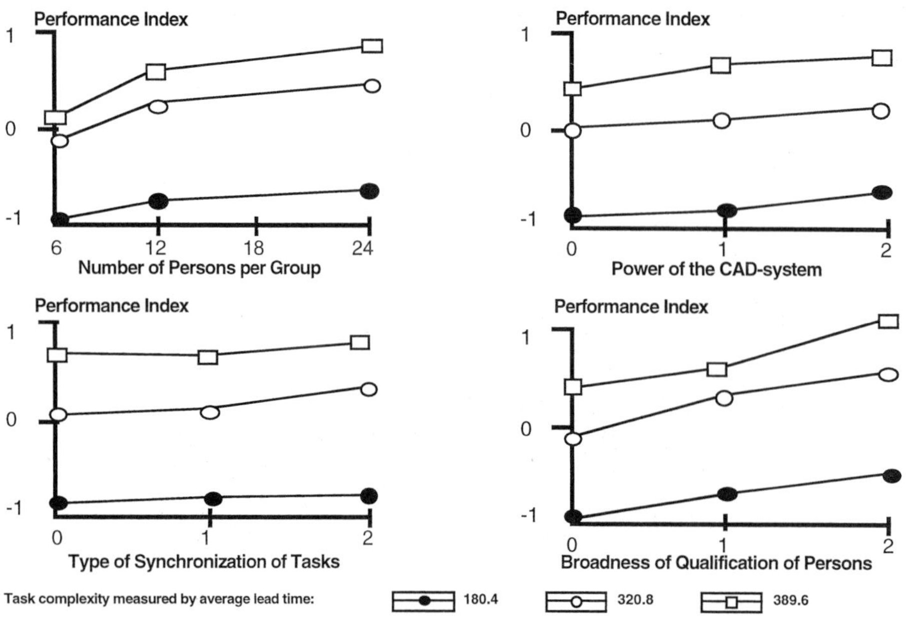

Figure 23. Combined influence of task complexity (measured by average lead time) and different parameters of organization on a performance index of the design department. *(Steidel, 1994).*

ented", that means every (electronic) result will be used by another person in the organization (customer); the designer has to perform the task not only with his own requirements, but he has to consider the entire demands of the process.

The drawings produced are used for CAM and CAP systems to define data for numerically controlled machines. Quality control and measurement procedures need the geometrical and technological data of parts or the product to be quality controlled. All data specifying the product as well as the technological (or economic) parameters of the product and necessary production processes are stored in data bases like EDM systems. Based on the drawings the designer derives part lists which are used by PPC systems to plan and control the necessary production processes. These and other functions force the designer to navigate, to interact and to interchange information with other company functions (persons) and other applications.

Dependent on the functional characteristics of the different applications, the qualification of the designer, the task to be performed, and the organizational structure of the company the allocation of functions between humans, but also between applications can be established. It means that the characteristics of the system have implications on macro ergonomic (organizational structures) as well as micro ergonomic factors (e.g. preparation of data before or revising data after the interchange between applications). figure 25 shows for example 5 different types of work organization in a design department and its related department for preparing the data for numerical control. If data can be transformed without information loss, no revision has to be done by the designer. But the situation in practise is characterized by information transfer problems and therefore by efforts for data revisioning.

Using the data produced in the design department in other processes the designer has to take into account the requirements of other departments not only on information but also on data quality. figure 26 shows an example of geometrical description of a surface, which is sufficient for the designer's purpose but induces problems for preparation of NC data: surfaces of higher order are limited for milling. Especially for the data exchange between companies a large effort is made to ensure data quality. Special programs, e.g. the VDA-checker (VDA - Assoc. of German Automobile Industry) control the CAD data by different quality criteria. Thus the designer is responsible for a "good design" as well as for high quality data. This inner (and inter) company exploitation of data forces the designer to invest effort to the de-

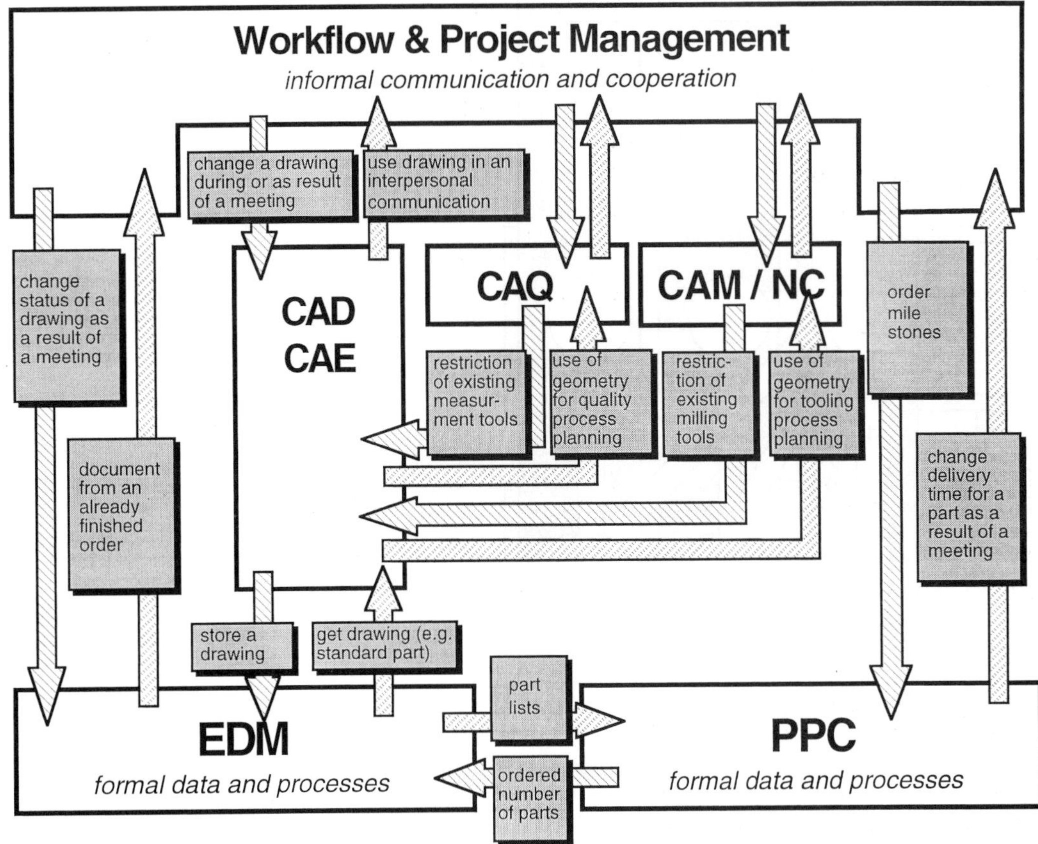

Figure 24. CAD in the information and communication infrastructure of a company and examples for information transfer between the applications

scription of the geometry. If this effort is not compensated by time or capacity it will lead to higher stress of the designer.

56.7 Intercompany Related Focus

An increasing amount of maker-supplier-relations, e.g. in the automotive industry, change their design departments to cooperative partnerships called product development cooperations. In development cooperations the maker develops products with one or more component suppliers, while he concentrates on his core competence. The suppliers directly apply their specific knowledge to the development of entire components. At the same time "Concurrent Engineering" (CE) as an organizational concept is used to shorten development time and improve the quality of the product and the production process.

A major obstacle to a successful cooperation is an obstructed communication due to the spatial separation of the partners on the one hand and the limits of presently common technical resources like telephone and fax on the other. In addition, heterogeneous EDP-systems in the partner companies complicate communication. The consequences are higher efforts by the involved employees, which partially compensate the benefits of applying CE. Even a permanent or temporary presence of employees of the supplier at the maker's location solely shifts the communication problem to the supplier.

At the moment large efforts are made to develop technical and organizational solutions to overcome the communication problem of product development cooperations. This goal will be achieved by the conception and introduction of a modern communication system with special respect to work routines, tasks, demands and needs of the employees. The functions of such a system must fit for the needs of the employees to be accepted by them. A person only will accept the system, if his personal gain is larger than the additional effort imposed by the operation of the communication system.

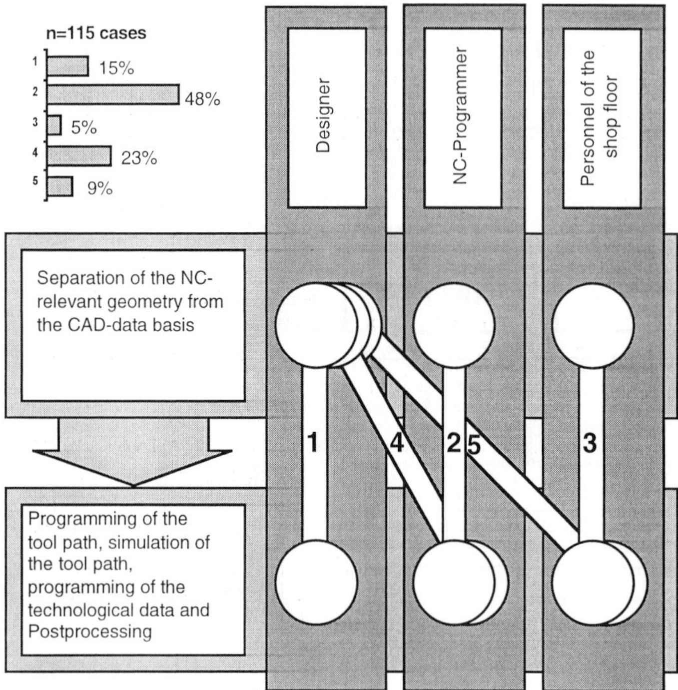

Figure 25. Types of work organization in CAD-NC coupling *(Lay et al., 1987).*

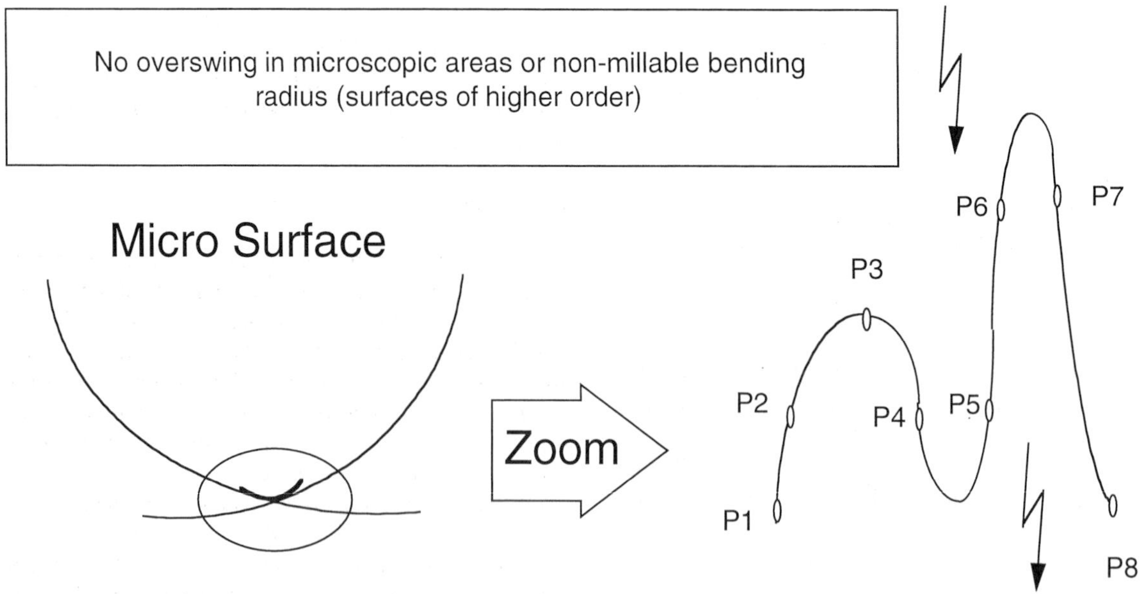

Figure 26. Quality of data (example) necessary for CAD-NC coupling.

In order to do this it is necessary to firstly analyze the working processes in the development process with respect to different types of communication. From there the various types and problems of communication in selected cooperation processes are examined with respect to qualitative and quantitative aspects following a participative approach. Based on that the user requirements can be derived. On the inter company process level a typical communication scenario is given in figure 27.

Functions for inner- and inter-company telecooperation can be split into the dimensions of synchronous and asynchronous communication (same / different time) and the type of information necessary for communication that is personal communication or shared documents (figure 28).

In product design the amount of creative work (as defined in chapter 1) is remarkably high. Because of the necessary division of labour a high demand of information, communication and cooperation emerges, which takes up to 40% of the working time (Springer et al., 1996). This was determined by numerous empirical studies (e.g. Hales, 1987). The systematic consideration of communication during the design process is the basis for the development of a telecooperative CAD-system. The considered criteria are:

- Persons
- Resources for the information utterance
- Media of the information transfer

Environment of the information exchange

Using these criteria the communication and cooperation between persons is defined as follows:

> "Between persons pieces of information uttered by resources, synchronously or asynchronously, are exchanged by means of media, received by modalities within an environment."

Persons

The criterion "persons" is essential, because it is the employees who drive the operational process. The criterion is defined by the number of partners, the number of locations (including the number of persons at each location), the continuity of the communication, and the intensity of the participation in the communication. The continuity of communication refers to the amount of time a person participates in a communication. The last can be distinguished between equally shared and one-sided participation. An example of one-sided participation is the informing of a person by another.

Resources for the Information Utterance

According to a general structure of communication the utterances of one partner lead to "innerances" of the receiving partner (e.g. Schulz v. Thun, 1994). They lead in turn to utterances by the latter. "Innerance" is an artificial word, which refers to information internally represented by a communicating person, which is not directly accessible by the partner. They only can be expressed by the use of human resources like language, facial expressions and gestures, and technical resources like technical drawings, sketches, documents or physical models. Technical resources are passive, because they do not utter information by themselves.

At the time of use, resources may utter information in various ways (e.g. physically or electronically). In this context a distinction with respect to the availability of resources is necessary. For example, a physically existing plot of a CAD-model with added written remarks and sketches can not be sent directly by electronic means, because the additional information would be lost. At this time the plot with the remarks is a composed resource that only exists physically. For an electronic transfer it must be digitized again.

Media of information transfer

Media of information transfer is either synchronous or asynchronous. Examples for synchronous media are face-to-face conversation while mailing services (physically or electronically) are asynchronous.

Modalities

The information transferred by media is received by the sensory modalities of the receiver. In product design the visual and auditory perceptions are the most important. Tactile perception is also relevant, e.g. to judge the condition of surfaces.

Environment

The criterion "environment" refers to the fact that personal communication and cooperation are influenced by spatial, organizational, and social boundary conditions. For instance, communication between different time zones requires the scheduling of conferences with respect to the local time of each partner. Social relationships between communicating persons strongly influence the exchanged information.

The communication process between partners can be described by the semiotic model (see chapter 1.2). interfered by the telecooperation system. figure 29 shows the process of information transfer between transmitting and receiving persons supported by a technical medium in

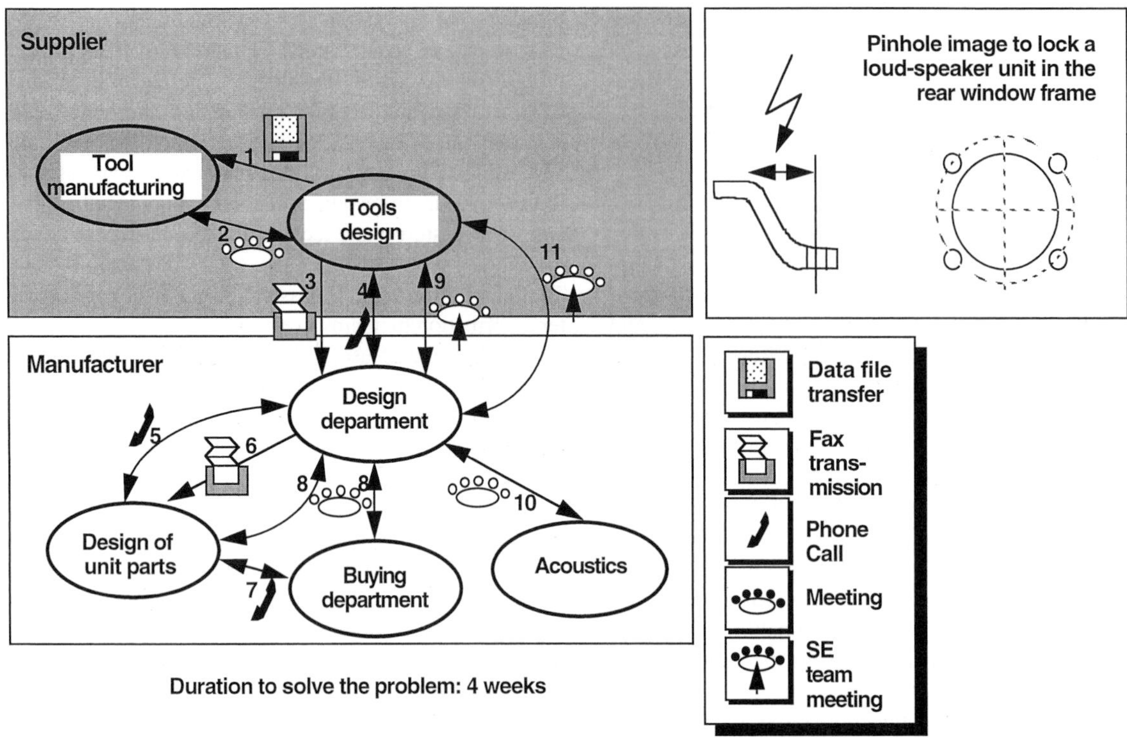

Figure 27. Example of a communication problem on the process level: the pinhole diameter (see sketch) must be changed due to technological requirements. *The duration to solve (such a "simple" problem) was approx. 3 months (Springer et al., 1995).*

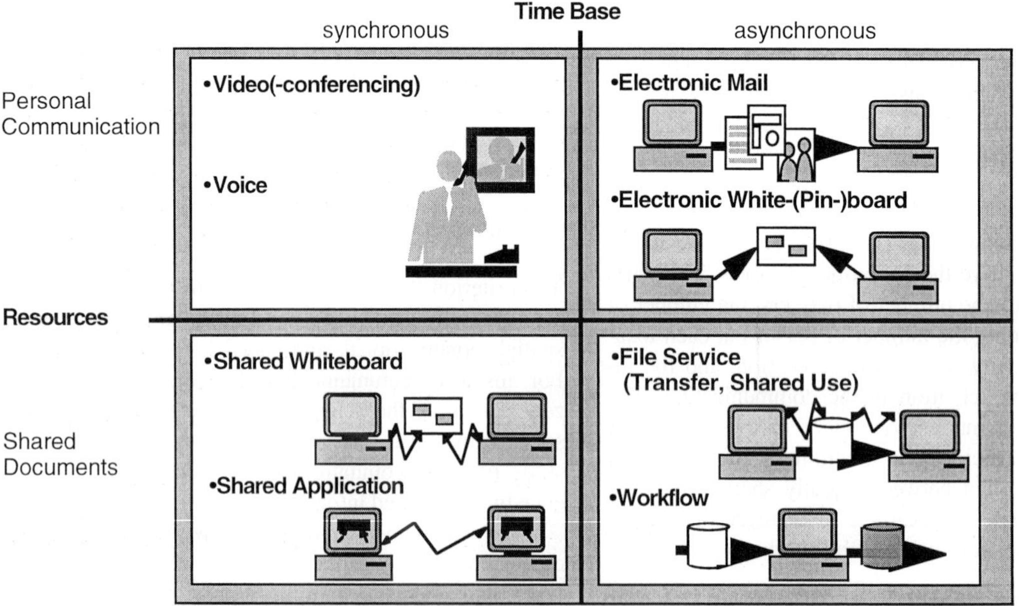

Figure 28. Components of computer supported cooperative design systems (CSC(D)W systems) *(Springer et al., 1995).*

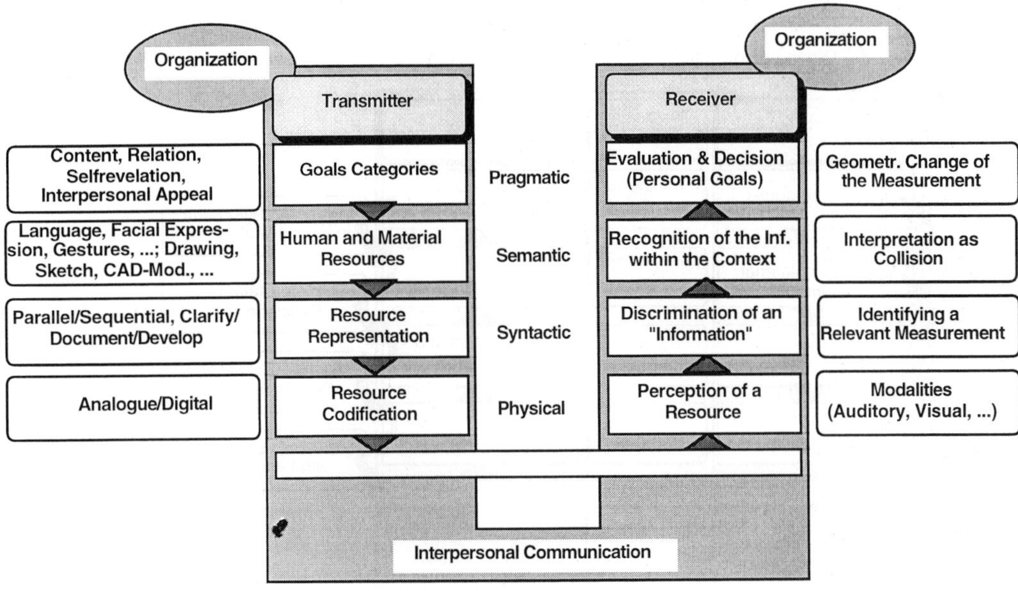

Figure 29. Semiotic Transmitter - Receiver Model and Examples for Communication Operations *(Springer et al., 1996).*

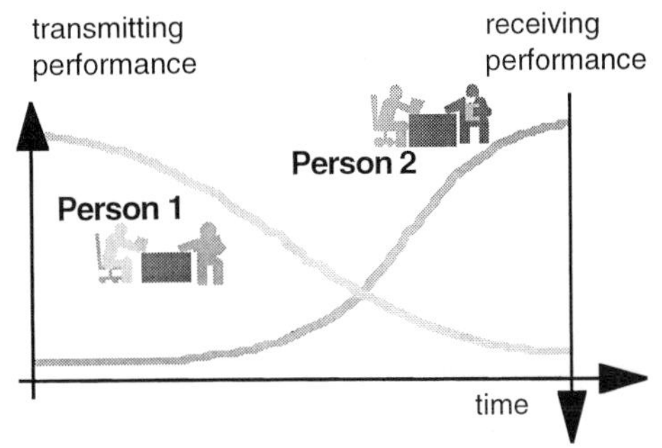

Figure 30. Transceiver Characteristic *(Springer et al., 1996).*

terms of the system presented above. But it should be stated, that at the same time the receiver transmits also information which is received by transmitter (transceiver characteristic, figure 30).

This is a characteristic for self reflexive systems like communication (Maturana/ Varela, 1985, Medina-Mora et al., 1992). The model also describes the interpersonal and interorganizational requirements for and communication problems hindering effective communication (figure 31) as well as deficiencies of today's existing CAD conferencing tools. These are for example:

- on the pragmatic level the lack of sketching application
- on the semantic level the non-availability of the "cut and paste"-function
- on the syntactic level the different dialogue structure of "shared application" and
- on the physical level the H320 compatibility, screen solution, mouse, keyboard characteristics, etc.

The results of an exemplary communication analysis are shown by the following scenario (figure 32). From these results basic types of communication that are used by designers can be derived. Focus of the communication in the scenario is a component that is abstractly characterized as "object". The problem consists of a contour change of the considered object for the purpose to adjust it to another object. Both objects exist as CAD-models, but not physically.

Three persons participate in the communication: Employees of the supplier *(S)*, the maker *(M)*, and a consulting engineering office *(E)*. At first *(M)* and *(E)* discuss the contour change of the object (*(E)* is responsible for the generation of the surfaces of the CAD-model). They use a plot with the cross-section of the object. *(S)* joins the conversation after six minutes and points out a mould opening angle that must be kept in limits for the production process.

For clarification *(E)* makes a sketch on a sheet of paper, which is then discussed and supplemented with additional sketches. After 30 minutes the discussion

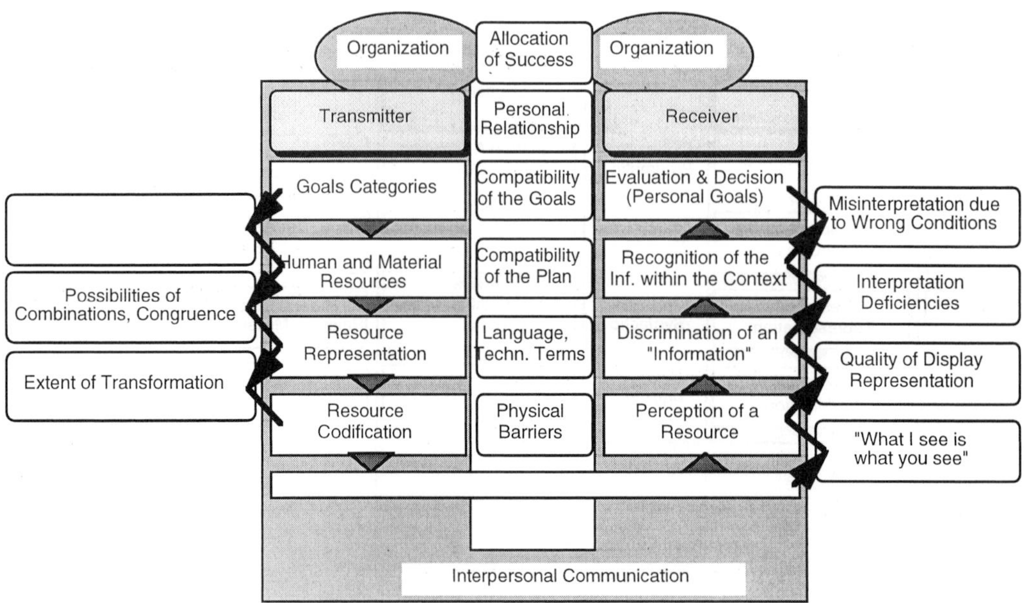

***Figure 31. Transmitter / receiver model and examples of interpersonal and interorganizational communication problems** (Springer et al., 1996).*

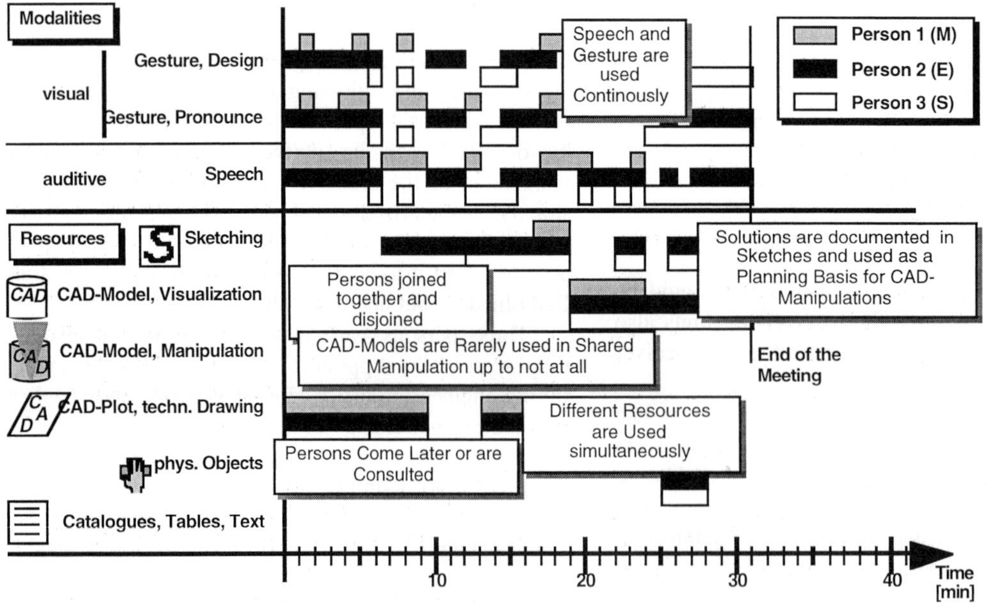

Figure 32. Communication scenario on the activity level and exemplary conclusions.

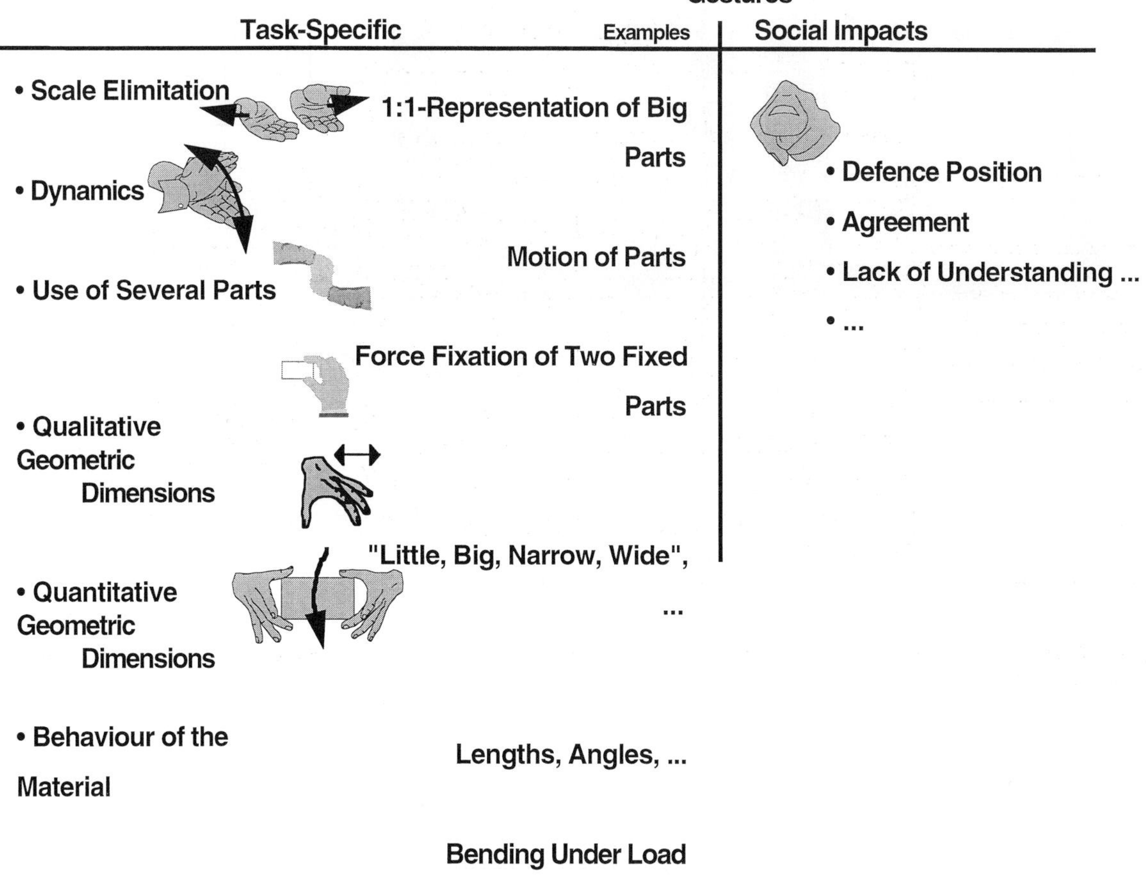

Figure 33. Gestures: task specific and social communicative aspects in communication about designs.

ends and five sketches of different sizes were drawn. During the conversation the employees outline production processes and contours of the object by hand movements. Because plot and sketches do not contain all necessary pieces of information, the CAD-model is viewed on a screen. Problematic areas are pointed out with fingers and the cursor. The rotation and zooming of the model are done by the principal user of the work station. The participants decide to make changes to the CAD-model, but these changes are not made during the conference.

This scenario demonstrates that visualization of design problems and possible solutions are of great importance. In addition most of the resources presented in the communication system have to be visualized. Types of communication were "sketching", "gestures", "communi-cation at CAD-models", „communication at the plot of CAD-models" and "communication at objects". The presently common means of telecommunication, telephone and fax, only partly serve this purpose. Gestures, esp. in product design, never have only social functions but a high task relevancy (figure 33).

For the development of a telecooperative CAD system the "natural" communication between designers (without a technical medium for transfer) must be used as reference. It is necessary that the designers use the system intuitively in order to maintain an undisturbed communication. From the scenario the following technical components are identified for the on-line communication of designers (see figure 34):

- Shared CAD-system
- Shared electronic sketch pad
- Video component to visualize gestures and facial expressions of partners
- Scanner (or document camera) to digitize and show plots and documents
- Video component to show physical objects

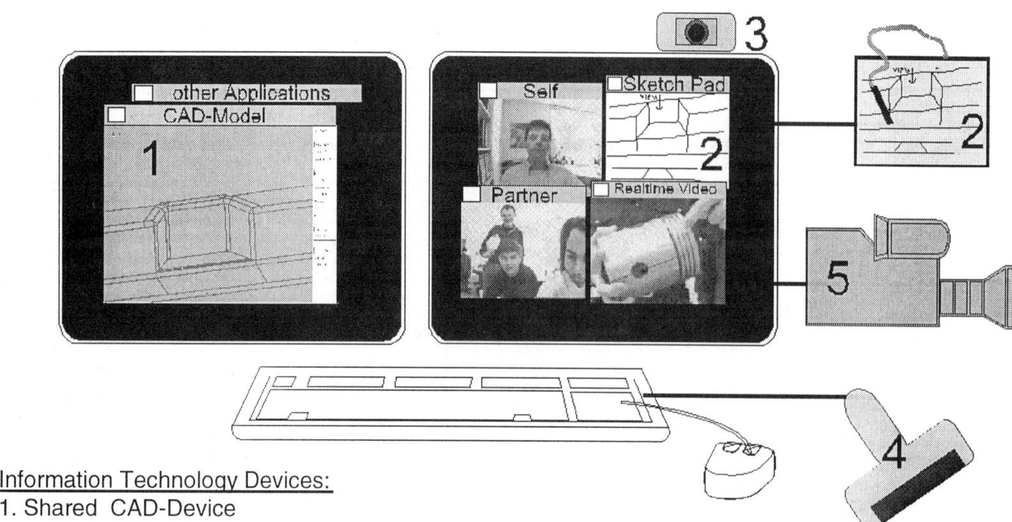

Figure 34. Technological Components of a Telecooperative CAD system.

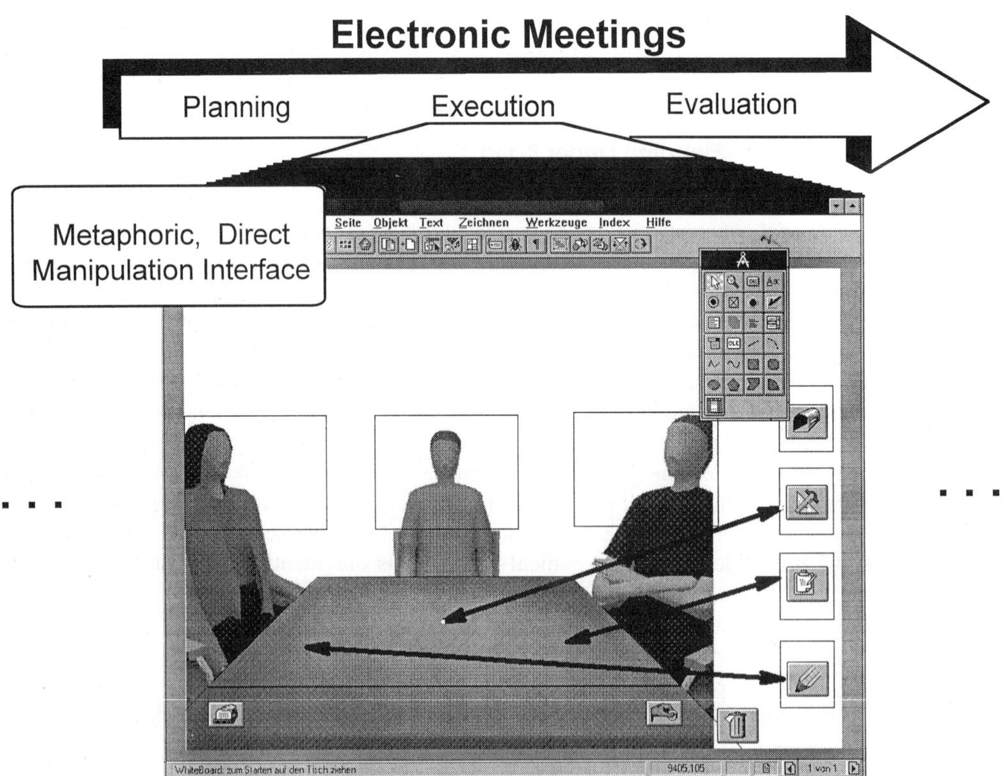

Figure 35. Metaphoric interfaces of advanced CSC(D)W systems

Shared CAD-component

The essential need to visualize CAD-models demands a shared CAD-system. Features like zooming, turning, fading in and out of layers, etc. must be accessible to all participants. However, it is not necessary to change the model during a communication session. The CAD-system should be used with an extra screen, because the users rate a shared CAD-system at the highest priority.

Shared electronic sketch pad

The shared electronic sketch pad should provide the opportunity to make sketches in the most natural way possible. That means that electronic pads and pens should be used which show the sketch on both the screen and the pad. Furthermore the thickness of the lines should correspond to the pressure applied on the pen. Elements drawn by different persons should indicate their origin.

Video Device to visualize gestures and facial expressions (of partners)

During the design conference the gestures and facial expressions of all participants must be visible clearly. A sufficient quality of the picture is necessary to show details and/or fast movements.

Scanner device (or document camera) to visualize plots / papers

If needed electronically, physically existing documents, e.g. plots with hand-written remarks, can quickly be transformed by a hand scanner.

Real time video device to visualize physical objects

An extra screen window should serve the purpose of visualizing physical objects such as clay models, single parts or components. Due to the fact that these objects are not always available at the workplace, it is necessary to have additional cameras, e.g. on the shop floor. Important features are suitable fixings, simple usage and design of the camera as well as lighting conditions.

The system can be enhanced by metaphorical interfaces for meeting planing, execution and examination (figure 35).

Further (macro-)ergonomic factors become relevant in inter-company cooperations:

- The data between different CAD systems is exchanged via standardized interfaces, e.g. IGES, VDA-FS or STEP. Because nearly every data exchange produces some kind of data loss, the designer (or another person) has to perform a substantial after-treatment of the exchanged data. This produces blind effort between the companies.
- The globalization of markets lead to world-wide cooperation. Because of the time lags shift work becomes necessary to enable the partners for synchronous communication.
- An increasing amount of work can be done at home (tele-home-working) or near home (tele-centre). On the one hand this type of work organization offers flexibility to the designers as well as to the companies needs, but it also requires a lot of regulations concerning privacy, working hours, working conditions and safety at home, alternation between home work and attendance in the company, etc.

56.8 Guidelines and Recommendations for Ergonomic CAD Systems

Work with display units is part of legislation in diverse regulations: Agreements between labour unions and employers regulate working hours and working conditions at VDU workplaces, thus also be valid for CAD workplaces. Normally the public legislation defines regulations for VDU work too. Since 1992 in Europe the "EU directive on the minimum health and safety requirements for work with display units" was launched and must be transformed into national law by every member state. The directive gives a general guideline on responsibilities and identifies different domains for legislation. It does not provide any measurements for ergonomic system design, but it refers directly to established ergonomic standards such as ISO 9241 and its European equivalent, the EN 29241.

The International Standards Organization (ISO) has worked out a set of standards (ISO 9241) which provide a scientific basis for planning and evaluating VDU workplaces based on ergonomic criteria. The standard currently comprises 17 parts: General introduction (part 1), task design (part 2), hardware and environmental factors (parts 3-9), and software and usability (parts 10-17). A fundamental condition for an improved design of CAD hard- and software, which especially takes into account the needs of the designers, is that on the one hand their needs are recognized, and on the other hand they must be formulated clearly for the system developers. With this requirement the ISO standards as well as the EU directive provides only a general guideline which must be specified to the needs of designers and the tasks and working conditions in the design department.

With this aim the working team "User interfaces of CAD systems" ("Benutzungsoberflächen von CAD-Systemen") of the study group "Computer Aided Design" ("Rechnerunterstütztes Entwerfen und Konstruieren (CAD)") of the German "Society for Computing Machinery" ("Gesellschaft für Informatik", GI) elaborated recommendations for the ergonomic design of user interfaces of CAD systems (Heinecke et al., 1996 a,b).

The GI recommendations should be a help to evaluate CAD software so that from a users point of view one

- can control if the needs of the users are satisfied in the software,
- can determine if and how he can adapt the software according to his needs,
- can describe where and in which respect individual software parts have to be changed in order to satisfy the needs of the users.

On the other hand the software developers need guidelines, with which they themselves or they together with the users

- can analyse and formulate requirements upon their software
- can assign requirements to particular software elements, and thus can relate the requirements directly to design improvements, and
- can evaluate design solutions, eventually also in a comparative way.

Thus, an improvement of the software which is oriented to the user problems is strongly based upon different prerequisites:

- competent users, who recognize and describe design deficits,
- organizational conditions, which guarantee that design improvements are realized within sight,
- an information and evaluation system, with which users, system experts of the company and the developers themselves are enabled to assess particular design aspects of the software considering user points of view and to show improvements of the design,
- software design recommendations, which are based upon scientific knowledge and must be secured in order to be able to create the necessary "pressure of improvement".

Design recommendations, which are used with such supporting measures, thus enable as well under the interest of the user an optimized use as well under economic points of view an efficient use of the CAD system in working processes.

The ergonomic design of the user interfaces of CAD systems refers to different levels of the development, the adaptation and the use of CAD. Therefore, different target groups are addressed by the recommendations:

- Developers for User Interface Tools
  The structure and the functionality of development tools, with the help of which CAD systems are developed, i.e. User Interface Management Systems (UIMS) for the user surface, influence partially the attributes of CAD user interfaces. Developers of software development tools receive information about the state of the technique and the perspectives of the further development.

- CAD Developers
  Developers can use the recommendations as a framework concept for the development and extension of CAD systems, i.e. for branch specific applications and by that for the in-process quality assurance of CAD systems.

- Quality control
  Before especially greater enterprises decide to obtain a new CAD system or the subsequent version of an existing system, they normally test the system with extensive test methods. Test centres receive with the GI recommendations a methodical guideline, with which they can define ergonomic test criteria while the users and their real working requirements are included.

- Service companies
  Before a CAD system is being used productively it should be adapted to the requirements, which are specific for the enterprise and its tasks. Empirical examinations and the Technical Guideline No. 2216 of the German Engineers' Association (VDI-Richtlinie, 1992) concerning the economic efficiency of CAD systems show that an adaptation not only increases the quality of use but also achieves the main part of the economic benefit of a CAD application. Software developers in the users enterprises, as well as in the consulting service companies, which adapt CAD systems to the special needs of their customers, receive with the GI recommendations a methodical guideline for the definition of requirements.

- Purchasers
  Purchasers of CAD systems, above all forced by a shifting from the seller to the purchaser market, in future will require for ergonomically acceptable CAD systems. In this connection on the one hand the products themselves can be examined by the customer, and on the other hand a comparison of different products can be realized before being a product.

- Representatives of the employees
  The representatives of the employees have and in future will have, the more because of the passing of the EU VDU directive and its conversion into national law, the responsibility to watch the standards and validated scientific knowledge. The present consolidation of international standards concerning the design of VDU workplaces in the ISO 9241 shows that the ergonomic knowledge meanwhile has reached a stable position in the consent forming. The representatives of the employees and consulting institutions receive with the GI recommendations a methodical guideline, with which they can together with the users define ergonomic test criteria for the CAD application and realize an examination.

- Users
  The users of a CAD system who know the details of the concrete user context best, normally adapt the CAD application to their specific demands. For that the CAD systems provide adaptation tools (i.e. for menu structures, pictograms, macros). The GI recommendations are a help for the definition of requirements upon such adaptation tools, and they give the users recommendations for the use of such tools.

From the users point of view the evaluation of the user interfaces according to four aspects turned out to be advantageous. The GI recommendations describe these aspects in a model of the user interfaces, similar to the semiotic model (see chapter 1.2.). This reference model is useful for a structure of design recommendations and the quality assurance process. Also the international standards (ISO 9241, parts 3 to 17) are implicitly adjusted to this model so that the reader gets a help for the fast finding of the appropriate standard.

The structure of the recommendations is adjusted to the semiotic model for user interfaces. Thus the reader finds i.e. recommendations for the design of in-/output devices (physical level) separated from recommendations for the design of the dialogue (syntactic level). In addition, the requirements upon the tools and those upon the organization are separated (semantic and pragmatic level). As standards normally are application neutral, it is obvious that requirements upon tools and organization are difficult to define. The GI recommendations try to fill at least partially this gap with CAD specific requirements on these levels from task domains (exemplary tasks), and thus complete the requirements of the standards upon the in-/output and the dialogue.

The requirements are based on 4 different information levels which are structured in columns of a table:

- The first column presents the general recommendation,
- the second give the reasons and basic principles (e.g. standard, scientific knowledge),
- the third includes one or more clear scenarios to enable the users of the recommendation to check whether the criterion reflects requirements from their special conditions (scenario-based evaluation, see Carroll, 1995), and
- the fourth column includes one or more precise test criteria.

Thus the tabular information lead the reader from each general design recommendation to a concrete test criterion.

This structure of the offered information is useful because design recommendations in the literature often are offered in an unclear and not well-founded and referenced form. Thus in the GI recommendations the concretization steps are represented which are necessary for each practical application. It occurs that instead of general recommendations the precise design criteria can be mentioned (i.e. at the input equipment or concerning the representation of information). In such cases not the task-oriented scenario is needed to formulate test criteria because the characteristics are the criteria themselves. In other cases test criteria are revealed in a special way. They are formulated in an interrogative form to activate the software designer or quality controller to make a precise remark about the fulfillment of a criterion. So the GI recommendations are no check list for the inspection of a user interface, and certainly no "bag of tricks" for design engineers - as far as those really would appreciate one - but they are conceived as a guideline for the consideration of ergonomic criteria on different levels of human-computer interaction.

56.9 References

Abeln, O. (1990). CAD-Systeme der 90er Jahre - Vision und Realität. In: *Datenverarbeitung in der Konstruktion '90. VDI-Bericht* 861.1. Düsseldorf: VDI-Verlag.

Beitz, W., Ehrlenspiel, K. (1984). Modellvorstellung für Entwicklung und Konstruktion. *VDI-Z*, 126 (7), 201-207.

Blume, H.-J., Boelke, R. (1990). Mechanokutane Sprachvermittlung. Fortschrittsberichte VDI, *Reihe* 10, Nr. 137. Düsseldorf: VDI-Verlag.

Burdea, G., Zhuang, J. (1991). Dextrous tele-robotics with force feedback - an overview. *Part 1: Human Factors, Robotica,* 9, 171-178., Part 2: Control and Implementation, *Robotica* 9, 291-298.

Burdea, G., Zhuang, J., Roskos, E., Silver, D., Langrana, N. (1992). A Portable Dextrous Master with Force Feedback, *Presence*, 1 (1), 18-28.

Burdea, G., Coiffet, P. (1994). *Virtual Reality Technology*. New York: John Wiley.

Carroll, J.M. (Ed.), (1995). *Scenario-based design*. New York: John Wiley.

Chen, M., Mountford, S.J., Sellen, A. (1988). A Study in Interactive 3-D Rotation Using 2-D Control Devices. *Computer Graphics*, 22 (4), 121-129.

Craig, J.C. (1963). Difference Threshold for intensity of tactile stimuli. *Perceptions and Psychophysics*, 11, 150-152.

Dorner, F. (1993). Beitrag zur Beurteilung der Wirksamkeit organisatorischer Maßnahmen am Beispiel der Zeitwirtschaft in der Konstruktion. Diss. RWTH Aachen. Aachener Beiträge zur Humanisierung und Rationalisierung, Band 7. Aachen: Augustinus.

Drisis, L. (1996). Rationalisierung der rechnerunterstützten Konstruktion durch softwareergonomische Interaktionsgestaltung. *VDI-Fortschritt-Berichte*, Reihe 1, Nr. 258. Düsseldorf: VDI Verlag.

Foley, J.D., van Dam, A., Feiner, S.K., Hughes, J.F. (1990). *Computer Graphics - Principles and Practice (2nd edition),* Reading: Addison Wesley.

Frieling, E., Klein, H., Schliep, W., Scholz, R. (1987). Gestaltung von CAD-Arbeitsplätzen und ihrer Umgebung. Bundesanstalt für Arbeitsschutz, Forschung Fb 503. Bremerhaven: WirtschaftsverlagNW.

Frieling, E., Pfitzmann, J. (1987): Neuentwicklung einer Menütablett-Vorlage. In: Schönpflug, W.; Wittstock, M. (Hrsg.): *Software-Ergonomie* '87. Stuttgart: Teubner.

Gescheider, G.A., Caparo, A.J., Frisina, R.D., Hamer, R.D., Verillo, R.T. (1978). The effects of a surround on vibrotactile thresholds. *Sensory Processes*, 2, 99ff.

Göbel, M., Springer, J., Hedicke, V., Rötting, M., Luczak, H. (1995a): Tactile feedback applied to Computer-Mice. *International Journal of Human Computer Interaction* 71, p. 1-24.

Göbel, M., Rötting, M., Springer, J. (1995): Eingabevorrichtung für Bildschirmgeräte mit taktilem Feedback., Deutsche Patenturkunde Nr. 41 40 780, Tag der Anmeldung: 06.12.1991, Tag der Erteilung: 18.05.1995b.

Hales, C. (1987): Analysis of the engineering design process in an industrial context. University of Cambridge Diss. 1987 Department of Engineering. Gants Hill Publications: Eastleigh.

Heinecke, A.-M., Dzida, W., Pfitzmann, J., Springer, J. (1996a). Gestaltungsempfehlungen für CAD-Benutzungsoberflächen. Empfehlungen der FG 4.2.1, AK 2 der Gesellschaft für Informatik. Bonn.

Heinecke, A.-M., Dzida, W., Pfitzmann, J., Springer, J. (1996b): Empfehlungen der GI für Benutzungsschnittstellen von CAD-Systemen. In: *CAD '96*. München: Hanser.

Heinecke, A.M. (1991): Developing recommendations for CAD user interfaces. In: Bullinger, H.-J. (Ed.), Human Aspects in Computing: Design and Use of Interactive Systems and Work with Terminals (Advances in Human Factors/Ergonomics 18A). Amsterdam: Elsevier.

Hill, J.W. (1967). *The perception of multiple tactile stimuli. Technical Report No. 4823-1*, Stanford University, Electronic Laboratory. Palo Alto, CA.

Iwata, H. (1993). A Six Degree-of-Freedom Pen-Based Force Display, In: Smith, M. J.; Salvendy, G. (Eds.), Human-Computer Interaction: Applications and Case Studies, *Proceedings 5th International Conference HCI '93,* Vol. 1, Amsterdam: Elsevier.

Jansen, H., Krause, F.-L. (1984). Interpretation of Freehand Drawings for Mechanical Design Processes. *Computer and Graphics*, 8 (4), 351-369.

Jones, R., Mitchell, S., Newman, S. (1993). Feature-based systems for the design and manufacture of sculptured products, *International Journal of Production Research*, 31 (6), 1441-1452.

Klaus, M. (1992). Zweckorientierte Datenermittlung in der Zeitwirtschaft. *VDI-Z*, 134 (4), 42-44.

Lay, G., Boffo, M., Schneider, R.J. (1987). Integration von rechnergestützter Konstruktion und NC-Programmierung. ZwF CIM Zeitschrift für wirtschaftliche Fertigung und Automatisierung, 82 (6), 325-332.

Luczak, H., Volpert, W. (1987). *Arbeitswissenschaft. Kerndefinition - Gegenstandskatalog - Forschungsgebiete*. Eschborn: RKW-Verlag.

Luczak, H., Reuschenbach, Th., Steidel, F. (1989). Simulation als Gestaltungsinstrument der Arbeitsorganisation rechnerunterstützter Konstruktion. Internationales Wissenschaftliches Kolloquium, Technische Hochschule Ilmenau, 34, 67-70.

Luczak, H., Beitz, W., Springer, J., Langner, T. (1991). Frictions and frustrations in creative-informatory work with computer aided design - CAD-systems -. In: Bullinger, H.-J. (Ed.): *Human Aspects in Computing: Design and Use of Interactive Systems and Work with Terminals*. Amsterdam: Elsevier.

Luczak, H., Steidel, F., Reuschenbach, Th., Müller, Th., Frädrich, J. (1992). Personelle Flexibilität in der rechnerunterstützten Konstruktion, Sonderforschungsbereich 203 der TU Berlin (Ed.), *Rechnerunterstützte Konstruktionsmodelle im Maschinenwesen (Final Report),* Teilprojekt B 6. Berlin: Technische Universität Berlin.

McAllister, D. (Ed.) (1993). *Stereo Computer Graphics and other true 3D technologies*. Princeton: Princeton Univ. Press.

McCartney, J., Hinds, B.K., Zhang, J.J., Hamilton, W. (1993). Dedicated CAD for Apparel Design, In: Smith, M. J.; Salvendy, G. (Eds.), Human-Computer Interaction: Applications and Case Studies, *Proceedings 5th International Conference HCI '93, Vol. 1*. Amsterdam: Elsevier.

Maturana, H., Varela, F. (1985). Autopoitische Systeme: eine Bestimmung der lebendigen Organisation. In: Maturana, H. (Ed.), *Erkennen: die Organisation und Verkörperung von Wirklichkeit. Ausgewählte Arbeiten zur biologischen Epistemiologie*. 2. Auflage, Braunschweig: Vieweg, 170-235.

Medina-Mora, R., Winograd, T., Flores, R., Flores, F. (1992). The Action Workflow Approach to Workflow Management Technology. In: Turner, J.; Kraut, R. (Eds.), *CSCW '92 - Sharing Perspectives, Proc. of the Conference on Computer Supported Cooperative Work*. Baltimore, MD: ACM Press.

Miwa, M., Fukino, M., Kato, M., Oyama, T. (1993). A Method of Communication between CAD and VR interfaces, In: Smith, M. J.; Salvendy, G. (Eds.), Human-Computer Interaction: Applications and Case Studies, *Proceedings 5th International Conference HCI '93, Vol. 1*. Amsterdam: Elsevier.

Morris, C.W. (1946). *Signs, language and behavior*. New York: Prentice-Hall.

Rasmussen, J. (1983). Skills, rules, and knowledge: Signals, signs, and symbols, and other distinctions in human performance models. *IEEE Transactions on Systems, Man and Cybernetics*, SMC-13, 257-266.

Richter, W. (1987). Gestalten nach dem Skizzierverfahren. *Konstruktion,* 39 (6), 227-237.

Richter, W. (1990). Wünsche an die Konstruktionslehre. *Konstruktion*, 42 (10), 313-319.

Rückert, C., Springer, J. (1994). Testing Design Methodology through Task Performance. In: Hight, T.K.; Mistree, F. (Eds.): *International Conference on Design Theory and Methodology, DTM '94, Minneapolis 1994*. New York: American Society of Mechanical Engineers, 161-168.

Scherff, J., Springer, J. (1994): Speech Input as a Special Mean of Adapting Man-Machine Interface. In: Proceedings of the 12th Triennal Congress of the International Ergonomics Association, Volume 4, Ergonomics and Design. Mississauga, Ontario: Human Factors Association of Canada 1994, 390-392.

Schulz von Thun, F. (1994). Miteinander Reden: Stile, Werte und Persönlichkeitsentwicklung, Rowohlt: Reinbeck.

Speeter, T. H. (1992). Transforming Human Hand Motion for Telemanipulation. Presence, 1 (1), 63-79.

Springer, J. (1992). Systematik zur ergonomischen Gestaltung von CAD-Software. Dissertation Technische Universität Berlin. VDI Fortschritt-Berichte, Reihe 20 Nr. 60. Düsseldorf: VDI-Verlag.

Springer, J. (1993). Systematic Evaluation and Optimization of CAD Systems. In: Luczak, H.; Çakir, A.; Çakir, G. (Eds.): Work with display units'92 - *Selected Proceedings of the 3rd International Conference WWDU'92,* Berlin 1992. Amsterdam: Elsevier, 442 - 448.

Springer, J., Müller, Th., Langner, Th., Luczak, H., Beitz, W. (1990). Stress and strain caused by CAD-work - results of a laboratory study. In: *L. Berlinguet and D. Berthelette (Eds)., Proceedings of the work with display units conference* 1989. Amsterdam: Elsevier.

Springer, J., Langner, Th., Luczak, H., Beitz, W. (1991). Experimental Comparison of CAD Systems by Stressor Variables. *International Journal of Human-Computer Interaction,* 3 (4), 375-405.

Springer, J., Herbst, D., Schlick, C., Stahl, J. (1995): Personal Communication and Telecooperation in Product Design - Requirements for Telecooperative CAD-Systems. In: Anzai, Y; Ogawa, K.; Mori, H. (Eds.): Symbiosis of Human and Artefact, *6th International Conference on Human-Computer Interaction,* Yokohama, July 1995. Amsterdam: Elsevier, 793-798.

Springer, J., Herbst, D., Schlick, C. (1996: Persönliche Kommunikation und Telekooperation - Anforderungen an telekooperative CAD-Systeme. In: Brödner, P; Paul, H.; Hamburg, I.: (Hrsg.): *Kooperative Konstruktion und Entwicklung - Nutzungsperspektiven von CAD-Systemen.* München: Hampp-Verlag .

Steidel, F., Reuschenbach, Th., Luczak, H. (1990). Simulation of organization in CAD-using design departments. In: Noro, K.; Brown, O. (Eds.), *Human Factors in Organizational Design and Management-III.* Amsterdam: North-Holland.

Steidel, F. (1994). *Modellierung arbeitsteilig ausgeführter, rechnerunterstützter Konstruktionsarbeit - Möglichkeiten und Grenzen personenzentrierter Simulation.* Dissertation Technische Universität Berlin, Fachbereich Konstruktion und Fertigung.

Taghavi, A., Penning, J. (1970). Über die menschliche Reaktionszeit nach periodischen und aperiodischen optischen und akustischen Reizen. Pflügers Arch. ges. *Physiol.,* 319.

Tekano K., Student, C. (1989). Bewegungsorganisation und Reaktionszeit. In: *Handbuch der Ergonomie,* Bd.1. München, Wien. Carl Hanser Verlag.

VDI-Richtlinie 2216 (1992). *Datenverarbeitung in der Konstruktion - Einführungsstrategien und Wirtschaftlichkeit von CAD-Systemen.* Düsseldorf: VDI-Verlag.

VDI-Richtlinie 2221 (1993). *Methodik zum Entwickeln und Konstruieren technischer Systeme und Produkte.* Düsseldorf: VDI-Verlag.

Handbook of Human-Computer Interaction
Second, completely revised edition
M. Helander, T.K. Landauer, P. Prabhu (eds.)

Chapter 57

Design of the Computer Workstation

Karl H. E. Kroemer
Virginia Tech, ISE Department
Blacksburg, Virginia , USA

57.1 Introduction

Complaints related to posture and vision are frequently voiced by computer operators. Musculo-skeletal pain and discomfort, eye "fatigue and strain" constitute the majority of all subjective and objective symptoms. Many of these complaints are related: difficulties in viewing (focusing distance, angle of gaze, etc.), together with straining curvatures of the spinal column (particularly in the neck and lumbar region), joined by fatiguing postures of shoulders and arms result in a stress-strain combination where cause and effect intermix, alternate and build upon each other (Helander, Billingsley and Schurick, 1984; Karwowski, Eberts, Salvendy, and Noland, 1994; Stock, 1991).

The postural problem appears to be largely caused by improperly designed and ill arranged workstation furniture. The old convention of "sitting straight" at the desk has been carried over to computer work places. "Egyptial tomb reliefs illustrate clearly that, even at this time, dignified man had to sit with back straight, thighs horizontal and lower legs vertical. How was it, in spite of all the evidence against it being either comfortable or natural, that this stilted posture came to be accepted as standard, whether for sitting on a throne, for dining, for contemplation in the privacy of the boudoir or for working in an office?" (In the editorial introduction of the March 1986 issue of Ergonomics.) Yet, the 1988 version of ANSI-100 Standard (Human Factors Society, 1988) concerning visual display terminal workstations presumed an "upright, or near straight" posture for deriving furniture dimensions.

Another inherited problem is the habit of putting the computer screen "at or slightly below eye height". Apparently, this false dictum stems from design recommendations for control consoles of the late 1950s/early 60s, where the space at elbow height had already been given away for control buttons, switches, and levers. This left only console space above, i.e., near eye height, for locating displays (Morgan, Cook, Chapanis, and Lund, 1963). Yet, computer workstations are different from consoles, and they do not require all this space for hand-operated controls.

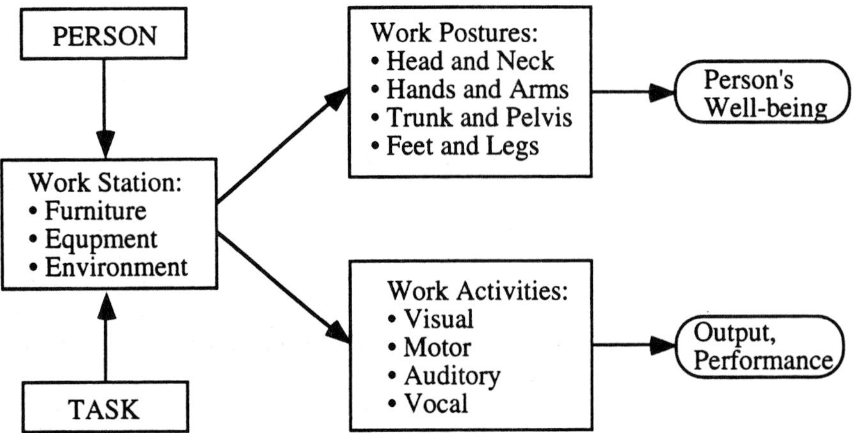

Figure 1. Ergonomic interactions at computer workstations.

The third inherited problem is the conventional keyboard, now usually containing about a hundred or more keys, located in a essentially flat (horizontal) "board", traditional placed on a support table. This antiquated input device requires motions of the hand's digits and of the wrist, and postures of hands, arms, shoulders and hence of the trunk that are often constraining, fatiguing, and possibly unhealthy.

No wonder that many operators, when left alone, arrange components of their workstation in various "unconventional" configurations. The monitor has been placed high atop a "tower" of CPU unit and swivel stand, or placed flat on a support surface to the side of the keyboard. Keyboards have been propped up, sloped up or down, put on the lap, or propped upon the arm rest of the chair. Instead of using common office chairs, rocking chairs, easy chairs, even automobile seats have been employed by users, especially if the office supervisor did not insist on the regular layout of the workstation. Workstations at home have become rather popular, and might become more so with increasing tele-commuting, where the home office replaces the space required in the employer's building. In the home office, the person is free to use any workstation design, good or bad in the traditional sense, which suits the individual.

57.2 Interactions

Successful ergonomic design of the VDT workstation depends on proper consideration of several interrelated aspects, sketched in Figure 1. A person performing a "work task" assumes related "work postures" and performs "work activities". These are influenced by the workstation conditions which include furniture; input and control devices; display and other equipment; and the environment; all of which shall fit the person and the task. Existing workstation components strongly affect work postures assumed by the person, and the actual work activities. The ergonomist, of course, would prefer that desired work postures and appropriate activities determine workstation design

The actual work posture affects the physical well-being while the work activities determine the output of the person working with the equipment. "Feeling well" both physically and about one's performance has effects on health and work attitudes, and on work output. Of course, these interactive relationships are not static but vary with time, persons, and circumstances.

This very brief discussion of the relationships among work variables is meant to emphasize the need for carefully designing the workstation, especially its furniture, equipment, and lighting so that the desired results of well-being and high performance are achieved.

57.3 The Work Task

The widespread use of computers has changed office work profoundly (McIntosh, 1994). As a result of computerizing systems, the tasks associated with many job categories have changed, in some cases dramatically. In modern offices, traditional "typing" has been transferred from a typewriter to a text processor. Hence, different and more complex skills, more control functions and more responsibility are required from a person doing text processing than from a traditional typist. Similar changes have been introduced, for example, for engineering draftsmen who use computer-aided design techniques instead of "paper and pencil". The computer also influences many tasks of providing and controlling information on the supervisory level: managers receive information about daily activities, budget status, personnel data, etc., via computer, and interact with each other by computer ("E-mail replaces snail mail").

In the computerized workplace, the interactions between the human and the computer establish special requirements on human visual and motoric capabilities. The eyes scan source documents (for input into the computer) and the display screen on the monitor (either as information input to the human, or as feedback about information being transmitted to the computer system). The fingers input information to the system via keyboard, mouse, stick and rotary controls, light-pen, touch panels, trackball, etc. Voice communication with the computer, both as input and output, is also developing rapidly. The intensity of these links between the human and the computer is characteristic of certain work tasks. Those links that are especially frequent and tight establish ergonomic design priorities.

57.4 The Person

Anthropometric characteristics of the computer user, including physiological and biomechanical aspects, are important for the design of VDT workstations. While one always desires even more exact and detailed data, particularly on variables related to gender, age, and ethnic origin, there is sufficient anthropometric information for many regional and national user populations. Table 1 presents the best currently available information for U.S. female and male civilians.

Certain body dimensions of the human operator determine related dimensions of the workstation, for example:

- Eye Height primarily determines the location (distance from the eye, and height) of visual targets: monitor, source document, note pad, keyboard, etc.
- Elbow Height and Forearm Length are related to the location of motor activities such as keying and writing with a pen, and the operation of hand controls such as keys, mouse, trackball, etc.
- Knee Height and Thigh Thickness determine the needed height of the leg room underneath tables or support surfaces. The forward protrusions of the knee (Buttock-Knee Depth) and of the foot determine the needed depth of the leg room under the equipment.
- Thigh Breadth determines the minimal width for the open leg room and of the width of the seat.
- Buttock-Popliteal Depth determines the depth of the seat pan.
- Lower Leg Length (Popliteal Height) determines the height of the seat.

Of course, other dimensions also have significant effects on workstation design dimensions, such as Functional Reach. In some cases, the application of anthropometric information to the design task is straight-forward, for example in stating that the seat pan depth must be shorter than Buttock-Popliteal Depth to avoid uncomfortable pressure of the seat front on the soft tissues behind the knee.

Many design applications require the assumption of certain body postures; for example, the height of the elbow or the location of the eyes depend on the sitting or standing posture assumed by the person. Several postures - instead of one posture - and the motions of the body at work must be considered to accommodate the need and preferences of the operator. The revision of the 1988 ANSI-100 Standard considers three different seated postures, and a standing position, for the design and use of furniture for the computer office. The seated reference positions range from forward leaning and high sitting to reclined sitting, with the traditional "upright" posture between those two.

57.5 Positioning the Body Relative to the Computer

The human interfaces with the VDT through several senses (mostly vision, audition and taction) and responds to received stimuli by motor outputs. (Voice interaction seems imminent.) Within the human, the nervous system transmits the signals to/from the brain which decides upon inputs and generates output activities.

Important sensory reception occurs through the eyes fixing their sight on the monitor, on the source document, even on the keys. (Current complex computer keyboards require visual search and identification of keys, "blind" touch typing is often not feasible.) Of course, handwriting requires visual control, as does the search for other items on the work surface. Preferences for the angle of the line of sight and for focusing distance vary among and within individuals. They vary with the work tasks and are often dependent on visual deficiencies and their correction by lenses. Unfortunately, many current computer work stations require the position of the person's eyes to be relatively fixed with respect to the visual target. This eye fixation has rather stringent consequences for trunk posture, as discussed later.

Table 1. Body dimensions of U.S. civilians. *With permission from Kroemer, Kroemer, and Kroemer-Elbert, 1994). Ergonomics: How to Design for Ease and Efficiency. Englewood Cliffs, NJ: Prentice Hall.*

	Percentiles			Std. Deviation
	fem. 5th *male*	*fem.* 50th *male*	*fem.* 95th *male*	*fem.* S *male*
HEIGHTS				
(f above floor, s above seat)				
Stature ("Height")^f	152.78 / 164.69	162.94 / 175.58	173.73 / 186.65	6.36 / 6.68
Eye Height^f	141.52 / 152.82	151.61 / 163.39	162.13 / 174.29	6.25 / 6.57
Shoulder (acromial) Height^f	124.09 / 134.16	133.36 / 144.25	143.20 / 154.56	5.79 / 6.20
Elbow Height^f	92.63 / 99.52	99.79 / 107.25	107.40 / 115.28	4.48 / 4.81
Wrist Height^f	72.79 / 77.79	79.03 / 84.65	85.51 / 91.52	3.86 / 4.15
Crotch Height^f	70.02 / 76.44	77.14 / 83.72	84.58 / 91.64	4.41 / 4.62
Height (sitting)^s	79.53 / 85.45	85.20 / 91.39	91.02 / 97.19	3.49 / 3.56
Eye Height (sitting)^s	68.46 / 73.50	73.87 / 79.20	79.43 / 84.80	3.32 / 3.42
Shoulder (acromial) Ht (sitting)^s	50.91 / 54.85	55.55 / 59.78	60.36 / 64.63	2.86 / 2.96
Elbow Height (sitting)^s	17.57 / 18.41	22.05 / 23.06	26.44 / 27.37	2.68 / 2.72
Thigh Height (sitting)^s	14.04 / 14.86	15.89 / 16.82	18.02 / 18.99	1.21 / 1.26
Knee Height (sitting)^f	47.40 / 51.44	51.54 / 55.88	56.02 / 60.57	2.63 / 2.79
Popliteal Height (sitting)^f	35.13 / 39.46	38.94 / 43.41	42.94 / 47.63	2.37 / 2.49
DEPTHS				
Forward (thumbtip) Reach	67.67 / 73.92	73.46 / 80.08	79.67 / 86.70	3.64 / 3.92
Buttock-Knee Distance (sitting)	54.21 / 56.90	58.89 / 61.64	63.98 / 66.74	2.96 / 2.99
Buttock-Popliteal Distance (sitting)	44.00 / 45.81	48.17 / 50.04	52.77 / 54.55	2.66 / 2.66
Elbow-Fingertip Distance	40.62 / 44.79	44.29 / 48.40	48.25 / 52.42	2.34 / 2.33
Chest Depth	20.86 / 20.96	23.94 / 24.32	27.78 / 28.04	2.11 / 2.15
BREADTHS				
Forearm-Forearm Breadth	41.47 / 47.74	46.85 / 54.61	52.84 / 62.06	3.47 / 4.36
Hip Breadth (sitting)	34.25 / 32.87	38.45 / 36.68	43.22 / 41.16	2.72 / 2.52
HEAD DIMENSIONS				
Head Circumference	52.25 / 54.27	54.62 / 56.77	57.05 / 59.35	1.46 / 1.54
Head Breadth	13.66 / 14.31	14.44 / 15.17	15.27 / 16.08	0.49 / 0.54
Interpupillary Breadth	5.66 / 5.88	6.23 / 6.47	6.85 / 7.10	0.36 / 0.37
FOOT DIMENSIONS				
Foot Length	22.44 / 24.88	24.44 / 26.97	26.46 / 29.20	1.22 / 1.31
Foot Breadth	8.16 / 9.23	8.97 / 10.06	9.78 / 10.95	0.49 / 0.53
Lateral Malleolus Height^f	5.23 / 5.84	6.06 / 6.71	6.97 / 7.64	0.53 / 0.55
HAND DIMENSIONS				
Circumference, Metacarpale	17.25 / 19.85	18.62 / 21.38	20.03 / 23.03	0.85 / 0.97
Hand Length	16.50 / 17.87	18.05 / 19.38	19.69 / 21.06	0.97 / 0.98
Hand Breadth, Metacarpale	7.34 / 8.36	7.94 / 9.04	8.56 / 9.76	0.38 / 0.42
Thumb Breadth, Interphalangeal	1.86 / 2.19	2.07 / 2.41	2.29 / 2.65	0.13 / 0.14
WEIGHT (in kg)	39.2* / 57.7*	62.01 / 78.49	84.8* / 99.3*	13.8* / 12.6*

*Estimated (by Kroemer)

NOTE: In this table, the entries in the 50th percentile column are actually "mean" (average) values. The 5th and 95th percentile values are from measured data, not calculated (except for weight). Thus, the values given may be slightly different from those obtained by subtracting 1.65 S from the mean (50th percentile), or by adding 1.65 S to it.

The hands are the major output interface from the human to the computer: they operate keys and other devices such as mouse, trackball, joystick, light pen or touch panel. If these controls are fixed within the workstation, the operator has no choice but to keep the hands at this location. (Examples are fixed keyboard, fixed touch panel or a fixed mouse pad.) If such input devices are moveable within the workstation area, the locations of the hands with respect to the body are also more variable. However, with current technology, controls and hands are usually in front of the body, below chest and above lap height. Again, this has consequences for trunk posture, as will be discussed.

Foot controls are not used frequently with current

*Table 2. **Links Between Human and Computer Influencing Work Posture.** With permission from Kroemer, K. H. E., Kroemer, H. B., and Kroemer-Elbert, K. E. (1994) Ergonomics: How to Design for Ease and Efficiency. Englewood Cliffs, NJ: Prentice Hall. All rights retained.*

Input to the Human	Output from the Human	Requirement of Locating the Human Relative to the Computer
Eyes	—	High
—	Hands, Feet	Medium to High
Ears	—	Low
—	Mouth	Low

designs. If present, they obviously require locating the foot at them, hence also limit body postures.

The ear is another input channel to the human, and the mouth an output device. However, sound or speech signals (not yet often used with current computer systems) usually do not restrict the location of the head to any specified location since acoustic signals travel through the air or can be transmitted through speakers or phones attached to the head.

Table 2 lists primary input and output modalities between human and computer, and also indicates how they affect the relative positioning of body and computer.

Controls for hand or foot operation which are rigidly attached to the equipment require strictly defined locations of hands or feet. If the controls are made moveable these restrictions are less severe. The visual link defines the position of the eyes rather strictly, most severely if the operator has limited visual capabilities, or wears corrective lenses that are ground for certain focusing distances and prescribe the direction of the line of sight. Aural and vocal links allow relatively much freedom for positioning the body.

57.6 Body Postures

Various methods and techniques have been developed to describe body postures and to make judgments about their suitability. Priel (1974) developed a "posturegram" which records the levels at which limbs and joints are located and the direction and magnitude of their movements. This system relies on "basic" postures of the body, deviations from which are recorded. The OWAS system (Ovaco Working Posture Analysis System) is similar in such that it postulates basic body segment positions to which one compares to actually observed working postures. This system also includes an evaluation of the suitability of the working postures (Karhu, Haerkoenen, Sorvali, and Vepsaelaeinen, 1981). Based on the OWAS system, the RULA (Rapid Upper Limb Assessment) procedure was developed to investigate work places where work-related upper limb disorders are reported (McAtamney and Corlett, 1993). A related method was used in the TRAM system (Berns and Milner, 1980) where, like with OWAS, postures at the work place are recorded at regular intervals on prepared recording forms. TRAM also includes estimates of forces and of the suitability of body positions. The ARBAN system (Holzmann, 1982) stressed the ergonomic analysis of the work conditions. It uses videotaping, coding the posture and work load, and includes computerization of the results and their evaluation. The computer routine and evaluation is based on heuristic rules. "Posture targeting" (refined by Corlett, Madeley, and Manenica, 1979) uses prepared sketches of the human body, with "targets" (like in shooting competitions) associated with each major body joint. On these targets, deviations from a standard posture are recorded so that they show the direction and magnitude of displacement of body segments. These posture codes can be combined with assessments of the postural loading (Wilson, Corlett, and Manenica, 1986). Keyserling (1986) used a computer-aided procedure which has a menu of standard postures for trunk and shoulders. Gross deviations from these are read from video-tapes and recorded in their frequency of occurrence. Malone (1991) developed a taxonomy which also used diagrammatic depictions to record posture, while Paul and Douwes (1993) used photographs. The PEO technique uses a "portable" (e.g., hand-held) computer for in situ (on-line) observation at the work place. The program calculates the number and direction of the body postures (Fransson-Hall, Gloria, Kilbom, Winkel, Karlqvist, and Wictorin, 1995). The "Nordic Questionnaire" is a well-standardized inquiry tool on body discomfort (Kuorinka, Jonsson, Kilbom et al., 1987; Van der Grinten, 1991).

57.7 "Healthy" Body Postures

Ergonomic design recommendations for geometric relations between human and workstation components rely on the concept of "good" (or "healthy") body postures, as opposed to "awkward" postures.

It has often been said, usually in connection with spinal column problems, that the human is neither designed for standing on two legs nor for continuous sitting. Obviously, this observation does not help to design ergonomically correct workstations and will not bring us back onto four legs. However, it raises the question of whether there is one healthy (sitting) posture, and if this posture should or could be maintained for many hours.

A generally accepted tenet has been that an upright and "straight" trunk and neck are part of a healthy posture. Since the late 1800s, this assumption was used, usually together with presuming right angles at hips, knees, and ankles, to design office chairs and other furniture. Yet, what physiologic or orthopedic reasons do exist to make children and adults "sit straight" in the spite of the fact that, if left alone, hardly anybody chooses to maintain this posture?

Standing or sitting "straight" means that, in the lateral view, the spinal column in fact forms an S-curve showing forward bends (lordoses) in the neck and low back regions and a rearward bulge (kyphosis) in the chest region. While there appears to be no reason to doubt that this is - in the current evolutionary condition of the civilized human - a normal and desirable curvature of the spine which keeps the trunk and its organs in acceptable order, it needs to be discussed how such a posture should be achieved, supported, or even enforced.

When one sits down on a hard flat surface, not using a backrest, the ischial tuberosities (inferior protuberances of the pelvic bones) act as fulcra around which the pelvic girdle rotates under the weight of the upper body. The bones of the pelvic girdle are linked by connective tissue to the lower spine. Thus, a rotation of the pelvis about the ischial tuberosities can affect the posture of the spinal column, particularly in the lumbar region (Keegan, 1952). If the pelvis rotation is rearward, the normal lordosis of the lumbar spine is flattened. This was deemed highly undesirable by orthopedists and physiologists; hence, avoidance of this pelvic rotation is a rationale of theories of seat design.

There are many tissue connections between hip and thigh, particularly the muscles spanning the hip joint or both knee and hip joints (e.g., hamstrings, quadriceps, rectus femoris, sartorius, tensor fasciae latae, psoas major). Therefore, as Keegan showed in 1952, the chosen hip angle affects the location of the pelvis and hence the curvature of the lumbar spine. At a small hip angle, the pelvic girdle is likely to be rotated backwards (flattening the lumbar spine) while at a large hip angle a forward rotation of the pelvis on the ischial tuberosities, accompanied by lumbar lordosis, is likely. "Opening the hip angle" is another aim of some theories of seat design.

Staffel (1884) and seven decades later Schlegel (1956) proposed a forward-declining seat surface to open up the hip angle and to bring about lordosis in the lumbar area. This idea lead to a seat pan design with a "Schneider Wedge" on its rear edge which was popular for about a decade in Europe (Schneider and Decker, 1961). More recently, Mandal (1975, 1982) and Congleton, Ayoub and Smith (1985) have promoted seat surfaces that slope downward and forward.

The underlying idea is that the desired lumbar lordosis be achieved by opening the hip angle to more than 90° and by rotating the pelvis forward. Most proponents of the forward declination of the seat pan deem a backrest desirable or necessary. To prevent the buttocks from sliding off a strongly forward-declined seat, the seat surface may be shaped to fit the human underside (Congleton), or one may counteract the downward-forward thrust by either bearing down on the feet (Mandal) or by propping knees or upper shins on special pads ("balans chair"). Chaffin and Andersson (1991) call this posture "semi-sitting".

Another way to bring about lordosis of the lumbar area is to push this section of the back and spinal column forward with a specially designed backrest. Old wooden school benches simply had a horizontal wood slot at lumbar height which forced the seated pupil to bend the lower back forward to avoid painful contact: hence, to the satisfaction of the teacher, the child sat "up". There are more subtle and agreeable ways to promote lumbar concavity: The "Akerblom pad" (Akerblom, 1948) and adjustable or inflatable lumbar cushions incorporated in the seat back of some car and airplane seats are examples for such design features.

Of course, one can shape the total backrest: Apparently independently of each other, Ridder (1959) in the USA and Grandjean (1963) and co-workers in Switzerland found rather similar backrest shapes to be acceptable by experimental subjects. In essence, these backrest shapes follow the curvature of the rear side of the human body: at the bottom concave or open to accept the buttocks, above slightly convex to fill in the lumbar lordosis, than raising nearly straight but declined backwards to support the thoracic area, at the top again convex to follow the neck lordosis. This shape (with more or less pronounced curvatures depending on the designer's assumptions about body size and body posture) has been used successfully for seats in automobiles, aircraft, passenger trains, cars, and for easy chairs; in the traditional office these "first class" shapes were thoughtfully provided for managers while other employers had to use simpler designs, down to the miserable small board attached to so-called secretarial chairs. - Extensive bibliographies and reviews of recommendations for seat designs encompassing the last three decades can be found in the publications by Bradford and Prete (1978), Grandjean (1963, 1969, 1987, 1988), Kroemer, Kroemer, and Kroemer-Elbert (1994), Kroemer and Robinette (1968), Lueder (1983), Lueder and Noro (1995), Zacharkow (1988), and Wilson, Corlett, and Manenica (1986).

57.8 Experimental Studies

In addition to empirical studies, such as done by Ridder and Grandjean, many analytic experiments have been performed to measure physiologic responses of the human body to certain postures. Lundervold (1951, 1958) was apparently the first to extensively record and interpret electromyograms (EMGs) which represent activities of (upper body) muscles associated with defined body positions. EMG amplitudes increase with stronger muscle tension, and flatten when the muscle relaxes. Their frequencies change with muscle fatigue (Soderberg, 1992).

57.8.1 Trunk and Low Back

Sitting postures may not only be subjectively comfortable (or not), but are often associated with more or less defined back pain, often in the lumbar region (Williams, Hawley, McKenzie, and Wijmen, 1991). EMG measurements have been performed on seated persons, summarized by Chaffin and Andersson (1991), Grieco (1986), Lueder and Noro (1995), Soderberg, Blanco, Consentino, and Kurdelmeier (1986), Winkel and Bendix (1986). As to be expected, varying EMG activities were found in the muscles stabilizing the sitting body, particularly the trunk. However, involvement of muscles in the hip and lower trunk regions does not seem to be very important for "regular" seated postures because the observed EMG activities indicate rather low demands on muscular capabilities (Andersson, Schultz, and Oertengren, 1986), typically well below one tenth of the maximal contraction capabilities. However, muscular strains in the low back area could be important in unusual conditions and postures, such as leaning over the desk at which one is seated, or to lift an object such as a computer monitor with extended arms.

Furthermore, the interpretation of these weak EMG signals is controversial since one cannot necessarily assume that little muscle use (i.e., flat EMG signals) should be preferable over more intensive use. Maintenance of the same posture over long periods of time, i.e. continued "static" muscle tension (even at the low levels just mentioned), becomes uncomfortable and should be avoided by introducing rest periods (Sundelin, Hagberg and Hammarstrom, 1986; Zwahlen, Hartmann, and Kothari, 1986) or by physical activities and exercises (Lee and Waikar, 1986; Lee, Swanson, Sauter, Wickstrom, Waikar, and Mangum, 1992). Occasional or repeated bursts of muscular activities ("dynamic sitting") are desired by some physiologists to obtain suitable muscle tone and training; for electrolyte and fluid balance (Grieco, 1986; Kilbom, 1986); for intervertebral disk metabolism (Hansson, 1986); to improve the circulation of blood (Winkel, 1986) and to prevent blood pooling (Thompson, Yates and Franzen, 1986). While "common sense" indicates that twisted body postures are uncomfortable and possibly harmful (as has been shown for lifting tasks), substantial experimental work has not yet been published on this topic.

57.8.2 Neck and Shoulders

Muscular tensions observed in the shoulder/neck region appear, in contrast to those observed in the lower trunk, often to be of critical magnitude and importance. Tension and pain in the neck area are among the most frequently mentioned health complaints of computer operators. The relative intensity of muscle tension is often considerably higher than the ten or less percent reported for lower trunk muscles, and may be maintained over long periods of time when the head must be kept in a fixed relation to the visual object (Ekholm, Schuldt, and Harms-Ringdhal, 1986; Harms-Ringdhal and Ekholm, 1986; Hansson and Attebrant, 1986; Zwahlen, Hartmann, and Kothari, 1986), or the shoulders or arms are elevated (Fernstroem, Ericson, and Malker, 1994; Lundervold, 1951, 1958; Sauter, Schleifer and Knutson, 1991). Intensity, frequency, and length of time of such muscle contractions can generate intense discomfort, pain and related musculo-skeletal health complaints which may persist over long periods of time. In some contrast to the events in the lumbar region, EMG activities in the neck/shoulder area do provide important information on the appropriateness or distress of head, neck and shoulder postures.

57.8.3 Disk Pressure

Other analytical studies addressed the pressure in the intervertebral disks dependent on trunk posture. High disk pressure is presumed to translate into a variety of possible health problems, such as herniation of the fibrous retaining layers and their displacement toward the spinal cord. Disk compression and trunk muscle activities are related: the stability of the stacked vertebrae is achieved by contraction of muscles which generate essentially vertical forces in the trunk (primarily m. latissimus dorsi, erector spinae, internal and external oblique, rectus abdominus). Together, these pull "down on the spine" and keep the vertebrae aligned on top of each other. Each vertebra rests upon its lower one cushioned by the spinal disk between their main bodies, and also supported lateral-posteriorly in the two facet joints of the articulation processes. Since the downward pull of the muscles generates disk and facet joint compression (in response to upper body weight and external forces), one should expect close relationships between trunk muscle activities and disk pressures. Experiments were performed in the 1960's in Scandinavia where the pressure transducers were pushed into spinal disks of three subjects (Andersson and Oertengren, 1974; Nachemson, 1966; for a compilation and review see Chaffin and Andersson, 1991). The experiments showed that the amount of intra-disk force in the lumbar region was dependent upon trunk posture and support.

When standing at ease, the forces in the lumbar spine were in the neighborhood of 330 N. This force increased by about 100 N when sitting on a stool without backrest. It made little difference if one sat erect with the arms hanging, or relaxed with the lower arms on the thighs. (Sitting relaxed but letting the arms hang down increased the internal force to nearly 500 N.) Thus, there was an increase in spinal compression force in the lumbar region when sitting down from standing; but the differences among sitting postures were not very pronounced. About the same force values were found when sitting on an office chair with a small lumbar support. Sitting with the arms hanging, writing with the arms supported on the table and activating a pedal lead to forces around 500 N. The spinal forces were increased by typing, when the forearms and hands must be lifted to keyboard height. (A further increase was seen when a weight was lifted in the hands with the arms extended forward - see also the biomechanical calculations by Eklund, Corlett, and Johnson, 1983.) None of these postures made use of the backrest. However, if one leaned back decidedly over a small backrest, and let the arms hang down, the internal compression forces were reduced to approximately 400 N.

When the backrest is upright, it cannot support the body, and disk forces between about 350 and 660 N may occur. Declining the straight backrest behind vertical brings about dramatic decreases in internal force, because part of the upper body weight is now transmitted to the backrest and hence does not rest on the spinal column. An even more pronounced effect can be brought about by making the backrest protrude towards the lumbar lordosis. A protrusion of 5 centimeters nearly halves the internal disk forces from the values associated with the flat backrest; protrusions of four to one cm in the lumbar region bring about proportionally smaller effects (Chaffin and Andersson, 1991).

In a series of more recent studies (summarized by Andersson, Schultz, and Oertengren, 1986), disk pressures were measured and calculated for various desk tasks and for sitting and standing postures. One of the conclusions is: "In a well designed chair the disk pressure is lower than when standing." (p. 1113).

These experimental results yield three important findings. The first is that sitting without use of backrest or of armrests may increase disk pressure significantly over standing. The second is that there are no dramatic disk pressure differences between sitting straight, sitting relaxed, or sitting with supported arms, if there is no backrest or only a small lumbar board. The third finding is that leaning on a well designed backrest can bring about disk pressures that are as low as found in a standing person. Certainly, these findings do not support the belief that sitting upright reduces disk pressure, as opposed to sitting relaxed or leaning back.

If the backrest consists only of a small lumbar board, a dramatic beneficial effect requires that one nearly "drapes oneself on it" by learning backwards over it, as depicted in Figure 3. Even a large backrest that can support the total trunk is nearly useless when upright, but highly beneficial when leaned back behind vertical (Corlett and Eklund, 1984). Its positive effects are dramatically enhanced if it is shaped to bring about the S-curve of the spinal column (Branton, 1984), particularly the lumbar lordosis.

"... [A]n impression which many observers have already perceived when visiting offices or workshops with VDT workstations: Most of the operators do not maintain an upright trunk posture . . . In fact, the great majority of the operators lean backwards even if the chairs are not suitable for such a posture." (Grandjean, Huenting, and Nishiyama, 1984, p. 100-101). Relaxed leaning against a declined backrest is the least stressful sitting posture. This is a condition that is often freely chosen by persons working in the office if there is a suitable backrest available (Laeubli, 1986).

One approach to determine subjectively comfortable postures is to allow subjects to relax their muscles by providing them support in any chosen posture. This can be done under water, or in weightlessness (Kroemer, Kroemer, and Kroemer-Elbert, 1994). The relaxed postures are remarkably similar and show a rear contour found in some "easy chairs" such as the famous Eames Lounge Chair (Bradford and Prete, 1978).

57.8.4 Hand and Wrist

Keyboard operation has long been known to be mentally and physically stressful. Especially the highly repetitive activity of pressing keys with digits of the hand often overexerts the human motor system. Aches and pains in the hand/wrist/forearm region are common in typists and players of musical instruments; tendinitis and tenosynovitis are common medical diagnoses (Armstrong, 1991; Armstrong, Fine, and Silverstein, 1986; Fry, 1986; Hochberg, Leffert, Heller, and Merriman, 1983; Kuorinka and Forcier, 1995; Lockwood, 1989). These overexertions, especially of the tendon/sheath unit, often in the wrist area, are basically a mechanical overuse problem (Armstrong and Chaffin, 1979; Rempel, Harrison, and Barnhart, 1992). The tendon is akin to a cable under tension rubbing against the inner surface of a sleeve (the tendon sheath) under different conditions of lubrication by synovial fluid. The condition is worsened if tension and transmitted force are increased, frequency elevated, viscosity of the lubricant reduced, and the tendon bent such as with a flexed, extended, or laterally deviated wrist. Biomechanically, these conditions are similar, whether existent on the shop floor in manufacture or assembly, on the construction site by carpenters or bricklayers, or experienced in the office while keying or mousing.

"Epidemics" of health complaints, mostly in the hand-wrist-forearm area, have been reported among keyboard users: first in the 1960s and 70s in Japan, then in the early 1980s in Australia, followed by outbreaks especially among newspaper reporters in the USA in the 1990s. While the biomechanical stress due to keyboard use is basic, the contributions of psychosocial conditions, and possibly of medical misdiagnoses are still argued (Armstrong, 1983; Armstrong and Lackey, 1994; Ayoub and Wittels, 1989; Burnette and Ayoub, 1989; Carayon, 1994; Hadler, 1992; Kiesler and Finholt, 1988; Kroemer, 1989, 1992; Lim and Carayon, 1994; Low, 1990; Moore, Wells, and Ranney, 1991; Putz-Anderson, 1988; Rempel, Harrison and Barnhart, 1992). Injury occurs often in the carpal tunnel, with syndromes related particularly to increased pressure affecting the functioning of the median nerve (Armstrong and Chaffin, 1979; Chatterjee, 1987; Goldstein, Armstrong, Chaffin, and Mathews, 1987; Pascarelli and Kella, 1993; Pfeffer, Gelberman, Boyes, and Rydevik, 1988). In the USA, such cumulative trauma disorders have become a major legal issue in products liability disputes (Owen, 1994).

Measurement of arm/wrist/hand motions and postures is often done with goniometers, with data taken either by sampling (Price, Fayzmehr, Haas, and Beaton, 1982) or continuous recording (Damann and Kroemer, 1995; Jedrziewski, 1992; Kruithof, 1995; Marras and Schoenmarklin, 1993). The posture classification systems discussed earlier, such as RULA, are also useful (Rudakewych, Valent, and Hedge, 1994). In addition, various kinds of subjective judgment scales can be used to make assessments of the perceived strain, related work, and equipment including keyboard or mouse (e.g., Burastero, Tittiranonda, Chen, Shin, and Rempel, 1994; Swanson, Falinsky, Steward, and Pan, 1994). Among the objective but invasive measures is the assessment of pressure inside the carpal tunnel via insertion of pressure transducers (Armstrong, Werner, Waring, and Foulke, 1991; Rempel and Horie 1994a) which can also be used to assess the effects of wrist rests while keyboarding (Rempel and Horie, 1994b).

Speaking in the terminology of experimental design, measures of dependent variables (such as EMG, carpal tunnel pressure, subjective judgments, or performance outcomes such as numbers of correct or incorrect inputs, or work endurance time) can be used to assess the effects of changes in the independent variables, such as different keyboards, different mice, different locations or spatial arrangements of keyboards or mouse pads, wrist or arm supports, location of display monitors, or different chairs (Armstrong, Martin, Arbor, Rempel, and Johnson, 1994; Erdelyi, Sihvonen, Helin, and Haenninen, 1988; Genaidy and Karwowski, 1993; Haslegrave, 1994; Kroemer, 1994a; Kruithof, 1995; Martin, 1994; McMulkin and Kroemer, 1994; Paquet, 1995; Thompson, 1994; Wells, Moore, and Ranney, 1992).

57.9 Sitting Postures and Work-station Design

By tradition, the leg position "thigh horizontal, lower leg vertical and feet on the floor" (i.e., hip, knee and ankle angles of 90°) is used to determine the "desirable" seat height. The assumption is that with the seat adjusted so the front edge of the seat pan is slightly below the individual's popliteal height, there would be no pressure between the undersides of the thigh near the knee fold and the front section of the seat pan. This avoids compression of sensitive leg tissue and of blood vessels which may impede venous blood return and cause irritation of nerves. However, if the feet are not placed directly underneath the knees, pressure between seat edge and tissue could still occur.

Another traditional procedure is to assume an essentially upright (vertical) trunk with the head balanced on top of it; upper arms hanging down vertically, and the elbow angle about 90°, i.e., forearms and hands held essentially horizontal. For decades, this was deemed the "proper" posture for sitting, particularly for typewriting, because of the presumably healthy curvature of the spine; the transferal of head, trunk and upper arm weights to the buttocks (particularly the ischial tuberosities); and the assumed minimization of muscle tension around the shoulder and elbow joints to keep the hands in place. However, as mentioned earlier, persons sitting at their preference seldom assume these positions, but select various "bent" postures, often using backrests.

Rotation of the pelvis and curvature of the spinal column are closely associated, as discussed above. When sitting on a flat surface with the hip angle at approximately 90°, the pelvis tends to rotate backwards and to flatten the lumbar spine lordosis. Such flattening can be avoided, if desired, by muscle tension, by design of the backrest (for example by providing a pad at the location of the lumbar lordosis) or by providing a seat surface that mechanically tilts the pelvis forward. Such lumbar lordosis can also be facilitated by opening the hip angle, for example by thrusting the feet forward and knees down. This is helped by elevating the seat pan and by tilting it so that the front section is lower than the rear part.

Disk compression and trunk muscle activities are related: The stability of the stack of vertebrae is achieved by contraction of trunk muscles which essentially pull "down on the spine" and keep the vertebrae aligned on top of each other. The downward pull of the muscles generates spinal disk and facet joint compression. These strains are reduced when trunk, neck, head and arm weights are at least partially supported by resting against a suitable backrest or by propping the arms upon armrests or table.

57.10 Design Strategies for Computer Workstations

The preceding discussions should have made it clear that several variables combine to determine the "ergonomics of computer workstations". These include psychological and organizational conditions as well as the physical environment, which includes climate, illumination, and general facility and work space design (Human Factors Society, 1988; Grandjean, 1987; Kroemer, Kroemer, and Kroemer-Elbert, 1990; Sauter, Schleifer, and Knutson, 1991). A discussion of all these variables is beyond this text, but theoretical and practical information can be found, e.g., in the publications by Kroemer, Kroemer, and Kroemer-Elbert (1994), Lueder and Noro (1995), and Oestberg, Warrell, and Nordell (1984). Highly specific, unusual work tasks and conditions may prevail, and individual preferences may lead to rather unconventional solutions.

The human is the most important component of the system since she or he drives the output. Hence, the human must be accommodated first: the design of the workplace components should fit all operators, and allow many personally preferred variations in working posture. The myth of "one healthy upright posture, good for everybody, anytime" is not true.

The large majority of computer workstations consist of a display unit, a data entry unit, support(s) on which these rest, and chair. These are the system components that the following ergonomic design recommendations consider.

Among the first steps in designing office furniture for human use is to establish the main clearance and external dimensions which can be derived from human body measurements. The basic principles are to make all clearances ("inside" dimensions) large to fit large persons; and to make all outside measures small to suit small persons. Compromises between these two aims are often needed, with adjustability a common solution.

A compilation of American anthropometric data was presented in Table 1. Three major strategies can be pursued to determine major equipment dimensions (Kroemer, 1985). The first strategy assumes that all components are adjustable in height. The adjustability ranges for the seat height as well as support heights for the equipment (primarily the keyboard and other working surfaces) and for the display are then calculated. The second strategy assumes that the support height must be fixed (like table heights in traditional offices usually are), but that seat height and display height are adjustable. The third strategy presumes a fixed seat height, but

Table 3. Adjustment Ranges for Computer Workstation Heights in cm. *These data apply to North Americans, with the seat pan adjusted so that the thighs are horizontal while the lower legs are vertical.*

	First Strategy	**Second Strategy**	**Third Strategy**
Height of ... Above Floor	All adjustable	Support for keyboard fixed, all other adjustable	Seat fixed, all other adjustable
Seat Pan	37.0 to 51.2	49.5 to 54.5	fixed at 49.5
Support Surface for keyboard or other data entry device	52.9 to 70.4	fixed at 70.4	65.4 to 70.4
Center of Display	93.1 to 122.0	105.6 to 127.0	105.6 to 122.0
Footrest	not needed	0 to 17.5	0 to 12.5

that support and display height are adjustable. The results of the ensuing calculations are compiled in Table 3. It contains the height adjustment necessary to fit about 90% of the U.S. civilian population by excluding only females who are smaller that 5th percentile in the relevant dimension, and males who are larger than the 95th percentile, see Table 1. The only assumptions made is that heels worn are of 2 cm height, and that the thickness of support structures (i.e., table thickness) is 2 cm as well. All heights given in Table 3 are counted from the floor to 51 cm, thereby accommodating the 5th percentile through the 95th percentile users. Then thigh thickness is added to calculate the necessary clearance height underneath the support structure; also adding 2 cm for the support structure results in support surface heights of 53 cm to 70 cm. The next step is to determine eye height, using sitting eye height above the seat (from Table 1). From this, the center height of the display is determined using values for the preferred viewing distance and the preferred angle of sight. (For more detail see Kroemer, 1985, 1994b; Hill and Kroemer, 1986.) Accordingly, the height of the center of the computer display should be between 93 and 122 cm above the floor. A footrest is not needed in this design approach.

In the second design strategy, the support for the keyboard is held fixed at 70 cm above the floor so that all users, even the tallest considered (95th percentile) fit underneath, as shown in Table 3. If the seat heights are adjusted according to thigh thickness, many persons will need footrests. Also the display must be arranged slightly higher than in the previous strategy where most people used lower seats and keyboard heights.

The third strategy starts with the assumption that seat height is fixed at 50 cm above the floor to accommodate even persons with long legs; persons with shorter legs need to use footrest; see Table 3. Following the same logic as before results in intermediate heights of the support surfaces for the keyboard and for the display.

Each of these strategies brings about design solutions with specific advantages and disadvantages. The first strategy, requiring complete adjustability, easily accommodates all persons and does not require footrests. However, the adjustment ranges needed for seat pan height, support surface height, and display height are the largest of all strategies.

The second approach allows support surface height ("table height") to be kept constant for all workstations, but requires the tallest seat height, yet with relatively little adjustment needed. Footrests are often necessary, in fact to considerable heights. The display needs to be adjusted up and down considerably, however slightly less than in the first design strategy.

The third design approach allows to use chairs of constant height, but requires widespread use of footrests which, however, need not to be as high as in the second design strategy. Of course, the support surfaces for keyboard and display must be independently adjustable, but the adjustment ranges needed for each are the narrowest of all approaches.

Either of these approaches will provide "fit" to nearly all computer users but, given the adjustments that can be made to suit personal preferences, does not assume or require certain postures, such as upright trunk or horizontal forearms. In fact, all of these design solutions provide freedom to sit (nearly) any way one likes, from bending forward to learning back, holding the legs in any postures within the leg room provided, and using either conventional seats, chairs with large backrests, or forward-declining seat surfaces for semi-sitting.

Either one of the three design strategies also permits the use of a multitude of data entry devices, such as keyboards, trackballs, voice, etc. Likewise, it accommodates any display units, since its specifies only the height of the center of the screen without making limiting assumptions about the specifics of housing and support of the display.

Of course, the strategy example presented above relies on certain (stated) assumptions, such as that the desired seat height is related to popliteal height, or that heel height is 2 cm. Individual preferences may be different, such as adjusting the seat higher to facilitate opening the hip angle. Furthermore, given working conditions, such as preset heights of the keyboard or of the display may make people adjust their seats higher than the presumed in the example above. Thus, field surveys (e.g., by Grandjean, 1969, 1987; Grandjean, Huenting, and Nishiyama, 1984; Grieco, 1986; Helander and Little, 1993; Lueder and Noro, 1995) have frequently reported higher settings of office chairs than calculated in the examples above. These observations and experiences simply stress the

- individual variability and preferences, which must be accommodated in the design of adjustment ranges; and that
- various interactions exist among the components of the work place situation, including the geometric parameters of the furniture and workplace dimensions.

The sample design strategies exercised above may not be suitable or acceptable in every case. But they do show that rational and practical design approaches are feasible that accommodate the actual range of body sizes, of body postures, and of work utensils at the computer workstation.

57.10.1 Seat Design

Ergonomic design of the seat is of primary importance for reducing the physiological and biomechanical stresses on the seated body; for providing a wide range of adjustments and postures to suit the individual, and for promoting well-being and performance. Given these far-ranging goals and the wide personal variability, it is clearly impossible to recommend one given seat design. In fact, it is obvious that various designs with varying features are needed. Hence, only some basic features and dimensions can be mentioned here.

The height of the seat surface should be adjustable in the range of 37 to 55 cm, depending on the strategy actually selected (see Table 3). The seat surface should be between approximately 38 and 43 cm deep, and at least 45 cm wide. These recommendations apply to a conventional seat, with its pan horizontal or inclined or declined by only a few degrees from horizontal. Less conventional designs, such as for semi-sitting, deviate from these measures. The seat surface should be comfortably but firmly elastic to distribute pressure and to allow various sitting postures. Particular attention should be paid to the front of the seat surface which must not generate undue pressure to the thighs of the seated person.

Seat surfaces which slope down as much as 30 degrees in the forward direction may require either a specially shaped seat pan or pads upon which knees or shins are propped. This prevents the buttocks from sliding down and out. While some users prefer such body supports, others do not like them (Drury and Francher, 1985; Lueder and Noro, 1995).

The backrest should provide a large and well-formed surface to support back and possibly the neck. At its lowest part, the backrest must provide room for the buttocks, but should have a slight protrusion (not to exceed 5 cm, preferably adjustable) to fit into the lumbar concavity of the body. The height of this lumbar pad should be adjustable between 15 and 23 cm above the seat pan. Above, the backrest can be nearly flat, but must be able to be inclined from a near upright position to 20, possibly 30 degrees behind vertical. In its upper part, the seat surface should follow the concave form of the neck. This cervical pad should be adjustable to heights between 50 and 70 cm above the seat surface, and should also be adjustable in the amount by which it protrudes to allow individual variations. The width of the backrest is not critical.

Obviously, many seat dimensions need to be adjustable to suit body form and preferences of the individual (Brienza, Chung, Brewbaker, and Kwiatkowski, 1993). It has been shown in the laboratory and in the real world (Kroemer, 1988; Lueder and Noro, 1995; Occhipinti, Colombini, Molteni, and Grieco, 1993; Tougas and Nordin, 1987) that adjustment devices will

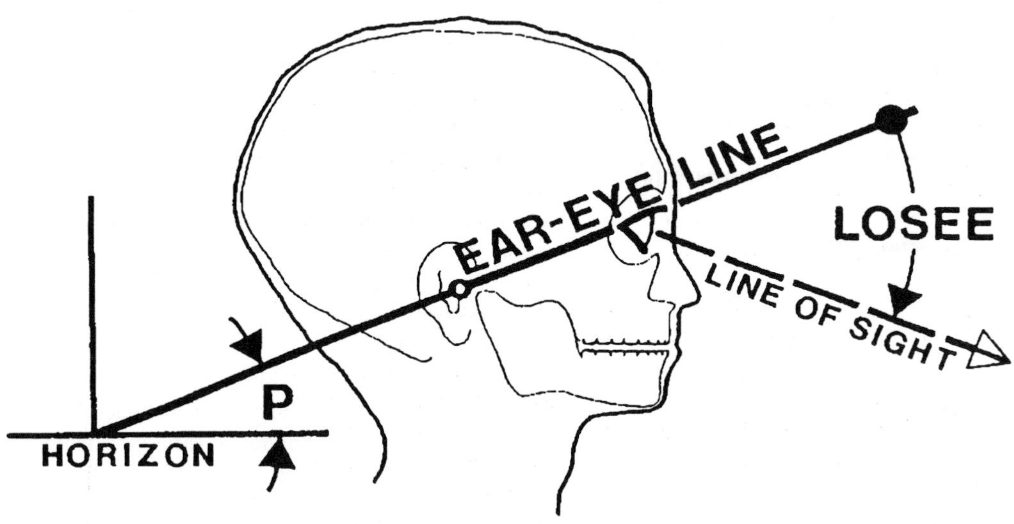

Figure 2. The Ear-Eye Line passes through the right auditory meatus (ear hole) and the right external canthus (juncture of the eye lids) *with both eyes on the same level. The angle of the line of sight against the ear-eye line (LOSEE) is on average 45 degrees with a standard deviation of 12 degrees. The head is held "erect" ("upright") when the angle P between the ear eye line and horizon is 15 degrees.*

be used if "easy and natural", but otherwise disregarded. Whether adjustment features should be coupled (for example backrest tilt linked with seat pan tilt) is a matter of preference and convenience. The same hold true for armrests, which may or may not be deemed desirable; however, the data shown in Figure 2 indicate that propping the arm on a support can reduce the compression load on the spinal column.

Another matter of design concern is to provide the opportunity and means to change body posture frequently during the work period. Maintaining a given posture, even if it appears comfortable in the beginning, becomes stressful as time goes on. Changes in posture are necessary, best by a brief period of physical activity.

Hence, the workstation should be so designed and be so easily adjustable that the operator can assume a variety of postures.

To permit changes in hand/arm and eye locations as well, the input device (e.g., keyboard) should be moveable within the work space. Also, one should be able to move the display screen to various heights, which requires an easily changeable, possibly motorized system of the support surface.

57.10.2 Stand-up Workstations

Another way to change working posture is to allow the computer operator, at his or her own choosing, to work for some period of time while standing up. Such stand-up workstations can often use a spare computer in the office, to which work activities can be switched from the sit-down workstation for a while. Stand-up workstations should be adjustable to have the input device at approximately elbow height when standing, i.e., between 90 and 120 cm. As in the sit-down workstation, the display should be located close to the other visual targets, such as source document and keyboard. For standing, a footrest at about 2/3 knee height (approximately 30 cm) is often well liked so that one can prop one foot up on it temporally. This brings about changes in pelvis rotation and in spine curvature.

57.10.3 Visual Targets

If vision must be focused on the screen as well as on the source document and on the keyboard, all these visual targets should be located close to each other, at the same distance from the eyes and in about the same direction of gaze. If the visual targets are spaced apart in direction or distance, the eyes must continuously refocus while sweeping from one target to another. This is particularly critical if reading glasses (or any other eye correction lenses) are worn because these are usually shaped for one particular focusing distance and for an assumed direction of sight. Often, the computer screen is arranged too high forcing the operator

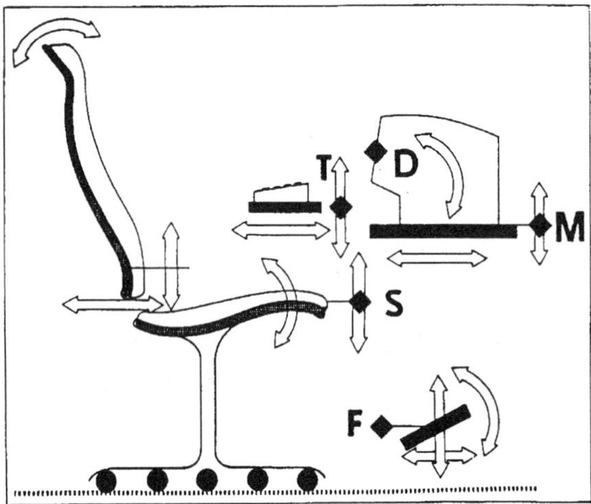

*Figure 3. **Main adjustment features of the computer workstation.** (S) Seat height, (T) Table height, (F) Foot rest height, (D) Display height on the (M) Monitor support.*

(particularly when wearing reading glasses) to tilt the neck severely backwards which requires muscle tension and generates strain on the cervical part of the spinal column, which, in turn, regularly lead to complaints about headaches and pains in the neck/shoulder region. Similar postural complaints are often voiced by persons who have the display placed to the side of the keyboard, hence have to turn the head sideways, leading to neck and trunk twisting.

As mentioned earlier, the traditional idea of placing the computer screen "at eye height" is usually false. The angle of the line of sight, connecting the pupil with the visual target should be declined, with most people preferring a gaze angle of about 45¡ against the Ear-Eye line; however the individual preferences are quite diverse. This angle is best described against the Ear-Eye line, which in the side view of the head runs through the ear hole and the corner where the eye lids meet. This is a more easily determined reference line than the traditional Frankfurt line. Furthermore, the use of the Ear-Eye line also allows a description of the posture of the head against an external reference, such as the horizon (Ankrum and Nemeth, 1995; Lie and Fostervold, 1994; Jampel and Shi, 1992; Karwowski, Eberts, Salvendy, and Noland, 1994; Kroemer, 1994b; Kumar, 1994). The angle of incidence (the angle formed between the line of sight and the plane of the screen), should be about 90° (Ankrum, Hansen, and Holahan, 1994). Figure 2 shows the relations.

57.10.4 Adjustment Features

All components of the VDT workstation must "fit each other", and each must suit the operator. This requires easy adjustability. Figure 3 sketches various adjustment features which allow to match seat height (S) with the height of support of the input devices or table (T), possibly while using a footrest (F); and to match eye position with the monitor display (D) resting on its support (M).

57.11 Summary

Proper design and use of furniture assume flexibility in work organization and management attitudes. Indeed, providing freedom for individual variations from the conventional norm requires to consider that persons working with computers differ in their physiques and work preferences. The ergonomic design of VDT workstations, their adjustability and proper use can determine, via many and subtle interactions, the person's well-being and the related work performance.

The output of the human-computer system is driven by the human. With current computers, the main interactions are through eyes and hands. Thus, the body posture is largely determined by visual targets (screen, source document, keyboard) and by input devices (keyboard, mouse, etc.), and of course by the seat. Improperly designed and ill arranged computer workstations lead to health complaints and attitude problems, while "ergonomic" conditions can further well-being, both physically and psychologically. With conventional computer systems, three major linkages exist to the operator.

- The first linkage is "motoric", mostly by hand operation of keyboard, mouse, and possibly other devices. If these are placed as usual on a support structure (table), it must be adjustable in height and distance to allow suitable arm posture (especially a straight wrist, a mostly horizontal forearm and vertical upper arm).
- The second linkage is "visual", where one must look at the display, keyboard and source document. These visual targets should all be located at proper viewing distance (less than 1m) and at suitable viewing angles (LOSEE of 45 + 12¡), in the medial (mid-sagittal) plane of the human.
- The third linkage is by "body support", primarily by the seat. Large variations in preferred sitting postures exist, which can be supported by a variety

of seat designs. Besides the seat pan, back and head rests are important design considerations, as is ease of adjustment. A foot rest may be desired and arm rests including wrist rests (either related to the keyboard or the mouse pad) can help both in achieving suitable body posture but avoiding conditions which contribute to the risk of cumulative trauma disorders.

With quickly advancing computer technology, new design solutions for the office workstation may be feasible, desired, even necessary. Consider the introduction of non-conventional keyboards (split, chord, non-binary keys), or of increased mouse use, of employing mouth and ear for inputs and feedback, of changes in software and tasks. With technology, job expectations, and management practices changing so rapidly, many of the workstation design tenets derived from the typist's workstation of the first half of the 20th century do not apply any more.

The phantom of the "average person sitting upright with right angles at elbows, hips and knees" is abolished and replaced by a design model that incorporates ranges of body sizes and of working postures, and the diversity of individual preferences. To facilitate posture changes is a major task in the design of computerized workstations. This goes beyond the traditional seat adjustment feature and other conventional and rather unimaginative concepts. The keyboard is no longer attached to the display unit but is rather freely movable; it is often put on lap or thighs instead of placed on the table; consider the increasing use of "laptop" computers. Many home offices are quite different from the traditional office arrangement. As already practiced by innovative solutions for toys and computer game equipment, the ergonomist should consider radical departures from the traditional configurations of displays, input devices, and other workstation components. Freedom of choice is an overriding design principle - see Figure 4.

Figure 4. Computer workstation design should facilitate "free posturing".

Ergonomic design approaches and solutions, discussed in this chapter, show that the computer workstation can be engineered to accommodate the human for achieving "ease" and "efficiency". Yet, the discussions in this chapter also show that conventional measures of the strain in the body of the computer operator may be difficult to perform, and to interpret. Consider, for example, the assessment and interpretation of spinal disk pressure.

Not much progress has been made in the scientific assessment of "stresses and strains" of the computer operator since the first version of this chapter appeared in 1988. It is still difficult to merge "objective" measures (such as of postures, body segment angles, muscle tension, tissue compression, fluid pressures, spinal column and disk strains) with "subjective" evaluations and opinions by the various ergonomic, biomechanical, and medical experts and, most important, by the computer users. For example, objective measures do not explain sufficiently why so many computer operators complain about low back problems. On the other hand, some biomechanic findings do coincide with, and explain, physiologic outcomes, such as tendon and tendon-sheath strains (tendonitis, or carpal tunnel syndrome, for example). A concerted scientific effort of ergonomists with physiologic, psychologic, biomechanic and engineering background could provide missing support for human factors solutions in the design and organization of computer workstations, traditional or emerging.

57.12 References

Akerblom, B. (1948). *Standing and Sitting Posture.* Stockholm: Nordiska Bokhandeln.

Andersson, G B. J. and Oertengren, R. (1974). Lumbar Disc Pressure and Myoelectric Back Muscle Activity During Sitting. *Scand. J. Rehabilitation Medicine*, 6, 115-121.

Andersson, G. B. J., Schultz, A. B., and Oertengren, R. (1986). Trunk Muscle Forces During Desk Work. *Ergonomics*, 29(9), 1113-1127.

Ankrum, D. R. and Nemeth, K. J. (1995). Posture, Comfort, and Monitor Placement. *Ergonomics in Design*, April issue, 7-9.

Ankrum, D. R., Hansen, E. E., and Holahan, K. J. (1994). The Vertical Horopter and the Angle of View. In *Proceedings of the Work With Display Units WWDU'94 Conference* (pp. D38-D39). Milano, Italy: University of Milan, Institute of Occupational Health "Clinica del Lavoro L. Devoto".

Armstrong, T. J. (1983). *An Ergonomics Guide for Carpal Tunnel Syndrome*. Akron, OH: American Industrial Hygiene Association.

Armstrong, T. J. (1991). Upper Limb Cumulative Trauma Disorders, Localized Fatigue, and Ergonomic Control Programs. In Proceedings, Occupational Ergonomics: Work Related Upper Limb and Back Disorders (pp. 1-1 to 1-25). San Diego, CA: AIHA, San Diego Local Section.

Armstrong, T. J. and Chaffin, D. B. (1979). Some Biomechanical Aspects of the Carpal Tunnel. *Biomechanics, 12*, 567-570.

Armstrong, T. J., Fine, L. J., and Silverstein, B. A. (1986). Cumulative Trauma Disorders and Keyboard Workstations. *A Literature Review for IBM Purchase*, New York. Ann Arbor, MI: The University of Michigan.

Armstrong, T. J. and Lackey, E. A. (1994). *An Ergonomics Guide to Cumulative Trauma Disorders of the Hand and Wrist.* Fairfax, VA: American Industrial Hygiene Association.

Armstrong, T. J., Martin, B. J., Arbor, A., Rempel, D. M., and Johnson, P. W. (1994). Mouse Input Devices and Work-Related Upper Limb Disorders. In *Proceedings of the Work With Display Units WWDU'94 Conference* (pp. C20-C21). Milano, Italy: University of Milan, Institute of Occupational Health "Clinica del Lavoro L. Devoto".

Armstrong, T. J., Werner, R. A., Waring, W. P., and Foulke, J. A. (1991). Intra-Carpal Canal Pressure in Selected Hand Tasks: a pilot study. In *Proceedings, 11th Congress of the International Ergonomics Association* (pp. 156-158). London, UK: Taylor & Francis.

Ayoub, M. A. and Wittels, N. E. (1989). Cumulative Trauma Disorders. *International Reviews of Ergonomics*, 2, 217-272.

Berns, T. A. R. and Milner, N. P. (1980). *TRAM: A Technique for the Recording and Analysis of Moving Work Posture.* (Report 80:23, pages 22-26). Stockholm, Sweden: Ergolab.

Bradford, P. and Prete, B. (Eds.) (1978). *Chair.* New York, NY: Crowell.

Branton, P. (1984). Backshapes of Seated Persons-How Close can the Interface be Designed? Applied Ergonomics, 15(2), 105-107.

Brienza, D. M., Chung, K. C., Brewbaker, C. E., and Kwiatkowski, R. J. (1993). Design of a Computer-controlled Seating Surface for Research Applications. *IEEE Transactions on Rehabilitation Engineering*, 1(1), 63-66.

Burastero, S., Tittiranonda, P., Chen, C. Shin, M., and Rempel, D. (1994). Ergonomic Evaluation of Alternative Computer Keyboards. In *Proceedings of the Work With Display Units WWDU'94 Conference* (pp. C15-C16). Milano, Italy: University of Milan, Institute of Occupational Health "Clinica del Lavoro L. Devoto".

Burnette, J. T. and Ayoub, M. A. (1989). Cumulative Trauma Disorders. Pain Management, 196-264 and 256-264.

Carayon, P. (1994). Stressful Jobs and Non-stressful Jobs: A Cluster Analysis of Office. *Ergonomics,* 37(2), 311-323.

Chaffin, D. B. and Andersson, G. B. J. (1991). *Occupational Biomechanics*. New York, NY: Wiley.

Chatterjee, D. S. (1987). Repetition Strain Injury - A Recent Review. *J. Society of Occupational Medicine*, 37, 100-105.

Congleton, J. J., Ayoub, M. M., and Smith, J. L. (1985). The Design and Evaluation of the Neutral Posture Chair for Surgeons. *Human Factors*, 27(5), 589-600.

Corlett, E. N. and Eklund, J. A. (1984). How Does a Backrest Work? *Applied Ergonomics*, 15, 111-114.

Corlett, E. N., Madeley, S. J., and Manenica, I. (1979). Postural Targetting: A Technique for Recording Working Postures. *Ergonomics*, 22(3), 357-366.

Damann, E. A. and Kroemer, K. H. E. (1995). Wrist Posture during Computer Mouse Usage. In *Proceedings of the Human Factors and Ergonomics Society 39th Annual Meeting* (in press). Santa Monica, CA: Human Factors and Ergonomics Society.

Drury, C. G. and Francher, M. (1985). Evaluation of a Forward Sloping Chair. *Applied Ergonomics*, 16(1), 41-47.

Ekholm, J., Schuldt, K., and Harms-Ringdahl, K. (1986). Arm Suspension and Elbow Support in Sitting Work Postures: Effects on Neck and Shoulder Muscular Activity. In *Proceedings of the Conference "Work*

With Display Units, (333-335). Stockholm: Swedish National Board of Occupational Safety and Health.

Eklund, J. A. E., Corlett, E. N., and Johnson, F. (1983). A Method for Measuring the Load Imposed on the Back of a Sitting Person. *Ergonomics*, 26(11), 1063-1076.

Erdelyi, A., Sihvonen, T., Helin, P., and Hanninen, O. (1988). Shoulder Strain in Keyboard Workers and its Allevation by Arm Supports. *Occupational Environmental Health,* 119-124.

Fernstroem, E., Ericson, M. O., and Malker, H. (1994). Electromyographic Activity During Typewriter and Keyboard Use. *Ergonomics*, 37, 3, 477-484.

Fransson-Hall, C., Gloria, R. Kilbom, Asa, Winkel, J., Karlqvist, L., and Wiktorin, C. (1995). A Portable Ergonomic Observation Method (PEO) for Computerized On-line Recording of Postures and Manual Handling. *Applied Ergonomics*, 26(2), 93-100.

Fry, H. J. H. (1986). Overuse Syndrome in Musicians - 100 Years Ago. *Lancet*, Sept. issue, 728-731 and *Medical J. of Australia*, Dec. issue, 620-625.

Genaidy, A. M. and Karwowski, W. (1993). The Effects of Neutral Posture Deviations on Perceived Joint Discomfort Ratings in Sitting and Standing Postures. Ergonomics, 36(7), 785-792.

Goldstein, S. A., Armstrong, T. J., Chaffin, D. B., and Mathews, L. S. (1987). Analysis of Cumulative Strain in Tendons and Tendon Sheaths. *J. Biomechanics*, 20(1), 1-6.

Grandjean, E. (1963). *Physiologische Arbeitsgestaltung*. Thun-Muenchen: Otto.

Grandjean, E. (Ed.) (1969). *Sitting Posture.* London: Taylor & Francis.

Grandjean, E. (1987). *Ergonomics in Computerized Offices*. London, UK: Taylor & Francis.

Grandjean, E. (1988). *Fitting the Task to the Man.* London, UK: Taylor & Francis.

Grandjean, E., Huenting, W., and Nishiyama, K. (1984). Preferred VDT Workstation Settings, Body Posture and Physical Impairments. *Applied Ergonomics*, 15(2), 99-104.

Grieco, A. (1986). *Sitting Posture: An Old Problem and a New One.* Ergonomics, 29(3), 345-362.

Hadler, N. M. (1992). Arm Pain in the Workplace: A Small Area Analysis. *JOM,* February, 113-119.

Hansson, T. (1986). Prolonged Sitting and the Back. In *Proceedings of the Conference Work with Display Units.* Stockholm, May 12-15, 1986 (491-492). Stockholm: Swedish National Board of Occupational Safety and Health.

Hansson, J. E. and Attebrant, M. (1986). The Effect of Table Height and Table Top Angle on Head Position and Reading Distance. In *Proceedings of the Conference "Work with Display Units."* Stockholm: Swedish National Board of Occupational Safety and Health.

Harms-Ringdahl, K. and Ekholm, J. (1986). Pain and Extreme Position of Lower Cervical Spine in Sitting Postures. In *Proceedings of the Conference "Work with Display Units",* (341-342). Stockholm: Swedish National Board of Occupational Safety and Health.

Haslegrave, C. M. (1994). What Do We Mean by a "Working Posture"? *Ergonomics,* 37(4), 781-799.

Helander, M. G. and Little, S. E. (1993). Preferred Settings in Chair Adjustments. In *Proceedings of the Human Factors and Ergonomics Society 37th Annual Meeting*, 448-452. Santa Monica, CA: Human Factors Society.

Helander, M. G., Billingsley, P. A., and Schurick, J. M. (1984). An Evaluation of Human Factors Research on Visual Display Terminals in the Workplace. *Human Factors Review*, 55-129. Westlake Village, CA: Canyon.

Hill, S. G. and Kroemer, K. H. E. (1986). Preferred Declination of the Line of Sight. *Human Factors*, 28(2), 127-134.

Hochberg, F. H., Leffert, R. D., Heller, M. D., and Merriman, L. (1983). Hand Difficulties Among Musicians. *JAMA*, 14(249), 1869-1872.

Holzmann, P. (1982). ARBAN-A New Method of Analysis of Ergonomic Effort. *Applied Ergonomics*, 13(2), 82-86.

Human Factors Society (Ed.) (1988). *ANSI Standard HFS 100 American National Standard for Human Factors Engineering of Visual Display Terminal Workstation.* Santa Monica, CA: Human Factors Society.

Jampel, R. S. and Shi, D. S. (1992). The Primary Position of the Eyes, The Resetting Saccade, and the Transverse Visual Head Plane. *Investigative Ophtalmology and Visual Science*, 38(8), 2501-2510.

Jedrziewski, M. (1992). Initial Wrist Posture During Typing as a Function of Keyboard Height and Slope. Unpublished Master Thesis, Virginia Tech, Blacksburg, VA.

Karhu, O., Haerkoenen, R., Sorvali, P., and Vepsaelaeinen, P. (1981). Observing Working Postures in Industry: Examples of OWAS Application. *Applied Ergonomics*, 12(1), 13-17.

Karwowski, W., Eberts, R., Salvendy, G., and Noland, S. (1994). The Effects of Computer Interface Design on Human Postural Dynamics. *Ergonomics*, 37(4), 703-724.

Keegan, J. J. (1952). Alternations to the Lumbar Curve Related to Posture and Sitting. *Journal of Bone and Joint Surgery,* 35(A3), 589-603.

Keyserling, W. M. (1986). A Computer-Aided System to Evaluate Postural Stress in the Workplace. *Am. Industrial Hygiene Assoc. Journal*, 10, 641-649.

Kiesler, S. and Finholt, T. (1988). The Mystery of RSI. *American Psychologist*, 43(12), 1004-1015.

Kilbom, A. (1986). Physiological Effects of Extreme Physical Inactivity. In *Proceedings of the Conference "Work with Display Units"*. Stockholm, May 12-15, 1986 (486-489). Stockholm: Swedish National Board of Occupational Safety and Health.

Kroemer, K. H. E. (1985). Office Ergonomics: Work Station Dimensions. Chapter 18 in D.C. Alexander, and B. M. Pulat (Eds.) *Industrial Ergonomics* (187-201). Norcross, GA: Institute of Industrial Engineers.

Kroemer, K. H. E. (1988). Ergonomic Seats for Computer Workstations (313-320). In *Trends in Ergonomics/Human Factors V* (F. Aghazadeh, ed.) Amsterdam and New York: North Holland.

Kroemer, K. H. E. (1989). Cumulative Trauma Disorders. *Applied Ergonomics*, 20, 274-280.

Kroemer, K. H. E. (1992). Avoiding Cumulative Trauma Disorders in Shop and Office. *American Industrial Hygiene Association Journal*, 53(9), 596-604.

Kroemer, K. H. E. (1994a). Alternative Keyboards and Alternatives to Keyboards. In *Proceedings of the Work With Display Units WWDU'94 Conference* (pp. C1-C7). Milano, Italy: University of Milan, Institute of Occupational Health "Clinica del Lavoro L. Devoto".

Kroemer, K. H. E. (1994b). Locating the Computer Screen: How High, How Far? Ergonomics in Design, January issue, page 40.

Kroemer, K. H. E., Kroemer, H. J., and Kroemer-Elbert, K. E. (1990). *Engineering Physiology: Physiologic Bases of Ergonomics.* (2nd ed.) New York, NY: Van Nostrand Reinhold.

Kroemer, K. H. E., Kroemer, H. B., and Kroemer-Elbert, K. E. (1994). *Ergonomics - How to Design for Ease and Efficiency.* Inglewood Cliffs, NJ: Prentice Hall.

Kroemer, K. H. E. and Robinette, J. C. (1968). Ergonomics in the Design of Office Furniture. AMRL-TR 68-80. Wright-Patterson AFB, OH. Also published with shortened list of references 1969 in *Industrial Medicine*, 38(4), 115-125.

Kruithof, P. C. (1995). Evaluation of Wrist Posture During the Operation of Four Electromagnet Mice. Unpublished Master Thesis, Virginia Tech, Blacksburg, VA.

Kumar, S. (1994). A Computer Desk for Bifocal Lens Wearers, with Special Emphasis on Selected Telecommunication Tasks. *Ergonomics*, 37(10), 1669-1678.

Kuorinka, I, Jonsson, B. Kilbom, A., Vinterberg, H., Biering-Sorensen, F., Andersson, G., and Jorgensen, K. (1987). Standardized Nordic Questionnaires for the Analysis of Musculoskeletal Symptoms. *Applied Ergonomics*, 18, 233-237.

Kuorinka, I. and Forcier, L. (1995). *Work Related Musculoskeletal Disorders (WRMDs): A Reference Book for Prevention.* London, UK: Taylor & Francis.

Laeubli, T. (1986). Review on Working Conditions and Postural Discomfort in VDT Work. In *Proceedings of the Conference "Work with Display Units." Stockholm,* May 12-15, 1986 (3-6). Stockholm: Swedish National Board of Occupational Safety and Health.

Lee, K., Swanson, N., Sauter, S., Wickstrom, R., Waikar, A., and Mangum, M. (1992). A Review of Physical Exercises Recommended for VDT Operators. *Applied Ergonomics*, 23(6), 387-408.

Lee, K. S. and Waikar, A. M. (1986). Reduction of Physical Stress Experienced by VDT Operators. In *Proceedings of the Conference "Work with Display Units."* Stockholm, May 12-15 (505-510). Stockholm: Swedish National Board of Occupational Safety and Health.

Lie, I. and Fostervold, K. I. (1994). VDT-Work with Different Gaze Inclinations. *Proceedings of the Work With Display Units WWDU'94 Conference* (pp. D40-D42). Milano, Italy: University of Milan, Institute of Occupational Health "Clinica del Lavoro L. Devoto".

Lim, S. Y. and Carayon, P. (1994). Psychosocial Work Factors and Upper Extremity Musculoskeletal Discomfort Among Office Workers. In *Proceedings of the Work With Display Units WWDU'94 Conference* (pp. C9-C11). Milano, Italy: University of Milan, Institute of Occupational Health "Clinica del Lavoro L. Devoto".

Lockwood, A. H. (1989). Medical Problems of Musicians. *New England Journal of Medicine*, 320(4), 221-227.

Low, I. (1990). Musculoskeletal Complaints in Keyboard Operators. *Occupational Health Safety*, 6(3), 205-211.

Lueder, R. K. (1983). Seat Comfort. A Review of the Construct in the Office Environment. *Human Factors*, 25, 701-711.

Lueder, R. and Noro, (1995) (Eds.). *Hard Facts About Soft Machines*. London, UK: Taylor & Francis.

Lundervold, A. (1951). Electromyographic Investigations of Position and Manner of Working in Typewriting. *Acta Physiologica Scandinavica*, 24, 84.

Lundervold, A. (1958). Electromyographic Investigations During Typewriting. *Ergonomics*, 1, 226-233.

Malone, R. L. (1991). Posture Taxonomy. Unpublished Master Thesis, Virginia Tech, Blacksburg, VA.

Mandal, A. C. (1975). Work-Chair with Tilting Seat. *Lancet*, 642-643.

Mandal, A. C. (1982). The Correct Height of School Furniture. *Human Factors*, 24, 257-269.

Marras, W. S. and Schoenmarklin, R. W. (1993). Wrist Motions in Industry. *Ergonomics*, 36(4), 341-351.

Martin, M. G. (1994). Healthy Ergonomic Keying/Mousing Principles. In *Proceedings of the Work With Display Units WWDU'94 Conference* (pp. C11-C12). Milano, Italy: University of Milan, Institute of Occupational Health "Clinica del Lavoro L. Devoto".

McAtamney, L. and Corlett, E. N. (1993). RULA: A Survey Method for the Investigation of Work-Related Upper Limb Disorders. *Applied Ergonomics*, 24(2), 91-99.

McIntosh, D. J. (1994). Integration of VDUs into the US Office Work Environment. In *Proceedings of the Work With Display Units WWDU'94 Conference* (pp. F19-F27). Milano, Italy: University of Milan, Institute of Occupational Health "Clinica del Lavoro L. Devoto".

McMulkin, M. L. and Kroemer, K. H. E. (1994). Usability of a One-Hand Ternary Chord Keyboard. *Applied Ergonomics*, 25(3), 177-181.

Moore, A., Wells, R., and Ranney, D. (1991). Quantifying Exposure in Occupational Manual Tasks with Cumulative Trauma Disorder Potential. *Ergonomics*, 34(12), 1433-1453.

Morgan, C. T., Cook, J. S., Chapanis, A., and Lund, M. W. (Eds.) (1963). *Human Engineering Guide to Equipment Design*. New York, NY: McGraw-Hill.

Nachemson, A. (1966). The Load on Lumbar Disks in Different Positions of the Body. *Clinical Orthopaedics and Related Research*, 45, 107-122.

Occhipinti, E., Colombini, D., Molteni, G., and Grieco, A. (1993). Criteria for the Ergonomic Evaluation of Work Chairs. *Medicina Lavaro*, 84(4), 274-285.

Oestberg, O., Warrell, B., and Nordell, L. (1984). ComforTable-A Generic Desk for the Automated Office. *Behavior and Information Technology*, 4, 411-416.

Owen, R. D. (1994). Carpal Tunnel Syndrome: A Products Liability Prospective. Ergonomics, 37(3), 449-476.

Paquet, V. L. (1995). The Effects of Keyboard Height, Wrist Support and Keying Time on Wrist Posture and Trapezias EMG during Keyboarding. Unpublished Master Thesis, Virginia Tech, Blacksburg, VA.

Pascarelli, E. F. and Kella, J. J. (1993). Soft-Tissue Injuries Related to Use of the Computer Keyboard. *JOM*, 35(5), 522-532.

Paul, J. A. and Douwes, M. (1993). Two-dimensional Photographic Posture Recording and Description: A Validity Study. *Applied Ergonomics*, 24(2), 83-90.

Pfeffer, G. B., Gelberman, R. H., Boyes, J. H., and Rydevik, B. (1988). The History of Carpal Tunnel Syndrome. *Journal of Hand Surgery*, 13-B(1), 28-34.

Price, D. L., Fayzmehr, F., Haas, E., and Beaton, R. (1982). *Ergonomics of Typewriting, Phase I Executive Summary*. (Report IBM/SPO-3, November 12, 1982). Blacksburg, VA: Human Factors Laboratory, Virginia Polytechnic Institute and State University.

Priel, V. Z. (1974). A Numerical Definition of Posture. *Human Factors,* 16(6), 576-584.

Putz-Anderson, V. (1988). Cumulative Trauma Disorders: *A Manual for Musculoskeletal Diseases of the Upper Limbs*. London: Taylor & Francis.

Rempel, D. and Horie, S. (1994a). Effect of Wrist Posture During Typing on Carpal Tunnel Pressure. In *Proceedings of the Work With Display Units WWDU'94 Conference* (pp. C27-C28). Milano, Italy: University of Milan, Institute of Occupational Health "Clinica del Lavoro L. Devoto".

Rempel, D. and Horie, S. (1994b). Effect of Keyboard Wrist Rest on Carpal Tunnel Pressure. In *Proceedings of the Work With Display Units WWDU'94 Conference* (pp. C29-C30). Milano, Italy: University of Milan, Institute of Occupational Health "Clinica del Lavoro L. Devoto".

Rempel, D. M., Harrison, R. J., and Barnhart, (1992). Work-Related Cumulative Trauma Disorders of the Upper Extremity. *JAMA*, 267(6), 838-842.

Ridder, C. A. (1959). *Basic Design Measurements for*

Sitting. (Bulletin 616, Agricultural Experiment Station). Fayetteville, AR: University of Arkansas.

Rudakewych, M. Z., Valent, L., and Hedge, A. (1994). Field Evaluation of a Negative Slope Keyboard System Designed to Minimise Postural Risks to Computer Workers. In *Proceedings of the Work With Display Units WWDU'94 Conference* (pp C17-C19). Milano, Italy: University of Milan, Institute of Occupational Health "Clinica del Lavoro L. Devoto".

Sauter, S. L., Schleifer, L. M., and Knutson, S. J. (1991). Work Posture, Workstation Design, and Musculoskeletal Discomfort in a VDT Data Entry Task. *Human Factors*, 32, 151-167.

Schlegel, K. F. (1956). Sitzschaeden und deren Vermeidung durch eine neuartige Sitzkonstrunktion. *Medizinische Klinik*, 51(46), 1940-1942.

Schneider, H. J. and Decker, K. (1961). Gedanken zur Gestaltung des Sitzes. *Deutsche Medizinische Wochenschrift*, 86(38), 1816-1820.

Soderberg, G. L. (1992). *Selected Topics in Surface Electromyography for Use in the Occupational Setting: Expert Perspectives* (DDHS-NIOSH Publication 91-100). Washington, DC: U.S. Department of Health and Human Service.

Soderberg, G. L., Blanco, M. K., Consentino, and Kurdelmeier, K. A. (1986). An EMG Analysis of Posterior Trunk Musculature During Flat and Anteriorly Inclined Sitting. *Human Factors*, 28(4), 483-491.

Staffel, F. (1984). Zur Hygiene des Sitzens. Zbl. *Allgemeine Gesundheitspflege*, 3(403), 403-421.

Stock, S. R. (1991). Workplace Ergonomic Factors and the Development of Musculoskeletal Disorders of the Neck and Upper Limbs: A Meta-Analysis. *American Journal of Industrial Medicine*, 19, 87-101.

Sundelin, G., Hagberg, M. and Hammarstrom, U. (1986). The Effects of Pauses and Perceived Discomfort when Working at a VDT Wordprocessor. *In Proceedings of the Conference "Work with Display Units."* Stockholm: Swedish National Board of Occupational Safety and Health.

Swanson, N. G., Falinsky, T. L., Steward, L. L., and Pan, C. S. (1994). The Effects of Keyboard Design Features on Comfort and Productivity. In *Proceedings of the Work With Display Units WWDU'94 Conference* (pp. C13-C14). Milano, Italy: University of Milan, Institute of Occupational Health "Clinica del Lavoro L. Devoto".

Thompson, F. J., Yates, B. J., and Franzen, O. G. (1986). Blood Pooling in Leg Skeletal Muscles Prevented by a "New" Venopressor Reflex Mechanism. In *Proceedings of the Conference "Work with Display Units."* Stockholm: Swedish National Board of Occupational Safety and Health.

Thompson, D. (1994). Effects of Type of Keyboard Tactile Feedback on VDT Keying Forces. In *Proceedings of the Work With Display Units WWDU'94 Conference* (pp. C22-C23). Milano, Italy: University of Milan, Institute of Occupational Health "Clinica del Lavoro L. Devoto".

Tougas, G. and Nordin, M. C. (1987). Seat Features Recommendations for Workstations. *Applied Ergonomics*, 18(3), 207-210.

Van der Grinten, M. P. (1991). Test-Retest Reliability of a Practical Method for Measuring Body Part Discomfort. In *Proceedings, 11th Congress of the International Ergonomics Association* (pp. 54-56). London, UK: Taylor & Francis.

Wells, R., Moore, A., and Ranney, D. (1992). Relationship Between Forearm Muscle Pain/Tenderness and Work Exposures: Results from Repetitive Manual Tasks. In *Proceedings of the of the International Conference on Occupational Disorders of the Upper Extremities*. University of Michigan, September/ October.

Williams, M. M., Hawley, J. A., McKenzie, R. A., and Wijmen, P. M. (1991). A Comparison of the Effects of Two Sitting Postures on Back and Referred Pain. *Spine*, 16(10), 1185-1191.

Wilson, J., Corlett, N., and Manenica, I. (1986). *Ergonomics of Working Postures*. Philadelphia, PA: Taylor & Francis.

Winkel, J. (1986). Macro- and Micro-Circulatory Changes During Prolonged Sedentary Work and the Need for Lower Limit Valves for Leg Activity. In *Proceedings of the Conference "Work with Display Units."* Stockholm: Swedish National Board of Occupational Safety and Health.

Winkel, J. and Bendix, T. (1986). Muscular Performance During Seated Work Evaluated by Two Different EMG Methods. European Journal of Applied Physiology, 55, 167-173

Zacharkow, D. (1988). *Posture: Lifting, Standing, Chair Design and Exercise*. Springfield, IL: Thomas.

Zwahlen, H. T., Hartmann, A. L., and Kothari, N. (1986). How Much do Rest Breaks Help to Alleviate VDT Operation Subjective Ocular and Musculoskeletal Discomfort? In *Proceedings of the Conference "Work with Display Units"*. Stockholm: National Swedish Board of Occupational Safety and Health.

Handbook of Human-Computer Interaction
Second, completely revised edition
M. Helander, T.K. Landauer, P. Prabhu (eds.)

Chapter 58

Work-related Disorders and the Operation of Computer VDT's

Mats Hagberg
National Institute for Working Life,
Solna, Sweden

David Rempel
University of California San Francisco - University of California at Berkeley Ergonomics program,
California, USA

58.1 Introduction

58.1.1 Scope of the Chapter

The rapid growth of computers in all aspects of work has exposed a large part of the world population exposed to VDT's and dramatically increased the number of hours per day that people sit in front of a VDT. The VDT demand on the operator may vary with tasks and computer-station set up. Adverse health effects are often attributed to the VDT use by the computer operators. VDT operation usually involves daily exposure of long duration. Therefore, any symptoms from slight headache to adverse pregnancy outcome will rightfully or wrongfully be linked to the VDT use. The ongoing debate concerning health effects of VDTs has made everyone aware of the possible hazard of operating a VDT. Especially when new techniques in computer operations are introduced the public concern is expressed in newspaper headlines and magazines. The lag time for scientists to evaluate the possible health effects attributed to the technique is a problem for a balanced discussion on VDT health related issues .

The main scope of this brief overview is to present the current scientific view on common health problems related to VDT use. This overview will mainly focus on work-related musculoskeletal problems. For details the reader should consult reviews in the reference list. Medical terms are used infrequently but sometimes they are impossible to avoid.

58.1.2 Work-related Disorders vs. Occupational Diseases and Injuries

The diseases related to VDT operation are not unique to VDT use but can be caused by other occupational and home exposures. In addition, there are symptoms and other adverse health effects related to VDT use that can not be labelled disease. The World Health Organization defines work-related diseases as multifactorial - the work environment and the performance of work can contribute significantly; but is one factors of a number of different types of factors to the causation of disease (WHO, 1985). An occupational disease has a specificity in either the cause or in the effect, for example, asbestosis is an occupational lung disease caused by exposure to asbestos fibers only. Thus diseases related to VDT should be considered as work-related diseases and not occupational diseases.

In the last years the use of terms such as RSI (repetitive strain injuries) and CTD (cumulative trauma disorders) have been strongly criticised (Hadler, 1989;1990). Sometimes the terms have inappropriately been used as synonyms for disease terms such as CTS (carpal tunnel syndrome, which is compression of the median nerve at the wrist) or De Quervain´s disease (an inflammation of the tendons to the long thumb abductor and the short thumb extensor at the wrist) or other specific disorders. This is not correct since both CTS and De Quervain are not necessarily related to repetitive strain or to cumulative trauma. The terms cumulative trauma disorders and repetitive strain have also have been criticized because they suggest a pathological mechanism that is may not be proven. A work-related musculoskeletal disorder may be caused by a single strain or trauma not necessarily a repetitive or cumulative one. Furthermore both psychological and social factors play an important role in genesis and perpetuation work-related musculoskeletal disorders. Job demand and lack of control in VDT task may cause a psychological strain causing muscle tension and symptoms (Bongers, de Winter, Kompier and Hildebranndt, 1993).

Work-related musculoskeletal disorder is the preferred term for conditions that may be subjectively or objectively influenced or caused by work (Hagberg, 1996). Work-related musculoskeletal disorder is an umbrella term that neither defines the pathological mechanism nor the diagnostic criteria.

58.1.3 A Brief Historic Perspective of VDT as Health Hazard

VDTs has been in use since the 1960´s. In the 1980´s VDTs spread rapidly coincident with the introduction of personal computers in the office.. Although many keypunch operators in the 1960's were female, most of the early computer operators were male. In the 1980's large groups of women became computer operators. The hazards of the electro-magnetic fields associated with VDTs were in focus in the mid 1980's. Pregnancy effects such as malformation and miscarriage were major concerns including skin effects. Many newspapers carried headlines about VDT's as major health hazards. In the 1990's the focus has shifted towards musculoskeletal effects of VDT's.

In the mid- and late 1980s an "epidemic" of compensation claims for work-related upper limb pain (termed RSI and mainly wrist pain) among keyboard operators swept Australia. Several explanations for this phenomenon have been offered including longer hours sitting in a fixed posture at the VDT, labor unrest, and increased presence of females in the labor market.. Approved claims grew to such a magnitude that the Australian government had to revert back to stricter rules. Approved claims were reduced and eventually a change of the compensation system was forced. It is likely that work-related symptoms associated with keyboard use still occurred but were not compensated.

Still in the 1990's there are books which address the health hazard in a speculative way e.g. "VDU terminal sickness" (Bentham, 1991) may increase worry about VDT work rather than prevent adverse health effects.

58.1.4 Risk Assessment of Disorders Related to VDT Use

Risk assessment is the process of determining risks to health attributable to environmental or other hazards. The four steps in the process are: 1. Hazard identification. 2. Risk characterization. 3. Exposure assessment. 4. Risk estimation. In risk assessment both epidemiologic and experimental data are used. To determine causal effects one must consider magnitude of effect, specificity of exposure and effect, consistency across studies, predictive performance and coherence (Susser, 1991) . These aspects of causal inference in the health effects have been used in this chapter.

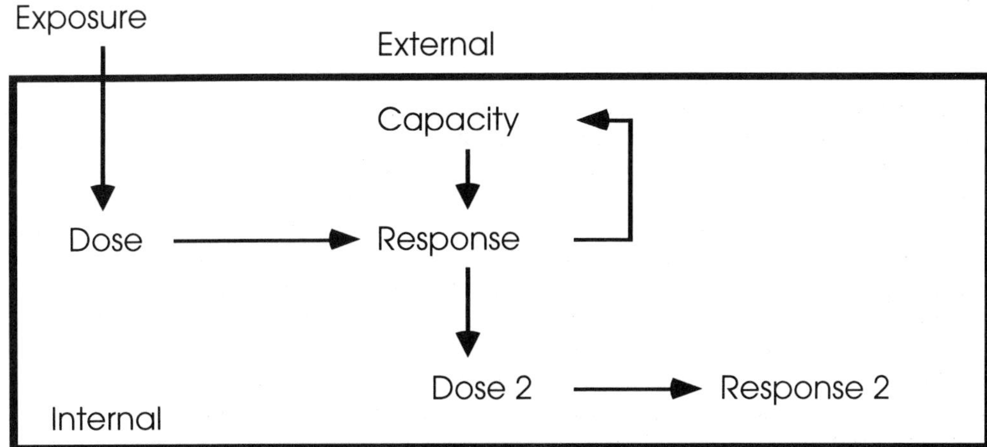

Figure 1. The conceptual model for work-related musculoskeletal disorders.

58.2 Common Work-related Musculoskeletal Disorders Related to VDT Use

58.2.1 Model

In a recent review a multinational scientific group published a model for work related musculoskeletal disorders (Armstrong, Buckle and Fine, 1993) . The model conformed to the terminology used in occupational epidemiology (Checkoway, Pearce and Crawford-Brown, 1989). Exposure is external to the worker. Exposure is the requirements of the job. The requirements can be both physical and psychological. The exposure determines a dose in the worker which is modified by the capacity to a physiologic response. The physiologic response can be harmful strain that constitutes a second dose which leads on to a second physiologic response or can be beneficial such as physical training and adaptation with a resultant increase the individual capacity (Figure 1). Work demand with sustained awkward postures assumed during keyboard use may cause a dose on the wrist tendons and muscles. This dose may cause a second dose of elevated pressure and edema. Individual capacity of tissue susceptibility and blood pressure may determine the magnitude of pressure change in the carpal tunnel at the wrist and whether symptoms from the median nerve (carpal tunnel syndrome) or tendons will develop.

Another example: work requirements with the exposure of high demands and little control may result in a dose of stress that cause a physiologic response of muscle tension (Theorell, Harms-Ringdahl, Ahlberg-Hultin and Westin, 1991). The individual capacity of coping may determine the magnitude of muscle tension.

The conceptual model work-related musculoskeletal disorder conformed to the terminology used in occupational epidemiology (Checkoway, Pearce and Crawford-Brown, 1989) that is defined exposure as external to the worker. Exposure is the requirements of the job. The requirements can be both physical and psychological. The exposure determines a dose in the worker which is modified by the capacity to a physiologic response. The response can be harmful strain that constitutes a second dose which leads on to a second response. Work requirements with the exposure of high demands and little control may result in a dose of stress that cause a physiologic response of muscle tension.

At first thought VDT work may be viewed as optimal with low load compared to industrial assembly work. However, both assembly work and VDT work may give exposure that can be related to upper extremity pain. The pain may be due to different disorders caused by different exposure characteristics (Table 1).

58.2.2 Tendinitis

The tendon is a rope like tissue that connects the muscle to the bone or fascia, transferring force from the muscle to produce a joint motion. The tendon consists of parallel arranged collagen fibers with the strength of about 50% that of cortical bones (Frankel and Nordin, 1980). Fibrous tissue surrounding the tendon forming a

***Table 1. Comparison of examples of upper extremity pain between assembly line worker and VDT operator** (Hagberg, 1996).*

	Assembly line worker	**Visual display unit (VDT) - operator**
Shoulder pain	Shoulder tendinitis due to work with the hands above shoulder height	Myofascial type of pain which may be caused by task invariability e.g. static tension of the trapezius muscle
Hand-wrist pain	Repetitive power grips causing repetitive strain on the extensor tendons and tendinitis. Carpal tunnel syndrome may also relate to repetitive power grips	Intensive keying causing increased load on the extensor tendons and tendinitis Carpal tunnel syndrome may also relate to intensive keying.

tendon sheath protects the tendons against mechanical friction when crossing joints. The tendon sheath consists of a synovial membrane that reduces the friction against the bone (Figure 2).

Tendinitis and tenosynovitis or tendovaginitis are irritations or swelling of the tendon and the synovial membrane of tendon sheath (Kurppa, Waris and Rokkanen, 1979). Common sites for the inflammation are the tendons to the rotator cuff muscles (shoulder) consisting of the supraspinatus, infraspinatus, subscapularis, and the teres minor muscles. Other sites are the long head of the biceps brachii at the shoulder, the insertion of the wrist extensor muscles at the elbow (tennis elbow) and the wrist flexor muscles at the elbow (golfer's elbow). Sites at the wrist are the tendons at the base of the thumb, the abductor pollicis longus and extensor pollicis brevis muscles (De Quervain disease) and the tendons on the back of the wrist that pull the fingers back (extensor comminis). A common characteristic for the tendons at these sites is that the tendons perform large movement as it bends around a pulley point at the joint. Peritendinitis is inflammation of the tendon and adjacent tissues most often muscle or synovial tissue, leading to local swelling and edema (Kurppa, Waris and Rokkanen, 1979).

In keyboard work repetitive finger motion may induce tendinitis of tendons at the dorsum of the wrist. In a study of 533 telecommunication employees working with VDTs, there were 76 cases (15%) with musculoskeletal disorders in the upper extremity that were probable tendon related (Hales, Sauter and Peterson, 1994). Two percent of the cases were probable De Quervain's disease. A case history of "Mouse joint" associated mouse operating devices with a flexor tendinitis in the hand (Norman, 1991).

58.2.3 Carpal Tunnel Syndrome

Peripheral Nerve Injuries. Compression injuries are the most common work-related disorders of nerve tissue. They can occur as acute injuries or chronic lesions. The chronic lesions are often termed nerve entrapments or tunnel syndromes.

In a nerve compression fiber deformation or ischemia may lead to nerve dysfunction within minutes. Repeated nerve compression may cause an oedema (Lundborg, 1987). At 30 mm Hg the intra neural micro vascular flow is impaired (Rydevik, Lundborg and Bagge, 1981). At 80 mm mercury it stops. The resultant block in blood flow may also damage the endothelial cells of the intra neural or synovial micro vessels resulting in an increased permeability (Lundborg, 1987) leading to intra neural oedema. Inflammation with fibroblast invasion may cause tissue scarring. Tissue scarring alters the function of the nerve and may also lead to further pressure elevation. A permanent pressure increase may lead to nerve degeneration due to impaired blood perfusion. The pressure increase may also block the outward and inward axoplasmic flows in the nerve (Lundborg, 1987). In a study of decreased conduction velocity of the median nerve, a 2,8 relative risk must be seen for operators with more than 4 hours of keying compared to those with less than 4 hours of keying per day (Nathan, Meadows and Doyle, 1988). This interpretation was not done by the author but other reviewers recalculating Nathan and coworkers data (Hagberg, Morgenstern and Kelsh, 1992; Stock, 1991). In a cross sectional study of 533 telecommunication employees using video display terminals (VDT), 111 (22%) cases of upper extremity musculoskeletal disorders were identified (Hales, Sauter

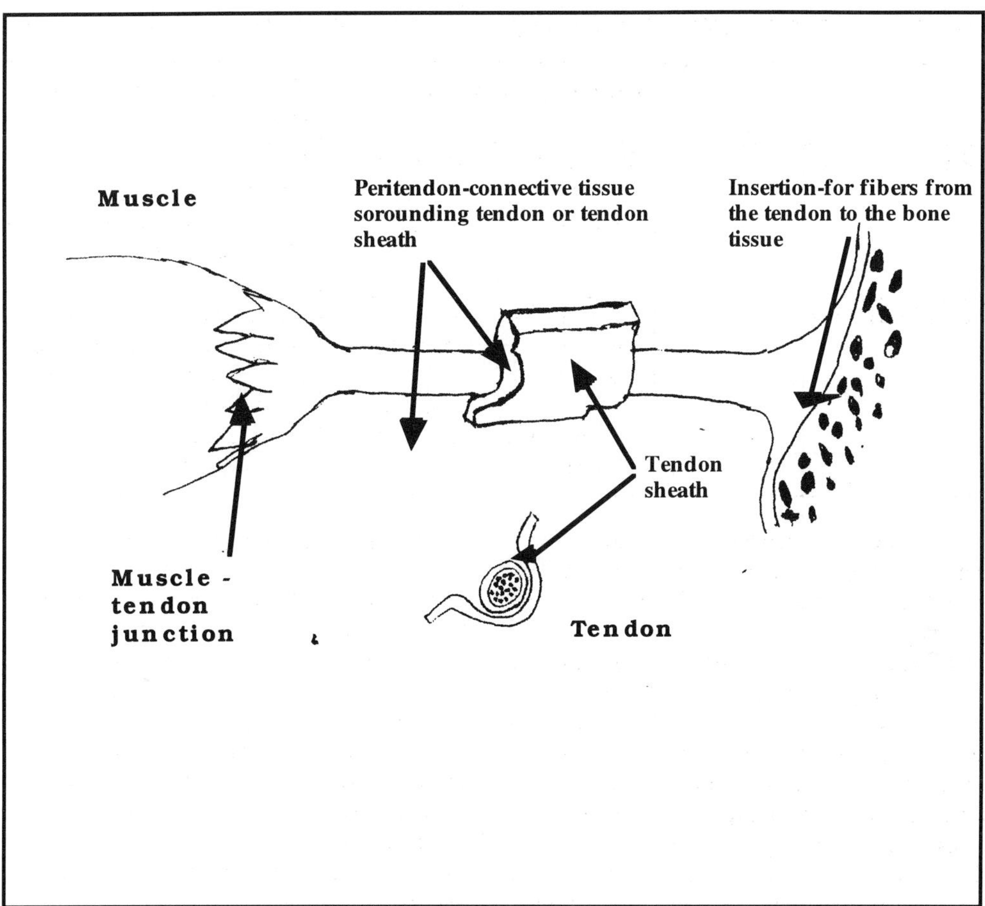

Figure 2. The anatomy of a tendon.

and Peterson, 1994), suspected nerve entrapment syndromes were found in 4% of the employees.

Carpal Tunnel Pressure in Wrist Extension and Flexion. Exposures are likely to affect the median nerve both directly by mechanical stress (e.g. stretching and compression) and indirectly by ischemia eventually causing paresthesia or a nerve conduction block. Sustained extension of the wrist can cause an increase of pressure in the carpal tunnel that can affect the blood perfusion of the median nerve (Rempel, 1995). Microscopic studies of tissues in the carpal tunnel in wrist specimens revealed changes, e.g., increased thickening of fibrocytes and fibrous connective tissue in the radial and ulnar bursa and the median nerve (Armstrong and Chaffin, 1979a,b; Armstrong, Castelli, Evans and Diaz-Perez, 1984) . The pattern of these changes corresponded with the pattern of stresses produced between the tendons, nerves and adjacent flexor retinaculum and carpal bones. It was suggested that repeated exertions with a flexed or an extended wrist are important factors in the etiology. It was concluded that these stresses and tissues changes were involved in the pathogenesis of activity related carpal tunnel syndrome.

An increase of carpal tunnel pressure by three to six times the resting value was found during isometric or isotonic maximal contractions of wrist and finger muscles (Werner, Elmquist and Ohlin, 1983). These changes relate to mechanical pressure and perfusion of the median nerve. In considering material handling, it is evident that poor ergonomic design of tools with respect to weight, shape and size may impose extreme wrist positions on the worker and the use of high forces. Holding an object requires a power grip and high tension in the finger flexor tendons causing an increased pressure in the carpal tunnel. The heavier the

Table 2. Some characteristics of non-specific neck-shoulder pain *(Hagberg, 1996).*

Neck-shoulder muscle pain/ non-specific neck-shoulder pain	
History	Gradual increase of neck stiffness and pain during the work day and worst at the end of the work-day and week. Pain felt localised to cervical spine and neck-shoulder angle. Usually no radiation of pain. Improvement by heat and deterioration by cold draught.
Signs	Tenderness over neck shoulder muscle. Impaired range of active cervical spine motion (normal passive motion). No neurological deficits.
Medical management	NSAIDs may reduce the pain and the inflammatory component. Acupuncture can be used to reduce pain. Strength training of neck-shoulder muscles. Aerobic training to reduce pain and improve circulatory capacity
Differential diagnosis	Thoracic outlet syndrome other nerve entrapments. Systemic diseases.
Work-place factors	Incorrect glasses or need for glasses may cause neck-shoulder pain in work with visual display terminals. Lay-out and work technique should be checked. Forward flexion posture of the cervical spine may cause pain and stiffness. Frequent rests and breaks may be introduced.

object then the greater the power required to hold the object.

Keyboard operation has been identified as a risk factor for carpal tunnel syndrome in some studies. Typists had a relative risk of 3.8 compared to non-typist (Hagberg, Morgenstern and Kelsh, 1992). In the study of 533 telecommunication employees there were 4 cases (1%) of probable CTS (Hales, Sauter and Peterson, 1994). Cluster of work related musculoskeletal disorders was noted in white collar workers employed in medical illustration and graphic arts (Franzblau, Flaschner, Albers, Blitz, Werner and Armstrong, 1993) . Among the graphic artists, (N=7) there were 3 cases of carpal tunnel syndrome in comparison to no such reports among other workers in the department (N=39). This specific work element was found to be performed more frequently by graphic artists where the cutting and pasting and using of computer mouse (Franzblau, Flaschner, Albers, Blitz, Werner and Armstrong, 1993).

58.2.4 Neck and Shoulder Symptoms (Non-Specific Neck-Shoulder Pain)

Symptoms of recurring or persistent pain, numbness, aching, burning, stiffness in the neck and upper extremity is common without any specific diagnosis (Hagberg, Silverstein and Wells, 1995). These conditions have previously been lumped together in broad categories, for example Occupational Cervicalbrachial Disorder, CTD, RSI (Hagberg, Silverstein and Wells, 1995). Usually both the injured structure and the pathogenesis mechanism is unclear. The symptoms may increase gradually. Ergonomic interventions are an important aspect of medical management in these cases (Table 2).

Most literature concerning VDTs and health concerns symptoms without knowledge of the origin of the symptoms. The prevalence of neck and shoulder symptoms varies in different reports reflecting difference in exposures and in the investigated population of operators but also difference in the definition of symptoms and the anatomical area. The neck and the right upper extremity are the most common location for symptoms especially if intense mouse use is involved (Karlqvist, Hagberg, Köster, Wenemark and Ånell, 1996). .

In a study of 150 Video Display Terminal (VDT) operators in the editorial department of a large metropolitan newspaper 28% were categorized by symptom criteria potentially to have musculoskeletal disorders (Faucett and Rempel, 1994). More hours per day of VDT use and less decision latitude on the job were risk factors for potential musculoskeletal disorders. Increased sustained head rotation and elevated keyboard height were related to pain severity and stiffness in the shoulders, neck and upper-back (Faucett and Rempel, 1994). Lower management and co-worker support were associated with more severe hand and arm numbness.

Table 3. Work factors associated with musculoskeletal disorders in the neck (logistic regression model)*(Hales, Sauter and Peterson, 1994).*

	Relative risk	95% Confidence interval
Routine work lacking decision making opportunities	4.2	2.1-8.6
Use of bifocals	3.8	1.5-9.4
Lack of a productivity standard	3.5	1.5-8.3
Fear of being replaced by computers	3.0	1.5-6.1
High information processing demands	3.0	1.4-6.2
Job requires a variety of tasks	2.9	1.5-5.8
Increasing work procedure	2.4	1.1-5.5

There were high levels of neck and shoulder discomfort observed in the questionnaire study population of 905 VDT users which suggested a need for further attention to control cervicalbracial (neck and arm) pain syndrome in VDT work (Sauter, Schleifer and Knutson, 1991). In this population arm discomfort increased with increased keyboard height above elbow level supporting arguments for low placement of the keyboard in an observational study of 40 VDT users (Sauter, Schleifer and Knutson, 1991).

In a cross-sectional study of 1545 clerical workers increased prevalence of adverse condition related to vision, musculoskeletal discomfort and headaches among clerical workers who used VDT were seen (Rossignol, Morse, Summers and Pagnotto, 1987). Musculoskeletal discomfort and headaches were higher among VDT worker in computer and data processing services, public utilities than among workers in banking, communications and hospitals (Rossignol, Morse, Summers and Pagnotto, 1987).

In a cross sectional study of 533 telecommunication employees using video display terminals (VDT), 111 (22%) cases of upper extremity disorders were defined (Hales, Sauter and Peterson, 1994). In a logistic regression model the following associations were noted; diagnosis of period condition, usage of bifocals at work and seven pyschosocial variables (fear of being replaced by computers, increasing work pressure, search in workload, routine work, lack in decision making opportunities, high information processing demands, job which required a variety of task a lack of production standard) (Hales, Sauter and Peterson, 1994). The highest odds ratios were found for near work related factors and musculoskeletal disorders located in the neck (Table 3) (Hales, Sauter and Peterson, 1994).

Individual Factors - Age and Gender

An increasing prevalence of neck and shoulder symptoms is usually seen with increasing age. Females reported more symptoms than males even in the same VDT work tasks (Karlqvist, Hagberg, Köster, Wenemark and Ånell, 1996). Possible explanations for gender difference in symptom reporting are difference working techniques (Karlqvist et al in press), difference in exposure at non-occupational activities e.g. household work, or difference in genetic e.g. there are gender differences in muscles fiber type composition (Lindman, Eriksson and Thornell, 1991).

Intensity of VDT Use

An increase of symptom was seen with the duration of VDT use measured as hours per day (Karlqvist, Hagberg, Köster, Wenemark and Ånell, 1996; Faucett and Rempel, 1994; Bernard, Sauter and Fine, 1994; Bergqvist, Wolgast, Nilsson and Voss, 1994) ,29, 33, 34. In a study of journalists increasing hours on the computer was related to symptoms in the hand-wrists and neck/shoulder (Bernard, Sauter and Fine, 1994). Entry working at least 30 hours per week on deadline and job pressure were related to symptoms. The risks for neck/shoulders symptoms were elevated for data and entry work with limited opportunity to take wrist breaks and VDT use for at least 20 hours per week (Bergqvist, Wolgast, Nilsson and Voss, 1994) .

Posture

Within a study of VDT operators at a bank Hunting and co-workers (Hunting, Läubli and Grandjean, 1981) reported a dose-response relationship between the neck-

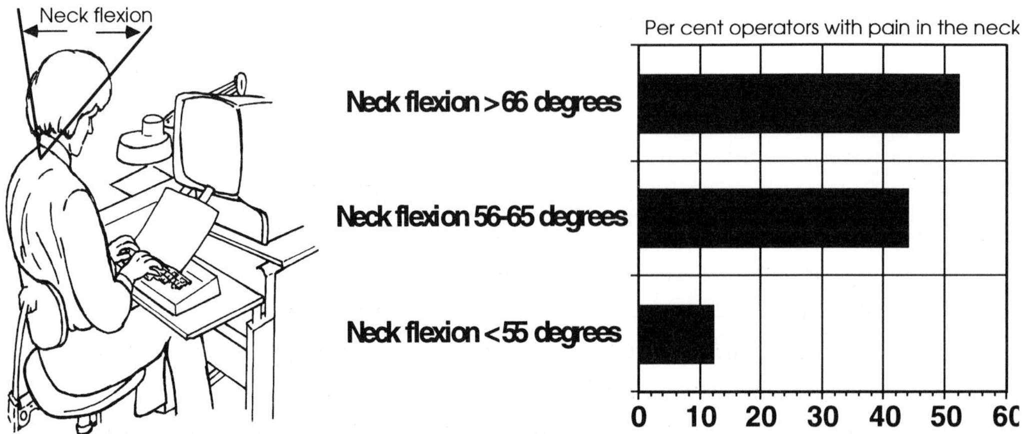

Figure 3. Prevalence of neck stiffness and neck pains for different work postures involving neck flexion.

flexion angle the prevalence of reported neck pains (Figure 3). The prevalence of neck symptoms increased with the angle of neck-flexion (Figure 3). A possible explanation for this can be the increased load on the neck/shoulder muscle (Chaffin, 1973). In a study of 260 VDT workers (Bergqvist, Wolgast, Nilsson and Voss, 1994) found an increasing risk of neck/shoulder discomfort with increasing keyboard height. Possible explanation for this was an increased shoulder joint torque and shoulder non-neutral position with increasing keyboard height.

58.2.5 Non Specific Wrist Pain

In a cross sectional study of 533 telecommunication employees using video display terminals (VDT), 111 (22%) cases of upper extremity disorders were defined (Hales, Sauter and Peterson, 1994). The most common anatomical location for symptoms were the hand and wrists (12% of the employees).

A longitudinal study on use of VDTs with cross-sectional examinations 1981 and 1987-88 suggested that VDT use was related to the risk of developing hand and wrist problems (Bergqvist, Knave, Voss and Wibom, 1992). In a study of 53 disabled keyboard operators it was suggested that the patients had ligament's hypermobility of finger joints (42%) and harmful and inefficient keyboard styles (Pascarelli and Kella, 1993).

An increased risk of hand-wrist symptoms when keying 60% of the workday was found both in cross-sectional and the prospective phase in the investigation of newspaper employees (Bernard, Sauter and Fine, 1994). Relative risks of hand-wrist symptoms from 2,3 to 9,1 were seen with increase of keying from the previous year (Bernard, Sauter and Fine, 1994).

In the study of 260 VDT workers Bergqvist and co-workers (Bergqvist, Wolgast, Nilsson and Voss, 1994) noted an increase of arm/hand discomfort and disorders with lower keyboard heights. A possible explanation for this may be that with an decreasing keyboard height the wrist angle increases in extension. In a posture with a low keyboard height an extension in the wrist was noted (Bergqvist, Wolgast, Nilsson and Voss, 1994; Honan, Serina, Tal and Rempel, 1995) ,65.

58.2.6 Hand and Arm Pain in Keyboard Operators- Principles of Management

There is few if any studies on the management of upper extremity pain in VDT operators. Some principles are outlined in Table 4.

58.2.7 Activity Related Low-back Pain and Leg Pain

Prevalence of low-back pain is related to the duration of sitting posture. Long duration of sitting posture throughout the workday is reported as a risk factor for low-back pain (Jayson, 1996). Alternating standing and sitting posture has been related to a decrease in low-back symptoms prevalence as well as a decrease in symptoms in the shoulder/neck (Oxenburgh, 1987). An variation of posture will decrease symptoms and swelling from the lower extremity (Winkel, 1987).

Leg discomfort increased with low, soft seat pans, suggesting that posture constrained is more important than thigh compression as a risk factor for leg discomfort in VDT work (Sauter, Schleifer and Knutson, 1991).

***Table 4. Outline of management of upper extremity pain in VDT operators** (Hagberg, 1996).*

Principles of Management – Hand and Arm Pain in Keyboard Operators

- Identify clear pathological cases of hand/arm pain (e.g., CTS)
- Reassure the patient that with appropriate action recovery will occur although it may take months or years
- Keep the patient at work if possible but limit time on aggravating tasks (keyboard use)
- Monitor the patient with regular follow-ups and expect continued improvement
- When symptoms have died down, advise gradual reintroduction of precipitating activity
- Explore the psychosocial situation including attitudes to work, support from management and colleagues
- Liaise with the patient's workplace (with an Occupational Physician or Nurse if possible)
- Ensure that workstation ergonomics have been evaluated and are satisfactory and that the patient has been taught to use the equipment properly and has the right glasses. --Enquire about the variation of work tasks, work intensity and whether there are rules or opportunity for breaks from the keyboard or job rotation
- Surgery is rarely necessary
- Those few cases who fail to respond to this plan of multi-disciplinary management may need eventually to be retrained in the use of voice activated word processors etc.

58.3 Hazards in VDT Operation

58.3.1 Sitting Work Posture

In a sitting position the lumber spine straightens from its normal lordotic curvature. This posture will increase the force on the intervertibral disc of the spine (Andersson, 1987). In addition the operator in a sitting position tends to lean forward. This causes stress to the ligamental muscles in the lumber region. If a standing work posture can be obtained less strain on the low back is seen. Attempts with alternating sitting and standing work results in a lower discomfort of the low back (Winkel, 1987).

58.3.2 Non Neutral Postures

Non-neutral neck posture was associated with neck pain (figure 3). The normal qwerty keyboard will cause a posture of ulnar deviations in the hand. For mouse operators ulnar deviation in the mouse operating hand has been reported (Figure 4). Also in outward shoulder rotation a difference between mouse and non-mouse operators have been reported (Karlqvist, Hagberg and Selin, 1994).

58.3.3 Static (Constrained) Work

Working at a VDT terminal causes a low variation in muscle contraction levels which may cause muscle fatigue discomfort (Hagberg, 1996; Winkel, 1987; Hagberg and Sundelin, 1986). It used to be argued that to prevent work-related musculoskeletal disorders it was necessary to minimise the load. When the arms are held in a position for the keyboard with the shoulders slightly flexed and abducted and also sometimes an elevated shoulder girdle a low static contraction in the trapezius muscle occurs (Hagberg and Sundelin, 1986; Sundelin, 1993). Screen position and document position are also determinant of a neck posture and neck muscle load (Arndt, 1983). A VDT operators moves less frequently than in other types of jobs (Kilbom, 1987).

The mechanism of health effects caused by task invariability may be that prolonged static contraction of the trapezius muscle - during work or daily activity results in an overload of type 1 muscle fibres - one hypothesis which might explain neck myalgia. At a low contraction level the low threshold motor units are used (type 1 fibres). A low static contraction during work may result in a recruitment pattern or motor program where *only* the type 1 muscle fibres are used (Figure 5) which causes a selective motor unit fatigue and damage to the type 1 fibres (Hagberg, 1994). In trapezius muscle biopsies in patients with work-related trapezius myalgia, enlarged oversized type 1 fibres and a reduced ratio of type 1 fibres area to capillary area have been reported (Lindman, Hagberg, Ängqvist, Söderlund, Hultman and Thornell, 1991; Lindman, Hagberg, Bengtsson, Henriksson and Thornell, 1995) .

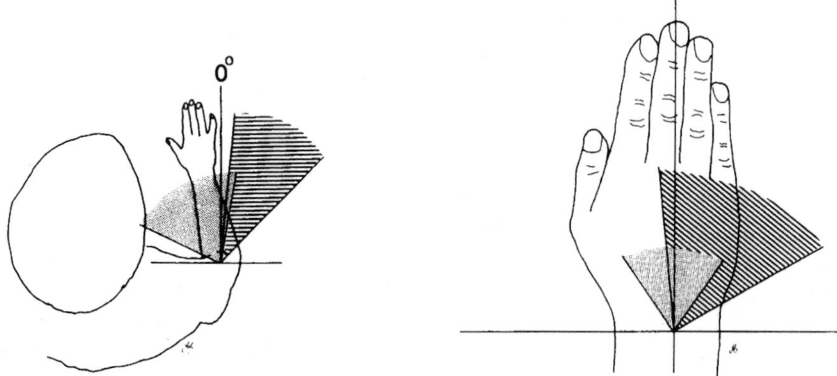

Figure 4. Comparison of postures between keyboard operators not using a mouse and keyboard operators using a mouse in the shoulder (outward rotation) and in the wrist (deviation). *Wrist deviation between -5 degrees and +60 degrees for mouse operators (striped sectors) and between -35 degrees and +35 degrees for non mouse operators (dotted sector). Negative values are radial deviation and positive values indicate ulnar deviation. Modified from (Karlqvist, Hagberg and Selin, 1994).*

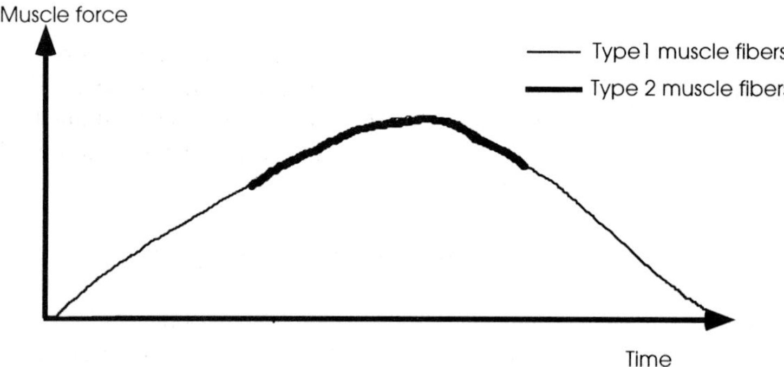

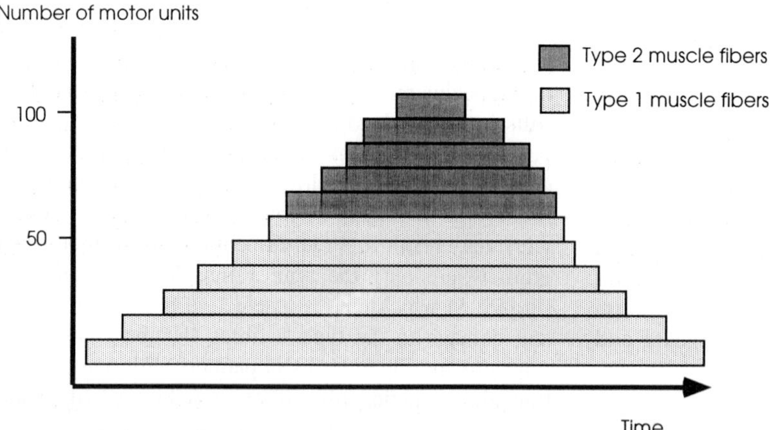

Figure 5. At low contraction levels the type 1 muscle fibres are recruited. *A low static contraction level during work may result in a recruitment pattern or motor program where only the type 1 muscle fibres are used. This may cause a selective motor unit fatigue and damage to the type 1 fibres.*

58.3.4 Strategies in Minimizing Work Related Disorders at VDT Workstations

The objective with designing a VDT work both from a VDT workstation but also from an organizational view is to create a workstation and work environment that is not only healthy but also promotes health and productivity for the operator. Furthermore it is important to create a job where a development of skill and competence can be achieved. In the following some aspects of prevention of work-related musculoskeletal disorders among VDT keying and promoting workers health will be discussed.

Selection of Workers

So far there is no scientific evidence that pre-employment screening of musculoskeletal disorders on applicants will prevent work-related musculoskeletal disorders (Hagberg, Silverstein and Wells, 1995). It is important to remember that there is no scientific evidence that shows that pre-employment and pre-placement screening can predict the risk of developing a work-related musculoskeletal disorder. Results from scientific evaluation of pre-employment and pre-placement screening have often evoked protests from practising physicians as seen in "Letters to the editor (Hagberg, Silverstein and Wells, 1995) . At lastly mention should be made of the legal status of pre-employment screening. In most countries the anti-discrimination laws to practise the pre-employment screening could come under legal scrutiny. Different attempts to do screening of individual factors in workers are being made by using medical history, strength testing, ultrasonic and radiographic examination of the back, physical fitness and biological markers. Non of the published reports deals specifically with the VDT workers. When using a medical history as a screening tool a previous history of back pain is a predictor of a new episode of back pain. Strength testing in physical strenuous jobs have been in some studies shown as a way to predict musculoskeletal disorders (Hagberg, Silverstein and Wells, 1995). Empirical evidence from work place studies are consistent: the use of low back X-rays as a pre-placement screen is a poorly predictive of future back pain. There are biological markers that have been suggested for screening but there are no empirical evidence of its usefulness . In conclusion there are few weak determinants which may predict musculoskeletal disorders in physical demanding jobs. However, these variables are all of low magnitude compared to workplace related risk factors (Hagberg, Silverstein and Wells, 1995).

Physical Fitness Training

Physical fitness training among VDT workers was found to decrease the severity and prevalence of symptoms in the neck and should among VDT operators (Dyrssen, Svendenkrans and Paasikivi, 1989). Whether physical fitness training prevents VDT without symptoms to develop symptoms is unclear. However, since musculoskeletal symptoms are common in the general population and among VDT operators physical fitness training program as a part of workers health and safety program may be an efficient way of both primary and secondary prevention. The physical training of VDT operators symptoms can be regarded as an early rehabilitation program.

Rests, Breaks and Job Rotation

Frequent breaks during the VDT work may reduce and prevent symptoms. In the Italian National Telecom company a 15 minutes long physiological break for 75 minutes of work reduced and prevented musculoskeletal symptoms (Grieco, 1986).

Palm, Wrist and Forearm Supports

There are lots of different ergonomic aids out on the market. Palm-, wrist- and forearm supports are marketed as instruments for reducing discomfort and preventing musculoskeletal disorders. There is little or no scientific evaluation of the use of these tools. Palm-/wrist support may provide the opportunity to rest the wrist and forearm and are preferred by some VDT operators (Bendix and Jessen, 1986; Grandjean, 1984). Ordinary touch typists preferred to operate without wrist support (Bendix and Jessen, 1986) . The proposed explanation for this was that it interfered with rapid accurate movement. Resting the forearm on the desk when performing an editing task using a computer mouse showed less muscle activity compared to not resting an arm (Karlqvist et al in press).

Keyboard Design

A variety of ergonomic keyboard designs are available. Minor advantages in posuture with ergonomic keyboard designs have been reported (Kroemer, 1972; Honan, Serina, Tal and Rempel, 1995),.

58.3.5 Non Keyboard Input Devices

Symptoms in the neck, shoulder, forearm and wrist have been related to the introduction of to the use of the non-keyboard computer input device such as the computer mouse in case histories from occupational health care personnel in Sweden. The symptoms among mouse users in Sweden have been termed "mouse-syndrome" or "mouse-arm syndrome" by the patients and occupational health care personnel.

There was a good internal consistency for symptoms in neck, shoulder-scapular region, shoulder joint region, elbow - forearm, wrist and hand-fingers in a study of mouse operators (Hagberg, 1995).

The risk ratio was 1,3 for having the single symptom in the shoulder - scapular region among the intense mouse users, 1,4 for having the single symptom in the wrist and 2,8 for the single symptom in the hand -fingers. If instead the outcome of grouped symptoms was studied the risk ratio was 5,6 for having symptoms in all three regions the shoulder-scapular region, the wrist and in the hand-fingers for the intense mouse users (Hagberg, 1995). Similar the risk ratio for having symptoms in combination wrist and hand-finger region was 7,4 for the intense mouse users (Hagberg, 1995).

Traditional analysis of occurrence and association of work-related musculoskeletal symptoms usually focus on one body part at a time. Ergonomic exposure e.g. computer mouse use may cause symptoms not only in one part of the body but in many parts in specific combinations. The combination of symptoms may be an efficient way to assess the occurrence and associations of exposure - effect relationships and to evaluate preventive measures.

58.4 Vision Related Disorders

A longitudinal study on use of VDTs with cross-sectional examinations 1981 and 1987-88 suggested that VDT use was related to the risk of developing eye discomfort (Bergqvist, Knave, Voss and Wibom, 1992). In cross sectional studies association between VDT use and different eye discomforts symptoms have been reported (Bergqvist, 1993a). There has been consistent association reported for the combined symptoms of smarting, gritty feelings and readness (SGR) and for sensitive to light symptoms (Bergqvist, 1993a). There are several VDT work parameters that can be associated with eye discomfort; time spent viewing the screen, the screen factors such as contrast, age, sharpness, readability factors etc., time spent viewing other objects than the screen, the frequency of glance changes between screen and manuscript and luminance difference between them, time spent at the VDT working station (Bergqvist, 1993a). Findings of another association between eye discomforts or SGR symptoms and low age sharpness on the display characters have been seen in several studies (Bergqvist, 1993a). Flicker has been reported associated with SRG and sensitivity to light and dryness symptoms in the eyes (Bergqvist, 1993a).

58.5 Pregnancy Related Problems

Clusters of malformations were reported to be associated with VDT work in newspapers. Later review claimed that the clusters could be reasonably achieved due to random variations (Bergqvist, 1993b). Since there is an emission of radiation from VDTs, great attention was gained by report on the possible theratogenic effects of low frequency magnetic fields (Delgado, Leal, Monteagudo and Garcia, 1982). There are at least 16 epidemiological studies that have made comparisons between VDT and non VDT work . From these epidemiological studies could be concluded that there is no association between spontaneous abortions, serious malformations or foetal growth retardation and the mothers VDT work during pregnancy (Bergqvist, 1993b). Furthermore at present an effect on line frequency magnetic fields from VDT work on the risk of spontaneous abortion is not established nor strong supported (Bergqvist, 1993b). However, there are different results dependent on comparison group, restriction of positive finding concerning net/image frequency magnetic fields, but there is nor firm evidence or an effect. There was one study with a positive association. Those who during pregnancy had worked with a VDU-model which had high net/image frequency magnetic field levels were significantly of higher risk of spontaneous abortion compared to those working with VDU-model showing low field levels (Bergqvist, 1993b).

58.6 Skin Disorders and VDT Work

Skin symptoms located to the face, related to VDT work have been reported from many countries. In a survey with the VDT operators complaining of skin symptoms were examined by occupational dermatologists, subjects with seborrhoeic eczema, acne and rosacea were over represented in the VDT exposed group (Lidén and Wahlberg, 1985). Another cross-sectional investigation did not reconfirm the former findings, there were no association between objective skin signs and VDT work (Berg, Lidén and Axelson, 1990) . In a longitudinal study an increased incidence of skin symptoms were found in VDT workers with intensive work (Bergqvist, Knave, Voss and Wibom, 1992). In a cross-sectional study psychosocial and organizational conditions were associated with skin symptoms and facial erythema while photosensitive skin type and low relative humidity were related to an increased prevalence of seborroeic eczema (Bergqvist and Wahlberg, 1985). Experimental studies have so far failed in double blind provocation tests with electromagnetic field to present evidence for alternating field as the cause of skin symptoms (Stenberg, 1995).

Skin problems and headache risk for VDT and non VDT users were similar but an indication of increased risk were found for certain groups and situations (Bergqvist, Knave, Voss and Wibom, 1992).

Stress have been suggested as one of the important determinants of skin of reactions. Higher levels of stress sensitive hormones during work were seen in employees with skin symptoms compared to VDT operators without skin symptoms (Stenberg, 1995). The findings were explained as a techno-stress in which the working conditions rather than the VDT work itself caused the symptoms (Berg, Arnetz, Lidén, Eneroth and Kallner, 1992) .

In summary there is a consistent pattern showing an exposure relationship between the amount of VDT work and prevalence of self reported skin symptoms (Stenberg, 1995). The cause of the symptom is still obscure. Stress as a risk factor is not reputed by any study (Stenberg, 1995).

58.7 References

Andersson G. B. J. (1987). Biomechanical aspects of sitting: an application to VDT terminals. *Behaviour and Information Technology*. 6:257-69.

Armstrong T.J., Chaffin D.B. (1979). Some biomechanical aspects of the carpal tunnel. *J Biomechanics*. 12:567-570.

Armstrong TJ, Chaffin D.B. (1979). Carpal tunnel syndrome and selected personal attributes. *J Occup Med*. 21:481-486.

Armstrong T.J., Castelli W.A., Evans F.G., Diaz-Perez R. (1984). Some histological changes in carpal tunnel contents and their biomechanical implications. *J Occup Med.*;26:197-201.

Armstrong T., Buckle P., Fine L., et al. (1993).A conceptual model for work-related neck and upper limb musculoskeletal disorders. *Scand J Work Environ Health*.19:73-84.

Arndt R. (1983). Working posture and musculoskeletal problems of video display terminal operators - review and reappraisal. *Am Ind Hyg Assoc J*. 44:437-446.

Bendix T, Jessen F. (1986). Wrist support during typing - a controlled, electromyographic study. *Applied Ergonomics*. 17:162-168.

Bentham P. (1991). *VDU terminal sickness*. London: Green Prin.

Berg M, Arnetz B, Lidén S, Eneroth P, Kallner A. (1992). Techno-stress. A psychophysiological study of employees with VDU-associated skin complaints. *JOM*.34:698-701.

Berg M, Lidén S, Axelson O. (1990).Facial skin complaints and work at visual display units; an epidemiologic study of office employees. *J Am Acad Dermatol*. 22:621-5.

Bergqvist U., Wahlberg J. E. (1994). Skin symptoms and disease during work with visual display terminals. *Contact Dermatitis*. 1994;30:197-204.

Bergqvist U, Knave B, Voss M, Wibom R. (1992).A longitudinal study of VDT work and health. *International Journal of Human Computer Interaction*. 4:197-219.

Bergqvist U, Wolgast E, Nilsson B, Voss M. (1995).Musculoskeletal disorders among visual display terminal workers – individual, ergonomic and work organizational factors. *Ergonomics*. 38:763-76.

Bergqvist U. (1993).Health problems during work with visual display terminals. *Arbete och Hälsa*. 28:1-59.

Bergqvist U. (1993). Pregnancy outcome and VDU work - a review. In: Luczak H, Cakir A, Cakir G, eds. *Work with display units 92*. Amsterdam: Elsevier Science Publisher B.V.

Bernard B., Sauter S., Fine L. J. (1994). Job task and psychosocial risk factors for work-related musculoskeletal disorders among newspaper employees. *Scand J Work Environ Health*. 20:417-26.

Bongers P. M., de Winter C. R. , Kompier M. A. , Hildebranndt V. H. (1993).Psychosocial factors at work and musculoskeletal disease. *Scand J Work Environ Health*. 19:297-312.

Chaffin D. B. (1973).Localized muscle fatigue - definition and measurement. *J Occup Med*. 15:346-54.

Checkoway H., Pearce N., Crawford-Brown D. J. (1989). *Research methods in occupational epidemiology*. New York: Oxford University Press.

Delgado J.M.R., Leal L., Monteagudo J.L., Garcia M.G. (1982). Embryological changes induced by weak, extremely low frequency electromagnetic fields. *Journal of Anatomy*. 134:533-51.

Dyrssen T, Svedenkrans M, Paasikivi J. (1989).Muskelträning vid besvär i nacke och skuldror effektiv behandling för att minska smärtan. *Läkartidningen*. (22):2216-2120.

Faucett J, Rempel D. (1994).VDT-related musculoskeletal symptoms: interactions between work posture and psychosocial work factors. *Am J Indust Med*. 26:597-612.

Frankel VH, Nordin M. (1980). *Basic biomechanics of the skeletal system*. Philadelphia: Lea & Febiger.

Franzblau A., Flaschner D., Albers J.W., Blitz S, Werner R., Armstrong T. (1993).Medical screening of office workers for upper extremity cumulative trauma disorders. *Arch Environ Health*. 48:164-70.

Grandjean E. (1984). Postures and design of VDT work-stations. *Behaviour and Information Technology*. 3:301-11.

Grieco A. (1986). Sitting posture: an old problem and a new one. *Ergonomics*. 1986;29:345-62.

Hadler N.M. (1989).Work-related disorders of the upper extremity Part II. *Occupational Problems in Medical Practice (Pfizer Laboratories)*. 1989;4:2-11.

Hadler N.M.(1990). Cumulative trauma disorders an iatrogenic concept. *J Occup Med.* 1990;32:38-41.

Hagberg M. (1994).Neck and shoulders disorders. In: Rosenstock L, Cullen MR, eds. *Textbook of occupational and environmental medicine*. Philadelphia: W.B. Saunders Company; 1994.

Hagberg M. (1996). Exposure considerations when evaluating musculoskeletal diagnoses. In: Mital A, Kreuger H, Kumar S, Menozzi M, Fernandez J, eds. *Advances in occupational ergonomics and safety*. Cincinnati: International Society for Occupational Ergonomics and Safety.

Hagberg M. (1996). Neck and arm disorders. *BMJ*. 313:419-22.

Hagberg M. (1995). The "mouse-arm syndrome" - concurrence of musculoskeletal symptoms and possible pathogenesis among VDU operators. In: Grieco A, Molteni G, Piccoli B, Occhipinti E, eds. *Work with display units 94*. Amsterdam: Elsevier Science B.V.

Hagberg M, Morgenstern H, Kelsh M. (1992). Impact of occupations and job tasks on the prevalence of carpal tunnel syndrome. *Scand J Work Environ Health*. 18:337-45.

Hagberg M, Silverstein B, Wells R, et al. (1995). *Work related musculoskeletal disorders (WMSDs): a reference book for prevention*. London: Taylor & Francis Ltd.

Hagberg M, Sundelin G. (1986). Discomfort and load on the upper trapezius muscle when operating a word-processor. *Ergonomics*. 1986;29(12):1637-1645.

Hales TR, Sauter S.L., Peterson M. R., et al. (1994). Musculoskeletal disorders among visual display terminal users in a telecommunications company. *Ergonomics*. 37:1603-21.

Honan M, Serina E, Tal R, Rempel D. (1995).Wrist Postures While Typing on a Standard and Split Keyboard. *Human Factors and Ergonomics Society 39th Annual Meeting*, October 1995, San Diego, California.

Hunting W, Läubli T, Grandjean E. (1981). Postural and visual loads at VDT workplaces. *Ergonomics*. 24:917-931.

Jayson M. I. (1996). Back pain. *BMJ*.313:355-8.

Karlqvist L, Hagberg M, Köster M, Wenemark M, Ånell R. (1996). Musculoskeletal symptoms among computer-assisted design (CAD) operators and evaluation of a self-assessment questionnaire. *Int J Occup Environ Health*. 2:185-94.

Karlqvist L, Hagberg M, Selin K. (1994). Variation in upper limb posture and movement during word processing with and without mouse use. *Ergonomics*. 37:1261-7.

Kilbom Å. (1987). Short- and long term effects of extreme physical inactivity: a review. In: Knave B, Widebäck PG, eds. *Work with display units 86*. Ansterdam: North-Holland.

Kurppa K, Waris P, Rokkanen P. (1979). Peritendinitis and tenosynovitis. *Scand J Work Environ & Health*. 5 Suppl 5:19-24.

Kroemer K. H. E. (1972). Human engineering the keyboard. *Human Factors*. 14:51-63.

Lidén C, Wahlberg J.E. (1985). Work with video display terminals among office employees. *Scand J Work Environ Health*. 11:489-93.

Lindman R., Eriksson A., Thornell L. E. (1991). Fiber type composition of the human female trapezius muscle. *Am J Anat*. 190:385-92.

Lindman R, Hagberg M, Ängqvist K-A, Söderlund K, Hultman E, Thornell L-E. (1991). Changes in muscle morphology in chronic trapezius myalgia. *Scand J Work Environ Health*. 17:347-55.

Lindman R, Hagberg M, Bengtsson A, Henriksson KG, Thornell L-E. (1995). Capillary structure and mitochondrial volume density in the trapezius muscle of chronic trapezius myalgia, fibromyalgia and healthy subjects. *J Musculoskeletal Pain*. 3:5-22.

Lundborg G. (1987). Nerve regeneration and repair. A review. *Acta Orthop Scand*. 58:145-169.

Rydevik B, Lundborg G, Bagge U. (1981). Effects of graded compression on intraneural blood flow. *Hand Surg*. 6:3-12.

Nathan P. A., Meadows K. D. , Doyle L. S. (1988). Occupation as a risk factor for impaired sensory conduction of the median nerve at the carpal tunnel. *Journal of Hand Surg*. 13:167-170.

Norman L. A. (1991). Mouse joint – another manifestation of an occupational epidemic. *West J Med*. 155:413-5.

Oxenburgh M. S. (1987). Musculoskeletal injuries occurring in word processor operators. In: Stevenson M, ed. *Readings in RSI: The ergonomics approach to repetition strain injuries*. New South Wales: University Press; 1987.

Pascarelli E. F., Kella J. J.(1993). Soft-tissue injuries related to use of the computer keyboard. *JOM*. 35:522-32.

Rempel D. (1995).Musculoskeletal Loading and Carpal Tunnel Pressure. Chapter 9, pp 123-132, in *Repetitive Motion Disorders of the Upper Extremity*. S. L. Gordon, et al. (Eds.). Am Acad Orthopaedic Surgeons, Rosemont, Illinois.

Rossignol A. M., Morse E. P., Summers V. M., Pagnotto L. D. (1987). Video display terminal use and reported health symptoms among Massachusetts clerical workers. *JOM*. 1987;29:112-8.

Sauter S. L., Schleifer L. M., Knutson S. J. (1987).Work posture, workstation design, and musculoskeletal discomfort in a VDT data entry task. *Human Factors*.33:151-67.

Stenberg B. (1995). Skin symptoms and VDT work - reports from three continents. In: Grieco A, Molteni G, Piccoli B, Occhipinti E, eds. *Work with display units 94*. Amsterdam: Elsevier Science B.V.

Stock S. R. (1991). Workplace ergonomic factors and the development of musculoskeletal disorders of the neck and upper limbs a meta-analysis. *Am J Indust Med*.19:87-107.

Sundelin G. (1993). Patterns of electromyographic shoulder muscle fatigue during MTM-paced repetitive arm work with and without pauses. *Int Arch Occup Environ Health*. 1993;64:485-93.

Susser M. (1991). What is cause and how do we know one? A grammar for pragmatic epidemiology. *Am J Epidemiol*. 1991;133:635-48.

Theorell T, Harms-Ringdahl K, Ahlberg-Hultin G, Westin B. (1991). Psychosocial job factors and symptoms from the locomotor system: a multicausal analysis. *Scand J Rehabil Med*. 23:165-73.

Werner C. O., (1983). Elmquist D, Ohlin T. Pressure and nerve lesions in the carpal tunnel. *Acta Orthop Scand*. 54:312-316.

WHO. (1985). Identification and control of work-related diseases. *Geneva: WHO Technical report*. 174:7-11.

Winkel J. (1987). On the significance of physical activity in sedentary work. In: Knave B., Wideback P. G, eds. *Work with display units 86*. Ansterdam: North-Holland.

Part IX

CSCW and Organizational Issues in HCI

Handbook of Human-Computer Interaction
Second, completely revised edition
M. Helander, T.K. Landauer, P. Prabhu (eds.)

Chapter 59

Research on Computer Supported Cooperative Work

Gary M. Olson and Judith S. Olson
University of Michigan
Michigan, USA

59.1 Introduction

The emergence of ubiquitous computer networking and the blurring of distinctions between computing and communication technologies have made possible many new ways for people to interact and work together. Information in many forms can be shared worldwide. It is possible for teams whose members are geographically dispersed to carry out coordinated work. Organizations can undertake complex information-intensive activities that span time and distance. Computer Supported Cooperative Work (CSCW) is the name of the research area that studies the use of computing and communication technologies to support group and organizational activity. Other terms used for this concept have included collaboration technology, organizational computing, and group support systems (GSS). Other chapters in this volume review these new technologies. Our goal is to review the research that illuminates how these technologies affect human behavior. Because the area is new, we will first review the methods used to do such research and then review a representative sample of results that have used these methods.

CSCW as a field has emerged more recently than human-computer interaction (HCI), and therefore in many ways is less mature. Card (1991) has characterized the growth of the field of HCI as following four schematic stages typical of development of systems technologies in general. The four stages are illustrated in Figure 1. According to this scheme, HCI has moved through the following stages:

- *Stage 1* Building illustrative *point systems*, or examples of what can be done to support work with computers.
- *Stage 2* Evaluating, comparing, and reviewing systems so that we understand the *dimensions* by which systems and work vary, affecting the ultimate success of a system.
- *Stage 3* Analyzing the dimensions so that we can characterize the *relationships* in more detail.
- *Stage 4* Articulating the *models and laws* that govern behavior with systems.

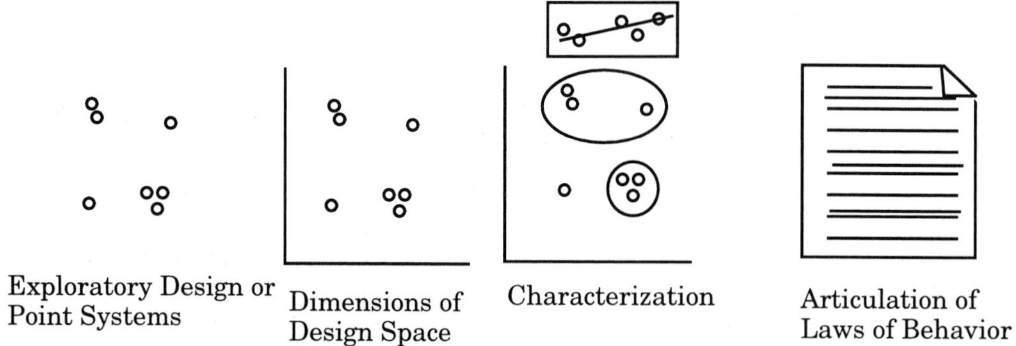

Figure 1. The four stages of the development of the field of HCI, from building example systems to articulating laws of behavior.

The field of CSCW has mostly been at the stage of building point systems. Many more systems have been built than have been evaluated. Some attempts at understanding the dimensions by which the systems and impacts vary have been proposed, but the efforts to turn these dimensionalizations into deeper understanding are scattered and inconclusive.

Proponents of user-centered design argue that an understanding of the work situation, the group members, and the task specifics is critical for designing new systems (e.g., Olson and Olson, 1991). This is difficult when the antecedent knowledge is missing. One reason for this state of affairs is that the prerequisite understanding of groups and organizations is itself only just emerging. There is a weaker base of understanding from social and organizational psychology than HCI had from cognitive psychology at a similar stage of development. As a result, a considerable amount of research that appears under the rubric of CSCW is basic research about the nature of groups, organizations, and work But trial and error from creative system builders is too slow a discovery process. What is required is a better understanding of the nature of group and organizational work, a better articulation of the design space of technology features, and evaluation of systems in use that leads to a theory of CSCW. These in turn can help direct subsequent invention of new ways to do group work.

In the review of CSCW research that follows, we first describe some of the methods and issues involved in CSCW research. We next consider a conceptual perspective that provides a framework for describing the human use of CSCW systems. We then turn to a brief survey of recent research results. Finally, we discuss some general research issues for the future.

59.2 Varieties of Research Methods

Research on CSCW technologies has as its goal learning about what people do with the technologies (process) and what effects these have on the people, their tasks, their relationships, and their organizations (outcome). The methods we review in this section represent a variety of approaches to achieving these goals. Each method has strengths and weaknesses, and each has substantial methodological literatures about how to use them. We can only briefly describe each method, but include references to more extensive discussions of each of them.

CSCW research comes from many different traditions: anthropology, sociology, organizational psychology, cognitive psychology, social psychology, management science, information systems, computer science, and others. As a result, the research literature on CSCW is diverse, and can be difficult to assimilate. Controversies in the field are often as much methodological as conceptual. It is important to understand the range of methods used, both to conduct research and to interpret the emerging literature.

Survey. A survey is the administration of a set of questions to a large sample of respondents. Often the questions provide fixed alternatives from which the respondent chooses one. They can be administered through a written document presented to the respondent on paper or, increasingly, on-line. Alternatively, they can be administered verbally, either in person or over the telephone. Surveys put a premium on gathering a very large sample, and the data from surveys are often subjected to extensive statistical analyses. There typically is no opportunity for a respondent to expand

upon their answer (in contrast, say, to an interview). There is an extensive literature on survey construction, administration, and analysis (e.g., Hessler, 1992; Schwarz and Sudman, 1996; Bradburn and Sudman, 1988; Sudman, Bradburn and Schwarz, 1996). For example, it is well known that survey results can be influenced dramatically by the precise wording of questions and alternatives (Sudman and Bradburn, 1982; Clark and Schober, 1992).

Interview. In comparison to a survey, an interview often involves more open-ended queries of respondents. An interview can be quite formal, with the questions all specified in advance and asked in a standard order. Alternatively, the interview can be unstructured, with only a general set of topics to guide the interviewer and the detailed questions arising from the conversation with the respondent. As with surveys, there is an extensive literature on how to design, conduct, and analyze interviews (e.g., Whyte and Whyte, 1984; Sommer and Sommer, 1991).

Diaries. An individual can keep a detailed record of what they did and what they observed in their work. This can be an effective way to capture long-term processes in a group or organization. However, diaries have the obvious limitation that they depend on the vagaries of self-reporting and selectivity (Conrath, 1973; Higgins, McClean and Conrath, 1985).

Ethnography. The ethnographic method comes from anthropology. It is the most misunderstood method among CSCW researchers, who tend to call any unstructured field observations an ethnographic study. But it has a much more precise meaning than this. As Spradley (1979) defines it, "Ethnography is the work of describing a culture. The essential core of this activity aims to understand another way of life *from the native point of view* [p. 3, emphasis added]." Ethnographic methods were at first applied almost exclusively to cultures very different from our own. But more recently these methods have been used to study work settings and other special environments within our own Western culture. For instance, Vaughan (1996) reported an ethnographic study of the history of decision making in the U.S. space shuttle program, providing an in-depth view of the way the world looked to the engineers and managers involved in the decision to launch the Challenger that led to its accident. Reports of ethnographic studies are usually qualitative and narrative in form, and indeed Anderson (1994) makes this point in some detail using CSCW examples. Spradley (1979, 1980) and Emerson, Fretz and Shaw (1995) offer practical advice on how to conduct ethnographic studies.

Analytic Field Study. An analytic field study is an observational study where events that are observed are coded for the purpose of developing a quantitative characterization of the observations. For instance, in a series of field studies, we have made video tapes of meetings of software design groups, transcribed these video tapes, developed coding schemes for the content of the conversations, and described and analyzed this material quantitatively through these coding categories (Olson, Olson, Carter, and Storrøsten, 1992; Olson, Herbsleb and Rueter, 1994). Importantly, the coding schemes were developed with extensive attention to their validity and reliability.

Case Studies. At one extreme, surveys or polls often interrogate hundreds or even thousands of respondents in order to obtain statistical precision about some question. At the other extreme, a case study examines a single or small number of cases in great depth. It is still a very useful research method, especially for the early exploratory phases of investigation. The detailed analyses of a case study can expose potential unexpected relationships that had not been noticed before, or can find counterexamples to claims made by theories. For example, Orlikowski (1992b; Orlikowski and Gash, 1994) conducted an in-depth study of the adoption of Lotus Notes at a large professional consulting services company, uncovering the importance of the fit of a system to the organization's incentive schemes. Yin (1989) is an excellent resource regarding the conduct of case studies.

Experiment. An experiment is a controlled set of observations in which subjects are given a specific task to do under one of several different conditions, and quantitative comparisons are made of performance. Subjects are assigned randomly to experimental conditions, and many other precautions are taken to avoid confounding unintentional variables with the independent variables of interest. Because true experiments control for extraneous variables and can follow time courses of effects, they generally allow us to make inferences about causality. There is an extensive literature on how to design, conduct, and analyze experiments (e.g., Bower and Clapper, 1989). On the down side, the laboratory, while giving the researcher control over many aspects of the setting, is often quite different from the field. Generally the laboratory is a setting to be used for singular effects for small groups, though imaginative researchers have brought aspects of organizations into the laboratory as well (Weick, 1965; Cohen and Bacdayan, 1994). We have often advocated a mixed strategy in which laboratory and field studies are linked in explicit ways within a program of research (Olson and Olson, in press a).

Quasi-experiment. A quasi-experiment is an experiment in the field where subjects are not randomly assigned to conditions. Such studies take advantage of differences that occur in the real world. For instance, we might compare the productivity of two organizations in the same industry that adopted different CSCW technologies. Or we might look at the performance of groups before and after they adopted a particular meeting room technology. Turner (1984) studied the effects of two different user interfaces used in the Social Security Administration, finding that claims representatives with a more efficient user interface were substantially less satisfied with their working conditions because they had to process so many more claims. Quasi-experiments can be extremely useful but, in contrast to true experiments, do not allow clear inference of causality because a myriad of potentially confounding factors differ between the conditions from natural causes.

Longitudinal Studies. A cross-sectional study is one that looks at phenomena at a particular point in time, whereas a longitudinal study is one that traces phenomena over time. As a number of theorists have noted (e.g., Orlikowski, 1992a; DeSanctis and Poole, 1994;), technology effects are often slow to emerge and depend on the interplay of complex social and organizational factors, making longitudinal research critical to understanding the effects of new technology systems.

Longitudinal studies can be expensive to carry out for phenomena that change slowly. To ameliorate this problem a variety of hybrid paradigms have been developed that allow mixtures of cross-sectional and longitudinal data collection (Baltes, Reese and Nesselroade, 1977). When the behavior of different entities are examined at different points in their individual histories there is always the risk of confounding developmental stage with cohort effects. In a cross section of people that differ in their age, each cohort developed in a different historical period, and the unique factors of these periods can have strong effects independent of developmental stage. For example, Baby Boomers and people who grew up in the Depression differ not only on age but on many attitudes about risk that reflect the historical periods in which they grew up. As a concrete example, these cohort effects could have substantial effects on their patterns of use of the Internet.

Historical Studies. Looking at technology historically can often reveal patterns that suggest important social and cultural factors. Indeed, long-term effects of technologies on organizations can only be studied this way. An example of this kind of study comes from the management literature, where Yates (1989) looked at the role of office technologies in the development of organizations in several industries.

Simulation and Formal Modeling. Computer simulations and mathematical models of groups or organizations have a number of uses. They can provide precise, testable theories of complex phenomena that can be evaluated against empirical data. Once validated they can be used to derive predictions about phenomena not yet observed, guiding subsequent empirical investigations that can lead to further theory validation or revision. They can also be used to do sensitivity analyses and other purely theoretical investigations about the character of collections of theories. These methods are not yet widespread in CSCW, but some interesting recent examples are Levitt, Cohen, Kunz, Nass, Christiansen and Jin (1994) and Prietula and Carley (1994).

59.2.1 Level of Analysis

There are a number of different levels of analysis possible in CSCW studies. Some common levels are:

Individual. Systems designed to support groups and organizations can be examined from the perspective of an individual. How is an individual's work affected by use of such systems? Questions of user interface, learnabilty, participation, leadership, etc., focus on the individual level.

Group, team. This is one of the most common levels of analysis in CSCW research, since many systems have been developed to support the kinds of teams that have become so popular in industry.

Organization. This can cover a number of different grain sizes, from a division or department of a company to something as broad as General Motors or IBM or the University of Michigan.

Industry. This is a level of analysis that is common in economics. It is seen in CSCW research that tracks the spread of new tools in different segments or looks at issues such as the "productivity paradox" (Landauer, 1995).

Other levels of analysis include family, occupation, nation, or culture. We will focus on groups and organizations since these are the most common in CSCW research.

59.2.2 Measures of Group or Organizational Performance

All of the various methods just described can be used to learn more about what people do with the technologies (process) and what effects these had on the people, their tasks, their relationships, and their organizations (outcome). Information technology effects can be complex, and therefore it is important to look at multiple measures of performance in order to understand fully what has happened. For instance, measures of task *outcome* and individual or group *satisfaction* often go in different directions (McLeod, 1992; Olson, Olson, Storrøsten and Carter, 1993), suggesting that relying on just one or the other measure would give a misleading picture of what was going on.

Outcome. The initial focus in studying CSCW systems is often the outcome or result of using a new technology. For groups, this could be a measure of the quality of the work they performed, assessed either by having judges score the work for overall quality or by assessing some characteristic of the work (e.g., number of ideas). In contrast to *task outcome*, we could assess *group outcome*. Individuals in the group might vary in how well they understand and/or agree with the group's product, and how satisfied they were about the process they engaged in (e.g., frustrations about not being heard). Particular experiences also change the individuals in the group in what they know (some acquire new skills or knowledge), how willing they are to work with each other again, loyalty to the organization, and individual status.

We can also measure outcomes at the organizational level. There has been extensive discussion about organizational *productivity* in relation to information technology (e.g., Strassmann, 1990; Landauer, 1995). Other organizational characteristics of interest include learning, flexibility, and innovation (e.g., Nonaka and Takeuchi, 1995), customer satisfaction (Fornell, 1995), any of a variety of economic indicators, or human resource outcomes (hiring, retention). The extent to which a technology is actually adopted and used is another organizational outcome of interest (e.g., Grudin, 1988; Orlikowski, 1992b).

Process. If we want to understand not just what happened as a result of deploying technology but why, we must examine the details of how the technology was used and how it changed what people do. Process analysis is usually more difficult than measuring outcomes, but it is only through process analysis that we can learn why outcomes were affected in the way they were. Recent discussions of structuration theory have emphasized how subtle and multidimensional process analysis can be (e.g., DeSanctis and Poole, 1994; Orlikowski, 1992a). When looking at how groups or organizations behave, we can focus on several kinds of factors: the progress of the task, the communication process, and the interpersonal process, such as role taking.

For groups, task progress includes how time is spent (e.g., Olson, Olson, Carter and Storrøsten, 1992, activity "state transition diagrams"), the content of the discussion (the argument structure, how many ideas are generated and evaluated, etc.), the general task allocation across group members (whether the work is done interactively or in parallel), and some measure of efficiency.

Communication processes include how much clarification is needed, the turntaking and management of work flow, what non-verbal communication occurs, and measures of social bonding or affect (digressions, attacks, socializing). One can also identify episodes of cooperation and conflict (e.g., Process Analysis, Bales, 1950), general judgment of the affect of an interchange, and simple measures of participation.

The easiest processes to measure are those involving overt, explicit activity, such as conversation, gestures, and general activity. It is more difficult to assess the long-term, more gradual changes in knowledge, routines, or social structure. These more covert characteristics of groups and organizations may be among the most important in determining the ultimate effectiveness of information technology.

Process can also be examined at a number of time scales. Studies of group interaction typically focus on the unfolding of group process over minutes and hours, whereas organizational processes unfold over days, weeks, and months. Very different observational strategies are needed for these different time scales. It has become quite common in studies of groups to use video taped records of their activity to study process. With appropriate time sampling such methods can be used over longer terms, but it is more common to study organizational processes though such methods as dia-

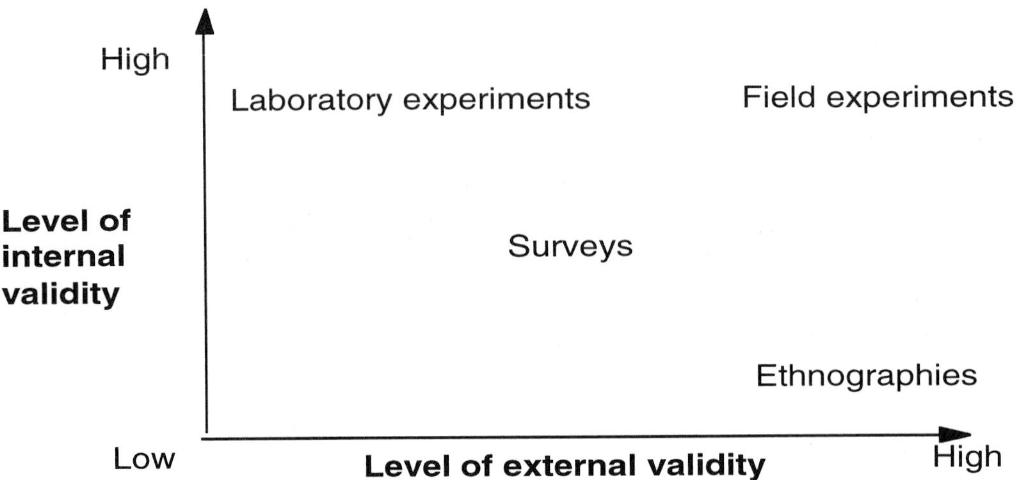

Figure 2. Validity grid.

ries, interviews, communication networks (e.g., Baker, 1994), and tracking of various kinds of records.

59.2.3 Internal and External Validity

Methods differ in how validly they reveal phenomena. There are two important kinds of validity. *External* validity refers to the generalizability of the findings from the setting that was investigated to other settings or situations. Research in natural settings such as ethnographies has high external validity, while laboratory experiments often have low external validity. *Internal* validity refers to the extent to which alternative explanations for the behavior observed can be eliminated. Laboratory experiments have high internal validity whereas ethnographies have low. Figure 2 suggests how various methods generally compare on these two forms of validity.

It is possible to move methods a bit in this space. For instance, some programs of research have taken great pains to develop laboratory situations that mimic what is observed in the field in an effort to increase the external validity of the lab work (e.g., Olson, Olson, Storrøsten and Carter, 1993), moving it up the external validity dimension. Specialized research methods such as causal analysis (Heise, 1975) allow causal inferences in field studies, moving it up on the internal validity dimension.

Different audiences for research view the two kinds of validities differently. Managers or customers usually rate external validity very high, whereas researchers are often especially concerned with internal validity. Of course this picture hides a lot of additional complexity. A manager may want to know how closely a result fits his or her exact situation, a very specific level of external validity. A researcher or designer or marketer might most want to know how wide a range of situations a result fits, a very broad kind of external validity.

59.2.4 Special Problems in Doing CSCW Research

As hard as it is to do research on HCI, it is even harder in CSCW. There are a number of special problems in carrying out research on CSCW systems that contribute to this.

Critical Mass of Users. Evaluation of systems whose principal function is to share information within an organization usually requires that a critical mass of users adopt the technology. For instance, the value of systems like e-mail, fax, or desktop video for an organization can be difficult to evaluate until enough people have them. This mass adoption can be difficult to achieve for prototype systems or those that do not yet smoothly fit the full work context.

System Reliability. Whether one is doing laboratory studies of small teams or field studies in large organizations, system reliability is critical in order to be able to proceed with usage studies. This requires a degree of system hardening not usual in computer science research. For instance, in our own laboratory we have been prevented from carrying out empirical studies of

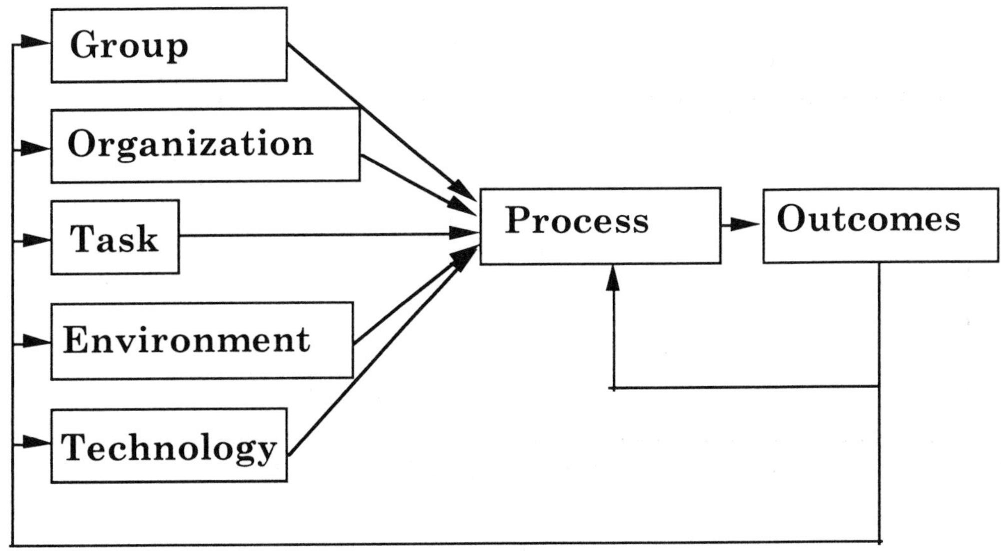

Figure 3. Overall view of aspects important in understanding groupware.

small groups using shared editors when the groups could not finish a 90-minute task because the software crashed. Studies of new kinds of electronic mail filtering systems were precluded because the systems were not reliable enough for users in an organization to be willing to adopt. The cost of this can be quite high, since getting networked software to be reliable can be extremely difficult. Yet without such reliability empirical studies are difficult to do.

Indirect Effects. The introduction of new technologies into groups or organizations often produces indirect effects that were not anticipated (Sproull and Kiesler, 1991; Tenner, 1996). Researchers usually focus their attention on those areas where they expect effects, and as a result may miss the indirect effects that can be more important. Moreover, many of the indirect effects may involve tacit phenomena that take special efforts to measure. It is not enough to focus on the efficiency of work. The environment into which technologies are placed is reactive, and it changes as people change their behavior, as new roles emerge, and as organizations themselves change. People no longer behave the same way they did before the technology appeared. It often takes a while for the second-level effects to appear, making it all the harder to anticipate them. For example, ATMs were introduced to reduce the labor costs associated with banking transactions. But by making transactions easier customers radically changed their behavior, *increasing* the number of transactions (Attewell, 1994). The resulting increase in back office activity to handle all of the transactions washed out the cost savings in tellers. Similarly, word processing led to more time and effort spent on revising manuscripts and CAD software led to greater numbers of intermediate designs, with no improvement in either case in the overall quality of the work (Attewell, 1994).

59.3 Conceptual Framework for CSCW Studies

One reason it is difficult to make progress in this field is that research has been done in a myriad of situations, making systematic comparisons very difficult. Groups, organizations, tasks, and tools vary in many ways, and various combinations of these affect the success of work with technology. Figure 3 presents a scheme for describing the ways situations differ whose aim is to help clarify research contributions and allow them to be compared appropriately. This scheme, developed by Olson and Olson (in press b), is based on earlier frameworks, especially those of Shaw (1981), McGrath, (1984), Hackman (1987), Morgan and Lassiter (1992), and Kraemer and Pinsonneault (1990). Although most studies have looked at the left-to-right flow of effects, we have included feedback loops to account for complexities of process that have been stressed in structuration theory, wherein the use of a technology itself changes the context of subsequent technology usage

(Giddens, 1979; Cohen, 1989; Orlikowski, 1992a; DeSanctis and Poole, 1994). This framework is a step toward the dimensionalization of CSCW research, a key step on the way toward maturity (Olson, Card, Landauer, Olson, Malone and Leggett, 1993).

It is all too easy to focus on the interesting properties of new technologies and not think very deeply about the human contexts into which this technology will be placed. Despite repeated pleas for user-centered design (e.g., Norman and Draper, 1986; Olson and Olson, 1991), most technologies are still designed and installed into human settings with little or no attention to the subtle details of human groups and organizations. As a result, we acquire stories of failure and frustration at a faster rate than success cases.

This problem is especially salient for systems intended to support groups and organizations. Our level of understanding of groups and organizations is much more limited than our understanding of individual behavior. This is because the study of groups and organizations is inherently more difficult. Experiments which can lead to the understanding of causality are difficult or impossible to do. Many relevant processes unfold over long periods of time, making their capture and analysis hard. And much that happens is implicit, requiring difficult analysis to tease out. But as we will see, progress is being made on all these fronts.

59.3.1 Characteristics of Work Groups

Groups themselves differ on a number of important features that determine the success or failure not only of the group's work itself but also of the adoption of the technology. Individuals in the groups differ in their skill, ability and knowledge, their personalities, and their enduring motivations and agendas. These determine, among other things, the amount of effort the person will expend in a setting, which in turn can determine their tolerance for various new, but as yet imperfect tools.

Much of the ensuing behavior is then determined by how these individuals relate in the group. The individuals in the group may be homogeneous or not, they may have different levels of knowledge of each other's abilities and motivations, their personalities may mesh or not, and they will have an established or unknown level of trust. Over time groups establish patterns about how they communicate with each other (e.g., whether they are generally approachable and available). And, the roles, status or power of the individuals can influence expectations and behavior (Hackman and Morris, 1975).

These group characteristics change systematically as a group develops (Kraut, Galegher and Egido, 1988). Early in their formation, groups spend time learning about each other--each member's knowledge and skills, as well as coming to trust each other. Krauss and Fussell (1990) and Gabarro (1990) reported that groups that know each other well use shorthand language to communicate, and are much more successful than newly formed groups in communicating over a variety of channels (e.g., by e-mail, delayed video conferencing).

As groups mature, roles, power relationships and communication patterns also develop. The fit between group characteristics and the demand characteristics of the technology is among the major determinants of the success or failure of groupware (e.g., DeSanctis and Poole, 1994). For example, some decision support systems allow anonymous entries, allowing people to contribute regardless of their status or power. This presumably makes the end product of the discussion better, since all expertise in the group can be contributed. However, there is no advantage of this anonymity in a group of peers who know and trust each other. Similarly, The Coordinator, an e-mail system that requires the communicants to declare what they expect the reader of the message to do (acknowledge, accept) is seen as a success in some highly structured groups and a failure in more free-flowing groups (Winograd, 1988).

59.3.2 Characteristics of Organizations

Organizations represent a key level of aggregation in the study of CSCW systems. One definition of an organization is that it is a system comprised of people and technology for developing shared purposes and translating them into action.[1] Social technology includes such things as rules, procedures, and routines, whereas physical technology includes such things as buildings, layout, furnishings, and communication infrastructure. Organizations are comprised of multiple actors most often having diverse capabilities and goals. Organizations are characterized by a series of relations among these actors (such as authority), with communication and shared meaning as crucial elements of these relations. Since organizations depend on communication, advances in communication technology are inevitably a key component in the emergence of new organizational forms. The large government and business organizations that are the hallmark of this century

[1] Our characterization of organizations in this paragraph comes from conversations with our colleague Michael Cohen.

are the products of telegraphy, telephony, and the plethora of modern information technologies. It is hardly surprising, therefore, that new CSCW technologies are candidates for producing changes in organizations.

While there are many views of organizations and organizing that one could raise with respect to CSCW technologies, we briefly describe some of the key ideas having to do with information processing and coordination. March and Simon (1958) stressed that the function of organizations is the management and processing of large amounts of information. This is a useful perspective for thinking about computer support of organizations, since computing's most natural role in an organization is to facilitate this information processing function through modifying the constraints on the sharing of information.

The description of organizations as information processing entities has led to the adoption of a broad range of cognitive constructs to characterize them. In both the scholarly and popular literature one finds extensive discussions of the characteristics of organizational cognition: knowledge (e.g., Nonaka and Takeuchi, 1995), collective intelligence (e.g., Weick, 1993; Weick and Roberts, 1993), routines (e.g., Cyert and March, 1963; Cohen and Bacdayan, 1994), learning (e.g., Senge, 1990; Argyris, 1992), and memory (e.g., Walsh and Ungson,1991; Walsh, 1995). These descriptions fit in nicely with general discussions of distributed cognition (e.g., Hutchins, 1990, 1991, 1995a, 1995b; Norman, 1993). Such descriptions are natural ones for analysts of CSCW systems.

One important characteristic of cognitive activity that is as true of organizations as of individual minds is that some of the knowledge is explicit and easily accessible while other knowledge is more tacit and procedural (Anderson, 1982). Organizational *routines* are "multi-actor, interlocking, reciprocally-triggered sequences of actions" that are "a major source of the reliability and speed of organizational performance (Cohen and Bacdayan, 1994, p. 554)." One example they give comes from the Cuban missile crisis. Russian troops were being brought to Cuba on civilian transport ships and were dressed in civilian clothes to hide the fact that they were soldiers. Nonetheless, when they disembarked on the piers in Havana they formed into orderly columns and marched away in formation, in full view of the cameras of the U.S. spy planes that were observing all of these comings and goings. Marching in formation was how the soldiers knew to move, an organizational routine that was difficult to overcome even when instructed to do so.

As Cohen and Bacdayan (1994) describe, routines at the organizational level are naturally built from cognitive procedures at the individual level, and share the characteristics of tacitness and automaticity. They report an ingenious study in which they brought the phenomena of routines into the laboratory for careful examination. Pairs of subjects silently played a card game that required cooperation, and over time the pairs learned patterns of movements for the cards that they effortlessly employed as different situations came up. The play of the pairs of subjects exhibited many of the properties of routines seen in organizations, such as gradual acquisition, resistance to change, automatic invocation in response to social and physical cues, and limited access to verbal descriptions by the participants. More generally, these behaviors are important aspects of the organizational response to new technologies.

Another key aspect of organizational life is the multiplicity of goals that the participants in the organization are pursuing. These goals are reflected in the culture of the organization, including such things as authority relationships, reward systems, and career paths. The complexity of goals and rewards has often been ignored in decisions to adopt CSCW systems. In an already classic study, Orlikowski's (1992b) case study of the introduction of Lotus Notes into a consulting organization highlighted the conflict between the information sharing assumptions of Notes and the career-enhancing retention of information by individual consultants. Grudin (1988) pointed out that a common problem in organizations is that those who benefit from information technology may be different from those whose work is changed by it, leading to differential incentives for using the technology.

59.3.3 Characteristics of the Task

There are a number of ways in everyday English to describe tasks, such as brainstorming, design, teaching, or decision making. But these are at the wrong level of granularity for determining exactly how various kinds of technology can help or hinder what people do. We use here a more fine-grained set of descriptors, types of activities that can be matched with appropriate technologies. This is the list from the synthesis developed for the framework in Olson and Olson (in press b).

Tasks involve different types of material. For example, the objects of work could be physical (e.g., the brain in neurosurgery, Nardi, Kuchinsky, Whittaker, Leichner and Schwarz, 1995), digital (e.g., in CAD models or code walkthroughs), or ethereal (e.g., gestures, such as diagrams on "airboards", Olson and Olson, 1991). Video may be needed to share physical or gestural objects, but is less well suited to sharing digital objects (though we and others have seen subjects point cameras at computer screens as a cheap and fast way to share screens). Tasks also differ on how difficult or easy they are, whether the problem or goal has a large number of interconnected constraints and whether or not it has familiar components. The usefulness of accessible knowledge stores (a digital library, for example, or a set of similar cases on which one can draw) or modeling systems (e.g., an expert advisor or a financial model) are dependent on these features of the work.

Tasks also differ on the core activity, which can determine the style of interaction required among group members. These core activities can involve planning and orchestrating the team members work, gathering and/or generating information, explaining and sharing information, discussing in order to come to agreement, and planning and producing a product. Some of these core activities require tight interaction (e.g., discussing to come to agreement) and others do not (e.g., generating information or ideas). These may determine whether the group needs to be interacting in real time or could work asynchronously. This in turn will affect the success of the work if done asynchronously, for example, through Lotus Notes, or by real-time conversation (e.g., over the phone).

The relationships between various subtasks given to individuals in groups are similarly either tightly coupled (one cannot begin or continue without the output of the other) or loosely coupled (work can effectively proceed in parallel) (see Weick, 1979). Again, technologies can either support or inhibit these aspects of work.

One somewhat difficult aspect to fit into a framework such as this is the cooperative/conflictful nature of the task/group interaction. If the individuals have incompatible goals or motivations (as labor negotiations do), then a policy or planning situation can have a great deal more discussion and affect than in groups engaged in cooperative planning. Again, one can imagine ways in which various communication technologies (e.g., the presence or absence of video) would fit or not fit depending on the contentiousness of the task/group.

59.3.4 Characteristics of the Environment

Many aspects of the physical environment affect group work and the technologies' effectiveness for support. The most important is the physical distance between group members. Allen (1977) and more recently Kraut, Egido, and Galegher (1990) showed elegantly that the closer people are together physically the more likely they are to collaborate. Many CSCW technologies are designed to overcome these barriers. But nothing today has yet duplicated the richness and ease of co-located work. Interestingly, even when people are co-located, distance and angle of regard affect interaction and thus work. Hall (1966) has shown that people prefer to sit at 90 degrees when they are collaborative, and that any seated distance over 6 feet changes who people will talk with. For instance, in meeting rooms (computer supported or not) people will talk to the person next to them as opposed to the people across the table if the table is more than 6 feet across.

Interestingly, the one variable about distance work that technology cannot overcome is contextual *time*, such as when in the day the interaction occurs (early morning for those in Hong Kong is early evening for those in Ann Arbor, both participating in a "simultaneous" video-based distance learning experience). Furthermore, holidays, celebrations, and moods of weather affect the local participant in ways that may be opaque to the distant group member.

59.3.5 Characteristics of the Technology

Technology to support group work today has become increasingly varied. We separate here technologies that support *conversation* from those that support the *shared work object*. People co-develop work products, like proposals, white papers, budgets, etc. In today's world of distributed group members, these products are often faxed, sent by FTP or e-mail attachments, or stored on a shared file server so others can retrieve them. In addition, the group will converse about those objects, using face-to-face meetings, e-mail, voice mail, and discussion databases. The features that groups need in these technologies differ.

Technologies to Support Conversation. Conversation conducted face-to-face has some natural characteristics that are severely disturbed when we converse using technology at long distances (Clark, 1996). What changes is what is visible (both the field of view and its clarity, if something is visible at all) and what is audible (again its clarity and conveyance of the spatial origin). Most important, perhaps, is the delay that technologies impose. We know that decoupling the auditory and visible streams disrupts comprehension of the meaning, and that if the auditory stream is delayed more than a half second, conversational turn taking is disrupted (Fussell and Benimoff, 1995). When we connect remotely, there are control and reciprocity issues as well (e.g., who initiates a conversation, your ability to signal willingness to converse, control over what can be seen with remote video, and whether I see you when you see me). In addition, there are issues about the effect on conversation or status if one has a narrower channel in which to communicate than others do (e.g., having an only audio teleconference, when others are face-to-face). These issues are likely to come into strong play when the group includes individuals with different power and status.

Although we often think that the richer the channel the more effective it will be for group communication (e.g., Daft and Lengel, 1986), there are striking counter examples. People are better at detecting a remote liar if they hear rather than see the person (Krauss, 1981), and inappropriate judgments from dress or demeanor are prevented if one cannot see the remote person. Often, the more leisurely pace in production of an e-mail message allows a non-native speaker time to compose well-formed sentences.

Technologies to Support the Shared Work Object. Group work involves not only conversation, but the objects to support the work (e.g., meeting minutes, project plan, draft proposal, item to be repaired, CAD drawing). Tools that have been built for creating and editing shared objects vary widely on important features that interact with group members' style and the task they are engaged in. Whether everyone has equal access to see and edit the work object likely interacts importantly with power, status, and skill differences in groups. The fit of the tool to the material of the work also determines its success. For example, although linear text is effective for orchestrated presentations such as a proposal, it is not an effective representation for groups doing project management. Subtle differences can emerge in the correspondence between the participants' views of the object and the ability to align their work. Turntaking and the ability to capture others' attention vary in systems that have no telepointer and those that allow only one person to edit at a time. Furthermore, today's technology is woefully inadequate when one wishes to move from one phase of work to the other, from asynchronous to synchronous and back, and from brainstorming to organizing to discussing.

59.4 Research on Specific CSCW Systems

We turn now to a brief review of the kinds of CSCW systems that have been built and evaluated. We have sampled the research literature in order to illustrate some of the issues. These studies are typical of Stage 1 in Figure 1, where the focus is on evaluating a specific system. Happily, in some areas, enough studies have been done for general results to emerge.

Group Support Systems for Face-to-Face Work. A wide variety of systems have been developed to support different kinds of face-to-face group work. Because a lot of this work arose from Management Information Systems departments in Business Schools, these systems often embody prescriptions about how to help groups of managers solve business problems.

Group Decision Support Systems (GDSS) are one very common kind of face-to-face system. They emerged from decision support systems designed to aid individual decision makers by adding a series of group tools to combine the ideas of many, to coordinate the criteria used, and to make a collective decision. Most GDSSs structure the interaction among group members. For example, they require the group to separate their brainstorming activity from organizing the ideas and evaluating them. The systems prescribe groups not only to phase their work but to use various tools to help them in each phase. (e.g., Nunamaker, Dennis, Valacich, Vogel and George, 1991). Some GDSSs require the services of a facilitator and someone to retrieve, run, and store results from one subtask to the other.

Other group support systems, such as Colab (Stefik, Foster, Bobrow, Kahn, Lanning and Suchman, 1987), ShrEdit (McGuffin and Olson, 1992), and a commercial product, Aspects (Group Technologies, 1990) are more free form, allowing groups to use a shared workspace as they wish. Application sharing through the use of Shared-X, Timbuktu, or Point-to-Point is a simple but powerful collaborative tool. These more permissive systems are often based on the analogy of traditional group tools such as shared whiteboards or flipcharts, allowing the groups to determine flexibly when they want to engage in various phases of work and how they wish to orchestrate themselves.

A number of experimental evaluations of group support systems and several literature reviews attempt to draw general conclusions from this work (McLeod, 1992; Kraemer and Pinsoneault, 1990; Hollingshead and McGrath, in press). McLeod (1992) used the methodologically important approach of a formal meta-analysis (Rosenthal, 1984) to survey a series of experimental studies mostly conducted in the 1980s. These studies looked at a range of GDSS and other face-to-face systems. She found that such systems typically increase decision quality, equality of participation, and degree of task focus, while they increase the time needed to make a decision, decrease consensus and satisfaction among the participants.

More recent studies have found similar results, but have extended the analysis to include process as well as outcome measures. For instance, Olson, Olson, Storrøsten and Carter (1993) found groups using an unstructured group editor had higher quality outcomes but lower satisfaction than groups using a whiteboard and paper. A detailed process analysis showed that the computer-supported groups explored fewer options than the whiteboard groups, suggesting that the tool helped to keep the groups more focused on the core issues, to waste less time on less important topics, and to capture what was said as they went (reduced process losses, in the sense of Steiner, 1972).

Group Authoring Systems. Much group work currently consists of individuals writing documents (e.g., system requirements, policy proposals, project proposals) and then soliciting comments from many different people and making changes, iterating the comment/change cycle again. Today this activity involves circulating multiple paper drafts and spending time entering agreed upon edits. Numerous systems have been developed to support collaborative writing (e.g., ForComment — Edwards, Levine, Kurland, 1986; Quilt — Leland, Fish, and Kraut, 1988; the PREP Editor — Neuwirth, Kaufer, Chandhok, and Morris, 1990; SEPIA, Haake and Wilson, 1992; Posner and Baecker, 1993, present an extensive list of such tools).

Writing consists of several kinds of activities: generating the ideas, planning the text, generating the text, and revising the text (Flower and Hayes, 1978). While these activities are often intermingled, one could imagine that different kinds of tools might be needed during the different phases, and that moving easily between the phases would be important. In studies of individual writing it is well known that using computers versus paper-and-pencil has dramatic effects on the process of writing, particularly upon the amount of time spent in the different kinds of activities described above (Haas, 1989).

Plowman (1995) describes how talk and writing interact as collaborative authors develop the ideas for their text, stressing the need for informal support that gives authors the opportunity for developing their ideas. A study of the use of the PREP editor also supported the need for flexibility in the technology to support the difference phases and preferences of collaborating authors (Kaufer, Neuwirth, Chandhok and Morris, 1995).

More specialized systems support groups whose tasks involve not just authoring text, but designing something, such as a computer system or architectural plan for a kitchen or building. Most of these systems are designed to capture the argumentation during the design process, linking the questions of consideration with the alternative solutions that were proposed as well as the evaluative discussion that accompanied it. The most well known of these is gIBIS (Conklin and Begeman, 1988) which uses a hypertext linking structure to organize the various issues, alternatives and criteria in the design rationale. A great deal of interest has followed this early line. There is a strong belief that this kind of system would help designers in two ways. It would help designers consider more alternatives and consider them more fully, and it would help those other team members that later have to maintain and/or alter the system (Moran and Carroll, 1996). However, various studies of the use of these notations highlight the frustration of capturing issues as design progresses, and the frequent mismatch between the design process and the notation (Shum, 1996).

Electronic Mail and Conferencing. It is generally agreed that electronic mail is the one groupware application that has seen wide success (Sproull and Kiesler, 1991; Satzinger and Olfman, 1992; O'Hara-Devereaux and Johansen, 1994; Anderson, Bikson, Law and Mitchell, 1995). The widespread dissemination of networks and personal computers have led to extensive use of e-mail in organizations and from home. E-mail by now has many of the characteristics of other widespread communication technologies such as the telephone, in that in its most basic form it works across heterogeneous hardware and software, offering the possibility of universal service (Anderson et al, 1995). The use of standard attachments (e.g., MIME) and common representation formats (e.g., Postscript, binhex, uucode, rtf) makes it increasingly easy to send complex, multimedia documents through e-mail. E-mail spans the barriers of space and time, and the use of distribution lists offers broadcast access to widespread communities. Demographic data on network connections, e-mail use, and general connectivity all show the wide adoption of electronic communication as a common form of human contact.

Electronic mail has a number of well-known effects on human behavior. Because of e-mail's power to reach many subscribers quickly, it has changed the culture of the organizations in which it resides: it changes who talks to whom (Sproull and Kiesler, 1991), what kind of person is heard from (Finholt,

Sproull, and Kiesler, 1990), and the tone of what is said (Sproull and Kiesler, 1991). That is, some people, forgetting that there is a human reading the message at the other end, and in the absence of feedback from the recipient, tend to "flame," to write a-social emotive messages that are either shocking, upsetting or offensive to the reader. On the more positive side, several studies have found that e-mail is especially useful for managing time, tasks, and information flow (Mackay, 1988; Carley and Wendt, 1991), though people also vary widely in how they use it (Mackay, 1988).

Another well-known property of e-mail is the rapid growth in messages handled by an individual user. The fact that electronic mail is cheap and that sending a single message to a distribution list is easy, people send out a lot of it. Subscribing to bulletin boards or news lists can clog the e-mail pipeline and make the task of examining and answering e-mail aversive. Furthermore since mail arrives in chronological sequence, it can become difficult to follow the thread of a conversation; people do not fully explain referents (e.g., they say only "OK. Friday" in the message as opposed to setting the confirmation in context); readers get confused.

In response to these problems, some e-mail systems organize messages by topic. Early systems such as Information LENS (Malone, Grant, Lai, Rao, Rosenblitt, 1987) allowed users to generate rules by which the incoming mail could be sorted into folders that can be later examined by the reader in some priority order. These characteristics are now included in many commercial products. Another early attempt to provide structure to electronic conversations was the Coordinator (Winograd, 1988), which asked the sender of a message to declare the action that the recipient is expected to make, by designating the message as a request, a commitment or promise, background information, etc. One can imagine that this kind of formalization of conversational patterns at best fits only some kinds of organizational situations, and is problematic in many others.

In a recent interesting monograph, a group of researchers examined the implications of e-mail becoming a universal resource like the telephone or television (Anderson et al., 1995). The demographics of the current penetration of e-mail show that while it has become widely used among an information elite, it still has limited penetration to the broader society. There are substantial gaps in the availability of personal computers and network connections based on income, education, and race. The authors explore the technical and social infrastructures for universal e-mail access, and in the course of doing so review a wide range of research literature on the topic of e-mail. They also list a number of recommendations for further research on e-mail.

Communication Support for Remote Connectivity. Ever since Picturephone (Wish, 1975), designers have been exploring the use of video connections to support people working at a distance. In spite of the commercial failure of Picturephone and the lack of evidence that video connectivity does anything to enhance simultaneous group work at a distance (Chapanis, 1973; Egido, 1988), people persist in trying it. Room-based video conferencing systems are commercially available (e.g.,. Picturetel) and continue to be extensively deployed in organizations to support distributed meetings where group members view their remote colleagues as well as a presentation outline, viewgraphs, or diagrams. Desktop video conferencing systems running over networks or ISDN lines have become available (e.g., Intel's ProShare system). Some experimental video systems are intended to support two or more co-workers while they engage in close work (Tang and Minneman, 1991). The VideoWhiteboard focuses the video only on the object under discussion and the hands drawing; others, like CAVECAT (Mantei, Baecker, Sellen, Buxton, and Milligan, 1991) put the faces of the co-workers on the screen in small windows. Commune (Minneman and Bly, 1991) show both user and drawing surface, whereas the ClearBoard (Ishii and Kobayashi, 1992) blends the two by arranging people on either side of the object under discussion, as if looking through glass. Unfortunately, not very many of these systems have been evaluated with careful studies. However, a study with a well-designed video conferencing set up showed that small groups can produce output that is indistinguishable in quality from face-to-face groups, though the video supported groups are less satisfied and the details of their behavior are quite different (Olson, Olson and Meader, 1995).

Another use of video is for general awareness of one's colleagues during the course of long term group work. Cruiser (Fish, Kraut, Root, and Rice, 1992) allowed quick glances into people's offices to see if they are there and/or interruptible. The VideoWindow at Bellcore was intended to encourage both ordinary meeting and casual interactions from remote sites over coffee (Fish, Kraut, Chalfonte, 1990). The RAVE suite of systems at Rank Xerox EuroPARC (Gaver, Moran, MacLean, Lovstrand, Dourish, Carter, and Buxton, 1992) was intended to support awareness of global activity, glances into individuals' offices, and point-to-point contact for close intense work. Montage is a system that provided awareness and the option of making easy connections to a colleague if he or she is willing to be interrupted (Tang, Isaacs and Rua, 1994). Long-term use of video connectivity was analyzed in the Portland Experiment (Olson and Bly, 1991). All of these systems have been studied within research lab settings, where modest amounts of sustained use were found. It would be extremely useful to have studies of these systems carried out in other kinds of organizational settings.

A number of attempts have been made to provide a conceptual framework for research on different kinds of communication media. Two of the better known are media richness theory (Daft and Lengel, 1986; criticized by Weick and Meader, 1994) and the common ground perspective (Clark and Brennan, 1991; Clark, 1996; O'Conaill, Whittaker and Wilbur, in press). These perspectives suggest that we should analyze the details of conversation among group members and how it affects their work (see also Heath and Luff, 1991, in press). Olson and Olson (in press b) have applied the framework we presented earlier to research on the role of video in collaboration, which revealed a number of significant gaps in our understanding of the factors that contribute to the potential usefulness of video connections. A broad survey of research and theory on video mediated communication appears in Finn, Sellen and Wilbur (in press).

Collaboratories. A collaboratory is the "...combination of technology, tools and infrastructure that allow scientists to work with remote facilities and each other as if they were co-located." (Lederberg and Uncapher, 1989, p. 6) A National Research Council (1993) report defines a collaboratory as a "...center without walls, in which the nation's researchers can perform their research without regard to geographical location — interacting with colleagues, accessing instrumentation, sharing data and computational resources [and] accessing information in digital libraries." (National Research Council, 1993, p. 7) A simplified form of these definitions describes a collaboratory as the use of computing and communication technology to achieve the enhanced access to colleagues and instruments provided by a shared physical location, but in a domain where potential collaborations are not constrained by temporal or geographic barriers.

Finholt and Olson (in press) and Kouzes, Myers and Wulf (1996) have reviewed the collaboratory concept and described some preliminary findings. It is likely that collaboratory interactions in science will become a routine aspect of scientific practice, with important implications not just for the practices of scientists but also for the training of graduate students.

59.5 Research Challenges in CSCW

Research on CSCW systems is still relatively recent, and there are lots of research challenges remaining. In this section we mention only a few prominent challenges. Many of the issues described in Olson et al (1993) remain. We note below both new ones and extensions to issues raised earlier.

59.5.1 Systems that Use Widespread Networking

The 1990s have seen the emergence of broad access to wide area computer networks, and this infrastructure is being used for a variety of interesting purposes. So far, the research done on these recent phenomena is mostly in the form of statistical descriptions of the extent of such developments and case studies of interesting uses. Much more research on the significance and meaning of these rapidly growing phenomena is needed.

The WorldWide Web. The most astounding electronic phenomenon of the 1990s is the explosive growth of the World Wide Web (WWW), a general infrastructure for the sharing of information through HTML documents. The early acceleration of use of the WWW was through Mosaic, a system developed at the National Center for Supercomputing Applications (NCSA) (Schatz and Hardin, 1994), though subsequent explosive growth has been through commercial software like Netscape Navigator and Microsoft Explorer. While we can plot the growth of Web sites, home pages, and hits, we as of yet know very little about the social and organizational effects of the WWW.

Multi-user virtual spaces. MUDs (multi-user domains or multi-user dungeons) and their many variants (e.g., MOOs, MUSEs, MUSHs) are a popular form of social interaction over the network that have devoted communities of users (Curtis, 1996; Turkle, 1995). MUDs are a kind of virtual reality, with the unusual property that the interface to them is typically quite simple: a text-based, command oriented system which of course allows the widest possible array of network users to participate. MUDs use spatially rich metaphors of rooms, doors, hallways, and the like to construct complex virtual worlds through which the participants wander and interact with each other.

Community Support Systems. A special case of the use of networked computing is the support of both existing and emerging communities. The Blacksburg Electronic Village (BEV) is perhaps the best example of a community support system for an existing community (Carroll, Rosson, Cohill and Schorger, 1995). Blacksburg, Virginia, is a community of roughly 36,000 people (extended to 70,000 if one includes the entire county). The BEV, open since 1993, uses e-mail and WWW facilities to provide a community network in which members of the community can communicate and exchange ideas about anything of interest to members. There are statistics on the extent of participation and on the use of BEV (e.g., on their Web site), but as of yet there is no in-depth research.

The Internet is also the location for a variety of virtual communities, that is, communities of people whose principal or sole links are electronic. There are a number of descriptions of such communities, including some in-depth case studies (e.g., Rheingold, 1993; Hiltz, 1994; Turkle, 1995), but no systematic research.

New Organizational Forms. Historically, organizational forms have been linked to the emergence of new communication technologies (e.g., telegraph, telephones). Thus, there is every reason to believe that CSCW systems will impact how organizations evolve. There is much speculation about the emergence of virtual organizations (e.g., Davidow and Malone, 1992), the flattening of organizational hierarchies (e.g., Malone, 1987; Malone, Benjamin and Yates, 1987), and the appearance of such specialized organizational forms as research collaboratories (Finholt and Olson, in press).

Behavioral Economics of the Internet. It is widely agreed that the Internet offers interesting new possibilities for commerce (e.g., Tapscott, 1996). While not all aspects of the enabling infrastructure are fully in place (e.g., reliable security systems), there are many important questions about how people will behave in light of new options for commercial activity. Similarly, pricing schemes for digital information have been explored (e.g., Varian and MacKie-Mason, in press a, b), but as so often happens we are often surprised at how people behave when any system is deployed. It is still quite unclear how privacy issues will play out. As a result, there is important research to be done on these matters.

59.5.2 Large Scale Coordinated Studies

CSCW research is inherently difficult to do, whether in the field or in the lab. The requirement for the systems to be robust and reliable means that getting a system ready to evaluate can take a long time. Locating groups or organizations with the right characteristics can take a long time. Collecting and analyzing process data is also time consuming. Finally, it can be difficult to gather large numbers of cases in order to be confident in ones results through the use of powerful statistics (Cohen, 1988).

As a result, much of the research literature in CSCW consists of small, inconclusive studies. The number of careful, definitive studies is very small. Evaluations of systems often consist of trying a prototype with a small number of users, and reporting "preliminary" results. But follow-on non-preliminary results seldom appear.

Several things could be done to improve this. First, some standardization of methods, tasks, and concept definitions would help. Second, the use of a shared conceptual framework could help with drawing generalizations across studies. Third, different sites could coordinate their studies so data could be pooled, a strategy that has been used successfully in other sciences.

This third option, carrying out coordinated studies, could be quite useful. The coordination could begin by development of standard, robust research prototypes, spreading the workload involved in getting prototypes to sufficient degrees of reliability. Then agreed upon research protocols could be developed and used by a consortium of investigators in order to gather sufficient numbers of cases to allow generalization and comparisons. In fields like molecular biology such coordinated attacks on complex problems are common, and indeed CSCW researchers have built systems in an effort to assist in the coordination (Schatz, 1991). Research on collaboration technology could well be coordinated through collaboration technology.

59.5.3 Interfaces to CSCW Technologies

In many cases the design strategies for single-user interfaces apply to those for group interfaces. However, interfaces to CSCW software must deal with many new and unusual features (Ellis, Gibbs, and Rein, 1991; Olson, Olson, Mack and Wellner, 1990; Olson, McGuffin, Kuwana, and Olson, 1993), and thus much research is needed on new ways of designing group interfaces (Madsen, 1989; Olson and Olson, 1992). This is particularly important as toolkits for building group systems are emerging (e.g., Hill, Brinck, Rohall, Patterson and Wilner, 1994; Dewan and Choudhary, 1992). We look at two examples of special issues.

In some current systems, group members are no longer in full control of the changes to their system; co-workers are adding to the shared database (as in hypertext) perhaps without the knowledge of the individual, and things appear and disappear in real time in group editing systems. Users report that they are out of control and uncertain, far more than in single user systems, where the only active agent other than the user is the buggy software or crashing hardware. Furthermore, users ask for some indication of what the other members of the group are doing if they are working simultaneously (called having a "sense of presence" of others). Also, if conversation is focused, they seek a way to coordinate their views, to be able to point to things in a short-hand style ("over here we need to..."). Clearly, various interface controls of the coordination of views and the telepointer feature are important.

To support the flow of work when the group members are not working simultaneously, there is a need for a way to convey the progress or changes made to the object since last time. There has to be smooth coordination between joint work and individual work, so that the shared document, or pieces of it, can be transferred to the single participants' workstations and back, and merged in a graceful fashion, both mechanically and in terms of the logic and expressive style of discourse. In a similar vein, people need to be able to control who sees what of their work, whether the annotations they are making are strictly private, shared among a subset of group members to read and/or change, or whether they are for public viewing or editing.

59.5.4 Design of Physical Space

Even though group and organizational work is increasingly facilitated by electronic means, the participants are still located in some physical space. Detailed studies of coordinated work have revealed how important the details of physical space are for all kinds of work (Hutchins, 1991; Heath and Luff, 1991, 1992; Suchman, in press). Thus, as we think about supporting group work it is essential we think about the physical space in which the work is situated. This applies equally whether the participants are co-located or distributed.

From all we know about proxemics (Hall, 1966) it is not surprising that such details should matter for face-to-face meetings. Mantei (1988) described many of the interesting details of face-to-face meetings in the Capture Lab. Conversation patterns are directly affected by spatial arrangements of the participants, and when computing technology is introduced into meeting rooms the placement of monitors and keyboards also has a big influence. Given the increasing appearance of such physical spaces in organizations we need a much more thoroughly articulated set of principles about how such spaces should be laid out.

These details are also important for virtual spaces of various kinds. Such factors as angles of regard, eye contact, and the spatial distribution of images and voices have important effects on video conferencing (Heath and Luff, 1991; Olson, Olson and Meader, 1995). It disrupts one's normal learned responses of interpreting what others are doing when the video presentation of remote participants is not spatially sensible. That is, if the camera is placed in the upper corner instead of at eye level, or if two or more cameras' outputs are juxtaposed (so they look like bleachers full of meeting participants), the participants can no longer use their well-learned, "natural" recognition processes to easily monitor the ambiance of the group. The timing and pacing of multimedia cues is crucial for coherent conversations among remote participants (Krauss, Garlock, Bricker, and McMahon, 1977; Clark and Brennan, 1991). Our ability to interpret the spatial location from sound is also potentially important to the design of the audio connection, to determine who is speaking, what background conversations might be taking place, and what sound distractions might be disrupting the remote participants.

59.5.5 Theory

We have both too much and too little theory in CSCW. The referent disciplines from which CSCW has emerged are full of rich theories, and practitioners have introduced these theories into the field. But these theories are seldom assimilated into the broader community, and as a result there are numerous theories but none that are widely accepted.

There are several theories that are closely associated with work in CSCW. The theory of situated action, made most famous by Suchman's (1987) pioneering research, has received widespread attention (e.g., an entire issue of the journal *Cognitive Science* was devoted to debate triggered by a critical article by Vera and Simon, 1993; see a summary by Olson, 1994). The basic idea is that an adequate description of activity must include details of how it is situated in its physical, social, cultural, and historical environment. This theory has led to sharp critiques of modern theories of cognitive psychology and artificial intelligence (e.g., Bobrow, 1991; Brooks, 1991).

A closely related set of ideas is known as distributed cognition, and its most elegant articulation has come from the work of Hutchins (1990, 1991, 1995a, b). This line of theorizing has examined in detail how the cognitive activity of small groups is intertwined with the social and material environments in which it is practiced. Hutchins has examined technical activities like navigating a ship through a channel or landing a modern airliner. A more general discussion by Norman (1993) stresses the importance of "cognitive artifacts" in making human activity intelligent.

Another theory closely associated with the field of CSCW is the coordination theory of Malone and Crowston (1990; 1994; Crowston, in press). Their theory explicates the coordination mechanisms that are used in organizations to facilitate the accomplishment of goals. Emphasis is on coordination of the individual agent activities, whether the coordination takes the form of expectations, norms, or internalized procedures. Focus is often on how coordinating messages are passed from agent to agent, how agents perform their activities, and how certain kinds of organizational forms (e.g., hierarchies or markets) favor certain kinds of coordination over others (Levitt, Cohen, Kunz, Nass, Christiansen and Jin, 1994; Malone, Benjamin, and Yates, 1987; Malone, 1987).

In contrast, the view that organizations are collections of individuals examines the task being accomplished by a set of individuals, each of whom has certain built-in strengths (e.g., ability to learn, make allowances for error, solve problems intelligently, etc.) and limits (e.g., slow to learn, inaccurate in communicating both sending and receiving messages, having conflicting motivations, etc.) In this view the emphasis is commonly micro: on the stage of problem solving or activity the collection of individuals is in, how they blend their experiences and divide their attention, and how they move from individual to coordinated work and back. Additional emphasis is on the ways in which the individuals communicate their ideas, requests, and misunderstandings to each other, and the ways in which various technologies and media either help or hinder that coordination. Many of the work situations that are the focus of this approach are synchronous, either face-to-face or remote, with shared workobjects and video or audio channels. The theoretical machinery is borrowed from cognitive psychology and communications. Some interplay of the roles people take and their interaction style are from social psychology (e.g., Bales, 1950), some from cognitive science (e.g., Fikes, 1982).

The structuration theory of Giddens (1979; Cohen, 1989) has influenced several CSCW researchers to look at the complex interactions of social structure and practice with information technology. Structuration theory holds that social activity is due to the interplay of social structure and practice, particularly as they unfold over time. It is a highly contextual, "situated" (Olson, 1994) view of social action. In the adaptations of structuration theory to CSCW, information technology is viewed as one element of the complex of structure and process that work together over time to produce social or organizational change. For instance, Orlikowski (1992a, 1992b; Orlikowski and Cash, 1994) has looked at the interplay of technology and social context in several field experiments, while DeSanctis and Poole (1994) have looked at the use of GDSS systems. These theorists have rightly cautioned us against simplistic views of how technology is used in organizations. So far structuration theories in CSCW have been highly qualitative in their methods, but there are statistical techniques for examining complex, interactionist conceptualizations of social processes over time. This is clearly a ripe area for further research.

It is probably premature to expect a newly formed field like CSCW that has such diverse intellectual roots to coalesce around widely accepted theoretical ideas. The observational base of findings from CSCW research still seriously underdetermines theory, so the further evolution of empirical research and theory development must go hand in hand.

59.6 Conclusions

Research on CSCW systems is proliferating, and we have only been able in this chapter to touch on some representative highlights. Our goal has been to offer a critical methodological framework and some conceptual guidelines on how to approach this research. We encourage readers to examine this literature themselves directly. The best sources of current research are the proceedings of such major conferences as CHI, CSCW, and E-CSCW (the European CSCW meetings), and journals such as *Human-Computer Interaction*, *ACM Transactions on Information Systems* (TOIS), *ACM Transactions on Computer Human Interaction* (TOCHI), *Computer Supported Cooperative Work*, *Communications of the ACM*, *Organizational Computing*, *Organizational Science*, *Information Systems Research*, and *Management Information Systems Quarterly* (MISQ). We are confident that our understanding of the use of CSCW systems in groups and organizations will advance considerably in the coming decades.

59.7 Acknowledgments

Preparation of this chapter was made possible by grants IRI-9320543 and IRI-9216848 from the National Science Foundation, the Ameritech Foundation, and the Intel Natural Data Types Research Council. We are grateful to Tom Brinck, Michael Cohen, Kevin Crowston, James Eng, Tom Finholt, Susan McDaniel, and Stephanie Teasley for comments on earlier drafts of this chapter.

59.8 References

Allen, T.J. (1977). *Managing the flow of technology.* Cambridge, MA: MIT Press.

Anderson, J.R. (1982) Acquisition of cognitive skill. *Psychological Review, 89*, 369-406.

Anderson, R.H., Bikson, T.K., Law, S.A., and Mitchell, B.M. (1995) *Universal access to e-mail: Feasibility and societal implications.* Santa Monica, CA: RAND.

Anderson, R.J. (1994) Representations and requirements: The value of ethnography in system design. *Human-Computer Interaction, 9*, 151-182.

Argyris, C. (1992) *On organizational learning.* Cambridge, MA: Blackwell.

Attewell, P. (1994) Information technology and the productivity paradox (pp. 13-53). In D.H. Harris (Ed.), *Organizational linkages: Understanding the productivity paradox.* Washington, DC: National Academy Press.

Baker, W.E. (1994) *Networking smart: How to build relationships for personal and organizational success.* New York: McGraw-Hill.

Bales, R. F. (1950) *Interaction process analysis: A method for the study of small groups.* Cambridge, MA: Addison-Wesley.

Baltes, P.B., Reese, H.W., and Nesselroade, J.R. (1977) *Life-span developmental psychology: Introduction to research methods.* Monterey, CA: Brooks/Cole.

Bobrow, D.G. (1991) Dimensions of interaction: A shift in perspective in artificial intelligence. *AI Magazine, 12*, 64-80.

Bower, G.H., and Clapper, J.P. (1989) Experimental methods in cognitive science (245-300). In M.I. Posner (Ed.), *Foundations of cognitive science.* Cambridge, MA: MIT Press.

Bradburn, N.M., and Sudman, S. (1988) *Polls and surveys: Understanding what they tell us.* San Francisco: Jossey-Bass.

Brooks, R. (1991) Intelligence without representations. *Artificial Intelligence, 47*, 139-159.

Card, S. (1991) Presentation on the Theories of HCI at the NSF Workshop on Human Computer Interaction, Washington, D.C.

Carley, K., and Wendt, K. (1991) Electronic mail and scientific communication: A study of the Soar extended research group. *Knowledge: Creation, Diffusion, Utilization, 12*, 406-440.

Carroll, J.M., Rosson, M.B., Cohill, A.M., and Schorger, J. (1995) Building a history of the Blacksburg Electronic Village. In *Proceedings of the ACM Symposium on Designing Interactive Systems* (August 23-25, Ann Arbor, Michigan). New York: ACM Press, pp. 1-6.

Chapanis , A. (1973) Interactive human communication. *Scientific American, 232*(3), 36-42.

Clark, H.H. (1996). *Using language.* New York: Cambridge University Press.

Clark, H. H. and Brennan, S. E. (1991) Grounding in communication (pp. 127-149). In L. Resnick, J. M. Levine, and S. D. Teasley (Eds.) *Perspectives on socially shared cognition.* Washington, DC: APA.

Clark, H.H., and Schober, M.F. (1992) Asking questions and influencing answers. In J. Tanur (Ed.), *Questions about questions: Inquiries into the cognitive basis of surveys.* New York: Russell Sage.

Cohen, I.J. (1989) *Structuration theory: Anthony Giddens and the constitution of social life.* New York: St. Martin's Press.

Cohen, J. (1988) *Statistical power analysis for the behavioral sciences* (2nd Ed.). Hillsdale, NJ: Lawrence Erlbaum Associates.

Cohen, M.D., and Bacdayan, P. (1994) Organizational routines are stored as procedural memory: Evidence from a laboratory study. *Organizational Science, 5*, 554-568.

Conklin, J., and Begeman, J. L. (1988) gIBIS: A hypertext tool for exploratory policy discussion (pp. 140-152). *Proceedings of the Conference on Computer Supported Cooperative Work.*

Conrath, D.W. (1973) Communication patterns, organizational structure, and man: Some relationships. *Human Factors, 15*, 459-470.

Crowston, K. (in press), "A coordination theory approach to organizational process design," *Organization Science.*

Curtis, P. (1996) MUDding: Social phenomena in text-based virtual realities (pp. 347-373). In P. Ludlow (Ed.), High noon on the electronic frontier: Conceptual issues in cyberspace. Cambridge, MA: MIT Press.

Cyert, R.M., and March, J.G. (1963) *A behavioral theory of the firm.* Englewood Cliffs, NJ: Prentice-Hall.

Daft, R.L., and Lengel, R.H. (1986) Organizational information requirements, media richness and structural design. *Management Science, 32,* 554-571.

Davidow, W.H., and Malone, M.S. (1992) *The vitural corporation: Structuring and revitalizing the corporation for the 21st century.* New York: Harper Collins.

DeSanctis, G., and Poole, M.S. (1994) Capturing the complexity in advanced technology use: Adaptive structuration theory. *Organizational Science, 5,* 121-147.

Dewan, P., and Choudhary, R. (in press) A high-level and flexible framework for implementing multi-user user-interfaces. *ACM Transactions on Information Systems, 10,* 345-380.

Edwards, M. U., Levine, J. A., and Kurland, D. M. (1986) ForComment, Broderbund.

Egido, C. (1988) Videoconferencing as a technology to support group work: A review of its failures (pp. 13-24). *Proceedings of the Conference on Computer Supported Cooperative Work.*

Ellis, C. A., Gibbs, S. J., and Rein, G. L. (1991) Groupware: Some issues and experiences. *Communications of the ACM, 34*(1), 38-58..

Emerson, R.M., Fretz, R.I., and Shaw, L.L. (1995) *Writing ethnographic fieldnotes.* Chicago: University of Chicago Press.

Fikes, R. E. (1982) A commitment-based framework for describing informal cooperative work. *Cognitive Science, 6,* 331-347.

Finholt, T.A., and Olson, G.M. (in press) From laboratories to collaboratories: A new organizational form for scientific collaboration. *Psychological Science.*

Finholt, T., Sproull, L., and Kiesler, S. (1990) Communication and performance in ad hoc task groups. in J. Galegher, R Kraut, and C. Egido (Eds.), *Intellectual teamwork.: Social and technological foundations of cooperative work.* Hillsdale, NJ: Lawrence Erlbaum Associates.

Finn, K., Sellen, A., and Wilbur, S. (Eds.) . (in press). *Video-mediated communication.* Hillsdale NJ: Lawrence Erlbaum Associates.

Fish, R. S., Kraut, R. E., Chalfonte, B. L. (1990) The VideoWindow system in informal communications (pp. 1-11). *Proceedings of the Conference on Computer Supported Cooperative Work.*

Fish, R. S. , Kraut, R. E., Root, R. W., and Rice, R. E. (1992) Evaluating video as a technology for informal communication (pp. 37-48). In Bauersfeld, P., Bennett, J., and Lynch, G. (Eds.) CHI'92 Human Factors in Computing Systems New York: ACM.

Flower, L., and Hayes, J.R. (1978) A cognitive process theory of writing. *College Composition and Communication, 32,* 365-387.

Fornell, C. (1995) Productivity, quality, and customer satisfaction as strategic success indicators at firm and national levels. *Advances in Strategic Management, 11A,* 217-229.

Fussel, S. R., and Benimoff, N. I. (1995) Social and cognitive processes in interpersonal communication: Implications for advanced telecommunications technologies. *Human Factors, 37*(2), 228-250.

Gabarro, J. J. (1990) The Development of Working Relationships, in J. Galegher, R. E. Kraut, and C Egido (Eds.), *Intellectual teamwork,* Hillsdale, NJ: Lawrence Erlbaum Associates.

Gaver, W.W., Moran, T., MacLean, A., Lovstrand, L., Dourish, P., Carter, K. A., and Buxton, W. (1992) Realizing a video environment: EuroPARC's RAVE system. *Proceedings of CHI'92.*

Giddens, A. (1979) *Central problems in social theory: Action, structure and contradiction in social analysis.* Berkeley, CA: University of California Press.

Group Technologies, Inc. (1990) Aspects.

Grudin, J. (1988) Why CSCW applications fail: Problems in the design and evaluation of organizational interfaces (pp. 85-93). *Proceedings of the Conference on Computer Supported Cooperative Work.*

Haake, J.M., and Wilson, B. (1992) Supporting collaborative writing of hyperdocuments in SEPIA. In *Proceedings of CSCW '92.* New York: ACM Press.

Haas, C. (1989) Does the medium make a difference? Two studies of writing with pen and paper and with computers. *Human-Computer Interaction, 4,* 149-169.

Hackman, J. R. (1987) The design of work teams (pp. 315-342). in J. W. Lorsch (Ed.) *Handbook of organizational behavior.* Englewood Cliffs, NJ: Prentice-Hall.

Hackman, J.R., and Morris, C.G. (1975) Group tasks, group interaction process, and group performance effectiveness: A review and proposed integration (Vol. 8, pp. 47-99). In L. Berkowitz (Ed.), *Advances in experimental social psychology.* New York: Academic Press.

Hall, E. T., (1966) *The hidden dimension*. NY: Anchor Books.

Heath, C., and Luff, P. (1991) Disembodied conduct: Communication through video in a multi-media office environment (pp. 99-103). In *Proceedings of CHI '91*. New York: ACM.

Heath, C., and Luff, P. (1992) Collaboration and control: Crisis management and multimedia technology in London Underground line control rooms. *Computer Supported Cooperative Work, 1*, 69-94

Heath, C. and Luff, P. (in press) Media space and communicative asymmetries. *Human Computer Interaction.*

Heise, D.R. (1975) *Causal analysis*. New York: Wiley.

Hessler, R.M. (1992) *Social research methods*. St. Paul, MN: West Publishing.

Higgins, C.A., McClean, R.J., and Conrath, D.W. (1985) The accuracy and biases of diary communication data. *Social Networks, 7*, 173-187.

Hill, R.D., Brinck, T., Rohall, S.L., Patterson, J.F., and Wilner, W. (1994) The *Rendezvous* architecture and language for constructing multi-user applications. *ACM Transactions on Computer-Human Interaction, 1*, 81-125.

Hiltz, S.R. (1994) *The virtual classroom: Learning without limits via computer networks*. Norwood, NJ: Ablex.

Hollingshead, A.B., and McGrath, J.E. (in press) The whole is less than the sum of its parts: A critical review of research on computer-assisted groups. In R. Guzzo (Ed.), *Team decision making in organizations*. San Francisco: Jossey-Bass.

Hutchins, E. (1990). The technology of team navigation (pp. 191-220). In J. Galegher, R. E. Kraut, and C. Egido (Ed.), *Intellectual teamwork: Social and technological foundations of cooperative work*. Hillsdale, NJ: Lawrence Erlbaum Associates.

Hutchins, E. (1991) The social organization of distributed cognition (pp. 283-307). In L. B. Resnick, J.M. Levine and S.D. Teasley (Eds.), *Perspectives on socially shared cognition*. Washington: American Psychological Association.

Hutchins, E. (1995a) *Cognition in the wild*. Cambridge, MA: MIT Press.

Hutchins, E. (1995b) How a cockpit remembers its speeds. *Cognitive Science, 19*, 265-288.

Ishii, H, and Kobayashi, M. (1992) Clearboard: A seamless medium for shared drawing and conversation with eye contact. *Proceedings of CHI'92.*

Kaufer, D.S., Neuwirth, C.M., Chandhok, R., and Morris, J. (1995) Accommodating mixed sensory modal preferences in collaborative writing systems. *Computer Supported Collaborative Work, 3*, 271-295.

Kouzes, R.T., Myers, J.D., and Wulf, W.A. (1996) Collaboratories: Doing science on the Internet. *IEEE Computer, 29*(8), 40-46.

Kraemer, K. L., and Pinsonneault, A. (1990) Technology and groups: Assessments of empirical research. In J. Galegher, R Kraut, and C. Egido (Eds.), *Intellectual teamwork.: Social and technological foundations of cooperative work.* Hillsdale, NJ: Lawrence Erlbaum Associates.

Krauss, R. M. (1991) Impression formation, impression management, and nonverbal behaviors. In E. T. Higgins, C. P. Herman, and M. Zanna (Eds.) *Social Cognition: The Ontario Symposium.* Hillsdale, NJ: Lawrence Erlbaum Associates.

Krauss, R.M., and Fussell, S.R. (1990) Mutual knowledge and communication effectiveness. In J. Galegher, R Kraut, and C. Egido (Eds.), *Intellectual teamwork.: Social and technological foundations of cooperative work.* Hillsdale, NJ: Lawrence Erlbaum Associates.

Krauss, R. M., Garlock, C. M., Bricker, P. D., and McMahon, L. E. (1977) The role of audible and visible backchannel responses in interpersonal communication. *Journal of Personality and Social Psychology, 35*, 523-529.

Kraut, R.E., Egido, C., and Galegher, J. (1990) Patterns of contact and communication in scientific research collaboration. In J. Galegher, R Kraut, and C. Egido (Eds.), *Intellectual teamwork.: Social and technological foundations of cooperative work.* Hillsdale, NJ: Lawrence Erlbaum Associates.

Kraut, R.E., Galegher, J., and Egido, C. (1988) Relationships and tasks in scientific research collaboration. *Human-Computer Interaction, 3*, 31-58.

Landauer, T.K. (1995) *The trouble with computers: Usefulness, usability, and productivity*. Cambridge, MA: MIT Press.

Lederberg, J., and Uncapher, K. (1989). *Towards a national collaboratory: Report of an invitational workshop at the Rockefeller University*. Washington, D.C.: National Science Foundation.

Leland, M. D. P., Fish, R. S., and Kraut, R. E. (1988) Collaborative document production using Quilt (pp

206-215). *Proceedings of the Conference on Computer Supported Cooperative Work.*

Levitt, R. E., Cohen, G. P., Kunz, J. C., Nass, C. I., Christiansen, T., and Jin, Y. (1994). The "virtual design team": Simulating how organization structure and information processing tools affect team performance (pp. 1-18). In K. M. Carley and M. J. Prietula (Eds.), *Computational organizational theory.* Hillsdale, NJ: Lawrence Erlbaum Associates.

Mackay, W.E. (1988) More than just a communication system: Diversity in the use of electronic mail (pp. 344-353). In *Proceedings of CSCW '88.* New York: ACM.

Madsen, C. M. (1989) Approaching group communication by means of an office building metaphor (pp. 449-460). *First European Conference on Computer Supported Cooperative Work.*

Malone, T. W. (1987) Modeling coordination in organizations and markets. *Management Science, 33,* 1317-1332.

Malone, T. W., Benjamin, R. I., and Yates, J. (1987) Electronic markets and electronic hierarchies. *Communication of the ACM, 30,* 484-497.

Malone, T. W., Grant, K. R., Lai, K-Y., Rao, R., and Rosenblitt, D. (1987) Semi-structured messages are surprisingly useful for computer-supported coordination. *ACM: Transactions On Information Systems, 5,* 115-131.

Malone, T., and Crowston, K. (1990) What is coordination theory and how can it help design cooperative work systems (pp. 357-370). *Proceedings of the Conference on Computer Supported Cooperative Work.*

Malone, T. W. and K. Crowston. (1994), The interdisciplinary study of coordination, *Computing Surveys, 26,* 87-119.

Mantei, M. M. (1988) Capturing the Capture Lab concepts: A case study in the design of computer supported meeting environments (pp. 257-270). Proceedings of the conference on Computer Supported Cooperative Work.

Mantei, M. M., Baecker, R. M., Sellen, A. J., Buxton, W. A. S., and Milligan, T. (1991) Experiences in the use of media space (pp. 203-208). In Robertson, S., Olson, G. M., and Olson, J. S. (Eds.) CHI'91 Human Factors in Computing Systems New York: ACM.

March, J.G., and Simon, H.A. (1958) *Organizations.* New York: Wiley.

McGrath, J. E. (1984). *Groups: Interaction and performance.* Englewood Cliffs, NJ: Prentice-Hall.

McGuffin, L., and Olson, G. M. (1992) ShrEdit: A shared electronic workspace. CSMIL Technical Report #45, The University of Michigan.

McLeod, P. L. (1992). An assessment of the experimental literature on electronic group support: Results of a meta-analysis. *Human-Computer Interaction, 7,* 257-280.

Minneman, S. L., and Bly, S. A. (1991) Managing a trois: A study of a multi-user drawing tool in distributed design work (pp. 217-224). In Robertson, S. P., Olson, G. M., and Olson, J. S. (Eds.) *CHI'91: Human Factors in Computing Systems* New York: ACM.

Moran, T.P., and Carroll, J.M. (1996). *Design rationale: Concepts, techniques, and use.* Mahwah, NJ: Erlbaum.

Morgan, B. B., Jr., and Lassiter, D. L. (1992) Team composition and staffing. In R. W. Swezey and E. Salas, (Eds) *Teams, their training and performance.* Norwood, NJ: Ablex Publishing Company.

Nardi, B.A., Kuchinsky, A., Whittaker, S., Leichner, R., and Schwarz, H. (1995) Video-as-data: Technical and social aspects of a collaborative multimedia application. *Computer Supported Cooperative Work, 4,* 73-100.

National Research Council (1993). *National collaboratories: Applying information technology for scientific research.* Washington, D.C.: National Academy Press.

Neuwirth. C.M., Kaufer, D. S., Chandhok, R. and Morris, J. H. (1990) Issues in the design of computer support for co-authoring and commenting (pp. 183-195). *Proceedings of the Conference on Computer Supported Cooperative Work.*

Nonaka, I., and Takeuchi, H. (1995) *The knowledge-creating company: How Japanese companies create the dynamics of innovation.* New York: Oxford University Press.

Norman, D.A. (1993) *Things that make us smart.* Reading, MA: Addison-Wesley.

Norman, D.A., and Draper, S.W. (Eds.) (1986) *User centered system design: New perspectives on human-computer interaction.* Hillsdale, NJ: Lawrence Erlbaum Associates.

Nunamaker, J. F., Dennis, A. R., Valacich, J. S., Vogel, D. R., and George, J. F. (1991) Electronic meeting systems to support group work. *Communications of the ACM, 34*(7), 40-61.

O'Conaill, B., Whittaker, S., and Wilbur, S. (in press) Conversations over video-conferences: An evaluation of the spoken aspects of video mediated communication. *Human-Computer Interaction.*

O'Hara-Devereaux, M., and Johansen, R. (1994) *Global work: Bridging distance, culture and time*. San Francisco: Jossey-Bass.

Olson, G.M. (1994) Situated cognition (pp. 971-973). In R.J. Sternberg (Ed.), *Encyclopedia of human intelligence*. New York: Macmillan.

Olson, G.M., Herbsleb, J.D., and Rueter, H.H. (1994) Characterizing the sequential structure of interactive behaviors through statistical and grammatical techniques. *Human-Computer Interaction, 9*, 427-472.

Olson, G.M., McGuffin, L.S., Kuwana, E., and Olson, J.S. (1993) Designing software for a group's needs: A functional analysis of synchronous groupware (pp. 129-148). In L. Bass and P. Dewan (Eds.), *User interface software*. New York: Wiley.

Olson, G.M., and Olson, J.R. (1991). User-centered design of collaboration technology. *Journal of Organizational Computing. 1*, 61-83

Olson, G.M., and Olson, J.S. (1992) Defining a metaphor for group work. *IEEE Software, 9*(3), 93-95.

Olson, G.M., and Olson, J.S. (in press a) Technology support for collaborative workgroups. In G.M. Olson, T. Malone and J. Smith (Eds.), *Coordination theory and collaboration technology*. Hillsdale, NJ: Lawrence Erlbaum Associates.

Olson, G.M., and Olson, J.S. (in press b) Making sense of the findings: Common vocabulary leads to the synthesis necessary for theory building. In Finn, K., Sellen, A., and Wilbur, S. (Eds.) . *Video-mediated communication*. Hillsdale NJ: Lawrence Erlbaum Associates.

Olson, G. M., Olson, J. S., Carter, M. and Storrøsten, M., (1992) Small group design meetings: An analysis of collaboration. *Human Computer Interaction, 7*, 347-374.

Olson, J.S., Card, S., Landauer, T., Olson, G.M., Malone, T., and Leggett, J.. (1993) Computer-supported cooperative work: Research issues for the 90s. *Behavior and Information Technology, 12*, 115-129.

Olson. J.S., Olson, G.M., Mack. L.A., and Wellner, P. (1990) Concurrent editing: the group's interface (pp. 835-840). In D. Diaper (Ed.), *INTERACT '90 - Third IFIP Conference on Human-Computer Interaction* Elsevier.

Olson, J.S., Olson, G.M., and Meader, D.K. (1995) What mix of video and audio is useful for remote real-time work? *Proceedings of CHI '95*, ACM SIGCHI, 362-368.

Olson, J.S., Olson, G.M., Storrøsten, M., and Carter, M. (1993) Groupwork close up: A comparison of the group design process with and without a simple group editor. *ACM Transactions on Information Systems, 11*, 321-348.

Olson, M.H., and Bly, S.A. (1991) The Portland experience: A report on a distributed research group. *International Journal of Man-Machine Studies, 34*, 211-228.

Orlikowski, W.J. (1992a) The duality of technology: Rethinking the concept of technology in organizations. *Organizational Science, 3*, 398-427.

Orlikowski, W.J. (1992b) Learning from Notes: Organizational issues in groupware implementation (pp. 362-369). In *Proceedings of CSCW '94*. New York: ACM.

Orlikowski, W.J., and Gash, D.C. (1994) Technological frames: Making sense of information technology in organizations. *ACM Transactions on Information Systems, 12*, 174-207.

Plowman, L. (1995) The interfunctionality of talk and text. *Computer Supported Cooperative Work, 3*, 229-246.

Posner, I., and Baecker, R.M. (1993) How people write together. In R.M. Baecker (Ed.), *Readings in Groupware and Computer-Supported Cooperative Work*. San Mateo, CA: Morgan Kaufmann.

Prietula, M. J., and Carley, K. M. (1994). Computational organization theory: Autonomous agents and emergent behavior. *Journal of Organizational Computing, 4*, 41-83.

Rheingold, H., (1993) *The virtual community*. Reading, MA: Addison-Wesley.

Rosenthal, R. (1984) *Meta-analytic procedures for social research*. Newbury Park, CA: Sage.

Satzinger, J., and Olfman, L. (1992) A research program to assess user perceptions of group work support (pp. 99-106). In P. Bauersfeld, J. Bennett, and G. Lynch (Eds.) CHI'92: Human Factors in Computing Systems New York: ACM.

Schatz, B. R. (1991) Building an electronic scientific community. 24th Hawaii International Conference on System Sciences. 3, 739-748.

Schatz, B.R., and Hardin, J.B. (1994) NCSA Mosaic and the World Wide Web: Global hypermedia protocols for the Internet. *Science, 265*, 895-901.

Schwarz, N., and Sudman, S. (Eds.) (1996) *Answering questions: Methodology for determining cognitive and communicative processes in survey research*. San Francisco: Jossey-Bass.

Senge, P.M. (1990) *The fifth discipline: The art and practice of the learning organization.* New York: Doubleday Currency.

Shaw, M. E. (1981) *Group dynamics, The psychology of small group behavior.* New York: McGraw Hill.

Shum, S.B. (1996) Analyzing the usability of a design rationale notation (pp. 185-215). In T.P. Moran and J.M. Carroll (Eds.), *Design rationale: Concepts, techniques, and use*. Mahwah, NJ: Lawrence Erlbaum Associates.

Sommer, B., and Sommer, R. (1991) *A practical guide to behavioral research: Tools and techniques* (3rd ed). New York: Oxford.

Spradley, J.P. (1979) *The ethnographic interview*. New York: Harcourt Brace Jovanovich.

Spradley, J.P. (1980) *Participant observation.* New York: Holt, Rinehart and Winston.

Sproull, L., and Kiesler, S. (1991) *Connections: New ways of working in the networked organization.* Cambridge, MA: MIT Press.

Stefik, M., Foster, G., Bobrow, D., Kahn, K., Lanning, S., and Suchman, L. (1987) Beyond the chalkboard: Computer support for collaboration and problem solving in meetings. *Communications of the ACM, 30*, 32-47.

Steiner, I. D. (1972) *Group processes and productivity.* New York: Academic Press.

Strassmann, P.A. (1990) *The business value of computers: An executive's guide.* New Canaan, CT: The Information Economics Press.

Suchman, L. A. (1987) *Plans and situated actions.* Cambridge, UK: Cambridge University Press.

Suchman, L.A. (in press) Centers of coordination: A case and some themes. In L. Resnick (Ed.), *Discourse, tools, and reasoning.*

Sudman, S., and Bradburn, N.M. (1982) *Asking questions: A practical guide to questionnaire design.* San Francisco: Jossey-Bass.

Sudman, S., Bradburn, N.M., and Schwarz, N. (1996) *Thinking about answers: The application of cognitive processes to survey methodology.* San Francisco: Jossey-Bass.

Tang, J.C., Isaacs, E.A., and Rua, M. (1994) Supporting distributed groups with a montage of lightweight interactions. In CSCW'94, New York: ACM.

Tang, J. C., and Minneman, S. L. (1991) VideoWhiteboard: Video shadows to support remote collaboration. In Robertson, S. P., Olson, G. M., and Olson, J. S. (Eds.) CHI'91: Human Factors in Computing Systems New York: ACM.

Tapscott, D. (1996) *The digital economy: Promise and peril in the age of networked intelligence.* New York: McGraw-Hill.

Tenner, E. (1996) *Why things bite back: Technology and the revenge of unintended consequences.* New York: Alfred A. Knopf.

Turkle, S. (1995) *Life on the screen: Identity in the age of the Internet.* New York: Simon and Schuster.

Turner, J.A. (1984) Computer mediated work: The interplay between technology and structured jobs. *Communications of the ACM, 27*, 1210-1217.

Varian, H., and MacKie-Mason, J. (in press a) Some economics of the Internet, To appear in W. Sichel (Ed.), *Networks, infrastructure and the new task for regulation.* Ann Arbor: University of Michigan Press.

Varian, H., and MacKie-Mason, J. (in press b) Pricing the Internet, To appear in Brian Kahin and James Keller (Eds.) *Public access to the Internet.* Cambridge, MA: MIT Press.

Vaughan, D. (1996) *The Challenger launch decision: Risky technology, culture, and deviance at NASA.* Chicago: University of Chicago Press.

Vera, A.H., and Simon, H.A. (1993) Situated action: A symbolic interpretation. *Cognitive Science, 17*, 7-48.

Walsh, J.P. (1995) Managerial and organizational cognition: Notes from a trip down memory lane. *Organizational Science, 6*, 280-321.

Walsh, J.P., and Ungson, G.R. (1991) Organizational memory. *Academy of Management Review, 16*, 57-91.

Weick, K. E. (1965) Laboratory experimentation with organizations (pp. 194-260). In J. G. March (Ed.) *Handbook of organizations.* Chicago, IL: Rand-McNally.

Weick, K. E. (1979) *The social psychology of organizing* (2nd Ed.) Reading, MA: Addison-Wesley.

Weick, K.E. (1993) The collapse of sensemaking in organizations: The Mann Gulch disaster. *Administrative Science Quarterly, 38*, 628-652.

Weick, K., E., and Meader, D. K. (1994) Sensemaking and group support systems. In L. Jessup and J. Valacich, (Eds.) *Group Support Systems.* Macmillan Publishers.

Weick, K.E., and Roberts, K.H. (1993) Collective mind in organizations: Heedful interrelating on flight decks. *Administrative Science Quarterly, 38*, 357-381.

Whyte, W.F., and Whyte, K.K. (1984) *Learning from the field: A guide from experience*. Beverly Hills, CA: Sage Publications.

Winograd, T. (1988) A language/action perspective on the design of cooperative work. *Human Computer Interaction, 3*, 3-30.

Wish, M. (1975) User and non-user conceptions of PICTUREPHONE® service. *Proceedings of the 19th Annual Convention of the Human Factors Society.*

Yates, J. (1989) *Control through communication: The rise of system in American management*. Baltimore: Johns Hopkins University Press.

Yin, R.K. (1989) *Case study research: Design and methods*. (Rev. ed). Beverly Hills, CA: Sage.

Handbook of Human-Computer Interaction
Second, completely revised edition
M. Helander, T.K. Landauer, P. Prabhu (eds.)

Chapter 60

Organizational Issues in Development and Implementation of Interactive Systems

Jonathan Grudin
Information and Computer Science
University of California, Irvine
Irvine, California, USA

M. Lynne Markus
Programs in Information Science
The Claremont Graduate School
Claremont, California, USA

60.1 Introduction

The expression *human-computer interaction* usually brings to mind one person with a display alongside a keyboard and mouse. This is in a sense the "basic unit" of human-computer interaction today. We know that most computer use occurs in settings that greatly influence the interaction, but because those settings vary so widely—schools, universities, large companies, small companies, an airplane seat, home—most of this handbook focuses on what can be said about computer use in general. But a few chapters are devoted to individual differences and individuals with special characteristics. Similarly, a few chapters cover differences in organizational context. This chapter focuses on the effect of organizational differences on system and application *implementation*—by which we mean the process of bringing systems into organizations, including adoption and use—and on *development*, which also takes place in a broad range of settings.

Human-computer interaction has drawn on a tradition of ergonomics and human factors that includes some attention to organizational influences, but this has been muted, especially in North America. The success of the PC brought a great need to address problems of visual displays and input devices. This attracted the perceptual and cognitive psychologists who were instrumental in forming the ACM Special Interest Group in Computer and Human Interaction (SIGCHI) and giving HCI its present shape.

Early PCs were not designed to be networked. As a result, PC use was largely insulated from group and organizational activity. For a decade, designers had the luxury of focusing exclusively on individual users, "the basic unit" of human-computer interaction.

By the early 1990s, consensus was reached on many perceptual and low-level cognitive issues—Windows'95 was a final nod to the graphical user interface. Of course, perceptual and cognitive issues persist, and new ones arise. But they must share the stage, because the networking challenges have been met. Virtually all PCs will soon have some network access. Interactive software use will almost invariably be immersed in group, organizational, and interorganizational activity.

The organizational context of computer use is often clear. A computer is used in a particular workplace, for particular tasks, by one member of a group working under specified conditions. The organization has considerable influence on the nature of the interaction: What software is provided? Is training provided? What level of technical support is available? How much attention is given to lighting and furniture? Where are printers and other peripherals placed? In addition, a wide range of communication and coordination issues are introduced. How is relevant information entered into the system? Who has access to it? How does it reach them at appropriate times? And so on.

Even in an apparently "organization-free" setting, group and organizational influence is felt. Consider those who use personal computers at home. They rely on others to guide hardware and software choices. They are influenced by the level of support provided by manufacturers and distributors. Vendor decisions about interoperability affect them.

We have noted that the organizational context affects the implementation of computer systems—their introduction and use. Below, we will argue that understanding the organizational context of use is critical for designers and developers. In addition organizational context affects interactive system development because development, like use, takes place in different kinds of organizations.

Small software start-up companies provide certain possibilities, constraints, priorities, and pressures. Development labs that employ thousands of people are a very different context. And still other experiences are encountered in the systems group of a large "user organization," such as a hospital, bank, or government agency. Organizational differences affect all aspects of development, including the design of human-computer dialogues and interfaces.

How do these two aspects of organizational knowledge—organizational effects on use and organizational effects on development—influence design? Knowledge of system introduction and use can provide critical insight in formulating requirements, finding characteristic users, and identifying salient interface constituents, where the interface is broadly defined to include documentation, training, and support. Knowledge of the development context can help one anticipate challenges, select appropriate techniques, and avoid the tendency, when obstacles are encountered, to blame individuals rather than organizational structures and processes.

Organizations themselves operate in a broader context. As world attention fastens on issues of computer access and use, HCI is affected by national policies, legislation, litigation, negotiations among governments, and so forth. Organizations may respond first to these influences, but ultimately the effect is felt by individuals using computers.

Organizational issues have been considered more carefully by Europeans working in an ergonomic tradition. In North America, organizational concerns are a focus of the Information Systems field (also called Data Processing, Management Information Systems, Informatics, and increasingly often Information Technology). They are also considered by some human factors professionals. Organizational issues have not been prominent in SIGCHI, which has primarily focused on issues relevant to "mass market" software. The marketplace tends to insulate developers from organizational issues affecting computer use. Customers are expected to fit "shrinkwrap software" into their homes or organizations. They may expect some help from marketing or customer support of major vendors, but not from the designers or developers of mass market products. As noted, HCI usability specialists focus more on the perceptual and cognitive capabilities common to most users, and less on social and organizational influences that are more variable across users.

The boundaries are breaking down between the two groups, one focused on information systems and one on commercial products. In the past, many organizations developed all their software in-house; today software products are used everywhere and users expect higher quality interfaces. Commercial software is increasingly designed to support group activity and must be accepted by groups, not by individuals, forcing recognition of organizational issues long grappled with by in-house developers. Grudin (1990) suggested that the North American human-computer interaction field could be seen as a gradual "outward" movement away from computer hardware (1 in Figure 1), focusing next on software (2), then perceptual aspects of input and display devices (3), then cognitive aspects of gradually higher level (4), and finally to group-level interactions (5). The next step in this progression is to the organizational contexts in which groups function. Neglected by HCI, this organizational context of computer use has long been the focus of the Information Systems field. This chapter presents the case for bringing together insights from HCI and IS.

Figure 1. Five foci of human-computer interaction development *(Grudin, 1990).*

60.2 Case Study: An Interface Project Misses the Organizational Point

Markus and Keil (1994) illustrate the benefit of a careful organizational analysis by demonstrating that a well-executed interface design project can produce a highly usable system that is not useful—and not used. A major computer company employing leading interface designers, given the pseudonym "CompuSys," initiated a project to redesign the interface to an application developed for internal use by the sales force. The application was an expert system of the kind made famous in the mid-1980s by Digital's XCON (Barker and O'Connor, 1989). Sales representatives, trying to work out complex system configurations for customers, frequently made errors. Because the company often swallowed the cost of fixing these errors, an expert system to help configure products could be of great benefit. An expert system capable of accurately configuring products was built, but it was used with only a fraction of the orders. Costly errors continued to plague other orders.

Why wasn't the system used? The sales force complained about its usability, leading to the major redesign of the awkward interface. The project employed many techniques advocated in chapters of this handbook, including iterative design with user feedback. Users from five pilot sites were trained on the new system. After an investment of millions of dollars, a much improved interface was introduced.

The new version was not used much more than the one it replaced.

Why? The design was based on this model of the sales process: i) a customer identifies system requirements; ii) the sales representative works out a system configuration that will meet the requirements; iii) the price for the system is calculated. Logical, but not how things usually work. Most customers have a general sense of what they need done and a fixed budget for technology. They indicate how much they have to spend, and the sales rep tries to identify a useful system that can be acquired for that amount. The application did not support this "backwards" reasoning from price to configuration—it worked only in one direction, from configuration to price. Lacking this key functionality, the application did not help the sales force. The new interface made it easier to work from the configuration to the price, but this missed the point. It was usable but not useful.

The developers did not understand why the usable system was neglected. It was an organizational (in fact, interorganizational) analysis that discovered the "counterintuitive" work process.

How can we avoid such mistakes? Developers can examine work settings and test prototypes in conditions as work-like as possible, as encouraged by advocates of contextual and participatory or collaborative approaches (e.g., Beyer and Holtzblatt, 1995; Bødker, Grønbæk and Kyng, 1993). We can build our intuition by studying the literature on organizational theory and practice. The next section of this chapter summarizes insights from this literature. Subsequent sections describe the importance of organizational issues for the use and development of interactive systems.

60.3 What is an Organization?

Organizations are often defined as collections of people with a common purpose or task. But this definition applies equally well to groups, which have become the focus of so much interest with the popularity of groupware technologies. If we know about groups, is there anything else we have to know in order to understand organizations? The answer, we believe, is yes.

It is often said that a group is more than its members. When we say this, we means that the relationships among the members, the "group dynamics" if you will, are an important factor that differentiates a group from a random collection of individuals. By analogy, organizations can be thought of as "groups of groups." In the organization, the formal structure and the dynamic processes defining the relationships among the groups are important factors that differentiate organizations from random collections of groups.

General systems theory suggests that the best way to understand a human-machine "system" (whether it involves an individual, a group, or an organization) is to start at least one level up to look at the role or function or purpose of the system in the larger whole of which it is a part. Then, one has the background knowledge needed to get the most out of an understanding of the component parts. Thus, if one is trying to learn about a unique "human-computer interaction" one would first want to know what the purpose and context of that interaction was, before looking at the components: individuals with display, keyboard and mouse. Similarly, to understand an organization, we examine the role that organization plays in the networks of organizations in which it participates before looking at its component parts: groups and individuals with structured relationships and dynamic interactions.

60.3.1 Organizations in Context

Organizations do not exist in isolation, any more than individuals do. They operate in a larger societal context or environment than can usefully be considered a network of organizations.

Consider AutoCorp, an automobile manufacturing company. This organization interacts with many other organizations of several different kinds: suppliers of raw materials, employment agencies for personnel, banks and financial institutions of all types, marketing services firms (e.g., advertising agencies), distribution channel firms (e.g., automobile dealerships), large customers (e.g., auto rental agencies), competitors, individual customers, and the public at large. In this network of interacting organizations, each organization performs a different role. Each organization has unique goals or "interests" that are sometimes compatible with those of the other organizations, and sometimes in conflict. Some organizations are much larger and richer than the others, controlling more resources, and thus are more likely to "win" when there are conflicts of interests. For example, AutoCorp may wish to court auto rental companies as customers, since they buy many cars, and may therefore decide to give them prices as good or better than they give to smaller individual auto dealers. (On the other hand, AutoCorp may begin to worry about the sales of used cars by the auto rental companies cutting into their dealers' sales of new and used cars, and therefore may decide to terminate the advantageous purchase terms that they give to auto rental companies.)

Similarly, in the software development industry, we find networks of organizations with different roles involved in the sale and support of various products and services. If AutoCorp decided that all its managerial and technical personnel should use Lotus Notes, for example, it might contract with Compaq for computer hardware, with Lotus Development Corp. for the Notes software, with a small "Notes development company" for a specialized custom application based on the Lotus Notes platform, and a university department for consulting advice, training, and other support. This, too, is a network of organizations, in which the individual member organizations have different interests, different types of relationships with each other, and different resources to bear on any particular issue of the moment. The various vendors and services providers in the AutoCorp Lotus Notes network might interact quite harmoniously until AutoCorp experiences a tricky technical problem for which there is no simple fix. Then, each organization may claim that the problem is some other party's fault.

Because each organization in a network has different goals and interests, there are opportunities for conflict in their relationships with each other. Some organizations both cooperate and compete, as in the case of the automobile companies and the car rental companies. Some organizations seek success in short- or long-term financial terms (e.g., profitability, market share); others, like universities, hospitals, governments, social-service agencies and voluntary organizations, may define success in non-financial terms, such as knowledge creation and transfer, health, social welfare, the satisfaction of members. Rich dynamics result from the interaction of organizations with different goals and interests.

60.3.2 Organizational Components

Within most organizations of any size, things are just as complex and dynamic on the inside as they are on the outside. Organizations consist of people organized in various kinds of work groups, which in turn are organized in larger structural arrangements. AutoCorp, for example, may be internally organized by product divisions (cars, with subcategories including sport cars and luxury cars; sport/utility vehicles and minivans; trucks and industrial vehicles). Alternatively, it might be organized by geography (North America, Europe, Asia, Africa, and South America). Then again, it might be organized by the technology or the vehicle component that it makes (e.g., engine, power train, chassis, body etc.). Similarly, computer manufacturing companies can be organized by product (mainframes, minis, workstations, PCs) or by function (hardware, systems software, applications software, support) or with some other basis.[1]

There is nothing sacred about bases of organization. In some industries, virtually all organizations in the same size class have a similar organizational structure. In others, there is a great deal of local variation. Large organizations have multiple choices in the organizational structures they adopt, and may shift from one to another. However, their choices can determine what the organization can do easily and well compared to similar organizations. For instance, the large AutoCorp that is organized by product line will probably be much less responsive to geographical differences in customer preferences for auto styling than a similar company with geographic divisions. And the computer manufacturer, ComputerCorp, that is organized by function may have a harder time delivering new PC models to market than a similar company with a product organization.

Just as the different organizations in a network have different goals and interests based on their positions and functions in the network, so do different organizational groups, departments, divisions, and other types of units. Even though the organization as a whole may have a single, clear set of goals and interests, individuals, groups, and subunits within the organization may not share these goals and interests fully. For instance, members of the systems software unit of ComputerCorp may differ substantially from members of the hardware unit in terms of prior education and work experience. In addition, the heads of these units may be subject to widely different goals, performance measures, and rewards. For example, the software unit may be evaluated on development schedules and budgets, whereas the hardware group may be evaluated largely on manufacturing cost. Such differences can make it hard for the units to cooperate to achieve the total organization's goals. This could be seen in the case of CompuSys discussed at the beginning of this chapter: Errors in computer system configuration originated with the Sales department, which was rewarded for sales volume, but the manufacturing unit had to bear the costs associated with fixing incorrect orders. Naturally, given the incentives and rewards, the Sales department did not devote much time and energy to insuring that the orders were correct at the outset.

To some extent, problems of this sort can be prevented through good communication of organizational purpose by the organization's leaders. However, it is generally also necessary for the leaders to motivate and reinforce behavior in keeping with organizational goals by means of good measures, rewards and punishments. Unfortunately, the complexity of many large organizations makes it difficult to design these "management systems" so that they are both efficient and effective, yielding desired behavior with few undesired negative consequences. Generally speaking, in organizations of any size and structural complexity, subunits exhibit a fair degree of "goal displacement," pursuing goals and values that make sense to the subunit, but that do not necessarily advance the overall interests of the organization. For instance, the applications development and hardware manufacturing units in ComputerCorp might each meet their unit goals without necessarily positioning ComputerCorp to achieve its overall marketing strategy.

Within organizations, work groups and larger organizational units can develop distinct "cultures" (assumptions, beliefs, and language systems) that make it difficult for members to communicate clearly and effectively with members of other groups and units. There are endless stories of companies that try to establish data management discipline only to learn that

[1] Other bases of organization include project (common in the aerospace and construction industries as well as in software development firms), technology (disk drives, memory, processors; electronics, pneumatics, thermodynamics; radiology, obstetrics, orthopedics), time frame (first, second and third shift; development, maintenance, operations), and discipline (mathematics, physics, social science, humanities).

the same terms are used in very different ways in different parts of the organization. For instance, it's a "sale" to Sales when the customer gives a verbal OK to an order, but it's not a "sale" to Legal until a contract is signed, and it's not a "sale" to Manufacturing until the purchase order is entered into the manufacturing control system, and the Accounting department only acknowledges a "sale" when the invoice has been prepared. Intra-company language differences contribute to widely differing points of view on key organizational decisions. Conflict as well as cooperation occurs in organizational decision-making (both often occurring at the same time), producing a rich set of behavioral dynamics inside organizations similar to those observable when organizations interact.

60.3.3 Summary of Ways in Which Organizations Differ

In general, it is useful to think of at least three levels of reality operating simultaneously in and among organizations. The first can be called rational, technical, or economic reality. This level of reality takes a stated goal as given; the concern is with the most efficient and effective means of achieving it. The second level of reality can be called socio-emotional task reality. People have social needs and organizations are vehicles through which they attempt to meet them. In addition, people become habituated to particular ways of thinking and behaving in organizations due in part to their membership in organizational groups and subunits. These ways of thinking and acting may differ, sometimes dramatically from what an outside observer believes to be the rational, techno-economic optimum. The third level of reality is the structural/political level, which concerns goals and interests created by resources and positions in units and task chains (often called business processes) or interorganizational networks. Keeping all three realities in mind helps in comprehending the complex dynamics of organizational behavior.

This has necessarily been a highly simplified overview of organizational behavior. In the next section, we show how these organizational issues can have enormous implications for the adoption, deployment, use, and consequences of information technology in organizations. However, first we will review some major categories of differences between organizations and their component work groups and subunits that can significantly shape the use of information technology:

- size in number of members
- size in terms of financial resources, particularly "slack" (uncommitted resources) that come from past financial success or powerful backers
- geography (scope of operations) and space (e.g., in buildings)
- age of organization, demography of members, average tenure of employees — experience working together
- stated or implicit goals or strategies (e.g., least cost producer versus product innovator) which can determine the "key business processes"
- structure/basis of organization (product, geographic, function, technology, time)
- culture (beliefs, assumptions, language systems, characteristic behavior patterns)
- "management systems" (measures, rewards, promotion patterns, etc.)
- information technology infrastructure (history of prior investments in and commitments to particular technology directions, patterns of IT governance)

With this long list of differences, it should not be surprising that organizations, as well as sub-units and groups, can react quite differently to the "same" technology.

60.4 What are the Organizational Issues in Interactive System Use?

In this section, we will examine the organizational issues in interactive system use from the perspective of organizations adopting systems for internal use, rather than the perspective of organizations who develop systems for sale to other organizations. (This is a somewhat artificial distinction, because developers often use the systems they develop, and user companies often develop applications for their own use and then find it attractive to offer them for sale to other companies. Nevertheless, as we elaborate below in Part 3, development process can differ quite substantially when the system is intended primarily for in-house use and when it is developed for external consumption, so we believe the distinction is an important one to make.)

We organize our discussion by broad phases in a *life cycle of system use*. The phases we consider are: initiation (when an idea originates and a project is funded), acquisition (when the user organization acquires or builds the system), implementation and use (when the user organization deploys the system internally and people begin to use it or reject it), and impacts and consequences (when the organization experiences the effects of system use and takes steps to augment, mitigate, or otherwise manage them).

60.4.1 Initiation Phase

In the initiation phase, an organizational decision is made to adopt a new computer-based technology or to adopt an organizational change requiring IT support. The decision process is often complex. The impetus for an innovation may come from outside the organization, as when management consultants recommend that the client company adopt Lotus Notes as a way to "manage intellectual capital" and to "support knowledge work" or when a vendor convinces the company's Chief Information Officer (CIO) of a groupware product's potential as an infrastructure for electronic communication, document management, and teamwork. Alternatively, the impetus for the innovation may come from inside the organization, as when the Chief Executive Officer (CEO) visits a supplier and is impressed by the benefits that company achieved from the adoption of Lotus Notes, or when the technology scanning or portfolio planning group within the IS department identifies groupware as a high priority technology for investment.

The source of a technology investment idea can have important influences on downstream events. It can, for instance, affect: the features of the technology or software package purchased, built or used; how the innovation is used by various parties in the organization; and what its impacts are. The person or group that initially proposes the innovation may not have the formal organizational authority or resource control to proceed with acquisition or development. Instead, an initiator may have to seek approval from authorized decision-makers. The process by which this occurs may be highly informal, requiring only a personal appeal to a "line" executive who controls a large enough budget to fund the project.[2] Other organizations, however, have specially designated approval boards and formal processes for reviewing and approving technology expenditures. There is substantial variation from one organization to the next in how these boards and processes are structured.[3]

Organizational policy may require the initiators to prepare a formal proposal justifying the investment, actually "selling" the idea to decision-makers by demonstrating that the innovation meets pre-established investment criteria (e.g., financial return on investment or fit with an existing strategic IT plan). Some of the investment criteria may not fit the innovation, perhaps because they were developed for investing in new manufacturing equipment or new retail sales locations, rather than new information technologies. Technology champions may find that applying the investment criteria to a groupware acquisition decision requires some distortion in descriptions of technology use, risks, and benefits. (See Dean, 1987 for a discussion of the technology justification process.)

During the justification process, various people and groups in an organization can develop a shared understanding of what the technology is good for. Building consensus about the value of a technology can substantially ease downstream implementation and acceptance. However, the shared understanding that develops during the justification process may not conform closely to the objective capabilities of the technology and the ways in which it must be used for the organization to achieve maximum benefit. Thus, a technology like Lotus Notes may come to be seen as a low cost solution to the problems of an aging architecture of desktop computing or to the problem of an expensive-to-maintain home-grown email system. Subsequently, individuals in organizations sharing this view of Lotus Notes may never take full advantage of the tool's discussion databases.[4]

On the other hand, the initial impetus for an innovative interactive system can come from a CEO or another highly placed line corporate officer. The CEO may have been influenced by a vendor's sales pitch, by articles in the press, or by first hand knowledge of what sister companies are doing. Thus, advertising, business fads, and public image may affect the outcome of what many people believe should be rational decision making based on sound technical and economic criteria (Cohen, March and Olson, 1972). For instance, Kling (1978) gives a wonderful example of a welfare case tracking system that was adopted and used despite its lack of operational benefits because the system made the agency look good to potential funders.

When the impetus for a technology acquisition comes from powerful organizational decision-makers, the innovation is unlikely to be subjected to rigorous justification, review and approval. The initiator can directly provide access to the resources required to acquire and develop the technology. However, when de-

---

[2] "Line" refers to managers in the core businesses or functions of the organization, as opposed to those in "staff" functions. In most organizations, IS is viewed as a "staff" function. This is frequently true even in software development firms, where the IS people who provide support for the internal operations of the business are organizationally separate from "line" software developers who work on the products the company sells.

[3] Literature on this issue is found under such headings as "IT Management," "IT Governance," and "Management of the IS function." (See Markus and Soh, 1993; Davenport, Eccles, and Prusak, 1993.)

[4] We have seen two such companies in which this has occurred.

cisions are made without formal review by knowledgeable technologists and intended users, there is no guarantee that the technology will address real organizational needs, fit the organization's preferred ways of working, and actually be used. For instance, the IS department might already be committed to a different technological solution and may not give the CEO's project wholehearted support. Similarly, potential users of the innovation may fail to see any personal advantages in the technology and refuse to use it.[5]

During the initiation phase a project's schedule, its level of funding, and the allocation of funds to different project activities are usually set. These decisions can sometimes be revisited when a project that continues to look promising runs behind schedule or over budget. But the schedule, scope, and funding decisions made during the initiation phase often have lasting, and not entirely positive, influences downstream. For instance, an organizational decision to limit access to Lotus Notes to one particular work unit can create difficulties later for activities that cross the boundaries between work units. Or the decision-makers may allocate enough resources to acquire or develop a technology but significantly underfund training and support for users, creating predictably negative consequences when the technology is "up and running" (see Walton, 1989).

In short, the initiation phase of the life cycle can involve political negotiations between people and groups who propose new technologies and people and groups who control essential resources (both technical and financial). These negotiations can result in the selection of inappropriate solutions to organizational problems, or they can result in perceptions and decisions that subsequently have negative effects on system features, use, and impacts. As we see below, additional problems and errors can be introduced at each subsequent phase in the life cycle.

60.4.2 Acquisition

Once a technology investment proposal has received formal approval and funding, a project leader is usually appointed to oversee the next phase of the project. The major activities of this phase are to acquire the capabilities required by the innovation and make the capabilities operational. Several difficulties can arise in this phase.

[5] See Grudin, 1994, on electronic calendaring systems proposed by managers but resisted by team members who have to input their schedules.

The first and most important problem is that the project team may define the capabilities required by the interactive system in purely technical terms (Stinchcombe, 1990). The project team may focus on software features, access hardware, and networking requirements, but neglect to provide for the training and support of users and necessary changes in such organizational aspects as their job descriptions, their performance evaluations, and their rewards. When the project team defines its work in purely technical terms, downstream problems, such as limited user acceptance, low levels of use, and poor quality use almost always occur (Walton, 1989).

But even if the project team includes "implementation planning" in its charter, problems may still arise.[6] If the technology has been poorly designed or selected, acceptance and use problems will often occur regardless of training, support, or user involvement in design or selection. Therefore, it is important to examine the design/selection processes in some detail.

As previously mentioned, the initiation decision may specify what technology is to be used and how it is to be obtained (e.g., acquired from a vendor versus built in-house). If these decisions have not been made, the project team generally decides them, perhaps under the oversight of an executive steering committee that requires regular reports. In making these decisions, the project team is often subjected to influence attempts by various interested parties internal and external to the project team. For example, several members of the project team may have strong desires to build the technology in-house, even though there are perfectly acceptable packages available from external vendors. Some team members may wish to customize a package to unique organizational needs rather than to change the way the organization works. Project team members may have different personal preferences for a technology vendor, a software package, or an infrastructural platform or architecture. Or they may demand that the solution incorporate certain features. Or, in the interests of meeting schedule and budgets, certain aspects of the project included in the original proposal may be postponed or dropped altogether.

[6] "Implementation" is an ambiguous term in the IS community. Developers often use the term to mean software development, or "coding." Social scientists and line managers often use the word to refer to the set of activities involved in ensuring user acceptance and appropriate use of a technology. These activities include participation in technology design or selection as well as training and support. We use the term "implementation" in the latter sense, while noting that many conflicts occur in organizations because IS specialists and line managers use this term in very dissimilar ways.

The outcomes of these negotiations will depend on various factors including the composition of the project team (whether or not it includes users, for example), organizational policies and practices applicable to the project (e.g., mandated system development methodologies or a corporate policy to buy software rather than build it in-house), and unique project team dynamics. For instance, in the CompuSys case described earlier in this chapter, technologist members of the project team did not hear, or refused to listen to, user members' repeated requests for the full and immediate integration of CONFIG with their Automatic Quotation System (Markus and Keil, 1994).

The net result of the acquisition phase is that the innovation becomes more real and more resistant to change than it was in the initiation phase. In the process of writing detailed specifications, obtaining input from potential users, contracting with vendors, and making arrangements with facilities specialists, installers, operations and support personnel, trainers and users' managers, various organizational changes occur. First, the technical characteristics of the innovation become "fixed," at least for some period of time.[7] Second, plans are made and executed (or *not* made and *not* executed) to improve the capacity of organization and its human resources to use the technology effectively. Third, perceptions of what the technology is good for and how it should be used often stabilize and carry over into the use phase.

These changes can take place in any direction, relative to the initiation phase. On the one hand, the design team may take a poorly thought-through executive decision to invest in coordination technology and craft from it an eminently workable plan for building the organization's intellectual capital. On the other hand, a well-reasoned executive goal to encourage information sharing with the aid of information technology may be transformed, during the acquisition phase, into an expensive infrastructure project without the applications and skilled users required to deliver measurable business value (Markus and Soh, 1993, Soh and Markus, 1995).

Finally, another output of the acquisition phase is a set of social relations among various groups inside and outside the organization who will work with or support the technology during the "use" phase. The acquisition phase creates or formalizes linkages among technology vendors, third-party developers, in-house developers, in-house computer operations and support personnel, or an outsourcing firm, and users and their managers. These social relations can have far reaching consequences in subsequent phases of the project life cycle. For instance, users' ability to resolve the "recurrent dilemmas of routine computer use" (Kling and Scacchi, 1982) may depend critically on various maintenance and support personnel (see also Gasser, 1986). Thorny support issues may remain unresolved due to the incentives built into outsourcers' "service level agreements" as negotiated during the acquisition phase. User skills may stagnate or decline, because a one-shot training program did not address the need for advanced training or for initial training for new hires. In short, what gets "set in place" during the acquisition phase may or may not be adequate for the organization's future needs.

60.4.3 Implementation and Use

It may seem as though the decisions made during the acquisition phase completely determine the outcome from there on out. But again we find that activities occurring during the implementation and use phase can quite substantially alter (for better or worse) the capabilities previously acquired and thereby affect the downstream phase of the technology use life cycle.

As earlier mentioned, some project teams do not make adequate provisions during the acquisition phase to involve users in design, to upgrade users' technology skills, or to change organizational structures and policies. In effect, they make or buy a technological product and throw it "over the wall" to users and their managers. While this usually results in a failure of the technology to be used at all or to be used well enough to yield hoped-for organizational benefits, it is sometimes the case that line managers and users see some potential in the technologies tossed at them and adopt these technologies as their own. Doing so may, of course, require line managers to make significant investments in training, facilitation, support, and changes in policies, procedures, and structures (investments, we add, that usually were not budgeted as part of the initial project proposal).

When users and their managers take technologies as their own, there is no guarantee that they will use them in ways consistent with either the initiator's or the project team's original vision. Technologists often assume that the appropriate use of an information technology is synonymous with its features and that both the features and the appropriate use of a technology can be easily inferred during a casual browsing proc-

[7] Over time, of course, major changes in system capability occur through maintenance and enhancement. cf. Swanson and Beath, 1989; Stinchcombe, 1990.

ess. But this assumption depends on a seriously flawed view of users and of the processes by which typical users learn about new information technologies. Studies show that the average user of even a modestly complex information technology like the digital telephone system uses only a small fraction of the technology's features (Manross and Rice, 1986). Typical users (as opposed to the "power users" that technologists often are) don't enjoy the process of learning a new technology, and may even experience moderate to severe phobic reactions. They usually learn only as much of a technology as they need to do the task at hand, and they often learn by asking their co-workers (who may be little more skilled than they are) to help them, rather than by consulting manuals, on-line tutorials, specialists, or help desks. Once they acquire some level of proficiency, they often stop learning new features unless a new release, a conversion, or a major change in work pressures fairly demands new learning (Tyre and Orlikowski, 1994). Often users will enact time-consuming and inefficient "workarounds" (Gasser, 1986), rather than invest the time, energy, and pain required to learn a more efficient procedure.

One implication of these learning dynamics is that users may quite easily acquire a very different idea about what a technological innovation is good for than those of technology vendors, initiators, developers, or implementors. Just as there was no guarantee that the CEO would "value" an information technology she reads about in an airplane seatback magazine the same way that the development company does, and just as there is no guarantee that project team members will view the innovation in the same light as the person or group who championed it, there is no guarantee that users and their managers will see technologies "objectively" in terms of their features or value them in the same way that vendors, initiators, or internal developers do. So, for example, we have studied organizations in which people use neither Lotus Notes' email capabilities nor its distribution lists, but do value it as a document repository and a source of "news feeds." Similarly, we have also seen organizations in which people use Lotus Notes exclusively as an email and personal file management system without employing any shared document databases or discussion lists.

Whereas the previous examples have concerned significant *underuse* of a complex information technology, it is also the case that users sometimes take simple information technologies and considerably *overuse* them, getting more out of them than designers ever intended. For instance, we know of at least two organizations (Harvard Business School, 1994; Markus, 1994) in which very simple email systems were effectively used as if they were full-functioned groupware systems. In both organizations, people with the goal of better managing geographically-dispersed organizational activities jointly discovered ways to support many-to-many group-oriented communications via a technology that is better able to support one-to-one private and one-to-many broadcast communications.

In settings where "overuses" of technology occur, we believe that people first substitute the new technology in activities and processes they were already doing in some other way. These initial uses of the technology may not be economic — that is, the new technology may have no real relative advantage compared to the older technologies for these uses. However, some users learn more about the technology from these early trials and eventually experiment with valuable new uses for it. Some of these new uses involve employing the new technology in complementarity with older technologies (rather than as substitutions for them) (Soe, 1994). For instance, managers at one company we studied (HCP Inc.) used email in conjunction with the telephone. Subordinates would first fully document problems or decision situations in email, and then would telephone their managers, achieving much more rapid discussion and approval than possible via either a phone call or email alone (Markus, 1994). It is these new uses, unanticipated when the technology was first acquired, rather than the initially planned uses, that often result in what are subsequently called organizational "transformations:" radical improvements in business processes, first-in-the-world new products and services, and so forth.

The technical term for the process we have been describing here, in which users take a technology and redefine it, using it differently than developers, initiators and implementors intended, is *reinvention* (Rogers, 1995). Reinvention is significant, because it means that the use and hence the impacts of a technology can never fully be determined during the acquisition phase. Even when the project team involves users in design and fashion a careful technology implementation plan, both users and developers may fail to see the real organizational implications of a technology until the technology itself is real, installed and up and running in an organization.[8] While it's easy after the fact the spot the design flaw in CONFIG, for example,

[8] Social scientists repeatedly warn that user participation in design does not ensure success, since participation can lead to "incrementalism" or recreation of the status quo (Walton, 1989; Leonard-Barton, 1988, 1990; Markus and Keil, 1994).

it probably did not seem like a fatal flaw at the time to either the developers or the users. Otherwise, the users would have been well within their rights to threaten to withdraw their support and participation in the project team unless the designers agreed to first-release integration of CONFIG and AQS. Something similar could have occurred in Orlikowski's widely-cited case study of Lotus Notes at Alpha Corp. (Orlikowski and Gash, 1994). After the fact, it may seem quite obvious that consultants would not want to enter data into Lotus Notes databases because of their intense job pressures and time use targets and their fear that someone else would take credit for their ideas in the up-or-out world of management consulting. But the high-level partners who approved Alpha Corp's huge financial investment in Notes must themselves have been persuaded by the technologists that "if we build it they will come."

Reinvention during the use phase of the life cycle means that, to a certain extent, use patterns (and the subsequent organizational impacts) just happen. Good design practice (e.g., user involvement) and holistic design (i.e., design that addresses the social and political aspects of work in addition to the technical and economic aspects) are certainly important, and we strongly advocate their use by project teams. Nevertheless, we recognize that what happens when users get their hands on a technology can never be fully predicted or controlled. We call this phenomenon *emergence* (Markus and Robey, 1988). Sometimes what emerges during use is much less than vendors, initiators, and implementors had hoped; sometimes it is much, much more.

60.4.4 Impacts and Performance

The use of an information technology is an on-going process. Even if the technology stays relatively stable, use can evolve over time as people experiment with features in the context of their organizational problems and invent new uses for it. However, it is rare for the technology itself or the context in which it is used to remain stable.

Recall the case of the CONFIG system. Developers were disappointed with the low initial level of use; to address this perceived problem, they developed a completely new interface to the system and "reimplemented" it, devoting substantial resources both to the technological platform and to user training and support. This effort did not pay off for CompuSys, but in many other organizations it does. The old rule "if at first you don't succeed, try, try again" applies nowhere better than in the field of innovation, where "sticking to it" and "trying again" are well known success factors (Kanter, Stein, and Jick, 1992). Some experts estimate the majority of the benefits obtainable from an innovation come from subsequent modifications and enhancements, rather than from the initial change itself (Stinchcombe, 1990). So, for example, Frito-Lay did not reap full advantages from its handheld computer project until it developed analytic tools to improve product promotion decision making and changed the organizational level at which promotion decisions were made (Harvard Business School, 1993). This occurred some 10 years after the initial technology investment decisions were made! Similarly, it may take some years before an organization develops the "killer app" document database that makes its investment in Lotus Notes pay off.

Of course, a key point to bear in mind is that the subsequent improvements to the innovation must be carefully tracked and managed. As in many other avenues of human endeavor the subsequent enhancements on the basic innovation may be superficial "bells and whistles" that please users or developers but do not necessarily enhance the effectiveness of work processes, organizational communication and decision making or customer service. In fact, one of the major reasons given for the failure of IT investments to pay off in terms of improved organizational performance is a tendency for organizations to make non-value added improvements in their IT environments (Baily, 1986; Baily and Gordon, 1988).[9] The people at VeriFone believe, "If you're just using email, there's no reason to have a Pentium. You don't need a Ferrari to drive to the supermarket." (Harvard Business School, 1994).

When technologies are used to at least some threshold level, impacts begin to be observable. Positive organizational impacts from information technology are said to fall into four categories: new products and services enabled by IT, improved business processes, better organizational decision-making attributable to databases and analytic tools, and increased organizational flexibility attributable to communication, collaboration, and coordination technologies (Sambamurthy and Zmud, 1992). However, two issues regarding the impacts of technology must be borne in mind.

First, positive organizational impacts due to technology investments do not always result in improved organizational performance, measured in terms important to various organizational stakeholders (Soh and

[9] This issue and its relationship to usability is explored in detail by Landauer (1995).

Markus, 1995). For example, a computer manufacturing company like CompuSys may realize improved business processes (reduced errors on customer shipments) and yet may not be able to realize any improvements in overall profitability, market share, or customer retention. Lack of performance improvement despite positive impacts will occur if the innovation is quickly duplicated by competitors or if the improvements only bring company performance up to existing customer expectations. Similarly, a university that attracts new students via its distance learning program may find its own traditional geographic market "poached" by distant universities with similar programs, ultimately leaving it no better off than it was before the innovation. Ultimately, the ability to turn impacts into organizational performance depends on many factors, not all of which are under the control of the innovating organization, such as the behavior of competitors (Arthur, 1990; Clemons, 1991).

Second, positive organizational impacts are almost invariably accompanied by negative impacts on some dimensions of organizational life (Pool, 1983, Rogers, 1995). For instance, the improved organizational efficiency and flexibility attributed to electronic communications technologies like email may be accompanied by depersonalization, stress, overload, and accountability politics (Sproull and Kiesler, 1991; Markus, 1994b). The organization may find ways to reduce the negative impacts or may conclude that the negative impacts are a small price to pay for the positive benefits achieved. Nevertheless, the organization can find it impossible to eliminate negative effects entirely, even if it wishes to do so. For organizations to adopt new ways of working, they must often abandon the social interaction patterns associated with prior ways of working. No matter how much people in the organization may value the improvements in organizational functioning they may still mourn the passing of traditional ways that gave meaning and quality to their working lives (Bridges, 1994).

Furthermore, negative impacts may be ineradicable because they prop up or enable the positive impacts. For example, managers at HCP Inc. preserved email as a useful tool for strategic discussions that were painful to conduct in writing (but beneficial since this allowed additional parties to be "added" to the strategic discussions later without explaining everything again, because of the email archive) by discouraging the use of the telephone for work-related purposes. But this resulted in people feeling alienated and depersonalized. To counter this, the telephone was used extensively to remain in personal contact with people (but not for business reasons, since this might have eroded the discipline of conducting business in email) (Markus, 1994b).

Similarly, one of the great strengths of email is the ability to document what has been done on projects and to compare progress to commitments. The same features of email enable a distinctly negative use pattern (as perceived by those who have had it done to them). People at HCP Inc. tended to keep track of others' promises and fulfillments. When promises were broken and organizational results suffered, it was easy for individuals to show themselves blameless and others at fault by forwarding copies of the email correspondence to their own and the offender's bosses (Markus, 1994b). Naturally, this practice can corrode organizational climate quickly.

In short, impacts can change over time, growing in contribution to organizational performance or diminishing, frittered away through lack of focused management attention. In addition, positive impacts can occur without making lasting effects on important indicators of organizational performance, because they are "competed away" through the actions of competitors and the reactions of customers in the marketplace. Finally, whatever positive effects occur may be accompanied inseparably by negative impacts, often affecting the social relationships in the workplace.

These organizational issues in interactive system deployment are summarized in Table 1. In the next section, we discuss more fully how organizational issues affect interactive system development.

60.5 What are the Organizational Issues in Interactive System Development?

The previous sections provide software developers with insight into organizational issues that affect the customers and users of systems. Organizational issues also affect developers directly, through issues that arise in the specific organizational contexts in which they work. Indirectly, organizations mediate between developer and user organizations, and organizations contribute to the economic, cultural, political, and societal conditions that influence design and development.

Developers are well aware that organizations constrain their work through time pressures, approval processes, formal specifications, and other management practices. Less evident is that these constraints differ markedly across organizations and that some of the differences are systematic, based on historical fac-

Table 1. Summary of lifecycle phases.

Lifecycle Phases	Description	Challenges and Effects
Initiation	Idea generation Project justification Project funding decision	Idea unworkable or not best use of technology Features may be selected before analysis Implementation may be underfunded
Acquisition	Project leader identified Solutions specified in greater detail User organization acquires or builds system	Design process can promote or limit acceptance Solution may be poorly specified Network of support relationships is created
Implementation and Use	Internal deployment First use or rejection	Training may not be sufficient Use may not conform to plan Users may reinvent technology
Impacts and Consequences	Organization experiences effects Acts to augment, mitigate, manage them	System is modified and enhanced Training needs evolve Consequences emerge

tors and on the conditions governing development in different segments of the industry. These differences help determine which techniques and tools will be useful. Organizational structures and practices have obvious and subtle effects on the human-computer interfaces that are developed.

Organizational differences that influence technology use also affect development: size, geographical placement, age, function, culture, environment. In a small start-up company, all employees see one another regularly; in a large organization, software, documentation, and training developers may work in different states or countries. At the societal level, American court decisions regarding "look and feel" infringement and European co-determination laws can affect the process and product of development.

Relationships of developers and the eventual users of their technology is central to human-computer interface design, so we focus here on examining development contexts in which organizational function and structure greatly influence the possibilities for interaction among developers and users. Drawing on Grudin (1991a, 1996) we consider four development contexts: competitively bid contract development, internal or in-house development, product or package development, and custom development. The first three organizational contexts differ radically. The fourth, custom development, shares features with each of the others. This set is not exhaustive, and important organizational distinctions (such as size, age, and culture) provide further variation within each.

Differences in development contexts are often overlooked; we tend to identify "the computer industry" as a single entity. Academic training tends to be general, with specialization coming later in a developer's career. Nevertheless, different research disciplines have emerged around the concerns of contract, internal, and product development. Software Engineering formed to address issues in managing large projects, often the result of competitive contract awards; Information Systems has focused on the internal development of systems by large user organizations; and Human-Computer Interaction has focused on issues arising from developing commercial off-the-shelf software.

The distinctions that permitted separate disciplines are eroding. Contracted and internally developed software is no longer self-contained, it must co-exist with commercial products and provide human-computer interfaces of comparable quality. Commercial software developers focusing on groupware applications or features must be more sensitive to the social factors in user organizations that in-house developers have long struggled with. Unfortunately, we now find different disciplines with distinct literatures and terminologies, and communicating across them is a challenge.

60.5.1 The Emergence of Distinct Development Contexts

The historical emergence of development contexts illuminates their differences (Grudin and Poltrock, 1995).

Contract Development

Prior to the emergence of computers based on integrated circuits in the mid-1960s, systems were extremely expensive. Most large systems were contracted by the U.S. government. Government agencies defined the requirements and geographically distant organizations bid for contracts. Different contracts might be awarded for design, development, and maintenance. Developers and users were in different organizations, usually separated by geography and by legal restrictions on communication to prevent unfair advantage to any bidder. This created substantial organizational barriers to the direct contact among developers and users that is at the heart of methodologies endorsed throughout this handbook. However, this mattered less at the time, because not much software was interactive. Most computers were batch processors: Program and data were loaded, the computer computed, and punched or printed output emerged.

In this environment, stage models of development evolved naturally, culminating in the waterfall model (Royce, 1970) at the dawn of software engineering. This specification-based, design-it-first approach, with little provision for feedback or iteration, became the dominant development methodology.

Its limitations were recognized when interactive software became widespread (e.g., Gundry, 1988). Boehm (1988) and others introduced spiral models explicitly to incorporate prototyping and iterative design for interactive software development.

Nevertheless, the separation of developers and users remains a major organizational obstacle to interface design in contract development. Winkler and Buie (1995) summarize the challenges and possible approaches, which include standards that can be included in requests for proposals (RFPs) but primarily focus on raising awareness in both user and developer organizations. The user organization can better specify interface requirements, but even more important is to specify an interface development *process*. Until development organizations are familiar with these processes, cost estimation is difficult, so acceptance of this approach will not be immediate. However, Winkler and Buie clearly identify organizational change as the key to developing better interfaces in government contracting.

Internal Development

With more reliable and less expensive mainframe computers available in the mid-1960s, business use of computers expanded. In-house development of software by user organizations became the principal focus of system development and may still account for most development. The history of systems development in this organizational context is described in detail in Friedman (1989).

Although most processing remained batch rather than interactive, with "end users" engaged in data entry and system operator tasks, the waterfall development model was soon challenged in this organizational context. Barriers to interaction among users and developers that mark contract development are less evident in internal development, where both groups have the same employer and often work in greater proximity. Nevertheless, organizational and cultural barriers often blocked user involvement. Some information systems groups, imbued with the prevailing "design-it-right-up-front" development ideology, fail to seek ongoing user involvement. Young, highly-paid information systems staff may clash "culturally" with other workers. As change agents invested with power and authority, they encountered resistance.

Nevertheless, methodologies were developed to provide greater user involvement. These included the sociotechnical approach (Mumford, 1983; 1993) and Scandinavian participatory design approaches (Bjerknes, Ehn and Kyng, 1987; Greenbaum and Kyng, 1991). They stress developer awareness of worker preferences and actual work processes and emphasize the education of prospective users in technical possibilities.

Product Development

With the arrival of PCs in the early 1980s, commercial, off-the-shelf product development became a major industry, focusing on highly interactive systems and applications. The competitive marketplace for these applications leads to greater emphasis on the human-computer interface and greater time pressures. Contrasted with contract and internal development, product development organizations present yet a different set of constraints on developers. As with contract development, product users and developers are in different organizations, but here the situation is reversed: development organizations define the requirements and users are only firmly identified later, after development is complete.

The inadequacy of the waterfall development methodology was clear in this organizational context. Prototyping and iterative design, with heavy user involvement, were promoted from the outset by researchers including John Gould, whose work appears in this volume. Although these principles were widely accepted, they were not widely practiced, due to organ-

Table 2. Summary of four development contexts.

Development Context	Description	Usability Issues
Competitive Contract	Users, developers in different organizations Users identified before developers Contract often for single development phase	Extreme barriers to ongoing user involvement Reliance on mediators: consultants, standards Need for HCI awareness and a process focus
Internal or In-house	Users and developers are in same organization Users, developers identified at outset Development team handles all phases	Good opportunities for user involvement Cultural and organizational barriers may block Tools can help overcome resource limitations
Product or Package	Users, developers in different organizations Developers identified before specific users Development team may hand off revisions	Leads in usability, but utility often neglected Workplace studies needed but can be difficult Challenges: time pressure, installed base, etc.
Custom	Different orgs. but ongoing relationship Users, developers identified early in project Development team handles multiple revisions	Good opportunities for user feedback over time Smaller niche -> less resources for interfaces Largest growth area for usability work?

izational constraints detailed in Grudin (1991b) and Poltrock and Grudin (1994). When developers are motivated to seek user involvement—which is not always the case—they can have difficulty identifying appropriate users, obtaining access to them, and motivating users who work in other organizations and may never use the final product. If these barriers are overcome, there are often obstacles to using the information that is gathered. Development schedules rarely provide time for iteration, and changes in the interface can be visible and unsettling to management, as well as to those working on product documentation and training, which are dependent on the interface.

In the absence of user involvement, however, the many individual, team, and organizational pressures on product developers distort the human-computer interface design (Grudin, 1991b).

To overcome these obstacles, product developers have sought to adapt participatory design and related techniques (e.g., Muller, 1992). A particularly influential approach is contextual analysis and design (Holtzblatt and Beyer, 1993; Holtzblatt and Jones, 1993, Beyer and Holtzblatt, 1995).

Custom Development

A fourth organizational context for development, custom development blends characteristics of the three preceding contexts. The custom development organization is distinct from the user organization. It works under contract, but the contract is not necessarily competitively bid; selection may in part be based on geographic proximity. There are no prohibitions against long-term, close involvement; in fact, these can serve to mutual advantage, infusing aspects of internal development into the process. The development organization generally focuses on a market niche, amortizing their investment across similar custom jobs. If successful at finding customers with the same needs, they approach product development; in fact, they may evolve their software into a commercial product. Many small Lotus Notes application developers follow this pattern.

Custom development is likely to thrive as demands for software become increasingly diverse and specialized. Custom development could be particularly promising for HCI tools that focus on documenting upstream design process for subsequent use in redesign or maintenance, because it is a context in which design, redesign and maintenance are often done by the same people (Grudin, 1996).

Table 2 summarizes some of the factors differentiating the four development contexts described above.

60.5.2 Other Organizational Factors Affecting Development

Organization size is a significant factor affecting interactive systems development. The previous section implicitly assumed large development organizations, apart from custom development. A small start-up has few resources and less division of labor, with greater flexibility. A small company that intends to move into producing products may start off in a custom development mode, working with a few potential customers to fine-tune their system.

Age is also important, in part because younger organizations are less likely to have organizational practices or structures that are historical legacies. For example, Apple and Microsoft matured in the era of highly interactive software, and today both have an unusual stress on user involvement in design. Apple does considerable usability testing, which Microsoft has recently supplemented with heavy use of contextual analysis.

Organizational structures and processes can vary markedly across a single development context. For example, some organizations are driven by their marketing division, others are engineering-driven. The opportunities and constraints faced by a developer vary accordingly.

The nature of the intended user population is another important variable. If the users are technically savvy, developers' intuitions about a system interface may be more accurate; they may risk pilot testing in their own organization. The homogeneity or heterogeneity of user populations also affects the design process.

Two further factors are the novelty of the system or application being developed and the availability of third-party mediators—external consultants, subcontractors, value-added resellers, independent software vendors, standards organizations, and so forth. Through the 1980s myriad mediators arose to help communicate technical possibilities to users and user requirements to developers. These two factors interact, in that consultants and other mediators are more useful in established product areas than in novel ones.

This list is not exhaustive, but it serves as an indicator that organizational factors within a development environment have a strong bearing on systems development. Thoughtful developers will consider these factors carefully. Knowledge of organizational influences can alert developers to obstacles and biases.

60.6 Conclusion

The field of Human-computer Interaction could avoid reckoning with organizational issues when PCs were computational islands. But as PCs are networked locally and used to access the Internet, the day of reckoning arrives. Designers, developers, acquirers, users, and researchers must now be cognizant of group and organizational issues. The rapidity of this change can scarcely be exaggerated, even in a field and era given to hyperbole. HCI and IS are merging whether or not they realize it. In this chapter, we introduced the study of organizations and detailed two areas in which organizational issues influence many who work on human-computer interaction: The organizational contexts of system introduction and adoption, and the organizational contexts of system development. With this knowledge, readers are in a position to explore the different literatures, plan their acquisition of systems, develop more usable and useful software, position their research, and manage their careers in interactive systems development.

60.7 References

Arthur, W. B. (1990). Positive Feedback in the Economy. *Scientific American*, (February): 92-99.

Baily, M. N. (1986). What Has Happened to Productivity Growth? *Science*, 234, (October 24): 443-451.

Baily, M. N., and Gordon, R.J. (1988). The Productivity Slowdown, Measurement Issues and the Explosion of Computer Power, in W.C. Brainard, and G.L. Perry (Eds.).*Brookings Papers on Economic Activity,* Washington, DC: The Brookings Institute.

Barker, V. and O'Connor, D. (1989). Expert systems for configuration at Digital: XCON and beyond. Communications of the ACM, *32*(3), 298-318.

Beyer, H. and Holtzblatt, K. (1995). Apprenticing with the customer. *Communications of the ACM*, 38(5), 45-52.

Bjerknes, G., Ehn, P. and Kyng, M. (Eds.) (1987). *Computers and democracy - a Scandinavian challenge.* Alder shot, UK: Gower.

Boehm, B. (1988). A spiral model of software development and enhancement. IEEE Computer, 21(5), 61-72.Bridges, W. *Managing Transitions*, Addison Wesley, 1991.

Bødker, S., Grønbæk, K. and Kyng, M. (1993). Cooperative design: Techniques and experiences from the Scandinavian scene. In Schuler and Namioka, Participatory design. Hillsdale, NJ: Lawrence Erlbaum, 157-175. Republished in R.M. Baecker, J. Grudin, W.A.S. Buxton, and S. Greenberg (Eds.), *Readings in Human-Computer Interaction: Toward the Year 2000.* San Mateo, CA: Morgan Kaufmann.

Clemons, Eric K. (1991). Evaluation of Strategic Investments in Information Technology. Communications of the ACM, 34(1), (January): 22-36.

Cohen, M.D., March, J.G., and Olsen, J.P., (1972). A Garbage Can Model of Organizational Choice. *Administrative Science Quarterly*, 17: 1-25.

Dean, J.W., Jr. (1987). Building for the Future: The Justification Process for New Technology. In Johannes M. Pennings and Arend Buitendam (Eds.), *New Technology as Organizational Innovation*, Cambridge, MA: Ballinger, pp. 35-58.

Davenport, T. H., Eccles, R.C., and Prusak, L. (1992). Information Politics, *Sloan Management Review*, 34(1), (Fall): 53-65.

Friedman, A.L. (1989). *Computer systems development: History, organization and implementation.* Chichester, UK: Wiley.

Gasser, L. (1986). The Integration of Computing and Routine Work. *ACM Transactions on Office Information Systems,* 4(3), (July): 205-225.

Greenbaum, J. and Kyng, M. (Eds.)(1991). *Design at work: Cooperative design of computer systems.* Hillsdale, NJ: Lawrence Erlbaum Associates.

Grudin, J. (1990). The computer reaches out: The historical continuity of interface design. *Proc. CHI'90,* 261-268. New York: ACM.

Grudin, J. (1991a). Interactive systems: Bridging the gaps between developers and users. IEEE Computer, *24(*4), 59-69. Republished in R.M. Baecker, J. Grudin, W.A.S. Buxton, and S. Greenberg (Eds.), *Readings in Human-Computer Interaction: Toward the Year 2000.* San Mateo, CA: Morgan Kaufmann.

Grudin, J. (1991b). Systematic sources of suboptimal interface design in large product development organizations. *Human-Computer Interaction*, *6*(2), 147-196.

Grudin, J. (1994). Groupware and social dynamics: Eight challenges for developers. *Communications of the ACM,* 37*(*1), 92-105.

Grudin, J. (1996). Evaluating opportunities for design capture. In T. Moran and J. Carroll (Eds.), *Design Rationale: concepts, techniques, and use* (pp. 453-470). Hillsdale, NJ: Lawrence Erlbaum.

Grudin, J. and Poltrock, S.(1995). Software Engineering and the CHI and CSCW Communities. In R. N. Taylor and J. Coutaz (Eds.), *Lecture Notes in Computer Science 896: Software Engineering and Human-Computer Interaction* (pp. 93-112). Berlin: Springer-Verlag.

Gundry, A.J. (1988). Humans, computers, and contracts. In D.M. Jones and R. Winder (Eds.) *People and computers IV. Cambridge*, UK: Cambridge University Press.

Harvard Business School (1993). *Frito-Lay, Inc.: A Strategic Transition Case* (D) 9-193-004

Harvard Business School (1994). VeriFone: The Transaction Automation Company, Case 9-195-088.

Holtzblatt, K. and Beyer, H.(1993). Making customer-centered design work for teams. *Communications of the ACM,* 36(10), 92-103.

Holtzblatt, K. and Jones, S. (1993). Contextual inquiry: A participatory technique for system design. In D. Schuler and A. Namioka (Eds.), *Participatory design: Principles and practices.* Hillsdale, NJ: Lawrence Erlbaum Associates.

Kanter, R. M., Stein, B.A., and Jick, T.D. (1992). *The Challenge of Organizational Change: How Companies Experience It and Leaders Guide It.* New York, NY: The Free Press.

Kling, R. (1978). Automated Welfare Client-tracking and Service Integration: The Political Economy of Computing. *Communications of the ACM*, 21(6) (June): 484-493.

Kling, R., and Scacchi, W. (1982). The Web of Computing: Computer Technology as Social Organization. In M. C. Yovits (Ed.). *Advances in Computers,* Orlando, FL: Academic Press, 1-89.

Landauer, T. K. (1995). *The Trouble with Computers: Usefulness, Usability, and Productivity.* Cambridge: MIT Press.

Leonard-Barton, D. (1988). Implementation as Mutual Adaptation of Technology and Organization, *Research Policy*, 17: 251-267.

Leonard-Barton, D. (1990). Implementing New Production Technologies: Exercises in Corporate Learning, pp. 160-215, in Mary Ann Von Glinow and Susan Albers Mohrman (Eds.). *Managing Complexity in High Technology Organizations*, New York: Oxford University Press.

Manross, G.G., and Rice, R.E.. (1986). Don't Hang Up: Organizational Diffusion of the Intelligent Telephone. *Information and Management,* 10(3): 161-175.

Markus, M. L. (1994). Electronic Mail as the Medium of Managerial Choice, *Organization Science*, (5)4 (November): 502-527.

Markus, M. L. (1994). Finding a Happy Medium: Explaining the Negative Effects of Electronic Mail on Social Life at Work, *ACM Transactions on Information Systems,* 12(2) (April): 119-149. (b)

Markus, M. L. and Keil, M. (1994). If We Build It They Will Come: Designing Information Systems That Users Want To Use, *Sloan Management Review* (Summer): 11-25.

Markus, M. L. and Robey, D. (1988). Information Technology and Organizational Change: Causal

Structure in Theory and Research, *Management Science*, 34(5)(May): 583-598.

Markus, M. L., and Soh, C. (1993). Banking on Information Technology: Converting IT Spending Into Firm Performance. In Rajiv D. Banker, Robert J. Kauffman, and Mo Adam Mahmood (Eds.). *Perspectives on the Strategic and Economic Value of Information Technology Investment,* Middletown, PA: Idea Group Publishing, pp. 364-392.

Muller, M.J. (1992). Retrospective on a Year of Participatory Design using the PICTIVE Technique. *Proc. CHI'92*, 455-462. NY: ACM.

Mumford, E. (1983). Designing Human Systems. Manchester Business School.

Mumford, E. (1993). The Participation of Users in Systems Design: An Account of the Origin, Evolution, and Use of the ETHICS Method. In Schuler, D. and Namioka, A. (Eds.), *Participatory Design: Principles and Practice*. Lawrence Erlbaum Associatess, pp. 257-270.

Orlikowski, W. J., and Gash, D.C. (1994). Technological Frames: Making Sense of Information Technology in Organizations. *ACM Transactions on Information Systems*, 12(2) (April): 174-207.

Poltrock, S.E. and Grudin, J. (1994). Organizational obstacles to interface design and development: Two participant observer studies. *ACM Transactions on Computer-Human Interaction*, 1(1), 52-80.

Pool, I.S. (1983). *Forecasting the Telephone: A Retrospective Technology Assessment of the Telephone,* Norwood, NJ: Ablex.

Rogers, E.M. (1995). *Diffusion of Innovations* (4th ed.), New York, NY: The Free Press.

Royce, W.W. (1970). Managing the Development of Large Software Systems: Concepts and Techniques. Proc. *IEEE Wescon*, 1-9.

Sambamurthy, V., and Zmud, R.S. (1992). *Managing IT for Success: The Empowering Business Partnership*, Morristown, NY: Financial Executives Research Foundation.

Soe, L.L. (1994). *Substitution and Complementarity in the Diffusion of Multiple Electronic Communication Media: An Evolutionary Approach.* Unpublished Doctoral Dissertation, University of California, Los Angeles.

Soh, C., and Markus, M.L. (1995). How IT Creates Business Value: A Process Theory Synthesis, *Proceedings of the International Conference on Information Systems*, Amsterdam, The Netherlands, pp. 29-41.

Sproull, L., and Kiesler, S. (1991). *Connections: New Ways of Working in the Networked Organization*, Cambridge, MA: MIT Press.

Stinchcombe, A.L. (1990). *Information and Organizations*, Berkeley, CA: University of California Press.

Swanson, E. B., and Beath, C. M. (1989). *Maintaining Information Systems in Organizations.* NY: John Wiley and Sons.

Tyre, M.J., and W.J. Orlikowski. (1994). Windows of Opportunity: Temporal Patterns of Technological Adaptation in Organizations, *Organization Science*, 5(1) (February).

Walton, R. E. (1989). *Up and Running: Integrating Information Technology and the Organization*, Boston, MA: Harvard Business School Press.

Winkler, I., and Buie, E. (1995). HCI Challenges in Government Contracting. *SIGCHI Bulletin*, 27(4), 35-37.

Handbook of Human-Computer Interaction
Second, completely revised edition
M. Helander, T.K. Landauer, P. Prabhu (eds.)

Chapter 61

Understanding the Organisational Ramifications of Implementing Information Technology Systems

Ken Eason
HUSAT Research Institute
Loughborough University
Leicestershire, U.K.

61.1 Abstract

Information technology is a major force for organisational change. Every organisation that applies the technology experiences organisational ramifications. This chapter charts the development of different models of organisational effects over a 40-year period. In the 1950s, before there were major applications, model one offered predictions of impact. It was a deterministic model in which the application of the technology led to irrevocable consequences, although the nature of the consequences was disputed. During the 1960s and 1970s many studies of organisational impact were undertaken which produced conflicting results. As a result a contingency model of computer impact emerged (model two) which accounted for the different impacts by reference to different forms of technology and application. In the last decade it has become clear that this is also an inadequate model because it does not allow for the active nature of organisations which act to shape the impact of the technology. Nine case studies are examined to explore the processes by which organisational impact takes place. The active manner in which these processes operate is summarised in model three. This is an organisational assimilation model in which the three sub-systems of an enterprise (the business function, the social system and the technical system) interact and create outcomes in each sub-system. The design implications of this model are explored and the proposition offered that the technology can be used to create any form of organisational impact that is desired. The design process for achieving this end must have as its target the creation of a new socio-technical system rather than the implementation of a technical system. The chapter ends with a review of the many methods now available to support this approach and highlights the need for organisational stakeholders to play significant roles in new system developments.

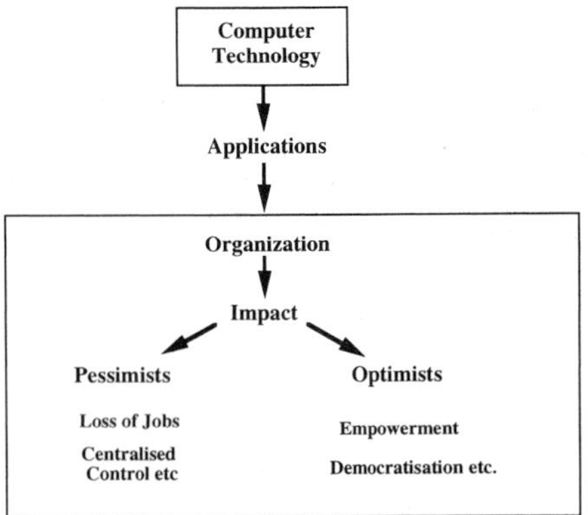

Figure 1. Model 1 - The deterministic effects of computer technology.

61.2 Introduction

Toffler (1980, 1990) has characterised the huge changes we are seeing at the end of the twentieth century as 'the Third Age'. Following the agricultural and industrial revolution we are embarking upon an information age in which communication and information technologies are providing the stimulus for massive societal change. The signs of change are everywhere; satellite communications and the internet challenge national boundaries, the 'virtual class-room' is changing the nature of education, mass communication and electronically based products transform domestic life, etc. Nowhere is the pace of change greater than in the world of work where every feature of the organisation from the workplace to the boardroom is affected by applications of new technology.

The purpose of this chapter is to look beyond the way information technology serves the individual user at work and to examine the wider ramifications for the organisation. The chapter begins with the early predictions of the organisational impact of computers and traces, through the development of three models, the changes in our understanding of the way information technology can affect organisations as we have gained more experience of its application. A number of case illustrations are used to demonstrate the mechanisms by which organisations may seek positive and avoid negative outcomes for their future structures and processes. The chapter ends with a review of design methods which can help organisations plan for integrated technical system development and organisational change.

61.3 Predictions About Organisational Effects

When computer technology first began to find widespread application in business and industry, there was a spate of predictions about the long term effects. There were sharp differences of view in the predictions. Forecasters fell neatly into optimists and pessimists. For the optimists the technology would pave the way to an information rich society in which people at work would be empowered by the computer to greater heights of task performance (Evans 1979). The greater spread of information would also be a major force for democracy at work as more were able to influence organisational decision making. For the pessimists, by contrast, the computer was the bringer of automation and, because this would replace human labour, was the destroyer of jobs. There were many predictions that the computer would first destroy jobs in manufacturing because of the development of automated factories and then office automation would destroy the jobs of clerks, secretaries, etc. (Jenkins and Sherman 1979). Where jobs remained, there were predictions that they would become simplified, made more routine and bureaucratised by computers that demanded discipline and rule following. Job satisfaction was expected to decrease, as all challenge, interest and human control of the work declined.

At the managerial level there were also predictions of change. Leavitt and Whisler (1958) predicted that management in the 1980s would be much more centralised. With the availability of much more information through computer systems, it was predicted that those with the greatest power would attract even greater power. Leavitt and Whisler suggested that the conventional pyramidal structure of an organisation would be replaced by an hour-glass structure in which senior managers controlled operational staff through the use of information systems without the benefit of armies of middle managers. These predictions were closely related to the 'big brother is watching you' predictions; that governmental and other agencies would be able to control the lives of citizens because of the rich array of information they could access about each individual.

These predictions are summarised in Figure 1. Although the optimists and pessimists differed markedly in their predictions, they shared one assumption; that computers would have a deterministic effect on organisations. If you used the technology in your business it would lead to an inevitable set of outcomes. The only issue was the disagreement about the nature of the outcomes.

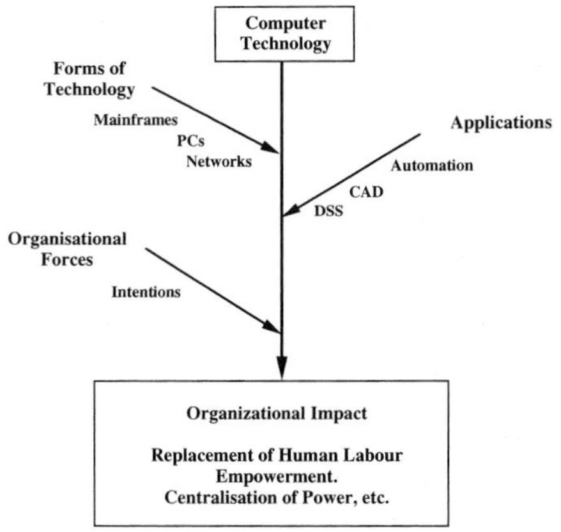

Figure 2. Model 2 - A contingency framework for organizational impact.

61.4 Computer Impact Studies

As computer applications in organisations became more widespread, a flourishing research community studied the effects to determine whether the predictions were accurate. There were two striking findings from these studies. First there was widespread evidence that computer technology was having an effect on organisational life; it was indeed the case that a revolution was under way. Second, for every study that confirmed a prediction, there was another one that found quite the opposite. Whisler (1970) found centralisation of power; Blau and Schoenherr (1971) found decentralisation; Downing (1980) found evidence of job simplification and dissatisfaction through office automation, whilst Bjørn- Andersen et. al. (1979) found increases in job satisfaction in banking as a result of computer applications. Whilst there were major examples of job losses, there were many studies which showed that job numbers were not being devastated to the degree predicted.

How can the diversity of influences be explained? Model 1, the deterministic model is too limited to explain this diversity. An alternative (model 2) is presented in Figure 2. This is a contingency framework model which identifies the major variables that could produce the diversity. One important variable is the nature of computer technology which was changing dramatically through this period. The early applications in business were based on large mainframes with networks of dumb terminals which invited centralisation and standardisation. The advent of the personal computer gave individual employees the opportunity to use a standalone work station as a flexible and powerful aid to the work, as an 'empowerment' device, expanding what was possible and adding to job satisfaction. Undoubtedly the flexibility and breadth of the technology contributes to the diversity of outcomes. It is not, however, the only factor at work. There are examples of mainframe systems that support job satisfaction and networks of personal computers that provide controlling and dissatisfying work environments.

Another variable affecting the outcome is the specific application to which the technology is being put. Automation of a work process tends to displace human labour and to routinize the work that remains to be done. By contrast the various computer-aided and support applications (for example, computer-aided design (CAD), computer-aided instruction (CAI) and decision support systems (DSS)) are tools to support human beings as they perform complex tasks and tend to have empowerment effects. However, even the definition of an application will not enable us to predict organisational applications with any confidence. There are many examples of the liberating effects of automation and of the constraining effects of support tools.

The final variable to consider is the organisation itself. Deterministic models of computer impact treat the organisation as a passive entity that can be changed by an external stimulus. In practice an organisation is an active system of human agents who are seeking ways to fulfil individual and collective goals. They will see the technology as a force to help or hinder the achievement of these goals. The organisational impact of a system may be shaped by the actions of these agents before and after implementation. If these agents have the power their actions may also shape the extent of use of the technology. Since these forces are acting within a single organisation, the same application implemented in two different organisations can have different outcomes. The intention of those who commission the system may in one case be to reduce costs by eliminating some of the labour force whilst in another it may be to improve the productivity of each employee. Every implementation has organisational side-effects - on payment systems, career paths etc. - and these vary with the work practice and culture of each organisation.

The original model of the impact of computer technology on organisations was a deterministic one. Introduce a computer system and it would have certain

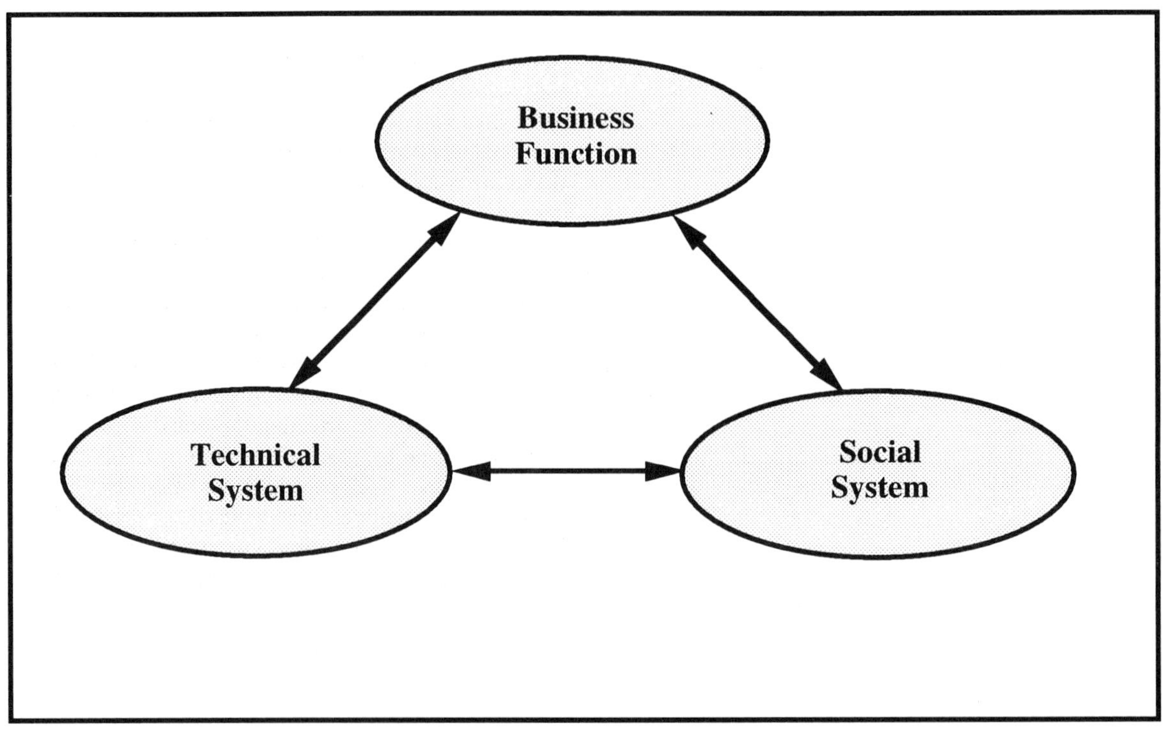

Figure 3. An integrated system view of organisational performance.

irrevocable implications for the organisation. As a result of the impact studies we have to change this model. We need an enabling model of technology which recognises that the technology is a powerful force for reshaping the way an organisation functions but that it is not deterministic. The particular outcomes are the result of decisions made about the form of technology, the type of application, and the intentions of those who commission the system.

Model two, however, is also a rather limited representation of what occurs in practice. Although it represents a less deterministic view of computer technology, it is still framed in terms of technology as cause of change and organisational ramifications as effects. Other approaches regard this as an inadequate framework; it is equally appropriate to have a model in which it is possible for changes in the social system of the organisation to have an impact on whether a specific technical system is effective. Socio-technical systems theory, first formulated in the 1950s (Trist et. al, 1962; Emery and Trist, 1969), advances a view of organisations in which social and technical subsystems need to work in harmony to produce effective overall system performance. A change in one subsystem has to be accommodated by changes in the other. A related approach is the integrated systems movement, represented in Figure 3, which considers the work system as three sub-systems; a business function or domain which sets the goals to be achieved and social and technical sub-systems which provide the resources to achieve these goals (see Walton, 1989). Success requires the integration of all these subsystems. Change can be initiated from any one of the sub-systems and will have ramifications for the other sub-systems and overall performance. It is very difficult, for example, for model 1 or model 2 to account for the high level of failure of computer applications which, in many instances, is caused by the inability or unwillingness of users in organisations to make use of them (see, for example, Long, 1987).

If there are three sub-systems from which change can be initiated, a model of computer impact, which has computer technology as cause and organisational structure and process as effect, is only one of the possible frameworks for cause and effect. In the next section a number of case studies in the application of information technology are examined to explore how these three sub-systems interact.

A retail company has a number of centres which customers can telephone to order products. A new computer system was purchased to enable order entry clerks to record customer orders on-line. It was intended that the system would increase the speed of transactions with customers, render clerks more productive and facilitate the filling of orders because data entered could be used to draw products from the warehouse, prepare invoices, etc. In operation, the clerks found that the system constrained and delayed their conversations with customers. The system required the clerk to complete fields of information in a strict sequence in a form filling mode of interaction. They had to start, for example, with the customer's name, address, etc. before entering details of product order, etc. The data collected was appropriate but customers often gave information in different ways; they started with product information before giving personal details. Regular customers expected the clerk to know their personal details. Some had regular orders and simply wished to confirm it or make minor variations. In order to cope with the new system, the clerks adopted one of two strategies. Either they took down the information from the customer manually and entered it into the system later, or they asked the customer to give the information in the sequence required by the system. In the former case performance became slower. In the latter case customers often became frustrated and complained to management. The clerks and the management expressed disappointment that the system did not achieve the intended goals. The designers reported that they had studied the data required and constructed an optimum way in which order entry tasks could be completed. The users felt they needed a flexible system into which they could put data in any sequence and, for regular customers, a system which retained details of past orders from a customer which could be retrieved and modified.

Box 1. An order entry system.

61.5 Case Studies in Technical and Organisational Change

In this section brief summaries are offered of nine case studies of the application of information technology. They are of a variety of applications but in every case a technical system was implemented in an organisational setting with some degree of success. There are more dramatic examples that could be used where, for example, implementation failed because of organisational issues, but the examples chosen offer more evidence of the dynamics of technological uptake. Only a brief synopsis of the full case study is provided. References are provided where a fuller account of the case has been published.

For each account the aim is to describe the nature of the application and the intention for its development, to identify task, system and organizational outcomes and to describe the mechanisms by which these outcomes came about. Some details are given of the design method employed and in section 61.7 we will examine the way design methods handle these mechanisms.

Box 1 presents an example of a fairly typical business application of information technology with a fairly typical effect upon its principal user. The order entry clerk has been given a system which is supposed to facilitate the order entry task but has to struggle with the system because it is not sufficiently flexible to cope with the variety of ways in which customers present information. The designers have studied the data to be collected and have created an optimal generic method for getting this data into a database. There is no evidence that they studied the work practice of order entry clerks and understood the diversity of the task. It is common in investigations of seemingly routine tasks, to discover that operators have developed a range of skilled strategies to cope with unsuspected diversity in the task. It is the adaptability of human beings to the immediate demands made upon them that enables or-ganisations to function in varied and changeable conditions. The technical system was deterministic in the assumptions it contained about the nature of the task and forced the clerk into new adaptation strategies which either doubled the length of the transaction or irritated the customer. Either way it left management and clerks dissatisfied by the failure of the system to facilitate task performance. From the analysis of the outcome it is possible to begin specifying a more useful system; with flexibility of data input, and rapid retrieval facilities to obtain previous customer records and modify them for new orders.

This example has negative consequences for task performance but all of the technical system was in use. Another common finding is that after implementation, only part of the functionality of a system is actually being used. The hospital example in Box 2 is a case

A hospital introduced a patient information system. The intention was to create a database which could store all the information about a patient's stay in the hospital. It had fields for administrative information (patient name and address, date of entry and departure, ward, etc.) and for medical information (initial diagnosis, test results, treatment, etc.). Terminals for the system were placed in all wards, consulting rooms and administrative offices. In use, the system soon contained a good record of patient administrative information but there were wide gaps in the medical records provided. The medical staff were responsible for entering the medical information. Some reported they did not enter information because it was time consuming and the system served no function for them. Others reported concern for the privacy of information confidential to their patients. Medical information was sensitive and should only be available to medical staff treating the patient. The system designers felt they had incorporated sufficient security arrangements to protect patient confidentiality. The doctors, however, felt the widespread access points to the system made it vulnerable and did not enter information in order to protect their patients. Other staff felt the reluctance of the medical staff might have more to do with the requirement that they have to formally record early diagnosis which might prove to be wrong. Neither administrators nor systems staff were in a position to enforce the co-operation of the medical staff and as a result of the system developed as a patient administrative information system.

Box 2. A patient information system *(Bjørn - Andersen, Eason and Robey, 1986).*

where an unexpected pattern of use developed because of organisational issues.

In this example the facilities for creating administrative patient records were in use but those for medical records were under-used. An important group of users, the medical staff, were expected to provide this data but in many cases failed to do so.

This situation has the characteristics of other situations where under-use has occurred. First, the staff in question are discretionary users, i.e. they cannot be forced to use the system or specific features of it. They are free to engage in their tasks by other methods if they choose. In this respect they are unlike the order entry clerks who had to use the system to do the job. Secondly the medical staff could see no benefit to them if they devoted time to inputting the data. Indeed all they could see were costs (or disadvantages). It took extra time, could potentially lead to a breach of customer confidentiality and created records which could be used to judge the competence of medical staff. Discretionary users of this kind are in a position to make a personal cost-benefit assessment of a system and, as here, when the judgement is negative they may opt-out of system usage. There are other examples in the literature. Grudin (1989) describes the non-acceptance by a group of managers of an automatic diary keeping system. The system would have facilitated the arrangement of meetings but it meant a loss of personal control over time management to the potential users which they were not prepared to accept.

Avoiding these kinds of outcomes requires the involvement of the users in the development of the application in order that everybody can perceive benefits and that perceived costs can be detected early and suitable actions taken. The aim would be that each group of users can make a positive cost-benefit assessment of the system before it is introduced.

These two cases led to unexpected outcomes for the task and the usage of the system but they did not lead to changes in organizational structure. It is often the case that the new system destabilises the organization to such a degree that structural changes occur even if they were not intended. In the next case, in Box 3, the organization had an explicit policy not to make organizational changes but found them inevitable.

The legal firm in this case announced a 'no organisational change' policy to allay the fears of staff about new technology and because it was their aim to use the technology as new and better tools to support the existing work of staff. However, the technology also enabled the secretaries to get their normal work done faster and the lawyers were quick to find ways of using the surplus capacity this created.

Those that did so by giving legal documents to their secretaries rather than the word processing centre destabilised the existing working arrangements to the dislike of the secretaries and the anxiety of the centre. By decentralising the centre to the various departments the legal firm solved the problem to the satisfaction of all parties. But this was an unplanned change decided upon after considerable stress and conflict amongst the staff concerned.

A large legal partnership had a word processing centre for producing complex legal documents. It wished to introduce office automation to the secretarial staff who served the lawyers. The intention was to improve the quality of the output from the secretaries. The firm explicitly announced that it was not trying to reduce the number of secretaries or to change their roles or the role of the word processing centre. The secretaries were given personal computers with powerful electronic publishing software and were networked with the word processing centre. Shortly after implementation the secretaries found they were working faster and had spare capacity. Some lawyers used this capacity for additional administrative tasks but others found it more convenient to ask secretaries to create and modify legal documents than to send them to the word processing centre. These secretaries felt they were being reduced to word processing operators and the future of the word processing centre was called into question. The firm resolved the problem by decentralising the word processing centre so that each department had a small centre local to their lawyers enabling the secretary's role to be expanded as an assistant to the lawyer.

Box 3. A word processing system for secretaries in a legal firm.

In an electricity distribution company the power engineers had to prepare plans to isolate parts of network for maintenance and repair work. The plans, which could involve 50 switching activities, were developed by one engineer and checked by another before a 'permit to work' was issued. This was a time consuming and largely routine activity. Since altering the state of a network involved logical steps, management commissioned the development on an expert system to automatically generate the switching schedule. They hoped to release the power engineers for more important duties and get less qualified staff to undertake the residual duties necessary to create the plans. The development plan was iterative and the power engineers were involved at all stages. A prototype was developed based upon the logic of the network and it was tested by the power engineers. They came to two conclusions. Firstly, a good switching schedule involved much more knowledge than the logic of the network. The planner needed to understand the geographical distribution of the switching stations, the equipment found in specific stations, the work practices of the staff who would work on the network, etc. Secondly, the power engineers became concerned about responsibility for safety. When a schedule is produced manually the power engineer takes responsibility for the safety of these staff. If production was automatic who took this responsibility and who would be held to account if anything went wrong? After discussion in the user community a different development route was taken. A switching schedule production assistant was developed which generated and checked parts of the plan and acted as a recorder of decisions taken by the power engineer. The task of producing the overall plan remained with the engineers but they could concentrate upon strategic issues and leave the routine to the system.

Box 4. An expert system for electricity network switching *(Eason et. al., 1996).*

Developments of this kind are not uncommon. The technology changes what can be done, existing role relations are challenged and gradually there is recognition that a new organisational form is required. It could be even more dramatic for support staff. If the principals (the lawyers in this case) also used the technology there would be even more questions about the role of the support staff. In one sense it is desirable that an organisation gains experience of the effect of technology and then decides by which form of organisation it can best exploit the new potential. However, this kind of evolutionary process has to be within a planned framework because, if it is unexpected, it leads to the build up of stress and conflict and is dysfunctional for the staff and the organisation.

There are, of course, many examples where a system is planned not just to change task performance but to change the roles of staff in the organisational structure. Often the outcome is not what was intended. The case described in Box 4 started as an iterative development of an expert system and finished in quite a different way.

An electricity distribution company provides a service to its consumers. They can telephone a service enquiry unit if they are off-supply or need maintenance work for central heating, cookers, etc. The clerks who take the call refer it to the foreman of the depot nearest the consumer and the foreman arranges for an electrician to visit the consumer. If the problem is an emergency (off-supply, danger of fire, etc.), the clerk refers the enquiry to a radio operator who can notify an electrician on the road to visit the consumer immediately. The company wished to improve the rate of response. They wanted more enquiries to go directly via the radio operator to the electrician. The radio was, however, a poor means of communication. When the electrician was on the consumer's premises he could not be contacted. The company did not allow electricians to carry mobile telephones because it would be a breach of privacy to receive or make calls on a customer's premises. A system was introduced which provided an electronic link between the radio operator and the electricians van. Terminals were placed in the vans which could receive and store up to 25 enquiries. The system was used in a pilot implementation and the clerks found they could distribute emergency calls and many non-emergency calls by this means up to the limit of an electricians load each day. The electricians rapidly found that they had lost most of their discretion over the way they organised their rounds. At any time they could find, on returning to their vans, that they had been ordered somewhere else. They also complained that the job allocation process now took no account of distances, local road conditions, etc. The foremen who were responsible for the electricians now found they did not know what the electricians were doing. Reviewing the pilot, management concluded that the depots had lost too much of their flexibility. They sought a revised version of the system that would give the foreman ultimate responsibility for job allocation and allow the electricians to negotiate jobs allocated to them.

Box 5. A mobile communications system for electricity service engineers (Eason, 1996).

In this case the development began with the intention of automating the generation of switching schedules in order that power engineers could be deployed to duties that made more use of their professional skills. The original belief was that the schedules were largely a matter of applying the logic by which the power distribution system was constructed and that an expert system could be devised which could do all or most of this task. Fortunately, by testing an early prototype, the users and the development team quickly discovered the latent knowledge the engineers used to construct switching schedules in addition to the logic of the distribution system. The process also alerted the potential users to very significant non-functional requirements; the need to preserve safety in the creation of the schedules and the issue of accountability should the schedule be faulty. There is no doubt that any system devised to generate switching schedules that did not address these issues would not be acceptable in the organisation. The use of a user-centred iterative development strategy enabled users to identify these issues very early in the design process. As a result an informed, realistic and acceptable plan was developed to create a switching schedule production assistant which would leave responsibility squarely with the power engineers but offer wide ranging assistance in the task. The literature is full of examples of applications that involved grandiose plans to replace human labour that proved unrealistic when implemented, many of them involving the development of expert systems. Berry and Hart (1990) report a number of case studies of expert systems which went through a similar pattern to the switching schedule system. They began with grand plans but, after implementation, the systems were reduced to much more limited roles in the support of human roles. Unfortunately many of these cases did not use an iterative design process and large scale investment went into the creation of systems that proved unworkable before the realistic systems were developed.

The examples so far have primarily affected the roles of the principal users but, as the example of the work processing centre in the legal firm demonstrates, the effects can reach beyond immediate users to affect the work roles of others. The next case in Box 5, also from the electricity supply industry, illustrates the mechanisms by which knock-on effects are transmitted through an organisation.

The system in this case was intended for a well defined purpose; to enable the electricity company to respond more quickly and effectively to consumer service enquiries. The solution seemed very sensible. It followed the principles of 'business process re-engineering' (Hammer and Champy, 1990) by transmitting the information about the enquiry directly from

A national freight forwarding company arranged for goods to be imported and exported through all the major ports of the country. It had branches in all major cities and branch managers had autonomy to serve the needs of local businesses in any way that would be profitable. Freight forwarding involves the completion of many documents (for shipping, insurance, payments, etc.) and the company planned a network system which would enable staff to capture information about a consignment electronically and re-use the information to generate the many documents. Management planned to use the system to solve another problem. The branches operated independently and, as a result, partial loads were often sent from neighbouring cities to the same port on the same day. Since this information would now be available on the network, they planned to identify loads that could be consolidated and cut down the number of journeys. A pilot system was implemented in three neighbouring branches to test the load consolidation possibilities. The staff found that there were loads that could be consolidated but that negotiations between the branch managers were fraught with difficulties. Whose load was it? Which city would be the collecting point? How would profits be shared between the branches? The major difficulty was that working across branches interfered with the local deals managers had made with customers and hauliers. It seemed that the only way it would work would be for regional office to select and take control of consignments that could be consolidated. Having reviewed the results of the pilot, management dropped the plan for load consolidation and concentrated upon giving each branch good support for its own work. They recognised that the energy of the company came from the entrepreneurial zeal of its branches which needed local independence. They were in danger of threatening this vital organizational characteristic for a limited business gain and they concluded it was a risk not worth taking.

Box 6. A local consolidation system for freight forwarding *(Klein and Eason 1991).*

the point of contact with the consumer to the electrician who would make the service visit. This cuts out time wasting, intermediate steps. The problem was that this short cut also had major implications for the ability of staff in two significant work roles to fulfil their responsibilities effectively. The electricians became 'slaves to their vans' and could not plan their journeys to take account of local distances, road conditions etc. The foremen no longer allocated work to the electricians or knew what work they were doing and their opportunity to supervise and control the electrician work force virtually disappeared. Neither of these effects were intended or predicted. The secondary impact of systems on work roles associated with users appears to be poorly predicted in most system design processes. In this case the operation of a live trial quickly made these issues apparent and users, management and the development team were able to examine several variants of the system which achieved the business purpose and sustained the work roles of all the staff concerned before major investment in systems development was incurred. If the system had been implemented as originally conceived it would have created an inflexible business process and would have led to major conflicts with several groups of staff.

Many applications are undertaken because information technology can be used to improve the performance of major business tasks but with relatively little understanding of the organizational consequences that can ensue. One way of interpreting what occurred in the example of electricity service enquires was that power over enquiry allocation was being centralised - not to senior management but to the central enquiry centre - leaving the local depot staff less discretion over allocation and scheduling of service visits. Another example of an unwitting move towards centralisation with other unwanted consequences is given in the freight forwarding case in Box 6.

This case also features another common occurrence in the business application of information technology. The primary purpose of the freight forwarding system was the electronic capture of information about consignments which could then be used for the generation of various documents. Management recognised, however, that the existence of this data on the network provided the opportunity for load consolidation between branches. It is often the case that user organisations come to appreciate that data collected for one purpose can be used for another. Load consolidation has considerable business advantages to the company and laudable 'green' consequences as it reduces the number of truck journeys. The problem was that to accomplish load consolidation meant either formulating a set of rules about how it would be done or giving

The salaries of teachers in a county were paid by 28 regional salary units. As part of a Government plan to restructure educational administration, a centralized payroll system was implemented in two stages. In the first phase the 28 salary centres sent details of each teacher's pay to the central department for entry into the system. In the second phase staff in the 28 centres would be able to input data direct to the system. The objectives of the system were to save money both through efficient data input and by interest savings on salary payments. In the previous system teachers had been paid holiday pay in advance as a lump sum. The centralized system credited the bank accounts of employee's on a fortnightly basis regardless of holidays, saving the interest on large lump sums.

When the centralized system was introduced, thousands of teachers found they had not been paid or had been paid incorrectly. This problem persisted for several months and became a national scandal. The blame was variously ascribed to software problems, to the quality of the staff entering the data and to the move from semi-formal local arrangements to the stringent formal requirements of a centralized system.

The public outcry persisted even though, after 5 months, the head of the centralized system was able to announce that it was working as intended. Representatives of the teachers remained unhappy about the effects of the system, which were seen as part of a general centralization policy of the Government. Teachers were particularly unhappy about the loss of the lump sum payments. Six months later the central payroll system was abandoned and teachers' salaries were again paid from regional centres.

Box 7. A centralised payroll system for teachers (Myers, 1995).

a manager a regional level responsibility for loads that could be consolidated both examples of the centralisation of decision making. This company had been successful because each branch was an independent profit centre able to make its own decisions about how to make money out of freight forwarding. As soon as the pilot system revealed the way in which the applications might disrupt this fundamental characteristic of the company culture, management abandoned load consolidation. This is a further example where a pilot study revealed implications which the staff and development team had not appreciated. We should note here that it was not the technical system that created centralisation - it was one particular application of the system which the user community could abandon whilst still seeking the major benefits of office automation at branch level.

The use of information technology to centralise power is a very common theme and in the next example it was a deliberate policy. This example, in Box 7, is set in a national educational authority.

In this instance a large and complex systems development has been used as an instrument for centralising some highly sensitive personnel payment procedures. It led to many errors which suggests that local diversity in custom and practice was not understood or adhered to when the central system was launched. In addition, significant advantages to significant stakeholders (the teachers) were lost when the system was introduced - they no longer get lump sum advances to pay for their holidays. These factors led to widespread condemnation of the system and even though initial operational problems were overcome, the lack of user acceptance led in the end to its abandonment as politically unacceptable. This case serves well to show how people can organise what Keen (1981) calls 'counter-implementation strategies' when they consider that their vital interests are at risk. In other circumstances counter-implementation may mean strikes but, in this case, public debate was sufficient to raise awareness of the impact of the system and cause its ultimate downfall.

On some occasions it is not the organisational intention of those who commission a system that leads to problems but the organisational assumptions built into the technical system by the system designers. The case described in Box 8 is an example of this process.

The concept of automated support for meetings was obviously attractive to this company. The meetings needed to have a clear and documented outcome that could be quickly distributed for action and the system offered this opportunity. However, the meetings also needed to be responsive to recent events and the concerns of participants. The need to structure and organise the meeting beforehand in order that the system could give maximum support made it difficult to intro-

The managers of a company with several sites in different parts of the country meet monthly to review achievements and agree policies and targets for the future. They needed a full, accurate and speedy account of the meetings to direct actions in the different sites after the meeting. They sought an automated means of capturing the content of the meeting to replace the slow manual process. They purchased an automated meetings system which provided a 'war room' environment for the meetings. The room had large displays for text, graphics and video and each participant had a personal computer from which they could provide input. The system designers had created the system to support a democratic process and each participant could vote on motions put to the meeting. The agenda, issues and documents for the meeting had to be predetermined which enabled a record of decisions to be maintained on-line and agreed before the end of the meeting. Initially the participants found the system an exciting new way of running the meetings but rapidly many of them became disillusioned. The chairman found he had to spend a great deal of time pre-planning the meeting and he needed a technical expert available before and during the meeting. The administrators welcomed the completed and agreed minutes at the end of the meeting but found they had to work very hard much earlier before the meeting to gather the documents and put them into the system. The participants resented having to supply information and documents much earlier and found they could not include late developments so characteristic of the fast moving nature of the business. More seriously they found they could not include debate of new issues at the meeting because the agenda was predetermined. They found they had to create various ad hoc informal meetings around the main meeting which led to great uncertainty about the decisions that had been taken. The voting mechanism was a distraction because there was an unequal power distribution among participants. Over a period of time the role of the system diminished until it was primarily being used as a minute taking assistant for the administrators.

Box 8. A system for supporting meetings.

duce new items during the meeting. The experience of the participants was that the meeting was being organised for the system rather than for their needs. The structure of the system incorporated a number of assumptions about meetings that were not appropriate for this company. One assumption was that a meeting could be pre-structured. Another was that voting was a necessary part of agreeing on issues. This may be true of elected assemblies; it is not the case in many business settings. This company acquired a generic system for one purpose and found it constrained what they could do and made assumptions about how they would do it. It took the company a long time to find a way of operating the system which met their needs and in so doing they rejected most of the functionality it provided.

The last example is one that many organisations are beginning to explore. With the advent of telecommunications people can, in theory, 'work from anywhere'. If they are information workers they can have access to the information and tools of their trade through computers which they can operate from a work place, home, whilst travelling, etc. They can also use the same medium to communicate with colleagues. Why then have the staff of an organisation in one physical location; why not have a 'virtual organisation' in which people work and communicate from wherever they are? Box 9 offers a summary of one company's experiences with this form of working.

The sales team of a company is an obvious candidate for 'virtual' organisation because it needs to be on-the-road and visiting customers as much as possible. An analysis of the business process, as in this case, shows that it is possible to undertake the work of winning and processing orders via a telecommunications system. However, this is also a fundamental change in the organisation. People working co-operatively from the same site have many opportunities to develop a wide understanding of one another that transcends immediate task goals. They develop shared attitudes and aspirations, commit themselves to common targets, understand and perhaps share company culture, mission, etc. They are able to work at collective work strategies which may achieve more than they could individually. All of this is lost when people are not in personal touch on a continuous basis. It could be argued that the telecommunications system should be able to sustain this sense of being part of the team and the corporate identity. The current practice, however, does not support this and in many organisations staff who have worked in this way have become semi-detached, often becoming sub-contractors not regarded as part of the core competence of the organisation.

The regional sales team of a large organization had offices on one of the main manufacturing sites. They typically spent 2 days of the week in the office (attending weekly sales meetings, progressing orders, etc.) and 3 days away visiting customers. The company decided that these staff could work through a 'virtual organization'. Their homes and cars would be equipped for teleworking and a few 'hot desks' (work spaces with the same equipment) would be provided at the main site to be used on a 'first come, first served' basis by staff who had to visit the site. Orders could be processed through the system, all company databases could be accessed by it and meetings could be held via a teleconferencing facility. After implementation there were immediate problems because staff had difficulty operating complex technology and had no immediate support available to them. They were able, after a period of adjustment, to undertake their work in this way but they and their management became concerned about a number of long term implications. Working from home for a lot of the time, the division between work time and leisure became increasingly blurred. When visiting customers, with no office base, the home became the base to which all enquiries were directed. Those communicated via the system could be stored automatically but if other customers wanted to make contact, other family members became unwitting assistants. Out of day-to-day contact with colleagues the staff increasingly lost contact with the informal news, the politics of the company, the grapevine. They saw more of their customers than their colleagues and as the management remarked some of them became agents for the customer rather than agents for the company. Management were concerned that staff now worked totally independent and any concept of a sales team achieving targets through co-operation had been lost. Various team events were held to recapture the sharing of goals, culture, aspirations, etc. but were not wholly successful. Some of the staff became independent contractors performing defined activities for the company and also offering their services to other organizations.

Box 9. A teleworking system for a virtual sales organisation.

61.6 The Model of Organisational Impact Revisited

The summary of nine cases of system implementation provides a rich variety of organisational outcomes and further, more detailed, evidence of the processes by which these outcomes occur. In section 61.3 we modified the original model of technological determinism to provide for contingencies due to the different forms of technology, different applications and intended organisational changes. We will now use the data from the examples to add more substance to the model under three headings:

61.6.1 Intended and unintended outcomes

Most of these cases began as a result of an attempt to improve performance of a business function by use of technology. In most cases there was no deliberate intention to make organisational changes; indeed, in box 3, the legal firm, it was explicitly ruled out. In every case, however, there were changes that went beyond those intended and produced outcomes elsewhere in the organisation. Some outcomes are effects upon the immediate user of technology, as in box 1 (order entry) and box 4 (switching schedules). Other effects demonstrate the organisation as a system in which a change in one part has implications elsewhere, for example, the effect on the foreman in electricity service enquiries (box 5) and the effect on the word processor centre in the legal firm (box 3). The kind of effects are at many levels and of various kinds, for the performance of a particular task, for the centralisation of power, for the redistribution of responsibilities, for the sustaining of significant company culture, mission and process, etc. In some instances, organisational change was a deliberate intent (box 6: freight forwarding, and box 9: the virtual organisation of a sales team). In these cases the organisational effects were much more far reaching than expected. We can draw two conclusions. Firstly that, even when no organisational effects are intended, the technology destabilises the existing system and some changes will occur. Secondly, development methods are poor at predicting these outcomes and many unintended outcomes result which are unwanted by all members of the organisation.

61.6.2 Positive and Negative Outcomes; Winners and Losers

In these cases there were usually explicit overall business reasons for senior management to embark upon system development. However, an organisation is a collection of people in work roles and each person judges the development from their own perspective. Of the unintended outcomes some were positive or created opportunities which staff could exploit for positive advantage. The lawyers (box 3) for example, saw opportunities to use their secretaries in different ways. In most of the cases, some of the outcomes were regarded by those affected as negative; the effects on the doctors, the electricians, the order entry clerks, the secretaries, the freight forwarders etc. In most of the cases these outcomes were not intended by those responsible for the development. In some cases there are staff who experience positive outcomes whilst others experience negative outcomes. One way of conceptualising this process is to recognise that the organisation has many 'stakeholders', people in roles with a vested interest in the change (see Mitroff, 1980) and that some stakeholders will be winners whilst others are losers. Boehm et. al. (1994) believe that a major goal for systems implementation is the search for 'win-win' outcomes in which all stakeholders achieve benefit. Where there are major losers amongst stakeholders who have power and influence, the future of the system will be in jeopardy.

Change as a Continuing Process

It is customary to conceive of systems development as a period of design, an implementation phase during which change will occur and then a period of stability. These cases do not fit this model. In some of them there was a major point of technical implementation but the process by which the human actors assimilated the new situation and acted upon it, evolved over a period of time thereafterwards. For example, the lawyers saw the opportunity in box 3 to change the work of their secretaries which in time led to pressure for organisational change. The sales staff, working from home, gradually lost touch with company culture and efforts were made to restore the situation (box 9). Unlike the technical sub-system, the social sub-system continues to adapt and evolve through the actions of its human agents. In some instances the development process created a technical system which was sufficiently flexible to cope as the users changed their behaviour. In some cases the iterative process, working through trials and prototypes, meant the technical system could be changed to meet the emerging requirements. In others, however, notably order entry (box 1) and the meetings organiser (box 8) the design of the system provided a set of constraints around which the human agents had to work to find ways of performing their tasks.

Summary: An Organisational Assimilation Model

The case study data carries us even further away from model 1, the deterministic model of the effects of computer technology. Comparing the cases with model 2; the contingency model it is possible in the data to see different impacts of different types of technology and particularly different types of application (compare for example the human replacement possibilities of expert systems (box 4) and the centralisation possibilities of networked databases (box 6). However, model 2 does not recognise the strongest factor shaping, not just the organisational ramifications, but also the use of the system, i.e. the reaction of the stakeholders in the user organisation to the opportunities and treats they perceive. In order to understand the outcomes of implementing information technology it is necessary to have an active model of the social sub-system; to recognise that it is a collection of human agents capable of being both proactive and reactive in pursuit of opportunities and in defending against treat. Model 3 in Figure 4 is a summary of the forces of organisational assimilation that govern the outcomes that result.

This model develops the framework given in Figure 3 which portrays the organisation as a system having three significant elements; the business function or task that constitutes its goals and two sub-systems which enable it to work towards these goals, the technical system and the social system. Five processes have been shown to connect these sub-systems which are the processes found in the case studies. They are in the sequence found in some of the case studies but the sequence is not immutable. Process A is an identification of a business or task function which can be significantly improved by the use of a technical system. Process B is the creation of a technical system to meet this purpose and its implementation. Process C is the way the technical system impacts the social system and process D is the way the change in the business function impacts upon the social system. Process E is the way the agents in the social system respond to the changes in business function and to the technical system. Any of these processes may lead to outcomes, i.e. B may lead to an improvement in the business process, C may lead to centralisation of power and E may lead to non-use of significant parts of the technical system.

Many developments seem to follow this pattern. They start with the narrow agenda of finding a technical system to solve a business problem (A and B) and

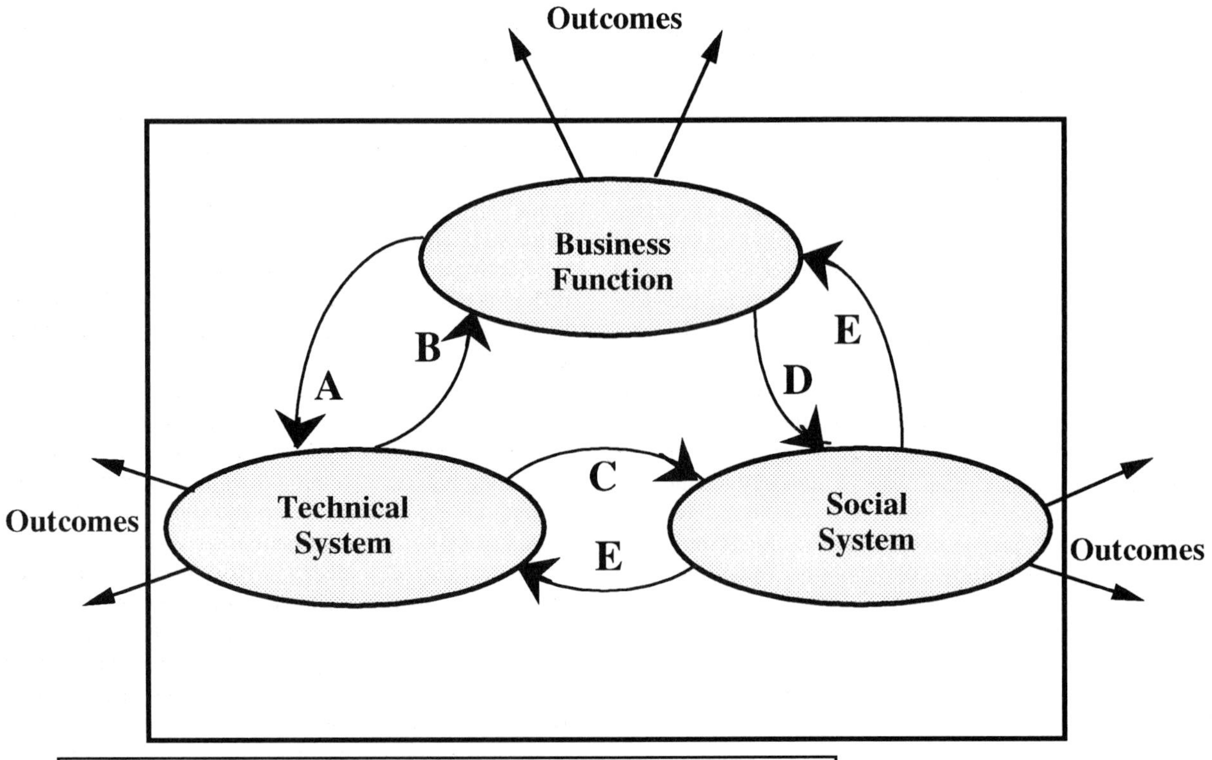

Figure 4. Forces of organisational assimilation.

only after implementation do processes C, D and E come into the equation as the agenda is broadened by other stakeholders to include the implications for the social system. In some of the cases, however, there is an early recognition that changing a business process changes the social system and these changes influence the search for an appropriate technical system. The overall process may also involve several iterations of these processes as initial technical systems create new opportunities or are found wanting and a revised system is tried with another round of responses. In practice there is likely to be a rich array of these processes occurring at different levels of detail and in different timescales as the influential agents in the organization work to achieve their collective and individual goals. We can conceptualise this development process as a primary (formal, planned) process followed by a secondary (informal, unplanned) process. The primary process is characterised by an agreed, costed programme giving specific responsibilities to 'designers' who use analytic and design tools to accomplish agreed goals. The secondary process is usually a reaction to the output of the primary process, is the result of actions by affected stakeholders and may be largely uncoordinated. In most of the cases (but not all) the primary process is restricted to A and B. In some cases aspects of C, D and E were included in the primary process. It is tempting to define the activities in the secondary process as defensive and negative, limiting the impact of the new system or coping with dysfunctions the change produces. Undoubtedly this is a dominant effect and is responsible for many major system failures. However, the secondary process can also be positive. Users may appreciate the new opportunities provided and may exploit the technology in new ways, take advantage of the new organisational options made available. There is some evidence that, where the primary process embraces business, technical and organisational issues, the result is an implementation users and stakeholders can assimilate and exploit to advantage. Where the initial agenda of the primary process is narrow, the impact is often negative, unplanned and dysfunctional.

61.7 The Implications for Design Practice

61.7.1 The Design Implications of the Three Models

The movement from model 1, through model 2 to model 3, has practical implications for the design process as well as theoretical implications for understanding how technical systems impact upon organisational processes. Under model 1, the deterministic model, once a decision has been taken to implement information technology, the organisational changes are fixed and inevitable. The implications are that the primary design process can be wholly devoted to processes A and B in Figure 4 (the business goals and technical solutions to meet them). The implications for the social system were fixed and the resolution of issues arising could be left to the social system management processes in the organisation, e.g. negotiating the consequences of the loss of jobs through downsizing.

Model 2, the contingency model, has different implications for design practice. It means that it is possible to choose the organisational effects of implementing new technology. A technical system developed on a mainframe computer with a network of dumb terminals and a series of centralised databases supporting fixed operational procedures can be used, for example, to create a centralised, tightly controlled bureaucratic structure. A technical system developed upon a network of powerful personal computers each with a suite of software packages including communication facilities, desk top publishing, spreadsheets etc., offers, by contrast, a route to the creation of a flat, networked organisation of empowered knowledge workers. There are also many other scenarios. The implication is that the designers in the primary process who select the architecture for the technical system have to be aware of the kind of social system that is required as well as the business goals to be served. The agenda for the design process needs to be extended beyond processes A and B to include C and D which are respectively the perceived consequences of the technical system and the business function for the social system.

The contingency approach therefore recognises that it is possible to use information technology to achieve a wide range of business and organisational outcomes and can extend the design agenda to seek planned outcomes in these sub-systems. However, it has two implications which limit its coverage of organisational issues. It presumes organisational choices are the result of different kinds of technical choices and it presumes these decisions can be made at the beginning of the design process by the limited number of people engaged in the primary design process (those who commission and develop the system).

Model 3, the organisational assimilation model, treats the social system as a collection of active agents who will interpret proposed changes in the technical and business systems as opportunities or threats and act to secure outcomes in their own interests. The implications of this view for the design process are considerable. If the design is created by the process described for model 2 (i.e. those who commission and build the system seek to achieve a particular set of outcomes in the business, technical and social subsystems) model 3 would predict that this would be followed by an unplanned, political process in which the stakeholders in the social system accept or reject different features of the planned system. This two part version of the design process is what characterises many of the case examples presented in section 61.5. The formal part of the design process embraces some of the business and organisational goals but it produces effects that are often unplanned and unwanted by stakeholders. As a result the social system acts to marginalise unwanted effects and develop the potential of positive effects. This process can extend over time and result in considerable organisational stress and marginal gain from the investment in technology.

The alternative to this approach is to embrace the active population of stakeholders from the social system in the formally recognised parts of the design process. The intention would be to ensure that the outcomes in the business, technical and social systems are planned and represent a consensus of the views of the significant stakeholders. This broad-based approach to design, broad in both scope and in participants, appears to be the only way in which the huge potential of modern technology can be exploited to create wanted and intended business and organisational outcomes.

61.7.2 Approaches to Integrated Socio-technical Systems Design.

The conventional approach to the implementation of technical systems within organisational settings is best characterised, as above, as a two stage process. The first, formal and recognised part of the process analyses the business needs and plans a technical system solution and the informal, secondary part of the process constitutes the unplanned responses of the stakeholders in the social system to the planned changes. Although this is the norm there are many methods and concepts which attempt to embrace the broad agenda and to bring the social system stakeholders into the recognised design process. The purpose of this section is to review the variety of approaches that could contribute to this different approach to implementing systems.

The need for an integrated approach to avoid major system development failures has been widely recognised. In a search for critical success factors Walton (1989), for example, undertook a secondary analysis to the documentation of 19 development processes for implementing systems in organisational settings. He concluded that success depended upon three factors (1) the degree to which planning embraced the need to produce an integrated system (including the business, technical and social sub-systems), (2) the degree to which all the significant stakeholders were able to participate in the development of the integrated system, and (3) the ability of the users in the resultant social system to exploit the capability of the technical system to achieve the business goals.

The development of socio-technical systems theory as a systems development methodology (see Weisbord, 1990) has also emphasised these three critical factors. In this approach emphasis is given to the requirement that the overall, integrated, system can cope as an open system in transaction with a turbulent and changing world. The implication is that the system has to be flexible and adaptive over time. The overall system has two sub-systems to do the work and it is the social system which can provide resource for flexibility because it is composed of human agents capable of learning and development. In socio-technical systems approaches the primary consideration is the construction of organisational structures (often based upon the creation of semi-autonomous work groups) which can provide the overall system with short-term flexibility and long-term adaptiveness. Within this framework the critical requirements are the empowerment of individuals and groups and the achievement of 'learning organisations' which can review themselves and meet new challenges. The development of technical systems in this approach is seen as the creation of the tools as a flexible resource for the social system to sue to achieve organisational aims. This is exemplified in the development by Volvo in Sweden of car assembly plants without assembly lines. In its place relevant technology was placed in assembly cells for autonomous work groups to utilise in the undertaking of major sub-assembly tasks (Blackler and Brown, 1980).

The participation of stakeholders in the design process is an integral part of socio-technical systems approaches. One vehicle for participation is the 'search conference' (Emery, 1983). This is a process whereby stakeholders explore the problems and opportunities available to their organisation, identify and agree major goals, investigate means of achieving goals and plan the transition from existing systems to the systems needed in the future. The emphasis is upon the stakeholders doing the significant work and taking the significant decisions and not relying on external experts.

One of the most well developed socio-technical systems design methodologies for information technology applications is the ETHICS methodology (Effective Technical and Human Implementation of Computer Systems) (Mumford, 1983a, 1983b). This is a multi-stage process in which stakeholders can analyse their current situation and explore alternative social systems and technical systems before identifying a compatible socio-technical system which can meet their future needs.

Although these integrated socio-technical systems approaches have been used successfully in significant developments they have not been widely adopted in information technology developments. Other methods have made specific contributions to handling organisational issues in information technology systems development and we now turn to a review of these methods.

61.7.3 Methods for Specific Organisational Issues

One approach that has made significant advances is to broaden the base of analysis of systems requirements at the beginning of the development process. Traditionally systems analysis has concentrated upon the functions to be performed by the technical system and has paid little attention to requirements of the users. Systems analysis techniques have been expanded by such methods as Soft Systems Methodology (Checkland, 1981) which provide a rich picture of the context within which new systems will have to operate. Task analysis methods of a variety of forms have existed for many years which focus on the activities users have to undertake and more recently, ethnomethodological approaches (Suchman, 1987) are in widespread use to provide a rich account of the culture of work organisations

The rich array of methods for analysing work settings can provide detailed information about the current work system, how, for example, the current human and technical resources operate together to achieve business purposes. It provides a good base for integrated design but the next issue is how this information can be used in the design process. There are two issues to consider. First, how can this information serve the development not just of a new technical system but an alternative socio-technical system? Secondly, since the emphasis is upon change, how is the information about the current work system relevant to future systems that may be developed?

One approach that goes beyond the mere development of a technical system and which is enjoying great popularity at the moment is Business Process Re-engineering (Hammer and Champy, 1990). This approach focuses upon the business goals of the organisation and examines the current processes by which these goals are addressed. It then seeks other methods by which these goals may be achieved more effectively and efficiently and most of the solutions involve the use of new technology or changes in the social system. It may be possible, for example, to outsource non-core activities and to use modern communication technology to control the quality of the external work. Business process re-engineering does seek integrated system solutions but they are usually created by a small team and there is growing evidence that, when implemented, they are often resisted by the many stakeholders whose interests were not considered in the development of the new system. This approach has a clear agenda for processes A, B, C and D from Model 3 but creates yet again a secondary action from the social system invoking processes E and F.

What methods exist then that can engage the wider population of stakeholders in the primary phase of the system development? Since the existing methods provide the opportunity for those who commission new systems to influence the development, one approach is to create opportunities for the workforce who are disenfranchised in this process, to create systems in their own interests. This has been the approach adopted by the Scandinavian worker democratisation studies, exemplified by project Utopia (Ehn, 1988). The aim is to identify technical tools which could assist workers in various crafts to extend and develop their skills. As a result their value as resources is enhanced whereas other systems may only serve to marginalise them. The design process for achieving these ends involves the creation of rough prototypes of possible tools which potential users can study to determine the development route of greatest value.

This approach has a clear political objective and although it has created great interest it has not been widely copied although there is evidence that more technical systems developments involve wider user participation. In structured systems design methods such as SSADM (Structured Systems Analysis and Design Methodology) (Cutts, 1987) each phase of the linear process has to be 'signed off' by representatives of the user population. In theory users can have a powerful influence over the development. There are also specific procedures for user participation, for example, JAD (Joint Application Design) (August 1991) which provides a workshop forum for users to work through requirements and review opportunities.

There has now been considerable experience with a variety of forms of user participation in system development and one of the major outcomes is the realisation that it is not an easy task for users to undertake. Users can be confronted with questions about the requirements they have of a technology about which they know very little or asked about the implications of proposals couched in technical language. In the conventional linear or waterfall approach to systems development these questions have to be asked and answered early in the process before major investment decisions are made which is the time when the user is least prepared to make informed judgement (Eason, 1988). It is unfortunately too often the case that even when user participation has occurred during the primary phase of development many of the implications are not identified by users until after implementation and there may still be tertiary reactions from the social system.

To avoid this outcome there is a need for user-centred tools, which in this instance means tools which help users express their requirements assess the implications of proposals and select routes forward that represent their interests in the development of both the technical and social sub-systems. The problem of asking users about organisational implications is that they have to extrapolate from one universe of discourse to another - from a technical description to their world of work or from a business process description to their own responsibilities and concerns etc. It may be hard to understand a description presented in what may seem like a foreign language and even harder to work out the implications. One solution is to use early prototypes of the technical interface to provide a concrete manifestation of the technical abstractions. A working prototype may also demonstrate how some aspects of the business process may be processed by the technology in the future. Prototypes are employed in this way in the democratisation at work approach advocated by Ehn (1988) and it was a prototype version of the switching schedule system in box 4 which led electricity supply engineers to questions the organisational implications of this development. A physical prototype of this kind can often help to make explicit questions about the future role of the human in the system by focusing on what the technical system could contribute in the future. Such approaches are less helpful is assessing the implications of larger scale changes in the business process or of introducing multi-user technical systems. The assessment of implications here depends upon seeing the new system elements in relation to existing social systems structures, processes and culture. Ideally this evaluation is conducted by introducing pilot or trial versions of the new system into real settings. This was the process used in the mobile communications case (box 5) and the freightforwarding case (box 6) and in both cases the stakeholders quickly appreciated significant organisational implications which changed the nature of the subsequent development. These examples of 'organisational prototyping' are very effective but they are expensive to mount. An alternative is to produce a paper-based organisational scenario of the future system i.e. a business process with a statement of the roles of users in the process and the technical system that supports them. Users can then assess the implications for their own roles of this new mode of operation. This process has been embodied in the 'user cost-benefit assessment method' described by Eason and Olphert (1995). It serves like Beohm's (1994) methods to provide early warning of the winners and losers in any change process whilst there is still the opportunity to develop alternative scenarios which reduce the impact upon losers

To assess the implications of a development in any one of the sub-systems involved in integrated socio-technical systems requires methods which enable stakeholders to move easily and systematically between the different universes of discourse. An attempt to provide a methodology which embraces both a form of representation for socio-technical systems and a process for stakeholders to engage with it is the ORDIT methodology (Olphert and Harker, 1994). The form of representation is based upon responsibility analysis which provides the integrating concept for the socio-technical system , i.e. undertaking the business task requires the allocation of responsibilities to work roles in the social system and the fulfilment of these responsibilities requires information resource provision from the technical system. Alternative scenarios can be developed by different allocations of responsibilities and can be evaluated from different stakeholder perspectives.

61.7.4 Implications for the Systems Development Process

Once it is accepted that design is about the development of new integrated socio-technical systems and that a wide range of stakeholders need to be involved in the design, the overall concept of the form of the design process has to be reviewed. It has traditionally had three characteristics (1) the agenda has been to create a technical system to serve a business purpose, (2) design is undertaken by technical specialists on behalf of those who commission the system and (3) the process will follow a linear or waterfall structure in which analysis establishes requirements which are followed by the design of solutions to meet these requirements. Integrated socio-technical systems development involves a much broader agenda and a wide range of stakeholders exploring the implications of proposals for one sub-system upon the other subsystems. It is essentially a learning and exploring process which leads to users in the social system able to exploit new technology to better achieve business purposes. The linear process does not give stakeholders the opportunity to explore alternatives in order to arrive at informed decisions and a number of alternatives have been proposed to provide this opportunity. The iterative approach (Eason, 1988) seeks early scenarios or prototypes of possible socio-technical system futures to enable stakeholders to review the way forward. As a result design proceeds through a series of design and review loops towards the formulation a new system. The spiral model (Beohm, 1988) works through a similar series of design and review loops where the decisions about what to prototype and review are based on assessments of greatest risk. The evolutionary approach is perhaps de facto emerging as an alternative because of the manner in which modern technical systems can be initiated with a limited number of components and added to over time. This provides the opportunity for users to learn what is possible and to seek ways of developing systems in their own interests. The danger of this approach is that a chaotic structure can result that would be difficult to describe as an integrated socio-technical system.

Changing views about the shape of the design process are being accompanied by a major shift in the locus of decision making in design. In early applications of computer technology in business the design of the technical system was bespoke: a unique system was created often by internal teams of programmers for each organisation. All decisions (about business processes, technical and social sub-systems) were therefore taken in the organisation. Today more and more components of the technical system are 'brought in' and result from generic design processes undertaken in vendor organisations. The locus of decision making for the business processes and the social sub-system remains in the organisation but local technical design is about purchase decisions and the configuration and customisation of technical systems to meet local requirements. Whether this is successful depends upon the foresight of the designers of the generic products. The case of the system to support meetings (box 8) is an example where organisational assumptions were built into a generic product which were inappropriate in the organisation that purchased the system. This danger will become greater as more generic products are created which define forms of communication and cooperation between users (as in Computer Support for Cooperative Work (CSCW) applications) because such systems have direct impacts upon the network of work roles in the social system (Eason, 1996). This could be a way in which technical determinism appears: the assumptions in the technical system determine the form a social system must take - which will almost inevitably create a reaction from local stakeholders. A foundation concept in socio-technical systems theory is the principle of 'minimum critical specification' (Cherns, 1976) which asserts that systems design decisions should be made as locally as possible. By this means users are given the autonomy to find the best way of coping with the demands upon them. This principle needs to be applied to the design of generic products in order that the creation of the integrated socio-technical system is in the hands of local designers and stakeholders. Chapter 60 by Grudin and Markus explores the implications of organisational issues for the generic system developer in greater detail.

61.8 Conclusions

Over a period of 40 years we have gradually learned more about how the information revolution is coming about and how organisational life is being transformed by developments in information and communication technologies. The earlier models which presumed that the application of the technology lead to fixed and inevitable consequences for organisations have been shown to be inadequate for two reasons. The first is that the technology is extremely flexible and could be used to achieve any organisational effect that is desired. The second is the recognition the design requirements is not just to create a technical system but to create an integrated socio-technical system capable of achieving new business purposes. The creation of broad systems of this kind is not the prerogative of technical systems designers; there are many powerful stakeholders in organisations who expect and demand a role in the creation of these new systems. Where new systems have been created on a narrow technical agenda the best way of representing the outcome is to show the way the stakeholders in the social system act subsequently to protect their interests. A formal process with a narrow agenda promoted by a limited number of the interested parties followed by a informal reactive process lead by the other interested parties is no way to achieve an integrated socio-technical system. Many methods now exist which can make a contribution to the achievement of broad based socio-technical systems design in organisations and can involve a much wider array of the stakeholders in the formal part of the process. The main task we confront is to ensure these methods become the norm in the implementation of new technology in organisations. To accomplish this we need to ensure that the stakeholders and the users in the organisation can play an effective part in determining their own destiny. Many of us have the desire to use the technology as an empowerment tool in human affairs: we cannot achieve this unless we can empower stakeholders and potential users in the design process so that they can choose and develop the tools that will empower them in the pursuit of their goals.

61.9 References

August, J.H. (1991). *Joint Application Design; The Group Session Approach to Systems Design*. Yourdon Press, Englewood Cliffs, N.J.

Berry, D. and Hart, A. (1990). *Expert Systems; Human Issues*. Chapman and Hall, London.

Bjørn-Andersen, N., Hedberg, B., Mercer, D., Mumford, E. and Sole, A. (1979). *The Impact of Systems Change in Organisations.* Sijthoff and Noordhoff, Amsterdam.

Bjørn-Andersen, N., Eason, K.D. and Robey, D. (1986). *Managing Computer Impact.* Ablex, Norwood, New Jersey.

Blackler, F.H.M. and Brown, C.A. (1980). 'Job Design and Social Change: Case Studies at Volvo'. In Duncan, K.D., Gruneberg, M.M. and Wallis, D. (eds.) *Changes in Working Life.* Wiley, Chichester.

Blau, P.M. and Schoenherr, R.A. (1971). *The Structure of Organisations.* Basic Books, New York.

Boehm, B.W. (1988). A Spiral Model of Software Development and Enhancement. *Computer,* May pp. 61-72.

Boehm, B.W., Bose, P., Horowitz, E. and Lee, M-J. (1994). Software Requirements as Negotiated Win Conditions. *Proceedings of the First International Conference on Requirements Engineering.* IEEE Computer Society Press, Los Alamitos, California, pp 74-83.

Checkland, P.B. *(1981). Systems Thinking, Systems Practice.* Wiley, Chichester.

Cherns, A.B. (1976). The Principles of Socio-Technical Design.*Human Relations,* 29, 783-792.

Cutts, G. (1987). *SSADM,* Paradigm, London.

Downing, H. (1980). Word Processors and the Oppression of Women. In: Forester, T. (ed.) *The Microelectronics Revolution.* Basil Blackwell, Oxford.

Eason, K.D., Harker, S.D.P., Raven, P.F., Brailsford, J.R. and Cross, A.D. (1987). A User-Centred Approach to the Design of a Knowledge-Based System. *Proceedings of INTERACT'87; the Second IFIP Conference on Human-Computer Interaction,* pp 341-347.

Eason, K.D. (1988). *Information Technology and Organisational Change.* Taylor and Francis, London.

Eason, K.D. (1990). 'New Systems Implementation'. In John R. Wilson and E. Nigel Corlett (eds). *Evaluation of Human Work,* pp 835-849, Taylor and Francis, London.

Eason, K.D. and Olphert, C.W. (1995). Early Evaluation of the Organisational Implications of CSCW Systems. In Thomas, P.J. (ed.) *CSCW Requirements and Evaluation.* Springer, London, pp 75-90.

Eason, K.D. (1996). Division of Labour and the Design of Systems for Computer Support for Co-operative Work. *Journal of Information Technology,* 11, pp 39-50.

Ehn, P. (1988). *Work-Oriented Design of Computer Artifacts.* Arbetslivcentrum, Stockholm.

Emery, F.E. and Trist, E.L. (1969). Socio-Technical Systems. In Emery F.E. (ed) *Systems Thinking,* Penguin, London.

Emery, M. (1983). 'Learning and the Quality of Working Life'. QWL Focus, Feb. 3(1), 1-7.

Evans, C. (1979). *The Mighty Micro.* Hodder and Stoughton, London.

Galer, M.D., Harker, S.D.P. and Ziegler, J. (1992). *Methods and Tools in User-Centred Design for Information Technology.* North Holland, Amsterdam.

Greenbaum, J. and Kyng, M. (1991). *Design at Work; Cooperative Design of Computer Systems.* Erlbaum, Hillsdale, N.J.

Grudin, J. (1989). 'Why Groupware Applications Fail: Problems in Design and Evaluation'. Office, Technology and People, Vol.4., No.3. pp 245-264.

Hammer, M. and Champy, J. (1990). *Re-engineering the Corporation: A Manifesto for Business Revolution.* Nicholas Brealey, London.

Hornby, P. and Clegg, C. (1992). User Participation in Context; A Case Study in a UK Bank. *Behaviour and Information Technology,* Vol.11, No. 5, pp 293-307.

Jenkins, C. and Sherman, B. (1979). *The Collapse of Work.* Eyre Methuen, London.

Keen, P. (1981). Information Systems and Organisational Change. *Communications of the ACM,* 24.1.

Klein, L. and Eason, K.D. (1991). *Putting Social Science to Work.* Cambridge University Press, Cambridge.

Long, R.J. (1987). *New Office Information Technology: Human and Managerial Implications.* Croom Helm, London.

Mitroff, I.I. (1980). 'Management Myth Information Systems Revisited: A Strategic Approach to Asking Nasty Questions about Systems Design'. In Bjørn-Andersen, N. (ed.), *The Human Side of Enterprise* , North-Holland, Amsterdam.

Mumford, E. (1983a). *Designing Human Systems.* Manchester Business School Publications, Manchester.

Mumford, E. (1983b). *Designing Secretaries.* Manchester Business School Publications, Manchester.

Myers, M.D. (1995). Dialectical Hermeneutics: A Theoretical Framework for the Implementation of Information Systems. *Information Systems Journal,* Vol.5, No. 1, 51-70.

Olphert, C.W. and Harker, S.D.P. (1994). The ORDIT Method for Organisational Requirements Definition. In Bradley, G.E. and Hendrick, H.W. (eds). *Human Factors in Organisational Design and Management IV*. Elsevier, Amsterdam, pp 421-426.

Suchman, L. (1987). *Plans and Situated Actions: The Problem of Human-Machine Communication*. Cambridge University Press, Cambridge.

Toffler, A. (1980). *The Third Wave*. Collins, London.

Toffler, A. (1990). *Power Shift*. Bantan Books.

Trist, E.L., Higgin, G.W., Murray, H. and Pollack, A.B. (1962). *Organisational Choice*. Tavistock, London.

Walton, R.E. (1989). *Up and Running: Integrating Information Technology and the Organisation.* Harvard Business School, Boston, Mass.

Weisbord, M.R. (1990). *Productive Workplaces; Organising and Managing for Dignity, Meaning and Community*. Jossey-Bass, Oxford.

Whisler, T.L. (1970). *The Impact of Computers on Organisations.* Praeger, New York.

Handbook of Human-Computer Interaction
Second, completely revised edition
M. Helander, T.K. Landauer, P. Prabhu (eds.)

Chapter 62

Psychosocial Aspects of Computerized Office Work

Michael J. Smith and Frank T. Conway
Department of Industrial Engineering
University of Wisconsin-Madison
Madison, Wisconsin, USA

62.1 Introduction

The introduction of computers at work has had as profound an impact on work processes and the design of work as the Industrial Revolution some 250 years ago. As with the Industrial Revolution, the way in which employees have responded to the changes produced by computer automation has differed depending on how the technology affected their quality of life, employment, working conditions and the nature of job tasks. As is typically the case, those employees with low paying, simple jobs have been less satisfied with the changes that computer automation brought about than highly paid, skilled professionals and technical experts (OTA, 1985)

By the year two thousand more than one-half of the workforce in developed countries will be working with computers a substantial part of their working day (OTA, 1985). In economically developing countries the trend toward computerization has been accelerating, and computer use is expected to be comparable to the developed countries by the middle to the end of the next century. Computers provide advantages in manufacturing process control, inventory management, records management, complex systems control and office automation. They produce efficiencies, competitive advantages and the ability to carry-out work processes that would not be possible without their use.

As Smith and Carayon (1995a) indicated there are several reasons for companies to use computer automation. These include: (1) lowered production costs through the use of more efficient machines, (2) reduced workforce, (3) a less skilled and cheaper workforce in the vast majority of redesigned jobs, (4) improved product quality and conformity, (5) increased "up-time" or productive time, and (6) enhanced flexibility of the production system to meet changing market needs. These can produce outcomes that adversely affect the quality of working life of employees, and may be in conflict with the best interests of the employees' welfare. The reasons underlying a company's decision to automate, and the basic philosophy and approach taken to automate have major effects on employee satisfaction and with and the acceptance of the computer automation (Eason, 1988; Bikson and Eveland, 1990).

Computers require substantial support from architectural and electrical infrastructure, employee knowledge and skills, and new methods of managing work (OTA, 1985). The demands placed on jobs which use computers are very different from traditional jobs that do not use computers. Computerized jobs tend to be more sedentary, require more cognitive processing and mental attention, and require less physical energy expenditure than traditional manufacturing jobs with high physical demands. Yet the production demands can be high, with constant work pressure and little decision making possibilities. These are conditions that have been shown to produce occupational stress (Cooper and Marshall, 1976; Karasek, 1979; Smith et al., 1981; Smith, 1987; Dainoff, 1982; Smith and Sainfort, 1989; Smith and Carayon, 1995a).

The economic advantages of computers at work have overshadowed potential problems that can occur which may influence the health and safety of employees. Computing has brought a host of problems including reduced quality of working life, job loss, cumulative trauma disorders and increased psychological stress (Smith, 1984; OTA, 1985; Berlinguet and Berthlette, 1990; Bullinger, 1991; Smith and Salvendy, 1989, 1993). The transition from more traditional forms of work to computerization has been difficult in many workplaces, and has resulted in significant psychosocial and sociotechnical problems for the workforce. These issues will be discussed in detail below, as well as recommendations for more effective computer automation implementation strategies and work design improvements. The purpose of this chapter is to examine how the use of computers at work affects the satisfaction and stress levels of employees who use computers, and how to design computerized work systems for the best possible result.

In the last two decades millions of video display terminals (VDT's) have been deployed in thousands of offices around the world. There has been a groundswell of complaints from workers about the visual and musculoskeletal demands imposed by working at a VDT's (Grandjean and Vigliani, 1980; Dainoff, 1982; NAS, 1983; Bergqvist, 1984; Knave and Wideback, 1987; Smith, 1987; Bergqvist et al., 1992; Smith and Salvendy, 1993; Luczak, Cakir and Cakir, 1993; Grieco et al., 1995). After several years of debate and research there is a growing consensus that poor workstation design coupled with workload, postural demands and job demands can contribute to shoulder, neck, back and wrist/hand discomfort, fatigue and pain for many VDT users. Improper illumination and glare, work demands, VDT screen design, and task characteristics can contribute to visual discomfort. And, improper work organization and job design can lead to psychological stress.

The claims that working at a VDT creates user psychological distress are not new (Gunnarsson and Ostberg, 1977; Smith et al., 1981; Elias et. al., 1980). There has been extensive debate on the role of the VDT technology in producing these stress effects as contrasted to the role of poor management procedures (Smith, 1984; Smith et al., 1986). Early research on the job stress aspects of VDT use indicated mixed results that created debate (Bergqvist, 1984; Smith, 1987). Some studies indicated that VDT use was linked to greater job dissatisfaction and distress (Smith et al., 1980, 1981; Elias et al., 1980; Ghiringelli, 1980). While others found no additional distress due to VDT use (Sauter et al, 1983; Starr et al, 1982, 1985; Starr, 1984). More recent findings suggest that the role of VDT's in influencing job design, organizational policies, management practices and career opportunities is a determining factor in the creation of distress (Smith and Sainfort, 1989; Smith and Carayon, 1995a).

62.2 What Is Job Satisfaction ?

There are many characteristics of the concept of whether employees are happy and satisfied with their work. In an overall sense, employees have a "global" impression of their job which relates to the job in its totality, as opposed to specific characteristics or "facets" of the job. When asked the question, "Do you like your job?", an employee can give a generalized response such as, "I like my job." In fact, it is possible to define "how much" an employee likes the job, such as, "I like my job a lot." This type of "job satisfaction" reflects a weighing of the good and poor aspects of the job to come up with an overall impression. But the weighing is not necessarily a linear process since one critically important aspect of the job may be the single defining factor of satisfaction, or conversely, many equally important smaller aspects of the job may add up to determine satisfaction. The point is that this global satisfaction is critically important for employee attitude and motivation about the job.

The second aspect of job satisfaction deals with specific characteristics of the job which the employee may or may not like, such as the interaction with the supervisor, or the operational characteristics of the computer system, or the level of workload. These are referred to as "facets" of the job, and are examined individually, rather than as a composite as with global satisfaction. These facets of satisfaction will also affect attitude and motivation, but in a different way than global satisfaction. Global satisfaction defines the underlying structure of attitude and motivation of employees toward the job. Facet satisfaction defines situational, often transient feelings about a small "piece" of the job. As we shall see, an employee can be very dissatisfied with job facets, such as the computer hardware capabilities and software glitches, but still be very happy with the job, and be motivated to work very hard.

" A satisfied employee is a productive employee." This premise is one that has led to a vast number of studies to test the statement's validity. For such a study, an important consideration is the relationship between employee satisfaction and workplace performance. The focus on employee satisfaction has subsequently led to the study of the satisfaction that an individual derives from the work that they do. Given the great amount of time that an individual spends on the job, it is reasoned that characteristics of the job will play an important role in the determination of the employee's satisfaction, which in turn will influence that person's ability and willingness to function on the job. Consequently, it is presumed that by understanding those factors that cause an employee to be satisfied with the job, we can better design jobs to enhance employee performance. Happy and productive employees will be the combined result. Although this point is not universally held as a truth, the next section will endeavor to provide some theoretical context for job satisfaction.

62.3 Theories of Job Satisfaction

This section will provide a brief overview of select theories of job satisfaction. The theories are presented to provide some alternative views with which to examine job satisfaction, and do not represent a complete survey of job satisfaction concepts. A more complete review on job satisfaction concepts can be found in Locke (1976).

Locke (1976) identified two distinct categories of job satisfaction theories which he defined as causal models and content theories of job satisfaction. Causal models attempt to specify those factors that are relevant to job satisfaction and determine how the factors combine to determine overall job satisfaction. Conversely, content theories attempt to identify the specific needs or values that are most important for job satisfaction. Each category will be briefly explained below.

62.3.1 Causal Models

One causal model of job satisfaction proposes that the individual's affective reactions depend on the discrepancy between what his/her environment provides and what that individual has adapted to or expects. This is referred to as Expectancy Theory. The expectancy of the individual could also be influenced by the expectation of the pleasantness or unpleasantness of a situation. These expectations can lead the person to prepare for the situation by taking specific actions. When an expected pleasant event does not occur, the individual may devalue the experience because there is a difference between the anticipated success or pleasure and the resultant failure. A person expecting failure may have time to build defenses against the failure, or to begin exercising coping mechanisms that would lessen the disappointment. The person's expectancy can influence the timing of the evaluation of the situation, and may also impact the intensity of the evaluation.

A second causal model focuses on the degree to which the job fulfills personal needs, which then determines how satisfied the individual is with the job. This is referred to as the Need Theory. Needs are conceptualized as arising from conditions necessary to maintain life and assure well-being. These needs cause an individual to act in a goal-directed manner for their fulfillment. Two interrelated categories of needs are physical needs, which are conditions to maintain a functioning body; and psychological needs, which are required for a properly functioning consciousness. Needs are objective requirements of a person's survival and well-being. They exist whether or not the person desires them.

A third causal model focuses on the values of the person. A value is defined as a condition which a person consciously or subconsciously desires, wants or strives to attain. Values are subjective since they are derived from the perceptions of the person. This Value Theory further postulates that values are acquired/learned from social situations, while needs are innate drives. Values can be broken into attributes of content and intensity. Content refers to what is wanted or valued, and intensity is how much it is wanted or valued. A ranking of an individual's values would produce a value hierarchy.

62.3.2 Content Theories

Content theories specify those particular needs that have to be satisfied in the job situation, or those values that must be acquired in order for the individual to be satisfied in his/her job. Two well known content theories are Maslow's Need Hierarchy Theory and Herzberg's Motivator-Hygiene theory.

Maslow (1943) postulated a needs hierarchy in which higher order needs would not be desired or sought until lower order needs were satisfied or fulfilled. The need progression hierarchy began with physiological needs such as the need for water and food at the lowest level. Safety needs followed the physiological needs and included the freedom from physical threats and economic security. Belongingness and love needs were at the next level, followed by esteem needs. The highest order need was self-actualization, a level at which the person achieved the highest capability. Maslow did not claim that the lower needs had to be fully satisfied before the next level began to motivate the person, however, the lower needs would always be relatively more fulfilled than the higher order needs.

Herzberg and his colleagues proposed a two-factor theory of job satisfaction (Herzberg, Mausner, and Snyderman, 1959). They found five factors that had an influence on job satisfaction: (1) achievement, (2) recognition, (3) the work itself, (4) responsibility, and (5) advancement. Three of these, work itself, responsibility and advancement were of most importance for influencing attitudes that persisted. These five factors rarely appeared when respondents described what made them dissatisfied about their jobs. An entirely different set of factors emerged from the analysis of the dissatisfiers of work. The major dissatisfiers were company policy and administration, supervision, salary, interpersonal relations and working conditions. These factors were similar to the satisfiers in that they served only to influence job dissatisfaction, and rarely led to job satisfaction. The dissatisfiers were different than the satisfiers because they consistently produced short-term changes in job attitudes.

Herzberg et al. (1959) determined that the central theme of the satisfiers was an employee's relationship to the activities performed. For the dissatisfiers the emphasis was on the context or environment in which the employee carried out the activities. Herzberg referred to these dissatisfiers as hygiene factors, while he referred to the satisfiers as motivators. This model of job satisfaction provided two unipolar traits, motivators and hygiene factors.

These models have provided a general orientation to job satisfaction, and this orientation will help in the examination of the use of technology such as computers and how people respond to them. The next section will provide a perspective on sociotechnical issues and computer use.

62.4 Socio-technical Aspects of Computer Use and Job Satisfaction

The sociotechnical system approach emphasizes viewing organizations in terms of the interrelationships of how the social and technological subsystems of that organization function. This perspective asserts that the people that produce products or services are affected by the technology they use, and likewise that the technology is affected by the people using it (Trist and Bamforth, 1951; Trist et. al. 1963, Trist, 1978; Emery and Trist 1965). This approach does not accept technology as a given, and focuses on finding ways to redesign each system in order to benefit all aspects of the work setting.

There are a variety of perspectives regarding the "technological determinism" of workplace automation (OTA, 1985, 1987). Some experts believe that innovation drives the application, while others believe that social processes define the nature of applications. Kling (1980) has stressed that computing applications are not "deterministic", but are influenced by the "social context" in which technology is used. Thus, the social context will affect the philosophy and implementation approach, rather than the technological capabilities of the equipment. As Kling states, "....., speaking about the 'impacts of technology' often detracts attention from the social processes by which they are developed, adopted, and used." From our perspective, the underlying processes that define the application are less important than the impact itself, especially on the design of work and the satisfaction that employees derive from their work. It makes no difference if the application is determined by social convention, business practice or individual initiative if the end result is a substantial reduction in the quality of working life.

Research studies by Aronsson (1989), Bradley (1983, 1989), Carayon (1993, 1994), Huuhtanen and

Leino (1992), Johansson and Aronsson (1984), Korunka and Weiss (1995), Lindstrom (1991), Sainfort (1990), Smith et al. (1981,1992), Stellman et al. (1985), Westlander (1994), have demonstrated that the introduction of computers into the workplace brings substantial changes in the work processes, social relationships, management style, and the nature and content of job tasks. In the 1980's, the process of implementation of technological change from paper and pen to computerization was most often a top down process (OTA, 1985; Eason, 1988). Management determined the type of hardware and software, the interfaces, and the workstations, when and where implementation would take place, the staffing levels, the structures of new job tasks and the style of supervision. There have been instances in which employees came to work one day only to find that new computers had been installed and their jobs had changed overnight. In some cases, there was no warning that this would happen and it caught many employees by surprise. These employees had no input to the decisions regarding the new technology or the new work structures. As a rule, employees reacted poorly to this implementation strategy and many labor relations problems occurred, as did physical and mental health problems.

62.5 Job Stress Effects of Computerization

62.5.1 What Is Stress ?

The basis of stress theory lies in the works of Cannon (1914) and Selye (1956), who developed the foundation for a physiological concept of stress. Stress was described as a pattern of physiological reactions called "general adaptation syndrome" (GAS) which is activated in a non-specific, stereotyped form by any environmental demand (Selye 1956, 1983). The syndrome is characterized by a mobilization of energy resources and proceeds along three stages: alarm, resistance (adaptation), and exhaustion. The initial arousal leads to an elevated activation of bodily resources to maintain or achieve adaptation. Elevation of blood pressure and an increase in heart rate are recognized among a multitude of changes, such as an increased discharge of hormones controlled by the sympathetic nervous system and the pituitary and adrenal glands. The end results of this syndrome, if prolonged, were exhaustion and disease.

One of the characteristic features of the physiological theory was that stress was understood as a stimulus-response phenomenon. The concept of stress described the organism's reaction, which was activated in the same manner by any environmental demand which would be called the stressor. The response-based definition is limited because the same reaction pattern can be evoked by a wide array of stimulus conditions, including physical exercise.

Grounds for the development of the cognitive theory of stress were based on the criticism of the physiological stimulus-response theory of stress which was first challenged most profoundly by Lazarus (1977, 1993), who claimed that stress could not be understood on the basis of a stimulus-response model. Support for the adoption of the cognitive theory of stress was gained from empirical research on work, stress and health, which indicated that within the same work conditions not all workers experienced stress.

Individual differences in cognition are thought to intervene between the stressor and the reaction (Dewe, 1991; Lazarus, 1974; 1993). Cognitive processes determine the quality and the intensity of the reactions to the environment. A stressor will not have an effect unless it is recognized and assessed by the person. Thus, an appraisal phase is added as a third component in the stimulus-response stress model. The appraisal phase is characterized by two consecutive steps. In the primary phase, a stressor is detected and its possible harmfulness is assessed. Three different kinds of stress situations are acknowledged: harm, threat, and challenge. Harm refers to psychological damage that has already taken place, e.g. an irrevocable loss. Threat is the anticipation of harm that has not yet taken place but may happen. Challenge results from difficult demands that one feels confident about overcoming by effective mobilization of resources. The second step involves the assessment of the resources available to confront the stressor. Resources are then activated and manifested as coping strategies to counteract the stressors.

Stress has been defined as the body's reactions to adverse environmental stimulation (Selye, 1956). It has also been defined as the psychological reactions to a perceived threat (Lazarus, 1974). In most instances, stress is felt to be a dysfunctional reaction that can lead to adverse performance and health outcomes. Because stress is a psychological process, there are close ties with satisfaction, attitude and motivation. Stress can be acute or chronic. Acute stress is like facet satisfaction in that it is situational and typically of short duration. Chronic stress is more like global satisfaction in that it defines an underlying structural process that is more permanent. The reader is referred to Smith, Carayon and Miezio (1986) and Smith (1984,1987) for reviews of the early literature on job stress and the use of VDT's. The following will discuss some of the more current research on stress associated with computer use at work, with an emphasis on office work.

62.5.2 Select Studies of Psychosocial Effects of Computerization

Aronsson (1989) studied the stress effects of introducing computers for office employees in three job categories which reflected the degree of difficulty of the job. The employees in the lowest job stratum reported that the intensity of demands of their work had increased the most, while the middle stratum reported an increase to a lesser extent than the lowest stratum experienced, and the highest stratum reported no changes in demands. The lowest stratum had the most negative opinions about changes in socialization resulting from the computerization. As the intensity of demands increased, employees reported greater impairment in social contacts and less cooperation. This relationship was strongest in the lowest stratum. Employees were asked their perception about their job stability over the next five years. There were significant differences between the groups with 95% of those in the lowest stratum forecasting job loss, while 49% of the middle strata and 31% of those in the upper strata foresaw job loss.

Korunka and Weiss (1995) conducted a longitudinal investigation of the effects of introducing a new computer technology on psychosomatic complaints and job satisfaction. Measurements were taken two months before and twelve months after the conversion of the job environment to new computer technology. A self-report questionnaire was used to collect information from 171 employees that were working in seven different companies. The results showed that highly monotonous work was associated with increased psychosomatic complaints and less job satisfaction. A higher level of participation in the change process was associated with greater job satisfaction after the introduction of the new technology. There were no substantial effects of attitudes towards the job or individual differences in the level of change and the resultant levels of psychosomatic complaints and job satisfaction after the implementation of the new technology. In those companies with low participation of employees in the implementation, there was a significant increase in psychosomatic complaints and a significant decrease in job satisfaction after technology implementation. Job satisfaction increased when the work with new technology was diversified and called for high skill qualifications, but tended to decrease for employees with low skill qualifications who were doing monotonous work at visual display units.

Majchrzak and Cotton (1988) conducted a longitudinal study of employee responses as their jobs were changed from low automation, mass assembly technology positions to computer-automated batch (CAB) manufacturing technology positions. The CAB jobs demanded more mental and visual skills and less physical skills than the old assembly jobs. Those employees who took the new positions were volunteers and were given no special training classes to acquaint them with the new technology. Their job grades and pay scales were not changed by taking the new jobs. However, the company was in the process of reducing its assembly operations, and employees were aware that this new batch circuit production would be one of the last operations to close because of high production demands. Consequently, many employees took these new jobs in hope of keeping their jobs longer.

The change from mass production to CAB technology increased the level of automation and informal communication opportunities, and decreased the workflow integration and employee control over the quality of the process. An equal number of employees responded positively and negative to the technological change. Interestingly, a large proportion of employees reported experiencing no changes. For example, even though the transfer from mass to CAB yielded a significant average increase in input/output unpredictability, 35 percent of the employees reported no change in this aspect of their job. For some employees there were psychological stress disturbances. Psychological adjustment was enhanced by job changes that promoted both input/output variety and communication for social non-task-relevant purposes.

Job satisfaction was enhanced to the extent that work-cycles were sufficiently short and sufficiently predictable to preclude the need to work with others. This finding is unusual since it would be expected that short cycle work would be monotonous, and lack of socialization would reduce social support. Work commitment was increased when job transfers fostered more operator process control (which was manifested by more quality control, less equipment automation, and more buffer space for self-paced work). A generalized feeling of a better quality of life was created when the job transfer provided for more control, more routine, and more coordination. Employees who had less work experience and more positive attitudes about the impact of automation were more committed to the technological change. When management helped to clarify the requirements of the new jobs, there was higher employee commitment following the job transfer.

Another extensive analysis was conducted on VDT use and its effects on job design for banking and insurance employees (Lindstrom, 1991). This study examined the association of VDT use, job demands, and job characteristics to the well-being of employees. The study evaluated these considerations in 1,124 banking and insurance employees using a self-report questionnaire. Specific analysis was conducted on the differences between the occupational subgroups of customer service employees, office employees, ADP experts, and managers and supervisors. Being young was related to a greater daily VDT use among ADP experts, while females with low educational level among office employees reported greater VDT use. Female managers, supervisors and office employees had more daily VDT use than men.

Women had more health complaints than men. In particular, psychic symptoms and fatigue were more frequent among women. Across the job categories, psychic symptoms and fatigue were least frequent among managers and supervisors. Managers and supervisors reported the most control over their work, as well as the highest variety in task content. Customer service personnel reported the least control over their work, while office employees reported the least variety in task content. Lack of autonomy was reported most often by customer service employees and least often by ADP experts. Haste at work was about the same for all groups. For the entire group, a large daily amount of VDT work, computer breakdowns, slow computer response times and poor access to the data terminal were related to psychic symptoms and fatigue, feelings of a lack of competence, and nonspecific somatic health complaints.

Task difficulty and poor supervisory practices had the largest correlations with psychic symptoms and fatigue. Among ADP experts, haste and poor supervisory practices correlated with psychic symptoms and fatigue. For managers and supervisors, the difficulty of the tasks, lack of content variety and lack of control had the strongest correlations to psychic symptoms and fatigue. Feelings of a lack of competence were related to the difficulty of the tasks in all groups, except the ADP experts. For the customer service personnel, poor coworker relations were related to feelings of a lack of competence. For office employees, poor supervisory practices, lack of control, and lack of content variety were associated with feelings of a lack of competence.

The difficulty of tasks was one of the main predictors of stress and health complaints for all the groups except ADP experts, for whom the main predictor was haste at work. Of the VDT variables, the unsatisfactory mastery of VDT applications was among the factors for three groups. VDT use was more common and intense among occupational groups other than the supervisors and managers, who also had fewer interruptions and problems associated with VDT work. Psychic symptoms and fatigue were related to job characteristics, including haste at work, poor supervisory practices, difficulty of tasks, and lack of variety in work content. Also, unsatisfactory mastery of VDT applications was an consideration for many jobs. Unsatisfactory mastery of VDT applications was the most common explanatory factor for feelings of a lack of competence. The extent of VDT use and problems related to the use were associated with nonspecific somatic symptoms for the entire group.

Huuhtanen and Leino (1992) conducted a three-year longitudinal research program examining technology changes in banking and insurance companies. Two insurance companies and four banks were examined, with 1,744 employees taking part in 1985 and 2,134 responding in 1987. During the study period, new electronic payment systems that were based on customer self-service were installed in the banks. Microcomputer networks at the branch offices were developed, which created new and more services possible through bank teller micros. Questionnaires were used as the data collection method and the response rates were 75% in 1985 and 69% in 1987. Employees were asked to estimate the impact of the new technology on job characteristics as they related to the mental well-being of employees. The questions were asked before the systems were installed and then again two years after the new technology had been implemented.

The findings presented here represent those 803 employees who participated in both the 1985 and the 1987 data collections. The occupational groups studied were customer service workers, office workers, data experts, sales personnel, supervisors, VDT workers, and miscellaneous others such as porters and messengers. The largest groups of workers were the customer service workers and office workers, with the smallest groups being the VDT workers and data experts. The results indicated that employee perceptions about the effects of the new technology before it was installed changed after the technology was actually introduced. The level of interest in work and opportunities to use the worker's abilities were perceived as increasing more than expected. The monotony of work did not increase as much as expected. The work pace increased more than was expected. The way that the jobs were organized by the technology had an influence on both the quantity and quality of the work production after implementation. Various occupations were differentially affected by the new technology. The data experts felt that their work pace had increased as a result of the new systems. Whereas, the customer service employees, office workers, and the VDT workers felt the difficulty of the tasks increased more than was expected.

There were differences between the various age groups in the perceptions of technology effects. In 1987 the youngest age group felt more interested in their work, more productive, more of a master of the work, more in control of the order in which work was done, and more appreciative of the work than the oldest age group. The monotony of work and the difficulty of tasks increased more in the oldest age group. Things to be remembered and contacts with coworkers decreased more in the oldest than in the youngest age group. The youngest age group had the best mastery of applications in both years. The evaluation of the opportunities to use one's abilities as a result of the new technologies was most positive in the youngest age group, for both customer service employees and office workers. The oldest age groups estimated that the difficulty of their tasks had increased.

Carayon, Yang, and Lim (1995) conducted a three-year longitudinal study of office workers in a public organization to determine the relationship between job factors and employee stress. The results indicated that employee perception's of job design and the extent of stress varied over time. For the first year of data collection, quantitative workload, work pressure, and supervisor social support were the most important predictors of employee stress. For the second year, task clarity, supervisor social support, and job future ambiguity were the most important predictors. For the third year, task clarity, attention, and job future ambiguity were the most consistent predictors. This shows that while there was some consistency in the structure of the relationships between job design considerations and the level of employee stress, the specific job design factors that were related to particular stress outcomes such as anxiety or somatic complaints differed over time.

Carayon-Sainfort and Smith (1991) studied the effects of the frequency of computer problems and computer use intensity on employee perceptions of task characteristics and worker stress. The study was cross sectional in design, and sampled 262 office workers from three organizations using a self-report questionnaire. Results indicated that computer problems (such as break downs) and computer use intensity had indirect effects on worker stress through their influence on task characteristics, such as workload, work pressure, and job control. A high frequency of computer problems and computer use intensity was related to feelings of high workload, high work pressure, and low job control. High workload and work pressure, and low job control were associated with high daily life stress.

62.5.3 Summary of Select Study Findings

Compilation of the research evidence on VDT use, work organization changes and psychosocial stress into an integrated picture provides the following general conclusions:

- Computer users in low paying, less skilled jobs have greater amounts of psychological distress than those in higher paying, more skilled jobs.
- When jobs are transitioned from one technology to a new one, those employees in lower paying less skilled jobs report more stress due to the new technology than employees in more skilled, higher paying jobs.
- Older employees perceive greater job changes than younger employees, and also report more stress when technology changes.
- The specific job factors that produced stress varied according to the job category. However, there were several job stressors that were consistent across different job categories in many of the studies. These were: (1) high job demands, such as heavy workload, work pressure and increased work pace, (2) a lack of control over the work process and/or an inability to participate in decisions, (3) a high level of task difficulty, (4) monotony, lack of variety or lack of task content, (5) poor supervision or lack of supervisory support, and (6) technology problems, such as slowdowns or break downs, which increase the perception of higher work load and less control.

62.6 Psychosocial Aspects of VDT's and Cumulative Trauma Disorders in Keyboarding

Recently, there has been interest in the role of occupational psychosocial stress in the causation and aggravation of upper extremity cumulative trauma disorders for VDT users (Smith, 1984; Bammer and Blignault, 1988; Smith and Carayon, 1995b; Hagberg, et al., 1995). Hadler (1990, 1992) has stated that psychological stress may be the primary cause of the symptomology associated with many upper extremity CTD's, especially in VDT users. Smith and Carayon (1995b) proposed that work organization factors define ergonomic risks to upper extremity musculoskeletal problems by specifying the nature of the work activities (variety or repetition), the extent of loads, the exposure to loads, the number and duration of actions, ergonomic considerations such as workstation design, tool and equipment design, and environmental features. These factors interact as a system to produce an overall load on the person (Smith and Sainfort, 1989; Smith and Carayon, 1995a), and this load may lead to an increased risk for upper extremity musculoskeletal problems (Smith and Carayon, 1995b).

There are psycho-biological mechanisms that make a connection between psychological stress and upper extremity CTD's plausible and likely. At the personal level psychological stress can lead to an increased physiological susceptibility to CTD's by affecting hormonal responses (Levi, 1972) and circulatory responses that exacerbate the influences of the traditional biomechanical risk factors (Selye, 1956). In addition, psychological stress can affect employee attitude, motivation and behavior that can lead to risky actions which may increase CTD risk (Smith and Carayon, 1995b). At the organizational level, the policies and procedures of a company can affect CTD risk through the design of jobs, the length of exposures to stressors, establishing work-rest cycles, defining the extent of work pressures and establishing the psychological climate regarding socialization, career and job security (Smith et al, 1992; NIOSH, 1992, 1993).

Smith et al (1992), Theorell et al (1991) and Faucett and Rempel (1994) have demonstrated that some of these organizational features can influence the level of self reported upper extremity musculoskeletal health complaints. In addition, the organization defines the nature of the task activities (work methods), employee training, availability of assistance, supervisory relations and workstation design. All of these factors have been shown to influence the risk of upper extremity musculoskeletal symptoms (Linton and Kamwendo, 1989; Smith et al, 1992; Lim et al, 1989; Lim and Carayon, 1995; NIOSH, 1990, 1992, 1993; Smith and Carayon, 1995b).

A related issue is a social psychological aspect of illness behavior. It is possible that a person under psychological stress could develop specific physical symptoms (such as sore wrists) that would "legitimate" their general psychological discomfort and pain. Having pain in the wrists and fingers may be a more socially acceptable disorder than feeling depressed. Thus, the effects of psychological disturbances may be reflected in physical disorders of the musculoskeletal system.

This may be likened to mass psychogenic illness (Colligan and Murphy, 1979) or psychosomatic disorders (Wolf, 1986) where psychologically induced disturbances lead to physical impairment. Mass psychogenic illness has been defined as "the collective occurrence of a set of physical symptoms and related beliefs among two or more individuals in the absence of an identifiable pathogen" (Colligan and Murphy, 1979). The illness is perceived as being caused by a physical agent and the affected individual can then escape the hazardous environment (Colligan and Murphy, 1979). It may be that the reporting of muscular pain and CTD's are more socially acceptable than psychological stress reactions to difficult working conditions (Kiesler and Finholt, 1988). Like mass psychogenic illness, CTD's have often been observed in low-pay, high-pressure, repetitive jobs (Putz-Anderson, 1988; Silverstein et al., 1987; NIOSH, 1992).

62.7 A Model of Psychosocial Stress and VDT Use

To fully understand the health and safety implications of computerization it must be realized that many working conditions jointly influence the VDT user. Smith and Sainfort (1989) and Smith and Carayon (1995) have proposed a comprehensive job design model which illustrates the various facets of working conditions which can produce psychosocial stress. Figure 1 illustrates these facets of working conditions, and as is implied by the diagram there is an interaction among all of these facets during the work process. We believe that it is an accumulation of demands from and cognitions about several facets of work that leads to employee satisfaction, motivation, health and safety problems and VDT user stress. A short description of this model of working facets as defined by Smith and Sainfort (1989) follows:

Figure 1 illustrates a model for conceptualizing the various elements of a work system that can exert demands on employees which may influence psychological and physiological reactions. At the center of this model is the individual with his/her unique physical characteristics, perceptions, personality and behavior. The individual uses technologies, such as computers (VDT's), to perform specific job tasks. The characteristics and capabilities of the technologies affect em-

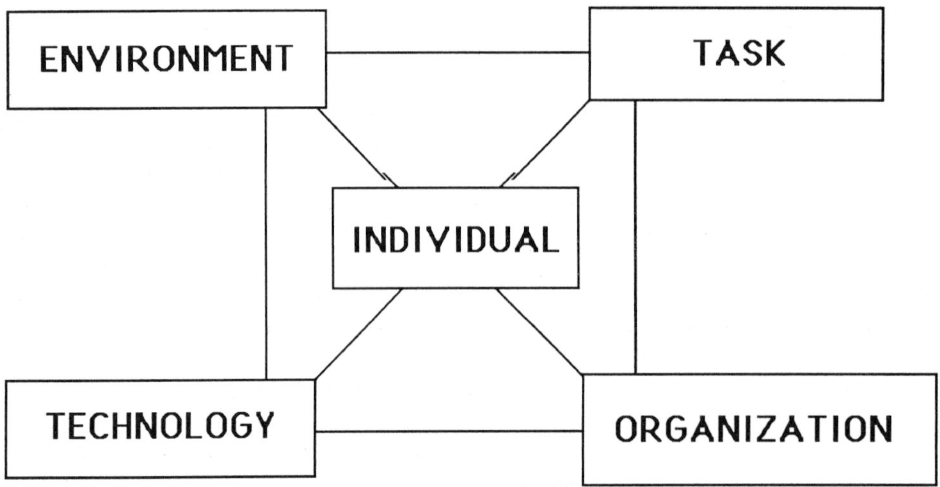

Figure 1. Model of VDT working conditions and their impact on the employee.

ployee performance and the required skills and knowledge to effectively use the technology. The task requirements also affect the skills and knowledge needed, while both the tasks and technologies affect the content (variety and skill use) of the job and the cognitive and physical demands. The tasks define the use of technologies and are carried out in a worksetting that comprises the physical and the social environment. The environment can affect employee comfort, psychological moods and attitudes. Finally, there is an organizational structure that defines the nature and level of individual involvement, interaction, control , supervision and standards of performance.

This model can be used to establish relationships between job requirements, psychological and physical loads and job satisfaction, motivation, and stress. Harmful demands lead to stress responses that can produce adverse satisfaction and motivational effects. In this model these various elements interact to determine the way in which work is accomplished and the effectiveness of the work in achieving individual and organizational needs and goals. This is a systems concept in that any one element will have influences on any other element(s). Each element in this model and some examples of the potential adverse aspects that have been identified for VDT users are described below.

62.7.1 The Individual

A number of personal considerations determine the physical and psychological effects that the previous elements of the model will produce. These include personality, physical health status, skills and abilities, physical conditioning, prior experiences and learning, motives, goals and needs (see for example Levi, 1972). This is not an exhaustive list, but illustrates the potential influences.

The individual working at a computer serves as a central focus for most inquiry into the study of computer use, job satisfaction, and employee stress. (Steffy and Jones, 1989) examined influences of individual factors and found that younger employees reported greater video display terminal strain, job dissatisfaction, and job tension, though older employees were more prone to psychosomatic problems. Another interesting finding was that women reported higher levels of video display terminal strain, job dissatisfaction, and job tension. Zeffane (1994) found older employees to be more satisfied than younger employees, whereas Huuhtanen and Leino (1992) found that older employees had a harder time adapting to new technology.

Length of time with an organization has been shown to moderate the relationships between role stress variables and overall job satisfaction (Igbaria and Guimaraes, 1992). Zeffane (1994) found that tenure with a company was positively correlated with job satisfaction. Education moderated the relationship between role ambiguity and three facets of job satisfaction: (1) work, (2) supervision, and (3) promotion (Igbaria and Guimaraes,1992).

62.7.2 The Environment

Various aspects of the physical environment have been implicated as job stressors in the office. Noise is the most well known environmental stressor which can cause increases in arousal, blood pressure, and negative psychological mood (Glass and Singer,1972; Cohen and Spacapan, 1984). General air quality and housekeeping have been shown to be important considerations in the occurrence of "mass psychogenic illness", "stuffy office syndrome" and other stress responses, such as health symptoms (Colligan and Murphy, 1979; Stellman et al., 1985). Finally, environmental conditions that produce sensory disruption and make it more difficult to carry out tasks increase the level of employee stress and emotional irritation (Gunnarsson and Ostberg, 1977; Cakir et al, 1979; Smith et al., 1981; Sauter et al., 1983; Grandjean, 1979). These can lead to decreased job satisfaction and lower motivation.

62.7.3 The Technology

The ability to accomplish tasks and the extent of physiological and psychological load are often defined by the technology being used by the employee. When the technology produces too much or too little load, then increased stress and adverse physical health outcomes can occur (Smith et al., 1981; Johansson and Aronsson,1984; Ostberg and Nilsson, 1985; Carayon and Sainfort, 1992). New technology often creates employee fears of inadequate skills and obsolescence. It also creates a fear over potential job loss due to increased efficiency of technology (Ostberg and Nilsson, 1985; Smith et al., 1987; Lindstrom, 1991).

On the other hand, new computer technology can also enhance job content by providing performance feedback and more cognitive requirements (Kalimo and Leppanen, 1985). Travers and Stanton, (1984) found that VDT users had higher satisfaction, lower tension, lower fatigue, lower confusion, lower anger and lower depression levels than employees at the same job who did not use a VDT. Starr et al. (1982) found that directory assistance operators using VDTs did not report lower overall job satisfaction than those not using VDT's. Zeffane (1994) found increased job satisfaction as an employees had greater computer use over a range of management functions.

Steffy and Jones (1989) found that hours of video display terminal use were not predictors of job satisfaction. Additionally, employees who spent more hours at a video display terminal experienced greater video display terminal-related strains and job dissatisfaction, though hours of use was not related to general psychosomatic distress and job tension. VDT users experienced greater tension, dissatisfaction, and psychosomatic distress than nonusers. Other studies have found that increased hours working at the VDT were related to increased somatic complaints (Sauter et al, 1983; Smith et al, 1981; NIOSH, 1992). Steffy and Jones (1989) found that workstation discomfort contributed to VDT operator strain, psychosomatic distress, job dissatisfaction and job tension. Carey (1992) also found that more VDT use was significantly correlated with lower job satisfaction. Travers and Stanton (1984) found that eye-related health problems increased as employees spent more time at the VDT, and that these problems existed even when the employees had more control over their work stations.

62.7.4 Organizational Factors

The organizational context in which work tasks are carried out often has considerations that influence employee satisfaction, motivation and stress. As mentioned earlier, new computer technology often requires new skills for proficient performance. The way in which employees are introduced to new technology and the organizational support they receive, such as training and time to acclimate, has been tied to stress and emotional disturbances (Smith and Sainfort, 1989; Amick and Celentano, 1991; Smith et al., 1987; Amick and Smith, 1992). The ability to grow in a job and to be promoted (career development) has a stress connection (Arthur and Gunderson, 1965; Smith et al, 1981; Smith et al., 1992). Possible job loss also can create stress (Caplan et al., 1975; Cobb and Kasl, 1977; Kasl, 1978; Smith et al., 1981; Smith et al, 1992).

Employees functioning in an organizational climate that they perceive as poor experience more psychological strain (Cohen et al, 1987; Piotrkowski et al., 1992). Relationships with co-employees have been shown to be potentially problematic for stress (Piotrkowski, et al., 1992; Billette and Bouchard, 1993). A contrary finding was that co-employee support was not important in predicting job satisfaction (Amick and Celentano, 1991).

The size of the organization has been studied for its influence on employee satisfaction and (Idson, 1990) determined that the low job satisfaction in larger establishments can largely be explained by the fact that production is organized in an inflexible manner. It was the case that employees with higher wages in the larger establishments that lacked control over the nature of the work environment were less satisfied in their jobs.

Yang and Carayon (1995) found that supervisor support was a significant predictor of workload dissatisfaction, tension-anxiety and daily life stress. Results also showed that supervisor support was much more relevant to reducing employee stress than co-employee support. Amick and Celentano (1991) found that supervisor support is important in predicting job satisfaction, in fact, supervisor support was the most important predictor of job satisfaction.

Zeffane (1994) found those employees more certain about the future directions of the organization were significantly more satisfied about their jobs than those who were not.

62.7.5 The Task

Aspects of the work task have been studied more than any other element in this model. A wide variety of influences have been studied including content considerations such as repetitiveness (Cox, 1985), meaningfulness (Hackman and Oldham, 1976; Smith et al., 1992) and workload (Smith et al., 1981; Sauter et al, 1983; Carayon and Sainfort, 1991). Machine paced work tasks are more stressful than non-paced tasks (Salvendy and Smith, 1981). Lack of participation (French, 1963; Caplan et al., 1975) and control (Karasek et al., 1981; Fisher, 1984; Carayon-Sainfort, 1992; Carayon, 1993; Smith et al., 1992; Amick and Smith, 1992; Sauter, Hurrell and Cooper, 1989) can produce emotional problems and decreased job satisfaction.

Office employees in jobs that lack control experience psychological strain (Piotrkowski, et al., 1992), workload dissatisfaction and daily life stress (Carayon-Sainfort, 1991). In a longitudinal study, Greenberger, Strasser, and Cummings (1989) found that personal control significantly predicted job satisfaction and performance. Carayon (1994) found that people who perceived themselves as having control over their job and who perceived that electronic performance monitoring is accurate tended to be more satisfied with their jobs. Amick and Celentano (1991) found that low autonomy (a lack of control) was associated with decreased job satisfaction.

Frese (1989) supports the concept of increasing employee control instead of focusing on reducing stressors such as high work demands and low job content. He proposes that when a person has control, she can directly influence the stressors. Technological innovations change workplaces quickly and therefore the stressors also change quickly. By giving employees control over stressors, stressors that the employees perceive to be most problematic are reduced in a more timely fashion.

Korunka and Weiss (1995) conducted a longitudinal study that found that highly monotonous work was associated with increased psychosomatic complaints lower job satisfaction and that a higher level of participation was associated with greater job satisfaction. It was also noted that job satisfaction increased in the work with new technologies which was diversified and called for high qualifications, but tended to decrease for persons with low qualifications doing mental monotonous work at VDUs. Billette and Bouchard (1993) found that pressures to perform and work monotony were related to negative mental health. Zeffane (1994) found that task variety and participation in decisions were positively correlated with job satisfaction.

Role ambiguity and confusion over what the individual is to do on the job has been shown to be related to employee stress and strain. Igbaria and Guimaraes (1992) found that role ambiguity was the most dysfunctional variable for information center employees in relation to job satisfaction. Glisson and Durick (1988) found there were significantly negative correlations between job satisfaction and each of the following problems: role ambiguity, task identity, and task significance. Skill variety also had a significant positive effect on job satisfaction.

Work overload has been shown to affect employee mental health (Smith et al., 1981, 1992; Piotrkowski, et al., 1992). Carayon-Sainfort (1992) found that high workload was significantly correlated with workload dissatisfaction and daily life stress. Yang and Carayon (1995) found that quantitative workload and computer-related problems significantly contributed to employee boredom and daily life stress. Quantitative workload was also a significant predictor of workload dissatisfaction. Amick and Celentano (1991) found that increased job demands were associated with less job satisfaction.

Carayon-Sainfort and Smith (1991) and Carayon-Sainfort (1992) found that high workload and work pressure, and low job control were related to high workload dissatisfaction and daily life stress. Carayon-Sainfort and Smith (1991) found that high frequency of computer problems and intense use of a computer were related to increases in perceived workload and work pressure, and a decrease in perceived job control. Results supported an indirect effect, but not the direct effect of computer system performance on employee stress. The indirect effects mediated the stress outcomes through task characteristics such as workload, work pressure, and job control.

Smith, Cohen, Stammerjohn and Happ (1981) compared the stress factors for video display terminal operators versus non-operators doing the same jobs. They found that the clerical VDT operators reported more workload dissatisfaction, boredom, qualitative workload, job future ambiguity, and role ambiguity than non-operators or professionals that used the

VDT's. The clerical VDT operators reported higher psychological distress and more somatic health complaints such as sore eyes and muscles.

These five elements of the system work in concert to provide the resources for achievement of individual and organizational goals. The potential negative attributes of each of the elements have been indicated from the studies cited above, but there are also positive aspects of each that can counteract the negative influences. A major advantage of this model is that it does not highlight any one factor, or a small set of factors, rather it examines the design of work from a holistic perspective.

62.8 Improving the Psychosocial Characteristics of VDT Work

62.8.1 A Systems Perspective

Work organization and job design features of VDT work that adversely influence job satisfaction, stress and health can be improved to reduce their negative consequences. However, it is essential to realize that VDT work design problems that can lead to job dissatisfaction and stress are seldom single aspects of the organization or of job design. Rather, they are most often the combination of many aspects of improper workplace design. Thus, solutions for reducing or eliminating job stress and enhancing job satisfaction must be comprehensive, and simultaneously deal with several different aspects of improper work design. Solutions that focus on only one or two work design considerations will probably not succeed in controlling job stress problems. In the following sections we will describe methods for improving work design to reduce VDT user job stress. The positive aspects for each individual factor will be examined separately to highlight the critical aspects of each factor. However, the overall strategy is to approach improvements as a global process that improves many factors simultaneously.

62.8.2 Organizational Support

Improvements in job design should start with the organization providing a supportive environment for employees. Such an environment enhances employees' motivation to work, feelings of security, and reduces employees' feelings of stress (Lawler, 1986,1992; Hendrick, 1986; Eason, 1988; Smith and Carayon, 1995a). Organizations can begin by making a policy statement that defines the importance of employees and their substantial value to the enterprise. Further the policy should be explicit on how the organization will provide a supportive environment for employees, and specific on the means through which this will be achieved.

One very effective means for providing support to employees is to have supervisors and managers who have been indoctrinated and trained in methods for being supportive. First-line supervisors are a critical link between the technology, organizational structure and employees. Supportive supervisors can serve as buffers that "protect" employees from "hassles" from the organization or technology. This support serves to limit the extent of stressors that employees are exposed to. In addition supervisors can provide social support which has been shown to be helpful in reducing stress reactions (House, 1981). Job improvements should start at the top of the organization since this establishes the power base for improvements to travel down to other levels.

62.8.3 Job Content

The content of job tasks has long been defined as an important consideration in employee motivation, productivity (Herzberg et al., 1959; Hackman and Oldham, 1976) and more recently in job stress reactions (Cooper and Marshall, 1976; Smith, 1987; Kalimo et al., 1996). There are three main aspects of job content that are of specific relevance in VDT work, task complexity, employee skills and career opportunities. In some respects, these are all related to the concept of developing the motivational climate for employee job satisfaction and psychological growth. Psychological growth encompasses improvement of employee intellectual capabilities and skills, increased ego enhancement or self image and increased social group recognition of individual achievement.

The primary means for enhancing job content is to increase the extent of skill use in performing job tasks. This typically means enlarging the scope of job tasks (increasing variety), as well as enriching the elements of each specific task. Enlarging the number of tasks increases the repertoire of skills needed for successful performance, and also increases the number of decisions made by the employee in defining task sequences and activities. This increased "skilling" of the job content promotes an employee's self image of personal worth and of value to the organization. It also enhances the social work group's positive image of the individual.

Since many VDT jobs require little knowledge or skill use, how can this job "skilling" be achieved? The first step is to enlarge the number of tasks carried out by an individual employee which can lead to increased skill requirements. This also reduces the psychological "boredom" that comes from repetitive work. However, there is no guarantee that enlargement alone will lead to increased skill use. If increasing the number of tasks does not increase the knowledge and skill level required to do the job, then the psychological benefits are greatly reduced. While there is still the benefit of reduced boredom due to enlargement, there is only small ego enhancement.

The next step is to increase the complexity of the tasks. This means increasing the amount of thinking and decision making. This can be achieved by combining simple tasks into sets of related activities that have to be coordinated, or by adding mental requirements that take addition knowledge and cognitive skills. Understanding how this process works is best illustrated with an example. Let us assume that we have a VDT user who enters health insurance codes from paper claims forms into a computer database for eight hours per day. The task is simple, entering subscriber numbers through a keypad, and we want to increase the content of this job.

The first step would be to enlarge the number of tasks being performed by the employee. We could add the tasks of entering additional data such as medical provider codes and the type of medical procedures codes. In addition, we could add the task of verifying the entered codes. These additional tasks would not require substantially more mental skill than the original task, but they would increase task variety. However, this may not be sufficient to deal with the boredom of such a simple job. We can also enrich the job tasks by adding cognitive content. This can be achieved by providing opportunities for the employee to make decisions about the task activities. For instance, the employee could evaluate each claim for proper payment, contact claimants for follow-up information, resolve claims disputes from the claimants, or assist claimants in filing proper forms and paperwork. These activities utilize greater intellectual capability than just the data entry task and provide greater satisfaction and self esteem.

There are instances when computerized technology is implemented when the new task activities have greater mental requirements than previous tasks, and these requirements exceed the current knowledge and skills of the employee. These jobs usually already have high content and do not need to be redesigned to add more content. However, the new cognitive demands can cause psychological stress. When intellectual requirements of the job exceed employee knowledge or skills, or when additional knowledge requirements are added to the job which the employee has to learn, then there is the need to provide training so that employees have the added knowledge and skills necessary to perform the tasks well (adequately). Training has more than one benefit. First it can improve employee's knowledge and skills so that performance is better. But it has the added benefit of enhancing employee self-esteem and confidence by adding value to the employee's skills. Providing training also shows the employee that the employer is willing to invest in skill enhancement. This promotes employee confidence in employment stability and value to the company.

62.8.4 Career Opportunities

Another aspect of job content enhancement is the development of career opportunities for employees. Recent organizational strategies for enhancing profitability have tended to flatten organizational structure by reducing middle management and administrative staff (See Lawler, 1986 and 1992). This strategy provides fewer opportunities for employees to advance through a career in supervision and management. New concepts of career growth and advancement are aimed at increasing employee knowledge and skills, and then providing job opportunities for applying the added skills. Such opportunities require enriched jobs in which the employee can use new technical skills, and where the employee has decision making responsibility about task activities. With this approach, career paths and additional compensation are based on the level of employee knowledge and skills (pay based on knowledge), the skill requirements of the new job and employee performance. Advancement is through technical and performance merit rather than through supervisory responsibilities. Such systems can only be successful where enriched jobs can be developed.

For more traditional organizations where restructuring is not occurring, there are limitations on the number of employees who can be promoted into management positions. In such a situation, it is not unusual for there to be ten or more qualified employees for each supervisory position available. This type of organizational career path can be frustrating for good employees who do not get selected for management positions. These employees should have opportunities to develop a career through a means separate from promotion into management. Here again, job enrichment and developing employee knowledge and skills can provide a different sort of career ladder that can enhance individual employee esteem and financial needs.

62.8.5 Job Control

An aspect of job design that has a powerful psychosocial influence is the amount of control an employee has over the job. Various aspects of control are important and can be defined by the questions, "what, how and when?" These specify the nature of the task(s) to be undertaken, the need for coordination among employees, the methods to be used to carry-out the task(s) and the scheduling of the task(s). Control can be designed into jobs at the levels of the task, the work unit and the company. At the task level the employee can be given autonomy in the methods and procedures used in completing the task. In the example of the data entry clerk at the insurance company, the employee can determine the order of entering the codes, can initiate contact with the medical provider for further information or with the subscriber.

At the work unit level groups of employees can self-manage several inter-related tasks. The group can decide who will perform particular tasks, the scheduling of tasks, coordination of tasks and production standards to meet company goals. At the company level employees can participate in structured activities that provide input to management about employee opinions or quality improvement suggestions. An important concept in providing control to employees is, the greater the levels and extent of employee involvement (task, work unit, company), the greater the benefit for self management. If there is a limitation on the levels of control available, then it is better to start at the task level and work up the organizational structure later.

62.8.6 Workload

A concern for employees when computer automation occurs is an increase in their work load. Such an increase is logical since one main purpose of automation is to enhance the quantity and quality of work output. The increase is often necessary to pay for the automation. The problem that can occur is in establishing the appropriate work load that accommodates both economic needs and the human factors needs of the employee. For the human factors needs, there are scientific methods that have been developed in industrial engineering for determining appropriate work methods and work loads (the performance requirements of jobs). These have been used successfully in manufacturing industries for decades, but have had little application in office settings, especially for VDT work.

The use of scientific methods to establish work load for VDT operators should be a high priority for every company. Such methods set reasonable production standards or work output requirements, help to protect employees from excessive work load, and help to ensure the quality of products. These methods are thoroughly described in the books Introduction to Work Study, Third (revised) Edition, 1979, G. Kanawaty (Editor), International Labour Office, Geneva, and Handbook of Industrial Engineering, Second Edition,1992, G. Salvendy (Editor), John Wiley & Sons , New York.

Computers can assist employees to work faster and more effectively. We must ensure that in making employees more productive that they are not overworked. While we generally have substantial experience and knowledge about factory work standards for employee performance, we have very little knowledge about what reasonable workloads are for office employees who are using computers. Factory work often does not entail mental workload which is a new dimension in dealing with performance requirements for computer users. In addition, ergonomic conditions that cause fatigue in factories are typically from loading the muscles dynamically, while in offices they are from static postures, long-term close viewing of computer screens and mental demands. New ways of assessing workload have to be developed for computerized jobs because of these new job demands which are not prevalent in other types of work. As Henning, et al., (1989. 1992, 1993, 1994) have shown different approaches to rest breaks may be more effective for computer users than traditional work/rest cycles. Self-determined breaks and mini-breaks may provide greater benefits.

62.8.7 Socialization

Computerized tasks often have high concentration demands which diminish the amount of social interaction during work. This can lead to social isolation of employees. To counter this social isolation, there should be structured opportunities for socialization when employees are not engaged in computerized tasks, or when employees are on rest breaks. Non-computerized tasks that do not require extensive concentration should be organized so that employees are close to each other to provide the opportunity to talk with each other. Such socialization provides social support which is an essential modifier of adverse psychological disturbances and cardiovascular disorders. Socialization also reduces social isolation and promotes improved mental health.

62.8.8 Proper Ergonomics

It is important to recognize that poor ergonomic conditions can lead to psychosocial problems for VDT users.

Thus, for complete job design there is also the need for proper ergonomic conditions. Since the focus of this section is on the psychosocial aspects of computer work, we will not provide a detailed discussion of how to achieve ergonomic improvements. Rather we refer you to other chapters in this Handbook that deal with workstation ergonomics and the following articles: (1) Smith (1984), (2) Smith et al, (1992,) and (3) Smith, Cohen and Grandjean (1996) for a discussion of ways to improve ergonomic conditions for human-computer interaction and VDT work.

62.8.9 Finding the Proper Balance in VDT Work Design

There are no "perfect" jobs or "perfect" workplaces which are free of all psychosocial and ergonomic stressors. Often, we must consider the need to compromise when making improvements at the workplace. In any redesign process there are "trade-offs" which require us to think about how to get the best "balance" to have the greatest positive benefit for employee health and productivity. There are many factors that can produce adverse psychosocial conditions that lead to stress. Each of these factors are inter-related, so that making modifications in one factor may not be beneficial if concomitant changes are not made in other factors that are related.

There are two aspects of "balance" that need to be addressed. These are (1) the balance of the total system, and (2) compensatory balance. System balance is based on the idea that a workplace or process or job is more than the sum of the individual components of the system. The interplay among the various components of the system produce results that are greater (or lesser) than the additive aspects of the individual parts. It is the way in which the system components relate to each other that determines the potential for the system to produce positive results. If an organization concentrates solely on the technological component of the system, then there is an "imbalance" because the personal and psychosocial factors are neglected. Thus, job improvements must take account of and accommodate the entire work system. Our model of the work system can be used to establish relationships between job demands, job design factors, and stress.

The second type of balance is "compensatory" in nature. It is seldom possible to eliminate all psychosocial factors that cause stress. This may be due to financial considerations, or it may be because it is impossible to change inherent aspects of job tasks. The essence of this "balance" is to reduce psychological stress by making changes in aspects of work that can be positively changed to help improve those negative aspects that cannot be changed. In one strategy, proper job design can be achieved by providing all of those characteristics of each work element that meet recognized criteria for physical loads, work cycles, job content, control, and socialization, and that provide for individual physiological and psychological needs. With this approach, the best designs will eliminate all sources of stress. However, such a perfect job cannot often be achieved in reality, so a second strategy is to use positive work elements to compensate for poor work elements which can balance the stress by moderating those negative factors to reduce the total demands (loads).

The five elements of the work system function in concert to provide the resources for achieving individual and organizational goals. We have described some of the potential negative attributes of the elements in terms of job stress, but there are also positive aspects of each that can counteract the negative influences of others. For instance, the negative influences of inadequate skill to use new technology can be offset by training employees. Or the adverse influences of low job content that creates repetition and boredom can be balanced by an organizational supervisory structure that promotes employee involvement and control over tasks, and job enlargement that introduces task variety. Our approach proposes to balance the loads that are potentially stressful by considering all of the work elements. For instance, organizational structure could be adapted to enriched jobs in order to provide support to the individual such as increased staff or shared responsibilities or increased financial resources.

In conclusion, there are several aspects of the design of computerized work activities that can influence the satisfaction, motivation, performance and health of employees. Research has shown that the organizational methods used to implement new technology, the extent of employees' control, task content, work pressures, career opportunities, job security, the quality of environmental and ergonomic considerations, supervisory support, socialization at work, and many other work design issues all affect employee psychological and physical well-being. Theories of proper job design coupled with intervention studies provide a basis for proper organizational and job design concepts. As a foundation, a total systems approach that includes multiple aspects of the work process needs to be applied to obtain a proper design perspective. Interventions need to examine organizational issues, task characteristics, technology design, environmental design and individual employee characteristics for the best possible results for job satisfaction, performance and health.

62.9 References

Amick III, B. C. and Celentano, D. D. (1991). Structural determinants of the psychosocial work environment: introducing technology in the work stress framework. *Ergonomics*, 34 (5), 625-646.

Amick, B.C. III and Smith, M.J., 1992, Stress, computer-based work monitoring and measurement systems: A conceptual overview. *Applied Ergonomics*, 23, 6-16.

Aronsson, G. (1989). Changed Qualification Demands in Computer-mediated Work. *Applied Psychology*: An International Review, 38 (1), 57-71.

Arthur, R.J. and Gunderson, E.K., 1965. Promotion and mental illness in the Navy. *Journal of Occupational Medicine*, 7: 452-456.

Bammer, G. and Blignault, I. (1988). More than a pain in the arms: A review of the consequences of developing occupational overuse syndromes (OOSs). *Journal of Occupational Health and Safety - Australia and New-Zealand* 4(5): 389-397.

Bergqvist, U., Knave, B., Voss, M. and Wibom, R. (1992). A longitudinal study of VDT work and health. *International Journal of Human-Computer Interaction,* 4(2), 197-219.

Bergqvist, U. O. (1984). Video display terminals and health: A technical and medical appraisal of the state of the art. Scandinavian Journal of Work, *Environment and Health*, 10 (Suppl 2).

Berlinguet, L. and Berthelette, D. (Eds.). (1990). *Work With Display Units 89*. Amsterdam: Elsevier Science Publishers.

Bikson, T.K. and Eveland, J.D. (1990). *Technology transfer as a framework for understanding social impacts of computerization.* Santa Monica: RAND Corporation.

Billette, A. and Bouchard, R. (1993). Pool Size, Job Stressors, and Health Problems: A Study of Data Entry Clerks. *International Journal of Human-Computer Interaction*, 5 (2), 101-113.

Bradley, G. (1983). Effects of computerization on work environment and health: from a perspective of equality between sexes. *Occupational Health Nursing*, 31, 35-39.

Bradley, G. (1989). *Computers and the Psychosocial Work Environment*, London: Taylor and Francis.

Bullinger, H. J. (1991). *Human Aspects in Computing: Design and Use of Interactive Systems and Work with Terminals*. (Vol. 18A). Amsterdam: Elsevier Science Publishers.

Cakir, A., Hart, D. J. and Stewart, T. F. M. (1979). *The VDT Manual.* Darmstadt: Inca-Fiej Research Association.

Cannon, W.B. (1914). The interrelations of emotions as suggested by recent physiological researchers. *American Journal of Psychology*, 25, 256-282.

Caplan, R.D., Cobb, S., French, J.R.P., Harrison, R.V. and Pinneau, S.R. (1975). *Job demands and worker health.* Government Printing Office, Washington DC.

Carayon, P. (1993). Chronic effects of job control, supervisor social support and work pressure on office worker stress. In G. Keita and S. Sauter (Eds.) *Job Stress 2000: Emerging Issues*. Washington, DC: American Psychological Association.

Carayon, P. (1994). A longitudinal study of quality of working life among computer users: Preliminary results. In A. Grieco, G. Molteni, E. Occhipinti and B. Piccoli (Eds.), *Proceedings of the Fourth International Scientific Conference on Work with Display Units.* Amsterdam: Elsevier Science Publishers, 39-44.

Carayon, P. (1994). Effects of Electronic Performance Monitoring On Job Design and Employee Stress: Results of Two Studies. *International Journal of Human-Computer Interaction*, 6 (2), 177-190.

Carayon, P. C., Yang, C.-L. and Lim, S.-Y. (1995). Examining the relationship between job design and employee strain over time in a sample of office employees. *Ergonomics*, 38 (6), 1199-1211.

Carayon-Sainfort, P. (1992). *The Use of Computers in Offices*: Impact

on Task Characteristics and Employee Stress. *International Journal of Human-Computer Interaction,* 4 (3), 245-261.

Carayon-Sainfort, P. and Smith, M. J. (1991). Impact of Computer System Performance on Task Characteristics and Employee Stress. In H. J. Bullinger (Ed.), *Human Aspects in Computing: Design and Use of Interactive Systems and Work with Terminals*. Amsterdam: Elsevier Science Publishers,195-199.

Carey, J. M. (1992). Job Satisfaction and visual display unit (VDU) usage: an explanatory model. *Behaviour and Information Technology,* 11 (6), 338-344.

Cobb, S. and Kasl, S. (1977). *Termination: The Consequences of Job Loss*. Washington, D.C.: U.S. Government Printing Office.

Cohen, S., and Spacapan, S. (1984). The social psychology of noise. In D.M. Jones and A.J. Chapman (eds.) *Noise as a Public Health Problem*, Milan: Centro Ricerche e Stdui Amplifon.

Cohen, B. G. F., Piotrkowski, C. S. and Coray, K. E. (1987). Working conditions and health complaints of women office workers. In G. Salvendy, S. L. Sauter, and J. J. Hurrell (Eds.), *Social, Ergonomic and Stress Aspects of Work with Computers*. Amsterdam: Elsevier Science Publishers, 365-372.

Colligan, M.J. and Murphy, L.R. (1979). Mass psychogenic illness in organizations: An overview. *Journal of Occupational Psychology* 52: 77-90.

Cooper, C.L. and Marshall, J., 1976, Occupational sources of stress: A review of the literature relating to coronary heart disease and mental ill health. *Journal of Occupational Psychology,* 49, 11-28.

Cox, T. (1985). Repetitive work: Occupational stress and health. In C.L. Cooper and M.J. Smith (Eds.), *Job Stress and Blue-Collar Work* . New York: John Wiley and Sons, 85-112.

Dainoff, M. J. (1982). Occupational stress factors in visual display terminal (VDT) operation: A review of empirical research. *Behaviour and Information Technology*, 1(2), 141-176.

Dewe, P. (1991). Primary appraisal, secondary appraisal and coping: Their role in stressful work encounters. *Journal of Occupational Psychology*, 64, 331-351.

Eason, K. (1988). *Information Technology and Organizational Change.* London: Taylor and Francis, Ltd.

Elias, R., Cail, F., Tisserand, M. and Christman, M. (1980). Investigations in operators working with CRT display terminals: relationships between task content and psychophysiological alterations. In E. Grandjean and E. Vigliani (Eds.) *Ergonomic Aspects of Visual Display Terminals*, London: Taylor & Francis, Ltd., 211-218.

Emery, F., and Trist, E. (1965). The causal texture of organizational environments. *Human Relations*, 18, 21-31.

Faucett, J. and Rempel, D. (1994). VDT-related musculoskeletal symptoms: Interactions between work posture and psychosocial work factors. *American Journal of Industrial Medicine*, 26, 597-612.

French, J.R.P. Jr., 1963. The social environment and mental health. *Journal of Social Issues*, 19: 39-56.

Fisher, S. *Stress and the perception of control.* Lawrence Erlbaum Associates Publishers, New Jersey 1984.

Frese, M. J. (1989). Human Computer Interaction within an Industrial Psychology Framework. *Applied Psychology: An International Review*, 38 (1), 29-44.

Ghiringhelli, L. (1980). Collection of subjective opinions on use of VDUs. In E. Grandjean and E. Vigliani (Eds.) *Ergonomic Aspects of Visual Display Terminals*, London: England: Taylor & Francis, Ltd, 227-232.

Glass, D.C. and Singer, J.E. (1972). *Urban Stress: Experiments on Noise and Social Stressors*, New York: Academic Press.

Glisson, C. and Durick, M. (1988). Predictors of Job Satisfaction and Organizational Commitment in Human Service Organizations. *Administrative Quarterly*, 33, 61-81.

Grandjean and E. Vigliani. (1980). *Ergonomic Aspects of Visual Display Terminals*, London: Taylor & Francis, Ltd.

Grandjean, E. (1979). Ergonomical and medical aspects of cathode ray tube displays . Zurich, Switzerland: Federal Institute of Technology.

Greenberger, D. B., Strasser, S. and Cummings, L. L. (1989). The Impact of Personal Control on Performance and Satisfaction. *Organizational Behavior and Human Decision Processes*, 43, 29-51.

Grieco, A., Molteni, G., Occhipinti, E. and Piccoli, B. (1995). *Work with Display Units 94*. Amsterdam: Elsevier Science Publishers.

Gunnarsson, E. and Ostberg, O. (1977). Physical and emotional job environment in a terminal-based data system. Stockholm: Department of Occupational Safety, Occupational Medical Division, Section for Physical Occupational Hygiene.

Hackman, J.R. and Oldham, G.R. (1976). Motivation through the design of work: test of a theory. *Organ. Behav. and Human Perf.,* 16, 250-279.

Hadler, N.M. (1990). Cumulative trauma disorders - An iatrogenic concept. *Journal of Occupational Medicine* 32(1): 38-41.

Hadler, N.M. (1992). Arm pain in the workplace - A small area analysis. *Journal of Occupational Medicine,* 34, 113-119.

Hagberg, M., Silverstein, B., Wells, R., Smith, M.J., Hendrick, H.W., Carayon, P., Perusse, M. (1995). *Work Related Musculoskeletal Disorders (WMDSs): A Reference Book for Prevention.* London: Taylor and Francis.

Hendrick, H. (1986). Macroergonomics: A conceptual model for integrating human factors with organizational design. In O. Brown and H. Hendrick (Eds.),

Human Factors in Organizational Design and Management, Amsterdam: Elsevier Science Publishers,467-477.

Henning, R. A., Ortega, A., Callaghan, E. and Kissel, G. (1994). Self management of rest breaks by VDT users. In *Proceedings of the Human Factors and Ergonomics Society 38th Annual Meeting*, 2. Santa Monica: Human Factors and Ergonomics Society, 754-758.

Henning, R. A., Alteras-Webb, S. M., Jacques, P., Kissel, G. and Sullivan, A. (1993). Frequent, short breaks during computer work: The effects on productivity and well-being in a field study. In H. Luczak, A. Cakir, and G. Cakir (Eds.), *Work With Display Units 92*. Berlin, Germany: Elsevier Science Publishers, 292-295.

Henning, R. A., Sauter, S. L. and Krief, E. F. (1992). Work Rhythm and Physiological Rhythms in Repetitive Computer Work: Effects of Synchronization on Well-Being. *International Journal of Human-Computer Interaction,* 4 (3), 233-244.

Henning, R. A., Sauter, S. L., Salvendy, G. and Krieg Jr., E. F. (1989). Microbreak length, performance, and stress in a data entry task. *Ergonomics,* 32 (7), 855-864.

Herzberg, F., Mausner, B. and Snyderman, B. B. (1959). *The Motivation to Work* (2nd ed.). New York: John Wiley & Sons.

House, J.S. (1981). *Work Stress and Social Support.* Addison-Wesley, Reading, MA.

Huuhtanen, P. and Leino, T. (1992). The Impact of New Technology by Occupation and Age on Work in Financial Firms: A 2-Year Follow-Up. *International Journal of Human-Computer Interaction*, 4 (2), 123-142.

Idson, T. L. (1990). Establishment size, job satisfaction and the structure of work. Applied Ergonomics, 22 , 1007-1018.

Igbaria, M. and Guimaraes, T. (1992). Antecedents and Consequences of Job Satisfaction Among Information Center Employees. *Communications of the ACM* , 35, 352-369.

Johansson, G. and Aronnson, G. (1984). Stress reactions in computerized administrative work. *J. Occup. Behav.*, 58, 159-181.

Kalimo, R. and Leppanen, A. (1987). Visual display units - psychosocial factors in health. In M.J. Davidson and C.L. Cooper (Eds.) *Women and Information Technology*. Chichester: John Wiley and Sons Ltd, 193-224.

Kalimo, R., Lindstrom, K., and Smith, M.J. (1996). Psychosocial approach in occupational health. In G. Salvendy (Ed.) *Handbook of Human Factors and Ergonomics*, New York: John Wiley & Sons.

Kanawaty, G. (1986). *Introduction to Work Study.* Geneva: International Labour Office.

Karasek, R., 1979, Job demands, job decision latitude, and mental strain: implications for job redesign, Administrative Science Quarterly, 24, 295-308.

Karasek, R.A. (1981). Job decision latitude, job design, and coronary heart disease. In G. Salvendy and M.J. Smith (Eds.) *Machine Pacing and Occupational Stress.* London: Taylor & Francis, 45-56.

Kasl, S.V., 1978. Epidemiological contributions to the study of work stress. In: Cooper, C.L. and Payne, R. (Eds.), *Stress at Work.* John Wiley & Sons, New York.

Kiesler, S. and Finholt, T. (1988). The mystery of RSI. *American Psychologist* 43(12): 1004-1015.

Kling, R. (1980). Social analyses of computing: theoretical perspectives in recent empirical research. *Computing Surveys,* 12 (1), 61-110.

Korunka, C. and Weiss, A. (1995). The Effect of New Technologies on Job Satisfaction and Psychosomatic Complaints. *Applied Psychology: An International Review*, 44 (2), 123-142.

Knave, B. and Wideback, P. G. (1987). *Work with Display Units.* Amsterdam: Elsevier Science Publishers.

Lawler, E. E. (1986). *High-Involvement Management.* San Francisco, CA: Jossey-Bass Publishers.

Lawler, E. E. (1992). *The Ultimate Advantange: Creating the High-Involvement Organization* (1st ed.). San Francisco: Jossey-Bass Inc.

Lazarus, R.S. (1974). Psychological stress and coping in adaptation and illness. *International Journal of Psychiatry in Medicine*, 5: 321-333.

Lazarus, R.S. (1977). Cognitive and coping processes in emotion. In A. Monat and R.S. Lazarus, Eds., *Stress and Coping.* New York: Columbia University Press, 145-158.

Lazarus, R.S. (1993). From psychological stress to emotions: A history of changing outlooks. *Annual Reviews Psychology*, 44, 1-21.

Levi, L. (1972). *Stress and Distress in Response to Psychosocial Stimuli.* New York: Pergamon Press.

Lim, S. Y. and Carayon, P. (1995). Psychosocial and work stress perspectives on musculoskeletal discomfort. In *Proceedings of PREMUS 95.* Montreal: Institute for Research on Safety and Security (IRSST).

Lim, S. Y., Rogers, K. J. S., Smith, M. J. and Sainfort, P. C. (1989). A study of the direct and indirect effects of office ergonomics on psychological stress outcomes. In M. J. Smith and G. Salvendy (Eds.), *Work with Computers: Organizational, Management, Stress and Health Aspects*. Amsterdam: Elsevier Science Publishers, 248-255.

Lindstrom, K. (1991). Well-Being and Computer-Mediated Work of Various Occupational Groups in Banking and Insurance. *International Journal of Human-Computer Interaction*, 3 (4), 339-361.

Linton, S.J. and Kamwendo, K. (1989). Riskfactors in the psychosocial work environment for neck and shoulder pain in secretaries. *Journal of Occupational Medicine* 31(7): 609-613.

Locke, E. A. (1976). The Nature and Causes of Job Satisfaction. In M. D. Dunnette (Ed.), *Handbook of Industrial and Organizational Psychology*. Chicago: Rand McNally College Publishing Company, 1297-1349.

Luczak, H., Cakir, A. and Cakir, G. (1993). *Work with Display Units 92*. Amsterdam: Elsevier Science Publishers.

Majchrzak, A. and Cotton, J. (1988). A longitudinal study of adjustment to technological change: From mass to computer-automated batch production. *Journal of Occupational Psychology*, 61 , 43-66.

Maslow, A. H. (1943). A Theory of Human Motivation. *Psychological Review*, 50 , 370-396.

NAS. (1983). *Video Terminals, Work and Vision*. Washington, DC: National Academy Press.

NIOSH (1990). *Health Hazard Evaluation Report - HETA 89-250-2046 - Newsday, Inc.*.Washington, D.C., U.S. Department of Health and Human Services.

NIOSH (1992). *Health Hazard Evaluation Report - HETA 89-299-2230 - US West Communications*. Washington, D.C., U.S. Department of Health and Human Services.

NIOSH (1993). *Health Hazard Evaluation Report - HETA 90-013-2277- Los Angeles Times*. Washington, D.C., U.S. Department of Health and Human Services.

Ostberg, O. and Nilsson, C. (1985). Emerging technology and stress. In C.L. Cooper and M.J. Smith (Eds.) *Job Stress in Blue Collar Work*. New York: John Wiley & Sons, 149-169.

OTA. (1985). *Automation of America's Offices*. Washington, DC: Office of Technology Assessment, Congress of the United States.

OTA. (1987). *The Electronic Supervisor*. Washington, DC: Office of Technology Assessment, Congress of the United States.

Piotrkowski, C. S., Cohen, B. G. F. and Coray, K. E. (1992). Working Conditions and Well-Being Among Women Office Employees. *International Journal of Human-Computer Interaction,* 4 (3), 263-281.

Putz-Anderson, V. (1988). *Cumulative Trauma Disorders - A Manual for Musculoskeletal Diseases of the Upper Limbs*. London: Taylor and Francis.

Sainfort, P. C. (1990). Job design predictors of stress in automated offices. *Behaviour and Information Technology*, 9 (1), 3-16.

Salvendy, G. (1992). *Handbook of Industrial Engineering*. New York: John Wiley and Sons.

Salvendy, G. and Smith, M.J. (Eds) (1981). Machine-Pacing and Occupational Stress. London: Taylor and Francis.

Sauter, S. L., Gottlieb, M. S., Jones, K. C., Dodson, V. N. and Rohrer, K. M. (1983). Job and health implications of VDT use: Initial results of the Wisconsin-NIOSH study. *Communications of the ACM*, 26(4), 284-294.

Sauter, S.L., Hurrell, J. and Cooper, C. (1989). *Job Control and Worker Health*. New York: John Wiley and Sons.

Selye, H. (1956). *The Stress of Life*. New York: McGraw-Hill.

Selye, H. (1983). The stress concept: Past, present, and future. In C.L. Cooper, Ed., *Stress research: Issues for the Eighties*. New York: Wiley & Sons, 1-20.

Silverstein, B.A., Fine, L.J. and Armstrong, T.J. (1987). Occupational factors and carpal tunnel syndrome. American Journal of Industrial Medicine 11: 343-358.

Smith, M.J. (1984). The physical, mental and emotional stress effects of VDT work. Computer Graphics and Applications, 4, 23-27.

Smith, M.J. (1987). Mental and physical strain at VDT workstations. Behaviour and Information Technology, 6, 243-255.

Smith, M.J. (1987). Occupational Stress. In G. Salvendy (Ed.) *Handbook of Human Factors*. New York: John Wiley and Sons, 844-860.

Smith, M.J., Cohen, B.G.F., Stammerjohn, L.W and Lalich, N. (1980). Video display operator stress. In E. Grandjean and E. Vigliani (Eds.) *Ergonomic Aspects of*

Visual Display Terminals, London: Taylor and Francis, 201-210.

Smith, M.J. and Carayon (1995a). New technology, automation and work organization: Stress problems and improved technology implementation strategies. International Journal of Human Factors in Manufacturing, 5, 99-116.

Smith, M.J. and Carayon, P. (1995b) Work organization, stress and cumulative trauma disorders. In S. Moon and S. Sauter (Eds.) *Beyond Biomechanics: Psychosocial Aspects of Cumulative Trauma Disorders*. London: Taylor and Francis.

Smith, M. J., Cohen, B. G., Stammerjohn, L. W. and Happ, A. (1981). An Investigation of Health Complaints and Job Stress in Video Display Operations. *Human Factors*, 23 (4), 387-400.

Smith, M. J. (1984). Health issues in VDT work. In J. Bennet, D. Case, J. Sandlin and M. J. Smith (Eds.), *Visual Display Terminals*, New Jersey: Prentice Hall, 193-228.

Smith, M. J., Carayon, P. and Miezio, K. (1986). Job Stress and VDUs: Is technology a problem? In *Proceedings of the International Scientific Conference: Work with Display Units*, Stockholm, Sweden: Swedish National Board of Occupational Safety and Health, 189-195.

Smith, M. J., Carayon, P., Eberts, R. and Salvendy, G. (1992). Human-Computer Interaction. In G. Salvendy (Ed.), *Handbook of Industrial Engineering*, New York: John Wiley and Sons,1107-1144.

Smith, M. J. and Sainfort, P. C. (1989). A balance theory of job design for stress reduction. International Journal of Industrial Ergonomics, 4, 67-79.

Smith, M. J. and Salvendy, G. (1989). *Work with Computers: Organizational, Management, Stress and Health Aspects*. (Vol. 12A). Amsterdam: Elsevier Science Publishers.

Smith, M. J. and Salvendy, G. (1993). *Human-Computer Interaction: Applications and Case Studies*. (Vol. 19A). Amsterdam: Elsevier Science Publishers.

Smith, M.J., Cohen, W. and Grandjean, E. (1996). Design of Computer Terminal Workstations. In G. Salvendy (Ed.) *Handbook of Human Factors and Ergonomics*. New York: John Wiley and Sons.

Starr, S. J., Thompson, C. R. and Shute, S. J. (1982). Effects of Video Display Terminals on Telephone Operators. Human Factors, 24 (6), 699-711.

Starr, S. J. (1984). Effects of video display terminals in a business office. Human Factors, 26(3), 347-356.

Starr, S. J., Shute, S. J. and Thompson, C. R. (1985). Relating posture to discomfort in VDT use. Journal of Occupational Medicine, 27(4), 269-271.

Steffy, B. D. and Jones, J. W. (1989). The Psychological Impact of Video Display Terminals on Employees' Well-Being. *American Journal of Health Promotion*, 4 (2), 101-107.

Stellman, J.M., Klitzman, S., Gordon, G.C. and Snow, B.R. (1985). Work environment and the well-being of clerical and VDT workers. *Journal of Occupational Behavior*, 8, 95-102.

Theorell, T., Ringdahl-Harms, K., Ahlberg-Hulten, G. and Westin, B. (1991). Psychosocial job factors and symptoms from the locomotor system - A multicausal analysis. *Scandinavian Journal of Rehabilitation Medicine* 23: 165-173.

Travers, P. H. and Stanton, B. A. (1984). Office Employees and Video Display Terminals: Physical, Psychological, and Ergonomic Factors. *Occupational Health Nursing* 11, 586-591.

Trist, E. (1978). On sociotechnical systems. In W. Pasmore and J. Sherwood (Eds.), *Sociotechnical systems: A sourcebook*. San Diego: University Associates.

Trist, E., and Bamforth, K. (1951). Some social and psychological consequences of the long wall method of coal-gettting. Human Relations 1, 3-38.

Trist, E., Higgin, C., Murray, H., and Pollack, A. (1963). *Organizational choice*. London: Tavistock Publications.

Westlander, G. (1994). The full-time VDT operator as a working person: Musculoskeletal work discomfort and life situation. International Journal of Human-Computer Interaction, 6(4), 339-364.

Wolf, S. (1986). Common disorders and grave disorders identified with occupational stress. In S. Wolf and A.J. Finestone (Eds.), *Occupational Stress - Health and Performance*. Littleton, MA: PSG Publishing Company, 47-53.

Yang, C.-L. and Carayon, P. (1995). Effect of job demands and social support on employee stress: a study of VDT users. Behaviour and Information Technology, 14 (1), 32-40.

Zeffane, R. M. (1994). Correlates of Job Satisfaction and their Implications for Work Redesign: A Focus on the Australian Telecommunications Industry. *Public Personnel Management,* 23 (1), 61-75.

Author Index

Subject Index